New York City Subways

Subways

Stops are not served by all trains at all times.
Refer to Transit Authority map for descriptions
of express, local, and limited service.

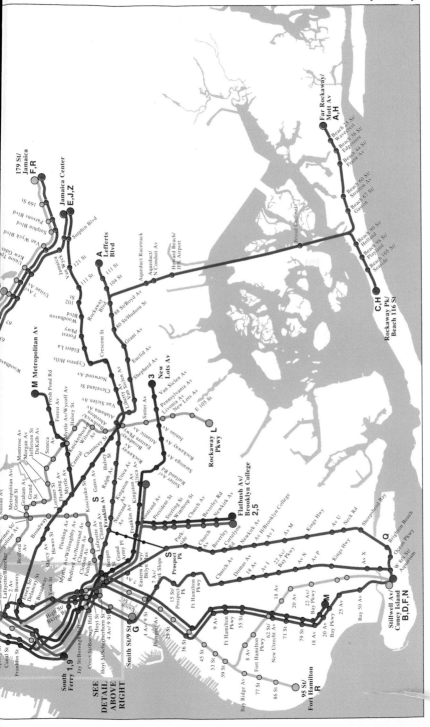

Downtown Manhattan

New Museum of Contemporary Art, 31
New School of Social Research, 46
New York Stock Exchange, 14
New York University, 37
Puck Building, 32
St. John's Episcopal Methodist Church, 19
St. Luke's Chapel, 35
St. Mark's in the Bowery Church, 40
St. Paul's Chapel, 20
South Street Seaport Museum, 18
Staten Island Ferry Terminal, 7
Statue of Liberty and Ellis Island Ferry Terminal, 3
Strand Bookstore, 42
Tower Records, 36
Trinity Church, 12
Umberto's Clam House, 30
U.S. Customs House, 11
Woolworth Building, 23
World Financial Center, 22
World Trade Center, 21

Downtown

Alternative Museum, 28
Anthology Film Archives, 33
Buddhist Temple, 27
Castle Clinton, 1
Cherry Lane Theatre, 34
Chinatown Fair, 26
Church of the Ascension, 44
Church of Our Lady of the Rosary, 8
City Hall, 24
Clocktower Gallery, 25
Cooper Union, 39
Downtown Heliport, 9
East Coast Memorial, 2
Federal Hall, 15
Federal Reserve Bank, 16
Forbes Magazine Galleries, 47
Forbidden Planet, 43
Fraunces Tavern, 10
Fulton Fish Market, 17
Grace Church, 41
Jefferson Market Library, 45
Joseph Papp Public Theater, 38
Morgan Guaranty Trust Company, 13
Museum of Holography, 29

Midtown Manhattan

East River

Queens-Midtown Tunnel

FDR Dr.

United Nations

TURTLE BAY

Queensboro Bridge

First Ave.

Second Ave.

Third Ave.

Lexington Ave.

Park Ave.

Madison Ave.

Fifth Ave.

Citicorp Center

Grand Army Plaza

Park South

Central

Carnegie Hall

Museum of Modern Art

Rockefeller Center

Grand Central Terminal

New York Public Library

Bryant Park

MURRAY HILL

Empire State Building

Second Ave.

Third Ave.

Park Ave.

HERALD SQUARE

GARMENT DISTRICT

Broadway

Seventh Ave.

TIMES SQUARE

Eighth Ave.

Ninth Ave.

New York Convention & Visitors Bureau

COLUMBUS CIRCLE

A,B,C,D, 1,2,3,9

Port Authority Bus Terminal

General Post Office

Dyer Ave.

Tenth Ave.

HELL'S KITCHEN

Lincoln Tunnel

Eleventh Ave.

Twelfth Ave.

E. 56th St.
E. 55th St.
E. 54th St.
E. 53rd St.
E. 52nd St.
E. 51st St.
E. 50th St.
E. 49th St.
E. 48th St.
E. 47th St.
E. 46th St.
E. 45th St.
E. 44th St.
E. 43rd St.
E. 42nd St.
E. 41st St.
E. 40th St.
E. 39th St.
E. 38th St.
E. 37th St.
E. 36th St.
E. 35th St.
E. 34th St.
E. 33rd St.
E. 32nd St.

E. 60th St.
E. 59th St.
E. 58th St.
E. 57th St.

W. 60th St.
W. 59th St.
W. 58th St.
W. 57th St.
W. 56th St.
W. 55th St.
W. 54th St.
W. 53rd St.
W. 52nd St.
W. 51st St.
W. 50th St.
W. 49th St.
W. 48th St.
W. 47th St.
W. 46th St.
W. 45th St.
W. 44th St.
W. 43rd St.
W. 42nd St.
W. 41st St.
W. 40th St.
W. 39th St.
W. 38th St.
W. 37th St.
W. 36th St.
W. 35th St.
W. 34th St.
W. 33rd St.

N,R
B,Q
4,5,6
N,R
B,Q
N,R
B,D,E
B,D,F,Q
N,R
1,2,3,9
C,E
A,C,E
A,C,E
N,R
B,D,F,Q
1,2,3,9
1,2,3, N,R,9
B,D,F, Q,7
6
E,F
4,5, 6,S,7
1 2 3 4 5 6 7 8 9 10 11 12 13 14 15 16 17
28 29 30 31 32 33 34 35 36 37 38 39 40 41 42 43 44 45 46 47 48 49 50 51 52 53 54 55 56 57 58 59 60 61 62 63 64 65 66 67 68

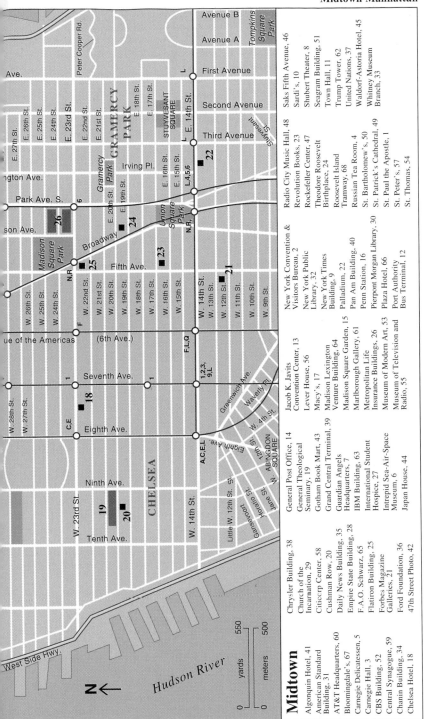

Midtown

Algonquin Hotel, 41
American Standard Building, 31
AT&T Headquarters, 60
Bloomingdale's, 67
Carnegie Delicatessen, 5
Carnegie Hall, 3
CBS Building, 52
Central Synagogue, 59
Chanin Building, 34
Chelsea Hotel, 18
Chrysler Building, 38
Church of the Incarnation, 29
Citicorp Center, 58
Cushman Row, 20
Daily News Building, 35
Empire State Building, 28
F.A.O. Schwarz, 65
Flatiron Building, 25
Forbes Magazine Galleries, 21
Ford Foundation, 36
47th Street Photo, 42
General Post Office, 14
General Theological Seminary, 19
Gotham Book Mart, 43
Grand Central Terminal, 39
Guardian Angels Headquarters, 7
IBM Building, 63
International Student Hospice, 27
Intrepid Sea-Air-Space Museum, 6
Japan House, 44
Jacob K. Javits Convention Center, 13
Lever House, 56
Macy's, 17
Madison Lexington Venture Building, 64
Madison Square Garden, 15
Marlborough Gallery, 61
Metropolitan Life Insurance Buildings, 26
Museum of Modern Art, 53
Museum of Television and Radio, 55
New York Convention & Visitors Bureau, 2
New York Public Library, 32
New York Times Building, 9
Palladium, 22
Pan Am Building, 40
Penn Station, 16
Pierpont Morgan Library, 30
Plaza Hotel, 66
Port Authority Bus Terminal, 12
Radio City Music Hall, 48
Revolution Books, 23
Rockefeller Center, 47
Theodore Roosevelt Birthplace, 24
Roosevelt Island Tramway, 68
Russian Tea Room, 4
St. Bartholomew's, 50
St. Patrick's Cathedral, 49
St. Paul the Apostle, 1
St. Peter's, 57
St. Thomas, 54
Saks Fifth Avenue, 46
Sardi's, 10
Shubert Theater, 8
Seagram Building, 51
Town Hall, 11
Trump Tower, 62
United Nations, 37
Waldorf-Astoria Hotel, 45
Whitney Museum Branch, 33

Uptown

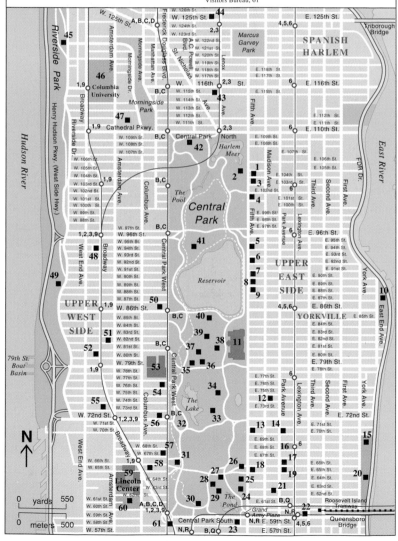

Downtown Washington, D.C.

Central Washington, D.C.

Central Washington, D.C.

Washington National Cathedral
CLEVELAND PARK
Klingle St.
Cathedral Ave.
MT. PLEASANT
16th St.
14th St.
13th St.
Columbia F
Harvard St
National Zoo
Adams Mill Rd.
Irving St.

GLOVER PARK
Massachusetts
Woodley Rd.
WOODLEY PARK-ZOO M
15th St.

Calvert St.
Vice Presidential Mansion
Calvert St.
Euclid St.
ADAMS-MORGAN

Observatory La.
37th St.
U.S. Naval Observatory
Rock Creek Park
Rock Creek Pkwy.
KALORAMA CIRCLE
Columbia Rd.
Florida Ave.

Whitehaven Park
EMBASSY ROW
Dumbarton Oaks Park
Waterside Dr.
Ave.
U St.
U ST/CARDOZO

R St.
Montrose Park
Rock Creek
DUPONT CIRCLE
Florida
New Hampshire Ave.
16th St.
15th St.
Vermont

Georgetown University
R St.
28th St.
Q St.
SHERIDAN CIRCLE
Q St.
20th St.
DUPONT CIRCLE M
P St.
LOGAN CIRCLE

Wisconsin Ave.
34th St.
P St.
DUPONT CIRCLE M
Connecticut Ave.
SCOTT CIRCLE
14th St.
13th St.

GEORGETOWN
30th St.
M St.
NEW DOWNTOWN
THOMAS CIRCLE

C&O Canal
White hurst Fwy.
26th St.
23rd St.
WASHINGTON CIRCLE
FARRAGUT NORTH
FARRAGUT SQUARE
MCPHERSON SQUARE
McPHERSON S

66
FOGGY BOTTOM-GWU
K St.
FARRAGUT WEST M
M

Key Br.
George Washington Pkwy.
Theodore Roosevelt Memorial
Rock Creek Pkwy.
JAUREZ CIRCLE
GWU
Pennsylvania Ave.
H St.
LAFAYETTE SQUARE
New York Av

ROSSLYN M
Theodore Roosevelt Island
G St.
FOGGY BOTTOM
F St.
E St.
Virginia Ave.
18th St.
White House
15th St.
METRO CENT

ROSSLYN
66
Roosevelt Bridge
17th St.
The Ellipse
E St.
OLD DOWNTO
M

50
66 50
Constitution Ave.
FEDERAL TRIANGL
14th St.

50
George Washington Pkwy.
Memorial Bridge
Lincoln Memorial
Washington Monument
U.S. Holocaust Memorial Museum
SMITHSONIAN
M

ARLINGTON CEMETERY M
Memorial Dr.
Lady bird Johnson Park
Columbia Island
Independence Ave.
West Potomac Park
Kutz Br.
Raoul Wallenberg Pl.
Tidal Basin
Outlet Br.
East Basin Dr.
Maine Ave.

Visitors Center
ARLINGTON CEMETERY
Potomac River
Jefferson Memorial
Francis Memoria
395

VIRGINIA
Jefferson Davis Hwy.
East Potomac Par

Pentagon
PENTAGON M
395
1

Central Washington, D.C.

The Mall Area, Washington, D.C.

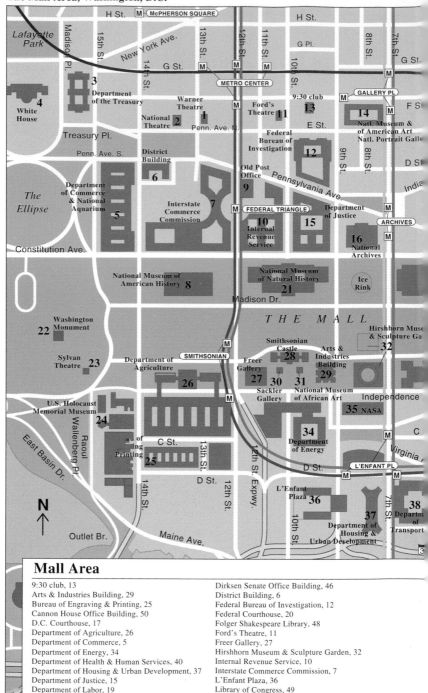

Mall Area

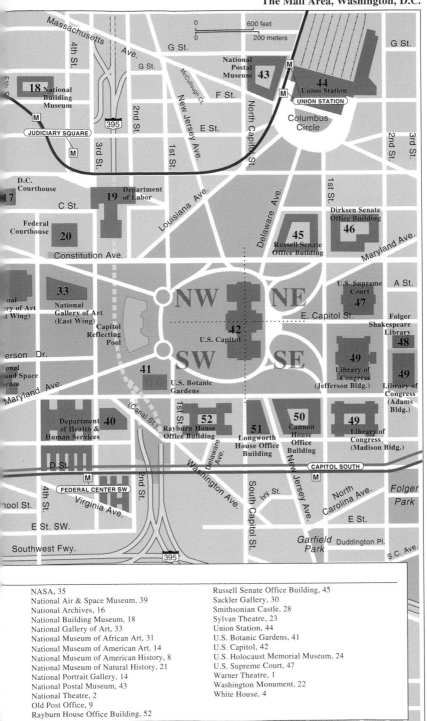

The Mall Area, Washington, D.C.

White House Area, Foggy Bottom, and Nearby Arlington

N

GEORGETOWN

Prospect St.
33rd St.
N St.
Old Stone House
Olive St.
24th St.
Rock Creek
31st St.
M St.
26th St.
25th St.
L St.
New H. Ave.
C&O Creek
South St.
WASHINGTON CIRCLE
Whitehurst Fwy.
29
K St. (under expressway)
G.W. Hosp.
FOGGY BOTTOM-GWU
66
Geo. Wash. Univ.

Potomac River
Thompson Boat Center
Watergate Hotel
JUAREZ CIRCLE
24th St.
23rd St.
FOGGY BOTTOM
Watergate Hotel Complex
Francis Scott Key Br.
Rock Creek Pkwy.
Kennedy Center for the Performing Arts
Theodore Roosevelt Memorial

Fort Myer Dr.
N. Lynn St.
N. Moore St.
19th St.
George Washington Pkwy.
Theodore Roosevelt Island
ROSSLYN
M
N. Kent St.
Wilson Blvd
Depart.
ROSSLYN
Fairfax Dr.
Arlington Ridge Rd.
66
Theodore Roosevelt Br.
66 50
50
Natl. Acad. of Sc.

N. Nash St.
50
NW
SW
Linco. Mem.

Mead Dr.
Marine Corps War Memorial (Two Jima Statue)
George Washington Memorial Pkwy.
Arlington Memorial Br.
Ericsson Memorial
12th St.
Netherlands Carillon
ARLINGTON
Ladybird Johnson Park
M
Memorial Dr.
ARLINGTON CEMETERY
Columbia Island
Grave of President John F. Kennedy
Arlington House
Robert E. Lee Memorial
Visitor Center
Jefferson Davis Hwy.
ARLINGTON NATIONAL CEMETERY
Tomb of the Unknown Soldier
Lyndon B. Johnson Memorial

V I R G I N I A

0   1500 feet
0   500 meters

Pentagon, National Airport

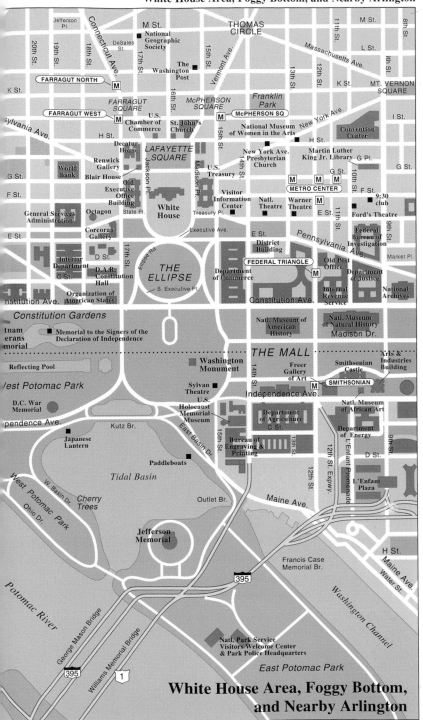

White House Area, Foggy Bottom, and Nearby Arlington

Metrorail System, Washington, D.C.

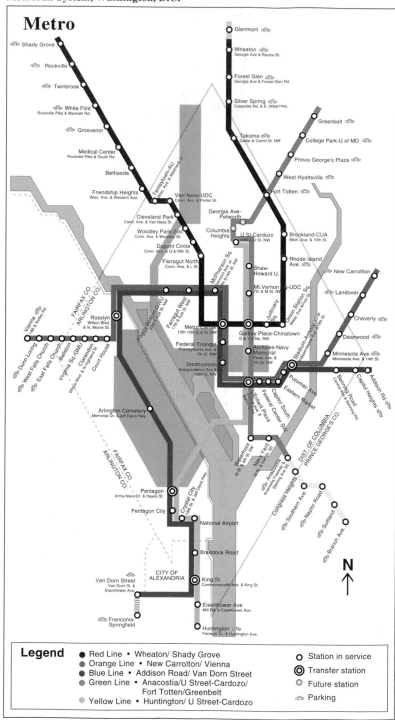

Metro

Legend
- ● Red Line • Wheaton/ Shady Grove
- ● Orange Line • New Carrolton/ Vienna
- ● Blue Line • Addison Road/ Van Dorn Street
- ● Green Line • Anacostia/U Street-Cardozo/ Fort Totten/Greenbelt
- ● Yellow Line • Huntington/ U Street-Cardozo

- ○ Station in service
- ◎ Transfer station
- ○ Future station
- 🚗 Parking

Let's Go:
USA

"Its yearly revision by a new crop of Harvard students makes it as valuable as ever." **—The New York Times**

"Value-packed, unbeatable, accurate, and comprehensive." **—The Los Angeles Times**

"A world-wise traveling companion—always ready with friendly advice and helpful hints, all sprinkled with a bit of wit." **—The Philadelphia Inquirer**

"Lighthearted and sophisticated, informative and fun to read. [Let's Go] helps the novice traveler navigate like a knowledgeable old hand." **—Atlanta Journal-Constitution**

"All the essential information you need, from making a phone call to exchanging money to contacting your embassy. [Let's Go] provides maps to help you find your way from every train station to a full range of youth hostels and hotels." **—Minneapolis Star Tribune**

"Unbeatable: good sight-seeing advice; up-to-date info on restaurants, hotels, and inns; a commitment to money-saving travel; and a wry style that brightens nearly every page." **—The Washington Post**

■ Let's Go researchers have to make it on their own.

"The writers seem to have experienced every rooster-packed bus and lunar-surfaced mattress about which they write." **—The New York Times**

"Retains the spirit of the student-written publication it is: candid, opinionated, resourceful, amusing info for the traveler of limited means but broad curiosity." **—Mademoiselle**

■ No other guidebook is as comprehensive.

"Whether you're touring the United States, Europe, Southeast Asia, or Central America, a Let's Go guide will clue you in to the cheapest, yet safe, hotels and hostels, food and transportation. Going beyond the call of duty, the guides reveal a country's latest news, cultural hints, and off-beat information that any tourist is likely to miss." **—Tulsa World**

■ Let's Go is completely revised each year.

"Up-to-date travel tips for touring four continents on skimpy budgets." **—Time**

"Inimitable.... Let's Go's 24 guides are updated yearly (as opposed to the general guidebook standard of every two to three years), and in a marvelously spunky way." **—The New York Times**

Let's Go Publications

Let's Go: Alaska & The Pacific Northwest
Let's Go: Britain & Ireland
Let's Go: California
Let's Go: Central America
Let's Go: Eastern Europe
Let's Go: Ecuador & The Galápagos Islands
Let's Go: Europe
Let's Go: France
Let's Go: Germany
Let's Go: Greece & Turkey
Let's Go: India & Nepal
Let's Go: Ireland
Let's Go: Israel & Egypt
Let's Go: Italy
Let's Go: London
Let's Go: Mexico
Let's Go: New York City
Let's Go: Paris
Let's Go: Rome
Let's Go: Southeast Asia
Let's Go: Spain & Portugal
Let's Go: Switzerland & Austria
Let's Go: USA
Let's Go: Washington, D.C.

Let's Go **Map Guide:** Boston
Let's Go **Map Guide:** London
Let's Go **Map Guide:** New York City
Let's Go **Map Guide:** Paris
Let's Go **Map Guide:** San Francisco
Let's Go **Map Guide:** Washington, D.C.

LET'S GO

The Budget Guide to
USA
1997

Nicholas Corman
Editor

Elissa L. Gootman
Associate Editor

Melissa M. Reyen
Associate Editor

St. Martin's Press ✺ New York

HELPING LET'S GO

If you want to share your discoveries, suggestions, or corrections, please drop us a line. We read every piece of correspondence, whether a postcard, a 10-page e-mail, or a coconut. All suggestions are passed along to our researcher-writers. Please note that mail received after May 1997 may be too late for the 1998 book, but will be retained for the following edition. **Address mail to:**

> **Let's Go: USA**
> **67 Mt. Auburn Street**
> **Cambridge, MA 02138**
> **USA**

Visit Let's Go at **http://www.letsgo.com,** or send e-mail to:

> **Fanmail@letsgo.com**
> **Subject: "Let's Go: USA"**

In addition to the invaluable travel advice our readers share with us, many are kind enough to offer their services as researchers or editors. Unfortunately, the charter of Let's Go, Inc. enables us to employ only currently enrolled Harvard-Radcliffe students.

About Let's Go

THIRTY-SIX YEARS OF WISDOM

Back in 1960, a few students at Harvard University banded together to produce a 20-page pamphlet offering a collection of tips on budget travel in Europe. This modest, mimeographed packet, offered as an extra to passengers on student charter flights to Europe, met with instant popularity. The following year, students traveling to Europe researched the first, full-fledged edition of *Let's Go: Europe*, a pocket-sized book featuring honest, irreverent writing and a decidedly youthful outlook on the world. Throughout the 60s, our guides reflected the times; the 1969 guide to America led off by inviting travelers to "dig the scene" at San Francisco's Haight-Ashbury. During the 70s and 80s, we gradually added regional guides and expanded coverage into the Middle East and Central America. With the addition of our in-depth city guides, handy map guides, and extensive coverage of Asia, the 90s are also proving to be a time of explosive growth for Let's Go, and there's certainly no end in sight. The first editions of *Let's Go: India & Nepal* and *Let's Go: Ecuador & The Galápagos Islands* hit the shelves this year, and research for next year's series has already begun.

We've seen a lot in 37 years. *Let's Go: Europe* is now the world's bestselling international guide, translated into seven languages. And our new guides bring Let's Go's total number of titles, with their spirit of adventure and their reputation for honesty, accuracy, and editorial integrity, to 30. But some things never change: our guides are still researched, written, and produced entirely by students who know first-hand how to see the world on the cheap.

HOW WE DO IT

Each guide is completely revised and thoroughly updated every year by a well-traveled set of 200 students. Every winter, we recruit over 120 researchers and 60 editors to write the books anew. After several months of training, Researcher-Writers hit the road for seven weeks of exploration, from Anchorage to Ankara, Estonia to El Salvador, Iceland to Indonesia. Hired for their rare combination of budget travel sense, writing ability, stamina, and courage, these adventurous travelers know what train strikes, stolen luggage, food poisoning, and marriage proposals are all part of a day's work. Back at our offices, editors work from spring to fall, massaging copy written on Himalayan bus rides into witty yet informative prose. A student staff of typesetters, cartographers, publicists, and managers keeps our lively team together. In September, the collected efforts of the summer are delivered to our printer, who turns them into books in record time, so that you have the most up-to-date information available for *your* vacation. And even as you read this, work on next year's editions is well underway.

WHY WE DO IT

At Let's Go, our goal is to give you a great vacation. We don't think of budget travel as the last recourse of the destitute; we believe that it's the only way to travel. Living cheaply and simply brings you closer to the people and places you've been saving up to visit. Our books will ease your anxieties and answer your questions about the basics—so you can get off the beaten track and explore. Once you learn the ropes, we encourage you to put Let's Go away now and then to strike out on your own. As any seasoned traveler will tell you, the best discoveries are often those you make yourself. When you find something worth sharing, drop us a line. We're Let's Go Publications, 67 Mt. Auburn St., Cambridge, MA 02138, USA (e-mail: fanmail@letsgo.com).

HAPPY TRAVELS!

Contents

Maps

Color Maps

Researcher-Writers

Frank Beidler   *Great Lakes and Upper South*
In the tradition of Casey Jones, Frank built a reputation of timeliness and excellence. The Chicago native bewildered Indiana authorities after displaying his mug, which had mysteriously morphed into that of a 21-year-old, discovered Oxford in all its sound and fury, and fell in love with Mississippi. Frank's copy was a half-pound of meaty, succulent, and well-done splendor; Dave Thomas would be proud.

Scott M. Brown   *The Carolinas, Georgia, Florida, Alabama*
Scott "Odysseus of the Southern Highways" Brown scoured his native region in a tireless quest for the juiciest of barbecues and the most surreal of museums. Stunned by the unparalleled debauchery of Key West (which he assiduously detailed nonetheless), our shrewd Carolinian darling stunned us in turn, braving gargantuan mosquitoes and pesky towing companies to ensure that the South had its day in the sun.

Sam Bull   *Michigan, Wisconsin, Minnesota, Missouri, Iowa, Kansas*
With a prolific pen, an unfaltering wit, and an itinerary straddling the Great Lakes and the Great Plains, Sam was an R/W of superlatives. After nearly ODing on state parks, our brewery tour connoisseur tackled Midwestern metropoli like a true Packer, then sent back copybatches so meticulous we thought they were already typeset and so clever we wish we'd written them ourselves.

Kirsten Valentine Cadieux   *New England and Maritime Provinces*
Embarking on her journey before many of us had started taking exams, Valentine took the Northeast by storm. Not even transmission blues in Maine or black flies in Canada could hold her back. She brought new meaning to the words "lobster sensitivity," schooled us in the longevity of time zones, and developed an intriguing predilection for the Plymouth & Brockton bus lines. Thanks for the postcards: you win!

Ethan Drogin   *Maryland, Virginia, West Virginia, Washington, D.C.*
Ethan played pick-up hoops with Annapolites, drank Virginian microbrew with bartenders in Williamsburg, offered tidings to "Ryan" outside a 7-Eleven at 3am, and chivalrously escorted an Argentinian girl to her first Orioles game. When not procuring his posse, Ethan conquered an itinerary that, at times—at best—was merciless. But he endured it all, with magnificent marginalia and pristine prose.

Stephen Gordon   *Mid-Atlantic, Southern New England, Michigan, Toronto*
Armed with a powerbook on his shoulder and a beeper on his belt, Steve tore through the Mid-Atlantic, braving backcountry roads like a cross between Mario Andretti and Sir Edmund Hillary. He had us longing for the waters of Niagara, the coasts of Connecticut, and the verdant splendor of the Berkshires. With insightful prose, our L.A. kid showed us what this side of the country is all about.

Nicole Gresham   *The Dakotas, Wyoming, Nebraska, Montana*
Tackling a route legendary for its endless highway miles, Nicole gobbled up our nation's heartland with nary a hitch. She waxed eloquent on everything from Montana's speed limits (or lack thereof) to the Native American Nez Perce campaign. In July, Nicole took to the mountains, churning out history-filled coverage of the Rockies. Lewis & Clark would be proud—but not as proud as we are.

Maria Guerra　　　　　　　　　*Louisiana, Arkansas, Texas, Oklahoma, Mississippi*
So dedicated that she dreamt Let's Go dreams, Maria's copy was the stuff of our own
fantasies. Supplementing her meticulous research with inside scoops gathered during
surreptitious ladies' room chats, this Texan graced her state and its neighbors with
her unfathomably upbeat 'tude. To our delight, she agreed to an extended stint in
New Orleans, where she ate her crawfish the local way and rhapsodized on jazz.

David Lerch　　　　　　　　　　　　　　　　*The Rocky Mountains*
Cranking out impeccable copy with his liberal hand and frontier spirit, David left no
peak of the Rockies unexplored. His voluminous batches were a testament to his
Über research, as he unearthed wineries in the desert, conspiracy at the Continental
Divide, Basques in Boise, polygamy in Salt Lake, hotsprings in Thermopolis, a bear in
the deep woods, and burritos. *¡Muchos burritos!*

Stephanie Stein　　　　　　　　　　　　　　　*The Southwest*
A two-time R/W, Stephanie brought experience and an English teacher's touch to her
brilliant write-ups. A hard-core shopper with a budget traveler's eye, the money she
saved on travel went toward her purchases—which were huge. This Virginia native
crossed the country, got her kicks on Route 66, hiked the Grand Canyon in a day,
and, in all her glory, found the texture your feet have been longing for.

Jace Clayton	*Manhattan, Brooklyn, Staten Island*
Vanessa Gil	*Manhattan, Queens, Long Island, The Catskills*
Maika Pollack	*Manhattan, The Bronx, Atlantic City*
Neil Lawande	*Virginia, Washington, D.C.*
Eunice Park	*Maryland, Virginia, Washington, D.C.*
Robyn Kali Bacon	*Southern British Columbia, Alberta*
Brian Ericson	*Southcentral Alaska, Northern British Columbia*
Mary S. Hatcher	*Oregon*
Raymond D. Heary	*Alaska, Northern British Columbia*
Lindsey M. Turrentine	*Washington*
Stephanie L. Smith	*Los Angeles Sprawl, Santa Barbara, San Luis Obispo*
Maren Lau	*Hawai'i*
Lee Koffler	*Las Vegas, Sierra Nevada, the Desert, San Diego*
Ted Gideonse	*Tahoe, Wine Country, NoCal, Gold Country, Frisco Nightlife*
Dan Appel	*San Francisco Bay Area, Sacramento, Santa Cruz, Monterey*
Ben Eilenberg	*San Mateo Coast*
Alberto Hazan	*El Paso and Ciudad Juárez*

Kevin C. Murphy	*Editor, New York City*
Lisa Ann Halliday	*Editor, Washington, D.C.*
Elizabeth M. Angell	*Editor, Alaska & the Pacific Northwest*
Sara K. Smith	*Associate Editor, Alaska & the Pacific Northwest*
Kenton H. Beerman	*Editor, California*
Natalie A. Landreth	*Associate Editor, California*

Acknowledgments

Happily, we didn't work on this book alone. Our R/Ws did us proud, crafting copy that made us muse, giggle, and tear. David F. had an encyclopedic knowledge of all things beneficent and scurrilous, not to mention *punctuatio*. The trivia-proffering domestic room proved that even non-issues have two sides. Michelle led the way, the Regional Guides crunched away, Anne Chisholm kept things sane, Patrick Chung Canadized, and Peter Ndung'u preserved the order.**—Team USA**

My sincerest thanks go to Melissa and Elissa, for their hard work, indispensable advice, and fun spirit. I couldn't possibly have asked for better partners in this project. Special thanks to Michelle, David F., and all the managing editors; to Kate & Dean, who trusted me with their home; and to Julie J., for her infinite generosity. Finally, thanks and love to my entire family. Roz and Ben: this book is for you.**—NC**

Nick and Melissa, I adore you guys. You never failed to amuse or impress me. Thanks and love to my precious friends, whom I mention only by association—with Athens, Harvard '95 and '96, Israel, Bronfman, the mag, Dunster, 71 Walker, Story St., family, and life in general. And especially to Mommy, Daddy, Jenny, & Mike, who've been with me thru all of the above and couldn't be more wonderful.**—ELG**

A heartfelt "you go" to Nick and Elissa, who did their thing with grace and style, while helping me do mine. Love to Mom, Dad, and Matti-boom, whose affection and support have meant everything. Thanks to Megan for listening, Katina for Charleying, Garyun for laughing, and Kim for discovering what it's all about. Finally, to my roommates, softball team, friends, and the one I'll be waiting for at the end.**—MMR**

Editor	Nicholas Corman
Associate Editor	Elissa L. Gootman
Associate Editor	Melissa M. Reyen
Managing Editor	David Fagundes
Publishing Director	Michelle C. Sullivan
Production Manager	Daniel O. Williams
Associate Production Manager	Michael S. Campbell
Cartography Manager	Amanda K. Bean
Editorial Manager	John R. Brooks
Editorial Manager	Allison Crapo
Financial Manager	Stephen P. Janiak
Personnel Manager	Alexander H. Travelli
Publicity Manager	SoRelle B. Braun
Associate Publicity Manager	David Fagundes
Associate Publicity Manager	Elisabeth Mayer
Assistant Cartographer	Jonathan D. Kibera
Assistant Cartographer	Mark C. Staloff
Office Coordinator	Jennifer L. Schuberth
Director of Advertising and Sales	Amit Tiwari
Senior Sales Executives	Andrew T. Rourke
	Nicholas A. Valtz, Charles E. Varner
General Manager	Richard Olken
Assistant General Manager	Anne E. Chisholm

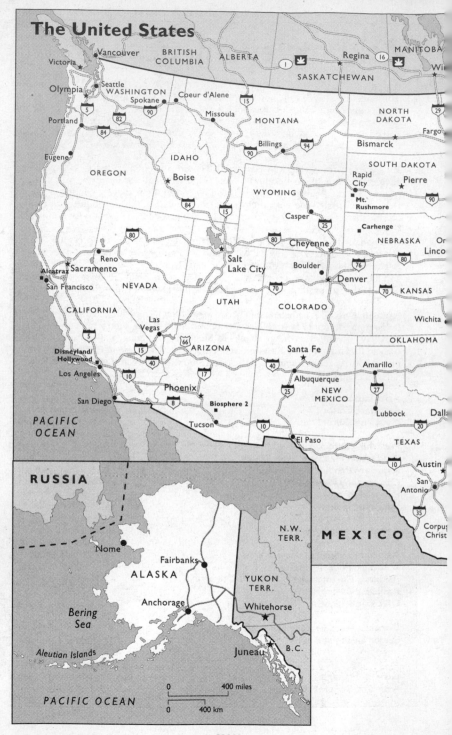

The United States

Victoria
Vancouver
BRITISH COLUMBIA
ALBERTA
Regina
MANITOBA
SASKATCHEWAN
Wi

Olympia
Seattle
WASHINGTON
Spokane
Coeur d'Alene
Missoula
MONTANA
NORTH DAKOTA
Fargo

Portland
Eugene
OREGON
Boise
IDAHO
Billings
Bismarck
SOUTH DAKOTA

Rapid City
Pierre
Mt. Rushmore

WYOMING
Casper
Carhenge
NEBRASKA
Linco

Reno
Sacramento
Alcatraz
San Francisco
Salt Lake City
Cheyenne
Boulder
Denver
KANSAS
Or

NEVADA
CALIFORNIA
UTAH
COLORADO
Wichita

Las Vegas
Disneyland/ Hollywood
Los Angeles
San Diego
ARIZONA
Santa Fe
Albuquerque
Amarillo
OKLAHOMA

PACIFIC OCEAN
Phoenix
Biosphere 2
Tucson
El Paso
NEW MEXICO
Lubbock
Dall

TEXAS
Austin
San Antonio
Corpus Christ

MEXICO

RUSSIA
Nome
Fairbanks
ALASKA
Anchorage
N.W. TERR.
YUKON TERR.
Whitehorse

Bering Sea
Juneau
B.C.

Aleutian Islands

PACIFIC OCEAN

0   400 miles
0   400 km

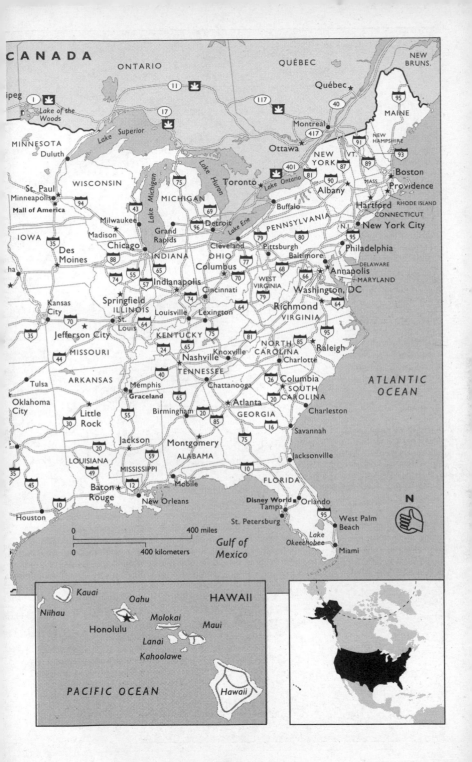

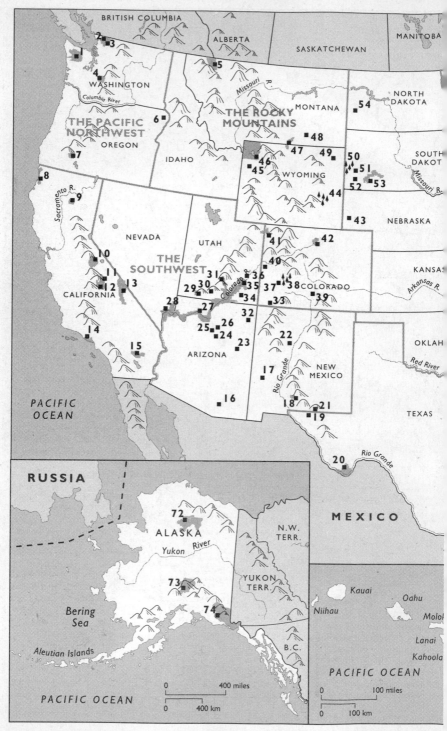

USA National Park System

National Monuments
Black Canyon, CO, 37
Canyon de Chelly, AZ, 32
Colorado, CO, 40
Devils Tower, WY, 49
Dinosaur, CO, 41
Gila Cliff Dwellings, NM, 17
Great Sand Dunes, CO, 39
Lassen Volcanic, CA, 9
Little Bighorn, MT, 48
Mt. Rushmore, SD, 51
Natural Bridges, UT, 34
Scotts Bluff, NE, 43
Sunset Crater Volcanic, AZ, 25
Walnut Canyon, AZ, 24
White Sands, NM, 18
Wupatki, AZ, 26
Petroglyph, NM, 22

National Parks
Acadia, ME, 71
Arches, UT, 36
Badlands, SD, 53
Big Bend, TX, 20
Bryce Canyon, UT, 30
Canyonlands, UT, 35
Capitol Reef, UT, 31
Carlsbad Caverns, NM, 21

Colonial, VA, 66
Crater Lake, OR, 7
Death Valley, CA, 13
Denali, AK, 73
Everglades, FL, 62
Gates of the Arctic, AK, 72
Glacier, MT, 5
Grand Canyon, AZ, 27
Grand Teton, WY, 45
Great Smoky Mts., TN, 63
Guadalupe Mts., TX, 19
Haleakala, HI, 75
Hot Springs, AR, 60
Isle Royale, MI, 57
Joshua Tree, CA, 15
Kings Canyon, CA, 11
Mammoth Cave, KY, 64
Mesa Verde, CO, 33
Mt. Rainier, WA, 4
New River Gorge, WV, 65
North Cascades, WA, 2
Olympic, WA, 1
Petrified Forest, AZ, 23
Redwood, CA, 8
Rocky Mt., CO, 42
Saguaro, AZ, 16
Sequoia, CA, 12
Shenandoah, VA, 67

Theodore Roosevelt, ND, 54
Voyageurs, MN, 56
Wind Cave, SD, 52
Wrangell-St. Elias, AK, 74
Yellowstone, WY, 46
Yosemite, CA, 10
Zion, UT, 29

National Recreation Areas
Bighorn Canyon, MT, 47
Hell's Canyon, OR, 6
Lake Mead, NV, 28
Ross Lake, WA, 3
Santa Monica Mts., CA, 14

National Forests
Allegheny, PA, 69
Black Hills, SD, 50
Chippewa, MN, 55
Grand Mesa, CO, 38
Manistee, MI, 58
Medicine Bow, WY, 44
Monongahela, WV, 68
Ozark, AR, 59
White Mts., NH, 70

National Seashores
Padre Island, TX, 61

How to Use This Book

The big disclaimer: this book does not contain everything there is to know about traveling in the USA. We went, we saw, we picked out the most helpful resources for travelers trying to see the U.S. on a tight budget, but we did not cover it all. Stray from our directions; see the sights between the places we mention—the U.S. is chock full of restaurants, inns, and roadside kitsch waiting to be found.

Let's Go: USA is divided into three parts. The first portion, **Essentials,** further splits in three. The chapter starts with information for planning a trip in the USA or Canada; this section includes details on necessary documents, entrance requirements, and exchange rates, a description of certain laws and customs, health and safety advice, packing tips, and travel advice addressed to the concerns of women, senior citizens, bisexuals, gays, and lesbians, disabled travelers, and older travelers. Information on getting to the USA and Canada, including listings for budget travel agencies, comes next. Finally, look for advice on getting around (including descriptions of charter flights, ticket consolidators, and couriers), finding a bed, exploring the outdoors, and keeping in touch once you've arrived.

The **United States,** the book's second part, begins with a short chapter on **American Culture** and history and continues for most of the pages to come. Thirteen chapters, named for geographic regions, make up the coverage of the 50 states. The regions run north to south and progress east to west in the following order: **New England, Mid-Atlantic, The South, Florida, Great Lakes, Great Plains, Texas, Rocky Mountains, The Southwest, The Pacific Northwest, California, Alaska,** and **Hawaii.** Within a chapter, the order of states advances toward the next region. Each state's text opens with the largest, or most accessible, destination and fans outward. Look in the index for an alphabetized list of the destinations covered in each state.

The third section of the book contains locations in **Canada** which travelers often include in trips to the U.S. or make excursions from the U.S. to visit. Following a description of **Canadian Culture** and history, coverage runs from east to west: **Nova Scotia, New Brunswick, Prince Edward Island, Québec, Ontario, Alberta, British Columbia,** and the **Yukon Territory.** Entries within the provinces generally move away from the American border.

We cap things off with an **appendix,** filled with the scoop on climate, electricity, weights and measures, distances between cities, and national holidays.

For all of the destinations in the USA and in Canada, we normally include **Accommodations, Camping, Food, Sights,** and **Entertainment.** Our **Practical Information** will help you get around, find help, and keep in touch; tourist offices provide further help and, often, free maps. **Near** sections include suggestions for daytrips.

If you intend to travel extensively in one area, consider buying one of our regional guides, *Let's Go: Alaska & the Pacific Northwest* and *Let's Go: California,* or one of our city guides, *Let's Go: New York City* and *Let's Go: Washington, D.C.* And now, without further ado ("raise the curtain, kids!"), we present to you the best guidebook ever written. Enjoy.

A NOTE TO OUR READERS

The information for this book is gathered by *Let's Go*'s researchers during the late spring and summer months. Each listing is derived from the assigned researcher's opinion based upon his or her visit at a particular time. The opinions are expressed in a candid and forthright manner. Other travelers might disagree. Those traveling at a different time may have different experiences since prices, dates, hours, and conditions are always subject to change. You are urged to check beforehand to avoid inconvenience and surprises. Travel always involves a certain degree of risk, especially in low-cost areas. When traveling, especially on a budget, always take particular care to ensure your safety.

ESSENTIALS

PLANNING YOUR TRIP

▓ When to Go

Going to the right place at the right time makes all the difference when traveling. In most of the U.S., **tourist season** is from **Memorial Day** to **Labor Day** (May 26 to Sept. 1 in 1997); expect things to be in full, camera-clicking swing. In the off-season, hotels might be cheaper and sights less crowded, but it's called the off-season for a reason—those sights you traveled so far to see might be closed. Also remember that on national holidays many sights will be closed. In general, tourist offices are great resources for travelers—call ahead for information on local festivals. For a **climate chart** and information on **national holidays,** see p. 904.

▓ Useful Information

GOVERNMENT INFORMATION OFFICES

General info for foreigners planning to travel to the U.S. is provided by the **United States Travel & Tourism Administration,** Department of Commerce, 14th St. and Constitution Ave. NW, Washington, D.C., 20230 (202-482-4003 or 202-482-3811). The USTTA has branches in Australia, Canada, and the United Kingdom; contact the Washington office for details on the branch in your country. Information on state tourism offices is listed in the state introductions below.

HITTING THE BOOKS

On the road, knowledge is power. The mail-order travel shops below offer books and supplies catering to special travel interests.

Adventurous Traveler Bookstore, P.O. Box 1468, Williston, VT 05495 (802-860-6776, fax 802-860-6607, or both at 800-282-3963; email books@atbook.com; http://www.gorp.com/atbook.htm). Free 40-page catalog upon request. Specializes in outdoor adventure travel books and maps for the U.S. and abroad. Their World Wide Web site offers extensive browsing opportunities.

Bon Voyage!, 2069 W. Bullard Ave., Fresno, CA 93711-1200 (800-995-9716; from abroad 209-447-8441, email 70754.3511@compuserve.com). Annual mail order catalog offers a range of products for everyone from the luxury traveler to the diehard trekker. Books, travel accessories, luggage, electrical converters, maps, videos, more. All merchandise may be returned for exchange or refund within 30 days of purchase, and prices are guaranteed. (Lower advertised prices will be matched and merchandise shipped free.)

Rand McNally, 150 S. Wacker Dr., Chicago, IL 60606 (800-333-0136), publishes one of the most comprehensive road atlases of the U.S. and Canada. Available in their stores throughout the country, and most other bookstores for $9.

Travel Books & Language Center, Inc., 4931 Cordell Ave., Bethesda, MD 20814 (800-220-2665; fax 301-951-8546; email travelbks@aol.com). Sells over 75,000 items, including books, cassettes, atlases, dictionaries, and a wide range of specialty travel maps, including wine and cheese maps of France, Michelin maps, and beer maps of the U.S. Free comprehensive catalog upon request.

On-line data services can be a gold mine for the prospective traveler looking to find general info on an area, book airline reservations, hunt for rental car bargains, or chat with people thousands of miles away. On the vast **Internet** computer network, all kinds of preparation is possible. Commercial services such as **America Online, CompuServe,** and **Prodigy** offer both internet access and their own resources. To become a part of the information highway, pick up a computer magazine and find an advertisement which offers instructions on how to join the rapidly expanding masses in cyberspace.

While navigating the Net is not extraordinarily difficult, the system's overwhelming size can make trying to find useful information troublesome. If you have **World Wide Web (WWW)** access, try one of the Web's search engines, such as **Webcrawler** (http://webcrawler.com), or **Yahoo** (http://www.yahoo.com/Entertainment/ Travel); type in one or more keywords (e.g. "Boston travel"), and the engine will generate a list of information headings. The **Student and Budget Travel Resource Guide** is among the most helpful Web pages; it has links to the CIA world factbook, consular information sheets, state travel advisories, Amtrak train schedules, the Internet Guide to Hostelling, a subway navigator, a jet lag diet, and more (http:// asa.ugl.lib.umich.edu/chdocs/travel/travel-guide.html, or send e-mail to travel-guide@umich.edu). **City_Net** gives information on a wide array of cities and regions (http://www.city.net). Try **newsgroups** and **mailing lists** if you're really in the mood to browse; unfortunately, their "signal-to-noise ratio" (the percentage of useful information) is often depressingly low. **IRC** (Internet Relay Chat) allows real-time typed conversation with users around the world; from most UNIX systems, type "irc" and then "/help newuser."

■ Documents and Formalities

PASSPORTS

Be sure to file all applications several months in advance of your planned departure date. Remember, you are relying on government agencies to complete these transactions. A backlog in processing can spoil your plans. *Before you leave* be sure to photocopy the page of your passport that contains your photograph and identifying information, especially your passport number; this will help prove your citizenship and facilitate the issuing of a new passport if your old one is **lost** or **stolen.** Carry this photocopy in a safe place apart from your passport, and leave another copy at home. Consulates recommend that you also carry an expired passport or an official copy of your birth certificate. If you do lose your passport, notify the local police and the nearest embassy or consulate of your home government *immediately.* If you have the information that was on your passport, identification, and proof of citizenship, some consulates can issue a new passport within two days; of course, it may take weeks. In an emergency, ask for immediate temporary traveling papers which will permit you to return to your home country. Remember: your passport is a public document that belongs to your nation's government; you may have to surrender it to a foreign government official. If you don't get it back in a reasonable amount of time, inform the nearest embassy or consulate of your home country.

> **U.S. and Canadian citizens** may cross the U.S.-Canada border with only proof of citizenship (e.g. a birth certificate or a voter's registration card along with a photo ID; a driver's license alone will not be enough). U.S. citizens under 18 need the written consent of a parent or guardian; Canadian citizens under 16 need notarized permission from both parents.
>
> **British citizens** can apply in person or by mail to a passport office for a full passport, which is valid for 10 years. The fee is UK£18. Children under 16 may be included on a parent's passport. Processing by mail usually takes four to six weeks. The London office offers same-day, walk-in rush service; arrive early.
>
> **Irish citizens** can apply for a passport by mail to either the Department of Foreign Affairs, Passport Office, Setanta Centre, Molesworth St., Dublin 2 (01 671 16 33), or the Passport Office, 1A South Mall, Cork (021 627 25 25). Obtain an application at a local Garda station or request one from a passport office. The new Passport

Express Service offers a two week turn-around and is available for an extra IR£3. Passports cost IR£45 and are valid for 10 years. Citizens under 18 or over 65 can request a three-year passport that costs IR£10.

Australian citizens must apply for a passport in person at either a post office, a passport office, or an Australian diplomatic mission. An appointment may be necessary. A parent may file an application for a child who is under 18 and unmarried. Application fees are frequently adjusted. For more info, call toll-free (in Australia) 13 12 32.

New Zealand citizens can obtain passport application forms from travel agents or the Department of Internal Affairs Link Centre. Completed applications may be lodged at Link Centres and at overseas posts, or forwarded to the Passport Office, PO Box 10-526, Wellington, New Zealand. Processing time is 10 working days from receipt of a correctly completed application. The application fee for an adult passport is NZ$80 in New Zealand, and NZ$130 overseas. An urgent passport service is also available.

South African citizens can apply for a passport at any Home Affairs Office. Two photos, either a birth certificate or an identity book, and a $12 fee must accompany a completed application. Passports are valid for 10 years.

U.S. AND CANADIAN ENTRANCE REQUIREMENTS

Foreign visitors to the United States and Canada are required to have a **passport** and **visa/proof of intent to leave.** To visit Canada, you must be healthy and law-abiding, and demonstrate the ability to support yourself financially during your stay. A visa, stamped into a traveler's passport by the government of a host country, allows the bearer to stay in that country for a specified purpose and period of time. To obtain a U.S. visa, contact the nearest U.S. embassy or consulate.

United States Travelers from certain nations may enter the U.S. without a visa through the **Visa Waiver Pilot Program.** Visitors qualify as long as they are traveling for business or pleasure, are staying for 90 days or less, have proof of intent to leave (e.g., a returning plane ticket), a completed I-94W, and enter aboard particular air or sea carriers. Participating countries are Andorra, Austria, Belgium, Brunei, Denmark, Finland, France, Germany, Iceland, Italy, Japan, Liechtenstein, Luxembourg, Monaco, the Netherlands, New Zealand, Norway, San Marino, Spain, Sweden, Switzerland, and the UK. Contact a U.S. consulate for more info; countries are added frequently.

Most visitors obtain a **B-2,** or "pleasure tourist," visa, usually valid for six months. Don't lose your visa. If you do lose your I-94 form (arrival/departure certificate attached to your visa upon arrival), you can replace it at the nearest **U.S. Immigration and Naturalization Service** office, though it's very unlikely that the form will be replaced within the time of your stay. **Extensions** for visas vary; there are approximately 25 sub-categories available. For more info, look up the Federal Government Dept. of Justice, INS in the Blue Pages. The **Center for International Business and Travel (CIBT),** 25 W. 43rd St., Ste. 1420, New York, NY 10036 (800-925-2428), secures travel visas to and from all possible countries.

Canada Citizens of Australia, Ireland, Mexico, New Zealand, the U.K., and the U.S., may enter Canada without visas, as long as they plan to stay for 90 days or less and carry proof of intent to leave. South Africans do need a visa to enter Canada. Citizens of all other countries should contact their Canadian consulate for more information

EMBASSIES AND CONSULATES

Contact your nearest embassy or consulate to obtain information regarding visas and passports to the United States and Canada.

U.S. Embassies and Consulates

Embassies in Canada, 100 Wellington St., Ottawa, Ontario K1P 5T1 (613-238-5335)
United Kingdom, 24 Grosvenor Sq., London W1A 1AE (011 44 171 499 9000)

Ireland, 42 Elgin Rd., Ballsbridge, Dublin 4 (011 353 1 668 7122)

Australia, Moonah Place, Canberra, ACT 2600 (011 61 6 270 5000)

New Zealand, 29 Fitzherbert Terr., Thorndon, Wellington (011 64 4 472 2068)

South Africa, 225 Pretorius St., PO Box 9536, Pretoria (011 27 12 342 1048)

Consulates in Canada, 1155 Saint Alexandre St., Montreal, Quebec, PO Box 65 Station Desjardins, H5Z 1Z1 (514-398-9695)

United Kingdom, Queen's House, 14 Queen St., BT1 6EQ, Belfast, N. Ireland (011 44 23 232 8239)

Australia, MLC Centre, 19-29 Martin Place, 59th Fl., Sydney NSW 2000 (011 612 373 9200)

New Zealand, 4th Fl., Yorkshire General Bldg., corner of Shortland and O'Connell St., PO Box 42022 Auckland 1 (011 64 9 303 2724)

South Africa, PO Box 6773, Roggebaai 8012 (011 27 21 25 4151)

Canadian Embassies and Consulates

Embassies in United States, 501 Pennsylvania Ave., Washington, D.C. 20001 (202-682-1740)

United Kingdom, McDonald House, 38 Grosvenor Square, W1X 0AA (011 44 71 258 6600)

Ireland, Canada House, 65 St. Stephen's Green, Dublin 2 (011 353 14 78 19 88)

Australia, Commonwealth Ave., Canberra ACT 2600 (011 61 6 273 3844)

New Zealand, 61 Molesworth St., Thorndon, Wellington (011 64 4 473 9577)

South Africa, 5th Floor, Nedbank Plaza, Corner of Church and Beatrix St., Arcadia, Pretoria 0083 (011 27 12 324 3970)

Consulates in Australia, Level 5 Quay West, 111 Harrington St., Sydney NSW, 2000 (011 612 364-3000)

New Zealand, Princes Court, 2 Princes St., Auckland (011 54 9 309 3690)

CUSTOMS: ENTERING

United States Passing customs should be routine, but take it seriously; don't joke around with customs officials or airport security personnel. It is illegal to transport perishable food like fruit and nuts, which may carry pests. Officials may seize articles made from certain protected species, so be ready to part with your illegally purchased cowboy boots or fur coat. For more information on carrying prescription drugs, see Health, p. 14.

You may bring the following into the U.S.: $200 in gifts; 200 cigarettes (1 carton) or 100 cigars; and personal belongings such as clothes and jewelry. Travelers ages 21 and over may also bring up to one liter of alcohol, although state laws may further restrict the amount of alcohol you can carry. Money (cash or traveler's checks) can be transported, but amounts over $10,000 must be reported. Customs officers may ask how much money you're carrying and your planned departure date in order to ensure that you'll be able to support yourself while in the U.S.

The **U.S. Customs Service,** 1301 Constitution Ave., Washington, D.C. 20229 (202-927-5580), publishes a helpful brochure entitled, *Know Before You Go*. It details everything the international traveler needs to know about customs requirements.

Canada Besides items of a personal nature that you plan to use in Canada during your visit, the following items may be brought in free of duty: up to 1.14L of alcohol or a 24-pack of beer (as long you are of age in the province you are visiting), 50 cigars, 200 cigarettes (1 carton), 1kg of manufactured tobacco, and gifts valued less than CDN$60. As in the U.S., if you exceed the limited amounts, you will be asked to pay a fine. For detailed info on Canadian customs and booklets on other Canadian travel information, write Revenue Canada, Customs, Excise and Taxation, Communication Branch, Ottawa, Ont., Canada K1A 0L5 (613-954-7125; fax 957-9039).

CUSTOMS: GOING HOME

Upon returning home, you must declare all articles you acquired abroad and must pay a duty on the value of those articles that exceed the allowance established by

The World At a Discount

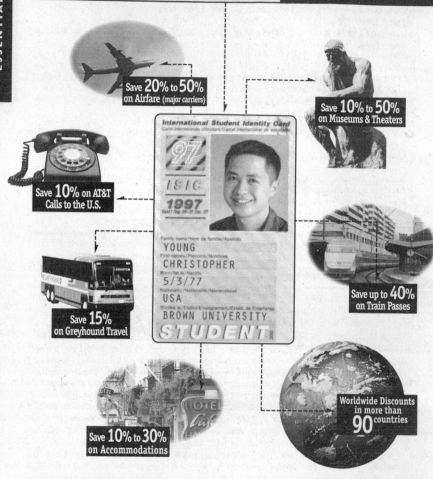

Save **20%** to **50%** on Airfare (major carriers)

Save **10%** to **50%** on Museums & Theaters

Save **10%** on AT&T Calls to the U.S.

Save **15%** on Greyhound Travel

Save up to **40%** on Train Passes

Save **10%** to **30%** on Accommodations

Worldwide Discounts in more than **90** countries

The International Student Identity Card
Your Passport to Discounts & Benefits

With the ISIC, you'll receive discounts on airfare, hotels, transportation, computer services, foreign currency exchange, phone calls, major attractions, and more. You'll also receive basic accident and sickness insurance coverage when traveling outside the U.S. and access to a 24-hour, toll-free Help Line. Call now to locate the issuing office nearest you (over 555 across the U.S.) at:

Free 40-page handbook with each card!

1-888-COUNCIL (toll-free)

For an application and complete discount list, you can also visit us at **http://www.ciee.org/**

Council

CIEE: Council on International Educational Exchange

your country's customs service. Goods and gifts purchased at duty-free shops abroad are not exempt from duty or sales tax at your point of return; you must declare these items, as well. "Duty-free" merely means that you need not pay a tax in the country of purchase. Each country allows the importation of specific amounts of alcohol, tobacco, gifts, and cash, but the quantities vary per country.

British Citizens: Her Majesty's Customs and Excise, Custom House, Nettleton Road, Heathrow Airport, Hounslow, Middlesex TW6 2LA (011 01 81 910 3744; fax 910 3765).

Irish Citizens: The Revenue Commissioners, Dublin Castle (011 01 679 27 77; fax 671 20 21; e-mail taxes@ior.ie; WWW http:ttwww.revenue.ie) or The Collector of Customs and Excise, The Custom House, Dublin 1.

Australian Citizens: Australian Customs Service, GPO Box 8, Sydney NSW 2001 (02 213 2000; fax 213 4000).

New Zealand Citizens: Consult the New Zealand Customs Guide for Travelers, available from customs offices, or contact New Zealand Customs, 50 Anzac Ave., Box 29, Auckland (011 09 377 35 20; fax 309 29 78).

South African Citizens: Commissioner for Customs and Excise, Private Bag X47, Pretoria 0001, distributes the pamphlet *South African Customs Information,* for visitors and residents who travel abroad. South Africans residing in the U.S. should contact the Embassy of South Africa, 3051 Massachusetts Ave., NW, Washington, D.C. 20008 (202-232-4400; fax 202-244-9417).

YOUTH, STUDENT, & TEACHER IDENTIFICATION

Many U.S. establishments will honor an ordinary university student ID for student discounts. Still, two main forms of student and youth identification are extremely useful, especially for the insurance packages that accompany them.

International Student Identity Card (ISIC). The 1997 card is valid from Sept. 1996-Dec. 1997 and costs $18. Flashing this card can procure you discounts for sights, theaters, museums, accommodations, train, ferry, and airplane travel, and other services. Present the card wherever you go, and ask about discounts even when none are advertised. Applicants must be at least 12 years old and degree-seeking students of a secondary or post-secondary school. Because of the proliferation of phony ISICs, many airlines and some other services require other proof of student identity: a signed letter from the registrar attesting to your student status and stamped with the school seal and/or your school ID card. The card provides accident insurance of up to $3000 with no daily limit, as well as $100 per day of in-hospital care for up to 60 days. In addition, cardholders have access to a toll-free **Traveler's Assistance Hotline** (800-626-2427 in U.S. and Canada, elsewhere call collect 713-267-2525) whose multilingual staff can provide help in medical, legal, and financial emergencies overseas. When you apply for the card, ask for a copy of the *International Student Identity Card Handbook,* which lists some available discounts. Most of the Budget Travel Agencies listed below issue the ISIC. The **International Teacher Identity Card (ITIC)** is $19 and offers similar but limited discounts, as well as medical insurance coverage. For more info on these handy cards consult the organization's new web site (http:\\www.istc.org).

International Youth Discount Travel Card or **GO25 Card** is issued by the **Federation of International Youth Travel Organizations (FIYTO),** Bredgade 25H, 1260, Copenhagen K, Denmark, (45 33 33 96 00; fax 45 33 93 96 76). Issues a discount card to travelers who are under 26 but not students. This 1-year card offers many of the same benefits as the ISIC, and most organizations that sell the ISIC also sell the GO25 card. A brochure that lists discounts is free when you purchase the card. US$10, CDN$15, UK£5 (without travel insurance), US$16 (with insurance); prices subject to change.

INTERNATIONAL DRIVING PERMIT

Although not required in the U.S. or Canada, the International Driving Permit (IDP) can smooth out difficulties with American and Canadian police officers and serves as an additional piece of identification. A valid driver's license from your home country must always accompany the IDP. Your IDP must be issued in your own country before you depart; check with your national automobile association. Some foreign driver's licenses are valid in the U.S. for up to one year; check before you leave.

■ Money Matters

If you stay in hostels and prepare your own food, expect to spend anywhere from $10-60 per person per day, depending on the local cost of living and your needs. Transportation will increase these figures. No matter how low your budget, if you plan to travel for more than a couple of days, you will need to keep handy a larger amount of cash than usual. Carrying it around with you, even in a money belt, is risky and personal checks from home will probably not be accepted no matter how many forms of identification you have (even some banks shy away from accepting checks).

Many Canadian shops, as well as vending machines and parking meters, accept U.S. coins at face value (which is a small loss for you). Many stores will even convert the price of your purchase for you, but they are under no legal obligation to offer you a fair exchange. During the past several years, the Canadian dollar has been worth roughly 20% less than the U.S. dollar. All prices in the Canada section of this book are listed in Canadian dollars unless otherwise noted.

CURRENCY AND EXCHANGE

Note: the following advice applies to Canada as well. You'll get better rates exchanging for U.S. dollars in the U.S. than at home, and wholesale rates offered at banks will be lower than those offered by other exchange agencies. However, converting some money before you go will allow you to zip through the airport while others languish in exchange lines. It's a good idea to bring enough foreign currency to last for the first 24-72 hours of a trip, depending on the day of the week you will be

arriving. If you are planning to visit a little-touristed area, where bank tellers may not recognize or be willing to exchange foreign currencies, carry U.S. dollars from early on. Most international airports in the U.S. have currency exchange booths.

The Greenback (the U.S. dollar)

CDN$1 = US$.73	US$1= CDN$1.37
UK£1 = US$1.55	US$1 = UK£0.64
IR£1 = US$1.61	US$1 = IR£0.62
AUS$1 = US$0.78	US$1 = AUS$1.29
NZ$1 = US$0.68	US$1 = NZ$1.46

The main unit of currency in the U.S. is the **dollar;** the dollar is divided into 100 cents. The color of paper money is green in the U.S; bills come in denominations of $1, $5, $10, $20, $50, and $100. The U.S. has 1¢ (penny), 5¢ (nickel), 10¢ (dime), and 25¢ (quarter) coins.

The Loony (The Canadian Dollar)

US$1 = CDN$1.37	CDN$1 = US$0.73
UK£1 = CDN$2.10	CDN$1 = UK£0.48
IR£1 = CDN$2.15	CDN$1 = IR£0.46
AUS$1 = CDN$1.08	CDN$1 = AUS$0.93
NZ$1 = CDN$0.92	CDN$1 = NZ$1.09

The main unit of currency in Canada is the **dollar,** which is identical to the U.S. dollar in name only. You will need to exchange money when you go over the border, although in many places you may use American currency. Paper money comes in denominations of $2, $5, $10, $20, $50, and $100, which are all the same size but color-coded by denomination. Coins come in denominations of 1¢, 5¢, 10¢, 25¢, and $1. Many years ago, the Canadian government phased out the $1 bill and replaced it with a $1 coin, known as the **loony** for the loon which graces its reverse.

TRAVELER'S CHECKS

Traveler's checks are one of the safest and least troublesome means of carrying funds. Several agencies and many banks sell them, usually for face value plus a 1% commission. (Members of the American Automobile Association can get American Express checks commission-free through AAA.) Keep in mind that in small towns, traveler's checks are less readily accepted than in cities with large tourist industries. Nonetheless, there will probably be at least one place in every town where you can exchange them for local currency. If you're ordering your checks, do so well in advance, especially if large sums are being requested.

Each agency provides refunds if your checks are lost or stolen, and many provide additional services. (You may need a police report verifying the loss or theft.) Inquire about toll-free refund hotlines (in the countries you're visiting), emergency message relay services, and stolen credit card assistance when you purchase your checks.

Always keep your check receipts separate from your checks and store them in a safe place or with a traveling companion; record check numbers when you cash them and leave a list of check numbers with someone at home; and ask for a list of refund centers when you buy your checks. Keep a separate supply of cash or traveler's checks for emergencies. Be sure never to countersign your checks until you're prepared to cash them. And always be sure to bring your passport with you when you plan to use the checks.

American Express: Call 800-221-7282 in the U.S. and Canada, in the U.K. 011 0800 52 13 13, in New Zealand 011 0800 44 10 68, in Australia 011 008 25 19 02). Elsewhere, call U.S. collect 801-964-6665. American Express traveler's cheques are now available in 11 currencies including Australian, British, Canadian, and U.S. They are the most widely recognized worldwide and the easiest to replace if lost or

stolen. Checks can be purchased for a small fee at American Express Travel Service offices, banks, and American Automobile Association offices. Cardmembers can also purchase cheques at American Express Dispensers at Travel Service Offices at airports, by ordering them via phone (800-ORDER-TC (673-3782)), and through America OnLine. American Express offices cash their cheques commission-free, although they often offer slightly worse rates than banks. You can also buy *Cheques for Two* which can be signed by either of two people travelling together.

Citicorp: Call 800-645-6556 in the U.S. and Canada; in the U.K. 01144 181 297 4781; from elsewhere call U.S. collect 813-623-1709. Sells both Citicorp and Citicorp Visa traveler's checks in Australian, Canadian, U.S., and British currency. Commission is 1-2% on check purchases. Checkholders are automatically enrolled for 45 days in the Travel Assist Program (hotline 800-250-4377 or collect 202-296-8728) which provides travelers with English-speaking doctor, lawyer, and interpreter referrals as well as check refund assistance and general travel information. Citicorp's World Courier Service guarantees hand-delivery of traveler's checks when a refund location is not convenient. Call 24 hr. a day, seven days a week.

Thomas Cook MasterCard: Call 800-223-9920 in the U.S. and Canada; elsewhere call U.S. collect 609-987-7300; from the U.K. call 011 0800 622 101 free or 011 1733 502 995 collect or 011 44 1733 318 950 collect. Offers checks in U.S., Canadian, and Australian dollars, British pounds, and ECUs. Commission 1-2% for purchases. Try buying the checks at a Thomas Cook office for potentially lower commissions. If you cash your checks at a Thomas Cook Office they will not charge you commission.

CREDIT CARDS

Credit cards are not accepted at many small, cheap locations where traveler's checks are welcomed, and pricey establishments which cheerfully accept them can quickly deplete your account. Still, credit cards can be invaluable in the U.S., and are sometimes expected or required (for example, at many car rental agencies). Credit cards are also useful when an emergency, such as necessary car repairs, leaves you temporarily without other resources. In addition, some cards carry services for users, which range from personal or car rental insurance to emergency assistance. Major credit cards can be used to instantly extract cash advances from associated banks and ATM machines; this can be a great bargain for foreign travelers because credit card companies get the wholesale exchange rate, which is generally 5% better than the retail rate used by banks. However, you will be charged ruinous interest rates if you don't pay off the bill quickly, so be careful when using this service.

MasterCard (outside North America, "EuroCard" or "Access") and **Visa** (or "Barclaycard") are the most widely accepted. Both sell credit cards through banks. For lost or stolen cards: Visa, (800-336-8472); Mastercard, (800-999-0454).

American Express cards also work in some ATMs, as well as at AmEx offices and major airports. This card has a hefty annual fee ($55), unless you are a student, in which case you have the option of obtaining the free Optima card. Both of these American Express cards offer extensive travel-related services. For a lost or stolen card, call (800-CASH-NOW/528-4800).

ATM CARDS

There are tens of thousands of ATMs (automatic teller machines) everywhere in the U.S., offering 24-hr. service in banks, airports, grocery stores, gas stations, etc. ATMs allow you to withdraw cash from your bank account wherever you are, and happily get the same wholesale exchange rate as credit cards. Two major ATM networks in the U.S. are **Mastercard/Cirrus** (800-4-CIRRUS/424-7787) and **PLUS** (800-843-7587). Inquire at your bank about fees charged for ATM transactions.

MONEY FROM HOME

If you run out of money on the road, you can have more mailed to you in the form of traveler's checks bought in your name, a certified check, or through postal money orders. Certified checks are redeemable at any bank, while postal money orders can be cashed at post offices upon display of two IDs (one of which must be a photo ID). Keep receipts, since money orders are refundable if lost. **Personal checks** from home will probably not be acceptable no matter how many forms of identification you have.

Wiring money can cost from around $15 (for domestic service) to $35 (international), depending on the bank, plus there will be a fee ($7-15) for receiving the money. Once you've found a bank that will accept a wire, write or telegram your home bank with your account number, the name and address of the bank to receive the wire, and a routing number. Also notify the bank of the form of ID that the second bank should accept before paying the money. As a very last resort, consulates will wire home for you and deduct the cost from the money you receive.

Western Union (800-225-5227) is a well-known and expensive service that can be used to cable money with your Visa or MasterCard within the domestic United States. You or someone else can phone in a credit card number or bring cash to a Western Union office for pick-up at another Western Union location. The rates for sending cash are generally $10 cheaper than with a credit card. Rates to send cash from a local office are $29 to send $250, $40 to send $500, and $50 to send $1000. You will need ID to pick up the money.

American Express is one of the easiest ways to get money from home. AmEx allows green card holders to draw cash from their checking accounts at any of its major offices and many of its representatives' offices, up to $1000 every 21 days (no service charge, no interest). AmEx also offers Express Cash, with over 100,000 ATMs located in airports, hotels, banks, office complexes, and shopping areas around the world. Express Cash withdrawals are automatically debited from the Cardmember's specified bank account or line of credit. Green card holders may withdraw up to $1000 in a seven day period. There is a 2% transaction fee for each cash withdrawal with a $2.50 minimum. To enroll in Express Cash, Cardmembers

may call 1-800-227-4669. Outside the U.S. call collect (904) 565-7875. Unless using the AmEx service, avoid cashing checks in foreign currencies; they usually take weeks and a $30 fee to clear.

TAXES

The U.S. **sales tax** is the equivalent of the European Value-Added Tax. Expect to pay 4-10% depending on the item and the place; in most states, groceries are not taxed. *Let's Go* lists sales tax rates in the introduction to each state.

Prices tend to be higher in Canada than in the U.S., as are taxes; you'll quickly notice the 7% **goods and services tax (GST)** and an additional **sales tax** in some provinces. See the provinces' introductions for info on local taxes. Visitors can claim a rebate of the GST they pay on accommodations of less than one month and on most goods they buy and take home, so be sure to save your receipts and pick up a GST rebate form while in Canada. The total claim must be at least CDN$7 of GST (equal to $100 in purchases) and must be made within one year of the date on which you purchased the goods and/or accommodations for which you are claiming your rebate; further goods must be exported from Canada within 60 days of purchase. A brochure detailing restrictions is available from local tourist offices or through **Revenue Canada, Customs, Excise, and Taxation, Visitor's Rebate Program,** 275 Pope Rd., Summerside, Prince Edward Island, Canada C1N 6C6 (800-668-4748 in Canada, 613-991-3346 outside Canada).

TIPPING AND BARGAINING

In the U.S., it is customary to **tip** waitstaff and cab drivers 15%. Tip more for unusually good service, less for unusually bad. At the airport, try to carry your own bags; porters expect a customary $1 per bag tip. Tipping is less compulsory in Canada, and a good tip signifies remarkable service. **Bargaining** is generally frowned upon and fruitless in the U.S. and in Canada.

■ Safety and Security

STREET SMARTS

Trust your instincts. The gawking camera-toter is a more obvious target than the low-profile local look-alike. Look like you know what you are doing and where you are going, even if you don't. Do not keep money or anything precious in your back pocket or a fanny pack; use a neck pouch or money belt instead. Always keep an eye on your belongings; on trains and buses, put a leg through the straps of your bag if you can. Walking directly into a cafe or shop to check you map beats checking it on a street corner, however, look over your map before leaving the hotel room so that you can act as if you know where you are going. Muggings are more often impromptu than planned. Walking with nervous, over-the-shoulder glances can be a tip that you have something valuable to protect. Be aware of your surroundings; in cities, a single block can separate safe and unsafe areas. Do not respond or make eye contact with people who harass you.

In most places in the U.S. and Canada, **call 911 for emergency medical help, police, or fire** toll-free (you don't have to put a coin in the pay phone). In some rural areas, the 911 system has not yet been introduced; if 911 doesn't work, dial the **operator (0),** who will contact the appropriate emergency service. For official **United States Department of State** travel advisories on the U.S. and/or Canada, including crime and security, call their 24 hr. hotline at 202-647-5225. To order publications, including a pamphlet entitled *A Safe Trip Abroad,* write them at Superintendent of Documents, U.S. Government Printing Office, Washington, D.C. 20402, or call 202-783-3238.

ALCOHOL AND DRUGS

You must be 21 to drink in the U.S. Even foreigners accustomed to observing no drinking age *will be carded* and will not be served without proper ID (preferably some government document; a driver's license suffices, but a passport is best). **In Canada, you must be 19,** except in Alberta, Manitoba, and Quebec, where you must be 18. Some areas of the United States are "dry," meaning they do not permit the sale of alcohol at all, while other places do not allow it to be sold on Sundays. The possession or sale of marijuana, cocaine, LSD, and most opiates are serious crimes in the U.S. and Canada.

■ Health

BEFORE YOU GO

A compact **first-aid kit** should suffice for minor problems on the road. The following items are useful in many situations: multi-sized bandages, aspirin or other pain killers, antibiotic cream, a thermometer, a Swiss Army knife with tweezers, moleskin, a decongestant for colds, motion sickness remedy, medicine for diarrhea or stomach problems, sunscreen, insect repellent, and burn ointment.

In your **passport** or other document, write the names of any people you wish to be contacted in case of a medical emergency and list any allergies or medical conditions of which doctors should be aware. Bring any **medication** you regularly take and may need while traveling, as well as a copy of the **prescription** and a statement of any pre-existing medical conditions, especially if you will be bringing insulin, syringes, or any narcotics into the U.S. or Canada. It is always a good idea to get a **check-up** before traveling, especially if you will be abroad for more than a month or two, or if you will be hiking, camping, or visiting rural or unindustrialized regions. Allergy sufferers

should find out if their conditions are likely to be aggravated in the regions they plan to visit, and obtain a full supply of any necessary medication before the trip, since matching a prescription to a foreign equivalent is not always easy, safe, or possible. If you wear **glasses** or **contact lenses,** carry an extra prescription and arrange to have your doctor or a family member send a replacement pair in an emergency. If you wear contacts, be sure to carry a pair of glasses in case your eyes are tired or you lose a lens. The following organizations have helpful medical information:

American Diabetes Association, 1600 Duke St., Alexandria, VA 22314 (800-232-3472). Call or write to receive a copy of *Travel and Diabetes.*

American Red Cross, 285 Columbus Ave., Boston, MA 02116-5114 (800-564-1234). Call to purchase the Red Cross's invaluable First-Aid and Safety Handbook ($15). The American Red Cross also offers many well-taught and inexpensive first-aid and CPR courses.

Global Emergency Medical Services (GEMS), 2001 Westside Dr., Ste. 120, Alpharetta, GA 30201 (800-860-1111; fax 770-475-0058). Subscribers have immediate 24-hr. access to an emergency room registered nurse with on-line access to your personal medical history, your primary physician, and a worldwide network of English-speaking medical providers.

International Association for Medical Assistance to Travelers (IAMAT) offers a membership ID card, and a directory of doctors who treat members for a set fee schedule. Membership is free, though donations are appreciated and used for further research. In the **U.S.,** 417 Center St., Lewiston, NY 14092 (716-754-4883; fax 519-836-3412; e-mail iamat@sentex.net; http://www.sentex.net/iamat). In Canada, 40 Regal Road, Guelph, Ontario, N1K 1B5 (519-836-0102) or 1287 St. Clair Avenue West, Toronto, M6E 1B8 (416-652-0137; fax 519-836-3412).

Medic Alert Foundation, 2323 Colorado Ave., Turlock, CA, 95382 (24-hr. hotline 800-432-5378). For travelers with medical conditions that cannot be easily recognized (diabetes, epilepsy, heart conditions, allergies to antibiotics, etc.). Membership provides the internationally recognized Medic Alert Identification Tag and an annually updated wallet card. Lifetime membership is $35 the first year, and $15 annually thereafter.

ON-THE-ROAD AILMENTS

Always eat well, drink lots of fluids, and get enough sleep. Keep some power chow handy, like trail mix, granola bars, bananas, or candy bars. About 95% of headaches are caused by dehydration—drink even if you're not thirsty. Pure water is best. Many travelers experience fatigue, discomfort, or mild diarrhea upon arriving in a new area; unless symptoms are severe, allow time for your body to adjust before becoming worried. Travelers in high-altitude areas should expect some drowsiness and wait to adjust to the lower atmospheric oxygen levels before engaging in any strenuous activity; also, alcoholic beverages will have heightened effects. Of course, many real health problems are common on the road. If you suffer from any of these ailments in a severe form, seek medical help as soon as possible:

Diarrhea: Traveler's diarrhea is common. The illness can last from three to seven days, and symptoms include diarrhea, nausea, bloating, urgency, and malaise. The most dangerous side effect of any diarrhea is dehydration; a simple and effective anti-dehydration formula is 8oz. of water with a ½ tsp. of sugar or honey and a pinch of salt taken several times daily. Also good are soft drinks without caffeine, and salted crackers. Down several of these remedies a day, rest, and wait for the disease to run its course. If you develop a fever or your symptoms don't go away after four or five days, consult a doctor.

Frostbite: Skin affected by frostbite turns white, then waxy and cold. Victims should drink warm beverages, stay or get dry, and *gently and slowly* warm the frostbitten area with dry fabric or, better, with steady body contact. *Never rub frostbite;* the skin is easily damaged when frozen.

Giardia: Found in many rivers and lakes, giardia is a bacteria which causes gas, painful cramps, loss of appetite, and violent diarrhea; it can stay in your system for

FOR LESS THAN THE PRICE OF THIS BOOK, YOU COULD BE STAYING HERE.

For just $14-16 you could wake up in a National Park overlooking the San Francisco Bay and Golden Gate Bridge. Or stay in the heart of downtown San Francisco just a block from the big city excitement of Union Square. And for even less per night choose one of the other spectacular hostels in Northern California. Spend a night at a hostel and share experiences with travelers from around the world! For reservations call:

Pigeon Point Lighthouse. 415/879-0633		Hidden Villa Ranch 415/949-8648
San Francisco - Fisherman's Wharf 415/771-7277		Marin Headlands 415/331-2777
San Francisco Downtown 415/788-5604		Redwood National Park 707/482-8265
Point Montara Lighthouse 415/728-7177		Sacramento 916/443-1691
Point Reyes National Seashore . . .415/663-8811		

HOSTELLING INTERNATIONAL

The new seal of approval of the International Youth Hostel Federation.

HOSTELLING
INTERNATIONAL ®

weeks. To protect yourself, bring your water to a rolling boil, or purify it with iodine tablets before drinking or cooking with it.

Insects: While insects can be annoying, they are rarely deadly. Wear long pants and long sleeves and buy a bednet for camping. Use insect repellents; DEET can be bought in spray or liquid form, but use it sparingly, especially on children. Soak or spray your gear with permethrin, which is licensed in the U.S. for use on clothing. Calamine lotion or topical cortisones may stop insect bites from itching, as can a bath with a half-cup of baking soda or oatmeal.

Heatstroke: In the early stages of heatstroke, sweating stops, body temperature rises, and an intense headache develops, which if untreated can be followed by mental confusion and, eventually, ultimately, death. Cool the victim off immediately with fruit juice or salted water, wet towels, and shade. In the desert, the body loses 1-2 gallons of water per day, so keep on drinking. Whether you're driving or hiking, *tote two gallons of water per person per day.*

Hypothermia: Hypothermia results from exposure to cold and can occur even in the middle of the summer, especially in rainy or windy conditions or at night. The signs are easy to detect: body temperature drops rapidly, resulting in the failure to produce body heat; you may shiver, have poor coordination, feel exhausted, or have slurred speech, sleepiness, hallucinations, or amnesia. *Do not let victims of advanced hypothermia fall asleep*—their body temperatures will drop further, and if they lose consciousness they may die. To avoid hypothermia, keep dry and out of the wind. Wool keeps insulating even when wet.

Poison Ivy, Poison Oak, Poison Sumac: These three-leafed plants secrete oils that can cause unbearable itchiness, hives, and sometimes inflammation of the infected areas. If you think you have come into contact with one of these plants, wash your skin in cold water and soap (heat dilates the pores, driving the poison deeper). If rashes occur, calamine lotion, topical cortisone, or antihistamines may stop the itching. *Never scratch the affected area;* this will only spread the oil to other locations. Some people have allergic reactions that cause serious asthma-like symptoms; find medical help if this occurs.

Rabies: If you are bitten by any animal, clean your wound thoroughly and seek medical help. Although the danger of rabies is greater in rural areas, the threat exists in the city as well.

Sunburn: Carry sunscreen with you and apply it liberally and often. Sunscreens of SPF (sun protection factor) 20 are strong enough for the fairest skin; higher ratings generally won't help and are more expensive. If you do get sunburned, drinking more fluids than usual will cool you down and help your skin recover faster.

Ticks/Lyme Disease: Tick-borne diseases, such as Lyme disease, are problems for hikers in the U.S., especially (but not only) on the East Coast. Lyme is characterized by a circular rash of 2 inches or more which looks like a bull's-eye. Other symptoms are flu-like: fever, headache, fatigue, or aches and pains. Untreated, Lyme disease can lead to heart, joint, nervous system problems, or even death. There is no vaccine, but Lyme can be treated with antibiotics if caught early. Removing a tick within 24 hr. greatly reduces the risk of infection. If you find a tick, grasp the tick's head parts with tweezers as close to your skin as possible and apply slow, steady traction. Do not attempt to get ticks out of your skin by burning them or coating them with nail polish remover or petroleum jelly. Tropical cortisones may help quell the itching.

AIDS, HIV AND STDS

Acquired Immune Deficiency Syndrome (AIDS) is a growing problem around the world. In the U.S. it is estimated that more than 1 million people are infected with HIV, and that 80% of those people do not realize that they infected. The easiest mode of HIV transmission is through direct blood to blood contact with an HIV+ person; never share intravenous drug, tattooing, or other needles. The most common mode of transmission is sexual intercourse. In order to lessen your chances of contracting HIV or any other Sexually Transmitted Disease (STD), such as gonorrhea, chlamydia, genital warts, syphilis, and herpes (which are a lot easier to catch than HIV, and can be just as deadly), use a latex condom every time you have sex. Condoms are widely

available in the U.S. and Canada, but it doesn't hurt to stock up before you set out. The **U.S. Center for Disease Control** (800-342-2437) can provide more info.

■ Alternatives to Tourism

There's no better way to submerge yourself in a culture than to become part of its economy. Job leads often come from local residents, hostel owners, employment offices, and chambers of commerce. Temporary agencies often hire for non-secretarial placement as well as for standard typing assignments. Marketable skills, i.e. touch-typing, dictation, computer knowledge, and experience with children, will prove very helpful (even necessary) in your search for a temporary job. Consult local newspapers and bulletin boards on college campuses for job listings.

STUDY OPPORTUNITIES

If you are interested in studying in the U.S. or in Canada, there are a number of different paths you can take. One possibility is to enroll in a language education program, particularly if you are interested in a short-term stay. Almost all U.S. institutions accept applications from foreign students directly. If English is not your native language, you will likely be required to take the Test of English as a Foreign Language (TOEFL), which is administered in many countries. Requirements are set by each school. Contact the **TOEFL/TSE Publications,** P.O. Box 6154, Princeton, NJ 08541-6154 (609-771-7100; http://www.toefl.org).

World Learning, Inc., P.O. Box 676, Brattleboro, VT 05302 (800-345-2929 or 802-257-7751; http://www.worldlearning.org), runs the International Students of English program, which offers intensive language courses at select U.S. campuses. The price of a four-week program averages $1800.

Institute of International Education (IIE), 809 United Nations Plaza, New York, NY 10017-3580 (212-984-5413 for recorded information; fax 212-984-5358). For book orders: IIE Books, Institute of International Educations, PO Box 371, Annapolis Junction, MD 20701 (800-445-0443; fax 301-953-2838; e-mail iiebooks@iie.org). A nonprofit, international and cultural exchange agency, the IIE is an excellent source of information on studying in the U.S., Canada, and abroad. Publishes *Academic Year Abroad* ($43 plus $4 shipping) detailing over 2300 semester and year-long programs worldwide and *Vacation Study Abroad* ($37 plus $4 shipping) which lists over 1800 short-term, summer, and language school programs.

Eurocentres, 101 N. Union St. #300, Alexandria, VA 22314 (800-648-4809; fax 703-684-1495; http://www.clark.net/pub/eurocent/home.htn) or Eurocentres, Head Office, Seestrasse 247, CH-8038 Zurich, Switzerland (01 485 50 40; fax 481 61 24). Coordinates language programs and homestays for college students and adults in Alexandria/Washington, D.C., and New York City. Programs cost about $500-5000 and last from 2 weeks to 3 months. Some financial aid is available.

Language Immersion Institute, 75 South Manheim Blvd., The College at New Paltz, New Paltz, NY 12561 (914-257-3500; fax 914-257-3569; e-mail lii@new-paltz.edu), provides language instruction in 20 different languages at all levels. Weekend courses offered at New Paltz and in NYC. They also conduct 2-week summer courses and some overseas courses. Program fees are about $275 for a weekend or $625 per week for the longer courses.

U.S. Student Visas

Foreign students who wish to study in the United States must apply for either a J-1 visa (for exchange students) or an F-1 visa (for full-time students enrolled in an academic or language program). To obtain a J-1, you must fill out an IAP-66 eligibility form, issued by the program in which you will enroll. Both are valid for the duration of stay, which includes the length of your particular program and a brief grace period thereafter. In order to extend a student visa, submit an I-538 form 15-60 days before your original departure date.

If you are studying in the U.S., you can take any on-campus job to help pay the bills once you have applied for a social security number and have completed an Employment Eligibility Form (I-9). If you are studying full-time in the U.S. on an F-1 visa, you can take any on-campus job provided you do not displace a U.S. resident. On-campus employment is limited to 20 hrs. per week while school is in session, but you may work full-time during vacation if you plan to return to school. For further info, contact the international students office at the institution you will be attending.

Canadian Student Visas

To study in Canada, you will need a **Student Authorization Certificate** in addition to any entry visa you may need. To obtain one, contact the nearest Canadian consulate or embassy. Be sure to apply at least four months ahead of time; it can take a long time for the paperwork to go through, and there is a processing fee. You will also need to prove to the Canadian government that you are able to support yourself financially. A student authorization is good for one year. If you plan to stay longer, it is very important that you do not let it expire before you apply for renewal. Canadian immigration laws do permit full-time students to seek on-campus employment. For specifics, contact a Canadian Immigration Center (CIC) or consulate. Residents of the U.S., Greenland, and St. Pierre/Miquelon may apply for Student Authorization at a port of entry.

WORKING IN THE U.S.

Volunteer (unpaid) jobs are readily available almost everywhere in the U.S. Some jobs provide room and board in exchange for labor. The place to start getting specific information on the jungle of paperwork surrounding **work visas** is your nearest U.S. embassy or consulate. Write to **Council Travel** (see Budget Travel Agencies, p. 27) for *Volunteer! The Comprehensive Guide to Voluntary Service in the U.S. and Abroad* ($14.50 including postage). Council also runs a summer travel/work pro-

gram designed to provide students with the opportunity to spend their summers working in the U.S.; university students from the following countries are eligible: **Australia,** NUS Services, 220 Faraday St., 1st floor, Carlton, Melbourne, Victoria 3053 (tel. 61 3 348 1777); **Canada,** Travel CUTS, 187 College St., Toronto, Ontario, M5T 1P7 (416-979-2406); **Costa Rica,** OTEC, Calle 3, Avenida ly 3, Edificio Ferencz, San Jose (tel. 506 22 28 66); **France,** Council Travel, 22 rue des Pyramides, 75001 Paris (tel. 33 1 44 55 55 44); **Germany,** Council, Graf Adolph Strasse 64, 40210 Dusseldorf (tel. 49 211 32 9088); **Ireland,** USIT, Aston Quay 19, O'Connell Bridge, Dublin 2 (353 1 679 8833); **New Zealand,** STA Travel Limited, 10 High St., P.O. Box 4156, Auckland (tel. 64 9 309 0458); **Spain,** TIVE, Jose Ortega y Gasset, 71, 3rd floor, 28006, Madrid (tel. 34 1 347 7778); **United Kingdom,** BUNAC, 16 Bowling Green Ln., London EC1R OBD (tel. 44 171 251 2472).

U.S. Work Visas

You **must** apply for a work visa. Working or studying in the U.S. with only a B-2 (tourist) visa is grounds for deportation.

WORKING IN CANADA

Most of the organizations and the literature discussed above are not aimed solely at those interested in working in the U.S.; many of the same programs which arrange volunteer and work programs in the U.S. are also active in Canada. Contact individual organizations and write for the publications which interest you most. Travel CUTS may also help you out. For more information, see Budget Travel Agencies (p. 27).

Canadian Work Visas

If you intend to work in Canada, you will need an **Employment Authorization,** obtained before you enter the country; visitors ordinarily are not allowed to change status once they have arrived. A processing fee applies. Employment authorizations are only issued after it has been determined that qualified Canadian citizens and residents will not be adversely affected by the admission of a foreign worker. Your potential employer must contact the nearest **Canadian Employment Centre (CEC)** for approval of the employment offer. For more info, contact the consulate or embassy in your home country. Residents of the U.S., Greenland, and St. Pierre/Miquelon may apply for an Employment Authorization at a port of entry.

■ Specific Concerns

WOMEN TRAVELERS

Women exploring any area on their own often face heightened threats to personal safety. In all situations, it's best to trust your instincts; if you'd feel better somewhere else, move on. Hitchhiking is never safe for lone women, or even for women traveling in pairs and groups. You may want to consider staying in hostels which offer single rooms which lock from the inside, YWCAs, or other establishments that offer rooms for women only. Stick to centrally located accommodations; avoid late-night treks or subway rides. Always carry change for the phone and money for a bus or taxi. Carry a whistle on your keychain, and don't hesitate to use it in an emergency.

The less you look like a tourist, the better off you'll be. Look as if you know where you're going (even when you don't) and consider approaching women or couples for directions if you're lost or feel uncomfortable. If you spend time in cities, you may be harassed no matter how you're dressed. Your best answer to verbal harassment is no answer at all. Don't hesitate to seek out a police officer or a passerby if you are being harassed. *Let's Go* lists emergency numbers (including rape crisis lines) in the Practical Information listings of most cities. These warnings and suggestions should not discourage women from traveling alone. Be adventurous, but avoid unnecessary risks.

The **National Organization for Women (NOW)** has branches across the country and can refer women travelers to rape crisis centers and counseling services and provide lists of feminist events in the area. Main offices include 22 W 21st, 7th floor, New York, NY 10010 (212-260-4422); 1000 16th St. NW, 7th Fl., Washington, D.C. 20004 (202-331-0066); and 3543 18th St., San Francisco, CA 94110 (415-861-8960).

A Journey of One's Own, by Thalia Zepatos (Eighth Mountain Press $17). The latest thing on the market, interesting and full of good advice, plus a specific and manageable bibliography of books and resources.

Ferrari Guides' Women's Travel in Your Pocket, Ferrari Publications, PO Box 37887, Phoenix, AZ 85069 (602-863-2408), an annual guide for women (especially lesbians) traveling worldwide ($14).

Women Going Places, a women's travel and resource guide emphasizing women-owned enterprises. Geared towards lesbians, but offers advice appropriate for all women. $14 from Inland Book Company, 1436 W. Randolph St. Chicago, IL 60607 (800-243-0138) or order from a local bookstore.

OLDER TRAVELERS

Senior citizens are eligible for a wide range of discounts on transportation, museums, movies, theaters, concerts, restaurants, and accommodations. If you don't see a senior citizen price listed, ask and you may be delightfully surprised.

AARP (American Association of Retired Persons), 601 E St., NW, Washington, D.C. 20049 (202-434-2277). Members 50 and over receive benefits and services including the AARP Motoring Plan from AMOCO (800-334-3300), and discounts on lodging, car rental, and sight-seeing. Annual fee $8 per couple; lifetime membership $75.

Elderhostel, 75 Federal St., 3rd Fl., Boston, MA 02110-1941 (617-426-7788; fax 617-426-8351; www at http://www.elderhostel.org). For those 55 or over (spouse of

any age). Programs at colleges, universities, and other learning centers on varied subjects lasting one to four weeks.

National Council of Senior Citizens, 1331 F St. NW, Washington, D.C. 20004 (202-347-8800). Memberships are $12 a year, $30 for three years, or $150 for a lifetime. Individuals or couples can receive hotel and auto rental discounts, a senior citizen newspaper, use of a discount travel agency, supplemental Medicare insurance (if you're over 65), and a mail-order prescription drug service.

BISEXUAL, GAY, AND LESBIAN TRAVELERS

Prejudice against bisexuals, gays, and lesbians still exists in the U.S. and Canada, but acceptance is growing. Still, in many areas, public displays of homosexual affection are illegal. Most major cities have large, active gay and lesbian communities.

Whenever available, *Let's Go* lists local gay and lesbian hotline numbers, which can provide counseling and social information for bisexual, gay, and lesbian visitors. *Let's Go* also lists local gay and lesbian hotspots whenever possible.

Damron Travel Guides, PO Box 422458, San Francisco, CA 94142 (415-255-0404 or 800-462-6654). Publishers of the *Damron Address Book* ($15), which lists bars, restaurants, guest houses, and services in the United States, Canada, and Mexico which cater to gay men. The *Damron Road Atlas* ($15) contains color maps of 56 major U.S. and Canadian cities and gay and lesbian resorts and listings of bars and accommodations. *The Women's Traveller* ($12) includes maps of 50 major U.S. cities and lists bars, restaurants, accommodations, bookstores, and services catering to lesbians. Forthcoming in 1997 is *Damron's Accomodations*, listing gay and lesbian hotels around the world ($19).

Ferrari Guides, PO Box 37887, Phoenix, AZ 85069 (602-863-2408; fax 439-3952; e-mail ferrari@q-nct.com). Gay and lesbian travel guides: *Ferrari Guides' Gay Travel A to Z* ($16), *Ferrari Guides' Men's Travel in Your Pocket* ($14), *Ferrari Guides' Women's Travel in Your Pocket* ($14), and *Ferrari Guides' Inn Places* ($16). Available in bookstores or by mail order (postage/handling $4.50 for the first item, $1 for each additional item mailed within the U.S. Overseas, call or write for shipping cost.)

Gayellow Pages, PO Box 533, Village Station, New York, NY 10014. (212-674-0120; fax 420-1126). An annually updated listing of accommodations, resorts, hotlines, and other items of interest to the gay traveler. U.S./Canada edition $16.

Giovanni's Room, 345 S. 12th St., Philadelphia, PA 19107 (215-923-2960; fax 923-0813; e-mail gilphilp@netaxs.com). An international feminist, lesbian, and gay bookstore with mail-order service. Carries many of the publications listed here.

Spartacus International Gay Guides ($33), published by Bruno Gmunder, Postfach 110729, D-10837 Berlin, Germany (30 615 00 30; fax 30 615 9134). Lists bars, restaurants, hotels, and bookstores around the world catering to gays. Available in bookstores or by mail from Giovanni's Room.

DISABLED TRAVELERS

Hotels and motels in the U.S. and Canada have become more and more accessible to disabled persons, and many attractions are trying to make exploring the outdoors more feasible. Call ahead to restaurants, hotels, parks, and other facilities to find out about the existence of ramps, the widths of doors, the dimensions of elevators, etc.

Hertz, Avis, and National **car rental agencies** have hand-controlled vehicles at some locations (see Renting, p. 41). Amtrak **trains** and all **airlines** can better serve disabled passengers if notified at least 72 hours in advance; tell the ticket agent when making reservations which services you'll need. Hearing-impaired travelers may contact Amtrak (tel. 800-872-7245, in PA 800-322-9537) using teletype printers. Greyhound buses will also provide free travel for a companion, with a doctor's statement confirming a companion is necessary; if you are without a fellow traveler, call Greyhound (tel. 800-752-4841) at least 48 hours but no more than one week before you plan to leave, and they will make arrangements to assist you. Wheelchairs, seeing-eye dogs, and oxygen tanks are not deducted from your luggage allowance. For informa-

WHO SAYS YOU NEED A CAR IN L.A. ?

At Hostelling International–Los Angeles/Santa Monica everything is convenient and hassle-free.

- Open 24 hours
- 1 block from one of California's legendary beaches
- 2 blocks from more than 100 chic sidewalk cafes and restaurants, comedy and movie theaters, popular pubs, and trendy shops
- Complimentary shuttle from Los Angeles International Airport. Call hostel on arrival for details.
- Daily doings at the hostel, including barbecues, movies and more
- Regularly scheduled trips to Disneyland, Universal Studios, Las Vegas, Grand Canyon, Mexico and more
- Couples rooms available with advance reservations
- Easy Reservations via telephone, fax, IBN

For information and reservations write Hostelling International–Los Angeles/Santa Monica, 1436 Second Street, Santa Monica, California USA 90401, FAX (310) 393-1769; call (310) 393-9913; or visit our website at http://www.hihostels.com.

HOSTELLING INTERNATIONAL

The new seal of approval of the International Youth Hostel Federation.

HOSTELLING
INTERNATIONAL

tion on discounts available with the Golden Access Passport, see National Parks, p. 53. For information on special transportation availability in particular cities, contact the local chapter of the Easter Seals Society.

American Foundation for the Blind, 11 Penn Plaza, New York, NY 10011, 212-502-7600. Provides information and services for the visually impaired. For a catalogue of products, contact Lighthouse, Inc. (800-829-0500). Open Mon.-Fri. 8:30am-4:30pm.

Facts on File, 11 Penn Plaza, 15th Floor, New York, NY 10001 (212-967-8800). Publishers of *Disability Resource,* a reference guide for travelers with disabilities ($45 plus shipping). Retail bookstores or by mail order.

Mobility International, USA (MIUSA), PO Box 10767, Eugene, OR 97440 (514-343-1284 voice and TDD; fax 343-6812). International headquarters in Brussels, rue de Manchester 25, Brussels, Belgium, B-1070 (322 410 62 97; fax 410 68 74). Information on travel programs, international work camps, accommodations, access guides, and organized tours for those with physical disabilities. Membership costs $25 per year, newsletter $15.

Moss Rehab Hospital Travel Information Service, 1200 W. Tabor Rd., Philadelphia, PA 19141 (215-456-9600, TDD 456-9602). Telephone info resource center on travel accessibility and other travel-related concerns for those with disabilities.

Society for the Advancement of Travel for the Handicapped (SATH), 347 Fifth Ave. #610, New York, NY 10016 (212-447-7284; fax 725-8253). Publishes quarterly travel newsletter *SATH News* and information booklets (free for members, $13 each for nonmembers) with advice on trip planning for people with disabilities. Annual membership $45, students and seniors $25.

Twin Peaks Press, PO Box 129, Vancouver, WA 98666-0129 (360-694-2462, orders only MC and Visa 800-637-2256; fax 360-696-3210). Publishers of *Travel for the Disabled,* which provides travel tips, lists of accessible tourist attractions, and advice on other resources for disabled travelers ($20). Also publishes *Directory for Travel Agencies of the Disabled* ($20), *Wheelchair Vagabond* ($15), and *Directory of Accessible Van Rentals* ($10). Postage $3 for first book, $1.50 for each additional book.

The following organizations arrange tours or trips for disabled travelers:

Directions Unlimited, 720 N. Bedford Rd., Bedford Hills, NY 10507 (800-533-5343 or 914-241-1700; fax 914-241-0243). Specializes in arranging individual and group vacations, tours, and cruises for the physically disabled.

Flying Wheels Travel Service, 143 W. Bridge St., Owatonna, MN 55060 (800-535-6790; fax 507-451-1685). Arranges trips in the USA and abroad for groups or individuals in wheelchairs or with other sorts of limited mobility.

The Guided Tour Inc., Elkins Park House, Suite 114B, 7900 Old York Rd., Elkins Park, PA 19027-2339 (215-782-1370 or 800-783-5841; fax 635-2637). Organizes travel programs for persons with developmental and physical challenges and those requiring renal dialysis. Call, fax, or write for a free brochure.

■ Nuts and Bolts

TIME ZONES

North Americans tell **time** on a 12-hour clock cycle. Hours before noon are "am" *(ante meridiem);* hours after noon are "pm" *(post meridiem).* Due to the easy confusion of 12pm and 12am, *Let's Go* uses "noon" and "midnight" instead. The four time zones in the continental U.S. are (east to west): **Eastern, Central, Mountain,** and **Pacific. Alaska, Hawaii** and the **Aleutian Islands** have their own time zones. Most of the U.S. and all of Canada observe **daylight savings time** from the last Sunday in April (April 27th in 1997) to the last Sunday in October (Oct. 26th in 1997) by advancing clocks ahead one hour.

ELECTRICAL CURRENT

Electric outlets in North America provide current at 117 volts, 60 cycles (Hertz). Appliances designed for the European electrical system (220 volts) will not operate without a transformer and a plug adapter (this includes electric systems for disinfecting contact lenses). Transformers are sold to convert specific wattages (e.g. 0-50 watt transformers for razors and radios).

■ Packing

Pack lightly...that means you. Even if you have a car. The more you bring, the more you have to worry about. If you'll be traveling by foot, before you leave, pack your bag, strap it on, and take it for a walk. At the slightest sign of heaviness, unpack something. A good general rule is to pack only what you absolutely need, then take half the clothes and more money than you thought you'd need. Packing need not be as permanent as it seems; things that you didn't bring can usually be found along the way.

LUGGAGE

If you intend to do a lot of hiking, biking, or walking, you should have a frame backpack. Internal-frame packs are best for general traveling; they are flexible enough to survive contortions borne of twisting trails and crowded subways. If you'll be doing extensive camping or hiking, you may want to consider an external-frame pack, which offers added support, distributes weight better, and allows for a sleeping bag to be strapped on. In any case, get a pack with a strong, padded hip belt to transfer weight from your shoulders to your legs. Remember, you get what you pay for; quality packs cost anywhere from $125-$300. When checking a backpack on a flight, tape down loose straps that can catch in the conveyer belt. Wrap sharper items in clothing so they won't stab you or puncture your luggage. Also, bringing a smaller bag in addi-

tion to your pack or suitcase allows you to leave your big bag in the hotel while you explore the area.

ETCETERA, ETCETERA, ETCETERA

Random Useful Stuff: umbrella, resealable plastic bags (for damp clothes, soap, food), plastic trash bags (for rain protection), alarm clock, strike-anywhere matches, sun hat, sunglasses, needle and thread, safety pins, whistle, personal stereo, pocketknife, notebook and pens, water bottle, tweezers, flashlight, string (makeshift clothesline and lashing material), clothespins, padlock, earplugs, compass, deodorant, razors, condoms, tampons, maps, an electrical transformer and plug adapter for North American outlets.

Sleepsacks: If planning to stay in **youth hostels,** make a sleepsack instead of paying the hostel's linen charge. Fold a full size sheet in half the long way, then sew it closed along the open long side and one of the short sides.

GETTING THERE

■ Budget Travel Agencies

Council Travel (800-2-COUNCIL/226-8624), is a full-service travel agency specializing in student, youth, and budget travel. They offer discount airfares on scheduled airlines, railpasses, hosteling cards, and international student (ISIC), youth (Go25), and teacher (ITIC) identity cards. Offices in most major U.S. cities, and a main office at 205 E. 42nd St., **New York,** NY 10017 (212-822-2700). Overseas offices include: 28A Poland St. (Oxford Circus), **London,** W1V 3DB, (0171) 437 7767; 22 rue des Pyramides, 75001 **Paris,** (1) 44 55 55 65; **Munich,** tel. (089) 39 50 22; **Tokyo,** 81 (3) 3 777 7752; **Singapore,** (65) 7387-066; **Bangkok,** (66) 2-282-7705.

STA Travel, 6560 North Scottsdale Rd. #F100, Scottsdale, AZ 85253 (800-777-0112). Student and youth travel organization with over 100 offices worldwide, including 16 U.S. locations. Offers discount airfare for young travelers, railpasses, accommodations, tours, insurance, and ISIC. Offices include: 429 S. Dearborn St., **Chicago,** IL 60605 (312-786-9050); 4341 University Way NE, **Seattle,** WA 98105 (206-633-5000); 10 Downing St., Ste. G, **New York,** NY 10003 (212-627-3111); 297 Newbury St., **Boston,** MA 02115 (617-266-6014); 3730 Walnut St. **Philadelphia,** PA 19104 (215-382-2928); 2401 Pennsylvania Ave., **Washington, D.C.** 20037 (202-887-0912); 7202 Melrose Ave., **Los Angeles,** CA 90046 (213-934-8722); 51 Grant Ave., **San Francisco,** CA 94108 (415-391-8407); **UK:** Priory House, 6 Wrights Ln., London W8 6TA, (0171) 938 4711. **New Zealand:** 10 High St., Auckland, tel. (09) 309 9723. **Australia:** 222 Faraday St., Melbourne VIC 3050, tel. (03) 349 6911.

Let's Go Travel, Harvard Student Agencies, 67 Mount Auburn St., **Cambridge,** MA 02138 (617-495-9649 or 800-5-LETS GO/553-8746). Offers railpasses, HI-AYH memberships, ISIC, ITIC, FIYTO cards, guidebooks (including all *Let's Go* titles), maps, bargain flights, and a complete line of budget travel gear. All items available by mail; call or write for a catalog (or see the one inside this very book).

Campus Travel, 52 Grosvenor Gardens, **London** SW1W OAG (http://www.campustravel.co.uk). 41 branches in the U.K. Student and youth fares on plane, train, boat, and bus travel. Flexible airline tickets. Discount and ID cards for youths, travel insurance for students and those under 35, and maps and guides. Puts out travel suggestion booklets. Telephone booking service: in Europe call (0171) 730 3402; in North America call (0171) 730 2101; worldwide call (0171) 730 8111; in Manchester call (0161) 273 1721; in Scotland (0131) 668 3303.

Travel CUTS (Canadian University Travel Services, Ltd.), 187 College St., Toronto, Ont. M5T 1P7 (416-979-2406; fax 979-8167; email mail@travelcuts). Canada's national student travel bureau; its version of Council, with 40 offices across Canada. In the **U.K.,** 295-A Regent St., London W1R 7YA, (0171 637 3161). Discounted

domestic and international flights; ISIC, FIYTO, GO25, HI hostel cards; and rail-passes. Special fares with valid ISIC or FIYTO cards. Free *Student Traveller* maga-zine, and info on Student Work Abroad Program (SWAP).

Usit, 19-21 Aston Quay, O'Connell Bridge, **Dublin** 2 (677 8117; fax 679 8833). Spe-cializes in youth and student travel. Offers low-cost tickets and flexible travel arrangements all over the world. Sells ISIC, FIYTO-GO25 cards.

■ From Europe

Travelers from Europe will experience the least competition for inexpensive seats during the off-season. Peak-season rates generally take effect between mid-May and early June and run until mid-September. Don't count on getting a seat right away dur-ing these months. The worst crunch leaving Europe takes place from mid-June to early July; August is uniformly tight for returning flights. Take advantage of cheap off-season flights within Europe to reach an advantageous point of departure for North America. (London is a major connecting point for budget flights to the U.S.; New York City is often the destination.) To make your way out West, catch a coast-to-coast flight once you're in the U.S.

Charter companies, courier services, and ticket consolidators all offer low rates, but often with restrictions or risks. Many major airlines offer reduced-fare options or youth fares, available only to persons under a certain age (often 24) within 72 hours of the flight's departure.

Major airlines that tend to offer relatively inexpensive fares for a round-trip ticket from Europe include: **British Airways** (800-247-9297), **Continental, Northwest, TWA,** and **United** (800-538-2929). Smaller, budget airlines often undercut major car-riers by offering bargain fares on regularly scheduled flights. Competition for seats on these smaller carriers can be fierce—book early. Other trans-Atlantic airlines include **Virgin Atlantic Airways** (800-862-8621) and **IcelandAir** (800-223-5500).

■ From Asia, Africa, and Australia

Whereas European travelers may choose from a variety of regular reduced fares, Asian, Australian, and African travelers must rely on APEX. A good place to start searching for tickets is the local branch of an international budget travel agency (see Budget Travel Agencies p. 27). **STA Travel,** with offices in Sydney, Melbourne, and Auckland, is probably the largest international agency you will find.

Qantas (800-227-4500), **United,** and **Northwest** fly between Australia or New Zealand and the United States. Advance purchase fares from Australia have extremely tough restrictions. If you are uncertain about your plans, pay extra for an advance purchase ticket that has only a 50% penalty for cancellation. Many travelers from Aus-tralia and New Zealand take **Singapore Air** (800-742-3333) or other East Asian-based carriers for the initial leg of their trip.

Delta Airlines (800-241-4141), **Japan Airlines** (800-525-3663), **Northwest** (800-225-2525) and **United Airlines** (800-538-2929) offer service from Japan. A round-trip ticket from Tokyo to L.A. usually ranges from $1250-2500.

South African Airways (800-722-9675), **American** (800-433-7300), and **North-west** connect South Africa with North America.

ONCE THERE

■ Embassies and Consulates

FOREIGN EMBASSIES AND CONSULATES IN THE U.S. AND CANADA

Embassies in U.S.: Canada, 501 Pennsylvania Ave. NW, Washington, D.C. 20001 (202-682-1740); **United Kingdom,** 3100 Massachusetts Ave. NW, Washington, D.C. 20008 (202-462-1340); **Ireland,** 2234 Massachusetts Ave. NW, Washington, D.C. 20008 (202-462-3939); **Australia,** 1601 Massachusetts Ave. NW, Washington, D.C. 20036 (202-797-3000); **New Zealand,** 37 Observatory Circle NW, Washington, D.C. 20008 (202-328-4800); **South Africa,** 3051 Massachusetts Ave. NW, Washington, D.C. 20008 (202-232-4400).

Consulates in U.S.: Canada, 1251 Ave. of the Americas, Exxon Building, 16th Floor, New York, NY 10020-1175 (212-596-1600) and 300 S. Grand Ave.,10th floor, California Plaza, Los Angeles, CA 90071 (213-346-2700); **United Kingdom,** 845 3rd Ave., New York, NY 10022 (212-745-0200); 11766 Wilshire Blvd., Suite 400, Los Angeles, CA 9002-6538 (310-477-3322); **Ireland,** 345 Park Ave., 17th Floor, New York, NY 10154 (212-319-2555) and 44 Montgomery St., Suite 3830, San Francisco, CA 94101 (415-392-4214); **Australia,** 630 5th Ave., New York, NY 10111 (212-408-8400) and Century Plaza Towers, 19th floor, 2049 Century Park East, Los Angeles, CA 90067 (310-229-4800); **New Zealand,** 12400 Wilshire Blvd., Suite 1150, Los Angeles, CA 90025 (310-207-1605); **South Africa,** 333 E. 38th St., 9th Floor, New York, NY 10016 (212-213-4880) and 50 N. La Cienega Blvd., Ste. 300, Beverly Hills, CA 90211 (310-657-9200).

Embassies in Canada: United States, 100 Wellington St., Ottawa, Ontario K1P 5T1 (613-238-5335); **United Kingdom,** 80 Elgin St., Ottawa, Ontario K1P 5K7 (613-237-1530); **Ireland,** 130 Albert St., suite 1105, Ottawa, Ontario K1P 5G4 (613-233-6281); **Australia,** 50 O'Connor St., suite 710, Ottawa, Ontario K1P 6L2 (613-236-0841); **New Zealand,** 99 Bank St., suite 727, Ottawa, Ontario K1P 6G3 (613-238-5991); **South Africa,** 15 Sussex Dr., Ottawa, Ontario K1M 1M8 (613-744-0330).

Consulates in Canada: United States, 2 Place Terrasse Dufferin, CP 939, Québec, G1R 4T9 (418-692-2095), 1095 Pender St. West, Vancouver, British Columbia V6E 2M6 (604-685-4311). For U.S. visa and immigration services, call 900-451-6663 (open Mon.-Fri. 7am-8pm); to schedule an appointment with the U.S. consulate, call 900-451-2778; **United Kingdom,** 1000 de la Gauchetiere West, Suite 4200, Montreal, Québec H3B 4W5 (514-866-5863) and 1111 Melville St., suite 800, Vancouver, British Columbia V6E 3V6 (604-683-4421); **Australia,** 175 Bloor St. East, suite 314, Toronto, Ontario M4W 3R8, (416-323-1155) and World Trade Center office complex, suite 602, 999 Canada Place, Vancouver, British Columbia V6C 3E1 (604-684-1177); **New Zealand,** 888 Dunsmuir St., suite 1200, Vancouver, British Columbia V6C 3K4 (604-684-7388); **South Africa,** 1 Place Ville Marie, suite 2615, Montreal, Québec H3B 4S3 (514-878-9217) and Stock Exchange Tower, suite 2300, 2 First Canadian Place, Toronto, Ontario M5X 1E3 (416-364-0314).

■ Getting Around

BY PLANE

When dealing with any commercial airline, buying in advance is best. Periodic **price wars** may lower prices in spring and early summer months, but they're are unpredictable; don't delay your purchase in hopes of catching one. To obtain the cheapest fare, buy a roundtrip ticket, stay over at least one Saturday, and travel on off-peak days (Mon.-Thurs. morning) and off-peak hours (overnight **"red-eye" flights** can be cheaper and faster than primetime). Chances of receiving discount fares increase on

competitive routes. Fees for changing flight dates range from $25 (for some domestic flights) to $150 (for many international flights). Most airlines allow children under two to fly free (on the lap of an adult).

Since travel peaks June to August and around holidays, reserve a seat several months in advance for these times. Call the airline the day before your departure to confirm your flight reservation, and get to the airport early to ensure you have a seat; airlines often overbook. (Of course, being "bumped" from a flight doesn't spell doom if your travel plans are flexible—you will probably leave on the next flight and receive a free ticket or cash bonus. If you would like to be bumped to win a free ticket, check in early and let the airline officials know.)

The following programs, services, and fares may be helpful for planning a reasonably-priced airtrip, but always be wary of deals that seem too good to be true:

Advance Purchase Excursion Fare (APEX): The commercial carriers' lowest regular offer; specials advertised in newspapers may be cheaper, but have more restrictions and fewer seats. APEX fares provide you with confirmed reservations and often allow "open-jaw" tickets (landing and returning from different cities). Call as early as possible; these fares often require a two- to three-week advance purchase. Be sure to inquire about any restrictions on length of stay.

Frequent flyer tickets: It is not wise to buy frequent flyer tickets from others—it is standard policy on most commercial airlines to check a photo ID, and you could find yourself paying for a new, full-fare ticket. If you have a frequent flyer account, make sure you're getting credit when you check in.

Air Passes: Many major U.S. airlines offer special **Visit USA** air passes and fares to international travelers. You must purchase these passes outside of North America, paying one price for a certain number of flight vouchers. Each voucher is good for one flight on an airline's domestic system; typically, all travel must be completed within 30-60 days. The point of departure and destination for each coupon must be specified at the time of purchase, and once in the U.S., changes carry a $50-$75 fee. Dates of travel may be changed once travel has begun, usually at no extra charge. **USAir** offers packages for the East coast (from $199) and for all 48 states (from around $359). **United, Continental, Delta, Air Ontario, Air BC,** and **TWA** sell vouchers as well. TWA's **Youth Travel Pak** offers a similar deal to students 14-24, including North Americans. Canadian Regional Airlines (England office 011-44-1737-55-53-00; fax 01737 555300) offer one- and two-week unlimited flight air passes for Eastern Canada (one-week EastPass $249, two-week $349); Western Canada (one-week WestPass $249, two-week $349); and the entire Canadian Regional network (one-week NationalPass $325, two-week $425).

Major Airlines

Air Canada, (800-776-3000). Discounts for ages 12-24 on stand-by tickets for flights within Canada; still, advance-purchase tickets may be cheaper.

Alaska Airlines, P.O. Box 68900, Seattle, WA 98168 (800-426-0333).

America West, 4000 E. Sky Harbor Blvd. Phoenix, AZ 85034 (800-235-9292). Serves primarily the western United States.

Continental, 2929 Allen Parkway, Houston, TX 77210 (800-525-0280; fax 713-590-2150).

Delta, Hartsfield International Airport, Atlanta, GA 30320 (800-241-4141).

Northwest, 5101 Northwest Dr., St. Paul, MN 55111-3034 (800-225-2525).

Southwest, P.O. Box 36611, Dallas, TX 75235-1611 (800-435-9792).

TWA, 1 City Center, 515 N. 6th St., St. Louis, MO 63101 (800-221-2000).

United, P.O. Box 66100, Chicago, IL 60666 (800-241-6522).

USAir, Crystal Park Four Dr., Arlington, VA 22227 (800-428-4322).

Charter Flights

Charters save you a lot of money on peak-season flights if you can be flexible. Companies reserve the right to change the dates of your flight or even cancel the flight a mere 48 hours in advance. Delays are not uncommon. Restrictions on the length of your trip and the timeframe for reservations may also apply. To be safe, get your

SEATTLE

AMERICAN INTERNATIONAL BACKPACKERS
HOSTEL

126 Broadway Ave East
Seattle, Washington 98102
FREE CALL DIAL: 1 800 600 2965
Local: 206 720 2965 Fax: 206 322 2576

Tours:
-> Camping trip to Olympic National Park
-> Visit graves of Jimi Hendrix, Bruce & Brandon Lee
   and Kurt Cobain's House

Facilities Include:
-> Lounge with Cable TV (Showtime, Cinemax, Movie
   Channel), Stereo System,
-> Free use of Pool Table
-> Parking, Full Kitchen, Laundry and Weight Set
-> Absolutely No Curfew

FREE Beer Nights Monday, Wednesday and Friday

FREE Breakfast everyday; eggs, bread, coffee and tea

**FREE Pick-up from anywhere downtown, Greyhound,
      Amtrak, Visitors Information and Ferry Terminals**

FREE Spaghetti dinner on Sundays

FREE Use of Pool Table, Linen, Blankets and Locker

Prices

$12.^{50}to $14.^{50} shared

$35.00 sgl to $40.00 dbls

BACKPACKERS ADVENTURE AND TOUR SERVICE

126 Broadway Avenue East, Seattle, Washington 98102

FREE CALL FROM ANYWHERE IN US AND CANADA 1 800 785-7581
RESERVATIONS ACCEPTED WITH VISA OR MC Fax : 206 322-2576
Local: 206 322-2602

FREE BEER AND FOOD AT
CAMPGROUND

San Francisco---->Seattle
Two day camping and hiking trip from
San Francisco through the Redwood
National Forest to Seattle $75.00 per
person. Price includes camping & food

Seattle-------> Vancouver
$24.00
Bus will pick-up and drop-off from
all Hostels in each city

ticket as early as possible, and arrive at the airport several hours before departure time. Think carefully when you book your departure and return dates; you will lose all or most of your money if you cancel your ticket. Prices and destinations can change markedly from season to season, so be sure to contact as many organizations as possible in order to get the best deal.

Ticket Consolidators

Ticket consolidators sell unbooked commercial and charter airline seats for very low prices, but deals include some risks. Tickets are sold on a space-available basis which does not guarantee you a seat; you get priority over those flying stand-by but below regularly-booked passengers. The earlier you arrive at the airport the better, since passengers are seated in the order they check in. Consolidators tend to be more reliable on domestic flights, both in getting you on the flight and in getting you exactly where you want to go. This may be a good route to take if you are traveling: on short notice (you bypass advance purchase requirements, since you aren't tangled in airline bureaucracy); on a high-priced trip; to an offbeat destination; or in the peak season, when published fares are jacked way up. If possible, deal with consolidators close to home so you can visit in person, if necessary. Get the company's policy in writing: insist on a receipt that gives full details about the tickets, refunds, and restrictions, and record who you talked to and when. For more info and a list of consolidators, consult Kelly Monaghan's *Consolidators: Air Travel's Bargain Basement* (US$7 plus US$2 shipping) from the Intrepid Traveler, P.O. Box 438, New York, NY 10034 (email intreptrav@aol.com).

Cheap Tickets, (800-377-1000). Offices in Los Angeles, CA (310-645-5054), San Francisco, CA (415-896-5023), Honolulu (808-947-3717), Overland Park, KS, and NYC (212-570-1179).

Mr. Cheap's Travel, (800-636-3273 or 800-672-4327). Offices in El Cajon, CA (619-442-1100), Denver, CO (303-758-3833) and Clackamas, OR (503-557-9101).

NOW Voyager, (primarily a courier company; see below), does consolidation with reliability which rivals that of most charter companies (97% of customers get on flights the first time) and at prices which are considerably lower.

STA Travel, Los Angeles, CA (213-934-8722, fax 213-937-6008) or San Francisco, CA (415-391-8407, fax 415-391-4105). Also has offices in Berkeley, Santa Monica, and Westwood, CA. Specializes in student travel.

Courier Companies and Freighters

Courier travel works like this: you are a traveler seeking an inexpensive ticket to a particular location; the courier service is a company seeking to transport merchandise to a particular location. If your destinations and schedules coincide, the courier service will sell you a cheap ticket in exchange for use of the luggage space which accompanies it. Courier services offer some great prices, but with restrictions: their schedules may be confining, luggage is limited to carry-on bags only. For a practical guide to the air courier scene, check out Kelly Monaghan's Insider's Guide to Air Courier Bargains ($15 plus $3 shipping), available from Upper Access Publishing (UAP), P.O. Box 457, Hinesburg, VT 05461 (800-356-9315), or consult the Courier Air Travel Handbook ($10 plus $3.50 shipping), published by Bookmasters, Inc., P.O. Box 2039, Mansfield, OH 44905 (800-507-2665; fax 419-281-6883).

NOW Voyager, 74 Varick St. #307, New York, NY 10013 (212-431-1616), offers courier service. 70% off a ticket, but remember, only carry-on luggage (one item). Subject to stays of very limited duration on round-trip flights. Flights originate primarily in NYC. (Phones open Mon.-Fri. 10am-5:30pm, Sat. noon-4:30pm, EST.)

Standby Brokers

Standby brokers do not sell tickets, but rather, the promise that you will get to a destination near where you're intending to go, within a window of time (usually 5 days), from a location in a region you've specified. You call in before your date-range to hear

all of your flight options for the next seven days and your probability of boarding. You then decide which flights you want to try to make and present a voucher at the airport which grants you the right to board a flight on a space-available basis. This procedure must be followed again for the return trip. Flexibility of schedule and destination is often necessary, but all companies guarantee you a flight or a refund if all available flights that fit your date and destination range were full. Be aware that delays of up to several days have been reported; if you are delayed, you could incur costs that outweigh savings.

Airhitch, 100 North Sepulveda Blvd. 903, El Segundo, CA 90245 (800-326-2009 or 212-864-2000 on the East Coast; 800-397-1098 or 310-726-5000 on the West Coast), works to and from a greater number of cities than most courier companies, but you must often list 3 cities within a given region to which you are willing to fly; Airhitch guarantees that you will get to one of them. You must also give a 5-day travel window for domestic flights. Be sure to read *all* the fine print. The "USA-hitch" program connects the northeastern United States with the West (NYC to Seattle or Baltimore to L.A. $129), and California to Hawaii ($129). "Sunhitch" program offers round-trip tickets from the East coast to the Caribbean or Mexico for $189. Programs change frequently; call for the latest information.

Air Tech, 584 Broadway #1007, New York, NY 10012 (212-219-7000). Space available flights and last-minute confirmed flights at discounts. Domestic travelers must give a 2-day travel window. Flights primarily from NYC (Boston departures possible). One way to L.A. or San Francisco $129; West Coast to Hawaii $129. To Europe $169 each way with a 5-day window. One-year open tickets to Europe (NYC-Paris $595).

BY TRAIN

Locomotion is still one of the cheapest ways to tour the U.S. and Canada, but keep in mind that discounted air travel, particularly on longer trips, may be cheaper than train travel. As with airlines, you can save lots of money by purchasing your tickets as far in advance as possible, so plan ahead and make reservations early. It is essential to travel light on trains; not all stations will check your baggage.

Amtrak (800-872-7245, or 800-USA-RAIL) is the only provider of intercity passenger train service in the U.S. Most cities have Amtrak offices which directly sell tickets, but tickets must be bought through an agent in some small towns. **Discounts on full rail fares:** senior citizens (15% off); travelers with disabilities (15% off); children under 15 accompanied by a parent (50% off); children under age two (free); current members of the U.S. armed forces, active-duty veterans, and their dependents (25% off). Circle trips, and holiday packages can also save money. Call for up-to-date info and reservations. Amtrak also offers some special packages: **All-Aboard America** offers unlimited travel within a given region ($228 during the summer). The **Air-Rail Travel Plan** lets you travel in one direction by train and return by plane.

The **USA Rail Pass,** a discount option available only to those who aren't citizens of North America, allows unlimited travel and unlimited stops over a period of either 15 or 30 days. A 30-day nationwide travel pass sells for $440 during peak season (June 17-Aug. 21) and $350 during the off-season (except late Dec.); a 15-day nationwide pass is $355/$245. A 30-day pass limited to travel in the western region (as far east as Denver) is $330/290; the 15-day pass for the west is $265/$215; a 30-day pass to the eastern region (as far west as Chicago) is $265/$240; and the 15-day version is $205/$185.

VIA Rail, Place Ville Marie, Lobby Level, Montreal, Québec H3B 2G6 (800-561-3949), is Amtrak's Canadian analog. Regular fare tickets are discounted 40% with 7-day advance-purchase, and fares vary with seasons. **Discounts on full fares:** students, youths under 24, and seniors (10% off); children ages two to 15, accompanied by an adult (50% off); children under two (free on the lap of an adult). Reservations are required for first-class seats and sleeping car accommodations. Call for details. The **Canrail Pass** allows unlimited travel on 12 to 15 days within a 30-day period.

Between early June and late September, a 12-day pass costs $420, senior citizens and youths under 24 pay $377. Off-season passes cost $287, seniors and youths pay $258. Add $35 for each additional day of travel desired. Call for information on seasonal promotions.

BY BUS

Buses generally offer the most frequent and complete service between cities and towns in the U.S. and Canada. Often a bus is the only way to reach smaller locales without a car. In rural areas and across open spaces, however, bus lines tend to be sparse. Russell's Official National Motor *Coach Guide* ($14.45 including postage) is an indispensable tool for constructing an itinerary. Updated each month, *Russell's Guide* contains schedules of every bus route (including Greyhound) between any two towns in the United States and Canada. Russell's also publishes two semi-annual *Supplements,* one which includes a directory of bus lines and bus stations ($6), and one which offers a series of Route Maps ($6.45). To order any of the above, write Russell's Guides, Inc., P.O. Box 278, Cedar Rapids, IA 52406 (319-364-6138; fax 319-364-4853).

Greyhound (800-231-2222), operates the largest number of routes in the U.S., though local bus companies may provide more extensive services within specific regions. Schedule info is available at any Greyhound terminal or by calling the 800 number. Reserve with a credit card over the phone at least ten days in advance, and the ticket can be mailed anywhere in the U.S. Otherwise, reservations are available only up to 24 hours in advance. You can buy your ticket at the terminal, but arrive early. *Advance purchase is cheaper, so make reservations early.* **Discounts on full fares:** senior citizens (15% off); children ages two to 11 (50% off); travelers with disabilities and special needs, and their companions ride together for the price of one (call 800-752-4841 for more information); active and retired U.S. military personnel and National Guard Reserves (with valid ID), and their spouses and dependents, may

take a roundtrip between any two points in the U.S. for $169. If **boarding at a remote "flag stop,"** be sure you know exactly where the bus stops. It's a good idea to call the nearest agency and let them know you'll be waiting and at what time. Catch the driver's attention by standing on the side of the road and flailing your arms wildly—better to be embarrassed than stranded. If a bus passes (usually because of overcrowding), a later, less crowded bus should stop. Whatever you stow in compartments underneath the bus should be clearly marked; be sure to get a claim check for it, and watch to make sure your luggage is on the same bus as you.

Ameripass: Allows adults unlimited travel for 7 days ($179), 15 days ($289), 30 days ($399), or 60 days ($599). Prices for students with a valid college ID, and senior citizens are slightly less; 7 days ($159), 15 days ($259), 30 days ($359), or 60 days ($359). Children's passes are half the price of adults. The pass takes effect the first day used. Before purchasing an Ameripass, total up the separate bus fares between towns to make sure that the pass is really more economical, or at least worth the unlimited flexibility it provides. **TNMO Coaches, Vermont Transit,** and **Continental Panhandle Line** are Greyhound subsidiaries, and as such will honor Ameripasses; actually most bus companies in the U.S. will do so, but check for specifics.

International Ameripass: For travelers from outside North America. Primarily peddled in foreign countries, they can also be purchased in either of Greyhound's International Offices, located in New York City and Los Angeles (800-246-8572). A 4-day pass, which can not be used during a weekend, is $99, 5-day pass $119, 7-day pass $159, 15-day pass $219, 30-day pass $299, 60-day pass $499.

Greyhound Lines of Canada (800-661-8747 in Canada or 403-265-9111 in the United States) is a Canadian bus company with no relation to Greyhound.

Green Tortolse, 494 Broadway, San Francisco, CA 94133 (415-956-7500 or 800-867-8647), has "hostels on wheels" in remodeled diesel buses done up for living and eating on the road; meals are prepared communally. Prices include transportation, sleeping space on the bus, and tours of the regions through which you pass. Deposits ($100 most trips) are generally required since space is tight. Trips run June to October. From Hartford, Boston, or New York to San Francisco takes 10-14 days and costs about $300-380 plus $76-81 for food. There are also roundtrip vacation loops that start and finish in San Francisco winding through Yosemite National Park, Northern California, Baja California, the Grand Canyon, or Alaska along the way. Prepare for an earthy trip; the buses have no toilets and little privacy. Reserve one to two months in advance; however, many trips have space available at departure.

East Coast Explorer (718-694-9667 or 800-610-2680 outside NYC) is an inexpensive way to tour the East Coast between NYC and Boston or Washington, D.C. For $3-7 more than Greyhound, you and 13 other passengers will travel all day (10-11 hr.) on back roads stopping at natural and historic sites. One trip per week runs in each direction between NYC and Washington, D.C. ($32), as between NYC and Boston ($29). The air-conditioned bus will pick up and drop off at most hostels and budget hotels. Reservations are required.

BY CAR

Let's Go lists U.S. highways thus: "I" (as in "I-90") refers to Interstate highways, "U.S." (as in "U.S. 1") to United States highways, and "Rte." (as in "Rte. 7") to state and local highways. For Canadian highways, "TCH" refers to the Trans-Canada Highway, "Hwy." or "autoroute" refers to standard automobile routes.

Automobile Clubs

American Automobile Association (AAA), 1050 Hingham St., Rocklin, MA 02370 (800-AAA-HELP/222-4357) is the best-known of the auto clubs. It offers free trip-planning services, roadmaps and guidebooks, discounts on car rentals, emergency road service anywhere in the U.S., free towing, and commission-free traveler's cheques from American Express. AAA has reciprocal agreements with the auto associations of many other countries which often provide you with full benefits while in the U.S.

AAA has two types of membership, basic and plus, but the two services do not differ greatly. Basic membership fees are $54 for the first year with $40 annual renewal; $23 yearly for associate (a family member in household).

On the Road

Tune up the car before you leave, and make sure the tires are in good repair and have enough air. Get good maps: **Rand McNally's Road Atlas,** covering all of the USA and Canada, is one of the best (available at bookstores and gas stations, $10). A **compass** and a **car manual** can also be very useful.

In general, you should always carry a spare tire and jack, jumper cables, extra oil, flares, a flashlight, and blankets (in case you break down at night or in the winter). When traveling in the summer or in the desert bring five gallons of water for drinking and for the radiator. In extremely hot weather, use the air conditioner with restraint; if you see the car's temperature gauge climbing, turn it off. Turning the heater on full blast will help cool the engine. If radiator fluid is steaming, turn off the car for half an hour. *Never pour water over the engine to cool it.* Never lift a searing hot hood. In remote areas, remember to bring emergency food and water.

Gas in the U.S. runs about $1.25 per gallon (33¢ per litre), but prices vary widely according to state gasoline taxes. In Canada, gas costs CDN55-60¢ per litre (CDN$2-2.25 per gallon). **Sleeping in a car or van parked in a city is extremely dangerous—** even the most dedicated budget traveler should not consider it an option. **Be sure to buckle up**—seat belts are required by law in many regions of the U.S. and Canada. The **speed limit in the U.S.** is either 55 or 65 mph in most places. Heed the limit; not only does it save gas, but most local police forces and state troopers make frequent use of radar to catch speed demons. **Speed limit in Canada** is 100km/hr.

How to Navigate the Interstates

In the 1950s, President Eisenhower envisioned an **interstate system,** a federally funded network of highways designed primarily to subsidize American commerce. His dream has been realized, and there is actually an easily comprehensible, consistent system for numbering interstates. Even numbered interstates run east-west and odd ones run north-south, decreasing in number toward the south and the west. North-south routes begin on the West Coast with I-5 and end with I-95 on the East Coast. The southernmost east-west route is I-4 in Florida. The northernmost east-west route is I-94, stretching from Montana to Wisconsin. Three-digit numbers signify branches of other interstates (e.g., I-285 is a branch of I-85), often a bypass skirting around a large city.

Renting

Although the cost of renting a car is often prohibitive for long distances, renting for local trips may be reasonable. **Auto rental agencies** fall into two categories: national companies with hundreds of branches, and local agencies which serve only one city.

National chains usually allow cars to be picked up in one city and dropped off in another (for a hefty charge). By calling a toll-free number you can reserve a reliable car anywhere in the country. Drawbacks include steep prices and high minimum ages for rentals (usually 25). If you're 21 or older and have a major credit card in your name, you may be able to rent where the minimum age would otherwise rule you out. **Alamo** (800-327-9633) rents to ages 21-24 with a major credit card for an additional $20 per day. **Avis** (800-331-1212) and **Hertz** (800-654-3131) enforce a minimum age of 25, unless the renter has a corporate account. Some branches of **Budget** (800-527-0700) rent to ages 21-24 with a credit card, but it's not the norm. Most **Dollar** (800-800-4000) branches and some **Thrifty** (800-367-2277 or 703-658-2200) locations allow ages 21-24 to rent for an additional daily fee of about $20. **Rent-A-Wreck** (800-421-7253) specializes in supplying vehicles that are past their prime for lower-than-average prices. Most branches rent to ages 21-24 with an additional fee, but policies and prices vary from agency to agency.

Most packages allow you a certain number of miles free before the usual charge of 30-40¢ per mile takes effect; if you'll be driving a long distance (a few hundred miles or more), ask for an unlimited mileage package. Always be sure to ask whether the price includes insurance against theft and collision. There may be an additional charge, the collision and damage waiver (CDW), which usually comes to about $12-15 per day. If you use **American Express** to rent the car, they will generally cover the CDW; call AmEx's car division (800-338-1670) for more info.

Buying

Adventures on Wheels, 42 Hwy 36, Middletown, NJ 07748 (908-583-8714; fax 583-8932), will sell domestic and international travelers a camper or station wagon, organize its registration and provide insurance, and guarantee that they will buy it back from you after you have finished your travels. Buy a camper for $6000-8000, use it for 5-6 months, and sell it back for $4000-4500. The main office is in New York/New Jersey; there are other offices in Los Angeles, San Francisco, and Miami. Vehicles can be picked up at one office and dropped off at another.

Auto Transport Companies

These services match drivers with car owners who need cars moved from one city to another. Would-be travelers give the company their desired destination and the company finds a car which needs to go there. The only expenses are gas, tolls, and your own living expenses. Some companies insure their cars; with others, your security deposit covers any breakdowns or damage. You must be at least 21, have a valid license, and agree to drive about 400 mi. per day on a fairly direct route. Companies regularly inspect current and past job references, take your fingerprints, and require a cash bond. Cars are available between most points, although it's easiest to find cars for traveling from coast to coast; New York and Los Angeles are popular transfer points. If offered a car, look it over first. Think twice about accepting a gas guzzler since you'll be paying for the gas. With the company's approval you may be able to share the cost with several companions.

Auto Driveaway, 310 S. Michigan Ave., Chicago, IL 60604 (800-346-2277; e-mail jsonl@aol.com; http://www.autodriveaway.com).
A. Anthony's Driveaway, 4391 NW 19th Ave., Pompano Beach, FL 33064 (305-970-7384; fax 970-3881).
Across America Driveaway, 3626 Calumet Ave., Hammond, IN 46320 (800-964-7874; 310-798-3377 in L.A.; 312-889-7737 in Chicago).

BY BICYCLE

Before you rush onto the byways of America pedaling furiously away on your banana-seat Huffy Desperado, remember that safe and secure cycling requires a quality helmet and lock. A good helmet costs about $40—much cheaper than critical head surgery. U-shaped **Kryptonite** or **Citadel** locks run about $30 and carry insurance against theft for one or two years if your bike is registered with the police. **Bike Nashbar,** 4111 Simon Rd., Youngstown, OH 44512 (800-627-4227; fax 330-782-2856), is the leading mail-order catalog for cycling equipment.

Adventure Cycling Association, P.O. Box 8308-P, Missoula, MT 59807 (406-721-1776; fax 721-8754; e-mail acabike@aol.com). A national, non-profit organization that researches and maps long-distance routes and organizes bike tours for members. Membership $128 in the U.S., $35 in Canada and Mexico.
The Canadian Cycling Association, 1600 James Naismith Dr., #212A, Gloucester, Ont. K1B 5N4 (613-748-5629; fax 748-5692; email cycling@cdnsport.ca). Distributes *The Canadian Cycling Association's Complete Guide to Bicycle Touring in Canada* (CDN$20), plus guides to specific regions of Canada, Alaska and the Pacific Coast. Also sells maps and books.

ESSENTIALS

BY MOTORCYCLE

It may be cheaper than car travel, but it takes a tenacious soul (and ass) to endure a motorcycle tour. If you must carry a load, keep it low and forward where it won't distort the cycle's center of gravity. Fasten it either to the seat or over the rear axle in saddle or tank bags. Those considering a long journey should contact the **American Motorcyclist Association** (800-AMA-JOIN/262-5646), the linchpin of U.S. biker culture. A full membership ($29 per year) includes a subscription to the extremely informative *American Motorcyclist* magazine and a kick-ass patch for your riding jacket.

Of course, safety should be your primary concern. Motorcycles are incredibly vulnerable to crosswinds, drunk drivers, and the blind spots of cars and trucks. *Always ride defensively.* Dangers skyrocket at night; travel in the daytime. Wear the best helmet you can find; helmets are required by law in many states. Americans should ask their State Departments of Motor Vehicles for a motorcycle operator's manual.

Americade is an enormous week-long annual touring rally. In 1997 it will be held June 2-7 in Lake George, NY. Registration is $50 per person for the week or $12 per day. Call 518-656-3696 to register.

BY THUMB

Brace yourself for a whitebox:

> *Let's Go* urges you to consider the great risks and disadvantages of hitchhiking before thumbing it. Hitching means entrusting your life to a randomly selected person who happens to stop beside you on the road. While this may be comparatively safe in some areas of Europe and Australia, it is generally *not* so in the U.S. We do not recommend it. We strongly urge you to find other means of transportation and to avoid situations where hitching is the only option.

■ Accommodations

You have to sleep somewhere. Wherever you go, try to make reservations in advance, especially if you'll be traveling during peak tourist season. If you find yourself in truly dire financial straits, you can call the **Traveler's Aid Society** in some larger cities as a last resort; they will likely send you to a shelter. Local crisis hotlines may also be able to help.

HOTELS AND MOTELS

Many visitors centers, especially ones off major thoroughfares entering a state, have hotel coupons that can save you a bundle; if you don't see any, ask. Budget motels are usually clustered off the highway several miles outside of town, but the carless (and the light of wallet) may do better to try the hostels, YMCAs, YWCAs, and dorms downtown. The annually updated *National Directory of Budget Motels* ($6, plus $2 shipping), from **Pilot Books,** 103 Copper St., Babylon NY 11702 (516-422-2225 or 516-422-2227; fax 516-422-2227), covers over 2200 low-cost chain motels in the U.S. Pilot Books also publishes *The Hotel/Motel Special Program and Discount Guide* ($6, plus $2 shipping), which lists hotels and motels offering special discounts. Also look for the comprehensive *State by State Guide to Budget Motels* ($13), from Marlor Press, Inc., 4304 Brigadoon Dr., St. Paul, MN 55126 (800-669-4908 or 612-484-4600; fax 612-490-1182; email marlor@ix.netcom.com).

Chains usually adhere to a level of cleanliness and comfort more consistent than locally operated budget competitors. The cellar-level price of a single is about $30. Some budget chains are **Motel 6** (800-466-8356), **Super 8 Motels** (800-800-8000, 605-229-8708; fax 605-229-8900; http://www.super8motels.com/super8.html; call for their International Directory), **Choice Hotels International** (800-453-4511), and **Best Western International** (800-528-1234 or 602-957-4200; fax 602-957-5505; inquire

ESSENTIALS

about discounts for seniors, families, frequent travelers, groups, or government personnel).

HOSTELS

For tight budgets and those lonesome traveling blues, hostels can't be beat. Hostels are generally dorm-style accommodations, often in single-sex large rooms with bunk beds; some hostels offer private rooms for families and couples. They often have kitchens and utensils for your use, bike or moped rentals, storage areas, and laundry facilities. There can be drawbacks; some hostels close during certain daytime "lock-out" hours, have a curfew, impose a maximum stay or, less frequently, require that you do chores. Fees range from $5 to $25 per night, hostels associated with one of the large hostel associations often have lower rates for members. *The Hostel Handbook for the U.S.A. & Canada* (Jim Williams, Ed.; available for $3 from Dept: IGH, 722 Saint Nicholas Ave., NY, NY 10031; email Hostel@aol.com) lists over 500 hostels. If you have Internet access, check out the **Internet Guide to Hostelling** (http://hostels.com). Reservations for HI hostels may be made via the International Booking Network (IBN), a computerized system which allows you to book to and from HI hostels months in advance for a nominal fee. If you plan to stay in hostels, consider joining one of these associations:

Hostelling International-American Youth Hostels (HI-AYH), 733 15th St. NW, Suite 840, Washington, D.C. 20005 (202-783-6161; fax 202-783-6171; http://www.taponline.com/tap/travel/hostels/pages/hosthp.html). Maintains 34 offices and over 150 hostels in the U.S. Memberships can be purchased at many travel agencies (see p. 27) or the national office in Washington, D.C. 1-year membership $25, under 18 $10, over 54 $15, family cards $35; includes *Hostelling North America: The Official Guide to Hostels in Canada and the United States.* Reserve by letter, phone, fax, or through the International Booking Network (IBN), a computerized reservation system which lets you book from other HI hostels worldwide up to six months in advance. Basic rules (with much local variation): check-in 5-8pm, check-out 9:30am (although most urban hostels have 24-hr. access), max. stay 3 days, no pets or alcohol allowed on the premises. Fees $5-22 per night.

Hostelling International-Canada (HI-C), 400-205 Catherine St., Ottawa, Ontario K2P 1C3, Canada (613-237-7884; fax 237-7868). Maintains 73 hostels throughout Canada. IBN booking centers in Edmonton, Montreal, Ottawa, and Vancouver; expect CDN$9-22.50/night. Membership packages: 1-yr, under 18 CDN$12; 1-yr., over 18 CDN$25; 2-yr., over 18 CDN$35; lifetime CDN$175.

Rucksackers North America, 1412 Cerrillos Rd., Santa Fe, NM 87505 (505-988-1153); ask for Preston Ellsworth.

Backpackers Hostels Canada, a very helpful service, can be reached by sending an e-mail message to ljones@mail.foxnet.net.

BED AND BREAKFASTS

For a cozy alternative to impersonal hotel rooms, B&Bs (private homes with rooms available to travelers) range from the acceptable to the sublime. Hosts will sometimes go out of their way to be accommodating by accepting travelers with pets, giving personalized tours, or offering home-cooked meals. On the other hand, many B&Bs do not provide phones, TVs, or private bathrooms.

Several travel guides and reservation services specialize in B&Bs. Among the more extensive guides are *Bed & Breakfast, USA* ($16), from Tourist House Associates, Inc., RR 1, Box 12-A, Greentown, PA 18426, *The Complete Guide to Bed and Breakfasts, Inns and Guesthouses in the U.S. and Canada* ($17), which lists over 11,000 B&Bs plus inns (available through Lanier Publications, P.O. Box D, Petaluma, CA 94952, tel. 707-763-0271; fax 707-763-5762; email lanier@travelguides; or CompuServe ["Go B&B"] or America Online ["Bed & Breakfast Guide Online"]), and *America's Favorite Inns, B&Bs, and Small Hotels* ($20, CDN$27). All three can be

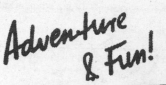

found in bookstores. The following services book rooms in B&Bs throughout the U.S. and Canada:

Bed and Breakfast International, P.O. Box 282910, San Francisco, CA 94128-2910 (800-872-4500 or 415-696-1690; fax 415-696-1699). Rates range $60-$150 per night per room and include breakfast; 2-night min. stay. Discounts for singles, families with children, and stays over one week.

Bed and Breakfast: The National Network (TNN) of Reservation Services, Box 4616, Springfield, MA 01101 (800-884-4288; fax 401-847-7309; email anna's@wsii.com; http://www.bandbnet.com) can book reservations at over 7000 B&Bs throughout America and Canada. A travel kit will be mailed upon request.

YMCAS AND YWCAS

Not all **Young Men's Christian Association (YMCA)** locations offer lodging; those that do are often located in urban downtowns, which can be convenient but a little gritty. YMCA rates are usually lower than a hotel's but higher than a hostel's and may include use of libraries, pools, air conditioning, and other facilities. Many YMCAs accept women and families (group rates often available), and some (as in Los Angeles) will not lodge people under 18 without parental permission. All reservations must be made and paid for in advance, with a traveler's check (signed top and bottom), U.S. money order, certified check, Visa, or MasterCard. Call the local YMCA in question for fee information. For info or reservations (reservation fee $3), contact **Y's Way International,** 224 E. 47th St., New York, NY 10017 (212-308-2899; fax 212-308-3161; http://www.ymca.org/ for links to branches worldwide).

Most **Young Women's Christian Associations (YWCAs)** accommodate only women or, sometimes, couples. Nonmembers are often required to join when lodging. For more information or a world-wide directory ($10), write **YWCA-USA,** 726 Broadway, New York, NY 10003 (212-614-2700). For Y's in **Canada,** contact the Montreal YMCA at 1450 Stanley St., Montreal, PQ H3A 2W6 (514-849-8393; fax 514-849-8017) or YMCA Canada, 2160 Yonge St., Toronto, Ontario M4S 2A9 (416-485-9447; fax 417-485-8228).

ALTERNATIVE ACCOMODATIONS

Barclay International Group, 150 West 52nd Street, New York, NY 10022 (800-845-6636 or 212-832-3777; fax 212-753-1139), arranges hotel alternative accommodations (apartment, condo, cottage, B&B or villa rentals) in over 20 countries, including the U.S. and Canada. Most are equipped with kitchens, telephones, TV, and concierge and maid service. Rentals are pricey, starting around $500/week off-season. Generally less expensive than hotels with comparable amenities, these accomodations may suit families with children, business travelers, or Kosher or vegetarian travelers.

Homestay/USA, 25 Bay State Rd., Boston, MA 02215 (East Coast office: 800-662-2967 or 617-247-0350, fax 247-2967; West Coast Office: 800-858-0292 or 415-288-1380, fax 288-1381). World Learning's Homestay/USA arranges homestays with U.S. families for international visitors ages 15 and up. The East Coast office handles placements in the northeast and southeast United States while the west Coast office handles other regions.

■ Camping and the Outdoors

The Health and Packing sections both contain valuable advice for outdoor travelers.

ROUGHING IT SAFELY

Stay warm, stay dry, stay hydrated. The vast majority of life-threatening wilderness problems stem from a failure to follow this advice. If you're going into an area that is not well traveled or well marked, let someone know where you're hiking and how long you intend to be out. *Never go camping or hiking by yourself for any signifi-*

cant time or distance. On any hike, overnight or for the day, that will take you more than one mile from civilization, you should pack enough equipment to keep you alive in case of disaster: raingear, warm layers (not cotton!), a hat, mittens, a first-aid kit, high energy food, and water. Whether you're bound for a densely populated campground or deep wilderness, a good guide to outdoor survival is *How to Stay Alive in the Woods,* by Bradford Angier (Macmillan, $8). For information on outdoor ailments, such as rabies, giardia and insects, see On-the-Road Ailments (see Health, p. 14).

While safety from the environment is your main concern, you should also be concerned about safety from other people. Keep your gear nearby at all times; campgrounds can be ideal spots for thieves or worse. A well-lit and well-monitored campground can minimize this problem, but you should still be wary. Groups should try to stay together after dark.

It is also important to consider your effect on the environment. Because firewood is scarce in popular parks, campers are asked to make small fires using only dead branches or brush; using a campstove is a safe way to cook. Check ahead to see if the park prohibits campfires altogether. To avoid digging a rain trench for your tent, pitch it on high, dry ground. Don't cut vegetation, and don't clear campsites. Make sure your campsite is at least 150 ft. from any water supply or body of water. If there are no toilet facilities, bury human waste at least four inches deep and 150 ft. or more from any water supply or campsite. Always pack your trash in a plastic bag and carry it with you until you reach the next trash can; burning and burying pollute the environment.

BEAR IN MIND

The aggressiveness of bears varies from region to region. Rangers and other local authorities will always be your best resource for learning the details of bear behavior (and how best to deal with it) in a particular region. As a basic rule of thumb, if you're close enough for a bear to be observing you, you're too close. To avoid a grizzly experience, never feed a bear, or tempt it with such delectables as open trash cans. Keep your camp clean, and keep your trash high off the ground. Avoid indulging in greasy foods, especially bacon and ham. Bears are also attracted to perfume smells; do without cologne, scented soap, and hairspray while camping. Leave your packs empty and open on the ground so that a bear can nose through them without shredding them. When you sleep, don't even think about leaving food or any scented items (trash, toiletries) near your tent.

Always shine a flashlight when walking at night: the bears will clear out before you arrive if given sufficient warning. If you see a bear at a distance, calmly walk (don't run) in the other direction. If you stumble upon a bear cub, leave immediately, lest its over-protective mother stumble upon you. If you are attacked by a bear, assume the fetal position, put your arms over the back of your neck, and play dead.

EQUIPMENT

At the core of your equipment is the **sleeping bag.** Your purchase should depend on the climate in which you plan to camp; sleeping bags are rated according to the lowest outdoor temperature at which they will still keep you warm. If a bag's rating is not a temperature but a seasonal description, keep in mind that "summer" translates to a rating of 30-40°F, "three-season" means 20°F, and "winter" means below 0°F. Bags are made either of down (warmer and lighter) or of synthetic material (cheaper, heavier, more durable, and warmer when wet). Low prices for good sleeping bags: $65-100 for a summer synthetic, $135-200 for a three-season synthetic, $150-225 for a three-season down bag, and upwards of $250-550 for a down winter-bag. **Sleeping bag pads** range from $13 to $30, while **air mattresses** go for $25-50. Another option is the part-foam, part air-mattress **Therm-A-Rest,** which inflates to full padding when unrolled.

When you select a **tent,** your major considerations should be shape and size. The easiest tents are free-standing, with their own frames and suspension systems. They

set up quickly and require no staking (though staking adds security on windy days). Low profile dome tents are especially efficient; when pitched, their internal space is almost entirely usable, which means little unnecessary bulk. Be sure your tent has a rain fly; seal the tent's seams with waterproofer. Regarding size, two people *can* fit in a two-person tent but will find life more pleasant in a four-person. Good two-person tents start at about $135; $200 will fetch a four-person. Backpackers and cyclists prefer small, lightweight models (from $145). You can often cut your costs in half by finding outdated models. **Sierra Design,** 1255 Powell St., Emeryville, CA, 94608 (510-450-9555), sells excellent tents, including the two-person "Clip Flashlight" ($170) that weighs less than 4 lbs.

Other necessities include a **plastic groundcloth** to protect the tent floor and a **battery-operated lantern** (*never* gas). When camping in autumn, winter, or spring, bring along a "space blanket," an amazingly compact technological wonder that helps you retain your body heat ($3.50-13; doubles as a groundcloth). Large, collapsible **water sacks** will significantly improve your lot in primitive campgrounds. They weigh practically nothing when empty, but can get bulky. **Campstoves** come in all sizes, weights, and fuel types, but none are truly cheap ($30-85). Beware: stove gas can be heavy and bulky if you bring too much.

Recreational Equipment, Inc. (REI), 1700 45th St. E, Sumner, WA 98390 (800-426-4840; http://www.rei.com). Stocks a wide range of the latest in camping gear and holds great seasonal sales. Many items guaranteed for life (excluding normal wear and tear).

L.L. Bean, Casco St., Freeport, ME 04033-0001 (800-341-4341). Supplies its own equipment and national-brand merchandise. 100% satisfaction guaranteed on all purchases. Freeport outlet open Sun.-Thurs. 8am-10pm, Fri. and Sat. 8am-11pm.

Campmor, Inc. P.O. Box 700, Saddle River, NJ 07458-0700 (800-526-4784; http://www.campmore.com). A wide selection of name-brand equipment at low prices. One-yr. guarantee on unused or defective merchandise.

Eastern Mountain Sports (EMS), One Vose Farm Rd., Peterborough, NH 03458 (603-924-7231). Stores nationwide (Colorado to Virginia to Maine) provide excellent service and guaranteed customer satisfaction on all items sold, though the prices are slightly higher. They don't have a catalog, and they generally don't take mail or phone orders; call above number for the nearest branch.

Cheaper equipment is sold on the used market, but make sure you know what you're buying. Consult want ads and student bulletin boards, and take someone knowledgeable along. Spending a little more money up front may save you from having to replace equipment later.

A good source of info on **camping vehicles (RVs)** is the **Recreational Vehicle Industry Association,** P.O. Box 2999, Reston, VA 20195-0999; 1896 Preston White Dr., Reston, VA 20191-4363 (703-620-6003). For info regarding RV camping publications and state campground associations, call the **Go Camping America Committee,** (800-47-SUNNY/78669).

NATIONAL PARKS

National Parks protect some of the most spectacular scenery in North America. Though their primary purpose is preservation, the parks also host recreational activities like ranger talks, guided hikes, skiing, and snowshoe expeditions. Generally, internal roads allow you to reach the interior and major sights even if you are not a hiker. For info pertaining to the national park system, contact the **National Park Service,** Office of Public Inquiries, P.O. Box 37127, Washington, D.C. 20013-7127 (202-208-4747). The **National Park Foundation,** 1101 17th St. NW, Suite 1102 Washington, D.C. 20036 (202-785-4500), distributes *The Complete Guide to America's National Parks* by mail-order ($16, plus $3 shipping).

Entrance fees vary. The larger and more popular parks charge a $4-10 entry fee for cars and sometimes a nominal fee for pedestrians and cyclists. The **Golden Eagle**

Passport ($25), available at park entrances, allows entry into all national parks for one year. Visitors ages 62 and over qualify for the **Golden Age Passport** ($10 one-time fee), which entitles the passport-holder's party to free park entry, a 50% discount on camping, and 50% reductions on various recreational fees for the passport holder. Persons eligible for federal benefits on account of disabilities can enjoy the same privileges with the **Golden Access Passport** (free). Golden Age and Golden Access Passports must be purchased at a park entrance with proof of age or federal eligibility, respectively. All passports are also valid at National Monuments, Forests, Wildlife Preserves, and other national recreation sites.

Most national parks have both backcountry and developed tent **camping;** some welcome RVs, and a few offer grand lodges. At the more popular parks in the U.S. and Canada, reservations are essential, available through **DESTINET** (800-365-2267 in U.S.; 619-452-8787 outside the U.S.) no sooner than seven months in advance. Lodges and indoor accommodations should be reserved months in advance. Campgrounds often observe first-come, first-camp policies. Arrive early; many campgrounds fill up by late morning. Some limit your stay and/or the number of people in a group.

Often less accessible and less crowded, **National Forests** provide a purist's alternative to parks. While some have recreation facilities, most are equipped only for primitive camping—pit toilets and no water are the norm. Entrance fees, when charged, are $10-20, but camping is generally free, or $3-4. Backpackers can take advantage of specially designated wilderness areas, which have regulations barring all vehicles; the necessary wilderness permits can be obtained at the U.S. Forest Service field office in the area. If you are interested in exploring a National Forest, call or write for a copy of *A Guide to Your National Forests* (publication *FS* #418); **U.S. Forest Service,** U.S. Department of Agriculture, P.A.O., 2 CEN, P.O. Box 96090, Washington, D.C. 20090-6090 (202-205-1760). This booklet includes a list of all national forest addresses; request maps and other information directly from the forest(s) you plan to visit.

■ Lines of Communication

U.S. MAIL

Offices of the **U.S. Postal Service** are usually open Monday to Friday from 9am to 5pm and sometimes on Saturday until about noon; branches in many larger cities open earlier and close later. All are closed on national holidays. If you don't want to make the trip to the post office, most **hotels** and **hostel owners** will send stamped postcards or letters home for you if you ask. Postal rates in the U.S.: **within the U.S.,** postcards 20¢, letters: 1oz. 32¢, 23¢ per additional ounce. Because of recent mail bomb scares, the U.S. Postal Service now requires that **overseas** letters be mailed directly from the post office and accompanied by a customs form. **Overseas rates:** postcards 50¢, ½oz. 60¢, 1oz. $1, 40¢ per additional ounce. **Aerogrammes,** sheets that fold into envelopes and travel via air mail, are available at post offices for 50¢. Domestic mail generally takes 3-5 days; overseas mail, 7-14 days. Write **"AIR MAIL"** on the front of the envelope for speediest delivery.

If people want to get in touch with you, mail can be sent **General Delivery** to a city's main post office in the U.S. or Canada. You should bring a passport or other ID to pick up General Delivery mail. *Always write "Hold for 30 Days" in a conspicuous spot on the envelope.* Family and friends can send letters to you labeled like this:

> Michael J. <u>Fox</u> (underline last name for accurate filing)
> c/o General Delivery
> Post Office Street Address
> Sitcomsville, GA 30605
> USA (if from another country)

In both the U.S. and Canada, **American Express** offices will act as a mail service for cardholders if you contact them in advance. For information and a complete list of offices, call 800-528-4800 and ask for the *Traveler's Companion* booklet.

TELEPHONES

Telephone numbers in the U.S. and Canada consist of a three-digit area code, a three-digit exchange, and a four-digit number, written as 123-456-7890. Numbers with an **800** area code are toll-free numbers. A quick guide:

Local calls: Dial the last 7 digits.
Long-distance calls within the U.S./Canada: 1 + area code + 7-digit number. Same area code calls are not always local; for long-distance calls within an area code: 1 + 7-digit number. For toll-free 800 numbers: 1 + 800 + 7-digit number.
International calls: Dial the universal international access code (011) followed by the country code, the city code, and the local number. Country codes and city codes may sometimes be listed with a zero in front (e.g. 033 for France), but when using 011, drop successive zeros (e.g., 011-33). In some areas you will need to give the number to the operator, who will then place the call for you.

Evening rates are considerably less than weekday rates (generally Sun.-Fri. 5-11pm); **night and weekend rates** are cheaper than evening rates (generally Mon.-Fri. 11pm-8am, all day Sat., and all day Sun. except 5-11pm).

Dialing **"0"** will get you the **operator,** who is omnipotent in all matters remotely connected with phones. To obtain local phone numbers for a specific place or to find area codes for other cities, call **directory assistance** at **411** or look in the local **white pages** telephone directory; for **long-distance directory assistance,** dial **1-(area code)-555-1212.**

Pay phones are plentiful, most often stationed on street corners and in public areas. Put your coins (10-25¢ for a local call depending on the region) into the slot and before dialing. If there is no answer or if you get a busy signal, you will get your money back after hanging up, but if you connect with an answering machine the phone will gobble your coins. If you are at a pay phone and don't have barrels of change, you can dial "0" for the operator and ask to place one of the following types of calls:

Collect call: If whoever picks up the phone call accepts the charges, he or she will be billed for the call. The cheapest is MCI's 800-COLLECT (205-5328) service, which is 20-44% less expensive than other collect rates. AT&T's collect service, 800-CALL-ATT, guarantees AT&T lines and rates for the call.

Person-to-person collect call: A little more expensive than a normal collect call, but a charge appears only if the person you wish to speak to is there (for example, if you want to speak to Michelle but not her parents).

Third-party billing: Bills the call to a third party. Have the number of the place you want to call and the number of the place you want to bill the call to (e.g., home).

Alternatively, you may want to consider getting a **calling card number,** which is much cheaper. If you live in the U.S., contact **AT&T** (800-225-5288 for U.S.residents; others call 800-451-4341) or **MCI** (800-444-3333) for more information. In other countries, call your local phone company. In **Canada,** contact Bell Canada's Canada Direct (800-565-4708), in **Australia,** contact Telsta Australia Direct (tel. 13 22 00); in **Ireland,** Telecom Eireann Ireland Direct (800 250-250); in **New Zealand,** Telecom New Zealand (tel. 123); in South Africa **Telkom South Africa** (0903); in the **U.K.,** British Telecom BT Direct (800-345-144). Travelers with British Telecom, Telecom Eireann, New Zealand Telecom, Telkom South Africa, or Telecom Australia accounts at home can use special **access numbers** to place calls from the U.S. through their home systems. All companies except Telkom South Africa have different access numbers depending on whether their cooperative partner in the U.S. is AT&T, MCI, or Sprint. Access numbers are: British Telecom (800-445-5667 AT&T, 800-444-2162 MCI, 800-800-0008 Sprint); Telecom Australia (800-682-2878 AT&T, 800-937-6822 MCI, 800-676-0061 Sprint); Telkom South Africa (800-949-7027).

Let's Go Picks

Were we limited to a single page, it would look a little bit like this one here, on which we tear off our veneer of objectivity and shamelessly declare our personal favorites—the sights, bites, and hostels we liked best. Enjoy! For more extensive listings, see the pages that follow. All Let's Go Picks are indexed.

Naturally Splendid: Waipi'o Valley, Big Island of HI. The vista is worth a thousand pictures. **Arches National Park,** UT. The most beautiful place on Earth according to author Edward Abbey; we say it's definitely up there. **Grand Canyon,** AZ. Makes the so-entitled movie seem like Child's Play. **Cedar Breaks National Monument,** UT. A relatively undiscovered natural beauty.

Human-Made Wonders: Gateway Arch, St. Louis, MO. Like a big silver rainbow, but enduring and elevator-equipped. **Carhenge,** NE. Read all about it on p. 487. **Mount Rushmore,** SD. Four stoned Presidents. **Corn Palace,** Mitchell, SD. The only house of grain that's fit for princes.

Hospitable Hostels: Winter Park Hostel, Winter Park, CO. Friendliness, amenities, superb location—Winter Park Hostel, will you marry us? **Shagawa Sam's,** Ely, MN. So what if it's in the boondocks? There's a barbecue downstairs. **Lowenstein-Long House/Castle Hostelry,** Memphis, TN. Quirkily pleasant. **St. Augustine Hostel,** FL. Jean and Peter light up the Sunshine State. **Ottawa International Hostel,** Ontario. In a former prison. A kinder, gentler slammer.

Camp Here: Jenny Lake, Grand Teton National Park, WY. This may be the most spectacular spot in the nation to pitch a tent, with not one but two views of the Tetons: look up, or down at their reflection in said lake. **King Creek,** near Bryce Canyon, UT. There's water, there are pine trees, it's off a dirt road—what more could a peace-seeker want? **Anywhere in Kentucky.** Stop the car and treat yourself to a night in a Kentucky State Park campground.

Towns We Hate to Leave: Chattanooga, TN. Some may call it Chattavegas—we call it a little-touristed pocket of nice campgrounds and people, cheap eats, and cool attractions. **Chapel Hill, NC.** Music and cyclists galore. Chapel Hill, take us away. **New York City.** Hardly undiscovered, but wow! What a treasure!

Scenic Drives: Telluride to Durango, via Silverton, CO. This is what roadtripping is all about. **Mt. Evans Road,** CO. Watch the sun set over the Continental Divide to the West as the lights go on in Denver, 10,000 ft. below your wheels.

Filling Up: Old Town Café, Missoula, MT. Gourmet oatmeal. **Jacob Lake Inn,** Grand Canyon North Rim, AZ. Shakes you need a spoon for. **Tomasita's,** Santa Fe, NM. Strawberry margaritas as smooth as the Macarena. **Arthur Bryant's,** Kansas City, MO. BBQ tasty enough for Jimmy Carter.

Sustenance in Style: Virginia's, Atlanta, GA. Pull out that black turtleneck—now is the time on Sprockets when we caffeinate. **The Red Crane,** San Francisco, CA. Award-winning Chinese cuisine in the city with the best Chinese food in America. **Ramsi's Café on the World,** Louisville, KY. Down-home blues, cosmopolitan eats, otherworldly reception. **The Grit,** Athens, GA. Crunchity crunch crunch.

Fab Festivals: Montréal International Fireworks Festival, Québec. Shame on you for strictly associating fireworks with U.S. patriotism. **Mardi Gras,** Mobile, AL. The New Orleans version does draw more crowds...but that just makes it crowded. Mobile's more intimate celebration is the vibrant original.

Watering Holes: Safehouse, Milwaukee, WI. The excitement starts at the door, where those who don't know the password must give an impromptu performance. **Sunset Grill and Tap,** Boston, MA. 500 microbrews, 110 taps. 'Nuff said. **Key West, FL.** The whole goshforsaken town.

The Foot's Fetish: Sand Dunes National Monument, NM. Peds-down winner of the Most Interesting Texture Beneath Bare Feet award. Hike barefoot if not naked.

Classy Cans: Ruby Tequila's, Amarillo, TX. Their restroom is a sensory treat, with Spanish language tapes playing and brightly-painted flowers adorning the walls. The fajitas are also excellent. **Sage Creek Campground,** Badlands National Park, SD. Such pit toilets you have never seen.

UNITED STATES

Reaching from below the Tropic of Cancer to above the Arctic Circle and handily spanning the North American continent, the United States is undeniably big. It is a country defined by open spaces and an amazing breadth of terrain. Above and beyond its physical presence, the culture of the U.S. creeps across the globe, making the country unavoidable as well. American culture has grown from the seed of a government dedicated to individualism in a land large enough to allow for every person's personal space. Through decades of open-door immigration, the United States has absorbed and integrated millions of immigrants (4 million foreign-born settlers arrived between 1830 and 1850 alone) to create the melting pot which now defines the population. These days, some prefer the salad bowl metaphor, which allows for cultural particularism within the unified whole. The individuals and groups who compose the country's diverse character often chafe as they step into each other's space, but most will acknowledge that the conflict comes with the freedom. In recent years, the country which knew no bounds has been forced to become acquainted with physical, social, and economic constraints to its growth.

Perhaps the best thing any visitor or disenchanted American can do to regain hope in the whole experiment is to explore. Outside of the cities, the land that inspired this cross-continental adventure still awaits, and huge spaces assure us that there's still room to breathe and to move, and to let one another do the same.

■ History

IN THE BEGINNING

It is not known exactly when people first set foot in the Americas. Until recently, scientists estimated that the first Americans crossed the Bering Sea from Siberia on a land bridge during the last Ice Age, about 15,000 years ago. Recent archaeological digs have uncovered evidence of earlier habitation, but the validity of these findings is still questioned. It is certain that by 9000BC, scattered populations of hunter-gatherers lived in every corner of North America. These settlers adapted remarkably to their new environment; on the Plains, Native Americans hunted by forcing buffalo over ravines, and in the West, Aleuts and Eskimos hunted whales and other sea mammals. By the time of European colonization, around a hundred major groups composed nine cultural areas of North America.

EUROPEAN EXPLORATION AND COLONIZATION

The date of the first European exploration of North America is similarly disputed. The earliest Europeans to alight upon the "New World" were likely sea voyagers blown off course by storms. Two tales record the first deliberate explorations of North America: *The Saga of the Greenlanders* and *The Saga of Erik the Red* describe the travels of Icelanders who sailed to Greenland, and possibly as far south as northern New England, in 982AD. Northern Newfoundland was discovered and settled by the Vikings around the same time. But the most lasting "discovery" of the Americas occurred in 1492. Christopher Columbus found his voyage to the east blocked by Hispaniola in the Caribbean Sea. He believed he had reached the spice islands of the East Indies, and erroneously dubbed the inhabitants "Indians." Columbus' arrival launched one of the greatest cultural clashes in human history, one which the Native Americans undeniably lost.

Many Europeans came to the Americas in search of gold and silver; most were unsuccessful, but European colonization persisted. The Spanish boasted the most extensive American empire, based in South America and eventually spreading north into what are today New Mexico, Arizona, and Florida. St. Augustine (p. 320), founded in Florida in 1565, was the first permanent European settlement in the present-day United States. Meanwhile, the French and Dutch founded more modest empires to the north. It was the English, however, who most successfully settled the vast New World. After a few unsuccessful attempts, like the "lost colony" at Roanoke in North Carolina (p. 294), the English finally managed to establish a colony at Jamestown in 1607 (p. 246). The colonists struggled to survive in the New World. In 15 years, 8000 of the original 10,000 immigrants were dead. Luckily, friendly Powahatans introduced the colonists to a strain of Indian weed called tobacco, which achieved wild popularity in England. With an industry finally established, the economy improved, and the death rate fell. The Chesapeake Bay area became a land of opportunity for poor English; land was cheap, and passage to the New World could be paid for by indentured servitude. Not all labor was provided by indentured servants, however; the first African slaves were imported to Jamestown in 1619, and the slave trade became truly profitable in the later 17th century.

Not all English colonists sought wealth; many groups, including the English Puritans, came to escape religious persecution. Finding life intolerable under the Stuart reign, the Puritans sought to realize their hopes for a godly community in the New World. In 1620, they landed in Provincetown (p. 113) (*not* Plymouth Rock, p. 109) in what is now Massachusetts. Native Americans helped them to survive in a harsh land, inspiring one of the most treasured holidays in modern American culture, Thanksgiving. Though Britain's Empire grew to encompass 13 colonies along the eastern seaboard, the New England Puritans exerted a strong political and cultural influence until well after the Revolution.

CONSOLIDATION AND REVOLUTION

Throughout the first half of the 18th century, the English colonies expanded as people moved west into unsettled regions searching for more arable land. Valleys were settled, fields plowed, and babies born. A quarter-million settlers had grown into 2½ million by 1775. The British colonies experienced growing pains as the French attempted to expand their nearby empire. Several military clashes resulted; the greatest of these encounters was the Seven Years War, known in the U.S. as the French and Indian War. From 1756 to 1763, English colonists and British troops fought the French and their Native American allies, who joined the battle in exchange for French aid in inter-tribal conflicts. The British emerged victorious, and the 1763 Peace of Paris ceded French Canada to King George III, securing the colonies' boundaries from French incursion.

Enormous debts accompanied Britain's victory. Determined to make the colonists help pay the debts incurred in assuring their safety, the British government levied a number of taxes in the 1760s and early 1770s. The taxes were very unpopular; two of the most hated were the Stamp Act, which placed a tax on paper products and documents, and the tax on tea. The colonists felt they had a right to participate in decisions affecting their welfare, as they had grown accustomed to participating in colonial government, and they vigorously protested "taxation without representation." The British government repealed the Stamp Act in 1766, only to impose the Townshend Duties, tariffs on imported goods, a year later. Agitation over the taxes brought about the Boston Massacre in 1770 (p. 93). The Townshend Act was repealed, except for the tax on tea. The colonists protested the tea tax with the Boston Tea Party in December of 1774, in which a group dressed as Native Americans dumped several shiploads of English tea into Boston Harbor. The British response, dubbed the Intolerable Acts, was swift and harsh. Boston was effectively placed under siege, and the red-coated British soldiers who poured into town were met with armed rebellion. On July 4, 1776, the Continental Congress formally issued the *Declaration of Independence*, announcing the thirteen colonies' desire to be free of British rule. Initially a guerilla army composed of home-spun militia known as Minutemen, the Continental forces eventually grew into an effective army under the leadership of George Washington. Despite many setbacks, the Continental forces prevailed, sealing their victory by vanquishing British General Lord Cornwallis at Yorktown, Virginia (p. 246) in 1781 with the help of the French fleet.

Until 1787, the newly independent states functioned as a loose confederation. This arrangement proved unstable and problematic, so a Constitutional Convention was convened in Philadelphia (p. 194) to draw up a plan for a stronger central government and a more powerful executive. The debates of the men who worked at this convention, known as the Founding Fathers, resulted in the world's oldest written constitution. The document divides power between three separate branches of government—legislative, executive, and judicial. A system of checks and balances safeguards each branch against domination by any other. The first ten amendments were added immediately, so that all the states would ratify the document. These additions, known as the Bill of Rights, include the rights to free speech, freedom of the press, and freedom of religion. They are inalienable and cannot be infringed upon by the government. The *Constitution* is open to interpretation, and also provides for its own amendment. This flexibility is one of its greatest strengths; the *Constitution* has changed 27 times.

During the debate over the *Constitution*, the two-party system began to develop. The Federalists supported a strong central government which would encourage economic growth by providing aid to capitalists. Their opposition, the Jeffersonians, favored states' rights and feared the degenerative aspects of industrial capitalism. These issues are still central to America's sociopolitical debate, albeit in altered form—modern Republicans abhor big government but support capitalist pursuits, while today's Democrats side with centralized government and labor interests.

ONWARD AND OUTWARD: MANIFEST DESTINY

With the original thirteen states under stable federal rule, America began to expand westward. In 1803, President Thomas Jefferson purchased the Louisiana Territory (one-quarter of the present-day United States) from Napoleon for less than 3¢ an acre. Curious about what lay in this tract and eager to tap the northwest fur trade, Jefferson sent explorers Meriwether Lewis and William Clark to chart the region. With the aid of a Native American woman called Sacajawea, they reached Seaside, Oregon in October 1805. The work of Lewis and Clark strengthened American claims to the Oregon country, also claimed by Britain and Spain.

After the War of 1812 (a war over trade with Great Britain), the westward movement gained momentum. Manifest Destiny, a belief that the United States was destined by God to rule the continent, captured the ideological imagination of the era. Droves of people moved west in search of cheap, fertile land and a new life. America's annexation of Texas led Mexico to declare war in 1846. After American forces were cut down at the Alamo (p. 530), the war gained a rallying cry and strength of purpose. The U.S. won in 1848, forcing Mexico to cede most of the southwest and California—$15 million bought 1 million square mi. The money quickly paid large dividends; settlers discovered gold in the California hills, and the gold rush was on.

White settlers continued moving west, requisitioning land rapidly. The Homestead Act of 1862, which distributed tracts of government land to those who would develop and live on it, prompted the cultivation of the Great Plains. This large-scale settlement led to bloody battles with the Native Americans who had long inhabited these lands. Much of the legend of the Wild West revolves around tales of brave white settlers and stoic cowboys fending off attacks by Indians. These stories are largely distortions, created to justify the actions of the government in exploiting and displacing Native Americans. Nevertheless, expansion into wild frontier territory retains a significant place in America's self-image.

"A HOUSE DIVIDED"—THE CIVIL WAR

It became increasingly difficult for the United States to ease the tensions created by the existence of slavery within its borders. Although the *Declaration of Independence* nobly asserted that "all men are created equal," the *Constitution* allowed the slave trade to continue unrestricted for several years. Cultural, economic, and political differences divided North and South; slavery remained the basis of Southern agriculture, while the industrialized North was largely weaned from its dependence on slave labor by the mid-18th century. Compromises made while drawing up the *Constitution* were strained by westward expansion. The growing nation had to decide whether new territories would become free or slave states. The nation tried to work out its difficulties in laws like the Missouri Compromise of 1821, which legislated that all states north of latitude 36° 34' would be admitted to the Union as free states, except Missouri. But many did not want to compromise.

The 1860 election of Abraham Lincoln, who did not support the extension of slavery into the territories, pushed the southern states over the edge. South Carolina went first, seceding in late 1860. Twelve states (AL, AR, FL, GA, KY, LA, MS, MO, NC, TN, TX, and VA) followed in 1861. These states formed a Confederacy allowing greater autonomy and the freedom to pursue their agrarian, slave-based economy. For four years, the country endured a savage and bloody war, fought by the North to restore the Union, and by the South to break free from the North. The Civil War claimed more American lives than any other war in history. Finally, the North's greater industrialization and population overcame the South, and on April 9, 1865, General Robert E. Lee, the commander of the southern army, surrendered to General Ulysses S. Grant, leader of the northern forces, at Appomatox Court House, Virginia. Lincoln had led the North to victory, but the price was high. He was assassinated on April 14 by a Southern sympathizer. His legacy, the 13th Amendment, ended slavery in 1865, but the fight for black equality is still being fought.

INDUSTRIALIZATION AND WORLD WAR I

The period after the war brought Reconstruction to the South, and Industrial Revolution to the North. For twelve years, troops were stationed in the South to suppress violence, regulate elections, and impose penalties for violation of federal law. As the South strained under the punishment inflicted by the North, the economy in the North flourished. Rapid investment by captains of industry such as George Vanderbilt, Andrew Carnegie, and John D. Rockefeller boosted the American economy and increased American influence abroad. This industrial expansion occurred at great cost to workers and farmers, and trade unions grew in response to poor working conditions and low wages. The 19th-century form of unabashed "free market" capitalism soon began to collapse under its own weight, as witnessed by the recessions of the 1890s and the 1930s. The superficial high which the U.S. rode in the decades leading up to the turn of the century is known as the Gilded Age.

Politically, the United States was coming of age. Through victory in the Spanish-American War in 1898, the United States acquired colonies in the Philippines, Puerto Rico, and Cuba. The imperial spirit was embodied by President Theodore Roosevelt, who assumed the office upon the assassination of President McKinley in 1901. Roosevelt also embraced another dominant turn-of-the century phenomenon: progressivism, a movement that sought to create a more just social order by attacking the corruption and monopolistic practices of big business. The efforts of the progressives resulted in such accomplishments as an increase in public works spending, the 1906 Pure Food and Drug Act, and the direct election of U.S. senators. These trends brought Democrat Woodrow Wilson to the White House in 1912. Wilson passed an economic reform program that was highlighted by the Clayton Anti-Trust Act and the establishment of the first peacetime income tax in American history. Wilson also created the National Park Service (p. 53) to protect the 40 national parks and monuments already in existence, and those to yet to be created.

The relative stability of the early years of the century was crushed beneath the steel weight of World War I. President Wilson overcame a strong isolationist sentiment among his constituents, and the United States eventually saw tardy but serious involvement in the war. When victory was won, Wilson was instrumental in drafting the peace, which included creation of the League of Nations, a forerunner of the United Nations. Domestic opposition prevented the U.S. from joining, and the League was a flop. Onerous terms imposed on Germany by the Versailles Treaty, which ended the war, would bear bitter fruit in the coming decades.

ROARING 20S, GREAT DEPRESSION, AND WWII

Women were granted the right to vote in 1920 by the 19th Amendment to the *Constitution*. The 18th Amendment, calling for the prohibition of alcohol, was a miserable failure of an amendment introduced at a time when the nation wanted to celebrate its prosperity. Pro-capital Republican policies encouraged American business. President Calvin Coolidge proclaimed that the "business of America is business," and proceeded to assume an arch-indifference towards the operation of the economy. A general (if false) prosperity settled in and fueled an unprecedented fit of conspicuous consumption. The economic euphoria of the "Roaring 20s," however, was largely supported by overextended credit. The façade came tumbling down on Black Thursday, October 24, 1929, when the New York Stock Exchange crashed to the ground and launched the Great Depression. America suffered another harsh blow as the long-abused soil of the Great Plains literally blew away in one of the worst droughts in history, replacing the bread basket with a dust bowl, and ruining thousands of farmers.

Under the firm hand of President Franklin D. Roosevelt, the United States began a decade-long recovery. His New Deal program created work for hundreds of thousands, building monuments, bridges, and parks with public funds through the Works Progress Administration (WPA). Farm prices were subsidized, plantings were centrally planned, and financial institutions (including the stock market) were put under federal jurisdiction. Agencies like the Tennessee Valley Authority supplied power to entire regions while private utility monopolies were broken up and placed under public regulation. Minimum wages were set, child labor was prohibited, and the Social Security Act brought the United States somewhat reluctantly into the era of the welfare state.

A crisis in foreign affairs gripped the national attention late in the decade. Hitler and his Nazi regime horrified the West; territorial gluttony in central Europe finally launched the second global war of the century. The Japanese attack on Pearl Harbor, Hawaii (p. 817) on December 7, 1941, a "day that will live in infamy" in the words of Roosevelt, unified the American people behind the allied cause. America entered World War II. The productive capacity of the nation's war-time economy was critical in assuring allied victory over the Axis powers. During the war, Hitler's regime systematically brutalized and exterminated most of the Jewish, gay, and mentally ill population of Germany and Poland. Many of those who survived later immigrated to the U.S. The war ended in Europe in April of 1945, when Hitler committed suicide. The war in the Pacific continued until August, when the United States dropped two newly developed nuclear bombs on Japan, killing 80,000 civilians. The war will always be remembered for the Holocaust, which killed 6 million Jews and others, and for the United States' terrifying use of nuclear power.

COLD WAR AND THE NEW FRONTIER

Spared the war-time devastation of Europe and East Asia, the U.S. economy boomed in the post-war era, solidifying the status of the United States as the world's foremost economic and military power. But an ideological polarity was developing between America and the other nuclear power, the Soviet Union. Fears of Soviet expansion led to the Red Scare of the 1950s. Congressional committees saw communists everywhere, thousands of civil servants, writers, actors, and academics were blacklisted, and two American citizens, the Rosenbergs, were tried and sentenced to death during this time for allegedly selling nuclear secrets to the Soviets. Suspicion of communism had grown in the U.S. since the Russian Revolution in 1917, but the feverish intensity it gained during the Cold War ultimately led to American military involvement in the Korean and Vietnam Wars. Tensions between the U.S. and the USSR reached their peak during the Cuban Missile Crisis of 1962, when President John Kennedy and Nikita Khrushchev brought the world to the brink of nuclear war in a showdown over the deployment of Soviet nuclear missiles in Cuba.

Despite the nuclear shadow, the early 1960s were characterized domestically by an optimism embodied by the President himself. Kennedy's Peace Corps, NASA's program to place Americans on the moon, and the "New Frontier" to eliminate poverty and racism all contributed to what many see as the nation's last period of large-scale activism. Optimism waned as the Vietnam conflict escalated, and all but disappeared with Kennedy's 1963 assassination in Dallas (p. 514). As the 60s progressed, social unrest increased. The nation witnessed public protests against involvement in Vietnam and against the continuing discrimination against African-Americans. Dr. Martin Luther King, Jr. led peaceful demonstrations, marches, and sit-ins for civil rights. Unfortunately, these were often met with violence; civil rights activists were drenched with fire hoses, arrested, and sometimes even killed. Dr. King himself was assassinated in Memphis (p. 282) in 1968.

The second wave of the women's movement accompanied the civil rights movement. Sparked by Betty Friedan's landmark book, *The Feminine Mystique,* American women sought to change the delineation between men's and women's roles in society, demanding access to male-dominated professions and equal pay. The sexual revolution, fueled by the development of the birth control pill, brought a woman's right to choose to the forefront of national debate; the 1973 Supreme Court decision *Roe v. Wade* legalized abortion, initiating a battle between abortion opponents and pro-choice advocates that divides the nation today.

LATELY...

In 1980, actor and former California governor Ronald Reagan was elected to the White House riding a tidal wave of conservatism, and a materialistic ethic gripped the nation. College campuses became quieter and more conservative as graduates flocked to Wall Street to become investment bankers. Though the decade's conservatives did embrace certain right-wing social goals such as prayer in schools and the campaign against abortion, the Reagan Revolution was essentially economic. Reaganomics gave tax breaks to big business and the rich, spurred short term consumption, de-regulated savings and loans, and laid the ground work for economic disaster in the 1990s.

Today, America is dealing with a massive deficit, an insufficient education system, crumbling infrastructure, and issues such as abortion, AIDS, gay rights, and racism. Hoping for change, Americans elected Democrat Bill Clinton to the presidency in 1992. The youngest elected president in United States' history, saxophone-toting Clinton promised a new era of government interest and activism after years of laissez-faire rule. The promise of universal health care, the most ambitious of Clinton's policy goals, best captured the new attitude. By 1995, however, health care legislation was dead, and the American Congress, a democratic stronghold since mid-century, had been taken over by the Republican party, the most apparent backlash to Clinton's inability to gain consensus for major pieces of legislation.

■ Government and Politics

The U.S. federal government has three branches, the executive, legislative, and judicial. The executive branch is headed by the president and vice-president, who are elected every four years. The executive branch administers many federal agencies, which fall under the jurisdiction of 13 departments of the government. The heads of these 13 departments are known as the Cabinet. They aid the president in policy decisions.

The legislative branch has two arms, the House of Representatives and the Senate. In the House of Representatives, each state is allocated a number of seats proportional to its population, while in the Senate, each state has two representatives regardless of its size or population. Both Senators and Representatives are directly elected by the people of their state. Budget appropriations originate in the House of Representatives, but the Senate must concur. The Senate approves presidential appointees and treaties with foreign governments.

The judicial branch consists of the Supreme Court of the United States and 90 district courts. The Supreme Court has nine justices, who are appointed to life terms by the President. These courts consider violations of federal law and certain civil cases. Decisions of the district courts may be appealed to one of the 12 appellate courts. Appellate court decisions may be appealed to the Supreme Court. In the U.S., the accused is innocent until proven guilty.

Elected representatives in the U.S. are usually members of the Republican or Democratic parties. The Republicans are conservative, or right-wing, while the Democrats are liberal, or to the left of the political spectrum.

■ Architecture

Early settlers brought the architectures of their countries to the Americas. Dutch, English, Spanish, and French influence meshed with native knowledge to shape the American landscape. The small windows and steep-pitched roofs of the John Ward House in Salem, MA, reflect the English medieval heritage prevalent in New England. In St. Augustine, Florida, the Castillo de San Marcos exemplifies traditional medieval Spanish building. Further west, the Spanish tradition became intertwined with that of the native pueblo; the Palace of the Governors in Santa Fe combines European order with native forms. The most important architectural movement of the early 18th century was Neoclassicism. Two of the best examples of this style are Monticello, and the University of Virginia, both designed by Thomas Jefferson. Many plantation homes in the south were built along these stylistic lines.

The 19th century was dominated by romantic and eclectic architecture that drew from a spectrum of styles. In the middle of the century McKim, Mead, and White became the most important architectural firm in the U.S. These men brought the ideas of the Ecole des Beaux-Arts in Paris to the United States and applied classical style to the large buildings of the emerging American megalopolis. Their work can be seen at the Boston Public Library and the J. Pierpont Morgan Library in New York City. At the same time, Frederick Law Olmstead achieved equivalent stature in landscape architecture. He sculpted New York's Central Park and the grounds of the Biltmore estate in Asheville, North Carolina.

Louis Sullivan, the first modern architect, gave new form to the tall late 19th century buildings of Chicago. Frank Lloyd Wright, Sullivan's student, was more interested in the home and designed Fallingwater, in Ohiopyle, PA, demonstrating his interest in integrating landscape and house. In the 1930s, skyscrapers rose to new heights; the Empire State Building grew thousands of feet into the New York City sky. Mies van der Rohe next innovated the skyscraper by revealing the skeleton of steel and concrete. The Seagram Building, built in 1950s New York City is an elegant example. Eero Saarinen was a member of van der Rohe's school, but branched off to develop his own style, designing the TWA terminal at Kennedy Airport. The most famous living American architect is I.M. Pei, whose work includes the East Building of the National Gallery of Art in Washington, D.C. A recent addition to the ranks of internationally renowned American architects is Frank Gehry; check out his copper-clad art center at the University of Toledo. More information on these buildings is available in individual city listings.

■ The Arts

LITERATURE

The first best-seller printed in America, the *Bay Psalm Book,* was published in Cambridge in 1640. Like much of the literature read and published in 17th- and 18th-century America, this chart buster was religious in nature. The early 1800s saw the rise of works that told the tale of the strong, yet innocent American individual. Herman Melville's *Moby Dick,* Walt Whitman's *Leaves of Grass,* and Nathaniel Hawthorne's *Scarlet Letter* all revolved around characters made unique by the American experience. These works were contemporary to lyrical philosophical essays like Henry David Thoreau's *Walden* (written at Walden Pond, p. 108) and Ralph Waldo Emerson's *Self-Reliance.* While New England writers tried to portray a culture distinct from that of their European forebears, Midwestern humorists attempted to define the American character with larger-than-life tall tales set in the landscapes of the new continent. The most sophisticated practitioner of this genre was Mark Twain. His works include the *Adventures of Huckleberry Finn,* which explores coming-of-age on the Mississippi River. As pioneers traveled farther west, authors like Willa Cather captured the stark beauty of the Plains.

The Industrial Revolution inspired works that portrayed the declining morals of society. Stephen Crane's *Maggie: A Girl of the Streets* captured the life of the tenement dwellers in the expanding cities, while Upton Sinclair's *The Jungle* portrayed abominable factory conditions. The novels of Henry James and Edith Wharton showed how the affluent half lived, portraying the intricate mannerisms of late 19th century high society.

The early 20th century marked a reflective, self-centered movement in American literature. F. Scott Fitzgerald's works portray restless individuals, financially secure, but empty inside. Many writers were caught in the tumult of the new century; some moved abroad in search of inner peace. This "lost generation" included Ernest Hemingway, William Faulkner, Eudora Welty, T.S. Eliot, Ezra Pound, Robert Frost, and Wallace Stevens. The 1920s also saw an important rise in black literature. Prefigured by the narratives of Fredrick Douglass, W.E.B. DuBois, and Booker T. Washington, the "Harlem Renaissance" matched the excitement of the Jazz Age with the works of Langston Hughes, Jean Toomer, and Zora Neale Hurston.

The Beatniks of the 50s, spearheaded by cult heroes Jack Kerouac and Allen Ginsberg, lived wildly through postwar America's dull conformity—Kerouac's *On the Road* (1955), though dated, nonetheless makes a fine companion to this guidebook for the contemporary road scholar.

Some of the greatest modern American novels have examined the tensions in American society. Books such as Ralph Ellison's *Invisible Man,* Richard Wright's *Black Boy,* Toni Morrison's *Beloved,* and Oliver LaFarge's portrayal of a Navajo youth, *Laughin' Boy,* all reflect this ongoing examination.

MUSIC

Although America is best known for its contribution to popular music—country, bluegrass, big band, jazz, blues, rock 'n' roll, and rap—America has also nurtured classical composers of note, as well as some truly great classical musicians and ensembles. Leonard Bernstein, George Gershwin, Aaron Copeland, and Charles Ives have made their marks on the international score, blending classical forms and popular American genres. Yo-Yo Ma, Joshua Bell, and Robert Levin are world-recognized players. The orchestras in most major U.S. cities range from excellent to world-renowned. The San Francisco Symphony, the New York Philharmonic, and the Philadelphia Orchestra are some of the best.

While classical music exists in the U.S., popular music flourishes. Jazz has been called America's classical music. The blues, ragtime, and military brass bands combined in New Orleans to create the music we call jazz. This music of the American soul has been sounded by greats like Louis Armstrong, Ella Fitzgerald, Miles Davis, Billie Holiday, Charlie Parker, John Coltrane, and Wynton Marsalis, to name a few. A baby of the blues, rock 'n' roll produced many of America's music icons—first Chubby Checker and Jerry Lee Lewis, and eventually the King of Rock, Elvis Presley. Now, rock spans from punk (The Ramones) to grunge (Nirvana) to pop (Madonna and Michael Jackson).

FILM

American film has come a long way since viewers were first amazed by Thomas Edison's 30-second film of a galloping horse. Edison's technology was originally used in peep shows, but the medium quickly developed more lofty goals. Today's movies are works of art and entertainment, crafted by well-known and undiscovered directors and actors alike, and are increasingly filled with stunning computer-generated special effects. The influence of the multi-billion dollar American movie industry is undisputed as year after year records on openings, earnings, and fastest grossing movies are overturned. Celebrated movies of each genre include: **sci-fi** (*Star Wars, Alien*), **adventure** (*Independence Day, Jurassic Park*), **thriller** (*Psycho, Silence of the Lambs*), **drama** (*Casablanca, Citizen Kane*), **horror** (*Texas Chainsaw Massacre, Friday the 13th*), **cult** (*Easy Rider, The Rocky Horror Picture Show*), and the quintessential American **western** (*True Grit, Unforgiven*).

VISUAL ART

The works of artists in the 19th century such as Thomas Cole and Winslow Homer expressed the beauty and power of the American continent. In the early twentieth century, Edward Hopper and Thomas Hart Benton explored the innocence and mythic values of the United States during its emergence as a superpower. The Abstract Expressionism of Arshile Gorky and Jackson Pollock displays both the swaggering confidence and frenetic insecurity rampant in cold-war America. Pop Art, created by Jasper Johns, Robert Rauschenberg, Roy Lichtenstein, and Andy Warhol, satirizes the icons of American life and pop culture.

Since the 1890s, when Eastman-Kodak revolutionized the camera, photography has provided an important medium for American artists. Stieglitz's views of the city used a new method of framing the physical world to create art. Photography became an excellent medium for artists concerned with improving desperate social conditions. The Farm Security Administration (FSA), part of the WPA, paid photographers to document the Great Depression. Dorothea Lange and Walker Evans took photos which transcended this documentary purpose and can only be called art. American photographers have also used their medium to capture the remarkable natural environment. Ansel Adams revealed the grandiose beauty of the National Parks with his black and white photographs, now immortalized in every poster store in America. Abstraction and surrealism have also worked their way into photography; Diane Arbus took pictures of "freaks," making the interaction of normality and abnormality the theme of her art. Robert Mapplethorpe framed nudes and flowers to create abstract forms.

Mapplethorpe's work also played with social conventions, especially the perceptions and manifestations of sexuality. His work often involves nudity and homoerotic imagery. When Congressional members learned an exhibit of Mapplethorpe's work had been funded in part by the National Endowment for the Arts (NEA), a furor ensued, causing the Corcoran Gallery in Washington, D.C. (p. 220) to withdraw the exhibit from its gallery. Protesters had the last laugh, as they projected Mapplethorpe's photos on the side of the building, but the NEA has remained controversial. In 1996, the Republican congress cut NEAs budget nearly 40% (from $162.4 million to $99.5 million). The organization is struggling to survive this massive blow by streamlining bureaucracy.

■ The Media

TELEVISION

There are television sets in almost 98% of U.S. homes, and the competition between the four national networks **(ABC, CBS, NBC,** and **Fox)** and cable television has led to an exponential growth in TV culture over the last few years. During prime time (8-11pm EST) you can find the most popular shows: the drama *ER,* the farcical yet popular *Melrose Place,* and *The Simpsons,* the wittiest animation ever to leave Springfield. On cable you'll discover around-the-clock channels offering news, sports, movies, weather, and home shopping. **MTV,** offering dazzling displays of calculatedly random visceral images, affords a glimpse into what parents country-wide fear represents the psyche of their wide-eyed children.

Television is the point of entry to world-wide news for most Americans. Twenty-four hour news coverage is available on **CNN,** a cable station. All the networks have politically moderate to liberal coverage. Perhaps the most in-depth, if underwatched, news programs in the U.S. are those on public television, or **PBS.** These programs are funded by viewer contributions and have no commercials.

PRINT MEDIA

The most influential newspapers in the U.S. are the *New York Times, The Washington Post,* and the *Los Angeles Times.* These publications are all liberal in slant, and have wide distributions throughout the U.S. *The Christian Science Monitor* and the *Wall Street Journal* are well-respected publications.

There are three major weekly newsmagazines. Liberal readers prefer *Time* and *Newsweek,* while conservatives favor *U.S. News & World Report.* Other widely-read magazines in the U.S. include *People,* which chronicles American gossip, *Spin,* which focuses on the music industry, and the *New Yorker,* which combines New York happenings with short stories and essays on current events. Most European fashion magazines have an American counterpart. There are hundreds of other magazines aimed at audiences ranging from computer junkies to body builders. Find a good bookstore or newsstand and check them out.

■ This Year's News

The United States lived out 1996 in anticipation of two competitive events which will have unfolded by the time this book hits the shelves; the Atlanta summer Olympic Games and November Presidential elections. Major contenders in the latter included incumbent Democrat Bill Clinton, whose reputation was marred by ongoing investigation into the Whitewater scandal and allegations of ideological wishy-washiness, and cardboard conservative Bob Dole, famed for his pragmatism and doltishness.

The postal service and those who love it breathed a sigh of relief when a 15-year string of mail bombings ended with the arrest of the suspected "Unabomber;" misanthropic mathematician Theodore Kazcinski. Meanwhile, O.J. Simpson was acquitted of the murder of his ex-wife and her acquaintance Ronald Goldman. Everyone had an opinion about the case, including the media, which insisted that perception of the outcome's fairness was split along racial lines—i.e., that African-Americans tended to profess O.J.'s innocence, while most whites were convinced of the athelete's guilt.

On the lighter side, the marriage between Michael Jackson (King of Pop) and Lisa Marie Presley (daughter of the King of Rock) proved ill-fated, highlighting at least one parallel between British and American royalty.

UNITED STATES

NEW ENGLAND

With a centuries-old commitment to education and an unending fascination with government, New England has counted itself an intellectual and political center since before the States were even United. Students and scholars from across the country funnel into New England's colleges each fall, and town meetings in many rural villages still evoke the feeling of public government which inspired the American colonists to create a nation so many years ago. The region supports countless historical attractions which commemorate every step in the formation of this nation as it broke with the old world.

Geographically, the region seems an unlikely cradle for any sort of civilization. Mountains wrinkle the land, while the soil at their feet lies barren. Mark Twain once said that if you don't like the weather in New England, wait 15 minutes. Unpredictable at best, the region's climate can be particularly dismal starting in November, when winds blow in off rocky shores bringing the harsh, wet winter, which lasts through March. Be warned that everything from rivers to state campgrounds to tourist attractions may slow down or freeze up during these months.

Though the climate gave early settlers a tough time, today's visitors find adventure in the region's rough edges. New England's dramatic, salty coastline calls urbanites to spend their summers on the sand; the slopes of the Green and White Mountains, with their many rivers and lakes, inspire skiers, hikers, cyclists, and canoers. In the fall, the nation's most brilliant foliage bleeds and burns, transforming the entire region into a giant kaleidoscope.

Maine

Nearly a thousand years ago, Leif Ericson and his band of Viking explorers set foot on the coasts of Maine. Moose roamed as kings of the sprawling evergreen wilderness, the cry of the Maine coon cat echoed through towering mountains, and countless lobsters crawled in the ocean deep. A millennium has not changed much. Forests still cover nearly 90% of Maine's land, an area larger than the entire neat stack of New England states below, and the inner reaches of the state stretch on for mile after uninhabited mile. The more populated shore areas embrace a harsh and jagged coastline. Rather than trying to conquer the wilderness like the urbanites to the south, the deeply independent Maine "Downeaster" has adapted to this rough wilderness with rugged pragmatism. The rugged beauty of the place has inspired writers as various as Stephen King, Henry Wadsworth Longfellow, and Edna St. Vincent Millay, and beckons all.

PRACTICAL INFORMATION

Capital: Augusta.
Maine Publicity Bureau: 325B Water St., Hallowell (623-0363 or 800-533-9595). Send mail to P.O. Box 2300, Halowell 04347. **Bureau of Parks and Recreation,** State House Station #22 (1st floor Harlow Bldg.), Augusta 04333 (287-3821). **Maine Forest Service,** Bureau of Forestry, State House Station #22 (2nd floor Harlow Bldg.), Augusta 04333 (287-2791). All agencies open Mon.-Fri. 8am-5pm.
Time Zone: Eastern. **Postal Abbreviation:** ME.
Sales Tax: 6%.

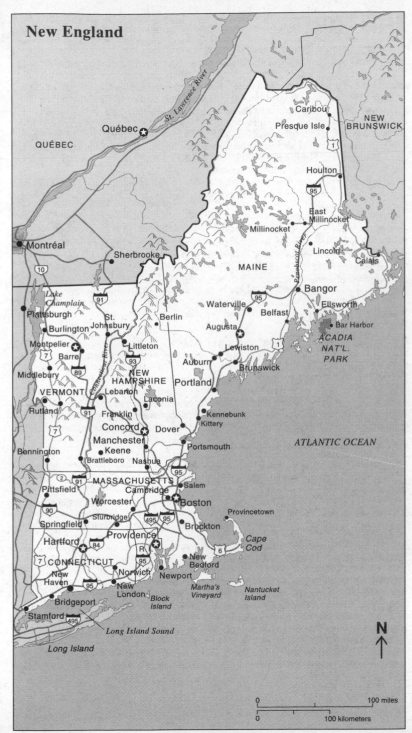

New England

MAINE COAST

As the bird flies, the length of the Maine coast from Kittery to Lubec measures 228 miles, but if untangled, all of the convoluted inlets and rocky promontories would stretch out to a whopping 3478 miles. Fishing, the earliest business here, was later augmented by a vigorous shipbuilding industry; both traditions are still visible today. Unfortunately, rampant overfishing has catastrophically depleted the North Atlantic cod population and left fishermen wondering about the future of their livelihood. Lobsters are still plentiful, however, and lobsters by the pound are ubiquitous in coastal Maine. Stop under one of the innumerable makeshift red wooden lobster signs that speckle the roadsides, set yourself down on a gray wooden bench and chow. Keep in mind that lobsters are tastiest before July, when most start to molt. Also be forewarned that lobster poaching is treated seriously here; the color codings and designs on the buoy markers are as distinct as a cattle rancher's brand and serve the same purpose.

U.S. I hugs the coastline, stringing the port towns together. Lesser roads and small ferry lines connect the remote villages and offshore islands. Get your bearings at the **Maine Information Center** (439-1319), in Kittery, 3 mi. north of the Maine-New Hampshire bridge (open daily 8am-6pm; mid-Oct. to June daily 9am-5pm). **Greyhound** (800-231-2222) serves points between Portland and Bangor along I-95, the coastal town of Brunswick, and connecting routes to Boston. Reaching most coastal points of interest is virtually impossible by bus; a car or bike is necessary.

■ Portland

During the July 4th fireworks celebration of 1866, a young boy playing on Portland's wharf inadvertently started a fire which destroyed over three-fourths of the city before it was extinguished. Portland had to be rebuilt—for the fourth time (the old Portland fort had first been razed to the ground by Indians in 1632). Today, the Victorian reconstruction that survives in what is now called the Old Port Exchange stands in stark contrast to Portland's spirited youth culture. Ferries run to the nearby Casco Bay Islands; Sebago Lake provides sunning and water skiing opportunities; and Freeport, the outlet capital of the free world, offers budget shopping galore.

PRACTICAL INFORMATION

Tourist Office: Visitors Information Bureau, 305 Commercial St. (772-5800), at the corner of Center St. Open Mon.-Fri. 8am-5pm, Sat.-Sun. 10am-6pm; Oct. 16-May 14 Mon.-Fri. 9am-5pm, Sat.-Sun. 10am-3pm.

American Express: 480 Congress St. (772-8450). Open Mon.-Fri. 8:30am-5:30pm.

Buses: Concord Trailways, 161 Marginal Way (828-1151), a 15-min. walk from downtown. Office open daily 5:30am-8:30pm. To: Boston (8 per day, 2hr., $15); Bangor (3 per day, 2hr., $20). Offers discounts on round-trip fares for college students with ID. Metro bus #8 will transport you from the station to downtown, but you must call (774-0351). **Greyhound/Vermont Trailways,** 950 Congress St. (772-6587 or 800-231-2222), on the western outskirts of town. Be cautious here at night. Take the Congress St. bus (#1) downtown. Office open daily 6:30am-7:15pm. To: Boston (7 per day, 2hr., $12); Bangor (3 per day, 2hr., $17).

Ferries: Prince of Fundy Cruises, P.O. Box 4216, 468 Commercial St. (800-341-7540 or 800-482-0955 in ME). Ferries to Yarmouth in southern Nova Scotia leave from the Portland Marine Terminal, on Commercial St. near the Million Dollar Bridge. Prices vary; call for details.

Public Transportation: Metro Bus (774-0351) offers service within and beyond the downtown area. Most routes run only 7am-7pm. $1, seniors and disabled 50¢, under 6 free, transfers free.

Crisis Lines: Rape Crisis, 774-3613. **Crisis Intervention Hotline,** 800-660-8500. Both operate 24hr.

Emergency: 911.
Police: 874-8300.
Post Office: 622 Congress St. (871-8449). Open Mon.-Fri. 8:30am-5pm, Sat. 9am-noon. The 125 Forest Ave. office (871-8410) handles passports. Open Mon.-Fri. 7:30am-7pm, Sat. 7:30am-5pm. **ZIP code:** 04104.
Area Code: 207.

Downtown sits near the bay, along **Congress St.** between State and Franklin St. A few blocks south lies the Old Port on Commercial and Fore St. These two districts contain most of the city's sights and attractions. I-295 (off I-95) forms the western boundary of downtown.

ACCOMMODATIONS AND CAMPING

Portland has some inexpensive accommodations, but prices jump during the summer season. You can always try Exit 8 off I-95, where **Super 8** (854-1881) and other budget staples (singles around $40-45) proliferate.

Portland Youth Hostel (HI-AYH), 645 Congress St. (874-3281). Centrally located in a university dorm. 48 beds in clean doubles with bath and shower. The staff is energetic and helpful; plans include locker space for storage during lockout (11am-3pm) and efforts to make this a "green" hostel. Check-in 5pm-midnight. Check-out 11am. $15, nonmembers $18. $10 key deposit required. Reservations recommended.

The Inn at St. John, 939 Congress St. (773-6481), across from the bus station. Reasonable prices in a comfortable inn make for a great alternative to the hostel. Tidy, tasteful singles ($35, with private bath $40) and doubles ($45/$50). Free local calls. Continental breakfast included. Kitchen, laundry facilities, and bike storage available. Rates go up July-Oct.

YWCA, 87 Spring St. (874-1130), downtown near the Civic Center. Women only. The small rooms verge on sterile, but the amiable atmosphere more than compensates. Fills up in summer. Check-out 11am. Singles $25, doubles $40. Lounge, pool, and kitchen (bring utensils). Phone in reservations with Visa or MasterCard.

YMCA, 70 Forest Ave. (874-1111), on the north side of Congress St., 1 block from the post office. Access to kitchen, pool, and exercise facilities.Cash only. 85 rooms, all for men only. Check-in 11am-10pm. Singles $27 per night, $88 per week. Key deposit $10.

Wassamki Springs, 855 Saco St. (839-4276), in Westbrook. Closest campground (15-min. drive) to Portland. Drive 6mi. west on Congress St. (becomes Rte. 22, then County Rd.), then turn right on Saco St. Full facilities plus a sandy beach. Flocks of migrant Winnebagos nest among cozy, fairly private sites that go right up to the lake. Sites $18 for 2 people, hookup $21, $4 per additional person; $2 additional for lakefront sites. Showers 25¢. Reservations recommended 4-6 weeks in advance, especially July-Aug. Open May to mid-Oct.

FOOD

Life is de bubbles for seafood lovers in Portland. One of the nation's leaders in restaurants per capita, Portland loves to chop *le poisson* and make it taste nice, as well as to boil lobsters and sauté clams in ze spice. Do-it-yourselfers can buy seafood, dead or alive, on the active port on Commercial St.

Seamen's Club, 375 Fore St. (772-7311), at Exchange St. in the Old Port with a harbor view. Top-notch seafood dining steeped in briny lore. Salads and sandwiches $6-8, dinner $10 and up. Fresh lobster year-round. Open Mon.-Thurs. 11am-10pm, Fri. 11am-11pm, Sat.-Sun. 10:30am-11pm.

Federal Spice, 225 Federal St. (774-6404), just off Congress St. Whips up cheap, bold home-cooking in a hurry using spicy hot elements from Caribbean, South American, and Asian cuisine. Healthsmart menu features burritos and tacos, all under $6. Eat in or take out.

Bella Bella, 606 Congress St. (780-1260). Specializes in Mediterranean country food. Italian, Spanish, Greek, and North African entrees ($8.75-12.75) served in a psychedelic flower-painted café. Open 5-10pm daily.

SIGHTS

Many of Portland's most spectacular sights lie outside the city proper, along the rugged coast or on the beautiful, secluded islands a short ferry ride offshore. **Two Lights State Park** (799-5871), across the Million Dollar Bridge on State St. and south along Rte. 77 to Cape Elizabeth, is a wonderful place to picnic and relax. **Casco Bay Lines** (774-7871), on State Pier near the corner of Commercial and Franklin, America's oldest ferry service, runs year-round to the nearby islands. Daily **ferries** depart approximately every hour (5:45am-10:30pm) for nearby **Peaks Island** ($5, bikes $3.40). On the island you can rent a bike at **Brad's Recycled Bike Shop,** 115 Island Ave. (766-5631), for $10 per day. If your feet aren't up to pedaling, try the quiet, unpopulated beach on **Long Island.** (Departures daily 6am-9pm. $6.35.) If you start at Long Island, you can island-hop by catching later ferries to other islands (same price as Peaks ferry). Getting to more than two islands will take all day, though; start early and pay close attention to the schedule.

You may feel the call of the sea the instant you arrive in Portland, but the city does have a full slate of activities for landlubbers. The **Portland Museum of Art,** 7 Congress Sq. (775-6148), at the intersection of Congress, High, and Free St., collects American art by notables such as John Singer Sargent and Winslow Homer. (Open Tues.-Wed. and Sat. 10am-5pm, Thurs.-Fri. 10am-9pm, Sun. noon-5pm. $6, students $5, ages 6-12 $1, under 6 free.) At 487 Congress St., the **Wadsworth-Longfellow House** (879-0427), a museum of social history and U.S. literature, zeroes in on late 18th- and 19th-century antiques as well as on the life of the poet. Henry lived in the house from birth to his early 20s. (Tours every ½hr. $4, under 12 $1; purchase tickets at 489 Congress St. Open June-Oct. Tues.-Sun. 10am-4pm. Gallery and museum store also open Oct.-June Wed.-Sat. noon-4pm.)

ENTERTAINMENT AND NIGHTLIFE

After a not-so-brief respite spanning back to its days as a Vaudeville venue, the **State Theater,** 609 Congress St. (879-1111; for tickets 879-1112), is back in business, presenting both concerts and theatrical productions. (Tickets $15-25. Info line open 24 hr.; box office open Mon.-Fri. 9:30am-5pm, Sat. 10am-4pm, Sun. noon-showtime on performance days.) The **Portland Symphony,** under the direction of Toschiyuki Shimada, will move to the Portland City Hall Auditorium in early 1997. Call for details (773-8191, 800-639-2309 in ME and NH; 50% student discount available).

Traditionally held on the first Sunday in June, the **Old Port Festival** (772-6828) begins the summer with a bang, filling several blocks from Federal to Commercial St. with as many as 50,000 people. On summer afternoons, enjoy the **Noontime Performance Series** (772-6828) during which a variety of bands performs in Portland's Monument Square (late June-early July Mon.-Fri. noon-1pm). The **6-Alive Sidewalk Arts Festival** (828-6666), generally held around mid-August, lines Congress St. with booths featuring artists from all over the country.

For a taste of the hometown spirit, check out the **Portland Pirates,** Portland's own ice-kicking professional hockey team, at the Civic Center, 1 Civic Center Sq. (season runs Sept.-May; call 828-4665 for tickets; $8-13, under 12 and seniors ½-price). The **Portland Seadogs,** the local minor-league pro baseball team, takes the field from Apr. 6 to Sept. 4 at Hadlock Field on Park Ave. (tickets 874-9300; $4, under 16 and seniors $2).

After dark, head toward the Old Port area, especially **Fore St.** between Union and Exchange St. Known as "the strip," this part of town boasts a high proportion of pleasant "shoppes" and a few good pubs. **Gritty MacDuff's,** 396 Fore St. (772-2739), brews its own sweet beer for adoring locals. These tasty pints are worth the $2.50. (Open Mon.-Fri. 11:30am-1am, Sun. noon-1am.) You'll find an English pub around the corner at **Three Dollar Dewey's,** 446 Fore St. (772-3310), on the corner of Commercial and Union. Dewey's serves 65 varieties of beer and ale (30 on tap at $3), along with great chili and free popcorn. It also has a few fairly cheap dinner options—like BBQ for $6. (Open Mon.-Sat. 11am-1am, Sun. noon-1am.) **Brian Boru,** 57 Center St. (780-1506), provides a more mellow pub scene (open daily noon-1am). Try the Irish nachos ($5.50), or stop by on Sunday for a traditional Irish breakfast and chug $1.50 pints all day. Find info on Portland's jazz, blues, and club scene in either the *Casco Bay Weekly* or *FACE,* both of which are free in many restaurants and stores.

■ South of Portland

When weather permits, biking may be the best way to travel Maine's rocky shores and spare yourself the aggravation of thick summer traffic. In **Biddeford,** 17 mi. south of Portland on U.S. 1, **Quinn's Bike and Fitness,** 140 U.S. 1/Elm St. (284-4632), rents 10-, 5-, and 3-speed bikes. ($10 per day, $30 per week, with $20 deposit; $1.25 lock rental. Open Mon.-Sat. 9am-5:30pm.)

A few minutes south on U.S. 1, you'll find the town of **Kennebunk,** and, several miles east on Rte. 35, its coastal counterpart **Kennebunkport.** If you want to bypass busy U.S. 1, take the Maine Turnpike south of Portland to Exit 3, then take Fletcher St. east into Kennebunk.

Both of these towns are popular hideaways for wealthy authors and artists. A number of rare and used bookstores lines U.S. 1 just south of Kennebunk, while art galleries fill the town itself. The blue-blooded (and blue-haired) resort of Kennebunkport reluctantly grew famous as the summer home of former President Bush, who owns an estate on Walker's Point. The **Kennebunk-Kennebunkport Chamber of Commerce,** 173 Port Road (967-0857), in Kennebunkport, distributes a free guide to area sights. (Open Mon.-Thurs. 9am-6pm, Fri. 9am-7pm, Sat.-Sun. 10am-4pm; mid-Oct. to June, Mon.-Fri. 9am-5pm.)

Spending the night in Kennebunk will make your trip significantly more expensive; avoid poverty by camping. **Salty Acres Campground** (967-8623), 4½ mi. northeast of Kennebunkport on winding Rte. 9, offers swimming, a grocery store, laundry, phones, showers, and a convenient location about 1 mi. from beaches. Be prepared for a communal camping experience; sites are small and closely packed. (300 sites $15, with electricity and water $20, full hookup $22; $8 per additional adult after 2; $2 per additional child after 2. Open mid-May to mid-Oct. Reservations not accepted.) For cheap, fresh greens close by, check out **Patten's Berry Farm** (967-2418), where fruit (watermelon 39¢/lb.), vegetables, milk, bottled water, and eggs are all sold at reasonable prices (from Kennebunkport, take Rte. 9 to North St.; open May-Dec. daily 8am-6pm). A little farther out is the **Mousam River Campground** (985-2507), on Alfred Rd. just west of Exit 3 off I-95 in west Kennebunk. (115 sites $16, $15 with AAA; RV sites $21/$20; $4 per additional adult after 2; $3 per additional person age 13-17. Free showers, small swimming pool, tightly packed but very tidy campsites. Open mid-May to mid-Oct.)

The **Rachel Carson National Wildlife Refuge** (646-9226, Mon.-Fri. 8am-4:30pm), ½ mile off U.S. 1 on Rte. 9, provides a secluded escape from tourist throngs west. A self-guided trail winds through the salt marsh home of over 200 species of shorebirds and waterfowl. The refuge is a tribute to the naturalist and author who wrote *Silent Spring,* which helped launch the environmental movement (open daily sunrise to sunset; free). In nearby Wells the **National Estuarine Research Reserve,** junction of Rte. 1 and Rte. 9, sprawls over meadows and beaches and offers tours of the estuary, bird life, and wildflowers (open daily 8am-5pm).

South of Kennebunk on U.S. 1 lies **Ogunquit,** meaning "beautiful place by the sea." The long, sandy shoreline is a definite must-see. Stop in at the **Ogunquit Information Bureau,** on the left side of the road when driving south (646-2939; open Mon.-Fri. 11am-4pm, Sat.-Sun. 10am-4pm). Grab some wheels at **Bikes By the Sea,** Rte. 1 in Ogunquit. Bike with helmet starts at $16 per day (open daily 9am-6pm). In the summer, a vibrant gay community inhabits Ogunquit. **Moody,** just south of Ogunquit, hosts some of the least expensive lodgings in the region.

Nearby **Perkins Cove** charms the plaid socks off the polo shirt crowd with boutiques hawking seashell sculptures. The two **Barnacle Billy's** restaurants (646-5575), 20 yards apart on Oar Weed Rd., practice an interesting division of labor. Go to the original for lobster (broiled, baked or sauteed), especially their delicious lobster rolls ($10), and look to the newer location for a fuller menu. (Both open daily 11am-9:30pm.)

■ North of Portland

Much like the coastal region south of Portland, the north offers the traveler unforgettable beaches, windswept ocean vistas, and verdant forests—for a price. Lodging in L.L. Bean country isn't cheap, but camping or just passing through can give all the flavor, without the guilt of spending $70 at a hotel. Much of the region is unserviced by public transportation, but if you have a car, the drive along U.S. 1 offers a charming, unadulterated view of coastal Maine. Don't expect to speed through; congested traffic and winding roads make the drive up Maine's coast slow at times. Get a good map, and plan to move slowly.

Freeport About 20 mi. north of Portland on I-95, Freeport once garnered glory as the "birthplace of Maine." The 1820 signing of documents declaring the state's independence from Massachusetts took place at the historic **Jameson Tavern,** 115 Main St. (865-4196), right next to L. L. Bean. Dinner here will run you $12-22; lighter fare can be had in the tap room for $6-9. Freeport is now known as the factory outlet capital of the world, with over 100 downtown stores. The grandaddy of them all, **L.L. Bean,** began manufacturing Maine Hunting Shoes in Freeport in 1912. Bean sells everything from clothes epitomizing preppy *haute couture* to sturdy tenting gear. The factory outlet, 11 Depot St. (865-4761, ext. 2929), behind Bannister Shoes, is the place for bargains (open daily 10am-9pm). The retail store, 95 Main St. (865-4761 or 800-341-4341), stays open 24 hr., 365 days a year. Only three events have ever caused the store to close (and only for a few hours each time): a nearby fire in the late 1980s, the death of President Kennedy, and the death of L.L. Bean founder Leon Leonwood (no wonder he went by L.L.) Bean.

In a town where even the fast food is fancy (McDonald's and Arby's are housed in stately Victorian mansions), unpretentious eateries are welcome sights. **DeRosier's,** 120 Main St. (865-6290), across from L. L. Bean, has quality pizza and sandwiches, as well as ice cream, candy bars, and soda. If you want to spend a night in the area, **Desert of Maine Campground,** Exit 19 off I-95 (head 2 mi. west), accommodates with 50 sites, nature trails, amazing dunes, a museum, and shuttles into downtown Freeport ($16, hookup $20).

Camden In the summer, the khaki crowd flock to friendly Camden, 100 mi. north of Portland, to dock their yachts alongside the tall-masted schooners in Penobscot Bay. Many of the cruises are out of the budgeteer's price range, but the Rockport-Camden-Lincolnville **Chamber of Commerce** (236-4404; outside ME 800-223-5459), on the public landing in Camden behind Cappy's Chowder House (see below), can tell you which are most affordable. They also have info on a few rooms in local private homes for $30; otherwise, expect to pay $50 or more. (Open Mon.-Fri. 9am-5pm, Sat. 10am-4pm, Sun. noon-4pm.) Cheaper still, the **Camden Hills State Park** (287-3824; outside ME 800-332-1501), 1¼ mi. north of town on U.S. 1, is almost always full in July and August, but you can be fairly certain to get a site if you arrive before 2pm. This beautiful coastal retreat offers more than 25 mi. of trails, including one trail which leads up to **Mt. Battie** and has a harbor view. Make reservations by phone with a credit card. Showers are 25¢ and toilets are available. (Open May 15-Oct. 15. Day use $2. Sites $15, ME residents $11.50.) The folks at **Ducktrap**

Sea Kayak Tours (236-8608) will put you alongside the schooners. Keep an eye out for dolphins, seals, and loons. (Two-hour tour $25; reservations recommended.)

Eating in Camden will never be cheap, but the oceanside experience may be worth it. Cut your losses by sticking to lighter fare. In the heart of downtown Camden is **Cappy's Chowder House,** 1 Main St. (236-2254), a kindly, comfortable hangout where great seafood draws tourists and townspeople alike (open daily 7:30am-midnight, off-season 8:30am-9pm). The seasonal seafood pie ($8), made with scallops, shrimp, mussels, and clams, is absolutely exquisite. **Fitzpatrick's,** on Sharp's Wharf (236-2041), has breakfast omelettes, lunch sandwiches, and burgers all for less than $5 (open daily 7am-3pm).

The **Maine State Ferry Service** (789-5611), 5 mi. north of Camden in Lincolnville, takes you across the Bay to Islesboro Island (9 per day; round-trip $4, ages 5-11 $2, under 5 free, bike $2, car and driver $12). Don't miss the last return at 4:30pm, or you'll be stranded. The ferry also has an agency on U.S. 1 in **Rockland,** 517A Main St. (596-2202), that runs boats to North Haven, Vinalhaven, and Matinicus. Always confirm ahead of time; rates and schedules change with the weather.

Belfast Seventeen miles north of Camden on U.S. 1, Belfast is "real life" coastal Maine at its best. The **Belfast Area Chamber of Commerce,** 31 Front St. (338-5900), on the water, can help you with planning. (Open mid-May to mid.-Oct. daily 10am-6pm.) When the chamber is closed for the season, call the director, Jim Lovejoy, at home at the **Hiram Alden Inn,** 19 Church St. (338-2151). The inn is also Belfast's most affordable accommodation, and a luxurious one at that (singles $30, doubles $45, additional adult $10; breakfast included). Stroll by the waterfront and watch the fishing boats come in, or enjoy the innumerable antique sales, flea markets, and plain old junk sales that line Rte. 1 in Belfast and the surrounding towns on summer weekends. **The Gothic,** 4 Main St. (338-4933), serves homemade baked goods and ice cream. If you're lucky, they'll have blueberry sorbet ($1.20) while you're in town (open Mon.-Fri. 8am-5:30pm, Sat. 9am-5pm).

■ Mount Desert Island

Mt. Desert Island is anything but deserted. During the summer, the island swarms with tourists lured by the thick forests and mountainous landscape. Roughly half of the island is covered by Acadia National Park, which harbors some of the last protected marine, mountain, and forest environments on the New England coast. To be the first person in the U.S. to see the sunrise, climb Cadillac Mountain just before dawn (4 or 4:30am in summer). Then descend into the lively town of Bar Harbor, on the eastern side of the island, for your obligatory Maine lobster. Rte. 3 runs through Bar Harbor, becoming Mt. Desert St.; it and Cottage St. are the major east-west arteries. Rte. 102 circuits the western half of the island.

PRACTICAL INFORMATION

Tourist Office: Acadia National Park Visitors Center (288-4932 or 288-5262), 3mi. north of Bar Harbor on Rte. 3. Open May-June and mid-Sept. to Oct. daily 8am-4:30pm; July to mid-Sept. daily 8am-6pm. **Park Headquarters** (288-3338), 3mi. west of Bar Harbor on Rte. 233. Open Oct.-May Mon.-Fri. 8am-4:30pm. **Bar Harbor Chamber of Commerce** (288-5103), in the Marine Atlantic Ferry Terminal, Rte. 3. Open Mon.-Fri. 8am-5pm. **Mount Desert Island Regional Chamber of Commerce** (288-3411), on Rte. 3 at the entrance to Thompson Island. Open daily 10am-6pm. In the same building you'll find an **Acadia National Park Information Center** (288-9702). Open June-Sept. daily 9:30am-2:30pm.
Buses: Greyhound/Vermont Transit (800-451-3292) leaves for Bangor daily at 6:45am in front of the Post Office, 55 Cottage St. Station open June-Labor Day; $9. Buy tickets at **Fox Run Travel,** 4 Kennebec St. (288-3366). Open Mon.-Fri. 8:30am-5pm. The owner of Fox Run comes to meet the bus (Mon.-Fri. 6:15-6:45am, Sat.-Sun. 6:15-7am) for last-minute ticket purchases.

Ferries: Beal & Bunker, from Northeast Harbor on the town dock (244-3575). To: Cranberry Islands (5-7 per day, 25min., $8, under 12 $4). Open Mon.-Fri. 8am-4:30pm. **Marine Atlantic** (288-3395 or 800-341-7981), Bar Harbor. To: Yarmouth, Nova Scotia (1 per day June 24-Oct. 14; call for availability during the rest of the year; 6hr.; $41.50, car $55, bike $9.25; $3 port tax per person).

Bike Rental: Bar Harbor Bicycle Shop, 141 Cottage St. (288-3886). Mountain bikes $9 for 4hr., $14 per day. Rentals include helmet, lock, and map. Driver's license, cash deposit, or credit card required. Open daily 10am-5:30pm.

National Park Canoe Rentals (244-5854), north end of Long Pond off Rte. 102. Canoes: 4-hr. morning rental (until 1:30pm) $20, 4-hr. pm $22, full day $30. Open May to mid-Oct. daily 8:30am-5pm.

Crisis Lines: Downeast Sexual Assault Helpline, 800-228-2470; **Mental Health Crisis Line,** 800-245-8889. Both 24hr.

Emergency: 911. **Acadia National Park Emergency,** 288-3369. **Mt. Desert Police,** 276-5111.

Post Office: 55 Cottage St. (288-3122). Open Mon.-Fri. 8am-4:45pm, Sat. 9am-noon (in summer Sat. 9am-1pm). **ZIP code:** 04609. **Area code:** 207.

ACCOMMODATIONS AND CAMPING

Grand hotels with grand prices linger from the island's exclusive resort days. Still, a few reasonable establishments do exist, particularly on Rte. 3 north of Bar Harbor. Camping spots cover the island, especially Rte. 198 and 102, well west of town.

Mt. Desert Island Hostel (HI-AYH), 27 Kennebec St. (288-5587), Bar Harbor, behind St. Saviour's Episcopal Church, adjacent to the bus stop. Two large dorm rooms which accommodate 24 in cheery red-and-white bunks. Common room, full kitchen, and a perfect location. Organized activities include movie nights and comedy performances. Breakfast and dinner available ($3 each). Lockout 9am-5pm. Curfew 11pm. $12, nonmembers $15. Linen $1. Call 800-444-6111 for reservations; essential July-Aug. Open mid-June to Aug.

Mt. Desert Island YWCA, 36 Mt. Desert St. (288-5008), Bar Harbor, near downtown. Women only. Extensive common space, full kitchen, laundry. Dorm-style singles with hallway bath $25 per night, doubles $40; glassed-in porch with 7 beds $18 per bed. $25 key/security deposit. Fills quickly; make reservations early. In summer, open daily 8:30am-10pm.

Acadia Hotel, 20 Mt. Desert St. (288-5721), Bar Harbor. A homey place overlooking the park. Cable TV, private bath. Room for 1 or 2 people $59-95 late June-early Sept.; $45-65 May to late June and early Sept. to Oct. (The expensive rooms feature whirlpools.) In summer, breakfast included and reservations recommended.

White Birches Campground, (244-3797), Southwest Harbor, on Seal Cove Rd. 1½mi. west of Rte. 102. 60 wooded sites offer an escape from the touristy areas. $16 for up to 4 people, $20 with hookup; weekly $96/120; $2 per additional person. Free hot showers, stove, bathrooms. Open May 15-Oct. 15 daily 8:30am-10pm for check-in. Reservations recommended, especially in July-Aug.

Acadia National Park Campgrounds: Blackwoods (288-3274), 5mi. south of Bar Harbor on Rte. 3. Over 300 sites. Mid-May to mid-June and mid-Sept. to mid-Oct. $13, mid-June to mid-Sept. $14, free mid-Dec. to mid-March. Large group sites also available. Reservations recommended in summer; call 800-365-2267. **Seawall** (244-3600), Rte. 102A on the western side of the island, 4mi. south of Southwest Harbor. A 10-min. walk from the ocean. Toilets but no hookups. Pay-to-cleanse showers available nearby; bring quarters. Walk-in sites $8, drive-in $13. Office open May-Sept. daily 8am-8pm. First come, first served.

FOOD, NIGHTLIFE, AND ENTERTAINMENT

Seafood is all the rage here. 'Nuff said.

Beal's (244-7178 or 800-245-7178), Southwest Harbor, at the end of Clark Point Rd. Superb prices for lobster. Pick your own live crustacean from a tank ($10-15); Beal's does the rest. Dine on the dock with munchies and beverages from a nearby stand. Open Memorial Day-Labor Day 9am-8pm. Off-season, dining area closed, but fresh seafood sold. Hours vary with weather.

Cottage St. Bakery and Deli, 59 Cottage St. (288-3010), Bar Harbor. Memorably delicious muffins (85¢), pancakes ($2.85), and breads (loaf $2.25-3.50) baked fresh on the premises. Box lunches $7.50. Open May-Oct. daily 6:30am-10pm.

Jordan's, 80 Cottage St. (288-3586), Bar Harbor. A favorite of locals and visitors, especially those who love muffins (6 for $3.75) and plate-sized blueberry pancakes ($2.85). Their popular breakfast is served all day. Open daily 5am-2pm.

The Colonel's Deli Bakery and Restaurant (276-5147), on Main St. in Northeast Harbor. Sate thyself with sandwiches so big you'll have to squash the fresh baked bread to get one into your mouth ($3-5). The desserts are unusual and delicious ($2-3). Open April-Oct. daily 7am-9pm.

Most after-dinner pleasures on the island are simple. For a treat, try **Ben and Bill's Chocolate Emporium,** 66 Main St. (288-3281), near Cottage St., which boasts 50 flavors of homemade ice cream (cone $2) and enough luscious chocolates, fudges, and candy to challenge Willy Wonka (open March-Dec. daily 9:30am-11:30pm). **Geddy's Pub,** 19 Main St. (288-5077), is a three-tiered entertainment complex with a bar, pool tables, dancing, and occasional live music. Dance to a DJ Friday and Saturday nights (no cover; open Apr.-Oct. daily noon-1am). Locals prefer the less touristy **Lompoc Café & Brew Pub,** 36 Rodick St. (288-9392), off Cottage St., which features homebrewed Bar Harbor Real Ale and live jazz, blues, Celtic, rock, or folk nightly (shows June-Sept. at 9pm; cover $1-2; open May-Oct. 11:30am-1am). The Art Deco **Criterion Theatre** (288-3441), on Cottage St., recently declared a national landmark, shows movies in the summer. (Shows daily 7:30pm. $6, under 12 $3.50, balcony seats $7. Box office open ½hr. before show.)

SIGHTS

Mt. Desert Island is shaped roughly like a lobster claw, 14 mi. long and 12 mi. wide. To the east on Rte. 3 lie Bar Harbor and Seal Harbor. South on Rte. 198 near the cleft is **Northeast Harbor.** Across Somes Sound on Rte. 102 is **Southwest Harbor,** where fishing and shipbuilding thrive without the taint of tacky tourism. **Bar Harbor** is by far the most crowded part of the island, sandwiched between the Blue Hill and Frenchmen Bays. Once a summer hamlet for the very wealthy, the town now welcomes a motley melange of R&R-seekers; the monied have fled to the more secluded Northeast and Seal Harbor.

The staff at the **Mt. Desert Oceanarium** (244-7330), at the end of Clark Pt. Rd. in Southwest Harbor, know their sea stuff. The main museum, reminiscent of a grammar-school science fair, fascinates children and some adults. (Open mid-May to late Oct. Mon.-Sat. 9am-5pm. Ticket for all three facilities $11.50, ages 4-12 $8.25, under 4 free; inquire about individual rates.) Call for directions to the lobster hatchery or Salt Marsh Walk (288-5005). Cruises head out to sea from a number of points on the island. In Bar Harbor, **Whale Watcher, Inc.,** 1 West St. (288-3322), Harbor Place, offers sailing trips (2hr.; $14), lobster fishing, seal watching (1½hr.; $16.75), and whale watching trips. (4hr. $28. Open May-Oct. Reservations recommended. Call for schedule.) The **Acadian Whale Watcher** (288-9794), Golden Anchor Pier, West St., has slightly lower prices and offers food and beer aboard. (Buy tickets at corner of Cottage and Main St. 5 trips per day, including sunset cruises. $28. Open mid-May to mid-Oct.) Bundle up—temperatures can drop dramatically on the water.

Wildwood Stables (276-3622), along the Park Loop Rd. in Seal Harbor, lets tourists explore the island via horse and carriage. (1hr. tour $12, seniors $11, ages 6-12 $7, ages 2-5 $4. 2hr. $15/$14/$8/$5. Reservations recommended.)

Acadia National Park The 33,000 acres that comprise **Acadia National Park** are a landlubber's dream, offering easy trails and challenging hikes. Millionaire and expert horseman John D. Rockefeller, fearing the island would someday be overrun by cars, funded all of the park's 120 mi. of trails. These **carriage roads** make for easy

NEW ENGLAND

walking, fun mountain biking, and pleasant carriage rides, and are accessible to disabled persons.

Be realistic about your abilities here; the majority of injuries in the park occur in hiking accidents. *Biking and Hiking Guide to the Carriage Roads* (free), available at the visitors center, offers invaluable safety advice for the more labyrinthine trails. **Precipice Trail,** one of the most popular hikes, is closed June to late Aug. to accommodate nesting peregrine falcons. The 5-mi. **Eagle Lake Carriage Road** is graded for bicyclists. Touring the park by auto costs $5 per week, $3 per pedestrian or cyclist. Seniors can purchase a lifetime pass ($10), and disabled are admitted free.

About 4 mi. south of Bar Harbor on Rte. 3, **Park Loop Rd.** runs along the shore of the island, where great waves crash against steep granite cliffs. The sea comes into **Thunder Hole** with a bang at half-tide, sending plumes of spray high into the air and onto tourists. Swimming waters can be found in the relatively warm **Echo Lake** or at **Sand Beach,** both of which have lifeguards in the summer.

New Hampshire

"The Switzerland of America," New Hampshire bears little resemblance to the English county for which it is named. The White Mountains dominate the central and northern regions, while Mt. Washington, the highest point in the Appalachians (6288 ft.), surveys the Atlantic and five states. The first state to declare independence from Great Britain, New Hampshire still embraces an individualistic ideal; the state motto, "Live Free or Die," is emblazoned on every license plate. Today, eager hordes descend upon the state year-round, drawn by a wealth of wilderness activities and an abundance of tax-free outlet shopping.

PRACTICAL INFORMATION

Capital: Concord.
Office of Travel and Tourism: Box 856, Concord 03302 (603-271-2666, 800-262-6660, or 800-258-3608). A 24-hr. recording provides fall foliage reports, daily ski conditions, weekly snowmobile conditions, and weekly special events. **Fish and Game Department,** 2 Hazen Dr., Concord 03301 (603-271-3421), provides info on hunting and fishing regulations and license fees. **U.S. Forest Service,** 719 Main St., Laconia 03246 (603-528-8721). Open Mon.-Fri. 8am-4:30pm.
Time Zone: Eastern. **Postal Abbreviation:** NH.
Sales Tax: 0%. Live Tax-Free or Die. 8% tax on rooms and meals.

■ White Mountains

In the late 19th century, the White Mountains became an immensely popular summer retreat for wealthy New Englanders. Grand hotels peppered the rolling green landscape, and as many as 50 trains per day bore tourists through the region. The mountains are not quite as busy nor as fashionable these days, and hiking and skiing have mostly replaced train travel. Unfortunately, the economics of vacationing here have not changed quite as drastically; affordable lodgings are as scarce as public transportation, and the notoriously unpredictable weather makes camping risky. The area is divided by the notches between the mountains.

Getting There and Getting Around Boston is a good starting point for trips into the White Mountains, but getting around the area itself can be problematic. **Concord Trailways** (228-3300 or 800-639-3317) runs from Boston's South Station bus terminal, 555 Atlantic Ave., Boston, MA (617-426-8080), to Concord (Storrs St., 228-3300; open daily 4:45am-8pm; $11), Conway (First Stop store on Main St.; 447-8444; open daily 5:30am-10pm; $25), and Franconia (Kelly's Foodtown; 823-7795;

open daily 9am-9pm; $26). **Vermont Transit** (800-451-3292) stops its Boston-to-Vermont buses in Concord ($11) at the Trailways terminal, 10 St. James Ave. (617-423-5810). The **Appalachian Mountains Club (AMC)** runs a **shuttle service** (466-2727) among points within the mountains. Consult **AMC's** *The Guide* for a complete map of routes and times; reservations are recommended for all stops and required for some. (Early June to early Oct. daily 8:45am-3:30pm. $6, nonmembers $8.) For **trail and weather info** call the **Pinkham Notch Visitors Center** (466-2725), on Rte. 16 (open daily 6:30am-10pm). Regional **ZIP codes:** Franconia, 03580; Jackson, 03846; Gorham, 03587. **Area code:** 603.

Useful Organizations and Accommodations

Travel info can be obtained at local travel offices or from the **White Mountain Attraction Center,** P.O. Box 10, N. Woodstock 03262 (745-8720), on Rte. 112 in North Woodstock. The main area office of the **U.S. Forest Service,** 719 Main St., Laconia 03247 (528-8721), lies south of the mountains. **Forest service ranger stations** dot the main highways through the forest: **Androscoggin** (466-2713), on Rte. 16, ½ mi. south of the U.S. 2 junction in Gorham; **Ammonoosuc** (869-2626), on Trudeau Rd., in Bethlehem, west of U.S. 3 on U.S. 302; and **Saco** (447-5448), on the Kancamangus Hwy. in Conway 100 yards off Rte. 16. Each station provides info on trail locations and conditions, and a handy free guide to the **backcountry facilities** in its area (stations open daily 8am-4:30pm).

The **Appalachian Mountains Club (AMC)** has its main base in the mountains at the Pinkham Notch Visitors Center, on Rte. 16 between Gorham and Jackson (see Pinkham Notch, below). The area's primary source of info on camping, food, and lodging, the AMC also sells an assortment of camping and hiking accessories. The club runs two car-accessible lodgings in the White Mountains: **Joe Dodge Lodge** (see Pinkham Notch, below) and the **Crawford Hostel** (846-7773; 466-2721 for reservations), adjoining the **Crawford Notch Depot,** east of Bretton Woods on U.S. 302. (24 bunkbeds, toilets, metered showers, full kitchen. Bring a sleeping bag and food. Curfew 9:30pm. $10, nonmembers $15. Reservations recommended.) The Depot has trail guides, maps, food, camping necessities, film, and restrooms (open late May to Labor Day daily 9am-5pm). The AMC also operates a system of eight **huts,** spaced about a day's hike apart along the Appalachian Trail, inaccessible by car or by phone. Breakfast, dinner, or both must be taken with each night's lodging, and guests must provide their own sleeping bags or sheets. Meals at the huts, while not as good as those back at the lodge, are ample and appetizing. (Bunk with 2 meals $50, child $20; nonmembers $57/$27. $5 less without breakfast, $10 less without dinner.) All huts stay open for **full service** June-Oct.; **self-service rates** (caretaker in residence but no meals provided) are available at other times ($12, nonmembers $18; call for reservations).

Camping, Hiking, and Biking

Camping is free in a number of backcountry areas throughout the **White Mountains National Forest (WMNF).** The forest allows neither camping nor fires above the tree line (approximately 4000 ft.), within 200 ft. of a trail, or within ¼ mi. of roads, huts, shelters, tent platforms, lakes, or streams. Rules vary depending on forest conditions; call the **U.S. Forest Service** (528-8721) before settling into a campsite. The Forest Service can also direct you to one of their 22 designated **campgrounds.** (Bathrooms and firewood usually available. Sites $10-14. Call 800-280-2267 two weeks in advance to reserve a site, especially July-Aug.; reservation fee $7.85.)

If you intend to spend a lot of time in the area, and especially if you are planning to do some significant **hiking,** invest in the invaluable *AMC White Mountain Guide* ($17; available in most bookstores and huts). The guide includes full maps and descriptions of all trails in the mountains—you can pinpoint precisely where you are at any given time. When hiking, be careful and come prepared; many an unprepared hiker has died among the treacherous peaks, where weather conditions change at a moment's notice. Bring three layers of clothing in *all* seasons: one for wind, one for rain, and one for warmth. Beware of black flies, particularly in June.

Next to hiking, **bicycling** is the best way to see the mountains close up. According to some bikers, the approach to the WMNF from the north is slightly less steep than others. Consult the *New Hampshire Bicycle* guide and map, available at information centers, the U.S. Forests Service's bike trail guides, or *30 Bicycle Tours in New Hampshire* ($11), available at local bookstores and outdoor equipment stores.

■ Franconia Notch Area

Formed by glacial movements which began during an ice age 400 million years ago, Franconia Notch is more than just old. Imposing granite cliffs, waterfalls, endless woodlands, and the famous rocky profile of the "Old Man of the Mountain" attract droves of summer campers. The nearest town, **Lincoln,** lies just south of I-93 where Rte. 112 becomes the scenic Kancamagus Hwy. From Lincoln, the Kancamagus Hwy. branches east to Conway, twisting 35 scenic mi. through the **Pemigewasset Wilderness.** Four-thousand-foot peaks rim the large basin, attracting backpackers and skiers galore. South of the highway, trails head into the **Sandwich Ranges,** including **Mount Chocorua** (south along Rte. 16 near Ossippee), a dramatic peak and a favorite of 19th-century naturalist painters.

Sights and Activities The **Flume Visitors Center** (745-8391), off I-93 north of Lincoln, screens an excellent, free 15-min. film that acquaints visitors with the landscape (open daily 9am-6pm). While at the center, purchase tickets to **The Flume,** a 2-mi. nature walk over hills, through a covered bridge, and to a boardwalk over a fantastic gorge walled by 90-ft. granite cliffs ($6, ages 6-12 $3). A 9-mi. recreational **bike path** begins at the visitors center and runs through the park.

The westernmost of the notches, Franconia is best known for the **Old Man of the Mountain,** a 40-ft.-high human profile formed by five ledges of stone atop a 1200-ft. cliff north of The Flume. Nathaniel Hawthorne addressed this geological visage in his 1850 story "The Great Stone Face," and P.T. Barnum once offered to purchase the rock. Today, the Old Man is rather doddering; cables and turnbuckles support his forehead. **Profile Lake,** a 10-min. walk from the base of the Cannon Mountain Aerial Tramway, has the best view of the geezer.

Unlike the Old Man, the **Great Cannon Cliff,** a 1000-ft. sheer drop into the cleft between **Mount Lafayette** and **Cannon Mountain,** beckons more than just onlookers. Hands-on types test their technical skill and climb the cliff via the "Sticky Fingers" or "Meat Grinder" routes; less daring visitors opt to let the 80-passenger **Cannon Mountain Aerial Tramway** (823-5563) do the work. (Open Memorial Day-Aug. daily 9am-7pm; Sept.-Oct. 21 9am-5pm; early Dec. to mid-April 8:30am-4:30pm. $8, ages 6-12 $4; one-way $6; Mon.-Fri. senior NH residents free.)

Myriad trails lead up into the mountains on both sides of the notch, providing excellent day hikes and spectacular views. Be prepared for severe weather, especially above 4000 ft. The **Lonesome Lake Trail,** a relatively easy hike, winds its way 1½ mi. from Lafayette Place to **Lonesome Lake** (bring your own prozac), where the AMC operates its westernmost summer hut (see White Mountains: Useful Organizations, above). The **Greenleaf Trail** (2½mi.), which starts at the Aerial Tramway parking lot, and the **Old Bridle Path** (3mi.), from Lafayette Place, are much more ambitious. Both lead up to the AMC's Greenleaf Hut near the summit of Mt. Lafayette overlooking Echo Lake, a favorite destination for sunset photographers. From Greenleaf, trudge the next 7½ mi. east along **Garfield Ridge** to the AMC's most remote hut, the Galehead. Hikes from this base can keep you occupied for days. A campsite on Garfield ridge costs $5; a number of other campsites, mainly lean-tos and tent platforms with no showers or toilets, scatter throughout the mountains. Most run $5 per night on a first come, first served basis, but many are free. Contact the U.S. Forest Service or consult the AMC's free two-page handout, *Backpacker Shelters, Tent sites, Campsites, and Cabins in the White Mountains.*

North of the south end of Franconia Notch, **The Basin,** a waterfall in the Pemige-wasset River, drops into a 15-ft. granite pool. The Basin's walls, smoothed by 25,000 years of sandy scouring, seem almost too perfect to be natural. One of the park's most popular attractions, The Basin is fully wheelchair-accessible.

After any exertion, cool off at the lifeguard-protected **beach** on the northern shore of **Echo Lake State Park** (356-2672), just north of Franconia Notch. (Open daily mid-June to Sept. 9am-8pm. $2.50, under 12 and over 65 free.)

Skiing Less renowned than the resorts of Mt. Washington Valley, the ski areas of Franconia Notch, collectively known as **Ski-93,** P.O. Box 517, Lincoln 13251 (745-8101 or 800-937-5493), offer multiple-area packages. **Loon Mountain** (745-8111), 3 mi. east of I-93 on Rt. 112, has a free beginner's rope tow and, by limiting lift ticket sales, promises crowd-free skiing. (Lift tickets $38, Sat.-Sun. $45; ages 13-21 $32/$40; ages 6-12 $25/$28.) For cross-country skiing plus some great downhill runs, try **Waterville Valley** (236-8311. Lift tickets $37/$43, ages 13-18 $34/$39, ages 6-12 $25/$29. Prices go down during value seasons: Nov. 8-Dec. 20 and late March to April.) **Cannon Mountain** (823-5563), in the Notch on I-93, sports decent slopes and the New England Ski Museum. (Lift tickets $28/$37, ages 13-18 and students $25/$32, ages 6-12 $20/$27.) Rates rise on weekends.

Camping **Lafayette Campground** (823-9513), is nestled smack in the middle of Franconia Notch. (Showers. Sites for 2 $14, $7 per additional person. Call ahead for reservations. Open mid-May to mid-Oct., weather permitting.) If Lafayette is full, try the more suburban **Fransted Campground** (823-5675), 1 mi. south of the village and 3 mi. north of the notch. (Showers, bathroom. Sites $13, on the river $16. Open May-Columbus Day.)

■ North Conway

At first glance, North Conway, strung along the stretch of land shared by Rte. 16 and Rte. 302, seems like just another strip of motels and fast food joints on the way to somewhere else. Look again. This town, the largest city around, capitalizes on two of New Hampshire's most striking features: the taxes and the terrain. Factory outlet stores, including most major clothing labels, teem with voracious bargain hunters, while mountain men and women crowd in the region's best outdoor equipment stores. A number of very good cross-country and downhill ski centers await nearby.

Accommodations and Food Four miles north of North Conway, the **Sham-rock Village Hostel** (356-5153), on Rte. 16A in Intervale off Rte. 16/302 (from N. Conway, turn left onto the first bridge on 16A), provides beds, kitchen access, laundry facilities, and breakfast ($12, students and seniors $10; call ahead). The **Maple Leaf Motel** (356-5388), on Main St., south of the North Conway city park, has clean, spacious rooms with private bath, TV, and perhaps phone for reasonable rates. (Singles $58, doubles $62; foliage and ski seasons $78/82; in spring $30/34.)

Breakfast and lunch spots line North Conway's Main St.; **Gunther's** (356-5200), above Campbell's Books, serves up food devised by owner and cook George Gunther (meals $3-7, open daily 7am-2pm). The *après* crowd reconvenes at the pricey **Valley Square** (formerly Café Rubino), in the Eastern Slope Inn. (Nightly dinner specials $7-9. Dancing Fri.-Sat. Open Sun.-Thurs. 11:30am-midnight, Fri.-Sat. 11:30am-1am. In summer open also for breakfast.)

Skiing and Outdoor Activities Though close to many ski areas, North Conway is proudest of its own local mountain, **Cranmore** (356-5543). (Two-day lift tickets Sun.-Fri. $55, Sat. and holidays $72; kids $29/$39. Open mid-Nov. to April daily 10am-6pm.) At **Attitash** (374-2368) ask about the "smart credit ticket," as well as short-term options. (Open mid-April to Nov. Mon.-Fri. 9am-4pm, Sat.-Sun. 8am-4pm.) **Wildcat** (466-3326), known for having the area's largest lift capacity and a free novice skiing area, fronts Rte. 16 just south of Pinkham Notch State Park (lift tickets $25, Sat.-Sun. $37; ages 6-12 $19/$22). During the summer, Wildcat offers gondola rides. ($9, ages 4-10 $4.50. Mid-June to mid-Oct. 9:30am-4:30pm.) All three areas offer special rates for groups and multi-day visitors; call ahead. During the summer, speed demons enjoy the **Alpine Slide** at Attitash, a wild ¾-mi. sled ride down the mountain to test the most adventurous souls. A one-day pass ($16) includes unlimited rides on the alpine slide and nearby waterslides (open daily 9:30am-6pm).

A number of stores in the North Conway area rent outdoor equipment. For downhill and cross-country skis, try **Joe Jones** (356-9411), in North Conway on Main St. at Mechanic. (Alpine skis, boots, and poles $15 for 1 day, $25 for 2 days. Cross-country equipment $10/$16. Open daily 9am-9pm; Sept.-Nov. and April-June Sun.-Thurs. 10am-8pm, Fri.-Sat. 9am-8pm.) **Eastern Mountain Sports (EMS)** (356-5433), on Main St. inside the Eastern Slope Inn, distributes free mountaineering pamphlets and books on the area, including *30 Bicycle Tours in New Hampshire* ($11). EMS also sells camping equipment and rents tents and sleeping bags. The knowledgeable staff can give assistance and recommendations for climbing and hiking in North Conway. (Open in summer Mon.-Sat. 9am-9pm, Sun. 9am-6pm; Oct.-May Sun.-Wed. 9am-6pm, Thurs.-Sat. 9am-9pm.)

■ Pinkham Notch

Practical Information New Hampshire's easternmost notch lies in the shadow of Mt. Washington between Gorham and Jackson on Rte. 16. The home of AMC's main info center in the White Mountains, and the starting point for most trips up Mt. Washington, Pinkham Notch's practicality gets more publicity than its beauty, although both deserve reknown. To get to Pinkham Notch from I-93 south, take Exit 42 to U.S. 302E, then follow Rte. 116N to U.S. 2E to Rte. 16S. From I-93 north, take Exit 32 onto Rte. 112E to Rte. 16N. AMC's **Pinkham Notch Visitors Center** (466-2721, ext. 116 or 466-2727 for reservations), 10 mi. north of Jackson on Rte. 16, is the area's best source of info on weather and trail conditions. The center also handles reservations at any of the AMC lodgings and sells the complete line of AMC books, trail maps ($3, weatherproofed $5), and camping and hiking accessories (open daily 6:30am-10pm).

Accommodations AMC's huts offer the best lodging on the mountain. At **Joe Dodge Lodge,** immediately behind the Pinkham Notch visitors center, get a comfy bunk with a delicious and sizeable breakfast and dinner. ($42, kids $24; nonmembers $35/$17; $6 less without breakfast, $12 less without dinner. Lodging $5 more on Sat. and in Aug.) **Hermit's Lake Shelter,** situated about two hours up the Tuckerman Ravine Trail, has bathrooms but no shower and sleeps 72 people in eight lean-tos and three tent platforms ($7 per night; buy nightly passes at the visitors center). **Carter Notch Hut** lies to the east of the visitors center, a 4-mi. hike up the 19-mi. **Brook Trail.** Just 1½ mi. from Mt. Washington's summit sits **Lakes of the Clouds,** the largest (room for 90), highest, and most popular of the AMC's huts; additional sleeping space for six backpackers in its basement refuge room can be reserved from any other hut ($12, nonmembers $18). Bring food—there's a stove.

If all the AMC facilities are booked, head to the **Berkshire Manor,** 133 Main St. (466-2186), in Gorham. The outside appears somewhat dated, but inside, guests have access to a full kitchen, a spacious living room, cozy bedrooms, and hall bathrooms. (Singles $15, doubles $30; rates sometimes negotiable.)

Mt. Washington From just behind the Pinkham Notch Visitors Center all the way up to the summit of Mt. Washington, **Tuckerman's Ravine Trail** takes four to five hours of steep hiking each way. Use caution when climbing—every year, Mt. Washington claims at least one life. A gorgeous day can suddenly turn into a chilling storm, with whipping winds and rumbling thunderclouds. It has never been warmer than 72°F atop Mt. Washington, and the average temperature on the peak is a bone-chilling 26.7°F. With an *average* wind speed of 35mph and gusts that have been measured up to an astounding 231mph, Mt. Washington ranks as the windiest place in the country by far. All risks aside, the climb *is* stellar, and the view well worth it. Motorists can take the **Mount Washington Auto Road** (466-3988), a paved and dirt road that winds 8 mi. to the summit. At the top, buy a bumper sticker boasting "This Car Climbed Mt. Washington"—it's certain to impress folks when you cruise back through town, particularly if you're driving a Ford Model T. The road begins at Glen House, a short distance north of the visitors center on Rte. 16. ($15 per car and driver, $6 per passenger, ages 5-12 $4. Road open mid-June to mid-Sept. daily 7:30am-6pm; mid-May to mid-June and mid-Sept. to mid-Oct. 8:30am-5pm.) **Guided van tours** to the summit include a 30-minute presentation on the mountain's natural history ($20, ages 5-12 $10). On the summit you'll find strong wind, an info center and snack bar (466-3347; open Memorial Day-Columbus Day daily 8am-8pm), and a museum run by the **Mt. Washington Observatory** (466-3388; museum open Memorial Day-Columbus Day daily 9am-7pm).

Vermont

Perhaps no other state is as aptly named as Vermont. The lineage of the name extends back to Samuel de Champlain, who in 1609 dubbed the area "green mountain" in his native French *(vert mont);* the Green Mountain range shapes and defines Vermont, spanning the length of the state from north to south and covering most of its width as well. Over the past few decades, ex-urbanite yuppies have invaded, creating some tension between the original, pristine Vermont and the packaged Vermont of organic food stores and mountaineering shops. Happily, the former still seems to prevail; visitors can frolic in any of the 30 state forests, 80 state parks, or the mammoth 186,000-acre Green Mountain National Forest.

PRACTICAL INFORMATION

Capital: Montpelier.
Vermont Travel Division: 134 State St., Montpelier 05602 (802-828-3237). Open Mon.-Fri. 7:45am-4:30pm. **Department of Forests, Parks and Recreation,** 103 S. Main St., Waterbury 05676 (802-241-3670). Open Mon.-Fri. 8am-4:30pm. **Vermont Snowline** (229-0531). 24-hr. recording on snow conditions Nov.-May. **Travel Division Fall Foliage Hotline** (828-3239). Fall leaf colors info Sept.-Oct.
Time Zone: Eastern. **Postal Abbreviation:** VT.
Sales Tax: 5%; 7% on meals and lodgings.

SKIING

Twenty-four downhill resorts and 47 cross-country trail systems lace Vermont. For a free winter attractions packet, call the Vermont Travel Division (see Practical Information, above). Also contact the **Vermont Ski Areas Association,** 26 State St. (P.O. Box 368), Montpelier 05601 (802-223-2439; open Mon.-Fri. 8am-4:30pm). The **Lake Champlain Regional Chamber of Commerce** (802-863-3489), 60 Main St., Ste. 100, Burlington 05401 (open Mon.-Fri. 9am-5pm) has much helpful info as well.

Vermont's famous **downhill** ski resorts offer a great range of terrain and accommodations. Always inquire about shared rooms with bunks, which cost significantly less than private rooms. The better resorts include: **Killington** (802-773-1330 or 800-621-6867; 155 trails, 19 lifts, 6 mountains, and one of the most extensive snowmaking systems in the world); **Stratton** (802-297-2200 or 800-787-2886; 92 trails, 12 lifts); **Sugarbush** (802-583-2381 or 800-537-8427; 111 trails, 16 lifts, 2 mountains); **Stowe** (802-253-3000 or 800-253-4754; 46 trails, 11 lifts); **Middlebury College Snow Bowl** (802-388-4356; 14 trails, 3 lifts); and **Jay Peak** (802-988-2611 or 800-451-4449; 50 trails, 6 lifts). **Cross-country** resorts include the **Trapp Family Lodge,** Stowe (802-253-8511, lodging 800-826-7000; 60km of trails); **Mountain Meadows,** Killington (802-757-7077; 25km of trails); **Woodstock** (457-2114; 47km of trails); and **Sugarbush-Rossignol** (802-583-3333 or 800-451-4320; 25km of trails).

■ Burlington

Tucked between Lake Champlain and the Green Mountains, the largest city in Vermont—a state known for its laid-back love of nature—successfully bridges the gap between the urban and the outdoors. Five colleges, including the University of Vermont (UVM), give the area a youthful, progressive flair; bead shops pop up next door to mainstream clothing stores without disrupting local harmony. Stroll along Church St. for a taste of the middle-class hippie atmosphere, which transcends its oxymoronic nature and colors the reality of this city at ease.

PRACTICAL INFORMATION

Tourist Office: Lake Champlain Regional Chamber of Commerce, 60 Main St. (863-3489), provides free maps of the Burlington Bike Path and parks. Open Mon.-Fri. 8:30am-5pm, June-Oct. also Sat.-Sun. 10am-2pm. **Church St. Marketplace Information Gallery,** in a more central location at Church and Bank St. Open May-June and Sept. Mon.-Sat. 11am-4pm, Sun. noon-4pm; July-Aug. and Oct. Mon.-Thurs. 11am-5pm, Fri.-Sat. 11am-7pm, Sun. noon-4pm.

Trains: Amtrak, 29 Railroad Ave., Essex Jct. (879-7298 or 800-872-7245), 5mi. east of the center of Burlington on Rte. 15. To: Montreal (1 per day, 3hr., $17-20); New York (2 per day, 9¾hr., $53-66); White River Junction (1 per day, 2hr., $13-21). Open Mon.-Sat. 6-10:15am and 6:30-7:30pm, Sun. 8:30am-1pm and 6:30-7:30pm. CCTA bus to downtown runs Mon.-Sat. every ½hr. 6am-9:30pm; 75¢.

Buses: Vermont Transit, 137 St. Paul St. (864-6811 or 800-451-3292; 800-642-3133 in VT), at Main St. To: Boston ($45); Montreal ($20); White River Junction ($14.50); Middlebury ($7.50); Bennington ($19); Montpelier ($7.50); Albany ($34). Sept.-May 25% student discount, with ID. Connections made with Greyhound; Ameripasses accepted. Open daily 6am-7:30pm; tickets sold 7:30am-8pm.

Public Transportation: Chittenden County Transit Authority (CCTA) (864-0211). Frequent, reliable service. Downtown hub at Cherry and Church St. Connections with Shelburne and other outlying areas. Buses operate every ½hr. Mon.-Sat. roughly 6:15am-9:20pm, depending on routes. 75¢, seniors and disabled 35¢, under 18 50¢, under 5 free. **Special Services Transportation Agency,** 655-7880, has info and advice about travel for the disabled and elderly.

Bike Rental: Ski Rack, 85 Main St. (658-3313). Road bikes $8 per hr., $18 per day, $65 per week; mountain bikes $8/22/70. Helmet and lock included. In-line skates $8 per hr., $12 per day. Credit card required for rental. Open Mon.-Thurs. 10am-8pm, Fri. 9am-9pm, Sat. 9am-6pm, Sun. 11am-5pm.

Crisis Lines: Women's Rape Crisis Center, 863-1236. **Crises Services of Chittenden County,** 863-2400. Both open 24hr.

Emergency: 911.

Post Office: 11 Elmwood Ave. (863-6033), at Pearl St. Open Mon.-Fri. 8am-5pm, Sat. 9am-noon. **ZIP code:** 05401. **Area code:** 802.

ACCOMMODATIONS AND CAMPING

Inquire at the chamber of commerce for a complete rundown on area accommodations. B&Bs are generally found in the outlying suburbs. Reasonably priced hotels and guest houses line **Shelburne Rd.** south of downtown. **Mrs. Farrell's Home Hostel (HI-AYH)** (865-3730), 3 mi. from downtown, is accessible by public transportation. Ask for directions when you call for reservations or confirmation. The six beds are split between a clean, comfortable basement and a lovely garden porch. The friendly, adventurous owner is sometimes hard to reach; call around 7-8am or 5-7pm. (Free linens, showers, coffee, and bagels. Strict 10pm curfew. $15, nonmembers $18. Disabled accessible room available for summer.) Proprietor Bruce Howden created the original art that adorns the walls of the charming **Howden Cottage,** 32 N. Champlain (864-7198); he also bakes breakfast muffins at this B&B, and he recently added a solarium to boot. (Singles $39, doubles $49; mid-Oct. to mid-May $49/$59. Double bedrooms with a shared bath $39-59. Pricier suites available for $59-89. Reservations by credit card recommended.)

North Beach Campsites (862-0942), on Institute Rd. 1½ mi. north of town by North Ave., has access to a beach on Lake Champlain; take the "North Ave." bus from the main terminal on Saint Paul St. (67 sites. $16, with electricity $19, with full hookup $21. VT residents $4 less. Showers 25¢ per 5min. Beach is free, but it closes at 9pm and parking costs $3. Open mid-May to mid-Sept.) You can have your MTV at **Shelburne Campground** (985-2540), on Shelburne Rd., 1 mi. north of Shelburne and 5 mi. south of Burlington by Rte. 7; buses to Shelburne South stop right next to the campground. (Pool, laundry facilities, free showers. Sites for 2 $16, with water and electricity $20, with full hookup, including cable TV $24; $2 per additional person. Open May-Oct.) See Near Burlington, below, for more camping options.

FOOD

Immortalized by ex-regulars Phish on their album *A Picture of Nectar,* **Nectar's,** 188 Main St. (658-4771), rocks with inexpensive food and nightly live music. (Famous fries $3. No cover. Open Mon.-Fri. 5:30am-2am, Sat. 7am-1am, Sun. 7am-2am.) Upstairs, **Club Metronome** (865-4563) invites live music acts to perform, and those willing to pay a $7-8 cover to listen and dance (some shows 21+). At **Sweetwater's,** 118 Church St. (864-9800), incredibly high ceilings and vast wall paintings dwarf those who come for delicious soups ($2-4) and sandwiches ($5-7). When in Vermont, try the Vermonter ($6; open daily 11:30am-10pm). The **Oasis Diner,** 189 Bank St. (864-5308), has provided the ultimate American diner experience since 1954. Hamburger, fries and a small soda goes for $4.75. (Open Mon.-Sat. 5am-3pm, Sun. 8am-3pm.) The **Vermont Pub and Brewery,** 144 College St. (865-0500), at St. Paul's, offers affordable sandwiches, delicious homemade beers (pint $3), and English pub favorites like Cornish pasties (similar to a pot pie, $5). To learn more about Original Vermont Lager, go on the free brewery tour. (Tours Wed. 8pm, Sat. 4pm. Pub open Mon.-Thurs. and Sat. 11:30am-1am, Fri. 11:30am-2am, Sun. 10am-1pm. Live entertainment June-Aug. Thurs.-Sat. 9:30pm.) Buy a bottle of wine for $4 in the odorific warehouse of the **Cheese Outlet,** 400 Pine St. (863-3968 or 800-447-1205). Gnaw on a hunk of glorious cheese or nibble at their café fare (open daily 8am-7pm, Sun. 10am-5pm). Finally, of course, top off any meal with the ultimate Vermont experience. Although the converted gas station has burned down, the first **Ben and Jerry's** (862-9620) still sits on its original site at 169 Cherry St., serving Cherry Garcia or Chocolate Chip Cookie Dough ice cream cones for $2. (Open in summer Sun.-Thurs. 11:30am-11:30pm, Fri.-Sat. 11:30am-midnight; in off season Sun.-Thurs. 11:30am-10:30pm, Fri.-Sat. 11:30am-11:30pm.)

SIGHTS AND ENTERTAINMENT

Despite its suburban appearance, Burlington offers lively cultural and artistic entertainment. The popular pedestrian mall at historic **Church Street Marketplace** provides a haven for tie-dye and ice cream lovers and sells works by local artists. Amateur historians delight in Victorian **South Willard St.,** where you'll find **Champlain College** and the **University of Vermont** (656-3480), founded in 1797. **City Hall Park,** in the heart of downtown, and **Battery Street Park,** on Lake Champlain near the edge of downtown, are beautiful places to relax. The **Burlington Community Boathouse** (865-3377), at the base of College St. at Lake Champlain, rents sailboats ($20-40 per hr.; $5 discount for VT residents) and rowboats ($5 per hr.; Mon.-Thurs. only) for a cruise on the lake (open mid-May to mid-Sept. daily 9am-7pm). The **Spirit of Ethan Allen** scenic cruise (862-9685) departs from the Burlington Boathouse at the bottom of College St. The boat cruises along the Vermont coast, giving passengers a close-up view of the famous Thrust Fault, which is not visible from land. (Late May to

NEW ENGLAND

mid-Oct. daily 10am, noon, 2, and 4pm. $8, ages 3-11 $4. Call about the more costly theme dinner and sunset cruises.)

The **Shelburne Museum** (985-3346), 7 mi. south of Burlington, in Shelburne, houses one of the best collections of Americana in the country. Beside 35 buildings transported from all over New England, 45-acre Shelburne has a covered bridge from Cambridge, MA and a steamboat and lighthouse from Lake Champlain. Don't miss the Degas, Cassatt, Manet, Monet, Rembrandt, and Whistler paintings. Tickets are valid for two consecutive days; you'll need the time to cover the mile-long exhibit. (Open daily 10am-5pm; mid-Oct. to mid-May by reservation. $17.50, students $10.50, ages 6-12 $6, under 6 free. ½-price tickets available, valid 3-5pm on a single day. AAA discount.) Five mi. farther south on U.S. 7, the **Vermont Wildflower Farm** (425-3500), has a seed shop and 6½ acres of wildflower gardens. (Open May to late Oct. daily 10am-5pm. $3, seniors $2.50, under 12 free.)

The **Ethan Allen Homestead** (865-4556) rests northeast of Burlington on Rte. 127. In the 1780s, Allen, who forced the surrender of Fort Ticonderoga during the American Revolution and helped establish the state of Vermont, built his cabin in what is now the Winooski Valley Park. A multimedia show and tour give insight into the hero and his era. (Open mid-June to mid-Oct. Mon.-Sat. 10am-5pm, Sun. 1-5pm; mid-May to mid-June daily 1-5pm; late Oct. to mid-May reserved tours available. Last tour 4:15. $3.50, seniors $3, ages 5-17 $2, families $10, under 5 free.)

Summer culture vultures won't want to miss the many festivities Burlington has to offer. The **Vermont Mozart Festival** (862-7352 or 800-639-9097) sends Bach, Beethoven, and Mozart to barns, farms, and meadows throughout the area in late July and early August; the **Discover Jazz Festival** (863-7992 or 800-639-1916) features over 200 international and VT musicians, during June, in both free and ticketed performances; and the **Champlain Valley Folk Festival** (656-3311) entertains in early August. The Flynn Theatre Box Office, 153 Main St. (863-5966), handles sales for the Mozart and jazz performances (open Mon.-Fri. 10am-5pm, Sat. 11am-4pm).

■ Near Burlington: Champlain Valley

Lake Champlain, a 100-mi.-long lake between Vermont's Green Mountains and New York's Adirondacks, is often referred to as "Vermont's West Coast." **Lake Champlain Ferry** (864-9804), located on the dock at the bottom of King St., crosses from Burlington to Port Kent, NY and back. (Late June to Aug. daily 13 per day 8am-7:45pm; Sept. to mid-Oct. 8-11 per day 8am-5:30pm. $3, ages 6-12 $1, car $12. The trip takes 1hr.) Lake Champlain Ferry also sails from Grand Isle to Plattsburg, NY; and 14 mi. south of Burlington, from Charlotte, VT, to Essex, NY (either fare $2, ages 6-12 50¢, with car $6.75). Only the Grand Isle Ferry runs year-round.

Mt. Philo State Park (425-2390), 15 mi. south of Burlington on Rte. 7, offers pleasant camping and gorgeous views of the Champlain Valley; take the Vermont Transit bus from Burlington south along U.S. 7 toward Vergennes. (Open Memorial Day-Columbus Day daily 10am-sunset. 16 sites with no hookup $10. Lean-tos $14. Entrance fee $1.50, ages 4-14 $1.) The marsh of the **Missisquoi National Wildlife Refuge** sits at northern end of the Lake near Swanton, VT. Also north of the Lake, **Burton Island State Park** (524-6353) is accessible only by ferry (8:30am-6:30pm; $1.50; call for schedule) from Kill Kare State Park, 35 mi. north of Burlington and 3½ mi. southwest off U.S. 7 near St. Albans Bay. The campground has 21 tent sites ($12) and 25 lean-tos ($16/$4). The state park on **Grand Isle** (372-4300), just off U.S. 2 north of Keeler Bay, also offers camping. (155 sites $12, $3 each additional person after 4. 34 lean-tos $16/$4. Open late May to mid-Oct.)

■ Middlebury

Unlike the many Vermont towns that seem to shy away from association with local colleges, Middlebury, "Vermont's Landmark College Town," welcomes the energy and culture stimulated by Middlebury College. The result is a traditional Vermont atmosphere tinged with vitality, historical attractions, and an active nightlife.

Practical Information Middlebury stretches along U.S. 7, 42 mi. south of Burlington. Ask the friendly staff at the **Addison County Chamber of Commerce,** 2 Court St. (388-7951), in the historic Gamaliel Painter House, for area info. (Open Mon.-Fri. 9am-5pm; limited weekend hours during summer.) **Vermont Transit** stops at the Exxon station at 16 Court St. (388-4373), west of Main St. Buses run to Burlington (3 per day, 1hr., $7.50); Rutland (3 per day, 1½hr., $7.50); Albany (3 per day, 3hr., $28); and Boston (3 per day, 6hr., $43). (Open Mon.-Sat. 6am-10pm, Sun. 7am-9pm.) There is no public transportation in Middlebury, but the **Bike and Ski Touring Center,** 74 Main St. (388-6666), rents bikes on the cheap ($10 per day, $50 per week). Middlebury's **post office:** 10 Main St. (388-2681; open Mon.-Fri. 8am-5pm, Sat. 8am-12:30pm). **ZIP code:** 05753. **Area code:** 802.

Accommodations and Camping Lodging does not come cheaply in Middlebury; prepare to trade in a few lesser vital organs for an extended stay. Middlebury's best budget accommodations chill several mi. from the center of town and require a love of the great outdoors. The **Sugar House Motor Inn** (388-2770 or 388-4330), just south of the Horn Farnsworth House on Rte. 7, offers basic motel rooms from which you can make free local calls to your heart's content. (Singles from $39, doubles $49; prices jump to $90/$95 during the turning of the leaves and Middlebury graduation.) On the southern edge of Middlebury, the **Greystone Motel** (388-4935), 2 mi. south of the town center on Rte. 7, has 10 reasonably priced rooms (singles $45-55, doubles $55-65). Situated on a lake, **Branbury State Park** (247-5925), 7 mi. south on U.S. 7, then 4 mi. south on Rte. 53, is all abuzz with campers, picnickers, and water lovers. (44 sites $12. Lean-tos $16. No hookups. Canoe rentals $5 per hr., $20 per day; paddleboats $5 per ½hr. Reservations recommended July-Aug. Open late May to mid-Oct.) **River's Bend Campground** (388-9092), 2 mi. north of Middlebury on the Pog Team Rd. in New Haven, is meticulous and appropriately named; it sits at the bend of the New Haven River. Conveniently close to the **Dog Team Tavern**, where gargantuan portions of chow sell for around $13, Rivers Bend offers 156 neatly placed sites on a semi-wooded lawn. (Free showers. Sites with water and electricity $18, river sites $22; $6 per adult after 2. Use fishing, swimming, picnicking facilities for $3. Canoe rental $7 per hr.) **Lake Dunmore Kampersville** (352-4501 or 388-2661) is located 10 mi. south of Middlebury (take Rte. 125 straight from Middlebury or off Rte. 7 in Vergennes). Lake Dunmore is a camping resort, with two pools, minigolf, organized games and activities, and a snack bar that will deliver pizza directly to your site. (180 sites. Tent sites $17, with water and electricity $19. RV with water and electricity $23.50; with full hookup $26.)

Food and Nightlife Middlebury's many fine restaurants cater chiefly to plump wallets, but the year-round presence of students ensures the survival of cheaper places. **Calvi's,** 42 Main St. (388-4182), is an old-fashioned soda fountain with good-old-days prices; try a cone of their homemade ice cream. ($1.50. Open Mon.-Sat. 8am-9pm; mid-Sept.-early June 8am-6pm.) Students also flock to **Mister Up's** (388-6724), on Bakery Ln. just off Main St., for an impressively eclectic menu including sandwiches ($5-7) and an extensive salad bar ($6.50; open daily 11:30am-midnight). **Fire and Ice,** 26 Seymour St. (388-7166), down the hill from the Congregationalist Church downtown, quenches the appetites of students and locals with well-prepared American fare and a great salad and bread bar. (Open Tues.-Fri. 11:30am-9pm, Sat.-Sun. 11:30am-9:30pm. Entrees $10-$17.50; lunch menu $5-12.) **Noonie's Deli** (388-0014), in the Marbleworks building just behind Main St., makes terrific sandwiches on homemade bread ($4-5) and follows up with fresh baked desserts (open Mon.-Sat. 9am-9pm, Sun. 11am-9pm).

Thanks to the college, the town has nightlife. Overlooking Otter Creek, trendy **Woody's,** 5 Bakery Ln. (388-4182), off Main St., carves out delicious (if somewhat upscale) dishes and drinks. Lunch prices are reasonable ($4-7) and Sunday brunch rocks (open Mon.-Sat. 11:30am-midnight, Sun. 10:30am-3pm and 5-9:30pm). **Amigos,** 4 Merchants Row (388-3624), befriends weary travelers with Mexican food ($2.50-12) and live local music on Fridays and Saturday in summer (10pm-1am). Get happy with free chicken wings 4-6pm Monday through Thursday. (Open Mon.-Sat. 11:30am-10pm, Sun. 4-9pm. Bar open nightly until midnight.)

Sights The **Vermont State Craft Center** (388-3177), at Frog Hollow, exhibits and sells the artistic productions of Vermonters. (Open Mon.-Thurs. 9:30am-5:30pm, Fri. 9:30am-6:30pm, Sat. 9:30am-6pm, Sun. noon-5pm; in winter Mon.-Sat. 10am-6pm.) The nearby **Sheldon Museum,** 1 Park St. (388-2117), houses an extensive, sometimes macabre collection of Americana, including a set of teeth extracted in the 19th century and a disturbingly well-preserved stuffed cat from the same period. (Open June.-Oct. Mon.-Fri. 10am-5pm, Sat. 10am-4pm; Nov.-May by appt. Guided tour $3.50, students and seniors $3, under 12 50¢. Self-guided tour of first floor exhibition $1.50/$1/free.) **Middlebury College** hosts year-round cultural events; the architecturally striking concert hall in the college **Arts Center,** just outside of town, resonates with a terrific concert series. Call the campus **box office** (388-3711, ext. 7469) for details on events sponsored by the college (open Tues.-Sat. 11am-4pm). The **University of Vermont's Morgan Horse Farm** (388-2011), west of Middlebury on Rte. 23, 2 mi. from Rte. 125, conducts a tour that will neither bruise the behind (no riding) nor thrill and excite (open May-Oct. daily 9am-4pm. $3.50, teenagers $2, under 12 free).

■ Stowe

The village of Stowe winds gracefully up the side of Mount Mansfield (Vermont's highest peak, at 4393 ft.). Ostentatiously quaint, the town fancies itself an American skiing hotspot on par with its ritzier European counterparts. Stowe scoffs at the idea of being a bargain, but behind the façade, travelers can find some unbeatable values.

Practical Information Stowe is 12 mi. north of I-89's Exit 10, which is 27 mi. southwest of Burlington. The ski slopes lie along Rte. 108 northwest of Stowe. **Vermont Transit** only comes as close as the **Gateway Motel,** on S. Main St. in Waterbury, 10 mi. from Stowe (open Mon.-Fri. 8:30am-7pm, Sat. 8am-6pm, Sun. 9am-3pm). From there, **Lamoille County Taxi** (253-9433) will drive you to Stowe village for $20. In the winter, **The Stowe Trolley** (253-7585) runs on an irregular schedule between the important locations in the village. (Every 30min. 7:30-10:30am and 2-3pm; every hr. 11:30am-1:30pm. $1.) In summer, the trolley does that tour thang (75-min. guided tours Mon., Wed., and Fri. 11am; $5).

In addition to providing info on area attractions, the **Stowe Area Association** (253-7321 or 800-247-8693), on Main St. in the center of the village, runs a free booking service for member hotels and restaurants. (Open Mon.-Fri. 9am-5pm, Sat.-Sun. 10am-5pm; in winter Mon.-Fri. 9am-9pm, Sat.-Sun. 10am-6pm.) The **Stowe Mountain Resort's** booking service (253-3000) does the same. Stowe's **post office:** 105 Depot St. (253-7521), off Main St. (open Mon.-Fri. 8:30am-5pm, Sat. 7am-4:30pm). **ZIP code:** 05672. **Area code:** 802.

Accommodations and Camping The **Vermont State Ski Dorm** (253-4010), at the base of Mt. Mansfield, 7 mi. from town on Mountain Rd. (shuttles run to town during ski season), is Stowe's best lodging bargain by far. The manager will call town to get you special deals on bike, snowshoe, ski, in-line skate, and canoe rentals. He's also a great chef; order ahead for breakfast ($4) and dinner ($6). (Beds $15, in ski season $20. Reserve by phone far in advance for ski and foliage seasons. Closed June-July.) The friendly, eccentric **Golden Kitz** (253-4217 or 800-548-7568), Mountain Rd., comes complete with a room for "flirty dancing." This lodge/motel offers parlor areas, an art studio, and bedrooms varying in theme and price. Call ahead. (Singles with shared bath $20-$30 in lowest season, $40-50 during Christmas week and fall foliage; doubles with private bath $35-45/$45-80. Multi-day packages available.) The committed budget traveler should ask for the "dungeon" double ($20 per night, $120 per week), though it is often rented out long-term.

Gold Brook Campground (253-7683), 1½ mi. south of the town center on Rte. 100, offers the experience of camping without all that roughing-it business. (Showers, laundry, volleyball, badminton, horseshoes, skateboard ramp. Tent sites for 2 $14, with electrical hookup $18-25; $3 per additional person.) **Smuggler's Notch State Park** (253-4014) keeps it simple with hot showers, tent sites, and lean-tos. (Sites for 4 $11; $3 per additional person up to 8; lean-tos $15/$4. Reservations recommended. Open mid-May to mid-Oct.)

Join locals from all walks of life but with one thing in common—a love for cheaply priced gargantuan deli sandwiches ($2.50-4) at the **IGA Deli** (253-4576), S. Main St. Salads include the seafood salad, which runs $6 per lb.; in winter, they also serve soups ($2.25 per piping hot pint; open daily 9am-6pm). At the **Depot Street Malt Shoppe,** 57 Depot St. (253-4269), visitors enjoy classic diner fare and salivate over hot fudge sundaes in an artfully recreated 50s soda shop. (Meals $3-8. Open daily 11am-9pm.) The **Sunset Grille and Tap Room** (253-9281), on Cottage Club Rd. off Mountain Rd., sells generous meals ($5-15) and a vast selection of domestic beers in a friendly, down-home barbecue bar/restaurant. (Open for dining daily 11:30am-10pm; bar open Mon.-Fri. 11:30am-2am, Sat. 11:30am-1am.)

Skiing and Activities Stowe's ski offerings consist of the **Stowe Mountain Resort** (253-3000 or 800-253-4754) and **Smuggler's Notch** (664-8851 or 800-451-8752). Both areas are expensive; lift tickets cost about $45 per day. Nearby, the hills are alive with the sound of the area's best cross-country skiing at the **Von Trapp Family Lodge** (253-8511), on Luce Hill Rd. Yes, it *is* the family from *Sound of Music,* and it is divine. The lodge also offers rentals and lessons. (Trail fee $12. Ski rentals $12. Lessons $14. Discounts for kids.) **A.J.'s Ski and Sports** (253-4593), at the base of Mountain Rd., rents snow equipment. (Skis, boots, and poles: downhill $18 per day, 2 days $32; cross-country $12/$20; snowboard and boots $24 per day. Discount with advance reservations. Open daily 9am-6pm; Nov.-April 8am-6pm.)

In summer, Stowe's frenetic pace drops off—as do its prices. Rent mountain bikes ($6 per hr., $14 per ½day, $20 per day) and in-line skates ($6/$12/$18) at **Action Outfitters,** 2280 Mountain Rd. (253-7975; open in summer Mon.-Fri. 9am-5pm, Sat.-Sun. 9am-6pm; in winter daily 8am-6pm.) **The Mountain Bike Shop** (253-7919 or 800-MTBIKE4/682-4534) on the Mountain Rd. near Stowe Center, rents bikes and in-line skates ($6 per hr., $16 for 4hr.; kids $4/$10; helmet included); cross-country skis ($8 for ½day, $12 per day; kids $6/$10); and snowshoes ($8/$12). (Open Sun.-Mon. 9am-5pm, Tues.-Sat. 9am-6pm.) Stowe's 5½-mi. asphalt recreation path, perfect for cross-country skiing in the winter and biking, skating, or strolling in the summer, runs parallel to the Mountain Road's ascent.

Fly fisherfolk should head to the **Fly Rod Shop** (253-7346), 3 mi. south of Stowe on Rte. 100, to rent fly rods and reels ($10 per day) and pick up the necessary **fishing**

Ben & Jerry: Two Men, One Dream, and Lots of Chunks

In 1978, Ben Cohen and Jerry Greenfield enrolled in a Penn State correspondence course in ice cream making, converted a gas station into their first shop, and launched themselves on the road to the ice cream hall of fame. Today, **Ben and Jerry's Ice Cream Factory** (244-5641), a few miles north of Waterbury on Rte. 100, is a cow-spotted mecca for ice cream lovers. On a 20-min. tour of the facilities, taste the sweet success of the men who brought "Lemongrad" to Moscow and "Economic Chunk" to Wall Street. The tour tells the history of the operation and showcases the policies which have given the company a reputation for social consciousness. (Tours daily every 15min. 9am-9pm, Sept. to late June tours every 30min. 9am-6pm. $1.)

NEW ENGLAND

licenses (non-residents 3-day $18, season $35). The owner can show you how to tie a fly, or you can stick around for free fly-fishing classes on the shop's own pond (April-Oct. Wed. 4-6pm, Sat. 9-10am). If you're looking to canoe on the nearby Lamoille River, visit **Umiak** (253-2317), Rte. 100, 1 mi. south of Stowe Center. The store (named after a unique type of kayak used by the Inuit) rents regular ol' kayaks and canoes in the summer ($20 per ½day, $30 per day) and offers a full-day river trip for $24, under 12 $12. (Rental and transportation to the river included. Open May-Sept. daily 9am-6pm; otherwise Wed.-Sun. 10am-5pm.) Located in a rustic red barn on Mountain Rd., **Topnotch Stowe** (253-8585) offers 1-hr. horseback-riding tours. (May-Nov. daily 11am, 1, and 3pm; $25.)

The absence of any significant body of water doesn't stop the **Stowe Yacht Club** at the Commodore's Inn (253-7131), just south of the village on Rte. 100, from hosting a full summer racing season, albeit with remote-controlled models. The races are free and public (May-Oct. Mon. and Wed. 4pm, Sun. 1pm).

■ White River Junction

Named for its location at the confluence of the White and Connecticut Rivers, White River Junction was once the focus of railroad transportation in the northeastern U.S. Today, near the intersection of I-89 and I-91, the Junction preserves its status as a travel hub by serving as the bus center for most of Vermont. **Vermont Transit** (295-3011 or 800-552-8737), on U.S. 5 adjoining the William Tally House Restaurant, makes connections to New York City (3 per day, 8hr., $50-52), Burlington (4 per day, 2hr., $14.50), Montréal (1 per day, 5hr., $45), and smaller centers on a less regular basis (office open Sun.-Fri. 7am-8:30pm, Sat. 7am-5pm). **Amtrak** (800-872-7245), on Railroad Rd. (go figure) off N. Main St., rockets once per day to New York (7½hr., $54), Essex Junction (near Burlington; 2hr., $13-21), Montréal (4½hr., $27-35), and Philadelphia (9½hr., $63-78). (Open nightly 9:15pm-6am.)

If you must stay here, the **info booth,** at the intersection of Sykes and U.S. 5 off I-89 and 91 across from the bus station, will apprise you of any possible distractions. (Open late June to Labor Day and first 2 weeks of Oct. daily 9am-4pm; otherwise sporadically on weekends.) In town, the **chamber of commerce** (295-6200), Main St., in the Gates-Briggs Bldg., has area info (open daily, roughly 9am-5pm). White River's **post office:** 9 Main St. (295-2803; open Mon.-Fri. 8-10am and 3-5pm, Sat. 8-10am). **ZIP code:** 05001. **Area code:** 802.

The best, and virtually only, bet for lodging is the old-style **Hotel Coolidge,** 17 S. Main St. (295-3118 or 800-622-1124), across the road from the retired Boston and Maine steam engine. From the bus station, walk to the right on U.S. 5 and down the hill past two stop lights (1mi.) into town. Renamed in honor of frequent guest "Silent Cal" Coolidge's pop, the Coolidge boasts a dorm-style budget hostel-ette and neatly kept rooms at fair prices. (Hostel beds with shared bath $20; economy singles from $39.50, doubles from $45.) For a quick bite, stop at local favorite, the **Polkadot Restaurant,** 1 N. Main St. (295-9722). This authentic diner cooks up sandwiches ($1.50-4.50) and full sit-down meals (pork chop plate $5.50; open daily 5am-8pm). At the **Catamount Brewery,** 58 S. Main St. (296-2248), sample other-worldly unpasteurized amber ale produced by British brewing methods. (Free tours July-Oct. Mon.-Sat. 11am, 1, 3pm and Sun. 1, 3pm; Nov.-June Sat. 11am, 1, 3pm. Open Mon.-Sat. 9am-5pm, Sun. noon-5pm.)

■ Brattleboro

Southeast Vermont is often accused of living too much in its colonial past, but Brattleboro seems to be more a captive of the Age of Aquarius than the War for Independence. Whether camouflaged in Birkenstocks and tie-dye or adorned more conventionally, visitors feel right at home in this town, where the vibes are groovy and the organic produce is even better. Nature-worship peaks in the fall foliage season, when tourists invade the area to take part in the ultimate earth fest.

Practical Information Get the *Brattleboro Main Street Walking Tour* and a detailed town map at the **chamber of commerce,** 180 Main St. (254-4565; open Mon.-Fri. 8:30am-5pm). In summer and foliage seasons, an **info booth** (257-1112), on the Town Common off Putney Rd., operates from 9am to 5pm (sometimes closed Tues.). On the busiest summer weekends, an additional booth (257-4801) opens on Western Ave. just beyond the historic Creamery Bridge (open Thurs.-Sun. 10am-6pm). The **Amtrak** (800-835-8725) *Montrealer* train from New York and Springfield, MA stops in Brattleboro, behind the museum on Vernon Rd. Trains go once daily to Montréal (6hr., $39-55), New York (5½hr., $44-48), and Washington D.C. (10hr., $75-93). Arrange tickets and reservations at **Lyon Travel,** 10 Elliot St. (254-6033; open Mon.-Fri. 8:30am-5pm). **Greyhound** and **Vermont Transit** (254-6066) come into town at the parking lot behind the Citgo station at the U.S. 5/Rte. 9/I-91 junction on Putney Rd. (Open Mon.-Fri. 8am-5pm, Sat.-Sun. open for departures.) Brattleboro is on Vermont Transit's Burlington-New York City route (to New York, 3 per day, $37-39). Other destinations include White River Junction (3 per day, 1½hr., $11.50), Burlington (3 per day, 3½hr., $26.50), Montréal (2 per day, 6½hr., $50), and Boston (1 per day, 3hr., $22). To get downtown from the bus station, you can take the infrequent **Brattleboro Town Bus** (257-1761), which runs on Putney Rd. to Main St., then goes up High St. to West Brattleboro (Mon.-Fri. 6:30am-5:45pm. 75¢, students 25¢). Brattleboro's **post office:** 204 Main St. (254-4100; open Mon.-Fri. 8am-5pm, Sat. 8am-noon). **ZIP code:** 05301. **Area code:** 802.

Accommodations and Camping Economy lodgings such as **Super 8** and **Motel 6** proliferate on Rte. 9 (singles generally $32-37). Renovated in the 1930s, the Art Deco **Latchis Hotel** (254-6300), on the corner of Flat and Main St., rents decent rooms in an unbeatable location. (Singles $45-65, doubles $52-75. Reservations recommended, especially in summer.) **West Village,** 480 Western Ave. (254-5610), about 3 mi. out of town on Rte. 9 in West Brattleboro, caters more to the long-term visitor. (Some rooms have kitchenette and microwave. Singles $40, doubles $45; weekly $160. No reservations more than 1 week in advance.) If you're really short on cash, grab your bug repellent and flashlight and wander to the **Vagabond Hostel (HI-AYH)** (874-4096), 25 mi. north on Rte. 30. The hostel offers decent bunks and extensive facilities, but not much lighting and many mosquitoes. (96 bunks, game room, kitchen. $12, nonmembers $15; group rates available. Open May 15-Nov. 16.) **Fort Dummer State Park** (254-2610) is 2 mi. south of town on U.S. 5; turn left on Fairground Ave. just before the I-91 interchange, then right on S. Main St. until you hit the park. This "stupid" fort offers campsites with fireplaces, picnic tables, bathroom facilities, and a lean-to with wheelchair access. (Sites $10, $3 per additional person. Lean-tos $14, $4 per additional human. Day use of park $1.50 each, kids $1. Firewood $2 per armload. Hot showers 25¢. Reservations accepted up to 21 days in advance for 2-day min. stay; $3 non-refundable reservation fee. Open late May to Labor Day.) **Molly Stark State Park** (464-5460), 15 mi. west of town on Rte. 9., has much the same facilities. (Office open daily 10am-6pm. 24 sites $10; 11 lean-tos $14; RV sites without hookups $10. Hot showers 25¢ per 5min. Reservations accepted up to 21 days in advance for 2-day min. stay; $3 non-refundable reservation fee. Open Memorial Day-Columbus Day.) Just 32 mi. west of Bennington, the **Greenwood Lodge (HI-AYH)** (442-2547) rents bunks and private rooms in a 20-bed lodge in the **Prospect Cross-Country Ski Center.** (Beds $15-19, private rooms for 1 or 2 $25-35. Open May-Oct.) Camping is also available. (Sites $12, with hookup $15.75; $2.10 per additional person.)

Food and Nightlife Just across Putney Rd. from the Connecticut River Safari, the **Marina Restaurant** (257-7563) overlooks the West River, offering a cool breeze and a beautiful view. Try the shrimp and chip basket ($4), or the garden burger ($4.75), and see why the locals rave. (Open Mon.-Sat. 11:30am-2:30pm and 4-10pm, Sun. brunch 10am-2pm and 2:30pm-6:30pm. In summer, live music daily 3-7pm.) **Common Ground,** 25 Eliot St. (257-0855), where the town's laid-back "granolas" cluster, supports organic farmers by featuring a wide range of affordable veggie dishes; you might try a soup, salad, bread, and beverage combo for $4.75, or stick with PB&J for $3. (Open Mon. and Wed.-Sat. for lunch and dinner—hours are irregular, so call ahead; Sun. 10:30am-2pm and 5:30-8pm.) The **Backside Café,** 24 High St. (257-5056), inside the Mid-town Mall, serves delicious food in an artsy loft with roof-top dining. Breakfast features farm-fresh eggs cooked to perfection; later in the day, dive into a $6 pasta and herb salad or a $4 egg and cucumber sandwich. (Open Mon. 7:30am-4pm, Tues.-Fri. 7:30am-4pm and 5-9pm, Sat. 8am-3pm, Sun. 10am-3pm; in winter, no lunch on Fri.) At the **Latchis Grill,** 6 Flat St. (254-4747), next to the Latchis Hotel, patrons dine in inexpensive elegance and sample beer brewed on the premises by **Windham Brewery.** (Lunch and dinner $5-15. 7oz. beer sampler $1.75. Open Tues.-Thurs. and Sun. noon-4pm and 5:30-9:30pm; Fri.-Sat. noon-4pm and 5:30-10:30pm.) For locally grown fruits, vegetables, and cider, stop by the **farmers markets** (254-9657), on the Town Common on Main St. (open mid-June to mid-Sept. Sat. 10am-2pm), and on Western Ave. near the Creamery Bridge (open mid-May to mid-Oct. Wed. 3-6pm, Sat. 9am-2pm). At night, rock, blues, R&B, and reggae tunnel through the **Mole's Eye Café** (257-0771), at the corner of High and Main St. (Music Wed. and Fri.-Sat. 9pm. Cover Fri.-Sat. $3. Open Mon.-Fri. 11:30am-1am, Sat. 4pm-midnight or 1am.)

Entertainment Brattleboro chills at the confluence of the West and Connecticut Rivers, both of which can be explored by **canoe.** Rentals are available at **Connecticut River Safari** (257-5008 or 254-3908), on Putney Rd. just across the West River Bridge. (2hr. min. rental $10, $15 per ½day, $20 per day. Two not-necessarily-consecutive days $30. Open mid-May to mid-Sept. daily 8:30am-6pm, mid-Sept. to mid-Oct. weekends and by appointment.)

The **Brattleboro Museum** and **Brattleboro Art Center** (257-0124) reside in the old Union Railroad Station at the lower end of Main St. (Open mid-May to Oct. Tues.-Sun. noon-6pm. $2, students and seniors $1, under 18 free.) The **Windham Gallery,** 69 Main St. (257-1881), hosts local art openings on the first Friday of every month, as well as poetry readings and discussions by artists about their works. (Open Fri.-Sat. noon-8pm, Wed.-Thurs. and Sun. noon-4pm. Suggested donation $1.)

Brattleboro's internationally renowned **New England Bach Festival** (257-4526; Mon.-Fri. 9am-5pm for ticket info) runs throughout October, happily coinciding with the high season for fall foliage; plan your trip well in advance. Thousands cram the common for **Village Days,** the last weekend in July, and **Apple Days,** the last weekend in September, to browse through displays of local arts and crafts. Village Days also features the **Anything That Floats River Parade,** where man-made, non-motorized rafts (two kegs strung together will do) stop at nothing to win the race.

Massachusetts

Massachusetts sees itself as the intellectual center of the nation, and this belief is not entirely unfounded. From the 1636 establishment of Harvard, the oldest university in America, until today, Massachusetts has attracted countless intellectuals and literati. More than thinkers though, Massachusetts has attracted activists, including the men and women who fought the American Revolution. Today, the state remains rich in colonial and revolutionary history, while encouraging the ongoing pursuit of academics and liberal politics.

This little state also offers a large variety of cultural and scenic attractions. Boston, the revolutionary "cradle of liberty," has become an ethnically diverse urban center. Resplendent during the fall foliage season, the Berkshire Mountains fill western Massachusetts with a charm that attracts thousands of visitors. The seaside areas from

Nantucket to Northern Bristol feature the stark oceanic beauty which first attracted settlers to the North American shore.

PRACTICAL INFORMATION

Capital: Boston.
Massachusetts Division of Tourism: Department of Commerce and Development, 100 Cambridge St., Boston 02202 (617-727-3201; 800-632-8038 for guides). Offers a complimentary, comprehensive *Spirit of Massachusetts Guidebook.* Open Mon.-Fri. 8:30am-5pm.
Time Zone: Eastern. **Postal Abbreviation:** MA.
Sales Tax: 5%; 0% on clothing and pre-packaged food.

EASTERN MASSACHUSETTS

■ Boston

As one of the United States' oldest cities, Boston has deep roots in early America and a host of memorials and monuments to prove it. A jam-packed tour of revolutionary landmarks and historic neighborhoods, the Freedom Trail winds its way through downtown Boston. The Black Heritage Trail tells another story about this city which, despite an outspoken abolitionist history, has been torn by ethnic and racial controversy. Irish, East Asian, Portuguese, and African-American communities have found homes throughout the city, creating a sometimes uneasy cultural mosaic. Meanwhile a seasonal population of 100,000 college students tugs the average age in Boston into the mid-20s. While most residents have a less Boston-centric view of the cosmos than Paul McCartney, who recently proclaimed the city "the hub of the universe," few would deny that Boston is an intriguing microcosm of the American melting pot.

PRACTICAL INFORMATION

Tourist Office: Boston Common Information Center, 147 Tremont St., Boston Common. T: Park St. A good place to start a tour of the city. Free maps and brochures of Boston, Freedom Trail maps ($1.50), and *The Official Guidebook to Boston* ($3), which has useful coupons. Open Mon.-Sat. 8:30am-5pm, Sun. 9am-5pm. **Boston Visitors Information,** 800 Boylston St. (536-4100), in the Prudential Plaza's customer service booth. T: Prudential. Open Mon.-Fri. 8:30am-5pm, Sat.-Sun. 10am-5pm. **National Historical Park Visitor's Center,** 15 State St. (242-5642). T: State. Info on historical sights and accommodations. One ranger speaks French. Open Mon.-Fri. 8am-5pm, Sat.-Sun. 9am-5pm.
Airport: Logan International (561-1800 or 800-235-6426), in East Boston. Easily accessible by public transport. The free **Massport Shuttle** connects all terminals with the "Airport" T stop on the blue line. **City Transportation** (596-1177) runs shuttle buses between Logan and major downtown hotels ($7.50 one way, under 12 free; service daily every 30min. 7am-11pm). A **water shuttle** (330-8680) provides a more scenic 7-min. journey to the downtown area. The shuttle runs from the airport to Rowes Wharf near the New England Aquarium and many hotels. Mon.-Fri. every 15min. 6am-8pm; Fri. every 30min. 8-11pm also; Sat. every 30min. 10am-11pm; Sun. every 30min. 10am-8pm. $8, seniors $4, under 12 free; purchase tickets downtown. Taxi to downtown costs $15-20, depending on traffic.
Trains: Amtrak (345-7442 or 800-872-7245), South Station, Atlantic Ave. and Summer St. T: South Station. Frequent daily service to: New York City (5hr., $49); Washington, D.C. (9hr., $66); Philadelphia (7hr., $55); Baltimore (8½hr., $66). Avoid travel on Fri. and Sun. to get lower fares. Station open daily 5:45am-10pm.
Buses: The recently completed South Station bus terminal (T: South Station), right next to the train station, is used by several bus companies. **Greyhound** (800-231-2222). To: New York City (15 per day, 4½hr., $25); Washington, D.C. (17 per day, 9½hr., $43); Philadelphia (12 per day, 7hr., $43); Baltimore (11 per day, 9hr., $43).

Vermont Transit (802-862-9671), administered by Greyhound, buses north to ME, NH, VT, and Montréal. To Burlington, VT (6 per day, 5hr., $45) and Portland, ME (8 per day, $12). **Peter Pan,** 155 Atlantic Ave. (800-343-9999), runs to Western MA and Albany, NY ($25), and New York City ($25). **Concord Trailways** (800-639-3317) goes north to NH and ME; stops include Concord ($11) and Portland ($15). **Bonanza** (800-556-3815) provides frequent daily service to Providence ($7.75); Fall River ($8); Newport ($13); Falmouth ($13); Woods Hole ($13). **Plymouth & Brockton** (508-746-0378) travels between the south shore of Boston and Cape Cod. Station open 24hr. **East Coast Explorer,** 245 Eighth Ave., NYC (718-694-9667, Mon.-Fri. 8-11pm), offers all-day, scenic budget bus trips between New York, Boston, and Washington, D.C.

Ferries: Bay State Cruise (723-7800) departs from Long Wharf; ticket sales in a red building across from the Marriot Hotel. T: Aquarium. Cruises late June to Labor Day leave for Provincetown at 9:30am ($29 same-day roundtrip) and George's Island (Mon.-Fri. 10-11am and 1-4pm on the hr.; Sat.-Sun. 10am-5pm on the hr.; $7, seniors and under 13 $5). Labor Day to late June call for schedule.

Public Transportation: Massachusetts Bay Transportation Authority (MBTA), 722-3200 or 800-392-6100. The **subway** system, known as the **T**, consists of the Red, Green, Blue, and Orange lines. "Inbound" trains run into the center of Boston, while "outbound" trains travel from the city into the outlying areas. Useful maps available at information centers and T stops. Lines run daily 5:30am-12:30am (get there at midnight to be safe). 85¢, seniors 20¢, ages 5-11 40¢. Some automated T entrances in outlying areas require tokens and don't sell them; buy several tokens at a time and have them handy. **MBTA Bus** service covers the city and suburbs more closely than the subway. Fare, generally 60¢, may vary with destination. Bus schedules available at Park St. or Harvard Sq. T stations. The **MBTA Commuter Rail** reaches suburbs and the North Shore, leaving from the North Station, Porter Sq., and South Station T stops. A new South Shore commuter rail is planned to open in Sept. 1997. A "T passport," sold at the visitors center, offers discounts at local businesses and unlimited travel on all subway and bus lines and some commuter rail zones; only worthwhile for frequent users of public transportation. 1-day pass $5, 3-day $9, 7-day $18.

Taxis: Red Cab, 734-5000. Base fare $1.50; $2 per mi. **Checker Taxi,** 536-7000. Base fare $2.70, $1.60 per mi.

Car Rental: Merchants Rent a Car, 20 Rex Dr. (356-5656). T: Braintree. Rents to drivers 18 and over. Compact cars $29 per day, $180 per week, with unlimited mileage in New England. Under 21 25% surcharge per day. Customer must supply auto insurance or credit card with coverage. Open Mon.-Fri. 8am-5:30pm, Sat. 8am-noon. **Dollar Rent-a-Car** (569-5300), in Logan Airport. T: Airport. Rates vary daily depending on availability. Under 25 $20 surcharge per day. Must be 21 with major credit card. 5% AAA discount. Open 24hr. Other offices throughout Boston, including the Sheraton Hotel (523-5098), keep more limited hours.

Bike Rental: Community Bike Shop, 496 Tremont St. (542-8623). $5 per hr., $20 per day (24 hrs.), $75 per week. Must have major credit card. Open Mon.-Fri. 9:30am-8pm, Sat. 9:30am-6pm., Sun. noon-5pm.

Hotlines: Rape Hotline, 492-7273. **Alcohol and Drug Hotline,** 445-1500. Both open 24hr. **Gay and Lesbian Helpline,** 267-9001. Open Mon.-Fri. 4-11pm, Sat. 6-8:30pm, Sun. 8:30-11pm.

Emergency: 911.

Post Office: 24 Dorchester Ave. (654-5327). Open 24hr. **ZIP code:** 02205. **Area code:** 617.

Boston owes its layout as much to the clomping of colonial cows as to urban designers. Avoid driving—the public transportation system is excellent, parking expensive, and Boston drivers somewhat maniacal. Several outlying T-stops offer park-and-ride services. The North Quincy T stop charges $2 per day. Alternatively, there is free parking on Memorial Dr. in Cambridge. If you do choose to drive, be defensive and alert; Boston's pedestrians can be as aggressive as its drivers. Finally, to avoid getting lost in Boston's labyrinth, ask for detailed directions wherever you go.

Boston

Boston Garden, 3
Boston Public Library, 12
Children's Museum, 7
Greyhound / Trailways
Bus Terminal, 9
Hancock Building, 10
Mass. Genl. Hospital, 2
MIT, 13
Museum of Science, 1
New England Aquarium, 5
North Station, 4
Post Office, 6
South Station, 8
Trinity Church, 11

Freedom Trail:
State House, 14
Robert Goud Shaw & 54th
Regiment Memorial, 15
Park St. Church/ Old Granary
Burying Ground, 16
King's Chapel & Burying
Ground, 17
Old North Church, 18
Paul Revere House, 22
Old State House, 19
Quincy Market, 20
Old South Meeting House, 21
Old Corner Book Store, 23

TO LOGAN AIRPORT

Callahan Tunnel →
Sumner Tunnel →

NORTH END
Commercial St.
Charlestown Br.
Fitzgerald Expressway
Atlantic Ave.

Freedom Trail

AQUARIUM

Inner Harbor

Northern Ave.

Fort Point Channel

Summer St.

1/4 mile
250 meters

SOUTH STATION

NORTH STATION

HAY-MARKET

BOWDOIN

GOVERNMENT CENTER

STATE

GOVT CENTER

PARK ST.

DOWNTOWN CROSSING

Washington St.

CHINA-TOWN

CHINATOWN

NE MEDICAL CENTER

Shawmut Ave.

Herald St.

Essex St.

Tremont St.

Boylston St.

BOYLSTON

Charles River Park

Blossom St.

Cambridge St.

SCIENCE PARK

Staniford St.

Charles St.

CHARLES

Embankment Rd.

Longfellow Br.

BEACON HILL

Pinckney St.

Mt. Vernon St.

Joy St.

Beacon St.

Boston Common

Charles St.

ARLINGTON

Arlington St.

Berkeley St.

Clarendon St.

COPLEY

COPLEY SQUARE

BACK BAY

Marlborough St.

Commonwealth Ave.

Newbury St.

Boylston St.

Dartmouth St.

Exeter St.

Fairfield St.

Gloucester St.

Hereford St.

Columbus Avenue

Huntington Ave.

PRUDENTIAL CENTER

BACK BAY

HYNES

Massachusetts Ave

Harvard Br.

CAMBRIDGE

Storrow Drive

Beacon St.

Charles River

N

90

93

90

State St.

Milk St.

Franklin St.

Somerset St.

New Chardon St.

Sudbury St.

Let's Go's compendium **The Unofficial Guide to Life at Harvard** ($8) has the inside scoop and up-to-date listings for Boston/Cambridge area restaurants, history, entertainment, sights, transportation and services. Inquire at bookstores in Harvard Sq. (see Cambridge, below).

ACCOMMODATIONS

Cheap accommodations are hard to come by in Boston. In September, Boston fills with parents depositing their college-bound children; in June parents help remove their graduated, unemployment-bound children. Reserve a room six months to a year in advance during those times. Those with cars should investigate the motels along highways in outlying areas. **Boston Reservations,** 1643 Beacon St. #23, Waban, 02168 (332-4199; fax 332-5751), presides over scores of Boston area accommodations. (Open Mon.-Fri. 9am-5pm. Bed and breakfast singles $70-80, doubles $85-90; hotel rooms $75-250.)

Hostelling International-Boston (HI-AYH), 12 Hemenway St. (536-9455). T: Hynes/ICA. This cheery, colorful hostel has clean but crowded rooms, some with sinks. Shared bath. Great location. Lockers, common rooms, kitchens, laundry, and Internet access. Wheelchair accessible. Over 200 beds in summer, 100 in winter. Planned activities nightly. Ask about discounts at local establishments. Check-in 24hr. Check-out 11am. Lockout 11am-3:30pm. $17, nonmembers $20. Private rooms available. $10 linen deposit. Reservations highly recommended; IBN reservations available.

Back Bay Summer Hostel (HI-AYH), 512 Beacon St. (353-3294), in Boston University's Danielsen Hall. T: Copley. Located in a pretty section of town, Back Bay picks up overflow from its sister in the Fenway. Close to 200 beds. 7-day max. stay. Check-in 7am-noon and 3pm-2am. Check-out 9:30am. $17, nonmembers $20. Reservations highly recommended. Open June 15-Aug 25.

Irish Embassy Hostel, 232 Friend St. (973-4841), above the Irish Embassy Pub. T: North Station. Small, clean, comfortable dorm rooms. 3 free barbecues per week and free admission to the pub; a lively place to stay and make friends. In summer, hostelers take advantage of the free public pool nearby. Common area with TV and kitchen. Check-in daily 9am-2pm and 5-9pm; otherwise ask in the pub. 24-hr access. 48 beds. $15; 1 private double $15 per person. Reservations recommended. Lockers free; lock rental $1. Linens free. No sleeping bags.

Garden Halls Residences, 260 Commonwealth Ave. (267-0079; fax 536-1735), in Back Bay. T: Copley. The rooms in these Boston brownstones are clean, bright, and attractively furnished. Outstanding location just a few blocks from Copley Sq. Vending machines, TV/VCR (during term-time), laundry, microwaves, and linen service. Singles, doubles, triples, and quads; some private baths. Check-in 10am-4pm. $40 per person per night, $230 per week; ask about monthly rates. Breakfast $3, dinner $5. Key and linen deposit $40. Reservations recommended.

Greater Boston YMCA, 316 Huntington Ave. (536-7800). Down the street from Symphony Hall on Mass. Ave. T: Northeastern. Elegant lobby and friendly atmosphere, with access to cafeteria, pool, and recreational facilities. Most rooms are bare, drab singles, but you might get stuck with a walk-through. Must be 18. Shared hall bathroom. Breakfast included. Should be disabled accessible by 1997. 10-day max. stay. ID required for check-in. Office staffed 24hr. Check-out 11am. With HI-AYH ID singles $33, doubles $51; nonmembers $38/$56. Key deposit $5.

Berkeley Residence Club (YWCA), 40 Berkeley St. (482-8850). T: Arlington or Back Bay, on Orange Line. In the South End. In a tough neighborhood. Solid, clean, industrial accommodations for women only; men can visit the lobby. Grand piano, patio, pool, TV room, sun deck, laundry facilities, library. Hall baths. Some doubles with sinks are available. Singles $38, doubles $58. Breakfast included; dinner $6.50.

Anthony's Town House, 1085 Beacon St. (566-3972), Brookline. T: Hawes, Green Line-C. Very convenient to the T stop. 12 ornately furnished rooms for 20 guests, who range from trim professionals to scruffy backpackers. Check-out noon. Singles and doubles $30-70; mid.-Nov. to mid-March $5 less. Ask about weekly rates during the off season.

The Farrington Inn, 23 Farrington Ave. (787-1860 or 800-767-5337), Allston Station. T: Harvard Ave. on Green Line-B, or bus #66. From intersection of Harvard and Commonwealth Ave., stand on Harvard with Marty's Liquors on your left. Farrington is the third street on the right. Located 10min. from downtown by public transit; in Allston, near many pubs and restaurants. Functional rooms with local phone, parking, and breakfast. Most rooms have TVs. Shared baths. Singles $40-50, doubles $50-60. 3-4-bedroom apartments with living room available; $15-20 per person (weekly rates available).

FOOD

Boston ain't called Beantown for nothing. You can sample the real thing at **Durgin Park,** 340 Faneuil Hall Marketplace (227-2038; T: Government Center). Durgin was serving Yankee cuisine in Faneuil Hall (see Sights, below) long before the tourists arrived, and maintains its integrity with such delights as Indian pudding ($2.75) and Yankee pot roast ($7.50). Durgin Park's downstairs **Oyster Bar** highlights another Boston specialty with frequent seafood specials, including a modest lobster dinner for around $10. Find the city's celebrated seafood in the numerous (mostly expensive) seafood restaurants lining Boston Harbor by the wharf (T: Aquarium).

Beyond seafood and baked beans, Boston dishes out an impressive variety of international cuisines. The scent of garlic filters through the **North End** (T: Haymarket), where an endless array of Italian groceries, bakeries, cafés, and restaurants line Hanover and Salem St. **Café Vittoria,** 294 Hanover St. (227-7606), serves especially tasty cappuccino (open Sun.-Thurs. 8am-midnight, Fri.-Sat. 8am-1am). Chinese Fu dogs guard the entrance to **Chinatown** and watch over the countless delectable restaurants packed in behind the gates (T: Chinatown). It's easier to walk through the crowded streets, but if you're driving, Kneeland and Washington St. are two main arteries. A Sunday brunch of *Dim Sum* ("to point to the heart's desire") is an inexpensive Chinese tradition; try **The China Pearl,** 9 Tyler St. (426-4338), for a good variety (around $2 each). The open-air stalls of **Haymarket** sell fresh produce, fish, fruits, cheeses, and pigs' eyes at well below supermarket prices. Get there early for the good stuff. (Indoor stores open daily dawn-dusk; outdoor stalls Fri.-Sat. only. T: Government Center or Haymarket.) Just up Congress St. from Haymarket, the restored **Quincy Market** houses a cornucopia of food booths peddling interesting but over-priced fare.

Addis Red Sea, 544 Tremont St. (426-8727). T: Back Bay. Walk 5 blocks south on Clarendon St. from the T stop, then turn left on Tremont (10-min. walk). Boston's best Ethiopian. The *mesob* (woven table) will soon groan under the colossal platters piled with marvelous mush and the incredible *injera* (flatbread) used to scoop it up. Entrees $8-9, 5-dish communal platters around $12. The Winnie Mandela Combination Platter, $17, commemorates her visit to the restaurant. Open Mon.-Tues. 5-10pm, Wed.-Thurs. 5-10:30pm, Fri. 5-11pm, Sat. noon-11pm, Sun. noon-10pm.

Pho Pasteur, 8 Kneeland St. (451-0247). T: Chinatown. Exit T on Washington St., turn left, walk 2 blocks, then turn left on Kneeland. Ridiculously good, *huge* bowls of pho (traditional Vietnamese noodle soup) for absurdly cheap prices (entrees $3-7; both carnivore- and veggie-friendly). The flavorful dishes and rich chatter of the multi-ethnic fan base more than make up for the bare, mirror-lined decor. Ask about other locations, on Washington St. and in Brighton. Try the jackfruit or pineapple shake. Open daily 9:30am-9:30pm.

No Name, 15 Fish Pier (338-7539), on the waterfront. T: South Station, then a 15-min. walk. This hole-in-the-pier restaurant has been serving up some of the best fried seafood in Boston since 1917; bigshots like the Kennedys and more obscure patrons from all walks of life swear by it. No awards here for snazzy flavorings, spices, or presentation, but the freshness and quality of the seafood cannot be beat. The harbor view allows you to watch tomorrow's dinner emerging from the boats. Entrees $9-15. Open Mon.-Sat. 11am-10pm, Sun. 1-9pm.

Bob the Chef's, 604 Columbus Ave. (536-6204). T: Mass. Ave. From the T, turn right on Mass. Ave., and right onto Columbus Ave. Southern food that's unchallenged in

Boston, especially in these days of rampant veganism and fat anxiety. Smokin' sweet potato pie, fried fish, chicken livers, corn bread, and famed "glorifried chicken" have soul to spare. Entrees $6-12. Open Mon.-Thurs. 11am-9pm, Fri.-Sat. 8am-11pm, Sun. 8am-10pm.

Grand Chau Chow, 41-45 Beach St. (292-5166), in Chinatown. T: South Station. Follow Atlantic Ave. south to Beach St. A primarily local clientele dines on some of the best Chinese food in Boston, between marble walls and stacked tanks rife with displaced deep-sea dwellers. The menu includes over 300 well-sized entrees, averaging $6-7. Open Sun.-Thurs. 10am-3am, Fri.-Sat. 10am-4am.

La Famiglia Giorgio's, 112 Salem St. (367-6711), in the North End. T: Haymarket. Notorious for serving two meals: the one you eat in the restaurant and the one you take home. Portions are enormous and tasty; the garden salad contains more than one head of lettuce. Vegetarians have boundless options, including a towering tribute to eggplant. Entrees $6-15; purchase of an entree per person required. Open Mon.-Sat. 11am-10:30pm, Sun. noon-10:30pm. No reservations.

Trident Booksellers and Café, 338 Newbury St. (267-8688). T: Hynes/ICA. A parade of vegetables manifest themselves throughout the menu, in a variety of guises. Standards like the veggie burger are supplemented with the more creative Tibetan dumplings, New Moon Lasagna, and delicious portabello mushroom sandwich. Entrees around $10. Open daily 9am-midnight.

SIGHTS

The Freedom Trail

A great introduction to Boston's history lies along the red-painted line of the Freedom Trail, a 2½-mi. path through downtown Boston which passes many of the city's historic landmarks. Even on a trail dedicated to the land of the free, some sights charge admission; bring some money if you're bent on doing the whole thing. The National Park Service offers free guided tours of the trail's free attractions starting at their **visitors center,** 15 State St. (242-5642. Open July-Labor Day daily 9am-5pm. Tours in summer daily on the hr. 10am-3pm.)

The Freedom Trail begins at another **visitors center,** in **Boston Common** (T: Park St.; open Mon.-Fri. 8:30am-6pm, Sat. 10am-6pm, Sun. 11am-6pm). You can pick up maps here, in varying degrees of detail (free, $2, or $5). The trail runs uphill to the **Robert Gould Shaw and 54th Regiment Memorial,** on Beacon St. The memorial honors the first black regiment of the Union Army in the American Civil War and their Bostonian leader, all made famous by the movie *Glory.* The trail then crosses the street to the **State House** (727-3676; free tours Mon.-Fri. every 30min. 10am-noon, every hr. noon-4pm; open Mon.-Fri. 9am-5pm). Next, the trail proceeds to the **Park Street Church** and passes the **Old Granary Burial Ground** on the way to **King's Chapel and Burial Ground** (523-1749), on Tremont St. Boston's oldest Anglican church, the Chapel housed a congregation as early as 1688; more recently, the cemetery has come to house Governor Bradford and William Dawes. (Tours $1, students and seniors 50¢, under 12 free. Open Mon. and Fri.-Sat. 9:30am-4pm, Tues. and Thurs. 11:30am-1pm. Classical music recitals Tues. 12:15pm.)

Closed for renovations until spring of 1997, the **Old South Meeting House** (482-6439), was the site of the pre-party get together which set the mood for the Boston Tea Party. Formerly the seat of British government in Boston, the **Old State House** (720-3290) now serves as a museum and the next stop on the trail. (Open daily 9:30am-5pm; $3, students and seniors $2, ages 6-18 $1.50, under 6 free.) The trail proceeds past the site of the **Boston Massacre** and through **Faneuil Hall,** a former meeting hall and current mega-mall where the National Park Service operates a desk and conducts talks in the upstairs Great Hall (open daily 9am-5pm; talks every 30min.). As you head into the North End, the **Paul Revere House** (523-1676) is the next landmark on the path. (Open in summer daily 9:30am-5:15pm; Nov. to mid-April 9:30am-4:15pm; Jan.-March closed Mon. $2.50, students and seniors $2, ages 5-17 $1.) The **Old North Church** follows (523-6676; open Mon.-Sat. 9am-5pm, Sun. services 9, 11am, and 4pm). **Copp's Hill Burial Ground** provides a resting place for lots of colonial Bostonians and a nice view of the Old North Church. Nearing its end, the Freedom Trail heads over the Charlestown Bridge to the newly renovated **U.S.S. Constitution** (426-1812). The Navy gives free tours from 9:30am to 3:50pm. (Open daily 9:30-sunset.) The final stop on the trail, the **Bunker Hill Monument** (242-5641), isn't on loan from Washington. The fraudulent obelisk—nearby Breed's Hill was the real site of the battle in question—has a grand view of the city. Come prepared and do some stretches; the monument doubles as a Stairmaster (294 steps and no elevator). To return to Boston, follow the red line back over the bridge or hop on a water taxi from one of the piers near the *Constitution*. (Open daily 9am-4:30pm. Water taxis every 30min., every 15min. after 3:30pm. $1, exact change required.)

Downtown

In 1634, early inhabitants designated the **Boston Common** (T: Park Street), now bounded by Tremont, Boylston, Charles, Beacon, and Park St., as a place to let their cattle graze. These days, street vendors, not cows, live off the fat of this land. Though bustling in the daytime, the Common is dangerous at night—don't walk alone here after dark. Across from the Common on Charles St., the title characters from the children's book *Make Way for Ducklings* (immortalized in bronze) point the way to the **Public Gardens,** where peddle-powered **Swan Boats** (522-1966) glide around a quiet pond lined with shady willows. (T: Arlington. Boats open mid-April to mid-June daily 10am-4pm; mid-June-Labor Day 10am-5pm; Labor Day to mid-Sept. Mon.-Fri. noon-4pm, Sat.-Sun. 10am-4pm. $1.50, seniors $1.25, under 12 95¢.)

The city's neighborhoods cluster in a loose circle around the Common and Gardens. Directly above the Common lies **Beacon Hill,** an exclusive residential neighborhood originally settled by the Puritans. Significantly smaller today than when the Puritans resided here, the Hill gave tons of earth to fill in the marshes that are now the Back Bay (see Back Bay and Beyond, below). Art galleries, antique shops, and cafés line the cobblestone streets and brick sidewalks of the hill; Charles St. makes an especially nice setting for a stroll. The **State House** sits atop the Hill (see Freedom Trail, above). The **Harrison Gray Otis House,** 141 Cambridge St. (227-3956), is a Charles Bulfinch original. (Tours Tues.-Fri. on the hr. noon-4pm, Sat. 10am-4pm. $4, seniors $3.50, under 12 $2.) The nearby **Boston Athenaeum,** 10½ Beacon St. (227-0270), offers hours of its art gallery and print room, and of the collection, which contains over 700,000 books, including most of George Washington's library. (Free tours Tues. and Thurs. 3pm; reservations required. Open in summer Mon.-Fri. 9am-5:30pm; Sept.-May Sat. 9am-4pm also.)

The **Black Heritage Trail** begins at the **Boston African-American National Historic Site,** 46 Joy St. (742-1854; T: Park Street), where you can pick up a free map and visit the museum inside (open daily 10am-4pm; donation requested). Fourteen fascinating stops, each marked by a red, black, and green logo, make up the trail. Landmarks in the development of Boston's African-American community include North America's first black church, the **African Meeting House** (1805), the **Robert Gould Shaw and 54th Regiment Memorial** (see Freedom Trail, above), and the **Lewis and Harriet Hayden House,** a station on the Underground Railroad.

East of Beacon Hill on Cambridge St., the red brick plaza of **Government Center** (T: Government Center) surrounds the monstrous concrete **City Hall** (725-4000), designed by I.M. Pei (open to the public Mon.-Fri.). A few blocks south, its more aesthetically pleasing relative, the **Old State House,** 206 Washington St. (720-1713 or 720-3290; T: State), once rocked with a revolution (see Freedom Trail, above).

Set amidst Boston's business district, the pedestrian mall at **Downtown Crossing,** south of City Hall at Washington St. (T: Downtown Crossing), centers around **Filene's,** 426 Washington St., (357-2100), the mild-mannered department store that conceals the chaotic bargain-feeding frenzy that is **Filene's Basement.** Even if you don't plan to shop, check out the Basement—it's a cultural institution.

Southwest of the Common, Boston's **Chinatown** (T: Chinatown) demarcates itself with an arch and huge Fu dogs at its Beach St. entrance, and pagoda-style telephone booths and streetlamps throughout. Within this small area cluster many restaurants,

NEW ENGLAND

food stores, and novelty shops; this is the place for good Chinese food, Chinese slippers, and 1000-year-old eggs. *Do not walk alone here at night.* Chinatown holds two big festivals each year. The first, **New Year,** usually celebrated on a Sunday in February, includes lion dances, fireworks, and Kung Fu exhibitions. The **August Moon Festival** honors a mythological pair of lovers at the time of the full moon, usually on the second or third Sunday in August. Call 542-2574 for details.

The east tip of Boston contains the historic **North End** (T: Haymarket). Now an Italian neighborhood, the city's oldest residential district overflows with window-boxes, Italian flags, fragrant pastry shops, créches, Sicilian restaurants, and Catholic churches. The most famous of the last, **Old St. Stephen's Church,** 401 Hanover St. (523-1230), is the classic colonial brainchild of Charles Bulfinch. (Open daily 8:30am-5pm; services Mon.-Sat. 5:15pm, Sun. 8:30 and 11am.) Down the street, the sweet-smelling **Peace Gardens** attempt to drown out the clamor of the North End with beautiful flora. (For more sights, see Freedom Trail, above.)

The Waterfront

The **waterfront area,** bounded by Atlantic and Commercial St., runs along Boston Harbor from South Station to the North End Park. Stroll down Commercial, Lewis, or Museum Wharf for a view of the harbor and a breath of sea air. The excellent **New England Aquarium** (973-5200; T: Aquarium), on Central Wharf at the Waterfront, presents cavorting penguins, giant sea turtles, and a bevy of briny beasts all in a 187,000 gallon tank. Dolphins and sea lions perform in the ship *Discovery,* moored alongside the Aquarium. Lines tend to be long on weekends; pass the time for free, watching harbor seals frolic in the tank outside. (Open July-Labor Day Mon.-Tues. and Fri. 9am-6pm, Wed.-Thurs. 9am-8pm, Sat.-Sun. and holidays 9am-7pm; otherwise Mon.-Wed. and Fri. 9am-5pm, Thurs. 9am-8pm, Sat.-Sun. and holidays 9am-6pm. $8.75, students and seniors $7.75, ages 3-11 $4.75; Thurs. after 4pm $1 off, seniors free Mon. noon-4:30pm.) The aquarium also offers **whale-watching cruises** (973-5277) from April to October. (Sightings guaranteed. Generally 2 trips daily; call for times. $24, students and seniors $19, ages 12-18 $17.50, ages 3-11 $16.50. Under 36" not allowed. Reservations suggested.) The **Bay State Cruise Company** (723-7800) conducts cheap lunch cruises of the harbor and longer cruises to the **Boston Harbor Islands** for a picnic or a tour of Civil War Fort Warren (see Practical Information, above).

Back Bay and Beyond

In **Back Bay,** north of the South End and west of Beacon Hill, three-story brownstone row houses line some of the only gridded streets in Boston. Originally the marshy, uninhabitable "back bay" on the Charles River, the area was filled in during the 19th century. Architectural styles progress chronologically through 19th-century popular design as you travel from east to west, reflecting the gradual process of filling in the marsh. Statues and benches punctuate the large, grassy median of **Commonwealth Ave.** ("Comm. Ave."). Boston's most flamboyant promenade, **Newbury St.** (T: Arlington, Copley, or Hynes/ICA) may inspire you to ask yourself some serious questions about your credit rating; the dozens of small art galleries, boutiques, bookstores, and cafés that line the street exude exclusivity and swank, and offer unparalleled people-watching. The riverside **Esplanade** (T: Charles) extends from the Longfellow Bridge to the Harvard Bridge, parallel to Newbury St. Boston's answer to the beach, the park fills with sun-seekers and sailors in the summer. It may look nice, but don't go in the water. Pick up the bike path along the river and pedal to the posh suburb of **Wellesley** for a terrific afternoon ride.

Beyond Back Bay, west on Commonwealth Ave., the huge landmark **Citgo sign** watches over **Kenmore Sq.** (T: Kenmore). The area around Kenmore has more than its share of neon, with many of the city's most popular nightclubs hovering on **Lansdowne St.** (see Nightlife, below). Near Kenmore Sq., the **Fenway** area contains some of the country's best museums. Ubiquitous landscaper Frederick Law Olmsted of Central Park fame designed the **Fens** area at the center of the Fenway as part of his

"Emerald Necklace" vision for Boston. Although the necklace was never completed, the park remains a gem; fragrant rose gardens and neighborhood vegetable patches make perfect picnic turf. As you might well suspect, the Fenway also houses Fenway Park (see Curse of the Bambino, below).

The rest of Olmsted's **Emerald Necklace Parks** make up a free five-hour walking tour given by the Boston Park Rangers (635-7383; tour reservations required). Visiting the parks individually—the Boston Common (T: Park St.; see Downtown, above), the Public Garden (T: Arlington; see Downtown, above), Commonwealth Avenue Mall (T: Arlington), Back Bay Fens (T: Kenmore), Muddy River, Olmsted Park, Jamaica Pond, the Arnold Arboretum (T: Arborway), and Franklin Park—requires a bit less time. Call the Park Rangers for info and directions.

Copley

In the Back Bay on commercial Boylston St., handsome **Copley Sq.** (T: Copley) accommodates a range of seasonal activities, including summertime concerts, folk dancing, a food pavilion, and people-watching. The massive and imposing **Boston Public Library,** 666 Boylston St. (536-5400), serves as a permanent memorial to the hundreds of literati whose names are inscribed upon it. Relax on a bench or window seat overlooking the tranquil courtyard or in the vaulted reading room. The auditorium gives a program of lectures and films, and often displays collections of art. (Open Mon.-Thurs. 9am-9pm, Fri.-Sat. 9am-5pm.) Across the square next to I.M. Pei's Hancock Tower (see below), stands H.H. Richardson's Romanesque fantasy, **Trinity Church** (536-0944). Many consider Trinity, built in 1877, a masterpiece of U.S. church architecture—the interior justifies this opinion. (T: Copley. Open Mon.-Sat. 8am-6pm.) The ritzy mall on the corner is **Copley Place,** right next door to the renovated **Prudential Building.** The **Prudential Skywalk,** on the 50th floor of the Prudential Building, 800 Boylston St. (236-3318), grants a full 360° view from New Hampshire to the Cape. (T: Prudential. Open daily 10am-10pm. $4, seniors and kids $3.) The **John Hancock Observatory,** 200 Clarendon St. (572-6429; 247-1977 for a recording; T: Copley or Back Bay), the tallest building in New England at 60 floors (740 ft.), also lets you take in the city skyline (open Mon.-Sat. 9am-10pm, Sun. 10am-10pm. $4.25, seniors and ages 5-17 $3.25). The partially gentrified **South End,** south of Copley, makes for good brownstone viewing and casual dining.

Two blocks down Massachusetts Ave. from Boylston St., the **Mother Church of the First Church of Christ, Scientist,** 1 Norway St. (450-2000), at Mass. Ave. and Huntington, headquarters the international movement founded in Boston by Mary Baker Eddy. Both the Mother Church and the smaller, older one out back can be seen by guided tour only. Use the catwalk to pass through the **Mapparium,** a 30-ft.-wide stained glass globe, in the Christian Science Publishing Society next door. The globe, built in the 1930s, features highly unusual acoustics; sound waves bounce off the sphere in any and all directions. Whisper in the ear of Pakistan while standing next to Surinam (tours Mon.-Sat. 10am-4pm; free).

Museums

The free *Guide to Museums of Boston* has details on museums not mentioned here.

Museum of Fine Arts (MFA), 465 Huntington Ave. (267-9300), near Massachusetts Ave. T: Ruggles/Museum on Green line-E. Boston's most famous museum contains one of the world's finest collections of Asian ceramics, outstanding Egyptian art, a showing of Impressionists, and superb American art. Two famous unfinished portraits of George and Martha Washington, begun by Gilbert Stuart in 1796, merit a gander. Open Tues. and Thurs.-Sat. 10am-4:45pm, Wed. 10am-9:45pm, Sun. 10am-5:45pm; Memorial Day-Labor Day also Mon. 10am-4:45pm.

Isabella Stewart Gardner Museum, 280 Fenway (566-1401), a few hundred yards from the MFA. T: Ruggles/Museum. In what ranks as one of the greatest art heists in history, a 1990 break-in relieved the museum of works by Rembrandt, Vermeer, Dégas, and others. Many masterpieces remain, however, in Ms. Gardner's Venetian-style palace, and the courtyard garden soothes a weary traveler's soul. Open Tues.-

Sun. 11am-5pm. Chamber music on 1st floor Sept.-May Sat. and Sun. afternoons ($15, seniors and students $12). $7, students and seniors $5, ages 12-17 $3, under 12 free; Wed. students $3. See the courtyard only for free.

Museum of Science (723-2500), Science Park. T: Science Park. At the far east end of the Esplanade on the Charles River Dam. Contains, among other wonders, the largest "lightning machine" (a Van de Graaff generator, for all you science buffs) in the world. A multi-story roller-coaster for small metal balls explains energy states. Within the museum, the **Hayden Planetarium** features models, lectures, films, and laser and star shows; the **Mugar Omni Theatre** shows films on scientific subjects on a four-story-domed screen. Museum open in summer Sat.-Thurs. 9am-7pm, Fri. 9am-9pm; otherwise Sun.-Thurs. 9am-5pm, Fri. 9am-9pm. Exhibits $8, seniors and ages 3-14 $6; Sept.-April Wed. 1-5pm free. Planetarium, laser show, and Omni each $7.50, seniors and ages 3-14 $5.50. Museum, Omni, and Planetarium combo $16, seniors and ages 3-14 $12.

Children's Museum, 300 Congress St. (426-8855), in south Boston on Museum Wharf. T: South Station. Follow the signs with milk bottles. Kids of all ages paw way-cool hands-on exhibits and learn a little something to boot. Open Sat.-Thurs. 10am-5pm, Fri. 10am-9pm; Sept.-June closed Mon. $7, seniors and ages 2-15 $6, age 1 $2, under 1 free; Fri. 5-9pm $1.

John F. Kennedy Presidential Library (929-4567), Columbia Point on Morrissey Blvd. in Dorchester. T: JFK/UMass; free MBTA shuttle to U Mass campus and from the library. Dedicated "to all those who through the art of politics seek a new and better world." The looming white structure, designed by I.M. Pei, contains exhibits tracing Kennedy's career from the campaign trail to his tragic death. Open daily 9am-5pm. $6, seniors and students with ID $4, ages 6-16 $2, under 6 free.

Institute of Contemporary Art (ICA), 955 Boylston St. (266-5152). T: Hynes/ICA. Boston's lone outpost of the avant-garde attracts major contemporary artists while aggressively promoting lesser-known work. Innovative, sometimes controversial exhibits change every 8 weeks. The museum also presents experimental theater, music, dance, and film. Prices vary; call for details. Open Wed.-Sun. noon-5pm. $5.25, students $3.25, seniors and under 16 $2.25; free Thurs. 5-9pm.

ENTERTAINMENT

Musicians, dancers, actors, and *artistes* of every description reside in Boston. An unusually large and diverse community of **street performers** ("buskers") juggle steak knives, swallow torches, wax poetic, and sing folk tunes in the subways and squares of Boston and Cambridge. The *Boston Phoenix* and the "Calendar" section of Thursday's *Boston Globe* list activities for the coming week. Also check the free *Where: Boston* booklet available at the visitors center. What Boston doesn't have, Cambridge probably does (see Cambridge: Entertainment and Nightlife, p. 106). **Bostix** (482-BTIX/2849), a Ticketmaster outlet in Faneuil Hall and at Copley Sq. (at Boylston and Dartmouth St.), sells ½-price tickets to performing arts events starting at 11am on the day of performance. (Service charge $1.50-2.50 per ticket. Cash and traveler's checks only. Copley Sq. open Mon. 10am-6pm; both locations open Tues.-Sat. 10am-6pm, Sun. 11am-4pm.)

Actors in town cluster around Washington St. and Harrison Ave. in the **Theater District** (T: Boylston). The **Wang Center for the Performing Arts,** 270 Tremont St. (482-9393), produces theater, classical music, and opera in its gorgeous baroque complex. Here, the renowned **Boston Ballet** (695-6950), one of the nation's best, annually revives classics like the *Nutcracker* and *Swan Lake.* The **Shubert Theater,** 265 Tremont St. (426-4520), hosts Broadway hits touring through town. Tickets for these and for shows at the **Charles Playhouse,** 74 Warrenton St. (426-5225), home of the ongoing Blue Man Group and *Shear Madness,* cost around $30.

The area's regional companies cost less and may make for a more interesting evening. Both the **New Theater,** 66 Marlborough St. (247-7388), and **Huntington Theater Co.,** 264 Huntington Ave. (266-7900; 266-0800 for box office), at Boston University, have solid artistic reputations (tickets $8-35). During termtime, affordable student theater is always up; watch students tread the boards at **Tufts Theater**

Arena (627-3493), the **BU Theater** (353-3320), the **MIT Drama Shop** (253-2908), and the **MIT Shakespeare Ensemble** (253-2903). For student musical performances, try the **New England Conservatory** (262-1120; box office 536-2412).

The **Boston Symphony Orchestra,** 201 Mass. Ave. (266-1492; T: Symphony), at Huntington, holds its concert season October through April ($20-57). Rush seats ($7) go on sale three hours before concerts. During July and August, the symphony takes a vacation at **Tanglewood** (413-637-1666), in western Massachusetts. Though difficult to reach by public transportation, Tanglewood defines music *en plein air*. Peter Pan (see Practical Information, above) buses to Lenox; from there, it's a 1½-mi. walk. Mid-May through July, while the BSO's away, the **Boston Pops Orchestra** (266-1492) plays in **Symphony Hall**, 301 Mass. Ave. (Box office and concert info 266-1200; open Mon.-Sat. 10am-6pm, Sun. 1-6pm on concert days. Recorded message 266-2378. Tickets $11-36.50.) You can also see the Pops at the **Hatch Shell** (266-1200) on the Esplanade any night in the first week of July; arrive early to sit within earshot of the orchestra (concert 8pm; free). On the **4th of July,** hundreds of thousands of patriotic thrillseekers pack the Esplanade to hear the Pops concert (broadcast by loudspeaker throughout the area) and watch the fireworks display. Arrive before noon for a seat on the Esplanade, although you can watch the fireworks from almost anywhere along the river.

The **Berklee Performance Center,** 136 Mass. Ave. (266-7455; box office 266-1400, ext. 261), an adjunct of the Berklee School of Music, holds concerts featuring students, faculty, and jazz and classical luminaries.

For info on other special events, such as the **St. Patrick's Day Parade** (March 17), **Patriot's Day** celebrations (third Mon. in April), the week-long **Boston Common Dairy Festival** (June), the **Boston Harbor Fest** (early July), the North End's **Festival of St. Anthony** (mid-Aug.), and **First Night** (New Year's Eve), see the *Boston Phoenix* or *Globe* calendars.

Singing Beach, 40 min. out of downtown, on the commuter line (see Practical Information, above) to Manchester-by-the-Sea, gained its name from the sound made when you drag your feet through the sand. It's very cool. The beach charges a $1 entrance fee, but playing in the sand is free after that. You can swim too. Park your car in town and walk the ½ mi. to the beach. By car, take Rte. 127 to Exit 16.

The Curse of the Bambino and Other Sports

Ever since the Red Sox traded Babe Ruth to the Yankees in 1918, Boston sports fans have learned to take the good with the bad. They have seen more basketball championships than any other city (16) but haven't boasted a World Series title in over 75 years. Yet through it all, they follow their teams with Puritanical fervor. On summer nights, thousands of baseball fans make the pilgrimage to **Fenway Park** (T: Kenmore). Home of the infamous outfield wall known as the "Green Monster," Fenway is the nation's oldest Major League ballpark and center stage for the perennially heart-rending **Boston Red Sox** (box office 267-8661; open Mon.-Sat. 9am-5pm, Sun. 9am-5pm if there's a game) baseball club. Most grandstand tickets sell out far in advance, but bleacher seats are often available on game day.

The famous **Boston Garden** (T: North Station), located off the JFK Expwy. between the West and North Ends, has been replaced by the FleetCenter (T: North Station). Call 624-1000 for FleetCenter info. The storied **Boston Celtics** basketball team (season Oct.-May) and **Boston Bruins** hockey team (season Oct.-April) play here. A fair distance outside Boston, **Foxboro Stadium,** 16 Washington St., Foxboro, hosts the **New England Patriots** NFL team (season Sept.-Jan.; call 508-543-3900 for info). The stadium also stages concerts. Rail service to the games and some concerts runs from South Station; call for details.

In October, the **Head of the Charles** rowing regatta, the largest such single-day event in the world, attracts rowing clubs, baseball caps, and beer-stained college sweatshirts from across the country. The 3-mi. races begin at Boston University Bridge; the best vantage points are atop Weeks Footbridge and Anderson Bridge near Harvard University. On the third Monday in April the 10,000 runners competing in the **Boston Marathon** battle Boston area boulevards and the infamous Heartbreak Hill. Call the **Massachusetts Division of Tourism** (727-3201) for details.

NIGHTLIFE

Remnants of the city's Puritan heritage temper Boston's nightlife ("blue laws" prohibit the sale of alcohol after certain hours and on Sundays), along with the lack of public transportation after midnight. Nearly all bars and most clubs close between 1 and 2am, and bar admittance for anyone under 21 is hard-won. Boston's local music scene runs the gamut from folk to funk; Beantown natives-gone-national include the Pixies, Aerosmith, Tracy Chapman, Dinosaur Jr., The Lemonheads, Bobby Brown, and the Mighty Mighty Bosstones. Cruise down **Landsdowne St.** (T: Kenmore) and **Boylston Place** (T: Boylston) to find concentrated action. The weekly *Boston Phoenix* has comprehensive club and concert listings (out on Thurs.; $1.50). Call the *Phoenix* **club line** (859-3300) to hear about scheduled events at most clubs.

Avalon (262-2424), **Axis** (262-2437), **Venus de Milo** (421-9595), 5-13 Lansdowne St. T: Kenmore. Upscale 80s-style pre-yuppie, neo-punk/industrial, relentlessly techno and outrageously attired, respectively. All three open mid-week through the weekend 10pm-2am; exact hours for each vary, as does cover ($3-10). Axis and Venus have 18+ nights; call for details. Avalon stages live shows. Axis and Avalon join together for gay night on Sundays. Those over 21 can get in for $0-8 from rowdy **Bill's Bar** (421-9678), next door to Venus.

Bull and Finch Pub, 84 Beacon St. (227-9605). T: Arlington. If you must see the bar that inspired *Cheers,* we can't stop you. Large crowds. The interior bears no resemblance to the set. Open daily 11am-1:30am.

Wally's Café, 427 Mass Ave. (424-1408). T: bus #1 ("Dudley") to Columbus Ave. A great hole-in-the-wall bar frequented by the Berklee School of Music's aspirants. Best to go with friends at night; HI-Boston hostel makes frequent outings here. Live music nightly; no cover. Open Mon.-Sat. 9am-2am, Sun. noon-2am.

Sunset Grill and Tap, 130 Brighton Ave. (254-1331), in Allston. T: Harvard on Green line-B or bus #66 from the corner of Harvard St. and Brighton Ave. One of the country's largest selections of beer (over 400, more than 70 on tap). College students dig the buenos nachos ($7). Free late-night buffets Sun.-Tues. Open daily 11:30am-1am.

Zanzibar, 1 Boylston Place (351-7000). T: Boylston. Huts and palm trees a la Gilligan's Island aside, tropical heat is sure to sizzle from the small dance floor, where patrons thrash to house and classic European hits (Thurs.) or progressive Top 40 (Fri.-Sat.). Open Wed. 9pm-2am, Thurs. 10pm-2am. Cover Wed. and Fri.-Sat. $5, Thurs. $10. No sneakers or torn jeans. 19 plus with college ID Thurs.; otherwise 21 plus.

Nick's Comedy Stop, 100 Warrenton St. (482-0930), is funny. Jay Leno, who is not, got his start here. Wed.-Thurs., Sun. 8:30pm ($8), Fri.-Sat. 8:15 and 10:30pm ($12).

For those seeking the gay scene, **Coco's,** 965 Mass. Ave. (427-7807), clientele is predominantly women (cover $5; open Fri.-Sat. 9pm-2am). Adjoining **The Jungle** hosts women on Fridays, gay men and women on Saturdays. **Chaps** (266-7778; open daily 1pm-2am; $5 after 10pm), and **Club Café,** 209 Columbus Ave. (536-0966; T: Back Bay), are gay clubs. Club Café has a largely yuppie clientele, live music nightly, and no cover. (Open Thurs.-Sat. 2pm-2am, Sun.-Wed. 2pm-1am; Sun. brunch 11:30am-3pm.) Boston's favorite leather and Levi's bar, **Boston Ramrod,** 1254 Boylston St. (266-2986; T: Kenmore), behind Fenway Park on Boylston St., designates the last Saturday of the month Fetish Night—but why wait until then? (Cover Sun. $2, unless you're wearing leather. Open daily noon-2am.) Pick up a copy of *Bay Windows* for more info (available at many music stores).

■ Cambridge

Cambridge began its career as an intellectual and publishing center in the colonial era. Harvard, the nation's first university, was founded as a college of divinity here in 1636. Massachusetts Institute of Technology (MIT), founded in Boston in 1861, moved to Cambridge in 1916, giving the small city a second academic heavyweight. Today the city takes on the character of both the universities and the tax-paying Cantabridgians. Local and collegiate identity mingle and contrast, creating a patchwork of diverse flavors that change as you move from square to square. Bio-tech labs and computer science buildings radiate out from MIT through Kendall Sq. Harvard Sq., on the other side of the city, offers Georgian buildings, stellar bookstores, coffee houses, street musicians, and prime people-watching opportunities.

Practical Information Cambridge is best reached by a ten-minute T-ride outbound from the heart of Boston. The city's main artery, **Massachusetts Ave.** ("Mass. Ave."), parallels the Red Line, which makes stops at a series of squares along the avenue. The **Kendall Sq.** stop corresponds to MIT, just across the Mass. Ave. Bridge from Boston. The subway continues outbound through **Central Sq., Harvard Sq.,** and **Porter Sq.** The **Cambridge Discovery Booth** (497-1630), in Harvard Sq., has the best and most comprehensive information about Cambridge, as well as MBTA bus and subway schedules. Pick up the *Old Cambridge Walking Guide,* an excellent self-guided tour ($1.25); during the summer, ask about guided walking tours of Harvard and the surrounding area. (Open Mon.-Sat. 9am-5pm, Sun. 1-5pm.) **Harvard Sq. post office:** 125 Mt. Auburn St. (876-6483); open Mon.-Fri. 7:30am-6pm, Sat. 7:30am-3pm. **ZIP code:** 02138. **Area code:** 617. For budget **accommodations,** turn around and go back to Boston.

Food Every night, hundreds of college students renounce cafeteria fare and head to the funky eateries of Harvard Sq. Pick up the weekly *Square Deal,* usually thrust in your face by distributors near the T stop, for coupons on local fare. The only 24-hr. eatery in Harvard Sq., the **Tasty Sandwich Shop,** 2 JFK St. (354-9016; T: Harvard) is a 12-seater, fluorescent-lit, formica-countered, all-night diner (entrees $2-6). Between Harvard and Porter Sq., **Boca Grande,** 1728 Mass. Ave. (354-7400; T: Harvard or Porter, and a 10-min. walk), makes Mexican food to order right before your eyes, including enchiladas ($4), and spicy tamales ($4). The burritos grandes ($3.50) are certainly *grande,* but the bill stays *muy poco* (open daily 11am-10pm). **Café of India,** 52a Brattle St. (661-0683), in Harvard Sq., is *Let's Go's* collective fave. Try the Saag Paneer (entrees around $7.50-9.50; lunch specials $5). (Open Mon.-Thurs. 11:30am-11pm, Fri. 11:30am-midnight, Sat.-Sun. noon-11pm.) The **Border Café,** 32 Church St. (864-6100), in Harvard Sq., has tasty, filling Tex-Mex and Cajun entrees ($5-13), and long lines. (Open Sun. noon-11pm, Mon.-Thurs. 11am-11pm, Fri.-Sat. 11am-midnight. No reservations.) Follow the fading Busch sign to enormous sandwich supplier **Darwin's, Ltd.,** 148 Mt. Auburn St. (354-5233). Sandwiches are named after nearby streets: the "Brattle" has smoked salmon, cucumber, tomato, capers, and onion. (Open Mon.-Sat. 6:30am-9pm, Sun. 7am-7pm.) **Scoops and Beans,** 56 JFK St. (576-3532), in Harvard Sq., dishes out generous portions of rich Christina's Homemade Ice Cream (small $2); their more unique flavors include Green Tea and Red Bean, surprisingly delish (open daily 11:30am-midnight). Out towards Somerville, the **S&S Restaurant and Deli,** 1334 Cambridge St. (354-0777; take the #69 bus to the intersection of Cambridge and Beacon/Hampshire St.), dishes up sandwiches ($3-6), bonafide potato knishes ($2), and related delights, as well as less deli-oriented entrees ($5-12). "Ess and ess" means "eat and eat" in Yiddish. (Open Mon.-Tues. 7am-11pm, Wed.-Sat. 7am-midnight, Sun. 8am-11pm.)

Sights The **Massachusetts Institute of Technology (MIT)** supports cutting-edge work in the sciences. Campus tours (Mon.-Fri. 10am and 2pm) highlight the Chapel, designed by Eero Saarinen, and the impressive collection of modern outdoor sculpture which graces the grounds. Contact **MIT Information,** 77 Mass. Ave. (253-1000), for more information (open Mon.-Fri. 9am-5pm). The **MIT Museum,** 265 Mass. Ave. (253-4444), contains a slide rule collection and wonderful photography exhibits, including the famous stop-action photos of Harold Edgerton (open Tues.-Fri. 10am-5pm, Sat.-Sun. noon-5pm; $3, students and seniors $1, under 5 free).

In all its red brick-and-ivy dignity, **Harvard University,** farther down Mass. Ave. from Boston, finds space for Nobel laureates, students from around the world, and, contrary to popular belief, the occasional party. The **Harvard University Information Center,** 1350 Mass. Ave. (495-1573), at Holyoke Center in Harvard Sq., distributes free guides to the university and its museums, and offers tours of the campus. (Tours in summer Mon.-Sat. 10, 11:15am, 2 and 3:15pm, Sun. 1:30 and 3pm; Sept.-May Mon.-Fri. 10am and 2pm, Sat. 2pm.) The university revolves around **Harvard Yard,** a grassy oasis amidst the Cantabridgian bustle. The Yard's eastern half holds classroom buildings, **Memorial Church,** and the **Harry Elkins Widener Memorial Library** (495-2411). Widener, named by Eleanor Widener for her son, who perished on the Titanic, stands as the largest academic library in the world, containing 4½ million of the university's 12 million books. To visit the library, you'll need a temporary pass from the library privileges office (495-4166) on the main floor (open Mon.-Fri. 9am-5pm). Some of the school's first buildings still grace the western half of the yard ("The Old Yard").

The most noted of Harvard's museums, the **Fogg Art Museum,** 32 Quincy St. (495-9400), gathers a considerable collection of works ranging from ancient Chinese jade to contemporary photography, as well as the largest Ingres collection outside of France. Across the street, the modern exterior of the **Arthur M. Sackler Museum,** 485 Broadway (495-9400), holds a rich collection of ancient Asian and Islamic art. The third of Harvard's art museums, the **Busch-Reisinger Museum,** 32 Quincy St. (495-9400), displays Northern and Central European sculpture, painting, and decorative arts. (All three open Mon.-Sat. 10am-5pm, Sun. 1-5pm. Each $5, students $3, seniors $4; free Sat. mornings.) Peering down at the Fogg, Le Corbusier's piano-shaped **Carpenter Center,** 24 Quincy St. (495-3251), shows student and professional work with especially strong photo exhibits and a great film series at the **Harvard Film Archives** (open Mon.-Sat. 9am-midnight, Sun. noon-10pm). The **Botanical Museum,** one of Harvard's several **Museums of Natural History,** 24 Oxford St. (495-3045), draws huge crowds to view the Ware collection of "glass flowers." A German glassblower and his son alone created these remarkably accurate, enlarged reproductions of over 840 plant species. (Open Mon.-Sat. 9am-5pm, Sun. 1-5pm. $5, students and seniors $4, ages 3-13 $3. Admission includes all the natural history museums.)

The restored **Longfellow House,** 105 Brattle St. (876-4491), now a National Historic Site, headquartered the Continental Army during the early stages of the Revolution. The poet Henry Wadsworth Longfellow, for whom the house is named, lived here later. The staff can give you info on other local historic sights. (Tours May-Oct. Wed.-Sun. 10:45am-4pm. $2, under 17 free.) The **Mt. Auburn Cemetery** (547-7105) lies about 1 mi. up the road at the end of Brattle St. The first botanical-garden/cemetery in the U.S. has 170 acres of beautifully landscaped grounds fertilized by Louis Agassiz, Charles Bulfinch, Dorothea Dix, Mary Baker Eddy, and H.W. Longfellow among others. Locals say it's the best birdwatching site in Cambridge.

Entertainment and Nightlife In warm weather, street musicians ranging from Andean folk singers to jazz trios staff every corner of Harvard Sq.

The **American Repertory Theater,** 64 Brattle St. (547-8300), in the Loeb Drama Center, produces shows from September through June. Planned 1996-97 productions include *Superman, Six Characters in Search of an Author, Punch and Judy Get Divorced,* and *The Wild Duck.* (Box office open daily 11am-5pm, until 9pm on show days. Tickets $20-50; student rush tickets, available ½hr. before shows, $12 cash only.)

Cambridge's many cafés attract crowds at all times of year for lunch or after-hours coffee. **Algiers Coffee House,** 40 Brattle St. (492-1557), has two beautiful floors of airy, wood-latticed seating, and exceptional food to boot. Enjoy an exotic coffee drink (about $3) or a falafel sandwich ($7). (Open Mon.-Thurs. 8am-midnight, Fri.-Sat. 8am-1am, Sun. 8am-midnight.)

If spending your evening discussing Proust over java doesn't sound appealing, Cambridge provides other options. The **Middle East,** 472 Mass. Ave. (354-8238), in Central Sq., a three-stage nirvana for the musically adventurous, books some of the best shows in the Boston area. Indie shows draw a somewhat alternateen audience. (Cover varies. Open Sun.-Wed. 11am-1am, Thurs.-Sat. 11am-2am.) Around the corner, **T.T. The Bear's Place,** 10 Brookline St. (492-0082), in Central Sq., brings really live, really loud rock bands to its intimate, seemingly makeshift stage (Cover $5-8. Open Mon. 7:30pm-midnight, Tues.-Thurs. 8pm-1am, Fri.-Sun. 4pm-1am. 18+ welcome.) **Ryles,** 212 Hampshire St. (876-9330), in Inman Sq. accessible by bus #69, is a Boston jazz scene standby with nightly live music and a jazz brunch on Sunday from 10am to 3pm (open Sun. and Tues.-Thurs. 7pm-1am, Fri.-Sat. 7pm-2am). Try **Johnny D's,** 17 Holland St. (776-9667; T: Davis), in neighboring Somerville, for more live music. For over 10 years, Little Joe Cook and his blues band have been packing the **Cantab Lounge,** 738 Mass. Ave. (354-2685), in Central Sq., with local fans and recently enlightened college students. (Cover Thurs. $3, Fri.-Sat. $5. Open Mon.-Wed. 8am-1am, Thurs.-Sat. 8am-2am, Sun. noon-1am.)

■ Salem

Salem possesses a rich and varied history that stretches beyond the sensational **witch trials** of 1692. The city, once the sixth largest in the U.S., also features historic homes, a robust maritime heritage, and strong literary roots. Lodging in town is very expensive; plan your visit as a daytrip from Boston.

The **Witch Museum,** 19½ Washington Sq. (744-1692—note the number), gives a melodramatic but informative multi-media presentation that details the history of the trials. (Open daily 10am-5pm. $4, seniors $3.50, ages 6-14 $2.50.) Never actually a dungeon, the **Witch Dungeon,** 16 Lynde St. (741-3570), has re-enactments which amplify the toil and trouble of the proceedings. (Shows every 30min. $4.50, ages 6-14 $2.50. Open April-Dec. daily 10am-5pm.) Escape the sea of witch kitsch at the **Witch Trials Memorial,** off Charter St., where simple engraved stones commemorate the trials' victims.

Salem's **Peabody Museum** (745-1876; 745-9500 for recorded info), in East India Sq., recalls the port's former leading role in Atlantic whaling and merchant shipping. Ask for a free pass to the museum café and you can slip into the Oriental Garden, just beside the Museum on Liberty St. (Open Mon.-Sat. 10am-5pm, Sun. noon-5pm. $7, students $6.) The **Salem Maritime National Historic Site,** consisting of three wharves and several historic buildings jutting out into Salem Harbor on Derby St., is a quiet respite from the barrage of commercial tourist attractions. Derby Wharf is currently being restored, but you can still walk to the lighthouse on the end. Built in 1668, Salem's **House of Seven Gables,** 54 Turner St. (744-0991), became the "second most famous house in America" sometime after the release of Nathaniel Hawthorne's Gothic romance of the same name. The price is steeper than the famed roof, but the tour is thorough and informative. (Guided tour only. Open daily 10am-4:30pm. $7, ages 13-17 $4, ages 6-12 $3, under 6 free.)

Salem has two **information centers,** located at 2 New Liberty St. (740-1650; open daily 9am-5pm; Nov.-May 10am-4pm), and 174 Derby St. (740-1660; open daily 9am-5pm). Both provide a free map of Salem and the New Liberty location shows a movie on three screens about Salem and Essex County. The town is packed during Halloween with a two-week-long festival called **Haunted Happenings;** book at least a year in advance. Salem, 20 mi. northeast of Boston, is accessible by the Rockport/Ipswich commuter train from North Station (722-3200; $2.50) or bus #450 from Haymarket ($2.25). Salem's **area code** is 508.

■ Lexington and Concord

Lexington "Stand your ground. Don't fire unless fired upon, but if they mean to have a war, let it begin here," said Captain John Parker to the colonial Minutemen on April 19, 1775. Although no one is certain who fired the first shot, the American Revolution did indeed erupt in downtown Lexington. The fateful command was issued from the **Buckman Tavern,** 1 Bedford St. (862-5598), which housed the Minutemen on the eve of their decisive battle. The tavern now dispenses information instead of ale, but has otherwise been restored to its 1775 appearance. The site of the fracas lies across the street at the **Battle Green** where a **Minuteman Statue** still watches over Lexington. The nearby **Hancock-Clarke House,** 36 Hancock St. (861-0928), and the **Munroe Tavern,** 1332 Mass. Ave. (674-9238), also played significant roles in the birth of the Revolution. (Must be seen on a 30-min. tour that runs continuously. House and Taverns open mid-April to Oct. Mon.-Sat. 10am-5pm, Sun. 1-5pm. $3 per site, ages 6-16 $1, under 6 free. Combination ticket $7/$2.) You can also survey an exhibit on the Revolution at the **Museum of Our National Heritage,** 33 Marrett Rd./Rte. 2A (861-6559), which emphasizes historical and popular American life (open Mon.-Sat. 10am-5pm, Sun. noon-5pm; disabled access; free). An excellent model and description of the Battle of Lexington decorates the **visitors center,** 1875 Mass. Ave. (862-1450), behind the Buckman Tavern (open May-Oct. daily 9am-5pm; Nov. 9am-3pm; Dec.-Feb. Mon.-Fri. 10am-2pm; March-April daily 9am-3pm). When the Minutemen retreated from Lexington, they made their way to Concord via the **Battle Road;** the road now forms the spine of **Minuteman National Historical Park.** The **Battle Road Visitors Center** (862-7753), on Rte. 2A in Lexington, distributes maps and screens a film that sets the stage for the Revolutionary War (open mid-April-Oct. daily 9am-5pm).

For those not traveling on horseback, the road from Boston to Lexington is easy. Drive straight up Mass. Ave. from Boston or Cambridge, or take your bike up the **Minuteman Commuter Bike Trail,** which runs into downtown Lexington (access off Mass. Ave. in Arlington). MBTA buses from Alewife station in Cambridge run several times daily to Lexington (60¢). Lexington's **area code:** 617.

Concord Concord, the site of the second conflict of the American Revolution, is famous for both its military history and its status as a 19th-century American intellectual center. Past **The Minuteman** and over the **Old North Bridge,** you'll find the spot where "the shot heard round the world" rang out. From the parking lot, a five-minute walk brings you to the **North Bridge Visitors Center,** 174 Liberty St. (369-6993), where rangers will gladly surrender hosts of pamphlets and brochures (open April-Oct. 9am-5:30pm, call for winter hrs.).

The Alcotts and the Hawthornes once inhabited **Wayside,** 455 Lexington Rd. (369-6975). Now part of the **Minute Man National Historical Park,** the house is open for public viewing. (Guided tour only; tours leave on the ½hr. Open May-Oct. Thurs.-Tues. 9:30am-5pm. $3, under 17 free.) During the latter half of the 19th century, Ralph Waldo Emerson lived down the road, and the **Concord Museum** (369-9763), directly across the street from Wayside, houses a reconstruction of his study alongside Paul Revere's lantern and items from Henry David Thoreau's cabin. (Open Mon.-Sat. 9am-5pm, Sun. noon-5pm; Jan.-March Mon.-Sat. 10am-4pm, Sun. 1-4pm. $6, seniors $5, students $3, under 18 $3.) Today, Emerson, Hawthorne, Alcott, and Thoreau reside on "Author's Ridge" in the **Sleepy Hollow Cemetery** on Rte. 62, 3 blocks from the center of town. Concord, 20 mi. north of Boston, is served by commuter rail trains from North Station (722-3200; $2.75). Concord's **area code:** 508.

Walden Pond In 1845, Thoreau retreated 1½ mi. south of Concord on Rte. 126, "to live deliberately, to front only the essential facts of life." He did so and produced his famous book *Walden*. The **Walden Pond State Reservation** (508-369-3254), on Rte. 126, draws picnickers, swimmers, and boaters (open daily 5am-7:30pm; parking $2, daily in summer and Sat.-Sun. in spring). The Pond holds only 1000 visitors; call before going or risk being turned away. There are no pets or open grills allowed. When Walden Pond swarms with crowds, head east from Concord center on Rte. 62 to another of Thoreau's haunts, **Great Meadows National Wildlife Refuge** (508-443-4661), on Monson Rd. (open daily dawn-dusk; free).

■ Plymouth

Despite what American high school textbooks say, the Pilgrims did *not* step first onto the New World at Plymouth—they stopped first at Provincetown, but promptly left because the soil was inadequate. **Plymouth Rock** itself is a rather anti-climactically diminutive stone that has dubiously been identified as the actual rock on which the Pilgrims disembarked. Since that first Puritan foot was credited to the rock, it served as a symbol of liberty during the American Revolution, was moved three times, and was chipped away by tourists before landing at its current home beneath an extravagant portico on Water St., at the foot of North St.

On Warren Ave., **Plymouth Plantation** (746-1622), superbly recreates the Pilgrims' early settlement. In the **Pilgrim Village,** costumed actors play the roles of actual villagers carrying out their daily tasks, based upon William Bradford's record of the year 1627. To make sure they know their stuff, the plantation sends a historian to England each summer to gather more info about each villager. (Open April-Nov. daily 9am-5pm. $18.50, students and seniors $16.50, ages 6-17 $11; pass good for 2 consecutive days.) The adjacent **Wampanoag Summer Encampment** represents a Native American village of the same period. Admission to the plantation includes entry to the **Mayflower II,** built in the 1950s to recapture the atmosphere of the original ship and docked off Water St. (Open July-Aug. daily 9am-7pm; Sept.-Nov. and April-June 9am-5pm. Mayflower only $5.75, ages 6-17 $3.75.) The nation's oldest museum in continuous existence, the **Pilgrim Hall Museum,** 75 Court St. (746-1620), houses Puritan crafts, furniture, books, paintings, and weapons (open daily 9:30am-4:30pm; $5, seniors $4, ages 5-12 $2.50).

When you feel bogged down in history, head for **Cranberry World,** 225 Water St. (747-2350), and celebrate one of the five indigenous American fruits (the others are the tomato, the blueberry, the boysenberry and the Concord grape). Exhibits, including a small cranberry bog in front of the museum, show how cranberries are grown, harvested, and sold (open May-Nov. 9:30am-5pm; free).

The **Plymouth Visitor's Information Center,** 130 Water St. (800-USA-1620/872-1620), gives out brochures, useful maps, and hotel and B&B info. (Open April-May daily 9am-5pm, June daily 9am-6pm, July-Aug. daily 9am-9pm.) Considering the proximity of Cape Cod's soft sand beaches, you may not want to spend more than a day here. Only a few blocks from the center of town, the **Bunk and Bagel** (830-0914), has a cheerful, homey atmosphere and the cheapest beds in Plymouth. Private and hostel rooms come with a continental breakfast. (5-8 hostel beds with common bath. Office open daily 7-9:30am and 5-9pm. Hostel beds $15. Linens provided. Open May-Nov.) Majestic **Myles Standish Forest** (866-2526), 7 mi. south of Plymouth via Rte. 3, offers wooded ground for bedding down (sites $5, showers $1).

CAPE COD

Henry David Thoreau once said: "At present [this coast] is wholly unknown to the fashionable world, and probably it will never be agreeable to them." Think again, Henry. In 1602, when English navigator and Jamestown colonist Bartholomew Gosnold landed on this peninsula in southeastern Massachusetts, he named it in honor of all the codfish he caught in the surrounding waters. In recent decades, tourists have replaced the plentiful cod and the area has as many fudge and taffy stores as fishermen. This small strip of land supports a diverse set of landscapes—long unbroken stretches of beach, salt marshes, hardwood forests, deep freshwater ponds carved by glaciers, and desert-like dunes sculpted by the wind. Thankfully, the Cape's natural landscape has been protected from the tide of commercialism by the establishment of the **Cape Cod National Seashore.** Blessed with an excellent hostel system, Cape Cod is a popular budget seaside getaway, used by many cross-country travelers as a resting place at the end of a tour of urban America. The Cape also serves as the gateway to **Martha's Vineyard** and **Nantucket.**

Terminology for locations on the cape is sometimes confusing. **Upper Cape** refers to the part of Cape Cod closer to the mainland, the most suburbanized and developed section of the Cape. Proceeding away from the mainland, you travel "down Cape" until you reach the **Lower Cape;** the National Seashore encompasses much of this area. Cape Cod resembles a bent arm, with **Woods Hole** at its armpit, **Chatham** at the elbow, and **Provincetown** at its clenched fist.

If you're up for some exercise, cycling is the best way to travel the Cape's gentle slopes. The park service can give you a free map of trails or sell you the detailed **Cape Cod Bike Book** ($2.50; available at most Cape bookstores). The 135-mi. **Boston-Cape Cod Bikeway** connects Boston to Provincetown at land's end. If you want to bike this route, pick up a bicycle trail map of the area, available at some bookstores and most bike shops. The trails which line either side of the **Cape Cod Canal** in the National Seashore rank among the country's most scenic, as does the 14-mi. **Cape Cod Rail Trail** from Dennis to Eastham. Cape Cod's **area code:** 508.

■ Upper Cape

Hyannis Hyannis is not the Cape Cod most people expect. JFK spent his summers on the beach in nearby Hyannisport, but the town itself sees more action as a transportation hub than as a scenic mecca. Island ferries and buses to destinations throughout the Cape emanate from Hyannis; hop on one and get out of town—the Kennedys *aren't* going to meet you at the bus station.

The **Hyannis Area Chamber of Commerce,** 1481 Rte. 132 (362-5230), about 3 mi. up the road from the bus station, distributes the free *Hyannis Guidebook* and has a campground guide for the whole cape. (Open Mon.-Thurs. 9am-5pm, Fri. 9am-7pm, Sat. 9am-4:30pm, Sun. 11am-3pm; Sept.-May closed Sun.) In an **emergency,** call 775-1212 for police or 775-2323 for the fire department or an ambulance. **ZIP code:** 02601.

Hyannis doesn't know the meaning of the term "budget accommodations." The closest affordable places to stay are the campgrounds near Sandwich, about 15 mi. from Hyannis, and the hostel in Eastham.

Hyannis is tattooed midway across the Cape's upper arm, 3 mi. south of U.S. 6 on Nantucket Sound. **Plymouth & Brockton** (775-5524) runs five Boston-to-Provincetown buses per day with ½-hr. layovers at the **Hyannis Bus Station,** 17 Elm St. (775-5524). Other stops include Plymouth, Sagamore, Yarmouth, Orleans, Wellfleet, and Truro. (To Boston 3½hr., $10, and Provincetown 1½hr., $9.) **Bonanza Bus Lines** (800-556-3815) operates a line through Providence, RI to New York City (6 per day, 6hr., $40). **Amtrak,** 252 Main St. (800-872-7245), sends a direct train from New York City to Hyannis on Friday, and one from Hyannis to New York on Sunday (6hr., $65). See the listings for Martha's Vineyard (p. 115) and Nantucket (p. 117) for info on ferry service to the islands.

Sandwich The oldest town on the Cape, Sandwich cultivates charm unmatched by its neighbors. The beauty and workmanship of Sandwich glass was made famous by the Boston & Sandwich Glass Company, founded in Sandwich in 1825. Though the original company is gone, you can still see Sandwich's master glassblowers shape works of art from blobs of molten sand. The artisans at **Pairpoint Crystal** (888-2344), on Rte. 6A just across the town border in Sagamore, do their thing Mon.- Fri. 9am-noon and 1-4:30pm (free). To enjoy the town's considerable collection of older pieces, tiptoe through the unparalleled menagerie at **The Sandwich Glass Museum,**

129 Main St. (888-0251), in Sandwich Center (open daily 9:30am-4:30pm; Nov.-March Wed.-Sun. 9:30am-4pm; closed in Jan.; $3.50, under 12 $1).

The **Thornton W. Burgess Museum** (888-4668), on Water St., pays tribute to the Sandwich-born, self-taught naturalist who spun tales about Peter Cottontail and Reddy Fox. Take a gander at the herb garden outside—from one end, the outline mimics a "tussie-mussie" bouquet of flowers; from the other end it's Peter Cottontail's head. (Open Mon.-Sat. 10am-4pm, Sun. 1-4pm. Free; donations accepted.) **The Green Briar Nature Center and Jam Kitchen,** 6 Discovery Rd. (888-6870), is where you can wander through a briar patch and wildflower gardens. On Wednesdays and Saturdays, the center kitchen churns out jam before the eyes of hungry visitors. (Open Mon.-Sat. 10am-4pm, Sun. 1-4pm; Jan.-March Tues.-Sat. 10am-4pm. Free; donations accepted.) The best beach on the Upper Cape, **Sandy Neck Beach,** on Sandy Neck Rd. 3 mi. east of Sandwich off Rte. 6A, extends 6 mi. along Cape Cod Bay with beautifully polished egg-sized granite pebbles and verdant dunes. Hike only on marked trails; the plants are very fragile.

Across the Sagamore Bridge, **Scusset Beach** (888-0859), on the canal near the junction of U.S. 6 and Rte. 3, offers fishing and camping (tent sites $6, with hookup $9; day use $2 per car). The **Shawme-Crowell State Forest** (888-0351), at Rte. 130 and U.S. 6, provides 285 wooded campsites with showers and campfires, but no hookups ($6, including parking at Scusset Beach; open April to late Nov.). **Peters Pond Park Campground** (477-1775), on Cotuit Rd. in south Sandwich, combines waterside sites with swimming, fishing, rowboat rentals ($15 per day), showers, and a grocery store (sites $20-32; open mid-April to mid-Oct).

Sandwich lies at the intersection of Rte. 6A and Rte. 130, about 13 mi. from Hyannis. The **Plymouth & Brockton** bus makes its closest stop in Sagamore, 3 mi. west. From Sandwich, the **Cape Cod Railroad** (771-3788), takes a scenic two-hour ride through cranberry bogs and marshes. (3 roundtrips per day from Main and Center St. in Hyannis to the Cape Cod Canal. $11.50, ages 3-12 $7.50.)

■ Lower Cape

Cape Cod National Seashore As early as 1825, the Cape had suffered so much man-made damage that the town of Truro required that local residents plant beach grass and keep their cows off the dunes. Further efforts toward conservation culminated in 1961 with the creation of the Cape Cod National Seashore, which includes much of the Lower Cape from Provincetown south to Chatham. Over 30 mi. of wide, soft, uninterrupted beaches lie under the tall clay cliffs and towering 19th-century lighthouses of this protected area. Thanks to conservationists, the area has largely escaped the boardwalk commercialism which afflicts most American seacoasts. Just a short walk away from the lifeguards, the sea of umbrellas and coolers fades into the distance. Hike one of the seashore's seldom used nature trails; the wide variety of habitats that huddle together on this narrow slice of land is truly impressive. Grassy dunes give way to forests as you move away from the water. Salt marshes play host to migrating and native waterfowl. When the waves or the crowds at the beach become too intense, warm fresh-water ponds, such as **Gull Pond** in Wellfleet, or **Pilgrim Lake** in Truro, are perfect for secluded swimming.

Most beachgoers face one eternal question: ocean or bay. The ocean beaches attract with whistling winds and surging waves; the water on the bay side rests calmer and gets a bit warmer. The National Seashore oversees six beaches: **Coast Guard** and **Nauset Light** in Eastham; **Marconi** in Wellfleet; **Head of the Meadow** in Truro; **Race Point** and **Herring Cove** in Provincetown. (Parking at all beaches $5 per day, $15 per season; pedestrian and cyclist entrance $3.)

To park at any other beach, you'll need a town permit. Each town has a different beach-parking policy, but permits generally cost $25-30 per week, $75 per season, or $10 per day. Call the appropriate Town Hall before trying to get around the parking permit; beaches are sometimes miles from any other legal parking and police with tow trucks roam the area like vultures. On sunny days, parking lots fill up by 11am or earlier; it's often easier to rent a bike and ride in. Most town beaches do not require bikers and walkers to pay an entrance fee. Wellfleet and Truro stand out among the ocean beaches as great examples of the Cape's famous endangered sand dunes. **Cahoon Hollow Beach** in Wellfleet separates itself from the rest with spectacular, cliff-like dunes, a particularly young crowd, and day parking.

Among the best of the seashore's nine self-guiding **nature trails**, the **Great Island Trail**, in Wellfleet, traces an 8-mi. loop through pine forests and grassy marshes and along a ridge with a view of the bay and Provincetown. The **Buttonbush Trail**, a ¼-mi. walk with braille guides and a guide rope for the blind, starts at the Salt Pond Visitors Center. There are also three park **bike trails:** Nauset Trail (1.6mi.), Head of the Meadow Trail (2mi.), and Province Lands Trail (5mi.).

Start your exploration at the **National Seashore's Salt Pond Visitors Center** (255-1301), at Salt Pond off U.S. 6 in Eastham (open daily 9am-6pm; Sept.-June 9am-4:30pm). The center offers a free 10-minute film every ½ hr. and a free museum with exhibits on the Cape's human and natural history. Camping on the national seashore is illegal.

Eastham The **Eastham Windmill**, on Rte. 6 at Samoset Rd. in Eastham, has had its nose to the grindstone since 1680. The windmill continues to function and demonstrates how the native American crop of corn was put to use by industrious Cape Codders. (Open July-Aug. Mon.-Sat. 10am-5pm, Sun. 1-5pm. Free.) Off Rte. 6, **Fort Hill** grants a survey of Nauset Marsh and the surrounding forest and ocean, as well as the paths which access them. For a classic view of the dunes and sea, drive to **Nauset Light**, on Salt Pond Rd. Popular with Cape bikers, the excellent **Mid-Cape Hostel (HI-AYH)**, 75 Goody Hallet Dr. (255-2785), occupies a quiet, wooded spot in Eastham, convenient to the lower part of the Cape. The hostel has six cabins, a kitchen, and a relaxed atmosphere that attracts groups. On the Plymouth-Brockton bus to Provincetown, ask to be let off at the traffic circle in Orleans (not the Eastham stop). Walk out on the exit to Rock Harbor, turn right on Bridge Rd., and take a right onto Goody Hallet Rd. ½ mi. from U.S. 6. (Office open daily 7:30-9:30am and 5-10:30pm. $12. Reservations essential July-Aug. Open mid-May to mid-Sept.) **Atlantic Oaks** (255-1437 or 800-332-2267) has about 100 tent and RV sites, a bathhouse, playground, and basketball courts. (Office open daily 8am-9pm; off season 9am-6pm. Tent sites for 2 $23, with hookup $31; off season $16/$22. Open May-Nov.)

Wellfleet **Gull Pond,** off Gull Pond Rd. in Wellfleet, connected by a series of shallow channels to three more secluded ponds, provides the setting for some of the Cape's best paddling. From **Higgins Pond,** look for the home of the Wellfleet Oysterman; Thoreau based a chapter in *Cape Cod* on his stay there. In the spring, the **herring run** clogs the rivers of the Cape as the amorous creatures head inland to spawn, blindly ignoring the glut of potential mates swimming along with them. For an overnight stay, check out one of South Wellfleet's two **campgrounds: Maurice's** (349-2029) and **Paine's** (349-3007). The **Bayside Lobster Hut,** 91 Commercial St. (349-6333), lets you "see 'em swim." While it's questionable how inviting *that* is, cheap lobster ($12-19 by weight) and a casual setting with picnic tables are more certain enticements (open July-Aug. daily noon-10pm; Sept. and June 4:30-9pm).

Truro Built in 1827 and little-changed, the **First Congregation Parish of Truro** (349-7735) transports visitors back to the 19th century; electricity was installed just 30 years ago, and the outhouse still serves in place of a new-fangled toilet. Take the Bridge Rd. exit off U.S. 6 and turn right onto Town Hall Rd. (services Sun. 10am). The picturesque **Cranberry Bog Trail,** North Pamet Rd., provides a secluded, spectacular setting for a walk, criss-crossing the National Seashore; get a map at the National Seashore's Salt Pond Visitors Center (see above). During the winter it's a school, but in summer it's the **Truro Hostel (HI-AYH)** (349-3889), on North Pamet Rd. Take North Pamet Rd. exit off U.S. Hwy 6, follow 1½ mi. to the east. The hostel offers an escape from the crowds with plenty of space, a large kitchen, great ocean views, and access to a secluded beach. (42 beds. Office open daily 7:30-10am and 5-10pm. $12, non-members $15. Reservations essential. Open late June-early Sept.) Several popular campgrounds nestle among the dwarf pines by the dunelands of North Truro, just 7 mi. southeast of Provincetown on U.S. 6; **North Truro Camping Area** (487-1847), on Highland Rd. ½ mi. east of U.S. 6., has small sandy sites, heated restrooms, hot showers, and free cable TV. (Sites for 2 $15, full hookup $21; $7.50 per additional person.) Call **Horton's Park** (487-1220) or **North of Highland** (487-1191) for more sites in North Truro.

■ Provincetown

At Provincetown, Cape Cod ends and the wide Atlantic begins. The National Seashore protects two-thirds of "P-Town" as conservation land; the inhabited sliver touches the harbor on the south side of town. Still, Provincetown finds room for plenty of activity in that tiny space. **Commercial St.,** the city's main drag, has seen the whalers of years past replaced by specialty shops, Portuguese bakeries, art galleries, nightclubs, and lots of people. For over a century, Provincetown has been known for its broad acceptance of many lifestyles, and a sizeable gay and lesbian community has flowered here. Over half the couples on the street are same-sex, and a walk here makes it quietly plain that homosexuality does not adhere to any stereotype of size, shape, color, or dress.

Practical Information Provincetown rests in the cupped hand at the end of the Cape Cod arm, 123 mi. from Boston by car or three hours by ferry across Massachusetts Bay. Parking spots are hard won, especially on cloudy days when the Cape's frustrated sun-worshippers flock to Provincetown. Follow the parking signs on **Bradford St.,** the auto-friendly thoroughfare, to dock your car for $5-7 per day, or try the lots closer to the action off Commercial St. or those up the hill by the monument. Whale-watching boats, the Boston ferry, and buses depart from **MacMillan Wharf,** at the center of town, just down the hill from the Pilgrim Monument.

You'll find the exceptionally helpful **Provincetown Chamber of Commerce,** 307 Commercial St. (487-3424), on MacMillan Wharf. (Open July-Labor Day daily 9am-5pm; April to June and mid-Sept. to Nov. Mon.-Sat. 10am-4pm.) **Province Lands Visitors Center** (487-1256), Race Point Rd., has info on the national seashore and free guides to the nature and bike trails (open daily 9am-5pm). Hop on a **Plymouth and Brockton Bus** (746-0378) to Boston (in summer 4 per day, 4hr., $19) at the stop on MacMillan Wharf. **Bay State Cruises** (617-723-7800) sends a ferry to Boston (3hr., $16); from MacMillan wharf. (Ferries mid-June to Labor Day daily; Memorial Day to mid-June and Labor Day-Columbus Day weekends only.) To get around in Provincetown and Herring Cove Beach, take the **Provincetown Shuttle Bus** (487-3353). One route travels the length of Bradford St.; the other goes from MacMillan Wharf to Herring Cove Beach. (Operates late June to early Sept. daily on the hour 8am-11pm; 10am-6pm for the beach. $1.25, seniors 75¢.) Rented bikes from **Arnold's Where You Rent the Bicycles,** 329 Commercial St. (487-0844), are another workable mode of transport. ($2.50-3.50 per hr., 2-hr. min.; $10-15 per day; 24hr. rental $2 more. Deposit and ID required; credit cards accepted. Open daily 8:30am-5:30pm. Daily rentals due back by 5pm.) **Emergency:** 911. Provincetown's **post office:** 211 Commercial St. (487-0163; open Mon.-Fri. 8:30am-5pm, Sat. 9:30-11:30am). **ZIP code:** 02657. **Area code:** 508.

Accommodations and Camping Provincetown teems with expensive places to lay your head. Your most affordable options are the wonderful hostels 10 mi. away in nearby Truro and a bit further away in Eastham. Still, the roaring Provincetown nightlife may make you unhappy with a late-night drive home and, fortunately, a few decent quasi-budget accommodations exist. In the quiet east end of town, the excellent **Cape Codder,** 570 Commercial St. (487-0131; call 9am-3pm or 9-11pm), welcomes you with archetypal Cape Cod decor, right down to the wicker furniture, and private beach access. (Singles and doubles $30-60; mid-Sept. to mid-June about $10 less. Continental breakfast included in-season. Open May-Oct. Reservations recommended.) For the cheapest beds in town try **The Outermost Hostel,** 28 Winslow St. (487-4378), barely 100 yards from the Pilgrim monument. Thirty beds in five cramped cottages go for $14 each, including kitchen access and free parking. (Office open daily 8-10am and 6-9:30pm. Check-out 10am. Key deposit $5. Reservations recommended for weekends. Open mid-May to mid-Oct.) When the great American Realist Edward Hopper wanted to paint a guest house, he chose what is now the **Sunset Inn,** 142 Bradford St. (487-9810), which he painted in his famous Rooms For Tourists. The house has changed little and the warmth and light he depicted in it still welcome weary travelers (2 guests in summer $60, includes continental breakfast). Catering to a slightly older clientele, **Alice Dunham's Guest House,** 3 Dyer St. (487-3330), has four rooms (named for squares on a Monopoly board) available in a Victorian house near the beach, a five-minute walk from the center of town. (Check-out 11am. Singles $44, doubles $54; rates vary on holidays. 1 free night per week of stay.)

Camping in Provincetown will cost you. The western part of **Coastal Acres Camping Court** (487-1700), a 1-mi. walk from the center of town, west on Bradford or Commercial St. and right on West Vine St., has over 100 crowded sites; try to snag one on the waterside. (Office open 24hr.; Sept.-June daily 8am-4pm and 8pm-9:30pm. Sites $20, with water and electricity $27. Open April-Oct.)

Food Sit-down meals in Provincetown cost a bundle; grab a bite at one of the Portuguese bakeries on Commercial St. or at a seafood shack on MacMillan Wharf. If you're hankerin' for a blue plate special, dine at **Dodie's Diner,** 401½ Commercial St. (487-3868), where they put together meatloaf ($8) and chicken-fried steak ($9) that would make a mother proud (entrees $7-10; open daily 8am-10pm). Since 1921, **Mayflower Family Dining,** 300 Commercial St. (487-0121), has given visitors walls lined with ancient caricatures and a stomach lined with solid food. Try the Portuguese beef tips ($8), the Italian spaghetti ($4), or the crab cakes ($6; open daily 11:30am-10pm; cash only). **George's Pizza,** 275 Commercial St. (487-3744), serves up excellent deep-dish pizza ($5) on an outdoor deck (open daily 11am-1am).

Sights Provincetown has long been a refuge for artists and artisans; there are over 20 galleries. Most are free and lie east of MacMillan Wharf on Commercial St. In general, galleries stay open in the afternoon and evening until 11pm, but close during a two-hour dinner break. Get the free *Provincetown Gallery Guide* for complete details. The kingpin of the artsy district, the **Provincetown Art Association and Museum,** 460 Commercial St. (487-1750), exhibits works by new Provincetown artists alongside a permanent 500-piece collection. (Open late June to Sept. daily noon-5pm and 7-9pm; call for winter hours. $3 suggested donation, seniors and kids $1.)

Contrary to popular belief, the Pilgrims first landed at Provincetown, not Plymouth; they moved on after a two week stay, in search of more welcoming soil. The **Pilgrim Monument and Provincetown Museum** (487-1310), on High Pole Hill, looms over Provincetown and commemorates that 17-day Pilgrim layover. The nation's tallest granite structure (255 ft.) also serves as a useful navigation aid to mariners. For a gorgeous panoramic view of the Cape, ascend the 253 ft. on stairs and ramps. The **Provincetown Museum,** at the tower's base, covers a broad swath of Cape history, from whaling artifacts to dollhouses. (Open daily 9am-5pm. $5, ages 4-12 $3.) At the **Provincetown Heritage Museum,** 356 Commercial St. (487-0666), you can see a half-scale model of a fishing schooner, paintings and other exhibits (open mid-June to mid-Oct. daily 10am-6pm; $3, under 12 free with adult).

Entertainment and Nightlife Today, Provincetown seafarers carry telephoto lenses, not harpoons, when they go whale hunting. **Whale-watch cruises** are some of P-town's most popular attractions. Several companies take you out to the feeding waters in about 40 minutes, and cruise around them for two hours. The companies claim that whales are sighted on 99% of the journeys. Tickets cost about $18;

discount coupons can be found in most local publications. **Dolphin Fleet** (255-3857 or 800-826-9300), **Portuguese Princess** (487-2651 or 800-442-3188), and **Ranger V** (487-3322 or 800-992-9333), leave from and operate ticket booths on MacMillan Wharf, while **Superwhale** (800-942-5334) runs off Fisherman's Pier.

Provincetown's nightlife is almost totally gay- and lesbian-oriented, but all are welcome. Most of the clubs and bars on Commercial St. charge around $5, and shut down at 1am. Uninhibited dancing shakes the ground nightly for a mixed crowd at the **Backroom,** 247 Commercial St. (487-1430; cover $5; open 10pm-1am). Live music drives **Club Euro,** 258 Commercial St. (487-2505), in the Euro Island Grille. Sway to live reggae on Saturdays. (Sat. cover $2. Open May-Oct. daily 11am-2am.) Proud to be the "oldest gay bar on the seacoast," **Atlantic House,** 6 Masonic Ave. (487–3821), more commonly known as the "A House," offers dancing and two bars (cover $3-5; open daily noon-1am). The **Crown and Anchor,** 247 Commercial St. (487-1430), offers five bars primarily targeted to a gay clientele. All are free except the Disco Bar. The lively **Governor Bradford,** 312 Commercial St. (487-2781), has karaoke, female impersonators, and other entertainment (cover varies; 11am-1pm).

■ Martha's Vineyard

Martha's Vineyard provides a haven for many vacationing luminaries. From Princess Di to President Clinton, visitors seek out this secluded island for its dunes, inland woods, pastel houses, and weathered cottages. Try coming in the fall, when the tourist season wanes and the foliage flares with autumnal hues. Seven communities comprise Martha's Vineyard. The western end of the island is called "up island," from the nautical days when sailors had to tack upwind to get there. The three largest towns, Oak Bluffs, Vineyard Haven, and Edgartown, are "down island" and have flatter terrain. Oak Bluffs and Edgartown are the only "wet" (alcohol-selling) towns on the island.

Practical Information Oak Bluffs, 3 mi. west of Vineyard Haven on State Rd., is the most youth-oriented of the Vineyard villages. Tour **Trinity Park** near the harbor and see the famous "Gingerbread Houses" (minutely detailed, elaborate pastel Victorian cottages), or Oak Bluffs' **Flying Horses Carousel** (693-9481), on Circuit Ave. It's the oldest in the nation (built in 1876), and composed of 20 handcrafted horses with real horsehair (open daily 10am-10pm; fare $1). **Gay Head,** 12mi. off West Tisbury, offers just about the best view in all of New England. The local Wampanoag frequently saved sailors whose ships wrecked on the breathtaking **Gay Head Cliffs.** The 100,000-year-old precipice contains a collage of clay in brilliant colors and supports one of five lighthouses on the island. **Menemsha and Chilmark,** a little northeast of Gay Head, has a good coastline and claims to be the only working fishing town on the island; tourists can fish off the pier or purchase lobster straight from the sea. **Vineyard Haven** has more tacky t-shirt shops and fewer charming old homes than other towns.

Though small (30mi. across at its widest point), the Vineyard packs 15 beaches and a state forest in its bounds. A free map is available at the **Martha's Vineyard Chamber of Commerce,** Beach Rd., Vineyard Haven (693-0085; open Mon.-Fri. 9am-5pm. **Bonanza** buses (800-556-3815) stop at the Ferry Terminal in Woods Hole and depart, via Bourne, for Boston (11 per day, 2hr., $12) and New York (5 per day, 6hr., $39). Most **taxis** are vans with negotiable fares; set a price before you get in. In Oak Bluffs, call 693-0037; in Edgartown, 627-4677; in Vineyard Haven, 693-3705. The **Island Transport** (693-1589 or 693-0058) runs shuttle buses between Vineyard Haven (Union St.), Oak Bluffs (Ocean Park), and Edgartown (Church St.) late June through August. (Daily every 15min. 10am-7pm, every 30min. 7-10am and 7pm-midnight. Vineyard Haven to Oak Bluffs $1.50, to Edgartown $2.)

Ferries serve the island from Hyannis (778-2600 or 693-0112), New Bedford (997-1688), Falmouth (548-4800), and Nantucket (778-2600), but the shortest and cheapest ride, as well as the only one that transports cars, leaves from Woods Hole on Cape

Cod. The **Steamship Authority** (477-8600) sends 13 boats per day on the 45-minute ride to Vineyard Haven and Oak Bluffs. (Ticket office open Mon.-Thurs. and Sat. 5am-9:45pm, Fri. and Sun 5am-10:45 pm. $4.75, ages 5-12 $2.40, bike $3, car $38; reservation necessary weeks in advance.) The ferry company has three parking lots ($7.50 per day) and shuttle service to the dock. The **Chappy "On Time" Ferry** (627-9427) connects Edgartown Town Dock and Chappaquiddick Island. (Runs June to mid-Oct. daily 7:30-midnight; mid-Oct. to May reduced hours. Round-trip $1, car $4, bicycle $2.50, motorcycle $3.50.)

The Vineyard is designed for bicycles. Bring one or rent one at **Martha's Vineyard Scooter and Bike** (693-0782), at the Steamship Authority Dock in Vineyard Haven. (Open July-Aug. daily 8am-8pm; call for off season hours; $10-12 per day for a three-speed, $15-18 per day for a mountain bike or hybrid; deposit required.) Martha's Vineyard's **area code: 508.**

Accommodations and Camping While cheap places to stay may lure you to the outskirts of town and beyond, the expensive taxi rates to and from are not worth it. Anyone hoping to partake in the island's social life is best off spending the extra money to stay in town. The fantastic **Martha's Vineyard Hostel (HI-AYH),** Edgartown-West Tisbury Rd. (693-2665), West Tisbury, provides the 78 cheapest beds on the island. Located right next to the bike path, the hostel has a great kitchen with an illuminated stained glass hearth and recreational facilities. (Open April to mid-May 7-9:30am and 5-10:30pm. Curfew 11pm. Light chore required. $12, nonmembers $15. Linen $2. Reservations essential.) In town, the **Nashua House** (693-0043), Oak Bluffs, offers clean, comfortable beds with a Van Gogh in every room (singles and doubles $35-45 in early season, $50-65 in season; check in before 10pm.) The chamber of commerce provides a list of inns and guest houses; all recommend reservations in July and August, especially for weekends.

Martha's Vineyard Family Campground (693-3772), 1½ mi. from Vineyard Haven on Edgartown Rd., keeps 185 shaded sites in an oak tree forest. Groceries and metered showers are available nearby. (Sites for 2 $26; each additional person $9, ages 2-18 $2. Open mid-May to mid-Oct.) **Webb's Camping Area** (693-0233), Barnes Rd., Oak Bluffs, has 150 shaded and spacious sites. (Sites for 2 $27-29, depending on degree of privacy, with hookup $2 extra; each additional person $8, ages 5-17 $1. Open mid-May to mid-Sept.)

Food Cheap sandwich and lunch places speckle the Vineyard. Vineyard Haven and Oak Bluffs best accommodate the traveler who watches the bottom line, though the options may not be so kind to the waistline. Fried-food shacks across the island sell clams, shrimp, and potatoes, which generally cost at least $15. **Shindigs,** 32 Kennebec Ave. (696-7727), in Oak Bluffs, serves generous portions of tasty BBQ ($6-7) and sandwiches ($4-7; open daily 10am-10pm). Prospective revelers should note that alcohol is tightly controlled on the Vineyard.

Considering the outdoor beauty, you may want to grab your food and run at one of a number of take-out joints. **Louis',** 102 State Rd. (693-3255), Vineyard Haven, serves take-out Italian food that won't break the bank. Try the fresh pasta with meat sauce ($4) or the vegetable calzone ($4.50; open Mon.-Thurs. 11am-8:30pm, Fri.-Sat. 11am-9pm, Sun. 4-8:30pm). Sample a range of creative and delicious pastries and breads (75¢-$3.50) at the **Black Dog Bakery** (693-4786), on Beach St. exit in Vineyard Haven, but **for the love of God,** please don't buy another sweatshirt (open daily 5:30am-8pm). An island institution, **Mad Martha's** scoops out homemade ice cream and frozen yogurt. The main store (693-9151), on Circuit Ave. in Oak Bluffs (open daily 11am-midnight), is only one of eight throughout the island. Several **farm stands** on the island sell inexpensive produce; the chamber of commerce map shows their locations.

Sights Exploring the Vineyard can involve much more than zipping around on a moped. Take time to head out to the countryside, hit the beach, or trek down one of the great walking trails. **Felix Neck Wildlife Sanctuary** (627-4850), on the Edgartown-Vineyard Haven Rd., offers a variety of terrains and habitats for exploration (open daily 8am-sunset; off season closed Mon.; $3, seniors $1, under 12 $2). **Cedar Tree Neck** on the western shore harbors 250 acres of headland off Indian Hill Rd. with trails throughout, while the **Long Point** park in West Tisbury preserves 550 acres and a shore on the Tisbury Great Pond. The largest conservation area on the island, **Cape Pogue Wildlife Refuge and Wasque Reservation** (693-7662), floats on Chappaquiddick Island.

Two of the best beaches on the island, **South Beach,** at the end of Katama Rd. 3 mi. south of Edgartown, and **State Beach,** on Beach Rd. between Edgartown and Oak Bluffs, are free and open to the public. South boasts sizeable surf and an occasionally nasty undertow, while the warmer, gentler waters of State set the stage for parts of *Jaws,* the grandaddy of classic beach-horror films. For the best sunsets on the island stake out a spot at **Gay Head** or the **Manemsha Town Beach;** enjoy the sun's descent while dining on seafood from nearby stands.

■ Nantucket

Once the home of the biggest whaling port in the world, Nantucket saw one of its whaling ships, the *Essex,* rammed by a whale in 1820; the incident inspired Herman Melville's *Moby Dick.* Though Nantucket is today a secluded outpost of privilege and establishment, it is possible to enjoy a stay on the island without holding up a convenience store to do so. Nantucket's 82 mi. of beach are always free. If possible, visit during the last weeks of the tourist season, when prices drop. Only a few places stay open during the cold, rainy winter months, when awesome storms churn the slate colored seas.

Practical Information The **visitor services center,** 25 Federal St. (228-0925), can help you find a place to stay (open daily 9am-9pm, winters daily 9am-5pm). **Barrett's Bus Lines,** 20 Federal St. (228-0174 or 800-773-0174), opposite the visitors center, runs buses, on sunny days only, to Jetty's Beach (every ½hr. 10am-5pm, $1), Surfside Beach (hourly 10am-5pm), and Sconset (every hr. 10am-4pm, $3 round-trip, ages 5-12 $1.50). **Hyline** (778-2600) operates ferry service to Nantucket's Straight Wharf from Hyannis (6 per day, $11) and from Martha's Vineyard (mid-June to mid-Sept. 3 per day, $11). **Steamship Authority** (540-2022), docked at Steamboat Wharf on Nantucket, runs ferries from Hyannis only (6 per day, $10). Both charge $5 for bikes and take about two hours.

People say that hitchhiking is the best way to get around Nantucket. Those who prefer to pedal rent bikes at **Young's Bicycle Shop** (228-1151), Steamboat Wharf; mountain bikes and hybrids cost $20 per day. Young's distributes free maps of the island, but for an extended stay buy the $3 *Complete Map of Nantucket.* (Open daily 10am-8pm, Sept.-June 10am-6pm.) Nantucket's **area code: 508.**

Accommodations and Food Occupying an old life-saving station, the **Nantucket Hostel (HI-AYH),** 31 Western Ave. (228-0433), sits at Surfside Beach, 3½ mi. from town at the end of the Surfside Bike Path. (49 beds, full kitchen. Open daily 7:30-10am and 5-11pm. Curfew 11pm. Lockout 9:30am-5pm. $12, nonmembers $15. Linens $2. Reservations essential. Open late April to early Oct.) In the heart of Nantucket Town, **Nesbitt Inn,** 21 Broad St. (228-2446), offers 13 rooms, each with a sink and shared baths in a gorgeous Victorian guest house. The friendly owners make sure guests are comfortable with a fireplace, deck, kitchen access, and free continental breakfast. (Office open daily 7am-10pm. Check-in noon; check-out 11am. Singles $42, doubles $65, triples $85; Oct.-April $8-10 less. Reservations essential; deposit required.)

Meals on Nantucket are pricey. The standard entree runs about $12-14, but the frugal gourmet can still dine well. **Black Eyed Susan's,** 10 India St., offers a rotating breakfast and dinner menu with interesting dishes such as sourdough French toast with orange Jack Daniel's butter. (Full order $6.50, short $5. Breakfast daily 7am-1pm, dinner Fri.-Wed. 6-10pm. Reservations accepted.) Steal away to the **Brother-hood of Thieves,** 23 Broad St., a subterranean haven for those who don't like light interfering with their meals. Down a jumbo sandwich ($5) and mellow out to the sounds of local bands Tues.-Sun. nights. (Open Mon. 11:30am-11pm, Tues.-Thurs. 11:30am-11pm, Fri.-Sat. 11:30am-midnight, Sun. noon-11pm.) **Nantucket Nectars** was born on a boat based at the **Nantucket Allserve General Store** (228-8170), at the end of straight wharf. Today the store has all the Nantucket Nectar flavors in addition to snacks, propane refills, and boat bottom cleaning services.

Sights and Activities The remarkable natural beauty of Nantucket is well-protected; over 36% of the island's land can never be built upon. For a great **bike trip,** head east from Nantucket Town on Milestone Rd. and turn left onto any path that looks promising, and pedal in lush moors of heather, huckleberries, bayberries, and wild roses. **Sea Nantucket** (228-7499), at the end of Washington St. at the waterfront, will set you up in a rental **sea kayak** for an aquatic adventure ($25 for 4½hr.; open daily 8:30am-5:30pm). The boats aren't difficult to maneuver, but paddling works up a sweat. Take one out to a nearby salt marsh, or head across the harbor to an isolated beach on the Coatue peninsula to enjoy a picnic undisturbed by other beachgoers. If you'd rather stand on the strand between land and sea, rent **surf fish-ing** equipment from **Barry Thurston's** (228-9595), at Harbor Sq. near the A&P (necessary equipment $20 for 24hr.; open Mon.-Sat. 8am-9pm, Sun. 9am-6pm).

The fascinating **Nantucket Whaling Museum** (228-1736), Broad St. in Nantucket Town, recreates the old whaling community through exhibits on whales and methods of whaling, and a complete whale skeleton. The **Museum of Nantucket History** (228-3889), in the Thomas Macy Warehouse, gives insight into the island's boom years as a whaling port and describes other island industries such as candlemaking and sheep raising. Catch a lecture by a Nantucket old-timer. (Call for lecture times. $5, children $3. Both museums open early June to mid-Oct. daily 10am-5pm; late April-early June and mid-Oct. to early Dec. Sat.-Sun. 11am-3pm.) The best deal is a visitor's pass which gets you into both museums and seven other historical sights run by the historical association ($8, children $4). Pick up a free copy of *Yesterday's Island* for listings of nature walks, concerts, lectures, and art exhibitions.

WESTERN MASSACHUSETTS

Famous for cultural events in the summer, rich foliage in the fall, and skiing in the winter, the Berkshire Mountains have long been a vacation destination for Boston and New York urbanites seeking a relaxing country escape. Filling approximately the western third of Massachusetts, the Berkshire Region is bordered to the north by Rte. 2 (the Mohawk Trail) and Vermont, to the west by Rte. 7 and New York, to the south by the Mass Pike and Connecticut, and to the east by I-91. As well as natural beauty, the area is home to the Basketball Hall of Fame, a high-tech facility which pays tribute to the sport that originated in Springfield in 1891. A host of affordable bed and breakfasts, restaurants, and campgrounds adorn the area, making it both financially and logistically accessible for the budget traveler.

■ The Berkshires

Practical Information The Berkshires are sprinkled with quintessential New England towns. Churches, fudge shops, antique boutiques, and country stores are all here in full force. To see sights located far from the town centers, you'll have to drive. The roads are slow and sometimes pocked with potholes, but they are certainly scenic. The **Berkshire Visitors Bureau,** 2 Berkshire Common, Plaza Level (443-9186 or 800-237-5747), Pittsfield, is open Mon.-Fri. 8:30-4:30pm. An **information booth** on the east side of **Pittsfield's** rotary circle will give you the scoop on restaurants and accommodations in the surrounding cities (open Mon.-Fri. 9am-5pm). Berkshire County's dozen state parks and forests cover 100,000 acres and offer numerous camping options. For info on all that jazz, stop by the **Region 5 Headquarters,** 740 South St. (442-8928; open Mon.-Fri. 8am-5pm, Sat.-Sun. 8am-4:30pm). The Berkshires' **area code:** 413.

The Mohawk Trail Perhaps the most famous highway in the state, the Mohawk Trail (Rte. 2) provides a meandering and scenic drive which showcases the beauty of the Berkshires. During fall foliage weekends, the awe-inspiring reds and golds of the surrounding mountains draw crowds of leaf-peepers. **Millers Falls, MA** is the trail's eastern terminus. Five mi. west of Charlemont, off Rte. 2, lies the **Mohawk Trail State Forest** (339-5504), which offers campsites along a river ($6) and rents cabins (electricity but no hookups; small $8, large $10). **Whitewater Rafting** on the **Deerfield River** can be done through **Crabapple Whitewater** (800-553-7238), Charlemont. Trip times vary, and there are multiple trips for differing skill levels. **North Adams** is home to the **Western Gateway** (663-6312), on Furnace St. bypass of Rte. 8, a railroad museum which is also one of Massachusetts' five **Heritage State Parks.** (Open daily 10am-4:30pm; Labor Day-Memorial Day Thurs.-Mon. 10am-4:30pm. Free, donations encouraged. Summer Thursdays there's live music at 7pm.) The **Freight Yard Pub** (663-6547), within the Western Gateway park, is a good bargain, serving salads ($2-6) and "Berkshire's best" french dip sandwiches ($8; open daily 11:30am-1am; café dining available outside). On Rte. 8, ½ mi. north, is the **Natural Bridge** (663-6392 or 663-6312), a white marble bridge formed during the last Ice Age and the only natural, water-eroded bridge on the continent. (One-mi. self-guided walking tour. Open Memorial Day-Columbus Day, Mon.-Fri. 8:30am-4pm, Sat.-Sun. 10am-6pm. $5 per vehicle.)

   Mt. Greylock, the highest peak in Massachusetts (3491 ft.), is south of the Mohawk Trail, and accessible by Rte. 2 to the north and U.S. 7 to the west. By car, take Notch Rd. from Rte. 2 between North Adams and Williamstown, or take Rockwell Rd. from Lanesboro on U.S. 7. The roads up are rough but offer magnificent greenery and solitude. Hiking trails begin from nearly all the towns around the mountain; get free maps at the **Mount Greylock Visitors Information Center** (499-4262), Rockwell Rd. (open daily 9am-5pm). Once at the top, climb the **War Memorial** for a breathtaking view. Sleep high in nearby **Bascom Lodge** (743-1591), built from the rock excavated for the monument. (Members of the Appalachian Mountain Club Sun.-Thurs. $13, Fri.-Sat. $18, nonmembers $20/25, member under 15 $3/8, nonmember under 12 $10/15; Fri.-Sat. rates apply daily in Aug.) The lodge offers breakfast ($5) and dinner ($10), and is open daily 10am-5pm.

   The Mohawk Trail ends in **Williamstown** at its junction with U.S. 7; here, an **information booth** (458-4922) provides an abundance of free local maps and seasonal brochures, and can help you find a place to stay in one of Williamstown's many reasonably priced B&Bs (open summers daily 10am-6pm, winter weekends 10am-6pm). At **Williams College,** the second oldest in Massachusetts (est. 1793), lecturers compete with the beautiful scenery of surrounding mountains for their students' attention. Campus maps are available from the **Admissions Office,** 988 Main St. (597-2211; open Mon.-Fri. 8:30am-4:30pm). First among the college's many cultural resources, **Chapin Library** (597-2462), in Stetson Hall, displays a number of rare U.S. manuscripts, including early copies of the Declaration of Independence, Articles of Confederation, Constitution, and Bill of Rights (open Mon.-Fri. 10am-noon and 1-5pm; free). The small but impressive **Williams College Museum of Art** (597-2429), off Main St. (Rte. 2), between Spring and Water St., merits a visit. Rotating exhibits have included Soviet graphic art, postmodern architecture, and Impressionist works (open Mon.-Sat. 10am-5pm, Sun. 1-5pm; free). Also free in Williamstown, the **Sterling and Francine Clark Art Institute,** 225 South St. (458-9545), houses Impressionist paintings and collections of silver and sculpture (open Tues.-Sun. 10am-5pm; summers daily). For tasty eats, head to **Pappa Charlie's Deli,** 28 Spring St. (458-5969), a popular deli offering sandwiches such as the "Dick Cavett" and the "Dr. Johnny Fever" (under $4; open Mon.-Sat. 8am-11pm, Sun. 9am-11pm).

Williamstown's surrounding wooded hills beckon from the moment you arrive. The **Hopkins Memorial Forest** (597-2346) has over 2250 acres that are free to the public for hiking and cross-country skiing. Take U.S. 7 north, turn left on Bulkley St., go to the end and turn right onto Northwest Hill Rd. **Spoke Bicycles and Repairs,** 618 Main St. (458-3456), rents 10-speed bikes ($10-12 per day) and can give you advice on the best rides in the area (open Mon.-Fri. 10-6pm, Sat. 10am-5pm).

Route 7 South of Williamstown, the first major town along Rte. 7 is Pittsfield, the county seat of Berkshire County and the town credited with the creation of the county fair. Recreational possibilities abound at the **Pittsfield State Forest,** 4 mi. northwest of town, off Rte. 20 (442-8992). The Forest offers modern campsites ($8-10) and schedules outdoor activities. The Berkshire's rich literary history can be sampled at Herman Melville's home **Arrowhead,** 780 Holmes Rd. (442-1793), 3½ mi. south of Pittsfield. The building houses the Berkshire County Historical Society, and has displays on 19th-century country life and the role of women on the farm. (Open daily Memorial Day-Labor Day 10am-5pm, Oct. Mon., Thurs.-Sat. 10am-4:30pm, Sun. 11am-3:30pm, May Sat.-Sun. 10am-5pm. Tours of the house are conducted every ½-hour. Admission $4.50, seniors $4, ages 6-16 $3.) The **Berkshire Museum,** 39 South St. (443-7171), Pittsfield, displays Hudson River School paintings, natural history exhibits, and has an aquarium. (Open July-Aug. Mon.-Sat. 10am-5pm, Sun. 1-5pm; Sept.-June Tues.-Sat. 10am-5pm, Sun. 1-5pm. $3, seniors/students $2, children 12-18 $1. Free Wed. and Sat. 10am-noon.) The **Edith Wharton Restoration at the Mount,** at the junction of Rte. 7 and 7A in Lenox, was the home of the great turn-of-the-century Pulitzer Prize winner. (Tours on the hour. $6, seniors $5.50, ages 13-18 $4.50. Open May 28 to early Sept. Tues.-Sun. 10am-3pm.) **Stockbridge** is home to the **Norman Rockwell Museum** (298-4100), on Rte. 183, ½ mi. south from the junction of Rte. 7 and 102. Containing more that 1000 items, including many of Rockwell's *Saturday Evening Post* covers, the museum is a must-see for visitors to the area. (Open May-Oct. daily 10am-5pm. $8, children $2; Nov.-April Mon.-Fri. 11am-4pm, Sat.-Sun. 10am-5pm, $7.50, children $2.)

Tanglewood, the famed summer home of the **Boston Symphony Orchestra,** is one of the Berkshires' greatest treasures. South on Rte. 7, a short distance west of Lenox Center on Rte. 183 (West St.), Tanglewood concerts show off a variety of music, from Ray Charles to Wynton Marsalis to James Taylor, but its bread-and-butter is world-class classical music. Buy a lawn ticket, bring a picnic dinner, and listen to your favorites under the stars or in the Sunday afternoon sunshine. Orchestral concerts held July-Aug. Fri. 8:30pm, with 6:30 prelude, Sat. 8:30pm, Sun. 2:30pm. (Recorded concert line 637-1666. Tickets $13.50-67, lawn seats $11.50-12.50. Open rehearsals held Sat. 10:30am. Call for schedule of special events and prices. There are also chamber concerts on Thursday evenings and the Boston Pops give two summer concerts. The summer concludes with a jazz festival over Labor Day weekend.

Following Rte. 7 south will take you past the **Wagon Wheel Motel** (445-4532), at the junction of Rte. 20. Off-season rooms are $42 and vary in the summer. Summer weekend rates are high throughout the Berkshires (starting at $100). A cheaper option is to continue north on U.S. 20, about 3 mi., until you reach **October Mountain State Forest** (243-1778) with toilets, showers, and $6 sites.

Northampton and Amherst The last two sides of the Berkshire square are major interstate roads. Therefore, although it saves time, visitors don't see as much great natural scenery. There are alternate routes for beauty-seekers with time on their hands. Rte. 20 meanders above, below, and around the Mass Pike (Rte. 90), and in the north-south direction, Rte. 91 can be substitutes for Rtes. 47 and 63, which snake along the Connecticut River.

On Rte. 91, about 15 min. north of Springfield, lie educational meccas **Northampton** and **Amherst.** Northampton is a beautiful town that boasts a surprising number of restaurants and shops. For more info on the area, visit or call the **Greater Northampton Chamber of Commerce,** 62 State St. (584-1900). The **Peter Pan Trailways** terminal is located at 1 Roundhouse Plaza (536-1030). For a comfortable bed, try the **Motel 6,** (665-7161 or 800-4MOTEL6/466-8356), at the junction of Rte. 5 and 10, near south Deerfield (singles $40, doubles $46).

In Northampton, the **Smith College Museum of Art,** on Elm St. at Bedford Terrace, has a collection of 19th- and 20th-century European and American paintings, and offers tours and gallery talks (open Tues.-Sat. noon-5pm, Sun. 2-5pm, free). **Look Memorial Park** (584-5457), on the Berkshire Trail (Rte. 9) not far from downtown Northampton, is bordered by the Mill River. Its 200 acres make a pleasant picnic spot. (Open daily dawn-dusk; facilities open Memorial Day-Labor Day daily 11am-6pm. $2 per vehicle weekends, $1 Mon.-Fri.) For excellent wood-fired, brick oven pizza, head to **Pizzeria Paradiso,** 12 Crafts Ave. (586-1468), which offers gourmet vegetable, meat, and seafood creations ($6-7).

The **Five-College Consortium** is spread randomly across western Massachusetts and consists of five schools in which students may cross-register as part of a larger academic community. By far the largest is the gargantuan **UMass Amherst** (545-0222), in Amherst (tours summers Mon.-Fri. and daily in Aug.). The prestigious **Amherst College** (542-2328) shares the town with the main UMass campus (tours every 2hr. Mon.-Fri. 10am-4pm). Also in town is **Hampshire College** (582-5471). The all-woman **Smith College** (585-2500), in Northampton, and **Mt. Holyoke College** (538-2000), in South Hadley, complete the consortium. Springfield's **area code: 413.**

■ Springfield

As the largest city in the western half of Massachusetts, Springfield serves the region as an industrial and transportation center, and is worth a visit en route to or from the rest of the state. Springfield fills the southeast quadrant of the intersection of I-90 and I-91, the main north-south artery in western Mass. The **Greater Springfield Convention and Visitors Bureau,** 34 Boland Way (787-1548), can help you find accommodations. Trusty **Motel 6,** 106 Capital Dr. (800-4MOTEL6/466-8356), off I-91 at Exit 13A, offers clean, comfortable rooms, at equally comfortable prices (singles $36, doubles $42). Inexpensive eateries catering to the large working class of Springfield abound.

In 1891, with the help of Dr. James Naismith, the game of basketball was invented in Springfield. Today, the **Basketball Hall of Fame,** 1150 W. Columbus Ave. (781-5759), serves as a shrine to the sport and its birth (open daily 9am-6pm; $8, kids 7-15 and seniors $5, under 7 free). Once in town, check out the **Indian Motorcycle Museum,** 33 Hendee St. (737-2624), for a look at some great old bikes.

Rhode Island

Rhode Island, despite its diminutive stature (it's the smallest state in the Union), has always been a trendsetter. The first colony to declare independence from Great Britain became the first state to pass laws against slavery. Most Rhode Islanders are proud of their compact, non-conformist heritage. From founder Roger Williams, a religious outcast during colonial days, to Buddy Cianci, convicted felon and two-time mayor of Providence—he served one term while still on probation—Rhode Island has always lured a different crowd. Though you can drive through the body of Rhode Island in 45 minutes, the state's 400 mile coastline deserves a longer look. Small, provincial spots speckle the shores winding to Connecticut, and the inland roads remain quiet, unpaved thoroughfares lined with family fruit stands.

PRACTICAL INFORMATION

Capital: Providence.
Rhode Island Department of Tourism: 7 Jackson Walkway, Providence 02903 (277-2601 or 800-556-2484). Open Mon.-Fri. 8:30am-4:30pm. **Division of Parks and Recreation,** 2321 Hartford Pike, Johnston 02919 (277-2632). Open Mon.-Fri. 8:30am-4pm.
State Drink: coffee milk.
Time Zone: Eastern. **Postal Abbreviation:** RI.
Sales Tax: 7%.

■ Providence

Like Rome, Providence sits aloft seven hills. Seven colleges inhabit these hills, luring a community of students, artists, and academics to join the native working class and state representatives. Providence has cobbled sidewalks and colonial buildings, a college-town identity, and more than its share of bookstores and cafés. Head for the area around the colleges where students on tight budgets support a plethora of inexpensive restaurants and shops.

Practical Information The state capitol and the downtown business district cluster just east of the intersection of I-95 and I-195. **Brown University** and the **Rhode Island School of Design (RISD)** (RIZZ-dee) sit atop of a steep hill, a 10-min. walk east of downtown. For a self-guided walking tour map and tourist literature, visit the **Greater Providence Convention and Visitors Bureau,** 30 Exchange Terrace (274-1636 or 800-233-1636), on the first floor, next to City Hall (open Mon.-Fri. 8:30am-5pm). The **Providence Preservation Society,** 21 Meeting St. (831-7440), at the foot of College Hill, gives detailed info on historic Providence (self-guided tour map $1, audio cassette tour $5; open Mon.-Fri. 9am-5pm).
Amtrak, 100 Gaspee St. (800-872-7245), operates from a gleaming white structure behind the state capitol, a 10-min. walk from Brown or downtown. Trains set out for Boston (1hr., $8) and New York (4hr., $33-41) nine times per day (open daily 5:30am-11:45pm). **Greyhound** and **Bonanza,** 1 Bonanza Way (751-8800), off Exit 25 of I-95, have frequent service to Boston (17 per day, 1hr., $7.75) and New York (7 per day, 4hr., $35). (Station open 5am-midnight.) All Boston and New York buses make a stop at the Kennedy Plaza downtown, where Bonanza also has a ticket office (open daily 7am-6pm). **Rhode Island Public Transit Authority (RIPTA),** 265 Melrose St. (781-9400; Mon.-Fri. 7am-7pm, Sat. 8am-6pm), runs an **information booth,** on Kennedy Plaza across from the visitors center, which provides in-person route and schedule assistance and free bus maps Mon.-Fri. 7am-6pm. RIPTA's service includes Newport ($2.50) and other points south. (Buses run daily 4:30am-1:30am; hours vary by route. Fare 25¢ to $2.50; within Providence, generally 85¢; seniors ride free Mon.-Fri. 4:30-6am, 9am-3pm and 6pm-midnight, Sat.-Sun. all day.) **Emergency:** 911. Providence's **post office:** 2 Exchange Terrace (421-4361; open Mon.-Fri. 7:30am-5:30pm, Sat. 8am-2pm). **ZIP code:** 02903. **Area code:** 401.

Accommodations and Camping High downtown motel rates make Providence an expensive overnight stay. Rooms book far in advance for the graduation season in May and early June. Catering largely to international visitors to the universities, the stained-glass-windowed **International House of Rhode Island,** 8 Stimson Ave. (421-7181), near the Brown campus, has two comfortable rooms, but they're often full. Amenities include kitchen facilities, shared bath, TV, and a fridge. (2-night min. stay. Office open Mon.-Fri. 9:30am-5pm. Singles $45, students $30; doubles $50/$35; $5 off for stays of 5 nights or more. Reservations required.) Clean, comfortable **Motel 6,** 20 Jefferson Blvd. (467-9800), at Exit 14-15 off I-95, waits like an old friend (singles $50, doubles $56). The **New Yorker Motor Lodge,** 400 Newport Ave. (434-8000), in East Providence, rents the cheapest rooms around. It's a typical motel, but the price is right (singles $40, doubles $44). The nearest campgrounds lie a 30-minute drive from downtown. One of the closest, **Colwell's Campground** (397-4614), provides showers and hookups for 75 sites on the shore of the Flat River Reservoir. From Providence, take I-95S to Exit 10, then head west 8.5 mi. on Rte. 117 to Coventry. (Tent sites $10-15, depending on proximity to the waterfront.)

Food Good food is found in three areas in Providence: **Atwells Ave.** in the Italian district, on Federal Hill just west of downtown; **Thayer St.,** on College Hill to the east, home to off-beat student hangouts and ethnic restaurants; and the **Union St.** area, near downtown, with its beautiful old diners. **Geoff's,** 163 Benefit St. (751-2248), combines bread and ingredients in 60 different ways and names them all after stars like Buddy Ciani (sandwiches $4-6; open Mon.-Fri. 8am-10pm, Sat.-Sun. 10am-10pm). Sit down on a swivel stool for some good home cookin' at the **Seaplane Diner** (941-9547), on Allens Ave. Around "since Grandma was a girl," Seaplane has perfected cheap stick-to-your-ribs dinners. ($3.50-5.50. Open Mon.-Fri. 5:30am-3pm, Sat. 5:30am-1pm, Fri.-Sat. midnight-4am.) **Louis' Family Restaurant,** 286 Brook St. (861-5225), has made the entire community its family with friendly service. Students swear by the prices and donate artwork for the walls. Try the #1 special: two eggs, homefries, toast, and coffee for $2.30 (open daily 5:30am-3pm).

Sights The most notable historic sights in Providence cluster around the 350-year-old neighborhood around **College Hill. Brown University,** established in 1764, includes several 18th-century buildings and provides the best information about the area. The Office of Admissions, housed in the historic **Carliss-Brackett House,** 45 Prospect St. (863-2378), gives free hour-long walking tours of the campus (tours daily 10, 11am, 1, 3, and 4pm; office open Mon.-Fri. 8am-4pm). In addition to founding Rhode Island, Roger Williams founded the *first* **First Baptist Church of America,** 75 N. Main St. (454-3418), built in 1775 (open Mon.-Fri. 9am-4pm; free). Down the hill, the **Rhode Island State Capitol** (277-2357) supports the fourth largest free-standing marble dome in the world. (Free guided tours Mon.-Tues. and Thurs. 10 and 11am; reserve a spot months in advance. Free self-guide booklets available in room 218. Open Mon.-Fri. 8:30am-4:30pm.)

The nearby **RISD Museum of Art,** 224 Benefit St. (454-6500), gathers a fine collection of Greek, Roman, Asian, and Impressionist art, as well as a gigantic 10th-century Japanese Buddha. (Open Wed.-Sat. noon-5pm; Sept.-June Tues.-Wed. and Fri.-Sat. 10:30am-5pm, Thurs. noon-8pm, Sun. 2-5pm. $2, seniors $1, ages 5-18 50¢.) The New England textile industry was born in 1793 when Samuel Slater used plans smuggled out of Britain to build the first water-powered factory in America. The **Slater Mill Historic Site** (725-8638), on Roosevelt Ave. in Pawtucket, preserves the fabric heritage with operating machinery. The mill must be seen on a tour that leaves roughly every two hours. (Open June-Oct. Tues.-Sat. 10am-5pm, Sun. 1-5pm; March-June and Nov.-Dec. Sat.-Sun. 1-5pm. $6, under 12 $5.)

Entertainment and Nightlife The nationally acclaimed **Trinity Repertory Company,** 201 Washington St. (351-4242), offers $10 student rush tickets two hours before performances, except on Saturday (tickets $24-32). For splashier productions, contact the **Providence Performing Arts Center,** 220 Weybosset St. (421-2787), which hosts a variety of concerts and Broadway musicals. The **Cable Car Cinema and Café,** 204 S. Main St. (272-3970), shows artsy and foreign films in a kinder, gentler setting—recline on couches instead of regular seats (tickets $6).

If you're in the mood for a little hardball, check out the **Pawtucket Red Sox** (AAA farm team for their Boston big brothers) April-Aug. in Pawtucket's **McCoy Stadium,** 1 Columbus Ave. (724-7300; box seats $6, seniors and under 12 $5; general admission $4/$3). Stock cars race at **Seekonk Speedway,** 1756 Fall River Ave. (336-8488), a few mi. east on Rte. 6 in Massachusetts ($15, under 13 $5).

Read the free *New Paper* (distributed Thurs.), the "Weekend" section of the *Friday Providence Journal,* or the *Providence Phoenix* for film, theater, and nightlife listings. Brownies, townies, and RISDs rock the night away at several hot spots throughout town. Mingle with the local artist community at **AS220,** 115 Empire St. (831-9327), a café/bar/gallery/performance space popular with local artists. (Cover $2-5. Open daily 11am-1am. Second floor gallery open Mon.-Fri. 11am-4pm, Sat. 1-4pm. Free.) **The Living Room,** 23 Rathbone St. (521-5200), hosts both dancing and live alternative bands (open Mon.-Thurs. 8pm-1am, Fri.-Sun. 8pm-2am). **Club Baby-head,** 73 Richmond St. (421-1698), is "loud, dark, and dirty"—what more could you ask for in an alternative club? The gay community favors **Gerardo's,** 1 Franklin Sq. (274-5560; cover Thurs.-Sat. $3; open Sun.-Thurs. 4pm-1am, Fri.-Sat. 4pm-2am).

■ Newport

Money has always found its way into Newport. Once supported by slave trade profits, the town later became the summer home of society's elite and the site of some of the nation's most opulent mansions. The city's monied residents played the first game of polo in North America, hosted the America's Cup race for 35 years, and watched President Kennedy wed Jacqueline Bouvier. Today, the city attracts beautiful people (with deep pockets) from all over the world. For those with fewer funds, seasonal events such as the jazz and folk festivals are reason enough to visit. Keep in mind, though, that there's a 25-year waiting period to get a slip at the marina.

Practical Information The place to start any visit to Newport is the **Newport County Convention and Visitors Bureau,** 23 America's Cup Ave. (849-8048 or 800-326-6030), in the Newport Gateway Center. This fantastic visitors center offers exhibits on the town's history, and the *Best-Read Guide Newport* and *Newport This Week* (open Sun.-Thurs. 9am-5pm, Fri.-Sat. 9am-6pm). **Bonanza Buses** (846-1820) depart from the center, as do the buses of **Rhode Island Public Transit Authority (RIPTA)** (847-0209; open daily 4:30am-8:30pm). RIPTA routes run daily 10am-7pm. Fare, generally 85¢, is free on Route #59 Mon.-Fri. 9am-3pm and 6-7pm, and all day on weekends. RIPTA also heads north to Providence (1hr., $2.50) and points on Rte. 114. Rent bikes at **Ten Speed Spokes,** 18 Elm St. (847-5609)—surprisingly, there are no 10-speeds. (Mountain bikes $5 per hr., $25 per day. Must have credit card and photo ID. Open Mon.-Sat. 9:30am-6pm, Sun. 9:30am-5pm.) **Emergency:** 911. Newport's **post office:** 320 Thames St. (847-2329), opposite Perry Mill Market (open Mon.-Fri. 8:30am-5pm, Sat. 9am-1pm). **ZIP code:** 02840. **Area code:** 401.

Accommodations, Camping, and Food Guest houses account for the bulk of Newport's accommodations. Most offer a bed and continental breakfast with colonial intimacy. Those willing to share a bathroom or forego a sea view might find a double for $65; singles are almost nonexistent. Be warned that many hotels and guest houses book solid two months in advance for summer weekends. Fortunately for the budget traveler Newport is blessed with a **Motel 6,** 249 JT Connel Hwy. (848-0600), offering clean, comfortable rooms at equally comfortable prices (singles $30-40, doubles $6 more). **Campsites** await at **Fort Getty Recreation Area** (423-7264), on Conanicut Island. Walk to the nearby Fox Hill Salt Marsh for great birdwatching. (100 trailer sites; 20 year-round. 15-18 tent sites. Showers and beach access. Sites $17, hookup $22.)

Despite what you might expect, cheap food *does* exist in Newport. Most of Newport's restaurants line up on **Thames St.** A booth and some solid food beckon you to the **Franklin Spa,** 229 Spring St. Try the banana pancakes ($4) or lunch on the cajun chicken ($4; open Mon.-Sat. 6:30am-3pm, Sun. 6:30am-2pm). **Dry Dock Seafood,** 448 Thames St. (847-3974), fries 'em and serves 'em with a minimum of fuss (entrees $6-11; open daily 11am-10pm). Shack up with some choice mollusks at **Flo's Clam Shack,** 4 Wave Ave. (847-8141), across from Newport Beach, or enjoy the clam product of your choice (fried clams $9) alongside a severely incapacitated lobster boat labeled the *S.S. Minnow* (open Thurs.-Sun. 11am-9pm).

Sights Newport takes "keeping up with the Joneses" to new heights. The Jones in question, George Noble Jones, built the first "summer cottage" here in 1839, thereby kicking off an extravagant string of palatial summer estates. The different mansions are maintained and managed by different organizations; different tour options can be found at the visitors center. A self-guided walking tour or a guided tour by the **Preservation Society of Newport,** 424 Bellevue Ave. (847-1000; open Mon.-Fri. 9am-5pm), will allow you to ogle at the extravagance; purchase tickets at any mansion daily 10am-5pm. The 1765 **Wanton-Lyman Hazard House,** 17 Broadway (846-0813), the oldest standing house in Newport, has been restored in different period styles (open mid-June to Labor Day Thurs.-Sat. 10am-4pm, Sun. 1-4pm; $4). The father of William Mayes, a notorious Red Sea pirate, opened the **White Horse Tavern** (849-3600), on Marlborough and Farewell St., as a tavern in 1687, making it the oldest continuously operated drinking establishment in the country (beer $3-4). The oldest synagogue in the U.S., the beautifully restored Georgian **Touro Synagogue,** 85 Touro St. (847-4794), dates back to 1763. (Visits by free tour only. Tours mid-June to July 3 Sun. 1 and 2pm; July 4-Labor Day tours Sun.-Fri. every ½hr. 10am-4pm; call for off season tour schedule.) Die-hard tennis fans will feel right at home in Newport, where the newly renovated **Tennis Hall of Fame,** 194 Bellevue Ave. (849-3990), hosts grass court tournaments and dedicates a museum to the game (open daily 9:30am-5pm; $6, under 16 $3, family $12).

Newport's gorgeous beaches are frequently as crowded as the streets. The most popular, **First Beach** (848-6491), or Easton's Beach, on Memorial Blvd., features enchanting old beach houses and a carousel (open Memorial Day-Labor Day daily 8:30am-4pm; parking $8, weekends $10). **Fort Adams State Park** (847-2400), south of town on Ocean Dr. 2½ mi. from Gateway Center, lets visitors take advantage of showers, picnic areas, and two fishing piers. (Entrance booth open Mon.-Fri. 7:30am-4pm, Sat.-Sun. 7:30am-6pm; park open sunrise to sunset. $4 per car entrance fee.) Good beaches also line Little Compton, Narragansett, and the shore between Watch Hill and Point Judith; for more details, consult the free *Ocean State Beach Guide,* available at the visitors center.

Entertainment In July and August, Newport gives lovers of classical, folk, and jazz each a festival to call their own. The oldest and best-known jazz festival in the world, the **Newport Jazz Festival** (847-3700, after May) has seen the likes of Duke Ellington and Count Basie; bring your beach chairs and coolers to Fort Adams State Park to join the fun in mid-August (Sat.-Sun. tickets $33, under 12 $15). The **Newport Music Festival** (846-1133; box office 849-0700), July 12-27 in 1997, attracts pianists, violinists, and other classical musicians from around the world for two weeks of concerts in the ballrooms and on the lawns of the mansions. The next two years will feature the "Beethoveniad"—a major retrospective of Beethoven's works. (Box office open daily 9am-6pm; tickets $15-40.) In August, folksingers such as Joan Baez and the Indigo Girls entertain at the legendary **Newport Folk Festival** (June-Aug. 847-3709), which runs two days, noon to dusk, rain or shine (tickets $28).

Newport's nightlife is easy to find. By the water, **Pelham East,** 2 Pelham St. (849-3888), at the corner of Thames, books bands for straight rock 'n' roll (live music nightly; cover Fri.-Sat. $5; open daily noon-1am). For an alternative scene, hop over to **Señor Frogg's,** 108 William St. (849-4747), across from the Tennis Hall of Fame (cover varies; open Wed.-Thurs. 8:30am-1pm, Fri.-Sun. 5pm-1am). **Bad Bob's** (848-9840) rocks the boat at Waite's Wharf with a DJ and live bands playing rock, soul, and reggae (cover $1-7; open June to mid.-Sept. Fri.-Mon. 7pm-midnight).

■ Near Newport: Block Island

A popular daytrip 10 mi. southeast of Newport in the Atlantic, sand-blown **Block Island** possesses an untamed natural beauty. One quarter of the island is protected open space; local conservationists hope to increase that to 50%. From Old Harbor where the ferry lets you off, a 4-mi. hike or bike ride brings you to the **National**

Wildlife Refuge, a great spot for a picnic. Two miles south of Old Harbor, the **Mohegan Bluffs** invite the adventurous, cautious, and strong to wind their way down to the Atlantic waters 200 ft. below. High in the cliffs, the **Southeast Lighthouse** has warned fog-bound fisherfolk since 1875; its beacon shines the brightest of any on the Atlantic coast.

The **Block Island Chamber of Commerce** (466-2982) welcomes you at the ferry dock in Old Harbor Drawer D, Block Island (open daily 10am-4pm; mid-Oct. to mid-May Mon-Sat. 10am-4pm). Rhode Island rest stop info centers supply the free *Block Island Travel Planner.* **Cycling** is the ideal way to explore the tiny (7mi. by 3mi.) island; the **Old Harbor Bike Shop** (466-2029), to the left of the ferry exit, rents just about anything on wheels (mountain bikes $4 per hr., $20 per day; mopeds $15/$50, license required. Cars $60 per day; 20¢ per mi. Must be 21 with credit card. Insurance optional; $3 per day for mopeds, $10 per day for cars. Open daily 9:30am-7pm.) The **Interstate Navigation Co.** (783-4613) provides year-round **ferry service** to Block Island from Point Judith, RI (8-10 per day, off season 1-3 per day, 1¼hr., $6.60, ages 5-11 $3.15, cars by reservation $20.25, bikes $1.75), and summer service from Newport, RI (late June to early Sept. 1 per day, 2hr., $6.45) and New London, CT (mid-June to mid-Sept. 1 per day, 2hr., $13.50). If possible, leave from Galilee State Pier in Point Judith for the most frequent, cheapest, and shortest ride. **Coast Guard:** 466-2462.

The island does not permit camping; make it a daytrip unless you're willing to shell out $60 or more for a room in a guest house. Most restaurants hover near the ferry dock in Old Harbor; several cluster at New Harbor one mi. inland.

Connecticut

Connecticut, the third smallest state in the Union, resembles a patchwork quilt, stitched from industrialized centers (like Hartford and New Haven), serene New England villages, and lush woodland beauty. Perhaps it is this diversity that attracted such famous residents as Mark Twain, Harriet Beecher Stowe, Noah Webster, and Eugene O'Neill, and inspired the birth of the American Impressionist movement and the American musical—both Connecticut originals. Home to Yale University and the nation's first law school, Connecticut has an equally rich intellectual history. This doesn't mean that the people of Connecticut don't know how to let their hair down—hey, this is the state that brought us the lollipop, the three-ring circus, the frisbee, and one of the largest casinos in the Western Hemisphere.

PRACTICAL INFORMATION

Capital: Hartford.
Connecticut Vacation Center: 865 Brook St., Rocky Hill 06067 (800-282-6863). **Department of Environmental Protection-State Parks Division,** 203-424-3015. Call for an application for a state parks and forests camping permit and brochures describing sites. Open Mon.-Fri. 9am-4:30pm. **Connecticut Forest and Park Association,** 16 Meriden Rd., Rockfall 06481 (203-346-2372), has outdoor activities info.
Time Zone: Eastern. **Postal Abbreviation:** CT.
Sales Tax: 6%.

■ Hartford

The citizens of Connecticut's capital have not always been law-abiding. In 1687, the English governor demanded the surrender of the charter that Charles II had granted Hartford 25 years before. Obstinate, Hartfordians hid the charter in a tree trunk until the infuriated governor returned to England. Today, a plaque marks the spot at Charter Oak Place. Sometime over these last three centuries, Hartford has grown into the world's insurance capital; the city's skyline is shaped by architectural wonders financed by some of the larger firms, including the monolithic oval of the Boat Building (America's first two-sided building).

Practical Information Hartford marks the intersection of I-91 and I-84. The **Greater Hartford Convention and Visitors Bureau,** 1 Civic Center Plaza (728-6789 or 800-446-7811), and on Main St. in the Pavilion (522-6766), offer dozens of maps, booklets, and guides to local resorts, campgrounds, and historical sights (open Mon.-Fri. 10am-6pm, Sat. 10am-5pm). For info on the streets, look for one of the red-capped and khaki-clad Hartford guides, all of whom are knowledgable about the history, services, events, and geography of the city. (Guides on duty Mon.-Sat. from mid-morning until late night.) In front of the Old State House, **Connecticut Transit's Information Center** (525-9181), at State and Market St., doles out helpful down-town maps and public transportation info (basic bus fare 95¢). Union Place is home to **Amtrak** (727-1776 or 800-872-7245), which runs eight trains daily both north and south (office open daily 5:30am-9pm), and **Peter Pan Trailways** (800-237-8747), which connects to New York (2½hr., $17) and Boston (2½hr., $16) 10 times daily (ticket office open daily 5:45am-10pm). **Greyhound** (800-231-2222), at Union Place, buses to New York (16 per day, 2½hr., $14) and Boston (10 per day, 2½hr., $14; open daily 7am-10:30pm). Hartford's **post office:** 141 Weston St. (524-6001; open Mon.-Fri. 7am-6pm, Sat. 7am-3pm). **ZIP code:** 06101. **Area code:** 860.

Accommodations, Food, and Nightlife The excellent **Mark Twain Hostel (HI-AYH),** 131 Tremont St. (523-7255), offers great accommodations near the center of town ($12, nonmembers $15). In the heart of downtown, the **YMCA,** 160 Jewell St. (522-4183), offers small, dorm-like rooms at reasonable rates, including use of a gym, pool, and racquetball courts, as well as access to a cafeteria. (Singles $16.60, with private bath $20.60. $5 key deposit. No reservations accepted. Check-in 5am-midnight, check-out noon.) Just north of Hartford, the sleepy **Windsor Home Hostel (HI-AYH)** (683-2847) resides in Connecticut's oldest town. Hostelers stay in beds in rooms with 70s decor and share a bath, common area, and kitchen facilities. ($14, nonmembers $17. Reservations required; directions given upon confirmation.) For camping enthusiasts who don't mind a 30-minute drive out of the city, **Burr Pond State Park** (379-0172), five minutes north of Torrington off Rte. 8 on Burr Mountain Rd., provides 40 wooded sites ($10) with showers and swimming (registration 8am-sunset).

Many restaurants hover within a few blocks of the downtown area. The **Municipal Café,** 485 Main St. (278-4844; 527-5044 for entertainment info), at Elm, is a popular and friendly place to catch a good breakfast or lunch. The breakfast special means bacon, ham, or sausage with two eggs, toast, coffee or tea for $3.50. Hot dinners go for $6. At night, the "Muni" is big, big, big on the local music scene. (Bands Wed.-Thurs. and Sun. 8pm-1am, Fri.-Sat. 8pm-2am. Open daily for breakfast and lunch 7am-3:30pm, bar menu after 8pm.) **The Hartford Brewery, Ltd.,** 35 Pearl St. (246-2337), one of Connecticut's only brew-pubs, serves up sandwiches ($5-7), burgers ($7), and six freshly brewed beers. Tours available by appointment. (Open Mon.-Thurs. 11:30am-1am, Fri. 11:30am-2am, Sat. noon-2am.) Downtown, Hartford's oldest bar, the **Russian Lady,** 191 Ann St. (525-3003), has original antiques, from burnished wood counters to Tiffany lamps. Live modern music rocks this unlikely setting and the overpopulated mosh pit upstairs. (Cover for second floor $3-4. Open Wed.-Thurs. 5pm-1am, Fri. 5pm-2am, Sat. 7pm-2am, Sun. 7pm-1am.)

Sights Designed by Charles Bullfinch in 1796, the gold-domed **Old State House,** 800 Main St. (522-6766), housed the state government until 1914 (open Mon.-Fri. 10am-4pm, Sat. 10am-3pm). A block or so west, park 'n' ride at **Bushnell Park,** supposedly the first public American park, on one of the country's few extant hand-crafted merry-go-rounds. The **Bushnell Park Carousel** (246-7739), built in 1914, spins 48 horses and two lovers' chariots to the tunes of a 1925 Wurlitzer Organ. (Open May-Aug. Tues.-Sun. 11am-5pm; April and Sept. Sat.-Sun. 11am-5pm. 50¢.) Overlooking the park, the gold-domed (isn't everything?) **State Capitol,** 210 Capitol Ave. (240-0222), houses Lafayette's camp bed and a war-ravaged tree trunk from the Civil War Battle of Chickamauga, among other historic artifacts. Free one-hour tours begin at the west entrance of the neighboring **Legislative Office Building;** look for free parking behind the building. (Tours Mon.-Fri. 9:15am-1:15pm, Sat. tours from the capitol's SW entrance 10:15am-2:15pm.)

The **Wadsworth Athenaeum,** 600 Main St. (278-2670), the oldest public art museum in the country, has absorbing collections of contemporary and Baroque art, including Monet, Renoir, Degas, and one of only three Caravaggios in the United States. (Tours Thurs. at 1pm and Sat.-Sun. noon-2pm. Open Tues.-Sun. 11am-5pm. $5, seniors and students $4, under 13 free; free Thurs., and Sat. before noon.)

Lovers of American literature won't want to miss the engaging tours at **Mark Twain House,** 351 Farmington Ave. (493-6411), and **Harriet Beecher Stowe House,** 79 Forest St. (525-9317), both just west of the city center on Farmington Ave.; from the Old State House take any "Farmington Ave." bus east. The rambling, richly colored Mark Twain Mansion housed the Missouri-born author for 17 years, during which Twain composed his masterpiece *Huckleberry Finn.* (Open Mon.-Sat. 9:30am-4pm, Sun. noon-4pm; Oct.-May closed Tues. $7.50, seniors $7, ages 6-12 $3.50.) Harriet Beecher Stowe lived next door on Nook Farm from 1873, after the publication of *Uncle Tom's Cabin,* until her death. (Open Mon.-Sat. 9:30am-4pm, Sun. noon-4pm; Jan.-Nov. closed Mon. $6.50, seniors $6, ages 6-16 $2.75.)

■ New Haven

Simultaneously university town and depressed city, New Haven has gained a reputation as something of a battleground—academic types and a working-class population live uneasily side by side. Yalies tend to stick to their campus, widening the rift between town and gown. Every facet of life in the city, from architecture to safety, reflects this difference. While most of New Haven continues to decay, Yale has begun to renovate its neo-Gothic buildings and convert its concrete sidewalks to brick, and has largely succeeded in creating a young and thriving collegiate coffeehouse, bar, and bookstore scene around the university.

Practical Information New Haven lies at the intersection of I-95 and I-91, 40 mi. from Hartford. The **Greater New Haven Convention and Visitors Bureau,** 1 Long Wharf Dr. (777-8550 or 800-332-7829), provides free maps and info on current events (open Mon.-Fri. 8:30am-5pm). For a weekly recorded events update, call 498-5050, ext. 1310. The **Yale Visitors Center,** 149 Elm St. (432-2300), facing the Green, distributes free campus maps, a $1 walking guide, bus maps, and *The Yale,* a guide to undergraduate life ($3.50). (Free 1-hr. tours Mon.-Fri. 10:30am and 2pm, Sat.-Sun. 1:30pm. Open Mon.-Fri. 9am-4:45pm, Sat.-Sun. 10am-4pm.) **Amtrak** (786-2888 or 800-872-7245), Union Station on Union Ave., runs out of a newly renovated station. Be careful; the area is unsafe at night. (To: New York City $25; Boston $31; Washington, D.C. $78; Mystic $18. Ticket office open daily 6am-10pm.) Also at Union Station, **Greyhound** (772-2470 or 800-231-2222) runs frequent service to New York ($13), Boston ($16), Providence ($16), and New London ($12). The ticket office is open daily 7:30am-8pm. New Haven's **area code:** 203.

At night, don't wander too far from the immediate downtown and campus areas; surrounding sections are notably less safe. New Haven is laid out in nine squares. Between **Yale University** and City Hall, **Green,** the central square, provides a pleasant escape from the hassles of city life. A small but thriving business district of bookstores, boutiques, cheap sandwich places, and other services catering to students and professors borders the Green.

Accommodations and Food Inexpensive accommodations are sparse in New Haven; the hunt quickens around Yale Parents Weekend (mid-Oct.) and commencement (early June). **Hotel Duncan,** 1151 Chapel St. (787-1273), contains the oldest manually operated elevator in the state, as well as plush rooms with cable TV and mini fridges (singles $40, doubles $60; reservations recommended on weekends). Trusty **Motel 6** (469-0343) waits like an old friend at Exit 8 off I-91 (singles $52, doubles $58). **Bed & Breakfast/Nutmeg,** 222 Girard Ave. (236-6698), in W. Hartford, reserves doubles ($35-45) in New Haven B&Bs (open Mon.-Fri. 9am-5pm). **Hammonasset Beach** (245-1817), 20 minutes from town, offers camping as close as it gets (sites $12).

The university's coffee-and-cigarette set haunt the mural-clad **Daily Caffe,** 316 Elm St. (776-5063), a psychedelic joint opened by a Yale alum. Sandwiches start at $3.50. Top off your meal with awesome chocolate mousse cake ($3). (Open Mon.-Sat. 7am-midnight, Sat.-Sun. 9am-midnight; Sept.-May Mon.-Sat. 7am-1am, Sat.-Sun. 9am-1am.) **Rainbow Gardens,** 1022 Chapel St. (777-2390), is a shiny, happy, veggie-friendly hangout with heart-shaped decor, good service, and great sandwiches ($4-7; open Mon.-Thurs. 9am-8pm, Fri. 9am-9pm, Sat. 10am-9pm, Sun. 10am-7pm).

Sights Modeling their work on the colleges of Oxford, architects took great pains to artificially age the buildings on Yale's campus. Bricks were buried in different soils to give them that tarnished-by-the-centuries look, windows were shattered, and acid was sprayed on the facades. All this to give Yale that wonderful going-to-shambles aura. James Gambel Rodgers, a firm believer in the sanctity of printed material, designed **Sterling Memorial Library,** 120 High St. (432-1775). The building looks much like a monastery; even the telephone booths are shaped like confessionals. Rodgers spared no expense in making Yale's library look "authentic," even decapitating the figurines on the library's exterior to replicate those at Oxford. (Open Mon.-Wed. and Fri. 8:30am-5pm, Thurs. 8:30am-10pm, Sat. 8:30am-5pm.)

The creator of the massive **Beinecke Rare Book and Manuscript Library,** 121 Wall St. (432-2977), decided to skip the windows. Instead, this intriguing modern structure is paneled with Vermont marble cut thin enough to be translucent; supposedly its volumes (including one Gutenberg Bible and an extensive collection of William Carlos Williams's writings) could survive a nuclear war. (Open Mon.-Fri. 8:30am-5pm, Sat. 10am-5pm.) On New Haven's own Wall St., between High and Yale St., take a moment to notice the Neo-Gothic gargoyles perched on the **Law School** building which portray cops and robbers.

Open since 1832, the **Yale University Art Gallery,** 1111 Chapel St. (432-0600), on the corner of York, claims to be the oldest university art museum in the Western Hemisphere. The university holds especially notable collections of John Trumbull paintings and Italian Renaissance works, as well as several of Edward Hopper's finest oil paintings. (Open Sept.-July Tues.-Sat. 10am-4:45pm, Sun. 2-4:45pm. Free.) The **Peabody Museum of Natural History,** 170 Whitney Ave. (432-5050), off I-91 at Exit 3, houses Rudolph F. Zallinger's Pulitzer Prize-winning mural portraying the North American continent as it appeared 70 to 350 million years ago. Other exhibits include a dinosaur hall displaying the skeleton of a brontosaurus. (Open Mon.-Sat. 10am-5pm, Sun. noon-5pm. $5, over 64 and ages 3-15 $3.)

Entertainment and Nightlife Pick up a free copy of *The Advocate* to find out what's up in New Haven. Once a famous testing ground for Broadway-bound plays, New Haven's thespian community has scaled down in recent years. The **Schubert Theater,** 247 College St. (562-5666 or 800-228-6622), a significant figure in the town's on-stage tradition, still mounts shows (box office open Mon.-Fri. 10am-5pm, Sat. 11am-3pm). The **Yale Repertory Theater,** 222 York St. (432-1234), boasts such illustrious alums as Meryl Streep, Glenn Close, and James Earl Jones and continues to produce excellent shows (open Oct.-May; tickets $10-30; ½-price student rush tickets on the day of a show). In summer, the city hosts concerts on the Green (787-8956), including **New Haven Symphony** concerts (865-0831; box office 776-1444; open Mon.-Fri. 9am-5pm).

Toad's Place, 300 York St. (562-5694; 624-8623 for recorded info), has hosted gigs by Bob Dylan and the Stones, and still stages great live shows. (Box office open daily 11am-6pm; buy tickets at the bar after 8pm. Bar open Sun.-Thurs. 8pm-1am, Fri.-Sat. 8pm-2am, depending on shows.) The **Anchor Bar,** 272 College St. (865-1512), off the Green, holds its ground with the area's best jukebox (bottled beer $2.50-3; open Mon.-Thurs. 11:30am-1am, Fri.-Sat. 11:30am-2am). Yalie jocks and fratboys get drunk on $2.75 beer at the **Union League Café,** 1032 Chapel St. (562-4299; open daily 5:30pm-2am). **Bar,** 254 Crown St. (495-8924), is anything but generic—*the* place for drinking is also *the* gay hotspot on Tuesdays, and they make their own beer and brick oven pizzas (open Mon.-Thurs. 4pm-1am, Fri.-Sat. 4pm-2am, Sun. 1pm-1am).

■ Mystic and the Connecticut Coast

Connecticut's coastal towns along the Long Island Sound were busy seaports in the days of Melville and Richard Henry Dana, but the dark, musty inns filled with tattooed sailors swapping sea journeys have been consigned to history. Today, the coast is important mainly as a resort and sailing base. **Mystic Seaport** (572-5315), 1 mi. south on Rte. 27 from I-95 at Exit 95, commemorates the region's nautical past with a maritime museum, tall ships, restored homes, shops, arts and crafts collections, and locals in funny costumes (open daily 9am-7pm; 2-day admission $16, ages 6-15 $8, under 5 free). Seaport admission also entitles you to take a **Mystic River** cruise offered by **Sabino Charters** (572-5351) for a few dollars more. (30-min. trips mid-May to early Oct. daily on the hr. 11am-4pm. $3.50, ages 6-15 $2.50.) The 1½-hr. evening excursions do not require museum admission. (Runs mid-May to late Sept. daily 5pm; June 30-early Sept. Fri.-Sat. also 7pm. $8.50, ages 6-15 $7.)

New London is the site of the **U.S. Coast Guard Academy** (444-8270), a five-minute drive up Rte. 32. Take a free tour through its museum and, when it's in port, the cadet training vessel *U.S.S. Eagle* (444-8511; open May-Oct. Mon.-Wed. and Fri. 9am-4:30pm, Thurs. 9am-8pm, Sat. 10am-5pm, Sun. noon-5pm). One of Mystic's oft missed treasures is the great **Mystic Drawbridge,** off Main St. It was built in 1922 and is one of only a few working drawbridges east of the Mississippi. (May-Oct. every 15 min. past the hr. 7:15am-7:15pm.)

The **Tourist and Information Center,** Building 1d, Olde Mysticke Village, 06355 (536-1641), in **Olde Mysticke Village,** has oodles of info on area sights and accommodations (open Mon.-Sat. 9am-6:30pm, Sun. 9am-6pm). It may be difficult to secure cheap lodgings in tourist-infested Mystic; **Stonington** makes a more affordable base from which to explore the shore. If you plan to splurge on the pricey offerings in Mystic itself, call well ahead for reservations. The only option in Mystic is **Seaport Campgrounds** (536-4044), on Rte. 184, 3 mi. from Mystic. (Tent sites for 2 adults and 2 children $25.50, with water and electricity $28.50; $4 per additional person; over 60 10% discount. Open mid-April to late Oct.) In Stonington, the **Sea Breeze Motel,** 812 Stonington Rd. (535-2843), rents big, clean rooms with A/C. (Singles $50, Fri.-Sun. $85; $10 per additional person; rates much lower in winter.) **Cove Ledge Resort Motel** (599-4130), Whewell Circle, has hardwood-floored rooms with A/C, TV, and an outdoor pool. (Singles $60, with microwave and fridge $80, doubles $70; Fri.-Sat. $5 more. Rates lower in winter.)

Though most people think of seafood when they think of coastal Connecticut, Mystic's most renowned eatery is **Mystic Pizza,** 56 W. Main St. (536-3737 or 536-3700). Since the popular 80s movie, loved by MC and MR, was filmed nearby, the pizza place has remodeled its façade to resemble the Hollywood set. (Unremarkable slices $2; small pizza $5; large $9.25. Open daily 10am-midnight.) **Trader Jack's,** 14 Holmes St. (572-8550), near downtown, pours $2 domestic beers. Happy hour (Mon.-Fri. 5-7pm) will have you smiling with ½-priced appetizers and 50¢ off all drinks. Frequent live music (no cover) will spice up your burger ($4.50). (Food daily 5pm-midnight. Last call for drinks Sun.-Thurs. 1am, Fri.-Sat. 2am.) **Area code:** 860.

MID-ATLANTIC

Ranging up from the almost-Southern state of Virginia through the Eastern seaboard to New York, the mid-Atlantic states claim not only a large slice of the nation's population, but several of the nation's major historical, political, and economic centers. This region is home to every capital the U.S. has ever known; first settled in Philadelphia, PA, the U.S. government moved through Princeton, NJ, Annapolis, MD, Trenton, NJ, and New York City, before coming to rest in Washington, D.C. During the Civil War, the mid-Atlantic even hosted the capital of the Confederacy, Richmond, VA. The legislative heart of the U.S., the area witnessed some of the war's bloodiest fighting, as it had in the American Revolution; today, countless historical attractions mark every step in the struggles. In addition to the region's central place in government and finance, two centuries of immigration have flooded the mid-Atlantic's shores to create a fun, crowded, ethnically diverse area which presents many of the challenges of preserving cultural variety while striving for national unity.

Though urban centers (and suburban sprawl) cover much of the mid-Atlantic, the great outdoors have survived. The celebrated Appalachian Trail meanders through the area. In northern New York, the Adirondacks make up the largest park in the U.S. outside of Alaska. Campers prance among pinecones in the untouched wilds of Pennsylvania's Allegheny Mountains, and wildlife refuges scattered along the coast protect birdlife and wild ponies alike.

New York

Surrounded by the beauty of New York's landscape, you may find it difficult to remember that smog and traffic exist. The cities that dot upstate New York have a sweet natural flavor that holds its own against the seedy core of the Big Apple. Whether in the crassly commercial Niagara Falls, the idyllic Finger Lakes, or in Albany (Albany?) you will have little doubt that nature is king in upstate New York.

The City, on the other hand, is an entirely different kettle of fish. According to Ed Koch, former mayor of New York: "This rural America thing. It's a joke." New York City, the eighth most populated city in the world, would claim to be grander than the other seven. With a diverse population, a spectacular skyline, towering financial power, and a range of cultural enterprises, New Yorkers may have a point.

PRACTICAL INFORMATION

Capital: Albany.
Division of Tourism: 1 Commerce Plaza, Albany 12245 (518-474-4116 or 800-225-5697). Operators available Mon.-Fri. 8:30am-5pm; voice mail system all other times. Excellent, comprehensive *I Love NY Travel Guide* includes disabled access and resource information. **New York State Office of Parks and Recreation and Historic Preservation,** Empire State Plaza, Agency Bldg. 1, Albany 12238-0001 (518-474-0456), has literature on camping and biking. The **Bureau of Preserve Protection and Management** of the **Division of Lands and Forests,** DEC, 50 Wolf Rd., Room 438, Albany 12233-4255 (518-457-7433) has information on hiking and canoeing.
Time Zone: Eastern. **Postal Abbreviation:** NY
Sales Tax: 8.25%.

Sea Breeze Notel $75 + Tax
Mon + Tues

■ New York City

Nowhere in the nation is the rhythm of urban life more hammering than in New York City. Crammed into tiny spaces, millions of people find themselves in constant confrontation. Perhaps because of this crush, the denizens of New York are some of the loudest, pushiest, most neurotic, and loneliest in the world, although they may also be the most vibrant, energetic, and talented as well. Much that is unique, attractive, awe-inspiring, and repulsive about the Big Apple is a function of the city's scale—too big, too heterogeneous, too jumbled, and too exciting.

In 1624, the Dutch West Indies Company founded a trading colony. Two years later, in the first of the city's shady transactions, Peter Minuit bought Manhattan from the natives for just under $24. As the early colonists were less than enthralled by Dutch rule, they put up only token resistance when the British invaded the settlement in 1664. By the late 1770s the city was an active port with a population of 20,000. New York's primary concern was maintaining its prosperity, and the city reacted apathetically to the emerging revolutionary cause. As a result, the new Continental Army understandably made no great efforts to protect New York, and she fell to the British in September 1776 and remained in their hands until late November 1783.

Throughout turmoil, New York continued to grow. By the 19th century, she had emerged as the nation's pre-eminent city. As space filled up, Manhattan went vertical to house the growing population streaming in from Western Europe. Immigrants hoping to escape famine, persecution, and political unrest faced the perils of the sea for the promise of America, landing on Ellis Island in New York Harbor. Post-WWII prosperity brought still more arrivals, especially African-Americans from the rural South and Hispanics from the Caribbean. By the 60s, crises in public transportation, education, and housing fanned the flames of ethnic tensions and fostered the rise of a criminal underclass. City officials raised taxes to improve services, but in the process drove away middle-class residents and corporations.

In the 80s, New York rebounded, but the tragically hip Wall Street of the 80s soon faded to a gray 90s malaise, and the city once again confronted old problems—too many people, too little money, and not enough kindness. The first African-American mayor, David Dinkins, was elected in 1989 on a platform of harmonious growth, but the "melting pot" of New York continued to burn, smolder, and belch. In 1993, new mayor Rudy Giuliani enacted strict new anti-crime measures that have both significantly reduced crime three years running and exacerbated racial tensions throughout the five boroughs. Still, there are signs of life and renewed commitment in the urban blightscape. In 1997, the words of former Mayor Ed Koch still ring true. "New York is not a problem," he declared, "New York is a stroke of genius."

For the ultimate coverage of New York City, see our city guide, *Let's Go: New York City*, available wherever fine books are sold.

PRACTICAL INFORMATION

Tourist Office: New York Convention and Visitors Bureau, 2 Columbus Circle (397-8222 or 484-1200), 59th St. and Broadway. Subway: #1, 9, A, B, C, or D to 59th St.-Columbus Circle. Multilingual staff helps with directions, hotel listings, entertainment ideas, safety tips, and descriptions of neighborhoods. Try to show up in person; the phone lines tend to be busy. Open Mon.-Fri. 9am-6pm, Sat.-Sun. and holidays 10am-3pm.

Police: 212-374-5000. Use this for inquiries that are not urgent. Open 24hr.

American Express: Multi-task agency providing tourists with traveler's checks, gift checks, cashing services, you name it. Branches in Manhattan include: **American Express Tower,** 200 Vesey St. (640-2000), near the World Financial Center (open Mon.-Fri. 9:30am-5:30pm); **Macy's Herald Square,** 151 W. 34th St. (695-8075), at Seventh Ave. inside Macy's (open Mon.-Sat. 10am-6pm); **150 E. 42nd St.** (687-3700), between Lexington and Third Ave. (open Mon.-Fri 9am-5pm); in **Bloomingdale's,** 59th St. and Lexington Ave. (705-3171; open Mon.-Sat. 10am-6pm); **822**

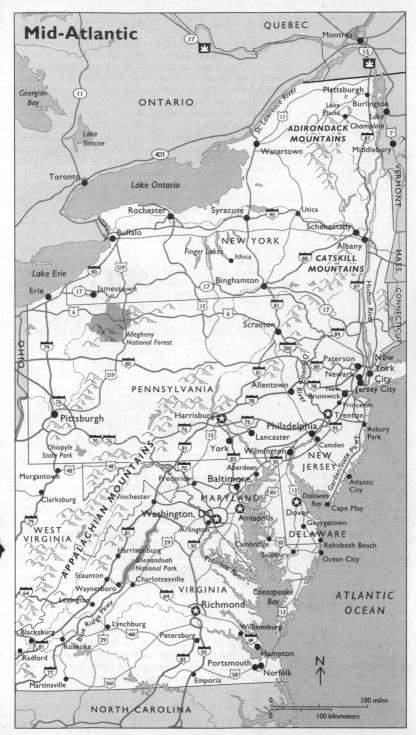

Mid-Atlantic

Lexington Ave. (758-6510), near 63rd St. (open Mon.-Fri. 9am-6pm, Sat. 10am-4pm).

Taxis: Most people in Manhattan hail yellow (licensed) cabs on the street: $2 base, 30¢ each one-fifth mi. or every 75 seconds; a 50¢ surcharge is levied from 8pm to 6am; passengers pay for all tolls. Don't forget to tip 15%. Ask for a receipt, which will have the taxi's ID number. This is necessary to trace lost articles or to make a complaint to the **Taxi Commission,** 221 W. 41st St. (221-TAXI/8294). For radio-dispatched cabs, check the Yellow Pages under "Taxicabs."

Car Rental: All agencies have min. age requirements and ask for deposits. Call in advance to reserve, especially near weekends. **Nationwide,** 220 E. 9th St. (867-1234), between Second and Third Ave. Reputable nationwide chain. Mid-sized domestic sedan $59 per day, $289 per week, 150 free mi. per day, 1000 free mi. per week. Open Mon.-Fri. 8am-6pm. Must be 23 with a major credit card.

Auto Transport Companies: New York serves as a major departure point. The length of time for application processing varies; these 2 process immediately. Nearly all agencies require references and a refundable cash deposit. **Dependable Car Services,** 801 E. Edgar Rd., Linden, NJ (840-6262 or 908-474-8080). Must be 21, have 3 personal references, and a valid license without major violations. $150-200 deposit. Open Mon.-Fri. 8:30am-4:30pm, Sat. 9am-1pm. **Auto Driveaway,** 264 W. 35th St., Suite 500 (967-2344); 33-70 Prince St., Flushing, Queens (718-762-3800). Must be 21, with 2 local references and a valid driver's license. $250 deposit, $10 application fee. Open Mon.-Fri. 9am-5pm.

Bicycle Rentals: Bike and Fitness, 242 E. 79th St. (249-9344), near Second Ave., rents 3-speeds for $3 per hr., $10.50 per day; mountain bikes and rollerblades $6 per hr., $21 per day. $40 for mountain bikes, plus driver's license and credit card. Overnight rentals ($8 plus cash deposit of $250). 2-hr. min. Open Mon.-Fri. 9:30am-8pm, Sat.-Sun. 7:30am-7pm. May-Oct. weekdays 10am-3pm and 7-10pm and from Fri. 7pm to Mon. 6am, Central Park closes its main loops to cars, allowing bicycles to rule its roads.

Help Lines: Crime Victim's Hotline, 577-7777. 24-hr. counseling and referrals. **Sex Crimes Report Line,** New York Police Dept., 267-7273. Open 24hr.

Walk-in Medical Clinic, 57 E. 34th St. (252-6000), between Park and Madison. Open Mon.-Fri. 8am-6pm, Sat. 10am-2pm. Affiliated with Beth Israel Hospital.

Emergency: 911.

Post Office: Central branch, 421 Eighth Ave. (967-8585; open Mon.-Fri. 8:30am-5pm), across from Madison Square Garden. Open 24hr. For General Delivery, mail to and use the entrance at 390 Ninth Ave. C.O.D.s, money orders, and passport applications are also processed at some branches. **ZIP code:** 10001. **Area codes:** 212 (Manhattan); 718 (Brooklyn, Bronx, Queens, Staten Island).

GETTING THERE

Plane Three airports service the New York Metro Region. **John F. Kennedy Airport (JFK)** (718-244-4444), 12 mi. from Midtown in southern Queens, is the largest, handling most international flights. **LaGuardia Airport** (718-533-3400), 6 mi. from Midtown in northwestern Queens, is the smallest, offering domestic flights and air shuttles. **Newark International Airport** (201-961-6000 or 201-762-5100), 12 mi. from Midtown in Newark, NJ, offers both domestic and international flights at better budget fares (though getting to and from Newark can be expensive).

JFK to midtown Manhattan can easily be covered by public transportation. Catch a brown and white JFK long-term parking lot bus from any airport terminal (every 15min.) to the **Howard Beach-JFK subway station,** where you can take the A train to the city (1hr.). Or you can take one of the city buses (Q10 or Q3; $1.50, exact change required) into Queens. The Q10 and Q3 connect with subway lines to Manhattan. Ask the bus driver where to get off, and make sure you know which subway line you want. The **Carey Airport Express** (718-632-0500), a private line, runs between JFK and Grand Central Station and the Port Authority Terminal (leaves every 30min. 5am-1am, 1hr., $13). A cab from JFK costs around $35-40.

LaGuardia can be reached from Manhattan two ways. If you have extra time and light luggage, you can take the MTA Q33 bus ($1.50, exact change or token) to the

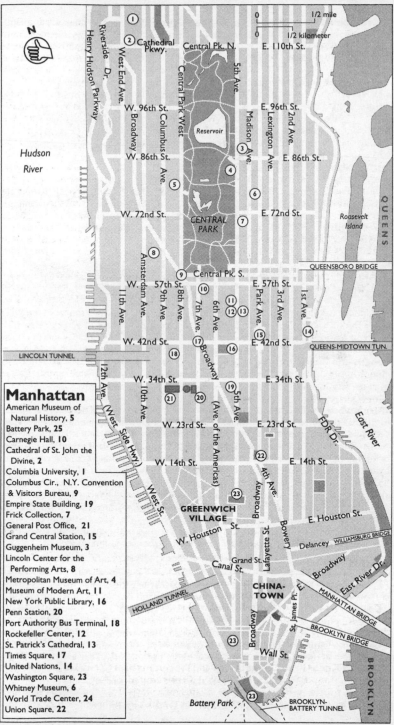

N

Hudson
River

① Cathedral
② Pkwy.
Cathedral
Central Pk. N.
E. 110th St.

0 ____ 1/2 mile
0 ____ 1/2 kilometer

Central Park West
Riverside Dr.
West End Ave.
Henry Hudson Parkway
Broadway
Columbus Ave.

W. 96th St.
E. 96th St.

Reservoir

W. 86th St.
5th Ave.
Madison Ave.
Lexington Ave.
2nd Ave.
③
E. 86th St.

④
⑤
⑥
W. 72nd St.
E. 72nd St.
⑦
CENTRAL
PARK

Roosevelt
Island

QUEENS

⑧

Amsterdam Ave.
11th Ave.

⑨ Central Pk. S.
QUEENSBORO BRIDGE

W. 57th St.
59th St.
8th Ave.
7th Ave.
6th Ave.
⑩ Carnegie
⑪ ⑫ ⑬
⑮
E. 57th St.
3rd Ave.
Park Ave.
1st Ave.

W. 42nd St.
⑰
⑯
⑱
E. 42nd St.
⑭
QUEENS-MIDTOWN TUN.

LINCOLN TUNNEL

12th Ave.
10th Ave.
West Side Hwy.

W. 34th St.
E. 34th St.
⑲
⑳ ㉑
Broadway
5th Ave.
(Ave. of the Americas)

W. 23rd St.
E. 23rd St.

FDR Dr.
East River

W. 14th St.
E. 14th St.
㉒

4th Ave.

㉓
GREENWICH
VILLAGE
E. Houston St.

W. Houston St.
Broadway
Lafayette St.
Bowery
Delancey
WILLIAMSBURG BRIDGE

Grand St.
Canal St.
East River Dr.

HOLLAND TUNNEL
CHINA-
TOWN
MANHATTAN BRIDGE

㉓
St. James Pl.
BROOKLYN BRIDGE
Broadway
Wall St.

BROOKLYN

㉓
Battery Park
BROOKLYN-
BATTERY TUNNEL

Manhattan
American Museum of
  Natural History, **5**
Battery Park, **25**
Carnegie Hall, **10**
Cathedral of St. John the
  Divine, **2**
Columbia University, **1**
Columbus Cir., N.Y. Convention
  & Visitors Bureau, **9**
Empire State Building, **19**
Frick Collection, **7**
General Post Office, **21**
Grand Central Station, **15**
Guggenheim Museum, **3**
Lincoln Center for the
  Performing Arts, **8**
Metropolitan Museum of Art, **4**
Museum of Modern Art, **11**
New York Public Library, **16**
Penn Station, **20**
Port Authority Bus Terminal, **18**
Rockefeller Center, **12**
St. Patrick's Cathedral, **13**
Times Square, **17**
United Nations, **14**
Washington Square, **23**
Whitney Museum, **6**
World Trade Center, **24**
Union Square, **22**

MID-ATLANTIC

74th St./Broadway/Roosevelt Ave./Jackson Hts. subway stop in Queens, and from there, take the #7, E, F, G or R train into Manhattan ($1.50). Allow at least 90 min. travel time. The second option, the Carey bus, stops at Grand Central Station and the Port Authority Terminal (every ½hr., 30min., $9). A cab from LaGuardia costs around $25.

Newark Airport to Manhattan takes about as long as from JFK. **New Jersey Transit (NJTA)** (201-762-5100 or 212-629-8767) runs a fast, efficient bus (NJTA #300) between the airport and Port Authority every 15 min. during the day, less often at night ($7). For the same fare, the **Olympia Trails Coach** (212-964-6233) travels between the airport and either Grand Central or the World Trade Center (every 20-30min. daily 5am-11pm; 25-60min. depending on traffic; $7).

Bus Greyhound (800-231-2222) grooves out of their major Northeastern hub, the **Port Authority Terminal,** 41st. St. and Eighth Ave. (435-7000; Subway: A, C, or E to 42nd St.-Port Authority). Be careful—with so many tourists, there are plenty of scam artists around. *This neighborhood is especially unsafe at night.* Avoid the terminal's bathrooms at all times. To: Boston (4½hr., $27); Philadelphia (2hr., $14); Washington, D.C. (4½hr., $27); Montréal (8hr., $65). **East Coast Explorer,** 245 Eighth Ave. (718-694-9667), offers budget full-day, scenic bus trips between New York, Boston, and Washington, D.C. (NYC to Boston $29, to Washington $32).

Train Train service in New York runs primarily through two stations. On the East side, **Grand Central Station,** 42nd St. and Park Ave. (Subway: #4, 5, 6, 7, or S to 42nd St./Grand Central), handles **Metro-North** (532-4900 or 800-638-7646) commuter lines to Connecticut and New York suburbs. Longer routes run from the West Side's **Penn Station,** 33rd St. and Eighth Ave. (Subway: #1, 2, 3, 9, A, C, or E to 34th St./Penn Station), courtesy of **Amtrak** (582-6875 or 800-872-7245), serving most major cities in the U.S., especially in the Northeast. (Washington, D.C. 4hr., $51). The **Long Island Railroad (LIRR)** (718-822-5477), and **NJ Transit** (201-762-5100) also chug from Penn Station. Nearby at 33rd St. and Sixth Ave., you can catch a **PATH** train to New Jersey (435-7000 or 800-234-7284, Mon.-Fri. 8am-5pm).

Car From New Jersey there are three ways to reach the city. The **George Washington Bridge,** which crosses the Hudson River into northern Manhattan, gives easy access to either Harlem River Dr. or the West Side Hwy. From the N.J. Turnpike you'll probably end up going through Weehawken, N.J. at the **Lincoln Tunnel,** which exits in Midtown in the West 40s. The **Holland Tunnel** connects to lower Manhattan, exiting into the SoHo and TriBeCa area. Coming from New England or Connecticut on I-95, follow signs for the **Triboro Bridge.** From there get onto FDR Dr., which runs along the east side of Manhattan and exits onto city streets every 10 blocks or so. Another option is to look for the **Willis Avenue Bridge exit** on I-95 to avoid the toll, and enter Manhattan north on the FDR Drive.

Hitchhiking is illegal in New York state and cops strictly enforce the law within NYC. *Hitching in and around New York City is suicidal.* Don't do it.

ORIENTATION

Five **boroughs** comprise New York City: Brooklyn, the Bronx, Queens, Staten Island, and Manhattan. For all its notoriety, **Manhattan** Island's length is only half that of a marathon; 13 mi. long and 2.5 mi. wide, it houses the third largest population of the five boroughs, after Brooklyn and Queens. Though small, Manhattan has all the advantages; it is surrounded by water and adjacent to the other four boroughs. **Queens,** the largest and most ethnically diverse of the boroughs, beckons to the east of midtown Manhattan. **Brooklyn** lies due south of Queens. **Staten Island,** to the south of Manhattan, has remained defiantly residential, like the suburban communities of outer Long Island. North of Manhattan nests the **Bronx,** the only borough connected by land to the rest of the U.S., home of the lovely suburb Riverdale as well as New York's most economically depressed area, the South Bronx.

Manhattan's Neighborhoods

Glimpsed from the window of an approaching plane, New York City can seem a monolithic concrete jungle. Up close, New York breaks down into manageable neighborhoods, each with history and personality. Boundaries between these neighborhoods can often be abrupt.

The city began at the southern tip of Manhattan, in the area around **Battery Park** where the first Dutch settlers made their homes. The nearby harbor, now jazzed up by the **South Street Seaport** tourist magnet, provided the growing city with the commercial opportunities that helped it to succeed. Historic Manhattan, however, lies in the shadows of the imposing financial buildings around **Wall St.** and the civic offices around **City Hall.** A little farther north, neighborhoods rich in the cultures brought by late 19th-century immigrants, **Little Italy, Chinatown,** and the southern blocks of the **Lower East Side,** rub elbows below Houston St. (pronounced "HOW-ston," not like the Texan city). Formerly the home of Eastern European and Russian Jews, Delancey and Elizabeth St. now offer pasta and silks. To the west lies the newly fashionable **TriBeCa** ("Triangle Below Canal St."). **SoHo** (for "South of Houston"), a former warehouse district west of Little Italy, now shelters a pocket of art studios and galleries. Above SoHo thrives **Greenwich Village,** where jumbled streets, trendy shops, and cafés have for decades been home to intense political and artistic activity.

A few blocks north of Greenwich Village, stretching across the west teens and twenties, lies **Chelsea,** the late artist Andy Warhol's favorite hangout and former home of Dylan Thomas and Arthur Miller. East of Chelsea, presiding over the East River, is **Gramercy Park,** a pastoral collection of elegant brownstones immortalized in Edith Wharton's *Age of Innocence.* **Midtown Manhattan** towers from 34th to 59th St., where traditional and controversial new skyscrapers share the skies, supporting over a million elevated offices. Here department stores outfit New York while the nearby **Theater District** attempts to entertain the world. North of Midtown, **Central Park** slices Manhattan into East and West. On the **Upper West Side,** the gracious museums and residences of Central Park West neighbor the chic boutiques and sidewalk cafés of Columbus Ave. On the **Upper East Side,** the galleries and museums scattered among the elegant apartments of Fifth and Park Ave. create an even more rarefied atmosphere.

Above 97th St., the Upper East Side's opulence ends with a whimper where commuter trains emerge from the tunnel and the *barrio* begins. Above 110th St. on the Upper West Side sits majestic **Columbia University** (founded as King's College in 1754), an urban member of the Ivy League. The communities of **Harlem** and **Morningside Heights** produced the Harlem Renaissance of black artists and writers in the 1920s and the revolutionary Black Power movement of the 1960s. Now torn by crime, these areas are historically interesting, but not to be explored after dark. **Washington Heights,** just north of St. Nicholas Park, is home to Fort Tryon Park, the Medieval Cloisters museum, and a community of Old World immigrants.

Manhattan's Street Plan

New York's east/west division refers to an establishment's location in relation to the two borders of Central Park—**Fifth Ave.** on the east side and **Central Park West** on the west. Below 59th St. where the park ends, the West Side begins at the western half of Fifth Ave. **Midtown** presides between 34th and 59th St. **Uptown** (59th St. and *up*) refers to the area north of Midtown. **Downtown** (34th St. and *down*) means the area south of Midtown. **Streets run east-west. Avenues run north-south.**

Manhattan's grid makes calculating distances fairly easy. Numbers increase from south to north along the avenues, but you should always ask for a cross street when getting an avenue address. This plan does not work in Greenwich Village or in lower Manhattan; just get a good map and ask for directions.

GETTING AROUND

Get a free subway map from station token booths or the visitors bureau, which also has a free street map. For a more detailed program of interborough travel, find a Man-

MID-ATLANTIC

hattan Yellow Pages, which contains detailed subway, PATH, and bus maps. In the city, the round-the-clock staff at the **NYC Transit Information Bureau** (718-330-1234) dispenses subway and bus info. For info on taxis and biking, see Practical Information (above).

Subways The fare for **Metropolitan Transit Authority (MTA)** subways and buses is $1.50; groups of four or more may find cabs cheaper for short rides. Once underground you may transfer to any train without restrictions. Most buses have access ramps, but steep stairs make subway transit more difficult for disabled people. Call for specifics on public transportation Mon.-Fri 9am-5pm (see Practical Information, above).

In crowded stations (notably those around 42nd St.), pickpockets find plenty of work; in deserted stations, more violent crimes can occur. *Always watch yourself and your belongings.* Try to stay in lit areas near a transit cop or token clerk. When boarding the train, make sure to pick a car with a number of other passengers on it—for long subway rides, the conductor's car is usually the best idea.

For safety, avoid riding the subways between 11pm and 7am, especially above E. 96th St. and W. 120th St. and outside Manhattan. Riding the subway at night can be dangerous—don't ride alone. During rush-hour you'll be fortunate to find air, let alone seating; on an average morning, more commuters take the E and the F than use the entire rapid-transit system of Chicago (the nation's second-largest system). Buy several tokens at once at the booth or, preferably, at the new token-vending machines now at most stations. You'll not only avoid a long line, but you'll be able to use any station—some token booths close at night.

Buses The **Metropolitan Transit Authority (MTA)** also runs buses for $1.50 a ride. Because buses sit in traffic, during the day they often move much more slowly than subways, but they also stay relatively safe and clean—and are always windowed. They'll also probably get you closer to your destination, since they stop roughly every two blocks and run crosstown (east-west), as well as uptown and downtown (north-south), unlike the subway which mostly travels north-south. The MTA transfer system provides north-south bus riders with a slip for a free east-west bus ride, or vice-versa. Just ask the driver for a transfer slip when you pay. Ring when you want to get off. A yellow-painted curb indicates bus stops, but you're better off looking for the blue signpost announcing the bus number or for a glass-walled shelter displaying a map of the bus's route and a schedule of arrival times. Either exact change or a subway token is required; drivers will not accept bills.

ACCOMMODATIONS

If you know someone who knows someone who lives in New York, get that person's phone number. The cost of living in New York is out of sight. Don't expect to fall into a hotel; if you do, odds are it will be a pit. At true full-service establishments, a night will cost you around $125 plus the hefty 14.25% hotel tax. Some choices are available for under $60 a night, but it depends on your priorities. People traveling alone may want to spend more to stay in a safer neighborhood. The outgoing student may prefer a crowded budget-style place; honeymooning couples may not.

Hostels and Student Organizations

New York International HI-AYH Hostel, 891 Amsterdam Ave. (932-2300; fax 932-2574), at 103rd St. Subway: #1, 9, B, or C to 102nd St. Located in a block-long, landmark building, this is the largest hostel in the U.S., with 90 dorm-style rooms and 480 beds. Shares site with the **CIEE Student Center** (666-3619), an info depot for travelers, as well as a Council Travel office. Members' kitchens and dining rooms, laundry facilities ($1), TV lounges, and an outdoor garden. Walking tours and outings. Secure storage area and individual lockers. 7-night max. stay in summer. Open 24hr. Check-in any time, check-out 11am (late check-out fee $5). No curfew. Members $22 per night, nonmembers $25. Family room $66. Groups of

4-12 may get private rooms; groups of 10 or above definitely will. Linen rental $3. Towel $2. Excellent wheelchair access.

International Student Center, 38 W. 88th St. (787-7706; fax 580-9283), between Central Park West and Columbus Ave. Subway: B or C to 86th St. Open only to foreigners (but not Canadians) aged 20-30; you must show a foreign passport or valid visa to be admitted. A welcoming brownstone. Single-sex, no-frills bunk rooms. Large basement TV lounge. 5-day max. stay when full in the summer, 7-day max the rest of the year. Open daily 8am-11pm. No curfew. $15. Key deposit $10. No reservations, and generally full in summer, but call by 10pm for a bed, and they'll hold it for you for two hours. Call before your arrival.

Sugar Hill International House, 722 Saint Nicholas Ave. (926-7030; fax 283-0108), at 146th St. Subway: A, B, C, or D to 145th St. Located on Sugar Hill in Harlem, across from the subway station. Reassuring, lively neighborhood. Converted brownstone with huge, well-lit, comfortable rooms. 2-10 people per room in bunkbeds. Staff is friendly and helpful, with a vast knowledge of NYC and the Harlem area. Facilities include kitchens, TV, stereo, and paperback library. Beautiful garden in back. All-female room available. Check-in 9am-10pm. 24-hr. access. $16 per person. Call in advance. The owners of Sugar Hill also run the new 4-floor hostel next door at 730 Saint Nicholas Ave., the **Blue Rabbit Hostel** (491-3892). Similar to the Sugar Hill, but with more doubles and more privacy. Backyard garden, friendly cats, common room, kitchen. Amazingly spacious rooms. Check-in 9am-10pm. $16; $18 for a bed in a double. Call in advance.

Banana Bungalow (AAIH/Rucksackers), 250 W. 77th St. (800-6-HOSTEL/646-7835 or 769-2441; fax 877-5733), between Broadway and 11th Ave. Subway: #1 or 9 to 79th St. Walk two blocks south and turn right. A continually expanding and renovating hostel, with sun deck on the top floor, tropical-themed lounge/kitchen, and dorm-style rooms sleeping 4-7; some rooms have private baths. Beds $18. Reservations recommended. Wheelchair access.

De Hirsch Residence, 1395 Lexington Ave. (415-5650 or 800-858-4692; fax 415-5578), at 92nd St. Subway: #6 to 96th St. Affiliated with the 92nd St. YMHA/YWHA. Some of the largest, cleanest, and most convenient housing in the city. Hall bathrooms, kitchens, and laundry facilities on every other floor; a collegiate feel. Single-sex floors, strictly enforced. A/C available for $3 per day or $45 per month. Access to the many facilities of the 92nd St. Y—free Nautilus and reduced rates for concerts. Organized activities such as walking tours of New York. Singles $294 per week ($42 per night); beds in doubles $210 per week ($30 per night). 3-day min. stay. Application required at least a month in advance; must be a student or working in the city, and must supply references. Wheelchair access.

International Student Hospice, 154 E. 33rd St. (228-7470), between Lexington and Third Ave. Subway: #6 to 33rd St. Up a flight of stairs in an inconspicuous converted brownstone with a brass plaque reading "I.S.H." Homey hostel with helpful owner exudes friendliness and community. Populated by a predominantly European crowd of backpackers. Good location in Murray Hill. Twenty very small rooms with bunk beds bursting with antiques, Old World memorabilia, and clunky oak night tables. The ceilings are crumbling and the stairs slant precariously, but the house is slowly being restored by residents. Rooms for 2-4 people and hall bathroom. Large common room, lounge, and enough dusty books to last a summer. Strict midnight curfew. $25 per night, with some weekly discounts.

Big Apple Hostel (AAIH/Rucksackers), 119th W. 45th St. (302-2603), between Sixth and Seventh Ave. Subway: #1, 2, 3, 9, N, or R to 42nd St.; or B, D, or E to Seventh Ave. Centrally located, this hostel offers clean, comfortable, carpeted rooms, full kitchen, back deck, luggage room, grill for barbecuing, a few common rooms, and laundry facilities. Passport nominally required; Americans accepted with out-of-state photo ID. Open 24hr. Bunk in dorm-style room with shared bath $22. Singles $58. Lockers in some rooms; bring a lock. Free coffee and tea in the kitchen. No reservations July-Aug., but they'll hold a bed if you call after 11am on the day you want to arrive. Reservations accepted Oct.-July; make them a few weeks in advance for the summer months.

Chelsea International Hostel (AAIH/Rucksackers), 251 W. 20th St. (647-0010), between Seventh and Eighth Ave. Subway: #1, 9, C, or E to 23rd St. The congenial staff at this 47-bed hostel offers their guests free beer and pizza on Wed. nights, and free beer (bring your own pizza) on Sun. Located in south Chelsea on a block with a police precinct, this hostel is fairly safe. Adequate 4-person dorm rooms $20 per bed; private rooms $45. Reservations recommended; call ahead.

Gershwin Hotel, 3 E. 27th St. (545-8000; fax 684-5546), between Fifth and Madison Ave. Subway: N or R to 28th St. With a large building full of pop art and twenty-somethings, the Gershwin seems more like a living MTV show idea than a place to stay. A next-door gallery, amateur band night (Sat.), artsy bar, and rooftop terrace complete the ambience of carefully cultivated hip. Out-of-state or foreign passport required. Free tea and coffee. 24-hr. reception. Check-out 11am. No curfew. 4-bed dorms $20 per bed. Private rooms are also available: doubles and triples $75-105. Continental breakfast $2.50.

Mid-City Hostel, 608 Eighth Ave. (704-0562), between 39th and 40th St. on the 3rd and 4th floors. Subway: #1, 2, 3, 9, N, or R to 42nd St.-Seventh Ave.; or A, C, or E to 42nd St.-Ninth Ave. No sign: just look for the street number on the small door. Lively neighborhood. Brick walls, skylights, and wooden beams across the ceiling. Caters to an international backpacking crowd—a passport or valid student ID is required. Small breakfast included. 7-day max. stay in summer. Lockout noon-6pm. Curfew Sun.-Thurs. midnight, Fri.-Sat. 1am. Bunk in dorm-style room with shared bath $20; Oct. to late June $18. Reservations are required and should be made far in advance for summer. Strictly no smoking.

Chelsea Center Hostel, 313 W. 29th St. (643-0214), between Eighth and Ninth Ave. Subway: #1, 2, 3, 9, A, C, E to 34th St. Knowledgeable staff will give advice in multiple languages (including Gaelic). 22 bunks in a low-ceilinged room make for a slightly cramped setup. Two showers. Tiny backyard garden, replete with ivy and a picnic table. Check in anytime, but lockout 11am-5pm. Dorm beds $20 in summer, $18 in winter, light breakfast included. Blankets and sheets provided as well. Be sure to call ahead; usually full in summer.

Uptown Hostel, 239 Lenox/Malcolm X Ave. (666-0559), at 122nd St. Bunk beds, sparkling clean and comfy rooms, and spacious hall bathrooms. $12 a night. Call 1-2 weeks in advance in summer, and at least 2 days in advance any other time.

YMCA—Vanderbilt, 224 E. 47th St. (756-9600; fax 752-0210), between Second and Third Ave. Subway: #6 to 51st St. or E, F to Lexington-Third Ave. Five blocks from Grand Central Station. Convenient and well-run, with vigilant security. Clean, brightly lit lobby bustles with internationals touting internal-frame backpacks. Rooms are quite small, and bathroom-to-people ratio is pretty low, but lodgers can use the copious athletic facilities (Stairmasters, aerobics classes, Nautilus machines, pool, and sauna), safe-deposit boxes, and guided tours of the city. No NYC residents. Five shuttles per day to the airports. Check-in 1-6pm; after 6pm must have major credit card to check in. Check-out noon, but luggage storage until departure ($1/bag). Singles $51, doubles $63. Key deposit $10 (refundable). Make reservations 1-2 weeks in advance and guarantee them with a deposit.

Hotels

Carlton Arms Hotel, 160 E. 25th St. (684-8337 or 679-0680), between Lexington and Third Ave. Subway: #6 to 23rd St. Stay inside a submarine and peer through windows at the lost city of Atlantis or stow your clothes in a dresser suspended on an astroturf wall. Each room has been designed in a different motif by a different avant-garde artist. The decoration doesn't completely obscure the age of these budget rooms, or their lack of air, but does provide distractions. Singles $49, with bath $57, doubles $62/$69, triples $74/$84. Pay for 7 or more nights up front and get a 10% discount. Make reservations for summer at least 2 months in advance. Substantial discounts for students and foreign travelers.

Roger Williams Hotel, 28 E. 31st St. (684-7500, reservations 800-637-9773; fax 576-4343), at Madison Ave. in pleasant Murray Hill neighborhood. Subway: #6 to 33rd St. This hotel, with its spacious, clean rooms, should suit your every need (though the elevator's tiny). Small refrigerators in each room. All rooms with toilet, bath, cable TV, phone, stove, and kitchenette. 24-hr. security. Singles $79, doubles or twins $89, triples $99, quads $109.

Portland Square Hotel, 132 W. 47th St. (382-0600 or 800-388-8988; fax 382-0684), between Sixth and Seventh Ave. Subway: B, D, F, or Q to 50th St.-Sixth Ave. Rooms are carpeted, clean, and comfortable, with A/C and cable TV, but the hotel's main asset is its great location. Attracts mostly foreigners. Singles with shared bath $50, with private bath $70, doubles $94, triples $99, quads $104.

Herald Square Hotel, 19 W. 31st St. (279-4017 or 800-727-1888, fax 643-9208), at Fifth Ave. Subway: B, D, F, N, or R to 34th St. In the original Beaux Arts home (built in 1893) of Life magazine. Work by some of America's most noted illustrators adorns the lobby, halls, and rooms. Tiny, clean, newly renovated rooms with color TV, small refrigerators, phones, and A/C. Singles with shared bath $45, with private bath $60; doubles $65, with 2 beds $99. International students get a 10% discount. Reservations recommended.

Pioneer Hotel, 341 Broome St. (226-1482), between Elizabeth St. and the Bowery. Located between Little Italy and the Lower East Side in a century-old (but recently renovated) building. Close to the nightlife of SoHo and the East Village. NYU film students shoot their film projects in this hotel's classic rooms. All rooms have TVs. Public telephones in the lobby. Singles $34, with A/C $40, doubles $48/$56, with bath $60. Singles also rent for $210 for the week

Pickwick Arms Hotel, 230 E. 51st St. (355-0300 or 800-PICKWIK/742-5945, fax 755-5029), between Second and Third Ave. Subway: #6 to 51st St.; or E, F to Lexington-Third Ave. Business types congregate in this well-located mid-sized hotel. Chandeliered marble lobby filled with the silken strains of Top 40 Muzak contrasts with tiny rooms and microscopic hall bathrooms. Roof garden, airport service available. Check-in 2pm; check-out 1pm. Singles $50, with shared bath $60. Doubles with bath $99, Studios (two double beds) $148. Additional person in room $12. Reservations recommended.

Hotel Wolcott, 4 W. 31st St. (268-2900; fax 563-0096), between Fifth and Sixth Ave. Subway: B, D, F, N, or R to 34th St. An ornately mirrored and marbled entrance hall leads into this inexpensive, newly renovated hotel. New furniture and carpeting, cable TV, and A/C. Singles $80, doubles $85, triples $95. Reservations recommended a month or more in advance for summer.

Washington Square Hotel, 103 Waverly Pl. (777-9515 or 800-222-0418; fax 979-8373), at MacDougal St. Subway: A, B, C, D, E, F, or Q to W. 4th St. Fantastic location. Glitzy marble and brass lobby, with a cool medieval gate in front. TV, A/C, and key-card entry to individual rooms. Recent additions include a restaurant/bar, lounge, and exercise room. Clean and comfortable; friendly and multilingual staff. Singles $85; doubles $110, with two twin beds $117; quads $138. Reservation required 2-3 weeks in advance.

Hotel Iroquois, 49 W. 44th St. (840-3080 or 800-332-7220; fax 398-1754), near Fifth Ave. Subway: B, D, or F to 47th St.-Rockefeller Ctr. Slightly worn but spacious rooms in an old pre-war building. This hotel once hosted James Dean and is now the stop of choice for Greenpeace and other environmental activists when in town. Check-out noon. Singles and doubles $75-100. Suites (up to 5 people) $125-150. Student discounts available, and prices negotiable during winter. Reservations advisable a few weeks in advance in the summer.

Mansfield Hotel, 12 W. 44th St. (944-6050 or 800-255-5167; fax 764-4477), at Fifth Ave. Subway: B, D, or F to 47th St.-Rockefeller Ctr. A dignified establishment housed in a turn-of-the-century building with comfortable leather couches in the lobby and beautiful oak doors in the hallways. Rooms have recently been renovated; the new ones have new lighting, paint, and furniture, and some of the larger ones have whirlpool tubs. Specifically request a renovated room when making reservations (1 month in advance for summer). Check-out noon. Singles and doubles $145, triples and quads $160. Large suites $195 for 5 or 6 people. Ask about student discounts.

Hotel Grand Union, 34 E. 32nd St. (683-5890; fax 689-7397), between Madison and Park Ave. Subway: #6 to 33rd St. Centrally located and reasonably priced. Large, comfy rooms equipped with cable TV, phone, A/C, mini-fridge, and full bathroom. Friendly, 24-hr. security. Singles and doubles $79-95, triples $90-104, quads $105+. 2-room suite from $105. Major credit cards accepted.

FOOD

This city takes its food seriously. New York will dazzle you with its culinary bounty, serving the needs of its diverse (and hungry) population. Ranging from mom-and-pop diners to elegant five-star restaurants, the food offered here will suit all appetites and pocketbooks. New York's restaurants do more than the United Nations to promote international goodwill and cross-cultural exchanges. City dining spans the globe, with eateries ranging from sushi bars to wild combinations like Afghani/Italian and Mexican/Lebanese. Listed below are some choice places divided by neighborhood, but feel free to explore and take a bite out of the Big Apple yourself.

East Midtown

East Midtown teems with restaurants. Around noon to 2pm, the many delis and cafés become swamped with harried junior executives trying to eat quickly and get back to work. The 50s on **Second Ave.** and the area immediately surrounding Grand Central Station are filled with good, cheap fare. You might also check out grocery stores, such as the **Food Emporium,** 969 Second Ave. (593-2224), between 51st and 52nd St., **D'Agostino,** Third Ave. (684-3133), between 35th and 36th St., or **Associated Group Grocers,** 1396 Second Ave., between E. 48th and E. 49th St. This part of town has many public spaces (plazas, lobbies, parks) for picnicking; try **Greenacre Park,** 51st St. between Second and Third Ave.; **Paley Park,** 53rd St. between Fifth and Madison Ave.; or the **United Nations Plaza,** 48th St. at First Ave.

Dosanko, 423 Madison Ave. (688-8575), at E. 47th St. Japanese fast food—very cheap, very fast, and very good. All is tranquil at this aromatic pit-stop; the food is so tasty it seems criminal to waste time talking. The scrumptious *gyoza* ($4.50) is a favorite, as are the many varieties of ramen ($5.30-7). Another Dosanko with more seating sits a few blocks away at 217 E. 59th St. (752-3936) between Second and Third Ave. Open Mon.-Fri. 11:30am-10pm, Sat.-Sun. noon-8pm.

Coldwaters, 988 Second Ave. (888-2122), between E. 52nd and E. 53rd St. Seafood ($6-11) is served under nautical paraphernalia and stained-glass lamps. Lunch is a bargain: two drinks (alcoholic or non-), choice of entree, salad, and fries for $8 (daily 11:30am-4pm). Dinner is also a good deal: soup, salad, entree, and dessert for $12 (Mon.-Thurs. 4-7pm). Try the Idaho Rainbow Trout ($9), Cajun Catfish ($9), or Boston Cod ($9). Open daily 11am-3am.

West Midtown

Your best bets here are generally along Eighth Ave. between 34th and 59th St. in the area known as **Hell's Kitchen.** Once deserving of its name, this area has given birth to an array of ethnic restaurants. The area's cheapest meals are of the **fast food** variety, on the east side of **Seventh Ave.** between 33rd and 34th Those with deeper pockets should take a meal on **Restaurant Row,** on 46th St. between Eighth and Ninth Ave., which offers a solid block of dining primarily to a pre-theater crowd (arriving after 8pm will make getting a table easier).

Ariana Afghan Kebab, 787 Ninth Ave. (262-2323), between 52nd and 53rd St. With the approximate dimensions of a shoebox, this family-run restaurant serves up excellent Afghani food at reasonable prices. The beef *tikka kebab,* chunks of beef marinated and cooked over wood charcoal, is excellent served with rice, bread, and salad ($7), as is the *aushak,* leek-filled dumplings topped with yogurt and a spicy meat sauce. Vegetarian entrees range from $5.50-7.25. Open Mon.-Sat. noon-10:30pm, Sun. 3-10pm.

Poseidon Bakery, 629 Ninth Ave. (757-6173), near 44th St. This fifty-year-old bakery serves up authentic Greek pastries and delicacies. They even make their own filo dough for their sweet, sweet *baklava,* their *kreatopita* (meat pie), *tiropita* (cheese pie), and *spanakopita* (spinach pie)—all delicious and sold for around $2. Open July-Aug. Tues.-Sat. 9am-7pm; Sept.-June also Sun. 10am-4pm.

Carnegie Delicatessen, 854 Seventh Ave. (757-2245), at 55th St. Eat elbow-to-elbow at long tables, and chomp on free dill pickles. The "Woody Allen," an incredible pastrami and corned beef sandwich, could easily stuff two people ($12.45). Don't leave without trying the sinfully rich cheesecake topped with strawberries, blueberries, or cherries ($5.45). Open daily 6:30am-4am. Cash only.

Lower Midtown and Chelsea

Straddling the extremes, the lower Midtown dining scene is neither fast-food commercial nor *haute cuisine* trendy. East of Fifth Ave. on **Lexington Ave.**, Pakistani and Indian restaurants battle for customers. Liberally sprinkled throughout, Korean corner shops that are equal parts grocery and buffet offer hot and cold salad bars.

Finding food in Chelsea isn't always easy. Good food tends not to be cheap, and cheap food is rarely good. The neighborhood is dotted with fake-retro diners that offer unexceptional $6 hamburgers and $7 omelettes. The best offerings are the products of the large Mexican and Central American community in the southern section of the neighborhood. **Eighth Ave.** provides the best restaurant browsing.

Jaiya, 396 Third Ave. (889-1330), between 28th and 29th St. Critics rave over Thai and other Asian food, with three degrees of spiciness, from mild to "help-me-I'm-on-fire." *Pad thai* $7.25—a definite steal. Lunch specials Mon.-Fri. 11:30am-3pm. Most dishes $5-6. Open Mon.-Fri. 11:30am-midnight, Sat. noon-midnight, Sun. 5pm-midnight. Another location at 81-11 Broadway in Elmhurst, Queens.

Zen Palate, 34 E. Union Sq. (614-9345), across from the park. Fantastic Asian-inspired vegetarian cuisine, including soothing, healthy, and fabulously fresh treats like "shredded heaven" (assorted veggies and spring rolls with brown rice) for $8, stir fried rice fettuccini with mushrooms $7, or other concoctions on the brown rice/seaweed/kale and soy tip. Fresh-squeezed juices and soy milkshakes $1.50. Crazy desserts like tofu-honey pie. Open Mon.-Sat. 11am-11pm, Sun. noon-10:30pm. Other locations at 663 9th Ave. (582-1669) at 46th St., and 2170 Broadway (501-7768) at 76th St.

Kitchen, 218 Eighth Ave. (243-4433), near 21st St. A real kitchen specializing in Mexican food, with hot red peppers dangling from the ceiling. All food to go; there's no dining room. Try the burrito stuffed with pinto beans, rice, and green salsa ($5.70). Dried fruit, nuts, and shrimp by the pound ($1-5), as well as other grocery items, are available in Kitchen's authentic Mexican grocery. Very serious about chilis and chips. Open daily 11:30am-10:30pm.

Big Cup, 228 8th Ave. (206-0059), between 21st and 22nd St. Lots of colorful and comfy velvet couches and overstuffed chairs make this a great place to curl up with a cup of joe ($1), plug in a powerbook, or cruise for cute guys. Predominantly gay clientele. Crazy coffee flavors like toffee-coffee and sandwiches like cactus, red pepper, and chipotle ($5) for daring tongues. Tarot readings in house Tues. nights at 8pm. Open Sun.-Thurs. 7am-2am, Fri.-Sat. 8am-3am.

Upper East Side

Meals on the Upper East Side descend in price as you move east from **Fifth Ave.'s** glitzy, overpriced museum cafés towards **Lexington, Third** and **Second Ave.** Hot dog hounds shouldn't miss the 100% beef "better than filet mignon" $1.50 franks and exotic fruit drinks at **Papaya King,** 179 E. 86th St. (369-0648), off Third Ave. (open Sun.-Thurs. 8am-1am, Fri.-Sat. 9am-3am). Visitors aiming to experience the classic New York bagel should try **H&H East,** 1551 Second Ave. (734-7441), between 80th and 81st St. Open 24 hr., H&H still uses a century-old formula to send you to bagel heaven. But don't feel confined to restaurant dining; grocery stores, delis, and bakeries speckle every block. You can buy provisions here and picnic in Central Park.

EJ's Luncheonette, 1271 Third Ave. (472-0600), at 73rd St. The understated American elegance and huge portions of good food in this hip 50s-style diner have fostered a legion of devoted Upper East Siders—the scrumptious fare (buttermilk pancakes $5, hamburgers $5.75) is rumored to have attracted such neighborhood luminaries as JFK, Jr. Open Mon.-Thurs. 8am-11pm, Fri.-Sat. 8am-midnight, Sun. 8am-10:30pm.

Brother Jimmy's BBQ, 1461 First Ave. (545-7427), at 76th St. The sign proclaims "BBQ and booze, the stuff that makes America strong," and this greasy-chops Carolina kitchen serves up plenty of both, along with a healthy dose of southern hospitality, in the form of free food for kids under 12, 25% off entrees for southerners on Wednesday nights, and free margaritas with dinner on Monday nights. Ribs $13, with 2 side dishes and corn bread. Sandwiches, for the less strong, $6-7. Kitchen open Sun.-Thurs. 5pm-midnight, Fri.-Sat. 11am-1am. Bar open "until you finish your last drink" or until around 4am.

Barking Dog Luncheonette, 1678 Third Ave. (831-1800), at 94th St. As the staff's shirts command, "SIT–STAY!" and satisfy your hunger pangs with helpings fit for the biggest dog on the block. The breakfast special ($4.50), with 2 eggs, hash browns, and your choice of bacon or sausage biscuit, tastes delicious, while late risers may prefer the burger platter ($6.50). With huge bay windows overlooking Third Ave., this charming corner restaurant features delightful dog decor and a peaceful atmosphere not unlike canine heaven. Open daily 8am-11pm.

Upper West Side

Unlike many other New York neighborhoods, the Upper West Side lacks a definitive typology of restaurants. Cheap pizza joints often neighbor chic eateries; street vendors hawk sausages in the shadow of pricey specialty stores. **Columbus Ave.** provides lots of options within a budgeter's realm. Wander down the tempting aisles of **Zabar's,** 2245 Broadway (787-2002), at 81st St., the gourmet deli and grocery that never ends.

Cleopatra's Needle, 2485 Broadway (769-6969), between 92nd and 93rd St. Jazz and authentic Middle Eastern fare served up nightly to faithful locals. Take-out lunch counter also available to those who can't stop at dinner. *Baba ghanoush* or Egyptian burrito for less than $4. Patrons have fun pronouncing exotic dishes like *Kibbehsinaya* ($8) and *Imam Bayildi* ($9), or else stick to familiar friends like roast cornish hen ($8.25). Takeout/deli open daily 8am-11pm, dinner Sun.-Thurs. 5-11pm, Fri.-Sat. 5pm-midnight.

La Caridad, 2199 Broadway (874-2780), at 78th St. One of New York's most successful Chinese-Spanish hybrids. You could eat here 160 times and never have the same dish twice. The ebullient waiters charm in three languages. The decor isn't elaborate, but the delicious homestyle cooking should remind you of your *abuelita.* Prices stay decidedly south of the $10 border. Open Mon.-Sat. 11:30am-1am, Sun. 11:30am-10:30pm.

Soutine, 104 W.70th St. (496-1450), at Amsterdam Ave. This thimble of a bakery has packed a punch since 1983—its lovingly baked treats even gained the approval of food critic Ed Levine. Try their sacristans (puff pastries) or fruit tarts for under $2. Sandwiches $3.50. Open Mon.-Fri. 8am-7pm, Sat. 9am-5pm. **H&H Bagels,** 2239 Broadway (595-8000), at 80th St. With bagels that are cheap (70¢) and baked fresh daily, H&H has been nourishing the huddled masses of the Upper West Side for years. Open 24hr.

Morningside Heights and Harlem

The cafés and restaurants in Morningside Heights cater to Columbia students, faculty, and their families. This usually means that hours run late and the price range fits that of a starving student. But college students aren't without discernment; the old-style coffeeshops and restaurants serve up delicious food with atmosphere.

Massawa, 1239 Amsterdam Ave. (663-0505), at 121st St. You'll want to make sure your hands are spotless before heading here, a restaurant that specializes in cheap well-prepared Ethiopian and Eritrean cuisine—traditionally eaten by hand. The various vegetarian dishes range from $5-6, and are served with spongy *ingera* bread or rice. Between 11:30am and 3pm, they offer kicking lunch specials like lamb stew and collard-green/potato platters ($4-5.75). Open daily noon-midnight.

Tom's Restaurant, 2880 Broadway (864-6137), at 112th St. "Doo-doo-doo-doo...." Suzanne Vega wrote that darn catchy tune about this diner, and Tom's is featured in most episodes of *Seinfeld,* but this eatery is mainly known for its luxurious milkshakes ($2.45). Greasy burgers for $3-5, dinner under $6.50. Open Mon.-Wed. 6am-1:30am and open continuously from Thurs. 6am to Sun. 1:30am. "Doo-doo-doo-doo...."

Copeland's, 547 W. 145th St. (234-2357), between Broadway and Amsterdam Ave. Subway: #1 or 9 to 145th St. Excellent soul food without the slick presentation of the more famous Sylvia's. Smothered chicken $6.50; fried pork chop $7.20. Smorgasbord next door—cafeteria-style but just as good. The Southern-style breakfast and Sunday brunch are simply amazing. Open Tues.-Thurs. 4:30-11pm, Fri.-Sat. 4:30pm-midnight, Sun. 11am-9:30pm.

Greenwich Village

Whatever your take on the West Village's bohemian authenticity, it's undeniable that all the free-floating artistic angst does result in many creative (and inexpensive) food venues. The aggressive and entertaining street life makes stumbling around and deciding where to go almost as much fun as eating. Try the major avenues for cheap, decent food. The European-style bistros of **Bleecker St.** and **MacDougal St.,** south of Washington Square Park, have perfected the homey "antique" look. You can't eat inside the **Murray Cheese Shop,** 257 Bleecker St. (243-3289; open Mon.-Sat. 8am-7pm, Sun. 9am-5pm), at Cornelia St., but the 400-plus kinds of cheese justify a picnic. Try the camembert in rosemary and sage ($4), and get the bread next door at **A. Zito Bread.** Late night in the Village is a unique New York treat; as the sky grows dark, the streets quicken. Explore twisting side streets and alleyways where you can drop into a jazz club or join Off-Broadway theater-goers as they settle down over a burger and a beer to write their own reviews. Or ditch the high life and slump down 8th St. to **Sixth Ave.** to find some of the best pizza in the city.

Cucina Stagionale, 275 Bleecker St. (924-2707), at Jones St. Unpretentious Italian dining in a pretty environment. Packed on weekends—the lines reach the street at times. A sample of the soft *calimari* in spicy red sauce ($6) or the spinach and cheese ravioli ($7) will tell you why. Pasta dishes $6-8; veal, chicken, and fish dishes $8-10. Once you've been seated, might as well get a dessert too; the bill still won't be over $15. Open Sun.-Thurs. noon-midnight, Fri.-Sat. noon-1am.

Florent, 69 Gansevoort St. (489-5779), between Washington and Greenwich Ave. In the terminally hip bowels of this meat-packing district is a 24-hr French diner that's not to be missed. Clientele ranges from drag queens to rastafarians, the food is fab, and the place is full even at 4am. Goat cheese and apple or portabello mushroom salads $6. Entrees range from burgers to gourmet, $9-20. Good wine list. It may not be very budget, but it's the best place to celebrate Bastille Day this side of Paris. Open 24hr.

Caffè Reggio, 119 MacDougal St. (475-9557), south of W. 3rd St. Celebs, wannabes, and students crowd the oldest café in the Village. Open since 1927, this place showcases busts and madonnas in every corner, and pours a mean cup of cappuccino ($2.25). Choose from a wide selection of pastries ($2.50-3.50). You'll bounce off the walls. Open Sun.-Thurs. 10am-2am, Fri.-Sat 10am-4am.

Caffè Borgia, 185 Bleecker St. (673-2290), at MacDougal St. Moody, dark café has the look and feel of mother Italy. Cult figures who frequent the place include Pacino and De Niro. Virtually endless coffee list ($1.50-2.75) and many sweet desserts. Open Sun.-Thurs. 10am-2am, Fri. 10am-4am, Sat. 10am-5am.

SoHo and TriBeCa

In SoHo, food, like life, is all about image. Most of the restaurants here tend to be preoccupied with decor, and most aim to serve a stylishly healthful cuisine.The image lifestyle, however, takes money, so don't be surprised if you find it hard to get a cheap meal. Often the best deal in SoHo is brunch, when the neighborhood shows its most good-natured front.

Dining in TriBeCa is generally a much funkier (and blessedly cheaper) experience than in chic SoHo. The restaurants here have a dressed-down, folksy, flea marketish flavor. TriBeCa is much more industrial than SoHo, and restaurants are often hidden like little oases among the hulking warehouses and decaying buildings.

MID-ATLANTIC

Bell Caffè, 310 Spring St. (334-BELL/2355), between Hudson and Greenwich. This low-key restaurant in an old bell factory may be off the beaten path, but there are good reasons to walk the extra blocks. Bell sports a global-village-meets-garage-sale aesthetic with a delicious multicultural menu to match, offering Indian, African, Mexican, Jewish, and Japanese "ethno-healthy" cuisine, including "Spring Street Rolls" made with shrimp, ginger, port vinaigrette, and couscous. Always laid back, always healthy, and everything on the menu is under $10. Free live music nightly 9:30pm-midnight and monthly receptions for the new art that goes up on the restaurant's walls. Open Sun.-Thurs. noon-2am, Fri.-Sat. noon-4am.

Lucky's Juice Joint, 75 W. Houston St. (388-0300), near W. Broadway. *Three's Company* meets SoHo at this small restaurant specializing in fresh juice combinations. Smoothies ($3.50) are made with a whole banana and a choice of everything from soy milk to peaches; a variety of other additions—from ginseng to bee pollen—can be put into your smoothie for under a dollar more. Lucky's is not just a vegetarian's dream; it also serves up fresh and tasty food to the weary gallery-goer. Veggie sandwiches $4-5, chilled 10-oz. "shots" of wheat grass $1.50. Open Mon-Sat. 9am-8pm; Sun. 10am-8pm.

Yaffa's Tea Room, 19 Harrison St. (274-9403), near Greenwich St. Situated in a pleasingly uncommercial and hidden corner of TriBeCa, Yaffa's is one of the few places in Manhattan that serves high tea—and definitely the coolest. The decor is straight out of yard sales and used furniture stores—not ratty, just "unusual." Wide selection of healthful sandwiches ($7.50) and entrees ($7-15). Brunch served daily 8:30am-5pm (omelettes and main selections $4.50-6.50, pastries $4-6). High tea ($15, reservations required) served Mon.-Fri. 2-6pm, and includes a "savory course" (cucumber, salmon, or watercress finger sandwiches), fresh baked scones, dessert sampler, and a pot of tea. Bar open daily 8:30am-4am, restaurant open 8:30am-midnight.

East Village, Lower East Side, and Alphabet City

Culinary cultures clash on the lower end of the East Side, where pasty-faced punks and starving artists dine alongside an older generation conversing in Polish, Hungarian, and Yiddish. The neighborhood took in the huddled masses, and, in return, immigrant culture after immigrant culture has left its mark in the form of cheap restaurants. **First** and **Second Ave.** are the best for restaurant-exploring, and sidewalk cafés and bars line **Avenue A.** Check out **6th St.** between First and Second Ave., a block composed of several Indian restaurants offering $3 lunch specials. For kosher eating, head on down to the Lower East Side south of East Houston St. **Kossar's Hot Bialys,** 367 Grand St. at Essex St. (473-4810; open 24hr.), makes bialys that recall the heyday of the Lower East Side.

Dojo Restaurant, 24 St. Mark's Pl. (674-9821), between Second and Third Ave. Dojo is one of the most popular restaurants and hangouts in the East Village, and rightly so; it offers an incredible variety of vegetarian and Japanese food that manages to be simultaneously healthy, delicious, and inexplicably inexpensive. Tasty soyburgers with brown rice and salad $3. Spinach and pita sandwich with assorted veggies $3. Outdoor tables allow for interaction with slick passers-by. New location (same menu) on Washington Square South at 14 W. 4th St. (505-8934). Open Sun.-Thurs. 11am-1am, Fri.-Sat. 11am-2am.

Benny's Burritos, 93 Ave. A (254-2054), at 6th St. This colorful, shiny Cal-Mex hot spot is dirt-cheap and always hoppin'. Trendy, tasteful decor, lots of windows for excellent people-watching, and great food—plump, tasty burritos with black or pinto beans $5-6. Fab frozen margaritas $5. Locals swear by it. Open Sun.-Thurs. 11am-midnight, Fri.-Sat. 11am-1am. No credit cards accepted.

Damask Falafel, 85 Ave. A. (673-5016) between 5th and 6th St. This closet-sized stand serves the cheapest and best falafel in the area—$1.75 for a sandwich, $3.50 for a falafel platter with tabouli, chick peas, salad, and pita bread. $1.25 for two succulent stuffed grape leaves. Banana milk shakes $1.25. Open Mon.-Fri. 11am-2am, Sat.-Sun. 11am-4am.

Veselka, 144 Second Ave. (228-9682), at 9th St. Down-to-earth, soup-and-bread, Polish-Ukrainian joint. Traditional food served in a friendly, untraditional setting. Big, beautiful murals cover everything, including the dumpster around the corner. Enormous menu includes about 10 varieties of soups, as well as salads, blintzes, meats, and other Eastern European fare. Blintzes $3.50, soup $1.95 a cup (the chicken noodle is sumptuous). Combination special gets you soup, salad, stuffed cabbage, and four melt-in-your-mouth *pirogi* ($7.95). Great breakfast specials: challah french toast, OJ, and coffee for $3.75. Open 24hr.

Ratner's Restaurant, 138 Delancey St. (677-5588), just west of the Manhattan Bridge. The most famous of the kosher restaurants, partly because of its frozen-food line. In odd contrast to its run-down surroundings, this place is large, shiny, and popular. Jewish dietary laws are strictly followed and only dairy food is served—but oy vey! Such matzah brei ($8.95)! Also feast on fruit blintzes and sour cream ($9) or simmering vegetarian soups ($4). Open Sun.-Thurs. 6am-midnight, Fri. 6am-3pm, Sat. sundown-2am.

Chinatown

If you're looking for cheap, authentic Asian fare, join the crowds that push through the narrow, chaotic streets of one of the oldest Chinatowns in the U.S. The neighborhood's 200-plus restaurants cook up some of the best Chinese, Thai, and Vietnamese eats around. Once predominantly Cantonese cooking has now burgeoned into different cuisines from the various regions of China: hot and spicy Hunan or Szechuan, the sweet and mildly spiced seafood of Soochow, or the hearty and filling fare of Beijing. Cantonese *dim sum* is still a Sunday afternoon tradition, when waiters roll carts filled with assorted dishes of bite-sized goodies up and down the aisles. Simply point at what you want (beware of "Chinese Bubblegum," a euphemism for tripe), and at the end of the meal, the empty dishes on your table are tallied up. For dessert, check out the **Chinatown Ice Cream Factory,** 65 Bayard St. (608-4171), at Mott St., for flavors like lychee, mango, ginger, red bean, and green tea. (Open Mon.-Thurs. 11:30am-11pm, Fri. and Sun. 11:30am-11:30pm, Sat. 11:30am-midnight.)

Excellent Dumpling House, 111 Lafayette St. (219-0212 or 219-0213), just south of Canal. True to its name, this restaurant offers absolutely terrific vegetarian and meat dumplings fried, steamed, or boiled ($4 for 8 sizeable pieces). Also great pan-fried noodles ($5-6.50) and huge bowls of noodle soups (mostly $3.50-4). Lunch specials (served Mon.-Fri. 11am-3pm) include entree such as shredded pork with garlic sauce or chicken with black bean sauce, choice of soup, fried rice, and a wonton (all specials $5.50). Small, unassuming, and populated with tourists. Nevertheless, splendid food and fast service. Open daily 11am-9pm.

House of Vegetarian, 68 Mott St. (226-6572), between Canal and Bayard St. Faux chicken, faux beef, faux lamb, and faux fish comprise the huge menu of this small and appropriately green eatery; all the animals are ersatz here, made from soy and wheat by-products. Great *lo mein* (with three kinds of mushrooms $6.75) and gluten with black bean sauce ($7). Most entrees $6-10. An ice-cold lotus-seed or lychee drink ($2) hits the spot on summer days. Open daily 11am-11pm.

HSF (Hee Sheung Fung), 46 Bowery (374-1319), just south of Canal St. Tasteful, large, crowded, and festooned with Chinese neon placards and rotating poultry in the window. Well known for its fantastic *dim sum* (served daily 7:30am-5pm) and

---

Foul Play?

The **Chinatown Fair,** 8 Mott St., features old-school video games and one clever chicken. Take on the fair's resident chicken genius. For 50¢, the fowl in question will engage you in an arduous battle of wits, tic-tac-toe style. Don't write off the bird just yet—remember, this is its livelihood. When we say that the Chinatown Fair chicken is tough to beat, we're not kidding. One disgruntled sore loser, upon falling to the mighty bird, was overheard to remark: "I'm not normally so terrible at tic-tac-toe—the chicken confused me." Hmmm. Keep that cockiness to yourself; you just might walk away a loser.

for its "Hot Pot" buffet. The Hot Pot is the Asian equivalent of fondue, in which a huge pot of boiling broth is placed in the center of your table with a platter of more than 50 raw ingredients spread around it for dipping. Ingredients are unlimited ($18 per person) and range from fresh scallops, squid, shrimp, clams, mussels, and periwinkles to spinach, watercress, and Chinese cabbage. Range of other entrees ($7.50-17) as well, including delicacies like prawns in Yushan garlic sauce ($13). Open daily 7:30am-5am.

Little Italy

A chunk of Naples has migrated to this lively yet very compact quarter roughly bounded by Canal, Lafayette, Houston St., and the Bowery. **Mulberry St.** is the main drag and the appetite avenue of Little Italy. Stroll here after 7pm to catch street life, but arrive earlier to get one of the better tables. For the sake of variety and thrift, dine at a restaurant but get your just dessert at a café.

Ballato, 55 E. Houston St. (274-8881), at Mott St. Gracefully stemmed wine glasses and glistening chocolate-covered cherries greet you. Although clearly cross-bred with SoHo style, Ballato serves impeccable southern Italian cooking to a small crowd of couples, tourists, and students. Pasta $7.50-11.50, trout in olive oil $12.50. *Antipasti* $5.50-8. Two-course lunch (Mon.-Fri. noon-4pm; $7.50) includes choice from a wide selection of entrees and either an appetizer or dessert. *Prix fixe* dinner (Sun.-Fri. 4-6:30pm, Sat. 5-6:30pm; $14.50) includes all 3 courses. Open Mon.-Fri. noon-11pm, Sat. 4pm-midnight, Sun. 4-11pm.

La Mela, 167 Mulberry St. (431-9493), between Broome and Grand St. Kitschy photos and postcards dot the walls; tables and chairs endlessly shift and merge to accommodate large groups and families, and super-friendly waitstaff merrily chortle as you chew. Equally rambunctious outdoor seating in their backyard, complete with a guitar-touting bard. A wide assortment of pasta and *gnocchi* ($6.50-10), along with a large number of entrees ($12-15). Always specials; the waiters love to shout you through your order. Open daily noon-11pm.

Caffè Roma, 385 Broome St. (226-8413), at Mulberry St. A good *caffè* gets better with time. A full-fledged saloon in the 1890s, Roma has kept its original furnishings intact: dark green walls with polished brass ornaments, sinuous wire chairs, marble tables, chandeliers, and darkwood cabinets where liquor bottles used to roost. The pastries and coffee, Roma's *raison d'être*, prove as refined as the setting. Try the neapolitan *cannoli* or the *baba au rhum* ($1.50 to take out, $2.25 to eat in). Potent espresso $1.75, obligatory cappuccino, with a tiara of foamed milk, $2.50. Open Sun.-Thurs. 8am-midnight, Fri.-Sat. 9am-1am.

Financial District

Lower Manhattan is luncheon heaven to sharply-clad Wall St. brokers and bankers—it offers cheap food prepared lightning-fast at ultra-low prices and always available as take-out. Bargain-basement cafeterias here can fill you up with everything from gazpacho to Italian sausages. Fast-food joints pepper Broadway near Dey and John St. just a few feet from the overpriced offerings of the Main Concourse of the World Trade Center. In the summer, ethnic food pushcarts form a solid wall along Broadway between Cedar and Liberty St.

Zigolini's, 66 Pearl St. (425-7171), at Coenties Alley. One of the few places in the area where indoor air-conditioned seating abounds, this authentically Italian restaurant serves huge and filling sandwiches ($5-7), as well as some great pasta dishes. Try the tomato spirals with sundried tomatoes, artichokes, roasted peppers, and parsley ($6.50). Come up with an appealing combo of your own and they might add it to the menu—it's happened before. Open Mon.-Fri. 7am-7pm.

Frank's Papaya, 192 Broadway (693-2763), at John St. Excellent value, quick service. Very close to the World Trade Center. Jumbo turkey burger $1.60, all-beef hot dog 50¢. Breakfast (egg, ham, cheese, coffee) $1.50. Stand and eat at one of the counters inside. Open Mon.-Sat. 5:30am-10pm, Sun. 5:30am-5:30pm.

Hamburger Harry's, 157 Chambers St. (267-4446), between West and Greenwich St. Gourmet burgers for the connoisseur: 7-oz. beef patty or chicken broiled over applewood with exotic toppings like avocado, alfalfa sprouts, chili, salsa, and béarnaise sauce ($6, with red slaw and fries or potato salad $8). Regular burger $4, nacho cheese fries $3. Open Mon.-Sat. 11:30am-10pm, Sun. 11:30am-9pm.

Brooklyn

Ethnic flavor changes every two blocks in Brooklyn. **Brooklyn Heights** offers nouvelle cuisine, but specializes in pita bread and *baba ghanoush*. **Williamsburg** is dotted with kosher and cheap Italian restaurants, **Greenpoint** is a borscht-lover's paradise, and **Flatbush** serves up Jamaican and other West Indian cuisine. Brooklyn now has its own Chinatown in Sunset Park.

Moroccan Star, 205 Atlantic Ave. (718-643-0800), in Brooklyn Heights. Subway: #2, 3, 4, 5, M, N, or R to Borough Hall, then 4 blocks on Court St. Ensconced in the local Arab community, this restaurant serves delicious and reasonably cheap food. Try the *pastello*, a delicate semi-sweet chicken pie with almonds ($8.75, lunch $6). Open Sun. noon-10pm, Tues.-Thurs. 10am-11pm, Fri.-Sat. 11am-11pm.

Teresa's, 80 Montague St. (718-797-3996), in Brooklyn Heights. Subway: #2, 3, 4, 5, M, or R to Borough Hall; Montague St. is right there, and Teresa's is at the Promenade end. Good, cheap Polish food in a pleasant wood and off-white interior. Stuffed peppers $6.75. *A pierogi* ($3.50) stuffed with cheese, potatoes, meat, or sauerkraut and mushrooms makes a filling meal. Weekday lunch specials (Mon.-Fri. 11am-4pm): entree, soup, and beverage for $6. Open daily 9am-11pm.

Oznaut's Dish, 79 Berry St. (718-599-6596). Subway: L to Bedford Ave. From the subway, walk west to Berry St. and head north. Beautiful, beautiful, beautiful, with good food to boot. Scene: Antoni Gaudi meets ex-Manhattanite artists in laid-back Williamsburg and they build a restaurant in *kif*-dream Morocco. Lamb burger on peasant bread $6.50. Granola, yogurt, and fruit $4. Forty teas (and lots of wine) to choose from, like Iron Goddess of Mercy and Lapsang Crocodile. North African/American-eclectic fare, with plenty of cross-pollinated goodies like coconut Indian curry ($8). Open Tues.-Sun. 6am-midnight.

PlanEat Thailand, 184 Bedford Ave. (718-599-5758). Subway: L to Bedford Ave. A restaurant that could only exist in Brooklyn: the city's best inexpensive Thai food served in a small restaurant decorated with high-quality graffiti on the walls. All beef dishes under $6, all chicken dishes under $7, and a killer pad thai for only $5.25. If you ask for spicy, they'll give you medium—it'll be enough to clear your sinuses (unlike most eateries, hot means *hot!* and is reserved for those who know what they're getting into). Open Mon.-Sat. 11:30am-11:30pm, Sun. 1pm-11pm.

Primorski Restaurant, 282 Brighton Beach Ave. (718-891-3111), between Brighton Beach 2nd St. and Brighton Beach 3rd St. Subway: D or Q to Brighton Beach, then four blocks east on Brighton Beach Ave. Populated by Russian-speaking Brooklynites, this vaguely nautically themed restaurant serves some of the Western Hemisphere's best Ukrainian borscht ($2.25) in an atmosphere of gritty Slavic decadence. Eminently affordable lunch special (Mon.-Fri. 11am-5pm, Sat.-Sun. 11am-4pm; $4) is one of the best lunch deals in NYC—your choice of among three soups and about 15 entrees, bread, salad, and coffee or tea. At night, prices rise as the disco ball begins to spin. Nightly entertainment, including live disco music. Open daily 11am-2am.

Queens

With nearly every ethnic group represented in Queens, this often overlooked borough offers visitors authentic and reasonably priced international cuisine away from Manhattan's urban neighborhoods. **Astoria** specializes in discount shopping and cheap eats. Take the G or R train to Steinway St. and Broadway and start browsing— the pickings are good in every direction. In **Flushing,** excellent Chinese, Japanese, and Korean restaurants flourish, often making use of authentic ingredients such as skatefish, squid, and tripe. **Bell Blvd.** in Bayside, out east near the Nassau border, is the center of Queens nightlife for the young, white, and semi-affluent; on most weekends you can find crowds of natives bar-hopping here. **Jamaica Ave.** in downtown

Jamaica and **Linden Blvd.** in neighboring St. Albans are lined with restaurants specializing in African-American and West Indian food.

Pastrami King, 124-24 Queens Blvd. (718-263-1717), near 82nd Ave., in Kew Gardens. Subway: E or F to Union Tpke./Kew Gardens. Exit station following sign that says "Courthouse" and "Q10 bus," then go left past the sign to the north side of Queens Blvd. It's 2 blocks ahead and across the street. Everything here, from the meats to the slaw to the pickles, is made on the premises. Meat-lovers will be full for days on the open grilled-salami sandwich ($7.25), while the fat-averse can stick to salads ($5.75-9) and omelettes ($4-9). Open Tues.-Sun. 9:30am-11pm.

Uncle George's, 33-19 Broadway, Astoria (718-626-0593), at 33rd St. Subway: N to Broadway, then 2 blocks east; or G or R to Steinway St., then 4 blocks west. This popular Greek restaurant, known as "Barba Yiogis O Ksenihtis" to the locals, serves inexpensive and hearty Greek delicacies around the clock. Almost all entrees are under $10; die-hard fans feed on roast leg of lamb with potatoes ($8), or octopus sauteed with vinegar ($7). Goat soup ($6) and chick pea soup ($3) are part of the lighter fare. Excellent Greek salad with feta cheese ($6). Open 24hr.

Anand Bhavan, 35-66 73rd St., Jackson Heights (718-507-1600). Subway: F, G, H, R, or 7 to 74th St./Broadway, then walk 2 blocks down 73rd St. Tasty vegetarian South Indian restaurant—you'll wonder if you're in Queens or Bombay. Picant lunch specials ($6-8; served noon-4pm) are an incredible bargain, as is the Madras special, a filling 4-course meal that includes *sambar* (spicy lentil soup) and a choice of *iddly* (rice crepe with peppers and onions) or *vada* (stuffed lentil dough). When they say spicy, they mean spicy. Open daily 11am-9:30pm.

The Bronx

When Italian immigrants settled the Bronx, they brought their recipes and a tradition of hearty communal dining. While much of the Bronx is a culinary disaster zone, the New York *cognoscenti* soon discovered the few oases along **Arthur Ave.** With a sexy interior, and inviting outdoor tables, **Egidio Pastry Shop,** 622 E. 187th St., makes the best *gelato* in the Bronx.

Mario's, 2342 Arthur Ave. (718-584-1188), near 186th St. Five generations of the Migliucci *famiglia* have worked the kitchen of this celebrated southern Italian *trattoria*. The original clan left Naples in the early 1900s and opened the first Italian restaurant in Egypt, then came to the U.S. and cooked themselves into local lore; unsurprisingly, Mario's appears in Puzo's *The Godfather*. A room-length couch embraces patrons with familial arms amid an out-of-this-world pink decor. Proudly serves such delicacies as escargot ($5.50) and *spiedini alla romana*, a deep-fried sandwich made with anchovy sauce and mozzarella ($8). Traditional pasta $9.50-11.50, eggplant stuffed with ricotta $6.25. Open Tues.-Thurs. noon-11pm, Fri.-Sat. noon-midnight, Sun. noon-10pm.

Ann & Tony's, 2407 Arthur Ave. (718-933-1469), at 187th St. This bistro established in 1927 may specialize in comfy, no-frills decor like its Arthur Ave. compatriots—but unlike most restaurants in the area, Ann & Tony's has specials for dinner that run as low as $6, salad included. For lunch, sandwiches begin at $5. Open Mon.-Thurs. 11am-10pm, Fri. 11am-11pm, Sat. 1pm-midnight, Sun. 1-9pm.

SIGHTS

You can tell tourists in New York City from a mile away—they're all looking up. The internationally famous New York skyline is deceptive and elusive; while it can be seen miles away, the tallest skyscraper seems like just another building when you're standing next to it. This sightseeing quandary may explain why many New Yorkers have never visited some of the major sights in their hometown. In this densely-packed city, even the most mind-boggling landmarks become backdrops for everyday life. The beauty of New York City goes beyond its museums, parks, and sights. In New York you can get anything you could want, need, or dream of within a few city blocks. Explore, explore, explore. The city moves faster than we do—there will always be something new around the corner. Seeing New York takes a lifetime.

Lower Manhattan

The southern tip of Manhattan is a motley assortment of cobblestones and financial powerhouses. The Wall St. area is the densest in all New York, although Wall St. itself measures less than a ½-mi. long. This narrow state of affairs has driven the neighborhood into the air, creating one of the highest concentrations of skyscrapers in the world. With density comes history; lower Manhattan was the first part of the island to be settled by Europeans, and many of the city's historically significant sights lie in the concrete chasms here. Its crooked streets serve as a reminder of what New York City was like before it grew up and tidied out into a neat grid.

Battery Park, named for a battery of guns that the British stored there from 1683 to 1687, is now a chaotic chunk of green forming the southernmost toenail of Manhattan Island. The #1 and 9 trains to South Ferry terminate at the southeastern tip of the park; the #4 and 5 stop at Bowling Green, just off the northern tip. On weekends the park is often mobbed with people on their way to the Liberty and Ellis Island ferries, which depart from here.

Once the northern border of the New Amsterdam settlement, **Wall St.** takes its name from the wall built in 1653 to shield the Dutch colony from a British invasion from the north. By the early 19th century, the area was the financial capital of the United States. At Wall and Broad St. rests **Federal Hall** (825-6888), the original City Hall, where the trial of John Peter Zenger helped to establish freedom of the press in 1735. On the southwest corner of Wall and Broad St. stands the current home of the **New York Stock Exchange** (656-5168; open to the public Mon.-Fri. 9am-4pm). The Stock Exchange was first created as a marketplace for handling the $80 million in U.S. bonds that were issued in 1789 and 1790 to pay Revolutionary War debts. Arrive early in the morning, preferably before 9am, because tickets usually run out by 1pm. The observation gallery that overlooks the exchange's zoo-like main trading floor draws many observers.

Around the corner, at the end of Wall St., rises the seemingly ancient **Trinity Church** (602-0872). Its Gothic spire was the tallest structure in the city when first erected in 1846. The vaulted interior feels positively medieval.

Walk up Broadway to Liberty Park, and in the distance you'll see the twin towers of the city's tallest buildings, the **World Trade Center.** Two World Trade Center has an **observation deck** (323-2340) on the 107th floor. (Open daily June-Sept. 9:30am-11:30pm, Oct.-May 9:30am-9:30pm. $8, seniors and ages 6-12 $3.)

Farther north on Broadway, City Hall Park and **City Hall** serve as the focus of the city's administration. The Colonial chateau-style structure, completed in 1811, may be the finest piece of architecture in the city. North of the park, at 111 Centre St., between Leonard and White St., sits the **Criminal Court Building.** Here you can sit in on every kind of trial from misdemeanor to murder—visit the clerk's office in Room 150 for a schedule of what's taking place where, or call 374-6261.

One of the most sublime and ornate commercial buildings in the world, the Gothic **Woolworth Building** towers at 233 Broadway, off the southern tip of the park. Erected in 1913 by F.W. Woolworth to house the offices of his corner-store empire, it stood as the world's tallest until the Chrysler Building opened in 1930. Gothic arches and flourishes litter the lobby of this five-and-dime Versailles, including a caricature of Woolworth himself counting change. A block and a half farther south on Broadway, **St. Paul's Chapel** was inspired by London's St. Martin-in-the-Fields. St. Paul's is Manhattan's oldest public building in continuous use. For info on the chapel, call the office of the Trinity Museum (602-0773; chapel open Mon.-Fri. 9am-3pm, Sun. 7am-3pm).

Turn left off Broadway onto Fulton St. and head for the **South Street Seaport.** New York's shipping industry thrived here for most of the 19th century. The process of revitalization recently turned the historic district, in all its fishy and foul-smelling glory, into the ritzy South Street Seaport complex, an 18th-century market, graceful galleries, seafaring schooners, and **Pier 16,** a shopping mall and food court. At the end of Fulton St., as the river comes suddenly into view, so does the smell of dead fish waft through your nostrils. The stench comes from the **Fulton Fish Market,** the largest fresh-fish mart in the country, hidden right on South St. on the other side of the overpass. Those who can stomach wriggling scaly things might be interested in the behind-the-scenes tour of the market given some Thursday mornings June to October (market opens at 4am). The Pier 16 kiosk, the main ticket booth for the seaport, is open from 10am to 7pm (open 1hr. later on summer weekends).

The Statue of Liberty and Ellis Island

The **Statue of Liberty** (363-3200) remembers decades of immigrant crossings. The statue was given by the French in 1886 as a sign of goodwill. Since it has stood at the entrance to New York Harbor, the Statue of Liberty has welcomed millions of immigrants to America. Today, the statue welcomes tourists galore, as everyone and their sixteen cousins make the ferry voyage to Liberty Island. The other ferry stop is **Ellis Island.** Once the processing center for the 15 million Europeans who came to the U.S via New York, Ellis Island was shut down after the large waves of immigration were over. Recently redone, Ellis Island now houses an excellent **museum** telling the tale of many Americans' ancestors. (Ferries leave for Liberty Island from Battery Park every ½hr. Mon.-Fri. 9am-3:30pm, Sat.-Sun. 9am-4:30pm. Last ferry back at 7pm; Sept.-June 5:15pm. Ferry info 269-5755. $7, seniors $5, ages 3-17 $3, under 2 free.)

Lower East Side

Down below Houston lurks the trendily seedy Lower East Side, where old-timers rub shoulders with heroin dealers and hip twentysomethings. Two million Jews swelled the population of the Lower East Side in the 20 years before World War I; immigrants still live in the Lower East Side, although now they are mostly Asian and Hispanic. Chinatown has expanded across the Bowery and along the stretch of East Broadway, one of the district's main thoroughfares. A lot of East Village-type artists and musicians have recently moved in as well, especially near Houston St., but despite the influx of artists, a down-at-heel element remains.

Despite the population shift, remnants of the Jewish ghetto that inspired Jacob Riis's compelling work *How the Other Half Lives* still remain. New York's oldest synagogue building, the red-painted **Congregation Anshe Chesed** at 172-176 Norfolk St., just off Stanton St., now houses a Hispanic social service organization. Further down Norfolk, at #60 between Grand and Broome St., sits the **Beth Hamedrash Hagadol Synagogue,** the best-preserved of the Lower East Side houses of worship. From Grand St., follow Essex St. three blocks south to **East Broadway.** This street epitomizes the Lower East Side's flux of cultures. You will find Buddhist prayer centers next to (mostly boarded up) Jewish religious supply stores, and the offices of several Jewish civic organizations.

The area around Orchard and Delancey St. is one of Manhattan's bargain shopping centers. At 97 Orchard St., between Broome and Delancey St., you can visit the **Lower East Side Tenement Museum** (431-0233), a preserved tenement house of the type that proliferated in this neighborhood in the early part of the century. Buy tickets for a slide show, video, and guided tour at 90 Orchard St., at the corner of Broome St. (Tours are conducted Tues.-Fri. at 1, 2, and 3pm, Sat.-Sun. every 45min. 11am-4:15pm. $7, students and seniors $6.) The museum gallery at 90 Orchard St. offers free exhibits and photographs documenting Jewish life on the Lower East Side (open Tues.-Sun. 11am-5pm). Guided historical walking tours depart from the corner at 90 Orchard St. on Saturday and Sunday.

SoHo and TriBeCa

SoHo ("SOuth of HOw-ston Street") is bounded by Houston St., Canal, Lafayette, and Sullivan St. The architecture here is American Industrial (1860-1890), notable for its cast-iron façades. While its roots are industrial, its inhabitants are New York's prospering artistic community. Here, **galleries** reign supreme and experimental theaters and designer clothing stores fill the voids. This is a great place for star-gazing, too, but don't bother the celebrities—they really don't like that.

Greene St. offers the best of SoHo's lofty architecture. Genuine starving artists hang out in **TriBeCa** ("Triangle Below Canal St."), an area bounded by Chambers St., Broadway, Canal St., and the West Side Hwy. Admire the cast-iron edifices lining White St., Thomas St., and Broadway, the 19th-century Federal-style buildings on Harrison St., and the shops, galleries, and bars on Church and Reade St.

Greenwich Village and Washington Square Park

Located between Chelsea and SoHo on the lower West side of Manhattan, Greenwich Village (or, more simply put, "the Village") and its residents have defied convention for almost two centuries. Greenwich Village is the nexus of New York bohemia and counter-culture capital of the East Coast. In direct contrast to the orderly, skyscraper encrusted streets of greater Manhattan, narrow thoroughfares meander haphazardly through the Village without regard to artificial grids. Tall buildings give way to brownstones of varying ages and architectural styles. Village residents embody the alternative spectrum, with punks, hippies, ravers, rastas, guppies, goths, beatniks, and virtually every other imaginable group coexisting amidst a myriad of cafés, bars, shops, and theaters.

The bulk of Greenwich Village lies west of Sixth Ave. The West Village boasts an eclectic summer street life and excellent nightlife. The area has a large and visible gay community around **Sheridan Sq.** These are the home waters of the Guppie (Gay Urban Professional), and many gay men and lesbians shop, eat, and live here. **Christopher St.,** the main byway, swims in novelty restaurants and specialty shops. (Subway: #1 or 9 to Christopher St./Sheridan Sq.) A few street signs refer to Christopher St. as "Stonewall Place," alluding to the **Stonewall Inn,** the club where police raids in 1969 prompted riots that sparked the U.S. gay rights movement.

Washington Square Park beats at the heart of the Village, as it has since the district's days as a suburb. (Subway: A, B, C, D, E, F, or Q to W. 4th St./Washington Sq.) The marshland here served as home to Native Americans and freed slaves, and later as a colonial cemetery, but in the 1820s the area was converted into a park and parade ground. Soon chi-chi residences made the area the center of New York's social scene. Society has long since gone north, and **New York University** has moved in. The country's largest private university and one of the city's biggest landowners (along with the city government, the Catholic Church, and Columbia University), NYU has dispersed its buildings and eccentric students throughout the Village.

In the late 1970s and early 80s Washington Square Park became a base for low-level drug dealers and a rough resident scene. The mid-80s saw a noisy clean-up campaign that has made the park fairly safe and allowed a more diverse cast of characters to return. Today musicians play, misunderstood teenagers congregate, dealers mutter cryptic code words, homeless people try to sleep, and children romp in the playground. In the southwest corner of the park, a dozen perpetual games of chess clock their ways toward checkmate while circles of youths engage in hours of hacky-sacking. The fountain in the center of the park provides an amphitheater for comics and musicians of widely varying degrees of talent.

On the south side of Washington Square Park, at 133 MacDougal St. lies the dislocated **Provincetown Playhouse,** a theatrical landmark. Originally based on Cape Cod, the Provincetown Players were joined by the young Eugene O'Neill in 1916 and went on to premiere many of his works. Farther south on MacDougal are the Village's finest coffeehouses, which saw their glory days in the 1950s when beatnik heroes and coffee-bean connoisseurs Jack Kerouac and Allen Ginsberg attended jazz-accompanied poetry readings at **Le Figaro** and **Café Borgia.** These sidewalk cafés still provide some of the best coffee and people-watching in the city.

The north side of the park, called **The Row,** showcases a stretch of elegant Federal-style brick residences built largely in the 1830s. Up Fifth Ave., at the corner of 10th St., the **Church of the Ascension,** a fine 1841 Gothic church with a notable altar and stained-glass windows, looks heavenward (open daily noon-2pm and 5-7pm). **The**

Pen and Brush Club, located at 16 E. 10th St., was founded to promote female intelligentsia networking; Pearl Buck, Eleanor Roosevelt, Marianne Moore, and muckraker Ida Tarbell counted among its members.

At Fifth Ave. and 11th St. **The Salmagundi Club,** New York's oldest club for artists, has sheltered the sensitive since the 1870s. The club's building is the sole remaining mansion from the area's heyday. (Open daily 1-5pm. Call 255-7740 for details.) **Forbes Magazine Galleries** (206-5548) dominate the corner of Fifth Ave. and 12th St. The galleries present eccentric Malcolm Forbes's vast collection of *stuff*. (Open Tues.-Sat. 10am-4pm. Free.)

East Village and Alphabet City

The East Village, a comparatively new creation, was carved out of the Bowery and the Lower East Side as rents in the West Village soared and its residents sought accommodations elsewhere. Allen Ginsberg, Jack Kerouac, and William Burroughs all eschewed the Village establishment to develop their junked-up "beat" sensibility east of Washington Square Park. A fun but touristy stretch of Broadway runs through the Village, marking the western boundary.

One of the world's most famous bookstores, the **Strand,** at the corner of 12th St. and Broadway, bills itself as the "largest used bookstore in the world" with over two million books on 8 mi. of shelves. In 1853, John Jacob Astor constructed the **Joseph Papp Public Theatre,** 425 Lafayette St. (598-7150), to serve as the city's first free library. In 1967, Joseph Papp's **New York Shakespeare Festival** converted the building to its current use as a theatrical center.

The intersection of **Astor Place** (at the juncture of Lafayette, Fourth Ave., Astor Pl., and E. 8th St.) is distinguished by a sculpture of a large black cube balanced on its corner. Astor Place prominently features the rear of the **Cooper Union Foundation Building,** 41 Cooper Sq. (353-4199), built in 1859 to house the Cooper Union for the Advancement of Science and Art, a tuition-free technical and design school founded by self-educated industrialist Peter Cooper. The school's free lecture series has hosted almost every notable American since the mid-19th century. Cooper Union was the first college intended for the underprivileged and the first to offer free adult education classes. Across from a church at 156 Second Ave. stands a famous Jewish landmark, the **Second Avenue Deli** (677-0606). This is all that remains of the "Yiddish Rialto," the stretch of Second Ave. between Houston and 14th St. that comprised the Yiddish theater district in the early part of this century. The Stars of David embedded in the sidewalk in front of the restaurant contain the names of some of the great actors and actresses who spent their lives entertaining the poor Jewish immigrants of the city.

St. Mark's Place, running from Third Ave. at 8th St. down to Tompkins Square Park, is the geographical and spiritual center of the East Village. In the 1960s, the street was the Haight-Ashbury of the East Coast, full of weed-smoking flower children waiting for the next concert at the Electric Circus. In the late 1970s it became the King's Rd. of New York, as mohawked youths hassled passers-by from the brownstone steps of Astor Place. Things are changing again; a Gap store sells its color-me-matching combos across the street from a shop stocking "You Make Me Sick" T-shirts. Many Villagers now shun this commercialized and crowded street.

In **Alphabet City,** east of First Ave., south of 14th St., and north of Houston, the avenues run out of numbers and adopt letters. This part of the East Village has so far escaped the escalating yuppification that has claimed much of St. Mark's Place; during the area's heyday in the 60s, Jimi Hendrix would play open-air shows to bright-eyed Love Children. There has been a great deal of drug-related crime in the recent past, although the community has done an admirable job of making the area livable. Alphabet City is generally safe during the day, and the addictive nightlife on Avenue A ensures some protection there, but try to avoid straying east of Avenue B at night. Alphabet City's extremist Boho activism has made the neighborhood chronically ungovernable; a few years ago, police officers set off a riot when they attempted to forcibly evict a band of the homeless and their supporters in **Tompkins Square**

Park, at E. 7th St. and Ave. A. The park has just reopened after a two-year hiatus, and still serves as a psycho-geographical epicenter for many a churlish misfit.

Lower Midtown and Chelsea

Madison Ave. ends at 27th St. and **Madison Square Park.** The park, opened in 1847, originally served as a public cemetery. The area near the park sparkles with funky architectural gems. Another member of the "I-used-to-be-the-world's-tallest-building" club, the eminently photogenic **Flatiron Building** sits off the southwest corner of the park. Often considered the world's first skyscraper, it was originally named the Fuller Building, but its dramatic wedge shape, imposed by the intersection of Broadway, Fifth Ave., 22nd St., and 23rd St., quickly earned it its current *nom de plume*. St. Martin's Press, publisher of such fine books as *Let's Go: USA*, currently occupies roughly half the famed building's space.

A few blocks away, **Union Square** (so named because it was a union of two main roads), between Broadway and Park Ave. South, and 17th and 14th St., sizzled with High Society intrigue before the Civil War. Early in this century, the name gained dual significance when the neighborhood became a focal point of New York's Socialist movement, which held its May Day celebrations in **Union Square Park.** Later, the workers and everyone else abandoned the park to drug dealers and derelicts, but in 1989 the city attempted to reclaim it. The park is now pleasant and safe, though not necessarily pristine. The scents of herbs and fresh bread waft through the park every Wednesday, Friday, and Saturday, courtesy of the **Union Square Greenmarket.** Farmers and bakers from all over the region come here to hawk their produce, jellies, and baked goods.

Home to some of the most fashionable clubs, bars, and restaurants in the city, **Chelsea** has lately witnessed something of a rebirth. A large and visible gay and lesbian community and an increasing artsy-yuppie population have given the area, west of Fifth Ave. between 14th and 30th St., the flavor of a lower-rent West Village. Chelsea's continuing gentrification has prompted many of its newer, more upscale residents to rename the area **Clinton.** The historic **Hotel Chelsea,** 222 W. 23rd St. between Seventh and Eighth Ave., has sheltered many an artist, most famously Sid Vicious of the Sex Pistols. Edie Sedgwick made stops here between Warhol films before torching the place with a cigarette. Countless writers, as the plaques outside attest, spent their days searching for inspiration and mail in the lobby. Arthur Miller, Vladimir Nabokov, Arthur C. Clarke, and Dylan Thomas all sojourned here. Chelsea's **flower district,** on 28th St. between Sixth and Seventh Ave., colorfully blooms during the wee hours of the morning.

East Midtown and Fifth Avenue

The Empire State Building, on Fifth Ave. between 33rd and 34th St. (736-3100), has style. It retains its place in the hearts and minds of New Yorkers even though it is no longer the tallest building in the U.S., or even the tallest building in New York (stood up by the twin towers of the World Trade Center). It doesn't even have the best looks (the Chrysler building is more delicate, the Woolworth more ornate). But the Empire State remains arguably New York's best-known and best-loved landmark and continues to dominate the postcards, the movies, and the skyline. The limestone and granite structure, with glistening ribbons of stainless steel, stretches 1454 ft. into the sky; its 73 elevators run through two mi. of shafts; the nighttime view from the top will leave you gasping. The Empire State was among the first of the truly spectacular skyscrapers, benefiting from innovations like Eiffel's pioneering work with steel frames and Otis's perfection of the "safety elevator." In Midtown it towers in relative solitude, away from the forest of monoliths that has grown around Wall St. (Observatory open daily 9:30am-midnight, tickets sold until 11:30pm. $4.50, under 12 and seniors $2.25.) The nearest subway stations are at 34th St. (subway: B, D, F, N, Q, and R), 33rd St. (#6), and 28th St. (R).

In the **Pierpont Morgan Library,** 29 E. 36th St. (685-0610), at Madison Ave., the J. Pierpont Morgan clan developed the concept of the book as fetish object. With regular exhibitions and lots and lots of books inside, this Low Renaissance-style *palazzo* attracts many a bibliophile. (Subway: #6 to 33rd St. Open Tues.-Sat. 10:30am-5pm, Sun. 1-5pm. Suggested contribution $5, students and seniors $3. Free tours on various topics Tues.-Fri. 2:30pm.)

The **New York Public Library** (661-7220) reposes on the west side of Fifth Ave. between 40th and 42nd St., near Bryant Park. On sunny afternoons, throngs of people perch on the marble steps, under the watchful eyes of the mighty stone lions Patience and Fortitude. This is the world's seventh-largest research library; witness the immense third-floor reading room. (Free tours Tues.-Sat. 12:30 and 2:30pm. Open Mon. and Thurs.-Sat. 10am-6pm, Tues.-Wed. 11am-7:30pm.)

Spread out against the back of the library along 42nd St. to Sixth Ave., **Bryant Park** soothes with large, grassy, tree-rimmed expanses. The stage that sits at the head of the park plays host to a variety of free cultural events throughout the summer, including screenings of classic films, jazz concerts, and live comedy. Call 397-8222 for an up-to-date schedule of events.

To the east along 42nd St., **Grand Central Terminal** sits where Park Ave. would be, between Madison and Lexington Ave. A former transportation hub where dazed tourists first got a glimpse of the glorious city, Grand Central has since been partially supplanted by Penn Station and the Wright Brothers, but it maintains its dignity. The massive Beaux Arts front, with the famed 13-ft. clock, gives way to the Main Concourse, a huge lobby area. Constellations are depicted on the sweeping, arched expanse of green roof, while egg-shaped ribbed chandeliers light the secondary apses to the sides. (Free tours Wed. at 12:30pm from the Chemical Bank in the Main Concourse and Fri. from the Phillip Morris building across the street.)

The New York skyline would be incomplete without the familiar Art Deco headdress of the **Chrysler Building**, at 42nd St. and Lexington Ave., built by William Van Allen as an ode to the automobile and topped by a spire modeled on a radiator grille. When completed in 1929, this elegantly seductive building stood as the world's tallest. The Empire State Building topped it a year later. East on 42nd St. about 1½ blocks, between Park and Second Ave., stands the **Daily News Building** home to the country's first successful tabloid. The paper and building supposedly served as the inspiration for the *Daily Planet* of Superman fame. A gigantic rotating globe, which still features East Germany, Yugoslavia, and the U.S.S.R., dominates the lobby.

If you feel an urgent need to get out of the city, head for the **United Nations Building** (963-4475), located along New York's First Ave. between 42nd and 48th St. Outside, a multicultural rose garden and a statuary park provide a lovely view of the East River. Inside, go through security check and work your way to the back of the lobby for the informative tours of the **General Assembly. (Visitor's entrance** at First Ave. and 46th St. Daily tours about 45min., leaving every 15min. 9:15am-4:45pm, available in 20 languages. $6.50, over 60 and students $4.50, under 16 $3.50.) You must take the tour to get past the lobby. Sometimes free tickets to G.A. sessions can be obtained when the U.N. is in session (Oct.-May); call 963-1234.

Between 48th and 51st St. and Fifth and Sixth Ave. stretches **Rockefeller Center,** a monument to the conjunction of business and art. On Fifth Ave., between 49th and 50th St., the famous gold-leaf statue of Prometheus sprawls on a ledge of the sunken **Tower Plaza** while jet streams of water pulse around it. The Plaza serves as an open-air café in the spring and summer and as a world-famous ice-skating rink in the winter. The 70-story **RCA Building,** seated at Sixth Ave., remains the most accomplished artistic creation in this complex. Every chair in the building sits less than 28 feet from natural light. The **NBC Television Network** makes its headquarters here, allowing you to take a behind-the-scenes look at their operations. The network offers an hour-long tour which traces the history of NBC, from their first radio broadcast in 1926 through the heyday of TV programming in the 50s and 60s. The tour visits the studios of *Conan O'Brien* and the infamous 8H studio, home of *Saturday Night Live.* (Tours run every 15min. Mon.-Sat 9:30am-4:30pm. $8.25.)

Despite an illustrious history and a wealth of Art Deco treasures, **Radio City Music Hall** (632-4041) was almost demolished in 1979 to make way for new office high-rises. However, the public rallied and the place was declared a national landmark. First opened in 1932, at the corner of Sixth Ave. and 51st St., the 5874-seat theater remains the largest in the world. The brainchild of Roxy Rothafel (originator of the Rockettes), it was originally intended as a variety showcase. Yet the hall functioned primarily as a movie theater; over 650 feature films debuted here from 1933 to 1979, including *King Kong, Breakfast at Tiffany's,* and *Doctor Zhivago.* The Rockettes, Radio City's vertically endowed chorus line, still dance on. Tours of the great hall are given daily 10am-5pm ($12, under 7 $6).

At 25 W. 52nd St., the **Museum of Television and Radio** (621-6800) works almost entirely as a "viewing museum," allowing visitors to attend scheduled screenings in one of its theaters or to choose and enjoy privately a TV or radio show from its library of 60,000. Continue over a block down W. 53rd St. towards Sixth Ave. and take in masterpieces in the **American Craft Museum** and the **Museum of Modern Art** (see Museums). Rest your tired feet with a visit to the sculpture garden of MoMA, and contemplate the works of Rodin, Renoir, Miró, Lipschitz, and Picasso.

St. Patrick's Cathedral (753-2261), New York's most famous church and the largest Catholic cathedral in America, stands at 51st St. and Fifth Ave. Designed by James Renwick, the structure captures the essence of great European cathedrals like Reims and Cologne yet retains its own spirit. The twin spires on the Fifth Ave. façade stretch 330 ft. into the air.

One of the monuments to modern architecture, Ludwig Mies Van der Rohe's dark and gracious **Seagram Building** looms over 375 Park Ave., between 52nd and 53rd St. Pure skyscraper, fronted by a plaza and two fountains, the Seagram stands as a paragon of the austere International Style. Van der Rohe envisioned it as an oasis from the tight canyon of skyscrapers on Park Ave.

The stores on Fifth Ave. from Rockefeller Center to Central Park are the ritziest in the city. Take time to worship at the shrines to capitalism. At **Tiffany & Co.** (755-8000), get rid of the mean reds; everything from jewelry to housewares shines, especially the window displays, which can be art in themselves, especially around Christmas (open Mon.-Wed. and Fri.-Sat. 10am-5:30pm, Thurs. 10am-7:30pm). **F.A.O. Schwarz,** 767 Fifth Ave. (644-9400) at 58th St. impresses kids and adults with one of the world's largest toy stores, including complex Lego constructions, life-sized stuffed animals, and a separate annex exclusively for Barbie dolls. (Open Mon.-Wed. 10am-6pm, Thurs.-Sat. 10am-7pm, Sun. 11am-6pm.)

On Fifth Ave. and 59th St., at the southeast corner of Central Park, sits the legendary **Plaza Hotel,** built in 1907 at the then-astronomical cost of $12.5 million. Its 18-story, 800-room French Renaissance interior flaunts five marble staircases, countless ludicrously named suites, and a two-story Grand Ballroom. Past guests and residents have included Frank Lloyd Wright, the Beatles, F. Scott Fitzgerald, and, of course, the eminent Eloise. *Let's Go* recommends the $15,000-per-night suite.

West Midtown

Penn Station, at 33rd St. and Seventh Ave., is one of the less engrossing pieces of architecture in West Midtown, but as a major subway stop and train terminal, it can at least claim to be functional. (Subway: #1, 2, 3, 9, A, C, or E to 34th St./Penn Station.) The original Penn Station, a classical marble building modeled on the Roman Baths of Caracalla, was demolished in the 60s. The railway tracks were then covered with the equally uninspiring **Madison Square Garden** complex. Facing the Garden at 421 Eighth Ave., New York's immense main post office, the **James A. Farley Building,** luxuriates in its 10001 ZIP code. A lengthy swath of Corinthian columns muscles broadly across the front, and a 280-ft. frieze tops the broad portico with the motto of the U.S. Postal Service: "Neither snow nor rain nor heat nor gloom of night stays these couriers from the swift completion of their appointed rounds."

East on 34th St., between Seventh Ave. and Broadway, stands monolithic **Macy's** (695-4400). This giant, which occupies a full city block, was recently forced to relinquish its title as the "World's Largest Department Store" and change its billing to the "World's Finest Department Store" when a new store in Germany was built one square foot larger. With nine floors (plus a lower level) and some two million square feet of merchandise, Macy's has come a long way since 1857, when it grossed $11.06 on its first day of business. The store was recently forced to revisit its humble roots when it filed for bankruptcy, and its fate still remains uncertain. The store sponsors the **Macy's Thanksgiving Day Parade,** a New York tradition buoyed by helium-filled 10-story Snoopies, marching bands, floats, and general hoopla. (Open Mon.-Sat. 10am-8:30pm, Sun. 11am-7pm. Subway: #1, 2, 3, or 9 to Penn Station; or B, D, F, N, Q, or R to 34th St.)

The streets of **Times Square** flicker at the intersection of 42nd St. and Broadway. Still considered the dark and seedy core of the Big Apple by most New Yorkers, the Square has worked hard in the past few years to improve its image. Robberies have decreased by 40%, pick-pocketing and purse-snatching by 43%, and the number of area porn shops has plummeted by more than 100 from its late-70s climax of 140. The historic Victory Theater is undergoing restoration and will be the site of a new children's theater, and Disney has big plans for the aging New Amsterdam Theater, where the Ziegfeld Follies performed their original chorus line routine for more than twenty years. Still, Times Square is Times Square. Teens continue to roam about in search of fake IDs, hustlers wait eagerly to scam suckers, and every New Year's Eve, millions booze and schmooze and watch an electronic ball drop. One-and-a-half million people pass through Times Square every day. Lots of subway lines stop in the square (#1, 2, 3, 7, 9, and A, C, E, N, R, S).

On 42nd St. between Ninth and Tenth Ave. lies **Theater Row,** a block of renovated Broadway theaters that many consider the heart of American theater. The nearby **Theater District** stretches from 41st to 57th St. along Broadway, Eighth Ave., and the streets which connect them. Approximately 37 theaters remain active, most of them grouped around 45th St.

How do you get to **Carnegie Hall?** Practice, practice, practice. Or simply walk to 57th St. and Seventh Ave. The hall was founded in 1891 and remains New York's foremost soundstage. Tchaikovsky, Caruso, Toscanini, and Bernstein have played Carnegie, as have the Beatles and the Rolling Stones. Other notable events from Carnegie's playlist include the world premiere of Dvořák's *Symphony No. 9 (From the New World)* on December 16, 1893, and a lecture by Albert Einstein in 1934. Carnegie Hall almost faced the wrecking ball in the 50s, but outraged citizens managed to stop the impending destruction through special legislation in 1960. (Tours are given Mon.-Tues. and Thurs.-Fri. at 11:30am, 2, and 3pm. $6, students and seniors $5; call 903-9790 for info.) Carnegie Hall's **museum** displays artifacts and memorabilia from its illustrious century of existence (open daily 11am-4:30pm; free).

Upper East Side

The Golden Age of the East Side society epic began in the 1860s and progressed until the outbreak of World War I. Scores of wealthy people moved into the area and refused to budge, even during the Great Depression, when armies of the unemployed pitched their tents across the way in Central Park. These days parades, millionaires, and unbearably slow buses share Fifth Ave. Upper Fifth Ave. is home to **Museum Mile,** which includes the **Metropolitan,** the **Guggenheim,** the **ICP,** the **Cooper-Hewitt,** and the **Jewish Museum,** among others.

The Upper East Side drips with money along the length of the Park. Start your journey at 59th St. and Third Ave., where **Bloomingdale's** sits in regal splendor. **Madison Ave.** graces New York with luxurious boutiques and most of the country's advertising agencies. **Park Ave.,** the street that time forgot, maintains a regal austerity with gracious buildings and landscaped medians. **Gracie Mansion,** at the north end of Carl Schurz Park, between 84th and 90th St. along East End Ave., has been the residence of every New York mayor since Fiorello LaGuardia moved in during World War II. Now Rudolph Giuliani occupies this hottest of hot seats. (Tours Wed.; suggested admission $3, seniors $2. To make a reservation for a tour, call 570-4751.)

Central Park

Central Park rolls from Grand Army Plaza all the way up to 110th St. between Fifth and Eighth Ave. Twenty years of construction turned these 843 acres, laid out by Frederick Law Olmsted and Calvert Vaux in 1850-60, into a compressed sequence of infinite landscapes. The park contains lakes, ponds, fountains, skating rinks, ball fields, tennis courts, a castle, an outdoor theater, a bandshell, and two zoos.

The Park may be roughly divided between north and south at the main reservoir; the southern section affords more intimate settings, serene lakes, and graceful promenades, while the northern end has a few ragged edges. Nearly 1400 species of trees, shrubs, and flowers grow here, the work of distinguished horticulturist Ignaz Anton Pilat. When you wander amidst the shrubbery, look to the nearest lamppost for guidance and check the small metal four-digit plaque bolted to it. The first two digits tell you what street you're nearest (e.g., 89), and the second two whether you're on the east or west side of the Park (even numbers mean east, odds west). In an emergency, call the **24-hr. Park Hotline** from boxes in the park (570-4820). **Bite of the Apple Tours** (541-8759) offers leisurely 2-hr. guided **bicycle tours** through Central Park. (3 tours daily leave from 2 Columbus Circle, in front of the visitors center. Call for reservations. $25, which includes bicycle rental fee.)

At the renovated **Central Park Wildlife Center** (861-6030), Fifth Ave. at 64th St., the monkeys effortlessly ape their visitors. (Open April-Oct. Mon.-Fri. 10am-5pm, Sat.-Sun. 10:30am-5:30pm; Nov.-March daily 10am-4:30pm. Last entry ½-hr. before closing. $2.50, seniors $1.25, ages 3-12 50¢.)

The Dairy building now houses the **Central Park Reception Center** (794-6564). Pick up the free map of Central Park and the seasonal list of events. (Open Tues.-Thurs. and Sat.-Sun. 11am-5pm, Fri. 1-5pm; Nov.-Feb. Tues.-Thurs. and Sat.-Sun. 11am-4pm, Fri. 1-4pm.) The **Wollman Skating Rink** (396-1010) doubles as a **miniature golf course** in late spring. (Ice- or roller-skating $4, seniors and kids $3, plus $6.50 skate or rollerblade rental; 9-hole mini-golf $5, kids $2.50; bankshot $6, kids $3; discounts for combining activities. Whole complex open Mon.-Thurs. 10am-6pm, Fri. 10am-10pm, Sat. 11am-11pm, Sun. 11am-7pm.)

The **Friedsam Memorial Carousel** (879-0244) turns at 65th St. west of Center Dr. The 58-horsepower carousel was brought from Coney Island and fully restored in 1983. (Open daily 10:30am-6pm; Thanksgiving to mid-March Sun. 10:30am-4:30pm. 90¢.) Directly north of the Carousel, **Sheep Meadow** grows from about 66th to 69th St. on the western side of the Park. This is the largest chunk of greensward, exemplifying the pastoral ideals of the Park's designers.Spreading out to the west, the **Lake** provides a dramatic patch of blue in the heart of the City. The 1954 **Loeb Boathouse** (517-2233) supplies all necessary romantic nautical equipment. (Open daily April-Sept. 10am-5:30pm, weather permitting. Rowboats $10 per hr., $30 deposit.)

Strawberry Fields was sculpted by Yoko Ono as a memorial to John Lennon. The Fields are located to the west of the Lake at 72nd St. and West Dr., directly across from the Dakota Apartments where Lennon was assassinated and where Ono still lives. Ono battled valiantly for this space against city council members who had planned a Bing Crosby memorial on the same spot. Picnickers and 161 varieties of plants now bloom over the rolling hills around the star-shaped "Imagine" mosaic on sunny spring days.

The **Swedish Cottage Marionette Theater** (988-9093), at the base of Vista Rock near the 79th St. Transverse, puts on regular puppet shows (Sat. noon and 3pm; $5, kids $4). Climb the hill to the round wooden space of the **Delacorte Theater**, which hosts the wildly popular **Shakespeare in the Park** series each midsummer. These plays often feature celebrities and are always free. Come early: the theater seats only 1936 lucky souls (see Theater). Large concerts often take place north of the theater, on the **Great Lawn.** Here, Paul Simon sang, the Stonewall 25 marchers rallied, *Pocahontas* premiered, and the New York Philharmonic and the Metropolitan Opera Company frequently give free summer performances.

Although fairly safe during the day, parts of Central Park can be dangerous at night.

Upper West Side

Broadway leads uptown to **Columbus Circle,** at 59th St. and Broadway, the symbolic entrance to the Upper West Side and the end of Midtown. A statue of Christopher marks the border. One of the Circle's landmarks, the **New York Coliseum,** has been relatively empty since the construction of the **Javits Center** in 1990.

Broadway intersects Columbus Ave. at **Lincoln Center,** the cultural hub of the city, between 62nd and 66th St. The seven facilities that constitute Lincoln Center—Avery Fisher Hall, the New York State Theater, the Metropolitan Opera House, the Library and Museum of Performing Arts, the Vivian Beaumont Theater, the Walter Reade Theater, and the Juilliard School of Music—accommodate over 13,000 spectators at a time. At night, the Metropolitan Opera House lights up, making its chandeliers and huge Chagall murals visible through its glass-panel façade. **Columbus Ave.** leads to the **Museum of Natural History** (see Museums). **Broadway** pulses with energy all day (and all night) long. The Upper West Side is covered with residential brownstones, scenic enough for a pleasant (and free) stroll. See Upper West Side food section for info on **Zabar's,** a sight as well as a store.

Harlem

Half a million people are packed into the 3 square mi. of greater Harlem. On the East Side above 96th St. lies **Spanish Harlem,** known as El Barrio ("the neighborhood"), and on the West Side lies Harlem proper, stretching from 110th to 155th St. Columbia University controls the area west of Morningside Ave. and south of 125th St., commonly known as **Morningside Heights.** On the West Side, from 125th to 160th St., much of the cultural and social life of the area takes place in **Central Harlem.** To the far north, from 160th St. to 220th St., **Washington Heights** and **Inwood** are areas populated by thriving Dominican and Jewish communities. All these neighborhoods heat up with street activity, not always of the wholesome variety; visit Harlem during the day or go there with someone who knows the area. If you lack street wisdom or can't find your own guide, opt for a commercial tour.

Yet, don't let Harlem's problems overshadow its positive aspects. Although an extremely poor neighborhood, it is culturally rich; and, contrary to popular opinion, much of it is relatively safe. Known to locals as the "city within the City," Harlem is considered by many to be the black capital of the Western world. Over the years Harlem has often been viewed as the archetype of America's frayed cities—you won't believe that hype after you've visited. The 1920s were Harlem's Renaissance; a thriving scene of artists, writers, and scholars lived fast and loose, producing cultural masterworks in the process. The Cotton Club and the Apollo Theater, along with numerous other jazz clubs, were on the musical vanguard, while Langston Hughes and Zora Neale Hurston changed the face of literature.

Columbia University, chartered in 1754, huddles between Morningside Dr. and Broadway, 114th and 120th St. Now co-ed, Columbia also has cross-registration across the street with all-female **Barnard College** (call 854-2842 for info or a tour). The **Cathedral of St. John the Divine** (316-7540), along Amsterdam Ave. between 110th and 113th, promises to be the world's largest cathedral when finished. Construction, begun in 1812, continues and should not be completed for another century or two. Near Columbia, at 120th St. and Riverside Dr., is the **Riverside Church.** The observation deck in the tower commands an amazing view of the bells within and the expanse of the Hudson River and Riverside Park below. You can hear concerts on the world's largest carillon (74 bells), a gift of John D. Rockefeller, Jr. (Tours of the tower given Sun. 12:30pm; call for tickets. Open Mon.-Sat. 9am-4:30pm, Sun. service 10:45am.) Diagonally across Riverside Dr. lies **Grant's Tomb** (666-1640). Once a popular monument, it now attracts only a few brave souls willing to make the hike. (Open daily 9am-5pm. Free.)

125th St., also known as Martin Luther King, Jr. Blvd., spans the heart of traditional Harlem. Fast-food joints, jazz bars, and the **Apollo Theater** (222-0992, box office 749-5838) keep the street humming day and night. 125th St. has recently experienced a resurgence. Off 125th St., at 328 Lenox Ave., **Sylvia's** (966-0660) has magnetized New York for 22 years with enticing soul-food dishes (open Mon.-Sat. 7am-10pm, Sun. 1-7pm). The silver dome of the **Masjid Malcolm Shabazz,** where Malcolm X was once a minister, glitters on 116th St. and Lenox Ave. (visit Fri. at 1pm and Sun. at 10am for services and info, or call 662-2200).

In Washington Heights, north of 155th St., the **George Washington Bridge** has spanned the Hudson since 1931, connecting New York with New Jersey.

Brooklyn

If you need an escape from tourist-infested Manhattan, it may be time to explore the streets of the borough called Brooklyn. What goes on in gregarious Brooklyn tends to happen on the streets and out of doors, whether it's neighborhood banter, baseball games in the park, or ethnic festivals. The Dutch originally settled the borough in the 17th century. When asked to join New York in 1833, Brooklyn refused, saying that the two cities shared no interests except common waterways. Not until 1898 did Brooklyn decide, in a close vote, to become a borough of New York City. The visitors bureau (see Practical Information, above) publishes an excellent free guide to Brooklyn's rich historical past that outlines ten walking tours of the borough.

The Brooklyn Bridge spans the East River from lower Manhattan to Brooklyn. Built in 1883, the bridge was one of the greatest engineering feats of the 19th century. The one-mi. walk along the pedestrian path (make sure to walk on the left side, as the right is reserved for bicycles) will show you why every New York poet feels compelled to write at least one verse about it, why photographers snap the bridge's airy spider-web cables, and why people jump off. Once on the bridge, you can look straight up at the cables and Gothic arches. To get to the entrance on Park Row, walk a couple of blocks west from the East River to the city hall area. Plaques on the bridge towers commemorate John Augustus Roebling, its builder, who, along with 20 of his workers, died during its construction.

Head south on Henry St. after the Brooklyn Bridge, then turn right on Clark St. toward the river for a synapse-shorting view of Manhattan. Many prize-winning photographs have been taken from the **Brooklyn Promenade,** overlooking the southern tip of Manhattan and New York Harbor. George Washington's headquarters during the Battle of Long Island, now-posh **Brooklyn Heights** has hosted many authors, from Walt Whitman to Norman Mailer, with beautiful old brownstones, tree-lined streets, and proximity to Manhattan. The **New York Transit Museum,** (718-243- 3060) at Boerum and Schermerhorn, is one of the best museums in the city. Located in a now defunct subway station, the museum houses subway cars, turnstiles, and maps from years past, and has exhibits on the construction of the entire system. ($3, kids 17 and under $1.50. There's only one way you should get there: take the 2, 3, 4 or 5 to Borough Hall; the A, C or F to Jay St./Borough Hall; or the M, N, or R to Court St.) Continuing south, you'll find **Atlantic Ave.,** home to a large Arab community. Atlantic runs from the river to Flatbush Ave. At the Flatbush Ave. Extension, pick up the **Fulton St.** pedestrian mall.

Williamsburg, several blocks north of downtown Brooklyn, has retained its Hasidic Jewish culture. The quarter encloses Broadway, Bedford, and Union Ave. It closes on *Shabbat* (Saturday), the Jewish holy day.

Prospect Park, designed by Frederick Law Olmsted in the mid-1800s, was supposedly his favorite creation. He was even more pleased with it than with his Manhattan project—Central Park. At the north corner of the park **Grand Army Plaza** provides an island in the midst of the borough's busiest thoroughfares, designed to shield surrounding apartment buildings from traffic. (Subway: 2 or 3 to Grand Army Plaza.) The nearby **Botanic Gardens** (718-622-4433) are more secluded and include a lovely rose garden. (Open in summer Tues.-Fri. 8am-6pm, Sat.-Sun. and holidays 10am-6pm; Oct.-March Tues.-Fri. 8am-4:30pm, Sat.-Sun. and holidays 10am-4:30pm. Free.) The mammoth **Brooklyn Museum** (718-638-5000) rests behind the gardens (open Wed.-Sun. 10am-5pm; suggested donation $4, students $2, seniors $1.50).

Both a body of water (really part of the Atlantic) and a mass of land, **Sheepshead Bay** lies on the southern edge of Brooklyn. Walk along Emmons Ave. and peruse menus for daily seafood specials. Nearby **Brighton Beach,** nicknamed "Little Odessa by the Sea," has been homeland to Russian emigrés since the turn of the century. (Subway: D or Q.)

Once a resort for the City's elite, made accessible to the rest of the Apple because of the subway, fading **Coney Island** still warrants a visit. The **Boardwalk,** once one of the most seductive of Brooklyn's charms, now squeaks nostalgically as tourists are jostled by roughnecks. Enjoy a hot dog and crinkle-cut fries at historic **Nathan's,** at Surf and Sitwell Ave. The **Cyclone,** 834 Surf Ave. (718-266-3434), at W. 10th St., built in 1927, was once the most terrifying roller coaster ride in the world. Hurtle through the 100-second-long screamer; with nine hills of rickety wooden tracks the ride's well worth $3. (Open mid-June to Labor Day daily noon-midnight; Easter weekend to mid-June Fri.-Sun. noon-midnight.) Go meet a walrus, dolphin, sea lion, shark, or other ocean critter in the tanks of the **New York Aquarium** (718-265-3474), at Surf and West 8th St. (Open daily 10am-5pm, holidays and summer weekends 10am-7pm. $7.75, seniors and kids $3.55.)

Queens

In this urban suburbia, the American melting pot bubbles away with a more than 30% foreign-born population. Immigrants from Korea, China, India, and the West Indies rapidly sort themselves out into neighborhoods where they try to maintain the memory of their homeland while living "the American Dream."

Queens is easily New York's largest borough, covering over a third of the city's total area. You need to understand Queens's kaleidoscope of communities to understand the borough. If you visit only one place in Queens, let it be **Flushing.** Here you will find some of the most important colonial neighborhood landmarks, a bustling downtown, and the largest rose garden in the Northeast. (Subway: #7 to Main St., Flushing.) Nearby **Flushing Meadows-Corona Park** was the site of the 1964-1965 World's Fair, and now holds Shea Stadium (home of the Mets) and several museums.

The Bronx

While the media present "Da Bronx" as a crime-ravaged husk, the borough offers its few tourists over 2000 acres of parkland, a great zoo, turn-of-the-century riverfront mansions, grand boulevards evocative of Europe, and thriving ethnic neighborhoods, including a Little Italy to shame its counterpart to the south. If you're not heading for Yankee Stadium, stay out of the **South Bronx** unless you're in a car and with someone who knows the area.

The most obvious reason to come to the Bronx is the **Bronx Zoo/Wildlife Conservation Park** (718-367-1010 or 718-220-5100), also known as the New York Zoological Society. The largest urban zoo in the United States, it houses over 4000 animals. You can explore the zoo by foot or ride like the king of the jungle aboard the Safari Train, which runs between the elephant house and Wild Asia ($1). Soar into the air for a funky cool view of the zoo from the **Skyfari** aerial tramway that runs between Wild Asia and the Children's Zoo (one-way $2, kids $1). The **Bengali Express Monorail** glides round Wild Asia (20min.; $2). If you find the pace too hurried, saddle up a camel in the Wild Asia area ($3). Call 220-5142 three weeks in advance to reserve a place on a **walking tour.** Pamphlets containing self-guided tours are available at the Zoo Center for 75¢. Parts of the zoo close down during the winter (Nov.-April). (Open Mon.-Fri. 10am-5pm, Sat.-Sun. 10am-5:30pm; Nov.-Jan. daily 10am-4:30pm. $6.75, seniors and kids $3; free Wed. For disabled-access, call 718-220-5188. Subway: #2 or 5 to E. Tremont Ave.)

North across East Fordham Rd. from the zoo, the **New York Botanical Garden** (718-817-8705) sprawls over snatches of forest and virgin waterways. (Garden grounds open in summer Tues.-Sun. 10am-7pm; Nov.-March 10am-6pm. Suggested donation $3; seniors, students, and kids $1. Parking $4. Subway: #4 or D to Bedford Park Blvd. and Bx26 bus 8 blocks east.)

The **Museum of Bronx History** (881-8900), at Bainbridge Ave. and 208th St. (subway: D to 205th St., or #4 to Mosholu Pkwy; walk 4 blocks east on 210th St. and then south a block) is run by the Bronx Historical Society on the premises of the landmark Valentine-Varian House. The museum presents historical narratives explaining the borough of the Bronx. (Open Sat. 10am-4pm, Sun. 1-5pm. $2.)

Staten Island

Getting there is half the fun. At 50¢ (roundtrip), the ½-hr. ferry ride from Manhattan's Battery Park to Staten Island is as unforgettable as it is inexpensive. Or you can drive from Brooklyn over the **Verrazano-Narrows Bridge**, the world's second-longest (4260 ft.) suspension span. Because of the hills and the distances (and some very dangerous neighborhoods in between), it's a bad idea to walk from one site to the next. Make sure to plan your excursion with the bus schedule in mind.

The most concentrated number of sights on the island cluster around the beautiful 19th-century **Snug Harbor Cultural Center,** at 1000 Richmond Terrace. Picnic and see its catch: the **Newhouse Center for Contemporary Art** (718-448-2500), a small gallery displaying American art with an indoor/outdoor sculpture show in the summer (open Wed.-Sun. noon-5pm; free), the **Staten Island Children's Museum** (718-273-2060), with participation exhibits for the five- to 12-year-old in you (open Tues.-Sun. noon-5pm; $4), and the **Staten Island Botanical Gardens.**

Live Free or Die

The Staten Island secession movement is a lot more serious than one might think. Virtually every municipal election on the island in recent memory has included the petition to make New York City four boroughs instead of five. When one referendum showed that a majority of residents wanted to leave the Big Apple, the Borough President, Guy Molinari, got so excited that he set up four cannons, pointed them at each of the other four boroughs, and fired off a round. "Just warning shots," he said. Brooklyn, Manhattan, Queens, and the Bronx did not return fire.

MUSEUMS AND GALLERIES

For museum and gallery listings consult the following publications: *The New Yorker* (which has the most accurate and extensive listing), *New York* magazine, and the Friday *New York Times* (in the Weekend section). Most museums and all galleries close on Mondays, and are jam-packed on the weekends. Many museums require a "donation" in place of an admission fee—you can give less than the suggested amount. Most museums are free one weeknight; call ahead to confirm.

Major Collections

Metropolitan Museum of Art, (879-5500), Fifth Ave. at 82nd St. Subway: #4, 5, or 6 to 86th St. If you see only one, see this. The largest in the Western Hemisphere, the Met's art collection encompasses 3.3 million works from almost every period through Impressionism; particularly strong in Egyptian and non-Western sculpture and European painting. Contemplate infinity in the secluded Japanese Rock Garden. When blockbuster exhibits tour the world they usually stop at the Met—get tickets in advance through Ticketron. Open Sun. and Tues.-Thurs. 9:30am-5:15pm, Fri.-Sat. 9:30am-8:45pm. Donation $7, students and seniors $3.50.

Museum of Modern Art (MoMA), 11 W. 53rd St. (708-9400), off Fifth Ave. in Midtown. Subway: E or F to Fifth Ave./53rd St. One of the most extensive contemporary (post-Impressionist) collections in the world, founded in 1929 by scholar Alfred Barr in response to the Met's reluctance to embrace modern art. Cesar Pelli's structural glass additions flood the masterpieces with natural light. See Monet's sublime *Water Lily* room, and many Picassos. Gorgeous sculpture garden. Open Sat.-Tues. 11am-6pm, Thurs.-Fri. noon-8:30pm. $8, students and seniors $5, under 16 free. Films require free tickets in advance. Pay-what-you-wish Thurs.-Fri. 5:30-8:30pm.

American Museum of Natural History (769-5100), Central Park West, at 79th to 81st St. Subway: B or C to 81st St. The largest science museum in the world, in a suitably imposing Romanesque structure. Newly reopened dinosaur exhibit is worth the lines you'll inevitably face. Locals recommend seeing things from a new perspective by lying down under the whale in the Ocean Life room. Open Sun.-Thurs. 10am-5:45pm, Fri.-Sat. 10am-8:45pm. Donation $6, students and seniors $4, children $3. Free Fri.-Sat. 5-8:45pm. The museum also houses **Naturemax** (769-5650), a cinematic extravaganza on a huge movie screen (4 stories). $6, students and seniors $5, children $3, Fri.-Sat. double features $7.50, children $4. The **Hayden Planetarium** (769-5100) offers multi-media presentations. Seasonal celestial light shows twinkle in the dome of its **Theater of the Stars,** accompanied by astronomy lectures. Admission $5, seniors and students $4, kids $2.50. Electrify your senses with the theater's Laser Floyd or Laser Grunge.

Guggenheim Museum, 1071 Fifth Ave. and 89th St. (423-3500). Many have called this controversial construction a giant turnip, Frank Lloyd Wright's joke on the Big Apple. The museum closed from 1990-92 while a ten-story "tower gallery" sprouted behind the original structure, allowing the museum to show more of its rich permanent collection of mostly 20th-century art. Open Sun.-Wed. 10am-6pm, Fri.-Sat. 10am-8pm. $7, students and seniors $4, under 12 free. Pay what you wish Fri. 6-8pm. Two-day pass to this museum and **Guggenheim Museum SoHo,** 575 Broadway (423-3500) at Prince St. Open Sun. and Wed.-Fri. 11am-6pm, Sat. 11am-8pm. $6, students and seniors $4, and under 12 free.

Whitney Museum of American Art, 945 Madison Ave. (570-3676), at 75th St. Subway: #6 to 77th St. Futuristic fortress featuring the largest collection of 20th-century American art in the world, with works by Hopper, Soyer, de Kooning, Motherwell, Warhol, and Calder. Controversial political art has infiltrated what was once a bastion of high-modernism, with food, trash, and video becoming accepted media. Open Wed. 11am-6pm, Thurs. 1-8pm, Fri.-Sun. 11am-6pm. $7, students and seniors $5, under 12 free. Thurs. 6-8pm $3.50.

Cooper-Hewitt Museum, 2 E. 91st St. (860-6868), at Fifth Ave. Subway: #4, 5 or 6 to 86th St. Andrew Carnegie's majestic, Georgian mansion now houses the Smithsonian Institute's National Museum of Design. The playful special exhibits focus on such topics as doghouses and the history of the pop-up book. Open Tues. 10am-9pm, Wed.-Sat. 10am-5pm, Sun. noon-5pm. $3, students and seniors $1.50, under 12 free. Free Tues. 5-9pm.

The Frick Collection, 1 E. 70th St. (288-0700), at Fifth Ave. Subway: #6 to 68th St. Robber-baron Henry Clay Frick left his house and art collection to the city, and the museum retains the elegance of his French "Classic Eclectic" château. Impressive grounds. The Living Hall displays 17th-century furniture, Persian rugs, Holbein portraits, and paintings by El Greco, Rembrandt, Velázquez, and Titian. Relax in a courtyard inhabited by elegant statues surrounding the garden pool and fountain. Open Tues.-Sat. 10am-6pm, Sun. 1-6pm. $5, students and seniors $3. Under 10 not allowed, under 16 must be accompanied by an adult.

Smaller and Specialized Collections

American Craft Museum, 40 W. 53rd St. (956-3535), across from MoMA. Subway: E or F to Fifth Ave.-53rd St. Offering more than quilts, this museum revises the notion of crafts with its modern media, including metal and plastic. Open Tues. 10am-8pm, Wed.-Sun. 10am-5pm. $5, students and seniors $2.50.

The Cloisters (923-3700), Fort Tryon Park, upper Manhattan. Subway: A through Harlem to 190th St.; or take the M4 bus that departs from the Met. This monastery, built from pieces of 12th- and 13th-century French and Spanish cloisters, was assembled at John D. Rockefeller's behest by Charles Collens in 1938 as a setting for the Met's medieval art collection. Highlights include the Unicorn Tapestries, the Cuxa Cloister, and the Treasury, with 15th-century playing cards. Museum tours Tues.-Fri. 3pm, Sun. noon, in winter Wed. 3pm. Open Tues.-Sun. 9:30am-5:15pm. Donation $6, students and seniors $3 (includes admission to the Metropolitan Museum of Art).

International Center of Photography, 1130 Fifth Ave. (860-1777), at 94th St. Subway: #6 to 96th St. Housed in a landmark townhouse built in 1914 for *New Repub-*

lic founder Willard Straight. The foremost exhibitor of photography in the city, and a gathering-place for its practitioners. Historical, thematic, contemporary, and experimental works, running from fine art to photo-journalism. Midtown branch at 1133 Sixth Ave. (768-4680), at 43rd St. Both open Tues. 11am-8pm, Wed.-Sun. 11am-6pm. $4, students and seniors $2.50.

Intrepid Sea-Air-Space Museum, Pier 86 (245-0072), at 46th St. and Twelfth Ave. Bus: M42 or M50 to W. 46th St. One ticket admits you to the veteran World War II and Vietnam War aircraft carrier *Intrepid,* the Vietnam War destroyer *Edson,* the only publicly displayed guided-missile submarine, *Growler,* and the lightship *Nantucket.* A breathtaking wide-screen flick puts the viewer on a flight deck as jets take off and land. The Iraqi tanks near the gift shop were captured in the Gulf War. Open May-Oct. daily 10am-5pm; Oct.-Apr. Wed.-Sun. 10am-5pm. $10, seniors, students, and veterans $7.50, ages 6-11 $5.

Jacques Marchais Center of Tibetan Art, 338 Lighthouse Ave. (718-987-3478), Staten Island. Take bus S74 from Staten Island Ferry to Lighthouse Ave., turn right and walk up the hill. One of the finest Tibetan collections in the U.S. Exuding serenity, the center replicates a Tibetan temple set amid sculpture gardens. Open May-Oct. Wed.-Sun. 1-5pm. $3, seniors $2.50, children $1.

The Jewish Museum, 1109 Fifth Ave. (423-3200), at 92nd St. Subway: #6 to 96th St. Over 14,000 works detail the Jewish experience throughout history. Open Sun.-Mon. and Wed.-Thurs. 11am-5:45pm, Tues. 11am-9pm. $7, students and seniors $5, under 12 free; Tues. pay what you wish after 5pm.

The Museum for African Art, 593 Broadway (966-1313), between Houston and Prince St. in SoHo. Subway: N or R to Prince and Broadway. Formerly the Center for African Art, the museum has changed its name and expanded to feature two major exhibits of stunning African and African-American art. Open Tues.-Fri. 10am-5:30pm, Sat.-Sun. noon-6pm. $4, students and seniors with ID $2.

El Museo del Barrio, 1230 Fifth Ave. (831-7272), at 104th St. Subway: #6 to 103rd St. El Museo del Barrio is the only museum in the U.S. devoted exclusively to the art and culture of Puerto Rico and Latin America. Open Wed.-Sun. 11am-5pm; May-Sept. Wed. and Fri.-Sun. 9am-5pm, Thurs. noon-7pm. Suggested contribution $4, students and seniors $2.

Museum of the City of New York (534-1672), 103rd St. and Fifth Ave. next door to El Museo del Barrio. Subway: #6 to 103rd St. Premier museum chronicling New York City presents the city's story from the 16th century to the present through historical paintings, Currier and Ives prints, period rooms, and artifacts. Open Wed.-Sat. 10am-5pm, Sun. 1-5pm. Contribution requested.

Museum of Television and Radio, 25 W. 52nd St. (621-6600), between Fifth and Sixth Ave. Subway: B, D, F, Q to Rockefeller Center; E or F to 53rd St. Boob tube relics and memorabilia, as well as over 50,000 programs in the museum's permanent collection. With admission you can watch or listen to anything from the *Twilight Zone* to *Saturday Night Live.* Open Tues.-Wed. and Fri.-Sun. noon-6pm, Thurs. noon-8pm. $6, students $4, seniors and children $3.

National Museum of the American Indian, 1 Bowling Green (668-6624), in the U.S. Customs House. Subway: #4 or 5 to Bowling Green. This newly re-opened museum exhibits the best of the Smithsonian's vast collection of Native American artifacts, in galleries and exhibitions designed by Native American artists and craftsmen as well as historians. Also shows works by contemporary artists. Open daily 10am-5pm. Free.

New Museum of Contemporary Art, 583 Broadway (219-1355), between Prince and Houston St. Subway: R to Prince, #6 to Bleecker, or B, D or F to Broadway/Lafayette. Dedicated to the destruction of the canon and of conventional ideas of "art," supports the hottest, the newest, and the most controversial. Many works deal with politics of identity—sexual, racial, and ethnic. Once a month, an artist sits in the front window and converses with passers-by. Open Wed.-Fri. and Sun. noon-6pm, Sat. noon-8pm. $4; students, seniors, and artists $3; under 12 free; Sat. 6-8pm free.

ENTERTAINMENT AND NIGHTLIFE

Although always an exhilarating, incomparable city, New York only becomes *New York* when the sun goes down. From the blindingly bright lights of Times Square to the dark, impenetrably smoky atmosphere of a Greenwich Village or SoHo bar, the Big Apple pulls you in a million directions at once. Find some performance art, hear some jazz, go to an all-night diner, twist the night away—heck, even get a tattoo. A cab ride home at 4:30am through empty streets with the windows down is always sure to make your spirits soar. This city never sleeps and, at least for a few nights, neither should you.

Publications with especially noteworthy sections on nightlife include the *Village Voice, New York* magazine, and the Sunday edition of the *New York Times*. The most comprehensive survey of the current theater scene can be found in *The New Yorker*. An **entertainment hotline** (360-3456; 24hr.) covers weekly activities by both borough and genre.

Theater

Broadway is currently undergoing a revival—ticket sales are booming, and mainstream musicals are receiving more than their fair share of attention. Broadway tickets cost about $50 each when purchased through regular channels. **TKTS** (768-1818 for recorded info) sells half-price tickets to many Broadway shows on the same day of the performance. TKTS has a booth in the middle of Duffy Square (the northern part of Times Square, at 47th and Broadway). TKTS tickets are usually about $25 each plus a $2.50 service charge per ticket. (Tickets are sold Mon.-Sat. 3-8pm for evening performances, Wed. and Sat. 10am-2pm for matinees, Sun. noon-8pm for matinees and evening performances.) For info on shows and ticket availability, call the **NYC/ON STAGE** hotline at 768-1818. **Ticketmaster** (307-7171) deals in everything from Broadway shows to mud-truck races; they charge at least $2 more than other outlets, but take most major credit cards. *Listings,* a weekly guide to entertainment in Manhattan ($1), has listings of Broadway, Off-Broadway, and Off-Off-Broadway shows.

Off-Broadway theaters have between 100 and 499 seats; only Broadway houses have over 500. Off-Broadway houses frequently offer more offbeat, quirky shows, with shorter runs. Occasionally these shows have long runs or make the jump to Broadway houses. Tickets cost $10-20. The best of the Off-Broadway houses huddle in the Sheridan Square area of the West Village. TKTS also sells tickets for the larger Off-Broadway houses. **Off-Off-Broadway** means cheaper, younger theaters.

For years, the **Joseph Papp Public Theater,** 425 Lafayette St. (598-7150), was inextricably linked with its namesake founder, one of the city's leading producers. The theater recently produced an exhaustive and exhausting Shakespeare Marathon—every single one of the Bard's plays was shown, down to *Timon of Athens*. Tickets cost $15-35. About a quarter of the seats are sold for $10 on the day of performance (starting at 6pm for evening performances and 1pm for matinees). Papp also founded **Shakespeare in the Park** (861-7277), a New York summer tradition. From June through August, two Shakespeare plays are presented at the **Delacorte Theater** in Central Park, near the 81st St. entrance on the Upper West Side, just north of the main road. Tickets are free, but lines form early. Call for info.

Movies

If Hollywood is *the* place to make films, New York City is *the* place to see them. Most movies open in New York weeks before they're distributed across the country, and the response of Manhattan audiences and critics can shape a film's success or failure nationwide. Dozens of revival houses show motion picture classics, and independent filmmakers from around the reel world come to New York to flaunt their work. Big-screen fanatics should check out the cavernous **Ziegfeld,** 141 W. 54th St. (765-7600), one of the largest screens left in America, which shows first-run films. **MoviePhone** (777-FILM/3456) allows you to reserve tickets for most major movie-houses and pick them up at showtime from the theater's automated ticket dispenser; you charge the ticket price plus a small fee over the phone. **The Kitchen,** 512 W. 19th St. (255-5793), between Tenth and Eleventh Ave., (subway: C or E to 23rd St.), is a world-renowned showcase for the off-beat from New York-based struggling artists (prices vary). See eight screens of alternative (not quite underground) cinema at the **Angelika Film Center,** 18 W. Houston St. (995-2000), at Mercer St. (subway: #6 to Bleecker St. or B, D, F, or Q to Broadway-Lafayette). The café upstairs has excellent espresso. **Anthology Film Archives,** 32 Second Ave. (505-5181) at E. 2nd St., is a forum for independent filmmaking. The **New York International Film Festival** packs 'em in every October; check the *Voice* or the *Times* for dates and times.

Opera and Dance

You can do it all at **Lincoln Center** (875-5000), New York's one-stop shopping mall for high-culture consumers; there's usually opera or dance at one of its many venues. Write Lincoln Center Plaza, NYC 10023, or drop by its Performing Arts Library (870-1930) for a full schedule and a press kit as long as the *Ring* cycle. The **Metropolitan Opera Company** (362-6000), opera's premier outfit, plays on a Lincoln Center stage as big as a football field. Regular tickets run as high as $100—go for the upper balcony (around $15; the cheapest seats have an obstructed view), unless you're prone to vertigo. You can stand in the orchestra ($14) along with the opera freakazoids, or all the way back in the Family Circle ($15). (Regular season runs Sept.-April Mon.-Sat.; box office open Mon.-Sat. 10am-8pm, Sun. noon-6pm.) In the summer, watch for free concerts in city parks (362-6000).

At right angles to the Met, the **New York City Opera** (870-5570) has a new sound under the direction of Christopher Keene. "City" now has a split season (Sept.-Nov. and March-April) and keeps its ticket prices low year-round ($15-73). For rush tickets, call the night before and wait in line the morning of. In July, look for free performances by the **New York Grand Opera** (360-2777) at Central Park Summerstage every Wednesday night. Check the papers for performances of the old warhorses by the **Amato Opera Company,** 319 Bowery (228-8200; Sept.-May). Music schools often stage opera as well; see Music for further details.

The New York State Theater (870-5570) is home to the late, great George Balanchine's **New York City Ballet,** the country's oldest dance company. Decent tickets for the *Nutcracker* in December sell out almost immediately. (Performances Nov.-Feb. and April-June. Tickets $12-57, standing room $8.) Gaining ever more accolades these days, the **American Ballet Theater** (477-3030), under Kevin McKinsey's guidance, dances at the Met every May and June (tickets $16-95). The **Alvin Ailey American Dance Theater** (767-0940) bases its repertoire of modern dance on jazz, spirituals, and contemporary music. Often on the road, it always performs at the **City Center** in December. Tickets ($15-40) can be difficult to obtain. Write or call the City Center, 131 W. 55th St. (581-7907), weeks in advance. Look for ½-price tickets at the Bryant Park ticket booth (see below).

Other companies include the **Martha Graham Dance Co.,** 316 E. 63rd St. (832-9166), performing original Graham pieces during its October New York season, and the **Merce Cunningham Dance Company** (255-8240), of John Cage fame. Half-price tickets for many music and dance events can be purchased on the day of performance at the **Bryant Park** ticket booth, 42nd St. (382-2323), between Fifth and Sixth Ave. (Open Tues.-Sun. noon-2pm and 3-7pm; cash and traveler's checks only.) Concert tickets to Monday shows are available on the preceding Sunday.

Classical Music

As always, start with the ample listings in the *New York Times, The New Yorker,* or *New York* magazine. Remember that many events, like outdoor music, are seasonal.

The **Lincoln Center Halls** have a wide, year-round selection of concerts. The **Great Performers Series,** featuring famous and foreign musicians, packs the Avery Fisher and Alice Tully Halls and the Walter Reade Theater from October until May (call 875-5020; tickets from $11). **Avery Fisher Hall** (875-5030; wheelchair accessible) paints the town ecstatic with its annual **Mostly Mozart Festival.** Show up early; there are usually pre-concert recitals beginning one hour before the main concert

MID-ATLANTIC

which are free to ticketholders. The festival runs from July to August, with tickets to individual events costing $12-30. The **New York Philharmonic** (875-5656) begins its regular season in mid-September (tickets $10-60; call 721-6500 Mon.-Sat. 10am-8pm, Sun. noon-8pm). Students and seniors can sometimes get $5 tickets; call ahead (Tues.-Thurs. only). Anyone can get $10 tickets for the odd morning rehearsal; again, call ahead. For a couple of weeks in late June, Kurt Masur and friends lead the posse at **free concerts** (875-5709) on the Great Lawn in Central Park, in Prospect Park in Brooklyn, in Van Cortland Park in the Bronx, and elsewhere. Free outdoor events at Lincoln Center occur all summer; call 875-4000.

    Carnegie Hall (247-7800), Seventh Ave. at 57th St., is still the favorite coming-out locale of musical debutantes (box office open Mon.-Sat. 11am-6pm, Sun. noon-6pm; tickets $10-60). One of the best ways for the budget traveler to absorb New York musical culture is to visit a **music school.** Except for opera and ballet productions ($5-12), concerts at the following schools are free and frequent: The **Juilliard School of Music,** Lincoln Center (769-7406), the **Mannes School of Music** (580-0210), and the **Manhattan School of Music** (749-2802).

Jazz Joints

The **JVC Jazz Festival** (787-2020) blows into the city in June. All-star performances have included Ray Charles and Mel Torme. Tickets go on sale in early May.

    Apollo Theatre, 253 W. 125th St. (749-5838, box office 864-0372), between Frederick Douglass Blvd. and Adam Clayton Powell Blvd. Subway: #1, 2, 3, or 9 to 125th St. Historic Harlem landmark has heard Duke Ellington, Count Basie, Ella Fitzgerald, and Billie Holliday. Legendary Amateur Night (where the audience boos acts off the stage, à la *Gong Show*) $5.

    Birdland, 2745 Broadway (749-2228), at 105th St. Subway: #1 or 9 to 103rd St. Good food and top jazz. Cover Fri.-Sat $5 plus $5 min. per set at bar, $10/$20 at tables; Sun.-Thurs. $5 plus $5 min. per set at tables; no cover at bar. No cover for brunch Sun. noon-4pm. Open Mon.-Sat. 5pm-2am, Sun. noon-4pm and 5pm-2am. First set nightly at 9pm.

    Blue Note, 131 W. 3rd St. (475-8592), near MacDougal St. Subway: A, B, C, D, E, F, or Q to Washington Sq. The Carnegie Hall of jazz clubs. Now a commercialized concert space with crowded tables and a sedate audience. Often books top performers. Cover $20 and up, $5 drink min. Sets daily 9 and 11:30pm.

    Village Vanguard, 178 Seventh Ave. (255-4037), south of 11th St. Subway: #1, 2, 3, or 9 to 14th St. A windowless, wedge-shaped cavern, as old and hip as jazz itself. Every Mon. the Vanguard Orchestra unleashes its torrential Big Band sound at 10pm and midnight. Cover Sun.-Thurs. $15 plus $10 min., Fri.-Sat. $15 plus $8 min. Sets Sun.-Thurs. 9:30 and 11:30pm, Fri.-Sat. 9:30, 11:30pm, and 1am.

Clubs

In addition to the venues listed below, check the *Village Voice* for shows at the **Bottom Line** (228-7880), the **Cooler** (229-0785), the **Knitting Factory** (219-3055), and **Wetlands** (966-4225), all fine clubs for live music of all varieties.

    CBGB/OMFUG (CBGB's), 313 Bowery (982-4052), at Bleecker St. Subway: #6 to Bleecker St. The initials stand for "country, bluegrass, blues, and other music for uplifting gourmandizers," but everyone knows that since 1976 this club has been all about punk rock. Blondie and the Talking Heads got their starts here, and the club continues to be *the* place to see great alternative rock. Shows nightly at around 8pm. Cover $5-10.

    Maxwell's, 1039 Washington St. (201-798-4064), in nearby Hoboken, NJ. Subway: B, D, F, N, Q, or R to 34th St., then PATH train ($1), or simply take the PATH train ($1) to the Hoboken stop; walk down Washington to 11th St. High-quality underground rockers from America and abroad have plied their trade in the back room of a Hoboken restaurant for about 15 years. Cover $5-10; shows sometimes sell out, so get tix in advance from Maxwell's or Ticketmaster.

MID-ATLANTIC

Mercury Lounge, 217 E. Houston St. (260-4700), at Ave. A. Subway: F to 2nd Ave.-E. Houston St. The Mercury has attracted an amazing number of big-name acts to its fairly small-time room, running the gamut from folk to noise to pop. Past standouts have included Lenny Kravitz, Morphine, They Might Be Giants, and Bikini Kill. Music nightly; cover usually $5-15.

Bars

The White Horse Tavern, 567 Hudson St. (243-9260), at W. 11th St. Dylan Thomas drank himself to death here. Boisterous crowd pays a strange and twisted homage to the poet. Beer $4, ½-price during happy hour. Open Sun.-Thurs. 11am-2am, Fri.-Sat. 11am-4am.

The Ear Inn, 326 Spring St. (226-9060), near the Hudson. Established in 1817 and once a big bohemian/activist hangout, this bar now tends to the TriBeCa young-and-wistful crowd. Mellow jazz and blues at low volume so as not to stem the flow of conversation. Appetizers and salads $2-6. Food served from 11am-4:30pm and 6pm-1am. Bar open till 4am.

10th Street Lounge, 212 E. 10th St. (473-5252), between Second and Third Ave. Chic East Village hotspot favored by an artsy young crowd. Dim red lighting and music ranging from reggae to hip-hop lure them to this inconspicuous, unmarked hole-in-the-wall. Thurs.-Sat. evenings have a $10 cover. Open daily until 3am.

The Shark Bar, 307 Amsterdam Ave. (496-6600), at 75th. Classy and enjoyable bar and soul-food restaurant. After-work crowd nurses stiff drinks. Live jazz Tues. with a $5 cover; "gospel brunch" Sat. 12:30 and 2pm (no cover). Beer from $3. Open Mon.-Wed. 5:30pm-midnight, Thurs.-Sat. 5:30pm-1am, Sun. 5:30-11pm.

Max Fish, 178 Ludlow St. (529-3959), at Houston St. in the Lower East Side. The crowd is hip, if a bit pretentious, and the all-CD jukebox is easily the best in town: The Fall, The Minutemen, and Superchunk. Beer $2.50. Open daily 5:30pm-4am.

Polly Esther's, 21 E. 8th St. (979-1970), near University Pl. Grab those bell bottoms and platform shoes—it's a bar dedicated to the 1970s! Beer $3. Two-for-one happy hour 1-9pm on weekdays and 1-7pm on weekends. Open Mon.-Fri. 11am-2am, Sat.-Sun. 11am-4am. Another location at 249 W. 26th St. (929-4782).

McSorley's Old Ale House, 15 E. 7th St. (473-9148), at Third Ave. One of the oldest bars in the city, McSorley's has hosted Abe Lincoln, the Roosevelts, and John Kennedy since it opened in 1854—women weren't allowed in until 1970. Great selection of beers. Open Mon.-Sat. 11am-1am, Sun. 1pm-1am.

The Westend Gate, 2911 Broadway (662-8830), between 113th and 114th St. Subway: #1 or 9 to 116th St. Once frequented by Kerouac, now a hangout for the Columbia set. Small dance room with rock and funk bands in the back—bands every Fri.-Sat. night (cover $5 and up). Cheap pitchers with a great beer selection. Food served until 11pm. Open daily 11:30am-2am.

Dance Clubs

Tunnel, 220 Twelfth Ave. (695-7292), near 28th St. Subway: C or E to 23rd St. Immense club; 3 floors packed with 2 dance floors, lounges, glass-walled live shows, and a skateboarding cage. Enough room for a multitude of parties in this labyrinthine club. Cover $20. Open Fri.-Sat.; Sat. nights lure a mostly gay crowd.

Webster Hall, 125 E. 11th St. (353-1600), between Third and Fourth Ave. Subway: #4, 5, 6, N, or R to Union Sq.-14th St. Walk 3 blocks south and a block east. New and popular club offers dancing, a reggae room and a coffee shop. "Psychedelic Thursdays" often feature live bands. Cover $5-15. Open Wed.-Sat. 10pm-4am.

Limelight, 47 W. 20th St. (807-7850), at Sixth Ave. Subway: F or R to 23rd St. Huge club in a converted church. Several rooms for dancing. Big suburban crowd. Men may have trouble getting in without women. Queer Wed. and Fri. nights. Sun. night is live heavy metal. Cover $15, but look for discount fliers everywhere.

Robots, 25 Ave. B (995-0968), at 3rd Ave. Subway: F to Second Ave. For 14 years, Robot has been the place to go when other clubs have closed but your energy has yet to wear off. Open bar before midnight; most guests arrive around 4am and stay until 10am. Thursday's **Killer** offers a strong dose of acid trance and progressive house. Open Wed.-Thurs. 10pm-7am, Fri.-Sat. 10pm-noon. Cover $6-15.

MID-ATLANTIC

Palladium, 126 E. 14th St. (473-7171), at Third Ave. Subway: #4, 5, 6, L, N, or R to 14th St. Once Madonna and her friends set the pace—now big hair has replaced big crowds. But the music is still good and the space is still cool. Look in Village stores for discount invites. Cover $20. Open Fri.-Sat. 10pm-4am.

Gay and Lesbian Clubs

Clit Club, 432 W. 14th St. (529-3300), at Washington St. This is *the* place to be for young, beautiful, queer girls. Host Julie throws the hottest party around every Fri. night. Cover $3 before 11pm, $5 after 11pm. Doors open at 9:30pm.

Jackie 60, 432 W. 14th St. (366-5680), at Washington St. Drag queens and sometimes celebrity crowd. Cover $10. Open at 10pm.

Uncle Charlie's, 56 Greenwich Ave. (255-8787), at Perry St. Subway: #1 or 9 to Christopher St. Biggest and best-known gay club in the city. Guppies galore. Women welcome, but few come. Open daily 4pm-4am.

The Pyramid, 101 Ave. A (420-1590), at 6th St. Subway: #6 to Astor Pl. Also known by its street address, this dance club mixes gay, lesbian, and straight folks. Vibrant drag scene. Fri. is straight night. Cover $5-10. Open daily 9pm-4am.

Hipster Hangouts and Must-Sees

Nuyorican Poets Café, 236 E. 3rd St. (505-8183), between Ave. B and Ave. C. Subway: F to Second Ave. Walk 3 blocks north and 3 blocks east. New York's leading venue for the currently in-vogue "poetry slams" and spoken word performances. Cover $5-10.

Collective Unconscious, 28 Ave. B (254-5277), between 2nd and 3rd St. Subway: F to Second Ave. Walk 3 blocks east and 2 blocks north. Plays, rock shows, and other performances (cover usually $5-7). Open-mike night Sun. at 9pm ($3). Ongoing serial play on Sat. at 8pm ($5). Bring your own refreshments.

Blue Man Group-Tubes, 434 Lafayette St. (254-4370), at the Astor Place Theater. Not a hangout, but a quirky Off-Broadway show with a cult following. Definitely worth the ticket price if you dig wacky "performance art."

Giant Step and **Soul Kitchen,** mobile parties that move from club to club, drawing ardent followers of their funk-jazz-hip-hop hybrid. Check the *Voice* for locations and dates.

Sports

While most cities would be content to field a major-league team in each big-time sport, New York opts for the Noah's Ark approach: two baseball teams, two hockey teams, and two NFL football teams. In addition to local teams' regularly scheduled games, New York hosts a number of celebrated world-class events. Get tickets three months in advance for the prestigious **U. S. Open** (718-760-6200; tickets from $12), held in late August and early September at the USTA Tennis Center in Flushing Meadows, Queens. On the third Sunday in October, two million spectators witness the 22,000 runners of the **New York City Marathon** (only 16,000 finish). The race begins on the Verrazzano Bridge and ends at Central Park's Tavern on the Green.

On the **baseball** diamond, the **New York Mets** bat at **Shea Stadium** in Queens (718-507-8499; tickets $6.50-15). The legendary but mortal **New York Yankees** play ball at Yankee Stadium in the Bronx (293-6000; tickets $6.50-17). Both the **New York Giants** and the **Jets** play **football** across the river at **Giants Stadium** (201-935-3900) in East Rutherford, NJ. Tickets start at $25. Speaking of football, the **New York/New Jersey Metrostars** play the real thing—**soccer**— in the same venue. The **New York Knickerbockers** (that's the Knicks to you) dribble the **basketball** at **Madison Square Garden** (465-6751, 751-6130 off season; tickets from $13). The **New York Rangers** play **hockey** at **Madison Square Garden** (465-6741 or 308-6977); the **New York Islanders** hang their skates at the **Nassau Coliseum** (516-794-9300), in Uniondale, Long Island. Tickets begin at $12 and $14, respectively.

■ Long Island

For some, Long Island evokes images of sprawling suburbia dotted with malls and office parks; others see it as a retreat for privileged New Yorkers, a summer refuge of white sand and open spaces. Yet between the malls and beaches lie both vital cultural centers and pockets of poverty. Although the New York City boroughs of Brooklyn and Queens are technically part of the island, practically speaking, Nassau and Suffolk Counties constitute the real Long Island. East of the Queens-Nassau line, people back the Islanders, not the Rangers, and they enjoy their role as neighbor to the great metropolis. The Hamptons, on the South Fork, are mainly ritzy summer homes. The North Fork is home to many farms. Besides great beaches, Long Island offers good camping just outside the City. The Long Island Expressway (LIE, officially State Hwy. 495), stretches 73 exits over 85 mi. from Manhattan to Riverhead. Traffic jams are seemingly incessant on the expressway during rush hour (which basically lasts from 7am-midnight). Many Islanders commute to the city by train, but the sights of Long Island are most easily accessible by car.

PRACTICAL INFORMATION

Get Long Island info at the **Long Island Convention and Visitors Bureau** (951-2423), which operates a visitors booth on the LIE South between Exits 51 and 52 in Commack, and on the Southern State Pkwy. between Exits 13 and 14. The Island's main public transportation, **Long Island Railroad (LIRR)** (822-5477), has five central lines. Depending on how far you want to go, peak fares range from $4.75 to 15.25, and off-peak fares range from $3.25 to 10.25. Call for connection directions from NYC subways. Daytime bus service is provided by **Long Island Bus** in Queens, Nassau, and western Suffolk (766-6722). The routes are complex and irregular—make sure you confirm your destination with the driver. (Fare $1.50, crossing into Queens an additional 50¢, transfers 25¢. Disabled travelers and senior citizens pay ½-fare.) The S-92 bus of **Suffolk Transit** (852-5200) loops back and forth between the tips of the north and south forks, with nine runs daily, most of them between East Hampton and Orient Point. Call to confirm stops and schedules. (Open Mon.-Fri. 8am-4:30pm.) The route also connects with the LIRR at Riverhead, where the forks meet. (No service Sun. Fare $1.50, transfers 25¢, seniors and disabled 50¢, under 5 free.) **Hampton Express** (212-861-6800, on Long Island 286-4600) runs to and through the South Fork, while **Sunrise Express** (800-527-7709, in Suffolk 477-1200) covers the North Fork. Long Island's **area code: 516**.

ACCOMMODATIONS AND CAMPING

Finding a place to stay on the island can be daunting. Daytrippers in Nassau would do best to return to the city. Suffolk County provides a wider variety of mostly touristy accommodations. In Montauk, sleep at **Montauket,** Tuthill Rd. (668-5992). Follow the Montauk Hwy. to Montauk; at the traffic circle take Edgemere, then left onto Fleming, then another left. Make reservations for summer weekends starting March 1—it fills up quickly. (Doubles $35, with private bath $40.) For **camping,** dig your trenches at **Battle Row** (572-8690), in Bethpage, Nassau. Eight tent sites and 50 trailer sites are available on first come, first served basis. Electricity, restrooms, showers, grills, and a playground are available. (Tent sites $8.75, trailer sites $15.) Also try **Heckscher Park** (581-4433 or 800-456-2267), in East Islip, Suffolk. Take LIE Exit 53 and go south on the Sagtikos State Pkwy. Follow signs onto the Southern State Pkwy. east, and follow this as it turns south and becomes the Heckscher Spur Pkwy. The Park is at the end of the Pkwy. The state-run facility has 69 tent and trailer sites, restrooms, showers, food, grills, a pool, and a beach. ($15 first night, $14 per additional night. Make reservations at least 7 days in advance. Open May-Sept.) **Wildwood Park** (668-7600 or 800-456-2267), at Wading River. LIE Exit 68 and go north onto Rte. 46 (Wm. Floyd Pkwy.). Follow it to its end and go right (east) on Rte. 25A. Follow the signs from there. The former estate of Charles and John Arbuckle, multi-millionaire coffee dealers, has 300 tent sites and 80 trailer sites with full hook-ups, restrooms, showers, food, and a beach. (Sites $13 first night, $10 each additional night; sites with a concrete platform $14/11. Reservations urged for summer weekends and must be made at least a week in advance.) **A Reasonable Alternative, Inc.** (928-4034), offers rooms in private homes all along the shores of Nassau and Suffolk (singles and doubles $50-100).

SIGHTS

Nassau At **Old Westbury Gardens** (333-0048), on Old Westbury Rd., nature overwhelms architecture. The elegant house, modeled after 19th-century English country manors, sits in the shadow of its surroundings of gardens and tall evergreens. A vast rose garden adjoins a number of stunning theme gardens. (Open Wed.-Mon. 10am-5pm. House and garden $10, seniors $7, children $6. Take LIE to Exit 39S (Glen Cove Rd.), turn right on Old Westbury Rd., and continue ¼ mi.)

Jones Beach State Park (785-1600) is the best compromise between convenience and crowd for city daytrippers. There are nearly 2500 acres of beachfront here, and the parking area accommodates 23,000 cars. Only 40 min. from the city, Jones Beach packs in the crowds during the summer months. Along the 1½-mi. boardwalk you can find deck games, roller-skating, miniature golf, basketball, and nightly dancing. The **Marine Theater** in the park hosts big-name rock concerts. There are eight different bathing areas on the rough Atlantic Ocean and the calmer Zach's Bay, plus a number of beaches restricted to residents of certain towns in Nassau County. In the summer take the LIRR to Freeport or Wantaugh, where you can get a bus to the beach. Call 212-739-4200 or 212-526-0900 for info. **Recreation Lines** (718-788-8000) provides bus service straight from mid-Manhattan. If you are driving, take the LIE east to the Northern State Pkwy., go east to the Meadowbrook (or Wantaugh) Pkwy., and then south to Jones Beach.

Suffolk The peaceful villages of Suffolk County, only a few hours's drive from Manhattan, are New York's version of the tradition-steeped towns of New England. Many of Suffolk's colonial roots have been successfully preserved, and the county offers some fine colonial house-museums. Salty old towns, full of shady streets—refreshing retreats from the din of New York—line the lazy coast.

After shopping at the **Walt Whitman Mall,** the nearby **Walt Whitman's Birthplace,** 246 Old Walt Whitman Rd. (427-5240), will seem a more appropriate memorial to the great American poet. (Open Wed.-Fri. 1-4pm, Sat.-Sun. 10am-4pm. Free. Take LIE to Exit 49N, drive 1¾ mi. on Rte. 110, then left on Old Walt Whitman Rd.)

Fire Island A 32-mi.-long barrier island buffering the South Shore from the roaring waters of the Atlantic, Fire Island has both summer communities and federally protected wilderness. Cars are allowed only on the easternmost and westernmost tips of the island; there are no streets, only "walks." Fire Island was a hip counterculture spot during the 60s and still maintains a laid-back atmosphere. The **Fire Island National Seashore** (289-4810 for the headquarters in Patchogue) is the main draw here, and in summer it offers fishing, clamming, and guided nature walks. The facilities at **Sailor's Haven** (just west of the Cherry Grove community) include a marina, a nature trail, and a famous beach. Similar facilities at **Watch Hill** (597-6455) include a 20-unit **campground,** where reservations are required. **Smith Point West,** on the eastern tip of the island, has a small visitors info center and a nature trail with disabled access (281-3010; center open daily 9am-5pm). Here you can spot horseshoe crabs, whitetail deer, and monarch butterflies, which flit across the country every year to winter in Baja California. **Wilderness camping** is available near Smith Point West on Fire Island. Camping is free but requires a hike of about 1½ mi. to get into the camping area. You must pick up a permit from Smith Point Visitors Center (281-3010; open daily 9am-5pm) on the day you go down. To get to Smith Point, take Exit 68, head south, and follow the signs.

The **Sunken Forest,** so called because of its location down behind the dunes, is another of the Island's natural wonders. Located directly west of Sailor's Haven, its soils support an unusual and attractive combination of gnarled holly, sassafras, and poison ivy. From the summit of the dunes, you can see the forest's trees laced together in a hulky, uninterrupted mesh.

To get to Fire Island from **Bay Shore** (665-3600), take one of the ferries which sail to Fair Harbor, Ocean Beach, Ocean Bay Park, Saltaire, and Kismet (roundtrip $11, under 12 $5). From **Sayville** (589-8980), ferries leave for Sailor's Haven (roundtrip $8, under 12 $4.50) and Cherry Grove and Fire Island Pines (roundtrip to either $10, under 12 $5). From **Patchogue** (475-1665), ferries go to Davis Park and Watch Hill (roundtrip to either $10, under 12 $5.50). LIRR stations lie within a short distance of the three ferry terminals, making access from New York City relatively simple (all ferries May-Nov.).

Wine Country Long Island does not readily conjure up images of plump wine-grapes just waiting to be plucked by epicurean Islanders. But a visit to one of the North Fork's 40 vineyards can be a pleasant and interesting surprise. The wineries and vineyards here produce the best Chardonnay, Cabernet Sauvignon, Merlot, Pinot Noir, and Riesling in New York State. Many of the Island wineries offer free tours and tastings. To get to there, take the LIE to Exit 73, then Rte. 58, which becomes Rte. 25 (Main Rd.). North of and parallel to Rte. 25, Rte. 48 (North Rd. or Middle Rd.), claims a number of wineries. Road signs announce tours and tastings. Of note is **Palmer Vineyards,** 108 Sound Ave. (722-9463), in Riverhead. Take a self-guided tour of the most advanced equipment on the Island and see a tasting room with an interior assembled from two 18th-century English pubs.

Hamptons Composed of **West, South, Bridge,** and **East Hampton,** this area is famous for its ritzy homes for rich New Yorkers who "summer" and great beaches. Each town offers a quaint Main St. with shops, restaurants, and good people watching in the summer. Historians and sadists should check out the **Southampton Historical Museum** (283-2494), located near the center of town at the corner of Meeting House Ln. and Main St. Start with the pillory, where thieves and those *accused* of adultery were publicly flayed. Or try your neck in the stocks, the clever device used to humiliate (and hurt) drunkards and disrespectful children. (Open in summer Tues.-Sun. 11am-5pm. $3, ages 6-11 50¢. Take Rte. 27E to Southampton Center.) The **Guild Hall Museum,** 158 Main St. (324-0806), in East Hampton, specializes in well-known artists of the eastern Island region, from the late 19th century to the present. (Open in summer daily 11am-5pm; Sept.-May Wed.-Sun. 11am-5pm. $2.) The East Hampton beach is known to be one of the most beautiful in the world.

At **East Hampton Bowl,** 71 Montauk Hwy. (324-1950), just west of East Hampton, the bowling alley and attached bar stay open until at least midnight every night, and Saturday nights feature "Rock-'n'-Bowl." (Bowling $3.40 per game; shoe rental $2.)

Sag Harbor Out on the South Fork's north shore droops Sag Harbor, one of the best-kept secrets of Long Island. Founded in 1707, this port used to be more important than New York Harbor since its deep shore made for easy navigation. The legacy of Sag Harbor's former grandeur survives in the second-largest collection of Colonial buildings in the U.S., and in cemeteries lined with the gravestones of Revolutionary soldiers and sailors. Check out the **Sag Harbor Whaling Museum** (725-0770). Enter the museum through the jawbones of a whale. Note the antique 1864 washing machine and the excellent scrimshaw collection. (Open May-Sept. Mon.-Sat. 10am-5pm, Sun. 1-5pm. $4, children $1. Call for tours.)

Montauk At the easternmost tip of the South Fork, Montauk is one of the most popular destinations on Long Island. The trip from Manhattan takes four hours by car. Take the LIE to Exit 70 (Manorville), then go south to Sunrise Hwy. (Rte. 27), which becomes Montauk Hwy., and drive east.

The **Montauk Point Lighthouse and Museum** (668-2544) is the high point of a trip here. The 86-ft. structure went up by special order of President George Washington. On a clear day, you should climb the 138 spiralling steps to the top, where you can see across the Long Island Sound to Connecticut and Rhode Island. The best seasons for viewing are spring and fall; the thick summer air can haze over the view. But even on a foggy day, you may want to climb up to see if you can spot the *Will o' the Wisp,* a ghostly clipper ship sometimes sighted on hazy days under full sail with a lantern hanging from its mast. Experts claim that the ship is a mirage resulting from the presence of phosphorus in the atmosphere. (Open May-June and Oct.-Nov. Sat.-Sun. 10:30am-4pm; June-Sept. daily 10:30am-6pm; Sept.-Oct. Fri.-Mon. 10:30am-5pm. $2.50, children $1. Parking $3.)

Try **Viking** (668-5700) or **Lazybones'** (668-5671) for half-day fishing cruises ($20-25). **Okeanos Whale Watch Cruise** (728-4522) offers excellent six-hour trips for spotting fin, minke, and humpback whales ($30 and up).

Shelter Island Shelter Island bobs in the protected body of water between the north and south forks. Accessible by ferry or by private boat, this island of about 12 square mi. offers wonderful beaches (locals tend to favor Wades Beach and Hay Beach) and a serene sense of removal from the intrusions of the city. A detailed map of the island is available from most inns and other places of business. **The Belle Crest House,** 163 North Ferry Rd. (749-2041), in Shelter Island Heights just up the hill from the north ferry, is a beautiful old country home with large rooms—a great spot for a romantic getaway. (From May 1-Oct. 31: Mon.-Thurs. doubles $65-70 with shared bath, $95 with private bath; Fri.-Sun. $80 and $165. 2-night min. for summer weekends. Off-season rates dip as low as $45.) **North Fork: Greenport Ferry** (749-0139), North Ferry Rd., on the dock, takes passenger and driver for $6.50, roundtrip $7, each additional passenger $1, walk-on (without a car) $1. Ferries run daily every 15 min., with the first ferry leaving Greenport at 6am and the last ferry departing the island at 11:45pm. **South Fork: North Haven Ferry** (749-1200), 3 mi. north of Sag Harbor on Rte. 114, on the dock, takes car and driver for $6 one-way, $6.50 roundtrip, additional passengers $1 each, walk-ons $1 roundtrip. Ferries run daily at approximately 10-min. intervals from 6am to 1:45am.

■ Catskills

The Catskills are widely known as the site of the century-long repose of Rip Van Winkle, but these sleepy bucolic parts aren't just for napping—these mountains are home to quiet villages, sparkling streams, and miles of hiking and skiing trails, all of which can be found in the state-managed Catskill Preserve. Amid the Catskill's purple haze lies Woodstock, site of the famous 1969 rock festival (and of the 1994 marketing rehash). Music history aside, Woodstock is a small, peaceful city that offers a welcoming contrast to the metropolis to the South.

Practical Information **Adirondack Pine Hill Trailways** provides excellent service through the Catskills. The main stop is in **Kingston,** at 400 Washington Ave. on the corner of Front St. (914-331-0744 or 800-858-8555). Buses run to New York City (11 per day, 2hr., $18.50; same-day roundtrip $25 or $35, depending on the day). Other stops in the area include Woodstock, Pine Hill, Saugerties, and Hunter; each connects with New York City, Albany, and Utica. (Ticket office open daily 6am-11:30pm.) The **Ulster County Public Information Office,** 244 Fair St., 5th fl. (914-340-3566 or 800-342-5826), six blocks from the Kingston bus station, has a helpful travel guide and a list of Catskill hiking trails (open Mon.-Fri. 9am-5pm). Four stationary **tourist cabooses** dispense info at the traffic circle in Kingston, on Rte. 28 in Shandaken, on Rte. 209 in Ellenville, and on Rte. 9W in Milton (open in summer Fri.-Sun.; hours vary depending on volunteer availability). Rest stop **visitors centers** along I-87 can advise you on area sights.

■ Catskill Forest Preserve

The 250,000-acre **Catskill Forest Preserve** contains many small towns which host travelers looking for outdoor adventure. The required permits for **fishing** (non-NY residents, $20 per 5 days) are available in any sporting goods store. Ranger stations distribute free permits for **back-country camping** necessary for stays of more than three days. Although trails are maintained year-round, lean-to's are sometimes dilapidated and crowded. Always boil or treat water with chemicals, and remember to pack out your garbage. For more info on fishing, hunting, or environmental issues, call the **Department of Environmental Conservation** (914-256-3000). **Adirondack Trailways'** buses from Kingston service most trail heads—drivers will let you out anywhere along secondary bus routes.

Accessible by bus from Kingston, **Phoenicia** is a fine place to anchor a trip to the Catskills. The **Esopus River,** to the west, has great trout fishing, and **The Town Tinker,** 10 Bridge St. (688-5553), rents inner-tubes for summertime river-riding. (Inner-tubes $7 per day, with a seat $15. Driver's license or $15 required as a deposit. Transportation $4. Life jackets provided. Open May-Sept. daily 9am-6pm; last rental 4:30pm.) Artifacts from the late-19th-century glory days of the steam engine fill the **Empire State Railway Museum** (688-7501), on High St. off Rte. 28. It features train rides on the Catskill Mountain Railroad (open weekends and holidays 10am-6pm). At the 65-foot-high **Sundance Rappel Tower** (688-5640), off Rte. 214, visitors climb up and return to earth the hard way. (4 levels of lessons; beginner, 3-4hr., $20. Lessons only held when a group of 4 is present. Reservations required.)

If your karma is running out of gasma, you can stop at **Woodstock,** between Phoenicia and Kingston. A haven for artists and writers since the turn of the century, Woodstock is best known for the concert which bore its name, an event which actually took place in nearby Saugerties. Since then, the tie-dyed legacy has faded, and Woodstock has become an expensive, touristed town. You can soothe your soul and chant your mantra at the **Zen Mountain Monastery** (688-2228), on S. Plank Rd., a few mi. from Woodstock off Rte. 28N from Mt. Tremper. The 8:45am Sunday services include an AM-azing demonstration of zazen meditation (weekend and week-long retreats from $175).

What is now **Historic Kingston** was once a defensive stockade built by Peter Stuyvesant. Stroll down Wall St., Fair St., or North Front St. and defend yourself against the cutesy shops that have taken its place. Live out your childhood firefighting fantasies at the **Volunteer Fireman's Hall and Museum,** 265 Fair St. (331-0866; open Wed.-Fri. 11am-3pm, Sat. 10am-4pm). Head to the **Woodstock Brewing Company,** 20 James St. (331-2810), for a taste of beer brewed right in the Hudson Valley. Nat Collins, the owner and brewmaster, will give you a free tour and tasting in his (and one of the state's only) complete microbrewery (tours 1pm on the first and third Sat. of each month).

Camping and Accommodations Huddle around the fire and shiver to ghost stories at any of the **state campgrounds.** Reservations (800-456-2267) are vital during the summer, especially Thursday through Sunday. (Sites $9-12; $1.50 registration fee; phone reservation fee $7; $2 more for partial hook-up. Open May-Sept.) The **Office of Parks** (518-474-0456) distributes brochures on the campgrounds. **North Lake/South Lake** (518-589-5058), Rte. 23A three mi. northeast of Haines Falls, rents canoes ($15 per day) and features two lakes, a waterfall, hiking, and 219 campsites ($15, reserve 7 days in advance; day use $5). **Kenneth L. Wilson** (914-679-7020), an 8-mi. hike from the Bearsville bus stop, has well-wooded campsites ($12), showers, a pond-front beach, and family atmosphere. A bit more primitive, **Woodland Valley** (914-688-7647), 5 mi. southeast of Phoenicia, does have flush toilets and showers, and sits on a good 16-mi. hiking trail (sites $9).

If the thought of sleeping outside in the land of the headless horseman makes your blood run cold, you can take refuge in a giant room with cable TV at the **Super 8 Motel,** 487 Washington Ave. (338-3078), in Kingston two blocks from the bus station. (Weekdays singles from $55, doubles from $57; weekends from $60/$62. Senior discounts available. Reserve for summer weekends.) In Phoenicia, the **Cobblestone Motel** (688-7871), on Rte. 214, has an outdoor pool and well-worn but very clean rooms (singles $40, doubles $44, rooms with kitchenette $55). Countless other motels, motor inns, economy cabins, and the like line Rte. 28 between Kingston and Phoenicia. For a true bargain, follow Rte. 28 off the beaten path to the **Belleayre Hostel** (254-4200). Bunks and private rooms, in a rustic setting not far from Phoenicia, all have sinks, radios, kitchen access, a picnic area, and sporting equipment. Call for directions. (Bunks in summer $9, in winter $12. Private rooms $20-25. Efficiency cabins for up to 4 $35-45.)

■ Albany

Although the English took Albany in 1664, the city was actually founded in 1614 as a trading post for the Dutch West Indies Company; established six years before the Pilgrims landed on the New England shore, it is the oldest continuous European settlement in the original 13 colonies. Today, Albany, New York's state capital since 1797, is the site of the largest state government in the nation and can justly claim the status of a major northeastern transportation hub. Even so, the city once named Fort Orange has never matched the growth of its southern sibling, the Big Apple, and the quaint multicolored streets, inexplicably named for birds—Dove, Lark, Peacock—make comparing Albany to New York City like trying to compare...oh, never mind.

Practical Information The **Albany Visitors Center,** 25 Quackenbush Sq. (434-5132), at Clinton Ave. and Broadway, runs trolley tours (Thurs.-Fri. July to Sept.; $4, seniors and kids $2) and free guided walking tours (Sat. June to Sept.; call for times). **Amtrak,** 555 East St. (462-5763 or 800-872-7245), in Rensselaer across the Hudson from downtown Albany, has service to New York City (6-8 per day, 2½hr., $31) and Buffalo (3 per day, 5hr., $71), and offers discounts for advance purchase (open Mon.-Fri. 5:30am-11pm, Sat.-Sun. 6am-midnight). **Greyhound,** 34 Hamilton St. (434-8095 or 800-231-2222), runs buses to Utica (1½hr., $13), Syracuse (3hr., $18), Rochester (4hr., $31), and Buffalo (5hr., $35), with substantial student discounts. *Be careful in this neighborhood at night.* (Station open 6am-1am.) Across the street, **Adirondack Trailways,** 34 Hamilton Ave. (436-9651), connects to other upstate locales: Lake George (3-5 per day, 2hr., $10); Lake Placid (1-2 per day, 4hr., $22.50); Tupper Lake (1 per day, 4hr., $27). Discounts for students and seniors are available for some routes. For local travel, the **Capital District Transportation Authority (CDTA)** (482-8822) serves Albany, Troy, and Schenectady (fare $1). The main office gives out info, and schedules are available at the Amtrak and Trailways stations. Albany's **post office:** 30 Old Karner Rd. (452-2499; open Mon.-Fri. 8:30am-6pm, Sat. 9am-2pm). **ZIP code:** 12212. **Area code:** 518.

Accommodations and Food The **College of Saint Rose,** 432 Western Ave., has large rooms and clean bathrooms in dorms on a relatively safe campus. The dining hall is open for use, and rooms with kitchen facilities are available. (Rooms $20 per person. For reservations contact Renee Besanson at Conferences and Special Events; 454-5171. Open May 15-Aug. 15 daily 8:30am-4:30pm.) Spectacular accommodations in a pleasant neighborhood come with a sizable discount for HI-AYH members at **Pine Haven Bed & Breakfast,** 531 Western Ave. (482-1574). Look for a big Victorian house at the convergence of Madison and Western Ave.; parking is in the rear. (Members $25, $10 each additional; nonmembers singles $49, doubles $64. Excellent hostel accommodations available in the basement for $15 per night.) Large, comfortable rooms can be found at trusty **Motel 6,** 100 Watervliet Ave. (438-7447), off I-91 at Exit 5 (singles $40, doubles $48). Nearby Schenectady (accessible via CDTA) provides a couple of reasonable rooming options. The **YWCA,** 44 Washington Ave. (374-3394), rents single rooms to women only ($20). **Thompson's Lake State Park** (872-1674), on Rte. 157 4 mi. north of East Berne, has the area's closest outdoor living (18mi. southwest of Albany). Expect 140 primitive sites ($13) and some natural perks, including nearby fishing, hiking trails, and a swimming beach.

The hill above downtown Albany is stocked with affordable eats. **Shades of Green,** 187 Lark St. (434-1830), located in a small nook near Western Ave., serves delicious vegetarian cuisine; wash down your tempeh reuben ($4.25) with a cool fruit or vegetable shake ($3; open Mon.-Sat. 11am-6pm). Around the corner, at **Torino Café** (434-3540), downtown office workers stain their ties eating veal marsala ($8.75) and spaghetti with red or white clam sauce ($6.75; open Sun.-Thurs. 8am-9pm, Fri.-Sat. 8am-10pm). Students and other locals foment pacifist revolution while slurping *pasta e fagioli* ($5.50) and biting into bagel melts ($3) uptown at **Mother Earth's Café,** 217 Western Ave. (434-0944), at Quail St. Live music, poetry readings, and plays provide radical entertainment every night (open daily 11am-11pm; no cover).

Sights Albany offers about a day's worth of sight-seeing activity. The **Rockefeller Empire State Plaza,** on State St., is a $1.9 billion towering, modernist Stonehenge. The platform has two main levels—the open air plaza on top of the concourse—with parking garages beneath (free parking after 2pm on weekdays). The plaza houses state offices and any sort of store or service one might want, including a **bus terminal, post office,** cleaners, a cafeteria, and the **New York State Museum** (474-5877). In addition to exhibits on state history, the museum displays an original set for "Sesame Street" (open daily 10am-5pm; $5 suggested donation). Hanging throughout the Plaza concourse, across from the museum, the **Empire State Collection** features works by innovative New York School artists such as Jackson Pollock, Mark Rothko, and David Smith (concourse level open daily 6am-11pm; tours by appointment; free). Don't be alarmed by the huge flying saucer at one end of the Plaza; it's just the **Empire Center for the Performing Arts** (473-1845), also known as "the Egg," a venue for theater, dance, and tasty concerts (box office open Mon.-Fri. noon-3pm). For a spectacular bird's-eye view of Albany, the Hudson River, and surrounding areas, take the elevator up to the ear-popping 42nd floor observation deck of the **Corning Tower** (open Mon.-Fri. 9am-4pm, weekends 10am-4pm).

Bounded by State St. and Madison Ave. north of downtown, **Washington Park** has tennis courts, paddle boats, and plenty of room for celebrations and performances. On Mother's Day weekend, music, dancing, and food accompany a colorful show of Albany's Dutch heritage during the **Tulip Festival** (434-2032). The **Park Playhouse** (434-2035) stages free musical theater in the park from July to mid-August Tues.-Sun. at 8pm. On Thursdays during June and July, come **Alive at Five** (434-2032) with the sound of free concerts at the **Tercentennial Plaza,** across from Fleet Bank on Broadway. For a list of events, call the **Albany Alive Line** (434-1217, ext. 409). The city also hosts **River Festival** in late Sept.

Home to the **Albany Roverats** and **Firebirds, Knickerbocker Arena,** 51 South Pearl St. (487-2000), also hosts large musical shows and sporting events (call Ticketmaster at 476-1000 for info on events). Bikers should check out the **Mohawk-Hudson Bikeway,** which passes along old railroad grades and canal towpaths as it weaves through the capital area (maps available at the visitors center).

▓ Cooperstown

To an earlier generation, Cooperstown evoked images of James Fenimore Cooper's frontiersman hero, Leatherstocking, who roamed the woods around the gleaming waters of Lake Otsego. Today, Cooperstown recalls a different source of American legend—baseball. Tourists file in every summer to visit the Baseball Hall of Fame, buy baseball memorabilia, eat in baseball-themed restaurants, and sleep in baseball-themed motels. Fortunately for the tepid fan, baseball's mecca is surrounded by rural beauty and some of New York state's best (non-baseball) rural tourist attractions.

Practical Information Cooperstown is accessible from I-90 and I-88 via Rte. 28. Street parking is rare in Cooperstown; your best bets are the free parking lots just outside of town on Rte. 28 south of Cooperstown, on Glen Ave. at Maple St., and near the Fenimore House. Take a **trolley** into town from any of these lots (runs July-Sept. daily 8:30am-9pm; weekends only Memorial Day-June and Labor Day-Columbus Day; 50¢). **Adirondack Trailways** (800-858-8555) picks up at Chestnut and Elm St. for two trips per day to New York City (5½ hr., $40). The **Cooperstown Area Chamber of Commerce,** 31 Chestnut St. (547-9983), on Rte. 80 near Main St., has accommodation listings (open daily June-Sept. 9am-8pm, daily Sept.-Oct. 9am-5pm, winter hours vary). Cooperstown's **post office:** 40 Main St. (547-2311; open Mon.-Fri. 8:30am-5pm, Sat. 9:30am-1pm). **ZIP code:** 13326. **Area code:** 607.

Accommodations, Food, and Nightlife Summertime lodging in Cooperstown seems to require the salary of a Major Leaguer; fortunately, there are alternatives to endless negotiation. If it's not full, try **Lindsay House,** 56 Chestnut St. (547-5618), a B&B near the center of town. As long as he lives, proprietor and bluegrass guitar picker Doug Lindsay vows he will provide a haven for the budget traveler (rooms from $30). Otherwise, camping will help you avoid bankruptcy. **Glimmerglass State Park,** 8 mi. north of Cooperstown on Rte. 31 (a.k.a. Main St. in Cooperstown) on the east side of Lake Otsego, has 36 pristine campsites in a gorgeous lakeside park. Swimming, fishing, and boating reward daytime visitors (for $5 per vehicle) from 11am-7pm. (Sites $13; showers, dumping station, disabled access; no hookups. Register Sun.-Wed. 8am-9pm, Thurs.-Sat. 8am-11pm. Call 800-456-2267 for reservations and a heinous $7 service charge.) **Shadowbrook** (264-8431), 10 mi. north on Rte. 31, offers reasonable sites, a pool, and a pond. (Sites $20, electricity and water $23. Showers and laundry facilities. Office open daily 9am-10pm; make reservations for summer weekends.) **KOA** (315-858-0236 or 800-562-3402), 20 minutes from Cooperstown on Rte. 20, accommodates families with kids' facilities, a pool, and nightly entertainment. (Sites $18, hookup $25, cabins $36. Office open Mon.-Fri. 8am-6pm, Sat.-Sun. 8am-8pm; nighttime registration possible. Fills up in summer.)

For hearty grub, sidle into **Black Bart's BBQ,** 64 Main St. (547-5656), across from the Baseball Hall of Fame, a bad-ass Tex-Mex restaurant whose burritos ($5.50), cajun (half-chicken $8), and hydroponically grown greens "ain't for sissies." (Open Sun.-Thurs 11am-8pm, Fri.-Sat. 11am-10pm.) A Cooperstown institution, **Schneider's Bakery,** 157 Main St. (547-9631), has been serving locals since 1887; try the delicious "old-fashioneds," donuts which are less sweet and greasy than their conventional cousins (38¢), or the equally spectacular onion rolls (25¢; open Memorial Day-Labor Day Mon.-Sat. 6:30am-5:30pm, Sun. 7am-1pm).

Although it caters largely to family vacations, Cooperstown does have a lively and spirited nightlife with a great bar scene. Try the excellent **Sherman's Tavern,** 48-50 Pioneer St. (547-4000), near Main St. Thursday night karaoke, and Friday night DJs add to this bar's friendly and lively atmosphere. Beer ($2.50), mixed drinks ($2.50), and sandwiches ($5) will satiate. (Open Sun.-Thurs. 11am-2am, Fri.-Sat. 11am-3am.)

Take me out to the **National Baseball Hall of Fame and Museum** (547-7200) on Main St., an enormous monument to America's favorite pastime. In addition to memorabilia from the immortals—including the bat with which Babe Ruth hit his famous "called shot" home run in the 1932 World Series—the museum displays a moving multimedia tribute to the sport and a history that traces baseball's roots back to ancient Egyptian religious ceremonies. The museum never fails to wax elegant. As one exhibit reads, "In the beginning, shortly after God created Heaven and Earth, there were stones to throw and sticks to swing." The annual ceremonies for new inductees are held in **Cooper Park,** next to the building (July or Aug.; call ahead). There are special exhibits for hearing and visually impaired fans. (Open daily 9am-9pm; Oct.-April 9am-5pm. $9.50, ages 7-12 $4, under 7 free.)

Aficionados of American culture should also see the **Corvette Americana Hall of Fame** (547-4135), on Rte. 28 4½ mi. south of Cooperstown—probably the only place you'll ever see two 1963 Corvettes framed by a backdrop depicting the Lost Continent of Atlantis. The museum features 'Vettes through the years,' including the car used in the movie *Death Race 2000.* (Open Memorial Day-Labor Day daily 9am-9pm, winters daily 10am-6pm, closed Jan. to mid-Feb. $9.50, ages 5-13 $6.50.)

■ Ithaca and the Finger Lakes

According to Iroquois legend, the Great Spirit laid his hand upon the earth, and the impression of his fingers made the Finger Lakes: Canandaigua, Keuka, Seneca, Cayuga, Owasco, and Skaneateles, and so on. Others credit the glaciers of the last Ice Age for these formations. Regardless of their origins, the results are spectacular. Visitors can stand beneath waterfalls in Ithaca's gorgeous gorges or gorge themselves on another of nature's divine liquids—the rich wine of the Finger Lakes Region's acclaimed vineyards.

PRACTICAL INFORMATION

The **Ithaca/Tompkins County Convention and Visitors Bureau,** 904 E. Shore Dr., Ithaca 14850 (272-1313 or 800-284-8422), has the best map of the area ($3.25), complete hotel and B&B listings, and a zillion brochures on New York. (Open Memorial Day-Labor Day Mon.-Fri. 8am-5:30pm, Sat.-Sun. 10am-5pm, Labor Day-Memorial Day Mon.-Fri. 9am-5pm.) Get a copy of the *Finger Lakes Travel Guide* from **The Finger Lakes Association,** 309 Lake St., Penn Yan 14527 (315-536-7488 or 800-548-4386). **Ithaca Bus Terminal** (272-7930; open Mon.-Sat 7am-6pm, Sun. noon-5pm), W. State and N. Fulton St., houses **Short Line** and **Greyhound** (800-231-2222), with service to New York City (12 per day, $33), Philadelphia (3 per day, $50), and Buffalo (4 per day, $20). **T-CAT (Tompkins Consolidated Area Transit)** (277-7433) is your only choice for getting out to Cayuga Lake without wheels. Buses stop at Ithaca Commons, westbound on Seneca St. and eastbound on Green. (60¢, more distant zones $1.25. Buses run Mon.-Fri.) **Emergency:** 911. Ithaca's **post office:** 213 N. Tioga St. (272-5455), at E. Buffalo (open Mon.-Fri. 8:30am-5pm, Sat. 8:30am-1pm). **ZIP code:** 14850. **Area code:** 607.

ACCOMMODATIONS AND CAMPING

Elmshade Guest House, 402 S. Albany St. (273-1707), at Center St. 3 blocks from the Ithaca Commons, is a B&B, and by far the best budget place in Ithaca. From the bus station, walk up State St. and turn right onto Albany St. Impeccably clean, well-decorated, large rooms with shared bath. You'll feel like a guest at a rich relative's house. Cable TV in every room, refrigerator, microwave in hall. Singles from $25, doubles $50. Generous continental breakfast served. Reservations recommended.

The Wonderland Motel, 654 Elmira Rd. (272-5252). Follow the talking white rabbit saying "I'm late! I'm late! For a very important date!" down Rte. 13 south. Outdoor pool, A/C, HBO, free coffee and Danish breakfast, and local calls. Family atmosphere. Singles from $36, doubles from $45; in winter $30/$36.

Three of the nearby state parks which offer camping are **Robert H. Treman** (273-3440), on Rte. 327 off Rte. 13; **Buttermilk Falls** (273-5761); and **Taughannock Falls** (387-6739), north on Rte. 89. (Sites $10-12; $1.50 walk-on fee or $7 reservation fee by calling 800-456-2267. Cabins $122 per week.) The brochure *Finger Lakes State Parks* describes the location and services of all area state parks; pick it up from any tourist office or park, or contact the **Finger Lakes State Park Region,** 2221 Taughannock Park Rd., P.O. Box 1055, Trumansburg 14886 (387-7041).

FOOD AND NIGHTLIFE

Restaurants in Ithaca cluster along Aurora St. and in Ithaca Commons and Collegetown. The *Ithaca Dining Guide* pamphlet available from the visitors center (see above) lists more options.

MID-ATLANTIC

Moosewood Restaurant, 215 N. Cayuga (273-9610), at Seneca St. The legendary vegetarian collective and home of the *Moosewood Cookbook*. Long-time veggies genuflect before Moosewood's ever-changing menu of yummy meals. Lunch $5; dinner $9-11. Open in summer Mon.-Sat. 11:30am-4pm and 6-9pm, Sun. 6-9pm; off season Mon.-Thurs. 11:30am-4pm and 5:30-8:30pm, Fri.-Sat. 11:30am-4pm and 5:30-9pm, Sun. 5:30-8:30pm. No reservations.

Joe's Restaurant, 602 W. Buffalo St. (273-2693), at Rte. 13 (Meadow St.), a 10-min. walk from Ithaca Commons. This is a *big* student spot. Original Art Deco interior dates from 1932. Italian and American entrees ($7-15) come with Joe's much beloved bottomless salad. Open daily 4-10pm.

Just a Taste, 116 N. Aurora (277-9463), near Ithaca Commons. Taste an extensive selection of fine wines (2½oz. $1.75-3.75), 80 beers, and tempting *tapas* (Spanish "appetizers," $2.50-5.25). Open Mon.-Sun. 11:30am-3:30pm, and Sun.-Thurs. 5:30-10pm, Fri.-Sat. 5:30-11pm.

Rongovian Embassy to the USA ("The Rongo") (387-3334), on Rte. 96 on the main strip in Trumansburg about 10mi. from Ithaca; worth the drive. Seek asylum in amazing Mexican entrees at this classic restaurant/bar, and plot a trip to "Bee-free," "Nearvarna," or "Freelonch" on their huge wall map. Try the *Pescado Verde*. Tacos $2.75. Mug of beer $1.75. Open Tues.-Thurs. and Sun. 5-9pm, Fri.-Sat. 5-10pm; bar open Tues.-Sun. 4pm-1am. Bands Wed.-Sat.; cover $5.

Station Restaurant, 806 W. Buffalo (272-2609), in a plush, renovated train station, registered as a National Historical Landmark. Pasta, poultry, and seafood specials $9-14. Open Mon.-Sat. 4-9:30pm, Sun. noon-8:30pm.

The area near Cornell called **Collegetown,** centering on College Ave., harbors student hangouts and access to a romantic path along the gorge. Maintain your Bohemian cachet in smoky, red-walled **Stella's,** 403 College Ave. (277-8731), one café that wears its pretension well. Try the Italian soda ($2) with heavy cream (open daily 7:30am-1:30am). Skulk down to **The Haunt,** 114 W. Green St. (273-3355), for live bands. Crowds grind to 80s dance music on Saturday, reggae on Tuesday, and techno on Wednesday.

SIGHTS AND ENTERTAINMENT

Ithaca **Cornell University,** youngest of the Ivy League schools, sits on a *steep* hill in downtown Ithaca between two tremendous gorges. Stop by the **Information and Referral Center** in the Day Hall Lobby for info on campus sights and activities (254-4636; open Mon.-Sat. 8am-5pm). The strangely pleasing cement edifice rising from the top of the hill houses Cornell's **Herbert F. Johnson Museum of Art** (255-6464), at the corner of University and Central. The small collection of European and American painting and sculpture includes works by Giacometti, Matisse, O'Keeffe, de Kooning, Hopper, and Benton; the rooftop sculpture garden has a magnificent view of Ithaca. (Open Tues.-Sun. 10am-5pm. Free. Wheelchair accessible.) The magnificent **Cornell Plantations,** a series of botanical gardens surrounding Cornell's great geological wonders, offer adventurous hikes into the Cornell gorge. The 1½-mi. long **Founder's Loop** takes only an hour and is well worth the time. **Ithaca College** (274-3011 for campus info), located on South Hill, also offers more campus-style entertainment.

Discriminating moviegoers should head to the **Cornell Cinema,** 104 Willard Straight Hall (255-3522), at the College; its programming and prices will thrill even the most jaded art-house movie junkie (tickets $4.50). The **Historic State Theatre,** 109 W. State St. (273-1037 or 274-2781), hosts dance and other live performances as well as movies in a vintage 1928 faux Spanish castle/movie palace. The architect, legend has it, went insane shortly after the completion of its construction. (Monthly classic film festivals $2-4.)

Finger Lakes The fertile soil of the Finger Lakes area has made this region the heart of New York's wine industry. The three designated **wine trails** provide opportunities for wine tasting and vineyard touring; locals say that the fall harvest is the best time to visit. All of the area's vineyards and eight wineries lie on the **Cayuga Trail,**

located along Rte. 89 between Seneca Falls and Trumansburg; call the visitors center for details (see Practical Information, above). For info on the **Seneca Trail,** 14 wineries split into those on the east side of the lake (Rte. 414) and those on the west side (Rte. 14), or the **Keuka Trail,** seven wineries along Rte. 54 and Rte. 76, contact The Finger Lakes Association (see Practical Information, above). Some wineries offer free picnic facilities, and all conduct free tours and tastings, though several require purchase of a glass ($1.50-2). **Americana Vineyards Winery,** 4367 East Covert Rd., Interlaken (387-6801), ferments 2 mi. from Trumansburg. If you're driving, take Rte. 96 or 89 north of Trumansburg to E. Covert Rd. A family of four operates this winery from grape-picking to bottle-corking; one of them will give you a personal tour and free tasting. Pick up a bottle for about $5-8. (Open May-Oct. Mon.-Sat. 10am-5pm, Sun. noon-5pm; April and Nov.-Dec. weekends only.)

   Seneca Falls saw the birth of the women's rights movement at the 1848 Seneca Falls Convention. Elizabeth Cady Stanton, and other leading suffragists, organized the meeting of those seeking the vote for women. Today, the **Women's Rights National Historical Park** commemorates their efforts. Begin your visit at the **visitors center,** 136 Fall St. (315-568-2991; open daily 9am-5pm). The **National Women's Hall of Fame,** 76 Fall St. (315-568-2936), commemorates outstanding U.S. women with photographs and biographies (open Mon.-Sat. 9:30am-5pm, Sun. noon-4pm; $3, students and seniors $1.50).

   The town of **Corning,** home to the Corning Glass Works, awaits 40 mi. outside Ithaca on Rte. 17W off Rte. 13S. Watch glassworkers blow glass at the **Corning Glass Center,** 151 Centerway (607-974-2000), which chronicles the 3500-year history of glass-making with over 20,000 pieces—sopranos beware! (Open daily 9am-8pm; Sept.-June 9am-5pm. $7, seniors $6, under 18 $5.) The nearby **Rockwell Museum,** 111 Cedar St., Rte. 17 (607-937-5386), shows pieces by Frederick Carder (founder of the Steuben Glass Work) and an excellent collection of American Western art (open Mon.-Sat. 10am-5pm, Sun. noon-5pm; $4, seniors $3.60, youth $2).

■ Niagara Falls

One of the seven natural wonders of the world, Niagara Falls also claims the title of one of the world's largest sources of hydro-electric power. Originally, 5½ billion gallons of water tumbled over the falls every hour; now, ¾ of this volume is diverted to supply the United States and Canada with power. Coincidentally, the work by hydro-electricians to regulate water flow has slowed the erosion which was rapidly eating away at the falls. It is believed that the falls now move back at a rate of 1 ft. per decade, down from 6 ft. per year. Admired not only for their beauty, the Falls have attracted thrill-seeking barrel-riders since 1901, when 63-year-old Annie Taylor successfully completed the drop. Modern day adventurers beware—heavy fines are levied for barrel attempts, and as park officials note, "chances for survival are slim."

PRACTICAL INFORMATION

   Tourist Office: Niagara Falls Convention and Visitors Bureau, 310 4th St., Niagara Falls, NY 14303 (285-2400 or 800-421-5223; 24hr. Niagara City Events Line 285-8711). Open daily 9am-5pm. To receive the excellent *Niagara USA* travel guide by mail, call 800-338-7890. An **information center** adjoins the bus station on 4th and Niagara St., a 10-min. walk from the Falls; free 1-hr. parking. Open daily 8am-8pm, mid-Sept. to mid-May daily 9am-5pm. The state runs the **Niagara Reservation State Park Visitors Center** (278-1796), in front of the Falls' observation deck; the entrance is marked by a garden. Open daily 8am-10pm; Oct.-Dec. 8am-8pm, mid-Nov. to Dec. 8am-10pm; Dec.-April 8am-6:30pm. **Niagara Falls Canada Visitor and Convention Bureau,** 5433 Victoria Ave., Niagara Falls, ON L2E 3L1 (905-356-6061), has info on the Canadian side. Open Mon.-Fri. 8:30am-8pm, Sat.-Sun. 10am-8pm; off season Mon.-Fri. 9am-5pm. **Ontario Travel Information Center,** 5355 Stanley Ave. (905-358-3221), at Rte. 420, provides tourism info for the province.

Trains: Amtrak (285-4224 or 800-872-7245), at 27th St. and Lockport 1 block east of Hyde Park Blvd. Take #52 bus to Falls/Downtown. To New York City (2-3 per day, $52) and Toronto (1 per day, $16). Open Thurs.-Mon. 6:20am-11:30pm, Tues.-Wed. 6:20am-3pm. Closed daily 10:45-11:30am.

Buses: Niagara Falls Bus Terminal (282-1331), 4th and Niagara St., sells **Greyhound** and **Trailways** tickets for use in Buffalo. Open Mon.-Fri. 8am-4pm. To get a bus in Buffalo, take a 1-hr. trip on bus #40 from the Niagara Falls bus terminal to the **Buffalo Transportation Center,** 181 Ellicott St. (800-231-2222; 12-17 per day, 1hr., $1.85). To: New York City (9 per day, 8hr., $40-50); Boston (4 per day, 12hr., $50-60); Chicago (6 per day, 12hr., $75); Rochester (8 per day, 1½hr., $10); Albany (5 per day, 7hr., $32). Open daily 6:30am-11:45pm.

Public Transportation: Niagara Frontier Metro Transit System, 343 4th St. (285-9319), provides local city transit. Fare $1.25. **ITA Buffalo Shuttle** (800-551-9369) provides service from Niagara Falls info center and major hotels to Buffalo Airport ($15).

Taxis: Rainbow Taxicab, 282-3221. **United Cab,** 285-9331. Both charge $1.50 base fee, $1.50 per additional mi. A taxi from Buffalo Airport to Niagara costs $36.

Emergency: 911.

Post Office: 615 Main St. (285-7561). Open Mon.-Fri. 7:30am-5pm, Sat. 9am-2pm. **ZIP code:** 14302. **Area code:** 716 (NY), 905 (ON).

Niagara Falls does its thang in both the U.S. and Canada; addresses given here are in NY, unless otherwise noted. Visitors approaching Niagara Falls should take U.S. 190 to the Robert Moses Pkwy., or else skirt the tolls (but suffer traffic and commercialism) by taking Exit 3 to Rte. 62. In town, Niagara St. is the main east-west artery, ending in the west at Rainbow Bridge, which crosses to Canada (pedestrian crossings 25¢, cars 75¢). Numbered north-south streets increase towards the east. Outside of town, stores, restaurants, and motels line Rte. 62 (Niagara Falls Blvd.). The gorgeous state park which includes Falls Park lies at the west edge of the city. Parking in town is plentiful; most lots near the Falls charge $3, but you can park in an equivalent spot for less on streets bordering the park. The free parking lot on Goat Island fills early.

ACCOMMODATIONS AND CAMPING

Niagara Falls International Hostel (HI-C), 4549 Cataract Ave., Niagara Falls, Ont. (357-0770), just off Bridge St. An excellent hostel near the falls, about 2 blocks from the bus station and VIA Rail. 68 beds; can be cramped when full. Family rooms, laundry facilities, and parking available. Bike rentals $12 per day. Friendly managers lead bike trips and hikes along the Niagara gorge. Office open 9-11am and 5pm-1am; kitchen and lounge open all day. Check-out 11am. CDN$17, nonmembers CDN$21. Linen CDN$1. Reservations recommended.

Niagara Falls International Hostel (HI-AYH), 1101 Ferry Ave. (282-3700). From bus station, walk east on Niagara St., turn left on Memorial Pkwy.; the hostel is at the corner of Ferry Ave. Walking from the falls, *avoid the area on Ferry Ave., between 4th and 5th St., particularly at night.* 44 beds, kitchen, TV lounge, limited parking. Owners will shuttle you to airport, train, or bus station on request; rate depends on group size. The daily Sunset Tour runs by the Power Project to Fort Niagara State Park, where the sun sets over Lake Ontario (weather and interest permitting, $4). Family rooms available. Check-in 7:30-9:30am and 4-11pm. Lockout 9:30am-4pm. Curfew 11:30pm; lights out midnight. Required sleepsack $1.50. $13, in winter $11; nonmembers $16/$14. Reservations essential. Closed mid-Dec. to early Jan.

All Tucked Inn, 574 3rd St. (282-0919 or 800-797-0919). Nice clean rooms close to the attractions. Singles and doubles around $40. Discounts for Let's Goers. Reservations suggested.

Olde Niagara House, 610 4th St. (285-9408). A country B&B just 4 blocks from the falls. Free pickup at the Amtrak or bus station. Rooms come with a delicious, hearty breakfast. Rooms $45-55, in winter $35-45; student singles $25-35/$20-25. Per person rates available, $15 and up.

YMCA, 1317 Portage Rd. (285-8491), a 20-min. walk from the Falls; at night take bus #54 from Main St. 58 beds. 24-hr. check-in. Fee includes use of full YMCA facilities; no laundry. *Dorm rooms for men only;* singles $25, key deposit $10. Men and women can sleep on mats in the gym, $15.

Four Mile Creek State Park (745-3802), on Robert Moses Pkwy. in the Ft. Niagara Area about 15mi. from downtown, 4mi. east of Youngstown. Affordable camping in sparsely wooded sites at the edge of Lake Ontario. Hiking and fishing on the premises. Showers. Sites $13, with electricity $15. Reserve in advance.

Niagara Glen-View Tent & Trailer Park, 3950 Victoria Ave., Niagara Falls, ON (800-263-2570). The closest sites to the Falls, but bare and unwooded; hiking trail across the street. Ice, showers, laundry facilities, and a pool. Shuttle from driveway to the bottom of Clifton Hill every ½hr. during the day. Office open daily 8am-11pm. CDN$26, with full hookup CDN$30. Open May to mid-Oct.

There are plans to open a new **HI-AYH Hostel** in the fall of 1996 in the theatre district of nearby Buffalo. Call 852-5222 for more info.

FOOD

Chomp options are slim here. The flagship restaurants of Niagara's pricey **Little Italy** have seen better days. Fortunately, there are a few other places which aren't over the falls. One popular spot, **The Press Box Bar,** 324 Niagara St. (284-5447), between 3rd and 4th St., lets patrons leave their mark by adding a dollar bill to the several thousand taped to the wall; every winter the owner takes them down and gives them to a cancer-fighting charity. From Monday to Wednesday, go for the spaghetti special (99¢, meatballs 25¢ each); otherwise, burgers ($1.85) and the trademark porterhouse steak ($8.75) are good bets. (Food served Sun.-Thurs. 11am-11pm, Fri.-Sat. 11am-midnight. Bar open Mon.-Thurs. 10am-2am, Fri.-Sat. 10am-3am, Sun. noon-2am.) **Sinatra's Sunrise Diner,** 829 Main St. (284-0959), serves genuine diner cuisine just a few blocks from the falls (2 eggs and toast 99¢, sandwiches $2-4; open Mon.-Thurs. 7am-8pm, Fri.-Sat. 7am-10pm, Sun. 7am-3pm). For a bite on the Canadian side, there's **Simon's Restaurant,** 4116 Bridge St., Niagara Falls, ON (356-5310), across from the whirlpool bridge, the oldest restaurant in Niagara Falls. Enjoy big breakfasts with giant homemade muffins (CDN74¢) or hearty diner dinners. (Open Mon.-Sat. 5:30am-9pm, Sun. 5:30am-3pm.) Farther inland, locals chow on pancakes, hot sandwiches, and full-meal specials (CDN$4-7) at **Basell's Restaurant,** 4880 Victoria Ave., Niagara Falls, ON (356-5310; open daily 6am-11pm). Near the falls and the Clifton Hill area, run home to **Mama Leone Restaurant,** 5705 Victoria Ave., Niagara Falls, ON (357-5220), for award-winning Northern Italian cuisine (CDN$7-10; open daily 4-11:30pm).

SIGHTS AND ENTERTAINMENT

The natural Canadian-U.S. border at the Niagara River divides the attractions at the falls. Either side can be seen in an afternoon. As early as the 1870s, gaudy commercialism had overrun the falls; officials on the American side responded in 1885 by making the immediate vicinity a state reservation park, the nation's first. Thus, though tourist snares abound on both sides, they're less rampant on the American shore. Stick to the official sights and you'll get more for your money.

From late November to early January, Niagara Falls holds the annual **Festival of Lights.** Bright bulbs line the trees and create brilliant, animated, outdoor scenes. The illumination of the falls caps the spectacle. This year, the Canadian festival (800-563-2557) includes Disney performances, a country music night, and a car show.

American Side **Niagara Wonders** (278-1792), a 20-min. movie on the Falls, plays in the info center. (Shows in summer daily on the hr. 10am-8pm; in fall Wed.-Sun. 10am-6pm; in spring daily 10am-6pm. $2, ages 6-12 $1.) The **Maid of the Mist Tour** (284-8897) consists of a 30-min. boat ride to the foot of both falls; don't bring anything that isn't waterproof. (Tours in summer daily every 15min. 9:15am-8pm; in fall and spring 10am-5pm. $7.75 plus 50¢ elevator fee, ages 6-12 $4.25, under 6 free.)

MID-ATLANTIC

The **Viewmobile** (278-1730), an open-sided people transporter, does a guided tour of the park, including stops at Goat Island, the brink of the falls, the visitors center, Schoellkopf's Museum, and the Aquarium. (Tours in summer daily every 15min. 10am-8pm, in winter 10am-6:30pm. $3.50, children $2.50.) The Viewmobile will drop off passengers on Goat Island for the **Caves of the Wind Tour**, which outfits visitors with yellow raincoats for a thrilling body-soaking ride to the base of the Bridal Veil Falls, including an optional walk to Hurricane Deck, putting you as close to the falls as you'll ever (want to) get. **Schoellkopf's Geological Museum** (278-1780), in Prospect Park, depicts the birth of the falls with slide shows every ½ hr. (Open daily 9:30am-7pm; Labor Day-Oct. 10am-5pm; Nov.-Memorial Day Thurs.-Sun. 10am-5pm. 50¢.) The **Master Pass** (278-1796), available at the park visitors center, covers admission to the theater, Maid of the Mist, the Viewmobile, the observation tower, Caves of the Wind, the Aquarium, and the geological museum ($20, ages 6-12 $15).

Outside the park, sharks, penguins, otters, and performing sea lions strut their stuff at the **Aquarium**, 701 Whirlpool St. (285-3575; open daily 9am-5pm, Labor Day-Memorial Day 9am-7pm; $6.25, ages 4-12 $4.25; included in the Master Pass). **Devils Hole State Park**, in the area, is home to the Niagara Gorge; on your hike down check out the rock where spiritual guru Jason Sperry's name is immortalized. Continuing north, the **Niagara Power Project**, 5777 Lewiston Rd. (285-3211), features interactive demonstrations, short videos, and displays on energy, hydropower, and local history (free); take Robert Moses Pkwy. north to Rte. 104. While you're there, stop at the fishing platform and catch salmon, trout, or bass for dinner. (Open daily 9am-6pm; Labor Day-June 10am-5pm.) The 200-acre state **Artpark** (800-659-PARK/7275), at the foot of 4th St., focuses on visual and performing arts, with a variety of workshops, classes, and demonstrations. The theater presents opera, pops concerts, and jazz festivals ($26-30; open July-Aug. Tues.-Sun; call for schedule).

The French, British, and American flags have all flown over **Old Fort Niagara** (745-7611), a French castle built in 1726 to guard the entrance to the Niagara River; follow Robert Moses Pkwy. north from Niagara Falls. (Open daily 9am-6:30pm; Labor Day-Dec. and April-May 9am-4:30pm; Jan.-Mar. 9am-5:30pm. $6, seniors $4.75, ages 6-12 $3.75.) Wander into **Artisans Alley**, 10 Rainbow Blvd. (282-0196), at 1st St., to see the works of over 600 American craftsmen (open daily 10am-9pm, Jan.-April Mon.-Sat. 10am-5pm, Sun. noon-5pm; free). The 4-time AFC Champ/Super Bowl bust **Buffalo Bills** (649-0015 for ticket info) play at Rich Stadium in Orchard Park, south of the falls.

Canadian Side On the Canadian side of Niagara Falls (across Rainbow Bridge), **Queen Victoria Park** provides the best view of Horseshoe Falls. The falls are illuminated for three hours every night, starting one hour after sunset. Parking is expensive (CDN$8). Once you park, air-conditioned buses called **People Movers** (357-9340) will take you through the 19-mi. area on the Canadian side of the Falls, stopping at points of interest along the way. (Early May to mid-Oct. Mon.-Fri. 10am-6pm, Sat.-Sun. 10am-10pm. CDN$4, children CDN$2.) You can save a buck by using **Park 'N' Ride**; park at Rapids View, at the south end of Niagara Pkwy., and take People Movers from there. Parking and all-day people mover pass $4 per person, $11 for 3 or more people. **Skylon Tower**, 5200 Robinson St. (356-2651), has the highest view of the Falls at 775 ft.; on a clear day you can see as far as Toronto (CDN$7, kids CDN$3.90). Its 552-ft. **Observation Deck** offers an unhindered view of the falls (open daily 8am-midnight, in winter hours change monthly). Canada's version of the Master Pass, the **Explorer's Passport** (CDN$13.25, children CDN$6.65), includes passage to **Journey Behind the Falls** (354-1551), a gripping tour behind the rushing waters of Horseshoe Falls (CDN$5.50, children CDN$2.75); **Great Gorge Adventure** (374-1221), a descent into the Niagara River Rapids (open late April-late Oct.; CDN$4.50, children CDN$2.25); and the **Spanish Aero Car** (354-5711), an aerial cable ride over the turbulent whirlpool waters (open mid-March to Oct.; CDN$4.75, children CDN$2.40).

The **Niagara Falls Brewing Company**, 6863 Lundy's Lane (374-1166), hosts free touring and tasting (open daily 10am-6pm). **Vincor International** (formerly Bright's

Winery), 4887 Dorchester Rd. (357-2400), is Canada's oldest and largest winery. (Tours Mon.-Sat. 10:30am, 2pm, and 3:30pm, Sun. 2 and 3:30pm; Nov. to April Mon.-Fri. 2pm, Sat.-Sun. 2 and 3:30pm. CDN$2 to taste 4 wines.) Bikers, rollerbladers, and leisurely walkers enjoy the 56-km **Niagara River Recreation Trail,** which runs from Ft. Erie to Ft. George and passes many interesting historical and geological sights.

For the happy few who realize that tourist commercialism can be as much a thing of beauty as any natural wonder, Niagara Falls offers the delightfully tasteless **Clifton Hill,** a collection of wax museums, funhouses, and other overpriced freak shows. One jewel in this tourist strip's crown, **Ripley's Believe It or Not Museum,** 4960 Clifton Hill (356-2238), displays such wonders as wax models of unicorn men and a genuine Jivaro shrunken head from Ecuador (open summers daily 9am-1:30am, off-season 10am-10pm; CDN$7, seniors CDN$5.50, kids CDN$3.40, under 5 free). While in Niagara Falls tune to 91.9FM CFL2 for tourist info on the Canadian side.

NORTHERN NEW YORK

■ The Adirondacks

In 1892, the New York State legislature demonstrated uncommon foresight in establishing the **Adirondacks State Park**—the largest U.S. park outside Alaska and one of the few places left where hikers can spend days without seeing another soul. In recent years, unfortunately, pollution and development have left a harsh imprint; acid rain has damaged the tree and fish populations, especially in the fragile high-altitude environments, and tourist meccas like **Lake George** have continued to expand rapidly. Despite these urban intrusions, much of the area retains the beauty visitors have enjoyed for over a century.

Of the six million acres in the Adirondacks Park, 40% are open to the public, offering an unsurpassed range of outdoor activities. Whether hiking, snow-shoeing, or cross-country skiing, the 2000 mi. of trails that traverse the forest provide spectacular mountain scenery. Canoers paddle through an interlocking network of lakes and streams, while mountain climbers conquer **Mt. Marcy,** the state's highest peak (5344 ft.) and skiers take advantage of a dozen well-known alpine centers. **Lake Placid** hosted the winter Olympics in 1932 and 1980, and frequently welcomes national and international sports competitions. **Tupper Lake** and Lake George have carnivals every January and February; Tupper also hosts the Tin Man Triathlon in mid-July. In September, the hot air balloons of the Adirondack Balloon Festival paint the sky over Glens Falls.

Practical Information The **Adirondack Mountain Club (ADK)** is the best source of info on hiking and other outdoor activities in the region. In its 74th year, the ADK has over 22,000 members. Their offices are located at RR3, Box 3055, Lake George 12845 (668-4447), and at Adirondack Loj Rd., P.O. Box 867, Lake Placid 12946 (523-3441; open Sat.-Thurs. 8am-8pm, Fri. 8am-10pm). Call the Lake Placid number for the scoop on outdoors skills classes such as canoeing, rock climbing, whitewater kayaking, and wilderness medicine ($20-200). For the latest backcountry info, visit ADK's **High Peaks Information Center,** 3 mi. south of Lake Placid on Rte. 73, then 5 mi. down Adirondak Loj Rd. The center also has washrooms (open daily 8am-7pm) and sells basic outdoor equipment, trail snacks, and the club's extremely helpful guides to the mountains ($18). Rock climbers should consult the experienced mountaineers at the **Mountaineer** (576-2281), in Keene Valley between I-87 and Lake Placid on Rte. 73. Snowshoes rent for $15 per day; ice-climbing equipment (boots and crampons) goes for $20 per day. (Open in summer Fri. 9am-7pm, Sat. 8am-7pm, Sun. 9am-6pm; otherwise Mon.-Fri. 9am-5:30pm, Sat. 8am-5:30pm, Sun. 10am-5:30pm.) The ADK and the Mountaineer are better equipped to give you details, but the **State Office of Parks and Recreation,** Agency Bldg. 1, Empire State

Place, Albany 12238 (474-0456), can provide basic info on the conditions and concerns of backwoods travel.

Adirondacks Trailways serves the Adirondacks with frequent stops along I-87. From Albany, buses go to Lake Placid, Tupper Lake, and Lake George. From the Lake George bus stop at the Mobil station, 320 Canada St. (668-9511; 800-858-8555 for bus info), buses set out for Lake Placid (1 per day, 2:50pm, $13), Albany (3 per day, $9.75), and New York City ($37.50). The gas station may close Dec.-May but buses still run. (Open June-Nov. Mon.-Wed. 7am-10pm, Thurs. 7am-midnight, Fri.-Sun. 7am-2am.) The Adirondacks' **area code: 518.**

Accommodations and Camping Two lodges near Lake Placid are also run by the ADK. The **Adirondak Loj** (523-3441), 8 mi. east of Lake Placid off Rte. 73, fills a beautiful log cabin on Heart Lake with comfortable bunk facilities and a family atmosphere. Guests can swim, fish, canoe, and use rowboats on the premises (canoe or boat rental $5 per hr.), and in winter, explore the wilderness trails on rented snowshoes ($15 per day) or cross-country skis ($20 per day). (B&B $30 in bunk room, with dinner $41; linen included. Tent sites for 2 $15, in winter $8, $2 per additional person. Lean-tos for 2 $18/$12/$2.50.) Call ahead for weekends and peak holiday seasons. For an even better mix of rustic comfort and wilderness experience, hike 3½ mi. to the **John's Brook Lodge** from the closest trailhead, in Keene Valley (call the Adirondak Loj for reservations); from Lake Placid, follow Rte. 73 15 mi. through Keene to Keene Valley and turn right at the Ausable Inn. The hike runs slightly uphill, but the meal which awaits you justifies the effort; the staff packs in groceries every day and cooks on a gas stove. A great place to meet friendly New Yorkers, John's Brook is no secret; beds fill completely on weekends. Make reservations one day in advance for dinner, longer for a weekend. Bring sheets or a sleeping bag. (B&B $26, with dinner $37. Lean-tos $10. Bunks $12; full kitchen access.)

If ADK facilities are too pricey, try the **High Peaks Base Camp**, P.O. Box 91, Upper Jay 12987 (946-2133), a charming restaurant/lodge/campground just a 20-min. drive from Lake Placid; take Rte. 86 E. to Wilmington, turn right on Fox Farm Rd. (just before the Hungry Trout Tackle Shop), then go right 2½ mi. on Springfield Rd. You'll get a bed for the night ($15-18 Fri.-Sat.) and a huge breakfast in the morning. Sometimes rides can be arranged from Keene; call ahead. (Free hot showers. Check-in until 10pm; later with reservations. Tent sites $5; $3 per additional person. Cabins for 4 $30, private rooms $40.) **Free camping** is easy to come by. Always inquire about the location of free trailside shelters before you plan a hike in the forest. Better still, camp for free anywhere on public land in the **backcountry** as long as you are at least 150 ft. away from a trail, road, water source, or campground and below 4000 ft. in altitude. The State Office of Parks and Recreation (see Practical Information, above) has more details.

In **Lake George**, 45 mi. south of the junction of Rte. 73 and I-87, off I-87 Exit 22, the basement of **St. James Episcopal Church Hall** (668-2634), on Montcalm St. at Ottawa a few blocks from the lake, doubles as the **Lake George Youth Hostel (HI-AYH)**. From the bus terminal, walk south 1 block to Montcalm, turn right, and go 1 block to Ottawa; you'll find a slightly musty bunkroom and a decent kitchen behind an HI-AYH sign in the parking lot. Limited parking available. (Check-in 5-9pm; later only with reservations. Curfew 10pm. $10, nonmembers $13. Sleepsack required; rental $1. Open late May to early Sept.; spring and fall by reservation.)

■ Lake Placid

Home of the Olympic Winter Games in both 1932 and 1980, Lake Placid keeps the memory and the dream of Olympic glory alive. World-class athletes train year-round in the town's extensive sporting facilities, lending an international flavor which distinguishes Lake Placid from its Adirondack neighbors. The natural setting of the Adirondack High Peaks Region draws droves of hikers and backpackers each year.

Practical Information Lake Placid sits at the intersection of Rte. 86 and 73. The town's Olympic past has left its mark; the **Olympic Regional Development Authority,** 216 Main St., Olympic Center (523-1655 or 800-462-6236), operates the sporting facilities and sells tickets for self-guided tours. (Available July to mid-Oct daily 9am-4pm. $16, seniors and ages 6-12 $12, under 6 free.) Information on food, lodging, and area attractions can be obtained from the **Lake Placid-Essex County Visitors Bureau** (523-2445), also in Olympic Center. (Open Mon.-Fri. 9am-5pm; late June to Labor Day also Sat.-Sun. 9am-4pm.) **Adirondack Trailways** (523-4309 for bus info) stops at the **326 Main St. Deli,** and has extensive service in the area. Buses run to New York City (1 per day, $50), making 13 stops along the way, including one at Lake George ($13). For **weather info,** call 523-1363 or 523-3518. Lake Placid's **post office:** 201 Main St. (523-3071; open Mon.-Fri. 9am-5pm, Sat. 8:30am-2pm). **ZIP code:** 12946. **Area code:** 518.

Accommodations, Camping, and Food As long as you avoid the resorts on the west end of town, both accommodations and food can be had cheaply in Lake Placid. Eight mi. from town, the **White Sled** (523-9314; on Rte. 73 between the Sports Complex at Mt. Hoevenberg and the ski jumps) is the best bargain around—for $17 you get a comfortable, clean bed in the bunkhouse, which includes a full kitchen, a spacious living room with TV, and a quiet setting to collect your thoughts (private rooms $38-50). **Meadowbrook State Park** (891-4351), 5 mi. west on Rte. 86 in Ray Brook, and **Wilmington Notch State Campground** (946-7172), off Rte. 86E between Wilmington and Lake Placid, have the area's nearest campsites. Both offer sites without hookups which accommodate two tents ($10 first night, $9 per additional night).

In Lake Placid Village, **Main St.** offers reasonably priced pickings to suit any palate. The lunch buffet (Mon.-Sat. noon-2pm) at the **Hilton Hotel,** 1 Mirror Lake Dr. (523-4411), includes a sandwich and all-you-can-eat soup and salad ($5.25). At the **Black Bear Restaurant,** 157 Main St. (523-9886), enjoy a $5 lunch or $4 breakfast special and a $2.75 Saranac lager (the Adirondacks' own beer) in the company of stuffed animals. (Bottomless java $1. Open Sun.-Thurs. 6am-10:30pm, Fri.-Sat. 24hr.) **The Cottage,** 5 Mirror Lake Dr. (523-9845), serves up sandwiches, salads ($4-6), and Lake Placid's best views of Mirror Lake, where the U.S. canoe and kayaking teams practice (open Sun.-Thurs. 11:30am-9pm, Fri.-Sat. 11:30am-10pm; bar open daily 11:30am-1am). **Mud Puddles,** 3 School St. (523-4446), below the speed skating rink, is a splash with the pop music crowd (open daily 8am-3am; cover $0-3).

Sights You can't miss the 70 and 90-m runs of the Olympic ski jumps which, along with the **Kodak Sports Park,** make up the **Olympic Jumping Complex,** just outside of town on Rte. 73. The $7 admission fee includes a chairlift and elevator ride to the top of the spectator towers, where you can catch summer (June to mid-Oct.) jumpers flipping and sailing into a swimming pool. (Open daily 9am-5pm, Sept.-June 9am-4pm.) Three mi. farther along Rte. 73, the **Olympic Sports Complex** (523-4436) at Mt. Van Hoevenberg has a summer trolley that coasts to the top of the bobsled run ($3, kids and seniors $2; mid-June to mid-Oct.). In the winter, you can bobsled down the Olympic run ($25), or try the luge ($10; open Dec.-March Tues.-Sun. 1-3pm). Contact the Olympic Regional Development Authority (see above) for a tour of the facilities.

The west branch of the **Ausable River,** just east of Lake Placid, lures anglers to its shores. **Fishing licenses** (1-day $11, 5-day $20, season $35; resident 3-day $6, season $14) are sold at **Town Hall,** 301 Main St. (523-2162), or **Jones Outfitters,** 37 Main St. (523-3468). Jones rents the necessary equipment as well, including rod, reel, line, tackle, and bait. (Package $15 per day, fly-fishing outfit $25 per day. Open daily 9am-6pm.) If you'd like to join the fish rather than beat them, Jones also rents canoes, kayaks, and rowboats ($12 per hr., $35 per day). The **Fishing Hotline** (891-5413) plays an in-depth recording with straight talk on fishing hotspots.

MID-ATLANTIC

■ Thousand Island Seaway

The Thousand Island region of St. Lawrence Seaway spans 100 miles from the mouth of Lake Ontario to the first of the many locks on the St. Lawrence River. Some 250 wooded islands and countless rocky shoals make navigation tricky in this area. Locals divide people into two groups: those who *have* hit a shoal and those who *will* hit a shoal. But don't let this dire prediction deter you; not only is the Thousand Island region a fisherman's paradise, with some of the world's best bass and muskie catch, it's the only area in the nation with a salad dressing named after it.

Practical Information The Thousand Islands region hugs the coast just two hours from Syracuse by way of I-81N. **Clayton, Alexandria Bay,** and **Cape Vincent** are the main cities in the area. For Welleslet Island, Alexandria Bay, and the eastern 500 islands, stay on I-81 until you reach Rte. 12E. For Clayton and points west, take Exit 47 and follow Rte. 12 until you reach 12E. Write or visit the **Clayton Chamber of Commerce,** 510 Riverside Dr., Clayton 13624 (686-3771), for the free *Clayton Vacation Guide* and *Thousand Islands Seaway Region Travel Guide.* (Open July-Aug. daily 9am-4pm, otherwise Mon.-Fri. 9am-4pm.) The **Alexandria Bay Chamber of Commerce,** 24 Market St., Alexandria Bay 13607 (482-9531), is just off James St. on the right. (Open mid-May to mid-Oct. daily 9am-5pm, otherwise Mon.-Fri. 9am-5pm.) The **Cape Vincent Chamber of Commerce** (654-2481) receives mail and visitors at James St., Cape Vincent 13618, by the ferry landing. (Open May-Oct. Tues.-Sat. 9am-5pm.) Access the region by bus with **Greyhound,** 540 State St., Watertown (788-8110). Two buses run daily to New York City (8½hr., $39-42), Syracuse (1¾ hr., $10-11), and Albany (5½hr., $31-34). From the same station, **Thousand Islands Bus Lines** (287-2782) leaves for Alexandria Bay and Clayton Monday to Friday at 1pm ($5.60 to Alexandria, $3.55 to Clayton); return trips leave Clayton from the **Nutshell Florist,** 234 James St. (686-5791), at 8:45am, and Alexandria from the **Dockside Café,** 17 Market St. (482-9849), at 8:30am. (Station open 9:15am-2:30pm and 6-8pm, give or take.)

Clayton's **post office:** 236 John St. (686-3311; open Mon.-Fri. 9am-5pm, Sat. 9am-noon). **ZIP code:** 13624. Alexandria Bay's **post office:** 13 Bethune St. (482-9521; open Mon.-Fri. 8:30am-5:30pm, Sat. 8:30am-1pm). **ZIP code:** 13607. Cape Vincent's **post office:** 360 Broadway St. (654-2424; open Mon.-Fri. 8:30am-1pm and 2-5:30pm). **ZIP code:** 13618. Thousand Island's **area code:** 315.

Accommodations and Camping George and Jean Couglar lovingly care for the idyllic **Tibbetts Point Lighthouse Hostel (HI-AYH),** RR 1 Box 330 (654-3450), on the western edge of the seaway on Cape Vincent, situated where Lake Ontario meets the St. Lawrence River. Take Rte. 12E into town, turn left on Broadway, and follow the river until the road ends. There is no public transportation to Cape Vincent, but with enough advance notice, George or Jean will pick you up in Clayton. (2 houses with 31 beds. Full kitchen with microwave. Check-in 5-10pm. Curfew 11pm. $10, nonmembers $13. Linen $1. Open May 15-Oct. 25.) **Burnham Point State Park** (654-2324), on Rte. 12E 4 mi. east of Cape Vincent and 11 mi. west of Clayton, sports 50 tent sites and boat docking facilities. (No showers. Sites for up to 2 tents and 6 people $13, with hookup $15. Use of car $4; of horse and wagon $1. Open Memorial Day-Labor Day daily 8am-9pm.) **Keewaydin State Park** (482-3331), just south of Alexandria Bay, maintains 41 sites along the St. Lawrence River. Campers have free access to an Olympic-size swimming pool. (Showers available. $14 first night, $13 per additional night. No hookups. Open Memorial Day-Labor Day.)

Exploring the Seaway Any of the small towns that dot Rte. 12 will serve as a fine base for exploring the region, although Clayton and Cape Vincent tend to be less expensive than Alexandria Bay. **Uncle Sam Boat Tours,** 604 Riverside Dr. (686-3511), in Clayton, and on James St. in Alexandria Bay (482-2611), gives a good look at most of the islands and the plush estates situated atop them. (2½-hr. tours April-Dec.

daily. From Clayton $13.50, ages 4-12 $7.75. From Alexandria Bay $12/$6.50. Seniors and AAA members $1 off.) Tours highlight **Heart Island** and its famous **Boldt Castle** (482-9724 or 800-847-526) and make unlimited stops so that visitors can get off and stay as long as they would like before being picked up; they do not cover the price of admission to the castle. George Boldt, former owner of New York City's elegant Wal-dorf-Astoria Hotel, financed this six-story replica of a Rhineland castle as a gift for his wife, who died before its completion. In his grief, Boldt stopped construction on the 365-bedroom, 52-bathroom behemoth, which remains unfinished today. After extensive renovations, this exorbitant monument is now open to the public. (Open May-Oct. $3.25, seniors $2.75, ages 6-12 $1.75.) In Clayton, **French Creek Marina,** 98 Wahl St. (686-3621), rents 14-ft. fishing boats ($50 per day) and pontoon boats ($200 per day), launches boats ($5), and provides overnight docking ($20 per night). **O'Brien's U-Drive Boat Rentals,** 51 Walton St. (482-9548), handles boat rentals in Alexandria Bay with 16-ft. fishing boats ($60 per day, $100 deposit) and 18-ft. run-abouts ($150 per day, $300 deposit; open April-Oct.; mechanic on duty daily). In Cape Vincent, **Sunset Trailer Park** (654-2482), 2 mi. beyond town on Rte. 12E, offers motor boats ($40 per day) and is convenient to Tibbets Point Hostel (see Accommodations, above).

Fishing licenses (5-day $20, season $35; resident 3-day $6, season $14) are available at sporting goods stores or at the **Town Clerk's Office,** 405 Riverside Dr., Clay ton (686-3512; open Mon.-Fri. 9am-noon and 1-4pm). No local store rents equipment; bring your own rods and reels or plan to buy them.

New Jersey

New Jersey was once called the Garden State for a reason, but with the advent of sub-urbia (NJ serves both New York City and Philadelphia), and tax-free shopping (giving rise to outlets and major mall country), travelers who refuse to get off the interstates envision the state as a conglomeration of belching chemical plants and ocean beaches strewn with garbage and gamblers. This picture, however, belies the state's quieter delights (off the highway). A closer look reveals that there is more to New Jersey than commuters, chemicals, and craps; the interior blooms with countless fields of corn, tomatoes, and peaches, while quiet sandy beaches outline the southern tip of the state. New Jersey also shelters quiet hamlets, the Pine Barrens forest, and two world-class universities: Rutgers and Princeton. Certainly, Atlantic City continues its gaudy existence, and the New Jersey Turnpike remains the zone of the road warrior, but those who stray from the path will be pleasantly surprised.

PRACTICAL INFORMATION

Capital: Trenton.
State Division of Tourism: CN 826, Trenton 08625 (609-292-2470). **New Jersey Department of Environmental Protection and Energy, State Park Service,** 401 East State St., Trenton, 08625-0404.
Time Zone: Eastern. **Postal Abbreviation:** NJ.
Sales Tax: 6%; no tax on clothing.

▨ Atlantic City

For over 50 years, coffee-table high rollers have been struggling for control of the likes of St. James Place and Ventnor Avenue. When these thoroughfares were immortalized in *Monopoly,* Atlantic City was a beachside hotspot tops among resort towns, frequented by wealthy families like the Vanderbilts and the Girards. The opulence has since faded; with the rise of competition from Florida resorts, the community chest closed, and Atlantic City suffered decades of decline. Then, with the legalization of gambling in 1976, casinos rose from the rubble of Boardwalk. Velvet-lined temples of tackiness now blight the beach, drawing international jet-setters and small-time slot-players alike.

PRACTICAL INFORMATION

Tourist Office: Atlantic City Convention Center and Visitors Bureau, 2314 Pacific Ave. (499-7130 or 800-262-7395); main entrance on the Boardwalk between Mississippi and Florida Ave. Home of the Miss America Pageant. Also a booth on the Boardwalk at Mississippi Ave. Personal assistance daily 9am-5pm; leaflets available 24hr.

Tours: Gray Line Tours, 900 Eighth Ave., New York City (397-2600), between 53rd and 54th St. Several daily roundtrip excursions to Atlantic City (3hr., $21, on weekends $23). Redeem your ticket receipt for up to $15 in cash, chips, or food from a casino when you arrive. Caesar's, the Taj Mahal, and TropWorld have the best offers ($15 in cold, flexible cash). The bus drops you off at the designated casino and picks you up 3hr. later.

Trains: Amtrak (800-872-7245), at Kirkman Blvd. near Michigan Ave. Follow Kirkman to its end, bear right, and follow the signs. To: New York (1 per day, 2½hr., $28). Open Sun.-Fri. 9:30am-7:40pm, Sat. 9:30am-10pm.

Buses: Greyhound (345-6617 or 800-231-2222), in the **Atlantic City Municipal Bus Terminal,** at Arkansas and Arctic Ave. Buses every hr. to New York (2½hr., $20). **New Jersey Transit** (800-582-5946) operates from the same station. Service to New York City daily every hr. 6am-10pm ($21). Both bus lines offer casino-sponsored roundtrip discounts, including cash back in Atlantic City; Bally's has a particularly good deal—you get your full fare ($15) back in quarters upon arrival. Terminal 24hr.

Public Transportation: A **yellow tram** runs continuously. Fare $2, all-day pass $5. **Jitneys** run up and down Pacific Ave. 24hr.; $1.25. **NJ Transit** buses up and down Atlantic Ave. Fare $1.

Crisis Lines: Rape and Abuse Hotline, 646-6767. **Gambling Abuse,** 800-GAMBLER/800-426-2537. Both open 24hr. **AIDS Hotline,** 800-281-2437. Open Mon.-Fri. 9am-5pm.

Emergency: 911.

Post Office: (345-4212), at Martin Luther King and Pacific Ave. Open Mon.-Fri. 8:30am-6pm, Sat. 8:30am-noon. **ZIP code:** 08401. **Area code:** 609.

Atlantic City lies about half-way down New Jersey's coast, accessible via the **Garden State Pkwy.** and the **Atlantic City Expwy.,** and easily reached by train from Philadelphia and New York. Atlantic City's attractions cluster on and around the Boardwalk, which runs east-west along the Atlantic Ocean. Running parallel to the Boardwalk, Pacific and Atlantic Ave. offer cheap restaurants, hotels, and convenience stores. Atlantic Ave. can be dangerous after dark, and any street farther out can be dangerous even by day.

Getting around Atlantic City is easy on foot. **Parking** at the Sands Hotel is free, but "for patrons only"; go spend a dollar at the slots after enjoying this little-known convenience. If you want to park in a **lot,** park as close to the boardwalk as possible. It'll run about $5-7 per hr., but the $3 lots several blocks away offer dubious security.

ACCOMMODATIONS AND CAMPING

Large, red-carpeted beachfront hotels have bumped smaller operators a few streets back. Smaller hotels along **Pacific Ave.,** 1 block from the Boardwalk, charge about $60-95 in the summer. Reserve ahead, especially on weekends. Many hotels lower their rates mid-week and in the winter, when water temperature and gambling fervor drop significantly. Rooms in guest houses are reasonably priced, though facilities can be dismal. If you have a car it pays to stay in **Absecon,** about 8 mi. from Atlantic City; Exit 40 from the Garden Sate Pkwy. leads to Rte. 30 and cheap rooms.

Inn of the Irish Pub, 164 St. James Pl. (344-9063), near the Ramada Tower, just off the Boardwalk. Big, clean, pretty rooms, decorated with antiques. No TVs, phone, or A/C, but the summer breeze from the beach keeps things cool. Some rooms have a view of the sea. Plush lobby with TV and pay phone. Coin-op laundry in hotel next door. Singles with shared bath $29, with private bath $51.40, doubles $45.80/$80. Breakfast and dinner $10, children $8. Key deposit $5.

Hotel Cassino, 28 Georgia Ave. (344-0747), at Pacific Ave. behind Trump Plaza. Slightly run-down, but clean, cheap, and family-run. Small gaudy green and orange-painted rooms with shared bath. Rates negotiable. Singles $25-35, doubles $30-45. Key deposit $10. Open May to early Nov.

Birch Grove Park Campground (641-3778), on Mill Rd. in Northfield. About 6mi. from Atlantic City, off Rte. 9. 50 sites. Attractive and secluded. Sites for 4 $15, with hookup $20. Reservations recommended July-Aug.

FOOD

After you cash in your chips, visit a **casino buffet** for a cheap meal (about $10 for dinner, $6-7 for lunch), but don't expect gourmet quality. The cheapest casino buffet in town is on the sixth floor of the **Claridge;** all-you-can-eat breakfast goes for $3.77, lunch and dinner cost $4.72. Yes, the town does provide higher-quality meals in a less noxious atmosphere. For a complete rundown of local dining, pick up a copy of *TV Atlantic Magazine, At the Shore,* or *Whoot* (all free) from a hotel lobby, restaurant, or local store.

An inviting pub with a century's worth of Irish memorabilia draped on the walls, the **Inn of the Irish Pub,** 164 St. James Pl. (345-9613), serves hearty, modestly priced dishes such as deep-fried crab cakes ($4.50), honey-dipped chicken ($4.50), and Dublin beef stew ($5). The lunch special (Mon.-Fri. 11am-2pm) gets you a pre-selected sandwich and cup of soup for $2 (open 24hr.). Frank Sinatra is rumored to have had the immense subs ($4.50-9) from **White House Sub Shop** (345-1564 or 345-8599), at Mississippi and Arctic Ave., flown to him while on tour (open Mon.-Sat. 10am-midnight, Sun. 11am-midnight). For renowned Italian food, including the best pizza in town, hit **Tony's Baltimore Grille,** 2800 Atlantic Ave. (345-5766), at Iowa Ave. (Pasta around $5; pizza $5-8. Open daily 11am-3am; bar open 24hr.) For a traditional oceanside dessert, try custard ice cream or saltwater taffy, both available from vendors along the Boardwalk. **Custard and Snackcups,** between South Carolina and Ocean Ave. (345-5151), makes 37 flavors of soft-serve ice cream and yogurt, ranging from peach to pineapple to tutti-frutti. (Cones $2.25. Open Sun.-Thurs. 10am-midnight, Fri.-Sat. 10am-3am.)

CASINOS, THE BOARDWALK, AND BEACHES

You don't have to spend a penny to enjoy yourself in Atlantic City's casinos; their vast, plush interiors and spotless marble bathrooms can entertain a resourceful and voyeuristic budget traveler for hours. Watch blue-haired ladies shove quarter after quarter in the slot machines with a vacant, zombie-like stare. Open nearly all the time, casinos lack windows and clocks, denying you the time cues that signal the hours slipping away; keep your eyes on your watch or you'll have spent five hours and five digits before you know what hit you. To curb inevitable losses, stick to the cheaper games—blackjack and slot machines—and stay away from the cash machines. If you're on a really tight budget, the **5¢ slots,** available only at Trump Plaza, Trop-World, Bally's Grand, and Taj Mahal (see below), will allow you to gamble for hours on less than $10. The minimum gambling age of 21 is strictly enforced.

All casinos on the Boardwalk fall within a dice toss of one another. The farthest south is **The Grand** (347-7111), at Iowa Ave., and the farthest north is **Showboat** (343-4000), at States Ave. If you liked *Aladdin,* you'll love the **Taj Mahal** (449-1000), at Pennsylvania Ave. Donald Trump's huge and glittering jewel is too out there (and too large) to be missed—it was missed payments on this tasteless tallboy that cast the financier into his billion-dollar tailspin. It will feel like *Monopoly* when you realize Trump owns three other hotel casinos in the city: **Trump Plaza** (441-6000) and **Trump Regency** (344-4000) on the Boardwalk, and **Trump Castle** (441-2000) at the Marina. The outdoor Caesar at **Caesar's Boardwalk Resort and Casino** (348-4411) at

Arkansas Ave., has moved indoors, replaced by a kneeling Roman gladiator heralding the entrance to **Planet Hollywood.** Come, see, and conquer at the only casino with 25¢ video blackjack, and play slots at the feet of a huge **Statue of David.** The **Sands** (441-4000) at Indiana Ave. goes for a more "natural" effect with a decor of huge, ostentatious pink and green seashells.

There's something for everyone in Atlantic City, thanks to the Boardwalk. Those under 21 (or those tired of the endless cycle of winning and losing) **gamble for prizes** at one of the many arcades that line the Boardwalk. It feels like real gambling, but the teddy bear in the window is easier to get than the grand prize at a resort. The **Steel Pier,** an extension in front of the Taj Mahal, has the usual amusement park standbys: roller coaster, ferris wheel, tilt-a-whirl, carousel, kiddie rides, and many a game of "skill." Rides cost $1.50-3 each (open in summer daily noon-midnight; call the Taj Mahal for winter hours).

When you tire of spending money, check out the **beach.** Although older couples, families, and defunct gamblers often litter the dunes, the sand and water are generally clean, and a nice breeze blows over a beautiful view of the ocean. **Ventnor City,** just west of Atlantic City, has quieter shores.

■ Cape May

Lying at the southern extreme of New Jersey's coastline, Cape May is the oldest sea-shore resort in the United States. Isolated when the railroad connected Philadelphia to Atlantic City, this small vacation community retained much of its history, in the form of countless 19th-century Victorian homes. Indeed, the unique architecture of Cape May has proven to be its greatest asset. Although the Atlantic still beckons, the charming bed and breakfasts which line the brick sidewalks are unparalleled.

Practical Information Despite its geographic isolation, Cape May is very accessible. By car from the north, Cape May is literally the end of the road. Follow the toll-heavy Garden State Pkwy. south as far as it goes, watch for signs to Center City, and you'll end up on Lafayette St. From the south, take a 70-minute **ferry** from Lewes, DE (302-644-6030) to Cape May (889-7200 or 800-643-3779 for recorded schedule info). In summer months, 10 to 12 ferries cross daily; the rest of the year, expect only five to seven per day. ($18 one way per vehicle and driver. Passengers $4.50; ages 6-12 $2.25, motorcyclists $15, bicyclists $5.) Take a **shuttle** to the ferry from the Cape May Bus Depot ($1). The **welcome center,** 405 Lafayette St. (884-9562), provides a wagonload of helpful info about Cape May, and free hotlines to B&Bs (open daily 9am-4:30pm). As its name indicates, the **Chamber of Commerce and Bus Depot,** 609 Lafayette St. (884-5508), near Ocean St. across from the Acme, provides tourist info and is a local stop for **New Jersey Transit** (215-569-3752 or 800-582-5946). Buses run to: Atlantic City (16 per day, 2hr., $3.50); Philadelphia (6 per day, 3hr., $13.50); New York City (3 per day, 4½hr., $27). (Open Mon.-Fri. 9am-8pm, Sat. 9am-5pm; mid-Oct. to mid-May Mon.-Thurs. 9am-5pm, Fri. 9am-8pm.) Pick up another form of wheeled transportation at the **Village Bike Shop** (884-8500), at Washington and Ocean St. adjacent to the mall. Ask about the four-person surrey bike. (One-seaters $3.50 per hr., $9 per day. Open daily 7am-8pm.) Cape May's **post office:** 700 Washington St. (884-3578; open Mon.-Fri. 9am-5pm, Sat. 9am-noon). **ZIP code:** 08204. **Area code:** 609.

Accommodations and Camping Look for specials on hotel rooms along Beach Dr., or try one of the many seaside homes which take in nightly guests. The Victorian homes cater to the B&B set with rooms for $80-100 per night. Still, some reasonably priced inns persevere. Although the **Hotel Clinton,** 202 Perry St. (884-3993; 516-799-8889 in winter), lacks presidential suites, the family owned establishment has decent sized singles ($25-35) and doubles ($35-45) with a shared bath (16 rooms with sinks and fans; reservations recommended; open mid-June to Sept.). Next door, the **Parris Inn,** 204 Perry St. (884-8015 or 884-6363), near Lafayette St., rents spacious though simple rooms, most of which have private baths, all of which are equipped with TV and A/C (singles $65-105; doubles $75-120).

Campgrounds line U.S. 9 south of Atlantic City. See the stars at **Cold Springs Campground,** 541 New England Rd. (884-8717; 450 fairly private sites; $16.50, with hookup $20; open May to mid-Oct.). **Cape Island Campground,** 709 U.S. 9 (884-5777 or 800-437-7443), is slightly ritzier with a pool, store, and athletic facilities (sites with water and electricity $26, full hookup $31; open May to late Sept.).

Food Cape May's cheapest food is the pizza and burger fare along **Beach Ave.** You'll have to shell out a few more clams for a sit-down meal. Bustling with pedestrians shopping for fudge and saltwater taffy, the **Washington St. Mall** supports several popular food stores and eateries. The **Cape May Popcorn Factory,** 43 Perry St. (898-1315 or 800-453-4855), has the largest and most exotic selection of flavored popcorn you're likely to find anywhere (open daily 10am-10pm). **The Ugly Mug,** 426 Washington St. Mall (884-3459), serves a dozen clams for half as many dollars. Clam chowder goes for $2 a cup or $2.30 a bowl. (Open Mon.-Sat. 11am-2am, Sun. noon-2am. Food served until 11pm.) One of the most popular pubs in southern Jersey, **The Shire,** 315 Washington St. Mall (884-4700), just off Perry St., features $1 domestic drafts for a lively crowd while reggae, rock, and jazz bands play nightly. (No cover; 2 drink min. while bands play. Sandwiches $5-6; dinner entrees $10-14. Open Mon.-Sat. 10am-2am, Sun. 10am-1am.) **La Patisserie,** at the corner of the mall and Ocean St., offers authentic French baked goods, including brioche ($1.50), baguette ($1.60), and large slices of gatean ($3.50). (Open daily 7am-10pm.)

Hitting the Beach Fine beaches bless the entire Jersey shore, and Cape May's glisten, dotted with the famous Cape May diamonds (actually quartz pebbles). Unroll your beach towel on a city-protected beach (off Beach Ave.), but make sure you have the **beach tag** required for beachgoers over 11 from June to September between 10am and 5pm daily. Pick up a tag from the vendors roaming the shore (daily $3, weekly $9, seasonal $15), or the Beach Tag Office (884-9522).

The **Mid-Atlantic Center for the Arts,** 1048 Washington St. (884-5404), offers tours and activities such as a Victorian Week and the Music and Tulip Festivals. Pick up *This Week in Cape May* in any public building or store for a detailed listing. (Guided walking and trolley tours $5, ages 3-12 $2.50.) The beacon of the **Cape May Light House** in **Cape May Point State Park** (884-2159), west of town at the end of the point, guides tourists, not ships. A 199-step climb to the top of the lighthouse, built in 1859, offers a magnificent panorama of the New Jersey and Delaware shore. ($3.50, ages 2-12 $1. Park open 8am-dusk.)

Due to prevailing winds and location, thousands of birds make a pit stop in Cape May every year on their way to warmer climates. The **Cape May Bird Observatory,** 707 E. Lake Dr. (884-2736), on Cape May Point, serves as the center of knowledge for this bird watching mecca of North America. They distribute bird maps and run field trips and workshops. (Open Tues.-Sun. 9am-5pm. Recorded birding hotline, 884-2661.) For those looking for a respite from the seashore, Cape May boasts several golf and mini-golf courses, as well as tennis courts. **The Cape May Tennis Club,** 1020 Washington St. (884-8986), offers exquisitely maintained hard and clay courts for reasonable rates ($5 per person per hr.; open daily 8am-7pm).

Pennsylvania

Driven to protect his fellow Quakers from persecution, William Penn, Jr. petitioned the English crown for a slice of North America in 1680. King Charles II owed the Penns a considerable sum of money, so in 1681 he granted the Quakers a vast tract of land between present-day Maryland and New York. By making his colony a bastion of

MID-ATLANTIC

religious tolerance, Penn attracted settlers of all ethnicities and beliefs to Pennsylvania (which literally means "Penn's woods"), and the state promptly grew in population. The site of the First Continental Congress and the birthplace of the Declaration of Independence, Philadelphia, the country's first capital, was soon overshadowed—New York City rapidly grew into the nation's most important commercial and cultural center, while Washington, D.C. became the country's capital.

In the face of adversity, Pennsylvania, a state accustomed to revolution, has rallied. In 1976, Philadelphia groomed its historic shrines for the nation's bicentennial celebration, and they are now the centerpiece of the city's ambitious urban renewal program. Pittsburgh, a steel city once dirty enough to fool streetlights into burning during the day, has also initiated a cultural renaissance. Away from the cities, Pennsylvania's landscape—from the farms of Lancaster County to the deep river gorges of the Allegheny Plateau—retains much of the natural beauty that the area's first colonists discovered centuries ago.

PRACTICAL INFORMATION

Capital: Harrisburg.
Pennsylvania Travel & Tourism: 453 Forum Bldg., Harrisburg 17120 (800-237-4363). Info on hotels, restaurants, and sights. **Bureau of State Parks,** Rachel Carson State Office Bldg., 400 Market St., Harrisburg 17108 (717-787-8800). The detailed *Recreational Guide* is available free from all visitors centers.
Time Zone: Eastern. **Postal Abbreviation:** PA.
Sales Tax: 6%.

■ Philadelphia

The first capital of the United States, Philadelphia has a strong and proud patriotic history. "The City of Brotherly Love" played a pivotal role in forging the fledgling nation. Look beyond the red brick and cracked Liberty Bell, and you'll find sophistication. A large metropolis, Philadelphia has the museums, concert halls, galleries, and universities of a world-class urban center, and a throbbing club scene to complement its star-spangled historic district.

PRACTICAL INFORMATION

Tourist Office: 1525 John F. Kennedy Blvd. (636-1666), at 16th St. Pick up a free *Philadelphia Visitor's Guide* and the *Philadelphia Quarterly Calendar of Events*. Open daily 9am-5pm, except Thanksgiving and Christmas. The **National Park Service Visitors Center** (597-8974, 627-1776 for recording), at 3rd and Chestnut St., has info on **Independence Park,** including maps, schedules, the film *Independence* (shown daily 9:30am-4pm), and the above brochures. Tour assistance for non-English-speaking and disabled travelers. Open daily 9am-5pm. The **Gay Community Center** (732-2220), provides info about events and activities for Philly's homosexual population.
Airport: Philadelphia International (24-hr. info line 937-6800), 8mi. southwest of Center City on I-76. The 20-min. **SEPTA Airport Rail Line** runs from Center City to the airport. Trains leave 30th St., Suburban, and Market East Stations daily every 30 min. from 5:25am-11:25pm; $5 at window, $7 on train. Last train from airport 12:10am. **Airport Limelight Limousine** (342-5557) will deliver you to a hotel or a specific address downtown ($8 per person). Taxi downtown $20.
Trains: Amtrak, 30th St. Station (824-1600 or 800-872-7245), at 30th and Market St., in University City. To: New York (19 per day, 2hr., $30-39); Boston (9 per day, 7hr., $55-75); Washington, D.C. (19 per day, 2¼hr., $28); Pittsburgh (2 per day, 8hr., $67). Office open Mon.-Fri. 5:10am-10:45pm, Sat.-Sun. 6:10am-10:45pm. Station open 24hr.
Buses: Greyhound, 10th and Filbert St. (931-4075 or 800-231-2222), 1 block north of Market near the 10th and Market St. subway/commuter rail stop in the heart of Philadelphia. To: New York (17 per day, 2½hr., $14); Boston (16 per day, 8½hr., $40); Baltimore (6 per day, 2½hr., $13); Washington, D.C. (8 per day, 3hr., $15);

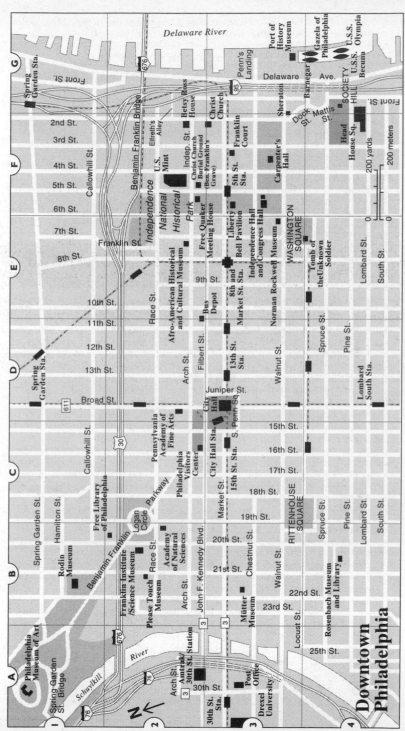

MID-ATLANTIC

Delaware River

Port of History Museum

Gazela of Philadelphia

U.S.S. Olympia

676

Penn's Landing

95

Delaware Ave.

Betsy Ross House

Christ Church

Sheraton

U.S.S. Becuna

SOCIETY HILL

Elfreth's Alley

Indep. St.

Franklin Court

Dock St.

Mattis St.

Head House Sq.

Front St.

2nd St.

3rd St.

U.S. Mint

Christ Church Burial Ground (Ben. Franklin's Grave)

5th St.

Carpenter's Hall

200 yards

Callowhill St.

4th St.

National

5th St. Sta.

200 meters

Spring Garden Sta.

Front St.

Benjamin Franklin Bridge

6th St.

Historical

Free Quaker Meeting House

Liberty Bell Pavilion

Independence Hall and Congress Hall

Norman Rockwell Museum

WASHINGTON SQUARE

0

0

7th St.

Franklin St.

Independence

Park

8th St.

9th St.

8th and Market St. Sta.

Tomb of the Unknown Soldier

Lombard St.

South St.

Afro-American Historical and Cultural Museum

Race St.

10th St.

Bus Depot

Spruce St.

Pine St.

11th St.

Filbert St.

13th St. Sta.

Walnut St.

Lombard South Sta.

12th St.

Arch St.

13th St.

Juniper St.

611

Spring Garden Sta.

Broad St.

City Hall

S. Penn Sq.

15th St.

30

Callowhill St.

Pennsylvania Academy of Fine Arts

City Hall Sta.

15th St. Sta.

16th St.

Philadelphia Visitors Center

17th St.

RITTENHOUSE SQUARE

Spruce St.

Pine St.

Lombard St.

South St.

Free Library of Philadelphia

18th St.

Market St.

19th St.

Spring Garden St.

Hamilton St.

Logan Circle

Benjamin Franklin Parkway

20th St.

Rodin Museum

Academy of Natural Sciences

Race St.

John F. Kennedy Blvd.

21st St.

Chestnut St.

Walnut St.

Rosenbach Museum and Library

Franklin Institute /Science Museum

Arch St.

22nd St.

Please Touch Museum

23rd St.

Mütter Museum

Locust St.

Downtown Philadelphia

676

River

3

3

Philadelphia Museum of Art

Spring Garden St.

Spring Garden St. Sta.

Schuylkill

Arch St.

Amtrak 30th St. Station

30th St. Sta.

3

Post Office

25th St.

76

76

N

2

30th St.

Drexel University

Delaware River

Pittsburgh (7 per day, 6½hr., $30); Atlantic City (10 per day, 2½hr., $11). Station open daily 7am-1am. **New Jersey Transit** (569-3752), in the same station. To: Atlantic City (1½hr., $10); Ocean City (2hr., $10.60), and other points on the New Jersey shore. Operates daily with buses to Atlantic City nearly every ½hr.

Public Transportation: Southeastern Pennsylvania Transportation Authority (SEPTA), 580-7800. Extensive bus and rail service to the suburbs. Buses serve the 5-county area; most operate 5am-2am, some all night. Two major subway routes: the east-west **Market St. line** (including 30th St. Station and the historic area) and the north-south **Broad St. line** (including the stadium complex in south Philadelphia). *The subway is unsafe after dark;* buses are usually okay. Subway connects with commuter rails—the main line local runs through the western suburb of Paoli ($3.75-4.25); SEPTA runs north to Trenton, NJ ($5). Pick up a free SEPTA system map and a good street map at any subway stop. Fare $1.60, 2 tokens for $2.30, transfers 40¢. Unlimited all-day pass for both $5.

Taxis: Yellow Cab, 922-8400. **United Cab,** 238-9500. $1.80 base, $1.80 per mi.

Car Rental: Courtesy Rent-a-Car, 7704 Westchester Pike (446-6200). $19 per day with unlimited mi. Must be 21 with major credit card. **Budget** (492-9400), at 21st and Market St. Downtown and easy to find, but more expensive. $38 per day with unlimited mi. Drivers must be 24.

Crisis Lines: Suicide and Crisis Intervention, 686-4420. **Youth Crisis Line,** 787-0633. Both 24hr. **Gay and Lesbian Counseling Services,** 732-8255.

Emergency: 911.

Post Office: 2970 Market St. (895-8000), at 30th St. across from the Amtrak station. Open Mon.-Fri. 9am-5pm. **ZIP code:** 19102. **Area code:** 215.

William Penn, Jr., planned his city as a logical and easily accessible grid of wide streets. The north-south streets ascend numerically from the **Delaware River,** flowing near **Penn's Landing** and **Independence Hall** on the east side, to the **Schuylkill River** (pronounced SKOO-kill) on the west. The first street is **Front;** the others follow consecutively from 2 to 69. **Center City** runs from 8th Street to the Schuylkill River. From north to south, the primary streets are Race, Arch, JFK, Market, Chestnut, and South. The intersection of Broad (14th) St. and Market marks the focal point of Center City. The **Historic District** stretches from Front to 8th St. and from Vine to South St. The **University of Pennsylvania** sprawls on the far side of the Schuylkill River, about 1 mi. west of Center City. **University City** includes the Penn/Drexel area west of the Schuylkill River. When getting directions, make sure they include numbered streets.

Due to the proliferation of one-way streets and horrendous traffic, **driving** is not a good way to get around town. Parking in Philly will cost you an arm and a leg. Try the city-run **Visitors Parking** (entrance on Dock and Walnut). The $1.50 per ½ hr. price is crazy, but the value kicks in at 24 hrs. for $9. If you lose your ticket, parking will automatically cost you $9. Philly's system of **buses** and its **subway** will take you almost anywhere you'll want to go. Pick up transit maps at the tourist office.

ACCOMMODATIONS AND CAMPING

Inexpensive lodging in Philadelphia is popular and hard to find, but if you make arrangements a few days in advance you should be able to find comfortable lodging close to Center City for around $50. The motels near the airport at Exit 9A on I-95 are the least expensive in the area. **Bed and Breakfast Center City,** 1804 Pine St. (735-1137 or 800-354-8401), will rent you a room ($45-85) or find you a room in a private home. **Bed & Breakfast Connections/Bed & Breakfast of Philadelphia** (610-687-3565), in Devon, PA, also books in Philadelphia and throughout southeastern Pennsylvania. (Singles $40-75, doubles $60-220. Make reservations at least a week in advance. Best to call 9am-7pm.) The closest camping lies across the Delaware River in New Jersey. Try the **Timberline Campground,** 117 Timber Ln. (609-423-6677), 15 mi. from Center City. Take U.S. 295S to exit 18B (Clarksboro), go straight through the traffic light ½ mi. and turn right on Friendship Rd. Timber Ln. is 1 block on the right. (Sites $17, with water, electric, and sewer hookup $22.)

Chamounix Mansion International Youth Hostel (HI-AYH) (878-3676 or 800-379-0017; fax 871-4313), in West Fairmount Park. Take bus #38 from Market St. to Ford and Cranston Rd., follow Ford to Chamounix Dr., then turn left and follow the road to the hostel (about a 20 min. walk). A deluxe hostel in a former country estate with clean, beautifully furnished rooms and lots of perks—showers, a recently remodeled kitchen, coin-op laundry, chess table, TV/VCR, and a piano. Some basic groceries for sale. Very friendly, helpful staff. Free parking. 64 beds. Make reservations one week in advance. Check-in 8-11am and 4:30pm-midnight. Lockout 11am-4:30pm. Curfew midnight. $11, nonmembers $14. Linen $2.

Bank Street Hostel (HI-AYH), 32 S. Bank St. (922-0222 or 800-392-4678), from the bus station, walk down Market St.; it's between 2nd and 3rd. Subway: 2nd St. A great hostel in a great location in the historic district. A/C, big-screen TV and VCR in lobby, free coffee and tea, laundry facilities, kitchen, pool table, and a musical morning wakeup (9am, usually jazz, blues, or big band). Super-convenient to South St., Penn's Landing, and Chinatown. Like-new facilities. Single-sex dorms. 70 beds. Lockout 10am-4:30pm, but they'll hold baggage. Curfew Sun.-Thurs. 12:30am, Fri.-Sat. 1am. $16 members, $19 nonmembers. Linen $2.

Old First Reformed Church (922-4566), at 4th and Race St. in Center City, 1 block from the Independence Mall and 4 blocks from Penn's Landing. A historic church that converts its social hall to a youth hostel that sleeps around 30. Foam pads on the floor, showers, A/C. Ages 18-26 only. 3 night max. stay. Check-in 5-10pm. Curfew 11pm. $15. Breakfast included. Open July 4-Labor Day.

Motel 6, 43 Industrial Hwy. (610-521-6650), in Essington, Exit 9A off I-95. Clean, large, standard rooms with A/C and cable. Singles $50-55, doubles $56-60.

FOOD

Philadelphia likes to eat, and eat well. Known largely for its fare, Philly's specialties include **cheesesteaks, hoagies,** and **soft pretzels.** Inexpensive food fills the carts of the ubiquitous city street vendors, and ethnic eateries gather in several specific areas: very hip **South St.,** between Front and 7th; **Sansom St.,** between 17th and 18th; and **2nd St.,** between Chestnut and Market. **Chinatown,** bounded by 11th, 8th, Arch, and Vine St., offers an abundance of moderately priced restaurants. The quintessential Philly Cheesesteak can be found at **Pat's Steaks** (468-1546), 12th and Passyunk, in **South Philadelphia.** It's a big cheese in the world of steaks and worth the trek (basic cheesesteak $4.75, open 24hr.).

For fresh fruit and other foodstuffs, visit the **Italian Market,** on 9th St. below Christian St. The **Reading Terminal Market** (922-2317), 12th and Arch St., is by far the best place to go for lunch in Center City. Since 1893, food stands have clustered in the indoor market selling fresh produce and meats. (Open Mon.-Sat. 8am-6pm.)

Historic District

Famous 4th St. Delicatessen (922-3274), 4th and Bainbridge St. A Philadelphia landmark since 1923, this traditional Jewish deli serves everything from corned beef sandwiches ($6) to egg creams from the soda fountain ($1.50). A self-proclaimed "living museum," the family operated business recalls Brooklyn of yesteryear, offering knishes ($1.50), lox ($8), and fried matzos ($5). Open Mon.-Sat. 7am-6pm, Sun. 7am-4pm.

DiNardo's, 312 Race St. (925-5115). DiNardo's specializes in hard shell crabs, flying them into Philly daily from the Gulf of Mexico. One pound of sauteed garlic crabs costs $9. Dinner entrees $12-18. Lunch is cheaper, varying from $5-8. Mon. and Tues. all-you-can-eat crabs ($18). Open Mon.-Thurs. 11am-10pm, Fri.-Sat. 11am-11pm, Sun. 3-9pm.

Rib-It, 52 S. 2nd St. (568-1555). This small Philadelphia chain claims to have the best ribs in town ($9-12). All-you-can-eat ribfest which attracts young couples and families Mon.-Thurs. until 10pm ($12-16). Burgers $6. Open Mon.-Thurs. noon-11pm, Fri.-Sat. noon-1am, Sun. noon-10:30pm.

MID-ATLANTIC

Center City

Rangoon, 112 9th St. (829-8939), Chinatown. This intimate and unique restaurant serves wonderful Burmese cuisine. The proprietor nourishes a love of good food, low prices, and spice. Entrees $4-10, most around $6.50. Open Tues.-Thurs. 11:30am-3pm and 5-9pm, Fri. 11:30am-10pm, Sat. 1-10pm, Sun. 1-9pm.

Harmony, 135 N. 9th St. (627-4520), Chinatown. The chefs in this small, popular establishment dupe health-conscious carnivores with a variety of meatless Chinese dishes, including imitation beef, poultry, seafood, and pork. Most entrees $7-12. Open Sun.-Thurs. 11:30am-10:30pm, Fri.-Sat. 11:30am-midnight.

Lee's Hoagie House, 44 S. 17th St. (564-1264). Hoagies ($3.75-6, giant $7.50-11) since 1953. The 3-ft. hoagie ($39) feeds you and your 11 best friends. Delivery available (2 sandwich min.). Open Mon.-Fri. 10:30am-6pm, Sat. 10:30am-5pm.

Seafood Unlimited, 270 S. 20th St. (732-3663), has a variety of fresh seafood. Lobster only $11. Entrees $7-12. Open Mon.-Thurs. 11am-9pm, Fri.-Sat. 11am-10pm.

University City

Smoky Joe's, 210 S. 40th St. (222-0770), between Locust and Walnut. This family-run restaurant and bar has been a student hang out for over 50 years. Personally autographed photos of Penn's top athletes adorn the walls. House specialties include eggs benedict ($4.50), mushroom soup ($1.50), and burgers ($4.50). Occasional live music. Open daily 11am-2am. No lunch served on weekends.

Abner's Cheesesteaks (662-0100), at 38th and Chestnut. Cheesesteak, large soda, and small fries for $5.87. Attracts businesspeople for lunch, and college students during late-night. Healthy cuisine (chicken, pasta salad) was recently added to the menu. Open Mon.-Thurs. 11am-midnight, Fri.-Sat. 11am-3am, Sun. 11am-11pm.

Tandoor India Restaurant, 106 S. 40th St. (222-7122). Northern Indian cuisine straight from the clay oven. Lunch buffet $6, dinner buffet $9. 20% student discount with valid ID. Open for lunch Mon.-Fri. noon-3pm, Sat.-Sun. noon-3:30pm; for dinner daily 4:30-9:45pm.

Le Bus, 3402 Sansom St. (387-3800). You'll think you have stumbled into the dining hall when you have to grab a tray, but good food awaits. Sandwiches $3-5.50; entrees $6-8. Café with outdoor seating as well. Open June-Aug. Mon.-Fri. 7:30am-9pm; Sept.-May Mon.-Fri. 7:30am-10pm, Sat. 9am-10pm, Sun. 10am-10pm.

SIGHTS

Independence Hall and the Historic District

The buildings of the **Independence National Historical Park** (597-8974), bounded by Market, Walnut, 2nd, and 6th St., witnessed many landmark events in U.S. history. (Open daily 9am-6pm; Sept.-May 9am-5pm; free.) The **visitors center,** at 3rd and Chestnut St., makes a good starting point. The grandiose building across the street is the **First Bank of the U.S.** Located at Chestnut and 4th St., the **Second Bank of the U.S.** presents a stunning example of Greek Revival architecture. Arguably one of the most beautiful buildings in Philly, the Bank now contains an expansive portrait gallery, which houses paintings of Washington, Jefferson, and Franklin, among others. Delegates signed the Declaration of Independence in 1776 and drafted and signed the 1787 Constitution in **Independence Hall,** between 5th and 6th St. on Chestnut. (Open Mon.-Fri. 9am-5pm, Sat.-Sun. 9am-6pm, but arrive before 11am in the summer to avoid a long line. Free guided tours daily every 15-20 min.) The U.S. Congress first assembled in nearby **Congress Hall** (free self-guided tours available); its predecessor, the First Continental Congress, convened in **Carpenters' Hall,** in the middle of the block bounded by 3rd, 4th, Walnut and Chestnut St. (open Tues.-Sun. 10am-4pm). North of Independence Hall, the **Liberty Bell Pavilion** contains the **Liberty Bell,** one of America's most famous symbols.

The remainder of the park contains preserved residential and commercial buildings of the Revolutionary era. To the north, Ben Franklin's home presides over **Franklin Court,** on Market between 3rd and 4th St. The home contains an underground museum, a 20-min. movie, a replica of Franklin's printing office, and phones which allow you to confer with long–dead political luminaries. (Open daily 9am-5pm. Free.) At nearby **Washington Sq.,** an eternal flame commemorates the fallen heroes of the Revolutionary War at the **Tomb of the Unknown Soldier.** Philadelphia's branch of the **U.S. Mint** (597-7350), at 5th and Arch St. across from Independence Hall, offers a free, self-guided tour to explain the mechanized coin-making procedure. No free samples here. (Open Mon.-Sat. 9am-4:30pm.)

Just behind Independence Hall, the **Norman Rockwell Museum** (922-4345), 6th and Sansom St., offers a sight and sound presentation and exhibits over 600 works, including many of the artist's *Saturday Evening Post* covers (open Mon.-Sat. 10am-4pm, Sun. 11am-4pm; $2). Walk onto the powder-blue marvel near the mint **Benjamin Franklin Bridge,** off Race and 5th, to observe boat traffic on the Delaware and get a great view of both Philadelphia and Camden, NJ. It's bound to make you wonder how safe it is to put so much faith in engineers—not for those with vertigo.

In 1723, a penniless Ben Franklin arrived in Philadelphia and walked along **Elfreth's Alley,** near 2nd and Arch St., allegedly "the oldest street in America." Betsy Ross sewed the first flag of the original 13 states at the tiny **Betsy Ross House,** 239 Arch St. (627-5343), near 3rd. (Open Tues.-Sun. 10am-5pm. $1 donation requested.) Two Quaker meeting houses grace the streets of Philadelphia: the original **Free Quaker Meeting House** (923-6777), at 5th and Arch St., and a new one at 4th and Arch St. (open Tues.-Sat. 10am-4pm, Sun. noon-4pm). **Christ Church** (922-1695), on 2nd near Market, served the Quakers who sought a more fashionable way of life. Ben Franklin lies buried in the nearby **Christ Church cemetery,** at 5th and Arch St.

Mikveh Israel (922-5446), the first Jewish congregation of Philadelphia, has a burial ground on Spruce near 8th St. (Services Fri. 7pm, Sat. 9am and 8pm.) The **Afro-American Historical and Cultural Museum** (574-0381), 7th and Arch St., was the first U.S. museum devoted solely to the history of African-Americans. (Open Tues.-Sat. 10am-5pm, Sun. noon-5pm. $4, students $2.)

Society Hill proper begins where the park ends, on Walnut between Front and 7th St. Townhouses dating back 200 years line the picturesque cobblestone walks illuminated by old-fashioned streetlights. **Head House Sq.,** at 2nd and Pine St., claims America's oldest firehouse and marketplace, and now houses restaurants, boutiques, and craft shops. An outdoor flea market moves in on summer weekends.

South of Head House Sq., the **Mario Lanza Museum,** 416 Queen St. (468-3623), enshrines a collection of artifacts and memorabilia from the life of opera singer Mario Lanza. (Vintage films shown daily Mon.-Sat. 10am-3:30pm.) Farther south, the **Mummer's Museum,** 1100 S. 2nd St. (336-3050), at Washington Ave., gives you a peek inside the closets of the construction workers, policemen, and others who follow the tradition of Philly's mummers, dressing in feathers and sequins for a bizarre New Year's Day parade. (Open Tues.-Sat. 9:30am-5pm, Sun. noon-5pm. $2.50.)

Located on the Delaware River, **Penn's Landing** (923-8181) is the largest freshwater port in the world. Docked here you'll find the *Gazela,* a three-masted, 178-ft. Portuguese square rigger built in 1883; the *U.S.S. Olympia,* Commodore Dewey's flagship during the Spanish-American War (922-1898; tours daily 10am-5pm; $5); and the *U.S.S. Becuna,* a WWII submarine. The landing also hosts waterfront concerts April-Oct. (629-3257). Big bands play Thurs. nights, while Fri. evenings feature children's theatre. Call for the free Waterfront Club shuttle bus (629-3000).

On the corner of 8th and Race St., the Pennsylvania College of Podiatric Medicine contains the **Shoe Museum** (625-5243). This 6th-floor collection contains footwear fashions from the famous feet of Reggie Jackson, Lady Bird Johnson, Dr. J, Nancy Reagan, and more. (Tours Wed. and Fri. 9am-5pm, call for appointment.) **Tattoo Museum,** 3216 Kensington Ave. (426-9477), has historical artifacts and a large quantity of tattooing info. If you're looking to do more than research the history of tattooing, there are tattoo shops on some street corners.

Center City

Center City, the area bounded by 12th, 23rd, Vine, and Pine St., bustles with activity. An ornate structure of granite and marble with 20-ft. thick foundation walls, **City**

Hall (686-9074), at Broad and Market St., is the nation's largest municipal building and truly an American chateau. Until 1908, it also reigned as the tallest building in the U.S., with the help of the 37-ft. statue of William Penn, Jr. on top. A municipal statute prohibited building higher than the top of Penn's hat until Reagan-era entrepreneurs overturned the law in the mid-80s, finally launching Philadelphia into the skyscraper era. For a commanding view of the city, take an elevator up to the tower. Call ahead for tickets or you might have to wait. (Open Mon.-Fri. 10am-3pm. Last elevator 2:45pm. Free.) The **Pennsylvania Academy of Fine Arts** (972-7600), at Broad and Cherry, the country's first art museum, has an extensive collection of American and British art, including works by Charles Wilson Peale, Thomas Eakins, Winslow Homer, and some contemporary artists, along with changing exhibitions. (Open Mon.-Sat. 10am-5pm, Sun. 11am-5pm. Tours daily 12:15 and 2pm. $6, students and seniors $5.) Across from City Hall, the **Masonic Temple**, 1 N. Broad St. (988-1917), contains collections of books and other artifacts dating back to 1873. (Must be seen on a 45-min. tour. Mon.-Fri. 10, 11am, 1, 2, and 3pm, Sat. 10 and 11am. Closed Sat. July-Aug. Free.)

Just south of **Rittenhouse Sq.**, the **Rosenbach Museum and Library**, 2010 Delancey St. (732-1600), houses rare manuscripts and paintings, including some of the earliest known copies of Cervantes' *Don Quixote*, the original manuscript of James Joyce's *Ulysses*, and the original musical score to *Yankee Doodle Dandy*. (Open Sept.-July Tues.-Sun. 11am-4pm. Guided tours $3.50; students, seniors, and children $2.50.) Ben Franklin founded the **Library Company of Philadelphia**, 1314 Locust St. (546-3181), near 13th St., over 250 years ago so that colonists could order books from England; the club's members still pay for books from the mother country today (open Mon.-Fri. 9am-4:45pm; free).

Benjamin Franklin Parkway

Nicknamed "America's Champs-Elysées," the Benjamin Franklin Pkwy. cuts a wide, diagonal deviation from William Penn's original grid of city streets. Built in the 1920s, this tree- and flag-lined boulevard connects Center City with Fairmount Park and the Schuylkill River. The street is flanked by elegant architecture, including the twin buildings at Logan Sq., 19th and Ben Franklin Pkwy., which house the Free Library of Philadelphia and the Municipal Court.

The **Academy of Natural Sciences** (299-1000), at 19th and Ben Franklin Pkwy., showcases live animal exhibits and a 65-million-year-old dinosaur skeleton. (Open Mon.-Fri. 10am-4:30pm, Sat.-Sun. and holidays 10am-5pm. $6.50.) Farther down 26th St., the **Philadelphia Museum of Art** (763-8100) holds one of the world's major art collections, including Rubens's *Prometheus Bound*, Picasso's *Three Musicians*, and Duchamp's *Nude Descending a Staircase*, as well as extensive Asian, Egyptian, and decorative art collections. Hosts traveling exhibitions (recently Cézanne) which tend to attract droves of tourists and require special tickets. (Open Tues. and Thurs.-Sun. 10am-5pm, Wed. 10am-8:45pm. Call for prices.) Three blocks from the museum, **Eastern State Penitentiary** (236-7236), on Fairmount Ave. at 22nd St., once a ground-breaking institution in the field of criminal rehabilitation, conducts tours of the solitary quarters which prisoners (including Al Capone) inhabited many years ago. Tours include an exhibit of artwork addressing life in confinement. (Open May to early Nov. Thurs.-Sun. 10am-6pm; until late May Sat.-Sun. 10am-6pm. $7.) The **Free Library of Philadelphia** (686-5322) scores with a library of orchestral music and one of the nation's largest rare book collections. (Open Mon.-Wed. 9am-9pm, Thurs.-Fri. 9am-6pm, Sat. 9am-5pm; Oct.-May also Sun. 1-5pm.)

A casting of the *Gates of Hell* outside the **Rodin Museum** (563-1948), 22nd St., guards the portal of the most complete collection of the artist's works this side of the Seine, including one of the gazillion versions of *The Thinker* (open Tues.-Sun. 10am-5pm; $1 donation).

The fantastic **Science Center** in the **Franklin Institute** (448-1200), at 20th and Ben Franklin Pkwy., amazes visitors with four floors of gadgets and games depicting the intricacies of space, time, motion, and the human body. The 20-ft. **Benjamin**

Franklin National Memorial statue divines lightning at the entrance. In 1990, to commemorate the 200th anniversary of Franklin's death, the Institute unveiled the **Futures Center,** which houses a timely set of exhibits on the changing global environment. (Futures Center open Mon.-Wed. 9:30am-5pm, Thurs.-Sat. 9:30am-9pm, Sun. 9:30am-6pm. Science Center daily 9:30am-5pm. Admission to both $9.50, over 62 and ages 4-11 $8.50.) The **Omniverse Theater** (448-1111), provides 180° and 4½ stories of optical oohs and aahs. (Shows on the hr. Mon.-Wed. 10am-4pm, Thurs. 10am-4pm and 7-8pm, Fri. 10am-4pm and 7-9pm, Sat. 5 and 7-9pm, Sun. 5-6pm. $7.50, seniors and kids $6.50. Advance tickets recommended.) **Fels Planetarium** (448-1388), boasts an advanced computer-driven system that projects a simulation of life billions of years beyond ours. Drop in for a lively rock music and multi-colored laser show on Friday or Saturday night. (Shows daily every hr. 11:15am-4:15pm. $7.50, seniors and kids $6.50; exhibits and a show $12, seniors and kids $10.50; exhibits and both shows $14.50/$12.50.)

Covered with bike trails and picnic areas, **Fairmount Park** sprawls behind the Philadelphia Museum of Art on both sides of the Schuylkill River. At night, gaze at the spectacular lights of **Boathouse Row,** where the shells of local crew teams are kept. But be alert—while the park itself is safe, some of the surrounding neighborhoods are not. In the northern arm of Fairmount Park trails leave the Schuylkill and wind along secluded Wissahickon Creek for 5 mi. The **Japanese House and Garden** (878-5097), off Montgomery Dr. near Belmont Ave., is built in the style of a 17th-century *shoin* and surrounded by a grand, authentic garden. (Open May-Labor Day 11am-4pm daily; Sept.-Oct. Sat.-Sun. only 11am-4pm.)

West Philadelphia (University City)

The **University of Pennsylvania (UPenn)** and **Drexel University,** located across the Schuylkill from Center City, reside in west Philadelphia within easy walking distance of the 30th St. station. The Penn campus provides a haven of green lawns and red brick quadrangles in contrast to the deteriorating community surrounding it. Ritzy shops and cafés line Chestnut St. and boisterous fraternities line Spruce. Warm weather brings out a variety of street vendors along the Drexel and Penn borders. Enter the Penn campus at 34th and Walnut, where you'll be greeted by a statue of Benjamin Franklin, who founded the university in 1740. Much of the area surrounding University City is unsafe—each year several students and tourists are shot. Try not to travel alone at night.

However, University City is home to one of Philly's most extraordinary treasures, the elegantly landscaped **University Museum of Archeology and Anthropology** (894-4000), at 33rd and Spruce St. *Discover* magazine considers it one of the world's top ten science museums. Peruse the outstanding East Asian art collection under the beautiful stone-and-glass rotunda, and stop to puzzle over the museum's Egyptian mummy and 12-ton sphinx. (Open Tues.-Sat. 10am-4:30pm; Sept.-May Tues.-Sat. 10am-4:30pm, Sun. 1-5pm. Requested admission $5, students and over 62 $2.50.) In 1965, Andy Warhol had his first one-man show at the **Institute of Contemporary Art** (898-7108), at 36th and Sansom St., and the gallery has stayed on the cutting edge to this day with changing exhibitions featuring all media. (Open Thurs.-Sun. 10am-5pm, Wed. 10am-7pm. $3; free Sun. 10am-noon.)

ENTERTAINMENT

The **Academy of Music** (893-1999), Broad and Locust St., modeled after Milan's *La Scala,* houses the **Philadelphia Orchestra.** Under the direction of Wolfgang Sawallisch, the orchestra, among the nation's best, performs Sept. through May. General admission tickets ($5) go on sale at the Locust St. entrance 45 min. before Fri. and Sat. concerts; check with the box office for availability. (Regular tickets $15-78.)

The **Mann Music Center** (567-0707), on George's Hill near 52nd St. and Parkside Ave. in Fairmount Park, hosts summer Philadelphia Orchestra concerts and jazz and rock events with 5000 seats under cover and 10,000 on outdoor benches and lawns. From June through August, pick up free lawn tickets for the orchestra from the visitors center at 16th St. and JFK Blvd. on the day of a performance. For the big-name shows, sit just outside the theater and soak in the sounds gratis (real seats $12-35). The **Robin Hood Dell East** (477-8810), Strawberry Mansion Dr. in Fairmount Park, brings in top names in pop, jazz, gospel, and ethnic dance in July and August. The Philadelphia Orchestra holds several free performances here in summer, and as many as 30,000 people gather on the lawn. Inquire at the visitors center (636-1666) about upcoming events.

More free concerts fill summer evenings at **Penn's Landing** (629-3237). During the school year, the outstanding students of the world-renowned **Curtis Institute of Music,** 1726 Locust St., give free concerts on Mondays, Wednesdays, and Fridays at 8pm (893-5997; concerts mid-Oct. to April). **Merriam Theater,** 250 S. Broad St., Center City (732-5446), stages a variety of both student and professional dance, musical, and comedy performances September through May. The **Old City,** from Chestnut to Vine and Front to 4th St., comes alive on the first Friday of every month (Oct.-June) for the fantastic **First Friday** celebration. The streets fill with people and the music of live bands, as the area's many art galleries open their doors, enticing visitors with offers of free food.

In addition to the wide array of cultural centers, Philadelphia is a great sports town. Philly's four professional teams play a short ride away on the Broad St. subway line. The **Phillies** (baseball; 463-1000) and **Eagles** (football; 463-5500) hold games at **Veterans Stadium,** Broad St. and Pattison Ave.; while the **Spectrum,** across the street, houses the **76ers** (basketball; 339-7676) and the **Flyers** (hockey; 755-9700). General admission tickets for baseball and hockey run from $5 to $20; football and basketball tickets ($15-50). The city also hosts both men's and women's professional tennis tournaments, the prestigious Core State Cycling Championship, and a Senior PGA tourney.

NIGHTLIFE

Check Friday's weekend magazine section in the Philadelphia *Inquirer* for entertainment listings. *City Paper,* distributed on Thursdays, and the *Philadelphia Weekly,* distributed on Wednesdays, have weekly listings of city events (free at newsstands and markets). *Au Courant* (free) and *PGN* (75¢), gay and lesbian weekly newspapers, list events taking place throughout the Delaware Valley region. Along **South St.,** clubbers dance and live music plays on weekends. Many pubs line 2nd St. near Chestnut, close to the Bank St. hostel. **Columbus Blvd.,** running along Penn's Landing, has recently become a local hotspot, with tons of nightclubs and restaurants attracting droves of young urban professionals. Most bars and clubs that cater to a gay clientele congregate along Camac St., S. 12th St., and S. 13th St.

Gothum, 1 Brown St. (928-9319), at Columbus Blvd. Hardcore dancing to an acid techno beat. Claims Philly's two largest dance floors. Includes 5 lounge bars, VIP section, and outdoor deck. Open Tues.-Sun. Hours and times vary.

Katmandu, Pier 25 (629-1724), at North Columbus Blvd. A hopping bar and restaurant with nightly live music, including rock and reggae. Tropical gardens and open-air decks. Drafts $2.75. Cover Mon.-Thurs. after 8:30pm $5; Fri.-Sat. $7; Sun. $2, after 5pm $5. Open daily noon-2am.

Trocadero (923-ROCK/7625), 10th and Arch St. Nationally known bands perform to a mostly college-age crowd. Fri. night Industrial-Dance-Gothic with DJ. Cover $6-16. Advance tickets through Ticketmaster. Doors usually open around 10pm.

Woody's, 202 S. 13th St. (545-1893). A good-looking, young gay male crowd frequents this aptly named club. Happy hour 5-7pm daily with 25¢ off all drinks. Dance to country tunes Tues., Fri., and Sun., or grind to house music Thurs.-Sat. Wed. is all ages night. Videos shown after 9pm. Lunch Mon.-Sat. noon-3:30pm. Sunday brunch noon-4pm. Bar open Mon.-Sat. 11am-2am, Sunday noon-2am.

Khyber Pass Pub, 56 S. 2nd St. (440-9683). One of Philly's best live music venues, this small club (150 people max.) has managed to attract groups like Smashing Pumpkins and Hole. Eclectic assortment of twenty-somethings enjoy alternative, country, grunge, and thrash metal bands. Cover varies. Open daily noon-2am.

Xero, 613 S. 4th St. (629-0565). Popular bar attracts young audience (21-25) intent on drinking cheaply ($2.50 drafts). Happy hour Fri.-Sat. 7-10:30pm includes 75¢ drafts and free chicken wings until 9pm. Weekends also feature techno, industrial, and gothic music. All-you-can-drink Thurs. cover $7. Open Mon.-Wed. 5pm-2am, Thurs.-Fri. 4pm-2am, Sat.-Sun. 2pm-2am.

Blue Man Jazz Café (413-2272), on 4th St. between Market and Chestnut St., is one of the best jazz clubs in Philly. The venue attracts such names as Betty Carter and Gloria Lynn on Fri. and Sat. nights. Tues. night is blues; Wed. night is Latin/jazz fusion. Entrees $14-20. Cover $5 on weekends. Lunch Mon.-Fri. 11am-2pm. Dinner Sun.-Thurs. 5pm-1am. The club is open daily 5pm-2am.

Jake and Oliver's, 222 South 3rd St. (627-4825). A Lutheran Church until the mid-1920s, this "House of Brews" functions as a restaurant, bar, and dance hall. Forty microbrews on tap ($3.50-$4.75). Entrees $8-15. Happy hour 5-7pm daily ($1 off drinks, ½-price appetizers). Techno music throbs in air-conditioned dance hall upstairs. Open daily 11:30am-2am.

■ Near Philadelphia: Valley Forge

American troops during the Revolutionary War waged a fierce battle at Valley Forge, but not against the British; during the winter of 1777-78, the 12,000 men under General George Washington's command spent agonizing months fighting starvation, bitter cold, and disease. Only 8000 survived. Nonetheless, inspired by Washington's fierce spirit and the news of an American alliance with France, the troops left Valley Forge stronger and better trained. They went on to win victories in New Jersey, to reoccupy Philadelphia, and to help create the independent nation.

Valley Forge National Historic Park encompasses over 3600 beautiful acres of rolling hills and lush forests (open daily 6am-10pm). Self-guided tours begin at the **visitors center** (610-783-1077), which also features a museum and film (18-min. shows twice per hr. 9am-4:30pm; center open daily 9am-5pm). The tour visits Washington's headquarters, reconstructed soldier huts and fortifications, and the Grand Parade Ground where the Continental Army drilled. Admission to **Washington's headquarters** costs $2 (under 17 free), but the grounds of the park are free to all. Audio tapes rent for $8. The park has three picnic areas but no camping; the visitors center distributes a list of nearby campgrounds. Nature lovers and joggers alike flock to take advantage of a paved 6-mi. bike trail which winds through the park and offers occasional glimpses of the deer which inhabit the area.

To get to Valley Forge, take the Schuylkill Expressway westbound from Philadelphia for about 12 mi. Get off at the Valley Forge Exit, then take Rte. 202S for 1 mi. and Rte. 422W for 1½ mi. to another Valley Forge Exit. SEPTA runs buses to the visitors center Monday through Friday only; catch #125 at 16th and JFK ($3.10).

■ Lancaster County

The Amish, the Mennonites, and the Brethren, three groups of German Anabaptists who fled persecution in Deutschland (thus the misnomer "Pennsylvania Dutch" by confused locals), sought freedom to pursue their own religion in the rolling countryside of Lancaster County. They successfully escaped censorship, but they have not escaped attention. Although originally farmers, the "Plain Peoples'" chief industry is now tourism. Thousands of visitors flock to this pastoral area every year to glimpse a way of life that eschews modern conveniences like motorized vehicles, television, and cellular phones, in favor of modest amenities.

PRACTICAL INFORMATION

Tourist Office: Lancaster Chamber of Commerce and Industry, 100 Queen St. (397-3531 or 800-735-2629), in the Southern Market Center. Pick up guided walking tours of Lancaster City or buy a self-guided booklet ($1.50). To reserve a tour in the off season call 653-8225 or 394-2339. Open Mon.-Fri. 8:30am-5pm. **Pennsylvania Dutch Visitors Bureau Information Center,** 501 Greenfield Rd. (299-8901),

MID-ATLANTIC

on the east side of Lancaster City off Rte. 30. Open Mon.-Sat. 8am-6pm, Sun. 8am-5pm; Sept.-May daily 9am-5pm.

Trains: Amtrak, 53 McGovern Ave. (291-5080 or 800-872-7245), in Lancaster City. To: Philadelphia (4-7 per day, 1¼hr., $9).

Buses: Capitol Trailways, 22 W. Clay St. (397-4861). 3 buses per day to Philadelphia (2hr., $12.35). Open daily 7am-4:45pm.

Public Transportation: Red Rose Transit, 45 Erick Rd. (397-4246). Service around Lancaster and the surrounding countryside. Base fare $1; over 65 free Mon.-Fri. 9am-3:30pm, after 6:30pm, and all day on weekends.

Post Office: 1400 Harrisburg Pike (396-6900). Open Mon.-Fri. 7:30am-7pm, Sat. 9am-2pm. **ZIP code:** 17604. **Area code:** 717.

Lancaster County covers a huge area. It's difficult to get around without a car (unless you've got a horse and buggy). Red Rose Transit shuttles between major sights. The sideroads off U.S. 30 are the best places to explore the area. You always thought **Intercourse** would lead to **Paradise,** and on the country roads of Lancaster County, it does. All addresses given here are found in Lancaster City, unless noted.

ACCOMMODATIONS AND CAMPING

Hundreds of hotels and B&Bs cluster in this area. Stop by a visitors center for help finding a room. About the only thing that outnumber cows here is **campgrounds;** there's little difference between them, so choose the location you like best.

Pennsylvania Dutch Motel, 2275 N. Reading Rd. (336-5559), at Exit 21 off Pennsylvania Turnpike. Big clean rooms with cable and A/C. Friendly hostess has written directions to major sights. Singles $42, doubles $46; Nov.-March $8-10 less.

Conestoga Wagon Motel (286-5061), Rte. 23E in Morgantown. Spotless rooms with cable TV, A/C, and free local calls. Singles $40, doubles $45; $5 each additional person.

Old Mill Stream Camping Manor, 2249 U.S. 30E (299-2314). The closest year-round facility, 4mi. east of Lancaster City. Includes gameroom, laundry, playground, and general store. Office open daily 8am-8pm. Sites $17, with hookup $20. Reservations recommended.

Roamers Retreat, 5005 Lincoln Hwy. (442-4287 or 800-525-5605), off U.S. 30, 7½mi. east of Rte. 896. Offers laundry and gameroom. Three night min. stay holiday weekends. Sites $18, with hookup $20. Call for reservations. Open April-Oct.

FOOD

A good alternative to high priced "family-style" restaurants exists at the **farmers markets** which dot the roadways. Don't miss the **Central Market,** in Lancaster City at the northwest corner of Penn Sq., a huge food bazaar which has provided inexpen-

---

Hershey's Candyland

Milton S. Hershey, a Mennonite resident of eastern Pennsylvania, discovered how to mass market chocolate, previously a rare and expensive luxury. Today, the company that bears his name operates the world's largest chocolate factory, in **Hershey,** about 45 minutes from Lancaster. East of town at **Hersheypark** (800-437-7439), the **Chocolate World Visitors Center** presents a free, automated tour through a simulated chocolate factory. After the tour, visitors emerge into a pavilion full of chocolate cookies, discounted chocolate candy, and fashionable Hershey sportswear. Beware: to take this "free" tour, you must pay $4 to park in a Hershey lot. (Open Sun.-Fri. 9am-10pm, Sat. 9am-7:45pm; Labor Day to mid-June daily 9am-5pm.) Hersheypark's **amusement center** (534-3900) has heart-stopping rides and short lines. Don't miss the Sidewinder or the new wooden rollercoaster, the Wildcat. (Open late May-early Sept. daily 10am-10pm. $25, over 55 and ages 3-8 $16.) **Trailways** (397-4861) provides transportation from Lancaster City to Hershey (1 per day, 2½hr., $8.15).

sive meats, cheeses, vegetables, and sandwiches since 1899 (open Tues. and Fri. 6am-4:30pm, Sat. 6am-2pm). Many fun and inexpensive restaurants surround the market. The huge **Farmers Market** complex in Bird-in-the-Hand, on Rte. 340, charges more than the Amish road stands, but is centralized and has parking (open Wed.-Sat. 8:30am-5:30pm, July-Oct. Wed., Fri.-Sat. 8:30am-5:30pm; April-June Fri.-Sat. 8:30am-5:30pm). **The Amish Barn**, 3029 Old Philadelphia Pike (768-8886), serves all-you-can-eat fare for $13 (kids $5; open daily 7:30am-9pm). **Isaac's**, 44 N. Queen St. (394-5544), in the Central Mall, creates imaginative sandwiches with avian names ($4-6; open daily 10am-9pm).

The most distinctive culinary specialty of Lancaster County is the traditional Amish dessert, **shoofly pie.** The pie was popularized in the days before the refrigerator because of its resistance to spoiling. Nevertheless, upon being removed from the oven, it attracted droves of flies and thus gained its name from the constant "shoo fly" calls of its baker.

SIGHTS

The **People's Place** (768-7171), on Main St./Rte. 340, in Intercourse, 11 mi. east of Lancaster City, covers an entire block with bookstores, craft shops, and an art gallery. The film *Who Are the Amish?* runs every half hour 9:30am-5pm. (Film $3.50, under 12 $1.75. Open Mon.-Sat. 9:30am-8pm; Labor Day-Memorial Day Mon.-Sat. 9:30am-5pm.) **Amish World**, also in Intercourse, has charming hands-on exhibits on Amish and Mennonite life, from barn raising to hat styles ($6.50, children $3.25). There are plenty of bus tours through the Amish countryside from which to choose; **Amish Country Tours** (786-3600) offers 2½-hr. trips which include visits to one-room schools, Amish cottage industries, authentic farms, and a vineyard for wine tasting. ($16, children 4-11 $11. Tours given at 10am and 1:30pm daily April-Oct.) There is nothing cooler than a postcard that says "I am in Intercourse, having a good time, and wishing you were here." Hell, send us one. County seat **Lancaster City,** in the heart of Dutch country, has red-brick row houses huddled around historic **Penn Sq.**

■ Gettysburg

In early July of 1863, Union and Confederate forces met at Gettysburg in one of the bloodiest and most decisive battles of the Civil War. The ultimate victory of the Union forces dealt a dire blow to the hopes of the South, but at a horrible price for both sides: there were over 50,000 casualties. Four months later, President Lincoln arrived in Gettysburg to dedicate the **Gettysburg National Cemetery** (many Union soldiers lie buried where they fell) and to give "a few appropriate remarks." Lincoln emphasized the preservation of the union in a speech that, though only two minutes long, was a watershed in American history. Each year thousands of visitors head for these Pennsylvania fields, heeding the President's call to "resolve that these dead shall not have died in vain."

For a great overview of the area, take a high-speed elevator up the 300-ft. **National Tower** (334-6754; open Easter-Aug. daily 9am-6:30pm; Sept.-Nov. 9am-5:30pm; $4.90, seniors $4.35, ages 6-15 $2.65). The **Cyclorama Center,** across from the tower, holds the second draft of Lincoln's speech, a 20-min. film on the battle, and, of course, the cyclorama, a 356-by-26-ft. mural depicting this turning point in the Civil War. A sound and light show runs every 30 min. (Open daily 9am-4:30pm. $2.50, seniors $2, children 6-15 $1, under 5 free.)

Before attacking Gettysburg's Civil War memorabilia, get your bearings at the **National Military Park Visitors Information Center** (334-1124), 1 mi. south of town on Taneytown Rd. (open daily 8am-6pm; Labor Day-Memorial Day 8am-5pm). A large collection of pistols, rifles, and artillery draws war buffs, and there are also exhibits on familial tragedies. Drive the 18-mi. **self-guided auto tour** on your own, letting the free map navigate you through the monuments and landmarks, or pay a park guide to show you the sights (2-hr. tour $25). Rangers lead free guided walking tours, including rotation "Battle Walls" which describe the opening clash, Pickers Chase, and the battle for Little Round Top. The visitors center also houses a 750-sq.-ft. **electric map;** lights represent the advances and withdrawals of the dueling armies, giving visitors a more defined vision of the physical layout of the battlefield ($2, over 61 $1.50, under 15 free). You can rent a **bike** at Artillery Ridge campground (see below; $4 per hr., $16 full day, $10 ½day). Gettysburg's **area code:** 717.

The **Gettysburg Travel Council,** 35 Carlisle St. (334-6274), in Lincoln Sq., stocks a full line of motel brochures, as well as maps and info on local sights (open daily 9am-5pm). For cheap, large rooms with A/C, try **Cleveland's Motel** (334-3473), just off U.S. 15 about 2 mi. from the park (singles $30, doubles $45; Sept.-April rates drop). The closest hostel is 20 mi. away; follow Rte. 34N to Rte. 233. Next to the entrance of **Pine Grove Furnace State Park,** the incredibly large and luxurious **Ironmasters Mansion Hostel (HI-AYH)** (717-486-7585) has 44 beds in a gorgeous area, close to swimming, fishing, and hiking and even a sliver of the Appalachian Trail. Play a game of pool or volleyball, work out the kinks in the jacuzzi, and marvel at the life-sized chess set. (Open 7:30-9:30am and 5-10pm. $10, nonmembers $13.) **Artillery Ridge,** 610 Taneytown Rd. (334-1288), 1 mi. south on Rte. 134, maintains campsites with access to showers, a riding stable, laundry facilities, and a pool. Also features nightly movies, fishing pond, and bike rentals. Horseback tours offered (sites for 2 $12.50, with hookup $17; open April-Nov.).

Gettysburg is a quiet, remote community with three distinct sections; the touristy strip lined with motels and fast food near the highway, a charming red-brick downtown area, and the historic battlefield just outside of town. Most tasty restaurants are located in the center of town or along the road connecting the center to the battlefield. The candle-lit **Springhouse Tavern,** 89 Steinwehr Ave. (334-2100), hides in the basement of the **Dobben House,** Gettysburg's first building (c. 1776) and an Underground Railroad shelter for runaway slaves during the Civil War. Create your own grilled burger ($6) or try "Mason's Mile High" ($6.25), a double-decker with ham, roast beef, and turkey (open daily 11:30am-9pm). **Food for Thought,** 46 Baltimore St. (337-2221), serves huge salads, sandwiches, and other organic fare. (Meals $2.50-5.25; open Tues.-Thurs. 8:30am-9pm, Fri.-Sat. 8:30am-11pm, Sun. 10am-6pm.)

When the Union and the Confederacy decided to lock horns here, they didn't have the traveler in mind. Inaccessible by Greyhound or Amtrak, Gettysburg is in south-central PA, off U.S. 15, about 30 mi. south of Harrisburg.

■ Pittsburgh

Charles Dickens called this city "Hell with the lid off" for a reason. As late as the 1950s, smoke from area steel mills made street lamps essential even during the day. Thankfully, the decline of the steel industry has meant cleaner air and rivers, and a recent renaissance in Pittsburgh's economy has produced a brighter urban landscape. Private-public partnerships have created shiny new architecture like Phillip Johnson's Pittsburgh Plate Glass Building, a Gothic black-glass cathedral. Throughout these renewals, Pittsburgh's individual neighborhoods have maintained strong and diverse identities; Oakland, Southside, and the Strip District vie for visitors' attention as much as downtown. Admittedly, some of the old, sooty Pittsburgh lives on in the suburbs; but one need only ride up the Duquesne Incline and view downtown from atop Mount Washington to see how thoroughly Pittsburgh has entered a new age—and to understand why locals are so justly proud of "The 'Burgh."

PRACTICAL INFORMATION

Tourist Office: Pittsburgh Convention and Visitors Bureau, 4 Gateway Center, 18th fl. (281-7711 or 800-359-0758), downtown on Liberty Ave. Open Mon.-Fri. 9am-5pm. There are four visitors centers: downtown, Oakland, Mt. Washington, and the airport. The **Downtown Visitors Center,** on Liberty Ave. adjacent to Gateway Center, is open Mon.-Fri. 9am-5pm, Sat.-Sun. 9am-3pm.

Airport: Pittsburgh International (472-3525), 15mi. west of downtown by I-279 and Rte. 60 in Findlay Township. **Airline Transportation Company** (471-2250) runs shuttles to downtown (Mon.-Fri. every ½hr. 7am-11:40pm; $12, roundtrip $20), Oakland (Mon.-Fri. every hr. 9am-10pm, Sat. every 2hr. from 9am-5pm, Sun. every 2hr. 10am-2pm; $21 roundtrip), and Monroeville (Mon.-Fri. every 2hr. 9am-3pm, every hr. 3pm-10pm, Sun. at 2, 4, 7, and 9pm; $18, $32 roundtrip).

Trains: Amtrak, 1100 Liberty Ave. (471-6170 or 800-872-7245), at Grant on the northern edge of downtown next to Greyhound and the post office. Generally safe inside, but be careful walking from here to the city center at night. To: Philadelphia (2 per day, 7hr., $77); Chicago (1 per day, 9hr., $96). Open 24hr.

Buses: Greyhound, (391-2300 or 800-231-2222), on 11th St. at Liberty Ave. near Amtrak. Large and fairly clean, with police on duty. To: Philadelphia (7hr., $42); Chicago (12hr., $62). Station and ticket office open 24hr.

Public Transportation: Port Authority of Allegheny County (PAT) (442-2000). Within the Golden Triangle: bus fare free until 7pm, 75¢ after 7pm; subway (between the 3 downtown stops) free. Beyond the Triangle: bus fare $1.25, weekend all-day pass $3; subway $1.25-1.60. Schedules and maps at most subway stations and in the Community Interest section of the yellow pages.

Taxis: Peoples Cab, 681-3131. $1.40 base fare, $1.40 per mi.

Car Rental: Rent-A-Wreck, 101 Hargrove St. (488-3440), 1 block from Liberty tunnels. $20-28 per day with 50 free mi.; 18¢ per additional mi. Must be 21 with credit card or $300 cash deposit. Open Mon.-Sat. 8am-8pm; winters 8am-6pm.

Crisis Lines: Rape Action Hotline, 765-2731. Open 24hr.

Emergency: 911.

Post Office: (642-4475; 642-4478 for general delivery), at 7th and Grant St. Open Mon.-Fri. 7am-6pm, Sat. 7am-2:30pm. **ZIP code:** 15219. **Area code:** 412.

Pittsburgh's downtown, the **Golden Triangle,** is shaped by two rivers—the Allegheny to the north, and the Monongahela to the south—which flow together to form a third, the Ohio. Streets in the Triangle parallel to the Monongahela are numbered 1 through 7. The **University of Pittsburgh** and **Carnegie-Mellon University** can be found east of the Triangle in **Oakland.** With one of the lowest crime rates in the nation for a city of its size, Pittsburgh is fairly safe, even downtown at night.

ACCOMMODATIONS AND CAMPING

More a hotel than a hostel, **Point Park College,** 201 Wood St. (392-3824), at Blvd. of the Allies eight blocks from the Greyhound Station, provides clean rooms, some of which have private baths, to HI-AYH members and college students. The third-floor cafeteria serves an all-you-can-eat breakfast ($4) daily 7-9:30am. (3-day max stay. Office open daily 8am-4pm. Check-in until 11pm; tell the guards you're a hosteler. $15; linen included. Reservations recommended. Open May 15-Aug. 15.) Several inexpensive motels can be found in the city's outskirts. **Motel 6,** 211 Beecham Dr. (922-9400), off I-79 at Exit 16/16B, about 10mi. from downtown, is faithful as always. (Singles $32, doubles $38. Reservations suggested for summer weekends.) A 30-minute (11-mi.) drive from downtown, the **Red Roof Inn,** 6404 Stubenville Pike (787-7870), south on I-279 past the Rte. 22/Rte. 30 junction at the Moon Run exit, offers the comfort of a clean, quiet chain motel. (Check-in 24hr. Check out by noon. Singles $45, doubles $65. In summer, reserve 2 weeks in advance.) **Pittsburgh North Campground,** 6610 Mars Rd., Cranberry Township 16066 (776-1150), has the area's closest camping, 20 min. from downtown; take I-79 to the Mars exit. (110 campsites; showers, swimming. Tent sites for 2 $17, hookup $24; $3 per extra adult, $2 per extra child.)

FOOD

Aside from the pizza joints and bars downtown, **Oakland** is the best place to look for a good, inexpensive meal. Collegiate watering holes and cafés pack **Forbes Ave.** around the University of Pittsburgh, while colorful eateries and shops line **Walnut St.** in Shadyside and **East Carson St.** in South Side. The **Strip District** on Penn Ave.

between 16th and 22nd St. (north of downtown along the Allegheny) bustles with Italian, Greek, and Asian cuisine, vendors, grocers, and craftsmen. On Saturday mornings, fresh produce, fish, and street performers vie for business.

Original Hot Dog Shops, Inc., 3901 Forbes Ave. (687-8327), at Bouquet St. in Oakland. A rowdy (actually, very rowdy), greasy Pittsburgh institution with lots and lots of fries, burgers, dogs, and pizza. Call it "the O" like a local. 16in. pizza $4. Open Sun.-Wed. 10am-3:30am, Thurs. 10am-4:30am, Fri.-Sat. 10am-5am.

Beehive Coffeehouse and Theater, 3807 Forbes Ave. (683-HIVE/4483), just steps from "the O." A quirky coffeehouse brimming with cool wall paintings, cool staff, cool clientele, and hot cappuccino ($1.75). The theater in the back features current films. Poetry and an occasional open-mike improv night buzz upstairs. Mon.-Fri. 7am-midnight, Sat. 8:30am-midnight, Sun. 9:30am-midnight. Another location in Southside, 1327 E. Carson St. (488-HIVE/4483).

The Elbow Room, 5744 Ellsworth Ave. (441-5222), in Shadyside. The relaxed clientele take advantage of garden seating, free refills, and Crayolas for paper tablecloths. Spicy chicken sandwiches ($6.75), Charles pasta ($8.25), and a hybrid southwest/front parlor decor make it worth the trip. Open Sun.-Thurs. 11am-midnight, Fri.-Sat. 11am-1am.

Harris' Grill-A Café, 5747 Ellsworth Ave. (363-0833), across the street from The Elbow Room. Chomp on inexpensive Greek specialties ($5-11) beneath the European-style umbrellas on the outdoor deck. Open daily 11am-2am.

SIGHTS

The **Golden Triangle** is home to **Point State Park** and its famous 200-ft. fountain. A ride up the **Duquesne Incline,** 1220 Grandview Ave. (381-1665), in the South Side, affords a spectacular view of the city ($2, ages 6-11 $1, under 6 free). Founded in 1787, the **University of Pittsburgh** (621-4141; 648-9402 for tours) stands in the shadow of the 42-story **Cathedral of Learning** (624-6000) at Bigelow Blvd. between Forbes and 5th Ave. The cathedral, an academic building dedicated in 1934, features 23 "nationality classrooms" designed and decorated by artisans from Pittsburgh's many ethnic traditions. **Carnegie-Mellon University** (268-2000) welcomes scholars right down the street on Forbes Ave.

The **Andy Warhol Museum,** 117 Sandusky St. (237-8300), on the North Side, is the world's largest museum dedicated to a single artist, housing seven floors of the Pittsburgh native's material, from pop portraits of Marilyn, Jackie, and Grace to continuous screenings of films like *Eat,* a 39-min. film of a man eating, and a series of pieces entitled *Oxidation,* made from synthetic polymer paint and urine on canvas. (Open Wed. and Sun. 11am-6pm, Thurs.-Sat. 11am-8pm. $5, seniors $4, students and children $3.) A 20-min. walk into the North Side, **The Mattress Factory,** 500 Sampsonia Way (231-3169), is actually a modern art museum (very sneaky!) which specializes in temporary site-specific installations that surround and engage the audience; don't miss the three spectacular permanent exhibits by James Turrell, the mythic lightworker (open Tues.-Sat. 10am-5pm, Sun. 1-5pm; donation suggested).

Two of America's greatest financial legends, Andrew Carnegie and Henry Clay Frick, made their fortunes in Pittsburgh; today, their bequests enrich the city's cultural fortune. Carnegie's most spectacular gift, **The Carnegie,** 4400 Forbes Ave. (622-3131; 622-3289 for guided tours), across the street from the Cathedral of Learning (take any bus to Oakland), comprises both an art museum and a natural history collection. Five hundred famous dinosaur specimens stalk the natural history section, including an 84-ft. giant dubbed *Diplodocus Carnegii* (the things money will buy...), and one of only two full *Tyrannosaurus Rex* fossils in the nation. The modern art wing hosts an impressive collection of Impressionist, Post-Impressionist, and 20th-century work. (Open Tues.-Sat. 10am-5pm, Sun. 1-5pm. $5, seniors $4, students and children $3.) Though most people know Henry Clay Frick for his art collection in New York, the **Frick Art Museum,** 7227 Reynolds St., Point Breeze (371-0600), 20 min. from downtown, displays some of his earlier, less famous acquisitions. The permanent collection contains Italian, Flemish, and French works from the 13th to 18th centuries. Call about chamber music concerts October through April. (Open Tues.-Sat. 10am-5:30pm, Sun. noon-6pm. Donations accepted.)

ENTERTAINMENT AND NIGHTLIFE

Most restaurants and shops carry the weekly *In Pittsburgh*, a great source for free, up-to-date entertainment listings, nightclubs, and racy personals. The internationally acclaimed **Pittsburgh Symphony Orchestra** (392-4900) performs September through May at **Heinz Hall**, 600 Penn Ave., downtown, and gives free outdoor concerts on summer evenings in Point State Park. The **Pittsburgh Public Theater** (321-9800) is quite renowned, but charges a pretty penny (performances Oct.-July; tickets $25.50-$34.50).

Punk rockers, blues mavens, and anyone else over 21 looking for a relaxing place to sit down with a bottled beer ($2) can mark the passage of time at **Tobacco Road,** 223 Atwood St. (682-7707), in Oakland. Live music starts at 10pm nightly. (Open Mon.-Fri. 10am-2am, Sat. 11am-2am, Sun. 1pm-2am.) **The Metropol,** 1600 Smallman St. (261-4512), in the Strip District, fills a spacious warehouse with raving natives and other dancing species (cover $2-15; doors generally open 8-9pm).

▨ Allegheny

Heaven for hikers and those who prefer Nature unsullied and non-commercial, the **Allegheny National Forest** encompasses half a million acres of virgin woodland in northwest Pennsylvania. While fishing, hunting, mountain trail biking, and cross-country skiing opportunities make it an outdoor lover's ideal year-round vacation destination, its location—only 20 mi. from I-80 at its southern border—makes it also an excellent stopover for car-weary travelers looking for some sylvan R&R.

Practical Information The forest divides into four quadrants, each with its own ranger station providing forest maps ($3) and info about facilities within the region. **NE: Bradford Ranger District** (362-4613), on Rte. 59 west of Marshburg (open Mon.-Fri. 7am-4:30pm, summers also Sat.-Sun. 8:30am-5pm). **NW: Sheffield Ranger District** (968-3232), on U.S. 6 (open Mon.-Fri. 8am-4:30pm, summers also Sat. 9am-5:30pm). **SE: Ridgway Ranger District** (776-6172), on Montmorenci Rd. (open Mon.-Fri. 8am-4:30pm). **SW: Marienville Ranger District** (927-6628), on Rte. 66 (open Mon.-Fri. 7:30am-4pm). For general forest info, call the Bradford ranger station or write to **Forest Service**, USDA, P.O. Box 847, Warren 16365. When driving in the forest, be very careful during wet weather; about half the region is served only by dirt roads. Allegheny's **area code:** 814.

Accommodations and Camping From whatever direction you approach the Allegheny Forest, you'll encounter a small community near the park that offers groceries and accommodations. **Ridgway**, 25 mi. from I-80's Exit 16 at the southeast corner, and **Warren**, on the northeastern fringe of the forest at the U.S. 6/U.S. 62 junction, provide comparable services. Trusty **Motel 6**, 1980 E. Main St. (716-665-3670), sits just north of Allegheny in Jamestown (singles $38, doubles $44). Closer to the park in the town of Warren, the **Conewango Motel**, 1665 Market St. (723-7410), offers typical cheap motel rooms (singles $35, doubles $45; reservations encouraged on weekends). The forest administers 34 **campgrounds;** 10 stay open year-round, albeit with no services in the winter (sites $11-13, parking $3). **Red Bridge, Dew Drop, Kiasutha,** and **Heart's Content** are the most popular areas. You can call 800-280-2267 to reserve sites up to 240 days in advance (reservation fee $7.85), although half are allotted on a first come, first served basis. You don't need a site to crash in the Allegheny; stay 1500 ft. from a major road or body of water and you can partake of **free backcountry camping** anywhere. There are also five free boat- or hiking-accessible camping sites along the 95-mi. shore of the Allegheny Reservoir (see below) which do not require reservations or a permit (fresh water, toilets, no showers).

Sights and Activities Each summer, the **Allegheny Reservoir,** located in the northern section of the forest, is stocked with fish and then with tourists who enjoy fishing, boating, swimming, or touring the **Kinzua Dam. Allegheny Outfitters** (723-1203), on Rte. 6 in Warren next to the Allegheny River Motel, handles canoe rentals for the reservoir and the Allegheny River ($20 per day, weekends $24 per day; open Mon.-Fri. by appt., Sat.-Sun. 9am-5pm). **Kinzua Boat Rentals and Marina** (726-1650), 4 mi. east of Kinzua Dam on Rte. 59, rents canoes ($5.50 per hr., $20 per day), rowboats ($5.50/$20), and motorboats ($12/$50; open Memorial Day-Sept. daily 8am-8pm). **Fishers** should dial the 24-hr. fishing hotline for lake conditions (726-0164). **Hikers** will find the free pamphlet describing the forest's 10 trails quite helpful. Twelve mi. of trails meander through the wildlife refuge at **Buzzard Swamp,** near Marienville; no motor vehicles are permitted.

■ Ohiopyle

Lifted by steep hills and cut by cascading rivers, southwest Pennsylvania encompasses some of the loveliest forests in the East. Native Americans dubbed this region "Ohiopehhle" ("white frothy water") for the grand Youghiogheny River Gorge (yock-a-gay-nee—"The Yock" to locals), now the focal point of Pennsylvania's **Ohiopyle State Park.** The park's 19,000 acres offer hiking, fishing, hunting, whitewater rafting, and a variety of winter activities. The latest addition to the banks of the Yock, a graveled bike trail that winds 28 mi. north from the town of Confluence to Connellsville, was converted from a riverside railroad bed. Recently named one of the 19 best walks in the world, the trail is just one section of the "rails to trails" project that will eventually connect Pittsburgh and Washington, D.C.

Practical Information Ohiopyle borders on Rte. 381, 64 mi. southeast of Pittsburgh via Rte. 51 and U.S. 40. The **Park Information Center,** P.O. Box 105 (329-8591), lies just off Rte. 381 on Dinnerbell Rd. (open daily 8am-4pm; Nov.-April Mon.-Fri. 8am-4pm). To receive a free booklet on the Laurel Highlands region, which includes Ohiopyle, call 800-925-7669. **Greyhound** serves **Uniontown,** a large town 20 mi. to the west on U.S. 40, and travels to Pittsburgh (2 per day, 1½hr., $11). Ohiopyle's **post office:** 47 E. Fayette St. (438-2522; open Mon.-Fri. 8am-6pm, Sat. 8am-noon). **ZIP code:** 15470. **Area code:** 412.

Accommodations and Camping Motels around Ohiopyle are few and far between, but the excellent **Ohiopyle State Park Hostel (HI-AYH)** (329-4476), on Ferncliffe Rd., sits right in the center of town off Rte. 381. Bob Utz has 24 bunks, a kitchen, a washer and dryer, and an extreme fondness for chess—he's unbeatable. (Check-in 6-11pm. $9, nonmembers $12. Linen not provided.) Just down the street, **Falls Market and Overnight Inn,** P.O. Box 101 (329-4973), rents surprisingly nice singles ($25) and doubles ($40) with shared baths (laundry facilities, fridge, access to TV/VCR). The downstairs store has groceries and a restaurant/snackbar (burgers $1.75, pancakes $2.25; open daily 7am-9pm). There are 226 **campsites** in Ohiopyle and 8 sites for groups up to 12 (PA residents $10, out-of-staters $12, group sites more; $3 reservation fee). The park recommends calling at least 30 days in advance for summer weekend reservations.

The Yock Throngs of tourists come each year to raft Ohiopyle's 8-mi.-long class III rapids. Some of the best whitewater rafting in the East, the rapids take about five hours to conquer. Four outfitters front Rte. 381 in "downtown" Ohiopyle: **White Water Adventurers** (800-992-7238), **Wilderness Voyageurs** (800-272-4141), **Laurel Highlands River Tours** (800-472-3846), and **Mountain Streams and Trails** (800-245-4090). The price for a guided trip on the Yock varies dramatically ($28-57 per person per day), depending on the season, day of the week, and difficulty. If you're an experienced river rat (or if you just happen to *enjoy* flipping boats), any of the above companies will rent you equipment. (Rafts about $11-14 per person; canoes $20; "duckies"—inflatable kayaks—about $20-25.) **Bike rental** prices vary with bike styles (generally $3-4 per hr.). In order to float just about anything on the river, you must get a **launch permit** at the park (Mon.-Fri. free; weekend passes $2.50, call at least 30 days in advance). You'll also need a $2 token for the park shuttle-bus which will take you to the launch area. Be forewarned that to get back to your car, you'll need transportation from your destination to the parking lot. The market in the Falls Market and Overnight Inn (see above) sells the **fishing licenses** required in the park ($15 for 3 days, $5 extra for season-long pass).

Near Ohiopyle Fallingwater (329-8501), 8 mi. north of Ohiopyle on Rte. 381, is a cantilevered masterpiece by the father of modern architecture, Frank Lloyd Wright. Designed in 1936 for the wealthy Kaufmann family, "the most famous private residence ever built" blends into the surrounding terrain; huge boulders that predate the house are part of the structure's architecture. The family originally wanted the house to be near the Bear Run Waterfall, around which they spent many of their summer vacations. Instead of designing the residence to face the cascading water, however, Wright built the house over the waterfall, so you can hear the water's roar in every room but can only see it from one terrace. This site can only be seen on a one-hr. guided tour; make reservations. (Open Tues.-Sun. 10am-4pm; Nov.-March weekends only. Tours Tues.-Fri. $8, students $6, ages 9-18 with parents $5; Sat.-Sun. $12/$8/$6. Children under 9 must be left in child care, $2 per hr.)

Fort Necessity National Battlefield, on U.S. 40 near Rte. 381, is a replica of the original fort built by George Washington. In July 1754, young George, then of the British army, was trounced in an attack on Fort Necessity that began the French and Indian War. Check out the fort's **Visitors Information Center** (329-5512) for more info (open daily 8:30am-6:30pm; Labor Day-Memorial Day 8:30am-5pm). Entrance to the park $2; those under 17 get in free. **Braddock's Grave** lies 1 mi. northwest of the fort on U.S. 40. Another mi. down the road, the singular **Museum of Early American Farm Machines and Very Old Horse Saddles with a History** (438-5180) exhibits rusted and zany Americana, including a 12-ton cast iron steam engine from 1905 and saddles from the Civil War, all strewn about a motel lawn.

Delaware

Delaware, a small state with the feel of a small town, comes as a welcome sanctuary from the sprawling cities of the upper east coast. Delaware's particular charm is well represented by the story of the state bug, the ladybug, adopted in 1974 after an ardent campaign by elementary school children. Quiet seaside communities and rolling dunes lure vacationers to Delaware from all along the country's eastern shores.

PRACTICAL INFORMATION

Capital: Dover.
State Visitors Service: P.O. Box 1401, 99 King's Hwy., Dover 19903 (800-282-8667 in DE, 800-441-8846 outside DE). Open Mon.-Fri. 8am-4:30pm. **Division of Fish and Wildlife,** P.O. Box 1401, 89 King's Hwy., Dover 19903 (739-5297).
Time Zone: Eastern. **Postal Abbreviation:** DE
Sales Tax: 8% on accommodations, 2.75% on motorized vehicles. 0% on everything else; you gotta love it.

■ Delaware Seashore

Lewes Founded in 1613 by the Zwaanendael colony from Hoorn, Holland, **Lewes** (LOO-IS) touts itself as Delaware's first town. More than 350 years later, the town is a sleepy burg on the Delaware Bay, across the Delaware River from Cape May, NJ. Lewes' history and its calm shores attract an annual influx of antique hunters and vacationing families who seek a safe retreat from the rough Atlantic waters. With produce stands sporadically lining the streets, the small-town atmosphere in Lewes is upscale and reserved, but well-kept beaches and welcoming natives make the town inviting for budget travelers.

The **Lewes Chamber of Commerce** (645-8078), on King's Hwy., operates out of the Fisher Martin House (open Mon.-Fri. 10am-4pm, Sat.-Sun. 10am-2pm). Secluded 4000-acre **Cape Henlopen State Park** (645-8983), east of Lewes, on the Atlantic Ocean, is home to a seabird nesting colony, sparkling white "walking dunes," and a beach with a bathhouse (open daily 8am-sunset; $5 per car, bikes and walkers free). Sandy campsites are available on a first come, first served basis (645-2103; sites $15; open April-Oct.). **Oby Lee Coffee Roasters and Café,** 124 2nd. St. (645-0733), in the Lewes Bake Shoppe, has sandwiches ($2-4) and fat-free, caffeine-free Vanilla Dreams ($1.25; open Sun.-Fri. 7:30am-10pm, Sat. 7:30am-11pm).

Carolina Trailways (227-7223), in the Ace Hardware on Rte. 1, serves Lewes with buses to Washington, D.C. (3½hr., $31), Baltimore (3½hr., $27), and Philadelphia (4hr., $29). Lewes is one end of the 70-min. **Cape May, NJ/Lewes, DE Ferry** route (644-6030; one-way $18). In Lewes and Rehoboth, the Delaware Resort Transit (DRT) **shuttle bus** (800-292-7665) runs from the ferry terminal, through Lewes to Rehoboth and Dewey Beach, every ½hr. ($1 per day; open Memorial Day-Labor Day daily 7am-3am.) Lewes and Rehoboth's **ZIP code** is 19971; the **area code** is 302.

Rehoboth Beach Despite their proximity, Lewes and Rehoboth Beach foster such opposite auras that they might as well be in different countries. Rehoboth Beach is both a resort for young, blue-collar families and home to a burgeoning gay community. The once pristine seashore has been littered with mini-golf courses, discount T-shirt shops, and countless fast-food places; however, the beach maintains its allure due to Rehoboth's cheap lodgings and inexpensive lifestyle. From the plastic "strip" that is Rte. 1, follow Rehoboth Ave. until it hits the water at Rehoboth Beach, or follow Rte. 1 south to **Dewey Beach.** The **Rehoboth Beach Chamber of Commerce,** 501 Rehoboth Ave. (800-441-1329 or 227-2233), near the imitation lighthouse, has info (open Mon.-Fri. 9am-5pm, Sat. 9am-noon). **Carolina Trailways,** 251 Rehoboth Ave. (227-7223), runs through Rehoboth Beach. Buses go to Washington, D.C. (3½hr., $31), Baltimore (3½hr., $27), and Philadelphia (4hr., $29).

Inexpensive lodging abounds in Rehoboth. **The Abbey Inn,** 31 Maryland Ave. (227-7023), always has a conversation waiting on the porch, and a two-day minimum stay. (Singles from $32, doubles from $40, 15% surcharge on weekends. Open Memorial Day-Labor Day. Call for reservations a week in advance.) **The Whitson,** 30 Maryland Ave. (227-7966), offers plush rooms for a bit more money. (Two day min. stay on weekends. Singles $43-53, doubles $58-63.) **The Lord Baltimore,** 16 Baltimore Ave. (227-2855), one block from the boardwalk, has clean, antiquated, practically beachfront rooms, TV, and A/C (singles and doubles $35-65; reservations recommended). The **Big Oaks Family Campground** (645-6838), at the intersection of Rte. 1 and 270, is secluded with open sites (with hookup $21.50).

In a town of plastic, **Cafe Papillion,** 42 Rehoboth Ave. (227-7568), in the Penny Lane Mall, provides a haven of authenticity, and the healthiest fare around, with croissants and specialty coffee ($1.50-2), and baguette sandwiches ($5-6; open Mon.-Fri. 8am-midnight, Sat.-Sun. 9am-midnight). **Thrasher's,** 7 and 26 Rehoboth Ave., has served fries and only fries ($3-6) in enormous paper tubs, for over 60 years. Don't expect ketchup, just vinegar and salt (open daily 11am-11pm).

The **Blue Moon,** 35 Baltimore Ave. (227-6515), rises at 4pm daily and rocks a predominantly gay crowd until 1am (no cover). **Irish Eyes,** 15 Wilmington Ave. (227-2888), are smiling because they feature live rock in the week and ol' Irish on the weekends (open Mon.-Fri. 5pm-1am, Sat.-Sun. noon-1am).

Maryland

Once upon a time, the picturesque, shellfish-rich estuary of Chesapeake Bay ruled the Maryland economy. On the rural eastern shore, small-town Marylanders captured crabs and raised tobacco. Across the bay in Baltimore, workers ate the crabs, loaded ships, and ran factories. Then the federal government expanded, industry shrank, and Maryland had a new, more slender core: not the bay, but the Baltimore-Washington Parkway. Suburbs grew up and down the corridor, Baltimore revitalized, and the Old Line State acquired a new, liberal urbanity.

As Washington, D.C.'s homogenized commuter suburbs swell beyond the limits of Maryland's Montgomery and Prince Georges counties, Baltimore revels in its immensity while Annapolis, the capital, remains a small-town commune for sailors. The mountains and mines of the state's western panhandle—geographic and cultural kin to West Virginia—are to this day largely undeveloped. If anything brings this state together, it may be a sense of proportion: forests and fields encompass but never overwhelm, rivers and islands are not too big to be thoroughly explored, and cities are too small to engulf even the most provincial person.

PRACTICAL INFORMATION

Capital: Annapolis.
Office of Tourism: 217 E. Redwood St., Baltimore 21202 (800-543-1036). **Forest and Parks Service,** Dept. of Natural Resources, Tawes State Office Building, Annapolis 21401 (410-974-3771; Mon.-Fri. 8am-4:30pm).
Time Zone: Eastern. **Postal Abbreviation:** MD.
Sales Tax: 5%.

■ Baltimore

> Of the external embellishments of life there is a plenty there—as great a supply, indeed, to any rational taste, as in New York itself. But there is also something much better: a tradition of sound and comfortable living.
> —H.L. Mencken, "On Living in Baltimore," 1926

Seventy years later, Mencken's Baltimore-New York City parallel still holds true. Baltimore maintains a well-touristed waterfront district adjacent to its commercially oriented downtown—though on a scale much smaller than that of the Big Apple. And amidst Baltimore's modern, industrial harbor are reminders of a distinguished past and a glorious present: historic stone drawbridges compete with new steel structures, and the old Baltimore & Ohio Railroad contrasts with the sleek, glass-windowed skyline. Modern Baltimore still serves as Maryland's urban core, and old-time shirtsleeve Bawlmer endures in the quiet limelight of Anne Tyler's novels and John Waters' films. Near the downtown skyscrapers, old ethnic neighborhoods like Little Italy front Baltimore's signature rowhouses, whose unique façades are microcosms of the larger city. Baltimore's treasures—the National Aquarium, Camden Yards, and crabs—more than atone for gritty urban environs and hostile race relations.

PRACTICAL INFORMATION

Visitor Information: Baltimore Area Visitors Centers, 300 W. Pratt St. (837-INFO/4636 or 800-282-6632), at S. Howard St., 4 blocks from Harborplace. Pick up a map and a *Quick City Guide,* a quarterly glossy with excellent maps and events listings. Open daily 9am-5:30pm.
Baltimore-Washington International Airport (BWI): 859-7111, on I-195 off the Baltimore-Washington Expressway (I-295), 10mi. south of the city. Use BWI as a gateway to Baltimore or Washington, D.C. Take MTA bus #17 to the N. Linthicum

Light rail station. Airport shuttles (724-0009) run daily to hotels every ½hr. 5:45am-11:30pm ($10 to downtown Baltimore, $15 roundtrip). For Washington, D.C., shuttles leave every hr. 5:45am-11:30pm ($21-29). Trains from BWI Airport run to Baltimore ($5), and Washington, D.C. ($10).

Amtrak: Penn Station, 1500 N. Charles St. (800-872-7245), at Mt. Royal Ave. Easily accessible by bus #3 or 11 from Charles Station downtown. Trains run every ½hr. to: New York ($58-74), Washington, D.C. ($16-18), and Philadelphia ($31-36). Ticket window open daily 5:30am-9:30pm, self-serve 24hr. (credit card only).

Greyhound: 2 locations: 210 W. Fayette St. (752-1393), near N. Howard St.; and 5625 O'Donnell St. (744-9311), 3mi. east of downtown near I-95. Frequent connections to New York ($23.50), Washington, D.C. ($6), and Philadelphia ($12).

Public Transport: Mass Transit Administration (MTA), 300 W. Lexington St. (539-5000 or 333-2700 or 800-543-9809). Bus, Metro, and light-rail service to most major sights in the city; service to outlying areas more complicated. Some buses run 24hr. **Metro** operates Mon.-Fri. 5am-midnight, Sat. 6am-midnight. Light rail operates Mon.-Fri. 6am-11pm, Sat. 8am-11pm, Sun. 11am-7pm. Base fare for all of these $1.25, but may increase with distance traveled.

Taxi: Yellow Cab (685-1212); **Royal Cab** (327-0330).

Crisis Lines: Suicide Hotline (531-6677). **Sexual Assault and Domestic Violence Center** (391-2396).

Emergency: 911.

Post Office: 900 E. Fayette St. (347-4425). Open Mon.-Fri. 7:30am-9pm, Sat. 8:30am-5pm. **ZIP Code:** 21233. **Area Code:** 410.

Baltimore dangles in central Maryland, 100 mi. south of Philadelphia and about 150 mi. up the Chesapeake Bay from the Atlantic Ocean. The Jones Falls Expressway (I-83) halves the city with its southern end at the Inner Harbor, while the Baltimore Beltway (I-695) encircles it. I-95 cuts across the southwest corner of the city.

Baltimore is full of one-way streets. **Baltimore Street** (running east across the Inner Harbor) and **Charles Street** (running north from the west side of the Harbor) divide the city into quarters. Streets parallel to Baltimore St. get "West" or "East" tacked onto their names, depending on which side of Charles St. they are on. Streets are dubbed "North" or "South" according to their relation to Baltimore St.

ACCOMMODATIONS AND CAMPING

Baltimore International Youth Hostel (HI-AYH), 17 W. Mulberry St. (576-8880), at Cathedral St. Near bus and Amtrak terminals. Take MTA bus #3, 11, or 18. Don't walk in the surrounding neighborhood at night. Elegant, centrally located 19th-century brownstone with 48 dorm style beds. Kitchen, laundry, and lounge with baby grand piano. There's also a cat. Friendly managers allow a 3-night max. stay. Curfew 11pm, but house keys are available for a $2 rental fee. $13, nonmembers $16. Reservations recommended.

Mount Vernon Hotel, 24 W. Franklin St. (727-2000), near Cathedral St. in Mount Vernon. Standard, comfortable rooms with A/C. Terrific location. Singles from $70, doubles from $85. Parking $6 per day.

Capitol KOA, 768 Cecil Ave. (410-923-2771 or 987-7477), near Millersville. Tent site for two $24, with electricity $28. RV site with full hookup $29.75. Each additional adult $4. Off-season prices are lower. Open April-Nov.

FOOD AND DRINK

Virginia may be for lovers, but Maryland is for crabs—every self-respecting restaurant offers **crab cakes,** and most claim to serve Baltimore's best.

The **Light Street Pavilion** (332-4191), Pratt and Light St. at Harborplace, has manifold foodstuffs to suit every taste bud (open Mon.-Thurs. 10am-10pm, Fri.-Sat. 10am-11pm, Sun. 10am-8pm). **Lexington Market,** 400 W. Lexington (685-6169), at Eutaw St., provides endless produce, fresh meat, and seafood (open Mon.-Sat. 8:30am-6pm; subway: Lexington Station or bus #7). **Cross Street Market,** between S. Charles and Light St. in South Baltimore, provides produce, as well as one of the best raw bars in the city. In Fells Point, the two-building **Broadway Market** sits in the middle of S. Broadway St., three blocks from the dock (open Mon.-Sat. 7am-6pm). **One World Café,** 904 S. Charles St. (234-0235), in the Federal Hill district, serves vegetarian cuisine to those seeking an alternative to seafood (open Mon.-Thurs. 7am-11pm, Fri. 7am-12:30am, Sat. 8am-12:30am, Sun. 8:30am-10pm).

The Helmand, 806 N. Charles St. (752-0311). Despite the white linen tablecloths, there's nary a thing on the menu over $10. Acclaimed by some local magazines as one of the 10 best restaurants in the city, this Afghan restaurant serves authentic dishes in which meat garnishes vegetables and yogurt sauces garnish all. Try the *kaddo borani,* pan-fried and baked baby pumpkin in a yogurt-garlic sauce. Open Sun.-Thurs. 5-10pm, Fri.-Sat. 5-11pm.

Bertha's Dining Room, 734 S. Broadway (327-5795), at Lancaster. The bumper stickers say "Eat Bertha's Mussels": black-shelled bivalves ($7.75-10) served upon butcher-block tables—best with chunky vegetable mussel chowder (cup $1.75). Jazz bands play Tues.-Wed. and Fri.-Sat. nights. 20 kinds of beer on tap (½-pint $2.50, pint $3.50). Afternoon tea Mon.-Sat. 3-4:30pm, offers scones, tarts, and other pastries (tea reservations necessary; call one day in advance). Kitchen open Sun.-Thurs. 11:30am-11pm, Fri.-Sat. 11:30am-midnight. Bar until 2am.

Ikaros, 4805 Eastern Ave. (633-3750), 2mi. east of downtown; take bus #10. Like its Greek mythological namesake, this restaurant has fallen from heaven. In a romantic, Mediterranean atmosphere, this Baltimore institution has been serving the city's best *souvlaki* ($5) for 27 years. The Greek salads ($6-7) are a meal in themselves. Open Sun.-Mon. and Wed.-Thurs. 11am-10pm, Fri.-Sat. 11am-11pm.

Haussner's, 3242 Eastern Ave. (327-8365), at S. Clinton; take bus #10. Hundreds of oil paintings crowd the dining room, where Central European cuisine including fresh pig knuckles and *Sauerbraten* ($10.60) is served. Wear long pants after 3pm. Open Tues.-Sat. 11am-10pm.

SIGHTS

The **National Aquarium,** 501 E. Pratt St. (576-3800), Pier 3, makes the Inner Harbor worthwhile. Multi-level exhibits and tanks show off rare fish, big fish, red fish, and blue fish along with the biology and ecology of oceans, rivers, and rainforests. The Children's Cove (level 4) lets visitors handle intertidal marine animals. (Open March-Oct. Sun.-Thurs. 9am-6pm, Fri.-Sat. 9am-8pm; Nov.-Feb. Sat.-Thurs. 10am-5pm, Fri. 10am-8pm. $11.50, seniors $9.50, children 3-11 $7.50, under 3 free; Oct.-March Fri. 5-8pm $3.50.)

Baltimore's gray harbor ends with a colorful bang in a five-square-block body of water bounded on three sides by the aquarium, Harborplace, the Maryland Science Museum, and a bevy of boardable ships. **The Clipper City** (539-6277), a beautiful topsail schooner, provides a scenic, two-hour jaunt around the Inner Harbor. The cruise offers a full bar, as well as an opportunity to see the 19th-century replica raise its sails. (Departs Mon.-Sat. at noon and 3pm. $12, children $2.) The **Baltimore Maritime Museum** (396-3453), awaits at Piers III and IV. (Open Mon.-Fri. 10am-5pm, Fri.-Sat. 9:30am-6pm; winters Fri.-Sun. 9:30am-5pm. $4.50, seniors $4, children under 13 $1.75, active military free.)

At the Inner Harbor's far edge lurks the **Maryland Science Center,** 601 Light St. (685-5225), whose five-story IMAX screen, 38-speaker sound system, and Davis Planetarium's 50-ft. dome stun audiences. (Open Memorial Day-Labor Day Mon.-Thurs. 10am-6pm, Fri. and Sun. 10am-8pm; Sept.-May Mon.-Fri. 10am-5pm, Sat.-Sun. 10am-6pm. Admission $9, ages 4-17, seniors, and military $7, under 4 free.)

A fantastic Baltimore museum, the **Walters Art Gallery,** 600 N. Charles St. (547-9000), at Centre, keeps one of the largest private art collections in the world, spanning 50 centuries. The museum's apex is the Ancient Art collection (level 2); its seven marble sarcophagi with intricate relief carvings are found in only two known collections; the other is in the National Museum in Rome. (Open Tues.-Sun. 11am-5pm. $4, seniors $3, students and kids under 18 free; Sat. free before noon.) The **Baltimore Museum of Art** (396-7100), at N. Charles and 31st St., picks up where the Walters leaves off, exhibiting a fine collection of Americana and modern art. Two adjacent 20th-century **sculpture gardens** make wonderful picnic grounds. (Open Wed.-Fri. 10am-4pm, Sat.-Sun. 11am-6pm. Admission $5.50, students and seniors $3.50, ages 7-18 $1.50, under 7 free. Thurs. free.) At the museum, the **Baltimore Film Forum** (889-1993) shows classic and current American, foreign, and independent films on Thursdays and Fridays at 8pm ($5, students and seniors $4).

The **Baltimore Zoo** (366-5466), off I-83 at Exit 7, offers a new Chimpanzee Forest exhibit, the spectacular Palm Tree Conservatory, a lake surrounded by lush greenery, and an "African Watering Hole," which is a simulated savannah with elephants, Siberian tigers, and a waterfall. The **Children's Zoo** imports animals from nearby farms and the Maryland wilds. (Open Mon.-Fri. 10am-4pm, Sat.-Sun. 10am-5:30pm; everything closes at 4pm in winter. $7.50, seniors and ages 2-15 $4, under 2 free.) **Fort McHenry National Monument** (962-4290), at the foot of E. Fort Ave. off Rte. 2 and Lawrence Ave. (take bus #1), commemorates the American victory against the British in the War of 1812. This famous battle inspired Francis Scott Key to write the "Star Spangled Banner." (Open daily 8am-8pm; Sept.-May 8am-5pm. $2, seniors and under 17 free.)

Once a station for the Baltimore & Ohio Railroad, the **B&O Railroad Museum,** 901 W. Pratt St. (752-2490), looks out on train tracks where dining cars, Pullman sleepers, and mail cars park themselves for a touring frenzy. The Roundhouse captures historic trains and a replica of the 1829 "Tom Thumb," the first American steam-driven locomotive. Don't miss the extensive model-train display. (Open daily 10am-5pm. $6, seniors $5, kids 5-12 $3, under 5 free. Train rides on weekends for an additional $2.)

Baltimore is home to the **Babe Ruth Birthplace and Baltimore Orioles Museum,** 216 Emory St. (727-1539. Open daily 10am-5pm, Nov.-March 10am-4pm. $5, seniors $3, kids 5-16 $2, under 4 free.) **Oriole Park at Camden Yards** (547-6234), just west of the Inner Harbor at Eutaw and Camden St., is the home to the Orioles. (Tours leave hourly Mon.-Fri. 11am-2pm, on the ½-hour Sat. 10:30am-2pm and Sun. 12:30-2pm. $5, seniors and children under 12 $4.)

ENTERTAINMENT AND NIGHTLIFE

The **Showcase of Nations Ethnic Festivals** (837-4636 or 800-282-632), at **Festival Hall,** W. Pratt and Sharp St., celebrates the culture of a different Baltimore neighborhood each week (June-Sept.). The **Pier Six Concert Pavilion** (625-4230), at Pier VI at the Inner Harbor, presents big-name music nightly from late July through Sept. Tickets are available at the pavilion or through TeleCharge (625-1400 or 800-638-2444; $15-30). If you don't have the cash for a ticket, but want to hear the show, head to Pier V for free eavesdropping. The **Left Bank Jazz Society** (466-0600) sponsors jazz shows Sept.-May. The **Theatre Project,** 45 W. Preston St. (752-8558), experiments with theater, poetry, music, and dance. (Performances Wed.-Sat. 8pm, Sun. 3pm. Tickets $5-14. Box office open Tues. noon-5pm, Wed.-Sat. 1-9pm, Sun. noon-4pm.) The beloved **Baltimore Orioles** play at their new stadium at Camden Yards, a few blocks from the Inner Harbor, at the corner of Russell and Camden St. In 1997, the Orioles will be joined by the **Ravens,** when Baltimore gets a second chance at profes-

---

Nevermore, Nevermore

Edgar Allan Poe, a short-lived, mustached, opium-addicted 1830s author, virtually invented the horror tale and the detective story. Poe, whose most famous works include *The Tell-Tale Heart, The Pit and the Pendulum* and *The Raven,* never envisioned that they would be lauded as innovative or deemed worthy of careful study. Poe wrote for the money and considered his stories trash. Visit the macabre writer's original haunting ground at **Edgar Allan Poe House,** 203 N. Amity St. (396-7932), near Saratoga St. (bus #15 or 23). The tour ushers Poe-heads through the writer's biography and around the tell-tale original furniture. (Open Wed.-Sat. noon-3:45pm; Aug.-Sept. Sat. noon-3:45pm. $3, under 13 $1.)

sional football. The Ravens, formerly the Cleveland Browns, will play in **Memorial Stadium** until a new venue is built.

Baltimore has a large number of bar and nightclub options. At **Baltimore Brewing Co.,** 104 Albermarle St. (837-5000), west of the Inner Harbor on the outskirts of Little Italy, Brewmaster Theo de Groen has captured the hearts and livers of Baltimoreans with his original and distinctive lagers, brewed right on the premises. (Open Mon.-Thurs. 11am-11pm, Fri.-Sat. 11am-midnight. Happy hour daily 4-7pm, ½-liters of beer $2.) **8 X 10,** 10 E. Cross St. (625-2000), is *small.* But, it's popular, and overflowing with locals. Local bands play everything here, including blues, reggae, and jazz (open nightly 9pm-2am; cover $8-12).

The Midtown Yacht Club, 15 E. Centre St. (837-1300), off N. Charles in Mount Vernon, draws locals and homesick English tourists with its daily specials, Happy Hour, and 11 beers on tap (open daily 11am-2am). **Hippo,** 1 W. Eager St. (547-0069), is Baltimore's largest and most popular gay bar, and provides pool tables, videos, and a packed dance floor. The first Sun. of every month is Ladies' Tea (6-10pm), and Thurs. is Men's Night. (Saloon open daily 3pm-2am. Dance bar open Wed.-Sat. 10pm-2am. Video bar open Thurs.-Sat. 10pm-2am. Cover Thurs.-Fri. $3, Sat. $5.) **Hammerjacks,** 1101 S. Howard St. (481-7328), is a commercial concert venue, and *the* place in Baltimore for nationally recognized bands.

■ Annapolis

Walking the fine line between nostalgia and anachronism, the capital of Maryland boasts a historic waterfront, narrow streets flanked by 18th-century brick antique shops, and peaceful docks. Settled in 1649, Annapolis' Georgian townhouses once held Colonial aristocrats (and their slaves). It was here that the 1783-1784 Continental Congress ratified the *Treaty of Paris,* and the city made headlines again in 1790 during its stint as temporary capital of the U.S.

Practical Information and Orientation Annapolis lies southeast of U.S. 50 (a.k.a. U.S. 301), 30 mi. east of Washington, D.C. and 30 mi. south of Baltimore. From Washington, D.C., take U.S. 50E. (In Washington, D.C., 50 begins at New York Ave.) From Baltimore, follow Rte. 2S to U.S. 50W, cross the Severn River Bridge, then take Rowe Blvd. **Greyhound/Trailways** (800-231-2222) connect Annapolis to Washington, D.C. (2 per day, 1hr., $7.50) and towns on the far side of the Chesapeake Bay. Baltimore's **Mass Transit Administration** (539-5000) links Baltimore with Annapolis. (Express bus #210 runs Mon.-Fri., 1hr., $2.85. Local bus #14 daily, 90min., $2.25.) The **Annapolis Department of Public Transportation,** 160 Duke of Gloucester St. (263-7964), operates a web of buses connecting the historic district with the rest of town (Mon.-Sat. 5:30am-10pm, Sun. 8am-7pm). The **Annapolis and Anne Arundel County Conference & Visitors Bureau,** 26 West St. (268-8687), has brochures and info (open daily 9am-5pm). **Information desks** field questions at the State House (841-3810; open daily 10am-5pm). The city extends south and east from Church Circle and State Circle. School St., in a blatantly unconstitutional move, connects Church and State. Maryland Ave. runs from the State House to the Naval Academy. Main St. (where food and entertainment are found) starts at Church Circle and ends at the docks. Those lost in Annapolis can re-orient themselves by looking for the State House dome or St. Anne's spire. Annapolis is compact and easily walkable; save yourself a headache by parking in a lot or garage ($4-10). For **emergencies** dial 911. The **area code** is 410.

Accommodations and Food Bed and breakfasts abound in this self-consciously quaint town, while motels are harder to come by. The visitors information centers have brochures on B&Bs and hotels in the area. Rooms should be reserved in advance, especially for the busy summer months. **Bed and Breakfasts of Maryland** (800-736-4667) aids in arranging accommodations in Annapolis. **Middleton Tavern,** 2 Market Space (263-3323), at Randall St., was established in 1750 and frequented by members of the Continental Congress; today it offers Maryland's specialties, seafood lasagna ($8) or oysters from the raw bar. Nightly music accompanies the marine delights (open Mon.-Fri. 11:30am-1am, Sat.-Sun. 10am-1am; food served until midnight). **Chick & Ruth's Delly,** 165 Main St. (269-6737), offers dishes named after politicians. Omelettes ($3-6), corned beef sandwiches ($4), and malted milkshakes ($2.50) highlight an inexpensive and delicious menu (open 24hr.).

Sights and Nightlife The Corinthian-columned **State House** offers maps and houses the state legislature and a fine silver collection. *The Treaty of Paris* was signed here on January 14, 1874 (open daily 9am-5pm; free tours 11am and 3pm). Restaurants and tacky tourist shops line the waterfront at **City Dock,** where Naval Academy ships ply the waters and civilian yachtsmen congregate. Main St., full of tiny shops and eateries, stretches from here back up to Church Circle. The **Banneker-Douglass Museum,** 84 Franklin St. (974-2893), outlines African-American cultural history (open Tues.-Fri. 10am-3pm, Sat. noon-4pm; free). The **U.S. Naval Academy** holds its fort at the end of King George St. Tours begin at the **Armel-Leftwich Visitors Center** (263-6933), inside the academy gates at the end of King George St. ($5, seniors $4, students $3).

Locals and tourists generally engage in one of two activities: wandering along City Dock or schmoozing/boozing at upscale Annapolitan pubs. **The Colonial Players, Inc.,** 108 East St. (268-7373), is the place for theater-goers. (Performances Thurs.-Sun. 8pm, additional Sun. show at 2:30pm. Thurs. and Sun. $7, students and seniors $5; Fri.-Sat. $10.) Bars and taverns line downtown Annapolis, drawing crowds every night. The fact that you just had dinner at the **Middleton Tavern,** 2 Market Space (263-3323), shouldn't stop you from partying there later. At the **New Moon Café,** 137 Prince George St. (280-1955), local jazz bands occasionally perform (open Mon.-Fri. 9am-3pm and 5pm-midnight, Sat.-Sun. 8am-midnight).

■ Eastern Shore

The long arm of land known as the Eastern Shore is claimed by Maryland in the north and Virginia in the south. Though the Chesapeake Bay is the only physical divide between the shore and its mother states, the gulf between these areas is cultural as well. The Eastern Shore harbors a lifestyle last found in most of Virginia and Maryland decades ago. Untouched marshlands and expansive fields punctuate the forests and dunes of this tranquil landscape. Here, tractors are more common than commuters on the roads, and wild ponies still go unpenned. The Eastern Shore is a remarkable port of American natural history, a wilderness which is truly sublime.

■ Assateague, MD and Chincoteague, VA

Local legend has it that horses first came to Assateague Island by swimming ashore after escaping a sinking Spanish galleon. A more likely story is that a few centuries ago, several miserly mainland farmers put their horses out to graze on Assateague to avoid taxes and fencing expenses. Whatever their origins, the descendents of Assateague's original horses, the famous wild ponies, now roam free across the unspoiled beaches and forests of the island.

Assateague Island is divided into three parts. The **Assateague State Park** (410-641-2120), on Rte. 611 in southeast Maryland, is a two-mi. stretch of picnic areas, beaches, bathhouses, and campsites. (Park open daily April-Oct. 8am-sunset. $2, seniors free. Campsite registration 8am-11pm. Sites $20; reservations available only in one-week blocks, Sat.-Sat.) The **Assateague Island National Seashore** claims most of the long sandbar north and south of the park and has its own campground and beaches, most of which are inaccessible by car (sites $12, Nov. to mid-May $8). The **ranger station** (410-641-3030) distributes free back-country camping permits, but only before 2pm. The **Barrier Island Visitors Center** (410-641-1441), on Rte. 611, provides an introduction to the park and gives day-use info (open daily 9am-5pm; $4 per car). Of the meandering 1-mi. nature trails, Forest Trail offers the best viewing tower, but Marsh Trail (ironically) has fewer mosquitoes.

The **Chincoteague National Wildlife Refuge** stretches across the Virginia side of the island. Avid bird-watchers flock here to see rare species such as peregrine falcons, snowy egrets, and black-crowned night herons. During slack tide (the last Wed. in July), the Chincoteague wild ponies are herded together and made to swim from Assateague to Chincoteague Island, where the local fire department auctions off the foals the following day. The adults swim back to Assateague and reproduce, providing next year's crop. Thus, the best time for pony-sighting on Assateague Island is in mid-July, just before they're sold. For more info, visit the **Chincoteague Refuge Visitor Contact Station** on the island (804-336-6122; open daily 9am-4:30pm; $4 per car). The **Wildlife Loop** begins at the visitors center and provides ideal pony-viewing (open 5am-sunset; open to cars 3pm-sunset).

The best way to get to Assateague Island is by car—buses and taxis can be sporadic. If a car is out of the question, take **Carolina Trailways** (410-289-9307) to Ocean City via daily express or local routes from Greyhound stations in Baltimore ($22) and Washington, D.C. ($36.50). From Ocean City, take a taxi to Assateague (289-1313; about $20). For more area info, call or write to the **Chincoteague Chamber of Commerce,** P.O. Box 258, Chincoteague, VA 23336 (804-336-6161; open summers daily 9am-4:30pm, winters Mon.-Sat. 9am-4:30pm).

■ Ocean City

Ocean City is a lot like a kiddie pool. It's shallow and plastic, but can be a lot of fun if you're the right age. This 10-mi. strip of land packs endless bars, all-you-can-eat buffets, hotels, mini-golf courses, boardwalks, flashing lights, and tourists into a thin region between the Atlantic Ocean and the Assawoman Bay. Tourism is the town's only industry; in-season the population swells from 12,000 to 300,000, with a large migratory population of "June bugs," high school seniors that descend in swarms during the week after graduation to celebrate (read: to drink beer).

PRACTICAL INFORMATION

Ocean City runs north-south, with numbered streets linking the ocean to the bay. The **Ocean City Visitors Center** (800-626-2326), at 40th St. in the Convention Center, will welcome you (open Mon.-Thurs. 8am-5pm, Fri. 8am-6pm, Sat. 9am-5:30pm, Sun. 9am-5pm; Sept.-May daily 8:30am-5:30pm). **Carolina Trailways** (289-9307), at 2nd St. and Philadelphia Ave., sends buses to Baltimore (7 per day, 3hr., $22) and Washington, D.C. (4hr., $36.50). (Open daily 7am-8am and 10am-5pm; Sept.-May 10am-3pm.) In town, the **bus** (723-1607) is the best way to get around ($1 per day for unlimited rides). The bus runs 24hr. and travels the length of the town. **Parking** in Ocean City is a nightmare, although the beach is accessible on foot from most hotels, and free parking is available during the day at the Convention Center on 40th St. Ocean City's **post office:** 408 N. Philadelphia Ave. (289-7819; open Mon.-Fri. 9am-5pm, Sat. 9am-noon). **ZIP code:** 21842. **Area code:** 410.

ACCOMMODATIONS AND FOOD

If you're going to stay in Ocean City, make every effort to secure a room at the **Summer Place Youth Hostel,** 104 Dorchester St. (289-4542), in the south end of town. This exceptional establishment has great proprietors, tasteful southwestern decor, and gives you more bang for your buck than do most hostels. Private rooms have access to kitchen, TV, common areas, deck, hammock, and grill ($18 per person; no lockout; shared bath; reservations necessary; open April-Oct.). If the hostel's full, try **Whispering Sands** (289-5759), oceanside at 45th St. The amicable owner rents out rooms with kitchen access ($15; open May-Oct.). Most **motels** charge $35-50 per room on weekdays, and rates double on weekends. **Assateague National Seashore** (641-1441) or **Assateague State Park** (641-2120) provide tent-pitching facilities.

Dining in Ocean City is a glutton's delight. The streets are lined with seemingly identical restaurants hosting all-you-can-eat specials and featuring Maryland's specialty: crabs. **The Crab Bag** (250-3337), at 130th and Coastal Hwy., is a local favorite. It may look like a shanty, but the all-you-can-eat crabs ($17) are unbeatable. Limited seating encourages take-out (open daily 4-9pm). **Food Lion** (524-9039), on 120th St., has what you need to prepare a tasty meal (open daily 6am-midnight).

SIGHTS AND ENTERTAINMENT

Ocean City's star attraction is its beautiful beach. It runs the entire 10-mi. length of town and is wide and sandy the entire way (open 6am-10pm; free). When the sun goes down, hard-earned tans are put to work at Ocean City's league of bars and nightclubs. The most popular is **Seacrets** (524-4900), on 49th St., bayside. This huge complex brings a taste of Jamaica *sans* Rastas to the mid-Atlantic. Barefoot barflies wander between floats to the strains of the live reggae bands which play nightly (open Mon.-Sat. 11am-2am, Sun. noon-2am; cover $3-5). Seek refuge from the meat market at **Macky's Bayside Bar & Grill,** 5309 Coastal Hwy. (723-5565), bayside, behind Tio Gringo's. Macky's offers an all-wood interior and the opportunity to rub elbows with locals (open daily 11:30am-2am).

Washington, D.C.

After winning independence from Great Britain in 1783, the United States was faced with the challenge of finding a home for its fledgling government. Both Northern and Southern states wanted the capital on their turf. The final location—100 sq. mi. pinched from Virginia and Maryland—was a compromise resulting in what President Kennedy later termed "a city of Northern charm and Southern efficiency."

Nineteenth-century Washington was a "city of magnificent distances"—a smattering of slave markets, elegant government buildings, and boarding houses along the large-scale avenues designed by French engineer Pierre L'Enfant. The city had hardly begun to expand when the British torched it in 1814; a post-war vote to give up and move the capital failed in Congress by just eight votes. Washington continued to grow, but so did its problems—a port city squeezed between two plantation states, the district was a logical first stop for slave traders, whose shackled cargo awaited sales on the Mall and near the White House. Foreign diplomats were properly disgusted. The Civil War altered this forever, transforming Washington from the Union's embarrassing appendix to its jugular vein.

During the 1960s, Washington hosted a series of demonstrations advocating civil rights and condemning America's role in Vietnam. Martin Luther King, Jr. delivered his "I Have a Dream" speech in 1963 to the 250,000 people gathered on the Mall. In 1968, an anti-war gathering ringed the Pentagon with chants and shouts. Later the same year, riots touched off by King's assassination torched parts of the city; some blocks still await rebuilding. 1993 saw the inauguration of Bill Clinton, America's first baby boomer president, and 1997 marks a new presidential term.

Despite Washington's current problems with crime, the ambitious and strange experiment of an infant nation building a capital from scratch has matured into one of America's most intriguing urban centers. A conglomerate of political powerhouse, sleepy Southern town, decaying metropolis, and vigorous urban center yields Washington, D.C.'s intimidating and distinctive character.

The two discrete cities of Federal Washington and local Washington, D.C. coexist in the diamond-shaped District without much conflict or contradiction. Only blocks away from the National Mall's haven of tourism, Washington, D.C. communities—yuppie, gay, Latino, black—dwell and prosper, separate from the government grind.

Central Washington, D.C.

MUSEUMS
1 National Museum of Art/
  National Portrait Gallery
2 Natl. Mus. of American History
3 Natl. Mus. of Natural History
4 National Gallery of Art
5 Air & Space Museum
6 Hirshhorn Museum

1500 feet
500 meters

N

MID-ATLANTIC

Gallaudet University

CAPITOL HILL

EASTERN MARKET

K St.
H St.
7th St.
6th St.
4th St.

Maryland Ave.

Stanton Park

Union Station

UNION STATION

Supreme Court

Library of Congress

Seward Park

CAPITOL SOUTH

G St.
F St.

1st St.
E. Capitol St.
4th St.
New Jersey Ave.

North Capitol St.

South Capitol St.

NE

Florida Ave.

New Jersey Ave.

P St.

New Jersey Ave.

M St.

Rhode Island Ave.

7th St.

Massachusetts Ave.

E St.

2nd St.

3rd St.

Louisiana Ave.

Pennsylvania Ave.

US Capitol

NW

SHAW

SHAW/HU

MT VERNON SQ-UDC

Mt. Vernon Square

CHINATOWN

GALLERY PLACE

JUDICIARY SQ

ARCHIVES

H St.

FBI

THE MALL

Smithsonian Museums

Independence Ave.
Maryland Ave.

FEDERAL CENTER SW

L'ENFANT PLAZA

2nd St.

395

4th St.

Southwest Fwy.

Vermont Ave.

Logan Circle

12th St.
13th St.
14th St.

Thomas Circle

New York Ave.

METRO CENTER

McPHERSON SQ

15th St.

E St.

FEDERAL TRIANGLE

SMITHSONIAN

12th St.
14th St.

C St.

12th St Expwy

D St.

395

Scott Circle

16th St.

K St.

White House

The Ellipse

17th St.

Washington Monument

East Basin Dr.

Kutz Br.

Tidal Basin

Jefferson Memorial

DUPONT CIRCLE

New Hampshire Ave.

Florida Ave.

Q St.
P St.

20th St.

Dupont Circle

Connecticut Ave.

FARRAGUT NORTH

FARRAGUT WEST

H St.

18th St.

FOGGY BOTTOM

Pennsylvania Ave.

GWU

Constitution Ave.

Lincoln Memorial

Independence Ave.

West Potomac Park

Ohio Dr.

Potomac River

Sheridan Circle

Mass. Ave.

23rd St.

Washington Circle

M St.

26th St

FOGGY BOTTOM-GWU

G St.
F St.
Virginia Ave.
E St.

66

50

Roosevelt Bridge

Rock Creek Pkwy.

Memorial Bridge

Columbia Island

Rock Creek

Montrose Park

Dumbarton Oaks

R St.
R St.
P St.

28th St.
30th St.

GEORGETOWN

Wisconsin Ave.

C&O Canal

Whitehurst Fwy.

Roosevelt Island

George Washington Pkwy

Ladybird Johnson Park

VIRGINIA

R St.

Georgetown University

34th St.

Key Br.

George Washington Pkwy.

66

50

ROSSLYN

ARLINGTON CEMETERY

ARLINGTON CEMETERY

From the bars and businesses around Dupont Circle and the ethnic delights of Adams-Morgan to the collegiate-types in Georgetown and Foggy Bottom, Washington's second city has more to offer than downtown can possibly put on display, and more to see than any tour guide could ever expound upon.

For more comprehensive, detailed Washington, D.C. budget coverage, see *Let's Go: Washington, D.C. 1997,* available at bookstores everywhere.

PRACTICAL INFORMATION

Tourist Office: Washington, D.C. Convention and Visitors Association (WCVA), 1212 New York Ave., Ste. 600 NW (789-7000). Does not expect walk-ins. Write or call for copies of *The Washington, D.C. Visitor's Guide and Visitor Map* and a calendar of events. **Meridian International Center,** 1630 Crescent Pl. NW (667-6800). Metro: Dupont Circle. Call or write for brochures in a variety of languages. Office open Mon.-Fri. 9am-5pm.

Airport: National Airport (703-419-8000). It's best to fly here from within the U.S., since National is on the Metro and closer to Washington. Metro: National Airport. Taxi $10-15 from downtown. **Dulles International Airport** (703-419-8000) is Washington, D.C.'s international airport and much further from the city; some domestic flights also land here. Taxi to Dulles $40+. From Dulles to downtown Washington, D.C., the **Washington Flyer Dulles Express Bus** hits the West Falls Church Metro every 20-30 min. Mon.-Fri. 6am-10pm, Sat.-Sun. 7:30am-10pm; last bus from Metro 11pm. $8. Non-express buses to the city center leave every ½hr. 5:20am-10:20pm on weekdays; on weekends every hr. 5:20am-12:20pm, every ½hr. 12:50-10:20pm (45-60min.; $16, under 6 free).

Trains: Amtrak, Union Station, 50 Massachusetts Ave. NE (484-7540 or 800-872-7245; 800-523-8720 for Metroliner). To: New York City (3½hr., $60-75); Baltimore (45min., $15-17); Philadelphia (2hr., $33); Boston (9hr., $61). Maryland's commuter trains, **MARC** (410-859-7400), also depart from Union Station. These offer weekday commuter service to Baltimore ($5.75) and Harpers Ferry, WV ($7.25).

Buses: Greyhound, 1005 1st St. NE (800-231-2222) at L St. To: Philadelphia ($15); New York City ($26); Baltimore ($6).

Public Transportation: Metrorail, 600 5th St. NW (637-7000), is a relatively safe mode of transportation, accessed via a computerized fare card bought from a machine. If you plan to use the Metro several times, buy at least a $20 farecard; you will get a 10% bonus. Trains run Mon.-Fri. 5:30am-midnight, Sat.-Sun. 8am-midnight. Fare $1.10-3.25, depending on distance traveled and whether travel is during peak-hour. 1-day Metro pass $5. **Flash Pass** allows unlimited bus (and sometimes Metro) rides for 2 weeks or a month. To make a bus transfer, get a pass from machines on the platform *before* boarding the train. The extensive **Metrobus** (same address, phone, and hours as Metrorail) system reliably serves Georgetown, downtown, and the suburbs. Fare $1.10. A comprehensive bus map is available from the main Metro office.

Taxis: Yellow Cab (544-1212). Fares are not based on a meter but on a map which splits the city into five zones and 27 subzones. Zone prices are fixed; ask how much the fare will be at the beginning of your trip.

Car Rental: Bargain Buggies Rent-a-Car, 912 N. Lincoln St. (703-841-0000), in Arlington. $24.95 per day plus 15¢ per mile, with 100 free miles. $125.95 per week (local rental), with 500 free miles. $69.95 per weekend, with 200 free miles. Rates differ from branch to branch. Min. age 18, with major credit card or cash deposit of $250. Those under 21 need full insurance coverage of their own. Rates may be contingent on rental length and make of car. Open Mon.-Fri. 8am-7pm, Sat. 9am-3pm, Sun. 9am-noon.

Bike Rental: Big Wheel Bikes, 315 7th St. SE (543-1600). Metro: Eastern Market. Mountain bikes for $5 per hr., $25 per business day; 3-hr. min. For an extra $5, you can keep the bike overnight. Major credit card required for deposit. Open Tues.-Fri. 11am-7pm, Sat. 10am-6pm, Sun. 11am-5pm.

Hotlines: Rape Crisis Center: 333-7273. **Washington Post News Line:** 334-9000. **Gay and Lesbian Hotline:** 833-3234. 7pm-11pm. **Traveler's Aid Society:** 546-3120. Helpful in emergencies. Open Mon.-Fri. 9am-5pm.

Emergency: 911.
Post Office: 900 Brentwood Rd. NE (682-9595). Open Mon.-Fri. 8am-8pm, Sat. 10am-6pm, Sun. noon-6pm. **ZIP code:** 20090. **Area code:** 202.

ORIENTATION

Washington, D.C. is ringed by the **Capital Beltway,** or I-495 (except where it's part of I-95); the Beltway is bisected by **U.S. 1,** and meets **I-395,** coming from Virginia. **I-95** shoots up from Florida, links Richmond, VA, to Washington and Baltimore, then rockets up the East Coast past Boston. The high-speed **Baltimore-Washington Parkway** connects Washington, D.C. to Baltimore. **I-595** trickles off the Capital Beltway east to Annapolis. **I-66** heads west through Virginia.

The city is roughly diamond-shaped, with the four tips of the diamond pointed in the four compass directions, and the street names and addresses split into four quadrants: NW, NE, SE, and SW, as defined by their relation to the U.S. Capitol, Washington's geographic as well as spiritual heart. The names of the four quadrants distinguish otherwise identical addresses—pay very, *very* close attention to them.

Washington, D.C. designer Pierre L'Enfant's basic street plan is a rectilinear grid. Streets running from east to west are named in alphabetical order running north and south from the Capitol, from two A Streets two blocks apart (nearest the Capitol) out to two W Streets dozens of blocks apart. (There is no A or B St. in NW and SW, and no J St. anywhere.) After W St., east-west streets take on two-syllable names, then three-syllable names, then (at the north end of NW) names of trees and flowers in alphabetical order (roughly—some letters get repeated, and others skipped entirely). Streets running north-south get numbers (1st St., 2nd St., etc.). Numbered and lettered streets sometimes disappear for a block, then keep going as if nothing happened. Addresses on lettered streets indicate the numbered cross street (1100 D St. SE will be between 11th and 12th St.). State-named avenues radiate outward from the U.S. Capitol and the White House. The city added streets as the U.S. added states, and ultimately acquired avenues named for all 50.

Some **major roads** are **Pennsylvania Ave.,** which runs SE-NE from Anacostia to Capitol Hill to the Capitol, through downtown, past the White House (#1600), and ends finally at 28th and M St. NW in Georgetown; **Connecticut Ave.,** which runs north-northwest from the White House through Dupont Circle and past the Zoo; **Wisconsin Ave.,** running north from Georgetown past the Cathedral to Friendship Heights; **16th St. NW,** which zooms from the White House north through offices, townhouses, Adams-Morgan, and Mt. Pleasant; **K St. NW,** a major artery downtown; **Constitution and Independence Ave.,** just north and south of the Mall; **Massachusetts Ave.,** reaching from American University past the Cathedral, then through Dupont and Old Downtown to Capitol Hill; **New York Ave.,** whose principal arm runs from the White House through NE; and high-speed **North Capitol St.**

Over 600,000 residents inhabit the federal city and more than double that number live in suburban areas surrounding the city. Black, white, Asian, Hispanic, gay, bisexual, straight, Democrats, and Republicans are all well-represented. Escape the touristy **Mall** to get a true feel for the city. **Capitol Hill** extends east from the Capitol; its townhouses and bars mix white- and blue-collar locals with legislation-minded politicians. The area south of the Mall begins as federal offices that lead to the **Navy Yard** with its surrounding clubs and bars and terminates at the **waterfront.** North of the Mall, **Old Downtown** goes about its business accompanied by **Foggy Bottom** (sometimes called the "West End") on the other side of the White House and **Farragut** around K St., west of 15th St. NW. **Georgetown** draws crowds and sucks away bucks nightly from its center at Wisconsin and M St. NW. Business and pleasure, embassies and streetlife, and a huge gay scene converge around **Dupont Circle;** east of 16th St. the Dupont Circle character changes to struggling **Logan Circle,** then to the clubby **Shaw/U District,** and finally to Howard University and **LeDroit Park,** an early residence for Washington's African-American elite. A strong Hispanic community coexists with black, white, and cool in **Adams-Morgan,** north of Dupont and east of Rock Creek Park. West of the park begins **Upper Northwest,** a big stretch of spread-out, residential territory that includes the National Zoo and the Cathedral. Across the Anacostia River, the **Southeast** (including **Anacostia**), has been damaged and further isolated by poverty, crack, and guns.

ACCOMMODATIONS

Business hotels discount deeply and swell with tourists on summer weekends. Hostels, guest houses, and university dorms get particularly packed; reservations are a good idea. Check the *New York Times* Sunday Travel section for summer weekend deals. Washington, D.C. automatically adds an **13% occupancy surcharge** and another **$1.50 per room per night** to your bill. Prices listed below *do not* include taxes, unless otherwise noted. **Bed & Breakfast Accommodations, Ltd.,** P.O. Box 12011, Washington, D.C. 20005 (328-3510), reserves rooms in private homes (singles start at $45, doubles at $55; $15 per additional person).

Washington International Hostel (HI-AYH), 1009 11 St. NW 20001 (737-2333). Metro: Metro Center; take the 11th St. exit, then walk 3 blocks north. International travelers appreciate the college-aged staff, bunk beds, bulletin boards, kitchen, A/C, lockers, game room, laundry facilities, and common rooms. Rooms hold 4-12 beds. Wheelchair accessible. Be careful to the northeast of the hostel. $18, non-members $21. Open 24hr. Reservations recommended.

Kalorama Guest House at Kalorama Park, 1854 Mintwood Place NW (667-6369) and at **Woodley Park,** 2700 Cathedral Ave. NW (328-0860). Metro (both): Woodley Park-Zoo. Well-run, impeccably decorated guest rooms in Victorian townhouses; the first is in the upscale western slice of Adams-Morgan near Rock Creek Park, the second in a high-class neighborhood near the zoo. Both have laundry facilities and free local calls. Free continental breakfast. Office open Mon.-Fri. 8am-8pm, Sat.-Sun. 8:30am-7pm. Rooms with shared bath $40-65, $5 per additional person. Rooms with private baths $55-85, $60-95 per two. Reserve 1-2 weeks in advance.

Washington International Student Center, 2451 18th St. NW (800-567-4150 or 667-7681). Metro: Woodley Park-Zoo (15-min. walk). Clean, relatively safe hostel located amidst some of Adams-Morgan's best restaurants and clubs. Young guests and friendly staff, large common room with cable TV, two kitchens, and three bathrooms. Each of the four bedrooms has A/C and 6-8 beds. Bicycle rental $7 per day. No lock-out. $15 per night, breakfast included. Lockers available. Call for free pick-up from the Greyhound Bus or Union Stations.

Hereford House, 604 South Carolina Ave. SE (543-0102). Metro: Eastern Market. British-style B&B in a Capitol Hill townhouse. Downtown convenience with quiet B&B charm. Two shared baths, laundry, A/C, refrigerator, and garden patio. Singles $40-50, doubles $55-60. Senior discount. Reservations recommended.

Adams Inn, 1744 Lanier Place NW (745-3600 or 800-578-6807), near Ontario Rd. behind the Columbia Rd. Safeway supermarket, 2 blocks from the center of Adams-Morgan. Metro: Woodley Park-Zoo, then a 12 min. walk; or #42 bus to Columbia Rd. from Dupont Circle. Elegant Victorian townhouses run by a super-nice staff. All rooms have A/C; all shared-bath rooms have private sinks. Patio, laundry facilities, phones, and eating facilities. TV in lounge. Office open Mon.-Sat. 8am-9pm, Sun. 1-9pm. Singles with shared bath $45, with private bath $60. Doubles with shared bath $55, with private bath $70. Breakfast included. Reservations require deposit. Limited parking $7 per night.

Tabard Inn, 1739 N St. NW (785-1277), at 17th St. Metro: Dupont Circle. Romantic inn offers complimentary breakfast in a maze of slightly dim lounges. Singles $59-79, with private bath $99-135. $12 per additional person.

Connecticut Woodley Guest House, 2647 Woodley Rd. NW (667-0218). Metro: Woodley Park-Zoo; across the street from the Washington Sheraton. Tidy rooms, modestly furnished. Office open daily 7:30am-midnight. Singles with shared bath $42-46, with private bath $53-60. Doubles with shared bath $48-51, with private bath $58-66. Max. stay 4 weeks. Group, family, and long-term rates available.

Davis House, 1822 R St. NW (232-3196), near 19th St. Metro: Dupont Circle. Charming and spacious wood-floored building. Common room, sun room, patio, and microwave. Accepts international visitors, staff of Quaker organizations, and "representatives of other organizations working on peace and justice concerns." Other visitors occasionally accepted on a same-day, space-available basis. Max. stay 2 weeks. Open daily 8am-10pm. Singles in shared room $30, private singles $35, doubles $60 (with hall bath). One night's deposit required. Reserve as early as possible. No credit cards accepted.

Brickskeller Inn, 1523 22nd St. NW (293-1885), between P and Q St. Metro: Dupont Circle. Small, clean, recently renovated rooms, usually with private sinks and shared bathrooms; some rooms have private bath, A/C, and TV. Singles $45-60, doubles $65-75. Weekly rates: singles from $150, doubles from $225.

Swiss Inn, 1204 Massachusetts Ave. NW (371-1816 or 800-955-7947). Metro: Metro Center. Four blocks from Metro Center; close to downtown. Offers 7 clean, quiet studio apartments with refrigerators, private baths, high ceilings, kitchenettes, and A/C. Free local calls and laundry. Singles and doubles $98 ($78 in summer), with 20% discount for *Let's Go* readers. Weekly rates: singles and doubles $78 per night. Parking $5 per day weekdays (free weekends); managers will pick up patrons from the bus stop, Metro station, or downtown airport terminal.

HoJo Inn, 600 New York Ave. NE (546-9200). Metro: Union Station. A long (½-hr.) walk from the Metro; take N. Capitol St., then turn right on New York Ave. Clean, carpeted rooms with A/C and TV. Pool and free continental breakfast. Shuttle bus service to downtown. Singles $56, doubles $60. Seniors and military discount.

Georgetown University Summer Housing, available only for summer educational pursuits; they gladly take college-aged interns but *will not house self-declared tourists.* Housing is single-sex. 3-week min. stay. Singles $17, with carpeting $19. Available early June-early Aug. Contact G.U. Office of Housing and Conferences Services, Washington, D.C. 20057 (687-4560).

American University Summer Housing, available for students and interns. Metro: Tenleytown-AU. Simple dorm rooms with A/C. Available late May-mid-Aug. 3-week min. stay. Doubles with hall bathrooms $119 per week per person; triples $98 per week per person. Valid ID from any university and full payment for stay must be presented at check-in. $300 deposit required. Reserve early for check-in dates in early June; after that call 24hr. ahead to get a room if the dorms aren't full. Write to 407 Butler Pavilion, 4400 Massachusetts Ave. NW 20016-8039, attn.: Housing Management (885-2669).

Howard University Housing, (806-5661 or 806-5653) has hostel-like rates for interns and students in Washington, D.C. for the summer. Rooms available June 1-July 31. Singles $14, with A/C $18. Call and ask for Rev. James Coleman.

Cherry Hill Park, 9800 Cherry Hill Rd. (301-937-7116; fax 595-7181), in Maryland. Metrobus from the Metrorail runs to and from the grounds every 30 min., every 15 min. during rush hour. The closest campground to Washington. Most of the 400 sites are for RVs. Cable hookup available, coin-operated laundry, and heated swimming pool with whirlpool and sauna. Tent site $25; RV site with full hookup $33. $3 per additional person. $25 deposit required. Reserve at least 5 days ahead. Seniors, AAA, military, and KOA members 10% discount.

FOOD

Washington, D.C. makes up for its days as a "sleepy Southern town" with a kaleidoscope of international restaurants. Smithsonian-goers should plan to eat dinner far away from the triceratops and the biplanes; visitors to the Mall get stuffed at mediocre institutional cafeterias mere blocks from the better food on Capitol Hill. It's an open secret among interns that **happy hours** provide the cheapest dinners in Washington. Bars attract early-evening drinkers with plates, platters, and tables of free appetizers; the best concentrate on Capitol Hill or south of Dupont Circle.

Capitol Hill

Heart & Soul Café, 424 8th Street SE (547-1892), off Pennsylvania Ave. Metro: Eastern Market. It's an experience in fine Southern cuisine. Sandwiches $4.50-5, entrees $9-13. Specialties include the Heart & Soul Gumbo (cup $4) and the country fried chicken ($9). Buffet brunch Sat. 10am-2pm and Sun. 11:30am-4pm for $9.

MID-ATLANTIC

10% discount for *Let's Go*ers. Open Mon.-Thurs. 11:30am-10pm, Fri. 11:30am-11pm, Sat. 10am-11pm, Sun. 11:30am-10pm.

The Market Lunch, 225 7th St. SE (547-8444), in the Eastern Market complex. Metro: Eastern Market. One of the best deals in town. Strong smells of fresh fish and meat waft over a dozen stools. Crab cakes ($6-9) are the local specialty, but the Blue Bucks (buckwheat blueberry pancakes $3) have people lining up around the corner on Sat. mornings. Open Tues.-Sat. 7:30am-3pm.

Misha's Deli, 210 7th St. SE (547-5858), north of Pennsylvania Ave. on 7th St., across from the Eastern Market building. Metro: Eastern Market. Inexpensive Russian and Eastern European food. Tasty knishes ($2) and blintzes ($1.75). Plenty of meats, cheeses, and breads to buy for your very own sandwich. Borscht ($2-2.50); wide array of sweets and desserts. Some outdoor seating available. Open Mon.-Fri. 8am-7:30pm, Sat. 7am-6pm, Sun. 9am-5pm.

Chinatown

Burma Restaurant, 740 6th St. NW (638-1280). Burma is a deviation from China-town's somewhat repetitive menus. The owner, a retired Burmese diplomat and former U.N. delegate, loves to talk about Burma's rare cuisine, which replaces soy sauce with pickles, mild curries, and unique spices. Anything served in the *Kotang* sauce, made from sesame, soya, cilantro, ginger, garlic, onions, and lemon juice, demands a try. Most entrees $8, noodle dishes $7.50. Open Mon.-Fri. 11am-3pm, Fri.-Sat. 6pm-10:30pm, Sun.-Thurs. 6-10pm.

Georgetown

Aditi, 3299 M St. NW (625-6825), at 33rd St. The Sanskrit name translates as "creative power" or "abundance"; here it also means great food. The $14 Aditi dinner challenges any appetite; or eat light with a vegetarian entree, $5-8. Meat dishes $9-13. Open for lunch Mon.-Sat. 11:30am-2:30pm, Sun. noon-2:30pm; for dinner Sun.-Thurs. 5:30-10pm, Fri.-Sat. 5:30-10:30pm.

Booeymonger, 3265 Prospect St. NW (333-4810), at Potomac St. Breakfast ($3 for the special); quick 'n' tasty giant sandwiches (such as the Pita Pan or Tuna Turner), under $5. The $6 dinner special (available 5pm-closing) includes a specialty sandwich, beverage, and choice of salad or soup. Free coffee refills (until 11am) jumpstart your weekday morning. Open daily 8am-midnight.

Paolo's, 1303 Wisconsin Ave. NW (333-7353), near N St. Huge, elegant Italian dishes well worth the price (pasta $10-17, pizza $7-10, other entrees $13-17). Open Sun.-Thurs. 11:30am-1am, Fri.-Sat. 11:30am-2am.

Sarinah, 1338 Wisconsin Ave. NW (337-2955), near O St. Delicious Indonesian food includes *satays,* grilled and skewered lamb, beef, chicken, or shrimp with spicy sauces ($9-10), and vegetarian entrees ($7-8). Long list of exotic desserts ($3.25-4.25). Open Tues.-Sat. noon-3pm and 6-10:30pm, Sun. 6-10:30pm.

Zed's Ethiopian Cuisine, 3318 M St. NW (333-4710), near 33rd St. Award-winning cuisine eaten amid basket-woven tables and a youthful, savvy, local clientele. Appetizers $4. Entrees $6-12. $5 weekday lunch specials. Open daily 11am-11pm.

Farragut

The Star of Siam, 1136 19th St. NW (785-2839), between L and M St. Metro: Farragut West or Farragut North. This critically acclaimed restaurant is a favorite of both businesspeople and true connoisseurs. The green curry *Gang Keo-Wan* ($7.50 lunch, $8.50 dinner) will raise your oral temperature to new heights. Outdoor seating available. Open Mon.-Sat. 11:30am-11pm, Sun. 5-10pm.

Tokyo Terrace, 1025 Vermont Ave. NW (628-7304), near K St. Metro: McPherson Square. Tokyo Terrace caters to the area's sushi-lovers with a serious variety of both Japanese and Chinese fare. All-you-can-eat sushi, tempura, and miso soup buffet ($11) is available Fri. 6-9pm. Open Mon.-Thurs. 9:30am-7:30pm, Fri. 9:30am-9pm, Sat. noon-7:30pm.

Dupont Circle

City Lights of China, 1731 Connecticut Ave. NW (265-6688), between R and S St. Perhaps the District's best Chinese restaurant. The carefully prepared Szechuan-Hunan standards ($9-22, most around $10) and widely acclaimed house specialties, such as the crispy fried shredded beef ($13) make a good case. Open Mon.-Thurs. 11:30am-10:30pm, Fri. 11:30am-11pm, Sat. noon-11pm, Sun. noon-10:30pm.

Food for Thought, 1738 Connecticut Ave. NW (797-1095), three blocks north of the Circle. Casual coffeehouse atmosphere attracts alternative youth, and veggie dishes satisfy the healthiest appetites. Local acoustic musicians add a Bohemian touch; open mike every Mon. 9-11:30pm. Bulletin boards announce everything from rallies to rides to L.A. Pool table upstairs. Gazpacho (cup $3). Lunch combos ($4.75-6.75) offered Mon.-Fri. until 4:30pm. Dinner ($6-10). Open Mon.-Thurs. 11:30am-12:30am, Fri. 11:30am-2am, Sat. noon-2am. Sun. 5pm-12:30am.

Pizzeria Paradiso, 2029 P St. NW (223-1245), near 21st St. The lines are perpetually long most nights, but the wait is for the best pizza in the city. The crispy crust is out-of-this-world. Sides include tangy *panzanella* (Tuscan bread and vegetable salad) and elegant salads. Biscotti ($3), *gelati* ($4). Open Mon.-Thurs. 11am-11pm, Fri.-Sat. 11am-midnight, Sun. noon-10pm.

The Pop Stop, 1513 17th St. NW (328-0880), near P St. The price of a cup of coffee buys you several hours in the easy chairs upstairs at this hippest of Washington, D.C. cafés. The structural diversity attracts a varied crowd, though it's weighted toward the local, gay, and young; many stop by on their way to or from bars and clubs—that espresso breathes a second wind into a Saturday night. Wide variety of café drinks ($1-3) and sandwiches ($4). Open Sun.-Thurs. 7:30am-2am, Fri.-Sat. 7:30am-4am.

Skewers, 1633 P St. NW (387-7400), near 17th St. Skewers defies the neighborhood tendency toward multi-ethnic menus and sticks exclusively to Middle Eastern fare, to go with its tapestry-hung, pottery-filled interior. Chicken kabob ($7). Open Sun.-Thurs. 11am-11pm, Fri.-Sat. 11am-midnight.

Soho Tea & Coffee, 2150 P St. NW (463-7646), *en route* to the bars and clubs near P St. west of the Circle. This hip coffeehouse benefits from its strategic location, drawing crowds of bar-and-club-hoppers in the wee hours of the morning and serving a steady stream of patrons all day long. Veggie bowls ($4.25), sandwiches ($5.25). Espresso $1.25-3.50. Open daily 6am-4am.

Zorba's Café, 1612 20th St. NW (387-8555), near Connecticut Ave., by the Q St. entrance to the Dupont Circle Metro. Mediterranean folk music soothes customers enjoying fantastic Greek food. The restaurant is self-service; place your order with the cashier. *Yero* plate, with excellent french fries and a salad ($5.40). Open Mon.-Wed. 11am-11:30pm, Thurs.-Sat. 11am-2:30am, Sun. noon-10:30pm.

Shaw / U District

Ben's Chili Bowl, 1213 U St. NW (667-0909), at 13th St. Self-declared "Home of the Famous Chili Dog," this venerable (30-year-old) neighborhood hangout was the filming site of *The Pelican Brief.* Spicy homemade chili—on a hotdog (with chips, $2), on a half-smoke ($3), or on a ¼-lb. burger ($2.50). Die-hards eat it plain: small bowl $2, large bowl $2.55. Open Mon.-Thurs. 6am-2am, Fri.-Sat. 6am-4am, Sun. noon-8pm. Breakfast served Mon.-Sat. until 11am.

Florida Avenue Grill, 1100 Florida Ave. NW (265-1586), at 11th St. Fantastic Southern-style food: breakfast (served until 1pm) with salmon cakes or spicy half-smoked sausage, grits, apples, or biscuits ($2-6). Lunch and dinner dishes (with 2 vegetables, $6.50-10). Open Tues.-Sat. 6am-9pm.

Adams-Morgan

The Islander, 1762 Columbia Rd. NW (234-4955), upstairs. Some of Washington, D.C.'s best food is made in this Trinidadian and Caribbean restaurant, which has been winning regulars for over 15 years with its exotic but unpretentious cuisine. Curried goat ($8.75), Calypso chicken ($8.50). Nine kinds of *roti* (thin pancakes stuffed with vegetables/meat, $3.50-7). Appetizers $1.50-4. Sweet ginger beer ($1.50). Open Mon. 5-10pm, Tues.-Thurs. noon-10pm, Fri.-Sat. noon-11pm.

Meskerem, 2434 18th St. NW (462-4100), near Columbia Rd. Fine Ethiopian cuisine served in a beautiful setting: cheery yellow 3-level interior incorporates an upstairs dining gallery with Ethiopian woven tables and a view of the diners below. Lunch entrees $7.25-11, dinner $9-12. Open daily noon-midnight.

MID-ATLANTIC

Mixtec, 1792 Columbia Rd. NW (332-1011), near 18th St., is a cheap, friendly, and refreshing bastion of hearty Mexican food. A neon light flashes the specialty—*tacos al carbon.* The $3 version consists of two small tortillas filled with beef and served with three kinds of garnish. Chicken *mole* ($10). Entrees $9-10. Open Sun.-Thurs. 11am-10pm, Fri.-Sat. 11am-11pm.

Red Sea, 2463 18th St. NW (483-5000), near Columbia Rd. The first of Adams-Morgan's famous Ethiopian restaurants is still among the best. *Sambusa,* pastry filled with tasty ground beef and spices ($2.50). Traditional pancake bread, *injera,* accompanied by tender lamb, beef, chicken, and vegetable *wats*—entrees $7-11. Open Sun.-Thurs. 11:45am-11pm, Fri.-Sat. 11am-midnight.

Upper Northwest

Austin Grill, 2404 Wisconsin Ave. NW (337-8080). The Austin Grill sets the standard for Tex-Mex in Washington. Try the *carnitas,* melt-in-your-mouth braised pork fajitas ($9.75), or the Austin special, a pair of enchiladas striped with a trio of house sauces ($8.50). The place is small and hip, so lines are long. The wait for a table can be made more pleasant with the Stars and Bars, a powerful margarita worth its $4.75 price tag. Open Mon. 11:30am-10:30pm, Tues.-Thurs. 11:30am-11pm, Fri. 11:30am-midnight, Sat. 11am-midnight, Sun. 11am-10:30pm.

Faccia Luna, 2400 Wisconsin Ave. NW (337-3132). Pizza-crust connoisseurs, this small local chain is your Mecca, your Delhi, your Jerusalem. The wood-fired oven produces crisp-yet-tender crust, accompanied by subtly seasoned sauce and steaming cheese. Forget pepperoni and top it with eggplant, spinach, or pesto. Intriguing pastas and piping-hot calzones amid sunlit, blond-wood booths. Basic pie $6.05-11.50. Open Sun.-Thurs. 11:30am-11pm, Fri.-Sat. 11:30am-midnight.

Rocklands, 2418 Wisconsin Ave. NW (333-2558). Rocklands serves up South Carolina/Florida-style tangy grilled BBQ. Quarter-rack of pork ribs $4.50, BBQ pork sandwich $4. Raid owner John Snedden's shelf of 100 different hot sauces; sample as extensively as your deviously little mouth will permit. Open Mon.-Sat. 11:30am-10pm, Sun. 11am-9pm.

SIGHTS

Every first-time visitor is compelled to go to the Capitol and the Smithsonian, but away from the grassy expanses of the manicured Mall, the rest of Washington, D.C. is a veritable thicket of art museums, ethnic communities, parks, public events, and nightlife. Adams-Morgan, Dupont Circle, Connecticut Ave., and Georgetown are all good bets for those sick of the standard tourist circuit.

The most popular tour company is **Tourmobile Sight-seeing,** 1000 Ohio Dr. SW (554-7950 or 554-5100), near the Washington Monument, which takes passengers on the standard 18-sight loop. Get on the blue-and-white bus at any stop and buy tickets from the driver. (Tours run 9:30am-4:30pm, 9am-6:30pm from mid-April to mid-September. $12, children 3-11 $6.) **Scandal Tours** (800-758-8687) schleps tourists from one place of infamy to the next, stopping at Gary Hart's townhouse, Watergate, and the Vista Hotel, where Mayor Barry was (ahem) caught with his pants down (75 min., $27). **Capitol Entertainment Services** (636-9203) features a **Black History Tour** through Lincoln Park, Anacostia, and the Frederick Douglass home. (3hr. tours begin at area hotels. $22, children 5-12 $12.) Anthony S. Pitch's nationally recognized **walking tours** (301-294-9514) offer a 1-hr. Lafayette Square tour (group of 15 people or more required; $6 per person) and a two-hour Adams-Morgan tour (Sun. at 11am; $5 per person). Also offered is a two-hour motorized tour of the **Presidents' Homes** which visits the pre- and post-White House residences of all 17 20th-century American presidents (20 people per bus; $23 each).

Capitol Hill

The scale and style of the **U.S. Capitol** (224-3121) still evoke the power of the republic. (Metro: Capitol South.) The **East Front** faces the Supreme Court; from Jackson (1829) to Carter (1977), most Presidents were inaugurated here. For Reagan's 1981 inauguration, Congress moved the ceremony to the newly renovated **West Front,** overlooking the Mall. If there's light shining in the dome at night, Congress is still meeting. The public East Front entrance brings you into the 180-ft.-high rotunda. Pick up a map from the tourist desk (free guided tours begin here daily every 15 min. 9am-4pm). To view the congress' deliberations first hand, climb to the House and Senate **visitors galleries.** Americans should request a gallery pass (valid for the whole 2-yr. session of Congress) from the office of their representative, delegate, or senator. Foreign nationals may get one-day passes by presenting a photocopy or a passport, driver's licence, or birth certificate at the desk immediately outside the House visitors gallery (for a House pass) or at the "Appointments desk" located at the extreme North End of the main hallway of the crypt level (for a Senate pass). Expect to see a few bored-looking elected officials failing to listen to the person on the podium who is probably speaking for the benefit of home-district cable TV viewers. The real business of Congress is conducted in **committee hearings.** Most are open to the public; check the *Washington Post's* "Today in Congress" box for times and locations. The free **Capitol subway** shuttles between the basement of the Capitol and the House and Senate office buildings; a buzzer and flashing red light signals an imminent vote. (Open daily 9am-4:30pm, Memorial Day-Labor Day daily 8am-8pm.)

The nine justices of the **Supreme Court,** 1 1st St. NE (479-3000), across from the East Front of the Capitol building (Metro: Capitol South or Union Station), are the final interpreters of the U.S. Constitution. Oral arguments are open to the public; show up before 8:30am to be seated, or walk through the standing gallery to hear 5 min. of the argument. (Court is in session Oct.-June Mon.-Wed. 10am-3pm for 2 weeks each month.) The *Washington Post's* A-section can tell you what case is up. You can still walk through the courtroom itself when the Justices are on vacation. Brief lectures cover the history, duties, and architecture of the court and its building. (Every hr. on the ½-hr. 9:30am-3:30pm. Open Mon.-Fri. 9am-4:30pm. Free.)

The **Library of Congress,** 1st St. SE (707-5000 or 707-8000), between East Capitol and Independence Ave. (Metro: Capitol South), is the world's largest library, with 26 million books and over 80 million other holdings occupying three buildings: the 1897 Beaux Arts Jefferson Building; the 1939 Adams Building across 2nd St.; and the 1980 Madison Building. The entire collection, including rare items, is open to those of college age or older with a legitimate research purpose, but anyone can take the tour that starts in the Madison Building lobby. After a brief film, the tour winds through tunnels to the Jefferson Building, which is otherwise closed for renovations. The octagonal Main Reading Room, under a spectacular dome, remains open to scholars despite renovations. (Most reading rooms open Mon.-Fri. 8:30am-9:30pm, Sat. 8:30am-6pm.)

Folger Shakespeare Library, 201 East Capitol St. SE (544-4600), houses the world's largest collection of Shakespeare stuff (about 275,000 books and manuscripts). The Folger also sponsors readings, lectures, and concerts such as the PEN/Faulkner poetry and fiction readings and the Folger Consort, a chamber music group specializing in Renaissance music. Stop for a rest in the authentic Elizabethan "knot" garden, on the building's 3rd St. side. (Exhibits open Mon.-Sat. 10am-4pm; library open Mon.-Fri. 8:45am-4:45pm.)

The trains converge at **Union Station,** 50 Massachusetts Ave. NE (484-7540), 2 blocks north of the Capitol (Metro: Union Station). Colonnades, archways, and domed ceilings equate Burnham's Washington with imperial Rome; today the station is an ornament in the crown of capitalism, with chic stores and a food court.

Directly west of Union Station is the **National Postal Museum,** 1st St. and Massachusetts Ave. NE (357-2700), on the lower level of the City Post Office (Metro: Union Station). The Smithsonian's collection of stamps and other philatelic materials was relocated here in July 1993. The collection includes such postal flotsam as airmail planes hung from a 90-ft.-high atrium, half of a fake mustache used by a train robber, and the letter-carrier uniform worn by Cliff Claven in TV's "Cheers" (open daily 10am-5:30pm; free). Northeast of Union Station is the red-brick **Capital Children's Museum,** 800 3rd St. NE (675-4125; Metro: Union Station). Touch and feel the exhibits in this huge interactive experiment; walk through the life-sized cave, learn how a

MID-ATLANTIC

printing press works, grind and brew your own hot chocolate, or wander through the room-sized maze. Or just watch cartoons. (Open daily 10am-5pm. $6, seniors $4, under 2 free. All kids must be accompanied by an adult.)

The **Sewall-Belmont House,** 144 Constitution Ave. NE (546-3989; Metro: Union Station), one of the oldest houses in Washington, D.C. and headquarters of the National Woman's Party, now houses a museum of the women's movement. (Open Tues.-Fri. 11am-3pm, Sat.-Sun. noon-4pm; ring the bell. Free.)

Southeast

Three museums and a boardable destroyer are docked among the booms at the **Washington Navy Yard,** 9th and M St. SE (Metro: Navy Yard). The best of the lot, the **Navy Museum,** Building 76 (433-4882), allows you to climb inside the space capsule, play human cannonball inside huge ship guns, jam yourself into a bathysphere used to explore the sea floor, or give orders on the bridge (open Mon.-Fri. 9am-4pm, Sat.-Sun. 10am-5pm). Tour the **U.S.S. Barry,** a decommissioned destroyer, docked a few steps from the Navy Museum. The **Marine Corps Historical Museum,** Building 58 (433-3534), marches through Marine Corps time from the American Revolution to the present, touting the guns, uniforms, swords, and other memorabilia of marines from the halls of Montezuma to the shores of Kuwait—they even have the original flag raised at Iwo Jima, complete with bullet holes (open Mon., Wed.-Thurs., and Sat. 10am-4pm, Fri. 10am-8pm, Sun., noon-5pm).

The neighborhood of **Anacostia** was begun after the Civil War when one-acre plots sold by the Freedmen's Bureau drew freed slaves to the area. *Use caution in this neighborhood.* Despite the opening of the Anacostia Metro, this neglected neighborhood remains largely unattractive to tourists, despite community struggles to overcome drug-related violence. If you prefer exploring on foot, do so here only during the day and with a friend or two. The **Anacostia Museum,** 1901 Fort Place SE (287-3369 or 357-2700; take W-1 or W-2 bus from Howard Rd. near the Metro Station to Fort Place), focuses on African-American history and culture. Pick up a flier at the Smithsonian Castle to see what's showing at the museum (open daily 10am-5:30pm; free).

Museums on and around the Mall

The U.S. Holocaust Memorial Museum, 100 Raoul Wallenberg Pl. SW (488-0400; Metro: Smithsonian), houses displays that move beyond historical narrative, and put the Holocaust on a personal level. The permanent exhibit chronicles the rise of Nazism, the events leading up to the war in Europe, and the history of antisemitism. Films show Soviet, British, and American troops entering the concentration camps, shocked by the mass graves and emaciated prisoners they encounter. "The Hall of Remembrance" contains an eternal flame. The main exhibit is not recommended for children under 12, but the exhibit "Daniel's Story: Remember the Children" was designed for younger folk. Museum draws *immense* crowds; get in line by 9am to acquire same-day tickets. Open daily 10am-5:30pm. Free.

The National Gallery of Art: West Building (737-4215 or 842-6176), houses its pre-1900 art in a domed marble temple in the Western Tradition, including important works by El Greco, Raphael, Rembrandt, Vermeer, and Monet. Leonardo da Vinci's earliest surviving portrait, *Ginevra de' Benci,* the only one of his works in the U.S., hangs amongst a fine collection of Italian Renaissance Art. Open Mon.-Sat. 10am-5pm, Sun. 11am-6pm.

The National Gallery Of Art: East Building (737-4215 or 842-6176), houses the museum's plentiful 20th-century collection in I. M. Pei's celebrated, sunlit structure. The gallery owns works by a parade of modern artists, including Picasso, Matisse, Mondrian, Miró, Magritte, Pollock, Warhol, Lichtenstein, and Rothko. Don't expect to see all of them, however; the East Building constantly rearranges, closes, opens, and remodels itself for temporary exhibits. Open Mon.-Sat. 10am-5pm, Sun. 11am-6pm.

Smithsonian Museums On and Around the Mall

The **Smithsonian** (357-2700 or 357-1729) is the catalogued attic of the United States. The world's largest museum complex stretches along Washington's longest lawn, the Mall. **Constitution Ave.** (on the north) and **Independence Ave.** (on the south) fence the double row of museums. All Smithsonian museums are free and wheelchair-accessible, and all offer written guides in various languages. The museums are open daily 10am-5:30pm; extended summer hours are determined annually.

The National Museum of American History (357-1300). Henry Ford said "History is bunk." This museum thinks history is junk—several centuries' worth of machines, photographs, vehicles, harmonicas, and uncategorizable U.S. detritus reside here. When the Smithsonian inherits quirky artifacts of popular history, like Dorothy's slippers from *The Wizard of Oz* or Archie's armchair, they end up here. The original "Star Spangled Banner" hangs behind Foucault's pendulum.

The Museum of Natural History (357-1300). This golden-domed, neoclassical museum considers the earth and its life in 2½ big, crowded floors of exhibits. Inside, the largest African elephant ever captured stands under dome-filtered sunshine. Dinosaur skeletons dwarf it in a nearby gallery. Upstairs, cases of naturally occurring crystals (including glow-in-the-dark rocks) make the final plush room of cut gems anticlimactic, despite the famously cursed Hope Diamond. The Insect Zoo pleases with live creepy-crawlies, from cockroaches to walking sticks.

The National Air and Space Museum (357-1686). Gigantic, and the world's most popular museum to boot, with 7.5 million visitors per year. Airplanes and space vehicles dangle from the ceiling; the Wright brothers' biplane in the entrance gallery looks intimidated by all its younger kin. The space-age atrium holds a moon rock, worn smooth by two decades of tourists' fingertips. Walk through the Skylab space station, the Apollo XI command module, and a DC-7. IMAX movies on Langley Theater's 5-story screen are so realistic that some viewers suffer motion sickness. Films 10:10am-5:25pm. Tickets $4, youth (21 and under) and seniors $2.75; available at the box office on the ground floor.

Hirshhorn Museum and Sculpture Garden (357-1300). This four-story, slide-carousel-shaped brown building has outraged traditionalists since 1966. Each floor consists of 2 concentric circles, an outer ring of rooms and paintings, and an inner corridor of sculptures. The Hirshhorn's best shows feature art since 1960; no other gallery or museum in Washington, D.C. even pretends to keep up with the Hirshhorn's avant-garde paintings, mind-bending sculptures, and mixed-media installations. The museum claims the world's most comprehensive set of 19th- and 20th-century Western sculpture, including small works by Rodin and Giacometti. Sculpture Garden open daily 7:30am-dusk.

The Arts and Industries Building (357-1300). An exhibition of the 1876 Centennial Exhibition of American technology in Philadelphia. Check out the exterior: a polychromatic, multi-style chaos of gables, arches, rails, shingles, and bricks. Inside, furniture and candy-making equipment congregate near the Mall entrance; further back, heavy machinery will delight fans of steam (isn't that everyone?).

The National Museum of African Art (357-4600 or 357-4814). Underground at 950 Independence Ave. SW, the site displays artifacts from sub-Saharan Africa such as masks, textiles, ceremonial figures, and fascinating musical instruments like a harp made partly of pangolin scales. One permanent display contains bronzes from what is today Nigeria; another focuses on pottery.

The Arthur M. Sackler Gallery (357-2031 or 786-2374). Underground at 1050 Independence Ave. SW, the museum showcases an extensive collection of art from China, South and Southeast Asia, and Persia. Exhibits include illuminated manuscripts, Chinese and Japanese painting, jade miniatures, carvings and friezes from Egypt, Phoenicia, and Sumeria, Hindu statues, and the Sackler Library.

The Freer Gallery of Art (357-1300). The small, delicate pearl on a Mall-encircling necklace of big, showy gems. The Freer displays Asian and Asian-influenced art, including Chinese bronzes, precious manuscripts, jade carvings, and James McNeill Whistler's beautiful, opulent *Peacock Room*. Free tours at 1:30pm.

Monuments on and around the Mall

The **Washington Monument** (Metro: Smithsonian) is a vertical shrine to America's first president. The stairs up the monument were a famous (and strenuous) tourist exercise until the Park Service closed them after too many heart attacks occurred on the way up, and vandalism marred the steps. The wind experts say the thing could withstand a super-tornado blowing at 145 mi. per hour. The line takes 45 min. to circle the monument; people with disabilities can bypass it. (Open April-Aug. daily 8am-midnight; Sept.-March daily 9am-5pm. Free.) The **Reflecting Pool** mirrors Washington's obelisk in 7 million gallons of lit-up water 24 hr. a day.

Maya Ying Lin, who designed the **Vietnam Veterans Memorial,** south of Constitution Ave. at 22nd St. NW (Metro: Foggy Bottom/GWU), called it "a rift in the earth—a long, polished black stone wall, emerging from and receding into the earth." 58,132 Americans died in Vietnam, and each of their names is chiseled onto the memorial's stark black edifice. Books at both ends of the structure serve as indexes to the memorial's numbered panels. Many families and veterans make rubbings of their loved ones' names from the walls (open 24hr.).

The **Lincoln Memorial,** at the west end of the Mall (Metro: Smithsonian or Foggy Bottom-GWU), recalls the rectangular grandeur of Athens' Parthenon. From these steps, Martin Luther King, Jr. gave his "I Have a Dream" speech to the 1963 March on Washington. A seated Lincoln presides over the memorial, keeping watch over protesters and Fourth of July fireworks. Climbing the 19-ft. president is a federal offense; a camera will catch you if the rangers don't (open 24hr.).

Dedicated in July 1995, the 19 colossal polished steel statues of the **Korean War Memorial** trudge up a hill, rifles in hand, an eternal expression of weariness mixed with fear frozen upon their faces. The statue of the 14 Army men, 3 Marines, Navy Medic, and Air Force officer is accompanied by a black granite wall with over 2000 sandblasted photographic images from this war in which 54,000 Americans lost their lives. The memorial is at the west end of the Mall, near Lincoln.

A 19-ft. bronze Thomas Jefferson stands enshrined in the domed rotunda of the **Jefferson Memorial** (Metro: L'Enfant Plaza). The memorial's design pays tribute to Jefferson's home, Monticello, which he designed. Interior walls quote from Jefferson's writings: the *Declaration of Independence,* the *Virginia Statute of Religious Freedom, Notes on Virginia,* and an 1815 letter (open 24hr.). The memorial overlooks the **Tidal Basin,** where pedalboats float in and out of the shrine's shadow.

South of the Mall, exotic foliage from all continents and climates vegetates inside and outside the **U.S. Botanical Garden** (225-8333), 1st St. and Maryland Ave. SW (Metro: Federal Center SW). Cacti, bromeliads, and other plants flourish inside. (Guided tours Tues. and Thurs. at 9 and 11:30am, call ahead; open 9am-5pm.) Further west, the **Bureau of Engraving and Printing** (a.k.a. **The Mint**) (662-2000), 14th St. and C St. SW, offers tours of the presses that annually print over $20 billion worth of money and stamps. Money-love has made this the area's longest line; arrive mega-early or expect to grow old while you wait (open Mon.-Fri. 9am-2pm; free).

Downtown and North of the Mall

It's only proper that an architectural marvel should house the Smithsonian's **National Building Museum** (272-2448), towering above F St. NW between 4th and 5th St. (Metro: Judiciary Square). Montgomery Meigs's Italian-inspired edifice remains one of Washington's most beautiful; the Great Hall could hold a 15-story building. "Washington: Symbol and City," one of the NBM's first permanent exhibits, is a display on Washington, D.C. architecture. Other highlights include rejected designs for the Washington Monument and the chance to design your own Capitol Hill rowhouse. (Open Mon.-Sat. 10am-4pm, Sun. noon-4pm; open summers until 5pm daily. Tours Mon.-Fri. 12:30pm, Sat.-Sun. 12:30pm, 1:30pm.)

The Smithsonian's **National Museum of American Art** and **National Portrait Gallery** (357-2700) share the Old Patent Office Building, a neoclassical edifice 2 blocks long (American Art entrance at 8th and G St., Portrait Gallery entrance at 8th and F; Metro: Gallery Place-Chinatown). The NMAA's corridors contain a diverse collection of major 19th- and 20th-century painters, as well as folk and ethnic artists. Washington, D.C. janitor James Hampton stayed up nights in an unheated garage for 15 years to create the *Throne of the Third Heaven of the Nations' Millennium General Assembly,* to the right of the main entrance. "Art of the American West" puts the U.S.'s westward expansion in perspective, while Edward Hopper competes with the abstractions of Franz Kline on the third floor (open daily 10am-5:30pm; tours Mon.-Fri. noon, Sat.-Sun. 2pm; free). The wide range of media, periods, and styles represent make the National Portrait Gallery a museum of the American character (open 10am-5:30pm; tours daily 10:15am and 1:15pm; free).

The U.S.'s founding documents can still be found at the **National Archives** (501-5000 or 501-5404, guided tours 501-5205), at 8th St. and Constitution Ave. NW (Metro: Archives-Navy Memorial). Visitors line up outside to view the original *Declaration of Independence, U.S. Constitution,* and *Bill of Rights.* Humidity-controlled, helium-filled glass cases preserve and exhibit all three documents in the central rotunda (open daily April-Labor Day 10am-9pm, Labor Day-March 10am-5:30pm; free). The **Federal Bureau of Investigation** (324-3000) still hunts Commies, freaks, druggies, and interstate felons with undiminished vigor. Tour lines form on the beige-but-brutal J. Edgar Hoover building's outdoor plaza (tour entrance from 10th St. NW at Pennsylvania Ave.; Metro: Federal Triangle or Archives-Navy Memorial). Real FBI agents sport walkie-talkies as they speed you through gangster paraphernalia, confiscated drugs, gun displays, and mugshots of the nation's 10 most wanted criminals. John Dillinger's death mask hangs alongside his machine gun (tours Mon.-Fri 9am-4:15pm; free).

"*Sic semper tyrannis!*" shouted assassin John Wilkes Booth after shooting President Abraham Lincoln during a performance at **Ford's Theatre,** 511 10th St. NW (426-6924 or 426-1749; Metro: Metro Center). National Park rangers narrate the events of the April 14, 1865 assassination (open daily 9am-5pm; free). The **Old Post Office** (606-8691 or 606-8694), at Pennsylvania Ave. and 12th St. NW (Metro: Federal Triangle), sheathes a shopping mall in architectural wonder. Its arched windows, conical turrets, and 315-ft. clock tower rebuke its sleeker contemporary neighbors. The National Park Service shows you around the clock tower; the view from the top may be Washington's best. (Tower open mid-April to mid-Sept. 8am-10:45pm; otherwise 10am-6pm. Shops open Mon.-Sat. 10am-8pm, Sun. noon-6pm.)

The **National Museum of Women in the Arts,** 1250 New York Ave. NW (783-5000; Metro: Metro Center), houses works by the likes of Mary Cassatt, Georgia O'Keeffe, Lilla Cabot Perry, Frida Kahlo, and Alma Thomas in a former Masonic Temple. The hunt for the museum's permanent collection, which begins on the third floor, is something like an initiation rite. (Open Mon.-Sat. 10am-5pm, Sun. noon-5pm. Suggested donation $3, seniors and students $2.)

White House and Foggy Bottom

The **White House,** 1600 Pennsylvania Ave. NW (456-7041 or 456-6213), isn't Versailles; the President's house, with its simple columns and expansive lawns, seems a compromise between patrician lavishness and democratic simplicity. The President's personal staff works in the West Wing, while the First Lady's cohorts occupy the East Wing. Get a free ticket for a short tour at the ticket booth at the northeast corner of the **Ellipse,** the park due south of the White House. Get in line for a ticket *before 7:30am;* expect a 2½ hour wait after you have ticket in hand (tours Tues.-Sat. 10am-noon; tickets distribution begins at 7:30am). American citizens can arrange a better tour of the White House through their Congressperson.

Shoot 'Em Up!

At the end of the FBI tour, a marksman picks up an FBI-standard revolver and a German HNK-MP5 fully automatic submachine gun and blasts away at sinister cardboard evildoers. Tellingly, the largely American audience always applauds vigorously when the gunfire ends.

The **Renwick Gallery** (357-1300 or 357-2531), at 17th St. and Pennsylvania Ave. NW (Metro: Farragut West), is filled with "American crafts." The first floor's temporary exhibits often show fascinating mixed-media sculptures and constructions by important contemporary artists (open daily 10am-5:30pm; free). Once housed in the Renwick's mansion, the **Corcoran Gallery** (638-3211, 638-1439, or 638-1070) is now in much larger quarters on 17th St. between E St. and New York Ave. NW (Metro: Farragut West), and displays American artists such as John Singer Sargent, Mary Cassatt, and Winslow Homer. The gallery's temporary exhibits are on the cutting edge of contemporary art. (Open Wed. and Fri.-Mon. 10am-5pm, Thurs. 10am-9pm. Suggested donation $3, families $5, students and seniors $1, under 12 free.)

The **National Academy of Sciences** (334-2000), 21st and C St. NW, holds scientific and medical exhibits. Pay homage to the statue of Albert Einstein outside, and note that the man who formulated the Theory of Relativity seems to be wearing Tevas (open Mon.-Fri. 8:30am-5pm).

Above Rock Creek Parkway, the **John F. Kennedy Center for the Performing Arts** (467-4600), off 25th St. and New Hampshire Ave. NW (Metro: Foggy Bottom-GWU), rises like a marble sarcophagus. Built in the late 60s, the center boasts four major stages and a film theater. The flag-decked Hall of States and Hall of Nations lead to the Grand Foyer, which could swallow the Washington Monument with room to spare. An unsavory 7-ft. bronze bust of JFK stares up at 18 Swedish chandeliers. In the Opera House, snowflake-shaped chandeliers require 1735 electric light bulbs. (Open daily 10am-midnight. Free tours 10am-1pm, every 15min.)

Georgetown

When Archbishop John Carroll learned where the new capital would be built, he rushed to found **Georgetown University,** at 37th and O St., which opened in 1789 as the U.S.'s first Catholic institution of higher learning. Students live, study, and party in the townhouses lining the streets near the university. Georgetown's basketball team, the **Hoyas,** are perennial contenders for the national college championship. Buy tickets through TicketMaster (432-7328), the campus Ticket Office (687-4692), or Athletic Department (687-2449).

Philip Johnson's 1963 gallery, **Dumbarton Oaks,** 1703 32nd St. NW (339-6401 or 342-3212), between R and S St., holds a collection of beautifully-displayed carvings, tools, and other art from the Aztec and Mayan civilizations. In 1944, the Dumbarton Oaks Conference, held in the Music Room, helped write the United Nations charter (open Tues.-Sun. 2-5pm; suggested donation $1). Save at least 1 hr. for the Edenic Gardens. (Open daily April-Oct. 2-6pm, Nov.-March 2-5pm. Admission $3, seniors and children $2; Nov.-March free.)

Retired from commercial use since the 1800s, the **Chesapeake & Ohio Canal** (301-299-3613) extends 185 mi. from Georgetown to Cumberland, MD. The benches under the trees around 30th St. make a prime city lunch spot.

Dupont Circle

Dupont Circle used to be called Washington's most diverse neighborhood; then it became expensive. Nevertheless, the Circle and its environs remain a haven for Washington's artsy, international, and gay communities. Unless otherwise stated, the closest Metro to these sites is Dupont Circle. Massachusetts Ave. between Dupont Circle and Observatory Circle is also called **Embassy Row.** Identify an embassy by the national coat-of-arms or flag out front. The **Art Gallery District** is bounded by Connecticut Ave., Florida Ave., and Q St. More than 25 galleries (most of them on R St.) exhibit here. Call 232-3610 for more info.

The **Phillips Collection,** 1600 21st St. (387-2151), at Q St. NW, was the first museum of modern art in the U.S. Everyone gapes at Auguste Renoir's masterpiece *Luncheon of the Boating Party,* in the Renoir room. Among the other few permanent exhibitions are the Rothko room and the Klee room. A stroll up the annex and down through original mansion is a delightful parade of Delacroix, Matisses, Van Goghs, Mondrians, Degas, Mirós, Gris, Kandinskys, Turners, Courbets, Daumiers,

Prendergasts, O'Keeffes, and Hoppers—to name a few. (Open Tues.-Wed. and Fri.-Sat. 10am-5pm, Thurs. 10am-8:30pm, Sun. noon-5pm. Admission Sat.-Sun. $6.50, students and seniors $3.25, under 18 free. Tues.-Fri. admission by contribution.)

Anderson House, 2118 Massachusetts Ave. NW (785-2040), retains the robber-baron decadence of U.S. ambassador Larz Anderson, who built it in 1902-5. The Society of the Cincinnati makes this mansion its home base (open Tues.-Sat. 1-4pm; free). Flags line the entrance to the **Islamic Center,** 2551 Massachusetts Ave. NW (332-8343), a brilliant white building within which stunning designs stretch to the tips of spired ceilings. No shorts; women must cover their heads, arms, and legs. (Open daily 10:30am-5pm. Donation requested.)

Upper Northwest

Legend has it that the word "pandemonium" entered the vernacular when the first giant pandas left China for **Washington's National Zoological Park** (673-4800) as a gift from Mao to Nixon. After years of unsuccessful attempts to birth a baby panda in captivity, Ling-Ling died tragically; her life-mate Hsing-Hsing remains in the Panda House. The zoo spreads east from Connecticut Ave. a few blocks uphill from the Woodley Park-Zoo Metro; follow the crowds to the entrance at 3000 Connecticut Ave. NW. Steep forested paths and flat walks near the entrance pass plenty of outdoor exhibits in fields and cages, which visitors seeking the big attractions often ignore. Valley Trail (marked with blue bird tracks) connects the bird and sealife exhibits, while the red Olmsted Walk (marked with elephant feet) links land-animal houses. (Open daily 8am-8pm, Oct.-April 8am-6pm; buildings open daily 9am-6pm, Sept.-March 9am-4:30pm. Free.)

The **Washington National Cathedral** (537-6200 or 364-6616), at Massachusetts and Wisconsin Ave. NW (Metro: Tenleytown, then take the #30, 32, 34 or 36 bus toward Georgetown; or walk up Cathedral Ave. from the equidistant Woodley Park-Zoo Metro), took over 80 years (1907-90) to build, though the cathedral's interior spaces have been in use for decades. Rev. Martin Luther King, Jr. preached his last Sunday sermon from the Canterbury pulpit; more recently, the Dalai Lama spoke here. Take the elevator to the Pilgrim Observation Gallery and see Washington from the highest vantage point in the city (open daily 10am-3:15pm). Angels, gargoyles, and other grotesques glower outside. (Tours Mon.-Sat. 10am-3:15pm every 15 min., Sun. 12:30-2:45pm. Suggested donation $2, children $1.) The **National Arboretum** (245-2726), 24th and R St. NE (Metro: Stadium-Armory, then a B2 bus), is the U.S.'s living library of trees and flowers. Go berserk over the arboretum's world-class stock of *bonsai*. (Open daily 8am-5pm; July-March Mon.-Fri. 8am-5pm, Sat.-Sun. 10am-5pm. Bonsai collection open daily 10am-3:30pm. Free.)

Arlington, VA and Alexandria, VA

The silence of **Arlington National Cemetery** (692-0931; Metro: Arlington Cemetery) honors those who sacrificed their lives in war. The 612 acres of hills and tree-lined avenues hold the bodies of U.S. military veterans from five-star generals to unknown soldiers. Before you enter the main gate, get a map from the visitors center. The Kennedy Gravesites hold the remains of President John F. Kennedy, his brother Robert F. Kennedy, and his wife Jacqueline Kennedy Onassis. The Eternal Flame flickers above JFK's simple memorial stone. The Tomb of the Unknowns honors all servicemen who died fighting for the United States and is guarded by delegations from the Army's Third Infantry (changing of the guard every ½-hr., Oct.-March every hr. on the hr.). Robert E. Lee's home, **Arlington House,** overlooks the cemetery. Enter the pastel-peach mansion at the front door; tours are self-guided. Head down Custis Walk in front of Arlington House and exit the cemetery through Weitzel Gate to get to the **Iwo Jima Memorial,** based on Joe Rosenthal's Pulitzer Prize-winning photo of six Marines straining to raise the U.S. flag on Mount Suribachi (cemetery open April-Sept. daily 8am-7pm, Oct.-May daily 8am-5pm).

The **Pentagon** (695-1776), the world's largest office building, shows just how huge military bureaucracy can get (Metro: Pentagon). To take the guided tour, sign

MID-ATLANTIC

in, walk through a metal detector, get X-rayed, and show proper photo identification (passports for non-U.S. citizens). The guide keeps the pace of the tour brisk; hey, it's like a military music video. (Tours every ½-hr. Mon.-Fri. 9:30am-3:30pm, Oct.-May no tours at 10:30am, 1:30, and 3pm. Free.)

Old Town Alexandria (Metro: King St.) has cobblestone streets, brick sidewalks, over 1000 restored old facades, tall ships, and quaint shops. Come here to shop, stroll, and dine. A newly renovated info center, the **Lyceum,** 201 S. Washington St. (703-838-4994), has exhibitions and audio-visual presentations on historic Alexandria (open Mon.-Sat. 10am-5pm, Sun. 1-5pm). George Washington and Robert E. Lee prayed at **Christ Church,** 119 N. Washington St. (703-549-1450), at Cameron St., a red brick Colonial building with a domed steeple. Restored to its 18th-century good looks, **Gadsby's Tavern,** 134 N. Royal St. (838-4242), allows you to see how budget travelers did it 200 years ago, when as many as 4 people would be assigned to a bed. (Open Oct.-March Tues.-Sat. 10am-4pm, Sun. 1-4pm. Admission $3, children 11-17 $1.) See one of America's first indoor kitchens at **Robert E. Lee's Boyhood Home,** 607 Oronoco St. (548-8454), near Asaph St. (open Mon.-Sat. 10am-4pm, Sun. 1-4pm; $3, students 10-17 $1). The **George Washington Masonic National Memorial,** 101 Callahan Dr. (683-2007), has a museum and a lofty Greek-temple-style portico that supports a steep pyramid (open daily 9am-5pm).

Mount Vernon (703-780-2000), in Fairfax County, VA (Metro: Huntington, then take the Fairfax Connector 101 bus at the north end of the station), was George Washington's final estate. To drive, take the Beltway (I-495) to the George Washington Parkway and follow it to Mount Vernon. A key to the Bastille, a gift from the Marquis de Lafayette, is displayed in the main hall. Upstairs is the bedroom of George and Martha Washington; a gravel path outside leads to their tomb. The graveless slave burial ground is nearby. The estate's fields once grew corn, wheat, tobacco, and marijuana. (Open daily April-Aug. 8am-5pm; Sept.-Oct. and March 9am-5pm; Nov.-Feb. 9am-4pm. $8, over 62 $7.50, children 6-11 $4.)

ENTERTAINMENT AND NIGHTLIFE

Theater and Film

The **Kennedy Center** (416-8000), at 25th St. and New Hampshire Ave., offers ubiquitous performing-arts spaces. Tickets get expensive ($22-47), but most productions offer ½-price tickets the day of performance to students, seniors, military, and the disabled; call 467-4600 for details. Free events dot the Kennedy calendar. The prestigious **Shakespeare Theater,** 450 7th St. NW (393-2700; Metro: Archives-Navy Memorial), at the Lansburgh on Pennsylvania Ave., puts on...Shakespeare. Standing-room tickets ($10) are available two hours before curtain. Thespians thrive in Washington's **14th St. theater district,** where tiny repertory companies explore and experiment with enjoyable results. *City Paper* covers this scene. **Woolly Mammoth,** 1401 Church St. NW (393-3939), **Studio Theater,** 1333 P St. NW (332-3300), and **The Source Theater,** 1835 14th St. NW (462-1073), are all in this borderline neighborhood near Dupont Circle (tickets $12-29).

Key Theatre, 1222 Wisconsin Ave. NW (333-5100), near Prospect St. (1 block north of M St.) features first-run art films and subtitled foreign films. ($6.50, over 65 $4, children $3, matinees $3.50.) If the Key isn't showing what you're looking for, the **Outer Circle,** 4849 Wisconsin Ave. NW (244-3116), across the street from Safeway (Metro: Tenleytown), probably is. ($7.25, seniors and children $4.25. All shows before 6pm $4.25.)

Classical Music

Washington, D.C. is home to the well-respected **National Symphony Orchestra (NSO),** which performs in the **Kennedy Center.** Tickets are normally expensive ($18-45), but ½-price tickets are available. The NSO also gives concerts in celebration of Memorial Day, the Fourth of July, and Labor Day. The **Washington Opera** (416-

7890) also calls the Kennedy Center home. For a schedule of free events, call 467-4600. Check the *Washington Post's* "Weekend" section for more info.

Jazz

A free lunchtime summer jazz series takes place downtown at the **Corcoran Gallery** (638-3211), 17th St. between E St. and New York Ave. NW, in the Hammer Auditorium, every Wed. at 12:30pm (Metro: Farragut West). **Madame's Organ,** 2003 18th St. NW (667-5370), near Florida Ave. in Adams-Morgan, hosts eclectic clientele who can only be described as fab. This blues club features live music nearly every night, with Sat. reserved for "a DJ from outer space." (Open Sun.-Thurs. 6pm-2am, Fri.-Sat. 6pm-3am. Cover $3. Drafts $2.50, mixed drinks $3.50.) **Vegas Lounge,** 1415 P St. NW (483-3971), four blocks east of Dupont Circle (Metro: Dupont Circle), lights up the scene with professional jam sessions Tues.-Wed. (otherwise known as "open-mike nights," but these guys play like pros) and bands Thurs.-Sat. (cover $5-9) that churn out an assortment of styles. The manager, "Dr. Blues," enthusiastically describes the sound as Chicago-meets-New Orleans. Happy hour (Tues.-Sat.) offers $1 off beers. (Open Tues.-Thurs. 7pm-2am, Fri.-Sat. 7pm-3am.)

Bars and Other Live Music

If you don't mind a young crowd, squeeze into a *local* rock-and-roll show; the Washington, D.C. punk scene is one of the nation's finest. To see what's up with local bands, check *City Paper.* The newest of Washington, D.C.'s live music venues, colossal **Capitol Ballroom,** 1015 Half St. SE (703-549-7625; Metro: Navy Yard), boasts an impressive line-up of big-name alternative bands and small-name, big-draw local groups. Tickets $5-35, available from TicketMaster (432-7328); doors open at 7pm. In summer on Saturday and Sunday, jazz and R&B shows occupy the outdoor **Carter-Barron Amphitheater** (426-6837), in Rock Creek Park up 16th St. and Colorado Ave. NW (tickets about $16). From late June to August, rock, punk, and metal preempt soccer-playing at **Fort Reno Park** (282-1063), at Chesapeake and Belt St. NW above Wisconsin Ave. (Metro: Tenley Circle).

The Tombs, 1226 36th St. NW (337-6668), at Prospect St.; entrance to the right of 1789 Restaurant. Designers for the movie *St. Elmo's Fire* based a set on this bar. Georgetown students as well as some high profile clientele (Clinton, Beau Bridges, Chris O'Donnell) drop in for burgers and beer. $2-3 cover on Sun. nights (DJ and dancing). Mixed drinks $3.25 and up. Open Mon.-Thurs. 11:30am-2am, Fri. 11:30am-3am, Sat. 11am-3am, Sun. 9:30am-2am.

The Bayou, 3135 K St. NW (333-2897), under the Whitehurst Freeway in Georgetown; take any #30 Metrobus to M St. and walk 2 blocks down Wisconsin Ave. Music varies from metal and rock to blues and jazz. Comedy Sat. 6:30pm. Most shows 18+; the rest all ages. Cover $3-20. Reggae on Sun.; Mon. is Grateful Dead night ($4). Box office open 8pm-midnight. Open Sun.-Thurs. 8pm-1:30am, Fri. 8pm-2:30am, Sat. 6:30pm-2:30am, but call ahead; no band means no Bayou.

Crow Bar, 1006 20th St. NW (223-2972). Metro: Farragut North or Farragut West. Everyone from bikers to businessmen stops by for Crow Beer ($3.75, $3 during happy hour). The "Forbidden Planet" space-age dance room (open Thurs.-Sat. 9pm-close) heightens the off-beat decor. Two floors; a game room featuring foosball and pool; and a patio. Happy hour 4-7pm. Open Mon.-Thurs. 11:30am-1:45am, Fri. 11:30am-2:45am, Sat. noon-2:45am, Sun. noon-1:45am.

Brickskeller, 1523 22nd St. NW (293-1885), between P and Q St. Metro: Dupont Circle. *The* place for beer. If you drank a different beer every day, it would still take you nearly two years to work your way through Brickskeller's list of over 600 brews—the world's largest beer selection. The saloon's original "beer-tails" are mixed drinks made with beer, like the house classic Black Velvet (stout and champagne, $4.50) or the Ruddy Mary (beer instead of vodka, $3.25). Bi-monthly beer-tasting events, $24 for the night. Open Mon.-Thurs. 11:30am-2am, Fri. 11:30am-3am, Sat. 6pm-3am, Sun. 6pm-2am.

Planet Fred, 1221 Connecticut Ave. NW (331-3733 or 466-2336). A trip to Planet Fred may feel like an alien experience. Occasional live bands pack in wall-to-wall punks, while Wed. night's "Drag Freak Bingo" draws a zany bunch ($7 cover). "Female Trouble" every other Sun. is an ever-popular lesbian dance party. Mon. offers free salsa lessons (7-9pm) and $2.75 margaritas. Thurs. is DJ dancing and $10 all-you-can-drink. Happy hour Mon.-Fri. 4-7:30pm, includes $1.50 drafts and $1.75 rails. Open Sun.-Thurs. 11:30am-2am, Fri. 11:30am-3am, Sat. 8pm-3am.

9:30 club, 815 V St. NW (393-0930 or 265-0930). Metro: U St.-Cardozo; use the Vermont Ave. exit. Washington, D.C.'s most established local and alternative rock venue. Occasionally $3 to see three local bands; $5-20 for nationally known acts, which often sell out weeks in advance. Crowd ages and styles vary according to concert line-up (under-21 admitted and hand-stamped). Cash-only box office open Mon.-Fri. 1-6pm, until 11pm on show-days, Sat.-Sun. 6-11pm. Door time Sun.-Thurs. 7:30pm-midnight, Fri.-Sat. 9pm-2am. 50¢ surcharge for advance tickets from 9:30 club box office. Tickets also available from ProTix (800-955-5566).

Asylum in Exile, 1210 U St. NW (319-9353 or 232-9354). Metro: U St.-Cardozo. An alternative to Washington, D.C.'s bigger and badder band clubs. The death-goth decor doubles as an intimate setting, with DJ dance beats and an outdoor patio. Bands Wed.-Fri.; acoustic music Wed. for no cover. $3 cover on Thurs., $5 on Fri. When there's no band, there's still drinking and dancing. Nightly specials 8-11pm, with varying $2 pints and $2 Rolling Rock pitchers on Tues. 18+. Open Sun.-Thurs. 8pm-2am, Fri.-Sat. 8pm-3am.

Oxford Tavern "Zoo Bar," 3000 Connecticut Ave. NW (232-4225), across the street from the zoo. Metro: Woodley Park-Zoo. Washington's oldest saloon with a cheery wildlife mural and a bright neon subtitle, but Steely Dan and Duke Ellington are still on the jukebox (so everything is okay). Tourists and locals mix and mingle at happy hour (Mon.-Fri. 3-7pm) and chug $1.50 drafts, $2.50 rails, and $1.75 domestics. A DJ plays on Fri. nights, and live jazz, rock, and blues bands rock Tues.-Thurs. and Sat. Open Sun.-Thurs. 9:30am-2am, Fri.-Sat. 9am-3am.

Bardo, 2000 Wilson Blvd. (703-527-9399). Metro: Court House. One block east (downhill) from the Metro. This is the bah where William Kennedy Smith got a beatin' from a bounsah. Hugely popular 20-something haunt is the self-proclaimed "largest microbrewery on the continent." Happy hour (weekdays before 8pm and all day Sun.) offer $1.50 mugs and $2 pints of Bardo beer. Billiard room with 24 tables opens daily at 5pm. Free brewery tours Thurs. 7pm. Open Mon.-Fri. 11:30am-2am, Sat. 1pm-2am, Sun. 4:30pm-2am.

Dance Clubs

Tracks, 1111 1st St. SE (488-3320). Metro: Navy Yard. The hottest dance club in Washington, D.C. Two dance floors, three bars, a patio, an outdoor volleyball court, and a set of bleachers overlooking the main dance floor (all packed into an old warehouse) ensure that there's something for every type of club-goer to do. Thurs. is college night: alternative youth with baggy pants and small knapsacks pay the $5 cover to enjoy the open bar 9-10:30pm. Fri.'s music is deep house with no cover 8-9pm, $5 9-10pm, $8-10 after 10pm; bar serves $1 drinks and $4 pitchers until midnight in the summer. Sat. is gay. Sun. brings R&B and hip-hop with a $2 cover after 7pm. Both are free and run 4-8pm. At 8pm, the club opens for an evening of house beats with a $3 cover until 9pm, $3-5 9-11pm, and $5 after 11pm. All drinks $2.25. Doors open at 8pm; no cover before 9pm, $3 after. Open Thurs.-Fri. at 9pm, Sat. 8pm, Sun. 7pm; no set closing time. Always 18+.

Bent, upstairs at 1344 U St. NW (986-6364), near 13th St. Metro: U St.-Cardozo. Big Dali-esque clocks melt off the roof. Happy hour Thurs.-Fri. 6-9pm: free fondue and salsa, $2 rails, and $1.50 domestic beers. Wed.-Sat. DJ 70s-90s disco with a $2 cover after 11pm. Sun. 70s funk soul with no cover but $7 all-you-can-drink. Open Wed. and Sun. 9pm-2am, Thurs. 6pm-2am, Fri. 6pm-3am, Sat. 9pm-3am.

Club Heaven and **Club Hell,** 2327 18th St. NW (667-4355), near Columbia Rd. Hell is downstairs, Heaven is upstairs—the ground-floor Italian café must be *il Purgatorio*. In Hell, smoke blurs the gold tables and loud music emanates from yellow-backlit masks. Heaven looks like an old townhouse, but the dance floor throbs to pounding beats and the back patio is crowded with timid souls who can't take the noise. Thurs. 80s dance party in Heaven with $4 cover. No cover other nights. Domestic beer $3, imports $3.75; $1 off during happy hour (daily 6-8:30pm in

Hell). Dancing starts about 10pm. Heaven open Sun.-Thurs. 10pm-2am, Fri.-Sat. 10pm-3am. Hell open Tues.-Thurs. 9pm-2am, Fri.-Sat. 6pm-3am.

Gay Bars and Clubs

The *Washington Blade* is the best source of gay news, reviews, and club listings; published every Friday, it's available in virtually every storefront in Dupont Circle. **Tracks,** 111 First St. SE (488-3320; Metro: Navy Yard), becomes the hottest gay dance club in Washington, D.C. on Sat. nights.

The Circle Bar, 1629 Connecticut Ave. NW (462-5575). Metro: Dupont Circle. A three-in-one social emporium with a ground-floor restaurant, a top-floor bar, and an underground dance club. Happy hour Mon.-Fri. 5-9pm, drops Bacardi and Skyy Vodka prices to $2, while Sat.-Sun. happy hour 11am-10pm, keeps all vodkas at $2. Wed. is ladies' night. Open Sun.-Thurs. 11am-2am, Fri.-Sat. 11am-3am.

Hung Jury, 1819 H St. NW (279-3212). Metro: Farragut West. Believe it or not, no one's hung here. Lesbians from all over Washington, D.C. spend their weekend nights bopping to Top 40. $5 cover. Men must be accompanied by a woman to enter; gay men are admitted but occasionally must "prove" they're gay. Shooter $1. "Grab bags" (whatever a bartender pulls out of a box) $1.50. Open Fri.-Sat. 9pm-3:30am.

J.R.'s, 1519 17th St. NW (328-0090). Metro: Dupont Circle. Upscale but down-home brick and varnished-wood bar full of "guppies" (gay urban professionals). Happy hour Mon.-Thurs. 2-8pm, Fri. 2-9pm: $2 domestic bottled beer, Sat. noon-8pm and Sun. all day: 75¢ vodka. S&M ("Stand and Model") at night. Mon.-Thurs. 3pm-2am, Fri. 2pm-3am, Sat. noon-3am, Sun. noon-2am.

SPORTS

Opportunities for sports addicts abound in the Washington, D.C. area. The **Georgetown Hoyas** (college basketball) pack the **USAir Arena** (formerly the Capital Centre). The Hoyas won it all in 1987. Their professional counterparts, the **Bullets,** also fire away here, as do the **Capitals** (hockey). (Call USAir Arena at 301-350-3400, located between Landover Rd. and Central Ave. in Landover, MD. Take the Beltway (I-95) to Exits 15A or 17A and follow signs.) The **Redskins** won the Super Bowl in 1982, 1987, and 1992, and fans flock religiously to **RFK Stadium** (547-9077) to see them, as well as to root for the **Washington, D.C. United,** the District's new Major League Soccer (MLS) team. Call the **Department of Recreation** (673-7660 or 673-7671) for info on public pools, biking and hiking trails, jogging, and ice skating.

Virginia

If Virginia seems obsessed with its past, it has good reason: many of America's formative experiences—the white settlement of North America, the shameful legacy of the slave trade, American independence, the aristocratic farsightedness of the early U.S., and even the Civil War—all took root in Virginia. English colonists founded Jamestown in 1607; the New World's first black slaves joined them unwillingly 12 years later. While George Washington was still battling Native Americans in the French and Indian War, Thomas Jefferson wrote about religious and political freedom in the colonial capital, Williamsburg. Washington later returned to deal the British a table-turning defeat at Yorktown. Virginian James Madison traveled to Philadelphia in 1787 with drafts of the *Constitution,* and Virginian George Mason led the Bill of Rights campaign. Meanwhile, eastern Virginia's Tidewater aristocracy dominated the state for a century with its culture of slave-dependent plantations—a culture that imploded during the Civil War, when Union and Confederate armies pushed one another around Virginia on the way to Appomattox.

MID-ATLANTIC

While eastern Virginia celebrates its Revolutionary and Confederate history, Shenandoah National Park and the geologically stunning caverns of the west provide a respite from the state's barrage of nostalgia (and heat). The western region is not entirely without history, however; Jefferson's masterpieces (UVA and Monticello, in Charlottesville) and Harpers Ferry provide bastions of culture. Virginia has, for the most part, pulled up its Old Southern roots for a more cosmopolitan existence; Virginia is home to many of Washington, D.C.'s political elite, as plantation life yields to the strong traditional influence of government. Still, Virginia relishes its role as the cradle of American independence and an icon of Southern culture.

PRACTICAL INFORMATION

Capital: Richmond.
Virginia Division of Tourism: 901 E. Byrd St., 19th Floor, Richmond 23219 (804-786-4484 or 800-VISIT-VA/847-4882). **Division of State Parks,** 203 Governor St., Richmond 23219 (804-786-1712).
Time Zone: Eastern. **Postal Abbreviation:** VA.
Sales Tax: 4.5%.

■ Richmond

Once the capital of the rebel Confederacy, Richmond is by no means shy when it comes to its history. Civil War leaders Robert E. Lee and Stonewall Jackson are worshipped through Richmond's museums and restored homes, which showcase anything and everything Confederate. But Richmond is not entirely mired in its own history; indeed, Richmond honors a significant African-American heritage as well, commemorating such figures as entertainer Bill "Bojangles" Robinson, banker Maggie Walker, and tennis Hall-of-Famer Arthur Ashe (see page 242). With districts like the sprawling, residential Fan and formerly industrial Shockoe Bottom, this state capital sports its more inclusive, renovated 20th-century face.

PRACTICAL INFORMATION AND ORIENTATION

Visitor Information: Richmond Visitors Center, 1710 Robin Hood Rd. (358-5511), Exit 78 off I-95/64, in a converted train depot. Helpful 6-min. video introduces the city's attractions. Walking tours and maps of downtown and the metro region. Can also arrange for same-day discounted accommodations. Open Memorial Day-Labor Day daily 9am-7pm; off-season 9am-5pm.
Amtrak: far away at 7519 Staple Mills Rd. (264-9194 or 800-872-7245). To: Washington, D.C. (8 per day, 2hr., $18-23); Williamsburg (8 per day, 1¼hr., $9-10); Virginia Beach (2 per day, 3hr., $16-19, the last third of the trip is on a shuttle); New York City (8 per day, 7hr., $81); Baltimore (5 per day, 3hr., $26-31); Philadelphia (5 per day, 4¾hr., $38-48). Taxi fare to downtown $12. Open 24hr.
Greyhound: 2910 N. Boulevard (254-5910 or 800-231-2222), 2 blocks from downtown; take GRTC bus #24 north. To: Washington, D.C. (16 per day, 2½hr., $10-12); Charlottesville (2 per day, 1½hr., $18); Williamsburg (8 per day, 1hr., $11); Norfolk (10 per day, 3hr., $16); New York City (26 per day, 6½hr., $53); Baltimore (8 per day, 3½hr., $22); Philadelphia (9 per day, 7hr., $40).
Public Transport: Greater Richmond Transit Co., 101 S. Davis Ave. (358-4782). Maps available in the basement of City Hall, 900 E. Broad St., and in the Yellow Pages. Buses infrequently serve most of Richmond, downtown frequently; most leave from Broad St. downtown. Bus #24 goes south to Broad St. and downtown. Fare $1.15, transfers 15¢. Seniors 50¢ during off-peak hours. Free **trolleys** provide dependable, if limited, service to downtown and Shockoe Slip daily 10am-4pm, with an extended Shockoe Slip schedule 5pm-midnight.
Taxi: Veterans Cab Association (329-3333). **Yellow Cab Co.** (222-7300).
Hotlines: Traveler's Aid, 643-0279 or 648-1767. **Rape Crisis Hotline,** 643-0888. **Psychiatric Crisis Intervention,** 648-9224. **Gay Information,** 353-3626. **AIDS/HIV Info.,** 359-4783. Mon.-Fri. 8am-6pm, Sat. noon-5pm, Sun. noon-8pm.
Emergency: 911.

Post Office: 1801 Brook Rd. (775-6133). Open Mon.-Fri. 7am-6pm, Sat. 10am-1pm. **ZIP Code:** 23219. **Area Code:** 804.

Imaginative locals have invented novel names for Richmond's neighborhoods. **Carytown** is an upscale district in the northwest between Thompson St. and the Boulevard. The **Fan,** named for its questionable resemblance to a lady's fan, is bounded by the Boulevard, I-95, Monument Ave., and Virginia Commonwealth University, and harbors many of Richmond's oldest homes. **Jackson Ward,** in the heart of downtown (bounded by Belvedere, Leigh, Broad, and 5th St.), and **Shockoe Slip** and **Shockoe Bottom** to the east, are more urban areas. **Broad St.,** not Main St., is the city's central artery, and the streets that cross it are numbered from west to east. Both I-95, leading north to Washington, D.C., and I-295 encircle the urban section.

ACCOMMODATIONS AND CAMPING

Budget motels cluster on **Williamsburg Rd.,** the edge of town, and along **Midlothian Turnpike,** south of the James River. However, public transport to these areas is infrequent at best. The farther from downtown you stay, the less you pay. The visitors center can reserve accommodations, sometimes at $10-20 discounts.

Massad House Hotel, 11 N. 4th St. (648-2893), five blocks from the capitol, in the commercial downtown area. A 1940s elevator shuttles guests to clean rooms with showers, A/C, and cable TV. Singles $43, doubles $46.

Cadillac Motel, 11418 Washington Hwy. (798-4049), 10mi. from the city. Take I-95 to Exit 89. Sparse rooms with A/C and cable TV. Singles $36, doubles $45.

Executive Inn, 5215 W. Broad St. (288-4011), 3mi. from center of town; take bus #6. Once the Red Carpet Inn, Executive still sports the same red carpet in its grand (by motel standards), slightly faded rooms. Provides A/C, cable TV, and a pool/health club. Singles $43, doubles $45-49. Weekly rate $165.

Pocahontas State Park, 10301 State Park Rd. (796-4255), 10mi. south on Rte. 10 and Rte. 655 in Chesterfield. Offers showers, biking, boating, picnic areas, and a huge pool. Sites $11. No hookups. Pool admission $2.25, ages 3-12 $1.75. For free reservations, call 225-3867 or 800-933-PARK.

FOOD

At once a college town and a Southern capital, Richmond offers cheap student eateries and affordable down-home fare. At the **farmers market,** at N. 17th and E. Main St., pick up fresh fruit, vegetables, meat, or even a pot swine. For student haunts, head for the area around Virginia Commonwealth University (VCU), just west of downtown. For fried apples, grits, and cornbread, try downtown itself.

Coppola's, 2900 W. Cary St. (359-6969). A popular NYC-style deli crowded with happy locals and Italian food. Dinners ($5-7) and fantastic sandwiches ($3-6). Outdoor seating available. Open Mon.-Wed. 10am-8pm, Thurs.-Sat. 10am-9pm.

3rd St. Diner (788-4750), at the corner of 3rd and Main. Old-time locals on the mint-green balcony are served cheap eats—the $2.25 breakfast special (2 eggs, biscuit or toast, and homefries, grits, or Virginia fried apples), or dinner sandwiches ($3-6)—by tattooed waitresses in combat boots. Open 24hr.

Texas-Wisconsin Border Café, 1501 W. Main St. (355-2907). Owned by a pair of art professors, this isn't your typical Tex-Mex place; the walls feature monthly exhibits of local artwork. The cuisine is more traditional, with chili (bowl $4) and fajitas ($8). Open daily 11am-2am.

Oceans, 414 E. Main St. (649-3456), serves excellent, filling breakfasts and lunches. All items under $5. Open daily 7am-2:30pm.

Bottom's Up, 1700 Dock St. (644-4400), at 17th and Cary. This popular hangout serves the best pizza in Richmond ($8, will feed two) and will ply you with drinks after dark (drafts $1.50-3, bottles $2.75-3.25). Open Mon.-Wed. 11:30am-11pm, Thurs. 11:30am-midnight, Fri. 11:30am-2am, Sat. noon-2am, Sun. noon-11pm.

SIGHTS

Ever since Patrick Henry declared "Give me liberty or give me death" in Richmond's **St. John's Church,** 2401 E. Broad St. (648-5015), this river city has been quoting, memorializing, and bronzing its heroes; actors recreate the famous 1775 speech each Sunday (late May to early Sept., 2pm). You must take a tour to see the church. (Tours Mon.-Sat. 10am-3:30pm, Sun. 1-3:30pm; $3, seniors $2, students under 18 $1.) The Thomas Jefferson-designed **State Capitol** (786-4344), at 9th and Grace St., is a Neoclassical masterpiece that served as the home of the Confederate government during the Civil War and today houses the only statue of George Washington that he actually posed for (open daily 9am-5pm; Dec.-March Mon.-Sat. 9am-5pm, Sun. 1-5pm). **Monument Avenue,** a boulevard lined with trees, gracious old houses, and towering statues of Confederate heroes, is a virtual Richmond memory lane. Robert E. Lee faces his beloved South; Stonewall Jackson scowls at the Yankees. The recently commissioned statue of local hero Arthur Ashe provides an anomalous, though inspiring, addition to the avenue.

The **Court End** district stretches north and east of the capitol to Clay and College St. and guards Richmond's most distinctive historical sights. The **Museum of the Confederacy,** 1201 E. Clay St. (649-1861), is the world's largest Confederate artifact collection. The main floor leads visitors through the military history of the Great War of Northern Aggression, the basement displays guns and over 500 flags of the Confederacy, and the top floor houses temporary exhibits. The museum also runs 1-hr. tours through the **White House of the Confederacy,** next door. Statues of Tragedy, Comedy, and Irony grace the White House's entrance. (Museum open Mon.-Sat. 10am-5pm, Sun. 1-5pm. Tours of the White House Mon., Wed., and Fri.-Sat. 10:30am-4:30pm, Tues. and Thurs. 11:30am-4:30pm, Sun. 1:15-4:30pm. Museum $5, seniors $4, students $3, under 6 free; White House $5.50, seniors $4.50, students $3.50; for both: $8, $5, $3.50.)

The **Valentine Museum,** 1015 E. Clay St. (649-0711), enamors visitors with exhibits on local and Southern social and cultural history, plus the South's largest collection of costumes and textiles. Admission price includes a tour of the Neoclassical **Wickham-Valentine House** (built in 1812), next door. (Museum open Mon.-Sat. 10am-5pm, Sun. noon-5pm. House tours on the hr., 10am-4pm. $5, seniors and students $4, children 7-12 $3.) Combination tickets to the Museum of the Confederacy, White House of the Confederacy, Valentine Museum, and **John Marshall House,** 818 E. Marshall St. (648-7998), which contains period and family furnishings of the Chief Justice, are available. ($11, seniors and students $10, ages 7-12 $5; tickets available at any of the sights, all of which are within walking distance of each other. John Marshall House is open Tues.-Sat. 10am-5pm, Sun. 1-5pm.)

East of the Capitol, follow your tell-tale heart to the **Edgar Allan Poe Museum,** 1914 E. Main St. (648-5523). Poe memorabilia stuffs five buildings, including the

---

Arthur Ashe: A True Ace

On July 11, 1996, the city of Richmond unveiled a stirring memorial to Arthur Ashe, depicting the AIDS victim with a tennis racket in one hand and books in the other, surrounded by smiling children. The statue stands in stark contrast to such traditional Southern heroes as Jeb Stuart, Robert E. Lee, and Jefferson Davis. One of the most famous black tennis players in history, Ashe was a pioneer in bringing tennis clinics to the inner city. His prowess on the court, leading to a Wimbledon victory in 1975, was matched by his humanism off of it. The memorial is located at the intersection of Monument Ave. and Roseneath Rd.

Stone House, the oldest extant structure within the original city boundaries. (Open Tues.-Sat. 10am-4pm, Sun.-Mon. noon-4pm. $5, seniors $4, students $3.)

Four blocks from Monument Ave. and N. Boulevard rests the Southeast's largest art museum, the **Virginia Museum of Fine Arts,** 2800 Grove Ave. (367-0844). The Museum contains pieces ranging from ancient Egyptian works to Picasso and Warhol to Fabergé's ornate Russian eggs. (Open Tues.-Sat. 11am-5pm, Thurs. 11am-8pm in the North Wing Galleries, Sun. 1-5pm. $4 donation requested.)

The **Maggie L. Walker National Historic Site,** 110½ E. Leigh St. (780-1380), commemorates the founder and president of the oldest surviving black-operated U.S. bank. Physically disabled and the daughter of an ex-slave, Walker spent her life fighting for black women's rights (tours Wed.-Sun. 9am-5pm; free). The **Black History Museum and Cultural Center of Virginia,** 00 (yes, 00) Clay St. (780-9093), has rotating exhibits (open Tues. and Thurs.-Sat. 11am-4pm; $2, children $1).

To the west lies the **Science Museum of Virginia,** 2500 W. Broad St. (367-1080). The museum houses more than 250 hands-on exhibits, and most prominently, the **Universe Theater,** which doubles as a planetarium and an Omni theater. (Museum open Mon.-Sat. 9:30am-5pm, Sun. noon-5pm. Planetarium and Omni shows daily; call for times. $4.50, seniors and children 4-17 $4. $2-3 extra for shows.)

The **Shockoe Slip** district from Main, Canal, and Cary St. between 10th and 14th St., features fancy shops in restored and newly painted warehouses, but few bargains. **Cary St.,** from the Boulevard to Thompson St., is crowded with vintage clothing stores, antique boutiques, and entertaining crowds.

ENTERTAINMENT AND NIGHTLIFE

One of Richmond's most entertaining and delightful diversions is the **Byrd Theater,** 2908 W. Cary St. (353-9911). Movie buffs buy tickets from a tuxedoed agent, are ushered into an opulent, chandeliered theater, and treated to a pre-movie concert, played on an ornate and cavernous Wurlitzer organ that rises out of the floor. All shows 99¢; on Saturdays the balcony opens for $1 extra. **Free concerts** abound near the farmers market at N. 17th and E. Main St. in the summer; check *Style Weekly,* a free magazine available at the visitors center. Baseball fans can watch the minor-league **Richmond Braves** (Atlanta's AAA affiliate) for a fraction of major-league prices (field boxes $7, reserved seats $5, general $4). Nightlife enlivens Shockoe Slip and sprinkles itself in a less hectic manner throughout the Fan. In addition to the following nightlife venues, the **Texas-Wisconsin Border Café** (see above) rolls up its rug to become a popular bar.

Tobacco Company Club, 1201 E. Cary St. (782-9555). This local institution caters to 25+ professionals, with dance tunes, hip-hop, and a happy hour (upstairs, 5-7pm): cheap beer and a free buffet. Open Tues.-Sat. 8pm-2am; rarely a cover.

Matt's British Pub and Comedy Club, 1045 12th St. (643-5653), pours out a bit of Brit wit Fri. at 8 and 10:30pm and Sat. at 8 and 11pm. Microbrews and drafts $2.75-$3.60, rails $3.40. Open Mon.-Sat. 1:30pm-2am, Sun. 4pm-2am.

Penny Lane Pub, 207 N. 7th St. (780-1682). Irish tavern with live bands nightly—traditional Irish music on Fri. Cuisine includes Bangers 'n' Mash ($10), fish 'n' chips ($8), and Cornish pastries ($10). Open Mon.-Sat. 11am-2am, Sun. 4pm-2am.

Flood Zone, 11 S. 18th St. (643-6006), south of Shockoe Slip, hosts both big name and off-beat local rock bands. Ticket office open Tues.-Fri. 10am-6pm. Tickets $6-20, depending upon the show.

Paramyd, 1008 North Blvd. (358-3838). One of Richmond's few gay bars is a hopping gay dance club on weekends. Happy hour Mon.-Fri. 6-9pm. Drafts $2. Fri.-Sat. cover varies, Sun. $4.

■ Williamsburg

At the end of the 17th century, when women were women and men wore wigs, Williamsburg was the capital of Virginia. During the Revolutionary War, the capital moved to Richmond, along with much of Williamsburg's grandeur. The depressed city was rescued in 1926 by John D. Rockefeller, Jr., who showered the area with money and restored a large chunk of the historical district as a colonial village.

Street-side performers, evenings of 18th-century theater, and militia revues are just part of everyday business in Williamsburg. But although the ex-capital claims to be a faithfully restored version of its 18th-century self, don't look for dirt roads, open sewers, or African slaves. Williamsburg also prides itself on being home to **William and Mary,** the second-oldest college in the United States.

PRACTICAL INFORMATION AND ORIENTATION

Visitor Information: Williamsburg Area Convention & Visitors Bureau, 201 Penniman Rd. (253-0192), ½mi. northwest of the transportation center. Free *Visitor's Guide to Virginia's Historic Triangle.* Open Mon.-Fri. 8:30am-5pm. **Tourist Visitors Center,** 102 Information Dr. (800-447-8679), 1mi. northeast of the train station. Tickets and transportation to Colonial Williamsburg. Maps and guides to historic district, including a guide for the disabled. Info on prices and discounts on Virginia sights. Open daily 8:30am-8pm.

Transportation Center: 408 N. Boundary St. across from the fire station at the end of the road. **Amtrak,** (229-8750 or 800-872-7245). To: New York (1 per day, 7½hr., $56); Washington, D.C. (1 per day, 3½hr., $29-34); Philadelphia (1 per day, 6hr., $40); Baltimore (1 per day, 5hr., $33-40); Richmond (1 per day, 1½hr., $10-12). Open Tues.-Thurs. 7:15am-2:45pm, Fri.-Mon. 7:15am-9:30pm. **Greyhound/ Trailways,** (229-1460). Ticket office open Mon.-Fri. 8:30am-6pm, Sat.-Sun. 8:30am-2pm. To: Richmond (7 per day, 1hr., $11); Norfolk (8 per day, 2hr., $11); Washington, D.C. (7 per day, 4hr., $29); Baltimore (via Washington, D.C.; 7 per day, 4hr., $48); Virginia Beach (4 per day, 2½hr., $15). **James City County Transit (JCCT),** (220-1621). Service along Rte. 60, from Merchants Sq. in the historic district west to Williamsburg Pottery or east past Busch Gardens. Operates Mon.-Sat. 6:15am-6:20pm. Fare $1 plus 25¢ per zone-change.

Bike Rentals: Bikes Unlimited, 759 Scotland St. (229-4620), rents for $10 per day, with $5 deposit (includes lock). Open Mon.-Fri. 9am-7pm, Sat. 9am-5pm, Sun. noon-4pm. **Bikesmith of Williamsburg,** 515 York Rd. (229-9858), rents single-speed bikes at $8.50 per 4hr., $11.50 per day. Open Mon.-Sat. 10am-6pm.

Taxi: Williamsburg Limousine Service (877-0279). To Busch Gardens or Carter's Grove $6 roundtrip. To Jamestown and Yorktown $15 roundtrip. Call between 8:30am-10pm.

Emergency: 911.

Post Office: 425 N. Boundary St. (229-4668). Open Mon.-Fri. 8am-5pm, Sat. 10am-2pm. **ZIP Codes:** 23185 (Williamsburg), 23690 (Yorktown), and 23081 (Jamestown). **Area Code:** 804 (Hampton Rd. peninsula area: 757).

Williamsburg lies 50 mi. southeast of Richmond between **Jamestown** (10 mi. away) and **Yorktown** (14 mi. away). The Colonial Parkway, which connects the three towns, has no commercial buildings along its route, helping to preserve an unspoiled atmosphere.

ACCOMMODATIONS AND CAMPING

Budget motels line Rte. 60 west and Rte. 31 south. Avoid the expensive hotels operated by the Colonial Williamsburg Foundation. A cheaper, friendlier, and more comfortable alternative is guest houses. All expect you to call ahead.

Only five minutes from the historic district, **Lewis Guest House,** 809 Lafayette St. (229-6116), rents several comfortable rooms, including an upstairs unit with a private entrance, kitchen, and bath as a single ($25) or double ($30). The friendly proprietor keeps a yappy dog. A few doors down is the **Carter Guest House,** 903 Lafayette St. (229-1117). Two spacious rooms each have two beds and a shared bath. (Singles $25, doubles $26-30.) Be forewarned: Mrs. Carter —a woman of very traditional Southern values—will not let unmarried men and women sleep in the same bed. Hotels around the historic district, especially chain- or foundation-owned hotels, are not cheap. The **Southern Inn,** 1220 Richmond Rd. (229-8913), a 10-minute walk from William & Mary, has clean, ordinary rooms with colonial-looking façades and a pool (singles and doubles $35; office open daily 8am-1pm, 4-11pm).

Several campsites blanket the area. **Anvil Campgrounds,** 5243 Moretown Rd. (565-2300), 3mi. north of the Colonial Williamsburg Information Center on Rte. 60, boasts 73 shaded sites, a swimming pool, bathhouse, recreational hall, and store. (Sites $15, with water and electricity $23, full hookup $25.)

FOOD AND DRINK

Most of the authentic-looking "taverns" are overpriced and packed with sweaty tourists. For a fraction of the cost, you can still enjoy a colonial culinary experience by fixing a picnic with food from the **Williamsburg Shopping Center,** at the intersection of Richmond Rd. and Lafayette St. Rte. 60 also collects a bevy of fast-food places and far more pancake houses than any sane person might expect.

Beethoven's Inn, 467 Merrimac Trail (229-7069). Great sandwiches, subs, and other light fare with music-related names. Try the Titanic Sub, a combination of turkey, roast beef, grilled veggies, and feta cheese ($5.50). A variety of board games passes the wait for your food. Open Mon.-Sat. 11am-9pm, Sun. noon-8pm.

Green Leafe Café, 465 Scotland St. (220-3405), next door to Paul's Deli. Always mellow, Green Leafe cultivates a subdued atmosphere while serving sandwiches and salads ($3.50-5.50) and swaying on Tues. (after 9pm) to the quiet sounds of live folk music. The café's slogan is "Life's too short to drink bad beer." You won't get any here: 20 delicious brews on tap, including savory Virginia micros ($3 per pint, $3.25 per bottle). Open daily 9am-2am.

The Old Chickahominy House, 1211 Jamestown Rd. (229-4689), rests over a mile from the historic district. Share the antiques and dried-flower decor with pewter-haired locals whose ancestors survived "Starvation Winter" in Jamestown. Miss Melinda's complete luncheon includes Virginia ham served on hot biscuits, fruit salad, a slice of delectable homemade pie, and iced tea or coffee ($5). 20 to 30-min. wait for lunch. Open daily 8:30-10:15am and 11:30am-2:15pm.

Paul's Deli Restaurant and Pizza, 761 Scotland St. (229-8976), a lively summer hangout for errant, leftover W&M students, sells crisp stromboli for 2 ($6.15-9) and filling subs ($4-5). Nightly specials on pasta and seafood. Wed.-Sat. 7-9pm features ½-price on selected beer. Great jukebox. Open daily 10:30am-2am.

SIGHTS

Unless you plan to apply to W&M, you've probably come to see the restored gardens and buildings, crafts, tours, and costumed actors in the historic district also known as **Colonial Williamsburg.** The Colonial Williamsburg Foundation (CWF) owns nearly everything in the historic district, from the **Governor's Palace** to the lemonade stands and even most of the houses marked "private home." A **Patriot's Pass** allows unlimited admission for one year, in addition to special programs and discounts ($33, children 6-12 $19, under 6 free). The **Basic Plus Ticket** is valid for two consecutive days, offering unlimited access to all sights except **Basset Hall**—the restored 18th-century home once inhabited by the Rockefellers ($29, children 6-12 $17, under 6 free). The **Basic Admission Ticket,** good only on the day of purchase, allows access to everything but the museums and **Carter's Grove** ($25, children under 12 $15, under 6 free). Tickets are available at the **CWF Visitors Center** (220-7645; open daily 8:30am-8pm).

Though the historic district does not require a ticket (for no charge you can walk the streets, ogle the buildings, march behind the fife-and-drum corps, lock yourself in the stocks, and use the restrooms), the experience of immersing one's self in sights and speaking with the "People of the Past" should not be undervalued. Some old-time shops that actually sell goods—notably the **Colonial Post Office** and **M. Dubois Grocer** by the Palace Green—are open to the public. Two of the buildings on the CWF map, the **Wren Building** and the **Bruton Parish Church**—are made to look like regular exhibits but in fact are free. The weekly *Visitor's Companion* lists all outdoor events, evening programs, and provides a map of the colonial area.

The real beauty of Colonial Williamsburg lies in interacting with its history; People of the Past include Martha Washington, Thomas Jefferson, and other once-local men and women. The trade shops afford a wonderful opportunity to learn from skilled artisans such as cabinet-makers and smithies, as well as actors who are eager to talk about the growing conflict between the colonies and Britain. (Watch out for the bartender in **Raleigh Tavern;** he readily upbraids "urchins" with poor manners.)

Those willing to pay shouldn't miss the **Governor's Palace,** on the Palace Green. This mansion housed the appointed governors of the Virginia colony until the last one fled in 1775. Reconstructed Colonial sidearms and ceremonial sabers line the reconstructed walls, and the extensive gardens include a hedge maze (open daily 9am-5pm; separate admission $17). Most sights in town are open 9:30am-5:30pm; a complete list of hours is provided in the *Visitor's Companion.*

Spreading west from the corner of Richmond and Jamestown Rd., **The College of William & Mary** is the second-oldest college in the U.S., having educated Presidents Jefferson, Monroe, and Tyler. The **Sir Christopher Wren Building** (built in 1695, two years after the college received its charter), also restored with Rockefeller money, is the nation's oldest classroom building. Nearby, the shops at **Merchant Square** sprawl a hair's breadth from the historic district.

■ Near Williamsburg

Jamestown and Yorktown At the **Jamestown National Historic Site** you'll see the remains of the first permanent English settlement (1607) as well as exhibits explaining colonial life. At the **visitors center** (229-1733), skip the hokey film and catch a 30-min. "living history" walking tour (free with admission to the site), on which a guide portraying one of the colonists describes the Jamestown way of life. Among other sights, you'll visit the **Old Church Tower;** built in 1639 it's the only 17th-century structure still standing. Also featured is a statue of **Pocahontas.** Call ahead for tour info, since "living history" guides get occasional off-days. You can also rent a 45-min. audio tape ($2) and drive or hike the 5-mi. **Island Loop Route** through woodlands and marsh. In the remains of the settlement itself, archeologists work to uncover the original site of the triangular **Jamestown Fort.** (The National Historic Site is open daily 9am-6pm; off-season 8am-5:30pm. The park opens and closes a ½hr. before the visitors center. Entrance fee $8 per car, $2 per bike.)

The nearby **Jamestown Settlement** (229-1607) is a commemorative museum commemorating with changing exhibits, a reconstruction of James Fort, a Native American village, and full-scale replicas of the three ships that brought the original settlers to Jamestown in 1607. The 20-min. dramatic film lives up to its name and fills tourists in on the settlement's history, including a discussion of settler relations with the indigenous Powhatan tribe. (Open daily 9am-5pm. $9, children 6-12 $4.25, under 6 free. Combination ticket, also good for Yorktown Victory Center $12.50, children under 12 $6, under 6 free.)

The British defeat at **Yorktown** signaled the end of the Revolutionary War. British General Charles Lord Cornwallis and his men seized the town for use as a port in 1781, but were stranded when the French fleet blocked their sea approaches. Colonists and French troops attacked and the British soldiers surrendered, dealing a devastating blow to the British cause. The Yorktown branch of **Colonial National Park** (898-3400) vividly recreates this last significant battle of the war with an engaging film, dioramas, and a smart-looking electric map (behind the information center). Take a 7-mi. automobile journey around the battlefield; you can rent a tape cassette and recorder to listen to while you drive ($2; **visitors center** open daily 8:30am-6pm; last tape rented at 5pm). The **Yorktown Victory Center** (887-1776), one block from Rte. 17 on Rte. 238, offers a museum brimming with Revolutionary War items and an intriguing living history exhibit: in an encampment in front of the center, a troop of soldiers from the Continental Army of 1781 takes a well-deserved break from active combat. (Open daily 9am-5pm. $6.75, kids 6-12 $3.25.)

Williamsburg Limousine (877-0279) offers daily round-trip transportation from Williamsburg to Jamestown, Yorktown ($15), and Carter's Grove ($8), but if you can, bike from South England St. in Colonial Williamsburg along the one-way, 7-mi., wooded **Carter's Grove Country Road** to Carter's Grove and the other James River plantations. The unlined **Colonial Parkway** to both Jamestown and Yorktown makes a beautiful bike route.

James River Plantations Built near the water to facilitate the planters' commercial and social lives, these country houses buttressed the slave-holding Virginia aristocracy. Tour guides at **Carter's Grove Plantation** (229-1000), six mi. east of Williamsburg on Rte. 60, describe the restored house and fields. The last owners doubled the size of the original 18th-century building while maintaining the colonial feel. Also reconstructed were slave quarters and an archaeological dig. The brand-new **Winthrop Rockefeller Archaeological Museum,** built unobtrusively into a hillside, provides a fascinating case-study look at archaeology. (Plantation open Tues.-Sun. 9am-5pm; Nov.-Dec. 9am-4pm. Museum and slave quarters open March-Dec. Tues.-Sun. 9am-5pm. $13, kids 6-12 $9, free with CWF Patriot's Pass.) The **Country Road,** an 8-mi., one-way scenic route from Carter's Grove to the historic district, makes for a great bike ride (open Tues.-Sun. 8:30am-4pm; Nov.-Dec. 8:30am-3pm).

Berkeley Plantation (829-6018), halfway between Richmond and Williamsburg on Rte. 5, was—contrary to popular belief—the site of the first official Thanksgiving in 1619. It later saw the birth of President William Henry Harrison. Union soldiers camped on the grounds here in 1862; one of them wrote the famous bugle tune *Taps*. The beautiful, terraced box-wood gardens stretch from the original 1726 brick building to the James River. (House and grounds open daily 8am-5pm. $8.50, seniors $6.65, ages 6-12 $9. Grounds only $5, seniors $3.60, ages 6-16 $2.50.)

Busch Gardens, Water Country: USA, and Anheuser-Busch Brewery When you've filled your colonial quotient, head to **Busch Gardens: The Old Country** (253-3350), three mi. east of Williamsburg on Rte. 60. Each part of the park represents a European nation; trains and sky-cars connect the sections. Recently opened is **Escape from Pompeii,** a water coaster ride which re-creates the city's destruction by Mt. Vesuvius. (Open April-mid-June and Sept.-Oct. daily 10am-7pm; mid-June-Aug. Sun.-Fri. 10am-10pm, Sat. 10am-midnight. $30, children 3-6 $23. $5 off after 5pm. A three-day ticket, $45 is good for both Busch Gardens and Water Country: USA. Parking $4.) Owned and operated by Busch Gardens (and about 2mi. away), **Water Country: USA** is a mammoth 40-acre water park. (Open weekends in May and June-Sept. 10am-dusk. $22, ages 3-6 $16, under 3 free. After 3pm, $12 for all.) A free monorail from Busch Gardens takes you to the **Anheuser-Busch Brewery** (253-3036). Self-guided walking tours include visits to the brewhouse, the high-speed packaging lines, and the newest promotional displays. The **Hospitality Center** offers free beer and pizza, in addition to gift shops, films, and a gallery of artifacts from the company's history (accessible from I-64; open daily 10am-4pm; free).

■ Virginia Beach

After years of attracting a cruising collegiate crowd, Virginia Beach is shedding its playground image and maturing into a family-oriented vacation spot. While the beach and boardwalk still draw hundreds of students, nightlife venues are being systematically pushed off the main drag by the town's inhabitants; residents have become so concerned about crime and youthful irreverence that they recently had security cameras installed on the boardwalk, a measure which has made the area an extremely safe community, relative to its size. But Virginia Beach is no retirement community; it remains a beach town, with the usual honky-tonk menagerie—shops, fast-food joints, and motels—that often besmirch touristed seaside towns.

PRACTICAL INFORMATION

Tourist Office: Virginia Beach Visitors Center, 2100 Parks Ave. (437-4888 or 800-446-8038), at 22nd St. Info on budget accommodations and area sights, as well as the Virginia Beach Bikeway Map. Open daily 9am-8pm; Labor Day-Memorial Day 9am-5pm.

MID-ATLANTIC

Trains: Amtrak, (245-3589 or 800-872-7245). The nearest station, in Newport News, provides free 45-min. bus service to and from the corner of 24½ and Pacific St.; you must have a train ticket to get on the bus. To: Washington, D.C. (6hr., $42); New York City (10hr., $85); Philadelphia (8½hr., $70); Baltimore (7hr., $49); Richmond (4hr., $18); Williamsburg (2hr., $13).

Buses: Greyhound, 1017 Laskin Rd. (422-2998 or 800-231-2222). Connects with Maryland via the Bridge Tunnel. To: Washington, D.C. (6½hr., $35); Richmond (3½hr., $23); Williamsburg (2½hr., $14).

Public Transportation: Virginia Beach Transit/Trolley Information Center (640-6300). Info on area transportation and tours, including trolleys, buses, and ferries. The **Atlantic Avenue Trolley** runs from Rudee Inlet to 42nd St. (summer daily noon-midnight; 50¢, seniors and disabled 25¢, day passes $2.50). Other trolleys run along the boardwalk, the North Seashore, and to Lynnhaven Mall.

Bike/Moped Rental: Atlantic Convenient Mart (491-6143), at 28th St. and Atlantic Ave. Bikes $3 per hr., $13 per day. In-line skates $5 per hr., $15 per day. Open daily 7am-midnight. **Moped Rentals, Inc.** (437-8629), 21st St. and Pacific Ave. Mopeds $23.50 per 1½hr. Open summers daily 10am-midnight.

Emergency: 911.

Post Office: (428-2821), 24th St. and Atlantic Ave. Open Mon.-Fri. 8am-4:30pm.

ZIP Code: 23458. **Area Code:** 757.

Virginia Beach is hard to get to, but easy to get around. Drivers from the Washington, D.C. area may take I-64 east from Richmond through the Hampton Roads Bridge Tunnel into Norfolk, then get on Rte. 44 (the Virginia Beach-Norfolk Expressway), which leads straight to 22nd St. and the beach. From the northern coast (near Ocean City, MD), take Rte. 13 south through the Chesapeake Bay Bridge Tunnel (toll $10). Follow Rte. 60 East into the Virginia Beach resort community. In Virginia Beach east-west streets are numbered; north-south avenues (Atlantic and Pacific comprise the main "drag") are parallel to the beach.

ACCOMMODATIONS

The number of motels in Virginia Beach is unreasonably high; unfortunately, so are most of the rates. Atlantic Ave. and Pacific Ave. buzz with activity during the summer and boast the most desirable hotels; reserve as far in advance as possible. If you're traveling in a group, look for "efficiency rate" apartments, which are rented cheaply by the week (see below).

Angie's Guest Cottage-Bed and Breakfast and HI-AYH Hostel, 302 24th St. (428-4690), ranks as the best place to stay on the entire Virginia Coast. Barbara Yates (a.k.a. Angie) and her team welcome guests with exceptional warmth. (Check-in 10am-9pm. Memorial Day-Labor Day $12.50, nonmembers $15.50; off-season $8.50, nonmembers $11.50. Overflow camping at off-season rates. Kitchen and lockers available. Linen $2. Reservations helpful, but not required. Open April 1-Oct. 1, March with reservations.) In the bed and breakfast, rooms ($54-78) have A/C and shared baths. Accommodations at the **Ocean Palms Motel** (428-8362), 30th St. and Arctic Ave., consist of two-room apartments with refrigerators ($30-45 per night). Right next door, the **Cherry Motel,** 2903 Arctic Ave. (428-3911), rents tidy one- and two-bedroom apartments by the day and by the week, each with four beds and a kitchen. (Weekly rates May 15-June 15 one-bedroom $300, two-bedroom $375; June 16-Labor Day $375/$525. Daily rates from $50.) The **TraveLodge,** 4600 Bonney Rd. (473-9745), off Rte. 44 (Exit 3-B), offers a special $40 rate Sun.-Thurs. Only eight miles from the seashore, this motel offers cable TV, an outdoor pool, fitness center, and complimentary continental breakfast.

Camp at the **First Landings** (481-2131 or 490-3939), about eight mi. north of town on U.S. 60, where choice sites go for $19. Because of its desirable location amid sand dunes and cypress trees, the park is very popular; call two to three weeks ahead for reservations. (Park open 8am-dusk. Take the North Seashore Trolley.) **KOA,** 1240 General Booth Blvd. (428-1444 or 800-665-8420), runs a quiet campground with open sites and free bus service to the beach and boardwalk. The campground is hard

MID-ATLANTIC

to find; look for the red and yellow KOA sign. (Sites $24, electricity $26, full hook-up $33; comfortable and spacious one-room cabins $46.)

FOOD, DRINK, AND NIGHTLIFE

Junk-food aficionados will love Virginia Beach. Beyond the neon glare, **The Jewish Mother**, 3108 Pacific Ave. (422-5430), dotes on her customers with deli sandwiches ($4-6), omelettes ($5-7), salads ($4.75-6.50), and an array of delicious desserts. At night the restaurant becomes a popular (and cheap) bar with live music; happy hour (4-7pm) features $1-1.50 domestic drafts. The Wed. night "Blues Jam" is popular. (Cover $3-5; Thurs. no cover for "ladies." Open Mon.-Fri. 8:30am-3am, Sat. 8am-3am, Sun. 7:30am-3am.) **The Raven**, 1200 Atlantic Ave. (425-1200), lays out tasty seafood and steaks in a tinted-glass greenhouse. (Sandwiches and burgers $5-7, dinners $12-17. Happy hour Sat.-Sun. noon-3pm: Bloody Marys and mimosas $1.50. Open daily 11:30am-2am.) **Giovanni's Pasta Pizza Palace**, 2006 Atlantic Ave. (425-1575), serves tasty, inexpensive Italian pastas, pizzas, and hot grinders. (Lunch and dinner $5-8. Open daily noon-11pm.)

Organic produce, vegetarian goodies, vegan-philosophy, and a particularly tasty Garden Burger ($5) are available at **The Heritage Store**, 314 Laskin Rd. (428-0100; open Mon.-Sat. 10am-7pm, Sun. 12-6pm). The **Farm Fresh Supermarket** (428-0344), at Laskin Rd. and Baltic Ave., has a salad bar, stocked with fresh fruit, pasta salads, and desserts ($3 per lb.;open 24hr.).

At night the beach becomes a haunt for lovers. **Chicho's** (422-6011), on Atlantic Ave. between 20th and 21st St., is one hot spot left from the days when bars clustered near the water. Bartenders shout over the din of videos of surfing competitions and bungee jumping (open Mon.-Fri. 5pm-2am, Sat.-Sun. 1pm-2am; no cover). Increasingly, the bar scene has retreated from the main arteries to places like **H₂O**, 1069 19th St. (425-5684). Massive columns filled with burbling blue water flank the walls and give the club the atmosphere of a posh, tasteful fish tank. A $3-5 cover lets you mingle with other tanned and well-groomed fish. (Open daily 11am-3pm for lunch, 5pm-10pm for dinner, 5pm-2am for drinks. Live DJ and a dance floor.) Across the way, **The Bayou**, 1900 Pavillion Dr. (422-8900), on the first floor of the Radisson Hotel, will drown you in the deafening sounds of live alternative bands five nights a week (cover $3-5; open daily 6pm-2am). The **Virginia Beach Amphitheater** (368-3000 for listings, 872-8100 or 262-8100 for tickets), on Concert Dr. off Princess Anne Rd., hosts big names in rock, folk, and pop music—including the Eagles and James Taylor—and seats up to 20,000 people.

■ Charlottesville

The renowned renaissance man Thomas Jefferson, when writing his own epitaph, was careful to point out his role as "father of the University of Virginia." The college he founded sustains Charlottesville economically, geographically, and culturally, perpetuating both a community of writers—such as Pulitzer Prize-winning poet Rita Dove—and a community of pubs. Even the friendly, hip, and down-to-earth population of this Blue Ridge foothills town seems to embody the third U.S. President's dream of a well-informed, culturally aware citizenry which chooses to live close to the land. Indeed, it is largely because of Jefferson that Charlottesville is the intellectual capital of Virginia.

PRACTICAL INFORMATION AND ORIENTATION

Visitor Information: Chamber of Commerce, 415 E. Market St. (295-3141), within walking distance of Amtrak, Greyhound, and town. Open Mon.-Fri. 9am-5pm. **Charlottesville/Albermarle Convention and Visitors Bureau**, P.O. Box 161 (977-1783), on Rte. 20 near I-64. Take bus #8 (Piedmont College) from 5th and Market St. Arranges same-day discount accommodations; Monticello, Michie Tavern, and Ash Lawn-Highland combination tickets ($17, seniors $15.50, under 12 $7.50). Open daily March-Oct. 9am-5:30pm, Nov.-Feb. 9am-5pm.

University of Virginia Information Center (924-7969), at the rotunda in the center of campus. Brochures, university map, and tour info. Open daily 9am-4:45pm. Open daily 8am-10pm. The larger **University Center** (924-7166), off U.S. 250W, is home to the campus police. Transport schedules, entertainment guides, and hints on budget accommodations. Campus maps. Open 24hr.

Amtrak: 810 W. Main St. (296-4559or 800-872-7245), 7 blocks from downtown. To: Washington, D.C. (1 per day, 3hr., $28); New York (1 per day, 7-8hr., $94); Baltimore (1 per day, 4hr., $45); Philadelphia (1 per day, 5½hr., $68). Open daily 5:30am-9pm.

Greyhound: 310 W. Main St. (295-5131), within 3 blocks of downtown. To: Richmond (1 per day, 1½hr., $17); Washington, D.C. (3 per day, 3hr., $29); Norfolk (1 per day, 4hr., $32); Baltimore (4 per day, 4-5hr., $41); Philadelphia (3 per day, 7-11hr., $48). Open Mon.-Sat. 7am-8:30pm, Sun. noon-8:30pm.

Public Transport: Charlottesville Transit Service (296-7433). Bus service within city limits. Maps available at both info centers, Chamber of Commerce, and the UVA student center in Newcomb Hall. Buses operate Mon.-Sat. 6:30am-6:30pm. Fare 60¢, seniors and disabled 30¢, under 6 free. The more frequent UVA buses technically require UVA ID, but in practice, a studious look usually suffices.

Taxi: Yellow Cab, 295-4131. 25¢ base fare, $1.50 each additional mi.

Hotlines: Region 10 Community Services Hotline, 972-1800. **Lesbian and Gay Hotline,** 971-4942. Open Mon.-Thurs. 5-9pm.

Emergency: 911. **Campus Police:** dial 4-7166 on a UVA campus phone.

Post Office: 513 E. Main St. (978-7610). Open Mon.-Fri. 8:30am-5pm, Sat. 10am-1pm. **ZIP Code:** 22902. **Area Code:** 804.

Charlottesville streets are numbered east to west, using compass directions; 5th St. N.W. is 10 blocks from (and parallel to) 5th St. N.E. Streets running east-west across the numbered streets are neither parallel nor logically named. C-ville has two downtowns: one on the west side near the university called **The Corner,** and **Historic Downtown** about a mile east. The two are connected by **University Ave.,** running east-west, which becomes **Main St.** after the Corner ends at a bridge. Rte. 64, which runs east-west all the way to Richmond, is Charlottesville's main feeder.

ACCOMMODATIONS AND CAMPING

Budget accommodations are scarce in Charlottesville. **Budget Inn,** 140 Emmett St. (293-5141), near the university, is relatively inexpensive. (Singles $42, doubles $46. $5 per additional person. Office open daily 8am-midnight.) **Acknowledge,** 400 Emmett St. (296-2104), has standard rooms (singles $45, doubles $49). **Charlottesville KOA Kampground,** Rte. 708 (296-9881 or 800-336-9881 for reservations), from Charlottesville, take U.S. 29 south to Rte. 708 southeast, has shaded campsites, a rec hall with video games, a pavilion, free movies and laundry facilities, and a pool (Sites $17, with water and electric $21, full hookup $23. Open daily March 13-Nov. 15 10am-8pm. Sites $17, with water and electric $21, full hookup $23.)

FOOD

The Corner neighborhood near UVA boasts bookstores and countless cheap eats, with good Southern grub in Charlottesville's unpretentious diners. The Emmett strip is lined with fast food franchises. The Downtown Mall (off-limits to cars) serves more upscale fare.

The Hardware Store, 316 E. Main St. (977-1518), near the middle of the outdoor mall. Slightly off-beat bar atmosphere: beers served in glass boots, appetizers in miniature basketball courts, and condiments in toolboxes. American grille and an eclectic set of entrees, from *ratatouille gratinée* ($5.75) to crepes both sweet ($2-5) and savory ($6-7). Sandwiches ($3-7). Quality desserts. Open Mon.-Thurs. 11am-9pm, Fri.-Sat. 11am-10pm.

Macado's, 1505 University Ave. (971-3558). Great sandwiches ($4-5), a handful of entrees ($5-7), and homemade desserts are surrounded by walls full of UVA football memorabilia. Pool tables, pinball, and foosball. Happy hour 4-7pm. Upstairs is a rockin' bar where Edgar Allen Poe once lived. Tell-tale jukebox. Open Sun.-Thurs. 9am-1am, Fri.-Sat. 9am-2am.

Littlejohn's, 427 University Ave. (977-0588). This deli serves students great sandwiches ($3-6), soups, and gigantic muffins ($1.10). The Nuclear Sub ($4) is a potent combo of barbecued beef, coleslaw, and melted cheese calculated to cause internal meltdown. Maybe Robin Hood will save you. Large selection of beers and NYC photos. Open 24hr.

Coupe DeVille's, 9 Elliewood Ave. (977-3966). Students cross the road for specialty chicken (½ rotisserie chicken $6.50). Burgers $5-6. Open Mon.-Fri. 11:30am-2pm and 5:30-10pm, Sat. 5:30-10pm. Pub open Mon.-Sat. 10pm-2am.

SIGHTS

Most activity on the spacious **University of Virginia** campus clusters around the **Lawn** and fraternity-lined **Rugby Road.** Jefferson watched the university being built through his telescope at Monticello; return the gaze with a glimpse of Monticello from the Lawn, a terraced green carpet that is one of the prettiest spots in American academia. Professors live in the Lawn's pavilions; Jefferson designed each one in a different architectural style. Lawn tours leave from the Rotunda (on the hr. 10am-4pm); self-guided tour maps are provided for those who prefer to find their own way. **The Rotunda** (924-7969) once housed a bell that was shot for the crime of waking students up early (open daily 9am-4:45pm). The **Bayley Art Museum,** Rugby Rd. (924-3592), features visiting exhibits and a small permanent collection including one of Rodin's casts of *The Kiss* (open Tues.-Sun. 1-5pm).

The **Downtown Mall,** about five blocks off E. Main St., is a brick pedestrian thoroughfare lined with restaurants and shops catering to a diverse crowd. A kiosk near the fountain in the center of the mall has posters with club schedules.

Jefferson oversaw every stage of development of his beloved **Monticello** (984-9800), a home that truly reflects the personality of its creator. The house is a Neoclassical jewel filled with fascinating innovations (such as a fireplace dumbwaiter to the wine cellar) compiled or conceived by Jefferson. A unique all-weather passage links the kitchen and dining room so that neither rain nor snow nor gloom of night could keep dinner from its appointed rounds, while an indoor compass registers wind direction via a weathervane on the roof. The cleverly laid-out grounds include orchards and flower gardens, and afford magnificent views in every direction. (Tours offered daily. Open daily March-Oct. 8am-5pm; Nov.-Feb. 9am-4:30pm. $8, seniors $7, ages 6-11 $4, students $3, Nov.-Feb $1.)

Minutes away is **Ashlawn** (293-9539), on Rte. 795, the 500-acre plantation home of President James Monroe, who was not only a neighbor, but a close friend of Jefferson. (Open daily 9am-6pm; Nov.-Feb. daily 10am-5pm. Tour $6, seniors $5.50, children 6-11 $3.)

Down the road from Monticello on Rte. 53 is **Michie Tavern** (as in the mouse; 977-1234), with an operating grist mill, a general store, and a tour of the 200-year-old establishment (open daily 9am-5pm; $5, under 6 $1).

ENTERTAINMENT AND NIGHTLIFE

The town loves jazz, likes rock, and thrives on pubs. Ubiquitous posters in the Downtown Mall and the free *Charlottesville Review* can tell you who plays where and when. In the **Box Gardens** behind Ashlawn June-Aug., English-language opera and musical theater highlight the **Summer Festival of the Arts** (293-4500, open Tues.-Sun. 10am-5pm). Ashlawn hosts **Music at Twilight** on Wed. evenings, including New Orleans jazz, Cajun music, blues, and swing ($10, seniors $9, students $6). During the school year, the town cheers for the **UVA Cavaliers,** who compete in the intense Atlantic Coastal Conference (ACC) against perennial powers Duke, North Carolina, and Florida State Universities.

The Max, 12 11 St. SW (295-6299). One of the largest and most popular bars in the city. Tues. features Top-40 DJ and dancing (cover: men 21+ $4, women 18+ $3); Wed. is two-steppin' and line dancing with free lessons until 9:30pm ($4 cover); Thurs.-Sat. brings live bands of all genres next door to **Trax.** (For info about live shows call 295-TRAX/8729; $5 cover for men.) Drafts $1.85. Open Tues., and Thurs.-Sat. 8pm-2am, Wed. 7pm-midnight.

Outback Lodge, 917 Preston Ave. (979-7211). Happenin' pub with a pool table, foosball, and a jukebox. Philly cheesesteak ($5) and fajitas ($8) are popular, as is happy hour (Mon.-Fri. 4-7pm). Live music Wed.-Sat. with a cover ($2-10). Call for bands and times. Open Mon.-Fri. 11am-2am, Sat.-Sun. 5pm-2am.

Dürty Nelly's, 2200 Jefferson Park Ave. (295-1278). Bar/deli. More than 50 beers: domestic drafts $1.50, $1.10 during happy hour (Mon.-Fri. 4-7pm). Tues. nights and weekends feature live music with a $2-4 cover. Open daily 11am-2am.

Tryangles, 212 W. Water St. (246-8783). The only gay bar in the city. Entrance requires a $25 membership which entitles you to free admission Sun.-Thurs. Fri.-Sat. features a DJ and dancing ($3 cover). Domestic drafts $1.25. Open Sun.-Thurs. 9pm-1am, Fri.-Sat. 9pm-4am.

■ Shenandoah National Park

Shenandoah National Park was America's first great natural reclamation project; in 1926, Congress authorized Virginia to purchase a 280-acre tract of over-logged, over-hunted land. The small population of reclusive trappers was relocated and President Franklin D. Roosevelt dedicated the park to wildlife preservation in 1936. The experiment remains one of his greatest successes; today, residents include not-so-reclusive deer, bears, and other critters who make their home in the lush forest that has prospered over the last 60 years. Fields have given way to woodland, transforming the park into a spectacular ridgetop preserve. A trip along its spine via Skyline Drive allows glimpses of the Blue Ridge Mountains, the fertile plains below, and some of the park's furry and inquisitive inhabitants.

Shenandoah's natural beauty comes in the form of sweeping vistas and an abundance of life. On clear days, drivers and hikers can see miles of unspoiled ridges and treetops, home to more plant species than all of Europe. In the summer, the cool mountain air offers a respite from Virginia's oppressive heat and humidity. Early in June, see the blooming mountain laurel in the highlands. In the fall, Skyline Drive and its lodges are choked with tourists who come to enjoy the magnificent autumn foliage. Of course, outdoorsmen can be found almost any season, trekking along the Appalachian Trail. The narrow park stretches almost 75 mi. along the Blue Ridge Mountains, parallel to and south of the wilder George Washington National Forest.

PRACTICAL INFORMATION

Dickey Ridge Visitors Center: Mile 4.6 (635-3566), closest to the north entrance. Daily programs. Open April-Nov. daily 9am-5pm. **Byrd Visitors Center:** Mile 51 (999-3283), in the center of the park. Open April-Oct. daily 9am-5pm. Byrd offers an historical-minded museum and movie; both stations offer exhibits, free hiking pamphlets, daily weather updates, and ranger-led nature hikes.

Park Information: (999-2243; daily 8am-4:30pm, or 999-3500 for 24-hr. recorded message). Superintendent, Park Headquarters, Shenandoah National Park, Rte. 4, P.O. Box 348, Luray, VA 22835.

Greyhound (800-231-2222) sends buses once per morning from Washington, D.C. to Waynesboro, near the park's southern entrance ($40), but no bus or train serves Front Royal.

Emergency: 800-732-0911. **Area Code:** 540.

Shenandoah's amazing technicolor mountains—bluish and covered with deciduous flora in the summer, streaked with brilliant reds, oranges, and yellows in the fall—can be enjoyed from the many overlooking areas along **Skyline Drive** (speed limit 35 mph), which runs 105 mi. south from Front Royal to Rockfish Gap. (Miles along Skyline Dr. are measured north to south, beginning at Front Royal.) The rest stops provide picnic areas for hikers; map boards also carry data about trail conditions. The drive closes during and following bad weather. Most facilities also hibernate in the winter. ($5 per vehicle, $3 per hiker, biker, or bus passenger, disabled persons free; pass is good for 7 days and is necessary for re-admittance.) Containing park regulations, trail lists, and a description of the area's geological history, the *Park Guide* ($2) is invaluable to those on an extended visit. Few brochures are displayed, but rangers will provide free literature upon request.

ACCOMMODATIONS AND CAMPING

The **Bear's Den (HI-AYH)** (554-8708), 35 mi. north of Shenandoah on Rte. 601S, provides a woodsy stone lodge with two 10-bed dorm rooms and one room with one double bed and two bunks. Drivers should exit from Rte. 7 onto Rte. 601S; after ½ mi., turn right at the stone-gate entrance, and proceed up the hostel driveway for another ½ mi. No bus or train service is available. The hostel has a dining room, kitchen, on-site parking, and a laundry room. The proprietor sells snacks, drinks, and hiking and camping supplies. (Check-in 5-10pm. Lock-out 10pm. Check-out 9:30am. $12, nonmembers $15. Camping $6 per person. Reservations recommended; Bear's Den (HI-AYH), Postal Rte. 1, Box 288, Bluemont, VA 22135.)

The park maintains two affordable lodges: motel-esque rooms within cabin-esque exteriors. **Skyland** (999-2211 or 800-999-4714), Mile 42 on Skyline Drive, offers brown and green wood-furnished cabins ($46-79, $5-7 more in Oct., open April-Oct.,) and slightly more upscale motel rooms ($77-88; open April-Nov.). **Lewis Mountain,** Mile 57 (999-2255 or 800-999-4714), also gets cabin fever with a set of its own ($52-55, $7 more in Oct.). Reservations needed; up to six months in advance.

The park service also maintains three major **campgrounds: Big Meadows** (Mile 51); **Lewis Mountain** (Mile 58); and **Loft Mountain** (Mile 80). All have stores, laundry facilities, and showers (no hookups). Heavily wooded and uncluttered by mobile homes, Lewis Mountain makes for the happiest tenters. (Sites at Lewis Mountain and Loft Mountain $12, at Big Meadows $14; reservations 800-365-2267.)

Back-country camping is free, but you must obtain a permit at a park entrance, visitors center, ranger station, or the park headquarters. Since open fires are prohibited, bring cold food or a stove; boil water or bring your own—some creeks are oozing with microscopic beasties. Illegal camping carries a hefty fine. Hikers on the **Appalachian Trail** can make use of primitive open shelters, three-sided structures with stone fireplaces, strewn along the trail at approximate 7-mi. intervals. Shelters are reserved for hikers with at least three nights in different locations stamped on their camping permits; casual hikers are banned from them. ($1 per night donation). The **Potomac Appalachian Trail Club (PATC)** maintains six cabins in back-country areas of the park. You must reserve in advance by writing to the club at 118 Park St., SE, Vienna, VA 22180-4609, or calling 703-242-0693. Bring lanterns and food; the cabins contain only bunk beds, water, and stoves. (Sun.-Thurs. $3 per person, Fri.-Sat. $14 per group; one group member must be at least 21.)

HIKES AND ACTIVITIES

The **Appalachian Trail** runs the length of the park. Trail maps and the PATC guide can be obtained at the visitors center (see Practical Information, p. 252). The PATC puts out three topographical maps ($5), each of a different part of the park. When purchased as a package, the maps come with a trail guide, descriptions, and suggestions for budgeting time ($16). Brochures covering the hikes are free. Overnight hikers should keep in mind the unpredictability of mountain weather. Both park visitors centers offer a variety of programs: talks on local wildlife, short guided walks among the flora, and lantern-lit discussions of the mountaineers' culture and lifestyle. Slide presentations on the park's natural wonders are given regularly.

MID-ATLANTIC

Old Rag Mountain, five mi. from Mile 45, reaches a height of 3268 ft.—not an intimidating summit—but the 8.8-mi. loop up the mountain is deceptively difficult. This six- to eight-hr. hike is steep, involves scrambling over and between granite, and at many points flaunts disappointing false summits. Bring lots of water, food, and stamina. Camping is banned above 2800 ft. (The National Park Service charges $3 to hikers 16 and older, unless they have already paid the Shenandoah admission fee.) The **Whiteoak Canyon Trail** beckons from its own parking lot at Mile 42.6. The trail to the canyon is easy; the six waterfalls and trout-filled streams below are spectacular. (5-day non-resident permit, $6.50.) From Whiteoak Canyon, the **Limberlost** trail (5-mi. roundtrip) slithers into a hemlock forest. **Lewis Spring Falls Trail,** at Mile 51.4, takes only ¾-mi. to reach a gorgeous array of falls. The trail descends farther (about an hour's walk) to the base of the falls, where water drops 80 ft. over the crumbling stone of an ancient lava flow. **Hogback Overlook,** from Mile 20.8 to Mile 21, bristles with easy hikes and idyllic views of the smooth Shenandoah River and Valley. At **Dark Hollow Falls,** Mile 50.7, a 1½-mi. hike takes you to the base of scenic cascades.

Take a break from hiking or driving at one of Shenandoah's seven **picnic areas,** located at Dickey Ridge (Mile 5), Elkwallow (Mile 24), Pinnacles (Mile 37), Big Meadows (Mile 51), Lewis Mountain (Mile 58), South River (Mile 63), and Loft Mountain (Mile 80). All have tables, fireplaces, water fountains, and comfort stations.

Outside the Park

Western Virginia boasts some of the most stunning geological formations in the east. Discovered in 1878, **Luray Caverns** (743-6551) features a "Stalagpipe Organ." (Take Exit 264 off I-81. $12, children 7-13 $6, under 7 free.) Admission to the antique carriage and car museum is included (open daily 9am-6pm). The **Shenandoah Caverns** (477-3115) tout iridescent stalactites and stalagmites that thrive in the 56°F air. Take U.S. 211 to Newmarket, get on I-81 North, go 4 mi. to the Shenandoah Caverns exit, and follow the signs for the caverns—not the town of the same name. ($8, ages 8-14 $4, under 8 free. Open 9am-5pm, mid-April to mid-June and Labor Day-Oct. 9am-6pm.) **Skyline Caverns** (635-4545 or 800-635-4599), in Front Royal, 15 min. from the junction of Skyline Drive and U.S. 211, has built a reputation on its anthodites, whose white spikes defy gravity and grow in all directions at the rate of an inch every 7000 yr. (Open mid-June-Aug. daily 9am-6pm; spring and fall Mon.-Fri. 9am-5pm, Sat.-Sun. 9am-6pm; winters daily 9am-4pm. $10, ages 6-12 $5.)

The area north of the park is home to several vineyards offering pleasant picnic spots. **Piedmont Vineyards** (687-5528), on Rte. 626N, offers free tours and samples from its ten vines. If a scenic paddle floats your boat, contact the **Downriver Canoe Co.** (635-5526 or 800-338-1963), Rte. 613, Bentonville. (3-mi. trip $29 per canoe; 3-day trip $122 per canoe. Kayak and tube trips available. 25% discount weekdays.)

Blue Ridge Parkway

If you don't believe that the best things in life are free, this ride could change your mind. The 469-mi. Blue Ridge Parkway, continuous with Skyline Drive, runs through Virginia and North Carolina, connecting the **Shenandoah** and **Great Smoky Mountains National Parks** (in Tennessee). Administered by the National Park Service, the parkway joins hiking trails, campsites, and picnic grounds. Every bit as scenic as Skyline Drive, the Parkway remains much wilder and less crowded. From Shenandoah National Park, the road winds south through Virginia's **George Washington National Forest** from Waynesboro to Roanoke. The forest beckons motorists off the road with spacious campgrounds, canoeing opportunities, and swimming in the cold, clear mountain water at **Sherando Lake** (Mile 16).

Nature trails range from the **Mountain Farm Trail** (Mile 5.9), a 20-min. hike to a reconstructed homestead, to the **Rock Castle Gorge Trail** (Mile 167), a 3-hr. excursion. At **Mabry Mill** (Mile 176.1) you can visit a mountain farm, and at **Crabtree Meadows** (Mile 339) you can purchase local crafts. **Humpback Rocks** (Mile 5.8) is an easy hike with a spectacular view. Of course, real go-getters will venture onto the **Appalachian Trail,** which will take you in scenic style all the way to Georgia. In addition to these trails, the Park Service hosts a variety of ranger-led interpretive activities. Info is available at the visitors centers.

The **Blue Ridge Country HI-AYH Hostel** (703-236-4962), Rte. 2, Galax, rests only 100 ft. from the parkway at Mile 214.5. Located in the world capital of old-time mountain music, this reproduction of a 1690 colonial building houses 22 beds. ($15, nonmembers $12 nonmembers. Lockout 9:30am-5pm, curfew 11pm. Open Feb.-Dec.) There are nine **campgrounds** along the parkway, each with water and restrooms, located at Miles 61, 86, 120, 167, 239, 297, 316, 339, and 408 ($9, reservations not accepted). The cities and villages along the parkway offer a range of accommodations. For a complete listing, pick up a *Blue Ridge Parkway Directory* at one of the visitors centers.

For general info on the parkway, call **visitor information**. For additional details call the park service in Roanoke, VA (540-857-2490), or in Montebello, VA (703-857-2490). For info write to **Blue Ridge Parkway Headquarters,** 400 BB&T Bldg., Asheville, NC 28801 (704-271-4779). Eleven **visitors centers** line the parkway at Miles 5.8, 63.8, 86, 169, 217.5, 294, 304.5, 316.4, 331, 364.6, and 382, located at entry points where highways intersect the Blue Ridge (most open daily 9am-5pm).

West Virginia

Geography and history have collided to keep West Virginia among the poorest and most isolated states in the Union. The Appalachians, at their highest and most rugged, physically wall off the state, while mining in West Virginia has been synonymous with the worst excesses of industrial capitalism. Still, West Virginia has had proud moments. The state was formed during the Civil War when the Virginia counties which remained loyal to the Union shunned the Confederacy. Having suffered in the mines, West Virginians also helped start the American Labor movement.

With the decline of heavy industry in the last 30 years, West Virginia has turned to another resource—abundant natural beauty. Thanks to great skiing, hiking, and fishing, and the best whitewater rafting in the east, tourism has become one of the state's main sources of employment and revenue. West Virginians remain people of sturdy character, and in the face of irrepressible tourism, hold firmly their traditional, early 20th-century values and lifestyles.

PRACTICAL INFORMATION

Capital: Charleston.
Department of Tourism: 1900 Kanawah Blvd. E., Bldg. 6, #B564, Charleston 25305 (304-348-2286 or 800-CALL-WVA/225-5982). **Division of Parks and Recreation,** State Capitol Complex, Bldg. 3, #714, Charleston 25305 (304-558-2764). **U.S. Forest Service Supervisor's Office,** 200 Sycamore St., Elkins 26241 (304-636-1800).
Time Zone: Eastern. **Postal Abbreviation:** WV
Sales Tax: 6%.

■ Harpers Ferry

Harpers Ferry's stunning location—at the junction of the Potomac and Shenandoah rivers—has time and again provided a beautiful backdrop to the events of history. This town witnessed John Brown's famous 1859 raid on the U.S. Armory—an attempt to start a war to liberate the slaves. Although Brown and his fellow attackers were captured, and in some cases killed, the raid brought the nation's sharp moral divisions over slavery to the revolutionary forefront. (Ironically, Storer University—one of the U.S.'s first integrated colleges—was founded upon the Armory's paymaster's quarters in 1865, and endured for more than 80 years.) No longer a revolutionary hotbed, Harpers Ferry today provides excellent hiking, biking, canoeing, rafting, and surveying of nature's beauty. Thomas Jefferson called the view from a Harpers Ferry overlook "worth a voyage across the Atlantic," and while that may seem a bit extreme, if you're already across it's certainly worth the journey.

PRACTICAL INFORMATION

Park Information: 535-6223, Harpers Ferry National Historical Park, P.O. Box 65, Harpers Ferry, WV 25425.

Visitors Center: (535-6298), just inside the park entrance off Rte. 340. Open daily 8am-5pm, Memorial Day-Labor Day 8am-6pm. The center offers info on area hiking, lodging, and food, as well as free historical literature. $5 per car, $3 per hiker or bicyclist; good for 7 consecutive days. Free parking. A bus shuttles from the parking lot to town every 15min.

West Virginia Welcome Center: (535-2482), across the street from the entrance to Harpers Ferry, unaffiliated with the town but great for in-state travelers; get info on accommodations, restaurants, and activities such as white-water rafting. Open daily 9am-5pm.

Emergency: 911, or contact a ranger at 535-6455.

Area Code: 304 (in West Virginia; 301 in Maryland).

Amtrak (800-872-7245), on Potomac St., goes to Washington, D.C. once per morning. Reservations *required* ($15 one-way, $24 roundtrip, depending on availability). The **Maryland Rail Commuter (MARC)** (800-325-7245) offers a cheaper and more frequent rail-ride; on Mon.-Fri., two trains run to Union Station in Washington, D.C. and three return to Harpers Ferry. ($6.75, seniors, disabled travelers, and children 5-15 $3.50. Ticket office open Mon., Wed., and Fri. 6am-9pm, Tues. and Thurs. 5am-8pm. You can also buy tickets on the train, for $3 more.) The closest **Greyhound** bus stations are ½-hr. drives in Winchester, VA, and Frederick, MD.

ACCOMMODATIONS AND CAMPING

Hikers can try the **Harpers Ferry Hostel (HI-AYH)**, 19123 Sandy Hook Rd. (301-834-7652), at Keep Tryst Rd. in Knoxville, MD, for cheap accommodations. Meet a rugged through-hiker or two about halfway along their 2020-mi. Appalachian Trail odyssey. This renovated auction house, standing high above the Potomac, has 28 beds in two large dormitory rooms, and two smaller rooms with 11 beds. Train service is available to Harpers Ferry, two mi. from the hostel, and Brunswick, three mi. away. Proprietor will pick you up at the station for $5, although the two-mi. hike is spectacular. (Lockout 9:30am-5pm. Check-in 7:30am-9am and 5-9pm; curfew 11pm. Limited parking. $11, nonmembers $14. Sleepsack $1. Camping member or ATC hiker $6, nonmember $9; includes use of hostel kitchen and bathrooms. Max. stay 3 nights. 50% reservation deposit.)

The **Hillside Motel,** 340 Keep Tryst Rd. (301-834-8144), in Knoxville, MD, has 19 rooms that are just what you'd expect for their low rates (singles $30, doubles $35). You can **camp** along the C&O Canal, where sites lie five mi. apart, or in one of the five Maryland state-park campgrounds that lie within 30 mi. of Harpers Ferry (for more info, call the ranger station 301-739-4200). **Greenbrier State Park** (301-791-4767), is a few miles north of Boonsboro on Rte. 66 between Exits 35 and 42 on I-70 ($16; open April-Nov.). Far closer is the commercial **Camp Resort** (304-535-6895), on Rte. 3, adjacent to the entrance to Harpers Ferry National Park (sites $25 for 2 people, with water and electric hookup $28; each additional person $4, under 17 $2; registration fee $3 per person). They also rent cabins: $75 for a two-room cabin that sleeps eight.

HIKES AND ACTIVITIES

Park rangers at the visitors center provide free 45-min. to 1-hr. tours, daily from 10:30am to 4pm throughout the summer. Other special events range from battlefield re-enactments to parades (304-535-6298 for a schedule of activities).

The bus from the parking lot stops at **Shenandoah Street,** where visitors may browse through the renovated blacksmith's shop (you'll wince as the blacksmith hammers at furnace-fired iron), ready-made clothing store, and general store; the stores contain replicas of 19th-century goods. Guides in period costume explain the vagaries of the Industrial Revolution. A turn onto High St. reveals many of Harpers Ferry's most interesting exhibits. **Black Voices from Harpers Ferry,** on the corner of High and Shenandoah St., is an exhibit on the history of local African-Americans from slavery to Storer University. Also on High St., the **Civil War Story** chronicles the town's role in the national conflict through displays and a 20-ft. time line.

Uphill, stairs on High St. follow the Appalachian Trail to **Upper Harpers Ferry.** Ascend past **Harper's House,** the restored home of town founder Robert Harper; **St. Peter's Church,** where a sagacious pastor flew the Union Jack during the Civil War to protect the church; and **Jefferson's Rock,** where Tom had his Atlantic-crossing inspiration. At the top of the climb moulders **Storer University,** one of America's first desegregated colleges (closed now for over 40 years due to bankruptcy).

Visitors hoping to reconcile history with nature can hike or boat. The **Maryland Heights Trail** offers some great views in the Blue Ridge Mountains, including formidable cliffs and glimpses of crumbling Civil War-era forts and bivouacs. Climbers must register at the visitors center. The **Bolivar Heights Trail** follows a Civil War battle line and features trail-side exhibits and a three-gun battery. The **Appalachian Trail Conference Headquarters** (304-535-6331), at the corner of Washington and Jackson St., offers catalogues to its members featuring good deals on hiking books, as well as trail info, and a maildrop for hikers. (Open May-Oct. Mon.-Fri. 9am-5pm, Sat.-Sun. 9am-4pm; Nov. to mid-May Mon.-Fri. 9am-5pm. Membership $25, seniors and students $18.) The less adventurous can walk along the **Chesapeake & Ohio Canal Towpath,** off the end of Shenandoah St. and over the bridge. The Towpath is also popular with bikers and hikers.

Water fanatics may contact **Blue Ridge Outfitters** (304-725-3444), a few miles west of Harpers Ferry on Rte. 340N in Charles Town, who arrange excursions ranging from 4-hr. canoe trips on the Shenandoah to 3-day white-water raft rides on Virginia's toughest waterways (canoe or a seat on a ½-day raft trip from $45; open daily 8am-7pm). **River & Trail Outfitters,** 604 Valley Rd. (301-695-5177), at Rte. 340, in Knoxville, MD, rents canoes, inner tubes, and rafts in addition to organizing guided trips (canoes $45 per day, raft trips $45 per person, tubing $28.50 per day). It also organizes weekend ($199) and day ($60) cross-country ski trips (open daily 9am-5pm). If you're staying at the hostel, tubing and upstream transportation are provided for free.

Antietam National Battlefield

A few miles north of Harpers Ferry, the bloodiest one-day battle of the Civil War was fought at Antietam. On September 17, 1862, 12,410 Union and 10,700 Confederate soldiers lost their lives as Confederate General Robert E. Lee tried and failed to overcome the army of Union General George B. McClellan. However, McClellan's typical failure to follow the retreating Confederates and crush them decisively tainted the victory, and eventually led to his relief of duty. Still, the nominal Union triumph provided President Lincoln with the opportunity to issue the Emancipation Proclamation, freeing all slaves in those states still in rebellion against the U. S. on January 1, 1863. The **visitors center** (301-432-5124) has a museum of artifacts used in the battle, free maps for self-guided tours, and tapes to rent ($5) with a detailed account of the battle. Park rangers explain with dramatic gusto the retreats and advances of the battle, providing visual aids. (26-min. film 9am-5pm on the hr. Center open daily May-Sept. 8:30am-6pm, Oct.-April 8:30am-5pm. $2, family $4.)

▓ New River Gorge

The New River Gorge is a mixture of raw beauty, raw resources, and raw power. One of the oldest rivers in the world, the river cuts a narrow gouge in the Appalachian

Mountains, leaving valley walls which tower an average of 1000 ft. above the white waters. Industrialists bled the region until coal and timber virtually disappeared in the early and middle parts of this century. The **New River Gorge National Park** now protects the area and oversees the fishing, climbing, canoeing, mountain biking, and world-class rafting that go on in the gorge. There are a number of excellent hiking trails in the park; among them, the **Kaymoor Trail** runs 2 mi. into the abandoned town of Kaymoor, a coal-mining community that shut down in 1962. The park operates three visitors centers: **Canyon Rim,** (574-2115; open daily 9am-5pm), off Rte. 19 near Fayetteville at the northern extreme of the park; **Grandview,** (763-3715; open daily noon-8pm), on Rte. 9 near Beckley; and **Hinton,** (466-0417; open daily 9am-5pm), on Rte. 20. Stop at Canyon Rim, which has info on all activities in the park, including free, detailed hiking guides, and an 11-minute slide presentation that's not to be missed. (Canyon Rim and Grandview open daily 9am-8pm; Sept.-May 9am-5pm. Hinton open daily 9am-5pm; Sept.-May Sat.-Sun 9am-5pm.)

The area's main draw, **whitewater rafting,** has become one of the state's leading industries. A general info service at 800-225-5982 can connect you to some of the nearly 20 outfitters who operate on the New River and the nearby Gauley River. **American Whitewater Tours** (800-787-3982), on Rte. 19 in Fayetteville, runs all-day trips on the New River (Mon.-Fri. $68, Sat. $88). In the summer, **New River Rafting** (800-639-7238), does ½-day New River trips (Mon.-Fri. $39, Sat. $49). The company also runs trips on the rowdier **Gauley River,** which is only open six weeks in the fall. An express trip on the Upper Gauley (for experienced rafters only) covers some of the country's wildest whitewater—including the "Pure Screaming Hell Rapids" and the "Heaven Help You Rapids" (trips Mon. and Fri. $59), while the lower Gauley makes a mellower all-day trip (trips Mon.-Fri. $59, Sat.-Sun. $69).

Where Rte. 19 crosses the river at the park's northern end, the engineered grace of the **New River Gorge Bridge** complements the natural beauty of the gorge itself. Take a walk down to the overlook at the Canyon Rim Visitors Center for a good gander. Towering 876 ft. above New River, the bridge claims the world's largest single steel arch span. On **Bridge Day,** the third Saturday of October, you can walk across the bridge and parachute off. Old time coal miners lead you down into an actual mine at the **Beckly Exhibition Coal Mine** (256-1747), New River Park in Beckley. Ride in a "men trip" car through over 150 ft. of underground passages, viewing both manual and automated mining (open April-Oct. daily 10am-5:30pm; $6.50, seniors $5.50, ages 4-12 $3, under 4 free).

Camping abounds in the area. Many of the raft companies operate private campgrounds and four public campgrounds are scattered in the general area. The most central, **Babcock State Park** (800-225-5982), Rte. 41 south of U.S. 60, 15 mi. west of Rainelle, has shaded, sometimes slanted sites ($11, with water and electricity $14). The park also rents 26 cabins, which range from deluxe to economy sizes. **Greyhound** stops in Beckley, at 105 Third Ave. (253-8333 or 800-231-2222; open Mon.-Fri. 7-11am and 4-8pm, Sat.-Sun. 7-9am and 4-8pm). **Amtrak** (253-6651 or 800-872-7245), stops on Rte. 41N, in Prince. (Trains Sun., Wed., and Fri. Open Sun., Wed., and Fri. 9am-1pm and 7-9:30pm, Thurs. and Sat. 7am-2:30pm.) **Area code:** 304.

■ Monongahela National Forest

Popular with canoers, fly fishermen, and spelunkers, mammoth **Monongahela National Forest** supports deer, bears, wild turkeys, and magnificent limestone caverns. Over 500 campsites and 600 mi. of well maintained hiking trails lure additional outdoor adventurers to this camping mecca, where much of West Virginia's most scenic country can be experienced, relatively unspoiled by noisy crowds. Each of the forest's six districts comes complete with its own campground and recreation area. The forest **Supervisor's Office,** 200 Sycamore St. (636-1800), in Elkins, distributes a full list of sites and fees, and provides info about fishing and hunting seasons and licenses (open Mon.-Fri. 8am-4:45pm). Established sites run $7-15, but the adventurous can sleep in the backcountry for free. If you're going into the backcountry, drop by the **Cranberry Visitors Center** (653-4826), at the junction of Rte. 150 and Rte. 39/55; they like to know you're out there. (Open daily 9am-5pm; Sept.-Nov. and Jan.-May Sat.-Sun. 10am-4pm.) The forest's **Lake Sherwood Area** (536-3660), 25 mi. north of I-64 on Rte. 92 in the south of the forest, offers fishing, hunting, swimming, hiking, boating, and camping, but few roving Merry Men to spoil your stay; the campsites often fill on summer weekends (2-week max. stay; sites $10). **Cranberry Mountain** (846-2695), in the Gauley district 6 mi. west of U.S. 219 on Rte. 39/55, has hiking trails through cranberry bogs and campsites for $5-8. The **Middle Mountain Cabins** (456-3335), on Rte. 10, feature fireplaces, kitchens, drinking water, and resident field mice. Three cabins, which sleep a total of 11 people, rent as a group regardless of the number of cabins in use. (1-week max. stay. $30 per night, $168 per week. These are popular; call well in advance. Open May-Oct.)

The only public transportation in the forest area comes into White Sulphur Springs at the forest's southern tip. **Greyhound** (800-231-2222) has a flag stop at the Village Inn, 38 W. Main St. (536-2323; 1 eastbound bus to Clifton Forge at 9am, and 1 westbound bus per day to Beckly at 4pm). **Amtrak** (800-872-7245) stops trains at an unmanned station on W. Main St., across from the Greenbriar, on Sunday, Wednesday, and Friday (To Washington, D.C. $51 and Charlottesville, VA $28). The Monongahela National Forest's **area code:** 304.

MID-ATLANTIC

THE SOUTH

The American South has always fought to maintain a unique identity in the face of the more economically powerful North. That tension produced the bloodiest war in the nation's history. Now North and South battle against stereotypes and conventional wisdom. Today's South has adopted the industry and urbanity of the North while retaining genteel hospitality, an easy-going pace, and a *carpe diem* philosophy. The rapid economic growth of the southern metropoli—Atlanta, Nashville, Charlotte, Orlando, and New Orleans—has disproved the Northern stereotypes of rednecks, racists, and impoverished hayseeds. The cities have infused much of the region with a modern flavor. But the past lingers on for good, in the genuine warmth of Southern hospitality, and for bad, in the division of wealth between whites and blacks.

This region's history and culture—a mélange of Native American, English, African, French, and Spanish—are reflected in its architecture, cuisine, language, and people. Landscapes are equally varied. Nature blessed the region with overwhelming mountains, lush marshlands, sparkling beaches, and fertile soil. From the Atlantic's Sea Islands to the rolling Ozarks, the Gulf's bayous to the Mississippi Delta, the South's beauty will awe, entice, and enchant.

Kentucky

Legendary for the duels, feuds, and stubborn frontier spirit of its earlier inhabitants (such as Daniel Boone, for whom almost everything in the state is named), Kentucky presents a gentler face to travelers. Kick back, take a shot of local bourbon, grab a plate of burgoo (a spicy meat stew), and relax amidst rolling hills and bluegrass. These days, Kentuckians' fire erupts on the highways—they aren't ungracious, but they do drive *fast*. Of course, the most respected mode of transportation in the state remains the horse; Louisville ignores its vibrant cultural scene and active nightlife for a full week at Derby time, and Lexington devotes much of its most beautiful farmland to breeding champion racehorses. Farther east, the Daniel Boone National Forest preserves the virgin woods of the Kentucky Highlands, where trailblazers first discovered a route across the mountains to what was then the West.

PRACTICAL INFORMATION

Capital: Frankfort.
Kentucky Department of Travel Development: 500 Mero St. #2200, Frankfort 40601 (502-564-4930 or 800-225-8747). **Kentucky State Parks,** 500 Mero St., 10th Floor, Frankfort 40601 (800-255-7275).
Time Zones: Mostly Eastern; *Let's Go* makes note of areas in Central (1hr. behind Eastern). **Postal Abbreviation:** KY.
Sales Tax: 6%.

■ Louisville

Perched on the Ohio River, hovering between the North and the South, Louisville feels like a town caught between two pasts. One past has left a legacy of smokestacks, meat-packing yards, and the occasional crumbling edifice; the other still entices visitors with beautiful Victorian neighborhoods, ornate cast-iron buildings, and the elegance of twin-spired Churchill Downs. Each year, the nation's most prestigious horse race, the Kentucky Derby, caps a week-long extravaganza drawing more than half a million visitors. When it comes down to the big event, the party stands still for one thunderous moment and Kentuckians become deadly serious; many fortunes ride on the $15 million wagered each Derby Day.

Upper South

THE SOUTH

PRACTICAL INFORMATION

Tourist Office: Louisville Convention and Visitors Bureau, 400 S. 1st St. (582-3732 or 800-792-5595), at Liberty St. downtown. The standard goodies, including some bus schedules. Open Mon.-Fri. 8:30am-5pm, Sat. 9am-4pm, Sun. 11am-4pm.
Airport: Louisville International Airport (367-4636), 15min. south of downtown on I-65. Take bus #2 into the city.
Buses: Greyhound, 720 W. Muhammad Ali Blvd. (800-231-2222), at 7th St. To: Indianapolis (5 per day, 2hr., $20); Cincinnati (6 per day, 2hr., $16); Chicago (8 per day, 6hr., $31). Lockers $1 first day, $3 per each additional day. Open 24hr.
Public Transportation: Transit Authority River City (TARC), 585-1234. Extensive system of air-conditioned buses serves most of the metro area; buses run daily 5am-11:30pm. Fare 75¢, $1 during peak hours (Mon.-Fri. 6:30-8:30am and 3:30-5:30pm).
Taxis: Yellow Cab, 636-5511. $1.50 base fare ($1.80 suburbs), $1.50 per mi. 24hr.
Car Rental: Budget Rent-a-Car, 4330 Crittenden Dr. (363-4300). From $50 per day; from $30 per day on weekends. Must be 21 with a major credit card, or 25 without one. Open daily 6:30am-9pm.
Bicycle Rental: Highland Cycle, 1737 Bardstown Rd. (458-7832). $4.25 per hr., $15 per day. Open Mon.-Wed. and Fri. 9am-8pm, Thurs. 9am-5:30pm, Sat. 9am-4:30pm.
Hotlines: Rape Hotline, 581-7273. **Crisis Center,** 589-4313. **Gay/Lesbian Hotline,** 897-2475. Open daily 6-10pm.
Emergency: 911.
Post Office: 1420 Gardner Ln. (454-1650). Open Mon.-Fri. 7:30am-7pm, Sat. 7:30am-1pm. **ZIP code:** 40231. **Area code:** 502.

Major highways through the city include **I-65** (north-south expressway), **I-71,** and **I-64.** The easily accessible **Watterson Expressway,** also called **I-264,** rings the city, while the **Gene Snyder Freeway (I-265)** circles farther out. The central downtown area is defined by **Main St.** and **Broadway** running east-west, and **Preston Hwy.** and **19th St.** running north-south. The **West End,** beyond 20th St., is a rough area.

ACCOMMODATIONS AND CAMPING

Though easy to find, accommodations in downtown Louisville are not particularly cheap. For a bargain, try the budget motels on I-65 near the airport or head to **Newburg** (6mi. away) or **Bardstown** (39mi. away; see South of Louisville, p. 265). To get Derby Week lodging, make reservations six months to a year in advance and prepare to pay big bucks; the visitors bureau will help after March 13.

Red Roof Inn, 4704 Preston Hwy. (968-0151), off I-65 at Exit 130, 1mi. from the airport and 15min. from downtown. Small, clean rooms in a swell motel but a drab neighborhood. A/C, cable TV, free local calls. Singles $40, doubles $55.
Collier's Motor Court, 4812 Bardstown Rd. (499-1238), south of I-264, 30min. from downtown by car; TARC buses serve this inconvenient area. Well-maintained, cheap rooms with HBO, Showtime, and A/C. Singles $32, doubles $37.50.
Emily Boone Hostel, 1027 E. Franklin St. (585-3430), take Market St. east to Wenzell, then Wenzell North to Franklin. Despite its small size (maximum occupancy 3 visitors) and a frighteningly large dog (Irish wolfhound), the Boone abode is a pleasant place to spend a night in Louisville. Must call ahead.
KOA, 900 Marriot Dr. (812-282-4474), across the river from downtown. Follow I-65 north across the bridge and take the Stansifer Ave. exit. Paved camping, but *very* convenient to downtown. Grocery, playground, free use of the next door motel's pool, mini golf, and fishing lake. Sites for 2 $17, with hookup $22.50; each additional person $4, under 18 $2.50. Cabins for 2 $31.

FOOD

Louisville's chefs whip up a wide variety of cuisines, though good budget fare can be hard to find in the heart of downtown. **Bardstown Rd.** offers easy access to cafés,

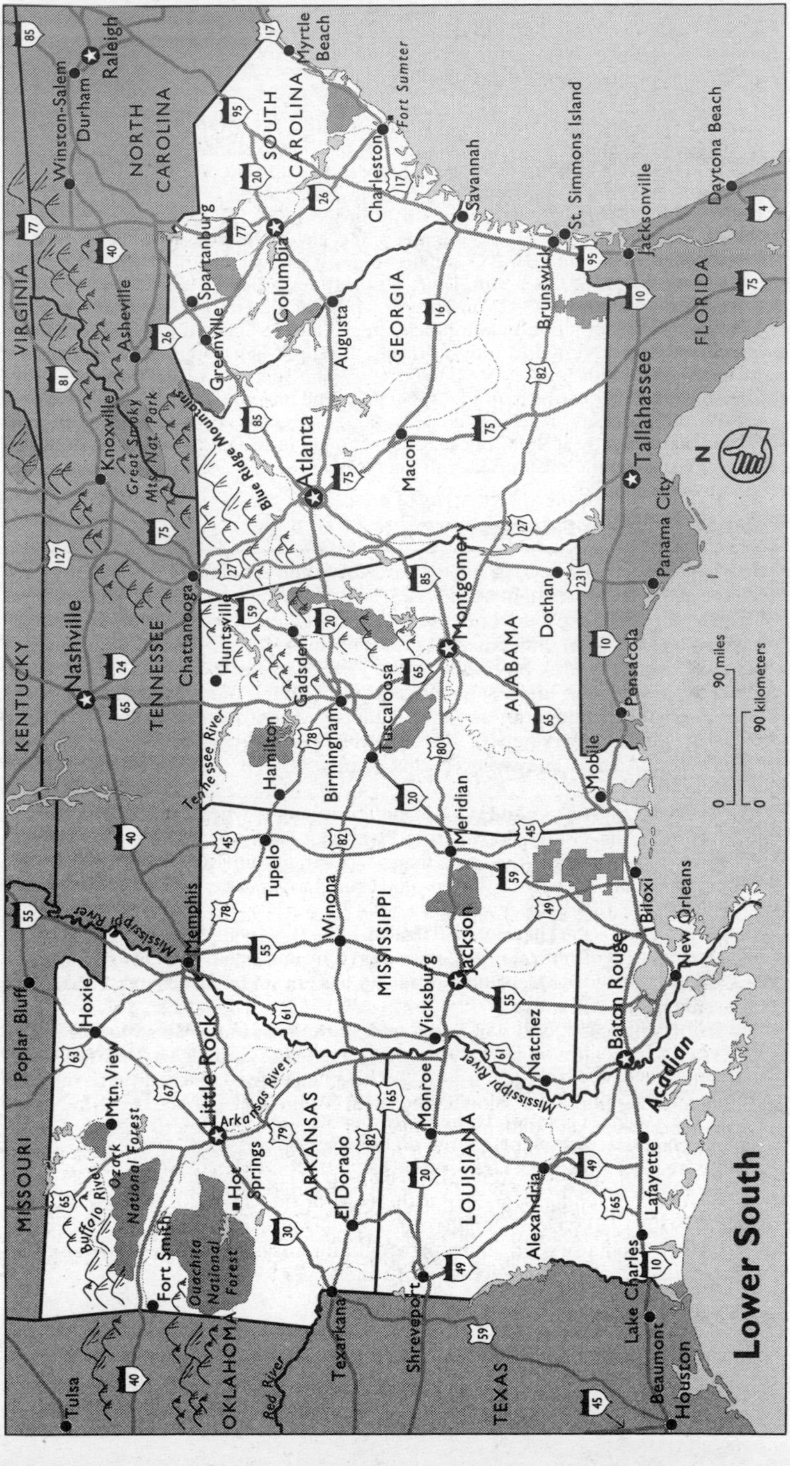

THE SOUTH

Lower South

Acadian

Cities and places (map labels):

Raleigh, Winston-Salem, Durham, Myrtle Beach, Fort Sumter, NORTH CAROLINA, SOUTH CAROLINA, Charleston, Savannah, St. Simmons Island, Jacksonville, Daytona Beach, VIRGINIA, Asheville, Spartanburg, Greenville, Columbia, Augusta, GEORGIA, Brunswick, FLORIDA, Knoxville, Great Smoky Mts. Nat. Park, Blue Ridge Mountains, Atlanta, Macon, Tallahassee, Panama City, Nashville, KENTUCKY, TENNESSEE, Chattanooga, Huntsville, Gadsden, Montgomery, Dothan, Pensacola, Tennessee River, Hamilton, Birmingham, Tuscaloosa, ALABAMA, Meridian, Mobile, Memphis, Tupelo, Winona, MISSISSIPPI, Jackson, Vicksburg, Biloxi, New Orleans, Poplar Bluff, Hoxie, MISSOURI, Mississippi River, Natchez, Baton Rouge, Little Rock, Mtn. View, Ozark National Forest, Buffalo River, Hot Springs, Ouachita National Forest, ARKANSAS, El Dorado, Monroe, LOUISIANA, Alexandria, Lafayette, Tulsa, Fort Smith, OKLAHOMA, Red River, Texarkana, Shreveport, Lake Charles, Beaumont, Houston, TEXAS, Arkansas River, New Orleans

N

90 miles

90 kilometers

budget eateries, and local and global cuisine, while **Frankfort Rd.** is rapidly becoming Bardstown-ized with restaurants and chi-chi cafés of its own. Downtown, **Theatre Sq.** provides plenty of good lunch options.

Ramsi's Café on the World, 1293 Bardstown Rd. (451-0700). This intimate restaurant peddles "ethnic non-regional cuisine" to a mix of hipsters and local families. Good vegetarian options. Chipolte con queso $4; salad Niçoise $6.50. Entrees $5-9. Open Mon.-Thurs. 11am-1am, Fri.-Sat. 11am-2am, Sun. 3-11pm.

Mark's Feed Store, 1514 Bardstown Rd. (458-1570). Award-winning barbecue served up on the cheap. If the weather's fine, eat on the patio with the metal pigs. Bodacious Burgoo and Bar-B-Q combo $8; pork sandwich $3.50; large ½ basket of onion straws $1.79. Open Sun.-Thurs. 11am-10pm, Fri.-Sat. 11am-11pm.

Cafe Kilimanjaro (583-4332), in Theater Sq. Jamaican, Ethiopian, and international cuisine. Jamaican jerk chicken lunch special $4.75; Chicken jerk dinner $9 and well worth it. Live world music Fri.-Sat. 10:30pm-3am. Open Mon. 11am-3pm, Tues.-Thurs. 11am-3pm and 4-9pm, Fri.-Sat. 11am-3pm and 5-10:30pm.

Twice Told, 1604 Bardstown Rd. (456-0507). The first coffeehouse to open in Louisville. Offers poetry readings, comedy, jazz, blues, and art exhibitions. Entertainment starts nightly at 9pm, but make sure to get in earlier for a Portabella burger ($3.75) made with mushrooms, not beef. Cover for shows $2-4. Open Sun.-Thurs. 10am-midnight, Fri.-Sat. 10am-1am.

NOT JUST A ONE-HORSE TOWN

The **Highlands** strip runs along Baxter/Bardstown and is bounded by Broadway and Trevilian Way on the south. Buses #17, 23, and 44 can all take you to this "anti-mall" of largely unfranchised, independent businesses. Cafés, pizza pubs, antique shops, record stores, and other enticements beckon to strollers. Farther south, in University of Louisville territory (take bus #2 or 4), the **J.B. Speed Art Museum,** 2035 S. 3rd St. (636-2893), houses an impressive collection of Dutch paintings and tapestries, Renaissance and contemporary art, and a sculpture court (open Tues.-Sat. 10am-4pm, Sun. noon-5pm; free; parking $2). The **Louisville Visual Arts Association** (896-2146) has info on local artists' shows and events. (Open Mon.-Fri. 9am-5pm, Sat. 9am-3pm, Sun. noon-4pm.)

The **Belle of Louisville** (574-2355), an authentic paddle-wheel craft, floats at 4th St. and River Rd. (2-hr. cruises depart from Riverfront Plaza late May-early Sept. Tues.-Sun. 2pm; sunset cruises Tues. and Thurs. 7pm; nighttime dance cruise Sat. 8:30-11:30pm. Boarding begins 1hr. before departure; arrive early, especially in July. $8, seniors $7, under 13 $4; dance cruise $12.)

Also downtown is the **Hillerich and Bradsby Co. (Louisville Slugger),** 800 W. Main (585-5226). A recent returnee to Louisville (from the Indiana suburb of Jeffersonville), the world-famous baseball bat producer has not yet published exact tour times or museum hours. Call ahead.

Lovers of American kitsch will find a treat at the **Harlan Sanders Museum,** Kentucky Fried Chicken International Headquarters, 1441 Gardiner Ln. (456-8607), off the Watterson Expwy. at Newburg Rd. S. The smell of fried chicken permeates this monument to the honorary Colonel who, with his pressure cooker, secret recipe of 11 herbs and spices, and trademark white suit, brought chicken to the masses. His autobiography, *Life As I Have Known It Has Been Finger Lickin' Good,* is on display but, sadly, *not* for sale (open Mon.-Thurs. 8am-5pm, Fri. 8am-3pm).

As for natural splendor, a gander at the **Falls of the Ohio,** 201 W. Riverside Dr. (812-280-9970), Clarksville, IN, might be just the ticket. The interpretive center at the Falls can help you find a good hiking path, hunt for fossils, or explore the river's geology (open daily 7am-11pm; $2, children 12 and under $1).

ENTERTAINMENT AND NIGHTLIFE

Start any entertainment search with the free weekly arts and entertainment newspaper, *Leo,* available at most downtown restaurants or at the visitors center. The **Ken-**

tucky Center for the Arts, 5 Riverfront Plaza (tickets and info 584-7777 or 800-775-7777), off Main St., hosts the **Louisville Orchestra,** the **Louisville Ballet,** the **Broadway Series,** and other major productions (open Mon.-Sat. 9am-6pm, Sun. noon-5pm). The **Lonesome Pines** series showcases indigenous Kentucky music, including bluegrass, as well as national jazz and various eccentric acts (ticket prices vary; student discounts available). Downtown, the **Actors Theater,** 316 W. Main St. (584-1265), a Tony award-winning repertory company, gives evening performances (8pm) and some matinees. (Sept. to mid-June. Box office open Mon.-Fri. 9am-5pm. Tickets from $15; student and senior rush tickets 15min. before each show $10.) Bring a picnic dinner to the **Kentucky Shakespeare Festival** (583-8738), in Central Park, which takes place over eight summer weekends starting in early June; don't forget bug spray (performances 8pm).

Butchertown Pub, 1335 Story Ave. (583-2242), presents three stages of alternative music and blues from local and national bands (cover $1-4; open Mon. 4-11:30pm, Tues. 4pm-1am, Wed.-Sat. 4pm-2am). A multi-faceted entertainment machine, **The Brewery,** 426 Baxter Ave. (583-3420), hosts college bands like Collective Soul and Toad the Wet Sprocket on Thursday nights. When there's no show, hang out on the Brewery's four volleyball courts or catch the monthly boxing night. (Cover for live shows only. Open Sun.-Thurs. 11am-2am, Fri.-Sat. 11am-4am.) **Phoenix Hill Tavern,** 644 Baxter Ave. (589-4957), cooks with nightly blues, rock, and reggae on four stages including a deck and a roof garden (cover $2-3; open Wed.-Thurs. and Sat. 8pm-4am, Fri. 5pm-4am). Members of the Techno Alliance take heart; **Sparks,** 104 W. Main St. (587-8566), throbs 'til the early morn (cover Fri.-Sat. $3-5, Sun. $3; open daily 10pm-4am). For gay nightlife, check out **The Connection,** 120 S. Floyd St. (585-5752; cover $2-5; open Tues.-Sun. 9pm-4am).

HORSIN' AROUND

Even if you miss the Kentucky Derby, make a visit to **Churchill Downs,** 700 Central Ave. (636-4400), 3 mi. south of downtown; take bus #4 ("4th St.") to Central Ave. You don't have to bet to admire the twin spires, the colonial columns, the gardens, and the sheer scale of the track—but it sure does make things exciting. (Races April-July 1 Wed.-Fri. 3-7pm, Sat.-Sun. 1-5:30pm; Oct.-Nov. Tues.-Sun. 1-5pm. Grandstand seats $2, clubhouse $3.50, reserved clubhouse $5.50. Grounds open in racing season daily 10am-4pm. Parking $2.)

The **Kentucky Derby Festival** celebrates with balloon and steamboat races, concerts, and parades for a full week before the climactic **Run for the Roses** on the first Saturday in May. A one- to five-year waiting list stands between you and a ticket for the Derby ($20-30), but never fear; on Derby morning, tickets are sold for standing room only spots in the grandstand or infield. Get in line early for good seats lest the other 80,000 spectators get there first. Amazingly, no one is turned away. The **Kentucky Derby Museum** (637-1111), at Churchill Downs, offers a slide presentation on a 360° screen, tours of the stadium, profiles of famous stables and trainers, a simulated horse race for betting practice, and tips on exactly what makes a horse a "sure thing." (Open daily 9am-5pm. $5, seniors $4, ages 5-12 $1.50, under 5 free.)

■ South of Louisville

Bardstown Kentucky's second-oldest city hosts **The Stephen Foster Story** (800-626-1563 or 348-5971), a mawkish, heavily promoted outdoor musical about America's first major songwriter, the author of "My Old Kentucky Home." (Mid-June to Labor Day Tues.-Sun. 8:30pm, indoor matinee Sat. 2:30pm. $12, under 13 $6, Sat. matinee $10, Sun. evening $5.)

In 1791, Kentucky Baptist Reverend Elijah Craig left a fire unattended while heating oak boards to make a barrel for his aging whiskey. The boards were charred but Rev. Craig carried on. Bourbon was born in that first charred wood barrel, and Bardstown became the "Bourbon Capital of the World." Ninety percent of the nation's bourbon hails from Kentucky, and 60% of that is distilled in Nelson and Bullitt Counties. **Jim Beam's American Outpost** (543-9877), 15 mi. west of Bardstown in Clermont off Rte. 245, features "master distiller emeritus" himself, Jim Beam's grandson, Booker Noe, who narrates a film about bourbon. Don't miss the free lemonade, coffee, and sampler bourbon candies. From Louisville, take I-65 south to Exit 112, then Rte. 245 east for 1½ mi. (open Mon.-Sat. 9am-4:30pm, Sun. 1-4pm; free). You can't actually tour Beam's huge distillery, but **Maker's Mark Distillery** (865-2099), 19 mi. southeast of Bardstown in Loretto, will show you how bourbon was made in the 19th century (sorry, no Funky Bunch). Take Rte. 49 south to Rte. 52 east. (Tours Mon.-Sat. on the hr. 10am-3pm, Sun. on the hr. 1-3pm; Jan.-Feb. Mon.-Fri. only. Free.) Neither site has a license to sell its liquors. **Bardstown Visitors Center,** 107 E. Stephen Foster Ave. (348-4877 or 800-638-4877), gives a free 1-hr. tour, taking visitors by **My Old Kentucky Home** and **Heaven Hill Distillery** in an open-air trolley. (Tours in summer daily 9:30am, 11am, 1:30pm, and 3pm; visitors center open Mon.-Sat. 8am-7pm, Sun. noon-5pm; Nov.-Mar. Mon.-Sat. 8am-5pm.)

Abraham Lincoln's Birthplace Near Hodgenville, 45 mi. south of Louisville on U.S. 31 east, this national historic site marks the birthplace of Honest Abe. From Louisville, take I-65 down to Rte. 61; public transportation does not serve the area. Fifty-six steps representing the 56 years of Lincoln's tragically shortened life lead up to a stone monument sheltering the small log cabin. Set in a beautiful location, the site offers many examples of frontier architecture as well as an 18-min. video about Lincoln in Kentucky. (358-3137. Open June-Aug. daily 8am-6:45pm; Labor Day-Oct. and May 8am-5:45pm; Nov.-April 8am-4:45pm. Free.)

Mammoth Cave Hundreds of enormous caves and narrow passageways cut through **Mammoth Cave National Park** (758-2328 or 800-967-2283), 80 mi. south of Louisville off I-65, then west on Rte. 70. Mammoth Cave comprises the world's longest network of cavern corridors—over 325 mi. in length. Start your exploration at the **visitors center** (open summers daily 7:30am-7:30pm; off season 7:30am-5:30pm). Devoted spelunkers should try the 6-hr. "Wild Cave Tour" during the summer (must be 16; $31); less ambitious types generally take the 2-hr., 2-mi. historical walking tour ($5.50, seniors $3.25, ages 6-15 $3, under 5 free). Ninety-minute tours accommodate disabled visitors ($4). The caves stay at 54°F year-round; bring a sweater. **Greyhound** comes only as close as **Cave City,** just east of I-65 on Rte. 70. **Time zone:** Central (1hr. behind Eastern).

■ Lexington

Lexington, Kentucky's second-largest city, revels in its Southern heritage. Even recent growth spurts have left the city's town-like atmosphere intact. Historic mansions show through the skyscrapers downtown, and a 20-minute drive from the city will set you squarely in bluegrass country. Like the rest of Kentucky, Lexington has horse fever; the Kentucky Horse Park gets top billing, while shopping complexes and small industries at the outskirts of town share space with 150-odd quaint, green horse farms. These farms have nurtured such equine greats as Citation, Lucky Debonair, Seattle Slew, and Whirlaway, giving good reason for the city's passion.

PRACTICAL INFORMATION

Tourist Office: Greater Lexington Convention and Visitors Bureau, 301 E. Vine St. (233-1221 or 800-848-1224), at Rose St. Open Mon.-Fri. 8:30am-6pm, Sat. 10am-5pm.

Buses: Greyhound, 477 New Circle Rd. N.W. (299-8804 or 800-231-2222); take Lex-Tran bus #6 downtown. To: Louisville (1 per day, 1¾hr., $19); Cincinnati (4 per day, 1hr., $19); Knoxville (4 per day, 3hr., $39). Open daily 7:30am-11pm.

Public Transportation: Lex-Tran, 109 W. London Ave. (253-4636). Buses leave from the **Transit Center,** 220 W. Vine St., between M.L. King and Stone Ave. Sys-

tem serves the university and city outskirts. Service is erratic. Buses run 6:15am-
6:15pm; evening service on some routes until 10pm. Fare 80¢.
Taxis: Lexington Yellow Cab, 231-8294. $1.90 base fare, $1.60 per mi. 24hr.
Hotlines: Crisis Intervention, 233-0444. **Rape Crisis,** 253-2511. **AIDS Volun-
teers of Lexington,** 254-2865.
Emergency: 911.
Post Office: 1088 Nandino Blvd. (231-6700); take bus #1 ("Georgetown"). Open
Mon.-Fri. 8am-5pm, Sat. 9am-1pm. General delivery to 111 Barr St. (254-6156).
Open Mon.-Fri. 8am-4:30pm. **ZIP code:** 40511. **Area code:** 606.

New Circle Rd. (Rte. 4/U.S. 60 bypass) loops the city, intersecting with many roads
that connect the downtown district to the surrounding towns. **High, Vine,** and **Main
St.** running east-west and **Limestone St.** and **Broadway** running north-south provide
the best routes through downtown.

ACCOMMODATIONS AND CAMPING

A concentration of horse-related wealth in the Lexington area pushes accommodation prices up. The cheapest places lurk outside the city, beyond New Circle Rd. **Dial
Accommodations,** 301 E. Vine St. (233-1221 or 800-848-1224), at the visitors center,
can help you find a room. (Open Mon.-Fri. 8:30am-6pm, Sat. 10am-6pm, Sun. noon-
5pm; off season reduced hours.)

Catalina Motel, 208 New Circle Rd. (299-6281), take Newton Pike north of the city,
and turn east onto New Circle Rd. Large, clean rooms with A/C, cable, and HBO
(singles $30, doubles $36).
Microtel, 2240 Buena Vista Dr. (299-9600), near I-75 and Winchester Rd. Pleasant,
new motel rooms with window seats—yeah, window seats (singles $33).
Bryan Station Inn, 273 New Circle Rd. (299-4162); take bus #4 or Limestone St.
north from downtown, and turn right onto Rte. 4. Clean rooms on a motel/fast-
food strip. No phones. Must be 21. Singles $32, doubles $34; Fri.-Sat. rates higher.
Kimball House Motel, 267 S. Limestone St. (252-9565), between downtown and
the university. Look for the grungy sign and peeling paint, and step into a mid-20th
century timewarp. Parking in back. No phones in rooms. Ask specifically for one of
the 1st-floor singles (no A/C, shared bath) which go for $28; they often fill by late
afternoon. Otherwise, singles from $34, doubles $38. Key deposit $5.
Kentucky Horse Park Campground, 4089 Ironworks Pike (233-43030), 10mi.
north of downtown off Newton Pike. Great camping plus laundry, showers, athletic courts, swimming pool, and a free shuttle to the KY Horse Park and Museum
next door. Wide open tent sites, but the 200 RV sites have a good mix of shade and
lawn. 2-wk. max stay. Sites $11, with hookup $15. Senior discounts available.

FOOD AND NIGHTLIFE

Ramsey's, 496 E. High St. (259-2708). Real Southern grease. Vegetarians beware:
even the vegetables are cooked with pork parts. One meat and 3 vegetables $9.50.
Sandwiches under $6. Open Sun.-Mon. 11am-11pm, Tues.-Sat. 11am-12pm.
Alfalfa Restaurant, 557 S. Limestone St. (253-0014), across from Memorial Hall at
the university; take bus #9. Menu of fantastic international and veggie meals
change nightly. Complete dinners with salad and bread under $10. Filling soups
and salads from $2. Live jazz, folk, and other music. Fri.-Sat. 8-10pm; no cover.
Open Mon. 11am-5:30pm, Tues.-Thurs. 11am-9pm, Fri. 11am-10pm, Sat. 10am-2pm
and 5:30pm-10pm, Sun. 10am-2pm.
Parkette Drive-In, 1216 New Circle Rd. (254-8723). Drive-up, 50s-style eatery with
bargain food, but no rollerskating waitresses. Giant "Poor Boy" burger plate $2.50;
chicken box with 3 pieces, gravy, fries, cole slaw, and roll $4.10. A few booths
inside give carless folks an equal opportunity to join in the nostalgia. Open Mon.-
Thurs. 11am-11pm, Fri.-Sat. 11am-1am.
Everybody's Natural Foods and Deli, 503 Euclid Ave. (255-4162). A health-food
store which sets out a few tables and serves excellent gazpacho, sandwiches

($2.75-3.65), and a daily lunch special ($4.75). Veggie delight $3.75; fruit smoothies $2.75. Open Mon.-Fri. 8am-8pm, Sat. 10am-8pm, Sun. noon-5pm.

Lexington's nightlife surpasses most expectations for a town its size. For current entertainment info, read the "Weekender" section of Friday's *Herald-Leader*. **Sundance** and **The Brewery,** both at 509 W. Main St. (255-2822), provide a lively country and western bar and music scene (both open daily 8am-1am). Stand-up comics do their thing at **Comedy off Broadway,** 3199 Nicholsville Rd. (271-5653), at Lexington Green Mall. **The Bar,** 224 E. Main St. (255-1551), a popular disco cabaret/lounge complex, caters to gays and lesbians. (Cover Fri. $4, Sat. $5. Must be 21. Lounge open Mon.-Sat. 4pm-1am; disco open Mon.-Thurs. 10pm-1am, Fri. 10pm-2am, Sat. 10pm-3:30am.) For a bit o' the Irish, stop in at **Lynagh's Pub and Club** (255-1292), in University Plaza at Woodland and Euclid St. The pub offers superior burgers ($4.75; open Mon.-Sat. 11am-1am, Sun. noon-11pm), while the club has music next door (cover from $3; open Tues.-Sat. 8pm-1am).

SIGHTS

To escape the stifling swamp conditions farther south, antebellum plantation owners built beautiful summer retreats in milder Lexington. The most attractive of these stately houses preen only a few blocks northeast of the town center in the **Gratz Park** area near the old public library. Wrap-around porches, wooden minarets, stone foundations, and rose-covered trellises distinguish these old estates from the neighborhood's newer homes. The **Hunt Morgan House,** 201 N. Mill St. (253-0362), stands at the end of the park across from the old library. Built in 1814 by John Wesley Hunt, the first millionaire west of the Alleghenies, the house witnessed the birth of Thomas Hunt Morgan, who won a 1933 Nobel Prize for proving the existence of the gene. The house's most colorful inhabitant, however, was Confederate General John Hunt Morgan who, pursued by Union troops, rode his horse up the front steps and into the house, leaned down to kiss his mother, and rode out the back door. (Tours Tues.-Sat. 10am-4pm, Sun. 2-5pm. $5, under 12 $2.) Mary Todd, the future wife of Abraham Lincoln, grew up just five blocks away in the **Mary Todd Lincoln House,** 578 W. Main St. (233-9999); you can see the house on a one-hour tour (open April-Dec. 15 Tues.-Sat. 10am-4pm; last tour 3:15pm; $5, ages 6-12 $2). Senator Henry Clay and John Hunt Morgan now lie buried at the **Lexington Cemetery,** 833 W. Main St. (255-5522. Open daily 8am-5pm. Free cemetery scavenger hunts available for children, but you don't have to dig anything up.) During his lifetime, Clay resided at **Ashland,** 120 Sycamore Rd. (266-8581), a 20-acre estate across town at the corner of Sycamore and Richmond Rd.; take the "Woodhall" bus. (Open Tues.-Sat. 10am-4:30pm, Sun. 1-4:30pm. 1-hr. tours $5, students $3, ages 6-12 $2.)

HORSES

Lexington horse farms are among the most beautiful places on earth. Visit **Three Chimneys Farm** (873-7053), at Rte. 1 and Old Frankfort Pike 4 mi. from I-64 and 8½ mi. from New Circle Rd., the home of 1977 Triple Crown winner Seattle Slew (tours daily 10am and 1pm, by appointment only). **Kentucky Horse Park,** 4089 Ironworks Pike (800-368-8813), 10 mi. north at Exit 120 off I-75, has full facilities for equestrians, a museum, a film, and the Man O' War Monument. (Open daily 9am-5pm. $10, ages 7-12 $5; live horse shows and horse-drawn vehicle tours included. A 50-min. horse ride and tour is in addition to entrance fee, pony rides $3.25.) The last weekend in April, the horse park hosts the annual **Rolex** tournament qualifier for the U.S. equestrian team. Every April, the **Keeneland Race Track,** 4201 Versailles Rd. (254-3412 or 800-456-3412), west on U.S. 60, holds the final prep race for the Kentucky Derby (races Oct. and April; post time 1pm; $2.50; workouts open to the public). At **Red Mile Harness Track,** 847 S. Broadway (255-0752), take bus #3 on S. Broadway, harness racing takes center stage. (Races April-June and late Sept.-early Oct.; in spring post time 7:30pm, in fall 1pm. $3. Parking free. Morning workouts open to the public in racing season 7:30am-noon.)

■ Near Lexington

Harrodsburg, the oldest permanent English settlement west of the Alleghenies, is nestled 32 mi. southwest of Lexington on U.S. 68. Relive the legacy of Fort Harrod, founded in 1774, at **Old Fort Harrod State Park,** S. College St. (734-3314), an active replica in which craftspeople clothed in 18th-century garb demonstrate skills like blacksmithing and quilting. (Open 8:30am-8pm; off season 8am-4:30pm. $3.50, ages 6-12 $2.) Pick up a tour booklet for historic downtown Harrodsburg at the **visitors center,** 1035 Main St. (734-2364), on the corner of U.S. 68 and Main (open Mon.-Fri. 8:30am-4:30pm).

The Shakers, a 19th-century celibate religious sect, practiced the simple life at **Shaker Village** (734-5411), about 25 mi. southwest of Lexington and north of Harrodsburg on U.S. 68. The 5000-acre farm features 27 restored Shaker buildings; a tour includes demonstrations of everything from making apple butter to coopering (barrel-making). Riverboat excursions on the Kentucky River can be added into the deal. (Open daily 9am-6pm. $9.50, students 12-17 $4.50, ages 6-11 $2.50; with river trip $12/$6.50/$3.50. Oct.-March reduced hours and prices.)

In **Richmond,** Exit 95 off I-75, the elegant Georgian-Italianate mansion **White Hall** (623-9178) was the home of the abolitionist (not the boxer) Cassius M. Clay, cousin of Senator Henry Clay. (45-min. guided tours only. Open April-Oct. daily 9am-4:30pm; Labor Day-Oct. Wed.-Sun. only. $4, under 13 $2.50, under 6 free.) A re-creation of one of Daniel Boone's forts, **Fort Boonesborough State Park** (527-3131), also in Richmond, has samples of 18th-century crafts, a small museum collection, and films about the pioneers. (Open April-Aug. daily 9am-5:30pm; Sept.-Oct. Wed.-Sun. 9am-5:30pm. $4.50, ages 6-12 $2.50, under 6 free. Combination White Hall/Boonesborough tickets available.)

▓ Daniel Boone National Forest

The **Daniel Boone National Forest** cuts a vast green swath through Kentucky's Eastern Highlands. Enclosing 670,000 acres of mountains and valleys, the forest is layered with a gorgeous tangle of chestnut, oak, hemlock, and pine, as well as pristine lakes, waterfalls, and extraordinary natural bridges. This is Bluegrass country, where seasoned backpackers and Lexington's day trippers still find the heart of old Appalachia deep in the forest—though, by some reports, you're less likely these days to stumble onto feuding Hatfields and McCoys than into some farmer's hidden field of marijuana, reputedly Kentucky's #1 cash crop.

Practical Information Seven U.S. Forest Service Ranger Districts administer the National Forest. Ranger offices offer trail maps and details on which portions of the 254-mi. **Sheltowee Trace,** the forest's most significant trail, pass through their districts. **Stanton Ranger District,** 705 W. College Ave. (663-2852), Stanton, includes the Red River Gorge and Natural Bridge (open Mon.-Fri. 8am-4:30pm). To the north, **Morehead Ranger District,** 2375 KY 801 S. (784-5624), includes Cave Run Lake. Contact the **Morehead Tourism Commission,** 168 E. Main St., Morehead 40351 (784-6221) for more info. To the south, **London Ranger District** (864-4163 or 864-4164), on U.S. 25S, covers Laurel River Lake, close to **Cumberland Falls;** Laurel River Lake's **visitors center** (878-6900 or 800-348-0095) is at Exit 41 off I-75 (open Mon-Sat. 9am-5pm). For forest-wide info, contact the Forest Supervisor, 1700 Bypass Rd. (745-3100). **Greyhound** (800-231-2222) serves several towns with buses to and from Lexington, KY: Morehead (1 per day, 1hr., $16); London (3 per day, 1½hr., $17); Corbin (4 per day, 2hr., $19). **Emergency:** 911. **Area code:** 606.

THE SOUTH

Stanton Ranger District Split by the Mountain Pkwy., **Stanton Ranger District** divides into two parts, with **Natural Bridge State Resort Park** on the south side, and **Red River Gorge Geological Area** on the north. **Natural Bridge,** off Rte. 11, is the area's absolute must-see site. It takes a hike through the forest to reach the bridge, but the expansive view awaiting at the top of the bridge's vast span proves worth the walk. The **Red River Gorge** area contains some of the most varied and ecologically rich terrain in this part of the country. The circuit runs through the single-lane **Nada Tunnel,** an old railroad tunnel cut directly through the rock (scary as hell!), and past the restored **Gladie Historic Site Log House,** which illuminates turn-of-the-century rural logging life. Along the way, it takes in buffalo, curving mountain roads, forests, and picturesque wooden and metal bridges. If you don't mind driving down a 3-mi. gravel road, make a stop at the beautiful **Rock Bridge,** down Rock Bridge Rd. near the junction of Rte. 715 and Rte. 15.

Slade, 52 mi. southeast of Lexington (take I-64 to Mountain Pkwy.), makes a good base for a tour of this portion of the forest. A red **tourist caboose,** run by the **Natural Bridge/Powell County Chamber of Commerce** (663-9229), sits at the Slade Exit off Mountain Pkwy. (open Mon.-Fri. 10am-6pm, Sat.-Sun. 10am-5pm). The town itself contains almost nothing except the forest and the lavish **Natural Bridge State Resort Park,** 2135 Natural Bridge Rd. (663-2214 or 800-325-1710), off Rte. 11. Avoid the park's pricey lodge, and patronize its **campgrounds: Whittletown** has 40 well shaded sites; and **Middle Fork** 39 open sites. (Sites for 2 with hookup $12; $1 per additional adult, under 17 free. Primitive camping $8.50.) Off Rte. 15, **Koomer Ridge** offers wooded primitive camping (sites $6, double sites $10). You can also pitch a tent anywhere in the forest, as long as you stay more than 300 ft. from roads or marked trails. Those who prefer the great indoors should lay down their burdens in one of the large, clean, slightly dim rooms at **Li'l Abners** (663-5384), 2½mi. from Red River Gorge on Rte. 11 in Slade (singles $44, doubles $49; in July and Aug. book a room in advance).

While wandering this part of the state, be sure to try **Ale-8-1** ("A Late One"), the local soft drink in the tall green bottle, and the regional staple of soup beans and cornbread. Good restaurants are hard to come by, but many **general stores** peddle cheap, filling sandwiches. The particularly well stocked **Pine Ridge General Store,** 6023 Rte. 15 (668-3498), near the Koomer Ridge campground, has ham and cheese sandwiches ($1.85) and 12" pizzas ($7; open Sun.-Thurs. 8am-10pm, Fri.-Sat. 8am-midnight). In nearby Stanton, **Bruen's Restaurant,** on Sipple St. at Exit 22 off Mountain Pkwy., makes greasy spoon fare in an authentic down-home atmosphere. Breakfast is served all day; have two eggs, bacon, and a biscuit with gravy for just $2.55, or a cheeseburger for $1.50. (Open Sun.-Thurs. 4:30am-9pm, Fri.-Sat. 4:30am-10pm.)

London Ranger District For boating, fishing, hiking, and just hanging out, try **Laurel River Lake. Camping** is available at two spacious and densely wooded Forest Service campgrounds on the lake, both off Rte. 1193 and adjacent to marinas: **Grove** (528-6156 or 800-280-2266), with 52 sites; and **Holly Bay** (878-8134), with 90 sites (all sites have hookups; sites for 1 $12, for 2 $18). Visitors to giant **Cumberland Falls,** 18 mi. west of Corbin on Rte. 90—"The Niagara of the South"—camp at the state park which surrounds the falls (528-4121; 50 sites with hookup $8.50; open Apr.-Oct.). If you stay, check out the falls' famous moonbows. **Sheltowee Trace Outfitters** (800-541-RAFT/7238), in Parker's Lake behind Holiday Motor Lodge at Hwy. 90, 1 mi. west of the state park, arranges guided, six-hour whitewater rafting trips down the Cumberland Falls' Class III rapids ($40, ages 5-12 $30).

■ Cumberland Gap

Stretching from Maine to Georgia, the majestic Appalachian Mountain Range proved a formidable obstacle to the movement of early American settlers, but not to buffalo; by following herds of buffalo, Native Americans learned of the Cumberland Gap, a natural break in the mountains allowing passage west. Frontiersman Daniel Boone became famous when he blazed the Wilderness Trail through the Gap in 1775, thereby opening the west to colonization. Today, the **Cumberland Gap National Historic Park,** best reached by U.S. 25E from Kentucky or U.S. 58 from Virginia, sits on 20,000 acres shared by Kentucky, Virginia, and Tennessee. The Cumberland Gap **visitors center** (606-248-2817), on U.S. 25E in Middleboro, KY, has a 10-min. film, and a brief slide presentation on the history of the Gap. (Park and center open daily 8am-6pm; Labor Day-Memorial Day Mon.-Fri. 9am-5pm.) The Park's 160-site **campground,** on U.S. 58 in Virginia, has hot showers (primitive sites $10). From either the campground or the visitors center take a difficult 4-mi. hike to **Pinnacle Rock** for breathtaking aerial circumspection. **Backcountry camping** requires a free permit from the visitors center.

Tennessee

Sloping from the majestic Great Smoky Mountains to the verdant Mississippi lowlands, Tennessee makes and breaks stereotypes with the smooth ease of Jack Daniels. Those enchanted with the last state to secede from the Union, and the first to rejoin, often express their affection in the form of song—an ode to Davy Crockett deems this Southern parallelogram "greatest state in the land of the free," Arrested Development come to quench their thirst, and there ain't no place the Grateful Dead would rather be. Tennessee's economy is industry-based, with the world's largest Bible-producing business. Music fuels the state's artistic life; country western twangs from Nashville, while the blues wail in Memphis.

PRACTICAL INFORMATION

Capital: Nashville.
Visitor Information: Tennessee Dept. of Tourist Development, 320 6th Ave., Nashville (741-2158). Open Mon.-Fri. 8am-4:30pm. **Tennessee State Parks Information,** 401 Church St., Nashville (800-421-6683).
Time Zones: Eastern and Central (1hr. behind Eastern); *Let's Go* makes note of areas which lie in Central. **Postal Abbreviation:** TN.
Sales Tax: 7.75-9%, by county.

■ Nashville

Long-forgotten Francis Nash is one of only four Revolutionary War heroes honored with U.S. city names (Washington, Wayne, and Knox are the others), but his tenuous foothold in history pales in comparison to Nashville's notoriety as the banjo pickin', foot stompin' capital of country music. Large, eclectic, and unapologetically heterogeneous, Tennessee's capital is not only the home of the Country Music Hall of Fame, but a slick financial hub as well ("the Wall Street of the South"). The city headquarters the Southern Baptists and finds room for centers of fine arts and higher learning such as Fisk University and Vanderbilt.

PRACTICAL INFORMATION

Tourist Office: Nashville Area Convention and Visitors Bureau, 161 4th Ave. N. (259-4700), between Commerce and Church St. downtown. Ask for the free *Music City Vacation Guide.* Open Mon.-Fri. 8am-5pm. **Nashville Tourist Information Center** (259-4747), I-65 at Exit 85, James Robertson Pkwy., ½mi. east of the capitol just over the bridge. Complete maps marked with attractions. Open daily 8am-8pm.
Airport: Metropolitan (275-1675), 8mi. south of downtown. Bus fare downtown $1.40 with a transfer. An airport shuttle (275-1180) operates out of major downtown hotels ($8, $15 roundtrip). Taxis downtown run $15-17.

Buses: Greyhound, 200 8th Ave. S. (255-1691 or 800-231-2222), at Broadway downtown. Borders on a rough neighborhood, but the station is bright. To: Memphis (12 per day, 4-5hr., $30); Chattanooga (4 per day, 3hr., $21); Birmingham (5 per day, 3½hr., $30); Knoxville (6 per day, 3hr., $30). Open 24hr.

Public Transportation: Metropolitan Transit Authority (MTA) (862-5950). Buses operate Mon.-Fri. 5am-midnight, less frequent service Sat.-Sun. Fare $1.30, transfers 10¢. MTA runs 2 **tourist trolleys** from Riverfront Park and Downtown Circle daily every 10-15min. 11am to early evening (90¢).

Taxis: Nashville Cab, 242-7070. 90¢ base fare, $1.50 per mi.

Car Rental: Alamo Rent-A-Car (800-327-9633), at the airport. $40 per day, on weekends $16 per day. Under 25 surcharge $20 per day.

Hotlines: Crisis Line, 244-7444. **Rape Hotline,** 256-8526. Both 24hr. **Gay and Lesbian Switchboard,** 297-0008. Opens nightly 5pm.

Emergency: 911.

Post Office: 901 Broadway (255-9447 or 255-9451), across from the Park Plaza Hotel and next to Union Station. Open Mon.-Fri. 7:30am-7pm, Sat. 9am-2pm. **ZIP code:** 37202. **Area code:** 615.

Nashville's streets are fickle, often interrupted by curving parkways and one-ways. Names change constantly and without warning; **Broadway,** the main east-west thoroughfare, melts into **West End Ave.** just outside downtown at Vanderbilt and I-40. Downtown, numbered avenues run north-south, parallel to the Cumberland River. The curve of **James Robertson Pkwy.** encloses the north end, becoming **Main St.** on the other side of the river (later **Gallatin Pike**) and **McGavock St.** at the south end. The area south of Broadway between 2nd and 7th Ave. and the region north of James Robertson Pkwy. are both unsafe at night.

ACCOMMODATIONS AND CAMPING

Finding a room in Nashville isn't difficult, just expensive. Make reservations well in advance, especially for weekend stays. Budget motels concentrate around **W. Trinity Ln.** and **Brick Church Pike,** off I-65 at Exit 87B. Dirt-cheap hotels inhabit the area around **Dickerson Rd.** and **Murfreesboro,** but the neighborhood is seedy at best. Closer to downtown (but still sketchy), several motels huddle on **Interstate Dr.** just over the Woodland St. Bridge.

The Cumberland Inn, 150 W. Trinity Ln. (226-1600), Exit 87A off I-65N north of downtown. Cheerful rooms with bright, modern furnishings, HBO, laundry facilities, and a free continental breakfast. Unlimited local calls $1 per day. Singles $30, doubles $38; Fri.-Sat. $35/$48.

Hallmark Inn, 309 W. Trinity Ln. (228-2624 or 800-251-3294). Comfortable, well-kept rooms, with cable TV, free continental breakfast, and a pool. Singles $28-38, doubles $38-58. Another location on Dickerson Rd. (356-6005).

Motel 6, 4 locations. 311 W. Trinity Ln. (227-9696), at Exit 87B off I-65; 323 Cartwright St. (859-9674), Goodlettsville, off Long Hollow Pike west from I-65; 95 Wallace Rd. (333-9933), off Exit 56 from I-24; 420 Metroplex Dr. (833-8887), near the airport. Decent rooms with HBO, outdoor pool, free local calls. Singles $32, doubles $36. Under 18 free with parents. Wallace and Metroplex locations are slightly ritzier and more expensive.

The Liberty Inn, 2400 Brick Church Pike (228-2567). Presents its guests with spacious rooms, but small closets. Cable, A/C, local calls 35¢. Singles $30, doubles $42; Fri.-Sat. $42/$65.

Two campgrounds lie within the range of public transportation near Opryland USA; by car, take Briley Pkwy. north to McGavock Pike and exit west onto Music Valley Dr. **Nashville Holiday Travel Park,** 2572 Music Valley Dr. (889-4225), provides a wooded area for tenting and densely packed RV sites (sites for 2 $17, with hookup $26; $4 per additional person over age 11). **Opryland KOA,** 2626 Music Valley Dr. (889-0282), exit at 12B off I55 north and go north at Music Valley Dr., has 50 tent sites ($20) and tons of crowded sites with hookups ($30); perks include a pool and live summer music.

FOOD

In Nashville, music even influences the local delicacies; pick up a Goo-Goo Cluster (peanuts, pecans, chocolate, caramel, and marshmallow), sold at practically any store, and you'll bite into the initials of the Grand Ole Opry. Nashville's other finger-lickin' traditions, barbecue or fried chicken followed by pecan pie, are no less sinful. Restaurants for collegiate tastes and budgets cram West End Ave. and the 2000 block of Elliston Pl., near Vanderbilt.

Slice of Life, 1811 Division St. (329-2525), next to music studios. Hang out with country musicians and celebs (visitors include ZZ Top and Lily Tomlin) in this cool yuppie hangout. Features fresh bread, wholesome Tex-Mex, and macrobiotic foods like 16-bean gumbo. Dinner entrees $7-11; lunches $5-7. Giant cookies and muffins ($1.25) steam in the bakery. Open Mon. 7am-4pm, Tues.-Thurs. 7am-9pm, Fri. 7am-10pm, Sat. 8am-10pm, Sun. 8am-4pm.

Iguana, 1910 Belcourt (383-8920). Iguana does it right—good food, great service, and *the best* chicken fajitas, hands-down, no questions asked ($10). Young crowd, outdoor deck. Open Mon.-Fri. 11am-2am, Sat.-Sun. 5pm-2am.

The World's End, 1713 Church St. (329-3480). It's the end of the world as we know it, and I feel like a burger or a salad ($5-8), or maybe a beer ($2.50). Caters to a primarily gay crowd, but no one need feel unwelcome. Open Sun.-Thurs. 4pm-12:30am, Fri.-Sat. 4pm-1:30am.

Garden Allegro, 1805 Church St. (327-3834). Just north of Vanderbilt, this veggie joint grabs rave reviews from its clients. Try the exquisite vegetarian curry ($7). Open daily 9am-9pm.

SIGHTS

Music Row, home of Nashville's signature industry, centers around Division and Demonbreun St. from 16th to 19th Ave. S., bounded to the south by Grand Ave. (take bus #3 to 17th Ave. and walk south). After surviving the mobs outside the must-see **Country Music Hall of Fame,** 4 Music Sq. E. (256-1639), at Division St., you can marvel at classic memorabilia such as Elvis's "solid gold" Cadillac and 24-karat gold piano, evocative photos from the early days of country music, and aggressively colored costumes from more recent performances. Though Tennessee is the birthplace of bluegrass, the Hall of Fame shows off Cajun, cowboy, western swing, and honky-tonk styles of country music as well. Admission includes a tour of RCA's historic **Studio B,** where stars like Dolly Parton and Chet Atkins—not to mention The King—recorded their first hits. (Hall of Fame open daily 8am-6pm in summer; off season daily 9am-5pm. $10, ages 6-11 $5, under 6 free.) When you get inspired enough to record your own hit, the **Recording Studio of America,** 1510 Division St. (254-1282), underneath the **Barbara Mandrell Country Museum** (242-7800), lets you karaoke and record popular country and pop tunes with 24-track backgrounds (open Sun.-Thurs. 9am-6pm, Fri.-Sat. 9am-8pm; audio $15, video $25). See Elvis' evergreen Cadillac and special exhibit cars like the Batmobile at **World Famous Car Collectors' Hall of Fame,** 1534 Demonbreun St. (255-6804; open daily 8am-9pm; $5, ages 4-11 $3.25).

Nashville's pride and joy awaits in **Centennial Park,** a 15-minute walk west along West End Ave. from Music Row. The "Athens of the South" boasts a full-scale replica of the **Parthenon** (862-8431), complete with a towering Athena surrounded by her fellow Olympians. Originally built as a temporary exhibit for the Tennessee Centennial in 1897, the Parthenon met with such Olympian success that the model was rebuilt to last. The Nashville Parthenon also houses the **Cowan Collection of American Paintings** in its first floor galleries, a refreshing but erratic selection of 19th- and early 20th-century American art. (Open Tues.-Sat. 9am-4:30pm, Sun. 12:30-4pm. $2.50, seniors and kids $1.25, under 4 free.) But soft! what light on yonder Parthenon steps breaks? It's **Shakespeare in the Park,** performed in mid-July and August as part of the annual **Shakespeare Festival** (229-2273).The **Upper Room Chapel Museum,** 1908 Grand Ave. (340-7207), also in the park area off 21st Ave. S., houses a spectacular 20-ft. floor-to-ceiling stained glass window with over 9000 pieces of glass (open Mon.-Fri. 8am-4:30pm; $2 contribution recommended).

The **Tennessee State Capitol** (741-1621), a comely Greek Revival structure atop the hill on Charlotte Ave. next to downtown, offers, among other things, free guided tours of the tomb of James Knox Polk (tours hourly Mon.-Fri. 9-11am and 1-3pm). Across the street, the **Tennessee State Museum,** 505 Deaderick (741-2692), depicts the history of Tennessee from the early Native American era to the time of "overlander" pioneers; imaginative and interactive displays enhance the sometimes whitewashed version of Tennessee history. A new War Memorial Building recounts America's wartime history from the Spanish-American War through World War II (open Tues.-Sat. 10am-5pm, Sun. 1-5pm; free). Don't miss the gift shop.

The **Museum of Tobacco Art and History,** 800 Harrison St. (271-2349), off 8th Ave., pays tribute to Tennessee's most important crop. From a dual-purpose Indian pipe/tomahawk (a slow and a quick way to death) to giant glass-blown pipes, the museum's exhibits expound upon the unexpectedly captivating history of tobacco, pipes, and cigars (open Mon.-Sat. 9am-4pm; free).

Fisk University's **Van Vechten Gallery** (329-8543), at the corner of Jackson St. and D.B. Todd Blvd. off Jefferson St., exhibits a small but distinguished collection of art by Picasso, Renoir, and Cézanne among others. The gallery also displays African sculpture and many works by Alfred Steiglitz and Georgia O'Keeffe. (Open Tues.-Fri. 10am-5pm, Sat.-Sun. 1-5pm. Recommended donation $4.)

If you tire of the downtown area, rest at the **Cheekwood Museum of Art** and **Tennessee Botanical Gardens** (356-8000), 7 mi. southwest of town on Forest Park Dr.; take bus #3 ("West End/Belle Meade") from downtown to Belle Meade Blvd. and Page Rd. The leisurely, well-kept Japanese and rose gardens are a welcome change from Nashville glitz and are a wonderful compliment to the 19th-century art of the museum. (Open Mon.-Sat. 9am-5pm, Sun. 11am-5pm. $6, students and seniors $5, ages 6-17 $3, under 6 free.) The nearby **Belle Meade Mansion,** 5025 Harding Rd. (356-0501), dubbed "The Queen of Tennessee Plantations," offers a second respite. This 1853 plantation has the works: gorgeous grounds, smokehouse, dollhouse, and dairy (most buildings open to tours). Belle Meade was also the site of the nation's first thoroughbred and Tennessee walking-horse breeding farm. (Two great tours per hr., led by guides in period costume; last tour 4pm. Open Mon.-Sat. 9am-5pm, Sun. 1-5pm. $7, ages 6-12 $2.)

Andrew Jackson's beautiful manor house, the **Hermitage,** 4580 Rachel's Ln. (889-2941), off Exit 221 from I-40, sits atop 625 gloriously shaded acres 13 mi. from downtown Nashville. Admission includes a terrific 15-min. film, a museum, access to the house and grounds, and a visit to nearby Tulip Grove Mansion and church. Allow yourself 1½-2 hours for the whole shebang; it's worth it. One of the city's more popular attractions, the Hermitage gets crowded in the summer. (Open daily 9am-5pm. $7.50, seniors $6.50, kids 6-12 $4.)

ENTERTAINMENT AND NIGHTLIFE

Opryland USA, 2808 Opryland Dr., Rm. 4787, Nashville 37214 (889-6611 for info), Exit 11 off Briley Pkwy., cross-pollinates Las Vegas schmaltz and Disneyland purity (or maybe vice versa) with the best in country music thrown in the middle. This amusement park contains all the requisite family attractions, from the outlandish new Hangman roller coaster to a state fair midway, but the music sets it apart: Opryland stages seven slickly produced live music spectaculars daily. Tune your radio to 580AM for more info. (Open April-May Sat.-Sun.; May-early Oct. daily; call for changing hours. $28, ages 4-11 $18; 2 days $38. Celebrity concert series $15-22.) The **Grand Ole Opry (GOO),** the setting for America's longest-running radio show, moved here from the town center in 1976. *The* place to hear country music, the Opry howls every Friday and Saturday night ($16.50); matinees are held on various days during peak tourist season (April-Oct. Tues. and Thurs. 3pm; $14.50, tours of the Opry take place daily for $11). Call or write for reservations. Check the Friday *Tennessean* for a list of performers.

Set aside the first weekend in June for the outdoor **Summer Lights** downtown, when top rock, jazz, reggae, classical, and (of course) country performers jam simultaneously (performances Mon.-Thurs. 4pm-12:30am). For info on **Nashville Symphony** tickets and performances, call Ticketmaster (741-2787).

Whether it's a corner honky-tonk joint or the Grand Ole Opry, Nashville offers a wealth of opportunities to hear country and western, jazz, rock, bluegrass, and folk. The Nashville *Key,* available at the chamber of commerce, opens many entertainment doors. Comprehensive listings for all live music and events in the area can be found in free copies of *Nashville Scene,* or in the Thursday or Friday *Tennessean* (35¢). Pick up *Bone* for more music info, and *Q (Query)* for gay and lesbian news and listings. Muse over these publications plus many more at **Moskós,** 2204-B Elliston Place (327-2658), a newsstand and luncheonette (sandwiches $4-5.25; open Mon.-Fri. 7am-midnight, Sat. 8am-midnight, Sun. 8:30am-midnight). Enjoy some maritime madness aboard **General Jackson** (889-6611), America's largest showboat. Board ye deck at 11:45am for the midday cruise or 7pm for the dinner cruise (prices from $18-45).

Bluebird Café, 4104 Hillsboro Rd. (383-1461), in Green Hills. This famous bird sings country, blues, and folk; Garth Brooks got his start here. Women traveling solo will generally feel safe in this mellow, clean-cut establishment. Dinners of salads and sandwiches ($4-6.50) until 11pm. Early shows 7pm; cover begins around 9:30pm ($4-7). Open Mon.-Sat. 5:30pm-1am, Sun. 6pm-midnight. No cover on Sundays.

Tootsie's Orchid Lounge, 422 Broadway (726-0463). For years, owner Tootsie Bess lent money to struggling musicians until they shot to stardom on the Grand Ole Opry. These days, the Lounge still has good C&W music and affordable drinks (domestic beer $2.25). Women should think twice about braving the sometimes rowdy bar alone at night. Open Mon.-Sat. 10am-2am, Sun. noon-2am.

Lucy's Record Shop, 1707 Church St. (321-0882), vends wicked vinyl during the day to the same young crowd that shows up for indie, national, and local shows at night. Cover $5. All ages welcome.

Ace of Clubs, 114 2nd Ave. S. (254-2237), in a huge warehouse. Packs 'em in Mon.-Thurs. for live blues and rock, Fri.-Sat for retro and disco. Cover after 9pm $5. Open Mon.-Fri. 5:30pm-3am, Sat. 8pm-3am. The party really starts after 11pm.

The Connection, 901 Cowen St. (726-8718). Nashville's top gay club, imported from—Louisville? Anyway, high-energy dance music! Open Wed.-Sun. 6pm-3am.

■ Near Nashville: Chattanooga

A bustling city, tucked into a meander on the **Tennessee River,** Chattanooga cultivates more than its choo-choo image. The city that began as a trading post in 1815 has kept its commercial tradition, evolving into a major factory outlet center. **Hunter Museum of Art,** 10 Bluff View (423-267-0968), houses the South's most complete American art collection and impressive traveling exhibits (open Tues.-Sat. 10am-4:30pm, Sun. 1-4:30pm; $5, students $3). The **riverwalk** pathway connects the museum to the **Tennessee Aquarium** (800-322-3344), on Ross's Landing, with over 7000 animals, one of the world's largest aquariums, focusing on freshwater life and the Tennessee River. (Open Mon.-Fri. 10am-6pm, Sat.-Sun. 10am-8pm; Oct.-April daily 10am-6pm. $9.75, ages 3-11 $5.25.)

A few miles outside Chattanooga the world's steepest passenger railway, the **Incline** ($7, ages 3-12 $4), which takes passengers up a ridiculous 72.7-degree grade to **Lookout Mountain,** where seven states can be seen on a clear day. Before ascending, partake of Chattanooga's military heritage at the **Battles for Chattanooga Museum,** 3742 Tennessee Ave. (423-821-2812; open daily 8:30am-8:30pm; $5, children $2). Also on Lookout Mountain, **Rock City Gardens** (706-820-2531), attracts families and hardcore aficionados of kitsch with subterranean black-lit gnome dioramas and Mother Goose theme areas built around several interesting rock formations. (Open daily 8am-sundown; Labor Day-Memorial Day 8:30am-sundown. $9, ages 3-12

$5.) To get down, ride the **alpine slide** (423-825-5666), take I-24W, Lookout Valley, Exit 174 and follow the signs ($4.25). Purchase tickets for all these sights and watch a 22-min. video on Chattanooga ($1) at the space-age **visitors center**, 2 Broad St. (800-322-3344; open daily 8:30am-5:30pm), next to the Aquarium.

Budget motels congregate on the highways coming into the city and on **Broad St.** at the base of Lookout Mountain. **Holiday Trav-l-Park**, 1769 Mack Smith Rd. (706-891-9766), in Rossville ½ mi. off I-75 at the East Ridge Exit, enlivens sites for tents and RVs with a Civil War theme and a nightly Civil War show in the summer (2-person site $13.50, with hookup $17.50). Two nearby lakes, Chickamauga and Nickajack, are equipped with **campgrounds.**

A **free shuttle** scuttles from the Chattanooga Choo Choo Holiday Inn to the Aquarium, with stops on every block. (Runs Mon.-Sat. 7am-9:45pm, Sun. 10am-8pm; off-season hrs. shorter. Summer service to Lookout Mountain $1, children 50¢.)

■ Great Smoky Mountains

The largest wilderness area in the eastern U.S., the **Great Smoky Mountains National Park** encompasses a half-million acres of gray-green Appalachian peaks bounded on either side by misty North Carolina and Tennessee valleys. This park welcomes more visitors per year than any other national park. Bears, wild hogs, white-tailed deer, groundhogs, wild turkeys, a handful of red wolves, and more than 1500 species of flowering plants make their homes here despite the human invasion. Whispering conifer forests line the mountain ridges at elevations of over 6000 ft. Rhododendrons burst into their full glory in June and July; by mid-October the sloping mountains become a giant, crazy quilt of color.

Practical Information Start any exploration of the area at one of the park's three visitors centers: **Sugarlands** (423-436-1200), on Newfound Gap Rd., 2 mi. south of Gatlinburg, TN, next to the park's headquarters; **Cades Cove** (423-453-4200), on Cades Cove loop, just southeast of Townsend, TN; and **Oconaluftee** (704-497-1900), 4 mi. north of Cherokee, NC. Be sure to ask for *The Smokies Guide*, which details the park's tours, lectures, activities, and changing natural graces (25¢). All the visitors centers have the same hours (daily 8am-4:30pm). The park's **information line** (423-436-1200; open daily 8:30am-4:30pm) links all three visitors centers. Park **emergency** can be reached at 423-436-1230.

Sleeping and Eating After a Long Day of Hiking Eight campgrounds lie scattered throughout the park, each with tent sites, limited trailer space, water, and bathrooms (no showers or hookups). **Smokemont, Elkmont,** and **Cades Cove** accept reservations (sites $11); the rest are first come, first served (sites $6-11). In summer, RV drivers or those who wish to stay at one of the campgrounds near the main roads should reserve at least eight weeks in advance (800-365-2267).

Motels lining Rte. 441 and Rte. 321 decrease in price with distance from the park. Small motels also cluster in both **Cherokee** and **Gatlinburg.** Prices vary wildly depending on the season and the economy. In general, Cherokee motels are cheaper ($35+) and Gatlinburg motels are nicer ($45+); prices soar to even greater heights on weekends. But fear not, brave heart: two hostels service the park. **Smoky Mountain Ranch Camp (HI-AYH)**, 3248 Manis Rd. (429-8563 or 800-851-6715), a terrific hostel, nestles in the mountains, 9.7 mi. southwest of Pigeon Forge on Rte. 321 and 6 mi. northeast of Cades Cove on Rte. 321. Crash at the top of the hill in the comfortable hostel dorm with A/C, cable TV, and a kicking stereo. Spend a day, spend a month, good times lay ahead in this haven of Tennessee comfort ($13.25, nonmembers $15; linen included). Closer to Gatlinburg is **Bell's Wa-Floy Retreat**, 3610 East Pkwy. (423-436-5575), 10 mi. east of Gatlinburg on Rte. 321. From Gatlinburg proper, catch the eastbound trolley (25¢) to the end of the line; from there, hop, skip, or jump the 5 mi. to Wa-Floy. The lovely grounds of this Christian retreat community envelop a pool, tennis courts, meditation area, chapel, and bubbling brook. Friendly proprietor

Mrs. Floy Bell recites poetry and rents spaces in dark apartment-style buildings. (Check-in before 10pm. HI-AYH members $10, nonmembers $12. Linens $1. Reservations required.)

Sights and Activities Over 900 mi. of hiking trails and 170 mi. of road meander through the park. Rangers at the visitors centers will help you devise a trip appropriate for your ability. Some of the most popular trails wind 5 mi. to **Rainbow Falls,** 4 mi. to **Chimney Tops,** and 2½ mi. to **Laurel Falls.** To hike off the marked trails, you'll need a free backcountry camping permit from a visitors center. Wherever you go, bring water and *don't feed the bears.* For gorgeous scenery without the sweat, drive the 11-mi. **Cades Cove** loop, which circles the vestiges of a mountain community that occupied the area from the 1850s to the 1920s, before the park took over. In the summer, grist is ground at the 1876 **Mingus Mill,** on Newfound Gap Rd. 1 mi. north of the Oconaluftee Visitors Center. **Mountain Farm Museum,** right next to the Oconaluftee center, re-creates a turn-of-the-century settlement, including a blacksmith shop and a corncrib. (Both sights free.)

■ Knoxville

Settled as a frontier outpost in the years after the Revolution and named for Washington's Secretary of War Henry Knox, the former capital of Tennessee hosted the 1982 World's Fair (which attracted 10 million visitors) and continues to be home to the 26,000 students of the University of Tennessee. A pleasant day-trip from the stunning Smoky Mountains, Knoxville and hemmed by vast lakes created by the Tennessee Valley Authority, Knoxville offers friendly, sparkling-clean urbanity and a hopping nightlife for city slickers looking for a taste of the outdoors.

Practical Information Downtown stretches north from the Tennessee River, bordered by **Henley St.,** and the **World's Fair Park,** to the west. The University of Tennessee, student hangouts, restaurants, bars, shopping, and sights revolve around it. The highly visible **Sunsphere** within the park houses **Knoxville Visitor's Information,** 810 Clinch Ave. (523-2316; open Mon.-Fri. 8:30am-5pm). **Greyhound,** 100 Magnolia Ave. (522-5144 or 800-231-2222), in a sketchy neighborhood at Central St., sends buses to Nashville (3 per day, 2hr., $31), Chattanooga (3 per day, 2½hr., $19), and Lexington (4 per day, 3½hr., $38). Public transportation is provided by **KAT** (637-3000); buses run from 6:15am-6:15pm or later, depending on the route ($1, transfers 20¢). Knoxville's main **post office:** 1237 E. Wisegarber Rd. (558-4502), at Middlebrook Pike (Mon.-Fri. 8am-4:30pm). **ZIP code:** 37950. **Area code:** 423.

Accommodations, Food, and Nightlife Many not-quite-budget motels sit along I-75 and I-40 just outside the city. It's hard to find anything distinctly Scottish at the **Scottish Inns,** 301 Callahan Rd. (689-7777), at Exit 110 off I-75, but the rooms are clean and well-equipped (cable, HBO, outdoor pool; singles $32, doubles $36, prices increase by $13 on weekends). If **camping** is your game, head to **KOA North,** 908 E.

Dollywood

A mythical American village created by Dolly Parton in the Tennessee hills, **Dollywood,** 1020 Dollywood Ln. (800-365-5996), dominates Pigeon Forge, celebrating the cultural legacy of the East Tennessee Mountains and the country songmistress herself (famous for some mountainous topography of her own). In Dolly's world, craftspeople demonstrate their skills and sell their wares, thirty rides offer thrills and chills, and country favorites perform. While Dolly asserts that she wants to preserve the culture of the Tennessee Mountains, she also seems to want you to pay to come again—Dollywood's motto is "Create Memories Worth Repeating." Generally open daily 10am-6pm, but hours change constantly. ($29, over 59 $25, ages 4-11 $20.)

Raccoon Valley Rd. (947-9776), at Exit 117 off I-75, which is located closer to the city than most other campgrounds. (50 tent sites with more than enough room for RVs. $13, with hookup $15.)

Known for its good parties and low crime rate, **The Fort,** the set of numbered cross-streets west of World's Fair Park, houses the majority of students from the **University of Tennessee. The Strip,** the stretch of Cumberland Ave. separating The Fort from campus proper, offers student hangouts, bars, and restaurants. **Falafel Hut,** 601 15th St. (522-4963), the middle eastern brother of Jabba and a major center of collegiate hipsters, cooks a few blocks off The Strip. Slobber over the lentil soup ($1.70) or a falafel sandwich ($2.55; open Mon.-Thurs. 9am-9pm, Fri.-Sat. 9am-10pm, Sun. 11am-9pm). **Longbranch Saloon,** 1848 Cumberland Ave. (546-9914), offers a casual neighborhood bar atmosphere (no chaps and spurs) and a mellow twentysomething crowd. Take a domestic bottle ($1.75) or draft ($1.25) out to the patio in nice weather (open daily 3pm-3am).

Market Sq., a popular pedestrian plaza to the east of World's Fair Park, offers restaurants, fountains, and shade. **Mercury Theater,** 28 Market Sq. (637-8634), hosts punkish and alternative bands. The other center of chowing, browsing, and carousing, **Old City,** spreads north up Central St. **Java,** 109½ S. Central St. (525-1600), in the middle of Old City, serves up steaming cups of you-know-what ($1.25, refills 25¢), slices of amazing cake ($3.50), and thick, funky atmosphere (open Sun.-Thurs. 8am-11pm, Fri.-Sat. 9am-1am). Two clubs duke it out for the title of Soul Central in Knoxville: **Bullfrog's,** 131 S. Central (673-0411), pumps out reggae nightly (open 10pm-3am; cover varies); while **Lucille's,** 106 N. Central (546-3742), dishes out jazz (open Tues.-Sat. 6pm-2am). **The Underground,** 214 W. Jackson Ave. (525-3675), a dance club, houses the **Boiler Room,** an after-hours club that keeps things cooking until the wee hours and hosts a partially gay crowd. (Underground open Mon.-Wed. and Fri.-Sat. 10am-3am; Boiler open Sat.-Sun. mornings 1am-6am, with a $5 cover.) For goings-on around town, pick up a free *Metro Pulse.*

Sights Knoxville offers about a day's worth of sightseeing. **World's Fair Park** makes a fine stroll with a reflecting pool, grassy expanses, a playground, and more national flags than sands through the hourglass—so are the Days of our Lives. Within the park, the **Knoxville Museum of Art,** 1050 World's Fair Park Dr. (525-6101), houses changing exhibits of high caliber. (Open Tues.-Thurs. 10am-5pm, Fri. 10am-9pm, Sat. 10am-5pm, Sun. 11:30am-5pm. Most exhibits free.) Downtown rides the **Blount Mansion,** 200 W. Hill (525-2375), a National Historic Landmark, the 1792 frame house of governor William Blount (pronounced as if there were no "o"—as in "M. Poirot, it seems the victim was struck with a Blount object"). One-hour tours of the period-furnished home leave on the hour; last tour at 4pm. (Open Mar.-Oct. Tues.-Sat. 9:30am-5pm, Sun. 2-5pm; Nov.-Feb. Tues.-Fri. 9:30am-5pm. $4, ages 6-12 $2.) Nearby, the **James White Fort,** 205 E. Hill Ave. (525-6514), still preserves portions of the original stockade built in 1786 by Knoxville's first citizen and founder. (Tours run continuously until 3:30pm. Open Mon.-Sat. 9:30am-4:30pm. $4, children $2.) The small **Museum of East Tennessee History,** 600 Market St. (544-5732), at Clinch, covers the cultural history of East Tennessee from its founding to the World's Fair. (Open Tues.-Sat. 10am-4pm, Sun. 1-5pm. $3, students $2.) Picnickers will appreciate **Kirch Park,** across the street, a tiny, perfectly manicured oasis of green in the midst of downtown.

For a taste of down-home Appalachia, visit the **Farmer's Market** (524-3276), 15 mi. from downtown on I-640 off Exit 8. The pavilion peddles local produce, plants, jams and jellies, arts and crafts, ice cream, soft pretzels, and more. Don't leave the area without visiting the **Museum of Appalachia** (494-7680 or 494-0514), 16 mi. north of Knoxville on I-75 at Exit 22 in **Norris.** The "museum" is actually a vast village with authentic houses, barns, a school, a spectacular Hall of Fame building replete with a dulcimer exhibit, livestock—even jail cells. In the display barn, don't miss the incredible story of Brother Harrison Mayes, the evangelist who planted signs advertising God in all 50 states and hoped to land one on the moon. The museum avoids schmaltz and fustiness. (Open daily dawn to dusk year-round except Christmas Day. $6, ages 6-15 $4.) Cleanse the aesthetic palate with a beautiful trip to **Norris Dam** and the accompanying **Grist Mill,** just east of the museum, exit left onto Rte. 61 then turn left onto 441, about 4.5 mi.

■ Memphis

In 1912, a Memphis musician named W.C. Handy shocked the music world with his 12-bar blues. Decades later, Elvis Presley shocked the world with his gyrating pelvis and amazingly versatile voice. Though the King may be dead (we think?) his image lives on throughout the city. Every year roadtrippers from around the country make a pilgrimage to the mecca of tackiness—Graceland, Elvis's former home.

PRACTICAL INFORMATION

Tourist Office: Visitor Information Center, 340 Beale St. (543-5300), 2 blocks south on 2nd St. and 2 blocks south of the Greyhound station on Beale. Open Mon.-Sat. 9am-6pm, Sun. noon-6pm.

Airport: Memphis International, 2491 Winchester Rd. (922-8000), south of the southern loop of I-240. Taxi fare to the city $16—negotiate in advance. Hotel express **shuttles** (922-8238) cost $8 (service 8:20am-11pm). Public transport to and from the airport $1.10; service is sporadic and the trip can be confusing for a traveler unfamiliar with the area.

Trains: Amtrak, 545 S. Main St. (526-0052 or 800-872-7245), at Calhoun on the southern edge of downtown. *Take a taxi—the surrounding area is very unsafe even during the day.* To: New Orleans (5 per week, 8hr., $83); Chicago (5 per week, 10½hr., $116); Jackson (2 per week, 4hr., $51).

Buses: Greyhound, 203 Union Ave. (523-1184 or 800-231-2222), at 4th St. downtown. Unsafe area at night, but it beats the Amtrak station. To: Nashville (12 per day, 4hr., $31); Chattanooga (4 per day, 3hr., $35.50); Jackson (9 per day, 4hr., $31). Open Mon.-Fri. 7am-8:30pm, Sat.-Sun. 7am-3:30pm.

Public Transportation: Memphis Area Transit Authority (MATA; 274-6282), corner of Union Ave. and Main St. Bus routes cover most suburbs, but don't run frequently. The major downtown stops are at the intersections of Front and Jefferson St., and 2nd St. and Madison Ave.; the major routes run on Front, 2nd, and 3rd St. Buses run Mon.-Fri. 7am, Sat.-Sun. 10am; until 6pm-11pm, depending on route. Fare $1.10, transfers 10¢. Refurbished 19th-century Portuguese **trolley** cars (run by MATA) cruise Main St. Mon.-Thurs. 6:30am-9pm., Fri. 6:30am-1am, Sat. 9:30am-1am, Sun. 10am-6pm. 50¢. The visitors center sells 3-day trolley passes.

Taxis: Yellow Cab, 526-2121. $2.35 first mi., $1.10 each additional mi. Open 24hr.

Crisis Lines: Crisis Line, 274-7477. **Sexual Assault Crisis,** 528-2161. **Gay/Lesbian Switchboard,** 728-4297. **HIV/AIDS Switchboard,** 278-2437.

Time Zone: Central (1hr. behind Eastern).

Emergency: 911.

Post Office: 555 S. 3rd St. (521-2186). Open Mon.-Fri. 8:30am-5:30pm, Sat. 10am-2pm. **ZIP code:** 38101. **Area code:** 901.

Downtown, named avenues run east-west and numbered ones north-south. **Madison Ave.** divides north and south addresses. Two main thoroughfares, **Poplar** and **Union Ave.,** pierce the heart of the city from the east; 2nd and 3rd St. arrive from the south. **I-240** and **I-55** encircle the city. **Bellevue** becomes **Elvis Presley Blvd.** and leads you straight to Graceland. If you're traveling by car, take advantage of the free, unmetered parking along the river.

SINCE M'BABY LEFT ME, I FOUND A NEW PLACE T'DWELL

Memphis offers a fine hostel (the budget traveler's best option), and not much else. A few downtown motels have prices in the budget range; otherwise, more distant lodgings are available near Graceland at Elvis Presley Blvd. and Brooks Rd. For the celebration of the earth-shattering days of Elvis's birth (Jan. 8) and death (Aug. 15), as well as for **Memphis in May** and **Memphis Music in July** festivals, book 6 months to 1 year in advance. The visitors center has a thorough listing of lodgings.

> **Lowenstein-Long House/Castle Hostelry (AAIH/Rucksackers),** 217 N. Waldran (527-7174), parking lot at 1084 Poplar. Take bus #50 from 3rd St. A good location, but sketchy neighborhood makes lodging here a drawback for those without cars. The house rises out of its dilapidated surroundings with sheer Victorian elegance. Women's rooms on the 3rd floor are pleasant and homey; men's rooms out back can be a bit less neat. $12; stay 3 nights, get 1 free. Private doubles $33. Camping on lawn out back, $6 per person; includes access to kitchen and bath. Work (when available) can be exchanged for price of stay. Towels $1, linens $2. Key deposit $20.
>
> **Hernando Inn,** 900 E. Commerce St. (601-429-7811), just across the Mississippi border in Hernando (about 15mi. south of Memphis). Take Exit 280 of I-55. Must be 21 to occupy these big rooms, with cable TV, HBO, and A/C. $20 phone deposit. Singles $38, doubles $42; prices may vary. $2 key deposit.
>
> **Motel 6,** 1117 E. Brooks Rd. (346-0992), near intersection of Elvis and Brooks Rd. close to Graceland. HBO, pool, and small, clean rooms with stall showers and free local calls. $34, 2 adults $40, under 17 free, $3 per extra adult.
>
> **Memphis/Graceland KOA,** 3691 Elvis Presley Blvd. (396-7125), right next door to Graceland. The location makes up for the lack of trees and privacy. Sites $19, with hookup $21.
>
> **Memphis South Campground,** 460 Byhalia Rd. (601-429-1878), Hernando, MS, 15 mi. south of Memphis, at Exit 280 off I-55 in Mississippi. A relaxing spot with some greenery, a pool and laundry. Tent sites $12, with water and wattage $15, with full hookup $17.

MEALS FIT FOR THE KING

In Memphis, barbecue is as common as rhinestone-studded jumpsuits; the city even hosts the World Championship Barbecue Cooking Contest in May. But don't fret if gnawing on ribs isn't your thing—Memphis has plenty of other Southern-style restaurants with down-home favorites like fried chicken, catfish, chitlins, and grits.

> **The Rendezvous** (523-2746), Downtown Alley, between the Ramada and Days Inn. A Memphis legend, serving large portions of ribs ($6.50-10), and cheaper sandwiches ($3-4). Open Tues.-Thurs. 4:30pm-midnight, Fri.-Sat. noon-midnight.
>
> **The North End,** 346 N. Main St. (526-0319 or 527-3663), at Jackson St. downtown, specializes in tamales, wild rice, stuffed potatoes, and creole dishes ($3-8). The hot fudge pie is known as "sex on a plate" ($3.50). Happy Hour daily 4-7pm. Live music starts at 10:30pm Wed.-Sun. with a $2 cover. Open daily 10:30am-3am.
>
> **P and H Café,** 1532 Madison Ave. (726-0906). The initials aptly stand for Poor and Hungry. The self-proclaimed "beer joint of your dreams" serves huge burgers and grill food ($3-5) to students and locals; try the patty melt with grilled onions ($3). Waitresses are a friendly Memphis institution. During Death Week in Aug., P and H hosts the infamous "Dead Elvis Ball." Open Mon.-Fri. 11am-3am, Sat. 5pm-3am.
>
> **Corky's,** 5259 Poplar Ave. (685-9744), about 25min. from downtown. Nationally famous BBQ, is justifiably popular with the locals. Top-notch BBQ dinner and ribs served with baked beans, cole slaw, and bread ($6-9). Scrumptious pies and cobbler. Arrive early and expect to wait, or use the drive-thru. Corky's mails ribs overnight anywhere in the continental U.S.: call 800-9-CORKYS/926-7597. Open Mon.-Thurs. 11am-10pm, Fri.-Sat. 11am-10:30pm, Sun. 11am-10pm.
>
> **Public Eye,** 175 Cooper St. (726-4040), just off Broadway in Overton Square. A pork-o-phile's paradise, the Eye offers great pork and rib options for under $10. Open Sun.-Thurs. 11am-10pm, Fri.-Sat. 11am-midnight.
>
> **Squash Blossom Market,** 11801 Union St. (725-4823). An upscale health food store (with a tasty café in back) that seems a little out of place in a city dripping with sauces, grease, and above all, meat. Veggie delights about $4 during Sun. brunch. Open Mon.-Fri. 9am-9pm, Sat. 9am-8pm, Sun. 11am-6pm.

Front St. Delicatessen, 77 S. Front St. (522-8943). A lunchtime streetside deli in the heart of downtown. Sandwiches $2.50-$3.50. Open Mon.-Fri. 8am-4pm, Sat. 11am-3pm.

MEMPHIS MUSIC AND MARVELS

Elvis Sightings: Graceland

You'll laugh. You'll cry. You'll want to see it again and again. Bow down before **Graceland,** 3763 Elvis Presley Blvd. (332-3322 or 800-238-2000), take I-55 South, Elvis Presley's home and the paragon of Americana that every Memphis visitor must see. Unfortunately, any desire to learn about the man, to share his dream, or to feel his music requires the ability to transcend the mansion's crowd-control methods and required audio-tape tour, to reach beyond the tacky commercialism and ignore the employees who seem to adhere to the Elvis motto "Taking Care of Business in a Flash." Still, you'll never forget the mirrored ceilings, carpeted walls, and yellow-and-orange decor of Elvis' 1974 renovations. By tour's end, even those who aren't die-hard Elvis fans may be genuinely moved. Be sure to gawk audibly at the Trophy Building where hundreds of gold and platinum records line the wall. The King and his court are buried next door in the **Meditation Gardens,** where you can seek enlightenment while reciting a mantra to the tune of "You're So Square." (Ticket office open 7:30am-6pm; Labor Day-Memorial Day 8:30am-5pm. Attractions open 2hr. after ticket office closes. $9, seniors $8, ages 5-12 $5.)

If you love him tender, love him true—visit several Elvis museums, and several more Elvis souvenir shops. The **Elvis Presley Automobile Museum** houses a score of pink and purple Elvis-mobiles in a huge hall, while an indoor drive-in movie theater shows clips from 31 Elvis movies ($5, ages 5-12 $2.75). A free 20-minute film, *Walk a Mile in My Shoes,* with performance footage, contrasts the early (slim) years with the later ones. **Elvis Airplanes** features—you got it—the two Elvis planes: the *Lisa Marie* (named for Elvis' daughter) and the tiny *Hound Dog II Jetstar* ($4.50, children $2.75). The **Sincerely Elvis** exhibit glimpses into Elvis's private side; see the books he

---

Driving That Train: A Graybox in Three Acts

Act I. On the night of April 29, 1900, Jonathan Jones, known to history as "Casey," pulled engine 638 into the Memphis depot right on time. This was an ordinary feat for Casey, who, since his first passenger run only 60 days before, had quickly gained a reputation for punctuality on the rails. Thus, it had come as a small surprise to the Station Master in Memphis that Casey, ever wise to improving his record of timeliness and in need of some extra cash, offered his services to replace the sick-listed engineer of the late-running New Orleans Special. By the time Casey and his fireman, Jim Webb, finally kicked the New Orleans engine #382 out of the station, the train was already 95 min. behind schedule. **Act II.** In that particular engine and on that particular track gauge, speeds for the route usually ran about 35 mph, but the determined Casey opened the throttle at over 70 mph, reportedly saying "the old lady's got her high-heeled slippers on tonight." Unfortunately, as the "old lady" danced down through Tennessee, trouble was brewing in Mississippi. At Vaughn, an airhose had broken, locking several cars on the track. Even worse, a dense fog had set in. When Jim finally caught sight of the brake lights at Vaughn, little time was left to act. Jim jumped to save himself, but Casey held on, closing the throttle, throwing the brakes, and thrusting the train into reverse. **Act III.** Casey's actions brought the train down to 25 mph, but in the collision he was thrown from the engine to his death. For his heroism, which prevented anyone else from being hurt, the young man from Cayce, KT was honored with a ballad by a black engine-wiper named Wallace Saunders. In that song, and in the songs which have followed—most famously that of the Grateful Dead—Casey Jones continues to drive that train. He is a lasting image of the railroads and a true Tennessee hero.

read, the shirts he wore, and home movies with his wife Priscilla ($3.50, children $2.25). The **Platinum Tour Package** discounts admission to the mansion and all attractions ($17, seniors $15.30, ages 5-12 $11).

Every year on the week of August 15 (the date of Elvis' death), millions of the King's cortege get all shook up for **Elvis Week,** an extended celebration that includes a pilgrimage to his junior high school and a candlelight vigil. The days surrounding his birthday (Jan. 8) also see some Kingly activities.

Elvis Who?: The Blues, B.B. King, and more...

Long before Sam Phillips and Sun Studio produced Elvis, Jerry Lee Lewis, U2, and Bonnie Raitt, historic **Beale St.** saw the invention of the blues. The **W.C. Handy Home and Museum,** 352 Beale St. (527-3427), exhibits the music and photographs of the man, the myth, the legend who first put a blues melody to paper (open Tues.-Sat. 10am-6pm, Sun. 1-5pm; $2, students $1). The **Beale Street Blues Museum,** 329 Beale St. (527-6008), sings the blues story from slavery to the 1940s ($5, under 13 $2). The **Center for Southern Folklore,** 130 Beale St. (525-3655), documents various aspects of music history, including a tribute to Memphis's WDIA—the first radio station in the nation to play only music performed by black artists. Notables like B.B. King and Rufus Thomas began their musical careers on these airwaves (open daily 10am-8pm; free). Call the center for info on the **Music and Heritage Festival** (525-3655) which fills the Main St. Mall downtown during the 3rd weekend of July. Gospel, country, blues, and jazz accompany dance troupes and craft booths. Some booths offer oral histories on everything from life on the Mississippi to playing in segregated baseball leagues. (Open 11am-11pm. Free.) Of course, Memphis music history includes the soul hits of the Stax label and rockers like Big Star as well as the blues. The **Memphis Music Hall of Fame,** 97 S. 2nd St. (525-4007), showcases the city's music history from 1945 to the 1970s (open Mon.-Sat. 10am-6pm, Sun. noon-6pm), while **Sun Studio,** 706 Union Ave. (521-0664), shows off the city's rock 'n' roll roots. (30-min. tours every ½ hr. Open daily 9am-6:30pm; Oct.-April 10am-6pm. $7.50, under 13 free.)

...and still more: Civil Rights, Mud, and Miscellany

The **National Civil Rights Museum** is housed at the site of Martin Luther King, Jr.'s assassination at the **Lorraine Motel,** 450 Mulberry St. (521-9699), at 2nd St. The museum offers a 10-minute movie, graphic photographs of lynching victims, and life-size exhibits vividly tracing the progress of the Civil Rights Movement. (Open Mon.-Sat. 10am-6pm, Sun. 1-5pm; in winter Mon. and Wed.-Sat. 10am-5pm, Sun. 1-5pm. $5, students with ID and seniors $4, ages 6-12 $3; free Mon. 3-5pm.)

Mud Island, 125 Front St. (576-7241), a quick monorail ride over the picturesque Mississippi, has it all: a museum, the renowned World War II B-17 **Memphis Belle,** and a five-block scale model of the Mississippi River that you can swim in or stroll along. Free tours of the Riverwalk and Memphis Belle Pavilion run several times daily. Thursday evenings on the island are free; arrive before 6pm and catch the sunset. (Open daily 9am-7pm; pool open Tues.-Sun. noon-7pm. $4, seniors $3. Parking $3.) At the **Mississippi River Museum,** 125 N. Front St. (576-7241), spy on a Union iron-clad gunboat from the lookout of a Confederate bluff, or relax to the blues in the Yellow Dog Café ($6, seniors and under 12 $4).

On the waterfront, you won't miss the 32-story, six-acre **Great American Pyramid,** 1 Auction St. (526-5177), which houses a 20,000-seat arena. Tours cover the "Entertainment Hallway" and a University of Memphis basketball locker room. (Open Mon.-Sat. 10am-4pm, Sun. noon-5pm. $3.75, seniors and under 13 $2.75.)

A. Schwab, 163 Beale St. (523-9782), a small department store run by the same family since 1876, still offers old-fashioned bargains. A "museum" of relics-never-sold gathers dust on the mezzanine floor, including an array of voodoo potions, elixirs, and powders. Elvis bought some of his flashier ensembles here. (Open Mon.-Sat. 9am-5pm. Free guided tours.) Next door on Beale St., the **Memphis Police Museum** (528-

2370) summons visitors to gawk at 150 years' worth of confiscated drugs, homemade weapons, and officer uniforms (open 24hr.; free).

The Pink Palace Museum and Planetarium, 3050 Central Ave. (320-6320), which is, by the way, gray, details the natural history of the mid-South and expounds upon the development of Memphis; check out the sharp and sparkling crystal and mineral collection or experience the vertigo of the IMAX theater. (Open summers Mon.-Wed. 9am-5pm, Thurs.-Sat. 9am-9pm, Sun. noon-5pm. $5.50, seniors $5, ages 3-12 $3.50. Call for IMAX times: $5.50/$5/$4. Planetarium: $3/ $2.50/$2.)

Victorian Village consists of 18 mansions in various stages of restoration and preservation. **Mallory-Neeley House,** 652 Adams Ave. (523-1484), is open to the public and was built in the mid-19th century. Most of its original furniture remains intact for visitors to see. (Open Tues.-Sat. 10am-4pm, Sun. 1-4pm, closed Jan.-Feb. 40-min. tour $4, seniors and students $3, under 5 free. Last tour 3:30pm.) French Victorian architecture and an antique/textile collection live on in **Woodruff-Fontaine House,** 680 Adams Ave. (526-1469; open Mon.-Sat. 10am-3:30pm, Sun. 1-3:30pm; $5, students $2, seniors $4). **Magevney House,** 198 Adams Ave. (526-4464), once held the clapboard cottage of Eugene Magevney, who helped establish Memphis's first public schools. (Open Tues.-Sat. 10am-4pm; Labor Day-Memorial Day Mon.-Fri. 10am-2pm, Sat. 10am-4pm. Free. Reservations required.)

Memphis has almost as many parks as museums, each offering a slightly different natural setting. Brilliant wildflowers and a marvelous heinz of roses (57 varieties) bloom and grow forever at the **Memphis Botanical Garden,** 750 Cherry Rd. (685-1566), in Audubon Park off Park Ave. (Open Mon.-Sat. 11am-6pm. $2, ages 6-17 $1.) Across the street, the **Dixon Galleries and Garden,** 4339 Park Ave. (761-2409), flaunts its manicured landscape and a collection of European art which included works by Renoir, Degas, and Monet. (Open Tues.-Sat. 10am-5pm, Sun. 1-5pm. $5, students $3, seniors $4, ages 1-12 $1. Mon. only the gardens are open, and admission is ½ the above prices.) **Lichterman Nature Center,** 5992 Quince Rd. (767-7322), is a 65-acre wildscape with forests and wildlife and a picnic area (open Tues.-Sat. 9:30am-5pm, Sun. 1-5pm. $2, students ages 4-18 and seniors $1).

The **Chucalissa Archaeological Museum,** 1987 Indian Village Dr. (785-3160), recaptures the past of America's earliest residents with its reconstructed prehistoric village and museum. Local Choctaw Native Americans sell pottery and beaded jewelry. (Open Tues.-Sat. 9am-4:30pm, Sun. 1-5pm. $3, children $2.)

ARE YOU LONESOME TONIGHT?

If you don't know what to do while you're in Memphis, the visitors center's *Key* magazine, the *Memphis Flyer,* or the "Playbook" section of the Friday morning *Memphis Commercial Appeal* can tell you what's goin' down 'round town. Also, swing by **Sun Café,** 710 Union Ave. (521-0664), adjacent to the Sun Studios, for a tall, cool glass of lemonade ($1.75) and a talk with the young waiters and cashiers about what to do (open daily 9am-7pm; Sept.-May 10am-6pm).

Beale St. sways with the most happening, hip nightlife. Blues wafts up and down the street. Save a few bucks by buying a drink at one of the many outdoor stands and meandering from doorway to doorway, park to park. **B.B. King's Blues Club,** 143 Beale St. (527-5464), where the club's namesake still makes appearances, happily mixes young and old, tourist and native. Wash down a catfish sandwich ($7) with a beer ($3). (Cover $4-10; when B.B. himself plays $30. Open daily from 11:30am-til the show stops.) **Rum Boogie Café,** 182 Beale St. (528-0150), presents a friendly,

---

Rubber Ducky, you make...wait, those ducks are real!

William Faulkner once said of Memphis that "the Delta meets in the lobby of the **Peabody Hotel,"** 149 Union St. (529-4000), in the heart of downtown. While you're there, gobble the Peabody Cheesecake with Strawberry Sauce ($4). Every day at 11am and 5pm, the hotel rolls out the red carpet and the **ducks** that live in its indoor fountain waddle about the premises to a piano accompaniment.

THE SOUTH

relaxed atmosphere and honest homegrown blues to a touristy crowd. Check out the celebrity guitars on the wall, including blues great Willie Dixon's. (Cover $5. Full menu; domestic beer $2.50. Open daily 11:30am-very late, music begins around 8pm.) For pool, **Peoples,** 323 Beale St. (523-7627), racks 'em up from noon-at least 2am (tables $7.35, Fri.-Sat. $8.40). **Silky O'Sullivan's,** 183 Beale St. (522-9596), is a big Irish bar behind the façade of an almost completely razed historic landmark. Outside, chill out with the goats and munch on burgers ($4-6) to the tune of LOUD piano music or blues emanating from next door. (Cover Fri.-Sat. $3. Open Mon. 6pm-1am, Tues.-Thurs. 3pm-2:30am, Fri.-Sat. noon-5am, Sun. noon-1am.)

Just up the street from Sun Studio, **"616,"** 600 Marshall (526-6552), has a huge dance floor, local and national bands, and occasional 10¢ longnecks. (Cover around $8). A hot gay spot, **J. Wags,** 1268 Madison (725-1909) has been open 24 hr. since way back. (All-you-can-drink beer busts 10pm-3am for $4. Live music Fri.-Sat. Drag shows Fri.-Sat. at 1:30am.) Up, up, and away to the **Daily Planet,** 3439 Park Ave. (327-1270), where live bands play everything from rock to country (open Tues.-Sun. 5pm-2am). For a collegiate atmosphere, try the Highland St. strip near Memphis State University, with hopping bars like **Newby's,** 539 S. Highland St. (452-8408), which has backgammon tables and hosts rock and blues (domestic beer $2.25; open Mon.-Sat. 11am-3am, Sun. 4pm-3am; music Fri.-Sat. around 10:30pm).

The majestic **Orpheum Theater,** 203 S. Main St. (525-3000), shows classic movies beginning at 7:30pm on summer weekends, along with an organ prelude and a cartoon ($6, seniors and under 13 $5). The grand old theater, with 15-ft.-high chandeliers and a pipe organ, has occasional live music (box office open Mon.-Fri. 9am-5pm and before shows). **Memphis in May** (525-4611) celebrates through the month with concerts, art exhibits, food contests, and sporting events. The **Memphis Chicks** (who are, by the way, men), 800 Home Run Ln. (272-1687), near Libertyland, are a big hit with fans of Southern League baseball. ($5, box seats $6; $2 off for seniors and under 13. Call Ticketmaster or the box office Mon.-Fri. 9am-5pm.)

North Carolina

North Carolina can be split into three neat regions: down-to-earth mountain culture in the west, mellow sophistication in the Research Triangle of the central piedmont, and placid coastal towns in the east. Often untouched by development, the Old North State's natural beauty continues to be one of its greatest assets. From Mt. Mitchell to Monteo, North Carolina is dotted with state and national parks, nature preserves, and countless historic sites.

Confederate soldiers from Mississippi first called their allies from North Carolina Tar Heels after they failed to maintain their position in the face of Union troops, meaning that they forgot to tar their heels in order to really stick to their ground. Carolinians see it differently. They claim the nickname refers to the tenacity they displayed in both the Revolutionary and Civil wars—while they may have faltered in body, they remained steadfast in spirit. Dubious origins aside, the Tar Heel has become a North Carolina rallying point—especially during the NCAA men's basketball tournament, an event that commands a quasi-religious reverence in residents during yearly "March Madness."

PRACTICAL INFORMATION

Capital: Raleigh.
Travel and Tourism Division: 430 N. Salisbury St., Raleigh 27611 (919-733-4171 or 800-847-4862). **Department of Natural Resources and Community Development,** Division of Parks and Recreation, P.O. Box 27687, Raleigh 27611 (919-733-4181).

Time Zone: Eastern. **Postal Abbreviation:** NC.
Sales Tax: 6%.

■ The Research Triangle

Large universities and their students dominate the cities of the research triangle, commonly referred to as "the triangle." **Raleigh,** the state capital, is an easygoing, historic town, boasting a vibrant art community and providing a home for North Carolina State University (NC State). **Durham,** formerly a major tobacco producer, now (ironically) supports multiple hospitals, diet clinics, and medical research projects devoted to finding cancer cures. Duke University, one of the most prestigious schools in the nation, adds a share of PhDs to Durham's doctoral mix. The nation's first state university, the University of North Carolina (UNC), can be found just 20 mi. down the road in **Chapel Hill.** College culture predominates here—a sea of bicycles provides environment-friendly student transport, and the Hill's music scene thrives—*Ben Folds Five, Bus Stop, The Squirrel Nut Zippers,* and *Mike* are just a few of the local bands starting to receive national attention.

PRACTICAL INFORMATION

Tourist Office: Raleigh Capitol Area Visitors Center, 301 N. Blount St. (733-3456). Daily slide shows; in summer, tours Sun. at 2pm. Open Mon.-Fri. 8am-5pm, Sat. 9am-5pm, Sun. 1-5pm. **Durham Convention Center and Visitors Bureau,** 101 E. Morgan St. (687-0288). Open Mon.-Fri. 8:30am-5pm, Sat. 10am-2pm. **Chapel Hill Chamber of Commerce,** 104 S. Estes Dr. (967-7075). Open Mon.-Fri. 9am-5pm.

Airport: Raleigh-Durham International (460-1383), 15mi. northwest of Raleigh on U.S. 70. Many hotels and rental car agencies provide free airport limousine service if you have reservations.

Trains: Amtrak, 320 W. Cabarrus St., Raleigh (833-7594 or 800-872-7245). To: Washington, D.C. (2 per day, 6hr., $50); Richmond (2 per day, 4hr., $39); Miami (1 per day, 17hr., $149). Open daily 6am-10pm.

Buses: Greyhound (800-231-2222) has a station in each city. **In Raleigh,** 314 W. Jones St. (834-8275). To: Durham (5 per day, 35min., $7); Chapel Hill (4 per day, 80min., $8); North Charleston (3 per day, 8hr., $46). Open daily 7am-12:30am. **In Durham,** 820 W. Morgan St. (687-4800), 1 block off Chapel Hill St. downtown, 2½mi. northeast of Duke University. To: Chapel Hill (4 per day, 35min., $3.40); Washington, D.C. (3 per day, 6hr., $49). Open daily 7am-11:30pm. **In Chapel Hill,** 311 W. Franklin St. (942-3356), 2 blocks from the UNC campus. To: Durham (3 per day, 35min., $4.50); Washington, D.C. (2 per day, 8-10hr., $52). Open Mon.-Sat. 8:30am-4:20pm.

Public Transportation: Capital Area Transit, Raleigh (828-7228). Buses run Mon.-Sat. Fare 50¢. **Durham Area Transit Authority (DATA),** Durham (683-DATA/3282). Most routes start downtown at the corner of Main and Morgan St. on the loop. Operates daily; hours vary for each route; fewer on Sun. Fare 60¢, students/seniors 30¢; transfers 10¢; kids under 12 free. **Chapel Hill Transit,** Chapel Hill (968-2769). Operates Mon.-Fri. 6am-6pm. Fare 60¢, on campus 30¢.

Taxis: Safety Taxi, 832-8800. **Cardinal Cab,** 828-3228. Both charge $1.35, plus $1.50 each mi. 24-hr. service.

Crisis Line: Rape Crisis, 828-3005. Operates 24hr.

Emergency: 911.

Post Office: In Raleigh, 311 New Bern Ave. (420-5333). Open Mon.-Fri. 8am-5:30pm, Sat. 8am-noon; **ZIP code:** 27611. **In Durham,** 323 E. Chapel Hill St. (683-1976). Open Mon.-Fri. 7:30am-5pm; **ZIP code:** 27701. **In Chapel Hill,** 179 E. Franklin St. (967-6297). Open Mon.-Fri. 8:30am-5:30pm, Sat. 8:30am-noon; **ZIP code:** 27514. **Area code:** 919.

ACCOMMODATIONS AND CAMPING

Carolina-Duke Motor Inn, 2517 Guess Rd. (286-0771 or 800-438-1158), Durham (next to I-85). Clean rooms with wood furnishings, A/C, and heat. Access to swimming pool and laundry facilities. Free Movie Channel, local calls, local maps, and shuttle to Duke Medical Center on the main campus. Singles $34, doubles $40; $3 each additional person. 10% discount for *Let's Go* users, seniors, and AAA members. Next door, the **Wabash Express** (286-0020) serves cheap, filling breakfasts (6 pancakes for $3.75) in an old railway car. Open Sat.-Sun. 7-11am.

Red Roof Inns, 5623 Chapel Hill Blvd. (489-9421 or 800-THE-ROOF/843-7663), off U.S. 64E (Bus stop ¼mi. south on Chapel Hill Blvd.) Large, clean rooms. Disabled access, free local calls, cable TV, A/C, and heat. Singles $41, doubles $50.

Clairmont, 2639 S. Saunders St. (828-5151), Raleigh, off I-40 (City bus stop ½-block away.) Clean, mid-sized rooms. Cable TV, 5 free local calls, A/C, heat, and 24-hr. free coffee and juice. One room with disabled access. Singles $45, doubles $52. 10% discount for AAA members.

Umstead State Park (787-3033), 2mi. northwest of Raleigh, on U.S. 70. Tent and trailer sites in pristine woodland. Large lake for fishing, trails for hiking and horseback riding (BYO Horse). Open 8am-9pm; Sept.-May shorter hours. Closed to camping Mon.-Wed. Sites $9; no hookups.

FOOD

In Raleigh, **Hillsborough Street,** across from NC State, has a wide array of inexpensive eateries and bakeries staffed largely by students; the same is true of **Franklin Street** in Chapel Hill and, to a lesser degree, of **9th Street** in Durham. The **Well-Spring Grocery,** at the Ridgewood Shopping Center on Wade Ave. in Raleigh (286-2290), sells organic fruits and vegetables and whole grain baked goods (open daily 9am-9pm). The Chapel Hill WellSpring, at Franklin and Elliott St., also houses **Penguins,** a small café serving a variety of gourmet coffees and the best ham and gruyère croissant $1.25 can buy (open 8:30am-8pm).

Bullock's Barbeque, 3330 Quebec St., Durham (383-3211); turn left off Hillsborough Rd. into LaSalle, then immediately right on Quebec. Meet Durham inside this unassuming little eatery. Everyone who is anyone eats here, including out-of-towners such as Jay Leno, Magic Johnson, and Billy Joel. Signed photos and memorabilia crowd the pine-paneled walls. Mr. and Mrs. W.B. Bullock's famous barbecue goes for $5.85 per lb., ½lb. $3.10; all you can eat for $7.50.

Clyde Cooper's Barbeque, 109 E. Davie St., Raleigh (832-7614), 1 block east of the Fayetteville Street Mall downtown. Beckons you to "Eat Mo' Pig" NC-style. Locals favor the baby back ribs ($5.25 per lb.) and the barbeque chicken ($5.25). Open Mon.-Sat. 10am-6pm.

The Ninth Street Bakery Shop, 776 9th St., Durham (286-0303). More than a bakery; sandwiches from $3. Try the dense bran or blueberry muffins (baked goods start at 45¢). Weekend nights feature vegan and seafood dinners 5:30-9pm and acoustic music 8-11pm. Open Mon.-Thurs. 7am-6pm, Fri. 7am-11pm, Sat. 8am-11pm, Sun. 8am-4pm.

Ramshead Rath-Skeller, 157 A E. Franklin St., Chapel Hill (942-5158), directly across from UNC. A student hangout featuring pizza, sandwiches, and hot Apple Pie Louise. Ships' mastheads, German beer steins, and old Italian wine bottles adorn 6 dining rooms with names like the Rat Trap Lounge. "Reverend" Jim Cotton, here since 1947, may cook your steak. Meals $7-8. Open Mon.-Thurs. 11am-2:30pm and 5-9:30pm, Fri.-Sat. 11am-2:30pm and 5-10:30pm, Sun. 11am-10pm.

Skylight Exchange, 405½ W. Rosemary St., Chapel Hill (933-5550). An eclectic den where used books and records are sold, as well as sandwiches ($2-3). Live music on weekends makes it an effortlessly hip operation. Open Sun.-Thurs. 11am-11pm, Fri-Sat. 11am-midnight.

Owens 501 Diner, 1500 N. Fordham Blvd. (933-3505), Chapel Hill (the continuation of US 15-105), adjacent to Eastgate Shopping Center. A friendly staff and Elvis wall clock with gyrating pendulum welcome you to this bastion of 50s nostalgia. Slide into a stainless steel bench, listen to Chuck Berry, and watch Greg Owens cook your burger ($4.50). Open Tues.-Sat. 7am-10pm, Sun. 8:30am-3pm.

SIGHTS AND ENTERTAINMENT

Raleigh's historical attractions are a welcome break from the academic pursuits of the research triangle. The **capitol building** (846-2263), in Union Square at Edenton and Salisbury St., was built in 1840. (Open Mon.-Fri. 8am-5pm, Sat. 9am-5pm, Sun. 1-5pm. Free.) Across from the capitol, the **North Carolina Museum of History,** 1 E. Edenton St. (715-0200), exhibits memorabilia from the earliest settlement to the present (open Tues.-Sat. 9am-5pm, Sun. 1-6pm; free). Pick up a brochure at the visitors center for a self-guided tour of the beautifully renovated 19th-century homes of **Historic Oak-wood** and **Oakwood Cemetery,** where several North Carolina governors and statesmen are buried, as well as four Confederate generals. Across the street and around the corner at Bicentennial Square, the **Museum of Natural Sciences** (733-7450) displays fossils, gems, and animal exhibits, including an extensive wetlands exhibit (open Mon.-Sat. 9am-5pm, Sun. 1-5pm; free). The **North Carolina Museum of Art,** 2110 Blue Ridge Blvd. (839-6262), off I-40 at the Wade Ave. exit, has eight galleries, with works by Raphael, Botticelli, Rubens, Monet, Wyeth, and O'Keeffe. (Tours Tues.-Sun. 1:30pm. Open Tues.-Thurs. 9am-5pm, Fri. 9am-9pm, Sat. 9am-5pm, Sun. 11am-6pm. Free.) To see local artists in action, visit the galleries and craft shops of the **Moore Square Art District** (828-4555), which occupies a 3-block radius around Moore Square. Near the Square is **City Market,** a collection of shops, cafés, and bars. **Mordecai Historic Park,** 1 Mimosa St. (834-4844), recreates 19th-century life in Raleigh on the grounds of an antebellum plantation ($3).

Duke University is Durham's main draw, and the admissions office, 2138 Campus Dr. (684-3214), doubles as a **visitors center** (open Mon.-Fri. 8am-5pm, Sat. 9am-1pm). **Duke Chapel** (684-2921), in the center of the university, has more than a million pieces of stained glass depicting almost 900 figures in 77 windows. (Open July-Aug. daily 8am-8pm, Sept.-June 8am-10pm; services Sun. 11am.) The **Sarah Duke Gardens** (684-3698), near West Campus on Anderson St., have over 15 acres of landscaping and tiered flower beds (open daily 8am-dusk). Take the free Duke campus shuttle bus to East Campus, where the **Duke Museum of Art** (684-5135) shows a small but impressive collection of Italian and Dutch oils, classical sculptures, and African art (open Tues.-Fri. 9am-5pm, Sat. 11am-2pm, Sun. 2-5pm; free). Also take time to enjoy Duke's 7700-acre **forest** (682-9319).

The **Duke Homestead,** 2828 Duke Homestead Rd. (477-5498), is on the other side of Durham, up Guess Rd. Washington Duke started his tobacco business on this beautiful estate before endowing a certain university. (Open Mon.-Sat. 9am-5pm, Sun. 1-5pm; Nov.-March Tues.-Sat. 10am-4pm, Sun. 1-4pm. Free.)

Duke-free Durham does exist: **Bennett Place,** 4408 Bennett Memorial Rd., North Durham (383-4345), is the site of Confederate general Joseph Johnston's surrender to Union general William T. Sherman. The **Museum of Life and Science,** 433 Murray Ave. (220-5429), is a nationally acclaimed assemblage of hands-on exhibits from the geological to the astronomical, with the occasional animatronic dinosaur ($5.50, under 12 $3.50; open Mon.-Sat. 10am-6pm, Sun. 1-6pm). Nightlife in Durham is notoriously nonexistent, though **The Power Company** (683-1151), on the Downtown Loop across from the train station, breaks up the nocturnal monotony with Top 40 hits, Sunday drag shows, and Thursday "college nights." The clientele is primarily gay and lesbian, except Thurs. (members $4, guests $6; 18+).

Chapel Hill and neighboring Carrboro are virtually inseparable from the **University of North Carolina at Chapel Hill** (962-2211), an area residents call "the Southern part of heaven." The university's Smith Center hosts sporting events and concerts. Until 1975, astronauts practiced celestial navigation at the UNC **Morehead Planetarium** (962-1236), which now puts up six different shows per year, each conceived and produced while you watch. (Open Sun.-Fri. 12:30-5pm and 7-9:45pm, Sat. 10am-5pm and 7-9:45pm. $3.50, students, seniors, and children $2.50.)

Pick up a free copy of the *Spectator* and *Independent* weekly magazines, available at most restaurants, bookstores, and hotels, for complete listings of Triangle special events. Students often frequent bars along **9th Street** in Durham, and **Franklin**

Street in Chapel Hill. The **Cat's Cradle, 300** E. Main St., Carrboro (967-9053), the quasi-legendary rock club where R.E.M. and Pearl Jam once played, is the place to hear burgeoning local and national talent. Students throng to **ComedySportz** (968-3922), Franklin St., across from NCNB Plaza, Chapel Hill, to catch competitive team improv and local favorites Anthony King and Ross White. (cover $6; $1 discount with college ID. Shows Fri. 8:30pm, Sat. 7:30 and 8:45pm.) Raleigh's City Market sportz another branch (829-0822).

The **Durham Bulls** (688-8211), a class-A farm team for the Atlanta Braves, became famous after the 1988 movie *Bull Durham* was filmed in their ballpark. They still play here. (General admission $4.25. Students, seniors, and under 18 $3.25.)

■ Charlotte

In 1799, a fortunate fellow stubbed his toe while strolling through Charlotte. Moments later he was heard howling and screaming—not because of the pain (although that might have been part of it), but because he realized he had hurt his toe on a 17-pound golden nugget. Mines sprung up, prospectors poured in, and gold speculation boomed. The rush lasted about 50 years, until folks in California began finding smaller nuggets in larger quantities. The 19th-century mines are gone, but Charlotte, which began as a village on the Catawba Indian trade route, is now the largest city in the Carolinas and the nation's third largest banking center.

Practical Information Info **Charlotte,** 330 S. Tryon St. (331-2700 or 800-231-4636), awaits uptown for brochure-browsing, and offers free parking off 2nd St. Ask for the *A Walk Through Historic Forth Ward* guide. (Open Mon.-Fri. 8:30am-5pm, Sat. 10am-4pm, Sun. 1-4pm.) Heed the "All Aboard" at **Amtrak,** 1914 N. Tryon St. (376-4416 or 800-872-7245), or ride **Greyhound,** 601 W. Trade St. (372-0456 or 800-231-2222). Both are open 24 hr. **Charlotte Transit,** 901 N. Davidson St. (336-3366), runs local buses (85¢, $1.15 for outlying areas; transfers free; 24hr. unlimited ride pass $1.50). In an **emergency,** call 911. Charlotte's **post office:** 201 N. McDowell (333-5135; open Mon.-Fri. 7am-5:30pm). **ZIP code:** 28202. **Area code:** 704.

Accommodations and Food Charlotte's budget motels thrive along the I-85 Service Rd. **Red Roof Inn** (596-8222), I-85 at Sugar Creek Rd., has large rooms, new wood furniture, A/C, heat, cable TV, free local calls, coffee, and daily papers (singles $32, doubles $39). South of the city, try the **Motel 6,** 3430 Vardell Ln. (527-0144); take I-77 south, Exit 7 at Clanton Rd. Amenities include cable TV, HBO, A/C, laundry, pool, and free local calls (singles $32, doubles $40).

South from uptown, the **Dilworth** neighborhood cooks with a generous number of restaurants serving everything from ethnic cuisine to pizza and pub fare. Part yuppie, part gay, and continuously upbeat, the area and its residents are well heeled; yet some places won't turn away, or bankrupt, unwashed backpackers. **Café 521,** 521 N. College St. (377-9100), is a coffeehouse with a Euro image and outstanding lunchtime fare ($4-6). Portions are small, but everything comes with free bread and olive oil to dip it in. (Open Tues.-Fri. 11:30am-3:30pm and 5pm-1am, Sat.-Mon. 5pm-1am; bar closes nightly 2am.) The **Charlotte Regional Farmer's Market,** 1801 Yorkmont Rd. (357-1269), hawks local produce, baked goods, and crafts year-round (Tues.-Sat. 8am-6pm). **Talleys Green Grocery,** 1408 East Blvd. (334-9200), serves organic health food, and sandwiches ($5) and hot soups to go, onward to Talleys with a heave and a ho (open Mon.-Sat. 9am-9pm, Sun. 10am-7pm).

Sights, Entertainment, and Nightlife The **Mint Museum of Art,** 2730 Randolph Rd. (337-2000), a 5-min. drive from uptown, is particularly proud of its pottery, porcelain, and American art collections. (Open Tues. 10am-10pm, Wed.-Sat. 10am-5pm, Sun. noon-5pm. Guided tours daily 2pm. $4, students $2, under 13 free; free Tues. after 5pm.) The **Discovery Place,** 301 N. Tryon St. (845-6664 or 800-935-0553), draws crowds with its hands-on science and technology museum, OmniMax theater, and planetarium. (Open Mon.-Sat. 9am-6pm, Sun. 1-6pm; Sept.-May Mon.-Fri. 9am-5pm, Sat. 9am-6pm, Sun. 1-6pm. Exhibit halls, OmniMax, or planetarium $5.50, seniors and ages 6-12 $4.50, ages 3-5 $2.75; any two $7.50/$6.50/$4.50.)

Paramount's Carowinds Entertainments Complex (588-2600 or 800-888-4FUN/ 4386), 10 mi. south of Charlotte off Exit 90 from I-77, is an amusement park which pays tribute to *Wayne's World* with the "Hurler" roller coaster. (Open daily 10am-8pm. $28, seniors and ages 4-6 $14, under 4 free; after 5pm $13. Parking $3.) The **Charlotte Knights** play minor league baseball April through July at Knights Castle (357-8071), off I-77S at Exit 88 (tickets $5, seniors and children $3.50).

For nightlife, arts, and entertainment listings, grab a free copy of either *Creative Loafing* or *Break* in one of Charlotte's shops or restaurants. The **Moon Room,** 431 S. Tryon St. (342-2003), has live music on weekends and occasionally explodes into bohemian funkiness with Thursday theme nights; watch for Poetry Night and Psychic Night (open Thurs. 5:30-11:30pm, Fri.-Sat. 5:30pm-1am). Quench your thirst with homemade brew from **Dilworth Brewing Co.,** 1301 East Blvd. (377-2739), where local rock and blues play on weekends. (Hearty pub food $4-6; Thurs. all-you-can-eat spaghetti $7). Late night dancing can be found at **The Baha,** 4369 S. Tryon St. (525-3343), a "progressive dance complex" with nights like Disco Hump and College Quake. Arrive before 11pm for a short line and a low cover (open Fri.-Sat. until 4am). Call about occasional all-age live music shows.

CAROLINA MOUNTAINS

The sharp ridges and rolling slopes of the southern Appalachian range create some of the most spectacular scenery in the Southeast. Amidst this beauty flourishes a melange of diverse personalities. In the hills, scholars chat with ski bums, hippie enclaves merge with farming communities, and artists encourage the impulsive spending of cash-toting tourists. Enjoy the area's rugged wilderness while backpacking, canoeing, rafting, mountain biking, cross-country skiing, or just driving the **Blue Ridge Parkway.** The Blue Ridge Mountains divide into two areas. The north area is the **High Country,** which includes the territory between Boone and Asheville, 100 mi. to the southwest. The south includes the **Great Smoky Mountains National Park** (see p. 276) and the **Nanatahala National Forest.**

■ Boone and Blowing Rock

Nestled among the breathtaking mountains of the High Country, **Boone,** named for frontiersman Daniel Boone, has two faces. Tourist attractions such as Mast General Store, Tweetsie Railroad, and the many antiques shops lure young and old to eat family-style, flatten coins on railroad ties, and, of course, shop. But this small town lives year-round, populated by locals and the students of **Appalachian State University (ASU).** Downtown beckons with a soda fountain and numerous student hang-outs. **Blowing Rock,** 7 mi. south at the entrance to the Blue Ridge Parkway, is a friendly mountain villa with a large population of craftmakers and folk artists. The rock which blows overhangs **Johns River Gorge;** chuck a piece of paper (biodegradable, please) over the edge, and it will blow right back at you.

PRACTICAL INFORMATION

Tourist Office: Boone Area Chamber of Commerce, 208 Howard St. (264-2225 or 800-852-9506), has info on accommodations and sights. Turn from Rte. 321S onto River St., drive behind the university, turn right onto Depot St., then take the first left onto Howard St. Open Mon.-Fri. 9am-5pm. The **Blowing Rock Chamber of Commerce** (295-7851) is on Main St. Open Mon.-Sat. 9am-5pm. **North Carolina High Country Host Visitor Center,** 1700 Blowing Rock Rd. (264-1299 or 800-438-7500), distributes free copies of the *High Country Host Area Travel*

Guide, a detailed map of the area, and the *Blue Ridge Parkway Directory,* a mile-by-mile description of services and attractions located on or near the Parkway. Open daily 9am-5pm.

Public Transportation: Boone AppalCart, 274 Winkler's Creek Rd. (264-2278). Local bus and van service with 3 main routes: Red links downtown Boone with ASU and motels and restaurants on Blowing Rock Rd.; Green serves Rte. 421; Crosstown runs between ASU and the marketplace. Red route every hr. Mon.-Fri. 7am-6:30pm; Green Mon.-Fri. 7am-7pm; crosstown Mon.-Fri. 6:30am-11pm, Sat. 9am-8pm. Fare 50¢.

Taxis: Boone Taxi (264-9322). $6 flat rate. Open Mon.-Thurs. 7am-midnight, Fri.-Sat. 7am-3am. Call ahead for an earlier pick-up.

Bike Rental: Rock and Roll Sports, 208 E. King St. Bikes $15, helmets $5, car racks $2. Ask for a trail map. Open Mon.-Sat. 10am-6pm, Sun. noon-4pm.

Emergency: 911. **National Park Service/Blue Ridge Parkway Emergency,** 800-727-5928.

Post Office: 637 Blowing Rock Rd. (264-3813), and 678 W. King St. (262-1171). Both open Mon.-Fri. 9am-5pm, Sat. 9am-noon. **ZIP code:** 28607. **Area code:** 704.

ACCOMMODATIONS, CAMPING, AND FOOD

Catering primarily to vacationing families, the area fronts more than its share of expensive motels and B&Bs. Scratch the surface, though, and you'll find enough inexpensive rooms and campsites to keep you comfy. Weekends in July and August tend to be very expensive.

Blowing Rock Assembly Grounds (295-7813), near the Blue Ridge Pkwy., has clean hostel rooms, shared bathrooms, sports facilities, and a cheap cafeteria, in a gorgeous setting with access to hiking trails. Call for a pick-up, or follow Rte. 321S from Boone (left at the Shoppes on the Pkwy. onto Possum Hollow Rd., left at the first stop sign, left at the golf course). "BRAG" is primarily a retreat for religious groups, but everyone is welcome. (Reception daily 9am-5pm. Check-in 4pm, check-out noon. $14, motel-like rooms in new building $46. Reservations required.)

Most inexpensive hotels are concentrated along **Blowing Rock Rd.** (Rte. 321) or Rte. 105. The red-brick **Red Carpet Inn,** 862 Blowing Rock Rd. (264-2457 or 800-443-7179), has spacious rooms that come with TV, VCR, A/C, heat, a playground, and a pool. Prices vary drastically with seasonal availability. Some holiday weekends have a two-night minimum stay. (Singles $53, doubles $57. Reservations recommended.) The **Boone Trail Motel,** 275 E. King St./U.S. 421 (264-8839), south of downtown, has brightly painted rooms with quaint country baskets to hold the T.P. (Singles $25, doubles $30; Fri.-Sat. $35/$38.)

Boone and **Pisgah National Forest** offer developed and well equipped **campsites** as well as **primitive camping** options for those looking to rough it. Along the Blue Ridge Pkwy., spectacular tent sites ($10) are available at the **Julian Price Campground,** Mile 297 (963-5911); sites around Loop A are on a lake. **Linville Falls,** Mile 316 (963-5911), and **Crabtree Meadows,** Mile 340 (675-4444; open May-Oct.), are your other options (both $10).

Route 321 boasts countless fast-food options and family-style eateries. College students and professors alike hang out on **West King Street** (U.S. 441/221). **Our Daily Bread,** 627 West King St. (264-0173), offers sandwiches, salads, and super vegetarian specials for $3-5 (open Mon.-Fri. 8am-6:30pm, Sat. 9am-5pm). The **Daniel Boone Inn** (264-8657), at the Rte. 321/421 junction, does hefty, sit-down, all-you-can-eat meals, country-style (open daily 11am-9pm for dinner, $10; also Sat.-Sun. 8am-11am for breakfast, $6). Choose a soup ($2) from five or six made daily at **Piccadeli's,** 2161 Blowing Rock Rd. (262-3500), or build your own deli sandwich ($4-5) with all the fixin's (open Sun.-Thurs. 11am-10pm, Fri.-Sat. 11am-10:30pm). The **Appalachian Soda Shop,** 516 West King St. (262-1500), gives you an awful lot of grease at a low, low price (huge, juicy burgers $2-4; open Mon.-Sat. 11am-5pm).

SIGHTS AND ENTERTAINMENT

Horn in the West (264-2120), in an open-air amphitheater located near Boone off Rte. 105, dramatizes the American Revolution as it was fought in the south Appalachians. (Shows late June-late Aug. Tues.-Sun. 8:30pm. $12, under 13 $6; group rates upon request. Reservations recommended.) Adjacent to the theater, the **Daniel Boone Native Gardens** celebrate mountain foliage (open May-Oct. daily 9am-6pm, $2), and the **Hickory Ridge Homestead** documents 18th-century mountain life. (Open while the Horn is in session, 9am-5pm; included in Horn admission price, or $2 alone.) **An Appalachian Summer** (800-843-2787) is a month-long festival of high-caliber music, art, theater, and dance sponsored by ASU. Held May through September, Roan Mountain's **Summer in the Park** festival features cloggers and storytellers at the State Park Amphitheater; call the **Roan Mountain Visitors Center** (423-772-3314 or 423-772-3303) for info.

In Blowing Rock, stop by **Parkway Craft Center,** Mile 294 Blue Ridge Pkwy. (295-7938), 2 mi. south of Blowing Rock Village in the Cone Manor House, where members of the Southern Highland Craft Guild demonstrate their skills (open daily 9am-6pm). The craft center is on the grounds of the **Moses H. Cone Memorial Park,** 3600 acres of shaded walking trails and magnificent views. Check the **National Park Service** desk in the center for a copy of *This Week's Activities.* (Open May-Oct. daily 9am-5:30pm; free.) Guided horseback rides from **Blowing Rock Stables** (295-7847) let you tour the park without hoofing it yourself. To find the stables, get off the Blue Ridge Pkwy. at the Blowing Rock sign, turn left onto Rte. 221/Yonahlossee Rd. and follow the signs. (Open March-Dec. daily 9am-4pm. 1-hr. tour $20, 2-hr. $35. No kids under 9 permitted. Call 1 day in advance to reserve.) The **Cosmic Coffee House** (295-4762), N. Main St., shows local artwork and hosts local bands several times a month, all the while brewing coffee that's "out-of-this-world" ($1 for cup and a refill; open Mon.-Sat. 8am-11pm, Sun. 9am-9pm).

Hikers should arm themselves with the invaluable, large-scale map *100 Favorite Trails* ($3.50). **Edge of the World,** P.O. Box 1137, Banner Elk (898-9550), on Rte. 184 downtown, is a complete outdoor equipment and clothing store which rents equipment and gives regional hiking info. The staff also lead day-long backpacking, whitewater canoeing, spelunking, and rock climbing trips throughout the High Country for about $65. (Open Sun.-Thurs. 9am-6pm, Fri.-Sat. 9am-10pm.)

Downhill skiers enjoy the Southeast's largest concentration of alpine resorts, with four in the area: **Appalachian Ski Mountain,** off U.S. 221/321 (800-322-2373; lift tickets $20, Sat.-Sun. $29; rentals $9/$12); **Ski Beech,** 1007 Beech Mt. Pkwy. (387-2011 or 800-438-2093), Beech Mountain 28604 off Rte. 184 in Bonner Elk (lift tickets $25, Sat.-Sun. $37; rentals $12/$16); **Ski Hawknest,** Town of Seven Devils, 1800 Skyland Dr. (963-6561; lift tickets $20, Sat.-Sun. $33; rentals $12/$14); and **Sugar Mountain,** Banner Elk off Rte. 184 (898-4521; lift tickets $25, Sat.-Sun. $39; rentals $12/$15). It's best to call ahead to the resort for specific ski package prices. The Boone AppalCart (264-2278) runs a free **shuttle** in winter to Sugar Mountain and Ski Beech. Call the High Country Host (264-1299) for **ski reports.**

The 5-mi. road to **Grandfather Mountain** (800-468-7325), off Rte. 221, provides an unparalleled view of the entire High Country area. At the top, a private park features a 1-mi.-high suspension bridge; a museum displaying minerals, birds, and plants indigenous to North Carolina; and a small zoo ($9, ages 4-12 $5, under 4 free). To hike or camp on Grandfather Mt. requires a permit, available at the **Grandfather Mt. Country Store** on Rte. 221 or at the park entrance (day use $4.50, camping $9). Pick up a trail map at the entrance to learn which trails are available for overnight use, and inform the **Backcountry Manager,** Grandfather Mt., Linville 28646, of your plans. This can be done at the park entrance as well. (Mountain open daily 8am-7pm; Dec.-March 8am-5pm, weather permitting.)

■ Asheville

Hazy blue mountains, deep valleys, spectacular waterfalls, and plunging gorges draw a diverse crowd to this Appalachian Mountain hub. Students of the University of North Carolina at Asheville (UNC-Asheville), a thriving gay and lesbian community, nature lovers, and artists provide a human landscape to complement the terrain. While natural beauty prevails, the Biltmore Estate, as well as nearby Cherokee museums and cultural exhibitions, keep tourists busy. Asheville's craggy vistas are best seen from the Blue Ridge Pkwy.

PRACTICAL INFORMATION

Tourist Office: Chamber of Commerce, 151 Haywood St. (258-3858 or 800-257-1300), off I-240 on the northwest end of downtown. Ask at the desk for detailed city and transit route maps and the free *Asheville Urban Trail Guide*. Open Mon.-Fri. 8:30am-5:30pm, Sat.-Sun. 9am-5pm.

Buses: Greyhound, 2 Tunnel Rd. (253-5353 or 800-231-2222), 2mi. east of downtown, near the Beaucatcher Tunnel. Asheville Transit buses #13 and 14 run to and from downtown every ½hr.; last bus 5:50pm. To: Charlotte (3 per day, 3hr., $29); Knoxville (6 per day, 3hr., $26); Atlanta (1 per day, 7hr., $41); Raleigh (1 per day, 5hr., $50). Open Mon.-Fri. 8am-5:30pm, Sat. 8-11:30am and 3-5:30pm.

Public Transportation: Asheville Transit, 360 W. Haywood (253-5691). Bus service within city limits. All routes converge on Pritchard Park downtown. Operates Mon.-Fri. (and some Sat.) 5:30am-7pm, most at ½-hr. intervals. Fare 60¢, transfers 10¢. Discounts for seniors, disabled, and multi-fare tickets. Short trips within the downtown area are free.

Crisis Line: Rape Crisis, 255-7576.

Emergency: 911.

Post Office: 33 Coxe Ave. (257-4112), at Patton Ave. Open Mon.-Fri. 7:30am-5:30pm, Sat. 9am-noon. **ZIP code:** 28802. **Area code:** 704.

ACCOMMODATIONS AND CAMPING

Asheville's reasonably priced motels cluster in two spots—on **Merrimon Ave.** near downtown, and **Tunnel Rd.,** east of downtown. The **In Town Motor Lodge,** 100 Tunnel Rd. (252-1811), provides light, clean rooms with cable, A/C, pool, and free local calls (singles $27, doubles $32; Sat.-Sun. $32/$39). The **Down Town Motel,** 65 Merrimon Ave. (253-9841), just north of the I-240 expressway (bus #2), offers cable, A/C, and large rooms a 10-min. walk from downtown (singles $38, doubles $40; multi-night discounts possible). If you dug Lincoln Logs as a kid, you'll love **Log Cabin Motor Court,** 330 Weaverville Hwy. (645-6546). Take Rte. 240 to Rte. 19/23/70N to the New Bridge Exit, turn right, then left at the light; it's 1 mi. down on the right. Each log cabin has TV, heat, and pool access (singles $31, doubles $35).

With the vista-laden Blue Ridge Pkwy., Pisgah National Forest, and the Great Smokies easily accessible by car, campsites are far from scarce. Close to town, **Bear Creek RV Park and Campground,** 81 S. Bear Creek Rd. (253-0798), takes the camp out of camping with a pool, laundry facilities, groceries, and a game room. Take I-40 Exit 47, and look for the sign ($18, with hookup $20). The nearest campground in the national forest, **Powhatan** (667-8429), 12 mi. southwest of Asheville off Rte. 191, has wooded sites on an 8-acre trout lake, with hiking trails and a swimming lake to entertain you (gates close 10pm; $10, no hookups; open May 15-Oct.).

FOOD

You'll find the greasy links of most major fast-food chains on **Tunnel Rd.** and **Biltmore Ave.** The **Western North Carolina Farmers Market** (253-1691), at the intersection of I-40 and Rte. 191 near I-26, sells fresh produce and crafts. Take bus #16 to I-40, then walk ½mi. (Open daily 8am-6pm.)

Malaprops Bookstore/Café, 61 Haywood St. (254-6734 or 800-441-9829), downtown in the basement of the bookstore. Gourmet coffees, bagels, and great smells found here. Check out the scintillating readings upstairs and the Malaprops staff art on the walls. Open Mon.-Thurs. 9am-8pm, Fri.-Sat. 9am-10pm, Sun. noon-6pm.

Superette, 78 Patton Ave. (254-0255), in the heart of downtown, serves good, fast, cheap Middle Eastern food. Salads from $1.50, sandwiches $2.50-$3.50. Open Mon.-Fri. 8am-5pm, Sat. 10am-4pm.

Smokehouse Mountain BBQ, 205 Spruce St. (234-4871 or 800-850-3718), on the southeast corner of downtown, serves up classic southern barbeque at affordable prices (most entrees under $10). Go for the food but stay for the music; country, mountain, and bluegrass bands start playing about 7:30pm on Thurs.-Sat. nights. Open Tues.-Sat. 5:30pm-varied closing times.

SIGHTS AND ENTERTAINMENT

Four free weekly papers, *Mountain Express, Community Connections, Asheville Traveler,* and *What's Happening* (Re-Run and Dwayne not included) feature entertainment listings; pick them up to find out what's going on around town.

It does not seem possible that George Vanderbilt could have **Biltmore Estate,** 1 North Pack Sq. (255-1700 or 800-543-2961), three blocks north of I-40's exit 50. The ostentatious abode was built in the 1890s under the supervision of architect Richard Morris Hunt and landscaper Fredrick Law Olmstead, and remains the largest private home in America. A tour of this Neo-classical castle can take all day if it's crowded; try to arrive early. The self-guided tour winds through some of the 250 rooms, around the indoor pool, through a bowling alley, into rooms lined with Sargent paintings and Dürer prints, and through the immense rare book libraries. Tours of the surrounding gardens, and of the Biltmore winery (with sour-wine tasting for those 21 and over) are included in the hefty admission price. (Open daily 9am-5pm. Winery opens Mon.-Sat. 11am, Sun. 1pm. $25, ages 10-15 $19, under 9 free. Nov.-Dec. $2-3 more to defray the cost of Christmas decorations.)

Travelers Henry Ford, Thomas Edison, and F. Scott Fitzgerald all stayed in the towering **Grove Park Inn** (252-2711), on Macon St. off Charlotte St. Look for the bright red-tile roof peeking through the trees. The hotel, made of stone quarried from the surrounding mountains, is expensive lodging but cheap sightseeing with early-20th-century fireplaces so immense you could walk into them. Next door is the **Estes-Winn Memorial Museum,** which houses about 20 vintage automobiles ranging from a Model T Ford to a 1959 Edsel. Check out the 1922 candy-red America La France fire engine. (Open Mon.-Sat. 10am-5pm, Sun. 1-5pm. Free.)

The **Thomas Wolfe Memorial,** 48 Spruce St. (253-8304), between Woodfin and Walnut St., the site of the novelist's boyhood home, was a boarding house run by his mother, perhaps the inspiration for the guest house in Wolfe's novel *Look Homeward, Angel.* (Open Mon.-Sat. 9am-5pm, Sun. 1-5pm; hours vary in winter. Tours every ½hr. $1, students 50¢.)

Asheville's artistic tradition extends beyond literature; visit the **Folk Art Center,** Mile 382 Blue Ridge Pkwy. (704-298-7928), east of Asheville and north of U.S. 70, to see the outstanding work of the Southern Highland Handicraft Guild (open daily 9am-5pm; free). The center's **Guild Fair** fills the Asheville Civic Center, off I-240 on Haywood St., with craft demonstrations, dancing, and music for one weekend in mid-July ($5). To know this deal, twere best not know thyself, it's free **Shakespeare** in Montford Amphitheater (June-Aug. Fri.-Sat. 7:30pm).

■ Near Asheville: Nantahala National Forest

The **Cherokee Indian Reservation** (800-438-1601) lies about 30 mi. outside Asheville on U.S. 441. "Unto these Hills," an outdoor drama, retells the story of the Cherokees and climaxes with a moving re-enactment of the Trail of Tears (June-Aug., Mon.-Sat 8pm; $9, children $5). From May to October, the reservation offers a guided tour of the **Ocunaluftee Indian Village,** a re-created mid-18th century Native American village ($9, children $5). At the **Museum of the Cherokee Indian** (704-497-3481), on

Drama Rd. off U.S. 441, hear the Cherokee language spoken, view artifacts and films, and learn about the past and the present of the Cherokee. This place is fascinating and well worth a visit. (Open Mon.-Sat. 9am-8pm, Sun. 9am-5pm; Sept. to mid-June daily 9am-5pm. $4, under 13 $2.) The **Cherokee Visitors Center** (800-438-1601), on U.S. 441, is open daily from 9am-5pm.

The **Nantahala Outdoor Center (NOC),** 13077 Hwy. 19 W., Bryson City, NC (704-488-2175), 13 mi. southwest of Bryson City on U.S. 19/74 just south of GSM Park, beckons with cheap beds and the great outdoors. (Bunks in simple cabins. Showers, kitchen, laundry facilities. $11.50. Call ahead.) The NOC's whitewater rafting expeditions are pricey, but you can rent your own raft for a trip down the Nantahala River. (Sun.-Fri. $16, Sat. $22. 1-person inflatable "duckies" $27 weekdays, $30 on Sat. Group rates available. Higher prices July-Aug. Prices include transportation to site and all necessary equipment.) The NOC also offers trips with slightly higher price tags on the **Ocoee, Nolichucky, Chattoga,** and **French Broad Rivers.** If you're a Gremlin, skip the river and hike a thousandth of the 2144-mi. **Appalachian Trail;** the NOC staff will assist if you need help charting an appropriate daytrip.

CAROLINA COAST

■ Outer Banks

Known as the "barrier islands" by the inlanders they shield from Atlantic squalls, the Outer Banks have a history as stormy as the hurricanes that annually pummel their beaches. England's first attempt to colonize North America ended in 1590 with the peculiar disappearance of the Roanoke Island settlement (see graybox, below). Over 600 ships have foundered on the Banks' southern shores, but the weather is not entirely culpable. Early inhabitants of Nags Head would string lanterns over their horses' necks and walk them along the beach; convinced that the lights signified boats safe in harbor, captains trying to make port crashed into the shore. The townspeople looted these vessels and their scheme earned the town its name.

Today, the Outer Banks descend from touristy beach towns southward into heavenly wilderness. Highly developed Bodie Island, on the Outer Banks' northern end, includes the towns of Nags Head, Kitty Hawk, and Kill Devil Hills. Crowds become less overpowering as you travel south on Rte. 12 through magnificent wildlife preserves and across Hatteras Inlet to Ocracoke Island and its isolated beaches.

Colony Lost

After the failure of his party's first expedition to the New World, Sir Walter Raleigh decided to sponsor a new colony in "Virginia," the Elizabethan name for what is now the Carolina Coast. The colonists settled on **Roanoke Island** in 1587. Among the 116 adventurers were 17 women and nine children. This demographic makeup, along with the appointment of graphic artist John White as governor, reflected Raleigh's desire to build a colony on something more substantial than military might. Unfortunately, it was not to be—a series of skirmishes and misunderstandings with local Algonquin tribes made for an uneasy relationship between colonists and the indigenous residents. In need of supplies, Governor White returned to England, leaving behind his wife and child. When he next set foot on the sands of Roanoke, nearly three years later, he found the island deserted. The only hint of the nascent colony's whereabouts were the letters "CRO" carved into a tree, and a military palisade bearing the word "CROATOAN." Weather and low provisions prevented White from sailing for the alluded-to island, and the colony was never located. The dream of a peaceful colony in the New World vanished along with the Roanoke settlement.

PRACTICAL INFORMATION

Tourist Office: Aycock Brown Visitors Center (261-4644), off U.S. 158 across the Wright Memorial Bridge on Bodie Island, has info on lodging and picnic areas. Open daily 8:30am-6:30pm; in winter 9am-5pm. **Cape Hatteras National Seashore Information Centers: Bodie Island** (441-5711), Rte. 12 at Bodie Island Lighthouse. **Ocracoke Island** (928-4531), next to the ferry terminal at the south end of the island. Both open Easter-Columbus Day daily 9am-5pm. **Hatteras Island** (995-4474), Rte. 12 at Cape Hatteras Lighthouse. Open daily 9am-5pm.

Ferries: Toll ferries run to Ocracoke (800-345-1665) from **Cedar Island** (800-856-0343; 4-8 per day, 2¼hr.), east of New Bern on U.S. 70, and from **Swan Quarter** (800-773-1094), on the north side of Pamlico. $1, $10 per car (reserve ahead), $2 per biker. Free ferries cross Hatteras Inlet between Hatteras and Ocracoke. (Daily 5am-11pm, 40min.) Call 800-BY-FERRY/293-3779 for all ferry times.

Taxis: Beach Cab (441-2500), serves Bodie Island and Manteo. $1.50 first mi., $1.20 each additional mi.

Car Rental: U-Save Auto Rental (800-685-9938), 1mi. north of Wright Memorial Bridge in Point Harbor. $25 per day with 50 free mi. 15¢ each additional mi. Drivers must be 21 with MasterCard, Visa, or $250 cash deposit. Open Mon.-Fri. 8am-6:30pm, Sat. 8am-2pm.

Bike Rental: Pony Island Motel (928-4411). $2 per hr., $10 per day. Open daily 8am-dusk.

Emergency: 911.

ZIP codes: Manteo 27954, Nags Head 27959, Ocracoke 27960, Kill Devil Hills 27948, Kitty Hawk 27949. **Area code:** 919.

The Outer Banks are comprised of four narrow islands strung along half the length of the North Carolina coast. In the north, **Bodie Island** is accessible via U.S. 158 from Elizabeth, NC, and Norfolk, VA. **Roanoke Island** lies between Bodie and the mainland on U.S. 64 and includes the town of **Manteo. Hatteras Island,** connected to Bodie by a bridge, stretches like a great sandy elbow. **Ocracoke Island,** the southernmost island, is linked (by ferry) to Hatteras Island and to towns on the mainland. **Cape Hatteras National Seashore** encompasses Hatteras, Ocracoke, and the southern end of Bodie Island. On Bodie Island, U.S. 158 and Rte. 12 run parallel to each other until the north edge of the preserve. After that, Rte. 12 (also called Beach Rd.) continues south, stringing together Bodie and Hatteras. Addresses on Bodie Island are determined by their distance in miles from the Wright Memorial Bridge.

There is no public transportation available on the Outer Banks. The **Beach Bus** (255-0550) is a tourist attraction with matching prices (Bodie to Ocracoke $30). Nags Head and Ocracoke lie 76 mi. apart. The flat terrain makes hiking and biking pleasant, but the Outer Banks' ferocious traffic calls for extra caution.

ACCOMMODATIONS AND CAMPING

Most motels cling to Rte. 12 on crowded Bodie Island; for more privacy, try **Ocracoke.** On all three islands, rooming rates are highest from Memorial Day to Labor Day. Reserve seven to ten days ahead for weeknights and up to a month in advance for weekends. Bring long tent spikes to accommodate the loose dirt, tents with fine screens to keep out flea-sized, biting "no-see-ums," and strong insect repellent. Sleep on the beach and you may get fined.

Kill Devil Hills

Outer Banks International Hostel (HI-AYH), 1004 Kitty Hawk Rd. (261-2294), off Rte. 158. Quite possibly the best deal on the Outer Banks. The building, with 53 beds, single-gender dorms, and "honeymoon suite," was once the old Kitty Hawk school. Three communal kitchens, A/C, heat, volleyball, basketball, and shuffleboard. No lockout, no curfew. Members $15, nonmembers $18.

The Ebbtide, Mile 10, Beach Rd. (441-4913). Plushly carpeted, sparsely furnished rooms with A/C, heat, cable TV, refrigerator, microwave, and pool. Guests can eat a generous Southern breakfast for 99¢ at nearby **Ship's Wheel** restaurant. Singles or doubles $49-95; off season $29-70. Open March-Oct.

Nettlewood Motel, Mile 7, Beach Rd. (441-5039), on both sides of the highway. Private beach access. Bright, clean, cozy rooms. TV, A/C, heat, refrigerator, telephone, and pool. Singles or doubles $46-65; off season $30-35.

Manteo

Scarborough Inn (473-3979), U.S. 64/264. Romantic inn with 4-poster canopy beds, flowered linens, and wrap-around porches. Telephone, A/C, heat, refrigerator, continental breakfast, and free use of bicycles. One queen bed $50, 2 double beds $55, 1 king bed $60. Off season (Labor Day to Memorial Day) up to $8 less.

Ocracoke

Sand Dollar Motel (928-5571), off Rte. 12. Turn right at the Pirate's Chest gift shop, right again at the Back Porch Restaurant, and left at the Edwards Motel. Beautiful juniper paneling lends rooms a beach cabin feel. Refrigerator, A/C, heat, and pool. One queen bed $55, 2 queen beds $65. Off season $40/$45. Continental breakfast included. Open April-Thanksgiving.

Edwards Motel (928-4801), off Rte. 12 by the Back Porch Restaurant. Bright assortment of rooms, all with TV, A/C, and heat. Fish cleaning facilities on premises. Two double beds $45, off season $40; 2 double beds and 1 single, with refrigerator and screened porch $52/$45; efficiencies $62/$58; cottages $75-85/$71-77.

Three oceanside **campgrounds** on Cape Hatteras National Seashore are open Memorial Day to Labor Day: **Cape Point** (in Buxton) and **Frisco,** near the elbow of Hatteras Island, and **Ocracoke,** in the middle of Ocracoke Island. **Oregon Inlet,** on the southern tip of Bodie Island, opens in mid-April. Landlocked **Salvo** campground is nestled on the Pamlico Sound side of Hatteras Island. All have restrooms, cold running water, and grills. All sites (except Ocracoke's) cost $12, and are rented on a first-come, first-served basis. Ocracoke sites ($13) can be reserved by calling 800-365-CAMP/2267. Contact **Cape Hatteras National Seashore** (473-2111), for other deep woods concerns.

SIGHTS AND ACTIVITIES

The **Wright Brothers National Memorial,** Mile 8, U.S. 158 (441-7430), marks the spot where Orville and Wilbur Wright took to the skies. You can see models of their planes, hear a detailed account of the day of the first flight, and view the dramatic monument dedicated to the brothers in 1932. (Open daily 9am-6pm; in winter 9am-5pm. Presentations every hr. 10am-4pm. $2 per person, $4 per car.)

On **Roanoke Island,** the **Fort Raleigh National Historic Site,** off U.S. 64, offers several attractions. *The Lost Colony* (473-3414 or 800-488-5012), the longest-running outdoor drama in the U.S., has been performed here since 1937. (Early June-late Aug., Mon.-Fri. and Sun. 8:30pm. $14, seniors and military $13, under 12 $7. Bring insect repellent.) In the **Elizabethan Gardens** (473-3234), antique statues and fountains punctuate a beautiful display of flowers, herbs, and trees. (Open early June-late Aug. daily 9am-8pm; off season 9am-dusk. $3, ages 12-17 $1, under 12 free.) **Fort Raleigh** (473-5772) is a reconstructed 1585 battery—basically a pile of dirt. The nearby **visi-**

"Damned if they ain't flew!"

So exclaimed one eyewitness to humankind's first controlled, sustained flight. On December 17, 1903, two bicycle repairmen from Dayton, Ohio launched the world's first true airplane in 27mph headwinds from an obscure location on the NC coast called **Kill Devil Hills.** Orville Wright, with his brother Wilbur watching anxiously from the ground, held on with his right hand and steered the 605 lb. **Flyer** with his left. 852 feet and 57 seconds later, the **Wright brothers** had flown their craft into history—and then oblivion: the original Flyer was destroyed on the ground by a strong gust of wind.

tors center contains a tiny museum and shows a short film recalling the earliest days of English activity in North America. (Open Mon.-Fri. and Sun. 9am-8pm, Sat. 9am-6pm. Free.) Horseshoe crabs and marine monsters await at the **North Carolina Aquarium** (473-3493), 1 mi. west of U.S. 64. Watch for the sport fishing exhibit, planned for 1997. (In summer, open daily 9am-7pm; off season Mon.-Sat. 9am-5pm, Sun. 1-5pm. $3, seniors $2, ages 6-17 $1.)

Majestic lighthouses dot the Outer Banks; **Cape Hatteras,** run by the Cape Hatteras National seashore, is North America's tallest at 208 ft. As of summer 1996, all lighthouses closed until further notice. Special programs at the Hatteras Island Visitors Center in Buxton include **Maritime Woods Walk** (Mon. 2pm) and **Morning Bird Walk** (Wed. 7:30am). At Soundside Snorkel, park rangers teach visitors to **snorkel** (like, no duh); bring sneakers and a swimsuit. (Thurs. 2:30pm. Would-be participants chosen by lottery, Wed. 4:15pm, at the Cape Hatteras Visitors Center.)

South Carolina

The first state to secede from the Union in 1860, South Carolina continues to take great pride in its Confederate history. Civil War monuments dot virtually every public green or city square, and Confederate "patriots" periodically protest legislative efforts to remove the Confederate flag from the statehouse.

However, the timbre of the state is generally more laid-back than this would suggest. The capital, Columbia, is slow-paced with little to see—it was demolished during the Civil War along with everything else in Sherman's path. Charleston was spared, and despite nature's repeated assaults, still boasts stately, antebellum style. You may need to "do the Charleston" for a few days to take in the city's full flavor. Those who slow to South Carolina's languid pace find that this state preserves a grace and charm which often render more enjoyable the rituals of daily life.

PRACTICAL INFORMATION

Capital: Columbia.
Department of Parks, Recreation, and Tourism: Edgar A. Brown Bldg., 1205 Pendleton St. #106, Columbia 29021 (803-734-0122). **U.S. Forest Service,** 4931 Broad River Rd., Columbia 29210 (803-561-4000).
Time Zone: Eastern. **Postal Abbreviation:** SC.
Sales Tax: 6%.

■ Charleston

Dukes, barons, and earls once presided over Charleston's great coastal plantations, building an extensive, downtown district. In recent years natural disasters, including five fires and 10 hurricanes—the latest in 1989—have necessitated repeated rebuilding in the city. New storefronts and tree stumps mix with beautifully refurbished antebellum homes, old churches, and hidden gardens. The area also offers access to the nearby Atlantic coastal islands. While you're in Charleston meet the locals, some of the friendliest people you'll find in the South.

PRACTICAL INFORMATION

Tourist Office: Charleston Visitors Center, 375 Meeting St. (853-8000), across from Charleston Museum. Walking tour map ($4.50) has historical info and good directions. The free *Charleston Area Visitors Guide* is comprehensive, and the film, *Forever Charleston,* gives an overview of the city past and present ($2.50, children $1). Open daily 8:30am-5:30pm.

Trains: Amtrak, 4565 Gaynor Ave. (744-8263 or 800-872-7245), 8mi. west of downtown. One train per day to: Richmond (8hr., $112); Savannah (2hr., $32); Washington, D.C. (8hr., $144). Open daily 4:15am-noon and 1:30-8:30pm.

Buses: Greyhound, 3610 Dorchester Rd. (747-5341 or 800-231-2222), in N. Charleston. Avoid this area at night. To: Savannah (2 per day, 3hr., $30); Charlotte (2 per day, 6hr., $41.50). The South Carolina Electric and Gas Company "Dorchester/Waylyn" bus goes to town from the station area. Return on the "Navy Yard: 5 Mile Dorchester Rd." bus. Open daily 6am-9:30pm.

Public Transportation: South Carolina Electric and Gas Company (SCE&G) City Bus Service, 3664 Leeds Ave. (747-0922). Operates Mon.-Sat. 5:30am-midnight. Fare 75¢. **Downtown Area Shuttle (DASH)** (724-7420) operates Mon.-Fri. 8am-5pm. Fare 75¢, transfers to other SCE&G buses free. Shuttles to some parts of town also run Sat.-Sun. Pick up a free brochure at the visitors center.

Car Rental: Thrifty Car Rental, 3565 W. Montague Ave. (552-7531 or 800-367-2277). Must be 21 with major credit card. Under 25 surcharge $12 per day. Open daily 5:30am-11pm.

Bike Rental: The Bicycle Shoppe, 280 Meeting St. (722-8168). $3 per hr., $15 per day. Open Mon.-Sat. 9am-8pm, Sun. 1-5pm.

Taxis: North Area Taxi, 554-7575. Base fare $2.50 per person per zone.

Crisis Lines: Hotline, 744-HELP/4357. General counseling and info on transient accommodations. **People Against Rape,** 722-7273. Both operate 24hr.

Emergency: 911.

Post Office: 83 Broad St. (577-0690). Open Mon.-Fri. 8:30am-5:30pm, Sat. 9:30am-2pm. **ZIP code:** 29402. **Area code:** 803.

Old Charleston lies at the southernmost point of the mile-wide peninsula below **Calhoun Street. Meeting, King,** and **East Bay St.** are major north-south routes through the city. North of Calhoun St. runs the **Savannah Hwy. (U.S. 17).**

ACCOMMODATIONS AND CAMPING

Motel rooms in historic downtown Charleston are expensive. Cheap motels are a few mi. out of the city or across the Ashley River on U.S. 17S—not a practical option for those without cars. The **Rutledge Victoria Inn,** 114 Rutledge Ave. (722-7551), is a beautiful historic home that functions as a B&B on its upper floors and a hostel on the ground level. (Shared coed room with shared bath, free local calls, TV, A/C, and fridge $20 per person, $15 each additional day.) Only 6 beds available, so call ahead for reservations and specify that you want a hostel room. **Motel 6,** 2058 Savannah Hwy. (556-5144), 4 mi. south of town, is clean and pleasant, but far from downtown and frequently filled. Call ahead in summer (singles $28, additional person $4).

There are several inexpensive campgrounds in the Charleston area, including **The Campground at James Island County Park** (795-9884 or 800-743-7275). Take U.S. 17S to Rte. 171 and follow the signs. This spectacular park offers full hookups in addition to 16 acres of lakes, miles of bicycle and walking trails, and a small water park. (Tent sites, in limited number, $13; full hookup $18.) **Oak Plantation Campground** (766-5936), 8 mi. south on U.S. 17, has 350 sites and a free shuttle to the visitors center (office open daily 7:30am-9pm; sites $9-17).

FOOD AND NIGHTLIFE

BJ's at the Farm, 32-C Ann St. (722-0559), across from the visitors center. Home of the BJ Burger ($5.50), considered by many Charleston's best burger. Prices hover around $5-6. Open for lunch Mon.-Fri. 11am-3pm; delivery Mon.-Sat. after 5pm. Live music nightly at **The Music Farm** (853-FARM/3276; same bldg., same room), where Hootie and the Blowfish got their start and still play regularly.

T-Bonz Gill and Grill, 80 N. Market St. (517-2511). From T-bone to stir-fry, all in an open-beam building in the historic district. Popular Tues. night live music. Lunch or dinner $3-12. Potato with chili $3, steaks pricier ($10-14). Open daily 11am-2am (late-night menu only, midnight-2am).

Hyman's Seafood Company, 215 Meeting St. (723-6000). Kudos to the proprietor, who manages to serve 15-25 different kinds of fresh fish daily ($8). The snow crabs ($10) are a must for shellfish lovers. Open daily 11am-11pm. Adjoining **Aaron's Deli** serves kosher-style fare (open daily 7am-11pm).

Baker Café, 214 King St. (577-2694). Serves gourmet sandwiches (like the enticing blackened grouper with cayenne tartar sauce) and eggs just about any way imaginable ($6-8). Open Mon.-Fri. 8am-late afternoon and Sat.-Sun. 9am-late afternoon. Lunch starts at 11:30am; eggs served through the afternoon.

Craig Cafeteria (953-5539), corner of St. Philip and George St., is *the* place to chow in Chaz. Serves all-you-can-eat buffets at Charleston College. Breakfast (7-9am, $4.25), lunch (11am-2pm, $4.50), dinner (4:30-6:30pm, $4.75).

Locals rarely dance the Charleston anymore, and the city's nightlife suffers for it. Before going out, pick up a free copy of *Poor Richard's Omnibus,* available at grocery stores and street corners all over town, for listings of concerts and other events. Most bars and clubs are in the **Market St.** area. The **Music Farm,** 32 Ann St. (853-3276), has everything from rave to disco to live bands (hours and cover vary; call ahead). Find eclectic live music at the **Acme Bar and Grill,** 5 Faber St. (577-7383; open Sun. and Tues. 8pm-3am, Wed. and Sat. 8pm-2am, Thurs.-Fri. 8pm-wee hours). The bars and clubs between **George St.** and **Colhan St.** are less tourist-oriented and licensed to remain open until 5am.

SIGHTS AND ENTERTAINMENT

Charleston's ancient homes, historical monuments, churches, galleries, and gardens can be seen by foot, car, bus, boat, trolley, or carriage; ask about organized tours at the visitors center. The 2-hr. **Gray Line Water Tours** (722-1112) boat trip is not only longer but less expensive than most others (daily 10am, 12:30pm, and 3pm; $9.50, ages 6-11 $4.75, under 6 free; reservations recommended).

The open-air **City Market,** downtown at Meeting St., has a deal on everything from porcelain sea lions to handwoven sweetgrass baskets (open daily 9:30am-sunset). **Gibbes Museum of Art,** 135 Meeting St. (722-2706), displays a fine collection of portraits by prominent American artists (open Sun.-Mon. 1-5pm, Tues.-Sat. 10am-5pm; $5). Founded in 1773, the **Charleston Museum,** 360 Meeting St. (722-2996), maintains collections ranging from natural history specimens to old sheet music (open Mon.-Sat. 9am-5pm, Sun. 1-5pm). Charleston's mansions are pricey, so a good bet is the package deal with the Charleston Museum. A combination ticket is available for the museum and two historic homes located nearby: the 18th-century **Heyward-Washington House,** 87 Church St., and the **Joseph Manigault House,** 350 Meeting St. (Both homes open Mon.-Sat. 10am-5pm, Sun. 1-5pm. Museum and two homes $15, children $5; call the museum for separate prices.) To see how Charleston's wealthy merchant class lived in the early 19th century, visit the **Nathaniel Russell House,** 51 Meeting St. (724-8481), where a magnificent staircase spirals from floor to floor without visible support. (Open Mon.-Sat. 10am-5pm; Sun. 2-5pm.)

Gone But Not Forgotten

Ask a local where the Slave Market was located, and they will likely direct you to City Market. But as officials of this restored public market are quick to point out, there is no proof that slaves were quartered or sold here. You may then be directed to an old warehouse on Chalmers St. bearing the words "Old Slave Mart"...only to find that ambiguity persists. Local lore has it that two elderly ladies concocted a story about this building's alleged history in order to create a lucrative tourist trap. Slaves were indeed sold somewhere on the block, but no specific records exist. Unlike almost every other shred of Charleston history, documentation of slave trafficking has all but disappeared, indicating that there are some aspects of history that even historic Charleston would prefer to forget. The bare stone walls of the Chalmers warehouses and the spiked rods stretched menacingly over iron gates are apparently reminders enough.

The **Battery** offers a good view of the harbor and **Fort Sumter,** where an attack by rebel forces on April 12, 1861 touched off the Civil War. Over seven million pounds of metal were fired against the fort before it was finally abandoned in February, 1865. To walk the sacred ground, call **Fort Sumter Tours** (722-1691). Boat tours leave several times daily from the Municipal Marina, at the foot of Calhoun St. and Lockwood Blvd. ($10, ages 6-12 $5.) They also offers tours to **Patriots' Point,** the world's largest naval and maritime museum, where you can stroke the destroyer *Laffey's* aft cannons. Touring the ships will take several hours ($9, under 12 $4.50).

One of several majestic plantations in the area, the 300-year-old **Magnolia Plantation and Magnolia Gardens** (571-1266), 10 mi. out of town on Rte. 61 off U.S. 17, treats visitors to 50 acres of gorgeous gardens with 900 varieties of camelia and 250 varieties of azalea. Get lost in the hedge maze, or rent bicycles or canoes ($2 per hr.) to explore the neighboring swamp and bird sanctuary. (Open daily 8am-5pm. $9, seniors, military, and AAA $8, ages 13-19 $7, ages 4-12 $4.)

From mid-March to mid-April, the **Festival of Houses and Gardens** (723-1623) celebrates Charleston's architecture and traditions. Many private homes open their doors to the public (10 houses $25). Music, theater, dance, and opera fill the city during **Spoleto Festival U.S.A.** (800-255-4659) in late May and early June ($7 and up). The **Charleston Maritime Festival** (800-221-5273), in mid-September, celebrates America's water heritage with parades, artists, and a regatta. **Christmas in Charleston** (853-8000), is all a-jingle with tours, performances, and craft sales.

■ Columbia

One of America's first planned cities, Columbia sprung up in 1786 when Charleston's bureaucrats decided their territory needed a proper capital. Surveyors found some land by the Congaree River, and soon more than 1000 people had poured in. The students of the University of South Carolina (USC) now call the city home. In many ways, Columbia's college-town flavor overshadows its state politics, but the bronze stars on the State House, which mark General Sherman's cannonball strikes, indicate strong links to a Confederate past.

PRACTICAL INFORMATION

Tourist Office: Columbia Metropolitan Convention and Visitors Bureau, 1012 Gervais St. (254-0479). Pick up maps for self-guided walking tours of *Historic Columbia* or *African-American Historic Sites in Columbia.* Open Mon.-Fri. 9am-5pm, Sat. 10am-4pm, Sun. 1-5pm except in winter. **University of South Carolina Visitors Center,** 937 Assembly St. (800-922-9755). Free visitors parking pass and extensive info on USC and Columbia. Also assists with arranging tours. Open Mon.-Fri. 8:30am-5pm, Sat. 9:30am-2pm.

Airport: Columbia Metropolitan Airport, 3000 Aviation Way (822-5010). Taxis to downtown run $10-$12 (**Gamecock Cab,** 796-7700).

Trains: Amtrak, 850 Pulaski St. (252-8246 or 800-872-7245). One per day to: Washington, D.C. (10hr., $104); Miami (13hr., $124); Savannah (2hr., $36). Open daily 11am-7pm. Northbound train departs 1:36am, southbound 12:53am.

Buses: Greyhound, 2015 Gervais St. (256-6465 or 800-231-2222), at Harden about 1mi. east of the capital. To: Charlotte (3 per day, 105min., $15, weekends $16); Atlanta (6 per day, 5hr., $43). Most East Coast buses stop here. 24hr.

Public Transportation: South Carolina Electric and Gas (SCE&G) (748-3019). Local buses 75¢, 40¢ with coupon (call for details), 25¢ elderly and disabled. Most routes start from the transfer depot at Assembly and Gervais St.

Crisis Lines: Helpline of the Midlands, 790-4357. **Rape Crisis,** 771-7273. 24hr.

Emergency: 911.

Post Office: 1601 Assembly St. (733-4643). Open Mon.-Fri. 7:30am-5pm. **ZIP code:** 29202. **Area code:** 803.

The city is laid out in a square, with borders **Huger** (running north-south), **Harden** (north-south), **Blossom** (east-west), and **Calhoun** (east-west). **Assembly St.** is the main drag, running north-south through the heart of the city. **Gervais St.** is its east-west equivalent. The **Congaree River** marks the city's western edge.

ACCOMMODATIONS, CAMPING, AND FOOD

Just outside of downtown across the Congaree River, a number of inexpensive motels line **I-26** and **I-77.** One is **Masters Inn Economy** (791-5850 or 800-633-3434); off I-26E at Exit 113, take a left then an immediate right onto Frontage Rd. Fresh paint, free local calls, a pool, and cable TV brighten these rooms. (Disabled access available. Singles $26, doubles $36.) On the same road, try **Knights Inn** (794-0222), where rooms stenciled with castle scenes keep the knight theme going. All rooms have refrigerators, microwaves, cable TV, A/C, heat, and pool access. (Singles $34, doubles $37.) The **Sesquicentennial State Park** (788-2706) has a lake for swimming, a nature center, hiking and biking trails, and 87 wooded sites with electricity and water (gate closes 9pm; $13). Public transportation does not serve the park; take I-20 to the Two Notch Rd./Rte. 1 exit and head northeast for 4 mi.

The **Five Points** business district, at the junction of Harden, Devine, and Blossom St. ("Veterans Hospital" bus from downtown), caters to Columbia's large student population with bars, nightclubs, and coffeehouses. **Groucho's,** 611 Harden St. (799-5708), started out as a New York-style deli in the 50s, but has carved out its own identity with the invention of the dipper, a large deli sandwich featuring Groucho's own "45" sauce ($4-6; open daily 11am-4pm). **Adriana's,** 721 Saluda Ave. (799-7595), serves a super selection of Italian ice cream (massive serving $1.60), coffees, home-made Italian pastries, and incredible kiwi sorbetto (open Mon.-Thurs. 10:30am-mid-night, Fri.-Sat. 10:30am-12:30am, Sun. noon-11pm). Students and locals frequent USC's renowned deli **Stuffy's Famous,** 629 S. Main St. (771-4098), down Main St. from the State House (cheeseburger, fries, and iced tea $3.45). Happy hour (Mon.-Fri. 4-7pm) spells 15¢ wings. (Open Mon.-Fri. 10am-11pm, Sat. 11am-11pm, Sun. noon-10pm.) Stock up on fresh stuff at the **Columbia State Farmers Market** (253-4041), Bluff Rd. across from the football stadium (open Mon.-Sat. 6am-9pm).

SIGHTS AND ENTERTAINMENT

One of the finest zoos in the country, **Riverbanks Zoo and Garden** (779-8717), on I-26 at Greystone Blvd., northwest of downtown, shows visitors a rainforest, a desert, an undersea kingdom, and a southern farm. Over 2000 animals roam in open habitats. (Open Mon.-Fri. 9am-4pm, in summer also Sat.-Sun. 9am-5pm. $5.75, students $4.50, seniors $4.25, ages 3-12 $3.25.)

Columbia's 18th-century elegance remains intact at the **Robert Mills Historic House and Park,** 1616 Blanding St. (252-1770), three blocks east of Sumter St. One of America's first federal architects, Mills designed the Washington Monument and 30 of South Carolina's public buildings. His Neoclassical home is said to be haunted. Across the street at #1615, the **Hampton-Preston Mansion** (252-0938) not only served as headquarters for Sherman's Union forces during the Civil War, but also once housed Confederate general Wade Hampton. (Both open Tues.-Sat. 10:15am-3:15pm, Sun. 1:15-4:15pm. Tours $3, students $1.50, under 6 free.) The **South Carolina State Museum,** 301 Gervais St. (737-4595), beside the Gervais St. Bridge, is in the historic Columbia Mills building. Exhibits include a prehistoric great white shark—far more impressive than its modern cousin. (Open Mon.-Sat. 10am-5pm, Sun. 1-5pm. $4, students with ID and seniors $3, ages 6-17 $1.50, under 6 free.)

Stroll through the USC **Horseshoe,** at the junction of College and Sumter St., to admire the university's oldest buildings. The **McKissick Museum** (777-7251), at the top of the Horseshoe, shows scientific exhibits and selections from an extensive collection of Twentieth Century-Fox newsreels. (Open Mon.-Fri. 9am-4pm, Sat.-Sun. 1-5pm. Free.) **Finlay Park,** behind the post office on Assembly and Laurel St., is large and manicured, with playing fields, fountains, and swinging benches (closes daily 11pm). The weekly publication *Free Times* gives details on Columbia's club and **nightlife** scene. *In Unison* is a weekly paper listing ads for gay-friendly nightspots.

■ Myrtle Beach and the Grand Strand

Stretching 60 mi. from Little River near the North Carolina border to the tidelands of historic Georgetown, the Grand Strand is a long, wide ribbon of land bathed in beaches, tourists, restaurants, and small villages. In the middle of it all basks Myrtle Beach, full of mini-golf courses, tennis courts, water parks, and white sand. During spring break and in early June, Myrtle Beach (especially North Myrtle Beach) is jam-packed with leering, sunburned students who revel in the area's commercialism and the call of the deep blue.

The pace slows significantly south of Myrtle Beach. **Murrell's Inlet,** a quaint port stocked with good seafood, and **Pawley's Island** are both dominated by private homes. **Georgetown,** once a critical Southern port city, showcases its history via white-pillared homes on 18th-century-era rice and indigo plantations.

PRACTICAL INFORMATION

Tourist Office: Myrtle Beach Chamber of Commerce, 1200 N. Oak St. (626-7444), provides entertainment listings, coupons, and details on accommodations. Open Mon.-Fri. 8:30am-5pm, Sat. 9am-5pm, Sun. noon-5pm.

Buses: Greyhound, 508 9th Ave. N. (448-2471 or 800-231-2222). Open daily 8:30am-1pm and 3-7:30pm.

Public Transportation: Coastal Rapid Public Transit (CRPTA) (248-7277) provides minimal busing. Local 75¢; Conway to Myrtle Beach $1.25.

Bike Rental: The Bike Shoppe, 711 Broadway (448-5335). $10 per day, $5 per ½ day. License or credit card required. Open daily 8am-6pm.

Emergency: 911.

Post Office: 505 N. Kings Hwy. (626-9533). Open Mon.-Fri. 8:30am-5pm, Sat. 9am-1pm. **ZIP code: 29577. Area code: 803.**

A series of **avenues** running in numerical order bridges **U.S. 17** and **Ocean Blvd.,** also called **Kings Hwy.** Avenue numbers repeat themselves after reaching 1st Ave. in the middle of town, so note whether the avenue is "north" or "south." Also, take care not to confuse north **Myrtle Beach** with the town **North Myrtle Beach,** which has an almost identical street layout (and character). **Rte. 501** runs west towards Conway, U.S. 95, and, more importantly, the popular factory outlet stores. Unless otherwise stated, addresses on the Grand Strand are for Myrtle Beach.

ACCOMMODATIONS AND CAMPING

Couples and families take over in summer, Myrtle Beach's most expensive season. In fact, many motels and campgrounds accept only families or couples. Cheap motels lurk just west of the beach in the 3rd St. area or on U.S. 17. Prices plunge October through March when they need your business; you can often bargain for a lower hotel rate. A free 'n' easy way to find the most economical rooms is to call the **Beach Hotel and Motel Reservation Service,** 1551 21st Ave. N. Ste. #20 (626-7477 or 800-626-7477). For the best deals, ask for the "second row" string of hotels across the street from the ocean front. (Open daily 8am-8pm.) The Grand Strand has been called the "camping capital of the world;" Myrtle Beach alone is laden with nine campgrounds and two state parks.

Roving bands of sometimes rowdy bar-hoppers make safety on Ocean Blvd. a serious issue, and thousands of dollars worth of property are stolen from motel rooms every season. Lock all valuables and be wary of the **Strand's** hard-partying masses.

Sea Banks Motor Inn, 2200 S. Ocean Blvd. (448-2434 or 800-523-0603), across the street from the ocean. Family-run establishment with laundry facilities, a pool, beach access, new carpet, large windows, and TV. Some rooms have balconies. Rooms with 1 double bed from $23 (March and Sept.-Oct.) to $39 (in summer).

Grand Strand Motel, 1804 S. Ocean Blvd. (448-1461 or 800-433-1461). Similar to Sea Banks. Small rooms with 1 double bed for 2 adults from $63 (summer weekends; weeknights $53) to $18 (in winter). Golf packages available.

Lazy G Motel, 405 27th Ave. N (448-6333 or 800-633-2163), has 2-bed apartments with mini-kitchens, attractive decor, TV, A/C, a pool, and heat. From $23 (mid-Oct.-mid-March) to $61 (in summer).

Myrtle Beach State Park Campground (238-5325), 3mi. south of town off U.S. 17. 350 sites with full hookup on 312 acres of unspoiled land with a cool beach, fishing, a pool, and a nature trail. Showers and bathrooms are close by. Office open Mon.-Fri. 8am-5pm, Sat.-Sun. may not be open. $16, Oct.-March $12.

Huntington Beach State Park Campground (237-4440), 5mi. south of Murrell's Inlet on U.S. 17. A diverse environment with lagoons, salt marshes, and, of course, a beach. 127 sites with full hookup, convenient showers and rest rooms. Office open Mon.-Fri. 9am-5pm. $17, Oct.-March. $11. Call ahead for reservations.

ALL-YOU-CAN-EAT

Over 1600 restaurants, serving anything you can imagine, can be found (or, can't be missed) on the Grand Strand. Massive, family-style, all-you-can-eat joints await at every traffic light. Seafood is best on Murrell's Inlet, while Ocean Blvd. and U.S. 17 offer endless steakhouses, fast food joints, and buffets.

River City Café, 404 21st Ave. N. (448-1990), also on Business 17 in Murrell's Inlet, serves juicy burgers ($3), homemade fries, beer, and free peanuts (toss the shells on the floor) in a fun, collegiate atmosphere. Open daily 11am-10pm.

Mammy's Kitchen (448-7242), 11th Ave. N. at King's Hwy., grills up a breakfast deal and a half—hash browns, toast, eggs, and bacon for $2.19. Open daily 7am-noon and 4:30-9:30pm.

The Filling Station (626-9435), U.S. 17 at 17th Ave. N. One great menu idea: all-you-can-eat pizza, soup, sandwich bar, and dessert. Fill 'er up at lunch ($5) or dinner ($7). Children eat for $2-3, including drink.

SIGHTS AND ENTERTAINMENT

The cheapest and most amusing entertainment here is people-watching. Families, newlyweds, foreigners, and students flock to this incredibly popular area to lie out, eat out, and live out the myth of American beach culture. The boulevard and the length of the beach are called the **strand.** Cruising it at night is illegal—look for "You may not cross this point more than twice in 2 hours" signs.

White sand beaches and refreshing water are Myrtle Beach's classic attractions. The mind-boggling number of golf and mini-golf courses (45!) and amusement and water parks (13!) could make the Las Vegas Strip seem tasteful. The largest of the amusement parks is the **Myrtle Beach Pavilion** (448-6456), on Ocean Blvd. and 9th Ave. N. (Open daily 1pm-midnight. Unlimited rides $18.25, under 42" $11.75. Individual tickets 50¢; rides use 2-7 tickets, depending on the number of loops, droops, and spins.) The **Myrtle Waves Water Park** (448-1026), 10th Ave. N. and U.S. 17 bypass, will water-log you with 30 water rides, including the world's largest tubular slide (open daily 10am-7pm; $16, under 42" $10).

Myrtle Beach is a mecca for country music shows. The **Alabama Theater at Barefoot Landing,** 4750 U.S. 17S (272-1111), has it all—singin', swingin', and comedy, complete with an aptly named production called the American Pride Show (Mon.-Sat. 8pm; $17, ages 3-11 $7; reservations required).

Studebakers, 2000 N. Kings Hwy. (626-3855), is a casual, young (18 and up) hangout with a 50s theme, a lifeguard stand by the dance floor, and frequent contests and theme nights. (Open nightly 8pm-2am. Cover $8-10.) **2001,** 920 Lake Arrowhead Rd. (449-9434), in Restaurant Row, is three clubs in one: a contemporary country club, a "shag" club, and a high energy dance club. (Open daily 8pm-2am. Live entertainment Thurs.-Sat. Cover $6-8.) Grand Strand fests include the **Canadian-American Days Festival** in mid-March, the huge **Sun Fun Festival** in early June, and Christmas partying, which starts in November. Pick up free copies of *Beachcomber* and *Kicks* for upcoming events.

Georgia

From the North Georgia mountains to coastal plains and swamps, Georgia thrives on such alliterative industries as paper products, popcorn, peanuts, pecans, peaches, poultry, and politicians. President Jimmy Carter's hometown and the only house ever owned by President Franklin D. Roosevelt both stand on red Georgia clay. Coca-Cola was invented here in 1886; since then, it has gone on to carbonate and caffeinate the world over. The world has collegiate Athens to thank for the Bulldogs and REM, and costal Savannah to visit for a taste of antebellum romanticism. Ted Turner and CNN have brought world news and folks from all over the globe, making Georgia's capital a diverse, sophisticated metropolis. As host to the centennial Olympiad, Atlanta's image bombarded the universe via tube, paper, and radio wave; in 1997, the state is bound both to suffer from post-partum depression and to revel in freedom from those inspiring but ubiquitous linked, colored rings. Georgia blooms in the spring, glistens in the summer, and mellows in the autumn, all the while welcoming y'all with peachy Southern hospitality. Stay here long and you'll *never* be able to shake Georgia from your mind.

PRACTICAL INFORMATION

Capital: Atlanta.
Department of Industry and Trade, Tourist Division, 285 Peachtree St., Atlanta 30301 (656-3590), across from Atlanta Convention and Visitors Bureau. Write for or pick up the comprehensive *Georgia Travel Guide.* Open Mon.-Fri. 8am-5pm. **Department of Natural Resources,** 205 Butler St. SE, Atlanta 30334 (800-542-7275; 404-656-3530 in GA). **U.S. Forest Service,** 1720 Peachtree Rd. NW, Atlanta 30367 (347-2384), has info on the Chattahoochee and Oconee National Forests. Open Mon.-Fri. 10am-4:30pm.
Time Zone: Eastern. **Postal Abbreviation:** GA.
Sales Tax: 4-6%, depending on county.

■ Atlanta

An increasingly popular destination for 20- and 30-somethings craving big city life but weary of the country's more manic metropoli, Atlanta manages to be cosmopolitan with a smile. An influx of Northerners, Californians, the third-largest gay population in the U.S., and a host of ethnicities have diversified the capital not just of the state but of the New South. A nationwide economic powerhouse, Atlanta contains offices for 400 of the Fortune 500 companies, including the headquarters of Coca-Cola and CNN. Nineteen institutions of higher learning, including Georgia Tech, Morehouse College, Spelman College, and Emory University, call "Hotlanta" home. Razed by the fire of Union General William Sherman in the Civil War, Atlanta met with a more peaceful flame last year—one lit by boxer Mohammed Ali in the opening ceremonies of the 1996 Olympic Games.

PRACTICAL INFORMATION

Tourist Office: Atlanta Convention and Visitors Bureau, 233 Peachtree St. NE #2000 (521-6600 or 1-800-ATLANTA/285-2682), Peachtree Center, 20th fl. of Harris Tower, downtown; stop by for a free copy of *Atlanta Heritage, Atlanta Now,* or the *Atlanta and Georgia Visitors' Guide.* Open Mon.-Fri. 8:30am-5:30pm. Also at **Underground Atlanta** (577-2148), Pryor and Alabama St. Open Mon.-Sat.

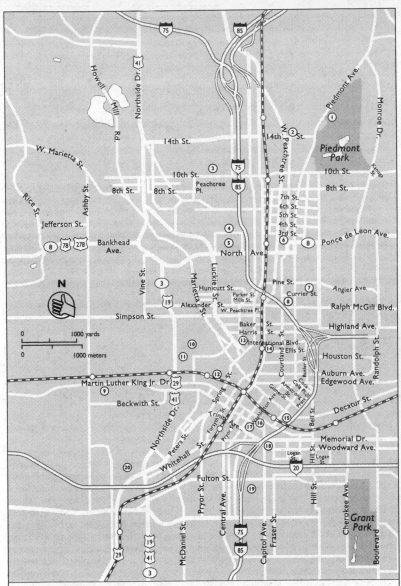

Downtown Atlanta

Alexander Memorial Coliseum, 3
Atlanta Botanical Garden, 1
Atlanta Fulton County Stadium, 19
City Hall, 17
Civic Center, 8
Clark Atlanta University, 9
CNN Center, 12
Georgia Dome, 11
Georgia Institute of Technology, 4
Grant Field / Bobby Dodd Stadium, 5

Exhibition & SciTrek Museum, 7
Fox Theatre, 6
Georgia Dept. of Archives & History, 18
Georgia State University, 15
Greyhound Bus Depot, 13
Peachtree Center, 14
Peachtree Community Playhouse, 2
Spelman College, 20
State Capitol, 16
World Congress Center, 10

10am-6pm, Sun. noon-6pm. **Gay Center Help Line,** 892-0661. 24hr. Center located at 71 12th St. (876-5372) provides community info and short-term counseling. Open daily 6-11pm.

Airport: Hartsfield International (222-6688 for general info; international services and flight info 530-2081), south of the city. Get phone assistance in 6 languages at the **Calling Assistance Center** in the international terminal (240-0042). MARTA (see Public Transportation, below) is the easiest way to get downtown, with 15-min. rides departing every 8min. daily 5am-1am, with baggage space available ($1.25). **Atlanta Airport Shuttle** (524-3400) runs vans from the airport to over 100 locations in the metropolitan and outlying area, including Stone Mountain, Marietta, and Dunwoody. (Every 15min. daily 4:30am-11pm. $8-30.) Taxi to downtown: $10.

Train: Amtrak, 1688 Peachtree St. NW (881-3061), 3mi. north of downtown at I-85. Take bus #23 from "Arts Center" MARTA station. To New York (1 per day, 19hr., $169) and New Orleans (3 per week, 11hr., $113). Open 6:30am-9:15pm.

Buses: Greyhound, 81 International Blvd. NW (584-1728), 1 block from Peachtree Center (a MARTA stop). To: New York (15 per day, 17hr., $83); Washington, D.C. (10 per day, 13hr., $94); Savannah (4 per day, 6hr., $43). Open Mon.-Fri. 24hr., Sat.-Sun. 8am-5pm.

Public Transportation: Metropolitan Atlanta Rapid Transit Authority (MARTA) (848-4711; schedule info Mon.-Fri. 6am-10pm, Sat.-Sun. 8am-4pm). Combined rail and bus system serves virtually all area attractions and hotels. Operates Mon.-Sat. 5am-1:30am, Sun. 6am-12:30am in most areas. Fare $1.50 exact change, or buy a token at station machines; transfers free. Unlimited weekly pass $11. Pick up a system map at the **MARTA Ride Store,** Five Points Station downtown, or at one of the satellite visitors bureaus. If you get confused, just find the nearest MARTA courtesy phone in each rail station.

Taxis: Checker, 351-1111. $2 per person downtown. **Rapid,** 222-9888. $1.50 base fare, $1.20 per mi. 24hr.

Car Rental: Atlanta Rent-a-Car, 3185 Camp Creek Pkwy. (763-1160), just inside I-285 3mi. east of the airport. 9 other locations in the area including Cheshire Bridge Rd. and I-85, 1mi. west of the Lindberg Center Railstop. $20 per day, 100 free mi., 19¢ per additional mi. Must be 21 with major credit card.

Help Lines: Rape Crisis Counseling, 616-4861. Open 24hr. **Gay Center Help Line,** 892-0661. Open daily 6-11pm.

Emergency: 911.

Post Office: 3900 Crown Rd. (768-4126). Open 10am-4pm. **ZIP code:** 30321. **Area code:** 404 roughly inside the I-285 perimeter, 770 outside.

Atlanta sprawls across the northwest quadrant of the state, 150 mi. east of Birmingham, AL and 113 mi. south of Chattanooga, TN, at the junctures of I-75, I-85, and I-20. I-285 ("the perimeter") circumscribes the city.

Getting around is confusing—*everything* seems to be named Peachtree. However, of the 40-odd roads bearing that name, only one, **Peachtree St.,** is a major north-south thoroughfare; other significant north-south roads are **Spring St.** and **Piedmont Ave.** Major east-west roads include **Ponce De Leon Ave.** and **North Ave.** In the heart of downtown—west of I-75/85, south of International Blvd. and north of the capitol, around the district known as Five Points—angled streets and shopping plazas run amok, making navigation difficult.

Most tourists frequent **Underground Atlanta** and **Peachtree Center,** shopping and entertainment complexes. The **Midtown** area (from Ponce de Leon Ave. to 26th St.) holds Atlanta's art museums. Directly southwest of downtown is the **West End**—an African-American area and the city's oldest historical quarter. North of Auburn Ave. lies the **Little Five Points** (L5P) district, which brims with galleries, theaters, bookstores, and a plethora of restaurants and nightclubs.

ACCOMMODATIONS AND CAMPING

Atlanta lodging lords had their own set of Olympic-related hoop dreams. Now you can benefit from the hostel renovations and expansions intended for weary fans.

Hostelling International Atlanta (HI-AYH), 223 Ponce de Leon Ave. (875-2882). From MARTA: North Ave. station, exit onto Ponce de Leon, about 3½ blocks east on the corner of Myrtle St. Part of a converted Victorian B&B in the middle of historic downtown, livened up with goldfish, dogs, and a collection of champion homing pigeons. Clean, dorm-style rooms. No sleeping bags allowed, but they distribute free blankets. Laundry facilities, gameroom, and kitchen. $16.25, nonmembers $25. Spacious private doubles $32.50. Luggage storage $1. Linens $1. Sheets $1. Free lockers.

Atlanta Dream Hostel, 115 Church St., Decatur 30030 (370-0380 or 800-DREAM96/373-2696 for reservations only). From MARTA: Decatur, go right on Church St. for 2 blocks. Located in a generally safe neighborhood yet convenient to downtown. A funky communal joint complete with 2 peacocks, a bus that serves as an Elvis shrine, a *biergärten,* and private "theme" rooms with names like "Jesus Room" and "Bad Taste Room" (add $10), this a hostel for the adventurous soul. *Un vrai poème bohème.* Showers, kitchen, TV, free linen, local calls, restaurant on premises ($2-6). Dorm rooms with roomy wooden bunks $12.

Economy Inns of America, 3092 Presidential Pkwy (454-8373), exit Chamblee Tucker Rd. off I-85. Large rooms with king-size beds available, satellite TV, and pool. 1-4 people $36 weekdays, $46 weekends.

Motel 6, 3 perimeter locations: 3585 Chamblee Tucker Rd. (455-8000), in Chamblee, Exit 27 off I-285; 6015 Oakbrook Pkwy. (446-2311), in Norcross, Exit 37 off I-85; and 2565 Weseley Chapel Rd. (288-6911), in Decatur, Exit 36 off I-20. Spacious and immaculate rooms. Each location offers free movie channel, free local calls, A/C, pool. Under 18 stay free with their parents. All locations $34, $6 per additional person.

Atlanta Midtown Manor, 811 Piedmont Ave. NE (872-5846). Three Victorian houses located in a relatively safe spot, convenient to downtown. Lovely rooms with floral shams, big round windows, A/C, TV. Free coffee, donuts, and local calls. Singles $33-45, doubles $55-85.

Villager Lodge, 144 14th St. NW (873-4171). A fence separates you from the highway. Tidy rooms in a dark decor. Chinese restaurant. Optional phone ($10 deposit); local calls 30¢. Laundry facilities. Pool. All rooms $48. Key deposit $5.

Red Roof Inn, 1960 Druid Hills (321-1653), Exit 31 off I-85, offers rooms with clean, modern decor and a pleasant tree-cloistered location. Convenient to downtown. Look carefully for the sign; it's partially hidden by branches. Singles $49 and up, doubles $59 and up.

Stone Mountain Family Campground (498-5710), on U.S. 78, 16mi. east of town. Exit 30B off I-285, or subway to Avondale then "Stone Mountain" bus. Gorgeous sites, most on the lake. Tent sites $15. RV sites with hookup $16, full hookup $17. Entrance fee $6 per car.

KOA South Atlanta (957-2610), on Mt. Olive Rd. in McDonough, Exit 72 off I-75. Showers, pool, laundry, and fishing pond on the premises. Tent sites with water $16, full hookup $23. You can also try **KOA North Atlanta,** 2000 Old U.S. 41 (427-2406), in Kennesaw. Sites with water and electric $18.

FOOD

From Russian to Ethiopian, al fresco to underground, Atlanta dining provides ample treats to tantalize your tastebuds. But since y'all are, here you may want to savor some home-style cookin'. Some favorite dishes to sample include fried chicken, black-eyed peas, okra, sweet-potato pie, and mustard greens. Dip a hunk of cornbread into "pot likker," water used to cook greens. For a cheap breakfast, you can't beat the Atlanta-based **Krispy Kreme Doughnuts** whose baked delights are a Southern institution. Eat 'em hot! The factory store is at 295 Ponce de Leon Ave. NE (876-7307; open 24hr.).

The internationally inclined food shopper should take the subway to Avondale and then the "Stone Mountain" bus to the **Dekalb County Farmers Market,** 3000 E. Ponce De Leon Ave. (377-6400), where the famished can run the gustatory gamut from Chinese to Middle Eastern and everything in between (open daily 9am-9pm).

Bridgetown Grill, 1156 Euclid Ave. (653-0110), in L5P. Reggae and salsa make for a hopping hole in the wall. Jerk chicken dinner ($8.50). Open Sun.-Thurs. 11am-10:30pm, Fri.-Sat. 11am-midnight.

The Varsity, 61 North Ave. NW (881-1706), at I-85. MARTA: North Ave. The world's largest drive-in. Best known for chili dogs ($1-2) and the greasiest onion rings in the South ($1.10). Ice cream cones (90¢). Open Sun.-Thurs. 9am-11:30pm, Fri.-Sat. 9am-1:30am.

Crescent Moon, 254 W. Ponce de Leon (377-5623), in Decatur. A heavenly and healthful breakfast spot. Indulge in luscious Belgian waffle pancakes ($5), or try the Elvis: seasoned potatoes with smoked chicken, mozzarella, and 2 scrambled eggs ($6). Whopping portions. Open for lunch Mon.-Fri. 7:30-10:45am and 11am-3pm, for dinner Tues.-Sat. 5:30-10pm. Weekend brunch 8am-2:30pm.

Mary Mac's Tea Room, 224 Ponce De Leon Ave. (876-1800), at Myrtle NE. Take the "Georgia Tech" bus north. 40s atmosphere with amazing cinnamon rolls ($4 a dozen). A "revival of Southern hospitality" for over 51 years. Entrees $5-6. Open for breakfast Mon.-Fri. 7-11am, Sat.-Sun. 9am-noon, for dinner Mon.-Sat. 11am-4pm, Sun. 11am-3pm; for "supper" Mon.-Sat. 4-9pm.

Virginia's, 1243 Virginia Ave. (875-4453), in residential Virginia Highlands. This character-filled coffeehouse features an endless variety of teas and coffees, as well as a signature brie melt ($6.50) and the strummings of a live guitar. Open Mon.-Fri. 11am-11pm, Sat.-Sun. 9am-11pm (weekend brunch 9am-3pm).

Everybody's, 1040 N. Highland Ave. (873-4545). Come here for the mouth-watering pizza and Italian dishes. Everybody's doing it. Large pie $12.50. Open Mon.-Thurs. 11:30am-11pm, Fri.-Sat. 11:30am-1am, Sun. noon-11pm.

Tortillas, 774 Ponce de Leon Ave. (892-0193). Student crowd munches dirt-cheap (and thoroughly yummy) Mexican food. Try the upstairs patio for open-air eating. Big vegetarian burritos $2. Soft chicken taco $3. Open Mon.-Sat. 11am-11pm.

Manuel's Tavern, 602 N. Highland Ave. (525-3447), prime spot between L5P and Virginia Highlands. Chicken salad melt $5.50. Jimmy and Rosalyn Carter are regulars. Open Mon.-Sat. 11am-2am, Sun. 3pm-midnight.

Eat Your Vegetables Café, 438 Moreland Ave. NE (523-2671), in the L5P area. Vegetarian entrees $7-8, including macrobiotic dinner special. Open Mon.-Thurs. 11:30am-10pm, Fri. 11:30am-10:30pm, Sat. 11am-10:30pm, Sun. 11am-3pm.

Touch of India, 1037 Peachtree St. (876-7777). Three-course lunch buffet $7. Dinners $8-10. Open Mon.-Sat. 11:30am-2:30pm and 5:30-10:30pm.

SIGHTS

Downtown and Around

Atlanta's sights may seem scattered, but the effort it takes to find them usually pays off. The **Atlanta Preservation Center,** 156 7th St. NE (876-2040), offers ten walking

---

Waffle Good

Labor Day 1955 was a glorious moment in the otherwise innocuous existence of Avondale Estates, Georgia. Two neighbors "dedicated to people," be they customers or employees, realized their dreams in the form of a little yellow hut that opened in the Atlanta suburb on this day, and hasn't closed since (though the original did move a block down the road, to 2850 E. College, Avondale; 404-294-8758). The **Waffle House** is open 24 hours a day, 365 days a year, in over a thousand locations in 21 lucky states. So take an exit, almost any exit, and go for the yellow. Slip a quarter in the jukebox and choose from among the "Waffle House Family Songs." Or perhaps if you're in a friskier mood, groove to the **bootie-bumpin' "Waffle Doo Wop."** Treat yourself to a side of hashbrowns—scattered, smothered, covered, chunked, topped, and diced. Discover for yourself why Waffle House is the friendliest franchise in the universe, and the world's leading server of waffles, T-bone steaks, omelettes, cheese 'n' eggs, raisin toast, and apple butter. Here, the South rises again, not in the form of a brutal war, but in the form of tasty cookin'.

tours of popular areas from March through November: Fox Theatre District, West End and the Wren's Nest, Historic Downtown, Miss Daisy's Druid Hills, Inman Park, Underground and Capitol area, Ansley Park, Sweet Auburn (MLK District), Piedmont Park, and Vine City; the 1½-hour Fox Theatre tour is given year-round. ($5, students $3, seniors $4. Call for more info.) Of course, you can just hop on MARTA and take in the sights on your own.

Reverend Martin Luther King, Jr.'s birthplace, church, and grave are all part of a 23-acre **Martin Luther King, Jr. National Historic Site.** The **birthplace of MLK** offers guided tours (331-3920) starting every ½ hour from 501 Auburn Ave. (open daily 9am-5pm). **Ebenezer Baptist Church,** 407 Auburn Ave. (688-7263), the church where Martin Luther King, Jr. was pastor from 1960 to 1968, now serves as a visitors center for the National Park Service (open Mon.-Fri. 9am-5pm). Plaques lining Sweet Auburn point out the Queen Anne architecture and eminent past residents of this historically African-American neighborhood. King's **grave** rests at the **Martin Luther King Center for Nonviolent Social Exchange,** 449 Auburn Ave. NE (524-1956); take bus #3 from Five Points. The center also holds a collection of King's personal effects and shows a film about his life. (Open daily 9am-8pm; Nov.-March 9am-5:30pm. Entrance and film free.)

The **APEX Museum,** 135 Auburn Ave. (521-2739), recognizes the cultural heritage of the African-Americans who helped build this country as slaves and as freemen. (Open daily 10am-6pm; in Aug. only Sun. 1-6pm. $3, students and seniors $2, children under 5 free.)

True fans of Rhett Butler and Scarlett O'Hara should also visit the Margaret Mitchell Room in the **Atlanta-Fulton Public Library,** 1 Margaret Mitchell (730-1700). The collection of memorabilia includes autographed copies of her famous novel. (Open Mon., Fri.-Sat. 10am-5pm, Tues.-Thurs. 10am-8pm, Sun. 2-6pm.) On the corner of 10th and Crescent, you can see the three-story house where Mitchell used to live—its renovation is the subject of ongoing controversy.

In **Grant Park,** directly south of Oakland Cemetery and Cherokee Ave., a 100-year-old **Cyclorama** (658-7625), a massive panoramic painting (42ft. high and 358ft. around), recreates the 1864 Battle of Atlanta with 3D sound and light effects. (Open in summer daily 9:30am-5:30pm; Oct.-May 9:30am-4:30pm. $5, students and seniors $4, ages 6-12 $3.) Next door, **Zoo Atlanta,** 800 Cherokee Ave. SE (624-5678), mounts displays stressing conservation and environmental awareness. Among the special exhibits are the Masai Mara, Sumatran Tiger Forest, and the Ford African Rain Forest. (Open daily 10am-4:30pm, until 5:30pm on weekends during Daylight Savings Time. $7.50, seniors $6.75, ages 3-11 $5, under 3 free.)

High-tech "Hotlanta" reigns with multinational business powerhouses situated in the business section of the **Five Points District. Turner Broadcasting System** offers an insider's peek with its **Cable News Network (CNN) Studio Tour** (827-2300), at corner of Techwood Dr. and Marietta St. Witness anchorfolk broadcasting live while writers toil in the background. Take MARTA west to the Omni/Dome/GWCC Station at W1. (45-min. tours given on the ½hr. Open daily 9am-6pm. $7, seniors $5, ages 5-12 $4.50.)

Redeveloped **Underground Atlanta** gets down with six subterranean blocks filled with over 120 shops, restaurants, and night spots behind restored 19th-century Victorian storefronts. Descend at the entrance beside the Five Points subway station. (Shops open Mon.-Sat. 10am-9:30pm, Sun. noon-6pm. Bars and restaurants open later.) **Atlanta Heritage Row,** 55 Upper Alabama St. (584-7879), Underground, documents the city's past and looks into the future with exhibits and films (open Tues.-Sat. 10am-5pm, Sun. 1-5pm; $2). Adjacent to the shopping complex, the **World of Coca-Cola Pavilion,** 55 Martin Luther King, Jr. Dr. (676-5151), highlights "the real thing's" humble beginnings in Atlanta in a $15 million facility. Over 1000 artifacts and interactive displays tell the powerhouse's tale. (Open Mon.-Sat. 10am-8:30pm, Sun. noon-5pm. $3.50, seniors $3, ages 6-12 $2.50.)

The politically minded revel in the **Georgia State Capitol** (656-2844; MARTA: Georgia State, then walk 1 block south), Capitol Hill at Washington St. (Tours Mon.-

Fri. on the hr. 10am-2pm except noon. Open Mon.-Fri. 8am-5pm, Sat. 10am-4pm, Sun. noon-4pm. Free.) Farther out, the **Carter Presidential Center,** 1 Copenhill (331-3942), north of Little Five Points, documents the Carter Administration (1977-1981) through exhibits and films. Take bus #16 to Cleburne Ave. (Open Mon.-Sat. 9am-4:45pm, Sun. noon-4:45pm. $4, seniors $3, under 16 free.)

In the **West End**—Atlanta's oldest neighborhood, dating from 1835—discover the **Wren's Nest,** 1050 R.D. Abernathy Blvd. (753-7735), home to Joel Chandler Harris, who popularized the African folktale trickster Br'er Rabbit through the stereotypical slave character Uncle Remus. Take bus #71 from West End Station South. (Tours $4, teens and seniors $3, ages 4-12 $2. ½-hr. storytelling June-Aug. 11:30am, 12:30, 1:30pm; Sept.-May Sat. 2pm; $2 extra. Open Tues.-Sat. 10am-4pm, Sun. 1-4pm.) The **Hammonds House,** 503 Peeples St. SW (752-8730), displays a fantastic collection of African-American and Haitian art. Take bus #67 from West End Station South to the corner of Oak and Peeples. (Open Tues.-Fri. 10am-6pm, Sat.-Sun. 1-5pm. $2, students and seniors $1.) Built by slave-born Alonzo F. Herndon, the **Herndon Home,** 587 University Place NW (581-9813), a 1910 Beaux-Arts Classical mansion, deserves a look; take bus #3 from Five Points station to the corner of Martin Luther King, Jr. Dr. and Maple, and walk one block north. Herndon, a prominent barber, became Atlanta's wealthiest African-American in the early 1900s. View the house's original furnishings, glass and silver collections, and family photographs. (Free tours every hr. Open Tues.-Sat. 10am-4pm.)

North of Midtown

Piedmont Park sprawls around the 60-acre **Atlanta Botanical Garden** (876-5859), Piedmont Ave. at the Prado. Stroll through five acres of landscaped gardens, a 15-acre hardwood forest with walking trails, and an exhibition hall. The **Dorothy Chapman Fugua Conservatory** houses hundreds of species of rare tropical plants; take bus #36 "North Decatur" from the Arts Center subway stop (open Tues.-Sun. 9am-7pm; $6, students $3, seniors $5, Thurs. free after 1pm).

Near the park, **Scitrek** (The Science and Technology Museum of Atlanta), 395 Piedmont Ave. NE (522-5500), with over 100 interactive exhibits for all ages, makes it one of the top ten science centers in the country. Take bus #2 from North Ave. Station. (Open Mon.-Sat. 10am-5pm, Sun. noon-5pm; call for summer hours. $7.50, students and seniors $5.)

Just to the west of Piedmont Park, the **Woodruff Arts Center,** 1280 Peachtree St. NE (733-5000; take the subway to Arts Center), contains the **High Museum of Art** (733-4200), Richard Meier's award-winning building of glass, steel, and white porcelain. (Open Tues.-Sat. 10am-5pm, Fri. 5-9pm, Sun. noon-5pm. $6, students with ID and seniors $4, children $2; free Thurs. 1-5pm.) The museum branch at **Georgia-Pacific Center** (577-6940), 1 block south of Peachtree Center Station, houses folk art and photography galleries (open Mon.-Fri. 11am-5pm; free).

The **Center for Puppetry Arts,** 1404 Spring St. NW (873-3391), at 18th St., has a museum featuring Wayland Flower's "Madame," traditional Punch and Judy figures, and some of Jim Henson's original Muppets. (Museum open Mon.-Sat. 9am-5pm. $5, students, seniors, and kids $4. Shows $5.75, students, seniors, and kids $4.75. $2 per person for museum and show on the same day.)

A drive through **Buckhead** (north of midtown and Piedmont Park off Peachtree near W. Paces Ferry Rd.) uncovers the "Beverly Hills of Atlanta"—the sprawling mansions of Coca-Cola CEOs and other specimens of yuppie culture. This area is also a hub of local grub and grog (see Entertainment, below). One of the most exquisite residences in the Southeast, the Greek Revival **Governor's Mansion,** 391 W. Paces Ferry Rd. (261-1776), has elaborate gardens and furniture from the Federal period. Take bus #40 "West Paces Ferry" from Linbergh Station. (Free tours Tues.-Thurs. 10-11:30am.) In the same neighborhood, discover the **Atlanta History Center/Buckhead,** 130 W. Paces Ferry Rd. NW (814-4000). On the grounds are the **Swan House,** a lavish Anglo-Palladian Revival home, and the **Tullie Smith House,** an antebellum farmhouse. Don't miss the intriguing *"Atlanta Resurgens"* exhibit. The **New**

Museum of Atlanta History features a Civil War Gallery. (Open Mon.-Sat. 9am-5:30pm, Sun. noon-5:30pm. $7, students and seniors $5, ages 6-17 $4, under 6 free.)

East of Midtown

A respite from the city is available at **Stone Mountain Park** (498-5702), 16 mi. east on U.S. 78, where a fabulous Confederate Memorial is carved into the world's largest mass of granite. The "Mount Rushmore of the South" features Jefferson Davis, Robert E. Lee, and Stonewall Jackson and measures 90 ft. by 190 ft. Surrounded by a 3200-acre recreational area and historic park, the mountain dwarfs the enormous statue. Check out the dazzling laser show on the side of the mountain every summer night at 9:30pm (free). Take bus #120 "Stone Mountain" from the Avondale subway stop. (Buses leave Mon.-Fri. only at 4:30 and 7:50pm. Park gates open daily 6am-midnight; attractions open daily 10am-9pm, off season 10am-5:30pm. $5 per car. Admission to beach complex $4.)

The **Fernbank Museum of Natural History,** 767 Clifton Rd. NE (378-0127), near Ponce de Leon Ave., has a 65-acre forest, a display of the Apollo 6 command module, and an IMAX theater, among other exhibits. (Open Mon.-Sat. 10am-5pm, Fri. 5-9pm, Sun. noon-5pm. Museum $9.50, students and over 61 $8.50, ages 3-12 $6.50, or IMAX theater $5.50/$4.50/$4; both $13.50/$11.50/$9.50.)

ENTERTAINMENT AND NIGHTLIFE

For sure-fire fun in Atlanta, buy a MARTA pass (see Practical Information, above) and pick up one of the city's free publications on music and events. *Creative Loafing, Music Atlanta,* the *Hudspeth Report,* or "Leisure" in the Friday edition of the *Atlanta Journal* will all give you the low-down. *Southern Voice* has complete listings on gay and lesbian news and nightclubs throughout Atlanta; stop by **Charls,** 1189 Euclid St. (524-0304), for your free copy. (Open Mon.-Tue. 10:30am-6:30pm, Wed. 10:30am-8pm, Thu. 10:30am-7:30pm, Fri.-Sat. 10:30am-9pm, Sun. noon-6pm.) Look for free summer concerts in Atlanta's parks.

The **Woodruff Arts Center,** 1280 Peachtree St. NE (733-4200), houses the Atlanta Symphony, the Alliance Theater Company, Atlanta College of Art, and the High Museum of Art. For more performances, check the **Moorish and Egyptian Revival Movie Palace,** the **Fox Theatre,** 660 Peachtree St. (881-2100), or the **Atlanta Civic Center,** 395 Piedmont Ave. NE (658-7159), home to the Atlanta ballet.

Six Flags Over Georgia, 7561 Six Flags Pkwy. (948-9290), at I-20W, one of the largest theme amusement parks in the nation, includes several rollercoasters and a plethora of other rides. Take bus #201 "Six Flags" from Hightower Station. (Open Memorial Day-Labor Day Sun.-Thurs. 10am-10pm, Fri.-Sat. 10am-midnight. Open weekends rest of year. 1-day admission $30, ages 3-9, $20; 2-day pass for adults or kids $33; be sure to check local grocery stores and soda cans for discounts.)

For drink or dance, hotspots center in **Little Five Points; Virginia Highlands,** a trendy, hip neighborhood east of downtown; **Buckhead;** and **Underground Atlanta.** A college-age crowd usually fills Little Five Points; many head for **The Point,** 420 Moreland Ave. (659-3522), where live music plays all the time (cover $3-6; open Mon.-Fri. 4pm-4am, Sat. 1pm-3am, Sun. 1pm-4am). For blues, go to **Blind Willie's,** 828 N. Highland Ave. NE (873-2583), a dim, usually packed club with Cajun food and occasional big name acts (open 8pm-3am; live music starts around 9pm; cover $5-10). In Virginia Highlands, big name acts using assumed names try out new material at the **Dark Horse Tavern,** 816 N. Highland Ave. (873-3607; music starts downstairs 10pm; cover free-$8; open daily 6pm-'til). For a laid-back and often international crowd, move next door to **Limerick Junction Pub,** 822 N. Highland Ave. (874-7147), where contagious Irish music jigs nightly (open daily 5pm-2am). Cool off with a 96-oz. fishbowl at **Lu Lu's Bait Shack,** 3057 Peachtree St. (262-5220; open Sun.-Thurs. 5pm-3am, Fri.-Sat. 5pm-4am).

Kenny's Alley, a street in The Underground, is composed solely of bars—a blues club, a dance emporium, a jazz bar, a country-western place, a New Orleans-style dai-quiri bar, and an oldies dancing spot. Towards downtown, **Masquerade,** 695 North

Ave. NE (577-8026), occupies an original turn-of-the-century mill. The bar has three different levels: heaven, with live dance music; purgatory, a more laid-back coffee house; and hell, offering techno and industrial. A recently added outside dance space provides dancing with lights and celestial views. (Cover $4-8 or more, depending on band. Open Wed.-Sun. 9pm-4am. 18+.) **Backstreet,** 845 Peachtree St. NE (873-1986), a hot, 24-hr., gay dance spot, prides itself on being straight-friendly. The bar picks a different theme for every night; disco rules on Wednesdays. (Extra-special hoppin' "X-rated" drag cabaret Thurs.-Sun. at midnight. Cover Mon.-Thurs. $2, Fri. $5, Sat. $7, Sun. $3.)

■ Athens

The peach state's "Classic City" (as in "Classic City Car Wash") is indisputedly the Athens of Georgia. Home to over 30,000 University of Georgia (UGA) students, Athens boasts the Georgia Bulldogs, the State Botanical Garden, and a collegiate downtown full of hacky-sackers and record stores. Athens' main draw is its prolific music scene—REM, the B-52s, Vic Chesnutt, and Widespread Panic are just a few of the bands whose success was launched in this quintessential college town.

Practical Information Situated 70 mi. northeast of Atlanta, Athens can be reached from I-85 via U.S. 316 (Exit 4), which runs into U.S. 29. Two blocks north of the UGA campus is the **Athens Welcome Center,** 280 E. Dougherty St. (353-1820), in the Church-Brumby House, the city's oldest surviving residence (open Mon.-Sat. 10am-5pm). The **Athens Transit System** (613-3430) runs buses every ½ hr. on the hr. (Mon.-Fri. 6am-7pm, Sat. 7:30am-7pm). Schedules are available at the Welcome Center, City Hall at College and Hancock Ave., and the bus garage on Pound St. and Prince Ave. (75¢, ages 6-18 50¢, seniors 35¢). The **Athens Airport** (613-3420) offers a commuter shuttle (725-5573) to various points in and around Atlanta ($15-25). **Greyhound,** 222 W. Broad St. (549-2255 or 800-231-2222), buses to Atlanta (3 per day, 2hr., $13). (Station open daily 7:30am-9:30pm.) The **Rape Crisis Line** (353-1912) takes calls 7pm to 7am daily. The **health center** (546-5526) is open by appointment (Mon.-Fri. 8am-5pm). **Athens' post office:** 575 Olympic Dr. (800-275-8777; open Mon.-Fri. 8:30am-5pm). **ZIP code:** 30601. **Area code:** 706.

Accommodations, Camping, and Sights Broad St., Athens' main artery, continues south of town as Rte. 29. Motels line this strip; most are both affordable and convenient to downtown. If you simply must stay near sorority/fraternity row, the **Downtowner Motor Inn,** 1198 S. Milledge Ave. (549-2626), has rooms in 70s colors near campus with A/C, continental breakfast, TV, and pool. (Singles $44, doubles $50, $2 each additional person.) A full-service campground with secluded sites, **Pine Lake RV Campground,** Rte. 186 (769-5486), in nearby Bishop, has full hookups and fishing lakes (tent sites $14, with full hookup $18).

For a walking tour of Athens's historical neighborhood, pick up a copy of *Athens of Old* at the Welcome Center. For an in-depth look at Athens old and new take the two-hour **Classic City Tour.** This fascinating driving tour tells the stories of the antebellum homes, the Civil War, and the University of Georgia. (Tours leave from the Welcome Center Tues.-Sat. 11am and 2pm, Sun. 2pm. $9, under 12 $5. Walk-ins welcome; reservations 208-8687.) You'll see more than a thumbnail sketch at the **Georgia Museum of Art,** in historic North University Campus off Jackson St. and in a new location off Carleton St. on East Campus (542-3255). The museums house a collection of over 7000 works. (Open Mon.-Sat. 10am-5pm, Sun. 1-5pm; East Campus location open Fri. until 8pm. Free.) Look for the flowers of Guatemala at the **State Botanical Garden of Georgia,** 2450 S. Milledge Ave. (542-1244), a paradise for lay-aesthete and botanist alike. (Open daily 8am-sunset; conservatory open Mon.-Sat. 8am-4:30pm. Free.) The **Morton Theater,** 195 West Washington St. (613-3771), was the first theater in the U.S. to be owned and run by African-Americans. Ticket prices vary with the show, but are usually low ($4-10). Tour the **Taylor-Grady House,** 634

Prince Ave. (549-8688), Athens' oldest Greek Revival mansion. (Open Tues.-Fri. 10am-3:30pm. Free; informative guided tours $2.50, leave every ½hr.) Some bizarre Athenian sights include the city's symbol, a double-barreled cannon at City Hall Plaza that literally backfired and hence could not be put towards the Civil War effort, and the **the tree that owns itself.** According to local legend, Prof. W.H. Jackson deeded that the white oak standing at the corner of Dearling and Finley streets should own itself and its 8-ft. radius of shade. The original oak died in 1942 but was reborn from one of its own acorns.

Food and Nightlife **The Grit,** 199 Prince Ave. (543-6592), is Athens at its crunchiest and coolest, serving up scrumptious, healthy, *au natural* meals, including a great weekend brunch. Eat a bagel grilled with olive oil and herbs ($2), or try the excellent Middle Eastern food. (Entrees around $5. Open Mon.-Thurs. 11am-10pm, Fri. 11am-10:30pm, Sat.-Sun. brunch 10am-3pm and 5-10:30pm.) Less healthy but gosh-darned good is **Weaver D.'s,** 1016 E. Broad St. (353-7797), where solid soul food meals cost under $5. The sign outside reads "Automatic For the People," owner Dexter Weaver's favorite expression; it inspired the title of REM's 1992 album. The **Last Resort Grill,** 174 W. Clayton St. (549-0810), serves up massive quesadillas piled with fresh veggies ($3). The mural outside hints at the artfully prepared delicacies within. (Entrees $6-12. Open Sun.-Fri. 11am-3pm and 5-10pm, Sat.-Sun. 11am-11pm.) For the kind of food that kept Lewis Grizzard full and smiling before killing him, try the **Varsity,** 1000 W. Broad St. (548-6325), where the staff fry up onion rings, burgers, and chili dogs in record time, all for well under $2. (Open daily 4pm-late.) If you're scrounging for change on a growling stomach, one of three **Taco Stand** locations (including one downtown, 247 E. Broad St., 549-1446), can make it all better with deluxe burritos for under $2. (Open Mon.-Sat. 11am-2am, Sun. 11am-midnight. Kitchen closes at 11pm.) Top off your Athenian culinary experience with a 25¢ scoop from **Hodgson's Pharmacy,** 420 S. Milledge Ave. (543-7386), which may be the last place where ice cream comes so cheap. (Open Mon.-Sat. 9am-7pm, Sun. 2-7pm.)

Those on an REM pilgrimage must check out the **40 Watt Club,** 285 W. Washington St. (549-7871), where the group started out and where many bands today try to follow their lead (open daily 10pm-3am). The **Georgia Theatre** (353-3405), at the corner of Lumpkin and Clayton St., attracts shiny, happy people with local and national acts (cover usually $1-5; open daily 4pm-'til). With Guinness on tap and a smoke-free zone on the second floor, grad students love **The Globe,** 199 N. Lumpkin St. (353-4721; open Mon.-Sat. 4pm-1am). For Pop Tarts or latté at any hour, swing by **Jittery Joe's,** 243 W. Washington St. (548-3116), a 24-hr. retro java joint replete with lava lamps and vinyl couches. Across the street, **Manhattan** caters to a crowd of those who wish they lived there, but can't bear to part with $1 beers.

■ Savannah

In February 1733, General James Oglethorpe and a rag-tag band of 120 colonists founded the state of Georgia at Tamacraw Bluff on the Savannah River and the city of Savannah was born. When the price of cotton crashed at the turn of the century, many of the city's buildings fell into disrepair, and its proudest mansions became boarding houses or rubble. In the mid-1950s, a group of seven concerned women mobilized to restore the downtown area and preserve its numerous Federalist and English Regency houses as historic monuments. Today, broad streets, four historic forts, and trees dripping with Spanish moss enhance the city's classic Southern aura. Savannah has long rivaled the history and beauty of cities like New Orleans and Charleston while remaining relatively untouristed. Of course, things can always change—Forrest Gump mania has popularized a certain bench in Chippewa Square, and the bestseller *Midnight in the Garden of Good and Evil* is set here.

THE SOUTH

PRACTICAL INFORMATION

Tourist Office: Savannah Visitors Center, 301 Martin Luther King, Jr. Blvd. (944-0455), at Liberty St. in a lavish former train station. Excellent free maps and guides, especially the *Savannah Map Guide.* Reservation service for local inns and hostels. Open Mon.-Fri. 8:30am-5pm, Sat.-Sun. 9am-5pm. The **Savannah History Museum,** in the same building, has exhibits depicting the city's past. Open daily 9am-5pm. $3, students and seniors $2.50, ages 6-12 $1.75.

Trains: Amtrak, 2611 Seaboard Coastline Dr. (234-2611 or 800-872-7245), 4mi. out of the city. Taxis to town run about $5. To: Charleston, SC (1 per day, 2hr., $28); Washington, D.C. (2 per day, 11hr., $138). Open 3:30pm-7:30am.

Buses: Greyhound, 610 W. Oglethorpe Ave. (232-2135 or 800-231-2222), near downtown. To: Jacksonville (8 per day, 3hr., $19); Columbia, SC (4 per day, 4-6hr., $35); Washington, D.C. (5 per day, 12hr., $89). Open daily 5:30am-1:30am.

Public Transportation: Chatham Area Transit (CAT) (233-5767). Operates daily 6am-midnight. Fare 50¢, transfers 5¢; one-day passes $1.50. **C&H Bus,** 530 Montgomery St. (232-7099). From the civic center to Tybee Beach in summer 8:15am, 1:30pm, and 3:30pm; returns 9:25am, 2:30pm, and 4:30pm. Fare $1.75.

Taxis: Adam Cab (927-7466). 60¢ initial fee, $1.20 per mi.

Crisis Line: Rape Crisis Center, 233-7273. 24hr.

Emergency: 911.

Post Office: 2 N. Fahm St. (235-4646). Open Mon.-Fri. 8:30am-5pm. **ZIP code:** 31402. **Area code:** 912.

Savannah rests on the coast of Georgia at the mouth of the **Savannah River,** which runs north of the city along the border with South Carolina. The city stretches south from bluffs overlooking the river. The restored 2½-square-mi. **downtown historic district,** bordered by East Broad, Martin Luther King, Jr. Blvd., Gwinnett Street, and the river, is best explored on foot. **Tybee Island,** Savannah's beach, 18 mi. east on U.S. 80 and Rte. 26, makes a fine daytrip. Try to visit at the beginning of spring, the most beautiful season in Savannah.

ACCOMMODATIONS AND CAMPING

The **downtown** motels cluster near the historic area, visitors center, and Greyhound station. Do not stray south of Gwinnett St.; the historic district quickly deteriorates into an unsafe and seedy area. For those with cars, **Ogeechee Rd. (U.S. 17)** has several independently owned budget options.

Savannah International Youth Hostel (HI-AYH), 304 E. Hall St. (236-7744), in the historic district 2 blocks east of Forsyth Park. The best deal in town by far. Located in a restored Victorian mansion with a kitchen and laundry facilities. Flexible 3-night max. stay. Check-in 7:30-10am and 5-10pm; call the manager, Brian, for late check-in. Lockout 10am-5pm; no curfew. Dorm beds $11.50, private rooms $25.

Bed and Breakfast Inn, 117 W. Gordon St. (238-0518), at Chatham Sq. in the historic district. 10 rooms decorated with antiques, poster beds, and oriental rugs. All have TV, A/C, phones, and full Southern breakfast; some with shared bath. Singles $35, doubles $49. Two-night minimum on weekends.

Fort McAllister State Park (727-2339), take Exit 15 off I-95. Wooded sites with water and electricity, some with a water view. Office open daily 8am-5pm. Check-in before 10pm. Sites $12. Parking $2.

Skidaway Island State Park (598-2300), 13mi. southeast of downtown off Diamond Causeway. Inaccessible by public transportation. Follow Liberty St. east from downtown until it becomes Wheaton St.; turn right on Waters Ave. and follow it to the Diamond Causeway. Generally more noisy and crowded than Fort McAllister. Bathrooms and heated showers. Check-in before 10pm. Sites $17, additional nights $15; off season $15/$12. Parking $2.

FOOD AND NIGHTLIFE

Mrs. Wilkes Boarding House, 107 W. Jones St. (232-5997), is truly a Southern institution. Sit with friendly strangers around a large table and help yourself to luscious fried chicken, sweet potatoes, and spinach. All you can eat (and then some) $8. Join the line; the wait can be up to 2 hr. Open Mon.-Fri. 8-9am and 11am-3pm.

Clary's Café, 404 Abercorn St. (233-0402). A local family spot since 1903 with a famous weekend brunch and friendly service. Malted waffle $3.50. Open Mon.-Fri. 6:30am-4pm and 5-10pm, Sat. 8am-4pm and 5pm-midnight, Sun. 8am-2pm.

Paper Moon, 152 Whitaker St. (236-6645). Prices hover around $6 at this local favorite. The walls are decked with shelves of books, and a jukebox plays the likes of *Nine Inch Nails.* Open Sun.-Wed. 11am-3am, Thurs.-Sat. 11am-5am.

Olympia Café, 5 E. River St. (233-3131), on the river. Great Greek specialities, including salads and pizzas. Lunch or dinner $5-13. Open daily 11am-11pm.

Try the waterfront area **(River St.)** for budget meals and pub ambience. **Kevin Barry's Irish Pub,** 117 W. River St. (233-9626), offers live Irish folk music (Wed.-Sun. after 8:30pm; cover $2), as well as cheap drinks during its endless happy hour (Mon.-Fri. 4pm-3am, Sat. 11:30pm-3am, Sun. 12:30-2am). For a drink that will keep you on your ear for days, check out **Wet Willies,** 101 E. River St. (233-5650), with its casual dining, young folks, and irresistible frozen daiquiris (open Sun.-Thurs. 11am-1am, Fri.-Sat. 11am-2am). Local college students eat, drink, and shop at **City Market.** One hot spot is **Malone's Bar and Grill,** 27 Barnard St. (234-3059), with dancing, drinks, live jazz, and rock Thursday through Sunday nights. (Open daily 11am-2am. Happy hour daily 5-8pm. Ladies night Wed.-Thurs.) Hustlers will enjoy the 10 new Gandi pool tables and 80+ types of beer at **B&B Billiards,** 411 W. Congress St. (233-7116), which recently won a city renovation prize for transforming a five-and-dime warehouse into an airy brick nightspot. (Open Mon.-Sat. 4pm-3am. Happy hour daily 4-8pm. Free pool Tues.) Lady Chablis, a character featured in *Midnight in the Garden of Good and Evil,* performs regularly at gay/lesbian hotspot **Club One,** 1 Jefferson St. (232-0200), near City Market, at intersection with Bay St.

SIGHTS AND EVENTS

In addition to restored antebellum houses, the downtown area includes over 20 small parks and gardens. Scads of bus, horse carriage, and van tours ($7-12) leave every 10-15 min. from outside the visitors center. The **Historic Savannah Foundation,** 210 Broughton St. (233-7703), gives a tour through **Gray Line Tours** (233-3597 for reservations; $14).

Savannah's best-known historic houses are the **Davenport House,** 324 E. State St. (236-8097), on Columbia Square, and the **Owens-Thomas House,** 124 Abercorn St. (233-9743), a block away on Oglethorpe Square. The Owens-Thomas House is one of the best examples of Federalist architecture in the U.S. (Open Tues.-Sat. 10am-4:30pm, Sun. 2-4:30pm. Last tour 4:30pm. $5, students $3, under 13 $2.) The Davenport House, earmarked to be razed for a parking lot, was saved in 1955. There are guided tours of the first floor every ½hour; explore the third floor at your leisure. (Open Mon.-Wed. and Fri.-Sat. 10am-4:30pm, Sun. 10am-4pm. Last tour 4pm. $5.) The **Green Meldrim House,** 1 W. Maco St. (232-1251), on Madison Sq., is a Gothic revival mansion that served as one of General Sherman's headquarters throughout the Civil War (open Tues. and Thurs.-Sat. 10am-4pm; $4, students $2). The **Telfair Mansion and Art Museum,** 121 Bernard St. (232-1177), displays a distinguished collection of decorative arts in an English Regency house. (Open Tues.-Sat. 10am-5pm, Sun. 2-5pm. $3, students and seniors $1, ages 6-12 50¢, under 6 free.)

Lovers of Thin Mints, Do-Si-Dos, and, of course, Savannahs, should make a pilgrimage to the **Juliette Gordon Low Girl Scout National Center,** 142 Bull St. (233-4501), near Wright Square. The Scouts' founder was born here on Halloween 1860, which may explain the Girl Scouts' door-to-door treat-selling technique. The "cookie shrine" contains an interesting collection of Girl Scout memorabilia. (Open Mon.-Tues. and Thurs.-Sat. 10am-4pm, Sun. 12:30-4:30pm. $4, under 18 $3; discounts for AAA, groups, and Girl Scouts.) The **Negro Heritage Trail** visits African-American historic sights from the days of slavery to the present. The Savannah branch of the **Association for the Study of Afro-American Life and History,** 514 E. Harris St. (234-8000), conducts three different tours beginning at the visitors center. (Mon.-Fri. 1 and 3pm, Sat.-Sun. 10am, 1pm, and 3pm. $10, under 13 $5.)

Savannah's four forts once protected the city's port from Spanish, British, and other invaders. The most interesting, **Fort Pulaski National Monument** (786-5787), 15 mi. east of Savannah on U.S. 80 and Rte. 26, marks the Civil War battle site where rifled cannons first pummeled walls, making Pulaski and similar forts obsolete. (Open daily 8:30am-5:15pm, off season 8:30am-5:30pm. $2, $4 maximum per car, over 62 free with Golden Age Passport, under 16 free.) Built in the early 1800s, **Fort Jackson** (232-3945), also along U.S. 80 and Rte. 26, contains exhibits on the American Revolution, the War of 1812, and the Civil War (open daily 9am-5:30pm; $2, students and seniors $1.50). Both make quick detours on a daytrip to Tybee Beach.

Special events in Savannah include the **Hidden Garden of Historic Savannah** (238-0248), in mid-April, when private walled gardens are opened to the public. The free **St. Patrick's Day Weekend Music Fest** (232-4903) blares jazz, blues, and rock 'n' roll from noon to midnight, Friday through Sunday in the City Market.

■ Brunswick and Environs

Brunswick Beyond one unique hostel and pleasant nearby beaches, laid-back Brunswick is of little interest to the traveler who expects more than a relaxing layover between destinations. The fantastic **Hostel in the Forest** (264-9738 or 638-2623) is located 9 mi. west of Brunswick on U.S. 82. Take I-95 to Exit 6 and travel west on U.S. 82/84 about 1½ mi. until you see a white-lettered wooden sign set back in the trees along the eastbound lane, just past a small convenience store. The hostel sits ½ mi. back from the highway; every effort is made to keep the area surrounding the complex of geodesic domes and treehouses as natural as possible. Try to stay in one of the hostel's seven treehouses, each with a ceiling fan and spacious double bed. In addition, there is a natural swimming pool made from a diverted stream, replete with rope swing and teepee sweat lodge. The atmosphere is communal, and a few residents seem to be permanent. The low-key managers will shuttle you to the bus station for $3; they can usually be convinced to make daytrips to Savannah, the Okefenokee Swamp, and the coastal islands. Bring insect repellent in the summer; mosquitoes and biting flies abound. After rainstorms, the ½-mi. dirt road to the hostel is virtually impassable in any vehicle other than a large truck or 4-wheel drive—be prepared for potholes up to a foot deep. (No lockout, no curfew, and few rules. $10. Linens $2.) **Twin Oaks Pit Barbecue,** 2618 Norwich St. (265-3131), 8 blocks from downtown Brunswick across from the Southern Bell building, features a chicken-and-pork combination ($6). The breaded french fries ($1) are deep fried and *deeeee*-licious. (Open Mon.-Fri. 10:30am-7:30pm, Sat. 10:30am-4pm.) **Greyhound,** 1101 Glouchester St. (265-2800), offers service to Jacksonville (4 per day, 1½hr., $17) and Savannah (4 per day, 1½hr., $14). (Open Mon.-Fri. 8am-noon and 2-6pm, Sat. 8am-noon and 2-4pm.) Brunswick's **area code:** 912.

Okefenokee Swamp The **Okefenokee Swamp Park,** 5700 Okefenokee Swamp Park Rd. (912-283-0583), on U.S. 1, 8 mi. south of Waycross, is a haven for snoozing alligators, snakes, and birds. There are several "packages" available, including a 25-min. guided boat trip ($12 per person) and a canoe rental option ($14). All packages include the live reptile presentation, showcasing Okefenokee's wide variety of snakes, lizards and, of course, alligators. It gives you something to think about as you're walking over the boardwalk built directly on the swamp. (In summer open 8am-8pm; off season 8am-5:30pm.)

Golden Isles The Golden Isles, **St. Simon's Island, Jekyll Island,** and **Sea Island,** have miles of white sand beaches. **Cumberland Island National Seashore,** near the isles, consists of 16 mi. of salt marsh, live oak forest, and sand dunes laced with trails and a few decaying mansions. Phone reservations (882-4335, **Mon.**-Fri. 10am-4pm) are necessary for entry into the parks. The effort is rewarded with seclusion; you can walk all day on these beaches without seeing a soul. Sites are also available on a stand-by basis 15 min. before ferry departures to Cumberland Island. The **ferry** leaves from St. Mary's, on the mainland at the terminus of Rte. 40 at the Florida border. (45min. In summer daily 9 and 11:45am, returning 10:15am, 2:45, and 4:45pm; off season Thurs.-Mon. with *no* 2:45 return. $10, kids $6.)

Florida

Ponce de León landed on the Florida coast in 1513, in search of the elusive Fountain of Youth. Although the multitudes who flock to Florida today aren't desperately seek-ing fountains, many find their youth restored in the Sunshine State—whether they're dazzled by Orlando's fantasia Disney World or bronzed by the sun on the state's seductive beaches. Droves of senior citizens also migrate to Florida, where they thrive in comfortable retirement communities, leaving one to wonder whether the unpolluted, sun-warmed air isn't just as good as Ponce de León's fabled magical elixir. Although he never found the legendary font, de León did live to age 61, twice the expected life span at the time.

Anything as attractive as Florida is bound to draw hordes of people, the nemesis of natural beauty. Florida's population boom has strained the state's resources; commer-cial strips and tremendous development have turned many pristine beaches into tour-ist traps. Still, it is possible to find a deserted spot on the peninsula. When you do, plop down, grab a paperback, and let your feet sink into the warm sand.

PRACTICAL INFORMATION

Capital: Tallahassee.
Florida Division of Tourism: 126 W. Van Buren St., Tallahassee 32399-2000 (904-487-1462). **Department of Environmental Protection—Division of Recre-ation and Parks,** 3900 Commonwealth Blvd. #506, Tallahassee 32399-3000 (904-488-9872).
Time Zones: Mostly Eastern; Central (1hr. behind Eastern) in the westernmost parts of the panhandle. **Postal Abbreviation:** FL.
Sales Tax: 6%.

■ Jacksonville

Originally known as "Cowford" because the British believed that cows could wade across the 90-ft.-deep St. Johns River here, Jacksonville was renamed in 1822 for Gen-eral Andrew Jackson. The river has proven less of an impediment to growth than it was to cows; the nation's largest city (by square mileage), Jacksonville now crosses the St. Johns and stretches well beyond. The city draws visitors and residents with its mild climate and abundant beaches; travelers looking for the eternal Florida beach party should move on down the coast.

Practical Information I-95 runs through downtown leading across the Fuller Warren Bridge to the beaches. **Main St.** is the main north-south route through down-town; **Union St.** crosses east-west. To find the beaches, take Beach Blvd. from I-95 until you hit Rte. A1A and slide into the sand.

The **Jacksonville and the Beaches Convention & Visitors Bureau,** 3 Independent Dr. (798-9148), provides maps, brochures, and accommodations coupons. (Open Mon.-Fri. 8am-5pm.) Fly into **Jacksonville International** (reservations 741-4902; info 741-3044), off I-95 from Exit 127B; a cab downtown will cost $19-21. **Amtrak,** 3570

Clifford Ln. (766-5108 or 800-872-7245), off I-95 at the 20th St. exit, sends trains to Orlando (3hr., $37) and Washington, D.C. (13hr., $182) two to three times a day (5am-11pm daily). **Greyhound,** 10 N. Pearl St. (356-9976 or 800-231-2222), connects Jacksonville with Orlando (6 per day, 3hr., $23) and Atlanta (8 per day, 6hr., $39) by bus (open daily 24hr.). **Jacksonville Transportation Authority** (630-3100) operates in-town buses from 5:30am-midnight daily. (Hours vary somewhat by route. 60¢, to the beach $1.10; no transfers.) $10 weekly passes can be obtained from the JTA office at 100 N. Myrtle Ave. If you want to cab it, **Gator City Taxi and Shuttle Service,** 5320 Springfield Blvd. (355-8294), will take you where you need to go—it is the *only* cab service that makes trips to the airport. ($1.25 base fare, $1.25 per mi. Open 24hr.) **Alamo** (741-4428 or 800-327-9633), at the airport, rents cars starting at $23 per day with unlimited mileage. $20 surcharge for under 25. 6% airport fee. Major credit card required for rental. Jacksonville's **post office:** 1100 King's Rd. (359-2838; info line 359-2711; open Mon.-Fri. 7am-7pm, Sat. 8:30am-2:30pm). **ZIP code:** 32203. **Area code:** 904.

Accommodations and Camping

Most budget chains offer inexpensive rooms at locations near the airport. **Admiral Benbow Inn,** 14691 Duval Rd. (741-4254 or 800-451-1986), I-95 and Airport Rd. Exit 127A, rents large rooms with a medieval motif, cable TV, and A/C; non-smoking and wheelchair-accessible rooms are available (singles $29.50, doubles $49, 10% discount for AAA members). In an excellent location right on Jacksonville Beach, **Eastwinds Motel,** 1505 1st St. S. (249-3858), offers a wide variety of rooms featuring A/C, cable TV, fridge, and free local calls. ($65 for one queen-sized bed in summer, $49 in winter. Three-room suite with kitchen goes for $94 in summer, $74 in winter.)

Across the street from the Atlantic and its white sandy beach, **Little Talbot Island State Park,** 12157 Heckscher Dr. (251-2320), has 40 sites under palmetto trees and oaks. Take I-95S to Rte. A1A and go north. (Sites with electricity $18; in winter $12; ½-price for senior or disabled FL residents. Open March-Sept.) **K.A. Hanna Park,** 500 Wonderwood Dr. (249-4700), has mountain bike trails, hiking, and access to a beach with lifeguard service, in addition to 300 wooded sites with full hookups. Hop on Rte. A1A going north and follow the signs to Mayport Naval Station. (Office open daily 8am-sunset. Tent sites $10, with full hookup $13.50.)

Food and Nightlife

Five Points, located south of downtown on Park St. and **The Landing,** a dining and shopping extravaganza on Independent Dr. by the St. Johns River, swarms with dining options. In Five Points, try **Heartworks Gallery & Café,** 820 Lomax St. (355-6210), off Park St. Vegetarian specials (such as the famous "carrot dog") and killer desserts spice up this small café behind an even smaller gallery. (Entrees $3-5.50. Open Mon.-Sat. 11am-3pm, Fri. also 6-10pm for dinner specials.) A Jacksonville institution, **The Old South Restaurant,** 3058 Beach Blvd. (396-1920), skips the fancy stuff and attracts a local crowd with homecooked lunches and dinners. The menu varies daily but always includes an entree (fried chicken, meatloaf, etc.) and two veggies ($5). Try the chocolate ice box pie ($1) for dessert. (Open daily 11am-9pm.) **The Pizza Italian Restaurant,** 1053 Park St. (355-3820), serves up one huge submarine sandwich (at lunch just $3). All lunch items come in under $4. (For dinner, chicken parmigiana with a side of spaghetti $6.50. Open Mon.-Thurs. and Sat. 11am-9pm, Fri. 11am-10pm.)

Nightlife in Jacksonville sprawls like the city itself. **The Milk Bar,** 128 W. Adams St. (356-6455), houses two clubs in one. The main club has live music and DJs, while the Green Room plays jazz and funk and is frequented by straight and gay clientele (open Mon., Wed., and Fri.-Sat. 9pm-3am). Modern art murals and other splashes of paint have transformed an old theater into **Club 5,** 1028 Park St. (356-5555), in Five Points. It features the latest "progressive dance music." (Open Tues. 9pm-2am, Thurs. 9pm-3am, Fri.-Sat. 9pm-4am.) Near the beach, the **Ragtime Tap Room and Brewery,** 207 Atlantic Blvd. (241-7877), hosts live jazz Thursday through Sunday. Come for a des-

Florida Peninsula

GEORGIA

TO TALLAHASSEE

Osceola National Forest

Jacksonville

St. John's River

Santa Fe R.

St. Augustine

Suwannee River

Gainesville

ATLANTIC OCEAN

Ocala

Ocala National Forest

Daytona Beach

Cedar Keys

NASA Kennedy Space Center

Walt Disney World

Orlando

Cape Canaveral

Tampa

Florida's Turnpike

Tampa Bay

St. Petersburg

Manatee R.

Fort Pierce

Sarasota

Peace R.

Kissimmee R.

Lake Okeechobee

West Palm Beach

Palm Beach

Caloosahatchee R.

Fort Myers

Loxahatchee Nat. Wildlife Refuge

GULF OF MEXICO

Seminole Indian Reservation

Naples

Big Cyprus National Preserve

Fort Lauderdale

Miami

Miami Beach

Biscayne Bay

N

Everglades National Park

Florida City

Key Largo

0   100 miles

0   100 kilometers

Florida Bay

Florida Keys

Key West

sert (gold brick sundae $3), stay for the tunes. (Open Sun.-Thurs. 11am-11pm, bar, music, and appetizers 'til midnight; Fri.-Sat. 11am-1:30am.)

Sights and Entertainment Jacksonville spares the wallet with a couple of top-notch free attractions. **The Anheuser-Busch Brewery Tour,** 111 Busch Dr. (751-8118), off I-95, explains the brewing process and the history of the company, but still leaves time for a complimentary tasting (open Mon-Fri. 10am-5pm). The **Kingsley Plantation,** 11676 Palmetto Ave. (251-3537), off Rte. A1A, originally fell into the hands of slave trader Zephonia Kingsley in 1812, when wealthy planter John H. McIntosh failed to repay the loan Kingsley gave him in support of a failed revolution against Spain. (Had he succeeded, McIntosh would have become president of the "Republic of Florida.") The Kingsley home is the oldest surviving plantation house in Florida (open daily 9am-5pm; free). The **Cummer Museum of Art & Gardens,** 829 Riverside Ave. (356-6857), shows a collection of Western art dating to 2000BC. In the gardens, planted in the 1920s, look for an oak with a limbspan of over 150 ft. (Open Tues.-Thurs. 10am-9pm, Wed. and Fri.-Sat. 10am-5pm, Sun. noon-5pm. $5; students, seniors, and military $1; under 6 free. Tues. 4-9pm free.) Interactive hands-on exhibits at the **Museum of Science and History,** 1025 Museum Cir. (396-7062), cover a range of subjects from the history of Native Americans on the St. Johns River to the functions of the body. New exhibits feature manatee and dolphin skeletons, and a direct-cast sculpture of a *real* right whale named "Fermata." (Open Mon.-Fri. 10am-5pm, Sat. 10am-6pm, Sun. 1-6pm. $5, seniors and ages 4-12 $3. Get 2-for-1 admission with their brochure.)

The **Jacksonville Jazz Festival** (353-7770; call for exact dates) attracts large crowds each fall with a piano competition, live performances, and food. Throughout the year, pick up a copy of *Folio Weekly* for the dirt on weekly events.

■ St. Augustine

Spanish adventurer Pedro Menéndez de Aviles founded St. Augustine in 1565, making it the first European colony in North America and the oldest continuous settlement in the United States. Thanks to preservation efforts, much of St. Augustine's Spanish flavor remains intact. Unlike most towns on Florida's east coast, beaches do not define the character of St. Augustine; small crowds, historic sights, and friendly people invite visitors to relax and settle in for a rejuvenating stay.

Practical Information St. Augustine has no public transportation (boooo…); fortunately, most points of interest lie within walking distance of one another (yay!!!). The major east-west axis, **King St.,** runs along the river and crosses the bay to the beaches. **Saint George St.,** also east-west, contains most of the shops and many sights in St. Augustine, but does not permit vehicular traffic. **San Marco Ave.** and **Cordova St.** travel north-south. The **visitors center,** 10 Castillo (825-1000), at San Marco Ave. (from the Greyhound station, walk north on Ribeira, then right on Orange), gives out a free map of attractions and a comprehensive city guide. A free 28-min. video presentation hits the high points of St. Augustine's rich historical heritage while the more comprehensive (seven years in the making) *Dream of Empire* is a 52-min. film detailing just about every significant event in St. Augustine's lengthy history. ($3, ages 6-17 and students $2, under 6 free. Showtimes 9am-4pm daily. Visitors center open Oct.-Apr. daily 8:30am-5:30pm, Memorial Day-Labor Day 8am-7:30pm.) **Greyhound,** 100 Malaga St. (829-6401 or 800-231-2222), has service to Jacksonville (45min., $10) and Daytona Beach (1hr., $12) six times per day. (Open daily 7:30am-6pm.) **Ancient City Taxi** (824-8161) can take you from the bus station to San Marco Ave. for about $2. St. Augustine's **post office:** 99 King St. (829-8716), at Martin Luther King Ave. (Open Mon.-Tues. and Thurs.-Fri. 8:30am-5pm, Wed. 8:30am-5pm, Sat. 9am-1pm.) **ZIP code:** 32084. **Area code:** 904.

Accommodations and Camping The immaculate **St. Augustine Hostel,** 32 Treasury St. (808-1999), at Charlotte, 6 blocks from the bus station, offers spacious rooms that sleep six ($12), hotel-quality private rooms ($28), *huge* beds, A/C, a nicely decorated common area, stocked kitchen, and a pleasant roof garden. Simply magnificent. Welcoming managers Jean and Peter will make special arrangements for arrivals outside of open hours (8-10am and 5-10pm) and will also provide shuttle service from the Amtrak station (call a day in advance) and to the beach. (No curfew, no chores, no lockout, no problem. Parking $2. Linens $2.) Just over the Bridge of Lions, east of the historic district, the **Seabreeze Motel,** 208 Anastasia Blvd. (829-8122), features clean rooms with 2 double beds, A/C, cable TV, and a pool. (Singles $28, doubles $30.) The **American Inn,** 42 San Marco Ave. (829-2292), near the visitors center, rents spacious rooms with new carpets, two double beds, TV, and A/C, in a location convenient to the restaurants and historic sights (singles $26, doubles $35). For a real treat, splurge on the **St. Francis Inn,** 279 Saint George St. (824-6068), a charming 16-room inn with a jungle of flowers, a tucked-away pool, and much of its original 18th-century interior. Juice and iced tea are served free all day, along with *sangria* in the summer and sherry in the winter between the hours of 5 and 8pm. (Free use of bikes, free parking. Rooms have cable TV, A/C, heat, and working gas fireplaces. $55 and up. Rooms with balconies $110.) Nearby, a salt run and the Atlantic Ocean provide opportunities for great windsurfing, fishing, swimming, and surfing near the 139 campsites of the **Anastasia State Recreation Area** (461-2033), on Rte. A1A, 4 mi. south of the historic district. From town, cross the Bridge of Lions and turn left just beyond the Alligator Farm. (Office open daily 8am-sunset. Sites $15; Oct.-Feb. $12. With full hookup an additional $2. Reservations accepted up to 60 days in advance.)

Food and Nightlife The bustle of daytime tourists and abundance of budget eateries make lunch in St. Augustine's historic district a delight. Stroll **Saint George St.** and check the daily specials scrawled on blackboards outside each restaurant. **Anastasia Blvd.** also holds a wealth of budget options for lunch and dinner. **Captain Jack's,** 410 Anastasia Blvd. (829-6846), serves up large surf 'n' turf dinners for $17—don't miss the house specialty, fried shrimp, for $7. (Open Mon.-Fri. 11:30am-9pm, Sat.-Sun. noon-9pm.) The sandwich and juice counter at **New Dawn,** 110 Anastasia Blvd. (824-1337), a health-conscious grocery store, makes delicious vegetarian sandwiches, including the savory tofu salad surprise ($3.75; banana smoothies $2.75; open Mon.-Sat. 9am-5:30pm). If you *do* give a damn, come to **Scarlett O'Hara's,** 70 Hypolita St. (824-6535), at Cordova St., where the barbecue chicken sandwiches are $4.75 and the drinks are refreshing. St. Augustine supports an impressive array of bars. Pick up a copy of the *Today Tonight* newspaper, available at most grocery and convenience stores, for a complete listing of current concerts and events. In the restored area, try the **Milltop,** 19½ Saint George St. (829-2329), a tiny bar situated above an old mill. Local string musicians play on the tiny stage. (Open daily 10:30am-12:30am. Music daily from 1pm until closing; cover varies from none whatsoever to a very slight charge.) Cheap flicks and cheap eats await the weary traveler at **Pot Belly's,** 36 Granada St. (829-3101), across from the Lightner Museum. This combination pub, deli, and cinema serves a vast array of junk food, with each item bearing the name of a famous film—"Dances With Wolves" ($5) is twelve spicy buffalo wings. Waitresses will serve you *in the theater,* so sit back in the reclining chair and enjoy the latest movies for only $2.50. Most food items run $2-4 (shows every 15-30min., 6:30pm-midnight). The new hot spot for the young beach crowd, the **Oasis Deck and Restaurant,** 4000 A1A/Beach Blvd. (471-3424), schedules nightly live entertainment and happy hours (happiness Mon.-Fri. 4-7pm; open daily 6:30am-1am).

Sights and Entertainment The historic district centers on **Saint George St.,** beginning at the Gates of the City near the visitors center and running south past Cadiz St. and the Oldest Store. Visit the **Spanish Quarter** (825-6830), on Saint George St., a living museum which includes Gallegos House. Artisans and villagers in period costumes describe the customs and crafts of the Spanish New World. (Open daily

9am-5pm. $5, students and ages 6-18 $2.50, seniors and AAA members $4.50.) While in the **Restored Area,** be sure to check out the other 18th-century homes and shops. The oldest masonry fortress in the continental U.S., **Castillo de San Marcos National Monument,** 1 Castillo Dr. (829-6506), off San Marco Ave., has 14-ft.-thick walls built of coquina, the local shellrock. Inside the fort itself, a four-pointed star complete with drawbridge and murky moat, you'll find a museum, a large courtyard surrounded by guardrooms, livery quarters for the garrison, a jail, a chapel, and the original cannon brought overseas by the Spanish. A cannon-firing ceremony occurs four times per day on weekends. (Open daily 8:45am-4:45pm. Tours at 10am and 2pm; $2.)

For two decades, St. Augustine was the end of the line—the railroad line, that is. Swarms of wealthy Northerners escaped to railroad owner Henry Flagler's Ponce de León Hotel, at King and Cordova St. The hotel, decorated entirely by Tiffany and out-fitted with electricity by Edison himself (the first hotel to feature this luxury), is now **Flagler College** (829-6481). In the summer, the college lies deserted, but students enliven the campus and the town during the school year. On summer days, free 25-min. tours pass through some of the recently restored rooms in the old hotel; go, if only to see the exquisite stained glass windows. (Tours on the hour 11am-4pm.) In 1947, Chicago publisher and art-lover Otto Lightner converted the Alcazar Hotel, across the street, into the **Lightner Museum** (824-2874), to hold an impressive collec-tion of cut, blown, and burnished glass, as well as old clothing and numerous oddities including nun and monk beer steins. (Open daily 9am-5pm. $5, AAA members $3, students with ID and ages 12-18 $1.)

Being the oldest continuous settlement in the U.S. entails having some of the oldest stuff in the U.S. The self-proclaimed **Oldest House,** 14 Saint Francis St. (824-2872), has been occupied continuously since its construction in the 1600s. (Open daily 9am-5pm. $5, students $3, seniors $4.50, couples with kids $12.) The **Oldest Store Museum,** 4 Artillery Ln. (829-9729), holds over 100,000 items from the 18th and 19th centuries (open Mon.-Sat. 9am-5pm, Sun. noon-5pm; $4, ages 6-12 $1.50).

Six blocks north of the info center, **La Leche Shrine and Mission of Nombre de Dios,** 27 Ocean St. (824-2809), sits just off San Marco Ave. It held the first Catholic ser-vice in the U.S. on September 8, 1565. Soaring over the moss- and vine-covered struc-ture, a 208-ft. steel cross commemorates the founding of the city. (Open 9am-5pm daily. Mass Mon.-Fri. 8:30am, Sat. 6pm, Sun. 8am. Admission by donation.) No trip to St. Augustine would be complete without a trek to the **Fountain of Youth,** 155 Mag-nolia Ave. (829-3168); go right on Williams St. from San Marco Ave. and continue a few blocks past Nombre de Dios. (Open daily 9am-5pm. $4.75, seniors $3.75, ages 6-12 $1.75, under 6 free.) Not only can you drink from the spring that Ponce de León thought would give him eternal youth, you can marvel at a statue of the explorer that doesn't age. While you're there, take in the huge oaks and hanging Spanish moss of Magnolia Ave., heralded as one of the prettiest streets in America.

■ Daytona Beach

Daytona's 500-ft.-wide beach is the city's *raison d'être*. During spring break, students from practically every college in the country come here to get a head start on sum-mer. The beach itself resembles a traffic jam; dozens of cars, motorcycles, and rental dune buggies crawl along the hot sand. During any season, a fleet of vehicles rolls past sunbathers, cruises down the Atlantic Ave. strip, or races up the appropriately named International Speedway Blvd. in search of Daytona's famous racetrack. If you're looking for scenery in Daytona Beach, go a few miles north to picturesque Ormond Beach. If not, slap on some sunblock (SPF 15 or higher, kids) and enjoy.

Practical Information Daytona Beach lies 53 mi. northeast of Orlando and 90 mi. south of Jacksonville. **Atlantic Ave.,** or **Rte. A1A,** crawls with budget motels, surf shops, and bars in **Beachside,** the main strip of land. **East International Speedway Blvd.** (U.S. 92) runs north-south. Pay attention when hunting down street addresses; Daytona Beach is a collection of smaller towns that have expanded and converged, but have also preserved their individual street-numbering systems. As a result, many street numbers are not consecutive. To avoid the gridlock on the beach, arrive early (6 or 7am) and leave early (3pm or so). You'll pay $5 to drive onto the beach (permitted from sunrise to sunset), and police strictly enforce the 10mph speed limit. Free parking is plentiful during most of the year, but difficult during peak seasons, especially Speed Week, Bike Week, Racefest, and the Pepsi 400 (see Entertainment, below), not to mention spring break (the week after Easter).

For tourist info, visit the **Daytona Beach Area Convention and Visitors Bureau,** 126 E. Orange Ave. (255-0415 or 800-854-1234), at the chamber of commerce on City Island (open Mon.-Fri. 9am-5pm). Flights into Daytona arrive at the **Daytona Beach International Airport,** 700 Catalina Dr. (248-8069), next to (and virtually indistinguishable from) the International Speedway directly off International Speedway Blvd. on the left. **Amtrak,** 2491 Old New York Ave. (734-2322 or 800-872-7245), 24 mi. west on Rte. 92, makes tracks to Miami (1-2 per day, 8hr., $50; open daily 7:40am-2pm and 4-7:30pm). **Greyhound** buses come and go from 138 S. Ridgewood Ave. (255-7076 or 800-231-2222), 4 mi. west of the beach (open daily 8am-10pm). **Voltran Transit Co.,** 950 Big Tree Rd. (761-7700), on the mainland, operates local buses. (Service Mon.-Sat. 5:30am-6:30pm, Sun. abbreviated schedule. 75¢, kids and seniors 35¢, transfers free. Free maps available at hotels.) **A&A Cab Co.** (253-2522) charges $1.80 for the first ½ mi. and $1.20 per additional mi. Rent an **Alamo** car (255-1511 or 800-327-9633) at the airport. A subcompact costs $25 per day or $109 per week with unlimited mileage. (Free drop-off in Jacksonville or Ft. Lauderdale. Must be 21 with credit card. Under 25 surcharge $20 per day. Open daily 6am-11pm.) Reach the 24-hr. **Rape Crisis and Sexual Abuse** line at 254-4106. **Emergency: 911.** Daytona Beach's **post office:** 220 N. Beach St. (253-5166; open Mon.-Fri. 8am-5pm., Sat. 9am-noon). **ZIP code:** 32115. **Area code:** 904.

Accommodations and Camping Almost all of Daytona's accommodations front **Atlantic Ave. (Rte. A1A),** either on the beach or across the street; those off the beach offer the best deals. During spring break and big race weekends, even the worst hotels become overpriced. Don't plan to sleep on these well-patrolled shores. Look for cheaper, quieter hotels along **Ridgewood Ave.** In summer and fall, prices plunge; most hotels offer special deals in June. **Daytona Beach International Youth Hostel (Rucksackers),** 140 S. Atlantic Ave. (258-6937), 1 block north of E. International Speedway Blvd., provides 100 beds, A/C, TV, kitchen facilities, free local calls, and a recreation room in close proximity to the beach. Don't expect luxury. A crowd of international students usually fills the place. Check out those redwood-root chairs in the lobby—gnarly! ($13.35, $60 weekly for members; $70 weekly for non-members. Lockers $1-2. Key deposit $5.) If you have a few extra dollars, the **Camellia Motel,** 1055 N. Atlantic Ave. (252-9963), across the street from the beach, is worth it. The maternal manager oversees cozy, bright rooms, with phones, free local calls, cable TV, and A/C; rooms with kitchens cost an extra $5. Four languages (English, Slovak, French, and German) are spoken here. Every effort is made to make you feel at home, including ice cream money, shuttle service (for groups of 3 or 4) from bus station and airport, and complimentary postcard, which the manager urges you to "send to your mama." Free maps and brochures await you at the desk. (Singles and doubles $25; $5 per additional person. During spring break singles $60; $10 per additional person.) The **Rio Beach Motel,** 843 S. Atlantic Ave. (253-6564), has large rooms decorated in dark plums and greens. Cable TV, A/C, pool, and a prime location directly on the ocean make it even better. (Singles and doubles $27; during spring break, Speed Week, and Bike Week $60-70.)

Camping options await at **Tomoka State Park,** 2099 N. Beach St. (676-4050), 8 mi. north of Daytona and 70 min. from Disney World. Take bus #3 "North Ridgewood" to Domicilio and walk 2 mi. north. You'll find 100 sites located under tropical foliage near a salt marsh, along with nature trails, a museum, and lots of shade. (Open daily 8am-sunset. Sites $15 per day with $2 electric fee.) **Nova Family Campground,** 1190 Herbert St. (767-0095; fax 767-1666), in Port Orange south of Daytona Beach and 10 min. from the shore, comes through for RVers with shady hookup-equipped sites, a grocery store, and a swimming pool. Take bus #7 or 15 from downtown or from the beach. Bike rental is $15 per day, $5 per hr. (Open daily 8am-8pm. Sites $16, with electric and water $18, full hookup $20. Open sites posted after hours; register the next day.)

Food "If it swims...we have it," boasts **B&B Fisheries,** 715 E. International Speedway Blvd. (252-6542). The oldest (since 1932) family-owned seafood house in Daytona. Take out your choice of 4-5 varieties of fresh fish for lunch starting around $5.15. (Open Mon.-Fri. 11am-8:30pm, Sat. 4-8:30pm. Take-out service Mon.-Sat. 11:30am-8:30pm.) Probably the most famous (and popular) seafood restaurant in the area is **Aunt Catfish's** (767-4768) which sits just to the left of Dunlawton Bridge as it connects to the mainland. Fried alligator appetizers are $3; fried Carolina-style salt and pepper catfish with rolls, salad and hot bar, and choice of veggie side goes for $10. Come early. (Open Mon.-Sat. 11:30am-9:30pm, Sun. 11:30am-10pm.) **St. Regis Bar and Restaurant,** 509 Seabreeze Blvd. (252-8743), in a historic home, is a good break from budget fare. Eat an eclectic array of edibles (dinner $13-25; cheaper "sunset dinners" Tues.-Thurs. 4:30-6:30pm) on the cool veranda while listening to live jazz (Fri.-Sat. 8pm-midnight). Happy hour 5-7pm means free hors d'oeuvres, $1 drafts, and $2.50 mixed drinks (open Tues.-Sat. 6pm-around 11pm).

Entertainment and Nightlife Bored with beachcombing? Get in touch with your primitive side and race off to the **Daytona International Speedway,** 1801 W. International Speedway Blvd. (254-2700 for info; 253-RACE/7223 for race tickets). **Speed Week** (Feb. 1-16) is two weeks of almost daily races, including the **Daytona 500** (Feb. 16), which draws the festivities to a close. (Tickets $60-160.) **Racefest** (July 3) and the **Pepsi 400** (July 6) provide the avid fan with even more opportunities to watch his or her favorite jalopy burst into flames (tickets $35-95). The day before the Pepsi 400, **Daytona USA,** a theme park dedicated to all things NASCAR, will have its grand opening. Located on the Speedway premises, Daytona USA is a self-described "interactive museum" where you can, among other things, design and drive your own virtual race car. ($10, seniors $8, ages 6-12 $5, under 6 free.) Call 947-6800 for info. **Bike Week** extends from February 28 until March 9. It ends with the **Daytona 200 Motorcycle Classic,** an event that draws every biker in the world to Daytona (tickets $30). The speedway itself houses a huge collection of racing memorabilia and early racing films and conducts 30-min. tours on days with no races (tours daily 9:30am-4pm; $5, ages 7-12 $2).

When spring break hits, concerts, hotel-sponsored parties, and other events cater to students questing for fun. News about these transient events and parties travels fastest by word of mouth, but check the *Calendar of Events* and *SEE Daytona Beach,* available at the chamber of commerce, for a starting point. On more mellow nights, head to the boardwalk, where you can play volleyball or pinball, listen to music at the Oceanfront Bandshell, or park (ahem) on the beach until 1am for $3. A virtually indistinguishable collection of dance clubs exists along **Seabreeze Blvd.** near the intersection with N. Atlantic Ave. Of all the nightclubs in Daytona, the **Ocean Deck,** 127 S. Ocean Ave. (253-5224), stands apart with its beachfront location and live reggae music. (Open daily 11am-2am. Music nightly 9:30pm-3am.)

■ Orlando

Call the Walt Disney World information hotline and you'll probably get this recorded message: "Thank you for calling Walt Disney World. All of our Disney operators are busy making magic with other customers. Please stay on the line." Besides sounding kind of kinky, this recording indicates how seriously Disney—and the city of Orlando—regards its own "magic." And why shouldn't it? Every year, millions descend upon this central Florida city for the sole purpose of visiting **Disney World,** the most popular tourist attraction on earth. Comprised of the original Magic Kingdom, Epcot Center, and Disney-MGM Studios, Disney holds its own against an onslaught of smaller parks that have sprung up all over the Orlando area. There are many ways to lighten your wallet in this land of illusions, so choose wisely. If you've seen Disney before, don't expect a vast number of changes to the park; it might be interesting to check out Orlando's other attractions.

PRACTICAL INFORMATION

Tourist Office: Orlando-Orange County Convention and Visitors Bureau, 8445 International Dr. (363-5871), several mi. southwest of downtown at the Mercado (Spanish-style mall); take bus #8 and ask the driver to make the stop. Maps and info on nearly all of the area's attractions, plus free bus system maps. Multilingual clerks will get you hotel referrals at discount prices. Brochures available in Spanish, French, and Japanese. Pick up the free *Orlando* for the skinny on the city. Ask for the free "Magic Card" and receive discounts at various attractions, shops, restaurants, and hotels. Open daily 8am-8pm.

Airport: Orlando International Airport, 1 Airport Blvd. (825-2001); from the airport take Rte. 436N, exit to Rte. 528W (the B-line Expwy.), then go east on I-4 to the exits for downtown. City bus #11 makes the trip for 75¢. **Mears Motor Shuttle,** 324 W. Gore St. (423-5566), has a booth at the airport for transportation to most hotels, including Plantation Manor (see Accommodations, below). One bus goes straight to Disney ($25 roundtrip, kids $17). No shuttle reservations necessary from airport (for return, call one day in advance). Also runs from most hotels to Disney ($7-14); call 1 day in advance to reserve a seat. Open 24hr.

Trains: Amtrak, 1400 Sligh Blvd. (843-7611 or 800-872-7245), 3 blocks east of I-4; take S. Orange Ave., turn west on Columbia, then right on Sligh. To: Tampa (1 per day, 2hr., $22); Jacksonville (2 per day, 2hr., $37). Open daily 7:30am-6:30pm.

Buses: Greyhound, 555 N. Magruder Blvd. (292-3424 or 800-231-2222), across from John Young Pkwy. To: Tampa (6 per day, 2½hr., $18); Jacksonville (9 per day, 3hr., $27). Open 24hr. **Gray Line Tours** (422-0744) offers bus transport to Busch Gardens (see p. 348). Roundtrip $49 plus admission, ages 3-9 $43. Pick-up at most major hotels.

Public Transportation: LYNX, 7800 W. Central Blvd. (841-8240; Mon.-Fri. 6am-8:15pm, Sat. 7:30am-6:15pm, Sun. 8am-4:15pm). Buses operate daily 6am-9pm (times vary with route). 75¢, under 18 25¢ (with ID), transfers 10¢. Downtown terminal at Central and Pine St., 1 block west of Orange Ave. and 1 block east of I-4. Schedules available at most shopping malls, banks, and at the downtown terminal. Serves the airport (bus #11 at side A, level 1) and Wet 'n' Wild.

Taxis: Yellow Cab, 422-4455. $2.75 first mi., $1.50 per additional mi.

Car Rental: Alamo, 324 W. Gore St. (857-8200 or 800-327-9633), near the airport. Compacts $19 per day, $95 per week. Under 25 surcharge $20 per day. Must have a major credit card. Open 24hr.

Crisis Lines: Rape Hotline, 740-5408. **Crisis Information,** 425-2624. **Rape Counseling**: 246-8007.

Emergency: 911.

Post Office: 46 E. Robinson St. (843-5673), at Magnolia downtown. Open Mon.-Fri. 7am-5pm, Sat. 9am-noon. **ZIP code:** 32801. **Area code:** 407.

Orlando lies at the center of hundreds of small lakes and amusement parks. **Lake Eola** is in the center of the city, east of I-4 and south of Colonial Dr. Streets divide north-south by **Rte. 17-92 (Orange Blossom Trail)** and east-west by **Colonial Dr.** Supposedly an east-west expressway, I-4 actually runs north-south through the center of town. To reach either downtown youth hostel (see Accommodations, below) by car, take the Robinson St. exit and turn right. **Disney World** and **Sea World** await 15 to 20 mi. south of downtown on I-4; **Cypress Gardens** is 30 mi. south of Disney off U.S. 27 near Winter Haven. Most hotels offer shuttle service to Disney. City buses, Gray Line, and Mears Motor Shuttle (see above) serve some parks.

ACCOMMODATIONS AND CAMPING

Orlando does not cater to the budget traveler. Prices for hotel rooms rise exponentially as you approach Disney World; plan to stay in a hostel or in downtown Orlando. Reservations are prudent, especially from December to January, March to April, late June to August, and on holidays.

Orlando International Youth Hostel at Plantation Manor (HI-AYH), 227 N. Eola Dr. (843-8888), at E. Robinson, downtown on the east shore of Lake Eola. Porch, TV room, A/C, kitchen facilities. Clean, no-frills dorms sleep 4-8. LYNX bus service stops here every 2 hours, 9 times daily, with 75¢ bus transport to Disney and all area attractions. Hospitable management runs free van service to Greyhound and Amtrak, and also reimburses bus fare from airport. Free access to nearby YMCA facilities, including Olympic-sized pool and gym. Must be a member or have non-U.S. passport to stay; there may be exceptions if they're not full. Flexible 3-day max. stay. Curfew 1am, weekend curfew 2am (flexible). Beds $12, private rooms $25 ($28.60 for 2 people). Breakfast (prepared by manager's mother) $2. Linen $1. Key deposit $5. Make reservations.

Hostelling International-Orlando Resort (HI-AYH), 4840 W. Irlo Bronson Memorial Hwy./Rte. 192 (396-8282), in Kissimmee. Super-clean rooms with new wooden bunk beds, A/C, pool, lake, and transportation to Disney ($12-14). Office open 24hr. Free maid service to dorms. Beds $13, non-members $16. Private rooms (with TV, A/C, phone) $28. Ages 6-17 ½-price, under 6 free. Linens $1. Make reservations.

Sun Motel, 5020 W. Irlo Bronson Memorial Hwy. (Rte. 192) (396-6666 or 800-541-2674; fax 407-396-0878), in Kissimmee. Very reasonable considering its proximity to Disney World (4mi.). Pretty rooms with floral bedspreads, cable TV, phone, pool, and A/C. Beware the cruel and unusual telephone deposit ($20), as well as the 45¢ local calls. Singles $45, doubles $70; off season $25/$28.

Disney's All-Star Resorts (934-7639), in Disney World. From I-4, take Exit 25B and follow the signs to Blizzard Beach—the resorts are just behind it. Not exactly cheap, but a great deal if you're in a group. Amazingly large cowboy boots and football helmets decorate large courtyards. Pools, A/C, phone, fridge ($5 extra per day), food court, free parking, free Disney transportation. $69-79 for 2 adults and 2 kids, $8 for each additional adult up to four. Disabled access available.

KOA, 4771 W. Irlo Bronson Memorial Hwy. (Rte. 192) (396-2400 or 800-KOA-7791/562-7791), in Kissimmee. Spacious sites with lots of trees, a pool, tennis courts, and a store (open 7am-9pm, til 11pm when crowds are big). Even in season you're bound to get a site, but arrive early. Free buses twice a day to Disney. Office open 24 hr. Tent sites with hookup (for 2) $22, $30 in peak season. Kamping kabins with A/C (for 2) $28, $40 in peak season. Extra adults $5 (up to 4). Under 18 free. Discount tickets through **Tickets N' Tours** (396-1182).

Stage Stop Campground, 14400 W. Colonial Dr. (Rte. 50) (656-8000), 8mi. north of Disney in Winter Garden. Coming from the north on the Florida Turnpike, take Exit 272 and travel 2½mi. east on Rte. 50. Family campground with a game room, pool, and laundry facilities. Office open in summer daily 8am-8pm. 248 sites (tent or RV) with full hookup $17; weekly $102.

Orlando has two municipal campgrounds, **Turkey Lake Park,** 3401 S. Hiawassee Rd. (299-5581), near Universal Studios (open daily 9:30am-7pm; sites with water and electricity $14.32, with full hookup $16.50), and **Moss Park,** 12901 Moss Park Rd. (273-2327), 10 mi. from the airport (open daily 8am-8pm; tent sites $11, with water and electricity $14; park entrance $1).

FOOD

Lilia's Grilled Delight, 3150 S. Orange Ave. (851-9087), 2 blocks south of Michigan St. 5min. from the downtown business district. Small, modestly decorated Polynesian restaurant—one of the best-kept secrets in town. Don't pass up the Huli Huli

Chicken, a twice-baked delight (½ chicken $4, pulled pork sandwich 99¢). Lunch $4-6. Dinner $5-9. Open Mon.-Fri. 11am-9pm, Sat. noon-9pm.

Bakely's, 345 W. Fairbanks Ave. (645-5767), in Winter Park. Take I-4 to Fairbanks Ave. exit. The variety at this restaurant/bake shop is as large as the portions. Lasagna with salad and bread $7. Save room for the six-layer Boston Cream cake ($3). Open Sun.-Thurs. 7am-11pm, Fri.-Sat. 7am-midnight.

Thai House, 2101 E. Colonial Dr. (898-0820). A small and charming family-run restaurant crowded with locals. The house specialty, Thai House Fried Rice, sizzles with a combination of pork, chicken, beef, shrimp, veggies, and spices ($7). Healthy portions for $5.50-8.50 (duck and seafood $9-15). Open Mon.-Fri. 11am-2pm and 5-9:30pm, Sat. 5-10pm.

Clarkie's Restaurant, 3110 S. Orange Ave. (859-1690). Serves up simple "Mom" food for under $5. Early Bird breakfast special: 2 eggs, grits, and toast or biscuit, $1.29 until 8am. Every kind of sandwich imaginable. Open Mon.-Fri. 6am-2:30pm, Sat. 6am-noon, Sun. 7am-1pm.

Francesco's Ristorante Italiano, 4920 W. Irlo Bronson Memorial Hwy./Rte. 192 (396-0889). Dine beneath Chianti bottles while Sinatra croons in the background, via stereo. Large portions of pasta, steak, or seafood complete with salad bar and bread $7-14. The breakfast special of two eggs, two bacon strips, and two pancakes runs $2.39. Open daily 7:30am-11pm.

ENTERTAINMENT AND NIGHTLIFE

N. Orange Ave., downtown, is the heart of Orlando nightlife. Relatively inexpensive bars line the city's main drag, including **Zuma Beach Club,** 46 N. Orange Ave. (648-8363). Home to a very mainstream college and twenty-something crowd, Zuma packs 'em in (3500 people on Sat. nights) with 2 stories of bars, beer tubs, and dance floors. Shaq stops by every once in while. (Open Mon. and Sat. 9pm-3am, Tues. 10pm-3:30am, Thurs. 9pm-2:30am, Fri. 8pm-2:30am.) For a more "alternative" (and mostly gay) club scene, try **The Club at Firestone,** 578 N. Orange Ave. (426-0005), at Concord. Built inside an old Firestone garage, The Club serves as the starting point for Orlando's gay pride parade. Times, cover, and events vary; call ahead.

Improvisational comedy shows will keep you in stitches at the **SAK Theater,** 45 E. Church St. (648-0001; shows Tues. 9pm, Wed.-Thurs. 8 and 9:45pm, Fri.-Sat. 7:30, 9:30, and 11:30pm; Fri.-Sat. $11, with FL ID $9, students and military $7).

The **Church Street Station,** 129 W. Church St. (422-2434), downtown on the corner of Church and Garland St., is a slick, block-long entertainment, shopping, and restaurant complex (open 11am-2am). Inside, boogie down and enjoy 5¢ beers (Wed. 6:30-7:30pm) at **Phineas Phogg's Balloon Works** (21+). At **yab-yum,** 25 Wall St. Plaza (422-3322), they sell 20 brands of cigarettes. (Live entertainment Tues.-Sat. Open Sun.-Thurs. 8am-1am, Fri.-Sat. 8am-2:30am.)

■ Disney World

Disney is the mother of all amusement parks—a sprawling three-park labyrinth of kiddie rides, movie sets, and futuristic world displays. If bigger is better, Disney World wins the prize for best park in the U.S. by a mile (824-4321, for info daily 8am-10pm). Disney World contains three sections: the **Magic Kingdom,** with seven theme regions; **Epcot Center,** part science fair, part World's Fair; and **Disney-MGM Studios,** a pseudo movie- and TV-studio with Magic Kingdom-style rides. All three cluster a few mi. from each other in the town of **Lake Buena Vista,** 20 mi. west of Orlando via I-4.

The one-day entrance fee of $38.50 (ages 3-9 $31) admits you to *one* of the three parks, and allows you to leave and return to the same park later in the day. A four-day **Value Pass** ($136.75, ages 3-9 $109.18) covers one day at each park, plus an extra day at any one of them. A four-day **Park-Hopper Pass** ($152.65, ages 3-9 $121) buys admission to all three parks for all four days. The five-day **World-Hopper Pass** ($186, ages 3-9 $148), includes admission to all other Disney attractions (see below). Both "Hopper" passes allow for unlimited transportation between attractions on the Disney monorail, boats, buses, and trains. Multi-day passes need not be used on consecutive days and they *never* expire. Attractions that charge separate admissions (unless you have a World-Hopper Pass) include **River Country** ($14.75, ages 3-9 $11.50), **Discovery Island** ($11, ages 3-9 $6), **Typhoon Lagoon** ($24, ages 3-11 $18), **Pleasure Island** ($17, over 18 only, unless with adult), and **Blizzard Beach** ($24, ages 3-11 $18). For descriptions, see Other Disney Attractions, below. *Warning: the prices listed above will almost certainly be higher when you actually purchase your tickets.* Disney's price inflation rates make college tuitions look stable.

Disney World opens its gates 365 days a year, but hours fluctuate with the season. Expect the parks to open at 9am and close at 8pm; these hours are often extended. The parks get busy during the summer when school is out, but the enormously crowded "peak times" are Christmas, Thanksgiving, spring break, and the month around Easter. More people visit between Christmas and New Year's than at any other time of year. The crowd hits the main gates at 10am; arrive before the 9am opening time and seek out your favorite rides or exhibits before noon. During peak periods (and often during the rest of the year), Disney World actually opens earlier than the stated time for guests staying at Disney resorts. To avoid the crowds, start at the rear of a park and work your way to the front. You'll be able to see the distant attractions while the masses cram the lines for those near the entrance. If you have extremely limited time, though, go on your "must-see" rides in spite of the lines. Persevere through dinner time (5:30-8pm), when a lot of cranky kids head home. Regardless of tactics, you'll often have to wait 45 min. to two hours at the biggies.

Mears Motor Shuttle offers transport from most hotels to Disney (see Practical Information, above). Major hotels and some campgrounds provide their own shuttles for guests. **Cyclists** can store their bikes at Epcot free of charge.

Magic Kingdom Seven "lands" comprise the Magic Kingdom. Enter on **Main Street, USA,** to capture the essence of turn-of-the-century hometown U.S. The architects employed "forced perspective" here, building the ground floor of the shops 9/10 of the normal size and making the second and third stories progressively smaller. Walt describes his vision in the "Walt Disney Movie" at the Hospitality House, to the right as you emerge from under the railroad station. The Main Street Cinema shows some great old silent films. Late in the afternoon, the "Mickey Mania Parade" down Main Street gives you a chance to see all the Disney characters, or find shorter lines at the more crowded attractions. Near the entrance, you'll find a steam train that huffs and puffs its way across the seven different lands.

Tomorrowland just received a neon and stainless steel facelift which skyrocketed it out of the space-race days of the 70s and into a futuristic intergalactic nation, **XS. Alien Encounter,** the newest Magic Kingdom attraction, chills without spins or drops, creating suspense in pitch blackness. The very cool indoor roller coaster **Space Mountain** still proves the high point of this section, if not the whole park, and absolutely merits the lengthy wait.

The golden-spired Cinderella Castle marks the gateway to **Fantasyland,** where you'll find Dumbo the Elephant and a twirling teacup ride. Two classic rides, **Peter Pan's Flight** and **Snow White's Adventures,** capture the original charm of the park; the evil Queen scares children like no one else. You know the song, so see what it means at **It's a Small World,** a saccharine but endearing boat tour celebrating the children of the world. Be warned: you may never, ever, get this tune out of your head. Killer A/C makes it a good bet for a hot day.

Liberty Square and **Frontierland** devote their resources to U.S. history and a celebration of Mark Twain. History buffs will enjoy the recently updated Hall of Presidents (President Clinton makes a cameo, Maya Angelou narrates), which focuses on our nation's quest for equality. Adventurers should catch the rickety, runaway **Big Thunder Mountain Railroad** rollercoaster or the truly dope **Splash Mountain,** which takes you on a voyage with Br'er Rabbit and leaves you chilled inside and out. Spooky and dorky, **Haunted Mansion** is a classic with a quick line. Also be sure to stop and watch the entertaining animatronics at the **Country Bear Jamboree,** or take a steamboat ride or canoe trip and rest your feet.

Adventureland romanticizes unexplored regions of the world. **The Jungle Cruise** takes a tongue-in-cheek tour through tropical waterways populated by not-so-authentic-looking wildlife. **Pirates of the Caribbean** explores caves where animated buccaneers spar, swig, and sing. The Swiss Family Robinson tree house, a replica of the eternally shipwrecked family's home, captures all the clever tricks the family used to survive.

Epcot Center In 1966, Walt dreamed up an "Experimental Prototype Community Of Tomorrow" (EPCOT) never intended to be completed, evolving constantly to incorporate new ideas from U.S. technology—a self-sufficient, futuristic utopia. At present, Epcot splits into **Future World** and **World Showcase.** For smaller crowds, visit the former in the evening and the latter in the morning.

The 180-ft.-high trademark geosphere that forms the entrance to Future World houses the **Spaceship Earth** attraction, where visitors board a "time machine" for a tour through the evolution of communications. At the **Wonders of Life, Body Wars** takes its visitors on a tour of the human body (with the help of a simulator). **Cranium Command** puts you at the helm of a 12-year-old boy as his animatronic "pilot" steers him around the pitfalls of daily life. **The Land** presents **The Circle of Life,** a live-action/animated film about the environment with characters from *The Lion King.* Fish, sharks, and manatees inhabit the re-created coral reef in **The Living Seas.** The immensely popular **Journey Into Imagination** pavilion recently replaced Michael Jackson's film "Captain Eo" with "Honey I Shrunk the Audience" which boasts stellar 3D effects. The **World of Motion** is currently undergoing renovation to introduce new exhibits on the future of transportation. **Universe of Energy,** sponsored by Exxon, will feature a new exhibit in the fall to replace its hopelessly outdated current exhibit, which is basically an advertisement for fossil fuels. The new ride will feature comedienne Ellen Degeneres and will probably avoid bragging about the Valdez—a rather disturbing feature of the old ride.

The **World Showcase** consists of a series of international pavilions surrounding an artificial lake. An architectural style or monument, as well as typical food and crafts, represent each country. People in indigenous costumes perform dances, theatrical skits, and other "cultural" entertainment at each country's pavilion. Before setting out around the lake, pick up a schedule of events at the **Global Information Station** located just behind Spaceship Earth as you enter the park. Just outside the info station are the World Key Terminals, computerized booths that dispense park info and make dinner reservations. Inside the station, live human beings from **Guest Relations** provide maps. The two 360° films made in China and Canada and the 180° film made in France rate among the best of the attractions; each includes spectacular landscapes, some national history, and an insider's look at the people of each country. **The American Adventure** gives a very enthusiastic and patriotic interpretation of American history. Save your pesos by shopping at Pier 1 rather than the marked-up Mexican marketplace. Norwegian life must be more exciting than the fishing, sailing, and oil exploring shown by the boat ride in the Norway Pavilion—but hey, it's the only ride in the World Showcase. Every night at 9pm (Sat. 10pm) Epcot presents a magnificent show called **Illuminations,** with music from the represented nations accompanied by dancing, lights, and fireworks.

The World Showcase pavilions specialize in regional cuisine. At the **Restaurant Marrakesh** in the Moroccan Pavilion, head chef Lahsen Abrache cooks delicious *brewat* (spicy minced beef fried in pastry) and *bastilla* (sweet and slightly spicy pie). A belly dancer performs in the restaurant every evening. (Lunch $10-15. Dinner $15-20.) The Mexican, French, and Italian pavilions serve up excellent food at similar prices. If you plan to eat a sit-down meal in the park, make reservations first thing in the morning at World Key Terminal, behind Spaceship Earth. The regional cafés (no reservations required) present cheaper options, but no real bargains. Unfortunately, all the food at Disney is scandalously overpriced—hot dogs go for $4.50. Eat outside "the World" to save your money for Goofy-eared hats.

Disney-MGM Studios Disney-MGM Studios set out to create a "living movie set," and they seem to have succeeded. Many familiar Disney characters stroll through the park, as do a host of characters dressed as directors, starlets, gossip columnists, and fans. Events such as stunt shows and mini-theatricals take place continually. And, every day, a different has-been star leads a parade across Hollywood Blvd.

The Twilight Zone Tower of Terror 2 climbs 13 flights in an old-time Hollywood hotel; when the cable snaps, the fastest ride at Disney begins. And just when you think the ride is over, WHAM! It drops you again (thus the "2"). **The Great Movie Ride,** inside the Chinese Theater, takes you on a simple but nostalgic trip through old and favorite films. Sites such as **Superstar Television,** which projects audience members alongside TV stars in classics like "I Love Lucy," and the **Monster Sound Show,** which asks volunteers to add special effects to a short movie, get the spectators involved in the process. One of the two biggest attractions at this park, the **Indiana Jones Epic Stunt Spectacular** lets you watch stuntmen and volunteers pull off amazing moves. The other biggie, the **Star Tours** ride, based on Star Wars, simulates turbulance or a space cargo ship caught in laser crossfire.

Other Disney Attractions For those who didn't get enough amusement at the three main parks, Disney also offers several other attractions on its grounds with different themes and separate admissions (see Disney World above). The newest, **Blizzard Beach,** one of several water parks, was built on the premise of a melting mountain. Ride a ski-lift to the peak of Mount Gushmore and take the fastest waterslide in the world (Summit Plummet) down the 120-ft. descent. **Typhoon Lagoon,** a 50-acre water park, centers around the world's largest wave-making pool and the 7-ft. waves it creates. Besides eight water slides, the lagoon has a creek on which you can take a low-key inner-tube ride, an anomaly at Disney, and a saltwater coral reef stocked with tropical fish and harmless sharks. Built to resemble a swimming hole, **River Country** offers water slides, rope swings, and plenty of room to swim. Parks fill up early on hot days, so you might get turned away. Across Bay Lake from River Country is **Discovery Island,** a zoological park. Those seeking more (relatively) sinful excitations should head to **Pleasure Island** when the sun goes down. Disney attempts to draw students and the thirty-something set with this conglomeration of theme nightclubs—country, comedy, live rock, and jazz. Those over 18 roam freely; those under 18 can enter only if they stay with their guardians.

■ Other Attractions

Sea World One of the country's largest marine parks, **Sea World** (407-351-3600), 12 mi. southwest of Orlando off I-4 at Rte. 528 (take bus #8), makes a splash with shows featuring whales, dolphins, sea lions, seals, and otters; all in all, the attractions should take about six hours to see. Though the Seal and Otter Show and the Baywatch water-ski show are enjoyable, the killer whales Baby Shamu and Baby Namu get the big raves. **Shamu: World Focus** continues to thrill with plenty of marine acrobatics executed smartly by a whole family of orcas and their trainers. Crowds gravitate towards Shamu Stadium, so arrive early to get a seat. The arctic exhibit features white beluga whales—somewhat less athletic than Shamu, but fascinating nonetheless. Retreat indoors for the **Golden Dragon Acrobats,** a set of flipping, twirling performers whose show will appeal to young and old audiences alike. The smallest crowds come in February and from September to October. Most hotel brochure displays and hostels have coupons for $2-3 off regular admission. (Open daily 9am-10pm; in winter 9am-9pm. $40, ages 3-9 $39. Sky Tower ride $3 extra.) Those stunning Anheuser-Busch Clydesdales can be viewed for free—with price of admission. They don't do flips, though.

Cypress Gardens Cypress Gardens (941-324-2111) lies southwest of Orlando in Winter Haven; take I-4 southwest to Rte. 27S, then Rte. 540W. The botanical gardens feature over 8000 varieties of plants and flowers with winding walkways and electric boat rides for touring. The plants, flowers, and sculptured mini-gardens of "The Gardens of the World" depict the horticultural styles of many countries and periods. Despite all the pretty flowers, the daily water-ski shows attract the biggest crowds and the loudest applause (daily 10am, noon, 2, and 4pm; times and frequency vary with crowd size). Look for coupons at motels. (Open daily 9:30am-10pm; call ahead for exact hours. $28, ages 6-12 $18.) **Greyhound** stops here once a day on its Tampa-West Palm Beach run ($20 from Tampa to Cypress Gardens).

Universal Studios Florida Opened in 1990, Universal Studios (363-8000; take I-4 to Exit 29 or 30B), is both amusement park and working film studio. Rides take on movie themes: **Kongfrontation,** in which a 35-ft. King Kong roughhouses with your cable car; the **E.T. Adventure** bike ride; and **Back to the Future...The Ride,** which utilizes seven-story OmniMax surround screens and spectacular special effects. **Terminator 2: Battle Across Time** is the park's newest attraction. Using 3D computer graphics and the matchless acting talent of Arnold, this ride takes you on, well, a battle across time.

Since the park also makes films, celebrity sightings are common. The studio recently produced *Apollo 13, Schindler's List,* and *Jurassic Park* (look for a display of dinosaurs from the film). You may recognize a number of Universal's back-lot locations at the park—Hollywood, Central Park, Beverly Hills, and the infamous Bates Motel from *Psycho.* Nickelodeon TV programs are in continuous production. (Open Sun.-Fri. 9am-9pm, Sat. 9am-10pm. $38.50, ages 3-9 $31.)

▩ Cocoa Beach and Cape Canaveral

Known primarily for rocket launches, space shuttle blast-offs, and **NASA's** enormous space center complex, the "Space Coast" also has uncrowded golden beaches and vast wildlife preserves. Even during spring break, the place remains placid; most vacationers and sunbathers here are Florida or Space Coast residents.

The Cocoa Beach area, 50 mi. east of Orlando, consists of mainland towns Cocoa and Rockledge, oceanfront towns Cocoa Beach and Cape Canaveral, and Merritt Island in between. **Route A1A** runs through Cocoa Beach and Cape Canaveral, while **North Atlantic Ave.** parallels the beach. The **Cocoa Beach Chamber of Commerce,** 400 Fortenberry Rd. (459-2200; open Mon.-Fri 8:30am-5pm), on Merritt Island, and the **Brevard County Tourist Development Council** (455-1309 or 800-872-1969; open Mon.-Fri. 8:30am-5pm, Sat. 8:30am-noon), at Kennedy Space Center, provide area info. **Greyhound,** 302 Main St. (636-3917), services Cocoa, 8 mi. inland. **Space Coast Area Transit** (633-1878) runs North Beach and South Beach routes and makes stops at every town in Brevard Co. Door-to-door service available ($1; students, seniors, and disabled 50¢; transfers free). From the bus station, a **taxi** to Cocoa Beach costs $15-20 (call **Yellow Cab,** 636-7017). **The Cocoa Shuttle** (784-3831) connects Cocoa Beach with Orlando International Airport, Disney World ($75 roundtrip for 1 or 2), and the Kennedy Space Center ($45 roundtrip for 1 or 2). Make reservations three days in advance. **Area code:** 407.

Accommodations, Camping, and Food Across from the beach, the **Luna Sea,** 3185 N. Atlantic Ave. (783-0500 or 800-586-2732), has tastefully decorated rooms with refrigerators, A/C, pool access, and a large continental breakfast. (Singles start at $34, $42 Jan.-Mar.; $6 each additional person.) If you need a place to spend the night between bus connections, walk right behind the Greyhound station to the **Dixie Motel,** 301 Forrest Ave. (632-1600), 1 block east of U.S. 1, where there are big, clean rooms with tile floors, pastel decor, and A/C, plus a swimming pool. Look for the DeLorean in the parking lot. (Singles $30, doubles $35. Key deposit $10.) Pitch your tent at scenic **Jetty Park Campgrounds,** 400 E. Jetty Rd. (868-1108), right on the beach in Cape Canaveral. (Sites $14.50, with hookup $20.35. Reservations recommended before shuttle launches.) At **Herbie K's Diner,** 2080 N. Atlantic Ave. (783-6740), south of Motel 6, a shiny chrome reproduction of a 50s diner, enjoy gargantuan "atomic" burgers (in the lingo, "One Blown Up and Jacked" is a $3 cheeseburger) served with a tiny side of orange sorbet ("to keep you sweet"). Select a classic tune from the jukebox on your table, but be careful when you choose "Locomotion": waitresses with names like Teddy Bear might just start dancing (open Sun.-Thurs. 6am-10pm, Fri.-Sat. 24hr.).

Beam Me Up, Scotty All of NASA's shuttle flights take off from the **Kennedy Space Center,** 18 mi. north of Cocoa Beach. If you don't have a car, you can reach Kennedy via the **Cocoa Shuttle** (see above). The **Kennedy Space Center Visitors Center** (452-2121 for info) provides a huge welcoming center for visitors and two different two-hour bus tours of the complex. The **red tour** takes you around the space sites, while the **blue tour** visits Cape Canaveral Air Force Station. There are also three IMAX films projected on 5½-story screens: *The Blue Planet* addresses environmental issues, *The Dream is Alive* tells the story of human and robotic space exploration, and *Destiny in Space* is about—you guessed it—space. (Tours depart daily every 15min. 9:45am-6pm. $7, ages 3-11 $4. Movie tickets $4, ages 3-11 $2.) Buy tickets to tours and IMAX movies immediately upon arriving at the complex to avoid a long line; the center itself is free, as are movies at the Spaceport Theater. In December 1996, the center will debut the **Apollo/Saturn V Center,** a $35 million, 100,000-sq.-ft. interactive museum, dedicated exclusively to the Apollo missions. A fully restored 363-ft. Saturn V rocket will stand as the centerpiece. The **Rocket Garden** and the **Astronauts Memorial,** the newest national memorial in the country, also deserve a visit. (Open daily 9am-8:30pm; in winter 9am-6pm; in spring and fall 9am-7:30pm.) The **NASA Pkwy.,** site of the visitors center, is accessible only by car via State Rd. 405; from Cocoa Beach, take Rte. A1AN until it turns west into Rte. 528, then follow Rte. 3N to the Spaceport. With NASA's ambitious launch schedule, you may have a chance to watch the space shuttles *Endeavor, Columbia, Atlantis,* or *Discovery* thunder off into the blue yonder above the cape. In Florida, call 800-KSC-INFO/572-4636 for **launch info** or send your name and address to the Public Affairs Office, PA-PASS, Kennedy Space Center 32899, for a viewing pass.

Surrounding the NASA complex, the marshy **Merritt Island Wildlife Refuge** (861-0667) stirs with deer, sea turtles, alligators, and eagles. (Open daily sunrise-sunset. Visitors center open Mon.-Fri. 9am-4:30pm, Sat. 9am-5pm.) Just north of Merritt Island, **Canaveral National Seashore** (407-267-1110), encompasses 67,000 acres of undeveloped beach and dunes, home to more than 300 species of birds and mammals. (Take Rte. 406E off U.S. 1 in Titusville. Open daily 8:30am-sunset. Closed 3 days before and 1 day after NASA launches.)

■ Fort Lauderdale

Fort Lauderdale's gleaming white sands stretch 23 miles down Florida's east coast, but it is the water that dominates the city's landscape. Dubbed the "Venice of America," Fort L. supports an intricate intra-coastal waterway with over 165 miles of navigable waters. Numerous inlets cut streets in two, carrying luxury yachts and serving as an arena for countless water sports. If marine activities don't float your boat, the number two activity in ritzy Fort Lauderdale is shopping. Join the ranks at Sawgrass Mills, the world's largest outlet mall, or window shop on Los Olas Blvd.

PRACTICAL INFORMATION

Tourist Office: Greater Fort Lauderdale Convention and Visitors Bureau, 1850 Eller Dr. (765-4466), in the Sentinel Building. Friendly advice and pamphlets galore. For published info, call 800-222-SUNY/7869. The **Chamber of Commerce,** 512 NE 3rd Ave. (462-6000), 3 blocks off Federal Hwy. at 5th St. Pick up the free *Visitor's Guide.* Open Mon.-Fri. 8am-5pm.

Airport: Fort Lauderdale/Hollywood International, 1400 Lee Wagoner Blvd. (call 359-1200 for recorded ramblings; to speak to a human being, dial 359-6100), 3½mi. south of downtown on U.S. 1, at Exits 26 and 27 on I-95. Take Bus #1 from downtown.

Trains: Amtrak, 200 SW 21st Terrace (587-6692 or 800-872-7245), just west of I-95, ¼mi. south of Broward Blvd. Take bus #22 from downtown. To: Miami (2 per day, 45min., $7); Orlando (1 per day, 4hr., $48). Open daily 6:45am-6:45pm.

Buses: Greyhound, 515 NE 3rd St. (764-6551 or 800-231-2222), 3 blocks north of Broward Blvd. downtown. *Be careful in the surrounding area, especially at night.* To: Orlando (8 per day, 4½hr., $34); Daytona Beach (6 per day, 6hr., $45); Miami (12 per day, 1hr., $5). Open 24hr.

Public Transportation: Broward County Transit (BCT) (357-8400; Mon.-Fri. 7am-8:30pm, Sat. 7am-8pm, Sun. 8:30am-5pm). Most routes go to the terminal at the corner of 1st St. NW and 1st Ave. NW, downtown. Operates daily 6am-9pm, every ½hr. on most routes. $1; seniors, college students, under 18, and disabled 50¢ (with ID). 7-day passes ($8) available at beachfront hotels. Pick up a handy system map at the terminal. **Tri-Rail** (728-8445 or 800-872-7245) connects West Palm Beach, Fort Lauderdale, and Miami. Trains run Mon.-Fri. 5am-10pm, Sat. 5am-midnight, Sun. limited schedule. Schedules available at the airport, motels, or Tri-Rail stops. Fare $3-5 (depending on destination), discount for students and seniors with Tri-Rail-issued ID.

Taxis: Yellow Cab, 565-5400. Open 24hr. **Public Service Taxi**, 587-9090. Open daily 7:30am-6:30pm. Both charge $3.65 base fare, $1.40 per mi.

Car Rental: Alamo, 2601 S. Federal Hwy. (525-4713 or 800-327-9633). $27.90 per day, $81 per week with unlimited mileage. Free drop-off in Daytona and Miami; shuttle to airport $3. Must be 21 with credit card deposit of $50 per day or $200 per week. Under 25 surcharge $20 per day.

Bike Rental: Mike's Cyclery, 5429 N. Federal Hwy. (493-5277). A variety of bicycles $20 per day, $50 per week. Some racing bikes cost slightly more. Credit card deposit required; amount varies according to bike. Open Mon.-Fri. 10am-7pm, Sat. 10am-5pm.

Crisis Lines: Crisis Hotline, 746-2756. **Rape Crisis**, 761-RAPE/7273.

Emergency: 911.

Post office: 1900 W. Oakland Park Blvd. (527-2028). Open Mon.-Fri. 7:30am-7pm, Sat. 8:30am-2pm. **ZIP code:** 33310. **Area code:** 954.

North-south **I-95** connects West Palm Beach, Fort Lauderdale, and Miami. **Rte. 84/I-75** (Alligator Alley) slithers 100 mi. west from Fort Lauderdale across the Everglades to Naples and other small cities on the Gulf Coast of Southern Florida. Fort Lauderdale is bigger than it looks—and it looks huge. The city extends westward from its 23 mi. of beach to encompass nearly 450 sq. mi. of land area. Roads come in two categories: streets and boulevards (east-west) and avenues (north-south). All are labeled NW, NE, SW, or SE according to their quadrant. **Broward Blvd.** divides the city east-west, **Andrews Ave.** cuts north-south. The unpleasant downtown centers around the intersection of **Federal Hwy. (U.S. 1)** and **Las Olas Blvd.**, about 2 mi. west of the oceanfront. Between downtown and the waterfront, yachts fill the ritzy inlets of the **Intracoastal Waterway. The strip** (variously called Rte. A1A, N. Atlantic Blvd., 17th St. Causeway, Ocean Blvd., and Seabreeze Blvd.) runs along the beach for 4 mi. between **Oakland Park Blvd.** to the north and Las Olas Blvd. to the south. Las Olas Blvd. has pricey shopping. **Sunrise Blvd.** offers shopping malls. Both degenerate into ugly commercial strips west of downtown.

ACCOMMODATIONS AND CAMPING

Hotel prices vary from slightly unreasonable to absolutely ridiculous, increasing exponentially as you approach prime beachfront and spring break. High season runs from mid-February to early April. Investigate package deals at the slightly worse-for-wear hotels along the strip in Fort Lauderdale. Many hotels offer off-season deals for under $35. Small motels, many with tiny kitchenettes, crowd each other 1 or 2 blocks off

THE SOUTH

the beach area; look along **Birch Rd.,** 1 block from Rte. A1A. The **Broward County Hotel and Motel Association,** 2701 E. Sunrise Blvd. (561-9333), provides a free directory of area hotels (open Mon.-Fri. 9am-5pm). Scan the *Fort Lauderdale News* and the Broward Section of the *Miami Herald* for occasional listings by local residents who rent rooms to tourists in spring. Sleeping on the well-patrolled beaches is illegal and virtually impossible between 9pm and sunrise.

International House, 3811 N. Ocean Blvd. (568-1615), one block from the beach. Take bus #10 to Coral Ridge Mall, then pick up bus #72 east, which stops at the hostel. Rooms with 4-6 beds, showers, A/C, cable TV, kitchen, and pool. Dive trips offered for guests with SCUBA certification ($35-70). Get your SCUBA certification for $135. Passport required. 96 beds. $15. Private rooms $33. Linen $2. Key deposit $5.

Floyd's Hostel/Crew House, (462-0631); call ahead for address. A home-like hostel catering to international travelers and boat crews. 40 beds, 5 kitchens, 5 living rooms, 8 bathrooms. Tranquil, international atmosphere. HBO and Showtime on living room TVs. Free daytime pickup from anywhere in the Ft. Lauderdale area. Free rice, tea, oatmeal, cereal, local calls, linens, and laundry. Check in by midnight or call for special arrangement. Passport required. Management has info on short-term employment opportunities in the area. The owners are engaged thanks to *Let's Go: USA 1995* (ask them for details). Beds $11, private rooms $30.

Estoril Apartments, 2648 NE 32nd St. (563-3840). From downtown, take bus #20, 10, 55, or 72 to Coral Ridge Shopping Center and walk 2 blocks east on Oakland; a 10-min. walk to the beach. Students can probably persuade the proprietors to pick them up from the bus station or airport. Very clean rooms with A/C, TV, and small kitchenette in some rooms. Pool and barbecue. Office closes 11pm. Singles $29, $6 per additional person; students and seniors $26. Dec. 15.-April 15 $34, $6 per additional person. 10% discount for *Let's Go* users and AAA members. Reservations recommended.

Quiet Waters County Park, 6601 N. Powerline Rd. (a.k.a. SW 9th Ave. in Pompano Beach) (360-1315), 10mi. north of Oakland Park Blvd. off I-95's Exit 37B. Take Hillsboro Blvd. west to Powerline Rd. From downtown, take bus #14. Fully equipped campsites (tent, mattresses, cooler, grill) for up to 6 people, all by the lake ("don't feed the gators!"). Normal water sports and see-it-to-believe-it 8-person "boatless water skiing" at the end of a cable. No electricity. No RVs. Check-in 2-6pm. Sites $17, Fri.-Sat. $25. $20 refundable deposit.

FOOD

The clubs along the strip offer massive quantities of free grub during happy hour: surfboard-sized platters of wieners, chips, and hors d'oeuvres, or all-you-can-eat pizza and buffets. However, these bars have hefty cover charges (from $5) and expect you to buy a drink once you're there (from $2). The quality of the cuisine serves as a reminder of the difference between a restaurant and a bar. For "real" food, try **La Spada's,** 4346 Seagrape Dr. (776-7893)—best and biggest subs in southern Florida. The foot-long Italian sub ($6.50) is an absolute must. (Open Mon.-Sat. 10am-8pm, Sun. 11am-8pm.) Popular with locals since 1951, **Tina's Spaghetti House,** 2110 S. Federal Hwy. (522-9943), just south of 17th St. (take bus #1 from downtown), has authentic red-checked tablecloths, hefty oak furniture, and bibs. Lunch specials run $4-5, while a spaghetti dinner costs $6-7. (Open Mon.-Fri. 11:30am-10pm, Sat.-Sun. 4-10pm.) In an aggressively marine decor, **Southport Raw Bar,** 1536 Cordova Rd. (525-2526), by the 17th St. causeway behind the Southport Mall (take bus #40 from the strip or #30 from downtown), serves spicy conch chowder ($2.50) and fried shrimp ($7). Try the tasty custom sandwiches. (Open Mon.-Fri. 11am-2am, Sat. 11am-3am, Sun. noon-2am.)

SIN, SIGHTS, AND ACTIVITIES

Fort Lauderdale offers all kinds of licit and illicit entertainment. Planes flying over the beach hawk hedonistic happy hours at local watering holes. Students frequent the night spots on the A1A strip along the beach—emphasis on "strip." Remember: you are dealing with the "A1A: Beachfront Avenue" of "Ice, Ice, Baby" fame. This area has the class and sophistication of, well, Vanilla Ice. When going out, bring a driver's license or a passport as proof of age; most bars and nightclubs won't accept college IDs. Be warned that this is *not* the place for cappuccino and conversation; expect nude jello wrestling and similarly lubricated entertainment.

For those who prefer garbed service, several popular nightspots line N. Atlantic Blvd. next to the beach. Hit **Banana Joe's on the Beach,** 837 N. Atlantic Blvd. (565-4446), at Sunrise and Rte. A1A, a tiny little bar directly on the beach, for happy hour Monday through Friday from 5 to 8pm. (Open Mon.-Sat. 7am-2am, Sun. noon-2am. Kitchen open 11:30am-7pm.) **Mombasa Bay,** 3051 NE 32nd Ave. (565-7441), on the Intracoastal Waterway, charges no cover but requires that everyone be 21 when there's live music. (Happy hour daily 4-7pm. Open 11:30am-2am weekdays, until 3am weekends. Reggae every night from 9:30pm.)

For daytime entertainment, take a tour of Fort Lauderdale's waterways aboard the **Jungle Queen,** located at the **Bahia Mar Yacht Center** (462-5596), on Rte. A1A 3 blocks south of Las Olas Blvd. Three-hr. tours leave daily at 10am, 2 ($10.55, ages 2-12 $7.40), and 7pm ($24.30, kids $11.65, dinner included). The **Water Taxi,** 651 Seabreeze Blvd. (467-6677), offers a different way to get around town and a fun place to dine in style. (One-way $7, under 12 $3.50. All-day service $15. Call ½hr. before pickup. Open daily 10am-midnight.) **Water Sports Unlimited,** 301 Seabreeze Blvd. (467-1316), on the beach, rents equipment for a variety of water sports including wave runners. ($35 per ½hr. on intercoastal highway, $50 per hr.; on ocean $45/$60.) Parasailing trips are $50 (500ft., 8min. duration) and a little more if you want them to "dip your feet in the water." Landlubbers can get closer to nature with a visit to **Butterfly World,** 3400 W. Sample Rd. (977-4400), just west of the Florida Turnpike in Coconut Creek, 3 acres of tropical gardens with thousands of live butterflies (open Mon.-Sat. 9am-5pm, Sun. 1-5pm; $10, ages 4-12 $5).

■ Miami

Long a hotspot for stars and a popular setting for TV shows and movies, Miami's Latin heart pulses to the beat of the largest Cuban population outside of Cuba. Only 7½ sq. mi., Miami Beach has an unbelievable number of hotels, which can accommodate three times the city's usual population. Tourists lie and fry by day, then dance the night away. Many small cultural communities distinguish Miami's residential areas: Little Havana, a well-established Cuban community; Coconut Grove, an eclectic enclave of wealthy intellectuals; placid, well-to-do Coral Gables; and the African-American communities of Liberty City and Overtown. Wherever you find yourself in Miami, a knowledge of Spanish is always helpful, sometimes necessary.

PRACTICAL INFORMATION

Tourist Office: A tourist **information booth,** 401 Biscayne Blvd. (539-2980), outside of Bayside Marketplace, downtown, has free maps and advice. Open daily 10am-6:30pm. **Coconut Grove Chamber of Commerce,** 2820 McFarlane Ave. (444-7270), has mountains of maps and advice. Open Mon.-Fri. 9am-5pm. **Greater Miami Convention and Visitors Bureau,** 701 Brickell Ave. (539-3000 or 800-283-2707 outside Miami), 27th fl. of the Barnett Bank bldg. downtown. Open Mon.-Fri. 7:30am-5:30pm. **Gay Community Hotline,** 759-3661.

Airport: Miami International (876-7000), at Le Jeune Rd. and NW 36th Ave., 7mi. northwest of downtown. Bus #7 runs downtown; many other buses make downtown stops. From downtown, take bus C or K to South Miami Beach. The airport's **information booth** doles out city and transportation maps.

Trains: Amtrak, 8303 NW 37th Ave. (835-1222 or 800-872-7245), not far from the Northside station of Metrorail. Bus L goes directly to Lincoln Rd. Mall in South Miami Beach. To: Orlando (2 per day, 5hr., $60); New Orleans (3 per week, 11hr., $200); Charleston (1 per day, 12hr., $150). Station open daily 6:15am-7:15pm.

Buses: Greyhound, Miami Station, 4111 NW 27th St. (871-1810 or 800-231-2222). To: Atlanta (6 per day, 16hr., $69); Orlando (8 per day, 6hr., $33); Fort Lauderdale (22 per day, 1hr., $4). Station open 24hr. A cheaper service to Key West and Orlando departs from the main HI youth hostel; call 534-2988 for more info.

Public Transportation: Metro Dade Transportation (638-6700; 6am-11pm for info). Complex system; buses often late. The extensive **Metrobus** network converges downtown, where most long trips transfer. Lettered bus routes A through X serve Miami Beach. After dark, some stops are patrolled by police (indicated with a sign). Buses run daily 4:30am-2am. $1.25; transfers 25¢, to Metrorail 50¢. The futuristic **Metrorail** services downtown. $1.25, rail to bus transfers 50¢. The **Metromover** loop downtown, which runs 6am-midnight, is linked to the Metrorail stations. 25¢, free transfers from Metrorail. **Tri-Rail** (800-872-7245) connects Miami, Ft. Lauderdale, and West Palm Beach. Trains run Mon.-Sat. 5am-9:30pm. Fare $3, daily $5, weekly $18; students and seniors 50% off.

Taxis: Yellow, 444-4444. **Metro,** 888-8888. Both $1.10 base fare and $1.75 per mi.

Bike Rental: Miami Beach Bicycle Center, 923 W. 39th St. (531-4161), Miami Beach. $5 for 1hr., $3 per additional hr.; $14 per day; $50 per week. Must be 18 with credit card or $100 deposit. Open Mon.-Sat. 9:30am-6pm.

Crisis Lines: Crisis Hotline, 358-4357. **Rape Treatment Center and Hotline,** 1611 NW 12th Ave. (585-7273). Both 24hr.

Emergency: 911.

Post Office: 500 NW 2nd Ave. (371-2911). Open Mon.-Fri. 8:30am-5pm, Sat. 9:30am-1:30pm. **ZIP code:** 33101. **Area code:** 305.

ORIENTATION

Three highways criss-cross the Miami area. **I-95,** the most direct route north-south, hits **U.S. I (Dixie Hwy.)** just south of **downtown.** U.S. 1 runs to the Everglades entrance at Florida City and then continues as the Overseas Hwy. to Key West. **Rte. 836,** a major east-west artery through town, connects I-95 to **Florida's Turnpike,** passing the airport in between. If you're headed to Florida City, take Rte. 36 and the Turnpike to avoid the traffic on Rte. 1.

Several causeways connect Miami to **Miami Beach.** The most useful is **MacArthur Causeway,** which becomes 5th St. in Miami Beach. Numbered streets run east-west across the island, increasing towards the north. The main north-south drag is **Collins Ave.** (or A1A). In South Miami Beach, north-south **Washington Ave.,** one block west of Collins, is the main commercial strip, while **Ocean Ave.,** on the waterfront, lies one block east. To reach **Key Biscayne,** take the **Rickenbacker Causeway** (toll).

When looking for street addresses, pay careful attention to the systematic street layout; it's *very* easy to confuse North Miami Beach, West Miami, North Miami Beach, and Miami addresses. Streets in Miami run east-west, avenues north-south; both are numbered. Miami divides into NE, NW, SE, and SW sections; the dividing lines (downtown) are **Flagler St.** (east-west) and **Miami Ave.** (north-south). Some numbered streets and avenues also have names—e.g., Le Jeune Rd. is SW 42nd Ave., and SW 40th St. is Bird Rd. Minimize headaches with a map that lists both numbers and names. **Little Havana** lies between SW 12th and SW 27th Ave; take bus #3, 11, 14, 15, 17, 25, or 37. The **Calle Ocho** (SW 8th St.) lies at the heart of this district; one block north, the corresponding section of **W. Flagler St.** is a center of Cuban business. A **car** can be an expensive liability in Miami. Carefully note the posted signs that indicate different parking zones; leave your car in a residential zone for even a few moments and you may return to find it towed. Never leave any remotely valuable objects visible in your parked car; automobile theft and break-ins are all too common here. Just ask Crockett and Tubbs.

ACCOMMODATIONS AND CAMPING

Cheap rooms abound in South Miami Beach's Art Deco hotels. For safety, convenience, and security, stay north of 5th St. Finding a "pullmanette" (in 1940s lingo), a room with a refrigerator, stove, and sink, and buying groceries will save you money.

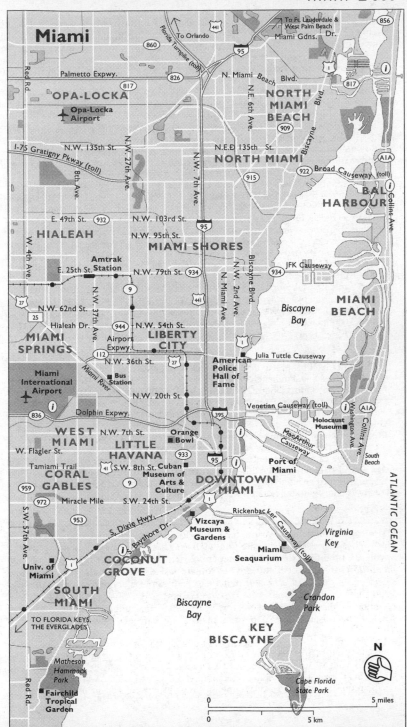

Miami

To Orlando

Florida Turnpike (toll)

To Ft. Lauderdale &
West Palm Beach

Miami Gdns. Dr.

Palmetto Expwy.

OPA-LOCKA

Opa-Locka
Airport

N. Miami Beach Blvd.

NORTH
MIAMI
BEACH

BAL
HARBOUR

I-75 Gratigny Pkway (toll)

N.W. 135th St.

N.E. 135th St.

NORTH MIAMI

Broad Causeway (toll)

E. 49th St.

N.W. 103rd St.

HIALEAH

N.W. 95th St.

MIAMI SHORES

JFK Causeway

MIAMI
BEACH

Amtrak
Station

E. 25th St.

N.W. 79th St.

Biscayne
Bay

N.W. 62nd St.

Hialeah Dr.

N.W. 54th St.

LIBERTY
CITY

MIAMI
SPRINGS

Airport
Expwy.

N.W. 36th St.

American
Police
Hall of
Fame

Julia Tuttle Causeway

Miami
International
Airport

Bus
Station

N.W. 20th St.

Venetian Causeway (toll)

Holocaust
Museum

Dolphin Expwy.

WEST
MIAMI

N.W. 7th St.

LITTLE
HAVANA

Orange
Bowl

MacArthur
Causeway

South
Beach

W. Flagler St.

S.W. 8th St.

Cuban
Museum of
Arts &
Culture

Port of
Miami

Tamiami Trail

CORAL
GABLES

DOWNTOWN
MIAMI

Miracle Mile

S.W. 24th St.

S. Dixie Hwy.

Rickenbacker Causeway (toll)

Virginia
Key

Vizcaya
Museum &
Gardens

Univ. of
Miami

S. Bayshore Dr.

COCONUT
GROVE

Miami
Seaquarium

SOUTH
MIAMI

Crandon
Park

TO FLORIDA KEYS,
THE EVERGLADES

Biscayne
Bay

KEY
BISCAYNE

ATLANTIC OCEAN

Matheson
Hammock
Park

N

Fairchild
Tropical
Garden

Cape Florida
State Park

0   5 miles

0   5 km

In South Florida, many inexpensive hotels are likely to have two- to three-inch cockroaches ("palmetto bugs"), so try not to take them as absolute indicators of quality. In general, high season for Miami Beach runs late December to mid-March; during the off season, when rooms are empty, hotel clerks are quick to bargain. The **Miami Beach Resort Hotel Association,** 407 Lincoln Rd. #10G (531-3553), can help you find a place to crash (open Mon.-Fri. 9am-4:30pm).

Camping is not allowed in Miami Beach. Those who can't bear to put their tents aside for a night or two should head to one of the nearby national parks.

The Clay Hotel and International Hostel (HI-AYH), 1438 Washington Ave. (534-2988), is in the heart of the Art Deco district, near nightlife; take bus C from downtown. Explore the halls and archways of this Mediterranean-style building. International crowd. Kitchen, laundry facilities, TV room, A/C, and a ride board. 180 beds; most rooms have 4. Two rooms share a bathroom. Open 24hr. No curfew. $12, nonmembers $13. Private rooms $28-50. Key deposit $5.

Miami Beach International Travelers Hostel (9th Street Hostel) (AAIH/Rucksackers), 236 9th St. (534-0268), at Washington Ave; from the airport, take bus J to 41st and Indian Creek, then transfer to bus C. Central location. Lively international atmosphere near the beach. Kitchen, laundry, common room with TV (4 movie nights a week). 29 clean, comfortable rooms (max. 4 people), all with A/C and bath. No curfew. Hostel rooms $12 with any hosteling membership or student ID; otherwise $14. Private singles or doubles $31. Must have either international passport, student ID, ISIC, or HI card.

The Tropics Hotel/Hostel, 1550 Collins Ave. (531-0361; fax 531-8676), across the street from the beach. From the airport, take bus J to 41st St., transfer to bus C to Lincoln Rd. and walk one block south on Collins Ave. Free on-site parking. Clean hostel rooms with 4 beds, A/C, private baths, phone, pool access, and free linens. No curfew. $14. Private rooms have A/C, cable TV, and free local calls. Singles $36, doubles $40.

Sea Deck Hotel and Apartments, 1530 Collins Ave. (538-4361). Cozy and clean pullmanettes with pretty floral bedspreads open onto a lush tropical courtyard. Pullmanettes $39, efficiencies $49.

Miami Airways Motel, 5001 NW 36th St. (883-4700 or 800-824-9910), near the airport but far from the action; take I-95 to Rte. 112W, which runs into 36th St. Free airport pickup. Clean, small rooms with breakfast, A/C, pool, HBO. Singles $36, doubles $42.

Larry & Penny Thompson Memorial Campground, 12451 SW 184th St. (232-1049). By car, drive 25min. south along Dixie Hwy. Pretty grounds with 240 sites in a grove of mango trees. Laundry, store, artificial lake with swimming beach, beautiful park, and waterslides. Lake open Memorial Day-Labor Day daily 10am-5pm; for further info, call 255-8251. Office open daily 9am-5:30pm but takes late arrivals. Sites with full hookup $17, weekly $90.

FOOD

If you eat nothing else in Miami, try Cuban food. Specialties include *media noche* sandwiches (a sort of Cuban club sandwich on a soft roll, heated and compressed); *mamey,* a bright red ice cream concoction; rich *frijoles negros* (black beans); and *picadillo* (shredded beef and peas in tomato sauce, served with white rice). For sweets, seek out a *dulcería,* and punctuate your rambles about town with thimble-sized shots of strong, sweet *café cubano* (around 25¢). Cheap restaurants are not common in Miami Beach, but an array of fresh bakeries and fruit stands can sustain you with melons, mangoes, papayas, tomatoes, and carrots for under $3 a day.

The Versailles, 3555 SW 8th St. (444-0240). Massive dining room, seemingly packed with Little Havana's entire population. Good Cuban fare. Breakfast $2-4, lunch from $2.50; entrees about $10. Open daily 8am-2am.

11th St. Diner, 1065 Washington Ave. (534-6373), at 11th St. A vintage diner with the requisite trimmings: soda fountain, straw dispensers, and an ancient Coca-Cola clock. Serves breakfast at all hours ($2-4), all sorts of sandwiches ($2.50-6), and grill items. Open daily 24hr.

King's Ice Cream, 1831 SW 8th St., a.k.a. Calle Ocho (643-1842). Tropical fruit *helado* (ice cream) flavors include coconut (served in its own shell), *mamey,* and mango ($2). Also try *churros* (thin Spanish donuts, 10 for $1), or *café cubano* (10¢). Open Mon.-Sat. 10am-11:30pm, Sun. 1-11:30pm.

Flamingo Restaurant, 1454 Washington Ave. (673-4302), near the Clay hostel. Friendly service, all in Spanish. Peck at the grilled chicken with pinto beans and rice ($5.50) or the *tostones con queso* ($2.75). Open Mon.-Sat. 7am-9:30pm.

La Rumba, 2008 Collins Ave. (534-0522), between 20th and 21st St. in Miami Beach. Noisy fun and huge portions of tasty Cuban and Spanish food. Try their *arroz con pollo* (chicken with yellow rice, $7.50). Open daily 7:30am-midnight.

Lulu's, 1053 Washington Ave. (532-6147), 1½ blocks from the 9th St. Hostel. $10 gets you tremendous portions of Southern cookin' with cornbread and two sides ("mess o' greens," for example). Live music Fri.-Sat. nights in the upstairs "Elvis room." Open Mon.-Thurs. 11am-midnight, Fri.-Sat. 11am-2am.

SIGHTS

South Miami Beach (or just South Beach), between 6th and 23rd St., teems with hundreds of hotels and apartments whose sun-faded pastel façades conform to 1920s ideals of a tropical paradise. An unusual mixture of people populates the area, including many retirees and first-generation Latins. **Walking tours** of the historic district start at the Oceanfront Auditorium, 1001 Ocean Dr. at 10th St. (Thurs. 6:30pm, Sat. 10:30am; $6); **bike tours** leave from the Miami Beach Bicycle Center at 601 5th St. (1st and 3rd Sun. of each month; $5, rental $5 extra). Call 672-2014 for info.

On the waterfront downtown, Miami's sleek **Bayside** shopping complex bursts with expensive shops, exotic food booths, and live reggae or salsa on Friday and Saturday nights. Near Bayside, visit the **American Police Hall of Fame and Museum,** 3801 Biscayne Blvd. (573-0070), and learn more than you ever wanted to know about the police; exhibits feature execution equipment, "specialty" cars, and jail cell replicas (open daily 10am-5:30pm; $6, seniors and ages 6-11 $3).

In **Little Havana,** the exhibits at the **Cuban Museum of Arts and Culture,** 1300 SW 12th Ave. (858-8006), reflect the bright colors and rhythms of Cuban art; take bus #27 (open Wed.-Sun. 10am-3pm; donation required). At **La Gloria Cubana,** 1106 SW 8th St. (858-4162), the art of Cuban cigar manufacturing lives on. (Open Mon.-Fri. 8am-6pm, Sat. 9am-4pm. Free.) In early March, **Carnaval Miami,** the largest Hispanic festival in the U.S., fills 23 blocks of Calle Ocho with salsa, music, and the world's longest conga line.

On the bayfront between the Grove and downtown stands the **Vizcaya Museum and Gardens,** 3251 S. Miami Ave. (250-9133); take bus #1 or the Metrorail to Vizcaya. Behold the array of European antiques within this 70-room Italianate mansion, surrounded by 10 acres of lush gardens. (Open daily 9:30am-5pm; last entry 4:30pm. $10, ages 6-12 $5.) The largest tropical botanical garden in the world, the **Fairchild Tropic Garden,** 10901 Old Cutler Rd., (667-1651), **Coral Gables,** covers 83 acres and features winding paths, a rain forest, a sunken garden, and a narrated train tour (open daily 9:30am-4:30pm; $8, under 13 free).

The new **Holocaust Memorial,** 1933-45 Meridian Ave. (538-1663), Miami Beach, recalls the six million Jews who perished during the Holocaust, through sculpture and historical displays (open daily 9am-9pm; free).

ENTERTAINMENT AND NIGHTLIFE

For the latest word on Miami entertainment, check the *Miami-South Florida Magazine;* the "Living Today," "Lively Arts," and Friday "Weekend" sections of the *Miami Herald;* or the *Miami New Times,* which comes out every Wednesday and can be found for free on street corners. **Performing Arts and Community Education (PACE)** manages more than 400 concerts each year (jazz, rock, soul, dixieland, reggae, *salsa,* and bluegrass), most of which are free.

THE SOUTH

Nightlife in the Art Deco district of South Miami Beach follows the Latin rhythms of the area—the party starts *late* (usually after midnight) and continues until well after sunrise. Gawk at models and stars while eating dinner at one of Ocean Blvd.'s open cafés and bars, then head down to Washington Ave. between 6th and 7th St. for some serious fun. Remember to put on your dancing shoes—these clubs have dress codes, and everyone dresses to the nines. The coolest of the cool, **Bash,** 655 Washington Ave. (538-2274), stands out among its neighbors; the large indoor dance floor grooves to dance music while the courtyard in back jams to the ocean beat of reggae (cover $10, Sun. free; open Tues.-Sun. 10pm-5am).

Those with dance fever can boogie on Sunday nights to 70s and 80s music on the huge multi-level dance floor of the **Cameo Theater,** 1445 Washington Ave. (532-0922 for showtimes and prices), at Española Way. The theater also rocks with national acts from Peter Frampton to the Beastie Boys. (Cover $5-10. Open Fri.-Sun. 11pm-5am.) Arrive before midnight to dodge the cover and long line at the **Groove Jet,** 323 23rd St. (532-2002). The front room of this massive dance hall plays popular dance tracks while the back room mellows out with blues and funk. (21+, Sun. women 18+. Cover midnight-2am $7, after 2am $10. Open Thurs.-Sun., sometimes Wed., 11pm-5am.) For gay nightlife, check out **Warsaw Ballroom,** 1450 Collins Ave. (531-4555), Miami Beach, where frequent theme nights (e.g., bubble bath night) liven up the two dance floors (Wed., Fri.-Sun. 9pm-5am; rarely a cover).

EVERGLADES REGION AND FLORIDA KEYS

■ Everglades

Encompassing the entire tip of Florida and spearing into Florida Bay, **Everglades National Park,** the next largest national park after Yellowstone, spans 1.6 million acres of one of the most beautiful and fragile ecosystems in the world. Vast prairies of sawgrass spike through broad expanses of shallow water, creating the famed "river of grass," while tangled mazes of mangrove swamps wind up the western coast. To the south, delicate coral reefs lie below the shimmering blue waters of the bay. A host of species found nowhere else in the world inhabits these lands and waters: American alligators, sea turtles, and various birds and fishes, as well as the endangered Florida panther, Florida manatee, and American crocodile.

Practical Information If you visit in the summertime, expect to get eaten alive by swarming mosquitoes. Visit the park in winter or spring, when heat, humidity, storms, and bugs are at a minimum and when wildlife congregates in shrinking pools of evaporating water. Whenever you go, be sure to bring mosquito repellent. There are three primary roads into the park, each of which is self-contained and separate from the others. Guarding the eastern section, the main **visitors center,** 40001 Rte. 9336 (305-242-7700), lies on **Rte. 9336** just inside the park. (Open daily 8am-5pm.) Rte. 9336 is the continuation of **Card Sound Rd.,** which runs west after crossing U.S. 1 at **Florida City;** watch for Everglades Park signs. Rte. 9336 cuts 40 mi. through the park past campgrounds, trailheads, and canoe waterways to the heavily developed **Flamingo** outpost resort. At the northern end of the park off U.S. 41 (Tamiami Trail), the **Shark Valley Visitors Center** provides access to a 15-mi. loop that can be seen by foot, bike, or a two-hr. tram. (Tram tours Christmas-April daily every hr. 9am-4pm; in summer 9:30, 11am, 1, and 3pm. $8, seniors $7.20, under 12 $4. Reservations recommended; call 305-221-8455.) The **Gulf Coast Visitors Center** (941-695-2591 or 800-445-7724), near Everglades City in the northwestern end of the park, provides access to the 99-mi. Wilderness Waterway, which winds down to Flamingo. **Park headquarters** (305-247-7272) handles **emergencies.** The park **entrance fee** is $5 per car, good for 7 days; the Shark Valley fee is $4 per car, $2 bike- or walk-in.

Accommodations Outside the eastern entrance to the park, Homestead and Florida City offer some cheap options along Rte. 997. In Flamingo, **Flamingo Lodge** (305-253-2241) offers large rooms with A/C, TV, private baths, pool, and a great bay view (singles and doubles $65, Nov.-Dec. and April $82, Jan.-March $96). A few first come, first served **campgrounds** line Rte. 9336; all have drinking water, grills, dump sites, and restrooms, but none have RV hookups (sites free in summer, in winter $10). **Backcountry camping** is accessible by foot or bike, but primarily by boat; most sites are on chickees (wooden platforms elevated above mangrove swamps). The required permits are available at the Flamingo and Everglades City ranger stations. Park campgrounds fill rapidly from December to April, so get there early.

Near the northwestern entrance, motels, RV parks, and campgrounds scatter around Everglades City. The **Barron River Villa, Marina, and RV Park** (941-695-3591) is an excellent deal, with 67 RV sites, 29 on the river (full hookup $16, on river $18; Oct.-April $22/$27), and precious motel rooms with TV and A/C (single or double $37, Dec. 15-April 30 $47). Another campsite rests beside **The Seas Store and Deli** and is owned by the proprietors (941-695-2746). Overlooking Chokoloskee Bay near the Gulf Coast Ranger Station are 54 sites with shower facilities, full hookups, cable hookups, marina, and dock (tent sites $15, RV $20).

Sights The park is positively swamped in fishing, hiking, canoeing, biking, and wilderness observation opportunities. Avoid swimming; hungry alligators, sharks, and barracuda patrol the waters. From November to April, the park sponsors amphitheater programs, canoe trips, and ranger-guided Swamp Tromps. Numerous trailheads lie off Rte. 9336; the ½-mi. **Mahogany Hammock Trail** passes the largest mahogany tree in the U.S., and the ¼-mi. **Pahayokee Overlook Trail** leads to a broad vista of grasslands and water. If you really want to experience the Everglades, though, start paddling. **Canoe trails** wind from Rte. 9336; the **Nine Mile Pond** canoe loop passes through alligator ponds and mazes of mangrove trees (allow 3-4 hr.), while the **Hell's Bay Canoe Trail** threads through mangrove swamps past primitive campsites like **Lard Can.** Rent a canoe at the **Flamingo Marina** (941-695-3101 or 800-600-3813; $8 per hr., $22 per ½-day, $27 per day; $40 deposit) or **Gulf Coast Visitors Center,** also the departure point for 1½-hr. wittily narrated boat tours often featuring **manatee** and **bottle-nosed dolphin** sightings (open daily 8:30am-5pm; $11.50, ages 6-12 $5.50). The 1½-hr. **Sunset Cruise** sails into Florida Bay ($9, ages 6-12 $4.50), while the **Back County Cruise** explores the thick mangrove forests of the southern Everglades ($14, ages 6-12 $6). Both leave from Flamingo Marina; call ahead for schedule.

■ Near Everglades: Big Cypress

Covering over 2400 sq. mi. of southwestern Florida, a third of which is patched with stands of cypress trees, **Big Cypress National Preserve** provides the freshwater supply crucial to the Everglades's survival. During the summer, deluges flood the reserve; this water slowly drains south through Everglades National Park into the Gulf of Mexico due to the land's average downward slope of two inches per mi.

U.S. 41 (Tamiami Trail) slices through the preserve. The **Loop Road Scenic Dr.** is a 26-mi. detour from U.S. 41 through the eastern half of the park; autos can pass year-round, but watch for potholes. Several **free, primitive campgrounds** dot the park. **Monument Lake** is picnic-area-happy, while **Dona Drive** is *the* place for potable water; both lie along U.S. 41. So does **Burns Lake,** with good fishing and abundant wildlife. Self-pampering campers will appreciate **Trail Lakes Campground** (941-695-2275), on U.S. 41 at the western end of the park in Ochopee, the only one in the preserve with electricity, water, a bathhouse, and laundry facilities (tent sites $10, hookup $12). For accommodations just outside the preserve or other nearby sights, check with the **Everglades City Chamber of Commerce** (941-695-3941).

■ Florida Keys

Intense popularity has transformed this long-time haven for pirates, smugglers, trea-sure hunters, and others deemed outside the moral order into supreme beach vaca-tionland. Whether smothered in tourists or outcasts, the Keys retain an "anything goes" mentality. When former Key West mayor Tony Tarracino arrived here decades ago, he did a quick inventory of bars and strip clubs, and concluded that he had reached heaven. (See graybox, p. 345.) If this sounds more like hell, just take a dive. Millions of colorful fish flash through gardens of coral 6 mi. off the coast, granting rel-ative solitude to scuba divers and snorkelers, and forming a 100-yd.-wide barrier reef between Keys Largo and West. Don't believe the hype; sharks are few here.

The **Overseas Highway (U.S. 1)** bridges the divide between the Keys and the southern tip of Florida, stitching the islands together. **Mile markers** section the high-way and replace street addresses. The first marker, Mile 126 in Florida City, begins the countdown to zero. **Greyhound** runs buses to the Keys from Miami ($27), stop-ping in Perrine (flag down the bus from U.S. 1), Homestead (247-2040), Key Largo (451-2908), Marathon (743-3488), Big Pine Key (872-4022), and Key West (296-9072). If you need to get off at a particular mile marker, most bus drivers can be con-vinced to stop at the side of the road. Watch for tiny Greyhound signs along the high-way; these indicate bus stops (usually hotels), where you can buy tickets or call the Greyhound **info line** on the red phones provided. Biking along U.S. 1 across the swamps between Florida City and Key Largo is treacherous due to fast cars and nar-row shoulders; instead of riding, bring your bike on the bus.

■ Key Largo

Baby why don't we go... Past the thick swamps and crocodile marshland of the Ever-glades, Key Largo opens the door to these Caribbean-esque islands. Dubbed "long island" by Spanish explorers, this 30-mi. island is the largest of the Florida Keys, but the carless shouldn't worry; everything important lies within a 6-mi. range. With 120-ft. visibility, the gin-clear waters off Key Largo are one of its biggest attractions. Twenty ft. down, an underwater statue of Jesus (meant to symbolize peace for man-kind) blesses all those who explore these depths. Fishing, swimming, and glass-bot-tom boats offer recreation without total submersion.

Practical Information The **Key Largo Chamber of Commerce/Florida Keys Welcome Center,** Mile 106 (451-1414), is stuffed with info; look for a large turquoise awning at 106 Plaza (open daily 9am-6pm). The dramatic mailroom scene from Bog-art and Bacall's *Key Largo* was filmed at the **post office:** Mile 100 (451-3155; open Mon.-Fri. 8am-4:30pm). **ZIP code:** 33037. **Area code:** 305.

Accommodations, Camping, and Food The free *Florida Traveler Lodg-ing Guide* and its money-saving coupons await at all chambers of commerce. **Ed and Ellen's Lodgings,** Mile 103.4 (451-9949, 888-889-5905; leave a message on Ed's beeper and he'll call right back), has only 3 units, so call ahead. E. and E. offer clean, spacious rooms with cable TV, A/C, free local calls, and kitchenette for $35 off sea-son, $45-75 in season ($5 per person after 2). **Hungry Pelican,** Mile 99.5 (451-3576), boasts beautiful bougainvillea vines, tropical birds in the trees, and tidy, cozy rooms and cottages with double beds ($45-130, $10 per person after 2). Reservations are a must for the popular **John Pennekamp State Park Campground** (see below); the sites are clean, convenient, and well worth the effort required to obtain them ($24, with electric $26). If you can't get a reservation there, the crowded but well-run **Key Largo Kampground,** Mile 101.5 (451-1431 or 800-KAMP-OUT/526-7688), behind Tradewinds shopping plaza, manages 170 RV and tent sites plus a heated pool, game room, laundry, bath house, and marina. (Waterfront sites available. $18-38, extra per-son $3.) The **Calusa Camp Resort,** Mile 101.5 (451-0232 or 800-457-CAMP/2267), on the bay side, has 400 sites (some waterfront), a pool, tennis courts, two bathhouses, and a marina ($25-31, extra person $3).

The 99-beer selection at **Crack'd Conch,** Mile 105 (451-0732), can quench any thirst. Great chasers are entire key lime pies ($8.50), once called "the secret to world peace and the alignment of the planets." (Open Thurs.-Tues. noon-10pm.) **The Italian Fisherman,** Mile 104 (451-4471), has fine food and a spectacular view of Florida Bay. Some scenes from *Key Largo* and the upcoming *Blood and Wine,* with Jack Nicholson, were shot in this once-illegal casino. (Lunch $4-8, dinner $7-15. Open daily 11am-10pm.) Also appearing in *Key Largo* is the **Caribbean Club,** Mile 104 (451-9970), a friendly local bar; snapshots of Bogart and Bacall grace the walls. (Beer $1.50, drinks $2-4. Live rock and reggae Thurs.-Sun. Open daily 7am-4am.)

John Pennekamp State Park The nation's first underwater sanctuary, Key Largo's **John Pennekamp State Park,** Mile 102.5 (451-1202), 60 mi. from Miami, safeguards a 21-nautical-mi. stretch of the 120-sq.-mi. coral reef that runs the length of the Florida Keys. (Park admission $4 per vehicle, $2 for vehicle with single occupant, $1 walk- or bike-in; 50¢ extra per person on all fees.) The park's **visitors center** (451-1202), about ¼ mi. past the entrance gate, provides maps of the reefs, info on boat and snorkeling tours, three aquariums, and films on the park. (Open daily 8am-5pm.) To see the reefs, visitors must take a boat or rent their own. **Boat rentals** (451-6322), unfortunately, are rather expensive (19' motor boat; 2-hr. min.; $25 per hr., $80 for 4hr.; deposit required; call for reservations). **Scuba trips** (9:30am and 1:30pm) are $37 per person for a two-tank dive. A **snorkeling tour** also allows you to partake of the underwater quiet. (2½hr. total, 1½hr. water time; tours 9am, noon, and 3pm; $25, under 18 $20.) If you're up for more snorkeling time, ask about the ½-day sailing/snorkeling combo trip, just a bit costlier than snorkel alone. To get a crystal clear view of the reefs without wetting your feet, take a **Glass Bottom Boat Tour** (451-1621), which leaves from the park shore at Mile 102.5. (Daily 9:15am, 12:15, and 3pm. $14, under 12 $9. For some tours, 2 kids free with an adult.)

■ Key West

Just 90 mi. from Cuba, this is the end of the road. Key West boasts the southernmost point of the continental U.S. at the end of Rte. 1 and dips farther into the Gulf of Mexico than much of the Bahamas. The island is cooler than mainland Florida in summer and far warmer in winter; the seeker of a year-round tropical paradise in the U.S. can do no better. Key West's balmy weather once drew authors such as Ernest Hemingway, Tennessee Williams, Elizabeth Bishop, and Robert Frost; today, an easygoing diversity lures a new generation of writers, artists, recluses, adventurers, and eccentrics, along with an out and swinging gay population. Visitors stream into the town, filling the small island to capacity. Key West's charm manages to shine through the gaggles of scooter-riding teenagers. Amble through the historic district, or take advantage of the island's feature attraction: the ocean that surrounds it.

PRACTICAL INFORMATION

Tourist Office: Key West Chamber of Commerce, 402 Wall St. (294-2587 or 800-527-8539), in old Mallory Sq. Dispenses the useful *Guide to the Florida Keys,* as well as a list of popular gay accommodations. Open daily 8:30am-5pm. **Key West Welcome Center,** 3840 N. Roosevelt Blvd. (296-4444 or 800-284-4482), just north of the intersection of U.S. 1 and Roosevelt Blvd. Call in advance for lodging, theater tickets, or reef trips. Open Mon.-Sat. 9am-9pm, Sun. 9am-6pm.

Airport: Key West International Airport (296-5439), on the southeast corner of the island. No public bus service.

Buses: Greyhound, 615½ Duval St. (296-9072). In an alley behind Antonio's restaurant. To: Miami (3 per day, 4½hr., $27). Open daily 7am-7pm.

Public Transportation: Key West Port and Transit Authority (292-8161), City Hall. One bus ("Old Town") runs clockwise around the island and Stock Island; the

other ("Mallory Sq. Rte.") runs counterclockwise. Service Mon.-Sat. 6:35am-10:15pm, Sun. 6:35am-10:05pm. Fare 75¢, students and seniors 35¢.
Disabled Transportation, 292-4424.
Taxis: Keys Taxi, 296-6666. Not divisible by 3. $1.40 base fare, $1.75 per mi.
Car Rental: Alamo, 2839 N. Roosevelt Blvd. (294-6675 or 800-327-9633), near the airport. $33 per day, $140 per week. Must be 21 with major credit card. Under 25 surcharge $20 per day. Miami drop-off free. Open daily 8am-7pm.
Moped/Bike Rental: Keys Moped & Scooter, Inc., 523 Truman Ave. (294-0399). Bikes $3 for 9am-5pm, $4 for 24hr., $20 per week. Mopeds $14 for 9am-5pm, $23 for 24hr. Open daily 9am-6pm. **Key West Hostel,** 718 South St. (296-5719). $4 per day, $30 per week. Credit card and deposit required. Open daily 9am-10pm.
Crisis Line: 296-4357, everything from general info to crises. 24hr.
Emergency: 911.
Post Office: 400 Whitehead St. (294-2557), 1 block west of Duval at Eaton. Open Mon.-Fri. 8:30am-5pm. **ZIP code:** 33040. **Area code:** 305.

Key West lies at the end of U.S. 1, 155 mi. southwest of Miami (3-3½hr.). Divided into two sectors, the eastern part of the island, known as **New Town,** harbors tract houses, chain motels, shopping malls, and the airport. Beautiful old conch houses clutter **Old Town,** west of White St. **Duval St.** is the main north-south thoroughfare in Old Town, **Truman Ave.** the major east-west route.

ACCOMMODATIONS AND CAMPING

Key West is packed virtually year-round, with a lull of sorts from mid-September to mid-December; even then, don't expect to find a room for less than $40. Try to bed down in **Old Key West;** the beautiful, 19th-century clapboard houses capture the flavor of the Keys. Some of the guest houses in the Old Town are for gay men exclusively. *Do not park overnight on the bridges*—this is illegal and dangerous.

Key West Hostel (HI-AYH), 718 South St. (296-5719), at Sea Shell Motel in Old Key West, 3 blocks east of Duval St. Call for airport or bus station pick-up. Thrift over luxury. Rooms with 4-8 beds, shared bath. A/C runs only at night. Kitchen open until 9pm. Office open 24hr. No curfew. $14.50, nonmembers $18; prices rise Oct.-May. Key deposit $5. Motel rooms $45, in winter $50-100. Lockers 75¢. Breakfast $2, dinner $1. Call ahead to check availability; also call for late arrival.

Caribbean House, 226 Petronia St. (296-1600 or 800-543-4518), at Thomas St. in Bahama Village. Caribbean-style rooms with cool tile floors, A/C, cable TV, free local calls, fridge, and ceiling fans. Comfy double beds. Continental breakfast included. The management may be able to place you in a completely furnished Caribbean cottage (sleeps 6) or an unfurnished low-rent apartment. Rooms $49 and up, cottages $59; winter $69/$79-89. Advance-payment reservations accepted, but rooms are usually available.

Wicker Guesthouse, 913 Duval St. (296-4275 or 800-880-4275). Excellent location on the main drag. Individually decorated rooms with pastel decor, hardwood floors, A/C; some have TV. Kitchen and pool access. Free parking. Breakfast included. Single or double with shared bath $45-69; Christmas to Easter $60-90.

Eden House, 1015 Fleming St. (296-6868 or 800-533-5397). Bright, clean, friendly hotel with very nice rooms, just 5 short blocks from downtown. Cool rooms with private or shared bath, some with balconies. Pool, jacuzzi, and kitchen. Join other guests for free happy hour by the pool, daily 4-5pm. $50-80, winter $80-145.

Boyd's Campground, 6401 Maloney Ave. (294-1465), at Mile 5. Take a left off U.S. 1 onto Macdonald, which becomes Maloney. 12 acres on the ocean. Full facilities, including showers. $26, in winter $31; each additional person $6. Waterfront sites $6 extra. Water and electricity $5, A/C or heat $5, full hookup $9 extra.

FOOD AND NIGHTLIFE

Expensive restaurants line festive **Duval St.** Side streets offer lower prices and fewer crowds. Sell your soul and stock up on supplies at **Fausto's Food Palace,** 522 Fleming

St. (296-5663), the best darn grocery store in Old Town. (Open Mon.-Sat. 8am-8pm, Sun. 8am-7pm.) When it was a pool hall, Hemingway used to drink beer and referee boxing matches at **Blue Heaven Fruit Market**, 729 Thomas St. (296-8666), 1 block from the Caribbean House. Today, Blue Heaven serves healthy breakfasts ($1.75-7.50), and mostly vegetarian lunches ($5-8) and dinners ($7.50-16; open daily 8am-3pm and 6-11pm). You won't have to bait a hook at **Angler's**, 3618 N. Roosevelt Blvd. (294-4717), which serves huge seafood platters and inexpensive lunches and entrees; lunch $4-7, dinner $6-22. (Open Sun.-Thurs. 11am-10pm, Fri.-Sat. 11am-11pm.) Finally, don't leave Key West without having a sliver of **key lime pie**, available everywhere.

Nightlife in Key West revs up at 11pm and winds down very late. **Captain Tony's Saloon**, 428 Greene St. (294-1838), the oldest bar in Key West and reputedly one of "Papa" Hemingway's preferred watering holes, has been chugging away since the early 30s. Tony Tarracino, the 80-year-old owner, enters nightly through a secret door. (Open Mon.-Thurs. 10am-1am, Fri.-Sat. 10am-2am, Sun. noon-1am. Live entertainment daily and nightly.) **Turtle Kraals** (294-2640), at the foot of Margaret St. on the waterfront at Lands End Village, was literally a zoo until recent legislation forced the restaurant to return its menagerie to the wild. It has retained its popularity, though (entrees $10-15). Alternative bars and clubs crowd Key West. Cruise the **500 block** of Duval St. to unearth the counterculture.

SIGHTS AND ENTERTAINMENT

Check out the daily *Key West Citizen* (sold in front of the post office) and the weekly *Solares Hill* (available at the Chamber of Commerce) for the latest in Key West entertainment. Most tourists take to Key West's streets aboard a bike or moped; alternatives include the **Conch Tour Train** (294-5161), a fascinating 1½-hr. narrated ride through Old Town, leaving from Mallory Sq. at 3840 N. or from Roosevelt Blvd. next to the Quality Inn (runs daily 9am-4:30pm; $14, ages 4-12 $6). **Old Town Trolley** (296-6688) runs a similar tour, but you can get on and off throughout the day at 14 stops (full tour 1½hr.; $15, ages 4-12 $6).

The **glass-bottomed boat** *Fireball* cruises to the reefs and back at noon, 2, and 6pm (296-6293; tickets $20, at sunset $25, ages 3-12 ½-price; 2hr.). The **Coral Princess Fleet**, 700 Front St. (296-3287), offers snorkeling trips daily at 10am, 1:30, and 5:30pm with free instruction for beginners ($20; open daily 8:30am-5:30pm). For a landlubber's view of the fish of Key West, the **Key West Aquarium**, 1 Whitehead St. (296-2051), in Mallory Sq., offers a 50,000 gallon Atlantic shore exhibit, a touch pool, and shark feedings ($6.50, ages 8-15 $3.50; open daily 10am-6pm).

"Brains Don't Mean a Shit"

This brief profundity sums up the philosophy of Captain Tony Tarracino, gun runner, mercenary, casino owner, and one-time mayor of Key West. "All you need in this world is a great ego and a huge sex drive," proclaimed the Captain, who escaped to the southernmost point over 40 years ago while evading the New Jersey bookies he cheated by using a **battered TV set to get racing results** before they came over the wire. Tarracino arrived in Key West to find an island populated by bar-hoppers, petty criminals, and other deviants. In this setting Tony T. thrived; he attempted to organize his local popularity into a political campaign. After four unsuccessful bids, Captain Tony was finally **voted mayor** in 1989, on the slogan "Fighting for your future: what's left of it." Although he was never re-elected, Tarracino is certain that history will exonerate him. "I'll be remembered," he vows and, with his own bar, countless t-shirts that bear his image, and even a feature film about his life, this is no idle assertion. But for now, Tony T. isn't going anywhere—he even mocks his own mortality. **"I know every stripper in this town,"** he boasts. "When I'm dead, I've asked them all to come to my casket and stand over it. If I don't wake up then, put me in the ground."

"Papa" wrote *For Whom the Bell Tolls* and *A Farewell to Arms* at the **Hemingway House,** 907 Whitehead St. (294-1575), off Olivia St. Take a tour, or traipse through on your own. About 50 cats (descendants of Hemingway's cats) prowl the grounds; ask the tour guides their names. (House open daily 9am-5pm. $6.50, ages 6-12 $4.) The **Audubon House,** 205 Whitehead St. (294-2116), built in the early 1800s, houses some fine antiques and a collection of the works of ornithologist John James Audubon (open daily 9:30am-5:30pm; $7.50, ages 6-12 $2). Down Whitehead St., past Hemingway House, you'll come to the **southernmost point** in the continental U.S. and the nearby **Southernmost Beach.** A small, conical monument and a few conch shell hawkers mark the spot, along with a sprinkling of hustlers who might offer to take your picture; beware, they may not give your camera back until you pay them. **Mel Fisher's Treasure Exhibit,** 200 Greene St. (294-2633), glitters with glorious gold and quite a few busts of M.F. himself; Fisher discovered the sunken treasures from the shipwrecked Spanish vessel *Atocha.* A *National Geographic* film is included in the entrance fee. (Open daily 9:30am-5pm; last film 4:30pm. $6, students and AAA members $4, ages 6-11 $2.) The **Monroe County Beach,** off Atlantic Ave., has an old pier allowing access past the weed line. The **Old U.S. Naval Air Station** offers deep water swimming on Truman Beach ($1). A paragon of Cuban architecture, the **San Carlos Institute,** 516 Duval St., built in 1871, houses a research center for Hispanic studies. The **Haitian Art Company,** 600 Frances St. (296-8932), six blocks east of Duval, explodes with vivid Haitian artworks. (Open daily 10am-6pm. Free.) Sunset connoisseurs will enjoy the view from **Mallory Sq. Dock.** Magicians, street entertainers, and hawkers of tacky wares work the crowd, while swimmers and speedboaters show off during the daily **Sunset Celebration.** The crowd always cheers when the sun slips into the Gulf with a blazing red farewell.

GULF COAST

■ Tampa

Even with perfect weather year-round and splendiferous beaches nearby, Tampa has managed to avoid the plastic pink flamingos and alligator beach floats of its Atlantic Coast counterparts. The city's existence doesn't hinge on tourism; Tampa is one of the nation's fastest growing cities and largest ports, with booming financial, industrial, and artistic communities. While this cosmopolitan flair strips the city of that party-'til-you-drop spunk endemic to West Palm Beach and Miami, it also makes Tampa a less tacky, more peaceful vacation destination.

PRACTICAL INFORMATION

Tourist Office: Tampa/Hillsborough Convention and Visitors Association, 111 Madison St. (223-1111 or 800-826-8358). Open Mon.-Sat. 9am-5pm.

Airport: Tampa International, (870-8700), 5mi. west of downtown. HARTline bus #30 runs between the airport and downtown Tampa. **The Limo Inc.** (572-1111 or 800-282-6817) offers schmantzy 24-hr. service from the airport to the city and to all the beaches between Ft. De Soto and Clearwater ($13). Make reservations 24hr. in advance.

Trains: Amtrak, 601 Nebraska Ave. (221-7600 or 800-872-7245), at the end of Zack St., 2 blocks north of Kennedy St. Open daily 8:30am-6:15pm. Trains to: Orlando (2 per day, 2hr., $19); Miami (1 per day, 6hr., $50). No trains run south from Tampa. There is no direct train link between Tampa and St. Petersburg.

Buses: Greyhound, 610 E. Polk St. (229-2174 or 800-231-2222), next to Burger King downtown. To Atlanta (7 per day, 12hr., $49) and Orlando (6 per day, 2½hr., $44). Open daily 4:45am-12:30am.

Public Transportation: Hillsborough Area Regional Transit (HARTline), 254-4278. $1.15, seniors 55¢, transfers 10¢. The Tampa Town Ferry (253-3076) has pick-up and drop-off points throughout downtown. Roundtrip $6.
Crisis Lines: Rape Crisis, 234-1234. AIDS, 800-352-2437. Helpline, 251-4000.
Emergency: 911.
Post Office: 5201 W. Spruce Rd. (879-1600), at the airport. Open 24hr. ZIP code: 33601. Area code: 813.

Tampa divides into quarters with Florida Ave. running north-south and Kennedy Blvd., which becomes Frank Adams Dr. (Rte. 60), running east-west. Even-numbered streets run north-south and odd-numbered streets run east-west. Ybor City, Tampa's Latin Quarter, is bounded roughly by 22nd St., Nebraska Ave., 5th Ave., and Columbus Dr. *Be careful not to stray more than two blocks north or south of 7th Ave. since the area can be extremely dangerous, even during the daytime.* You can reach Tampa on I-75 from the north, or I-4 from the east.

ACCOMMODATIONS AND CAMPING

Gram's Place Bed & Breakfast, 3109 N. Ola Ave. (221-0596), 2mi. from Ybor City; from I-275, take Martin Luther King Blvd. west to Ola Ave., and take a left on Ola. Dedicated to keeping the music and spirit of Gram Parsons alive, this artistic haven features a friendly owner, jacuzzi, sundeck, courtyard, cable TV, and continental breakfast. Call and a shuttle will pick you up from anywhere in Tampa for ½ the cab fare. *Do not walk in this area unaccompanied at night.* Rooms $45.
Budget Host, 3110 W. Hillborough Ave. (876-8673), near the airport and Busch Gardens. 33 small rooms with A/C, cable TV, pool. Singles $29, doubles $30.
Motel 6, 333 E. Fowler Ave. (932-4948), off I-275 near Busch Gardens. On the northern outskirts of Tampa, 30mi. from the beach. Big, clean rooms with free local calls, A/C, and pool. Singles $28, each additional person $4.
Americana Inn, 321 E. Fletcher Ave. (933-4545), 3mi. from Busch Gardens in northwest Tampa; from I-275, take the Fletcher exit west. Clean rooms, most with fridge and stove. Pool and cable TV. Regular rates (up to 4 people) Sun.-Thurs. $30, Fri.-Sat. $35-40. In high season, add $10. $5 discount for college students, seniors, military, and AAA, depending upon availability.

FOOD AND NIGHTLIFE

Cheap Cuban and Spanish establishments dot Tampa; black bean soup, gazpacho, and Cuban bread are affordable and tasty. Ybor City houses the best and cheapest food around. Make your own pasta combinations at The Spaghetti Warehouse (248-1720), at 9th and 13th St. in Ybor Sq. (entrees $4-9; open Mon.-Fri. 11am-10pm, Sat.-Sun noon-11pm). Across 9th Ave. from Ybor Sq. sits the historic El Pasaje building, where Café Creole (247-6283) features creole entrees (lunch $5-7) and dixie jazz hammered out on a vintage piano Fridays and Saturdays from 8:30pm to midnight. (Open Mon.-Wed. 11:30am-10pm, Thurs.-Fri. 11:30am-11:30pm, Sat. 5-11:30pm.) Downtown, The Loading Dock, 100 Madison St. (223-6905), hoists sandwiches like "flatbed" or "forklift" ($3-5; open Mon.-Fri. 8am-8pm, Sat. 10:30am-2:30pm). Skipper's Smokehouse, 910 Skipper Rd. (971-0666), off Nebraska Ave. in the northern outskirts of town, may look like a heap of wreckage washed up by last year's hurricane, but don't be fooled—it's a harbor for upstart Floridian bands and inexpensive meals. (Beans and rice $2.50, clam strip platter $5. Usually open Tues.-Sat. 10 or 11am-11pm, Sun. 1-11pm.) If you're in the mood for dueling pianos, check out Jelly Roll, 1812 N. 17th St. (247-2447), at 8th Ave. in Ybor City. (Cover $2, Fri.-Sat. $4. Open Wed.-Sat. 7pm-3am.) A collection of gay nightclubs populates the corner of 7th Ave. and 15th St. in Ybor City. Brief yourself on Tampan entertainment with the free *Tampa Tonight, Weekly Planet,* or *Stonewall.*

SIGHTS AND ACTIVITIES

Ybor City expanded rapidly after Vincent Martínez Ybor moved his cigar factories here from Key West in 1886. Although cigar manufacturing has since been mechanized, some people still roll the suckers by hand and sell them for $1 in **Ybor Sq.,** 1901 13th St. (247-4497), an upscale retail complex converted from three 19th-century cigar factories (open Mon.-Sat. 9:30am-5:30pm, Sun. noon-5:30pm). **Ybor City State Museum,** 1818 9th Ave. (247-6323), at 18th St., traces the development of Ybor City, Tampa, the cigar industry, and Cuban migration. (Open Tues.-Sat. 9am-noon and 1-5pm. $2.) Aside from the square, the Ybor City area has remained relatively unsullied by Tampa's rapid urban growth; **East 7th Ave.** serves up old-time jazz and Cuban cuisine. Buses #5, 12, and 18 run to Ybor City from downtown. Certain areas near Ybor City can be dangerous; stay on guard.

Before the Spanish-American War, Teddy Roosevelt trained his Rough Riders in the backyard of the Moorish **Tampa Bay Hotel,** 401 W. Kennedy Blvd. Now part of the University of Tampa, it once epitomized fashionable Florida coast motels. Gaze in awe at the **Henry B. Plant Museum** (254-1891), in a wing of a University of Tampa building. The exhibits, which include Victorian furniture and Wedgewood pottery, pale in comparison to the museum, a no-holds-barred orgy of Rococo architecture. (Tours at 1:30pm. Open Tues.-Sat. 10am-4pm, Sun. noon-4pm. $3, kids $1.)

Downtown, the **Tampa Museum of Art,** 600 N. Ashley Dr. (274-8130), houses a noted collection of ancient Greek and Roman works as well as a series of changing exhibitions. (Open Mon.-Sat. 10am-5pm, Wed. 10am-9pm, Sun. 1-5pm. $5, students with ID and seniors $4, ages 6-18 $3; free Sun. and Wed. 5-9pm.) Across from the University of South Florida, north of downtown, the **Museum of Science and Industry (MOSI),** 4801 E. Fowler Ave. (987-6300), features a simulated hurricane every hour on the hour and an IMAX dome theater. (Open Sun.-Thurs. 9am-5pm, Fri.-Sat. 9am-9pm, extended hours July and Aug. $8, students and seniors $7, ages 2-12 $5.) The **Museum of African-American Art,** 1308 N. Marion St. (272-2466), features the art history and culture of the classical Barnett-Aden collection. (Open Tues.-Fri. 10am-4:30pm, Sat. 10am-5pm. $3, seniors and under 12 $2.) The **Florida Aquarium,** 701 Channelside Dr. (273-4000), invites you to mash your face to the glass for a *tête-à-tête* with fish from Florida's various wet areas. (Open daily 9am-5pm; in summer, Fri. until 9pm. $14, seniors and ages 13-18 $13, ages 3-12 $7.)

For serious amusement-park fun among African wildlife, descend into **Busch Gardens—The Dark Continent,** E. 3000 Busch Blvd. (987-5171), at NE 40th St.; take I-275 to Busch Blvd., or bus #5 from downtown. Throw your stomach for a loop on Kumba, the largest drop (143ft.) in the world, or watch giraffes, zebras, ostriches, and antelope roam freely across the park's 60-acre plain; trains, boats, and walkways cater to the tamer crowd. Busch Gardens has two of an estimated 50 white Bengal tigers in existence. (Open daily 9am-8:30pm. $36, parking $4.) Inside the park, you can take advantage of the generous **Anheuser-Busch Hospitality House,** but you must stand in line for each of your two allotted beers. If the Dark Continent sears you, you can cool off at **Adventure Island,** 10001 McKinly Dr. (987-5660), a 13-acre water park about ¼ mi. north of Busch Gardens. ($21, ages 3-9 $19. Parking $2. Open Mon.-Thurs. 9am-7pm, Fri.-Sun. 9am-8pm; in winter daily 10am-5pm.)

Tampa is *the* place to "tally me banana." Banana boats from South and Central America unload and tally their cargo every day at the **waterfront** docks on 139 Twiggs St., near 13th St. and Kennedy Blvd. Every February the *Jose Gasparilla* (251-4500), a fully rigged pirate ship loaded with hundreds of exuberant "pirates," invades Tampa, kicking off a month of parades and festivals, such as the **Gasparilla Sidewalk Art Festival** (876-1747).

■ St. Petersburg and Clearwater

Twenty-two miles southwest of Tampa, across the bay, St. Petersburg caters to a relaxed community of retirees and young singles. The town enjoys 28 mi. of soft white beaches, emerald bathtub-warm water, melt-your-heart sunsets, and approximately 361 days of sunshine per year.

PRACTICAL INFORMATION

Tourist Office: St. Petersburg Area Chamber of Commerce, 100 2nd Ave. N. (821-4715). Open Mon.-Fri. 9am-5pm. **The Pier Information Center,** 800 2nd Ave. NE (821-6164). Open Mon.-Sat. 10am-8pm, Sun. noon-6pm.

Airport: St. Petersburg Clearwater International (535-7600) sits right across the bay from Tampa, off Roosevelt St.

Trains: Amtrak (522-9475 or 800-872-7245). Ticket office at Pinellas Sq. Mall, 7200 U.S. 19N. Open 8am-1:15pm and 2:20-6:45pm. St. Pete has no train station, but Amtrak will transport you from Tampa to St. Pete by bus ($10) or to Clearwater, stopping at 657 Court St. (441-1793), at E. Ave., on a free shuttle. Clearwater is inaccessible by train from Tampa, but not from other Florida cities.

Buses: Greyhound, 180 9th St. N. (898-1496), downtown St. Petersburg. To: Panama City (2 per day, 9hr., $57); Clearwater (3 per day, ½hr., $7). Open 6:45am-11:30pm. In Clearwater: 2111 Gulf-to-Bay Blvd. (796-7315). Open 6am-8pm.

Public Transportation: Pinnellas Suncoast Transit Authority (PSTA), 530-9911. Most routes depart from Williams Park at 1st Ave. N. and 3rd St. N. Fare $1, transfers free. To reach Tampa, take express bus #100 from downtown to the Gateway Mall ($1.50). A free shuttle loops through downtown.

Crisis Line: Rape Crisis, 530-7233. 24hr.

Emergency: 911.

Post Office: 3135 1st Ave. N. (323-6516), at 31st St. Open Mon.-Fri. 8am-6pm, Sat. 8am-12:30pm. **ZIP code:** 33737. **Area code:** 813.

In St. Petersburg, **Central Ave.** runs east-west. **34th St. (U.S. 19)** cuts north-south through the city and links up with the **Sunshine-Skyway Bridge,** connecting St. Pete with the Bradenton-Sarasota area to the south. The St. Pete beachfront is a chain of barrier islands accessible by bridges on the far west side of town, and extends from **Sand Key Beach** in the north to **Pass-a-Grille Beach** in the south. Many towns on the islands offer quiet beaches and reasonably priced hotels and restaurants. From north to south, these towns include: **Belleair, Indian Rocks Beach, Madiera Beach, Treasure Island,** and **St. Pete Beach.** The stretch of beach past the **Don Cesar Hotel** (luxury resort/pink monstrosity recently declared a historical landmark), in St. Pete Beach, and Pass-a-Grille Beach have the best sand, a devoted following, and less pedestrian and motor traffic. The town of **Clearwater,** connected by toll bridge to Sand Key in St. Petersburg, at the far north end of this island coastline, offers beaches, pricey motels and resorts, and not much else.

ACCOMMODATIONS AND CAMPING

St. Petersburg and Clearwater offer two hostels as well as many cheap motels lining 4th St. N. and U.S. 19 in St. Pete. Some establishments advertise singles for as little as $20, but these tend to be very worn down. To avoid the worst neighborhoods, stay on the north end of 4th St. and the south end of U.S. 19. Several inexpensive motels cluster along the St. Pete beach.

St. Petersburg Youth Hostel, 326 1st Ave. N. (822-4141), downtown in the McCarthy Hotel. Bunk rooms for a maximum of 4 people with in-suite bathrooms. Common room with kitchen, TV, A/C. 11pm curfew. $11 with any youth hostel card or student ID. $2 linen fee. Hostel rooms are available Nov.-May.; in the summer, rent historic hotel rooms with A/C and private bath for $15.

Clearwater Beach International Hostel (HI-AYH), 606 Bay Esplanade Ave. (443-1211), at the Sands Motel in Clearwater Beach; take Rte. 60W to Clearwater Beach, or catch the free bus from the Tampa Amtrak station to Clearwater Beach. (Clearwater has its own Amtrak and Greyhound stations for more direct arrivals.) Just 2 blocks from a superb white sand beach, or take a free canoe to the nearby state park, where sports fields and equipment are available for free and bike rental is $5 per day. Kitchen, common room, and pool. Bunk in shared room. $11, nonmembers $13. Linen $2. Private rooms with kitchen $35.

Grant Motel, 9046 4th St. N. (576-1369), 4mi. north of town on U.S. 92. Rooms with ruffled pillow shams and A/C; most have a fridge. Beautifully landscaped grounds. Pool. Singles and doubles $30; Jan. to mid-April singles $39, doubles $43.

Kentucky Motel, 4246 4th St. N. (526-7373). A little out of place, but hey. Large, clean rooms with friendly owners, cable TV, refrigerator, and free postcards. Singles $24, doubles $28; Jan.-March $10 more.

Treasure Island Motel, 10315 Gulf Blvd. (367-3055), across the street from beach. Big rooms with A/C, fridge, color TV, and pool access. Singles and doubles $32, Feb.-March $55; each additional person $4. Pirates not allowed.

Fort De Soto State Park (866-2662), composed of five islands at the southern end of a long chain of keys and islands, has the best camping with 233 wooded, private sites. (No alcohol; 2-day min. stay. Front gate locked at 9pm. Curfew 10pm. $16.50.) From January to April, you may want to make a reservation in person at the **St. Petersburg County Building,** 150 5th St. N. #125, or at least call ahead (582-7738). A wildlife sanctuary, the park also makes a great oceanside picnic spot.

FOOD AND NIGHTLIFE

St. Petersburg's cheap, health-conscious restaurants cater to its retired population, and generally close by 8 or 9pm. Hungry night owls should glide to St. Pete Beach and 4th St. If you're itching for crabs, try **Crabby Bills,** 407 Gulf Blvd. (360-8858), near Indian Rocks Beach. Seafood sandwiches run $4-7, while $9 buys a whole crab, two sides, and a hammer. (Open Mon.-Thurs. 11am-10pm, Fri.-Sat. 11am-11pm, Sun. noon-10pm.) For more crabs, head to **Tangelo's Bar and Grille,** 226 1st Ave. NE (894-1695), which serves tasty crab burgers ($5) and gazpacho ($2; open daily 11am-7pm). If you've had enough of those damned crabs, **Beach Nutts,** 9600 W. Gulf Blvd. (367-7427), Treasure Island, doesn't have much of a selection, but oh! what an atmosphere; the restaurant lies on the beach, and bands plays every night. (Live reggae Sat.-Sun. 4-8pm. Open daily 9am-2am.) Diner culture is alive at **Beach Diner,** 56 Causeway Blvd. (446-4747), on the median before the causeway connecting Clearwater Beach to the mainland (entrees $5-7). **Jamminz,** 470 Mondalay St. (441-2005), in Clearwater Beach, hosts every type of politically incorrect body contest you can imagine, plus dancing and pool (18+; open daily 6pm-late).

SIGHTS AND ACTIVITIES

Grab a copy of *See St. Pete and Beaches* or the *St. Petersburg Official Visitor's Guide* for the lowdown on area events, and many a useful map. **Pass-a-Grille Beach** may be the nicest beach, but its parking meters gobble quarters like Pac-Man in Vegas. For free parking, drive to the **Municipal Beach** at Treasure Island, accessible from Rte. 699 via Treasure Island Causeway. **Clearwater Beach,** at the northern end of the Gulf Blvd. strand, is mainstream beach culture at its unspectacular height. While here, visit the **Clearwater Marine Aquarium,** 249 Windword Passage (447-0980), the home of Sunset Sam, an Atlantic bottlenose dolphin who paints pictures. (Open Mon.-Fri. 9am-5pm, Sat. 9am-4pm, Sun. 11am-4pm. $5.75, kids $3.75.) Finish the day with **Sunsets at Pier 60,** a daily celebration with performers and vendors.

If you've got a hankerin' for some melting clocks, the **Salvador Dalí Museum,** 1000 3rd St. S. (823-3767), in Poynter Park on the Bayboro Harbor waterfront, will make things better. The museum contains the world's most comprehensive collection of Dalí works and memorabilia—94 oil paintings, 1300 graphics, and juvenalia from a 14-year-old Dalí. (Open Mon.-Sat. 9:30am-5:30pm, Sun. noon-5:30pm. $8, seniors $7, students $4, under 11 free.) If watching brawny men battle ferocious 'gators is more your speed, descend into the **Sunken Gardens,** 1825 4th St. N. (896-3187), home of over 7000 varieties of exotic flowers and plants. (Open daily 10am-5pm. $14, ages 3-11 $8.) **Great Explorations,** 1120 4th St. S. (821-8885), is an interactive educational museum with hands-on exhibits like the **Body Shop,** where you can see how your muscles compare to others' countrywide. (Open Mon.-Sat. 10am-5pm, Sun. noon-5pm. $6, ages 4-17 $5.) **The Pier** (821-6164), at the end of 2nd Ave. NE, downtown, extends into Tampa Bay from St. Pete, ending in a five-story inverted pyramid complex with a shopping center, aquarium, restaurants, and bars. (Open Mon.-Thurs. 10am-9pm, Fri.-Sat. 10am-10pm, Sun. 11am-7pm; bars and restaurants open later. Free trolley service from the parking area.)

■ Panama City Beach

Move over, Daytona—you're no longer "where the boys are." Suntan oil is the perfume of choice at Panama City Beach, the latest fad in spring break hotspots and a boldly rising meat market mecca. Here, along miles of snow-white beach, nearly bare bodies bask between a gulf and a party place. Still, PCB is not always a den of iniquity; while most attractions cater to the spring break beer and bikini mob, the Brady Bunch crowd claims its turf during the summer.

Practical Information After crossing Hathaway Bridge, Rte. 98 splits. Everything centers on **Front Beach Rd.**, also known as **The Strip** or **Miracle Mile.** To bypass the hubbub, take some of the smaller roads off Rte. 98. **Panama City Beach Convention and Visitors Bureau,** 12015 Front Beach Rd. (233-5070 or 800-PCBEACH/722-3224) will cram you with info (open daily 8am-5pm). **Bay Town Trolley** (769-0557) shuttles along the beach, making various flag stops (one-way $1; open Mon.-Fri. 8am-6pm). Taxis run on a grid system; fares increase as you move away from Harrison Ave. **AAA Taxi** (785-0533) or **Yellowcab** (763-4691) will take you from the airport to the visitors bureau for approximately $15. The **Domestic Violence and Rape Crisis Hotline** is 763-0706. **Crisis and Mental Health Emergency Hotline** is 769-9481; both are open 24 hr. **Emergency** is 911. Panama City's **post office:** 275 Rte. 79 (234-8888; open Mon.-Fri. 8:30am-5pm, Sat. 8:30am-12:30pm). **ZIP code:** 32407. **Area code:** 904.

Accommodations and Camping Depending on the time of year and strip location, rates range from can-do to outrageous. High season runs from the end of April until early September; rates drop in fall and winter. **La Brisa Inn,** 9424 Front Beach Rd. (235-1122 or 800-523-4369), off the beach, has spacious rooms with two double beds and free coffee, doughnuts, and local calls. (Singles or doubles $59, $10 surcharge on weekends; off season, singles $28.) **The Reef,** 12011 Front Beach Rd. (234-3396 or 800-847-7286), near the visitors center, has large rooms with bright decor, many with bay views. (Kitchens, TV, A/C available; singles weekend $79, weekdays $75, Sept.-Oct. weekend $49, weekday $45, Oct.-Feb. $35.) **Sea Breeze Motel,** 16810 Front Beach Rd. (234-3348), offers small rooms across the street from the beach; Cable TV, A/C, a pool, and reasonable rates will blow you away. (Single bed for 1 or 2 people $40, off season $20.)

Camp on the beach at **St. Andrews State Recreation Area,** 4607 State Park Lane (233-5140), 3 mi. east of PCB on Rte. 392. Call ahead (up to 60 days) for reservations at this popular campground to grab private sites right on the water beneath tall pine trees. Half of the 176 sites can be reserved. (Sites $15; on the water with electricity $19; winter $8/$12.) **Panama City Beach KOA,** 8800 Thomas Dr. (234-5731), two blocks south of Rte. 98, maintains 114 sites with showers, laundry, and a pool. (Tent sites with water $19, full hookup $23; winter $14/$18.)

Food and Nightlife Buffets stuff The Strip. **JP's Restaurant and Bar,** 4701 W. Rte. 98 (769-3711), serves homemade specialties in abundant portions (fettuccini and clams $9; open Mon.-Sat. 11am-11pm). **The Pickle Patch,** 5700 Thomas Dr. (235-2000), concocts delicious Greek cuisine in a homey atmosphere; $4 pita sandwiches for lunch and $6 plates for dinner. (Open Mon.-Fri. 6am-2pm, Thurs.-Sat. also open 6-9pm.) **Captain Anderson's Restaurant,** 5551 N. Lagoon Dr. (234-2225), off Thomas

Dr., has a rep for superb seafood and a panoramic view (dinners $9-20; open daily 4-10pm).

Cruisers and those who hope to be cruised will find a home on meat-market Miracle Mile. At **Spinnaker,** 8795 Thomas Dr. (234-7892), dive into the massive club's pool, visit one of the several clubs inside, or join one of the daily hot body contests; on the side, listen to major music acts (cover varies; open daily 10am-4pm). The largest club in the U.S. (capacity 8000), **Club LaVela,** 8813 Thomas Dr. (235-1061), jams on multiple dance floors to just about every kind of music (including national acts) all night. Ladies make out with no cover and free drinks on Tuesday, Friday, and Saturday nights; call for other frequent specials, including wet T-shirt, bikini, and hot bod contests on the weekends. (Cover $5-25. Open daily 10am-4am.) **Salty's Beach Bar,** 11073 Front Beach Rd. (234-1913), attracts a laid-back crowd with nautical decor and live music nightly (cover Fri.-Sat. $3; open 11am-2am).

Sights and Entertainment Over a thousand acres of gators, nature trails, and beaches make up the **St. Andrews State Recreation Area** (see Accommodations, above; open daily 8:30am-sunset; $2.35 per car). Take a glass-bottom boat trip to **Shell Island** from **Treasure Island Marina** (234-8944), on Thomas Dr. (3-hr. trips at 9am, 1, and 4:30pm; $10, under 13 $6). The **Museum of the Man in the Sea,** 17314 Panama City Beach Pkwy. (235-4101), explores the ocean deep. (Open daily 9am-5pm. $4, seniors $3.60, ages 6-16 $2.) Daredevils bungee jump, parasail, and scuba dive every day here. Check out the **Miracle Strip Amusement Park** (234-5810; open Mon.-Fri. 6-11:30pm, Sat. 1-11:30pm, Sun. 5-11pm; $15), adjacent to the **Shipwreck Island Water Park,** 2000 Front Beach Rd. (234-0368; $17, admission to both parks $25). Nearby **Alvin's Magic Mountain Mall,** 12010 Front Beach Rd. (234-3048), houses sharks and alligators in a 30,000-gallon tank (open daily 9am-11pm).

Alabama

The "Heart of Dixie" is best remembered for its critical role in the Civil Rights campaign of the 1960s. Once a stalwart defender of segregation (Governor George Wallace fought a vicious campaign opposing integration), Alabama now strives to broaden its image as a progressive Southern state without losing the charming aspects of its cultural heritage. Most visitors come to Alabama searching for legacies of its divided past, from Booker T. Washington's pioneering Tuskegee Institute (now a University), to the poignant statues in Birmingham's Kelly Ingram Park. But there is more to the state than its history. As one wry Alabaman put it, "Come for the long history of racial strife—stay for the food!"

PRACTICAL INFORMATION

Capital: Montgomery.
Alabama Bureau of Tourism and Travel: 401 Adams Ave. (334-242-4169; 800-252-2262 outside AL). Open Mon.-Fri. 8am-5pm. **Travel Council,** 702 Oliver Rd. #254, Montgomery (334-271-0050). Open Mon.-Fri. 8am-5pm. **Division of Parks,** 64 N. Union St., Montgomery (800-252-7275). Open daily 8:30am-4:30pm.
Time Zone: Central (1hr. behind Eastern). **Postal Abbreviation:** AL.
Sales Tax: 4% plus county tax.

■ Montgomery

While Montgomery was the first capital of the Confederacy, the city also played a key role in the birth of the New South. In 1955, local authorities arrested Rosa Parks, a black seamstress, because she refused to give up her seat on a local bus; a local minister named Dr. Martin Luther King, Jr. responded by calling a famed boycott. The nation took notice of his nonviolent approach to gaining racial equality, igniting a movement that radically transformed America. Today, Civil Rights movement battle-grounds are Montgomery's main draw (watch for signs proclaiming "Rosa Parks figu-rines sold here").

PRACTICAL INFORMATION

Tourist Office: Visitor Information Center, 401 Madison Ave. (262-0013). Open Mon.-Fri. 8:30am-5pm, Sat. 9am-4pm, Sun. noon-4pm. Free maps. **Chamber of Commerce,** 41 Commerce St. (834-5200). Open Mon.-Fri. 8:30am-5pm.

Buses: Greyhound, 950 W. South Blvd. (286-0658 or 800-231-2222). Take I-65 Exit 168 and turn right. To: Mobile (8 per day, 3hr., $27); Atlanta (9 per day, 3-5hr., $29); Tuskegee (7 per day, 1hr., $8). Open 24hr.

Trains: Amtrak, 335 Coosa St., downtown at Madison and Bibb St., in Riverfront Park. Take Coosa across the railroad tracks; the stop is on your left. No actual trains, but limited bus service to connecting cities of Atlanta, Pensacola, and New Orleans. *Be careful here at night.* Open Mon.-Fri. 9am-6pm, Sat. 10am-4pm.

Public Transportation: Montgomery Area Transit System (MATS), 2338 W. Fairview Ave. (262-7321). Due to cutbacks, buses run only during morning and afternoon rush hr. on weekdays and midday on Sat. $1.50, transfers 15¢.

Taxis: Yellow Cab, 262-5225. $1.50 first mi., $1.10 each additional mi. 24hr.

Crisis Lines: Council Against Rape, 286-5987. **Help-A-Crisis,** 279-7837. 24hr.

Emergency: 911.

Post Office: 135 Catoma St. (244-7576). Open Mon.-Fri. 7:30am-5:30pm, Sat. 8am-noon. **ZIP code:** 36104. **Area code:** 334.

Downtown Montgomery follows a grid pattern: **Madison Ave.** and **Dexter Ave.** are the major east-west routes; **Perry St.** and **Lawrence St.** run north-south.

ACCOMMODATIONS AND FOOD

Centrally located and well-maintained, two budget motels serve the downtown area: the comfortable and newly renovated **Town Plaza,** 743 Madison Ave. (269-1561), at N. Ripley St. near the visitors center (singles $22, doubles $26), which proffers maps and smiles upon arrival; and **Capitol Inn,** 205 N. Goldthwaite St. (265-0541), at Heron St. near the bus station, with spacious, clean rooms overlooking the city and a pool (singles $22, doubles $32). Those with a car will find it easy to procure accommoda-tions. **I-65** Exit 168, especially South Blvd., overflows with cheap motels—beware of the cheapest of the cheap, which are fairly seedy. Right next to I-65 on W. South Blvd., **The Inn South,** 4243 Inn South Ave. (288-7999), has nicely decorated rooms and a lobby with a grand double staircase and chandelier (singles $29, doubles $35). For other inns, contact **Bed and Breakfast Inns Montgomery,** P.O. Box 1026, Mont-gomery 36101 (264-0056). For the camping crowd, **Fort Toulouse Jackson Park** (205-567-3002), 7 mi. north of Montgomery on Rte. 6 off U.S. 231, has 39 rustic sites with water and electricity in beautiful woods (tents $8, RVs $10). **Martha's Place,** 458 Sayre St. (263-9135), a new but soon-to-be-legendary, family-run, down-home res-taurant serves a daily country-style lunch (entree, 2 veggies, lemonade and dessert $5.50) and a Sunday buffet. ($6.50. Open Mon.-Fri. 11am-3pm, Fri. 5-9pm, Sun. brunch 11am-3pm). Across from the visitors center at **Young House,** 231 N. Hull St. (262-0409), $5 procures two big pieces of fried chicken and two healthily-sized veg-gie sides (open Mon.-Fri. 11am-2pm). More Southern fare awaits you at the **Sassafras Tea Room,** 532 Clay St. (265-7277), a restaurant/antique dealership where you can gaze at murals while lunching on meat and/or greens ($4.25-5.25; open Mon.-Fri. 11am-2pm). At **The China Bowl,** 701 Madison Ave. (832-4004), 2 blocks from the Town Plaza Motel, large portions include a daily special of one entree, fried rice, egg roll, chicken wing, and a fried wonton for $4.20. (Open Mon.-Thurs. 11am-9pm, Fri. 11am-9:30pm.) For a great snack, make your way over to the **Montgomery State Farmers Market** (242-5350), at the corner of Federal Dr. (U.S. 231) and Coliseum Blvd., and snag a bag of peaches for a buck (open spring and summer daily 7am-

6pm). For a more filling meal, there is never an empty seat at **The State Market Cafeteria,** 1659 Federal Dr., which serves free iced tea with every Southern-style meal ($3-5; open Sun.-Fri. 5am-2pm).

SIGHTS AND ENTERTAINMENT

Maya Lin, the architect who designed the Vietnam Memorial in Washington, D.C. also designed Montgomery's newest sight, the **Civil Rights Memorial,** 400 Washington Ave. (264-0268), at Hull St. This dramatically minimalist tribute remembers 40 of the men, women, and children who died fighting for civil rights. The outdoor monument bears names and dates of significant events on a circular black marble table over which water continuously flows; a wall frames the table with Martin Luther King, Jr.'s words, "Until justice rolls down like waters and righteousness like a mighty stream" (open 24hr; free).

The legacy of African-American activism and faith lives on one block away at the 112-year-old **Dexter Avenue King Memorial Baptist Church,** 454 Dexter Ave. (263-3970), where King first preached, and where he and other Civil Rights leaders organized the 1955 Montgomery bus boycott; ten years later, King led a nationwide march past the church to the capitol building. The basement mural chronicles King's role in the nation's struggle during the 1950s and 60s. (Tours Mon.-Thurs. 10am and 2pm, Fri. 10am, Sat. every hr. 9am-2pm. Donations appreciated.)

Old Alabama Town, 310 N. Hull St. (240-4500), at Madison, encompasses a historic district of 19th-century buildings 3 blocks north of the church. The complex includes a pioneer homestead, an 1892 grocery, a schoolhouse, and an early African-American church. Renowned Alabama storyteller Kathryn Tucker Windham artfully recounts her family's past as she leads you through the quaint, reconstructed village. (Open Mon.-Sat. 9am-3:30pm. Sun. 1-3:30pm. Last tour at 3pm. $5, ages 6-18 $3.)

The **State Capitol** (242-3935), Bainbridge St. at Dexter Ave., has recently reopened after years of renovations. (Open Mon.-Sat. 9am-4pm for free, self-guided tours.) The nearby **Alabama State Archives and History Museum,** 624 Washington Ave. (242-4363), exhibits many Native American artifacts along with early military swords and medals. **Grandma's Attic** lets you try on antique furs and play with antique sewing machines and typewriters in a wooden-frame attic replica (open Mon.-Fri. 8am-5pm, Sat. 9am-5pm; free). Next door to the Archives, the elegant **First White House of the Confederacy,** 644 Washington Ave. (242-1861), contains many original furnishings from Jefferson Davis's presidency (open Mon.-Fri. 8am-4:30pm; free). Another restored home of interest, the **F. Scott and Zelda Fitzgerald Museum,** 919 Felder Ave. (264-4222), off Carter Hill Rd., contains a few of her paintings and some of his original manuscripts, as well as their strangely monogrammed bath towels. Zelda, originally from Montgomery, lived here with F. Scott from October 1931 until April 1932. (Open Wed.-Fri. 10am-2pm, Sat.-Sun. 1-5pm. Free.)

Country music fans might want to join the droves who make daily pilgrimages to the **Hank Williams Memorial,** 1304 Upper Wetumpka Rd. (262-0804), in the Oakwood Cemetery Annex off Upper Wetumpka Rd. near dowtown. A stone cowboy hat rests upon the grave, flanked by oversized music notes and other memorabilia. (Open Mon.-Fri. 10am-sunset.) For live entertainment, turn to the renowned **Alabama Shakespeare Festival** (271-5353 or 800-841-4ASF/4273), staged at the **State Theatre** on the grounds of the 250-acre private estate, **Wynton M. Blount Cultural Park;** take East Blvd. 15 min. southeast of downtown onto Woodmere Blvd. The theater also stages Broadway shows and other plays. (Tickets $19-24; previews the week before opening $15. Box office open Mon.-Sat. 10am-6pm, Sun. noon-4pm.) Also in Blount Cultural Park, the **Montgomery Museum of Fine Arts,** 1 Museum Dr. (244-5700), houses a substantial collection of 19th- and 20th-century paintings and graphics, as well as "Artworks," a hands-on gallery and art studio for kids. (Open Tues.-Wed. and Fri-Sat. 10am-5pm, Thurs. 10am-9pm, Sun. noon-5pm. Free.)

Montgomery shuts down fairly early, but if you're in the mood for some blues and beers, try **1048,** 1048 E. Fairview Ave. (834-1048), near Woodley Ave. (open Mon.-

Fri. 4pm 'til late, Sat.-Sun. 8pm 'til the cow walks in the door) or **Sinclair's,** 1051 Fairview Ave. (834-7462; open Mon-Thurs. 11am-10pm, Fri.-Sat. 11am-11pm).

■ Near Montgomery: Tuskegee

Even after Reconstruction, "emancipated" blacks in the South remained segregated and disenfranchised. Booker T. Washington, a former slave, believed that blacks could best improve their situation by educating themselves and learning a trade, as opposed to pursuing the classical, erudite education which W.E.B. Dubois proposed. The curriculum at the college Washington founded, **Tuskegee Institute,** revolved around such practical endeavors as agriculture and carpentry, with students constructing almost all of the campus buildings. Washington raised money for the college by giving lectures on social structure across the country. Artist, teacher, and scientist **George Washington Carver** became head of the Agricultural Department at Tuskegee, where he discovered many practical uses for the peanut, including axle grease and peanut butter.

Today, a more academically oriented Tuskegee University fills 160 buildings on 1500 acres and offers a wide range of subjects; the buildings of Washington's original institute comprise a national historical site. A walking tour of the campus begins near the entrance to the university at the **Carver Museum; the visitor orientation center** (334-727-3200) is inside (both open daily 9am-5pm; free). Down the street from the museum on old Montgomery Rd. lies **The Oaks,** a restored version of Washington's home. Free tours from the museum begin on the hour. (10am-4pm).

For a filling, delicious, and inexpensive meal after your tour, head to **Thomas Reed's Chicken Coop,** 527 Old Montgomery Rd. (334-727-3841). Chicken is sold by the piece or as a full dinner (all under $5)—and you *will* lick your fingers, unless you're feeling stubborn (open daily 10am-5pm).

To get to Tuskegee, take I-85 toward Atlanta and exit at Rte. 81 south. Turn right at the intersection of Rte. 81 and Old Montgomery Rd. onto Rte. 126. **Greyhound** (334-727-1290 or 800-231-2222) also runs from Montgomery (2 per day, 1hr., $9).

■ Birmingham

Like its English namesake, Birmingham sits on soil rich in coal, iron ore, and limestone—responsible for its lightning transformation into a premier steel industry center. No longer an industrial town, the University of Alabama now employs the majority of the city's workers. With the fires out, an easy, cosmopolitan version of Southern charm and hospitality has kicked in, visible in local art festivals and museums. For the past half-century, Birmingham has been "a place of revolution and reconciliation," trying in recent decades to heal the wounds left by Eugene "Bull" Connor, firehoses, bombings, and police dogs, images of which cluttered the American media in the early 1960s.

PRACTICAL INFORMATION

Tourist Office: Birmingham Visitors Center, 1200 University Blvd. (458-8001), at 12 St., I-65 Exit 259. Maps, calendars, and coupons for accommodations. Open Mon.-Sat. 8:30am-5pm, Sun. 1-5pm. Another location on the lower level of **Birmingham Municipal Airport** (458-8002). Open daily 7:45am-10pm. **Greater Birmingham Convention and Visitors Bureau,** 2200 9th Ave. N., 3rd fl. (252-9825), downtown. Open Mon.-Fri. 8:30am-5pm.

Trains: Amtrak, 1819 Morris Ave. (324-3033 or 800-872-7245). To Atlanta (3 per week, 5hr., $33) and New Orleans (3 per week, 7hr., $68). Open 8:30am-5pm.

Buses: Greyhound, 619 N. 19th St. (251-3210 or 800-231-2222). To: Montgomery (8 per day, 2hr., $15); Mobile (8 per day, 8hr., $39); Atlanta (6 per day, 2-3hr., $22). Open 24hr.

Public Transportation: Metropolitan Area Express (MAX), 322-7701. Runs Mon.-Fri. 5am-5pm. $1, transfers 25¢. **Downtown Area Runabout Transit (DART),** 252-0101. Runs Mon.-Fri. 10am-4pm. Fare 50¢.

Taxi: Yellow Cab, 252-1131. $3 base fare, $1.20 per additional mi.
Crisis Lines: Crisis Center, 323-7777. Open 24hr. **Rape Response,** 323-7273.
Emergency: 911.
Post Office: 351 24th St. N. (521-0302). Open Tues.-Fri. 24hr. Closes Sat. 4:30am
and reopens Mon 4:30am. **ZIP code:** 35203. **Area code:** 205.

The downtown area grid system has avenues running east-west and streets running
north-south. Each numbered avenue has a north and a south. Major cultural and government buildings surround **Linn Park,** located between 19th and 21st St. N. on 7th
Ave. N. The **University of Alabama in Birmingham (UAB)** extends along University
Blvd. (8th Ave. S.) from 11th to 20th St.

ACCOMMODATIONS AND CAMPING

Royal Inn, 821 20th St. S. (252-8041), 2 blocks from UAB hospital. Large, clean
rooms and tasteful decor in a convenient location. Singles and doubles $35.
Ranchhouse Inn, 2127 7th Ave. S. (322-0691). Near busy bars and restaurants. Pleasant rooms with cable TV and wood paneling. Local calls 25¢ each. Singles $30,
doubles $36.
Oak Mountain State Park (620-2527), 15mi. south of Birmingham off I-65 in Pelham (Exit 246). Alabama's largest state park, with nearly 10,000 heavily forested
acres. Horseback rides, golf, hiking, and an 85-acre lake. Sites for 1-4 $8.50, with
full hookup $15.

FOOD

Barbecue remains the local specialty, although more ethnic variations have sprung up
downtown. The best places to eat cheaply (and meet young people) are at **Five
Points South,** located at the intersection of Highland Ave. and 20th St. S. Choose
between pesto pizza with sun-dried tomatoes ($3 per slice) at **Cosmo's Pizza,** 2012
Magnolia Ave., in Pickwick Place (930-9971; open Mon.-Thurs. 11am-11pm, Fri.-Sat.
11am-midnight, Sun. noon-10pm), or health-conscious veggie lunches and groceries
at **The Golden Temple,** 1901 11th Ave. S. (933-6333; open Mon.-Fri. 8:30am-7pm,
Sat. 9:30am-5:30pm, Sun. noon-5:30pm; kitchen open Mon.-Sat. 11:30am-2pm).

Ollie's, 515 University Blvd. (324-9485), near Green Springs Hwy. Bible Belt dining
in an enormous circular 50s-style building. Pamphlets shout "Is there really a Hell?"
while you lustfully consume your beef. BBQ sandwich $2, homemade pie $1.50.
Diet plates available. Open Mon. 10am-3pm, Tues.-Sat. 10am-8am.
The Mill, 1035 20th St. S. (939-3001), sits at the center of Five Points South, serving
tasty pizzas ($6-8) and sandwiches ($5-6). Microbrewery, bakery, and restaurant in
one, this sidewalk café/restaurant/bar will sate any gastronomic need. Live entertainment Tues.-Sun. Open Mon.-Fri. 6:30am-1am, Sat.-Sun. 2pm-3am.
Bogue's, 3028 Clairmont Ave. (254-9780). A short-order diner with true, delicious
Southern fare (cheese omelette and biscuit $3). Always busy weekend mornings.
Open Mon.-Fri. 6am-2pm, Sat.-Sun. 6-11:30am.
Café Bottega, 2240 Highland Ave. S. (939-1000). High-ceilinged and sophisticated,
this café serves fresh bread to dip in olive oil and Italian specialties brimming with
fresh vegetables and herbs. Marinated pasta with sweet peas and mint $5.25.
Entrees $5-12. Open Mon.-Sat. 11am-11pm. Bar open until "everyone goes home."

SIGHTS

Part of Birmingham's efforts at reconciliation have culminated in the **Black Heritage
Tour** of the downtown area. The **Birmingham Civil Rights Institute,** 520 16th St.
N. (328-9696), at 6th Ave. N., rivals the museum in Memphis (see Memphis, p. 282)
in thoroughness, and surpasses it in visual and audio evocations, depictions, and footage of African-American history and the turbulent events of the civil rights movement. The Institute displays exhibits on human rights across the globe and serves as a
public research facility. A trip to Birmingham would be incomplete without a tour.

THE SOUTH

(Open Tues.-Sat. 10am-5pm, Sun. 1-5pm. $3 donations appreciated.) Other significant sights include the **Sixteenth Street Baptist Church,** 1530 6th Ave. N. (251-9402), at 16th St. N. (in the lower level), where four black girls died in a September 1963 bombing by white segregationists after a protest push which culminated in Dr. Martin Luther King Jr.'s "Letter From a Birmingham Jail." (Open Tues.-Fri. 10am-4pm, Sat. by appointment. Donations appreciated.) Many protests spurred by the death occurred in nearby **Kelly-Ingram Park,** corner of 6th Ave. and 16th St., where a bronze statue of Dr. Martin Luther King, Jr. and sculptures portraying the brutality and hope of the civil rights demonstrations now grace the green lawns.

Remnants of Birmingham's steel industry are best viewed at the gigantic **Sloss Furnaces National Historic Landmark** (324-1911), adjacent to the 2nd Ave. N. viaduct off 32nd St. downtown. Though the blast furnaces closed 20 years ago, they stand as the only preserved example of 20th-century iron-smelting in the world. Ballet and drama performances and music concerts are often held here at night. (Open Tues.-Sat. 10am-4pm, Sun. noon-4pm; free guided tours Sat.-Sun. at 1, 2, and 3pm.) To anthropomorphize the steel industry, Birmingham made a cast of **Vulcan** (Roman god of the forge), who overlooks the skyline as the largest cast-iron statue in the world. Visitors can watch over the city from its observation deck. The Vulcan's glowing torch burns red when a car fatality has occurred that day in the city, green when none occur (328-6198; open daily 8am-10:30pm. $1, under 7 free).

The **Alabama Sports Hall of Fame** (323-6665), corner of Civic Center Blvd. and 22nd St. N., honors the careers of outstanding sportsmen like Bear Bryant, Jesse Owens, Joe Louis, Joe Namath, and Willie Mays. (Open Mon.-Sat. 9am-5pm, Sun. 1-5pm. $5, students and seniors $3.) A few blocks down from the Hall of Fame, **Linn Park** refreshes visitors, and sits across from the **Birmingham Museum of Art,** 2000 8th Ave. N. (254-2565). The museum displays U.S. paintings and English Wedgewood ceramics, as well as a superb collection of African textiles and sculptures. (Open Tues.-Sat. 10am-5pm, Sun. noon-5pm. Free.)

For a breather from the downtown scene, revel in the marvelously sculpted grounds of the **Birmingham Botanical Gardens,** 2612 Lane Park Rd. (879-1227), whose spectacular floral displays, elegant Japanese gardens, and enormous greenhouse vegetate on 68 acres (open daily dawn-dusk; free).

Antebellum **Arlington,** 331 Cotton Ave. (780-5656), southwest of downtown, houses a fine array of 19th-century Southern decorative arts and holds crafts fairs in Birmingham's sole surviving Greek revival home. Go west on 1st Ave. N., which becomes Cotton Ave. (Open Tues.-Sat. 10am-4pm, Sun. 1-4pm. $3, ages 6-18 $2.)

If you don't know much 'bout geology, visit the **Red Mountain Museum and Cut,** 2230 22nd St. S (933-4104). Wander across a walkway to see different levels of rock formation inside Red Mountain, or check out exhibits on the prehistoric inhabitants of Alabama. (Open Mon.-Fri. 9am-4pm, Sat. 10am-4pm, Sun. 1-4pm. $2.)

ENTERTAINMENT AND NIGHTLIFE

Historic **Alabama Theater,** 1817 3rd Ave. N. (252-2262), shows old movies on occasional weekends; their organ, the "Mighty Wurlitzer," entertains the audience pre-show ($4, seniors $3, under 12 $2). The free *Fun and Stuff* and "Kudzu" section in Friday's edition of *The Birmingham Post Herald,* list movies, plays, and clubs.

Music lovers lucky or smart enough to visit Birmingham June 13-15, 1997 for **City Stages** (251-1272) will hear everything from country to gospel to big name rock groups, with headliners like James Brown, the Indigo Girls, and George Jones. The three-day festival, held in Linn Park, also includes food, crafts, and children's activities. (Daily pass $15, weekend pass $20.)

Nightclubs congregate in **Five Points South (Southside).** On cool summer nights many people grab outdoor tables in front of their favorite bars or hang by the fountain. Use caution here, and avoid parking or walking in dark alleys near the square. For the hippest licks year-round, check out **The Nick,** 2514 10th Ave. S. (252-3831). The poster-covered exterior says it clear and proud: "the Nick…rocks." (Cover $2-5. Open Mon.-Fri. 3pm-late, Sat. 8pm-later. Live music Wed.-Mon.) **Louie Louie's,** 2001

THE SOUTH

Highland Ave. (933-2778), at 21st St., has good cheap drinks and tunes; live bands play Wednesday, Friday, and Saturday, and disco plays on Thursday. (Tues.-Thurs. 75¢ cans and $1 drinks. Open Tues.-Sat. 7pm-'til.) **The Burly Earl,** 2109 7th Ave. S. (322-5848), specializes in fried finger-foods and local acoustic, blues, and rock sounds; sandwiches are $3-5. (Open Mon.-Thurs. 10am-11pm, Fri.-Sat. 10am-1am. Live music Thurs.-Sat. nights.)

■ Mobile

Though Bob Dylan lamented being stuck here while yearning for Memphis, Mobile (mo-BEEL) has had plenty of fans in its time—French, Spanish, English, Sovereign Alabama, Confederate, and American flags have each flown over the city since its 1702 founding. This historical diversity is revealed in local architecture; antebellum mansions, Italianate dwellings, Spanish and French historical forts, and Victorian homes line azalea-edged streets. The faded splendor of these buildings tell of a time in the not-so-distant past when cotton was king. Today, Mobile offers a laid-back and untouristed version of New Orleans; the site of the first Mardi Gras, the city still holds Fat Tuesday, without the hordes and MTV that plague its cajun counterpart.

PRACTICAL INFORMATION

Tourist Office: Fort Condé Information Center, 150 S. Royal St. (434-7304), in a reconstructed French fort near Government St. Open daily 8am-5pm.

Trains: Amtrak, 11 Government St. (432-4052 or 800-872-7245). The "Gulf Breeze" blows from Mobile to NYC via bus service to Birmingham or Atlanta. To: New Orleans (1 per day, 16hr., $45). Ticket office open daily 5:30am-midnight.

Buses: Greyhound, 2545 Government St. (478-9793 or 800-231-2222), at S. Conception downtown. To: Montgomery (8 per day, 4hr., $27); New Orleans (10 per day, 3hr., $24); Birmingham (7 per day, 6hr., $39). Open 24hr.

Public Transportation: Mobile Transit Authority (MTA), 344-5656. Major depots are at Bienville Sq., Royal St. parking garage, and Adams Mark Hotel. Runs Mon.-Fri. 6am-6pm, less Sat. $1.25, seniors and disabled 60¢, transfers 10¢.

Taxis: Yellow Cab, 476-7711. $1.30 base fare, $1.20 per additional mi.

Crisis Lines: Rape Crisis, 473-7273. **Crisis Counseling,** 666-7900. **Helpline,** 431-5111. All 24hr.

Emergency: 911.

Post Office: 250 Saint Joseph St. (694-5917). Open Mon.-Fri. 7am-5pm, Sat. 9am-4pm. **ZIP code:** 36601. **Area code:** 334.

The downtown district fronts the Mobile River. **Dauphin St.** and **Government Blvd.** (U.S. 90), which becomes Government St. downtown, are the major east-west routes. **Royal St.** and **Broad St.** are major north-south byways. **Water St.** runs along the bay in the downtown area, becoming the **I-10 causeway.** Some of Mobile's major attractions lie outside downtown. The *U.S.S. Alabama* is off the causeway (I-10) leading out of the city; **Dauphin Island** is 30 mi. south.

ACCOMMODATIONS AND CAMPING

Accommodations are both reasonable and accessible, but stop first at the Fort Condé Information Center (see above); they can make reservations for you at a 10-15% discount. **Family Inns,** 900 S. Beltline Rd. (344-5500), I-65 at Airport Blvd., sports new carpets, firm beds, and general comfort (singles $29, doubles $36). **Motel 6,** 400 Beltline Hwy. (343-8448), off Airport Blvd., has large, well-furnished rooms with HBO and pool access; among other branches is the near-downtown 1520 Mudslinger Dr. (473-1603), near I-10 and Dauphin Island Pkwy. (Singles $32, doubles $36; each additional person $2.) **I-10 Kampground,** 6430 Theodore Dawes Rd. E. (653-9816), lies 7½ mi. west on I-10 (Exit 13 and turn south). The kampground is not accessible by public transportation. (Pool, kiddie playground, laundry, and bath facilities. Tent sites $13; RVs $16; each additional person $1.)

FOOD AND NIGHTLIFE

Mobile's Gulf location means fresh seafood and Southern cookin'. **Dreamland,** 3314 Old Shell Rd. (479-9898), has two things on the menu: whole slab or half slab. That's ribs, y'all, smoked right here. (Open Mon.-Thurs. 10am-10pm, Fri.-Sat. 10am-midnight, Sun. 11am-9pm.) The **Lumber Yard,** 2617 Dauphin St. (476-4609), saws off healthy sandwiches, salads, and pizzas, and a full-service bar with happy hour Mon.-Sat. 4-7pm. ($1 domestic drafts. Open Mon.-Fri. 11am-10pm, Sat. 11am-11pm. Live music Thurs.-Fri.) Ten pool tables and mega-subs ($3) make **Solomon's,** 5753 Old Shell Rd. (344-0380), the quintessential brew and cue college hangout (open 24hr.). **Hayley's,** 278 Dauphin St. (433-4970), an alternative bar/hangout, adorns its tables with peaceful messages (beer $1.50, jello shots $1; open daily 3pm-3am). For after-hours dancing, **Exit,** 9 N. Jackson off Dauphin St. (433-9979), pulses until morning (open Wed.-Sat. 2am-'til).

SIGHTS

Mobile encompasses four historic districts: **Church St., DeTonti Square, Old Dauphin Way,** and **Oakleigh Garden.** Each offers an array of architectural styles. The info center provides maps for walking or driving tours of these areas. **Gray Line of Mobile** (432-2228) leads tours, and can get you to most main districts and sights.

Church St. divides into east and west subdistricts. The homes in the venerable **Church St. East District** showcase popular U.S. architectural styles of the mid to late 19th century, including Federal, Greek Revival, Queen Anne, and Victorian. While on Church St., pass through the **Spanish Plaza,** at Hamilton and Government St., which honors Mobile's sibling city—Málaga, Spain—while recalling Spain's early presence in Mobile. **Christ Episcopal Church,** 115 S. Conception St. (433-1842), sits opposite the tourist office at Fort Condé. Dedicated in 1842, the church contains beautiful German, Italian, and Tiffany stained glass windows. Call the office (weekdays 8am-5pm) or wander in when the church opens on weekends (Sunday services at 8 and 10am). The intriguingly named **Phoenix Fire Museum,** 203 S. Claiborne St. (434-7554), displays several antique fire engines including an 1898 steam-powered one (open Tues.-Sat. 10am-5pm, Sun. 1-5pm; free).

In the **DeTonti Historical District,** north of downtown, tour the restored **Richards-DAR House,** 256 North Joachim St. (434-7320); the stained glass and Rococo chandeliers blend beautifully with the antebellum Italianate architecture and ornate iron lace (tours $3, kids $1; open Tues.-Sun. 10am-4pm). Brick townhouses with wrought-iron balconies fill the rest of the district. **Oakleigh,** 350 Oakleigh Place (432-1281), 2½ blocks south of Government St., reigns as one of Mobile's grande dames, with a cantilevered staircase and enormous windows that open onto all the balconies upstairs. Inside, a museum contains furnishings of the early Victorian, Empire, and Regency periods. (Tours every ½hr.; last tour 3:30pm. Open Mon.-Sat. 10am-4pm, Sun. 2-4pm. $5, students $2, seniors $4.50, ages 6-18 $1.) Also tour the **Bragg-Mitchell,** 1906 Spring Hill Ave. (471-6364; open Mon.-Fri. 10am-4pm, Sun. 1-4pm) and **Condé-Charlotte,** 104 Theatre St. (432-4722; open Tues.-Sat. 10am-4pm), the former residences of cotton brokers and river pilots. (Package tour available at visitors center; $10 for four house museums. Last tour 3:30pm.)

The **Mobile Museum of Art,** 4850 Museum Dr. (343-2667), between Springhill Ave. and University Blvd., displays some fascinating African-American art. (Open Tues.-Sun. 10am-5pm. Free.) The **Exploreum,** 1906 Springhill Ave. (476-6873), offers hands-on scientific diversions kids will dig. (Open Tues.-Sat. 9am-5pm. $4, ages 2-17 $3.) The battleship *U.S.S. Alabama,* permanently moored at **Battleship Park** (433-2703), fought in every major battle in the Pacific during WWII; the famous submarine *U.S.S. Drum* rolled along its port side. The park is at the entrance of the Bankhead Tunnel, 2½ mi. east of town on I-10. (Open daily 8am-7:30pm. $8, ages 6-11 $4; flight simulator $3; parking $2.) **Bellingrath Gardens,** 12401 Bellingrath Gardens Rd. (973-2217), Exit 15A off I-10, includes some of the nation's premier gardens. The lush landscaped grounds feature a formal rose garden and Asian-American garden. Plants bloom year round, but March to November offer the most spectacular displays. (Open daily 8am-1hr. before sunset. Home and gardens $14, ages 5-11 $10. With river cruise $19/$14. Gardens only $7/$5.)

February is a big month for Mobile. Locals await the blooming of the 27-mi. **Azalea Trail** in February and March, and on February 11, 1997, Mobile's **Mardi Gras** will fill the streets. Enjoy parades, floats, costumes, and "throws" of the oldest (and, some say, best) Fat Tuesday around.

Mississippi

Perhaps more than any other state, Mississippi is known for its economic turmoil and racial strife. The state was devastated in the Civil War—the siege of Vicksburg and the near-destruction of Jackson left Mississippi in complete ruins—and in many ways, it never fully recovered. In the 1960s, whites in Mississippi reacted to black protests against segregation with campaigns of terror. In the last few decades, the state has been mired in rural poverty and below-average educational standards. The average income in Mississippi is the lowest in the nation.

At the same time, "The Magnolia State" boasts not only great physical beauty (towering weeping willows stand elegantly in the flat countryside) but also an impressive literary and cultural heritage. Writers William Faulkner, Eudora Welty, Tennessee Williams, and Richard Wright all considered Mississippi their home, as did blues musicians Bessie Smith, W.C. Handy, and B.B. King, who brought their riffs up the "Blues Highway" to Memphis, Chicago, and the world.

PRACTICAL INFORMATION

Capital: Jackson.
Division of Tourism: P.O. Box 1705, Ocean Springs, MS 39566 (800-927-6378).
Bureau of Parks and Recreation: P.O. Box 10600, Jackson 39209.
Time Zone: Central (1hr. behind Eastern). **Postal Abbreviation:** MS.
Sales Tax: 7-8%.

▒ Jackson

A sleepy Deep South town, Mississippi's commercial and political capital offers travelers a glimpse into life below the Mason-Dixon line without the usual plastic tourist traps. North Jackson's lush homes and plush country clubs epitomize traditional Southern living, while shaded campsites, cool reservoirs, national forests, and Native American burial mounds invite exploration only minutes away.

PRACTICAL INFORMATION

Tourist Office: Visitors Information Center, 1150 Lakeland Dr. (981-0019), off I-55S, Lakeland East exit. Located inside the Agricultural Museum. Open Mon.-Sat. 9am-5pm, Sun. 1-5pm. **Convention and Visitors Bureau,** 921 N. President St. (960-1891), downtown. Open Mon.-Fri. 8:30am-5pm.

Airport: Jackson Municipal (932-2859), east of downtown off I-20. Cab fare to downtown costs about $15.

Trains: Amtrak, 300 W. Capitol St. (355-6350 or 800-872-7245). The neighborhood is deserted at night. Walk downtown via Capitol St. To: Memphis (5 per week, 4hr., $46); New Orleans (5 per week, 4hr., $42). Open daily 8:30am-7pm.

Buses: Greyhound, 201 S. Jefferson (353-6342 or 800-231-2222). *Avoid this area at night.* To: Montgomery (3 per day, 7hr., $46); Memphis (5 per day, 4½hr., $32); New Orleans (4 per day, 4½hr., $34). Open 24hr.

Public Transportation: Jackson Transit System (JATRAN), 948-3840. Limited service Mon.-Fri. 5am-7pm, Sat. 7am-6pm. Fare 75¢, transfers free. Bus schedules and maps posted at most bus stops and available at JATRAN headquarters, 1025 Terry Rd. Open Mon.-Fri. 8am-4:30pm.

Taxis: City Cab, 355-8319. $1.10 base fare, $1 per mi.

Crisis Lines: Crisis Intervention, 355-8634. **Rape Hotline,** 982-7273. Both 24hr.

Emergency: 911.

Post Office: 401 E. South St. (968-1612). Open Mon.-Fri. 7am-6pm, Sat. 8am-noon. **ZIP code:** 39201. **Area code:** 601.

Downtown, just west of I-55, is bordered on the north by **High St.,** on the south by **Tombigbee St.,** and on the west by **Farish St.** North-south **State St.** bisects the city.

ACCOMMODATIONS AND CAMPING

In Jackson, hotel prices vary depending on location and comfort. If you have a car, head for the motels along I-20 and I-55. Expect to pay $25-30 for decent accommodations in the area, unless you go the bargain route and camp.

Sun 'n' Sand Motel, 401 N. Lamar St. (354-2501), downtown. Large, well-kept rooms with orange 'n' aqua plastic curtains—there's even a Polynesian room. Cable TV, pool, and in-house barber shop. Lounge/restaurant in motel serves a $5 lunch buffet. Singles $33, doubles $38; $5 per additional person.

Parkside Inn, 3720 I-55N (982-1122), at Exit 98B, close to downtown. Dark green furniture and wood-paneled walls spruce up these clean, somewhat small rooms. Pool, cable TV, free local calls, and some rooms with whirlpools available. Must be 21 to rent, 18 and under free with adult. Singles $29-32, doubles $35.

Timberlake Campgrounds, 143 Timberlake Dr. (992-9100). A popular summer camping site with both shaded and waterfront lots. Pool, video games, tennis courts, playground. Tent sites $9, with full hookup $14.

FOOD AND NIGHTLIFE

A waterfall trickles from the second floor of the converted smokehouse where **The Iron Horse Grill,** 320 W. Pearl St. (355-8419), at Gallatin, serves its Tex-Mex specialties ($8-11). Steak and seafood can be had for a bit more cash. (Open Mon.-Thurs. 11am-10pm, Fri.-Sat. 11am-11pm.) A 32-year Jackson institution, **Primo's Northgate,** 4330 N. State St. (982-2064), fills a spacious, quasi-romantic dining room with candlelight, jazz, and open-faced prime rib sandwiches ($8; open Mon.-Sat. 11am-10pm). Be prepared to wait in line during the lunch rush at **The Elite Restaurant,** 141 E. Capitol (352-5606). The daily-changing plate lunch special (with 2 veggies and bread, $5.25) make it worth the wait. The cheese-covered enchiladas ($5.70) are also a favorite (open Mon.-Fri. 7am-9:30pm, Sat. 5-9:30pm).

For a list of weekend events in Jackson, pick up a copy of the *Clarion-Ledger* on Thursday. **Hal & Mal's Restaurant and Oyster Bar,** 200 Commerce St. (948-0888), stages live music, from reggae to innovative rock, in a converted warehouse. (Bands Fri.-Sat. Cover $0-12. Restaurant open Mon.-Thurs. 11am-11pm, Fri. 11am-1am, Sat. 5pm-1am; bar open Fri.-Sat. until 1am.) **Cups,** 2757 Old Canton Rd. (362-7422), caters to an artsy crowd craving cappuccino and conversation (open Mon.-Thurs. 7am-10pm, Fri. 7am-midnight, Sat. 8am-midnight, Sun. 9am-10pm).

SIGHTS AND ENTERTAINMENT

Built in 1833, the **Old State Capitol** (359-6920), at the intersection of Capitol and State St., houses an excellent museum documenting Mississippi's turbulent history, including artifacts from original Native American settlements and documentaries on the Civil Rights Movement (open Mon.-Fri. 8am-5pm, Sat. 9:30am-4:30pm, Sun. 12:30-4:30pm; free). The **War Memorial Building,** 120 S. State St. (354-7207), tells the gruesome tale of American wars and the Mississippians who fought, distinguished themselves, and died in them (open Mon.-Fri. 8am-4:30pm; free). A tour of the **Governor's Mansion,** 300 E. Capitol St. (359-3175), gives an enlightening introduction to Mississippi politics. Because the governor still lives here, the touring hours are slim.

(Tours Tues.-Fri. every ½-hr. 9:30-11am; free.) During the siege of Jackson in 1863, General Sherman occupied an antebellum cottage called **The Oaks,** 823 N. Jefferson St. (353-9339). Today it displays period antiques including an original rocker and couch from Abraham Lincoln's office (open Tues.-Sat. 10am-4pm, Sun. 1:30-4pm; $2, students $1).

Though rich in history, Jackson hardly neglects the wonders of the present. The state legislature currently convenes in the beautiful **New State Capitol** (359-3114), at Mississippi and Congress, completed in 1903. A huge restoration project preserved the *beaux arts* grandeur of the building, complete with a gold-leaf eagle perched on the capitol dome, carnivalesque colors, and strings of lights which brighten the spacious interior. (Guided 1-hr. tours Mon.-Fri. 9, 10, 11am, 1:30, 2:30, and 3:30pm. Open Mon.-Fri. 8am-5pm. Free.) For more priceless beauty, the **Mississippi Museum of Arts,** 201 E. Pascagoula (960-1515), at Lamar St., has a fabulous collection of Americana and a fun participatory Impression Gallery for kids. (Open Tues.-Sun. 10am-5pm, Sun. noon-5pm. $3, kids $2; students free Tues. and Thurs.) Next door, the **Russell C. Davis Planetarium,** 201 E. Pascagoula (960-1550), ranks among the most stellar worldwide. (Shows Tues.-Sat. 7:30pm, Sat.-Sun. 2 and 4pm. Laser shows Thurs.-Sat. 8:30pm, Sat.-Sun. 3pm. $4, under 13 $2.50.)

Learn about the struggles and achievements of Mississippi's African-Americans at the **Smith-Robertson Museum and Cultural Center,** 528 Bloom St. (960-1457), behind the Sun 'n' Sand Motel. This large museum once housed the state's first African-American public school, which *Black Boy* author Richard Wright attended until the eighth grade. Now it displays folk art, photographs, and excellent exhibits on the Civil Rights Movement, particularly on the role of African-American women in Mississippi. (Open Mon.-Fri. 9am-5pm, Sat. 9am-noon, Sun. 2-5pm. $1, children 50¢.) Every Labor Day, the surrounding neighborhood celebrates African-American culture through art, theater, and food at the **Farish Street Festival** (944-1600).

Though a bit out of the way, the **Museum of the Southern Jewish Experience** (885-6042), 40 mi. south of Jackson at the UAHC Henry S. Jacobs Camp in Utica, is the most extensive museum focusing on this subject. A staggering map of the South shows where synagogues stood in the 18th and 19th centuries, but no longer operate due to the shrinking population of observant Jews in the area. (Call for directions and tour info. Open daily 8am-5pm. Free, but donations appreciated.)

▓ Vicksburg

Vicksburg's verdant hills and prime Mississippi River location made it the focus of much strategic planning during the Civil War. President Abraham Lincoln called the town the "key," and maintained that the war "can never be brought to a close until that key is in our pocket." The Confederates' Gibraltar fell to Union forces on July 4, 1863, after valiantly resisting a 47-day bombardment. The loss hit the city hard—until the late 1940s, Vicksburg refused to hold any 4th of July celebrations. Today, the city continues to embrace its history. Downtown, 19th-century mansions house museums, and Civil War monuments dominate the urban landscape. Lush parks lend Vicksburg a relaxed, pastoral feel.

Practical Information You'll need a car to see most of Vicksburg. The bus station, the information center, downtown, and the far end of the sprawling military park mark the city's extremes. The **Tourist Information Center** (636-9421 or 800-221-3536), across the street from the park, has a helpful map with info and locations for Vicksburg's sights (open daily 8am-5pm; in winter 9am-4pm). **Greyhound** (636-1230 or 800-231-2222) rides from a station inconveniently located at 1295 S. Frontage Rd. (open daily 7am-8:30pm). The **Rape and Sexual Assault Service** (638-0031) is open 24hr. Vicksburg's **post office:** (636-1071), on U.S. 61 at Pemberton Blvd. (open Mon.-Fri. 8:30am-5pm, Sat. 9am-noon). **ZIP code:** 39180. **Area code:** 601.

Accommodations, Food, and Nightlife Inexpensive accommodations come easy in Vicksburg, except during the military park's July Fourth weekend battle reenactment (see below). One of the best deals in town, the **Beechwood Motel,** 4449 Rte. 80E (636-2271), offers cable and clean rooms (singles $35, doubles $46). The well-worn rooms at the **Hillcrest Motel,** 40 Rte. 80E (638-1491), come with plastic furniture and pool access (singles $24, doubles $28). Most hotels cluster near the park; don't expect to stay downtown, unless you choose the **Relax Inn,** 1313 Walnut St. (638-3700; rooms $25-35). **River City RV Park,** 211 Miller St. (631-0388), provides 66 RV hookups, a pool, a game room, and a playground (sites $17).

While downtown, chow down at the **Burger Village,** 1220 Washington St. (638-0202), where a good meal costs under $5 (open Mon.-Sat. 9am-6pm). The popular **New Orleans Café,** 1100 Washington St. (638-8182), serves mouth-watering sandwiches (under $6), and Cajun specialties (specials $6-16; open Mon.-Sat. 11:30am-10pm). On weekends, the café's **Other Side Lounge** hosts live bands and a crowd of locals (open Fri.-Sat. 5:30pm-2am). Across the street, **Miller's Still Lounge,** 1101 Washington St. (638-8661), is a real Southern watering hole featuring blues and rock bands Thurs.-Sun (no cover; open Tues.-Sat. noon-2am, Sun. 5pm-2am).

Sights Memorials and markers of combat sites riddle the grassy 1700-acre **Vicksburg National Military Park** (636-0583; 800-221-3536 outside MS). The park blockades the eastern and northern edges of the city, with its entrance and visitors center on Clay St., about 1 mi. west of I-20's Exit 4 (center open daily 8am-5pm; park open daily 7am-8pm). Driving through the 16-mile path ($4 per car), you have three options: guide yourself with a free map available at the entrance, rent an informative cassette tape to guide you ($4.50), or have a live person take your carload through the sights ($20). Within the park, be sure to visit the **U.S.S. Cairo Museum** (636-2199). The Union boat, sunk in 1862, contains countless artifacts salvaged in the early 1960s (open daily 9:30am-6pm; off season 8am-5pm; free with park fee). Many consider the **Old Courthouse Museum,** 1008 Cherry St. (636-0741), one of the South's finest Civil War museums. During the siege of Vicksburg in 1863, Confederate troops used the cupola as a signal station and held Union prisoners in the upstairs courtroom. (Open Mon.-Sat. 8:30am-5pm, Sun. 1:30-5pm; early Oct.-early April Mon.-Sat. 8:30am-4:30pm, Sun. 1:30-4:30pm. $2, seniors $1.50, under 18 $1.)

Control of the mighty Mississippi River continues to preoccupy the military. A free tour of the **U.S. Army Engineer Waterways Experiment Station,** 3909 Halls Ferry Rd. (634-2502), the largest in the nation, explains the role of the Mississippi River in urban and rural development. A scale model of the dam system of Niagara Falls occupies the floor of one entire room. (1½-hour guided tours daily 10am and 2pm. Open daily 7:45am-4:30pm. Free.) Taste the lighter side of Vicksburg history, two blocks away, at the **Museum of Coca-Cola History and Memorabilia** and the **Biedenharn Candy Company,** 1107 Washington St. (638-6514), which first bottled the soft drink. The two-room museum displays Coke memorabilia from as far back as 1894, but since it takes 10 minutes to look around, the price is high. The museum does sell tasty Coke floats, along with over 100 different Coca-Cola items. (Open Mon.-Sat. 9am-5pm, Sun. 1:30-4:30pm. $1.75, under 12 $1.25.) Across the street from the Coke museum, a man known as **Johnny Reb** carves foot-tall caricatures of Civil War luminaries inside the **Gray and Blue Naval Museum,** 1102 Washington St. (638-6500). Johnny's work is a Vicksburg must-see. (Open daily 9am-5pm. $1.50.)

> **It's not easy being green...**
>
> The creator of the Muppets, Jim Henson, hung his hat in **Leland,** 90 mi. north of Vicksburg. His fuzzy, original creations (including the Swedish Chef and Chester the Rat) live on at the **Birthplace of the Frog Exhibit** (686-2687), intersection of Rte. 82 and S. Deer Creek, 7 mi. east in **Leland.** (Open Memorial Day-Labor Day Mon.-Fri. 10am-4pm, Sat.-Sun. 1-5pm. Free, but donations are appreciated.)

Vicksburg's finest contribution to the historical home circuit, the **Martha Vick House,** 1300 Grove St. (638-7036), was home to the daughter of the city's founder, Reverend Newitt Vick (open Mon.-Sat. 9am-5pm, Sun. 2pm-5pm; $5, children $2). The **Red Carpet Washateria and Lanes,** 2900 Clay St. (636-9682), on Rte. 80 near the river and Riverfront Park, shines with the sparkle of classic Americana—it's a bowling alley, pool room, and laundromat all in one! Bowl a game ($1.75 per person) and clean your socks (wash 75¢; dry 25¢) in one fell swoop. (Open Mon.-Fri. 9am-11pm, Sat. 10am-midnight, Sun. 1-10pm.)

■ Natchez

In the late 18th century, Natchez stood out as one of the wealthiest settlements on the Mississippi. Of the 13 millionaires in Mississippi at the time, 11 had their cotton plantations here. The custom was to build a manor on the Mississippi side of the river and till the soil on the Louisiana side. After the Civil War, the cotton-based economy of the South crumbled, and the days of the mansion-building magnates passed. Many of the homes remain, however, affording visitors to Natchez the opportunity to gaze at elegant dwellings from a vanished era.

Practical Information From inside an antique-filled home, the **Mississippi Welcome Center,** 370 Sergeant Prentiss Dr. (442-5849), does its thing with Southern hospitality. Pick up maps and discount books; they'll also suggest tours and book hotel rooms (open daily 8am-7pm; Labor Day-Memorial Day 8am-5pm). Make connections to Vicksburg (1 per day, 1hr., $14) and New Orleans (2 per day, 3hr., $35) at the **Natchez Bus Station,** 103 Lower Woodville Rd. (445-5291; open Mon.-Sat. 8am-5:30pm, Sun. 2-5pm). In-town transportation is available from **Natchez Ford Rental,** 199 St. Catherine St. (445-0060), for $38 per day plus 20¢ per mi. (must be 21 with major credit card or $250 cash deposit). The **Natchez Bicycling Center,** 334 Main St. (446-7794), rents vehicles of the two-wheeled variety. ($7.50 for 1-3hr., $10 for 3-5hr., $14 for all day. Must be 14 or accompanied by an adult 18 or older. Open Tues.-Fri. 10am-5:30pm, Sat. 10am-4pm; other times by appointment.) Natchez's **post office:** 214 N. Canal St. (442-4361; open Mon.-Fri. 8:30am-5pm, Sat. 10am-2pm); **ZIP code:** 39120; **area code:** 601.

Accommodations and Food The intersection of Rte. 61 and Highland Blvd. supports lots of good quality, high rooms. **Scottish Inns,** 40 Sgt. Prentiss Dr. (442-9141 or 800-251-1962), has spacious, clean rooms with wood furniture (singles $33, doubles $38). Close to the downtown area is the **Natchez Inn,** 218 John Junkie Rd. (442-0221), a friendly place with comfortable rooms, a pool, and cable TV (singles and doubles $40). Campers can settle in at the secluded **campground** in **Natchez State Park** (442-2658), less than 10 mi. north of Natchez on U.S. 61 in Stanton. The park has 22 sites, six with full RV hookup ($11) or just water and electricity ($10) and the rest for less evolved camping ($6).

A multitude of cafés and diners dish up budget eats in Natchez. **Cock of the Walk,** 200 N. Broadway (446-8920), earns its title and stature with spicy catfish and baked potatoes served in a dining room with ye olde worlde atmosphere. (Catfish fillet $9. Open Mon.-Thurs. 5-9pm, Fri.-Sat. 5-10pm, Sun. 5-8pm.) At the corner of State and Canal St., **Depot Deli** (442-6500) puts together po'boys ($5) and other deli-style sandwiches (open daily 10am-5pm). Try regional specialties such as Cajun boudin sausage, chili, peanut butter pie, and Gringo Pie (tamales with cheese, onions, and jalapeño peppers, $5) on the patio at **Fat Mama's Tamales,** 500 S. Canal St. (442-4548). The "knock-you-naked" margarita ($4) is a perfect way to wash it all down. (Open Mon.-Wed. 11am-7pm, Thurs.-Sat. 11am-9pm, Sun. noon-5pm.)

Sights Natchez Pilgrimage Tours, P.O. Box 347 (446-6631 or 800-647-6742), on the corner of Canal and State St., supervises tours of the restored manors left from Natchez's "white gold" days. Pick up free tour schedules, maps, and pamphlets, or their guidebook ($5) which details the histories of the homes. (Open Mon.-Sat. 9am-5pm, Sun. 12:30-5pm.) Pilgrimage Tours sells tickets for individual houses ($5) as well as discount packages for multiple manors (3 houses $14, 4 houses $17, 5 houses $19; children ½-price). For a speedier view of the city and the mansion exteriors, Pilgrimage Tours also sells tickets for a 35-minute horse-drawn carriage tour ($8) and a 55-minute air-conditioned bus tour ($10).

The largest octagonal house in America, **Longwood,** 140 Lower Woodville Rd. (442-5193), astounds visitors with its creative, elaborate decor and imaginative floorplan. Yet the six-story edifice, designed to be an "Arabian palace," remains unfinished; the builders, hired from the North, abandoned work at the beginning of the Civil War to fight for the Union. They never returned, and their discarded tools and undisturbed crates still lie as they were left. (Tours every 20min. Open daily 9am-4:30pm.) **Stanton Hall,** 401 High St. (442-6282), on the other hand, arose under the direction of local Natchez architects and artisans. Completed in 1857, the mansion features French mirrors, Italian marble mantels, and exquisitely cut chandeliers. (Tours every ½-hr. Open daily 9am-5pm.)

For centuries before the rise of such opulence, the Natchez Indians flourished on this fertile land. The arrival of the French incited fighting in the 1720s and 1730s, and French military successes brought an end to the thriving Natchez community. The **Grand Village of the Natchez Indians,** 400 Jefferson Davis Blvd. (446-6502), off 61S, pays homage to the tribe with a museum that documents their history and culture. The museum sits atop one of several huge tribal burial mounds which dominate the area. When the Great Sun, or chief, of the tribe died, his wife and others who so desired were strangled and buried in the same mound; the house of the chief's successor was then built on top. (Open Mon.-Sat. 9am-5pm, Sun. 1:30-5pm. Free.)

The first educational institution in the Mississippi Territory, historic **Jefferson College** (442-2901), 6 mi. east of Natchez off U.S. 61 near U.S. 84E, hosted the treason trial of Aaron Burr, Vice-President under Thomas Jefferson, in 1807. Fortunately for Burr, the judges couldn't be found for sentencing. Burr escaped into the night and was later acquitted in Virginia. (Grounds open daily sunrise-sunset. Buildings open Mon.-Sat. 9am-5pm, Sun. 1-5pm. Free.)

The 500-mile **Natchez Trace Parkway** leads north from Natchez to Nashville, TN. The Parkway rambles through lush forests, swamps, and shady countryside, passing through historic landmarks and a beautiful national park along the way. The Mississippi River floats nearby, a gentle companion in the sleepy, scenic South.

■ Oxford

Strolling along the covered sidewalks of **Courthouse Square,** window shopping, and relishing the shade of Oxford's tall cedar trees, a visitor can't help but feel the serene quality of this small town. It hasn't always been like this. Over the years, Oxford has seen several periods of racial unrest. In the 19th century the small Mississippi town played a critical role in the Cherokee evacuation from Georgia as a stopping point on the Trail of Tears. Over a century later, Oxford came to the country's attention when a federal court ruled that James Meredith should be the first black student to enroll at the **University of Mississippi,** just west of the city. The news resulted in rioting and the death of three civil rights workers.

For now, Oxford rests again, a fitting home for the unique **Center for the Study of Southern Culture** (601-232-5993), at Ole Miss, where visitors can pick up literature on southern culture or attend conferences that are held there. The **Elvis Conference** and the **Faulkner Conference** (both in Aug.) draw the largest crowds.

William Faulkner's home at **Rowan Oaks** (601-234-3284), lies just south of downtown on Old Taylor Rd. Faulkner named the property after the Rowan tree, a symbol of peace and security. The Rowan is not, in fact, a member of the Oak family. This botanical tidbit is a source of much amusement to Oxford locals, whose lifelong companionship may be gained by asking the simple question, "Does the Rowan Oak actually exist?" (Open Tues.-Sat. 10am-noon and 2-4pm, Sun. 2-4pm. Tours are self-guided and free. The grounds are open from sunup to sundown.)

The **tourist information center,** 107 S. Lamar (601-232-2419) provides sound advice and a fury of entertainment options (open daily 10am-5pm). At **Square Books,** 160 S. Lamar, a collection of Faulkner's works may be enjoyed on a balcony overlooking the downtown area. The bookstore sells ice cream and coffee (open Mon.-Thurs. 9am-9pm, Fri.-Sat. 9am-10pm, Sun. 10am-6pm). While downtown, stop in at **Smitty's Café,** 208 S. Lamar (601-234-9111), where most entrees are under $6, and the cornbread is delicious (open Mon.-Sat. 6am-9pm, Sun. 8am-9pm).

Louisiana

Legend has it that after exploring the Mississippi River valley in 1682, Frenchman René-Robert Cavalier stuck a cross in the ground and proclaimed the land "Louisiane," in honor of Louis XIV. The name remained, although King Louis' ownership of the region did not. For a little more than a century after Cavalier's journey, the area was tossed around (sometimes forcibly, sometimes secretly) between France, England, and Spain before arriving in the hands of Thomas Jefferson and the United States in 1803. Each successive reign lured a new group of settlers searching for a tolerant government: Spaniards came from the Canary Islands, French Acadians from Nova Scotia created Acadiana (see p. 382), and U.S. ownership attracted whites and free blacks from the West Indies. The descendants of these diverse populations mix and mingle here today—in Louisiana you'll find folks wailing the blues on one side of town and dancing to zydeco on the other, or a family cooking up pecan pie and chicken-fried steak while a neighbor's gumbo simmers next door.

PRACTICAL INFORMATION

Capital: Baton Rouge.
Louisiana Office of Tourism: P.O. Box 94291, Baton Rouge 70804-9291 (504-342-8119 or 800-633-6970). Open Mon.-Fri. 9am-5pm. **Office of State Parks,** P.O. Box 44426, Baton Rouge 70804-4426 (504-342-8111). Open Mon.-Fri. 9am-5pm.
Time Zone: Central (1hr. behind Eastern). **Postal Abbreviation:** LA.
Sales Tax: 8%.

■ New Orleans

New Orleans stands as a country unto itself. Originally explored by the French, *La Nouvelle Orleans* was secretly ceded to the Spanish in 1762 (the citizens didn't realize until four years later). Spain returned the city to France just in time for Thomas Jefferson to purchase it in 1803. N'Awlins stayed faithful, and in 1812, Louisiana was admitted to the Union. Multiculturalism rules here; Spanish courtyards, Victorian verandas, Acadian jambalaya, Caribbean gumbo, and French beignets mix and mingle to create an atmosphere unlike any other. Don't try to place the local accent—it's a combination found nowhere else. Similarly unique, New Orleans' internationally renowned jazz fuses African rhythms and modern brass.

New Orleans loves to party, and come late February there's no escaping the month-long celebration of Mardi Gras, the apotheosis of the city's already festive atmosphere. Anxious to accrue as much sin as spirit and flesh will allow before Lent, perfect strangers, in all stages of undress, embrace each other, ostensibly to acquire multi-colored beads and doubloons. The "city that care forgot" promenades, shuffles, sings, and swigs until Ash Wednesday. Afterwards, the soulful jazz melodies play on, comforting those who have forsaken drunken cavorting for the next 40 long and Lenten days. The New Orleans Jazz and Heritage Festival provides a post-Lenten party that rivals the excitement of Mardi Gras but stays a bit more mature.

New Orleans

PRACTICAL INFORMATION

Tourist Office: Write or call ahead to the very helpful **New Orleans Welcome Center**, 529 St. Ann (568-5661), at Jackson Sq. in the French Quarter. Free city and walking tour maps. Open daily 9am-5pm. **Greater New Orleans Tourist and Convention Commission**, 1520 Sugar Bowl Dr., New Orleans 70112 (566-5031), on the main floor of the Superdome. Open daily 9am-5pm.

Airport: Moisant International (464-0831), 15mi. west of the city. Cab fare to the Quarter is set at $21 for 2 people; $8 per person for 3 or more. **Louisiana Transit Authority** (737-9611; open Mon.-Fri. 9am-4pm) runs to downtown at Elk and Tulane Ave. (approx. 45min.); Mon.-Sat. every hr. 6am-6pm; $1.10 in exact change. Pick-up on the upper level, near the exit ramp.

Trains: Amtrak, Good morning America, how are ya? 1001 Loyola Ave. (528-1610 or 800-872-7245), in the Union Passenger Terminal, a 10-min. walk to Canal St. via Elk. To: Houston (3 per week, 8hr., $73); Jackson (5 per week, 4hr., $42); Atlanta (3 per week, 12hr., $95). Station open 24hr.; ticket office open Mon., Wed., and Fri. 5am-8pm, Tues., Thurs., and Sun. 8am-11pm, Sat. 8am-8pm. Dontcha know me, I'm your native son.

Buses: Greyhound, 1001 Loyola Ave. (524-7571 or 800-231-2222), in Union Passenger Terminal. To Austin (5 per day, 13hr., $79) and Baton Rouge (8 per day, 1½hr., $13). Open 24hr.

Public Transportation: Regional Transit Authority (RTA), 700 Plaza Dr. (248-3900). Most buses pass Canal St., at the edge of the French Quarter. Major buses and streetcars run 24hr. Fare $1, seniors and disabled passengers 40¢; transfers

10¢. 1-day passes $4, 3-day passes $8. Office has bus schedules and transit info; open Mon.-Fri. 8:30am-5pm.

Those with an Eastern Accent: It's not pronounced NU or-LEEEEns; elide the first two syllables; work on NOHR-lens—like *nor*-mal.

Taxis: United Cabs, 522-9771. **Checker Yellow Cabs,** 943-2411. $2.10 base fare, $1.20 per mi. 75¢ per additional person.

Car Rental: Budget, 1317 Canal St. (467-2277 or 800-527-0700), and 4 other locations. $37 per day with 100 free mi. Must be 25 with credit card. Open Mon.-Thurs. 8am-5pm, Fri. 8am-6pm, Sat. 8am-3pm. Reservations suggested.

Bike Rental: Michael's, 622 Frenchmen St. (945-9505), a few blocks west of the Quarter between Royal and Charles St. $3.50 per hr., $12.50 per day, weekly rates available. Car racks available. Must have major credit card for deposit. Open Mon.-Sat. 10am-7pm, Sun. 10am-5pm.

Crisis Lines: Crisis Line, 523-2673. **Rape Hotline,** 483-8888. Both 24hr.

Emergency: 911.

Post Office: 701 Loyola Ave. (589-1111 or 589-1112), near the Union Passenger Terminal. Open Mon.-Fri. 8am-6pm, Sat. 8am-noon. **ZIP code:** 70113. **Area code:** 504.

ORIENTATION

New Orleans, though fairly small, can be very confusing. The city's main streets follow the curve of the **Mississippi River,** hence its nickname "the crescent city." Directions from locals show further watery influences—lakeside means north, referring to **Lake Ponchartrain,** and riverside means south. Uptown lies to the west, up river; downtown lies down river. Many streets run only one way; watch out for drivers who make U-turns to cross intersections. Tourists flock to the small **French Quarter (Vieux Carré),** bounded by the Mississippi River, **Canal St., Esplanade Ave.,** and **Rampart St.** downtown. Streets in the Quarter follow a grid pattern, making foot travel easy. The best way to get downtown fast, the St. Charles Streetcar, runs 24 hr. between the Quarter and uptown areas ($1). Streetcars go out to **Lee Circle** at **Howard Ave.** (a convenient spot for shoppers to get off), through **Audubon Park,** and up **South Carrollton Ave.** Buses to all parts of the city pass by Canal St. at the edge of the Quarter. The **Garden District** is situated west of downtown.

New Orleans struggles to play down its high murder and crime rates, but avoid areas where you feel at all uncomfortable; do not walk around alone at night anywhere in this city. The tenement areas directly to the north of the French Quarter and directly northwest of Lee Circle pose particular threats to personal safety. At night, even quaint-looking side streets in the Quarter can be dangerous—stick to busy, well-lit roads and look as little like a tourist as possible (don't wear a t-shirt that has the words "New Orleans" anywhere on it). *Avoid all parks, cemeteries, and housing projects at night.* Take a cab to your lodgings when returning from the Quarter late at night.

Parking in New Orleans is easier than driving in it. To park near the French Quarter for as long as you like, head for the residential area around **Marigny St.** and **Royal St.,** where many streets have no meters and no restrictions.

ACCOMMODATIONS

Finding inexpensive yet decent rooms in the French Quarter is as difficult as finding a sober person on Mardi Gras; luckily, other parts of the city compensate for the dearth of cheap lodging downtown. Several **hostels** pepper the area and cater to the young and almost penniless, as do **B&Bs** near the Garden District.

Accommodations for **Mardi Gras** get booked up to a year in advance, and the **Jazz Festival** makes budget rooms reasonably scarce. During peak times, proprietors will rent out any extra space—be sure you know what you're paying for. Rates tend to sink in June and early December, when accommodations become desperate for business; use your negotiation skills.

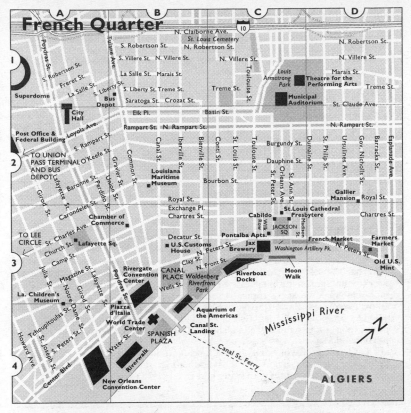

French Quarter

Marquette House New Orleans International Hostel (HI-AYH), 2253 Carondelet St. (523-3014). The cleanest hosteling experience in New Orleans. 160 new, comfy beds. Clean, homey kitchens and study rooms. Exceptionally quiet for a hostel. No alcohol permitted; smoking only in the courtyard. No curfew, no lockout. $14, nonmembers $17. Private rooms with queen-sized bed and pull-out sofa $39/$45. Linen $2.50. Key deposit $5.

India House, 124 S. Lopez St. (821-1904). If you've come to New Orleans for its bawdy entertainment, this bohemian haunt is party central. Spacious, comfortable common room with pictures and artwork from past visitors covering the walls. Free pickup at bus station or airport on request. 1pm check-out designed for those with "morning grogginess." $12 per night. Free linens. Key deposit $5.

St. Charles Guest House, 1748 Prytania St. (523-6556). In a serene neighborhood near the Garden District and St. Charles streetcar. A big three-building complex with 38 rooms, 8 with shared baths. Lovely pool and sunbathing deck, with (recorded) classical music. Small backpacker's singles with no A/C $15-25. Rooms with 1 queen-sized bed or 2 twins $45-65. Free breakfast.

Longpre House, 1726 Prytania St. (581-4540), in a 155-year-old house 1 block off the streetcar route; a 25-min. walk from the Quarter. Attracts travelers from all over the world with free coffee and a relaxed atmosphere. Dorm check-in 8am-10pm, after 11am for private rooms. No curfew. Dorms $16, with int'l passport or student ID $12. Singles and doubles with shared bath $35, with private bath $40.

Hotel LaSalle, 1113 Canal St. (523-5831 or 800-521-9450), 4 blocks from Bourbon St. downtown. Attractive lobby with coffee on an antique sideboard around the clock. Luxurious these rooms are not, but they are well-maintained. Singles $29, with bath $55; doubles $39/$59. Reservations recommended.

Old World Inn, 1330 Prytania St. (566-1330). A clean, comfortable house with multi-colored carpeting and painting-covered walls. The owners (New Orleans natives) can tell you what's hot, what's not, what's safe, what not. Complimentary breakfast. Singles $25, with bath $35; doubles $40/$50. $5 key deposit.

Prytania Inn, 1415 Prytania St. (566-1515). Includes 3 restored 19th-century homes about 5 blocks apart; stay in St. Vincent's if you can. Reasonable prices, multilingual staff (German, French, Italian, Spanish, and Japanese), homey atmosphere. Not for the couch potato—there's not a TV in sight. Singles $30-45, doubles $35-55. Breakfast served Mon.-Fri. 8-10am, Sat.-Sun. 8-10:30am ($5).

YMCA International Hostel, 920 St. Charles Ave. (568-9622). Clean, air-conditioned rooms for women, men, and couples. 20 rooms on the St. Charles side give an excellent view of Mardi Gras parades, but reserve early. Guests get free use of the Y's indoor pool, gym, and track. Shared baths. Singles $33, doubles $40.

CAMPING

The few campgrounds near New Orleans are tough to reach via public transportation. Travelers with wheels, however, have several options.

KOA West, 11129 Jefferson Hwy. (467-1792), in River Ridge; take Williams Blvd. exit off I-10; RTA bus transport available. Shuttle to French Quarter ($3) leaves 9am, returns 4pm. Pool, laundry facilities. Bathrooms new and very clean. Grounds shady and well-kept. 10 tent sites $22, 96 sites with full hookup $26.

St. Bernard State Park, (682-2101), 18mi. southeast of New Orleans in Violet; take Rte. 46S, go right on Rte. 39. Nearest public transport to the city ½mi. away. Register before 8pm, weekends 10pm. 51 sites with water and electricity $12.

Willow Mar Travel Park, 10910 Chef Menteur Hwy. (244-6611; 800-788-6787 outside LA), 3mi. east of the junction of I-10 and U.S. 90 (Chef Menteur Hwy.). Near public transport into the city. Pool, showers, and laundry facilities. Sites $12, with full hookup $16.

Parc D'Orleans Travel Park, 7676 Chef Menteur Hwy. (241-3167 or 800-535-2598), near the intersection of U.S. 90 and I-10. 71 small but orderly sites, a pool, and laundry facilities. Sites with water and electricity $14, with full hookup $16.

FOOD

New Orleans has more restaurants per capita than any major city in the world outside of Paris. In addition to the international options which entice hungry visitors, the city offers a long list of regional specialties which have evolved from the combination of Acadian, Spanish, Italian, African-American, and Native American ethnic cuisines. Here, the Acadian hot, spicy, **Cajun** culinary style—like a good stew—has a bit of everything thrown in. **Jambalaya** (a jumble of rice, shrimp, oysters, and ham or chicken mixed with spices) and the African **gumbo** grace practically every menu in New Orleans. A southern breakfast of grits, eggs, bacon, and corn bread satisfies even the most ardent eaters. **Creole cuisine,** a mixture of Spanish, French, and Carribean is famous for red beans and rice, **po'boys** (a french-bread sandwich filled with sliced meat, particularly seafood, and vegetables), and shrimp or crawfish **étouffé.** The daring go to **Ralph & Kacoos Seafood Restaurant,** 519 Toulouse St. (522-5226), between Decatur and Chartres St. Order the **crawfish,** and eat it the way the locals do: tear off the head and suck out the tasty juices. (Hey, when in Rome...) Finally, you must *not* leave New Orleans without dining on **beignets** and **café au lait** (or milk with a dash of coffee) at the world-famous, 1862 **Café du Monde** (see below).

Some of the best and cheapest **Creole pralines** ($1) come from **Laura's Candies,** 600 Conti St. (525-3880; open daily 9am-7pm). The **French Market,** between Decatur and N. Peters St. on the east side of the French Quarter, sells pricey fresh vegetables and everything else under the sun.

If the eats in the Quarter prove too trendy, touristy, or tough on your budget, take a jaunt down **Magazine St.,** where cafés, antique stores, and book fairs spill onto the sidewalk, or catch a streetcar uptown to the **Tulane University** area for some late-night grub and collegiate character.

French Quarter

Acme Oyster House, 724 Iberville (522-5973). Slurp fresh oysters shucked before your eyes (6 for $3.75, 12 for $6.50) or sit at the red checkered tables for a good ol' po'boy ($5-6). Open Mon.-Sat. 11am-10pm, Sun. noon-7pm.

Café du Monde, 800 Decatur St. (525-4544), near the French Market. The consummate people-watching paradise since 1862 really only does two things—café au lait ($1) and hot beignets ($1)—but boy, oh boy, they sure crank them out. Absolutely delicious. Open 24hr. To take home some of that chicory coffee, cross the street to the **Café du Monde Gift Shop,** 813 (also at 1039) Decatur St. (581-2914 or 800-772-2927). 15oz. of the grind $4.50. Open daily 9:30am-6pm.

Central Grocery, 923 Decatur St. (523-1620), between Dumaine and St. Philip St. Try an authentic **muffuletta** (deli meats, cheeses, and olive salad on Italian bread) at the place that invented them. A half ($3.75) serves 1, and a whole ($7) serves 2. Open Mon.-Sat. 8am-5:30pm, Sun. 9am-5:30pm.

Olde N'awlins Cookery, 729 Conti (529-3663), between Bourbon and Royal St. Scrumptious crawfish étouffé $17; sincere turtle soup $4; nice courtyard dining. Entrees $14-19, but top-notch. Open Mon-Fri. 11am-11pm, Sat.-Sun. 8am-11pm.

Gumbo Shop, 630 St. Peter (525-1486). Sit under a broad-leafed palm and savor a bowl of seafood okra or chicken andouille gumbo ($6). Entrees $6. Expect a line. Recipes available. Open Sun.-Thurs. 11am-11pm, Fri.-Sat. 11am-midnight.

Croissant d'Or, 617 Ursuline St. (524-4663). The historic building was the first ice cream parlor in New Orleans. Delicious, OK-priced French pastries, sandwiches, and quiches. Carré Mocca or chocolate mousse $1.75. Open daily 7am-5pm.

Country Flame, 620 Iberville St. (522-1138). No, it's not a country-western bar; it's a terrific Mexican restaurant with very low prices (2 tacos $2.25) and a laid-back atmosphere that beats Taco Bell any day. Dig those cafeteria-style plastic plates. Open Mon.-Thurs. 11am-10pm, Fri.-Sun. 11am-1am.

Mama Rosa's, 616 North Rampart (523-5546). Locals croon in praise over this Italian ristorante and gay hangout. Rosa's pizza was recently rated one of the nine best in the country by *People Magazine*...a true stamp of fine American dining. 14" cheese pie $9.25. Open daily 11am-9pm.

Tricou House, 711 Bourbon St. (525-8379). Enjoy "Bourbon Street's best deal"—red beans 'n' rice for $2.75—in the historic courtyard, circa 1832. All-you-can-eat deals include: BBQ ribs on Wed. and Sun. ($10), fried chicken on Tues. ($7), catfish on Thurs. ($10), and shrimp daily ($11.70). Open Sun.-Thurs. 11am-midnight, Fri.-Sat. 11am-2am.

Johnny's Po-Boys, 511 St. Louis St. (524-8129). The po'boy is *the* thing at this French Quarter institution, which offers 40 varieties of the famous sandwich (around $3.50), with a combo plate available for the indecisive. Decent Creole fare (jambalaya, gumbo, etc.) is also on the menu. Open Mon.-Fri. 7am-4:30pm, Sat.-Sun. 7am-4pm.

Sebastian's Little Garden, 538 St. Philip St. (524-2041). A romantic rendezvous for the dinnertime crowd. The pleasant, all-weather courtyard and gracious service add to da mood. Cajun and Creole dinners include soup and salad ($6-12). Open Sun.-Thurs. 5:30-10pm, Fri.-Sat. 5:30-11pm.

Original Papa Joe's, 600 Bourbon St. (529-1728). If you still can't get enough of that New Orleans cooking, papa will set you up with po-boys, fried seafood, and gumbo at reasonable prices (entrees $8-15). Watch the Bourbon St. crowd do their Bourbon St. thing as you dine. Open Thurs.-Mon. 11am-midnight.

Royal Blend, 623 Royal St. (523-2716). A quiet garden setting in which to escape the hustle and bustle of Royal St. Over 20 brewed and iced coffees available, as well as a mighty fine selection of teas—you can even brew your own. Light meals (croissant sandwiches, quiches) served daily; nosh on a bagel and lox for $5. Jazz guitarist Phil DeGruy performs Saturdays 3-5pm, weather permitting. Open Mon.-Thurs. 7am-8pm, Fri.-Sat. 7am-midnight, Sun. 7am-6pm.

Santa Fe, 801 Frenchmen St. (944-6854). One of the few places serving southwestern cuisine, this charming restaurant dishes up tasty dinners such as seafood fajitas, hickory-grilled tuna, crawfish popcorn, and coconut beer shrimp. Vegetarian options are plentiful. Entrees $9-14. Open Tues.-Thurs. 5-11pm, Fri.-Sat. 3-11pm.

Nola, 534 St. Louis St. (522-NOLA/6652). Watch gourmet pizzas being churned out of the wood-burning hearth at this oh so sleek and stylish restaurant. Delicious Creole dishes ($12-20) are prepared by world-renowned chef Emeril Lagasse. Open for lunch Mon.-Sat. 11:30am-2pm; for dinner Sun.-Thurs. 6-10pm, Fri. Sat. 6pm-midnight.

Outside the Quarter

Mother's Restaurant, 401 Poydras St. (523-9656), at Tchoupitoulas St., 4 blocks southwest of Bourbon St. Serving up roast beef and ham po'boys ($6-9) to locals for almost half a century. Try the crawfish or shrimp étouffé omelette ($8). Tremendous entrees $6-15. Open Mon.-Sat. 5am-10pm, Sun. 7am-10pm.

Pie in the Sky, 1818 Magazine St. (522-6291). Artwork by locals hangs on the pastel walls of this very hip, very tasty pizza joint. A traditional cheese pie goes for $10, but it's far more fun to make creative topping choices. Great salads and focaccia sandwiches too, or try the "buzzmatico" (4 scoops of ice cream with a double shot of espresso). Open Mon.-Sat. 11:30am-11pm, Sun. noon-10pm.

All Natural, 5517 Magazine St. (891-2651). This friendly neighborhood health store whips up fabulous vegetarian sandwiches, pizzas, and hot specials ($3-5). Probably the only place in the world that serves vegetarian jambalaya (with salad $5) and rye grass juice. Open Mon.-Thurs. 10am-8pm, Fri.-Sat. 9am-6pm.

Café Atchafalaya, 901 Louisiana Ave. (891-5271), at Laurel St. Take the "Magazine St." bus. This cozy cottage serves mouth-watering, traditional Southern cuisine. Simple dishes like red beans and rice ($6) or lamb chops will make you cry for joy, and question the cooking at home. Cobblers galore. Open Tues.-Thurs. 11:30am-2pm and 5:30-9pm, Fri. 11:30am-2pm and 5:30-10pm, Sat. 8:30am-2pm and 5:30-10pm, Sun. 8:30am-2pm.

Tee Eva's, 4430 Magazine St. (899-8350), between Napoleon and Jena St. Tee attracts locals with peerless pies and sizzlin' soul food. 3-in. sweet potato, cream cheese pecan, or plain pecan pie $1.25. Large 9-in. pies $8-12, by order only. Soul food lunches change daily ($5). Open daily 11am-8pm.

Dunbar's, 4927 Freret St. (899-0734), at Robert St. Breakfast, lunch, and dinner soul-food style, at incredibly low prices (breakfast $2, dinner $5-6). Sit next to the Tulane football team and gorge yourself on cabbage and candied yams or all-you-can-eat red beans and chicken (each $4). Free iced tea with student ID. Kind of a risky area; go when the sun shines. Open Mon.-Sat. 7am-9pm.

Franky and Johnny's, 321 Arabella (899-9146), southwest of downtown towards Tulane off Tchoupitoulas St. A hole-in-the-wall with great onion rings ($3.50) and boiled crawfish (2 lbs. $4, Nov.-June). Open daily 11am-11pm.

Camellia Grill, 626 S. Carrollton Ave. (866-9573). Take the St. Charles streetcar away from the Quarter to the Tulane area. One of the finest diners in America and New Orleans' safest, best late-night bet. Ask your bow-tied waiter for the chef's special omelette ($7) or partake of the pecan pie ($2.45). Expect a wait on weekend mornings. Open Mon.-Thurs. 9am-1am, Fri. 9am-3am, Sat. 8am-3am, Sun. 8am-1am.

Uglesich's, 1238 Baronne St. (523-8571), at Erato St. Their spicy, local dishes will certainly curl your toes. The neighborhood is a bit sketchy and the exterior shabby, but inside you'll find some of the city's best food. Family-owned and managed since 1924. Gumbo $4.75. Bring your wallet; entrees can get pricey. Open Mon.-Fri. 9:30am-4pm.

Joey K's Restaurant, 3001 Magazine St. (891-0997), at Seventh St. Locals congregate at this friendly neighborhood eatery, especially for the mid-day meal—lunch specials start at $3.25 and feature "Creole pot" cooking, stuffed eggplant, and fried seafood. Open Mon.-Fri. 11am-10pm, Sat. 8am-10pm.

The Praline Connection, 901 S. Peters St. (523-3973), at St. Joseph St. Why are there so many songs about pralines? And that's prah-leens, not pray-leens, according to those in the know. Either way you pronounce it, this place has some finger-lickin' good soul food. Baked and fried chicken, fried seafood, stuffed crab, or étouffées will please your palate if not your arteries. Entrees $8 and up. Open daily 11am-10pm.

Figaro's Pizzerie, 7900 Maple St. (866-0100), at Fern St. Figaro's is famous for its Neapolitan pizzas, which substitute garlic sauce for red sauce, but serves American-style pizzas and tasty pastas, too ($7-11). Dine indoors or on the patio, where white lights twinkle from the trees. Ask about nightly specials ($12-15). Open Mon.-Thurs. 11:30am-10:30pm, Fri.-Sat. 11:30am-11:30pm, Sun. noon-10pm.

Five Happiness, 3605 S. Carrollton Ave. (482-3935). You can't go wrong at the place *Gambit* newsweekly readers have voted best Chinese restaurant in New Orleans seven years in a row. Favorites include jumbo shrimp, juicy baked duck, and potstickers. Entrees start at $6.25. Open Mon.-Thurs. 11:30am-10:30pm, Fri.-Sat. 11:30am-11:30pm, Sun. noon-10:30pm.

Bennachin Restaurant, 133 N. Carrollton Ave. (486-1313), between Iberville and Canal St. Go ahead—don't be afraid to ask what exactly *shipa-shipa* is. (To answer your question, it's stewed shrimp with garlic and ginger.) Swing to the beat of African music as you peruse the selection of low-priced African dishes (before 4pm, specials are around $5). Try the *akara* (black-eyed pea fritters) or *domoda* (beef chunks in gravy thickened with peanuts). Open Mon.-Thurs. 11am-9pm, Fri. 11am-10pm, Sat. 5-10pm.

Joe's Crab Shack, 8000 Lakeshore Dr. (283-1010). A casual, fun restaurant overlooking Lake Pontchartrain. New Orleans flavor comes through in the delectable seafood platters, and in appetizers like crab fingers. Satisfying meals go for around $8. Open Sun.-Thurs. 11am-10pm, Fri.-Sat. 11am-11pm.

SIGHTS

French Quarter

Allow yourself *at least* a full day (some take a lifetime) in the Quarter. The oldest section of the city is famous for its ornate wrought-iron balconies, French, Spanish, and uniquely New Orleans architecture, and a joyous atmosphere. Known as the **Vieux Carré** (view-ca-RAY), meaning Old Square, the historic district of New Orleans offers interesting used book and record stores, museums, and about a zillion tourist shops. The farther you get from **Bourbon St.,** the more clearly you'll hear the variety of street musicians.

Some say that if New Orleans had a Main Street, it would be **Royal St.,** where a streetcar named *Desire* really did pass through. Two devastating fires, in 1788 and 1794, forced the neighborhood to rebuild. This was during the era of Spanish domination in the city, and the renovations took on the flavor of Spanish colonial architecture. Most notable are the intricate iron-lace balconies, which were either hand-wrought into patterns or cast in molds. At the corner of Royal and St. Peters St. is what may be the most photographed building in the French Quarter: **LaBranche House,** with balconies of wrought-iron oak leaves and acorns that span three tiers. Nearby is **M.S. Rau, Inc.,** 630 Royal St. (523-5660), where you can get an excellent aerial view of Royal St. by taking the rear stairs to the balcony. M.S. Rau houses an extensive antique collection and a wonderful display of huge mechanical music boxes. For some pictographic perspective, visit **A Gallery for Fine Photography,** 322 Royal St. (568-1313), which features New Orleans street scene shots and a century of photographs and original prints from masters like Ansel Adams and Edward Curtis.

The heart of the Quarter beats at **Jackson Sq.,** centered around a bronze equestrian statue of General Andrew Jackson, victor of the Battle of New Orleans. While the square jumps and jives with artists, mimes, musicians, psychics, magicians, and con artists, the **St. Louis Cathedral,** 615 Pere Antoine Alley (525-9585), presides at its head (cathedral tours every Mon.-Fri. 15-20min. 9am-5pm). Behind the cathedral, **St. Anthony's Garden,** shady only in the best and most literal sense of the word, was named in memory of Father Antonio de Sedella. The priest served in New Orleans for almost 50 years after his arrival in 1779, and was locally renowned for his dedication to helping the poor. His commemorative park was often the site of bloody duels, back in the colonial days. **Pirate's Alley** and **Père Antoine's Alley** border the garden. Legend has it that the former was the site of covert meetings between pirate Jean

Lafitte and President Andrew Jackson, as they conspired to plan the Battle of New Orleans.

The historic **French Market** (522-2621) takes up several city blocks just northeast of Jackson Sq. Vendors sell everything from watermelons to earrings. If you want touristy t-shirts that say "Mardi Gras" they'll have them, but the market is not a recently conceived tourist trap. On the contrary, the French Market has been operating in the same spot since 1791—long before tacky shorts, laminated maps, and disposable cameras (open daily 9am-8pm). Stop in at the market's **visitors center** (596-3424), on Dumaine St. at the river (open daily 9am-6pm). Admire natural wonders like fresh fruits, vegetables, herbs, and spices, and then buy some, at the **Farmer's Market,** which never closes. Those who dig scavenger hunts should head for the nearby **Community Flea Market,** where one person gathers what another one spills. Overflowing tables and stalls are piled high with everything from t-shirts to handmade furniture to antique glasses, and the scent of fish wafts through the air.

The **Jean Lafitte National Historical Park and Preserve,** 916-918 North Peters (589-2636), headquartered in the back section of the French Market at Dumaine and St. Phillip St., recognizes the rich cultural heritage of the French Quarter. The park conducts free 90-minute walking tours, which emphasize aspects of New Orleans' cultural, ethnic, and environmental history, through the Quarter (daily 10:30, 11:30am, and 2:30pm) and into the Garden District (2:30pm; reservations required). Call ahead for specific info.

It's always a great night to stroll the **Moon Walk,** a promenade stretching alongside the Big Muddy offering a fantastic riverside view and opportunities for Michael Jackson humor and/or emulation. It's actually named after former N.O. mayor Moon Landrieu, who oversaw renovations of the French Quarter in the 1970s.

Though the Park Service no longer leads tours of the city's cemeteries (these areas have been deemed unsafe), the **New Orleans Historic Voodoo Museum,** 724 Dumaine St. (523-7685), continues to bring visitors foul in heart and experienced with the evil eye right onto local burial grounds. (Open daily 10am-dusk. $5, college students and seniors $4, high school students $3, grade school students $2, under 5 free. Tours $12-18.) Tourists of pure heart should opt for the **Hidden Treasures Cemetery Tour** (529-4507), which visits New Orleans' original St. Louis cemetery #1. Tours ($12) last about an hour and depart at 9am daily from **The Ultimate Coffee Shop,** 417 Bienville St. (524-7417; reservations recommended; free coffee for those who live to see the next sunrise.)

At the very southwest corner of the Quarter, the **Aquarium of the Americas** (861-2538), Waldenberg Park by the World Trade Center, houses an amazing collection of sealife and birds. Among the 500 species, you'll see black-footed penguins, endangered sea turtles, and the world's only white alligators. ($9.75, seniors $7.50, ages 3-12 $5. Open Sun.-Thurs. 9:30am-6pm, Fri.-Sat. 9:30am-7pm.) The steamboat **John Audubon** (586-8777) shuttles between the aquarium and the Audubon Zoo (see below) four times each day. (From the aquarium 10am, noon, 2, and 4pm; from the zoo 11am, 1, 3, and 5pm. $9.50, kids $4.75. Roundtrip $12.50/$6.25. Package tours including cruise, zoo, and aquarium from $26.50/$13.25.)

Outside the Quarter

If you're not sure there's more to New Orleans than the French Quarter, take in the city from the 31st floor of the **World Trade Center,** 2 Canal St. (525-2185), in the southernmost corner of the Quarter ($2, seniors $1.50, ages 6-12 $1; open daily 9am-5pm). The **Riverwalk,** a multi-million dollar conglomeration of overpriced shops originally built as a venue for the 1984 World's Fair, ambles through this area overlooking the port. Combining entertainment and a cooking lesson with an unbeatable meal often spiced up with "onyons, green peppahs," the **Cookin' Cajun New Orleans Cooking School,** 116 Riverwalk (586-8832 or 523-6425), prepares Cajun or Creole creations before your eyes for your edification and consumption. Call ahead for the menu of the day, or just drop by and sample one of their 18 hot sauces. (Open Mon.-Sat. 11am-1pm. 2-hr. class $15.) For a 25-min. view of the Mississippi River and a bite of African-American history, take the wonderfully free **Canal Street Ferry** to Algiers Point; Algiers of old housed many of New Orleans' free people of color. The outdoor observation deck affords a panoramic view of the city's boldest and most beautiful sights. The ferry departs daily from the end of Canal St. (5:45am-9:30pm).

Relatively new in the downtown area, the **Warehouse Arts District,** on Julia St. between Commerce and Baronne, contains revitalized warehouse buildings which house contemporary art galleries inside historic architecture. Exhibits range from Southern folk art to experimental sculpture. Individual galleries distribute maps of the area. The **Contemporary Arts Center,** 900 Camp St. (523-1216), in an all brick building with a modern glass and chrome façade, mounts exhibits ranging from the cryptic to the puzzling; at least the architecture within is amazing and reasonably easy to appreciate. (Open Mon.-Sat. 10am-5pm, Sun. 11am-5pm. $3, students and seniors $2, under 12 free. Thurs. free.) Also in the Warehouse District is the **New Orleans School of Glassworks and Gallery,** 727 Magazine St. (529-7277). In the rear studio, watch so-inclined students and instructors transform blobs of molten glass into vases and sculptures. Magic. (Open Mon.-Sat. 11am-5pm. Free.) Nearby, pause in admiration of **Julia Row,** the 600 block of Julia St. When built in 1832, the series of 13 connected brick townhouses was dubbed "The Thirteen Sisters." In the mid-1800s, Julia Row was the Beverly Hills of New Orleans: a posh residence with a fashionable address. Most residents were newly arrived non-Creole immigrants.

Though much of the Crescent City's fame derives from the **Vieux Carré,** areas uptown have their fair share of beauty and action. The streetcar named "Desire" saw its day long ago, but the **St. Charles Streetcar** still runs west of the French Quarter, passing some of the city's finest buildings, including the elegant, mint-condition 19th-century homes along **St. Charles Ave.** ($1). *Gone With the Wind*-a-philes should recognize the whitewashed bricks and elegant doorway of the house on the far right corner of Arabella St. This is no ordinary plantation-style residence—it's a replica of **Tara.** Frankly, my dear, it's not open to the public.

Fans of fancy living should disembark the streetcar in the **Garden District,** an opulent neighborhood between Jackson and Louisiana Ave. The legacies of French, Italian, Spanish, and American architecture create an extraordinary combination of structures, colors, ironworks, and, of course, exquisite gardens. Watch for houses raised several feet above the ground for protection from the swamp on which New Orleans stands.

Forget your compass? Never fear—just look to **Lee Circle,** at the intersection of St. Charles and Howard Ave. A 60-ft. white marble column supports a bronze statue of Confederate General Robert E. Lee, who stands facing due north.

The St. Charles Streetcar eventually makes its way to **Audubon Park,** across from Tulane University. Designed by Frederick Law Olmsted—the architect who planned New York City's Central Park—Audubon contains lagoons, statues, stables, and the awesome and award-winning **Audubon Zoo** (861-2537), where the world's only white alligators (wait a second…) swim in a re-created Louisiana swamp. A free museum shuttle glides from the park entrance every 15 min. (streetcar stop #36) to the zoo. (Zoo open daily 9:30am-5pm. $7.75, seniors and ages 2-12 $3.75.)

Before You Die, Read This:

Being dead in New Orleans has always been a problem. Because the city lies 4 to 6 ft. below sea level, a 6-ft. hole in the earth fills up with 5 ft. of water. Coffins used to literally **float in the graves,** while cemetery workers pushed them down with long wooden poles. One early solution was to **bore holes in the coffins,** allowing them to sink. Unfortunately, the sight of a drowning coffin coupled with the **awful gargling sound** of its immersion proved too much for the squeamish families of the departed. Burial soon became passé, and stiffs were laid to rest in beautiful raised stone tombs. Miles and miles of **creepy, cool marble tombs** now fill the city's graveyards and its ghost stories.

One of the most unique sights in the New Orleans area, the coastal wetlands along Lake Salvador make up a segment of the **Jean Lafitte National Historical Park** called the **Barataria Preserve,** 7400 Hwy. 45 (589-2330), off the West Bank Expwy. across the Mississippi River down Barataria Blvd. (Rte. 45). The only park-sponsored foot tour through the swamp leaves at 2pm daily (free). Countless commercial boat tours operate outside and around the park; **Bayou Segnette Swamp Tours** (561-8244) does its 2-hr. bit for $20 per person, $12 for children. They'll pick you up from your hotel for an extra $20. Tour times change seasonally; call for details.

Museums

Louisiana State Museum, P.O. Box 2448 (568-6968), oversees 4 separate museums: the **Old U.S. Mint,** 400 Esplanade; **Cabildo,** 701 Chartres St.; **Presbytère,** 751 Chartres St.; and **1850 House,** 523 St. Ann St. All 4 contain artifacts, papers, and other changing exhibits on the history of Louisiana and New Orleans. The Old U.S. Mint is particularly interesting, focusing not on currency or fresh breath but on the history of jazz and the lives of jazz greats like Louis "Satchmo" Armstrong. And if you missed Mardi Gras, the "Carnival in New Orleans" recreates the festival, right down to models of inebriated party-goers. All open Tues.-Sun. 9am-5pm. Pass to 1 $4, seniors $3. Pass to all 4 $10/$7.50. Under 13 free.

New Orleans Museum of Art (488-2631), in City Park. Take the Esplanade bus from Canal and Rampart St. This magnificent museum houses the arts of North and South America, a small collection of local decorative arts, opulent works by the jeweler Fabergé, and a strong collection of French paintings with work by Degas. Two floors of exhibition space spotlight Asian, African, Oceanic, and contemporary art. Guided tours available. Open Tues.-Sat. 10am-5pm, Sun. 1-5pm. $6, seniors and ages 2-17 $3. Free to LA residents with valid ID Thurs. 10am-noon.

Historic New Orleans Collection, 533 Royal St. (523-4662). Located in the aristocratic 18th-century Merieult House, the contents of this impressive cultural and research center will teach you everything you wanted to know about Louisiana's history, but were afraid to ask. The History Tour explores New Orleans's past, while the interesting Williams Residence Tour showcases the eclectic home furnishings of the collection's founders, General and Mrs. L. Kemper Williams. Downstairs gallery displays changing exhibits. Tours 10, 11am, 2, and 3pm; each $2. Gallery open Tues.-Sat. 10am-4:45pm; free.

Musée Conti Wax Museum, 917 Conti St. (525-2605). One of the world's finest houses of wax, with figures from 300 years of Louisiana lore. The voodoo display and haunted dungeon are perennial favorites, along with the mock-up of Madame Lalaurie's torture attic. Open daily 10am-5pm; except Mardi Gras. $5.75, seniors and college students with ID $5.25, under 17 $3.50.

Confederate Museum, 929 Camp St. (523-4522), in a brownstone just west of Lee Circle. The oldest museum in the state houses an extensive collection of Civil War records and artifacts. Open Mon.-Sat. 10am-4pm. $4, under 16 $2.

New Orleans Pharmacy Museum, 514 Chartres St. (565-8027). This apothecary shop was built by America's first licensed pharmacist in 1923. On display are handmade apothecary jars, 19th-century "miracle drugs," voodoo powders, and the still-fertile botanical garden, where medicinal herbs were grown. Open Tues.-Sun. 10am-5pm. $2, seniors and students $1 (includes ½hr. tour), under 12 free.

K&B Plaza, 1055 St. Charles Ave. (586-1234), on Lee Circle. Houses an outstanding contemporary collection of art and sculpture from the Virlane Foundation, including sculpture by Henry Moore, mobiles by Alexander Calder, and a bust by Renoir. Open Mon.-Fri. 8am-5pm. Sculpture garden open 24hr. Free.

Louisiana Children's Museum, 420 Julia St. (523-1357). This place is really fun. Invites kids to play and learn, as they star in their own news shows, pretend to be streetcar drivers, or shop in a re-created mini-mart. Kids under 12 must be accompanied by an adult. Open Mon.-Sat. 9:30am-5:30pm; Labor Day-Memorial Day Tues.-Sat. 9:30am-5:30pm, Sun. noon-5:30pm. $5, under 1 free.

Louisiana Nature and Science Center, 11000 Lake Forest Blvd. (246-5672). Trail walks, exhibits, planetarium and laser shows, and 86 acres of natural wildlife preserve in Joe Brown Memorial Park. Hard to reach without a car, but a wonderful escape from the debauchery of the French Quarter. Open Tues.-Fri. 9am-5pm, Sat. 10am-5pm, Sun. noon-5pm. $4, seniors $3, kids $2. Planetarium shows $1.

Historic Homes and Plantations

Called the "Great Showplace of New Orleans," **Longue Vue House and Gardens,** 7 Bamboo Rd. (488-5488), off Metairie Rd., epitomizes the grand Southern estate with its lavish furnishings and opulent decor, fashioned after English country homes. The breathtaking sculpted gardens date back to the turn of the century. Take the Metairie Rd. exit off I-10 and pause for a peek at the 85-ft.-tall monument among the raised tombs in the Metairie Cemetery on the way. (Tours available in English, French, Spanish, Italian, and Japanese. Open Mon.-Sat. 10am-4:30pm, Sun. 1-5pm. $7, students $3, seniors $6, under 5 free. Gardens only $3, students $1.) **River Rd.** curves along the Mississippi across from downtown New Orleans, accessing several plantations preserved from the 19th century; pick up a copy of *Great River Road Plantation Parade: A River of Riches* at the New Orleans or Baton Rouge visitors centers for a good map and descriptions of the houses. Frequent free ferries cross the river at Plaquemines, White Castle, and between Lutcher and Vacherie. With each charging an individual entrance fee, a tour of all the privately owned plantations would be quite expensive. Those below are listed in order from New Orleans to Baton Rouge.

Hermann-Grima Historic House, 820 St. Louis St. (525-5661). Built in 1831, the house exemplifies early American influence on New Orleans architecture, replete with a large central hall, guillotine windows, a fan-lit entrance, and the original parterre beds. On Thurs. October-May, trained volunteer cooks prepare period meals in the only working 1830s Creole kitchen in the Quarter; call for details. Open Mon.-Sat. 10am-4pm; last tour 3:30pm. $5, students $4, seniors $4, ages 8-18 $3, under 7 free.

Gallier House Museum, 1118-1132 Royal St. (523-6722). The elegantly restored residence of James Gallier, Jr., the city's most famous architect, resuscitates the taste and lifestyle of the extremely wealthy in the 1860s. Tours every ½hr.; last tour 4pm. Open Mon.-Sat. 10am-4:30pm. $5, students and seniors $4, kids $2.50.

San Francisco Plantation House (535-2341), Rte. 44, 2mi. north of Reserve, 42mi. from New Orleans on the east bank of the Mississippi. Beautifully maintained plantation built in 1856. Laid out in the old Creole style with the main living room on the 2nd floor. The three-color exterior is restrained compared to the ceilings. Tours daily 10am-4pm. $7, seniors $5, ages 12-17 $4, ages 6-11 $2.75.

Houmas House, 40136 Rte. 942 (522-2262), in Burnside just over halfway to Baton Rouge on the west bank of the Mississippi. Setting for the movie *Hush, Hush, Sweet Charlotte,* starring Bette Davis and Olivia DeHavilland. Built in two sections: the rear constructed in the last quarter of the 18th century and the Greek Revival mansion in front built in 1840. Huge, moss-draped oaks shade the spacious grounds and beautiful gardens. "Southern Belle" guides lead tours in authentic antebellum dress. Open daily 10am-5pm; Nov.-Jan. 10am-4pm. $7, ages 13-17 $5, ages 6-12 $3.50.

Nottoway (545-2730 or 832-2093 in N.O.), Rte. 405, between Bayou Goula and White Castle, 18mi. south of Baton Rouge on the southern bank of the Mississippi. Largest plantation home in the South; often called the "White Castle of Louisiana." An incredible 64-room mansion with 22 columns, a large ballroom, and a 3-story stairway. The first choice of David O. Selznick for filming *Gone with the Wind,* but the owners wouldn't allow it. Open daily 9am-5pm. Admission and 1-hr. guided tour $8, under 13 $3.

Oak Alley (800-44-ALLEY/442-5539), Rte. 18 between St. James and Vacherie. Named for the magnificent alley of 28 evenly spaced oaks, which are nearly 300 years old. An amazing setting you'll want to see with your own eyes; the 28 columns of the Greek Revival house correspond with, yes, the 28 oak trees. Retinal candy. Mmmmm. Open daily 9am-5:30pm; tours every ½hr. $7, ages 13-18 $4, ages 6-12 $2, under 6 free.

ENTERTAINMENT AND NIGHTLIFE

If you've come to New Orleans to take advantage of drinking laws which let those over 18 buy and guzzle booze, you're about two years too late. Louisiana was the last state to relinquish the legal drinking age of 18. Until recently, it clung to its law even when this meant losing out on federal highway funds. In the summer of 1995, the state legislature finally bowed to the pressure and joined its peers—officially, *you now have to be 21 to buy and drink alcoholic beverages in Louisiana.*

Needless to say, life in New Orleans is and will always be a party. On any night of the week, at any time of the year, the masses converge on **Bourbon St.**, to drift in and out of bars and shop for a romantic interlude. Unfortunately, the many bars and clubs on Bourbon tend toward the sleazy and clothing optional. After exploring the more traditional jazz, blues, and brass sound of the Quarter, survey the rest of the city for less tourist-oriented bands playing to a more local clientele. Check *Off Beat* or the Friday *Times-Picayune* to find out who's playing where. The movements of New Orleans's large gay community fill the pages of *Impact* and *Ambush*, both available at **Faubourg Marigny Books,** 600 Frenchmen St. (943-9875; open Mon.-Fri. 10am-8pm, Sat.-Sun. 10am-6pm).

Born at the turn of the century in **Armstrong Park,** traditional New Orleans jazz still wails nightly at the tiny, dim, historic **Preservation Hall,** 726 Saint Peter St. (522-2841); expect jazz in its most fundamental element. Arrive early or be prepared for a lengthy wait in line, poor visibility, and sweaty standing-room only ($4). The Hall does not sell food or beverages. Doors open at 8pm; music begins at 8:30pm and goes on until midnight. If you don't get a seat, wait outside and listen for free.

Keep your ears open for **Cajun** and **zydeco** bands who use accordions, washboards, triangles, and drums to perform hot dance tunes (true locals two-step expertly) and sappy waltzes. Anyone who thinks couple-dancing went out in the 50s should try a *fais do-do*, a lengthy, wonderfully energetic traditional dance; just grab a partner and throw yourself into the rhythm. The locally based **Radiators** do it up real spicy-like in a rock-cajun-zydeco style.

Le Petit Théâtre du Vieux Carré, 616 St. Peter St. (522-9958), is one of the city's most beloved and historical theaters. The oldest continuously operating community theater in the U.S., the 1789 building replicates the early-18th-century abode of Joseph de Pontalba, Louisiana's last Spanish governor. Around six musicals and plays go up each year, as well as four fun productions in the "Children's Corner." The first Sunday of each month at 4pm, Le Petit hosts an open salon in which some of the city's most gifted poets, musicians, and performance artists showcase their talents in a relaxed atmosphere. (Box office open Tues.-Fri. 10am-5pm, Sat. 3-7pm.)

Festivals

New Orleans's Mardi Gras celebration is the biggest party of the year, a world-renowned, epic bout of lascivious debauchery that fills the three weeks leading up to Ash Wednesday. Parades, gala, balls, and general revelry take the streets, as tourists pour in by the planeful (flights into the city book up months in advance along with hotel rooms). In 1997, the day before Ash Wednesday, Fat Tuesday (literally *Mardi Gras*), falls on February 11; the biggest parades and the bulk of the partying will take place during the week of February 1-11. Remember: when it comes time to traffic in beads, anything goes, and a trade which sounds too good to be true probably carries some unspoken conditions.

The ever-expanding annual **New Orleans Jazz and Heritage Festival** (522-4786), from the last weekend in April to the first in May, attracts 4000 musicians from around the country to the city's fairgrounds. The likes of Aretha Franklin, Bob Dylan, Patti LaBelle, and Wynton Marsalis have graced this slightly "classier" fest, where music plays simultaneously on 11 stages in the midst of a huge Cajun food and crafts festival. The biggest names perform evening riverboat concerts. Exhilarating and fun, the festival grows more zoo-like each year. Book a room early.

New Orleans's festivals go beyond the biggies. From the **Tennessee Williams Literary Festival** (286-6688) to the **Gumbo Festival** (Oct. 11-12), you're likely to find a celebration of something year-round. Call the Tourist Convention Commission (see Practical Information, above) for further info.

Nightlife in the French Quarter

Bars in New Orleans stay open late, and few keep a strict schedule; in general, they open around 11am and close around 3am. Some places go the $3-5-per-drink route, but most blocks feature at least one establishment with cheap draft beer and Hurricanes, sweet drinks made of juice and rum. Beware of overly forward strangers and pickpockets, and always bring ID—the party's fun, but the law is enforced.

Pat O'Brien's, 718 Saint Peter St. (525-4823). The busiest bar and one of the best in the French Quarter, bursting with happy (read: drunk) tourists. Listen to the piano in one room, mix with local students in another, or lounge near the fountain in the courtyard. Home of the original Hurricane; purchase your first in a souvenir glass ($7). Open Sun.-Thurs. 10:30am-4am, Fri.-Sat. 10:30am-5am.

The Old Absinthe House, 240 Bourbon St. (525-8108). Reputed to be the oldest bar in the U.S., opened in 1807. The House has irrigated the likes of Mark Twain, Franklin D. Roosevelt, the Rolling Stones, and Humphrey Bogart. Reasonably priced drinks for the French Quarter. The Absinthe Frappe re-invents the infamous drink with anisette or Pernod liqueur ($4.75). Open daily noon-2am.

House of Blues, 225 Decatur St. (529-BLUE/2583). A sprawling complex with a large music/dance hall, and a balcony and bar which overlook the action. The restaurant serves everything from veggie pasta ($8) to Bayou Voodoo smothered chicken in Dixie's blackened voodoo beer (phew...$11). Cover $5-25; folks like Clapton get the big bucks. Concerts daily 9pm; stop by or call for the upcoming schedule. $1 longnecks and live music at Friday's happy hour (4-8pm). Restaurant open Sun.-Thurs. 11am-midnight, Fri.-Sat. 11am-2am.

The Napoleon House, 500 Chartres St. (524-9752). Located on the ground floor of the Old Girod House, which was built as an exile home for Napoleon in a plan to spirit him away from St. Helena. Movie buffs take note: the bar set the scene for one of the opening clips in Oliver Stones's "fictional documentary" *JFK*. New Orleans fare ($3-9) served to the tune of classical music. Open Mon.-Thurs. 11am-midnight, Fri.-Sat. 11am-1am, Sun. 11am-7pm.

Bourbon Pub/Parade, 801 Bourbon St. (529-2107). This gay dance bar sponsors a "tea dance" on Sun. with all the beer you can drink for $5. Dancing upstairs at the Paradise Disco, nightly 9pm until you fall off (no, not literally). Open 24hr.

Rubyfruit Jungle, 640 Frenchmen St. (947-4000). The biggest lesbian bar in New Orleans. High-energy music on weekends; other days usually have special themes. Mon. is seafood boil night (shrimp, crawfish, and a pitcher of beer $5), and Tues. is country/western. Open Mon.-Fri. 4pm-4am, Sat.-Sun. 1pm-4am.

Margaritaville, 1104 Decatur St. (592-2565; 592-2552 for music schedule). A solid mix of funk, R&B, and rock plays nightly at this café and club named after Jimmy Buffett's signature song—and yes, he is known to take the stage when in town. Key Lime pie and salt-rimmed margaritas are terrific companions for late-night listening. No cover. Music Sun.-Thurs. 2pm-midnight, Fri.-Sat. 2pm-2am. Food served Sun.-Thurs. 11am-10:30pm, Fri.-Sat. 11am-midnight.

Hog's Breath Saloon, 339 Chartes St. (522-1736), between Bienville and Conti St. Not for the faint of heart, the Hog's Breath is rowdy, spirited, and messy—the underwear dangling from the ceiling says it all. Pass the Hog Wings, please. Live music Fri. 9am-1am, Sat.-Sun. 3-7pm and 9pm-1am. Happy hour Mon.-Fri. 5-7pm. No cover. Open daily 11am-2am.

Crescent City Brewhouse, 527 Decatur St. (522-0571). The only microbrewery in New Orleans, this classy brewpub has 4 of its own blends, plus a multitude of darks, lights, and ambers. Glass walls and balcony make for good people-watching, a wonderful activity when set to live jazz. Open Sun.-Thurs. 11am-10pm, Fri.-Sat. 11am-midnight.

Kaldi's Coffeehouse, 941 Decatur St. (586-8989). A great escape from the local nocturnal frenzy, Kaldi's is all about chatting, postcard-writing, and cappuccino-sip-ping. The crowd is as varied as the night is long; the young and the old, gussied up and grunged down, gather here for live jazz on Friday and Saturday nights, gospel on Sundays, and Tues.-night poetry readings. Italian cream sodas are one of a kind ($2.25). Open Sun.-Thurs. 7am-midnight, Fri.-Sat. 7am-2am.

Bottom of the Cup Tearoom, 732 Royal St. (523-1204). If your cup of tea is, well, tea, you've come to the right place, although first you have to catch sight of the tiny sign. This tearoom is not only the site of much swirling conversation among friends, but also fortune-telling, palm-reading, and other soothsaying mediums. Psychic friends are on hand to describe *your* portent. Open Mon.-Sat. 9am-9pm, Sun. 11am-7pm.

O'Flaherty's Irish Channel Pub, 514 Toulouse St. (529-1317). Soak up some of that Irish culture in this watering hole that bills itself as the meeting-point of the disparate Celtic nations. Eavesdrop on Gaelic conversation while listening to Scottish bagpipes, watching Irish dances, and/or singing along to Irish tunes. Oh, and don't forget to eat your shepard's pie, Johnny. Open daily noon-3am.

Nightlife Outside the Quarter

Mid City Lanes, 4133 S. Carrolton Ave. (482-3133), at Tulane Ave. "Home of Rock n' Bowl;" bowling alley by day, dance club by night. (Don't worry, you can bowl at night too.) Featuring local zydeco, blues, and rock 'n' roll, this is where the locals party. Ignore the dingy exterior and walk inside for a true New Orleans experience. Thurs. is wild zydeco night. Music Wed.-Thurs. 9:30pm, Fri.-Sat. 10pm; cover $5-7. Pick up a *Rock n' Bowlletin* for specific band info (and a list of the regulars' birthdays). Lanes Sun.-Thurs. $8 per hr., Sat.-Sun. $10 per hr.

Cooter Brown's Tavern and Oyster Bar, 509 S. Carrolton Ave. (866-9104). Sporting a very mainstream-young-singles crowd, this rowdy blues bar (sorry folks, the tunes are recorded) lofts over 200 beers including a 3-liter Belgian ale for $60. Ground cow on a bun too ($4-7). Open Sun.-Mon. 11am-2am, Tues.-Thurs. 11am-3am, Fri.-Sat. 11am-4am.

Checkpoint Charlie's, 501 Esplanade (947-0979), in the Marigny. Grunges it up like the best of Seattle. Do your laundry while you listen to good live music 7 nights a week. Julia Roberts sat on these machines in *The Pelican Brief.* No cover. Open 24hr.

Tipitina's, 501 Napoleon Ave. (895-8477; 897-3943 for concert info). This famous establishment attracts both the best local bands and some big national names. The Neville Brothers, John Goodman, and Harry Connick Jr. stop in regularly. Favorite bar of late jazz pianist and scholar Professor Longhair; his bust now graces the front hall. Sunday evenings feature Cajun *fais-do-do's.* Cover $4-15; call ahead for times and prices.

Maple Leaf Bar, 8316 Oak St. (866-9359), near Tulane University. The best local dance bar offers zydeco and Cajun music; everyone does the two-step. Poetry readings Sun. 3pm. The party starts Sun.-Thurs. at 10pm, Fri.-Sat. at 10:30pm. Cover $3-5. Open daily 3pm-4am.

F&M Patio Bar, 4841 Tchoupitoulas St. (895-6784), near Napolean. Mellow twenty-somethings mix with college types, doctors, lawyers, and ne'er-do-wells. Serves food after 6pm, mostly fajitas ($3) and burgers ($4.25), from a mega-grill on the patio. Open Mon.-Thurs. 1pm-4am, Fri. 1pm-6am, Sat. 3pm-6am, Sun. 3pm-4am.

Michaul's, 840 St. Charles Ave. (522-5517). A huge floor for Cajun dancing; they'll even teach you how. In the evenings they teach for 30min., then dance for 30min.—alternating all night long. No cover. Open Mon.-Fri. 5pm-11pm, Sat. 6pm-midnight, Sun. 6pm-10pm. Dinner served Mon.-Thurs. 6-11pm, Fri.-Sat. 6pm-midnight.

Snug Harbor, 626 Frenchmen St. (949-0696), just east of the Quarter near Decatur St. Shows nightly 9 and 11pm. Regulars include Charmaine Neville, Amasa Miller, and Ellis Marsalis. The cover is steep ($6-14), but Mon. evening with Ms. Neville is worth it. Listen for soulful music from the bar in the front room. Bar open daily 5pm-2am; restaurant open Sun.-Thurs. 5-11pm, Fri.-Sat. 5pm-midnight.

Carrollton Station, 8140 Willow St. (865-9190), at Dublin St. A cozy neighborhood club with live music and friendly folks. Twelve beers on tap, behind the intricately carved wooden bar. Music Thurs.-Sat. nights; Sunday night acoustic jam sessions. Open daily 3:30pm-2am.

Vic's Kangaroo Café, 636 Tchoupitoulas St. (524-GDAY/4329). Shoot darts and kick back at this Australian pub, home of harmonica player Rockin' Jake. Live blues on Saturday nights, starting around 10pm. Open daily 11:30am-3:30am.

Muddy Waters, 8301 Oak St. (866-7174), at Dante St. This packed music club is famous for the funky blues performed live every night. Regulars include local faves like the Dirty Dozen Brass Band and Zydeco Twisters. A dance floor is downstairs, balcony and bar upstairs. Cover varies with band. Open daily noon-2am; music 10pm-2am.

Jimmy's, 8200 Willow St. (861-8200). Rock, rap, and reggae are just some of the musical genres that can be caught at this bare minimum bar and music club. There are no frills here—the walls are plain, there's no restaurant—but the varying cover covers the entire night's show, which may mean as many as five different bands performing in a continuous line-up. Open Tues.-Sat. 8pm-2am.

Mulate's, 201 Julia St. (522-1492). This large restaurant and bar packs 'em in nightly for Cajun dancing and live music. The bands are straight from Acadiana, and perform from 7:30 to 11pm. While the food is slightly pricey, the hungry can always fill up on appetizers. Open daily 11am-11pm.

Top of the Mart, World Trade Center, 2 Canal St. (522-9795). The nation's largest revolving bar, this 500-seat cocktail lounge spins 33 stories above the ground. The deck revolves three feet per min. and makes one revolution every hour and a half. The sunset view is mind-melting. No cover, but a one-drink minimum. Open Mon.-Fri. 10am-midnight, Sat. 11am-1am, Sun. 2pm-midnight.

■ Baton Rouge

Once a tall cypress tree marking the boundary between rival Native American tribes, Baton Rouge ("red stick") has grown into the capital of Louisiana. State politics have shaped the character of this city, once the home of "Kingfish" Huey P. Long. Today the rhythm and pace of this port city are defined by a state within the state: Louisiana State University (LSU). The downtown area of Baton Rouge has enough attractions to satisfy only the easily pleased tourist. For the party-happy visitor who can't make it to New Orleans, however, the sprawling campus of the state university offers cheap eateries, quite a few bars, and a few more bars. Enjoy.

The **State Capitol Visitors Center** (342-7317), on the first floor of the State Capitol, has helpful maps (open daily 8am-4:30pm). For more resources, stop by the **Baton Rouge Convention and Visitors Bureau,** 730 North Blvd. (383-1825 or 800-LAROUGE/527-6843; open Mon.-Fri. 8am-5pm). A short walk from downtown, **Greyhound,** 1253 Florida Blvd. (800-231-2222), at 13th St., sends buses to New Orleans (10 per day, 2hr., $15) and Lafayette (9 per day, 1hr., $12). Be careful; the area is unsafe at night. (Station and ticket booth open 24hr.) In an **emergency,** call 911. Baton Rouge's **post office:** 750 Florida Blvd. (381-0713), off River Rd. (open Mon.-Fri. 8:30am-5pm, Sat. 9am-noon); **ZIP code:** 70821; **area code:** 504.

The **Corporate Inn,** 2365 College Dr. (925-2451), at Exit 158 off I-10, has modest rooms and a hospitable staff (singles $37, doubles $42). **Motel 6,** 10445 Rieger Rd. (291-4912), at Exit 163 off I-10, throws you no surprises—cookie-cutter rooms, good

---

The Atchafalaya Basin

If you're driving through south-central Louisiana, you're probably driving over America's largest swamp, the Atchafalaya (a-CHAH-fa-LIE-a) Basin. The **Atchafalaya Freeway** (I-10 between Lafayette and Baton Rouge) crosses 32 mi. of swamp and cypress trees. To get down and dirty in the muck, exit at Henderson, 15 mi. east of Lafayette, and follow the signs to **McGee's Landing,** 1337 Henderson Rd. (228-2384 or 800-445-6681). This operation sends four 1½-hour **boat tours** into the Basin each day. (Tours daily 10am and 1, 3, and 5pm. $9, seniors $8, under 12 $5.)

security, soft beds, cable TV, and a pool (singles $37, doubles $44). The **KOA Campground,** 7628 Vincent Rd. (664-7281; reservations 800-292-8245), 12 mi. east of Baton Rouge (take the Denham Springs exit off I-12), keeps sites well-maintained, along with clean facilities and a big pool (sites for 2 $15.50, with hookup $21.50).

In a move reminiscent of Ramses II, Huey Long ordered the building of the unique **Louisiana State Capitol** (342-7317), a magnificent, modern skyscraper, completed over a mere 14 months in 1931 and '32. The **Magnolia Mound Plantation,** 2161 Nicholson Dr. (343-4955), built in 1791, is a restored French Creole mansion spanning 16 acres. (Open Tues.-Sat. 10am-4pm, Sun. 1-4pm; last tour 3:20pm. $3.50, students $1.50, seniors $2.50.) The **LSU Rural Life Museum,** 4600 Essen Ln. (765-2437), has authentically furnished shops, cabins, and storage houses; adjacent to the museum are the lakes, winding paths, roses, and azaleas of the Windrush Gardens. (Open daily 8:30am-5pm; $5, seniors $4, ages 5-11 $3.)

Head to LSU and around **Highland Rd.** for good cheap chow. **Louie's Café,** 209 W. State St. (246-8221), grills up fabulous omelettes ($5). Behind Louie's is **The Bayou,** 124 W. Chimes (346-1765), a pool hall and bar crowded with collegiate types (open Mon.-Sat. 5pm-2am; in winter 2pm-2am). When you want a place good enough for your parents, try **The Chimes,** 3357 Highland Rd. (383-1754), a big ol' restaurant and bar with more than 120 different beers. Louisiana alligator, farm-raised, marinated, and fried, served with dijon mustard sauce goes for $6—do you dare? (Open Mon.-Sat. 11am-2am, Sun. 11am-midnight.)

ACADIANA

Throughout the early eighteenth century, the English government in Nova Scotia became increasingly jealous of the prosperity of French settlers (*Acadiens*) and deeply offended by their refusal to swear allegiance to the British Crown. During the war with France in 1755, British frustration and hatred peaked; they rounded up the Acadians and deported them by the shipload in what came to be called *le Grand Dérangement,* "the Great Upheaval." Of the 7,000 Acadians who went to sea, one-third died of smallpox and hunger. Those who survived sought refuge along the Atlantic Coast in places like Massachusetts and South Carolina. As French Catholics they were met with fear and suspicion, and most were forced into indentured servitude. The Acadians soon realized that freedom waited only in the French territory of Louisiana. The "Cajuns" of St. Martin, Lafayette, Iberia, and St. Mary parishes are descended from these settlers.

Several factors have threatened Acadian culture since the relocation. In the 1920s, Louisiana passed laws forcing Acadian schools to teach in English. Later, during the oil boom of the 1970s and 80s, oil executives and developers envisioned the Acadian center of Lafayette (see below) as the Houston of Louisiana and threatened to flood the town and its neighbors with mass culture. Still, the proud people of southern Louisiana have resisted homogenization; today, the state is officially bilingual and a state agency preserves Acadian French in schools and in the media. "Cajun Country" spans the south of the state, from Houma in the east to the Texas border in the west.

■ Lafayette

The center of Acadiana, Lafayette is the perfect place to try some boiled crawfish or dance the two-step to a fiddle and accordion. Though the city's French roots are often obscured by the chain motels and service roads that have accompanied its growth, there is no question that the Cajuns still own the surrounding countryside, where zydeco music heats up dance floors every night of the week and locals continue to answer their phones with a proud *bonjour.*

PRACTICAL INFORMATION

Tourist Office: Lafayette Parish Tourist Information Bureau, 1400 Evangeline Thruway (232-3808), will swamp you with info. Open Mon.-Fri. 8:30am-5pm, Sat.-Sun. 9am-5pm.

Trains: Amtrak, 133 E. Grant St. (800-231-2222). 3 trains per week to: New Orleans (4hr., $29); Houston (5hr., $52); San Antonio (9hr., $81). The station does not sell tickets; buy in advance from **Bass Travel,** 1603 W. Pinhook Rd. (237-2177 or 800-777-7371; open Mon.-Fri. 8:30am-5pm), or another travel agent.

Buses: Greyhound, 315 Lee Ave. (235-1541 or 800-231-2222). To: New Orleans (7 per day, 3½hr., $19); Baton Rouge (7 per day, 1hr., $11); New Iberia (2 per day, ½hr., $6) and other small towns. Open 24hr.

Public Transportation: Lafayette Bus System, 400 Dorset Rd. (261-8570). Infrequent service Mon.-Sat. Fare 45¢, seniors and disabled 20¢, ages 5-12 30¢.

Taxis: Yellow/Checker Cab Inc., 237-6196. Runs on zones; from the bus or train station to downtown $4.

Car Rental: Thrifty Rent-a-Car, 401 E. Pinhook Rd. (237-1282). $25 per day with 100 free mi. Must be 25 with major credit card. Open Mon.-Fri. 7:30am-6pm, Sat.-Sun. 8am-5pm.

Crisis Line: Rape Crisis Center, 233-7273. Open Mon.-Fri. 8:30am-4:30pm.

Post Office: 1105 Moss St. (269-4800). Open Mon.-Fri. 8am-5:30pm, Sat. 8am-12:30pm. **ZIP code:** 70501. **Area code:** 318.

Lafayette stands at Louisiana's crossroads. **I-10** leads east to New Orleans (130mi.) and west to Lake Charles (76mi.); **U.S. 90** heads south to New Iberia (20mi.) and the Atchafalaya Basin; **U.S. 167** runs north into central Louisiana. The **Evangeline Thruway** runs north-south, splitting Lafayette in half. (The name comes from Henry Wadsworth Longfellow's epic poem, *Evangeline*, which portrays the plight of two ill-fated Acadian lovers who are separated on their wedding day in *le Grand Dérangement*.) You'll need a car to explore Acadiana and the Gulf Coast bayou country.

ACCOMMODATIONS AND CAMPING

Inexpensive hotels line the **Evangeline Thruway. Travel Host Inn South,** 1314 N. Evangeline Thruway (233-2090 or 800-677-1466), has large, attractive rooms with cable TV, pool, free Cajun breakfast, and a convenient location (singles $29, doubles $34). The ample but plain-looking rooms at **Super 8,** 2224 N. Evangeline Thruway (232-8826 or 800-800-8000), come with access to a pool and a stunning view of the highway (singles $31, doubles $36). Off the main drag, the **Travelodge Lafayette,** 1101 W. Pinhook Rd. (234-7402 or 800-578-7878), complements rooms with free breakfast, free local calls, and an in-room coffee maker and beans (single $38, double $43). Steal a glimpse at the raised marble crypts in the graveyard off Pinhook.

One campground close to the center of Lafayette, **Acadiana Park Campground,** 1201 E. Alexander (261-8388), off Louisiana Ave., features tennis courts and a soccer field. (Office open Mon.-Thurs. 9am-5pm, Fri.-Sat. 8am-8pm, Sun. 9am-5pm. Sites with full hookup $8.) The lakeside **KOA Lafayette** (235-2739), 5 mi. west of town on I-10 at Exit 97, has a komplete store, a mini-golf kourse, and a kool pool. (Office open daily 7:30am-8:30pm. Tent sites $16, with water and electricity $20, with full hookup $22.)

FOOD AND NIGHTLIFE

Cajun restaurants with live music and dancing have popped up all over Lafayette. Unfortunately, they cater to a tourist crowd with substantial funds. **Mulates** (MYOO-lots), 325 Mills Ave. (332-4648 or 800-42CAJUN/422-2586, 15 min. from Lafayette), near Breaux Bridge, calls itself the most famous Cajun restaurant in the world, and the autographs on the door corroborate its claim. Have them whip up some fried alligator ($5) or the special catfish. ($14; cajun music nightly 7:30-10pm, and Sat.-Sun. noon-2pm. Open Mon.-Sat. 7am-10:30pm, Sun. 11am-11pm.) In central Lafayette, **Chris' Po'Boys** offers seafood platters ($7) and—you guessed it—po'boys ($4-5; four locations, including 1941 Moss St.; 237-1095; open Mon.-Sat. 11am-2:30pm; and 631 Jefferson St.; 234-1696; open Mon.-Fri. 11am-2:30pm). **Randol's,** 2320 Kaliste Saloom Rd. (981-7080), romps with live music nightly in a rustic setting, and doubles as a restaurant (open Sun.-Thurs. 5-10pm, Fri.-Sat. 5-10:30pm). **Prejeans,** 3480 U.S. 167N (896-3247), may be hard to find (take Frontage Rd., which parallels Evangeline Rd.), but it sho' is good for savory Cajun food (dinners $8-12) and nightly music and dancing (7pm). Check out the 14-ft. alligator by the entrance. (Open Sun.-Thurs. 11am-10pm; Fri.-Sat. 11am-11pm.) Pick up a copy of *The Times,* available at restaurants and gas stations, to find out what's going on; Lafayette has a surprising variety of after-hours entertainment.

SIGHTS AND ENTERTAINMENT

First-time visitors to Lafayette should start at the **Acadian Cultural Center/Jean Lafitte National Park,** 501 Fisher Rd. (232-0789), which features a 40-min. documentary, *The Cajun Way: Echos of Acadia,* as well as a terrific exhibit on the exodus and migration of these French settlers (shows every hr. on the hr.; open daily 8am-5pm; free). The re-creation of an Acadian settlement at **Vermilionville,** 1600 Surrey St. (233-4077 or 800-992-2968), entertains as it educates with music, crafts, food, and dancing on the banks of the Bayou Vermilion (open daily 10am-5pm; $8, ages 6-18 $5). Unlike the grandiose mansions which populate the South, **Acadian Village,** 200 Greenleaf Rd. (981-2364 or 800-962-9133), offers a look at the unpretentious homes of common 19th-century Acadian settlers. Village visitors can also see a 400-year-old, 27-foot-long dugout canoe and other Native American artifacts at the **Mississippi Valley Museum** (no additional charge). Take U.S. 167N, turn right on Ridge Rd., then left on Mouton, and follow the signs. (Open daily 10am-5pm. $5.50, seniors $4.50, children $2.50.)

Check out **St. John's Cathedral Oak,** in the yard of St. John's Cathedral, 914 St. John St. This 450-year-old tree—one of the largest in the U.S.—shades the entire lawn with gargantuan, spidery limbs which spread 210 ft.; the weight of a single limb is estimated at 72 tons. (Free.) The **Lafayette Museum,** 1122 Lafayette St. (234-2208), exhibits heirlooms, antiques, and Mardi Gras costumes inside the 19th-century Alexandre Mouton House (named for Louisiana's first Democratic governor). (Open Tues.-Sat. 9am-5pm, Sun. 3-5pm. $3, students and children $1, seniors $2.)

Lafayette kicks off spring and fall weekends with **Downtown Alive!** (268-5566), a series of free concerts featuring everything from new wave to Cajun and zydeco (April-June and Sept.-Nov. Fri. 5:30pm; music from 6-8:30pm). The **Festival International de Louisiane** (232-8086), April 22-27 in 1997, highlights the music, visual arts, and cuisine of southwest Louisiana in a francophone tribute to the region.

■ New Iberia and Environs

While Lafayette was being invaded by oil magnates eager to build a Louisiana oil-business center, New Iberia kept right on with its daily business of being a picturesque bayou town. Though the area's attractions aren't numerous, several give visitors a better feel for the unique conditions of life on the bayou.

Unlike those which reaped fortunes from cotton, most plantations in southern Louisiana grew sugarcane. Most of these plantations are still private property, but **Shadows on the Teche,** 317 E. Main St. (318-369-6446), at the Rte. 14/Rte. 182 junction, welcomes visitors. A Southern aristocrat saved the plantation's crumbling mansion, built in 1831, from neglect after the Civil War. The collection of over 17,000 family documents—discovered in 40 trucks in the attic and spanning four generations—provides a first-hand look at antebellum life in the South. (Open daily 9am-4:30pm. $6, ages 6-11 $3.) A lone chimney protrudes from the lake next to **Live Oak Gardens,** 5505 Rip Van Winkle Rd. (318-365-3332), marking the existence of a mansion which was devoured by a whirlpool in 1980. Today, peaceful gardens and scenic boat tours belie the area's tempestuous past. (Open daily 9am-5pm. $10, seniors $9, ages 5-16 $5.50.) **Avery Island,** 7 mi. away on Rte. 329 off Rte. 90 (50¢ toll to enter the island), sizzles with the world-famous **Tabasco Pepper Sauce Factory,** where the McIlhenny family has produced the famous condiment for nearly a century. Guided tours include free recipes, samples, and tastings. *OOOOOeeeeeeee!!!!* (Open Mon.-Fri. 9am-4pm, Sat. 9am-noon. Free.) Before you leave New Iberia, be sure to take a one-hour **Airboat Tour** (318-229-4457) of the shallow water swamps and bayous of Lake Fausse Pointe. Look for snowy egrets, alligators, and the large, edible nutria rat. (Open Feb. 1-Oct. 31 Tues.-Sun. 8am-5:30pm. $10. Call for directions and required reservations.)

Picturesque campsites on the banks of the Bayou Teche are available at **Belmont Campgrounds,** 1000 Belmont Rd. at Rte. 31 and 86 (318-364-6020). Within the well-kept grounds are nature trails and fishing areas in the stocked pond (150 sites, with full hook-up, showers, and laundry; $13 per night).

New Iberia lies 21 mi. southeast of Lafayette on U.S. 90. See the **Iberia Parish Tourist Commission,** 2704 Rte. 14 (318-365-1540; open daily 9am-5pm), or the **Greater Iberia Chamber of Commerce,** 111 W. Main St. (318-364-1836; open Mon.-Fri. 9am-5pm), for maps. **Amtrak** (800-872-7245) stops in New Iberia, at an unstaffed station off Washington St., on the way between New Orleans and Lafayette. Three trains per week set out in each direction, for Lafayette (30min., $6) and New Orleans (3hr., $28). **Greyhound** (318-364-8571 or 800-231-2222) pulls into town at 101 Perry St. Buses run to Morgan City (1 per day, 1hr., $9), New Orleans (1 per day, 4hr., $23), and Lafayette (2 per day, 40min., $6). (Open Mon.-Fri. 7:30am-5pm, Sat.-Sun. 7:30am-noon.)

Arkansas

As you zip over the Mississippi River heading west into Arkansas, the landscape spreads into expansive green fields and hills that sparkle with the last rain. "The Natural State," as Arkansas license plates proclaim it, lives up to its boast, encompassing the ascents of the Ozarks, the clear waters of Hot Springs, and miles of highway twisting through lush pine forests.

As varied as Arkansas geography may be, one theme unites the entire state: Bill…er, President Clinton. Museums and exhibits, billboards, and posters everywhere celebrate and recount the life of this native son done good. While some folks here simply disdain the man ("I didn't vote for the dope from Hope," reads one bumper sticker), many wallow in praise for the Prez who (we are urged to remember) was once just a little lad from Arkansas. By the time you're using this book, we'll know who's in the majority.

PRACTICAL INFORMATION

Capital: Little Rock.
Arkansas Department of Parks and Tourism: 1 Capitol Mall, Little Rock 72201 (501-682-7777 or 800-NATURAL/628-8725). Open Mon.-Fri. 8am-5pm.
Time Zone: Central (1hr. behind Eastern). **Postal Abbreviation:** AR.
Sales Tax: 7%.

■ Little Rock

In the early 19th century, a small rock just a few feet high served as an important landmark for boats pushing their way upstream. Sailors and merchants began settling around this stone outcrop and, lo and behold, Little Rock was born. (Sadly enough, a nearby cliff called "Big Rock," another early river landmark, never amounted to anything.)

Trouble swept Little Rock in 1957 when it became the focus of a nationwide civil rights controversy. Governor Orval Faubus led a violent segregationist movement, using state troops to prevent nine black students from enrolling at Central High School. They entered only under protection from troops sent by President Eisenhower. Racial tension has cooled since then, and Little Rock is slowly becoming a more integrated community with a modest collection of historical attractions.

PRACTICAL INFORMATION

Tourist Office: Little Rock Convention and Visitors Bureau, 100 W. Markham St. (376-4781 or 800-844-4781), next door to the Excelsior Hotel. Open Mon.-Fri. 8:30am-5pm. Also try **Arkansas Dept. of Parks and Tourism.**

Airport: Little Rock Regional (372-3430), 5mi. east of downtown off I-440. Easily accessible from downtown (by bus 80¢, by Black and White Cab about $10).

Trains: Amtrak, Union Station, 1400 W. Markham St. (372-6841 or 800-872-7245), at Victory St. Three trains per week to: St. Louis (7hr., $74); Dallas (9hr., $81); Malvern, 20mi. east of Hot Springs (1hr., $11). Open Mon. and Wed. 6am-10pm, Tues. and Thurs. 6am-2pm and 5pm-1am, Fri.-Sat. 6am-2pm, Sun. 5pm-1am.

Buses: Greyhound, 118 E. Washington St. (372-3007 or 800-231-2222), across the river in North Little Rock. Use the walkway over the bridge to get downtown. To: St. Louis (2 per day, 7hr., $59); New Orleans (5 per day, 14hr., $69); Memphis (16 per day, 2hr., $21). Ticket prices higher on weekends. 25% discount for 14-day advance purchase. Open 24hr.

Public Transportation: Central Arkansas Transit (CAT) (375-1163). Little Rock has a fairly comprehensive local transport system (but no evening hours), with 21 bus routes running through the city Mon.-Sat. 6am-6pm. Maps available at the **Sterling Department Store** (375-8181), at 6th and Center St.

Taxis: Black and White Cabs, 374-0333. $1.10 initial fee; $1 per mi.

Car Rental: Budget Car and Truck Rental (375-5521 or 800-527-0700), at the airport or at 3701 E. Roosevelt Rd. rents vehicles for $37.50 per day, with 150 free mi.; $175 per week, with 1000 free mi.; 25¢ per additional mi. Must be 21; under 25 surcharge $5 per day. Open Sun.-Fri. 6am-11:30pm, Sat. 7am-10pm.

Crisis Lines: Rape Crisis, 663-3334. Open 24hr. **First Call for Help,** 376-4567. Open Mon.-Fri. 8am-5pm.

Emergency: 911.

Post Office: 600 E. Capitol (375-5155). Open Mon.-Fri. 7am-5:30pm. **ZIP code:** 72201. **Area code:** 501.

Downtown Little Rock is roughly grid-like, although the order deteriorates as you move away from the heart of the city. **Broadway** and **Main St.** are the major north-south arteries running to and from the river. **Markham St.** and all streets numbered 1 to 36 run east-west. **Third St.** turns into **W. Markham St.** just west of downtown.

ACCOMMODATIONS

Inexpensive motels in Little Rock tend to cluster around **I-30,** next to downtown, and **University Ave.** at the intersection of I-630 and I-430, a 5- to 10-min. drive from downtown. A few motels in town are cheaper but shabbier.

Master's Inn Economy (372-4392 or 800-633-3434), I-30 (Exit 140) and 9th St., *almost* downtown. Locations in North Little Rock as well. Spacious, well-lit rooms with a lovely pool, a restaurant, and even room service. Just one catch: you must be 21 to rent. Singles $33, $6 per extra person; under 18 free with adult.

Little Rock Inn, 601 S. Center St. (376-8301), at 6th St. half a block from downtown. Primarily a residential hotel, the Inn rents a limited number of well-worn rooms without TV or phone. $33 per night for 1-2 people, $75-90 per week with $20 security deposit. Call 2 days ahead.

Motel 6, 9525 Hwy I-30 (565-1388 or 800-466-8356). Simple, but clean and reliable rooms await. Singles $29, doubles $46.

KOA Campground (758-4598), on Crystal Hill Rd. in North Little Rock, 7mi. from downtown between exit 12 on I-430 and exit 148 on I-48. Well-kept grounds with 100 sites (some more public than others). You can "rough it" outdoors by the pool (sites $19, with hookup $25, cabins $28).

FOOD AND NIGHTLIFE

Vino's, 923 W. 7th St. (375-8466), at Chester St. The only micro-brewery in Little Rock gives Italian food a good name and price (pizza 95¢, calzones $5). Weekends bring live music of all types—folk, rock, alternative, you name it. Cover $5. Open Mon.-Wed. 11am-10pm, Thurs.-Fri. 11am-midnight, Sat. noon-midnight.

Juanita's, 1300 S. Main St. (372-1228), at 13th St. A local favorite for years, Juanita's serves up scrumptious Mexican food with nightly live music. Call or stop by for a jam-packed schedule. Open Mon. 11am-2:30pm, Tues.-Fri. 11am-2:30pm and 5:30-10:30pm, Sat. noon-10:30pm, Sun. 5:30-9pm.

Wallace Grill Café, 103 Main St. (372-3111), near the visitors center. Generous portions of rib-stickin' cuisine. BLT $1.70, fried catfish $5.25. Open Mon.-Fri. 6am-2:30pm, Sat. 7am-noon.

Olde World Pizza, 1706 Markham Blvd. (374-5504), will put anything from yellow squash to smoked turkey on your pie ($7). The atmosphere is relaxed. Be prepared to wait. Open Mon.-Thurs. 11am-10pm, Sat.-Sun. 11am-11pm.

The Minute Man, 322 Broadway (375-0392). If it were a chain, you could call it McTaco Bell. Good, greasy hamburgers ($1.40) and Mexican dishes (nacho salad $2.50), served at lightning speed. Open Mon.-Fri., 10:30am-9pm, Sat. 11am-8pm.

Backstreet, 1021 Jessie Rd. (664-2744), near Cantrell and Riverfront Rd., is a large complex with several gay and lesbian bars: **701** for women, **501** for men (rock and disco in each), and **Miss Kitty's,** which plays country *and* western. No cover except for special shows ($2.50). Open daily 9pm-5am.

Discovery (664-4784), next door to Backstreet. A big, loud, heavy-dancing gay bar, home to the Ms. Gay America pageant. Cover $12. Open Thurs.-Sat. 9pm-5am.

SIGHTS

Tourists can visit the eponymous "little rock" at **Riverfront Park,** a pleasant place for a walk along the Arkansas River. Pay close attention: the rock has had a long, hard life and is appropriately *little*, therefore easy to miss. For quick access, cut through the back of the Excelsior Hotel at Markham and Center St. The town celebrates its waterway with arts, crafts, bands, food, and a fireworks display at **Riverfest** (376-4781 for info), on the last evening of Memorial Day weekend (admission $1). The **state capitol** (682-5080), at the west end of Capitol St., may look familiar—it's a replica of the U.S. Capitol in Washington, D.C. At the front desk you can check out a tape and tape player for a free 45-min. audio tour. (Open Mon.-Fri. 9am-4pm.) To get an idea of the Clintons' pre-Presidential lifestyle, swing by the **Governor's Mansion,** S. Center at 18th St. in the middle of a gorgeous historic district. The **Arkansas Territorial Restoration,** 200 E. Third St. (324-9351), gives visitors a look at everyday life in 19th-century Little Rock through tours of four restored buildings including a print shop built in 1824. Though long (1 hr.), the tours are fascinating. (Open Mon.-Sat. 9am-5pm, Sun. 1-5pm. Tours begin every hr. on the hr. except for noon; last tour 4pm. $2, seniors $1, children 50¢; free 1st Sun. of the month.)

On the eastern edge of town lounges **MacArthur Park,** home to the **Museum of Science and History** (396-7050 or 800-880-6475). For kids and adults alike, the hands-on exhibits feature Arkansas history and wildlife, including a walk-through bear cave. (Open Mon.-Sat. 9am-4:30pm, Sun 1-4:30pm. $3, free the last Sat. of every month from 9-11am.) Next door the **Arkansas Art Center** (372-4000) offers outstanding collections by both European masters and contemporary artists. The 1997 season will showcase 20th-century Russian drawings, American still life paintings from the Metropolitan Museum of Art, and mid-Southern watercolorists (open Mon.-Thurs. and Sat. 10am-5pm, Fri. 10am-8:30pm, and Sun. noon-5pm; free). Northwest of the state capitol off I-30 at Fair Park Blvd., **War Memorial Park** houses the 40-acre **Little Rock**

Zoo, 1 Jonesboro Dr. (666-2406 or 663-4733), where animals are kept in areas which simulate their natural habitats (open daily 9am-5pm; $3, under 12 $1).

The **Toltec Mounds State Park** (961-9442), 15mi. east of North Little Rock on Rte. 386, brings you back to when the Mounds were a political and religious center for the Plum Bayou Native Americans. (Open Tues.-Sat. 8am-5pm, Sun. noon-5pm. 1-hr. guided tours, every ½hr. starting at 9:30am. $2.64, children $1.32.)

■ The Ozarks

Stretching from southern Missouri to northern Arkansas, the stunning **Ozark Mountains** gently ripple through the land, with a splendor matched only by the crystalline caves beneath them. Highways have bridged the natural boundaries that long isolated the lives and customs of American mountain natives, but the simple Ozark lifestyle manages to survive alongside the tourist trade.

Take caution when driving; the scenic highways that traverse these tall mountains expose curving, twisting danger as well as great views. Few buses venture into the area, and hitching is *not* recommended. Drivers should follow U.S. 71, or Rtes. 7 or 23 for the best access and jaw-dropping panoramas. Eureka Springs to Huntsville on Rte. 23 south is an especially scenic 1-hr. drive, and U.S. 62 east or west from Eureka Springs has some attractive stretches of road. Be sure to block off enough time to make it through the mountains—speed limits rarely exceed 35 mph. Contact the **Arkansas Department of Parks and Tourism** (see Arkansas Practical Information, p. 385) for info on camping, hiking, and canoeing.

MOUNTAIN VIEW

Despite the commercialism gradually seeping into Mountain View (Shop at Wal-Mart! Eat at Pizza Hut!), the village remains refreshingly unpretentious, authentically Ozark, and rather small (pop. 2400). Nearly every day, locals gather on a street corner to make music with banjos, dulcimers, fiddles, and guitars. Visit the Ozark Folk Center for another taste of Ozark charm.

Know that Mountain View is a dry county; beware of people selling renegade booze. Mountain View's **Chamber of Commerce** (269-8068) is located behind the Courthouse on the corner of Washington and Howard St. (open Mon.-Sat. 8am-5pm). Pick up one of their essential and easy-to-read maps. **Rental cars** are available at **Lackey Motors Car Rental** (269-3211 or 800-467-3214), at the corner of Main St. and Peabody Ave. You must be 23, with a credit card in your name if you're under 25. ($25 per day plus 25¢ per mi.; open Mon.-Sat. 8am-5pm.) Or for $1, the **Mountain View Shuttle** (269-2839) will provide rides in their 1935 vintage shuttle. (Hourly service around town 9am-midnight; after 6pm service to and from shows and by reservation.) In **emergencies,** dial 911. Mountain View's **post office** (269-3520), peddles stamps at 703 Sylamore Drive; **ZIP code:** 72560; **area code:** 501.

Mountain View offers many lodging options for the budget traveler. The owners of the **Wildflower Bed & Breakfast** (800-591-4879), on the northeast corner of the Courthouse square, are particularly hospitable; they welcome even those travelers who lack a Southern drawl. Eight florally decorated rooms with soft blue carpeting, multiple windows, and antique furniture lead off a common hallway. (Singles $37, doubles $42. Rooms with private bathrooms available. Reservations recommended.) The **Mountain View Motel,** 407 E. Main St. (269-3209), has 18 clean rooms sporting hot pots of free coffee (singles $30, doubles $37). A group of small cottages with rocking chairs make up the **Dry Creek Lodge** (269-3871 or 800-264-3655), spur 382 off Rte. 5, within the Ozark Folk Center (single or double $45-50, Nov.-Mar. $35-40).

Because Mountain View lies only 14 mi. south of the Ozark National Forest, the cheapest way to stay in the area is free **camping.** Pitch a tent anywhere within the forest—it's free, legal, and usually safe, as long as the campsite does not block any road, path, or thoroughfare. Campgrounds around the Blanchard Springs caverns, off Rte. 14E about 20min. from Mountain View, include **Blanchard Springs Recreation Area** (32 sites with hot showers and a swimming pool, $8), **Gunner Pool Recreation Area**

(27 sites, $5), and **Barkshed Recreation Area** (5 sites, free, but beware young idlers who bring their drink and wickedness). For more info about camping in the areas, contact the **Sylamore Ranger District** of the National Forest, P.O. Box 1279, Mountain View, AR 72560 (757-2211 or 269-3228).

Locals swear by **Tommy's Famous...a pizzeria** (269-FAST/3278), about ½mi. west of the courthouse square on Rte. 66. A small pie goes for $6; calzones start at $7. (Open Wed.-Sat. 3-10pm, Sun. 3-7pm.) The recently opened **Rhythm & Brew's,** 112 E. Main St. (269-5200), specializes in tasty desserts and sophisticated coffee drinks. It has the only cappuccino machine for 100mi. On Fridays and Saturdays, local musicians sign up to perform on the small stage. (Open for lunch Wed.-Sat. 11:30am-2pm, for dinner Thurs.-Sat. 6pm-midnight.)

Ozark culture thrives undiluted on the lush grounds of the **Ozark Folk Center** (269-3851), just minutes north of Mountain View off Rte. 9N. The center recreates a mountain village and showcases the cabin crafts, music, and lore of the Ozarks. In the **Crafts Forum,** over 25 artisans demonstrate everything from wheel-thrown ceramics to ironware forging and spoon carving. Hear original "unplugged" music as locals fiddle, pluck, and strum in the auditorium at lunchtime and nightly (shows at 7:30pm), while dancers implore the audience to jig and clog along. (Open May-Oct. daily 10am-5pm. Crafts area $7, ages 6-12 $4.50. Evening musical performances $7, ages 6-12 $4.50. Combination tickets and family rates available.) The center's seasonal events include the **Arkansas Folk Festival** (April 18-20, 1997), the **Annual Dulcimer Jamboree** (April 25-27, 1997), and the **National Fiddle Championships** (Oct. 31-Nov. 2, 1997). Revel in the musical charisma of triple Grammy Award winner Jimmy Driftwood, the quintessential Ozark artist, at the **Jimmy Driftwood Barn and Folk Museum** (269-8042), also on Rte. 9N (shows Fri. and Sun. 7pm; free). When you're ready to learn everything there is to know about the dulcimer, travel up Rte. 9N to the **Dulcimer Shoppe,** P.O. Box 1230 (269-4313). Visitors can watch craftsmen fashion these mellow music makers and even hammer a few strings themselves. (Open Apr.-Oct. Mon.-Fri. 9am-5pm, Sat. 10am-5pm.)

Fishing along the **White River** is one of many popular outdoor diversions in the area around Mountain View. Non-residents can purchase a 3-day **fishing license** ($10) from Wal-Mart, 314 Sylamore Ave. (269-4395). To experience the Ozarks from the saddle, contact the **OK Trading Post** (585-2217), 3½mi. west of the Rte. 5/9/14 junction (horse rentals $10 per hr.). The **Blanchard Springs Caverns** (757-2211), on the south border of the Ozark Forest, glisten with exquisite cave formations and glassy, cool springs. Trail guides navigate the caverns (frequent 45-min. tours; last tour leaves at 5pm). Blanchard has some great outdoor trails as well. (Open daily 9am-6:30pm; Nov.-March Wed.-Sun. 9:30am-4:30pm. $8, with Golden Age Passport and ages 6-15 $4.) Daytrips from Mountain View to the **Buffalo River** (1hr. northwest) are excellent for canoeing. **Crockett's Country Store and Canoe Rental** (800-355-6111), at the Rte. 14/27 junction in Harriet, can provide picnic lunches (about $5 per person), boats ($25), and maps of the waterways. (Life jackets and paddles come with boats. Open daily 6am until the Crocketts go to bed.)

EUREKA SPRINGS

Eureka! You've arrived at the "Little Switzerland" of the Ozarks. In the early 19th century, the native Osage spread reports of a wonderful spring with magical healing powers. Settlers quickly came to the site and established a small town from which they sold bottles of the miraculous water. Today, the tiny town in northwest Arkansas is filled with ritzy boutiques, native limestone walls, narrow streets, and Victorian buildings painted in brash colors fit only for citrus fruits. Tourists still come in droves, but no longer to experience the waters (they go to Hot Springs for that). Nowadays, Eureka's main attraction is the **Great Passion Play** (253-9200 or 800-882-PLAY/7529), off U.S. 62 on Passion Play Rd., modeled after Germany's *Oberammergau* Passion Play. Featuring a cast of 250 actors and countless live animals, this seasonal event built on piety, holy water, and slick marketing has drawn more than five million visitors to its depiction of Jesus Christ's life and death. Even if you miss the show, you can't miss the **Christ of the Ozarks** statue, seven stories of the messianic schtick used in the set…hallelujah, hallelujah. (Performances April 25-Oct. 25 Tues.-Wed. and Fri.-Sun. 8:30pm. Disabled access seating provided; sign language interpretation available on request. $12-13, ages 4-11 ½-price. For reservations write P.O. Box 471, Eureka Springs 72632.)

The **Chamber of Commerce** (253-8737 or 800-6EUREKA/638-7352) chills on U.S. 62 just north of Rte. 23 (open daily 9am-5:30pm, Nov-Mar. 9am-5pm). A **trolley** (253-9572) runs from local hotels to the downtown historic loop and to the play ($3 for an all-day pass, $1.50 for a one-trip pass). Eureka's **post office:** 101 Spring St. (253-9850), on the loop (open Mon.-Fri. 8:15am-4:15pm, Sat. 10am-noon); **ZIP code:** 72632; **area code:** 501.

Eureka Springs has more hotel beds than it does residents, and rates change almost daily. The **Dogwood Inn,** Rte 23S (253-7200 or 800-544-1884), offers pretty rooms beside an outdoor pool and hot tub (singles and doubles $28). Next door the **Colonial Mansion Inn** (253-7300 or 800-638-2622) rents spacious, green-carpeted rooms. Continental breakfast included (two beds $28). **Kettle Campgrounds** (253-9100), on Rte. 62 at the east edge of town, has 14 tent sites in a shaded, woodsy area, along with hot showers, a laundry room, and a pool (sites $15-16).

The town is filled with tourist-oriented restaurants. Escape the fast food and tourist glitz at the **Chuck Wagon,** 84 S. Main St. (253-5629), which serves "sandwiches stacked like Mae West" ($3.75-6.50) on a cozy patio jutting over a cliff (open daily 5am "until you stop coming"). After your meal, head downstairs, take off your hat, and stay a while at the **Wagon Wheel** (253-9934), a beer-drinker's country-western bar decorated with antiques (open Mon.-Fri. 10am-2am, Sat. 10am-midnight).

■ Hot Springs

Despite tourist traps like alligator farms, wax museums, and ubiquitous gift shops, the town of Hot Springs delivers precisely what it advertises—cleansing, soothing relaxation. Once you've bathed in the coils of these 143° springs, you'll realize why everybody, even the federal government (see below for info on **Hot Springs National Park**), got in on the bathhouse craze of the 20s.

Practical Information Before touring Hot Springs, stop by the **visitors center,** 626 Central Ave. (321-2277 or 800-772-2489), downtown off Spring St., and pick up *The Spring Magazine* (open daily 9am-5pm). Hot Springs's **post office:** 100 Reserve St. (623-7703), at the corner of Central in the Federal Reserve Building; **ZIP code:** 71901; **area code:** 501.

Accommodations, Camping, and Food Hot Springs has ample lodging, and the best deals can be found on the side streets off Central Ave., the town's main drag. The motels along Rte. 7 and 88 have similar prices, but rates rise for the tourist season (Feb.-Aug.). The **Tower Motel,** 755 Park Ave. (624-9555), has pleasant rooms with country landscape pictures and brightly colored tiles in the bathroom. (Singles $25, doubles $30). The **Margarete Motel,** 217 Fountain St. (623-1192), is just a stone's throw away from town and offers an excellent deal on large rooms (singles $26, doubles $34). Walk into gingerbread-like cabins at the **Best Motel,** 630 Ouachita (624-5736), which has moderately clean rooms organized around a small pool (singles $25, doubles $35). Those who can forsake the cuteness might look next door at the **Holiday Motel,** 642 Ouachita (624-9317; singles $27, doubles $31). The closest **campgrounds** are at **Gulpha Gorge** (624-3383 for info and emergencies), part of Hot Springs National Park; follow Rte. 70 to 70B about ½mi. northeast of town (sites $8, seniors $4; no hookups, no showers).

Granny's Kitchen, 322 Central Ave. (624-6183), cooks up good ol' country food (plate lunches $4), with old-fashioned Americana lining the walls. The **Dixie Café,** 3623 Central Ave. (624-2100), cooks up Southern food with fitting hospitality (entrees $4-7). **Cookin' with Jazz,** 101 Central Ave. (321-0555), serves New Orleans-style dishes—po' boys, creole, jambalaya, and gumbo—with live music on summer Thursdays (entrees $5-12). Wherever you dine, just remember to drink the water— after all, that's what made Hot Springs famous.

Sights and Entertainment After trickling through the earth for 4000 years, water gushes to the planet's crust in Hot Springs at a rate of 850,000 gallons a day. Let the baths begin! As the only operating house on "Bathouse Row," the **Buckstaff,** on Central Ave. (623-2308), retains the dignity and elegance of Hot Springs's heyday in the 1920s. (Open Mon.-Fri. 7-11:45am and 1:30-3pm, Sat. 7-11:45am. Bath $13, whirl-pool $1.50 extra; massage $15.50.) Around the corner, the **Hot Springs Health Spa,** N. 500 Reserve (321-9664), sports hot tubs and whirlpools. Not only does the spa offer the only coed baths in town (yes, suits are required!), but you can stay as long as you like and meander among many baths. Note the late hours. (Open daily 9am-9pm. Bath $12; massage $12-15.) The **Downtowner,** 135 Central Ave. (624-5521), has the town's cheapest hands-on, full treatment baths with no difference in quality (bath $10.50, whirlpool $1.50 extra; massage $12).

For info on **Hot Springs National Park,** contact the **Fordyce Bathhouse Visitors Center,** 369 Central Ave. (623-3383, TTD 624-2308), which distributes handy trail maps and a chart helpful for disabled and hearing-impaired visitors. The Center also has two self-guided tours: one on the history of the local baths, and one on the rise of President Clinton, who grew up in Hot Springs. Walking tours of the National Park are also offered. (Open daily 9am-6pm.) Diehard sightseers should take the 1½-hr. amphibious **National Park Duck Tour** (321-2911 or 800-682-7044), which leaves from 418 Central Ave. seven times a day to travel through Hot Springs and out into Lake Hamilton ($8.50, seniors $8, kids $5.50).

Hot Springs's natural beauty is unmissable. You can gaze up at the green-peaked mountains as you cruise Lake Hamilton on the **Belle of Hot Springs,** 5200 Central Hwy. (525-4438), during a 1½-hr. narrated tour alongside the Ouachita Mountains and Lake Hamilton mansions (trips during summer daily 1 and 3pm; $8.50, children $4.25). From the **Hot Springs Mountain Observatory Tower** (623-6035), located in the national park (turn off Central Ave. onto Fountain St. and follow the signs), view the beautiful panorama of the surrounding mountains and lakes. On clear days, it's possible to see as far as 140mi. (Open May 16-Labor Day daily 9am-9pm, day after Labor Day-Oct. and March-May 15 9am-6pm, Nov.-Feb. 9am-5pm. $2.75, ages 5-11 $1.75, under 5 free.) For outdoor frolicking, the clear and unpolluted waters of the **Ouachita River** entice you to hike, bike, fish, or canoe (326-5517 or 800-748-3718 for info). In Whittington Park, on Whittington St. off Central Ave., shops and bathhouses give way to an expanse of trees, grass, and shaded picnic tables.

Family entertainment fills Hot Springs's nights. The **Famous Bath House Show,** 701 Central Ave. (623-1415), features comedy skits and all kinds o' music—every-thing from Elvis spoofs to Motown grooves. (Show dates and times are sporadic; call for details. $9.45, under 13 $5; reservations recommended.) The **Music Mountain Jamboree,** 2720 Albert Pike, also at U.S. 270W (767-3841), is a 10-min. drive out of town. A country music shows take place here most days of the week during the sum-mer, and sporadically during the rest of the year. (Shows at 8pm. $10.50, kids $5; res-ervations recommended.)

Leaving Arkansas: Texarkana

Texarkana straddles the border between Texas and Arkansas; stand on the median of **State Line Ave.,** and you'll have a foot in each state. The **Texarkana Historical Museum,** 219 State Line Ave. (903-793-4831) between 3rd and Broad St., has exhibits on the area's Native Americans and Texarkana's most famous entertainer: the father of ragtime, **Scott Joplin** (open Tues.-Sat. 10am-4pm; $2, kids $1). Maps and info on sights in Texarkana are available at the **Arkansas Tourist Information Center** (501-772-4301), off I-30E between Exits 1 and 2 (open daily 8am-6pm).

GREAT LAKES

The world has glaciers to thank for this Midwestern freshwater paradise. During the Ice Age, massive sheets of ice flowed from the north, doing the work of countless bulldozers as they plowed the earth, carving out huge lake basins. At the end of the Ice Age, the glaciers receded and melted, leaving flat expanses of rich topsoil, numerous small pools, and five inland seas. These lands have yielded billions of bushels of grain and vegetables, acres of timber, and countless tons of iron and copper ore; the lakes have been the region's lifeline. Together, the Great Lakes comprise 15% of the earth's drinkable freshwater supply and an invaluable network of transport arteries for the surrounding states.

Lake Superior is the largest freshwater lake in the world, and its unpopulated, scenic coasts dance with one of the only significant wolf populations left in the lower 48 states. Lake Michigan proclaims itself a sports lover's paradise and delivers, with swimming, sailing, deep-water fishing, and sugar-fine sand dunes. Lake Erie has suffered the most from industrial pollution, but thanks to vigilant citizens and strict regulations, the shallowest Great Lake is gradually reclaiming its former beauty. The first Great Lake to be seen by Europeans, Lake Huron ironically lags behind in development, though not in size or recreational potential. The runt of the bunch, Lake Ontario still covers an area larger than New Jersey.

People have been drawn to the fertile plains and deep forests of the Great Lakes since prehistoric times. Today, the Great Lakes region's water and wilderness attract hostel and camping crowds, who revel in discovering areas that the talons of "progress" have never reached. The sophisticated urban traveler should not despair, however—Minneapolis and St. Paul have all the artsy panache of any coastal metropolis, while urban Chicago stands out as the focal point of Midwestern activity with world-class music, architecture, and cuisine.

Ohio

Contrary to popular belief, Ohio is not Iowa, Idaho, all cornfields, or grimy and industrial; it *is* the only state south of Lake Erie that borders Michigan and starts with an "O." Eons ago, the glaciers that carved out the Great Lakes flattened the northern half of the state, creating perfect farmland that is today patched with cornfields and soybean plants. The southern half, spared the bulldozing, still rolls with endless wooded hills. Columbus sits just north of the abrupt line dividing the regions. The state's other two metropoli, mortal enemies Cincinnati and Cleveland, lie on opposite ends of the state. Not only diverse, Ohio is innovative, as evidenced by the state beverage, tomato juice—until popularized in Reynoldsburg, a Columbus suburb, tomatoes were thought poisonous and inedible. Ohio's political tradition compliments its strong "middle-America" affiliation—in recent years Ohio has voted with the American majority in national elections more often than any other state.

PRACTICAL INFORMATION

Capital: Columbus.
State Office of Travel and Tourism: 77 S. High St., P.O. Box 1001, Columbus 43215 (614-466-8844). **Ohio Tourism Line:** 800-282-5393.
Time Zone: Eastern. **Postal Abbreviation:** OH.
Sales Tax: 5.5%.

Great Lakes

■ Cleveland

"Just drive north until the sky and all the buildings turn gray. Then you're in Cleveland." The critic who uttered this quote, hoping to achieve the "city cliché" honors normally reserved for Mark Twain, has remained obscure, much like any praise for beleaguered Cleveland—until recently. Despite a sometimes gloomy landscape, things have begun to look up; the city's old warehouses on the Cuyahoga River have been reworked into raving nightclubs, and the much-anticipated Rock and Roll Hall of Fame is finally open. The city's bicentennial celebrations in the summer of 1996 gave new spirit to a city still mourning the loss of the Cleveland Browns. While the future of Cleveland remains uncertain, it is clear that within its boundaries lies the potential to become one of America's metropolitan cultural centers.

PRACTICAL INFORMATION

Tourist Office: Cleveland Convention and Visitors Bureau, 3100 Tower City Center (621-4110 or 800-321-1001), on the 31st floor of Terminal Tower at Public Sq. Free maps. Write for the *Greater Cleveland Official Visitors Guide* for info on attractions. Open Mon.-Fri. 8:30am-5pm.

Airport: Cleveland Hopkins International (265-6030), 10mi. west of downtown in Brookpark. Take RTA's airport rapid transit line #66X ("Red Line") to Terminal Tower ($1.50).

Trains: Amtrak, 200 Cleveland Memorial Shoreway N.E. (696-5115 or 800-872-7245), across from Municipal Stadium east of City Hall. To New York City (1 per day, 11hr., $101) and Chicago (2 per day, 6hr., $76). Open 11pm-3:30pm.

Buses: Greyhound, 1465 Chester Ave. (781-0520 or 800-231-2222), at E. 14th St. 7 blocks from Terminal Tower. Near RTA bus lines. To: New York City (6 per day, 11hr., $61); Chicago (8 per day, 7½hr., $32); Pittsburgh (10 per day, 3hr., $19).

Public Transportation: Regional Transit Authority (RTA), 315 Euclid Ave. (566-5074; 24-hr. **answerline** 621-9500), across from Woolworth's. Bus lines, connecting with Rapid Transit trains, provide transport to most of the metropolitan area. Service daily 4:30am-midnight; call for info on "owl" after-midnight service. Train fare $1.50. Bus fare $1.25, express $1.50, all day pass $4; ask the driver for free transfer tickets when you get on.

Taxis: Yellow Cab, 623-1550; **Americab,** 429-1111. Both $1.50 base fare, $1.20 per mi. Both 24hr.

Crisis Line: Rape Crisis Line, 391-3912. Open 24hr.

Emergency: 911.

Post Office: 2400 Orange Ave. (443-4199; 443-4096 after 5pm). Open Mon.-Fri. 8am-7pm. **ZIP code:** 44101. **Area code:** 216.

Terminal Tower in **Public Sq.** cleaves the land into east and west. Many street numbers correspond to the distance of the street from Terminal Tower; e.g., E. 18th St. is 18 blocks east of the Tower. To reach Public Sq. from **I-90** or **I-71,** follow the Ontario Ave./Broadway exit. From **I-77,** take the 9th St. exit to Euclid Ave., which runs into Public Sq. From the Amtrak station, follow **Lakeside Ave.** to **Ontario Ave.,** which leads to the tower. Almost all RTA trains and buses run downtown, and the new **Waterfront Line** gives great access to the Science Museum, Rock and Roll Hall of Fame, and The Flats.

ACCOMMODATIONS AND CAMPING

With hotel taxes (not included in the prices listed below) as high as 14.5%, pickings are slim for good budget lodging in Cleveland. If you know your plans well in advance, **Cleveland Private Lodgings,** P.O. Box 18590, Cleveland 44118 (321-3213), can place you in a home around the city for as little as $35. (Leave 2-3 weeks for a letter of confirmation. Call Mon.-Fri.; messages will be promptly returned.) Otherwise, travelers with cars should head for the suburbs, where prices tend to be lower. The excellent and friendly, though somewhat distant, **Stanford House Hostel (HI-AYH),** 6093 Stanford Rd. (467-8711), 22 mi. south of Cleveland in Peninsula off Exit 12 from I-80, occupies a beautifully restored 19th-century Greek Revival farmhouse in the Cuyahoga Valley National Recreation Area. Gorgeous hiking and bike trails await nearby. (30 beds. 1-week max. stay. Check-in 5-10pm. Curfew 11pm. $10. Reservations recommended.) Closer to town, the suburb of Middleburg Heights offers many chain motels at reasonable prices. **Motel 6,** 7219 Engle Rd. (234-0990), offers clean, comfortable rooms (singles $40, doubles $46), as does the **Cross Country Inn,** 7233 Engle Rd. (243-2277), next door (singles $45, doubles $55). Both have A/C, cable, free local calls, and an insane 14.5% tax.

Woodside Lake Park, 2256 Frost Rd. (313-626-4251), off I-480 in Streetsboro 40 minutes east of downtown, has 300 wooded and unwooded sites. (Sites for 2 $20, with electricity $22; $2 per extra person, ages 3-17 $1. Reserve in summer.)

FOOD

Cleveland's culinary delights hide in tiny neighborhoods surrounding the downtown area. To satiate a craving for hot corned beef, step into one of the dozens of delis in the city center. Italian cafés and restaurants cluster in Little Italy, around **Mayfield Rd.** For fine food, cool shops, and a healthy dose of hipness, slouch toward nearby **Coventry Rd.** Over 100 vendors hawk produce, meat, cheese and other groceries at the indoor-outdoor **West Side Market,** 1995 W. 25th St. (771-8885), at Lorain Ave. (open Mon. and Wed. 7am-4pm, Fri.-Sat. 7am-6pm).

Tommy and the groovy health-conscious staff of **Tommy's,** 1824 Coventry Rd. (321-7757), up the hill from University Circle (take bus #9X east to Mayfield and Coventry Rd.), whip up scrumptious natural and vegetarian cuisine. Of course, you can also dodge all that health stuff and sock your gut with a Brownie Monster ($1.80; open Mon.-Thurs. 7:30am-10pm, Fri.-Sat. 7:30am-11pm, Sun. 9am-10pm). **Mama Santa's,** 12305 Mayfield Rd. (421-2159), in Little Italy just east of University Circle, serves Sicilian food in a dark, no-frills setting. (Medium pizza $3.70; spaghetti $4.50. Open Mon.-Thurs. 10:30am-11:45pm, Fri.-Sat. 10:30am-12:45am.)

SIGHTS AND ENTERTAINMENT

Downtown Cleveland has escaped the plight of other Great Lakes cities, such as Detroit and Erie, with a new baseball diamond, the first-class mall in Terminal Tower, and a rockin' new museum—life is good. **The Rock and Roll Hall of Fame,** 1 Key Plaza (515-8440 or 800-493-ROLL/7655), offers a dizzying exploration through the world of rock music. Listen to hundreds of history making tunes while learning all about the folks who made them. Spend hours gazing at Jimi Hendrix's original hand-written lyrics to *Purple Haze.* (Open Sun.-Thurs. 10am-5:30pm, Wed.-Sat. 10am-9pm, winters daily 10am-5:30pm, except Wed. when it's open until 9pm. $13, seniors and ages 4-11 $9.50. Tours take 3-4 hr.) **Cleveland Lakefront State Park** (881-8141), 2 mi. west of downtown and accessible from Lake Ave. or Cleveland Memorial Shore-way, is a 14-mi.-long park that includes a beach with great swimming and waterfront picnic areas (7mi. from downtown).

Seventy-five cultural institutions cluster in **University Circle,** 4 mi. east of the city. Check with the helpful visitors bureau for details on museums, live music, and drama. The world-class **Cleveland Museum of Art,** 11150 East Blvd. (421-7340), exhibits French and American Impressionist paintings, as well as a version of Rodin's "The Thinker." A beautiful plaza and pond face the museum. (Open Tues. and Thurs.-Fri. 10am-5:45pm, Wed. 10am-9:45pm, Sat. 9am-4:45pm, Sun. noon-5:45pm. Free.) Nearby, the **Cleveland Museum of Natural History,** 1 Wade Oval Dr. (231-4600), displays the only existing skull of the fearsome Pygmy Tyrant *(Nanatyrannus)* in all its malignant dimunition. (Open Mon.-Sat. 10am-5pm, Sun. noon-5pm. $6, students, seniors, and ages 5-17 $4, under 4 free; free Tues. and Thurs. 3-5pm except during special events.)

The **Cleveland Orchestra,** one of the nation's best, bows, plucks, and blows in University Circle at **Severance Hall,** 11001 Euclid Ave. (231-7300; tickets $14-26). In the summer, the orchestra moves to **Blossom Music Center,** 1145 W. Steels Corners Rd., Cuyahoga Falls (920-8040), about 45 min. south of the city (lawn seating $12-14). East of University Circle, the **Dobama Theatre,** 1846 Coventry Rd. (932-6838), Cleveland Hts., gives terrific, inexpensive (up to $15) performances in an intimate atmosphere. Though University Circle is generally safe, some nearby areas get a little rough, especially at night.

Playhouse Square Center, 1519 Euclid Ave. (771-4444), a 10-minute walk east of Terminal Tower, is the third-largest performing arts center in the nation. Inside, the **State Theater** hosts the **Cleveland Opera** (575-0900) and the famous **Cleveland Ballet** (621-2260) from October to June.

NIGHTLIFE

A great deal of Cleveland's nightlife is focused in the **Flats,** the former industrial core of the city, along both banks of the Cuyahoga River. Numerous nightclubs and restau-rants, some with a family atmosphere, populate the northernmost section of the Flats just west of Public Square. **Fagan's,** 996 Old River Rd. (241-6116), looks like a South Florida beach resort, not a den of iniquity which trains hungry English waifs to pick-pocket. "Please, Sir. Can I have some sandwiches for $5-9 or entrees starting at $11?" "Yes, son, you can, but please tell your friends not to dance on the gorgeous riverside deck." (Bands Fri.-Sat and Tues. Cover Sat.-Sun. $2-3. Open Sun.-Thurs. 11am-mid-night, Fri.-Sat. 11am-2am.) Happy memories of a childhood rec-room return in **The Basement,** 1078 Old River Rd. (344-0001), three floors of 60s-retro theme rooms and paraphernalia. (Domestic beer $2.25. Happy hour with $1.50 drinks daily 7-9pm. Open Sun.-Thurs. 7pm-2:30am, Fri.-Sat. 5pm-2am.) Gays and lesbians plot a course to

GREAT LAKES

The Grid, 1281 W. 9th St. (623-0113), near the East Flats. Come to relax in the comfortable bar and stay for the high-tech dance floor. (Bottled beer $2.25. Open daily 4pm-2:30am.)

Several other clubs front the boardwalk on the west side of the river. **Shooters,** 1148 Main Ave. (861-6900), a huge bar and restaurant with a smashing view of the river and Lake Erie, occasionally books major acts for an all-ages audience. Avoid the restaurant (dinners $11-20—ouch!) and take your drink to the outside deck. (No cover. Open daily 11:30am-2:30am.) Hard-core rockers should steer clear of the Flats and head for Coventry, where the **Grog Shop,** 1765 Coventry Rd. (321-5588), brings in local and national acts to entertain.

■ Near Cleveland

The self-proclaimed "best amusement park in the world," **Cedar Point Amusement Park** (419-627-2350 or 800-BEST-FUN/237-8386), off U.S. 6, 65 mi. west of Cleveland in **Sandusky,** earns superlatives over and over. Basically, it's just cool as all hell. Twelve rollercoasters, from the world's highest and fastest inverted rollercoasters (riders are suspended from above) to a "training coaster" for kids, offer a grand old adrenaline rush for all. Stick around for the patriotic laser light show which takes to the sky on summer nights at 10pm. (Open mid-May to early Sept. daily 9am-10pm; closes in May 8pm and on summer Sat. nights midnight. Open Sept. weekends only. $29, seniors $16, kids over 4 and under 48" $7.) The Lake Erie Coast around Sandusky is lined with numerous 50s-era roadside "amusements." **Train-O-Rama,** 6732 E. Harbor Rd. (419-734-5856), in Marblehead, consists of 1½ mi. of track through a miniature landscape with towns, villages, ski slopes, waterfalls, airports, monorails, and more. (Open Mon.-Sat. 10am-6pm, Sun. 1-6pm; Labor Day-Memorial Day Mon.-Sat. 11am-5pm, Sun. 1-5pm. $3.50, ages 4-11 $2.50.)

Sea World, 1100 Sea World Dr. (562-8101 or 800-63-SHAMU/637-4268), 30 mi. south of Cleveland off Rte. 43 at Rte. 91, presents Shark Encounter—sequel to the less menacing Penguin Encounter—along with numerous other aquatic exhibits. (Open summers daily 10am-11pm; off season call for hours. $24, ages 3-11 $19. Reduced prices on summer nights; senior discounts. Parking $3.)

Are you ready for some football? The **Pro Football Hall of Fame,** 2121 George Halas Dr. NW (330-456-8207), 60 mi. south of Cleveland in Canton, honors the pigskin greats; take Exit 107a at the junction of I-77 and U.S. 62. (Open daily 9am-8pm, Labor Day-Memorial Day 9am-5pm. $9, seniors $6, and ages 6-14 $4.)

The Amish communities of **Holmes County** make for an educational daytrip a bit farther south. In **Berlin,** 70 mi. south of Cleveland on I-77 and 17 pastoral mi. west on Rte. 39, the **Amish Farm** (303-893-2951) sheds some light on Amish life in the largest Amish community in the world. There are slide presentations, tours, demonstrations of non-electrical appliances, and buggy rides ($2.75; open April-Oct. Mon.-Fri. 10am-5pm, Sat. 10am-6pm).

■ Columbus

Rapid growth, a huge suburban sprawl, and some gerrymandering have recently pushed Columbus's population beyond that of Cincinnati or Cleveland. The main drag, High St., heads north from the towering office complexes of downtown, through the lively galleries in the Short North. It ends in the collegiate cool of Ohio State University (OSU), the largest university in the country, with over 60,000 students. Columbus is America without glitz, smog, pretension, or fame—the clean, wholesome land of *Family Ties* (Bexley, a Columbus suburb, was the model for the hit sitcom) and suburbanization.

Practical Information The **Greater Columbus Visitors Center** (220-6262 or 800-345-4386) is on the second floor of **City Center Mall,** 111 S. 3rd St. downtown. **Greyhound,** 111 E. Town St. (221-2389 or 800-231-2222), offers service from downtown to Cincinnati (10 per day, 2hr., $14), Cleveland (7 per day, 2½hr., $19), and Chicago (5 per day, 7-10hr., $35). There is no public transport to Ada, hometown of Wilson footballs. The **Central Ohio Transit Authority (COTA),** 177 S. High St. (228-1776; Mon.-Fri. 8:30am-5:30pm), runs in-town transportation until 11pm or midnight depending on the route (fare $1, express $1.35). The **Port Columbus International Airport** is just off Rte. 317 and Broad St. on the city's northwest side. Take the Broad St. bus or a taxi (about $12). In case of **emergency,** dial 911. For a taxi call **Yellow Cab,** 444-4444. Columbus's **post office:** 200 N. High St. (228-2816); **ZIP code:** 43202; **area code:** 614.

Accommodations and Food In the summer, when OSU students have vacated, check around the campus for apartment houses which advertise cheap, temporary rentals. Another resource, **Greater Columbus Bed & Breakfast Cooperative** (444-8488 or 800-383-7839), offers B&Bs in a wide radius around Columbus ($35 and up). The **Heart of Ohio Hostel (HI-AYH),** 95 E. 12th Ave. (294-7157), 1 block from OSU, has outstanding facilities, including a piano and a kitchen with an espresso machine, in a house designed by Frank Lloyd Wright. The management conducts numerous organized activities—biking, hiking, and rock climbing—and gives a free night's stay to anyone who puts on a one-hour concert. (Check-in 5-11pm. Curfew 11pm. $8, nonmembers $11. Weekly rates available.) For sensible prices and clean rooms, check out **Motel 6,** 5910 Scarborough Dr. (755-2250), off I-70 at Exit 110A. (Singles $30, doubles $36.) Visitors arriving at night may do well to look for cheap motels on the outskirts of the city where I-70 and I-71 meet I-270.

Chef-O-Nette, 2090 Tremont Center (488-8444), in Upper Arlington, has been serving up classic diner food for 46 years. Frequent lunch and dinner specials, like the Baked Marzetti, cost $4-5 (open Mon.-Sat. 7:30am-8pm). **Kahiki,** 3583 E. Broad St. (237-5425), has gourmet Polynesian and Chinese food. One local enthusiastically called it "an indescribable Polynesian pleasure palace." My oh my! (Open Sun.-Thurs. 11:30am-10pm, Fri. 11:30am-midnight, Sat. 4:30pm-midnight.)

High St. features scads of tasty budget restaurants. **Bernie's Bagels and Deli,** 1896 N. High St. (291-3448), offers a variety of sandwiches in a dark punk-rock cellar atmosphere ($1-3); live shows play in adjoining Bernie's Distillery. (See Nightlife below. Open Sun.-Mon. 11am-1am, Tues.-Sat. 11am-2:30am.) For pizza in bulk, try the **Pizza Outlet,** 1607 N. High St., at the corner of 11th and High St. (Open Mon.-Tues. 11am-2am, Wed.-Sun. 11am-3am.) Next door is the **Chuck-U Chicken Co.,** another wholesale food provider which has won the respect of OSU students. A small and well-loved Middle Eastern restaurant/grocery, **Firdous,** 1538 N. High St. (299-1844), makes tasty hummus plates ($5), fresh falafel, and shish kebabs (open Mon.-Thurs. 10am-9pm, Fri.-Sat. 10am-10pm, Sun. noon-8pm).

Sights **Ohio State University (OSU)** rests 2 mi. north of downtown. On campus, the architecturally impressive **Wexner Center for the Arts** (292-3535; box office 292-2354; open Mon.-Fri. 9am-5pm), on N. High St. at 15th Ave., shows avant-garde exhibits and films and hosts progressive music, dance, and other performances. (Exhibits open Tues. and Thurs.-Fri. 10am-6pm, Wed. and Sat. 10am-8pm, Sun. noon-5pm. Free.)

In 1991, the **Columbus Museum of Art,** 480 E. Broad St. (221-6801), acquired the Sirak Collection of Impressionist and European Modernist works. (Open Tues.-Wed. and Fri.-Sun. 10am-5:30pm, Thurs. 10am-8:30pm. Suggested donation $3, students $2.) Fire, water, explosions, nylon mittens, uranium, and kids mean good ol' fun at the **Center of Science and Industry (COSI),** 280 E. Broad St. (288-COSI/2674), ½ mi. west of I-71. (Open Mon.-Sat. 10am-5pm, Sun. noon-5:30pm. $6, ages 13-18 $5.) Look across the street to see the very first link in the **Wendy's** restaurant chain. Just east, James Thurber's childhood home, the **Thurber House,** 77 Jefferson Ave. (464-1032), is decorated with cartoons by the famous author and *New Yorker* cartoonist (open daily noon-4pm; free).

The huge **Franklin Park Conservatory,** 1777 E. Broad St. (645-8733), has a mammoth collection of self-contained plant environments including rain forests, deserts, and Himalayan mountains. (Open Tues.-Sun. 10am-5pm, Wed. 10am-8pm. $4.)

South of Capitol Square, the **German Village,** first settled in 1843, is now the largest privately funded historical restoration in the U.S., full of stately brick homes and old-style beer halls. At **Schmidt's Sausage Haus,** 240 E. Kossuth St. (444-5050), the oom-pah band **Schnickelfritz** leads polkas at 8pm nightly; between dances, try a plate of homemade sausage ($7; open Sun.-Thurs. 11am-10pm, Fri.-Sat. 11am-midnight). For dessert, try **Schmidt's Fudge Haus,** 1 block west of the Sausage Haus. On only one magical day each year, the last Sunday in June, visitors can tour everything in the village. Call or stop by the **German Village Society,** 588 S. 3rd St. (221-8888; open Mon.-Fri. 9am-4pm, Sat. 10am-2pm, Sun. noon-4pm).

Entertainment and Nightlife Four free weekly papers—*The Other Paper, Columbus Alive, The Guardian,* and *Moo*—available in many shops and restaurants, list arts and entertainment options. On the first Saturday night of each month, Columbus hosts the roaming art party known as **The Gallery Hop;** galleries in the Short North (the region between college town and downtown on High St.) display new exhibitions while socialites and art collectors admire the works (and each other) far into the night. A good place to start hopping is **Gallery V,** 694 N. High St. (228-8955), which exhibits contemporary paintings, sculptures, and works in less common media (open Tues.-Sat. 11am-5pm). The **Riley Hawk Galleries,** 642 N. High St. (228-6554), rank among the world's finest for glass sculpture (open Tues.-Sat. 11am-5pm, Sun. 1-4pm).

When you O.D. on art, Columbus has a sure cure: rock 'n' roll. Bar bands are a Columbus mainstay; it's hard to find a bar that *doesn't* have live music on the weekend. For rock, blues, and more, head to **Stache's,** 2404 N. High St. (263-5318). Bigger national acts stop at the **Newport,** 1722 N. High St. **Bernie's Distillery,** 1896 N. High St. (291-3448), intoxicates with 78 imported beers (domestic beer $1-2) and pounding live music all week (cover Fri.-Sat. $1). Twenty-one TV screens liven up the **Union Station Café and Gallery,** 630 N. High St. (228-3740), which entertains a primarily gay crowd. From this hip joint, trip a few blocks south to the **Brewery District.** Today, barley and hops have replaced the coal and iron of the once-industrial district. **High Beck,** 564 S. High St. (224-0886), grooves to rock and R&B, while **Hosters Brewing Co.,** 550 S. High St. (228-6066), at Livingston, attracts locals with homemade brew. Music enthusiasts should browse **Used Kids** or **Magnolia Thunderpussy,** both on High St. near the OSU campus, for some of the best used CD and cassette bargains in the nation.

On more mellow evenings, many of Columbia's denizens head for cafés. **Insomnia,** 1728 N. High St. (421-1234), near the OSU campus, serves up sweet caffeine in a homey atmosphere (if your home is filled with Bohemian students) with board games

---

Dave Thomas: An American Hero of Beef

When R. David Thomas was a little boy, he held the cartoon character Wimpy close to his heart. A mainstay on the Popeye show, Wimpy spent every episode gobbling hamburgers as if they were tiny, bite-size snacks. In doing so, he cut an inspiring figure for the future fast food entrepreneur. Born in 1932, Dave Thomas spent his early childhood in Atlantic City and dropped out of high school in the 10th grade to chase his culinary dreams. In 1969, he opened **the first Wendy's restaurant,** in Columbus. From there, the freckled face and red pigtails of his daughter spread across the U.S. like a midwest prairie fire. Today, Wendy's is an international fast food chain and Dave Thomas is a multi-millionaire who enjoys eating in his own commercials. Yet unlike many of his silver spoon-fed buddies, Thomas hasn't forgotten his humble beginnings and still loves to play the part of Wimpy, slipping out of board meetings and gold games to devour a quick burger...or three.

and a gas pump (iced flavored coffee $1). **Cup O' Joe,** 627 S. 3rd St. (221-1563), in German Village, adorns itself with futuristic lamps and a deliciously high level of pretention. Try the $2.50 Mocha Joe. (Open Mon.-Wed. and Thurs. 7am-11pm, Fri. 7am-10pm, Sat. 8am-1am, Sun. 8am-10pm.)

■ Near Columbus

A one-hour drive south of Columbus, the area around **Chillicothe** (pronounce chill-i-cozy with a lisp) features several interesting attractions. The **Hopewell Culture National Historic Park,** 16062 Rte. 104 (774-1125), swells with 25 enigmatic Hopewell burial mounds spread over 13 acres. The adjoining museum elucidates theories about Hopewell society based upon the mounds' configuration. (Museum open daily 8am-5pm; grounds open dawn-dusk. Entrance $4 per car, $2 per pedestrian.) Check with park officials for info on other nearby mounds. From mid-June to early September, the Sugarloaf Mountain Amphitheatre (775-0700), 7 mi. northeast of Chillicothe, presents **Tecumseh,** a drama re-enacting the life and death of the Shawnee leader (shows Mon.-Sat. 8pm. $13, Fri.-Sat. $15). A $3.50 behind-the-scenes tour, available hourly 2-5pm, will answer your questions about how the stunt men dive headfirst off the 21-ft. cliff. At **Scioto Trail State Park** (663-2125), 10 mi. south of Chillicothe off U.S. 23, a ¼-mi. walk leads to free 24-hr. walk-in **camping** behind Stuart Lake ($7, with electricity $11).

From Columbus, take U.S. 33 and then some very hilly, winding roads down to the stunning **Hocking Hills State Park,** 30 mi. east of Chillicothe; follow the signs. Waterfalls, gorges, cliffs, and "caves"—cavernous overhangs gouged in the rock by ancient rivers—scar the rugged terrain within the park. The park's main attraction is **Old Man's Cave** (385-6165), off Rte. 64, which takes its name from a hermit who lived, died, and was buried there in the 1800s. Be careful when exploring the cave area itself, especially in wet weather or in winter; people have died after slipping and falling. Old Man's Cave offers **camping** (primitive camping $10; sites with electricity and pool—don't try this at home!—$15).

■ Cincinnati

Longfellow called it the "Queen City of the West." Editor Horace Greeley once prophesied that it would become "the focus and mart for the grandest circle of manufacturing on this continent." Time and western progress, however, have proven both men wrong. The failure of Longfellow and Greeley to correctly address the lasting character of Cincinnati should serve as a warning for all those who seek to assign a singular identity to this swingin' riverfront town. The winged pigs which guard the entrance to downtown's Sawyer Point Park recall a distinct moniker bestowed on Cincinnati years ago—"Porkopolis." In the 1850s, the city led the planet in pork-packing. Today, in place of pigs roaming the streets, Cincinnati parades an excellent collection of museums, a pleasantly designed waterfront, and a jillion parks. Hidden in a valley surrounded by seven rolling hills and the Ohio River, Cincinnati seems to defy its isolation with prosperity.

PRACTICAL INFORMATION

Tourist Office: Cincinnati Convention and Visitors Bureau, 300 W. 6th St. (621-2142 or 800-246-2987). Open Mon.-Fri. 8:45am-5pm. Pick up the *Official Visitors Guide.* Also try the **Information Booth** in Fountain Sq. Open Mon.-Sat. 9am-5pm. **Info Line,** 528-9400, lists plays, operas, and symphonies.

Airport: Greater Cincinnati International, (606-767-3151) in Kentucky, 13mi. south of Cincinnati. **Jetport Express** (606-767-3702) shuttles to downtown ($10), or call the Transit Authority of Northern Kentucky (TANK; 606-825-3816) for alternate shuttling info.

Trains: Amtrak, 1301 Western Ave. (651-3337 or 800-872-7245), in Museum Center at Union Terminal. To: Indianapolis (3 per week, 3hr., $34); Chicago (3 per week, 8hr., $67). Open Mon. 9:30am-5pm, Tues.-Fri. 9:30am-5pm and 11pm-6:30am, Sat.-Sun. 11pm-6:30am. Avoid the neighborhood north of the station.

Buses: Greyhound, 1005 Gilbert Ave. (352-6041 or 800-231-2222), just past the intersection of E. Court and Broadway. To: Indianapolis (4 per day, 2-3hr., $17); Louisville (10 per day, 2hr., $16); Cleveland (10 per day, 4-6hr., $36); Columbus (10 per day, 2-3hr., $15). Open daily 7:30am-6:30am. Tickets open 24hr.

Public Transportation: Queen City Metro, 122 W. Fifth St. (621-4455; Mon.-Fri. 6:30am-6pm, Sat. 8am-5pm). Most buses run out of Government Sq., at 5th and Main St., to outlying communities. Rush-hour fare 65¢, other times 50¢; to suburbs 30¢ extra. Office has schedules and info.

Taxi: Yellow Cab, 241-2100. $1.50 base fare, $1.20 per mi. Open 24hr.

Crisis Lines: Rape Crisis Center, 216 E. 9th St. (381-5610), downtown. 24hr. **Gay/ Lesbian Community Switchboard:** 651-0070. Open Mon.-Fri. 6pm-11pm, Sat.-Sun. noon-7pm.

Emergency: 911.

Post Office: 525 Vine St. (684-5667), located in the Skywalk. Open Mon.-Fri. 8am-5pm, Sat. 8am-1pm. **ZIP code:** 45202. **Area code:** 513; Kentucky suburbs: 606.

The downtown business community centers on **Fountain Sq.,** on E. 5th at Vine St. Cross streets are numbered and designated East or West by their relation to Vine St. **Riverfront Stadium,** the **Serpentine Wall,** and the **Riverwalk** are down by the river. The **University of Cincinnati** spreads out from Clifton, north of the city.

ACCOMMODATIONS AND CAMPING

Few cheap hotels can be found in downtown Cincinnati. On the north side of town, in Sharonsville, off I-75 about 30 mi. north of Cincinnati is a cluster of low-priced accommodations on Chester Rd. About 12 mi. south of the city, inexpensive accommodations line I-75 at Exit 184. Closer still, the motels at Central Pkwy. and Hopple St. offer good lodging without high costs. Other options are the following:

College of Mount St. Joseph, 5701 Delhi Rd. (244-4327 or 244-4373), about 8mi. west of downtown off U.S. 50; take bus #32. A few immaculate rooms in a quiet, remote location available year-round; call ahead. Sinks in rooms, baths in the hall, lounge, no A/C. Singles $15, doubles $20; rates may rise. All-you-can-eat cafeteria lunch $3.50.

Motel 6, 7937 Dream St. (606-283-0909), in Florence, KY, just off I-75 at Exit 180. Only 12 mi. south of Cincinnati, the motel offers easy access to downtown as well as an outdoor pool, cable TV, HBO, and free local calls. Singles $33, doubles $39.

FOOD

The city that gave us the first soap opera, the first baseball franchise (the Redlegs), and the Heimlich maneuver presents its great culinary contribution—**Cincinnati chili.** Although this mixture of meat sauce, spaghetti, and cheese is an all-pervasive ritual in local culture, somehow no other city seems to have caught this gastronomical wave. Chili is cheap; antacid tablets cost extra.

Skyline Chili, everywhere. 65 locations in Cincinnati, including 643 Vine St. (241-2020), at 7th St. Better than other chains. The secret ingredient has been debated for years; some say chocolate, but curry is more likely. 5-way jumbo chili $4.90, cheese coney (hot dog) $1.15. Open Mon.-Fri. 10:30am-7pm, Sat. 11am-3pm.

Izzy's, 819 Elm St. (721-4241), also 610 Main St. This unpretentious deli, founded in 1901, is a Cincinnati institution. Overstuffed sandwiches $3-4. Addictive potato pancakes (99¢ each, and worth every penny). Izzy's famous Reuben $5. Open Mon.-Fri. 7am-9pm, Sat. 10am-7pm; Main St. location open Mon.-Sat. 7am-9pm.

Mullane's, 723 Race St. (381-1331). A streetside café and restaurant with terrific vegetarian food. Out-of-this world meatless entrees (lunch $5-6, dinner $6-10) and hearty salads. Tarot card reading nightly. Chicken or ham can be added to entrees for $2. Open Mon.-Thurs. 11:30am-11pm, Fri. 11:30am-midnight, Sat. 5pm-midnight.

Graeter's, 41 E. 4th St. (381-0653), between Walnut and Vine St. downtown, and 10 other locations. Since 1870, Graeter's has been pleasing sweet-toothed locals with candy and ice cream made with giant chocolate chips. A (not very) small cone $1.35, with chips $1.30. Open Mon.-Fri. 7am-6pm, Sat. 7am-5pm.

SIGHTS

Downtown Cincinnati orbits around the **Tyler Davidson Fountain,** a florid 19th-century masterpiece and an ideal spot to people-watch. If you squint, you can almost see Les Nesman rushing to WKRP to deliver the daily hog report. Check out the expansive gardens at **Proctor and Gamble Plaza,** just east of Fountain Sq., or walk along **Fountain Square South,** a shopping and business complex connected by a series of second-floor **skywalks.** In the square, the observation deck at the top of **Carew Tower** provides the best view in the city.

Close to Fountain Sq., the **Contemporary Arts Center,** 115 E. 5th St., 2nd fl. (345-8500), near Walnut St., carries a strong reputation in the national arts community. In 1990, the Center was indicted for showing Robert Mapplethorpe's risqué photographic works in an incident which touched off the national controversy over the NEA. Exhibits change frequently; call about current shows and evening films, music, and multimedia performances. (Open Mon.-Sat. 10am-6pm, Sun. 1-5pm. $3.50, seniors and students $2; free Mon.) Also downtown, the **Taft Museum,** 316 Pike St. (241-0343), has a beautiful collection of painted enamels, as well as pieces by Rembrandt and Whistler. (Open Mon.-Tues. and Thurs.-Sat. 10am-5pm, Sun. 1-5pm. $3.50, seniors and students $2.)

Cincinnati's answer to Paradise is **Eden Park,** northeast of downtown; take bus #49 to Eden Park Dr. The **Krohn Conservatory** (421-4086), one of the largest public greenhouses in the world, presents an indoor Eden (open daily 10am-5pm; $2, seniors and under 18 $1). The collections at the **Cincinnati Art Museum** (721-5204), within the park, span 5000 years, including musical instruments and Near Eastern artifacts. (Open Tues.-Sat. 10am-5pm, Sun. 11am-5pm. $5, students and seniors $4, under 17 free.)

Union Terminal, 1031 Western Ave. (287-7000 or 800-733-2077), 1 mi. west of downtown near the Ezzard Charles Dr. Exit off I-75 (take bus #1), functions more as a museum than as a bus terminal. A fine example of Art Deco architecture, the building boasts the world's largest permanent half-dome. Inside, cool down in an Ice Age world of simulated glaciers at the **Museum of Natural History** (287-7020), or investigate a carefully constructed artificial cavern, featuring a colony of real live bats. On the other side of the dome, the **Cincinnati Historical Society,** 1301 Western Ave. (287-7030), in Museum Center, houses exhibits on Cincinnati history and an **Omnimax Theater** (287-7081; call for showtimes). (Both museums open Mon.-Sat. 9am-5pm, Sun. 11am-6pm. 1 museum $5.50, ages 3-12 $3.50; both museums $9/$6; Omnimax $6.50/$4.50; all 3 $12/$8.)

ENTERTAINMENT AND NIGHTLIFE

Pick up the free newspapers *City Beat, Everybody's News,* and *Antenna* for happenings around town. The cliff-hanging communities on the steep streets of **Mt. Adams** support a vivacious arts and entertainment industry. Perched on its own wooded hill, the **Playhouse in the Park,** 962 Mt. Adams Circle (421-3888), does theater in the round with a wide range of dramatic style. (Performances mid-Sept. to June, Tues.-Sun. Tickets $19-31; student and senior rush 15min. before show $12.)

The University of Cincinnati's **Conservatory of Music** (556-9430) gives free pops concerts, as well as classical recitals. A tad more upscale, the **Music Hall,** 1243 Elm St. (721-8222), hosts the **Cincinnati Symphony Orchestra** (381-3300) Sept. through May (tickets $10-40). The orchestra's summer season (June-July) takes place at **Riverbend,** near Coney Island (tickets $12.50-29). The **Cincinnati Opera** (241-2742; limited summer schedule; tickets $15-60) performs in the Music Hall as well. For updates, call **Dial the Arts** (751-2787). The **Cincinnati Ballet Company** (621-5219; performances Oct.-May; tickets $9-48) has moved to the **Aronoff Center for the Arts,** 650 Walnut (621-2787), at the corner of 7th and Main.

Escape the highbrow and beat the summer heat in the world's largest recirculating pool at **Coney Island,** 6201 Kellogg Ave. (232-8230), off I-275 at the Kellogg Ave. Exit. Other amusements include waterslides, rides, and an 18-hole miniature golf course on which each hole replicates a famous hole on the PGA tour. (Pool open daily 10am-8pm; rides Mon.-Fri. noon-9pm, Sat.-Sun. 11am-9pm. Pool only $11, seniors and ages 4-11 $9; rides only $7/$7; both $15/$13.) **Summerfair** (531-0050), an art extravaganza, takes over the park for the first weekend in June.

Cincinnati's fanatical fans watch baseball's **Reds** (421-4510; tickets $6.50-11.50) and football's **Bengals** (621-3550; tickets $30) in **Riverfront Stadium,** 100 Broadway. The **Riverfront Coliseum** (241-1818), a Cincinnati landmark, hosts other sporting events and concerts year-round.

At the beginning of September, **Riverfest** (352-4001) commemorates the roles of the river and steamboats in Cincinnati's history. The city basks in its German heritage during **Oktoberfest-Zinzinnati** (579-3191), held the third weekend in September. For more info on festivals, contact the convention and visitors bureau.

Overlooking downtown from the east, Mt. Adams harbors Cincinnati's most active nightlife. For a drink that will transport you back to the 19th century, try Cincinnati's oldest tavern, **Arnold's,** 210 E. 8th St. (421-6234), between Main St. and Sycamore downtown. After 9pm, Arnold's does that ragtime, traditional jazz, bluegrass, and swing thing. Wash down a Thai chicken sandwich ($5.75) with a draft beer (domestic $1.25) and sit a spell. (Open Mon.-Fri. 11am-1am, Sat. 4pm-1am.) Antique toys adorn the inside of **Blind Lemon,** 936 Hatch St. (241-3885), at St. Gregory St. in Mt. Adams, while live jazz and blues fill the courtyard. (Domestic draft $2. Music daily 9:30pm; no cover. Open Mon.Fri. 5pm-2:30am, Sat. 3pm-2:30am, Sun. 3-8:30pm.) **Main Street Brewery,** 1203 Main St. (665-HOPS/4677), downtown, pours home-brewed Main Street Ale (pint $3) for crowds of youngish locals who come to be seen in this new hotspot (open Mon.-Thurs. 11am-11pm, Fri.-Sat. 11am-midnight, Sun. noon-11pm).

■ Near Cincinnati

If you can't get to California's Napa or Sonoma Valleys, the next best thing may be **Meiers Wine Cellars,** 6955 Plainfield Pike (891-2900); take I-71 to exit 12 or I-75 to Galbraith Rd. Free tours of Ohio's oldest and largest winery give you a chance to observe the entire wine-making operation and taste the fermented fruits of the labor. (Tours June-Oct. Mon.-Sat. every hr. 10am-3pm; Nov.-May by appointment.)

The town of **Mason,** 24 mi. north of Cincinnati off I-71 at exit #24, beckons with **Paramount's Kings Island** (573-5800 or 800-288-0808), an amusement park which cages **The Beast,** the world's longest wooden rollercoaster. Do you remember the now-classic 1974 Brady Bunch episodes in which the kids lost Mike Brady's architectural plans? Well, all the wild shenanigans took place at Kings Island. Admission to the park entitles you to unlimited rides and attractions and the opportunity to buy expensive food. Lines shrink after dark. (Open May 27-Sept. 4 Sun.-Fri. 10am-10pm, Sat. 10am-11pm. $29, seniors and ages 3-6 $16. Parking $4.)

Accommodations can be found at **Yogi Bear's Camp Resort,** 5688 Kings Island Dr. (800-832-1133), off I-71 Exit 25 at Mason. There's a pool, a playground, and 350 pricey sites for 2 $25, with full hookup $38. (Cabins for 2 $50. $5 per extra adult, $3.50 per extra child. Within a stone's throw of Kings Island amusement park. Reservations recommended.)

Michigan

Michigan's developed Lower Peninsula paws the Great Lakes like a huge mitten, while its pristine and oft-ignored Upper Peninsula hangs above, quietly nursing moose and a famed population of wolves. Together, they define over 3000 miles of coastline along four of the Great Lakes; their shores have the feel of an ocean coast—uniquely blended with the fresh water of the lakes—in the heart of America. Dunes, beaches, forests, and over 11,000 smaller inland lakes add to Michigan's coastal character, and the state, whose once-booming automotive industry now fills only a shadow of its former stature, is starting to make waves as a natural getaway.

PRACTICAL INFORMATION

Capital: Lansing.
Michigan Travel Bureau: 333 S. Capitol Ste. F, Lansing 48909 (517-335-1876 or 800-543-2937). Gives out info on the week's events and festivals. **Department of Natural Resources,** Information Services Center, P.O. Box 30028, Lansing 48909 (517-373-1270). Offers resources on state parks, forests, and campsites. Entry to all state parks requires a motor vehicle permit; $4 per day, $20 annually. Call 800-543-2937 for reservations at any state park campground.
Time Zones: Eastern, except a small sliver of the western Upper Peninsula which lies in Central (1hr. behind Eastern). All of *Let's Go's* Michigan coverage lies within Eastern. **Postal Abbreviation:** MI.
Sales Tax: 6%.

■ Detroit

An author recently proclaimed Detroit "America's first Third-World city"; indeed, the city has witnessed a quarter-century of hardship. In the 60s, as the country grooved to Motown's beat, Detroit erupted with some of the era's most violent race riots. Massive white flight to the suburbs has been the norm ever since; the population has more than halved since 1967, turning some neighborhoods into ghost towns. The decline of the auto industry in the late 70s added unemployment to the city's problems, causing frustration, violence, and hopelessness among its residents.

The five gleaming towers of the riverside Renaissance Center symbolize the hope of a city-wide comeback. Aggressive tourist media focuses attention on Detroit's attractions: Michigan's largest and most comprehensive museums, a fascinating ethnic history, and the still visible (though soot-blackened and slightly crumbling) evidence of the city's former architectural grandeur. Detroit may no longer be the city it once was, but it does its best to present an attractive face to the world.

PRACTICAL INFORMATION

Tourist Office: Detroit Convention and Visitors Bureau, 100 Renaissance Center #126 (800-338-7648). Pick up the free *Metro Detroit Visitors Guide.* Open Mon.-Fri. 9am-5pm, Sat. 10am-5pm, Sun. noon-5pm.
Airport: Detroit Metropolitan (942-3550 or 800-351-5466), 2mi. west of downtown off I-94 at Merriman Rd. in Romulus. **Commuter Transportation Company** (941-3252) runs shuttles downtown (45min.; $13), stopping at major hotels. Daily on the hour 7am-midnight. Make reservations. A taxi downtown costs $25.
Trains: Amtrak, 11 W. Baltimore (873-3442 or 800-872-7245), at Woodward. To Chicago (3 per day, 5hr., $35) and New York (1 per day, 16hr., $124). Open daily 6am-11:30pm. For Canadian destinations, you must go through **VIA Rail,** 298 Walker Rd., Windsor, ON (800-561-3949), across the river in Canada.
Buses: Greyhound, 1001 Howard St. (961-8011 or 800-231-2222). At night, the area is deserted and unsafe. To Chicago (7 per day, 7hr., $27) and St. Louis (7 per day, 13-15hr., $52). Station open 24hr.; ticket office open daily 4:30am-1am.

Public Transportation: Detroit Department of Transportation (DOT), 1301 E.
Warren (933-1300). Carefully policed public transport system serves downtown,
with limited service to the suburbs. Many buses stop service at midnight. Fare
$1.25, transfers 25¢. **DOT Attractions Shuttle** (259-8726) delivers camera-toting
tourists to the metro area's most popular sights 10am-5:45pm. All-day ticket $5.
People Mover, 150 Michigan Ave. (800-541-RAIL/7245). Ultramodern elevated
tramway circles the Central Business District on a 2.7-mi. loop; worth a ride just for
the view. Runs Mon.-Thurs. 7am-11pm, Fri. 7am-midnight, Sat. 9am-midnight, Sun.
noon-8pm. Fare 50¢. **Southeastern Michigan Area Regional Transit (SMART),**
962-5515. Bus service to the suburbs. Fare $1-2.50, transfers 10¢. Get free maps of
the system at the office on the first floor of First National Bank at Woodward and
Fort. Buses run 4am-midnight. All-day pass $1.50.
Taxis: Checker Cab, 963-7000. Flat fee $1.40 per mi.
Car Rental: Thrifty Rent-a-Car, 29111 Wick Rd. (946-7830), in Romulus. $35 per
day, $185 per week; unlimited mi. in Michigan and neighboring states. Optional
insurance $9. Must be 21 with credit card. Under 25 surcharge $20 per day.
Hotlines: 24-hr. Crisis Hotline, 224-7000. **Sexual Abuse Helpline,** 800-551-0008
or 800-234-0038. 24hr. **Gay and Lesbian Switchboard Line,** 810-398-4297. Sun.-
Fri. 4:30-11pm.
Emergency: 911.
Post Office: 1401 W. Ford St. (226-8304) handles general delivery; open 24hr. **ZIP
code:** 48233. **Area code:** 313, 810 (just a little north). All numbers are in area
code 313 unless otherwise noted.

Detroit lies on the Detroit River, which connects Lakes Erie and St. Clair. Across the
river to the south, the town of **Windsor, ON,** can be reached by tunnel just west of
the Renaissance Center, or by the Ambassador Bridge, 3500 Toledo St. Detroit is a
tough town—it was the fictional setting for *Robocop*—but you probably won't
encounter trouble during the day, especially within the People Mover loop.

Detroit's streets form a grid. The **Mile Roads** run east-west as major arteries. **Eight
Mile Rd.** is the city's northern boundary and the beginning of the suburbs. **Woodward Ave.** heads northwest from downtown, dividing city and suburbs into "east
side" and "west side." **Gratiot Ave.** flares out northeast from downtown, while
Grand River Ave. shoots west. **I-94** and **I-75** pass through downtown. For a particularly helpful map, check the pull-out in the *Detroit Metro Visitor's Guide.*

ACCOMMODATIONS AND CAMPING

Detroit's suburbs harbor cheap chain motels, especially near the airport in Romulus,
and along E. Jefferson near downtown. The *Detroit Metro Visitor's Guide* lists
accommodations by area and includes price ranges. Devoted campers should resign
themselves to a 45-min. commute if they insist on communing with nature.

Country Grandma's Home Hostel (HI-AYH), 22330 Bell Rd. (753-4901), in New
Boston, halfway between Detroit and Ann Arbor, inaccessible by public transportation. Small, friendly hostel with six beds in three rooms, a kitchen, free on-site
parking, and a homey atmosphere. $9, nonmembers $12. Call for required reservations and directions.
Shorecrest Motor Inn, 1316 E. Jefferson Ave. (568-3000 or 800-992-9616), lets you
sleep as close to downtown as the budget traveler can. Cable TV, A/C, and refrigerators. Nice, clean, comfortable singles $48, doubles $54. Key deposit $5. Reserva-
tions suggested.
Motel 6, 38300 Grand River Ave. (810-471-0590), offers cookie-cutter rooms with
free local calls and HBO. Singles $32, doubles $38. Reservations suggested.
The Villager-Lodge, 8500 Wickham Rd. (595-1990 or 800-328-7829), in Romulus.
Clean rooms and free airport shuttle. Rooms from $35. Reservations suggested.
Metro Inn-Airport, 8230 Merriman Rd. (729-7600), in Romulus. Free airport shut-
tle. Clean rooms from $35.
Algonac State Park (765-5605; 465-2160 Nov. to mid-April), on the shore of the
Detroit River 55mi. from downtown; take I-94E, then Rte. 29N. Watch the big ships

cruise the river at night, carrying cargo to and from Detroit, the country's fifth largest port. Two campgrounds: 76 inland sites $10, 220 river view sites $14. All have electricity. Vehicle permits $4.

FOOD

Although many of the restaurants downtown have migrated to the suburbs, the budget traveler still has some in-town dining options. **Greektown,** at the Greektown People Mover stop, has Greek restaurants and excellent bakeries on Monroe St., all on 1 block near Beaubien St. **Hamtramck,** a Polish neighborhood northeast of Detroit, serves up old-fashioned pirogies. East of the Renaissance Center in the old warehouse district, **Rivertown** hosts some of the city's best nightlife, though it is safest not to loiter in the streets. No budget traveler should miss the **Eastern Market** (833-1560), at Gratiot Ave. and Russell St., an 11-acre smorgasbord with almost every edible imaginable (open Mon.-Sat. 7am-4pm).

Cyprus Taverna, 579 Monroe St. (961-1550), is a local favorite for Greek cuisine (open Sun.-Thurs. 11am-2am, Fri.-Sat. 11am-4am).

Trapper's Alley (963-5445), once a tannery in Greektown, has been converted into a four-story mall of food and retail shops (open Mon.-Thurs. 10am-9pm, Fri.-Sat. 10am-11pm, Sun. noon-7pm).

Xochimilco, 3409 Bagley St. (843-0179); from downtown, take the "Baker St." bus to Lafayette and Washington Blvd. Chefs from Mexico give customers an authentic and inexpensive experience. 3 meat tacos, 3 enchiladas, or 3 burritos with rice and beans $5.25-5.75. Free chips and salsa. Open daily 11am-4am. No reservations on weekends; come early.

Soup Kitchen Saloon, 1585 Franklin St. (259-1374). Once home to a speakeasy and brothel, this Rivertown building now features some of the best live blues in town. Fresh seafood, steaks, and cajun. Have BBQ catfish or seafood creole (both $11), at lunch. 12 beers on tap and over 25 bottled. Shows Fri.-Sat.; cover varies. Open Mon.-Thurs. 11am-midnight, Fri. 11am-2am, Sat. 4pm-2am, Sun. 4pm-midnight.

The Clique Restaurant, 1326 East Jefferson St. (259-0922). Heralded city-wide for fast service and fabulous breakfasts served all day. French toast $3; 3-egg omelette $4.75. Open Mon.-Fri. 6am-10pm, Sat.-Sun. 7am-10pm.

Union Street, 4145 Woodward St. (831-3965). Spicy, mouth-watering cuisine in a popular mid-town beer hall. Rasta wings with hellfire sauce are a scorching success ($7.25). Although Union Street itself is nice, be careful in the surrounding area. Open Mon.-Fri. 11:30am-2am, Sat. 5pm-2am.

SIGHTS

For a reason to visit Detroit, look no farther than the colossal **Henry Ford Museum & Greenfield Village,** 20900 Oakwood Blvd. (271-1620; 271-1976 for 24-hr. info), off I-94 in nearby Dearborn; take SMART bus #200 or 250. The 12-acre museum showcases a comprehensive exhibit of the importance of the automobile in America, including the limousine in which President Kennedy was assassinated and a copy of the Apollo mission's Lunar Rover. Over 80 historic edifices from around the country have been moved to **Greenfield Village,** next to the museum; visit the workshop of the Wright Brothers or the factory where Thomas Edison researched. (Both open daily 9am-5pm. Museum or village $12.50, seniors $11.50, ages 5-12 $6.25. Combination ticket valid 2 consecutive days $22, ages 5-12 $11.) The most impressive of the auto barons' mansions, **Fisher Mansion and Bhaktiredanta Cultural Center,** 383 Lenox Ave. (331-6740), houses Indian cultural exhibits within an ornate stone, marble, and carved wood structure leafed with over 200 ounces of gold. By a strange twist of fate, the center and mansion were co-founded by Henry Ford's grandson and United Auto Workers President Walter Reuther's daughter. (Tours Fri.-Sun. 12:30, 2, 3:30, and 6pm. $6, seniors and students $5, under 13 $4.)

Detroit makes an effort to lure people to its **Cultural Center,** at Woodward and Warren St. (take bus #53 or the Attractions Shuttle)—and it's worth the time to take the bait. One of the nation's finest art museums, the **Detroit Institute of Arts,** 5200

Woodward (833-7900), houses Van Gogh's "Self-Portrait" and the nation's largest historic puppet collection (open Wed.-Fri. 11am-4pm, Sat.-Sun. 11am-5pm; suggested donation $4, children $1). Explore the history of the African experience in America at the **Museum of African American History,** 301 Frederick Douglass Rd. (833-9800; open Wed.-Sat. 9:30am-5pm, Sun. 1-5pm; suggested donation $3, kids $2). Succumb to vertigo at the Imax Dome in the **Detroit Science Center,** 5020 John R. St. (577-8400; open Mon.-Fri. 9:30am-2pm, Sat.-Sun. 12:30-5pm; $6.50, seniors, children, and students with ID $4.50).

Downtown Detroit can be seen in about a day. The futuristic, gleaming, steel-and-glass **Renaissance Center** strikes a shocking contrast to the downtown wasteland. A five-tower complex of office, hotel, and retail space, the Ren Cen encloses a maze of concrete walkways and spiraling stairs; the **World of Ford** on level two reminds visitors of Detroit's heyday as the center of an auto empire. At 73 stories, the **Westin Hotel** stands as the second tallest hotel in North America, affording incredible views of the city. Take a ride up and contrast the historical view with the city of today. (For general Ren Cen info call 568-5600; tour information 341-6810; lines open daily 9am-5pm. Building open Sun.-Thurs. 11am-11pm, Fri.-Sat. 11am-1:30am. Tours $3.)

Although Berry Gordy's Motown Record Company has moved to Los Angeles, the **Motown Museum,** 2648 W. Grand Blvd. (875-2264), preserves its memories. Downstairs, shop around the primitive studio in which the Jackson Five, Marvin Gaye, Smokey Robinson, and Diana Ross recorded their tunes. (Open Sun.-Mon. noon-5pm, Tues.-Sat. 11am-5pm. $6, seniors $5, ages 12-18 $4, under 12 $3.) The museum lies east of Rosa Parks Blvd. about 1 mi. west of the Lodge Freeway (Rte. 10); take the "Dexter Avenue" bus or the Attractions Shuttle from downtown.

The **Holocaust Memorial Center,** 6602 W. Maple Rd., West Bloomfield (810-661-0840), provides a historical and educational memorial to the victims of the Nazis. The museum's collection of rare documentaries and propaganda films, an invaluable resource for those studying the Holocaust, has made it an important research center as well. (Tours Sun. 1pm. Open Sun.-Thurs. 10am-3:30pm, and from Sept.-June Fri. 9am-noon. Free.)

One of Detroit's favorite escapes, **Belle Isle** (267-7121), 3 mi. from downtown via the MacArthur Bridge, maintains many attractions: a conservatory, a nature center, an aquarium, and a small zoo for animal lovers with short attention spans.

ENTERTAINMENT AND NIGHTLIFE

Newly renovated and restored, Detroit's theater district, around Woodward and Columbia, is witnessing a cultural revival. The **Fox Theater,** 2211 Woodward Ave. (396-7600), near Grand Circus Park, features high-profile performances (drama, comedy, and musicals) and some Broadway shows. The nation's largest movie theater hall (it holds 5000), the Fox also shows epic films occasionally. (Box office open Mon.-Fri. 10am-6pm. Tickets $25-100, movies under $10.) The **State Theater,** 2115 Woodward Ave. (961-5450; 810-932-3643 for event info), brings in a variety of popular concerts, including big-name rockers like Björk. The State Theater is also home to Club X, a giant 18+ raging party, which brings in DJs from a local radio station to play alternative dance music. (Open Sat. 10pm-2am. Cover $8, 21+ $5.)

Detroit's numerous festivals draw millions of visitors. Jazz fans jet to Hart Plaza during Labor Day weekend for the four-day **Montreux-Detroit Jazz Festival** (963-7622). With more than 70 acts on three stages and mountains of international food at the World Food Court, it's the largest free jazz festival on the continent. The nation's oldest state fair, the **Michigan State Fair** (368-1000 or 369-8250), at Eight Mile Rd. and Woodward, gathers together bake-offs, art exhibits, and livestock for the two weeks before Labor Day. A two-week extravaganza in late June, the international **Freedom Festival** (923-7400), held jointly with Windsor, Ontario, celebrates the friendship between the U.S. and Canada. During the festival, North America's largest annual fireworks display takes place over the Detroit River near the Renaissance Center, marking the birthdays of both nations. The **Concours d'Elegance** (810-370-3140), at the Meadow Brook Hall, exhibits elegant classic cars during the first Sunday in

August. In January, the gee-whiz **North American International Auto Show** (886-6750) showcases the new models, prototypes, and concept cars from manufacturers around the world in the **Cobo Center,** 1 Washington Blvd. The **Detroit Grand Prix** (393-7749) zooms by for three days in June as the streets of Belle Isle are transformed into a race course. The **Spirit of Detroit Thunderfest APBA Gold Cup** (259-7760), the speedboat equivalent of the Indy 500, churns the waters of the Detroit River June 6-8 in 1997. Detroit's **African World Festival** (833-9800) brings over a million people to Hart Plaza on the third weekend in August for an open-air market and free reggae, jazz, blues, and gospel concerts. **Orchestra Hall,** 3711 Woodward Ave. (962-1000), at Parsons St., houses the Detroit Symphony Orchestra (box office 833-3700; open Mon.-Fri. 9am-5pm). Pick up a copy of the weekly *Metro Times* for complete entertainment listings.

The Detroit **Pistons** shoot hoops at the Palace of Auburn Hills, 2 Championship Dr. (a.k.a. 3777 Lapeer Rd.), Auburn Hills (810-377-8600). Hockey's **Red Wings** face off in the Joe Louis Arena, 600 Civic Center Dr. (396-7444). The **Tigers** catch fly balls at Tiger Stadium, on Michigan and Trumball Ave. (962-4000). The **Lions** punt, pass, and tackle at the Pontiac Silverdome, 1200 Featherstone Rd., Pontiac (810-335-4151). For tickets to concerts or sporting events, call **Ticketmaster** (810-645-6666).

For the latest in nightlife, pick up a free copy of *Orbit* in record stores and restaurants. *Between the Lines,* also free, has entertainment info for lesbians, gays, and bisexuals. **St. Andrew's Hall,** 431 E. Congress (961-MELT/6358), hosts local and national alternative acts (shows Fri.-Sun.; usually 17+; advance tickets sold through Ticketmaster, 810-645-6666; $7-10). **Shelter,** the dance club downstairs, draws crowds on non-concert nights. Take advantage of Ontario's lower drinking age (19) at the **Zoo Club,** 800 Wellington (519-258-2582) in Windsor. Those with too much cash rid themselves of the burden with three floors of gambling at The **Windsor Casino,** 445 Riverside Dr. (800-991-7777; open 24hr.).

■ Ann Arbor

Named after Ann Rumsey and Ann Allen, wives of two of the area's early pioneers (who supposedly enjoyed sitting under grape arbors), Ann Arbor has certainly made tracks. In 1837, the University of Michigan moved to town. Since then, this gargantuan, well-respected institution has created a hip collage of leftists, granolas, yuppies, and middle Americans.

PRACTICAL INFORMATION

Tourist Office: Ann Arbor Convention and Visitors Bureau, 120 W. Huron St. (995-7281 or 800-888-9487), at Ashley. Has info on the city and the University of Michigan. Open Mon.-Fri. 8:30am-5pm.

Trains: Amtrak, 325 Depot St. (994-4906 or 800-872-7245). To Chicago (3 per day, 4½hr., $35) and Detroit (3 per day, 1hr., $11). Station open daily 7am-10:30pm; tickets sold 7am-last train.

Buses: Greyhound, 116 W. Huron St. (662-5511). To Detroit (6 per day, 1-1½hr., $9) and Chicago (5 per day, 5hr., $27). Office open Mon.-Sat. 8am-6:30pm.

Public Transportation: Ann Arbor Transportation Authority (AATA), Blake Transit Center, 331 S. 4th Ave. (996-0400 or 973-6500). Service in Ann Arbor and a few neighboring towns. Buses run Mon.-Fri. 6:45am-10:15pm, Sat.-Sun. 8am-6:15pm. Fare 75¢, seniors and students 35¢. Station open Mon.-Fri. 7:30am-9pm, Sat. noon-5:30pm. AATA's **Nightride,** 663-3888. Safe door-to-door transportation 11pm-6am. Call to book a trip; average wait 20min. Fare $2 per person, regardless of distance. **Commuter Transportation Company,** 941-9391 or 800-488-7433. Frequent shuttle service between Ann Arbor and Detroit Metro Airport. Vans depart Ann Arbor 5am-7pm; return 7am-midnight. $14.50, roundtrip $27. Door-to-door service for up to 4 $39; reserve at least 2 days in advance.

Car Rental: Campus Auto Rental, 202 S. Division St. (761-3768). $29 per day with 150 free mi., $145 per week with 1000 free mi.; 20¢ per additional mi. Optional insurance $9. Open Mon.-Fri. 8am-6pm, Sat.-Sun. 9am-1pm.

GREAT LAKES

Hotlines: **Sexual Assault Crisis Line**, 483-7273. **U. Michigan Sexual Assault Line**, 936-3333. Both 24hr. **Gay Crisis Line**, 662-1977. Open Mon.-Fri. 9am-7pm. **U. Michigan Gay/Lesbian Hotline**, 763-4186.
Most Important Thing in the World: Happiness.
Emergency: 911.
Post office: 2075 W. Stadium Blvd. (665-1100; open Mon.-Fri. 7:30am-5pm). **ZIP code:** 48106. **Area code:** 313.

Ann Arbor's streets usually lie in a grid, but watch out for the slant of Packard and Detroit St. **Main St.** divides the town east-west and **Huron St.** cuts it north-south. The central campus of the University of Michigan, where restaurants cluster, lies four blocks east of Main St., south of E. Huron (a 5-min. walk from downtown). Although street meter parking is plentiful, authorities ticket ruthlessly. One-way streets and unexpected dead ends also make driving near the campus stressful.

ACCOMMODATIONS

Expensive hotels, motels, and B&Bs dominate Ann Arbor due to the many business travelers and sports fans who flock to the town. Reasonable rates can be found at discount chains farther out of town or in Ypsilanti southeast of town along I-94. Within town, good ol' **Motel 6**, 3764 S. State St. (665-9900), rents nice, clean, comfortable rooms (singles $37, doubles $43). During the summer, the University of Michigan rents rooms in **Bursley Hall**, 1931 Duffield St. (763-1140), on North Campus, and offers free local calls and parking in a nearby lot for $3.50 per day (room $31). The **Embassy Hotel**, 200 E. Huron (662-7100), at Fourth Ave., offers clean singles for $32 and doubles for $43; $2 key deposit required. With seven campgrounds within a 20-mi. radius of Ann Arbor, **camping** is a very accessible option; call the campground offices of the **Pinckney Recreation Area**, 8555 Silver Hill, Pinckney (426-4913; open Mon.-Thurs. 8am-4:30pm, Fri.-Sat. 8am-8:30pm, Sun. 8am-8:30pm), or the **Waterloo Recreation Area**, 16345 McClure Rd., Chelsea (475-8307; open daily 8am-noon and 1-5pm). Call 800-543-2YES/2937, for reservations at these and all Michigan state parks.

FOOD AND NIGHTLIFE

Where there are students, there are cheap eats; restaurants cram the sidewalks of **State St.** and **S. University St.** Purchase fresh produce straight from the growers at the **farmers market**, 315 Detroit St. (761-1078), next to Kerrytown (open May-Dec. Wed. and Sat. 7am-3pm; Jan.-April Sat. 8am-3pm). The readers of *Ann Arbor News* voted **Cottage Inn Pizza**, 512 E. William St. (663-3379), at Thompson St., the "best pizza." (Pasta $4-7; pizza $7-14. Open Mon.-Thurs. 11am-midnight, Fri.-Sat. 11am-1am, Sun. noon-midnight.) Locals seek out **Del Rio**, 122 W. Washington (761-2530), at Ashley, for cheap burgers and Mexican food (burritos $2.50). A vestige of a fast-dying Ann Arbor tradition, Del Rio's employees manage the business cooperatively. (Free jazz Sun. Open Mon.-Fri. 11:30am-2am, Sat. noon-2am, Sun. 5:30am-2am.)

  The Blind Pig, 208 S. First St. (996-8555), showcases the rock 'n' roll, reggae, and blues offerings of local bands and acts from all over the country. (Open daily until 2am. No cover downstairs.) **Rick's American Café**, 611 Church St. (996-2747), plays Ann Arbor's blues, with live music and a packed dance floor almost nightly (19+, Tues. 18+; cover varies; open daily). The **Bird of Paradise**, 207 S. Ashley (662-8310), sings with live jazz every night; the big names come on Fridays and Saturdays (cover usually $3). **The Nectarine**, 510 F. Liberty (994-5436), offers DJ-controlled dance music, with gay nights on Tuesdays and Fridays. Though few clubs target a gay audience, many of Ann Arbor's clubs cater to mixed crowds.

SIGHTS AND ENTERTAINMENT

The university offers a handful of free museums which merit a walk-through. A small but impressive collection of artwork from around the world fills the **University of**

Michigan Arts Museum (UMAM), 525 S. State St. (764-0395), at the corner of University St. (open Tues.-Sat. 11am-5pm, Sun. noon-5pm, until Thurs. 9pm; free). Just down the street, the **Kelsey Museum of Archaeology,** 434 S. State St. (764-9304), presents pieces recovered from digs in the Middle East, Greece, and Italy (open Mon.-Fri. 9am-4pm, Sat.-Sun. 1-4pm; free). The **University of Michigan Exhibit Museum of Natural History,** 1109 Geddes Ave. (763-6085), at Washtenaw, displays a Hall of Evolution and other exhibits on Michigan wildlife, astronomy, and rocks. Within, the **Planetarium** (764-0478 or 763-6085) projects star-gazing weekend entertainment ($3, children $2; museum open Mon.-Sat. 9am-5pm, Sun. 1-5pm). Outside the University at the **Ann Arbor Hands-On Museum,** 219 E. Huron (995-5437), exhibits are designed to be felt, turned, touched, and pushed. (Open Tues.-Fri. 10am-5:30pm, Sat. 10am-5pm, Sun. 1-5pm. $4, seniors, students, and children $2.50.) Numerous local artists display their creations at the **artisan market,** 315 Detroit St. (open May-Dec. Sun. 11am-4pm).

The monthlies *Current, Agenda, Weekender Entertainment,* and the weekly *Metrotimes,* all free and available in restaurants, music stores, and elsewhere, print up-to-date entertainment listings. To hear classical music contact the **University Musical Society** (764-2538), in the Burton Memorial Clock Tower at N. University and Thouper; the society sponsors 40 to 50 professional concerts per season (tickets $10-50; open Mon.-Fri. 10am-5pm). Ann Arbor prides itself on live jazz; call the University Activities Office (763-1107) for info.

As tens of thousands of students depart for the summer (and rents plummet), locals indulge in a little celebrating. During late July, thousands pack the city to view the work of nearly 600 artists at the **Ann Arbor Summer Art Fair** (995-7281). The **Ann Arbor Summer Festival** (647-2278) draws crowds from mid-June to early July for a collection of comedy, dance, and theater productions, as well as musical performances including jazz, country, and classical. Outdoor movies conclude the festivities nightly at **Top of the Park,** on top of the Fletcher St. Parking Structure, next to the Heath Services Building. The **county events hotline** (930-6300) has info on all these events.

■ Grand Rapids

From its humble beginning as one among many fur trading posts, Grand Rapids worked hard to distinguish itself from its neighbors. While many towns opted for tourist chic with quaint, old-fashioned looks, Grand Rapids plowed ahead to become a city of concrete, pavement, and tall buildings. The city has gone on to further distinguish itself by claiming a couple of notable American firsts; Grand Rapids was the first city to put fluoride in its drinking water, and also earns distinction as the city that produced America's first (and only) unelected president, Gerald Ford.

Practical Information Most of Grand Rapids' streets are neatly gridded; **Division St.** (surprise!) divides the city east-west. For general area info, head to the **Grand Rapids-Kent County Convention and Visitors Bureau,** 140 Monroe Center NW #300 (459-8287 or 800-678-9859; open Mon.-Fri. 10am-5:30pm), or the **West Michigan Tourist Association,** 1253 Front St. (456-8557 or 800-442-2084; open Mon.-Thurs. 8:30am-5pm, Fri. 8:30am-6pm, Sat. 9am-1pm). Grand Rapids serves as a transportation hub for Western Michigan, providing **Greyhound,** 190 Wealthy St. (456-1707), connections to little towns like Detroit (4 per day, 3½hr., $21) and Chicago (5 per day, 4½hr., $24). (Open daily 6:40am-10pm.) **Amtrak** (800-872-7245), at Wealthy and Market, has service to the south and west, including Chicago (1 per day, 3½hr., $29). The station only opens when trains pass through. For eastern service, travelers have to get to the **Kalamazoo Station,** 459 N. Burdick St. (344-1841), Kalamazoo, 50 mi. south of Grand Rapids on Rte. 131, where trains leave for Detroit (3 per day, 3hr., $42-56). (Station open daily 9am-9pm.) **Grand Rapids Transit Authority (GRATA),** 333 Wealthy St. (776-1100), sends buses throughout the city and suburbs (Mon.-Fri. 6am-6pm, Sat. 9:30am-9:30pm. Fare $1.25, seniors 60¢, 10-

GREAT LAKES

ride pass $7, seniors $6.) **Yellow Cab** (458-4100) will get you where you want to go ($1.45 base fare, $1.40 per mi.; 24hr.). In a crisis, call the **Suicide, Drug, Alcohol, and Crisis Line,** 336-3535. **Emergency:** 911. Grand Rapids' **post office:** 225 Michigan Ave. NW (776-1519; open Mon.-Fri. 8:30am-6pm, Sat. 8am-noon). **ZIP code:** 49503. **Area code:** 616.

Accommodations and Food Most of the cheaper motels cluster south of the city along Division and 28th St. The **Knights Inn,** 5175 28th St. SE (956-6601 or 800-843-5644), offers 102 spacious rooms, some with VCRs (singles $38, doubles $44; reservations recommended). **Motel 6,** 3524 28th St. SE (957-3511), also offers the comfort and convenience of a national chain motel. Rooms have cable TV and HBO (singles $32, doubles $38). Women are out of luck at the **YMCA,** 33 Library St. NE (458-1141), within walking distance of downtown ($26 the first night, $15 each additional night). The *West Michigan Travel Planner* includes listings to help campers choose from the many area campgrounds; write or call the West Michigan Tourist Association (see Practical Information, above) for a copy. The *MARVAC RV and Campsite Guide* and the *Michigan Campground Directory* list state and private sites; inquire at the visitors bureau.

Grand Rapids' most popular Mexican food comes from the **Beltline Bar and Café,** 16 28th St. SE (245-0494). Plates of tacos go for $5.50, and burritos start at $5. (Open Mon.-Tues. 7am-midnight, Wed.-Sat. 7am-1am, Sun. noon-10:30pm.) **Pietro's Back Door Pizzeria,** 2780 Birchcrest Dr. (452-3228), off 28th St. SE, serves delicious wood-fired pizza with an array of gourmet toppings ($5-9). The *ristorante* in front concocts higher-end Italian food. ($7.50-12. Open Mon.-Thurs. 11:30am-10:30pm, Fri. 11:30am-11pm, Sun. noon-10pm; pizzeria Mon.-Thurs. 11:30am-2pm, Sun. 4-10pm.) Head to the **Grand Rapids Brewing Company,** 3689 28th St. SE (285-5970), for burgers ($5.50), pasta, and "hand-crafted" house beers ($3 per pint). Tours are available upon request. (Open Mon.-Thurs. 11am-10pm, bar until midnight; Fri.-Sat. 11am-11pm, bar until 1am; Sun. 11am-10pm, bar until 11pm.) The **Four Friends Coffeehouse,** 136 Monroe Center (456-5356), has cappuccino, espresso, a semi-artsy atmosphere, good muffins ($1.15), and live music on Saturdays. (Open Mon.-Wed. 7am-8pm, Thurs. 7am-10pm, Fri. 7am-midnight, Sat. 9:30am-midnight.)

Sights, Festivals, and Nightlife The **Van Andel Museum Center,** 272 Pearl St. NW (456-3977), houses the **Grand Rapids Public Museum,** a showcase for marvels such as the world's largest whale skeleton, a 50-animal carousel (which you can ride), and a planetarium. (Open daily 9am-5pm. $5, seniors $4, ages 3-17 $2; planetarium $1.50). The **Gerald R. Ford Museum,** 303 Pearl St. NW (451-9263), records the life and turbulent times of Grand Rapids' favorite native son. Above and beyond showcasing a respectable collection of art, the **Grand Rapids Art Museum,** 155 N. Division St. (459-4677), makes an effort to get children's attention with a special tour map designed to keep them occupied and engaged. (Open Sun. and Tues. noon-4pm, Wed. and Fri.-Sat. 10am-4pm, Thurs. 10am-9pm. $3, seniors $1.50, students $1.) The largest year-round conservatory in Michigan, the **Frederik Meijer Gardens** (957-1580), at the intersection of Beltline and Bradford St., keeps more than 70 bronze sculptures among numerous tropical plants spread out over 70 acres of wetlands. (Open Mon.-Tues. and Thurs.-Sat. 9am-5pm, Wed. 9am-9pm, Sun. noon-5pm. $4, seniors $3.50, ages 5-13 $1.50.)

Grand Rapids hosts a number of free ethnic festivals, each lasting two to three days: the **Afro-American Festival** in mid-July, the **Festa Italiana** in mid-August, the **Polish Festival** in late August, the **Hispanic Festival** in September, and the German **Oktoberfest.** For more info on any of the festivals, call 456-3361.

For detailed listings on events and nightlife in Grand Rapids, swipe a free copy of *On the Town* or *In the City,* both available just about everywhere—shops, restaurants, kiosks, etc. The 24-hr. **Fun Line** (439-8629) saves you the trouble of reading. Dance clubs overshadow other forms of nightlife in Grand Rapids. **The Reptile House,** 139 S. Division St. (242-9955), showcases loud alternative bands Wednesday through Friday and dances Tuesdays and Saturdays (some weekdays 18+, on weekends 21+). The largest dance club in Grand Rapids, **The Orbit Room** (942-1328), at E. Beltline and 28th St., packs in up to 1200 gyrating bodies for nightly music ranging from alternative to top 40, disco to country (Wed. 18+, other nights 19+ until 11pm; open Wed., Fri., and Sat.-Sun.). **The Anchor,** 447 Bridge St. (774-7177), is a good old American bar, filled with locals and relatively cheap drinks.

∎ Lake Michigan Shore

With dunes of sugary sand, superb fishing, abundant fruit harvests, and deep winter snows, the eastern shore of Lake Michigan has been a vacationer's dreamland for over a century. The coastline stretches 350 mi. north from the Indiana border to the Mackinaw Bridge; its southern end comes within a scant two hours from downtown Chicago. The freighters that once powered the rise of Chicago still steam along, but have long since been usurped by the pleasure boats that mob the coast.

Many of the region's attractions nestle in small coastal towns, which cluster around **Grand Traverse Bay** in the north. Coastal accommodations can be exorbitantly expensive; for cheaper lodging, head inland. **Traverse City,** at the south tip of the bay, is famous as the "cherry capital of the world," and fishing is best in the **Au Sable** and **Manistee Rivers.** However, the rich **Mackinac Island Fudge,** sold in numerous specialty shops, seems to have the biggest pull on tourists ("fudgies" to locals; see Mackinac Island, p. 415). The main north-south route along the coast is **U.S. 31.** Numerous detours twist closer to the shoreline, providing an excellent way to explore the coast. The **West Michigan Tourist Association,** 136 E. Fulton, Grand Rapids 49503 (456-8557), hands out free literature on the area (open Mon.-Fri. 8:45am-5pm). The entire Lake Michigan Shore's **area code:** 616.

∎ Southern Michigan Shore

Holland Southwest of Grand Rapids off I-196, Holland was founded in 1847 by Dutch religious dissenters and remained mostly Dutch until well into the 20th century. Today the town cashes in on its heritage with **The Wooden Shoe Factory** (396-6513), at U.S. 31 and 16th St.; **Windmill Island** (396-5433), at 7th St. and Lincoln Ave.; the **Holland Museum,** 310 W. 10th St. (392-9084); **Veldheer Tulip Gardens,** 12755 Quincy St. (399-1900); a recreated **Dutch Village** (396-1475), U.S. 31 at James St.; and a **Dutch Winter Fest** (396-4221), in late November/early December. The attractions (admission $1-4) attempt to paint a picture of life as it was once lived here, but a simple stroll around downtown will give any visitor a sense of how this tightly-knit community has survived and how it continues to function today. The **Wooden Shoe Motel** (392-8521), U.S. 31 Bypass at 16th St., rents single rooms starting at $49 (doubles $54), features a miniature golf course in the back ($2, motel guests $1.50), and boasts the world's only pool shaped like a wooden shoe. For more info visit the **Holland Convention and Visitors Bureau,** 100 E. 8th St. (396-4221 or 800-968-8590; open Mon.-Fri. 9am-5pm). **Greyhound,** 171 Lincoln Ave. (396-8664), runs through Holland to Detroit (3 per day, 4hr., $24), and Chicago (3 per day, 8hr., $22). (Open Mon.-Fri. 7-10am, noon-4pm.)

Grand Haven One of the best beaches on the Eastern Lake Michigan Shore, Grand Haven offers the weary traveler a beach resort-like atmosphere with a relaxed feel and lots of sand—so pure that auto manufacturers use it to make cores and molds for engine parts. The town lies about 25 mi. west of Grand Rapids off I-96, and features a cement "boardwalk" which connects the beach to the small downtown and makes for pleasant walks and romantic evening strolls. Washington St. serves as the core of downtown Grand Haven. **Butch's Beach Burritos,** 726 S. Harbor Ave. (842-3690), has burritos, chili dogs, and other greasy beach fare ($2-5; open May-Sept. 11am-9pm). The **Bij De Zee Motel,** 1030 Harbor Ave. (846-7431), may look a little ramshackle, but inside, the warm, friendly atmosphere makes for a pleasant stay.

Besides, it's right across from the beach and one of the cheapest places around (rooms from $40; some have kitchenettes). State Parks such as **Muskegon** (744-3480) and **Hoffmaster** (798-3711) line the coast near Grand Haven between Saugatuck and Muskegon. Campground sites run $10-14.

■ Central Michigan Shore

Manistee and Interlochen Manistee beckons tourists with Victorian shtick. The **A.H. Lyman Store,** 425 River St. (723-5531), has been transformed into a museum celebrating the area's ethnic heritage and history (open Mon.-Sat. 10am-5pm, Oct.-May Tues.-Sat. 10am-5pm; $1.50, kids 50¢). **Manistee National Forest** (800-543-2937 for suggested reservations) has copious camping (sites $4-10). Most areas are open year-round except when closed because of snowfall; for info on camping, hiking, canoeing, and the late June/early July **National Forest Festival,** call the **Manistee Ranger Station,** 1658 Manistee Hwy. (723-2211 or 800-999-7677; open Mon.-Fri. 8am-5pm) or the **Cadillac District Ranger Office** (775-8539), on Rte. 55, 4 mi. west of Cadillac (open Mon.-Fri. 8am-5pm).

There are several inexpensive motel options in and near Manistee. The **Riverside Motel,** 520 Water St. (723-2575), has dock space for boats and offers evening river tours (rooms $45-70; in winter around $35). The **Portage Lake Motel,** 4714 Main St. (889-4921), offers clean and comfortable rooms on the lake, close to town (rooms from $45; in winter around $35). If you're with friends, share one of the spacious kitchenette rooms at the **Traveller's Motel,** 5606 Eight Mile Rd. (889-4342), a half block from Rte. 22 in Onekama (kitchenettes sleep up to 6 people, $75).

The **Manistee County Chamber of Commerce,** 11 Cyprus St. (723-2575), has pamphlets on local attractions. A little south, the **Lake Michigan Car Ferry** (800-841-4243) shuttles people and cars between **Ludington** and **Manitowoc, WI** (4-hr. trips, 2 each way per day late June-Aug.; in spring and fall 1 per day. $35, seniors $32, ages 5-15 $15, cars an additional $45).

The renowned **Interlochen Center for the Arts** (276-6230), in **Interlochen,** 17 mi. south of Traverse City on Rte. 137, trains talented young artists in classical music, dance, theater, creative writing, etc. Here, the **International Arts Festival,** held year-round, has attracted the likes of Yo Yo Ma, Itzhak Perlman, the Boston Pops, the Emerson String Quartet, and Willie Nelson; faculty and students also put on top-notch concerts in the various arts throughout the year. (Box office open in summer Mon. 9am-4:30pm, Tues.-Sat. 9am-8:30pm, Sun. 11:15am-8:30pm; reduced hours off season. Tickets $5 for student performances, from $10 for professional; student and senior discounts available for many performances.) **Interlochen State Park** offers recreation and camping nearby (sites $8, with electricity and showers $10; daily vehicle permit $4); for directions and info, contact the ranger office (800-543-2937; open 8am-5pm), 1 mi. south of Interlochen along Rte. 137.

Sleeping Bear Dunes The Sleeping Bear Dunes rest along the western shores of the Leelanau Peninsula, 20 mi. west of Traverse City on Rte. 72. According to legend, the mammoth sand dunes represent a sleeping mother bear, waiting for her cubs—the **Manitou Islands**—to finish a swim across the lake. Local legend does not explain why the cubs didn't just take the ferry that services the islands from Leland. **Manitou Island Transit** (256-9061) makes daily trips to South Manitou and ventures five times per week to the larger, wilder North Manitou (check-in 9:30am; roundtrip $19, under 12 $13). Camping is free on both islands with a required permit (available at the visitors center); the Manitou islands do not permit cars.

The **Sleeping Bear Dunes National Lakeshore** (326-5134), of which the islands are one part, also includes 25 mi. of lakeshore on the mainland. When the glaciers came to a halt and melted, mountains of fine sand were left behind, creating a landscape that looks like a cross between an ocean coast and a desert. You can be king of the sandhill at **Dune Climb,** 5 mi. north of Empire on Rte. 109. From there, hike 2.8 strenuous mi. over sandy hills to reach an absolutely gorgeous sandy beach. The less adventurous can motor to an overlook along the **Pierce Stocking Scenic Drive,** off Rte. 109 just north of Empire, where there is a 450-ft. sand cliff leading to the cool water below (open mid-May to mid-Oct. daily 9am-10pm). For maps and info on the numerous cross-country skiing, hiking, and mountain biking trails, call the **National Parks Service Visitors Center,** 9922 Front St. (326-5134), Empire (open daily 9am-6pm; mid-Oct. to May 9:30am-4pm).

The **Platte River** (at the southern end) and the **Crystal River** (near Glen Arbor at the northern end) are great for canoeing or floating. **Riverside Canoes,** 5042 Scenic Hwy. Rte. 22 (325-5622), at Platte River Bridge in Honor, will equip you with an inner tube ($4-6 for 1hr., $9-11 for 2hr.), canoe ($23-27), or kayak ($14). Sleeping Bear Dunes has four campgrounds: **DH Day** (334-4634), in Glen Arbor, with 88 primitive sites ($10); **Platte River** (325-5881), in Honor, with 179 sites and showers ($12, with electricity $17); and two free backcountry campsites accessible by 1½-mi. trails (no reservations; required permit available at the visitors center or at either developed campground).

Traverse City Named after the "Grand Traverse" that French fur traders once made between the Lelanaw and Old Michigan Peninsulas, Traverse City offers the summer vacationer a slew of sandy beaches and more cherries than you can count (50% of the nation's cherries are produced in the surrounding area). The annual **Cherry Festival** (947-4230), held the first full week in July, serves as a tribute to the fruit's annual harvest. In early to mid-July, five orchards near Traverse City let you pick your own cherries, including **Amon Orchards** (938-9160), 10 mi. east on U.S. 31 ($1.25 per pound; eat while you pick for free; open 8am-7pm). The nearby sparkling bay and ancient sand dunes make this region a Great Lakes paradise, though a crowded and expensive one. In the summer, swimming, boating, and scuba diving focus on **Grand Traverse Bay;** free beaches and public access sites speckle the shore. Explore the coastline of the **Leelanau Peninsula,** between Grand Traverse Bay and Lake Michigan, on scenic **Rte. 22.** Get to **Leland,** a charming one-time fishing village which now launches the Manitou Island ferries (see Sleeping Bear Dunes, above), via M22. For local events and entertainment, pick up the weekly *Traverse City Record-Eagle Summer Magazine,* available in corner kiosks around the city.

There are many **campgrounds** near Traverse City—in state parks, the National Lakeshore, and various townships. The West Michigan Tourist Association's guide gives a comprehensive list of public and private sites and the tourist bureau has a helpful camping pamphlet. State parks usually charge $10-14, but national forests are the best deal at $5-8. **Northwestern Michigan Community College,** East Hall, 1701 E. Front St. (922-1406), has the cheapest beds in the city. (1 bedroom $25, additional person $35; 2-room suite with bathroom $50. Nearby parking is accessible via College Dr. Open late June-Aug. Reservations recommended.) The **Shoestring Resort** (946-7935), at the intersection of Garfield and River Rd., 12 mi. south of town, offers exceptionally nice one-, two-, and three-bedroom cabins with cable TV and A/C (cottages start at $35 per night; prices $10 lower in winter; weekly rates available). Only four blocks from downtown, the **Best Valu Motel,** 828 E. Front St. (947-8822), offers clean rooms (singles $45, weekends $75; lower in winter; reservations suggested).

The **Traverse City Convention and Visitors Bureau,** 101 West Grandview Pkwy./ U.S. 31N #200 (800-940-1120 or 947-1120), on the second floor of the brick Delta Center, dispenses the helpful *Traverse City Guide* ($2; open Mon.-Fri. 9am-5pm). **Indian Trails** and **Greyhound,** 3233 Cass Rd. (946-5180), tie Traverse City to Detroit (3 per day, 7½hr., $52) and to the Upper Peninsula via St. Ignace (1 per day, 2½hr., $16). The **Bay Area Transportation Authority** (941-2324) has demand response service; you call them and they'll pick you up (fare $2; daily pass $4). Traverse City's **post office:** 202 S. Union St. (946-9616; open Mon.-Fri. 8am-5pm). **ZIP code:** 49684.

GREAT LAKES

■ Northern Michigan Shore

Charlevoix and Petoskey Situated on the ½-mi.-wide ribbon of land between Lake Michigan and Lake Charlevoix, the stretch of coast near Charlevoix (SHAR-le-voy), north of Traverse City on U.S. 31, served as the setting for some of Hemingway's Nick Adams stories. The town now attracts more tourists than it did in Hemingway's time; the population triples in the summer. In Charlevoix the Beautiful, sailing is king. Join in the tacking and jibing on a two-hour afternoon or evening cruise on the **Appledor** (547-0024; $24, kids $11). For visitor info, head to the **Charlevoix Chamber of Commerce,** 408 Bridge St. (547-2101; open Mon.-Fri. 9am-5pm, Sat. 10am-5pm). Lodging rarely comes cheap in this resort-oriented area, but reasonably priced camping, RV stations, and cottages are available at **Uhrick's Lincoln Log Motel and Campground,** 800 Petoskey Ave. (547-4881), on U.S. 31 (tent sites $15, with full hookup $18; cottages from $48).

Petoskey, 18 mi. north of Charlevoix, is notorious for its **Petoskey Stones,** fossilized coral from an ancient sea which is now found heaped along the lakeshores. For info on beaches and other attractions, including canoeing, orchards, and walking tours, contact the **Petoskey Regional Chamber of Commerce,** 401 E. Mitchell (347-4150; open summers Mon.-Fri. 8am-5pm, Sat. 10am-3pm, Sun. noon-4pm; mid-Oct. to May Mon.-Fri. 8am-5pm). Greyhound affiliate **Indian Trails** (517-725-5105 or 800-292-3831 in MI) stops at the **Bookstop,** 301 W. Mitchell (347-4400; open Mon.-Sat. 8am-5:30pm), and sends buses once daily to St. Ignace ($8) and Detroit ($39).

North Central Michigan College, 1515 Howard St. (348-6611; 348-6612 for reservations), lets single dorm rooms within a suite. (Rooms $22.50, for 2 $28, 4-person suite $48. Linens provided. Reservations recommended.) The **EconoLodge,** 1858 U.S. 131S (348-3324 or 800-748-0417), offers remarkably nice rooms with cable TV and A/C (singles $45-80). Petoskey's **Gaslight District,** 1 block from the Chamber of Commerce, features local crafts and foods in period shops. Hop on the **Grain Train Natural Foods Co-op,** 421 Howard St. (347-2381), for soy pizza and other ever-changing delectables ($2.50-3.50; open Mon.-Thurs. 9am-7pm, Fri. 9am-8pm, Sat. 9am-5pm, Sun. 11am-5pm). **Petoskey State Park** (347-2311), 2 mi. east of town off Rte. 31, offers 190 campsites on Little Traverse Bay (sites $13; $4 vehicle fee).

North of Petoskey, **Rte. 119** winds along the lakeside through tunnels of trees, giving the smooth auto road hiking trail scenery. In Cross Village, **Legs Inn** (526-2281), the only restaurant for miles, serves Polish entrees ($9-16) amidst fantastic Native American decor. (Live blues, folk, reggae, polka, etc. Wed.-Sun. Cover Fri.-Sun. $3-4. Open daily noon-10pm.)

Straits of Mackinac Never say "mackinACK"; in the Land of the Great Turtle (as early native Americans called it), Mackinac and Mackinaw are both pronounced "mackinAW." Colonial **Fort Michilimackinac** still guards the straits between Lake Michigan and Lake Superior, as tourists, not troops, flock to **Mackinaw City,** the town that grew up around the fort. Along with Fort Michilimackinac, **Fort Mackinac** (on Mackinac Island) and **Historic Mill Creek** (3½mi. south of Mackinac on Rte. 23), form a trio of **State Historic Parks.** (436-5563. All open mid-June to Labor Day daily 9am-6pm; Labor Day-Oct. and mid-May to mid-June 10am-4pm. Each park $6.75, ages 6-12 $4, family $20; season pass to all three $12.50, kids $7.50.)

Pick up brochures at the **Mackinaw City Chamber of Commerce,** 706 S. Huron (436-5574; open Mon.-Fri. 9am-5pm, Sat. 9am-4pm, Sun. 9am-1pm; off season Mon.-Fri. 9am-5pm). Get more at the **Michigan Dept. of Transportation Welcome and Travel Information Center** (436-5566), on Nicolet Ave. off I-75 (free reservation service; open daily 8am-8pm; off season 9am-5pm). **Indian Trails** bus lines (517-725-5105 or 800-292-3831 in MI) has a flag stop at the Big Boy restaurant on Nicolet Ave. One bus runs north and one south each day; buy tickets at the next station.

Campers can hunker down at **Mackinaw Mill Creek Campground** (436-5584), 3 mi. south of town on Rte 23; most of its 600 sites lie near the lake (sites $11.25, with full hookup $13.25). Sites at the **Wilderness State Park** (436-5381), 11 mi. west on Wilderness Park Dr., come with showers and electricity ($14).

On **Mackinac Island,** tourists visit **Fort Mackinac** (906-847-3328), Victorian homes, and the **Grand Hotel** (906-847-3331). Connoisseurs will immediately recognize the island as the birthplace of **Mackinack Fudge,** sold in shops all over the Michigan coastline. Lodging is never cheap on the island, but the Grand Hotel carries the cost (and elegance) to an extreme; the average double goes for $390 per night. For $5 you can lurk on the estate grounds (daily 9am-5:30pm), for $10 you can dangle your feet in the pool, and for $15 you can even set foot on the tennis courts. Horse-drawn **carriages** cart guests all over the island (906-847-3325; open daily 8:30am-5pm; $12, ages 4-11 $6). **Saddle horses** ($20 per hr.) are also available. Encompassing 80% of the island, **Mackinac Island State Park** features a circular 8.2-mi. shoreline road for biking and hiking (free). Pick up the invaluable *Mackinac Island Locator Map and Business Directory* ($1) at the **Mackinac Island Chamber of Commerce** (906-847-3783; open summers daily 9am-7pm, winters 9am-4pm; off-season hours vary). Three competing **ferry lines** leave Mackinaw City and St. Ignace with overlapping schedules; during the summer, a ferry leaves every 15 minutes 7:30am-midnight ($12 roundtrip, under 11 $7, bike passage $4). Cars are not allowed on the island.

■ Upper Peninsula

A multi-million-acre forestland bordered by three of the world's largest lakes, Michigan's Upper Peninsula (U.P.) is among the most scenic, unspoiled stretches of land in the Great Lakes region. But in 1837, after Congress decided in favor of Ohio in the fight over Toledo, Michigan only grudgingly accepted this "wasteland to the north" in the unpopular deal which gave the territory statehood. From the start, Michigan made the most of the land, laying waste to huge tracts of forest destined for the treeless Great Plains and the fireplaces of Chicago. In the past century, however, the forests have been protected and returned to their former grandeur, and the U.P.'s spectacular waterfalls and miles of coastline have won the hearts of nature lovers.

Only 24,000 people live in the U.P.'s largest town, Marquette. The region is a paradise for fishing, camping, hiking, snowmobiling, and getting away from it all. Hikers enjoy numerous treks, including Michigan's 875 mi. of the **North Country Trail,** a national scenic trail extending from New York to North Dakota. (Contact the North Country Trail Association, 3777 Sparks Dr. SE, Ste. 105, Grand Rapids, MI 49546, for details.) A vibrant spectrum of foliage makes autumn a beautiful time to hike the U.P.; in the winter, skiers replace hikers. Dozens of rivers beckon canoers to the area as well; those who heed the call of the rapids should contact the **Michigan Recreational Canoe Association,** P.O. Box 357, Baldwin, MI 49304.

Welcome centers guard the U.P. at its six main entry points: **Ironwood,** 801 W. Cloverland Dr. (932-3330); **Iron Mountain,** 618 Stephenson Ave. (774-4201); **Menominee,** 1343 10th Ave. (863-6496); **Marquette,** 2201 U.S. 41S (249-9066; all open mid-June to Aug. daily 9am-5pm); **Sault Ste. Marie,** 1001 Eureka St. (632-8242; open June-Sept. daily 9am-5pm); and **St. Ignace** (643-6979), on I-75N (open mid-June to early Sept. daily 9am-7pm). Pick up the invaluable *Upper Peninsula Travel Planner,* published by the **Upper Peninsula Travel and Recreation Association** (800-

GREAT LAKES

Pasty anybody?

The pasty originated in Cornwall, England, where it was a regular staple of tin-miners and fishermen. Legend has it that pasty cooks would carve the initials of the intended eater into the dough. Fishermen would start eating their pasties at the uninitialized end. When the fish bit, they could put the dish down and immediately mind the catch. Afterwards, the **initials would reveal exactly whose meal was whose.** The Michigan version of the pasty usually contains flour, lard, steak, potatoes, turnips, onions, and ground pepper. So what does it taste like? As one native of Sault Ste. Marie put it, "Well...sort of like...beef stew pie."

562-7134; open Mon.-Fri. 8am-4:30pm). For additional help planning a trip into the wilderness, write to the **U.S. Forestry Service,** 2727 N. Lincoln Rd., Escanaba 49829 (786-4062). Upper Peninsula's **area code** is 906.

The peninsula has 200 **campgrounds,** including those at both national forests (call 800-543-2937 for reservations). Sleep with your dogs or bring extra blankets: temperatures in these parts drop to 40°F, even in July. Outside the major tourist towns, motel rooms start at around $24. For regional cuisine, indulge in the Friday night **fish-fry:** all-you-can-eat perch, walleye, or whitefish buffets available in nearly every restaurant in every town for about $7-10. The local ethnic specialty is a meat pie, imported by Cornish miners in the 19th century, called a **pasty** (PAY-stee).

Sault Ste. Marie and the Eastern U.P. Ask the locals why people come to Sault (pronounced "soo") Ste. Marie and they'll inevitably answer, "the locks." The St. Mary's River connects—and separates—Lake Huron and Lake Superior. Back in the day, there was a 21-ft. vertical drop over one mi., rendering the river impassible by boat. Native Americans simply picked up their canoes and walked the distance, but a 1000-ft. freighter needs a little more help; in 1855, entrepreneurs built the first lock here. The busiest in the world today, the city's four locks float over 12,000 ships annually. The **Locks Park Historic Walkway** parallels the water for a mi. On the waterfront at the end of Johnston St., the **Valley Camp** (632-3658), a 1917 steam-powered freighter, has been converted into the Great Lakes' largest maritime museum. Call ahead for group tours (open daily 10am-6pm; $6). Just up the block from the water, the concrete **Tower of History,** 326 E. Portage St. (632-3658), offers a panoramic view of the locks, bridges, and ships. (Open May 15-Oct. 15 daily 10am-6pm. $3.) The U.S. Army Corps of Engineers, which operates the locks, maintains a good **visitors center,** 10 Portage St. (632-1472; open 8am-10pm).

For burgers and sandwiches ($4-8), head down the street to **The Antlers,** 804 E. Portage St. (632-3571). Animal lovers beware—the walls have eyes (and heads: bear, deer, and hog, for example). The city's best lodging deals crowd the I-75 Business Spur. Sleepy **Buck's Motel,** 3501 I-75 Business Spur (632-1173 or 800-781-1102), has clean, fresh-smelling rooms with TV and phone for $30-47. A bit west of the city, frolic and camp in the uncrowded eastern branch of the **Hiawatha National Forest** (786-4062; no showers; sites $6-11; no reservations). For more modern camping (and larger crowds), try **Tahquamenon Falls State Park** (492-3415 or 800-543-2YES/2937), 90 min. west of the city. (Hookups available. Mid-May to mid-Oct. sites $12, off season without electricity $8. $4 vehicle permit required. Reservations recommended during holidays.) Rent a canoe ($6 for ½day) or rowboat ($1.50 per person) at the Lower Falls or gawk at the 50 ft. Upper Falls (no barrel riders here). North of Tahquamenon, over 300 shipwrecks lie off **Whitefish Point.** Today protected as the **Underwater Preserve,** they afford divers an opportunity to search for **sunken treasure.** For more info, contact the **Paradise Area Tourism Council,** Box 64, Paradise 49768 (492-3927). The **Great Lakes Shipwreck Historical Museum** (635-1742 or 492-3436) grippingly documents this "Graveyard of the Great Lakes." (Open mid-May to mid-Oct. daily 10am-6pm. $6, kids under 13 $4, families $17.)

Middle of the Peninsula The western branch of the **Hiawatha National Forest** dominates the middle of the Peninsula, offering limitless wilderness activities and many campsites (pit toilets, no showers; sites $6-11; no reservations). In the west branch, **Munising** has access to the forest and to **Pictured Rocks National Lakeshore,** where water saturated with copper, manganese, and iron oxide has painted the cliffs with multicolored bands. **Pictured Rocks Boat Cruise** (387-2379) gives the best view (approx. 3-hr. tours $21, ages 6-12 $7, under 6 free). The Forest and Lakeshore share a **visitors center** (387-3700) at the intersection of Rte. 28 and H58 in Munising (open daily 9am-5pm). From Munising, H58—a bumpy, unpaved gem of a road—weaves along the lakeshore past numerous trailheads and campsites. Free backcountry camping permits are available from the Munising or **Grand Sable Visitors Center** (494-2660), 1 mi. west of Grand Marais on H58 (open mid-May to early Sept. daily 10am-6pm). Stroll, birdwatch, or collect smooth stones along the shore at

Twelve Mile Beach and **Grand Sable Dunes.** Survey Lake Superior from atop the **Log Slide;** swim if you're fond of ice water. If all this liquid is making you thirsty, march down to **Dune's Saloon** in Grand Marais, home of the Lake Superior Brewing Company (at the junction of 77 and H58), for a Hematite Stout or an Agate Amber ($2.25). For more-than-a-tent shelter, the **Poplar Bluff Cabins** (452-6271), Star Route Box 3118, has rooms with a view and kitchens. (Cottages from $35 per night, $200 per week. Free use of boats on lake. Open May-Dec.) Drive 12 mi. east of Munising on Rte. 28, and head 6 mi. south from Shingleton on M94.

Equidistant from the north and south coasts and a little east of Hiawatha's west branch, the **Seney National Wildlife Refuge** (586-9851), on Rte. 77, shelters 95,000 acres for over 250 species of birds and mammals. Admission to the park is free and includes the 7-mi. **Marshland Wildlife Drive,** a self-guided auto tour replete with loon and eagle observation decks; the best times for viewing wildlife are early morning and early evening. The refuge also offers hiking, cross-country skiing, biking, canoeing, and fishing opportunities (visitors center open daily 9am-5pm). Before you fish, get a required state **fishing permit** ($5.25 per day, $20.35 annually, residents $9.85 annually; available at any convenience store, grocery, or tackle shop).

At the bottom of the peninsula, don't miss **Big Spring** (341-2355), called Kitch-iti-kipi by Native Americans, at **Palms Book State Park.** Take a self-operated raft to watch plump trout play among billowing clouds of silt in a forest of ancient tree trunks in the 45-ft.-deep, 200-ft.-wide spring (open daily 9am-7pm). At nearby **Indian Lake State Park** (800-543-2937), you can rent a teepee ($18), cabin ($30), or campsite with hookup ($14). Reservations are necessary for teepees and cabins, recommended for campsites. Farther south, the **Fayette State Historic Park** (644-2603) handles camping. (Hookup, no showers. $8. Open mid-May to mid-Oct.) All state parks require a $4 daily vehicle permit or $20 annual permit.

Keeweenaw Peninsula In 1840, Dr. Douglas Houghton's mineralogical survey of the Keeweenaw Peninsula, a curved finger of land on the U.P.'s northwest corner, incited a copper mining rush which sent the area booming. When mining petered out around 1969, the land was left barren and exploited. Today, reforestation and government support have helped Copper Country find new life as a tourist destination. Every year, 250 in. of snow fall on the towering pines, smooth-stone beaches, and low mountains of Keeweenaw. Visitors ski, snowshoe, and snowmobile through the winter and enjoy the gorgeous green coasts in the summer.

At the base of the peninsula, hugging the shore of Lake Superior, sits the **Porcupine Mountain Wilderness State Park** (885-5275), affectionately known as "The Porkies." The park sports campsites (hookups available; $6-12), cabins (sleep 2-8; $30), and paths into the **Old Growth Forest,** the largest tract of uncut forest between the Rockies and the Adirondacks. Reservations are required for cabins and recommended for campsites (800-543-2YES/2937). The **visitors center,** near the junction of M-107 and South Boundary Rd. (inside the park), provides camping permits (open in summer daily 10am-6pm). The **Houghton Visitors Center,** 326 Sheldon St. (482-5240), has info on the entire peninsula (open Mon.-Sat. 8am-5pm).

The **Brockway Mountain Drive,** between Eagle Harbor and Copper Harbor, is a must for those weary of relentlessly flat terrain. Rising 1337 ft. above sea level, its summit provides some of the best views on the peninsula. The northernmost town in Michigan, **Copper Harbor** functions as the main gateway to **Isle Royale National Park** (see below). The **Norland Motel** (289-4815), near the mouth of U.S. 41, north of Copper Harbor, has immaculate rooms with TV, fridge, and coffeemaker ($28-40; reservations recommended in summer). **The Gratiot Street Café** (289-4223), on U.S. 41 in Copper Harbor, serves up light fare for low prices (sandwiches, pasties $3-5) as well as breakfast (full stack of pancakes $2.75; open daily 8am-8pm). Just down the street, the **Keeweenaw Adventure Company** (289-4303) can make all your wilderness dreams come true with dog sled rides ($30 for two people, overnight trip with training $225 per person), adventure packages (sea kayaking, hiking, biking), bike rentals ($10 for 5hr., $18 full day), and more.

GREAT LAKES

■ Isle Royale

Around the turn of the century, moose swam from the Canadian coast to this pristine 45-mi.-long, 10-mi.-wide island. With no natural predators, the animals overran the land. Today, wild animals are the island's only permanent inhabitants; the fisherfolk who once lived here left after the island was designated **Isle Royale National Park** in 1940. For backcountry seclusion, this is where the wild things are; no cars, phones, or medical services pamper visitors. Come prepared.

Practical Information Despite the fact that it's closer to the Ontario and Minnesota mainlands, Isle Royale is part of Michigan. Accessible only by boat, the park has its **headquarters** on the Upper Peninsula, in **Houghton,** at 800 E. Lakeshore Dr., 49931 (906-482-0984; open Mon.-Sat. 8am-4:30pm). The headquarters operates a 6½-hr. ferry to the island (round-trip $85, under 12 $40), while **Isle Royale Ferry Service,** The Dock, Copper Harbor (906-289-4437; off season at 108 Center St., Hancock, 906-482-4950), makes 4½-hr. trips from Copper Harbor (round-trip $76, under 12 $38). Both ferries land at **Rock Harbor.** For access to other parts of the island, take any of several shuttles from Rock Harbor or leave from **Grand Portage, MN;** the **Grand Portage-Isle Royale Transportation Line Inc.,** 1507 N. First St., Superior, WI (715-392-2100), sends a boat to Windigo, which stops at trailheads around the island before reaching Rock Harbor six hours later. ($80-86 roundtrip to Rock Harbor, under 12 $50.) During the summer, additional trips go as far as Windigo ($60 roundtrip, under 12 $30). On the island, the park's **ranger stations** include **Windigo** on the west tip; **Rock Harbor,** the most developed, on the east tip; and **Malone Bay,** between Windigo and Rock Harbor on the south shore.

Camping, Accommodations, and Food Scattered **campgrounds** cover the island; required free permits are available at any ranger station. Some sites have three-sided, screened-in shelters. They go quickly on a first come, first served basis; bring your own tent just in case. Nights are always frigid (mid-40s°F in June), and biting bugs peak in June and July; bring warm clothes and insect repellent. Intestinal bacteria, tapeworms, and giardia lurk in the waters of Isle Royale; use a .4-micron filter or boil water for at least two minutes. Purified water is available at Rock Harbor and Windigo. Very few places on the island permit fires; bring a small campstove. The **Rock Harbor Lodge** (906-337-4993) controls most of the island's commercial activity; the store carries a decent selection of overpriced food and camping staples. The lodge and associated cabins are the only indoor accommodations on the island (from $68 per person, double occupancy).

Activities Streams, lakes, and 170 mi. of trails traverse the park. The **Greenstone Ridge Trail,** the main artery of the trail system, follows the backbone of the island from Rock Harbor Lodge, passing through several spectacular vistas. Serious backpackers will want to conquer the **Minong Ridge Trail,** which runs parallel to the Greenstone Trail to the north for 30 mi. from McCargoe Cove to Windigo; the remains of early Native American copper mines line the trail. Shorter hikes near Rock Harbor include **Scoville Point,** a 4.2-mi. loop out onto a small peninsula, and **Suzy's Cave,** a 3.8-mi. loop to an inland sea arch. Contact the park office for info on cruises, evening programs, and ranger-led interpretive walks. **Canoeing** and **kayaking** allow access to otherwise inaccessible parts of the island, and both Rock Harbor and Windigo have **boat** and **canoe rental** outfitters. (Motors $12 per ½day, $20 per day. Boats and canoes $10.50 per ½day, $18 per day.) **Scuba divers** explore shipwrecks in the treacherous reefs off the northeast and west ends of the island—after registering at the park office. There are no public air compressors; bring filled tanks.

Indiana

The seemingly endless cornfields of southern Indiana's Appalachian foothills give way to expansive plains in the industrialized north. Here, Gary's smokestacks spew black clouds over the waters of Lake Michigan, and urban travel hubs have earned the state its official nickname, "The Crossroads of America." The origin of Indiana's unofficial nickname, "The Hoosier State," is less certain; some speculate that it is a corruption of the pioneers' call to visitors at the door—"Who's there?"—while others claim that it spread from Louisville, where labor contractor Samuel Hoosier preferred to hire Indiana workers over Kentucky laborers. Whatever the nickname's derivation, Indiana's Hoosiers are generally considered a no-nonsense Midwestern breed. The Indiana General Assembly once nearly passed a law to make the official value of pi three instead of 3.14etc., just for the sake of simplicity. More recently, the pragmatic people of Indianapolis laughed a meteorologist named David Letterman out of town for forecasting hail "the size of canned hams."

PRACTICAL INFORMATION

Capital: Indianapolis.
Indiana Division of Tourism: 1 N. Capitol #700, Indianapolis 46204 (800-289-6646). **Division of State Parks,** 402 W. Washington #W-298, Indianapolis 46204 (232-4125).
Time Zones: Confusing. Mostly Eastern; Central near Gary in the northwest and Evansville in the southwest. Only the parts of the state near Louisville, KY and Cincinnati, OH observe daylight savings time. **Postal Abbreviation:** IN.
Sales Tax: 5%.

■ Indianapolis

Flat, dusty expanses of corn surround this calm Midwestern metropolis. Folks shop and work all day among downtown's skyscrapers and drive home to sprawling suburbs in the evening. Life moves at an amble here—until May. Then, an army of 350,000 spectators and countless crewmembers overruns the city, and the winged wheel of the Indianapolis 500 rises above clouds of turbocharged exhaust to claim its throne. Gentlemen, start your engines…and the city goes into a frenzy as modern-day chariots of fire strain toward the finish for a $7.5 million winner's purse.

PRACTICAL INFORMATION

Visitor Information: Indianapolis City Center, 201 S. Capitol Ave. (237-5200), in the Pan Am Plaza across from the RCA Dome, has a helpful model of the city; press marked buttons to light up tourist attractions. Open Mon.-Fri. 10am-5:30pm, Sat. 10am-5pm, Sun. noon-5pm. Also try 800-233-INDY/4639.
Airport: Indianapolis International (487-7243), 7mi. southwest of downtown off I-465, Exit 11B. To get to the airport, take bus #9 ("West Washington"), American Trailways ($6), or a cab ($7-9).
Trains: Amtrak, 350 S. Illinois (263-0550 or 800-872-7245), behind Union Station. Trains travel east-west only. To: Chicago (3 per week, 4½hr., from $31); Washington, D.C. (3 per week, 19hr., from $115); Cincinnati (3 per week, 3hr., from $34). Station hours vary daily; call ahead.
Buses: Greyhound, currently at 127 N. Capital Ave. (800-231-2222), the depot hopes to move to its new location in Union Station, 1 block south of the Pan Am Plaza, by spring of 1997. To: Chicago (14 per day, 4hr., $32), Cincinnati (4 per day, 2hr., $17). Open 24hr. **American Trailways** (635-4000 or 800-742-7806) operates out of the Greyhound station, but also plans to move to Union Station by spring 1997. To: Bloomington (4 per day, 1hr., $23), airport (4 per day, 15min., $9). Open 24hr.

Public Transportation: Metro Bus, 1501 W. Washington St. (635-3344). Open Mon.-Fri. 7:30am-5:30pm. Fare 75¢, rush hour (Mon.-Fri. 6-9am and 3-6pm) $1. Service to the Speedway area 25¢ extra. Transfers 25¢. Patchy coverage of outlying areas. For disabled service, call 632-3000.
Taxis: Barrington Cab (786-7994), $1.25 first mi., 72¢ each additional. **Yellow Cab** (487-7777), $2.70 first mi., $1.80 each additional.
Car Rental: Thrifty, 3030 W. 38th St. (636-5622), ½ block west of Georgetown St. Daily $37 with 300 free mi. Weekly $190 with 2000 free mi. Must be 21 with major credit card. Under 25 add $8 daily. Open Mon.-Fri. 8am-5pm, Sat. 9am-2pm.
Emergency: 911 or 236-3000.
Post Office: 125 W. South St. (464-6000), across from Amtrak. Open Mon.-Fri. 8am-4:30pm. **ZIP code:** 46206. **Area code:** 317.

The city is laid out in concentric circles, with a dense central cluster of skyscrapers and low-lying outskirts. The very center of Indianapolis is just south of **Monument Circle** at the intersection of **Washington St.** (U.S. 40) and **Meridian St.** Washington St. divides the city north-south; Meridian St. divides it east-west. **I-465** circles the city and provides access to downtown. **I-70** cuts through the city east-west and passes by the Speedway. Plentiful 2-hr. meter parking can be found along the edges of the downtown area, and there are numerous indoor and outdoor lots ($5-8 per day) in the center, especially along **Ohio St.**

ACCOMMODATIONS AND CAMPING

Budget motels line the **I-465 beltway,** 5 mi. from downtown. Make reservations a year in advance for the Indy 500, and expect to pay inflated rates throughout May.

Fall Creek YMCA, 860 W. 10th St. (634-2478), just north of downtown. Small and sparce rooms, but resources make them ideal; access to a pool, a gym, athletic and laundry facilities, and free parking included. 86 rooms for men, 10 for women. Singles $25, with bath $35; weekly $70/$80, students $60; all rooms require a $5 key deposit. Call for availability and reservations as early as possible.
American Inn, 5630 Crawfordsville Rd. (248-1471), about 1½mi. west of the Indianapolis Speedway at the east end of the Speedway Shopping Center. Catch the #13 bus to and from the shopping center. Well-kept rooms with fridges, phones, and cable TV. Singles $22, doubles $34.
Medical Tower Inn, 1633 N. Capitol Ave. (925-9831), an easy 5-min. drive from downtown. One- and two-room set-ups with standard hotel florals and a decent view of the city. Singles $48, doubles $63; students $46/$61.
Motel 6, 6330 Debonair Lane (293-3220), I-465 at Exit 16A, 3mi. from the Indy Speedway and 10mi. from downtown, or take the #13 bus. Clean, bright rooms and an outdoor pool. Singles $34, doubles $40. Fills up fast; call for reservations, especially on weekends.
Indiana State Fairgrounds Campgrounds, 1202 E. 38th St. (927-7510). If you want to get close to nature, go elsewhere. 170 sod and gravel sites, along a vast parking lot. Sites $10.50, full hookup $12.60. Especially busy during the state fair.

FOOD

Ethnic food stands, produce markets, and knick-knack sellers fill the spacious **City Market,** 222 E. Market St., in a renovated 19th-century building. **Union Station,** 39 Jackson Pl. (267-0070), a 13-acre refurbished rail depot 4 blocks south of Monument Circle near the Hoosier Dome, is crowded with shops, dance clubs, bars, hotels, and restaurants; at the Trackside Food Court and Market on the second floor, vendors hawk a variety of eats (entrees average $2.50-5).

Bazbeaux Pizza, 334 Massachusetts Ave. (636-7662), and 832 E. Westfields Blvd. (255-5712). Indianapolis' favorite pizza. The Xchoupitoulas pizza is a cajun masterpiece. Construct your own culinary wonder ($5-18) from a choice of 53 toppings. Open Mon.-Thurs. 11am-10pm, Fri.-Sat. 11am-11pm, Sun. 4:30-10pm.

Essential Edibles, 429 E. Vermont St., (266-8797). Incredibly difficult to find, this way cool veggie joint rests in the basement of the old St. Mary's School building across from St. Mary's church on the city's northeast side. Locals swear by the South Indian Plate (about $6) and highly recommend the bread ($3 per loaf), made fresh in the restaurant's bakery. Open Mon.-Sat. 11am-2:30pm and Thurs. 5:30pm-9pm, Fri.-Sat. 5:30pm-10pm. Live jazz Fri. and Sat.

Acapulco Joe's, 365 N. Illinois (637-5160). The first Mexican restaurant in Indianapolis greets its guests with a perplexing sign saying: "Acapulco Joe's has sold over 5 million tacos—do you realize that represents *over 6 pounds of ground beef?*" Heavy on flavor, atmosphere, and popularity. Entrees up to $7.65. Open Mon.-Thurs. 7am-9pm, Fri.-Sat. 7am-10pm.

SIGHTS

Gold chandeliers and a majestic stained glass dome grace the marbled interior of the **State House** (232-3131), between Capitol and Senate St. near W. Washington St.; self-guided tour brochures are available inside (open daily 8am-5pm, main floor only Sat.-Sun.; for guided tours call 233-5243). The **Eiteljorg Museum of American Indians' and Western Art,** 500 W. Washington St. (636-9378), features an impressive collection of Western art from the past century as well as Native American art and clothing from over seven regions of the U.S. (open Tues.-Sat. 10am-5pm, Sun. noon-5pm; in the summer Mon. 10am-5pm; $5, seniors $4, students $2 with ID). A 5-min. drive from the Eiteljorg, the seemingly cageless **Indianapolis Zoo,** 1200 W. Washington St. (630-2001), has one of the world's largest enclosed whale and dolphin pavilions (open daily 9am-5pm; $9, seniors $6.50, ages 3-12 $5.50, under 3 free).

Farther from the city center, but well worth a visit, is the **Indianapolis Museum of Art,** 1200 W. 38th St. (923-1331). The museum has beautifully landscaped 152-acre grounds which offer nature trails, art pavilions, the Eli Lily Botanical Garden, a greenhouse, and a theater. Visit the third floor of the **Krannert Pavilion** for interactive modern art installations. (Open Mon.-Wed. and Fri. 10am-5pm, Thurs. 10am-8:30pm, Sun. noon-5pm. Free. Special exhibits $3; free Thurs.) Dig for fossils, speed through the cosmos, or explore a maze at the **Children's Museum,** 3000 N. Meridian St. (924-5437), one of the country's largest (open daily 10am-5pm; closed Mon. Sept.-Feb.; $6 adults and children, $5 seniors).

Wolves and bison roam under researchers' supervision at **Wolf Park** (567-2265), on Jefferson St. in Battle Ground, IN (1hr. north of Indianapolis on I-65). The werewolves do their thing on Friday and Saturday nights at 7:30pm. (Open daily 1-5pm, open later Fri. for the wolf howl. Mon.-Sat. $4, Sun. $5, under 14 free.)

ENTERTAINMENT AND NIGHTLIFE

In its heyday, the **Walker Theatre,** 617 Indiana Ave. (236-2009, 236-2087 for tickets), a 15-min. walk northwest of downtown, booked jazz greats Louis Armstrong and Dinah Washington. Local and national artists still perform here as part of the weekly **Jazz on the Avenue** series (Fri. 6-10pm) and the annual **Jazz Festival** (3rd week in Aug.). The theater, erected in 1927 with stunning Egyptian and African decor, commemorates Madame Walker, an African-American beautician who invented the straightening comb and became America's first self-made woman millionaire. The **Indianapolis Symphony Orchestra,** 45 Monument Circle (box office 639-4300 or 800-366-8457), handles entertainment in classical style. The **Indianapolis Opera,** 250 E. 38th St. (283-3531, box office 940-6444; tickets $12-47, students and seniors $12-44), and the **Indianapolis Repertory Theatre,** 140 W. Washington St. (635-5252; tickets $6-30, student rush 1hr. before show $6), both perform September through May. Contact the **Arts Council Office,** 47 S. Pennsylvania St. (631-3301 or 800-865-ARTS/2787), for the schedules of other performances in the area.

By day an outlying cluster of art galleries, bead shops, and record shops, the **Broad Ripple** area (6mi. north of downtown at College Ave. and 62nd St.) transforms after dark into a nightlife mecca for anyone under 40. The party fills the clubs and bars and spills out onto the sidewalks and side streets off Broad Ripple Ave. until about 1am on weekdays and 3am on weekends. Check out the **Old Pro's Table,** or **O.P.T.,** 829 Broad Ripple Ave., for pool tables and a juke box. Chug nightly drink specials and sing an inebriated "Love Me Tender" to pictures of Elvis at **Rock Lobster,** 820 Broad Ripple Ave. (257-9001). **The Patio,** 6308 Guilford Ave. (255-2828), and **The Vogue,** 6259 N. College Ave. (255-2828), are music clubs featuring local and mid-size national acts, respectively. The Patio has free dancing on Wednesday nights which attracts a sizeable gay crowd. (Cover $2-7, more for big names.) Those interested in a more jocular evening should try the **Broad Ripple Comedy Club** (255-4211), on the corner of College and Broad Ripple. Shows daily, call ahead for price information. After the clubs close, make a run for tacos ($1.75) and burritos ($3) at **Paco's Cantina,** 737 Broad Ripple Ave. (251-6200; open until 4am or later, at the owner's whim).

GO, SPEED RACER, GO!

Most of the year, the **Indianapolis Motor Speedway,** 4790 W. 16th St. (481-8500), off I-465 at the Speedway exit (bus #25), lies dormant and waiting, as tourists ride buses around the 2½-mi. track ($2). The adjacent **Speedway Museum** (484-6747) houses Indy's Hall of Fame (open daily 9am-5pm; $2, under 17 free).

The country's passion for fast cars reaches a fevered pitch during the **500 Festival** (636-4556), a month of parades, a mini-marathon, and lots of hoopla leading up to the day when 33 aerodynamic race cars, specially designed not to go airborne, jet around the track at speeds exceeding 225mph. The festivities begin with time trials in mid-May and culminate with the bang of the **Indianapolis 500** starter's gun on the Sunday of Memorial Day Weekend (weather permitting). Think ahead; tickets for the race go on sale the day after the previous year's race and usually sell out within a week (from $30; call the Speedway for an order form, available in April). NASCAR's **Brickyard 400** (800-822-4639) sends stock cars zooming down the speedway in early August.

■ Bloomington

Bloomington is not much of a farming town. Untouched by the glaciers of the last ice age and burdened by large limestone deposits, its terrain remains hilly and its soil infertile. An anomaly in a region of heavy farming, the town has grown alongside its most prominent institution, Indiana University. Events like the Little 500 bike race, attract hundreds of visitors and the accolades of David Letterman's Top Ten staff. The town's many happenin' cafés, art exhibits, and IU itself make Bloomington an excellent destination for anyone interested in the culture of Hoosier guys and gals.

Practical Information Bloomington is south of Indianapolis on Rte. 37; **N. Walnut** and **College St.** are the main thoroughfares running north-south in town. The **visitors center** is located at 2855 N. Walnut St. (339-8900 or 800-800-0037; open Mon.-Fri. 8am-5pm, Sat. 9am-4pm, Sun. 10am-3pm; 24-hr. brochure area). Buses from **American Trailways,** 535 N. Walnut (332-1522), four blocks from the center of downtown, connect Bloomington to Chicago (3 per day, 6hr., round-trip $90) and Indianapolis (3 per day, 1hr., round-trip $23; open Mon.-Fri. 4:30am-5:30pm, weekends during bus times only). **Bloomington Transit** transports the public on seven routes. Service is infrequent; call 332-5688 for info (75¢, seniors and kids 5-17 35¢). Call **Yellow Cab** (336-4100) for a taxi. Bloomington's **post office:** 206 E. 4th St. (334-4030), two blocks east of Walnut St. (open Mon.-Fri. 8am-6pm, Sat. 8am-1pm). **ZIP code:** 47403. **Area code:** 812.

Accommodations, Food, and Nightlife Budget hotels cluster around the intersection of N. Walnut St. and Rte. 46. A bit further from town is the **Bauer House,** 4595 N. Maple Grove Rd. (336-4383). Hard to find, but worth the trip, this family run bed and breakfast is tucked into the hills to the west of the city, off Rte. 46. For $50, Mrs. Bauer will make up one of four large rooms and wake the house in the morning with a big country breakfast. (Open March-Oct. Reservations recommended, especially around the beginning and end of the school year.) **Motel 6,** 1800 N. Walnut St. (332-0820), offers clean, spacious rooms, a pool, free local calls, and free HBO (singles $32, doubles $37). The **Lake Monroe Village Campgrounds,** 8107 S. Fairfax Rd. (824-2267), 8 mi. south of Bloomington, allows campers to choose a spot on 60 wooded acres and throws in free showers and a pool (sites $18, hookup $23, log cabins for 2 $42).

The **Downtown Square,** or "The Square" as it's locally known, holds a wealth of restaurants in a two- block radius, most on Kirkwood Ave. near College and W. Walnut St. Laugh the hemp cheese ($1 per oz.) off your Mondo Burrito ($3.50) at **The Laughing Planet Café,** 322 E. Kirkwood Ave. (323-CAFE/2233), where they whip up "whole foods in a hurry" (open daily 11am-9pm). Enter a hall of mirrors at **Snow Lion,** 113 S. Grant St. (336-0835), just off Kirkwood Ave., to sample Tibetan and Oriental cuisine (lunch $3.75, entrees $7.50; open Mon.-Sun. 11:30am-2pm, daily 5-10pm). Bohemian and vegetarian visitors may do well to use their beet-seeking whistles in Bloomington. Such actions will probably lead to the **Wild Beet,** 123 S. Walmut (323-3000). A likeable establishment with interesting fare (they serve "orgasmic juices"), the Beet also provides live music for aprés-sight-seeing entertainment (Tues.-Thurs. 5pm-1am, Fri.-Sat. 5pm-2am). For dessert head east on Kirkland St., where **Jiffy-Treet,** 425 E. Kirkwood Ave. (332-3502), produces homemade ice-cream; the strawberry sherbert is dreamy (1 scoop $1.09).

Beer and alternative rock are the milk and ambrosia of college students, and IU is no exception. Taste 80 beers brewed from Jamaica to Japan at **The Crazy Horse,** 214 W. Kirkwood (336-8877; open Mon.-Thurs. 11am-1am, Fri.-Sat. 11am-2am, Sun. 11am-midnight). **Mars,** 479 N. Walnut St. (336-6277 concert line), is the planet for big-name regional and mid-size national acts; **Bluebird,** 216 N. Walnut St. (336-2473), stages local acts; and **Second Story,** 201 S. College Ave. (336-5827), hosts alternative groups. **Rhino's,** 225½ S. Walnut St. (333-3430), has lesser known acts and accepts people under 21, unlike the others. Check bulletin boards on the east side of town for concert flyers.

Sights IU's **Art Museum,** Fine Arts Plaza, E. 7th St. (855-5445), maintains an excellent collection of Oriental and African art works (open Wed.-Thurs. and Sat. 10am-5pm, Fri. 10am-8pm, Sun. noon-5pm; free). Browse three floors of old valuables downtown at the **Antique Mall,** 311 W. 7th St. (332-2290; open Mon.-Thurs. and Sat. 10am-5pm, Fri. 10am-8pm, Sun. noon-5pm). Indiana geologists believe **Lake Monroe** was once the bottom of a shallow sea that filled with limestone 230 million years ago. Enjoy the lake's cool waters and calm breezes 10 mi. south of town. Special Bloomington days include Labor Day Weekend, when the 4th St. **Festival of the Arts and Crafts** (800-800-0037) draws hundreds of Midwestern artisans to Bloomington, and, in June, **A Taste of Bloomington** gathers local bands and food from local restaurants together under a single tent while festival-goers eat their hearts out.

Illinois

In 1893, at Chicago's World Columbian Exposition, a young professor named Fredrick Jackson Turner gave a stirring speech in which he proclaimed the "closing of the American Frontier." That such a proclamation was made in Illinois seems only fitting; although once praised for its vast prairies and the arability of its soil, by the end of the nineteenth century, Illinois had become a land known for its thriving urban industry.

Today, four cities exemplify Illinois' diversity. Cairo, at the southern tip of the state, is so-called for its resemblance to the fertile Nile River Valley. Collinsville boasts the Cahokia Mounds, representing Illinois' Native American heritage. Springfield is the capital and the center of Lincoln-worship. Chicago, in the industrial north, rules the roost—the Midwest's ubiquitous cornfields come to an abrupt halt, and suits trade corn futures and pork bellies behind jungles of polished steel.

PRACTICAL INFORMATION

Capital: Springfield.
Office of Tourism: 620 E. Adams St., Springfield 62701 (217-782-7500).
Time Zone: Central (1hr. behind Eastern). **Postal Abbreviation:** IL.
Sales Tax: 6.25-8.75%, depending on the city.

■ Chicago

Over two centuries ago, Checagon ("place of the smelly onion" to its early Native American inhabitants) occupied a marsh at the southern tip of Lake Michigan. Despite its foul odors, westbound settlers saw potential along the banks of the Chicago River, and by the mid-1800s the small town had grown into a burgeoning commercial center. With the growth of the railroad industry, Chicago quickly became America's meat-packing hub, horrifyingly depicted in Upton Sinclair's *The Jungle*. Millions of immigrants flooded the city to meet the high demand for labor, creating a few vast fortunes and countless broken dreams. Machine politics flourished, blurring any distinction between organized government and organized crime.

Trading commodities ultimately displaced cattle slaughter as the city's economic mainstay, and narrow steel tracks gave way to the wide concrete runways of O'Hare, the world's busiest airport. Chicago began to export authors—Studs Terkel, Theodore Dreiser, and Ernest Hemingway to name a few—along with its Cracker Jacks and canned hams. Today, the city preens as an extremely diverse world-class metropolis. Its neighborhoods shelter many ethnic communities, and feature the work of Frank Lloyd Wright, Mies van der Rohe, and Louis Sullivan, as well as the art of Picasso, Chagall, and Joan Miró. The University of Chicago employs more Nobel Laureates than any other university in the world. The "City in a Garden" no longer reeks of onion, but of prestige.

PRACTICAL INFORMATION

Tourist Office: The **Chicago Office of Tourism,** 78 E. Washington St. (744-2400 or 800-2CONNECT/226-6632). Open Mon.-Fri. 10am-6pm, Sat. 10am-5pm, Sun. noon-5pm. In the same building is the **Chicago Cultural Center,** 77 E. Randolph St. at Michigan Ave., which has info on Chicago's ethnic groups. Open Mon.-Fri. 10am-6pm, Sat. 10am-5pm, Sun. noon-5pm. Another location a few min. north at 806 Michigan Ave. is the **Chicago Visitor Information Center** (744-2400), in the Water Tower Pumping Station. Open Mon.-Fri. 9:30am-6pm, Sat. 10am-6pm, Sun. 11am-5pm. On the lake, the **Navy Pier Info Center,** 700 E. Grand. Open Mon.-Thurs. 10am-9pm, Fri.-Sat. 10am-10pm, Sun. 10am-7pm.

Airports: O'Hare International (686-2200), off I-90. Inventor of the layover, the holding pattern, and the headache. Flights depart every 40-46 seconds. Depending on traffic, a trip between downtown and O'Hare can take up to 2hr. The blue line **Rapid Train** runs between the Airport El station and downtown ($1.50). The ride takes 40min-1hr. **Midway Airport** (767-0500), on the western edge of the South Side, often offers less expensive flights. To get downtown, take the El orange line from the Midway stop. Lockers $1 per day. **Continental Air Transport** (454-7800 or 800-654-7871) connects both airports to downtown hotels. From: O'Hare baggage terminal (every 30min. 5am-10:30pm; 60-75min.; $14.75), and Midway (every hr., 25min. after the hr., 6:25am-8:25pm; $10.75).

Trains: Amtrak, Union Station, 225 S. Canal (558-1075 or 800-872-7245), at Adams St. west of the Loop. Take the El to State and Adams, then walk 7 blocks west on Adams. Amtrak's main hub may look familiar; it was the backdrop for the final baby-buggy scene of *The Untouchables*. To: Milwaukee (5 per day, 1½hr., $25); Detroit (2 per day, 6½hr., $35); New York (2 per day, 18½hr., $141). Station open 6:15am-10pm; tickets sold daily 6am-9pm. Lockers $1 per day.

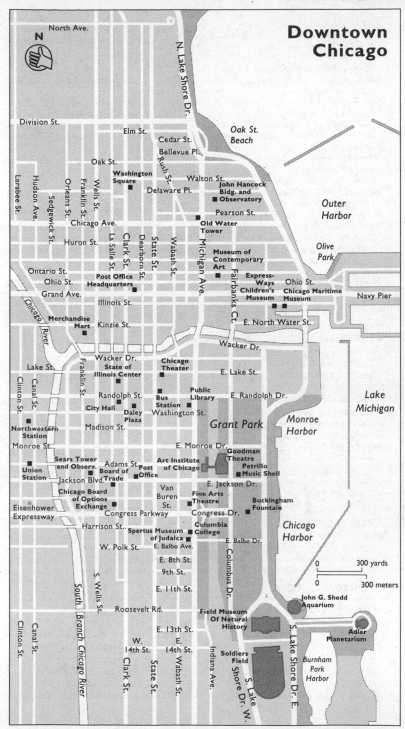

Downtown Chicago

North Ave.

Division St.

Elm St.

Cedar St.

Bellevue Pl.

Oak St.

Washington Square

Walton St.

Delaware Pl.

John Hancock Bldg. and Observatory

Pearson St.

Chicago Ave.

Old Water Tower

Huron St.

Museum of Contemporary Art

Ontario St.

Ohio St.

Post Office Headquarters

Express-Ways Children's Museum

Ohio St.

Chicago Maritime Museum

Grand Ave.

Illinois St.

E. North Water St.

Merchandise Mart

Kinzie St.

Wacker Dr.

Lake St.

Wacker Dr.

State of Illinois Center

Chicago Theater

E. Lake St.

Randolph St.

Bus Station

Public Library

E. Randolph Dr.

City Hall

Daley Plaza

Washington St.

Madison St.

Northwestern Station

Grant Park

Monroe Harbor

Monroe St.

E. Monroe Dr.

Sears Tower and Observ.

Adams St.

Art Institute of Chicago

Goodman Theatre

Petrillo Music Shell

Union Station

Board of Trade

Post Office

Jackson Blvd

E. Jackson Dr.

Chicago Board of Options Exchange

Van Buren St.

Fine Arts Theatre

Buckingham Fountain

Eisenhower Expressway

Congress Parkway

Congress Dr.

Chicago Harbor

Harrison St.

Spertus Museum of Judaica

Columbia College

W. Polk St.

E. Balbo Ave.

E. Balbo Dr.

E. 8th St.

9th St.

E. 11th St.

Roosevelt Rd.

John G. Shedd Aquarium

E. 13th St.

Field Museum Of Natural History

Adler Planetarium

W. 14th St.

E. 14th St.

Soldiers Field

Burnham Park Harbor

Oak St. Beach

Outer Harbor

Olive Park

Navy Pier

Lake Michigan

Chicago River

North Ave.

N. Lake Shore Dr.

Rush St.

Wells St.

Franklin St.

Orleans St.

Sedgewick St.

Hudson Ave.

Larabee St.

Chicago Ave.

La Salle St.

Clark St.

Dearborn St.

State St.

Wabash Ave.

Michigan Ave.

Fairbanks Ct.

Franklin St.

Canal St.

Clinton St.

S. Wells St.

South Branch Chicago River

Canal St.

Clinton St.

Clark St.

State St.

Wabash St.

Indiana Ave.

Columbus Dr.

S. Lake Shore Dr. W.

S. Lake Shore Dr. E.

0   300 yards

0   300 meters

GREAT LAKES

Buses: Greyhound, 630 W. Harrison St. (800-231-2222), at Jefferson and Desplaines. Take the El to Linton. *The* hub of the central U.S. Also home base for several smaller companies covering the Midwest. To: Detroit (12 per day, 8hr., $27); Milwaukee (14 per day, 2hr., $12); St. Louis (7 per day, 5-8hr., $31). Station open 24hr., ticket office open Mon.-Fri. 5am-2:30pm, Sat.-Sun. 6am-10am.

Taxis: Yellow Cab, 829-4222. **Flash Cab,** 561-1444. **American United Cab,** 248-7600. Average fare $1.50 for flag drop, $1.20 per mi.

Car Rental: Dollar Rent-a-Car (800-800-4000), at O'Hare and Midway. $47 per day, $135 per week; under 25 surcharge $12 per day. **Thrifty Car Rental** (800-367-2277), at O'Hare and Midway. $35 per day, $129 per week, $9 for liability insurance. Under 25 surcharge $10 per day. 100 free mi. per day, 15¢ per additional mi. Must be 21 with major credit card for both.

Hotlines: Rape Crisis Line, 847-872-7799. **Gay and Lesbian Hotline/Anti Violence Project,** 871-2273.

Police: 744-4000 (non-emergency).

Medical Services: Cook County Hospital, 1835 W. Harrison (633-6000). Take the Congress A train to the Medical Center Stop.

Emergency: 911.

Post Office: 433 W. Van Buren St. (697-6497), 2 blocks from Union Station. Open Mon.-Fri. 7am-9pm, Sat. 8am-5pm. **ZIP code:** 60607. **Area code:** 312 (Chicago), 708 or 847 (outside the city limits). Numbers given here are in area code 312 unless otherwise noted.

ORIENTATION

Chicago has overtaken the entire northeastern corner of Illinois, running north-south along 29 mi. of the southwest Lake Michigan shorefront. The city sits at the center of a web of interstates, rail lines, and airplane routes; most cross-country traffic swings through the city. A good map is essential for navigating Chicago; it was not planned on an orderly grid.

The one area that you *must* know is the **Loop,** Chicago's downtown and hub of the public transportation system. The Loop is bounded by the Chicago River to the north and west, Lake Michigan to the east, and Roosevelt Rd. to the south. Directions in *Let's Go* are generally from downtown. South of the Loop, numbered east-west streets increase towards the south. Many ethnic neighborhoods lie in this area. LaSalle Dr. loosely defines the west edge of the **Near North** area. The **Gold Coast** shimmers on N. Lakeshore Dr. **Lincoln Park** is bounded by Clark St., Lincoln Ave., and Halstead. Lincoln Park melts into **Wrigleyville,** near the 300s of N. Clark and N. Halstead St., and then becomes **Lakeview,** in the 4000s.

The city's north side is generally safe at all times, though at night you should avoid the area around Cabrini Green (bounded by W. Armitage Ave. on the north, W. Chicago Ave. on the south., Sedgwick on the west, and Halsted on the east). The west side of the Chicago River (north and south branches) is unsafe at night. South of the Loop, especially south of Cermak Rd., be careful. In general, know where you are going and go there; don't wander around aimlessly or ignorantly.

To avoid driving in the city, daytrippers can leave their cars in one of the suburban subway lots for 24 hr. ($1.75). There are a half-dozen such park-and-ride lots; call CTA (see below) for info. Parking downtown costs $8 per day for most lots.

GETTING AROUND

The **Chicago Transit Authority (CTA),** 350 N. Wells, 7th fl. (836-7000), runs rapid transit trains, subways, and buses. The **elevated rapid transit train** system, called the **El,** bounds the major downtown section of the city, known as the Loop. Some downtown routes run underground, but are still referred to as the El. The El operates 24 hr., but late-night service is infrequent and unsafe in many areas; stick with the crowds. Also, some buses do not run all night; call CTA for schedules and routes. CTA maps are available at many stations and the Water Tower Information Center. The CTA map can be your best friend; it includes a "Quick Ride" Guide with instructions to major attractions from downtown. Since buses and trains are everywhere, deciphering the map is worth the trouble. Don't just step blindly onto a train; many are express trains, and often different routes run along the same tracks. Train and bus fare is $1.50; add 25¢ for express routes. Remember to get a transfer (25¢) from bus drivers or when you enter the El stop, which will get you up to two more rides on different routes during the following two hours. Ten tokens good for one train or bus ride each at any time of day cost $12.50. Buy token rolls at *some* stations, supermarkets, and at the "Check Cashed" storefronts with the yellow sign; these places also carry $18.50 weekly passes (valid Sun.-Sat.) or $72 monthly passes.

On Saturdays from mid-June to mid-Oct. a Loop Tour Train departs on a 40-min. free tour at 12:15pm, 12:55pm, 1:35pm, and 2:15pm (tickets must be picked up at the Chicago Office of Tourism). **METRA** operates a vast commuter rail network; 11 rail lines and four downtown stations send trains snaking out into suburbs north, west, and south. (Free schedules and maps at their office at 547 W. Jackson. Route info, 322-6777 Mon.-Fri. 8am-5pm, 836-7000 evenings and weekends. Fare $1.75-5, depending on distance.) **PACE** (836-7000) is the suburban bus system.

Neighborhoods

In the late 19th century, Chicago's slaughterhouses, factories, and warehouses drew millions of immigrants from all areas of the world; the ethnic neighborhoods they created remain, though their borders have shifted due to gentrification, continued immigration, and university-building. Most are relatively safe during the day, but take a cab or get very good directions at night. For more info see Katherine Rodeglier's article *Ethnic Chicago,* which gives a detailed analysis of the city's neighborhoods (available at the Cultural Center; see Practical Information).

The center of the **Chinese** community lies out of the Loop, at Cermak Rd. and Wentworth Ave. New Chinatown, north of the Loop at Argyle St. offers a few more Chinese restaurants, but is mainly **Vietnamese.** The area of Argyle St. east of N. Broadway is known as Little Saigon. The **German** community has scattered, but the beer halls, restaurants, and shops in the 3000s and 4000s of N. Lincoln Ave. bear witness to their presence. The former residents of **Greektown** have moved to the suburbs, but S. Halsted St., just west of the Loop, offers a wide variety of Greek restaurants. **Little Italy** fell prey to the University of Illinois at Chicago (UIC), but a shadow of the old neighborhood remains along W. Taylor St. west of the UIC campus. The **Jewish** community leaves its mark on Devon Ave. from Western Ave. to the Chicago River. The area near Midway Airport is home to much of Chicago's **Lithuanian** population, one of the world's largest. The Pilsen neighborhood, south of downtown around 18th St., offers a slice of **Mexico.** Quell your hunger for Polish sausage along N. Milwaukee Ave. between blocks 2800 and 3100; Chicago's **Polish** population ranks as one of the largest outside of Warsaw. Andersonville, along Clark St. north of Foster Ave., is the historic center of the **Swedish** community, though immigrants from Asia and the Middle East have settled here in recent years.

ACCOMMODATIONS

A cheap, convenient bed awaits you at one of Chicago's hostels. If you have a car, you can also try the moderately priced motels on Lincoln Ave. Motel chains have locations off the interstates, about an hour's drive from downtown; they're inconvenient and expensive ($35 and up), but are a reliable option for late night arrivals. **Chicago Bed and Breakfast,** P.O. Box 14088, Chicago 60614 (951-0085), runs a referral service with over 150 rooms of varying prices throughout the city and outlying areas. Few have parking, but the majority are near public transit. (2-night min. stay. Singles from $65, doubles from $75. Reservations required.)

Chicago Summer Hostel (HI-AYH), 731 S. Plymouth Ct. (327-5350). Close to downtown and the lake. Clean, light, dorm-style housing filled with international students. Kitchen, laundry, exercise rooms, ride-sharing board. 2-3 beds per room; suites have 2-3 bedrooms, a bathroom, and a living room. $16, nonmembers $19.

Private double $60. Open mid-June to early Sept. Call ahead; the owners plan to move to another location sometime soon.

International House (HI-AYH), 1414 E. 59th St. (753-2270), Hyde Park, off Lake Shore Dr. Take the Illinois Central Railroad from the Michigan Ave. station (10-20min.) to 59th St. and walk ½ block west. Part of the University of Chicago. Isolated from the rest of the city; the neighborhood can be dangerous. Clean singles filled mostly by permanent residents. Cheap cafeteria with outdoor courtyard. Shared bath, linens provided. $21, nonmembers $34.50. Reservations required.

Chicago International Hostel, 6318 N. Winthrop (262-1011). Take the Howard St. northbound train to Loyola Station; walk 3 blocks south on Sheridan Rd. to Winthrop, and ½ block south. Slightly bland but sunny and clean rooms in a fairly safe location near the lake, beaches, and many fast food joints. Free parking in rear. Kitchen, laundry. Bike rental $8 per day. 4-6 beds per room. Check in 7-11am, 4pm-2am. Lockout 11am-4pm. $13, double with bath $40. Lockers $1. Key deposit $5. Reservations recommended.

Eleanor Residence, 1550 N. Dearborn Pkwy. (664-8245). *Women over 18 only.* Fantastic location near Lincoln Park and Gold Coast. Majestic common room and lobby, clean single rooms. $40 with breakfast and dinner included. Reserve at least 1 day in advance; 1-night deposit required.

Hotel Cass, 640 N. Wabash (787-4030), just north of the Loop. Take subway to State or Grand St. Convenient location. Clean rooms with wood trim and A/C. Coffee shop and lounge. No parking. Laundry room. Singles $50, doubles $55. $5 discount with ISIC. Key deposit $5. Reservations recommended.

Arlington House (AAIH/Rucksackers), 616 Arlington Pl. (929-5380 or 800-467-8355). Take the El to Fullerton, walk 2 blocks east, left on Orchard, then right on Arlington Place. Dorm-style rooms with 4, 6, or 10 beds. Ideal location in Lincoln Park, near the center of Chicago nightlife. Free parking in the street if you can find it. Laundry room, kitchen. Open 24hr. $15, nonmembers $18. Linen $2.

Hotel Wacker, 111 W. Huron (787-1386), at N. Clark. Insert your own joke, you lecherous swine. A large green sign on the corner as well as maps in the tourist office make this place easy to find. Clean, old-fashioned rooms. Convenient to downtown. No parking. TV, A/C, phone. 24hr. check-in. Singles $40, doubles $45. Weekly $210-225. Key and linen deposit $5.

Leaning Tower YMCA, 6300 W. Touhy (847-647-8222). From the Harvard St. El stop, take bus #290; 1hr. from the Loop. Inaccessible by public transport evenings and Sundays. Look for a half-scale replica of the Leaning Tower of Pisa (it's a water tower). Private baths, cafeteria. Use of YMCA facilities, including swimming pool and gym. Both men and women welcome. Must be over 21. Free parking. Singles $32, doubles $35. Key deposit $5.

Acres Motel, 5600 N. Lincoln Ave (561-7777), at Bryn Mawr Ave., offers free parking and singles or doubles for $35, $40 on the weekends.

FOOD

One of the best guides to city dining is *Chicago* magazine, which includes an extensive restaurant section, cross-indexed by price, cuisine, and quality. The monthly magazine can usually be picked up at tourist offices; ask at the desk.

Pizza

Chicago's pizza is known 'round the world. Try it standard-style, with the cheese on top, or stuffed, with toppings in the middle of the crust. Mmmm!

Pizzeria Uno, 29 E. Ohio (321-1000), and **Due,** 619 N. Wabash (943-2400). The newspaper clippings on the wall may look like any other Uno's, but this is where the delicious legacy of cheese, tomato, and deep-dish pizza began. Lines are long, and pizza takes 45min. to prepare. Same menu at younger sister Due (right up the street), with a terrace and more room than Uno's. Pizzas $5-18. Uno open Mon.-Fri. 11:30am-1am, Sat. 11:30am-2am, Sun. 11:30am-11:30pm. Due open Sun.-Thurs. 11:30am-1:30am, Fri. 11:30am-2:30am, Sat. noon-2:30am.

Giordano's, 730 N. Rush St. (951-0747). The downtown location is only one of 35 branches in the Chicago area. The stuffed pizza is worth the 35-min. wait. Call ahead to get your pizza cooking. Pizzas $4-18. Lunch specials $5. Open Sun.-Thurs. noon-midnight, Fri.-Sat. 11am-1am.

The Loop

Heaven on Seven, 111 N. Wabash (263-6443), on the 7th floor of the Garland Building. The mantlepiece painted with vegetables, alligators, and crabs means you're getting closer to Cajun nirvana. The line is long, but hell, the gumbo is great ($7-12). Cash only. Open Mon.-Fri. 7am-5pm, Sat. 7am-3pm.

The Berghoff, 17 W. Adams (427-3170). Dark, cavernous German restaurant filled with lunching traders. Bratwurst $4.75, beer stein of Berghoff's own beer $2.25. Open Mon.-Thurs. 11am-9:30pm, Fri. 11:30am-9:30pm, Sat. noon-10pm.

Russian Tea Time, 77 E. Adams (360-0000), across from the Art Institute, serves Russian delicacies from borscht to stroganoff in the heart of downtown Chicago. Start with a bottomless cup of tea for $1.85. Entrees under $10. Open Mon. 11am-9pm, Tues.-Thurs. 11am-11pm, Fri.-Sat. 11am-midnight, Sun. 11am-9pm.

Wishbone, 1001 W. Washington (850-2663), just west of the Loop. Take bus #20 "Madison" to Morgan St. A Southern cuisine extravaganza in a converted tire warehouse, with cornbread and banana bread on every table. Vegan and veggie specials vary daily ($5-9.50). Tues.-Fri. sit-down breakfast 7-11am, cafeteria-style lunch 11:30am-3pm, dinner Mon. 5-8pm, Tues.-Thurs. 5-10pm, Fri.-Sat. 5-11pm; brunch Sat.-Sun. 8am-2:30pm.

Near North

Billy Goat's Tavern, 430 N. Michigan (222-1525), underground on lower Michigan Ave. Descend through a seeming subway entrance in front of the Tribune building. The gruff service was the inspiration for the legendary *Saturday Night Live* "Cheezborger, cheezborger—no Coke, Pepsi" skit. Cheezborgers $2.40. Butt in anytime Mon.-Sat. 10am-midnight, Sun. 11am-2am.

The Original A-1, 401 E. Illinois (644-0300), in North Pier. A haven for the homesick Texan. No mere hamburgers; try a Durango burger ($6.50) instead. Open Mon.-Fri. 11:30am-10pm, Sat. noon-midnight, Sun. noon-9pm.

Frontera Grill, 445 N. Clark (661-1434). Avant-Tex-Mex for yuppies. The piñatas inside are worth seeing. Entrees $10-17. Open Tues.-Sat. after 9am.

Little Saigon

Mekong, 4953 N. Broadway (271-0206), at Argyle St. Busy, spotless Vietnamese restaurant. All-you-can-eat lunch buffet, Mon.-Fri. 11am-2:30pm, $5. Tasty soups $3.50-4. Open Sun.-Thurs. 10am-10pm, Fri.-Sat. 10am-11pm.

Chinatown

Hong Min, 221 W. Cermak (842-5026). El: Cermak. Attention paid to the food, *not* the furnishings—unlike some Chinese restaurants nearby. Duck of West Lake $10, steamed whitefish $7. Open daily 10am-2am.

Three Happiness, 2130 S. Wentworth Ave. (791-1228). Don't worry, be happy, happy, happy. Gulping fish greet you at the door; a dragon and crowds wait upstairs. Dim sum ($1.75) is served Mon.-Fri. 10am-2pm, Sat.-Sun. 10am-3pm. Open Mon.-Thurs. 10am-midnight, Fri.-Sat. 10am-midnight, Sun. 10am-10pm.

Little Italy

What is left of Little Italy can be reached by taking the El to UIC, then walking west on Taylor St. or taking bus #37 down Taylor St.

The Rosebud, 1500 W. Taylor (942-1117). Small, dark restaurant serves huge portions of pasta. Lunch specials $7-9, dinner from $9. Valet parking $5, reservations recommended. Open for lunch Mon.-Fri. 11am-3pm; dinner Mon.-Thurs. 5-10:30pm, Fri.-Sat. 5:30-11:30pm.

Al's Italian Beef, 1079 W. Taylor St. (226-4717), at Aberdeen near Little Italy; also at 169 W. Ontario. Churns out top-notch Italian beef, reddish with lots of spices. Join the crowd standing at the formica counter. Italian beef sandwich $3.30. Open Mon.-Sat. 9am-1am.

Mario's Italian Lemonade, 1074 W. Taylor St., across from Al's. A classic neighborhood stand that churns out sensational Italian ices (70¢-$4.50) in flavors ranging from cantaloupe to cherry. Open daily mid-May to mid-Sept. 10am-midnight.

Greektown

The Parthenon, 314 S. Halsted St. (726-2407). Don't look for the golden ratio in the architecture here. The staff converses in volleys of Greek, the murals and hangings transport you to the Mediterranean, and the food wins top awards. The Greek Feast, a family-style dinner ($12.25), includes everything from *saganaki* (flaming goat cheese) to *baklava* (glazed pastry). Open daily 11am-1am.

Greek Islands, 200 S. Halsted (782-9855). Stroll under the grape leaf awning and sit down at a blue-checked table for magnificent food. No reservations, so expect a ¾- to 1-hr. wait on weekends. Daily special $7-9. Open Sun.-Thurs. 11am-midnight, Fri.-Sat. 11am-1am.

North Side/Lincoln Park

Jada's, 1909 N. Lincoln Ave. (280-2326). Nondescript decor focuses attention on excellent Thai food. Most dishes can be cooked without meat. Entrees $5-8. Open Tues.-Sat. 5-11pm, Sun. 4-10pm.

Potbelly's, 2264 N. Lincoln (528-1405). Could be named for the stoves scattered around the deli or your stomach when you leave. 50s-style decor with wooden booths. Subs $3.29. Open daily 11am-11pm.

Kopi, A Traveller's Café, 5317 N. Clark (989-5674). A 10-min. walk from the Berwyn El, 4 blocks west on Berwyn. Peruse a travel guide over a few cups of java or just sit back and appreciate the art. On Mon. and Thurs. nights the café blends coffee and music (no cover). Open Mon.-Thurs. 8am-11pm, Fri. 8am-midnight, Sat. 9am-midnight, Sun. 10am-11pm.

Café Ba-Ba-Reeba!, 2024 N. Halsted (935-5000). Well marked by the colorful, glowing façade. Hearty Spanish cuisine with subtle spices; try the *paella valenciana* ($12) under clumps of hanging garlic or people-watch on the outdoor terrace. Open for lunch Tues.-Sun. 11:30am-2:30pm; open for dinner Sun.-Thurs. 5:30-10pm, Fri. 5:30pm-midnight, Sat. 5pm-midnight, Sun. 5:30-10:30pm.

Café Voltaire, 3231 N. Clark (528-3136). Named for the Zurich hangout of James Joyce and Picasso, this high-minded coffeehouse struggles to match the legend. Underground performance space (cover $5-10) for aspiring intellectuals. Grain-based planet burgers $6. Open Sun.-Thurs. 11:30am-11pm, Fri.-Sat. 11:30am-1am.

The Bourgeois Pig, 748 Fullerton Ave. (883-5282). Quiet, soothing coffee shop with faux marble tables, board games, and vegetarian specialties to boot. Cappuccino $1.75, scones $1.45. Open Mon.-Thurs. 6:30am-11pm, Fri. 6:30am-midnight, Sat. 8am-midnight, Sun. 8am-11pm.

SIGHTS

Chicago's "sights" range from well publicized museums to undiscovered back streets, from beaches and parks to towering skyscrapers. Begin with the tourist brochures, the bus tours, and the downtown area, but remember that they reveal only a fraction of Chicago. Believe the advice of a famous art historian, who said: "No one will learn the city of Chicago without using their feet." Walk north of the Magnificent Mile, south of the Loop, and west of the river; venture on the El and the buses, and enjoy Chicago in all its splendor—but be careful and use common sense.

Museums

Each of Chicago's major museums admits visitors free at least one day per week. The "Big Five"—The Art Institute of Chicago, the Museum of Science and Technology, and the closely clumped Lakefront Museums (Shedd Aquarium, Adler Planetarium, and the Field Museum of Natural History)—exhibit everything from Monet to mummies to marine mammals. A handful of smaller collections represent diverse ethnic groups and professional interests. Pick up brochures at the tourist info office (see Practical Information).

The Art Institute of Chicago, 111 S. Michigan Ave. (443-3600), at Adams St. in Grant Park. The city's premier art museum. Four millennia of art from China, Africa, Europe, and beyond. The Institute's Impressionist and Post-Impressionist collections win international acclaim. Highlight tour daily 2pm. Open Mon. and Wed.-Fri. 10:30am-4:30pm, Tues. 10:30am-8pm, Sat. 10am-5pm, Sun. and holidays noon-5pm. $7, seniors, students, and children $3.50; free Tues. Check out the free jazz in the courtyard Tues. after 4:30pm.

Museum of Science and Industry, 5700 S. Lake Shore Dr. (684-1414), housed in the only building left from the 1893 World's Columbian Exposition. In Hyde Park; take bus #6 "Jeffrey Express" to 57th St. Hands-on exhibits ensure a crowd of grabby kids. Highlights include the Apollo 8 command module, a German submarine, a full-sized replica of a coal mine, and an exhibit on learning disabilities. OmniMax Theater shows; call for showtimes and prices. Open Sun.-Thurs. 9:30am-5:30pm, Fri. 9:30am-9pm; Labor Day-Memorial Day Mon.-Fri. 9:30am-4pm, Sat.-Sun. 9:30am-5:30pm. $6, seniors $5, ages 5-12 $2; with Omnimax $10/$8/$3.50; free Thurs.

Field Museum of Natural History (922-9410), Roosevelt Rd. at Lake Shore Dr. in Grant Park. Take bus #146 from State St. Geological, anthropological, botanical, and zoological exhibits. Don't miss the Egyptian mummies, the Native American Halls, the Hall of Gems, and the dinosaur display. Open daily 9am-5pm. $5, students, seniors, and ages 3-17 $3, families $16; free Thurs.

The Adler Planetarium, 1300 S. Lake Shore Dr. (922-STAR/7827), in Grant Park. Discover your weight on Mars, read the news from space, and examine astronomy tools of the past. Don't forget the spectacular Skyshow. Open daily 9am-5pm, Fri. until 9pm. Skyshow daily 10am, and hourly 1-4pm; also Fri. hourly 6-8pm. $4, seniors and ages 4-17 $2; free Tues.

Shedd Aquarium, 1200 S. Lake Shore Dr. (939-2438), in Grant Park. The world's largest indoor aquarium with over 6600 species of fresh and saltwater fish in 206 tanks. The Oceanarium features small whales, dolphins, seals, and other marine mammals. Check out the Pacific Ocean exhibit, complete with simulated crashing waves. Parking available. Open daily 9am-6pm; Labor Day-Memorial Day Mon.-Fri. 9am-5pm, Sat.-Sun. 9am-6pm. Feedings Mon.-Fri. 11am and 2pm. Combined admission to Oceanarium and Aquarium $10, seniors and ages 3-11 $8; Thurs. Aquarium free, Oceanarium ½-price. Buy weekend tickets in advance through Hot Tix or Ticketmaster.

The Museum of Contemporary Art, 220 E. Chicago Ave. (280-2660), take the #66 Chicago Ave. bus. A splendid addition to Chicago's power-packed museum line-up, the MCA supplies both permanent and temporary collections of modern art (work since 1945). Warhol, Javer, and Nauman highlight a vibrant listing of artists. Open Tues. 11am-6pm, Wed. 11am-9pm, Thurs.-Sun. 11am-6pm. $6.50, students and seniors $4, children under 12 free.

Chicago Historical Society (642-4600), N. Clark St. at North Ave. A research center for scholars with a museum open to the public. Founded in 1856, 19 years after the city was incorporated, to record events. Permanent exhibit on America in the age of Lincoln, plus changing exhibits. Open Mon.-Sat. 9:30am-4:30pm, Sun. noon-5pm. $3, students and seniors $2; free Mon. Library and reading room closed Sun.-Mon.

Spertus Institute of Jewish Studies, 618 S. Michigan Ave. (322-1747), downtown. Upstairs, observe a fabulous collection of synagogue relics from around the world. Downstairs, dig in the sands of artifact hill, built inside the museum. $4, students and seniors $2. Open Sun.-Thurs. 10am-5pm, Fri. 10am-3pm. Artifact center open Sun.-Thurs. 1-4:30pm.

Terra Museum of American Art, 666 N. Michigan Ave. (664-3939), at Eric St. Excellent collection of American art from colonial times to the present, with a focus on 19th-century American Impressionism. Free tours Tues.-Sun. noon and 2pm. Open Tues. noon-8pm, Wed.-Sat. 10am-5pm, Sun. noon-5pm. $3, seniors $2, under 14, teachers, and students with ID free; free Tues.

Museum of Broadcast Communications (629-6000), at Michigan and Washington. Celebrate couch-potato culture with exhibits on America's pastime: zonking out with the tube. Open Mon.-Sat. 10am-4:30pm, Sun. noon-5pm. Free.

The Loop

When Mrs. O'Leary's cow kicked over a lantern and started the Great Fire of 1871, Chicago's downtown flamed into a pile of ashes. The city rebuilt with a vengeance, turning the functional into the fabulous to create one of the most concentrated clusters of architectural treasures in the world.

The downtown area, hemmed in by the Chicago River and Lake Michigan, rose up rather than out. Take a few hours to explore this street museum either at your own pace or on a **walking tour** organized by the Chicago Architectural Foundation. Tours start from the foundation's bookstore/gift shop at 224 S. Michigan Ave. (922-3432). Learn to recognize Louis Sullivan's arch, the Chicago window, and Mies van der Rohe's revolutionary skyscrapers. Two 2-hr. tours are offered: one of early skyscrapers, another of modern ($10 for one, $15 for both). The foundation also provides a 1½-hr. boat tour of the city departing from the Wendella pier at Michigan Ave. ($18).

You can watch the frantic trading of Midwestern farm goods at the world's oldest and largest commodity exchange, the **Futures Exchange** or the **Chicago Board of Options Exchange,** both located in **The Board of Trade Building,** 400 S. LaSalle (435-3590); just look for Ceres, the grain goddess, towering 609 ft. above street level. (Tours Mon.-Fri. 9:15am, every ½hr. 10am-12:30pm. Open Mon.-Fri. 9am-2pm. Free.) The third exchange is the **Chicago Mercantile Exchange,** 30 S. Wacker (930-8249), at Madison.

In the late 19th century, Sears and Roebuck, along with competitor Montgomery Ward, created the mail-order catalog business, undercutting many small general stores and permanently altering the face of American merchandising. Today, although the catalog business has faded, the **Sears Tower,** 233 W. Walker (875-9696) remains; more than an office building, at 1707 ft., it stands as a monument to the insatiable lust of the American consumer. Cars become peaceful, orderly ants viewed from the top of this, the second-tallest building in the world. (Open 9am-11pm, Oct.-Feb. 9am-10pm. $6.50, seniors $4.75, children $3.25, families $18. Lines can be long.) **The First National Bank Building and Plaza** rises about 2 blocks northeast at the corner of Clark and Monroe St. The world's largest bank building compels your gaze skyward with its diagonal slope. Marc Chagall's vivid mosaic, *The Four Seasons,* lines the block and sets off a public space often used for concerts and lunchtime entertainment. At the corner of Clark and Washington St. 2 blocks north, **Chicago Temple,** the world's tallest church, sends its steeples toward heaven.

State and Madison, the most famous intersection of "State Street that great street," forms the focal point of the Chicago street grid. Louis Sullivan's **Carson Pirie Scott** store building is adorned with exquisite ironwork and the famous extra-large Chicago window. Sullivan's other masterpiece, the **Auditorium Building,** awaits several blocks south at the corner of Congress and Michigan. Beautiful design and flawless acoustics highlight this Chicago landmark. Next door, the **Sony Fine Arts Theatre,** 418 S. Michigan (939-2119), screens current artistic and foreign films in the grandeur of the **Fine Arts Building** (open daily; $8, students $5.50, seniors or matinee $4.75). Tomorrow's master artists get their start today at **Gallery 37** (744-8925), on State St. between Randolf and Washington. An open-air gallery, staffed by aspiring artists from city schools, offers visitors free tours, art exhibitions, and live performances during the summer months.

Chicago is decorated with one of the country's premier collections of outdoor sculpture. Large, abstract designs punctuate many downtown corners. The Picasso at the foot of the **Daley Center Plaza** (346-3278), at Washington and Dearborn, enjoys the greatest fame. Free concerts play at noon on summer weekdays in the plaza. Across the street rests Joan Miró's *Chicago,* the sculptor's gift to the city. A great Debuffet sculpture sits across the way in front of the **State of Illinois Building.** The building is a postmodern version of a town square designed by Helmut Jahn in 1985;

take the elevator all the way up, where there is a thrilling (and free) view of the sloping atrium, circular floors, and hundreds of employees at work. A few years ago, the city held a contest to design a building costing less than $144 million in honor of the late mayor. The result is the **Harold Washington Library Center,** 400 S. State St. (747-4300), a researcher's dream and an architectural delight. (Tours Mon.-Sat. noon and 2pm, Sun. 2pm. Open Mon. 9am-7pm, Tues. and Thurs. 11am-7pm, Wed., Fri.-Sat. 9am-5pm.)

Near North

The city's ritziest district lies above the Loop along the lake, just past the Michigan Ave. Bridge. A hotly contested international design competition in the 1920s resulted in the **Tribune Tower,** 435 N. Michigan Ave., a Gothic skyscraper which overlooks this stretch. Chicago's largest newspaper, *The Chicago Tribune,* is written here; quotations exalting the freedom of the press adorn the inside lobby. Roam the 8.5 mi. corridors of **Merchandise Mart** (644-4664; entrances on N. Wells and Kinzie), the largest commercial building in the world (so big it needs its own zip code), 25 stories high and two city blocks long. The first two floors are a mall open to the public; the remainder contains showrooms where design professionals converge to choose home and office furnishings, from sofas to restroom signs. (Public tours Mon.-Fri. noon. $8, students over 15 and seniors $7.)

Big, bright, and always festive, Chicago's **Navy Pier** captures the carnival spirit 365 days a year. No small jetty, the mi.-long pier has it all, with a concert pavilion, dining options, nightspots, sight-seeing boats, a spectacular ferris wheel, a crystal garden with palm trees, and an Omnimax theater. Now *that's* America.

Chicago's showy **Magnificent Mile,** a row of glitzy shops along N. Michigan Ave. between Grand Ave. and Division St., can put a magnificent drain on the wallet. Several of these retail stores, including Banana Republic and Crate & Barrel, were designed by the country's foremost architects. Don't miss **Niketown,** 669 N. Michigan Ave. (642-6363), a glorified shoe store, where sports fans can pay homage to the pedicure of their heroes and heroines. The **Chicago Water Tower** and **Pumping Station** (467-7114) hide among the ritzy stores at the corner of Michigan and Pearson Ave. Built in 1867, these two structures survived the Great Chicago Fire. The pumping station houses the multimedia show *Here's Chicago* and a tourist center (see Practical Information, above). Across the street, expensive and trendy stores pack **Water Tower Place,** the first urban shopping mall in the U.S.

Urban renewal has made **Lincoln Park,** a neighborhood just west of the park which bears the same name, a popular choice for upscale residents. Bounded by Armitage to the south and Diversey Ave. to the north, lakeside Lincoln Park offers recreation and nightlife, with beautiful harbors and parks. Cafés, bookstores, and nightlife pack its tree-lined streets; some of Chicago's liveliest clubs and restaurants lie in the area around Clark St., Lincoln Ave., and N. Halsted.

The bells of St. Michael's Church ring in **Old Town,** a neighborhood where eclectic galleries, shops, and nightspots crowd gentrified streets. Absorb the architectural atmosphere while strolling the W. Menomonee and W. Eugenie St. area. In early June, the **Old Town Art Fair** attracts artists and craftsmen from across the country. (Take bus #151 to Lincoln Park and walk south down Clark or Wells St.)

North Side

North of Diversey Ave., the streets of Lincoln Park become increasingly diverse. Supermarket shopping plazas alternate with tiny markets and vintage clothing stores, while apartment towers and hotels spring up between aging two-story houses. In this ethnic no man's land, you can find a Polish diner next to a Korean restaurant, or a Mongolian eatery across the street from a Mexican bar.

Though they finally lost their battle against night baseball in 1988, Wrigleyville residents remain fiercely loyal to the Chicago Cubs. Tiny, ivy-covered **Wrigley Field,** 1060 W. Addison, just east of Graceland, at the corner of Clark, is the North Side's most famous institution (see Sports, p. 437). A pilgrimage here is a must for the serious or curious baseball fan, and for the *Blues Brothers* nut who wants to visit the famous pair's falsified address. After a game, walk along Clark St., one of the city's busiest nightlife districts, where restaurants, sports bars, and music clubs abound. Explore the neighborhood, window shop in the funk, junk, and 70s revival stores. Wrigleyville and Lakeview, around the 3000s and 4000s of N. Clark St. and N. Halsted, are the city's most concentrated gay areas. Partake of midwest tradition at **Waveland Bowl,** 4002 Northwestern, off Addison and Western. It's one of few bowling alleys that's open 24 hours a day, 365 days a year (single games start at $5).

Near West Side

The **Near West Side,** bounded by the Chicago River to the east and Ogden Ave. to the west, assembles a veritable cornucopia of tiny ethnic enclaves. Farther out, however, looms the West Side, one of the most dismal slums in the nation. Dangerous neighborhoods lie alongside safe ones, so always be aware of your location. Greektown, several blocks of authentic restaurants north of the Eisenhower on Halsted, draws people from all over the city.

A few blocks down Halsted (take the #8 Halsted bus), Jane Addams devoted her life to historic **Hull House.** This settlement house bears witness to Chicago's role in turn-of-the-century reform movements. Although the house no longer offers social services, painstaking restoration has made the **Hull House Museum,** 800 S. Halsted (413-5353), a fascinating part of a visit to Chicago. (Open Mon.-Fri. 10am-4pm, Sun. noon-5pm. Free.) The **Ukrainian Village,** centered at Chicago and Western, is no longer dominated by ethnic Ukrainians, but you can still visit the **Ukrainian National Museum,** 2453 W. Chicago Ave. (421-8020; open Thurs.-Sun. 11am-4pm; donations suggested).

Hyde Park and the University of Chicago

Seven mi. south of the Loop along the lake, the **University of Chicago's** (702-9192) beautiful campus dominates the **Hyde Park** neighborhood; get there via the METRA South Shore Line. A former retreat for the city's artists and musicians, the park's community underwent urban renewal in the 50s and now provides an island of intellectualism in a sea of degenerating neighborhoods. University police aggressively patrol the area bounded by 51st St. to the north, Lakeshore Dr. to the east, 61st St. to the south, and Cottage Grove to the west, but don't test the edges of these boundaries. Lakeside Burnham Park, to the east of campus, is relatively safe during the day but dangerous at night.

On campus, U. of Chicago's architecture ranges from knobby, gnarled, twisted Gothic to neo-streamlined high-octane Gothic. Frank Lloyd Wright's famous **Robie House,** 5757 S. Woodlawn (702-8374), at the corner of 58th St., blends into the surrounding trees. A seminal representative of Wright's Prairie School, which sought to integrate house with environment, its low horizontal lines now house university offices. Tours depart daily at noon ($3, students and seniors $1 on Sun.). The **Oriental Institute, Museum of Science and Industry,** and **DuSable Museum of African-American History** (see Museums) are all in or border on Hyde Park. From the Loop, take bus #6 "Jefferson Express" or the METRA Electric Line from the Randolph St. Station south to 59th St.

Oak Park

Oak Park sprouts 10 mi. west of downtown on the Eisenhower Expwy. (I-290). Frank Lloyd Wright endowed the community with 25 of his spectacular homes and buildings; don't miss the **Frank Lloyd Wright House and Studio,** 951 Chicago Ave., with his beautiful 1898 workplace. The neighborhood's **visitors center,** 158 Forest Ave. (708-848-1500), offers maps, guidebooks, and tours of the house and environs. (45-min. tours of the house Mon.-Fri. 11am, 1 and 3pm, Sat.-Sun. every 15min. 11am-4pm. 1-hr. self-guided tours of Wright's other Oak Park homes can be taken with a map and audio cassette available daily 10am-3pm. Guided tours Sat.-Sun. 10:30am, noon, and 2pm. All three types of tours $6, seniors and under 18 $4; combination interior/exterior tour tickets $9/$7. Open daily 10am-5pm.)

Outdoors

A string of lakefront parks fringe the area between Chicago proper and Lake Michigan. On a sunny afternoon, a cavalcade of sunbathers, dog walkers, roller skaters, and skateboarders storm the shore. The two major parks, both close to downtown, are Lincoln and Grant, operated by the Recreation Department (294-2200). **Lincoln Park** extends across 5 mi. of lakefront on the north side, and rolls in the style of a 19th-century English park: winding paths, natural groves of trees, and asymmetrical open spaces. The **Lincoln Park Conservatory** (249-4770) encloses fauna from desert to jungle eco-systems under its glass palace (open daily 9am-5pm; free).

Grant Park, covering 14 blocks of lakefront east of Michigan Ave., follows the 19th-century French park style: symmetrical, ordered, with squared corners, a fountain in the center, and wide promenades. The **Petrillo Music Shell** hosts free summer concerts here; contact the **Grant Park Concert Society,** 520 S. Michigan Ave. (819-0614). Bathe in the colored lights that illuminate **Buckingham Fountain** each night from 9-11pm. The **Field Museum of Natural History, Shedd Aquarium,** and **Adler Planetarium** beckon museum-hoppers to the southern end of the park (if you don't want to walk the mile from the fountain, take bus #146), while the **Art Institute** lies to the northwest (see Museums, p. 430).

On the north side, Lake Michigan lures swimmers to **Lincoln Park Beach** and **Oak St. Beach.** Popular swimming spots, both attract sun worshipers as well. The rock ledges are restricted areas, and swimming from them is illegal. Although the beaches are patrolled 9am-9:30pm, they are unsafe after dark. Call the Chicago Parks District (747-2200) for further info.

Farther Out

In 1885, George Pullman, inventor of the sleeping car, wanted to create a model working environment so that his Palace Car Company employees would be "healthier, happier, and more productive." The town of **Pullman,** the result of this quest, grew up 14 mi. southeast of downtown, and was considered the nation's ideal community until 1894 when a stubborn Pullman decided to fire workers and evict them from their homes. The community soon faded to unrest, eventually becoming the focus of a monumental strike. As the centerpiece of the town, Pullman built **Hotel Florence,** 1111 S. Forrestville Ave. (785-8181); today, the hotel houses a museum and conducts tours of the Pullman Historic District. (Tours leave the hotel on the first Sun. of each month May-Oct. at 12:30 and 1pm. $4, students and seniors $3. 20min. by car, take I-94 to W. 111th St.; by train, take the Illinois Central Gulf Railroad to 111th St. and Pullman or the METRA Rock Island Line to 111th St.)

In **Wilmette,** the **Baha'i House of Worship** (847-256-4400), at Shendan Rd. and Linden Ave., is topped by an 11-sided dome modeled on the House of Worship in Haifa, Israel (open daily 10am-10pm; Oct.-May 10am-5pm; services daily 12:15pm). The **Chicago Botanic Garden** (847-835-5440), on Lake Cook Rd. ½ mi. east of Edens Expwy., pampers vegetation 25 mi. from downtown (open daily 8am-sunset; parking $4 per car, includes admission). Spend an exhausting day at **Six Flags Great America** (847-249-1776), I-94 at Route 132 E., Gurnee, IL, the largest amusement park in the Midwest. (Open daily 10am-10pm; shorter hrs. in spring and fall. $31, over 59 $15.50, ages 4-10 $26; 2-day pass, not necessarily consecutive, $38.)

Steamboat gambling has been embraced by the Midwest as a way to avoid anti-betting laws. The action centers in Joliet, IL. Roll the bones on **Empress River Cruises,** 2300 Empress Dr. (708-345-6789), Rte. 6 off I-55 and I-80, (departs six times daily; Mon.-Fri. boarding is free) or **Harrah's Casino Cruises** (800-342-7724), which accommodates over 1000 "guests."

ENTERTAINMENT

To stay on top of Chicago events, grab a copy of the free weekly *Chicago Reader*, or *New City*, published Thursdays, and available in many bars, record stores, and restaurants. The *Reader* reviews all major shows, with show times and ticket prices. *Chicago* magazine has exhaustive club listings, theater reviews, and listings of music, dance, and opera performances throughout the city. The Friday edition of the *Chicago Tribune* includes a section with music, theater, and cultural listings.

Theater

One of the foremost theater centers of North America, Chicago is also a home to Improv and the Improv-orgy. The city's 150+ theaters show everything from blockbuster musicals to off-color parodies. Downtown theaters cluster around the intersection of Diversey, Belmont, and Halsted (just north of the Loop), and around Michigan Ave. and Madison Ave. Smaller, community-based theaters scatter throughout the city. The "Off-Loop" theaters on the North Side specialize in original drama, with tickets usually $17 and under.

Most theater tickets are expensive, though you can get half-price tickets on the day of performance at **Hot Tix Booths,** 108 N. State St. (977-1755), or at the 6th level of 700 N. Michigan Ave. Buy in person only. Show up 15-20 min. before the booth opens for first dibs. (Open Mon.-Fri. 10am-7pm, Sat. 10am-6pm, Sun noon-5pm.) Phone **Curtain Call** (977-1755) for info on ticket availability, schedules, and Hot Tix booths. **Ticketmaster** (559-0200) supplies tickets for many theaters. Ask about senior, student, and child discounts at all Chicago theaters.

Steppenwolf Theater, 1650 N. Halsted (335-1888), where David fucking Mamet got his goddamn start. Tickets $25-33; ½-price after 5pm Tues.-Fri., after noon Sat.-Sun. Office open Sun.-Mon. 11am-5pm, Tues.-Fri. 11am-8pm, Sat. 11am-9pm.

Goodman Theatre, 200 S. Columbus Dr. (443-3800), presents consistently good original works. Tickets around $28; ½-price after 6pm, or after 1pm for matinee. Box office open 10am-5pm, 10am-8pm show nights, usually Sat.-Sun.

Shubert Theater, 22 W. Monroe St. (902-1500), presents big-name Broadway touring productions. Tickets costs vary with show popularity $25-70. Box office open Sun.-Fri. 10am-6pm, Sat. 10am-4pm.

Victory Gardens Theater, 2257 N. Lincoln Ave. (871-3000). 3 theater spaces. Drama by Chicago playwrights. Tickets $23-28. Box office open 10am-8pm.

Center Theatre, 1346 W. Devon Ave. (508-5422). Solid, mainstream work. Ticket prices vary by show ($10-20). Box office hours vary; usually open noon-5pm.

Annoyance Theatre, 3747 N. Clark (929-6200). Original works that play off pop culture, 7 different shows per week. Often participatory comedy. Tickets ($7-10) sold just before showtime, which is usually 8 or 9pm.

Bailiwick Repertory, 1225 W. Belmont Ave. (327-5252), in the Theatre building. A mainstage and experimental studio space. Tickets from $6. Box office open Wed. noon-6pm, Thurs.-Sun. noon-showtime.

Live Bait Theatre, 3914 N. Clark St. (871-1212). Shows with titles like *Food, Fun, & Dead Relatives* and *Mass Murder II.* Launched a multi-play *Tribute to Jackie* (Onassis, that is). Tickets $6-12. Box office open Mon.-Fri. noon-5pm.

Comedy

Chicago boasts a plethora of comedy clubs. The most famous, **Second City,** 1616 N. Wells St. (337-3992), satirically spoofs Chicago life and politics. Second City graduated Bill Murray and late greats John Candy, John Belushi, and Gilda Radner, among others. Most nights a free improv session follows the show. **Second City Etc.** (642-8189) offers yet more comedy next door. (Shows Mon.-Thurs. 8:30pm, Fri.-Sat. 8 and 11pm, Sun. 9pm. Tickets $11-16, Mon. $5.50. Box office hours for both daily 10:30am-10pm. Reservations recommended; during the week you can often get in if you show up 1hr. early.) The big names drop by and make it up as they go along at **The Improv,** 504 N. Wells (782-6387. Shows Sun. and Thurs. 8pm, Fri.-Sat. 7, 9:30pm, and midnight; but season varies, so call ahead. Tickets $10-13.50.)

Dance, Classical Music, and Opera

Chicago philanthropists built the high-priced, high-art performance center of this metropolis. Ballet, comedy, live theater, and musicals are performed at **Auditorium Theater,** 50 E. Congress Pkwy. (922-2110). From October to May, the **Chicago Symphony Orchestra,** conducted by Daniel Barenboim, resonates at **Orchestra Hall,** 220 S. Michigan Ave. (435-6666). **Ballet Chicago** (251-8838) pirouettes in theaters throughout Chicago (performance times vary; tickets $20-32). The **Lyric Opera of Chicago** performs from September to February at the **Civic Opera House,** 20 N. Wacker Dr. (332-2244). While these places may suck your wallet dry, the **Grant Park Music Festival** affords the budget traveler a taste of the classical for free; from mid-June to late August, the acclaimed **Grant Park Symphony Orchestra** plays a few free evening concerts a week at the Grant Park Petrillo Music Shell (usually Wed.-Sun.; schedule varies; call 819-0614 for details).

Seasonal Events

Like Chicago's architecture, the city celebrates summer on a grand scale. The **Taste of Chicago** festival cooks the eight days up through July fourth. Seventy restaurants set up booths with endless samples in Grant Park while crowds chomp to the blast of big name bands (free entry, food tickets 50¢ each). The first week in June, the **Blues Festival** celebrates the city's soulful, gritty music; the **Chicago Gospel Festival** hums and hollers in mid-June; and Nashville moves north for the **Country Music Festival** at the end of June. The **¡Viva Chicago!** Latin music festival swings in late August, and the **Chicago Jazz Festival** scats Labor Day weekend. All festivals center at the Grant Park Petrillo Music Shell. Call the Mayor's Office Special Events Hotline (744-3370 or 800-487-2446) for more info on all six free events.

Chicago also offers several free summer festivals on the lakeshore, including the **Air and Water Show** in late August, when Lake Shore Park, Lake Shore Dr., and Chicago Ave. witness several days of boat races, parades, hang gliding, and stunt flying, as well as aerial acrobatics by the fabulously precise Blue Angels. In mid-July, the **Chicago to Mackinac Island Yacht Race** begins in the Monroe St. harbor. On Saturdays during the summer, Navy Pier lights the lake with a free fireworks show (595-7437 for times).

The regionally famous **Ravinia Festival** (728-4642), in the northern suburb of Highland Park, runs from late June to early September. The Chicago Symphony Orchestra, ballet troupes, folk and jazz musicians, and comedians perform throughout the festival's 14-week season. (Shows Mon.-Sat. 8pm, Sun. 7pm. Lawn seats $8; other tickets $15-35.) On certain nights the Chicago Symphony Orchestra allows students free lawn admission with a student ID. Call ahead. Roundtrip on the train (METRA) costs about $7; the festival runs charter buses for $12. The bus ride takes 1½ hr. each way.

Sports

The National League's **Cubs** play baseball at **Wrigley Field,** at Clark St. and Addison (831-2827), one of the few ballparks in America that has retained the early grace and intimate feel of the game; it's definitely worth a visit, especially for international visitors who haven't seen a baseball game (tickets $8-19). The **White Sox,** Chicago's American League team, swing on the South Side at the new **Comiskey Park,** 333 W. 35th St. (tickets, $4-18; 924-1000). Da **Bears** play football at **Soldier's Field Stadium,** McFetridge Dr. and S. Lakeshore Dr. (708-615-BEAR/2327). The **Blackhawks** hockey team skates and da **Bulls** basketball team slam-dunks at the **United Center,** 1901 W. Madison, known fondly as "the house that Michael Jordan built." (Blackhawks 455-4500, tickets $15-75; Bulls 943-5800, tickets $15-30) Beware of scalpers who illegally sell tickets at inflated prices outside of sports events. For current sports events, call **Sports Information** (976-1313). For tickets call Ticketmaster (Bulls and Blackhawks: 559-1212, White Sox: 831-1769, Cubs: 831-2827).

GREAT LAKES

NIGHTLIFE

"Sweet home Chicago" takes pride in the innumerable blues performers who have played here. Jazz, folk, reggae, and punk clubs throbulate all over the **North Side.** **Bucktown,** west of Halsted St. in North Chicago, stays open late with bucking bars and dance clubs. Aspiring pick-up artists swing over to Rush and Division, an intersection that has replaced the stockyards as one of the biggest **meat markets** in the world. To get away from the crowds, head to a little neighborhood spot for atmosphere. Full of bars, cafés, and bistros, **Lincoln Park** is influenced by singles and young married couples, as well as by the gay scene. For more raging, raving, and discoing, there are plenty of clubs in River N., in Riverwest, and on Fulton St.

Clubs and Bars

B.L.U.E.S., 2519 N. Halsted St. (528-1012); El to Fullerton, then take the eastbound bus "Fullerton." Cramped, but the music is unbeatable. Success here led to larger relative **B.L.U.E.S. etcetera,** 1124 W. Belmont Ave. (525-8989); El to Belmont, then 3 blocks west on Belmont. The place for huge names: Albert King, Bo Diddley, Dr. John, and Wolfman Washington have played here. Live music every night 9pm-1:30am. Cover for both places Mon.-Thurs. $5, Fri.-Sat. $8.

Buddy Guy's Legends, 754 S. Wabash (427-0333), downtown. Officially Buddy himself only plays in January, but he is known to stop by when he's not on tour. Blues 7 nights per week 5pm-2am, until 3am on Sat. Cover varies.

Metro, 3730 N. Clark (549-0203). Live alternative and alternateen music, ranging from local bands to Soul Asylum and Tom Jones. 18+; occasionally all ages are welcome upstairs. Cover $8-12. Downstairs, the **Smart Bar** (549-4140) is 21+. Cover $5-8. Opening times vary (around 10pm); closes around 4am on weekends.

Shelter, 564 W. Fulton (528-5500). Club kids immersed in pulsating rhythms and lava lamps congregate on several dance floors. Cover $8-10. Opens around 10pm and raves until the wee hours.

Wild Hare & Singing Armadillo Frog Sanctuary, 3350 N. Clark (327-0800), El: Addison. Near Wrigley Field. Live Rastafarian bands play to a swaying, bobbing mass of twentysomethings. Cover $3-5, Mon.-Tues. free. Open daily until 2-3am.

Butch McGuires, 20 W. Division St. (337-9080), at Rush St. Originator of the singles bar. Owner estimates that "over 6500 couples have met here over 23 million glasses of beer and gotten married" since 1961—he's a little fuzzier on divorce statistics. Once you're on Rush St., check out the other area hangouts. Drinks $2-5. Open Sun.-Thurs. 9:30am-2am, Fri. 10am-4am, Sat. 10am-5am.

Jazz Showcase, 636 S. Michigan (427-4846), in the Blackstone Hotel downtown. #1 choice for serious jazz. Big names heat up with impromptu jam sessions during the jazz festival. No smoking. Music Tues.-Thurs. 8 and 10pm, Fri.-Sat. 9 and 11pm, Sun. 4 and 8pm. Cover Tues.-Thurs. $12, Fri.-Sat. $15. Closing time varies.

Zebra Lounge, 1220 N. State St. (642-5140). Small piano bar lined with zebra skins and dark wood. Mostly thirtysomethings, but younger and older visitors drop in. Live music nightly at 9:30pm. Open Sun.-Thurs. 2pm-2am, Fri.-Sat. 2pm-3am.

Melvin B.'s, 1114 N. State St. (751-9897). "I built this place for people to have fun," says the owner. Obviously popular, in a prime downtown location with a pleasant outdoor terrace. Open Sun.-Thurs. 11am-2am, Fri.-Sat. 11am-3am. Wander next door to the **Cactus Cantina** to do battle with their margaritas. *En garde.*

Lounge Ax, 2438 N. Lincoln Ave. (525-6620), in Lincoln Park. Alternative industrial grunge in no particular order batted out Tues.-Sun. until 2am. Cover $5-10.

Roscoe's Bar and Café, 3354 N. Halsted. (281-3355). Primarily gay clientele, but all are welcome. Roscoe's has it all: a pool room, garden terrace, dance floor, café, even a clairvoyant. Occasional live performances. Long Island Iced Tea pitchers, $10. on Sun. Open Sun.-Fri. until 2am, Sat. until 3am.

■ Springfield

Springfield, or "the town that Lincoln loved," owes much to its most distinguished former resident. In 1837, it was Abraham Lincoln, along with eight other "long" legislators (they were all over six feet tall) who successfully moved the state capitol from

Vandalia to Springfield. A veritable hotbed of political activity during these years, the small town hosted the heated Lincoln-Douglas debates of 1858 and attracted the attention of the entire nation. Although the decades leading into and through the twentieth century did not bring the same economic or population growth to Springfield that occurred in either St. Louis or Chicago, the town continues to harbor an intense political environment and welcomes tourists to learn everything—and we mean *everything*—there is to know about Honest Abe.

Practical Information The **Springfield Convention and Visitors Bureau,** 109 N. 7th St. (789-2360 or 800-545-7300), will give you a detailed street map for your stroll through Lincolnland (open Mon.-Fri. 8am-5pm). Write ahead to request a comprehensive info packet. Springfield is accessible via **Amtrak** (753-2013 or 800-872-7245), at 3rd and Washington St. near downtown. Trains run to Chicago (3-4 per day, 4hr., $37) and St. Louis (3 per day, 2½hr., $26). (Open daily 6am-9:30pm.) **Greyhound** has a station at 2351 S. Dirksen Pkwy. (544-8466), on the eastern edge of town. Walk or take a cab to the nearby shopping center, where you can catch bus #10. Roll to Chicago (6 per day, 5hr., $34), Indianapolis (2 per day, 2hr., $46), or St. Louis (4 per day, 5hr., $53). (Open Mon.-Fri. 9am-8pm, Sat. 9am-noon and 2pm-4pm. Lockers $1 per day.) **Springfield Mass Transit District,** 928 S. 9th St. (522-5531), shuttles around town. Pick up maps at transit headquarters, most banks, or the Illinois State Museum. (Buses operate Mon.-Sat. 6am-6pm. Fare 50¢, transfers free.) The city also has authorized the creation of a downtown **trolley system,** designed to take tourists to places of historic interest. (Cost ranges from $1.50 per stop to $8 per day. 522-5531 for more info.) For taxi service, try **Lincoln Yellow Cab** (523-4545 or 522-7766; $1.25 base, $1.50 per mi.). Springfield's **post office:** G 411 E. Monroe (788-7200; open Mon.-Fri. 7:30am-5:30pm), at Wheeler St.; **ZIP code:** 62701; **area code:** 217.

Accommodations and Camping Cheap accommodations await off I-55 and U.S. 36 on Dirksen Pkwy., but bus service from downtown is limited. More expensive downtown hotels may be booked solid on weekdays when the legislature is in session, but ask the visitors bureau about finding reasonable weekend packages. Make reservations as early as possible for holiday weekends and during the State Fair in mid-Aug.

The **Dirksen Inn Motel/Shamrock Motel,** 900 N. Dirksen Pkwy. (522-4900; take bus #3 "Bergen Park" to Milton and Elm St. then walk a few blocks east), has clean, pleasant rooms, and refrigerators (office open 24hr.; singles $27, doubles $29). **Best Rest Inn,** 700 N. Dirksen Pkwy. (522-7961), offers full-sized beds, free local calls, and cable TV (singles $28, doubles $38). **Parkview Motel,** 3121 Clear Lake Ave. (789-1682), take bus #3 to Elm St. and walk 1 block east. The Parkview is well-maintained and is closer to downtown than most other budget accommodations (singles $30, doubles $40). **Mister Lincoln's Campground,** 3045 Stanton Ave. (529-8206), next to the car dealership 4 mi. southeast of downtown, has free showers, tent space ($7 per person, $2 per child), cabins (for 2 with A/C $23, $3 per additional adult, $2 per additional child), and an area for RVs (full hookup $19). Take bus #10.

Food and Nightlife If the urge to eat authentic Springfield cuisine should strike, head to the **Vinegar Hill Mall** area (southeast of downtown, at 1st and Cook St.) for a variety of moderately priced restaurants. In the mall, the **Capitol City Brewery Bar and Grill** (753-5720) cooks up lunch specials and homemade brew; daily specials include 50¢ homemade lagers on Wednesdays. The Grill chefs recommend the Springfield Horseshoe burger, fashioned from ham, prairie toast, cheddar cheese, french fries, and beer. (Open Mon. 11am-2pm, Tues.-Fri. 11am-9pm, Sat. noon-1am; stops serving food at 9pm.) Later at night, **The Atrium** (753-5710) merges with the Capitol City Brewery to provide a full-fledged dance-floor, disco-ball entertainment complex. DJs on weekdays, bands on weekends (21+; cover $5).

Farther north, across from the old state capitol, **The Feed Store,** 516 E. Adam S. St. (528-3355), has homemade soup, deli sandwiches ($2.75-4.50), and a great special—sandwich, soup, and drink for $4.65 (open Mon.-Sat. 11am-3pm). **Saputo's,** 801 E. Munroe at 8th St. (544-2323), 2 blocks from Lincoln's home, dishes up tasty southern Italian cuisine. Try the baked lasagna. (For lunch $4.75, for dinner $10. Open Mon.-Fri. 10:30am-midnight, Sat. 5pm-midnight, Sun. 5-10pm.)

Sights Springfield makes money by re-creating Lincoln's life, and it does so zealously. Park the car and walk from sight to sight, retracing the steps of the man himself (or so they keep telling you). Happily, all Lincoln sights are free. Call 800-545-7300 to verify site hours (winter weather often forces curtailed hours). The **Lincoln Home Visitors Center,** 426 S. 8th St. (492-4150), at Jackson, shows a 19-minute film on "Mr. Lincoln's Springfield" and doles out free tickets to see the **Lincoln Home** (492-4150), the only one Abe ever owned and the main Springfield attraction, sitting at 8th and Jackson in a restored 19th-century neighborhood. (10-min. tours every 5-10min. from the front of the house. Open daily 8:30am-5pm. Arrive early to avoid the crowds.)

A few blocks northwest, at 6th and Adams right before the Old State Capitol, the **Lincoln-Herndon Law Offices** (785-7289) let visitors see how Lincoln spent a day at the office, before the Presidency (open for tours only daily 9am-5pm; last tour at 4pm; donation suggested). Around the corner and to the left, across from the Downtown Mall, sits the magnificent limestone **Old State Capitol** (785-7691). In 1858, Lincoln delivered his stirring and prophetic "House Divided" speech here, warning that the nation's contradictory slavery policy risked dissolution. The rotunda houses a display of the manuscript copy of Lincoln's "Gettysburg Address." The capitol also witnessed the famous Lincoln-Douglas debates which catapulted Lincoln to national prominence. (Open daily 9am-5pm, last tour at 4pm. Donation suggested.) Opened in 1877, the **New State Capitol** (782-2099), 4 blocks away at 2nd and Capitol, engrosses with murals of Illinois pioneer history and an intricately designed dome. Sneak a closer peek at the façade through the free sidewalk telescopes in front of the building. (Tours by appointment only. Building open Mon.-Fri. 8:30am-4pm, Sat. first floor only 8am-3:30pm.) Enter at 1500 Monument Ave., north of town, to view the **Lincoln Tomb** (782-2717), at Oak Ridge Cemetery. Lincoln, his wife, and three sons rest here (open daily 9am-5pm).

If Lincoln-mania begins to bring you down, walk to the **Dana-Thomas House,** 301 E. Lawrence Ave. (782-6776), 6 blocks south of the Old State Capitol. Built in 1902, the stunning and well-preserved home was one of Frank Lloyd Wright's early experiments in Prairie Style and still features Frank's original fixtures. (1-hr. tours every 15-20min. $3, children $1. Open Wed.-Sun. 9am-5pm.) The **Illinois State Museum** (782-7386), Spring and Edwards St., houses contemporary Illinois art and displays on the area's Native American inhabitants (open Mon.-Sat. 8:30am-5pm, Sun. noon-5pm; free).

With 66 bells, the **Thomas Rees Carillon** (753-6219), in **Washington Park Botanical Gardens** (753-6228), rings true as the third largest carillon in the world and one of the few to offer visitors a view of the bells and playing mechanism (tours June-Aug. Tues.-Sun. noon-sunset; also spring and fall weekends). Springfield's renowned Fourth of July shebang, called (surprise!) **Lincolnfest,** more than doubles the town's population with fireworks and plenty of patriotism. For Lincoln's more ambitious fans, the **New Salem Historic Site** (632-4000), 20 mi. NW of Springfield near Petersburg on Rte. 97, can be accessed by Jefferson St. With real Lincoln logs, the site has been constructed to show the workings of a prairie town during the early 19th century. (Open Mar.-Oct. 9am-5pm, Nov.-Feb. 8am-4pm. Call ahead for summer theatre schedules.)

Wisconsin

Oceans of milk and beer flood the Great Lakes' most wholesome party state. French fur trappers first explored this area in search of lucrative furry creatures. Years later, miners burrowed homes in the hills during the 1820s lead rush (earning them the nickname "badgers") and hearty Norsemen set to clearing vast woodlands. By the time the forests fell and the mines were exhausted, German immigrant farmers had planted rolling fields of barley amidst the state's 15,000 lakes and made Wisconsin the beer capital of the nation. Today, visitors to "America's Dairyland" flock past cheese-filled country stores to delight in the ocean-like vistas of Door County, as well as the ethnic fêtes (and less refined beer bashes) of Madison and Milwaukee.

PRACTICAL INFORMATION

Capital: Madison.
Division of Tourism: 123 W. Washington St., P.O. Box 7606, Madison 53707 (608-266-2161; 800-432-8747 out of state).
Time Zone: Central (1hr. behind Eastern). **Postal Abbreviation:** WI.
Sales Tax: 5½%.

■ Milwaukee

A mecca of drink and festivals, Milwaukee is a city given to celebration. The influx of immigrants, especially German and Irish, gave the city its reputation for *gemütlich-keit (*hospitality). The ethnic communities take turns throwing city-wide parties each summer weekend; some bars even curtail weekend activities in the summer, realizing that the crowds will be at the fiestas. The city's notorious beer industry adds to the revelry, supplying the city's more than 1500 bars and taverns with as much brew as anyone could ever need. Aside from merrymaking, Milwaukee's attractions include top-notch museums, beautiful German-inspired architecture, delicious frozen custard, and a long expanse of scenic lakeshore.

PRACTICAL INFORMATION

Tourist Office: Greater Milwaukee Convention and Visitors Bureau, 510 W. Kilbourne (273-7222 or 800-231-0903), downtown. Open Mon.-Fri. 8am-5pm; in summer also Sat. 9am-2pm. Another location in Grand Avenue Mall at 3rd St. Open Mon.-Fri. 10am-8pm, Sat. 10am-7pm, Sun. 11am-5pm.
Airport: General Mitchell International, 5300 S. Howell Ave. (747-5300). Take bus #80 from 6th St. downtown (30min.). **Limousine Service,** 769-9100 or 800-236-5450. 24-hr. pick-up and drop-off from most downtown hotels with reservation. $7.50, roundtrip $14.
Trains: Amtrak, 433 W. St. Paul Ave. (271-0840 or 800-872-7245), at 5th St. 3 blocks from bus terminal. The area is fairly safe in daylight, less so at night. To: Chicago (6 per day, 2hr., $25); St. Paul (1 per day, 5hr., $72). Open daily 5:30am-9pm.
Buses: Greyhound, 606 N. 7th St. (272-2156 or 800-231-2222), off W. Michigan St. downtown. To: Chicago (17 per day, 2hr., $12); Minneapolis (5 per day, 7½hr., $47). Station open 24hr.; office open daily 6:30am-11:30pm. **Wisconsin Coach** (544-6503 or 542-8861), in the same terminal, services southeast Wisconsin. **Badger Bus,** 635 N. 7th St. (276-7490), across the street, burrows to Madison (6 per day, 1½hr., $9). Open daily 6:30am-10pm. Neither station is very safe at night.
Public Transportation: Milwaukee County Transit System, 1942 N. 17th St. (344-6711). Efficient metro area service. Most lines run 4:30am-2am. Fare $1.35, seniors with Medicare card and children under 12 65¢. Weekly pass $10.50/$6.50. Free maps at library or at Grand Ave. Mall info center. Call for schedules.
Taxi: Veteran, 291-8080. $1.75 base, $1.50 per mi., 50¢ per additional passenger.
Car Rental: Rent A Wreck, 4210 W. Silver Spring Dr. (464-1211). Rates from $15 per day with 50 free mi., 15¢ each additional mi. Insurance $3.50 per day. Ages 25

and up need major credit card or $150 cash deposit. Ages 21-25 add $10; need major credit card. Open Mon.-Fri. 8am-6pm, Sat. 8am-1pm.
Hotlines: Crisis Intervention, 257-7222. **Rape Crisis Line,** 542-3828. Both 24hr.
Gay People's Union Hotline, 562-7010. Open daily 7-10pm.
Emergency: 911.
Post Office: 345 W. St. Paul Ave. (270-2004), south along 4th Ave. from downtown next to the Amtrak station. Open Mon.-Fri. 7:30am-8pm. The airport post office is open 24hr. **ZIP code:** 53203. **Area code:** 414.

Most north-south streets are numbered, increasing from Lake Michigan toward the west. Downtown Milwaukee lies between **Lake Michigan** and 10th St. Addresses increase north and south from **Wisconsin Ave.,** the center of east-west travel.

ACCOMMODATIONS

Downtown lodging options tend toward the pricey; travelers with cars should head out to the city's two hostels. **Bed and Breakfast of Milwaukee** (277-8066) finds rooms in local B&Bs (from $55).

University of Wisconsin at Milwaukee (UWM), Sandburg Halls, 3400 N. Maryland Ave. (229-4065 or 299-6123). Take bus #30 north to Hartford St. Convenient to nightlife and east-side restaurants. Laundry facilities, cafeteria, nightclub, bar, free local calls. Singles with shared bath $25, doubles $33. Clean, bland suites with bath divided into single and double bedrooms: 4 beds $58, 5 beds $69. Parking $5 for 24hr. 2-day advance reservations required. Open June-Aug. 15.

Red Barn Hostel (HI-AYH), 6750 W. Loomis Rd. (529-3299), in Greendale 13mi. southwest of downtown via Rte. 894; take the Loomis exit. Public transportation takes forever and barely comes within a mile; not worth it without a car. Cool, dark rooms with stone walls on the bottom floor of an enormous red barn. Full kitchen, no laundry facilities, campground-quality bathroom. Check-in 5-10pm. $11, nonmembers $14. Open May-Oct.

Wellspring Hostel (HI-AYH), 4382 Hickory Rd. (675-6755), Newburg, take I-43N to Rte. 33W to Newburg; Hickory Rd. intersects Newburg's Main St. The setting, on a riverside vegetable farm, is worth the 45-min. drive if you're looking to get away from the city; 25 beds, kitchen, pool, nature trails, on-site parking. Office open daily 8am-8pm. $15, nonmembers $18. Private room with bath $37.50. Reservations required.

Hotel Wisconsin, 720 N. 3rd St. (271-4900), across from the Grand Avenue Mall. Occupies an impressive Germanesque brick building in the heart of downtown. 250 large, floral rooms with private bath, cable TV, fridge. Small rooms without TV or fridge also available ($49). Free parking. Singles $59, Nov.-Feb. $54; doubles $64; $8 per additional adult. Key deposit $5. Make reservations early.

Motel 6, 5037 S. Howell Ave. (482-4414), next to the airport, delivers a lot of bang for the buck in a remodeled building 15 min. from downtown. Open, airy rooms include AC and cable. Singles $34, doubles $40.

FOOD

Milwaukee is a premier town for food and drink. Don't expect *haute* cuisine, but what the city lacks in glamour it makes up for in grill skill. German brewery masterminds subjected a gold liquid that has been around since 4000BC to refrigeration, glass bottles, cans, and lots of PR, and made **beer** available to all. Milwaukeeans take advantage of nearby Lake Michigan with a local favorite called the Friday night **fish fry.** French ice cream, known as **frozen custard,** is the dairy state's special treat; Milwaukee stands vend flavors like Snow Job and Grand Marnier Blueberry Crisp.

For Italian restaurants, look on **Brady St.** You'll find heavy Polish influences in the **South Side** and good Mexican food sambas at National and S. 16th St. **East Side** eateries are a little more cosmopolitan.

John Hawk's Pub, 100 E. Wisconsin Ave. (272-3199). A riverside terrace and gleaming oak bar complement the wide range of traditional British pub fare (soups $2, sandwiches $4-6). Try the fish fry (2-piece basket $5.25). Live jazz Sat. 9pm; no cover. Open Sun.-Thurs. 10am-10:30pm, Fri.-Sat. 10am-2am.

Leon's, 3131 S. 27th St. (383-1784). A cross between *Grease* and *Starlight Express* (note the roller-skating waitresses). Great frozen custard; 2 scoops $1. Hot dogs 95¢. Open Sun.-Thurs. 11am-midnight, Fri. 11am-12:30am, Sat. 11am-1am.

Abu's Jerusalem of the Gold, 1978 N. Farwell (277-0485), at Lafayette on the East Side. A tiny pink corner restaurant with tapestries, trinkets, and tasty Middle Eastern delights for herbivore and carnivore alike. *Miklube* (rice and vegetables with secret spices) with bread, salad, hummus, and tabouli. Rosewater lemonade 85¢. Open Mon.-Thurs. 11:30am-9pm, Fri.-Sat. 11:30am-11pm, Sun. noon-9pm.

La Casita, 2014 N. Farwell Ave. (277-1177). A wide range of Mexican food served at simple wooden tables. Slightly trendy, with brightly colored walls and crowded outside patio. Entrees $5-8. Open Mon. 4-9:30pm, Tues.-Thurs. 11:30am-10:30pm, Fri.-Sat. 11:30am-midnight, Sun. 3-9pm; Sept.-Mar. Tues.-Thurs. 11:30am-9:30pm, Fri.-Sat. 11:30am-11pm, Sun. 4:30-9:30pm.

SIGHTS

Although many of Milwaukee's breweries have left, the city's name still evokes images of a cold one. No visit to the city would be complete without a look at the yeast in action. **The Miller Brewery,** 4251 W. State St. (931-2337), the corporate giant that produces 43 million barrels of beer annually, offers free one-hr. tours with free samples. (2 tours per hr. Mon.-Sat. 10am-3:30pm; call for winter schedule. Under 19 must be accompanied by adult.) **Pabst Brewing Company,** 915 W. Juneau Ave. (223-3709), offers free 40-min. tours with free tastings (on the hr. Mon.-Fri., 10am-3pm, Sat. 10am-2pm; call for winter schedule). The **Lakefront Brewery,** 818 E. Chambers St. (372-8800), produces five year-round beers and several seasonal specials including pumpkin beer and cherry lager (tours Fri. 5:30pm, Sat. 1:30, 2:30, and 3:30pm; $3—$1 goes to Vietnam Veterans Memorial).

The **Milwaukee County Transit System** (344-6711) runs four-hr. **bus tours** with stops at a brewery and several beautiful churches. (Tours leave the Grand Ave. 2nd St. entrance mid-June to Aug. Mon.-Sat. 12:15pm. $11, under 12 $8.)

A road warrior's nirvana, **Harley-Davidson Inc.,** 11700 W. Capitol Dr. (342-4680), gives one-hr. tours of its engine and transmission facility. (Mon.-Fri. 9, 10:30am, and 12:30pm, but call ahead. Reservations required for groups larger than 7.)

Several excellent museums grace the city of Milwaukee. The **Milwaukee Public Museum,** 800 W. Wells St. (278-2700; 278-2702 for recorded info), at N. 8th St., attracts visitors (especially kids) with dinosaur bones, a replicated Costa Rican rainforest, a Native American exhibit, and a re-created European village. (Open daily 9am-5pm. $5.50, students with ID and ages 4-17 $3.50, seniors $4.50. Parking available.) The lakefront **Milwaukee Art Museum,** 750 N. Lincoln Memorial Dr. (224-3200), in

GREAT LAKES

The Brew Crew

The cars roll in from all over. There are men donning football jerseys; there are shiny-faced families of four (Dad has a gleam in his eye); there are young couples holding hands. What's it all about? You can read it in the glazed-over eyes beholding **giant copper kettles**...BEER. Most tours start in the brewhouse (though the Lakefront Brewery cuts to the chase, starting at the tap). Next is the canning and bottling center, where desperate eyes watch liquid pour into cans as **parched tongues lick parched lips.** In the distribution warehouse, guests stare at freshly packed cases, mentally calculating exactly how long it would take them and their four best buddies to finish it all off. Finally, they get what they came for. At Miller, each guest gets two or three glasses to sample. At Lakefront, it's an **all-you-can-drink affair** while the tour lasts. At Pabst, you must choose two of four brews on tap. Ahh...the golden liquid gently tickles the back of the throat as it descends. The **beer gods** are smiling. Life is good.

the War Memorial Building, houses Haitian art, 19th-century German art, and American sculpture and painting, including two of Warhol's soup cans. (Open Tues.-Wed. and Fri.-Sat. 10am-5pm, Thurs. noon-9pm, Sun. noon-5pm. $5, students, seniors, and disabled $3.) The **Charles Allis Art Museum,** 1801 N. Prospect Ave. (278-8295), at Royal Ave. 1 block north of Brady (take bus #30 or 31), houses a fine collection of Chinese, Japanese, Korean, Persian, Greek, and Roman artifacts. (Open Wed. 1-5pm and 7-9pm, Thurs.-Sun. 1-5pm. $2.)

Better known as "The Domes," the **Mitchell Park Horticultural Conservatory,** 524 S. Layton Blvd. (649-9800), at 27th St., recreates a desert and a rain forest and mounts seasonal displays in a series of seven-story conical glass domes. (Open daily 9am-5pm. $3.25; students, seniors, and disabled $1.75. Take bus #10 west to 27th St., then #27 south to Layton.) The **Boerner Botanical Gardens,** 5879 S. 92nd St. (425-1130), in Whitnall Park between Grange and Rawsen St., boast billions of beautiful blossoms (open mid-April to Oct. daily 8am-sunset; free). County parks line much of Milwaukee's waterfront, providing free recreational areas and trails. **High Roller Bike and Skate Rental** (273-1343), at McKinley Marina in Veteran's Park, has in-line skates ($5 per hr, $17 per day) and bikes ($9 per hr., $33 per day) for your rental enjoyment. (Open daily 10am-8pm, weather permitting. Must be over 18 with ID.) Olympians and unwashed masses alike skate at the **Pettit National Ice Center,** 500 S. 84th St. (266-0100), next to the state fairgrounds.

ENTERTAINMENT

The modern white stone **Performing Art Center (PAC),** 929 N. Water St. (273-7206 or 800-472-4458), across the river from Père Marquette Park, hosts the **Milwaukee Symphony Orchestra,** the **Milwaukee Ballet,** and the **Florentine Opera Company.** (Symphony tickets $14-48, ballet $10-56, opera $12-75, ballet and symphony offer ½-price student and senior tickets on the day of any show.) During the summer, the PAC's Peck Pavilion hosts **Rainbow Summer** (273-7206), a series of free lunchtime concerts—jazz, bluegrass, country, you name it (Mon.-Fri. noon-1:15pm). The **Milwaukee Repertory Theater,** 108 East Wells St. (224-9490), stages shows from September to May (tickets $8-26; ½-price student rush tickets available ½hr. before shows). On summer Thursdays, **Jazz in the Park** (271-1416) presents free concerts in East Town's Cathedral Square Park, at N. Jackson St. between Wells and Kilbourn St. In Père Marquette Park, by the river between State and Kilbourn St., **River Flicks** (286-5700) screens free movies at dusk every Thursday in August.

Summerfest (273-3378; 800-837-3378 outside Milwaukee), the largest and most lavish of Milwaukee's festivals, spans 11 days in late June and early July; daily life halts as a potpourri of big-name musical acts, culinary specialities, and an arts and crafts bazaar take over Maier Festival Park. Locals line the streets for **The Great Circus Parade** (273-7877), in mid-July, a re-creation of turn-of-the-century processions with trained animals, daredevils, costumed performers, and 75 original wagons. In early August, the **Wisconsin State Fair** (266-7000) rolls into the fairgrounds toting big-name entertainment, 12 stages, exhibits, contests, rides, fireworks, and a pie-baking contest ($6, seniors and disabled $5, under 11 free). Ethnic festivals abound during festival season; the most popular are **Polishfest** (529-2140), **Asian Moon** (332-6544), both in mid-June; **Festa Italiana** (223-2180), in mid-July; **Bastille Days** (271-1416), near Bastille Day (July 14); **German Fest** (464-9444), in late July ($6, under 12 free); **Mexican Fiesta** (383-7066), in late August; and **Indian Summer Fest** (774-7119), in early September. Pick up a copy of the free weekly *Downtown Edition* for the full scoop on festivals and other events.

The **Milwaukee Brewers** baseball team plays at **County Stadium,** at the interchange of I-94 and Rte. 41 (933-9000 or 800-933-7890), as do the pigskin-tossing **Green Bay Packers** (342-2717) for some of their home games.

GREAT LAKES

NIGHTLIFE

Milwaukee never lacks for something to do after sundown. Downtown gets a bit seedy at night, but the area along **Water St.** between Juneau and Highland offers slightly yuppified bars and street life. Clubs and bars also cluster near the intersection of **North Ave.** and **N. Farwell St.**, near the UW Campus.

Safehouse, 779 N. Front St. (271-2007), across from the Pabst Theater downtown. A brass plate labeled "International Exports, Ltd." marks the entrance of this truly bizarre world of spy hideouts, James Bond music, mata hari outposts, and drinks with names like Rahab the Harlot. A briefing with "Moneypenny" in the foyer is just the beginning of the intrigue. Draft beer (code name: "liquid gold") $1.50; 24oz. specialty drinks $5 (the glass is a keeper); simple dinners $8-12. Cover $1-2. Open Mon.-Thurs. 11:30am-1:30am, Fri.-Sat. 11:30am-2am, Sun. 4pm-midnight.

Von Trier's, 2235 N. Farwell (272-1775), at North St. Murals, beer steins, and antlers crowd this small, overwhelmingly German establishment. 20 beers on tap (mostly imported) and 74 in bottles ($2.50-5), along with numerous hot drinks and coffees. Service in the lavish interior or on a large outdoor patio (the "beer garden"). Open Sun.-Thurs. 4pm-2am, Fri. Sat. 4pm-2:30am.

ESO$_2$, 1905 E. North Ave. (278-8118). Flashing lights and alternative dance mixes shower down on a large, ventilated dance floor. Look for theme nights (like Tues. retro), with special drink prices (like $3 pitchers). Cover usually $2.

Dance, Dance, Dance, part of **Lacage,** 801 S. 2nd Ave. (383-8330). Caters to a twenty to thirtysomething gay clientele, but all are welcome. Videos accompany dance mixes. Cover Wed.-Thurs. $2, Fri. $3, Sat. $5.

Wolski's Tavern, 1836 N. Pulaski St. (276-8130). The bar with seniority—it's the oldest in the city. Pool, darts, beer ($1.50-2.25), and low-key neighborliness.

■ Madison

The capitol crowns one of Madison's hilltops while the University of Wisconsin presides over the other; together, the two determine the city's character. Sandwiched between Lakes Mendota and Monona, Madison is both staid capital city and exuberant college town. Twentysomething culture (coffee shops, used clothing stores, record shops, bicycle paths on the streets) dominates the area, without completely edging out Wisconsin-centric museums and senators in suits.

Practical Information The **Greater Madison Convention and Visitors Bureau,** 615 E. Washington Ave. (255-2537 or 800-373-6376; open Mon.-Fri. 8am-5pm). **Greyhound,** 2 S. Bedford St. (257-3050 or 800-231-2222), has buses to Chicago (8 per day, 3-5hr., $17) and Minneapolis (6 per day, $37-39). **Badger Bus** (255-6771) departs from the same depot and has trips to Milwaukee (6+ per day, 1hr., $9). The station is open daily from 5:30am-10:30pm. **Madison Metro Transit System,** 1101 E. Washington Ave. (266-4466), travels through downtown, UW campus, and surrounding areas. ($1.25; free Mon.-Sat. 10am-3pm in capitol-UW campus area.) **Post office:** 3902 Milwaukee Ave. (246-1249; open Mon. 7:30am-7pm, Tues.-Fri. 7:30am-6pm, Sat. 8:30am-2pm). **ZIP code:** 53714. **Area code:** 608.

Accommodations and Camping Madison may seem a budget traveler's paradise in some ways, but its low-cost lodging department lacks. At motels stretching along Washington Ave. (U.S. 151), near the intersection with I-90, rates start at $40 per weeknight and rise dramatically on weekends. The **Select Inn,** 4845 Hayes Rd. (249-1815), near the junction of I-90 and U.S. 151, bucks the trend, offering large rooms with cable TV and A/C from $30; continental breakfast included, free local calls. Nearby **Motel 6,** 1754 Thierer Rd. (241-8101), is a solid second choice (from $39, with cable and A/C). Prices steepen downtown, starting around $60. The **Memorial Union,** 800 Langdon St. (265-3000), on the UW campus, has large, elegant rooms with excellent views and cable TV (from $55). **Campers** should head south on

I-90 to Stoughton, where **Lake Kegonsa State Park,** 2405 Door Creek Rd. (873-9695), has 80 sites (½ reserved for walk-ins) in a wooded area ½ mi. from the beach. (Showers, flush toilets. Wisconsin residents weekdays $7, weekends $9; non-residents $9/$11. Parking permits $5 per day, non-residents $7.)

Food and Nightlife Good restaurants pepper Madison; a cluster spice up the university and capitol areas. **State St.** hosts a wide variety of cheap restaurants, both chains and Madison originals. **Taqueria Gila Monster,** 106 King St. (225-6425), stomps out low-fat, high-flavor Mexican food with flair; try the catfish and cactus fillings in your two enchiladas ($3; open Mon.-Thurs. 11am-9pm). **Himal Chuli,** 318 State St. (251-9225), offers *tarkari, dal,* and other Nepali favorites for super-low prices—a full veggie meal goes for around $5, meat meals for $7. (Open Mon.-Sat. 11am-9pm.) **Dotty Dumpling's Dowry,** 116 N. Fairchild (255-3175), is where classic American chow meets the mobile. The award-winning burgers ($3.75, veggie burger $3.80), malts ($3), and 19 beers on tap ($2) are consumed under hanging wooden canoes, blimps, and airplanes. (Open Mon.-Wed. 11am-10pm, Thurs.-Sat. 11am-11pm, Sun. noon-8pm). On Friday nights, the **Essen Haus,** 514 E. Wilson St. (255-4674), plays host to live polka bands, semi-rowdy crowds, and two-gallon hats. At **Crystal's Corner Bar,** 1302 Williamson St. (256-2953), down a draught beer ($1.20-3.25), and groove to live bands, usually blues. (Schedule and cover vary. Open Sun.-Thurs. 11am-2am, Fri.-Sat. 11am-2:30am.)

Sights and Entertainment Between the university and the capitol area, Madison offers many options for sight-seeing. The imposing **State Capitol** (266-0382), in Capitol Square at the center of downtown, boasts beautiful ceiling frescoes and the only granite dome in the U.S. (Free guided tours from the ground floor info desk Mon.-Sat on the hr. 9-11am and 1-4pm, Sun. on the hr. 1-4pm. Open daily 6am-8pm.) Also on Capitol Sq., the **Wisconsin Veterans Museum,** 30 W. Mifflin St. (264-6086), honors Wisconsin soldiers. (Open Tues.-Sat. 9:30am-4:30pm; April-Sept. also Sun. noon-4pm. Free.) The **State Historical Museum,** 30 N. Carroll St. (264-6555), explores the history of Wisconsin's Native American population. (Open Tues.-Sat. 10am-5pm, Sun. noon-5pm. Free.) The **Madison Art Center** (257-0158), inside the civic center, exhibits modern and contemporary art and hosts traveling exhibitions. (Open Tues.-Thurs. 11am-5pm, Fri. 11am-9pm, Sat. 10am-5pm, Sun. 1-5pm. Most exhibits free.)

The **Madison Civic Center,** 211 State St. (266-6550), frequently stages arts and entertainment performances, including the **Madison Symphony Orchestra** (tickets from $20). (Office open Mon.-Fri. 11am-5:30pm, Sat. 11am-2pm. Most seasons run late Aug. to May.) The **Madison Repertory Theatre,** 122 State St. #201 (256-0029), performs classic and contemporary musicals. (Showtimes vary. Tickets $16.50-$19.50.) The free *Isthmus* (printed every Thurs.) covers the entertainment scene.

A few noteworthy museums grace the **University of Wisconsin.** Highlights include the **Geology Museum,** 215 W. Dayton (262-2399; open Mon.-Fri. 8:30am-4:30pm, Sat. 9am-noon) and the **Elvehjem Museum of Art,** 800 University Ave. (263-2246; open Tue.-Fri. 9am-5pm, Sat.-Sun. 11am-5pm; free). Also part of UW, the outdoor **Olbrich Botanical Gardens** and indoor **Bolz Conservatory,** 3330 Atwood Ave. (246-4550), offer a plethora of plants. Inside the conservatory dome, free-flying birds, waterfalls, and tropical plants ignore the Wisconsin weather. (Gardens open daily 8am-8pm; Sept.-May Mon.-Sat. 8am-5pm, Sun. 9am-5pm. Free. Conservatory open Mon.-Sat. 10am-4pm, Sun. 10am-5pm. $1, ages 6-18 50¢, under 5 free; free Wed. and Sat. 10am-noon.) For more info on any UW attraction, visit the **UW Visitors Center** at the corner of Observatory Dr. and N. Park St., on the west side of the Memorial Union.

Family Land (254-7766), off U.S. 12 at Wisconsin Dells just north of Baraboo, splashes with the world's fastest and steepest water slide, a wave pool, a mini golf course, and other instruments of water park fun ($17, water park alone $15, under 3 free). East of Madison, **House on the Rock,** 5754 U.S. 23 (935-3639), in Spring Green, offers spectacular views of the Wyoming Valley from its glass-walled Infinity Room, and a 40-acre complex of gardens and fantastic architecture. (Open daily mid-May to Aug. 9am-8pm, March to mid-May and Sept.-Oct. 9am-7pm. $13.50.)

■ Door County

Door County's 250 mi. of coastline, ten lighthouses, rocky shores, and sandy beaches give the peninsula the atmosphere of a New England seashore. Lake Michigan reinforces the comparison, sending ocean-like waves and riptides to pound the windy eastern shore. With miles of bike paths, acres of orchards, and stunning scenery, Door County—much like the towns of the Atlantic coast—swings open to visitors on a summer-oriented seasonal schedule.

Practical Information Door County Chamber of Commerce, 6443 Green Bay Rd. (743-4456 or 800-52-RELAX/73529), on Rte. 42/57 entering Sturgeon Bay, has free brochures for every village on the peninsula as well as biking maps. (Open Mon.-Fri. 8:30am-5pm, Sat.-Sun. 10am-4pm; mid-Oct. to mid-May. Mon.-Fri. 8:30am-4:30pm.) Just outside the center, the **Inline** computer/phone system lists hotel vacancies and allows free phone calls to listed lodgings. Look for a visitors center in each of the other villages as well. Public transportation comes only as close as **Green Bay,** 50 mi. southwest of Sturgeon Bay, where **Greyhound** has a station at 800 Cedar (414-432-4883). Every day, 5 buses head to Milwaukee; hop aboard for $18. (Station open Mon.-Fri. 6:15am-5:15pm, Sat.-Sun. 10am-1pm and 4-5:15pm.) In Green Bay, rent a car from **Advantage,** 1629 Velp (414-497-2152), 3 mi. from the Greyhound station. ($14 per day, $89 per week; 10¢ per mi.; insurance $5. Must be 25. Open Mon.-Fri. 8:30am-5:30pm, Sat. 8am-3pm.) **Emergency:** 911. Door County's **post office:** 359 Louisiana (743-2681), at 4th St. in Sturgeon Bay (open Mon.-Fri. 8:30am-5pm, Sat. 9:30am-noon). **ZIP code:** 54235. **Area code:** 414.

Door County truly begins north of **Sturgeon Bay,** where Rte. 42 and 57 converge and then split again—Rte. 57 running up the eastern coast of the peninsula, Rte. 42 up the western side. The peninsula juts out 200 mi. northeast of Madison and 150 mi. north of Milwaukee, with no land access except via Sturgeon Bay. Summer (especially July and August) is high season in Door County's 12 villages. The county is less developed and more traditional the farther north you go, and less commercialized in the east. **Fish Creek, Sister Bay,** and **Ephraim,** the county's largest towns, lie on the west side of the peninsula. Anywhere in the area, temperatures can dip to 40°F at night, even in July; dress warmly.

Accommodations and Camping Pricey resorts, hotels, and motels crowd Rte. 42 and Rte. 57 ($60 and up in summer). Camping is as plentiful, and much cheaper. Reserve for July and August as far in advance as possible. **Billerbecks,** 9864 Hidden Spring Rd. (854-2528), Ephraim, off Rte. 42, close to the beach, says hell no to high prices, accepting guests in three clean, beautiful rooms filled with antique furniture (shared bath; rooms $24-27; open late May to late Oct.). The **Century Farm Motel** (854-4069), on Rte. 57, 3 mi. south of Sister Bay, rents small two-room cottages with A/C, TV, private bath, and fridge ($40-55; open mid-May to mid-Oct.). One thousand Barbies, 600 animated store window mannequins, 35 cars, and a bevy of gnome statues grace the premises of the **Chal-A Motel,** 3910 Rte. 42/57 (743-6788), 3 mi. north of the bridge in Sturgeon Bay. Rooms are large. (July-Aug. singles $44, doubles $49; Nov. to mid-May $24/$29; mid-May to June $29/$34.)

Four out of the area's five **state parks** (all except Whitefish Dunes State Park) provide space for camping ($10, Wisconsin residents $8; Fri.-Sat. $12/$10). All state parks require a motor vehicle permit ($7 per day, Wisconsin residents $5; annually $25/$18). **Peninsula State Park,** P.O. Box 218, Fish Creek 54212 (868-3258), by Fish Creek village on Rte. 42, contains the largest of the campgrounds (469 sites), with showers and flush toilets, 20 mi. of shoreline, a golf course, a spectacular view from Eagle Tower, and 17 mi. of hiking trails. Make reservations well in advance (i.e.

6 months), or come in person and put your name on the waiting list for one of the 127 walk-in sites. **Potawatomi State Park,** 3740 Park Dr., Sturgeon Bay 54235 (746-2890), just outside Sturgeon Bay off Rte. 42/57, before you cross the bridge, maintains 125 campsites, half of which are open to walk-ins; write to make reservations for the other half. **Newport State Park** (854-2500) is a wildlife preserve at the tip of the peninsula, 7 mi. from Ellison Bay off Rte. 42. Although it permits entrance to vehicles, all 16 of its sites are accessible only by hiking. To get to **Rock Island State Park** (847-2235), take the ferry from Gill's Rock to Washington Island and another ferry (847-2252; roundtrip $6, campers with gear $7) to Rock Island (40 sites; open mid-April to mid-Nov.).

Private camping options are plentiful on the peninsula, The **Camp-Tel Family Campground,** 8164 Rte. 42 (868-3278), 1 mi. north of Egg Harbor, has tent sites and tiny A-frame cabins, each with two sets of bunks, a loft, and heat. (Sites $15, with water and electricity $17. A-frame $28. Each adult after 2 $5.) **Path of Pines,** 3709 Rte. F (868-3332), 1 mi. east of the ever-packed Peninsula off Rte. 42 in Fish Creek, rents 91 quiet, scenic sites. (Showers, laundry facilities. Tent sites $15-18; with water and electricity $20-23.)

Food and Drink Many people come to Door County just for **fishboils**—not trout blemishes, but a Scandinavian tradition dating back to 19th-century lumberjacks. Cooks toss potatoes, onions, and whitefish into an enormous kettle over a wood fire. To remove the fish oil from the top of the water, the boilmaster (often imported from Scandinavia) judges the proper time to throw kerosene into the fire, producing a massive fireball; the cauldron boils over, signaling chow time—it's much better than it sounds. Most fishboils conclude with a big slice of cherry pie. Door County's best-known fishboils take place at **Edgewater Restaurant** (854-4034), in Ephraim (May-Oct. Mon.-Sat. evenings; call for times; $12.50, under 12 $8.50; reservations recommended), and **The Viking** (854-2998), in Ellison Bay (mid-May to Oct. every ½hr. 4:30-8pm; $11, under 12 $8; indoor/outdoor). **Al Johnson's Swedish Restaurant** (854-2626), in Sister Bay on Rte. 42 down the hill and 2 blocks past the info center on the right, has excellent Swedish food ($8-17), waitstaff in traditional Swedish dress, and goats who dine daily (weather permitting) on the thick sod roof (open daily 6am-9pm; in winter Mon.-Sat. 6am-8pm, Sun. 7am-8pm). **Bayside Tavern** (868-3441), on Rte. 42 in Fish Creek, serves serious burgers ($2.50-4.75) and a delicious Friday perch fry ($9). At night, it's a crowded bar with live blues on Mondays (cover $2), Tuesday pint nights, and open-mike Wednesdays. (Open Sun.-Thurs. 11am-2am, Fri.-Sat. 11am-2:30pm.)

Sights and Activities Biking is the best way to take in the breathtaking scenery, lighthouses, rocks, and white sand beaches of Door's coastline; ask for free bike maps at tourist offices. **Whitefish Dunes State Park** heaps high with sand dunes, hiking/biking/skiing trails, and a well-kept wildlife preserve. (Open daily 8am-8pm. Vehicle permit required.) Just north on Cave Point Rd. off Rte. 57, **Cave Point County Park** stirs the soul with its rocky coastline and some of the most stunning views on the peninsula (open daily 6am-9pm; free). At Jacksonport, **Lakeside Park,** immortalized in song by the rock band *Rush,* offers a wide, sandy expanse of beach backed by a shady park and playground (open daily 6am-9pm; free). South of Bailey's Harbor off Rte. 57, follow Kangaroo Lake Rd. to **Kangaroo Lake,** the largest of the eight inland lakes on this thin peninsula; circle the lake to find your own secluded swimming spot in waters warmer than Lake Michigan's. Trails at the **Ridges Sanctuary** (839-2802), north of Bailey's Harbor off County Rte. Q, enable exploration of over 17 sand ridges and a type of forest unique to the area. (Nature center open daily 9am-4pm. Free.) At **Peninsula State Park,** in Fish Creek, visitors ride mopeds and bicycles along 20 mi. of shoreline road, rent boats, and sunbathe at **Nicolet Beach.** At the top of **Eagle Tower,** 1 mi. and 110 steps up from the beach, you can see clear across the lake to Michigan. (Open daily 6am-11pm. Vehicle permit required.) At the park entrance, **Edge of Park Bike Rentals,** 4007 Rte. 41 (868-3344), rents six-speed bikes ($5 per hr., $20 per day) and mopeds ($24 per hr.). For more satisfying hiking, try **Newport State Park,** 6 mi. east of Ellison Bay on Newport Dr. off Rte. 42. The park also encompasses a 3000-ft. swimming beach and 13 mi. of shoreline on Lake Michigan and inland Europe Lake (no vehicles).

There's more to Door County than parks. The award-winning **Door Peninsula Winery,** 5806 Rte. 42 (743-7431 or 800-551-5049), Sturgeon Bay, invites you to partake of 30 different wines (15-20min. tours and tastes in summer daily 9am-6pm; off season 9am-5pm). If you're dry-minded, the **Peninsula Players** (868-3287), off Rte. 42 in Fish Creek, do their thing in America's oldest professional resident summer theater (shows in summer Tues.-Fri.; call for details). The shipping and packing town of **Green Bay,** the largest city anywhere near Door County, is home to the oldest NFL team, the **Green Bay Packers** (496-5719 for tickets; $24-28). The city also packs pollution, noise, and industry, as well as plenty of bars and a little gambling. **The Oneida Bingo and Casino** (414-497-8118), County Rte. GG southwest of downtown, antes up with 1300 slot machines open 24 hr. and 47 blackjack tables open daily 10am-4am (18+). The **National Railroad Museum,** 2285 S. Broadway, Green Bay (414-435-7245), exhibits steam and diesel—yes, trains. (Open daily 9am-5pm; $6, ages 6-15 $3.)

■ Apostle Islands

Long ago, pious Frenchmen mistakenly believed there were only 12 islands off the coast of Wisconsin. They named them the Apostle Islands. Over the years, the area has been successively claimed by Native Americans, loggers, quarrymen, and fishermen. Today, a National Lakeshore protects 21 of the islands, as well as a 12-mi. stretch of mainland shore; summer tourists visit the islands' caves by the thousands, camping on the unspoiled sandstone bluffs and foraging for wild raspberries.

Practical Information All Apostle Islands excursions begin in the sleepy mainland town of **Bayfield** (pop. 686), in northwest Wisconsin on the Lake Superior coast. The nearest **bus** station, 101 W. Main St. (682-4010), in **Ashland,** 22 mi. southeast of Bayfield on U.S. 2, has service to Duluth (1 per day, 1½hr., $15). The **Bay Area Rural Transit (BART),** 300 Industrial Park Rd. (682-9664), in Ashland, offers a shuttle to Bayfield (4 per day; Mon.-Fri. 7am-3:20pm; $1.80, students $1.50, seniors $1.10). The **Bayfield Chamber of Commerce,** 42 S. Broad St. (779-3335 or 800-447-4094), has helpful info on the area, including accommodations. (Open Mon.-Sat. 9am-5pm, Sun. 10am-2pm.) **National Lakeshore Headquarters Visitors Center,** 410 Washington Ave. (779-3397), distributes hiking and camping info and free **camping** permits. Many sites are primitive (open daily 8am-6pm; in winter Mon.-Fri. 8am-4:30pm). For the latest assessment of the area's unpredictable **weather,** call 682-8822. The Apostle Island and Bayfield **area code** is 715.

Accommodations, Camping, and Food During summer months, the pickings are slim for the budget traveler in Bayfield. The best deal in town is the **Frostman Home,** 24 N. 3rd St., Bayfield (779-3239), with three large, comfy rooms (two with lake views) just a block from town. (Open mid-May to mid-Oct. Singles and doubles $30.) **The Seagull Bay Motel** (779-5558), off Rte. 13 at 7th St. in Bayfield, offers spacious, clean rooms (from $40; mid-Oct. to mid-May $25). **Dalrymple Park,** ¼ mi. north of town on Rte. 13, offers 30 **campsites** under tall pines on the lake (no showers; $10, with electricity $11; no reservations). **Apostle Islands View Campground** (779-5524), ½ mi. south of Bayfield on County Rd. J off Rte. 13, lives up to its name with modern sites which overlook the islands. (Sites $12, with hookup $15, with hookup and cable $19. Reservations recommended one month in advance in July-Aug.) For info on more expensive **guest houses** ($25-200), inquire at the chamber of commerce.

Maggie's, 257 Maypenny Ave. (779-5641), the local watering hole, prepares burgers ($5) and gourmet specials in flamingo-filled decor. (Open Sun.-Thurs. 11am-

10pm, Fri.-Sat. 11am-11pm.) For local flavor and any kind of pie (whole pies $6-10), try the **Gourmet Garage** (779-5365), just south of Bayfield on Rte. 13 (open daily 9am-6pm). **Greunke's Restaurant,** 17 Rittenhouse Ave. (779-5480), at 1st St., specializes in huge, cheap diner-style breakfasts ($3.25-5.75) by day and locally famous fishboils on summer nights at 6:30pm ($11, kids $5.50; call for additional times).

Getting Around and Activities Though often overshadowed by Bayfield and Madeline Island (see below), the other 21 islands have subtle charms of their own. The sandstone quarries of Basswood and Hermit Islands, as well as the abandoned logging and fishing camps on some of the other islands, serve as mute reminders of a more vigorous era. The restored **lighthouses** on Sand, Raspberry, Michigan, Outer, and Devil's Islands offer spectacular views of the surrounding country. Sea caves, carved out by thousands of years of winds and water, pocket the shores of several islands; a few on Devil's Island are large enough to explore by boat. The narrated three-hour cruises organized by the **Apostle Islands Cruise Service** (779-3925 or 800-323-7619) allow visitors a chance to see all of these sights without paying the exorbitant prices charged by other companies. (Tours depart the Bayfield City Dock mid-May to mid-Oct. daily 10am. $22, kids $11.) From late June to mid-August, the cruise service runs an inter-island shuttle that delivers campers and lighthouse-ophiles to their destinations. The best **beach** on the mainland is just south of Bayfield along Rte. 13, near Sioux Flats; watch for a poorly marked path to the left about 7 or 8 mi. out of town. Due to the extreme cold, **swimming** in Lake Superior can be quite uncomfortable. For alternative modes of transportation, stop by **Trek and Trail** (800-354-8735), on the corner of Rittenhouse and Broad St.

Not just a base town for the islands, Bayfield is the proud home of some awfully good apples. The town grows vibrant in early October, when up to 60,000 gather for the **Apple Festival.** For freshly picked orchard taste, make your way to the **Bayfield Apple Company** (779-5700), on Betzold Rd. (open Sept.-Jan. daily 9am-6pm).

Madeline Island A few hundred years ago, the Chippewa came to **Madeline Island** from the Atlantic in search of the *megis shell,* a light in the sky purported to bring prosperity and health. Today, the island maintains a more natural allure, as thousands of visitors each summer seek the clean and sandy beaches of this relaxing retreat. Towards the end of the day, head to **Sunset Bay** on the island's north side and see why the bay got its name.

With roughly five streets, Madeline Island is easy to navigate by foot, bike, or car. The **Madeline Island Chamber of Commerce** (747-2801), on Main St., can help you find accommodations (open daily 10am-4pm). **Madeline Island Ferry Line** (747-2051 or 747-6801) shuttles between Bayfield and **La Pointe,** on Madeline Island. (20-min. summer ferries daily every 30min. 7am-11pm. $3, ages 6-11 $1.75, bikes $1.50, cars $7—driver not included. March-June and Sept.-Dec. ferries run less frequently and prices drop.) In winter, the state highway dept. sets up a road across the ice. During transition periods the ferry service runs windsleds between the island and the mainland (take a hat). Rent a moped from "Moped Dave" at **Motion to Go,** 102 Lake View Pl. (747-6585), about 1 block from the ferry. ($10 per hr., $45 per day. Mountain bikes $5/$18. Tandem bikes $8/$30. Open mid-May to early Oct. 10am-8pm.) La Pointe's **post office:** (747-3712), just off the dock on Madeline Island (open Mon.-Fri. 9am-4:20pm, Sat. 9:30am-12:50pm). **ZIP code:** 54850.

Rooms in the area fill during the summer; call ahead for reservations. The **Madeline Island Motel** (747-3000) has clean rooms named for local historical personalities. (Singles $65, doubles $70. May to mid-June and Oct.-Nov. $55/$60. Dec.-April all rooms $40.) Madeline Island has two campgrounds. **Big Bay Town Park** (747-6913), 6½ mi. from La Pointe out Big Bay Rd., sits right next to beautiful Big Bay Lagoon (sites $9, with electricity $11). Across the lagoon, **Big Bay State Park** (747-6425; Bayfield office 779-4020) rents 55 primitive sites ($8-12; daily vehicle permit $7, $5 for Wisconsinites). Sites can be reserved by mail for an extra $3. The **Island Café** (747-6555), 1 block to the right from the ferry exit, knows how to serve up a hefty meal ($3-7), even to a vegetarian. The whitefish and trout meals ($10.50) are dinner classics (open daily 8am-10:30pm). **Grampa Tony's** (747-3911), next to the chamber of commerce, offers no-frills dining. (Sandwiches $4-5.25, salads $2.50-5.75, ice cream $1.25 and up.)

Minnesota

Overwhelming expanses of isolated wilderness blanket most of northern Minnesota. This is a land that spawns giants in the imagination, like Mesabi of Native American legends and, in more recent lore, Paul Bunyan and his blue ox Babe. In the south, the Twin Cities produce proud urban giants of their own, in defiance of the north's raw nature; pop star Prince casts a purple shadow over his hometown, and the Pillsbury Doughboy chuckles for the world. Hee, hee...

PRACTICAL INFORMATION

Capital: St. Paul.
Minnesota Office of Tourism: 100 Metro Sq., 121 7th Pl. E., St. Paul 55101-2112 (612-296-5029 or 800-657-3700). Open Mon.-Fri. 8am-5pm.
Time Zone: Central (1hr. behind Eastern). **Postal Abbreviation:** MN.
Sales Tax: 6.5-7%.

■ Minneapolis and St. Paul

From modest beginnings as a Mississippi River outpost to a tenure as transportation hub and then wheat and flour mecca, the Twin Cities have steadily and jointly evolved with the times. Today they possess many of the same characteristics as the rest of the state, but with an urban twist. The Minnesota accent is muted in this area, while collegiate spirit, nightlife, and high culture are more pronounced. Here, consumer yuppie culture (cruise the Mall of America), the wanna-be youth punk world (slink into any of the myriad cafés), and corporate America (check out downtown and the skyway systems) thrive in a state of peaceful coexistence.

PRACTICAL INFORMATION

Tourist Office: Minneapolis Convention and Visitors Association, 40 S. 7th St. (335-5827), in the **City Center Shopping Area,** 2nd level skyway. Open Mon.-Fri. 9:30am-8pm, Sat. 9:30am-6pm, Sun. noon-5pm. **St. Paul Convention and Visitors Bureau,** 101 Northwest Center, 55 E. 5th St. (297-6985 or 800-627-6101). Open Mon.-Fri. 8am-5pm. For 24-hr. info on local events, call **Cityline** (645-6060) or **The Connection** (922-9000).
Airport: Twin Cities International, south of the cities on I-494 in Bloomington (726-8100). Take bus #7 to Washington Ave. in Minneapolis or bus #54 to St. Paul. **Airport Express** (726-6400) shuttles to the downtowns and some hotels roughly every ½hr. 6am-11pm. To St. Paul $8, to Minneapolis $10.
Trains: Amtrak, 730 Transfer Rd. (644-1127 or 800-872-7245), on the east bank off University Ave. SE, between the Twin Cities. Bus #7 runs to St. Paul, #16 connects to both downtowns. To Chicago (1 per day, 7½hr., $75) and Milwaukee (1 per day, 6hr., $72). Open daily 7:15am-midnight.
Buses: Greyhound: In Minneapolis, 29 9th St. (371-3323), at 1st Ave. N. Very convenient. To Chicago (11 per day, 9-11hr., $52) and Milwaukee (9 per day, 7hr., $47). Open 24hr. with security. In **St. Paul** (222-0509), at 7th St. and St. Peter, 3 blocks east of the Civic Center. In a somewhat unsafe area. To Chicago (5 per day, 8-11hr., $51) and Milwaukee (6 per day, 7hr., $49). Open daily 5:30am-9pm.
Public Transportation: Metropolitan Transit Commission, 560 6th Ave. N. (373-3333). Buses service both cities Mon.-Fri. 6am-11pm, Sat.-Sun. 7am-11pm; some buses operate 4:30am-12:45am, others shut down earlier. Peak fare (Mon.-

Fri. 6-9am and 3:30-6:30pm) $1.50. Off peak $1; seniors, disabled, and ages 5-12 50¢. Express 50¢ extra. Bus #16 connects the 2 downtowns (50min.); express bus #94 is faster (25-30min.).

Car Rental: Thrifty Car Rental, 160 E. 5th St. (227-7690). Starting from $20 per day with 150 free mi.; 16¢ each additional mi. Must be 21 with major credit card. Under 25 surcharge $10 per day.

Taxis: In Minneapolis, **Yellow Taxi,** 824-4444. In St. Paul, **Town Taxi,** 331-8294. Both charge $1.75 base fare, $1.30 per mi.

Hotlines: Crime Victim Center, 822 S. 3rd St., St. Paul (340-5400). **Rape/Sexual Assault Line,** 825-4357. Both open 24hr. **Gay-Lesbian Helpline,** 822-8661 or 800-800-0907. Open Mon.-Fri. noon-midnight, Sat. 4pm-midnight. **Gay-Lesbian Information Line,** 822-0127. Open 8:30am-5pm.

Emergency: 911.

Post Office: In **Minneapolis** (349-4957), 1st St. and Marquette Ave., next to the Mississippi River. Open Mon.-Fri. 7am-11pm, Sat. 9am-1pm. **ZIP code:** 55401. In **St. Paul,** 180 E. Kellogg Blvd. (293-3268). Open Mon.-Fri. 8am-6pm, Sat. 8:30am-1pm. **ZIP code:** 55101. **Area code:** 612.

A loopy net of interstates covers the entire Minneapolis/St. Paul area. **I-94** connects the downtowns. **I-35** (north-south) splits in the Twin Cities, with **I-35W** serving Minneapolis and **I-35E** serving St. Paul. Curves and one-way streets tangle both of the downtown areas; even the numbered grids in the cities are skewed, making north-south and east-west designations tricky. Purchase a map and pay attention. **Skyways,** a second-story tunnel system, connect more than ten square blocks of buildings in each downtown area, protecting humans from the winter cold.

ACCOMMODATIONS AND CAMPING

Cost, safety, and cleanliness tend to go hand-in-hand-in-hand in the Twin Cities, with a few notable exceptions. The visitors bureaus have useful lists of **B&Bs** (but not a list of prices), while the **University of Minnesota Housing Office** (624-2994) keeps a list of local rooms which rent on a daily ($13-45) or weekly basis. Camping is an inconvenient option; private campgrounds lie about 15 mi. outside the city, and the closest state park camping is in the **Hennepin Park** system, 25 mi. out.

College of St. Catherine, Caecilian Hall (HI-AYH), 2004 Randolph Ave. (690-6604), St. Paul. Take I-94 to Snelling Ave., follow Snelling Ave. south to Randolph Ave. and take a right—it's about 5 blocks down, on the left. Or take St. Paul bus #14. The most convenient summer lodging for those with a car. Simple, quiet dorm rooms near the river in a generally safe residential neighborhood. Shared bath, laundry, kitchenette. Free local calls. Singles $14, doubles $26, triples $33. 2-week max. stay. Open June to mid-Aug.

Home Sweet Dome

It could be the spirit of Paul Bunyan watching over his boys of summer. Or perhaps it's nothing at all. But in its 15 years of existence, the **Hubert Humphrey Metrodome** has garnered a reputation as a powerful intangible in the success of the **Minnesota Twins.** The Twins won two World Series championships, in 1987 and 1991. Both victories were achieved without a single win on the road (each time, the team won all four home games). Visiting teams grew suspect, complaining that the white Metrodome ceiling obscured high fly balls—or contending that the giant vents behind home plate were rigged, blowing air out when the Twins were at bat, but sucking it in when their opponents came up. One manager, Bobby Valentine, then of the Texas Rangers, went so far as to **monitor airflow** by draping a piece of cloth in front of the vents. Today, the Twins are struggling to maintain respectability, mired in third place as this book goes to press. Oh, olde magic Metrodome, where art thy powers?

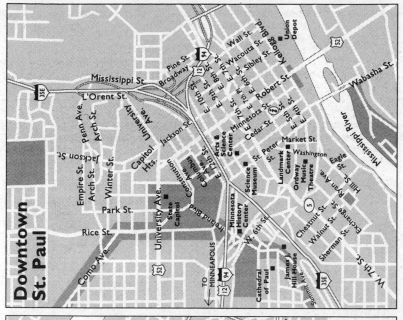

Downtown St. Paul

Downtown Minneapolis

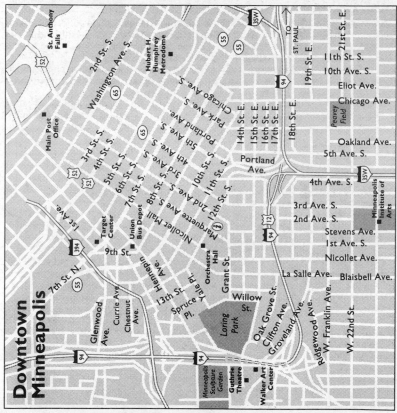

GREAT LAKES

City of Lakes International House, 2400 Stevens Ave. S. (871-3210), Minneapolis, south of downtown near the Institute of Arts. The best bet for carless budget travelers who dig community living. Owner gives suggestions for bars, restaurants, etc. Free local calls. Afternoon check-out. Beds $14; singles $28, 2 available. Linen $3. Key deposit $5. Bike rentals. Reservations strongly recommended.

Evelo's Bed and Breakfast, 2301 Bryant Ave. (374-9656), South Minneapolis, excellent location just off Hennepin, a 15-min. walk from uptown; take bus #4 from downtown. Friendly owners have 3 comfortable rooms in a beautiful house with elegant Victorian artifacts. Singles $40, doubles $50. Reservations required.

Minneapolis Northwest I-94 KOA (420-2255), 15mi. north of Minneapolis. Take Rte. 30W (I-94 Exit 213) to Rte. 101N. Pool, sauna, showers, game rooms. Sites for 2 $18.50, with water and electricity $26.50, with full hookup $23.50. Cabins for 2 $29; $3 per additional adult, kids $1.

FOOD

The Twin Cities' love of music and art carries over into their culinary choices—look for small cafés with nightly music, plush chairs, and poetry readings. **Uptown** Minneapolis, centered on the intersection of Lake St. and the 2900s of Hennepin Ave., has plenty of funky restaurants and bars without high prices. The **Warehouse District** and **Victoria Crossing** serve the dessert crowd with lavish pastries, meals themselves. Near the University of Minnesota campus, **Dinkytown** (on the same side of the river) and the **West Bank** (across the river, hence the name) cater to student appetites with many dark and intriguing low-end places. **St. Paul Farmers Market** (227-6856) sells fresh produce and baked goods in a main downtown location and various others citywide, every day except Monday; call for times and sites.

Minneapolis

Jitters, 1026 Nicollet Mall (333-8511). A cheerful, brightly painted coffeehouse with formica tables and unique lamps. Giant focaccia sandwiches ($4.60) and homemade cookies ($1.25). Great coffee. Sat.-Sun. omelettes $5.25; Sun. waffle bar $5. Open Mon.-Fri. 6:30am-1am, Sat.-Sun. 8am-1am.

Mud Pie, 2549 Lyndale Ave. S. (872-9435), at 26th St. A wide variety of vegetarian dishes with Mexican and Middle Eastern accents. Don't miss the town-renowned veggie burger ($4.75). Open daily 11am-10pm.

Urban Bean Coffeehouse, 2717 Hennepin Ave. (872-1419). Relax in a soft plush armchair, gaze at the fish (in a tank filled with water from the Red Sea), and enjoy a great cappuccino ($2). Live jazz Tues.; no cover. Open Sun.-Thurs. 7am-11pm, Fri.-Sat. 7am-midnight (hours may increase in near future).

Strudel and Nudel, 2605 Nicollet Ave. (874-0113). Specializes in soups ($1.75), sandwiches ($3.50), and desserts. Open Mon.-Sat. 7am-4pm, Sun. 8am-3pm.

Key's Café, 1007 Nicollet Mall (339-6399). What it lacks in personality Key's makes up for in breakfast duration—it's served all day. Omelettes $5.75, sandwiches $3.50-6. Open Mon.-Fri. 6:30am-8:30pm, Sat. 7am-9pm, Sun. 8am-3pm.

St. Paul

Mickey's Dining Car, 36 W. 7th St. (698-0259), diagonally across from the Greyhound station. Delicious, greasy, 24-hr. diner food. There should be one of these on every corner in America. Steak and eggs from $5; pancakes $2.50.

Café Latté, 850 Grand Ave. (224-5687), near Victoria Crossing. Enormous pastries and a steaming milk drink called Hot Moo ($1.85) overshadow the soups and sandwiches ($3-5); the Swedish Hot Moo is especially good. The long line moves quickly. Open Mon.-Thurs. 9am-11pm, Fri.-Sat. 9am-midnight, Sun. 9am-10pm.

Table of Contents and **Hungry Mind Bookstore,** 1648 Grand Ave. (699-6595), near Snelling Ave.; 1310 Hennepin Ave. (339-1133), Minneapolis (dressier, with a bar). An excellent gourmet café. The wafer-crust pizza ($5) is a tasty alternative to pricier dinners ($11-20). Open Mon.-Thurs. 9am-10pm, Fri.-Sat. 9am-11pm (bar in Minneapolis until 1am), Sun. 10am-7pm (in Minneapolis until 10pm).

SIGHTS

Minneapolis

Situated in the land of 10,000 lakes, Minneapolis boasts three of its own clumped together a couple of mi. southwest of downtown; take bus #28. Ringed by stately mansions, **Lake of the Isles** is an excellent place to meet Canadian geese. **Lake Calhoun,** on the west end of Lake St., south of Lake of the Isles, is a hectic social and recreational hotspot. Located in a more residential neighborhood, **Lake Harriet** features tiny paddleboats and a stage with occasional free concerts. The city keeps up 28 mi. of lakeside trails for strolling, biking, etc. Rent **skates** at **Rolling Soles,** 1700 W. Lake St. (823-5711; both $6 per hr., $12 per day; open daily 9am-10pm, weather permitting). **Calhoun Cycle Center** (827-8231), across the street, rents out **bikes.** ($6 per hr., $15 per ½day, $24 per day. Must have credit card and drivers' license. Open daily 9am-9pm.) At the northeast corner of Lake Calhoun, the **Minneapolis Park and Recreation Board** (370-4883 or 370-4964) handles **canoe** and **rowboat** rentals (canoes $5.50 per hr., rowboats $11 per hr.).

Home to two of the country's premiere art museums, Minneapolis is a true art hub. The **Minneapolis Institute of Arts,** 2400 3rd Ave. S. (870-3131; take bus #9), south of downtown, displays an outstanding collection of international art including the world-famous *Doryphoros,* a Roman sculpture of a perfectly proportioned man. (Open Tues.-Sat. 10am-5pm, Thurs. 10am-9pm, Sun. noon-5pm. Free.) The **Walker Art Center,** 725 Vineland Place (375-7622), a few blocks southwest of downtown, draws thousands with daring exhibits by Lichtenstein and Warhol, and temporary exhibits concentrating on specific eras. (Open Tues.-Sat. 10am-5pm, Thurs. 10am-8pm, Sun. 11am-5pm. $4; students with ID, seniors, and ages 12-18 $3; free Thurs. and first Sat. of the month.) Next to the Walker, the beautiful **Minneapolis Sculpture Garden,** the largest urban sculpture garden in the U.S., contains oodles of sculptures and a fountain in a maze of landscaped trees and flowers. To find a sure cure for absolutely anything, stop by the **Museum of Questionable Medical Devices,** 219 Main St. S.E. (379-4046), north of the river, near St. Anthony Falls. The Solorama Bedboard (meant to cure brain tumors) and phrenological equipment (phrenologists measure head bumps to determine personality) are among the more respectable highlights of the collection. (Open Tues.-Thurs. 5-9pm, Fri. 5-10pm, Sat. 11am-10pm, Sun. noon-5pm. Donation requested.)

The Twin Cities exist because of the Mississippi River, and you can get a good look at the Mighty Miss from several points in town. Off Portland Ave., **Stone Arch Bridge** offers a scenic view of **St. Anthony Falls;** several mi. downstream, Minnehaha Park (take bus #7 from Hennepin Ave. downtown) lets you to take a gander at the **Minnehaha Falls,** immortalized in Longfellow's *Song of Hiawatha.* The visitors center at the **Upper St. Anthony Lock and Dam** (332-3660), at Portland Ave. and West River Pkwy., provides a great view and a helpful explanation of the locks. (Observation tower open mid-March to mid-Dec. daily 9am-10pm.)

St. Paul

St. Paul's history and architecture are its greatest appeals. West of downtown along **Summit Ave.,** the nation's longest continuous stretch of Victorian homes, built on the tracks of an old railroad, include a former home of American novelist **F. Scott Fitzgerald,** the Governor's Mansion, and the home of railroad magnate **James J. Hill,** 240 Summit Ave. (297-2555; 1¼-hr. tours Wed.-Sat. every ½hr. 10am-3:30pm; $4, seniors $3, ages 6-15 $2). Overlooking the capitol on Summit Ave. stands **St. Paul's Cathedral,** 239 Selby Ave. (228-1766), a scaled-down version of St. Peter's in Rome. (Mon.-Fri. mass daily 7:30am and 5:15pm, no afternoon mass Wed.; Sat. mass 8am and 7pm; call for Sun. mass schedule.) Battle field-tripping schoolchildren to see the golden horses atop the ornate **State Capitol** (296-3962 or 297-1503), at Cedar and Aurora St. (Tours on the hr. Mon.-Fri. 9am-4pm, Sat. 10am-3pm, Sun. 1-3pm. Open Mon.-Fri. 9am-5pm, Sat. 10am-4pm, Sun. 1-4pm.) The nearby **Minnesota History Center,** 345 Kellogg Blvd. W. (296-1430), an organization older than the state itself, houses three exhibit galleries on Minnesota history, as well as a café and gift shop. (Open Tues.-Sat. 10am-5pm, Thurs. 10am-9pm, Sun. noon-5pm. Free.) The society also runs a re-creation of life in the fur-trapping era at **Fort Snelling** (725-2413), far to the southwest at the intersection of Rte. 5 and 55, where elaborately costumed artisans, soldiers, and guides lead you through the 18th-century French fort. (Infantry drills daily 11:30am and 2:30pm. Open Mon.-Sat. 10am-5pm, Sun. noon-5pm. $4, seniors $3, ages 6-15 $2.) The historic **Landmark Center**, 75 W. 5th St. (292-3225), a grandly restored 1894 Federal Court building replete with towers and turrets, contains the **Minnesota Museum of Art** along with a collection of pianos, a concert hall, and four restored courtrooms.

Shop 'Til You Drop

About 10 min. south of downtown, the **Mall of America**, 60 E. Broadway (883-8800), Bloomington, corrals an indoor rollercoaster, ferris wheel, mini-golf course, and 2 mi. of stores. Welcome to the largest mall in America. Shop until the funds run out, then try your luck panning for gold. Watch out: mind-boggling consumerism can be exhausting even when it's fun. (Take I-35E south to I-494W to the 24th Ave. exit. Open Mon.-Sat. 10am-9:30pm, Sun. 11am-7pm.)

ENTERTAINMENT

Second only to New York in number of theaters per capita, the Twin Cities bring musicals, comedy, opera, and experimental drama to the city. Almost all of the many Twin Cities parks feature free evening concerts in the summer; for info on dates and locales, check at one of the visitors centers. The thriving alternative, pop, and classical music scene fills out the wide range of entertainment options. For general info on the local music scene and other events, pick up the free and extremely useful *City Pages* or *Twin Cities Reader.*
    Guthrie Theater, 725 Vineland Pl. (377-2224), Minneapolis, adjacent to the Walker Art Center just off Hennepin Ave., stands out in the theater world. (Season fluctuates; call ahead. Box office open Mon.-Fri. 9am-8pm, Sat. 10am-8pm, Sun. 11am-7pm. Tickets $15-42; rush tickets 10min. before show $10, line starts 1-1½hr. before show.) For family-oriented shows, try the **Children's Theater Company** (874-0400), at 3rd Ave. and 24th St., next to the Minneapolis Institute of Arts. (Season Sept.-June. Box office open Mon.-Sat. 9am-4pm. Tickets $9.50-24; seniors, students, and kids $9-16. Rush tickets 15min. before show $8.) For experimental theater, try the **Theatre de la Jeune Lune** ("theater of the young moon"), which performs (in English) at the **Loring Playhouse**, 1645 Hennepin Ave. (333-6200; tickets $9-19, depending on day), and the **Illusion Theater**, 528 Hennepin Ave., 8th fl. (338-8371; tickets $12 and up). The **Penumbra Theatre Company,** 270 N. Kent St. (224-3180), St. Paul, is Minnesota's only professional African-American theater company (box office open Mon.-Fri. 11am-4pm). Dudley Riggs' **Brave New Workshop,** 2605 Hennepin Ave. (332-6620), stages consistently good musical comedy shows in an intimate club. (June-July box office open Mon. 5-8pm, Fri. and Sun. 4-9pm, Sat. 4pm-12:30am; tickets $5 for Mon. shows, $8-12 weekends. Aug.-May box office open Wed.-Fri. and Sun. 4-9pm, Sat. 4pm-12:15am; tickets $12-18.)
    The Twin Cities' music scene offers everything from the opera to Paisley. **Sommerfest,** a month-long celebration of Viennese music performed by the **Minnesota Orchestra,** marks the high point of the cities' classical scene during July and August; **Orchestra Hall,** 1111 Nicollet Mall, Minneapolis (371-5656 or 800-292-4141), downtown, hosts the event. (Box office open Mon.-Sat. 10am-6pm. Tickets $13-47; rush tickets for students with ID 30min. before show $7.50.) Nearby **Peavey Plaza,** in Nicollet Mall, holds free coffee concerts. The **St. Paul Chamber Orchestra,** the **Schubert Club,** and the **Minnesota Opera Company** all perform at St. Paul's glass-and-brick **Ordway Music Theater,** 345 Washington St. (224-4222; box office open Mon.-Fri. 10am-5:30pm, Sat.-Sun. 11am-3pm; tickets $20-55). The artist formerly known as **Prince** emerged from local status to make his mark on the world. Today,

his state-of-the-art **Paisley Park** studio complex outside the city draws bands from all over to the Great White North.

The Twin Cities' festivals span the seasons. In January, the 10-day **St. Paul Winter Carnival,** near the state capitol, cures cabin fever with ice sculptures, ice fishing, parades, and skating contests. June brings the 12-day **Fringe Festival** (770-2233) for the performing arts (tickets $4-5). On July 4, St. Paul celebrates **Taste of Minnesota** on the Capitol Mall; on its coattails rides the nine-day **Minneapolis Aquatennial,** with concerts, parades, art exhibits, and kids dripping sno-cones on their shirts. (Call **The Connection,** 922-9000, for festival info.) During late August and early September, spend a day at the **Minnesota State Fair,** at Snelling and Como, or the **Renaissance Festival** (445-7361), in the town of Shakopee.

The **Hubert H. Humphrey Metrodome,** 501 Chicago Ave. S. (332-0386), in downtown Minneapolis, houses the **Minnesota Twins,** the cities' baseball team, and the **Minnesota Vikings,** the resident football team. For the scoop on secret Twins' activities, see the graybox on p. 452. The **Timberwolves** kindle basketball hardwood at the **Target Center,** 600 1st Ave. (673-0900).

NIGHTLIFE

Minneapolis' vibrant youth culture spawns most of the Twin Cities' clubs and bars. The post-punk scene thrives in the Land of 10,000 Aches: **Soul Asylum** and **Hüsker Dü,** as well as the best bar band in the world, **The Replacements,** rocked here before it all went big (or bad). Nightlife blooms on **Hennepin Ave.,** around the **University of Minnesota Minneapolis,** and across the river on the **West Bank** (bounded on the west by I-35W and to the south by I-94), especially on **Cedar Ave.** The Twin Cities card hard, even for cigarettes, so carry your ID with you. After 1am, many clubs open their doors; call clubs for specifics.

Ground Zero, 15 4th St. N.E. (378-5115), off Hennepin Ave. just north of the river, is practically synonymous with local nightlife, mushrooming with live music on Wednesdays, techno and dance other nights; Mondays are for beatniks, Thursdays mean bondage and go-go (open until 1am). **NYE's Bar,** 112 E. Hennepin Ave. (379-2021), across the river from downtown, eases on in with a live polka band (Thurs.-Sat.) and a piano band every night. Prince's old court, **First Avenue and 7th St. Entry,** 701 First Ave. N. (332-1775), downtown, rocks with live music several nights a week; even Prince turns up occasionally. (Cover $1-5, for concerts $7-18. Open Mon.-Sat. 8pm-1am.) When the college crowd just wants to be, they do it at **BW-3,** 412 14th Ave. SE. (331-2999). When it's time to turn it up, they hit the **400 Bar** (332-2903), on 4th St. at Cedar Ave., featuring live music nightly on a miniscule stage; acts range from local garage bands to national acts. (Cover Fri.-Sat. $2-5. Open daily noon-1am.) **Red Sea,** 316 Cedar Ave. (333-1644), has live reggae nightly and serves Ethiopian food and ethnic burgers ($4-6) until 11pm; bar closes at 1am. Day or night, the **Uptown Bar and Café,** 3018 Hennepin Ave. (823-4719), packs 'em in. A yuppie-ish lunch crowd goes punk as the night rolls around. (Shows around 10:30pm. Weekend cover varies. Open 8am-1am.) **The Gay 90s** (333-7755), on Hennepin at 4th St., is a nightspot with popularity that transcends sexual orientation (open daily 8pm-3am). In St. Paul, **O'Gara's Garage,** 164 N. Snelling Ave. (644-3333), hosts big bands and jazz nightly in the Irish-theme front bar (no cover); live alternative and dance music play in the back Fridays and Saturdays. (Cover $2. Open daily until 1am. 21+ after 8pm.) The normally mellow crowd at **Plums** (699-2227), at Randolph and Snelling Ave., lets loose on Thursday $5 all-you-can-drink nights. The top floor of the **Mall of America** (see p. 456) invites bar-hopping after the screaming kids have gone to bed; start at **Fat Tuesdays** and go from there.

■ Duluth

The aura of Duluth hits the traveler before the city's smokestacks are even visible; a certain tingling of the nose indicates that one has just entered an area of intense industrial activity. Duluth was built on iron and continues to be dominated by industry—its 47 mi. of dockline make it the largest freshwater port in North America. Hidden behind all this is a city trying to evolve into more than just a gateway to the Great Lakes wilderness. Duluth has converted old factories into bars and nightclubs, former train depots now house museums, and visitors centers dot the city.

Practical Information Three Duluth locations distribute tourist literature and maps: **Convention and Visitors Bureau,** 100 Lake Place Dr. (722-4011), at Endion Station in Canal Park (open Mon.-Fri. 8:30am-5pm); the **Summer Visitors Center** (722-6024), at Vista dock on Harbor Dr. (open mid-May to mid-Oct. daily 8:30am-8pm, although hours are highly variable); and **The Depot,** 506 W. Michigan St. (727-8025; open daily 10am-5pm; mid-Oct. to April Mon.-Sat. 10am-5pm, Sun. 1-5pm). **Greyhound,** 2122 W. Superior (722-5591 or 800-231-2222), stops 2 mi. west of downtown; take bus #9 "Piedmont" from downtown. Buses run to Milwaukee (3 per day, 10hr., $70) and St. Paul (3 per day, 2hr., $20). Buy tickets daily 6:45am-7pm. The **Duluth Transit Authority,** 2402 W. Michigan St. (722-7283), sends buses throughout the city (peak fare Mon.-Fri. 7-9am and 2:30-6pm $1, high school students 75¢; off peak 50¢). For info on routes and times, visit their kiosk at the **Holiday Center,** 207 W. Superior St. (open Mon.-Fri. 9am-5:15pm). Tourist mover extraordinaire **Port Town Trolley** (722-7283) serves the downtown area, canal park, and waterfront (runs Memorial Day-Labor Day daily 11am-7pm and Sept. weekends; 50¢). Local help lines include the **24-Hour Sexual Assault Crisis Line** (726-1931) and the **Gay/Lesbian Resource Line** (722-4903; open Mon. 9am-2pm, Wed. 2-6pm, Tues. and Thurs.-Fri. noon-5pm). Duluth's **post office:** 2800 W. Michigan St. (723-2590), 6 blocks west and 1 block south of the Greyhound station (open Mon.-Fri. 8am-5pm, Sat. 9am-1pm). **ZIP code:** 55806. **Area code:** 218.

Accommodations and Camping Duluth motels depend on the summer migration of North Shore-bound tourists for their livelihood. Rates rise and rooms fill during the warm months; call as far ahead as possible. The **College of St. Scholastica,** 1200 Kenwood Ave. (723-6396, ask for the housing director), rents out large, quiet dorm rooms with free local phone calls, kitchen access, and laundry facilities, from early June to mid-August (singles $18, doubles $36; reservations recommended). Group rates and week-long apartment rentals can be arranged. **The Grand Motel,** 4312 Grand Ave. (624-4821), has clean, medium-sized rooms with fridge, cable, and A/C (June to mid-Oct. weekday $37, weekend $42; Oct.-May $29/$33). Some relatively reasonable motels line London Rd., west of downtown; try the **Chalet Motel,** 1801 London Rd. (728-4238 or 800-235-2957; May-Sept. $43 and up, lower rates in winter). You know you've come home when you see the big buffalo. **Buffalo Valley** (624-9901), 15 mi. from Duluth off I-35S at Exit 245, is a bit cluttered but makes up for it with its restaurant, bar, six ballfields, and trout pond. (Showers, bathrooms. 24-hr. patrol. Campground open mid-April to Sept. daily 11am-1am, restaurant open daily 11am-1am. Sites $11, with hookup $15.) **Jay Cooke State Park** (384-4610), southwest of Duluth on I-35 off Exit 242, has scenic campgrounds. There are 83 campsites (21 with electricity), 50 mi. of hiking trails, 12 mi. of snowmobile trails, and 32 mi. for cross-country skiing, all among the tall trees of the dramatic St. Louis River valley. (Open daily 9am-9pm. $8, with showers $12, with electricity $10.50/$14.50. Vehicle permit $4. Reservations highly recommended, 800-246-CAMP/2267. $6 reservation fee.) **Spirit Mountain,** 9500 Spirit Mountain Pl. (628-2891 or 800-642-6377, ext. 244), near the ski resort of the same name, stretches skyward 10 mi. south on I-35 off Exit 249 (beautiful, spacious sites $12, with electricity $15, plus water $17).

Food Upscale **Fitger's Brewery Complex,** 600 E. Superior St., and the **Canal Park** region, south from downtown along **Lake Ave.,** feature plenty of pleasant eateries, both chains and local. The **DeWitt-Seitz Marketplace,** on the south end of Canal St., has a number of slightly pricier restaurants for a variety of palates. **Hacienda del Sol,**

319 E. Superior St. (722-7296), drums up cheap, original Mexican recipes and may reintroduce live music and poetry reading events; call for details (entrees $4-7; open Mon.-Thurs. 11am-10pm, Fri.-Sat. 11am-midnight). In a mildly campy cottage, **Sir Benedict's Tavern on the Lake,** 805 E. Superior St. (728-1192), serves soups ($2-4), sandwiches ($4-7), and beer ($2-3) with an English flair. Those under 21 are not admitted without parents. (Live music, especially Celtic and Bluegrass, Wed.-Thurs. free. Open Sun.-Tues. 11am-11:30pm, Wed.-Sat. 11am-12:30am.) The **Blue Note Café,** 357 Canal Park Dr. (727-6549), creates delicious sandwiches ($4-5) and desserts ($2-3) in a yuppified coffeehouse setting. **Grandma's** restaurant (727-4192) and entertainment complex usurps nearly the entire wharf at the south end of Lake Ave. The saloon and deli serve sandwiches and pub fare, while **Grandma's Grill** specializes in steaks. In an old pipe-fitting factory, **Grandma's Garden** (722-4722) is the shining star of Duluthian nightlife, with dining, a huge dance floor, a bar, and an arcade. (Restaurant open daily 11am-10pm. Club open Sun. 5-10:30pm, Tues. 5-8pm, Wed.-Fri. 5pm-1am, Sat. 11:30am-1am.)

Sights and Entertainment Duluth's proximity to majestic Lake Superior is its biggest draw; many visitors just head right down to **Waterfront Canal Park** and watch the big ships go by. Call the **Boatwatcher's Hotline** (722-6489) for up-to-the-minute info on ship movements in the area. Accompanied by deafening horn blasts, the unique **Aerial Lift Bridge** climbs 138 ft. in 55 seconds to allow vessels to pass through the world's largest inland harbor; late afternoon is prime viewing time. Within Canal Park, the **Marine Museum** (727-2497), run by the U.S. Army Corps of Engineers, presents extensive exhibits on commercial shipping in Lake Superior. (Open daily 10am-4:30pm. Free.) International sculpture and art celebrating Duluth's sister cities in Sweden, Ontario, Russia, and Japan line the paths of the park. Pick up a free walking tour brochure at any info center. Across the Aerial Lift bridge, **Park Point** has excellent swimming areas and sandy beaches.

The **Ore Docks Observation Platform,** part of the Duluth, Missabe, and Iron Range Railway Co., extends out into the harbor, allowing for outstanding views of the shiploading process and the harbor itself. The **Willard Munger State Trail** links West Duluth to Jay Cooke State Park, providing 14 scenic mi. of paved path perfect for bikes and rollerblades—rent either from the Willard Munger Inn, 7408 Grand Ave. (624-4814 or 800-982-2453; bikes $13 for ½day, $17 per day; rollerblades $10/$14). For panoramic views of the city and harbor, visit **Skyline Pkwy.,** a 30-mi. road rising 600 ft. above the shoreline. A birdwatcher's paradise awaits at **Hawk Ridge,** 4 mi. north of downtown off Skyline Pkwy. In order to avoid flying over open water, hawks steer their migration over Duluth; in September and October they fly past this bluff in flocks. The five-story stone octagonal **Enger Tower,** on Skyline Pkwy. at 18th Ave. W., rises from the highest land in Duluth; the nearby Japanese flower gardens make a beautiful picnic area.

A 39-room neo-Jacobean mansion built on wealth created by iron-shipping, **Glensheen,** 3300 London Rd. (724-8864), lies on the northern outskirts of town. (Open late-May to early-Sept. 9:30am-5pm, off-season hours vary. $8.75, seniors and ages 12-15 $7.) For further evidence of Duluth's shipping past, take a tour of the most visited ship on the Great Lakes, the steamer **William A. Irvin** (722-7876 or 722-5573), downtown on the waterfront. (Tours late May to early Sept. Sun.-Thurs. 9am-6pm, Fri.-Sat. 9am-8pm. Call for spring and fall schedule. $6.50, ages 3-11 $4.)

Duluth's cultural calendar centers around **The Depot,** 506 W. Michigan St. (727-8025), a former railroad station housing four performing arts groups and several museums; the immense **Lake Superior Museum of Transportation** stands out with antique locomotives restored to shining splendor by retired railway workers. (Open daily 10am-5pm; mid-Oct. to April Mon.-Sat. 10am-5pm, Sun. 1-5pm. $5 includes all the museums and a trolley ride; families $15, ages 3-11 $3.) The **Duluth-Superior Symphony Orchestra** (727-7575, season Sept.-May, Mon.-Fri. 8:30am-4:30pm; call for details), **Minnesota Ballet, Duluth Playhouse,** and **Matinee Musicale** all strut their

GREAT LAKES

stuff in The Depot. On the waterfront, **Bayfront Park** hosts many events and festivals, most notably the mid-August **Bayfront Blues Festival.**

■ Chippewa National Forest

Gleaming white stands of birch lace the Norway pine forests of the **Chippewa National Forest.** Home to the highest density of breeding bald eagles in the continental U.S., the forest sees these proud birds soaring over the Mississippi River between Cass Lake and Lake Winnie from mid-March to November. Wetlands and lakes usurp nearly half of the forest land, providing ample opportunities for canoeing and watersports. The national forest shares territory with the **Leech Lake Indian Reservation,** home to 4560 members of the Minnesota Chippewa tribe, the fourth largest tribe in the U.S. The Chippewa migrated from the Atlantic coast in the 1700s, displacing the Sioux. In the mid-1800s, the government seized most of the Chippewa's land and established reservations like Leech Lake.

For the northbound traveler, Walker, a small town in the southwest corner of the park and reservation, serves as an ideal gateway to the area. Travelers can find info at the **Leech Lake Area Chamber of Commerce** (547-1313 or 800-833-1118), on Rte. 371 downtown. (Open May-Sept. Mon.-Thurs. and Sat. 9am-5pm, Fri. 9am-8pm, Sun. noon-4pm; in winter Mon.-Fri. 8:30am-4:30pm.) The **Forest Office** (547-1044; superintendent 335-8600), just east of town on Rte. 371, has the dirt on outdoor activities (open Mon.-Fri. 7:30am-5pm). **Greyhound** (751-7600) runs from Minneapolis to Walker (1 per day, 5½hr., $34), stopping at the **Lake View Laundrette** (547-9585), 1st and Michigan St. just east of the chamber of commerce. A southbound bus leaves daily at 8:30am, a northbound at 4:15pm; purchase tickets at the next station. Chippewa National Forest Area's **area code: 218.**

Camping—cheap, plentiful, and available in various degrees of modernity—is the way to stay. For info on forest campgrounds, over 400 of which are free, contact the forest office. North of Walker, billboards for private campgrounds string the edges of Rte. 371. **The Wedgewood Resort and Campground** (547-1443), offers shady sites on the shores of Leech Lake. (Open May-Feb. $12; with water and electricity $14; cabins $35 and up. Boat rentals start at $10.) Indoors, **Bailey's Resort** (547-1464), 4½ mi. north off Kabekona Bay Rd., rents comfortable cabins with full kitchens starting at $59 a night. The cabins at **Stoney Point Resort** (335-6311 or 800-332-6311), 16 mi. east of town on Rte. 2, sleep up to eight people; prices start at $78 per day for a four-person cabin. You can also camp next door at the **National Forest Campground** (800-280-CAMP/2267; $12, $14 with hookup, $8 reservation fee).

M I double-S I double-S I double-P I

Step across the mighty Mississippi at its source, officially (and cleverly) known as the **Beginning of the Mississippi,** at Lake Itasca State Park, 30 mi. west of Chippewa National Forest on Rte. 200. The park office (266-2100), through the north entrance and down County Rd. 38, has info on camping. (Office open Mon.-Fri. 8am-4:30pm, Sat.-Sun. 8am-4pm; mid-Oct. to Apr. Mon.-Fri. 8am-4:30pm. Ranger on call after hours.) The comfortable **Mississippi Headwaters HI-AYH Hostel** (266-3415) has 34 beds with some four-bed rooms for families. The hostel stays open in the winter to facilitate access to the park's excellent cross-country skiing. (Laundry, kitchen, multiple bathrooms. 2-night min. stay on certain weekends. Check-in Sun.-Thurs. 5-10pm, Fri.-Sat. 5-11pm. Check-out Mon.-Fri. 10am, Sat.-Sun. 1pm. Members $14, nonmembers $17. Linen $2-4. $4 vehicle permit required.) In the park, **Itasca Sports Rental** (266-2150) offers mountain bikes ($3.50 per hr., $20 per day), canoes ($3/$18), and 6-h.p. motorboats ($12 for 2hr.; open May-Oct. daily 7am-9pm).

■ Iron Range

It was the cry of *"Goald!"* that brought the flood of miners, but it was the staying power of iron that kept them here. The Iron Range was born in the 1880s with the discovery of huge deposits of hematite at Soudan, in the northeastern range. Today a mere stretch of 120 miles of wilderness and small towns along Minnesota Rte. 169 produces over 50% of the country's steel. Visitors come to the region not only to tour the old mines, but also for prime fishing, hiking, and camping.

Grand Rapids Toto, I don't think we're in Kansas anymore. The former home of **Judy Garland,** this small paper mill town stands at the southwest corner of the Iron Range, offering a convenient starting point for a trip through the mines. The town celebrates its native daughter with the **Judy Garland Historical Center,** 10 5th St. NW (326-6431), in the Central School. (Open June-Aug. Mon.-Fri. 9:30am-5pm, Sat. 9:30am-4pm, Sun. 11am-4pm; off season Mon.-Fri. 9:30am-5pm, Sat. 9:30am-4pm.) The **Judy Garland Birthplace** (327-9302), on Rte. 169 south of town, captures in precise detail the state of the house in which Garland spent her earliest years. (Open in summer daily 10am-5pm, in winter Mon.-Fri. 10am-5pm. $2.)

Moving off the yellow brick road, see a re-created turn-of-the-century mining camp at the **Forest History Center,** 2609 Country Rd. 76 (327-4482), off Rte. 2W or Rte. 169S. ($4, ages 6-15 $2. Open late May to mid-Oct. Mon.-Sat. 10am-5pm, Sun. noon-5pm; call for possible winter activities.) Fifteen mi. northeast of Grand Rapids in **Calumet,** drop in at the **Hill Mine Annex State Park** (247-7215), a now-retired natural iron ore pit mine. An exceptional 90-min. tour brings visitors through the buildings and shops, into the 500-ft.-deep mine, where former miners relive their experience for visitors. The $5 admission is money well-spent (ages 5-12 $3).

Motel Americana (326-0369 or 800-533-5148), just west of town at 1915 Rte. 2W, is cheap and convenient. Rooms start at $28; most have fridge, microwave, and coffee maker. **Prairie Lake Campground,** 400 Wabana Rd. (326-8486), 6½ mi. north of town on Rte. 38, has a nice, shady waterfront location with showers, flush toilets, and canoe and paddleboat rentals (Open May to early Sept. Tent sites $9.75, with varying degrees of hookup $11.75-$15.75. Canoe rentals $14 per day, paddle boat rentals $3 per hr.)

To get to Grand Rapids, click your heels together three times and say, "There's no place like home," or hop aboard a **Greyhound** bus from Duluth ($15.40) or Minneapolis ($29). Buses stop at the **Redding Bus Depot** (326-37226), on 4th St. next to Variety Cleaners (ticket office open daily 9-11am and 1-3pm). **Arrowhead Transit,** 308 2nd Ave. NE (326-3505), located off Rte. 169, serves the local area, with fares from 50¢ to $8. Grand Rapids' **area code:** 218.

Hibbing and Chisholm The answer, my friend, is blowing in **Hibbing,** the hometown of Robert Zimmerman (a.k.a. **Bob Dylan**). The **Hibbing Tourist Center,** 1202 E. Howard St. (262-4166), off Rte. 169, serves travelers with pride. (Open late May to early Sept. Mon.-Fri. 9am-5pm, Sat.-Sun. 9am-3pm; off season Mon.-Fri. 10am-4pm.) To reach the largest open-pit ore mine in the world, **Hull Rust Mahoning Mine** (262-4166), take 3rd Ave. E. to the north until it ends. (Open mid-May to Sept. daily 9am-7pm.) Greyhound spent its puppyhood here as a transport for miners in the Hibbing area; carless travelers in particular may wish to pay tribute at the **Greyhound Bus Origin Center** (263-5814), at 23rd St. and 5th Ave. E., where exhibits include antique buses and a zillion bus cartoons. (Open mid-May to mid-Sept. Mon.-Sat. 9am-5pm. $1, ages 6-12 50¢.) **Adams House,** 201 E. 23rd St. (263-9742 or 888-891-9742), lets double rooms in a beautiful Tudor-style B&B for $48 (light breakfast included). **Forest Heights,** 2240 E. 25th St. (263-5782), offers camping. (Tents $6, RVs $12. Showers $1.50.)

Flags from around the world fly on the **Longyear Lake Bridge of Peace,** which connects Hibbing to **Chisholm,** home to **Ironworld USA** (254-3321 or 800-372-6437), possibly the world's only mining theme park with displays on local ethnic groups. (Open Memorial Day-Labor Day daily 10am-7pm. $7, seniors $5.50, ages 7-17 $5; May and Sept. $4.25/$4/$2.25. Call for special daily rates and events.) In **Eveleth,** 20 mi. east, the **U.S. Hockey Hall of Fame** (744-5167), at Rte. 53 and Trick Ave., honors the hockey greats of Eveleth and elsewhere. (Open Mon.-Sat. 9am-5pm, Sun. 11am-5pm; Jan.-March closed Mon. $3, ages 13-17 $2, ages 6-12 $1.75.) Hibbing and Chisholm's **area code:** 218.

Soudan and Ely Plunge into the Iron Range's first mine, the **Soudan Underground Mine** (753-2245), in Soudan on Rte. 1, where visitors take a 90-min. tour to the 17th level of digging, ½ mi. beneath the earth's surface. (Tours Memorial Day-Labor Day every ½hr. 9:30am-4pm; off season by reservation. $6, ages 5-12 $4, plus $4 state park vehicle fee. Gates open until 6pm; off season by reservation.) Next to the mine, **McKinley Park Campground** (753-5921) rents semi-private campsites overlooking gorgeous Vermilion Lake. (Sites $10.50, with hookup $12. Canoe and paddleboat rentals $16 per day.)

Serving as a launching pad both into the **Boundary Waters Canoe Area Wilderness (BWCAW)** and the Iron Range, **Ely** supports its share of wilderness outfitters. Head to the **chamber of commerce,** 1600 E. Sheridan St. (365-6123 or 800-777-7281), for BWCAW permits and brochures on various guides. (Open in summer Mon.-Sat. 9am-6pm, Sun. noon-4pm; off season Mon.-Fri. 9am-5pm.) The **International Wolf Center,** 1396 Rte. 169 (365-4685), has informative displays on the history, habitat, and behaviors of these creatures. (Open July-Aug. daily 9am-6pm; Sept. to mid-Oct. and May-June 9am-5pm; mid-Oct. to April Fri.-Sat. 10am-5pm, Sun. 10am-3pm. $5, seniors $4, ages 6-12 $2.50.) Next door, the **Dorothy Molter Museum** (365-4451), honors the "Root Beer Lady of Knife Lake." Not only was Ms. Molter the last year-round resident of the BWCAW, but she brewed 11 to 12 *thousand* bottles of root beer each year. (Open May-Sept. daily 10am-6pm. $2, kids $1.) **Shagawa Sam's,** 60 W. Lakeview Pl. (365-6757), Ely, has a recently renovated, tidy loft full of bunks for $10 per night, including linen and showers, plus some RV campsites and cabins. (Tent sites $6, RV sites $10, $1.50 each for water and electricity. Cabins for 4 $60-65. Canoe rental $10 per day.) Even if you don't stay, you can still drop by the exceptional rib feast ($8.25) on Wednesdays and Fridays. While in town, let the **Chocolate Moose,** 101 N. Central (356-6343), a favorite of locals and canoeists alike, tempt you with blueberry pancakes ($4). A BBQ with ribs ($10) and chicken ($9.25) takes over on Friday and Saturday nights. (Open daily 6am-9pm, ice cream until 10pm. Breakfast served 6-11am.) Soudan and Ely's **area code:** 218.

▓ Lake Superior North Shore

Rte. 61 Although the true Lake Superior North Shore extends 646 mi. from Duluth, MN to Sault Ste. Marie, ONT, **Rte. 61 (North Shore Dr.),** winding along the coast from Duluth to Grand Portage, gives travelers an abbreviated version of the journey. Small, touristy fishing towns separate the 31,000-sq.-mi. inland sea (comprising 10% of the world's freshwater surface area) from the moose, bear, and wolves inland. Sunday drivers beware—in summer, especially weekends, Rte. 61 is often glutted with boat-towing pick-up trucks and family-filled campers. The cabins, cottages, and luxurious resorts that flank the roadside fill up fast in summer; make reservations early. Remember to bring warm clothes; temperatures can drop into the low 40s (°F) at night in summer.

Most towns along the shore maintain a visitors center. The **Lake County Information Center** (218-834-4005 or 800-554-2116), 30 mi. from Duluth up Rte. 61 in Two Harbors, has lodging guides and info for each town along the MN stretch of the North Shore. (Open June to mid-Oct. daily 9am-5pm, winter Fri.-Sun. 10am-2pm.) **Happy Times** bus lines runs four buses per week (Sun., Mon., Wed., Fri.) up the shore from the **Duluth Greyhound Station,** 2122 W. Superior St. (218-722-5591; open daily 7am-9pm) to Grand Marais ($28, round-trip $35).

LET'S GO® TRAVEL

1 9 9 7

CATALOG

WE GIVE YOU THE WORLD...AT A DISCOUNT

1 - 800 - 5 - LETSGO

TRAVEL GEAR

Let's Go carries a full line of Eagle Creek packs, accessories, and security items.

A. World Journey

Equipped with Eagle Creek Comfort Zone Carry System which includes Hydrofil nylon knit on backpanel and shoulder straps, molded torso adjustments, and spinal and lumbar pads. Parallel internal frame. Easy packing panel load design with internal cinch straps. Lockable zippers. Black, Evergreen, or Blue. The perfect Eurailing pack. $20 off with rail pass. $195

B. Continental Journey

Carry-on sized pack with internal frame suspension. Detachable front pack. Comfort zone padded shoulder straps and hip belt. Leather hand grip. Easy packing panel load design with internal cinch straps. Lockable zippers. Black, Evergreen, or Blue. Perfect for backpacking through Europe. $10 off with rail pass. $150

ACCESSORIES

C. Padded Toiletry Kit

Large padded main compartment to protect contents. Mesh lid pocket with metal hook to hang kit on a towel rod or bathroom hook. Features two separate small outside pockets and detachable mirror. 9" x 4¾" x 4¼". Black, Evergreen, or Blue. *As seen on cover in Blue.* $20

D. Padded Travel Pouch

Main zipper compartment is padded to protect a compact camera or mini binoculars. Carries as a belt pouch, or use 1" strap to convert into waist or shoulder pack. Front flap is secured by a quick release closure. 6" x 9" x 3". Black, Evergreen, or Blue. *As seen on cover in Evergreen.* $26

E. Departure Pouch

Great for travel or everyday use. Features a multitude of inside pockets to store passport, tickets, and monies. Includes see-thru mesh pocket, pen slots, and gusseted compartment. Can be worn over shoulder, around neck, or cinched around waist. 6" x 12". Black, Evergreen, or Blue. *As seen on cover in Black.* $16

SECURITY ITEMS

F. Undercover Neckpouch

Ripstop nylon with a soft Cambrelle back. Three pockets. 5¼" x 6½". Lifetime guarantee. Black or Tan. $9.95

G. Undercover Waistpouch

Ripstop nylon with a soft Cambrelle back. Two pockets. 4¾" x 12" with adjustable waistband. Lifetime guarantee. Black or Tan. $9.95

H. Travel Lock

Great for locking up your Continental or World Journey. Anodized copper two-key lock. $5

CLEARANCE

Call for clearance specials on a limited stock of travel packs, gear, and accessories from the 1996 season.

Prices and availability of products are subject to change.

1-800-5-LETS GO

EURAIL PASSES

Let's Go is one of the largest Eurail pass distributors in the nation. Benefit from our extensive knowledge of the European rail network. Free UPS standard shipping.

Eurail Pass (First Class)
Unlimited train travel in 17 European nations.
15 days	$522
21 days	$678
1 month	$838
2 months	$1148
3 months	$1468

EurailYouthpass (Second Class)
All the benefits of a Eurail pass for passengers under 26 on their first day of travel.
15 days	$418
1 month	$598
2 months	$798

Eurail Flexipass (First Class)
Individual travel days to be used at your convenience during a two month period.
10 days in 2 months	$616
15 days in 2 months	$812

EurailYouthpass Flexipass (Second Class)
All the benefits of a Flexipass for passengers under 26 on their first day of travel.
10 days in 2 months	$438
15 days in 2 months	$588

Europass
Purchase anywhere from 5 to 15 train days within a two month period for train travel in 3, 4, or 5 of the following countries: France, Germany, Italy, Spain, and Switzerland. Associate countries can be added. Call for details.

Pass Protection
For an additional $10, insure any railpass against theft or loss.

Call for details on Europasses, individual country passes, and reservations for the Chunnel train linking London to Paris, Brussels, and Calais. Rail prices are subject to change. Please call to verify price before ordering.

DISCOUNTED AIRFARES

Discounted international and domestic fares for students, teachers, and travelers under 26.
Purchase your 1997 International ID card and call 1-800-5-LETSGO for price quotes and reservations.

1997 INTERNATIONAL ID CARDS

Provides discounts on airfares, tourist attractions and more. Includes basic accident and medical insurance.

International Student ID Card (ISIC)	$19
International Teacher ID Card (ITIC)	$20
International Youth ID Card (GO25)	$19

See order form for details.

HOSTELLING ESSENTIALS

1997-8 Hostelling Membership
Cardholders receive priority and discounts at most international hostels.
Adult (ages 18-55)	$25.00
Youth (under 18)	$10.00

Call for details on Senior and Family memberships.

Sleepsack
Required at many hostels. Washable polyester/cotton.
Durable and compact. $13.95

InternationalYouth Hostel Guide
IYHG offers essential information concerning over 4000 European hostels $10.95

TRAVEL GUIDES
Let's Go Travel Guides
The Bible of the Budget Traveler
Regional & Country Guides (please specify)
USA $19.99
Eastern Europe, Europe, India & Nepal,
Southeast Asia $16.99
Alaska & The Pacific Northwest, Britain & Ireland, California, France, Germany, Greece & Turkey, Israel & Egypt, Italy, Mexico, Spain & Portugal, Switzerland & Austria $17.99
Central America, Ecuador & The Galapagos Islands, Ireland $16.99
City Guides (please specify) $11.99
London, New York, Paris, Rome, Washington, D.C.

Let's Go Map Guides
Fold out maps and up to 40 pages of text
Map Guides (please specify) $7.95
Berlin, Boston, Chicago, London, Los Angeles, Madrid, New Orleans, New York, Paris, Rome, San Francisco, Washington, D.C.

1-800-5-LETS GO

ORDER FORM

International Student/Teacher Identity Card (ISIC/ITIC) (ages 12 and up) enclose:

1. Proof of student/teacher status (letter from registrar or administrator, proof of tuition payment, or copy of student/faculty ID card. FULL-TIME only.)
2. One picture (1 ½" x 2") signed on the reverse side.
3. Proof of birthdate (copy of passport, birth certificate, or driver's license).

GO25 card (ages 12-25) enclose:

1. Proof of birthdate (copy of passport, birth certificate, or driver's license).
2. One picture (1 ½" x 2") signed on the reverse side.

Last Name   First Name   Date of Birth

Street   *We do not ship to P.O. Boxes.*

City   State   Zip Code

Phone (very important!)   Citizenship (Country)

School/College   Date of Travel

Description, Size	Color	Quantity	Unit Price	Total Price

Total Purchase Price	
Shipping and Handling (See box at left)	
MA Residents (Add 5% sales tax on gear & books)	
TOTAL	

SHIPPING & HANDLING

Eurail pass does not factor into merchandise value

Domestic 2-3 Weeks
Merchandise value under $30 .... $4
Merchandise value $30-100 .... $6
Merchandise value over $100 .... $8

Domestic 2-3 Days
Merchandise value under $30 .... $14
Merchandise value $30-100 .... $16
Merchandise value over $100 .... $18

Domestic Overnight
Merchandise value under $30 .... $24
Merchandise value $30-100 .... $26
Merchandise value over $100 .... $28

All International Shipping $30

From which Let's Go Guide are you ordering?   ☐ Europe ☐ USA ☐ Other_____

MASTERCARD ☐   VISA ☐

Cardholder Name:

Card Number:

Expiration Date:

Make check or money order payable to:

Let's Go Travel

http://hsa.net/travel

67 Mt. Auburn Street • Cambridge, MA 02138 • USA • (617) 495-9649

1-800-5-LETS GO

Boundary Waters Canoe Area Wilderness (BWCAW) At its northern end, Rte. 61 runs along BWCAW, a designated wilderness comprising 1.2 million acres of lakes, streams, and forests (including part of **Superior National Forest**) in which no human-made improvements—phones, roads, electricity, private dwellings—are allowed. Within the BWCAW, small waterways and portages string together 1100 lakes, allowing virtually limitless "canoe-camping." Running northwest from **Grand Marais**, the 60-mi., paved **Gunflint Trail** (County Rd. 12) is the only developed road offering access to the wilderness; resorts and outfitters gather around this lone strip of civilization. In summer 1996, BWCAW permitted the use of motorized boats only at Seagull Lake, at the far end of the trail; this may change, as the state legislature is currently debating the issue.

The **Tip of the Arrowhead Visitors Information Center** (218-387-2524 or 800-622-4014), on N. Broadway off Rte. 61 in Grand Marais, has info on BWCAW and the Minnesota part of the North Shore. (Open mid-May to Oct. Mon.-Sat. 9am-5pm, Sun. 11am-4pm. Call for winter hours.) The **Gunflint Ranger Station** (218-387-1750), one mi. south of town, distributes permits required to enter BWCAW from May to September (open daily 7am-5:30pm, Oct. to mid-May Mon.-Fri. 7:30am-4:30pm).

The **"Spirit of the Land" Island Hostel** (218-388-2241 or 800-454-2922), is located on an island in Seagull Lake, at the end of the Gunflint Trail. The well-kept cabins are seldom full. The Christian-oriented **Wilderness Canoe Base,** which leads canoe trips and summer island camps for various groups, administers the hostel. Call from Grand Marais to arrange a boat pick-up. (Full kitchen, outhouses. Beds $15. Meals $4-6. Hot showers $2. Saunas $3. Canoe rental $18 per day, $10 per ½day. Snowshoe rentals in winter. Closed Nov.-Dec.) Closer to civilization, the pine-paneled **Cobblestone Cabins** (218-663-7957), off Rte. 61 one mi. north of Tofte, come with access to a cobblestone beach, canoes, a woodburning sauna, and kitchenettes (cabins for 1-12 $40-85). Pack plaid if you plan to stay at the elegant **Naniboujou Lodge** (218-387-2688), 15 mi. northeast of Grand Marais on Rte. 61. The lodge offers summer/fall family rates on rooms with shared baths ($50, doubles $65). Cheap and popular with the fishermen, **South of the Border Café,** 4 W. Rte. 61 (218-387-1505), in Grand Marais, specializes in huge breakfasts and satisfying, greasy food (check your pulse). The bluefin herring sandwich (fried, of course) will run you $2.75. (Open daily 5am-2pm.)

■ Voyageurs

Voyageurs National Park sits on Minnesota's boundary with Ontario, accessible almost solely by boat. Named for the French Canadian fur traders who once traversed this area, the park invites today's voyagers to leave the auto-dominated world and push off into the longest inland lake waterway on the continent. While some hiking trails exist, boats and canoes provide most transportation within the park. Preservation efforts have kept the area much as it was in the late 18th century, and wolves, bear, deer, and moose roam freely. Remember that undeveloped often means unregulated; water should be boiled for at least two min. before consumption. Many fish in these waters contain mercury. Lyme-disease-bearing ticks have been found in the area as well; visitors should take precautions.

The park can be accessed through **Crane Lake, Ash River,** or **Kabetogama Lake,** all three are east of Rte. 53, or through **International Falls,** at the northern tip of Rte. 53 just below Ft. Frances, Ontario. Call **Crane Lake Visitor and Tourism Bureau,** 7238 Handberg Rd. (993-2234 or 800-362-7405; Mon.-Fri. 9am-5pm), or visit the **International Falls Visitors and Convention Bureau,** 200 Fourth St. (800-325-5766; open daily 8am-5pm). Within the park, three visitors centers serve tourists: **Rainy Lake** (286-5258), 12 mi. east of International Falls at the end of Rte. 11 (open May-Sept. daily 9am-5pm; off season Thurs.-Mon. 9am-5pm); **Ash River** (374-3221), 8mi. east of Rte. 53 on Rte. 129, then 4 mi. north (open late May to early Sept. Wed-Sun. 10am-4pm); and **Kabetogama Lake** (875-2111), 1 mi. north of Rte. 122, then follow the signs (open mid-May to Sept. daily 9am-5pm). Voyageurs' **area code:** 218.

GREAT LAKES

Many of the park's numerous **campsites** are accessible only by water. Car-accessible sites can be found in state forest campgrounds, including **Wooden Frog** (757-3274), about 4 mi. from Kabetogama Visitors Center Rd. 122 ($7, showers available at lodge $2), and **Ash River** (757-3274), 3 mi. from the visitors center and 2 mi. east on Rte. 129 ($7, no showers). Only 5 min. from International Falls, **International Voyageurs RV Campground** (283-4679), off Rte. 53 south of town, offers decent camping—cheap sites, showers, and laundry facilities. What more could you want? You said it—maybe a little shade. (Tent sites $8, RV with full hookup $12. Showers $3.) **Birch Point Camp** (286-3414), east of town on County Rd. 20 off Rte. 53, offers some shade and straightforward, non-luxurious campsites. (Open mid-May to mid-Sept. Sites $9, with hookup $9.50.) Rte. 53 in International Falls is loaded with motels—try the **Hilltop Motel** (283-2505 or 800-322-6671), Rte. 53. (Singles $33, Fri.-Sat. $39. Doubles $37/$43. Call for off-season rates.)

International Falls, the "Icebox of the Nation," former home of Bronco Ngurski and the inspiration for **Rocky and Bullwinkle's** hometown Frostbite Falls, hosts a few attractions outside of the park. The state's largest prehistoric burial ground, **Grand Mound History Center** (279-3332), 17 mi. west of town on Rte. 11, supposedly dates from 200BC. (Open May-Aug. Mon.-Sat. 10am-5pm, Sun. noon-5pm; Sept.-Oct. Sat. 10am-4pm, Sun. noon-4pm. $2.) **Smokey Bear Park,** home of a 22-ft.-tall thermometer and the 26-ft., 82-ton giant who asks you to help fight forest fires, rounds out the offerings with some lighter entertainment.

GREAT PLAINS

Between the big cities of the East and West Coasts, the Rocky Mountains and the Great Lakes, lies the Heartland of the United States—a vast land of prairies and farms, less developed and less appreciated than the rest of the country. Here, open sky stretches from horizon to horizon, broken only by long thin lines of trees–shelter belts, begun in the 1930's with enlightened land management. Grasses and grains paint the land green and gold; the plains breadbasket feeds the country and much of the world.

In 1803, young America suddenly doubled in size, acquiring lands west of the Mississippi when Thomas Jefferson purchased the Louisiana Territory from France at the bargain price of 4¢ per acre. Over time, the plains spawned legends of pioneers and cowboys seeking to conquer the frontier and of Native Americans struggling to defend their homes. In 1862 the Homestead Act sparked bloody battles over land rights, as the government handed territory to land-hungry settlers to farm. The building of the transcontinental railroad added to the conflict, but eventually the new transportation and the government's act began an economic boom that lasted until a drought during the Great Depression transformed the region into a devastated dust bowl. Modern farming techniques have since reclaimed the soil, and the heartland thrives on the trade of farm commodities.

Despite the touch of man, the land still rules here, and the most staggering sights in the region are the work of nature—the Badlands of the Dakotas, the prairies of North Dakota, the vast caverns of Missouri, the rolling hills of Iowa, the Willa Cather Memorial Prairie in Nebraska, and the rising Black Hills, which mark the transition from plains to mountains. The mighty Missouri and Mississippi Rivers trace their way through the thriving small towns of America, while amber waves of grain quietly reign among the greatest of American symbols.

North Dakota

An early visitor to the site of present-day Fargo declared, "It's a beautiful land, but I doubt that human beings will ever live here." Posterity begs to differ. The stark, haunting lands that so intimidated early settlers found an audience, and the territory became a state along with South Dakota on November 2, 1889. The inaugural event did not go off without confusion—Benjamin Harrison concealed the names when he signed the two bills, so both Dakotas claim to be the 39th state.

North Dakota has remained largely isolated geographically. In the western half, the colorful buttes of the Badlands rise in desolate beauty, while in the eastern half, mind-numbingly empty flatness rule; the 110 mi. of Rte. 46 from U.S. 81 to Rte. 30 is the longest stretch of highway in the U.S. without a single curve.

PRACTICAL INFORMATION

Capital: Bismarck.
Tourism Department: 604 East Blvd., Bismarck 58505 (701-328-2525 or 800-437-2077). **Parks and Recreation Department,** 1424 W. Century Ave. #202, Bismarck 58502 (701-221-5357). Both open Mon.-Fri. 8am-5pm.
Time Zones: Mostly Central (1hr. behind Eastern). *Let's Go* makes note of areas in Mountain (2hr. behind Eastern). **Postal Abbreviation:** ND.
Sales Tax: 5-7%, depending on the city.

■ Fargo

In the 1880s, easy divorce laws and a large concentration of lawyers made Fargo a premier divorce destination; unhappy couples from all over the U.S. and Europe traveled to Fargo for a ten-minute divorce. Though Fargo is no longer the favored site for a quickie divorce, people still pass through at a rapid pace.

Amtrak, 402 4th St. N (232-2197 or 800-872-7245), chugs four trains per week to Minneapolis (5hr., $54) and Williston (9hr., $69). (Open Mon.-Fri. 8am-3:30pm, and nightly midnight-7am.) **Greyhound,** 402 Northern Pacific (N.P.) Ave. (293-1222 or 800-231-2222), lopes to Minneapolis (5 per day, 4-7hr., $32) and Bismarck (3 per day, 5hr., $28). (Open daily 6:45am-6pm and 10:30pm-4am; closed Sun. and holidays 8-10:30am.)

Fargo's **Main Ave.** runs east-west and intersects **I-29, University Dr.,** and **Broadway.** If you find Fargo just too much, sort things out at the **Fargo-Moorhead Convention and Visitors Bureau,** 2001 44th St. SW (282-3653 or 800-235-7654; open daily 7am-9pm, Sept.-April daily 8am-6pm). For help, dial the 24-hr. **Crisis Line** at 232-4357. Fargo's main **post office:** 657 2nd Ave. N (241-6100; open Mon.-Fri. 7:30am-5:30pm, Sat. 8am-2pm); **ZIP code:** 58103; **area code:** 701.

Cheap chain motels line I-29 and 13th Ave. (Exit 343 off of I-29 from the west or take Main Ave. from the east.) **The Sunset Motel,** 731 W. Main (800-252-2207), in west Fargo, offers clean rooms, free local calls, a continental breakfast, and an indoor pool with a two-story waterslide. Call early on weekends. (Singles $22, doubles $35; kitchenettes $5 extra.) **Moorhead State University** (218-236-2231) rents rooms with linens and phones in Ballard Hall, just north of 9th Ave. on 14th St. (check-in 24 hrs., $10 per person). **Lindenwood Park** (232-3987), at 17th Ave. and 5th St. S, offers campsites close to the peaceful Red River and the not-so-peaceful train tracks ($8, with hookup $14). **Old Broadway,** 22 Broadway (237-6161), is the flagship microbrewery, serving burgers ($5-10), and beer cheese soup ($3). After 11pm it's a popular nightspot. (Open Mon.-Sat. 11am-1am.) At night, North Dakota State University students descend upon the bars along Broadway near Northern Pacific Ave.

■ Theodore Roosevelt National Park

After his mother and wife died on the same day, pre-White House Theodore Roosevelt moved to a ranch in the badlands for a dose of spiritual renewal. He was so influenced by the red-and brown-hued moon-like formations, horseback riding, big-game hunting, and cattle ranching in this unforgiving land that he later claimed, "I never would have been President if it weren't for my experiences in North Dakota." Today's visitor to **Theodore Roosevelt National Park** can achieve the same inspiration among the quiet canyons and dramatic rocky outcroppings which have earned the park the nickname "rough-rider country."

Practical Information The park is split into southern and northern units and bisected by the border between Mountain and Central time zones. The entrance to the better-developed southern unit is just north of I-94 in **Medora,** a frontier town revamped into a tourist mecca. (In Medora, even the newspaper vending machines are encased in wood to appear more authentically Western.) The park entrance fee ($4 per vehicle, $2 per pedestrian) covers admission to both units of the park for seven days. The **South Unit's Visitors Center** (623-4466), in Medora, maintains a mini-museum; see Teddy's guns, spurs, and old letters, as well as a beautiful film of winter in the Badlands. Pick up a copy of *Frontier Fragments,* the park newspaper, which has listings of ranger-led walks, talks, and demonstrations. (Open daily 8am-8pm; Sept. to mid-June 8am-4:30pm.) The **South Unit's Emergency** number is 623-4379. The **North Unit's Visitors Center** (842-2333) dispenses free overnight camping permits (open May-Sept. daily 9am-5:30pm). Call the ranger at 842-2137 in case of an **emergency** in the north unit. For more information, call 800-MEDORA-1/633-6721 or write to Theodore Roosevelt National Park, P.O. Box 7, Medora 58645-0007.

Great Plains

CANADA

SASKATCHEWAN

Regina

MANITOBA

Winnipeg

ONTARIO

Lake of the Woods

Thunder Bay

Williston   Minot

Lake Sakakawea

NORTH DAKOTA

Washburn

Devils Lake

Grand Forks

International Falls

Lake Superior

Mandan   Bismarck   Jamestown   Fargo

THEODORE ROOSEVELT NAT'L. PARK

Duluth

MINNESOTA

MONT.

Aberdeen

WISCONSIN

SOUTH DAKOTA

Watertown

Rapid City

Lake Oahe   Pierre

St. Paul

Minneapolis

Rochester

Mississippi River

Mitchell   Sioux Falls

BADLANDS NAT'L. PARK

WYO.

Mount Rushmore National Monument

Yankton

Sheldon

Effigy Mounds National Monument

Madison

Missouri River

Sioux City

IOWA

Dubuque

Ames

Cedar Rapids

Iowa City

Davenport

NEBRASKA

Des Moines

Grand Island

Omaha

Osceola

The Amana Colonies

Burlington

Peoria

Platte River

Kearney   Hastings   Lincoln

Missouri River

ILLINOIS

Springfield

MISSOURI

Hannibal

Waconda Lake

Oakley

KANSAS

Topeka

Independence   Columbia

Kansas City

Jefferson City

St. Louis

COLO.

Garden City   Great Bend

Hutchinson

Dodge City   Wichita

Springfield

Blackwell

Tulsa

ARKANSAS

Oklahoma City

Shawnee

Memphis   TENN.

Amarillo

Lawton   OKLAHOMA

Little Rock

Ardmore

MISS.

N

Lubbock

TEXAS   Ft. Worth   Dallas

Abilene

Shreveport

LOUISIANA

Jackson

0   150 miles
0   225 km

> ### YOU ARE NOW ONLY TWO PAGES FROM WALL DRUG.

Greyhound serves Medora from the Sully Inn (see p. 468), with buses to Bismarck (3 per day, 3½hr., $21) and Billings (2 per day, 6hr., $43), although there is no ticket office in Medora. Medora's **post office:** 355 3rd Ave. (open Mon.-Sat. 8am-7pm). Next door at 365 3rd Ave. is an ATM. **Zip code:** 58645; **area code:** 701. **South Unit time zone:** Mountain (2hr. behind Eastern).

Camping, Accommodations, and Food In the south unit, get a free camping permit at the Medora Visitors Center or try the **Cottonwood Campgrounds** in the park (toilets and running water; sites $8). Check in at the North Unit Visitors Center or go to **Squaw Creek Campground**, 5 mi. west of the north unit entrance (toilets and running water; sites $8). During mating season (i.e. early Spring), the campground is a popular buffalo night-spot—just so you know.

You can find expensive, non-camping accommodations in Medora. The **Sully Inn,** 401 Broadway (623-4455), offers tiny and clean rooms at the lowest rates in town, plus free local calls and 10% off in its bookstore (singles $40, doubles $45). Teddy Roosevelt himself was known to bunk down at the **Rough Riders Hotel** (623-4444, ext. 297), at 3rd St. and 3rd Ave. The hotel's restaurant serves pasta, omelettes, and burgers (buffalo and otherwise) for $5-7. Say "Hi" to the stuffed buffalo in the lobby. (Open Sun.-Thurs. 7am-9pm, Fri.-Sat. 7am-10pm, closed May to mid-June.)

Sights and Entertainment The **south unit** features a 36 mi. **scenic automobile loop,** a great way to see the park; many hiking trails start there and wander into the wilderness. **Wind Canyon,** located on the loop, is a constantly mutating canyon formed by winds blowing against the soft clay. The **Coal Vein Trail,** a ¾-mi. trail, follows a seam of lignite coal that caught fire here and burned from 1951 to 1977. For 26 years, the smoking, glowing vein was a tourist attraction; park visitors would come to gawk or to roast marshmallows. The third largest **petrified forest** in the U.S. lies a day's hike into the park; if you prefer to drive, ask at the visitors center for a map. **Painted Canyon Overlook,** 7 mi. east of Medora, has its own **visitors center** (575-4020) with picnic tables, and a breathtaking view of the Badlands. (Open Memorial Day-Labor Day daily 8am-6:30pm; mid-April to Memorial Day and Labor Day to mid-Nov. 8:30am-4:30pm.) The occasional buffalo roams through the parking lot. **Peaceful Valley Ranch** (623-4496), 7 mi. into the park, offers a variety of horseback riding excursions, starting at 1¼ hr. ($12). **Rough Rider Adventures** (623-4808) on 3rd St. in Medora, offers guided tours and rents mountain bikes ($15 for 4hr.; open mid-June to Labor Day daily 8am-8pm).

The less-visited **north unit** of the park is 75 mi. from the south unit on U.S. 85. Most of the land is wilderness, resulting in virtually unlimited **backcountry** hiking possibilities. Be careful not to surprise the buffalo; one ranger advises singing while hiking so they can hear you coming. The buffalo have been known to like Baroque classics, Barry White love ballads, and riffs from "Free to Be You and Me." The **Caprock Coulee Trail** journeys through prairie, river valley, mountain ridge, and juniper forest, all in the space of 4 mi.

The popular **Medora Musical** (623-4444), in the Burning Hills Amphitheater west of town, stages variety shows nightly at 8:30pm from early June to early September. Featured attractions range from "The Flaming Idiots" to "Arneberg's Sensational Canines," depending on your luck. Tickets are available on 4th St. at the **Harold Schafer Heritage Center** (623-4444; $13-14.50, students grades 1-12 $7.50-8.50).

South Dakota

From the forested granite crags of the Black Hills to the glacial lakes of the northeast, the Coyote State has more to offer than casual passers-by might expect. WALL DRUG. In fact, with only ten people per sq. mi., South Dakota has the highest ratio of sights-to-people in all of the Great Plains. Colossal man-made attractions like Mount Rushmore National Monument and the Crazy Horse Memorial compete with stunning natural spectacles such as the Black Hills and the Badlands, making tourism the state's largest industry after agriculture. WALL DRUG. Camera-toting tourists in search of nature have brought both dollars and development to South Dakota, which struggles to keep its balance between natural beauty and neon signs.

PRACTICAL INFORMATION

Capital: Pierre.
Division of Tourism: 711 E. Wells St., Pierre 57051 (773-3301 or 800-732-5682). Open Mon.-Fri. 8am-5pm. **U.S. Forest Service,** 330 Mt. Rushmore Rd., Custer 57730 (673-4853). Open Mon.-Fri. 7:30am-4:30pm. **Division of Parks and Recreation,** 523 E. Capitol Ave., Foss Building, Pierre 57501 (773-3371), has information on state parks and campgrounds. Open Mon.-Fri. 8am-noon and 1-5pm.
Time Zones: Mostly Mountain (2hr. behind Eastern). *Let's Go* makes note of areas in Central (1hr. behind Eastern). **Postal Abbreviation:** SD.
Sales Tax: 4-7%, depending on the city.

■ Sioux Falls

Sioux Falls is like a nice guy. Some will take this description to mean "boring," but those who value the quiet, friendly, and clean-cut will understand that "nice" truly is a compliment. As the largest city in the upper Midwest, many pass through Sioux Falls, but the city can't be appreciated from the inside of the Greyhound station. Downtown is sprinkled with historic buildings of pink quartzite, and the city is ringed by a series of riverside parks connected by bike trails.

You can visit the city's namesake rapids at **Falls Park,** just north of downtown on Falls Park Dr. Hike, bike, or skate on the **Sioux River Greenway Recreation Trail,** which rings the city from Falls Park in the northeast to the Elmwood golf course in the northwest. Legend says that in order to escape the law, Jesse James made a 20 ft. leap on horseback across **Devil's Gulch** in **Garretson,** 20 mi. northeast of Sioux Falls; take Rte. 11 10 mi. north from I-90 (open summer daily 9am-7pm; free).

In the first full weekend of June, the neighboring city of **Tea** hosts the **Great Plains Balloon Race,** visible from all over Sioux Falls (call 336-1620 for more info). A full scale cast of Michelangelo's David stands in Fawick Park on 2nd Ave. and 10th St. The only existing cast of Michelangelo's Moses stands on the grounds of Augustana College, 29th St. and Summit Ave. The **Corn Palace,** 604 N. Main St. (996-7311 or 995-4030), in Mitchell (from Sioux Falls, head 70 mi. west on I-90), stands as a regal testament to granular architecture. Dating back to 1892, the structure was decorated inside and out with thousands of bushels of native corn, grain, and grasses in an effort to encourage settlement by demonstrating the richness of South Dakota's soil (open in summer daily 8am-10pm, winter hours vary; free).

Main St. divides the city east-west, and **Minnesota Ave.** is the major north-south thoroughfare. **10th** and **12th St.** intersect them; 10th connects with **I-229** in the east and 12th connects with **I-29** in the west. The **Chamber of Commerce,** 200 N. Phillips (336-1620), at 8th, provides free city maps (open Mon.-Fri. 8am-5pm). **Greyhound,** 301 N. Dakota Ave. (336-0885; open daily 7:30am-5pm and 9-9:20pm), bolts to Minneapolis (1 per day, 6hr., $41), Omaha (2 per day, 4hr., $35), and Rapid City (1 per day, 8hr., $97). Flag a **Yellow Cab** (336-1616; $1.50 base fare, $1.25 per mi.).

GREAT PLAINS

Time zone: Central. Sioux Falls's **post office:** 320 S. Second St. (357-5000; open Mon.-
Fri. 7:30am-5:30pm, Sat. 8am-1pm). **ZIP code:** 57101. **Area code:** 605.

Every national motel chain has a location in this popular stopover; take your pick
along I-29. The **Arena Motel,** 2401 W. Russell St. (336-1470 or 800-204-1470), at Exit
81 off I-29, has clean, big rooms. Singles cost $25-28, doubles $32-35. The slightly
dog-eared **Albert House,** 333 N. Phillips (336-1680), offers cheap rooms downtown
(singles $24, doubles $29). There are a number of state parks nearby, but you can
camp for free at **Split Rock City Park,** 20 mi. northeast in Garretson. From I-90E, exit
north to Rte. 11 (Corson) and drive 10 mi. to Garretson; turn right at the sign for
Devil's Gulch, and it will be on your left before the tracks. Sites have pit toilets and
drinking water.

Every city needs a trendy downtown brewery, and the **Sioux Falls Brewing Co.,**
431 N. Phillips (332-4847), fits the bill. Grab a slice of buffalo pie (cheesecake with
stout beer and dark chocolate) with your sandwich, burger, or salad ($5-8; open
Mon.-Thurs. 11am-midnight, Fri.-Sat. 11am-2am, Sun. 1-9pm). **Minerva's,** 301 S. Phillips (334-0386), has upscale sandwiches, pasta, and a great salad bar ($6-7.50), but
pricey dinners ($10-12; open for lunch Mon.-Sat. 11am-2:30pm, for dinner Mon.-
Thurs. 5:30-10pm, Fri.-Sat. 5-11pm). **Metro Mix,** 215 S. Phillips (338-2698), a coffeehouse with $3-5 sandwiches by day, transforms into a DJ'd club by night; live blues,
dance, or jazz play Friday and Saturday nights (cover varies).

■ The Badlands

Some 60 million years ago, when much of the Great Plains was under water, tectonic
shifts thrust up the Rockies and the Black Hills. Mountain streams deposited silt from
these nascent highlands into the area now known as the Badlands, capturing and fos-
silizing the remains of wildlife that once wandered these flood plains in layer after
pink layer. Erosion has carved spires and steep gullies into the earth, creating a landscape that contrasts sharply with the prairies of eastern South Dakota, not to mention
the rest of the world. The Sioux first called these arid and treacherous formations
"mako sica," or "bad land;" General Alfred Sully called them "hell with the fires out."

Practical Information Badlands National Park smolders about 50 mi. east of
Rapid City on I-90. Begin a driving tour at either end of Rte. 240, which winds
through the wilderness in a 32-mi. detour off I-90 (Exit 110 or 131). The **Ben Reifel
Visitors Center** (433-5361; open daily 7am-8pm; Sept.-May hours vary), 5 mi. inside
the park's northeastern entrance, is larger and much more convenient than **White
River Visitors Center** (455-2878; open May 31-Sept. 9am-5pm), 55 mi. to the southwest off Rte. 27 in the park's less-visited southern section. Both visitors centers have
potable water. The **entrance fee,** collected at the visitors centers, is $5 per car, $2 per
person. **Jack Rabbit Buses,** 333 6th St. (348-3300), leaves Rapid City for Wall at
11:30am ($22.80). The Badlands experience extreme temperatures in midsummer
and winter; but late spring and fall offer pleasant weather and fewer insects. Always

---

Have You Dug Wall Drug?

There is almost no way to visit the Badlands without being importuned by adver-
tisements from **Wall Drug,** 510 Main St. (605-279-2175), a towering monument
to the success of saturation advertising. After seeing billboards for Wall Drug
from as far as 500 mi. away, travelers feel obligated to make a stop in Wall to see
what all the ruckus is about—much as they must have done 60 years ago, when
Wall enticed parched Plains travelers with free water. The "drug store" itself is
now a conglomeration of shops, containing Old West memorabilia, kitschy souvenirs, oodles of Western books, and numerous photo opportunities with statues of oversized animals. (Open daily 6am-10pm; mid-Sept. to April daily 6:30am-
6pm.) Wall itself is hardly worth a visit. All in all the town is just another brick in
the...oh, never mind.

watch (and listen) for rattlesnakes, and don't tease the bison. For **emergencies,** call 433-5361. **ZIP code:** 57757. **Area code:** 605.

Accommodations, Food, and Camping The **Fountain Motel,** 112 S. Blvd. (279-2488), in Wall, floweth with decent rooms (singles $31, doubles $35). In Interior, try the **Badlands Inn** (433-4501), just out of the park. For $33 (singles) or $45 (doubles), you too can sleep where the crew filming Robert Heinlein's *Starship Trooper* stayed in summer 1996. Next to the visitors center inside the park, **Cedar Pass Lodge** (433-5460), rents air-conditioned cabins with showers. (Singles $43, doubles $47; $4 per additional person. Open mid-April to mid-Oct. Fills up early; call ahead.) At the lodge's mid-priced **restaurant** (the only one in the park), brave diners try the **buffalo burger** ($3.45; open April-Sept. daily 6:45am-8:30pm; off-season hours vary). Two campgrounds lie within the park. **Cedar Pass Campground,** just south of the Ben Reifel Visitors Center, has sites with water and restrooms ($10). It fills up by afternoon in summer; get there early. At **Sage Creek Campground,** 11 mi. from the Pinnacles entrance south of Wall, you can sleep in an open field for free; there are outhouses, no water, and no fires allowed—but hey, it's free. Pitch your tent ½ mi. from the road and out of sight to enjoy a more intimate introduction to this austere landscape. Wherever you sleep, don't cozy up to the bison; especially in spring, nervous mothers can become just a tad protective.

Sights and Activities The 244,000-acre park protects large tracts of prairie and stark rock formations. The Reifel Visitors Center has a video on the Badlands, as well as a wealth of information on nearby parks, camping, and activities. Park rangers offer free star gazing programs, evening slide shows (call for times), and nature walks. Try one of the 1½-hr. walks from the Cedar Pass amphitheater (8am and 6pm)—you may find Oligocene fossils at your feet.

To hike through the Badlands on your own, pick up a trail guide from one of the visitors centers. Hike the bluffs via the short but steep **Saddle Pass Trail;** for more of a prairie walk, try the **Castle Trail** (10 mi. round-trip). Overnight hikers should ask for **backcountry camping** info. For stunning vistas without the sweat, a drive along Rte. 240 is an excellent way to see the park. Rte. 240 also passes the trailheads of the **Door, Window,** and **Notch Trails,** all brief excursions into the Badlands terrain. The gravel **Sage Creek Rim Rd.,** west of Rte. 240, has fewer people and more animals; highlights are **Roberts Prairie Dog Town** and the park's herds of bison, antelope, and prairie dogs. Across the river from the Sage Creek campground lies another prairie dog town and some popular bison territory. Check out the buffalo chips to detect recent activity. It is easy to lose your bearings in this territory, so consult with a ranger or tote a map.

BLACK HILLS REGION

The Black Hills, named for the dark hue that distance lends the green pines covering the hills, have long been considered sacred by the Sioux. The Treaty of 1868 gave the Black Hills and the rest of South Dakota west of the Missouri River to the tribe. But when gold was discovered in the 1870s, the U.S. government snatched back the land. The neighboring monuments of Mt. Rushmore (a national monument) and Crazy Horse (an independent project) strikingly illustrate the clash of the two cultures that reside among these hills. Today, white residents dominate the area, which contains a trove of natural treasures including Custer State Park, Wind Cave National Park, Jewel Cave National Monument, and the Black Hills National Forest.

I-90 skirts the northern border of the Black Hills from Spearfish in the west to Rapid City in the east; **U.S. 385** twists from Hot Springs in the south to Deadwood in the north. The road system that interconnects through the hills covers beautiful territory, but the roads are difficult to navigate without a good map; pick up one for free almost anywhere in the area. Don't expect to get anywhere fast—these convoluted routes will hold you to half the speed of the interstate.

Take advantage of the excellent and informative **Grayline tours,** P.O. Box 1106, Rapid City, 57709 (605-342-4461). Make reservations or call one hour before departure, and they will pick you up at your motel in Rapid City. Tour #1 is the most complete (mid-May to mid-Oct. daily, 8hr., $30 includes admission prices). **Affordable Adventures,** P.O. Box 546, Rapid City, 57709 (605-342-7691), offers guided mini-van tours of the area ($25-65).

■ Black Hills Forest

The majority of the land in the Black Hills area is part of the National Forest and exercises the "multiple use" principle—mining, logging, ranching, and tourism all take place in close proximity. "Don't-miss" attractions like reptile farms and Flintstone Campgrounds lurk around every bend of the narrow, sinuous roads. The forest itself provides unlimited opportunities for backcountry hiking and camping, as do park-run campgrounds and private tent sites. Contact the **Black Hills National Forest Visitors Center** (605-343-8755), on I-385 at Pactola Lake, for details on backcountry camping (open Memorial Day-Labor Day Sun.-Fri. 8am-6pm, Sat. 8am-7pm).

Camping Backcountry camping in the national forest is free. You must stay 1 mi. away from any campground or visitors center, off the side of the road (leave your car in a parking lot or pull off), and campfire-free. Good area campgrounds include **Pactola,** on the Pactola Reservoir just south of the junction of Rte. 44 and U.S. 385 (sites $12), **Sheridan Lake,** 5 mi. northeast of Hill City on U.S. 385 (sites $13), and **Roubaix Lake,** 30 miles south of Lead on U.S. 385 (sites $9). All campgrounds are quiet and wooded, offering fishing, swimming, and pit toilets, but no hookups. Many national forest campsites can and should be reserved by calling 800-280-CAMP/2267. For a $3 topographical map, contact the visitors center. The Black Hills National Forest extends into Wyoming, with a ranger station in Sundance (307-283-1361; open Mon.-Fri. 8am-5pm). The Wyoming side of the forest permits campfires, allows horses in more areas, and draws fewer visitors.

■ Mount Rushmore

After the overly advertised tourist traps elsewhere in the Black Hills, **Mount Rushmore National Monument** is a refreshing surprise. South Dakota historian Doane Robinson originally conceived this "shrine of democracy" in 1923 as a memorial for local Western heroes like Lewis and Clark and Kit Carson; sculptor Gutzon Borglum finally chose the four presidents. Borglum initially encountered opposition from those who felt the work of God could not be improved, but the tenacious sculptor defended the project's size, insisting that "there is not a monument in this country as big as a snuff box." Throughout the Depression, work progressed slowly and a great setback occurred when the nearly completed face of Thomas Jefferson had to be blasted off Washington's right side and moved to his left due to insufficient granite. In 1941, the 60-ft. heads of George Washington, Thomas Jefferson, Theodore Roosevelt, and Abraham Lincoln were completed; work ceased as the U.S. entered World War II. The planned 465-ft.-tall bodies were never completed, but the millions of visitors who come here every year don't seem to mind.

From Rapid City, take U.S. 16 and 16A to Keystone and Rte. 244 up to the mountain. Parking is free, but there may be a charge in 1997 (to raise money for a new parking area). The **visitors center** (605-574-4104) has exhibits and wheelchairs. (Open daily 8am-10pm; Labor Day-Memorial Day daily 8am-5pm. Ranger tours summers 10am-4pm.) **Borglum's Studio** holds a plaster model of the carving, tools, and plans (open daily 9am-5pm). During the summer, the **Mount Rushmore Memorial Amphitheater** hosts a monument-lighting program. A patriotic speech and slide show commence at 9pm, and light floods the monument 9:30-10:30pm.

The **Mt. Rushmore KOA Palmer Gulch Resort** (605-574-2525 or 800-233-4331), lies 5 mi. west of Mount Rushmore on Rte. 244. With cabins ($35-40) comes the use of showers, stoves, pool, laundry, free shuttle service to Mount Rushmore, movies, hayrides, basketball, volleyball, trail rides (on *Dances with Wolves* horses—$10.50 per hr.), a gas station, and of course, a gift shop. That's primitive camping for ya. Make reservations early. (Campsites for 2 $20, with water and electricity $26.)

■ Crazy Horse Memorial

If you thought Mount Rushmore was big, think again. The Crazy Horse Memorial is a wonder of the world in progress; an entire mountain is metamorphosing into a 563-ft.-high memorial sculpture of the great Lakota war leader Crazy Horse. His death was the result of infuriating miscommunication, treachery, and cowardice. He was stabbed by a soldier during an arrest attempt.

The project was initiated by Lakota Chief Henry Standing Bear in response to nearby Mount Rushmore. He wanted to let "the white man know the red man has heroes, too." The memorial stands as a bittersweet reminder that in the midst of the Black Hills gold rush the year before Crazy Horse died, the U.S. took back the Black Hills, which they had promised to the Sioux. The project began in 1947 and received no government funding of any kind. The sculptor, Korczak Ziolkowski, believed in the American spirit of free enterprise and went solo for years, twice refusing $10 million in federal funding. Crazy Horse's face and part of his arm are now visible; eventually, his entire torso and head will be carved into the mountain. The Memorial, 17 mi. southwest of Mount Rushmore on U.S. 16/385, includes the **Indian Museum of North America** as well as the mountain statue; don't miss the impressive 10-min. slide show. (605-673-4681. Open daily 6:30am-9pm; Oct.-April 8am-dusk. $6, $15 per carload, under 6 free. AAA discount.)

■ Custer State Park

Peter Norbeck, governor of South Dakota during the late 1910s, loved to hike among the thin, towering rock formations that haunt the area south of Sylvan Lake and Mt. Rushmore. In order to preserve the area, he created Custer State Park. The spectacular **Needles Hwy.** (Rte. 87) within the park follows his favorite hiking route. Norbeck designed this road to be especially narrow and winding so that newcomers could experience the pleasures of discovery. The highway does not have guard rails, so slow and cautious driving is essential; watch out for mountain goats and bighorn sheep. Custer's biggest attraction is its herd of **1500 buffalo,** which can best be seen near dawn or dusk wandering near Wildlife Loop Rd. If you're "lucky," they, along with some friendly burros will come right up to your car; don't get out of your car (605-255-4515; open Mon.-Fri. 7:30am-5pm). The park's **entrance fee** is $3 per person, $8 per carload for a 7-day pass. At the entrance, ask for a copy of *Tatanka* (Lakota for "bison"), the Custer State Park newspaper. The **Peter Norbeck Visitors Center** (605-255-4464), on U.S. 16A 1 mi. west of the State Game Lodge, serves as the park's info center. (Open Memorial Day-Labor Day daily 8am-8pm, Labor Day-Oct. 9am-5pm, May-Memorial Day 9am-5pm.) All seven park **campgrounds** charge $8-11 per night; most have showers and restrooms. About half of the park's 323 sites are reservable (800-710-2267), and the entire park fills by about 1pm in the summer. Food and concessions are available at all four park lodges, but the local general stores in Custer, Hermosa, or Keystone generally charge less.

At 7,242 ft., **Harney Peak** is the highest point east of the Rockies and west of the Pyrenees. At the top is an old lookout point, a few mountain goats, and a great view of the Black Hills—sightseeing helicopters hover below. Bring water and food, wear good shoes, and leave as early in the morning as possible to finish before dark. You can hike, fish, ride horses, paddle boats, or canoe at popular **Sylvan Lake,** on Needles Hwy. (605-574-2561; kayak rental $3.50 per person per ½hr.). Horse rides are available at **Blue Bell Lodge** (605-255-4531; stable 255-4571) on Rte. 87 about 8 mi.

from the south entrance ($14 per hr., under 12 $12). Rent mountain bikes ($7.50 per hr.) at the **State Game Lodge** (605-255-4541), on U.S. 16A near the visitors center. All lakes and streams permit fishing with a daily license ($6; 5-day nonresident license $14). Summer trout fishing is the best; call for limitations on the number of fish you can keep. Rental equipment is available at the four area lodges.

■ Wind Cave and Jewel Cave

In the cavern-riddled Black Hills, the subterranean scenery often rivals the above-ground sites. Private concessionaires will attempt to lure you into the holes in their backyards, but the government owns the area's prime underground real estate: **Wind Cave National Park** (605-745-4600), adjacent to Custer State Park on U.S. 385, and **Jewel Cave National Monument** (605-673-2288), 14 mi. west of Custer on Rte. 16. There is no public transportation to the caves. Bring a sweater on all tours—Wind Cave remains a constant 53°F, Jewel Cave 47°F.

Wind Cave Wind Cave was discovered in 1881 by Tom Bingham, who heard the sound of air rushing out of the cave's tiny single natural entrance—the wind was so strong it knocked his hat off. Air forcefully gusts in and out of the cave due to outside pressure changes, and when Tom went back to show his friends the cave, his hat got sucked in. Today, the amazing air pressure leads scientists to believe that only 5% of the cave passages have been discovered. The cave is known for its "boxwork," a honeycomb-like lattice of calcite covering its walls. There are five tours, all of which have more than 150 stairs. The **Garden of Eden Tour** is the least strenuous (1hr.; 6 per day, 8:40am-5:30pm; $3, seniors and ages 6-15 $1.50). The **Natural Entrance Tour** passes the original opening to the cave (1½hr.; each hour 9am-6pm; $5, seniors and ages 6-15 $2.50). The **Caving Tour** is limited to 10 people ages 16 and over (4-hr. tours depart 1pm; $15; seniors $7.50; reservations required). In the afternoon, all tours fill about an hour ahead of time, so buy tickets early. For info, contact Wind Cave National Park, RR1, Box 190-WCNP, Hot Springs 57747 (605-745-4600; open June to mid-Aug. daily 8am-7pm; winter hours vary). The park has a campground with free firewood, potable water, and restrooms (sites $11).

Jewel Cave In striking contrast to nearby Wind Cave's boxwork, the walls of this sprawling underground labyrinth (the second longest cave in the U.S.) are covered with a layer of gray calcite crystal—hence the name. The ½-mi. **Scenic Tour** includes 723 stairs (every ½hr. 8:30am-5:30pm; in winter 1 per day; $5, ages 6-15 $2.50). Make reservations for the 4-hr. **Spelunking Tour**, limited to 10 people ages 16 and over, and be sure to wear sturdy foot gear (summer Sun., Tues., Thurs., and Sat. 12:30pm; $15). For more info, contact the **visitors center** (605-638-2288; open daily 8am-7pm, mid-Oct. to mid-May 8am-4pm).

■ Rapid City

Rapid City's location makes it a convenient base from which to explore the Black Hills and the Badlands. Every summer the area welcomes about 3 million tourists, over 40 times the city's permanent population. Come here for a roof and a hot meal, then head to the nearby parks and monuments.

Practical Information The main east-west roads, **St. Joseph, Kansas City,** and **Main** (also **Business Loop 90**) are next to each other. **Mount Rushmore Rd.** (also Rte. 16) is the main north-south route. Pick up a free map at the **Rapid City Chamber of Commerce and Visitors Information Center,** 444 Mt. Rushmore Rd. N., in the Civic Center. (Visitors Info 348-2015; open mid-May to mid-Oct. daily 7:30am-6pm. Chamber of Commerce 343-1744, open Mon.-Fri. 8am-5pm.) Call 394-2255 to check on road conditions. **Jack Rabbit Lines** scurries east from the **Milo Barber Transportation Center,** 333 6th St. (348-3300), downtown, with one bus daily to Pierre (3hr.,

$53) and Sioux Falls (8hr., $97). **Powder River Lines,** also in the center, services Wyoming and Montana, running once per day to Billings (9hr., $54) and Cheyenne (8½hr., $59). The station is open Mon.-Fri. 8am-5pm, Sat. 10am-5pm, Sun. 10am-noon and 2-5pm. **Affordable Adventures** and **Greyline Tours** have regional tours based out of Rapid City (see the "Black Hills Region," p. 507). The **Rapid City Regional Airport,** 8 mi. SE of town on U.S. 44 (394-4195 or 393-9924), serves the area. **Airport Express Shuttle** (399-9999) charges $8-12 for a one-way trip from Rapid City to the airport. Public transportation (394-6631) runs **buses** 6am-6pm ($1, seniors 50¢). The **Rape and Assault Victims Helpline** (341-4808) is open 24hr. **Emergency** is 911. **Time zone:** Mountain (2hr. behind Eastern). Rapid City's **post office:** 500 East Blvd. (394-8600), several blocks east of downtown (open Mon.-Fri. 8am-5pm, Sat. 9am-12:30pm). **ZIP code:** 57701. **Area code:** 605.

Accommodations Rapid City accommodations are *considerably* more expensive during the summer. Make reservations; budget motels often fill up weeks in advance, especially during the first 2 weeks in August when nearby Sturgis hosts its annual motorcycle rally. Skiers and winter travelers are in luck—there are bargains in the off season (mid-Sept. to mid-May). **Kings X Lodge,** 525 E. Omaha St. (342-2236), boasts clean rooms, cable, and free local calls (June-Aug. singles $29, doubles $37). **Big Sky Motel,** 4080 Tower Rd. (800-318-3208), has a view (June-Sept. singles $29-37, doubles $36-42). **Camping** is available at Badlands National Park (p. 471), Black Hills National Forest (p. 472), and Custer State Park (p. 473).

Food and Nightlife Sixth St. **Bakery and Delicatessen,** 516 6th St. (342-6660), next to the $1.50 cinema, serves up delectable sandwiches ($3.50-4), biscuits (65¢), croissants, and espresso. (Open Mon.-Fri. 6:30am-8pm, Sat. 7am-8pm, Sun. 9am-6pm; in winter Mon.-Sat. 7am-6pm, Sun. 10am-4pm.) **Remington's,** 603 Omaha St. (348-4160), doesn't shave as close as a blade or your money back—it memorializes the late great cowboy and sculptor Frederic Remington and serves fine sandwiches, burgers, steak, and chicken ($4.50-11; open Mon.-Thurs. 11am-10:30pm, Fri.-Sat. 11am-11:30pm, Sun. 4:30pm-10pm).

Nightlife lines **Main St.** between 6th and Mt. Rushmore St. For a beer as black as the Hills, toss back a Rushmore Stout ($2.75) at the **Firehouse Brewing Co.,** 610 Main St. (348-1915), *the* bar in Rapid City. Located in a restored 1915 firehouse, the company brews 12 beers in-house and serves up sandwiches, burgers, pasta ($5-10), and occasional live music in the summer (open Mon.-Thurs. 10am-midnight, Fri.-Sat. 11am-2am, Sun. 4-10pm). The **Atomic Café,** 515 7th St. (399-1922), mushrooms with alternative and punk "most nights" in a laid-back atmosphere; sip a cappucino ($1-2.25) or try the "Atomic Bomb" ($4.50), four shots of espresso that will detonate in your stomach (cover varies; open Mon.-Thurs. 8am-midnight, Fri.-Sat. 9am-2am, Sun. 9am-10pm). For boot-stompin', knee-slappin' country-western music and dancing, head to **Boot Hill,** 526 Main St. (343-1931), where bands perform nightly (occasional $2 cover Fri.-Sat.; open Mon.-Sat. 1pm-2am).

Sights and Entertainment If you have a car, pick up a map of the **Rapid City Circle Tour** at the Civic Center or any motel; the route leads you to numerous free attractions and includes a jaunt up Skyline Dr. for a bird's-eye view of the city and seven concrete dinosaurs of **Dinosaur Park.** All of the tour's museums can be reached on foot: **The Museum of Geology** (free) and the children's **Museum in Motion** ($2), both at 501 E. St. Joseph St. (394-2467); the **Dahl Fine Arts Center** (394-4101; free), at 7th and Quincy St.; and the **Sioux Indian Museum** (348-0557) and **Pioneer Museum** (394-6099), at 515 W. Blvd. (free).

■ Spearfish and Deadwood

Spearfish Located on the northwest edge of the Black Hills, Spearfish makes a good base for exploring more expensive Lead and Deadwood. Nearby, the lovely

Spearfish Canyon Scenic Byway (U.S. 14A) winds through 18 mi. of forest along Spearfish Creek, passing one of the sites where *Dances with Wolves* was filmed (marked by a small sign 2mi. west of U.S. 14A on Rte. 222).

For free maps and hiking advice stop by the **Spearfish Ranger Station,** 2014 N. Main St. (605-642-4622; open Mon.-Fri. 8am-5pm, Sat. 7am-3pm). The **Chamber of Commerce,** 115 E. Hudson St. (800-626-8013), lies just east of Main St. (Open Mon.-Fri. 8am-7pm, Sat. 10am-3pm, Sun. noon-7pm; in winter Mon.-Fri. 8am-5pm.) The weary traveler can rest at **Bell's Motor Lodge** (605-642-3812), on Main St. at the east edge of town, with free local calls, TV, and a pool (singles $40; doubles $50; open May-Sept.). The **Canyon Gateway Hotel** (605-642-3402 or 800-281-3402), south of town on U.S. 14A, offers cozy rooms (singles $36, doubles $38.50). Four mi. west of U.S. 14A on Rte. 222 are two spectacular National Forest campgrounds among the pine and next to a rushing creek: **Rod and Gun Campground** (sites $5) and **Timon Campground** (sites $8). Both have pit toilets; Timon has potable water.

The vaguely Mediterranean **Bay Leaf Café,** 126 W. Hudson (605-642-5462), right off Main St., serves salads, sandwiches, and veggie dishes ($3-12; jazz and blues piano Fri.-Sat. 8pm; open daily 7am-10pm, Sept.-May 8am-9pm). Lunch on the lawn of **Lown House Restaurant** (605-642-5663), at 5th and Jackson, or feast on sandwiches, burgers, and steaks ($3-10) inside the 1893 mansion (open daily 7am-9pm; Labor Day-Memorial Day 9am-7pm).

Deadwood Continue along Main St. from Lead for 3 mi. and you'll find yourself in Deadwood. Gunslingers **Wild Bill Hickock** and **Calamity Jane** sauntered into town during the height of the Gold Rush. Bill stayed just long enough—two months—to spend eternity here. Deadwood is home to **Saloon #10,** 657 Main St. (605-578-3346), where legend has it that he was shot holding aces and eights, the infamous "dead man's hand." Every summer Bill has more lives than 60 cats; the shooting is morbidly re-enacted on location four times per day. The main attraction in Deadwood is **gambling,** with casinos lining **Main St.** The **Midnight Star,** 677 Main St. (800-999-6482), owned by Kevin Costner, displays memorabilia from his cinematic exploits. There is free parking on the north side of town; take the 25¢ trolley into town or walk three blocks. Budget digs are scarce in Deadwood; stay in nearby Spearfish or Rapid City, or try **Recreational Springs Resort** (605-584-1228), on Rte. 385 about 10 mi. south of Deadwood (sites $5, with hookup $10; single cabins $35, double $50). Food in Deadwood varies month to month as casinos try new hooks—the best deals are the ones advertised on the windows.

■ Hot Springs

Located on scenic **U.S. 385,** the well-to-do once flocked from the four corners to bathe in the mineral waters of this quaint town. Today, Hot Springs is just about the only town in the Black Hills untouched by glitz and neon; its charming pink sandstone buildings and less expensive lodgings make it a good base from which to explore the southern Black Hills. Wind Cave National Park lies just outside of town, but plan to give Hot Springs' sights a few hours before you head for the hills. For info, stop at the **visitors center,** 801 S. 6th St. (745-6974 or 800-325-6991), on U.S. 385, which runs right through downtown (open May-Oct. daily 8am-8pm).

The Sioux and Cheyenne used to fight over possession of the 87°F spring here; in 1890, a public pool was erected at the spring. Zip down the waterslide at **Evan's Plunge** (745-5165), on U.S. 385, into the world's largest naturally heated pool (open June-Aug. daily 5:30am-10pm; winter hours vary; $7, ages 3-12 $5). **Kidney Spring,** just to the right of the waterfall near U.S. 385 and Minnekahta Ave., is rumored to have healing powers. Drink from the public fountain at the gazebo or bring a jug and take some of the mineral water home. Woolly mammoths were sucked into a sinkhole and fossilized near Hot Springs about 26,000 years ago; see their bones at the **Mammoth Site** (745-6017), on the U.S. 18 bypass. (½-hr. tours $4.25, seniors $4, ages 6-12 $2.50. Open daily 8am-8pm; winter hours vary.)

At the **Historic Log Cabin Motel** (745-5166), on U.S. 385 at the north edge of town, real log cabins come in all shapes and sizes. Guests can partake of the communal outdoor hot tub (no phones; singles $39, doubles $49). **Hide Away Cabins,** 442 S. Chicago St. (745-5683), on U.S. 385, has rooms tucked away in the proprietors' backyard next to the flower garden (singles $25, doubles with kitchenettes around $40). **Katz Kafe** (745-6005), in the Minnekahta Block Mall on National and River St., has good soups and salads from $5-6. Live piano music and tea parlor atmosphere (open Mon.-Fri. 7am-4pm, Sat. 8am-4pm).

Iowa

"Boring" Iowa bears the brunt of the nation's jokes about farming, corn, and rednecks; Iowa Hawkeyes prefer the word "quiet." It's a fine distinction, but you'll have to get off I-80 to understand it. Along old country roads you can find fields of dreams, bridges of Madison County, barns of childhood fantasies, and the scenic Loess Hills in the west—created by wind-blown quartz silt, the hills are a geological rarity found only in Iowa and China. Iowa preserves its European heritage in the small towns that keep German, Dutch, and Swedish traditions alive. Of course, Iowa's farming reputation can't be ignored. Iowa contains a fourth of all U.S. Grade A farmland, and the familiar farmers of *American Gothic* were painted by native son Grant Wood. Clearly, Iowa can be proud.

PRACTICAL INFORMATION

Capital: Des Moines.
Iowa Department of Economic Development: 200 E. Grand Ave., Des Moines 50309 (515-242-4705 or 800-345-4692).
Time Zone: Central (1hr. behind Eastern). **Postal Abbreviation:** IA.
Sales Tax: 5%.

■ Des Moines

French explorers originally named the Des Moines river the "Rivière des Moingouenas," for a local Native American tribe, but then shortened the name to "Rivière des Moings." Because of its identical pronunciation (mwan), later French settlers mistakenly called the river and city by a name much more familiar to them: Des Moines (of the monks). Today, Des Moines ("da moyne") shows neither Native American nor monastic influence, but rather the imprint of the agricultural state that spawned it. The World Pork Expo is a red-letter event on the Iowan calendar and the city goes hog-wild for the Iowa State Fair every August. Des Moines also boasts a great art museum and countless local festivals.

PRACTICAL INFORMATION

Tourist Office: Greater Des Moines Convention and Visitors Bureau, 2 Ruan Center, #222 (286-4960 or 800-451-2625), at 6th and Locust in the skywalk. Open Mon.-Fri. 8:30am-5pm. For upcoming events, call 830-1451.
Airport: Des Moines International (256-5195), Fleur Dr. at Army Post Rd., about 5mi. southwest of downtown; take bus #8 "Havens." Taxi to downtown $10.
Buses: Greyhound, 1107 Keosauqua Way (243-1773 or 800-231-2222), at 12th St., just northwest of downtown; take bus #4 "Urbandale." To: Iowa City (6 per day, 2hr., $21); Omaha (9 per day, 2hr., $27); St. Louis (6 per day, 10hr., $40-74). Tickets sold daily 7am-midnight. Open in summer 24hr.; Sept.-May daily 7am-2am.
Public Transportation: Metropolitan Transit Authority (MTA), 1100 MTA Lane (283-8100), just south of the 9th St. viaduct. Open Mon.-Fri. 8am-5pm. Buses run Mon.-Sat. approx. 6am-6pm. $1, seniors 50¢ except weekdays 3-6pm; transfers

10¢. Routes converge at 6th and Walnut St. Get maps at the MTA office or any Dahl's market. A 25¢ **trolley** runs through downtown area Mon.-Fri. 11am-2pm.

Taxis: Yellow Cab, 243-1111. $1.70 base, $1.40 per mi. 50¢ surcharge 10pm-4am.

Car Rental: Budget (287-2612), at the airport. $21 weekend, $32 weekdays with 150 free mi. per day; 25¢ per additional mi. Must be 21 with major credit card. Under 25 surcharge $10 per day. Open Sun.-Fri. 6am-11pm, Sat. 6am-10pm. Airport office (287-6015) open daily 6:30am-11:30pm.

Crisis Lines: Rape/Sexual Assault Line, 288-1750. Open 24hr. **Suicide Hotline,** 244-1010. **Red Cross Crisis Line,** 244-1000. Both Mon.-Fri. 3pm-8am, weekends 24hr.

Gay and Lesbian Resource Center, 522 11th St. (281-0634).

Emergency: 911.

Post Office: 1165 2nd Ave. (283-7505), downtown just north of I-235. Open Mon.-Fri. 7:30am-5:30pm. **ZIP code:** 50318. **Area code:** 515.

Des Moines idles at the junction of I-35 and I-80. Numbered streets run north-south, named streets east-west. Numbering begins at the **Des Moines River** and increases as you move east or west; **Grand Ave.** divides addresses north-south. Other east-west thoroughfares are **Locust St.,** and, moving north, **University Ave.** (home to Drake University), **Hickman Rd.,** and **Euclid/Douglas Ave.** Most downtown buildings are connected by the **Skywalk,** a series of passages above the street, so many Des Moines businesspeople never have to go outdoors—except to smoke.

ACCOMMODATIONS AND CAMPING

Finding cheap accommodation in Des Moines is usually no problem, though you should make reservations for visits in August, when the State Fair comes to town, and during high school sports tournament season in March. Several cheap motels cluster around **I-80** and **Merle Hay Rd.,** 5 mi. northwest of downtown. Take bus #4 "Urbandale" or #6 "West 9th" from downtown.

YMCA, 101 Locust St. (288-2424), at 1st St. downtown on the west bank of the river. Convenient location. Small, somewhat clean rooms with a communal bathroom. Lounge, laundry, athletic facilities, pool. Men only. Singles $24.50, $75 per week. Key deposit $5. Call ahead; it fills quickly.

YWCA, 717 Grand Ave. (244-8961), across from the Marriott Hotel downtown in a fairly safe area. Moderately clean dorm-style rooms with access to lounge, kitchen, laundry, and pool. All rooms have two beds, a small fridge, sink, and microwave; its main purpose is to provide social services and emergency shelter. Women (and boys under 12) only. $8 per day, $46 per week. $7 for use of pool and facilities. Call ahead; it books up.

Motel 6, 4817 Fleur Dr. (287-6364), at the airport, 5min. south of downtown. Take bus #8, which runs on a limited schedule. Free local calls, cable TV with HBO. Singles $30, doubles $36.

Village Inn, 1348 E. Euclid (265-1674), at 14th St. E., offers large, recently renovated rooms. Take bus #4 "E. 14th." Singles $35, doubles $41.

Iowa State Fairgrounds Campgrounds, E. 30th St. (262-3111), at Grand Ave. Take bus #1 "Fairgrounds" to the Grand Ave. gate and follow Grand straight east through the park. No fires. Basic sites with water $10, with electricity $12. Fee collected in the morning. At fair time in August, the place books well in advance. Open mid-May to mid-Oct.

FOOD

Good eating places tend to congregate on **Court Ave.** downtown, or in antique-filled **Historic Valley Junction** in West Des Moines, on 5th St. south of Grand.

The Tavern, 205 5th St. (255-9827), in Historic Valley Junction, has the best pizza around—and everyone knows it, so you'll have to wait your turn. Pizzas with top-

GREAT PLAINS

pings from "bacon cheeseburger" to "taco fiesta" range $7-15. Open Mon.-Thurs. 11am-11pm, Fri.-Sat. 11am-midnight, Sun. noon-10pm.

Stella's Blue Sky Diner, 400 Locust St. (246-1953), at the Skywalk level in the Capital Square Mall. Settle into a 50s-style vinyl chair as loud waitresses serve up meatloaf and burgers. Have an order of neutron fries ($2) and a malt ($2.50); ask for it "Stella's way"—do you feel lucky? Open Mon.-Fri. 6:30am-6pm, Sat. 8am-6pm.

Billy Joe's Pitcher Show, 1701 25th (224-1709), at University in West Des Moines. A combination restaurant and movie theater. Waitresses serve beer (pitchers $5.75) and assorted grub ($4-10) while you watch the flick ($3, before 6pm $2). 4-5 shows per day, 12:30-9pm; weekend midnight shows; call for exact times.

The Iowa Machine Shed, 1151 Hickman Rd. (270-6818), in Urbandale. One of the loudest restaurants in all of Iowa, including a high volume of tourists. Cracks 3600 eggs every week. The overall-clad waitstaff serves breakfast ($3.50-7), sandwiches ($4-5), and cow- and pig-derived entrees ($8-17). Open Mon.-Sat. 6am-10pm, Sun. 7am-9pm.

SIGHTS

The most elaborate of its ilk, the copper- and gold-domed **state capitol** (281-5591), on E. 12th St. across the river and up Grand Ave., provides a spectacular view of Des Moines from its lofty hilltop position. Inside, an 18-ft. long scale model of the battleship *U.S.S. Iowa* graces the lobby; take bus #5 "E. 6th and 9th St.," #1 "Fairgrounds," #4 "E. 14th," or #7 "Walker." (Free tours Memorial Day-Labor Day Mon.-Sat. every ½hr. 9:30am-3pm; call for winter hours. Building open Mon.-Fri. 8am-4:30pm, Sat.-Sun. 8am-4pm.) Farther downhill, the modern **Iowa State Historical Museum and Archives,** 600 E. Locust (281-5111), houses displays on Iowa's natural, industrial, and social history, including an exhibit addressing the environmental overdevelopment of Iowa and the disappearance of the prairie. Take any bus that goes to the capitol. (Open Tues.-Sat. 9am-4:30pm, Sun. noon-4:30pm. Free.) The geodesic greenhouse dome of the **Botanical Center,** 909 E. River Dr. (242-2934), just north of I-235 and the capitol, encompasses a desert, rainforest, and bonsai exhibit. (Open Mon.-Thurs. 10am-6pm, Fri. 10am-9pm, Sat.-Sun. 10am-5pm. $1.50, seniors 75¢, students 50¢, under 6 free.)

Most cultural sights cluster west of downtown on Grand Ave. The **Des Moines Art Center,** 4700 Grand Ave. (277-4405), draws raves for its modern art collection as well as for its architecture; Eero Saarinen, I. M. Pei, and Richard Meier contributed to the design of the museum. Check out the statue *Pegasus and Man* in the courtyard; the museum planned to market a wine with the statue as their logo, but the Bureau of Alcohol, Tobacco, and Firearms said they would have to put shorts on the figure. Take bus #1 "West Des Moines." (Open Tues.-Wed. and Sat. 11am-4pm, Thurs.-Fri. 11am-9pm, Sun. noon-4pm. $4, students and seniors $2; free until 1pm and all day Thurs.) Only a few blocks south of the Art Center on 45th St., the **Science Center of Iowa,** 4500 Grand Ave. (274-6868), dazzles with simulated space shuttle flights, laser shows, and computer-generated planetarium shows. (Open Mon.-Sat. 10am-5pm, Sun. noon-5pm. $5, seniors and ages 3-12 $3.) Historic **Jordan House,** 2001 Fuller Rd. (225-1286), east of Grand, was a stop on the Underground Railroad (open May-Oct. Wed. 10am-3pm, Sat. 1-4pm, Sun. 2-5pm; $2, kids 50¢).

Ten mi. northwest of downtown in Urbandale, **Living History Farms** (278-5286) at Hickman Rd. and 111th St., sets the standard for re-created pioneer villages. (Last tour 2hr. before closing. Open May to mid-Oct. daily 9am-5pm. $8, seniors $7, ages 8-12 $5.) In **Indianola,** 12 mi. south on U.S. 69, the **National Balloon Museum,** 1601 N. Jefferson (961-3714), holds the annual **National Balloon Classic** with hot-air balloons from all over the world. (Classic held in late July. Museum open Mon.-Fri. 9am-4pm, Sat. 10am-4pm, Sun. 1-4pm. Free. Call to arrange a tour; $1.)

ENTERTAINMENT AND NIGHTLIFE

The **Civic Center,** 221 Walnut St. (243-1109), sponsors theater and concerts; call for info. For listings of free events, pick up a copy of *Cityview,* the free local weekly paper. The **Iowa State Fair,** one of the largest in the U.S., captivates Des Moines for ten days during the middle of August (7-17 in 1997) with prize cows, crafts, cakes, and corn ($6 per day, under 12 free); for the low-down, write to State House, 400 E. 14th St., Des Moines 50319-0198, or call the state fair hotline (800-545-FAIR/3247). From May to September, Des Moinians gather for **Seniom Sed** (Des Moines spelled backwards; 245-3880), a city-wide block party held Fridays from 4:45 to 7:15pm at Nollen Plaza downtown. **Jazz in July** (280-3222) presents a series of free concerts at locations throughout the city nearly every day of the month; pick up a schedule at area restaurants or the visitors bureau. **Pella,** 41 mi. east of Des Moines on Rte. 163, blooms in May with its annual **Tulip Time** festival (628-4311; May 8-10 in 1997), with traditional Dutch dancing, a parade, concerts, and *glöckenspiel* performances.

Court Ave., in the southeast corner of downtown, is a yuppified warehouse district packed with trendy restaurants and bars. At **Papa's Planet,** 208 3rd St. (284-0901), 20-30-somethings move to 80s and 90s dance music on two dance floors, and play pool on the patio outside. (21+. Live music Fri.-Sat. Thurs. 5¢ beers, cover $5; Fri.-Sat. cover $3-5, includes drink specials. Open Thurs.-Sat. 7pm-2am.) **Java Joe's,** 214 4th St. (288-JAVA/5282), sells coffee from locales like Kenya and Sumatra ($1-2.75). Wednesday to Saturday, there's live folk, with some Celtic and Irish music thrown in; on Sundays, catch jazz. (Cover Fri.-Sat. $3. Open Mon.-Thurs. 7:30am-11pm, Fri.-Sat. 7:30am-1am, Sun. 9am-11pm.) **The Garden,** 112 SE 4th St. (243-3965), is a gay and lesbian dance bar. (Drag shows Fri.-Sat. 11pm, Sun. 10pm. Cover Thurs.-Sat. $2-3. Open Mon.-Wed. 7pm-2am, Thurs.-Sun. 5pm-2am.)

■ Iowa City

Iowa City, the staid capital of Iowa until 1857, is now a classic college town and a mecca of liberalism in a conservative state. The main University of Iowa campus fills the city with schools of students who support a plethora of bars, frozen yogurt stands, and street musicians. Each autumn weekend, hordes of Iowans make a pilgrimage to the city to cheer on the university's football team, the Hawkeyes.

Practical Information Iowa City lies on I-80 about 112 mi. east of Des Moines. North-south **Madison** and **Gilbert** and east-west **Market** and **Burlington** bind the downtown. The **convention and visitors bureau,** 408 1st Ave. (800-283-6592), sits across the river in Coralville off U.S. 6. (Open Mon.-Fri. 8am-5pm, Sat.-Sun. 10am-4pm.) Downtown, **Iowa City Transit** (356-5151) buses run Monday to Saturday 6:30am-10:30pm (75¢, seniors 35¢). The free **Cambus** runs all over campus and downtown. The University of Iowa's **Campus Information Center** (335-3055), in the **Iowa Memorial Union** at Madison and Market St., has area info (reduced hours in summer; open termtime Mon.-Sat. 8am-9pm, Sun. noon-4pm). **Greyhound** and **Burlington Trailways** are both located at 404 E. College St. (337-2127 or 800-231-2222), at Gilbert St. Buses head out for Des Moines (7 per day, 2-4hr., $20), Chicago (6 per day, 5hr., $35), and St. Louis (1 per day, 9-13hr., $55); station open Mon.-Fri. 7:30am-7pm, Sat.-Sun. noon-6pm. **Help lines** include the **24-hr. Crisis Line** (335-0140), **Rape Crisis** (335-6000), and **Gayline** (335-3877). Iowa City's **post office:** 400 S. Clinton St. (354-1560; open Mon.-Fri. 8:30am-5pm, Sat. 9:30am-1pm). **ZIP code:** 52240. **Area code:** 319.

Accommodations, Camping, and Food Cheap motels line U.S. 6 in **Coralville,** 2 mi. west of downtown, and 1st Ave. at Exit 242 off I-80. Skip the chains, and choose the last of a dying breed: the **Blue Top Motel** (351-0900), at 5th St. and 10th Ave. in Coralville (take Coralville Express bus "B" to the post office). Rents ten homey, inexpensive white cottages on five acres of manicured lawns (singles $29.50, with kitchen $39.50). The **Wesley House Hostel (HI-AYH),** 120 N. Dubuque St. (338-1179), at Jefferson, has two small, nondescript seven-bed rooms with kitchen and lounge access, but an all-day lockout. (Check-in 7-9pm. Check-out Mon.-Sat. 9am, Sun. 8am. $12, nonmembers $24.) **Kent Park Campgrounds** (645-2315), 9 mi. west on U.S. 6, manages 86 secluded first come, first served sites in a pretty area near a lake ($4, with electricity $8).

Downtown boasts good, moderately priced restaurants and bars; at the open-air **Pedestrian Mall,** on College and Dubuque St., you can eat and shop among the melodies of street musicians. In the mall, **Gringo's,** 115 E. College St. (338-3000), slaps down Mexican dishes ($5-12), an all-you-can-eat buffet on Mondays ($7), a taco bar Tuesdays ($5; both 5-8pm), and margaritas ($1.25). (Open Mon.-Thurs. 11am-10pm, Fri.-Sat. 11am-11pm, Sun. 11:30am-10pm.) A college favorite, **Micky's Irish Pub,** 11 S. Dubuque St. (338-6860), whips up salads, mickwiches, and burgers ($4-7; open Mon.-Fri. 11am-10pm, Sat.-Sun. 8am-10pm; bar open later). At **The Java House,** 211½ E. Washington St. (341-0012), sip coffee ($1.30) on a cushy red chair, espresso ($1.25) atop a couch, or latte ($1.90) at a table (feel free to mix and match). (Open Mon.-Thurs. 7am-12:30am, Fri.-Sat. 7am-1am, Sun. 8am-midnight.)

Sights, Entertainment, and Nightlife Iowa City's main attraction, the **Old Capitol** building (335-0548), at Capitol and Iowa St., has been restored almost beyond recognition. (Open Mon.-Sat. 10am-3pm, Sun. noon-4pm. Free.) The capitol is the focal point of the **Pentacrest,** a five-building formation surrounded by lawns: a perfect place to hang out. One of the five buildings, the **Museum of Natural History** (335-0480), at Jefferson and Clinton St., displays killer dioramas on the Native Americans of Iowa (open Mon.-Sat. 9:30am-4:30pm, Sun. 12:30-4:30pm; free). Strange as it may seem, the **University of Iowa Hospitals and Clinics** (335-0480), on Hawkins Dr. in Coralville, feels more like Disney World than a sick ward; it features free concerts and an extensive art collection. Use the main entrance and take elevator D to the eighth floor **Medical Museum** (open Mon.-Fri. 8am-5pm, Sat.-Sun. 1-4pm).

Bars and nightspots are ubiquitous downtown. **Deadwood** (351-9417) is often lauded as the city's best bar. For live music six nights a week, slide by **Gunnerz,** 123 E. Washington St. (338-2010) or **Gabe's,** 330 E. Washington St. (354-4788; cover $2-6). Local jazz, folk, and blues musicians play Thursday through Saturday at 9:30pm in **The Sanctuary,** 405 S. Gilbert (351-5692), a cozy, wood-paneled restaurant and bar with 120 beers (cover varies; open Mon.-Sat. 4pm-2am, Sun. 4pm-midnight). **The Union Bar and Grill,** 121 E. College St. (339-7713), brags that it's the "biggest damn bar in college foorball's "Big Ten" (open Tues.-Sat 7pm-2am).

■ Amana Colonies

In 1714, German fundamentalists disillusioned with the established church formed the Community of True Inspiration. Facing persecution at home, they fled to the U.S. in 1843, settling near Buffalo, NY. Later, the growing community migrated again—this time to the rich lands along the Iowa River. They named their quiet, communal settlement the Amana Colonies (Amana means "to remain true"). Although the colonies have become a large tourist attraction, most of the stores are run by colonists' descendents, many of whom are still active in the church.

The Amana Colonies lie 5 mi. north of I-80, clustered around the intersection of U.S. 6, Rte. 220, and U.S. 151. The main thoroughfare, the **Amana Trail,** runs off U.S. 151 and goes through all seven villages; signs off this road point to the main attractions. **Main Amana** is the largest, most touristy town; farther out, the smaller villages offer a taste of earlier times. There is no public transportation in the Colonies. The **Amana Colonies Visitors Center** (800-245-5465), just west of Amana on Rte. 220, provides free calls to area motels and B&Bs. (Open Mon.-Sat. 9am-5pm, Sun. 10am-5pm; call for winter hours.) A private car **caravan tour** (622-6178) covering six villages begins from the visitors center every Saturday at 10am (3hr., $8). Throughout the colonies, look for the helpful *Guide Map.*

GREAT PLAINS

Most lodging options are pricey but personal B&Bs ($40-60); call from the visitors center. At the **Guest House Motor Inn** (622-3599), on 47th Ave. in downtown Main Amana, rooms in a 135-year-old former communal kitchen have charming quilts on the beds (singles $37, doubles $43). **Sudbury Court Motel** (642-5411), 5 mi. west of the colonies on U.S. 6 at M St. in Marengo, offers large, cheap rooms in a quiet locale (singles $25, doubles $30). Camp at the **Amana Community Park,** on 27th Ave. in Middle Amana (restrooms; no showers; sites $3 per vehicle, with hookup $4).

Restaurants throughout the colonies serve huge portions of heavy food family-style. **Homestead Kitchen** (622-3203), U.S. 151, Homestead, churns out diner food the Amana way. (Sandwiches $2-4, entrees $5-8.50. Open Sun.-Thurs. 7:30am-8pm, Fri.-Sat. 7:30am-9pm.) Middle Amana's **Hahn's Hearth Oven Bakery** (622-3439), at 25th and J St., sells the scrumptious products of the colonies' only functional open-hearth oven. (Open April-Oct. Tues.-Sat. 7am to sell-out, usually around 4:30pm; Nov.-Dec. and March Wed. and Sat. only.)

The **Amana Heritage Society** (622-3567) operates four local museums: Museum of Amana History, Communal Kitchen and Cooper Shop Museum, Communal Agriculture Museum, and Community Church. A combination ticket for all four is $5, ages 8-17 $2. The **Museum of Amana History** (622-3567), on 220th Trail in Main Amana, illuminates the colonists' lifestyle with restored buildings and a super-cool slide show. (Open mid-April to mid-Nov. Mon.-Sat. 10am-5pm, Sun. noon-5pm. $3, ages 8-17 $1.) **Mini Americana** (622-3058), in South Amana on 220th trail, has a quirky exhibit of rural history in miniature (open daily April-Oct. 9am-5pm; $3.50). The **High Amana Store** (622-3797), at 13th and G St., hasn't changed its interior or friendliness policy since 1857 (usually open daily 10am-5pm, less in winter). The Amana Colonies are also home to many fine wineries. Sample dandelion wine at the **Heritage Wine and Cheese Haus** (622-3564), in Main Amana. (Open Mon.-Sat. 9am-6pm, Sun. 10am-6pm.) At **Ehrle Bros.,** (622-3241), Homestead, you can venture into the wine cellar between sips (open Mon.-Sat. 9am-5pm, Sun. 11am-5pm).

Nebraska

Early travelers on the Oregon and Mormon trails rushed through Nebraska on their way towards western gold and greenery. Accustomed to the forested hills of New England, these pioneers nicknamed Nebraska Territory the "Great American Desert," mistakenly believing that if trees did not grow here, neither would crops. Eventually they caught on, and began to abandon their westward journeys to farm the fertile Nebraskan soil. Their settlements drove out the native tribes of Sioux and Pawnee, who had long understood the value of Nebraska's land. But neither these property-minded settlements, which have since grown into cities, nor the tourists who drive past Scotts Bluff in air-conditioned autos can truly master the land. "We come and go, but the land is always here," philosophized Willa Cather, "and the people who love it and understand it are the people who own it—for a little while."

PRACTICAL INFORMATION

Capital: Lincoln.
Tourist Information: Nebraska Department of Economic Development, P.O. Box 94666, Lincoln 68509 (402-471-3796 or 800-228-4307). Open Mon.-Fri. 8am-5pm. **Nebraska Game and Parks Commission,** 2200 N. 33rd St., Lincoln 68503 (471-0641). Open Mon.-Fri. 8am-5pm.
Time Zone: Central (1hr. behind Eastern). **Postal Abbreviation:** NE
Sales Tax: 5-6½%, depending on city.

■ Omaha

Omaha is not the type of place one associates with "Nebraska." The largest city in the state, this birthplace of Gerald Ford, Malcolm X, and Boys Town is also its most urban. From the quiet streetside cafés of the Old Market to the jumping gay clubs at 16th and Leavenworth, Omaha offers cosmopolitan glitz with midwestern manners, combining world-class museums and restaurants with the native friendliness and easy living of a Nebraska small town.

PRACTICAL INFORMATION

Tourist Office: Greater Omaha Convention and Visitors Bureau, 6800 Mercy Rd. #202 (800-332-1819). Open Mon.-Fri. 8:30am-4:30pm. The **visitors center** (595-3990), at 10th and Deer Park by the zoo, is much easier to find; get off I-80 at 13th St. Open daily 8am-5pm; Nov.-Feb. Mon.-Fri. 8am-5pm. **Events Hotline,** 444-6800. **Gay and Lesbian Hotline,** 558-5303.

Trains: Amtrak, 1003 S. 9th St. (800-872-7245), at Pacific. To: Chicago (1 per day, 9½hr., $106); Denver (1 per day, 8hr., $112). Open daily 10:30pm-7:30am, Mon.-Sat. 7:30-11:15am and 12:30-4pm.

Buses: Greyhound, 1601 Jackson (800-231-2222). To: Des Moines (9 per day, 2-3hr., $25); Cheyenne (3 per day, 9-10hr., $66); Kansas City (2 per day, 4-6hr., $37-43); Sioux Falls (2 per day, 3-4hr., $34-57). Open 24hr.

Public Transportation: Metro Area Transit (MAT), 2222 Cumming St. (341-0800). Open Mon.-Fri. 8am-4:30pm. Schedules available at the Park Fair Mall, at 16th and Douglas near the Greyhound station, and the library at 14th and Farnam. Fare 90¢, transfers 5¢.

Taxis: Happy Cab, 339-0110. $1.80 first mi., $1.25 per additional mi. 24hr.

Car Rental: Cheepers Rent-a-Car, 7700 L St. (331-8586). $19 per day with 100 free mi.; $25 per day with 300 free mi.; 20¢ per additional mi. Must be 21 with a major credit card and personal liability policy. Open Mon.-Fri. 7:30am-8pm, Sat. 8:30am-3pm.

Crisis Lines: Rape Crisis, 345-7273. **Suicide Hotline,** 449-4650. Both 24hr.

Emergency: 911.

Post Office: 1124 Pacific St. (348-2895). Open Mon.-Fri. 8am-6pm, Sat. 8am-noon. **ZIP code:** 68108. **Area code:** 402.

Numbered north-south streets begin at the river and go west; named roads run east-west. **Dodge St.** (Rte. 6) divides the city north-south. At night, avoid **N. 24th St.**

ACCOMMODATIONS AND CAMPING

Budget motels in Omaha proper are often not particularly budget. For better deals, head for the city outskirts or across the river into Council Bluffs, Iowa.

YMCA, 430 S. 20th St. (341-1600), at Howard. Plain, basic rooms. Co-ed by floor. Microwave. Men's and women's singles $9.50-11.50. Linen provided. Key deposit $10. $3.50 extra to use athletic facilities. Call ahead.

Colonial Hotel, 3804 Farnam St. (551-4543). Rough around the edges, but cheap: where the YMCA, when full, refers would-be guests. Singles w/ shared bath $10 and up.

Satellite Motel, 6006 L St. (733-7373), just south of I-80 Exit 450 (60th St.). The round building on the corner. Clean, wedge-shaped rooms equipped with fridge, TV with HBO. Singles $32, doubles $40.

Bellevue Campground (291-3379), Haworth Park, on the Missouri River 10mi. south of downtown at Rte. 370. Take the infrequent bus "Bellevue" from 17th and Dodge to Mission and Franklin, and walk down Mission. Sites are paved with concrete, but there are enough trees to eliminate that trailer park feel. Showers, toilets, shelters. Open daily 6am-10pm; quiet stragglers can enter after hours. Sites $5, with hookup $10.

FOOD

It's no fun being a chicken, cow, or vegetarian in Omaha, with a fried chicken joint on every block and a steakhouse in every district. Once a warehouse area, the brick streets of the **Old Market**, on Jones, Howard, and Harney St. between 10th and 13th, now feature popular shops, restaurants, and bars. While you're there, visit the eerie **Fountain of the Furies**, "Greek avengers of patricide and disrespect of ancestors," in a concealed grotto off Howard St.

Délice European Café, 1206 Howard St. (342-2276), in the Old Market. Scrumptious pastries and deli fare at reasonable prices ($1.50-5). Plus, the bulletin board inside lists goings-on about town. Ask about availability of day-old baked goods; they're often not advertised. Open Sun.-Thurs. 8am-10pm, Fri.-Sat. 8am-11pm.

The Bohemian Café, 1406 S. 13th St. (342-9838), in South Omaha's old Slavic neighborhood. The placemat poetry says it all: "Dumplings and kraut today/at Bohemian Café/draft beer that's sparkling/plenty of parking/see you at lunch, okay?" The sauerkraut is fantastic, but most dishes are meat-based ($6-8). Open daily 11am-10pm.

The Jones Street Brewery, 1316 Jones St. (344-3858). A trendy, clean-cut microbrewery that serves soups, salads, and the "Need a Brew Burger," with jalapeños and hot sauce ($7). Live music on weekends; cover varies. Open Mon.-Thurs. 11:30am-11pm, Fri.-Sat. 11:30am-midnight, Sun. 2-10pm.

McFoster's Natural Kind Café, 302 S. 38th St. (345-7477), at Farnam St. Healthier, kinder dishes ($6-14), including chicken (hey—it's free range!), vegan eggplant parmesan (with a choice of dairy or soy-based cheese), and artichoke mornay. Occasional live music; cover around $3. Open Mon.-Thurs. 7am-10pm, Fri. 7am-11pm, Sat. 11am-11pm, Sun. 10am-3pm.

SIGHTS

Omaha's **Joslyn Art Museum,** 2200 Dodge St. (342-3300), displays an excellent collection of 19th- and 20th-century European and American art within a monumental Art Deco masterpiece. The exterior is pink Georgian marble, the interior dazzles with 30 different types of stone. From mid-July to mid-August, the museum hosts free "Jazz on the Green" concerts each Thursday from 7 to 9pm. (Open Tues.-Sat. 10am-5pm, Thurs. 10am-8pm, Sun. noon-5pm. $4, seniors and ages 5-11 $2; free Sat. 10am-noon.)

The grand **Union Pacific Railroad Station** houses the **Western Heritage Museum,** 801 S. 10th St. (444-5071), which in turn houses a huge exhibit on historic life in Nebraska. (Open Mon.-Sat. 10am-5pm, Sun. 1-5pm; Labor Day-Memorial Day closed Mon. $3, seniors $2.50, ages 5-12 $2.)

The largest indoor jungle in the world has made the amazing **Henry Doorly Zoo,** 3701 S. 10th St. (733-8401), at Deer Park Blvd. (or exit at 13th St. off I-80), the number one tourist attraction between Chicago and Denver. At the Kingdom of the Seas Aquarium, brown sharks swim above the glass-enclosed walkway. (Open Mon.-Sat. 9:30am-5pm, Sun. 9:30am-6pm; Labor Day-Memorial Day daily 9:30am-5pm. $7.)

Catch sight of deer and birds galore at the **Fontenelle Forest Nature Center,** 1111 N. Bellevue Blvd. (731-3140), in Bellevue, a privately owned 1300-acre forest and wetland, with 17 mi. of walking and hiking trails. The center includes a one-mile eco-friendly disabled accessible boardwalk raised above the forest floor. The Hickory Trail off the boardwalk brings you right up to the Missouri River. (Open Mon.-Fri. 8am-5pm, Sat.-Sun. 8am-6pm. $3.50.)

In 1917, Father Edward Flanagan founded **Boys Town** (498-1140), west of Omaha at W. Dodge and 132nd St., as a home for troubled and neglected boys. Made famous by the 1938 Spencer Tracy movie of the same name, Boys Town has become a popular tourist attraction and still provides a home to more than 550 boys and girls. Visits are free; guided tours take place hourly from 9am-4pm. (Visitors center open daily 9am-5:30pm; Sept.-April 9am-4:30pm.)

ENTERTAINMENT AND NIGHTLIFE

In late June and early July, **Shakespeare on the Green** (280-2391) stages free performances in Elmwood Park, on 60th and Dodge, Sunday through Thursday at 8pm. The **Omaha Symphony** (342-3560) plays at the **Orpheum Theatre,** 409 S. 16th St. (Sept.-May usually Thurs.-Sun.; call for specific dates and times; tickets $10-32). **Omaha's Magic Theater,** 325 S. 16th St. (346-1227; call Mon.-Fri. 9am-4pm), nobly devotes itself to the development of new American musicals (evening performances Mon.-Sat.; tickets $12, children $7).

Punk and progressive folk have found a niche at the several area universities; check the window of the **Antiquarian Bookstore,** at 1215 Harney, in the Old Market, for the scoop on shows. Several good bars await nearby. **The Dubliner,** 1205 Harney (342-5887), down the stairs, stages live traditional Irish music Friday and Saturday nights (cover varies). **Downtown Grounds,** 1117 Jackson St. (342-1654), grinds with live music in a hip coffeehouse. (Double mocha $3. Live music Fri.-Sat. and Mon.; cover Fri.-Sat $2. Open Mon.-Thurs. 9am-10pm, Fri. 9am-midnight, Sat. 8am-midnight, Sun. 10am-10pm.) A string of gay bars hover within a block of 16th and Leavenworth. One of the most popular, **The Max,** 1417 Jackson (346-4110; no sign outside), caters to men and women with five bars, a disco dance floor, DJ, fountains, and patio (cover Fri.-Sat. $3; open daily 4pm-1am).

■ Lincoln

Friendly folk, happening nightlife, and a renovated downtown enliven Lincoln, christened in the name of the President in 1867. The University of Nebraska football team, the Cornhuskers, is a significant presence in town; the smiling face of Coach Osborne beams down on the city from a billboard on O St., and locals gnash their teeth in communal woe after every losing game. In its breathtaking capitol building, the "Tower on the Plains," Lincoln houses the only unicameral (one-house) state legislature in the U.S. The state switched from two houses during the Great Depression in order to save money and avoid red tape; today, the Nebraskan government is considered a model of efficiency.

PRACTICAL INFORMATION

Tourist Office: Lincoln Convention and Visitors Bureau, 1221 N St. #320 (434-5335 or 800-423-8212). Open Mon.-Fri. 8am-4:45pm.

Airport: Lincoln Airport (474-2770), 5mi. northwest of downtown on Cornhusker Hwy. A taxi to downtown costs about $10.

Trains: Amtrak, 201 N. 7th St. (476-1295 or 800-872-7245). Once daily to: Omaha (1hr., $14); Denver (7½hr., $106); Chicago (10½hr., $111); Kansas City (6½hr., $46). Open nightly 11:30pm-6:45am; Mon.-Wed. also 7:30-11am and 12:30-4pm.

Buses: Greyhound, 940 P St. (474-1071 or 800-231-2222), close to downtown and city campus. To: Omaha (4 per day, 1hr., $12); Chicago (4 per day, 12-14hr., $71); Kansas City (3 per day, 6½hr., $46); Denver (3 per day, 9-11hr., $66). Open Mon.-Fri. 8:30am-5:30pm, Sat. 9am-5pm.

Public Transportation: Star Trans, 710 J St. (476-1234). Schedules are available on the bus, at many downtown locations, and at the office. Buses run Mon.-Sat. 6am-6pm. Fare 75¢, seniors with Medicare card 35¢, ages 5-11 40¢.

Taxis: Husker Cabs, Inc., 447-4111. $1.75 initial fee, $1.60 per mi. 24hr.

Car Rental: U-Save Auto Rental, 2240 Q St. (477-5236). $25 per day with 100 free mi.; 10¢ per additional mi.; $145 per week. Must be 21. $100 deposit.

Bike Rental: Blue's Bike & Fitness Center, 427 S. 13th (435-2322), at K St. Bikes $10 per ½-day, $16 per day. Credit card deposit required. Open Mon.-Thurs. 9am-7pm, Fri. 9am-6pm, Sat. 9am-5pm, Sun. noon-4pm.
Quadratic Formula: $(-b \pm \sqrt{b^2 - 4ac})/2a)$.
Crisis Lines: Crisis Line, 475-5171. **Rape Crisis Line,** 475-7273. Both 24hr. **University of Nebraska Gay/Lesbian Resource Center,** 472-5644.
Emergency: 911.
Post Office: 700 R St. (473-1695). Open Mon.-Fri. 7:30am-6pm, Sat. 9am-noon. **ZIP code:** 68501. **Area code:** 402.

Getting around Lincoln is as easy as A,B,C, 1,2,3, cha cha cha. Numbered streets increase as you go west; lettered streets progress through the alphabet as you go north. **O St.** is the main east-west drag, splitting the town north-south. **R St.** runs along the south side of the **University of Nebraska-Lincoln (UNL)** campus. **Cornhusker Hwy. (U.S. 6)** shears the northwest edge of Lincoln.

ACCOMMODATIONS AND CAMPING

There are few inexpensive motels in downtown Lincoln; most abound east of downtown around the 5600 block of Cornhusker Hwy. **UNL, Smith Hall,** 1120 14th St. (472-3561), rents some rooms when school is not in session; sheets, towels, and blankets are included (singles $18.50, doubles $11.80 per person). **The Great Plains Budget Host Inn,** 2732 O St. (476-3253 or 800-288-8499), has large rooms with fridges and coffeemakers. Take bus #9 "O St. Shuttle" (free parking; singles $36, doubles $44; free continental breakfast). The **Cornerstone Hostel (HI-AYH),** 640 N. 16th St. (476-0355 or 476-0926), at Vine, located in the basement of a church in the university's downtown campus, rarely fills up. Take the #4 bus; from the Greyhound station, walk seven blocks east to 16th, then five blocks north. (2 single-sex rooms; 3 beds for women, 5 for men. Shower, full kitchen, laundry facilities. Free parking. Curfew 11pm. $8, nonmembers $10. Free linens.) To get to **Camp-A-Way,** corner of 1st and Superior St. (476-2282), take Exit 401 or 401a from I-80. Pleasant sites, but a trifle out of the way. ($10, with full hookup $15. Showers and laundry facilities available.) The **Nebraska State Fair Park Campground,** 2402 N. 14th St. (473-4287), offers a convenient location with a parking lot atmosphere; take bus #7 "Belmont." (Site for 2 $10, with electricity $12, with full hookup $15; $1 per additional person. Open mid-April to Nov. 1.)

FOOD AND NIGHTLIFE

A dandy collegiate hangout, the **Nebraska Union** (472-2181), on 14th and R St. on campus, has cheap and speedy food, a post office, an ATM, and a bank (hours vary, but usually in summer Mon.-Fri. 7am-5pm, academic year daily 7am-11pm). Cheap bars, eateries, and movie theaters cluster around one side of UNL's downtown campus, between N and P from 12th to 15th St. **Historic Haymarket,** 7th to 9th and O to R St., is a newly renovated warehouse district near the train tracks, with cafés, bars, several restaurants, and a **farmers market** (434-6900; open mid-May to mid-Oct. Sat. 8am-12:30pm). All downtown buses connect at 11th and O St., 2 blocks east of Historic Haymarket. Every renovated warehouse district has its yuppie brewery—**Lazlo's Brewery and Grill,** 710 P St. (474-BEER/2337), is the oldest brewery in Nebraska, founded in 1991. Chow down on salads, sandwiches, burgers, steak, and chicken entrees for $5-15 (open daily 11am-1am). Right next door, **Ja Brisco,** 700 P St. (474-7272), whips up pizzas, pasta, and deli sandwiches ($4-12) that locals adore (open daily 11am-10:30pm). **Valentino's,** 232 N. 13th St. (475-1501), a regional chain with roots in Lincoln, offers inexpensive Italian pizza and pasta ($3-10). Locals come to sample from six different all-you-can-eat buffets. ($5, after 4pm $7. Open Sun.-Thurs. 11am-2pm and 4-10pm, Fri.-Sat. 11am-2pm and 4-11pm.) **The Coffee House,** 1324 P St. (477-6611), overfloweth with those near-a-university, espresso-induced intellectual-esque conversations (coffee 75¢-$1.25; open Mon.-Sat. 7am-midnight, Sun. 11am-midnight).

Nightspots abound in Lincoln, particularly those of the sports bar variety; locals always take time to celebrate Nebraska football, Lincoln's pride and joy. For the biggest names in Lincoln's live music scene, try **The Zoo Bar,** 136 N. 14th St. (435-8754). Cover varies, as does the music, but the emphasis is *good* blues. (Must be 21. Fri. 5-7pm cover $1. Open Mon.-Fri. 3pm-1am, Sat. noon-1am.) **The Panic,** 200 S. 18th St. (435-8764), at N St., is a great gay dance/video/patio bar (open Mon.-Fri. 4pm-1am, Sat.-Sun. 1pm-1am). And now for something completely different...**Sidetrack Tavern,** 935 O St. (435-9171). Sing along with house band Joyce, Paul, and Fred—they play everything, and everyone joins in the ruckus (Fri.-Sat. 7pm-1am).

SIGHTS AND ENTERTAINMENT

The "Tower on the Plains," the 400-ft. **Nebraska State Capitol Building** (471-0448), 14th at K St., an unofficial architectural wonder of the world, wows with its streamlined exterior and detailed interior. Its mosaic floor is reminiscent of a Native American blanket. Take the elevator to the 14th floor for a view of the city. (Tours June-Aug. Mon.-Fri. every 30min.; Sept.-May daily every hr. Open Mon.-Fri. 8am-5pm, Sat. 10am-5pm, Sun. 1-5pm. Free, 'cause it's paid for.)

The **Museum of Nebraska History** (471-4754), 15th and P St., has a phenomenal, moving exhibit on the history of the Plains Indians (open Mon.-Sat. 9am-5pm, Sun. 1:30-5pm; free). The **University of Nebraska State Museum,** 14th and U St. (472-6302), in Morrill Hall, boasts an amazing fossil collection that includes the largest mounted mammoth in any American museum (open Mon.-Sat. 9:30am-4:30pm, Sun. 1:30-4:30pm; requested donation $1). In the same building, the **Mueller Planetarium** (472-2641) lights up the ceiling with several shows daily and laser shows Saturdays and Sundays. (Call for times; closed on home game days. Planetarium $3, students and under 13 $2; laser shows $5/$2). The **Sheldon Memorial Art Gallery,** 12th and R St. (472-2461), was designed by Phillip Johnson and houses a Warhol collection (open Tues.-Wed. 10am-5pm, Thurs.-Sat. 10am-5pm and 7-9pm, Sun. 2-9pm; free). Picturesque picnicking spots include **Van Dorn Park,** 9th and Van Dorn, and nearby **Wilderness Park,** stretching from 1st and Van Dorn to 27th and Saltillo Rd. The **Pioneer Park and Golf Course** (441-7895), ½ mi. south of W. Van Dorn and Coddington (watch for the signs along Van Dorn) harbors bison and elk within its wildlife sanctuary. (Open June-Aug. Mon.-Sat. 8:30am-8:30pm, Sun. noon-8:30pm; Sept.-May Mon.-Sat. 8:30am-5pm, Sun. noon-5pm. Free.)

■ Scotts Bluff

Known to the Plains Indians as "Me-a-pa-te" ("hill that is hard to go around"), the imposing clay and sandstone highlands of **Scotts Bluff National Monument** were landmarks for people traveling the Mormon and Oregon Trails in the 1840s. For some time the bluff was too dangerous to pass through, but in the 1850s a single-file wagon trail was opened through narrow **Mitchell's Pass,** where traffic wore deep marks in the sandstone. Evidence of the early pioneers can still be seen today on the ½-mi.

The Little Elves of Carhenge

Driving through the low plains and small bluffs of western Nebraska, things begin to look the same. Suddenly, a preternatural power sweeps the horizon as you come in view of the ultimate shrine to bizarre on-the-road Americana—Carhenge. Consisting of 36 old cars painted gray, this bizarre sculpture has the same orientation and dimensions as Stonehenge in England. Carhenge's creator, Jim Reinders, wants to be buried here someday. When asked why he built it, Reinders replied, "plane, loqui deprehendi," or "clearly, I spoke to be understood." Right on, Jimmy! This wonder of the cornhuskers can be found right off U.S. 385, 2 mi. north of Alliance, NE.

stretch of the original Oregon Trail preserved at the pass. The **visitors center** (308-436-4340), at the entrance on Rte. 92, will tell you of the mysterious death of Hiram Scott, the fur trader who gave the Bluffs their name (open daily 8am-8pm, in winter 8am-5pm; $4 per carload, $2 per pedestrian). To get to the top of the bluffs, hike challenging **Saddle Rock Trail** (1.6 mi. each way) or motor up **Summit Dr.** At the top, you'll find **nature trails** and a magnificent view. Take U.S. 26 to Rte. 92; the monument is on Rte. 92 about 2 mi. west of **Gering** (*not* in the town of Scottsbluff). In mid-July, the **Oregon Trail Days Festival** packs the towns near Scotts Bluff with trail-happy, festive folk.

The **Sands Motel,** 814 W. 27th St. (800-535-1075), Scottsbluff on Rte. 26 and 71, has spotless rooms perked up with coffee makers and complimentary filters (singles $27-29, doubles $36). The **Kiwanis Riverside Campground,** 1600 S. Beltline Hwy. W. and 1818 Avenue A (630-6235), offers campsites in a sparsely wooded area ($8, $12 with hookup; open May 1-Sept. 30). Twenty mi. east of Rte. 92, the 525-ft. spire of **Chimney Rock,** visible from more than 30 mi. away, was another landmark for travelers to the Oregon Trail. A gravel road leads from Rte. 92 to within ½ mi. of it.

Kansas

The geographic center of the contiguous U.S., Kansas has been a major link in the nation's chain since the 1820s. Families on the Oregon and Santa Fe Trails drove their wagons West in search of new homes, while cowboys on the Chisholm Trail drove their longhorns north in search of railroads and good times. Cowtowns such as Abilene and Dodge City were happy to oblige; these rip-roaring meccas of gambling and drinking made legends of lawmen like "Wild Bill" Hickok and Wyatt Earp. The influx of settlers resulted in fierce battles over land, as white settlers forced Native Americans to move into the arid regions farther west. More grueling feuds over Kansas' slavery status (Kansas joined the Union as a free state in 1861) gave rise to the term "Bleeding Kansas." The wound has healed, and Kansas today presents a peaceful blend of kitschy tourist attractions—the Kansas Teachers' Hall of Fame in Dodge City or the World's Largest Hand-Dug Well in Greensburg—and eons of farmland. Highway signs subtly remind travelers that "every Kansas farmer feeds 75 people—and *you.*"

PRACTICAL INFORMATION

Capital: Topeka.
Division of Travel and Tourism: 700 SW Harrison #1300, Topeka 66603-3712 (800-2KANSAS/252-6727). Open Mon.-Fri. 10am-6pm. **Kansas Wildlife and Parks,** 900 Jackson Ave. #502N, Topeka 66612 (913-296-2281).
Time Zone: Central (1hr. behind Eastern). **Postal Abbreviation:** KS.
Sales Tax: 4.9%.

■ Wichita

In 1541, Coronado came to the site of present-day Wichita in search of the mythical gold-laden city of Quivira. Upon arriving, he was so disappointed that he had his guide strangled for misleading him. The largest city in Kansas, Wichita is *the* place for airplane manufacturing: Lear, Boeing, Beech, and Cessna all have factories in town. Much of the downtown is painfully suburban in its tree-lined stillness. As the Old Town area gets revamped, though, its bars and cafés party farther and farther into the Kansas night.

Practical Information The **convention and visitors bureau** dispenses info at 100 S. Main St. (265-2800 or 800-288-9424), on the corner of Douglas Ave. (open

Mon.-Fri. 8am-5pm). The closest **Amtrak** station, 414 Main St. (283-7533 or 800-872-7245), 25 mi. north of Wichita, in the town of Newton, sends one very early train to Kansas City (4hr., $62) and Albuquerque (12hr., $144; ticket office open Wed.-Fri. 7:30am-4pm). **Greyhound,** 312 S. Broadway (265-7711 or 800-231-2222), barks 2 blocks east of Main St. and 1½ blocks southwest of the transit station (open daily 3am-7pm). Buses serve Kansas City (3 per day, 5hr., $25), Oklahoma City (3 per day, 4½hr., $36), Denver (2 per day, 14hr., $59-72), and Dodge City (1 per day, 3hr., $36). **WMTA,** 214 S. Topeka (265-7221), handles in-town transportation. (Buses run Mon.-Fri. 5:30am-6:30pm, Sat. 7:20am-5:20pm. $1, seniors 55¢, ages 6-17 75¢; transfers 25¢. Station open Mon.-Fri. 6am-6:30pm, Sat. 7am-5:30pm.) In the summer a **trolley** (25¢) runs from downtown to Old Town during lunch hours (Mon.-Fri. 11am-2pm) and from downtown to Old Town and the museums on the river on Saturdays (10am-3:40pm). **Thrifty Rent-A-Car,** 8619 W. Kellogg (721-9552), puts you in a car for $35 per day (250 free mi., 29¢ each additional mi.) or $145 per week (2000 free mi.). You must be 21; ages 21 to 24 pay a $5-per-day surcharge (open daily 6:30am-10pm). **Emergency:** 911. Wichita's **post office:** 330 W. Second St. (262-6245), at Waco (open Mon.-Fri. 7am-5:30pm, Sat. 7am-3pm; lobby open 24hr.). **ZIP code:** 67202. **Area code:** 316.

Wichita lies on I-35, 170 mi. north of Oklahoma City and about 200 mi. southwest of Kansas City. Small and quiet, downtown makes for easy walking or parking. **Main St.** is the major north-south artery. **Douglas Ave.** divides the numbered east-west streets to the north from the named east-west streets to the south. Many downtown businesses have moved out along **Kellogg Ave. (U.S. 54),** the main east-west route.

Accommodations and Food Wichita offers up a bounty of cheap hotels. South Broadway has plenty of mom-and-pop places, but be wary of the neighborhood. The chains line E. and W. Kellogg Ave. 5 to 8 mi. from downtown. Only ten blocks from downtown, the **Mark 8 Inn,** 1130 N. Broadway (265-4679), has small, comfortable rooms that come with free local calls, cable TV, A/C, fridge, and laundry facilities, though partakers should be careful in this neighborhood at night. (Singles $27, each additional person $3; no checks.) The **Royal Lodge,** 320 E. Kellogg Ave. (263-8877), near downtown and the bus station, has rooms on the dark side (dim, that is) with free local calls, cable TV, and a waterbed option. (Singles $30, doubles $35; key deposit $5; no checks.) **Blasi Campgrounds,** 11209 W. U.S. 54 (722-2681), about 8 mi. west of downtown, features a pool, tennis courts, and a small fishing pond in a next-to-the-highway setting. (Tent sites $14. Full hookups priced according to vehicular largess; start at $16.40. Weekly rates, AAA, and AARP discounts available.)

Wichita is flavored with *meat!!!* If you eat only one slab of it in Wichita, make it a slab from **Doc's Steakhouse,** 1515 N. Broadway (264-4735), where the most expensive entree—a 17-oz. T-bone with salad, potato, and bread—is only $9. (Open Mon.-Thurs. 11:30am-9:30pm, Fri. 11:30am-10pm, Sat. 4-10pm.) Doc's brother Ted opened a small drug store in South Dakota sometime in the 1930s, and he'd like you to know that, from Doc's, it's "676 mi. to Wall Drug" (for more on this roadside legend see p. 470). Veggie-philes get their fill on Chinese and Vietnamese dishes ($4-9) at **Saigon Oriental Restaurant,** 1103 N. Broadway (262-8134; open Sun.-Thurs. 10am-9pm, Fri.-Sat. 10am-10pm). In the **Old Town** area, at Douglas Ave. and Washington St., revitalized warehouses now house breweries and restaurants. **Station Square** (263-1950), at Mead St. and Douglas Ave., combines two restaurants, two bars, and an outdoor barbecue grill, for cuisine and atmosphere ranging from 50s-diner-style to fajitas and 'ritas. (Live music Fri.-Sat. Open Sun. and Tues.-Sat. 11am-midnight.)

Sights The museums of the **Museums-on-the-River** series are located within a few blocks of each other; take the trolley or bus #12 "Riverside." **Old Cowtown,** 1871 Sim Park Dr. (264-0671), walks you through the rough and tumble cattle days of the 1870s with an open-air history exhibit. (Open Mon.-Sat. 10am-5pm, Sun. noon-5pm; Nov.-Feb. weekends only. $5, seniors $4.50, ages 6-12 $2, under 6 free. Call for spe-

GREAT PLAINS

cial events info.) Across the way, **Botanica,** 701 Amidon (264-0448), presents an interesting and colorful series of gardens. (Open June-Aug. Mon.-Wed. 9am-8pm, Thurs.-Sat. 9am-5pm, Sun 1-5pm; April-May and Sept.-Dec. Mon.-Sat. 9am-5pm, Sun. 1-5pm; Jan.-March Mon.-Fri. 9am-5pm. $3, students $2; Jan.-March. free.) The **Mid-America All-Indian Center and Museum,** 650 N. Seneca (262-5221), just down the road, showcases traditional and modern works by Native American artists. The late Blackbear Bosin's awe-inspiring sculpture, *Keeper of the Plains,* stands guard over the grounds. (Open Mon.-Sat. 10am-5pm, Sun. 1-5pm. $2, ages 6-12 $1, under 6 free.) The **Mid-America All-Indian Intertribal Powwow** surrounds the museum with traditional dancing, foods, arts, and crafts during the last weekend in July. The **Wichita Art Museum,** 619 Stockman Dr. (268-4921), exhibits American art, including works by Mary Cassatt, Winslow Homer, and Edward Hopper, as well as an interactive gallery for kids (open Tues.-Sat. 10am-5pm, Sun. 12-5pm; free). The **Wichita-Sedgwick County Historical Museum,** 204 S. Main St. (265-9354), one block south of the visitors bureau, gives a look into Wichita's past and includes a cottage circa 1890 and a Jone Six car (one of five left in existence), which never did quite meet its dream of superseding Ford. (Open Tues.-Fri. 11am-4pm, Sat.-Sun. 1-5pm. $2, under 13 $1.)

Fifty-three sculptures adorn the campus of the **Wichita State University,** at N. Hillside and 17th St. (take the "East 17th" bus); the collection includes pieces by Moore, Nevelson, and Hepworth. If you've heard of any of these people, you're not only in luck—you're in the minority. Get free sculpture maps at the **Edwin A. Ulrich Museum of Art** office (689-3664), in the McKnight Arts Center, also on campus, and admire the gigantic glass mosaic mural by Joan Miró which forms one wall of the building (call for hours; free). Just north of campus, the **Center for the Improvement of Human Functioning,** 3100 N. Hillside (682-3100), on the "N. Hillside-Oliver Loop" bus route, features a 40-ft. pyramid, used for reflection and receptions, with the world's largest FDA food pyramid painted on its side. Tours of the biochemical research station include a chance to "de-stress" mind, body, and soul by hurling clay skeet pigeons at a wall (tours daily 1:30pm; $4).

Most of Wichita's museums and historic points of attraction are part of the **Wichita Western Heritage Tour,** which focuses on the city's contribution to the arts and environment in addition to things historical. If you visit all of the sites, you get a free **belt buckle.**

At the mid-May **River Festival,** over 100,000 people converge on the city of Wichita for concerts, sporting events, and culinary delights ($2). The **Winfield Bluegrass Festival** (221-3250), 45 min. southeast of Wichita on U.S. 77, draws big-name artists for a long weekend of folk fun in late September.

■ Lawrence

In the 1850s, travelers weary of the Oregon Trail were attracted to the lush, hilly lands of eastern Kansas. Lawrence was founded by travelers who'd had enough. Tired voyagers now enjoy the cafés and lively bars supported by students of the **University of Kansas.** The university's **Museum of Anthropology** (864-4245), right across from their **Museum of Natural History,** features traveling exhibits on American culture (open Mon.-Sat. 9am-5pm, Sun. 1-5pm; free). With exhibits like "Pin-up Girls, Hairy Guys, and Art," the **Spencer Museum of Art** (846-4710), on campus at 14th and Mississippi, proves that it's not just another stuffy art museum—look for the traveling exhibit "Ports of Entry: William S. Burroughs." (Open Tues.-Wed. and Fri.-Sat. 10am-5pm, Thurs. 10am-9pm, Sun. noon-5pm. Free.) Students and professionals present plays and concerts at the **Lied Center** (864-ARTS/2787), at 15th and Iowa

---

Geographic Center of the U.S.

Have you ever wanted to be the center of the action? Go 2 mi. northwest of **Lebanon,** KS. Sit by the stone monument and feel special—the entire contiguous U.S. is revolving around you.

(box office open Mon.-Fri. noon-5:30pm). **Liberty Hall,** 644 Massachusetts St. (749-1972), rents videos, hosts concerts, and shows artsy and independent flicks in an ornate theater, complete with constellations twinkling on the ceiling. Chat with the employees to find out what's happening in town.

The **convention and visitors bureau** (865-4411), at 8th and Vermont, has more local info (open Mon.-Fri. 8am-5pm), or you can try their other center at 2nd and Locust St., across the bridge from downtown in the renovated train depot (open Mon.-Sat. 8:30am-5:30pm, Sun. 1-5pm). **Greyhound** runs nine buses per day to Kansas City (1hr., $11) and three per day to Wichita (4hr., $26), out of the Conoco gas station at 2447 W. 6th St. (843-5622). Lawrence's **area code:** 913.

If you need to spend the night, a slew of motels settle on 6th St. The **Westminster Inn,** 2525 W. 6th St. (841-8410), looks like a charming English lodge and has a swimming pool ($38 singles, $44 doubles). The **College Motel,** 1703 W. 6th St. (843-0131), has large, clean, phoneless rooms and a pool (rooms start at $35). Die-hard Democrats can pitch their tents at **Clinton Lake Campground** (842-8562), 4 mi. west of town on 23rd St., and take advantage of fishing, hiking, and swimming in beautiful Clinton Lake State Park (sites $4, with water and electric $5; $4 vehicle permit required).

Fast food hangs out on 23rd, Iowa, and 6th St. **Massachusetts St.** is home to the funkier coffeehouses and bars. Cut through the bull and charge toward the **El Matador Café,** 446 Locust St. (841-3837), down the street from the visitors center. Large, excellent Mexican dinners are $3-10; daily lunch specials are $4.50. (Open Tues.-Sat. 11:30am-2pm and 5-10pm.) The **Full Moon Café,** 803 Massachusetts St. (832-0444), feeds the hip and the hippie alike with tofu burgers ($4.25), falafel ($4.35), and meat dishes with an international theme. It's smiley, sunny, crunchy, and in the back of a furniture store. (Free live music Tues.-Wed. 8pm, Thurs. 9pm, Fri.-Sat. 10pm. Open Tues.-Sat. 11am-midnight.) The **Paradise Café,** 728 Massachusetts St. (842-5199), specializes in good old American breakfasts (served until 2:30pm), lunches, and dinners. The pancakes of the day ($3) taste as good as this place smells. Dinners (mostly fish and steak) range from $4.75-13. (Open Mon.-Sat. 6:30am-2:30pm and 5-10pm, Sun. 8am-2:30pm.) Watch 'em make brew, then try it at **The Freestate Brewery Co.,** 636 Massachusetts St. (843-4555), the oldest legal brewery in Kansas. Chase your beer with sandwiches, gumbo, or pasta. (Meals $4-12. Open Mon.-Sat. 11am-midnight, Sun. noon-11pm.) Over 100 types of beer, some on the wall, crowd **The Bottleneck,** 737 New Hampshire (842-5483; cover $2; open daily 3pm-2am).

■ Dodge City

Legend haunts Dodge City, the "wickedest little city in America." Originally, soldiers built Fort Dodge with the hope that annihilating the buffalo would thereby annihilate the Native Americans. Rapidly, the city grew from the influx of buffalo hunters and the travelers on the Santa Fe Trail. By 1879, the buffalo were gone (over 3 million had been slaughtered), the railroad had arrived, and Dodge City had switched to cattle herding. With more gunfighters, prostitutes, and other lawless types than there are pages in this god-forsaken book, chaos reigned; at one time **Front St.,** the main drag, had a saloon for every 50 citizens. Legendary lawmen Wyatt Earp and Bat Masterson earned their fame cleaning up the streets of Dodge City. The city eventually burned, and has been replaced with a highly polished, touristy re-creation.

Saunter on down to the **Boot Hill Museum** (227-8188), at Front St. and 5th Ave., a block-long complex re-creating the Boot Hill cemetery and Front St. as they looked in the 1870s. A 1903 Santa Fe locomotive stands among the saloons, barber shops, and the restored and furnished **Hardesty House,** a rancher's Gothic Revival home. (Admission to the complex $6, seniors and ages 7-17 $5.50; early Sept. to late May $5/$4.50. Open in summer daily 8am-8pm; early Sept. to late May Mon.-Sat. 9am-5pm, Sun. 1-5pm.) Across from Boot Hill, you'll find gunslingers, presidents, and Count Dracula at the **Wax Museum,** 603 5th Ave. (225-7311). The building also houses the **Kansas Teachers' Hall of Fame.** (Open Mon.-Sat. 8:30am-6pm, Sun. 1-5pm; call for winter hours. $2, ages 6-13 $1.25.) **The Home of Stone,** 112 E. Vine St. (227-6791), is a house of stone but not glass built in 1881, and one of the few remaining buildings of its era. (Open June-Aug. Mon.-Sat. 9am-5pm, Sun. 2-5pm. Free.) Walk down 2nd Ave. to Front St. to check out **"El Capitan,"** an enormous longhorn cattle statue which commemorates the cattle drives of the 1870s. Today, longhorn cattle lumber through town only during **Dodge City Days** (227-3119), July 25 to August 3, 1997, when the city reminisces with a huge festival.

   Dodge City Convention and Visitors Dept., at 4th Ave. and Spruce; P.O. Box 1474, 67801 (225-8186 or 800-OLD-WEST/653-9378), has more info on the festival and rodeo. Their office is upstairs from the **chamber of commerce** (227-3119). (Open in summer daily 8:30am-6:30pm; early Sept. to late May Mon.-Fri. 8:30am-5pm. They may open a new seasonal office at 400 Front St., in spring 1997.) On the lawn outside, stop and see the town memorial **sculpture garden,** carved by the late dentist O.H. Simpson (the middle initial is critical here). Dodge City attractions are all within walking distance, but if you need to go beyond the immediate downtown, call the **Minibus Transportation System** (225-8119), and they will pick you up for free within the city limits (operates Mon.-Fri. 9am-4pm; $1 donation requested). Dodge City's **area code:** 316.

   The **Bel-Air Motel,** 2000 E. Wyatt Earp Blvd. (227-7155), quick-draws its way to what may be the best deal in town. (Cable TV, A/C, free local calls. Singles $24, doubles $29.) Most other motels tucker out about 4 mi. west along Wyatt Earp Blvd. (U.S. 50 outside of town). Dodge City's campgrounds are adequate but none too scenic. The slightly dusty **Gunsmoke Campground** (227-8247 or 800-789-8247), on W. U.S. 50, 3 mi. west of Boot Hill, has a pool, laundry facilities, an ice cream parlor, and an office that looks like a saloon (sites for 2 $11, with hookup $15; each additional person $1.50). The **Water Sports Campground,** 500 Cherry St. (225-9003), 10 blocks south of Front St. on 2nd Ave., has lakeside sites for fishing and swimming (sites for 2 $13, with full hookup $15, A/C $2 extra).

   The **Golden Pancake House,** 2110 E. Wyatt Earp Blvd. (227-6196), is a genuine roadside diner (not just recreated to look like one) that rustles up mass quantities for just few bits. (Breakfast all day $2-5, sandwiches and burgers $2-5, dinner entrees $5-10. Open daily 6am-10pm.) **Peppercorn's,** 1301 W. Wyatt Earp Blvd. (225-2335), rustles up sandwiches and salads ($2-5) as well as steaks ($7-14) in a dark bar-like atmosphere. (Open Mon.-Thurs. 11am-midnight, Fri.-Sat. 11am-1am, Sun. 3pm-midnight; bar open Mon.-Sat. 11am-2am.)

   North of the Oklahoma panhandle, Dodge City rides 150 mi. west of Wichita and 310 mi. east of Colorado Springs on U.S. 50. **Amtrak** (800-872-7245) runs out of the **Santa Fe Station,** a century-old national historic landmark at Central and Wyatt Earp Blvd.; contact a travel agent for tickets. One train goes to Kansas City (6½hr., $100) and Albuquerque (9hr., $123) each day. **TNM&O/Greyhound,** 2301 N. Central (227-9547 or 800-231-2222), in the Total Gas station at Plaza St., sends one bus per day to Wichita (3hr., $30), Denver (9hr., $51), and Oklahoma City (7½hr., $50).

Missouri

Pro-slavery Missouri applied for statehood in 1818, but, due to Congressional fears about upsetting the balance of free and slave states, was forced to wait. In 1821, Maine chose to enter the Union as a free state, evening the score and allowing for the admission of both. Missouri's troubled entry into the Union and its Civil War-era status as a border state were harbingers of its future ambiguity. Perhaps because it is so close to the center of the country, Missouri defies regional stereotyping. Its large, East-coast-style cities are defined by wide avenues, long and lazy rivers, numerous parks, humid summer afternoons, and the sounds of blues and jazz wailing deep into the Missouri night. In the countryside, Bible factory outlets stand amidst firework stands and barbecue pits. Residents welcome you to their state with midwestern friendliness and a hint of a southern drawl.

Missouri's patchwork geography further complicates characterization. In the north, near Iowa, amber waves of grain undulate. Along the Mississippi, towering bluffs inscribed with Native American pictographs evoke western canyonlands. Farther inland, spelunkers enjoy some of the world's largest limestone caves—made famous by Tom Sawyer and Becky Thatcher. In the south, the ancient and underrated Ozarks ripple into Arkansas.

PRACTICAL INFORMATION

Capital: Jefferson City.
Missouri Division of Tourism: Department MT-90, P.O. Box 1055, Jefferson City 65102 (314-751-4133). Open Mon.-Fri. 8am-5pm. **Missouri Department of Natural Resources,** Division of State Parks, 205 Jefferson St., Jefferson City 65101 (800-334-6946). Open Mon.-Fri. 8am-5pm.
Time Zone: Central (1hr. behind Eastern). **Postal Abbreviation:** MO.
Sales Tax: 6.225%.

■ St. Louis

In the early 1700s, Pierre Laclede set up a trading post directly below the junction of the Mississippi, Missouri, and Illinois rivers. A natural stopover, the "River City" of St. Louis gained prominence as the U.S. raced into the West. Today, Eero Saarinen's magnificent Gateway Arch, a silvery beacon to visitors and a landmark of America's westward expansion, gleams over one of America's largest inland trading ports.

St. Louis, Memphis, and New Orleans have together been dubbed "America's Music Corridor." In the early 1900s, showboats carrying ragtime and brassy Dixieland jazz bands regularly traveled between Chicago and New Orleans; the music floated through St. Louis and left the city addicted. St. Louis contributed to the development of the blues and saw the birth of ragtime during Scott Joplin's years in the city. Today, St. Louis carries with it much of the character of the surrounding area. Subject to neither the bustle nor the overcrowding of Eastern cities, it asserts its premier status in its parks, monuments, museums, sports teams, and music scene.

PRACTICAL INFORMATION

Tourist Office: St. Louis Visitors Center, 308 Washington Ave. (241-1764). Open daily 9:30am-4:30pm. Other locations at the **airport** and **America's Center** (421-1023), at 7th and Washington. Open Mon.-Fri. 9am-5pm, Sat.-Sun. 10am-2pm. The booklet *Where: St. Louis* has decent maps at no cost. A more complete map, put out by Gousha, is available throughout the city and at the visitors center.
Airport: Lambert-St. Louis International (426-8000), 12mi. northwest of the city on I-70. Hub for **TWA.** MetroLink provides easy access to downtown ($1). A few westbound Greyhound buses stop at the airport.
Trains: Amtrak, 550 S. 16th St. (331-3300 or 800-872-7245), 2 blocks south of Kiel Center. To: Chicago (3 per day, 6hr., $48) and Kansas City (2 per day, 5½hr., $45). Ticket office open daily 6am-8pm, 8:30pm-1am, 3:30am-4:30am.
Buses: Greyhound, 1450 N. 13th St. (231-4484 or 800-231-2222), at Cass Ave. Bi-state bus #30 takes less than 10min. from downtown. To: Chicago (6 per day, 6hr., $31) and Kansas City (6 per day, 5hr., $33). Open 24hr.
Public Transportation: Bi-State (231-2345). Extensive daily service; infrequent during off-peak hours. Maps and schedules available at the Bi-State Development Agency, 707 N. 1st St. (on Laclede's Landing, in the St. Louis Center; 982-1495) or the reference desk of the public library at 13th and Olive St. **MetroLink,** the light-rail system, runs from 5th and Missouri Ave. in East St. Louis to Lambert Airport Mon.-Fri. 5am-1:30am, Sat. 5am-1:20am, Sun. 5:30am-12:30am. Travel is free in the "Ride Free Zone" (from Laclede's Landing to Union Station) Mon.-Fri. 10am-3pm. Metrolink or bus fare $1, transfers 10¢; seniors and ages 5-12 50¢/5¢. 1-day passes $3, 3-day passes $7; available at Metrolink stations. **Shuttle Bug** is a small bus

painted like a ladybug which cruises around Forest Park and the Central West End. All-day fare (until 6pm) $1.

Taxis: County Cab, 991-5300. $1.45 initial fee, $1.10 per mi. **Yellow Cab,** 991-1200. $1 initial fee, $1.20 per mi. Both open 24hr.

Hotlines: Rape Crisis, 531-2003. **Suicide Hotline,** 647-4357. Both 24hr. **Gay and Lesbian Hotline,** 367-0084. Open daily 6-10pm.

Emergency: 911.

Post Office: 1720 Market St. (436-4458). Open Mon.-Fri. 7am-8pm, Sat. 8am-3pm.

ZIP code: 63155. **Area code:** 314 (in MO), 618 (in IL); in text, 314 unless noted.

I-44, I-55, I-64, and I-70 meet in St. Louis. The city is bounded on the west by I-170 and circled farther out by I-270. **U.S. 40/I-64** runs east-west through the entire metropolitan area. Downtown, **Market St.** divides the city north-south. Numbered streets run parallel to the river, increasing to the west. The historic **Soulard** district borders the river south of downtown. **Forest Park** and **University City,** home to **Washington University,** lie west of downtown; the Italian neighborhood called **The Hill** is south of these. Parking comes easy; wide streets allow for lots of meters, and private lots are cheap ($1-5). The city's dangerous sections include **East St. Louis** (across the river in IL), the **Near South Side,** and most of the **North Side.**

ACCOMMODATIONS AND CAMPING

Budget lodging is generally located several mi. from downtown. For chain motels, try **Lindbergh Blvd. (Rte. 67)** near the airport or the area north of the I-70/I-270 junction in **Bridgeton,** 5 mi. beyond the airport. **Watson Rd.** (old Rte. 66 in South County) is littered with cheap motels southwest of where it merges with Chippewa; take bus #11 ("Chippewa-Sunset Hills") or #20 ("Cherokee-Sunset Hills"). Bed and breakfasts (singles from $50, doubles from $60) are listed in the visitors guide, free at visitors centers and many hotels.

Huckleberry Finn Youth Hostel (HI-AYH), 1904-1906 S. 12th St. (241-0076), 2 blocks north of Russell Blvd. in the Soulard District. From downtown, take bus #73 ("Carondelet"), or walk south on Broadway to Russell Blvd. and over (30-40min.). Don't walk on Tucker Blvd.; the hostel is *just* past an unsafe neighborhood. Full kitchen, free parking, and friendly staff. Dorm-style rooms with 5-9 beds. Outdoor lockers. Office open daily 8-10am and 6-10pm. Check-out 9:30am. Ask about work opportunities. $14, nonmembers $17. Linen $2 for stay.

Washington University (935-4637), Shepley Hall, at Shepley Dr., near the corner of Big Bend and Forsyth Blvd. Buses #91 and 93 take 40min. from downtown. Small, spartan dorm rooms with A/C, free local calls, and laundry; near Mallinkrodt student center. Singles $21, doubles $23 per bed. Rooms fill quickly, so reserve well in advance (i.e., April). Open late May to early Aug.

University of Missouri, St. Louis, Honors Hall (516-6872). Take I-70 to Natural Bridge Rd., turn right onto Arlmont Dr.; stay left at split at end of Bellerive Dr. Or take Metrolink to either campus stop, then hop on the campus shuttle. Dorm rooms with free local calls, TV, VCR, laundry, and kitchen access. (Singles $20, doubles $25-30.) Call Mon.-Fri. 8am-5pm to arrange for someone to meet you.

Motel 6, 4576 Woodson Rd. (427-1313), near the airport. From downtown, take bus #4. Other motels in the area can match the price, but few can touch the cleanliness or room quality. A/C, cable, pool. Singles $38, doubles $44.

Horseshoe Lake State Park Campgrounds, 3321 Rte. 111 (618-931-0270), off I-70 in Granite City, IL near Cahokia Mounds. Sites are on an island (connected by a causeway) in a relatively secluded area. No electricity or water. Park closes daily at 10pm. Sites $7.

FOOD

I'm hungry. Skip the big silver arch; where are the golden arches? Because of St. Louis' many historical and ethnic districts, the difference of a few blocks can mean vastly different food styles. For beer, outdoor tables, and live music, often without a

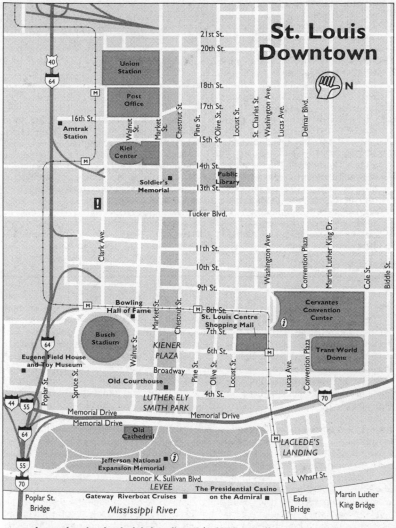

St. Louis Downtown

N

cover charge, head to **Laclede's Landing** (241-5875), a collection of restaurants, bars, and dance clubs housed in 19th-century buildings on the riverfront. Once an industrial wasteland, the Landing is now a hot nightspot (closed to minors midnight-6am). To get there, walk north along the river from the Gateway Arch, or toward the river on Washington St. The **Central West End** offers coffeehouses and outdoor cafés; a slew of impressive restaurants await just north of Lindell Blvd. along **Euclid Ave.** Take MetroLink to "Central West End" and walk north, or catch the Shuttlebug. St. Louis's historic Italian neighborhood, **The Hill,** southwest of downtown and just northwest of Tower Grove Park, produces plenty of inexpensive pasta; take bus #99 ("Lafayette"). Cheap Thai, Philippine, and Vietnamese restaurants spice up the **South Grand** area, at Grand Blvd. just south of Tower Grove Park. The hip intellectual set hangs out on **University City Loop** (not actually a loop, but Delmar Blvd. west of Skinker Blvd.), which features coffeehouses and a mixed bag of American and international restaurants.

Blueberry Hill, 6504 Delmar Blvd. (727-0880), on the Loop. A touristy rock 'n' roll restaurant similar to the Hard Rock—but much cooler. Record covers, Howdy Doody toys, giant baseball cards, and jukeboxes charm the premises. Live bands Thurs.-Sat. nights (cover $3-5). After 4pm, it's 16 and up; after 9pm, 21 and up. Open daily 11am-12:30am.

Pho Grand, 3191 S. Grand Blvd. (664-7435), in the South Grand area. Voted "Best Vietnamese" and "Best Value" in St. Louis. The real deal, not Americanized. Their specialty is the soup (pho, but not pronounced that way; $3.50-4); other entrees are $4-6. Open Sun.-Mon. and Wed.-Thurs. 11am-10pm, Fri.-Sat. 11am-11pm.

Cunnetto House of Pasta, 5453 Magnolia (781-1135), on The Hill. This acclaimed Italian favorite dishes up 30 kinds of pasta, veal, chicken, and steak (lunch $5-7, dinner $7-13). Slightly dressy. May be a long (1-2hr.) wait. Open Mon.-Thurs. 11am-2pm and 5-10:30pm, Fri. 11am-2pm and 5-11:30pm, Sat. 5-11:30pm.

Ted Drewe's Frozen Custard, 6726 Chippewa (352-7376), on old Rte. 66. Also at 4224 S. Grand Blvd. *The* place for the summertime St. Louis experience; custard is very popular here. Get in line for the chocolate-chip banana concrete; toppings are blended, as in a concrete mixer, but the ice cream stays hard enough to hang in an overturned cup ($2). Open Feb.-Dec. daily 11am-midnight.

Talayna's, 276 N. Skinker (863-2120), at Forest Park Pkwy. A local fave for pizza in all shapes and styles—choose from St. Louis, Boston, Chicago, or Talayna's own geographically neutral creations. Pizzas start at $5.45, calzones $5.65; entrees $5-10. Open Mon.-Thurs. 11am-2:15am, Fri.-Sat. 11am-3am, Sun. 11am-2am.

SIGHTS

Downtown

The nation's tallest monument at 630 ft., the **Gateway Arch** (425-4465), on Memorial Dr. within the **Jefferson National Expansion Memorial,** towers gracefully over all of southern Illinois. The most impressive view is from the ground looking up. Elevators straight out of a sci-fi film soar to the top of the arch every 5-10 min. To avoid long waits, go after dinner or in the morning—not on Saturday. The **Museum of Westward Expansion,** beneath the arch, shows a ½-hour film once an hour chronicling the arch's construction; **Odyssey Theater** arches your neck with films shown on a four-story screen every hour on the ½ hour. (Museum and arch open daily 8am-10pm; in winter 9am-6pm. Tickets for 1 attraction $5, ages 3-12 $2; 2 attractions $7.50/$3; 3 attractions $9.50/$3.50; all 4 $11/$4.) Scope out the city from the water with **Gateway Riverboat Cruises** (621-4040); one-hour tours leave from the docks in front of the arch (daily every 1½hr. 11am-3:30am; $7.50, ages 3-12 $3.50).

Within walking distance is the **Old Courthouse,** 11 N. 4th St. (425-6017), across the highway from the arch. Here, in 1847, Dred Scott sued for freedom from slavery (open daily 8am-4:30pm; tours usually on the hr; free). The **Old Cathedral,** 209 Walnut St. (231-3250), St. Louis' oldest church, still holds masses daily. The museum is around the corner (open daily 10am-4:30pm; 25¢).

If you don't know what an Algerian hook is (but might like to), visit the Chamber of Horrors in the **Wax Museum,** 720 N. 2nd St. (241-1155). Here's your chance to meet Liz Taylor and Ghandi, if not in the flesh, at least in the tallow. (Open Mon.-Sat. 10am-10pm, Sun. 1-8pm. $5, 13 and under $1.) Play Space Invaders, Pac-Man, Donkey Kong, and other classics (25¢) at the **National Video Game and Coin-Op Museum,** 801 N. 2nd St. (621-2900), which charts the rise of video games and pinball machines. (Open in summer Mon.-Sat. 10am-10pm, Sun. noon-6pm; Oct-March Mon.-Sat. noon-8pm, Sun. noon-6pm. Free.)

Stroll down the lane to the **National Bowling Hall of Fame and Museum,** 111 Stadium Plaza (231-6340), across from Busch Stadium. This well-organized museum is lined with funny panels on the history and development of bowling, with titles like "real men play quills and throw cheeses." For $2 you can play four frames in the old-fashioned lanes downstairs. (Open in summer Mon.-Sat. 9am-5pm, Sun. noon-5pm; Oct.-March daily 11am-4pm; baseball game days until 7pm. $5, ages 5-12 $2.50.) Historic **Union Station,** at 18th and Market St. 1 mi. west of downtown ("Levee" bus), houses a shopping mall, food court, and entertainment center in a magnificent structure. The Entertainer lives on at the **Scott Joplin House,** 12580 Rott Rd. (821-1209), just west of downtown at Geyer Rd., where the ragtime legend lived and composed from 1901 to 1903.

South and Southwest of Downtown

Soulard is bounded by I-55 and Seventh St.; walk south on Broadway or 7th St. from downtown, or take bus #73 ("Carondelet"). In the early 70s, the city proclaimed this area a historic district, because it once housed German and East European immigrants, many of whom worked in the breweries. Young couples and families are revitalizing the area, without displacing the older generation of immigrants. The historic district surrounds the **Soulard Farmers Market,** 730 Carroll St. (622-4180), on 7th St., which claims a more than 200-year tradition but *still* has fresh produce (open daily around 6am-5pm; hours vary among merchants). The end of 12th St. features the largest brewery in the world, the **Anheuser-Busch Brewery,** 1127 Pestalozzi St. (577-2626), at 12th and Lynch St. Take bus #40 ("Broadway") south from downtown. The 90-min. tour is markedly less thrilling than the chance to sample beer at the end. Don't get too excited about the free brew, though—you'll get booted after 15 min. (Tours June-Aug. Mon.-Sat. 9am-5pm; off season 9am-4pm. Get free tickets at the office.) A few blocks southwest of the brewery, Cherokee St.'s **Antique Row** is filled with antiques and used bookstores.

The internationally acclaimed 78-acre **Missouri Botanical Gardens,** 4344 Shaw Blvd. (800-642-8842), north of Tower Grove Park, thrive on grounds left by botanist Henry Shaw. From downtown, take I-44 west by car or catch bus #99 ("Lafayette") at 4th and Locust St.; get off at Shaw Blvd. and Tower Grove Ave. The gardens display flora and fauna from all over the globe; the Japanese Garden is guaranteed to soothe the weary budget traveler, while the Climatron is an excellent rainforest impersonator. (Open Memorial Day-Labor Day daily 9am-8pm; off season 9am-5pm. $3, seniors $1.50, under 12 free; free Wed. and Sat. until noon.) Much farther out this way, late President Ulysses S. once lived on **Grant's Farm,** 10501 Gravois Rd. (843-1700). Take I-55 to Reavis Barracks Rd., turn right onto Gravois Rd., then left onto the farm. The tour involves a train ride through a wildlife preserve where over 100 animals roam and interact freely, as evidenced by the donkey-zebra, and concludes with free beer in the historic Baurnhof area. (Open June-Aug. Tues. and Thurs.-Sun. 9am-3pm, Wed. 9am-5pm; other times vary. Call for reservations.)

West of Downtown

West of downtown, **Forest Park,** the country's largest urban park, was home to the 1904 World's Fair and St. Louis Exposition, where ice cream cones and hot dogs decorated kids' faces with sugar and ketchup for the first time ever. Take MetroLink to Forest Park or Central West End, then catch the Shuttle Bug, which stops at all the important sights. The park contains two museums, a zoo, a planetarium, a 12,000-seat amphitheater, a grand canal, and countless picnic areas, pathways, and flying golf balls. The **St. Louis Science Center,** 5050 Oakland Ave. (289-4400), in the park's south corner, has lots of hands-on exhibits, an OmniMax, and a planetarium. Learn how a laser printer works, watch an old Star Trek episode, practice surgery, or use police radars to clock the unusually high speeds of cars on I-40. (Museum open Sun.-Thurs. 9:30am-5pm, Fri.-Sat. 9:30am-9pm. Free. Call for show schedules and prices.) Marlin Perkins, the late, great host of TV's *Wild Kingdom,* turned the **St. Louis Zoo** (781-0900) into a world-class institution. You can even view computer-generated images of future human evolutionary stages (no, they don't all look like Kate Moss) at the "Living World" exhibit. (Open in summer Mon. and Wed.-Sat. 9am-5pm, Tues. 9am-8pm, Sun. 9am-5:30pm; Labor Day-Memorial Day daily 9am-5pm. Free.) The **History Museum** (746-4599), at Lindell Blvd. and DeBaliviere Ave. just north of the park, is filled with U.S. memorabilia, including a new exhibit on the 1904 St. Louis World's Fair. (Open Tues.-Sun. 9:30am-5pm. Free.) Atop **Art Hill,** just to the southwest, an equestrian statue of France's Louis IX, the city's namesake and the only Louis of

France to achieve sainthood, beckons with his raised sword toward the **St. Louis Art Museum** (721-0072), which contains masterpieces of Asian, Renaissance, and Impressionist art. (Open Tues. 1:30-8:30pm, Wed.-Sun. 10am-5pm. Main museum free, special exhibits $5, students and seniors $4.)

From Forest Park, head north a few blocks to gawk at the lavish residential sections of the **Central West End,** where every house is a turn-of-the-century version of a French château or Tudor mansion. The vast **Cathedral of St. Louis,** 4431 Lindell Blvd. (533-0544), is a strange amalgam of Romanesque, Byzantine, Gothic, and Baroque styles. Gold-flecked mosaics depict 19th-century church history in Missouri. Take bus #93 ("Lindell") from downtown, or walk from the Central West End MetroLink stop. (Open daily 7am-8pm, Labor Day-Memorial Day 7am-5pm. Guided tours Mon.-Fri. 10am-3pm, Sun. after the noon Mass. $2.) Northwest of Forest Park, **Washington University** makes things lively with a vibrant campus. The **Washington University Gallery of Art** (935-5490), in Steinberg Hall at the corner of Skinker and Forsyth Blvd., has a few Warhols within its diverse collection. Conrad Atkinson's *Critical Mats* welcome you to "the seductiveness of the end of the world." (Open during the school year Mon.-Fri. 10am-5pm, Sat.-Sun. 1-5pm. Free.)

ENTERTAINMENT

Founded in 1880, the **St. Louis Symphony Orchestra** is one of the country's finest. **Powell Hall,** 718 N. Grand Blvd. (534-1700), houses the 101-member orchestra in acoustic and visual splendor. Take bus #97 to Grand Blvd. or MetroLink to Grand Station and walk north. (Performances Sept. to early May Thurs. 8pm, Fri.-Sat. 8:30pm, Sun. 3 and 7:30pm. Box office open Mon.-Sat. 9am-5pm and before performances. Tickets $15-60; student and senior rush tickets ½-price on day of show.)

St. Louis offers theater-goers many choices. The outdoor **Municipal Opera** (361-1900), the "Muny," performs tour productions of hit musicals on summer nights in Forest Park. The back rows provide 1456 free seats on a first come, first served basis. The gates open at 7pm for 8:15pm shows; get there even earlier for popular shows and bring a picnic. (Box office open mid-June to Aug. daily 9am-9pm. Tickets $6-36.) Other productions are regularly staged by the **St. Louis Black Repertory,** 634 N. Grand Blvd. (534-3807), and the **Repertory Theatre of St. Louis,** 130 Edgar Rd. (968-4925). Call for current show info. Renovated and reopened in 1982, the **Fox Theatre** (534-1678) was originally a 1930s movie palace. Tour the Fox or pay a little more for Broadway shows, classic films, or Las Vegas, country, or rock stars. (Box office open Mon.-Sat. 10am-6pm, Sun. noon-4pm. Tours Tues., Thurs., Sat. at 10:30am. $2.50, under 12 $1.50; call for reservations.) The **Tivoli Theatre,** 6350 Delmar Blvd. (862-1100), shows artsy and lesser-known releases ($6, seniors $4). **Metrotix** (534-1111) has tickets to most of the city's theatrical events.

A recent St. Louis ordinance permits gambling on the rivers—the **Casino Queen** (800-777-0777) claims "the loosest slots in town." (10 cruises daily leave on odd-numbered hours from the riverfront near the arch. Admission $2-4; parking free.)

Six Flags over Mid-America (938-4800) is a popular amusement park, 30 min. southwest of St. Louis on I-44 at Exit 261 (hours vary by season; $29, seniors $14.50, ages 3-11 $24). The **St. Louis Cardinals** (421-3060) play ball downtown at **Busch Stadium** April through October (tickets $5-14). The recent arrival of the **Rams** (982-7267), formerly of L.A., has brought the ol' pigskin back to St. Louis. **Blues** hockey games (622-2500) slice ice at the **Kiel Center** at 14th St. and Clark Ave.

NIGHTLIFE

Music rules the night in St. Louis. The *Riverfront Times* (free at many bars and clubs) and the *Get Out* section of the Post-Dispatch list weekly entertainment. For seasonal events, check *St. Louis Magazine,* published annually, or the comprehensive calendar distributed at the tourist office.

The bohemian **Loop** parties hearty as students and intellectual types flock to the coffeehouses and bars of Delmar Blvd. for outdoor dining, conversation, and music.

Brandt's Market & Café, 6525 Delmar Blvd. (727-3773), does it all with wine, beer, espresso, tea, pizza, and health food (entrees $5-10). The live music outside, almost daily, runs the gamut from acoustic to lounge to Brazilian (open daily 9am-1am).

Most bars at **Laclede's Landing** offer mainstream rock and draw preppy, touristy crowds. In summer, bars take turns sponsoring "block parties," with outdoor food, drink, music, and dancing in the streets. Weekends see hordes of St. Louis University (SLU, pronounced "slew") students descending on the waterfront. **Boomerz** (621-8184), at N. 3rd St., is beloved for its classic rock and current alternative tunes (live music nightly; open 8pm-3am). **Kennedy's Second Street Co.,** 612 N. 2nd St. (421-3655), strikes a rawer chord with alternative music nightly and, occasionally, heavier punk, replete with mosh pit and stage diving. (Open 11:30am-3am. Cover $2-5.) **Mississippi Nights,** 914 N. 1st St. (421-3853), hosts big local and national bands (box office open Mon.-Fri. 11am-6pm).

The less touristy **Soulard** district has been known to ripple with the blues. **McGurk's** (776-8309), at 12th and Russell Blvd., has live Irish music nightly. (Open Mon.-Fri. 11am-1:30am, Sat. noon-1:30am, Sun. 1pm-midnight. No cover.) Soulard is also quite gay-friendly. The **1860's Hard Shell Café & Bar,** 1860 S. 9th St. (231-1860), hosts some pretty gritty blues and rock performances (music nightly and Sat. afternoon; no cover). **Clementine's,** 2001 Menard (664-7869), houses both a crowded restaurant and St. Louis's oldest gay bar (est. 1978). Sandwiches and entrees run $4.50-9.50. (Open Mon.-Fri. 10am-1:30am, Sat. 8am-1:30am, Sun. 11am-midnight.)

■ Near St. Louis

Cahokia Mounds State Historic Site Fifteen min. from the city in Collinsville, IL (8mi. east of downtown on I-55/70 to Rte. 111), over 120 earthen mounds mark the site of **Cahokia,** an extremely advanced Native American settlement inhabited from 700 to 1500AD, now the Cahokia Mounds State Historic Site. In constructing the foundations of important edifices, builders had to carry over 15 million loads of dirt on their backs; the largest, **Monk's Mound,** took 300 years to complete. The Cahokians, once a community of 20,000, faced the same problems of pollution, overcrowding, and resource depletion that we do today—which might help explain their mysterious disappearance. The **Interpretive Center** (618-346-5160) has a life-sized diorama and a 15-min. film illustrating this "City of the Sun" (shows every hr. 10am-4pm; center open daily 9am-5pm). Celebrate equinoxes and solstices at **Woodhenge,** a solar calendar much like Britain's stone one, at dawn on the Sunday closest to the big day. (Site open daily 8am-dusk. Free.)

St. Charles The town of St. Charles, just 20 min. northwest of St. Louis, has the dual distinction of being the starting point of Lewis and Clark's 1804 exploration of the Louisiana Purchase, and Missouri's first state capital. The **Lewis & Clark Center,** 701 Riverside Dr. (947-3199), traces the adventurers' trek across the continent through exhibits (open daily 10:30am-4:30pm; $1, kids 50¢). You can tour the **first Missouri State Capitol,** 200 S. Main St. (946-2882), and its surrounding green. (Open Mon.-Sat. 10am-4pm, Sun. noon-6pm. $2, under 13 $1.25.) Nestled along the Missouri River, St. Charles now supports numerous antique shops, cafés, and wineries. **Cavern Springs Winery,** 300 Water St. (947-1200), has wine tastings (Tues.-Sat. 10am-5pm) and tours of its extensive pre-Civil War caverns (Tues.-Sat. 3-5pm).

Other attractions lend themselves to not-so-peaceful days: outdoor festivals, riverboat gambling, and the **Goldenrod Showboat,** 1000 Riverside Dr. (946-2020), the nation's last surviving showboat and the inspiration for the musical (shows Wed.-Sun. $21-30; box office open Mon.-Sat. 9am-5pm, Sun. noon-7pm).

St. Charles marks the starting point of **KATY Trail State Park** (800-334-6946), an 1890s railroad route *cum* 138-mi. hiking and biking trail past bluffs, wetlands, and wildlife that even Lewis and Clark gawked at. Call for info on unfinished portions of the trail, which ends in Kansas City. South Main St. has many possibilities for bicycle rental; try **The Touring Cyclist,** 104 S. Main St. (949-9630). (Open Mon.-Fri. 9am-8pm, Sat. 9am-6pm, Sun. 9am-5pm. $5 per hr., $20 for 24hr.)

To see the St. Charles historic area, take I-70W and exit north at 5th St. A right on Boonslick Rd. takes you to **S. Main St.,** the main drag. The **visitors bureau** is at 230 W. Main (800-366-2427; open Mon.-Fri. 8am-5pm, Sat. 10am-5pm, Sun. noon-5pm).

▓ Hannibal

Hannibal hugs the Mississippi River 100 mi. west of Springfield, IL and 100 mi. north-west of St. Louis. Founded in 1819, the town remained a sleepy village until Samuel Clemens (a.k.a. Mark Twain) roused the world's attention to his boyhood home by making it the setting of *The Adventures of Tom Sawyer.* Today, tourists flock to Han-nibal, like gullible boys to a white-washed fence, for small-town hospitality, chain motels, and old brick buildings.

Practical Information The **Hannibal Visitors and Convention Bureau,** 505 N. 3rd St. (221-2477), offers info and free local calls (open Mon.-Sat. 8am-5pm, Sun. 9am-4:30pm; call for extended summer hours). On **Trailways Bus Lines,** 308 Mark Twain Ave. (221-0033 or 800-992-4618), in the Citgo Station, a northbound bus leaves for Chicago (2 per day, $41), a southbound bus for St. Louis (2 per day, $21). Station open daily 5:30am-1:30am. Hannibal's **post office:** 801 Broadway (221-0957; open Mon.-Fri. 8:30am-5pm, Sat. 8:30am-noon). **ZIP code:** 63401. **Area code:** 314.

Lean-Tos and Apple Cores Chain motels, some of which differ in name but share the same owner, swarm about Hannibal, particularly on **Mark Twain Ave.** (Rte. 36) and on **U.S. 61** near the Rte. 36 junction. Numerous **bed and breakfasts** are located downtown, but these tend to be more expensive (singles $50, doubles $60). Shiny and familiar, the recently renovated **Howard Johnson Lodge,** 3603 McMasters Ave. (221-7950), at the U.S. 36/61 junction, has potentially good but highly variable prices. Students should try to request an (unposted) rate of around $32 for a single. (A/C, cable TV, pool. Singles $30-45, doubles $35-60.) Two campgrounds offer relief from headaches induced by motel price inconsistencies. The **Mark Twain Cave Campgrounds** (221-1656), adjacent to the cave 1 mi. south of Hannibal on Rte. 79, are cheery and family-oriented, but not too secluded ($11, full hookup $15; $1.50 per person after 2). Sidestep Hannibal's unending fast food options, get your dental floss ready and head into **Ole Planters,** 316 N. Main St. (221-4410), where tasty BBQ beef sandwiches ($4) wait to be devoured. (Open Mon.-Sat. 11am-3pm and 4:30pm-close, Sun. 11am-3pm; call for Nov.-March hours.) **The Café,** 116 North St. (221-3355), serves up sandwiches ($4) and over 140 flavors of cheesecake (10 options per day; open Mon.-Sat. 10am-4pm, Sun. noon-4pm).

Jumping Frogs and Riverboats The **Mark Twain Boyhood Home and Museum,** 208 Hill St. (221-9010), highlights the downtown **historic district** with restored rooms and an assortment of memorabilia from the writer's life. Across the street sit the **Pilaster House** and **Clemens Law Office.** Further down the street, the museum's newest addition includes a collection of Tom and Huck Norman Rock-wells. (Open in summer daily 8am-6pm, in spring and fall 8am-5pm, Jan.-Feb. 10am-4pm. All sites included $4, ages 6-12 $2, under 6 free.) **The Mark Twain Riverboat Co.** (221-3222), Center St. Landing, steams down the Mississippi for a one-hour sight-seeing cruise that is part history, part folklore, part advertisement for the land attrac-tions. (Memorial Day-Labor Day 3 per day, May and Sept.-Oct. 1 per day. $8, ages 3-12 $5; dinner cruises $26/$16.) The **Mark Twain Cave** (221-1656), 1 mi. south of Hanni-bal on Hwy. 79, is allegedly the one Twain explored as a boy. (Open daily 8am-8pm, April-May and Sept.-Oct. 9am-6pm, Nov.-March 9am-4pm. 1-hr. tour $9, ages 4-12 $4.50, under 4 free.) Nearby **Cameron Cave** provides a slightly longer and far spook-ier lantern tour ($11, ages 4-12 $5.50). In early July, 100,000 fans converge on Hanni-bal for the fence-painting, frog-jumping fun of the **Tom Sawyer Days** festival. Twain, however, wasn't the only American icon to come through Hannibal. Mr. Davidson, **Harley Davidson** that is, rolls through every September as part of the Missouri State Harley Owners' Group Rally (call 573-221-2477 for details).

■ Kansas City

With over 200 public fountains and more miles of boulevard than Paris, Kansas City has a reputation for a heavy European influence. Nevertheless, this city can't hide its Heartland roots; Kansas City has twice been voted "Barbeque Capital of the World" and is considered a key player in the development of jazz. When Prohibition stifled many of the nation's parties in the 1930s, booze continued to flow here; KC's alcohol-induced nightlife brought jazz musicians from all over the country, and their music flourished. The Kansas City of today maintains its big bad blues-and-jazz rep in a metropolis spanning two states: the highly suburbanized half in Kansas (KCKS) and the quicker-paced commercial half in Missouri (KCMO).

PRACTICAL INFORMATION

Tourist Office: Convention and Visitors Bureau of Greater Kansas City, 1100 Main St. (221-5242 or 800-767-7700), 25th fl. of City Center Sq. Bldg. downtown. Grab *An Official Visitor's Guide to Kansas City.* Open Mon.-Fri. 8:30am-5pm.

Airport: Kansas City International (243-5237), 18mi. northwest of KC off I-29 (bus #29). **KCI Shuttle** (243-5000) departs every 30min., servicing downtown (KCMO), Westport, Overland Park, Mission, and Lenexa; $11-15. Taxi to downtown costs $23-26.

Trains: Amtrak, 2200 Main St. (421-3622 or 800-872-7245), at Grand Ave. directly across from Crown Center (bus #27). Two per day to: St. Louis (5½hr., $45) and Chicago (8hr., $89). Open 24hr.

Buses: Greyhound, 1101 N. Troost (221-2835 or 800-231-2222). Take bus #25. *The terminal is in an unsafe area.* To St. Louis (5 per day, 4-5hr., $33) and Chicago (5 per day, 10-15hr., $41.50). Open daily 5:30am-12:30am.

Public Transportation: Kansas City Area Transportation Authority (Metro), 1200 E. 18th St. (221-0660), near Troost. Excellent downtown coverage. 90¢, $1 for KCKS, $1.20 for Independence; seniors ½-price with Medicare card. Free transfers; free return receipt available downtown. Pick up maps and schedules at headquarters or on buses. Buses run 5am-6pm (outer routes) or midnight (downtown routes). The **trolley** (221-3399) loops from downtown to the City Market, Crown Center, Westport, and Country Club Plaza March-Dec. Mon.-Sat. 10am-10pm, Sun. noon-6pm; holiday hours vary. $4 for all day, seniors and ages 6-12 $3.

Taxis: Yellow Cab, 471-5000. $1.50 base fare, $1.20 per mi. 24hr.

Car Rental: Thrifty Car Rental, 2001 Baltimore (842-8550 or 800-367-2277), 1 block west of 20th and Main St. (bus #40). $28 per day, with 250 free mi.; 29¢ each additional mi. Under 25 surcharge $7.50 per day. Must be 21 with a major credit card. Open Mon.-Fri. 8am-8pm, Sat.-Sun. 9am-4pm. Free shuttle from the airport will take you to location at 11530 N.W. Prairie View Rd. (464-5670).

Crisis Line: 822-7272. 24hr.

Emergency: 911.

Post Office: 315 W. Pershing Rd. (374-9180), at Broadway (bus #40 or 51). Open Mon.-Fri. 8am-6:30pm, Sat. 9am-2:30pm. **ZIP code:** 64108. **Area codes:** 816 in Missouri, 913 in Kansas. Phone numbers given here lie in 816 area code unless otherwise noted.

The KC metropolitan area sprawls across two states, and travel may take a while, particularly without a car. Most sights worth visiting in KC lie south of downtown on the Missouri side; all listings are for Kansas City, MO unless otherwise indicated. Although parking around town is not as easy as in many midwestern towns, there are lots that charge $4 or less per day. KCMO is laid out on a grid with numbered streets running east-west and named streets running north-south. **Main St.** divides the city east-west.

GREAT PLAINS

ACCOMMODATIONS AND CAMPING

Kansas City can usually accommodate anyone who needs a room, but if there's a big convention or the Royals are in town, the whole city may be booked; call ahead. The least expensive lodgings are near the interstate highways, especially I-70. Unfortunately, the car-deprived budget traveler is not in luck here. Downtown, most hotels are either expensive, uninhabitable, or unsafe—sometimes all three. **Bed and Breakfast Kansas City** (913-888-3636) has over 40 listings at inns and homes throughout the city ($50 and up).

An excellent roadside deal is the **Interstate Inn,** (229-6311), off I-70 (what a surprise!) at Exit 18. With large, newly remodeled rooms, this place's greatest downfall is its name (singles $21, doubles $28). Owned by the same company, the **American Inn** (800-90-LODGE/905-6343) has multiple locations off I-70. Despite the gaudy red, white, and blue neon façade, the rooms inside are large, cheap, and good-lookin', and there are outdoor pools. The best prices are for a set of first come, first served rooms that go quickly; reserved rooms run considerably higher. Locations are on Woods Chapel Rd. (228-1080), 16 mi. east on I-70 off Exit 18 (singles $25, doubles $32) and Noland Rd. (373-8300), 12 mi. east on I-70 off Exit 12 ($30/$35).

Lake Jacomo (229-8980), 22 mi. southeast of KC, has forested campsites, fishing, swimming, and a damn cool dam across the street. (Sites $8, with electric $11, with full hookup $16.) Take I-470 south to Colbern, then go east on Colbern for 2 mi.

FOOD

Kansas City rustles up a herd of meaty, juicy barbecue restaurants that serve unusually tangy ribs. If midwestern meat dishes don't float your boat, the **Westport** area, at Westport Rd. and Broadway just south of 39th St., sports eclectic menus, cafés, and coffeehouses. For fresh produce year-round, visit the largest farmers market in the midwest: the **city market,** at 5th and Walnut St. in the River Quay area. Saturday and Wednesday are the busy days, although scattered shops stay open all week. (Open Mon.-Fri. 8am-4pm, Sat. 6am-6pm, Sun. noon-4pm.)

Arthur Bryant's, 1727 Brooklyn St. (231-1123). Take the Brooklyn exit off I-70 and turn right (bus #110 from downtown). Down-home, sloppy BBQ. The thin, orange, almost granular sauce is a spectacular blend of southern and western influences. A monstrous and messy sandwich is $5.65—choose beef, ham, pork, chicken, or turkey, but don't wear anything fancy. Open Mon.-Thurs. 10am-9:30pm, Fri.-Sat. 10am-10pm, Sun. 11am-8:30pm.

Strouds, 1015 E. 85th St. (333-2132), at Troost, 2mi. north of the Holmes exit off I-435; also at 5410 N. Oak Ridge Rd. (454-9600). Sign proclaims: "We choke our own chickens." Try them fried, with cinnamon rolls, biscuits, and honey. Enormous dinners ($4.25-13) in a weathered wooden hut crammed between the train tracks and an overpass. Arrive early to beat the crowd or you might have to wait. Open Mon.-Thurs. 4-10pm, Fri. 11am-11pm, Sat. 2-11pm, Sun. 11am-10pm.

Cascone's Grill, 20 E. 5th St. (471-1018), at the city market. They may just have the best breakfast in all of KC. ($2-4). Perfect for early birds who don't like worms. Sandwiches $1.50-3, lunch entrees $4.25. Open Tues.-Sat. 6am-2pm.

Rudy's Tenampa Tacqueria, 1611 Westport St. (931-9700). Less yuppified than its Westport counterparts, Rudy's is known for cheap, filling Mexican fare. Entrees $3.50-7. Open Mon.-Thurs. 11am-9pm, Fri.-Sat. 11am-11pm.

SIGHTS

For a taste of KC's masterpieces, try the **Nelson-Atkins Museum of Art,** 4525 Oak (751-1278 or 561-4000), at 45th, 3 blocks east of Country Club Plaza (bus #47 or 55). The museum contains one of the best East Asian art collections in the world. On Friday nights, the museum hosts world-class jazz acts. (5:30-8:30pm. Free tours Tues.-Sat. 10:30, 11am, 1, and 2pm; Sun. 1:30, 2, 2:30 and 3pm. Open Tues.-Thurs. 10am-4pm, Fri. 10am-9pm, Sat. 10am-5pm, Sun. 1-5pm. $4, students $2, ages 6-18 $1; free

Sat.) **Black Archives of Mid-America,** 2033 Vine (483-1300), holds a large and fine collection of paintings and sculpture by African-American artists. (Take the "Indiana" bus. Open Mon.-Fri. 9am-4:30pm. $2, under 18 50¢.)

A few blocks to the west at 47th and Southwest Trafficway, **Country Club Plaza** (753-0100), known as "the plaza," is the oldest and perhaps most picturesque shopping center in the U.S. Modeled after buildings in Seville, Spain, the plaza boasts fountains, sculptures, hand-painted tiles, and the reliefs of grinning gargoyles. You can pick up a free guide to the architecture at many shops and motels. A Country Club Plaza bus runs downtown until 11pm.

Crown Center, 2450 Grand Ave. (274-8444), sits 2 mi. north of the Plaza at Pershing; take bus #40, 56, or 57, or any trolley from downtown. The center, headquarters of Hallmark Cards, houses a maze of restaurants and shops, plus the **Coterie Theatre** (474-6552) and KC's only public outdoor ice skating rink, the **Ice Terrace** (274-8412; open Nov.-March daily 10am-9pm; $5.25, rentals $1.25). From mid-June to July, Crown Center has **Free Concerts in the Park** (889-7827, ext. 3378) every Friday (call for times). Run through a huge fountain designed for exactly that purpose—you can't have more fun on a hot summer night with your clothes on. To the west stands **Liberty Memorial,** 100 W. 26th St. (221-1918), a tribute to those who died in World War I. The memorial is closed indefinitely due to structural problems.

Nearby **Independence,** Missouri, a 15-minute drive east of KC, may have more claims to fame than KC; it's the hometown of former president Harry Truman, the starting point of the California, Oregon, and Santa Fe trails, and now, the world headquarters of the **Reorganized Church of Jesus Christ of Latter Day Saints** (833-1000), at River and Walnut St. Inspired by the chambered nautilus, the computer-designed building is a bizarre and beautiful seashell that spirals up nearly 200 ft. The interior is equally impressive, containing art representing the church's worldwide following as well as an enormous pipe organ. (Tours on the ½hr. Mon.-Sat. 9-11:30am and 1-4:30pm, Sun. 1-4:30pm. Organ recital Sun. 3:30pm. Free.) The town of Independence is accessible by bus #24 "Independence." Independence's **Dept. of Tourism,** 111 E. Maple (325-7111), has mucho info (open Mon.-Fri. 8am-5pm).

ENTERTAINMENT AND NIGHTLIFE

The **Missouri Repertory Theatre** (235-2700), at 50th and Oak, stages American classics. (Season Sept.-June. Tickets $19-32, seniors and students $3 off. Box office open Mon.-Fri. 10am-5pm; call for in-season weekend hours.) Quality Hill Playhouse, 303 W. 10th St. (235-2700) produces plays for summer crowds. (Tickets $14-19, seniors and students $2 off.) Huck Finn wanna-bes can take a one-hour cruise on the **Missouri River Queen** (281-5300 or 800-373-0027), at the Lewis and Clark viaduct. (Boards June-Aug. daily 2pm, Sept.-Dec. and March-May Sat.-Sun. 2pm. $7.50, seniors $6.30, ages 3-13 $3.50.) For more entertainment news, pick up a free copy of the *New Times* at area restaurants and bars.

Sports fans will be pierced to the heart by **Arrowhead Stadium,** at I-70 and Blue Ridge Cutoff, home to football's **Chiefs** (931-9400 or 800-676-5488; tickets $30-41). Next door, the water-fountained wonder of **Kauffman Stadium** (921-8800 or 800-422-1969) houses the **Royals** baseball team (tickets $6-14, Mon. and Thurs. $4.50). A stadium express bus runs from downtown on game days.

In the 20s, Kansas City played hot spot to the nation's best jazz. Count Basie and his "Kansas City Sound" reigned at the River City bars, while Charlie "Bird" Parker spread his wings and soared in the open environment. Stop by the **Grand Emporium,** 3832 Main St. (531-7557), twice voted the #1 blues night club in the U.S., to hear live jazz Fridays and Saturdays; weekdays feature rock, blues, and reggae bands (cover ranges $3-15; open Mon.-Sat. 10am-3am, Sun. noon-3am). Down the street, **Jardine's,** 4536 Main St. (561-6480), plays straight-up jazz six nights a week, with nary a cover. (Open Mon.-Fri. 11am-3am, Sat. 5pm-3am. Music starts at 5pm.) A few blocks west, noisy nightspots pack the restored **Westport** area (756-2789), near Broadway and Westport Rd. ½ mi. north of Country Club Plaza (see Sights, above). Don't expect a happy hour at **Blayney's,** but get there at around 10pm for intense rhythm and blues. (Cover

$2-5. Live music six nights a week. Open Mon.-Sat. 8pm-3am.) **Hurricane,** 4648 Broadway (753-0884), grinds out alternative rock five nights a week on their back deck. (Cover $3-5. Open daily 4pm-2:45am.) **Kiki's Bon-Ton Maison,** 1515 Westport Rd. (931-9417), features KC's best in-house soul band (Wed. 9:30pm and Sat. 10:30pm) and whips up cajun food with bayou flavor (jambalaya and crawfish $9-13; sandwiches $6). Kiki's also hosts the annual Crawfish Festival around the last weekend in May. (Open Mon.-Thurs. 11am-10pm, Fri. 11am-11pm, Sat. 11am-1:30am, Sun. 11:30am-8pm.) Big names in jazz and blues show up at the club downstairs from the ritzy **Plaza III Steakhouse,** 4749 Pennsylvania (753-0000), at Country Club Plaza. (Cover varies; Fri.-Sat. $5. Restaurant open Sun.-Thurs. 11:30am-10pm, Fri.-Sat. 11:30am-11pm. Club open Wed.-Sat. 7pm-1am.) Another jazz hotspot improvises toward the north of the city, just past downtown. **The Phoenix,** 302 W. 8th St. (561-9600), at Central St., blasts it out six nights a week, starting at 5pm (open Mon.-Sat. 11am-1am). **Gilhouly's,** 1721 39th St. (561-2899), at Bell St., doesn't host music, but has over 125 bottled imports and a large selection of Irish and Scottish beers on tap (open Mon.-Sat. 6am-1:30am). **The Edge,** 323 W. 8th St. (221-8900), is a popular gay bar and dance club. (Cover varies. Open Mon.-Thurs. 9pm-3am, Fri.-Sat. 8pm-3am.)

■ Branson

Scads of billboards, motels, and giant showplaces beckon the masses that visit Branson each year to embrace this modern-day mecca of country music and theater. The **Grand Palace,** 2700 W. Rte. 76 (334-7263 or 800-5-PALACE/572-5223), hears from big names like Vince Gill and Wynonna when they blow through town (shows April-Dec. $19-37). Japanese performer Shoji Tabuchi may not be a household name, but he's the most popular show in town. See him fiddle, sing, and crack jokes at none other than the **Shoji Tabuchi Show,** 3620 Shepherd of the Hills Expwy. (334-7469), near Rte. 76, a.k.a. Country Music Blvd. (shows March-Dec. $26-28, under 13 $18-19). Ever wonder what happened to the Osmond Brothers? Wonder no longer—they're still going strong at the **Osmond Family Theater** (336-6100), at the intersection of Rte. 76 and Rte. 165 (shows May-Dec. $21.50-23.50; under 13 $7, sometimes free). Other entertainment options include the **Andy Williams Show** (334-4500), the **Mel Tillis Show** (335-6635), the **Tony Orlando Yellow Ribbon Music Theater** (800-560-8669), and **Presley's** (334-4874), for a bit of Ozark humor.

If country music isn't your *thang* and you're in Branson anyway, never fear—this is the Ozarks, after all. **Table Rock Lake, Lake Taneycomo,** and a criss-crossing system of streams and creeks are perfect for canoeing, fishing, or just splashing along the shoreline. Try renting equipment at the state parks, or the **Indian Point Boat Dock** (338-2891), at the end of Indian Point Rd. You can get fishing boats ($16 per hr.), jet-skis, pontoon boats, and others, as long as you have a driver's license. Follow Rte. 76W for 5 mi. past the Strip and turn left on Indian Point Rd.

The **Branson Chamber of Commerce** (334-4136), on Rte. 248 just west of the Rte. 248/65 junction, has brochures and a computer/phone system great for making arrangements. (Open in summer Mon.-Fri. 8am-6pm, Sat. 8am-5pm, Sun. 11am-4pm; call for off-season hrs.) For crisis help, call the **Missouri Victim Center** at 889-4357. **Emergency:** 911. Branson's **post office:** 327 S. Commercial St. (334-3366), off Main St. (open Mon.-Fri. 8:30am-5pm, Sat. 9am-1pm). **ZIP code:** 65616. **Area code:** 417.

Motels along Rte. 76 generally start around $30; for tasteful, inexpensive motels, try Rte. 265, 4 mi. west of the Strip. The **Stonybrook Inn** (338-2344), on Rte. 265 just south of Rte. 76, has cheery, recently renovated rooms with A/C and cable but no phones (singles and doubles $30). **Indian Point** (338-2121), at the end of Indian Point Rd. south of Rte. 76, one of many campgrounds on Table Rock Lake run by the Corps of Engineers, has lakeside sites with swimming access and use of the boat launch. (2-day min. stay. Check-in by 9pm. Sites $10, with electricity $13; $3 administration fee. Open May-Oct.)

A few charming local restaurants stave off the fast-food invasion in the older section of town, on Rte. 76 near Business Rte. 65. For an Art Deco combination of old and new, visit the **Uptown Café** (336-3535), at Rte. 76 and 165, a nouveau diner with a mirrored-and-purple facade and an all-you-can-eat breakfast buffet (Mon.-Sat. 7:30-10:30am, Sun. 7:30am-2pm) for $5. Among their dinner entrees ($4-13) are chicken-fried steak and burgers (open daily 7:30am-midnight).

Greyhound (800-321-2222) runs two buses per day to Springfield (1hr., $9), Kansas City (5½hr., $40-45), and Memphis (6-8hr., $53), and one per day to St. Louis ($51.50). The bus stop is in front of the **5-Star Motel,** 424 N. Business 65.

Oklahoma

Between 1838 and 1839, President Andrew Jackson ordered the forced relocation of "The Five Civilized Tribes" from the southern states to the designated Oklahoma Indian Territory, in a tragic march which came to be known as the "Trail of Tears." The survivors rebuilt their tribes in Oklahoma, only to be moved again in 1889 to make way for whites rushing to stake claims on newly opened settlement lands. Ironically, when the territory was admitted to the Union in 1907, it adopted a Choctaw name (Oklahoma means "land of the red man"); today, many streets carry Indian names, and cultural life seems to center around Native American heritage and experiences. There are re-enactments and interpretations of the Trail of Tears throughout Oklahoma, and the world's largest collection of Western American art in Tulsa features 250,000 Native American artifacts. Visitors expecting a brown dustbowl of a state à la *The Grapes of Wrath* will be happily disappointed—thanks to improvements in farming technology, Oklahoma's rolling red hills are blanketed with green grass and crops.

PRACTICAL INFORMATION

Capital: Oklahoma City.
Oklahoma Tourism and Recreation Department: 500 Will Rogers Bldg., Oklahoma City 73105 (405-521-2409 or 800-652-6552), in the capitol. Open daily 8am-8pm.
Time Zone: Central (1hr. behind Eastern). **Postal Abbreviation:** OK.
Sales Tax: 7.65%.

▓ Tulsa

First settled by Creeks arriving from the Trail of Tears, Tulsa's location on the banks of the Arkansas River made it a logical trading outpost for Native Americans and Europeans. The discovery of huge oil deposits in the 1920s transformed the city into the oil capital of America. Today, Tulsa's Art Deco skyscrapers, French villas, and Georgian mansions, as well as its Native American population (the second largest among U.S. metropolitan areas) reflect its varied heritage—it's this diversity that lends Tulsa its status as the "cultural capital of Oklahoma."

PRACTICAL INFORMATION

Tourist Office: Convention and Visitors Division, Metropolitan Tulsa Chamber of Commerce, 616 S. Boston (585-1201 or 800-558-3311). Open Mon.-Fri. 8am-5pm.
Gay Information Line, 743-4297. Lists gay bars and social groups in Tulsa. Open daily 8am-10pm.
Airport: Tulsa International (838-5000) just northeast of downtown and accessible by I-244 or U.S. 169. Taxi to downtown costs approximately $15.
Buses: Greyhound, 317 S. Detroit (584-3717 or 800-231-2222). To: Oklahoma City (7 per day, 2hr., $17); St. Louis (4 per day, 7½-9½hr., $71); Kansas City (3 per day, 5hr., $38); Dallas (8 per day, 7hr., $34). Open 24hr.
Public Transportation: Metropolitan Tulsa Transit Authority, 510 S. Rockford (582-2100). Buses run 5am-7pm. Fare 75¢, transfers 5¢, seniors and disabled (dis-

abled card available at bus offices) 35¢, ages 5-18 60¢, under 5 free with adult. Maps and schedules, though not always reliable, are available at the main office (open Mon.-Fri. 8am-5pm), and at any library.

Taxis: Yellow Cab, 582-6161. $2.25 base fare, $1 per mi., $1 per extra passenger. 24hr. service.

Car Rental: Thrifty, 1506 N. Memorial Dr. (838-3333). $29 per day, $165 per week; unlimited mileage. Must be 21 with major credit card; under 25 surcharge $12 per day. Open 24hr. The state of OK does not honor the Int'l Driver's Permit.

Bike Rental: River Trail Bicycles, 6861 S. Peoria (481-1818). 5-speeds $4 per hr., $12 per day. In-line skates $5 per hr., $10 per day. Open Mon.-Thurs. 10am-7pm, Fri.-Sat. 10am-8pm, Sun. 11am-7pm. Driver's license or major credit card required.

Crisis Line: 836-HELP/4357. For info, referral, or crisis intervention. Open 24hr.

Emergency: 911.

Post Office: 333 W. 4th St. (599-6800). Open Mon.-Fri. 8:30am-5pm. **ZIP code:** 74101. **Area code:** 918.

Tulsa sections off into 1-sq.-mi. quadrants. Downtown rests at the intersection of **Main St.** (north-south) and **Admiral Blvd.** (east-west). Numbered streets lie in increasing order as you move north or south from Admiral. Named streets run north-south in alphabetical order. Those named after western cities are west of Main St.; eastern cities to the east. Every time the alphabetical order reaches the end, the cycle begins again. Always note whether an address is north, south, east, or west.

ACCOMMODATIONS AND CAMPING

Downtown motels are generally unclean and unsafe, especially north of I-244 near the airport. For more options, try the budget motels on I-44 and I-244. **Skelly Dr.,** which runs along I-44 to Exit 222, where I-44 and I-244 meet, features many motels of the non-chain variety; take bus #17 ("Southwest Blvd."). The **Budgetel Inn,** 4530 E. Skelly Dr. (488-8777 or 800-428-3438), off I-44, delivers a free continental breakfast to your door; you can brew some coffee with your in-room coffeemaker. (Singles $43, doubles $48). The **Georgetown Plaza Motel,** 8502 E. 27th St. (622-6616), off I-44 at 31st and Memorial St., has free local calls and cable (singles $26, doubles $32). The **Tulsa Inn,** 5554 S. 48th W. Ave. (446-1600), rents sparkling singles with free local calls, HBO, and cable; take Exit 222 (singles $23, doubles $33).

The **KOA Kampground,** 193 East Ave. (266-4227), ½ mi. west of I-44's Exit 240A, makes the outdoors less rough with a pool, laundry facilities, showers, and a game room (office open 8:30am-7pm; sites for 2 $15, with hookup $17). More picturesque but less convenient, the **Heyburn State Park** (247-6695), 20 mi. southwest of the city off I-44 at Rte. 33, provides lovely sites with shady trees on Heyburn Lake. (Fishing, swimming, bike rentals. Tent sites $6; RV sites $8, with electric $11.)

FOOD AND NIGHTLIFE

Many downtown restaurants cater to lunching businesspeople, closing at 3pm on weekdays and 1pm on Saturdays. **Nelson's Buffeteria,** 514 S. Boston (584-9969), is an old-fashioned diner serving their blue plate special (two scrambled eggs, hash browns, biscuit and gravy $2.50) and famous chicken-fried steak ($4.50) since 1929. Ask for extra gravy. (Open Mon.-Fri. 6am-2:30pm.) **Chimi's,** 1304 E. 15th St. (587-4411), at Peoria Ave., offers well-prepared standard Mexican fare, as well as good health-conscious menu selections. (Open Sun.-Thurs. 11am-10pm, Fri.-Sat. 11am-midnight.) For that old Rte. 66 feel, visit the **Metro Diner,** 3001 E. 11th St. (592-2616). The back end of a '57 Chevy greets you at the door. Salads, sandwiches, burgers, and pasta go for $4-8 (open daily 8am-10pm).

For up-to-date stats on arts and entertainment, pick up a free copy of *Urban Tulsa* at local restaurants. At night, head to the bars on **Cherry St.,** an area on 15th St. east of Peoria lined with restaurants and antique shops, or to those in the 3000s along S. Peoria. The **Blue Rose Café,** 3421 S. Peoria (742-3873), has great, cheap food (burgers $3-6) and an outdoor patio. *Tulsa People Magazine* voted it runner-up in the

"Best Place to Ride Your Harley" division. (Must be 21 at all times. Live blues and rock Sun.-Thurs. 9pm. No cover. Open daily 11am-2am.) The intersection of 18th and Boston makes noises in the night, catering to the young adult crowd; the college crowd flocks to **Hoffbraü,** 1738 Boston (583-9520), "the snob-free, dork-free, band-and-brewski place to be." (Burgers, sandwiches, Tex-Mex entrees $5-7. Must be 21. Local bands Fri.-Sat. 10pm; cover varies but usually around $3-10. Open Mon.-Thurs. 11am-10pm, Fri. 11am-2am, Sat. 5pm-2am.)

SIGHTS AND ENTERTAINMENT

The **Philbrook Art Center,** 2727 S. Rockford Rd. (749-7941 or 800-324-7941), combines a collection of Native American pottery and artifacts with Renaissance art in the recently renovated Italian Renaissance villa of an oil baron. Permanent collections of African and Asian art reside on these 23 acres surrounded by formal and informal gardens. (Open Tues.-Wed. and Fri.-Sat. 10am-5pm, Thurs. 10am-8pm, Sun. 11am-5pm. $4, students and seniors $2, under 13 free.) Take bus #5 ("Peoria") from downtown. Perched atop an Osage foothill two mi. northwest of downtown (take bus #47), the **Thomas Gilcrease Museum,** 1400 Gilcrease Museum Rd. (596-2700), houses the world's largest collection of Western American art, as well as 250,000 Native American artifacts and 10,000 paintings and sculptures by artists such as Remington and Russell. (Open Memorial Day-Labor Day Tues.-Wed. and Fri.-Sat. 9am-5pm, Thurs. 9am-8pm, Sun. 1-5pm. Labor Day-Memorial Day same hours but closed on Mon. $3 donation requested.)

The **Fenster Museum of Jewish Art,** 1223 E. 17th Pl. (582-3732), housed in B'nai Emunah Synagogue, contains an impressive collection of Judaica dating from 2000BC to the present (open Sun.-Thurs. 10am-4pm; free). The ultra-modern, gold-mirrored architecture of **Oral Roberts University,** 7777 S. Lewis (495-6161 or 800-678-8876), rises out of an Oklahoma plain about 6 mi. south of downtown Tulsa between Lewis and Harvard Ave.; take bus #9. In 1964, Oral had a dream in which God commanded him to "Build Me A University," and Tulsa's most-frequented tourist attraction was born. The 80-ft.-high sculpture of praying hands which guards the campus, and the hordes of believers flocking to visit, catapult the university beyond the realm of mere kitsch. Free **campus tours** (495-6807). (Visitors center open Mon.-Sat. 10:30am-4:30pm, Sun. 1-5pm.)

Rodgers and Hammerstein's *Oklahoma!* continues its run under the stars at the **Discoveryland Amphitheater** (245-6552), 10 mi. west of Tulsa on 41st St., accessible only by car. The musical presents a comedy and love story set during the time of statehood in the early 1900's. (Shows June-Aug. Mon.-Sat. 8pm. Mon.-Thurs. $12, seniors $11, under 12 $5; Fri.-Sat. $14/$13/$5.) Arrive early for the pre-show barbecue, starting at 5pm ($7, seniors $6.50, kids $5). For more cultural enlightenment, the **Tulsa Ballet** (585-2573), acclaimed as one of America's finest regional troupes, dances at the **Performing Arts Center** (596-7111), at 3rd and Cincinnati St. (Box office open Mon.-Fri. 10am-5:30pm, Sat. 10am-3pm.) The **Tulsa Philharmonic** (747-7445) and **Tulsa Opera** (582-4035) also perform at the PAC; the Philharmonic harmonizes most weekends September through May ($8-35), while the Opera stages three productions per year. Call for exact dates.

Trail of Tears National Historic Trail

President Andrew Jackson ignored a Supreme Court proclamation when he forced 16,000 Cherokee Indians to march from North Carolina, Tennessee, Georgia, and Alabama to the Indian Territories. Many walked the trail at gunpoint, and by the end tens of thousands had died of hunger and disease. The Historic Trail, established in December 1987, commemorates this journey. Though the trail is still under construction, an auto route follows as closely as possible the northern land trail taken by many of the Native Americans. For more info, contact Trail of Tears National Historic Trail, Southwest Region, National Park Service, P.O. Box 728, Santa Fe, NM 87504 (505-988-6888).

Tulsa shines during annual events like the **International Mayfest** (582-6435). This outdoor food, arts, and performance festival takes place in downtown Tulsa, (May 15-18 in 1997). The **Pow-Wow** (744-1113; usually in June, call for exact dates), at the Tulsa Fairground Pavilion, attracts Native Americans from dozens of tribes for a three-day festival of food, arts and crafts, and nightly dancing contests which visitors may attend ($2, seniors $1, under 10 free).

■ Near Tulsa: Tahlequah

A moving commemoration of Native American heritage, the **Trail of Tears Drama** re-enacts the Cherokees' tragic march, in **Tahlequah,** 66 mi. east of Tulsa on Rte. 51. The Cherokees' western capital, Tahlequah marks the end of the tribe's forced movement west; see below for more on the history of their journey. (Performances at 8:30pm Mon.-Sat. in June-Aug.; admission Mon.-Thurs. $9, ages 6-12 $4.50, Fri.Sat. $10, ages 6-12 $5. For tickets, call 456-6007, or write P.O. Box 515, Tahlequah 74465. Reservations recommended.) Visitors to Tahlequah can explore the **Tsa-La-Gi village,** a recreation of a 16th-century Cherokee settlement with ongoing demonstrations of skills such as flint knapping and basket weaving, and the **Cherokee National Museum.** (Village tours May-Aug. Mon.-Sat. 10am-5pm, Sun. 1-5pm. $4, kids $2. Museum open Mon.-Sat. 10am-8pm, Sun. 1pm-5pm; in winter Mon.-Sat. 10am-5pm, Sun. 1-5pm. $2.75, kids $1.50).

■ Oklahoma City

At noon on April 22, 1889, a gunshot sent settlers scrambling into Oklahoma Territory to claim land. By sundown, Oklahoma City, set strategically on the tracks of the Santa Fe Railroad, was home to over 10,000 homesteaders. The 1928 discovery of oil modernized the city, and elegant homes rose with the oil derricks. Oklahoma City plodded along fairly peacefully for the next 70 years—until the quiet was shattered on April 19, 1995, when a bomb at the Alfred R. Murrah federal office building exploded, killing 168. As the city slowly rebuilds itself, flowers and wreaths adorning the fence outside the federal building stand as memorials to the victims.

PRACTICAL INFORMATION

Tourist Office: Chamber of Commerce Tourist Information, 123 Park Ave. (297-8912), at Broadway. Open Mon.-Fri. 8:30am-5pm.

Airport: Will Rogers Memorial (680-3200), southwest of downtown. **Royal Coach,** 3800 S. Meridian (685-2638), has 24-hr. van service to downtown ($9 for 1 person; $3 per additional person). A taxi downtown costs $14.

Buses: Greyhound, 427 W. Sheridan Ave. (235-6425 or 800-231-2222), at Walker St. Take city bus #4, 5, 6, 8, or 10. *Be careful at night.* To: Tulsa (7 per day, 2hr., $17); Dallas (4 per day, 5hr., $32); Kansas City (6 per day, 10hr., $68). Open 24hr.

Public Transportation: Oklahoma Metro Transit, offices at Union Station, 300 S.W. 7th (235-RIDE/7433; open Mon.-Fri. 7am-5pm). Bus service Mon.-Sat. approximately 6am-6pm. All routes radiate from the station at Reno and Gaylord St., but don't expect to find a schedule here (or on the buses, for that matter)— they're hidden at the Union Station office (50¢). Route numbers vary depending on the direction of travel. Fare 75¢, seniors and ages 6-17 35¢.

Taxis: Yellow Cab, 232-6161. $2.50 base, $1.25 per mi, $1 per extra passenger.

Car Rental: Dub Richardson Ford Rent-a-Car, 2930 N.W. 39th Expwy. (946-9288 or 800-456-9288). Used cars $27 per day with unlimited in-state mileage. Must be 21 with major credit card. Open Mon.-Fri. 8am-6pm, Sat. 8:30am-noon. Oklahoma does not honor the International Driver's Permit.

Bike Rental: Miller's Bicycle Distribution, 3350 W. Main (360-3838), at I-35. 10-speeds and mountain bikes $5 per day, $54 per month. In-line skates $10 per day. Open Mon.-Sat. 9am-8pm, Sun. 1-6pm. Must have credit card.

Crisis Lines: Contact, 848-2273. For referrals or crisis intervention. **Rape Crisis,** 943-7273. Both open 24hr.

Emergency: 911.
Post Office: 320 S.W. 5th St. (278-6300). Open Mon.-Fri. 8:30am-5:30pm, Sat. 9am-noon. Emergency window open 24hr. **ZIP code:** 73125. **Area code:** 405.

Main St. divides the town north-south, while Broadway splits it east-west. Almost all of the city's attractions are outside the city center, but the all-encompassing Metro Transit reaches them. Use caution with public transportation, especially downtown after dark. Easy parking makes driving the best way to go.

ACCOMMODATIONS AND CAMPING

Accommodations in downtown OKC are scarce. **The Economy Inn,** 501 N.W. 5th St. (235-7455), is downtown near the bus station (cable TV; singles $25, doubles $35). The interstates offer a wider selection of inexpensive motels. Most are chains, but not all links are identical, as evidenced by the positively luxurious **Motel 6,** 4200 W. I-40 (947-6550), in Meridian (take bus #11 or #38). Palatial rooms come with access to a pool and a spa (singles $34, doubles $40).

Oklahoma City has two accessible campgrounds. **RCA,** 12115 Northeast Expwy. (478-0278), next to Frontier City Amusement Park 10 mi. north of the city on I-35, has a pool, laundry room, showers, and lots of fast food restaurants nearby (open 8am-9pm; sites $14, with full hookup $18). Much prettier (and farther from an amusement park), a state-run campground roosts on Lake Thunderbird, 30 mi. south of OKC at **Little River State Park** (360-3572). Take I-40 East to Choctaw Rd., then south until the road ends, and make a left. Swim or fish in the lake or hike the cliffs for a view. (Showers available. Open 8am-5pm. Tent sites $6.)

FOOD AND NIGHTLIFE

Oklahoma City contains the largest feeder cattle market in the U.S., and **beef** tops most menus. Aside from the turn-of-the-century warehouses yuppified into eating and drinking establishments, most places downtown close early in the afternoon after they've served business lunchers. **Cattleman's Steak House,** 1309 S. Agnew (236-0416), 1 block from the stockyards, may be a classy restaurant today, but its colorful past (est. 1910) includes a stint as a prohibition-era speakeasy. Steaks range from chopped sirloin ($7) to USDA prime ($18). (Open Sun.-Thurs. 6am-11pm, Fri.-Sat. 6am-midnight.) An Italian restaurant and wine bar, **Flip's,** 5801 N. Western (843-1527) serves their stuff ($5-19) in an artsy atmosphere (open daily 11am-2am). **Sweeney's Deli,** 900 N. Broadway (232-2510), is one of the few downtown places that stays up late. Enjoy a tasty dish in a friendly atmosphere. If you play enough pool here, everyone really *will* know your name. (Sandwiches $3-4; burgers $3. Open Mon.-Thurs. 11am-11pm; Fri. 11am-midnight.)

Nightlife in Oklahoma City is as rare as the elusive jackalope. For ideas, pick up a copy of the *Oklahoma Gazette,* or try the Bricktown district on Sheridan Ave.; many area restaurants have live music after dark. At the **Bricktown Brewery,** 1 N. Oklahoma St. (232-BREW/2739), at Sheridan Ave., you can watch the beer brew while dining on burgers, salads, and chicken dishes ($5-9). The second floor houses a bonanza of bar games, as well as live music. (Cover usually $3-10. 21+. Live music Tues. and Fri.-Sat. 8pm. Open Tues.-Sat. 11am-1am, Sun.-Mon. 11am-midnight.) For good dancing, the DJ at the **Wreck Room at the Habana Inn** (525-7610), at 39th and Barnes St., plays house and techno (open Thurs.-Sat. 10pm-5am; cover $3-7).

SIGHTS AND ENTERTAINMENT

Monday morning is *the* time to visit the **Oklahoma City Stockyards,** 2500 Exchange Ave. (235-8675), the busiest in the world. Cattle auctions (Mon.-Wed.) begin at 8am and sometimes last into the night. Visitors enter free of charge via a calfwalk over pens, leading from the parking lot east of the auction house. (Take bus #12 from the terminal to Agnew and Exchange.)

The **Kirkpatrick Center Museum Complex,** 2100 N.E. 52nd St. (427-5461), feels like an educational amusement park. A mall-like complex houses a pastiche of eight separate museums. Highlights are the **Air and Space Museum, International Photography Hall of Fame, Red Earth Indian Center,** and **Omniplex,** a hands-on science museum with free planetarium shows. (Take bus #22. Open Mon.-Sat. 9am-6pm, Sun. noon-6pm. Planetarium shows on the hour Sun.-Fri. 1-4pm, Sat. noon-4pm. Admission to all 8 museums $6.) The **Crystal Bridge** is a glass-enclosed cylinder 70 ft. in diameter containing both a desert and a rainforest. (Open daily 9am-6pm. $3, seniors $2, ages 4-12 $1.25. Outdoor gardens open daily 6am-11pm; free.) The **Festival of the Arts** (236-1426), held at Myriad Gardens (April 22-27 in 1997), highlights visual, culinary, and performing arts. The **Red Earth** festival (427-5228), June 6-8, 1997, is the country's largest celebration of Native America; the Myriad Convention Center hosts intense dance competitions in which dancers from different tribes perform for prize money (ticket prices vary).

TEXAS

Spanning an area as wide as Wisconsin to Montana and as long as North Carolina to Key West, Texas is more like its own country than a state; the fervently proud, can-do citizens of the "Lone Star State" seem to prefer it that way. In fact, after revolting against the Spanish in 1821, the Republic of Texas stood alone until 1845, when it entered the Union as the 28th state. The state's unofficial motto proclaims that "everything is bigger in Texas"; its truth is evident in prolific wide-brimmed hats, boat-sized American autos, and toweringly tall urban ranchers who seem ready and willing to conquer the frontier and fight for independence all over again.

Cotton, cattle, and oil built the Texan fortune, but the state's growing technology and tourism industries form the building blocks of the state's future. Regional cuisine, like most of Texan culture, is enriched by its age-old Mexican heritage. "Tex-Mex" is a restaurant epidemic ranging from 69¢ taco stands to elegant border cafés. Mexican pastries, longhorn beef, and chicken-fried steak are staples. And of course, BBQ with plenty of sauce.

PRACTICAL INFORMATION

Capital: Austin.
Texas Division of Tourism: P.O. Box 12728, Austin 78711-2728 (800-888-8839). **Texas Travel Information Center** (800-452-9292) helps visitors plan trips (open daily 8am-9pm). **U.S. Forest Service,** 701 N. First St., Lufkin 75901 (409-639-

TEXAS

8501). **Texas Parks and Wildlife Dept.,** Austin Headquarters Complex, 4200 Smith School Rd., Austin 78744 (512-389-8108 or 800-792-1112).
Time Zones: Mostly Central (1hr. behind Eastern); *Let's Go* makes note of areas in Mountain (2hr. behind Eastern). **Postal Abbreviation:** TX.
Sales Tax: 6-8%.

■ Dallas

Dallas mixes a little country, a little rock 'n' roll, rancher-businessmen, and cowgirl cheerleaders together in a "metroplex" mishmash of skyscrapers, neon lights, modern shopping malls, and miles upon miles of suburbs. In 1841 founding father John Neely Bryan, an ambitious Irish immigrant, built a tiny little loghouse outpost in the hope that one day it would grow into a bustling inland port on the Trinity River. The river, at times a raging torrent and at others a dusty little trickle, proved too unpredictable. This by no means hindered Dallas's development; the city rose to prominence in the 1870s when a major north-south railroad crossed a transcontinental line just south of town, and waves of settlers rode in on the rails to swell the population. Now the eighth-largest city in the United States, Dallas has since attracted flocks of immigrants from the Far East and Latin America. While the city's legendary preoccupation with commerce persists, recent campaigns for historic preservation have restored many run-down urban areas to their pre-petro glory.

PRACTICAL INFORMATION

Tourist Office: Dallas Convention and Visitors Bureau, 1201 Elm St. (746-6700), in the Renaissance Tower. Provides a slew of maps and brochures. Open Mon. 8:30am-5pm; Tues.-Fri. 8am-5pm. The bureau also oversees two **visitors centers:** 1303 Commerce St. (746-6603; open Mon.-Thurs. 8am-5:30pm, Fri. 8am-5pm, Sat. 9am-5pm, Sun. noon-5pm) and 603 Munger St. (880-0405), in the West End Market Place (open Mon.-Sat. 11am-8pm, Sun. noon-8pm). The **Gay and Lesbian Line** (368-6283) has recorded info. Internet Surfers contact http://www.pic.net/cityview/dallas.html for info on local entertainment.
Airport: Dallas-Ft. Worth International (574-8888), 17mi. northwest of downtown; take bus #409. **Love Field** (670-6080; take bus #39) has mostly intra-Texas flights. To get downtown from either airport, take the **Super Shuttle,** 729 E. Dallas Rd. (817-329-2000; in terminal, dial 02 on service phone located at ground transport services). Shuttle to downtown from DFW $15, from Love Field $11. 24hr. service. Taxi to downtown from DFW $25, from Love Field $15.
Trains: Amtrak, 401 S. Houston Ave. (653-1101 or 800-872-7245), in Union Station. To: L.A. (3 per day, 42hr., $217); Austin (3 per day, 6hr., $36); Little Rock (3 per day, 7½hr., $81). Open daily 9am-6:30pm.
Buses: Greyhound, 205 S. Lamar St. (655-7970 or 800-231-2222), 3 blocks east of Union Station. To: New Orleans (12 per day, 13hr., $69); Houston (9 per day, 5hr., $25); Austin (12 per day, 4hr., $23). Open 24hr.
Public Transportation: Dallas Area Rapid Transit (DART), 1401 Pacific Ave. (979-1111; open Mon.-Fri. 5am-10pm, Sat.-Sun. 8am-6pm). Routes radiate from downtown; serves most suburbs. Runs 5am-midnight; to suburbs 5am-8pm. Fare $1. Get maps at Elm and Ervay St. office (open Mon.-Fri. 7am-6pm). DART's downtown Dallas service **Hop-a-Bus** (979-1111) has a park-and-ride system. Three routes (blue, red, and green) run Mon.-Fri. about every 10min. 25¢; transfers free.
Taxis: Yellow Cab Co., 426-6262 or 800-749-9422. $2.70 first mi., $1.20 per additional mi. 24hr.
Car Rental: Rent-a-Wreck, 2025 S. Buckner Blvd. (800-398-2544). Extremely reliable service. Late-model used cars from $19 per day including unlimited mileage within 100mi. of downtown. Must be 18. Cash deposits accepted. Airport pick-up available. Open 9am-6pm, Sat. 9am-3:30pm.
Bike Rental: Bicycle Exchange, 11716 Ferguson Rd. (270-9269). From $60 per week. Must have a credit card. Open Mon.-Fri. 9am-7pm, Sat. 9am-5pm. Also at 1305 S. Broadway (242-4209) with same hours.

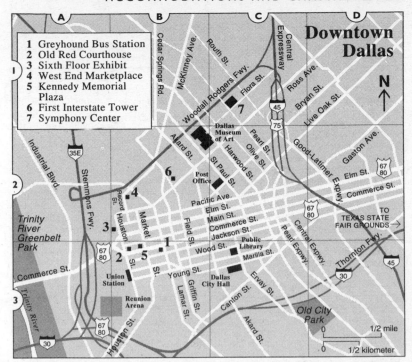

Downtown Dallas

N ↑

1 Greyhound Bus Station
2 Old Red Courthouse
3 Sixth Floor Exhibit
4 West End Marketplace
5 Kennedy Memorial Plaza
6 First Interstate Tower
7 Symphony Center

Crisis Lines: Rape Crisis and Child Abuse Hotline, 653-8740. **Suicide and Crisis Center,** 828-1000. **Contact 214,** 233-2233, for general counseling. All 24hr. **Emergency:** 911.

Post Office: 400 N. Ervay St. (953-3045), near Bryan St. downtown. Open Mon.-Fri. 8:30am-5pm. **ZIP code:** 75201; General Delivery, 75221. **Area code:** 214.

ACCOMMODATIONS AND CAMPING

Cheap lodging of the non-chain-motel variety doesn't come easy in Dallas; big events such as the Cotton Bowl (Jan. 1) and the State Fair in October exacerbate the problem. Look on **U.S. 75 (Central Expwy.), I-635 (LBJ Freeway),** and in the suburbs of **Irving, Mesquite,** and **Arlington,** for inexpensive motels. If you can afford it, **Bed and Breakfast Texas Style,** 4224 W. Red Bird Ln. (298-8586, daily 8:30am-4:30pm), will place you in a nice home, usually near town, with friendly residents who are anxious to make y'all as comfortable as possible. It's an especially good deal for groups of two. Be sure to call a few days ahead. (Singles from $50, doubles from $60.) The **Delux Inn,** 3817 Rte. 80E (681-0044), takes care of those with tighter wallets. All 133 units have key-card locks, A/C, and free HBO and ESPN. The Inn also sports a pool and restaurant. (Must be 18. Singles $20, doubles $25; each additional person $2. Free continental breakfast.) No matter where you find yourself, one of Dallas's 13 **Motel 6** locations (800-440-6000) should be nearby (singles $28-38).

Tent campers should take I-35E to Exit 460 and follow signs to the **KOA Kampground,** 7100 S. Stemmons Rd. (817-497-3353), 40min. north in Denton, for shady sites, free firewood, propane gas tanks, and a public hot tub and sauna. (Office open daily 8am-9pm. Tent sites for 2 $18, with full hookup $24.) **Sandy Lake Campground,** 1915 Sandy Lake Rd. (242-6808), has a grocery store, game room, two laundries, a small amusement park nearby, and 270 trailer sites ripe for RVs. Take I-635 to

I-35E and get off at Exit 444. (Office open Mon.-Fri. 7:30am-8pm, Sat. 8am-8pm, Sun. 1-6pm. RV sites $15-19, depending on vehicle size.)

FOOD

Cheap 'n' cheesy taco joints spring from every crack in the sidewalk here. For the low-down on more diverse dining, pick up the Friday weekend guide of the *Dallas Morning News*. The **West End Marketplace**, 603 Munger St. (748-4801), has fast but a bit pricey Tex-Mex food amidst a variety of touristy shops, while gourmet restaurants and low-priced authentic barbecue joints hang near **Greenville Ave.** In this desert of beef, **Farmers Produce Market**, 1010 S. Pearl Expwy., between Pearl and Central Expwy. near I-30, is a veggie oasis (open daily 5am-6pm).

Bubba's, 6617 Hillcrest Ave. (373-6527). A remodeled, '50s-style diner where you'll find the powerful and the plebian dining on the same turf. Homemade rolls come with sweet honey. Awful good fried chicken and chicken-fried steak dinners $5-6. Open daily 6:30am-10pm.

Terilli's, 2815 Greenville Ave. (827-3993). A sexy atmosphere with low-lit lamps and some of the best jazz nightly in Dallas. The goal is creative Italian; the result is their signature dish, Italchos—pizza crust nachos with a plethora of toppings ($10). Try the veggie lasagna ($9), and wash it down with a specialty martini ($5.50). Open daily 11:30am-2am.

Sonny Bryan's Smokehouse, 2202 Inwood (357-7120). This landmark of Dallas BBQ has a funky, run-down atmosphere where you can sit at school desks indoors. Try 1 meat on a bun ($6) or combine all 7 smokehouse delicacies ($14). Some vegetables available. Open Mon.-Fri. 10am-4pm, Sat. 10am-3pm, Sun. 11am-2pm.

Flying Burro, 2831 Greenville (827-2112). New Mexico-style dishes that would do Santa Fe proud. Hits include New Mexican pizza and fajita nachos; entrees around $10. Open Sun.-Wed. 11am-midnight, Thurs.-Sat. 11am-2am.

SIGHTS

A replica of the 1841 log cabin of **John Neely Bryan,** the City's founder, sits in the very heart of the city at Elm and Market St. Encircled by the present-day downtown, historic Dallas can easily be seen on a walking tour. Ride to the top of the **Reunion Tower,** 300 Reunion Blvd. (651-1234), 50 stories above the street, to get a feel for the city before you start walking. (Open Mon.-Thurs. 10am-10pm, Fri. 9am-midnight, Sat. 9am-midnight; $2, seniors and ages 3-12 $1.)

An underground walkway at the bottom of Reunion Tower leads to the adjoining **Union Station,** 400 S. Houston Ave. (746-6603), one of the city's few grand old buildings. The **West End Historic District and Marketplace,** full of broad sidewalks, funky shops, restaurants, and bars, lies north of the station. Pick up a pamphlet for a self-guided walking tour at the West End Foundation, 1801 N. Lamar. (702-7107. All stores open at least Mon. and Fri.-Sat. 11am-midnight, Tues.-Thurs. 11am-10pm, Sun. noon-6pm.)

Two blocks down and six flights up on Elm St., the notorious **Sixth Floor** of the former **Texas School Book Depository** (653-6666) still leaves people wondering how Lee Harvey Oswald could have fired the shot that killed President John F. Kennedy on November 22, 1963. This floor, now a fascinating museum devoted to the Kennedy legacy, traces the dramatic and macabre moments of the assassination in various media. (Open daily 9am-6pm. Self-guided tour $4, seniors $3, ages 6-8 $2. Audio cassette rental $2.) Below the depository, Elm St. runs through **Dealey Plaza,** a national landmark and site of the infamous grassy knoll, which the limo passed as the shots were fired. The area hasn't changed much and still bears an eerie resemblance to Abraham Zapruder's film of the assassination. Philip Johnson's **Memorial to Kennedy,** looms nearby, at Market and Main St. Just across the street is **The Conspiracy Museum,** 110 S. Market St. (771-3040). Exhibits in the museum, sporting CD-Rom technology and tons of maps and photographs, chronicle the deaths of famous figures (JFK and Lincoln, for example) and allege to expose the real truth. *Hard Copy*, anyone? (Open 10am-6pm. $7.)

Frightening gargoyles adorn the **Dallas County Courthouse**, on the corner of Houston and Main St. The building gained the nickname "Old Red" for its unique Pecos red sandstone. Just east, at the corner of Ross Ave. and Field St., stands Dallas's most impressive skyscraper, **The First Interstate Tower**, a multi-sided prism that towers above a glistening water garden. Farther east on Ross Ave., the **Dallas Museum of Art,** 1717 N. Harwood St. (922-1200), anchors the new **Arts District** with its excellent collections of Egyptian, Impressionist, modern, and decorative art. (Open Tues.-Wed. 11am-4pm, Thurs. 11am-9pm, Fri. 11am-4pm, Sat.-Sun. 11am-5pm. Free, except for special exhibits.) Closer to the downtown area, the imposing **Dallas City Hall,** 100 Marilla St. (670-3957), at Ervay St., was designed by the ubiquitous I.M. "Everywhere" Pei.

Thirty-seven late-19th-century buildings from around Dallas (including a dentists' office, a bank, and a schoolhouse) have been restored and moved to **Old City Park** (421-5141), about 9 blocks south of City Hall on Ervay St. at Gano. Pack a picnic and eat at the city's oldest and most popular recreation area and lunch spot. (Park open daily 9am-6pm. Exhibit buildings open Tues.-Sat. 10am-4pm, Sun. noon-4pm. $5, seniors $4, kids $2, families $12. Fee includes guided tours; free Mon. when exhibits are closed.)

Home to the state fair (Sept.-Oct.) since 1886, **Fair Park's** (670-8400) 30s Art Deco architecture, southeast of downtown on 2nd Ave., has gained national landmark status. The 277-acre park hosts the Cotton Bowl, and during the fair **Big Tex,** the 52-ft. smiling cowboy float, stands over the land Texas-tall; only the Texas Star, the largest ferris wheel in the Western hemisphere, looms taller. Inside the park, the **Dallas Aquarium** (670-8443) features swimming beasts that range from the ugly (although very edible) catfish to the fluorescent red empress. (Shark feedings Wed., Fri., and Sun. 2:30pm. Open daily 9am-4:30pm. $2, ages 3-11 $1.) The **Science Place** (428-5555) has toddlerish hands-on exhibits, but the planetarium and IMAX theatre are for young and old alike (open daily 9:30am-5:30pm; $6, seniors and ages 3-12 $3, under 3 free). Other attractions include the **Museum of Natural History** (421-3466; open daily 10am-5pm; $3, students and seniors $2, under 12 $1, under 3 free; Mon. 10am-1pm free); the **African-American Museum** (565-9026), a multi-media collection of folk art and sculpture (open Tues.-Fri. noon-5pm, Sat. 10am-5pm, Sun. 1-5pm; free); and the **Dallas Horticulture Center** (428-7476; open Tues.-Sat. 10am-5pm, Sun. 1-5pm; free).

Nearby **White Rock Lake** provides a haven for walkers, bikers, and in-line skaters. On the east shore of the lake, resplendent flowers and trees bloom and grow throughout the 66-acre **Dallas Arboretum,** 8617 Garland Rd. (327-8263). Take the #60N bus from downtown. (Open daily Mar.-Oct. 10am-6pm, Nov.-Feb. 10am-5pm. $6, seniors $5, ages 6-12 $3. Parking $2.) To gaze upon Dallas's mansions, drive up the **Swiss Avenue Historic District** or through the streets of the **Highland Park** area.

ENTERTAINMENT

Most Dallas establishments cater to the night owl; restaurants, bars, and fast food joints typically stay open until 2am. The free weekly *Dallas Observer* (out Wed.) can help you assess your entertainment options. The **Shakespeare in the Park** festival (497-1526), at Samuel-Grand Park just northeast of State Fair Park, presents two free plays every summer at 8:15pm (July-Aug.); each runs about two weeks and a $3 donation is suggested. At Fair Park, the **Music Hall** (565-1116) showcases **Dallas Summer Musicals** (421-0662; 373-8000 for tickets) June through October (tickets $5-45; call 696-HALF/4253 for ½-price tickets on performance days). The **Dallas Opera** (443-1043) takes residence November to February (tickets $20-95). The **Dallas Symphony Orchestra** (692-0203) plays in the new **Morton H. Meyerson Symphony Center,** at Pearl and Flora St. in the arts district. Take in a show if only to hear the world-class acoustics (tickets $12-50).

TEXAS

Six Flags Over Texas (817-640-8900), 15 mi. from downtown off I-30 in Arlington between Dallas and Fort Worth, maintains the original link in the nationwide amusement park chain with over 100 rides and attractions (Opens June-Labor Day daily 10am; Labor Day-Dec. and March-May Sat.-Sun. 10am. Closing times vary. $30, over 55 or under 4 ft. $24.) Across the highway lies the mammoth 47-acre **Wet 'n' Wild** (817-265-3356), America's largest waterpark. Experience simulated seasickness in the 1 million gallon wave pool. (Open daily Memorial Day-Labor Day 10am-9pm. $20, seniors $11, ages 3-9 $16.) Look for coupons for both parks on soda cans.

In Dallas, the moral order is God, country, and the **Cowboys.** Football devotees flock to **Cowboys Stadium** at the junction of Loop 12 and Rte. 183, west of Dallas in **Irving** (579-5000 for tickets; open Mon.-Fri. 9am-4pm). Sports fans will also want to visit the **Ballpark in Arlington,** 1000 Ballpark Way (817-273-5100), home of the Texas **Rangers** (ticket office open Mon.-Fri. 9am-6pm, Sat. 10am-4pm).

NIGHTLIFE

For alternative nightlife, head to **Deep Ellum,** east of the downtown. Eighties bohemians revitalized the area, which spent the 20s as a blues haven for the likes of Blind Lemon Jefferson, Lightnin' Hopkins, and Robert Johnson. Like almost everything in Dallas, it's commercial, but enjoyable. **Trees,** 2709 Elm St. (748-5009), recently rated the best live music venue in the city by the *Dallas Morning News,* occupies a converted warehouse with a loft full of pool tables. Bands tend to be alternative groups. (Cover $2-10. 17+. Open Tues.-Sat. 9pm-2am.) **Club Dada,** 2720 Elm St. (744-3232), former haunt of Edie Brickell, has added an outdoor patio and live local acts. Twentysomethings with pierced parts and ponytails as well as young adult preppies find common ground here. (Cover Thurs.-Sat. $3-5. 21+ Open daily 8pm-2am.) For more info on Deep Ellum, call the **What's Up Line** (747-DEEP/3337).

The trendy **West End** packs eight clubs into **Dallas Alley,** 2019 N. Lamar (988-0581), under one cover charge ($3-5). Inside, **Alley Cats** entertains with dueling piano sing-alongs. **110 Neon Beach** (988-9378) plays top 40, techno, and retro music for dancing. The **Outback Pub** (761-9355) and **Dick's Last Resort** (747-0001), both at 1701 N. Market, are popular with locals for having good beer selections, raucous crowds, and no beer. (Live music nightly out on the red brick marketplace. Both open Sun.Thurs. 11am-midnight, Fri.-Sat. 11am-2am.)

Greenville Ave. provides a refreshing change from the downtown crowds. **Poor David's Pub,** 1924 Greenville Ave. (821-9891), stages live music ranging from Irish folk tunes to reggae. Music is the main, and only, event: if there's no group booked, Poor David's doesn't open. (Open Mon.-Sat. 7:30pm-2am. Tickets available after 5pm at the door; cover $0-20.) A classic R&B bar, the **Greenville Bar and Grill,** 2821 Greenville Ave. (823-6691), has dollar beers Monday through Friday from 4 to 7pm (open daily 11am-2am). More popular nightspots line **Yale Blvd.,** home of Southern Methodist University's fraternity row. **Green Elephant,** 5612 Yale Blvd. (750-6625), a pseudo-60s extravaganza complete with lava lamps and tacky tapestries, is the bar of choice (open daily 10pm-2am). Many gay clubs rock north of downtown, in **Oak Lawn.** Among the more notable is **Roundup,** 3912 Cedar Springs Rd. (522-9611), at Throckmorton, a huge cover-free country and western bar which packs up to 1500 on weekends. Check out the shuffle board, pool tables, and game room for fun. Free dance lessons Thursdays and Sundays at 8:30pm (open Wed.-Sun. 8pm-2am).

■ Near Dallas: Fort Worth

If Dallas is the last Eastern city, Fort Worth is undoubtedly the first Western one. The historic **Stockyard District** (817-625-9715), 40 min. west on I-30, provides a worthwhile daytrip and some raw Texan entertainment. At the corner of N. Main and E. Exchange Ave., the Stockyards host weekly rodeos (817-625-1025; April-Sept. Sat. 8pm; $8) and **Pawnee Bill's Wild West Show** (817-625-1025; April-Sept. Sat. 2 and 4:30pm; $7, ages 3-12 $4), which features sharpshooting, bulldoggin', and a stagecoach robbery. At night, head for **Billy Bob's,** 2520 Rodeo Plaza (817-624-7117), in the Yards. At 100,000 sq. ft., the place bills itself as the world's largest honky tonk, with a bull ring, a BBQ restaurant, pool tables, video games, a country and western dance club, and 42 bar stations. On one night alone, during a Hank Williams, Jr. concert, Billy Bob's sold 16,000 bottles of beer. (Professional bull riding Fri.-Sat. 9 and 10pm. Free Texas Waltz lessons Thurs. 7-8pm. Cover $1, Sun.-Thurs. after 6pm $3, Fri.-Sat. $5.50-8.50. Open Mon.-Sat. 11am-2am, Sun. noon-2am. 18+ with ID or under 18 with parent.)

Board the **Tarantula** steam train (800-952-5717), at 2318 S. 8th Ave. or 140 E. Exchange Ave., for a 9-mi. roundtrip tour in and around the stockyards ($10, seniors $8, under 12 $5.50). Don't miss the **Sid Richardson Collection,** 309 Main St. (332-6554), in Sundance Sq. downtown, a great stash of paintings and bronzes by artists of the American West. (Open Tues.-Wed. 10am-5pm, Thurs.-Fri. 10am-8pm, Sat. 11am-8pm, Sun. 1-5pm. Free.) The **Chisholm Trail Round-Up** (817-625-7005), a three-day jamboree in the stockyards, June 13-15 in 1997, commemorates the heroism of cowhands who led the Civil War-time cattle drive to Kansas. The **Hog and Armadillo Races** are a round-up must-see; grandfather and grandson work together blowing at the beasts to make 'em move. For more on the stockyards, grab a copy of the *Stockyards Gazette* at the **visitors information center,** 130 Exchange Ave. (817-624-4741; open Sun.-Thurs. 9am-6pm, Fri. 9am-7pm, Sat. 9am-8pm).

Down Rodeo Plaza, a walk on **Exchange Ave.** provides a window on the wild west. Change from a livestock sale jingling in their pockets, cattlemen of yore would mosey down this street seeking entertainment. The strip still offers a plethora of saloons, restaurants, stores, and gambling parlors. Since 1906, a favorite stopping point has been the **White Elephant Saloon,** 106 E. Exchange Ave. (817-624-1887), with rough-hewn wood, brass footrails and photos of Old Fort Worth covering the walls. Live music—country-western, of course—plays during the week.

■ Austin

If the "Lone Star State" still inspires images of rough 'n' tumble cattle ranchers riding horses across the plains, Austin does its best to put the stereotype to rest. Here, high-tech whiz kids start Fortune 500 computer companies, artists make and sell exotic handicrafts, and bankers don sneakers for midday exercise on the city's downtown green belts. Austin's conspicuous student population keeps things youthful and energetic, while a thriving slacker population around the University of Texas campus ups the city's nose pierce to cowboy boot ratio. Ambitiously nicknamed the "Live Music Capital of the World," Austin's vibrant nightlife scene is heavy on live bands, with innovative variations on the city's strong blues tradition.

PRACTICAL INFORMATION

Tourist Office: Austin Convention Center/Visitor Information, 201 E. 2nd St. (474-5171 or 800-926-2282). Open Mon.-Fri. 8:30am-5pm, Sat. 9am-5pm, Sun. noon-5pm. **University of Texas Information Center,** 471-3434. **Texas Parks and Wildlife,** 4200 Smith School Rd. (389-8108 or 800-792-1112), has info on camping outside Austin. Open Mon.-Fri. 8am-5pm.

Airport: Robert Mueller Municipal, 4600 Manor Rd. (480-9091), 4mi. northeast of downtown. Taxi to downtown $12-14.

Trains: Amtrak, 250 N. Lamar Blvd. (476-5684 or 800-872-7245), take bus #1. To: Dallas (3 per week, 6hr., $36); San Antonio (3 per week, 3hr., $16; continues to Houston); El Paso (3 per week, 10hr., $129). Ticket office open Sun.-Thurs. 8am-10:30pm, Fri. 8am-5:30pm, Sat. 1-10:30pm.

Buses: Greyhound, 916 E. Koenig (800-231-2222), several mi. north of downtown off I-35. Easily accessible by public transportation. Bus #15 stops across the street and runs downtown. To: San Antonio (10 per day, 1½hr., $14); Houston (7 per day, 4hr., $19); Dallas (14 per day, 5hr., $23). Open 24hr.

Public Transportation: Capitol Metro, 106 E. 8th St. (474-1200 or 800-474-1201; info line open Mon.-Fri. 6am-10pm, Sat. 6am-8pm, Sun. 7am-6pm). 50¢, students

25¢, seniors, kids, and disabled free. Office has maps and schedules (Mon.-Fri. 8am-5pm). The **'Dillo Bus Service** (474-1200) serves downtown area; green trolleys run Mon.-Fri. every 15min. 6:30am-7pm, every 50min. 7-9pm (free). Park for free in the 'dillo lot at the City Coliseum at Bouldin and Barton Springs.

Taxis: Yellow Cab, 472-1111. $1.50 base fare, $1.50 per mi.

Car Rental: Rent-A-Wreck, 6820 Guadalupe (454-8621). $25 per day; 50 free mi. with cash deposit, 100 free mi. with credit card; 25¢ per additional mi. Open Mon.-Thurs. 8am-6pm, Fri. 8am-7pm, Sat. 9am-5pm. Must be 18; under 21 surcharge $10 per day.

Bike Rental: Austin Adventure Company, 706 B. Simonetti Dr. (209-6880). $15 for 2hr. Conducts 2-3-hr. bike tours ($30) and full-day mountain bike tours ($40-65). Van pick-up available. Reservations required; call and leave a message.

Crisis Lines: Crisis Intervention Hotline, 472-4357. **Austin Rape Crisis Center Hotline,** 440-7273. Both 24hr. **Outyouth Gay/Lesbian Helpline,** 708-1234 or 800-96-YOUTH/969-6884, for referrals and counseling. Open daily 5:30-9:30pm.

Emergency: 911.

Post Office: 209 W. 19th St. (929-1253). Open Mon.-Fri. 7am-6:30pm, Sat. 8am-3pm. **ZIP code:** 78701. **Area code:** 512.

UT students inhabit central **Guadalupe St.** ("The Drag"), where plentiful music stores and cheap restaurants thrive on their business. The state capitol governs the area a few blocks to the southeast. South of the dome, **Congress Ave.** features upscale eateries and classy shops. A plethora of bars and live music clubs front **6th St.** Lately, much nightlife has headed to the **Warehouse Area,** around 4th St., west of Congress. Away from the urban gridiron, **Town Lake** offers a verdant haven for the town's joggers, rowers, and cyclists.

ACCOMMODATIONS AND CAMPING

Cheap accommodations lie along **I-35,** running north and south of Austin. In town, three co-ops, run by college houses at UT, rent rooms and meals to hostelers. The co-ops work on a first come, first served basis and welcome everyone. Patrons have access to all their facilities including a fully stocked kitchen. Unfortunately, UT houses are open only from May to August.

Austin International Youth Hostel (HI-AYH), 2200 S. Lakeshore Blvd. (444-2294 or 800-725-2331), about 3mi. from downtown. From the Greyhound station, take bus #7 "Duval" to Lakeshore Blvd. and walk about ½mi. From I-35E, exit at Riverside, head east, and turn left at Lakeshore Blvd. Extremely clean, well-kept hostel with a cavernous 24-hr. common room overlooking Town Lake. Waterbeds available. Kitchen, with a convenient cubby for each guest. Located near grocery store. 40 barrack-style, single-sex rooms. No curfew. $12, nonmembers $15. No sleeping bags allowed; linen rental $1. Open daily 8-10am and 5-10pm.

Taos Hall, 2612 Guadalupe (474-6905), at 27th St. The UT co-op at which you're most likely to get a private room. Stay for dinner, and the residents will give you a welcoming round of applause; stay a week, and they'll vote you a member. Hallway bathrooms and linoleum floors. Three meals and a bed $15.

21st St. Co-op, 707 W. 21st St. (476-1857). From the bus stop take bus #39 on Airport St. to Koenig and Burnet, transfer to the #3 South, and ride to Nueces St.; walk 2 blocks west. Carpeted suites with A/C and a common room and co-ed bathroom on each floor. $10 per person, plus $5 for three meals and kitchen access. Fills up rapidly in summer; call ahead.

The Goodall Wooten, 2112 Guadalupe (472-1343). The "Woo" has nice rooms with small fridges and access to a TV room, laundry facilities, and basketball courts. Office open daily 9am-5pm and 8pm-midnight. Singles $20, doubles $25. Linen $5. Call ahead.

Motel 6, 8010 N. I-35 (837-9890 or 800-440-6000), 5mi. from downtown and Lake Austin; from I-35S take Exit 240A (Rundberg Ln.) and follow Frontage Rd. 112 units, a pool, new A/C, cable TV, and free local calls. Even if they're booked, show up at 6pm and you might get a room. Singles $32, doubles $38. Reservations necessary, particularly on weekends.

Pearl Street Co-op, 2000 Pearl St. (476-9478). Large, clean, sparsely furnished rooms. Laundry facilities, kitchen, and a beautiful courtyard pool. Open, friendly atmosphere with college students. Rooms include 3 square meals, shared bath, and access to cable TV/VCR room. 2-week max. stay. Singles $13, doubles $17.

A 15- to 45-min. drive separates Austin and the nearest **campgrounds.** The **Austin Capitol KOA** (444-6322 or 800-284-0206), 6 mi. south of the city along I-35, offers a pool, clean bathrooms, a game room, laundry facilities, a grocery store, and a playground. (Shady tent sites with water and electricity $24, with full hookup $27; $3 per additional person over 17. Cabins for 4 $34, for 6 $44. Get the third night free.)

FOOD

Scores of fast-food joints line the west side of the UT campus on **Guadalupe St.** Another area clusters around **Sixth St.,** south of the capitol; here the battle for happy hour business rages with unique intensity, and competitors employ such deadly weapons as three-for-one drink specials and free *hors d'oeuvres*. Though a bit removed from downtown, **Barton Springs Rd.** offers a diverse selection of inexpensive restaurants, including Mexican and Texas-style barbecue joints. The **Warehouse District** has seafood or Italian chow.

Threadgill's, 6416 N. Lamar St. (451-5440). A legend in Austin since 1933, serving up Southern soul food with the best of 'em. Creaky wooden floors, slow-moving ceiling fans, and antique beer signs set the stage. When former governor Ann Richards needed a caterer for her 60th birthday, she called Threadgill's. Southern fried chicken with all the veggies you can eat $7. Open daily 11am-10pm.

Ruby's BBQ, 512 W. 29th St. (477-1651). At Ruby's, Wild West meets the Jazz Age to form what may just be the best (and that means messiest) barbecue in all of Austin. The owners demand only farm-raised, grass-fed cows, none of that steroid crap. A grampus of a brisket sandwich goes for $3.55. Open Sun.-Thurs. 11am-midnight, Fri.-Sat. 11am-3am.

Trudy's Texas Star, 409 W. 30th St. (477-2935). Fine Tex-Mex dinner entrees ($5.25-8), and a fantastic array of margaritas. Famous for *migas*, a corn tortilla soufflé ($4). Pleasant outdoor porch bar with picnic tables open until 2am nightly. Open Mon.-Thurs. 7am-midnight, Fri.-Sat. 7am-2am, Sun. 8am-midnight. (Also at 8800 Burnet Rd., 454-1474.)

Mongolian BBQ, 9200 N. Lamar (837-4898), ½ block south of Rundberg St. Create your own stir-fry. Lunch $5, dinner $7; all you can eat $2 extra. Open Mon.-Fri. 11am-3pm and 5-9:30pm, Sat. 11:30am-3:30pm and 5-10pm.

Scholz Garden, 1607 San Jacinto Blvd. (477-4171), near the capitol. UT students and state politicians alike gather at this Austin landmark recognized by the legislature for "epitomizing the finest traditions of the German heritage of our state." German only in name, though—great chicken fried steaks and Tex-Mex meals $5-6. Live country-rock music. Open Mon.-Thurs. 11am-midnight, Fri.-Sat. 11am-2am.

Quackenbush's, 2120 Guadalupe St. (472-4477), at 21st St. A café/deli popular with UT students for espresso and other stylish drinks ($1-2.50). Bring Your Own Foucault Reader. Open daily 8am-11pm.

Metro's, 2222 Guadalupe St. (474-5730). Gourmet coffee drinks served all day and night amidst metal chairs, amoeba-shaped glass tables, and cement floors. Expect a tie-dyed-t-shirt-wearing crowd. Cup of espresso $1. Open 24hr.

SIGHTS

Not to be outdone by Washington, D.C., Texans built their **state capitol** (463-0063), Congress Ave. and 11th St., 7 ft. higher than the national one. (Free tours every 15min. Mon.-Fri. 8:30am-4:30pm, Sat.-Sun. 9:30am-4:30pm. Open Mon.-Fri.7am-10pm; Sat.-Sun. 9am-5pm.) The **Capitol Complex Visitors Center,** 112 E. 11th St. (463-8586), is located in the southeast corner of the capitol grounds. (Open Tues.-Fri.

TEXAS

9am-5pm, Sat. 10am-5pm.) Governor Hogg and his daughter Ima (Ura was just a myth) once lived across the street in the **Governor's Mansion** (463-5516), 11th and Colorado St., built in 1856 (free tours Mon.-Fri. every 20min. 10-11:40am). The Austin Convention Bureau offers free 1-hr. guided walking tours March through November (Sat. 2pm, Sun. 9am; call 454-1545 for info).

Both the wealthiest public university in the country, with an annual budget of almost a billion dollars, and the second largest university in the country, with over 50,000 students, the **University of Texas at Austin (UT)** forms the backbone of Austin's cultural life. The campus has two **visitors information centers,** one in Sid Richardson Hall, 2313 Red River St. (471-6498), and the other in the Nowtony Building (471-1420), at I-35 and Martin Luther King, Jr. Blvd. (Both open Mon.-Fri. 8am-4:30pm.) Campus tours leave from the base of the Tower (Mon.-Fri. 11am and 2pm, Sat. 1pm). Campus highlights include the **Lyndon B. Johnson Library and Museum,** 2313 Red River St. (482-5279), which houses 35 million documents (open daily 9am-5pm; free), and the **Harry Ransom Center,** corner of 21st and Guadalupe St. (471-8944), which hoards a copy of the Gutenberg Bible along with the world's first photograph and a vast collection of manuscripts and letters penned by Virginia Woolf, James Joyce, William Faulkner, D.H. Lawrence, and Evelyn Waugh. (Open Mon.-Sat. 9am-5pm, Sun. noon-5pm. Free.)

The **Austin Museum of Art at Laguna Gloria,** 3809 W. 35th St. (458-8191), 8 mi. from the capitol in a Mediterranean-villa look-alike, blends art, architecture, and nature. The rolling grounds overlook **Lake Austin,** while the museum displays 20th-century artwork and hosts **Fiesta Laguna Gloria** (835-2385), a yearly arts and crafts festival scheduled for May 17-18, 1997, with inexpensive evening concerts and plays. (Group tours Aug.-June by appointment. Open Tues.-Wed. and Fri.-Sat. 10am-5pm, Thurs. 10am-9pm, Sun. 1-5pm. $2, students $1, under 16 free; free Thurs.)

On hot afternoons, Austinites zip to riverside **Zilker Park,** 2201 Barton Springs Rd. (477-7273), just south of the Colorado River; take bus #30. Flanked by walnut and pecan trees, **Barton Springs Pool** (476-9044), a natural spring-fed swimming hole in the park, stretches 1000 ft. long and 200 ft. wide. Beware—the pool's temperature rarely rises above 60°F. Get away from the crowd and avoid the park fee ($2 per car on weekends March to early Sept.) by walking upstream and swimming at any spot that looks nice. (Hours vary seasonally. In general, the park is open Mon.-Fri. 5am-10pm, Sat.-Sun. and holidays 10am-6pm. Pool open Mar. 15-Oct. 15 Tues.-Wed. and Fri.-Sun. 5am-10pm, Mon. and Thurs. 5am-7:30pm. $2, Sat.-Sun. $2.25, ages 12-17 50¢, under 12 25¢.) The **Shoppe at Barton Springs** (476-6922), overlooking the lake, sells sundries and rents floats for $2 per hr. (Open Mon.-Fri. 10:30am-7pm, Sat. 9:30am-8pm, Sun. 11:30am-7pm.) For more fun and sun, drive to **Windy Point,** on Comanche Rd. 3 mi. west off the I-620 intersection and 20 min. from Austin, a picturesque sandy park on **Lake Travis.**

Just before dusk, head to the Congress Ave. Bridge and watch for the massive swarm of Mexican free-tail **bats** that emerge from their roosts to feed on the night's mosquitoes. When the bridge was reconstructed in 1980, the engineers unintentionally created crevices which formed ideal homes for the migrating bat colony. The city began exterminating the night-flying creatures until **Bat Conservation International** (327-9721; open Mon.-Fri. 8:30am-5:30pm), moved to Austin to educate people about bats' harmlessness and the benefits of their presence (the bats eat up to 30,000

Where Have All the Hippies Gone?

About 15 mi. northwest of downtown Austin, **Hippie Hollow,** 7000 Comanche Trail (266-1644), is Texas' only public nude swimming and sunbathing haven. The water of beautiful **Lake Travis** floats in the heart of Texas Hill Country, as everyone gets back to nature. Take Mopac (Loop 1) north to the exit for F.M. 2222. Follow 2222 west and turn onto Oasis Bluff. (17+ only. Open daily 9am-9pm. Entrance in summer and spring $5 per car; otherwise free.)

---

lbs. of insects each night). Today, the bats are among the biggest tourist attractions in Austin. The colony, seen from mid-March to November, peaks in July, when a fresh crop of babies hoists the population to around 1.5 million.

NIGHTLIFE

Nashville may be the queen of country music, but Austin is a renegade, funky princess with suitors including **Willie Nelson, Waylon Jennings,** and **Steve Earle.** On weekends fans converge to swing to the music on **6th St.,** an area bespeckled with warehouse nightclubs and fancy bars. The weekly *Austin Chronicle* and *XL-ent* provide detailed listings of current music performances, shows, and movies.

Famous for its blues, **Antone's,** 2915 Guadalupe St. (474-5314), at 29th St., has drawn the likes of B.B. King and Muddy Waters. (All ages welcome. Shows at 10pm. Cover $3-8. Open daily 8pm-2am.) The self-effacing name of **Hole in the Wall,** 2538 Guadalupe St. (472-5599), at 28th St., disguises another renowned music spot which features college alternative bands, and an occasional country and western or hardcore group. By day, the Hole is a sports bar with requisite pool tables. (Music nightly. Cover $3-5. Open Mon.-Fri. 11am-2am, Sat.-Sun. noon-2am.) The **Cactus Café** (471-8228), 24th and Guadalupe St. in the Texas Union, features adventurous acoustic music every night. Specializing in folk rock and Austin's own "New Country" sound, the Cactus gave Lyle Lovett his start. (Cover $2-15. Open roughly 9am-1am.)

In the 6th St. area, the **Chicago House,** 607 Trinity (499-8388), off 6th St., plays a different tune on weekends and hosts the occasional poetry reading. ($7, students and seniors $6. Open Fri.-Wed. 5pm-2am, Thurs. 8pm-2am.) For raunchy Texas-style rock 'n' roll and cheap beer, try **Joe's Generic Bar,** 315 E. 6th St. (480-0171; open daily 11am until the wayward crawl home; no cover). One of the biggest and best nightclubs on 6th St., **Toulouse's,** 402 E. 6th St. (478-0744), fills up to five stages with live music on the weekends. Professionals opt for the relaxed outside patio acoustic music, while raucous teenagers congregate inside for the "rougher" tunes. A karaoke machine upstairs spins vocal-free orchestrations every night at 10pm. (Cover $1-4. Open daily 8pm-2am.) **Paradox,** 311 E. 5th St. (469-7615), at Trinity, a warehouse-style dance club with retro-80s and some house music, draws twentysomethings by the pack (cover $3; open 9pm-4am; 17+). **404,** 404 Colorado (476-8297), is the city's most popular gay dance club ($5, under 21 $10; open Thurs.-Sun. 10pm-until people stop dancing).

For a quiet evening in Austin, visit the sophisticated **Copper Tank Brewing Company,** 504 Trinity St. (478-8444), probably the city's best microbrewery. On Wednesday a pint of any of the freshly brewed beers costs just $1—normally $3.50. (Open Mon.-Fri. 11am-2am, Sat.-Sun. 3pm-2am.)

▨ Houston

Houston was born when two brothers from the east, Augustus and John Allen, bought 2000 acres of land at $1.40 per acre on the Buffalo Bayou in 1836. As the story goes, Augustus stepped ashore at what is now called Allen's landing, drew a knife from his girdle and walked south, slicing through the weeds the path which would become Main St. Despite the Allens' elaborate plans for the city—first sketched out on the top of Augustus's stovepipe hat—Houston has come into its own only in the last half-century, due primarily to its status as the petrochemical capital of the nation. The fourth most populous city in the U.S., Houston sprawls over 5436 sq. mi. In recent years, the city has actively cultivated opera, theater, ballet, and museums, in an attempt to combat its image as a culturally devoid oil city. While Houston lacks natural beauty, it compensates with glass and steel skyscrapers that reflect the dazzling Texas sun and skies.

PRACTICAL INFORMATION

Tourist Office: Greater Houston Convention and Visitors Bureau, 801 Congress St. (227-3100 or 800-231-7799), at Milam St. Open Mon.-Fri. 8:30am-5pm.

Airport: Houston Intercontinental (230-3100), 25mi. north of downtown. Get to city center via **Airport Express** (523-8888); buses daily every 30min. 7am-11:30pm ($15-17, under 12 $5).

Trains: Amtrak, 902 Washington Ave. (224-1577 or 800-872-7245), in a rough neighborhood. During the day, catch a bus west on Washington (away from downtown) to Houston Ave.; at night, call a cab. To: San Antonio (4 per week, 5hr., $44); New Orleans (3 per week, 8hr., $73). Station and ticket office open Sat.-Wed. 7am-midnight, Thurs.-Fri. 7am-6pm.

Buses: Greyhound, 2121 S. Main St. (759-6565 or 800-231-2222). Late-night arrivals should call a cab—this is an unsafe neighborhood. To: Dallas (9 per day, 5hr., $25); Santa Fe (5 per day, 24hr., $99); San Antonio (10 per day, 4hr., $21). Open 24hr.

Public Transportation: Metropolitan Transit Authority (METRO Bus System) (739-4000). Provides reliable service anywhere between NASA (15mi. southeast of town) and Katy (25mi. west of town). Operates Mon.-Fri. 5am-11pm, Sat.-Sun. 8am-8pm; less frequently on weekends. Free maps available at the **Houston Public Library,** 500 McKinney (236-1313) at Bagby St. (open Mon.-Fri. 9am-9pm, Sat. 9am-6pm, Sun. 2-6pm), or at a Metro Rides Store. Fare $1; students and seniors (with $2 ID, available at Metro Ride stores) 25¢.

Taxis: Yellow Cab, 236-1111. $2.70 base fare, $1.35 per mi. *Be sure* to ask for a flat rate in advance.

Hotlines: Crisis Center Hotline, 228-1505. **Rape Crisis,** 528-7273. Both open 24hr. **Women's Center Hotline,** 528-2121. Open daily 9:30am-9pm. **Gay and Lesbian Switchboard of Houston** (529-3211) distributes entertainment info. Open daily 3pm-midnight.

Emergency: 911.

Post Office: 401 Franklin St. (227-1474). Open Mon.-Fri. 7am-7pm. **ZIP code:** 77052. **Area code:** 713.

Though the flat Texan terrain supports several mini-downtowns, true downtown Houston, a squarish grid of interlocking one-way streets, borders the **Buffalo Bayou** at the intersection of I-10 and I-45. **The Loop (I-610)** encircles the city center with a radius of 6 mi. Anything inside the Loop is easily accessible by car or bus. The shopping district of **Westheimer Blvd.** grows ritzier as you head west. Nearby, restaurants and shops line **Kirby Dr.** and **Richmond Ave.;** the upper portion of Kirby Dr. winds past some of Houston's most spectacular mansions. *Be careful in the south and east areas of Houston, which contain some risky neighborhoods.*

ACCOMMODATIONS AND CAMPING

Houston has plenty of cheap motels southwest of downtown along the **Katy Freeway (I-10W),** but better, more convenient rooms can be found along **South Main St. (90A-W).** Singles dip to $26, doubles to $30. (Bus #8 goes down S. Main; #119 and #72, "Westview," go out along the Katy Freeway.)

Perry House, Houston International Hostel (HI-AYH), 5302 Crawford St. (523-1009), at Oakdale St. In a residential neighborhood near Hermann Park and the museum district. From the Greyhound station, take bus #8 or #9 south to Southmore St.; walk 5 blocks east to Crawford St. and 1 block south to Oakdale St. 30 beds in 5 spacious rooms, well-equipped kitchen, choose-your-own chore, lock-out 10am-5pm. $11.25, nonmembers $14.25; linen $1.50.

YMCA, 1600 Louisiana Ave. (659-8501), between Pease and Leeland St. Downtown location features tiny cubicle-rooms with daily maid service, TV, common bath, and access to the Y's gym and health facilities. Singles $17.45. Key deposit $5. Another branch, 7903 South Loop (643-4396), is farther out but less expensive. Take Bus #50 at Broadway. Singles $14; key deposit $10.

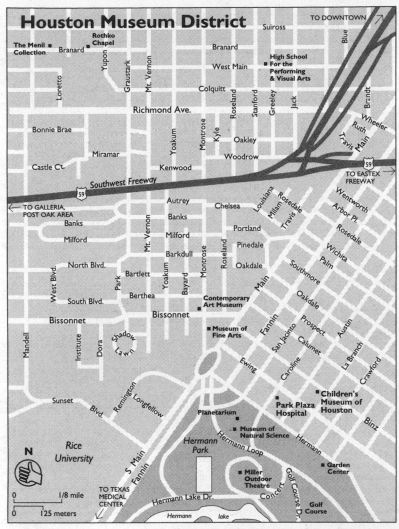

Houston Museum District

The Menil Collection ■
Rothko Chapel ■
Branard
Branard
West Main
High School For the Performing & Visual Arts ■
Suiross
TO DOWNTOWN
Blue
Loretto
Yupon
Graustark
Mt. Vernon
Colquitt
Roseland
Stanford
Greeley
Jack
Brandt
Richmond Ave.
Montrose
Kyle
Oakley
Woodrow
Wheeler
Ruth
Travis
Main
Bonnie Brae
Miramar
Castle Ct.
Kenwood
TO EASTEX FREEWAY
59
Southwest Freeway
59
← TO GALLERIA, POST OAK AREA
Autrey
Chelsea
Louisiana
Rosedale
Wentworth
Arbor Pl.
Banks
Banks
Portland
Milam
Travis
Rosedale
Milford
Milford
Pinedale
Wichita
Mt. Vernon
Barkdull
Roseland
Oakdale
Palm
North Blvd.
Montrose
Main
Southmore
West Blvd
Park
Bartlett
Yoakum
Bayard
Contemporary Art Museum ■
Fannin
Oakdale
Berthea
San Jacinto
Prospect
Austin
South Blvd.
Bissonnet
Bissonnet
■ Museum of Fine Arts
Calumet
La Branch
Crawford
Mandell
Institute
Dora
Shadow Lawn
Ewing
Caroline
Sunset
Remington
Longfellow
Planetarium
Park Plaza Hospital ■
■ Children's Museum of Houston
Binz
N
Rice University
Blvd.
S. Main
Fannin
Hermann Park
Hermann Loop
■ Museum of Natural Science
Hermann
■ Garden Center
0   1/8 mile
0   125 meters
TO TEXAS MEDICAL CENTER
Hermann Lake Dr.
■ Miller Outdoor Theatre
Concert
Golf Course Dr.
Golf Course
Hermann   lake

The Roadrunner, 8500 S. Main St. (666-4971), take bus #8. Friendly, helpful management, cable TV, mini-pool, free coffee, local calls, and ACME catalogs. Large, well-furnished rooms, but be careful of falling rock formations, crazy coyotes, and acme contraptions. Singles $24, doubles $30.

One campground graces the Houston area; it's in the boondocks, inaccessible by METRO Bus. **KOA Houston North,** 1620 Peachleaf (442-3700 or 800-440-2267), has sites with access to a pool and showers. From I-45, go east on Beltway 8N, then turn right on Aldine-Westfield Rd., and then right again on Peachleaf (tent sites for 2 $16, with electricity $18, full hookup $20; $2 per additional adult).

FOOD

Houston's port has witnessed the arrival of many immigrants (today the city's Indochinese population is the second largest in the nation), and its restaurants reflect this diversity. Houston's cuisine mingles Mexican, Greek, Cajun, and Vietnamese food. Look for reasonably priced restaurants along the chain-laden streets of **Westheimer** and **Richmond Ave.**, especially where they intersect with **Fountainview.** Houston has two **Chinatowns:** a district south of the George R. Brown Convention Center and a newer area on **Bellaire Blvd.** called **DiHo.**

Goode Company BBQ, 5109 Kirby Dr. (522-2530), near Bissonet. This might be the best (and most popular) BBQ in Texas, with a honky-tonk atmosphere to match. The mesquite smoked brisket, ribs, and sausage links (all smothered in homemade sauce) are great. Sandwiches $3; dinner $6-9. Open daily 11am-10pm.

Cadillac Bar, 1802 N. Shepherd Dr. (862-2020), at the Katy Freeway (I-10) northwest of downtown; take bus #75, change to #26 at Shepherd Dr. and Allen Pkwy. Wild, fun, authentic—and spicy—Mexican food. Tacos and enchiladas $5-10; heartier entrees $7-15. Drinks with sexy names $4. Open Mon.-Thurs. 10am-10:30pm, Sat. noon-midnight, Sun. noon-10pm.

The Buffalo Grille, 3116 Bissonnet (661-3663), at Buffalo Speedway. Famous for their Texas-sized breakfasts; favorites include pecan smoked bacon and Mexican breakfasts. Entrees ($5-10) served indoors or on the patio. Open Mon.-Fri. 7am-2pm; Sat.-Sun. 8am-2pm; lunch served Mon.-Sat.

Magnolia Bar & Grill, 6000 Richmond Ave. (781-2607). An upscale but reasonable Cajun seafood restaurant (chicken creole $9). The constant and varied crowd attests to the quality of the food and the relaxed, welcoming atmosphere. Late night jazz on Fri. and Sat., R&B on Sun. evenings. Open Mon.-Thurs. 11am-10pm, Fri.-Sat. 11am-11pm, Sun. 10:30am-10pm.

SIGHTS

The city's most popular attraction, **Space Center Houston,** 1601 NASA Rd. 1 (224-2100 or 800-972-0369), is technically not even in Houston, but 20 mi. from downtown in Clear Lake, TX; take I-45 south to NASA Rd. Exit, then head east 3 mi. The active Mission Control Center still serves as HQ for modern-day Major Toms. When astronauts ask, "Do you read me, Houston?" these folks answer. The complex also houses models of Gemini, Apollo, and Mercury as well as countless galleries and hands-on exhibits. You too can try to land the space shuttle on a computer simulator! (Open daily 9am-7pm; Labor Day to Memorial Day Mon.-Fri. 10am-5pm, Sat.-Sun. 10am-7pm. $12, seniors $10, ages 4-11 $8.50, under 4 free. Parking $3.)

Back in Houston, more earthly pleasures can be found underground. Hundreds of shops and restaurants line the 18-mile **Houston Tunnel System,** which connects all the major buildings in downtown Houston, extending from the Civic Center to the Tenneco Building and the Hyatt Regency. On hot days, duck into the air-conditioned passageways via any major building or hotel.

The 17th- to 19th-century American decorative art at **Bayou Bend Collection and Gardens,** 1 Westcott St. (639-7750), in **Memorial Park,** is an antique-lover's dream. The collection, housed in the mansion of millionaire Ima Hogg (we *swear*), daughter of turn-of-the-century Texas governor Jim "Boss" Hogg, includes more obscure Remington paintings. (90-min. tours every 15min. Open Tues.-Fri. 10am-2:45pm; Sat. 10-11:15am. $10, seniors $8.50, ages 10-18 $5, under 10 not admitted. Gardens open Tues.-Sat. 10am-5pm, Sun. 1-5pm. $3, under 11 free.)

Museums, gardens, paddleboats, and golfing are all part of **Hermann Park,** by Rice University and the Texas Medical Center. Within the 388 acres of beautifully landscaped grounds, you can visit the **Houston Museum of Natural Science,** 1 Hermann Circle Dr. (639-4600). The museum offers a splendid display of gems and minerals, permanent exhibits on petroleum, a hands-on gallery geared toward grabby children, a planetarium, and an IMAX theater. Inside the museum's **Cockrell Butterfly Centre,** a tropical paradise of 80°F, you'll find yourself surrounded by more than 2000 butterflies. Wear bright colors to attract them, and they will flutter your way, searching for nectar. (Hours fluctuate; call for details. Exhibits $3, seniors and under 12 $2; IMAX $9/$6; Planetarium $2/$1.50; Butterfly Center $3/$2.) At the southern end of the park, more flying critters—as well as gorillas, hippos, and reptiles—live in the **Hous-**

ton Zoological Gardens, 1513 N. MacGregor (525-3300). Crowds flock to see the rare white tigers that would make Sigfreid and Roy proud. (Open daily 10am-6pm. $2.50, seniors $2, ages 3-12 50¢.) The park grounds also encompass sports facilities, a kiddie train, a Japanese garden, and the Miller Outdoor Theater (see Entertainment, below).

The **Museum of Fine Arts,** 1001 Bissonet (639-7300), lies near the north side of Hermann Park. Designed by Mies van der Rohe, the museum boasts a collection of Impressionist and post-Impressionist art, as well as a slew of Remingtons. (Open Tues.-Wed. and Fri.-Sat. 10am-5pm, Thurs. 10am-9pm, Sun. 12.15-6pm. $3, students and seniors $1.50; free Thurs.) The museum's **Sculpture Garden,** 5101 Montrose St., includes pieces by artists such as Matisse and Rodin (open daily 9am-10pm; free). Across the street, the **Contemporary Arts Museum,** 5216 Montrose St. (526-3129), has multi-media exhibits. (Open Tues.-Wed. and Fri.-Sat. 10am-5pm, Thurs. 10am-9pm, Sun. noon-5pm. $3 suggested donation.)

About 1 mi. north of the park, a couple of Houston's highly acclaimed art museums are located within a block of one another. The **de Menil Collection,** 1515 Sul Ross (525-9400), includes an eclectic assortment of Surrealist paintings and sculptures, Byzantine and medieval artifacts, and European, American, and African art. The recently built **Cy Twombly Gallery,** inside the museum, is a permanent collection of work by the American artist…drum roll, please…Cy Twombly, whose minimalist art may elicit the common "I could have done that" response. (Open Wed.-Sun. 11am-7pm. Free.) A block away, the **Rothko Chapel,** 3900 Yupon (524-9839), houses 14 of the artist's paintings. Fans of modern art will delight in Rothko's ultra-simplicity; others will wonder where the paintings are (open daily 10am-6pm; free).

A tasteful tribute to citrus fruit can be found at the **Orange Show,** 2401 Munger St. (926-6368). This maze of strange shapes and painted tiles leads you past the artwork of retired postman Jeff McKissack, who opened this monument in 1954. Sculptures of various orange shades and shapes pay homage to the sticky fruit. (Open mid-Mar. to mid-Dec., Sat.-Sun. noon-5pm. $1, under 13 free.) Fans of folk art or booze should drive by **Beer Can House,** 222 Malone. Adorned with 50,000 beer cans, strings of beer-can tops, and a beer-can fence, the house was built by the late John Mikovisch, a retired upholsterer from the Southern Pacific Railroad. Conveniently, there's an **Anheuser-Busch Brewery,** 775 Gellhorn Rd. (670-1695), in town to satisfy any cravings which result from your visit; the free self-guided tour ends with a complimentary drink (open Mon.-Sat. 9am-4pm).

If you've got a car and a morbid sense of interest, head to the **American Funeral Service Museum,** 415 Barren Springs Dr. (876-3063 or 800-238-8861); from I-45, exit at Airtex, go west to Ella Blvd., turn right, and proceed to Barren Springs. The museum aims to "bring the history and facts behind our funeral service customs into the non-threatening light of day." It contains countless elaborate and ornate coffins, embalming artifacts, and two dozen coffin vehicles. Yes, it is a bit eerie, but also extremely interesting; check out the chicken-shaped caskets designed for die-hard farmers. (Open Mon.-Sat. 10am-4pm, Sun. noon-4pm. $5, seniors and under 12 $3.)

The **San Jacinto Battleground State Historical Park** (479-2431), 21 mi. east on Rte. 225 and 3 mi. north on Rte. 134, stands as the most important monument to Lone Star independence; the 18-minute battle which brought Texas freedom from Mexico was fought on this site on April 21, 1836. The **museum** in the Park celebrates Texas history with a dramatic multi-image presentation using 42 projectors (shown hourly 10am-5pm). Ride to the top of the 50-story **San Jacinto Monument** (479-2421) for a view of the area; at 570 ft., it is 15 ft. taller than the Washington Monument. (Both open daily 9am-6pm. Slide show $3.50, seniors $3, under 12 $1; elevator to top of monument $2.50/$2/$1; combo ticket $5.50/$4.50/$2.75.)

ENTERTAINMENT AND NIGHTLIFE

Jones Hall, 615 Louisiana Blvd. (853-8000), provides the stage for most of Houston's high-brow entertainment. The **Houston Symphony Orchestra** (227-ARTS/2787) performs here September through May (tickets $10-60); between October and May, the

Houston Grand Opera (546-0200) produces seven operas in the space (tickets $15-125; 50% student discount available at noon on the day of the show). In the summer, take advantage of the **Miller Outdoor Theater** (520-3292), in Hermann Park. The symphony, opera, and ballet companies and various professional theaters stage free concerts on the hillside most evenings April to October; the annual **Shakespeare Festival** struts and frets upon the stage from late July to early August. For an events update call 520-3290. The downtown **Alley Theater,** 615 Texas Ave. (228-8421), puts on Broadway-caliber productions at moderate prices (tickets $25-45; 50% student rush discount the day of the show).

The **Astrodome,** Loop 610 at Kirby Dr. (799-9555), the first mammoth indoor arena of its kind, is the home of the **Oilers** (799-1000) and the **Astros** (526-1709). Unfortunately, for the price of the tour, you're better off paying admission to a game; call for schedules and prices. (1¼-hr. tours daily 11am, 1, and 3pm. $4, seniors and ages 4-11 $3. Parking $4.)

Much of Houston's nightlife centers around a strip of **Richmond Ave.,** between Hillcroft and Chimney Rock. Dance to Top-40 music with local college students at the very chic, very dress-code-enforced **Blue Planet,** 6367 Richmond Ave. (978-5913); no baseball caps, t-shirts, or sneakers allowed. The bar features live acts Thursday nights. (Open Tues.-Fri. 6pm-2am, Sat.-Sun. 8pm-2am.) **City Streets,** 5078 Richmond Ave. (840-8555), is a multi-venue complex with six different clubs offering everything from country-western, live R&B, disco, and 80's music; you're sure to find something up your alley. (Open Tues.-Fri. 5pm-2am; Sat. 7:30pm-2am. $2-5 cover good for all 6 clubs.) Young professional twenty-somethings talk business and pleasure in the distinctly English atmosphere of **The Ale House,** 2425 W. Alabama (521-2333), at Kirby. The bi-level bar and beer garden offers over 130 brands of beer, some rather costly ($3-4). Upstairs you'll find old-time rock 'n roll or the blues on Sat. nights. (Open Mon.-Sat. 11am-2am, Sun. noon-2am.)

■ Galveston Island

In the 19th century, Galveston was the "Queen of the Gulf," Texas's most prominent port and wealthiest city. The glamour came to an abrupt end on Sept. 8, 1900, when a devastating hurricane ripped through the city and claimed 6,000 lives. The Galveston hurricane still ranks as one of the worst natural disasters in U.S. history. Now the narrow, sandy island of **Galveston** (pop. 65,000), 50 mi. southeast of Houston on I-45, meets the beach resort quotas for t-shirt shops, ice cream stands, and video arcades, but redeems itself with beautiful vintage homes, antique shops, and even some deserted beaches.

Practical Information Galveston's streets follow a grid; lettered avenues (A to U) run north-south, while numbered streets run east-west, with **Seawall** following the southern coastline. Most routes have two names; Avenue J and Broadway, for example, are the same street. The **Strand Visitors Center,** 2016 Strand St. (765-7834; open Mon.-Sat. 9:30am-6pm, Sun. 10am-6pm), and the **Galveston Island Convention and Visitors Bureau,** 2106 Seawall Blvd. (736-4311; open daily 8:30am-5pm), provide info about island activities. Greyhound affiliate **Texas Bus Lines,** 714 25th St. (765-7731), travels to Houston (4 per day, 1½hr., $11; open daily 8am-7pm). **Emergency** is 911. Galveston's **post office:** 601 25th St. (763-1527; open Mon.-Fri. 8:30am-5pm, Sat. 9am-noon); **ZIP code:** 77550; **area code:** 409.

Accommodations and Food Accommodation prices in Galveston fluctuate by season, rising to exorbitant heights during holidays and weekends. Money-minded folk should avoid lodging on the island; instead, make Galveston a daytrip from Houston. Nevertheless, RVs can find a reasonable resting place at any of several parks on the island. The closest to downtown, the **Bayou Haven Travel Park,** 6310 Heards Ln. (744-2837), off 61st St., is located on a peaceful waterfront with laundry facilities and bug-free restrooms and showers. (Sites for 2 with full hookup $14, waterfront sites

$17; $3 per additional person. Tents welcome.) **Galveston Island State Park** (737-1222), on 13½ Mile Rd., 6 mi. southwest of Galveston on FM3005 (it's not a radio station, it's a road—a continuation of Seawall Blvd.), rents sites for tents (sites $12, plus $5 entrance fee per vehicle; restrooms, showers, and screen shelters available).

Seafood and traditional Texas barbecue are bountiful in Galveston, especially along Seawall Blvd. **Hill's Pier 19** (763-7087), on the wharf at 20th St., serves seafood in a sprawling restaurant with tables upstairs, downstairs, inside and outside, as well as a comfortable cash bar. It's not cheap—a bowl of shrimp gumbo goes for $5. (Open Sun.-Thurs. 11am-9pm; Fri.-Sat. 11am-10pm.) The restaurant also has an in-house fish market, which makes things more affordable but less immediately edible (catfish $2.50 per lb., flounder $3.75 per lb.; open Sun.-Fri. 8:30am-5:30pm, Sat. 8:30am-6:30pm). The oldest restaurant on the island, **The Original Mexican Cafe**, 1401 Market (762-6001), cooks up Tex-Mex meals with homemade flour tortillas; go for their daily lunch specials ($4.25; open Mon.-Fri. 11am-10pm; Sat.-Sun. 8am-10pm). After a day at the beach, indulge your sweet tooth with a cherry phosphate ($1) at **LaKing's Confectionery**, 2323 Strand St. (762-6100), a large, old-fashioned ice cream and candy parlor (open Sun.-Fri. 10am-10pm; Sat. 10am-11pm).

Sights and Activities Galveston recently spent more than six million dollars to clean up and restore its shoreline. The money was well-spent—finding a beautiful beach is as easy as strolling along the seawall and picking a spot. The only beach in Galveston which permits alcoholic beverages, **Apffel Park,** on the far eastern edge of the island, attracts young partiers like flies. A more family-oriented atmosphere can be found at **Stewart Beach**, near 4th and Seawall, where a water slide keeps kids entertained. Three **Beach Pocket Parks** lie on the west end of the island, east of Pirates Beach, each with bathrooms, showers, playgrounds, and a concession stand. (Car entry for each of these beaches $5.)

Strand St., near the northern coastline, between 20th and 25th St., is a national landmark, with over 50 Victorian buildings which house a pastiche of cafés, restaurants, gift shops, and clothing stores. Once dubbed the "Wall Street of the Southwest," the district has been restored with authenticities such as gas lights and brick-paved walkways. The **Galveston Island Trolley** shuttles between the seawall beach area and the posh historic section of Strand St. (Operates from 6:30am-7pm. 60¢ for every 30 min.) Pick up the trolley and trolley tickets at either visitors center (see Practical Information, above). While in Galveston, stop by **Moody Gardens** (744-1745 or 800-582-4673); head up 81st from Seawall and you'll run right into it. The area, though filled with touristy spas and restaurants, makes room for a 10-story glass pyramid which encloses a tropical rainforest, 2000 exotic species of flora and fauna, and a 3D **IMAX Theater** with a six-story-high screen. Duck into the new **Bat Cave** to meet colonies of these nocturnal creatures. (Rainforest and IMAX open daily 10am-9pm; Nov.-Feb. Sun.-Thurs. 10am-6pm, Fri.-Sat. 10am-9pm. $6 each.)

■ San Antonio

Texas propaganda claims that every Texan has two homes—his own and San Antonio. The skyline may be dominated by soaring modern office buildings, but no Texan city seems more determined to preserve its rich heritage than San Antone. Founded in 1691 by Spanish missionaries, the city is home to the magnificent Alamo, historic Missions, and La Villita, once a village for San Antonio's original settlers and now a workshop for local artisans. Though both Native Americans and Germans have at one time claimed San Antonio as their own, Spanish speakers (55% of the population) today outnumber any other group and the city's food, architecture, and language reflect their influence. San Antonio is located on the most traveled route between the U.S. and Mexico, just 150 mi. from the Mexican border.

TEXAS

PRACTICAL INFORMATION

Tourist Office: 317 Alamo Plaza (270-8748), downtown across from the Alamo. Open daily 8:30am-6pm.

Airport: San Antonio International, 9800 Airport Blvd. (821-3411), north of town accessible by I-410 and U.S. 281. Bus #2 ("Airport") connects the airport to downtown at Market and Alamo. **Star Shuttle Service** (341-6000) travels from the airport to several locations near downtown for $6 per person. Cab fare $14.

Trains: Amtrak, 1174 E. Commerce St. (223-3226 or 800-872-7245), 2 blocks off the I-37 E. Commerce St. exit. To: Houston (3 per day, 4½hr., $44); Dallas (3 per day, 8hr., $44); Austin (3 per day, 2½hr., $16). Closed daily 6:30-10:30pm only.

Buses: Greyhound, 500 N. Saint Mary's St. (270-5824 or 800-231-2222). To: Houston (10 per day, 4hr., $21); Dallas (16 per day, 8hr., $32). Lockers $1. Open 24hr.

Public Transportation: VIA Metropolitan Transit, 800 W. Myrtle (227-2020; open Mon.-Sat. 6am-8pm, Sun. 8am-8pm), between Commerce and Houston. Buses operate daily 5am-10pm, but many routes stop at 5pm. Inconvenient service to outlying areas. Fare 40¢ (plus zone changes), express 75¢. VIA operates two **"cultural tour"** routes: Rte. 7 stops include the Zoo, McNay Art Museum, Witte Museum, Pioneer Hall, S.A. Botanical Gardens, and Alamo Pl.; Rte. 40 hits La Villita, Lone Star Brewery, and the missions. One-day "on-and-off" passes ($2) available at 112 Soledad St.

Taxis: Yellow Cab, 226-4242. $2.90 for first mi., $1.30 per additional mi.

Car Rental: Chuck's Rent-A-Clunker, 3249 S.W. Military Dr. (922-9464). $18 per day with 100 free mi., vans $35 per day. Must be 19 with credit card or cash deposit. Open Mon.-Fri. 8am-6pm, Sat. 9am-6pm, Sun. 10am-6pm.

Gay & Lesbian Switchboard, 733-73000. Open 24hr.

Crisis Lines: Rape Crisis Hotline, 349-7273. 24hr. **Presa Community Service Center,** 532-5295. Referrals and transport for elderly and disabled.

Emergency: 911.

Post Office: 615 E. Houston (227-3399), 1 block from the Alamo. Open Mon.-Fri. 8:30am-5:30pm. **ZIP code:** 78205. **Area code:** 210.

ACCOMMODATIONS AND CAMPING

In a city this popular, downtown hotel managers have no reason to keep prices low. Furthermore, San Antonio's dearth of rivers and lakes makes for few good campsites. For cheap motels, try **Roosevelt Ave.,** an extension of St. Mary's, and **Fredericksburg Rd.** Inexpensive motels also clutter **Broadway** between downtown and Brackenridge Park. Drivers should follow **I-35N** to find cheaper and often safer accommodations within 15 mi. of town.

Bullis House Inn San Antonio International Hostel (HI-AYH), 621 Pierce St. (223-9426), 2mi. northeast of the Alamo across from Fort Sam Houston. From the bus station, walk ½ block east on Pecan St. to Navarro St.; take bus #11 or #15 to Grayson and New Braunfels; walk west 2 blocks. A friendly ranch-style hostel in a quiet neighborhood. Pool, kitchen. Fills quickly in summer. Office open daily 7:30am-11pm. $13, nonmembers $16. Private rooms for 1 or 2 $30, nonmembers from $34. Sheets $2. Breakfast $4.

Elmira Motor Inn, 1126 E. Elmira (222-9463 or 800-584-0800), about 3 blocks east of St. Mary's a little over 1mi. north of downtown; take bus #8 and get off at Elmira St. Very large, well furnished, recently decorated rooms—the cleanest you'll get at this price. TV, 5 free local calls, and A/C (with in-room control). Very caring management. Room for 1 or 2 $38. Key deposit $2.

El Tejas Motel, 2727 Roosevelt Ave. (533-7123), at E. South Cross 3mi. south of downtown near the missions; take bus #42. Big, clean rooms with ye olde fashioned furniture. HBO and cable TV, pool. Singles $25-28, doubles $32-36.

Navarro Hotel, 116 Navarro St. (223-8453 or 224-0255). 43 rooms at a great location in the heart of town with free parking and A/C. Clean, irregularly shaped rooms with varying degrees of furniture quality. Singles $27, with bath $37; doubles $45, with or without bath.

Alamo KOA, 602 Gembler Rd. (224-9296 or 800-833-5267), 6mi. from downtown; take bus #24 ("Industrial Park") from the corner of Houston and Alamo downtown. Beautiful, well-kept grounds with lots of shade. Each site has a BBQ grill and patio. Showers, laundry facilities, A/C, heated pool, playground, free movies, and golf course. Open daily 7:30am-10:30pm. Sites for 2 $16, with full hookup $20; $2 per additional person over age 3.

FOOD

Explore the area east of S. Alamo and S. Saint Mary's St. for the best Mexican food and BBQ. Expensive cafés and restaurants cram the **River Walk**—breakfast alone could clean you out if you don't settle for a muffin and coffee. **Pig Stand** (227-1691) diners offer decent, cheap country-style food all over this part of Texas; the branches at 801 S. Presa, off S. Alamo, and 1508 Broadway, both near downtown stay open 24 hr. **Taco Cabana** does the best fast Mexican food in the area, with many locations across downtown. Visit the one at 101 Alamo Plaza (224-6158), at Commerce, any time (open 24hr.). North of town, Asian restaurants line **Broadway** across from Brackenridge. The **Farmers' Market** (207-8600), near Market Sq., sells produce, Mexican chiles, and candy. Come late in the day when prices drop and vendors are willing to haggle. (Open daily 10am-8pm; Sept.-May daily 10am-6pm.)

Josephine St. Steaks/Whiskey, 400 Josephine St. (224-6169), at McAllister. Away from the more touristy spots along the River Walk. Josephine's specializes in Texan steaks, but offers an assortment of chicken, seafood, and pork dishes (entrees $5-11). Great home-baked desserts; try the carrot cake or cookie pie (each $2.50). Open Mon.-Sat. 11am-10pm.

Rio Rio Cantina, 421 E. Commerce (CANTINA/226-8462). Funky upscale Mexican in a fancy, shaka-shaka setting with a riverside view. Order up a huge naked José Iguana ($8.50)—a 27-oz. monster of a beverage. Enchiladas go for $9. Open Sun.-Thurs. 11am-11pm., Fri.-Sat. 11am-midnight.

Earl Abel's, 4220 Broadway (822-3358). A professional organist for silent movies, Mr. Abel found himself out of work once the "talkies" hit the silver screen. His diner took off after Duncan Hines ate here and raved. Abel's family still runs the operation. Bacon, eggs, hash browns, and toast served with friendly smiles $4.25. Open daily 6:30am-1am. Breakfast until 11am.

Hung Fong Chinese and American Restaurant, 3624 Broadway (822-9211), at Queen Anne 2mi. north of downtown; take bus #14 or #9. The oldest Chinese restaurant in San Antonio. Consistently good and crowded. Big portions $5-7. Open Mon.-Thurs. 11am-10:30pm, Fri.-Sat. 11:30am-11:30pm, Sun. 11:30am-10:30pm.

SIGHTS

Much of historic San Antonio lies in the present-day downtown and surrounding areas. The city may seem diffuse, but almost every major site or park is within a few miles of downtown and accessible by public transportation.

The Missions

The five missions along the San Antonio River once formed the soul of San Antonio; the city preserves their remains in the **San Antonio Missions National Historical Park.** To reach the missions, follow the blue and white "Mission Trail" signs beginning on S. Saint Mary's St. downtown. **San Antonio City Tours** (228-9776), at the Alamo's visitors center on Crockett St., offers ½-day ($25) and full-day ($39) tours of the city. Bus #42 stops right in front of Mission San José, within walking distance of Mission Concepción. (All missions free and open daily 9am-5pm; Sept.-May 8am-5pm. For info on the missions, call 534-8833.) Every Saturday morning, a national park ranger leads a 10-mi. round-trip **bike tour** (229-4700) from Mission San José along the historic corridor (free; bring your own bike; call for schedule).

Mission Concepción, 807 Mission Rd. (229-5732), 4mi. south of the Alamo off E. Mitchell St. The oldest unrestored stone church in North America (1731). Traces of the once-colorful frescoes are still visible.

Mission San José, 6539 San José Dr. (229-4770). The "Queen of the Missions" (1720) has its own irrigation system, a gorgeous sculpted rose window, and numerous restored buildings. The largest of San Antonio's missions, it best conveys the self-sufficiency of these institutions. Four Catholic services held each Sun. (at 7:45, 9, and 10:30am, and a noon "Mariachi Mass").

Mission San Juan Capistrano, 9101 Graf (229-5734), at Ashley, and **Mission San Francisco de la Espada,** 10040 Espada Rd. (627-2021), both off Roosevelt Ave., 10mi. south of downtown as the Texas swallows fly. Smaller and simpler than the others, these two missions evoke the isolation of such outposts. Between them lies the Espada Aqueduct, the only remaining waterway built by the Spanish.

Remember the Alamo!

"Be silent, friend, here heroes died to blaze a trail for other men." Disobeying orders to retreat with their cannons, the 189 defenders of the Alamo, outnumbered 20 to one, held off the Mexican army for 12 days. Then, on the morning of the 13th day, the Mexicans commenced the infamous *deguello* (throat-cutting). The only survivors of the Alamo defenders were women, children, and slaves. Forty-six days later General Sam Houston's small army defeated the Mexicans at San Jacinto amidst cries of "Remember the Alamo!" These days, phalanxes of tourists attack the **Alamo** (225-1391), at the center of Alamo Plaza near Houston and Alamo St., and sno-cone vendors are the only defenders. A single chapel and barracks are all that remain of the former Spanish Mission. (Open Mon.-Sat. 9am-5:30pm, Sun. 10am-5:30pm.)

Southwest of the Alamo, black signs indicate access points to the 2.5-mi. **Paseo del Río (River Walk),** a series of well-patrolled shaded stone pathways which follow a winding canal built by the Works Progress Administration in the 1930s. Lined with picturesque gardens, shops, and cafés, and connecting most of the major downtown sights, the River Walk is the hub of San Antonio's nightlife. **Yanaguana Cruises** (244-5700 or 800-417-4139) offer a 30-min. narrated boat tour along the Paseo del Río; tickets are available at the River Center Mall, 849 E. Commerce St., or outside the Hilton Palacio del Rio, 200 S. Alamo St. ($4, children $1, seniors and military $3). The **Alamo IMAX Theater** (225-4629), in Rivercenter Mall, shows "The Price of Freedom," a 45-min. Alamo docudrama. (7 shows 9am-6pm. $6.75, seniors $6.25, ages 3-11 $4.50.) A few blocks south, **La Villita,** 418 Villita (207-8610), houses restaurants, craft shops, and art studios (open daily 10am-6pm).

The site of the 1968 World's Fair, **HemisFair Plaza,** on S. Alamo, draws tourists with nearby restaurants, museums, and historic houses. The **Tower of the Americas,** 600 Hemisphere Park (207-8615), rises 750 ft. above the dusty plains, dominating the meager skyline. Observe the city from the observation deck on top (open daily 8am-11pm; $3, seniors $2, ages 4-11 $1). Plaza museums include the **Institute of Texan Cultures,** 801 S. Bowie (558-2300), at Durango, with exhibits on the cultural groups who first settled Texas, and much touchable stuff for kids (open Tues.-Sun. 9am-5pm; $4, seniors and kids $2), and the **Mexican Cultural Institute,** 600 HemisFair Park (227-0123; open Tues.-Fri. 9:30am-5:30pm, Sat.-Sun. 11am-5pm).

Directly behind **City Hall,** between Commerce and Dolorosa St. at Laredo, the adobe-walled **Spanish Governor's Palace,** 105 Plaza de Armas (224-0601), built in 1772, displays Spanish Colonial-style architecture with carved doors and an enclosed patio and garden. (Open Mon.-Sat. 9am-5pm, Sun. 10am-5pm. $1, under 14 50¢, under 7 free.) Home to the San Antonio **Spurs** and the world's largest retractable seating system, the **Alamodome,** 100 Montana (207-3600), at Hoefgen St. downtown, resembles a Mississippi riverboat. Take bus #24 or #26; in a car, park at the south entrance in Lot A. (Tours Tues.-Sat. 10am, 1 and 3pm, except during scheduled events. $3, seniors and under 12 $1.50.)

San Antonio North and South

Head to **Brackenridge Park,** 3900 N. Saint Mary's St. (734-5401), 5 mi. north of the Alamo, for a day of unusual sight-seeing; from downtown, take bus #7 or #8. The 343-acre showground includes playgrounds, stables, a miniature train, an aerial tramway ($2.25, ages 1-11 $1.75), and a Japanese garden. (Open Mon.-Fri. 9:30am-5:30pm, Sat.-Sun. 9:30am-6:30pm.) Directly across the street, the **San Antonio Zoo,** 3903 N. Saint Mary's St. (734-7183), one of the country's largest, houses over 3500 animals from 800 species in reproductions of their natural settings, including an extensive African mammal exhibit. (Open daily 9:30am-5pm. $6, seniors $4, ages 3-11 $4.) Nearby **Pioneer Hall,** 3805 N. Broadway (822-9011), contains a splendid collection of artifacts, documents, portraits, and cowboy accessories which chronicle early Texas history (open daily 10am-5pm; $2, seniors and military $1.50). Next door, the **Witte Museum,** 3801 Broadway (820-2111), attempts to explain Texas wildlife and anthropology with everything from dinosaur bones to rock art. (Open Mon. and Wed.-Sat. 10am-6pm, Tues. 10am-9pm, Sun. noon-6pm; off season Tues. 10am-6pm. $4, seniors $2, ages 4-11 $1.75; free Tues. 3-9pm.)

The **San Antonio Museum of Art,** 200 W. Jones Ave. (978-8100), just north of the city center, showcases Texan furniture and pre-Columbian, Native American, Spanish, and Mexican folk art. (Open Mon. and Wed.-Sat. 10am-5pm, Tues. 10am-9pm, Sun. noon-5pm. $4, college students with ID and seniors $2, ages 4-11 $1.75; free Tues. 3-9pm. Free parking. Show your ticket from the Witte Museum within 3 days and get ½-price admission.) The former estate of Marion Koogler McNay, the **McNay Art Museum,** 6000 N. New Braunfels, on the bus #11 route (824-5368), flaunts a large collection of post-Impressionist European art, including works by Degas, Picasso, and Van Gogh (open Tues.-Sat. 10am-5pm, Sun. noon-5pm; free).

The **Lone Star Brewing Company,** 600 Lone Star Blvd. (270-9467), resides about 2 mi. south of the city, accessible by bus #7 or #40 (the VIA cultural route). Trigger-happy Albert Friedrich accumulated 3500 animal heads, horns, and antlers before he opened the Buckhorn in 1887. What better place to put them than in his bar? Now you can pity his prey and sample some beer on hourly tours. (Open daily 9:30am-5pm. $5, seniors $4, ages 6-12 $1.75.)

For intoxicating natural beauty, visit **Natural Bridge Caverns,** 26495 Natural Bridge Caverns Rd. (651-6101); take I-35N to Exit 175 and follow the signs. Discovered 36 years ago, the caverns' 140-million-year-old phallic rock formations will knock your socks off. (1½-hr. tours every ½hr. Open daily 9am-6pm; Labor Day-Memorial Day 9am-4pm. $7, ages 3-11 $5.)

ENTERTAINMENT AND NIGHTLIFE

On April 18-27, **Fiesta San Antonio** (227-5191) ushers in spring with concerts, parades, and plenty of Tex-Mex to commemorate the victory at San Jacinto and honor the heroes at the Alamo. For fun after dark any time, any season, stroll down the **River Walk.** The Friday *Express* or weekly *Current* will guide you to concerts and

---

How many words can YOU make from Schlitterbahn?

The entire local economy of the town of New Braunfels depends upon one doughnut-shaped object: the innertube. Almost two million visitors per year come to this town, hoping only to spend a day floating along the pea-green waters of the spring-fed Comal River. **Rockin' "R" River Rides,** 193 S. Liberty (210-620-6262), will drop you off upstream with a lifejacket and a trusty tube and pick you up downstream 1½ hr. later. (Open May-Sept. daily 9am-7pm. Tube rentals $8, $6 for bottomless floats, $25 deposit required.) If the Comal don't float your boat, head for the chlorinated waters of **Schlitterbahn,** 400 N. Liberty (210-625-2351), a 65-acre extravaganza of a waterpark with 17 water slides, nine tube chutes, and five giant hot tubs. (Open late May to Sept. Call for hours, which generally hover around 10am-8pm. $20, ages 3-11 $16.)

entertainment. The biggest dance club on the river, **Acapulco Sam's,** 212 College St. (212-SAMS/7267), features a Top-40 and reggae discotheque on one level, live rock 'n' roll music on the second, and a groovy DJ with a dance floor straight out of *Saturday Night Fever* on the third. (Music nightly 9:30pm. Cover around $4. Open Sun.-Fri. 6pm-2am, Sat. 6pm-3am.) For authentic *tejano* music, a Mexican and country amalgam, head to **Cadillac Bar,** 212 S. Flores (223-5533), where a different *tejano* band whips the huge crowd (anywhere from 500-1000 people) into a cheering and dancing frenzy every weeknight (open Mon.-Tues. 11am-midnight, Sat. 5pm-2am). Right around the corner from the Alamo, the **Bonahm Exchange,** 411 Bonahm (271-3811), San Antonio's biggest gay dance club, plays high-energy music with some house and techno thrown in. A younger, more mixed crowd comes on Wednesday and Thursday. (Open Mon.-Fri. 4pm-2:30am, Sat.-Sun. 8pm-4am.) Some of the best blues in the city plays at **Jim Cullum's Landing,** 123 Losoya (223-7266), in the Hyatt downtown. Cullum plays with his Happy Jazz Band Mon-Sat. 9pm-1am. The improv jazz quintet Small World performs on Sunday nights.

■ Corpus Christi

After you've taken in all of Corpus Christi's sights—in other words, after about half an hour—you may wonder what you're doing in the town named for the "body of Christ." Once you hit the beach, you'll understand why this area is divine.

Practical Information Touristy Corpus Christi (pop. 262,000) follows **Shoreline Dr.,** which borders the Gulf Coast, 1 mi. east of the downtown business district. The **Convention and Visitors Bureau,** 1201 N. Shoreline (881-1888 or 800-678-6232; open Mon.-Fri. 8:30am-5pm), where I-37 meets the water, has piles of pamphlets, bus schedules, and local maps, as does the **Corpus Christi Museum,** 1900 N. Chaparral (883-2862; open daily 10am-6pm). **Greyhound,** 702 N. Chaparral (882-2516 or 800-231-2222; open daily 7am-3am), at Starr, downtown, goes to Dallas (3 per day, 8-10hr., $38), Houston (4 per day, 4½hr., $21), and Austin (2 per day, 5-6hr., $29). **Regional Transit Authority (The "B")** (289-2600) bus schedule varies; pick up maps and schedules at the visitors bureau or at "B" headquarters, 1812 S. Alameda (883-2287; open Mon.-Fri. 8am-5pm). City Hall, Port Ayers, Six Points, and the Staples St. stations serve as central transfer points. (Fare 50¢; students, seniors, kids, and disabled 25¢, 10¢ off-peak. Sat. 25¢, transfers free.) The **Corpus Christi Beach Connector** follows the shoreline and stops at the aquarium daily 7am-6:30pm (same fares as buses). The free **Beach Shuttle** also travels to the beach, the Aquarium, and other nearby attractions. (Operates May-Sept. 10:30am-6:30pm.) If you need help, call the **Hope Line** (855-4673), for counseling and crisis service, or the **Battered Women and Rape Victims Shelter** (881-8888); both stay open 24hr. **Emergency:** 911. Corpus Christi's **post office:** 809 Nueces Bay Blvd. (886-2200; open Mon.-Fri. 7:30am-5:30pm, Sat. 8am-1pm). **ZIP code:** 78469. **Area code:** 512.

Accommodations, Food, and Nightlife Cheap accommodations are scarce downtown. Posh hotels and expensive motels take up much of the scenic and convenient shoreline. For the best motel bargains, drive several miles south on Leopard St. (take bus #27) or I-37 (take #27 Express). The rooms at **Ecomotel,** 6033 Leopard St. (289-1116; Exit I-37 at Corn Products Rd., head south, to Leopard St.), have A/C, ceiling fans, ample furniture, cable TV, and "massago-beds"—an excellent deal (singles $28, doubles $39). A haven in an area of expensive lodging is the **Sleep n' Save Motel,** 910 Corn Products Rd. (289-6919), off I-37. You *will* sleep and save in the no-frills rooms (free local calls, refrigerators, cable TV; singles $24, doubles $28). Campers should head for the **Padre Island National Seashore** or **Mustang State Park** (see Padre Island National Seashore, below). **Nueces River City Park** (884-7275), off I-37N from Exit 16, has free tent sites and three-day RV permits, but portable restrooms and no showers.

The mixed population and seaside locale of Corpus Christi have resulted in a wide range of cuisine. Restaurants of the non-chain type can be found on the "south side" of the city, around **Staples St.** and **S. Padre Island Dr.** The **Water St. Seafood Company,** 309 N. Water St. (882-8683), sells moderate to pricey edible marine life, such as deep fried Gulf oysters ($8) and shrimp and pasta salad ($5.50). Yum! (Open Sun.-Thurs. 11am-10pm, Fri.-Sat. 11am-11pm.) **Howard's BBQ,** 120 N. Water St. (882-1200), shells out a generous beef and sausage plate, an all-you-can-graze salad bar, and a drink for $5 (open Mon.-Fri. 11am-3pm). **Buckets Sports Bar & Grill,** 227 N. Water St. (883-7776), takes care of folks who need a TV fix. The eclectic menu sports American, Cajun, Italian, and Mexican dishes. (Hamburger $3.50; chef's salad $6. Open daily 11am-4am.) The city shuts down early, but several clubs manage to survive on **Water St.;** the **Yucatan Beach Club,** 208 N. Water St. (888-6800), visibly marked with a fluorescent blue and pink exterior, stages live nightly music, usually rock 'n' roll or reggae (no cover before 9pm, after $3; open daily 5pm-2am).

Sights Corpus Christi's most significant sight is the shoreline, bordered by miles of rocky seawall and wide sidewalks with graduated steps down to the water. Overpriced seaside restaurants, sail and shrimp boats, and hungry seagulls overrun the piers. Feeding the birds produces a Hitchcockian swarm; wear a hat and prepare to run for your life. Almost all of the beaches on **N. Shoreline Dr.** allow swimming; just follow the signs, or call the Beach Services (949-7023) for directions. Eight white *miradors* (Spanish for "lookouts") line the seawall; these Victorian-style gazebos are prime for Kodak moments.

Just offshore floats the aircraft carrier **U.S.S. Lexington** (888-4873 or 800-523-9539), a World War II relic now open to the public. In her day, the "Lady Lex" set more records than any carrier in the history of naval aviation. Be sure to check out the soldiers' quarters—you won't complain about small hostel rooms ever again. (Open daily 9am-5pm; Memorial Day-Labor Day 9am-8pm. $8, seniors and military personnel $6, ages 4-12 $4.) Built by the government of Spain in 1992, the **Columbus Fleet,** 1900 N. Chaparral St. (886-4492), near the Harbor Bridge, commemorates the 500th anniversary of Columbus's historic voyage with replicas of the *Niña,* the *Pinta,* and the *Santa María.* The fleet is adjacent to the **Museum of Science and History** (883-2862), which has an interesting exhibit on Spanish shipwrecks. Admission covers both the museum and the fleet. (Open Mon.-Sat. 10am-5pm, Sun. noon-5pm. $8, seniors and military $6.50, ages 13-17 $7, ages 6-12 $4.) To eke out a little art after a day in the sun, the **Art Museum of South Texas,** 1902 N. Shoreline (884-3844), at the north end of Shoreline Dr., is your only option. The collection changes every six to eight weeks; past exhibits have featured the works of Matisse, Remington, and Ansel Adams. (Open Tues.-Sat. 10am-5pm, Sun. 1-5pm. $3, students $2; seniors, military, and ages 2-12 $1; families $3 on Sun.) The **Texas Jazz Festival** (883-4500), July 25-27 in 1997, draws hundreds of musicians and thousands of fans from around the country (most performances free).

■ Padre Island

With over 80 mi. of perfectly preserved beaches, dunes, and wildlife refuge land, the **Padre Island National Seashore (PINS)** is a flawless gem sandwiched between the condos and tourists of North Padre Island and the spring break hordes of South Padre Island. The seashore provides excellent opportunities for windsurfing, beachcombing, swimming, or even surf fishing—an 850-lb. shark was once caught at the southern end of the island. Entry into PINS costs $4, though 7½ mi. of fine sand 'n' sun await at **North Beach,** which lies just before the checkpoint where fees are collected. Five mi. south of the entrance station, **Malaquite Beach** makes your day on the sand as easy as possible with picnic tables, restrooms, and a concession stand that rents it all (inner tubes $2.50 per hr., chairs $1.25 per hr., boogie boards $3 per hr.). The **Malaquite Visitors Center** (512-949-8068), has maps, exhibits, videos, and wildlife guidebooks (open daily 9am-6pm; Sept.-May 9am-4pm).

Visitors with four-wheel-drive and a taste for solitude should make the 60-mi. trek to the **Mansfield Cut**, the most remote and untraveled area of the seashore; loose sands prevent most vehicles from venturing far onto the beach. If you decide to go, be sure to tell the folks at the **Malaquite Ranger Station** (512-949-8173), 3½ mi. south of the park entrance; they handle emergency assistance and like to know who's out there. No wheels? Hike the **Grasslands Nature Trail**, a ¾-mi. loop through sand dunes and grasslands. Stop at the ranger station for a guide pamphlet.

Camping on the beach at PINS means falling asleep to the crashing of waves on the sand; if you're not careful, morning may mean waking up to the slurping noise of thousands of mosquitoes sucking you dry—bring insect repellent. The **PINS Campground** (512-949-8173), less than 1 mi. north of the visitors center, consists of an asphalt area for RVs, restrooms, and cold-rinse showers—no soap is permitted on PINS. Primitive camping occupies a 5-mi. section of beach (tent and RV sites $5). Wherever vehicles can go, camping is free. Near the national seashore, the **Balli County Park** (512-949-8121), on Park Rd. 22, 3½ mi. from the JFK Causeway, provides running water, electricity, and hot showers for campers. (3-day max. stay. Sites with water and electricity $10.50. Key deposit $5.) Those who value creature comforts should head a few mi. farther north to the **Mustang State Park Campground** (512-749-5246), on Park Rd. 53, 6 mi. from the JFK Causeway, for electricity, running water, dump stations, restrooms, hot showers, and picnic tables. (Entry fee $5. Tent sites $7; with water and electricity $12. RVs must reserve ahead. All must pick up a camping permit from the ranger station at the park entrance.)

Motorists enter the PINS via the JFK Causeway, from the Flour Bluff area of Corpus Christi. PINS is difficult to reach via Corpus Christi's public bus system.

WESTERN TEXAS

On the far side of the Río Pecos lies a region whose stereotypical Texan character verges on self-parody. This is the stomping ground of Pecos Bill—the mythical cowpoke who was raised by coyotes and grew to lasso a tornado. The land here was colonized in the days of the Republic of Texas, during an era when the "law west of the Pecos" meant a rough mix of vigilante violence and frontier gunslinger machismo. The border city of El Paso and its Chihuahuan neighbor, Ciudad Juárez, beckon way, *wayyyy* out west—700 mi. from the Louisiana border—while Big Bend National Park dips down into the desert cradled by a curve in the Río Grande.

■ Amarillo

Amarillo, named for the yellow clay of a nearby lake, opened for business as a railroad construction camp in 1887 and, within a decade, became the nation's largest cattle-shipping market. For years, the economy depended largely on the meat industry. In the 1920s the discovery of oil gave Amarillo's economy a kick, and "black gold" translated into enormous wealth for all involved. More recently, the city has gotten a boost from a relatively new industry—tourism. Amarillo successfully lures visitors to taste and experience the old West with chuck wagon rides through the flat plains and an impressive collection of museums which celebrate the culture of the bygone Western frontier.

Practical Information Amarillo sprawls at the intersection of I-27, I-40, and U.S. 287/87; you'll need a car to explore. Rte. 335 (the Loop) encircles the city. Amarillo Blvd. (Historic Rte. 66) runs east-west, parallel to I-40. The **Texas Travel Info Center,** 9400 I-40E (335-1441), at Exit 76, is open daily 8am-5pm. The **Amarillo Convention and Visitors Bureau,** 1000 S. Polk (374-1497 or 800-692-1338), at 10th St., distributes more specific info (open Mon.-Fri. 8am-5pm). **Amarillo International Airport,** 10801 Airport Blvd. (335-1671), sits about 7 mi. east of downtown off I-40.

Cab fare to the hotels on I-40 averages $4-6, to downtown $12-13. Go **Greyhound,** 700 S. Tyler (374-5371), to Albuquerque (6 per day, 5hr., $51) and Santa Fe (5 per day, 7½hr., $54). The station is open 24 hr. In town, buses from **Amarillo City Transit** (378-3094) operate Monday through Saturday, every ½ hr. 6am to 6pm; fare is 60¢. Ride like a king with **Royal Cab Co.** (376-4276; $1.30 base fare, $1 per mi). **Emergency:** 911. Amarillo's **post office:** 505 E. 9th Ave. (379-2148), in Downtown Station at Buchanan St. (open Mon.-Fri. 7:30am-5pm). **ZIP code:** 79105. **Area code:** 806.

Accommodations, Camping, and Food

Cheap motels lurk on the outskirts of town on I-40; be prepared to pay more as you near the downtown area. **Camelot Inn,** 2508 I-40E (373-3600), at Exit 72A, a pink castle-like hotel with big, recently renovated rooms and shiny wood furniture, ranks among the best of the I-40 offerings; ask for a room upstairs (single $26, double $40; no extra charge for 3 or 4 people). **Motel 6** (800-440-6000) has two locations along I-40 off Exit 72B (singles $32, doubles $37). Pitch your tent at the **KOA Kampground,** 111 Folsom St. (335-1792), 6 mi. east of downtown; take I-40 to Exit 75, go north 2 mi. to Rte. 60, then east 1 mi. The campground has a large pool, a basketball court, free morning coffee, and shady sites (open 7am-10pm, Labor Day to Memorial Day 8am-8pm; sites $17, full hookup $22).

Beef is what's for dinner at **The Big Texan** (372-6000 or 800-657-7177), at the Lakeside exit of I-40. Signs for miles around remind you that anyone who can eat a 72-oz. steak in an hour gets it free; the defeated pay $50. To date 23,342 have tried, but only 4,619 have succeeded (19.7%). The portions are as big as the state, but the bill won't whip you. Try the $4 rattlesnake appetizer. (Burgers $5-10; Texas steaks $15-26. Open daily 10:30am-10:30pm. Free Texas Opry concerts Tues.; reservations required.) **Ruby Tequila's,** 2108 Paramount (358-RUBY/7829), has seats out or inside, where you can plant yourself to drink the Ruby Tequila, a combination of sangria and margarita ($2). Go there, "because a visit to Ruby Tequila's is like a pretty painting on velvet—always in good taste and never overpriced."

Sights and Entertainment

The outstanding **Panhandle-Plains Historical Museums,** 2401 4th Ave. (656-2244), in nearby Canyon, have fossils, an old drilling rig, and exhibits galore on local history and geology (open Mon.-Sat. 9am-5pm, Sun. 1-6pm; free). The **Amarillo Zoo** (381-7911) spreads over 20 acres of open prairie with bison, roadrunners, and other Texas fauna. Take the Thompson Park exit on U.S. 287 (open Tues.-Sun. 9:30am-5:30pm; free). The **American Quarter Horse Heritage Center and Museum,** 2601 I-40E (376-5181), at Exit 72A, explores horse racing's cowboy origins, with additional exhibits on all things equine. (Open Mon.-Sat. 9am-5pm, Sun. noon-5pm, winters Sat.-Tues. 10am-5pm. $4, over 54 $3.50, ages 6-18 $2.50, under 6 free.) Amarillo celebrates its location, on top of the world's largest supply of helium, with the six-story stainless steel **Helium Monument,** 1200 Strait Dr. (355-2448). When the structure was erected in 1968, several contributors volunteered to put common items inside it to make a time capsule. One of the items is a $10 savings account deposit in an Oklahoma City bank which, when the monument is opened in 2968, will be worth over $1,000,000,000,000,000,000 (one quintillion dollars) payable to the U.S. Treasury. Get in some ropin', ridin', and brandin' at Figure 3 Ranch's **Cowboy Morning** (800-658-2613; $19, $14.50 for cowpokes; reservations required). The fee includes a wagon-ride to Palo Duro Canyon, a sausage, eggs 'n' biscuit breakfast served out of a chuck wagon, and lessons in various cowboyish activi-

---

Big Texan Women

Our intrepid researcher-writer reports that women are statistically more successful in their attempts to consume the Big Texan's 72-oz. monster steak (see Food, above). While 3977 of the 21,347 men who have tried (18.6%) have succeeded, 642 of only 1995 women (32.1%) have conquered the cow.

TEXAS

ties (horseback riding, branding, cow-chip throwing, and so on). In early August, mosey over to the **Civic Center** (378-4297), at 3rd and Buchanan, for **Old West Days,** a city-wide game of cops and robbers (open Mon.-Fri. 8am-5pm).

■ Palo Duro Canyon State Park

Rightly known as the "Grand Canyon of Texas," Palo Duro covers 16,000 acres of jaw-dropping beauty. The canyon—1200 ft. from rim to rugged floor—exposes red, yellow, and brown cliffs which are truly awesome. The park is 23 mi. south of Amarillo; take I-27 to Exit 106 and head east on Rte. 217 (from the south, get off I-27 at Exit 103). The **Visitor/Interpretive Center** (806-488-2227), just inside the park, has maps of hiking trails and info on all park activities (park and center open daily 7am-10pm). The park charges an entrance fee of $3 per person, under 12 free.

The pleasant 16-mi. scenic drive through the park provides many photo opportunities for the auto-inclined. If you want to experience the canyon from the saddle, **Goodnight Riding Stables** (806-488-2231), about 1 mi. into the park on the scenic drive, will rent you a horse/saddle/hard-hat combo for $9 per hour. **Goodnight Trading Post** (806-488-2760), also on the scenic drive, has a souvenir shop, a terrific restaurant (sliced BBQ sandwich $3.50), and mountain bikes to rent ($6.50 per hr.). Rangers allow and encourage **backcountry hiking** in Palo Duro. Most hikers can manage the 5-mi. **Lighthouse Trail,** but only experienced hikers should consider the rugged 9-mi. **Running Trail.** Temperatures in the canyon frequently climb to 100°F; *always* take at least two quarts of water on your hike. **Backcountry camping** is allowed in designated areas; primitive sites $9, with water $10; RV hookup $12-14. (Call 512-389-8900 for recommended reservations.)

Set in the heart of the park, Pulitzer Prize-winner Paul Green's musical drama **Texas,** Box 268, Canyon 79015 (806-655-2181 for tickets), takes the stage under the stars in an outdoor amphitheater (mid-June to mid-Aug. Mon.-Sat. 8:30pm).

■ Guadalupe Mountains

The Guadalupe Mountains rise out of the vast Texas desert to reach heights of unexplored grandeur. Early westbound pioneers avoided the area, fearful of the climate and the Mescalero Apaches who controlled the range. By the 1800s, when the Apaches had been driven out, only a few homesteaders and *guano* miners inhabited this rugged region. **Guadalupe Mountains National Park** covers 86,000 acres of desert, canyons, and highlands. Passing tourists will want to stop for the park's most renowned sights: **El Capitán,** a 2000-ft. limestone cliff, and **Guadalupe Peak,** the highest point in Texas at 8749 ft. Less hurried travelers should take the time to explore. With over 70 mi. of trails, the mountains promise challenging desert hikes for those willing to journey to this remote area. **Carlsbad, NM,** 55 mi. northeast, makes a good base town with several cheap motels, campgrounds, and restaurants.

Most major trails begin at the Headquarters Visitors Center (below). Guadalupe Peak presents a difficult three- to five-hour hike, depending on your mountaineering ability. Allow a full day to hike to the spring-fed stream of **McKittrick Canyon** or to **The Bowl,** a stunning high-country forest of Douglas fir and Ponderosa pine. The 2½-mi., 1½-hour **Spring Trail** leads from the **Frijole Ranch,** about 1 mi. north of the visitors center, to a mountain spring. The trail leading to the historic Pratt Cabin in the Canyon begins at the **McKittrick Visitors Center,** off U.S. 62/180. Free backcountry hiking is also permitted.

The **Headquarters Visitors Center** (828-3251) lies right off U.S. 62/180. (Open daily 7am-6pm; Sept.-May 8am-4:30pm. After-hours info posted on the bulletin board outside.) For more park info, get in touch with Guadalupe Mountains National Park, HC60, Box 400, Salt Flat 79847 (828-3251). **Emergency:** 911. Guadalupe's **area code: 915.** Guadalupe Mountains National Park sets its clocks to **Mountain time zone** (2hr. behind Eastern).

The park's two campgrounds, **Pine Springs Campgrounds** (828-3251), on the highway just past the headquarters, and **Dog Canyon Campground** (828-3251, ranger station 505-981-2418), just south of the New Mexico border at the north end of the park, have water and restrooms, but lack hookups and showers (sites $7 per night). Dog Canyon is accessible only by a 72-mi. drive from Carlsbad, NM on Rte. 137.

The park's lack of development may be a bonus for backpackers, but it makes daily existence tough. Bring water for even the shortest, most casual hike. There is no gas in the park; fill up ahead of time. *Hundreds of people run out of gas every season, so gas up before you enter the park.* Guadalupe Park is 120 mi. east of El Paso. **TNM&O Coaches** (505-887-1108), an affiliate of **Greyhound,** runs along U.S. 62/180 between Carlsbad, NM and El Paso, making flag stops at Guadalupe Mountains National Park en route (Carlsbad to El Paso, $30). Buses stop at the Headquarters Visitors Center.

▓ El Paso

With its arid climate and disparate architectural landscape, modern El Paso is part oversized strip mall, part Mexican mission town—a city caught between two states, two countries, and two languages. The largest of the U.S. border towns, El Paso grew up in the 17th century as a stop-over on an important east-west wagon route that trailed the Río Grande though "the pass" *(el paso)* between the Rockies and the Sierra Madres. As Spain extended its reach into the New World, El Paso became a center for missionary activity; missions from the period of Spanish colonization can still be seen today. More recently, the city has been dominated by Fort Bliss, the largest air defense base in the West, and the Biggs Army Airfield. For information on crossing the border, see p. 539.

PRACTICAL INFORMATION

Tourist Office: 1 Civic Center Plaza (544-0062), a small round building next to the Chamber of Commerce at the intersection of Santa Fe and San Francisco St. Easily identifiable by the thin, water-filled moat which surrounds it. Well-stocked with brochures; sells tickets for the **El Paso-Juárez Trolley Co.** (544-0061; 544-0062 for reservations), which conducts day-long tours across the border leaving on the hr. from the Convention Center ($10, ages 6-12 $8, children under 6 free; trolleys run 10am-4pm).

Mexican Consulate: 910 E. San Antonio St. (533-4082), on the corner of San Antonio and Virginia St. Dispenses **tourist cards.** Open Mon.-Fri. 9am-4:30pm.

Currency Exchange: Valuta, 301 E. Paisano (544-1152). Conveniently near the border. Open 24hr.

AmEx Office: 3100 N. Mesa St. (532-8900). Open Mon.-Fri. 8am-5pm.

Airport: El Paso International Airport, northeast of the city center. Take bus #33 from San Jacinto or any other central location. Daily flights to cities in Mexico, the U.S., and elsewhere, most with connections at Dallas/Ft. Worth.

Trains: Amtrak, 700 San Francisco St. (545-2247). Open Mon., Wed., and Sat. 11am-6:30pm, Tues., Thurs., and Sun. 9am-5pm.

Buses: Greyhound, 200 W. San Antonio (532-2365 or 800-231-2222), across from the Civic Center between Santa Fe and Chihuahua St. To: New York (7 per day, 48hr., $109) and L.A. (10-15 per day, 16hr., $35). **Lockers** up to 6hr. $2, 6-24hr. $4. Open 24hr.

Public Transportation: Sun Metro (533-3333) departs from San Jacinto Plaza, at Main and Oregon St. Fare 85¢, students and children 40¢, seniors 20¢.

Taxis: Yellow Cab, 533-3433. $1.20 base fare, $1.50 per mi. Wheelchair service.

Hotlines: Crisis Hotline, 779-1800. Open 24hr. **Lambda,** 562-4217. Gay and lesbian info 24hr.

Hospital: Providence Memorial Hospital, 2001 N. Oregon St. (577-6011). Open 24hr. For immunizations, visit **El Paso City County Health District,** 222 S. Campbell St. (543-3560); when approaching the Mexican border, turn left on Pai-

sano St. and walk 3 blocks. Immunizations (by appointment, Wed. only) are not required to enter Mexico, but are recommended. Open Mon.-Fri. 8am-5pm.
Emergency: 911.
Post Office: 219 E. Mills (532-2652). Open Mon.-Fri. 9am-5pm, Sat. 8am-noon. **ZIP code:** 79901. **Area code:** 915. To call **Ciudad Juárez,** dial 011-52-16, followed by the local number.
Time Zone: Mountain (2hr. behind Eastern.)

Approach El Paso from the east or west on **I-10** and from the north or south on **U.S. 54.** The intrusion of the Río Grande and the Franklin Mountains makes El Paso unusually confusing; get a map to get oriented. **Santa Fe St.** runs north-south, dividing El Paso into east and west; **San Antonio St.** crosses east-west, dividing the city into north and south. Near most hotels and restaurants, **San Jacinto Plaza** is right in the thick of things. To get to the city center from the airport, take the Sun Metro bus #33; the stop is across from the Delta ticket window (approximately every 30min., 40min., 85¢). Tourists should be wary of the streets between San Antonio and the border late at night.

ACCOMMODATIONS

El Paso offers more appealing budget accommodations than Juárez; stay north of the border if you can. Hotels cluster near Main St. and San Jacinto Square.

Gardner Hotel/Hostel (HI-AYH), 311 E. Franklin (532-3661), two blocks up Mesa St. from San Jacinto Park. Inexpensive, clean rooms in the heart of downtown. Amiable management is vigilant of security concerns. Reception open 24hr. **Hotel:** All rooms have color TV with cable (including HBO) and a phone. Singles $25-$30, with bath $40. Doubles $45. **Hostel:** Small, 4-person dorm rooms and shared bathrooms. Beautiful, spacious kitchen, common room with pool table and cable TV, and couches for lounging and socializing in the basement. HI members $14, non-members $17. Linen $2 extra. Reserve ahead.

Gateway Hotel, 104 S. Stanton St. (532-2611; fax 533-8100), at the corner of S. Stanton and San Antonio Ave. An excellent choice—a stone's throw from San Jacinto Square and a favorite stop for middle-class Mexicans. Clean and spacious rooms, large beds and closets, and thoroughly clean bathrooms, some with bathtubs. A/C upstairs; diner downstairs. Check-out 4pm. Parking $1.50 for 24hr. Singles $21, with TV $28. Doubles $33, with TV $35.

Budget Lodge Motel, 1301 N. Mesa (533-6821), a 10-min. walk from San Jacinto Square. Ample rooms are remarkably clean and have warm, strong running water, A/C, and cable TV. Small café serves breakfast and lunch at reasonable rates. Inviting pool. Singles $27. Doubles $32-41, including tax.

FOOD

El Paso is a hybrid species with North American and Mexican ancestors. Well known *gringo* chains coexist with small mom-and-pop restaurants; and burritos are the undisputed local specialty. Attention vegetarians: bean burritos and *chiles rellenos* are tasty meatless options, but beware of animal lard.

Sojourn's Coffeehouse, 127 Pioneer Plaza (532-2817), above the San Francisco Grille. Outstanding selection of coffees, veggie fare, salads, and a small but delicious choice of sandwiches ($4.95-6.50). Interesting decoration (Balinese) and crowd; pick up a calendar of special events to catch an open-mike poetry reading, listen to some eclectic gypsy music, or have your palm read. Open Mon.-Tues. 7:30am-3pm, Wed.-Fri. 7:30am-midnight, Sat.-Sun. 10am-1am.

The Tap Bar and Restaurant, 408 E. San Antonio St. (546-9049), near Stanton. Popular with Gardner Hostel-dwellers, and one of the only places open after 7pm, outlasting even McDonald's. Excellent breakfast *huevos rancheros* $4. The Mexican Plate #1 (tacos, *chiles rellenos,* enchilada, rice, beans, and nachos for $5.50) reminds you of what lies across the border. Other entrees $1.50-$7.50. Big-screen

TV, live *trio* every Thurs. 7-9pm, mariachis every Sat. 10:30-11:30pm. Full bar with endless varieties of beer. Open Mon.-Sat. 7am-2am, Sun. noon-2am.

Big Bun, 500 N. Stanton (tel. 533-3926). Dirt cheap tacos, burritos (US$1-2), hefty burgers (99¢), and sandwiches ($1.70-3). Soda refills 25¢, free for iced tea. Open Mon.-Fri. 7:30am-7pm, Sat. 7:30am-6pm.

SIGHTS AND ENTERTAINMENT

Most visitors to El Paso are either stopping off on the long drive through the desert or heading south to Ciudad Juárez and beyond. For a whirlwind tour of the city and its southern neighbor, hop aboard the Border Jumper Trolleys that depart every hour from El Paso.

Historic **San Jacinto Plaza** swarms daily with activity; street musicians play music that evokes El Paso's roots (*conquistadores* and cavalry). South of the square, on **El Paso Street,** hundreds of locals hurry along the thoroughfare and dash into stores in search of new bargains. To take in a complete picture of the Río Grande Valley, head northeast of downtown to Rim Rd. (which becomes Scenic Drive) to **Murchinson Park,** at the base of the mountains.

For nightlife, try **The Basement,** 127 Pioneer Plaza (532-7674). The gay hotspot is downtown at **The Old Plantation,** 219 S. Ochoa (533-6055), a dance club/bar (open Thurs.-Sun. 8pm-2am). For a wilder time, head to Juárez, with rowdiness, no minimum drinking age, and non-stop partying.

El Paso hosts the **Southwestern Livestock Show & Rodeo** (532-1401) in February and the **World's Finals Rodeo** (545-1188) in November. Fear not: El Paso's celebrations transcend its country-western roots. Another festival is the **Sun Bowl Parade** at **UTEP** (University of Texas at El Paso) which also offers historical campus tours (747-5000). During the spring and summer, the **El Paso Diablos** (755-2000), pride of the fabled Texas League, play the best minor-league baseball around. (Games April-May Mon.-Sun. 6:30pm; June-Aug. Mon.-Sat. 7pm, Sun. 6:30pm. Call to confirm. Tickets $4 general, $6 box seats.) To reach Cohen Stadium at 9700 Gateway North, take Sun Metro bus #42 from San Jacinto Plaza as far north as it goes and walk the rest of the way. Ask the driver for directions.

■ Near El Paso: Ciudad Juárez

Although Ciudad Juárez is separated from El Paso only by the narrow Río Grande, one truly steps into another dimension upon entering Mexico. Visitors are immediately bombarded by commotion on all sides and treated to a feast of bright paint and neon. Near the border, the city is hectic, loud, and cheap; bands of carousing *gringos* infiltrate the area in search of cheap booze and cheaper thrills. Fleeing in the face of the American advance, Mexican culture has withdrawn to the city's cathedral square and Parque Chamizal, a pleasant respite from the industrial production centers and poor residential areas that dot most of the cityscape.

Crossing the Border To reach the border from El Paso, take the north-south bus (every 10min., weekdays 6:30am-9pm, Sat. 8am-9pm, Sun. 9am-7pm, 30min., 25¢) to the **Santa Fe Bridge,** its last stop before turning around. Do not confuse the inexpensive bus with the costly trolley. Two pedestrian and motor roads cross the Río Grande: **El Paso Ave.,** an overcrowded one-way street, and **Santa Fe Ave.,** a parallel road lined with stores. If entering Mexico by foot, walk to the right side of the Santa Fe Bridge and pay the quarter to cross. Daytrippers, including foreign travelers with a multi-entry visa, should be prepared to flash their documents of citizenship in order to pass in and out of Mexico. You might even get your bag searched by a guard if you have a tendency to break off the short end of the wishbone, but normally you won't even have to show ID. After stepping off the bridge, head left to the tourist office, the large grey building on your left, for maps and information. Upon reentering the United States (30¢), be ready to deal with U.S. border guards and show a valid visa or proof of citizenship. If you have questions about crossings, call the **transit police** (12-31-97 or 14-17-04).

Practical Information As of August 1996, the **exchange rate** was US$1=7.56 pesos. Go left from the Santa Fe Bridge to find the **Coordinación de Turismo** (14-06-07), the gray building on the corner of Malecón and Francisco Villa. The amiable English-speaking staff has few truly helpful brochures. In Juárez, banks congregate near the bus station, on Juárez St., and on 16 de Septiembre. Most display their rates outside. One of the biggest, **Comisiones San Luis** (14-20-33), at 16 de Septiembre and Juárez, accepts traveler's checks (open Mon.-Thurs. 9am-9pm, Fri.-Sat. 9am-9:15pm, Sun. 9am-6:15pm). **Chequerama** (12-35-99), at Unión and Juárez, also takes traveler's checks (open Mon.-Sat. 10am-6pm). The **bus station** is on Blvd. Oscar Flores 4010 (10-72-97 or 10-74-04), north of the ProNaf center and next to the Río Grande mall. There is a **pharmacy** (12-08-24) on the corner of 16 de Septiembre and Noche Triste, across from the cathedral. **Hospital Latinoamericano** is at 250 N. López Mateos (16-14-67). In case of an **emergency** dial 06. The **police** can be reached at 15-15-51. The **post office** is on Lerdo at Ignacio Peña (open Mon.-Fri. 8am-5pm, Sat.-Sun. 9am-1pm). **Postal Code:** 32000. **Telephone Code:** 16.

Old Juárez, immediately adjoining the Santa Fe and Stanton bridges, can be covered on foot. Most city buses leave from the intersection of Insurgentes and Francisco Villa or thereabouts; always ask where the bus is going and tell the driver your destination. Taxis are available downtown, but fees are steep; set a price before getting in. The "Ruta 8" bus goes from *el centro* to the Americanized ProNaf for 1.50 pesos; taxis charge 30 times as much. During the day, Juárez is relatively safe for alert travelers. At night, however, women should not walk alone or in dark places; everyone should avoid the area more than 2 blocks west of Avenida Juárez.

Accommodations and Food In Juárez, a typical cheap hotel meets only minimal standards and charges some of the highest "budget" rates in Mexico. Inexpensive lodging can be found along Avenida Juárez; pricier places are located in the ProNaf area. **Hotel del Río,** Juárez 488 (12-37-76), is worth the climb upstairs for large, simple, clean rooms with comfortably thick beds, A/C, and color TVs. Room service and parking are available (singles, doubles, or tightly-squeezed triples about US$20). **Santa Fé** (14-02-70, 14-03-82, or 14-09-41), Lerdo Nte. 675 at Tlaxcala, offers nicely furnished rooms with A/C, color TV, and spotless bathrooms (singles US$22; doubles, some with balcony, US$25).

Expect a long quest for food that will not cause a bacteriological mutiny in a *gringo* belly; the prudent beat a path to Av. Juárez and Lerdo or to the ProNaf center. Weak-stomached travelers should avoid shacks. In general, *mariscos* (shellfish) are overpriced and less than fresh in Juárez. **Cafetería El Coyote Inválido,** Juárez 615 at Colón (14-27-27), offers a bustling, clean, American-diner atmosphere. Some come for the A/C alone. Hamburgers go for 14.50 pesos; an array of Mexican plates run 15-30 pesos. You can roll from here to there on the wheeled chairs at **Hotel Santa Fé Restaurante** (14-02-70), at the Hotel Santa Fé, but don't expect too many dining companions to share the fun. Wash down the *enchiladas de pollo* (17 pesos) with a beer (8 pesos; open daily 7am-11pm).

Sights and Entertainment The Aduana Fronteriza (12-47-07) stands in the *centro,* where Juárez and 16 de Septiembre cross. Built in 1889 as a trading outpost and later used for customs, it is now home to the **Museo Histórico de la Ex-Aduana,** which features exhibits on the region's history during the Mexican Revolution (museum open Tues.-Sun. 10am-6pm; free). At the ProNaf center, the **Museo de Arte e Historia** (16-74-14) displays Mexican art from the past and present (open Tues.-Sun. 11am-6pm; 1.50 pesos, students free). Also at the ProNaf center, the **Centro Artesanal** sells handmade goods at maximum prices; haggle and the prices will change. The

"Ruta 8" bus will take you from the *centro* to Pro Naf for 1.50 pesos; a taxi charges 20 times as much. Your call.

The *toro* and the *matador* battle in traditional bullfights on occasional evenings during the summer at the **Plaza Monumental de Toros,** Paseo Triunfo de la República and López Mateos (13-16-56 or 13-11-82). General admission seating begins at 25 pesos, 50 pesos in the shade (under 13 free). Call for dates and times. The **Lienzo de Charro,** on Av. Charro off República (27-05-55), also conducts bullfights and a *charreada* (rodeo) on Sunday afternoons during the summer.

Juárez has so many bars that counting them could make you dizzy even before you start drinking. Many of these establishments are unsavory, and even some of the better ones can become dangerous; stick to the glutted strip along Av. Juárez or in the ProNaf area. **Mr. Fog Bar,** Juárez Nte. 140 (14-29-48), is a popular spot for roving Americans looking for a weekend of excitement south of the border. A cartoon crocodile adorns the mirrored walls of this dark watering hole (dance floor in back; beer 7 pesos, liquor 6 pesos; open daily 11am-1am). For some live music, check out **Palacio Coin,** Juárez 130 (15-55-68), another popular hangout.

For more information on Ciudad Juárez and border towns, see *Let's Go: Mexico.*

■ Big Bend

Roadrunners, coyotes, wild pigs, mountain lions, and 350 species of birds make their home in Big Bend National Park, a 700,000-acre tract that lies in the curve of the Río Grande. Spectacular canyons, vast stretches of the Chihuahuan Desert, and the Chisos Mountains occupy this literally and figuratively far-out spot.

Practical Information Big Bend may be the most isolated spot you'll ever encounter. *You can only reach the park by car* via Rte. 118 or U.S. 385. There are few gas stations along the way; fill your tank before you leave urban areas. The **park headquarters** (915-477-2251) is at **Panther Junction,** about 26 mi. inside the park (open daily 8am-6pm; vehicle pass $5 per week). For info, write the Superintendent, Big Bend National Park, P.O. Box 129, 79834. The **Texas Travel Information Center** (800-452-9292) provides info on the park and helps visitors plan excursions (open daily 8am-9pm). Other **ranger stations** are located at Río Grande Village, Persimmon Gap, and Chisos Basin (Chisos open year-round daily 8am-3:30pm; other open seasonally). **Amtrak** (800-872-7245) serves the town of **Alpine,** 70 mi. north of Big Bend. **Emergency:** 915-477-2251 until 6pm; afterwards call 911.

Accommodations and Food The expensive **Chisos Mountain Lodge** (915-477-2291), 10 mi. from park headquarters, offers the only motel-style lodging within the park (singles $59, doubles $67; $11 per additional person). There are also lodges, equipped with showers and baths but no A/C (singles $56, doubles $66; $11 per additional person), and stone cottages which come with three double beds (1 or 2 people $70; $11 per additional person). Reservations are a must; the lodge often gets booked up to a year in advance. The restaurant and coffee shop at the lodge charge $5-12 for entrees (open daily 7am-8pm). Cheaper motels line Rte. 118 and Rte. 170 near Terlingua and Lajitas, 21 and 28 mi. from park headquarters. **Groceries, gas,** and green monkeys are available in Panther Junction, Río Grande Village, and the Chisos Basin at Castolon. The Río Grande Village Store has the park's only public **shower** (5min. 75¢).

Stay in **Terlingua, TX,** if you plan to spend more than a day at the Park. Terlingua, named for the three languages spoken in the town in the late 1800s (English, Spanish, and a Native American dialect), is accessible from Road 170 in Study Butte, about 35 mi. from park headquarters but only 7 mi. from the park's western entrance. The **Easter Egg Valley Motel** (915-371-2430), on Hwy. 70 1 mi. west of 170/118 junction, provides a good alternative to park sites (singles $36, doubles $45). Farther up Road 170, the **Starlight Theatre Bar and Grill** (915-371-2326) has large portions of cheap food ($3-8) and free live music (open daily 5:30pm-midnight).

Hiking, Rafting, and Camping Before you venture into the park, make sure you have plenty of water. If your stay is brief, take the 43-mi. **scenic drive** to Santa Elena Canyon; watch for flash floods. Park rangers at the visitors center can suggest other hikes and sights. The **Lost Mine Trail,** a 3-hr. hike up a peak in the Chisos, leads to an amazing summit-top view of the desert and the Sierra de Carmen in Mexico. Another easy walk ambles through the **Santa Elena Canyon** along the Río Grande. The canyon walls rise as high as 1000 ft. over the banks of the river. Four companies offer **river trips** down the 133-mi. stretch of the Río Grande owned by the park. **Far-Flung Adventures** (800-359-4138), next door to the Starlight Theatre Bar and Grill in Terlingua (see above), organizes one- to seven-day trips. A one-day trip to Santa Elena averages $100; call for exact prices. Park headquarters (see above) has more information on rafting and canoeing.

Designated **campsites** within the park are allotted on a first come, first served basis. **Chisos Basin** and **Río Grande Village** offer sites with restrooms and flush toilets ($7), while **Cottonwood** has water and pit toilets ($7). In summer, the sites in Chisos Basin are the best (and coolest) by far. In the park's peak season (Nov.-April) Río Grande Village fills first. Get to either campground early; sites fill quickly. For overnight backcountry camping or free sites along the hiking trails, obtain a free **backcountry permit** at the park headquarters.

TEXAS

ROCKY MOUNTAINS

Created by immense tectonic forces some sixty-five million years ago, the Rockies mark a vast wrinkle in the North American continent. Sculpted by wind, water, and glaciers over eons, their weathered peaks extend 3000 mi. from northern Alberta to New Mexico and soar to altitudes exceeding 2½ vertical miles. Cars overheat and humans stumble as they ascend the mountains, pausing between gasps to explore the aspen forests ruled by grizzly bears before reaching the thin air above the treeline, where mountain goats and bighorn sheep graze on flowers. Dominated by rock and ice, the highest peaks of the Rockies are accessible only to hard-core mountain climbers and wildlife prepared to survive in thin air and eternal snow.

Although the whole of the Rocky Mountain area supports less than five percent of the U.S. population, millions throng every year to its spectacular national parks, forests, and ski resorts. In the summer, hikers can follow the Continental Divide along the spine of the Rockies; a drop of water falling on the west side of the mountain will make its way to the Pacific Ocean while a drop of water on the east side will flow down to the Mississippi.

Idaho

When Lewis and Clark first laid eyes on Idaho in 1805, they witnessed pristine snow-capped mountains, clear lakes, frothing rivers, and dense pine forests. Little has changed since then and the state motto—*Esto perpetua,* Latin for "It is Forever"—suggests that nothing will anytime soon. Idaho remains nearly free of any heavy industry and large parts of the state are preserved as national forests and wilderness areas. The Rocky Mountains cross the Montana-Idaho border and divide Idaho into three distinct regions. To the southeast, world-famous potatoes thrive in volcanically rich valleys. To the north, dense pine forests envelop clear, cold lakes and harbor liberal sentiments befitting eastern Washington. In the center, ski slopes, hiking trails, and geothermal hot springs attract nature lovers. Like other Western states, Idaho fiercely values its freedom; it is the only state in the Union never to have had a foreign flag fly above it.

PRACTICAL INFORMATION

Capital: Boise.
Idaho Information Line: 800-635-7820. **Boise Convention and Visitors Bureau** (344-7777), corner of 9th and Idaho, 2nd floor. Open daily 8:30am-5pm. **Parks and Recreation Department,** 5657 Warm Springs Ave., Boise (334-4199). **Skier Info,** 800-243-2754. **Idaho Outfitters and Guide Association,** P.O. Box 95, Boise 83701 (342-1914). Provides free vacation directories and info about outdoor outfitters such as rafting companies and jet-boat operators.
Crisis Lines: Mental Health Emergency, 334-0808.
Time Zones: Pacific Time north of the Salmon River, Mountain Time to the south.
Postal Abbreviation: ID.
Sales Tax: 5%.

■ Boise

Small and hip, Boise (pronounced Boysee, not Boyzee) is a verdant residential oasis in the state's dry southern plateau. The easy, small-town familiarity of the residents, numerous grassy parks, and airy shopping plazas make for a relaxing way station on a cross-country jaunt. Most of the city's sights are within the ten square blocks between the capitol and the Boise River; you can easily manage on foot.

Practical Information The **visitors center,** 850 W. Front St. (388-0711), at the Boise Center Mall, dispenses tourist tips (open Mon.-Fri. 10am-4pm, Sat. 10am-2pm). When the visitors center isn't open, visit the information booth on the bottom floor of the **State Capitol Building,** (open weekdays 7am-6pm, weekends and holidays 9am-5pm). **Amtrak** (800-872-7245) serves Boise from the beautiful Spanish mission-style **Morrison-Knudsen Depot,** 2601 Eastover Terr. (336-5992), easily visible from Capitol Blvd., about a ten block walk from downtown Boise. To: Salt Lake City (3 per week, 8hr., $74); Portland (3 per week, 10hr., $92); Seattle (3 per week, 14hr., $92). **Greyhound** zips along I-84 from its terminal at 1212 W. Bannock (343-3681), a few blocks west of downtown. To: Salt Lake City (2 per day, 8hr., $34); Portland (2 per day, 8-10hr., $27); Seattle (2 per day, 14hr., $29); Missoula (1 per day, 14-18hr., $80). **Boise Urban Stages** (336-1010) runs several routes through the city, with maps available from any bus driver and displayed at each stop. (Buses operate Mon.-Fri. 6:45am-6:45pm, Sat. 7:45am-6:45pm. Fare 75¢, seniors 35¢.) **McU's Sports,** 822 W. Jefferson (342-7734), rents in-line skates ($5 per hr., $10 for 3 hr., $18 per day, $24 overnight) and mountain bikes ($14 per ½ day, $22 per day), as well as equipment for sports of all seasons. Boise's main **post office:** 770 S. 13th St. (383-4211; open Mon.-Fri. 7:30am-5:30pm, Sat. 10am-2pm). **ZIP code:** 83707. **Area code:** 208.

Accommodations and Camping Finding lodging in Boise is difficult; neither the YMCA nor the YWCA provide rooms, and even the cheapest hotels charge more than $20 per night. The more reasonable places tend to fill quickly, so make reservations. The friendly **Boisean,** 1300 S. Capitol Ave. (343-3645 or 800-365-3645), has spacious, clean rooms, a helpful staff, free local calls, free cable, spa, pool, and exercise room (singles $32, doubles $40-50; $4 per extra person). The **Sands Motel,** 1111 W. State St. (343-2533), within four blocks of the Capitol and the Greyhound Bus Depot, offers small, clean rooms, and free local calls (singles, $28, doubles $33, and $150 for the whole week). The **Sun Liner Motel,** 3433 Chinden Ave. (344-7647), offers plain, air-conditioned singles for $28. The **Boise National Forest Office,** 5493 Warm Springs Rd. (364-4241), provides information about campgrounds in the forest (open Mon.-Fri. 7:30-4:30pm). The **Boise KOA Kampground,** 7300 S. Federal Way (345-7673), has tent sites for $18.50, and full RV hookups for $23.50. Other campgrounds include: **Americana Kampground,** 3600 American Terrace Blvd. (344-5733; 90 sites, $17 includes full hookup, $2 each additional person); and **Fiesta Park,**

Boise's Basque Background

In 1848, the California Gold Rush brought a flood of immigrants to the U.S. Among them were the Basques, who moved from a small corner of Spain to the goldfields of the Sierras. The Basques, whose native language is unrelated to any in the world, had a particularly difficult time learning English. Unable to find jobs, the American Basques spread out into the western rangelands and mountains and became sheep herders. Although historians have recently found links between the mysterious language and Caucasian, the ancient language spoken in the Caucasus region, no conclusive evidence of a tie has been found and Basque remains without linguistic relatives. Basque culture is preserved at the **Basque Museum and Cultural Center,** at 6th and Grove St. (343-2671), in downtown Boise. This fascinating museum includes a gallery with changing exhibits, Basque art, and a replica of a Basque herder's house. Next door to the museum, try out Basque cuisine at **Bar Gernika,** 202 S. Capitol Blvd. (344-2175). The pub and eatery is named after the capitol of the Basque homeland. In the summer, enjoy the hearty meals outside on the patio. Authentic Basque dishes include Solomo sandwiches (marinated pork tenderloin $5.25-6.25) and lamb stew ($6). Open Mon.-Thurs. 11am-11pm, Fri. 11am-1am, Sat. 11:30am-1am.

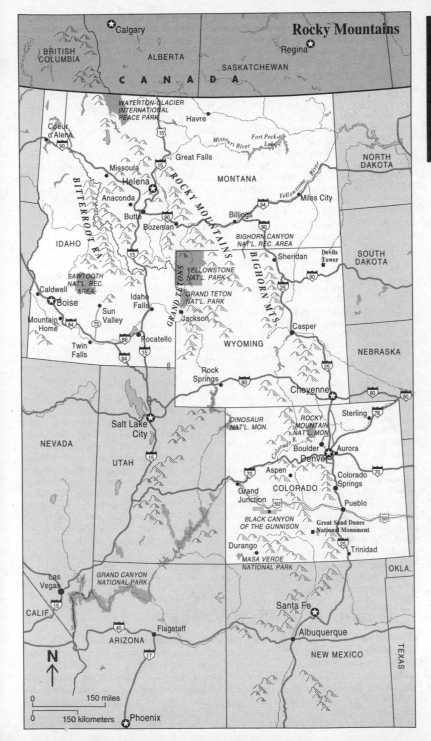

Rocky Mountains

11101 Fairview Ave. (375-8207; sites $16, with partial hookup $18.50, with full hookup $19.50).

Food and Nightlife Mr. Potatohead doesn't rule Boise food. The downtown area, centered around 6th and Main St., is bustling with lunchtime delis, coffee shops, ethnic cuisine, and several stylish bistros. **Moon's Kitchen,** 815 W. Bannock St. (385-0472), has been serving up classic American food to politicians and businessmen from the nearby capitol since 1955. (Breakfast specials around $4; famous shakes for $3. Open Mon.-Fri. 7am-3pm, Sat. 8am-3pm.) A more innovative menu and tastier sandwiches can be found at the **Raintree Deli,** 210 North Capitol Blvd. (336-4611), where half a sandwich is $3, a whole sandwich is $4.50, and a stuffed baked potato will cost you $4 (open Mon.-Fri. 9am-3:30pm). **The Beanery,** 107 8th St. (342-3456), carves up slow-roasted meats and serves them with bread, mashed potatoes, carrots, and a side salad for $5-6. In the summer, meals are served in the grove on a patio by the fountain. (Open Mon.-Fri. 11am-10pm, Sat. 11:30am-11pm, Sun. 11:30am-10pm.) Long live *Casablanca* at the combination restaurant and movie theater **Rick's Café American/The Flicks,** 646 Fulton St. (342-4222). Grab a snack or a light meal before the movie. (Italian and American sandwiches and salads, $4-6. Kitchen open 5-9:30pm. Movies daily 5, 5:20, 7, 7:15 and 9:45pm. $6, double feature $7.50.)

Although nightlife in Boise consists mainly of live music in coffeehouses and pubs, every Wednesday the town throws itself a party in the **Grove** (on Grove St. downtown). Local musicians perform for an hour, and are followed by several Budweiser trucks unloading kegs of beer by the dozen. That's when the real fun begins. Call the Chamber of Commerce (344-7777) for more info. Walk along Main St. from 5th to 11th to check out the scene. Treat all your senses to the smoky funk that wafts from the **Blues Bouquet,** 1010 Main St. (345-6605). Have a pint ($1.50-2.50) and sit back for live music Tues.-Sun. (Open daily 5pm until the blues take a walk.) **Dreamwalker,** 1015 Main St. (343-4196), offers coffee and live music late into the night. (Open Mon.-Thurs. 7am-2am, Fri. 7am-4am, Sat. 3pm-5am, Sun. 5pm-2am.)

Sights The **Boise Tour Train** (342-4796) shows you 75 sites around the city in one hour. Tours start and end in the parking lot of **Julia Davis Park,** departing every 75 min. starting at 10am. (5 tours per day, Mon.-Sat. 10am-3pm, Sun. noon-5pm. $6.50. Arrive 15min. early.) To learn about Idaho and the Old West at your own pace, walk through the **Historical Museum** (334-2120), in Julia Davis Park. (Open Mon.-Sat. 9am-5pm, Sun. 1-5pm. Free, donations encouraged.) Also in the park, the **Boise Art Museum,** 670 Julia Davis Dr. (345-8330), displays international and local works. (Open Tues.-Fri. 10am-5pm, Sat.-Sun. noon-5pm, and Mon. 10am-5pm in the summer. $3, students and seniors $2, grades 1-12 $1, under 6 free; free the first Thurs. of every month.) Take a self-guided tour through the country's only **state capitol** to be heated with natural geothermal hot water; be sure to pick up free maps at the conveniently located info booth on the ground floor (tour office 334-2470; open Mon.-Fri. 7am-6pm, weekends and holidays 9am-5pm). Raptors perch and dive at the **World Center for Birds of Prey,** 5666 W. Flying Hook Lane (362-3716), 6 mi. south of I-84 on Cole Rd. You must call ahead to arrange a tour ($4, seniors $3, children $2). For more back-to-nature fun, try the 22-mi. **Boise River Greenbelt,** a pleasant path ideal for a leisurely walk or picnic, or explore the **Boise State University** campus next to the river off of South Capitol Boulevard.

■ Ketchum and Sun Valley

In 1935, Union Pacific heir Averill Harriman sent Austrian Count Felix Schaffgotsch to scour the U.S. for a site to develop a ski resort area rivaling Europe's best. The Count dismissed Aspen, reasoning that its air was too thin for East Coasters, and selected the small mining and sheep herding town of Ketchum in Idaho's Wood River Valley. Sun Valley is the fancy resort village Harriman built one mile from Ketchum to entice such dashing celebrities as Ernest Hemingway, Claudette Colbert, and Errol Flynn to "rough it" amid the manicured ski slopes, haute cuisine, and nightly orchestra performances. An imported East Coast yacht-club feel remains in Ketchum, as celebrities and tourists continue to flock to the natural beauty and established amenities. The towering snowcapped peaks of the Sawtooth range still overshadow the brightest Hollywood stars, and one can escape from the artificial tans and fashionable stores to the gorgeous trails and lakes which abound in the surrounding mountains.

Practical Information The best time to visit the area is during "slack" (late Oct. to Thanksgiving and May to early June), when the tourists magically vanish. At the **Sun Valley/Ketchum Chamber of Commerce** (726-3423 or 800-634-3347), 4th and Main St. in Ketchum, an energetic staff points out good deals and interesting sights (open Mon. 9:30am-5pm, Tues.-Fri. 9am-5:30pm, weekends 9am-5pm; off season hours shorter). **Sawtooth National Recreation Area (SNRA) Headquarters** (726-7672; 727-5013 or 800-280-CAMP/2267 for reservations), 8 mi. north of Ketchum off Rte. 75, has detailed information on the recreation area, hot springs, and area forests and trails. (Open daily 9am-4:30pm.) Ketchum's **post office:** 301 1st Ave. (726-5161; open Mon.-Fri. 8am-5:30pm, Sat. 11am-2pm); **ZIP code:** 83340; **area code:** 208.

Camping and Food Prices here are for the Trumps. From early June to mid-October, **camping** is the best option for cheap sleep. Check with the Ketchum office of the **Sawtooth National Forest** to find out about free camping near Ketchum (622-3371). **Boundary Campground**, with restrooms and drinking water, is 3 mi. northeast of town on Trail Creek Rd. Two mi. further on the right, **Corral Creek Rd.** scatters its isolated sites along a rushing brook (no services). Up Rte. 75 into **Sawtooth National Recreation Area (SNRA)** (727-5013) lie several beautiful campgrounds; the cheapest are **Murdock** (11 sites) and **Caribou** (10 sites), which cost $5. They are respectively 2 and 4 mi. up a dirt road which begins as a paved road to the right of the visitors center. Water for these sites is available at the North Fork dump site. **North Fork** (26 sites) and **Wood River** (31 sites) are 7 and 10 mi. north of Ketchum. Each charges $9. **Easley Campground and Pool,** towards Stanley from SNRA headquarters, is adjacent to a tiny hot springs; showers are 50¢. For those who don't enjoy winter camping, **Ski View Lodge,** 409 S. Main St. (726-3441), rents out ten small, fake log cabins for $40-70, summer or winter. Call ahead to reserve one of these convenient motel rooms in disguise.

Ketchum's small confines bulge with over 65 restaurants, many of which serve inexpensive, well-prepared grub. **The Hot Dog Adventure Co.,** 210 N. Main (726-0017), offers a cosmopolitan selection of hot dogs ($1.75-3.75) and mouth-melting steak fries (open in the summer, noon-2:30am). **Desperado's** (726-3068), at the corner of 4th St. and Washington, offers delicious Mexican food at reasonable prices. ($5-7 for large plates of enchiladas and burritos.) Enjoy the view of Baldy while eating in the sun on their large patio. **Starrwood Bakery** (726-2253) takes pride in fresh breads, muffins, and salads; $5.50 buys a deli sandwich, side salad, and chips (open Mon.-Fri. 6:30am-6pm, Sat. 8am-4pm, Sun. 8am-3pm). **Whisky Jacques,** 209 N. Main St. (726-5297), Hemingway's old haunt, offers dollar mixed drinks nights Tues. and Sun. (Open daily 4pm-2am; live music schedule varies.)

Hemingway in Sun Valley

Ernest Hemingway's admiration of both rugged outdoor sports and famous, wealthy celebrities personifies the dualistic spirit of Ketchum. After spending many of his vacations hunting and fishing in the Sawtooth Range, Hemingway built a house in Sun Valley. He committed suicide there after a long struggle with alcoholism. While Hemingway's house is off-limits, the **Ketchum-Sun Valley Heritage and Ski Museum** (726-8118), at the corner of First St. and Washington Ave., offers exhibits on Hemingway's life in Sun Valley (open daily 1-5pm).

The Outdoors and Hot Springs The Sawtooth area is nationally renowned for its stunning **mountain bike trails,** which run through the gorgeous canyons and mountain passes of the SNRA. But beware! Trails can be snowed under well into July. Inquire about trail conditions at **Formula Sports,** 460 N. Main St. (726-3194; bikes $12 ½-day, $16 full day). The **Elephant's Perch,** 280 East Ave. (726-3497), off Sun Valley Rd. (open daily 9am-6pm), also rents mountain bikes and provides trail info. (Bikes $12 per ½-day, $20 per full day.)

Ketchum locals soak their buns after a "hard" day biking or hiking in their favorite geothermal hot spring. The **hot springs,** hidden in the hills and canyons of Ketchum, are largely a local secret; once you find them, they are usually free and uncrowded. Like the mining ruins in the surrounding mountains, many springs can be reached only by foot. For books and guidance, inquire at the Elephant's Perch or at SNRA headquarters. Always make sure the water is not too hot before going in.

Two of the more accessible, non-commercial springs are **Warfield Hot Springs,** on Warm Springs Creek, 11 mi. west of Ketchum on Warm Springs Rd., and **Russian John Hot Springs,** 8 mi. north of the SNRA headquarters on Rte. 75, just west of the highway. For the best information on fishing conditions and licenses, as well as equipment rentals (fly rods $12 per day), stop by **Silver Creek Outfitters,** 500 N. Main St. (726-5282 or 800-732-5687; open Mon.-Sat. 9am-6pm, Sun. 9am-5pm). The fly-fishing bible, *Curtis Creek Manifesto,* is available here ($8).

■ Sawtooth

Home to the **Sawtooth** and **White Cloud Mountains** in the north and the **Smokey** and **Boulder Ranges** in the south, the **Sawtooth National Recreation Area (SNRA)** sprawls over 756,000 acres of untouched land and is surrounded by four national forests, encompassing the headwaters of five of Idaho's major rivers. If you have a car, drive north on Rte. 75 to Stanley (a 60-mi. drive), pausing at the Galena Overlook, 25 mi. north of Ketchum and ¼ mile downhill from the 8701 ft. Galena Pass. The panoramic view of the Salmon River valley and the Sawtooth Range is almost surreal.

Practical Information The small frontier-style town of **Stanley,** located 60 mi. north of Ketchum at the intersection of Rte. 21 and Rte. 75, serves as a northern base for exploring Sawtooth. Stop by the **Stanley Chamber of Commerce** (774-3411 or 800-878-7950), on Rte. 21 in Stanley, to chat with the friendly staff about services in town and the park (open daily 9am-noon, 1-6pm; winter hours vary). Topographical maps ($2.50) and various trail books ($3-20) are available at McCoy's Tackle and at the **Stanley Ranger Station** (774-3000), 3 mi. south of Stanley on Rte. 75 (open Mon.-Fri. 8am-5pm, Sat.-Sun. 8:30am-4:30pm; in the off season Mon.-Fri. 8am-5pm). At the entrance to Redfish Lake (5 mi. south of Stanley and 55 mi. north of Ketchum), the Redfish Lake info booth (774-3673) dispenses a wide range of info about hiking, camping, and outdoor sports. Hours are sporadic; the booth is usually staffed during sunny, busy weekends. Two mi. west of the turnoff from Rte. 75 is the **Redfish Lake Lodge** (774-3536; open during the summer daily 7am-10pm). All the info centers have maps of Sawtooth ($3). Stanley's **post office** (774-2230) is on Ace of Diamonds St. (open Mon.-Fri. 8am-noon, 1-5pm). **ZIP code: 83278. Area code: 208.**

Accommodations, Camping, and Food Campgrounds continue to line Rte. 75 north of Wood River. Because there are so many campgrounds scattered around the SNRA, the free map of campsites available at SNRA headquarters is incredibly useful. Driving north on Rte. 75, the turnoff for **Alturas Lake** is marked about four mi. after Galena Pass. Campsites by the lake are available on a first come, first served basis and are $9. North of Alturas Lake, **Redfish Lake** (5 mi. south of Stanley, 55 mi. north of Ketchum) is considered the premier spot for camping in the SNRA, but beware of the ever-present lakeside mosquitoes. **Point Campground,** right next to a beach on Redfish Lake, can be reserved (800-280-CAMP/2267). Campsites are

$11 per night and accommodate 2 vehicles; no hookup. Free primitive camping with no water or hookups is available just outside the entrance to Redfish Lake on Rte. 75.

Further north on Rte. 75, past the town of Stanley, numerous sites are available adjacent to the Salmon River (first come, first served, $9, water available, no hookups). The town of Stanley provides more scenic and more reasonable lodging than Ketchum. On Ace of Diamonds St. in downtown Stanley, the **Sawtooth Hotel and Café** (774-9947) is a colorful, comfortable place to rest after a wilderness sojourn (singles $27, with private bath $45; doubles $30/50). More scenic is **McGowan's Resort** (774-2290), 1 mi. down Rte. 75 in Lower Stanley. Hand-built cabins ($50-95; Sept. to early June $40-75) sit directly on the banks of the Salmon River, house either four or six people, and usually contain kitchenettes. The **Sawtooth Cafe** (located in the eponymous hotel) lays a filling American meal out on the table. The Sawtooth Range out the back windows provides a feast for the eyes (burgers and salads $3-5 each). For evening entertainment, try **Casanova Jack's Rod and Gun Club** (774-9920), on Ace of Diamonds St. in Stanley. Casanova Jack will fill your gullet with a burger ($5.25 with fries) and steal your heart. On Thursday through Saturday nights, the spacious halls fill with a variety of live music and local crowds playing pool. (Open Thurs.-Mon. 11:30am-2am, Tues.-Wed. 4pm-2am.)

The Great Outdoors Hiking, boating, and fishing are unsurpassed in all four of the SNRA's little-known ranges. Be sure to pick up a free map of the area at SNRA headquarters before you hit the trail or the lake. Redfish Lake is the source of many trails; try the popular, leisurely hikes up to **Fishhook Creek** and **Bench Lakes.** The long, gentle loop around **Yellow Belly, Toxaway,** and **Petit Lakes** is an easy overnight suitable for novices. Two mi. northwest of Stanley on Rte. 21, take the 3-mi. Iron Creek Rd. which leads to the trailhead of the **Sawtooth Lake Hike.** This 5½-mi. trail is steep but well-worn, and not overly difficult if you stop to rest. Bionic hikers can try the steep 4-mi. hike to **Casino Lakes,** which begins at the **Broadway Creek** trailhead southeast of Stanley.

Mountain biking in the Sawtooths is almost unlimited. Beginners will enjoy riding the dirt road that accesses the North Fork campgrounds from the visitors center. This gorgeous road parallels the North Fork of the Wood River for 5 mi. before branching off into other narrower and steeper trails suitable for more advanced riders. These trails can be combined into loops of arbitrary size; consult the trail map or the ranger station. The **Boulder Creek Road,** 5 mi. from SNRA headquarters, leads to pristine **Boulder Lake** and an old mining camp. The steep 10-mi. road trip ride is suitable for advanced riders. Before venturing out into the wilderness on a backpacking trip, consult the detailed topographic maps in any of Margaret Fuller's **Trail Guides** ($13 for the Sawtooths and White Cloud guide), available at SNRA headquarters and McCoy's Tackle Shop. Groups of 10-20 need free wilderness permits which are available at SNRA headquarters. Always remember to keep fires small and within existing rings in wilderness areas. Stock up on eats for the trail at the **Mountain Village Grocery Store** (774-3350; open daily 7am-9pm).

In the heat of summer, cold rivers beg for **fishing, canoeing,** or **whitewater rafting. McCoy's Tackle Shop** (774-3377), on Ace of Diamonds St. in Stanley, rents gear, sells a full range of outdoor equipment, and has a gift shop. (Spinning rod $6 per day, $27 per 6 days; hours vary with the seasons; generally open in the summer daily 8am-8pm.) **Sawtooth Rentals** (774-3409), ¼ mi. north of the Rte. 21-Rte. 75 junction, lends vehicles for every terrain. (Mountain bikes $17-30 per day, kayaks $25 per day for a single or $35 for a double, rafts $15 per person per day, snowmobiles up to $100 per day.) The **Redfish Lake Lodge Marina** (774-3536) rents paddleboats ($5 per ½ hr.), canoes ($5 per hr., $15 per ½ day, $25 per day), and outboards ($10 per hr., $33.50 for ½ day, $60 per day; open in summer daily 7am-9pm). They also give pontoon boat tours of scenic Redfish Lake (1-hr. tours $6.50, children $4.50, schedule varies). **The River Company** (800-398-0346), based in Ketchum with an office in Stanley (774-2244), arranges expert whitewater rafting and floating trips. Full day trips ($80) feature gourmet campfire cuisine; ½-day trips (1:30pm-4:30pm) are $62.

(Ketchum office open late May-early Sept. 8am-6pm; Stanley office open in summer 7am-11pm.)

The most inexpensive way to enjoy the SNRA waters is to visit the **hot springs** just east of Stanley. **Sunbeam Hot Springs,** 13 mi. from town, is the best of the batch. Be sure to bring a bucket or cooler to the stone bathhouse; you'll need to add about 20 gallons of cold Salmon River water before you can get into these hot pools (120-130°F). High water can wash out the hot springs temporarily. Check with local stores for information about other hot springs.

■ Craters of the Moon

Astronauts once trained at the unearthly **Craters of the Moon National Monument,** an elevated lava field and group of craters that rises darkly from the sagebrush-covered rangelands 70 mi. southeast of Sun Valley on U.S. junction 20/26/93. Windswept and deathly quiet, the stark, twisted lava formations dominate sparse vegetation, a reminder of the volcanic eruptions that occurred here as recently as 2000 years ago.

Park admission is $4 per car, $2 per individual, and the bizarre campsites scattered among jagged lava formations cost $10 (52 sites without hookup). Wood fires are prohibited but charcoal fires are permitted. You can also camp for free in adjacent **Bureau of Land Management** land. Contact the BLM office in Shoshone Falls (886-2206) for info about the primitive camp sites. Camping in unmarked sites in the dry lava beds of the park itself is permitted with a free backcountry permit. **Echo Crater,** accessible by a 4-mi. hike, is the most frequented of these sites. Other comfortable sites are hard to find; the first explorers couldn't sleep in the lava fields for lack of bearable places to bed down.

The **visitors center** (527-3257), just off U.S. 20/26/93, has displays and videotapes on the process of lava formation, and printed guides for hikes to all points of interest within the park as well as a 7-mi. driving loop to the major sites. They also distribute backcountry camping permits. Rangers lead 5-6 guided hikes per day at the campground amphitheater. (Schedule varies, consult the visitors center. Open daily 8am-6pm; off season 8am-4:30pm.) Explore the **lava tubes,** caves formed when a surface layer of lava hardened and the rest of the molten rock drained out, creating a tunnel. Bring sturdy shoes and a flashlight.

Twenty miles east of the Craters of the Moon, a Chevron station offers gas on Rte. 20 in the town of Arco. (Sorry, no Arco station here.) The **Arco Deli and Sandwich Shop** (527-3757), east of the Chevron on Rte. 20, serves up (surprise) large sandwiches for small prices ($5 for a wide, foot-long sandwich; open daily 8am-8pm).

■ Coeur d'Alene, Idaho

When French and English fur traders passed through northern Idaho in the late 1800s, they attempted to trade with uninterested local Native Americans. The trappers' French-speaking Iroquois guides dubbed the dismissive natives "people with pointed hearts," which the trappers shortened to "hearts of awls"—Coeur d'Alene (kur-duh-Lane). The gaggle of tourists can do little to mar the rustic beauty of this town, 20 minutes from Spokane and known as CDA to locals.

Practical Information Get info at the **visitors center,** 414½ Mullan Ave. (667-4990; open Sun.-Tues. 9am-5pm, Wed.-Sat. 9am-7pm). The **bus station** lies at 1527 Northwest Blvd. (664-3343), 1 mi. north of the lake (open daily 8am-8pm). **Greyhound** serves Boise (1 per day, 11hr., $65), Spokane (3 per day, 45min., $9), Lewiston (2 per day, 3hr., $30), and Missoula (3 per day, 4hr., $31). **Crisis Services** can be reached at 664-1443 (24hr.). Coeur d'Alene's **post office,** is at 111 N. 7th St. (664-8126), 5 blocks east of the Chamber of Commerce (open Mon.-Fri. 8:30am-5pm). **ZIP code:** 83814. **Area code:** 208.

Accommodations, Camping, and Food Cheap lodgings are hard to find in this resort town. Try the motels on Sherman Ave., on the eastern edge of the city. **Star Motel,** 1516 E. Sherman Ave. (664-5035), fits phones and TVs with HBO in its tidy cubicles (singles $40, doubles $45). Across the street, **Budget Saver Motel,** 1519 Sherman Ave. (667-9505), competes with roomier accommodations (singles $35, doubles $42-47; late Sept.-early June $30/$37-40). There are five **campgrounds** within 20 mi. of town. **Robin Hood RV Park,** 703 Lincoln Way (664-2306, 800-280-CAMP/2267), lies within walking distance of downtown and just a few blocks from a beach (sites $7.50 for two; showers, laundry, hookups, no evil sheriffs). **Bell Bay,** on Lake Coeur d'Alene (off U.S. 95 south, then 14 mi to Forest Service Rd. 545), has 26 sites and good fishing ($9). Call the **Fernan Ranger District Office,** 2502 E. Sherman (769-3000), for info on Bell Bay and other forest campgrounds.

Coeur d'Alene has oysters aplenty. For the best and most entertaining shellfish slurp, go to **Cricket's Restaurant and Oyster Bar,** on Sherman Ave., with the car on the roof, to sup on six oysters for $7.50 and watch the toy train chug by on raised tracks. (Open Mon.-Fri. 11am-10pm, Sat. and Sun. 11am-11pm.) Revere the scorching power of the chile and the heroism of **Taco Dude,** 415 Sherman Ave. (666-9043). Everything on the menu is $1.25-$5. (Open Sun.-Thurs. 11am-9pm, Fri.-Sat. 11am-10pm.)

Sights and Activities The lake is Coeur d'Alene's *raison d'être.* Hike 2 mi. up **Tubbs Hill** to a scenic vantage point, or head for the **Coeur d'Alene Resort** and walk along the **world's longest floating boardwalk** (3300 ft.). You can tour the lake on a **Lake Coeur d'Alene Cruise** (765-4000) and see the world's only floating golf green. (Departs from the downtown dock May-Sept. 1:30, 3:30, and 5:30pm; 90min.; $10.75, seniors $9.75, kids $5.75.) Rent a canoe or a pedal boat at the city dock, and explore the lake ($7 per hr., $20 per ½day, $35 first whole day, $15 per day thereafter). A 3-mi. bike/foot path follows the lake shore. **Four Seasons Outfitting,** 200 Sherman Ave. (765-2863), organizes horse rides ($13 first 45min., $36 for 3hr.) and a variety of other expensive outdoor activities. Call in advance.

Montana

Despite the recent acquisition of large amounts of acreage by such Eastern celebrities as Ted Turner, Tom Brokaw, and Liz Claiborne, Montana still has 25 million acres of national forest and public lands. In Big Sky country, the population of pronghorn antelope seems to outnumber the humans. Copious fishing lakes, 500 species of wildlife (not including millions of insect types), beautiful rivers, mountains, glaciers, and thousands of ski trails make Montana a nature-lover's paradise.

PRACTICAL INFORMATION

Capital: Helena.
Travel Montana: For a free *Montana Travel Planner,* write P.O. Box 200533, Helena 59620 (406-444-2654 in MT or 800-541-1447). **National Forest Information,** Northern Region, Federal Bldg., 200 E. Broadway, Box 7669, Missoula 59801 (406-329-3511). Gay and lesbian tourists can contact **PRIDE!,** P.O. Box 775, Helena 59624 (406-442-9322), for info on Montana gay community activities.
Time Zone: Mountain (2hr. behind Eastern). **Postal Abbreviation:** MT.
Sales Tax: 0%. (But beware of steep gas taxes.)

■ Billings

The railstop town founded by Northern Pacific Railroad president Fredrick Billings in 1882 still rumbles with passing freight trains. Despite heavy development, Billings retains a deserted feel. Strip malls and chains punctuate the sparse, industrial atmosphere, and sights are few. Located at the junction of I-90 and I-94, Billings is more of a stopover than a destination. Both **Greyhound** and **Rimrock Trailways** operate from 2502 1st Ave. N. (245-5116); buses run to Bozeman (4 per day, $19), Missoula (3 per day, $41), and Bismarck (3 per day, $57.50). The station is open 24 hr.

Street names in Billings are confusing; three streets may have the same name, distinguished only by direction. The **visitors center,** 815 S. 27th St. (252-4016), offers a $1 map, but their basic free one should do the trick. (Open daily 8:30am-7:30pm, off season 8:30am-5pm.) Montana State University's **Lambda Alliance** (657-2951) has info on local gay and lesbian activities. See the town, or leave quickly, in a car from **Rent-a-Wreck,** 5002 Laurel Rd. (252-0219). Rentals start at $28.50 per day or $185 per week (less in winter), with 100 free mi. per day and a 19¢ charge per additional mi. (Must be 21 with credit card and liability insurance. Open Mon.-Fri. 8am-5:30pm, Sat. 9am-2pm, Sun. by appt.) Billings' **post office:** 2200 Grant Rd. (657-5732; open Mon.-Fri. 8am-5:30pm). **ZIP code:** 59108. **Area code:** 406.

Billings' lodgings are spread throughout the city. The **Picture Court,** 5146 Laurel Rd./W. I-90 (252-8478), rents cozy, well-kept, affordable rooms with A/C and TV. (Check-out 10:30am. Singles $29, doubles $36.) Though the **Rainbow Motel,** 421 St. Johns (259-4949; take Montana St. southwest until the St. Johns turnoff), is inexpensive, women and lone travelers should be advised that it is not in the safest part of town. (A/C, TV, laundry facilities; pot of gold not included. Singles $25, doubles $30. Weekly rooms with kitchenettes $120.) The **Cherry Tree Inn,** 823 N. Broadway (252-5603), across from Deaconess Hospital (take Exit 450 off I-90; go north on 27th St. then turn left onto 9th Ave.) was built around a Colonial America theme and has a small library. (A/C, phones, cable TV. Singles $32, doubles $37; AAA discount.)

You can try your luck all over the city; almost every public place offers some kind of video gambling, from poker to keno (a.k.a. bingo). Downtown, **Jake's,** 2701 1st Ave. N. (259-9375), has a few such machines, plus hearty soups ($3-5), burgers ($5.25), and a plentiful selection of microbrews and other less trendy liquids. (Open daily 11:30am-10:30pm.) Also downtown, **Café Jones,** 2712 2nd Ave. N. (259-7676), is a coffeehouse/juice bar with a rotating art exhibit. (Offerings $1-5. Open Mon.-Sat. 7am-midnight, Sun. 8am-10pm.) **Khanthaly's Laotian Cuisine,** 1301 Grand Ave. (259-7252), serves tasty Southeast Asian fast food (fried rice noodles, spring rolls, etc.) at rates more likely to be found in Laos than the U.S. ($1-4; open Mon.-Sat. 11am-9pm, Sun. noon-8pm).

■ Bozeman

Wedged between the Bridger and Madison Mountains, Bozeman thrives in Montana's broad Gallatin River Valley. Originally settled by farmers who sold food to Northern Pacific Railroad employees living in the neighboring town of Elliston, the valley now supplies food to a large portion of southern Montana. The presence of Montana State

---

The American Autobahn

This past year, Montana got loads of press coverage for being home to elements of the American lunatic fringe. While a traveler to the state is unlikely to run into militia captains or anti-technology zealots, he or she might notice the state's anti-government spirit in its approach to **highway speed limits.** This is the deal: during the day, as long as the weather is okay, traffic is flowing, and you've got a car that can take it, you're basically free to go as fast as you want. 'Tis a bold policy. In reality, however, traffic moves at about the same pace that it does in neighboring states: around 75mph on four-lane highways, and a bit slower on two-lane highways where one's speed is often dictated by that fifth-wheel trailer in the lead. Of course, as expected, there is still the lone helmet-wearing driver, attempting to break the speed of sound in a souped-up Porsche.

University makes Bozeman more accommodating to young wanderers and latter-day hippies than most Montana towns.

Practical Information The **Bozeman Area Chamber of Commerce,** 1205 E. Main St. (586-5421), provides ample info on local events (open Mon.-Fri. 8am-5pm). **Lambda Alliance** (994-4551) has local gay and lesbian info and an advocacy group. **Greyhound** and **RimRock Stages** serve Bozeman from 625 N. 7th St. (587-3110). Greyhound runs to Butte (3 per day, 1½hr., $13) and Billings (4 per day, 3hr., $19). RimRock buses to Helena (1 per day, 2hr., $14) and Missoula (3 per day, 5hr., $26). (Open Mon.-Fri. 7:30-11:30am, 12:30-5:30pm, and 8:30-10pm, Sat. 7:30-11:30am, 3:30-5:30pm, and 8:30-10pm, Sun. and holidays 7:30-9:15am, 3:30-5:30pm, and 8:30-10pm.) **Rent-a-Wreck,** 112 N. Tracey St. (587-4551), will put you in a well-worn auto for $30 per day. (100 free mi., 18¢ each additional mi. Must be 21 with major credit card. Open Mon.-Fri. 8am-6pm, Sat. 8am-5pm, Sun. by appt.) Bozeman's **post office:** 32 E. Babcock St. (586-1508; open Mon.-Fri. 9am-5pm). **ZIP code:** 59715. **Area code:** 406.

Accommodations Summer travelers in Bozeman support a number of budget motels along Main St. and on 7th Ave. north of Main. The **Sacajawea International Backpackers Hostel,** 405 West Olive St. (586-4659), offers travelers showers, laundry facilities, a full kitchen, and transportation to trailheads. There are only 10 beds, so call ahead ($10, kids $5). Owners can give advice on where to eat, drink, hang out, and hike; they even rent bikes (½ day $6, full day $10). The **Ranch House Motel,** 1201 E. Main St. (587-4278), has free HBO and A/C in standard, quiet rooms (singles $29, doubles $37; in winter $22/$27-32). The **Alpine Lodge,** 1017 E. Main St. (586-0356), provides clean, small rooms with soft carpets and venetian blinds (singles $31.25, doubles $37.50; cabins with kitchen $57.25, in winter $45).

Food and a Museum Whole sandwiches at **The Pickle Barrel,** 809 W. College (587-2411), consist of giant loaves of fresh sourdough bread stuffed with succulent deli meats and fresh vegetables. Ask the friendly collegian behind the counter for a hefty half sandwich ($4; open daily 10:30am-10pm; in winter 11am-10:30pm). **Brandi's,** 717 N. 7th (587-3848), has a great breakfast deal: two hotcakes for 50¢ or 2 eggs, hash browns, and toast for $1, with free coffee to boot (open 8am-9:30pm; breakfast 8am-noon). Hang out with the locals and create your own delicious deep-dish pizza (from $11.50) at **McKenzie's River Pizza,** 232 E. Main St. (587-0055; open Mon.-Sat. 11:30am-10pm, Sun 5-9pm). The **Haufbrau,** 22 S. 8th Ave. (587-4931), serves grilled delights (burger with fries and salad $3.30) at well-worn, carved wooden tables or at the bar. Wash down your meal with a pint of draft (10 beers on tap; pints $1.25-2.50, pitchers $6-9) and sit back for the nightly performance by a local musician. Led Zeppelin's Robert Plant recommends the Black Dog Ale at **Spanish Peaks Brewery,** 1290 N. 19th Ave. (585-2296). Pints are $2.50, and a sampler of all their beers goes for $5.

Yogi, Smokey, and a number of scarier, grizzlier bears prowl the halls of the **Museum of the Rockies,** 600 W. Kagy Blvd. (994-2251), immediately south of the MSU campus. Combining big-city quality with small-town charm, the museum contains a number of immaculately explained exhibits. The impressive dinosaur halls alone justify the visit; see the bones of the largest T. Rex ever found (excavated in Montana) and the world's only extant Triceratops family (actually, three scarily convincing life-sized robots). (Open 8am-8pm; Labor Day-Memorial Day Mon.-Sat. 9am-5pm, Sun. 12:30pm-5pm; $6.00—good for two days.)

Fishing Surrounded by three renowned trout-fishing rivers—Yellowstone, Madison, and Gardiner—the small town of **Livingston,** about 20 mi. east of Bozeman off I-90, is an angler's heaven. This is gorgeous country—*A River Runs Through It* was shot in Bozeman and Livingston. Livingston's Main Street is a great line of circa 1900 buildings housing bars (with video gambling), restaurants, fishing outfitters, and only a few new age additions. The **Yellowstone Angler** (222-7130), located ½ mi. south of Livingston on U.S. 89, provides licenses ($15 for 2 days) and rents and sells fishing gear and wear (rod and reel rental $15, waders $15, inner tubes $20). (Open in summer Mon.-Sat. 7am-6pm, Sun. 7am-5pm; Oct.-March Mon.-Sat. 7am-5pm.)

■ Little Big Horn

Little Big Horn National Monument, 60 mi. southeast of Billings off I-90 on the Crow Reservation, marks the site where Sioux and Cheyenne warriors annihilated five companies of the U.S. Seventh Cavalry under the command of Lt. Colonel George Armstrong Custer on June 25, 1876, in one of the most dramatic episodes in the conflict between Native Americans and the U.S. Government. White stone graves mark where the U.S soldiers fell; a somber stone monument, engraved with the names of the dead, covers the mass grave site where the soldiers are buried. The exact Native American casualties are not known, since their families and fellow warriors removed the bodies from the battlefield almost immediately. The renaming of the monument, formerly known as the Custer Battlefield Monument, signifies the U.S. Government's admission that Custer's behavior merits no glorification.

Rangers give great explanatory talks every hr. on the hr. A 5-mi. self-guided audio tour ($10) will narrate you through the battle movements of both sides; you can also see the park on a 45-min. bus tour ($4, kids $3). The **visitors center** (638-2621) contains a modest museum including a small movie theater, an electronic map of the battlefield, and displays of the weapons used in the battle. (Museum and visitors center open daily 8am-8pm; in fall 8am-6pm; in winter 8am-4:30pm. Free. Monument open daily 8am-7:30pm. Entrance $4 per car, $2 per person.)

■ Missoula

Home to the University of Montana, Missoula is the state at its most happening and most diverse. Downtown, chi-chi microbreweries share the view with tough old bars; health food stores and rafting outfitters look across the street to taxidermists and pork chop cafés.

Practical Information Traveling within Missoula is easy, thanks to reliable city **buses** (721-3333; buses operate Mon.-Fri. 6am-7pm, Sat. 9:30am-6pm; fare 50¢). The **Missoula Chamber of Commerce,** 825 E. Front St. (543-6623), at Van Buren, provides bus schedules. (Open Mon.-Fri. 8:30am-7pm, Sat.-Sun 10am-5pm; Labor Day-Memorial Day daily 8:30am-5pm.) **Greyhound,** 1660 W. Broadway (549-2339), shuffles off to Bozeman (4 per day, 5hr., $26) and Spokane (3 per day, 3½hr., $35). **Intermountain Transportation** serves Whitefish (1 per day, 3½hr., $18), and **RimRock Stages** buses to Helena (1 per day, 2½hr., $17) from the same terminal. **Enterprise Rent-a-Car,** 2201 W. Broadway (721-1888), rents year-old autos for low prices. ($27 per day with 150 free mi., 21¢ each additional mi.; rates go down in winter. Must be 21. Credit card deposit required.) The **Rape Crisis Line** (543-7606) is open 24 hr. Missoula's **post office:** 1100 W. Kent (329-2200), at Brooks and South St. (Open Mon.-Fri. 8am-6pm, Sat. 9am-1pm.) **ZIP code:** 59801. **Area code:** 406.

Accommodations Spend your nights in Missoula at the **Birchwood Hostel,** 600 S. Orange St. (728-9799), 13 blocks east of the bus station on Broadway, then 8 blocks south on Orange. The spacious, immaculate dorm rooms sleep 22. Laundry, kitchen, and bike storage facilities are available. (Open daily 5-10pm. HI members and cyclists $8, otherwise $9. Closed for 2 weeks in late Dec.) Cheap lodgings cluster along Broadway; check the quieter east end for a place to stay. Descend into the **Canyon Motel,** 1015 E. Broadway (543-4069 or 543-7251), for a roomy, comfortable, wood-paneled feel and queen-sized beds (A/C, cable TV; all rooms $25). **City Center Motel,** 338 E. Broadway (543-3193), sits on the deluxe side of the metaphorical lodging fence, flaunting a relatively new building, HBO, and rooms with phones (singles $31, doubles $38; AAA discount available). The year-round **Outpost Campground** (549-2016), 2 mi. north of I-90 on U.S. 93, provides showers, laundry facilities, and scattered woodsy shade (sites for 2 $10, with hookup $12).

Food and Nightlife Missoula's dining scene offers more than the West's usual steak and potatoes. Choice, thrifty eateries line the downtown area, particularly between Broadway and Railroad St. and north of the Clark Fork River. A few more places lurk about the perimeter of the university campus south of the river. At the **Food for Thought Café,** 540 Daly Ave., college kids eat and think about milkshakes ($3.25; open daily 7am-10pm). Choose from every breakfast dish you ever imagined, and several lunch numbers for under $6 at the **Old Town Café,** 127 W. Alder St. (728-9742). (Open Tues.-Sat. 6am-9pm, Sun.-Mon. 6am-3pm.) Both a restaurant and a natural food store, **Torrey's,** 1916 Brooks St. (721-2510), serves mouth-watering health food at absurdly low prices; seafood stir-fry is $3.50. (Open Mon.-Sat. 11am-8:30pm.) If you'd rather be happy than healthy, try the retro 1950s **Uptown Diner,** 120 N. Higgins Ave. (542-2449), where cheese fries and deluxe milkshakes run $3-5. Discerning palates wash down cheap, filling bar food with pilsner, amber, and dark brews of Bayern beer from the **Iron Horse Brew Pub,** 100 W. Railroad Ave. (728-8866), at Higgins Ave. S. (open daily noon-midnight). For a larger selection and a rowdier crowd, try one of the 50 beers on tap at **Rhinoceros (Rhino's),** 158 Ryman Ave. (721-6061), a local favorite (open daily 11am-2am).

Outdoor Activities The outdoors are Missoula's greatest attraction. Located at the intersection of the Trans-America and the Great Parks bicycle routes, the town swarms with cycling enthusiasts. **Adventure Cycling,** 150 E. Pine St. (721-1776), can provide info about bike trails in the area, and **New Era Bicycles,** 741 S. Higgins (728-2080), can help you join the pack with a rental. ($15 for 24hr.; leave credit card for deposit. Open Mon.-Thurs. 9am-6pm, Fri. 9am-7pm, Sat. 10am-6pm.)

Other popular Missoula diversions include skiing, rafting, backpacking, and hiking. For equipment rentals, stop by outdoor shops like **Trailhead,** 110 E. Pine St. (543-6966), at Higgins St. Although priority goes to University students, tourists can sometimes take part in day hikes, overnight trips, and classes on outdoor activities organized by the outdoor program of the **University of Montana Department of Recreation** (243-5172), at Field House 116. (Open Mon.-Fri. 9am-5pm, Sat. 9am-1pm.) The **Rattlesnake Wilderness National Recreation Area,** a few mi. northeast of town off the Van Buren St. exit from I-90, makes for a great day of hiking. Wilderness maps ($3) are available from the **U.S. Forest Service Information Office,** 200 E. Broadway (329-3511; open Mon.-Fri. 7:30am-4pm). The Clark Fork, Blackfoot, and Bitterroot Rivers overflow with opportunities for float trips. The **Montana State Regional Parks and Wildlife Office,** 3201 Spurgin Rd. (542-5500), sells float maps ($3.50; open Mon.-Fri. 8am-5pm). For rafting trips to a time when the continent thing wasn't so complicated, visit **Pangaea Expeditions,** 180 S. 3rd (721-7719; $15 for 2hr., $25 per ½ day, $45 per day).

Missoula's hottest sight is the **Aerial Fire Depot Visitors Center** (329-4934), 7 mi. west of town on Broadway (Rte. 10, past the airport), where you'll learn to appreciate the courage aerial firefighters need to jump into flaming, roadless forests. They parachute to work. Very studly. (Open daily 8:30am-5pm; Oct.-April by appointment for groups. Tours May.-Sept. on the hr. 10-11am and 1-4pm. Free.) The first Friday of every month occasions a touch of Missoula culture, with open houses at the town's 15 museums and galleries; artists are present at some.

■ From Missoula to Glacier

The **Miracle of America Museum,** off U.S. 93 between Missoula and Glacier before you enter the town of **Polson,** houses one of the greatest collections of Americana in the country. Look for the reconstructed general store, saddlery shop, barber shop, and gas station among the jumbled collection of classic American kitsch. (Open April-

Sept. daily 8am-8pm, Sun. 2-6pm; any other time by chance or appointment. $2.) The **National Bison Range,** about 40 mi. north of Missoula on U.S. 93, was established in 1908 to protect bison. Before they were hunted to near-extinction, 50 million of these animals roamed the plains; the range is home to 300-500 of the imposing creatures today, as well as several other indigenous life forms. (Range open 7am-9:30pm, ranger office open 8am-4:30pm. Free.)

■ Waterton-Glacier Peace Park

Waterton-Glacier transcends international boundaries to encompass one of the most strikingly beautiful portions of the Rockies. A geographical metaphor for the peace between the U.S. and Canada, the park provides sanctuary for many endangered bears, bighorn sheep, moose, mountain goats, and now grey wolves.

Technically one park, Waterton-Glacier is, for all practical purposes, two distinct areas: the small **Waterton Lakes National Park** in Alberta, and the enormous **Glacier National Park** in Montana. Each park charges its own admission fee (in Glacier, $5 per week; in Waterton Lakes, CDN$5 per day, CDN$8 per group of 2-10 people), and you must go through customs to pass from one to the other. Several **border crossings** pepper the park: **Chief Mountain** at Rte. 17 (open May 19-May 31 9am-6pm; June 1-Sept. 17 7am-10pm; closed Sept. 18 to mid-May in 1997); **Piegan/Carway** at U.S. 89 (open daily 7am-11pm); **Trail Creek** at North Fork Rd. (open June-Oct. daily 9am-5pm); and **Roosville** on U.S. 93 (open 24hr.).

Since snow melting is an unpredictable process, the parks are usually in full operation only from late May to early September. To find out which areas of the park, hotels, and campsites will be open when you visit, contact the headquarters of either Waterton (403-859-2203) or Glacier (406-888-5441). The *Waterton Glacier Guide* has dates and times of trail, campground, and border crossing openings. Mace, bear spray, and firewood are not allowed into Canada.

■ Glacier Park

Practical Information Glacier's layout is simple: one road enters through West Glacier on the west side, and three roads enter from the east at Many Glaciers, St. Mary, and Two Medicine. West Glacier and St. Mary serve as the two main points of entry into the park, connected by **Going-to-the-Sun Road** ("The Sun"), the only road traversing the park. **U.S. 2** runs between West and East Glacier along 82 mi. of the southern park border. Look for the "Goat Lick" signs off Rte. 2 near **Walton.** Mountain goats often descend to the lick for a salt fix in June and July.

Ask about trail and campsite availability and local weather and wildlife conditions at any of the three visitors centers. **St. Mary** (732-4424) guards the east entrance of the park. (Open late May to mid-June daily 8am-5pm; mid-June to early Sept. 8am-9pm; Sept. 8am-5pm.) **Apgar** aids at the west entrance. (Open late April to mid-June and Sept. daily 8am-5pm; mid-June to early Sept. 8am-8pm; Oct. 8am-4:30pm; after Oct. 31 open only on weekends.) A third visitors center graces **Logan Pass** on Going-to-the-Sun Rd. (Open early to mid-June daily 9am-5pm; mid- to late June 9am-6pm; early July to mid-Sept. 9am-8pm.)

Amtrak (226-4452 or 800-872-7245) traces a dramatic route along the southern edge of the park. Daily trains chug to West Glacier from Whitefish ($7), Seattle ($126), and Spokane ($63); Amtrak also runs from East Glacier to Chicago ($213) and Minneapolis ($189). **Rimrock Stages** (862-6700) is the only bus line that comes near the park (Kalispell). As with most of the Rockies, a car is the most convenient mode of transport, particularly within the park. **Rent-a-Wreck** rents used cars from two locations in the area: in Kalispell, 2425 U.S. 2 E. (755-4555; $30 per day); in East Glacier, at the Sears Motel (226-9293; $50 per day). Both locations offer 100 free mi. per day and charge 20¢ for each additional mile; you must be 21 with a major credit card. Glacier's **post office:** the Lake McDonald gas station, in the park. (Open Mon.-Fri. 9am-3:45pm.) **ZIP code:** 59921. **Area code:** 406.

Accommodations and Food Staying indoors within Glacier is absurd and expensive. **Glacier Park, Inc.** handles all in-park lodging, including one budget motel: the **Swiftcurrent Motor Inn** (732-5531), in Many Glacier Valley. The Swiftcurrent has cabins without bathrooms for $22. (With 2 bedrooms $37. Open mid-June to mid-Sept.) Reservations can be made through the distant offices of **Glacier Park, Inc.,** 925 Dial Corporate Center, Phoenix, AZ 85077-0928 (602-207-6000). Last-minute (1-2 day) reservations can be made at East Glacier Park (406-226-9311).

On the west side of the park, the cozy **North Fork Hostel** (888-5241), at the end of Beaver Dr. in the very cool, electricity-less town of **Polebridge,** makes an ideal base for exploring some of Glacier's most pristine areas. The bumpy 12-mi. trip up the dirt road is preparation for the propane and kerosene lamps, wood stoves, and outhouses that provide creature comforts at the hostel. (Dorm beds $12, $10 after 2 nights. Cabins $26. Linen $2. Log homes $40, weekly $225). The **Polebridge Mercantile Store** will replenish depleted supplies. They also rent out cabins and teepees for $20-35 a night; call 406-888-5105 for more info. A slice of homemade pie or a beer to revive flagged spirits can be had at the **Northern Lights Saloon.** (Open 4-9pm for food, 9pm-midnight for drinks.)

In the east, affordable lodging can be found just across the park border in **East Glacier,** on U.S. 2, 30 mi. south of the St. Mary entrance and about 5 mi. south of the Two Medicine entrance. **Brownies Grocery (HI-AYH),** 1020 Rte. 49 (226-4426), in East Glacier, has a yummy bakery and comfortable dorms in what is rumored to have once been a brothel. Brownies rents bunks ($11, nonmembers $13), private rooms (singles $15, nonmembers $18; doubles $20/$23), or a family room (sleeps 4-6; $30). Next door, the **Whistle Stop Café** is an oasis of local gourmet creations (Huckleberry French Toast $5) made with fresh ingredients and individual flair. The **Backpacker's Inn Hostel,** 29 Dawson Ave. (226-9392), offers 20 clean beds and hot showers for only $8 per night (bring a sleeping bag or rent one for $1).

Camping Camping is a cheaper and more scenic alternative to indoor accommodations. All developed campsites are available on a first come, first camped basis; the most popular sites fill by noon. However, "Campground Full" signs sometimes stay up for days on end; look carefully for empty sites. All 10 campgrounds accessible by car are easy to find. Just follow the map distributed at the park entrance. **Sprague Creek** and **Fish Creek** have peaceful lakeside sites. **Many Glacier** and **Two Medicine** are usually the last campsites on Sun Rd. to fill up. **Bowman Lake** (48 sites) and **Kintla Lake** (13 sites) rarely fill and offer pristine, lakeside sites. Neither has flush toilets, but they're the cheapest thing going ($10); the rest of the campgrounds cost $12 and you can flush to your little heart's content. Some sites at **Sprague, Apgar, Avalanche, Rising Sun,** and **St. Mary** remain reserved for bicyclists and pedestrians. Campgrounds in the surrounding national forests offer sites without running water for $5. Check at the Apgar or St. Mary visitors centers for up-to-date info on conditions and vacancies. Weather and the grizzlies adjust the operating dates at their whim; prepare for mosquitoes and chilly weather.

In Touch with Nature *There are bears out there. Familiarize yourself with the precautions necessary to avoid a run-in with a bear; consult rangers for advice.* **Backcountry trips** are the best way to appreciate the mountain scenery and the wildlife which make Glacier famous. The **Highline Trail** from Logan Pass is a good day-hike through prime bighorn sheep and mountain goat territory, although locals consider it too crowded. The visitors center's free *Nature with a Naturalist* pamphlet has a hiking map marked with distances and backcountry campsites. All backcountry campers must obtain, in person, a free wilderness permit from a visitors center or ranger station no more than 24 hr. in advance; backcountry camping is allowed only at designated campgrounds. The **Two Medicine** area in the southeast corner of the park is well traveled, while the treks to **Kintla Lake** and **Numa Lake** reward you with fantastic views of nearby peaks. **Belly River** is an isolated and pretty spot to stake a tent for an overnight wilderness stay.

Going-to-the-Sun Rd. runs a beautiful 52-mi. course through the park. Even on cloudy days, the constantly changing views of the peaks will have you struggling to keep your eyes on the road. But you'll have to—the road is narrow and vulnerable to rock slides and falling trees. Snow clogs the road until June, so check with rangers for exact opening dates. All vehicles must be under 21 ft. long and under 8 ft. wide to go over Logan Pass, a midpoint on the road.

Although "The Sun" is a popular **bike route,** only experienced cyclists with appropriate gear and legs of titanium should attempt this grueling ride. The sometimes nonexistent shoulder of the road creates a hazardous situation for cyclists: in the summer (June 15-Sept. 2), bike traffic is prohibited from 11am until 4pm from the Apgar turn-off at the west end of Lake McDonald to Sprague Creek, and from Logan Creek to Logan Pass. The east side of the park has no such restrictions. Bikes are not permitted on any hiking trails. **Equestrian** explorers should check to make sure trails are open; fines for riding on closed trails are steep. **Trail rides** ($29 for 2hr.) are available at Many Glacier, Apgar, and Lake McDonald. When in Glacier, don't overlook the park's interpretive programs. Ask about **the reds,** antique tour buses that snake around the area ($2-30). There are also regular shuttles for hikers ($2-14) that tour the length of The Sun. Get a schedule at any visitors center.

Boating and Fishing Boat tours explore all of Glacier's large lakes. Tours leave from **Lake McDonald** (4-5 per day, 1hr., $7, ages 4-12 $3.50) and **Two Medicine** (5 per day, 45min., $6.50). The tours from **St. Mary** (90min.) and **Many Glacier** (75min.) provide access to Glacier's backcountry (from St. Mary $8.50; from Many Glacier $8). The $7 sunset cruise proves a great way to see this quotidian phenomenon; it begins around 10pm in the middle of the summer. Call Lake McDonald (888-5727), Many Glacier (732-4480), or St. Mary (732-4430) for info. **Glacier Raft Co.** (888-5454 or 800-332-9995), in West Glacier, hawks trips down the middle fork of the Flathead River. A full-day trip (lunch included) costs $62, under 13 $33; ½-day trips ($32/$21) leave in the morning and afternoon.

Rent **rowboats** ($6 per hr., $30 per 10 hr.) at Lake McDonald, Many Glacier, and Two Medicine; **canoes** ($6.50 per hr.) at Many Glacier, Two Medicine, and Apgar; and **outboards** ($11 per hr., $55 per 10 hr.) at Lake McDonald. All require a $50 deposit. You need no permit to fish in the park. In an attempt to boost indigenous fish populations, the park stopped stocking its rivers in the 1970s. Limits are high and few seem in danger of exceeding them, but read the pamphlet *Fishing Regulations,* available at visitors centers. Outside the park, on Blackfoot Indian land, you *do* need a special permit, and everywhere else in Montana you need a state permit.

■ Waterton Lakes, AB

Only a fraction of the size of its Montana neighbor, Waterton Lakes National Park offers spectacular scenery and activities without the crowds that plague Glacier during the peak months of July and August.

Practical Information The only road from Waterton's park entrance leads 5 mi. south to **Waterton.** On the way, grab a copy of the *Waterton-Glacier Guide* at the **Waterton Visitor Center,** 215 Mountain View Rd. (859-2224), 5 mi. inside the park (open daily 8am-8pm; mid-May to June daily 10am-5:30pm). Rent **bikes** from **Pat's Texaco and Cycle Rental,** Mount View Rd., Waterton townsite (859-2266; mountain bikes CDN$6 per hr., CDN$30 per day, damage deposit CDN$20). In a medical **emergency,** call an **ambulance** (859-2636). The **police station** (859-2244) is on Waterton Ave. at Cameron Falls Dr. Waterton's **post office:** Fountain Ave. at Windflower. (Open Mon., Wed., and Fri. 8:30am-4:30pm, Tues. and Thurs. 8:30am-4pm.) **Postal code:** T0K 2M0. **Area code:** 403.

Accommodations, Camping, and Food As you enter the park, marvel at the enormous(ly pricey) **Prince of Wales Hotel** (859-2231 or 602-207-6000), where you can enjoy tea and a spectacular view. Then, settle into your affordable **tent** in one of the park's three campgrounds. **Townsite** offers tent sites for CDN$16, full hookups for CDN$21. **Crandell,** on Red Rock Canyon Rd., has sites for CDN$13; **Belly River,** on Chief Mountain Hwy., has primitive sites for CDN$10. **Backcountry camping** is CDN$6 per site and requires a permit from the visitors center (see above) or from **Park Headquarters and Information,** Waterton Lakes National Park, 215 Mount View Rd. (859-2224; open Mon.-Fri. 8am-4pm). The backcountry campsites are rarely full, and several, including beautiful **Crandell Lake,** are less than an hour's walk from the trailhead.

If you prefer to stay indoors, head straight for the **Mountain View Bed and Breakfast** (653-1882), 20 km east of the park on Hwy. 5 (the blue buildings), where you'll enjoy comfy beds, down-home hospitality, and a hearty breakfast, including homemade bread (singles CDN$25, doubles CDN$45). Don Anderson, the owner, also runs a fishing guide service and can supply you with gear. Don will keep you entertained and educated with stories of more than 50 years of living in the area. If you insist on having a bed in Waterton, drop by the **Waterton Pharmacy,** on Waterton Ave. (859-2335), and ask to sleep in one of the nine rooms of the **Stanley Hotel.** (Common washroom and shower access 3-8pm. Singles or doubles CDN$45.) Waterton is more than happy to serve as outpost for park visitors. **Waterton Pie Station,** 303 Windflower Ave. (859-2060), serves up sweet 'n' savory pies ($4.50-6.50; open daily 9am-10pm).

Outdoors If you've brought only hiking boots to Waterton, you can set out on the **International Lakeside Hike,** which leads along the west shore of Upper Waterton Lake and delivers you to Montana some 5 mi. after leaving the town. The **Crypt Lake Trail,** voted Canada's best hike, leads past waterfalls in a narrow canyon, and through a 20m natural tunnel bored through the mountainside to arrive after 4 mi. at icy, green Crypt Lake, which straddles the international border. To get to the trailhead, you must take the **water taxi** run by the **Waterton Shoreline Cruises** (859-2362). The boat runs twice a day (CDN$10, ages 4-12 CDN$5). The marina also runs a 2-hr. boat tour of Upper Waterton Lake. (CDN$17, ages 13-17 CDN$12, ages 4-12 CDN$8. Open mid-May to mid-Sept.)

Anglers will appreciate Waterton's **fishing.** Fishing in the park requires a **license** (CDN$4.50 per day, CDN$6.50 per week, CDN$13 per year), available from the park offices, campgrounds, wardens, and service stations in the area. Lake trout cruise the

---

The Nez Perce Campaign

"It is cold and we have no blankets. The little children are freezing to death. My people, some of them have run away to the hills and have no blankets, no food; no one knows where they are—perhaps freezing to death. I want time to look for my children and see how many of them I can find. Maybe I shall find them among the dead. Hear me, my chiefs. I am tired; my heart is sick and sad. From where the sun now stands, I will fight no more forever."

So spoke Chief Joseph, a leader of the Nez Perce tribe, shortly before surrendering to the U.S. Army on Oct. 5, 1877. A few months prior, gold had been discovered in the Nez Perce lands, exacerbating already existing land disputes; the tension climaxed in a violent spree in which young members of the Nez Perce tribe killed several white men and women. Fearing repercussions, Chief Joseph, a reknowned pacifist, fled with his tribe some 1700 mi., several times outwitting the Army forces. Finally, exhausted and cornered, the tribe surrendered in what is now northern Montana, approximately 40 mi. from the Canadian border. The site of the surrender, **Nez Perce National Historical Park: Bear Paw Battlefield** (406-357-2590), 16 mi. south of Chinook, MT, is open daily May-Sept. Mon.-Fri. 9am-5pm and is free to the public.

depths of **Cameron** and **Waterton Lakes,** while northern pike prowl the weedy channels of **Lower Waterton Lake** and **Maskinonge Lake.** Most of the backcountry lakes and creeks support populations of rainbow and brook trout. Try the nameless creek that spills from Cameron Lake about 200m to the east of the parking lot, or hike 1.5 km in to Crandell Lake for plentiful, hungry fish. You can rent a **rowboat, paddleboat,** or **canoe** at Cameron Lake for CDN$8 per hr. **Alpine Stables** (859-2462, in winter 403-653-2449), 2½ mi. north of the townsite, conducts trail rides of varying lengths (1-hr. ride CDN$15, all-day CDN$77).

In the evening, take in a free **interpretive program** at the **Falls** or **Crandell Theatre.** These interesting and quirkily entitled programs (e.g. *Bearying the Myths,* which offers straight talk about bears) change yearly. There are programs daily in summer at 8:30pm; contact the visitors center for schedule info.

Wyoming

The ninth-largest state in the Union, Wyoming is also the least populated. This is a place where livestock outnumbers citizens, and men wear cowboy hats and boots for *real.* Yet this rugged land was more than just a frontier during westward expansion; it was the first state to grant women the right to vote without later repealing it, and the first to have a national monument (Devils Tower) and a national park (Yellowstone) within its borders. Wyoming has everything you'd want to see in a state in the Rockies: a Frontier Days festival, spectacular mountain ranges, breath-taking panoramas, and, of course, cattle and beer.

PRACTICAL INFORMATION

Capital: Cheyenne.
Wyoming Information and Division of Tourism, I-25 and College Dr., Cheyenne 82002 (307-777-7777; 800-225-5996 outside WY; open daily 8am-5pm). Write for the free *Wyoming Vacation Guide.* **Department of Commerce, State Parks and Historic Sites Division,** 2301 Central Ave., Cheyenne 82002 (307-777-6323), has info on Wyoming's 10 state parks. Open Mon.-Fri. 8am-5pm. **Game and Fish Department,** 5400 Bishop Blvd., Cheyenne 82006 (307-777-4600). Open Mon.-Fri. 8am-5pm.
Time Zone: Mountain (2hr. behind Eastern). **Postal Abbreviation:** WY.
Sales Tax: 6%.

■ Yellowstone

Six hundred thousand years ago, intense volcanic activity fueled a catastrophic eruption that spewed out nearly 35 trillion cubic feet of debris, creating the central basin of what is now **Yellowstone National Park.** Although these geologic engines have downshifted, they still power boiling sulfuric pits, steaming geysers, and smelly mudpots. John Colter's descriptions of his 1807 explorations of this earthly inferno inspired fifty years of popular stories about "Colter's Hell." By 1872, popular opinion had swayed and President Grant declared Yellowstone a national park, the world's first. Today, Yellowstone's natural beauty is cluttered with cars, RVs, and thousands of snapshot-shooting, finger-pointing tourists. Still, in the backcountry, away from the crowds and geothermic anomalies that line the roads, you can survey the astounding number of bears, elk, moose, wolves, bison, and bighorn sheep that thrive in the park's quieter peaks and valleys. In 1988, a blaze charred a third of Yellowstone, and the land is slowly recovering. A tight budget led to one campground closure in 1996. New legislation may raise entrance fees to $25 in 1997.

PRACTICAL INFORMATION

Tourist Office: Most regions in this vast park have their own central station. The district rangers have a good deal of autonomy in making regulations for hiking and camping, so check in at each area. All centers offer backcountry permits and guides for the disabled, or a partner ranger station that does. Each center's display focuses on the attributes of its region of the park: **Albright Visitors Center** at **Mammoth Hot Springs** (344-2263), natural and human history; **Grant Village** (242-2650), wilderness; **Old Faithful/Madison** (545-2750), geysers; **Fishing Bridge** (242-2450), wildlife and Yellowstone Lake; **Canyon** (242-2550), natural history and history of the canyon area. All stations are open Memorial Day-Labor Day daily 8am-7pm; Nov.-Memorial Day 9am-5pm; call for hours between Labor Day and Nov. *Yellowstone Today,* the park's activities guide, has a thorough listing of tours and programs. For general park info and campground availability, call or write the Superintendent, Mammoth Hot Springs, Yellowstone National Park 82190 (344-7381). Headquarters open Mon.-Fri. 9am-5pm. **West Yellowstone Chamber of Commerce,** 100 Yellowstone Ave., West Yellowstone, MT 59758 (406-646-7701). Located 2 blocks west of the park entrance. Open daily 8am-8pm; Labor Day-Memorial Day 8am-5pm.

Tours: TW Services, Inc. (297-2757; TDD 344-5395). 9-hr. bus tour of the lower portion of the park leaves daily from lodges ($25, ages 12-16 $12, under 12 free). Similar tours of the northern region leave from Canyon Lodge, Lake Hotel, and Fishing Bridge RV Park ($17-22). Full-day tours around the park's figure-eight road system also available, leaving from Gardiner, MT and Mammoth Hot Springs ($25, ages 12-16 $12). Individual legs of this network of tour loops can get you as far as the Grand Tetons or Jackson, but using the system that way is inefficient and costs more than it's worth.

Buses: Greyhound (800-231-2222). No local office; pick-up at Chamber of Commerce at West Yellowstone. To Bozeman (1 per day, 2hr., $14) and Salt Lake City (1 per day, 9hr., $51).

Car Rental: Big Sky Car Rental, 429 Yellowstone Ave., West Yellowstone, MT (646-9564 or 800-426-7669). $30 per day, unlimited mi. Must be 21 with a credit card or passport. Open Mon.-Sat. 8am-5pm, Sun. 8am-noon; Nov.-April hours vary.

Bike Rental: Yellowstone Bicycles, 132 Madison Ave., West Yellowstone, MT (646-7815). Mountain bikes $3.50 per hr., $12.50 per ½ day, $18.50 per day; with helmet and water bottle. Open daily 8:30am-9:30pm; Nov.-April 10am-8pm.

Horse Rides: TW Services, Inc. (303-297-2757). From Mammoth Hot Springs Hotel, Roosevelt Lodge, and Canyon Lodge. Late May to early Sept. $17 per hr., $27 for 2hr.

Radio Information: Tune to 1610AM for park info.

Medical Services: Lake Clinic, Pharmacy, and **Hospital** (242-7241) at Lake Hotel. Clinic open late May to mid-Sept. daily 8:30am-8:30pm. Emergency room open May-Sept. 24hr. **Old Faithful Clinic,** at Old Faithful Inn (545-7325), open early May to mid-Oct. daily 8:30am-5pm; closed Thurs. and Fri. May 3-25 and Sept. 15-Oct. 20. **Mammoth Hot Springs Clinic** (344-7965), open daily 8:30am-5pm; Sept.-May Mon.-Fri. 8:30am-5pm. To reach a **ranger,** call 344-7381.

Emergency: 911.

Post Offices: Mammoth Hot Springs (334-7764), near the park headquarters. Open Mon.-Fri. 8:30am-5pm. **ZIP code:** 82190. In **West Yellowstone, MT,** 17 Madison Ave. (646-7704). Open Mon.-Fri. 8:30am-5pm. **ZIP code:** 59758. **Area codes:** 307 (in the park), 406 (in West Yellowstone and Gardiner). Unless otherwise listed, phone numbers have a 307 area code.

The bulk of Yellowstone National Park lies in the northwest corner of Wyoming, with slivers slicing into Montana and Idaho. **West Yellowstone, MT,** at the park's western entrance, and **Gardiner, MT,** at the northern entrance, are the most developed and expensive towns along the edge of the park. For a rustic stay, venture northeast to **Cooke City, MT.** The northeast entrance to the park leads to U.S. 212, a gorgeous stretch of road known as **Beartooth Highway,** which climbs to **Beartooth Pass** at 11,000 ft. and descends to **Red Lodge,** a former mining town. (Road open summer only because of heavy snowfall; ask at the chamber of commerce for exact dates.) The eastern entrance to the park from Cody is via Rte. 14/20. The southern entry to the park is through Grand Teton National Park.

The park's **entrance fee** is $10 for cars, $4 for pedestrians and bikers. The pass is good for one week at Yellowstone and Grand Teton National Parks.

Yellowstone's roads circulate its millions of visitors in a rough figure-eight configuration, with side roads branching off to park entrances and some of the lesser-known sites. The major natural wonders which make the park famous (e.g., Old Faithful) dot the Upper and Lower Loops. Construction and renovation of roads are planned for the next 80 years; call ahead to find out which sections will be closed during your visit…and your lifetime. It's unwise to bike or walk around the deserted roads at night, since you may risk startling large wild animals. The best time to see the roaming beasts is at dawn or dusk. When they're out, traffic stops and cars pull over. Approaching any wild animal at any time is illegal and extremely unsafe, and those who don't remain at least 25 yds. from moody and unpredictable bison or moose and 100 yds. from bears risk being mauled or gored to death. For more tips on avoiding fisticuffs with a bear, see Bear Necessities, p. 51. Near thermal areas, stay on marked trails, because "scalding water can ruin your vacation."

The park's high season extends from about June 15 to September 15. If you visit during this period expect large crowds, clogged roads, and motels and campsites filled to capacity.

ACCOMMODATIONS AND FOOD

Camping is far cheaper, but cabin-seekers will find many options within the park. Standard hotel and motel rooms for the nature-weary also abound, but if you plan to keep your budget in line, stick to the towns near the park's entry-points.

In the Park

TW Services (303-338-2751) controls all accommodations within the park with an iron fist, using a secret code for budget cabins: "Roughrider" means no bath, no facilities; "Economy" means with bath, somewhat furnished; "Eggplant Jello" means you are probably delirious. All cabins or rooms should be reserved well in advance of the June to September tourist season. Be very choosy when buying food in the park, as the restaurants, snack bars, and cafeterias are quite expensive. If possible, stick to the **general stores** at each lodging location (open daily 7:30am-10pm).

Old Faithful Inn and Lodge, near the west Yellowstone entrance. Pleasant Budget cabins with sink ($22), Economy cabins (toilet and sink, $34), and Frontier cabins ($38). Well-appointed hotel rooms from $47, with private bath $68.

Roosevelt Lodge, in the northwest corner. A favorite campsite of Teddy Roosevelt. Provides the cheapest and most scenic indoor accommodations around. Rustic shelters $24, each with a wood-burning stove (bring your own bedding and towel). Also Roughrider cabins ($27, bring your own towel) and more spacious "family" cabins with toilet ($41).

Mammoth Hot Springs, 18mi. west of Roosevelt area, near the north entrance. Unremarkable Budget cabins $34. Frontier cabins from $63.

Lake Yellowstone Hotel and Cabins, near the south entrance. Overpriced, but very close to the lake. Spacious, Frontier cabins $63.

Canyon Village, middle of the figure eight of the park loop. Less authentic and more expensive than Roosevelt Lodge's cabins, but slightly closer to the popular Old Faithful area. Frontier cabins $48. Roomier "Western" cabins $84.

West Yellowstone, MT

West Yellowstone International Hostel (AAIH/Rucksackers), 139 Yellowstone Ave. (406-646-7745 or 800-838-7745 outside MT), at the Madison Hotel and Motel. Friendly manager presides over old but clean, wood-adorned hotel. Hostel honors all memberships. Slightly crowded rooms; no kitchen. $15, nonmembers $17. Singles $24, with bath $37; doubles with bath $37-42. Rooms $2 cheaper in the spring. Open May 27 to mid-Oct.

Alpine Motel, 120 Madison (406-646-7544). Clean rooms with cable TV, a pool, and hand-crafted bed frames. Singles $44, doubles $47-59; off season $12 less.

Lazy G Motel, 123 Hayden St. (406-646-7586) has very pleasant, clean rooms. Singles $40, doubles $48.

Gardiner, MT

Located about 90 min. northeast of West Yellowstone, Gardiner served as the original entrance to the park and is smaller, more friendly, and less tacky than its neighbor. Pick a bundle of inexpensive food at **Food Farm,** 710 Scott St. W. (406-848-7524), across from the Super 8, or lasso some chow at the **Food Round-Up Grocery Store,** 107 Dunraven St. (406-646-7501), in W. Yellowstone. Right across from the park entrance, **Cecil's Fine Foods** offers 2 eggs, 2 pancakes, and 2 strips of bacon for $3.50.

The Town Café and Motel (406-848-7322), on Park St. across from the park's northern entrance. Pleasant, wood-paneled, carpeted rooms. TVs and baths but no showers or phones. Singles with kitchen $38, doubles $47.

Hillcrest Cottages (406-848-7353), on U.S. 89 near the crossing of the Yellowstone River. Singles with kitchen $45, doubles $56; $6 each additional adult, $3 each additional kid under 12.

Blue Haven Motel, on U.S. 89 (406-848-7719), has nice clean singles for $45 and doubles in private cabins for $50.

Cooke City, MT

Cooke City is located at the northeast corner of the park. The Nez Perce slipped right by the U.S. cavalry here (see graybox, p. 559), Lewis and Clark deemed the area impassable, and many tourists today still miss the mean plates of homefries, $4 soup-sandwich specials, and $3-6 breakfast combos at **Joan and Bill's Family Restaurant** (406-838-2280), at 214 Rte. 212 (open daily 6am-9:45pm).

After a day of tracking Yogi Bear, sniff out the bright, airy tent cabins at the **Yellowstone Yurt Hostel** (800-364-6242), at the corner of W. Broadway and Montana St., a quiet relief from the tourist traps which generally encrust the park. Cozy bunks, showers, and a kitchen are at your disposal for $10 a night. Check in before 9pm; call ahead if coming later. Ask about the shuttle to Bozeman, MT. You can also rest at the eastern end of town (there's only one street in Cooke, Rte. 212) at **Antler's Lodge** (406-838-2432), a renovated U.S. cavalry outpost where Teddy Roosevelt once stayed. (Singles $45, doubles $55; larger cabins for families equipped with kitchens from $60.)

CAMPING

Sites can be reserved at five of Yellowstone's 12 developed campgrounds. TW Recreational Services controls **Canyon, Grant Village, Madison** (all $12.50), and **Fishing Bridge RV** ($20). Reservations can be made up to a year in advance or on the same day (303-297-2757). **Bridge Bay Campground** (800-365-2267 or 619-452-5956) sits on treeless and non-scenic MISTIX turf, and accepts reservations up to eight weeks in advance for its 420 sites (open late May to mid-Sept.).

Seven campgrounds provide first come, first served sites ($8-12). During summer, most of these campgrounds fill by 10am. Arrive very early, especially on weekends and holidays. Bring a stove or plan to search for or buy firewood. Two of the most beautiful and tranquil areas are **Slough Creek Campground** (29 sites, 10mi. northeast of Tower Junction; open late May-Oct.) and **Pebble Creek Campground,** 36 sites, 15 mi. farther down the same road (no RVs; open mid-June to early Sept.). Both offer relatively uncrowded spots and have good fishing. You can also try **Canyon Village,** with 208 sites on pine-tree-laden Lewis Lake. **Indian Creek** (75 sites; open mid-June to mid-Sept.) and **Mammoth Campground** (85 sites; open year-round) campgrounds are none too scenic. Except for Mammoth, all camping areas close in winter. If all sites are full, try the $8 campgrounds outside the park in the **Area National Forests.** Good sites line U.S. 20, 287, 191, 89, and 212 (just out of Cooke City). These are often nearly empty—worth camping at even if there are spots open at Yellowstone. Call the Park Headquarters (344-7381) for info on any of Yellowstone's campgrounds.

The campgrounds at Grant, Fishing Bridge, and Canyon all have coin laundries and pay showers ($2, 50¢ for towel, 25¢ for soap). The lodges at Mammoth and Old Faithful have no laundry facilities but have showers for $2.

More than 95% (almost two million acres) of the park is backcountry. To venture overnight into the wilds of Yellowstone, you must obtain a free **wilderness permit** from a ranger station or visitors center. Pity the fool who doesn't consult a ranger before embarking on a trail. Rangers can give instructions on which trails and campgrounds you should avoid due to bears, ice, and other natural hindrances. Other backcountry regulations include sanitation rules, pet and firearms restrictions, campfire permits, and firewood rules. The more popular areas fill up in high season, but you can reserve a permit in person up to 48 hr. in advance; campfire permits are not required, but ask if fires at your site are allowed.

SIGHTS AND ACTIVITIES

For mountains of cash, **TW Services** will sell you tours, horseback rides, and chuckwagon dinners until the cows come home. But given enough time, your eyes and feet will do a better job than TW's tours, and you won't have to sell your firstborn. The main attractions all feature informative self-guiding tour pamphlets with maps (25¢). All are accessible from the road by wooden or paved walkways, usually extending ¼ to 1½ mi. through the various natural phenomena. All of the walkways are partially wheelchair-accessible, until they connect with longer hiking trails.

Like spaghetti sauce on a very hot range, where steam pressure builds up at the bottom and explodes through the surface, ruining your shirt, groundwater is superheated by rocks and explodes through holes in the earth's crust in the form of a **geyser.** The geysers that made Yellowstone famous are clustered on the western side of the park near the West Yellowstone entrance. The duration of the explosion depends on how much water is in the hole and the heat of the steam. **Old Faithful,** while neither the largest, the highest, nor the most regular geyser, is certainly the most photographed; it gushes in the **Upper Geyser Basin,** 16 mi. south of **Madison Junction** where the entry road splits north-south. Since its discovery in 1870, this granddaddy of geysers has consistently erupted with a whoosh of spray and steam (5000-8000 gallons worth) every 30 to 120 min. Enjoy other geysers (as well as elk) in the surrounding **Firehole Valley.** Swimming in any hot springs or geysers is prohibited, but you can swim in the **Firehole River,** three-quarters of the way up Firehole Canyon Dr. (turn south just after Madison Jct.), or in the **Boiling River,** 2½ mi. north of Mammoth, which is not really hot enough to cook ramen, let alone pasta. Never swim alone, and always beware of strong currents.

From Old Faithful, take the easy 1½-mi. walk to **Morning Glory Pool,** a park favorite, or head 8 mi. north to the **Lower Geyser Basin,** where examples of all four types of geothermal activity (geysers, mudpots, hot springs, and fumaroles) steam, bubble, and spray together in a cacophonous symphony. Farther north, 14 mi. past Madison, is the **Norris Geyser Basin,** the setting for **Echinus,** a park gem. About every hour, this geyser slowly mounts its furious display from a clear basin of water. Its neighbor, **Steamboat,** is the largest geyser in the world, topping 400 feet and erupting for up to 20 minutes. Its huge emissions used to occur about once a year. Lately, this steamer has been tooting on an erratic schedule—its last enormous eruption occurred on October 2, 1991.

Whether you're waiting for geysers to erupt or watching them shoot skyward, don't go too close, as the crust of earth around a geyser is only 2 ft. thick, and the Surgeon General has determined that falling into a boiling sulfuric pit *may* be hazardous to your health. Pets are not allowed in the basin. Check out the squirrel-type animals roaming around without much fur to understand why.

Shifting water sources, malleable limestone deposits, and temperature-sensitive, multicolored bacterial growth create the most rapidly changing natural structure in the park, the hot spring terraces at **Mammoth Hot Springs,** 20 mi. to the north. Ask a local ranger where the most active springs are on the day of your visit. Also ask about area trails, which feature some of the park's best wildlife viewing.

The east side's featured attraction, the **Grand Canyon of the Yellowstone,** wears rusty red-orange colors created by hot water acting on the volcanic rock. For a close-up view of the mighty Lower Falls, hike down the short but steep **Uncle Tom's Trail.** To survey the canyon from a broader vista, try **Artist Point** on the southern rim or **Lookout Point** on the northern rim. All along the canyon's 19-mi. rim, keep an eye out for bighorn sheep. At dawn or dusk, the bear-viewing area (at the intersection of Northern Rim and Tower roads) should be loaded with opportunities to dust off your binoculars.

Yellowstone Lake, 16 mi. south of the Canyon's rim at the southeastern corner of the park, contains tons o' trout but requires a Yellowstone **fishing permit,** available at visitors centers. ($5 per week, ages 12-15 free; under 12 may fish without a permit.) Catch a few and have the chef fry them for you in the Lake Yellowstone Hotel Dining Room. Some other lakes and streams allow catch-and-release fishing only. The **Hamilton Store** (242-7326), at Bridge Bay Dock, rents spinning rods ($7.50 per day, $20 deposit; open late May to mid-Sept. daily 7:30am-9pm). The expensive **Lake Yellowstone Hotel,** built in 1891 and renovated in 1989, merits a visit, if only for the magnificent view of the lake through the lobby's large windows. Walks around the lake are scenic and serene, not strenuous. Nearby **Mud Volcano,** close to Yellowstone Lake, features seething, warping sulfuric earth as well as the **Dragon's Mouth,** a vociferous steaming hole that early explorers reportedly heard all the way from Yellowstone River. You certainly can smell it from that far away.

Over 1200 mi. of trails crisscross the park, but many are poorly marked. Rangers of any visitor center are glad to recommend an array of **hikes** in their specific area for explorers of all levels. Most of the spectacular sights in the park are accessible by car, but only a hike will get you up close and personal with the multilayered petrified forest of **Specimen Ridge** and the geyser basins at **Shoshone** and **Heart Lake. Cascade Corner,** in the southwest, is a lovely area accessible by trails from Bechler. The already spectacular view from the summit of **Mt. Washburn,** between the **Canyon** and **Tower** areas, is enhanced when surveyed from the telescope inside the old fire lookout station. The **North Trail** is a mild incline; the **South Trail** is steeper. Trails in the **Tower-Roosevelt** area in the northeast of the park provide some of the most abundant wildlife watching. When planning a hike, pick up a topographical trail map ($7) at any visitors center and ask a ranger to describe forks in the trail. Allow yourself extra time (at least 1hr. per day) in case you lose the trail.

Federal Wolf Packs

In January 1995, after years of public debate, the federal government began to reintroduce gray wolves into the greater Yellowstone ecosystem. Before the program, the last known wolves in Yellowstone were killed in 1929 as part of a federally funded bounty hunt to eradicate the predators. Local and state response to the federal initiative has been mixed. Many ranchers have violently denounced the reappearance of wolves, fearing the wolves will kill livestock. Others hail the program as the first step in a return to a complete ecosystem. Montana's State Senate and House of Representatives responded with a caustic joint resolution that made their position clear: "Now, therefore, be it resolved that if the United States government is successful in its efforts to reintroduce wolves into the Yellowstone Park ecosystem, the U.S. Congress be urged to take the steps necessary to ensure that wolves are also reintroduced into every other ecosystem and region of the United States, including Central Park in New York City, the Presidio in San Francisco, and Washington, D.C."

ROCKY MOUNTAINS

■ Grand Teton

When French fur trappers first peered into Wyoming's wilderness from the eastern border of Idaho, they found themselves facing three craggy peaks, each over 12,000 ft. In an attempt to make the rugged landscape seem more trapper-friendly, they dubbed the mountains "Les Trois Tetons," French for "the three tits." When they found that these triple nipples had numerous smaller companions, they named the entire range "Les Grands Tetons." Today the snowy heights of **Grand Teton National Park** delight hikers and nature lovers with miles of strenuous trails. The less adventurous will appreciate the rugged appearance of the Tetons; the lofty pinnacles and glistening glaciers are just as impressive when viewed from the valley.

PRACTICAL INFORMATION

Tourist Offices: Moose (733-3399), Teton Park Rd. at the southern tip of the park. Open June to early Sept. daily 8am-7pm; early Sept. to late April daily 8am-5pm; May daily 8am-6pm. **Jenny Lake** (739-3392), next to the Jenny Lake Campground. Open June to early Sept. daily 8am-7pm. **Colter Bay** (739-3594), on Jackson Lake in the north part of the park. Open early June to early Sept. daily 8am-8pm; May and early Sept. to early Oct. 8am-5pm. Stop by the Moose Visitors Center (or Colter Bay if you're coming from Yellowstone) to pick up the free *Teewinot* newspaper at the entrance or at the visitors center for a gold mine of info about hiking trails, camping, and facilities. For general info contact the **Park Headquarters** (739-3600 or 733-3300) or write Superintendent Grand Teton National Park, P.O. Drawer 170, Moose 83012. Office at the Moose Visitors Center.
Park Information and Weather and Road Conditions: 733-3611. 24-hr. recording. **Wyoming Highway Info Center,** 733-3316 (winter only).
Medical Services: Grand Teton Medical Clinic, Jackson Lake Lodge (543-2514, after hours 733-8002), near the Chevron. Open late May to mid-Oct. daily 10am-6pm. **St. John's Hospital** (733-3636), in Jackson.
Emergency: 911 or Sheriff's office (733-2331) or park dispatch (739-3300).
Post Office: In Moose (733-3336), across from the Park HQ. Open Mon.-Fri. 9am-1pm and 1:30-5pm, Sat. 11am-12:30pm. **ZIP code:** 83012. **Area code:** 307.

The national park occupies most of the space between Jackson to the south and Yellowstone National Park to the north. **Rockefeller Pkwy.** runs the length of the valley between the Gros Ventre Mountains and the Tetons, connecting the two parks. The parkway offers dramatic views of the entire length of the Tetons. At dusk, moose, elk, and other big game are visible from the road. The park is accessible from all directions except the west, as those poor French trappers found out centuries ago. The park **entrance fee** is $10 per car, $4 per pedestrian or bicycle, $5 per family (non-motorized), under 16 (non-motorized) free. The pass is good for 7 days in both the Tetons and Yellowstone. There are several recreational areas; the most developed is **Colter Bay,** the most beautiful is **Jenny Lake.** These areas and their surrounding trailheads are excellent places to begin exploring the Tetons.

CAMPING

To stay in the Tetons without emptying your savings account, find a tent and pitch it; call 739-3603 for camping info. The park service maintains five campgrounds, all first come, first served. Vehicle sites are $10, bicycle group campsites $2, golden age discount $5. Maximum length of stay is 14 days at all sites except for Jenny Lake (7 day maximum). All have restrooms, cold water, fire rings, dump stations, and picnic tables. RVs are welcome in all but the Jenny Lake area, but there are no hookups. Large groups can go to Colter Bay and Gros Ventre; all others allow a maximum of six people and one vehicle per site. The 50 quiet, woodsy sites at Jenny Lake are among the most beautifully developed in the U.S. Mt. Teewnot towers over 6000 ft. above tents pitched in the pine forest at the edge of Jenny Lake. These sites often fill before 8 or 9am; get there early. **Lizard Creek,** closer to Yellowstone than the Tetons, has

60 spacious, secluded sites along the northern shore of Jackson Lake. The campsite fills up by about 2pm. **Colter Bay,** the most crowded campsite, with 310 sites, $2 showers, a grocery store, a laundromat, and two restaurants, is usually full by noon. At **Signal Mountain,** a few miles south of Colter Bay, the 86 sites are a bit more roomy than at Colter Bay, and are usually full by 10am. **Gros Ventre** is the biggest campsite (372 sites, 5 group sites) located along the edge of the Gros Ventre River at the southern border of the park, convenient to Jackson. Because the Tetons are hidden behind Elephant Butte, this campsite rarely fills and is the best bet for late arrivals. Reservations are required for camping groups.

For **backcountry camping,** reserve a spot in a camping zone in a mountain canyon or on the shores of a lake by submitting an itinerary from January 1 to May 15 to the **permit office,** Grand Teton National Park, Moose HQ, Attn: Permits, P.O. Box 170, Moose 83012. For more info, call 739-3309. Still, two-thirds of all spots are available first come, first served; get a permit up to 24 hr. before setting out at the Moose, Colter Bay, or Jenny Lake visitors center. Camping is unrestricted in some off-trail backcountry areas (though you must have a permit). Wood fires are not permitted above 7000 ft. in the backcountry and are generally not permitted at lower elevations either; be sure to check with rangers before singing 'round the campfire. Snow often remains into July at high elevation campsites and the weather can become severe (deadly to those unprepared for it) any time of the year. Be sure to take severe weather gear.

ACCOMMODATIONS AND FOOD

The Grand Teton Lodge Co. (543-3100 or 800-628-9988 outside WY) runs both of the Colter Bay accommodations, which are open late May to early October. **Colter Bay Tent Cabins** (543-2855) are the cheapest, but you don't want to be here when the temperature drops. You might as well camp if you have a tent; the "cabins" are canvas shelters with dusty floors, wood-burning stoves, tables, and four-person bunks. Sleeping bags, wood, and ice chests are available for rent. The tent cabins are $24 and include four cots. Restrooms and $2 showers nearby. The office is open 24 hr. daily June to early Sept. **Colter Bay Log Cabins** (543-2855) maintains 208 quaint log cabins near Jackson Lake. (Cabins with semi-private bath, sleeping two start at $29, with private bath start at $58, two room cabins with bath $79-99. Open mid-May to late Sept.) Friendly staff gives good recommendations about local hikes and excursions. Reservations are recommended. Make them up to a year in advance for any Grand Teton Lodge establishment by writing to: Reservations Manager, Grand Teton Lodge Co., P.O. Box 240, Moran 83013. Deposits are often required.

The best way to eat in the Tetons is to bring your own grub. Non-perishables are available at **Dornan's Grocery** in Moose (733-2415; open daily 8am-8pm, in winter 8am-6pm), or at **Colter Bay Village General Store.** In Jackson, stock up on provisions at **Albertson's** supermarket (733-5950; open daily 6am-midnight), on Broadway about ½ mi. south of downtown Jackson. Grab a reasonably priced burger at the **Colter Bay Grill** (543-2811; open daily 6:30am-10pm).

SIGHTS AND ACTIVITIES

While Yellowstone wows visitors with geysers and mudpots, Grand Teton's geology boasts some of the most scenic mountains in the U.S., if not the world. The youngest mountain range in North America, the Tetons stand alone, almost without foothills, providing hikers, climbers, and rafters with vistas not found in more weathered peaks. Enjoy the views from hiking trails, or if you're an experienced mountaineer, from the top of the Grand Teton itself, 13,771 ft. above sea level.

Jenny Lake's tranquility overcomes the steady tramp of its many visitors. The 2-mi. trail around the lake is gorgeous and relatively flat, and it leads to the **Cascade Canyon Trail.** The **Hidden Falls Waterfall** is located ½ mi. up the Cascade Canyon Trail. Hikers with more stamina can continue upwards towards inspiration point (another ¾ mi.) but only the lonely can trek 6¾ mi. further to **Lake Solitude,** which stands alone at 9,035 ft. Before hitting the trail or planning extended hikes, be sure to check in at the Ranger Station as trails at higher elevations may still be snow-covered. Prime hiking season does not begin until well into July during years with heavy snow.

Teton Boating (733-2703) shuttles across Jenny Lake every 20 min. (8am-6pm, $4 round-trip, 7-12 $2.25, under 7 free). Taking the boat cuts 4 mi. off the round-trip hike to the falls. Scenic cruises are offered hourly 10am-2pm ($7.50, children $4.50). They also rent boats ($10 for the first hr., $7 per additional hr., $45 per day). Free trail guides are available near the visitors center at the trailhead.

Other **hiking trails** abound. The 4-mi. walk from Colter Bay to **Hermitage Point** is popular for the scope of wildlife it encounters. Leave the crowds behind and hike the **Amphitheater Lake Trail,** beginning just south of Jenny Lake at the Lupine Meadows parking lot, which takes you 4.8 breathtaking miles to one of the park's glacial lakes. Those who were bighorn sheep in past lives can butt horns with **Static Peak Divide,** a steep 15-mi. trail up 4020 ft. from the Death Canyon trailhead (4½ mi. south of Moose visitors center), which offers some of the best lookouts in the park. All visitors centers provide pamphlets about the day hikes and sell the *Teton Trails* guide ($5). **National Park Tours** (733-4325) offers tours as well. (Open 7am-9pm. Prices vary greatly depending on where you want to start. Reservations required.)

Stop by **Adventure Sports** (733-3307), at Dornan's in Moose, to rent equipment for the mountains. They also give good advice on where to bike around the Tetons. No bikes are allowed on the trails in Teton National Park. (Open daily 9am-6pm. Credit card or deposit required.) **Fish-Moose** (733-3699), next to Venture Sports, rents spinning rods for $10 per day. (Adult mountain bikes $6 per hr., $24 per day; kids $4/$12; includes helmet. Open late May to mid-Sept. daily 8am-6pm.) **Mostly Seconds** (733-7176), in Jackson on 150 E. Broadway, rents crampons for $10 per day and ice axes for $6 per day. They also sell factory seconds of parkas and mountaineering wear. **Exum Mt. Guides** (733-2297) or **Jackson Hole Mt. Guides** (733-4979) offer four-day climbing trips to the top of Grand Teton. These trips include instruction, food, lodging, and necessary equipment ($500 for the whole shebang).

For a leisurely afternoon on Jackson Lake, **Signal Mountain Marina** (543-2831) rents boats. (Rowboats and canoes $8 per hr., $30 for 4hr., $55 for 8hr.; motorboats $15/$60/$100; water-ski boats $45/$150/$220 plus gas and oil; pontoons $40/$125/$175. Open daily early May to mid-Oct. 8am-7pm.) **Colter Bay Marina** has a somewhat smaller variety of boats at similar prices (open daily 8am-6pm). **Grand Teton Lodge Co.** (733-2811 or 543-2811) can also take you on scenic Snake River float trips (no whitewater) within the park (10½-mi. ½-day trip $31, ages 6-11 $16; with lunch $36/$26; with supper $42/$32). **Triangle X Float Trips** (733-5500) can float you on a 5-mi. river trip for less cost ($20, under 13 $15, gratuity not included). **Fishing** in the park's lakes, rivers, and streams is excellent. A Wyoming license ($5) is required; get one in Jackson, Moose General Store, Signal Mt., Colter Bay, Flagg Ranch, or Dornan's. **Horseback riding** is available through the Grand Teton Lodge Co. (1-5hr. rides; $17-45 per person).

The **American Indian Art Museum** (739-3594), in the Colter Bay Visitors Center, offers a private collection of Native American artwork, artifacts, movies, and workshops (open daily 8am-5pm; free). During July and August you can see Cheyenne, Cherokee, Apache, and Sioux dances at Jackson Lake Lodge (Fri. 8:30pm). At the **Moose** and **Colter Bay Visitors Centers,** rangers lead a variety of activities aimed at educating visitors about such subjects as the ecology, geology, wildlife, and history of the Tetons. Activities go on June through Sept.; for exact times, check the *Teewinot,* a free magazine available at the visitors centers.

In the **winter** all hiking trails and the unploughed sections of Teton Park Road are open to **cross-country skiers.** Pick up the trail map *Winter in the Tetons* or the *Teewinot* at the Moose Visitors Center. Naturalists lead **snowshoe hikes** from the Moose Visitors Center (739-3300; Jan.-Mar.; snowshoes distributed free; call for reservations). **Snowmobiling** along the park's well-powdered trails and up into Yellowstone is a noisy but popular winter activity; grab a map and guide at the Jackson Chamber of Commerce. For about $100 per day, you can rent snowmobiles at **Signal Mt.**

Lodge, Flagg Ranch Village, or in **Jackson;** an additional $10 registration fee is required for all snowmobile use in the park. A well-developed snowmobile trail runs from Moran to Flagg Ranch and numerous other snowmobiling opportunities exist in the valley. The Colter Bay and Moose parking lots are available for parking in the winter. All **campgrounds** close in winter, but **backcountry snow camping** (only for those who know what they're doing) is allowed with a free permit from the Moose Visitors Center. Before making plans consider that temperatures regularly drop below -20°F. Be sure to carry high-tech extreme weather clothing and check with a ranger station for current weather conditions (many early trappers froze to death in the 10-ft. drifts) and avalanche danger, and let them know where you're going.

■ Jackson

Jackson Hole—called a hole rather than a valley due to the high elevation of the surrounding mountains—describes the area bounded by the Teton and Gros Ventre ranges. Nearby Jackson is a ski village gone ballistic: its downtown streets are lined with Gucci, Ralph Lauren, and Polo shops, chic restaurants, and faux-western bars. Home to 5000 permanent residents, a dynamic mix of money and energy, international tourists and locals, people watchers and nature lovers, Jackson is a truly cosmopolitan place. Although a sliver of the area's beauty can be seen from town, striking out into the nearby Tetons or onto the Snake River—whether by foot, boat, horse, or llama—yields a richer experience.

PRACTICAL INFORMATION

Tourist Office: Jackson Hole Area Chamber of Commerce and Wyoming Information Center, 532 N. Cache St. (733-3316), in a modern, wooden split-level with grass on the roof. A crucial info stop. Open daily 8am-5pm. **Bridger-Teton National Forest Headquarters,** 340 N. Cache St. (739-5500), 2 blocks south of the Chamber of Commerce. Offers camping and hiking information, nature books, and paper maps ($3.75, waterproof $5). Open Mon. 8am-4:30pm, Tues.-Fri. 8am-5:30pm, Sat. 9am-5:30pm; late Sept. to late May Mon.-Fri. 8:30am-4:30pm.

Tours: Grayline Tours, 332 N. Glenwood St. (733-4325). Seven hour tours of Grand Teton National Park ($36) and 10 hr. tour of Yellowstone National Park's lower loop ($39). Call for reservations. Tour picks up at hotels. Office takes calls 9am-9pm.

Public Transportation: Jackson START (733-4521). $1 per ride, $2 outside of town limits; free for over 65 and under 9. **Grand Teton Lodge Co.** (733-2811) runs six shuttles per day in the summer, from Colter Bay to Jackson Lake Lodge ($2.50 each way).

Car Rental: Rent-A-Wreck, 1050 U.S. 89 (733-5014). $23-59 per day, $138-310 per week; 150 free mi. per day, 1000 free mi. weekly, 20¢ each additional mi. Must be 21 with credit card; under 25 need credit card or $300 cash deposit. Must stay within 500 mi. of Jackson. Open daily 8am-6pm.

Equipment Rental: Hoback Sports, 40 S. Millward (733-5335). A complete, professional outdoor sports store. Mountain bikes $15 for 4hr., $25 for 24hr.; lower rates for longer rentals. Skis, boots, and poles $13 per ½ day, $16 per day. Open peak summer daily 9am-7pm; peak winter daily 8am-9pm; off season daily 9am-7pm. Must have driver's license or credit card.

Weather and Road Conditions: Weather Line, 733-1731. 24-hr. recording. **Road Information,** Nov.-April 733-9966, outside WY 800-442-7850.

Crisis Lines: Rape Crisis Line, 733-7466.

Emergency: 911.

Post Office: (733-3650), corner of Powderhorn and Maple Way (1 block from McDonalds). Open Mon.-Fri. 8:30am-5pm, Sat. 10am-1pm. **ZIP code:** 83001. **Area code:** 307.

The southern route into Jackson, U.S. 191/I-80, becomes W. Broadway. The highway continues along Broadway, becoming Cache St. as it veers north into Grand Teton Park and eventually reaches Yellowstone, 70 mi. to the north. The intersection of Broadway and Cache St. at **Town Square Park** marks the center of town. The Jackson Hole ski resort draws snow bunnies to **Teton Village,** 12 mi. to the north via Rte. 22 and Teton Village Rd. The scenic Moose-Wilson Rd. connects the town of Wilson (at Rte. 22) with Teton Village and the Moose visitor area of Teton National Park; part of the road is unpaved and closed in the winter.

ACCOMMODATIONS AND CAMPING

Jackson's constant influx of tourists ensures that if you don't book ahead, rooms will be small and expensive at best and non-existent at worst. Fortunately, you can sleep affordably in one of two local hostels. **The Hostel X,** P.O. Box 546, Teton Village 83025 (733-3415), near the ski slopes 12 mi. northwest of Jackson, is a budgetary oasis among the wallet-parching condos and lodges of Teton Village and a favorite of skiers because of its location. It has a game room, TV room, ski waxing room, nursery room, and nightly ski movies in the winter. Accommodations range from dorm-style rooms to private rooms. (4 beds in dorm rooms. In summer honors HI-AYH cards. $35 for 1-2, nonmembers $38 for 1-2, $48 for 3-4. In winter, no member discount, $44 for 1-2, $56 for 3-4.) **The Bunkhouse,** 215 N. Cache St. (733-3668), in the basement of the Anvil Motel, has a lounge, kitchenette, laundromat, ski storage, and, as the name implies, one large but quiet sleeping room with comfortable bunks ($15). **The Pioneer,** 325 N. Cache St. (733-3673), is a good deal during the spring. In the summer, it offers lovely rooms with teddy bears and stupendous hand-made quilts (singles peak at $90 in July; off peak $45/$50).

While it doesn't offer scenery, Jackson's campground, the **Wagon Wheel Village,** 435 N. Cache St. (733-4588), welcomes tents and RVs on a first come, first served basis (8 tent sites $18; 38 RV sites $25 with full hookup; 25¢ showers). **KOA Kampground at Teton Village** (733-5354), on Teton Village Rd. 1 mi. south of Teton Village, offers shaded sites with a view of the Teton Range. 50 tent sites ($23), 150 RV sites ($23 no hookup, $30 full hookup), free showers and laundry machines available. Cheaper and more pleasant surroundings are available in the **Bridger-Teton National Forest** (800-342-2267) surrounding Jackson. Stop at Bridger-Teton Forest Headquarters for information about the sites and then drive toward Alpine Junction on U.S. 26/89 to find spots. (Sites $5-8 for one vehicle, water available at most sites, no showers.)

FOOD

The Bunnery, 130 N. Cache St. (733-5474), in the "Hole-in-the-Wall" mall, has hearty breakfasts. Two eggs, homefries, chili, cheese, and sprouts go for $6.25, and lunch sandwiches cost $5-6 (open daily 7am-3pm; late May to mid-Sept. 5:30pm-9pm). **Café a Mano,** 45 S. Glenwood (739-2500), offers excellent Mexican food with a chic twist. Sample the salsa bar and enjoy a shrimp burrito ($7). Chow down on barbecued chicken and spare ribs ($8) at the colorful and popular **Bubba's,** 515 W. Broadway (733-2288). They don't take reservations, so come early (open daily 7am-9pm). What **LeJay's 24 Hour Sportsmen Café** (733-3110), at the corner of Glenwood and Pearl, lacks in legitimate athletes, it makes up for in a good, cheap, and filling menu (burgers and sandwiches with fries $3-6; breakfast including 2 pancakes, 2 eggs, bacon, sausage, and coffee $5), and a lively, wrangler-meets-bohemian atmosphere (open 24hr...duh). At ½ pound each, muffins ($1.50-2) come fully loaded at **Bomber's Bump N' Grind** (739-2295) in the Grand Teton Plaza. (Sandwiches $4-6. Open Mon. 6:30am-3pm, Tues.-Fri. 6:30am-10pm, Sat. 7am-10pm, Sun. 7am-3pm.) For fresh, tasty bagels, latté, and a light menu of salads and sandwiches, seek out **Pearl St. Bagels,** 145 W. Pearl St. (739-1218; open daily 6:30am-6pm) at the corner of Glenwood and Pearl. Under the pteranodon, sit back with steak 'n potatoes and appreciate cowboy yodeling at the **Bar J Chuckwagon** (733-3370) supper and western show on Teton

Village Rd., 1 mi. from Rte. 22 ($13, under 8 $4.50, lap-sized free; opens 5:30pm, dinner show at 7:30pm).

OUTDOOR ADVENTURES

Whitewater rafting draws over 100,000 city slickers and backwoods folk to Jackson between May 15 and Labor Day. **Lone Eagle Expeditions** (377-1090 or 800-321-3800) is one of the best deals available among the myriad whitewater outfitters in Jackson. $24 buys a 3 hr., 8 mi. whitewater rafting trip, a hot meal, and free access to the company's hot tub, heated pool, and hot showers after the trip. **Mad River Boat Trips,** 1060 S. U.S. 89 (733-6203 or 800-458-7238) 25 mi. from Jackson, was the whitewater consultant for *A River Runs Through It.* A 3-hr., 8-mi. raft trip is $21 at 9am or 3pm. They also offer a steak dinner trip which takes 4 hr., leaves at 4pm, and costs $29. Cheaper thrills include a lift up to the summit of **Rendezvous Peak** at 10,450 ft. (Tram runs from May 24-June 14 and in Sept. 9am-5pm, June 15-Sept. 2 9am-7pm. $15, seniors $13, 13-17 $7.) The tram offers a great view of the Tetons and provides access to the Teton Crest trail without the climb to the top. Ride the **Snow King Chairlift** (733-5200) to the top of Snow King Mountain (7751 ft.) for a bird's eye view of Jackson and a great view of the Tetons. In winter, the **Jackson Hole Ski Resort** (733-2292) at Teton Village offers a huge 4139-ft. vertical drop, dry Wyoming powder, open bowls, tree skiing, and some of the best extreme skiing in the west. **Corbet's Couloir** is one of the steepest chutes accessible by lift in the U.S. ($45, $34 seniors and under 14). Right above the town of Jackson **Snow King** offers convenient skiing (1571-ft. drop; $25, $16 seniors and under 14).

ENTERTAINMENT AND NIGHTLIFE

Cultural activities in Jackson fall into two camps—rowdy, foot-stomping Western celebrations and more sedate presentations of music and art. Every summer evening (except Sunday), at 6:30pm, the Town Sq. at the corner of Broadway and Cache, hosts a kitschy episode of the **Longest-Running Shoot-Out in the World.** On Friday evenings at 6:30pm, you can do-si-do and swing your partner at the **Teton Twirlers Square Dance** (733-3316), on Snow King Rd. in the fair building on the rodeo grounds ($2.50). At the end of May, the town celebrates the opening of the **Jackson Hole Rodeo** (733-2805; open Memorial Day-Labor Day Wed. and Sat. 8pm; tickets $7). The **Grand Teton Music Festival** (733-1128) features some of the world's best orchestras from early July to late August. Festival orchestra concerts Fri. and Sat. at 8pm are $30; chamber music concerts Tues., Wed., and Thurs. at 8pm are $18; orchestra open rehearsal Thurs. at 9:30am is $5 (student discount 50%). On Memorial Day, the town bursts its britches as tourists, locals, and nearby Native American tribes pour in for the dances and parades of **Old West Days.** In the second half of September, the **Jackson Hole Fall Arts Festival** attracts crafters, painters, dancers, actors, and musicians to town. Learn the fine points of brewing from the knowledgeable owner of **Otto Brothers Brewery** (733-9000), in downtown Wilson on North St. Free tours include a sample of his unique homemade products, such as "Moose Juice Stout." This is Jackson's oldest brewery. (Open Mon.-Fri. 8am-8pm, Sat.-Sun. 4-8pm.)

The **Mangy Moose** (733-4913), in Teton Village at the base of Jackson Hole Ski Resort, is the quintessential aprés-ski bar. Moose racks and skis line the wooden walls, contrasting with the bright ski parkas of the patrons. Live music daily. Dinner is somewhat expensive (over $10; dinner daily 5:30-10:30pm, bar open 10pm-2am). Thursday brings popular disco night to tiny Wilson at the **Stagecoach Bar** (733-4407) on Rte. 22. Shed your sequins (or wear them again) and don a cowboy hat for the country music dancing on Sunday. A good selection of microbrews and a mix of locals and visitors make this an authentic Western bar. (Open Mon.-Sat. 10am-2am, Sun. noon-10pm.) For local ales, head to one of the most popular bars in the area, **Jackson Hole Pub and Brewery,** 265 Millward St. (739-BEER/2337), Wyoming's first brew-pub; the "Zonkers Stout" will put hair on your chest (pints $3, pitchers $10), while the pasta, sandwiches, and pizzas ($7-12) will fill your tummy (open Mon.-Thurs. until midnight, Fri.-Sat. until 1am, Sun. until 10pm). Western saddles serve as bar stools at the **Million Dollar Cowboy Bar,** 25 N. Cache St. (733-2207), Town Sq. This Jackson institution, attracting few locals or real cowboys, clearly caters to tourists. Still, you gotta see those saddle seats to believe 'em. (Live music Mon.-Sat. 9pm-2am. Cover $3-10 after 8pm. Open Mon.-Sat. 10am-2am, Sun. noon-10pm.)

■ Bighorn Mountains

The Bighorns erupt from the hilly pasture land of northern Wyoming, a dramatic backdrop to the grazing cattle, sprawling ranch houses, and valleys full of wildflowers. Visitors can hike through the woods or follow **scenic highways U.S. 14** and **U.S. 16** to waterfalls, layers of prehistoric rock, and views above the clouds. The **Medicine Wheel** on U.S. 14A is an ancient stone formation at 10,000 ft. dating from around 1300 A.D. For sheer solitude, poke your head above **Cloud Peak Wilderness** in the **Bighorn National Forest.** To get to Cloud Peak, a 13,175-ft. summit in the range, most hikers enter at **West Tensleep,** accessible from the town of Tensleep on the western slope, 55 mi. west of Buffalo on U.S. 16. Tensleep was so named because it took the Sioux 10 sleeps to travel from there to their main winter camps. You must register at major trailheads to enter the Cloud Peak area. The most convenient access to the wilderness area is from the trailheads near U.S. 16, 25 mi. west of Buffalo. From the **Hunter Corrals** trailhead, move to beautiful **Seven Brothers Lake,** an ideal base for dayhikes into the high peaks beyond. You can also enter the wilderness area from U.S. 14 from **Sheridan** in the north. Check with a forest office to find out about more out-of-the-way treks, and always check on local conditions with a ranger before any hike.

Campgrounds fill the forest (sites $8-10). Near the Buffalo entrance, **Middle Fork** has nine first come, first served sites (15mi. from Buffalo on U.S. 16; open mid-May to late Sept.), while **Lost Cabin,** 28 mi. from Buffalo on U.S. 16, furnishes 14 sites with water and toilets (14-day max. stay; 800-280-CAMP/2267; open mid-May to late Oct.). Both boast magnificent scenery. You can spend one night free just off Coffeen St. in Sheridan's grassy **Washington Park.** Camping is also available along the Bighorn River at Afterbay, Two Leggins, Bighorn, and Mallard's Landing.

■ Cody

William F. "Buffalo Bill" Cody was more than a Pony Express rider, scout, hunter, and sportsman. He also started "Buffalo Bill's Wild West Show," an extravaganza that catapulted the image of the cowboy into the world's imagination. Cody's show traveled all over the U.S. and Europe, attracting the attention of royalty and statesmen. Founded in 1896 by Cody, this "wild west" town is now a veritable tourist trap.

Cody lies at the junction of Rte. 120 and 14. The town's main street is **Sheridan Ave.** Otherwise, the streets running east-west have names, those running north-south are numbered. The **chamber of commerce,** 836 Sheridan Ave. (587-2297), can give

---

The World's Biggest Hot Tub

Smack-dab in the middle of Wyoming, **Thermopolis** is home to the most voluminous hot springs in the world. At the renowned "Big Spring," which is only as wide as a large hot tub, you can look down at least 100 feet into the aquamarine water. Local legend has it that when a ball and chain was lowered down into the spring, the bottom couldn't be found. In order to preserve the springs, no swimming is allowed in the natural pools. Who would want to soak in 135°F water reeking of sulfur anyway? But swimmers, soakers, and sliders can take their respective pleasures after all: some of the boiling hot water is mixed with icy cold water and pumped onto giant waterslides and into pools at **The Star Plunge** (864-3771), next to the natural springs ($7; open daily 9am-9pm). The whole shebang happens at the junction of U.S. 20 and Rte. 120.

you the lowdown (open Mon.-Sat. 8am-7pm, Sun. 10am-3pm). Cody's **post office:** 1301 Stampede Ave. (527-7161; open Mon.-Fri. 8am-5:30pm, Sat. 9am-noon). **ZIP code:** 82414. **Area code:** 307.

The **Buffalo Bill Historical Center,** 720 Sheridan Ave. (587-4771), is known affectionately as the "Smithsonian of the West" and composed of four museums under one roof. **The Buffalo Bill Museum** documents the life of you-know-who; the **Whitney Gallery of Western Art** shows off Western paintings, including a few Russells and Remingtons; the **Plains Indian Museum** contains several exhibits about its namesake group; and the **Cody Firearms Museum** shows off rifles that the white man brought here—the world's largest collection of American firearms. (Open June-Aug. daily 7am-8pm, May and Sept. 8am-8pm, Oct. 8am-5pm, March and Nov. Tues.-Sun. 10am-3pm, April Tues.-Sun. 8am-5pm. $8, students 13-21 $4, seniors $6.50, ages 6-12 $2, under 5 free. Tickets good for two consecutive days.) From June through August, Cody turns into "The Rodeo Capital of the World" with one every night at 8:30 (587-5155; tickets $7-9, ages 7-12 $4-6). On July 2nd, 3rd, and 4th the **Cody Stampede** rough-rides on into town (587-5155, $11). For free fun without the bullshit, drive about 6 mi. west on Rte. 20/14/16 toward Yellowstone and see the mighty **Buffalo Bill Dam** (325ft.), which was the highest dam in the world at the time of its completion in 1910. Go **rafting** on the Shoshone—a variety of trips are offered, from 2 hr. ($18) to ½ a day ($45). To make arrangements, call **River Runners,** 1491 Sheridan Ave. (800-535-7238) or **Wyoming River Trips** (800-586-6661), at Rte. 120 and 14 (both open May-Sept.).

Rates go up in the summertime, but a strip of reasonable motels lines **W. Yellowstone Ave.** The **Pawnee Hotel,** 1032 12th St. (587-2239), is just a block from downtown. (Small singles with shared bath $28, doubles with private bath and phone $38.) The **Gateway Motel and Campground,** 203 Yellowstone Ave. (587-2561), rents out precious little cabins with A/C and kitchenettes (singles $35, doubles $40). Campsites run $10 for one person, $12 for two; showers and laundry facilities are available (open May-Sept.). The **Irma Hotel and Restaurant,** 1192 Sheridan Ave. (587-4221), originally owned by Buffalo Bill and named after his daughter, has affordable eats if not rooms. Don't miss the original cherrywood bar, sent as a gift from Queen Victoria (open in summer daily 6am-10pm; Oct.-March 6am-9pm).

■ Buffalo

Not touristy enough to be a trap, not small enough for wayward travelers to feel like unwanted outsiders, Buffalo, at the crossroads of I-90 and I-25, is a charming, laid-back, friendly town and a perfect base for exploring the Bighorn Mountains.

Absorb some of the character of the Old West in the elegant, entertaining rooms of the **Occidental Hotel,** 10 N. Main St. (684-2788), which opened its doors as the town hall in 1880. Teddy Roosevelt and Buffalo Bill stayed here (open daily 10:30am-4:30pm and 6-8pm; free). If you're hankerin' after a bit o' frontier history, visit the **Jim Gatchell Museum of the West,** 10 Fort St. (684-9331; open daily 9am-8pm, Sept.-Nov. 9am-5pm; $2, under 18 free), or the museum and outdoor exhibits at the former site of **Fort Phil Kearny** (684-7629), on U.S. 87 between Buffalo and Sheridan (open daily 8am-6pm, mid-Oct. to mid-May Wed.-Sun. noon-4pm; $1). In nearby **Sheridan,** Buffalo Bill Cody used to sit on the porch of the once luxurious **Sheridan Inn,** at 5th and Broadway, as he interviewed cowboy hopefuls for his *Wild West Show.* Ernest Hemingway also stayed there for four days while writing *A Farewell to Arms.* The inn now gives tours ($3, seniors $2, under 12 free).

The **Buffalo Chamber of Commerce,** 55 N. Main St. (684-5544 or 800-227-5122), is at your service for town info (open June-Aug. Mon-Sat. 8am-6pm; May and Sept. Mon.-Fri. 8am-6pm; Nov.-April Mon.-Fri. 8:30am-4:30pm). The **U.S. Forest Service Offices,** 300 Spruce St. (684-7981), will sell you a map of the area for three greenbacks (open Mon.-Sat. 8am-4:30pm). There is no bus service in Buffalo; travel by **Greyhound** from either Sheridan or Gillette. In Sheridan, buses leave twice daily for Billings (3hr., $27) and Cheyenne (7hr., $45), from 1700 E. Hwy. 14/16 (office open daily 5:30am-5pm and 6:30-7:30pm). At **Alabam's,** 421 Fort St. (684-7452), you can buy topographical maps ($2.50); hunting, fishing, and camping supplies; and **fishing licenses** (1 day $5, 5 days $20; open daily Mon.-Sat. 8am-6pm, Sun. 8am-5pm). Buffalo's **post office:** 193 S. Main St. (684-7063; open Mon.-Fri. 8:30am-5pm, Sat. 10am-noon). **ZIP code:** 82801. **Area code:** 307.

In Buffalo, budget motels line Main St. (Rte. 90) and Fort St. The **Mountain View Motel,** 545 Fort St. (684-2881), keeps appealing pine cabins with TV, A/C, and heating (singles $34, doubles $40; winter $24/$30; big cabin with 3 double rooms $56, with kitchen $60). Next door, the **Z-Bar Motel** (684-5535 or 800-341-8000) has TV with HBO, refrigerators, and A/C (singles $37, doubles $45; Nov-April $29/36; kitchen $5 extra; reservations recommended). Eat at **Tom's Main Street Diner,** 41 N. Main St. (684-7444), a great little place in the heart of downtown. Lunch specials ($4-5, including beverage) and bread pudding are best ($2; open Mon., Wed.-Sat. 5:30am-2pm, Sun. 8am-2pm). **Dash Inn,** 620 E. Hart St. (684-7930), offers baked chicken, ribs meals, and great Texas Toast for $6-9 (open Tues.-Sun. 11am-9:30pm; in winter 11am-8:30pm).

■ Devils Tower

A Native American legend tells of seven sisters who were playing with their little brother when the boy turned into a bear and began to chase them. Terrified, the girls ran to a tree stump and prayed for help. The stump grew high into the sky, where the girls became the stars of the Big Dipper. The bear, infuriated, scraped the now-massive stump with his claws. Others tell of a core of fiery magma that shot up without breaking the surface sixty million years ago, and of centuries of wind, rain, and snow that eroded the surrounding sandstone, leaving a stunning spire. Still others, not of this world, have used the stone obelisk as a landing strip (*Close Encounters of the Third Kind*). The massive, stump-like column that figures so prominently in the myths of Native Americans, geologists, and space aliens is the centerpiece of **Devils Tower National Monument** in northeastern Wyoming.

The entrance fee to Devils Tower is $4 per car, $2 per pedestrian. The only way to get to the top is by climbing; nearly 6000 people attempt it yearly. Those interested in making the climb must register with a ranger at the **visitors center** (307-467-5283), 3 mi. from the entrance (open Memorial Day-Labor Day daily 8am-7:45pm; Labor Day-Oct. 8am-5pm). Cool **climbing demos** are given outside the visitors center (Memorial Day-Labor Day 11am and 4pm). Refrain from climbing the tower in June out of respect for the Native American ceremonies taking place there. For ground hikers, there are several **hiking trails;** the most popular 1.3-mi. **Tower Trail** loops the monument and provides great views. The park maintains a **campground** near the red banks of the Belle Fourche River. (Water, bathrooms, fireplaces, picnic tables, no showers. Sites $10. Open April-Oct.) **KOA** (307-467-5395), also on a scenic location near the river, camps right next to the park entrance and usually houses some kind of resident psychic. ($16, with full hookup $21. Cabins with no linen, 3 beds, and no bathroom $30.) To reach the monument from I-90, take U.S. 14, 25 mi. north to Rte. 24.

■ Casper

In its frontier heyday, Casper hosted mountain men, Mormons, friendly ghosts, Shoshone, and Sioux on their ventures. Eight pioneer trails intersected near Casper, including the famed Oregon, Bozeman, and Pony Express trails. The convergence of those famous paths lives on in the minds of those who call Casper by its nicknames, "the Hub" and "the Heart of Big Wyoming"—they also seem to have forgotten that most of those trailblazers kept on going.

Practical Information The **Casper Area Convention and Visitors Bureau,** 500 N. Center St. (234-5311 or 800-852-1889; fax 265-2643), will load you down with helpful info on camping and a good street map. (Open summers Mon.-Fri. 8am-6pm,

Sat.-Sun. 9am-6pm; winters Mon.-Fri. 9am-6pm.) **Powder River Transportation Services** (266-1904 or 800-433-2093 outside WY), at I-25 and Center St. in the Parkway Plaza Hotel, sends buses to: Buffalo (1 per day, 4hr., $24); Sheridan (1 per day, 5hr., $27); Rapid City (1 per day, overnight, $44); Cheyenne (2 per day, 3hr., $31); Billings (2 per day, 6hr., $47). (Ticket office open weekdays 6-10:30am and 11:30am-5pm, Sat. 6-10am and 3:30-4:30pm, Sun. 6-7:30am and 3:30-4:30pm.) **Casper Affordable Used Car Rental,** 131 E. 5th St. (237-1733), rents affordable used cars. ($27 per day with 50 free mi., $179 per week with 350 free mi., 18¢ per additional mi. Must be 22 with $200 or credit card deposit. Open Mon.-Fri. 8am-5:30pm.) Casper's main **post office:** 411 N. Forest Dr. (266-4000; open Mon.-Fri. 7am-6pm, Sat. 9am-noon). **ZIP code:** 82601. **Area code:** 307.

Accommodations and Camping Bunk down at **The Royal Inn,** 440 E. A St. (234-3501 or 800-96-ROYAL/967-6925), which has large, clean rooms decorated with tasteful modern art. Management has been known to pick up pale riders from the bus station. (Singles $26, doubles $33, or $29/$37 for slightly fancier rooms with microwave and fridge. All rooms have free cable, 4 free local calls and A/C. Tiny outdoor heated pool in the parking lot.) Pull up your covered wagon next to old Fort Casper at the **Fort Casper Campground,** 4205 Ft. Casper Rd. (234-3260). (RV site $16 with full hookup, tent site $11 for 2 people, each additional person $1.) Sleep under the big Wyoming sky at **Alcova Lake Campground** (473-2514 or 473-8853), 35 mi. southwest of Casper on County Rd. 407 off Rte. 220, a popular recreation area with beaches (tents $6, hookup $10).

Food Stop by the **Daily Grind Coffeehouse,** 328 E. A St. (234-7332), for the local scoop on everything from rock climbing to dancing (single cappuccino $2, house coffee $1). The joint sports a changing schedule of literary readings and live music, plus an open mike every Thursday night after 9:30pm. Surprisingly good Chinese food is the best bet for a cheap, satisfying meal in downtown Casper. The **Peking Restaurant,** 333 E. A St. (266-2207), offers lunch specials starting at $3.50 and dinner plates around $6.50 (open for lunch daily 11am-2pm, dinner 5pm-8:30pm). **La Costa,** 400 W. F St. (266-4288), in front of the Hampton Inn, makes some of the best Mexican food in town. Burritos go for $6, a complete Mexican dinner for $7. (Open Mon.-Thurs. 11am-10pm, Fri.-Sat. 11am-10:30pm, Sun. 11am-9pm.)

Sites Casper's pride and joy is fascinating **Fort Casper,** 4001 Ft. Casper Rd. (235-8462), a group of reconstructed cabins that replicate the old army fort which guarded the N. Platte River on the western side of town. (Open Mon.-Fri. 9am-6pm, Sat. 9am-5pm, Sun. noon-5pm; mid-Sept. to mid-May Mon.-Fri. 9am-5pm, Sun. 1-4pm. Free.) The **Nicolayson Art Museum,** 400 E. Collins Dr. (235-5247), called the "Nic" by those in the know, explores the aesthetics of the old and new west with exhibits such as a bison made of rusted auto parts and old tires (open Tues.-Sun. 10am-5pm, Thurs. until 8pm; $2, under 12 $1; free the 1st and 3rd Thurs. of every month from 4-8pm). A few mi. southeast of town on Rte. 251, **Lookout Point** (on top of **Casper Mountain**) and **Muddy Mountain** (6mi. farther) provide the best vantage points from which to survey the terrain. In early August, the week-long **Central Wyoming Fair and Rodeo,** 1700 Fairgrounds Rd. (235-5775), keeps the town excited with parades, livestock shows, and rodeos. The 4-mi. long **Platte River Parkway Bikepath** is a good place for an easy jog or bike ride through Casper.

■ Cheyenne

Originally the name of the Native American tribe that roamed the wilderness of the region, "Cheyenne" was considered a prime candidate for the name of the Wyoming Territory. The moniker was struck down by vigilant Senator Sherman, who pointed out that the pronunciation of Cheyenne closely resembled that of the French word *chienne* meaning, er, "bitch."

ROCKY MOUNTAINS

Practical Information Check with the **Cheyenne Area Convention and Visitors Bureau,** 309 W. Lincolnway (778-3133 or 800-426-5009), just west of Capitol Ave., for accommodations and restaurant listings, or the **Wyoming Information and Division of Tourism** (777-7777 or 800-225-5996), at I-25 and College Drive for statewide information and accommodations. **Greyhound,** 120 N. Greely Hwy. (634-7744), just off I-80, makes daily trips to: Salt Lake City (2 per day, 9hr., $60); Chicago (2 per day, 24hr., $131); Laramie (2 per day, 1hr., $12); Rock Springs (2 per day, 5hr., $46); Denver (6 per day, 3hr., $19). (Station open daily 10am-12:30pm and midnight-4am.) **Powder River Transportation** (634-7744), in the Greyhound terminal, honors Greyhound passes. Daily to Rapid City (1 per day, 10hr., $59); Casper (2 per day, 4hr., $31); Billings (2 per day, 12hr., $66). There is no **Amtrak** station in Cheyenne, although there is an unstaffed drop-off point in the lobby of the Plains Hotel (see Accommodations, below); from there, a free 15-min. shuttle bus ride is available to the **Borie** train stop. Trains chug three times per week to Denver (2½hr., $25) and Chicago (13½hr., $180). Reservations (800-USA-RAIL/872-7245) are required for trains from Borie. (Open daily 9:30am-5:30pm.) The **Rape Crisis Line** (637-SAFE/7233) is open 24 hr. **Emergency** is 911. Cheyenne's **post office:** 4800 Converse Ave. (772-6580; open Mon.-Fri. 7:30am-5:30pm, Sat. 7am-noon). **ZIP code:** 82009. **Area code:** 307.

Accommodations and Camping It's not hard to land a cheap room here among the plains and pioneers unless your visit coincides with Wyoming's enormous hootenanny **Frontier Days,** the last full week of July (see Sights and Entertainment, below). Beware of doubling rates and disappearing rooms in the days approaching this week.

Many budget motels line **Lincolnway** (U.S. 30/16th St.). **Plains Hotel,** 1600 Central Ave. (638-3311), conveniently located across from the I-180 on ramp and one block away from the center of downtown, offers cavernous, retro-stylish hotel rooms with marble sinks and free cable (winter singles $31, doubles $41; summer $34/43; $5 each additional person). Put your gun in your holster before walking into the **Frontier Motel,** 1400 W. Lincoln Way (634-7961), and grab a latté ($1.50) or an Italian soda ($1.50) at the front desk. A single with a living room, large bathroom, free cable, and A/C, starts at $20 in April and Sept. (prices rise towards mid-summer). **The Ranger Motel,** 909 W. 16th St. (634-7995), has small, beige rooms with phone and TV, and free local calls (summer singles $25, doubles $28; offseason $21/25). For **campers,** somewhat crowded spots blanket the **AB Campground,** 1503 W. College Rd. (634-7035; laundry, game room, free showers; tent sites $12.50). You might also try **Curt Gowdy State Park,** 1319 Hynds Lodge Rd. (632-7946), 23 mi. west of Cheyenne on Rte. 210. This year-round park is centered around two lakes with excellent fishing; horseback riding (B.Y.O. horse), and archery are also popular. ($4 per night in addition to a $2 entrance fee. $3 fee for out of state visitors.)

Food and Nightlife Cheyenne has a number of restaurants specializing in reasonably priced modern cuisine. **The Medicine Bow Brewing Company,** 115 E. 17th St. (778-BREW/2739), in the center of town, serves tasty sandwiches ($5) and enormous southwestern plates (smothered burrito, $6). Come to the bar at night to play darts, air hockey, pin ball, foosball, or pool on one of 10 tables. Medicine Bow Ale is just $1.75 per glass. If you're not sure what kind of beer to drink, try a free sample in a shot glass. (Open Mon.-Wed. 11am-midnight, Thurs.-Sat. 11am-2am, Sun. 11am-10pm; live music Thurs.-Sat.) **Lexie's Café,** 216 E. 17th St. (638-8712), has cheerful, cottage-style decor featuring wicker chairs and flowers. Its menu includes filling breakfast combos ($3-4), towering stacks of pancakes ($3), and burgers ($5). (Open Tues.-Thurs. 8am-8pm, Fri.-Sat. 8am-9pm.)

Those weary of the deer and antelope can play in **Joe Page's Bookstore and Coffeehouse,** 207 W. 17th St. (778-7134 or 800-338-7428), which offers occasional live music and poetry readings (open Mon.-Sat. 7am-10pm, Sun. 11am-5pm). A country night spot for the 21 and over crowd, **The Cheyenne Club,** 1617 Capitol Ave. (635-

7777), hosts live bands nightly at 8:30pm (open Mon.-Sat. 7pm-2am). When you want to guzzle, look for a pink elephant above **D.T.'s Liquor and Lounge,** 2121 E. Lincolnway (632-3458; open Mon.-Sat. 7am-2am, Sun. noon-10pm).

Festivals and Sights If you're within 500 mi. of Cheyenne during the last week in July, make every effort to attend the **Cheyenne Frontier Days,** nine days of nonstop Western hoopla. The town doubles in size as anyone worth a grain of Western salt comes to see the world's oldest and largest outdoor rodeo competition ($8 and up) and partake of the free pancake breakfasts (every other day in the parking lot across from the chamber of commerce), parades, concerts, and square dancing (778-7222 or 800-227-6336; open Mon.-Fri. 9am-5pm). Throughout June and July, a "gunfight is always possible," and the **Cheyenne Gunslingers** (635-1028) at W. 16th and Carey, make it happen (Mon.-Fri. 6pm, Sat. high noon). The **Wyoming State Capitol Building** (777-7220), at the base of Capitol Ave. on 24th St., shows off stained glass windows, yellowed photographs, and frontier history. Self-guided tours available along with free 1½-hr. guided tours twice daily. (Private group tours 777-7220; open Mon.-Fri. 8am-5pm.) The **Old West Museum** (778-7290), at 8th and Carey, houses a large collection of wagons, guns, and other old western memorabilia. (Open June-Sept. Mon.-Fri. 8am-6pm, Sat. 10am-5pm, Sun. 10am-5pm; winter Tues.-Fri. 9am-5pm, Sat.-Sun. 11am-4pm.)

■ West of Cheyenne

Laramie Laramie, the hoppin' home of the University of Wyoming (the state's only four-year college), serves up collegiate coffee-shop chic with cowboy grit. Drifters can get a dose of youthful spirit in town and then relax in nearby Medicine Bow National Forest or Curt Gowdy State Park. From Cheyenne, take the **"Happy Jack Road" (Rte. 210)** for the cow-filled scenic tour, or Rte. 80W for expedience. Laramie does its darndest to bring its rough and rugged 19th-century history back to life in **Wyoming Territorial Park,** 975 Snowy Range Rd. (800-845-2287), a reconstructed frontier town that sells a suspiciously large amount of candy and souvenirs (open daily mid-May to late Aug. 10am-6pm; free). The **Wyoming Territorial Prison** (hourly guided tours) and the **National U.S. Marshals Museum** offer fascinating glimpses into the relationship between the U.S. marshals, the labor movement, Native Americans, and Western outlaws. (Open daily early May to late Sept.; $6 for the museum and prison.)

The sprawling **Motel 8,** 501 Boswell (745-4856), down the street from the Caboose, contains large rooms for your motel comfort (A/C, pool; winter singles $22, doubles $25; summer $27/$30). **Ranger Hotel,** 453 N. 3rd St. (742-6677), patrols downtown and will send you back to the 1970s. (Phone, HBO, fridge, microwave. Singles around $24, prices negotiable.) Lined with hotels and fast food, **3rd St.** leads south into the heart of town, crossing **Ivinson** and **Grand St.;** both burst with student hangouts. **Jeffrey's Restaurant,** 123 Ivinson St. (742-7046), proffers heavenly homemade bread, and some of the best hot sandwiches, pasta dishes, and salads in Wyoming ($5-7; open Mon.-Sat. 11am-9pm, Sun. 9am-2pm). Next door, **Sara's Bakery** (472-7406) makes mouth-watering dessert specialties and light sandwiches (open Mon.-Sat. 7am-6pm). The air in **The Home Bakery,** 304 S. 2nd St. (742-2721), is musty with fresh flour and 100 years of bakery tradition (baked goods start at 40¢; daily sandwich specials $3; Mon.-Sat. 5am-5:30pm). Both students and Harleys steer their way into the **Buckhorn Bar,** 114 Ivinson St. (742-3554), a popular neighborhood hangout which features live music Sunday nights and busy pool tables (open Mon.-Sat. 6am-2am, Sun. noon-10pm). The **Cowboy Bar and Hooters Lounge,** 303 S. 3rd St. (745-3423), is filled with cowboys and um, well, you know... (Open Mon.-Sat. 4pm-2am, Sun. 4pm-10pm. Live music Wed.-Sat.)

The Snowy Range Local residents call the heavily forested granite mountains to the east of the Platte Valley the **Snowy Mountain Range** because snow falls nearly year round on the higher peaks. Even when the snow melts, quartz outcroppings reflect the sun, creating an illusion of a snowy peak. After Memorial Day, the **Snowy Range Scenic Byway (Rte. 130)** is cleared of snow and cars can drive 29 mi. through the mountains to elevations nearing two vertical miles. The Snowy Range is one part of the vast **Medicine Bow National Forest,** spread out over much of southeastern Wyoming.

The **Bush Creek Visitor Center** (326-5562) is at the west entrance (open from late May to late September daily 8am-5pm). The **Centennial Visitor Center** (742-6023), is 1 mi. west of Centennial at the east entrance (open late May to late Sept. daily 9:30am-5pm). Call the **Bush Creek Ranger District Office** (326-5258; open daily 7:30am-4:30pm) for general info about the Medicine Bow Forest.

Because of snow, campsites and hiking trails usually don't open until mid-July. In late summer, hike the challenging but short (2-mi.) **Medicine Bow Trail,** which climbs to **Medicine Bow Peak** (12,013ft.), the highest point in the forest. Nearby **Silver Lake** offers 19 first come, first served camping sites ($8). A little east, **Nash Fork** is another of several ideal, untrammeled camp settings, with 27 first come, first served sites ($9). All 23 of the park's developed campgrounds are open only in the summer and have toilets and water, but none have electric hookups or showers. Reservations for some campgrounds are available (800-280-2267; $7.50 reservation fee). A drive up **Kennaday Peak** (10,810ft.), at the end of Forest Rd. 215 off Rte. 130, takes you to an impressive vista of the park's forest from a fire lookout tower.

Mountain biking is generally not allowed on the high country trails because of the frail alpine plants and the rocky terrain. However, you can bike on four-wheel drive roads and jeep trails in the high country or on trails below about 10,000ft. The 7-mi. **Corner Mountain Loop,** just west of Centennial visitor center, is an exhilarating rollercoaster ride through a mixed forest of aspens, pines, and small meadows. During the winter, mountain biking and hiking trails are used for cross country skiing.

Saratoga On the far side of the Snowy Range, Saratoga, like its New York sister, is known for its **hot mineral springs.** At close to 120°F, these springs will definitely warm you up, and won't leave you reeking of sulfur. A few feet away from the hot springs, the **North Platte River** offers excellent fishing. The nearby **Hotel Wolf,** 101 E. Bridge St. (326-5525), a renovated Victorian inn, is still a howlin' good deal (singles from $26, doubles from $30). The local favorite **Wolf Hotel Restaurant** (326-5525) serves everything from expensive filet mignon to reasonably priced sandwiches and salads ($4-6; hours vary; open for lunch and dinner). For a more casual atmosphere, drop in on **Mom's Kitchen** (326-5236), three blocks down Rte. 130 from Bridge St., where the big daddy burger will definitely fill you up for $5. Next door to the Wolf, find **Lollypops,** 107 E. Bridge St. (326-5020), which sells ice cream ($1.35 single cone), coffee specialties ($2.25 for a latté), and $1.50 gourmet lollypops (open daily 7am-10pm). Across Rte. 130, **Classic Knead Bakery,** 113 W. Bridge St. (326-8932), works wonders with dough; delicious cinnamon rolls ($1), donuts (50¢), breads, and pastries will fill you up (open Tues.-Sat. 6am-2:30pm).

Colorado

The citizens of Colorado are rightly proud of their state's thin air, in which golf balls fly farther, eggs take longer to cook, and visitors tend to lose their breath just getting out of bed. Oxygen deprivation also lures athletes looking to loosen their lungs for a competitive edge, but most hikers, skiers, and climbers worship Colorado for its peaks, which give rise to enclaves such as Grand Junction and Crested Butte. Meanwhile, Denver—the country's highest capital—serves as the hub for the entire Rocky Mountain region, providing both an ideal resting place for cross-country travelers and a "culture fix" for those heading to the mountains. Colorado's extraordinary heights are balanced by its equally spectacular depths. For millions of years, the Gunnison and Colorado Rivers have been etching natural wonders such as the Black Canyon and the Colorado National Monument. Early settlers mined Colorado for its silver and gold, the U.S. military burrowed enormous intelligence installations into the mountains around Colorado Springs, but most travelers dig their feet into the state's soil simply to get down and dirty with Mother Nature.

PRACTICAL INFORMATION

Capital: Denver.
The Colorado Tourism and Travel Authority: CTTA, P.O. Box 3924, Englewood 80155 (800-265-6723). **U.S. Forest Service,** Rocky Mountain Region, 740 Sims St., Lakewood 80225 (303-275-5350). Free maps; topographic forest maps $3. Open Mon.-Fri. 7:30am-4:30pm. **Ski Country USA,** 1560 Broadway #1440, Denver 80202 (303-837-0793; open Mon.-Fri. 8am-5pm; recorded message 831-7669). **National Park Service,** 12795 W. Alameda Pkwy., P.O. Box 25287, Denver 80255 (969-2000). For reservations for Rocky Mountain National Park, call DESTINET at 800-365-2267. Open Mon.-Fri. 7am-4pm. **Colorado State Parks and Recreation,** 1313 Sherman St. #618, Denver 80203 (303-866-3437). Open Mon.-Fri. 8am-5pm. For reservations for any Colorado state park, call 470-1144 or 800-678-2267.
Time Zone: Mountain (2hr. behind Eastern). **Postal Abbreviation:** CO.
Sales Tax: 4%.
Speed Limit: 75 mph (yee hah!).

■ Denver

In 1858, the discovery of gold in the Rocky Mountains brought a rush of eager miners to northern Colorado. After the excruciating trek through the plains, the desperadoes set up camps for a breather and a stiff shot of whiskey before heading west into "them thar hills." In 1860, two of the camps consolidated to form a town named after then-governor of Kansas Territory James W. Denver. Between 1863 and 1867, Denver and nearby Golden played a political tug-of-war for the title of state capital. Today, Golden makes a lot of beer, while Denver, the "Queen City of the Plains," has become the Rockies' largest and fastest growing metropolis, serving as the commercial and cultural nexus of the region. The city has doubled in population since 1960 and continues to attract diversity—ski bums, sophisticated city-slickers from the coasts, and, of course, old-time cowpokes. The gold which originally drew people to Denver may be depleted, but the city retains its best asset—a combination of charming urban sophistication and the laid-back attitude of the West.

PRACTICAL INFORMATION

Tourist Office: Denver Metro Convention and Visitors Bureau, 225 W. Colfax Ave. (892-1112 or 892-1505), near Civic Center Park just south of the capitol. Open Mon.-Fri. 8am-5pm, Sat. 10am-4pm, Sun. 10am-2pm; in winter Mon.-Fri. 8am-5pm, Sat. 9am-1pm. Pick up a free copy of the comprehensive *Denver Official Visitors Guide.* **Big John's Information Center,** 1055 19th St. (892-1505 or 892-1112), at the Greyhound station. Big John, an ex-professional basketball player, enthusiastically offers info on hosteling, tours around Denver, and daytrips to the mountains. Open Mon.-Sat. 7-10am and 1-3pm. **16th St. Ticket Bus,** in the 16th St. Mall at Curtis St. is a double-decker bus with visitor info, ½-price tickets to local theater performances, and RTD bus info. Open Mon.-Fri. 10am-5pm, Sat. 11am-3pm.
Tours: Gray Line Tours (289-2841), at the bus station, runs tours daily in summer to: Rocky Mountain National Park (10hr.; $39, under 12 $29); the U.S. Air Force Academy (10hr.; $49, under 12 $29).
Airport: Denver International (342-2000), 25mi. northeast of downtown off I-70. Shuttles run from the airport to downtown Denver and ski resorts in the area. From the main terminal, **Airporter** (333-5833 or 800-355-5833) and **DASH** (342-5454 or 800-525-3177) shuttle to downtown hotels (35min.-1hr., $15). The **Sky Ride** (800-366-7433 or 299-6000) costs $6 to DIA from downtown, buses run hourly

from 5:45 am-10:45pm. **Taxis** from DIA to downtown are $40, shared cabs $20 each party. Call ground transportation (342-4059) for info on more shuttles serving the greater Denver area.

Trains: Amtrak, Union Station, 1701 Wynkoop St. (534-2812 or 800-872-7245) at 17th. To: St. Louis (1 per day, $215); Salt Lake City (1 per day, 13½hr., $113); Chicago (1 per day, 19hr., $167). Ticket office open 7am-9pm. The **Río Grande Ski Train,** 555 17th St. (296-4754), leaves from Amtrak Union Station and treks through the Rockies, stopping in Winter Park (Dec.-April only). Departs Denver 7:15am, Winter Park 4:15pm (2hr., $35 round-trip, reservations required).

Buses: Greyhound, 1055 E. 19th St. (293-6550 or 800-231-2222), downtown. To: Santa Fe (4 per day, 9hr., $60), Salt Lake City (4 per day, 12hr., $40), St. Louis (4 per day, 12-19hr., $95), Colorado Springs (7 per day, 2hr., $11.25), Chicago (6 per day, 15hr., $85). Ticket office open 6am-11:30pm.

Public Transportation: Regional Transportation District (RTD), 1600 Blake St. (299-6000). Service within Denver and to Longmont, Evergreen, Golden, and suburbs. Route hours vary; many shut down by 9pm or earlier. Fare Mon.-Fri. 6-9am and 4-6pm is $1; all other times 60¢; over 65 15¢. Must have exact change. Free 16th St. Mall Shuttle covers 14 blocks downtown.

Taxi: Metro Taxi (333-3333); **Yellow Cab** (777-7777); **Zone Cab** (444-8888). All $1.40 base fare, $1.40 per mi., 40¢ per additional passenger. Phone numbers designed for the memory impaired.

Car Rental: Thrifty (342-9400), in the airport. $33 per day, unlimited mi.; $189 per week. Under 25 surcharge $10 per day. Must be 21 with major credit card.

Auto Transport Company: Auto Driveaway, 5777 E. Evans Ave. (757-1211); take bus #21 to Holly and Evans. Must have $300 cash deposit, valid driver's license, and be at least 21. $10 fee. Open Mon.-Fri. 8:30am-5pm.

Crisis Lines: Rape Emergency Hotline (322-7273).

Gay and Lesbian Community Center (831-6268). Open Mon.-Fri. 10am-10pm, Sat. 10am-8pm, Sun. 1-4pm.

Emergency: 911.

Post Office: 951 20th St. (297-6000). Open Mon-Fri. 9am-5pm, Sat. 9am-noon. **ZIP code:** 80202. **Area code:** 303.

During rush hour, traffic sits at a virtual standstill along I-25 until about 15 mi. south of downtown. I-70 links Denver with Grand Junction (250 mi. west) and Kansas City (600 mi. east). Rte. 285 cuts south through the central Rockies, opening up the Saguache and Sangre de Cristo Ranges to easy exploration.

Running north-south, **Broadway** slices Denver into east and west. **Ellsworth Ave.,** running east-west, is the north-south dividing line. Streets west of Broadway progress in alphabetical order, while the streets north of Ellsworth are numbered. Streets downtown run diagonal to those in the rest of the metropolis. Many of the avenues on the eastern side of the city become numbered *streets* downtown. Most even-numbered thoroughfares downtown run only east-west. The hub of downtown is the **16th Street Mall.** Few crimes occur in the immediate area, but avoid the west end of Colfax Ave., the east side of town beyond the capitol, and the upper reaches of the **Barrio** (25th-34th St.) at night.

ACCOMMODATIONS AND CAMPING

Denver offers many affordable accommodations within easy reach of downtown. Hostelers with specific interests (or no ideas at all) should ask "Big John" Schrant at the Greyhound bus station for info and directions.

Melbourne International Hostel, 607 22nd St. (292-6386), at Welton St., near the center of the LoDo district and 6 blocks from the 16th St. mall. Owned by WWII pilot Leonard Schmitt and operated by his nephew Gary, the Melbourne has clean red-rugged rooms with fridges and communal kitchens. The international mix of hostelers can relax on the outside patio. Check-in 7am-midnight. Dorms $10, nonmembers $13. Private rooms $18/$21, couples $24/$27. Sheet rental $2. Key deposit $10. Reservations are needed June-Oct.

Downtown Denver

N

Grant St.
Sherman St.
Lincoln St.
Broadway
RTD Civic Center Station
State Capitol
Colorado History Museum
Library
22nd St.
California St.
Stout St.
Champa St.
21st St.
Curtis St.
20th St.
19th St.
Federal Bldg.
Museum of Western Art
Brown Palace
Cleveland Pl.
Cheyenne Pl.
Court Pl.
Tremont Pl.
Glenarm Pl.
Civic Center Park
Information Center
US Mint
Denver Art Museum
Byers/Evans House
Denver History Museum
Coors Field
Bus Terminal
18th St.
17th St.
Welton St.
California St.
Stout St.
Firefighter's Museum
Colfax Ave.
12th St.
Delaware St.
Union Station
RTD Market St. Bus Terminal
Skyline Park
16th St.
15th St.
14th St.
Arapahoe St.
Curtis St.
Champa St.
Colorado Convention Center
Denver Performing Arts Complex
Speer Blvd.
Klamath St.
Larimer St.
Lawrence St.
Market St.
Blake St.
Wazee St.
Wynkoop St.
Wewatta St.
Delgany St.
13th St.
Lipan St.
14th Ave.
Mariposa St.
University of Colorado–Denver
Auraria Campus
Denver Community College
9th Street Historic District
Cherry Creek
Speer Blvd.
Student Union
9th St.
8th St.
Larimer St.
Lawrence St.
Osage St.
Auraria Pkwy.
7th St.
Walnut
5th St.
Rio Ct.
Shoshone St.
287
Elitch Gardens
7th St.
South Platte River
Umatilla St.
Byron Pl.
Water St.
7th St.
Crescent Dr.
Children's Museum
Colfax Ave.
Zuni St.
River Dr.
Alcott St.
Bryant St.
Clay St.
Mile High Stadium
McNichols Arena
Bryant St.
Clay St.
25
25
0   .2 miles
0   .2 kilometers

ROCKY MOUNTAINS

Franklin House B&B, 1620 Franklin St. (331-9106). Cozy European-style inn within walking distance of downtown. Clean, spacious rooms. Free breakfast. Check in before 10pm. Check-out 11am. Singles $25, doubles $35, $10 for each additional person. Make reservations way ahead of time.

YMCA, 25 E. 16th St. (861-8300) at Lincoln St. Divided into sections for men, women, and families. Laundry and TV rooms. Singles without bath $25, shared bath $28, private bath $33; doubles with shared bath $47, with private bath $49. Weekly rates available.

Denver International Youth Hostel (AAIH/Rucksackers), 630 E. 16th Ave. (832-9996), 7 blocks east of downtown. Take AB or DIA bus to Market St., 1 block away, or take free 16th St. shuttle to Circle St. station at Broadway and walk 6 blocks east on 16th Ave. 140 beds, 4 or 6 to a room. Kitchen, laundry facilities, and communal fridge. Office open daily 8-10am and 5-10:30pm. Not the tidiest place around, but the price is right—$7.60, $1 discount with a copy of *Let's Go.* Sheet rental $1. Call to arrange arrival plans. The hostel is outside the well-traversed area; women and lone travelers should be cautious, but the police station across the street has significantly reduced safety concerns around the hostel.

Two state parks lie in the Denver metro area. **Cherry Creek State Park** (699-3860) has 102 crowded sites among a few strands of pine trees ($7, with electricity $10; daily entrance fee $4; $6.75 reservation fee); take I-25 to Exit 200, then go west on Rte. 225 for about ½ mi. and turn south on Parker Rd. **Chatfield State Park** (791-7275) maintains 153 well-developed sites (open April-Oct.; $7, with electricity $10; daily entrance fee $3); take I-25 or U.S. 85 south, turn west on Rte. 470, and then go south on Wadsworth Rd. A little farther away, **Golden Gate Canyon State Park,** take I-70 west to 6th Ave., go west towards Central City to Rte. 119, and then north 19 mi., offers 35 primitive year-round sites without water (sites $6, daily entrance fee $3). For reservations for any Colorado state park, call 470-1144 or 800-678-2267 (open Mon.-Fri. 7am-4:45pm).

FOOD

Downtown Denver is great for inexpensive Mexican and Southwestern food. Eat *al fresco* and people-watch at the cafés along the **16th St. Mall. Larimer Sq.,** southwest of the mall on Larimer St., has several more gourmet eateries. Along with sports bars and grilles, trendy restaurants cluster around **LoDo,** the neighborhood extending from Larimer Sq. out towards Coors Stadium. Colorado's distance from the ocean may make you wonder about *Rocky Mountain oysters;* this salty-sweet delicacy and other buffalo-meat specialties can be found at the **Denver Buffalo Company,** 1109 Lincoln St. (832-0080).

City Spirit Café, 1434 Blake St. (575-0022), a few blocks from the north end of the 16th St. Mall. Flamboyant decor with waitstaff to match. Serves delicious salads ($6), vegetarian dishes (try the burrito with sun dried tomatoes, basil, and goat

---

Mexican Madness

Denver has more Mexican food restaurants than you could shake a tamale at, but there's special reason to make a trip out to **Casa Bonita,** 6715 W. Colfax (232-5115), in Lakewood, west of Sheraton Blvd. in a shopping mall. This gigantic restaurant could only be conceived of in the U.S.; it encompasses over 52,000 square feet and seats 1100 guests amidst fake palm trees and real fake waterfalls. Every ten minutes tongue-in-cheek skits are enacted atop a thirty foot waterfall; someone always either gets pushed off or dives into the water below. Fire jugglers, mariachi bands, and fake gunfights round out the spectacle. While the food itself isn't exceptional, and all-you-can-eat dinner of enchiladas, tacos, rice, and sopapillas will definitely fill you up. (Open 11am-9:30pm.)

cheese, $7), and fresh desserts. Acid jazz on Tues. nights. Open Mon.-Thurs. 11am-midnight, Fri.-Sat. 11am-2am.

El Tacos Del Mexico, 714 Santa Fe (629-3926). Quickly prepared burritos will fill you up ($3-4). Open Sun.-Thurs. 8am-10pm, Fri.-Sat. 8am-2am.

Wynkoop Brewery, 1634 18th St. (297-2700), at Wynkoop across from Union Station in LoDo. Colorado's first brewpub is dedicated to brewing and serving beer (pint $3), alfalfa mead, homemade root beer, lunch, and dinner (burgers $6). Pool tables upstairs. Happy hour 3-6pm, $1.50 pints. Brewery open Mon.-Sat. 11am-2am, Sun. 11am-midnight. Free brewery tours Sat. 1-5pm.

Mercury Café, 2199 California (294-9258), across from the Melbourne Hostel. Inside is decorated like an old tea parlor. Homebaked wheat bread and reasonably priced lunch and dinner items. 10-oz. sirloin with bread and vegetable $10. Tues.-Fri. 11:30am-2:30pm and 5:30pm-2am, Sat.-Sun. 9am-3pm and 5:30pm-2am. Nightly events include live bands, open stage, and poetry readings until 2am.

The Market, 1445 Larimer Sq. (534-5140), downtown. Popular with a young, artsy, not-quite-bohemian crowd that people-watches alongside suits and hippies. Cappuccino $2, sandwiches $5, exotic salads $5-8 per lb. Open Mon.-Thurs. 6:30am-11pm, Fri. 6:30am-midnight, Sat. 7:30am-midnight, Sun. 7:30am-10pm.

SIGHTS

Denver's mild, dry climate promises 300 days of sunshine promise pleasant days. The **Denver Metro Visitors Bureau,** across from the U.S. Mint, is a good place to plan tours in the city or to the mountains. One of the best deals around is the **Cultural Connection Trolley** (299-6000), where $3 takes you to over 20 of the city's main attractions. The trolley runs daily May 5-Sept. 2 from 9:30am-6:30pm. The $3 fare is good all day and buses come every 30 min.; buy your ticket from the driver. The tour begins at the **Denver Performing Arts Complex,** follow the arches to the end of Curtis, at 14th St., but can be picked up near most local attractions; look for the green and red sign.

A modern reminder of Colorado's silver mining days, the **U.S. Mint,** 320 W. Colfax (844-3582), issues the majority of coins minted in the U.S.; look for the small "D" for Denver embossed beneath the date. Shake your money-maker while strutting by a million-dollar pile of gold bars, or jam to the deafening roar of countless machines churning out a total of 20 million shiny coins per day. No free samples. Arrive early; summer lines often reach around the block. (Free 15-min. tours every 15-20min. in summer and every 20min. in winter. Open Mon.-Fri. 8am-3pm. Tickets must be bought in person the day of the tour; get there before 11am.)

Don't be surprised if the 15th step on the west side of the **State Capitol Building** (866-2604) is crowded—it sits exactly 5280 ft. (1mi.) above sea level. The gallery under the 24-karat-gold-covered dome gives a great view of the Rocky Mountains. Free tours pass the Senate and House of Representatives chambers (tours every 30min.; Mon.-Fri. 9:30am-2:30pm).

Just a few blocks from the capitol and the U.S. Mint stands the **Denver Art Museum,** 100 W. 14th Ave. (640-2793), housing a world-class collection of Native American art. Architect Gio Ponti designed this six-story "vertical" museum to accommodate totem poles and period architecture. The fabulous third floor of pre-Columbian art of the Americas resembles an archaeological excavation site with temples, huts, and idols. (Open Tues.-Sat. 10am-5pm, Sun. noon-5pm. $3, seniors, students, and children $1.50, under 5 free; free Sat.) Housed in the Navarre Building, the **Museum of Western Art,** 1727 Tremont Place (296-1880), holds a stellar collection of Russell, Benton, O'Keefe, and Wood paintings and drawings (open Tues.-Sat. 10am-4:30pm; $3, students and seniors $2, children under 7 free). **The Black American West Museum and Heritage Center,** 3091 California St. (292-2566), presents a side of frontier history unexplored by John Wayne movies and textbooks. Learn, for example, that one-third of all cowboys were African-American (open Mon.-Fri. 10am-5pm, Sat.-Sun. noon-5pm; $3, students and seniors $2, ages 13-17 75¢, kids 4-12 50¢).

Aviation enthusiasts can visit old planes such as the rare B-1A bomber at **Wings Over the Rockies Air and Space Museum,** in hangar No.1 at Lowry Air Force Base

(360-5360 ext.21; adults $4, seniors and ages 6-17 $2, under 6 free; open Mon.-Sat. 10am-4pm, Sun. noon-4pm).

Red Rocks Amphitheater and Park, 12 mi. southwest of Denver on I-70 at the Morrison exit, is carved into red sandstone. As the sun sets over the city, even the best performers have to compete with the view behind them. The amphitheater is a regular stop on the tours of bands including R.E.M., U2, and the Denver Symphony. (For tickets call Ticketmaster 830-8497 Mon.-Fri. 9am-9pm, Sat.-Sun. 9am-8pm, or Tele-Seat at 800-444-SEAT/7328 Mon.-Sat. 6am-7pm, Sun. 7am-4pm. Park admission free. Shows $25-45.)

For outdoor folk, Denver has more public parks per sq. mi. than any other city, providing prime space for bicycling, walking, or lolling about in the sun; **Cheesman Park** (take bus #10) offers a view of the snow-capped peaks of the Rockies. Call 697-4565 for further info on Denver Parks. Nearby state parks also offer recreation. Check with the **Colorado Division of Parks and Outdoor Recreation** (866-3437; open Mon.-Fri. 8am-5pm). Forty mi. west of Denver, the road to the summit of **Mt. Evans** (14,260ft.) is the highest paved road in North America. (Generally open Memorial Day-Labor Day; take I-70 west to Rte. 103 in Idaho Springs.)

ENTERTAINMENT AND NIGHTLIFE

Every January, Denver hosts the world's largest rodeo, the **National Western Stock Show,** 4655 Humbolt St. (297-1166). Here, cowpokes compete for prize money while over 10,000 head of cattle compete for "Best of Breed." Hop on a rip snortin' bull, or purchase any combination of shiny spurs, day-glo necklaces, and leather whips. In the last weekend of August, **A Taste of Colorado** features a large outdoor celebration with food vendors and local bands at Civic Center Park, near the capitol. **Cinco De Mayo** (534-8342), um, yes, on the 5th of May, attracts over 200,000 visitors per year with live entertainment on six stages, food, and drink.

Denver's long-awaited baseball team, the **Colorado Rockies** (ROCKIES/702-5437), lofts home runs out of shiny new **Coors Field,** at 20th and Blake St. (tickets $8 and up). In the fall, the **Denver Broncos** (433-7466) put on the blitz at **Mile High Stadium,** as Broncoitis spreads throughout the state. Pan for Denver's NBA team, the **Nuggets,** at **McNichols Arena** (893-6700).

Denver's local restaurants and bars cater to a college-age and slightly older singles crowd. Pick up a copy of *Westword* for the lowdown on LoDo. At **Muddy's Java Café,** 2200 Champa St. (298-1631), eat dinner while listening to live music or reading a novel from their downstairs bookstore; then, after a long night of partying or reading James Joyce, contemplate their very early morning breakfast (jazz Tues., Fri., Sat.; open Sun.-Thurs. 11am-3am, Fri.-Sat. 11am-4am). The "Hill of the Grasshopper," **El Chapultepec** (295-9126), 20th and Market St., is an authentic hole-in-the-wall with jazz be-bopping that dates back to Denver's Beat heritage of the 1950s (nightly 9pm-1am; one drink min. per set; open daily 7am-2am). **Charlie's,** 900 E. Colfax (839-8890), at Emerson, is a popular gay bar swinging with country and western dancing (open daily 10am-4am). **Metro Express,** 314 E. 13th St. (894-0668), another gay nightspot, has non-alcoholic night on Thurs. for an under-21 crowd.

■ Mountain Resorts Near Denver

Winter Park Nestled among delicious-smelling mountain pines in the upper Fraser River valley, Winter Park is the closest ski and summer resort to Denver (68 mi.; take I-70 west to U.S. 40). In the summer, mountain biking and hiking trails climb the mountains of the Continental Divide, while in the winter **Winter Park Resort** opens with a 3,060 ft. vertical drop and 1,373 acres of glade skiing. The **Winter Park Mary Jane Ski Area** (800-453-2525) packs bowls all winter long, and has info on the resort; for snow conditions call 572-SNOW/7669. The **Winter Park-Fraser Valley Chamber of Commerce,** 78841 U.S. 40 (970-726-4118 or 800-903-7275), provides info about a diverse range of outdoor activities (open daily 8am-5pm). **Timber Rafting** offers an all-day rafting trip ($37 for hostelers, includes transportation and lunch).

The **Alpine Slide,** at 1½ mi. long, is Colorado's longest. (Open June-Labor Day Mon.-Fri. 10am-6pm, Sat.-Sun. 10am-5pm. $6, seniors and children $5.) You can take the **Zephyr Express** chairlift to the summit of Winter Park Mountain with your mountain bike, then ride down (open daily mid-June-Sept. 10am-5pm; $16 full day). Every Saturday at 6pm in July and August, get trampled underfoot at the **High Country Stampede Rodeo,** at the John Work Arena, west of Fraser on County Road 73 (adults $6, children $3).

On the town's southern boundary is the **Winter Park Hostel (HI-AYH)** (726-5356), 2½ blocks from the Greyhound stop and 2 mi. from Amtrak (free shuttle if you call ahead). The hostel is a cheery, homey village of converted trailer units, each with its own kitchen, bathroom, and spacious living room. In winter, free shuttles run to the ski area and supermarket. Hostelers save money on bike and ski rentals, raft trips, and restaurants. (Check-in 8am-noon and 4-8pm. May-Oct. $8, nonmembers $10; Nov.-April $13/$16. Private singles add $3; private doubles available. Linens $2. Closed April 15-June 30. Call for reservations.) **Le Ski Lab,** 7894 U.S. 40 (726-9841), offers discounts for hostelers (ski packages start at $7 per day, including skis, boots, and poles). Enjoy breakfast ($4-7) or lunch ($4-8) on the patio at **Carver's Bakery Café** (970-726-8202), at the end of the Cooper Creek Mall off U.S. 40. During peak season grab dinner from the bakery inside (open daily 7am-3pm).

The chamber of commerce (see above) also serves as the **Greyhound** depot (2 buses per day to Denver, 2hr., $15). **Home James Transportation Services** (303-726-5060 or 800-451-4844) runs door-to-door shuttles to and from Denver Airport. (Daily mid-April to mid-Nov.; every 2hr. mid-Nov. to mid-Dec. and early April; 11 per day mid-Dec. to April 1. $33. Call ahead for reservations.) From December to April, the perennially late **Río Grande Ski Train** (303-296-4754) leaves Denver's Union Station for Winter Park. (Mid-Dec. to April Sat.-Sun. 7:15am, arrive Winter Park 9:30am; depart 4:15pm. 2hr.; round-trip $35; reservations required).

Summit County Skiers, hikers, and mountain bikers can tap into a sportman's paradise in the highest county in the U.S., about 75 mi. west of Denver on I-70. The **Summit County Chamber of Commerce,** 110 Summit Blvd., P.O. Box 214, Frisco 80443 (970-668-2051), provides info on current area events (open Mon.-Fri. 9am-5pm). The **information center** ¼ mi. south of Silverthorne on Rte. 6 is also a convenient stop (262-0817; open Mon.-Fri. 9am-5pm). The ski resorts of **Breckenridge, Copper Mountain,** and **Keystone** are good alternatives to the more expensive resorts of Aspen and Vail. **Arapahoe Basin** has skiing until July 4 and sometimes into August, depending on snow conditions. The free **Summit Stage** shuttle bus connects all these resorts with the nearby towns of **Frisco, Dillon,** and **Silverthorne.**

The **Alpen Hütte (HI-AYH),** 471 Rainbow Dr. (970-468-6336), in Silverthorn, has welcoming hosts, a familial atmosphere, clean rooms with beautiful mountain views, and other year-round outdoor activities. Greyhound (from Denver) and Summit Stage both stop outside the door. (Free ski storage. Mountain bike rental. On-site parking. Office open 7am-noon and 4pm-midnight, located across the street in a huge recreation center. Lockout 9:30am-3:30pm. Curfew midnight. Summers $11, nonmembers $13; winter $13-23. Free lockers with $5 deposit. Linens and towels $2. Reservations recommended.) Several forest service campgrounds lie nearby; for instant seclusion, wing to **Eagle's Nest Wilderness.** For more info, contact **Dillon Ranger District Office,** 680 Blue River Parkway (970-468-5400; open winter Mon.-Fri. 8am-5pm, summers also Sat.-Sun. 9am-5pm).

Fashionable **Breckenridge** lies west of Silverton on I-70 and 9 mi. south of Frisco. Despite the many expensive restaurants and stores, you can still find reasonably priced accommodations at the **Fireside Inn,** 114 N. French St. (970-453-6456), parallel to and two blocks east of Main St. The indoor hot-tub is great for *apres-ski.* (Dorm $15, private rooms $45-65; in winter $25/$80-130. Reservations deposit—the first two nights lodging—due within 10 days of reservation; balance is due thirty days before your arrival. Closed in May.) To cut costs on ski gear, or to get the local scoop on restaurants and coffeehouses try the **The Near Gnu** (970-453-6026), on the north end of Main St. (open daily 10am-5pm).

■ Boulder

Almost painfully hip, Boulder lends itself to the pursuit of higher knowledge and better karma. It is home to both the central branch of the University of Colorado (CU) and the only accredited Buddhist university in the U.S., the Naropa Institute. Only here can you take summer poetry and mantra workshops lead by Beat guru Allen Ginsberg at the Jack Kerouac School of Disembodied Poets. Boulder is an aesthetic and athletic mecca. The nearby Flatiron Mountains, rising up as charcoal-colored slabs on the western horizon, beckon rock climbers, while to the east, the Great Plains float away into infinity. The town itself contains numerous multi-use paths; it is actually easier to get around on a bike than in a car. For those who do insist on driving, Boulder is *on the road* (U.S. Rte. 36) to the glorious Rocky Mountain National Park.

PRACTICAL INFORMATION

Tourist Office: Boulder Chamber of Commerce/Visitors Service, 2440 Pearl St. (442-1044), at Folsom about 10 blocks from downtown. Take bus #200. Open Mon.-Thurs. 8:30am-5pm, Fri. 9am-5pm. **University of Colorado Information** (492-1411), 2nd floor of University Memorial Center (UMC) student union. Open Mon.-Thurs. 7am-11pm, Fri.-Sat. 7am-midnight, Sun. 11am-11pm; term-time open Sun.-Thurs. 7am-midnight, Fri.-Sat. 7am-1am. The **CU Ride Board,** UMC 1st floor, advertises rides and riders—even in the summer.

Public Transportation: HOP, 2018 11th St. (447-8282). The HOP shuttles connect the Pearl St. Mall, The Hill, CU, and the Crossroads Mall in a two-way loop. Runs Mon.-Fri. 7am-7pm, with stops every 10min. 25¢, seniors 15¢. **RTD:** (299-6000 or 800-366-7433), at 14th and Walnut st. at the center of town. Mon.-Fri. 6am-8pm, Sat.-Sun. 8am-8pm. Fare 60¢, seniors 15¢. Denver Airport $8, under 12 $4; to Denver $2.50, Coors Field roundtrip $4.

Taxis: Boulder Yellow Cab (442-2277). $2.70 base fare, $1.20 per mi.

Car Rental: Budget Rent-a-Car, 1545 28th St. (444-9054), near the Clarion Harvest House. $32 per day with unlimited mi. Must be 25 with major credit card. Open Mon.-Fri. 7:30am-5:30pm, Sat.-Sun. 8am-1pm.

Bike Rental: University Bicycles, 839 Pearl St. (444-4196), downtown. Rents mountain bikes $14 per 4hr., $18 per 8hr., $24 overnight, with helmet and lock; 6-speeds $10/$12/$15. Open Mon.-Fri. 9am-7pm, Sat. 9am-7pm, Sun. 10am-5pm.

Crisis Lines: Rape Crisis, 443-7300. **Crisis Line,** 447-1665, for counseling.

Lesbian, Bisexual, Gay and Transgender Alliance, 492-8567; no regular hours during summer, but a recorded message has info. **Boulder Campus Gay, Lesbian, and Bisexual Resource Center,** 492-2966.

Emergency: 911.

Post Office: 1905 15th St. (938-1100), at Walnut St. Open Mon.-Fri. 7:30am-5:30pm, Sat. 10am-2pm. **ZIP code:** 80302. **Area code:** 303.

Boulder (pop. 83,000) is a small, manageable city. The most developed area lies between **Broadway** (Rte. 93) and **28th St.** (Rte. 36), two busy streets running parallel to each other north-south through the city. **Baseline Rd.,** which connects the Flatirons with the eastern plains, and **Canyon Blvd.** (Rte. 7), which follows the scenic Boulder Canyon up into the mountains, border the main part of the **University of Colorado** (CU) campus. The school's surroundings are known locally as **The Hill.** The pedestrian-only **Pearl St. Mall,** between 11th and 15th St., is the center of hip life in Boulder. Most east-west roads have names, while north-south streets have numbers; Broadway is a conspicuous exception.

ACCOMMODATIONS AND CAMPING

After spending your money at the Pearl St. Mall on tofu and yogurt, you may find yourself strapped for cash and without a room—Boulder doesn't offer many inexpensive places to spend the night. In the summer, you can rely on the hostel.

Boulder International Youth Hostel (AAIH/Rucksackers), 1107 12th St. (442-0522), two blocks west of the CU campus and 15min. south of the RTD station. From Denver take the A or B bus as close to College Ave. as possible. Located in the heart of CU housing and frats, the BIYH is a loud, youthful place. Shared hall bathrooms, kitchen, laundry, and TV. Lockout for dorms 10am-5pm. Curfew daily midnight. $13, CO residents $15. Private singles $27 per night, $150 per week; doubles $30/$180. Shower and towels free. Linen $4. Key deposit $4.

Chautauqua Association (442-3282), off Baseline Rd., turn at the Chautauqua Park sign and follow Kinnikinic to the administrative office, or take bus #203. Sits at the foot of the Flatirons. Stay in one of their suites (2-person $46, 4-person $59), or in a private cottage with a kitchen (4-night min. stay; 2 bedrooms $78; 3 bedrooms $98). Beware of coming here too often, lest you be labelled a Chautauquan. Make reservations months in advance.

The Boulder Mountain Lodge, 91 Four Mile Canyon Dr. (444-0882), 3mi. west on Canyon Rd. (which becomes Rte. 119). 25 beautiful sites in a grove of pines next to a creek. Pay phone, 2 hot tubs, seasonal pool, and free showers. Check-out by 10am; no reservations accepted. 3-person sites with or without hookup $14, $5 each additional person; $80 per week. Total vehicle length cannot exceed 25ft.

Camping info for **Arapahoe/Roosevelt National Forest** is available from the **Forest Service Station,** 2995 Baseline Rd. #10, Boulder 80303 (444-6600), at 32nd St. (open Mon.-Fri. 8am-5pm). Several campgrounds are available: **Kelly Dahl** (46 sites), 3 mi. south of Nederland on Rte. 119; **Rainbow Lakes** (18 sites), 13 mi. north of Nederland and 5 mi. west on unmaintained Arapahoe Glacier Rd. (no water; campground open late May to mid-Sept.). **Peaceful Valley** (15 sites) and **Camp Dick** (34 sites), both north on Rte. 72, offer cross-country skiing in the winter. All sites are $10, $5 per additional car, except Rainbow Lakes ($5).

FOOD AND HANGOUTS

The streets on The Hill surrounding CU and those along the Pearl St. Mall burst with good eateries, natural foods markets, cafés, and colorful bars, as well as bedraggled teens looking to supplement their parental allowance with the spare change of hapless travelers. Many more restaurants and bars line Baseline Rd. Boulder has more restaurants for vegetarians than for carnivores. For fresh produce and homemade breads and pies, head for the **Boulder County Farmer's Market** (494-4997), at 13th and Canyon; get there early (open May-Oct. Wed. 11am-4pm, Sat. 8am-2pm).

The Sink, 1165 13th St. (444-7465), on the Hill. When word went out in 1989 that the Sink had reopened, throngs of former "Sink Rats" commenced to travel back to Boulder; the restaurant still awaits the return of its former janitor, Robert Redford, who quit his job and headed to California in the late 50s. Surprisingly upscale new cuisine is served amidst wild graffiti and pipes. Burgers ($4), vegetarian, Mexican, and pizza. Call for info on live music (Tues. and Fri.). Open Mon.-Sun. 11am-2am; food served until 10pm.

Mountain Sun Pub and Brewery, 1535 Pearl St. (546-0886). A 21-tap salute to microbreweries near and far (pints $2.50) and upscale microbrewery fare; jalapeño cheeseburger $4.75, medium sized burritos $6. Open Mon.-Sat. 11:30am-1am, Sun. 2pm-midnight.

Boulder Salad Co., 2595 Canyon Blvd. (447-8272), revamps the cafeteria concept beyond your wildest dreams. Giant platters of salads, pastas, and grains settle onto your tray. All-you-can-eat lunch buffet $5, dinner $7-10. Open Mon.-Sat. 11am-9pm, Sun. 11am-8:30pm. Seniors 10% off, under 12 ½-price.

Creative Vegetarian Café (449-1952), on the corner of 19th and Pearl St, serves organic vegetarian food including portabello mushrooms, Indian curry, and tofu enchiladas ($6-10). Open for lunch Mon.-Fri. 11am-2pm, Sat.-Sun. 10am-3pm; for dinner Tues.-Thurs. and Sun. 5-9pm, Fri.-Sat. 5-10pm.

SIGHTS AND ENTERTAINMENT

The Boulder Museum of Contemporary Art, 1750 13th St. (443-2122), focuses on contemporary regional art (open Tues.-Fri. 11am-5pm, Sat. 9am-5pm, Sun. noon-5pm; free). The intimate and impressive **Leanin' Tree Museum,** 6055 Longbow Dr. (530-1442), presents 200 paintings and 80 bronze sculptures, focusing on western themes (open Mon.-Fri. 8am-4:30pm, Sat. 10am-4pm; free). Writers give readings in the Beat/ Buddhist tradition at the small **Naropa Institute,** 2130 Arapahoe Ave. (444-0202), or participate in a meditation workshop (open daily 9am-5pm). The **Rockies Brewing Company,** 2880 Wilderness Place (444-8448), between 30th St. and Foothills Pkwy., offers tours and free beer (25-min. tours Mon.-Sat. at 2pm; open Mon.-Sat. 11am-10pm).

University of Colorado intellectuals collaborate with wayward poets and back-to-nature crunchers to find innovative things to do. Check out the perennially outrageous street scene on the Mall and the Hill and watch the university's kiosks for the scoop on downtown happenings. The **University Memorial Center** (492-1411), at Broadway and 16th, hosts many events. On the third floor, its **Cultural Events Board** (492-3228) has the latest word on all CU-sponsored activities. In July and early August, the **Colorado Shakespeare Festival** (492-0554) suffers the slings and arrows of outrageous fortune (previews $9, tickets $12-36; student discounts available). The **Chautauqua Association** (442-3282) hosts the **Colorado Music Festival** (449-2413) from mid-July to August (tickets $6-33; students and seniors $2 off). During the second week of September, tunes wail at the **Boulder Blues Festival** (443-5858; $10-15). The **Parks and Recreation Department,** 3198 N. Broadway (441-3400), sponsors free summer performances in local parks; dance, classical and modern music, and children's theater are staples (open Mon.-Fri. 8am-5pm). **Running** and **biking** competitions dominate the Boulder sports scene.

■ Rocky Mountain Park

Of all the U.S. national parks, **Rocky Mountain National Park** is closest to heaven. A full third of the park lies above treeline, with Longs Peak piercing the sky at 14,255 ft. Here among the clouds, bitterly cold winds whip through a craggy landscape carpeted with tiny wildflowers, arctic shrubs, granite boulders, and crystalline lakes. The failure to find precious metal in these mountains in the late 1800s, and the area's subsequent designation as a national park in 1915, have allowed the region's delicate ecosystem to escape industrialization. Today, visitors mob the site, which has become the ultimate playground for the surrounding populace.

The city of **Estes Park,** located immediately east of the park, hosts the vast majority of would-be mountaineers and alpinists. As a result, the shopping malls and boulevards of Estes Park become painfully crowded in the summer. To the west of the park, the tranquil town of **Grand Lake,** located on the edges of two glacial lakes, is a quieter and more beautiful base from which to explore the park's less traversed but equally stunning western side. **Trail Ridge Rd. (U.S. 34),** which runs 45 mi. through the park from Grand Lake to Estes Park, is the highest continuous paved road in the U.S., rising to an altitude of 12,183 ft.

PRACTICAL INFORMATION

Tourist Office: Park Headquarters and Visitors Center (586-1206), 2½mi. west of Estes Park on Rte. 36 at the Beaver Meadows entrance to the park. Be sure to pick up a copy of the park newspaper, the *High Country Headlines.* (Open daily 8am-9pm; late Aug. to mid-June 8am-5pm. Summer evening programs are offered nightly at 7:30pm, and the park film is shown every ½hr. from 8:30am-4:30pm.)

Kawuneeche Visitors Center (627-3471), just outside the park's western entrance, 1¼ mi. north of Grand Lake, is the visitors center for the western half of the park. **Moraine Park Visitors Center and Museum** (586-3777), on Bear Lake Rd., handles educational programs in the park. The high altitude **Alpine Visitors Center,** at the crest of Trail Ridge Rd., has a great view of the tundra from the back window. **Lily Lake Visitors Center** is 6 mi. south of Park Headquarters on Rte. 7. The park entrance fee is $5 per vehicle, $3 per biker or pedestrian; the pass is valid for 7 days.
Police: Estes Park police, 586-4000. **Grand Lake police,** 627-3322.
Park Weather and Road Conditions: 586-1333 or 586-5555.
Emergency: 911. **Park Emergency:** 586-1399.
Post Offices: Grand Lake, 520 Center Dr. (627-3340). Open Mon.-Fri. 8:30am-5pm. **ZIP code:** 80447. **Estes Park,** 215 W. Riverside Dr. (586-8177). Open Mon.-Fri. 8:30am-5:30pm, Sat. 10am-2pm. **ZIP code:** 80517. **Area code:** 970.

You can reach the National Park from Boulder via U.S. 36 or from Loveland up the Big Thompson Canyon via U.S. 34. To get to Estes Park from Boulder, call the **Hostel Hauler** (586-3688) before 9pm and arrange a shuttle ($12, roundtrip $20).

ACCOMMODATIONS

Although Estes Park and Grand Lake have an abundance of expensive lodges and motels, there are few good deals on indoor beds near the national park, especially in winter when the temperatures drop and the tourists leave.

Estes Park

H Bar G Ranch Hostel (HI-AYH), 3500 H Bar G Rd., (586-3688; fax 586-5004). Turn off U.S. 34 onto Dry Gulch Rd. 1 mi. east of town next to Sombrero Stable; at H Bar G Rd. turn right to the hostel. With its spectacular views of the mountains and Estes Valley, this converted ranch could be a luxury resort. Instead, its hillside cabins, warm lodge, tennis court, recreation room, and kitchen shelter up to 100 hostelers. Proprieter Lou provides valuable info about the park and drives guests into town or the park entrance at 7:30am then retrieves them from the chamber of commerce in the afternoon. Members only. $9. Open late May to mid-Sept. Call ahead.

The Colorado Mountain School, 351 Moraine Ave. (586-5758). Tidy dorm-style accommodations are open to travelers unless already booked by mountain-climbing students. Wood bunks with comfortable mattresses, linens, and showers. Check-out 10am. 20 beds. $17. Reservations recommended 1 week in advance.

YMCA of the Rockies, 2515 Tunnel Rd., (586-3341), follow Rte. 66. It's fun to stay at the Y-M-C-A; extensive facilities on a 1400-acre complex, as well as daily hikes and other events for guests. A 4-person cabin with kitchen and bath from $51. 3 bedroom cabin with baths and kitchen from $133 per night. Guest membership $3, families $5. Call way ahead; they take reservations for members in early March, nonmembers in early April; booked for the summer by mid-May.

Grand Lake

Grand Lake draws fewer crowds than Estes Park in the summer. Though inaccessible without a car in the winter, the town is the "snowmobile capital of Colorado" and offers spectacular cross-country routes. Ask at the visitors center about seasonal events. Camping is available in the national forest campgrounds of **Stillwater Campground** located on the shores of **Lake Granby** (148 sites) or at **Green Ridge Campground,** located on the south end of Shadow Mountain Lake (81 campsites). Both sites have toilets, water, and boat ramps and the cost is $10 per night. Make reservations (800-260-2267) or arrive early to find a first come, first served spot.

Shadowcliff Hostel (HI-AYH), 405 Summerland Park Road (627-9220), from the western entrance, left to Grand Lake, then take the left fork ¼mi. into town on W. Portal Rd. Hand-built pine lodge perched on a cliff with a stunning view of Shadow Mountain Lake, Grand Lake, and the Rockies. Hiking trails, kitchen, andshowers.

$8, nonmembers $10, bedding rental $2. Private doubles $28, $4 per additional person. Cabins sleep 6-8; 6-day min. stay; $55-65 per day. Open June-Oct. Make reservations for the cabins a few *years* in advance.

Sunset Motel, 505 Grand Ave. (627-3318). Friendly owners plus cozy rooms equals a warm stay. Summer singles $40, doubles $45-55; winter $35/$45-55. 10% discount with *Let's Go: USA.*

Bluebird Motel, 30 River Dr. (627-9314), on Rte. 34 west of Grand Lake. Spiffy rooms with spotted carpets, fluffy pink curtains, TV, and fridges. Overlooks Shadow Mountain Lake and the snow-capped Continental Divide. Singles $40, doubles $49-55; rates go down $5 in winter.

CAMPING

National Park Campgrounds: Moraine Park (5½mi. from Estes; 247 sites; open all year) has secluded spots while **Glacier Basin** (9mi. from Estes; 150 sites; open in the summer only) has better views. Both require reservations in summer. Sites are $12; call DESTINET at 586-1206 or 800-365-2267; seven day max. stay. **Aspenglen,** 5mi. west of Estes Park near the Fall River entrance, has 56 sites ($10) and is open May 8-Sept. 30, with a 7 day max. stay. **Timber Creek,** 10mi. north of Grand Lake, the only national park campground on the western side of the park, is open year-round and has 100 woodsy sites ($10; in winter, no water, free, 7 day max. stay).

Olive Ridge Campground, 15mi. south of Estes Park on Rte. 7, has 56 first come, first served sites. Reservations are available (800-280-CAMP/2267; $10 per site, $5 per additional vehicle, 14 day max. stay). **Sprague Lake Handicamp** (586-1242), 7mi. from Estes Park Headquarters at Sprague Lake Picnic Area, is wheelchair accessible via a ½-mi. flat gravel path. The camp accommodates 6 wheelchairs and 12 campers. A $10 backcountry permit is required.

A **backcountry** camping permit is needed in the summer. On the east slope, contact the **Boulder Ranger District,** 2995 Baseline Rd. #110 (303-444-6600; open Mon.-Fri. 8am-5pm). On the west slope, contact the **Sulphur Ranger District,** 62429 Rte. 40 (887-3331), in Granby. (Open daily 8am-5pm; Sept.-May Mon.-Fri. 8am-5pm.)

FOOD

Both towns near the park have good restaurants and grocery stores where you can stock up on trail snacks. Look for "bulk foods" at **Safeway** in Estes' Stanley Village Mall across from the chamber of commerce.

Estes Park

Mama Rose's, 388 E. Elkhorn (586-3330), on the river-walk in Barlow Plaza, offers large portions of Italian food. Mama's special gives carbo-depleted mountain hoppers all-you-can-eat soup, salad, garlic bread, pasta, and spumoni for just $8. Also try the all-you-can-eat breakfast special ($6). Open daily 9am-4pm and 7pm-11pm.

Poppy's, 832 Elkhorn Ave. (586-8282), in Barlow Plaza, serves fresh individual-sized pizzas ($3), as well as fancy specialty pizzas, in a genteel fast-food atmosphere. 15" pizza $10-12, subs $4-7, all-you-can-eat salad/soup bar $6. Open Sun.-Fri. 11am-8pm, Sat. 11am-9pm.

Mountain Home Café (586-6624). Try Mike's waffles (from $2), made from scratch and served all day long, or the potato pancakes if you're too good for breakfast. Open Mon.-Sat. 7am-2:30pm, Sun. 8am-1pm.

Grand Lake

Cozy Corner, 825 Grand Ave. (627-5485), has friendly owners who serve large burgers ($5) and three crèpe breakfasts ($6) *al fresco.* Open daily summers 9am-9pm, winters closed on Thurs.

The Terrace Inn, 813 Grand Ave. (627-3079). Good homemade grub. Debby's special Italian sauce and huge fluffy pancakes ($4) are definite favorites. Open summers Sun.-Fri. 8am-9pm, Sat. 8am-10pm.

Marie's Grand Lake Café, 928 Grand Ave. (627-9475), located on the lake, is a watering hole for locals. Huge breakfast of 2 eggs, 2 sausage links, 2 pancakes, and hashbrowns for $3.50, burritos for $5. Open daily 6am-10pm.

SIGHTS AND ACTIVITIES

The star of this park is **Trail Ridge Rd.** (U.S. 34), a 50-mi. stretch that takes you up 12,183 ft. above sea level into frigid tundra. The roundtrip drive takes three hours by car, including stops to gaze at outrageous views of the Rockies and time spent sitting behind tour buses driving at 5mph. The road is closed Oct.-May for obvious reasons. For a closer look at the fragile environment, walk from roadside to the **Forest Canyon Overlook,** or take the ½-hour **Tundra Trail** roundtrip.

Serious mountaineers and hikers will be attracted to **Longs Peak** (14,255 ft.), the highest and most prominent mountain in the park. Athletic, acclimated hikers can climb the peak in late July or August by taking the 15 mi. round trip Keyhole route from the Longs Peak Ranger Station. The last 1½ mi. to the top involve scrambling over rock ledges and boulders. Make sure to leave before 6am to avoid the risk of thunderstorms and check in at the Long's Peak ranger station the day before you go.

For those in search of a calmer experience, rangers can help plan a hike to suit your interests and abilities. Since the trailheads in the park are already high, just a few hours of hiking will bring you into unbeatable alpine scenery along the Continental Divide. The 12,000 to 14,000-ft. altitudes can make your lungs feel like they're wrapped in rubber bands; give your body enough time to adjust before starting up the higher trails. Some easy trails include the 3.6-mi. roundtrip from Wild Basin Ranger Station to **Calypso Cascades** and the 2.8-mi. roundtrip from the Long Peaks Ranger Station to **Eugenia Mine.**

From Grand Lake, a trek into the scenic and remote **North** or **East Inlets** should leave camera-toting crowds behind. Climb to the superlative **Lake Nanita** (leave from North Inlet), which ascends 2240 ft. over the course of 11 mi. through pristine wilderness. From East Inlet, hike the 7 mi. to Lake Verna if you still feel strong. Plump trout swim in picturesque mountain lakes, offering excellent fishing.

While no biking is allowed on trails within the park itself, mountain bikers can head to the nearby national forests. **Colorado Bicycling Adventures,** 184 E. Elkhorn (586-4241 or 800-607-8765), rents bikes. ($5 per hr., $9 per 2hr., $15 per ½-day, $20 per day. Helmets included. 10% hosteler discounts.) They can also tell you where to find good mountain biking, or drive you up to the top of Trail Crest Road and guide you down the 5000-vertical-ft. paved descent. (2-hr. tour $20, 4-hr. tour $35, bike rental, helmet, and transport included. Open daily 9am-9pm, off-season 10am-5pm.)

■ Aspen

A world-renowned asylum for musicians and skiers, Aspen is a nightmare for the budget traveler. In this upper-class playground, where shoppers exclaim "I'll take it!" without asking for prices, low-budget living is a distant vision. To catch Aspen on the semi-cheap, stay in **Glenwood Springs** (40mi. north on Rte. 82; see p. 592) and make a daytrip here, or camp amidst aspen groves in the nearby national forest.

Pick up the free *Traveler's Guide* magazine at the **visitors center,** 320 E. Hyman Ave., in the **Wheeler Opera House** (open Mon.-Sat. 9am-7pm, Sun. 10am-7pm; winter daily 9am-5pm). For info on hikes and **camping** within 15 mi. of Aspen, contact the **Aspen Ranger District,** 806 W. Hallam (925-3445; **weather/avalanche info** 920-1664). They also sell a topographic map of the area ($3; open daily 8am-4:30pm, Sept.-May closed weekends). Aspen's **area code** is 970.

If you stay here, you'll have to bite the bullet and reach deep into your pockets. The **Little Red Ski Haüs,** 118 E. Cooper (925-3333), lies two blocks west of downtown in a cozy Victorian-style B&B (summer from $24 per person for a quad with shared bath, winter from $39 per person). The **St. Moritz Lodge,** 344 W. Hyman Ave. (925-3220 or 800-817-2069), charms ski bums with a pool, sauna, hot tub, fridge, and microwaves. (Dorm beds in summer $27, in early and late winter $30, peak winter from $39.) Unless six ft. of snow cover the ground, try **camping** in the one of the many **National Forest Campgrounds** that are within 5 mi. of Aspen. Reservable and first come, first served sites scatter just west of Aspen on Maroon Rd. (only accessible from 5pm-8:30am) and southeast of Aspen on Rte. 82. (3-5 day max. stay. $10 per night, $5 per additional vehicle. Sites fill before noon. Open June-early Sept. Reserve by calling 800-280-2267.) Free **backcountry camping** is also available by contacting the Aspen Ranger District.

The **Main Street Bakery,** 201 E. Main St. (925-6446), creates gourmet soups ($4-6), homemade granola with fruit ($4.25), and three-grain pancakes ($4-5; open Mon.-Sat. 7am-9:30pm, Sun. 7am-4pm). The **In and Out House,** 233 E. Main St. (925-6647), is just that—a revolving door of customers in an outhouse-sized space. They offer tasty sandwiches on freshly baked bread ($3-5; open Mon.-Fri. 8am-7pm, Sat. 9am-4pm, Sun. 10am-4pm). You'll find **Woody Creek Tavern,** 2 Woody Creek Pl. (923-4585), off Rte. 82 towards Glenwood Springs past the Snowmass turnoff, with burgers ($7) and burritos (open daily 11:30am-10pm). Even if you can't afford the slopes, you can probably buy a beer. The **Flying Dog Brew Pub,** 424 E. Cooper Ave. (925-7464), is a mini-brewery serving somewhat expensive American food and excellent beer; try a five-beer sampler for $3.75 (open daily 11:30am-2am; kitchen closes at 10pm). **The Red Onion,** 420 E. Cooper (925-9043), has a long, narrow bar and restaurant. Happy hour (daily 4-6pm) features selected ½-price appetizers (open daily 11:30am-2am; kitchen closes at 10pm).

Skiing is the main attraction in Aspen. The hills surrounding town contain four ski areas: **Aspen Mountain, Aspen Highlands, Buttermilk Mountain,** and **Snowmass Ski Area** (925-1220 or 800-525-6200). The resorts sell interchangeable lift tickets ($52, kids $31, over 70 or under 6 free). The **Glenwood Springs Hostel** offers a $36 full-day package for the Aspen ski resorts, including an interchangeable lift ticket, transportation, skis, and ski clothes. In the summer, ride the **Silver Queen Gondola** (925-1220 or 800-525-6200) to the top of the Aspen mountains (open daily 9:30am-4pm; $15, ages 13-19 $9, over 70 and under 13 free). At Snowmass Mountain, you can take a chairlift to the top and ride your mountain bike down (summers daily 10:30am-5pm; free). The **Maroon Bells** are not-to-be-missed mountains, but Maroon Creek Rd. is closed to public traffic from 8:30am-5pm daily. To avoid paying $5 for a long, slow bus ride, plan an early morning or a sunset hike. Aspen's most famous event, the **Aspen Music Festival** (925-9042) features jazz, opera, and classical music from late June to August. Free bus transportation takes listeners from Rubey Park downtown to "the Tent," before and after all concerts. The July 4 concert is free as are many others. Call for a schedule.

■ Glenwood Springs

Glenwood Springs, located along I-70, 40 mi. north of Aspen on Colorado Rte. 82, is a smart choice for the budget traveler. Renowned for its steaming hot springs and vapor caves, Glenwood is sprinkled with budget-friendly markets, cafés, pool/dance halls, and a great hostel. Contact **Glenwood Springs Chamber Resort Association,** 1102 Grand Ave. (945-6589), for town info. (Open Mon.-Fri. 8:30am-5pm, Sat.-Sun. 9am-3pm; Sept.-May closed weekends.) The gigantic **U.S. Forest Service** headquarters (945-2521), at 9th and Grand Ave., provides info about camping and outdoor activities (open Mon.-Fri. 8am-5pm). The **Aspen/Glenwood Bus** shuttles between Aspen and Glenwood daily. (Last bus leaves Glenwood at 3pm, Aspen at 5pm. $5 one way, children and seniors $4, within Glenwood $1.) The **Amtrak** station, 413 7th St. (945-9563 or 800-872-7245), chugs once per day to Denver (6½hr., $56) and Salt Lake City (9hr., $89). (Open daily 9am-5pm. Ticket office open daily 9:30am-4:30pm.) **Greyhound** runs from 118 W. 6th St. (945-8501). To: Denver (6 per day, 3½hr., $22); Grand Junction (5 per day, 2 hr., $9). (Open Mon.-Fri. 7am-2pm and 4-5:30pm, Sat. 8am-2pm.) Glenwood Springs's **area code** is 970.

Within walking distance of the springs, you'll find the **Glenwood Springs Hostel (HI-AYH),** 1021 Grand Ave. (945-8545 or 800-9-HOSTEL/946-7835), consisting of a spacious Victorian house and a newer building next door. Hostelers can ski at Sunlight, get big discounts at Aspen or Vail, go white-water rafting ($25), hike the Maroon Bells ($22), rent a mountain bike ($8), or go on an unforgettable caving trip through the labyrinthine Fulford Cavern ($22). (Free pickup from train/bus stations. Some free food. No curfew. Lockout 10am-4pm. $10, $12 for deluxe dorms, $18 for private single, $24 for a private double. Linen included.) The Victorian B&B next door is **Adducci's Inn,** 1023 Grand Ave. (945-9341). *Let's Go*-toting guests get $28-65 singles, $38-65 doubles, including breakfast; otherwise prices are slightly higher. (Free pick-up from bus and train stations. $10 per additional person.)

For a good and filling breakfast or lunch, try the **Daily Bread Café and Bakery,** 729 Grand Ave. (945-6253). They have a south of the border omelette with potatoes and toast for $6. (Open Mon.-Fri. 7am-2pm, Sat. 8am-2pm, Sun. 8am-noon.) **Doc Holliday's Saloon,** 724 Grand Ave. (945-9050), is the place for burgers ($7) and beers ($1.50-3). Weekdays (5-7pm) the Doc offers dollar drafts and food. (Food until 11pm, open daily 10am-2am.)

Glenwood Hot Springs Pool, 401 N. River Rd. (945-7131 or 800-537-7946), located in a huge resort complex and maintained at 90°F year-round, contains the world's largest outdoor hot springs pool, a waterslide, and spas with different water temperatures. (Open summers daily 7:30am-10pm, winters daily 9am-10pm. Day pass $6.50, after 9pm $4.75; ages 3-12 $4.25/$3.75.) Just one block from the large pools, the smelly gasses of **Yampah Spa and Vapor Caves,** 709 E. 6th St. (945-0667), along with 115°F steam, creates a relaxing experience amidst the dim underground caves. After sweating your brains out, relax to new age music in the Solarium ($7.75, hostelers $3.75; open daily 9am-9pm). Ski at uncrowded **Sunlight,** 10901 County Rd. 117 (945-7491 or 800-445-7931), 10 mi. west of town. (Hostelers Mon.-Fri. $17, Sat.-Sun. $21 per day. Non-hostelers, $28, under 12 $18.)

▓ Grand Junction

Grand Junction gets its hyperbolic name from its seat at the confluence of the Colorado and Gunnison Rivers and the conjunction-junction of the Río Grande and Denver Railroads. The city serves as a base from which to explore **Grand Mesa, Colorado National Monument, Arches National Park,** and **Moab.** Several **wineries** ferment to the east of town; to the west the red Utah desert bakes under blue skies.

Grand Junction lies at the intersection of U.S. 50 and U.S. 6 in northwestern Colorado. The **Grand Junction Visitor and Convention Bureau,** 740 Horizon Dr. (244-1480), on I-70, has a weekly lecture and slide show programs on the history and culture of southwest Colorado (open daily 8:30am-8pm, late Sept.-early May 8:30am-5pm). **Enterprise Car Rental,** 406 S. 5th St. (242-8103), rents compact cars for $35 per day, $180 per week. You must be 21. Denver is 228 mi. to the east; Salt Lake City 240 mi. to the west. The **Greyhound station,** 230 S. 5th St. (242-6012), has service to Denver (4 per day, 5½hr., $35); Durango (1 per day, 4hr., $34); Salt Lake City (1 per day, 6hr., $43); Los Angeles (5 per day, 15hr., $86). (Open daily 3:15am-5pm, 8pm-1:30am.) **Amtrak,** 337 S. 1st St. (241-2733 or 800-872-7245), has one trip a day to Denver ($74) and Salt Lake City ($72). (Open daily 10am-6pm.) Grand Junction's **post office:** 241 N. 4th St. (244-3401; open Mon.-Fri. 8am-5:15pm, Sat. 9am-12:30pm). **ZIP code:** 81502. **Area code:** 970.

Grand Junction's chief attribute is its location among several natural wonders. Fortunately, the smoothly running **Melrose Hotel (HI-AYH),** 337 Colorado Ave. (242-9636 or 800-430-4555), between 3rd and 4th St., assists travelers in navigating these sights. Owners Marcus and Sabrina will make you feel at home and direct you to the best deals in town. Tours to Arches National Park ($35), Colorado National Monument ($25), and Black Canyon plus Grand Mesa ($30) are great, taking you off tourist paths for serious sight-seeing (all three trips $75). In winter, $25 will buy a day trip to Powderhorn, including a lift ticket, skis, boots, poles, clothes, and transportation. (Kitchen facilities. Dorms $10, including light breakfast. Singles $22.50, with private bath $27.50; doubles $26.) **Le Master Motel,** 2858 North Ave. (243-3230), has singles for $32, and doubles for $36. Camp in **Highline State Park** (858-7208), 24 mi. from town and 7 mi. north of Exit 15 on I-70 (fishing access, restrooms; 25 sites $10), or **Island Acres State Park** (464-0548), 12 mi. east on the banks of the Colorado River (6 tent sites $6, 18 full hookups $11).

The **Rockslide Restaurant and Brew Pub,** 401 S. Main (245-2111), joins the avalanche of micro-breweries covering the nation. The home-brewed Big Bear Stout is $3 per pint. (Generous 10-in. pizza $6.75. During happy hour, the cost of your food will depend upon what time you entered; at 4:37pm, entrees are $4.37. Open Mon.-Fri. 11am-10pm, Sat.-Sun. 8am-11pm; bar open daily 11am-11pm.) The large and popular **Dos Hombres Restaurant,** 421 Brach Dr. (242-8861), just south of Broadway (Rte. 340) on the southern bank of the Colorado River, serves great Mexican food in a casual setting. ($4 lunch special includes two enchiladas or two tostadas plus rice, beans, chips, and salsa. Open daily 11am-10pm.) For all the fixins', head to **City Market** (243-0842), at the corner of 2nd St. and Rood Ave.

Grand Junction is surrounded by natural beauty, but there are sights to see in town as well. Most visitors will be surprised to find wineries amidst the spires and mesas of Grand Junction, but the 11 different sites and their free samples will get you tanked if you visit every one. To arrange tours pick up a free map at the Grand Junction Visitors Center or call the **Wine Industry Development Board,** 523-1232.

■ Colorado Monument

Colorado National Monument is a 32-sq.-mi. sculpture of steep cliff faces, canyon walls, and obelisk-like spires wrought by the forces of gravity, wind, and water. The **Rim Rock Dr.** runs along the edge of red canyons, providing views of awe-inspiring rock monoliths, the Grand Mesa, and the city of Grand Junction. **Window Rock Trail** and **Otto's Trail,** both ¼ mi., are easy walks to points from which you can gaze at the eerie, skeletal rock formations. The 6-mi. **Monument Canyon** trail gives a greater sense of grandeur, as it wanders amidst the giant rock formations. The monument charges an admission fee of $4 per vehicle or $2 per cyclist or hiker. Check in at the monument **headquarters and visitors center** (970-858-3617), near the western entrance (open daily May-Sept. 8am-7:30pm, off season daily 9am-5pm). **Saddlehorn Campground,** near the visitors center, provides 80 partially shaded sites on a first come, first served basis (restrooms, water, $9). The **Bureau of Land Management,** 2815 Horizon (970-244-3000; open Mon.-Fri. 7:30am-4:30pm), across from the airport, maintains three free primitive campgrounds near **Glade Park** at Mud Springs. Bring your own water.

■ Grand Mesa

Grand Mesa, or "the great table," is the world's largest flat-top mountain, looming 50 mi. east of Grand Junction (by road). A Native American story tells how the Mesa's many lakes were formed by fragments of a serpent torn to bits by a mad mother eagle who believed her young to be inside the serpent's belly. Recently, geologists have estimated that a 300-ft.-thick lava flow covered the entire region 6 billion years ago, and the Mesa is the only portion to have endured erosion. The numerous lakes on the Mesa that serve as spawning grounds for insects also provide fine fishing, as well as opportunities for pleasant hiking.

The Mesa not only has an excellent view, but excellent camping as well. The district **forest service,** 764 Horizon Dr. (970-242-8211), in Grand Junction off I-70, has maps ($3) and info on the **campsites** they maintain on the Mesa (open Mon.-Fri. 8am-5pm). **Island Lake** (41 sites, $6) and **Ward Lake** (27 sites, $7) are both on the water and have good fishing. **Jumbo** (26 sites, $7), **Little Bear** (37 sites, $7), and **Cottonwood** (42 sites, $7) are reasonably large campgrounds. Call the visitors center (856-4153) for more info on any site.

The **Mesa Lakes Resort** (303-268-5467), on Rte. 65 on the way to the summit, is an old fashioned mountain retreat. Feast on all-you-can-eat tacos for $5 in the lakeside restaurant from 5:30-8pm. The resort rents extremely rustic cabins for 2-4 people (stove, table, chairs, no running water; $40 per day), and more modern cabins for 6-12 people ($85-110 per day). A general store and fishing is available at the resort, horseback riding and motorboat rental is available nearby.

■ Colorado Springs

When pioneers rushed west toward Colorado in search of gold (shouting "Pikes Peak or Bust!") they were surprised to find towering red rocks and cave dwellings at the foot of the peak. The pioneers called the bizarre rock formations the Garden of the Gods, in part because of the Ute legend that the rocks were petrified bodies of enemies hurled down by the Gods above. Today, the United States Olympic Team, housed in Colorado Springs, are the ones looking for gold, while jets from United States Air Force Academy streak through wisps of clouds overhead.

PRACTICAL INFORMATION

Tourist Office: Colorado Springs Convention and Visitors Bureau, 104 S. Cascade #104 (635-7506 or 800-368-4748). Pick up the free *Colorado Springs Pikes Peak Region Official Visitors Guide* and the city bus map. Open summers daily 8:30am-5pm, winters Mon.-Fri. 8:30am-5pm.

Tours: Gray Line Tours, 3704 Colorado Ave. (633-1747 or 800-345-8197), at the Garden of the Gods Campgrounds. Trips to the U.S. Air Force Academy and Garden of the Gods (4hr., $20, under 13 $10), Pikes Peak (4hr., $25, under 13 $15). Offers a 10mi. whitewater rafting trip on the Arkansas River (7hr., includes lunch, $60, under 13 $40; must weigh at least 50 lbs). Office open daily 7am-10pm.

Buses: Greyhound, 120 S. Weber St. (635-1505). To: Denver (7 per day, 1¾hr., $11.25); Pueblo (5 per day, 50min., $7.50); Albuquerque (4 per day, 7-9hr., $60). Tickets sold daily 5:15am-9pm.

Public Transportation: Colorado Springs City Bus Service, 125 E. Kiowa (475-9733), at Nevada, 3 blocks from the Greyhound station. Serves Widefield, Manitou Springs, Fort Carson, Garden of the Gods, and Peterson AFB. Service Mon.-Sat. 6am-6pm every ½hr., irregular evening service until 10pm. Fare 75¢, seniors and kids 35¢, under 6 free; long trips 25¢ extra. Exact change required.

Taxis: Yellow Cab, 634-5000. $3 first mi., $1.35 per additional mi.

Car Rental: Ugly Duckling, 2021 E. Platte (634-1914). From $20 per day, $108 per week. 100 free mi. per day. Open Mon.-Fri. 8:30am-5:30pm, Sat. 8:30am-3pm. Must stay in Colorado and be 21 with major credit card or $350 deposit.

Crisis Lines: Crisis Emergency Services, 635-7000. 24hr. **Rape Crisis Line,** 444-7563 (day), 444-7000 (night).

Road Conditions: 635-7623 (recording).

Emergency: 911.

Post Office: 201 Pikes Peak Ave. (570-5336), at Nevada Ave. Open Mon.-Fri. 7:30am-5:30pm, Sat. 8am-1pm. **ZIP code:** 80903. **Area code:** 719.

Colorado Springs is laid out in a grid of broad thoroughfares. The mountains are to the west. **Nevada Ave.** is the main north-south strip running a few blocks east of I-25, known for its bars and restaurants. **Colorado Ave.** is the east-west axis, which connects with **U.S. 24** on the city's west side. **I-25** from Denver plows through downtown. East of Nevada Ave., there are mostly residential homes and large shopping centers. The numbered streets west of Nevada ascend as you move west.

ACCOMMODATIONS AND CAMPING

Avoid the mostly shabby motels along Nevada Ave. If the youth hostel is full, try a nearby campground or a place along W. Pikes Peak Ave. and W. Colorado Ave.

Garden of the Gods Youth Hostel and Campground (HI-AYH), 3704 W. Colorado Ave. (475-9450 or 800-248-9451). Twelve 4-bunk cabins hidden behind the massive 300-site campground. Hostelers have access to all the facilities of the campground including an 8-ft.-deep pool, jacuzzi, laundry, showers, and $3 all-you-can-eat pancake breakfast. The bunkrooms have no kitchens and are not heated, so bring a sleeping bag. Open April-Oct. Members only $14. Linens $4. The campground itself is probably a better deal for RVs ($25 full hookup, $23 partial) than for its tents (3 person sites $22, $2 per extra person). The sites are mostly on a gravel parking lot. Campers enjoy all amenities. Reservations recommended, particularly during summer weekends.

Apache Court Motel, 3401 W. Pikes Peak Ave. (471-9440), take bus #1 west down Colorado Ave. to 34th St. and walk 1 block north. Small, pink adobe rooms with friendly owners. A/C, TV, hot tub. Summer singles $43, doubles $45; winter $29/ $33.

Amarillo Motel, 2801 W. Colorado Ave. (635-8539). Take bus #1 west down Colorado Ave. to 28th St. Bunker-like rooms lack windows, but have clean kitchens and TV. Laundry available. Singles $28, doubles $45.

About ½ hr. from Colorado Springs, several **Pike National Forest** campgrounds lie in the mountains flanking Pikes Peak (generally open May-Sept.), but no local transportation serves this area. Campgrounds clutter Rte. 67 5-10 mi. north of **Woodland Park,** which is 18 mi. northwest of the Springs on U.S. 24. Others fringe U.S. 24 near the town of Lake George, 50 mi. west of the Springs. (All sites $8-10.) You can always camp off any road on national forest property for free if you are at least 150 yds. from a road or stream. The **Forest Service Office,** 601 S. Weber (636-1602), has maps of the area ($3; open Mon.-Fri. 8am-5pm). Farther afield, you can camp in the **Eleven Mile State Recreation Area** (748-3401 or 800-678-2267), off a spur road from U.S. 24 near Lake George, surrounds a reservoir (showers 50¢; sites $6, electricity $9; entrance fee $3).

FOOD AND NIGHTLIFE

Students and the young-at-heart perch among outdoor tables in front of the cafés and restaurants that line Tejon Ave. a few blocks east of downtown. **Poor Richard's Restaurant,** 326 North Tejon (632-7721), is the local coffeehouse/college hangout, serving pizza ($2.25 per slice; $9.50 per pie), sandwiches, and salads ($4-7; open daily 11am-10pm). Just across the street, **La Dolce Vita,** 33 N. Tejan (632-1369), is a coffeeshop/bookstore with an intellectual attitude, steaming up cappucino ($1.50) and serving croissant sandwiches ($4.25). They also have an extensive schedule of speakers, music, and workshops. (Open Mon.-Fri. 6:30am-10pm, Sat. 9am-10pm, Sun. 9am-3pm.) **La Baguette,** 2417 W. Colorado Ave. (577-4818), bakes bread and melts fondues a sight better than you might expect in a place so far from Paris. Soup and roll go for $3.75; cheese fondue with apple slices is $6. (Open Mon. 7am-6pm, Tues.-Sat. 7am-8:30pm, Sun. 8am-5pm.) Big crowds gather at **Henri's,** 2427 W. Colorado Ave. (634-9031), for fantastic margaritas and Mexican food, such as a trio of chicken tacos ($8) and enchiladas ($3 each; open daily 11:30am-10pm). The **Dublin House,** 1850 Dominion Way (528-1704), at Academy St., is a popular sports bar with occasional live tunes (open Mon.-Thurs. 4pm-2am, Fri.-Sun. 11am-2am).

Ground Zero

While most Cold War era bomb shelters are buried under 5-10 ft. of dirt, the **North American Air Defense Command Headquarters (NORAD)** (474-2239) was constructed 1800 feet below Cheyenne Mountain. The center looks like something out of a James Bond movie; a three mile tunnel leads to computers and detectors which scan the horizon for incoming inter-continental ballistic missiles. The center was designed to be operational even after a direct nuclear attack. Call way ahead to make reservations for a tour; security clearance can take up to six months. The **Peterson Air Force Base,** just east of Academy Blvd., houses a **visitors center** and the **Edward J. Peterson Space Command Museum** (556-4415; open Tues.-Fri. 8:30am-4:30pm, Sat. 9:30am-4:30pm, free).

SIGHTS

Pikes Peak From any part of the town, one can't help noticing the 14,110-ft. summit of Pikes Peak on the western horizon. You can climb the peak via the strenuous but well-maintained 13-mi. **Barr Burro Trail;** the trailhead is in Manitou Springs by the "Manitou Incline" sign (bus #1 to Ruxton). Don't despair if you don't reach the top—explorer Zebulon Pike never reached it either, and they named the whole mountain after him. Otherwise, pay the fee to drive up the gorgeous 19-mi. **Pikes Peak Highway** (684-9383), which is actually a well-maintained dirt road administered by the Colorado Department of Public Works. (Open June-Sept. 7am-7pm; Apr.-May, Dec.-Mar. Wed.-Sun. 9am-3pm, and Sept.-Nov. daily 9am-3pm, weather permitting. $5, ages 6-11 $2.) Five mi. west in Manitou Springs, you can also reserve a seat on the **Pikes Peak Cog Railway,** 515 Ruxton Ave. (685-5401), which takes you to the top from May to early October daily 8am-5:20pm, with departures every 80 minutes. (Call for times in May, Sept. and Oct. Roundtrip $22, ages 5-11 $10, under 5 free if held on lap.) From the summit, Kansas, the Sangre de Cristo Mountains, and the Continental Divide unfold before you. This lofty view inspired Kathy Lee Bates to write "America the Beautiful." Expect cold weather.

Cave of the Winds For more adventurous hiking through subterranean passages, head for the contorted caverns of the Cave of the Winds (685-5444) on Rte. 24, 6 mi. west of Exit 141 off I-25 (guided tours daily every 15min. Labor Day-Memorial Day 10am-5pm, summers daily 9am-9pm; $8, ages 6-15 $4). Just above Manitou Springs on Rte. 24 lies the **Manitou Cliff Dwellings Museum** (685-5242 or 685-5394) on the U.S. 24 bypass, where you can wander through a pueblo of ancient Anasazi buildings dating from 1100-1300AD. (Open daily June-Aug. 9am-8pm. $5, seniors $3.50, ages 7-11 $2.50.) **Seven Falls,** west on Cheyenne Blvd. from downtown, are lit up at night during the summer months; each fall is a different color.

Going for the Gold and Aiming High Olympic hopefuls train with some of the world's most high-tech sports equipment at the **U.S. Olympic Complex,** 750 E. Boulder St. (578-4644 or 578-4618), at I-25 Exit 156A; take bus #1 east to Farragut. Every ½ hr., the complex offers free 1¼-hr. tours that include a tear-jerking film. (Open Mon.-Sat. 9am-5pm, Sun. 10am-4pm; off season Mon.-Sat. 9am-4pm, Sun. noon-4pm.) Earlier searches for gold are recorded at the **Pioneers' Museum,** 215 S. Tejon St. (578-6650), downtown, which recounts the settling of Colorado Springs, and includes a display on the techniques and instruments of a pioneer doctor (open Tues.-Sat. 10am-5pm; free). Get your own yellow chunk at the **Western Museum of Mining and Industry,** 1025 N. Gate Rd. (488-0880), where you can learn how to pan for gold. (Open Mon.-Sat. 9am-4pm, Sun. noon-4pm. $5, students and seniors $4, ages 5-12 $2, under 5 free. Dec.-Feb. hours vary.)

Hosting over a million visitors yearly, the most popular attraction in the area is the **United States Air Force Academy,** 12 mi. north of town off I-25 Exit 156B (472-4515). The chapel was constructed of aluminum, steel, and other materials used in building airplanes (open Mon.-Sat. 8am-6pm, Sun. 1-6pm). On weekdays during the school year, cadets gather at 12:10pm near the chapel for the cadet lunch formation (i.e., to eat). The **visitors center** (472-2555 or 472-2025) has self-guided tour maps, info on special events, and a free 14-min. movie every ½-hr. (open daily 9am-6pm).

■ Great Sand Dunes

When Colorado's mountains all begin to look the same, make a path to the **Great Sand Dunes National Monument** at the northwest edge of the **San Luis Valley.** The monument drifts 32 mi. northeast of Alamosa and 112 mi. west of Pueblo on Rte. 150 off U.S. 160. There, a sea of 700-ft. sand dunes, representing thousands of years of wind-blown accumulation, laps silently at the base of the **Sangre de Cristo Range.** The progress of the dunes through passes in the range is checked by the shallow

Medano Creek; visitors can wade across the creek when it flows (April to mid-July). Those with 4WD can motor over the **Medano Pass Primitive Road.** The best way to enjoy the dunes is to just plow on in, but beware the intense afternoon heat. At the southern boundary of the monument, the **Oasis** complex (378-2222) offers 4WD tours that huff over Medano Pass Primitive Road to the nether regions of the dunes (2 tours daily; 2hr.; $18, ages 5-11 $9).

Rangers preside over daily activities. Full schedules are at the **visitors center** (378-2312), ½ mi. past the entrance gate. (Open daily 9am-6pm, Labor Day-Memorial Day hours vary. Entrance fee for vehicles $4, pedestrians and bikers $2.) Pick up the newspaper *Sand Dune Breezes,* at the entrance gate for suggestions on drives and hikes. For more info, contact the Superintendent, Great Sand Dunes National Monument, Mosca, CO 81146 (378-2312). For **emergencies** within the park, call 911.

Pinyon Flats (378-2312) is the monument's primitive, cactus-covered campground. Bring mosquito repellent in June. (88 first come, first served sites $8; arrive by early afternoon to get a site. Group sites reservable, $2 per person, $25 min.) Get free **backcountry camping** permits for the dunes from the visitors center. If the park's sites are full, Oasis (see above) will quench your needs with showers, two-person sites ($10, with hookup $15; each additional person $2.50), and cabins or tee-pees ($25 for 2 people). **San Luis State Park** (378-2020), 8 mi. away in Mosca, has showers and 51 electrical sites ($12; $3 vehicle entrance fee; closed in winter). For info on nearby National Forest Campgrounds (all sites $8), contact the Río Grande National Forest Service Office, 1803 W. U.S. 160, Monte Vista, CO 81144 (274-5193). Great Sand Dunes' **area code:** 719.

SAN JUAN MOUNTAINS

Ask Coloradans about their favorite mountain retreats, and they'll most likely name a peak, lake, stream, or town in the San Juan Range of southwestern Colorado. Four **national forests**—the **Uncompahgre** (un-cum-PAH-gray), the **Gunnison,** the **San Juan,** and the **Río Grande**—encircle this sprawling range. **Durango** is an ideal base camp for forays into these mountains. Northeast of Durango, the **Weminuche Wilderness** tempts the hardy backpacker with a vast expanse of rugged terrain where wide, sweeping vistas stretch for miles. Get maps and hiking info from **Pine Needle Mountaineering,** Main Mall, Durango 81301 (970-247-8728; open Mon.-Sat. 9am-6pm, summers until 9pm, Sun. 10am-5pm; maps $4).

The San Juan area is easily accessible on U.S. 50, which is traveled by hundreds of thousands of tourists each summer. **Greyhound** serves the area, but very poorly; traveling by car is the best option in this region. On a happier note, the San Juans are loaded with HI-AYH hostels and campgrounds, making them one of the more economical places to visit in Colorado.

▨ Black Canyon

Native American parents used to tell their children that the light-colored strands of rock streaking through the walls of the Black Canyon were the hair of a blond woman—and that if they got too close to the edge they would get tangled in it and fall. With or without folklore, the edge of **Black Canyon of the Gunnison National Monument** is a staggering place. The Gunnison River slowly gouged out the 53-mi.-long canyon, crafting a steep 2500-ft. gorge dominated by inky shadows (hence black); the Empire State Building, if placed at the bottom of the river, would reach barely halfway up the canyon walls.

Practical Information The Black Canyon lies 10 mi. east of the town of Montrose in Western Colorado. The **South Rim** is easily accessible via a five-mi. drive off U.S. 50 (entrance $4 per car); the wilder **North Rim** can only be reached by detouring around the canyon and taking a gravel road from Crawford off Rte. 92. The Canyon has two **visitors centers**—one on the South Rim (249-1915; open daily summers 8am-6pm, winters 8am-4pm), and another on the North Rim (open May-Sept. daily 8am-6pm). **Greyhound** serves Montrose at 132 N. 1st St. (249-6673), and **Gunnison,** 55 mi. east, at the Gunnison county airport, 711 Rio Grande (641-0060). Fare between Gunnison and Montrose is $12; buses run daily and will drop you off on U.S. 50, 6 mi. from the canyon. For $30, **Melrose Adventures** (800-430-4555) conducts tours of the Black Canyon and the Grand Mesa from Grand Junction. Trip includes transportation, entrance fees, and guided tours off the beaten path (trips on Thurs. and Sun., May-Oct.). Montrose's **ZIP code:** 81401. **Area code:** 970.

Accommodations and Food The South Rim has a campground with 102 small, somewhat crowded sites amidst sagebrush and tall shrubs ($8). Pit toilets, charcoal grills, water, and paved disabled accessible sites are available. On the North Rim, another campsite offers more space ($8, water and toilets available).

Many inexpensive motels line **Main St. /U.S. 30** in downtown Melrose. **The Traveler's B&B Inn,** 502 S. First (249-3472), parallel to Main St., lets simple, cozy rooms with TV and breakfast (singles $29, doubles $32; with private bath $32/$34; prices less in winter). **The Log Cabin Motel,** 1034 E. Main St. (249-7610), toward the end of town closest to the Monument, offers small but comfortable rooms (singles $32, doubles $34; $4 less in winter). **J.J.'s Restaurant and Halftime Lounge,** 613 E. Main St. (249-0439), serves generous portions of Mexican food ($6) and entertains at night with 5 pool tables, pin ball, air hockey, darts, and lots of beer (open daily noon-2am). **Starvin' Arvin's,** 1320 S. Townsend Ave. (249-7787), on U.S. 550, serves generous breakfasts all day. Feast on three-egg omelettes with hashbrowns and hotcakes for $5 (open daily 6am-10pm).

Exploring the Black Canyon The eight-mi. scenic drive along the South Rim boasts the spectacular **Chasm View,** where you can peer 2000 ft. down a sheer vertical drop at the Gunnison River. Don't throw stones; you might kill an exhausted hiker in the canyon below. There are no trails to the bottom, but you can scramble down the **Gunnison Route** which drops 2000 ft. over the course of one mi. A free **backcountry permit** (obtainable at the South Rim visitors center) is required for all trips down to the river. Make sure to bring at least three liters of water per person and be prepared to use your hands to climb back up. As long as you're down in the canyon, camp and enjoy the beauty; unimproved sites (no water) are available on a beach on the Gunnison River. The rock walls of the Black Canyon are a paradise for climbers. Register at the South Rim visitors center to climb some of the tallest rock faces in the Rocky Mountains. Less strenuous hikes follow the rims of the canyon, providing dizzying canyon views; talk with a ranger to plan a hike.

The **Ute Indian Museum,** 17253 Chipeta Dr. (249-3098), has informative exhibits about the culture of the Ute. (Open mid-May to Aug. Mon.-Fri. 9am-6pm, Sat. 10am-5pm, Sun. 1-5pm; in Sept. closed Mon.-Tues. $2.50.)

■ Crested Butte

Crested Butte (CREST-ed BYOOT, not Crusty Butt you meddling kids), 27 mi. north of **Gunnison** on Rte. 135, was once a mining town. The coal was exhausted in the 1950s, and a few years later the steep powder fields on the Butte began attracting skiers. While there are a lot more tourists today, the buildings of Crested Butte haven't changed much since the mining days, thanks to an ordinance banning franchises in the area. Crested Butte is one of the few unspoiled ski towns amidst such monstrosities as Vail and Aspen. The ski lifts lie 3 mi. north of town along Rte. 135. **Mt. Crested Butte Resort** (800-544-8448) offers excellent cruising runs that drop 3062 ft., but the mountain is most famous for its "extreme skiing" tempered with a decidedly backcountry flavor. Free skiing is sometimes available in Nov. and April, along with reasonably priced lodging packages.

Come summertime, Crested Butte becomes the **mountain bike** capital of Colorado. In 1976 a group of mountain bikers rode over Crested Butte as a commemorative event, celebrated these days in September, when a group of bikers make the same trek. Trails begin at the base of Mt. Crested Butte and extend into the exquisite Gothic area. **Trail 401** is a demanding and famous 24-mi. roundtrip loop with an excellent view. The **Gothic** area is also accessible with a car; just follow Rte. 135 past Mt. Crested Butte and keep driving. When bumpy Gothic Rd. begins to get medieval on your butt, park the car and explore the tiny town of Gothic.

The **Crested Butte Chamber of Commerce** (349-6438 or 800-545-4505) is just east of the intersection of Elk Ave. and Rte. 135 (open daily 9am-5pm). Pick up a trail map or one of numerous brochures. From the chamber of commerce, take a free **shuttle** (349-7381) to the mountain (every 30min. May-Sept., in winter every 15min. from 7:30am-10pm). Crested Butte's **post office:** 215 Elk Ave. (349-5568; open Mon.-Fri. 8am-4:30pm, Sat. 9am-1pm). **ZIP code:** 81224. **Area code:** 970.

You'll have as much luck finding budget lodging during peak winter season in Crested Butte as you will striking a major vein of gold; call the Crested Butte lodging hotline at 800-215-2226. **Gunnison National Forest's** office, 216 N. Colorado (641-0471), 30 mi. south in Gunnison, and the Chamber of Commerce, have info on a plethora of campgrounds. Camp for free in achingly beautiful surroundings at the **Gothic Campsite,** 3 mi. past the town of Gothic on Gothic Rd. (no water, unimproved sites) or park in one of the turnouts and find your own tent sites.

Brick Oven Pizza, 313 3rd St. (349-5044), dishes out authentic NY- and Chicago-style pizzas from a small window; tasty slices loaded with toppings $2, large pizzas $12 (open daily summers 11:30am-10pm, winters 4-10pm). **The Bakery Café,** at 3rd and Elk Ave., is a popular local breakfast place ($6; open daily 7am-6pm). **The Crested Butte Brewery,** 226 Elk Ave. (349-5026), features microbrews, American fare (burgers $6), and live music. Stop in at happy hour (daily 3-5pm) for pints of handcrafted brew ($2) and free chips and salsa.

■ Telluride

Site of the first bank Butch Cassidy ever robbed (the San Miguel), Telluride has a history right out of a 1930s black-and-white film. Prizefighter Jack Dempsey used to wash dishes in the Athenian Senate, a popular saloon/brothel that frequently required Dempsey to double as bouncer when he was between plates. Presidential candidate William Jennings Bryan delivered his "Cross of Gold" speech in Telluride from the front balcony of the Sheridan Hotel. Not so rare (especially after its devaluation) was the silver that attracted all the less aesthetically inclined hoodlums to Telluride in the first place. Today, skiers, hikers, and vacationers come to Telluride to put gold and silver *into* these mountains; the town is gaining popularity and may be the Aspen of the future. Still, a small-town feeling prevails; rocking chairs sit outside brightly painted, wood-shingled houses, and dogs are tied to storefront porches.

Practical Information The **visitors center** is upstairs at **Rose's,** near the entrance to town at demonic 666 W. Colorado Ave. (728-4431 or 800-525-3455; open summers daily 8am-9pm, winters daily 8am-7pm). Telluride is only accessible by car, on U.S. 550 or Rte. 145. The closest Greyhound stop is in Montrose, 132 N. 1st St. (249-6673), a 60-mi. drive. Telluride's **post office:** 101 E. Colorado Ave. (728-3900; open Mon.-Fri. 9am-5pm). **ZIP code:** 81435. **Area code:** 970.

Accommodations, Food, and Nightlife If you're visiting Telluride for a festival, bring a sleeping bag; the cost of a bed is outrageous. The **Oak Street Inn,** 134 N. Oak St. (728-3383), offers dorm-style lodging complete with a sauna. (Singles with shared bath $42, doubles $58, triples $72, quads $85. Showers $3. More expensive during festivals.) **Camp** at the east end of town in a town-operated facility with 46 sites, water, restrooms, and showers (728-3071; 2-week max. stay; $8, except during festivals). **Sunshine,** 6 mi. southwest on Rte. 145 toward Cortez, is a developed national forest campground (2-week max. stay; 14 sites, $8). For info on all **National Forest Campgrounds**, call the Forest Service (327-4261). Several free primitive sites huddle nearby, and are accessible by jeep roads. During festival times, you can crash anywhere; hot showers are available at the high school ($2).

Baked in Telluride, 127 S. Fir St. (728-4775), has enough rich coffee and delicious pastry, pizza, salad, and 50¢ bagels to get you through a festival weekend even if you *are* baked in Telluride (open daily 5:30am-10pm). **Steaming Bean Coffee,** 221 W. Colorado (800-230-BEAN/2326), has coffee by the cup or the bag (open Mon.-Fri. 7am-10pm, Sat.-Sun. 7:30am-10:30pm). Good breakfasts hide out at **Sofio's Mexican Café,** 110 E. Colorado (728-4882), where most breakfasts start at $4.25. (Open daily 7am-11:30am for breakfast; 5:30-10pm for dinner.)

For a great selection of beer, try **Floradera,** 103 W. Colorado (728-3888), where they have homebrewed beer on tap ($3.50; open daily 11am-midnight). Chug one of ten beers on tap at **The House, A Tavern,** 131 N. Fir St. (728-6207), where many college-students-gone-ski-bums hang out (drafts $2-4; happy hour 4-7pm, 75¢ off all beers). The cool, conversational **Last Dollar Saloon,** 100 E. Colorado (728-4800), near Pine, will take your last buck and smile (bottled beer $2.25-3.35). Although the continental cuisine is expensive, the welcoming bar at **Leimgruber's,** 573 W. Pacific Ave. (728-4663), is "the place to be for aprés-ski."

Festivals and Activities The quality and number of summer arts festivals in Telluride seem staggering when you consider that only 1500 people call the town home. For general festival info, contact the visitors center (see above). While get-togethers occur just about every weekend in summer and fall, the most renowned is the **Bluegrass Festival** (800-624-2422) in late June. In recent years, the likes of James Taylor and the Indigo Girls have attracted crowds of 19,000, although capacity is limited to 10,000 (tickets $30-45 per night). Telluride also hosts a **Talking Gourds** poetry fest (327-4767) and a **Jazz Celebration** (first weekend in Aug.), among others. Music festivals seem to jam all over town, all day, and deep into the night. The **Telluride International Film Festival** (603-643-1255), on Labor Day weekend, draws actors and directors from all over the globe, including Jodie Foster. It premiered such films as *The Crying Game* and *The Piano*. For some festivals, you can volunteer to usher, set up chairs, or perform other tasks in exchange for tickets.

Biking, hiking, and backpacking opportunities are endless; ghost towns and lakes are tucked behind almost every mountain crag. For an enjoyable day hike, trek up the San Miguel River Canyon to **Bridal Veil Falls,** which is visible from Telluride; drive to the end of Rte. 145 and hike the steep dirt road to the waterfall.

In winter, even self-proclaimed atheists can be spied crossing themselves before hitting the "Spiral Stairs" and the "Plunge," two of the Rockies' most gut-wrenching ski runs. For more info, contact the **Telluride Ski Resort,** P.O. Box 307, Telluride 81435 (728-3856). For a copy of the *Skier Services Brochure,* contact the visitors center. A free shuttle connects the mountain village with the rest of the town; pick up a current schedule at the visitors center. **Paragon Ski and Sport,** 213 W. Colorado Ave. (728-4525), rents camping supplies, bikes, roller blades, and skis and boots ($15 per day). The longer you rent, the cheaper it gets (open daily 9am-8pm; winters daily 8am-9pm).

■ Durango

As Will Rogers once put it, Durango is "out of the way and glad of it." Despite its popularity as a tourist destination, Durango retains a relaxed atmosphere. Come here to see Mesa Verde, raft down the Animas River, hike the beautiful San Juan Mountains, or ski at Purgatory.

Practical Information Durango parks at the intersection of U.S. 160 and U.S. 150. Streets run perpendicular to avenues, but everyone calls Main Ave. "Main Street." The **Durango Area Chamber Resort Association,** 111 S. Camino del Rio

(247-0312 or 800-525-8855), across from Gateway Dr., is extremely helpful and will answer questions about camping. (Open Mon.-Sat. 8am-7pm, Sun. 10am-4pm; winter Mon.-Sat. 8am-5pm, Sun. 10am-4pm.) **Greyhound,** 275 E. 8th Ave. (259-2755), runs once per day to Grand Junction (6hr., $30), Denver (12hr., $54), and Albuquerque (5hr., $39). (Open Mon.-Fri. 7:30am-noon and 3:30-5pm, Sat. 7:30am-noon, Sun. and holidays 7:30-10am.) The **Durango Lift** (259-5438) provides hourly bus service beginning at Main Ave. and Earl St. (7am-6:35pm, 75¢). **Emergency** is 911. Durango's **post office:** 222 W. 8th St. (247-3434; open Mon.-Fri. 8:30am-5:30pm, Sat. 9am-1pm). **ZIP code:** 81301. **Area code:** 970.

Accommodations, Food, and Nightlife

Durango Youth Hostel, 543 E. 2nd Ave. (247-9905), 1 block from downtown, has simple bunks and kitchen facilities in a large converted house that retains a cozy home-like feel. Ask the owners about local cafés, hangouts, and activities. (Check-in 7-10am and 5-10pm. Check-out 7-10am. $12. $5 key deposit.) Prices for other accommodations change rapidly in Durango; check ahead with the chamber resort association. The lowest price for a summer double hovers around $40. Even **Budget Inn,** 3077 Main Ave. (247-5222 or 800-257-5222), charges a lot for its spacious rooms—but it does have a nice pool and hot tub (one bed $45-52, two beds $62-64; winter $23-32/$28-36). **Cottonwood Camper Park,** on U.S. 160 (247-1977), ½ mi. west, is the closest campground to the train station (2-person site $14, full hookup $18; each additional person $2).

Although **Silverton,** 47 mi. north on U.S. 550, is a less popular (but cheaper) vacation spot than Durango, this small mining town lies at the base of some of the most beautiful mountains and hiking trails in the area. The **Teller House Hotel,** 1250 Greene St. (387-5423 or 800-342-4338), next to the French Bakery (which provides the hotel's complimentary breakfast), has comfy rooms in a well-maintained 1896 hotel. (Singles $26, with bath $38; doubles $33/$49, $8 per additional person.) Silverton is at the end of the Durango & Silverton RR (see below).

For fixins', head to **City Market** on U.S. 550 one block down 9th St., or at 3130 Main St. (both open 24hr.). Eat breakfast with locals at **Carver's Bakery and Brewpub,** 1022 Main Ave. (259-2545), which has delicious bread, breakfast specials ($2-5.50), fresh pasta ($5-7), and vegetarian dishes. Pints of home-brewed beer cost $3, pitchers $8. (Open Mon.-Sat. 6:30am-10pm, Sun. 6am-1pm.) **Farquhart's,** 725 Main Ave. (247-9861), serves up a hearty burrito plate for $6.50, along with the best live music in town. (Wed.-Sun. rock, world beat, and reggae. $5 cover Wed.-Fri. Open Sun.-Tues. 11am-11pm, Wed.-Thurs. 11am-midnight, Fri.-Sat. 11am-1:30am.) **Olde Tymer's,** 1000 Main Ave. (259-2990), wins Durango's Best Burger every year. Vegetarians will be happy with the salad options (open daily 11am-10pm).

Activities

Winter is Durango's busiest season, when nearby **Purgatory Resort** (247-9000), 27 mi. north on U.S. 550, hosts skiers of all levels. (Lift tickets $39, ages 6-12 $17, under 5 free.) When the heat is on, trade in your skis for a sled and test out the **Alpine Slide** (open summers daily 9:30am-6pm; 1 ride $8, 3 rides $21); or, take a **Scenic Chairlift Ride** (free).

Durango is best known for the **Durango and Silverton Narrow Gauge Train,** 479 Main St. (247-2733), which runs along the Animas River Valley to the glistening old town of **Silverton.** Old-fashioned, 100% coal-fed locomotives wheeze and cough through the San Juans, making a 2-hr. stop in Silverton before returning to Durango. (Trains at 7:30, 8:30, 9:15, and 10:10am; 8-9hr. $43, ages 5-11 $21.50.) From mid-July to mid-August, you can buy a one-way train ticket ($28.45) and return on a bus (1½hr., whole trip $42.70) which connects with the 8:30am train. The train can also drop off **backpackers** at various scenic points along the route and pick them up on return trips; call for more info on this service. (Office open daily June to mid-Aug. 6am-8pm, May and mid-Aug. to Oct. 7am-7pm, Nov.-May 8am-5pm.)

The entire Durango area is engulfed by **San Juan National Forest,** the headquarters of which are located in Durango (247-4874)—call for info on hiking and camping in the forest. In particular, backpackers planning trips in the massive **Weminuche Wil-**

derness northeast of Durango should contact the office. For river rafting, **Rivers West,** 520 Main St. (259-5077), has good rates (1hr. $12, 2hr. $19; kids 20% off; open daily 8am-9pm). **Durango Rivertrippers,** 720 Main St. (259-0289), also organizes trips (2hr. $19, 12 and under $14; 4hr. $29/$20; open daily 8am-9pm). **Southwest Adventures,** 780 Main Ave. (259-0370), offers a comparable deal. Biking gear is available from **Hassle Free Sports,** 2615 Main St. (259-3874 or 800-835-3800). Bikes rent at $16 per ½ day, $25 per day. (Open Mon.-Sat. 8:30am-6pm, Sun. 10am-5pm. Must have driver's license and major credit card.)

■ Near Durango: Pagosa Springs

The Ute people—the first to discover the waters of Pagosa—believed that the springs were a gift of the Great Spirit. Pagosa Springs, the hottest and largest in the world, bubble from the San Juan Mountains 62 mi. east of Durango on Rte. 160. The principal **hot baths** are located in two motels: **Spring Inn,** 165 Hot Springs Blvd. (264-5910 or 800-832-5523; outside baths $6.50; open 24hr.), and **Spa Motel,** 317 Hot Springs Blvd. (264-5910; $8 for outdoor pool and indoor hot tub; open 8am-9pm daily; must be 18). **Chimney Rock Archeological Area** (883-5359), 20 mi. west of Pagosa Springs on U.S. 160 and Rte. 151S, contains the ruins of a high-mesa Anasazi village. (2-hr. guided tour from May 15-Sept. 30 at 9:30, 10:30am, 1, and 2pm. $4, ages 6-12 $2, under 5 free.) Ski at **Wolf Creek,** 20 mi. east of Pagosa, which claims to have the most snow in Colorado (lift tickets $32, under 13 $20; rates often change). For fishing, hiking, and camping, contact the San Juan National Forest (247-4874; see Durango: Activities, above). The **visitors center** (264-2360) sits at the intersection of San Juan St. and Hot Springs Blvd. (open Mon.-Sat. 8am-5pm, Sun. 1-5pm; winters daily 9am-5pm). Except for the occasional mudslide and stampede, there is no public transportation in Pagosa Springs.

Lodging here won't break you. The **Sky View Motel** (264-5803), 1 mi. west of town on Rte. 160, offers singles with cable TV for $40, doubles for $45-55, and quads for $59. **Harvey's Motel,** 157 Pagosa St. (264-5715), one block from downtown, has cozy wood-paneled rooms with TVs and phones (singles $32-40, doubles $40-59). The **High Country Lodge** (264-4181 or 800-862-3707) lies 3 mi. east on Rte. 160. (Singles $37, cabin for 1 $62. For both, $5 each additional person up to 4. In winter $5 less.)

The **Moose River Pub,** 20 Village Dr. (731-5451), serves up Southwestern choplickin' goodies (open Mon.-Fri. 11am-2pm and 5-9pm, Sat. 5-9pm). **The Hog's Breath Saloon,** 157 Navajo Trail Dr. (731-2626), near Rte. 160W, features country western dancing (Fri.-Sat.) and a surf 'n' turf menu (entrees $8-11; open daily 11am-10pm). The award-winning green chili stew ($4) at the **Rolling Pin Bakery Café,** 214 Pagosa St. (274-2255), gets your attention with its unique combo of spices, chili, and chicken. Big breakfast flapjacks ($4) and sandwiches ($4-6) can cool your palate. (Open Mon.-Fri. 7am-5:30pm, Sat. 7am-2:30pm; winters Mon.-Sat. 7am-7:30pm.)

■ Mesa Verde

Mesa Verde (Green Table) rises from the deserts of southwestern Colorado, its flat top noticeably friendlier to vegetation than the dry lands below. Fourteen hundred

---

Four Corners

New Mexico, Arizona, Utah, and **Colorado** meet at an unnaturally neat intersection about 40 mi. northwest of **Shiprock,** NM, on the Navajo Reservation. **Four Corners** epitomizes American ideas about land; these state borders were drawn along scientifically determined lines of longitude and latitude, with no regard for natural boundaries. There isn't much to see, but die-hard tourists derive perverse thrills out of getting down on all fours and putting a limb in each state—a good story for a cocktail party. (Open summers daily 7am-8pm, winters daily 8am-5pm; $1.50.)

years ago, Native American tribes began to cultivate the area now known as **Mesa Verde National Park.** These people—today called the Anasazi, or "ancient ones"—constructed a series of elaborate cliff dwellings beneath the overhanging sandstone shelves surrounding the mesa. Then, around 1275AD, 700 years after their ancestors had arrived, the Anasazi abruptly and mysteriously vanished from the historical record, leaving behind their eerie and starkly beautiful dwellings.

The southern portion of the park divides into the **Chapin Mesa** and the **Wetherill Mesa.** To get an overview of the Anasazi lifestyle, visit the **Chapin Mesa Museum** (529-4475), at the south end of the park (open daily 8am-6:30pm; winters 8am-5pm). Rangers lead tours to **Cliff Palace,** the largest cliff dwelling in North America, and **Balcony House** (open summer only), a 40-room dwelling 600 ft. above the floor of the Soda Canyon (tours depart from the visitors center every ½hr. 9am-6pm; $1.25). **Step House,** on Weatherill Mesa, is one of the better-preserved ruins, as is **Spruce Tree House,** near the museum.

The Far View Lodge (see below) offers two half-day bus tours. One departs from the Lodge at 9am and visits Spruce Tree House; the second departs at 1pm and runs to Cliff Palace. The Lodge also offers a full-day tour, which departs at 9am and visits both sites. Be sure to arrive at least ½ hour before the tour departs. (½-day tours $15, under 12 $8. Full day $19/$8. No reservations.) **Mesa Verde Tours** (259-4818 or 800-626-2066) picks up travelers in Durango or Cortez for a 9-hr. bus tour of the park, leaving at 8:30am ($60, under 12 $30). Bring a lunch and make reservations the night before, as tours fill up.

The park's main entrance is off U.S. 160, 36 mi. from Durango and 10 mi. from **Cortez.** The **entrance fee** is $5 for vehicles, $3 for pedestrian and bikers. The **Far View Visitors Center** (529-4543), 20 mi. from the gate on the main road, publishes a comprehensive visitors guide with up-to-date and complete listings on park walks, drives, and trails (open summer daily 8am-5pm). During the winter, head to the museum (see above) or the **Colorado Welcome Center/Cortez Chamber of Commerce,** 928 E. Main (800-253-1616 or 565-3414), in Cortez, where you'll find the *Mesa Verde Country Visitors Guide* (open daily 8am-6pm; winter 8am-5pm). Since sights in the park lie up to 40 mi. apart, a car is helpful. For **emergencies,** call 911. Mesa Verde's **ZIP code:** 81331. **Area code:** 970.

Mesa Verde's only lodging, **Far View Lodge** (529-4421), across from the visitors center, is extremely expensive (from $70), but a few nearby motels can put you up for around $30. Try the **Ute Mountain Motel,** 531 S. Broadway (565-8507), in Cortez. (singles from $35, doubles $38-44; winter $24/$28-34). **North Broadway Motel,** 510 N. Broadway (565-2481), stocks its small rooms with AC, TV, fridge, microwave, and a big bath (singles $32, doubles $40; in winter $25/$30). The nearby **Durango Hostel** (see Durango, p. 602) has cheap beds. The only camping in Mesa Verde is 4 mi. inside the park at **Morfield Campground** (529-4400; off season 533-7731). The third-largest national park campground in America *has never been full* and boasts some beautiful, secluded sites. (Actually, it technically filled once, in 1989. Whatever. 450 sites $9, full hookup $17. Showers 75¢ for 5min.)

THE SOUTHWEST

Thomas Jefferson sent Meriwether Lewis on an exploratory expedition through the new Louisiana Territory, with instructions to investigate the region, its resources, the Indian populations, and to find a live mastodon. With the creature, Jefferson hoped to prove to European scientists that American creatures were just as large and powerful as those on other continents. The West—and in particular the Southwest—has always provided fodder for American myths such as the equation of size and quality. The area has led a double life as both a physical territory and a romantically-imagined land of savages, outlaws, and buffalo, settled by dint of American courage and ingenuity. In reality, Americans have played only a small part in the history of the region. The Anasazi of the 10th and 11th centuries were the first to discover that the arid lands of the Southwest could support an advanced agrarian civilization. The Navajo, Apache, and Pueblo nations later migrated into the region, sharing the land with descendents of the Anasazi, the Hopi. Today, reservation lands and ruins mark both the current and ancient presence of these peoples.

Spanish conquest began with the 16th-century forays of explorers based in Mexico, and continued at the hands of Catholic missionaries, who attempted to organize the Indians into a society of Christian village-dwellers. The United States first laid claim to parts of the Southwest with the 1803 Louisiana Purchase. The idealistic hope for a western "empire of liberty," where Americans could live the virtuous farm life, motivated further expansion, until the 1853 Gadsden Purchase set the last boundaries of today's Southwest. Since then, the individualist mythology of the region—of the lone gunslinger, the courageous lawman, and the rugged pioneer—has flourished. Ironically, in the past 200 years the American West has relied more than any other region on federal aid and bureaucracy and has become the country's most urban section, measuring by the percentage of the population living in urban areas. Nonetheless, explorers and cowboys continue to excite the national imagination in a way that the Bureau of Land Management never will.

The Southwest's natural grandeur lures visitors and keeps Kodak in business. The vastness of the desert and its peculiar colors—of red rock, sandstone, scrub brush, and pale sky—invite contemplation; farther north, Utah's mountains offer equally breathtaking vistas. The steel blue of the Superstition peaks, the rainbow expanse of the Painted Desert, the deep gorges of the Grand Canyon, the murky depths of Carlsbad Caverns, and the red stone arches and twisted spires of southern Utah and northern Arizona inspire awe and await exploration.

Nevada

Nevada once walked the straight and narrow. Explored by Spanish missionaries and settled by Mormons, the Nevada Territory's scorched expanses seemed a perfect place for ascetics to strive for moral uplift. The discovery of gold in 1850 and silver in 1859 changed all that; the state was won over permanently to the worship of filthy lucre. When the precious metals ran out, Nevadans shirked most vestiges of virtue, and gambling and marriage-licensing became big industries. The final moral cataclysms came when the state legalized prostitution on a county by county basis and built a crooning lounge idol named Wayne Newton.

Of course, there *is* another side to Nevada. Lake Mead National Recreation Area, only 25 mi. from Las Vegas, is an oasis in stunning desert surroundings, and the forested slopes of Lake Tahoe, shared with California, provide serene resort retreats for an escape from the cities.

PRACTICAL INFORMATION

Capital: Carson City.
Nevada Commission on Tourism: Capitol Complex, Carson City 89710 (702-687-4322 or 800-NEVADA8/638-2328). **Nevada Division of State Parks,** 123 W. Nye Lane, Carson City 89710 (702-687-4384). Both open Mon.-Fri. 8am-5pm.
Time Zone: Pacific (3hr. behind Eastern). **Postal Abbreviation:** NV.
Sales Tax: 6.75-7%; 8% room tax, in some counties.

■ Las Vegas

Not until Nevada made gambling legal in 1931 did Las Vegas begin to attract many visitors; even in 1940, the WPA guide to Nevada assured its readers that, despite increasing tourism, "no attempt has been made to introduce pseudo-romantic architectural themes, or to give artificial glamour and gaiety." Today, artificial glamour and gaiety dominate Vegas. Old West dreams of quick wealth meet the capitalist service-economy, as casino-hotels lure millions of visitors (and millions of dollars) with slot machines and Disneyesque attractions. Only in Vegas could there be a major museum devoted to Liberace.

PRACTICAL INFORMATION

Visitor Information: Las Vegas Convention and Visitor Authority, 3150 Paradise Rd. (892-0711), at the Convention Center, 4 blocks from the Strip by the Hilton. Up-to-date info on headliners, conventions, shows, hotel bargains and buffets. Open Mon.-Fri. 8am-6pm, Sat.-Sun. 8am-5pm. **Gay and Lesbian Community Center,** 912 E. Sahara Ave. (733-9800). Hours dependent on volunteer staff availability. **Nevada Association for the Handicapped,** (800-326-6888). **TDD** (800-326-6868).

Police: 795-3111.

Tours: Gambler's special bus tours leave L.A., San Francisco, and San Diego for Las Vegas early in the morning and return at night or the next day. Prices include everything but food and gambling. Ask at tourist offices in the departure cities or call casinos for info. **Gray Line,** 1550 S. Industrial Rd. (800-634-6579; fax 384-6549). Mini City Tours (1 per day, ½-day, $17.50). Bus tours from Las Vegas to: Hoover Dam/Lake Mead Express (2 per day, 8am and noon, 5hr., $18) and Grand Canyon's South Rim (spans 2 days, 1 night's lodging and park admission included; 3 per week, Mon., Wed., and Fri. 7am; with single room $147, double $111, triple or quad $99; runs Mar.-Oct.; reservations required). **Ray and Ross Tours,** 300 W. Owens St. (646-4661 or 800-338-8111). To Hoover Dam (1 per day, 5hr., $24) and Hoover Dam/Lake Mead (1 per day, 7hr., $32). Pick-up between 9:15 and 10:15am and drop-off at most hotels.

Airport: McCarran International (261-5743) at the southeast end of the Strip. Main terminal on Paradise Rd. Within walking distance of University of Nevada campus. Vans to hotels on the Strip and downtown $3-5; taxi to downtown $23.

Trains: Amtrak, 1 N. Main St. (386-6896 or 800-872-7245), in the Union Plaza Hotel. To L.A. (3 per week, 8hr., $68) and San Francisco (daily, 13hr., $120). Ticket office open daily 6:30-10am, 11am-3pm, and 4-7pm.

Buses: Greyhound, 200 S. Main St. (382-2292 or 800-231-2222), at Carson downtown. To L.A. (6 per day, 5hr., $37) and San Francisco (3 per day, 15hr., $54). Ticket office and terminal open daily 4:30am-1am.

Public Transportation: Citizens Area Transit (CAT) (228-7433; fax 455-5151). Route #301 serves downtown and the Strip 24hr. Routes #108 and #109 serve the airport. Both are $1.50, seniors & under 18 50¢; other routes $1. Routes other than #301 operate every 10-15 min. daily 5:30am-1:30am.

Taxis: Yellow, Checker and **Star Taxis** (873-2000). $2.20 initial fee, $1.50 per mi. Cabs run 24hr.

Car Rental: Rebel Rent-a-Car, 5021 Swenson (597-0427 or 800-372-1981). From $20 per day, with unlimited mi. within Clark County. Must be 21 with major credit card; under 25 surcharge $15 per day. Discounts in tourist publications.

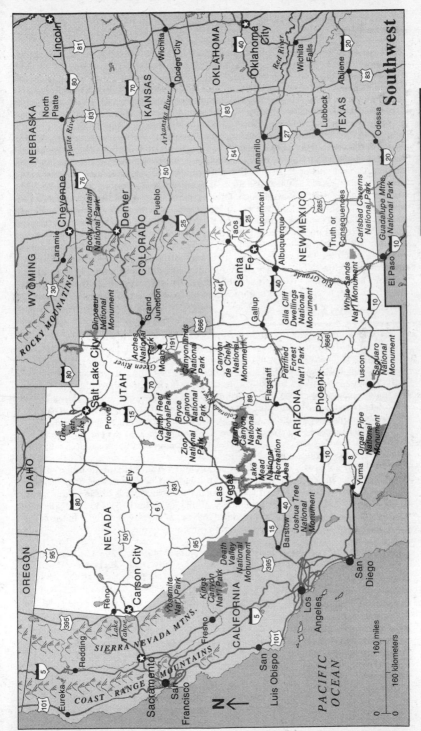

Kwik Marriage: Marriage License Bureau, 200 S. 3rd St. (455-4415). Must be 18 or obtain parental consent. Open Mon.-Thurs. 8am-midnight, Fri. 8am-Sun. midnight. $35, cash only. No waiting period or blood test required—that's healthy.

Crisis Lines: Rape Crisis Center Hotline, 366-1640. 24hr. **Gamblers Anonymous,** 385-7732. 24hr. **Suicide Prevention,** 731-2990. 24hr.

Emergency: 911.

Post Office: 2300 E. Tropicana in Lucky's groceries (736-5189). Open Mon.-Sat. 10:30am-7pm, Sun. 11am-7pm; general delivery Mon.-Fri. 10am-3pm; Customer service 24hr. **ZIP Code:** 89101. **Area code:** 702.

Getting to Vegas from Los Angeles involves a straight, 300-mi. shot on I-15 (5hr.). From Arizona, take I-40 west to Kingman and then U.S. 93/95 north. Las Vegas has two major casino areas. The **downtown** area, around Fremont and 2nd St., is foot-friendly; casinos cluster close together, and some of the sidewalks are even carpeted. The other main area, known as the **Strip,** is a collection of mammoth casinos on both sides of **Las Vegas Boulevard South.** Other casinos lie on **Paradise Blvd.,** parallel to Las Vegas Blvd. As in any city where money reigns supreme, many areas of Las Vegas are unsafe. Always stay on brightly lit pathways and do not wander too far from the major casinos and hotels. The neighborhoods just north and west of downtown can be especially dangerous.

For those under 18, Las Vegas has a **curfew.** Cruisers under 18 are not allowed unaccompanied in public places from midnight to 5am; those under 14 from 10pm to 5am. On weekends, no one under 18 is allowed on the Strip or in other designated areas from 9pm to 5am, unless accompanied by an adult.

ACCOMMODATIONS

Make reservations as far in advance as possible. Coming to town on a Friday or Saturday night without reservations is flirting with disaster. Even though Vegas has over 90,000 rooms, most hotels fill up on weekend nights. If you get stuck call the **Room Reservations Hotline** (800-332-5333). Remember too, the earlier you reserve, the better chance you have of snagging a special rate. Room rates at most hotels in Vegas fluctuate all the time. Many hotels use two rate ranges—one for weeknights, the other weekend nights. In addition, a room that costs $20 during a promotion can cost hundreds during a convention. Check local publications such as *What's On In Las Vegas, Today in Las Vegas, Vegas Visitor, Casino Player, Tour Guide Magazine,* and *Insider Viewpoint of Las Vegas* for discounts and coupons; they are all free and available at the visitor center, hotels, and attractions.

Strip hotels are at the center of the action and within walking distance of each other, but their inexpensive rooms sell out quickly: Cheaper motels line **Fremont St.,** from downtown south. Another option, if you have a car, is to stay at one of the hotel-casinos in Jean, NV (approximately 30mi. south on I-15). Public displays of affection by homosexual couples are illegal in Nevada. Members of the same sex sharing a hotel room may have to book a room containing two twin beds.

Las Vegas International Hostel (AAIH/Rucksackers), 1208 Las Vegas Blvd. South (385-9955). Tidy, spartan rooms with A/C and fresh sheets every day. Free lemonade, tea, coffee, Las Vegas guides, and advice about budget Vegas. Extremely helpful staff are excellent sources for cheap fun in Vegas. TV and laundry facilities. Tours to Zion, Bryce, and Grand Canyon (3 days, Mon. and Fri., $150). Office open daily 7am-11pm. Check-out 7-10am. Shared room and bath Sun.-Thurs. $12, Fri.-Sat. $14. Private room and shared bath $26. Rates lower Dec.-March. Key deposit $5.

Center Strip Inn, 3688 Las Vegas Blvd. South (739-6066; fax 736-2521). Attractive for its lack of Vegas gaudiness or high prices. Pleasant rooms include beds with floral spreads, TVs, refrigerators and safes (for those feeling especially lucky). Standard room with 2 double beds, Sun.-Thurs. $50-69, Fri.-Sat. $69-89.

Circus Circus, 2880 Las Vegas Blvd. South (734-0410 or 800-444-CIRCUS). Only hotel with its own clown shop. Rooms with TV and A/C for 1-4 people. Sun.-Thurs.

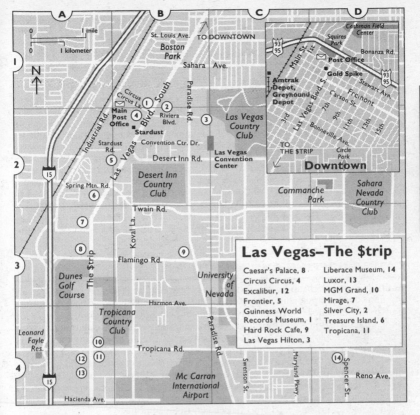

Las Vegas–The $trip

Caesar's Palace, 8	Liberace Museum, 14
Circus Circus, 4	Luxor, 13
Excalibur, 12	MGM Grand, 10
Frontier, 5	Mirage, 7
Guinness World	Silver City, 2
Records Museum, 1	Treasure Island, 6
Hard Rock Cafe, 9	Tropicana, 11
Las Vegas Hilton, 3	

$29-89, Fri.-Sat. $59-99, holidays $65-125. Roll-away bed $7. In summer, fills 2-3 months in advance for weeknights, 3-4 months for weekends.

Excalibur, 3850 Las Vegas Blvd. South (597-7700 or 800-937-7777). Camelot meets the Looney Tunes. A giant white castle of a hotel-casino with over 4000 rooms. Guests are paged as "Lady" or "Lord," as they beat the medieval thing into the ground again and again. Ah, the Dark Ages … Sun-Thurs. $69, Fri.-Sat. $89-125. Check-in 2pm, check-out 11pm.

Goldstrike, 1 Main St. in Jean, NV (800-634-1359; fax 874-1349). 30 miles south of Vegas on I-15 (Exit 12). A Vegas-style casino with a variety of inexpensive restaurants ($4 prime rib, $5 dinner buffet). Registration open 24hr. 1-2 person room Sun.-Thurs. $21, Fri.-Sat. $39. $3 for each additional person (up to 5).

CAMPING

Lake Mead National Recreation Area (293-8906), 25mi. south of town on U.S. 93/95. Sites $10, with hookup $14-18. See Lake Mead (see p.611) for details.

Circusland RV Park, 500 Circus Circus Dr. (734-0410), a part of the Circus Circus hotel on the strip. Laundry facilities, showers, pool, jacuzzi, and convenience store. Sun.-Thurs. $13, Fri.-Sat. $17.

FOOD, GLORIOUS FOOD

Almost every hotel-casino in Vegas courts tourists with cheap all-you-can-eat invitations, but expect greasy, cafeteria-quality food and long lines at peak hours. Alcoholic drinks in most casinos cost 75¢-$1 or come free to those who are gambling. For a tastier option, try one of the score of low-priced restaurants located a short drive west from the Strip, particularly along **Decatur Blvd.**

Rincon Criollo, 1145 Las Vegas Blvd. South (388-1906), across from the youth hostel. Dine on filling Cuban food beneath a wall-sized photograph of palm trees. Daily special includes steak prepared *palomillas*-style, rice, and black beans for an unbeatable $6. Hot sandwiches $3.50-4.50. Open Tues.-Sun. 11:30pm-9:30pm.

Poppa Gars, 1624 W. Oakey Ave. (384-4513). *Very* local joint. Lots of animal heads peer down on happily munching patrons. Poppa prepares a mean Country Sausage, made from a 100-year-old recipe ($5.25), and a filling buffalo burger ($8). Breakfast $3.95-$5.95. Open Mon.-Fri. 5am-9pm, Sat. 9am-2pm. No credit cards.

Circus Circus, 2800 Las Vegas Blvd. South (734-0410). The cheapest buffet in town. Rows of serving stations make you feel like a circus circus animal at a feed trough. Breakfast $3 (6-11:30am), brunch $4 (noon-4pm), dinner $5 (4:30-11pm).

Bally's Big Kitchen, 3645 Las Vegas Blvd. South (739-4930). Locals say it has the best buffets on the Strip. A bit pricier, but worth it if you dig casino buffet food. $9.58 breakfast and lunch, $13.86 dinner. Open daily 7:30am-2:30pm, 4-10pm.

Excalibur, 3850 Las Vegas Blvd. South (597-7777), has the Roundtable Buffet. The entrees are flashbacks to not-so-medieval dormitory food and the lavender booths give a decidedly 1970s, not 1370s, feel. Breakfast $4 (7-11am), lunch $5 (11am-4pm), dinner $6 (4-11pm).

CA$INO-HOPPING AND NIGHTLIFE

At first it was only cheap buffets, booze, and entertainment. Now, the casinos go all-out, introducing family amusement parks to woo parents and their tykes too. Contrary to the tendency to market to the young and vulnerable, *gambling is illegal for those under 21.* Hotels and most casinos give out "funbooks," with alluring gambling coupons which allow you to buy $50 in chips for $5. Do not bring more money than you're prepared to lose cheerfully. And always remember: *in the long run, you will almost definitely lose money.* Keep your wallet in your front pocket, and beware of the thieves who prowl casinos to nab big winnings from unwary jubilants. Most casinos offer free gambling lessons; check out *Today* in Las Vegas for current dates and times. More patient dealers may offer a tip or two (in exchange for one from you). Casinos, nightclubs, and wedding chapels stay open 24 hours.

The **Stratosphere Tower,** 2000 Las Vegas Blvd. South (800-998-6937), is the latest entry into the "I am flashier than thou" casino wars. A 100,000 sq. ft. casino lies at the base of the tallest observation tower in the U.S. (1149-ft. high; Elevator $7, open 24hr.). At the top, **High Rollers,** the highest rollercoaster in the world, wraps around the outside of the wind-swept tower, giving all riders bad hair days. If you'd rather get shot out of a cannon and dangle from a bungee cord, head for the indoors **Big Shot** ride (both rides $5; open Sun.-Thurs. 10am-midnight, Fri.-Sat. 10am-1am). **Caesar's Palace,** 3570 Las Vegas Blvd. South (731-7110), is one of the glitziest casinos in town. Marble statues grace the hallways and lobby, as actors dressed in Roman garb wander the casino day and night posing for pictures and uttering proclamations. In the **Festival Fountain show,** statues move, talk, battle, and shout amid a laser-light show (shows every hr., daily 10am-11pm). The majestic confines of the **Mirage,** 3400 Las Vegas Blvd. South (262-4000), are certainly no illusion. Among its attractions are a dolphin habitat (admission $3), Siegfried and Roy's white tigers (which have orange and black stripes if you come at the wrong time), and a "volcano" that erupts in fountains and flames every half hour (daily 8pm-1am), barring bad weather. At **Treasure Island,** 3300 Las Vegas Blvd. South (894-7111), pirates battle with cannons staged on giant wooden ships in a "bay" on the Strip (every 1½hr., daily 4:30pm-midnight). Before the watchful eyes of the sprawling sphinx and the towering black pyramid of **Luxor,** 3900 Las Vegas Blvd. South (262-4000), a dazzling laser light show is reminiscent of imperial ancient Egypt. Boat rides (every 20 min., daily 9am-12:30am; $4) stream through the "Nile" (a.k.a. hotel lobby). Wander into the depths of the desert at **King Tut Tomb and Museum,** which houses replicas of the artifacts uncovered at the king's grave (open daily 9am-11pm; $4). The hotel's three 3-D **holographic films,**

Search of the Obelisk, Luxor Live, and *The Theater of Time* have dazzling special effects ($4-5 each).

Relive the glory days of Hollywood at the **MGM Grand,** 3799 Las Vegas Blvd. South (891-1111). It features the Grand Adventures Amusement Park, complete with an indoor rollercoaster, an erupting volcano, and the *Temple of Gloom* (park open daily 10am-10pm; $17, seniors $9, ages 4-12 $10). **Circus Circus,** 2880 Las Vegas Blvd. South (734-0410), attempts to cultivate a (dysfunctional) family atmosphere; while parents run to the card tables and slot machines downstairs, their children spend their quarters upstairs on the souped-up carnival midway and in the titanic video game arcade. Two stories above the casino floor, tightrope-walkers, fire-eaters, and rather impressive acrobats perform (11am-midnight). Within the hotel complex, the **Grand Slam Canyon** is a Grand Canyon theme park with a rollercoaster and other rides—all enclosed in a glass shell. (Open Sun.-Thurs. 11am-6pm, Fri.-Sat. 10am-midnight. Admission and 2 small rides $4, seniors and under 3 free; additional rides $2-4. Unlimited rides $14, ages 3-9 $10.) **Excalibur,** 3850 Las Vegas Blvd. South (800-937-7777), has a medieval English theme which may make you nostalgic for the Black Plague. At *King Arthur's Tournament,* jousters and jesters entertain spectators while they eat a medieval banquet ($30). There are over 50 other casinos in Vegas, but they are generally less bombastic versions of the listed ones. Check with the visitor center for details.

Extra bucks will buy you a seat at a made-in-the-USA phenomenon—the **Vegas spectacular.** These stunning casino-sponsored productions happen twice per night and feature marvels such as waterfalls, explosions, fireworks, and casts of thousands (including animals). You can also see Broadway plays and musicals, ice revues, and individual entertainers in concert. All hotels have city-wide ticket booths in their lobbies. Some "production shows" are topless; most are tasteless. For a show by one of the musical stars who haunt the city, such as Diana Ross or Wayne Newton, you may have to fork over $40 or more. "Revues" featuring imitations of (generally deceased) performers are far more reasonable. But, why pay? You can't turn around in Vegas without bumping into an aspiring Elvis clone, or perhaps the real Elvis, pursuing anonymity in the brilliant disguise of an Elvis impersonator.

Nightlife in Vegas gets rolling around midnight and keeps going until everyone drops or runs out of money. At Caesar's Palace (731-7110), **Cleopatra's Barge** is a huge ship-disco (open Tues.-Sun. 10pm-4am; $5 cover Fri.-Sat.). Another popular disco, **Gipsy,** 4605 Paradise Rd. (731-1919), southeast of the Strip, may look deserted at 11pm, but by 1am the medium-sized dance floor packs in a gay, lesbian, and straight crowd (cover $4). Downtown, the **Fremont Street Blues and Reggae Club** (474-7209), at Fremont and 4th, provides live music every night (open Sun.-Thurs. 7pm-3am, Fri.-Sat. 7pm-5am).

■ Near Las Vegas: Lake Mead

Appearing as a turquoise oasis when you approach the Nevada desert on U.S. 93, Lake Mead has earned the nickname "The Jewel of the Desert" from its residents. The lake extends 110 miles behind **Hoover Dam,** the brainchild of its eponymous president, the Western Hemisphere's highest concrete dam. Harnessing the Colorado River, Hoover dam is a testament to Depression-era dreams of a better world achieved through engineering. The 727-ft. tall dam, made from 4.4 million cubic yds. of concrete, supplies hydroelectric power to over 500,000 homes. On the Nevada side, two androgynous winged statues, arms thrust skyward, sit above a tribute to the dam laborers. Guided 30-min. **tours** into the bowels of the dam are offered continuously throughout the day from the **Hoover Dam Visitor Center.** (293-8321; open 8:30am-6:30pm. $5, seniors and ages 10-16 $2.50, under 10 free. Wheelchairs available.)

Backcountry camping is permitted and free in most areas. Numerous National Park Service **campgrounds** lie within the recreation area as well (all sites $10 and first come, first served). The most popular is **Boulder Beach** (293-8990), accessible by

Lakeshore Rd. off U.S. 93. The **Lake Shore Trailer Village** (293-2540) has RV sites with showers for around $15. (Reservations required Memorial Day, July 4th, and Labor Day weekends; all other times first come, first served.)

U.S. 93 runs right over Hoover Dam. There are several free parking lots at intervals along the highway; the lots are crowded, but less so on the Arizona side. Shuttle bus service is available from the more remote lots. Public transportation does not serve Hoover Dam, but **Gray Line** buses and **Ray and Ross Tours** offer rides from Las Vegas (see Las Vegas Practical Information, above). For those bursting with energy, hop on a tour of the Dam power plant (293-8321; open daily).

■ Reno

If you were to cross *Showgirls* with *The Golden Girls,* the result would be Reno. Hoping to strike it rich at the card tables, busloads of the nation's elderly flock to "the biggest little city in the world" and all its hedonistic splendor. 24-hour bars, $5.99 sirloin steaks, seedy motels, mountain vistas, strip clubs full of young women who aspire to be dancers, and neon-lit pawnshops make Reno a strange place.

Practical Information Only 14 mi. from the California border and 443 mi. north of Las Vegas, Reno sits at the intersection of **I-80** and **U.S. 395,** which runs along the eastern slope of the Sierras. **Reno-Sparks Convention and Visitor Center,** 300 N. Center St. (800-FOR-RENO/367-7366), is located on the first floor of the National Bowling Stadium. (Open Mon.-Sat. 7am-8pm, Sun. 9am-6pm.) **Amtrak,** 135 E. Commercial Row (329-8638 or 800-USA-RAIL/800-872-7245), at Lake St., heads to: San Francisco (3 per day, $63); Sacramento (2 per day, $57); Salt Lake City (1 per day at 4:05 pm, $115); Chicago (1 per day at 4:05 pm, $225). **Greyhound,** 155 Stevenson St. (322-2970 or 800-231-2222), ½block from W. 2nd St, is open 24hr. Prices are lower when traveling Mon.-Thurs., slightly higher Fri.-Sun. To: San Francisco (17 per day, $34/36), Salt Lake City (4 per day, $46/49), L.A. (11 per day, $42/45), Vegas (1 per day, $51). The station has lockers (0-6hr. $2; 6-24hr. $4). **Reno Citifare,** (348-7433) at 4th and Center St., serves the Reno-Sparks area. Most routes operate 5am-7pm, though city center routes operate 24 hr. (Fare $1, seniors and disabled 50¢, ages 6-18 75¢.) Buses stop every 2 blocks. **Post Office:** 50 S. Virginia St. (786-5523), at Mill, two blocks south of city center. (Open Mon.-Fri. 7:30am-5pm, Sat. 10am-2pm.) **ZIP Code:** 89501. **Area Code:** 702.

Accommodations and Camping

Downtown Reno is compact, and its wide and well-lit streets are heavily patrolled in the summer. But be streetwise and avoid walking near the northeast corner alone after dark. Southwestern downtown has the cheapest accommodations. The prices listed don't include Reno's 9% hotel tax. The **El Cortez Hotel,** 239 W. 2nd St. (322-9161), is a clean, friendly hotel has A/C and a few long-time visitors (doubles Sun.-Thurs. $29, Fri.-Sat. $34, holidays $40). **Motel 6** has four locations in Reno: 866 N. Wells Ave. (786-0255); 1901 S. Virginia St. (827-0255); 1400 Stardust St. (747-7390) and 666 N. Wells Ave. (329-8681; no pool, but it is more centrally located. All locations: Sun.-Thurs. $30, weekends $38. Cheaper Oct.-May.) Those equipped to camp can make the drive to the woodland sites of **Davis Creek Park** (849-0684), 17 mi. south on U.S. 395 then ½ mi. west (follow the signs). Wrap yourself in a rustic blanket of pines and sage at the base of the Sierra Nevada's Mt. Rose. Showers, but no hookups. (63 sites available first come first served for $10 per site per vehicle, $1 per pet. Picnic area open 8am-9pm.)

Food Eating in Reno is cheap. To entice gamblers and to prevent them from wandering out in search of food, casinos offer a range of all-you-can-eat cuisine. But, there *are* alternatives. **Louis' Basque Corner,** 301 E. 4th St. (323-7203) is a local institution. Friendly waitstaff serves wonderfully spiced, hearty portions (full-course dinners $15, lunches $7-8; open Tues.-Sat. 11:30am-2:30pm and 5-9:30pm, Sun. 5-9:30pm). **The**

Blue Heron, 1091 S. Virginia St. (786-4110), is possibly the only restaurant in Reno without slot machines or video poker. It offers hearty and healthy vegetarian cuisine and is run by a friendly, down-to-earth staff. Filling entrees ($9) include soup or salad and delicious, freshly baked bread. Open Mon.-Sat. 11am-9pm, Sun. noon-9pm.

Sights and Entertainment Reno is a theme park. Usually, the theme of the day is "Casino!" so nightlife (and day life) revolve around the few dozen casinos downtown. They offer schmaltzy performances for the Wayne Newton crowd and generally aren't worth the steep admission prices. **Harrah's,** 219 N. Center St. (786-3232), tries hard to be hip with the addition of Planet Hollywood and a Playboy revue. Call for ticket prices and showtimes (open daily 10pm-5am). At **Circus Circus,** 500 N. Sierra (329-0711), a small circus hovers over the casino and performs "big-top" shows every ½ hr. Nearby **Virginia City** hosts **Camel Races** (847-0311) in September where camels and ostriches race through town. Take U.S. 395 south, then Rte. 341 about 25 mi. Reno's big new event, the **Reno Hilton Grand Prix** (789-2000 or 800-RENO-PAYS), also takes place in September. Vroom!

Near Reno: Pyramid Lake Thirty miles north of Reno, on the Paiute Indian Reservation, lies one of the most stunningly beautiful bodies of water in the U.S. The dichotomy of barren desert and pristine water makes Pyramid Lake a soothing respite from neon Reno. **Camping** is allowed anywhere on the lakeshore, but only designated areas have toilet facilities. A $5 **permit** is required for use of the park and the area is carefully patrolled by the Paiute tribe. Permits are available at the **Ranger Station** (476-1155; open Mon.-Sat. 9am-5pm). It contains a hot spring and a series of rocks on the north shore which beg to be climbed. Those looking for solitude should try the south and east shores; the areas north of the ranger station are clogged with RVs.

Utah

Beginning in 1848, persecuted Mormons settled on the land which is now Utah, intending to establish and govern their own theocratic state. U.S. President James Buchanan struggled to quash the Mormon's efforts in 1858, in a dispute which foreshadowed the states-rights conflicts leading up to the Civil War. Today the state's population is 70% Mormon—a religious presence felt particularly in Salt Lake City and the smaller cities surrounding the capital. Utah's citizens dwell primarily in the 100-mile corridor along I-15 stretching from Ogden to Provo. Outside this area, Utah's natural beauty dominates, intoxicating visitors in a way that watered-down 3.2% beer never can. Immediately east of Salt Lake City the Wasatch range beckons skiers in the winter and bikers in the summer. Southern Utah is like no other place on Earth: red canyons, river gorges, and crenellated cliffs attest to the creative powers of wind and water.

PRACTICAL INFORMATION

Capital: Salt Lake City.
Utah Travel Council: 300 N. State St., Salt Lake City 84114 (801-538-1030), across from the capitol building. Distributes the free *Utah Vacation Planner,* with complete lists of motels, national parks, and campgrounds, as well as statewide biking, rafting, and skiing vacation planners. **Utah Parks and Recreation,** 1636 W. North Temple, Salt Lake City 86116 (801-538-7220). Open Mon.-Fri. 8am-5pm.
Controlled Substances: Mormons eschew caffeine, nicotine, alcohol, and illegal drugs. While you won't have any trouble getting a pack of cigarettes, a cup of coffee or a coke, alcohol is another matter. State liquor stores are sprinkled sparsely about the state and have inconvenient hours. Only grocery and convenience stores

may sell beer for take-out. Because licenses and zoning laws can split a room, drinkers may have to move a few ft. down the bar to get a mixed drink.

State Holiday: July 24 is Pioneer Day, and most places of business are closed.
Time Zone: Mountain (2hr. behind Eastern). **Postal Abbreviation:** UT.
Sales Tax: 6.25%.

NORTHERN UTAH

■ Salt Lake City

Tired from five exhausting months of travel, Brigham Young looked out across the desolate valley of the Great Salt Lake and said, "this is the place." Young knew that his band of Mormon pioneers had finally reached a haven where they could practice their religion freely, away from the persecution they had faced in the east. Today, Salt Lake City is still dominated by Mormon influence. The Church of Latter Day Saints (LDS, not the hallucinogenic drug), owns the tallest office building downtown and welcomes visitors to Temple Square, a city block that includes the Mormon Temple and cool shady gardens. Despite its commitment to preserving traditions, Salt Lake is rapidly attracting high tech firms as well as outdoor enthusiasts drawn to world class ski resorts, rock climbing, and mountain trails. The city has already landed perhaps the biggest prize of all: the 2002 Winter Olympics.

PRACTICAL INFORMATION

Tourist Office: Salt Lake Valley Convention and Visitors Bureau, 180 S. West Temple (521-2868), 2 blocks from Temple Sq. Open Mon.-Fri. 8am-6pm, Sat. 9am-4pm, Labor Day-Memorial day Mon.-Fri. 8am-5pm, Sat. 9am-4pm. Distributes the *Salt Lake Visitors Guide*.

Airport: Salt Lake City International, 776 N. Terminal Dr. (575-2600), 4mi. west of Temple Sq. UTA bus #50 runs between the terminal and downtown for 65¢. Taxi to Temple Sq. costs about $14.

Trains: Amtrak, 325 S. Rio Grande (364-8562 or 800-872-7245), in an unsafe area. To: Las Vegas (3 per week, 8hr., $96) and L.A. (3 per week, 15½hr., $122). Open 24hr.; tickets sold Mon.-Sat. 4-9:30am, 10am-12:30pm, and 4:15pm-1am, Sun. 4pm-1am.

Buses: Greyhound, 160 W. South Temple (800-231-2222), 1 block west of Temple Sq. To: Las Vegas (2 per day, 8hr., $41); L.A. (3 per day, 15hr., $74); Denver (6 per day, $42). Open daily 5:30am-midnight; tickets sold 5:30am-11pm.

Public Transportation: Utah Transit Authority (UTA), 600 S. 700 West (287-4636). Frequent service to University of Utah campus; buses to Ogden (#70/72 express), suburbs, airport, mountain canyons, and Provo (#4 local or #1 express; fare $1.50). Buses every ½hr.-1hr. Mon.-Fri. 6am-11pm. Fare 65¢, seniors 30¢, under 5 free. Maps available at libraries and visitors bureau.

Taxis: Ute Cab, 359-7788. **Yellow Cab,** 521-2100. $1.25 base fare, $1.50 per mi.

Car Rental: Payless Car Rental, 1974 W. North Temple (596-2596). $30 per day, unlimited mi. within Utah, 200 free mi. outside the state. $140 per week, 1400 free mi. outside Utah. 16¢ per additional mi. Insurance $9 per day. Open Sun.-Fri. 6am-9pm, Sat. 6am-8pm. Must be 21 with a major credit card.

Bike Rental: Wasatch Touring, 702 E. 100 South (359-9361). 21-speed mountain bikes and helmets $20 per day. Call ahead to reserve a bike; they often rent all of their bikes by mid-day. Open Mon.-Sat. 9am-7pm.

Crisis Lines: Rape Crisis, 467-7273. Operates 24hr.

Emergency: 911.

Post Office: 230 W. 200 South (974-2200), 1 block west of the visitors bureau. Open Mon.-Fri. 8am-5:30pm, Sat. 10am-2pm. **ZIP code:** 84101. **Area code:** 801.

Salt Lake's grid system makes navigation simple. Brigham Young designated **Temple Sq.** as the heart of downtown. Street names indicate how many blocks east, west, north, or south they lie from Temple Sq.; the "0" points are **Main St.** (north-south) and **South Temple St.** (east-west). Local address listings often include two numerical cross streets leading to some confusion for visitors. A building on E. 8th St. (800 E.) might be listed as 825 E. 1300 S., meaning the cross street is 1300S (13th S.). Smaller streets and streets that do not fit the grid pattern often have non-numeric names. Downtown Salt Lake is equipped with audible traffic lights for the convenience of blind pedestrians.

ACCOMMODATIONS AND CAMPING

Ute Hostel (AAIH/Rucksackers), 21 E. Kelsey Ave. (595-1645), near the intersection of 13th S. and Main St. Young international crowd. Free pick-ups can be arranged from Amtrak, Greyhound, or the visitors information center. Free tea and coffee, parking, linen, and safe for valuables. 24hr. check-in. Dorm rooms $13-15. Comfortable doubles $30-35.

Ken-del Motel, 667 N. 300 West (355-0293), 10 blocks northwest of Temple Sq. in a transitional neighborhood. From the airport take bus #50 to N. Temple, then bus #70; from Greyhound or downtown catch bus #70. Huge dorm-style rooms *for women only* with nice bath and kitchen $15 per person. Well-kept singles with kitchens, TV, and A/C $30, doubles $40.

Temple View, 325 N. 300 West (525-9525), has clean, well-appointed rooms with cable, HBO, and unlimited free local calls. Singles $39.

Motel 6, 176 W. 600 South (531-1252). Relax in your room, by the pool, or meander downtown. Free local calls and HBO. Singles $43, doubles $49.

The Avenue's Hostel, 107 F. Street (359-3855 or 800-881-4785), 7 blocks east of temple square. Blankets and linens provided. Free pick-ups from Amtrak and Greyhound stations. Dorm rooms $12. Open 7:30am-12:30pm and 4-10:30pm.

The mountains rising to the east of Salt Lake City offer comfortable summer camping with warm days and cool nights. The **Wasatch-Cache National Forest** manages numerous campsites in the canyons and mountains of the Wasatch range. The **Mount Olympus Wilderness** (within the National Forest), in rocky **Little Cottonwood Canyon,** up Rte. 210 east of the city, features three of the closest campgrounds: **Box Elder** (35 sites), **Terraces** (25 sites), and **Bigwater Trailhead** (45 sites). Four more campgrounds lie just north of the city on I-15: **Sunset** (32 sites), **Bountiful Park** (79 sites), **Buckland Flat** (26 sites), and **Mueller Park** (63 sites). On weekends, go early to ensure a space (sites $9-11). If you need a hookup, try **KOA,** 1400 W. North Temple (355-1192; 60 tent sites, 290 RV sites; $18, with water and electricity $21, full hookup $23).

FOOD

Good, cheap restaurants are sprinkled all around the city and its suburbs. If you're in a hurry downtown, ZCMI Mall and Crossroads Mall, both located across from Temple Square, have standard food courts including a Cajun place in ZCMI that rocks.

The Pie, 1320 E. 200 South (582-0193), next to the University of Utah. This college hangout serves up big slices of pizza ($1.50) late into the night. Open Mon.-Thurs. 11am-1am, Fri.-Sat. 11am-3am, Sun. noon-11pm.

Park Café, 604 E. 1300 South (487-1670), near Liberty Park. A classy little joint with a patio and a view of a park. Lunches around $6. Open Mon.-Thurs. 7am-3pm and 5-9pm, Fri. 7am-3pm and 5-10pm.

Squatter's Salt Lake Brewing Company, 147 W. Broadway (363-BREW/2739), is a microbrewery with reasonably priced American cuisine, and a variety of sandwiches and salads ($5-7). Open daily 11:30am-1am.

Einstein Bagels, 147 S. Main (537-5033), near Temple Square. Grab a warm bagel (45¢) or a bagel sandwich ($3.60), read the newspaper, and people-watch in a bohemian meets bourgeoisie atmosphere.

SACRED SIGHTS

Followers of the **Church of Jesus Christ of Latter Day Saints** hold both the *Book of Mormon* and the *Bible* to be the Word of God. The seat of the highest Mormon authority and the central temple, **Temple Sq.** (240-2534), is the symbolic center of the Mormon religion. Feel free to wander around the pleasant, flowery, 10-acre square, but the sacred temple is off-limits to non-Mormons. Alighting on the highest of the temple's three towers, a golden statue of the angel Moroni watches over the city. The square has two **visitors centers** (north and south); the North visitors center displays Old and New Testament murals and videos about Temple Square. 25-min. **Book of Mormon** and **Purpose of Temple Presentations** begin alternately every 30 min. at the South visitors center (free). A 45-min. tour leaves from the flagpole every 10 min., showing off the highlights of Temple Square (free; both open daily 8am-10pm, off season 8am-9:30pm).

Visitors to Temple Sq. may also visit the **Mormon Tabernacle,** which houses the famed choir. Built in 1867, the structure is so acoustically sensitive that a pin hitting the floor at one end of the building can be heard 175 ft. away at the other end. Members of the choir are selected on the basis of character, musical competence, and sometimes family tradition. Rehearsals on Thursday evenings (8-9:30pm) and Sunday morning broadcasts from the tabernacle are open to the public (9:30-10am; doors close at 9:15am). No matter how forcefully they sing, however, the choir can't match the size and sound of the 11,623-pipe organ which accompanies them. (Organ recitals Mon.-Sat. noon-12:30pm, Sun. 2-2:30pm.) In the summer there are frequent concerts at **Assembly Hall,** next door to the tabernacle. The **Museum of Church History and Art,** 45 N. West Temple (240-3310), houses Mormon memorabilia from 1820 to the present, including an original 1830 copy of the Book of Mormon and a scale model of early Salt Lake City (open Mon.-Fri. 9am-9pm, Sat.-Sun. and holidays 10am-7pm; free). The **Beehive House,** 67 E. South Temple (240-2671), at State St., served as the official residence of Brigham Young while he served as "governor" of the Deseret Territory (a Mormon settlement unrecognized by the U.S. government) and president of the Church. (Open Mon.-Sat. 9:30am-4:30pm, Sun. 10am-1pm. ½-hr. guided tours every 10-15 min. Free.)

The moment when Brigham Young and his band of Mormons first came upon the Great Salt Lake is commemorated at **"This is the Place" State Park,** 2601 Sunnyside Ave. (584-8391), in Emigration Canyon on the eastern end of town. (Take bus #4. Park open in summer daily 8am-8pm.) The **"This is the Place" Monument** celebrates

It's All in the Family

Brigham Young and his Mormon followers originally settled in the Utah territory in order to escape the religious persecution which they experienced in the eastern U.S. Differences between Mormons and non-Mormons in the 19th-century, however, were cultural as well as religious: namely, Mormons believed in and practiced polygamy. Brigham Young had **over 15 wives** and many Mormon men had 4 or 5. In 1896, Utah applied for statehood and the federal government accepted with the caveat that the **LDS church had to disavow polygamy.** Although the deal was made and Utah became a state, many families simply hid their activities behind closed doors. As Utah grew less isolated from the national culture in the early 20th century, public pressure forced the LDS to begin excommunicating polygamists. Even today, despite both religious and modern pressures, polygamy continues to survive in certain fundamentalist sects of the LDS. Estimates of those living in multi-wived families in Utah range from a low figure of 5000 people, to upwards of 30,000 out of a total state population of 1,800,000 people. Curiously enough, **divorce rates** in polygamist families are unusually low (below 10%). Supporters of polygamy use this figure to justify plural marriage; others contest that the low divorce rate is probably due to the limited opportunities available to a wife in that kind of arrangement.

Brigham Young's decision to settle in Salt Lake City. The **visitors center** has been recently demolished to make way for a larger facility. Tour **Brigham Young's forest farmhouse,** where the leader held court with his numerous wives (open Tues.-Sun. 11am-5pm). Big business meets religion at the **Church of Jesus Christ of Latter Day Saints Office Building,** 50 E. North Temple (240-2842). This skyscraper is the tallest in Utah. Ride the elevator to the 26th floor (free) for a view of the Great Salt Lake in the west or the Wasatch Range in the east. Free tours are also offered (tours Mon.-Fri. 9am-4:30pm; observation deck Mon.-Sat. 9am-4:30pm).

SECULAR SIGHTS AND ENTERTAINMENT

Utah's original **capitol** was in the centrally located town of Fillmore, but since the population in the Salt Lake area was higher, the capitol was moved there in 1916. The gray granite building includes exhibits such as a race car that broke the land speed record at Bonneville Salt Flats. (538-3000. Open Mon.-Fri. 9am-3pm.) **Pioneer Memorial Museum,** 300 N. Main St. (538-1050), next to the capitol, has personal items belonging to the earliest settlers of the valley and info about prominent Mormon leaders: Brigham Young (open Mon.-Sat. 9am-5pm; free). While in the capitol area, hike up City Creek Canyon to **Memory Grove** and savor one of the city's best views. Also on capitol hill, the **Hansen Planetarium,** 15 S. State St. (538-2098), has fabulous free exhibits, in addition to laser shows set to Led Zeppelin and U2 (open Sun.-Thurs. 9am-10pm, Fri.-Sat. 9am-1am; $7.50).

Head for the **Children's Museum,** 840 N. 300 West (328-3383), to pilot a 727 jet or implant a Jarvik artificial heart in a life-sized "patient." (Open Mon.-Thurs. and Sat. 9:30am-5pm, Fri. 9:30am-9pm. $3, ages 2-13 $2.15; Mon. after 5pm $1.50/$1. Take bus #61.) For happenings at the **University of Utah,** contact the **Information Desk** in the U. of Utah Park Administration Building (581-6515; open Mon.-Fri. 9am-4pm), or **Olpin Student Center** (581-5888; open Mon.-Sat. 8am-9pm). Located at the University of Utah, the **Utah Museum of Fine Arts** (581-7332) hosts a permanent collection of world art (open Mon.-Fri. 10am-5pm, Sat.-Sun. 2-5pm).

The **Utah Symphony Orchestra** (533-6407) performs in Abravanel Hall, 123 W. South Temple (tickets in summer $10-25, in season $14-35; student rush $6). The neighboring **Salt Lake Art Center** (328-4201) stages dance and opera performances (open Tues.-Sat. 10am-5pm, Sun. 1-5pm; suggested donation $2). At 7:30pm every Tuesday and Friday in the summer, the **Temple Square Concert Series** (240-2534) puts on a free outdoor concert at Brigham Young Historic Park, with music ranging from string quartet to unplugged guitar. Call for a schedule of concerts.

In order to serve liquor, an establishment must be a private club. Most clubs sell a temporary membership card for $5 that is good for two weeks. However, a yearly membership at a club can sponsor an unlimited number of guests for free. Most members are glad to sponsor out of town guests. Pick up a free copy of *Private Eye Weekly, The Event,* or *Utah After Dark* at a bar or restaurant, for local club listings and events. The **Dead Goat Saloon,** 165 S. West Temple (328-4628), is a tavern (3.2% beer only) serving tourists and locals alike. (Open Mon.-Fri. 11:30am-2am, Sat. 6pm-2am, Sun. 7pm-1am. Cover $1-5, Fri.-Sun. $5.) Head over to the **X Wife's Place,** 465 S. 700 East (532-2353), to shoot stick. There's no cover, but you'll need a member to sponsor you. (Open Mon.-Sat. 4pm-1am. Normal beer and mixed drinks served.) **Club DV8,** 115 S. West Temple (539-8400), is one of the better dance clubs in Salt Lake City (also a private club) deviating from the straight and narrow, with 25¢ drafts on Saturdays (9-10pm) and "modern music" on Thursday nights. (Open Thurs.-Sat. 9pm-2am. ½-price drafts 9-10pm. 2-wk. membership $5; guest cover $3, before 10pm $1.) **The Zephyr,** 79 W. 300 South (355-2582), blows with live rock and reggae nightly (open daily 7pm-1am; get a member to sponsor you).

■ Near Salt Lake City

The **Great Salt Lake,** administered by Great Salt Lake State Park (250-1898), is a remnant of primordial Lake Bonneville, and is so salty that only blue-green algae and brine shrimp can survive in it. The salt content varies from 5% to 15%, providing unusual buoyancy; in fact, no one has ever drowned in the Great Salt Lake. Due to its chemical make-up, the water stinks. Oh well.

It is nearly impossible to get to the lake without a car; bus #37 ("Magna") will take you within 4 mi., but no closer. To get to the **south shore** of the lake, take I-80 17 mi. west of Salt Lake City to Exit 104. If flooding closes the south shore, drive north on I-15 past Ogden to fresh water **Willard Bay** (Exit 360) or further west on I-80 to **Saltair Beach.**

Some of the greatest skiing snow in the U.S., if not the world, falls on the Wasatch mountains, located just minutes from downtown Salt Lake. Rte. 210 heads east from I-25, climbing through the granite boulders of Little Cottonwood Canyon to **Snow-bird** (742-2222 or 800-453-3000) and **Alta** (572-3939). Rte. 190 climbs neighboring Big Cottonwood Canyon and leads to **Solitude** (534-1400) and **Brighton** (532-4731). **Park City** (649-8111) is located further east off of I-80. Alta is the best bet for the budget skier; $25 buys an all day lift ticket to wide open cruising runs, emerald glades, steep chutes, and champagne powder.

The **Alta Peruvian Lodge** (328-8589 or 800-453-8488) offers an excellent package for two people ($140-180) which includes a bed, all meals, service charges, tax, and lift tickets. **UTA** (see Salt Lake City Practical Information, p. 614) runs buses from the city to the resorts in winter, and has pickups at downtown motels. **Lewis Bros. Stages** (800-826-5844), one of the many shuttle services which provide transport to Park City, departs the airport every hour in winter and six times per day in summer ($18, $36 roundtrip). **Breeze Ski Rentals** (800-525-0314) rents equipment at Snow-bird and Park City ($18; 10% discount if reserved; lower rates for rentals over 3 days). Contact the Utah Travel Council (see Utah Practical Information, p. 613) and request the free *Ski Utah* for complete listings of ski packages and lodgings.

In the summer, outdoor lovers climb the Wasatch range to beat the desert heat of the city. Hiking, biking, and fishing are all prime attractions. Mountain bike rentals are available at Snowbird (bikes with helmet are $20 per ½day, $30 per day). Snowbird's **aerial tram** climbs to 11,000 ft., offering a spectacular view of the Wasatch Mountains and the Salt Lake Valley. (Open daily, hours vary with the season. $10, over 65 and 6-16 $8, under 6 free. With a bike $10, all day pass $15.) **Park City** offers a thrilling ½ mi. of curves and drops on their **alpine slide.** (Open Mon.-Fri. noon-10pm, Sat.-Sun. 10am-10pm. $6, seniors and children $4.50, under 7 $1.75.)

The town of **Wendover** (visitors center: 800-426-6862) lies 120 mi. east of Salt Lake City along I-80 on the Utah-Nevada border. The salt flats to the southeast are so amazingly flat that you can see the curvature of the earth. On the Nevada side of town, casinos tempt wayward Utahns who have strayed from Temple Square.

■ Dinosaur and Vernal

Dinosaur National Monument was created in 1915, seven years after paleontologist Earl Douglass happened upon an array of fossilized dinosaur bones. Since then, the monument has been enlarged to include the vast and colorful gorges created by the Green and Yampa Rivers, and the harsh terrain evokes eerie visions of its reptilian past. It is difficult to imagine that these harsh range lands, where temperatures can vary 150°F between winter and summer, was once the home to horsetail ferns and grazing dinosaurs. Nearby **Vernal**, 16 mi. west of Dinosaur on U.S. 40, is a popular base for exploring the Monument, Flaming Gorge, and the Uinta Mountains.

Practical Information The park collects an **entrance fee** of $5 per car, and $3 per biker, pedestrian, or tour bus passenger. The Monument's more interesting and varied west side lies along Rte. 149 off U.S. 40 just outside of **Jensen,** 30 mi. east of Vernal. The rugged east side of the park is accessible only from a road off U.S. 40, outside **Dinosaur, CO.** The **Dinosaur Quarry Visitors Center** (789-2115), near the fee collection booth, is accessible only by a free shuttle bus running every 15 min. or an uphill ½-mi. walk in the summer; in the winter you can drive up to the center (open daily 8am-7pm, in winter 8am-4:30pm). While you're there, pick up the Monument visitors guide *Echoes*. The **Dinosaur National Monument Headquarters** (970-374-3000), on the other side of the park at the intersection of U.S. 40 and the park road in Dinosaur, CO, provides orientation for exploring the canyonlands of the park. (Open daily 8am-4:30pm; Sept.-May Mon.-Fri. 8am-4:30pm.) In Vernal, stop at the **visitors center** in the **Utah Fieldhouse of Natural History and Dinosaur Garden,** 235 E. Main St. (789-4002), which offers helpful advice for daytrips in the area (open daily 8am-9pm). The **Ashley National Forest Service Offices,** 355 N. Vernal Ave. (789-1181), in Vernal, has info about hiking, biking, and camping in the surrounding forests (open Mon.-Fri. 8am-5pm).

Greyhound (800-231-2222) makes daily runs east and west along U.S. 40 (4 or 5 per day each way), stopping in Vernal and Dinosaur, CO, en route from Denver and Salt Lake City. Jensen is a flag stop, as is Monument Headquarters, 2 mi. west of Dinosaur, CO. In an **emergency,** call 789-2115 in UT or 303-374-2216 in CO. Vernal, UT's **post office:** 67 N. 800 West (789-2393; open Mon.-Fri. 9am-5pm, Sat. 10am-noon). **ZIP code:** 84078. **Area code:** 801.

Camping, Accommodations, and Food

For the low-down on campgrounds, contact the park visitors center. **Green River Campground,** consists of 88 shaded sites along the Green River (flush toilets, water, RVs, disabled sites; $10; open late spring-early fall). There are also several free primitive campsites in and around the park. Thirteen mi. east of Harper's Corner, off a 4-wheel drive road (impassable when wet) on the park's east side, **Echo Campground** (9 free sites), provides the perfect location for a crystalline evening under the stars. For **backcountry camping,** obtain a free permit from the headquarters or from Quarry Center.

Campground Dina RV Park, 930 N. Vernal Ave. (789-2148 or 800-245-2148), about 1 mi. north of Main St. on U.S. 191, is a great bet for those who want a shady, comfortable spot to pitch a tent (grassy sites $6.50, full hookup $19.50, heated pool, showers, convenience store, 10% off with *Let's Go*). **Vernal KOA,** 1800 W. Sheraton Ave. (789-8935 or 800-562-7574), off U.S. 40 south of town, has laundry facilities and a pool (tent sites $14, full hookups $18). In Vernal, the comfortable **Sage Motel,** 54 W. Main St. (789-1442), has big, clean rooms, A/C, cable TV, and unlimited free local calls (singles $35, 2 people $39, doubles $46). A plastic dino out front wards off intruders at the **Dine-A-Ville Motel,** 801 W. Main St. (789-9571), at the west end of town. The rooms feature color TV, and some have kitchenettes. (Singles $28.20, doubles $39.)

The **7-11 Ranch Restaurant,** 77 E. Main St. (789-1170), Vernal, serves resolutely American food, including big breakfasts with eggs, hash browns, and toast for $2.50 and dinners with a salad, vegetable, and bread from $7 (open Mon.-Sat. 6am-10pm). **La Cabaña,** 56 W. Main St. (789-3151), next to the Sage Motel, serves Mexican food and breakfast ($3 breakfast specials, $3 burritos; open daily 7am-10pm).

Sights and Activities

The star attraction is the dinosaur quarry display at the western visitors center. Some of the most complete dinosaur skeletons in the world can be seen still encased in the rock they were buried in. Excellent exhibits inform visitors about the life of dinosaurs and the excavation process. Also in the western section of the park, ancient petroglyphs can be seen along the road that accesses the campsites, both at **Club Creek** and beyond the campgrounds themselves.

In the eastern section of the park, the 25-mi. road (closed in winter) to majestic **Harper's Corner,** at the junction of the Green and Yampa River gorges, begins 2 mi. east of Dinosaur. From the road's terminus, a 2-mi. roundtrip nature hike leads to a view of the Green and Yampa Rivers and sculpted rock formations. **Dan River Hatch Expeditions,** 55 E. Main St. (789-4316 or 800-342-8243), in Vernal, arranges a wide variety of summer rafting trips along the rivers running through the monument (1-day voyage $60, under 12 $50).

In Vernal, the **Utah Fieldhouse of Natural History and Dinosaur Garden,** 235 Main St. (789-3799), houses the visitors center and offers excellent displays on the state's history. The dinosaur garden features life-size models. Check out the geological displays where fluorescent minerals make your shoelaces glow in the dark. (Open daily 8am-8pm; off season 9am-5pm. $1.50, ages 6-15 $1.)

■ Flaming Gorge

Seen at sunset, the contrast between the red canyonlands and the azure water of the Green River makes the landscape glow, hence the moniker "Flaming Gorge." In 1963 the Green River was dammed, giving rise to the creation of **Flaming Gorge National Recreation Area,** a diverse area stretching from cool pine and aspen forests to the beautiful deserts of Wyoming. Each year, doomed trout are placed in **Flaming Gorge Reservoir,** sacrificed to provide some of the best fishing in the state, if you enjoy catching fish without making any real effort. Waterskiing, boating, and hiking are also popular in the area.

Practical Information From Wyoming, travel on U.S. 191S to the gorge through the untouched high desert. The **Flaming Gorge Visitors Center** (885-3135), on U.S. 191 on the top of Flaming Gorge Dam, offers free guided tours of the dam (open daily 8am-6pm; off season 10am-5pm). The **Red Canyon Visitors Center** (889-3713), a few mi. off U.S. 191 on Rte. 44 to Manila, hangs 1360 ft. above Red Canyon and Flaming Gorge Lake (open daily 10am-5pm; closed in winter). Flaming Gorge's **ZIP code:** 84759. **Area code:** 801.

Camping and Accommodations Inexpensive **campgrounds** flourish in the Flaming Gorge area; ask for a pamphlet listing all the campgrounds at either visitors center. Reservations for large groups can be made by calling (800-280-CAMP/2267). For an excellent view of the Reservoir and Red Canyon, camp next to the visitors center in **Canyon Rim Campground** (18 sites $10; open mid-May to mid-Sept.), or in one of the numerous national forest campgrounds along U.S. 191 and Rte. 44 in the Utah portion of the park (2-week max. stay; sites $9-11). Farther north, **Buckboard Crossing** (68 sites $8) and **Lucerne Valley** (143 sites $10), are drier and unshaded, but their location, close to the marinas on the reservoir, is a bonus (both open mid-April to mid-Oct.). A number of free primitive campgrounds hide in the high country. You do not have to camp at a developed site; just be sure to check with the rangers to make sure the spot you pick is kosher.

If you'd rather sleep indoors, **Red Canyon Lodge** (889-3759), west on Rte. 44, 2 mi. before the visitors center, offers reasonably priced, rustic cabins. (Shared bathroom single cabins $30, doubles $40, with private bathroom $45/55, rollaway beds $5 per night, children under 12 free.) The resort also offers a private 20-acre lake stocked with trout, a free kids fishing pool, and a great restaurant (jalapeño chicken breast sandwich $7; open daily for all meals).

Sights and Activities Try your hand at fishing along the Green River Gorge below the dam. The lake teems with trout, and the Green River offers some of the best fly fishing in the country. To fish, you must obtain a **permit** (available at Flaming Gorge Lodge, the marinas, and most stores in Manila). For more info, call the **Utah Department of Wildlife Resources,** 152 E. 100 North, Salt Lake City (789-3103; open Mon.-Fri. 8am-5pm). **Cedar Springs Marina** (889-3795), 3 mi. before the dam in Dutch John, rents all kinds of boats. Pontoon boats accommodate 8 people and cost $70 for 3hr., $120 per day. Ski boats come fully equipped with water skis ($95 for 3hr., $170 per day; 6 people total; open 8am-6pm). Nearby Flaming Gorge Lodge (889-3773) rents fishing rods ($5 per day). At **Lucerne Valley Marina** (784-3483), 7 mi. east of Manila off Rte. 43, you can procure a small, 14-ft. fishing boat for $65 per day (open daily 8am-6pm).

The **Sheep Creek Geologic Loop,** an 11-mi. scenic drive off Rte. 44 just south of Manila, takes you past rock strata and wildlife. For a hide out from tourists, the valley of **Brown's Park,** 23 mi. east of Flaming Gorge, is perfect. Four-wheel drive is recommended. Nineteenth-century western outlaws Butch Cassidy and his Wild Bunch found the valley's isolation and its proximity to three state lines ideal for evading the law; today's visitors will find two free campsites (no water) on the river's shore: **Indian Crossing,** up the Green River, and **Indian Hollow,** downstream.

SOUTHERN UTAH

■ Moab

Moab first flourished in the 1950s as uranium miners rushed to the area, transforming the town from a quiet hamlet into a gritty desert outpost. Today the mountain bike has replaced the Geiger counter, as tourists rush into the town eager to bike the red slickrock, raft down whitewater rapids, or explore surrounding Arches and Canyonlands National Parks. The town itself has changed to accommodate the new visitors and athletes; microbreweries and T-shirt shops now fill the rooms of the old gray uranium building on Main Street.

Practical Information Moab sits 50 mi. southeast of I-70 on U.S. 191, 5 mi. south of Arches. **Amtrak** comes only as close as Thompson, 41 mi. northeast of town, and **Greyhound** plans its nearest stops in Green River, 52 mi. northwest. See if your hotel or hostel will pick you up from these distant points for a small fee; otherwise **Bighorn Express** (888-655-RIDE/7433 or 587-3061) makes trips from Salt Lake City airport to Moab ($35; open Mon.-Fri. 2-9pm, Sat.-Sun. 10am-2pm). **Coyote Shuttle** (259-8656) will take you where you want to go. Rates and hours vary.

The **Moab Information Center,** 3 Center St., provides info on the city and nearby parks and monuments (open daily 8am-9pm, Nov.-Feb. 8am-5pm). Moab's **post office:** 50 E. 100 North (259-7427; open Mon.-Fri. 8:30am-4pm, Sat. 9am-noon). **ZIP code:** 84532. **Area code:** 801.

Accommodations and Camping Although chain motels clutter Main St., Moab fills up fast in the summer, especially on weekends; call up to a month ahead to guarantee a reservation. Off-season rates can drop as much as 50%, and during that time the weather is more conducive to hiking. The owners of the **Lazy Lizard International Hostel (AAIH/Rucksackers),** 1213 S. U.S. 191 (259-6057; look for the "A1 Storage" sign just south of Moab on U.S. 191), go out of their way to be helpful— they'll pick you up (usually for $10-15), and arrange trips through local companies. The kitchen, VCR, laundry, and hot tub are at your beck and call. (Bunks $7 per person, private rooms for 1 or 2 $20; teepees for 1 or 2 $10.)

A birdcage, bowling pins, and a moose serve as decorative accents in the quirky and luxurious theme rooms of **Hotel Off Center,** 96 E. Center St. (259-4244 or 800-237-4685), ½ block off Main St. (Shared bathrooms. Open Mar. 1-Oct. 31. Dorm beds $15, singles $37, doubles $49; rates include continental breakfast.) **The Prospector Lodge,** 186 N. 1st West (259-5145), 1 block west of Main St., offers cool, comfy rooms with TV and free java. (Singles with a double bed $33, with queen-size $40, doubles $52, triples $60; $6 per additional person.) The **Sunset Motel,** 41 W. 100 N. (259-5191 or 800-421-5614), has standard motel rooms with free HBO and a pool (open year round; singles $30, doubles $35).

Arches National Park (see p. 623) has the area's best **campground.** In town, the **Canyonlands Campground,** 555 S. Main St. (259-6848 or 800-522-6648), next to the Shell Station, provides well-shaded sites and a pool. (Sites $14, with water and electricity $17, with full hookup $19; $2 per additional person.) **Slickrock Campground,** 1301½ N. Hwy. 191 (259-7660 or 800-448-8873), beckons the budget traveler with the enigmatic slogan "funpigs stay at Slickrock." (Pool, 3 hot tubs, and laundry machines. Tent sites $16, hookup $21.50, cabins with A/C for 4 $30.)

Food **The Poplar Place Pub and Eatery,** 100 N. Main St. (259-6018; open daily 11:30am-11pm), serves Southwestern style pizzas (from $8), Mexican dishes ($10), and fresh salads (around $5). For retro diner decor, visit **The Moab Diner and Ice Cream Shoppe,** 189 S. Main St. (259-4006), where you should try the veggie specials and the excellent french fries. (Burgers and sandwiches $4-5. Open daily 6am-10pm.) Grab dinner and a beer at **Eddie McStiff's,** 57 S. Main St. (259-BEER/2337), offering 12 homemade brews (pints $3), from "chestnut brown" to "passion fruit pale," along side pizza ($6-10), pasta ($7), and tourists (free; open daily 3-10pm).

Eclectic dining establishments dot Moab's streets, but when you need a drink, the **Moab Liquor Store,** 260 S. Main St. (259-5314), is the only place to purchase alcohol above 3.2% (open Mon.-Sat. 11am-7pm). Mixed drinks without food can be had at **The Rio Colorado Restaurant and Bar,** 2 S. 100 West (259-6666), off Main St. Try to find a year round member to sponsor you so you don't have to buy a temporary membership (open Mon.-Fri. 11:30am-11pm, Sat. 5pm-1am, Sun. 10am-midnight).

Sights and Activities Mountain biking and rafting, along with nearby national parks, are the big draws in Moab. The **Slickrock** trail is a 10-mi. loop which rolls up and down the slickrock outside of Moab. The trail has no big vertical gain, but it's technically difficult and temperatures often reach 100°F. **Rim Cyclery,** 94 W. 100 North (259-5333), one of the first mountain bike shops in southern Utah, rents bikes and distributes info about the slickrock trails. ($28-35 per day includes helmet. Open daily 9am-6pm, closed Sun. in winter.)

Countless raft companies are based in Moab. **Western River Expeditions** (800-453-7450) offers some of the best deals on the Colorado (full day $39, youth $29, includes lunch; ½-day trip $29/$23). **Trapax, Inc.** (259-5261) takes you for an evening boat ride along the Colorado River as their sound and light show ricochets off the canyon walls ($20, ages 6-16 $10, under 6 free). Various Moab outfitters also arrange horseback, motorboat, canoe, jeep, and helicopter rides. **Park Creek Ranch** (259-5505) offers **trail rides** into the La Sal Mountains (1hr. $17 per person; 2hr. $30) or the Arches National Park (1hr. $20 per person; 2hr. $35).

The museums of Moab attract art enthusiasts and those who are tired of the great outdoors. Albert Christensen spent 12 years creating the weird **Hole 'n the Rock** (668-2250), 15 mi. south of Moab on U.S. 191, a 14-room house carved out of a sandstone cliff. His wife Gladys kept the dream alive after his death in 1957 and opened the house to the public. Check out Christensen's nearby rendering of Franklin D. Roosevelt as well. (Open daily 9am-5pm. $2.) Utah's only winery, **Arches Vineyards,** 420 Kane Creek Blvd. (259-5397 or 800-723-8609), is located in the Moab area. (Tasting room open Mon.-Thurs. 11am-7pm, Fri.-Sat. 11am-9pm. Free.)

■ Finding the Fab Five

The five National Parks that cover this majestic area can be reached by several roads. From Moab, take U.S. 191N 4 miles to **Arches.** Continue north on U.S. 191 to Rte. 313S, which will lead to the Islands in the Sky area of **Canyonlands** (60mi.). To reach **Capitol Reef,** continue driving north on U.S. 191 and get on I-70 going west, leave I-70 at Exit 147, and follow Rte. 24S to Hanksville and then west to the park. Route 24W runs to Torrey where scenic Rte. 12 branches south and west through Dixie National Forest to **Bryce Canyon.** If you're looking for **Zion,** continue on Rte. 12W to U.S. 89S through Mt. Carmel Junction and pick up Rte. 9W.

The two national forests in Southern Utah are divided into districts, some of which lie near the national parks and serve as excellent places to stay on a cross-country jaunt. **Manti-La Sal National Forest** has two sections near Arches and the Needles area of Canyonlands. **Dixie National Forest** stretches from Capitol Reef, through Bryce, all the way to the western side of Zion.

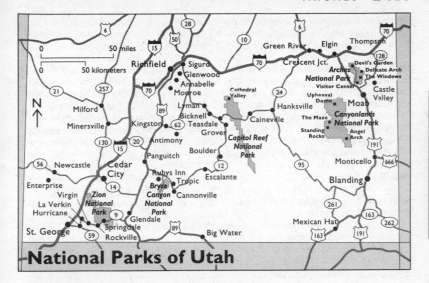

National Parks of Utah

■ Arches

"This is the most beautiful place on earth," novelist Edward Abbey wrote of **Arches National Park.** Thousands of sandstone arches, spires, pinnacles, and fins tower above the desert in overwhelming grandeur. Some arches are so perfect in form that early explorers believed they were constructed by a long-lost civilization. Deep red sandstone, green pinyon trees and juniper bushes, ominous grey thunderclouds, and a strikingly blue sky combine to etch an unforgettable panorama of color.

Practical Information The park entrance is on **U.S. 191,** 5 mi. north of Moab. Although no public transportation serves the park, **shuttle bus** companies travel to both the national park and Moab from surrounding towns and cities (see Moab practical information for details). While most visitors come in the summer, 100°F temperatures make hiking difficult. The weather is best in the spring and fall when warm days and cool nights combine to make a comfortable stay. In the winter, white snow provides a brilliant contrast to the red arches. The **visitors center** (259-8161), to the right of the entrance station, distributes free park service maps (open daily 8am-6pm; off season 8am-4:30pm). An **entrance pass** covers admission for a week ($4 per carload, $2 per pedestrian or biker). For more info, write the Superintendent, Arches National Park, P.O. Box 907, Moab 84532 (259-8161). **Water** is available in the park. For more details on accommodations, food, and activities, see p. 621. **Emergency:** 911. **Area code:** 801.

Camping The park's only campground, **Devil's Garden,** has 54 excellent campsites nestled amidst pinyon pines and giant red sandstone formations. The campsite is within walking distance of the Devil's Garden and Broken Arch Trailheads; however, it is a long 18 mi. from the visitors center. Because Devil's Garden doesn't take reservations, sites go quickly in season. Get there early in preparation for the rush; a line forms at the visitors center at 7:30am. (No wood-gathering. Running water April-Oct. 1-week max. stay. Sites $8.)

If the heat becomes unbearable at Arches, head to the aspen forests of the Manti La Sal National Forest. (Take Rte. 128 along the Colorado River and turn right at Castle Valley; at least a 1-hr. drive from Moab.) These beautiful sites sit 4000 ft. above the national park and are usually several degrees cooler. All sites cost $5, except the free sites at **Oowah Lake.** Oowah, 3 mi. down a dirt road, is a rainbow trout haven (fishing permits available at most stores in Moab and at the Forest Service office; $5 per day). For more info, contact the Manti-La Sal National Forest Service office in Moab, 125 W. 200 South 84532 (259-7155; open Mon.-Fri. 8am-4:30pm).

Sights and Activities The majority of Arches' natural beauty is not visible from the 18-mi. road. Bikes are only allowed on 2 wheel drive roads, so the best way to see the park is by foot. There are thousands of natural arches in the park, and each one is pinpointed on the free map and guide that is passed out at the fee collection booth. At the end of the paved road, **Devil's Garden** boasts an astounding 64 arches, while a challenging hike from the **Landscape Arch** leads across harrowing exposures to the secluded **Double O Arch.** The highlight of your visit should be the free-standing **Delicate Arch,** the symbol of the park; take the Delicate Arch turn-off from the main road, 2 mi. down a graded, unpaved road (impassable after rainstorms). Once you reach Wolf Range, a 1½-mi. foot trail leads to the arch. Beyond, you can catch a glimpse of the Colorado River gorge and the La Sal Mountains. Visitors occasionally come across petroglyphs left on the stone walls by the Anasazi and Ute who wandered the area centuries ago.

Arches aren't the only natural wonders here. One of the more popular trails, the moderately strenuous 2-mi. **Fiery Furnace Trail,** leads down into the canyon bottoms, providing new perspective on the imposing cliffs and monoliths above. Only experienced hikers should attempt this trail alone. Rangers lead groups from the visitors center into the labyrinth twice daily in the summer. Tours tend to fill up the day before; reservations can be made 48 hours in advance. Marcus and Sabrina of **Melrose Adventures** (800-430-4555) make trips out to Arches National Park on Fri. and Mon. ($45), from Grand Junction, CO. The price includes transportation and guided hikes off the beaten path.

■ Canyonlands

Those who make the trek to **Canyonlands National Park** are rewarded with a pleasant surprise: the absence of that overabundant, pestering species, homo Winnebagiens. The Green and Colorado Rivers divide the park into three sections, each with its own **visitors center.** (All three open daily 8am-5pm; hours change off season.) The **Needles** region (visitors center 259-4711) contains spires, arches, canyons, and Native American ruins, but is not as rough as the Maze area. To get to the Needles, take Rte. 211W from U.S. 191, about 40 mi. south of Moab. Farther north, **Island in the Sky** (visitors center 259-4712), a towering mesa which sits within the "Y" formed by the two rivers, affords fantastic views of the surrounding canyons and mountains; take Rte. 313W from U.S. 191 about 10 mi. north of Moab. The most remote district of the park, the rugged **Maze** area (visitors center 259-2652), is a veritable hurly-burly of twisted canyons made for *über*-pioneers with 4WD vehicles only. Be certain which area you want to visit; once you've entered a section of the park, getting to a different section involves retracing your steps and re-entering the park, a tedious trip which can last from several hours to a full day.

Practical Information Monticello's **Interagency Visitors Center,** 117 S. Main. St. (587-3235), sells area maps ($4-9; open Mon.-Fri. 8am-5pm, Sat.-Sun 10am-4pm). The park collects **entrance fees** of $4 per car and $2 per hiker or cyclist. For more info, write to the Superintendent, Canyonlands National Park, 125 W. 200 South, Moab 84532 (259-7164). Moab makes an excellent base town from which to explore the park (see p. 621).

There are no gas, water, or food services in the park. Just outside the boundary in the Needles district, however, the **Needles Outpost** (979-4007 or 259-8545) houses a limited, expensive grocery store and gas pump (open daily 8am-7pm). Hauling in groceries, water, and first-aid supplies from Moab or Monticello makes the most sense for travelers on a budget.

Camping and Hiking Before **backcountry camping** or **hiking,** register at the proper visitors center for one of a limited number of permits ($10 for backpack permit). Four-wheel drivers should also register at the visitors center ($25 permit).

Each region has its own official **campground.** In the Needles district, **Squaw Flat's** 26 sites occupy a sandy plain surrounded by giant sandstone towers, 40 mi. west of U.S. 191 on Rte. 211. Avoid this area in June, when insects swarm. Bring fuel and water, although the latter is usually available from mid-March to October. (Sites $6; Oct.-March free.) **Willow Flat Campground,** in the Island in the Sky district, sits high atop the mesa on Rte. 313, 41 mi. west off U.S. 191. You must bring your own water and insect repellent (12 free sites). Willow Flat and Squaw Flat both provide picnic tables, grills, and pit toilets. The backcountry campground at the **Maze Overlook** offers no amenities. All campgrounds operate on a first come, first served basis. (See Arches, p. 623, for more camping info.)

Each visitors center has a brochure of possible hikes including length and difficulty. With summer temperatures regularly climbing over 100°F, bring at least one gallon of water per person per day. Hiking options from the Needles area are probably the best developed, though Island in the Sky offers some spectacular views. In the Maze district, a six-hour, 6-mi. guided hike into Horseshoe Canyon leaves the visitors center at 8am on Fridays, Saturdays, and Sundays. If hiking in desert heat doesn't appeal to you, rent Jeeps or mountain bikes in Moab, or take a one-hour airplane tour from **Red Tail Aviation** (259-7421; $60 per person).

For some great overlooks at elevations above 8000 ft., head to the **Monticello District** of Manti-La Sal National Forest, south of Needles. This section of the forest has two campgrounds on **Blue Mountain. Buckboard,** 6.5 mi. west of Rte. 191 (9 sites and 2 group areas), and **Dalton Springs,** 5 mi. west of Rte. 191 (9 sites). Both campgrounds operate from late May to late October and charge $5 per site. From Moab, head south on U.S. 191 to Monticello and then west on Rte. 1S. For more info on the Monticello District, head to the **visitors center,** 117 S. Main St. (587-3235). From Moab, head south on U.S. 191 to Monticello and then west on Rte. 1S, or call the Manti-La Sal National Forest Service office in Monticello, 496 E. Central (587-2737), on U.S. 666 just east of town (open Mon.-Fri. 9am-5pm).

Farther away, **Dead Horse Point State Park** (entrance fee $3), perches on the rim of the Colorado Gorge. The park, south of Arches and 14 mi. south of U.S. 191, accessible from Rte. 313, offers more camping, with modern restrooms, water, hookups, and covered picnic tables. (Sites Sun.-Thurs. $8, Fri.-Sat. $10. ½ available on a first come, first served basis.) For more info, contact the Park Superintendent, Dead Horse Point State Park, P.O. Box 609, Moab 84532 (259-2614 or 800-322-3770; open daily 8am-6pm; call for off-season hours).

■ Capitol Reef

A geologist's fantasy and **Capitol Reef National Park's** feature attraction, the **Waterpocket Fold** bisects the park, presenting visitors with 65 million years of stratified natural history. This 100-mi. furrow in the earth's crust, with its rocky scales and spines, winds through Capitol Reef like a giant pre-Cambrian serpent. The sheer cliffs that border the fold were originally called a "reef," not for their oceanic origins, but because they posed a barrier to travel. Today, you can explore the reef from the seat of your car on the 25-mi. **scenic drive,** a 90-min. (roundtrip) jaunt next to the cliffs along paved and improved dirt roads. Pause along Rte. 24 and ponder the bathroom-sized **Fruita Schoolhouse** built by Mormon settlers, thousand-year-old petroglyphs etched on the stone walls, and **Panorama Point** where you can look through some of the clearest air in the continental U.S.

Stop at the **visitors center** (425-3791), on Rte. 24, for waterproof topographical maps ($8), regular maps ($4), free brochures on trails, info on daily activities such as ranger-led jaunts, and good ol' advice. Pick up the free park newspaper, *The Cliffline,* for a schedule of park activities. (Open daily 8am-7pm; Sept.-May 8am-4:30pm.) The middle link in the Fab Five chain, east of Zion and Bryce Canyon and west of Arches and Canyonlands, Capitol Reef is unreachable by major bus lines. **Entrance** to the park is free except for the scenic loop which costs $4 per vehicle. When **hiking,** keep in mind that summer temperatures average 95°F, and most water found in springs and rain-holding water pockets can only be used if purified.

Plentiful orchards lie within the park in the Fruita region. Feel free to consume as much fruit as you like while in the orchards, but cold hard cash is necessary to take extra home with you. The park's campgrounds give out sites on a first come, first served basis. The main campground, **Fruita,** 1.3 mi. south off Rte. 24, provides 73 sites (one reserved for the disabled), drinking water, and toilets ($8). **Cedar Mesa Campground,** in the park's south end, and **Cathedral Valley,** in the north, have only five sites each; neither has water or a paved road—but hey, they're free. To get to Cedar Mesa, take Rte. 24 past the visitors center to Notom-Bullfrog Rd. and go about 25 mi. south. Cathedral Valley is accessible only by 4WD or on foot. Both of these sites and unmarked backcountry campsites require a free **backcountry permit,** easily obtainable at the visitors center. For more info about the park, contact the Superintendent, Capitol Reef National Park, Torrey 84775 (425-3791).

For accommodations in the region, head to **Torrey,** 11 mi. west of the visitors center on Rte. 24. **The Chuck Wagon Motel and General Store** (425-3288 or 800-863-3288), in the center of Torrey on Rte. 24W, has a barbecue area, a beautiful pool, and attractive, wood-paneled rooms in a new building (A/C and phone; from $54) and in the older building above the store (no A/C or phone; from $39). The store comes through with a good selection of groceries, sports equipment, baked goods and picnic ware (open daily 7am-10pm). **The Boulder View Inn,** 385 W. Main St. (800-444-3980), provides comfortable rooms (no smoking or pets; summer from $45, winter from $30). Treat yourself to a meal at the **Capitol Reef Inn and Café,** 360 W. Main St. (425-3271), Torrey, which features local rainbow trout—smoked or grilled—and an enclosed porch dining room that looks out on the russet hills. The grilled trout sandwich ($6) comes with a ten-vegetable salad (open April-Oct. daily 7am-11pm). For a greasier repast, try **Brink's Burgers,** 165 E. Main St. (425-3710), Torrey (various burgers $2-4; open daily 11am-8pm). **The Redrock Restaurant and Campground** (542-3235 or 800-452-7971), in Hanksville, 37 mi. east of the visitors center on Rte. 24, provides both campsites and food. (Open daily 7am-10pm. Shaded tent sites $8 for 2 people, hookup $14; $2 each additional person. Showers $3.) For couples, **Joy's Bed and Breakfast,** 296 S. Center (542-3252 or 801-542-3255), Hanksville, accommodates with one room and a bath ($35, with breakfast $45).

Betwixt Boulder and Capitol Reef, off scenic Rte. 12, a stretch of Dixie National Forest shelters three lovely campgrounds. All perch at elevations over 8000 ft. and have drinking water and pit toilets (sites $7; first come, first served; open May-Sept.). The **Oak Creek Campground** includes seven sites, and the **Pleasant Creek Campground** has 16 sites. **Single Tree Campground** offers 22 sites, with two group sites (800-280-CAMP/2267 for group reservations), and two family sites, one of which can be reserved ahead of time. For more info, call the **Interagency** in Escalante (826-5499). Capitol Reef's **area code: 810.**

■ Bryce Canyon

The fragile spires of pink and red limestone which pepper **Bryce Canyon National Park** often seem more like the subjects of surrealist painting than the results of nature's art. Carved by millennia of wind and water, the canyons made life difficult for the Anasazi, Fremont, and Paiute who first navigated the region. Ebenezer Bryce, a Mormon carpenter who settled here in 1875, called the area "one hell of a place to lose a cow." For a solitary experience, hike into the canyons or visit between mid-October and mid-April when accommodation rates drop to as low as half-price.

Practical Information Approaching from the west, Bryce Canyon lies 1½ hr. east of Cedar City; take Rte. 14 to U.S. 89. From the east, take I-70 to U.S. 89, turn east on Rte. 12 at Bryce Junction (7mi. south of Panguitch), and drive 14 mi. to the Rte. 63

junction; go south 4 mi. to the park entrance. There is no public transportation to Bryce Canyon. The canyon's **entrance fee** is $5 per car, $3 per pedestrian.

Begin any tour at the **visitors center** (834-5322), on Rte. 63 inside the park. The free Bryce Canyon publication, *Hoo Doo,* available here, lists all park services, events, suggested hikes, and sight-seeing drives. (Open daily 8am-8pm; April-May and Sept.-Oct. 8am-6pm, Nov. March 8am-4:30pm.) For more info, write the Superintendent, Bryce Canyon National Park, Bryce Canyon 84717. **Emergency:** 911 or 676-2411. Bryce Canyon's **post office** (834-5361) is in Bryce Lodge. **Area code:** 801.

Accommodations, Camping, and Food Though very expensive for single travelers, **Bryce Lodge** (834-5361 or 586-7686), open April until Nov. 1, may be a good deal for a group. (Singles and doubles $74—heck, might as well get a double, triples $79, quads $84, quints $89.) The closest hostel is **Bryce Canyon International Hostel,** 190 Main St. in Panguitch, 21 mi from the park. From the park, take Rte. 12W to U.S. 89N. The hostel is in a house with clean bathrooms and a great kitchen ($12, private room $25). **Canyonlands International Youth Hostel (AAIH/Rucksackers)** (see p. 628), hosts travelers 60 mi. south of Bryce in **Kanab.**

North and **Sunset Campgrounds,** both within 3 mi. of the visitors center, offer toilets, picnic tables, potable water, and 210 sites on a first come, first served basis ($8; show up early in the morning to reserve). For free **backcountry camping,** obtain a permit from the ranger at the visitors center.

There are two campgrounds just west of Bryce on scenic Rte. 12, in the Dixie National Forest. The **King Creek Campground,** 11 mi. from Bryce on a dirt road off Rte. 12 (look for signs to Tropic Reservoir), features lakeside sites surrounded by pine trees ($8). Group sites are available with reservations (800-280-2267). At an elevation of 7400 ft., the **Red Canyon Campground** rents 36 sites on a first come, first served basis ($10). The **Powell District** of the Dixie National Forest has six campgrounds with toilets, running water, swimming, boating, and fishing, all within one hour's drive; of these, campers favor **Te-Ah** (800-280-2264), **Spruces,** and **Navajo Lake** (only Te-Ah accepts reservations; no fishing at Navajo Lake; sites at all campgrounds $9). Inquire at the visitors center or the forest service office in Panguitch, 225 E. Center St. (676-8815; open Mon.-Fri. 8am-4:30pm) for details.

The **grocery store** at Sunrise Point (834-5361, ext. 167) has the only reasonable in-park provisions (open spring-fall 8am-8pm, winter 7:30am-9pm). Behind the store, there are **showers** ($1.50 for 7 min.; available 7am-10pm).

Sights and Activities Popular scenery surrounds the visitors center; sunrises here are particularly astounding. The trail between **Sunrise Point** and **Sunset Point** are wheelchair accessible. The 3-mi. loop of the **Navajo** and **Queen's Garden** trails leads you into the canyon itself. If you feel up to a challenge, branch off onto the **Peek-A-Boo Trail,** a 4-mi. roundtrip. **Trail to the Hat Shop** descends four extremely steep mi. (And if you think climbing down is tough…) Ask about these and other trails at the visitors center. The 15-mi. main road winds past spectacular look-outs such as Sunrise Point, Sunset Point, **Inspiration Point,** and **Bryce Point** (see Practical Information, above for shuttle bus info). Due to construction, the park is closed south of **Farview Point.** Reserve a **van tour** along the main road at Bryce Lodge ($4, under 13 $2), or arrange for a guided horseback tour through **Canyon Trail Rides** (834-5500, off season 679-8665; $25-35 per person).

Near Bryce Truly daring hikers taunt death in a network of sandstone canyons in the ominously named **Phipps Death Hollow Outstanding Natural Area,** just north of **Escalante.** (Actually, it's not so bad as all that.) The **Escalante Interagency Office,** 755 W. Main St. (826-5499), on Rte. 12 just west of town, has free maps and backcountry permits (open daily 7am-6pm; off season Mon.-Fri. 8am-5pm). **Calf Creek** camping grounds, 15 mi. east of Escalante on Rte. 12, has a great hike near a cascading waterfall (with drinking water and toilets, sites $8).

West on Rte. 14, the flowered slopes of the **Cedar Breaks National Monument** descend 2000 ft. into its chiseled depths. The rim of this giant amphitheater stands a lofty 10,350 ft. above sea level. (Entrance $4 per car, $2 per pedestrian.) A 30-site **campground** (sites $8) and the **visitors center** (586-0787; open in summer daily 8am-6pm) await at **Point Supreme.** For more info, contact the Superintendent, Cedar Breaks National Monument, 82 N. 100 E, Cedar City 84720 (586-9451).

■ Zion

Some 13 million years ago, sea waters flowed over the cliffs and canyons of **Zion National Park.** Over the centuries the sea subsided, leaving only the powerful **Virgin River** whose watery fingers still carve into the russet sandstone. In the northwest corner of the park, the walls of Kolob Terrace tower thousands of feet above the river. Elsewhere, branching canyons and unusual rock formations show off erosion's unique artistry. In the 1860s, Mormon settlers came to the area and enthusiastically proclaimed that they had found the promised land. Brigham Young did not agree, however, and declared to his followers that the place was awfully nice, but "not Zion." The name "not Zion" stuck for years until a new wave of entranced explorers dropped the "not," giving the park its present name.

Practical Information The main entrance to Zion is in **Springdale,** on Rte. 9, which bounds the park to the south along the Virgin River. Approaching Zion from the west, take Rte. 9 from I-15 at Hurricane. In the east, pick up Rte. 9 from U.S. 89 at Mount Carmel Junction. The nearest **Greyhound** station (673-2933 or 800-231-2222), is in St. George (43mi. southwest of the park on I-15), in a McDonald's, 1235 S. Bluff St., at St. George Blvd. Buses run to Salt Lake City (1 per day, 6hr., $48), Los Angeles (9 per day, 15hr., $49), and Las Vegas (7 per day, 2hr., $23). The main **Zion Canyon Visitors Center** (772-3256), in the southeast corner of the park ½ mi. off Rte. 9, has an introductory slide program and a small but interesting museum (open daily 8am-8pm; off season 8am-6pm). The **Kolob Canyons Visitors Center** (586-9548), lies in the northwest corner of the park, off I-15 (open daily 9am-5pm; off season 9am-4pm). Pick up *The Sentinel,* at the main entrance, as well as the official Zion National Park guide. Both have excellent maps and hiking suggestions. The park charges an **entrance fee** of $5 per car, $2 per pedestrian. In an **emergency,** call 772-3256 during the day, 772-3322 after hours. **Area code:** 801.

Camping and Accommodations Over 300 sites are available on a first come, first served basis (come early) in the **South** and **Watchman Campgrounds** at the south gate. Both sites have water, toilets, and a sanitary disposal station for trailers. (2-week max. stay. Sites $8. Group sites for 9-40 people available for $2 per person. Open 24hr.) A primitive area at **Lava Point** can be accessed from a hiking trail in the mid-section of the park or from the gravel road which turns off Rte. 9 in **Virgin** (6 sites with toilets but no water; free; open June-Nov.).

One thousand ft. above the south entrance camping areas, **Mukuntuweep Campground** (644-5445 or 644-2154), near the east entrance, has altitude on its side. Not only is it cooler than the other sites, but a laundromat, toilets, showers, and a mountain backdrop enhance the area (70 tent sites $12.50, 30 full hookups $16.50).

Zion Canyon Campground, 479 Zion Park Blvd. (772-3237), in Springdale just south of the park, soothes the weary, hungry, and filthy with a convenience store, restaurant, grocery store (772-3402), showers, and coin-op laundry. (Registration 24hr. Sites for 2 $14, full hookup $18; extra adult $3.50, extra child under 15 50¢. Store open daily 8am-9pm, off season 8am-5pm.) The **Zion Canyon Lodge** (303-297-2757), along the park's main road, offers premium rooms at premium prices, with a dining room. (772-3213. Restaurant open daily 6:30-10am, 11:30am-3pm, and 5:30-9pm. Singles and doubles $75, $5 per additional person. Cabin singles and doubles $74, $5 per additional person. Lodge suite singles and doubles $109, $5 per addi-

THE SOUTHWEST

tional person.) For lodging alternatives, try **Springdale** or **Rockville,** 2-5 mi. south of the park, or **Cedar City,** north of the park on Rte. 15.

You need a free permit from the visitors center for **backcountry camping.** Camping along the rim is *not* allowed, but a free map from the visitors center will show you where you may and may not pitch a tent. Zion campgrounds don't take reservations and often fill on holidays and summer weekends; if you don't get in, try one of the six campgrounds in Dixie National Forest (see Bryce Canyon, p. 626). To the west of Zion lies another district of the Dixie National Forest—**Pine Valley.** At an elevation of 6683 ft., Pine Valley offers 57 sites with water and toilets (entrance $9, open May-Sept.). Groups can reserve sites by calling 800-280-CAMP/2267; the National Forest Service for this district (673-3431) has more details.

Treat yourself to more than a roof at **O'Toole's,** 980 Zion Park Blvd. (772-3457), Springdale, in a beautiful, recently renovated stucco-and-sandstone house. The gorgeous rooms, with great windows and sumptuous beds, include hot tub access and full breakfast; make reservations early. (Rooms for 2 $65-125, $10 per additional person.) The nearest hostel is the **Canyonlands International Youth Hostel (AAIH/ Rucksackers),** 143 E. 100 S., Kanab 84741 (801-644-5554), 20 mi. south in **Kanab.** The hostel's location, one hour north of the Grand Canyon on U.S. 89 and an equal distance south of Zion, Bryce, and Lake Powell, makes it a perfect base for exploring north Arizona and south Utah; roomy bunks, free linens, laundry facilities, TV, kitchen, parking, and a bountiful but bizarre breakfast banquet make it worth a trip from any of the parks. ($9. Reservations recommended.)

Sights If you love to walk or hike, you're in the right place. Paved and wheelchair accessible with assistance, the **Riverside Walk** stretches 1 mi. from the north end of Zion Canyon Dr. The refreshing **Emerald Pools** trail (1.2mi. roundtrip) is accessible to the disabled along its lower loop, but not on its middle and upper loops. The **Angel's Landing** trail (5mi. roundtrip) takes you 1488 ft. above the canyon; the last terrifying ½ mi. climbs a narrow ridge with guide chains blasted into the rock. Overnight hikers can spend days on the 27-mi. **West Rim Trail.** Even if you plan to visit **Kolob Canyon's** backcountry, be sure to make the pilgrimage to **Zion Canyon.** The 7-mi. dead-end road on the canyon floor rambles past the giant formations of **Sentinel, Mountain of the Sun,** and the overwhelming symbol of Zion, the **Great White Throne.** A shuttle from the lodge runs this route every hour on the hour in the summer (daily 9am-4pm; 1hr.; $3, children $2). Hikers enjoy the difficult trail to **Observation Point,** where steep switchbacks explore the unusually gouged canyon. Horseback tours arranged by **Canyon Trail Rides** (772-3810) leave from the lodge ($12-35 per person). **Bike Zion,** 445 Zion Park Blvd. (772-3929), rents rafts for $3 per day ($5 deposit) and bikes. ($23-35 per day, $17-27 per ½day, $9-11 per hr. Open daily 8am-8:30pm.)

■ Natural Bridges and Hovenweep

Natural Bridges National Monument Nearly 3000 years ago, the Paiutes who inhabited this region called it Ma-Vah-Talk-Tump, or "under the horse's belly." In 1909, President Taft renamed each bridge with a Hopi term like Sipapu "Place of Desolation" or Kachina "Ghost Dancer." Renamed once again in the less-imaginative present day, Utah's first national monument is simply called Natural Bridges. Despite the newer, blander moniker, these 200-ft.-high water-sculpted bridges set amidst white sandstone canyons still deserve a visit. To truly appreciate the size of the monuments, leave the overlooks and hike down to the bridges. The most impressive span is Sipapu Bridge. The hike from the road is 1.5 mi. roundtrip, but the trail drops over 600ft. in elevation as it descends underneath the bridge.

To reach Natural Bridges from northern Utah, follow U.S. 191S from Moab to its junction with **Scenic Rte. 95W** (north of Bluff and 4mi. south of Blanding). From Colorado, U.S. 66 heads west to U.S. 191S (junction in Monticello). From the south, Rte.

261 from Mexican Hat climbs a mesa in heart-wrenching 5mph gravel switchback, providing a spectacular view of Monument valley across the Arizona border.

The **visitors center** (692-1234), located a few miles off of Rte. 95, offers a slide show, small bookstore, and exhibits. (Open daily 8am-6pm; Nov.-Feb. 9am-4:30pm; March-April 8am-5pm. Park entrance $4 per vehicle, $2 per hiker or bicyclist; good for 7 days.) Sleep under the stars at the **campground** near the visitors center. 13 shaded sites set amidst pinyon pines accommodate up to 9 people each. RV length limit 26ft. Campground usually fills by 2pm. (Sites $5; first come, first served.) **Water** is available at the visitors center. For further info, contact the Superintendent, Natural Bridges, Box 1, Lake Powell 84533 (259-5174). If the park campground is full, primitive overflow camping is available off a gravel road originating at the intersection of Rte. 95 and Rte. 251, 6 mi. from the visitors center. The free sites are flat and shaded but have no facilities.

Hovenweep National Monument

Hovenweep, from the Ute meaning "deserted valley," features six groups of Pueblo ruins dating back more than 1000 years. The valley remains deserted today, and has only two rangers (one in Utah, one in Colorado) minding the monument's 784 acres. Immune to vacation swarms, or even small crowds, Hovenweep provides visitors space and time to ponder.

The best preserved and most impressive ruins, **Square Tower Ruins,** lie footsteps away from the visitors center (see below). The **Square Tower Loop Trail** (2mi.), loops around a small canyon, accessing **Hovenweep Castle,** built at the same time as European castles, and the **Twin Towers.** A shorter trail, the ½-mi. **Tower Point Loop,** accesses the ruins of a tower perched on a canyon. The outlying ruins—**Cujon Ruins** and **Huckberry Canyon** in Utah, and **Cutthroat Castle** and **Goodman Point Ruins** in Colorado—are isolated and difficult to reach.

Desolate but beautiful roads usher you to Hovenweep. In Utah or Arizona, follow U.S. 191 to its junction with Rte. 262E (14mi. south of Blanding, 11mi. north of Bluff). After about 30mi., watch for signs to the monument. Though unpaved for 2½ mi., the road in is accessible to all vehicles. From Cortez, CO, go south on U.S. 166/U.S. 160 to Country Rd. 6 (the airport road); follow the Hovenweep signs for 45 mi., including 15 mi. of gravel road. Call ahead to check road conditions at the **visitors center** (303-749-0510), accessible from both the Utah and Colorado sides (open daily 8am-5pm, except when the ranger is out on patrol). *There is no gasoline, telephone, or food at the monument.* There is no developed campsite at Hovenweep; for info about nearby camping, contact the visitors center. For more info, contact the Superintendent, Hovenweep National Monument, McElmo Rte., Cortez, CO 81321 (303-749-0510).

Nearby Civilization

Three small towns provide lodging and services for travelers to the monuments and the valley. In the agricultural town of **Blanding** (45mi. from Hovenweep, 60mi. from Natural Bridges), sleep at the **Prospector Motor Lodge,** 591 U.S. 191S (678-3231; rates $35-70; off season $27-50), or try the **Blanding Sunset Inn,** 88 W. Center St. (678-3323; basic rooms, $30 single, $40 double). The **Elk Ridge Restaurant,** 120 E. Center St. (678-3390), will pour your morning coffee (1 egg, potatoes, and toast $3; open daily 6am-9:30pm). Saddle up to **The Cedar Pony,** 191 U.S. 191 N. (678-2715), for a Navaho pizza topped with chili peppers, cheese, and tomatoes ($12) or a spaghetti, salad and garlic bread dinner ($3.75; open Mon.-Fri. 11am-8:30pm, Sat. 5-8:30pm).

Situated amidst the sandstone canyons, the town of **Bluff** (40mi. from Hovenweep, 65mi. from Natural Bridges) welcomes the budget traveler. Inexpensive and comfortable lodges and motels line U.S. 191, including **The Recapture Lodge** (672-2281; singles $32-42, doubles $34-48). Try the Navajo's sheepherder sandwich, consisting of roast beef and fried rice ($5) at the **Turquoise Restaurant** (672-2279), on U.S. 191 S (open daily 7am-10pm). The gigantic, austere sandstone sculptures of the **Valley of the Gods** provided the backdrop for some of the road scenes in *Thelma and Louise.*

A tough but scenic 17-mi. drive departs from U.S. 163W, 15 mi. south of Bluff on the right side of the road, and runs right through the valley.

Mexican Hat sits along the San Juan River on the border of the Navajo nation. The town is 20 mi. south of Fluff on U.S. 163 and 20 mi. north of Arizona. Rest your head at the newly renovated **Canyonlands Motel** (683-2230), on U.S. 163 (basic rooms; singles $34, double $47). **The Old Bridge Bar and Grille** (683-2220), on U.S. 163 next to the San Juan River, is the place for excellent Navajo specialties and filling sandwiches ($4-6).

Arizona

Populated primarily by Native Americans through the 19th century, Arizona has been hit in the past hundred years by waves of settlers—from the speculators and miners of the late 1800s, to the soldiers who trained here during World War II and returned after the war, to the more recent immigrants from Mexico. Deserted ghost towns scattered throughout the state illustrate the death of the mining lifestyle and the fast pace of urban development, while older monuments preserve settlements abandoned long before the existence of used car lots or postcards. Traces of lost Indian civilizations remain at Canyon de Chelly, Navajo National Monument, and Wupatki and Walnut Canyons. (The descendants of these tribes, almost one-seventh of the United States's Native Americans, now occupy reservations on one-half of the state's land.) However spectacular, neither ancient nor modern man-made memorials can overshadow Arizona's natural masterpieces—the Grand Canyon, Monument Valley, and the gorgeous landscapes seen from the state's highways.

PRACTICAL INFORMATION

Capital: Phoenix.
Arizona Tourism: 2702 N. 3rd St. Ste. 4015, Phoenix (602-230-7733). Open Mon.-Fri. 7am-5pm. **Arizona State Parks,** 1300 W. Washington St., Phoenix 85007 (602-542-4174). Open Mon.-Fri. 8am-5pm.
Time Zone: Mountain (2hr. behind Eastern). Arizona (with the exception of the reservations) does not observe Daylight Savings Time; in the summer, it is 1hr. behind the rest of the Mountain Time Zone. **Postal Abbreviation:** AZ.
Sales Tax: 6%.

NORTHERN ARIZONA

■ Grand Canyon

Even the weariest of travelers snap to attention upon first sight of the Grand Canyon (277mi. long, 10mi. wide, and over 1mi. deep). King of natural wonders and mecca of the American family vacation, the canyon descends past looming walls of limestone, sandstone, and shale as mothers cling to their children and fathers wear out their video cameras. The U.S. began designating its most daunting wild regions as national park sites for two reasons—first, to compensate with natural grandeur for the country's short cultural tradition, and second, to preserve unfarmable lands for recreation. Both breathtaking and hell on a plow, the Grand Canyon exemplifies the national park as it was originally conceived. Hike down into the gorge to get a real feeling for the immensity and beauty of this natural phenomenon. Many TV shows and movies have depicted its grandeur, including National Lampoon's *Vacation, Independence Day,* and a seminal two-part *Brady Bunch* episode, in which Bobby is rescued by Indians living in the canyon. All the Bradys are later inducted into the tribe (even though no Native Americans have lived in the gorge for over 100 years).

The **Grand Canyon National Park** is divided into three areas: the **South Rim,** including Grand Canyon Village; the **North Rim;** and the canyon gorge itself. The slightly lower, slightly more accessible South Rim draws 10 times as many visitors as the higher, more heavily forested North Rim. The 13-mi. trail that traverses the canyon floor makes a two-day adventure for sturdy hikers, while the 214-mi. perimeter road is a good five-hour drive for those who would rather explore from above. Despite commercial exploitation, the Grand Canyon is still untamed; every year several careless hikers take what locals morbidly call "the 12-second tour." Observe all safety precautions, use common sense, and drink lots and lots of water.

■ South Rim

In summer, everything on two legs or four wheels converges on this side of the Grand Canyon. If you plan to visit during the mobfest, make reservations for lodging, campsites, or mules well in advance—and prepare to battle the crowds. That said, it's much better than Disney World. A friendly Park Service staff, well-run facilities, and beautiful scenery help ease crowd anxiety. During winter there are fewer tourists; however, the weather is brisk and many hotels and facilities close.

PRACTICAL INFORMATION

Tourist Office: The **visitors center** (638-7888) is 6mi. north of the south entrance station. Open daily 8am-6pm, off season 8am-5pm. Ask for the *Trip Planner*. Free and informative, *The Guide* is available here, in case you somehow missed it at the entrance. Write the **Superintendent,** Grand Canyon National Park, P.O. Box 129, Grand Canyon, AZ 86023, for info before you go.

Buses: Nava-Hopi Bus Lines (800-892-8687), leaves Flagstaff Amtrak station for Grand Canyon daily 8:15am, 10:15am, 3pm; returns from Bright Angel Lodge 10am, 5:15pm, 6pm. $12.50, 14 and under $6.50; $4 canyon entrance fee not included. Times vary by season, so call ahead.

Transportation Information Desk: In **Bright Angel Lodge** (638-2631). Reservations for mule rides, bus tours, Phantom Ranch, taxis, backcountry camping, everything. Open daily 6am-7pm. A **free shuttle bus** rides the West Rim Loop (daily 7:30am-sunset) and the Village Loop (daily 6:30am-10:30pm) every 15min. A $3 **hiker's shuttle** runs every 15min. between Grand Canyon village and South Kaibab Trailhead near Yalci Point; leaves Bright Angel daily 6:30, 8:30, 11:30am.

Auto Repairs: Grand Canyon Garage (638-2631), east of the visitors center on the park's main road near Maswik Lodge. Garage open daily 8am-5pm. 24-hr. emergency service.

Equipment Rental: Babbit's General Store (638-2262 or 638-2234), in Mather Center, Grand Canyon Village near Yavapai Lodge and the visitors center. Rents comfortable hiking boots, socks included ($8 first day, $5 each additional); sleeping bags ($7-9/$5); tents ($15-16/$9); and other camping gear. Hefty deposits required on all items. Open daily 8am-8pm.

Weather and Road Conditions: 638-7888.

Medical Services: Grand Canyon Clinic (638-2551 or 638-2469), several mi. south on Center Rd. Open Mon.-Fri. 8am-5:30pm, Sat. 9am-noon.

Emergency: 911.

Post Office: (638-2512), next to Babbit's. Open Mon.-Fri. 9am-4:30pm, Sat. 11am-1pm. **ZIP code:** 86023. **Area code:** 520.

There are two entrances to the park: the main **south entrance** lies on U.S. 180N, the eastern **Desert View** entrance lies on I-40W. From Las Vegas, the fastest route to the Canyon is U.S. 93S to I-40E, and then Rte. 64N. From Flagstaff, I-40E to U.S. 89N is the most scenic; from there, Rte. 64N takes you to the Desert View entrance. Straight up U.S. 180N is more direct.

The Grand Canyon's **entrance fee** is $10 per car and $4 for travelers using other modes of transportation—even bus passengers must pay. The pass lasts for one week. If you're coming from Flagstaff, check noticeboards in hotels and hostels; travelers who have moved on sometimes leave their valid passes behind. **Pets** are allowed in the park, provided they are on a leash. They may not go below the rim; the **kennel** (638-2631, ext. 6039) on the South Rim will keep them while you hike.

Inside the park, posted maps and signs make orienting yourself easy. Lodges and services concentrate in **Grand Canyon Village,** at the end of Park Entrance Rd. The east half of the Village contains the visitors center and the general store, while most of the lodges and the **Bright Angel Trailhead** lie in the west section. The south **Kaibab Trailhead** is off East Rim Dr., to the east of the village.

ACCOMMODATIONS AND CAMPING

Compared to the six million years it took the Colorado River to carve the Grand Canyon, the 11 months it will take you to get a room on the South Rim will pass in the blink of an eye. It is almost impossible to sleep indoors anywhere near the South Rim without reservations or a wad of cash. If you arrive unprepared, check at the visitors center and the Bright Angel transportation desk after 4pm for vacancies.

Most accommodations on the South Rim are very expensive. The campsites listed here usually fill early in the day. Campground overflow generally winds up in the **Kaibab National Forest,** along the south border of the park, where you can pull off a dirt road and camp for free. No camping is allowed within ¼ mi. of U.S. 64. Sleeping in cars is *not* permitted within the park, but is allowed in the Kaibab Forest. For more info, contact the Tusayan Ranger District, Kaibab National Forest, P.O. Box 3088, Grand Canyon 86023 (638-2443). Any overnight hiking or camping within the park requires a free **Backcountry Use Permit,** which is available at the **Backcountry Office** (638-7875), ¼ mi. south of the visitors center (open daily 8am-noon; calls answered Mon.-Fri. 1-5pm). Permit requests are accepted by mail or in person only, up to four months in advance. The earlier you make your request, the better. Call the Backcountry Office for a list of the info you must include in a mail-in permit request. Once reserved, the permit must be picked up *no later than 9am* on the day you plan to camp, or it will be cancelled. While you're hiking, extra luggage may be checked at Bright Angel Lodge for 50¢ per day. Reservations for **Bright Angel Lodge, Maswik Lodge, Trailer Village,** and **Phantom Ranch** can be made through Grand Canyon National Park Lodges, P.O. Box 699, Grand Canyon 86023 (638-2401; fax 638-9247). All rooms should be reserved 11 months in advance for the summer. For same-day reservations (usually not available), call the Grand Canyon operator at 638-2631 and ask to be connected with the proper lodge.

Bright Angel Lodge (638-2401), Grand Canyon Village. Rustic cabins with plumbing but no heat. Very convenient to Bright Angel Trail and shuttle buses. Singles or doubles $35-53, depending on how much plumbing you want. "Historic" cabins for 1 or 2 people $61, $7 per additional person in rooms and cabins.

Maswik Lodge (638-2401), Grand Canyon Village. Small, clean cabins (singles or doubles) with showers $56, private room $72. $7 per additional person.

Phantom Ranch (638-2401; 303-297-2757 for reservations), on the canyon floor, a 4-hr. hike down the Kaibab Trail. Dorm beds $22; cabins for 1 or 2 people $54; $7 per additional person. As usual, reservations required 11 months in advance for April-Oct., but the Bright Angel transportation desk lists last-minute cancellations. Don't show up without reservations—they'll send you back up the trail, on foot.

Mather Campground (MISTIX 800-365-2267), Grand Canyon Village, 1mi. south of the visitors center. 320 shady, relatively isolated sites with no hookups. 7-day max. stay. $10. For March-Nov. reserve through MISTIX up to 8 weeks in advance; Dec.-Feb. sites go on a first come, first served basis. Check at the office, even if the sign says the campground is full.

Camper Village (638-2887), 7mi. south of the visitors center in Tusayan. RV and tent sites $15-22. First come, first served tent sites; reservations required for RVs.

Cottonwood Campground (638-7888), 17mi. from the Bright Angel trailhead on the North Kaibab trail. 14 free sites. Reservations recommended. Open May-Oct.

Indian Garden (638-7888), 4.6mi. from the South Rim Bright Angel trailhead and 3100ft. below the rim. 15 free sites, toilets, and water. Reservations needed.

Trailer Village (638-2401), next to Mather Campground. Clearly designed with the RV in mind. Showers and laundry nearby. 7-day max. stay. Office open daily 8am-noon and 1-5pm. 84 sites with hookup $18 for 2 people; $1.50 per additional person. Reservations required 6-9 months in advance.

Desert View Campsite (638-7888), 26mi. east of Grand Canyon Village. 50 sites with phone and restroom access, but no hookups. $10. No reservations; arrive early. Open mid-May to Oct.

Ten-X Campground (638-2443), in the Kaibab National Forest 10mi. south of Grand Canyon Village off Rte. 64. Shady sites surrounded by pine trees. Toilets, water, no hookups. Sites $10. Group sites for up to 100 people available with reservations. First come, first served. Open May-Sept.

FOOD

Fast food hasn't sunk its greasy talons into the rim of the Canyon, but you *can* find meals for fast-food prices. **Babbit's General Store** (638-2262), near the visitors center, has a deli counter (sandwiches $2-3.75) and a reasonably priced supermarket. Stock up on trail mix, water, and gear. (Open daily 8am-8pm; deli open 8am-7pm.) **The Maswik Cafeteria,** in Maswik Lodge, puts out a variety of inexpensive grill-made options (hot entrees $4.50-7, sandwiches $2-3.50) served in a wood-paneled cafeteria atmosphere (open daily 6am-10pm). **Bright Angel Dining Room** (638-2631), in Bright Angel Lodge, serves hot sandwiches ($5.50-7.50; open daily 6:30am-10pm). The soda fountain at Bright Angel Lodge chills 16 flavors of ice cream (1 scoop $1.60) for hot hikers emerging from trails (open daily 6am-8pm).

SIGHTS AND ACTIVITIES

From your first glimpse of the canyon, you will feel a compelling desire to see it from the inside, an enterprise which is much harder than it looks. Even the young at heart should remember that an easy downhill hike can become a nightmarish 100° incline on the return journey. Also keep in mind that the lower you go, the hotter it gets. Heat exhaustion, the second greatest threat after slipping, is marked by a monstrous headache and termination of sweating. (*Let's Go* offers basic advice about heatstroke on p. 14.) You *must* take two quarts of water per person; it's absolutely necessary. A list of hiking safety tips can be found in *The Guide*. Don't overestimate your limits; parents should think twice about bringing children more than a mile down any trail—kids remember well and may exact revenge when they get bigger.

The two most accessible trails into the Canyon are the **Bright Angel Trail,** originating at the Bright Angel Lodge, and **South Kaibab Trail,** from Yaki Point. Bright Angel is outfitted for the average tourist, with rest houses strategically stationed 1½ mi. and 3 mi. from the rim. **Indian Gardens,** 4½ mi. down, offers the tired hiker restrooms, picnic tables, and blessed shade; all three rest stops usually have water in the summer. Kaibab is trickier, steeper, and lacking in shade or water, but it rewards the intrepid with a better view of the canyon.

If you've made arrangements to spend the night on the canyon floor, the best route is the **South Kaibab Trail** (4-5hr., depending on conditions) and back up the Bright Angel (7-8hr.) the following day. Hikes down Bright Angel Trail to Indian Gardens and **Plateau Point,** 6 mi. out, where you can look down 1360 ft. to the river, make excellent daytrips (8-12hr.), but it's best to start early (around 7am).

If you're not up to descending into the canyon, follow the **Rim Trail** east to Grandeur Point and the **Yavapai Geological Museum,** or west to **Hermit's Rest,** using the shuttles. The Eastern Rim Trail swarms with sunset-watchers at dusk, and the observation deck at the Yavapai Museum, at the end of the trail, has a sweeping view of the canyon during the day. The Western Rim Trail leads to several vistas; **Hopi Point** is a favorite for sunsets, and the **Abyss** overlooks a nearly vertical cliff, leading to the **Tonto Plateau** 3000 ft. below. To watch a sunset (or sunrise), check *The*

Guide for the time. Show up at your chosen spot 45 min. beforehand and watch earth-tones and pastels melt into darkness.

The **Grand Canyon Railway** (800-THE-TRAIN/843-8724) leaves from Williams and offers tours for the whole family. The freedom tour takes passengers to great views in the Canyon ($3, children $7). The park service rangers present a variety of free, informative talks and hikes including a free talk at 8:30pm (in winter 7:30pm) in **Mather Amphitheater,** behind the visitors center.

■ North Rim

If you are coming from Utah or Nevada, or you simply want to avoid the crowds at the South Rim, the park's North Rim is a bit wilder, a bit cooler, and much more serene—all with a view as groovy as that from the South Rim. Unfortunately, because the North Rim is less frequented, it's hard to reach by public transportation.

PRACTICAL INFORMATION

Tourist Office: National Park Service Information Desk (638-7864; open daily 8am-8pm), in the lobby of Grand Canyon Lodge. Info on North Rim viewpoints, facilities, and some trails.

Public Transportation: Transcanyon, P.O. Box 348, Grand Canyon 86023 (638-2820). Buses to South Rim depart 7am, arrive 11:30am; return 1:30pm, arrive 6:30pm. $60, $100 round-trip. Call for reservations. Open late May-Oct.

Medical Services: North Rim Clinic (638-2611, ext. 222), located in cabin #7 at Grand Canyon Lodge. Staffed by a nurse practitioner. Walk-in or appointment service. Open Tues. 9am-noon and 2-5pm, Fri. 9am-noon and 2-6pm, Sat.-Mon. 9am-noon and 3-6pm.

Weather Info: 638-7888.

Emergency: 911.

Post Office: (638-2611), in Grand Canyon Lodge with everything else. Open Mon.-Fri. 8-11am and 11:30am-4pm, Sat. 8am-2pm. **ZIP code:** 86023. **Area code:** 520.

The **entrance fee** for the North Rim admits you to both rims for seven days ($10 per car, $4 per person on foot, bike, bus, or holy pilgrimage). From South Rim, take Rte. 64 east to U.S. 89N, which runs into Alt. 89; from Alt. 89, follow Rte. 67 south to the edge. Altogether, the drive is over 200 mi. and stunningly beautiful. Snow closes Rte. 67 from the middle of October to mid-May. Then, only a snowmobile can get you to the North Rim. Park visitor facilities close in the winter as well.

ACCOMMODATIONS, CAMPING, AND FOOD

Since camping within the confines of the Grand Canyon National Park is limited to designated campgrounds, only a lucky minority of North Rim visitors get to spend the night "right there." Advance reservations can be made through **MISTIX** (800-365-2267 or 619-452-5956). Otherwise, mark your territory by 10am. If you can't get in-park lodgings, visit the **Kaibab National Forest,** which runs from north of Jacob Lake to the park entrance. You can camp for free, as long as you're ½ mi. from official campgrounds and the road. The nearest low-priced motels are an hour's drive to the north, in **Kanab, UT** and **Fredonia.** Hotel rooms in Kanab hover around $40; the **Canyonlands International Youth Hostel (AAIH/Rucksackers)** puts you in a dorm for $9 (see Zion National Park Camping and Accommodations, p. 628).

Grand Canyon Lodge (303-297-2757), on the edge of the rim. Front desk open 24hr. Pioneer cabins shelter 4 people for $80. Singles or doubles in frontier cabins $58. Western cabins and motel rooms cost more. Reservations 801-586-7686; open daily 8am-7pm, late Oct. to mid-May Mon.-Fri. 8am-5pm.

Jacob Lake Inn (643-7232), 30mi. north of the North Rim entrance at Jacob Lake. Office open 6:30am-9:30pm. Cabins for 2 $66-71, for 3 $76-78, for 4 $81-84, for 5 $87, for 6 $96. Pricier motel units available. Reasonably priced dining room.

Jacob Lake RV Park (743-7804), ¼mi. south of the Inn. 50 tent sites $10, 60 sites with hookups for 2 people $20-22; $2 each additional person. Open May-Oct. 15.

North Rim Campground (MISTIX 800-365-2267), on Rte. 67 near the rim, the only campground in the park. You can't see into the canyon from the pine-covered site, but you know it's there. Near a food store, has laundry facilities, recreation room, and showers. 7-day max. stay. 82 sites $12. Closes Oct. 21.

DeMotte Park Campground, 5mi. north of the park entrance in the Kaibab National Forest. 25 woodsy sites $10. First come, first served.

Both feeding options on the North Rim are placed strategically at the **Grand Canyon Lodge** (638-2611). The restaurant serves dinners for $8 and up (reservations only) and breakfast for $3-7. A sandwich at the "buffeteria" costs $2.50. (Dining room open daily 6:30-10am, 11:30am-2:30pm, 5-9:30pm.) North Rim-ers are better off eating in Kanab or stopping at the **Jacob Lake Inn** for snacks and great milkshakes (lunch dishes about $5; open daily 6am-9pm).

SIGHTS AND ACTIVITIES

A ½-mi. paved trail takes you from the Grand Canyon Lodge to **Bright Angel Point,** which commands a seraphic view of the Canyon. **Point Imperial,** an 11-mi. drive from the lodge, overlooks **Marble Canyon** and the **Painted Desert.** The North Rim's *The Guide* lists trails in full. Only one trail, the **North Kaibab Trail,** leads into the Canyon from the North Rim; a shuttle runs to the trailhead from Grand Canyon Lodge (daily 6am-8pm; $5). Overnight hikers must get permits from the **Backcountry Office** in the Ranger Station (open daily 7:30am-noon), or write Backcountry Office, PO Box 129, Grand Canyon 86023; it may take a few days.

The North Rim offers nature walks, lectures, and evening programs at the North Rim Campground and at Grand Canyon Lodge. Check the info desk or campground bulletin boards for schedules. One-hr. ($12) or half-day **mule trips** ($35) descend into the canyon from the lodge (638-2292; open daily 7am-8pm). If you'd rather tour the Canyon wet, pick up a *Grand Canyon River Trip Operators* brochure and select from among the 20 companies which offer trips.

On warm evenings, the Grand Canyon Lodge fills with an eclectic group of international travelers, U.S. families, and rugged adventurers. Thirsty hikers will find a bar and a jukebox at **The Tea Room,** within the lodge complex (open 11am-10pm). Others look to the warm air rising from the canyon, a full moon, and the occasional shooting star for their intoxication at day's end.

■ Navajo and Hopi Reservations

As late as the 1830s, federal policymakers planned to create a permanent Indian country in the west; by mid-century those plans had been washed away by the tide of American expansion. Indian reservations evolved out of the U.S. government's subsequent ad hoc attempts to prevent fighting between Native Americans and whites while facilitating white settlement. Originally conceived as a means to detribalize Native Americans and prepare them for assimilation into Anglo-American society, the reservation system imposed a kind of wardship on the Indians for over a century, until a series of Supreme Court decisions, beginning in the 1960s, reasserted the tribes' legal standing as semi-sovereign nations.

The largest reservation in America, the **Navajo Nation** covers 17 million acres of northeastern Arizona, southern Utah, and northwestern New Mexico. Within its boundaries, the smaller **Hopi Reservation** is home to 6,000 Hopi ("Peaceable People"). Ruins mark the dwellings of the Anasazi, Indians who inhabited the area until the 13th century. Over 140,000 Navajo, or Dineh ("the People"), live here, one-tenth of the Native Americans in the entire U.S. The Navajo Nation has its own police force and its own laws. Possession and consumption of alcohol are prohibited on the reservation. Do not remove anything from the reservation and always respect the privacy of the people who live here. Photography requires a permission fee, and tourist photography is not permitted among the Hopi. Lively reservation politics are written up in the local *Navajo-Hopi Observer* and *Navajo Times* as well as in regional sections of Denver, Albuquerque, and Phoenix newspapers. For a taste of the Dineh's language and some Native American ritual songs, tune your radio to 660AM, "The Voice of the Navajo." Remember to advance your watch one hour during the summer; the Navajo Nation runs on **Mountain Daylight Time,** while the rest of Arizona remains on Mountain Standard Time.

Monument Valley, Canyon de Chelly, Navajo National Monument, Rainbow Bridge, and the roads which access these sights all lie on Navajo land. Driving off-road without a guide is considered trespassing. Fill up your gas tank before setting out to explore the reservation; stations are few and far between. *Discover Navajoland,* available from the **Navajoland Tourism Department,** P.O. Box 663, Window Rock 86515 (871-6436; open Mon.-Fri. 8am-5pm), has a full list of accommodations, and jeep and horseback tours. *The Visitors' Guide to the Navajo Nation* ($3) includes a detailed map. The "border towns" of **Gallup, NM,** and **Flagstaff** (p. 642) make good gateways to the reservations, with car rental agencies and frequent **Greyhound** service on I-40.

Window Rock is the seat of tribal government and features the geological formation for which the town is named. The limited lodging in town is expensive, but Navajo sights make Window Rock a good daytrip. The **Navajo Tribal Museum** (871-6673), on Rte. 264, has small exhibits (open Mon.-Fri. 8am-5pm; free). The **Navajo Council Tribal Chambers** (871-6417) offer free tours of the governing body's meeting place (open Mon.-Fri. 8am-noon and 1-5pm). The **Navajo Nation Zoo and Botanical Park** (871-6573), on Hwy. 264, ½mi. east of Rte. 12, features wildlife native to the reservation (open daily 8am-5pm; free). The oldest trading post in the U.S. and a national historic site, the **Hubbell Trading Post** (733-3475), 30 mi. west of Window Rock on Rte. 264, has functioned as a store since 1876 and now houses a museum (open daily 8am-6pm).

For further info contact the **Hopi Cultural Preservation Office,** P.O. Box 123, Kykotsmovi 86039 (734-2244), or the **Hopi Cultural Center,** P.O. Box 67, Second Mesa 86043 (734-2401), on Rte. 264 in the community of **Second Mesa.** The center consists of a museum of pottery, photography, and handicrafts, along with four gift shops, a motel, and a restaurant.

Inquire at the cultural center or at the Flagstaff Chamber of Commerce for the dates and sites of the Hopi **village dances.** Announced only a few days in advance, these religious ceremonies last from sunrise to sundown. The dances are highly formal occasions; do not wear shorts, tank tops, or other casual wear. Photographs, recordings, and sketches are strictly forbidden.

Area hotels charge quite a lot; plan to camp at the national monuments or the Navajo campgrounds. The **hotel** at the Hopi Cultural Center (734-2401) is expensive but decent (singles $60, doubles $70; reservations required 2 weeks to a month in advance). The **restaurant** is surprisingly reasonable (open daily 7am-9pm). Alternatively, you can make your visit a hard-driving day trip from Flagstaff or Gallup. Navaho and Hopi Reservation's **area code:** 520.

■ Canyon de Chelly

When compared with the Grand Canyon, Canyon de Chelly (pronounced "Canyon de Shay") more than makes up in beauty what it lacks in size. Sandstone cliffs of 30 to 1000 ft. surround the sandy, fertile, and aptly named **Beautiful Valley,** left by the Chelly River. Ruins in these eroded walls remind visitors of the architectural knowledge of the Anasazi civilization of the 12th century.

Canyon de Chelly National Monument lies on land owned by the Navajo Nation and administered by the National Park Service. (See Navajo and Hopi Reservations above for a brief explanation of reservation laws which affect tourists.) The park service offers **tours** three times per day during the summer (3-4hr., $10), or you can hire a private guide (minimum 3hr., $10 per hr.). Reservations for both can be made through the visitors center, but are not required. To drive into the canyon with a guide, you must provide your own four-wheel-drive vehicle and acquire a free permit from the visitors center. Horseback tours can be arranged at **Justin's Horse Rental** (674-5678), on South Rim Dr., at the mouth of the canyon (open daily 9am-sundown; horses $8 per hr.; mandatory guide $8 per hr.).

The 1¼-mi. trail to **White House Ruin,** 7 mi. from the visitors center off South Canyon Rd., is the only trail in the park you can walk without a guide. But what a trail—it winds down a 400-ft. face, past a Navajo farm and traditional *hogan* (log and clay shelter), through an orchard, and across a stream. You can also take one of the paved **Rim Drives** (North Rim 44mi., South Rim 36mi.), skirting the edge of the 300- to 700-ft. cliffs; the South Rim is more dramatic. Get booklets (50¢) on the White House Ruin and Rim Drives at the visitors center. **Spider Rock Overlook,** 16 mi. from the visitors center, is a narrow sandstone monolith towering hundreds of feet above the canyon floor. Native American lore says the whitish rock at the top contains the bleached bones of victims of the *kachina* spirit, Spider Woman.

During the 1800s, Canyon de Chelly saw repeated conflict between Indians and whites. In 1805, dozens of Native American women and children were shot by the Spanish, in what is now called **Massacre Cave.** Kit Carson starved the Navajo out of the Canyon in the 1860s, but the land was eventually returned. Navajo farmers once again inhabit the canyon, cultivating the lush soil and living in Navajo *hogans.*

The most common route to the park is from **Chambers,** 75 mi. south, at the intersection of I-40 and U.S. 191; you can also come from the north via U.S. 191. Entrance to the monument is free. The **visitors center** (674-5500) sits 2 mi. east of **Chinle** on Navajo Rte. 64 (open daily 8am-6pm; Oct.-April 8am-5pm). One of the larger towns on the reservation, Chinle, located adjacent to U.S. 191, has restaurants and gas stations. There is no public transportation to the park. For **emergencies,** contact the park ranger (674-5523 or 674-5524 after hours), the Navajo Police (674-2111), or an ambulance (674-5464).

Camp for free in the park's **Cottonwood Campground,** ½ mi. from the visitors center. This giant campground, in a pretty cottonwood grove, can get noisy with the din of the stray dogs who wander about the site at night. Sites are first come, first served, and facilities include restrooms, picnic tables, water (except in winter), and a dump station. (Max. RV length 35 ft.; 5-day max. stay. Group sites for 15-25 can be reserved 90 days in advance; 3-day max.; call 674-5500.) There are no budget accommodations anywhere in Navajo territory. **Farmington, NM,** and **Cortez, CO,** are the closest major cities with cheap lodging.

■ Monument Valley and Navajo Monument

Monument Valley Navajo Tribal Park You may have seen the red rock towers of Monument Valley in one of the numerous westerns filmed here. Some years before John Wayne hung out in the valley, Anasazi Indians managed to sustain small communities here, despite the hot, arid climate. The park's sights are natural rather than cultural; the breathtaking rust-hued sandstone formations can be seen from the park's looping 17-mi. **Valley Drive.** This dirt road winds in and out of the most dramatic monuments, including the famous pair of **Mittens** and the slender **Totem Pole.** The gaping ditches, large rocks, and mudholes on this road will do horrible things to your car—drive at your own risk, and hold your breath. Much of the valley can be reached only in a sturdy four-wheel-drive vehicle or by a long hike. In winter, snow laces the rocky towers, and most tourists flee. Inquire about snow and road conditions at the Flagstaff Chamber of Commerce (800-842-7293).

The park entrance is 24 mi. north of **Kayenta,** on U.S. 163 at the intersection with U.S. 160. The **visitors center** (801-727-3353), at the end of Rte. 564 across the Utah border 9 mi. west of U.S. 160, has a craft shop as well as displays of pottery and artifacts. (Park and visitors center open daily 8am-7pm; Oct.-April 8am-5pm. Entrance $2.50, seniors $1, under 7 free.)

Mitten View Campground, ¼ mi. southwest of the visitors center, offers 99 sites ($10), showers, and restrooms. First come, first served; groups of 6 or more may make reservations (group sites $20). The Navajo National Monument has more camping (see below). Alternate lodging options await in the small town of **Mexican Hat, UT** (see p. 631).

Navajo National Monument Home to some of the best preserved ruins in the southwest, the park is located off U.S. 160, 20 mi. west of Kayenta. From the park entrance, Rte. 564 takes you 9 mi. north to the Navajo National Monument. The site contains three Anasazi cliff dwellings, though one, **Inscription House,** has been closed to visitors. The other two, Keet Seel and Betatakin, admit a limited number of visitors. The stunning **Keet Seel** (open late May-early Sept.) requires a challenging 17-mi. roundtrip hike or a $55 horseback ride from the visitors center. A free campground near Keet Seel allows hikers to stay overnight, but it has no showers or drinking water. Reservations for permits to visit Keet Seel must be made in advance through the **visitors center** (672-2366), up to two months prior to the date of visit; total reservations are limited to 20 people per day (open daily 8am-6pm, off season 8am-4pm). **Betatakin,** a 135-room complex, is limited to 25 people per ranger-led tour. (In summer 2 per day, May 1 per day. A challenging 5-mi. hike, 5-6 hr. Sign-up is first come, first served on the day of the tour.) If you're not up for the trek to the ruins, the paved, 1-mi. roundtrip **Sandal Trail** lets you gaze down on Betatakin from a canyon-top overlook. The **Aspen Forest Trail,** another 1-mi. hike, overlooks canyons and aspens but no ruins. Write Navajo National Monument, HC 71 Box 3, Tonalea 86044 for more info.

The free campground, next to the visitors center, has 30 sites; an additional overflow campground nearby has no running water. Groups of 11 to 30 people may reserve spaces through the visitors center. Smaller groups or individuals must get sites on a first come, first served basis at either campground.

■ Lake Powell, Page, and Rainbow Bridge

In 1953, President Dwight Eisenhower said "dammit," and they did. Ten years and ten million tons of concrete later, Glen Canyon Dam, the second largest dam in the country, was completed. With no particular place to go, the Colorado River flooded a canyon in northern Arizona and southern Utah to form the 186-mi.-long Lake Powell. Named after John Wesley Powell, a one-armed Civil War veteran who led an exploratory expedition down the Colorado, the lake offers 1960 miles of national recreation shoreline. The town of Page sits near the southwest tip of Lake Powell, at the U.S. 89/Rte. 98 junction, and serves as a gateway to Lake Powell. Now thriving with over 3 million visitors a year, Page has come a long way since its founding in 1957 as a construction camp for the federal government. To turn the Page from Utah, take U.S. 89 south and east, past Big Water and across into Arizona.

Practical Information Visitors can descend into the cool inner workings of Glen Canyon Dam alone, or let the **Carl Hayden Visitors Center** (645-6404), on U.S. 89N, 1 mi. north of Page, act as guide. (Open daily 7am-6pm, off season 8am-5pm. Free self-guided dam tours every hr. on the ½hr. 8:30am-5:30pm.) In **Page,** seek the **Chamber of Commerce,** 106 S. Lake Powell Blvd. (645-2741; open summers Mon.-Sat. 8am-5pm, Sun. 10am-5pm; winters Mon.-Fri. 9am-5pm). **Skywest** (645-4200) connects the Page airport to Phoenix, Las Vegas, St. George, and Salt Lake City. The **Wahweep Marina Shuttle** (645-2333) runs from the airport to town (every hr. on the hr.; free). **Budget Rent-A-Car** (645-3977), at the airport, rents cars for $39 per day (100 free mi., 30¢ each additional mi.) or $191 per week (700 free mi., 30¢ each additional mi.). Those under 25 pay a $5 surcharge per day, and must have a major credit card. **Emergency** in Page is 911. Lake Powell and Page's area code: 520.

Accommodations, Camping, and Food Wahweep Campground, 100 Lake Shore Dr. (645-2433 or 800-528-6154), adjacent to the exorbitant **Wahweep**

Lodge, has 200 sites on a first come, first served basis ($10; group sites $3 per person, 9-person min.). The **Wahweep RV Park** next door takes care of the motorized set (sites $22; with full hook-up $48). In Page, the **Lake Powell International Hostel (AAIH/Rucksackers),** 141 8th Ave. (645-3898), has free pickup and delivery to Lake Powell, coffee, linens, a kitchen, BBQ grill, TV, volleyball court, outdoor eating area, and bathrooms in every unit. The hostel also offers a $15 shuttle (make arrangements in advance) to Flagstaff. Ask Jeff, the host, to arrange tours for you. (No curfew. Bunks $12-15.) Under the same management, **Pension at Lake Powell,** next door to the hostel, has more upscale rooms with 2-6 person suites of 3 rooms with a bathroom, a living room with cable TV, and a kitchen for $29-70. For a different kind of accommodation try **Uncle Bill's** (645-1224), 1 block farther down on 8th Ave., which boasts attractive rooms with kitchens adjoining, and a pretty patio out back (singles $33, doubles $40, 4-person apartment $69). **Bashful Bob's Motel,** 750 S. Navajo Dr. (645-3919), isn't embarrassed about its rooms with kitchens and cable TV (doubles $39, triples $44).

Head to **Strombolli's Restaurant and Pizzeria,** 711 N. Navajo Dr. (645-2605), for "calzones as big as your head" ($6; open daily 11am-10pm). Gulp a margarita ($3) at **Salsa Brava** (645-9058) on Elm St. across from Page Plaza. (Open daily 11am-10pm.)

Sights and Activities Lake Powell's man-made shores are rocky rather than sandy, with skimpy beaches that vanish when the water rises. However, recreation opportunities abound at **Wahweep Marina** (645-2433), where you can swim, rent a boat (6-person skiff $62 per day), or take a boat tour ($10-76). Many companies lead **Jeep tours** to the side canyons including the kaleidoscopic **Antelope Canyon;** check pamphlets at the Page Chamber of Commerce (see above) for more info. Sacred to the Navajo, **Rainbow Bridge National Monument** takes its name from a Navajo word, Nonnezoshi, meaning "rainbow turned to stone." Rainbow Bridge, the world's largest natural stone bridge, can be reached by a hike or a boat trip from Lake Powell. **ARA Leisure Services** (800-528-6154) conducts boat tours (full day $76, under 12 $43; ½-day $56/$33). Call for reservations well in advance.

■ Sunset, Wupatki, and Walnut Canyon

Sunset Crater Volcano National Monument The volcanic crater encompassed by Sunset Crater Volcano National Monument (520-556-7042), 12 mi. north of Flagstaff on U.S. 89, appeared in 1065AD when molten rock spurted from a crack in the ground, then fell back to earth in solid form. Over the next 200 years, a 1000-ft.-high cinder cone took shape as a result of periodic eruptions. The self-guided **Lava Flow Nature Trail** wanders 1 mi. through the surreal landscape surrounding the cone, 1½ mi. east of the visitors center, where gnarled trees lie uprooted amid the rocky black terrain. Lava tube tours have been permanently discontinued due to falling lava. The monument's **visitors center** is open daily 8am-5pm. (Park entrance $4 per car, $2 per person; includes Wupatki National Monument.) The **Bonito Campground,** in the Coconino National Forest at the entrance to Sunset Crater, provides the nearest camping (see p. 643).

Wupatki National Monument Eighteen mi. northeast of Sunset Crater, Wupatki National Monument possesses some of the Southwest's most scenic pueblo ruins, situated along a stunning road with views of the Painted Desert and the Grand Canyon. The Sinagua moved here in the late 11th century, after the Sunset Crater eruption forced them to evacuate the land to the south. In less than 200 years, however, droughts, disease, and over-farming led the Sinagua to abandon these stone houses perched on the sides of *arroyos* in view of the San Francisco Peaks. Five deserted pueblos front the 14-mi. road from U.S. 89 to the visitors center. Another road to the ruins begins on U.S. 89 about 30 mi. north of Flagstaff. The largest and most accessible, **Wupatki Ruin,** located on a ½-mi. roundtrip loop trail from the visitors center, rises three stories. Get info and trail guide brochures (50¢, or borrow one and bring it back) at the **Wupatki Ruin Visitors Center** (520-556-7040; open daily 8am-5pm); **backcountry hiking permits** are available. The monument is open daily from dawn to dusk; admission to Sunset Crater includes Wupatki.

Walnut Canyon National Monument Constructed within a 400-ft.-deep canyon, 7 mi. east of Flagstaff off I-40, the ruins of more than 300 rooms in 13th-century Sinagua dwellings make up the Walnut Canyon National Monument (520-526-3367; open summers daily 8am-6pm; winters daily 8am-5pm). From a glassed-in observation deck in the **visitors center** you can survey the whole canyon and the stunning variety of plants sprouting from its striated walls. The steep, self-guided **Island Trail** snakes down from the visitors center past 25 cliff dwellings. Markers along the 1-mi. trail describe aspects of Sinagua life and identify the plants the natives used for food, dyes, medicine, and hunting. Every Saturday morning, rangers lead 2-mi. hikes into Walnut Canyon, to the original Ranger Cabin and many remote cliff dwellings. Hiking boots and long pants are required for these challenging 2½-hr. hikes. (Call ahead, hours change frequently. Free with entrance.) The monument charges an entrance fee of $4 per car or $2 per person.

▓ Petrified Forest and Meteor Crater

Titanic and austere, **The Petrified Forest National Park** covers over 60,000 acres. This vast desert, dotted with fallen trees which turned into rock some 225 million years ago, resembles no other forest. The park's showpiece is a scenic chunk of the **Painted Desert,** so named for the stunning colors which stripe its rock formations.

The park road winds past the logs in their native habitat and by **Newspaper Rock,** covered with Native American petroglyphs. At **Blue Mesa,** a hiking trail ventures into the desert. **Long Logs Crystal** and **Jasper Forest** contain some of the most exquisite pieces of petrified wood in the park. Picking up fragments of the wood is illegal and traditionally unlucky; if the district attorney don't getcha then the demons will. Those who *must* have a piece should buy one at a store along I-40.

You can enter the park either from the north or the south (open daily 7am-7pm; $5 per vehicle, $3 per pedestrian); a 27-mi. road connects the two entrances. To enter the North Forest section of the park, exit I-40 at Holbrook and take U.S. 180 west to the **Rainbow Forest Museum** (524-6228). The museum lets you look at petrified logs up close and serves as a visitors center (open daily 8am-7pm, off season 8am-5pm; free). There are no established campgrounds in the park, but **free backcountry camping** is allowed in several areas with a permit from the museum.

To enter the Painted Desert section of the park, take I-40 to Exit 311 (107mi. east of Flagstaff). The **Painted Desert Visitors Center** (524-6228, ext. 236) is less than 5 mi. from the exit (open in summer daily 7am-7pm; off season 8am-5pm). There is no public transportation to either part of the park. **Nava-Hopi Bus Lines, Gray Line Tours,** and **Blue Goose Backpacker Tours** offer services from Flagstaff (see Flagstaff Practical Information, below). Lodging is available in **Holbrook** (27mi. from the museum), or **Gallup, NM,** but prices are not always cheap. Budgeteers should return to Flagstaff.

Meteor Crater (289-5898), 35 mi. east of Flagstaff off I-40 on the Meteor Crater Rd. exit, is a good stop on the way from Flagstaff to the Petrified Forest. Originally thought to be a volcanic cone, the crater is now believed to be the impact site of a giant nickel-iron meteorite that fell to earth 50,000 years ago. Visitors cannot hike down into the crater, but must peer over the guard-railed edge. (Open daily 6am-6pm; in winter 8am-5pm. $8, seniors $7, ages 6-17 $2.) The site was used to train Apollo astronauts in the 1960s, and a museum in the building near the admission booth patriotically celebrates the U.S. space program, as well as the sciences of astronomy and mineralogy (free with entrance to the crater).

■ Flagstaff

After a three-year stay among the Navajos and Apaches of south Arizona during the 1860s, Samuel Cozzens returned to New England and wrote *The Marvellous Country,* in which he promoted the *north* part of the territory as fertile, temperate, and ripe for settlement (although he had never actually been there). Colonists from Boston subsequently arrived in the San Francisco Mountains region; unable to locate the promised rich farmland and gold veins, they promptly departed. Before leaving, however, one group erected a stripped-pine flagpole as a marker for westward travelers. Presto change-o: Flagstaff was born! During the following decade, Flagstaff, designated a stop on the transcontinental railroad, became a permanent settlement; railroad tracks still cut through downtown. Flagstaff now provides a home for Northern Arizona University (NAU) students, retired cowboys, earthy Volvo owners, serious rock climbers, and Grand Canyon tourists.

PRACTICAL INFORMATION

Tourist Office: Flagstaff Visitors Center, 1 E. Rte. 66 (774-9541 or 800-842-7293), inside the Amtrak station. Open daily 8am-5pm.

Trains: Amtrak, 1 E. Rte. 66 (774-8679 or 800-872-7245). To Los Angeles (1 per day, 11hr., $87) and Albuquerque (1 per day, 6hr., $82). Daily connecting shuttle bus to the Grand Canyon ($12). Open daily 5:45am-11:15pm; ticket office closed 1:30-2:30pm and 6-7pm.

Buses: Greyhound, 399 S. Malpais Ln. (774-4573 or 800-231-2222), across from NAU campus, 5 blocks southwest of the train station on U.S. 89A. To: Phoenix (4 per day, 3hr., $20); Albuquerque (3 per day, 7hr., $52); Los Angeles (4 per day, 10-12hr., $73); Las Vegas (3 per day via Kingman, 6-7hr., $48). Terminal open 24hr.

Gray Line/Nava-Hopi, 114 W. Rte. 66 (774-5003 or 800-892-8687). *Use caution in this area at night.* Shuttle buses to the Grand Canyon (2 per day, $25 roundtrip) and Phoenix (3 per day, $43 roundtrip).

Public Transportation: Pine Country Transit, 970 W. Rte. 66 (779-6624). Routes cover most of town. Buses once per hr.; route map and schedule available at visitors center. Fare 75¢, seniors, children, and disabled 60¢. **Flagstaff Trolley** (774-5003) runs a hotel pickup route and a museum-shopping-history route (daily 8:45am-5pm). 1-day pass $4.

Taxis: Flagstaff Taxicab, 526-4123. Airport to downtown about $12.

Car Rental: Budget Rent-A-Car, 100 N. Humphreys St. (774-2763), within walking distance of the hostels. Guaranteed lowest rates. Cars from $33 per day with 100 free mi., 25¢ per additional mi.; $145 per week with 1050 free mi. Insurance $12 per day. Must be 21 with major credit card or a $200 cash deposit. Under 25 surcharge $5 per day. Open daily 7am-9pm. Ask Tom for *Let's Go* discount rates.

Camping Equipment Rental: Peace Surplus, 14 W. Rte. 66 (779-4521), 1 block from Grand Canyon Hostel. Daily tent rental ($5-8; $75 deposit), packs ($5; $100 deposit), stoves ($3; $3 deposit), plus a good stock of cheap outdoor gear. 3-day min. rental on all equipment. Credit card or cash deposit required. Open Mon.-Fri. 8am-9pm, Sat. 8am-8pm, Sun. 8am-6pm.

Emergency: 911.

Post Office: 2400 N. Postal Blvd. (527-2440), for general delivery. Open Mon.-Fri. 9am-5pm, Sat. 9am-noon. **ZIP code:** 86004. **Area code:** 520.

Flagstaff sits 138 mi. north of Phoenix (take I-17), 26 mi. north of Sedona (take U.S. 89A), and 81 mi. south of the Grand Canyon's south rim (take U.S. 180). Downtown surrounds the intersection of **Beaver St.** and **Rte. 66** (formerly Santa Fe Ave.). Both bus stations, four youth hostels, the chamber of commerce, and a number of inexpensive restaurants lie within ½ mi. of this spot. Other commercial establishments line **S. San Francisco St.,** 2 blocks east of Beaver. As a mountain town, Flagstaff stays relatively cool and receives frequent afternoon thundershowers.

ACCOMMODATIONS AND CAMPING

When swarms of summer tourists descend on Flagstaff, accommodation prices shoot up. Thankfully, the town is blessed with excellent hostels. Cruise historic Rte. 66 to find cheap motels. *The Flagsstaff Accommodations Guide*, available at the visitors center, lists all area hotels, motels, hostels, and B&Bs, with prices for each. If you're here to see the Grand Canyon, check the noticeboard in your hotel or hostel; some travelers leave their still-valid passes behind.

The Weatherford Hotel (HI-AYH), 23 N. Leroux St. (774-2731), downtown 1 block west of San Francisco St. Spacious rooms in a stately old hotel, with bay windows, bunk beds, and funky furniture. Convenient location. Dorm rooms have baths in rooms and halls. Access to kitchen. Open daily 7-10am and 5-11pm. Lockout 10am-5pm. Curfew 1am. Dorm beds $16; singles $30, Labor Day-Memorial Day $26; doubles $35/$28. Required sleepsack $1.

The Grand Canyon International Youth Hostel, 19 S. San Francisco St. (779-9421), in the 1930s Downtowner Motel just south of the train station. Sunny and clean. Free tea and coffee, breakfast, parking, and linen. Access to kitchen, TV room with cable, and laundry facilities. Free pickup from Greyhound and Amtrak stations. Shuttle to Page. Office open 7am-1am. Bunks $12; private doubles $30, $5 per additional person. Reservations accepted.

Motel Du Beau (AAIH/Rucksackers), 19 W. Phoenix St. (774-6731 or 800-398-7112), just behind the noisy train station. Carpeted dorm rooms with private bathrooms and showers. Social atmosphere lasts into the wee hours. Tea and coffee, breakfast, linen, parking. Rides to and from the airport, train, and bus stations are all gratis. Tours to Grand Canyon ($25), and Monument Valley (price varies) are available depending on interest. Office open 6am-midnight. Dorm beds $12; private rooms $25. Camping area out back $6 per person. Reservations accepted.

Hotel Monte Vista, 100 N. San Francisco St. (779-6971 or 800-545-3068), downtown. Charmingly quirky decor, with a coffee shop and a bar (featuring pool tables, video games, and off-track betting) downstairs. Dorms sleep 12 as of June 1996; management plans to add beds in the coming months. Beds in dorms with private baths $12; private rooms $40, weekends $55.

KOA Campground, 5803 N. U.S. 89 (526-9926), 6mi. northeast of Flagstaff. Local buses stop near this beautiful campground. Showers, restrooms, and free nightly movies. Tent sites for 2 $17, cabins $29; each additional person $4, under 18 $3.

Camping in the surrounding **Coconino National Forest** is a pleasant and inexpensive alternative, but you'll need a car to reach the designated camping areas. Pick up a forest map ($6) at the Flagstaff Visitors Center. Many campgrounds fill up quickly during the summer, particularly on weekends when Phoenicians flock to the mountains; those at high elevations close for the winter. All sites are handled on a first come, first served basis; stake out a site by 1pm. **Lake View,** 13 mi. southeast on Forest Hwy. 3 (U.S. 89A), has 30 sites ($10). **Bonito,** 10 mi. from downtown Flagstaff, off U.S. 89 on Forest Rd. 545, at the entrance to Sunset Crater (see p. 640), rents 44 sites ($8). Both feature running water and flush toilets. (Both 14-day max. stay. Open mid-May to Sept.) Those who can live without amenities can camp free anywhere in the national forest outside the designated campsites, unless otherwise marked. For info on campgrounds and backcountry camping, call the **Coconino Forest Service** (527-3600; open Mon.-Fri. 7:30am-4:30pm). Privately owned **Fort Tuthill Park** (774-5139), 3 mi. south of Flagstaff on U.S. 89A, offers 335 acres of Ponderosa pines and the 100-site **Fort Tuthill Campground** (774-5130; open May-Sept.; $8, no hookups; reservations accepted).

FOOD, NIGHTLIFE, AND ENTERTAINMENT

Macy's, 14 S. Beaver St. (774-2243), behind Motel Du Beau. This hippy, happy, touristed student hangout serves fresh pasta ($4-6), a wide variety of vegetarian entrees ($3-6), sandwiches ($4-6), pastries ($1-2), and espresso-based drinks ($1-4). Open Sun.-Wed. 6am-8pm, Thurs.-Sat. 6am-10pm; food served until 7pm.

Kathy's Café, 7 N. San Francisco St. (774-1951). Behind demure lace curtains, Kathy's prepares delicious breakfast entrees, accompanied by home fries and fresh fruit ($4-6). Also serves lunch. Open daily 6:30am-3pm.

Alpine Pizza, 7 Leroux St. (779-4109), and 2400 E. Rte. 66 (779-4138). A popular spot for beer, pool, and pizza. Large slices cooked to order ($2). Excellent, huge calzones $7; strombolis $7. Open Mon.-Thurs. 11am-11pm, Fri.-Sat. 11am-midnight, Sun. noon-11pm.

Main St. Bar and Grill, 14 S. San Francisco St. (774-1519), across from the Grand Canyon Hostel. When the vegetarian meals and non-alcoholic drinks of the cafés seem too healthy, try barbecued dishes ($6-14), complete with Buttery Texas Toast. Excellent selection of beers. Live music Tues.-Sat. 8pm; no cover. Open Mon.-Sat. 11am-midnight, Sun. noon-10pm.

Beaver St. Brewery, 11 S. Beaver St. (779-0079), has a fantastic menu and great beer. Dips and fondues ($7.25-9), huge sandwiches ($7-8.50), and pints of beer ($3). Open Sun.-Thurs. 11:30am-11pm, Wed.-Sat. 11:30am-midnight.

Beer flows freely in downtown Flagstaff; a number of bars line S. San Francisco St. The **Mad Italian,** 101 S. San Francisco St. (779-1820), has pool tables and daily happy hours (4-7pm) with drink specials and cheap munchies (open daily 11:30am-1am). Below the Weatherford Hotel, **Charly's,** 23 N. Leroux St. (779-1919), stages live music. Hostelers staying at the Weatherford get in free. (Open daily 11am-10pm; bar open daily 11am-1am.) A little outside of town, the **Museum Club,** 3404 E. Rte. 66 (526-9434), caters to party animals with a taste for the wild west. Also known as the **Zoo,** the club rocks cowboys and cowgirls with live country-western (cover $3; open daily noon-1am).

In early June, the annual **Flagstaff Rodeo** comes to town with competitions, barn dances, a carnival, and the Nackard Beverage cocktail waitress race. The **Flagstaff Symphony** (774-5107) plays from October to May (tickets $11-22, students ½-price). For the month of July, the **Festival of the Arts** attracts chamber concerts, orchestras, and individual performers.

■ Near Flagstaff

In 1894 Percival Lowell chose Flagstaff as the site for an astronomical observatory; he then spent the rest of his life here, culling data to support his theory that life exists on Mars. **The Lowell Observatory,** 1400 W. Mars Hill Rd. (774-2096), just west of downtown off Rte. 66, now has eight telescopes used in breakthrough studies of Mars and Pluto. Visitors get a tour of the facility with hands-on astronomy exhibits. On clear summer nights, you can peer through the 100-year-old Clark telescope at some heavenly goodie selected by the staff. (Open daily 9am-5pm, night sky viewings Mon.-Wed. and Fri.-Sat. 8, 8:45, and 9:30pm; Dec.-March Mon.-Sat. 10am-5pm, Sun. noon-5pm. $2.50, ages 5-17 $1.) **The Museum of Northern Arizona** (774-5213), on Fort Valley Rd. off U.S. 180 just north of town, houses a huge collection of Southwestern Native American art (open daily 9am-5pm; $5, seniors $4, students $3, ages 7-17 $2).

The huge, snow-capped mountains visible to the north of Flagstaff are the **San Francisco Peaks.** To reach the peaks, take U.S. 180 about 7 mi. north to the Fairfield Snow Bowl turnoff. Nearby **Mt. Agassiz** has the area's best skiing. The **Arizona Snow Bowl** (779-1951, daily 8am-5pm) operates four lifts from mid-December to mid-April; its 30 trails receive an average of 8½ ft. of powder each winter. Lift tickets cost $30. During the summer, these peaks are perfect for hiking. The Hopi believe **Humphrey's Peak**—the highest point in Arizona at 12,670 ft.—is the sacred home of the Kachina spirits. When the air is clear, you can see the North Rim of the Grand Canyon, the Painted Desert, and countless square mi. of Arizona and Utah from the top of the peak. Reluctant hikers will find the vista from the top of the Snow Bowl's **chairlift** almost as stunning. (20-30min. June 15-Labor Day daily 10am-4pm; Labor Day-April 15 Sat.-Sun. 10am-4pm. $9, seniors $6, ages 6-12 $5.) The mountains occupy national forest land, so camping is free, but there are no established campsites.

▓ Jerome

Perched on the side of Mingus Mountain, Jerome ranked as Arizona's third-largest city in 1920, and was populated by miners, speculators, saloon owners, and madams who came to the city following the copper boom of the late 1800s. The city never recovered from the stock market crash of 1929, however, and by mid-century Jerome was a ghost town. Now copperware boutiques and the hollow shells of stately old buildings vie for visitors' attention. Learn more about the area by heading over to **Jerome State Historic Park** (634-5381), ½ mi. off U.S. 89A just as you enter town. The park provides a panoramic view of the town, while helpful placards reveal the history of Jerome's decaying mansions. Inside the 80-year-old house of mine owner James Douglas, the park museum features exhibits on mining, minerals, and the early years of the town. (Open daily 8am-5pm. $2, ages 12-17 $1, under 12 free.) Enjoy period cars, trucks, machines, and props at **The Gold King Mine and Ghost Town** (634-0053), also on U.S. 89A just past Main St., even if it's not quite clear what period they're aiming to recreate. (Open daily 9am-5pm. $3, seniors $2.50, under 12 $2, under 5 free.) **The Mine Museum,** 200 Main St. (634-5477), displays a stock of rocks and old mining equipment (open daily 9am-4:30pm; 50¢).

Budget travelers should make Jerome a daytrip; lodging tends to be expensive. **The Inn at Jerome,** 309 Main St. (634-5094 or 800-634-5094), is one of the lower-priced joints in town; rooms run about $55-85. The oldest restaurant in Arizona, **The English Kitchen,** 119 Jerome Ave. (634-2132), has a large array of salads and sandwiches for under $8 (open Tues.-Sun. 8am-3:30pm). **Marcy's,** 363 Main St. (634-0417), offers ice cream, soups, and sandwiches (under $4) in a pleasant atmosphere (open Fri.-Wed. 11am-5pm). At night, float over to **The Spirit Room** (634-8809), at Main St. and Jerome Ave., for live music and mayhem (open daily 10am-1am). **Paul and Jerry's Saloon** (634-2603), also on Main St., has been helping people get sloppy in Jerome for three generations (open daily 10:30am-1am).

U.S. 89A slinks its way to Jerome 30 mi. southwest of Sedona; the drive between the two is simply gorgeous. Because there is no chamber of commerce, **The Station** (634-9621), on U.S. 89A across from the high school, serves as the unofficial visitors center (open daily 11am-6pm). Jerome's **area code:** 520.

▓ Sedona

The pines of the Coconino National Forest blanket Sedona's red sandstone formations, offering some of Arizona's most scent-sational scenery. Though a popular stopping point for vacationers, tourists, and the New Agers who believe the area to be a locus of "psychic vortices," the town itself consists of a cluster of gift shops and touring outfits. Ignore the upper-class shopping area and head for the state parks where the views, rather than the prices, will astound you.

Slide Rock Park (282-3034), 10 mi. north of Sedona on U.S. 89A, takes its name from a natural stone slide into the waters of Oak Creek. In the summer, locals swarm the slide. (Open summers daily 8am-7pm; closes earlier off season. Entrance $5 per car, $1 per pedestrian or cyclist.) An architectural wonder, **Chapel of the Holy Cross** (282-4069), on Chapel Rd., lies just outside a 1000-ft. rock wall in the middle of the red sandstone (call for appointments). Meditate amidst the splendor of **Red Rock State Park** (282-6907), on U.S. 89A about 15 mi. southwest of town. Rangers lead day-hikes into the nearby red rocks, including nature and bird walks. (Visitors center open daily 8am-5pm. Park open daily 8am-6pm; Oct.-April 8am-5pm. Entrance $5 per car, $1 per pedestrian or cyclist.)

The **Sedona Chamber of Commerce** (282-7722), at Forest Rd. and Rte. 89A, distributes listings for accommodations and private campgrounds in the area (open Mon.-Sat. 8:30am-5pm, Sun. 9am-3pm). Both the **Star Motel,** 295 Jordan Rd. (282-3641), and **La Vista,** 500 N. Rte. 89A (282-0000), can lodge you in comfy rooms with cable TV (1 bed $55-59, 2 beds $65-79). The **Sedona Motel,** 218 Rte. 179 (282-7187), features great views (rooms start at $59; prices slightly higher in the summer). There are a number of **campgrounds** within **Coconino National Forest** (527-3600), along Oak Creek Canyon on U.S. 89A (sites $10 per vehicle). The largest, **Cave Springs, 20** mi. north of town, administers 78 sites (for reservations call 800-283-CAMP/2267). For more info on Coconino, visit the **ranger station,** 250 Brewer Rd. (282-4119); turn off U.S. 89A at Burger King (open Mon.-Sat. 7:30am-4:30pm; in winter Mon.-Fri. 7:30am-4:30pm). Free **backcountry camping** is allowed in the forest, anywhere outside of Oak Creek and more than 1 mi. from any official campground. **Hawkeye RV Park,** 40 Art Barn Rd. (282-2222), has full hookups, water, electric, and showers, as well as tent sites (sites $17, with water and electric $22.50, full hookup $27.50).

The **Coffee Pot Restaurant,** 2050 W. U.S. 89A (282-6626), dishes up 101 varieties of omelettes ($4-9; open daily 5:30am-9pm). **Cups Bistro and Gallery,** 1670 W. U.S. 89A (282-2531), in west Sedona, serves organic, karmic food in a garden setting. Breakfast dishes run $3-7, sandwiches $5-6. (Open summers daily 8am-4pm; off season a bit later.) **Hot Rocks Pizza** (282-7753), in the Uptown Mall, has slices for $2 and entire pizzas from $6. Try the desert dancer, topped with fajita chicken, peppers, and onions ($7.50; open Sun.-Thurs. 10am-9pm, Fri.-Sat. 10am-10pm).

Sedona lies 120 mi. north of Phoenix (take I-17 north to Rte. 179W) and 30 mi. south of Flagstaff (take I-17S to Rte. 179W or use U.S. 89A southwest). The **Sedona-Phoenix Shuttle** (282-2066) offers three trips daily ($30, $55 roundtrip). Sedona's **area code: 520.**

■ Near Sedona

Montezuma Castle National Monument (567-3322), 10 mi. south of Sedona on I-17, is a 20-room abode. The dwellings, built into a cliff recess, date back to the 12th century. Visitors view the "castle" from a paved path below. (Open daily 8am-7pm. $2, under 16 free.) A beautiful lake formed by the collapse of an underground cavern, **Montezuma Well,** 11 mi. from the Castle off I-17 north of the Wall exit, once served as a source of water for the Sinagua who lived here (open daily 7am-7pm; free). Take U.S. 89A to Rte. 279 and continue through Cottonwood to reach **Tuzigoot National Monument** (634-5564), 20 mi. southwest of Sedona, a dramatic Sinaguan ruin overlooking the Verde Valley (open summers daily 8am-7pm, winters 8am-5pm; $2, under 17 free).

When finally completed, **Arcosanti** (632-7135), off I-17 at Exit 262, will be a self-sufficient community embodying Italian architect Paolo Soleri's concept of an "arcology" (defined as "architecture and ecology working together as one integral process"). Budgetarians will appreciate the architect's vision of a city where cars (and their expenses) are obsolete. The complete city, with its unusual geometric structures and subterranean parks, surprises even the most imaginative Legoland architects. (Tours daily every hr. 10am-4pm. Open daily 9am-5pm. $5 donation requested.)

SOUTHERN ARIZONA

■ Phoenix

Phoenix began as a small farming community in the late 1800s, but high tech jobs and shopping plazas have long since replaced the wheat fields. Shiny high-rises crowd the business district, while a vast web of six-lane strip mall highways surrounds the downtown. Sun, sun, sun, and sun are some of the city's main attractions. During the balmy winter months, tourists, golfers, and business conventioners flock to Phoenix. In the summer, the city crawls into its air-conditioned shell as temperatures climb to an average of 100°F and lodging prices drop by up to 70%. Summer visitors should carry water with them if they plan on walking for any length of time.

PRACTICAL INFORMATION

Tourist Office: Phoenix and Valley of the Sun Convention and Visitors Center, 400 E. Van Buren St. (254-6500), on the 6th floor of the Arizona Center. Open Mon.-Fri. 8am-5pm. **Weekly Events Hotline,** 252-5588.

Airport: Sky Harbor International (273-3300), only minutes southeast of downtown. Valley Metro bus #13 goes west into the city (5am-7pm). Shuttle service to downtown $7.

Trains: Amtrak, 401 W. Harrison (253-0121 or 800-872-7245); follow 4th Ave. south 2 blocks past Jefferson St. *Use caution at night.* To Los Angeles (7 per week, 20hr., $96) and San Antonio via El Paso (3 per week, 21hr., $99). Station and ticket office open Sun.-Wed. 4:15pm-9:45am, Thurs. 4:15pm-12:45am, Sat. 1:15-9:45am; closed daily 6:30-7:30am, 8:30-9:30pm.

Buses: Greyhound, 525 E. Washington St. (271-7425 or 800-231-2222). To: El Paso (15 per day, 8hr., $37.50); Los Angeles (12 per day, 8hr., $30); Tucson (13 per day, 2hr., $12); San Diego (4 per day, 8½hr., $36.50). Open 24hr.

Public Transportation: Valley Metro, 253-5000. Most lines run to and from the **City Bus Terminal,** at Central and Washington. Most routes operate Mon.-Fri. 5am-8pm; reduced service on Sat. Fare $1.25; disabled, seniors, and children 60¢. All-day $3.60, 10-ride pass $12. Bus passes and system maps at the Terminal.

Taxis: Ace Taxi, 254-1999. $2.45 base fare, $1.10 per mi.

Car Rental: Rent-a-Wreck, 1202 S. 24th St. (254-1000), in the Roadway Inn Hotel. Cars from $22 per day with 100 free mi.; 15¢ per additional mi. Must be 21 with credit card. Open Mon.-Sat. 7am-3pm; 24hr. pick up with reservation.

Hotlines: Center Against Sexual Assault, 241-9010. **Crisis Hotline,** 784-1500. Both 24hr. **Gay/Lesbian Hotline,** 234-2752. Open daily 10am-10pm.

Emergency: 911.

Post Office: 522 N. Central (407-2051), downtown. Open Mon.-Fri. 8:30am-5pm. General Delivery, 1441 E. Buckeye Rd. (407-2049). Open Mon.-Fri. 8am-5pm. **ZIP code:** 85026. **Area code:** 602.

The bus terminal at **Central Ave.** and **Washington St.** marks the heart of downtown. Central Ave. runs north-south; avenues are numbered west from Central and streets are numbered east. **Washington St.** divides streets north-south. For a price, parking is readily available downtown at one of the many meters or garages. You'll need a car or a bus pass to see much of Phoenix; this city is a sprawler.

ACCOMMODATIONS AND CAMPING

Budget travelers should visit Phoenix in the summer. Almost all downtown motels have vacancies discounted up to 70% during July and August. In the winter, when temperatures and vacancy signs go down, prices go up; be sure to make reservations if possible. The reservationless should cruise the rows of motels on **Van Buren St.** and **Main St.** (a.k.a. Apache Trail) in the suburbs. The strips are full of 50s ranch-style motels with names like "Deserama," as well as the requisite modern chains. Be advised that parts of these areas *can be quite dangerous;* investigate a hotel thoroughly before checking in. **Bed and Breakfast Inn Arizona,** 8900 E. Via Linda, #101, Scottsdale 85258 (860-9338 or 800-266-STAY/7829), matches visitors with accommodations in homes in Phoenix and throughout Arizona. However, they will only return your call collect—which could be very expensive. (Preferred 2-night min. stay. Singles $30, doubles $40. Reservations recommended.)

Metcalf House (HI-AYH), 1026 N. 9th St. (254-9803), a few blocks northeast of downtown. From the City Bus Terminal, take bus #7 down 7th St. to Roosevelt St., walk 2 blocks east to 9th St., and turn left—the hostel is ½ block north. In a residential area; shady and quiet. Dorm-style rooms, wooden bunks, and common showers. Kitchen, porch, common room, and laundry facilities. Can also help you with car rentals. Check-in 7-10am and 5-10pm. $12, nonmembers $15. Linen $1.

Economy Inn, 804 E. Van Buren St. (254-0181), close to downtown. Standard rooms with TV and phones. Singles $27, doubles $35; in winter $30/$38.

The American Lodge, 965 E. Van Buren St. (252-6823). Another basic motel close to downtown. More TV, more phones—imagine! Pool. Singles $25-30, doubles $35-38; in winter $35/$50.

KOA Phoenix West (853-0537), 11 mi. west of Phoenix on Citrus Rd. Take I-10 to Exit 124; go ¾mi. south to Van Buren St., then 1mi. west to Citrus Rd. 285 sites, heated pool and jacuzzi, and other perks. Tent sites $14.50, RV sites $15.50, electric and water $2.50 extra.

FOOD

Aside from malls, you will rarely find several restaurants together amid Phoenix's expanse. Downtowners feed mainly at small coffeeshops, most of which close on weekends. For more variety, try **McDowell St.** The **Arizona Center** (271-4000), on 3rd and Van Buren St., boasts food venues, fountains, and palm trees. The *New Times* gives extensive restaurant recommendations.

Macaya, 4001 N. Central (264-6141). Funky decor, terrific Mexican food, and big portions. They even serve breakfast. Fajitas $8-12, combo plates $5-9; the portions are large. Open Sun.-Thurs. 6am-11pm, Fri.-Sat. 6am-midnight.

Los Dos Molinos, 8646 S. Central Ave. (243-9113), features live music at lunch and dinner, a huge menu, and lemonade in a jelly jar. Enchiladas $3-3.50, burritos $3.25-5.25. Open Tues.-Sat. 11am-9pm.

Bill Johnson's Big Apple, 3757 E. Van Buren St. (275-2107), and 3 other locations. A down-South delight with sawdust on the floor. Sandwiches $3-10; hearty soups $1-2. Open Mon.-Sat. 6am-11pm.

SIGHTS

The **Heard Museum,** 22 E. Monte Vista Rd. (252-8840), 1 block east of Central Ave., has outstanding collections of Navajo handicrafts. The museum also promotes the work of contemporary Native American artists, and sponsors occasional lectures and Native American dances. (Guided tours daily. Open Mon.-Tues. and Thurs.-Sat. 9:30am-5pm, Wed. 9:30am-8pm, Sun. noon-5pm. $5, students $4, ages 13-18 $3; free Wed. 5-8pm.) The **Phoenix Art Museum,** 1625 N. Central Ave. (257-1880), 3 blocks south, exhibits American folk art, as well as classical and modern European art. (Open Tues. and Thurs.-Sat. 10am-5pm, Wed. 10am-9pm, Sun. noon-5pm. $4, seniors $3, students $1.50, under 6 free; free Wed.) The **Pueblo Grande Museum and Cultural Park,** 4619 E. Washington St. (495-0900), features the remains of a Hohokam pueblo (open Mon.-Sat. 9am-4:45pm, Sun. 1-4:45pm; $2, children $1).

The **Desert Botanical Gardens,** 1201 N. Galvin Pkwy. (941-1225), in Papago Park 5 mi. east of the downtown area, grow a beautifully colorful collection of cacti and other desert plants. (Take bus #3 east to Papago Park. Open daily 7am-10pm; in winter 8am-8pm. $6, seniors $5, ages 5-12 $1.) Also within the confines of Papago Park, the **Phoenix Zoo** (273-1341), at 62nd and E. Van Buren St., presents exhibits and a children's zoo. Walk around or take a guided tour via tram. (Open daily 7am-4pm; Labor Day-April 9am-5pm. $7, seniors $6, children $3.50.) In the summer, try to avoid outside attractions during the midday heat. The **Arizona Science Center,** 147 E. Adams St. (256-9388), offers interactive science exhibits aimed at children (open Mon.-Sat. 9am-5pm, Sun. noon-5pm; $4.50, seniors and ages 4-12 $3.50).

Taliesin West (860-8810 or 860-2700), on Frank Lloyd Wright Blvd. in nearby Scottsdale, served as the architectural studio and residence of Frank Lloyd Wright in his later years. Designed by Wright, the studio was meant to blend into the surrounding desert. (Guided tours only. Open June-Sept. daily 7:30-11am. $8, students and seniors $6, children $3.) To see more of Wright's work, check out the **Arizona Biltmore** (955-6600), on 24th St. and Missouri.

South of Phoenix across the dry Salt River lie Tempe's **Arizona State University (ASU)** and its sunny college atmosphere. Cafés and art galleries abound in this area. Another Frank Lloyd Wright creation, the **Gammage Memorial Auditorium** (965-3434), at Mill Ave. on campus (take bus #60, or #22 on weekends), one of the last major buildings designed by the architect, wears the pink and beige tones of the surrounding desert (20-min. tours daily in winter).

NIGHTLIFE AND ENTERTAINMENT

The free *New Times Weekly,* available on local magazine racks, lists club schedules for Phoenix's after-hours scene. Gay and lesbian nightlife spots can be found in *The Western Front,* available in some bars and clubs. The *Cultural Calender of Events* guide covers three months of area entertainment.

Recently rated the nation's best country nightclub, **Toolie's Country Saloon and Dance Hall,** 4231 W. Thomas Rd. (272-3100), has country-western music nightly. (Free dance lessons Mon., Wed., and Sun. Open Mon.-Thurs. 7am-1am, Fri.-Sat. 8am-1am, Sun. 11am-1am. Cover Thurs. $5, Fri.-Sat. $4.) **Char's Has the Blues,** 4631 N. 7th Ave. (230-0205), sports dozens of junior John Lee Hookers. (Doors open 7pm; music starts 9pm. Cover $3 on weekends.) **Phoenix Live,** 455 N. 3rd St. (252-2112), at Arizona Center, quakes the complex with three bars and a restaurant. The $5 weekend cover buys access to the entire building. Tuesday through Saturday, **LTL Ditty's** gets someone to tickle the ivories for sing-alongs with wild fans. **Ain't Nobody's Biz,** 3031 E. Indian School, #7 (224-9977), is a spacious lesbian bar with Thursday night beer busts ($1.50 pitchers Thurs. 9pm-midnight; open daily 2pm-1am). **The Country Club,** 4428 N. 7th Ave. (264-4553), is a gay bar occupying a house by the highway (happy hour Mon.-Sat. 11am-7pm; open daily 11am-1am).

Phoenix also has plenty for the sports lover. Catch NBA action with the **Phoenix Suns** (379-7867), at the America West Arena, or root for the NFL's **Phoenix Cardinals** (379-0101). Phoenix also hosts professional indoor tennis tournaments, a professional baseball team, and a hockey team.

■ From Phoenix to Tucson

Apache Junction and the Superstition Mountains A small mining town 40 mi. east of Phoenix at the junction of Rte. 88 and U.S. 60, **Apache Junction** serves as the "gateway to the **Superstition Mountains."** Steep, gray, and haunting, the mountains derived their name from Pima Native American legends, but they could easily have gained the name from the legends of the **Apache Trail,** which follows Rte. 88 into the mountains. In the 1840s, a Mexican explorer found gold in these hills but was killed before he could reveal the location. In the 1870s, Jacob Waltz apparently found the mine and promptly died. As you drive, remember the lost gold of the Apache Trail, but think twice before trying to find it.

The trail loops back to the town and U.S. 60 after about 6-8 hrs. of driving. Along the way, the partly unpaved road passes cliff dwellings, caves, ghost towns, and the man-made **Lake Canyon, Lake Apache,** and **Lake Roosevelt.** Leave the driving to **Apache Trail Tours** (602-982-7661), which offers jeep tours along the trail (1½-hr. tours $40 per person, 8-hr. tours $99). For more info head to **Apache Junction Chamber of Commerce,** 1001 N. Idaho (602-982-3141; open Mon.-Fri. 8am-5pm).

Many attractions vie for your attention along the loop. Among the best, the **Goldfield Ghost Town Mine Tours** (602-983-0333), 5 mi. north of the U.S. 60 junction on Rte. 88, offers tours of the nearby mines and some goldpanning from a refurbished ghost town (open daily 10am-6pm; mine tours $4, children $2; goldpanning $3). "Where the hell am I?" said Jacob Waltz when he came upon **Lost Dutchman State Park** (602-982-4485), 1½ mi. farther north on Rte. 88. At the base of the Superstitions, the park offers nature trails, picnic sites, and campsites (entrance $3 per vehicle; first come, first served campsites $8). **Tortilla Flat** (602-984-1776), an old ghost town on Rte. 88 18 mi. north of the U.S. 60 junction, keeps its spirits up with a restaurant, ice cream shop, and saloon. The **Tonto National Monument** (602-640-5250), 5 mi. east of Lake Roosevelt on Rte. 88W, manages a 700-year-old masonry and pueblo ruin from the prehistoric Salado people (open daily 8am-5pm; entrance $4 per car). **Tonto National Forest** (602-225-5200) has camping that is free in undeveloped sites, and $6-12 per developed site.

Biosphere 2 In 1991, eight research scientists sealed themselves inside this giant greenhouse to cultivate their own food and knit their own socks with no aid from the outside world, as they monitored the behavior of seven man-made ecosystems—savannah, tropical rainforest, marsh, 25-ft. deep ocean and coral reef, desert, and intensive agricultural area. After two years, they began having oxygen problems and difficulty with food production. Now no one lives in Biosphere 2, but teams of scientists still use it as a research facility.

The Biosphere is 30 minutes north of Tucson; take I-10 west to the "Miracle Mile" exit, follow the miracles to Oracle Rd., then go north until it becomes Rte. 77N. From Phoenix, take I-10 to Exit 185, follow Rte. 387 to Rte. 79 (Florence Hwy.), and ride Rte. 79 to Oracle Juntio, where you'll turn left onto Rte. 77. The two-hour guided tours include two short films, a walk through the laboratory's research and development models for the Biosphere 2 ecosystems, and a stroll around Biosphere 2 itself. (Open daily 9am-5pm. $13, seniors $11, ages 5-17 $6. AAA discount.) The **Inn at the Biosphere** (520-825-6222) offers deluxe accommodations on the same ranch as the Biosphere. (Cable TV, giant beds, and huge patios overlooking the Catalina mountains. Rooms for 1 or 2 $49; Oct.-April $80. A hefty $20 for each additional person.) Guests are sealed into their rooms at 8pm and taken out the subsequent leap year. Also within the complex, the **Canyon Café** serves up sandwiches and salads ($6).

■ Tucson

The Hohokan Indians inhabited the Tucson region 1200 years ago, but it was the Papago Indians who gave the city its name. Between 1776 and 1848, the region fell under Spanish, then Mexican, and ultimately, U.S. control. The arrival of Western civilization became manifest in 1864, when locals ruled that pigs could no longer roam freely on city streets; they would have to be chained. Smaller and friendlier than Phoenix, Tucson is now struggling to preserve its attractive, pigless downtown, and it remains to be seen whether the small band of cafés and artsy shops can compete with the city's suburban sprawl. In the meantime, travelers can take advantage of Tucson's varied environments—the walkable downtown, restaurant-and-shop-crammed highways, college scene, and national parks just outside the city.

PRACTICAL INFORMATION

Tourist Office: Metropolitan Tucson Convention and Visitors Bureau, 130 S. Scott Ave. (624-1817 or 800-638-8350). Ask for a bus map, the *Official Visitor's Guide,* and an Arizona campground directory. Open Mon.-Fri. 8am-5pm, Sat.-Sun. 9am-4pm.

Airport: Tucson International (573-8000), on Valencia Rd., south of downtown. Bus #25 runs every hr. to the Laos Transit Center; from there bus #16 goes downtown (last bus daily 7:48pm). **Arizona Stagecoach** (889-1000) will take you downtown for $12.50. Open 24hr. Reserve ahead.

Trains: Amtrak, 400 E. Toole Ave. (623-4442 or 800-872-7245), at 5th Ave., 1 block north of the Greyhound station. 3 trains per week to: Phoenix (2hr., $30); L.A. (9hr., $94). Open Sun.-Wed. 6:15am-1:45pm and 2:45-10:15pm, Thurs. 2:45-10:15pm, Sat. 6:15am-1:45pm.

Buses: Greyhound, 2 S. 4th Ave. (882-4386 or 800-231-2222), between Congress St. and Broadway. To: Phoenix (11 per day, 2hr., $12); L.A. (7 per day, 10hr., $32); Albuquerque (6 per day, 12hr., $70); El Paso (7 per day, 7hr., $32). Ticket office and terminal open daily 5:30am-2am.

Taxis: Yellow Cab, 624-6611. $1.10 base fare, $1.40 per mi. Open 24hr.

Public Transportation: Sun-Tran (792-9222). Buses run from the Ronstadt terminal downtown at Congress and 6th. Service roughly Mon.-Fri. 5:30am-10pm, Sat.-Sun. 8am-7pm. Fare 85¢, students under 19 60¢, seniors and disabled 35¢.

Car Rental: Care Free, 1760 S. Craycroft Rd. (790-2655). For the car-free. $18 per day with 100 free mi.; within Tucson only. 2-day min. rental. Must be 21 with major credit card. Open Mon.-Fri. 9am-5pm, Sat. 9am-2pm.

Bike Rental: The Bike Shack, 835 Park Ave. (624-3663), across from the UA campus. $25 first day, $10 each following day. Open Mon.-Fri. 9am-7pm, Sat. 10am-5pm, Sun. noon-5pm.

Hotlines: Rape Crisis, 327-7273. Open 24hr. Gay, Lesbian, and Bisexual Community Center, 422 N. 4th Ave. (624-1779).

Emergency: 911.

Post Office: 141 S. 6th St. (622-8454). Open Mon.-Fri. 8:30am-5pm, Sat. 9am-noon. Gen. Delivery, 1501 Cherry Bell (620-5157). ZIP code: 85726. Area code: 520.

Just east of I-10, Tucson's downtown area surrounds the intersection of **Broadway Blvd.** (running east-west) and **Stone Ave.**, 2 blocks from the train and bus terminals. The **University of Arizona** lies 1 mi. northeast of downtown at the intersection of **Park** and **Speedway Blvd.** Avenues run north-south, streets east-west; because some of each are numbered, intersections such as "6th and 6th" are possible—and probable. Speedway, Broadway Blvd., or **Grant** are the best east-west routes through town. To go north-south follow **Oracle Rd.** through the heart of the city, **Campbell Ave.** east of downtown, or **Swan Rd.** further east. The hip, young crowd is on **4th Ave.** at 6th St., and on **Congress St.,** where there are small shops, quirky restaurants, and bars, bars, bars.

ACCOMMODATIONS AND CAMPING

When summer arrives, Tucson opens its arms to budget travelers. Motel row runs along **South Freeway,** the frontage road along I-10, north of the I-19 junction. **Old Pueblo Homestays Bed and Breakfast,** P.O. Box 13603, Tucson 85732 (800-333-9776), arranges stays in private homes. Singles run $40-70, doubles $65 and up. (Open daily 8am-8pm. Winter reservations required 2 weeks in advance.)

The swank old **Hotel Congress and Hostel (AAIH/Rucksackers),** 311 E. Congress (622-8848), conveniently located across from the Greyhound and Amtrak stations, offers superb lodging to night-owl hostelers. Club Congress downstairs booms until 1am, making it a bit rough for early birds. Still, you get free earplugs and a real bed in a shared room with a private bath and a phone. The café downstairs serves great salads and some mean omelettes. ($12, nonmembers $14. Hotel singles $32, doubles $36. 10% discount for students.) **La Siesta Motel,** 1602 N. Oracle (624-1192), has clean rooms, a shaded picnic/BBQ area, a pool, and parking. (Singles $29, doubles $31, with 2 beds $35.)

Mount Lemmon Recreation Area in the **Coronado National Forest** offers beautiful campgrounds and free off-site camping in certain areas. Campgrounds and picnic areas are two minutes to two hours outside Tucson via the **Catalina Hwy. Rose Canyon,** 33 mi. northeast of Tucson via Hitchcock Hwy., at 7000 ft., is heavily wooded, comfortably cool, and has a small lake. Sites at higher elevations fill quickly on summer weekends. For more info, contact the **National Forest Service,** 300 W. Congress Ave. (670-4552), 7 blocks west of the Greyhound station (open Mon.-Fri. 8am-4:30pm). Among the commercial campgrounds near Tucson, try **Cactus Country RV Park** (574-3000), 10 mi. southeast of Tucson on I-10 off the Houghton Rd. Exit, which has showers, restrooms, and a pool. (Sites for 1 or 2 $15, with full hookup $24. $2.50 per additional person.)

FOOD

Good cheap Mexican restaurants are everywhere in Tucson; pick up a free *Tucson Weekly,* or just follow your nose. **Little Café Poca Cosa,** 20 S. Scott St. (622-6400), the (less expensive) *niño* of the Café Poca Cosa on Broadway, prides itself on fresh ingredients and an ever-changing menu—people literally walk in and say "give me something good" (lunch specials $5; open Mon.-Fri. 7:30am-2:30pm). **Café Margritte's,** 254 Congress (884-8004), has great art on its walls and features many levels of seating. Delicious food includes tea drinks ($1.60), appetizers from polenta pizza tart ($5) to tortilla bean soup ($2.75), and good vegetarian options. (Open Tues. and Sun. 4-10pm, Wed.-Thurs. 11am-10pm, Fri.-Sat. 11am-midnight.) **Geronimoz Restaurant**

and Bar, 800 E. University (623-1711), is where the business and family gangs eat lunch, and the home of the nighttime college crowd. Huge wooden bowls of salad ($5.25) and a large basket of sopapillas with honey start your meal. At night, shots start at $3.50, and margaritas at $2.75. (Open daily 11am-1am.) When you've had it up to your sombrero with Mexican food, head for **India Oven,** 2727 N. Campbell (326-8635). The garlic nan ($2.65) is exquisite. (Vegetarian dishes $5. Tandoori meats and curries $5-8. Open daily 11am-10pm.)

SIGHTS

Many of the sights associated with Tucson lie outside of the city, so be sure to read Near Tucson (652). Lined with cafés, restaurants, galleries, and vintage clothing shops, **4th Ave.** is an alternative, artsy magnet and a great place to take a stroll. Between Speedway and Broadway Blvd., the street becomes a historic shopping district with increasingly touristy shops. The **Tucson Museum of Art,** 140 N. Main Ave. (624-2333), shows an impressive collection of pre-Columbian art. (Open Tues.-Sat. 10am-4pm, Sun. noon-4pm. $2, students and seniors $1, under 12 free.)

Lovely for its varied—and elaborately irrigated—vegetation, the **University of Arizona's** mall sits where E. 3rd St. should be. The **Center for Creative Photography** (621-7968), on campus houses various exhibits, including the archives of the major American photographers Ansel Adams and Richard Avedon. (Open Mon.-Fri. 11am-5pm, Sun. noon-5pm. Free.) Shops catering to students cluster along **University Blvd.** at the west end of campus.

ENTERTAINMENT AND NIGHTLIFE

Tucson is a musical smorgasbord. While UA students rock and roll on Speedway Blvd., more subdued folks do the two-step in the country music clubs on N. Oracle. Pick up a copy of the free *Tucson Weekly* or the weekend sections of *The Star* or *The Citizen* for current entertainment listings. Throughout the year, the city of the sun presents **Music Under the Stars** (792-9155, for dates and times) a series of sunset concerts by the Tucson Symphony Orchestra. During **Downtown Saturday Night,** on the first and third Saturday of each month, Congress St. is blockaded for a celebration of the arts with outdoor singers, crafts, and galleries. On the last Thursday of every month, **Thursday Night Art Walk** lets you mosey through downtown galleries and studios. Call the **Tucson Arts District** (624-9977) for more info.

Club Congress, 311 E. Congress (622-8848), has DJs during the week and live bands on weekends (cover $4). The friendly hotel staff and a cast of regulars make it an especially good time. (Drink specials $1.50. Open daily 9pm-1am.) **The Rock,** 136 N. Park. (629-9211), caters to a college crowd with live shows and Friday night Battles of the Bands (cover $3-8; open 8pm-1am on show days; call ahead). A good place for a quiet drink, **Bar Toma,** 311 N. Cart Ave. (622-5465), offers a wide selection of tequilas (open Sun.-Thurs. 11am-9pm, Fri.-Sat. 11am-10pm). For live blues and rock, try **Berky's on Fourth,** 424 N. 4th Ave. (622-0376; cover $1-3; open Mon.-Fri. 4pm-1am, Sat.-Sun. 11am-1am). Hit **IBT's** (882-3053), on 4th Ave. at 6th St., for the gay scene. Locals hang out on 4th Ave. at night; most of the bars have live music (and cover charges). Try **3rd Stone** (628-8844), corner of 4th Ave. and 6th St., or head up 4th Ave. to **O'Malley's** (623-8600) which has food, pool tables, and pinball.

An authentic Old West saloon, **Wild Wild West,** 4385 W. Ina Rd. (744-7744), plays continuous country western music that will draw you to the largest dance floor (6000 sq. ft.) in Arizona. Bring your two left feet for free dance lessons on Tuesday, Thursday, or Sunday. (Cover Fri.-Sat. $3; Wed. men pay $2, women get in free. Open Tues.-Fri. and Sun. 4pm-1am, Sat. and Mon. 5pm-1am.)

■ Near Tucson

A museum, zoo, and nature preserve rolled into one, the **Arizona-Sonora Desert Museum,** 2021 N. Kinney Rd. (883-2702; follow Speedway Blvd. west of the city as it becomes Gates Pass Rd., then Kinney Rd.), recreates a range of desert habitats, from cave to mountain, and features over 300 kinds of animals. Take at least two hours to see the museum—preferably in the cool morning hours when the animals have not yet begun their afternoon siesta. (Open daily 8:30am-5pm; Oct.-Feb. daily 7:30am-6pm. $8.75, ages 6-12 $1.75.)

North of the museum, the western half of **Saguaro National Park,** also known as the Tucson Mountain District (883-6366), has limited hiking trails and an auto loop. The paved nature walk near the visitors center passes some of the best specimens of Saguaro cactus in the Tucson area. (Visitors center open daily 8am-5pm. Park open 24hr.) **Gates Pass,** on the way to the Tucson Mountain Unit and the Desert Museum, is an excellent spot for watching the sun as it rises and sets.

Saguaro National Park East (733-5153), a.k.a. Rincon Mountain District, lies east of the city on the Old Spanish Trail; take I-10 east to Exit 279 and follow Vail Rd. to the Old Spanish Trail. Within the park, 128 mi. of trails and an 8-mi. scenic drive lead through the cactus forest. (Visitors center open daily 8am-5pm. $4 per vehicle, $2 per pedestrian.) Get a free permit from the visitors center for **backcountry camping** (go before noon). The **Colossal Cave** (647-7275) on Vail Rd. is the only dormant cave in the U.S. Guided tours (45min.) involve flagstone walking, 70°F temperatures, and fluorescent lights. (Open Mon.-Sat. 8am-6pm, Sun. 8am-7pm; Sept. 15-March 16 Mon-Sat. 9am-5pm, Sun. 9am-6pm. $6.50, ages 11-16 $5, ages 6-10 $3.50.) In the shadow of the National Park, the cacti on Mt. Lemmon, just east of town, often go unsung; it's worth the time to drive up the mountain and see them.

Over 20,000 warplanes, from WWII fighters to Vietnam War jets, park in ominous, silent rows at the **Davis-Monthan Air Force Base** (750-4570), 15 mi. southeast of Tucson. Low humidity and sparse rainfall combine to preserve the relics. Take the Houghton Exit off I-10, then travel west on Irvington to Wilmont. (Free tours Mon. and Wed. 9am; call ahead for reservations.) You can also view the 2-mi. graveyard through the airfield fence.

North of Tucson, the cliffs and waterfalls of **Sabino Canyon** (749-2861) provide ideal scenery for picnics and day hikes (tram through the canyon daily every ½hr. 9am-4:30pm). Call the canyon folk for best directions. **Sabino Canyon Tours,** 5900 N. Sabino Canyon Rd. (749-2327), runs a shuttle bus through the canyon for a 45-min. tour; 3 nights per month there is a moonlight tour. (Mon.-Fri. every hr. on the hr. 9am-4pm; off-season Sat.-Sun. every ½hr. 9am-4:30pm.)

■ Tombstone

Founded in the wake of a gold and silver rush of the 1870s, Tombstone rebounded from two devastating fires before the failure of its mines spelled death for the town. Yet "the town too tough to die" has made another comeback. By inviting visitors to view the barnyard where Wyatt Earp and his brothers kicked some serious butt, Tombstone has turned the minutes-long showdown at the **O.K. Corral** (457-3456), on Allen next to City Park, into a year-round tourist industry (open daily 8:30am-5pm; $2). The Boothill Gunslingers, the Wild Bunch, and the Vigilantes/Vigilettes perform **re-enactments** of famous gunfights (Mon.-Sat. 2pm at 4th and Toughnut; $2.50, ages 6-12 $1.50). Call Lou at the Legends of the West Saloon (457-3055) to arrange with one of these groups to treat a friend or relative to a **public mock hanging.** The voice of Vincent Price narrates the town's history in the **Tombstone Historama** (457-3456), while a plastic mountain revolves onstage and a dramatization of the gunfight is shown on a movie screen—oh gee, did we give it away? (Shows daily every hr. on the ½hr. 9am-4pm. $2.) Marshals such as John Slaughter battled scores of outlaws at the **Tombstone Courthouse** (457-3311), at 3rd and Toughnut (open daily 8am-5pm; $2, ages 12-18 $1, under 12 free). See the **tombstones** of Tombstone—the result of all of this wanton gunplay—on Rte. 80 just north of town (open daily 7:30am-7pm; free). On an entirely different note, the **Rose Tree Museum** (457-3326), at 4th and Toughnut, houses the largest rose tree in the world (open daily 9am-5pm; $2, under

14 free). The **Tombstone Chamber of Commerce and Visitors Center** (457-3929) welcomes y'all at 4th and Allen St. (open Mon.-Fri. 9am-5pm, Sat.-Sun. 9am-4pm).

The **Larian Motel** (457-2272), Rte. 80, near Allen St. on Fremont, is clean and very close to downtown. (Summer single $35, double $40; winter $45/55.) Hit the hay at the **Hacienda Huachuca Motel,** 320 Bruce St. (457-2201 or 800-893-2201), where John Wayne stayed (in room 4) during the 1963 shooting of *McLintock*. Behind the peeling-paint exterior lie cute little rooms with cute little televisions and mini-fridges. (Singles or doubles $27.)

Don Teodoro's, 15 N. 4th St. (457-3647), serves Mexican plates for less than $6 (open Mon.-Fri. 11am-2pm and 5-9pm, Sat.-Sun. 11am-9pm). Get some victuals at **Ol' Miner's BBQ and Cafe,** 10 S. 5th St. (520-457-3488), where burgers and other sandwiches run $3-6. (Fickle hours.) **Blake's Char-Broiled Burgers and BBQ Ranch,** 511B Allen St. (457-3646), slaps the cow on the bun starting at $3.50 (open Tues.-Sat. 11am-7pm, Sun.-Mon. 11am-6pm). For a bit of moonshine and country music, smell your way to **Big Nose Kate's Saloon** (457-3107), on Allen St., named for "the girl that loved Doc Holliday and everyone else too." Cowboy bartenders serve such specialty drinks as "sex in the desert." (Open daily 10am-midnight.) The **OK Cafe,** 220 E. Allen St. (457-3980), has an all meat Buffalo Burger for $6.

To get to Tombstone, career your Conestoga to the Benson Exit off I-10, then go south on Rte. 80. The nearest **Greyhound** station (586-3141 or 800-231-2222), is in **Benson** at the Benson Flower Shop on 4th St., a block away from downtown; the **Amtrak** (800-872-7245) station is across the street. **Mr. Reynolds Taxi** (457-3897), makes the trip from Benson to Tombstone ($20). **Area code: 520.**

■ Near Tombstone: Bisbee

One hundred miles southeast of Tucson and 35 mi. east of Sierra Vista, Bisbee is a mellow, hip town, known throughout the southwest as a chic arts colony. Although it lures tourists by advertising picture-perfect weather every day of the year, visitors may revel in Bisbee's close proximity to Mexico and its excellent, relatively inexpensive accommodations. The **Chamber of Commerce,** 7 Main St. (432-5421), distributes the newspaper, *Bisbee Now,* and a map of downtown. (Both free. Open Mon.-Fri. 9am-5pm, Sat.-Sun. 10am-4pm.)

Rest your head at the pleasant **Bisbee Grand Hotel,** 61 Main St. (800-421-1909), which offers rooms furnished with turn-of-the-century antiques. Full breakfast included with a night's stay ($44 and up). For cheaper rates, try the **Jonquil Inn,** 317 Tombstone Canyon (432-7371). All the rooms are clean and smoke-free. Call ahead in the winter (singles $33, doubles $36). For good, all-American fare, head to **Miner's Diner,** 1 Brewery Gulch (432-8098), heralded as the provider of the world's best chicken wings. Choose carefully between mild, hot, and atomic! ($1.85 for 6, $12 for 50. Open Sun.-Mon. 7am-4pm, Wed.-Sat. 7am-10pm.)

On the way into town, the **Queen Mines** (432-2071), Rte. 80 interchange entering Old Bisbee, ceased its mining activities in 1943, but continues to give 1½-hr. educational tours. Put on the miner's hat and jacket. (Tours leave at 9, 10:30am, noon, 2, and 3:30pm. $8.) The **Mining and Historical Museum,** 5 Copper Queen (432-7071), highlights the discovery of Bisbee's copper surplus and the fortune-seeking miners who tapped this resource. (Open daily 10am-4pm. $3, seniors $2.50, children 18 and under free.)

New Mexico

In 1540, an expedition led by Francisco Vasquez de Coronado left Mexico City for what is now New Mexico, hoping to conquer the legendary city of Cibola. There, it was said, silversmiths occupied entire streets, while gold, sapphires, and turquoise decorated every house. Coronado and his men found only Indian pueblos; they returned to Mexico, none the richer, in 1542. Coronado may have failed in his quest, but he did start a trend—travelers have sought out New Mexico's riches ever since. Today, most explorers come in search of natural beauty and adobe architecture rather than gold, but the spirit of the conquistadors seems to live on in the purse-toting New Yorkers fingering turquoise jewelry in Taos Plaza.

New Mexico serves as a haven for hikers, backpackers, mountain-climbers, and skiers. Six national forests within the state provide miles and miles of beautiful and challenging opportunities for lovers of the outdoors, while Sandía, Mogollon, and Sangre de Cristo fulfill a mountain-climber's upward longings.

PRACTICAL INFORMATION

Capital: Santa Fe.
New Mexico Dept. of Tourism: 491 Old Santa Fe Trail, Santa Fe 87501 (800-545-2040), open Mon.-Fri. 8am-5pm. **Park and Recreation Division,** Villagra Bldg., P.O. Box 1147, Santa Fe 87504 (505-827-7465), open Mon.-Fri. 8am-5pm. **U.S. Forest Service,** 517 Gold Ave. SW, Albuquerque 87102 (505-842-3292). Open Mon.-Fri. 7:45am-4:30pm.
Time Zone: Mountain (2hr. behind Eastern). **Postal Abbreviation:** NM.
Sales Tax: 6.4%.

NORTHERN NEW MEXICO

■ Santa Fe

Santa Fe lies at the convergence of the **Santa Fe Trail,** running from Independence, MO, and **El Camino Réal** ("Royal Road"), running from Mexico City. The settlers who traveled these trails have left an indelible imprint on Santa Fe. During the Mexican War, the Americans wrested control of the city from the Mexicans. But the Mexican influence has not died; a 1957 zoning ordinance required all downtown edifices to conform to Spanish Pueblo style. On certain buildings, adobe plaster fails to cover traces of formerly Victorian façades. In spite of the illiberal uniformity of its architecture, free-thinkers and artists have flocked to Santa Fe, where they coexist with Native Americans, retirees, tourists, and jewelry hawkers. A casual *paseo* down Canyon Rd., the local artist's turf, will give you a better feel for the town than a visit to Santa Fe's plaza and museums.

PRACTICAL INFORMATION

Tourist Office: The Santa Fe Convention and Visitors Bureau, 201 W. Mary St. (800-777-2489). Pick up the useful *Santa Fe Visitors Guide.* Open Mon.-Fri. 8am-5pm. There's an **information booth** at Lincoln and Palace, open in summer Mon.-Sat. 9am-4:30pm. Visitors from abroad should gallop on down to **Santa Fe Council on International Relations,** 100 E. San Francisco St., in the La Fonda Hotel #281. Open Mon.-Fri. 9am-noon.
Buses: Greyhound, 858 St. Michael's Dr. (471-0008 or 800-231-2222). To Taos (2 per day, 1½hr., $16.80) and Albuquerque (4 per day, 1½hr., $11.30). Open Mon.-Fri. 7am-5:30pm and 7:30-9:35pm, Sat.-Sun., open when there are buses.
Trains: Amtrak, nearest station in **Lamy** (466-4511 or 800-872-7245), 13mi. away on Country Rd. 41. Call 982-8829 for shuttle to Santa Fe $14. Open daily 9am-5pm.
Public Transportation: Santa Fe Trails (984-6730) has 7 bus routes throughout the city (runs Mon.-Sat. 6:30am-7:30pm). Bus #6 leaves once every ½hr. from the downtown hub, on Sheridan Ave. 1 block from the plaza between Marcy St. and Palace Ave., going to the museums on Camino Lejo. 50¢, ages 6-12 25¢. **Shuttlejack** (982-4311) runs to the Albuquerque airport (12 per day, $20) and during the summer, to the opera (1 per day, $10 round-trip) from downtown hotels. Reserve 1 day in advance.

Car Rental: Budget Rent-a-Car, 1946 Cerrillos Rd. (984-8028). $42 per day, $185 per week. Must be 25 with major credit card. Open Mon.-Fri. 8am-6pm, Sat.-Sun. 8am-5pm.

Taxis: Capital City Taxi, 438-0000. $2 initial charge, $1.30 per mi.

Crisis Line: Rape Abuse Help Line, 800-551-0008.

Emergency: 911.

Post Office: 120 S. Federal Pl. (988-6351), in the Montoya Office Bldg., next to the Courthouse. Open Mon.-Fri. 7:30am-5:45pm, Sat. 9am-1pm. **ZIP code:** 87504. **Area code:** 505.

Except for the museums southeast of the city center, most restaurants and important sights in Santa Fe cluster within a few blocks of the **downtown plaza** and inside the loop formed by the **Paseo de Peralta.** Narrow streets make driving troublesome; park your car and pad the pavement. You'll find **parking lots** behind Santa Fe Village, near Sena Plaza, and one block east of the Federal Courthouse near the plaza, or use metered spaces (2 hr. max.) on the streets just south of the plaza. Pick up a *Downtown Parking Guide* at the visitors center. Parking is also available along the streets near the galleries on Canyon Road.

ACCOMMODATIONS AND CAMPING

For the low-down on budget accommodations, call the **Santa Fe Detours Accommodations Hotline** (986-0038). Hotels in Santa Fe tend to be very expensive. As early as May, they become swamped with requests for **Fiesta de Santa Fe** (early Sept.) and **Indian Market** (third week of Aug.). Make reservations early or plan to sleep standing up. At other times, look to the **Cerrillos Rd.** area for the best prices, but *use caution* and evaluate the motel (read: see the room) before checking in. At many of the less expensive motels, bargaining is acceptable. The adobe **Santa Fe Hostel (AAIH/ Rucksackers),** 1412 Cerrillos Rd. (988-1153), 1 mi. from the bus station and 2 mi. from the plaza, has a kitchen, a library, large dorm-style beds, and chores. (Office open daily 7am-11pm. $13, nonmembers $15; linen $2. B&B rooms $25 shared bath, $33 private bath; no discount for members; no credit cards; reservations needed in Aug.)

To camp around Santa Fe, you'll need a car. The **Santa Fe National Forest** (988-6940) has campsites and free backcountry camping in the beautiful Sangre de Cristo Mountains. The **Black Canyon Campground,** 8 mi. northeast of Santa Fe on Rte. 475, has 40 sites ($6). Four mi. farther, you can camp for free at one of **Big Tesuque's** seven sites. More free camping lurks at **Aspen Basin** (10 sites, 3mi. beyond Big Tesuque on Rte. 475). Neither Big Tesuque nor Aspen Basin has drinking water. (All three open May-Oct.; call the National Forest for info.) Another option is **KOA Santa Fe** (466-1419), Exit 290 on I-25N; follow the signs. (Sites $16, hookup $21. Open March-Oct.)

FOOD

Spicy Mexican food served on blue corn tortillas is the staple in Santa Fe. Bistros near the plaza dish up chilis to a mixture of government employees, well-heeled tourists, and local artists. Wander a few blocks away from the plaza to find smaller Mexican restaurants where the locals eat. Or, simply try the fragrant fajitas and fresh lemonade at one of the grill carts in the plaza.

Tomasita's Santa Fe Station, 500 S. Guadalupe (983-5721), near downtown. Locals and tourists line up for their blue corn tortillas and fiery green chili dishes ($5-8). Indoor and outdoor seating. Open Mon.-Sat. 11am-10pm.

Josie's, 225 E. Marcy St. (983-5311). The "J" is Spanish—say it like Hosie's. Incredible Mexican lunches and multifarious mouth-watering desserts worth the 20-min. wait. Specials $5.50-6.50. Open Mon.-Fri. 11am-3pm.

The Shed, 113½ E. Palas Ave. (982-9030), up the street from the plaza. The shed feels like an open garden, even in the enclosed section. Vegetarian quesadilla

($6.25) and amazing chicken enchilada verde ($8.50). Lunch 11am-2:30pm; dinner Wed.-Sat. 5:30-9pm.

Tia Sophia's, 210 W. San Francisco St. (983-9880), is where the locals eat. It looks and feels like a diner (the servers are quick and curt) but the food is exceptional. There is a new lunch special daily ($5.25-5.75), but the most popular item is the Atrisco ($5.75)—chile stew, cheese enchilada, beans, posole, and a sopapilla. Arrive before noon for the fastest service. Open Mon.-Sat for breakfast 7-11am, and lunch 11am-2pm.

SIGHTS

The **Plaza de Santa Fe** is a good starting point for exploring the museums, sanctuaries, and galleries of the city. Since 1609, the plaza has held religious ceremonies, military gatherings, markets, cockfights, and public punishments.

The four museums run by **The Museum of New Mexico** (827-6451; 24 hrs.) have identical hours. A three-day pass bought at one museum admits you to all four. (Open Tues.-Sun. 10am-5pm. Single visit $5, 4-day pass $8.) The **Palace of the Governors,** 100 Palace Ave. (827-6483), on the north side of the plaza, is the oldest public building in the U.S., and was the seat of seven successive governments after its construction in 1610. The *haciendas* palace is now a museum with exhibits on Native American, Southwestern, and New Mexican history. The craft and jewelry displays in front of the palace often have cheaper and better quality wares than you'll find in the "Indian Crafts" stores around town. Across Lincoln St., the **Museum of Fine Arts,** 107 W. Palace Ave. (827-4468), inhabits a large adobe building on the northwest corner of the plaza. Exhibits include works by major Southwestern artists, including Georgia O'Keeffe and Edward Weston, an amazing collection of 20th-century Native American art, and temporary exhibitions of more recent works. The other two museums lie southeast of town on **Camino Lejo,** just off Old Santa Fe Trail. The **Museum of International Folk Art,** 706 Camino Lejo (827-6350), 2 mi. south of the plaza, houses the Girard Collection which includes over 100,000 works of folk art from around the world. A gallery handout will help you appreciate the fascinating, though jumbled, exhibit. Next door, the **Museum of American Indian Arts and Culture,** 710 Camino Lejo (827-6344), displays Native American photographs and artifacts.

Although not part of the Museum of New Mexico, the **Institute of American Indian Arts Museum,** 108 Cathedral Place (988-6281), downtown, houses an extensive collection of contemporary Indian art. (Open March-Dec. Mon.-Sat. 10am-5pm, Sun. noon-5pm; Jan.-Feb. closed Mon. $4, students and seniors $2, under 16 free.)

About 5 blocks southeast of the Plaza lies the **San Miguel Mission** (983-3974), on the corner of DeVargas St. and the Old Santa Fe Trail. Built in 1710, the mission is the oldest functioning church in the U.S. Inside, glass windows at the altar look down upon the original altar built by Native Americans. (Open Mon.-Sat. 9am-4:15pm, Sun. 1:30-4:30pm; Nov.-April Mon.-Sat. 10am-3:45pm, Sun. 1:30-4:30pm. Donation suggested.) The United States' **Oldest House** (983-8206), just down DeVargas St. from the mission, dates from about 1200AD. The house, built by Pueblos, contains the remains of a Spaniard named Hidalgo, who allegedly bought a love potion from a woman who lived there and started kissing everything in sight. He was beheaded several days later—so much for free love. (Open Mon.-Sat. 9am-5pm. $1.) Take a picture for a buck, or buy a 20¢ postcard. Enter through the ice cream parlor and dessert shop (cones $2).

To find your way to where the **real artists live and sell their work,** head away from the Plaza; on San Francisco Dr., take a left on Alameda St., a right on Paseo de Paralta and a left on Canyon. Wander in and out of the galleries and indoor/outdoor cafés. Don't miss the **Hahn Ross Gallery,** 409 Canyon Rd. (984-8434), where the art is hip, affordable, and enjoyable (open 10am-5pm).

ENTERTAINMENT AND NIGHTLIFE

Native American ceremonies, fairs, and arts and crafts shows complement Santa Fe's active theater scene and the roster of world-famous musicians who frequently play in the city's clubs. The **El Farol,** 808 Canyon Rd. (983-9912), features up-and-coming rock and R&B musicians (shows nightly 9:30pm; cover changes for every band). **Old Santa Fe Trail** has several other night clubs. **414,** (986-9971) a gay/lesbian bar, is one of them. Find the *Santa Fe Reporter,* or *Pasatiempo* magazine in the Friday *Santa Fe New Mexican,* for more nightlife information.

The **Santa Fe Opera,** P.O. Box 2408, Santa Fe 87504-2408 (982-3855), 7 mi. north of Santa Fe on Rte. 84, performs in the open, against a gorgeous mountain backdrop. Nights are cool here; bring a blanket. The downtown box office is at the **El Dorado Hotel,** 309 W. San Francisco St. (986-5900), in the gift and news shop. ($20-110, standing-room $10-15—call the day of the show for specific prices.) **Shuttlejack** offers bus service from downtown for performances (see Practical Information, p. 655). The **Santa Fe Chamber Music Festival** (983-2075) celebrates the works of great baroque, classical, and 20th-century composers in the St. Francis Auditorium of the Museum of Fine Arts. (July to mid-Aug. Mon.-Thurs. 8pm, Fri.-Sat. 8pm, Sun. 6pm. Tickets $20-35.)

In August, the nation's largest and most impressive **Indian Market,** floods the plaza, as tribes from across the U.S. put up over 500 exhibits of fine arts and crafts. The **Southwestern Association on Indian Affairs** (983-5220) has more info.

Don Diego De Vargas' peaceful reconquest of New Mexico in 1692 marked the end of the 12-year Pueblo Rebellion, now celebrated in the three-day **Fiesta de Santa Fe** (988-7575). Held in early September, the celebration reaches its height with the burning of the 40-ft. *papier-mâché* **Zozobra** "Old Man Gloom." Festivities include street dancing, processions, and political satires. Most events are free. The *New Mexican* publishes a guide and a schedule for the fiesta's events.

■ Near Santa Fe

Bandelier National Monument, 40 mi. northwest of Santa Fe (take U.S. 285 to Rte. 4, then follow signs), features some of the most amazing pueblos and cliff dwellings in the state (accessible by 50mi. of hiking trails), as well as 50 square mi. of dramatic mesas, ancient ruins (*kivas* and remains of stone houses), and spectacular views of surrounding canyons. The most accessible, **Frijoles Canyon,** is the site of the **visitors**

"Now I Am Become Death, the Destroyer of Worlds."

At the outset of WWII, two scientists who had successfully tested fission at the University of Chicago asked Albert Einstein to write a letter to FDR requesting government support for research of atomic energy. Thus began the **Manhattan Project,** an intensely secret scientific enterprise with one explicit purpose: to build an atomic bomb for military use and, hopefully, to do it before the Germans. **Los Alamos, NM,** was chosen as a base for the endeavor because of its remote location, sparse population, and flat terrain—ideal conditions in which to test a nuclear device. Over the next few years, the most eminent scientists in the country convened in Los Alamos, laboring under exhilarating but also stressful and isolated conditions. Each scientist and his family had a pseudonym when they left town, and all identification claimed they lived at "PO Box 163, Santa Fe, NM." On July 16, 1945, at 5:30am, it was clear that the scientists had finally achieved their goal: a test bomb was detonated on top of a steel tower, generating an explosive power equivalent to **15,000 to 20,000 tons of TNT.** Elation and satisfaction quickly gave way to feelings of fear and hesitation—the workers had done their job, but the end product, capable of vast and instantaneous devastation, was rightfully frightening. Although many who had been involved in the project lobbied to prevent use of the weapon, their pleas could not reverse the momentum of the U.S. government, determined to end the war with a minimum of U.S. casualties. The bomb was used twice against the Japanese, at Hiroshima on Aug. 6 and at Nagasaki on Aug. 9, killing several hundred thousand civilians; Japan surrendered five days later.

center (672-3861, ext. 518; open summer 8am-6pm, spring and fall 9am-5:30pm, and winter 8am-4:30pm). A 5-mi. hike from the parking lot to the Río Grande takes you on a 700-ft. descent into the mouth of the canyon, past two waterfalls, and through fascinating mountain scenery. A two-day, 20-mi. hike leads from the visitors center to **Painted Cave**, decorated with over 50 Anasazi pictographs, then to the Río Grande. The hike is quite strenuous. Free permits are required for backcountry hiking and camping; pick up a topographical map ($9) of the monument area at the visitors center. A less taxing self-guided one-hour tour takes you through pueblo **cliff dwellings** near the visitors center. After the tour you can continue your hike by traversing the additional ½ mi. to the **ceremonial caves**, which offer an incredible view of the surrounding area. (Park entrance $5 per vehicle, $3 per pedestrian; good for 7 days.) The 95-site **Juniper Campground**, ¼ mi. off Rte. 4 at the entrance to the monument, has the area's only camping (sites $8, Golden Age passport ½-price; no reservations).

Pecos National Historical Park, located in the hill country 25 mi. southeast of Santa Fe on I-25 and Rte. 63, features ruins of a pueblo and a Spanish mission church. The small park includes an easy 1-mi. hike through various archaeological sites. Especially noteworthy are Pecos's renovated *kivas*—underground ceremonial chambers used in Pueblo rituals—built after the Rebellion of 1680. Off-limits at other ruins, the *kivas* in Pecos are open to the public. (Open daily 8am-dusk; Labor Day-Memorial Day 8am-6pm. Entrance $2 per person, $4 per car.) The monument's **visitors center** (757-6032) has a small, informative museum and a 10-min. film shown every ½ hour (open summer Mon.-Sat. 10am-4pm, Sun. 1-5pm; summer Mon.-Sat. 9:30am-4:30pm, Sun. 11am-5pm; free with park entrance). The park is not accessible by public transportation. If you make it there, you can pitch a tent in the backcountry of the **Santa Fe National Forest**, 6 mi. north on Rte. 63 (see Santa Fe Accommodations, p. 656).

If you find yourself on the road to Taos, stop by **La Iguana** (852-4540), on Rte. 68 in the town of **Embudo**. The place functions as a café, a gift shop, and an Elvis memorial, serving up Love Me Tender Burrito Plates ($6) and velvet portraits of the King ($13). Forget Las Vegas; ¡Viva La Iguana! (Open April-Oct. daily 10am-6pm.)

The **Bradbury Science Museum** (505-667-4444), 15th and Central, in Los Alamos, has exhibits and memorabilia from the Manhattan Project (see graybox, below) and World War II. (Sat.-Mon. 1-5pm, Tues.-Fri 9am-5pm. Free.)

■ Taos

The many artists who now inhabit Taos are but the latest in a diverse series of settlers lured by the fertility and stark beauty of the Taos Valley region. First came the Native American tribes, whose pueblos still speckle the valley. In the 17th century, Spanish missionaries and farmers attempted to convert the Native Americans to Christianity while farming alongside them. The 20th century has seen the town invaded by artists, such as Georgia O'Keeffe and R.C. Gorman, who have been captivated and inspired by Taos's untainted beauty. Aspiring artists still flock to the city, but recent trends indicate that the next generation of immigrants may be a mixed bag of pleasure-seekers and spiritualists who come to take advantage of Taos's natural surroundings. Each year a growing number of hikers and skiers infest the nearby mountains, more rafters brave the nearby whitewater of the Río Grande, and more New Agers get the vibe which draws them to the desert.

Practical Information In town, Rte. 68 becomes Paseo del Pueblo. Drivers should park on Placitas Rd., 1 block west of the plaza. Taos's **Chamber of Commerce**, 1139 Paseo del Pueblo Sur (758-3873 or 800-732-8267), just south of town at the Rte. 68/Rte. 64 junction, distributes maps and tourist literature from their office (open daily 9am-5pm). **Greyhound** (758-1144 or 800-231-2222), on Paseo del Pueblo Sur near the Chamber of Commerce, provides two buses per day to Albuquerque (3hr., $21.50), Santa Fe (1½hr., $17), and Denver (8hr., $50). Buy tickets from the bus driver (open Mon.-Sat. 8:30am-6pm). **Faust's Transportation** (758-3410) operates taxis daily 7am-6pm. In an **emergency**, call the **police** (758-2216) or an **ambu-**

lance (911). Taos's **post office:** 318 Paseo Del Pueblo Norte (758-2081), ¼ mi. north of the plaza (open Mon.-Fri. 8:30am-5pm). **ZIP code:** 87571. **Area code:** 505.

Accommodations and Camping

The **Rio Grande Hostel (HI-AYH)** (758-0090 or 800-999-PLUM/7586), 15 mi. south of Taos on Rte. 68 in Pilar, rests above the Río Grande. Greyhound and airport shuttle buses between Santa Fe and Taos use the hostel as a flagstop. Kitchen facilities are available, as well as discounts on Río Grande rafting trips. (Office open daily 5-9pm. Dorm beds $10.60, nonmembers $13.50. Private rooms with bath $29, nonmembers $32.50. Bungalows for 2 $22.50, nonmembers $26; must use shared bath in hostel.) Relatively inexpensive motel rooms await at the **Taos Motel,** 1799 Paseo de Pueblo Sur (758-2524 or 800-323-6009), on Rte. 68 (singles $34-50, doubles $42-57). Next door, the **Taos RV Park** (758-2524 or 800-323-6009) offers tent sites ($13 for 2 people) and full hookups ($19 for 2 people). Between the town of Taos and the Ski Valley is the **Abominable Snowmansion Hostel** (776-8298), Ski Valley Rd., Rte. 150 in Arroyo, which features nice rooms with huge common areas. (Rooms in the summer $16, in winter $22. Private rooms $20/28.)

Camping around Taos is easy for those with a car. Up in the mountains on wooded Rte. 64, 20 mi. east of Taos, the **Kit Carson National Forest** operates three campgrounds. **Las Petacas** is free but has no drinking water. **La Sombra** and **Capulin,** on the same road, charge $5. Additionally, four free campgrounds line Rte. 150 north of town. **Backcountry camping** requires no permit in the forest. For more info, including maps of area campgrounds, contact the **forest service office,** 208 Cruz Alta Rd. (758-6200; open Mon.-Fri. 8am-4:30pm), or stop by their visitors center (open daily 9am-4:30pm), on Rte. 64 west of town.

Food

Restaurants congregate at Taos Plaza and Bent St. **El Patio de Taos Restaurant and Cantina** (758-2121), on Teresina Ln. between Taos Plaza and Bent St., serves excellent New Mexican and Mexican cuisine out of the oldest building in Taos (lunch entrees $6.25-9.75; dinner entrees $6.50-19; open daily 11:30am-10pm). **Le Pascal Café-Deli,** 115 E. Plaza St. (758-4205), in Taos Plaza, serves eggs, bagels, and the $6 breakfast burrito with 2 eggs, green chili, cheese, and salsa. Lunches range from salads ($2.25) to sandwiches; make your own for $6.50. Huge portions include macaroni salad and a pickle (open Mon.-Sat. 8am-8pm, Sun. 9am-5pm). In the rear of **Amigo's Natural Foods,** 326 Pueblo Rd. (758-8493), across from Jack Donner's, lurks a small, holistic deli which serves such nutritionally correct dishes as tofu on polygranulated bread, and features a huge juice bar (open Mon.-Sat. 9am-7pm, Sun. 11am-5pm).

Sights and Activities

Many early Taos paintings hang at the **Harwood Foundation's Museum,** 238 Ledoux St. (758-9826), off Placitas Rd. (open Mon.-Fri. noon-5pm, Sat. 10am-5pm, Sun. noon-4pm; $2). Other galleries, with works by notable locals, can be found in the **Plaza,** on **Kit Carson Rd.** or **Ledoux St.,** and in the village of **El Prado,** just north of Taos. Taos's galleries range from high-quality operations of international renown to upscale curio shops. The **Taos Arts Festival** celebrates local art in early October each year.

Though not a part of the local gallery circuit, the **Mission of St. Francis of Assisi,** Ranchos de Taos Plaza (758-2754), displays a "miraculous" painting that changes into a shadowy figure of Christ when the lights go out (open Mon.-Sat. 9am-noon, 1-4pm; $2). Exhibits of Native American art, including a collection of beautiful black-on-black pottery, grace the **Millicent Rogers Museum** (758-2462), north of El Prado St., 4 mi. north of Taos off Rte. 522. (Open daily 10am-5pm; Nov.-March. closed Mon. $4, students and seniors $3, ages 6-16 $2, families $8.) A visit to the **Mabel Dodge Luhan Home** (758-9456) provides a quiet retreat from the tourist-packed plaza. The salon's hostess drew such luminaries as D.H. Lawrence, Robinson Jeffers, and Jean Toomer to Taos. ($2.50 admission includes a cup of coffee or tea.)

Taos Pueblo (758-9593), remarkable for its five-story pink-and-white adobe mission church and striking silhouette, is one of the last inhabited pueblos; thus much of the pueblo remains off-limits to visitors. (Open daily 8:30am-4:30pm. $5 per car, $3 per pedestrian, students $1, under 12 50 ¢. Camera permit $5, sketch and video camera permit $10, painting permit $15.) Feast days highlight beautiful tribal dances; **San Gerónimo's Feast Days** (Sept. 29-30) also feature a fair and races. Contact the **tribal office** (758-9593) for schedules of dances and other info. Best known for its sparkling pottery molded from mica and clay, **Picuris Pueblo** (587-2519), 20 mi. south of Taos on Rte. 75 near Peñasco, is smaller, less-touristed, and somewhat more accessible. Ask for a guide to Northern New Mexican Indian pueblos at the Taos Visitors Center.

The state's premier ski resort, **Taos Ski Valley** (776-2291; 800-776-1111 for lodging info; 776-2916 for ski conditions), about 5 mi. north of town on Rte. 150, offers powder conditions in bowl sections and short but steep downhill runs which rival those of Colorado. Reserve a room well in advance if you plan to come during the winter holiday season. (Lift tickets $39, equipment rental $12 per day.) There are two smaller, family ski areas: **Angel Fire** (800-446-8117), Central Plaza and Hwy. 434, and **Eagle Nest** (800-494-9117). In summer, the ski-valley area becomes a hiker's paradise.

Taos hums with every New Age service on earth: vibrasound relaxation, drum therapy, harmony massage, and cranial therapy for starters. **Taos Drums** (800-424-DRUM/3786), 5 mi. south of the plaza on Rte. 68, features the world's largest collection of Native American drums (open Mon.-Sat. 9am-6pm, Sun. 11am-6pm). A bulletin board outside **Merlin's Garden,** 127 Bent St. (758-0985), lists activities such as drum therapy and massage (open when Jupiter aligns with Mars).

■ Albuquerque

The Anasazi tribes settled here nearly 2000 years ago. Ever since, Albuquerque has been considered a stopover on the way to another destination. In search of the legendary seven cities of gold, the infamous Spaniard Coronado and his entourage camped here for the winter. Over the years, Spanish settlers, and later the United States government, routed major transportation lines through Albuquerque; Rte. 66 still splits the city in two. Smart travelers should linger long enough to enjoy the mellow neighborhood near the University, the adobe old town surrounding the historic plaza, and the dramatic Sandía Mountains.

PRACTICAL INFORMATION

Tourist Offices: Albuquerque Convention and Visitors Bureau, 21st St. Plaza, Galleria Level (800-284-2282). Free maps and the useful *The Art of Visiting Albuquerque.* Open Mon.-Fri. 8am-5pm. After hours, call for recorded events info. **Old Town Visitors Center** (243-3215), at Plaza Don Luís on Romero N.W. across from the church. Open Mon.-Sat. 9am-7pm, Sun. 10am-5pm. They also have an info booth at the airport. Open daily 9am-5pm.

Airport: Albuquerque International, 2200 Sunport Blvd. S.E. (842-4366), south of downtown. Take bus #50 from Yale Blvd. and Central Ave. **Checkered Airport Express** (765-1234) shuttles into the city (around $8). A taxi downtown costs under $10, to Old Town $8.

Trains: Amtrak, 214 1st St. S.W. (842-9650 or 800-872-7245). Open daily 9:30am-5:45pm. 1 train per day to: Los Angeles (13hr., $100); Kansas City (17hr., $173); Santa Fe (1hr. to Lamy, $25; 15min. shuttle to Santa Fe, $14); Flagstaff (5hr., $86). Reservations required.

Buses: Greyhound (243-4435 or 800-231-2222) and **TNM&O Coaches** (242-4998) run from 300 2nd St. S.W., 3 blocks south of Central Ave. Both lines go to: Santa Fe (4 per day, 1½hr., $11.30); Flagstaff (4 per day, 6hr., $53); Oklahoma City (4 per day, 12hr., $56); Denver (4 per day, 10hr., $61); Phoenix (4 per day, 9hr., $43); Los Angeles (4 per day, 18hr., $69).

Public Transportation: Sun-Tran Transit, 601 Yale Blvd. S.E. (843-9200; open Mon.-Fri. 7am-5pm). Most buses run Mon.-Sat. 6am-6pm. Pick up maps at visitors centers, the transit office, or the main library. Fare 75¢, seniors and ages 5-18 25¢.
Taxis: Albuquerque Cab, 883-4888. $3.60 first mi., $1.60 per additional mi.
Car Rental: Rent-a-Wreck, 501 Yale Blvd. S.E. (242-9556 or 800-247-9556). Cars with A/C from $23 per day with 150 free mi.; 20¢ per additional mi. $130 per week. Insurance $11 per day, $70 per week. Must be 21 with credit card; under 25 surcharge $3 per day. Open daily 8am-5pm.
Equipment Rental: Mountains & Rivers, 2320 Central Ave. S.E. (268-4876), across from the university. Rents canoes ($45 per day, $80 per weekend), and roller blades ($10 per day, $15 overnight, $20 per 2 days). Open Mon.-Fri. 9:30am-6:30pm, Sat. 9am-5pm, Sun. noon-5pm. Deposit required; reservations recommended.
Hotlines: Rape Crisis Center, 1025 Hermosa S.E. (266-7711). Center open Mon.-Fri. 8am-noon and 1-5pm; 24-hr. hotline. **Gay and Lesbian Information Line,** 266-8041. Open daily 6-9pm.
Emergency: 911.
Post Office: 1135 Broadway N.E. (245-9469). Open Mon.-Fri. 8am-6pm. **ZIP code:** 87104. **Area code:** 505.

Central Ave. and the **Santa Fe railroad tracks** create four quadrants used in city addresses: Northeast Heights (N.E.), Southeast Heights (S.E.), North Valley (N.W.), and South Valley (S.W.). The all-adobe campus of the **University of New Mexico (UNM)** rests along Central Ave. N.E. from University Ave. to Carlisle St. **The Plaza** lies between San Felipe, North Plaza, South Plaza, and Romero, off Central Ave.

ACCOMMODATIONS AND CAMPING

Cheap motels line Central Ave., even near downtown—*use caution; many are dangerous.* Avoid decrepit motels or any place which seems to house transients; at night, look for bright, outdoor lighting. Consider spending a bit more money here. **Motel 6,** 1701 University Blvd. N.E., has singles for $40 and doubles for $46. The **University Lodge,** 3711 Central Ave. N.E. (266-7663), near campus, has basic motel rooms and a basic motel pool (summer singles $21, winter $25; doubles $29/32).

The **Route 66 Youth Hostel,** 1012 Central Ave. S.W. (247-1813), at 10th St., offers bunks in sparse, clean rooms, as well as beautiful, newly renovated private rooms. (Well-stocked kitchen; free food. Office open daily 7-11am and 4-11pm. Check-out 11am. Chores required. Bunks $11 with any affiliation. Private singles with shared bath $16, huge doubles $26. Linen $1. Key deposit $5. No reservations.) Ask the Route 66 owner about his other hostel, **Oscuro** (648-4007), where you can live on an actual ranch, and do outside chores in the chicken coop or garden.

Albuquerque North KOA (867-5227), off I-25, close to the Sandía Parks, has a super friendly staff and a free pancake breakfast. (Tent sites $20, 2 people $25, full hookup $27. Always make reservations the 1st 2 weeks of Oct. during the hot air balloon festival.) **Coronado State Park Campground** (867-5589), 1 mi. west of Bernalillo on Rte. 44, about 20 mi. north of Albuquerque on I-25, provides a unique camping experience near the haunting Sandía Mountains. Adobe shelters on the sites are a respite from the heat. (Toilets, showers, drinking water. 1-week max. stay. Open daily 7am-10pm. Sites $7, with hookup $11. No reservations.)

FOOD AND NIGHTLIFE

Tasty, inexpensive eateries border the University of New Mexico. Browse and graze at **Best Price Books and Coffee,** 1800 Central Ave. S.E. (842-0624), where you can chase pastries ($1-2.25), sandwiches ($3-5.25), and gourmet burritos ($2-3), with 12 different kinds of coffee ($1) or a mind-blowing "Psuper Psonic Psyber Tonic" ($3.50). (Open daily 7am-11pm.) With a soft-strumming guitarist and outdoor seating, **El Patio,** 142 Harvard St. S.E. (268-4245), beckons passersby to sit, relax, and down a few enchiladas. (Mexican plates $3-6. Open Mon.-Thurs. 11am-9pm, Fri.-Sat. 11am-

9:30pm, Sun. noon-9pm.) **Olympia Café,** 2210 Central Ave. (266-5222), serves gyros and souvlaki (each $3.25), as well as vegetarian dishes and combination platters ($5-7; open Mon.-Fri. 11am-10pm, Sat. noon-10pm). **Double Rainbow,** 3416 Central S.E. (255-6633), is a bakery, coffee shop, and ice cream store. The salads are large, fresh, and delicious, and the calories you save from your entree can go towards your dessert—which will be huge. (Salads $3.25-7, sandwiches $5-6.25. Open daily 6:30am-midnight.) **Zane Graze,** 308 San Felipe (243-4377), a pleasant café near the plaza, has sesame chicken salad in a pita ($6) and fresh Taos cow ice cream ($1.75; open Wed.-Mon. 9am-5pm, Tues. 10am-3pm).

Dig in your spurs at **Caravan East,** 7605 Central Ave. N.E. (265-7877), "where there is always a dancin' partner," and live music. (Fri.-Sat. $3 cover. Drink specials for women daily 5:30-7:30pm. Open daily 4:30pm-2am.) Urban music lovers hear rock, blues, and reggae bands at **Dingo Bar,** 313 Gold St. S.W. (246-0663), where drafts run $2-3.50 (Fri.-Sat. after 8pm cover $2-8, depending on the band; open daily 4pm-1:30am). On the "Downtown Bar Crawl," get into the Dingo and five other bars on Central Ave. for one $5 cover charge; pay at any of the bars. **EJ's** (268-2233), at the intersection of Yale Blvd. and Silver St., satisfies late-night caffeine cravings in airy environs with live music. (Open Mon.-Thurs. 7am-11pm, Fri. 7am-midnight, Sat. 8am-midnight, Sun. 8am-9:30pm.)

SIGHTS

Located just north of Central Ave. and east of Rio Grande Blvd., 1 mi. south of I-40, **Old Town** clusters around Albuquerque's Spanish plaza. New Mexican art, Albuquerque history, and various temporary exhibits are displayed at the **Albuquerque Museum of Art and History,** 2000 Mountain Rd. N.W. (242-4600; open Tues.-Sun. 9am-5pm; free). The **Rattlesnake Museum,** 202 San Felipe N.W. (242-6569), houses the world's most diverse display of rattlesnakes (open daily 10am-6pm; $2, children $1). Spike and Alberta, two statuesque dinosaurs, greet you outside the **New Mexico Museum of Natural History and Science,** 1801 Mountain Rd. (841-2800). Inside the museum, exhibits present the geological and evolutionary history of New Mexico. (Open daily 9am-5pm. $4.20, students and seniors $3.15, children $1.)

The **National Atomic Museum,** 20358 Wyoming Blvd. (845-6670), on Kirtland Air Force Base, tells the story of "Little Boy" and "Fat Man," the atomic bombs dropped on Hiroshima and Nagasaki. *Ten Seconds that Shook the World,* a 1-hr. documentary on the making of the atomic bomb, shows daily; times vary. (Open daily 9am-5pm. Free.) The Air Force base is a few miles southeast of downtown, east of I-25. Ask at the visitor control gate on Wyoming Blvd. for a museum visitor's pass, and be prepared to show *several* forms of ID.

The **Indian Pueblo Cultural Center,** 2401 12th St. N.W. (843-7270), just north of I-40 (take bus #36 from downtown), provides an introduction to the Pueblo reservations (open daily 9am-5:30pm; $3, students $1, seniors $2). The center's cafeteria hosts Pueblo dance performances on weekends at 11am and 2pm; stay to eat authentic Pueblo food (fry-bread $1.75; open daily 7:30am-3:30pm).

■ Near Albuquerque

Located at the edge of suburbia on Albuquerque's west side, **Petroglyph National Monument** (897-8814) features over 15,000 images drawn on lava rocks by Native Americans and Spanish settlers over the course of centuries. Short paved trails access small sections of the park's **Boca Negra,** but most of the area can be explored only by off-trail hiking. Take 40N to Coors Rd. N.; turn left on Montano, right on Unser, and follow the signs to the park. Or, take bus #15 to Coors Blvd. and transfer to bus #93. (Open daily 9am-6pm; off season 8am-5pm. $1, weekends and holidays $2.)

The **Sandía Peaks** were named by the Spanish for the pink color they turn at sunset (*sandía* means watermelon). Take Tramway Rd. from either I-25 or I-40 to the **Sandía Peak Aerial Tramway** (296-9585 or 298-8518 for recorded info), the world's longest aerial tramway. The thrilling ride to the top of **Sandía Crest** allows you to ascend the west face of Sandía Peak and gaze out over Albuquerque, the Río Grande Valley, and western New Mexico; the ascent is especially striking at sunset. (½-hr. trip, times vary. $9.50; combination chairlift and tram ticket $17. Visitors center at the peak is open Sun.-Thurs. 10am-7pm, Fri.-Sat. 10am-9pm.) A 7-mi. toll road (Rte. 536) leads to the summit of **Sandía Crest,** where the dazzling 1½-mi. ridge hike to **Sandía Peak** (10,678ft.) begins.

The **Sandía Ski Area** provides a beautiful 58-mi. driving loop. Take I-40 east up Tijeras Canyon 17 mi., then turn north onto Rte. 44. The road winds through lovely forests of Piñon and Ponderosa pines, oaks, and spruce, then descends 18 mi. through a gorgeous canyon, to Bernalillo. Rangers lead guided hikes on Saturdays; you'll need reservations for the challenging winter snowshoe hikes (242-9052). During the summer, hiking and mountain biking trails are open to the public only during specific hours; call for details.

■ Chaco Canyon

Sun-scorched and water-poor, **Chaco Canyon** seems an improbable setting for the first great settlement of the Anasazi people. They developed complex irrigation techniques and constructed five-story rock buildings while some Europeans were still living in wooden hovels. By the 11th century, the canyon residents had set up a major trade network with dozens of small satellite towns in the surrounding desert. The system collapsed around 1150AD the system collapsed and, with no food and little water, the Chacoans abandoned the canyon for greener pastures.

Chaco Canyon's ruins are the best-preserved sites in the Southwest. **Pueblo Bonito,** the canyon's largest town, demonstrates the skill of Anasazi masons. Among many low structures, one four-story-tall wall still stands. Nearby **Chetro Ketl** houses one of the canyon's largest *kivas,* a prayer room used in Chacoan religious rituals.

Chaco Canyon is now part of the **Chaco Culture National Historical Park.** The **visitors center** (505-988-6727 or 505-786-7014), at the east end of the canyon, contains an excellent free museum which exhibits Anasazi art and architecture and explains the sophisticated economic network by which the Chacoan Anasazi traded with the smaller Anasazi tribes of modern Colorado and northern Mexico. (Open Sun.-Thurs. 10am-7pm, Fri.-Sat. 10am-9pm, Labor Day-Memorial Day 8am-5pm. $2 per person, $4 per carload.)

Camping in Chaco requires a backcountry permit and $8. Arrive by 11am; there are only 64 sites. You can also make Chaco a day trip from **Gallup,** 92 mi. away, where cheap accommodations come easy. Bring food and water. Be sure to fill up your car's tank; there is no gas in the park.

The canyon lies 160-mi. and a 3½-hr. drive northwest of Albuquerque and 120 mi. south of Durango, CO. At the turn of the century, it took a government archaeologist almost a year to get here from Washington, D.C. In January 1996, the northern route changed. Today's visitor takes country road 7900 (3mi. east of **Nageezi**) from NM Hwy. 44. Use NM 57 from the south.

Just west of the Continental Divide on Rte. 53, 12 mi. southeast of the Navajo town of **Ramah,** sits **Inscription Rock National Monument** (505-783-4226), where Native Americans, Spanish *conquistadores,* and later pioneers left their marks while traveling through the scenic valley. Self-guided trails allow access to the rock and ruins deeper in the park. The **visitors center** includes a small museum as well as several dire warnings against emulating the graffiti of old (open daily 9am-7pm; in winter 9am-5pm). For those unable to resist the urge to inscribe, an alternate boulder is provided. Trails close 1 hr. before the visitors center.

SOUTHERN NEW MEXICO

■ Gila Cliff Dwellings and Silver City

The spectacular **Gila Cliff Dwellings National Monument** (536-9461) preserves over 40 stone and timber rooms carved into the cliff's natural caves by the Pueblo around 1200 AD. Ten to 15 families lived here, farming the mesa top, until they mysteriously disappeared in the early 1300s. Accessible only by a 44-mi. drive on Rte. 15 from Silver City in the southwest part of the state, the stunning road to the park climbs up and down mountains to the canyon of the Gila River (open Memorial Day-Labor Day 8am-6pm; winter 9am-4pm). The **visitors center** (536-9461), 1 mi. from the dwellings at the end of Rte. 15, shows an informative 14-min. film, provides a $1 map, and is the trailhead for a picturesque 1-mi. round-trip hike to the dwellings (open daily 8am-5pm, off season 8am-4:30pm). The surrounding **Gila National Forest** (536-2250) hosts more great hiking, as well as **free backcountry camping**.

The **Chamber of Commerce**, 1103 N. Hudson (538-3785), makes a good starting point for a trip to the area (open Mon.-Sat. 9am-5pm, summers also Sun. noon-5pm). Twice daily, **Silver Stage Lines** (388-2586 or 800-522-0162) has bus service to Silver City from the El Paso airport ($25 round-trip, home pickup $3 extra). **Las Cruces Shuttle Service** (800-288-1784) offers daily trips between Silver City and Deming (4 per day, $15), Las Cruces (4 per day, $25), and El Paso (3 per day, $32). Gila's and Silver City's **area code** is 505.

Beds and restaurants await in **Silver City,** 80 mi. west of I-25 on Rte. 152W. The squeaky clean hostel at **Carter House (HI-AYH),** 101 N. Cooper St. (388-5485), has separate men's and women's dorms, a kitchen, laundry facilities, and a huge wrap-around porch; a B&B occupies the upstairs. Check-in is officially 4-9pm. ($12, non-members $15. B&B singles $52, doubles $58-69.) The **Palace Hotel,** 106 W. Broadway (388-1811), has beautiful antique rooms (doubles from $29.50). Bring a healthy appetite to the **Red Barn Steakhouse,** 708 Silver Heights Blvd. (538-5666), for sandwiches ($5) and an all-you-can-eat salad bar (open Mon.-Sat. 11am-10pm, Sun. 11am-9pm). The **Silver City Museum,** 312 W. Broadway (538-5921), houses exhibits on the history of the town and unusual collections of local residents' treasure troves, past and present, including one man's post-WWII neckties, another couple's buttons, and the exhibit curator's Def Leppard paraphernalia (open Tues.-Fri. 9am-4:30pm, Sat.-Sun. 10am-4pm; free). The **New Mexico Cowboy Poetry Gathering** (538-3694) convenes in Silver City every August.

Truth or Consequences

In 1950, the popular radio show "Truth or Consequences" sought to celebrate its tenth anniversary by persuading a small town to change its name to that of the program. Surprisingly, several towns across the U.S. volunteered. The producers chose a town called Hot Springs, NM—T or C, NM was born. The town lies 60 mi. west of Gila Cliff Dwellings National Monument on I-25, an impressive 150-mi. drive south of Albuquerque, and the surrounding area includes a great collection of natural hot springs. If you want to spend several days at the Monument, T or C's **Riverbend Hot Springs Hostel (HI-AYH),** 100 Austin St. (894-6183), offers a place to soak your weary bones and rest your weary head; the hostel's large earthen tubs on the balcony are filled twice daily with healing water from T or C's hot springs. Located on the banks of the Río Grande, the hostel offers tours to the holy grounds of the Apache. Ask about horseback riding at Leroy's. (Teepees $11, tent sites $8 per person, dorm beds $12. Full private apartment $40, or try the "love boat" anchored on the river right outside the hostel.)

■ White Sands

Remember the sandbox? Located on Rte. 70, 15 mi. southwest of Alamogordo and 52 mi. northeast of Las Cruces, **White Sands National Monument** contains the world's largest gypsum sand dunes, constituting 300 sq. mi. of beach without ocean. Located in the Tularosa Basin between the Sacramento and San Andres mountains, the dunes were formed when rainwater dissolved gypsum in a nearby mountain and then collected in the basin's Lake Lucero. As the desert weather evaporated the lake, the gypsum crystals were left behind and eventually formed the continually growing sand dunes. Hiking, walking, or just rolling through the dunes provides hours of mindless fun; the brilliant white sand is particularly awe-inspiring at sunset. Summer evening events include 7pm sunset strolls with a ranger and 8:45pm lectures. The basin is also home to a missile test range and the **Trinity Site**, where the world's first atomic bomb was detonated in July 1945. You'll find the **visitors center**, P.O. Box 1086, Holloman AFB 88330 (479-6124), as you enter the park from Rte. 70. (Open 8am-7pm; mid-Aug. to Memorial Day 8am-4:30pm. Dunes' drive open 7am-10pm; off season 7am-sunset. $2, $4 per vehicle. Disabled access.)

To use the park's free **backcountry campsites,** you must register at the park headquarters. More free backcountry camping can be found at **Lincoln National Forest** (437-6030), 13 mi. to the east. **Aguirre Springs** (525-4341), 30 mi. to the west, claims to have free camping, but you pay $3 to enter. For info contact the **Forest Supervisor,** Lincoln National Forest, 1101 New York Ave., Alamogordo 88310. **Oliver Lee Memorial State Park** (437-8284), 10 mi. south of Alamogordo on U.S. 54, then 5 mi. east on Dog Canyon Rd., has a campground at the canyon mouth on the west face of the Sacramento Mountains. (Sites $7, with hookup $11. Park open daily 6am-9pm; **visitors center** open daily 9am-4pm. $3 per vehicle.)

Nearby **Alamogordo** is a good place to stay. Motels and restaurants front White Sands Blvd. **Motel 6,** 251 Panorama Blvd. (434-5970), off Rte. 70, has clean rooms, TV, HBO, a pool, free local calls, and a view (singles $27, doubles $33). **All American Inn,** 508 S. White Sands Blvd. (437-1850), is clean and reasonable with A/C and a pool (singles $28, doubles $30). Camping is available at the **Alamogordo KOA,** 412 24th St. (437-3003); it's close to downtown, and has a pool. (Tent sites $16, RV base rate $17.) Reach for the stars at the **Space Center** (437-2840 or 800-545-4021), 2 mi. northeast of U.S. 54. (Open daily 9am-6pm; Sept.-May 9am-5pm. Museum and Omni-Max theater $5.25, seniors and ages 6-12 $3.50, family rate $15.50.)

■ Carlsbad Caverns

Imagine the surprise of the first Europeans to wander through southeastern New Mexico when 250,000 bats appeared at dusk. The legendary bat population of Carlsbad Caverns led to the discovery of the caverns at the turn of the century, when curious frontiersmen tracked the bats to their home. Once there, miners mapped the cave in search of bat *guano,* an excellent fertilizer found in 100-ft. deposits in the cave. By 1923, the caverns had been designated a national park, and herds of tourists were flocking to this desolate region. **Carlsbad Caverns National Park** marks one of the world's largest and oldest cave systems, and even the most jaded spelunker will stand in awe of the unusual creations beneath the surface.

Practical Information The **Carlsbad Visitors Center** (785-2232; 24-hr. recording 785-2107) has replaced dung-mining with a gift shop, nursery, and kennel. For 50¢ you can rent a small radio that transmits a guided tour. (Open daily 8am-7pm; Labor Day-Memorial Day 8am-5:30pm.) **White's City,** a tiny, expensive town, which seems to be run by Best Western, lies on U.S. 62/180 20 mi. southeast of Carlsbad and 7 mi. from the caverns along steep, winding mountain roads and serves as the access point to the park. Flash floods occasionally close the roads, so call ahead. El Paso, TX is the nearest major city, 150 mi. to the west past **Guadalupe Mountains National Park** (see p. 536), 35 mi. southwest of White's City. **Greyhound,** in cooperation with

TNM&O Coaches (887-1108), runs two buses per day to White's City from El Paso ($26, $52 roundtrip) or Carlsbad ($4.20 roundtrip). Some of these routes use White's City only as a flag stop. White's City's **post office:** 23 Carlsbad Caverns Hwy. (785-2220), next to the Best Western Visitors Center (open Mon.-Fri. 8am-noon and 1-5pm); **ZIP code:** 88268; **area code:** 505.

Camping and Accommodations The **Park Entrance Campground** (785-2291), just outside the park entrance, provides water, showers, restrooms, and a pool (tent sites or full hookup $16; up to 6 people). Backcountry camping is free in the park; get a permit at the visitors center. For more nearby camping, see Guadalupe Mountains National Park, TX on p. 536. Drive to **Carlsbad,** 20 mi. north, for cheap motels. **La Caverna Motel,** 224 S. Canal (885-4151), requires reservations in summer (singles $25.44, doubles $27.66). Even less expensive motels lie farther down the road.

Sights Backcountry hiking is allowed in the Carlsbad Caverns National Park, but talk to rangers first. Most visitors take tours into the caves. The **Natural Entrance Tour** and the **Big Room Tour** are self-guided and take one hour each; plaques guide you along the way. The Big Room Tour, open 8:30am-3:30pm, has some wheelchair accessible sections. The Natural Entrance Tour, a more strenuous journey, is open 8:30am-2pm. ($5 each, Golden Age Passport holders $2.50, ages 6-15 $3.) The ranger-guided **King's Palace Tour** goes through four scenic rooms in one-and-a-half hours (tours on the hr.; $5, Golden Age Passport holders and ages 6-15 $2.50). Plan your visit to the caves for the late afternoon, and see the magnificent nightly **bat flight.** A ranger talk precedes the amazing ritual, in which an army of hungry bats pours out of the cave at a rate of 6000 per minute. (May-Oct. daily just before sunset.) Early-birds can catch them on the pre-dawn return.

For a rugged caving experience, visit the undeveloped **Slaughter Canyon Cave** (785-2232), formerly **New Cave.** Take a lot of energy and a car (there's no public transportation); the parking lot is 23 mi. down a dirt road off U.S. 62/180S, and the cave entrance is a steep, strenuous ½ mi. from the lot. Flashlight tours (bring your own flashlight) traverse the difficult and slippery terrain inside; there are no paved trails or handrails. Call to reserve at least two days in advance; the park limits the number of people allowed inside. (Tours 2hr., 1¼mi., 2 per day; Labor Day-Memorial Day Sat.-Sun. only. $8, Golden Age Passport holders and ages 6-15 $4.)

THE PACIFIC NORTHWEST

The drive of "manifest destiny" brought 19th-century pioneers to the Pacific Northwest, some of the most beautiful and awe-inspiring territory in the United States. Lush rainforests, snow-capped peaks, and the deepest lake on the continent all reside in this corner of the country. Oregon's Mt. Hood and Columbia River Gorge, Washington's Cascade Mountains, miles and miles of the Pacific Crest Trail, and a long, stormy coast inhabited by sea lions and giant redwoods draw rugged individualists and escapist urbanites. Moving up from California, Coastal Highway 101 hugs the Pacific Ocean, rising above the mist with over 200 miles of salty spray and breathtaking scenery.

Settled like jewels amid the wet and wild lands of the Pacific Northwest, the cities of this region sparkle with all the urban flair of their Northeastern counterparts. But unlike New York, Washington, D.C., or Boston, the cosmopolitan communities of Seattle and Portland have spectacular mountain ranges in their backyards. The Northwestern traveler can hike the Cascade Range by day and club-hop by night, or eat breakfast at Pike Place Market in Seattle and have dinner deep in the rainforest of the Olympic Peninsula.

For more comprehensive coverage of the Pacific Northwest, consult the handsome and intrepid *Let's Go: Alaska & The Pacific Northwest, 1997*.

Washington

Geographically, politically, and culturally, Washington is divided by the Cascade Mountains. The personality difference between the state's eastern and western halves is pervasive and long-standing. To "wet-siders" who live near Washington's coast, the term "dry-siders" conjures images of rednecks tearing through the eastern deserts and farmlands in pickup trucks. In the minds of dry-siders, the residents of Seattle and the rest of western Washington might be yuppified, liberal freaks too wealthy to respect rural livelihoods or wildlife. These stereotypes are colorful, but can't capture the full range of political views represented by Washingtonians. Like its ideological spectrum, Washington's terrain is all-encompassing: deserts, volcanoes, and the world's only non-tropical rainforest all lie within state boundaries. You can raft on Washington's rivers, sea kayak around the San Juan Islands, and build sand castles on the Olympic Peninsula. Mount Rainier has fantastic hiking, while the Cascades boast perfect conditions for nearly every winter recreational activity. Seattle and Spokane are draped in handsome, green landscapes, proving that natural beauty can be its own selling point.

PRACTICAL INFORMATION

Capital: Olympia.
Washington State Tourism, Department of Community, Trade, and Economic Development, P.O. Box 42500, Olympia 98504-2500 (360-586-2088 or 800-544-1800). Open Mon.-Fri. 9am-4pm. **Washington State Parks and Recreation Commission,** 7150 Cleanwater Ln., Olympia 98504 (360-902-8500 or 800-233-0321). Write to P.O. Box 42650 for an info and reservation packet. **Outdoor Recreation Information Center,** 2nd Ave., at Marion and Madison, 915 2nd Ave. Suite 442, Seattle 98174 (206-220-7450). Information on national parks and forests.

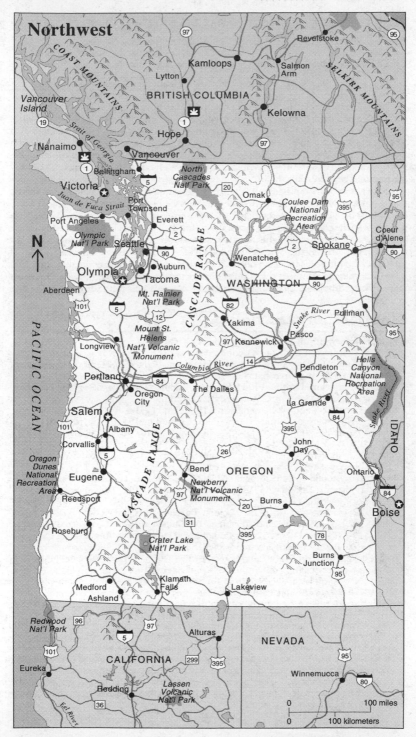

Northwest

Time Zone: Pacific (3 hr. behind Eastern). **Postal Abbreviation:** WA
Sales Tax: 8.1%

■ Seattle

Seattle's serendipitous mix of mountain views, clean streets, espresso stands, and rainy weather is the magic formula of the 1990s, attracting emigrants from across the U.S. Its seems that everyone living here today was born elsewhere. These newcomers come in droves, armed with college degrees and California license plates, hoping for job offers from Microsoft (in nearby Redmond) and a different lifestyle. Seattle has long been blessed with a magnificent setting and a vibrant artistic community, and the arrival of legions of energetic young people has made it one of the liveliest cities in the United States. A nearly epidemic fascination with coffee has also made it one of the most caffeinated.

Seattle sits on an isthmus, almost completely surrounded by water, with mountain ranges to the east and west. Every hilltop in Seattle offers an impressive view of Mt. Olympus, Mt. Baker, and Mt. Rainier. To the west, the waters of Puget Sound glint off downtown skyscrapers. The bright, watery light that reflects off Lake Washington and the Pacific Ocean highlights Seattle's spotless streets and graceful waterways. A daytrip in any direction leads travelers into wild and scenic country. But even the city itself, built on nine hills (Rome, you ask?) and separated into distinct neighborhoods, begs for exploration. Whatever you do in your travels around Seattle, *don't* be dismayed by the drizzle and *do* bring the umbrella. After all, you don't want to be tagged as an outsider.

PRACTICAL INFORMATION

Visitors Information: Seattle-King County Visitors Bureau (461-5840), 8th and Pike St., on the 1st floor of the **convention center.** Open Nov.-March Mon.-Fri. 8:30am-5pm; May-Oct. Mon.-Fri. 8:30am-5pm, Sat. 10am-4pm; Memorial Day-Labor Day Mon.-Fri. 8:30am-5pm, Sat.-Sun. 10am-4pm.

Parks Information: National Park Service, Pacific Northwest Region, 915 2nd Ave. #442 (220-7450). Open Mon.-Fri. 8am-4:30pm.

Airport: Seattle-Tacoma International (Sea-Tac) (431-4444 for general info) on Federal Way, south of Seattle proper. Take bus #174 or 194 from downtown.

Trains: Amtrak (800-USA-RAIL/872-7245, 382-4125 for arrival/departure times), King St. Station, at 3rd and Jackson St., next to the King Dome. To: Portland (3 per day, $26); Spokane (4 per day, $67); San Francisco (1 per day, $161); Vancouver, BC (4 per day, $29). Open daily 6am-10:15pm.

Buses: Greyhound (628-5526 or 800-231-2222), 8th Ave. and Stewart St. Daily to Sea-Tac Airport (2 per day, $5); Spokane (4 per day, $25); Vancouver, BC (8 per day, $25); Portland (9 per day, $15); Tacoma (6 per day, $4). Ticket office open daily 6:15am-9pm and 12:15-2am. **Green Tortoise Bus Service** (800-227-4766). Buses leave from 9th Ave. and Stewart St. on Thurs. and Sun. at 8am. To: Portland, OR ($15); Eugene, OR ($25); San Francisco, CA ($49); Los Angeles, CA (Thurs. only, $69). Reservations suggested 5 days in advance.

Ferries: Washington State Ferries (800-84-FERRY/33779) Colman Dock, Pier 52, downtown. Service from downtown to: Bainbridge Island, Bremerton in the Peninsula, and Vashon Island. Service from Fauntleroy in West Seattle to: Southworth in the Kitsap Peninsula and Vashon Island. Ferries leave daily, and frequently, 5am-2am. The **Victoria Line** (800-668-1167; 625-1880 for reservations), leaves Pier 48 daily at 1pm. The only auto ferry service available from Seattle to Victoria. One way: passengers $20.80, car and driver $46.15. Under 12 ½price.

Public Transportation: Metro Transit, Customer Assistance Office, 821 2nd Ave. (553-3000 for 24hr. info), in the Exchange Building downtown. Open Mon.-Fri. 8am-5pm. For 24hr. schedules and directions call 553-3000 or 800-542-7876. Fares are based on a 2-zone system. Zone 1 includes everything within the city limits ($1.10 during peak hours, 85¢ off peak). Zone 2 comprises anything outside the city limits ($1.60 peak, $1.10 off peak). Ages 5-18 always 75¢. Peak hours in both

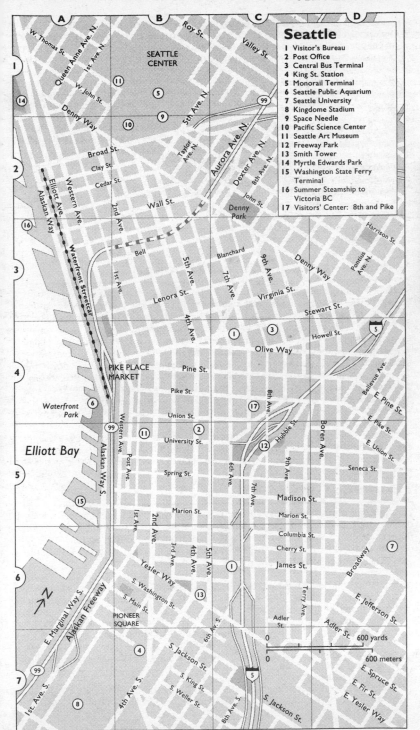

Seattle

1 Visitor's Bureau
2 Post Office
3 Central Bus Terminal
4 King St. Station
5 Monorail Terminal
6 Seattle Public Aquarium
7 Seattle University
8 Kingdome Stadium
9 Space Needle
10 Pacific Science Center
11 Seattle Art Museum
12 Freeway Park
13 Smith Tower
14 Myrtle Edwards Park
15 Washington State Ferry Terminal
16 Summer Steamship to Victoria BC
17 Visitors' Center: 8th and Pike

zones are Mon.-Fri. 6-9am and 3-6pm. Exact fare required. Transfers valid for 2hr. Weekend all-day passes $1.70. Ride free 5am-7pm daily in the downtown **ride free area,** bordered by S. Jackson St. on the south, 6th Ave. and I-5 on the east, Battery St. on the north, and the waterfront on the west. Always get a transfer. It can be used on any bus, including a return trip on the same bus within 2hr. All buses have free, easy-to-use **bike racks** and most are handicap accessible.

Car Rental: A-19.95-Rent-A-Car, 804 N. 145th St. (365-1995). $20 per day ($25 if under 21); 10¢ per mi. after 100 mi. Free delivery. Under 21 must have verifiable auto insurance. Credit card required.

Bicycle Rentals: The Bicycle Center, 4529 Sand Point Way (523-8300). $3 per hr. (2-hr. min.), $15 per 24hr. period. Credit card or license required as deposit. Open Mon.-Fri. 10am-8pm, Sat.-Sun. 10am-5pm.

Crisis Clinic: 461-3222. 24hr. **Seattle Rape Relief:** 1905 S. Jackson St., #102 (632-7273). Crisis counseling, advocacy, and prevention training. 24hr.

Gay Counseling: 1820 E. Pine (323-0220). Open Mon.-Fri. noon-9pm. **Lesbian Resource Center:** 1808 Bellview Ave. #204 (322-3953). Support groups, drop-in center, lending library, and workshops. Open Mon.-Fri. 9am-7pm.

Emergency: 911.

Post Office: 442-6340, at Union St. and 3rd Ave. downtown. Open Mon.-Fri. 8am-5:30pm. **General Delivery ZIP Code:** 98101.

Area Code: 206.

GETTING THERE AND GETTING AROUND

Seattle is a long, skinny city, stretched north to south on an isthmus between **Puget Sound** (to the west) and **Lake Washington** (to the east). The city is easily accessible by **car** via **I-5,** which runs north-south through the city, east of downtown; and by **I-90** from the east, which ends at I-5 southeast of downtown. From I-5, get to **downtown** (including **Pioneer Square, Pike Place Market,** and the **waterfront)** by taking any of the exits from James St. to Stewart St. Take the Mercer St./Fairview Ave. exit to the **Seattle Center.** The Denny Way exit leads to **Capitol Hill,** and farther north, the 45th St. exit will take you to the **University District.** The less crowded **Rte. 99,** also called **Aurora Ave.** or the Aurora Hwy., runs parallel to I-5 and skirts the western side of downtown, with great views from the **Alaskan Way Viaduct.** Rte. 99 is often the better choice when driving downtown, to Queen Anne, Green Lake, Fremont, or to the northwestern part of the city.

Downtown, avenues run northwest to southeast and streets southwest to northeast. Outside downtown, everything is simplified: with few exceptions, avenues run north-south and streets east-west. The city is split into **quadrants:** 1000 1st Ave. NW is a long walk from 1000 1st Ave. S.

ACCOMMODATIONS

The **Seattle International Hostel** is the best option for the budget traveler staying downtown. City-weary hostelers should head for the **Vashon Island Hostel** (sometimes called the "Seattle B"; see Vashon Island). **Pacific Bed and Breakfast,** 701 NW 60th St., Seattle 98107 (784-0539), can set you up with a single room in a B&B in the $45-70 range (open Mon.-Fri. 9am-5pm).

Seattle International Hostel (HI-AYH), 84 Union St. (622-5443), at Western Ave., right by the waterfront. Take bus #174, 184, or 194 from the airport (#194 from the north end of the baggage terminal is fastest), get off at Union St. and walk west. Free morning bagels and coffee, free linens, and a diverse crowd make up for the expanses of formica in this monstrously large hostel. Palatial lounge and library/TV room. Laundry ($1 wash, 75¢ dry), ride board in the lobby. Tickets for Aquarium, Omnidome, and passenger ferry. 7-day max. in summer. Front desk open 7am-2am. Checkout 11am. 24-hr. living room; no curfew. $16, nonmembers $19. Often full in summer; make reservations.

Green Tortoise Backpacker's Hostel, 1525 2nd Ave. (340-1222; fax 623-3207), between Pike St. and Pine St. Great location. 98 beds in 28 rooms plus 10 private rooms. Free breakfast and laundry. Pickup point for shuttle to Vancouver. No curfew. Beds $14, private rooms $30, private doubles $39.

Commodore Hotel, 2013 2nd Ave. (448-8868), at Virginia. Take bus #174 or 194 from airport. Get off at 4th Ave. and Virginia. Many rooms have pleasant decor and walnut furniture (with a few broken baseboards). Not the best area of downtown, but it's a great deal and 24-hr. security keeps out the riff-raff. Singles $31, with bath $45. 2 beds and bath $52. 2 hostel-style rooms offer a bare-bones bunk room and shared bath for $12. Weekly single $134.

Moore Motel, 1926 2nd Ave. (448-4851 or 448-4852), at Virginia. 1 block east from Pike Place Market. Next to the historic Moore Theater. Big rooms include 2 beds, TV, and a slightly moldy bathroom. A 24-hr. diner located off the lobby and cavernous halls with gargantuan heavy wooden doors makes the Moore seem like it hasn't changed since the 20s. Singles $34. Doubles $39. For HI members when the hostel is full, singles $30, doubles $35.

The College Inn, 4000 University Way NE (633-4441), at NE 40th St. For a place to crash near the University of Washington campus and its youthful environs, this is your best bet. Though singles are tiny and rooms have no TVs or private baths, turn-of-the-century bureaus and brass fixtures make a charming, if pricey, substitute. Private singles from $42. Doubles $60-75. Rates higher in summer. Credit card required.

FOOD

Though Seattlites appear to subsist on espresso and steamed milk, they have to eat sometimes. When they do, they seek out healthy cuisine—especially seafood. The best fish, produce, and baked goods can be purchased in the crowd-filled **Pike Place Market** (open Mon.-Sat. 6:30am-6pm, Sun. 6:30am-5pm). For excellent ethnic food, head for the **International District,** along King and Jackson St. between 5th and 8th Ave., which is packed with great eateries specializing in southeast Asian food. Fierce competition keeps prices low and quality high. Great food and interesting clubs abound in the **U District** near the University of Washington.

You can buy fish right off the boats at **Fisherman's Wharf,** at NW 54th St. and 30th Ave. NW in Ballard, along the route of bus #43. The wharf is usually open from 8am to 3 or 4pm. Seattle's cheapest food is available on University Ave. in the University district, where shops offer food from around the world for under $5. Or visit one of

---

I'll Have a Double Decaf Espresso—with a Twist of Lemon.

It all started in the early 70s, when Starbucks started roasting its coffee on the spot in Pike Place Market. Soon, Stewart Brothers Coffee, now "Seattle's Best Coffee," presented Starbucks with a rival, and the race was off for the best brew. Today, hundreds of bean-brands compete for the local market, and Seattle coffee drinkers often claim undying allegiance to one or another. Follow this basic guide to the lingo when ordering espresso drinks:

Short: 8oz.; **Tall:** 12oz.; **Grande:** 16oz.

Single: one shot of espresso; **Double:** two—add shots (usually about 60¢) until you feel you've reached your caffeine saturation point.

Espresso: the foundation of all espresso drinks—a small amount of coffee brewed by forcing steam through finely ground, dark-roasted coffee (pronounced es-PRESS-oh, not ex-PRESS-oh).

Cappuccino: espresso topped by the foam from steamed milk. Order "wet" for more liquid milk and big bubbles, or "dry" for stiff foam.

Latté: espresso with steamed milk and a little foam. More liquid than a "capp."

Americano: espresso with hot water—an alternative to classic drip coffee.

Macciato: steamed milk with a dollop of foam and espresso swirled onto the foam (not much coffee, but very pretty).

With skim (nonfat) milk, any of these drinks is called **skinny.** If all you want is a plain ol' cuppa joe, say "drip coffee," otherwise, shop workers will return your request for "coffee" with a blank stare.

Seattle's active **food coops,** at 6518 Fremont Ave. N (in Green Lake) and at 6504 20th NE (in the Ravenna District north of the university). While in Ravenna look for fine produce at **Rising Sun Farms and Produce,** 6505 15th Ave. NE at 65th St. (524-9741; open daily 8am-8pm). Capitol Hill, the U District, and Fremont all close off main thoroughfares on summer Saturdays for their farmer's markets.

Soundview Café (623-5700), on the mezzanine level in the Main Arcade down Flower Row. This wholesome, self-serve sandwich-and-salad bar offers fresh food, a spectacular view of Elliott Bay, and occasional poetry readings. Fill a $5 salad bar bowl with tabouli, pasta, salad, or fruit. The café also offers the most pleasant and accessible public seating in the market. Open daily 7am-5pm, Sun. 9am-3pm.

Piroshki, Piroshki, 1908 Pike Pl. (441-6068). For an ample, high-fat, and heavenly hands-on meal, try this Russian specialty. Piroshki are made of a croissant-like dough, baked around anything from sausage and mushrooms ($2.85) to apples doused in cinnamon ($3.50). Open daily 8am-7pm.

The Alibi Room, 85 Pike St. (623-3180), across from the Market Cinema in the Post Alley. Created by a local producer, The Alibi Room proclaims itself a local "indie filmmaker" hangout. Racks of screenplays, live music after 8pm (21+ only), and chic decor get an Oscar for ambience. Turkey/brie sandwiches for $6.50. Open daily 11am-2am.

Phnom Penh Noodle Soup House, 414 Maynard Ave. S. (682-5690). Head to the tiny upstairs dining room for a view of the pagoda in Hing Hay Park. The menu will help you decipher what you order. Try the Phnom Penh Noodle Special; some people come here weekly and never order anything else (of course, there are only 6 items on the menu). Everything $3.90. Open daily 8:30am-7pm.

House of Hong Restaurant, 409 8th Ave. S. (622-7997), at Jackson on the border of the International district. The most popular *dim sum* in town at $2 per dish; served daily 11am-5pm. Open Mon.-Thurs. 11am-10pm, Fri. 11am-midnight, Sat. 10:30am-midnight, Sun. 10:30am-10pm. Reservations recommended.

Mae Phim Thai Restaurant, 94 Columbia St. (624-2979), a few blocks north of Pioneer Sq., between 1st Ave. and Alaskan Way. Local businesspeople who pack this tiny, unassuming restaurant at lunch attest to the glory of good, inexpensive takeout. Close to the waterfront. All dishes $4.

Green Cat Café, 1514 E. Olive (726-8756), west of Broadway. This small coffee house is a favorite with locals for good reason. Wonderful breakfast and lunch fare; healthy diner food with a twist. Get down with the hobo scramble ($4.25). Open Mon.-Fri. 7am-7pm, Sat. 7:30am-7pm, Sun. 9am-7pm.

The Gravity Bar, 415 Broadway E. (325-7186), in the Broadway Market. Neo-healthy, organic food and crazy fruit and vegetable juices. Among the infamous fruit and vegetable drinks are Moonjuice (a melon/lime concoction, $3.50), Mr. Rogers on Amino Acid (16 fl. oz., $5), and the trendy new health elixir, **wheat grass juice.** Open Sun.-Thurs. 9am-10pm, Fri.-Sat. 10am-11pm.

Dick's, 115 Broadway Ave. E. (323-1300). A Broadway institution, made famous in Sir Mix-A-Lot's rap "Broadway." This pink, 50s-style, drive-in burger chain also has locations in Wallingford, Queen Anne, and Lake City. Try Dick's Deluxe Burger ($1.60). Soft serve kiddie cones cost 50¢. Open daily 10:30am-2am.

SIGHTS AND ACTIVITIES

The best way to take in the city skyline is from any one of the **ferries** that leave from the waterfront. It takes only two frenetic days to get a closer look at most of Seattle's major sights, as most are within walking distance of one another or are within the

Pop Quiz

What would you call a 12oz. espresso with an extra shot, steamed milk (skim, of course), and foam?
A: A tall, skinny, double latté.

Metro's Free Zone (see Getting Around, above). Beyond its cosmopolitan downtown, Seattle also boasts over 300 parks and recreation areas where you can enjoy the well-watered greenery. Don't pass up spending some time out of doors: take a rowboat out on Lake Union, bicycle along Lake Washington, or hike through the wilds of Discovery Park.

The new **Seattle Art Museum,** 100 University Way (654-3100 for a recording, TDD 654-3137), near 1st and University Way, boasts a stunning design by Philadelphian architect Robert Venturi. There's art *inside* the building, too. The museum has an entire floor dedicated to the art of Native Americans from the Pacific Northwest. Call for current info on films and lectures ($6, students and seniors $4, under 12 free; open Fri.-Wed. 10am-5pm, Thurs. 10am-9pm; free tours 12:30, 1, and 2pm; check for special tours at 7:15pm Thurs.). One block north of the museum on 1st Ave., inside the Alcade Plaza Building, is the free **Seattle Art Museum Gallery,** featuring current art, sculpture, and prints by local artists.

Westlake Park, with its Art Deco brick patterns and Wall of Water, is a good place to kick back and listen to steel drums. This small triangular park, on Pike St. between 5th and 4th Ave., is bordered by the original **Nordstrom's** and the gleaming new **Westlake Center,** where the monorail leaves for the Seattle Center. Nordstrom's is an upscale department store emphasizing customer service. (Travelers toting *Let's Go* may find **Nordstrom's Rack,** at 2nd and Pine, more appealing).

Bristling with excitement, and only a short walk down Pike St., is the **Pike Place Market,** a public market frequented by tourists and natives in equal proportions. (See Pike Place Market in Food, above.) The **Pike Place Hillclimb** descends from the south end of the Pike Place market down a set of staircases, past chic shops and ethnic restaurants to Alaskan Way and the **waterfront.** (An elevator is also available.) The **Seattle Aquarium** (386-4330) sits at the base of the Hillclimb at Pier 59, near Union St. Outdoor tanks re-create the ecosystems of salt marshes and tide pools. The aquarium's star attraction, the underwater dome featuring the fish of the Puget Sound and some playful harbor seals, fur seals, and otters, is worth the admission price. ($7.15, seniors $5.70, ages 6-18 $4.70, ages 3-5 $2.45; limited hours on holidays. Open daily 10am-5pm.)

Next to the aquarium is the **Omnidome** (622-1868), where movies play on a special rounded screen that produces a 3-D effect. ($7, seniors and students $6, ages 3-12 $5, second film $2; with admission to aquarium $11.95, seniors and ages 13-18 $9.25, ages 6-12 $8.50, under 12 $5.75. Films shown daily 9:30am-10pm.)

The 1962 World's Fair took place in Seattle, and the already entertainment-oriented city rose to the occasion by building the **Seattle Center.** Take the **monorail** from the third floor of the Westlake Center; for 90¢ (ages 5-12 70¢, seniors 35¢) it will ferry passengers to the Seattle Center every 15 minutes from 9am to midnight. The center stretches between Denny Way and W. Mercer St., and 1st and 5th Ave., and has eight gates, each with a model of the Center and a **map** of its facilities. The **Pacific Science Center** (443-2001), within the park, houses a **laserium** (443-2850) and an **IMAX theater** (443-4629). Evening IMAX shows run Thurs. through Sun. (tickets to IMAX *and* the museum $9.50, seniors and ages 6-13 $7.50, ages 2-5 $5.50). For info regarding special events and permanent attractions at the Center, call 684-8582 for recorded info or 684-7200 for a speaking human.

The **Space Needle** (443-2111), sometimes known as "the world's tackiest monument," is a useful landmark for the disoriented, and houses an observation tower and an expensive, 360° rotating restaurant. The Space Needle charges $8.50 (ages 5-12 $4) for a ride to its rotating top unless you have dinner reservations. (People have been known to make reservations with no intention of keeping them.)

Pioneer Square and Environs

From the waterfront or downtown, it's just a few blocks to historic Pioneer Square, at Yesler Way and 2nd Ave. The 19th-century warehouses and office buildings were restored in the 1970s and now house chic shops and trendy pubs. **Underground tours** (682-1511 for info or 682-4646 for reservations) take you into the subterranean rooms and passageways, explaining the sordid and soggy birth of Seattle. Be prepared for lots of tourists, comedy, and toilet jokes. Tours leave hourly from Doc Maynard's Pub, 610 1st Ave., and last 90 minutes ($6.50, seniors $5.50, students $5, and children $2.75; reservations recommended).

Klondike Gold Rush National Historic Park, 117 S. Main St. (553-7220), is an antique interpretive center that depicts the lives and fortunes of miners. Daily walking tours of Pioneer Square leave the park at 10am. Unlike the underground tours, these are free. To add some levity to this history of shattered dreams, the park screens Charlie Chaplin's 1925 classic, *The Gold Rush,* on the first Sunday of every month at 3pm (free; open daily 9am-5pm).

The International District

Three blocks east of Pioneer Square, up Jackson on King St., is Seattle's International District. Start your tour of the district by ducking into the **Wing Luke Memorial Museum,** 407 7th Ave. S (623-5124) to get a thorough description of life in an Asian-American community. This tiny museum houses a permanent exhibit on the different Asian nationalities in Seattle and temporary exhibits by local Asian artists. Thursdays are always free ($2.50, seniors and students $1.50, ages 5-12 75¢; open Tues.-Fri. 11am-4:30pm, Sat.-Sun. noon-4pm). The **community gardens** at Main and Maynard St. provide a peaceful and well tended retreat from the downtown sidewalks, though you may feel a bit like you're walking through someone else's back yard while you tiptoe through the turnips.

Capitol Hill

Capitol Hill is, in many ways, the pinnacle of Seattle's art culture, where alternative lifestyles and mainstream capitalism converge seamlessly. The district's leftist and gay communities set the tone for its nightspots, while the retail outlets include collectives and radical bookstores. Explore Broadway or walk a few blocks east and north for a stroll down the hill's residential streets, lined with well maintained Victorian homes. Bus #10 runs along 15th Ave. and makes more frequent stops; the #7 cruises Broadway, which is a more lively ride.

Volunteer Park, between 11th and 17th Ave. at E. Ward St., north of the main Broadway activity, lures tourists away from the city center. Bus #10 runs parkward up 15th Ave. To get to the park, it's better to take the #10 than the 7; it runs more frequently and stops closer to the fun stuff. The park boasts lovely lawns, an outdoor running track, and a playground. The outdoor stage often hosts free performances on summer Sundays. On rainy days, hide out amid the orchids inside the glass **conservatory** (free; open daily 10am-4pm, summer 10am-7pm). Be careful at night; the park has an unsavory reputation after dark. While in the park, visit the newly renovated **Seattle Asian Art Museum** (SAAM; 654-3100). A tour through the world-renowned collection of Asian art reveals Ming vases and ancient kimonos at every turn, as well as a hands-on exhibit on the current practise of traditional arts. Suggested admission $6, seniors and students $4, under age 12 free. Open Tues.-Sun. 10am-5pm, Thurs. 10am-9pm, closed Mon. Take bus #7 or 10 from downtown.

The **University of Washington Arboretum** (543-8800), 10 blocks east of Volunteer Park, houses the Graham Visitors Center, with exhibits on local plant life (visitors center is open daily 10am-4pm; winter Mon.-Fri. 10am-4pm and Sat.-Sun. noon-4pm) and is located at the southern end of the arboretum at Lake Washington Blvd. Take bus #11 from downtown. The Arboretum shelters superb **walking** and **running** trails, and boasts 4000 species of trees and shrubs and 43 species of flowers.

University District

With 33,000 students, the **University of Washington** is the state's cultural and educational center of gravity. To reach the district, take buses #71-74 from downtown, or #7, 43, or 48 from Capitol Hill. Stop by the friendly **visitors center,** 4014 University Way NE (543-9198), to pick up a campus **map,** and a self-guided tour book (open Mon.-Fri. 8am-5pm).

On the campus, visit the **Thomas Burke Memorial Washington State Museum** (543-5590), at NE 45th St. and 17th Ave. NE, in the northwest corner of the campus. The museum exhibits a superb collection on the Pacific Northwest's native nations, but it is slowly phasing out this collection to make room for its growing exhibit on Pacific Rim cultures. (Suggested donation $3, seniors and students $2, ages 6-18 $1.50; open daily 10am-5pm.)

WATERWAYS AND PARKS

A string of attractions festoon the waterways linking Lake Washington and Puget Sound. Houseboats and sailboats fill **Lake Union,** situated between Capitol Hill and the University District. **Gasworks Park,** a much-celebrated kite-flying spot at the north end of Lake Union, was recently converted to a park after its retirement from the oil refining business. **Gasworks Kite Shop,** 1915 N. 34th St. (633-4780), is one block north of the park (open Mon.-Fri. 10am-6pm, Sat. 10am-5pm, Sun. noon-5pm). To reach the park, take bus #26 from downtown to N. 35th St. and Wallingford Ave. N. If inspiration to go for a sail strikes while at the park, **Urban Surf,** across the street at 2100 N. Northlake Way (545-WIND/9463), rents windsurfing boards ($35 per day) and in-line skates ($5 per hr.).

Next to the lake is Woodland Park and the **Woodland Park Zoo,** 5500 Phinney Ave. N. (684-4800), best reached from Rte. 99 or N. 50th St. Take bus #5 from downtown. The park itself is overgrown, but the zoo habitats are realistic. The zoo specializes in conservation and research, and recently earned the Humane Society's highest standard of approval. The **elephant habitat** has enhanced the zoo's international reputation for creating natural settings. ($7.50; ages 6-17, seniors $5.75, students $5, ages 3-5 $4; parking $3, winter $1.50; open March 15-Oct. 15 daily 9:30am-6pm, Oct. 16-March 14 9:30am-4pm.)

Farther west, the **Hiram M. Chittenden Locks** (783-7059) along the Lake Washington Ship Canal on NW St., crowds to watch Seattle's boaters jockey for position. A circus atmosphere develops as boats traveling between Puget Sound and Lake Washington try to cross over (June 1-Sept. 30 daily 7am-9pm). If listening to the cries of frustrated skippers ("Gilligan, you nitwit!") doesn't amuse you, climb over to the **fish ladder** to watch homesick salmon hurl themselves up 21 concrete steps. Take bus #43 from the U District or #17 from downtown. The busiest salmon runs occur from June to September. Free tours of the locks start at 1, 2, and 3pm on summer weekends (open daily 10am-7pm; Sept.-June Thurs.-Mon. 11am-5pm).

Discovery Park (386-4236), on a lonely point west of the Magnolia District and south of Golden Gardens Park, at 36th Ave. W. and Government Way W. (take bus #24.), holds acres of minimally tended grassy fields and steep bluffs atop Puget Sound. The park is the largest in the Seattle area, with 534 bucolic acres. A **visitors center** looms large at the entrance (3801 W. Government Way), waiting to sell you a cheap and handy map (75¢). Shuttles ferry the elderly to the beach daily from 8:30am-5pm, June-Sept. At the park's northern end is the **Indian Cultural Center** (285-4425), operated by the United Indians of All Tribes Foundation, which houses the **Sacred Circle Gallery,** a rotating exhibit of Native American artwork (free; open Mon.-Fri. 9am-5pm, Sat.-Sun. noon-5pm).

Just south of **Lincoln Park,** along Fauntleroy Way in Fauntleroy, is the departure point for **passenger and auto ferries** to **Vashon Island** and **Southworth** (see Practical Information, above). Take bus #18 to Lincoln Park.

ENTERTAINMENT

If you're feeling sporty, you have many options. Two trade organizations, **PRO (Professional Rafters Organization)** (323-5485) and the **Washington State Outfitters and Guides Association** (392-6107), can provide advice and info on whitewater rafting. Whatever outfitter you use, be sure it lives up to basic safety standards. The **Northwest Outdoor Center,** 2100 Westlake Ave. (281-9694), on Lake Union, holds instructional programs in **whitewater** and **sea kayaking** during the spring, summer, and fall (2-evening intro to sea kayaking, including equipment $45). The center also leads sea kayaking trips through the San Juan Islands (open Mon.-Fri. 10am-8pm, Sat.-Sun. 9am-6pm). Visit **Recreational Equipment Inc. Coop (REI Coop),** 222 Yale Ave. for a 65ft. indoor climbing pinnacle and lessons on Northwest foliage. This paragon of woodsy wisdom (it also offers exploration and travel slide shows) can be seen from I-5. Take the Stewart St. exit. (Open Mon.-Sat. 10am-9pm, Sun. 11am-6pm. Rental area open 3hr. prior to store.)

More passive entertainment is available as well. During lunch hours in the summer-time, the free **"Out to Lunch"** series (623-0340) brings everything from reggae to folk dancing to the parks, squares, and office buildings of downtown Seattle. Pick up a schedule at the visitors center (see Practical Information). The **Seattle Opera** (389-7676, open Mon.-Fri. 9am-5pm, or Ticketmaster at 292-2787) performs at the Opera House in the Seattle Center throughout the year (students and seniors receive ½price tickets day-of performance, $15-30). Write to the Seattle Opera at P.O. Box 9248, Seattle 98109. The **Seattle Symphony Orchestra** (443-4747), also in Seattle Center's Opera House, performs a regular subscription series from September through June (rush tickets $6.50 and up) and a special popular and children's series. The **Pacific Northwest Ballet** (441-9411), one of only two ballet companies on the West Coast, runs a six-production, September to May season ($10 and up). The **University of Washington** offers a program of student recitals and concerts by visiting artists. Call the Meany Hall box office (543-4880; open Mon.-Fri. 10:30am-4:30pm).

Theater fans often get **rush tickets** at nearly half price on the day of the show (with cash only) from **Ticket/Ticket** (324-2744). The **Seattle Repertory Theater,** 155 W. Mercer St. (443-2222; open Mon. 10am-6pm, Tues.-Sat 10am-8pm), perform at the wonderful **Bagley Wright Theater** in Seattle Center ($10-38; Sun.-Fri. senior and student ½price tickets available30min. before each show). Other theaters to check out: **A Contemporary Theater (ACT),** 100 W. Roy St. (285-5110), at the base of Queen Anne Hill ($14-26; open Tues.-Thurs. noon-7:30pm, Fri.-Sat. noon-8pm, and Sun. noon-7pm); **Annex Theatre,** 1916 4th Ave. (728-0933; shows usually Thurs.-Sat. at 8pm and Sun. at 7pm; pay-what-you-can previews; tickets $10-12); and **Northwest Asian American Theater,** 409 7th Ave. S (340-1049), in the International District ($12, students, seniors, and handicapped $9; Thurs. $6).

Here's the scoop on movie theaters. **The Egyptian,** 801 E. Pine St. (32-EGYPT/34978), at Harvard Ave. on Capitol Hill, shows artsy films and is best known for host-ing the **Seattle International Film Festival** in the last week of May and the first week of June (regular tickets $6.75, seniors and children $4, matinee $4). **The Harvard Exit,** 807 E. Roy St. (323-8986), on Capitol Hill, shows quality classic and foreign films ($6.75, seniors and children $4, matinee $4). **Grand Illusion Cinema,** 1403 NE 50th St. (523-3935), in the U District at University Way, is one of the last independent the-aters in Seattle ($6, seniors and children $3, matinees $4). **United Artists Cinema,** 2131 6th Ave. and Blanchard, is known around Seattle as the $2 theater. Tickets to fairly recent Hollywood flicks cost $2, except for "midnight madness" shows which cost $5, but come with popcorn or a drink.

NIGHTLIFE

Many locals will tell you that the best spot to go for guaranteed good beer, live music, and big crowds is **Pioneer Square.** Most of the bars around the Square participate in a **joint cover** ($8) that will let you wander from bar to bar and sample the bands you like. **Fenix Café and Fenix Underground** (343-7740) and **Central Tavern** (622-0209) rock consistently, while **Larry's** (624-7665) and **New Orleans** (622-2563) fea-ture great jazz and blues nightly. **Kells** (728-1916) is a popular Irish pub with nightly celtic tunes. The **J and M Café** (624-1670) is in the center of Pioneer Square but has no music. All the Pioneer Square clubs shut down at 2am Friday and Saturday nights, and around midnight during the week.

Sit and Spin, 2219 4th St. This ain't no normal laundromat. Though the washers and dryers work, the real focus of this late-night café is the social scene. Bands with an alternative spin play on Fri. and Sat. nights. Café sells everything from local micro-brews on tap to urban style veggie bistro food (cashew chicken tarragon, $4.75) to boxes of laundry detergent. Open Sun.-Thurs. 9am-11pm, Fri.-Sat. 9am-2am. Kitchen opens daily at 11am.

Re-Bar, 1114 Howell (233-9873). A mixed gay and straight bar with a wide range of tunes and dancing on the wild side, depending on the night: Gay retro disco on Tues., hip-hop on Fri. Lots of acid jazz and **Greek Active** interactive theater on weekend nights. Cover $4. Open daily 9:30pm-2am.

Moe's Rockin' Café, 925 E. Pike St. (323-2373), 2 blocks east of Broadway. This new Seattle hotspot lures the best Seattle musicians to keep their corner of Capitol Hill hopping. Sun. and Mon. are dance nights—one floor R&B and one floor techno—and covers range from $4-12, depending on the show. Open daily 5pm-1:45am, and for brunch Sat.-Sun. 9am-3pm.

Kid Mohair, 1207 Pine St. (625-4444), south of Broadway on Capitol Hill. Dark wood and rich velvet in this new, cabaret-style gay club make for a glamorous scene. Dance to DJ'd house music with sequin bedecked drag queens for a $5 weekend cover. Open Mon.-Sat. 4pm-2am, Sun. 6pm-2am.

Red Door Alehouse, 3401 Fremont Ave. N. (547-7521), at N. 34th St., across from the Inner-Urban Statue. Throbbing with yuppified university students who attest to the good local ale selection and a mile-long beer menu. Hint: try the Pyramid Wheaton or Widmer Hefeweizen with a slice of lemon. Open daily 11am-2am. Kitchen closes at 11pm Sun.-Wed. and at midnight Thurs.-Sat.

The Trolleyman Pub, 3400 Phinney Ave. N. (548-8000). In the back of the **Red Hook Ale Brewery,** which rolls the most popular kegs on campus. Live blues on Sat. and jazz on Mon. Brewery open in summer, daily noon-5pm; pub open Mon.-Thurs. 9am-11pm, Fri. 9am-midnight, Sat. 11am-midnight, Sun. noon-7pm.

■ Near Seattle: Vashon Island

Only a short ferry ride from Seattle and an even shorter hop from Tacoma, Vashon (VASH-on) Island remains invisible to most Seattlites. Most of the island is undeveloped and covered in forests of Douglas firs, rolling cherry orchards, wildflowers, and strawberry fields, and almost any Vashon road eventually winds its way to a rocky beach. Four different **Washington State Ferries** (800-84-FERRY/33779) can get you to Vashon Island.

The island is wonderful for **biking,** and **Point Robinson Park** is a gorgeous spot for a picnic (from Vashon Hwy. take Ellisburg Rd. to Dockton Rd. to Pt. Robinson Rd.). More than 500 acres of woods in the middle of the island are interlaced with mild hiking trails, and several woodsy walks start from the **Vashon Island AYH Ranch Hostel (HI-AYH),** 12119 SW Cove Rd. (463-2592), west of Vashon Hwy. The hostel, sometimes called the **"Seattle B,"** is the island's only real budget accommodation and one of the main reasons to trek to Vashon. It's easy to reach: jump on any bus at the ferry terminal, ride to **Thriftway Market,** and call from the free phone inside the store, marked with an HI-AYH label. Judy will come pick you up if the hour is reasonable (note: she has never turned a hosteler away). A free pancake breakfast, free firewood, and a squadron of bikes available for borrowing await. Theme rooms add to the fun. The hostel accommodates 14 in bunk rooms. Hearty hostelers can also bed down under the stars in huge teepees or covered wagons. When all the beds are full, you can pitch a tent ($9, bicyclists $8, nonmembers $12; open May 1-Oct. 31). Get creative in the hostel kitchen with supplies from the large and slightly offbeat **Thriftway** downtown (open daily 8am-9pm).

■ San Juan Islands

The San Juan islands are an accessible treasure. Bald eagles spiral above haggard hillsides, pods of orcas spout offshore, and despite the lush vegetation it rains half as much as in Seattle. Two excellent guides to the area are *The San Juan Islands Afoot and Afloat* by Marge Mueller ($15) and *Emily's Guide,* a series of detailed descriptions of each island ($4, $11 for a set of three), available at bookstores and outfitting stores on the islands and in Seattle.

Washington State Ferries (800-84-FERRY/33779) depart Anacortes about nine times daily to **Lopez, Shaw, Orcas,** and **San Juan.** Not every ferry services all the islands. There are no reservations. Purchase tickets in Anacortes. Foot passengers travel in either direction between the islands free of charge. No charge is levied on eastbound traffic; pay for a vehicle only on **westbound** trips to or between the islands. To save on ferry fares, travel directly to the westernmost island on your itinerary and then make your way eastward to the mainland island by island. The ferries are packed in summer, so get there early. The ferry authorities accept only cash or in-state checks as payment. No credit cards. The **area code** in the San Juans is 360.

San Juan Island San Juan may be the last stop on the ferry route, but it is still the most frequently visited island. The **Whale Museum,** 62 1st St. (378-4710), exhibits skeletons, sculptures, and info on new research. ($4, seniors $3.50, ages 5-18 $1; under 5 free; open daily 10am-5pm; Oct. 1-Memorial Day daily 11am-4pm.) **Lime Kiln Point State Park,** on West Side Rd., provides the best ocean vista for **whale-watching** of all of the islands. Part of the **San Juan National Historic Park** is the **British Camp,** which lies on West Valley Rd. on the sheltered **Garrison Bay** (take Mitchell Bay Rd. east from West Side Rd.). Here, four original buildings have been preserved from the days of the bizarre "Pig War," including the barracks, now used as an **interpretive center.** If you're eager to **fish** or **clam,** pick up a copy of the Department of Fisheries pamphlet, *Salmon, Shellfish, Marine Fish Sport Fishing Guide,* for details on regulations and limits. The guide is available for free at **Ace Hardware and Marine,** 270 Spring St. (378-4622). Hunting and fishing licenses are required, and can be obtained from the hardware store (open Mon.-Sat. 8am-6pm, Sun. 9am-5pm). Check with the **red tide hotline** (800-562-5632) if you'll be gathering shellfish.

San Juan County Park, 380 Westside Rd. (378-2992), 10 mi. west of Friday Harbor on Smallpox and Andrews Bays, has cold water and flush toilets, but no RV hookups. (Vehicle sites $15. Hiker/biker sites $4.50.) **Lakedale Campgrounds,** 2627 Roche Harbor Rd. (378-2350), 4 mi. from Friday Harbor, has attractive grounds surrounded by 50 acres of lakes; boat rentals and swimming available. (Sites for 1-2 people with vehicle $16, July-Aug. $19, each additional person $3.50 (Open March 1-Oct. 15.) **La Cieba,** 395 Spring St. (378-8666), is a small Mexican joint supported by locals; join the feast with a fantastic burrito ($4.50; open Mon.-Sat. 11am-8pm, daily July 8-Aug).

Orcas Island Mt. Constitution overlooks Puget Sound from its 2409-ft. summit atop Orcas Island, the largest island of the San Juan group. A small population of retirees, artists, and farmers dwell here in understated homes surrounded by the red bark of madrona trees and green shrubs. With the largest state park in Washington and a youth hostel, Orcas has the best budget tourist facilities of all the islands. Unfortunately, much of the beach access is occupied by private resorts and is closed to the public. The trail to **Obstruction Pass Beach** is the best of the few ways to clamber down to the rocky shores. Because Orcas is shaped like a horseshoe, getting around is a chore. The ferry lands on the southwest tip. The island's main town, **Eastsound,** is 9 mi. northeast. Stop in a shop to get a free **map.** San Juan Transit (376-8887) provides bus service about every 90 minutes to most points on the island ($4-7).

Moran State Park, Star Rte. 22 (376-2326), in Eastsound, is unquestionably Orcas's star outdoor attraction. Over 21 mi. of hiking trails cover the park, ranging in difficulty from a one-hour jaunt around Mountain Lake to a day-long constitutional up the south face of **Mt. Constitution,** the highest peak on the islands. Pick up a copy of the trail guide from the **registration station** (376-2326). From the summit of Constitution, you can see other islands in the group, the Olympic and Cascade Ranges, Vancouver Island, and Mt. Rainier. Swim in two freshwater lakes easily accessible from the highway, or rent rowboats and paddleboats ($9 per hr.) from the park. Camping in the park offers all the best of San Juan fun: swimming, fishing, and hiking. There are four different campgrounds with a total of 151 sites. About 12 sites remain open year-round, as do the restrooms. Standard sites with hot showers cost $11. Hiker/ biker sites are $5.

For visitors info, call the Friday Harbor chamber of commerce (468-3663), or contact the Orcas Island chamber of commerce (376-2273). For Bike Rental go to Wildlife Cycle (376-4708), A St. and North Beach Rd., in Eastsound. (21-speeds $5 per hr., $20 per day. Open Mon.-Sat. 10:30am-5pm.). In an emergency, dial 911.

THE OLYMPIC PENINSULA

Due west of Seattle and its busy Puget Sound neighbors, the Olympic Peninsula is a remarkably different world. A smattering of logging and fishing communities and Indian reservations (along US Hwy. 101) lace the peninsula's coastline, but most of the ponderous land mass remains a remote backpacker's paradise. **Olympic National Park** dominates much of the peninsula and prevents the area's ferocious timber industry from threatening the glacier-capped mountains and temperate rainforests. However, the logging and fishing industries make living off the land the most common occupation on the peninsula. To the west the Pacific stretches to a distant horizon; to the north, the Strait of Juan de Fuca separates the Olympic Peninsula from Vancouver Island in Canada; and to the east, Hood Canal and the Kitsap Peninsula isolate this sparsely inhabited wilderness from the sprawl of Seattle.

■ Port Townsend

Unlike the salmon industry, the Victorian splendor of Port Townsend's buildings has survived the progression of time and weather. The entire business district has been restored and declared a national landmark. Port Townsend is a cultural oasis on an otherwise untamed peninsula. Walk down Water Street, and you'll be lured by cafes, book shops, and an immense ice cream parlor.

Port Townsend is full of huge Queen Anne and Victorian mansions. Of the more than 200 restored homes in the area, some have been converted into bed and breakfasts and are open for tours. The **Ann Starret Mansion,** 744 Clay St. (385-3205), has nationally renowned Victorian architecture, frescoed ceilings, and a free-hanging, three-tiered spiral staircase. Though it's now a bed and breakfast, people can take tours daily from noon-3pm ($2). **Point Hudson** is the hub of the small shipbuilding area and forms the corner of Port Townsend, where Admiralty Inlet and Port Townsend Bay meet. North of Point Hudson are several miles of beach, **Chetzemolka Park,** and the larger **Fort Worden State Park** (open daily 6:30amdusk). Port Townsend's **chamber of commerce,** 2437 E. Sims Way (385-2722), lies 10 blocks from the center of town on Rte. 20. Ask the helpful staff for a map and visitors guide. (Open Mon.-Fri. 9am-5pm, Sat. 10am-4pm, Sun. 11am-4pm.)

The Port Townsend area boasts two hostels. **Port Townsend Youth Hostel (HI-AYH),** Fort Worden State Park (385-0655), 2 mi. from downtown, is smack in the Fort, and has kitchen facilities. ($11, nonmembers $14, cyclists $9-13; family rooms available; July-Sept. $12, nonmembers $15; check-in 5-10pm, check-out 9:30am; no curfew.) **Fort Flagler Youth Hostel (HI-AYH),** Fort Flagler State Park (385-1288), is on handsome Marrowstone Island, 20 mi. from Port Townsend. From Port Townsend head south on Rte. 19, which connects to Rte. 116 east and leads directly into the park. It's fantastic for cyclists and solitude-seekers. ($11, nonmembers $13, cyclists $9-12; open by reservation only; check in 5-10pm, lockout 10am-5pm.)

By land, Port Townsend can be reached either from **U.S. 101** or from the **Kitsap Peninsula** across the Hood Canal Bridge. Washington State Ferries serve Winslow on Bainbridge Island; from there, several bus transfers will get you to Port Townsend; ask the Chamber of Commerce for details.

■ Olympic National Park

Amid the august Olympic Mountains, Olympic National Park unites 900,000 acres of velvet-green rainforest, jagged snow-covered peaks, and dense evergreen woodlands. This enormous region at the center of the peninsula allows limited access to four-wheeled traffic. There is no scenic loop, and only a handful of secondary roads attempt to penetrate the interior. The roads that do exist serve as trailheads for over 600 miles of hiking. The enormous amount of rain on the western side of the mountains supports rainforests dominated by Sitka spruce and western red cedars in the Hoh, Queets, and Quinault river valleys. The only people who seem not to enjoy this diverse and wet wilderness are those who come unprepared; a parka, good boots, and a waterproof tent are essential here.

Practical Information The **Olympic Visitors Center,** 3002 Mt. Angeles Rd. (452-0330), in Port Angeles, off Race St., fields questions about the whole park, including camping, backcountry hiking, and fishing, and displays a map of locations of other park ranger stations (open daily 9am-4pm; June-Sep. 8:30am-6pm). The park charges an **entrance fee** of $5 per car, $3 per hiker or biker, at the more built-up entrances, such as the Hoh, Heart o' the Hills, and Elwha—all of which have paved roads and toilet facilities. Entrance permit is good for 7 days. In an **emergency,** call 911. The **area code** in and around the park is 360.

The Park Service runs **interpretive programs** such as guided forest walks, **tidepool walks,** and campfire programs out of its ranger stations (all free). For a schedule of events, pick up a copy of the park newspaper from ranger stations or the visitors center.

July, August, and September are the best months to visit Olympic National Park, since much of the backcountry remains snowed in until late June, and only summers are consistently rainless (which, of course, brings flocks of fellow sightseers). Coming from Seattle, the best place to start an exploration of the park is the **Olympic Visitor's Center** (see above). **Backcountry camping** requires a free **backcountry permit,** available at ranger stations. Hwy. 101 continues on in a U shape, with Port Angeles at the top. From Port Angeles, many visitors drive down the western leg of the U and through the park quickly in one day.

Fishing within park boundaries does not require a permit, but you must obtain a state game department punch card for salmon and steelhead at local outfitting and hardware stores, or at the Fish and Game Department in Olympia. Though fishing is good in any of the park's 15 major rivers, the **Elwha River,** coursing through the northeastern part of the Park, is best for **trout.** The Hoh River, flowing west through the Park, is excellent for **salmon.** Ask at a fishing equipment store for current info.

Accommodations and Camping A roof can be a nice thing in the rainforest; find one at the **Rainforest Hostel,** 169312 U.S. 101 (374-2270), which has extremely knowledgeable proprietors. (Beds $10. Showers for non-guests $1.50.)

Olympic National Park, Olympic National Forest, and the State of Washington all maintain free **campgrounds.** The Washington Department of Natural Resources (DNR) publishes a guide to all its Washington sites which can be obtained at visitors centers and ranger stations. Pick up a **map** of the park and area from a ranger station. Free **National Park campgrounds** include **Ozette** (with drinking water) and **Queets** (no water). In addition, the National Park has many standard campgrounds (sites $10). Fees in **National Forest Campgrounds** range from $4-12; six campgrounds in the Hood Canal Ranger District are free. Reservations can be made for three Forest Service campgrounds (Seal Rock, Falls View, and Klahowga) by calling 800-280-CAMP/2267. Any ranger station can provide info on Park and Forest Service Campgrounds. Several **State Parks** are scattered along Hood Canal and the eastern rim of the peninsula (sites generally $10-16; occasionally $4-5). **Heart o' the Hills Campground** (452-2713; 105 sites), 5½ mi. from Port Angeles up Race Rd. inside Olympic National Park, is filled with vacationers poised to take **Hurricane Ridge** by storm the next day (sites $10, plus the $5 entrance fee). Farther west on U.S. 101, a short spur road to the south leads to two campgrounds along the waterfall-laced Elwha river: **Elwha Valley** (452-9191; 41 sites, $10), 5 mi. south off U.S. 101, and the nearby **Altaire** (452-9191; 30 sites, $10). Both have drinking water and flush toilets. **Fairholm Campground** (928-3380; 87 sites), 30 mi. west of Port Angeles at the western tip of Lake Crescent, has sites with drinking water ($10). **The Storm King Ranger Station** (928-3380) runs interpretive evening programs.

Farther west on U.S. 101, 13 mi. of paved road will get you to the **Sol Duc Hot Springs Campground** (327-3534), which has 80 sites with wheelchair-accessible restrooms. Nearby is the popular **Sol Duc Hot Springs Resort** (327-3583; open daily 9am-9pm, weekends in winter 9am-5pm, $6.25 per day, seniors $5.25), where retirees pay for a soak in the developed, chlorinated hot springs and eat at the restaurant or snack bar inside the lodge. Stop by the **Eagle Ranger Station** (327-3534; open June-Aug. daily 8am-5pm) for free backcountry permits. A better and less well-known way to harness the region's geothermal energy is to hike up to **Olympic Hot Springs.** Turn off at the Elwha River Road and follow it 12 mi. to the trailhead. The natural springs are about a 2½-mi. hike, but well worth it.

Outdoors Olympic National Park is home to one of the **world's only temperate rainforests.** Gigantic, thick old-growth trees, ferns, and mosses blanket the valleys of the Hoh, Queets, and Quinault Rivers, all on the west side of the Park. Although the forest floor is thickly carpeted with unusual foliage and fallen trees, rangers keep the many walking trails clear and well-marked. Many travelers seek out the **Hoh Rainforest Trail** which begins at the **Hoh Rainforest Visitor Center** (see below) and parallels the Hoh River for 18 mi. to Blue Glacier on the shoulder of Mount Olympus. Shy Roosevelt elk and northern spotted owl inhabit the area. The drive to the Hoh is stunning in some parts but some land belonging to the Department of Natural Resources has been, or is in the process of being, clear-cut. The first two campgrounds along the Hoh River Rd., which leaves U.S. 101 13 mi. south of Forks (see below), are administered by the DNR, accept no reservations, and are free. Drinking water is at the **Minnie Peterson** site only. DNR sites are uncrowded except in July and August; stay at one and drive to the Hoh trailhead to get a **map** and begin your rainforest exploration. You can obtain a separate **map** of the Hoh-Clearwater Multiple Use Area from the DNR main office, just off U.S. 101 on the north side of Forks. The **Hoh Rainforest Visitor Center** (374-6925) provides posters and permits (open daily 9am-6:30pm; Sept.-June daily 9am-3:30pm).

Several trailheads from U.S. 101 offer more solitude for the hiker as well as excellent opportunities to explore the **rainforest** amid surrounding ridges and mountains. The **Queets River Trail** follows the Queets River east from the free Queets Campground for 14 mi. The campground is at the end of a spur road that goes east from U.S. 101, 5 mi. south of the town of Queets (20 sites for tents only; open June-Sept.).

The Park and Forest Services and the Quinault Reservation share the land surrounding **Quinault Lake and River.** The Forest Service operates a day-use beach and an information center at the **Quinault Ranger Station,** South Shore Rd. (288-2444; open daily 9am-4:30pm; winter Mon.-Fri. 9am-4:30pm). From the Quinalt Ranger Station, it's 20 mi. to the **North Fork** trailhead, from which intrepid hikers can journey 44 mi. north across the entire park and finish at **Whiskey Bend.** Those with less time or energy have the dayhike options of one- to eight-mi. trails leaving from the Graves Creek Ranger Station. Between the coast and rainforest, the logging town of **Forks** on U.S. 101 offers cheap motels and food.

Piles of driftwood, imposing sea stacks, sculptured arches, and abundant wildlife lie along 57 mi. of rugged and deserted beaches. Bald eagles are often out on windy days, and whales and seals tear through the sea. The beaches are easily accessible from U.S. 101, between the Hoh and Quinault Reservations. The 15-mi. stretch of beaches begins in the north with **Ruby Beach** near Mile 165 on U.S. 101. South of Ruby Beach, at Mile 160, is **Beach #6,** a favorite whale-watching spot. Another three mi. south is **Beach #4,** with its beautiful tidepools. A unique 9-mi. loop trail starts at

Ozette Lake, north of Ruby Beach, heading through the rainforest along boardwalks, then along the beach.

Trivial Pursuiters take heed: Cape Flattery is the northwesternmost point in the contiguous U.S., and possesses enough interest outside of geographical trivia to make it worth the hour-long drive off U.S. 101. The town of Neah Bay, accessible from Rte. 112, is the westernmost point on the strait. In Neah Bay, the **Makah Cultural and Research Center** (645-2711), on Rte. 112, houses artifacts from an archaeological site at Cape Alava, where a huge mudslide 500 years ago buried and preserved a small Makah settlement. Once inside the reservation, the museum is on the first left, directly across from the Coast Guard station ($4, seniors and students $3; open daily 10am-5pm; Sep.-May Wed.-Sun. 10am-5pm). The Makah nation, whose recorded history goes back 2000 years, still lives, fishes, and produces artwork on this land.

■ Olympia

From the hilltop Capitol of Olympia, politicians keep an eye on the college students, local fishermen, and tourists below. The Evergreen State College campus lies just a few miles from the city center, and the super-liberal, highly pierced student body spills into town. Many locals scorn "Greeners," nostalgic for a time when Olympia was a small industrial city with a thriving fishing industry. But newcomers keep pouring into Olympia, and the capital of the Evergreen State continues to lure outsiders with more improvement projects, expanding local parks and wildlife refuges.

The crowning glory of Olympia is the **State Capitol Campus.** A free tour of the **Legislative Building** (586-8677) allows a peek at the public sphere. Only the tours can usher you into the legislative chambers, which are otherwise off-limits. (45-min. tours daily 10am-3pm; building open Mon.-Fri. 8am-5pm, Sat.-Sun. 10am-4pm.)

Every lunch hour, droves of state employees tumble forth from the capitol in spandex and sneakers and head for the various parks surrounding **Capitol Lake.** Trails begin in **Capitol Lake Park** at the west end of 7th Ave. and empty into the newly constructed **Heritage Park** with its $620,000 computerized, interactive fountain. Boats jam the Port in **Percival Landing Park** (743-8379), a reminder of Olympia's oyster-filled past. The **Yashiro Japanese Garden** (753-8380), at the intersection of Plum and Union, right next to City Hall, hoards hundreds of colorful plants behind its high walls, making it Olympia's very own secret garden. (Open 10am-dusk for picnickers and ponderers.)

Ten mi. south of the city is **Wolfhaven,** 3111 Offut Lake Rd. (264-4695 or 800-448-9653). Take Exit 99 off I-5, turn east, and follow the brown signs. The haven now hosts 40 wolves that have been reclaimed from zoos or illegal owners. Take a guided tour of the grounds ($5, ages 5-12 $2.50; May-Sep. 10am-4pm, Oct.-Apr. 10am-3pm) or join the Howl-In ($6, children $4; May-Sept. Fri.-Sat. 7-9:30pm). The **Nisqually National Wildlife Refuge** (753-9467), off I-5 between Olympia and Tacoma at Exit 114, offers a safe haven to 500 species of plants and animals as well as miles of open trail for the I-5-weary traveler to stop and meander. The trails are open daily during daylight hours ($2; office open Mon.-Fri. 7:30am-4pm).

Olympia State Capitol Visitors Center, P.O. Box 41020 (586-3460), on Capitol Way between 12th and 14th Ave. (signs on I-5 will direct you), provides detailed maps of both the capitol itself and the greater Olympia area (open Mon.-Fri. 8am-5pm). **Emergency** is 911. Olympia's **post office:** 900 S. Jefferson SE (357-2286; open Mon.-Fri. 7:30am-6pm, Sat. 9am-4pm). **ZIP code:** 98501. **Area code:** 360.

The motels in Olympia generally cater to lobbyists and lawyers rather than to budget tourists. Camping is the cheapest option. **The Grays Harbor Hostel,** 6 Ginny Ln. (482-3119), just off Rte. 8 in Elma, WA, 25 mi. west of Olympia, is a destination unto itself. A bed in this joint costs $10 and comes replete a hot tub, a spacious, 24hr. common room and a 3-hole golf course. Bikers can camp on the lawn for $6. To find the Klemps, take the fairground exit off Rte. 8 and make the first right. **Millersylvania State Park,** 12245 Tilly Rd. S. (753-1519), is 10 mi. south of Olympia. Take Exit 99 off I-5, then head south on Rte. 121. The park offers 216 tree-shrouded, reasonably spacious sites with pay showers and flush toilets (standard sites $11, RV hookups $16). **Capital Forest Multiple Use Area,** 15 mi. southwest of Olympia, off I-5 Exit 95, shelters 50 free campsites scattered among 6 campgrounds. The area is unsupervised, so lone travelers and women might be better off paying the $11 for Millersylvania.

There is potential for good eating along bohemian 4th Ave., east of Columbia, especially when the pace picks up during the school year. The **Olympia Farmer's Market,** 401 N. Capitol Way (352-9096), has a great selection of in-season fruits and berries; you can buy a fantastic cheap lunch here. (Open Mar.-Apr. Sat.-Sun. 10am-3pm, May-Sep. Thurs.-Sun. 10am-3pm, Oct. Fri.-Sun. 10am-3pm.) Try the "Legislator Dip" ($5.50) or a Spar burger ($6) at **The Spar Cafe & Bar,** 111 E. 4th Ave. (357-6444; open Mon.-Sat. 6am-9pm, Sun. 7am-8pm; bar open daily 11am-2am). Or dig the deluxe burrito ($4.50) and the vegetarian and vegan options at the **Smithfield Cafe,** 212 W. 4th Ave. (786-1725; open Tues.-Fri. 7am-8pm, Sat.-Sun. 9am-8pm).

Amtrak, 6600 Yelm Hwy. (800-872-7245), toots from Olympia to Seattle ($15) and Portland ($19) three times a day. **Greyhound,** 107 E. 7th Ave. (357-8667), at Capitol Way, runs buses to Seattle (6 per day, $8), Portland (7 per day, $15), and Spokane (3 per day, $29). (Open daily 7:30am-8pm.)

CASCADE RANGE

In 1859, an explorer making his way through the Cascade Range gushed: "Nowhere do the mountain masses and peaks present such strange, fantastic, dauntless, and startling outlines as here." Native people summed up their admiration more succinctly, dubbing the Cascades "Home of the Gods."

Intercepting the moist Pacific air, the Cascades divide Washington into the lush, wet green of the west and the low, dry plains of the east. The white-domed peaks of Mt. Baker, Vernon, Glacier, Rainier, Adams, and Mt. St. Helens are accessible by four major roads offering trailheads and impressive scenery. **U.S. 12** through White Pass approaches Mt. Rainier National Park and provides access to Mt. St. Helens from the north; **I-90** sends four lanes past the major ski resorts of Snoqualmie Pass; scenic **U.S. 2** leaves Everett for Stevens Pass and descends along the Wenatchee River, a favorite of whitewater rafters.

Rte. 20, better known as the **North Cascades Hwy.,** is the most breathtaking of the trans-Cascade highways and one of the most amazing drives in North America. From spring to fall it provides access to the wilderness of **North Cascades National Park.** Rte. 20 and U.S. 2 are often traveled in sequence as the **Cascade Loop.**

Greyhound runs on I-90 and U.S. 2 to and from Seattle, while **Amtrak** parallels I-90. The Cascades can only be explored properly with a car. The mountains are most accessible in July, August, and September; many high mountain passes are snowed in during the rest of the year. The Cascade range is attractive mainly to serious backpackers. Crowds are usually deterred by the day's climb to most flat spots. The best source of general info on the Cascades is the joint **National Park/National Forest Information Service,** 915 2nd Ave., Seattle 98174 (206-220-7450).

▓ Mount Rainier National Park

At 14,411 ft., Mt. Rainier (ray-NEER) presides over the Cascade Range. The Klickitat Native people called it *Tahoma,* "mountain of God," but Rainier is simply "the mountain" to most Washingtonians. Because of its height, Rainier creates its own weather. It juts up into the warm, wet ocean air and pulls down vast amounts of snow and rain. Clouds mask the mountain up to 200 days per year. Some 76 glaciers patch the slopes and combine with sharp ridges and steep gullies to make Rainier an inhospitable place for the 3000 determined climbers who clamber to its summit each year. Even for those who don't feel up to scaling the peak, there is plenty to explore in the old-growth forests and alpine meadows of Mt. Rainier National Park.

Practical Information Mt. Rainier is 90 mi. from Seattle. To reach the park from the west, drive south from Seattle on I-5 to Tacoma, then go east on Rte. 512, south on Rte. 7, and east on Rte. 706. **Rte. 706** is the only access road open year-round; snow usually closes all other park roads Nov.-May. The park **entrance fee** is $5 per car, $3 per hiker; the gates are open 24 hr. For **visitor information,** stop in at the **Longmire Hiker Information Center** (569-2211, ext. 3317), which distributes back-country permits (open Sun.-Thurs. 8am-4:30pm, Fri. 8am-7pm, Sat. 7am-7pm; closed in winter). **Paradise Visitors Center** (569-2211, ext. 2328) offers food, pay showers, and guided hikes. (Open Sun.-Fri. 9am-6pm; late Sept. to mid-Oct. 9:30am-6pm; mid-Oct. to winter 10am-5pm.) The **Sunrise Visitors Center** contains exhibits, snacks, and a gift shop (open June 25 to mid-Sept. Sun.-Fri. 9am-6pm, Sat. 9am-7pm). The **Ohanapecosh Visitors Center** offers info and wildlife displays (open daily 9am-6pm; May-June Sat.-Sun. 9am-6pm; closed mid-Oct. to April). All centers can be contacted by writing c/o Superintendent, Mt. Rainier National Park, Ashford 98304, or by calling 569-2211. **Rainier Mountaineering Inc. (RMI)** (569-2227), in Paradise, rents ice axes ($8.50), crampons ($8.50), boots ($16.50), packs ($16.50), and helmets ($6) by the day. Expert RMI guides also lead summit climbs, seminars, and special schools and programs. (Open May-Oct. daily 9am-5pm. Winter office: 535 Dock St. #209, Tacoma 98402; 627-6242.) In a park **emergency,** call 911 or 569-2211, ext. 2334. Rainier's **area code:** 360.

Accommodations and Food **Longmire, Paradise,** and **Sunrise** offer hotels and food that are often very costly. Stay in **Ashford** or **Packwood** if you must have a roof over your head. Otherwise, camp—isn't that what you're here for?

The **Hotel Packwood,** 102 Main St. (494-5431), is an old motel with good prices (singles $22, doubles from $25; no credit cards). The **Gateway Inn Motel,** 38820 Rte. 706, Ashford (569-2506), has cabins for two ($49; singles and doubles $35, with bath $40). **Whittaker's Bunkhouse,** 30205 SR 706 E., P.O. Box E, Ashford 98304 (569-2439), offers spiffy co-ed bunks (bring your own sleeping bag) and squeaky clean showers for $18. Traditional and costlier rooms are available.

Blanton's Market (494-6101), on Hwy. 123 in Packwood, is the closest decent supermarket to the Park and has an ATM in front (open daily 5am-10pm). **Ma & Pa Rucker's** (494-2651), on Hwy. 12 in Packwood, serves piping hot pizza (small $7, large $11), single scoops of ice cream for $1, and typical roadhouse burgers (open Mon.-Thurs. 8am-9pm, Fri.-Sun. 7am-10pm).

Camping Camping at the auto-accessible campsites from June through September is on a first come, first camped basis ($6-10). There are five such campgrounds in the park. Drive to **Ohanapecosh** (205 sites) for the serene high canopy of old-growth trees, to **Cougar Rock** (200 sites) for the strict quiet hours, to **Isput Creek** (29 sites) for the lush vegetation, and to **White River** (117 sites) or **Sunshine Point** (18 sites) for the panoramas. Sunshine Point is the only auto site open year-round.

With a **backcountry permit** (see Practical Information, above), hikers can use any of the free trailside camps scattered in the park's backcountry. Most have toilet facilities and a nearby water source, and some have shelters for groups of up to 12. Cross-country and alpine sites are high up the mountain on the glaciers and snow fields. *Fires are prohibited,* except in front-country campgrounds, and there size of a party is limited. **Glacier climbers** and **mountain climbers** intending to go above 10,000 ft. must register in person at ranger stations to be granted permits.

Outdoors All major roads offering scenic views of the mountain have numerous roadside sites for viewing. The roads to Paradise and Sunrise are especially pictur-esque. **Stevens Canyon Road** connects the southeast corner of the national park with Paradise, Longmire, and the Nisqually entrance, unfolding spectacular vistas of Rainier and the rugged Tatoosh Range.

Mt. Adams and Mt. St. Helens, not visible from the road, can be seen clearly from such **mountain trails** as **Paradise** (1½ mi.), **Pinnacle Peak** (2½ mi.), **Eagle Peak** (7 mi.), and **Van Trump Peak** (5½ mi.). For more info on these trails, pick up *Viewing Mount St. Helens* at one of the visitors centers.

A segment of the **Pacific Crest Trail (PCT),** running between the Columbia River and the Canadian border, crosses through the southeast corner of the park. The PCT is maintained by the U.S. Forest Service. Primitive **campsites** and **shelters** line the trail as it snakes through delightful wilderness areas. The **Wonderland Trail** winds 93 mi. up, down, and all around the Mountain. Hikers must get permits to make the arduous but stunning trek, and must complete the hike in 10-14 days. Call 569-2211, ext. 3317 for details on both hikes.

A trip to the **summit** of Mt. Rainier requires substantial preparation and expense. The ascent is a vertical rise of more than 9000 ft. over a distance of 9 or more mi.— usually taking two days. Permits for summit climbs now cost $15. Only experienced climbers should attempt the summit without a guide. Novices can sign up for a summit climb with **Rainier Mountaineering, Inc. (RMI)** (see Practical Information, above), which offers a one-day basic-climbing course followed by a two-day guided climb. For more info, contact Park Headquarters or RMI.

▓ Mount St. Helens

In a single cataclysmic blast on May 18, 1980, the summit of Washington's Mount St. Helens exploded into dust, creating a hole 2 mi. long and 1 mi. wide in what had been a perfect cone. Ash blackened the sky for hundreds of miles and blanketed the streets of nearby towns with inches of soot. Debris from the volcano flooded Spirit Lake, choked rivers with mud, and sent house-sized boulders tumbling down the mountainside. The blast leveled entire forests, leaving a stubble of trunks on the hills and millions of trees pointing arrow-like away from the crater.

Mount St. Helens National Volcanic Monument is steadily recovering from that explosion. Almost two decades later, the spectacle of disaster is freckled by signs of returning life—saplings push up past denuded logs, while insects and small mammals return to the blast zone. The mountain, like many other Cascade peaks, is still considered active and could erupt again, though the risk is now low.

Practical Information Because driving times around the Monument are long, a number of visitors centers and information stations line the highways surrounding the volcano, both inside and outside the monument itself. Plan the side you will approach the monument from, and find the most convenient visitors center. **Mount St. Helens National Volcanic Monument Visitors Center** (206-274-2100 or 206-274-2103 for 24-hr. recording), on Rte. 504, 5 mi. east of Castle Rock (Exit 49 off of I-5), is the first stop for most visitors. Interpretive talks and displays recount the mountain's eruption and regeneration, and are enhanced by a 22-min. film, and many hands-on activities. The center also provides info on lodgings, camping and mountain access (open May-Sept. daily 9am-5pm; call for winter hrs.). Both the **Pine Creek Information Center** (open June-Sept. daily 9am-6pm) in the south and the **Woods Creek Information Center** (open June-Sept. daily 9am-4pm) in the north are smaller than the main center, but are within 1 mi. of excellent viewpoints. Both offer displays, maps, and brochures on the area. In an **emergency,** call 911.

Following Rte. 504 from the west (Exit 40 off I-5), also know as the **Spirit Lake Memorial Hwy.,** is the quickest and easiest day trip to the mountain for most travelers—especially the Winnebago battalions and summer crowds. The **Mount St. Helens Visitors Center, the Coldwater Ridge Visitors Center,** and the **Johnston Ridge Observatory** line the way to the volcano. Along the **north** side, **U.S. 12** stretches from I-5 east, continuing to **Yakima.** Off U.S. 12 at Randle, Rte. 25 offers access to the **Iron Creek Campground, Windy Ridge,** and **Spirit Lake** (all laced with good hiking), and striking views of both the crater and the Blow Zone, where acres of blasted trees abut healthy forests. Rte. 503 parallels the **south** side of the volcano until it connects with **Rd. 90.** The Ape Cave lava formations and visitors center, as well as several campgrounds, are located along Rd. 90. Drivers should fill up their gas tanks before starting the journey, since fuel is not sold within the park. Mount St. Helens's **area code** is 360.

Camping There are two primitive **campgrounds** relatively near the crater. **Iron Creek Campground,** on Forest Service Rd. 25 near the junction with Rd. 76, has 98 sites ($8 each, call 800-280-2267 for reservations). **Swift Campground,** farther south on Forest Service Rd. 90, has 93 sites ($8 each, no reservations). Just west of Swift Campground on Yale Reservoir lie **Beaver Bay** and **Cougar Campgrounds,** both of which have toilets and showers (sites $8; for reservations call 503-464-5023). The monument itself contains no campground, but there are many in the surrounding national forest, and free dispersed camping (in unmaintained, primitive sites) is allowed in the monument and national forest.

Outdoors On the way west along Rd. 99, **Bear Meadow** provides the first interpretive stop, an excellent view of Mt. St. Helens, and the last restrooms before Rd. 99 ends at spectacular **Windy Ridge.** The monument begins just west of here, where Rd. 26 and Rd. 99 meet, at **Meta Lake.** Farther west along Rd. 99, frequent roadside turnouts reveal trees felled like match sticks and the stump-choked waters of **Spirit Lake.** For a serious hike, continue along **Independence Pass Trail #227** (3½ mi., 4-hr. roundtrip) to its intersection with **Norway Pass Trail,** which ends on Rte. 26. The entire hike is 6 mi. long, takes about five and a half hours, and requires a vehicle at both ends. The trail lies within the Blast Zone and fans say it's the best hike in the monument. Farther west, **Harmony Trail #224** (2 mi., 1½-hr. roundtrip) provides the only public access to Spirit Lake.

Even inside "the beast," there are accessible places. The **Pine Creek Information Station** lies 25 mi. south of the Rd. 25-Rd. 99 junction. Take Rd. 90 12 mi. west and then continue 2 mi. north on Rd. 83 to **Ape Cave,** a broken 2½-mi.-long lava tube formed in an ancient eruption. When exploring, wear a jacket and sturdy shoes. Lanterns may be rented for $3, or bring your own flashlights or Coleman lanterns.

The **Coldwater Ridge Visitors Center** (274-2131; fax 274-2129), 43 mi. east of Castle Rock and I-5 on Rte. 504, is a sprawling glass and copper building that's practically a free museum unto itself. The deck has a superb view of the cavity where the mountain's north side used to be and of **Coldwater Lake,** which was created by the eruption (open daily 10am-6pm; Sept.-April 9am-5pm).

Those with a strong legs and taste for conquest scale the stunted crater for unmatched views of the eruption's destruction and its source. The route is not a technical climb, but is steep and covered in loose scree. Average hiking time up is five hours, down is three hours. Permits for the hike are required; reserve in person or write to **The Monument Headquarters,** 1hr. north of Portland off Rte. 503 at 42218 NE Yale Bridge Rd., Amboy 98601 (750-3900).

■ North Cascades (Rte. 20)

A favorite stomping ground for Jack Kerouac (*The Dharma Bums*), deer, mountain goats, black bears, and grizzlies, the North Cascades remain one of the most rugged expanses of land in the continental U.S. The centerpiece of the area, **North Cascades National Park,** straddles the crest of the Cascades. Two designated wilderness areas attract backpackers and mountain climbers from around the world. **Rte. 20** (open April-Nov., weather permitting), a road designed for unadulterated driving pleasure, is the primary means of access to the area. Ira Springs's *100 Hikes in the North Cascades* is a readable guide for recreational hikers, while Fred Beckley's *Cascade Alpine Guide* targets the more serious high-country traveler.

Rte. 20 (Exit 230 on I-5) follows the Skagit River to the Skagit Dams and Lakes. The highway then enters the **Ross Lake National Recreation Area,** a buffer zone between the highway and North Cascades National Park. After crossing Washington Pass (5477 ft.), Rte. 20 descends to the Methow River and the dry Okanogan rangeland of Eastern Washington. The North Cascades National Park complex is bordered on the west by **Mt. Baker/Snoqualmie National Forest,** on the east by **Okanogan National Forest,** and on the south by **Wenatchee National Forest.**

Greyhound stops in Burlington once per day on the Seattle-Bellingham route. The fare is about $15 from Seattle to the East Cascades. No public transportation lines run within the park boundaries or along Rte. 20.

Sedro Woolley to Marblemount Though situated in the rich farmland of the lower Skagit Valley, **Sedro Woolley** is primarily a logging town. Stop by the **Chamber of Commerce,** 116 Woodsworth St. (360-855-0974), inside the train caboose (open daily 9am-5pm). Find the **North Cascades National Park Headquarters** at 2105 Rte. 20 (360-856-5700) in Sedro Woolley, as well as the headquarters for the **Mt. Baker/Snoqualmie National Forest.** Seek out the **Wilderness Information Center** (360-873-4590), in Marblemount, for a mandatory backcountry permit. Rte. 9 leads north of Sedro Woolley, providing indirect access to **Mt. Baker** through the forks at the Nooksack River and Rte. 542.

Rockport borders **Rockport State Park** (360-853-8461) farther east on Rte. 20, which rests among an old growth forest of Douglas firs and ferns. The park has a trail that accommodates wheelchairs and 62 fully developed campsites. ($10, with full hookup $15, each extra vehicle $5; three-sided adirondack cabins with bunk beds for 8 are $15, no reservations.) If Rockport is full, continue 1 mi. east to Skagit County's **Howard Miller Steelhead Park** (360-853-8808) on the Skagit River, where anglers come to catch the Park's tasty namesake (49 sites; tents $12, hookups $16, 3-sided Adirondack lean-tos $16). The surrounding **Snoqualmie National Forest** permits free camping closer to the high peaks.

At **Marblemount,** consider stopping at **Good Food** (360-873-2771), a small family diner at the east edge of town along Rte. 20. This pithy eatery boasts great vegetarian sandwiches ($3.25) and thick shakes ($2.25; open daily 9am-9pm). The **Marblemount Wilderness Information Center,** 728 Ranger Station Rd., Marblemount 98267 (873-4500, ext. 39), awaits 1 mi. north of Marblemount on a well-marked road from the west end of town. This is the place to go for a backcountry permit for the National Park (open summer Fri.-Sun. 7am-8pm, Mon.-Thurs. 7am-6pm; call for winter hr.). From Marblemount, it's 22 mi. up Cascade River Rd. to the trailhead for a 3½-mi. hike to the amazing **Cascade Pass.**

Ross Lake and North Cascades National Park **Newhalem** is the first town on Rte. 20 as you cross into the **Ross Lake National Recreation Area,** a buffer zone between the highway and North Cascades National Park. The newly rebuilt **North Cascades Visitors Center and Ranger Station** (206-386-4495), off Rte. 20 (open mid-April to mid-Nov. daily 8:30am-4:30pm; call for winter hr.), provides a peek at the diversity of flora and fauna in the Cascades.

The artificial and astoundingly blue expanse of **Ross Lake,** behind Ross Dam, snakes into the mountains as far as the Canadian border. The lake is ringed by 15 campgrounds, some accessible by trail, others only by boat. The National Park's **Goodell Creek Campground,** just south of Newhalem, has 22 leafy sites suitable for tents and trailers with drinking water and pit toilets, and a launch site for **whitewater rafting** on the Skagit River (sites $7; water turned off after Oct. when sites are free). **Colonial Creek** is both a campground and a trailhead for several hikes into the southern unit of the North Cascades National Park including the **Thunder Creek Trail,** which extends through old growth cedar and fir forests and remains flat for 1½ mi. until it starts to climb. Serious hikers often use the trail as a starting point for longer treks (open mid-May to Oct.; 164 sites, $10). **Newhalem Creek Campground,** near the visitors center, is especially good for trailers and RVs (129 sites that rarely fill, $10). The **Skagit General Store** (386-4489), east of the visitors center, sells fishing licenses and basic groceries, and is the only store within miles.

East to Mazama and Winthrop Leaving the basin of Ross Lake, Rte. 20 begins to climb, exposing the jagged, snowy peaks of the North Cascades. Thirty miles of astounding views east, the **Pacific Crest Trail** crosses Rte. 20 at **Rainy Pass** on one of the most scenic and difficult legs of its 2500-mi. Canada-to-Mexico route. Just off Rte. 20, an overlook at **Washington Pass** rewards a 5 mi. hike on a wheel-chair accessible paved trail with one of the state's most dramatic panoramas, an astonishing view of the red rocks exposed by Early Winters Creek in **Copper Basin.** The popular 2.2-mi. walk to **Blue Lake** begins just east of Washington Pass. An easier 2-mi. hike to **Cutthroat Lake** departs from an access road 4.6 mi. east of Washington Pass. From the lake, the trail continues 4 mi. farther (and almost 2,000 ft. higher) to **Cutthroat Pass,** which has a breathtaking view of towering, rugged peaks.

The hair-raising 23-mi. road to **Hart's Pass** begins at **Mazama,** on Rd. 1163, 10 mi. east of Washington Pass. The gravel road leads to the highest pass crossed by any road in the state. The road, open early July to late September, is **closed to trailers.** The **Mazama Store,** 50 Lost River Rd. (996-2855), is the last place for miles—stock up on gas and supplies (open daily 7am-7pm).

Winthrop to Twisp   Farther east is the town of **Winthrop,** the child of an unholy marriage between the television series *Bonanza* and Long Island yuppies who would eagerly claim a rusty horseshoe as an antique. Find the **Winthrop Information Station** (996-2125), on the corner of Rte. 20 and Riverside (open early May-mid-Oct. daily 10am-5pm). The shiny new **Methow** (MET-how) **Valley Visitors Center,** Building 49, Hwy. 20 (996-4000) hands out info on area camping, hiking and cross-country skiing (open summers daily 8am-5pm; call for winter hr.).

Flee Winthrop's prohibitively expensive hotels and restaurants to sleep 9 mi. south on Rte. 20 in **Twisp,** the town that should have been a breakfast cereal. Stay at **The Sportsman Motel,** 1010 E. Rte. 20 (997-2911), a hidden jewel, where a barracks-like façade masks tastefully decorated rooms and kitchens (singles $31, with 2 people $36, doubles $39). If you are in town during lunch hour, head to the **Glover Street Café,** 104 N. Glover St. (997-1323). This café offers gourmet sandwiches that won't bust your budget ($5.25 with soup or salad) as well as special salads ($3.75; open Mon.-Fri. 8am-3pm). The **Twisp Ranger Station,** 502 Glover St. (997-2131), employs a helpful staff ready to strafe you with trail and campground guides (open Mon.-Sat. 7:45am-4:30pm; winter Mon.-Fri. 7:45am-4:30pm). From Twisp, Rte. 20 continues east to Okanogan, and Rte. 153 runs south to **Lake Chelan.**

EASTERN WASHINGTON

■ Spokane

Spokane is the hub of a vast land-locked portion of the Pacific Northwest, and sup-ports a thriving service industry. Still, despite its inexpensive motels and massive quantities of cheap food, Spokane is still more of a gateway than a destination for most travelers.

The **Spokane Area Convention and Visitors Bureau,** 201 W. Main St. (747-3230 or 800-248-3230), Exit 281 off I-90, is overflowing with Spokane info (open Mon.-Fri. 8:30am-5pm; summers Sat. 8am-4pm, Sun. 9am-2pm). The **Spokane International Airport** (624-3218) is off I-90, 8 mi. southwest of town. **Amtrak,** W. 221 1st St. (624-5144, or 800-872-7245), at Bernard St., downtown, zips off to Chicago (1 per day, $219), Seattle (1 per day, $67), and Portland (1 per day, $67). (Station open 24 hr. Tickets Mon.-Fri. 11am-5:30am, Sat.-Sun. 7:15pm-5:30am). **Greyhound** (tickets 624-5251, info 624-5252), runs from the train station to Seattle (5 per day, $25) and Port-land (3 per day, $35). (Ticket office open daily 7:30am-9pm, midnight-2:30am.) **Northwestern Trailways** (838-5262 or 800-366-3830) also operates out of the train station with service to other parts of Washington, Oregon, Idaho, and Montana. Spo-kane lies 280 mi. east of Seattle on I-90. Avenues in Spokane run east-west parallel to the river, streets north-south, and both alternate one-way. The city is divided north and south by **Sprague Ave.**, east and west by **Division St. Emergency** is 911. Spokane's **post office:** W. 904 Riverside (626-6860; open Mon.-Fri. 6am-5pm). **ZIP code:** 99210. **Area code:** 509.

Spokane's best sights are outdoors. **Riverfront Park,** N. 507 Howard St. (625-6600), just north of downtown, is Spokane's civic center and greatest asset. Developed for the 1974 World's Fair, the park's 100 acres are divided by the roaring rapids that culminate in Spokane Falls. There are few long waits for the fair's remaining attractions. The **Arbor Crest Estate,** N. 4705 Fruithill Rd. (927-9894), is a beautiful compound atop a breezy bluff with stunning vistas overlooking the gorgeous valley below. Sample excellent Washington wine for free. Take I-90 to Exit 287, travel north on Argonne over the Spokane River, turn right on Upriver Dr., proceed 1 mi., and then bear left onto Fruithill Rd. Take a sharp left at the top of the hill.

Manito Park, 4 W. 21st Ave. (625-6622), has four sections for both hard-core botanists and those just wishing to spend time in one of the most beautiful spots in Spokane. Check out the carp in the **Nishinomiya Japanese Garden,** overdose on roses on Rosehill (they bloom in late June here), relax in the elegant Duncan Garden, or sniff the flowers in the David Graiser Conservatory. From downtown, go south on Stevens St. and turn left on 21st Ave. (free; open daily 8am-8pm).

Rodeway Inn City Center, W. 827 1st (838-8271 or 800-4-CHOICE/24-6423), at Lincoln, offers both a great location and pristine rooms (singles $44, doubles $54; rates fall by $10 in the off season).

The **Spokane County Market** (482-2627), on the north end of Riverside Park, sells fresh fruit, vegetables, and baked goods (open May-Oct. Wed., Fri., and Sat. 9am-5pm, Sun. 10am-4pm). A takeout burger phenom, **Dick's,** E. 103rd Ave. (747-2481), at Division, is an inexplicably inflation-free pocket of Washington. (Burgers 55¢, fries 49¢, sundaes 67¢. Open daily 9am-1am.) **Milford's Fish House and Oyster Bar,** N. 719 Monroe (326-7251), is one of the finest restaurants in the Pacific Northwest. And though it may sink your budget (specials run $13-19), the freshest seafood in town will certainly buoy your spirits. (Open Sun-Mon. 4-9pm, Tues.-Sat 5-10pm. Reservations recommended, especially on weekends.)

Oregon

One hundred years ago, entire families liquidated their possessions and sank their life savings into covered wagons, corn meal, and oxen. They hightailed it to Oregon in droves with little more than the shirts on their backs. Today, thousands of visitors are drawn each year by Oregon's remarkable natural beauty. While the coastal towns of Seaside and Cannon Beach are enticing, the waves and cliffs of Oregon's gorgeous Pacific should not blind the enterprising tourist to everything else the state has to offer. Don't miss out on the full Oregonian experience by clinging to the coast; venture inland to see other fabulous attractions—majestic Mt. Hood, the volcanic cinder-cones near Crater Lake, and the Shakespeare festival in Ashland. North America's deepest gorge and the towering Wallowa Mountains clash in the northeast, and the forested peaks of the Cascade Range stun visitors with their splendor. Both town and country are worth a closer look; Oregon's cities are as exciting and challenging as its wilderness. Portland is a casual and idiosyncratic city whose name was determined by a coin toss (one more turn of a coin and it would have been "Boston, Oregon"), while Eugene is a diverse college town with an attitude. Bend, a small interior city with an athletic, youthful crowd, is one of the liveliest towns in the state. Everything from excellent microbrews to accessible snow-capped peaks and lush forests make this state a seductive destination.

PRACTICAL INFORMATION

Capital: Salem.
Oregon Tourism Commission, 775 Summer St. NE, Salem 97310 (800-547-7842;
fax 503-986-0001). **Oregon State Parks,** 1115 Commercial St. NE, Salem 97310-
1001 (503-378-6305; fax 378-6447). For **reservations** in most state parks, call 800-
452-5687. **Department of Fish and Wildlife,** P.O. Box 59, Portland 97207 (503-
229-5222 for a recording of fishing seasons and legal sites).
Time Zone: Mountain and Pacific. **Postal Abbreviation:** OR
Sales Tax: None.

■ Portland

Casual and tolerant, Portland is the mellowest big city on the West Coast. Like the
popular poster depicting local tavern-owner "Bud" Clark in a trenchcoat flashing a
public sculpture (he was shortly thereafter elected mayor), Portland has nothing to
hide. Unhurried and uncongested, the downtown area is spotless and building height
is regulated to preserve views of the river, hills, and mountains. Portland's varied artistic scene is anchored by the city's venerable Symphony Orchestra, the oldest in the
country. On a July day you can ski Mt. Hood in the morning, watch the sun drop into
the Pacific Ocean from the cool sand of an empty beach, and still return to town in
time to catch an outdoor jazz concert at the zoo. Portland's first-rate flock of small
breweries pump out barrels of some of the nation's finest ale.

PRACTICAL INFORMATION

Visitors Information: Portland/Oregon Visitors Association, 25 SW Salmon St.
(222-2223 or 800-345-3214), at Front St. in the Two World Trade Center complex.
From I-5, follow the signs for City Center. Pick up the *Portland Book.* Open Mon.-
Fri. 8:30am-6:30pm, Sat. 9am-5pm; winter Mon.-Fri. 8:30am-5pm, Sat. 9am-4pm.
Airport: Portland International, 7000 NE Airport Way (335-1234). Take Tri-Met
bus #12 (a 45-min. ride), which arrives going south on SW 5th Ave. (95¢). **Raz
Tranz** (246-3301 for taped info) provides a shuttle that stops at most major hotels
downtown. Fare $8.50, ages 6-12 $2. Taxis to downtown $20-23.
Trains: Amtrak, 800 NW 6th Ave. (273-4866 or 800-872-7245, Union Station 273-
4865), at Hoyt St. To: Seattle (4 per day, $26); Eugene (2 per day, $20); Spokane (1
per day, $67), Boise (3 days per week, $104). Open daily 6:45am-6pm.
Buses: Greyhound, 550 NW 6th Ave. (243-2357 or 800-231-2222) at Glisan. in Fareless Sq. (see below). To: Seattle (9 per day; $15); Eugene (8 per day, $13); Spokane
(6 per day, $35). Lockers $2 for 6 hrs. Ticket window open daily 5am-11:45pm. Station open daily 5am-1am.
Public Transportation: Tri-Met, Customer Service Center, #1 Pioneer Courthouse
Sq., 701 SW 6th Ave. (238-7433). Fare info (231-3198); updates, changes, and
weather-related problems (231-3197); senior and disabled services (238-4952). Service generally 5am-midnight, reduced weekends. Fare 95¢-$1.25, ages 7-18 70¢,
over 65 and disabled 45¢; no fare in Fareless Sq. downtown. All-day pass $3.25. All
buses have bike racks (a $5 1-year permit can be obtained at area bike stores) and
are wheelchair accessible. Center open Mon.-Fri. 7:30am-5:30pm. **MAX** (228-
7246) is an efficient rail running between Gresham to the east and downtown.
Same fare system as buses.
Taxi: Broadway Cab, 227-1234. **Radio Cab,** 227-1212. Both 24hr.
Car Rental: Avis Rent-A-Car (800-331-1212 or 249-4950), at airport. Starting $28
per day, $195 weekly with unlimited free mi. Must be 25 or older with credit card.
Crisis Line: 223-6161. **Women's Crisis Line:** 235-5333. Both 24 hr. **Phoenix Ris-
ing** (223-8299). Gay and lesbian info and referrals. Open Mon.-Sat. 9am-9pm.
Emergency: 911.
Post Office: 715 NW Hoyt St. (294-2300). Open Mon.-Fri. 7am-6:30pm, Sat. 8:30am-
5pm. **General Delivery ZIP Code:** 97208-9999.
Area Code: 503.

Portland is in the northwest corner of Oregon, where the Willamette (wi-LAM-it) River flows into the Columbia River. I-5 connects Portland with San Francisco and Seattle; I-84 follows the route of the Oregon Trail through the Columbia River Gorge toward Boise. West of Portland, U.S. 30 follows the Columbia downstream to Astoria, but U.S. 26 is the fastest way to reach the coast. I-405 runs just west of downtown to link I-5 with U.S. 30 and 26.

Portland is divided into five districts. **Burnside St.** divides the city north and south; the Willamette River separates east and west. **Williams Ave.** cuts off a corner of the northeast which is called simply "North." All street signs are labeled by their districts: N, NE, NW, SE, and SW. **Southwest Portland** is known as downtown, but also includes the southern end of historic Old Town and a slice of the wealthier West Hills. The **transit mall** lies between SW 5th and 6th Ave., where car traffic is prohibited. The **Northwest** district contains most of **Old Town** and swanky West Hills. The **Southeast** is the hippest part of the city. Portland's best ethnic restaurants line **Hawthorne Boulevard,** along with small cafes and theaters catering to the artsy crowd—including nearby Reed College's students. The **North** and **Northeast** districts are chiefly residential, punctuated by a few quiet, small parks.

The award-winning **Tri-Met bus system** weaves together Portland's districts and suburbs. In the transit mall, 31 covered passenger shelters serve as both stops and information centers. Southbound buses pick up passengers along SW 5th Ave.; northbound passengers board on SW 6th Ave. Bus routes fall into seven regional service areas, each with its own individual "Lucky Charm": orange deer, yellow rose, green leaf, brown beaver, blue snow, red salmon, and purple raindrop. Shelters and buses are color-coded for their region. A few buses with black numbers on white backgrounds cross town north-south or east-west, ignoring color-coded boundaries.

Most of downtown, from NW Hoyt St. in the north to I-405 in the west and south and the Willamette River in the east, comprises **"Fareless Square."** As the name suggests, the buses and MAX are free in this zone. Pick up monthly passes, bus maps, and schedules at the visitors center or at the Tri-Met Customer Assistance Office.

ACCOMMODATIONS AND CAMPING

It's always wise to make reservations early, because places can fill in a flash, especially during the Rose Festival or a convention. Camping, though distant, is plentiful.

Hosteling International—Portland (HI-AYH), 3031 SE Hawthorne Blvd. (236-3380), at 31st Ave. Take bus #14 (brown beaver). Cheerful, clean, and crowded. Kitchen facilities; laundromat across the street. Fills up early in the summer (particularly the women's rooms), so make reservations (credit card required) or plan to arrive at 5pm to get one of the 12-15 beds saved for walk-ins. Don't miss the all-you-can-eat pancakes every morning (a paltry $1). Open daily 7:30-11am and 4-11pm. 34 beds. No curfew. $13, nonmembers $16. Members only July-Aug.

McMenamins Edgefield Hostel, 2126 SW Halsey St. (669-8610 or 800-669-8610), in Troutdale 20min. east of Portland off I-84. McMenamins converted this farm into its crown jewel. The lodge shares the estate with a winery (wine tasting!), brewery (beer tasting!), movie theater, and two restaurants (food tasting!). Elegant dark wood bunks and vast rooms. Two single-sex dorm-style rooms, each with 12 beds. Shower facilities down the hall include two claw-footed tubs. Save money by bringing food. $18 per night.

Ondine, 1912 SW 6th Ave. (725-4336), between College St. and Hall St. If you are in town on business with Portland State University, you are eligible for the budget travel experience of a lifetime! 24 big, clean rooms, each with 2 twin beds. Linen and towels provided. Private bathrooms. Microwaves available. Coin laundry. Excellent views. Within Fareless Square. Parking nightmarish. Reserve at least 1-2 wk. in advance. Cash, checks accepted. Singles $25, doubles $30.

Ben Stark International Hostel, 1022 SW Stark St. (274-1223; fax 274-1033). This old building is charming but run-down. 6 well kept hostel rooms, 2 bathrooms, common room down the hall. Laundry and lockers downstairs. No curfew; 24hr. desk service. Convenient location, but there are some shady characters around, and the club across the street is noisy on weekends. Reservations and passport or hostel membership required. $15 per night, $12 Nov.-May. Private rooms $36-45.

Champoeg State Park, 8239 NE Champoeg Rd. (678-1251). Take I-5 south 20 mi. to Exit 278, then follow the signs west for 6 mi. more. 19 shady RV sites ($19) have water and electricity. Tent sites ($15) do not afford much privacy. Two-day advance reservation required.

Ainsworth State Park, 37mi. east of Portland, at Exit 35 off I-84, in the Columbia Gorge. Proximity to expressway makes it convenient but noisy. Hardly a natural get-away, but the drive into Portland through the gorge is beautiful. Hot showers, flush toilets, hiking trails, and full hookup. All sites $19.

FOOD

Chang's Mongolian Grill, 1 SW 3rd St. (243-1991), at Burnside. All-you-can-eat lunches ($6) or dinners ($9). Select your meal from a buffet of fresh vegetables, meat, and fish, mix your own sauce to taste, and watch your chef cook it on a domed grill the size of a Volkswagen beetle. Rice, soup, and pancakes included. Open Mon.-Fri. 11:30am-2:30pm and 5-10pm, Sat.-Sun. noon-2:30pm and 5-10pm.

Western Culinary Institute Chef's Corner, 1239 SW Jefferson (242-2422 or 800-666-0312). Testing ground for the cooking school's adventures. Students in tall white hats will whip up a delicious, cheap meal. All lunches under $6. Mounth water pastries $1.25. Call ahead. Open Mon. 8am-2:30pm, Tues.-Fri. 8am-6pm.

Brasserie Montmartre, 626 SW Park Ave. (224-5552). Elegant, expensive restaurant with a subtle funny bone. Paper tablecloths, crayons, marauding magicians and nightly live jazz offer diversions for dull dates. Bistro section is slightly less expensive than the rest of the restaurant. Pasta and chicken $10, seafood and steak dishes $10-15, burgers $5. Open Mon.-Thurs. 11:30-2am, Fri. 11:30-3am, Sat. 10am-3am, Sun. 10am-2am.

Café Lena, 2239 SE Hawthorne Blvd. (238-7087). Take bus #5 (brown beaver). Local art on the wall. An eclectic menu features Thai, Italian, and American ($7-10). Vegetarian soup or salad with half a gargantuan sandwich is a good bet for $5.50-6.50. Spoken word or acoustic music every night. Breakfast served until 4pm. Open Tues.-Thurs. 7am-11pm, Fri.-Sat. 7am-midnight, Sun. 8am-3pm.

Accaurdi's Old Town Pizza, 226 NW Davis St. (222-9999). Relax on a couch, or at a table in this former whorehouse. Ghost sightings have not affected the staff's pizza-crafting abilities (small cheese, $4.55). Open daily 11:30am-11:30pm.

Garbonzo's, 922 NW 21st (227-4196), at Lovejoy. Quiet, delicious falafel bar. The falafel pita ($3.50) is a superb choice. Good hummus ($3), baba ghanoush ($3.50), and mouthwatering baklava ($1.25). Only 2 items over $7. Open Sun.-Thurs. 11:30am-1:30am, Fri.-Sat. 11:30am-3am.

Montage, 301 SE Morrison St. (234-1324). Take bus #15 (brown beaver) to the end of the Morrison Bridge and walk back toward the river. An oasis of Louisiana style and cooking. Unbelievable mac and cheese ($3), and gumbo you wish your mama made ($3). Open for lunch Mon.-Fri. 11am-2pm, dinner daily 6pm-2am.

SIGHTS AND ACTIVITIES

Shaded parks, magnificent gardens, innumerable museums and galleries, and bustling open-air markets beckon the city's tourists and residents alike. Catch the best of Portland's dizzying dramatic and visual arts scene on the first Thursday of each month when the small galleries in the Southwest and Northwest all stay open until 9pm. For info contact the **Metropolitan Arts Commission,** 1120 SW 5th Ave. (823-5111). Grab the *Art Gallery Guide* at the visitors center which pinpoints 65 art hot spots on a map. Or go to **Portland Art Museum,** 1219 SW Park Ave. (226-2811), to latch onto a **Public Art Walking Tour**.

Portland's downtown area centers on the pedestrian and bus **mall,** running north-south between 5th and 6th Ave., between W. Burnside St. on the north end and SW Madison St. to the south. At 5th Ave. and Morrison St. sits **Pioneer Courthouse,** a central downtown landmark. The monument is still a Federal courthouse and is the centerpiece for **Pioneer Courthouse Square,** 701 SW 6th Ave. (223-1613), which opened in 1983. Portlanders of every ilk hang out in this massive brick quadrangle that has a Starbucks in one corner and the travel branch of Powell's in the other. Area citizens purchased personalized bricks to support the construction of an amphitheater that hosts live jazz and folk music. In the summer the **Peanut Butter and Jam Sessions** draw thousands to enjoy the music (Tues. and Thurs. noon-1pm).

Anyone who doubts that mega-corporations rule the planet need only visit **Niketown,** 930 SW 6th (221-6453). TVs in the floor, life-size Andre Agassi and Michael Jordan sculptures, and hypnotic signs have tourists staggering around glassy eyed. Sports fans will enjoy the various artifacts: the jerseys and shoes of athletes, the balls they've played with, and even an autographed Jordan Wheaties Box. Advertising is art! Art is advertising! It's gotta be the shoes! (Open Mon.-Thurs. and Sat. 10am-7pm, Fri. 10am-8pm, Sun. 11:30am-6:30pm.)

The **Portland Art Museum,** 1219 SW Park (226-2811), at Jefferson St., houses Western painting and sculpture from the 1350s to the 1950s, as well as prints, photos, and contemporary works. The impressive collection of art from other cultures includes samples from Cameroon and Asia. The excellent Pacific Northwest Native American art exhibit includes masks, textiles, and sacred objects ($5, seniors and students over 16 $4.50, under 16 $2.50; open Tues.-Sun. 11am-5pm). The **Pacific Northwest College of Art** (226-4391) and the **Northwest Film Center** (221-1156) share space with the museum in the two buildings along the park. The Film Center shows classics, documentaries, and offbeat flicks Thurs.-Sun. Tickets are available at the box office for $6. **Museum After Hours** is a jazz and blues concert series popular with the after-work crowd (Oct.-April 5:30-9pm; prices vary; call the Museum).

If the kiddies get bored, take them to the **Portland Children's Museum,** 3037 SW 2nd Ave. (823-2227), at Wood St. (not in downtown; take bus #1, 12, 40, 41, 43, 45, or 55, all yellow rose), which schedules games, arts activities, and hands-on exhibits, including the ever-popular grocery store where plastic celery and bananas are currency. (Open daily 9am-5pm; $3.50 for all ages over 1. Infants admitted free.)

Old Town, north of the mall, resounded a century ago with the clamor of sailors whose ships filled the ports. The district has been revived by the large-scale restoration of store fronts, new "old brick," polished iron and brass, and a bevy of recently opened shops and restaurants. Old Town also marks the end of **Waterfront Park.** This 20-block-long swath of grass and flowers along the Willamette River provides locals with an excellent place to picnic, fish, stroll, and enjoy major community events. The festive **Saturday Market,** 108 W. Burnside St. (222-6072), by the Skidmore Fountain between 1st and Front St., is overrun with street musicians, artists, craftspeople, chefs, and greengrocers clogging the largest open-air crafts market in the country (March-Dec. Sat. 10am-5pm, Sun. 11am-4:30pm).

For a dose of fun that might go over youngsters' heads, pay a visit to the first and only 24hr. coin-operated **Church of Elvis,** 720 SW Ankeny St. (226-3671). Listen to

---

Don't Expect to Play Frisbee in This Park

No one knew that a hole cut through the sidewalk at the corner of SW Taylor St. and SW Front St. in 1948 was destined for greatness. Indeed, it was expected to accommodate a humble lamp post. But the post was never installed, and the 24-in. circle of earth was left empty until Dick Fagan, a columnist for the *Oregon Journal,* noticed it. Fagan used his column, called "Mill Ends," to publicize the patch of dirt, pointing out that it would make a great, though microscopic, park. After years of lobbying, the park was officially added to the city's roster in 1976. At 452.16 sq. in., **Mill Ends Park** is recognized by the *Guiness Book of World Records* as the **world's smallest park.** Locals have enthusiastically adopted the park, planting flowers and hosting a hotly contested **snail race** on St. Patrick's Day. Imagine all the things you can do there: eat your lunch (alone), wave at passing cars, read Habermas, meditate, develop a national healthcare plan everyone will accept, or just stand (in the place where you are).

synthetic oracles, witness satirical miracles, and, if you're lucky, experience a tour in the church's Art-o-Mobile.

Portland is the uncontested **microbrewery** capital of the United States and possibly the world, and Portlanders are proud of their beery city. The visitors center can give you a list of 26 metro area breweries, most of which will be happy to show you around their facilities. Henry Weinhard, a German brewmaster, started this tradition when he established the first brewery in the Northwest, outside of Fort Vancouver in 1856. Today **"Henry's"** has become an Oregon standard, outgrowing its status as a microbrew. Visit the **Blitz Weinhard Brewery,** 1133 W. Burnside (222-4351), for a ½-hour tour and samples in the hospitality room (free; open weekday afternoons).

The American Advertising Museum, 50 SW 2nd Ave. (226-0000) at the Skidmore stop on MAX, chronicles the fast-paced world of advertising. The gallery shows temporary exhibits; summer 1996 showcased a fascinating and informative retrospective on images of women in advertising. ($3, seniors and under 12 $1.50; open Wed.-Sun. 11am-5pm.)

Less than 2 mi. west of downtown, the posh neighborhoods of **West Hills** form a manicured buffer zone between soul-soothing parks and the turmoil of the city below. In the middle of West Hills, mammoth **Washington Park** and its nearby attractions typify the blend of urbanity and natural bounty which Portland has perfected. To get there, take the animated #63 (zoo bus) on SW Main St. or drive up SW Broadway to Clay St., turn right onto U.S. 26, and get off at the zoo exit. **Hoyt Arboretum,** 4000 SW Fairview Blvd. (228-8733 or 823-3655), at the crest of the hill above the other gardens, features 200 acres of trees and trails. Free nature walks (April-Nov. Sat.-Sun. at 2pm) last 90 min. and cover 1-2 mi. The **Rose Garden,** 400 SW Kingston Ave. (823-3636), on the way to the zoo entrance, is a gorgeous place to stroll on a lazy day or cool evening.

The **Washington Park Zoo,** 4001 SW Canyon Rd. (226-1561 or 226-7627), is renowned for its successful elephant-breeding and its scrupulous re-creation of natural habitats. The #63 (zoo bus) connects the park to SW Main St. in the downtown mall. A steam engine pulls passengers on a mini railway out to Washington Park gardens and back, giving a better view of flora and fauna (½hr. tour $2.75, seniors and ages 3-11 $2). The zoo features a number of "animal talks" on weekends and has a pet-the-animals **children's zoo.** If you're around in late June, July, or August, grab your picnic basket and head to the zoo's sculpture garden to catch live outdoor jazz at **Your Zoo and All That Jazz** (234-9695), Wed. nights. On Thurs. nights, the **Rhythm and Zoo Concerts** (234-9694) host a diverse range of international styles. Both events are free with zoo admission.

Hawthorne Boulevard is a hip strip where prices aren't yet too high and parking can still be found on weekends. It ends at the bottom of **Mt. Tabor Park,** one of two city parks in the world on the site of an extinct volcano. To get to the area, take bus #15 (brown beaver) from downtown, or hunt it down at SE 60th Ave. and Belmont Ave. Shops have also sprouted on **Belmont Ave.** (a few avenues north), which some have touted as the new Hawthorne, though locals are still waiting for the rest of Belmont to sprout.

ENTERTAINMENT AND NIGHTLIFE

Although once an uncouth and rowdy port town, Portland still maintains a fairly irreverent attitude. Nightclubs cater to everyone from the casual college student to the hard-core rocker. The best entertainment listings are in the Friday edition of the *Oregonian* and in a number of free handouts. The town's favorite cultural reader, the **Willamette Week** (put out each evening), the *Main Event, Clinton St. Quarterly, Just Out* (catering to gay and lesbian interests), the *Portland Guide,* and the *Downtowner* (friend of the upscale) are on street corners and in restaurants downtown.

Portland has its share of excellent concerts, but why bother with admission fees when you can find exciting talent playing for free in various public facilities around the city? Check the *Oregonian's* A&E (Arts and Entertainment) section or pick up a *Willamette Week* for up to date information (see above). For the best local rock, visit the **Satyricon** and **Laluna** (see below). The **Oregon Symphony Orchestra** plays classical and pop in Arlene Schnitzer Concert Hall, 1111 SW Broadway Ave. (228-1353 or 800-228-7343; Sept.-June; tickets $10-50; "Symphony Sunday" afternoon concerts $9-12), while **Chamber Music Northwest** performs summer concerts from late June through July at Reed College Commons, 3203 SE Woodstock Ave. (223-3202; Mon., Tues., and Thurs.-Sat. at 8pm. $12-26, ages 7-14 $5). **Sack Lunch Concerts,** 1422 SW 11th Ave. (222-2031), are free every Wed. at noon; you never know what kind of music you'll find.

Portland's many fine theaters produce everything from off-Broadway shows to experimental drama. **Portland Center Stage** (248-6309), at the Intermediate Theater of **Portland Center for the Performing Arts (PCPA)** (796-9293), at SW Broadway and SW Main, features classics from Oct.-April. (Fri.-Sat. $12.50-35, Sun. and Tues.-Thurs. $11-30.50. ½price tickets are sometimes available at the Intermediate Theater 1hr. before showtime.)

The best clubs in Portland are the hardest ones to find. Neighborhood taverns and pubs may be hidden, but they usually have the most character and best music. The clubs in Northwest Portland are easily accessible from downtown.

Biddy McGraw's, 3518 SE Hawthorne Blvd. (233-1178). Take bus #14 (brown beaver). With live Irish tunes and raucous dancing, weekends are always boisterous. Mon.-Tues. neither music nor table service will impose. Imports go for $3.25 a pint, micros $3, Henry's $2. Hours not set in stone, but should be open Mon. 6:30pm-2am, Tues.-Fri. 10am-2:30am, Sat.-Sun. 2pm-2:30am.

Produce Row Cafe, 204 SE Oak St. (232-8355), has 27 beers on tap, over 200 bottled domestic and imported beers. Bus #6 (red salmon) to SE Oak and SE Grand, then walk west along Oak towards the river. Live music Sat.-Mon. Cover varies. Open Mon.-Fri. 11am-midnight or 1am, Sat. noon-1am, Sun. noon-midnight.

La Luna, 215 SE 9th Ave. (241-LUNA/5862). Take bus #20 (purple raindrop), get off at 9th, walk 2 blocks south. Live concerts, 2 bars and a hip crowd. Open Thurs.-Sat. 8pm-2:30am, concerts and special events other nights.

Satyricon, 121 NW 6th Ave. (243-2380). Alternarock rumbles in the glowing back room every night. Old bar and a chic new sister restaurant, Felini. Veggie entrees start at $3, and Liberace's Libido goes for $7.50. No cover Mon. for New Band Night, otherwise $2-6. Food daily noon-2:30am; music 3pm-2:30am.

Bridgeport Brew Pub, 1313 NW Marshall (241-7179). Beer plus pizza equals fun. Brews are all Bridgeport; $1.65 for a 10oz pint, $2.75 for a 20oz. Open Mon.-Thurs. 11am-11pm, Fri. 11:30am-midnight, Sun. 1-9pm.

Lotus Card Room and Café, 932 SW 3rd Ave. (227-6185), at SW Salmon St. Groovy dance floor has a movie screen, glowing cartoon paintings, and a cage. Dance floor open 9pm-2am. Cover $2-4, sometimes free. Happy hour (Wed.-Sun.4-6:30pm) features micro-pints ($2). Open daily 11am-2am.

You Won't Find the Hendersons Here

John Lithgow has an Emmy and **"Sasquatch"** fever has subsided of late, but the mystery members of this hominid family, their existence shrouded in murky lore, remain inscrutable to the scientific community. Mt. Hood marks the southern boundary of the Dark Divide, the area most associated with the sightings of these large, hirsute creatures who lurk in the forests and eat nuts and twigs. This fearsome beast was known even before the white man got his grubby hands on the New World. The Salish called the creature *saskehavas,* from which comes the English term "Sasquatch." Many dismiss the possibility of any such mysterious **ape-man.** Why, they ask, is there no evidence of such a creature? Cryptozoologists (scientists who study undiscovered species) know better. They argue that numerous sightings and photographs *are* conclusive. If you do chance upon a **Bigfoot,** it will be easy to recognize. The big galoot stands roughly six to ten feet tall, weighs about 400 pounds, is covered in dark fur, and leaves behind a strong, fetid **odor.**

PACIFIC NORTHWEST

Panorama, Briggs, and **Boxes,** 341 SW 10th St. (221-RAMA/7262), form a network of interconnected clubs along Stark St. between 10th and 11th. Thriving gay and straight crowd. (Open Thurs. and Sun. 9pm-2:30am, Fri.-Sat. 9pm-4am, with a $3 cover on Fri.-Sat., $2 on Thurs.) After 11:30 pm, you can wander over to the smaller Briggs, or Boxes (both open daily til 2:30am).

■ Near Portland: Columbia River Gorge

Only an hour from Portland, the spectacular Columbia River Gorge stretches for 70 miles. The Columbia River has carved a canyon 1000 ft. deep through rumpled hills and sheer, rocky cliffs. Mt. Hood and Mt. Adams loom nearby while waterfalls plunge hundreds of feet over cliffs toward the Columbia. Traveling eastward, the river widens out and the wind picks up at the town of **Hood River.**

The famous **Vista House** (695-2230), completed in 1917 as a memorial to Oregon's pioneers, is now a visitors center in Crown Point State Park (open daily 9am-6pm). The house hangs on the edge of an outcropping high above the river. Crown Point is 3 mi. east of eastbound Exit 22 off I-84. A string of waterfalls adorns the scenic highway east of Crown Point. The granddaddy of them all, **Multnomah Falls,** attracts two million visitors annually. The falls crash 620 ft. into a tiny pool which then drains into a lower falls. Exit 31, on I-84, takes you to an island in the middle of the freeway from which you can see only the upper falls, but which provides access to walking trails through a pedestrian subway. A quick hike takes you to Benson Bridge wedged above the lower falls with views of the upper falls.

The wide Columbia and its 30mph winds make Hood River a **windsurfing** paradise. To fully experience Hood River, rent a board or take a lesson. At **Duck Jibe Pete's,** 1st and Oak St. (386-9434 or 386-1699), you can rent a high-quality sailboard including a car rack for $40 a day (open 9am-8pm daily). Beginners will want to sail at the **hook,** a shallow, sandy cove, and experts might try the **Spring Creek Fish Hatchery** on the Washington side. If the wind is up, the Hatchery is the place to watch the best in the business. The Event Center, toward the water off Exit 63, is another hub of activity. Parking all day is $3, but it's free if you just sit and watch. If you catch windsurfing mania, a 2½-3 hour class at **Rhonda Smith Port Marina Park** (386-WIND/9463)— take Exit 64 under the bridge and to the left—will get you started or bump you up a notch ($65-75). Rentals (right on the water) start at $25-35 for a half-day, with discounts for longer periods.

The town of Hood River, 76 mi. east of Portland on I-84, is the largest town in the gorge. The **Hood River County Chamber of Commerce,** 405 Portway Ave. (386-2000 or 800-366-3530), has the scoop on the gorge. Pick up the free *Gorge Vistas* and *The Visitor's Guide to Gorge Fun.* (Open Mon.-Thurs. 9am-5pm; mid-April-mid-Oct. Fri. 9am-4pm, Sat.-Sun. 10am-4pm; mid-Oct.-mid-April Fri. 9am-5pm.)

The outdoorsy **Bingen School Inn Hostel** (509-493-3363), 3 min. from Hood River across the Singing Bridge in Bingen, WA, is a converted schoolhouse. (Bike rental $15 per day. Sailboard rental $40 per day. 48 hostel beds, $11. 5 private rooms, $40.) Campgrounds surround Hood River. **Ainsworth State Park** (695-2301), at Exit 35 off I-84, caters to RVs but has many sites ($18). **Beacon Rock,** across the Bridge of the Gods (Exit 44) then 7 mi. west on Washington Hwy. 14, has more secluded sites for $10.

To follow the gorge, which divides Oregon and Washington, take I-84 east to Exit 22. Continue east up the hill on the only road possible, and you'll find yourself on Hwy. 30, a.k.a. the **Columbia River Scenic Highway.** Take Greyhound from Portland ($11) or Seattle ($37) to Hood River; the **station** (386-1212) is at 1205 B Ave., between 12th and 13th St. (open Mon.-Sat. and occasional Sun. 8:30am-7pm). **Amtrak** also runs trains from Portland to the station at Cascade and 1st St. ($14).

OREGON COAST

A renowned coastal highway, **U.S. 101** hugs the shore, occasionally rising to lofty viewpoints. From Astoria in the north to Brookings in the south, the highway laces together the resorts and fishing villages that cluster around the mouths of the rivers that feed into the Pacific. Its most breathtaking stretches lie between coastal towns, where hundreds of miles of state and national parks allow direct access to the beach. Gasoline and grocery **prices** on the coast are about 20% higher than in the inland cities. Motorists should try to stock up and fill up before reaching the coastal highways.

Astoria Astoria was Lewis and Clark's final stop at the end of their transcontinental trek; they reached the Pacific here in 1805. Six years later, John Astor, scion of one of 19th-century America's most wealthy families, established a fur-trading post, making Astoria the first permanent U.S. settlement on the West Coast. Today Astoria is a scenic getaway for inlanders and city-dwellers. **Astoria/Warrenton Area Chamber of Commerce,** 111 W. Marine Dr. (325-6311; fax 325-9767), just east of the bridge to Washington, is stocked with area info. (Open Mon.-Sat. 8am-6pm, Sun. 9am-5pm; Oct.-May Mon.-Fri. 8am-5pm, Sat.-Sun. 11am-4pm.)

Astoria is the most convenient connection between the Oregon coast and Washington. Two bridges run from the city: the **Youngs Bay Bridge,** to the southwest, on which Marine Drive becomes U.S. 101, and the **Astoria Bridge,** a scenic 4-mi. span over the Columbia River into Washington. The Astoria Bridge has narrow and hazardous bike lanes. Motels are crowded and expensive. The great, almost unknown **Fort Columbia State Park Hostel (HI-AYH),** Fort Columbia, Chinook, WA (360-777-8755), within Fort Stevens State Park, is across the 4-mi. bridge into Washington, then 3 mi. north on U.S. 101. This hospital-turned-hostel has 50¢ stuff-your-face pancake breakfasts. (Lockout10am-5pm, check-in 5-10pm. $10, nonmembers $13, bicyclists $8, under 18 with parent $5. Open April 1-Sept. 31.) The area is also a haven for campers; U.S. 101, south of Astoria, is littered with campgrounds. **Fort Stevens State Park** is by far the best (sites $17-20).

Tillamook Ever seen a cheese factory at work? Some of Oregon's finest, most famous cheeses are cultured on the shore of Tillamook Bay, where cow pastures predominate. Most visitors hanker for a hunk at the **Tillamook Cheese Factory,** 4175 U.S. 101 N. (842-4481). Watch from glass windows of this temple to dairy delights as cheese is made, cut, weighed, and packaged. Sample a tidbit in the tasting room. Try their ice cream too. (Open daily 8am-8pm; Sept. to mid-June 8am-6pm.)

Tillamook lies 49 mi. south of Seaside and 44 mi. north of Lincoln City on U.S. 101. The most direct route from Portland is U.S. 26 to Rte. 6. U.S. 101 is the main drag, and splits into two one-way streets in the downtown area. The Tillamook Cheese Factory is almost a downtown in itself, but is north of the major shops. The **visitors center** (842-7525), in the big red barn across from the cheese factory, has a map of all the camping spots in the are. For a cheap bed try the **Tillamook Inn,** 1810 U.S. 101N (842-4413), between the center of town and the Tillamook Cheese Factory. (Singles $35. Doubles $45. Winter rates lower. Call a few days in advance.)

Newport Part tourist mill, part fishing village, and part logging town, Newport offers the sights and smells of a classic seaport with kitschy shops. Newport's **chamber of commerce,** 555 SW Coast Hwy. (265-8801 or 800-262-7844) has a helpful office (open Mon.-Fri. 8:30am-5pm, Sat.-Sun. 10am-4pm; Oct.-April no weekends).

The strip along U.S. 101 provides plenty of affordable motels, with predictably noisy consequences. The **Brown Squirrel Hostel (HI-AYH),** 44 SW Brook St. (265-3729), has a bountifully outfitted kitchen. You can be out the door and at the beach in 2min. (22 beds. $12, couples $20. Couples should call ahead.) Campers should escape Newport to the many state campgrounds along U.S. 101. **South Beach State Park,** 5580 S. Coast Hwy. (867-4715), 2 mi. south of town, has a few yurts ($27), 25 electrical hookup sites ($19), several hiker/biker sites ($4.25), and showers. Just north of town lies the best option, **Beverly Beach State Park,** 198 N. 123rd St. (265-9278), which has 151 sites specifically for tents ($16) and 53 full hookup sites ($20).

Mo's Restaurant, 622 SW Bay Blvd. (265-2979), is a small local favorite with a reputation for the best clam chowder on the coast (with fish 'n' chips $7; open daily 11am-9pm). Head over to the **Oregon Coast Aquarium,** 2820 SE Ferry Slip Rd. (867-3474), a vast building featuring 2½ acres of exhibits. ($8.50, seniors $7.50, ages 4-13 $4.25. Open daily 9am-6pm; winter 10am-5pm.)

To sample local beer, cross the bay bridge, follow the signs to the Hatfield Center and turn off into the **Rogue Ale Brewery,** 2320 SE Oregon State University Dr. (867-3663). Their line of 12 brews includes the favorite Oregon Golden, American Amber, and Maierbock Ales. Sadly, the brewery has begun charging 50¢ for a 3oz. glass of brew (open daily 11am-6pm; sometimes later in the summer).

Oregon Sand Dunes For 50 mi. between Florence and Coos Bay, the beach widens to form the **Oregon Dunes National Recreation Area.** Shifting hills of sand rise to 500 ft. and extend up to 3 mi. inland (often to the shoulder of U.S. 101), clogging streams and forming many small lakes. Hiking trails wind around the lakes, through the coastal forests, and up to the dunes.

Siuslaw National Forest administers the national recreation area. **Campgrounds** fill up early with dune buggy and motorcycle junkies, especially on summer weekends. The blaring radios, thrumming engines, and staggering swarms of tipsy tourists might drive you into the sands to seek eternal truth, or at least a quiet place to crash. The campgrounds that allow dune buggy access, **Spinreel,** parking-lot style **Driftwood II,** and **Horsfall** (with showers), are generally loud and rowdy in the summer (sites $10). (Limited reservations for summer weekends are available; call 800-280-CAMP/2267 more than 5 days prior to arrival.) **Carter Lake** (23 sites) and **Tah Kenitch** (34 sites), both $10, are quiet sites for tenters and small RVs. The sites closest to Reedsport are in Winchester Bay and are either ugly, RV-infested, or both. The best campgrounds are between 1 and 4 mi. south of the Bay.

The dunes' shifting grip on the coastline is broken only once along the expanse, when the Umpqua and Smith Rivers empty into Winchester Bay about 1 mi. north of town. **Reedsport,** 21 mi. south of Florence, is a typical small highway town of motels, banks, and flashy restaurants, neatly subdivided by U.S. 101 and Rte. 38. In Reedsport, the **National Recreation Area Information Center** (271-3611), just south of the Umpqua River Bridge, will happily provide you with a map ($3) or *Sand Tracks,* the area recreation guide. (Open Sat.-Thurs. 8am-4:30pm, Fri. 8am-6pm; Sept.-May Mon.-Fri. 8am-4:30pm.) **Winchester Bay,** just south of Reedsport, has inexpensive rooms. The **Harbor View Motel** (271-3352), on U.S. 101, has clean, comfortable rooms. (Singles $28. Doubles $34. Off-season rates $2 lower.)

Those with little time or noise tolerance should at least stop at the **Oregon Dunes Overlook,** off U.S. 101, about halfway between Reedsport and Florence. Wooden ramps lead through the bushes for a peak at some pristine dunes and a glimpse of the ocean. Trails wander off from the overlook, as they do at several other points on U.S. 101. The **Tahkenitch Creek Loop** covers 2½ mi. from the overlook through forest, dunes, wetlands, and beach, and is marked by blue-ringed posts.

For an authentically silence-shattering dune experience, venture out on wheels. Plenty of places between Florence and Coos Bay rent and offer tours. **Pacific Coast Recreation,** 4121 U.S. 101 (756-7183), in Hauser, has direct dune access and restored World War II army vehicles out front. Take a **sand dune tour** in an old transport ($12, under 14 $8) or rent ATVs ($25 per hr.). **Spinreel Dune Buggy Rentals,** 9122 Wild Wood Dr. (759-3313), on U.S. 101, 7 mi. south of Reedsport, rents Honda Odysseys ($20 ½hr., $30 1st hr., $25 2nd hr.). They also have dune buggy rides, a good alternative to the monster dune tours ($15 ½hr., $25 per person per hr.). Family tours in a "VW Thing" are $35 for a half hour, $55 per hour.

When you tire of dune dawdling, you could try **deep-sea fishing** with one of the many charter companies that operate out of **Salmon Harbor,** in Winchester Bay. Like everywhere else on the coast, you can forget salmon fishing, but tuna and bottom-fishing are still available for die-hard enthusiasts. **Gee Gee Charters, Inc.** offers five-hour bottom-fishing trips ($50) daily at 6am and 1pm. Call the 24-hr. phone service several days before you wish to go for a reservation (271-3152). The required one-day license ($6.75) may be purchased at any of the charter offices. Three-hour crabbing trips are also available for $30.

CENTRAL AND EASTERN OREGON

■ Ashland

With an informal, rural setting near the California border, Ashland mixes hippiness and history, making it the perfect locale for the world-famous **Shakespeare Festival.** The brainchild of local college teacher Angus Bowmer, the festival began with two plays performed in the Chautauqua theater by schoolchildren as a complement to daytime boxing matches. Today, professional actors perform 11 plays—Shakespeare's share has shrunk to four; the other seven are classical and contemporary dramas. Performances run from mid-February through October on three Ashland stages—the **Elizabethan Stage,** the **Angus Bowmer,** and the **Black Swan.**

Due to the tremendous popularity of the productions, ticket purchases are recommended six months in advance. General mail-order ticket sales begin in January, but phone orders are not taken until February ($19-37 spring and fall, $22-42 in summer, plus a $3.50 handling fee per order for phone, fax, or mail orders; children under 5 not admitted to any of the shows). For complete ticket info, write Oregon Shakespeare Festival, P.O. Box 158, Ashland 97520 (482-4331; fax 482-8045). Although obtaining tickets can be difficult in the summertime, spontaneous theatergoers should not abandon hope. The **box office** at 15 S. Pioneer St. opens at 9:30am on theater days; prudence demands arriving a few hours early. Local patrons have been known to leave their shoes to hold their places in line, and you should respect this tradition. **Backstage tours** provide a wonderful glimpse of the festival from behind the curtain leaving from the Black Swan (2 hrs.; $8-9, ages 5-17 $6-6.75, children under 5 not admitted; Tues.-Sun. 10am).

The **Ashland Hostel (HI-AYH),** 150 N. Main St. (482-9217), is well-kept, cheery, and run by a wonderful staff that is ready to advise you on the ins and outs of Shakespeare ticket-hunting. (Laundry facilities, kitchen. $12, nonmembers $14. Check-in 5-11pm. Curfew midnight. Lockout 10am-5pm. Reservations advised March-Oct.) **Jackson Hot Springs** is located at 2253 Hwy. 99 N (482-3776), 2 mi. north of Ashland on Hwy. 99; from I-5 go west ½ mi from Exit 19 and turn right on 99. This is the campground nearest to downtown. (Laundry facilities, hot showers, and mineral baths $6 per person, $9 per couple. Sites $13, RV sites $16, with full hookup $18.)

■ Eugene

Situated between the **Siuslaw** (see-YU-slaw) and the **Willamette** (wil-LAM-it) **National Forests,** Oregon's second-largest city sits astride the Willamette River. Home to the **University of Oregon,** Eugene teems with museums, pizza joints, and all the trappings of a college town. The fleet-footed and free-spirited have dubbed Eugene "the running capital of the universe." Only in this city could the annual **Bach Festival,** in late June, be accompanied by the "Bach Run."

The **Eugene-Springfield Visitors Bureau,** 115 W. 8th (484-5307; outside OR 800-547-5445), at Olive St., has it all (open Mon.-Fri. 8:30am-5pm, Sat.-Sun. 10am-4pm; Sept.-April Mon.-Sat. 8:30am-5pm). Info on the area forests can be found at **Willamette National Forest,** 211 E. 7th Ave. (465-6522; open Mon.-Fri. 8am-4:30pm). Both **Amtrak,** 433 Willamette St. (800-USA-RAIL/872-7245), and **Greyhound,** 987 Pearl St. (344-6265 or 800-231-2222; open daily 8am-8pm), roll through town.

Eugene is 111 mi. south of Portland on the I-5 corridor. The University of Oregon campus lies in the southeastern corner of town, bordered on the north by Franklin Blvd., which runs from the city center to I-5. **Willamette Ave.** is the main drag dividing the city into east and west and is interrupted by the **pedestrian mall** on 7th, 8th, and Broadway downtown. The city is a motorist's nightmare of one-way streets; free parking is virtually nonexistent downtown.

The cheapest motels are on E. Broadway and W. 7th St. **Lost Valley Educational Center (HI-AYH),** 81868 Lost Valley Ln. (937-3351), in Dexter, is an educational experience. Take Rte. 58 east for 9 mi. toward Oakbridge, turn right on S. Rattlesnake Creek Rd.; after 4 mi., turn right onto Lost Valley Lane, and 1 mi. later you're there. Come in at night for the organic dinner. Call ahead for reservations. ($9, nonmembers $10. Campsites $6 per person. Dinner Mon.-Fri. $6.) Unfortunately, KOAs (Kampgrounds of America) and RV-only parks monopolize the camping scene around Eugene, but farther east on Rte. 58 and 126 the immense **Willamette National Forest** is packed with forested campsites ($3-16). The **Black Canyon Campground,** 28 mi. east of Eugene on Rte. 58 ($8-16), is another option.

The granola crowd shops at **Sundance Natural Foods,** 748 E. 24th Ave. (343-9142), at 24th and Hilyard (open daily 7am-11pm). **Keystone Cafe,** 395 W. 5th St. (342-2075), is an eclectic co-op serving vegetarian and vegan food (open daily 7am-3pm). At **Café Navarro,** 454 Willamette St. (344-0943), the mood is casual but the Caribbean and Latin cuisine is served with a gourmet flare. Vegetarian and seafood specialties complement a selection of dishes from Jamaica, Ethiopia, and Peru. Have Pozole ($7.50), or another lunch for only $5-6.50. (Open Tues.-Fri. 11am-2pm and 5-9:30pm. Also breakfast Sat.-Sun. 9am-2pm.) For some mellow nightlife, head to the **High St. Brewery Cafe,** 1243 High St. (345-4905; open Mon.-Sat. 11am-1am, Sun. noon-midnight). **Doc's Pad,** 165 W. 11th St. (683-8101), has good (strong) drinks and live music (open daily 7am-3am).

If you just have an afternoon hour to spare, canoe or kayak the **Millrace Canal,** which parallels the Willamette for 3 mi. Rent water craft from **The Water Works Canoe Company,** 1395 Franklin Blvd. (346-4386), which is run by University of Oregon students. (Open summer Mon.-Fri. 3pm-dusk, Sat.-Sun. noon-dusk; $4 per hr.; $14 for 24hr.; $30 deposit.) For a taste of the town, head to the **Saturday Market** (686-8885), at 8th and Oak, held weekly April through November (10am-5pm).

■ Crater Lake

Mirror-blue Crater Lake, the namesake of **Oregon's only national park,** was regarded as sacred by Native American shamans, who forbade their people to look upon it. Iceless in winter, though snowbanked until late July, the flawlessly circular lake plunges from its 6176-ft. elevation to a depth of nearly 2000 ft., making it the nation's deepest lake. It is also one of the most beautiful.

Practical Information In summer, **park admission** for cars is $5; hikers and bikers are charged $3 (free in winter). **William G. Steel Center** (594-2211, ext. 402), next to the park headquarters, provides free **backcountry camping permits,** details on the area, and road conditions. (Open daily 9am-5pm.) In Klamath Falls, find **Amtrak** at S. Spring St. depot (884-2822 or 800-872-7245; open daily 6:45-10:15am and 9-10:30pm), and **Greyhound** at 1200 Klamath Ave. (882-4616; open Mon.-Fri. 6-10am and 11:30am-5:30pm, Sat. 6am-3pm). **Emergency** is 911.

To reach the park from Portland, take I-5 to Eugene, then Rte. 58 east to U.S. 97 south. During the summer you can take Rte. 138 west from U.S. 97 and approach the lake from the park's north entrance, but this route is one of the last to be cleared. Before July, stay on U.S. 97 south to Rte. 62. *All of Crater Lake's services and operating hours are based on changing funding levels, which are not determined until April. Call the Steel Center to verify services and hours.*

Accommodations, Camping, and Food The park contains two campsites. **Mazama Campground** (594-2511) has 194 sites with no hookups (tents $11, RVs $12) and **Lost Creek Campground** (594-2211 ext. 402), at the southwest corner of the park, has just 16 tent-only sites ($10). You may be wise to make your foray to Crater Lake from the **Fort Klamath Lodge Motel** (381-2234), on Rte. 62, 6 mi. from the southern entrance to Crater Lake National Park. (Singles $32. Doubles $42.)

Eating cheaply in the Crater Lake area is hard. Buying food at the **Old Fort Store** (381-2345; open summer daily 9am-7pm) in **Fort Klamath,** is the best bet. In Klamath Falls, shop at the grocery store **Safeway** (882-2660) at Pine and 8th St. (open daily 6am-11pm), or grab a bun-less Buff Dog ($1.50) at **Hobo Junction**, 636 Main St. (882-8013), at 7th St. (open Mon.-Fri. 9am-4pm, Sat. 10am-3pm). **Cattle Crossing Café,** (381-9801) on Hwy. 62 in Fort Klamath, offers a rib-sticking breakfast ($4.25-5.10) and burgers ($4-5.25; open April-Oct. daily 6am-9pm).

Sights About 7700 years ago, Mt. Mazama created this pacific scene in a massive eruption that buried thousands of square miles of the western U.S. under a thick layer of ash. The cataclysmic eruption left a deep caldera which filled gradually with centuries of rain. The clear, reflective lake is the center of activity in the park.

Rim Drive, open only in summer, is a 33-mi. loop high above the lake and leads to some great trails, including **Garfield Peak Trail** (1.7 mi. one way), and **Watchman Lookout** (.8 mi. one way). If pressed for time, walk the easy 100 yd. from the visitors center down to the **Sinnott Memorial Overlook.** The view is the area's most panoramic and accessible. The steep but rewarding hike up **Mt. Scott** (2½ mi. one way), the park's highest peak (a tad under 9000 ft.), begins from the drive near the lake's eastern edge. The **Cleetwood Trail,** a 1-mi. switchback, is the only route to the lake's edge. From here, the **Lodge Company** (594-2511) offers two-hour boat tours on the lake. (Fare $11.75, under 12 $6.50; tour schedule varies; 3-9 tours per day June 18-Sept. 17; take Rim Drive clockwise from either park entrance to get there.) If you take an early tour, you can be left on **Wizard Island** and picked up later. Picnics and fishing are allowed, as is swimming, but the surface temperature reaches a maximum of 50°F (10°C). Park rangers lead free walking tours daily in the summer and periodically during the winter.

■ Bend

Nestled against the east slope of the Cascades, Bend is at the epicenter of a region with a kickin' array of accessible summertime activities. Put on the map in the 1820s by pioneers who found "Farewell Bend" a convenient river ford, the city has grown to become the state's largest urban center east of the Cascades. Bend's young, athletic crowd make the town one of the liveliest and least expensive in the Northwest.

Practical Information U.S. 97 (3rd St.) bisects Bend. The downtown area lies to the west along the Deschutes River; **Wall** and **Bond St.** are the two main arteries. **Central Oregon Welcome Center,** 63085 N. U.S. 97 (382-3221), has good info and free maps and coffee (open Mon.-Sat. 9am-5pm, Sun. 11am-3pm). **Deschutes National Forest Headquarters,** 1645 E. U.S. 20 (388-2715), can inform you on forests, recreation, and the wilderness (open Mon.-Fri. 7:45am-4:30pm). **Greyhound,** 2045 E. U.S. 20 (382-2151), east of town, runs one bus per day to Portland ($21) and Klamath Falls ($20). (Open Mon.-Fri. 7:30-11:30am and 12:30-5:30pm, Sat. 7:30am-noon, Sun. 8-11:30am.) Bend's **post office:** 2300 NE 4th St. (388-1971), at Webster (open Mon.-Fri. 8:30am-5:30pm, Sat. 10am-1pm). **ZIP code:** 97701. **Area code:** 541.

Accommodations Most of the cheapest motels are just outside town on 3rd St. **Bend Cascade Hostel,** 19 SW Century Dr. (389-3813 or 800-299-3813), is a beautiful facility with great management, 2 blocks from ski and bike rentals and the free shuttle to Mt. Bachelor. From 3rd St., take Franklin west, and follow the Cascade Lakes Tour signs to Century Drive (14th St.). (Laundry and kitchen, linen rental available. Lockout 9:30am-4:30pm, curfew 11pm. $14, seniors, students, cyclists, and members $13, under 18 $7.) **Mill Inn,** 642 NW Colorado (389-9198), on the corner of Bond St., is a B&B in a recently rebuilt hotel and boarding house. $15 gets you a bunk in the dorm-style "Locker Room" (capacity 4), or splurge for a trim, elegant private room for $32 for one or $40 for two, with shared bath. Reservations are recommended. **Deschutes National Forest** maintains a huge number of campgrounds in the Cascades to the west of town. All have pit toilets; those with drinking water cost $8-12 per night; those without are free. Contact the **Bend/Ft. Rock Ranger District Office** at 1230 NE 3rd St.,#A262 (388-5664).

Food While downtown Bend offers many pleasant cafés, 3rd St. also proffers a variety of good eateries. **Devore's,** 1124 NW Newport (389-6588), stocks healthy groceries and snacks, plus wine and beer. **West Side Bakery and Café,** 1005 NW Galveston (382-3426), is locally famous for its breakfasts and lunches. Virtually everything here is homemade, including the delicious bread (open daily 7am-3pm). **Taqueria Los Jalapeños,** 601 NE Greenwood Ave. (382-1402), hosts a steady stream of devoted locals coming through the screen door. A bean and cheese burrito costs a piddly $1.50 and the chimichanga plate ($4.75) is the priciest item on the menu (open Mon.-Sat. 7:30am-8pm).

Sights and Outdoors The **High Desert Museum** (382-4754), 6 mi south of Bend on U.S. 97, is a sight for sore eyes, offering indoor and outdoor exhibits on the fragile ecosystem of the Oregon plateau, and dioramas of life in the West in days past. Coming early in the day is your only hope of beating the crowds. Allow at least a few hours for the visit. The price of admission is high, but it's well worth it. (Open daily 9am-5pm. $6.25, seniors and ages 13-18 $5.75, ages 5-12 $3.)

In November 1990, **Newberry National Volcanic Monument** was established to link together and preserve the volcanic features south of Bend. For an introduction to the area, visit the **Lava Lands Visitor Center** (593-2421), 5 mi. south of the High Desert Museum on U.S. 97 (open March to mid-Oct., Wed.-Sun. 10am-4pm, late June-Labor Day daily 9:30am-5pm; off-season dates subject to weather and annual budget decisions). Immediately behind the visitors center is **Lava Butte,** a 500-ft. cinder cone from which much of the nearby lava flows. One mi. south of the visitors center on U.S. 97 is **Lava River Cave** (593-1456), a 100,000-year-old, 1-mi.-long subterranean lava tube. Bundle up before you descend and either bring a lantern or rent one at the cave for $1.50 (entrance $2.50, ages 13-17 $2, under 13 free; open mid-May to mid-Oct. 9am-6pm). The central component of the monument is **Newberry Crater,** 18 mi. south of Lava Butte on U.S. 97, then about 13 steep miles eastward and upward on Rte. 21. This diverse volcanic region covers some 500 sq. mi. and contains two lakes, **Paulina Lake** and **East Lake.** A collection of campgrounds lines the shores of the lakes.

If you can ski the 9075-ft. **Mt. Bachelor,** with its 3100-ft. vertical drop, you're in good company; Mt. Bachelor is one of the home mountains of the U.S. Ski Team (daily lift passes $35, ages 7-12 $19; call 800-829-2442 for more info). Chairlifts are open for sightseers during the summer (open daily 10am-4pm; $9.50, kids $4.75, seniors $6.50) and in the summer a U.S. Forest Service naturalist gives free presentations on local natural history on the summit daily at 11am and 1pm.

Whitewater rafting, although costly, is a favorite local recreational activity. Trips usually run around $70-80 per person per day, $35 per half day. Get a list of rafting outfits at the tourist office. **Cascade River Adventures** and **Sun Country Tours** (call 389-8370 or 800-770-2161 for both) run half-day ($34; under 12 $28) and full-day ($80; under 12 $70) trips out of the Sun River Resort (15 mi. south of Bend off U.S. 97) and out of an office in Bend (61115 S. Hwy. 97).

■ Hells Canyon

"The government bet you 160 acres that you couldn't live there three years without starving to death," said one early white settler of the region. Hells Canyon's endearing name comes from its legendary inaccessibility and hostility to human inhabitants. It is North America's deepest gorge: in some places the walls drop 5500 ft. to **Snake River** below. The fault and fold lines in the canyon walls make the cliffs seem to melt into great wrinkles of grass and rock. **Hells Canyon National Recreation Area** is a dumbfoundingly beautiful, insanely remote, and astoundingly rugged corner of the northwest.

The only way to even get close to the canyon without taking at least a full day is to drive the **Hells Canyon National Scenic Loop Drive,** which will only give you only the vaguest conception of what Hells Canyon is all about. The drive begins and ends in Baker City, following Rte. 86, Forest Service Rd. 39 and 350, Rte. 82, and finally I-84. Even this entirely paved route takes from six hours to two days to drive (and it covers nearly every mile of pavement in the area). Lookout points provide dramatic views of the rugged canyons. **Hells Canyon Overlook,** the most accessible (though least impressive), is reached by driving up Forest Rd. 3965. The road departs Rd. 39 about 5 mi. south of the Imnaha River crossing. The immense **Hells Canyon Dam** lies 23 mi. north of Oxbow on Rte. 86. The Snake's-eye views from the winding road become more dramatic the farther north you go. This drive is the only way to get near the bottom of the canyon by car.

The easiest way to see a lot of the canyon is to zip through on a jet boat tour or float through on a raft. A panoply of outfitters operate out of Oxbow and the dam area and run trips through the canyon. The Wallowa Mountains Visitor Center has a list of all the permittees, or pick up a brochure at any Chamber of Commerce office. **Hells Canyon Adventures,** (785-3352, outside Oregon 800-422-3568), 1½ mi. from the Hells Canyon Dam in Oxbow, runs a wide range of jet boat and raft trips through the Canyon. You can take a full day ($70) or three hour ($30) jet boat tour. A full day of whitewater rafting ($90) includes a jet boat ride back upstream.

Hiking is perhaps the best way to fully comprehend the vast emptiness of Hells Canyon, but to really get into the canyon requires a backpacking trip of at least a few days. There are over 1000 mi. of trails in the canyon, only a fraction of which are maintained regularly by the Forest Service. A wide array of dangers lurks below the rim; discuss your plans with rangers before heading out.

The largest town and service center in the area is Enterprise, 65 mi. from La Grande on Rte. 82. The **Wallowa Mountains Visitor Center,** 88401 Rte. 82 (426-5546), is on the west side of Enterprise. This is a good place to start for extensive information and tips on what to see and do, as well as museum exhibits and slide shows. Detailed maps are worth the $3 price (open Mon.-Sat. 8am-5pm). For info on **road and trail conditions,** call the Chamber of Commerce at 426-4622. In an **emergency,** dial 911.

Camping in the region can be a spiritual experience for those who have made adequate preparations. If you must have a roof over your head, the **Indian Lodge Motel,** 201 S. Main (432-2651), on Rte. 82 in Joseph, 6 mi. south of Enterprise, has elegant air conditioned rooms. (Singles $35. Doubles $45). The Hells Canyon area is covered with primitive campgrounds. Many have no drinking water, and none have showers. **Copperfield, McCormick,** and **Woodland** (all owned by Idaho Power) have tent and RV sites and restrooms, and are the only campgrounds open year round. These manicured campgrounds are located near Oxbow and Brownlee Dams, on Rte. 86 and Rte. 71 on the Snake (tent fee $6, RV fee $8).

Accessing the area without a vehicle or a horse is difficult. Some people hitchhike in from the gateway towns of Joseph or Halfway, and talk it up with people at campsites to get back out. *Let's Go* does not recommend hitchhiking.

PACIFIC NORTHWEST

CALIFORNIA

For hundreds of years, settlers have come to California in search of the ephemeral and the unattainable. The Spanish conquistadors came for the mythical land of El Dorado, crusty 49ers hunted for the Mother Lode, while the naïve and beautiful still search for stardom. Those fleeing a world devoid of dreams still believe that California is a bastion of eternal opportunity.

California's status as a land of bewildering possibility stems from its uniquely divergent blend of cultural influences. The glare of headlights, the clang of a trolley, the bustle of the barrio, the soft vanilla scent of Jeffery pines, and the ghostly shimmer of the desert floor are all California. The breezy liberalism of the Bay Area, the consciously chic stylization of L.A., and the trendy traditionalism of San Diego are all California. It is not without conflict that these visions collide. The anti-war movement of the 60s and 70s, the political tensions of the 80s, and the race riots of the 90s all testify to the delicate balance which exists in California and to the strength of the forces that bring the state together.

Literally the movers of the world, the tectonic plates that rumble far below the surface reflect the Earth's change and growth. Californians have learned to live with this phenomenon and now almost revel in its power. The periodic shakes can be survived and California drifts ever farther from the rest of the continent. They bring with them the volatile mix of personalities that both creates and destroys. To the north and south, people build their monuments to themselves.

This book is cool and all, but for the hippest, funniest inside scoop on the wacky Cali scene, check out the red-hot *Let's Go: California and Hawai'i 1997*.

PRACTICAL INFORMATION

Capital: Sacramento.
California Office of Tourism: 801 K St. #1600, Sacramento 95814 (call 800-862-2543 to have a package of tourism materials sent to you).
Time Zone: Pacific (3hr. behind Eastern). **Postal Abbreviation:** CA.
State Song: "I Love You, California."
Unofficial State Song: "California Über Alles."
Sales Tax: 7-8%, by county.

■ Los Angeles

Myth and anti-myth stand comfortably opposed in Los Angeles. Some see in its sweeping beaches and dazzling sun an extravagant demi-paradise, a bountiful land of opportunity where the most opulent dreams can be realized. Others point to its congestion, its smog, its increasing crime, and declare Los Angeles a sham, a converted wasteland where TV-numbed brain-dead masses go to wither in the sun.

Here is a wholly American urban phenomenon, one that developed not in the image and shadow of Europe, but contemporaneously with America's international ascendancy. It is this autonomy which gives L.A. its peculiar sense of pastlessness. In a city where nothing seems more than 30 years old, the latest trends curry more respect than the venerably ancient. Many come to this historical vacuum to make (or re-make) themselves. And what better place? Without the tiresome duty to kowtow to the gods of an established high culture, Angelenos are free to indulge not in what they must, but what they choose. The resulting atmosphere is deliciously rife with potential. Some may savor L.A.'s image-bound culture, others may be appalled by the shallowness of its unabashed excess—in any case, it's a hell of a show.

PRACTICAL INFORMATION

Tourist Office: Los Angeles Convention and Visitors Bureau, 685 S. Figueroa St. 90017 (213-689-8822), downtown. Hundreds of brochures. Publishes *Destina-*

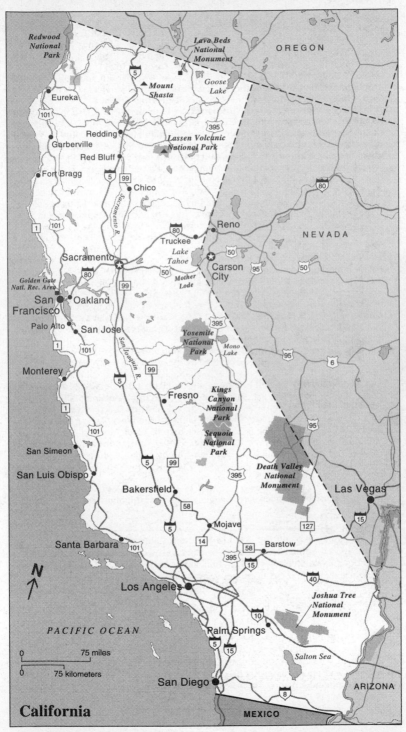

CALIFORNIA

California

tion Los Angeles, a free booklet including tourist information and a lodging guide. Open Mon.-Fri. 8am-5pm, Sat. 8:30am-5pm. In **Hollywood** at 6541 Hollywood Blvd. (213-689-8822). Open Mon.-Sat. 9am-1pm, 2-5pm. In **Santa Monica,** 1400 Ocean Ave. (213-393-7593), in Palisades Park. Open daily 10am-5pm; winter 10am-4pm. **Gay and Lesbian Community Services Center,** 1625 Schrader Ave., Hollywood (213-993-7400), 1 block from Hollywood Blvd. Youth and senior groups, employment, housing, educational, legal, and medical services. Open Mon.-Sat. 9am-10pm, Sun. 9am-6pm, but most offices close around 5pm.

Trains: Greyhound-Trailways Information Center: 1716 E. 7th St. (800-231-2222), at Alameda, downtown. Call for fares, schedules, and local ticket information. See neighborhood listings for other stations. In **Hollywood,** 1409 N. Vine St. (213-466-6384), 1 block south of Sunset; in **Santa Monica,** at 4th and Broadway.

Public Transportation: MTA Bus Information Line: 213-626-4455. You may be put on hold until the next ice age. Open Mon.-Fri. 8:30am-5pm. **Santa Monica Municipal (Big Blue) Bus Lines:** 1660 7th St. (310-451-5444), at Olympic. Faster and cheaper than the MTA. Fare 50¢ for most routes and 25¢ transfer tickets for MTA buses. Transfers to other Big Blue buses are free. **Important bus routes:** #1 and #2 connect Santa Monica and Venice. Bus #10 provides express service from Santa Monica (at 7th and Grand) to downtown L.A. Open Mon.-Fri. 8am-5pm.

Taxis: Checker Cab (482-3456), **Independent** (385-8294), **United Independent** (653-5050). If you need a cab, it's best to call.

Los Angeles County Commission on Disabilities: 500 W. Temple St. (213-974-1053). Information on transportation and recreational facilities for people with disabilities. Open Mon.-Fri. 8:30am-5pm. **California Relay Service for the Hearing Impaired:** 800-735-2929 (TTD/TTY). 24-hr. assistance.

Highway Conditions: 800-427-7623. AM radio stations offer frequent reports.

Crisis Lines: AIDS Hotline, 800-922-2437, or try the national hotline, 800-342-5971. For recorded information, call 976-4700. There is a small charge for this service. **Rape Crisis,** 310-392-9896. 24-hr. hotline.

Hospitals: Cedar-Sinai Medical Center, 8700 Beverly Blvd. (310-855-5000, emergency 310-855-6517). **Good Samaritan,** 616 S. Witmer St. (977-2121).

Emergency: 911.

Post Office: Centrally located branch at 900 N. Alameda, at 9th St. (310-431-6546). Open Mon.-Fri. 9am-5pm, Sat. 9am-noon. **ZIP code information:** 586-1737. **General Delivery ZIP code:** 90086. In Hollywood, at 1615 Wilcox Ave. (464-2194). Open Mon.-Fri. 8am-5pm, Sat. 8am-1pm. **General Delivery ZIP code:** 90028. In Santa Monica, at 1248 5th St. (576-2626), at Arizona. Open Mon.-Fri. 9am-5pm, Sat. 9am-1pm. **General Delivery ZIP Code:** 90401. **Area codes:** Downtown Los Angeles, Hollywood, Huntington Park, Santa Monica, and Montebello **213.** Malibu, Pacific Coast Highway, Beverly Hills, the Westside, southern Los Angeles County **310.** Northern Los Angeles County, San Fernando Valley, and Pasadena **818.** Orange County **714.** San Diego County **619.** Eastern border of L.A. County **909.** Ventura County **805.** Codes may change. Check with the operator.

ORIENTATION

Los Angeles sprawls along the coast of Southern California, 127 mi. north of San Diego and 403 mi. south of San Francisco. You can still be "in" L.A. even if you're 50 mi. from downtown. Before you even think about navigating Los Angeles's 6500 mi. of streets and 40,000 intersections, get yourself a good **map**—Los Angeles defies all human comprehension. A sound investment is the *Thomas Guide: Los Angeles County Street Guide and Directory* ($25).

The predominately Latino section of L.A. known as **East L.A.** begins east of downtown's Western Ave., with the districts of **Boyle Heights, Montebello,** and **El Monte.** South of downtown are the **University of Southern California (USC), Exposition Park,** and the districts of **Watts** and **Compton,** home to a large concentration of African-Americans. The area south of downtown, known as **South Central,** suffered the brunt of the fires and looting that erupted in 1992. South Central and East L.A. are considered crime-ridden and have little to attract tourists.

Los Angeles Area

Northwest of downtown is **Hollywood.** Sunset Boulevard presents a cross-section of virtually everything L.A. has to offer: lavish wealth, famous nightclubs along The Strip, sleazy motels, the old elegance of Silver Lake, and Chicano murals. Hollywood Boulevard runs just beneath the Hollywood Hills.

West of Hollywood, the **Westside** encompasses West Hollywood, Westwood, Century City, Culver City, Bel Air, Brentwood and (for our purposes) the independent city of **Beverly Hills.** The affluent Westside also is home to the University of California at Los Angeles and some trendy, off-beat Melrose Ave. hangouts. The area west of downtown is known as the **Wilshire District** after its main boulevard. **Hancock Park,** a green residential area, covers the northeast portion of the district.

The **Valley** spreads north of the Hollywood Hills and the Santa Monica Mountains. For most people, *the* valley is the **San Fernando Valley,** where more than a million people live in the suburbs, in a basin bounded to the north and west by the Santa Susanna Mountains and the Simi Freeway, to the south by the Ventura Freeway, and to the east by the Golden State Freeway. The valleys also contain the suburb of **San Gabriel** and the city of **Pasadena.**

Eighty miles of beach line L.A.'s **Coastal Region. Zuma** is northernmost, followed by **Malibu,** which lies 15 mi. up the coast from **Santa Monica.** Just a bit farther south is the funky and famous beach community of **Venice.** The beach towns south of Santa Monica, comprising the area called the **South Bay,** are Marina del Rey, Manhattan, Hermosa, and Redondo Beach. South across the **Palos Verdes Peninsula** is **Long Beach,** a port city of a half-million people. Finally, farthest south are the **Orange County** beach cities: Seal Beach, Sunset Beach, Huntington Beach, Newport Beach, and Laguna Beach. Confused yet? Everyone is. Invest in good maps.

GETTING AROUND

Nobody walks in L.A.

— Missing Persons

Public Transportation Nowhere in America is the automobile held in greater reverence than in L.A., though the **Metropolitan Transit Authority (MTA)** does work—sort of. The MTA was formerly known as the RTD (Rapid Transit District) and some older buses may still be labeled as such. Using the MTA to sightsee in L.A. can be frustrating simply because attractions tend to be spread out, and the system is not easily understood. Those determined to see *everything* in L.A. should get behind the wheel of a car. If this is not possible, base yourself in downtown or in Hollywood (where there are plenty of bus connections), make daytrips, and have plenty of change for the bus. Bus service is dismal in the outer reaches of the city, and two-hr. journeys are not unusual.

To familiarize yourself with the MTA, write for "sector maps," MTA, P.O. Box 194, Los Angeles 90053, or stop by one of the 10 **customer-service centers.** There are three downtown: Gateway Transit Center, Union Station (Mon.-Fri. 6am-6:30pm); Arco Plaza, 505 S. Flower St., Level C (daily 7:30am-3:30pm); and 5301 Wilshire (daily 8:30am-5pm); all dispense info and schedules. If you don't have time to map your route in advance, call 800-COMMUTE/266-6883 (TDD 800-252-9040; daily 5:30am-11:30pm) for transit info and schedules. Ninety percent of MTA's lines offer **wheel-chair-accessible buses** (call 1hr. in advance, 800-621-7828 daily 6am-10pm). Accessible bus stops are marked with the international symbol of disabled access.

Bus service is best downtown and along the major thoroughfares west of downtown. (There is 24-hr. service, for instance, on Wilshire Blvd.) The downtown **DASH shuttle** costs only 25¢ and serves Chinatown, Union Station, Gateway Transit Center, Olvera St., City Hall, Little Tokyo, the Music Center, ARCO Plaza, and more! They are extremely useful because downtown traffic is a disaster. DASH also operates a shuttle on Sunset Blvd. in Hollywood, as well as shuttles in Pacific Palisades, Watts, Fairfax, Midtown, Crenshaw, Van Nuys/Studio City, Warner Center, and Southeast L.A. (Downtown DASH operates Mon.-Fri. 6:30am-6:30pm, Sat. 10am-5pm; the Pacific Palisades shuttles do not run on Sat. Schedule information: 800-2LA-RIDE/252-7433.) Venice DASH operates every 10 min. on weekends during the busy summer season from 11am to 6pm. Call 213-485-7201 for pickup points. Parking costs $2.50, but this is much cheaper than at the beach. (MTA's basic fare is $1.35, seniors (62+) and passengers with disabilities 45¢, regular transfers 25¢, senior and disabled transfers 10¢, exact change required.) Transfers operate from one MTA line to another or to another transit authority. **All route numbers given are MTA unless otherwise designated.**

Freeways The freeway is perhaps the most enduring of L.A.'s images. When uncongested, these well-marked, 10- and 12-lane concrete roadways offer the ultimate in speed and convenience; the trip from downtown to Santa Monica can take as little as 20 min. A nighttime cruise along the I-10 past downtown—whizzing through the tangle of interchanges and on- and off-ramps, with the lights of L.A.'s skyscrapers as a backdrop—can be exhilarating.

The most frustrating aspect of driving is the sheer unpredictability of L.A. traffic. It goes without saying that rush hours, both morning and evening, are always a mess and well worth avoiding. But with construction performed at random hours there can be problems anytime. The solution? Patience. A little reminder: no matter how crowded the freeway is, it's almost always quicker and safer than taking surface streets to your destination. A good rule of thumb is that the same distance will take five times as long on surface streets as on the freeway.

Californians refer to their highways by names, numbers, or both. The names are little more than hints of a freeway's route, at best harmless, at worst misleading. For freeway information, call **CalTrans** (213-897-3693).

Do not hitchhike! In Los Angeles, it is tantamount to suicide. You could get picked up by a psycho, or run over by an absent-minded L.A. driver.

L.A. Westside

Armand Hammer Museum, 1
Beverly Hills High School, 2
Chateau Marmont, 3
Elvis' house: 2274 Hillcrest, 4
Farmer's Market, 5
Happy Days house: 565 N. Cahuenga, 6
Heidi Fleiss' house: 1270 Tower Grove Dr., 7
Hyatt on Sunset/ the Riot House, 8
Le Parc, 9
Los Angeles County Museum of Art, 10
Marilyn Monroe's house: 12305 Fifth Helena Dr., 11
Menendez/Prince/Elton John house: 722 N. Elm Dr., 12
O.J.'s house: 360 Rockingham Ave., 13
Playboy Mansion: 10236 Charing Cross, 14
Site of Hugh Grant's Arrest, 15
Spelling Mansion: 594 N. Mapleton Dr., 16
St. James Club, 17
Sunset Marquis, 18

TO GRIFFITH PARK AND MADONNA'S HOUSE
Franklin Ave.
Hollyhock House
Barnsdall Park
Vermont Ave.
Hollywood Frwy.
Western Ave.
Paramount Studios
HOLLYWOOD
DETAIL MAP
Vine
Cahuenga Blvd.
Highland
WEST HOLLYWOOD
Franklin Ave.
Hollywood Blvd.
Sunset Blvd.
Genessee
Fountain Ave.
Santa Monica Blvd.
Fairfax Ave.
Crescent Hts. Blvd.
Melrose Ave.
Ave.
Kings Rd.
Beverly Blvd.
Alta Loma Rd.
La Brea Blvd.
CBS Studios
Pan Pacific Park
Hancock Park
La Brea Tar Pits
3rd St.
Burton Way
Wilshire Blvd.
San Vicente
Fairfax Ave.
Venice
Crescent Hts. Blvd.
La Cienega
Pico Blvd.
Robertson Blvd.
Blvd.
Doheny Dr.
Hillcrest Rd.
Sunset Blvd.
Santa Monica Blvd.
Elm Dr.
Hillcrest Rd.
BEVERLY HILLS
Crescent Dr.
Canon Dr.
Beverly Dr.
Rodeo Dr.
Coldwater Canyon Drive
Franklin County Ranch
Lake Franklin
Olympic Blvd.
Century City Dr.
Moreno Dr.
Museum of Tolerance
Century Plaza Towers
Rancho Park
Santa Monica Frwy.
N
Roxbury Dr.
Beverly Hills Hotel
The Los Angeles Country Club
CENTURY CITY
Century Park E
Century Park W
Ave. of the Stars
Fox Studios
Little Santa Monica Blvd.
Tower Rd.
Benedict Canyon Rd.
Mapleton Dr.
Charing Cross
WESTWOOD
Century Square
Westwood Memorial Cemetery
Hilgard Ave.
Westwood Blvd.
Veteran Ave.
Sepulveda Blvd.
UCLA
Gayley Ave.
Le Conte Dr.
Sunset Blvd.
San Diego Frwy.
BRENTWOOD
Bristol Ave.
Bundy Dr.
San Vicente Blvd.
Santa Monica Blvd.
Barrington Ave.
Wilshire Blvd.
Olympic Blvd.
TO SANTA MONICA AND VENICE
TO SANTA MONICA AIRPORT

Vermont Ave.
Carmen Beachwood
Gower St.
Hollywood Memorial Park Cemetery
Yucca St.
Capitol Records Building
Frederick's of Hollywood Building
Hollywood Palladium
Cahuenga Blvd.
Vine St.
Sunset Blvd.
Franklin Ave.
Homewood Ave.
Fountain Ave.
Cole Ave.
Santa Monica Blvd.
Banana Bungalow Hollywood
Hollywood Int'l Guest House Hostel
Hollywood Wax Museum
Church of Scientology
Hollywood Int'l Youth Hostel
De Longpre Ave.
Cherokee Ave.
Lexington Ave.
June St.
McCadden Pl.
Las Palmas Ave.
Hollywood Bowl
Hollywood Hills Hostel
Highland Ave.
Mansfield Ave.
Orange Dr.
Mann's Chinese Theatre
Egyptian Theatre
Max Factor Beauty Museum
Walk of Fame
Hollywood Blvd.
Selma Ave.

ACCOMMODATIONS

As in any large city, cheap accommodations in Los Angeles may be unsafe as well. It can be difficult to gauge from the exterior whether a potential hotel is a dream bargain or a nightmare. Be suspicious of unusually low posted rates; they are rarely the bargains they seem. Ask to see a room before you plunk down any cash. Hotels in L.A. should cost at least $35 or they're probably not the kind of hotels in which most travelers would feel secure. For those willing to share a room and a bathroom, hostels (see below) are a saving grace. In choosing where to stay, the first consideration should be how much access you have to a car. If you don't have wheels, you would be wise to decide what element of L.A. appeals to you the most. Those visiting for the beaches would do well to choose lodgings in Venice or Santa Monica. Avid sightseers will probably be better off in Hollywood or the slightly more expensive (but cleaner and nicer) Westside. Downtown has lots of public transportation but is unsafe after dark. **Listed prices do not include L.A.'s 14% hotel tax.**

Hollywood

Although Tinseltown has worked up quite a bit of tarnish in recent years, its location, sights, and nightlife keep the tourists coming. Exercise caution if scouting out one of the many budget hotels on Hollywood or Sunset Blvd.—especially east of the main strips, the area can be frightening, particularly at night. The hostels here are generally excellent, a much better value than anything else downtown.

Orange Drive Manor, 1764 N. Orange Dr. (213-850-0350). Spiffy craftsman-style home in a low-key residential neighborhood just around the corner from Mann's Chinese Theater. $25 gets you a private room. The spacious $15 dorms only house 2-4 beds each and sport antique furniture. Some have private baths. Call ahead—they don't open the door unless you have a reservation. Kitchen, TV lounge, and free linens. Parking $5 per night. Check-out noon. No credit cards.

Student Inn International Hostel, 7038½ Hollywood Blvd. (213-469-6781). Comfy dorm rooms with 2-4 bunks and a private bath ($10-15). Doubles $30-34. Free linens and donut-stocked kitchen. Free pickup from LAX, Union Station, and the Greyhound station. Free parking. Free tickets to Disneyland, Universal Studios, and Magic Mountain. This is not a misprint. Call far in advance for reservations. No credit cards. **International passport required.**

Hollywood International Hostel, 6820 Hollywood Blvd. (800-750-6561 or 213-463-0797 outside the U.S.A.) Sparkling clean budget nirvana. Capacious lounge with free pool and a repro of Breugel's *Peasant Wedding*. Two kitchens, über-clean hall bathrooms, laundry, e-mail, and fax. Plenty of tours and parties. Locks on each room, but not on the front door. Bunks $12, private rooms $30. 28-day max. stay. 24-hr. check-in, but check-out 10am. Reserve ahead with a credit card.

Westside: Beverly Hills, Westwood, Wilshire

The Westside is a snazzy and relatively safe part of town with excellent public transportation to the beaches. Those planning to stay at least one month in summer or six months during the school year can call the **UCLA Off-Campus Housing Office** (310-825-4491; 350 Deneve Dr.; open Mon.-Fri. 8am-5pm) who can put you in touch with students who have a spare room through their "roommate share board."

The Little Inn, 10604 Santa Monica Blvd. (310-475-4422; fax 475-3236), West L.A. Found on "Little Santa Monica," the smaller road paralleling the divided boulevard to the south. The Little Inn has an unimpressive front, but step into the courtyard and you've reached budget-travel bliss. Rooms are sizable and very clean. A/C, TV, fridge. 24-hr. check-in. Check-out 11am. Singles $40; doubles $45-55.

Stars Inn, 10269 Santa Monica Blvd. (310-556-3076; fax 277-6202). Several blocks east of the Little Inn, the Stars is managed by the same group, and delivers a similarly high level of quality. Spacious and clean, with sparkling bathrooms. Rock-out location across from the Century City Shopping Center. A/C, cable TV, refrigerator. Check-out 11am. Singles $40 per night, $280 per week (sleeps 1-2); doubles $45-55, $350 per week (sleeps 2-4). $5 higher in July-Aug.

Bevonshire Lodge Motel, 7575 Beverly Blvd. (213-936-6154; fax 934-6640), near Farmer's Market. Clean motel with quiet, enclosed pool. Fridges and free parking. Singles $38.50; doubles $42.50. Room with kitchen $48.50. 10% ISIC discount.

Santa Monica and Venice

Venice Beach hostels beckon a cornucopia of young budget travelers. The panoply of cheap accommodations peppering the coast generally cater to raucous party kids, but there are some quiet gems in the mix. The hostels are a popular destination for foreign students, lured by a lively blend of indulgent beach culture and relentless nightlife, centered around Venice's Main St. and Santa Monica's 3rd St. Promenade.

HI-Los Angeles/Santa Monica, 1436 2nd St. (310-393-9913; fax 393-1769), Santa Monica, 2 blocks from the beach and across from the 3rd St. promenade. Take MTA #3 from downtown to 2nd and Broadway, Blue Bus #3 from airport to 4th and Broadway, or Blue Bus #10 from downtown. Exquisite hostel with tight security. Modern and clean lobby looks more like that of a swank office building than an inexpensive hostel. Colossal kitchen, huge laundry facilities, 2 nightly movies, gorgeous library, and a hot breakfast (75¢-$2.75). 28-day max. stay. $16 per night, private doubles $50; non-members add $3. Located next door to the associated Santa Monica Travelers Center (310-393-3413), which offers travel books, equipment, all types of rail passes, and an Air-Tech office.

Cadillac Hotel, 401 Ocean Front Walk (310-399-8876; fax 399-4536), Venice. An abfab art-deco landmark directly on the beachfront. Large and well-equipped gym, Finnish sauna. Rooftop sundeck and available parking (a real find in Venice). BYOB bar with pool table and authentic gondola from Venice's past as well as a piece of the Berlin wall. A bunk in a dorm-style room with bath is an absolute steal at $20. No reservations for bunks—show up around 11am and hope. Rooms are pricey but luxurious (from $55). Mention *Let's Go* for a discount. International crowd. Friendly staff. Wheelchair accessible.

Jim's at The Beach, 17 Brooks Ave. (310-399-4018), Venice. Outstanding location ½ block off the boardwalk. Run by Jim of *Backpacker's Bible* fame. **Passport required,** but recently traveled Americans welcome. Up to 6 beds per clean and sunny room. Kitchen and laundry. No curfew. Linen included. Voucher for a free dinner at Jim's choice of café on the Boardwalk. $20 key deposit. $20 per night, $130 per week. Discount for multi-night stays.

Downtown

Though extremely busy and relatively safe by day, the downtown area empties and becomes dangerous when the workday ends and on weekends. Both men and women should travel in groups after dark, especially in the area between Broadway and Main. The area is, however, home to some good bargain lodgings. Don't be afraid to haggle, especially during the off-season. Ask about cheaper weekly rates.

Hotel Stillwell, 838 S. Grand Ave. (213-627-1151 or 800-553-4774; fax 622-8940). Recently refurbished, this ultra-clean hotel is one of the most sensible downtown options. Rooms are bright and pleasantly decorated with new furniture and linens. Free Indian vegetarian breakfast in the restaurant downstairs. Parking area next door ($3 per day). Singles $39, $175 per week; doubles $49, $225 per week.

Motel de Ville, 1123 W. 7th St. (213-624-8474; fax 624-7652). If they can't house you, the City Center Motel next door will. Clean rooms with A/C and HBO. Pool, continental breakfast, free parking. Singles $35, doubles $40.

Park Plaza Hotel, 607 S. Park View St. (213-384-5281), on the west corner of 6th, across from green but unsafe MacArthur Park. Built in 1927, this grandiose Art Deco giant has a 3-story marble-floored lobby and a huge staircase seen in the ground-breaking post-modern opus *Newsies*. It has catered to the likes of Bing Crosby and Eleanor Roosevelt. Clean, small rooms have TVs; some have A/C. Olympic-size pool and weight room. Singles from $57, doubles $62.50.

CALIFORNIA

FOOD

The range of culinary options in L.A. mirrors the city's ethnic diversity—over 140 different languages are spoken here. Certain types of food are concentrated in specific areas. Jewish and Eastern European food is most prevalent in **Fairfax;** Mexican in **East L.A.;** Japanese, Chinese, Vietnamese, and Thai around **Little Tokyo, Chinatown,** and **Monterey Park,** and seafood along the coast. There are also restaurants where the main objective is to be seen, and the food is secondary, as well as those where the food itself seems too beautiful to be eaten—it was here, after all, that 80s *nouvelle cuisine* reached its zenith.

Fortunately for the budget traveler, Los Angeles elevates fast-food and chain restaurants to heights virtually unknown in the rest of the country. Many high-quality chains (most with take-out), each of which offers something special, cheap, and standardized in the most positive sense of the word. Chains are a way of life in L.A., and an attempt to localize a culture that is as diffuse as they come. For the optimal burger-and-fries experience, try **In 'n' Out Burger** (various locations, call 818-287-4377 for the one nearest you), a beloved chain evoking the halcyon 50s. Those who fear not gluts of grease should ask for the "4x4"—it's not on the menu, but they'll know. **Johnny Rocket's** (founded in 1986 AD) returns you to the never really lost era of American diners. Their chocolate shakes are *alimenta deorum.*

Hollywood

Hollywood and Sunset Blvd. have a range of excellent and diverse cuisines, while Fairfax has Mediterranean-style restaurants and delis. Melrose is full of chic cafés, many with outdoor seating perfect for people-watching. The proximity of Hollywood and West Hollywood causes the borders to blend together. It can be difficult to tell where the district (Hollywood) ends and the city (West Hollywood) begins. Visitors in search of good food would be wise to consider restaurants in both areas.

> **The Source,** 8301 Sunset Blvd. (213-659-6388). The health food restaurant where Woody Allen and Diane Keaton broke up in *Annie Hall.* Keep an eye out for Seinfeld (with Shoshana) or Fabio. Sandwiches ($5-6) and house specialty "magic mushrooms" ($8). Open Mon.-Fri. 8am-11pm, Sat. 9am-11pm, Sun. 9am-10pm.
>
> **Toi on Sunset,** 7505½ Sunset Blvd. (213-874-8062). Decor is a way-trendy mélange of posters, funky lamps, leopard-skin armchairs, and psychedelic murals. Clientele is as painfully hip as the interior decorating. Tarantino is a regular. *Pad thai* or vegetable curry $7. Lunch specials $5. Open daily 11-4am.
>
> **Duke's,** 8909 Sunset Blvd. (310-652-3100), at San Vicente in West Hollywood. Best place in L.A. to see **hung-over rock stars.** The walls are a kaleidoscope of posters and autographed album covers. Try the "Revenge"—eggs scrambled with avocado, sour cream, onions, tomatoes, and peppers. Entrees $4-7. Open Mon.-Fri. 7:30am-9pm, Sat.-Sun. 8am-4pm. No credit cards.
>
> **Pink's Famous Chili Dogs,** 711 N. La Brea Ave. (213-931-4223). More of an institution than a hot dog stand, Pink's has been serving up chili-slathered doggies ($2.10) to locals and celebs since 1939. Bruce Willis proposed to Demi here all those films ago. Open Sun.-Thurs. 8am-2am, Fri.-Sat. 8am-3am. No credit cards.
>
> **Chin Chin,** 8618 Sunset Blvd. (310-652-1818), in West Hollywood. Other locations in Brentwood, Studio City, and Woodland Hills. Immensely popular with the lunchtime set for its handmade *"dim sum* and then sum" (around $5). The shredded chicken salad ($6.50) is a perfect example of Sino-Californian cuisine. Outdoor seating and take-out. Special lite menu for the health-conscious. Open Sun.-Thurs. 11am-11pm, Fri.-Sat. 11am-midnight.

Wilshire District and Hancock Park

L.A.'s culture vultures convene in the Wilshire District to peruse the latest exhibitions, but its eateries are sadly out of step with its world-class museums. The museums line Wilshire Blvd., while inexpensive (and often kosher) restaurants dot Fairfax and Pico Blvd.

Cassell's Hamburgers, 3266 W. 6th St. (213-480-8668). Some say these burgers are the finest in the city. They're juicy, enormous, and come with as much potato salad and cottage cheese as you can fit on your sizable plate. Basic 1/3-lb. burger $4.60, more health-conscious folks can opt for the turkey burger ($4.60) or chicken breast ($5). Open Mon.-Sat. 10:30am-4pm. No credit cards.

Shalom Pizza, 8715 W. Pico Blvd. (213-271-2255). Kosher pizza in a quiet Jewish business district. Large cheese $11. RCC supervision. Open Sun. and Thurs. 11am-10pm, Mon.-Wed. 10am-9pm, Fri. 11am-2hr. before sundown, Sat. 1hr. after sunrise-2am. No credit cards.

Beverly Hills and Century City

Don't let the image fool you—Beverly Hills is a heavily touristed, accessible area in which, as in decayed Hollywood, it is possible to work with, not against, the glam. Accordingly, there is budget dining in Beverly Hills; it just takes a little looking.

Baja Fresh, 475 N. Beverly Dr. (658-6690) at Little Santa Monica. Join the crush of locals in the know and devour some of BH's healthiest, freshest, and cheapest Mexican food. Taco, rice, beans, chips, and fresh *pico de gallo* for $3. Open Mon.-Sat. 11am-9pm. No credit cards.

Finney's in the Alley, 8840 Olympic Blvd. (888-8787) Heading east on Olympic, turn right on Clark and immediately right into the alley and look for the yellow awning. You've probably never heard of it because the manager refuses to advertise for fear that "the secret will get out." Finney's most expensive offering is a steak sandwich ($4). Open Mon.-Sat. 11am-8pm.

Ed Debevic's, 134 N. La Cienega Blvd. (659-1952), Beverly Hills. This site of many a Sweet Sixteen party has large portions yummy food served by Elvis or Buddy Holly à la Jackrabbit Slim's in *Pulp Fiction.* Full bar. Open Sept.-May Mon.-Thurs. 11:30am-3pm and 5:30-10pm, Fri.-Sat. 11:30am-midnight, Sun. 11:30am-10pm, June-Aug. Sun.-Thurs. 11:30am-10pm, Fri.-Sat. 11:30am-midnight.

Westwood and UCLA

Westwood is home to tens of thousands of students, meaning that despite the surrounding high rents, this is budget traveler paradise. What do students want? Cheap food and beer. Consequently, both can be found in abundance. Ask about student discounts. The cheapest beer in town (99¢) can be imbibed at **Tacos Tacos,** 1084 Glendon Ave. in the Village.

Don Antonio's, 1136 Westwood Blvd. (310-209-1422), Westwood Village. Sinatra, red-checkered tablecloths, and huge portions of wonderful food make this expensive-looking establishment an all-hours fave with students and businessfolk alike. Drop in between 11am and 3pm (Mon.-Fri.) for the lunch special: a large slice of pizza, a salad, and all-you-can-drink for $3. Open daily 11am-3am. No credit cards.

Subbie's Roll-Inn, 972 Gayley Ave. (310-208-2354), Westwood Village. Also known as "$1.50 Subs." $2 buys you a foot-long (sub, of course). Open daily 10am-3am. No credit cards.

José Bernstein's, 935 Broxton Ave. (310-208-4992), Westwood Village. *Grande* Mexican and deli specialties. Breakfast special consists of 2 eggs, bacon or sausage, and potatoes, french toast or pancakes ($2.30). "The Tacominator" is 2 soft tacos, rice, beans, chips, and a drink ($3.25). Open Mon.-Fri. 9:30am-1am, Sat. 8am-2:30am, Sun. 9am-1am.

Headliner's Diner & Press Club, 10922 Kinross Ave. (310-208-2424), at Gayley in Westwood Village. Students, locals, and occasionally Magic Johnson. Burgers with fries or fruit ($4 and under) and huge breakfasts ($2.30). Open Mon.-Thurs. 7am-midnight, Fri. 7am-1am, Sat. 9am-1am, Sun. 9am-midnight.

Santa Monica

Santa Monica's restaurants fall unmistakably into the "see and be seen" category, especially along the 3rd St. Promenade. Prices are elevated accordingly, but so is the quality of the food.

Babalu, 1002 Montana Ave. (310-395-2500). Cuban specialties that would make Ricky proud ($7-8). Open Sun.-Thurs. 8am-10pm, Fri.-Sat. 8am-11pm.

Ye Olde King's Head, 116 Santa Monica Blvd. (310-451-1402), Santa Monica. An authentic British pub owned by a Birmingham expatriate. Ploughman's Plate of cheeses, chutneys, and bread is $6. Of course, what would a Brit establishment be without a broad assortment of English beers and ales? Open Mon.-Fri. 11am-1:30am, Sat.-Sun. 10am-1:30am.

Noah's New York Bagels, 320 Santa Monica Blvd. (310-394-3557) and 2710 Main St. (310-396-4339). This divine San Francisco-based chain offers some of the best bagels west of the Mississip'. They also have delectable knishes and hamantashen. Open Mon.-Fri. 7am-6pm, Sat. 6:30am-7pm, Sun. 7am-7pm. No credit cards.

Venice

Venetian cuisine runs the gamut from greasy to health-conscious, as befits its beachy-hippie population.

Van Go's Ear 24 Hour Restaurant & Gallery, 796 Main St. (310-314-0022). Quint-essential Venice—a psychedelic mural of the café's namesake complete with neon earring beckons you to dine on ridiculously large portions of tasty chow. All entrees named for celebs, such as the Kato Kaelin (a house salad; $3). The "Tight-wad Menu" has 8 breakfast combos under $3 (served weekdays 6-11am). The "Fruit Fuck" is a lewdly good smoothie concocted with oranges, apples, pears, kiwi, and bee pollen ($3.75). Always open in some capacity.

Windward Farms Market, 105 Windward Ave. (310-392-3566). Whole grain breads and fresh fruit. Sells deli sandwiches (50¢-$3.50), salads (50¢), and fresh juices ($2.50). Perfect picnic fare. Open daily 8am-7:30pm. No credit cards.

Rose Café, 220 Rose Ave. (310-399-0711). Artsy-fartsy gallery/café with massive rose murals. Deli specials ($5-6) are the best bet. Live jazz Fri.-Sat. 8-11pm. Open Mon.-Fri. 7am-11pm, Sat. 8am-11pm, Sun. 8am-5pm.

Robin Rose, 215 Rose Ave. (310-399-1774). World famous ice cream that comes in every flavor from kahlua to rose petal ($2.50). This is where to go for the DMV-licensed **Chocoholic's Traffic School.** It's $25 for an 8-hr. program with free-flowing (you guessed it) chocolate and ice cream. You might want to get a ticket just so you can come here. Open daily 8am-11pm.

Downtown

Financial District eateries vie for the coveted businessperson's lunchtime dollar. Their secret weapon, the lunch special, means more cheap food for budget travelers who come to this part of town. Finding a reasonably priced dinner can be a challenge, but you probably shouldn't hang out here that late anyway.

Philippe's, The Original, 1001 N. Alameda St. (213-628-3781), 2 blocks north of Union Station. The best place in L.A. to feel like Raymond Chandler. Philippe's claims to have originated the French-dip sandwich (don't argue); varieties include

---

Fruity!

Forget race riots, water shortages, or Divine Brown—one of the biggest nuisances Angelenos have recently faced is a pesky bug called the **Medfly** (Mediterranean fruit fly). One of the world's most destructive pests, the Medfly breeds by laying its eggs in healthy fruit. If it became established in California, it would decimate this agricultural breadbasket and result in nearly $1 billion of damage per year. Fears of an epidemic in the late 80s led the city to hire helicopters to fly overhead by night to dump insecticides. Unfortunately, the sprayings, depicted in the movie *Short Cuts,* maimed more pets than fruit flies and incited residents to sue the city for ruining their beloved cars' paint jobs. Signs denoting the boundaries of quarantine areas still exist on some freeways. The danger is less severe now, but Angelenos, ever mindful of disaster, have distributed cautionary pamphlets everywhere warning of the next big plague.

beef, ham, turkey, or lamb ($3-4). The mustard is hot, but good. Top it off with a large slice of pie ($1.90) and a 40¢ glass of iced tea or a 9¢ cup of coffee, and you've got a colossal lunch at this L.A. institution. Open daily 6am-10pm.

The Pantry, 877 S. Figueroa St. (213-972-9279). Open since the 20s, it hasn't closed once since—not for the earthquakes, not for the riots (when it served as a National Guard outpost), and not even when a taxicab drove through the front wall. Be prepared to wait for the giant breakfast specials ($6), especially on weekends. Sun. brunch at the Pantry is an L.A. tradition. Coincidentally owned by L.A.'s neat mayor, Dick "Dick" Riordan. Open 24hr. No credit cards.

La Luz Del Día, 1 W. Olvera St. (213-628-7495). This authentic and inexpensive Mexican restaurant is hidden amid the many tourist-trap Mexican joints along Olvera St. Tortillas are handmade on the premises, and the salsa's got some serious bite. Combination plates $4-5. Open Tues.-Fri. 6am-9pm, Sat.-Sun. 6am-10pm.

San Fernando Valley

Ventura Blvd. is lined with restaurants. Eating lunch near the studios in **Studio City** is your best stargazing opportunity. The famous are willing to dine outside the studios because of Studio City's unwritten law—you can stare all you want, but don't bother them *and don't ask for autographs.*

Dalt's Grill, 3500 W. Olive Ave. (818-953-7752), at the corner of Olive and Riverside in Burbank. Swank grill across from Warner Studios and frequented by the DJ's and music guests from the radio station upstairs, KROQ. Healthy chicken fajita Caesar salad $6.59. Burgers and sandwiches $4-5. Stocked lacquered oak bar. Open Mon.-Thurs. 11am-midnight, Fri.-Sat. 11am-1am, Sun. 10am-midnight

Miceli's, 3655 Cahuenga Blvd. (818-851-3444), Studio City. As close to L.A. as the Valley gets. Incredibly popular Italian restaurant with (of course) pizza (large $13-18), and other delectable delights sometimes served by singing waiters of varying talent. Sip a glass of good wine ($3.50), or a real cappuccino ($2.50) while enjoying the smooth sounds of cabaret, Broadway, and opera acts. Open Thurs. 5pm-midnight, Fri. 5pm-1am, Sat. 4pm-1am, Sun. noon-11pm.

Horseshoe Coffeehouse, 14568 Ventura Blvd. (818-986-4262), Sherman Oaks. Probably the only place with a coffee happy hour; a large "rocket fuel" (house blend) is 75¢ weekdays 5-8pm. More teas than there are cellular phones in L.A. Sandwiches ($3.75), and live music nightly, which could be anything from swing to Israeli folk music. Open daily 8am-2am. No credit cards.

Law Dogs, 14114 Sherman Way (818-989-2220), in Van Nuys. Just your average hot dog stand with legal advice. The attorney is available Wed. 7-9pm. Open Mon.-Tues. and Thurs. 10am-5pm, Wed. and Fri. 10am-9pm, Sat 10am-8pm.

SIGHTS

Hollywood

Modern Hollywood is no longer the upscale home of movie stars and production studios. In fact, all the major studios, save Paramount, have moved to the roomier San Fernando Valley. Left behind are those things that could not be taken: historic theaters and museums, a crowd of souvenir shops, several famous boulevards, and endless American fascination. With the exception of the seemingly endless string of movie premieres, the only star-studded part of Hollywood is the sidewalk. Wide-eyed (and often disappointed) tourists stroll Hollywood Boulevard among prostitutes and porn shops. Hollywood is still fascinating, but for different reasons.

The **Hollywood sign**—those 50-ft.-high, slightly erratic letters perched on Mt. Cahuenga north of Hollywood—stands with New York's Statue of Liberty and Paris's Eiffel Tower as a universally recognized symbol of its city. The original 1923 sign, which read HOLLYWOODLAND, was an advertisement for a new subdivision in the Hollywood Hills (a caretaker lived behind one of the "L"s). If you frolic on the sign like Robert Downey, Jr. did in *Chaplin,* or take a leap from it like all the faded 1920s starlets, you risk paying a $500 fine if you're caught (which is likely), but you can snap a great picture by driving north on Vine, turning right on Franklin, and left on

Beachwood to the supermarket parking lot. Resting beneath the Hollywood sign, at 6342 Mulholland Hwy. (at the corner of Canyon Lake Drive), is Castillo del Lago. Once the gambling den of gangster Bugsy Siegel, the red and yellow striped house now belongs to **Madonna.**

Hollywood Boulevard itself, lined with souvenir shops, clubs, and theaters, is busy day and night. Most sights in this area now focus around the intersection of Highland and Hollywood. To the east, things turn even seedier. If you want to stroll among the stars, have a look at the **Walk of Fame** along Hollywood and Vine. Many names will be meaningless to those under 40. To catch a glimpse of today's (or yesterday's) stars in person, call the Chamber of Commerce (213-469-8311) for times and locations of upcoming star-unveiling ceremonies.

The **Mann's Chinese Theater** (formerly Grauman's), 6925 Hollywood Blvd. (213-464-8111), between Highland and La Brea, is a garish rendition of a Chinese temple. There's always a crowd of tourists in the courtyard worshiping impressions made by movie stars in the cement, including Whoopi Goldberg's dreds, Betty Grable's legs, R2D2's wheels, Jimmy Durante's nose, and George Burns' cigar. Just across the street from Mann's is the **El Capitan Theatre,** 6838 Hollywood Blvd. (213-467-9545). This restored cinema house held the 1941 Hollywood premiere of *Citizen Kane,* and now only shows Disney films. It's a bit pricier than the other theaters in the area, but the ornate faux-exotic 1920's decoration inside is well worth it.

Two blocks east of Mann's is the **Hollywood Wax Museum,** 6767 Hollywood Blvd. (213-462-8860), where you'll meet 200 figures, from Jesus to Elvis—they all look good enough to eat. Delicious wax! (Open daily 10am-midnight. $9, children $7.) Down the street from the Wax Museum you'll find two touristy "Odd-itoriums:" the lingerie museum in **Frederick's of Hollywood,** 6608 Hollywood Blvd. (957-5953), has bras worn by Marilyn Monroe and Milton Berle (open Mon.-Thurs. 10am-8pm, Fri. 10am-9pm, Sat. 10am-6pm, Sun. noon-5pm), and **Ripley's Believe It or Not!** (466-6335), whose side-show mentality is harmoniously in keeping with the rest of Hollywood ($9, children $6; open daily 10am-11:30pm).

Music is another industry that, like film, finds a center in Los Angeles. The pre-eminent monument of the modern record industry is the 1954 **Capitol Records Tower,**

If I Were a Groupie

Long gone are the days when groupies could reach out and touch their favorite musicians by just telephoning backstage or hanging around after the show. It may have worked for Pamela Des Barres in the 70s, but today's groupie has to have skills which would put FBI agents to shame. It's a full-time occupation requiring insightful thinking, careful planning, and well-honed "people skills." *Let's Go* cannot give you the well-trained eyes and ears necessary for success, but we can point you in the right direction. The first thing you need to know is that stars tend to stay in the same hotels. Armed with this knowledge, you can narrow down your search. The **Rock 'n' Roll Hyatt** on the Sunset Strip was the site of Led Zeppelin's orgies and Jim Morrison's antics. It is now the preferred haunt of rising younger bands (Live, Smashing Pumpkins). Almost directly across the street is the **St. James Club,** a pricier and more refined spot which caters to older, established bands such as Duran Duran. By the base of the famous billboards on Sunset is a hotel for film groupies, the **Château Marmont.** Keanu Reeves and Dustin Hoffman have stayed here for extended periods of time. Further up the Strip, opposite Ben Frank's on Alta Loma, is the **Sunset Marquis.** This extremely expensive hotel houses the biggest musical acts (Rolling Stones, Peter Gabriel, George Michael). Hiding on a residential street near the corner of Melrose and La Cienega is **Le Parc,** which caters to the bigger groups who want peace and quiet (Morrissey) and most newer British acts (Blur, Elastica). Finally, as any savvy groupie knows, all bands register under fake names these days, so you'll have to rely on your big, bountiful, buxom wits—and charm.

1750 Vine St., just north of Hollywood. The building, which was designed to look like a stack of records, is cylindrical with fins sticking out at each floor (the "records") and a needle on top, which blinks H-O-L-L-Y-W-O-O-D in morse code.

Music fans of all types will want to at least see the **Hollywood Bowl** if they can't catch a rehearsal or concert. All sparkly after its recent facelift, the **Hollywood Bowl Museum** (213-850-2058) has several exhibits and listening stations where you can swoon to Stravinsky, Aron Copeland, and the Beatles, all of whom played the Bowl in the same week during the 60s (open Tues.-Sat. 10am-8:30pm; free).

The **Hollywood Studio Museum,** 2100 N. Highland Ave. (213-874-2276), across from the Hollywood Bowl, provides a refreshing look at the history of early Hollywood film-making. Back in 1913, when it was a barn, famed director Cecil B. DeMille rented the building as a studio and there shot Hollywood's first feature film, *The Squaw Man*. It went on to become the train station in *Bonanza*. Antique cameras, costumes worn by Douglas Fairbanks and Rudolph Valentino, props such as the chariot from *Ben Hur*, vintage film clips, and other memorabilia fill the museum (open Sat. 10am-4pm, Sun. noon-4pm, weekdays by appointment only; $4, seniors and students $3, ages 6-12 $2; ample free parking).

If you still haven't had enough showbiz glitz, visit the **Hollywood Memorial Park,** 6000 Santa Monica Blvd. (213-469-1181), between Vine and Western, a cemetery which has the remains of dead stars Rudolph Valentino, Douglas Fairbanks Sr., and many, many more!!! (Open Mon.-Fri. 8am-5pm; mausoleums close at 4:30pm.)

Wilshire and Hancock Park

The **Los Angeles County Museum of Art (LACMA),** 5905 Wilshire Blvd. (213-857-6000), at the west end of Hancock Park, has a distinguished, comprehensive collection which rebuts snooty Eastern types who insist that L.A.'s only culture is in its yogurt. Opened in 1965, the LACMA is the largest museum in the West. Five major buildings cluster around the **Times-Mirror Central Court:** a Japanese pavilion, the Ahmanson Building (the museum's original building and home to most of its non-modern permanent collection), the Hammer Building, the Bing Center, and the Robert O. Anderson Building, a spectacular 1986 addition to the museum. The **Steve Martin Gallery** in the Anderson Building houses the famed benefactor's collection of Dada and Surrealist works, including Rene Magritte's *Treachery of Images* ("Ceci n'est pas une pipe!"), which explains how he was able to roller skate through LACMA's halls in *L.A. Story*. There is free chamber music on Sunday. The museum offers a variety of tours and free talks daily. For schedules, check with the information desk in the Central Court (ticket office 857-6010) or contact the Docent Council at 857-6108. (Open Mon. and Wed. 10am-5pm, Fri. 10am-9pm, Sat.-Sun. 11am-6pm. $7, seniors and students $4, ages 6-17 $1; free 2nd Wed. of each month.)

Next door, in **Hancock Park,** an acrid petroleum stench pervades the vicinity of the **La Brea Tar Pits,** one of the most popular hangouts in the world for fossilized early mammals. Many of the beasties who came, thousands of years ago, to drink from the pools here found themselves stuck in the tar that lurks below a thin film of water. Most of the one million bones recovered from the pits from 1913-1915 are now housed in the **George C. Page Museum of La Brea Discoveries,** 5801 Wilshire Blvd. (recording 213-936-2230, operator 213-857-6311), at Curson. Wilshire buses stop in front of the museum. The museum includes reconstructed Ice Age animals and murals of L.A. Ice Age life, a laboratory where paleontologists work behind plate-glass windows, and a display that shows what it's like to stick around in the tar. Check out the holographic transformation of the **La Brea woman**—the only human unearthed in the tar. Holes were drilled into her skull to relieve her headache and release the evil spirits within before her body was presumably thrown into the tar. Archaeological digging continues in **Pit 91** behind the adjacent county art museum. (Open Tues.-Sun. 10am-5pm. $6, seniors and students $3.50, ages 5-10 $2, under 5 free. Free admission 1st Tues. of month. Parking $7.50. Museum tours Wed.-Sun. 2pm, tours of grounds 1pm.)

West Hollywood

Once considered a no-man's land between Beverly Hills and Hollywood, West Holly-wood, incorporated in 1985, was one of the first cities in the country to be governed by openly gay officials. The section of Santa Monica Blvd. around San Vincente is the city's oldest gay district. This thriving and welcoming **gay community** in the middle of L.A. is the center of much of the city's best nightlife. Its awesome **Gay Pride Weekend Celebration** is held in late June.

In the years before incorporation, lax zoning laws gave rise to today's **Sunset Strip.** It was originally lined with posh nightclubs frequented by stars, and today it is lined with pseudo-grungy rock clubs frequented by stars. The area's music scene is among the country's most fertile, and many world-famous bands from The Doors to Guns 'n Roses got their start here. Restaurants and comedy clubs flourish as well. The Strip **billboards** are famous for their audacious paeans to corporate glam. Just across the street, at 8218 Sunset Blvd., are the 15-ft.-high plaster effigies of **Rocky and Bullwinkle.** The courtyard is inscribed à la the Mann's Chinese theater with the signature of June Foray (the voice of Rocky *and* Natasha) and the elbow prints of the cartoon's writers. The converted house behind them was once the production office of the duo's creators, Jay Ward Productions, but is now the **Dudley Do-right Emporium** (213-654-3050; 8200 Sunset Blvd.; Tues., Thurs., and Sat. 11am-4:30pm), a quaint store teeming with (what else) Rocky and Bullwinkle pencils, cups, t-shirts, stickers, comics, and videos, alongside similar items featuring Jay Ward's other characters (George of the Jungle and Dudley Doo-right).

Melrose Avenue, running from the southern part of West Hollywood to Holly-wood, is lined with chi-chi restaurants, trendy boutiques, and art galleries. The choic-est stretch is between La Brea and Fairfax. The clothes in the often-temporary resident boutiques are a season behind and overpriced, but looking and laughing are always free. While much that is sold here is pre-owned ("vintage"), none of it is really cheap. **Retail Slut,** 7308 Melrose, is a mecca for punks, goths, and sluts of all ilks. It's the place to find that fetish gear you've been searching for, or just a cool spot to browse a huge selection of ear- and body-rings, hang out with local club kids, and hear word-of-mouth about the dark side of L.A.'s alternative scene. **Original Western Vintage,** 7377 Melrose, has used 501s for $6! **Aardvark's,** 7579 Melrose, is also a great place for used gear, from that pith helmet you can't go on safari without to cor-duroy sportshirts which weren't even popular in the 70s (open Mon.-Sat. 11am-9pm, Sun. 11am-7pm).

Beverly Hills and Century City

The very name Beverly Hills evokes images of palm-lined boulevards, tanned, taut skin, and million-dollar homes with guitar-shaped pools. While that may have been true in Hollywood's glamour days of the 40s and 50s, reality has set in and the civic icon of wealth has passed the crown to lesser-known and more exclusive enclaves. The reason why all the maps to stars' homes only seem to show dead stars is that while the privileged may still *shop* here, most no longer *live* here. The area may still house many a multi-millionaire and live up to the well-manicured ideal that many people expect when they come to L.A., but the real fame and money has long since moved away from the hype to areas which afford privacy.

Faking antiquity, the entire area—hill, lampposts and all—was constructed in the last decade, and it looks it. The heart of the city is in the **Golden Triangle,** a wedge formed by Wilshire and Santa Monica Blvd. centering on **Rodeo Drive,** known for its many opulent clothing boutiques and jewelry shops. After strolling through Tiffany and Dior, your mission, should you choose to accept it, is to go to the **Counter Spy Shop,** 9577 Wilshire Blvd. (310-274-7700). This is *the* place to get your lie detectors, surveillance equipment, and "completely legal weapons." Just don't ask too many questions (open Mon.-Fri. 9:30am-6pm, Sat. 10am-4pm). Across the way is the vener-able **Beverly Wilshire Hotel** (310-275-5200), whose old and new wings are con-nected by **El Camino Real,** a cobbled street with Louis XIV gates. Inside, hall mirrors reflect the glitter of crystal chandeliers and marble floors.

The new **Beverly Hills City Hall** (310-285-1000) stands, looking a bit out of place, on Crescent just below Santa Monica. This Spanish Renaissance building was erected during the heart of the Great Depression, and is now engulfed by Beverly Hills' new white phoenix of a **Civic Center.** Completed in September 1990, the Civic Center (which includes the Beverly Hills Fire Department, Police Station, and library) took nine years to build at a cost of $120 million.

Fans of *Beverly Hills 90210* should come to grips with the fact that West Beverly High, alas, is only a television construct (filmed, incidentally, at the considerably less glamorous Torrance High School). You can, however, cruise **Beverly Hills High** (located on Moreno, between Olympic and Spalding). Beverly Hills High may be the only high school in California with its own **oil well.** The **indoor swimming pool** is open for public use in summer (310-550-4796; open Mon.-Thurs. 1pm-5pm, Fri. 2-4pm), and has a sliding floor cover that converts the pool into a basketball court. This is where Jimmy Stewart and Donna Reed danced the aquatic Charleston in *It's a Wonderful Life.*

Moving farther north, the **Beverly Hills Hotel,** 9641 Sunset Blvd. (310-276-2251), is a pink, palm-treed collection of poolside cottages. Howard Hughes established his infamous germ-free apartment in this jungle-bungalow mix, while Marilyn Monroe reportedly had affairs with both JFK and RFK in other bungalows. It is also home to the famous **Polo Lounge,** where countless media industry deals have gone down. The Sultan of Brunei paid $185 million for the hotel in 1987, but ten years later you can get a room for a mere $275. Heading west on Sunset from the Strip, make a right onto Carolwood. **Barbara Streisand** lives at 301 Carolwood, and the house at 355 is where **Walt Disney** lived until his death. Turn back to Sunset and head towards Westwood, making a left on the tiny and windy Charing Cross. The estate at 10236 is **The Playboy Mansion.** Charing Cross becomes N. Mapleton, site of the largest and most extravagant residence in Beverly Hills (no mean feat). **Aaron Spelling's mansion,** 594 N. Mapleton, is larger than the Taj Mahal. Wife Candy Spelling's closets reportedly take up an entire wing.

Southwest of Beverly Hills is **Century City,** whose broad, awe-inspiring avenues frame the ABC Entertainment Center and the **Century City Shopping Center,** which features a 14-screen theater (310-289-4AMC/4262), and Steven Spielberg's yellow, submarine-themed restaurant, **The Dive!** (310-788-DIVE/3483; open Sun.-Thurs. 11:30am-10pm, Fri.-Sat. 11:30am-11pm). It specializes in, of course, sub sandwiches. This average-looking outdoor shopping plaza is one of the best places to **spot celebrities** desperately trying to go *incognito.* Action movie buffs may recognize **Fox Plaza** on the Avenue of the Stars from the thrill machine *Die Hard.*

South of Century Plaza is the very moving **Beit HaShoa Museum of Tolerance,** 9786 W. Pico Blvd. (310-553-8043), at Roxbury. The new museum (which opened in 1992) holds high-tech wizardry designed to help visitors explore their own prejudices, and offers displays on the Holocaust, the Croatian genocide, the L.A. Riots, and the U.S. Civil Rights movement. One room features unseen voices that hurl insults at visitors. Upstairs is the **Simon Weisenthal Center,** featuring interactive computers for Holocaust research and artifacts from concentration camps. Allow at least three hr. for your visit. Free parking. (Tours leave between 10am and 4pm on Mon.-Thurs., 10am and 3pm on Fri., and 10:30am-5pm on Sun. Admission $8, seniors $6, students $5, ages 3-11 $3.)

Westwood and UCLA

The gargantuan **University of California at Los Angeles (UCLA)** campus covers over 400 acres in the foothills of the Santa Monica Mountains. You can get a taste of the nexus of L.A. glam culture and academia by sitting in on a lecture like "History of the Motion Picture," which shows a movie every class meeting. Ask any student for directions. The illustrious film school's graduates include James Dean, Jim Morrison, Oliver Stone, Francis Ford Coppola, Kareem Abdul-Jabbar, Tim Robbins, and John Williams. To reach the campus by car, take the San Diego Fwy. (I-405) north to the Wilshire Blvd./Westwood exit, heading east into Westwood. Take Westwood Blvd. north off

Wilshire, heading straight through the center of the village and directly into the campus. By bus, take MTA routes #2, 3, 21, 22, 322, or 576 from downtown, or #20, 320, or 560 from outlying areas. Shell out the $5 to get a parking pass from campus information stands at all entrances—those in the most hated profession in America, parking ticket cops, *live* to cite unsuspecting visitors here. Pick up a brochure describing the brief **self-guided tour** of the central part of campus.

The **Wight Art Gallery** (825-3887) features the Grunwald Center for the Graphic Arts and various exhibits (open Tues. 11am-7pm, Wed.-Fri. 11am-5pm, Sat.-Sun. 1-5pm; tours Sat. and Sun. 1:30pm). The **Murphy Sculpture Garden,** which contains over 70 pieces scattered through five acres, lies directly in front of the Art Center. The collection includes works by such major artists as Rodin, Matisse, and Miró. Opposite the sculpture garden is **MacGowen Hall,** which contains the **Tower of Masks.** UCLA's **inverted fountain** is located between Knudsen Hall and Schoenberg Hall, directly south of Dickson Plaza. Water spurts from the innovative fountain's perimeter and rushes down through the gaping hole in the middle.

Ackerman Union, 308 Westwood Plaza (310-206-0833), stands southwest of the Quadrangle at the bottom of the hill. Ackerman is the campus information bank. A calendar lists the lengthy line-up of movies (first-runs often free), lectures, and campus activities. The ground floor is swallowed by the huge **Associated Students' Store** (310-825-0611), the perfect spot to buy a bevy of UCLA paraphernalia (open Mon.-Fri. 8:30am-6pm, Sat. 10am-5pm, Sun. noon-5pm).

Westwood Village, just south of the campus, with its myriad movie theaters, trendy boutiques, and upscale bistros, is geared more toward the residents of L.A.'s Westside than UCLA students. Like most college neighborhoods, however, Westwood is humming on Friday and Saturday nights. For the most part, the town is safe, and generally overrun by the high school and college crowd. Off the main drag at 1218 Glendon Ave. is the **Westwood Memorial Cemetery.** Flowers, teddy bears, and even sprouted Chia Pets are left by family and fans who make pilgrimages to the graves of Marilyn Monroe and Natalie Wood.

The **Armand Hammer Museum of Art and Cultural Center,** 10899 Wilshire Blvd. (310-443-7000), was opened to the public in November 1990. Hammer purportedly wanted to donate his collections to the L.A. County Museum of Art but demanded that the works be exhibited together in a separate wing. The museum refused, telling Hammer to build his own place—and he did just that. Impressive from the outside and light, airy, and marble-clad on the inside, Edwards Larrabee Barnes' tribute to Hammer's wealth is a welcome addition to the Westwood scene.

Science: Stranger Than Truth

The environs of the **Museum of Jurassic Technology,** 9341 Venice Blvd. (310-836-6131), in Culver City, are pretty damn strange. Not many museums are located among a strip of mini-malls behind a bedraggled façade. Prepare yourself; this aesthetic disjunction will be by far the most normal part of your experience here. Beyond the withered exterior lie a series of exhibits that range from mundane (the preserved skeleton of a European Mole) to fascinating (the tale of the Deeprong Mori, a bat that can pass through solid matter), to completely inscrutable (a lecture on the metaphysics of thought based on Geoffrey Sonnabend's work, *Obliscence: Theories of Forgetting and the Problem of Matter*). The point of this bizarre yet fascinating spectacle is to convince visitors that through scientific inquiry one can discover what is truly strange about this world. As the museum's intellectual forefather, 19th-century naturalist and curator C.W. Peale, said, "The learner must be led always from unfamiliar objects to the familiar, guided along, as it were, a chain of flowers into the mysteries of life." Is it genius or is it a joke? Is it science or is it a freak show? Is it a thoroughly unique if jarring experience? Absolutely. (Open Thurs. 2-8pm, Fri.-Sun. noon-6pm. Suggested donation $4, students and seniors $2.50.)

The museum houses a large collection of European and American works from the 16th to the 20th century. The museum's gem is **Van Gogh's** *Hospital at Saint-Rémy,* a startling, flame-like image of the private hospital in which Van Gogh died just a year after the painting's completion. The museum also holds the world's largest collection of works by acerbic French lithographer Honoré Daumier. (Parking in Westwood $2.75. Open Tues.-Wed. and Fri.-Sat. 11am-7pm, Thurs. 11am-9pm, Sun. 11am-5pm. Tours daily at 1pm. $4.50; free Thurs. after 6pm.)

Bel Air, Brentwood, and Pacific Palisades

Most stars today live in these three affluent communities, not in Beverly Hills farther downhill. Directly across from UCLA is the well-guarded community of **Bel Air,** where **Ronald Reagan** has retired to become the new Fresh Prince. His estate is at 668 St. Cloud, adjacent to the *Beverly Hillbillies* mansion, and a few blocks up from the former home of **Sonny and Cher,** at 364 St. Cloud. **Elizabeth Taylor** is literally around the (windy) corner, at 700 Nimes.

Farther west on Sunset Blvd. is **Brentwood,** home to many a young actor and that object of cultural obsession, **O.J. Simpson.** The Juice chills in his chi-chi digs at 360 Rockingham, as avid viewers of Court TV certainly know. **Marilyn Monroe** was found dead at her home (although *not* of a drug overdose) at 12305 Fifth Helena Dr. (off Carmelina) on August 4, 1962. Other celebs who own homes in Brentwood include Michelle Pfeiffer, Harrison Ford, Meryl Streep, and Rob Reiner.

The considerably more secluded **Pacific Palisades** is the place to live these days. Many entire streets are closed to anyone but residents and their guests, but you can try to catch a glimpse of **Tom Cruise** and **Nicole Kidman** outside 1525 Sorrento, or **Steven Spielberg** at 1515 Amalfi (this home, incidentally, belonged to David O. Selznick when he was producing *Gone with the Wind*). Arnold Schwarzenegger and Maria Shriver, Michael Keaton, Billy Crystal, Chevy Chase, and John Travolta all own homes in the area. The cliffs give way to the ocean at the popular **Will Rogers State Beach,** on the 16000 block of Pacific Coast Highway. At 1501 Will Rogers State Park Rd., hike around **Will Rogers State Historical Park** (310-454-8212) and take in the panoramic views of the city and the distant Pacific. You can visit the famous humorist's home and eat a picnic brunch while watching a Saturday afternoon **polo match.** (Matches Sat. 2-5pm and Sun. 10am-noon.) Follow Chatauqua Blvd. inland from PCH to Sunset Blvd., or take bus #2 which runs along Sunset.

Santa Monica

Santa Monica, the Bay City of Raymond Chandler's novels, was once known as the "Gold Coast" because of the fabulously wealthy stars who called it home. Today, the area is a lovely spot for the less pretentious, more hip crowd. The **3rd St. Promenade** has become the city's most popular nightspot, and the nearby beaches are jam-packed. Despite the resultant hassles (parking, prices, lines), there is much to do and see, especially at night. It takes about a half-hour (with no traffic) on express bus #10 or on the Santa Monica Fwy. (I-10) from downtown to reach Santa Monica.

Santa Monica is the place that put the "Bay" in *Baywatch.* Known more for its shoreside scene than its shore, Santa Monica is where **Route 66** meets the surf. Refurbished in 1996, the brand spankin' renewed **pier** now hosts a free Thursday night Twilight Dance Series in the summer. Among the bevy of corny rides lining the pier is the ferris wheel featured in *The Sting.* **Palisades Park** boasts the **Stairpath,** 189 steps of outdoor stairmaster both loved and feared. Located at 4th and Adelaide, it leads down to the beach. A mere three blocks from the beach is the **3rd Street Promenade,** one of the major walking thoroughfares in L.A. Once a quiet collection of used record stores and antique bookshops, it has recently de-evolved into a strip of over-priced bars and restaurants, and considerably more entertaining street performers. Note the mesh dinosaurs which light up at night. If a kid with a clipboard approaches you, don't run, you're probably just being offered **free movie passes.** This is, after all, the film screening capital of the world. Nearby 3110 Main St. houses the restaurant owned by **Arnold Schwarzenegger** and Maria Shriver, **Schatzi on Main** (310-399-4800).

Away from the main drag, but definitely worth a visit, is **The Museum of Flying** (272 Donald Douglas Loop North; 310-392-8822; open Wed.-Sun. 10am-5pm), on the airstrip of the Santa Monica Airport. This small hangar museum with Big Band background music has the *'24 New Orleans,* which made it around the world, among its rotating display of classic aircraft. It also has a fully equipped theater which shows aviation films.

Venice

Venice. A dredlocked crooner bobs through the parting crowd, amp strapped to his back, electric guitar draped with trinkets for sale. He rollerblades along, wailing away, pausing only to ogle and serenade the most alluring beachgoers. *Venice.* A forty-year-old quadruple amputee dances to a bongo drum's beat. Waddles, really—but look at the lustful gleam in his eyes as he does the only move he can—a pelvic thrust. *Venice.* Tattoo parlors filled with buzzing needles and half-choked gasps. Lips bitten to divert the pain from the needle site. *Venice.* Street vendors sleep on the beach at night. Makes it easier to get to work in the morning. *Venice.* Your name on a grain of rice. *Venice.* One of the most generative and interesting places on earth. A million causes, a million wild-eyed visionaries. *Venice.* Virtual ecstasy sold here.

Ocean Front Walk is Venice's main beachfront drag. Street people converge on shaded clusters of benches, evangelists drown out off-color comedians, and bodybuilders of both sexes pump iron in skimpy spandex outfits at the original **Muscle Beach** (1800 Ocean Front Walk, closest to 18th and Pacific). Fire-juggling cyclists, joggers, groovy elders (such as the **"skateboard grandma"**), and bards in Birkenstocks make up the balance of this playground population. Collect your wits and people-watch at one of the cafés or juice bars. During the day, things are relatively safe, but duck into the restroom around 6pm and the beach may be empty by the time you emerge. When the sun begins to fall, it's time to go.

Venice's **street murals** are another free show. Don't miss the brilliant, graffiti-disfigured homage to Botticelli's *Birth of Venus* on the beach pavilion at the end of Windward Ave.: a woman of ostensibly divine beauty wearing short shorts, a Band-aid top, and roller skates, boogies out of her seashell. The post office's mural sums up Venice's cluttered history in an appropriately jumbled way—with oil derricks seemingly perched on Kinney's shoulders. To look at paintings indoors, you might want to stop by **L.A. Louver,** 77 Market St. and 55 N. Venice Blvd. (310-822-4955), a gallery showing the work of some hip L.A. artists (open Tues.-Sat. noon-5pm).

To get to Venice from downtown L.A., take bus #33 or 333 (or 436 during rush hour). From downtown Santa Monica, take Santa Monica bus #1 or 2. Drivers can avoid hourly meter-feedings by parking in the $5 per day lot at Pacific and Venice.

The Pacific Coast Highway and Malibu

Begun in 1920, the **Pacific Coast Highway (PCH)** required $10 million and 17 years for completion. Many of the numerous bridges on the route were architectural wonders in their day; and some—such as the **Bixby Creek Bridge,** one of the longest single-span bridges in the world—still are. *Many* Californians like to drive the PCH stretch that plows through Malibu, especially on weekends when it can become an absolute parking lot. Although the loopy length of PCH makes it impractical for a complete journey up the California coast, those with access to a car should seek out this quintessentially Californian stretch.

From Santa Monica, where it temporarily merges with I-10, PCH runs northward along several of L.A. County's most popular beaches. Heading north from Santa Monica, the first major attraction is the **J. Paul Getty Museum,** 17985 PCH (310-458-2003), watch for the tiny sign just north of Sunset. This cliff-dwelling re-creation of the first-century Villa dei Papiri in Herculaneum is more than a set of walls on which to hang paintings. It's what Jupiter would have done had he made as much money as Getty. As a young oil man, Getty had a fascination with Caesar and all things Roman, a fascination which culminated in his choice of Malibu as the site of his own villa because it bore a striking resemblance to the Bay of Naples. He considered it to be a gift to the less culturally privileged people of SoCal. And what a gift it is. Gallery #228 is a must-see; it contains *some* of van Gogh's *Irises,* Monet's *Wheatstacks, Snow Effect,* and Munch's *Starry Night.* Call for updates and more specific information about the closing of the Getty in July 1997. Because of the museum's operating agreement with its residential neighbors, getting there is tricky. The parking lot is small and reservations are needed at least a day in advance, *weeks* in advance in summer. You are not permitted to park outside the museum unless you do so at the county lot. Bicyclists and motorcyclists are admitted without reservations. To avoid the parking hassle, take MTA #434 (which you can board at Sunset and PCH in Malibu or Ocean and Colorado in Santa Monica) to the museum. Remember to ask for a **free museum pass** from the bus driver or you will not be admitted. The museum gate is a half mi. from the bus stop, so be prepared to walk (open Tues.-Sun. 10am-5pm; free). There is an attractive garden **tea room** at the museum which serves delicious (and cheap) food and desserts (open same days 9:30am-4:30pm).

The **celebrity colony** of Malibu stretches along the low 20,000 blocks of PCH. With their multi-million-dollar homes and famous neighbors, Malibu residents can afford to be (and often are) hostile to outsiders. If you have a car, look at the homes and dare to dream. Mel Gibson, Janet Jackson, Jeffrey Katzenberg, Diana Ross, Tom Hanks, Sting, and Cher are just a handful of Malibu's more illustrious residents.

A public beach lies along the 23200 block of the PCH. You can walk onto the beach via the **Zonker Harris Beach** (named after the beach-obsessed Doonesbury character) access way at 22700 PCH. You can rent surfboards, wetsuits, and sailboards at nearby **Malibu Ocean Sports** (310-456-6302; open daily 10am-6 or 7pm). One of the best things about Malibu is the **Malibu Inn,** at 22969 PCH (310-456-6106). If it's good enough for the over 333 stars whose photos line the walls, then dammit, it's good enough for you. Succulent chicken teriyaki sandwich ($7) and broccoli cheese soup which will be your sin, your soul (open daily 7am-10pm).

Corral State Beach, an uncrowded windsurfing, swimming, and scuba-diving beach, lies on the 26000 block of PCH, followed by **Point Dume State Beach,** which is small and generally uncrowded. North of Point Dume, along the 30000 block of PCH, lies **Zuma,** L.A. County's northernmost, largest, and most popular county-owned sandbox, with lifeguards, restrooms, and a $5+ parking fee. Stations 8 to 12 belong to solitude seekers. 4, 6, and 7 are something different; valley high-schoolers have staked them out (mostly because 4 is where the food is), making them the most crowded and lively. Zuma 1,2, 3, and 5 are frequented by families who keep things more sedate. Swimmers should only dive in near manned lifeguard stations; because of the killer **riptide,** rescue counts are high. You might even get to live out your own *Baywatch* fantasy if you get saved by one of the **hot lifeguards.** For a less life threatening approach, strike up a conversation—they like to chat (about water safety of course).

Downtown

Mayor "Dick" Riordan and his band of jolly civil servants strive valiantly to project downtown as the font of L.A.'s diversity and culture. Actually, the only evident "diversity" is the stark contrast between the slick suited businesspeople and the cardboard domiciles which house delirious "Cappys" (homeless people). An uneasy truce prevails between the bustling financiers and the substantial street population, but visitors should be cautious; the area is especially unsafe after business hours and on weekends. Park in a secure lot, rather than on the streets. Parking is costly; try to arrive before 8am or park in one of the guarded lots around 9th and Figueroa ($2-3 per day) to avoid a $20 tab come 6pm.

The most striking (and chic) museum in the area is the **Museum of Contemporary Art (MOCA),** which showcases art from 1940 to the present. The main museum is located at California Plaza, 250 S. Grand Ave. (213-626-6222), and is a sleek and geometric architectural marvel. Its collection focuses on abstract expressionism, and

CALIFORNIA

includes works by Pollock, Calder, Miró, and Giacometti. Its interior is spacious and illuminated by pyramidal skylights. (Free tours noon, 1pm, and 2pm.) The second MOCA facility is the **Geffen Contemporary,** 152 N. Central Ave. (213-621-1727), in Little Tokyo. Originally intended to house exhibits only while the main museum was under construction, ironically, this building has since become a permanent part of the MOCA package. Park here and ride the DASH A shuttle to the main building. (Main MOCA, Tues.-Wed. and Fri.-Sun. 11am-5pm, Thurs. 11am-8pm. Admission to both places $6, seniors and students with ID $4, under 12 free. Free Thurs. 5-8pm. Wheelchair accessible.)

Across from City Hall East, between the Santa Ana Fwy. and Temple in the L.A. Mall, is the **L.A. Children's Museum,** 310 N. Main St. (213-687-8800), where everything can (and has been) touched. Children are invited to overcome the confusion of a hyper-technological society by participating in demonstrations of scientific principles. (Open Mon.-Fri. 11:30am-5pm, Sat.-Sun. 10am-5pm. Groups of 10 or more should call 213-687-8825, Mon.-Fri. 9am-5pm.)

The historic birthplace of L.A. lies farther north, bounded by Spring, Arcadia, and Macy. In the place where the original city center once stood, **El Pueblo de Los Angeles State Historic Park** (213-680-2525) preserves a number of historically important buildings from the Spanish and Mexican eras (open daily 9am-9pm). Start out at the **visitor center,** 622 N. Main St., in the Sepulveda House (213-628-1274), which offers free walking tours (Tues.-Sat. hourly 10am-1pm; call to check). Tours start at the **Old Plaza,** with its century-old Moreton Bay fig trees and huge bandstand, and wind their way past the **Avila Adobe,** 10 E. Olvera St., the "oldest" house in the city (the original adobe, true to L.A. style, has been replaced with concrete in order to meet earthquake regulations), followed by **Pico House,** 500 N. Main St., once L.A.'s most luxurious hotel. Farther down, at 535 N. Main St., the **Plaza Church,** established in 1818, has an incongruously soft, rose-adobe façade. The **visitor center** screens the film *Pueblo of Promise,* an 18-min. history of Los Angeles. **Olvera Street,** one of L.A.'s original roads, is now called Tijuana North by locals. The street is packed with touristy little stands selling Mexican handicrafts. Olvera St. is the sight of the Cinco de Mayo celebrations of L.A.'s Chicano population. Across Alameda St. from El Pueblo is the grand old **Union Station,** famous for its appearance in *Blade Runner.*

Near Downtown: Exposition Park

The museums of Exposition Park are generally safe and well-visited, and keep early hours—visitors should take the hint. The park is southwest of downtown, just off the Harbor Fwy., and is bounded by Exposition, Figueroa, Vermont, and Santa Barbara. From downtown, take DASH shuttle C, or MTA #40 or 42 (from Broadway between 5th and 6th) to the park's southern edge. From Hollywood, take MTA #204 down Vermont. From Santa Monica, take Blue Bus #20, 22, 320, or 322 on Wilshire, and transfer to #204 at Vermont.

The park is dominated by several major museums, including the **California Museum of Science and Industry,** 700 State Dr. (213-744-7400). Enter at the corner of Figueroa and Exposition next to the United DC-8 parked out front. IBM and Bell Telephone sponsor mathematics and communications exhibits, while McDonald's sponsors a display on nutrition. The **Aerospace Building,** as big as a hangar, exhibits $8 million worth of aircraft, including the Gemini 11 space capsule. (Museum open daily 10am-5pm. Free. Parking $5, bring quarters.) The five-story, 70-ft. wide **IMAX theater** (213-744-2014; $6.25, ages 13-17 $5, ages 4-12 $4, seniors $4.25) shows such features as the incredibly popular *Beavers: the Biggest Dam Adventure Ever Filmed,* a self-described "wild and wooly adventure film that follows a family of beavers as they build a new home," and *The Living Sea,* a panoramic portrait of Hawai'i with a soundtrack by Sting. In the same complex, but separate from the MSI, is the **California Afro-American Museum,** 600 State Dr. (213-744-7432), with a permanent sculpture collection, a research library, and exhibits focused on African-American contributions to science, humanities, and athletics. (Open Tues.-Sun. 10am-5pm. Free. Research library open by appointment only.)

Another of the park's attractions is the **Natural History Museum,** 900 Exposition Blvd. (213-744-3414). The museum has exhibits about pre-Columbian cultures, North American and African mammals, American history from 1472 to 1914, and dinosaurs. The **Hands-On Discovery Center** allows visitors to pet stuffed wild animals. Tours daily at 1pm during summer, on weekends only during winter. (Open daily 10am-5pm in July and Aug.; closed Mon. the rest of the year. $6, seniors and students $3.50, ages 5-12 $2, under 5 free.)

Exposition Park also includes the **Los Angeles Memorial Coliseum,** 3939 S. Figueroa St., home of the **USC Trojans** football team, and the **Sports Arena,** 2601 S. Figueroa St., home of the **Los Angeles Clippers** basketball team and a common venue for rock concerts. The colossal Coliseum, which seats over 100,000, was the main venue during the 1932 and 1984 Summer Olympic Games—the only stadium in the world to host them twice.

South of Exposition Park, to the west, is the city of **Inglewood.** This very rough neighborhood is home to many of the sporting events in L.A. At the corner of Manchester and Prairie is the **Great Western Forum,** home of the **Los Angeles Kings** hockey team, as well as the **Los Angeles Lakers** basketball team, both of whose tickets are in high demand. For Lakers and Kings tix (and for tickets for other Forum events) call the **Forum Box Office** (Kings tickets, 310-419-3160; Lakers tickets, 310-419-3182; open daily 10am-6pm) or **Ticketmaster** (213-480-3232). Kings tickets start at $11, and Lakers tickets jumped to a base of $21 after Shaq signed.

Griffith Park

One of few recreational parks in L.A., Griffith Park is the site of many outdoor diversions ranging from golf and tennis to hiking. The L.A. Zoo, Griffith Observatory and Planetarium, Travel Town, a bird sanctuary, and 52 mi. of hiking trails decorate the dry hills (open daily 5:30am-10pm). It stretches from the hills above North Hollywood to the intersection of the Ventura and Golden State Fwy. Several of the mountain roads through the park (especially the aptly named **Vista Del Valle Dr.**) offer panoramic views of downtown L.A., Hollywood, and the Westside. Unfortunately, heavy rains have made them unsafe for cars, but foot traffic is allowed on most. For **information,** stop by the **Visitor Center and Ranger Headquarters,** 4730 Crystal Spring Dr. (213-665-5188; open daily 5am-10pm).

The white stucco and copper domes of the Art Deco **Observatory and Planetarium** (213-664-1181, recording 664-1191) structure are visible from around the park. You might remember the planetarium from the climactic denouement of the James Dean film *Rebel Without A Cause.* Even if you don't, the planetarium is a must-see. A telescope with a 12-in. lens is open to the public every clear night. (Open for viewing daily dusk-9:45pm; winter Tues.-Sun. 7-9:45pm. Sky report and **information** 213-663-8171.) The planetarium presents popular **Laserium** light shows (818-901-9405), a psychotronic romp through the strawberry fields of your consciousness. (Observatory open daily 12:30-10pm; winter Tues.-Sun. 2-10pm. Planetarium show Mon.-Fri. at 1:30, 3, and 7:30pm, Sat.-Sun. also 4:30pm; in winter Tues.-Fri. 3 and 7:30pm, Sat.-Sun. also 1:30 and 4:30pm. $4, seniors $3, under 12 $2, under 5 not admitted. Kids 12 and under only admitted to the 1:30pm show. Laser shows blaze Sun. and Tues.-Sat. 6 and 8:30pm, summer also Fri.-Sat. 9:45pm. $7, children $6.) To get to the Observatory, take bus #203 from Hollywood.

The **L.A. Zoo,** 5332 Western Heritage Way (213-666-4090), is at the park's northern end. The zoo's 113 acres accommodate 2000 animals, and the facility is consistently ranked among the nation's best. Occasionally, the wacky keepers of the reptile house will toss a baby shoe into the anaconda exhibit (open daily 10am-5pm; $8, seniors $5.25, ages 2-12 $3.25). To reach the Zoo and Travel Town, take MTA #97 from downtown. There is no bus service between northern and southern Griffith Park.

To check out the wildest menagerie this side of the Pecos, drop in to the **Autry Museum of Western Heritage,** 4700 Western Heritage Way (213-667-2000), also located within Griffith Park at the junction of Golden State (I-5) and Ventura Fwy.

CALIFORNIA

(Rte. 134). The museum's collection covers both fact and fiction of the Old West, with exhibits on pioneer life and the history of Westerns, including costumes donated by Robert Redford, Gary Cooper, and Clint Eastwood (open Tues.-Sun. 10am-5pm. $7.50, seniors and students $5, children $3).

San Fernando Valley

The Valley is more than just a satellite of Los Angeles—it is suburban ritual elevated to its highest form. A third of L.A.'s population and all the **movie studios** (save one) reside here. From the Ventura Fwy. (Rte. 134) as it passes Burbank, you can see what are today the Valley's trademarks: the **NBC peacock,** the **Warner Bros. water tower,** and the carefully designed **Disney dwarves** which hold up the studio's roof in an updated parody of a Greek temple. If you drive by in the rain, you'll notice that architect Michael Graves seems to have orchestrated the runoff water pipes so that the seven dwarves appear to be pissing on daddy Disney. Although the story is now well known, Moushwitz, as Disney is sometimes called, has not gone to the expense to change the design. Most of the studios have **free TV show tapings** (see Entertainment, below).

The **Universal City Walk** is the yellow brick road to Universal Studios on top of the hill (take the Lankershim exit off the Hollywood Fwy.). It is a glitzy avenue of neon coursing with hot sex. The jewel in its silicone crown is definitely **B.B. King's Blues Club.** At the culmination of the City Walk is the movie-themed amusement park, **Universal Studios** (818-508-9600). Visit the Bates Hotel from Psycho, escape the raptors of Jurassic Park, ride the de Lorean from Back to the Future, survive an 8.3 earthquake, witness a variety of special effects and other demonstrations of movie-making magic, and don't you dare miss the Waterworld stage show. Allow 2½ hr. for the tour and at least one hr. to wander around afterward. (Open summer and holidays daily 8am-8pm. Last tram leaves at 5pm; Sept.-June 9am-6:30pm. $31, ages 3-11 and over 60 $25. Parking $6.)

Down in the residential area of Studio City lurks the epicenter of American 70s culture: the **Brady Bunch house.** It should be obvious that they did not live here at 11222 Dilling St. (just north of Ventura Blvd.), because it looks like a one-story house, and everyone knows the Bradys had that huge staircase up to the second floor from which Bobby threw down a ball and broke the vase. Alice always said, "Don't play ball in the house," but the scurrilous bastards never listened.

At the opposite end of the valley, 40 min. north of L.A. on the I-5 in Valencia is **Six Flags Magic Mountain** (818-367-5965; exit Magic Mountain Pkwy.), also known as *National Lampoon's* Wally World. Not for novices, Magic Mountain has the hairiest roller coasters in Southern California. (Open Sun.-Thurs. 10am-10pm, Fri.-Sat. 10am-midnight; mid-Sept. to Memorial Day Sat.-Sun. 10am-6pm only, save Christmas and Easter holiday weeks which follow summer hours. $33, seniors $19, kids under 48" $15, under 3 free. Parking $6.)

At the western end of the downtown area (also called Old Town Pasadena), is a structure as sleek and glassy as the modernism to which it is a shrine, the **Norton Simon Museum of Art,** 411 W. Colorado Blvd. (818-449-6840), at Orange Grove Blvd. Smooth and modern, it contrasts with the classic design of the Getty. There are numerous **Rodin, Moore,** and **Degas** bronzes, and the paintings include pieces by **Rembrandt, Raphael,** and **Picasso** (open Thurs.-Sun. noon-6pm; $4, seniors and students $2, under 12 free; wheelchair accessible). Take bus #180 west on Colorado between Lake and N. Orange or south on Lake between Washington and Colorado. Alternatively, take #181 west on Colorado between Lake and N. Orange.

The nearby **Huntington Library, Art Gallery,** and **Botanical Gardens,** are at 1151 Oxford Rd., San Marino 91108 (818-405-2100, ticket information 818-405-2275). The library houses one of the world's most important collections of rare books and English and American manuscripts, including a Gutenberg Bible, Benjamin Franklin's handwritten autobiography, a 1410 manuscript of Chaucer's *Canterbury Tales,* and numerous Shakespearean first folios. The art gallery is known for its 18th- and 19th-century British paintings. (Open Tues.-Fri. 1-4:30pm, Sat.-Sun. 10:30am-4:30pm; $4).

The Huntington Museum sits between Huntington Dr. and California Blvd. in San Marino, south of Pasadena. From downtown L.A., bus #79 leaves from Union Station and takes you straight to the library (40- to 45-min. trip).

ENTERTAINMENT

Many tourists feel a visit to the world's entertainment capital is not complete without some exposure to the actual business of making a movie or TV show. Fortunately, most production companies oblige. **Paramount** (213-956-5000) and **Warner Bros.** (818-954-1744) offer guided tours, but as they are *made* for tourists, they tend to be crowded and overpriced. The best way to get a feel for the industry is to land yourself some free tickets to a TV taping. You can see your fave-rave stars up close in an operating studio backlot without spending one cent.

NBC, 300 W. Alameda Dr. (recorded information 818-840-3537), in Burbank, is your best bet. You can pick up tickets here early in the morning for the **Leno** show taping that afternoon. Many of their "must see TV" shows tape over at **Paramount Pictures.** (Office open Mon.-Fri. 8am-5pm.) To secure VIP tickets for favorites like *Seinfeld,* write (far in advance) Paramount Guest Relations, 5555 Melrose Ave., Hollywood, CA 90038. If it's too late for that, unlimited tickets are given out on the morning of most tapings (so arrive early) at the Guest Relations Office Lot, 860 N. Gower St. (213-956-5575; open Mon.-Fri. 8am-4pm).

If all else fails, **Hollywood Group Services,** 1918 Magnolia Blvd. #203, Burbank, CA 91506 (818-556-1516), offers guaranteed seating, but will charge $10 if you don't show up. To find out what shows are available during your visit, send a SASE to either **Audiences Unlimited, Inc.,** 100 Universal City Plaza, Bldg. 153, Universal City, CA 91608 (818-506-0067). Keep in mind that any filming at **Universal Studios** is done on the backlot, and you won't see a thing from the tour. It's a studio. It's an amusement park. It is both—*at the same time.* If you're more interested in an **on-location movie shoot,** the City/County Film Office maintains a list of what movies are filming in the area. Call 213-957-1000 to find out, but be aware that film crews may not share your enthusiasm about audience participation.

Cinema

Countless theaters show films the way they were meant to be seen: in a big space, on a big screen, and with very high-quality sound. Angelenos are often amazed at the "primitive" sound at theaters they go to in the rest of the country. While here, you should take advantage of the incredible experience that is movie-going in L.A. The **Pacific Cinerama Dome,** 6360 Sunset Blvd. (213-466-3401), near Vine, boasts the ultimate movie screen: it stretches nearly 180° around the theater, while the surround-sound rumbles from one side to the other. This place can make almost any movie good, except for maybe ones starring Pauly Shore.

Watching a movie at one of the **Universal City** or **Century City** theaters can be an amazing experience. The theaters in **Westwood Village** near UCLA are also incredibly popular, especially on weekends. You *will* wait in line at all the best theaters, especially for new releases, but the lively crowds, state-of-the-art sound systems, and large screens more than justify the wait. In Santa Monica, 22 theaters rest between Santa Monica Pl. and the Third St. Promenade. **Silent Movie,** 611 N. Fairfax Ave. (213-653-2389), off Melrose in L.A. has the largest collection of pre-talkie gems. 250 seats creak to the live organ accompaniment to these silent film screenings. (Wed., Fri.-Sat. 8pm. $6, children $3.)

If you'd just like to stand outside and ogle the stars as they walk the red carpet into the theater for a **premiere,** call the four premiere-hounds: Mann's Chinese (about 2 per month), El Capitan (Disney films only), and the Village and Fox in Westwood. For **information** on where anything in L.A. is playing, call 213-777-FILM/3456, or pick up the Calendar section of the *Los Angeles Times.* Tickets at theaters are generally $7.50, seniors and children $4.

Theater and Concerts

In spite of the growing number of shows about L.A., very few Broadway/West End-style productions come out of this town. Instead, it has an abundance of smaller venues. 115 "equity waiver theaters" (under 100 seats) offer a dizzying choice for theater-goers, who can also take in small productions in museums, art galleries, universities, parks, and even garages. For the digs on what's hot, browse the listings in the *L.A. Weekly*.

L.A.'s concert venues range from small to massive. The **Wiltern Theater** (213-380-5005) shows alterna-rock/folk acts. The **Hollywood Palladium** (213-962-7600) is of comparable size with 3500 seats. Madness played here once—leave your offering at the door. Mid-size acts head for the **Universal Amphitheater** (818-777-3931) and the **Greek Theater** (213-665-1927). Huge indoor sports arenas, such as the **Sports Arena** (213-748-6131) or the **Forum** (310-673-1300), double as concert halls for large shows. Few dare to play at the 100,000+ seat **L.A. Coliseum.** Only U2, Depeche Mode, and Guns 'n Roses have filled the stands in recent years. Check out Ticketmaster at any one of the various Tower Records to find out who's playing.

NIGHTLIFE

Late-Night Restaurants

Club kids and café habitués alike share the need for the down tip on the happening after-hours. It's hard to explain the charm of eating greasy food and downing coffee in vinyl booths after an exhausting night of smoke and dancing; just do it. The ever-popular **Jerry's Deli** now has three locations: West Los Angeles, 8701 Beverly Blvd. (310-289-1811); Studio City, 12655 Ventura Blvd. (818-980-4245); and Encino (818-906-1800). The menu is longer than Methuselah's beard, so if you want it, they got it. If you're really lucky, you just might see Ian Ziering of *90210* fame. (Open 24hr.) **The Rainbow Grill,** 9015 Sunset Blvd. (310-278-4232), beside the Roxy on the Sunset Strip, has dark red vinyl booths which have cradled just about every famous butt in L.A. Marilyn Monroe met future husband Joe DiMaggio on a blind date here. Yummy pizza ($7) and calamari. (Open Mon.-Fri. 11am-2am, Sat.-Sun. 5pm-2am.) **Barney's Beanery,** 8447 Santa Monica Blvd. (213-654-2287), is L.A. at its best, but minus the pretension. Janis Joplin and Jim Morrison came all the time, and parts of *The Doors* were accordingly filmed at the bar. It hasn't changed much since then. $1 billiards. Strange mix of rock stars, international crowd, and local pool sharks. Over 600 items on the menu, 250 bottled beers, and 200 on tap. Mmmmm, beer. (Open daily 6am-2am.) **Ben Frank's,** 8585 Sunset Blvd. (310-652-8808), Sunset Strip, is more of a leg-

So You Wanna Be an Extra

Honey! Baby! Sweetheart! You don't have to be beautiful and proportionally perfect to grace celluloid these days—just look at Tom Arnold or Juliette Lewis. The quickest way to get noticed is to land yourself a job as an extra. It's an excellent short-term job which requires no experience and guarantees you $40-130 and two meals for one day's work. Step One is to stop calling yourself an extra—you're an "atmosphere actor" now (it's better for your ego and your résumé). Step Two is to contact a *reputable* casting service. **Cenex** (1700 W. Burbank Blvd., 2nd Floor, Burbank, CA 91506; 818-562-2888, ext. 3219) is the biggest, and accordingly, a good place to start. Do not call any place in the paper, lest your "acting career" end up like that of Mira Sorvino in *Mighty Aphrodite.* Step Three is to show up on time; you'll need the clout of DeNiro before you can waltz in after call. Step Four is to dress the part. This business hires purely on appearance, so don't wear red or white, which bleed on film and render you unusable. Finally, after you collect three SAG (Screen Actors Guild; 5757 Wilshire Blvd., Los Angeles, CA 90036; 213-937-3441) vouchers, you'll be eligible to pay the $1050 to join showbiz society. See you in the movies!

end than a restaurant. It looks tame, but it rocks. Madonna, Cindy Crawford, and every British band staying at the nearby hotels have been spotted here. The vanilla almond waffle ($4.75) is delish, but the younger set lives on the pile of fries with ranch dressing ($3; open 24hr.).

Coffeehouses

In this city where no one eats very much for fear of rounding out that bony figure, espresso, coffee, and air are the only options. **Highland Grounds,** 742 N. Highland Ave. (213-466-1507), Hollywood, has entertainment nightly from 8pm and an outdoor patio with continuously burning fire pit. Ah, ambience. They also have a full menu and beer. (Open Mon. 9am-6pm, Tues.-Thurs. 9am-12:30am, Fri.-Sat. 9am-1am, Sun. 10am-9pm.) **Wednesday's House,** 2409 Main St. (310-452-4486), downtown, is The Partridge Family on espresso. Popular joint with the self-consciously Gen-X crowd, who swap sex stories and yoga tips. Rethink those hot pants, lest you stick to the plastic slipcovered couches. Dig the delectable selection of pastries. (Open 8am-2am. No credit cards.) **Nova Express,** 426 N. Fairfax Ave. (213-658-7533), Fairfax, is like walking into the Star Wars cantina. Sci-fi books and comics which adorn the bookshelves are for reading and sale. Espresso $2, pizza $1.50 per slice or $13 for the "Spiral Galaxy." Live rock music on Fri., acoustic on Sat. They deliver until closing. (Open daily 9am-4am.) **The Coffee Bean and Tea Leaf,** 8951 Sunset Blvd. (310-659-1890), Sunset Strip, is a popular chain. This particular branch is frequented by the cast of *Friends.* Ice blends are $2.75. (Open Mon.-Fri. 6:30am-11pm, Sat.-Sun. 7am-midnight.)

Bars

Smoky cocktail lounges are all the rage in L.A. these days, but if martinis and mambo aren't your style, there are still plenty of no-nonsense watering holes around. The **Alligator Lounge,** 3321 Pico Blvd. (310-449-1844), Santa Monica, has a lounge-y atmosphere set apart from the stereotypical Hollywood scene. Live bands every night of the week and a full bar. Doors open at 8pm. The **Oar House,** 2941 Main St. (310-396-4725), Santa Monica, has a jam-packed dance floor beneath the antique-lined ceiling. Heavy carding, so bring every ID you've ever had. Happy hour 5-9pm. $1.50 shot, $1.75 pints. Wed. passport night, and Thurs. college ID night, and there are specials for those with them. (Open daily 5pm-2am.) **Atlas Bar and Grill,** 3760 Wilshire Blvd. (213-380-8400), Wilshire District, is a glamorous nightspot with retro decor, jazz and cabaret. Happy hour daily 3-7pm. ($5 cover on the weekends. Open Mon.-Fri. 11am-2am, Sat. 6pm-2am.) **The Snake Pit,** 7529 Melrose Ave. (213-852-9390), West Hollywood, is an unpretentious little hole amid many poser bars. It's crowded with a young, affable jetset. (Happy hour Mon.-Fri. 3-7pm, Sun. 9pm-midnight. Open Sun.-Thurs. 5pm-2am, Sat.-Sun. 11:30am-2am.)

Clubs

L.A. is famous, perhaps infamous, for its club scene. With the highest number of bands per capita in the world, most clubs are able to book top-notch acts night after night. The distinction between music clubs and dance clubs is a bit sketchy in L.A.—most music clubs have DJs a couple times a week, and most dance clubs have bands a couple times a week. Many clubs are simply host spaces for managements that change every night. These clubs can be the hottest thing in L.A. one month, and disappear the next. A recent issue of the *L.A. Weekly* reads, "Due to the erratic lives of L.A. musicians and the capricious personalities of booking agents, all of the following are subject to change for no apparent reason." So check the *L.A. Weekly* (free everywhere), before venturing out. **The Derby,** 4500 Los Feliz Blvd. (213-663-8979), Silver Lake, is a down new club. The kings of swing reign once again in this gregarious velvet joint. Ladies, grab your snoods—many dress the 40s part. They serve the menu from Louise's Trattoria (choice Italian fare) next door. (Full bar. Free pool. Free swing lessons Wed.-Thurs. 8pm, Sun. 7:30pm. Happy hour daily 4-7pm. Open Mon. 4pm-2am, Tues.-Sun. noon-2am.) **Luna Park,** 665 N. Robertson Blvd. (310-652-0611), West

Hollywood, is a swank newcomer which draws a crowd as eclectic as its music. Live funk, jazz, and rock. Supper club and full bar. (Cover $5-10.) **Club 1970s,** 836 N. Highland (213-957-4855), just north of Melrose in Hollywood, is hardcore bootie bumpin' for the leisure suit set. (Full bar. Sunday nights only. Open 9pm-2am. Do a little dance…) **The Viper Room,** 8852 Sunset Blvd. (310-358-1880), Sunset Strip, is Johnny Depp's infamous club and the site of River Phoenix's death. Music genre changes nightly, as does the DJ. Thurs. is Mr. Phat's Martini Lounge—say "the Sultan sent me," and you'll get in for ½ price. (Cover usually $10-15. Open 9pm-2am.) **Kingston 12,** 814 Broadway (310-451-4423), Santa Monica. is L.A.'s only full-time reggae club. Dredlocks flow freely. (Jamaican food, dance floor, 2 bars. Open Thurs.-Sun. 9pm-2am. Cover varies. 21 and over.)

Gay and Lesbian Bars and Clubs

Many ostensibly "straight" clubs have gay nights. Check the *L.A. Weekly* for additional listings or contact the Gay and Lesbian Community Services Center (see Practical Information). **Axis,** 652 N. La Peer Dr. (310-659-0471), West Hollywood, is the hub of West Hollywood's gay and lesbian scene. Music changes nightly. (Fri., Girl Bar; Sat., Axis for Men; Wed-Thurs. and Sun. 18 and over. Other nights 21 and over. Cover $5-10. Open nightly 9pm 'til everyone leaves.) **The Abbey,** 692 Robertson Blvd. (310-289-8410), West Hollywood, is a Spanish-revival coffeehouse that buzzes well into the night. Enormous double cappuccino $3. (Open Sun.-Thurs. 8am-2am, Fri.-Sat. 8am-3am. No credit cards.) **The Palms,** 8572 Santa Monica Blvd. (310-652-6188), is West Hollywood's oldest women's bar. Men are welcome, but may feel very alone. (Pool room. Dancing every night. Full bar. Lots of drink specials. Wed. $3 cover, $1 drinks. Thurs. $5 cover, 50¢ drinks. Open until 2am daily.) **Micky's,** 8857 Santa Monica Blvd. (657-1176), Santa Monica, is a large, popular wetspot filled with delectable men of all ages. On Thurs., male porno stars come to "hang around" and "dispense autographs." (Tues. 18 and up night, all others 21 and over only. Weekend beer bust 4-9pm. Cover $2-7. Open daily noon-2am.)

Comedy Clubs

The talent may be imported from New York and other parts of the country, but that doesn't change the fact that L.A.'s comedy clubs are the best in the world. Call ahead to check age restrictions. Cover charges are cheaper during the week; the clubs are less crowded, but just as drunk. **Comedy Store,** 8433 Sunset Blvd. (213-656-6225), West Hollywood, is the shopping mall of comedy clubs with three different rooms, each featuring a different type of comedy. (Each room charges its own cover.) Go to the Main Room for the big-name stuff and the most expensive cover charges ($10-12. Over 21 only. 2-drink minimum, with drinks starting at $4.50. Reservations taken all week.) **The Improvisation,** 8162 Melrose Ave. (213-651-2583), West Hollywood, offers L.A.'s best talent, including, on occasion, Robin Williams and Jerry Seinfeld. (Open nightly; check *L.A. Weekly* for times. Cover $8-11, 2-drink minimum. Reservations recommended.)

Seasonal Events

Tournament of Roses Parade and Rose Bowl (818-449-7673), Jan. 1, Pasadena. New Year's Day is always a perfect day in Southern California. The **Renaissance Pleasure Faire** (800-52-FAIRE/523-2473) lasts from the daffodil's first blossom to the day of the shortest night (weekends, late April to mid-June). The name is quite arousing, but save for the occasional kissing bridge, it's a pretty tame scene. From the haven angelic (L.A.), gallop apace on fiery-footed steeds (drive) to Phoebus' lodging (east) along I-10 to I-15 north and look for signs as you draw near the site of happy reveling (city of Devore). (Open 10am-6pm. $17.50, seniors and students $13.50, children $7.50.) **Cinco de Mayo** (213-625-5045), May 5, especially downtown at Olvera St. Huge celebrations mark the day the Mexicans kicked the French out of Mexico. **UCLA Mardi Gras** (310-825-8001), mid-May, at the athletic field. Billed as the world's largest collegiate activity (a terrifying thought). Proceeds benefit charity. During **Gay**

Pride Week (213860-0701), late June, Pacific Design Center, 8687 Melrose Ave., Hollywood. L.A.'s lesbian and gay communities celebrate in full effect. Art, politics, dances, and a big parade. (Tickets $10.)

■ Near Los Angeles: South Bay

South Bay life is beach life. **Hermosa Beach** wins both the bathing suit and congeniality competitions. **Manhattan Beach** exudes a yuppified charm, while **Redondo Beach** is by far the most commercially suburban. Richie Rich-esque **Rancho Palos Verdes** is a coast of a different breed. Its lighthouse, public gardens, and Lloyd Wright (*not* Frank Lloyd Wright) chapel have wowed many a visitor. From early morning to late evening, all these famed sandboxes are constantly overrun by gaggles of eager skaters, bladers, volleyball players, surfers, and sunbathers. At night, the crowds move off the beach and head toward the affordable clubs and restaurants which crowd Manhattan and Hermosa Ave. South Bay harbors two of L.A.'s finest hostels; the one in Hermosa Beach has a bitchin' social scene, while the one in San Pedro may make you want to take up *tai chi*. **Los Angeles Surf City Hostel,** 26 Pier Ave. (798-2323), is ½-block from the beach. Take the #439 bus from Union Station to 11th and Hermosa, walk 2 blocks north, and make a left on Pier. This good-natured place has free linens, bodyboards, and breakfast. (Discount car rentals, hall showers, laundry, kitchen, and TV lounge. 28-day max. stay. $10 key deposit. 4-6 bunk dorms $12 off-season, $15 in summer. No reservations; come in around noon. Private rooms $35.) **HI-Los Angeles South Bay (HI-AYH),** 3601 S. Gaffey St., Bldg. #613 (831-8109; fax 831-4635), is in Angels Gate Park (entrance by 34th) in San Pedro. Bus #446 runs from here to downtown and Union Station during rush hours. From the LAX transfer terminal, take MTA #232, get off at Avalon and Anaheim, where you can catch #446. These former army barracks are adjacent to Angels Gate Park. It has a kitchen, laundry, TV room, volleyball courts, free parking, and a mixed, slightly older clientele. (No sleeping bags allowed, linens available for $2. 7-day max. stay. Reception open 7-11am, 4pm-midnight. Private rooms $29, semi-private (2 people) $13 per person, dorms (3-6 beds) $11-14.)

■ Orange County

Orange County, or "O.C." as locals call it, is what many people associate with Southern California: beautiful beaches teeming with bronzed surfer dudes; boulevards of strip malls which stretch to the curve of the horizon and beyond; stunning homes perched high atop mottled hills; stately missions built by Spanish monks venturing north from Mexico; Walt Disney's expansive vision of what fun is and should be; and traffic snarls frustrating enough to make even the most jaded Angeleno weep. This most typically Californian of counties recently suffered perhaps a most typically American predicament: financial bankruptcy. More recently, many have called O.C.'s typically Californian reputation into question, as the county's homogeneously white population contrasts starkly with the vibrant heterogeneity of L.A. County. O.C. residents still refuse to believe they are a part of the L.A. sprawl—they click their heels three times and say, "We're not the suburbs of Los Angeles, we're not the suburbs of Los Angeles ..." Whatever. At least there's always Disneyland.

PRACTICAL INFORMATION

The **Anaheim Area Visitors and Convention Bureau,** 800 W. Katella Ave., Anaheim 92802 (999-8999), is open Mon.-Fri. 8:30am-5pm. **Amtrak** stops 5 times in O.C.: in **Irvine,** 15215 Barranca Ave. (753-9713); in **Santa Ana,** 1000 E. Santa Ana St. (547-8389); in **San Juan Capistrano,** 26762 Verdugo St. (240-2972); in **Anaheim,** 2150 E. Katella Ave. (385-1448); in **San Clemente** by the pier. **Greyhound** has stations at 100 W. Winston St. (999-1256), in **Anaheim,** 3 blocks south of Disneyland (open daily 6:30am-8pm); 1000 E. Santa Ana Blvd. (542-2215) in **Santa Ana** (open daily 7am-8pm); and 510 Avenida de la Estrella (492-1187) in **San Clemente** (open Mon.-Thurs.

7:45am-6:30pm, Fri. 7:45am-8pm). **Orange County Transportation Authority (OCTA),** 550 S. Main St. (636-7433), in Garden Grove, allows you to subvert traffic snarls and lets locals navigate the Byzantine highway system. Bus #1 travels the coast from Long Beach down to San Clemente, once per hr. early morning-8pm (fare $1, transfers free). Call for specific routes. Anaheim's **post office:** 701 N. Loara (520-2600), Anaheim. **ZIP code:** 92803. **Area code:** 714, 310 in Seal Beach.

ACCOMMODATIONS, CAMPING, AND FOOD

The Magic Kingdom is the sun around which the Anaheim universe revolves, so budget motels and garden variety "clean, comfortable rooms" flank it on all sides. Keep watch for family and group rates posted on marquees, and seek out establishments offering the "5 for 2" passport (5 days of Disney for the price of 2)—if you can stand five days of Mickey and Donald. The hostels have it all over the crowded motels and campgrounds. Those roughin' it should make reservations through Destinet (800-444-7275) a maximum of 7 months in advance, as soon as possible in the summer. There is a $6.75 *non-refundable* fee for every reservation made.

HI-Fullerton (HI-AYH), 1700 N. Harbor Blvd. (738-3721), in Fullerton, 15min. drive north of Disneyland. Wonderfully refurbished hostel with an international clientele. Modern kitchen, clean communal bathrooms, and spiffy single- and mixed-sex accommodations. 5-day max. stay. No curfew. Registration daily 7:30-10:30am and 4-10pm (winter) or 5-11pm (summer). $14, nonmembers $17.

Huntington Beach Colonial Inn Youth Hostel, 421 8th St. (536-3315), in Huntington Beach, 4 blocks inland at Pecan. Common showers, large kitchen, reading/TV room, and a lovable cat. Both the large deck and the surfboard shed out back are frequently used by the hostel's tan young guests. Free breakfast. No lockout. Multi-person dorms $12 per person; doubles $14. Must have picture ID. Call 2 days in advance for summer weekends.

Magic Carpet Motel, 1016 W. Katella Ave. (772-9450) and the **Magic Lamp Motel,** 1030 W. Katella Ave. (772-7242), both in Anaheim. These rugs can't show you a whole new world, but they do grant comfortable, affordable lodging across the street from Disneyland. $34 for 1-2 people, $2 each additional person. Deluxe suite ($65) sleeps up to 7. Reservations recommended (800-422-1556).

For a break from the otherwise pervasive mini-mall fare, try one of the various inexpensive ethnic restaurants tucked into the strip malls that line Anaheim's streets. A good choice is **El Pollo Inka,** 400 S. Euclid Blvd. (772-2263), where you can congregate with locals under a black light mural of Machu Picchu and devour filling Peruvian food (open Mon.-Thurs. 11:30am-9pm, Fri.-Sat. 11:30am-10pm).

■ Disneyland

Disneyland is the self-described "happiest place on earth." Should you decide to go on a weekend, rest assured you will wait in line to go happily anywhere, including the exit. Aim for a weekday and you'll be much happier. On your way in, grab a copy of *Disneyland Today!* which lists parade times. While screaming kids and their bedraggled parents crane to glimpse high schoolers parading by in plastic costumes, take advantage of the shorter lines and jump on as many rides as possible. The park was designed for kids, so if you consider yourself above such childish diversions, you won't enjoy yourself. Hey, there's a screaming kid in all of us.

Main Street, USA, a sugar-coated recreation of small-town America, has most of the park's shopping, but the prices prove that Disney execs know the advantage of a captive market. To the left of Main Street is **Adventureland,** home to the brand-spankin' new **Indiana Jones Adventure.** In order to ensure repeat riders by teasing the female contingent, the ride is punctuated by an animatronic Harrison Ford suggestively saying, "You were good in there...very good." The **Jungle Cruise** next door has added a new landing complete with a swing band to entertain you while you languish in the long line and contemplate returning to the Indiana Jones "ride."

Those with a Wild West fetish will find amusement galore in **Frontierland,** home to one of the most fun rides in the park, **Big Thunder Railroad.** Nearby, you can board the Mark Twain **riverboat** around **Tom Sawyer's Island,** which looks suspiciously like a clever way to isolate children away from everyone else. Way down yonder is **Critter Country,** home to **Splash Mountain,** a wet ride in a log past singing rodents to a thrilling vertical drop. Its host, Brer Rabbit, originated in the stories about racism in the post-Civil War South, written by a man called Uncle Remus, but the deepest message of the ride is instead, "Everybody's got a laughing place."

Fantasyland is the geographical and spiritual center of the park, containing the scintillating **Matterhorn Bobsleds** and kiddie rides like **It's A Small World,** which will fiendishly burn its happy happy song into your brain. **Tomorrowland** is where Disney meets the Jetsons circa 1960. This area houses some of the park's best rides, such as newly refurbished **Space Mountain** and **Star Tours.**

The Unlimited Use Passport ($34, senior $30, under 12 $26) allows you to enter and exit as much as you want in a single day. The park has two entrances, the main one on Harbor and a small one on Katella, and can be approached by car via I-5 to Katella. From L.A., take MTA bus #460 from 4th and Flower to the Disneyland Hotel (about 1½hr., 4:53am-1:20am.) Be forewarned that while parking in the morning should be painless, leaving in the evening often will not be. The park's hours vary, but are approximately Sun.-Thurs. 9am-10pm, Fri.-Sat. 9am-1am.

Not Disneyland

Buena Park offers a cavalcade of non-Disney diversions, some of which are better than others. The Knott family's answer to Disneyland, **Knott's Berry Farm,** 8039 Beach Blvd. (714-220-5200 for a recording) is at La Palma just 5 mi. north of Mickey and friends. Back in 1932, Walter Knott (no relation to Don) combined a raspberry, a blackberry, and a loganberry to invent a boysenberry. The seed of the area's first amusement park was born. Knott's offers a more exciting array of coasters to attract those bored of Disney's tamer rides. Highlights include Montezuma's Revenge, Boomerang, and the Birdcage Theater, where Steve Martin got his start. Their kiddie land is called Camp Snoopy, where you will encounter Woodstock who, at 6'4", is really much bigger than he looks on TV. (Hours vary; call the info line for details. Approximate hours are Sun.-Thurs. 9am-11pm, Fri.-Sat. 9am-midnight. $29, seniors and children under 12 $19.) Many Californians opt for amusement parks of the wetter variety, such as **Wild Rivers Waterpark,** 8770 Irvine Center Dr. (768-9453), in Irvine, off I-405 South. ($18, ages 55+ $10, ages 3-9 $14).

Farther inland is the highly uncritical monument to Tricky Dick—the **Richard Nixon Library and Birthplace,** 18001 Yorba Linda Blvd. (993-5075), in Yorba Linda. Listen to 18 min. of silence in the Watergate Room, where the tiny, poorly lit text is written white on black—making it impossible to read. Pat Nixon's peaceful rose garden outside is the site of many a high school prom. (Open Mon.-Sat. 10am-5pm, Sun. 11am-5pm; $6, seniors $4, kids 8-11 $2.)

■ Orange County Beach Communities

Orange County **beaches** are generally cleaner, less crowded, and more charming than those in L.A. County. **Huntington Beach** served as a point of entry for the surfing craze, which transformed California coast life in the early 1900s. It's still a fun, crowded hotspot for wave-shredders, with a pristine pier for ogling. **Newport Beach** is the Beverly Hills of beach towns, though the beach itself displays few signs of ostentatious wealth; it is crowded with young, rowdy hedonists cloaked in neon.

Laguna Beach, 4 mi. south of Newport, is nestled between canyons. Back in the old days, Laguna was a Bohemian artists' colony, but no properly starving artists can afford to live here now. The surviving galleries and art supply stores nevertheless add a unique twist to the standard SoCal beach culture that thrives on Laguna's sands. **Main Beach** and the shops nearby are the prime parading areas, though there are other, less crowded spots as well. One accessible beach (with a sizable gay crowd) is

Westry Beach, which spreads out south of Laguna just below **Aliso Beach Park.** Park on Pacific Coast Hwy. or on residential streets to the east and look for "Public Access" signs between private properties.

More tourists than swallows return every year to **Mission San Juan Capistrano** (248-2048), a half-hour south of Anaheim on I-5 (take Ortega Hwy. to Camino Capistrano). Established in 1776, it is somewhat run-down due to an 1812 earthquake. Father Junípero Serra, the mission's founder, officiated from inside the beautiful **Serra Chapel,** which at 218 years is the oldest building in the state. The dark chapel is warmed by the 17th-century Spanish cherrywood altar and the Native American designs painted on walls and ceiling. It's still used by the Catholic church, so enter quietly. (Open daily 8:30am-5pm. $4, seniors and ages 3-12 $3.)

■ Big Bear

Hibernating in the **San Bernardino Mountains,** the town of **Big Bear Lake** entertains visitors with winter skiing and summer boating. Call the **Big Bear Hotline** (909-866-7000) for recorded lodging and events information. To reach Big Bear Lake, take **I-10** to Junction 30/330. Follow **Rte. 30** to **Rte. 330,** also known as Mountain Rd., and continue to **Rte. 18.** There is a **bus service** between Big Bear and San Bernardino ($3.75) four times per day and twice per day on weekends. It picks up at the Greyhound station in San Bernardino and runs along Big Bear Blvd.

Big Bear has few budget accommodations, especially in the winter. The **Hillcrest Lodge,** 40241 Big Bear Blvd. (909-866-7330), offers cozy rooms an expensive feel at a budget price. The smallest rooms cost $32 in summer. Amenities include outdoor jacuzzi, free local calls, and HBO. Midweek chalet rates are not out of the budget traveler's reach, especially for groups of six or more. Camping is permitted at U.S. Forest Service sites throughout the area. Several of the grounds listed below accept reservations (800-280-2267). **Pineknot** (7000ft.), near the end of Summit Blvd., is surprisingly isolated, with 48 heavily wooded spots, half of which accept reservations. It's wheelchair accessible, with flush toilets and water (sites $15). Tent campers can avoid crowds and fees by camping outside of designated campgrounds on U.S. Forest Service land. Sites must be at least 200 ft. from streams and lakes. Obtain maps and free permits from the Big Bear Ranger Station. **Food** is pricey in the mountains. Groceries are available at **Vons,** 42170 Big Bear Blvd. (909-866-8459).

The **hiking** in Big Bear is both free and priceless. Stop at the Big Bear Ranger Station, Rte. 38 (909-866-3437) on opposite side of the lake. (Open Mon.-Sat. 8am-4:30pm in the summer, closed Sat. all winter.) Try the **Woodland Trail,** or for a more challenging hike, try the **Pineknot Trail,** which offers views of the lake. Beware of the high altitude and rarefied air here; expect to climb slowly.

Mountain biking is a popular activity in Big Bear when the snow melts. **Snow Mountain** (909-866-5766) operates lifts in summer so thrill-seeking bikers can plummet downhill without the grueling uphill ride. The chair lift costs $7 per ride or $18 for a day pass (helmet required). Save money and get a great workout by biking up yourself; trails are open and free to all riders. Beautiful national forest land to the east and west of ski country invites exploration. **Big Bear Bikes,** 41810 Big Bear Blvd. (866-2224), rents 'em for $6 per hr. or $21 per half-day

Fishing and **boating** are also popular Big Bear summer activities. Pick up an $8 fishing license at any area sporting goods store before you drop your line. **Holloway's Marina,** 398 Edgemor Rd. on the South Shore (800-448-5335), rents fishing boats for $28 per half-day. Big Bear Lake's **Fishing Association** (909-866-6260) handles all fishy queries. When conditions are favorable, ski areas sell out lift tickets quickly. **Tickets** for the resorts listed below may be purchased over the phone with Visa or MasterCard through TicketMaster (213-480-3232 or 714-740-2000). Call 800-427-7623 for information on road conditions and closures. The **Bear Mountain Ski (and Golf) Resort** (909-585-2519), has 11 lifts, 250 acres of terrain, 100- to 1300-ft. vertical drops, snowmaking, and more expert runs than other area slopes. Lift tickets cost $40, $30 for ages 65 and over. Equipment rental is $17 for skis, $27 for boots and

FOOD

Good restaurants cluster **downtown** along C St., Broadway, and in the Gaslamp. The best food near **Balboa Park** and the Zoo is north and west in nearby Hillcrest and University Heights. **Old Town** is *the* place to eat Mexican cuisine.

El Indio Mexican Restaurant, 409 F St. (239-8151), downtown. Damn good food at damn good prices. Combo plates $4, burritos $3. Open daily 11am-8pm.

Karl Strauss' Old Columbia Brewery and Grill, 1157 Columbia St. (234-2739), downtown. Pricier, but has won almost every restaurant award around. Entrees $6-10. Open Mon.-Sat. 11:30am-midnight, Sun. 11:30am-10pm.

The Golden Dragon, 414 University Ave. (296-4119), Hillcrest. Where Marilyn Monroe and Frank Sinatra ate when in town. Hugely varied menu offers over a hundred dishes (many vegetarian) $6-9. Open daily 4:30pm-3am.

Kansas City Barbecue, 610 W. Market St. (231-9680), Hillcrest. Site of the famous "You've Lost That Lovin' Feeling" bar scene in *Top Gun.* Giant BBQ lunches and dinners ($4.25-9) more than make up for the plain decor. Open daily 11am-1am.

Casa de Bandini, 2754 Calhoun St. (297-8211), Old Town. Incredible chimichangas ($7), combo plates ($7-8), and monster margaritas. Open Mon.-Thurs. 11am-9:30pm, Fri.-Sat. 11am-10pm, Sun. 10am-9:30pm.

Café Coyote, 2461 San Diego Ave. (295-2343), Old Town. Howling good food and 90 different tequilas. Burritos $5 and combo plates $6-9. Have some food with your margarita. Open Sun.-Thurs. 7:30am-10pm, Fri.-Sat. 7:30am-11pm.

SIGHTS

Downtown

South of Broadway, between 4th and 5th Ave., lie 16 blocks of antique shops, Victorian buildings, and trendy restaurants that comprise the historic **Gaslamp Quarter.** Gentrification has brought a number of new bars and bistros to the Quarter and the area is now frequented by upscale after-hours revelers. The area is a National Historic District, with several 19th-century landmarks worth a visit. The **Gaslamp Quarter Foundation** (233-4692) offers walking tours of the Quarter (Sat. 11am. 90-min. tours $5; seniors, students, ages 12-18 $3; under 12 free).

Moored windjammers, cruise ships, and the occasional naval destroyer face the boardwalk shops and museums along the **Embarcadero** (Spanish for "dock"). The magnificently restored 1863 sailing vessel, *Star of India,* is docked in front of the touristy **Maritime Museum,** 1306 N. Harbor Dr. (234-9153). Alongside are anchored both the 1904 British steam yacht *Medea* and the 1898 ferryboat *Berkeley,* a bay ferry that slipped away from its mooring after the 1906 earthquake. (Ship open daily 9am-9pm. $5, ages 13-17 and over 55 $4, 6-12 $2.) Along the harbor to the south, kitschy **Seaport Village** (235-4014) houses shingled shops.

From Harbor Drive, the **Coronado Bridge** stretches westward from Barrio Logan to the Coronado Island. High enough to allow the Navy's biggest ships to pass underneath, the sleek, sky-blue arc rests upon spindly piers and executes a graceful, swooping turn over the waters of San Diego Bay before touching down in Coronado. You've seen the bridge on *Simon and Simon.* When the bridge was built in 1969, its eastern end cut a swath through San Diego's largest Chicano community. In response, the community created **Chicano Park,** obtaining the land beneath the bridge and painting murals on the bridge's piers. The murals, best appreciated by a walk around the park, are heroic in scale and theme, drawing on Latino, Mayan, and Aztec imagery. Take bus #11 or the San Ysidro trolley to Barrio Logan station.

Balboa Park, the San Diego Zoo, and the El Prado Museums

Balboa Park was the creation of pioneering horticulturists whose plantings transformed a once-treeless pueblo tract into a botanical montage. Planting began in 1889, when San Diego's population was only 3000. Today, primitive Cycad and Coast Redwood trees tower above climbing roses and water lilies, and the city's population is over one million. Close to that number are drawn each year to Balboa Park for its concerts, cultural events, Spanish architecture, lush vegetation, and of course, the San Diego Zoo. Balboa Park is accessible by bus #7 or by driving east from downtown on Laurel St. Parking is free at museums and zoo lots. On Tuesdays, local businesses offer discounts and some cultural attractions offer free admission.

With over 100 acres of exquisite fenceless habitats, the **San Diego Zoo** (234-3153) deserves its reputation as one of the finest in the world. Joining the stunning **Tiger River** and **Sun Bear Forest** is the **Gorilla Tropics** enclosure, housing lowland gorillas and plant species imported from Africa. In addition to the usual elephants and zebras, the zoo houses such unusual creatures as Malay tapirs and aggressively cute koalas. Caloola, Sweeney, Blink Bill, Pangari, and Tabboo are perpetually stoned on eucalyptus leaves, so they don't jump around much, but they do look happy. This year's new attraction is the **Polar Bear Plunge,** where polar bears, Siberian reindeer, and arctic foxes can fish and tan tundra-style beside their very own chilled, Olympic-sized pool. The most efficient way to tour the zoo is to arrive very early and take the 40-min. open-air **double-decker bus tour,** which covers 80% of the park, but expect to wait in line. ($4, ages 3-11 $3. Sit on the left, given a choice.) Most of the zoo is wheelchair accessible, but steep hills make assistance necessary. (Open daily 9am-4pm, 9am-9pm in summer. $13, ages 3-11 $6, military in uniform free.) Look for discount coupons for zoo entrance in guidebooks.

Before exploring El Prado, stop by the **visitors center** in front of the Museum of Art (239-0512; open daily 9am-4pm). The center sells simple maps of the park for a well-spent 65¢, and the **Passport to Balboa Park,** which contains coupons for a week's worth of entry to all of the park's museums ($18). Passports are also available at participating museums.

The star of the western axis of the Plaza de Panama is the **Museum of Man** (239-2001). Inside the much-photographed tower, human evolution is traced through permanent exhibits on primates and early man. Several displays focus on Native American societies. Half of the museum is allotted to innovative temporary exhibits. (Open daily 10am-4:30pm. $4 or 2 coupons, ages 13-18 $2, 6-12 $1.)

Across the Plaza de Panama is the **San Diego Museum of Art** (232-7931), which maintains a comprehensive collection, ranging from ancient Asian to contemporary Californian. (Open Tues.-Sun. 10am-4:30pm. $7, seniors $5, military with ID $4, ages 6-17 $2, under 6 free. Free 3rd Tues. of each month.) Nearby is the outdoor **Sculpture Garden Court** (236-1725), with a sensuous Henry Moore piece presiding over other large abstract blocks. The **Timken Art Gallery,** 1500 El Prado (239-5548), features several superb portraits by David, Hals, Rubens, and others, and an excellent collection of large, abstract Russian church icons. (Open Oct.-Aug. Tues.-Sat. 10am-4:30pm, Sun 1:30-4:30pm; free.)

Farther east along the plaza stands the **Botanical Building** (234-8901), a wooden Quonset structure accented by tall palms which threaten to burst through the roof. The scent of jasmine and the splash of fountains make this an authentic oasis (open Fri.-Wed. 10am-4pm; free). The same botanists run the **Desert and Rose Gardens** one block east at 2200 Park Blvd. (235-1100; free). Cacti and stunted desert vegetation in one building provide a striking contrast to the abundant roses next door.

At the east end of El Prado lies the **Natural History Museum** (232-3821). Life-size robotic dinosaurs enhance the standard fossils and a recreated mine houses gem displays. (Open Fri.-Wed. 9:30am-5:30pm, Thurs. 9:30am-6:30pm. $6, seniors and military $5, ages 6-17 $3.) Across from the Natural History Museum is the **Reuben H. Fleet Space Theater and Science Center** (238-1233), with two **Omnimax** projectors, 153 speakers, and a hemispheric planetarium. (10-14 shows per day. $6.50, senior citizens $5, ages 5-15 $3.50, military and students $5.20.) Tickets to the space theater include admittance to the Science Center, where visitors can play with a cloud chamber, light-mixing booth, and other gadgets. (Open Sun.-Wed. 9:30am-9pm, Thurs.-Sat. 9:30am-10:30pm. $2.50, ages 5-15 $1.25.)

Old Town

In 1769, a group of Spanish soldiers accompanied by Father Junípero Serra established the first European settlement on the United States' western coast. Today the city's business takes place elsewhere. This area is for tourists and history buffs.

Presidio Park is most impressive of the historical areas. The park contains the **Serra Museum** (279-3258; open Tues.-Sat. 10am-4:30pm, Sun. noon-4:30pm ($3, 12 and under free). Exhibits tell the story of the initial settlement and interactions with the native Americans who lived nearby. Apparently the Spanish soldiers were a rough and unholy bunch, because in 1774 the padres moved their mission some six mi. away to its current location. **Mission Basilica San Diego de Alcalá** (281-8449) is still an active parish church where mass is held (daily 7am and 5:30pm). Mission San Diego has a chapel, a garden courtyard, a small museum of artifacts, and a reconstruction of the living quarters of boffo chap Junípero Serra. To find the park, use bus #43 or take I-8 east of Mission Grove Rd. and follow the signs.

West of the mission is **Jack Murphy Stadium**, home of the AFC champion **San Diego Chargers** football team and baseball's less successful **San Diego Padres** (Chargers tickets 280-2121, Padres tickets 525-8282).

Point Loma and Some Beaches

Point Loma walks a fine line between residential community and naval outpost. The **Cabrillo National Monument** (557-5450), at the tip of Point Loma, is dedicated to João Rodrigues Cabrillo, the first European to land in California, but is best known for the views of San Diego and migrating whales from December to February (whale information in winter 557-5450). **Ocean Beach (O.B.),** several miles north, caters to a surfing crowd that is slightly less upscale than farther up the coast. Although the waves here are considered miserable by hot-dog surfers, beginners will be fine. To go fishing yourself or just people-watch, join the anglers on the longest fishing pier in the Western Hemisphere. At Sunset Cliffs on O.B., timing can mean the difference between an afternoon of noisy children and a tranquil sojourn in the sun. Come at sunset. (Duh.) **Newport Avenue,** a three-block-long stretch of shops, restaurants, and bars for the beach-going set, is the main drag of O.B. The strands at **Mission Beach** and **Pacific Beach (P.B.)** are more respectable wave-wise than those at O.B. and consequently draw a younger, more surf-oriented crowd. There are tons of bars and grills along these shores—most are crowded and noisy. **Ocean Front Walk,** along Mission Beach, is packed with joggers, walkers, cyclists, and the usual beachfront shops, as well as a more recent proliferation of in-line skaters.

Sea World

Sea World (226-3901) is sort of like Disneyland plus fish and minus the rides. At **Shamu Stadium,** you can be amused and possibly drenched by cavorting orcas. If staying dry seems a little more appealing than the Shamu water treatment, consider the truly outstanding **Shark Encounter.** The highlight of this exhibit is the glass tunnel which leads you through the 700,000-gallon, shark-filled tank. The **Baywatch at Sea World** ski show was unveiled in 1995. Its lame plot is excused by exciting jet ski performances. Part of the event is narrated by none other than the international heartthrob **David Hasselhoff.** The hidden gem of the park is the **Anheuser-Busch Hospitality Tent,** which will give each (21 and over) guest up to **two free cups of beer.** Admission costs $31 for adults and $23 for children 3-11. It's open in summer Sun.-Thurs. 9am-10pm, Fri.-Sat. 9am-11pm. Hours are shorter off season.

NIGHTLIFE

Distinct pockets of action are scattered throughout the city. The Gaslamp is home to myriad upscale restaurants and bars that feature live music nightly. Hillcrest draws a largely gay crowd. The youthful beach areas host tons of bars. The free *San Diego Reader* is the definitive source of entertainment information.

Pacific Beach Grill and Club Tremors, 860 Garnet Ave. (2-PB-PARTY/272-7277), in Pacific Beach. Attracts the young and unattached with a nightly DJ. Open nightly 8:30pm-2am. Cover varies ($1-5). The upstairs bar is more quiet and has an ever-changing menu of cheap food. Open 11am-1:30am, kitchen 'til 11pm.

Dick's Last Resort, 345 4th Ave. (231-9100), in the Gaslamp. Buckets o' Southern grub and a wildly irreverent atmosphere. Beers from around the globe, like Dixieland Blackened Voodoo Lager. No cover for nightly rock or blues, but you'd better be buyin'! Burgers under $4, dinners $10-15. Open daily 11am-1:30am.

Café Lu Lu, 419 F. St. (238-0114), in the Gaslamp. Funky vegetarian coffee house designed by local artists. See and be seen as you dine for under $5 and sip raspberry-mocha espresso ($3.50). Open Sun.-Thurs. 9am-2am, Fri.-Sat. 9am-4am.

Club Sevilla, 555 4th Ave. (233-5979), downtown. Nightly live bands include Brazilian, flamenco, and salsa. *Tapas* bar upstairs. Open daily 5pm-2am. 21 and over.

Velvet, 2812 Kettner Blvd. (692-1080), near Old Town. Live and loud, plays host to local rock 'n' roll up-and-comers, as well as established bands. Alterna-rock 6 nights a week. $5 cover Wed.-Sat. Pool table. 21 and over. Open daily 8pm-2am.

Some of the more popular **lesbian** and **gay clubs** include: **The Flame,** 3780 Park Blvd. in Hillcrest (295-4163), a lesbian dance club; **Bourbon Street,** 4612 Park Blvd. in University Heights (291-0173), a gay piano bar; and **The Brass Rail,** 3796 5th Ave. in Hillcrest (298-2233; open daily 10am-2am).

SEASONAL EVENTS

At the **Penguin Day Ski Fest** (276-0830), New Year's Day, De Anza Cove on Mission Bay, the object is to go water-skiing in the ocean or lie on a block of ice without a wet suit; those who do are honored with a "penguin patch." Those who fail come away with a "chicken patch" (festivities 8am-1pm). The **Ocean Beach Kite Festival** (531-1527), on the first Saturday in March, 4741 Santa Monica Ave. in Ocean Beach, is great for the kiddies. Kite-making materials are provided free, and judging at 1pm is followed by a parade to the beach for the kite-flying competition. On Fri.-Sat. nights from June 1 through Labor Day, at San Diego State University's Mount Laguna Observatory, there's free **Summer Stargazing** (594-6182). **Surf, Sand, and Sandcastle Days** (424-6663), mid-July at Imperial Beach, by the pier at 9:30am, features "Castles of the Mind" and "Creatures of the Sea," as well as a parade and fireworks.

■ North of San Diego

La Jolla Pronounced "la HOY-a," this affluent locality houses few accommodations or eateries friendly to the budget traveler, but its beaches are largely open to the public and simply fabulous. The **La Jolla Cove** is popular with scuba divers, snorkelers, and brilliantly colored Garibaldi Goldfish. Surfers are especially fond of the waves at **Tourmaline Beach** and **Windansea Beach.** These waves can be too much for non-surfers. **La Jolla Shores,** next to Scripps/UCSD, has gentler swells ideal for bodysurfers, boogie-boarders, and swimmers and is exceptionally clean. **Black's Beach,** a public beach, is not officially a **nude beach,** but you wouldn't know it from the sun-kissed hue of most beachgoers' buns. The north end of the beach generally attracts gay patrons. To reach La Jolla, turn from I-5 and take a left at the Ardath exit or take buses #30 or 34 from downtown.

Escondido The **San Diego Wild Animal Park** (234-6541) is dedicated to the preservation and display of endangered species. Eight hundred of the park's 2200 acres have been landscaped to simulate four different geographical regions. A variety of African, European, and American animals range freely in their respective habitats. The entrance has shops, restaurants, and a 1¾-mi. trail—but most of the park is accessible only by the open-air **Wgasa Bush Line,** a 50-min. monorail tour through the four habitat areas. Sit on the right side, if possible. (Admission including Wgasa Bush Line tour and animal shows $19, seniors $15.50, ages 3-11 $12. Parking $3. Park open Mon.-Wed. 9am-7pm, Thurs.-Sun 9am-10pm.)

Visitors can poke through the late "wunnerful, wunnerful" champagne music conductor Lawrence Welk's personal barony, the **Welk Resort Center.** The lobby contains the **Lawrence Welk Museum,** 8860 Lawrence Welk Dr. (800-932-WELK/9355). All the majesty is open Sun.-Mon. and Wed. 10am-4:15pm, Tue.-Thurs. and Sat. 10am-7pm. It's all free. Those under the age of 60 may stand out in this crowd.

THE DESERT

Mystics, misanthropes, and hallucinogenophiles have long been drawn by the vast open spaces, austere scenery, and brutal heat of the desert. In the winter, the desert is a pleasantly warm refuge; in the spring, a technicolor floral landscape; and in the summer, a blistering wasteland. A barren place of overwhelming simplicity, the desert's beauty lies not so much in what it contains, but in what it lacks—congestion, pollution, and crowds of visitors craning to see the same sights.

■ Palm Springs

Palm Springs is the Fort Lauderdale of California. For years, the singularly lackadaisical brand of decadence offered by Palm Springs has attracted people from all walks of life. The Cahuillian Indians settled here for a winter respite and ever since, the area has drawn people hoping to snatch a piece of its glamorama lifestyle. While Palm Springs is home to gaggles of retirees, it is also a popular spring break destination for students and a winter destination for middle-aged, fat cat golfers and hip, young scene-seekers. With relatively warm temperatures, ubiquitous golf courses, symmetrical rows of palm trees, and more pink than a *Miami Vice* episode, the desert city teems with those seeking a sunny respite from their everyday lives.

Go to the **Chamber of Commerce,** 190 W. Amado Rd. (325-1577), for friendly advice and sexy maps ($1). Pick up *The Desert Guide,* a free monthly magazine outlining attractions and entertainment (open daily 9am-4pm). **Greyhound,** 311 N. Indian Canyon Dr. (800-231-2222), runs 7 buses per day to and from L.A. ($14 one-way, $21 roundtrip). The local bus system, **Sun Bus** (343-3451), connects all Coachella Valley cities daily 6am-6pm. Fare is 75¢ with 25¢ transfers (exact change). Line #111 stays on a straight course along Palm Canyon Dr. and from there along Rte. 111 to Palm Desert (1 bus every ½hr.). Lines #21 and #23 cover the downtown area. **Desert Cab,** 325-2868 and **Valley Cabousine,** 340-5845, both offer 24-hr. **taxi** service. **Emergency:** 911. Palm Springs' **post office:** 333 E. Amado Rd. (325-9631; open Mon.-Fri. 8am-5pm, Sat. 9am-1pm). **ZIP code:** 92263. **Area code:** 619.

Like most famous resort communities, Palm Springs caters mainly to those seeking a tax shelter, not a night's shelter—the cheapest way to stay here is to find an nearby state park or national forest campground. If you've gotta stay in town, **Budget Host Inn,** 1277 S. Palm Canyon Dr. (325-5574 or 800-829-8099), has large, clean rooms

---

Let's Not Go: The Fetid Salton Sea

This man-made "wonder" was formed in 1905-1907 when the aqueduct from the Colorado River broke and flooded the Coachella Valley. The accident resulted in a stagnant 35 mi. by 15 mi. lake covering a patch of desert. The lake festered for a while until the 60s, when someone thought it was a great idea to market the area as a tourist attraction. Fresh and saltwater fish were stocked in the sea, and marinas were built in ill-fated anticipation of a thriving resort and vacation industry. Hopes were cruelly dashed when decaying vegetation in the still water produced a foul odor and high salt content killed all but a few hardy species of fish. The sea is now ringed by abandoned buildings and **Salton City** is a defunct resort town withering in the desert sun. For more information, call the **West Shores Chamber of Commerce,** P.O. Box 5185, Salton City, CA 92705.

with fridges, phones, pool/jacuzzi access, and continental breakfast (rooms $29 summer weekdays and $79 winter weekdays, weekends $10-20 higher).

Las Casuelas-The Original, 368 N. Palm Canyon Dr. (325-3213), has some of the best Mexican food around. Combos start at $6 (open daily 10am-10pm). **Thai Smile,** 651 N. Palm Canyon Dr. (320-5503), offers tasty options for vegetarians. (Lunch $5-6, dinner $7-10. Open daily 11am-10pm.) Bars offer nightly drink specials to lure after-hours revelers. **La Taquería,** 125 E. Tahquitz Way (778-5391), attracts customers by covering its tile patio with mist and serving Moonlight Margaritas for $6.

The **Palm Springs Aerial Tramway** (325-1391) climbs the cliffs of Mt. San Jacinto to an observation deck that has excellent views of the Coachella Valley. The tramway station is located on Tramway Dr., which intersects Rte. 111 just north of Palm Springs (roundtrip $16, seniors $12, under 12 $10). A touch of true natural beauty has been marketed at the remarkable **Desert Museum,** 101 Museum Dr. (325-0189). The museum offers an impressive collection of Native American art, talking desert dioramas, and live animals. The **Living Desert Reserve** in Palm Desert, 1½ mi. south of Rte. 111 at 47900 Portola Ave. (346-5694), houses Arabian oryces, iguanas, desert unicorns, and Grevy's zebras alongside indigenous flora in the **Botanical Gardens.** The twilight reptile exhibit is a must-see. (Leer at the lizards daily Oct.-June 15 9am-5pm. $7, seniors $6, under 12 $3.50. Open June 16-Sept. 8am-noon. $5.50, children 3-12 $2.50. Wheelchair accessible.)

The **Indian Canyons** (325-5673), once home to the Agua Caliente Cahuilla Indians, are oases that contain a wide variety of desert life and remnants of the human communities they once supported. All four canyons can be accessed at the end of S. Palm Canyon Dr., 5 mi. from the center of town. (Open daily fall/winter 8am-5pm, spring/summer 8am-6pm. $5 adults, seniors $2.50, children $1, students $3.50.)

■ Joshua Tree National Park

When the Mormons crossed this desert area in the 1800s, they named the enigmatic desert tree they encountered after the Biblical prophet Joshua. Perhaps it was the heat, but the tree's crooked limbs reminded them of the Hebrew leader, who with his arms upraised, beckoned the weary traveler to the promised land. After crossing the more arid Arizona desert, finding the slightly cooler and wetter Mojave must have been like arriving in God's country. Joshua Tree contains an eerie panoply of high and low desert landscapes and life forms. Piles of quartz monzonite boulders, some over 100 ft. high, punctuate the desert terrain. Desert winds and floods have created textures and shapes majestic to the viewer and irresistible to the climber. Hardy fauna adapted to the unforgiving desert environment populate the park. Vestiges of human occupation, like ancient rock petroglyphs, dams built in the 19th century to catch the meager rainfall for livestock, and the ruins of gold mines, dot the park and offer tangible evidence of those who sought the majestic draw of the desert but, for one reason or another, still haven't found what they were looking for.

Practical Information Go to the **Headquarters and Oasis Visitor Center,** 74485 National Park Dr., Twentynine Palms (367-7511), ¼ mi. off Rte. 62, for displays, guidebooks, maps, access to water, and friendly rangers. Open daily 8am-5pm. Understanding the vicissitudes of **weather** is essential: summer highs are 95-115°F; winter highs are 60-70°F. It's hotter in the eastern area. Be careful of flash flood warnings in winter. The **Hi-Desert Medical Center,** 6601 White Feather Rd. (366-3711) in Joshua Tree, provides 24-hr. emergency care. In case of an **emergency,** call 911, or 367-3523 for a **ranger.** For the **24-hr. dispatch center,** call 909-383-5651 collect. The nearest **post office,** 73839 Gorgonio Dr. (367-3501), in Twentynine Palms, is open Mon.-Fri. 8:30am-5pm. **ZIP code:** 92277. **Area code:** 619.

Joshua Tree National Park covers 558,000 acres northeast of Palm Springs, about 160 mi. east of L.A. The park is ringed by three highways: **I-10** to the south, **Rte. 62** to the west and north, and **Rte. 177** to the east. From I-10, the best approaches are via Rte. 62 from the west, or from the south entrance at Cottonwood Springs.

Camping Most campgrounds in the park operate on a first-come, first-camped basis and accept no reservations. Exceptions are the group sites at Cottonwood, Sheep Pass, and Indian Cove and family sites at Black Rock Canyon. Destinet (800-365-2267) will set you up for reservations there. The **backcountry** is also open for unlimited camping. All campsites have tables, fireplaces, and pit toilets, and are free unless otherwise noted. Water and flush toilets are available only at Black Rock Canyon and Cottonwood campgrounds. Bring your own firewood because burning anything you find in the park is a major offense. Tents in the backcountry must be pitched at least 500 ft. from a trail and 1 mi. from a road. Your camping stay is limited to 14 days between October and May and to 30 days in the summer. Be sure to register first at a backcountry board found along the park's main roads so park staff knows where you are. **Hidden Valley** (4200ft.), in the center of the park, with secluded alcoves in which to pitch a tent, and shade provided by enormous boulders, is by far the best and most wooded of the campsites. The 39 sites in the Wonderland of Rocks fill quickly. Rock-climbers will be in heaven. **Jumbo Rocks** (4400ft.) is located near Skull Rock Trail on the eastern edge of Queen Valley. 125 well-spaced sites (65 in summer) surround (you guessed it) jumbo rocks. Front spots have best shade and protection. **Indian Cove** (3200ft.) has 107 sites (45 in summer) on the north edge of the Wonderland of Rocks. There are waterfalls after rain. Most of the 13 group sites are $15, but the two largest are $30. **Black Rock Canyon** (4000ft.), off Rte. 62, 2 mi. north of Yucca Valley, was the inspiration for **Jellystone Park,** the home of Yogi Bear and pals. The 100 wooded sites are conveniently near flush toilets and running water. (Sites $10. Wheelchair accessible.) If you want a roof over your head, consider staying at the **Twentynine Palms Inn,** 73950 Inn Dr. (367-3505), facing the Mara Oasis in Twentynine Palms. Robert Plant composed his hit "29 Palms" here. Rooms are $40-70 weekdays, $60-100 weekends.

Sights Over 80% of the park (mostly the southern and eastern areas) has been designated by Congress as a wilderness area—meaning trails but no roads, toilets, or campfires. For those seeking backcountry desert hiking and camping, Joshua Tree offers fantastic opportunities to explore truly remote territory. There is no water in the wilderness except when a flash flood comes roaring down a wash (beware your choice of campsite). Even then, it doesn't stay long. The most temperate weather is in late fall (Oct.-Dec.) and early spring (March-April). Temperatures in other months often span uncomfortable extremes.

Joshua Tree is world-renowned for **rock-climbing** and draws thousands of climbers each year. The visitors center can provide information on established top rope routes and will identify wilderness areas where placement of new bolts is restricted. The **Wonderland of Rocks** and **Hidden Valley** are particular hotspots. For instruction and equipment rentals contact **Ultimate Adventures,** Box 2072, Joshua Tree (366-4758) or **Wilderness Connection,** Box 29, Joshua Tree (366-4745).

A self-paced driving tour is an easy way to explore the magic of Joshua Tree without specialized equipment (although 4WD wouldn't hurt). Paved roads branch through the park's varied sights, and roadside signs indicate points of interest scattered throughout the park. Some of the most outstanding scenic points can be reached by the side roads. One sight that must not be missed is **Key's View** (5185ft.), 6 mi. off the park road just west of Ryan Campground. On a clear day, you can see to Palm Springs and the Salton Sea, and it's a fabulous spot to watch the sun rise. The **Cholla Cactus Garden,** off Pinto Basin Rd., also merits a visit. Four-wheel drive vehi-

---

Hangin' with Christ

For a simply divine experience, picnic with Jesus and friends at Yucca Valley's **Desert Christ Park,** 57090 Twentynine Palms Hwy. This array of 10- to 15-ft. concrete figures depicting Biblical stories can be reached by turning north from Twentynine Palms Hwy, and proceeding reverently to the end of Mohawk Trail. (No phone, God has an unlisted number. Open dawn-dusk and free as air.)

cles can access dirt roads, such as **Geology Tour Road,** which climbs through fascinating rock formations and ends in the Li'l San Bernardino Mountains.

Hiking through the park's trails is perhaps the best way to experience Joshua Tree. Hikers can tread through sand, scramble over boulders, and walk among the hardy Joshua trees themselves. Visitors will probably find the **Barker Dam Trail** packed with tourists. Painted petroglyphs and a tranquility that rises above the crowd make the reservoir worth a trip. Wildflowers, cooler temperatures, and the indelible picture of the encircling valleys reward the hardy hiker who climbs the 3 mi. to the summit of **Ryan Mountain** (5461ft.). Bring plenty of water for this strenuous, unshaded climb. Information on many other hikes, ranging from a 15-min. stroll to the **Oasis of Mara** (wheelchair accessible) to a 35-mi. circumambulation of the park's **California Riding and Hiking Trail,** is available at the park center.

Joshua Tree teems with flora and fauna that you're unlikely to see anywhere else in the world. You can see adaptations that plants have made in order to survive the severe climate and admire their delicate blooms. More animals can be seen at dawn and dusk than at high noon, but watch for kangaroo rats and lizards at all times. Look for the cactus wren in the branches of **Pinto Basin's** cholla. You may meet an enormous swarm of ladybugs near the oases; be aware that enormous swarms of bees are equally common. Golden eagles and bighorn sheep also live near the oases while coyote and bobcats stalk their prey at night. If you come equipped with time, patience, and a sharp set of eyes, the desert's beauty will gradually reveal itself. **Wildflower season** (mid-March to mid-May) is an especially colorful season.

■ Death Valley National Park

Dante and Milton would have found inspiration for further visions of hell in Death Valley. No place in the Old World approaches the searing temperatures that are the summer norm here. The highest temperature ever recorded in the Western Hemisphere (134°F in the shade) was measured at the Valley's Furnace Creek Ranch on July 10, 1913. Of that day, the ranch caretaker Oscar Denton said, "I thought the world was going to come to an end. Swallows in full flight fell to the ground dead, and when I went out to read the thermometer with a wet Turkish towel on my head, it was dry before I returned." During this most unusual year, the temperature also plummeted to 15°F and 4.54 inches of rain fell—all three figures remain as records today. Fortunately, the fatal threshold of 130°F is rarely crossed, and the region sustains a surprisingly intricate **web of life.** Since 1933, observers have reported seeing six types of fish, five types of amphibians, 36 types of reptiles, and 51 types of mammals. The elevation ranges from Telescope Peak at 11,049 ft. down to Badwater at 282 ft. below sea level. There are pure white salt flats on the valley floor, impassable mountain slopes, and enormous, shifting sand dunes. Nature focuses all of its extremes and varieties here at a single location, resulting in a landscape that is at once harshly majestic and improbably delicate.

Few venture to the valley floor during the summer and it is foolish to do so; the average high temperature in July is 116°F, with a nighttime low of 88°F. Ground temperatures hover near an egg-frying 200°F. When traveling through or visiting Death Valley in any season, follow the information given in the Health section, page 13, with care. In addition, check at the visitors center for the free pamphlet, *Hot Weather Hints.* To really enjoy the park, visit in winter, *not* summer.

Practical Information For **visitors information,** traipse on over to the **Furnace Creek Visitors Center** (786-2331), on Rte. 190 in the east-central section of the valley (open daily summer 8am-5pm, winter 8am-7pm); or write the Superintendent, Death Valley National Park, Death Valley 92328. For **TTY information,** call 786-2471, daily 8am-5pm. **Ranger Stations** are located at **Grapevine,** junction of Rte. 190 and 267 near Scotty's Castle; **Stove Pipe Wells,** on Rte. 190; and **Shoshone,** outside the southeast border of the valley at the junction of Rtes. 178 and 127. Weather report, weekly naturalist program, and park information are posted at each station (open daily 8am-5pm). The **$5 per vehicle** entrance fee is collected only at the visitors center in the middle of the park. Resist the temptation not to pay; the Park Service needs all the money it can get. **Get tanked** outside Death Valley at Olancha, Shoshone, or Beatty, NV. Otherwise, you'll pay about 20¢ per gallon more across from the Furnace Creek visitor center (open 7am-7pm), in Stove Pipe Wells Village (open 7am-8pm), and at Scotty's Castle (open 9am-5:30pm). **Groceries** and supplies can be had at **Furnace Creek Ranch Store** (786-2380), which is well-stocked and expensive (open daily 7am-9pm). **Post office:** Furnace Creek Ranch (786-2223). **ZIP code:** 92328. **Area code:** 619.

Getting Around There is no regularly scheduled public transportation into Death Valley. Bus tours are monopolized by **Fred Harvey's Death Valley Tours** (786-2345, ext. 222; tours only Oct.-May). A 3½-hr. tour of the lower valley costs $20 (children $12) and leaves at 9am, stopping briefly at Zabriskie Point, Devil's Golf Course, Badwater, and Artists' Drive. The best tour is the 5-hr. excursion into hard-to-access Titus Canyon ($30, children $20; leaves at 9am).

The best way to get around Death Valley is by car. The nearest agencies are in Las Vegas, Barstow, and Bishop. Death Valley is a 3½-hr. drive from Las Vegas and a 5-hr. drive from L.A. Of the nine **park entrances,** most visitors choose Rte. 190 from the east. The road is well-maintained, the pass is less steep, and you arrive more quickly at the visitors center. But the visitor with a trusty vehicle will be able to see more of the park by entering from the southeast (Rte. 178 west from Rte. 127 at Shoshone) or the north (direct to Scotty's Castle via NV Rte. 267 from U.S. 95). Unskilled mountain drivers should not attempt to enter via Titus Canyon or Emigrant Canyon Drive roads; neither has guard rails to prevent your car from sliding over **precipitous cliffs.**

Eighteen-wheelers have replaced 18-mule teams, but driving in Death Valley still takes stubborn determination. **Radiator water** (*not* for drinking) is available at critical points on Rte. 178 and 190 and NV Rte. 374, but not on unpaved roads. Believe the signs that say "4WD Only." Those who *do* bound along the backcountry trails should carry chains, extra tires, gas, oil, radiator and drinking water, and spare parts.

Accommodations In Death Valley, enclosed beds and fine meals within a budget traveler's reach are as elusive as the desert bighorn sheep. During the winter months, camping out with a stock of groceries is a good way to save both money and driving time. The wonderful **Johannesburg Death Valley Hostel** (HI-AYH; 374-2323 or 374-2473), is located in Johannesburg near the intersection of I-395 and Rte. 14. It's a great option for budget desert rats, offering 16 comfy beds, a friendly atmosphere, and several desert tour packages (bunks $16). **Stove Pipe Wells Village** (786-2387) is right in Death Valley, but will set you back $53 per night for one or two people, each additional person is $10.

The National Park Service maintains nine **campgrounds,** only two of which accept reservations. Call ahead to check availability and be prepared to battle for a space if you come during peak periods. Water availability is not completely reliable and supplies can at times be unsafe or unavailable; always pack your own. **Backcountry camping** is free and legal, provided you check in at the visitors center and pitch tents at least 1 mi. from main roads, 5 mi. from any established campsite, and ¼-mi. from any backcountry water source.

Sights Death Valley has hiking to bemuse the gentlest wanderer and to challenge the hardiest peregrinator. Backpackers and day hikers should inform the visitors center of their trip, and take along the appropriate topographic maps. The National Park Service recommends that valley floor hikers plan a route along roads where assistance is readily available, and outfit a party of at least two people. Do not wear sandals or lightweight footwear. Hiking in summer is a dumb-ass idea.

Artist's Drive is a one-way loop off Rte. 178, beginning 10 mi. south of the visitors center. The road snakes its sinuous way through craggy canyons on its way to **Artist's Palette,** a visually stunning array of green, yellow, and red mineral deposits in the hillside. 5 mi. south, you'll reach **Devil's Golf Course,** a plane of spiny salt crust composed of precipitate left from the evaporation of once-virile **Lake Manly.**

Three mi. south of Devil's Golf Course, on I-90, lies **Badwater,** an aptly named briny pool four times saltier than the ocean. The trek across the surrounding salt flat dips to the lowest point in the Western Hemisphere—282 ft. below sea level. Immortalized by Antonioni's film of the same name, **Zabriskie Point** is a marvelous place from which to view Death Valley's corrugated badlands. The view is particularly stunning when the setting sun fills the dried lake beds with burnt light. Perhaps the most spectacular sight in the entire park is the vista at **Dante's View,** reached by a 15-mi. paved road from Rte. 190. Just as the Italian poet stood with Virgil looking down on the damned, the modern observer gazes upon a vast inferno punctuated only by the perfect white expanse of the salt flats.

THE CENTRAL COAST

The spectacular stretch of coastline between L.A. and San Francisco known as the Central Coast may give you the sense of the awe felt by California's first settlers. The smogless sky meets the Pacific in a sweeping array of blue, while the shoreline runs the gamut from the dramatic plunge of Big Sur's cliffs to Carmel's white beaches.

■ Santa Barbara

Saint Babs is an enclave of wealth and privilege, but significantly less aggressively so than other Southern Californian enclaves of wealth and privilege. True to its soap opera image, the evening streets are thronged with lithe, thin-limbed young beauties walking hand in hand with guys named Rick or Stone. Yet the center of town, State St., is filled with inexpensive cafés and thrift stores as well as glamorous boutiques. The only common preoccupation here seems to be with perfecting a languorous lifestyle.

Practical Information and Orientation The **tourist office** is on Santa Barbara St. (965-3021), at Cabrillo by the beach. (Open Mon.-Sat. 9am-5pm, Sun. 10am-6pm. Closes at 4pm Dec.-Jan. and at 6pm July-Aug.) **Hotspots,** 36 State St. (963-4233) is a 24-hr. espresso bar with free tourist info and reservation service (open Mon.-Sat. 9am-9pm, Sun. 8am-4pm). To catch a train, try **Amtrak,** 209 State St. (800-872-7245), downtown, where tickets are sold until 9:30pm, and trips go to L.A. ($21) and San Francisco ($71). **Greyhound,** 34 W. Carrillo St. (962-2477), at Chapala, sends buses to L.A. ($12) and San Francisco ($38). **U-Save Auto Rental,** 510 Anacapa St. (963-3499) lets U save on car rentals. ($24 per day with 100 free mi., $129 per week with 1050 free mi.; 20¢ per additional mi. Must be 21 with major credit card. Open Mon.-Fri. 8am-6pm, Sat. 8am-2pm, Sun. 9am-1pm.) Bikes are 4 rent at **Cycles-4-Rent,** 101 State St. (966-3804) and at four other locations along the beach. (Open daily 9am-8pm.) **Emergency:** 911. **Post Office:** 836 Anacapa St. (564-2266), one block east of State. (Open Mon.-Fri. 8am-5:30pm, Sat. 10am-5pm.) **ZIP code:** 93102. **Area code:** 805.

Pick up **bus** route maps and schedules from the visitors center or the transit center behind the Greyhound station on Chapala. (75¢, disabled and over 61 30¢; free transfers.) A 25¢ **downtown-waterfront shuttle** runs along State St. **Biking** is a breeze, as most streets are equipped with special lanes. **Driving** can be bewildering; dead-ends and one-way streets abound, but free parking is also ubiquitous.

Accommodations and Camping A 10-min. drive north or south on U.S. 101 rewards you with cheaper lodgings than those in Santa Barbara proper. The **Hotel State Street,** 121 State St. (966-6586), just off the beach, is chock full of European travelers, cable TV, and nifty continental breakfast. ($40 for one double bed, $55 for two.) To get to the **Traveler's Motel,** 3222 State St. (687-6009), take the #6 or #11 bus from downtown, offers clean rooms with cable, A/C, and fridges. ($45 in summer, $30 in winter. $5 each additional person up to a max. of 4.) The free *Santa Barbara Campsite Directory* lists prices, directions to sites, and reservation numbers for all **campsites** in the area, and is available at the visitors center. State campsites can be reserved through Destinet (800-444-7275). **Carpinteria Beach State Park** (684-2811), 12 mi. southeast of Santa Barbara along U.S. 101, has 262 developed tent sites with hot showers (sites $16-25). There are two state beaches within 30 mi. of Santa Barbara: **El Capitan** (968-3294) and **Refugio** (968-1350).

Food State and Milpas St. both have many eateries, but State is hipper and pricier. **Super Cuca's Taquería,** 626 W. Micheltorena St. (962-4028), has an insanely delicious steak taco and drink special for $3.49. (Open daily 9am-10pm.) At **The Natural Café,** 508 State St. (962-9494), a healthy, attractive clientele dines on healthy, attractive food. (Smoothies $3, sandwiches $3.50-5. Open Sun.-Thurs. 11am-10pm, Fri.-Sat. 11am-11pm.) **Palace Express,** Center Court (899-9111), in Paseo Nuevo, has outstanding jambalaya, etouffées, and po' boys with four side orders for $5. Said to be some of the best soul food outside the south. (Open Mon.-Sat. 11am-10pm, Sun. 11am-8pm.) **R.G.'s Giant Hamburgers,** 922 State St. (963-1654). Voted best burgers in S.B. 6 years running. (Basic burger $3.11. Open daily 7am-9pm.)

Sights To get the full impact of the city's ubiquitous red tile motif, climb to the **observation deck** of the **Santa Barbara County Courthouse** at 1100 Anacapa St. (962-6464). The courthouse is one of the West's great public buildings (open Mon.-Fri. 8:30am-5pm, Sat.-Sun. 9am-5pm; tower closes at 4:45pm; free). Pick up *Santa Barbara's Red Tile Tour* at the Chamber of Commerce.

Mission Santa Barbara (682-4719), is on the northern side of town, at the end of Las Olivas St. (take bus #22). Praised as the "Queen of Missions" when built in 1786, the mission takes its beauty from a variety of architectural influences, among them Greco-Roman and Moorish (open daily 9am-5pm; $3). Two blocks north of the mission is the **Museum of Natural History,** 2559 Puesta del Sol Rd. (682-4711). This outstanding museum's noteworthy features include the largest collection of Chumash artifacts in the west, an extensive archive on the Channel Islands, and the only **planetarium** between L.A. and San Francisco. (Stargazing tours Mon.-Sat. 9am-5pm, Sun. 10am-5pm. Admission $5, seniors and ages 13-17 $4; off-season $1 less.)

Back downtown, at Montecito and Chapala St., stands the famed **Moreton Bay Fig Tree.** Brought from Australia by a sailor in 1877, the tree's gnarled branches now span 160 ft., and can provide shade for 1,000 mostly transient people.

The beach west of State St. is called **West Beach;** to the east, **East Beach.** The latter is preferable because **Chase Palm Park** acts as a buffer between it and Cabrillo Blvd. The park threads nearly 2 mi. of bike and foot paths through green lawns and tall palms. **East Beach,** with volleyball and biking trails, is universally popular. The beach

CALIFORNIA

Don't Keep Your Fool Head in the Sand!

When you think of weird California wildlife, what springs to mind? Condors? Elephant seals? Dogs? They're boring compared to some even funkier fauna. **Ostriches** populate the desert and inland central coast regions. They're not wild though. They've been imported by ranchers who want to market their lucrative hides (ostrich boots are all the rage among the line-dancin' crowd). At an ostrich farm, you'll have a rare chance to observe these nine-foot fowl, but you should honor ostrich etiquette. You can approach the birds' enclosure from a distance (provided the owners don't object), but **don't pet their dinky heads** and don't act like a weenie and taunt these gallant, long-necked beasts. They may look like they have their heads in the sand, but they've got really bad tempers, so stay cool. One particularly large concentration of ostrich ranches is along Refugio Rd., off Rte. 246 in Santa Ynez. Word in Let's Go circles is that you may also encounter one of these gangly beasts in Wisconsin, so watch the road.

at **Summerland,** east of Montecito (bus #20), is frequented by the **gay** and **hippie** communities. **Rincon Beach,** 3 mi. southeast of Carpinteria, has the best surfing in the county. **Gaviota State Beach,** 29 mi. west of Santa Barbara, offers good surf, and the western end is a (sometimes) **clothing-optional** beach. Keep in mind, however, that **nude** sunbathing is illegal in Santa Barbara. You can **whale-watch** from late November to early April, as the grays migrate.

Entertainment and Nightlife Even on Monday nights the clubs on State St. are packed. Be on the alert for happy hours, which often last from 5-8pm or 10-11pm and feature 50¢ drafts or 2-for-1 drink specials. Consult the *Independent* for the skinny on the S.B. scene. If you come on June 21, you should not miss the **Summer Solstice Parade and Fair** (965-3396), a pre-Bacchanal celebration where you won't feel out of place dressed as an 18-ft. dinosaur or a tidal wave. **Maikai Café and Bar,** 217 State St. (963-9276), becomes **Comedy Sportz** by night, a competitive improv team complete with a half-time referee. (All ages. Showtime 9pm, but come early. $5-7. Open daily 7am-10pm.) **Flying Dragon Art Studio and Espresso Bar,** 22 W. Mission St. (563-1937), is a funky coffeehouse in an old church offering local art, nightly entertainment, pastries ($1-3), and vegetarian and vegan fare ($2-5). (Open daily 8am-midnight.) **Vertigo,** 409 State St. (962-6818), is a techno dance club. Saturday is gay night. Catch the continuing saga of the live stage show "Blood Orgy on Hell Island." (Cover $5. Open Wed.-Sun. 9am-2am.) **Brickyard Ale House,** 525 State St. (899-2820), has bricks and beer. And more beer. And more bricks. And live bands Tues.-Sun. $1 pints on Thurs. There is no cover. This place is open Mon.-Sat. 11am-2am, Sun. 11am-midnight.

■ San Luis Obispo

At the crux of rolling hills and raging surf, San Luis Obispo grew into a full-fledged town only in 1894, after the Southern Pacific Railroad was built. Ranchers and oil-refinery employees make up a significant percentage of today's population, but Cal Poly State University supplies the town with some degree of vitality and charm. Those desperately seeking the soothing balm of small-town life can happily cool their heels in this affable burg—its acronym isn't SLO for nothin'.

What's on your mind? Pure information? Then grab brochures and maps at the **Chamber of Commerce,** 1039 Chorro St. (781-2777. Open Tues.-Fri. 8am-5pm, Sat.-Mon. 10am-5pm.) **Amtrak** chugs into town at 1011 Railroad Ave. (541-0505) and goes to both L.A. ($31) and S.F. ($67) twice daily. **Greyhound** is at 150 South St. (543-2121). To L.A. ($34) and S.F. ($37). The **post office** is bogged down at 893 Marsh St. (543-3062). **Zip Code:** 93405. **Area code:** 805.

Accommodations in SLO are on the pricey side, but fear not: **HI-San Luis Obispo,** 1292 Foothill Blvd. (544-4678), is here. Meditation room, organic garden, a dog, flexible 11pm curfew, and—new for 1997—a jacuzzi! make this a way cool place to stay. Bunks are $14 and family rooms $30. Bicycles rent for $5. **Pismo Beach State Park** (489-2684), is on Rte. 1, south of Pismo Beach. 143 tent sites ($16-18) in two campgrounds. Call 800-444-7275 for reservations.

When you need a SLO meal, head for Higuera and the streets running across it. **Big Sky Café,** 1121 Broad St. (545-5401) has good chow (sandwiches $5-6) and even better jazz. (Open Mon.-Sat. 7am-10pm, Sun. 8am-4pm.) **Woodstock's Pizza Parlor,** 1000 Higuera St. (541-4420), consistently wins annual best pizza awards. This popular student hangout has $4-11 pizzas. (Open Sun.-Thurs. 11am-1am, Fri.-Sat. 11am-2am.) SLO becomes a ragin' party town at night. **Mother's Tavern,** 725 Higuera St. (541-8733) draws in the Cal Poly kids. (Happy hour Mon.-Thurs. 3-6pm. Open Mon.-Fri. 10am-1:30am, Sat.-Sun. 9am-2am.)

There are few sights in SLO itself, but a wealth of natural beauty surrounds it on all sides. The gorgeous **Mission San Luis Obispo de Tolosa** (543-6850) still serves as the town's Catholic parish church (open daily 9am-5pm, 4pm in winter; $1 donation requested). **Morro Bay,** just north of town, is home to the **Seven Sisters,** a rocky chain of volcanic gnomes. Whales, seals, and otters frequent the relatively quiet **Montana de Oro State Park** (528-0513), 20 min. west of SLO on Los Osos Valley Rd. **Pirate's Cove** and **Shell Beach** are two adjoining beaches south of SLO near Avila. Take U.S. 101 south of SLO, exit at the Avila Rd. off-ramp, head west 2 mi., and turn left on Cave Landing Dr., just before the oil tanks. These beaches are more secluded than the more crowded **Avila** and **Pismo.**

■ Near San Luis Obispo: Hearst Castle

Hearst San Simeon Historic Monument (927-2010), located off Rte. 1, about 5 mi. east of Cambria, draws untold numbers of gawkers every year. It is an often graceful, always imposing building atop a hill high above the Pacific, a testament to the wealth and ostentation of William Randolph Hearst. The park is run by the state parks department, and the only way to view the Castle is on a guided tour led by a docent. **Tour One**—recommended for first-time visitors—covers the gardens, pools, and main rooms of the house. Other tours cover smaller areas in more detail. The building and grounds, the creation of Julia Morgan, are magnificent. Tours keep one moving along rather quickly, but the surroundings—natural and constructed—have a rarefied quality which only Hearst's millions and Morgan's talents could bring to life. The four daytime tours cost $14 each (ages 6-12 $8), and last about 1¾ hours. Call Destinet at 800-444-4445 for wheelchair accessible tours which must be reserved ten days in advance.

■ Big Sur

Upon beholding the startling scope of the Big Sur panorama, one might wish to say, "Golly, that *is* big, sir." Everyone will laugh. Your traveling companion may wish to interject, "It's big, sure." Everyone will laugh again. French friends may add, *"Bien sûr!"* They will be not nearly as funny. God will then smite you for your insolence. The locals will laugh their asses off and enjoy their little bit o' paradise alone.

Practical Information "Big Sur" signifies a coastal region bordered on the south by San Simeon and on the north by Carmel. For **visitors information,** go to the **Big Sur Station,** 667-2315, on Rte. 1, inside **Big Sur State Park,** a multi-agency that includes the **State Park Office,** the **U.S. Forest Service Office,** and the **Cal-Trans Office.** The station can provide information on all area State Parks, campgrounds, and local transit (open daily 8am-6pm). Big Sur's **Post Office:** (667-2305), Rte. 1, next to the Center Deli in Big Sur Center. **ZIP code:** 93920. **Area code:** 408.

Accommodations and Food Camping in Big Sur is heavenly. The cheapest way to stay in Big Sur is to camp for free in the **Ventana Wilderness** (pick up a permit at Big Sur Station). Ventana, at the northern end of Los Padres National Forest, is a backpack-only area—no automobiles. **Big Sur Campgrounds and Cabins** (667-2322), 26 mi. south of Carmel, has campsites ($24, with hookup $27) and tent cabins in summer ($44), as well as a store, laundry, playground, volleyball courts, and hot showers. **Pfeiffer Big Sur State Park** (667-2315), just south of Fernwood, is an inland park, but no less popular than those on the beach. The Big Sur River flows peacefully alongside the campground (hot showers; sites $17).

Grocery stores are located at River Inn, Ripplewood, Fernwood, Big Sur Lodge, Pacific Valley Center, and Gorda, but it's better to arrive prepared; prices are high. **Center Deli** (667-2225), beside the Big Sur Post Office, offers the most reasonably priced goods in the area (sandwiches $4) and a broad selection of groceries (open daily 8am-9pm; winter 8am-8:30pm). **Fernwood Burger Bar** (667-2422), Rte. 1, 2 mi. north of the post office, has juicy burgers from $4 (open daily 11:30am-10pm).

Sights and Activities The **state parks** and **wilderness areas** are exquisite settings for dozens of outdoor activities. **Hiking** on Big Sur is fantastic; the state parks and **Los Padres National Forest** all have trails that penetrate redwood forests and cross low chaparral, offering even grander views of Big Sur than those available from Rte. 1. **Pfeiffer Big Sur State Park** contains eight trails of varying lengths (50¢ map available at park entrance). Try the **Valley View Trail,** a short, steep path overlooking the valley below. **Buzzard's Roost Trail** is a rugged two-hour hike up tortuous switchbacks; if you can make it to the top, you'll be treated to a panorama of the Santa Lucia Mountains, the Big Sur Valley, and the Pacific.

Roughly at the midway point of Big Sur lies quiet **Julia Pfeiffer Burns Park** (day use only, $6), which features picnic tables among the redwoods and a chance to otter-watch in McWay Cove. Big Sur's most jealously guarded treasure is USFS-operated **Pfeiffer Beach,** 1 mi. south of Pfeiffer State Park. Turn off Rte. 1 at the "Narrow road not suitable for trailers" sign. Follow the road 2 mi. to the parking area and take the footpath to the beach. The small cove, partially protected from the Pacific by an offshore rock formation, is replete with sea caves and gulls.

■ Monterey

In the 1940s, Monterey was a coastal town geared toward sardine fishing and canning. But the sardines disappeared in the early 50s, and when John Steinbeck revisited his beloved Cannery Row around 1960, he wrote scornfully of how the district had become a tourist trap. Today, few traces of the Monterey described in *Cannery Row* remain; along the famous Row and Fisherman's Wharf, packing plants have been converted to multiplex souvenir malls, and the old bars where sailors used to drink and fight now feature sad wax recreations.

Practical Information Motorists can approach Monterey from **U.S. 101** (Munras Ave. exit), or **Rte. 1,** the coastal highway. **Visitors information** is available at 380 Alvarado St. (649-1770; open Mon.-Fri. 8:30am-5pm). **Monterey-Salinas Transit (MST),** 1 Ryan Ranch Rd. (899-2555 or 424-7695, TTY available), serves the region. Fare per zone is $1.50; ages 5-18, over 64, and people with disabilities 75¢ (each zone encompasses 1 or 2 towns, 4 zones total); exact change; transfers free. The free *Rider's Guide* to Monterey-Salinas Transit (MST) service contains complete schedules and route information. **Post Office:** 565 Hartnell St. (372-5803. Open Mon.-Fri. 8:45am-5:10pm.) **ZIP code:** 93940. **Area code:** 408.

Accommodations and Food Reasonably priced hotels cluster in the 2000 block of Fremont St. in Monterey and Lighthouse Ave. in Pacific Grove. **Del Monte Beach Inn,** 1110 Del Monte Blvd. (649-4410), is close to downtown, across the street from the beach. This Victorian-style inn offers pleasant rooms (shared bath) and a hearty breakfast for $40-60. (Check-in 2-6pm.) To get to **Veterans Memorial Park Campground** (646-3865), Via Del Rey, take Skyline Dr. off Rte. 68; from downtown, take Pacific St. south, turn right on Jefferson. It's perched on a hill with a view of the bay. 40 sites have hot showers (sites $15, no hookups). Although seafood is bountiful, it is often expensive—try chowing an early bird special (4-6:30pm or so). Head to **Fisherman's Wharf,** where the smoked salmon sandwiches ($6) are a local delicacy. **1001 Nights,** 444 Alvarado St. (372-3663), is an unassuming Middle Eastern restaurant with a great all-you-can-eat buffet ($8, lunch only; open Mon.-Sat. 11am-3pm and 5:30-10pm, Sun. 10am-3pm and 5:30-10pm).

Sights The best reason to visit Monterey is the magnificent **Monterey Bay Aquarium,** 886 Cannery Row (648-4800). The facility allows visitors a window into the most curious and fascinating marine life of the Pacific, with interactive displays that provide opportunities to learn about, see, and even touch real sea-life. Highlights include the slithering frenzy of sea otters at feeding time, a living kelp forest housed in a two-story-tall glass case, and a titillating petting zoo of deep-sea denizens (ever think you'd pet a stingray?). Gaze through the **world's largest window** at an enormous marine habitat containing green sea turtles, 7-foot ocean sunfish, large sharks, and the oozingly graceful Portuguese Man-o'-War. ($13.75, over 64 and 13-17 and college students $11.75, ages 3-12 $6. Open daily 10am-6pm.)

Cannery Row lies along the waterfront south of the aquarium. Once a depressed street of languishing sardine packing plants, this ¾-mi. row has been converted into glitzy mini-malls, bars, and discos. All that remains of the earthiness and gruff camaraderie celebrated by John Steinbeck in *Cannery Row* and *Sweet Thursday* are a few building façades. 835 Cannery Row once was the Wing Chong Market, the bright yellow building next door is where *Sweet Thursday* took place, and Doc Rickett's lab at 800 Cannery Row is now owned by a private men's club. For a stylized look at Steinbeck's Cannery Row, take a peek at the **Great Cannery Row Mural,** which stretches 400 ft. along the "700" blocks of Cannery Row. Fifty panels by local artists depict Monterey in the 30s.

17-Mile Drive meanders along the coast from Pacific Grove through **Pebble Beach** and the forests around Carmel. The Drive is rolling, looping, and often spectacular, though sometimes plagued by heavy tourist traffic and an outrageous $7 entrance fee. Save your money and bike it; bicyclists and pedestrians are allowed in at no cost. One point of interest along the drive is the **Lone Cypress**—an old, gnarled tree growing on a rock promontory. When viewed in the forgiving dimness of twilight, the tree is a silent testimony to perseverance and solitary strength.

■ Near Monterey: Pinnacles National Monument

If the banal farmland of the Salinas Valley is the leafy and delicious salad bowl of the nation, the **Pinnacles National Monument** is the cherry tomato. The usual **visitors information** is at the **King City Chamber of Commerce and Agriculture,** 203 Broadway, King City, CA 93930 (385-3814). **Area code:** 408.

Towering dramatically over the chaparral east of Soledad, **Pinnacles National Monument** contains the spectacular remnants of an ancient volcano. The **High Peaks Trail** runs a strenuous 5.3 mi. across the park and offers amazing views of the surrounding rock formations. For a less exhausting trek, try the **Balconies Trail,** a 1½-mi. promenade from the park's west entrance up to the Balconies Caves. Wildflowers bloom in the spring and Pinnacles offers excellent bird-watching all year long. Pinnacles also has the widest range of wildlife of any park in California, including a number of rare predators: mountain lions, bobcats, coyotes, golden eagles, and peregrine falcons ($4; free parking). The monument has a **campground** with firepits, restrooms, and picnic tables (sites $10). The park headquarters is located at the east side entrance (Rte. 25 to Rte. 146; 389-4485).

■ Santa Cruz

The city was born as one of foxy Father Junípero Serra's missions in 1791 (the name means "holy cross"), but today, Santa Cruz is nothing if not liberal. One of the few places where the old 60s catch-phrase "do your own thing" still applies, it simultaneously embraces macho surfers, a large lesbian community, and Neil Young.

PRACTICAL INFORMATION

Tourist Office: Santa Cruz County Conference and Visitors Council, 701 Front St. (425-1234 or 800-833-3494). Publishes free *Visitors Guide, Dining Guide,* and *Accommodations Guide.* Open Mon.-Sat. 9am-5pm, Sun. 10am-4pm.

Buses: Greyhound/Peerless Stages: 425 Front St. (423-1800 or 800-231-2222). To San Francisco (3 per day, $13), and L.A. via Salinas (3 per day, $51). Luggage lockers. Open daily 7-11am, 1-7pm.

Public Transportation: Santa Cruz Metro District Transit (SCMDT), 920 Pacific Ave. (425-8600), in the middle of the Pacific Garden Mall. Pick up a free copy of *Headways* for route information. Buses ($1) run daily 7am-10pm.

Taxis: Yellow Cab, 423-1234. $2.25 plus $2 per mi. 24hr.

Bicycle Rental: The Bicycle Rental Center, 131 Center St. (426-8687), at Laurel. First hr. $7, $50 per 3 days, $75 per week. Helmets and locks provided. Summer open daily 10am-6pm. Winter open daily 10am-5pm.
Post Office: 850 Front St. (426-5200). **ZIP code:** 95060. **Area code:** 408.

Santa Cruz is about two hr. south of San Francisco on the north lip of Monterey Bay. For a more scenic trip, take **U.S. 101** or **Rte. 1** from San Francisco. The Santa Cruz beach and its boardwalk run east-west, with Monterey Bay to the south.

ACCOMMODATIONS AND CAMPING

Like many a beach town, Santa Cruz gets crowded during the summer and on weekends and doubly crowded on summer weekends, when room rates skyrocket and availability plummets. Fortunately, a number of hotels, especially on San Lorenzo, East Cliff, Murry Dr. and on 2nd and 3rd St., hold an unreserved room or two.

Carmelita Cottage Santa Cruz Hostel (HI-AYH), 321 Main St. (423-8304), 4 blocks from Greyhound and 2 blocks from the beach. A 32-bed Victorian hostel with friendly staff. Kitchen, common room, cyclery; parking available. 11pm curfew. 3-day max. stay during summer. $12-14 per night. Reservations only via mail; write P.O. Box 1241, Santa Cruz 95061. Office open daily 8-10am and 5-10pm.

Harbor Inn, 645 7th Ave. (479-9731), near the harbor and a few blocks north of Eaton. A small and beautiful hotel well off the main drag. One queen bed per room (1 or 2 people). Rooms $35-55. In the winter, free breakfast is offered.

Santa Cruz Inn, 2950 Soquel Ave. (475-6322), located just off Rte. 1. Coffee and pastries for guests. Singles from $49, doubles from $59. Some rooms include private jacuzzis, A/C, and fireplaces.

Reservations for all state campgrounds can be made through Destinet (800-444-7275). To get to **Manresa Uplands State Beach Park** (761-1795), 12 mi. south of Santa Cruz, take Rte. 1 and exit Larkin Valley; veer right and follow San Andreas Rd. for 4 mi. then turn right on Sand Dollar. The pretty area overlooks the ocean. There are 64 campsites for tents only ($18). **New Brighton State Beach** (464-6329), is 4 mi. south of Santa Cruz off Rte. 1. Fall asleep to the murmur of the breakers in one of 112 campsites on a bluff overlooking the beach. Tall pines and shrubs maintain privacy. Showers get crowded from 7-9am (1-week max. stay; $18, winter $14).

FOOD

Santa Cruz offers the traveler an astounding number of restaurants in budget range. Fine local produce is sold at the **farmer's market,** at Pacific and Cathcart (open May-Sept. Wed. 3-7pm, Oct.-April Wed. 2-6pm).

Saturn Café, 1230 Mission St. (429-8505). A few blocks from downtown, but you'll be rewarded with vegetarian meals at their Santa Cruz best (generally under $5). Every dish is a winner and every milkshake a joy. The men's room wall text is sassier than average. Open daily noon-midnight.

The Jahva House, 120 Union St. (459-9876). Lush indoor and outdoor vegetation, live jazz, and high quality make this a standout among Santa Cruz's cafés. Cappuccino $1.80; fresh apple pie $3. Open Mon.-Sat. 6am-midnight, Sun. 7am-8pm.

Royal Taj, 270 Soquel Ave. (427-2400). You'll be murmuring "namaste" (I bow to you) after being treated like a king (with food to match) at this Indian restaurant. Daily lunch buffet (11:30am-2:30pm) $6.50. Veggie and meatie entrees $6-8. Stellar lassi $2. Open daily 11:30am-2:30pm and 5:30-10pm.

Ceylon Café, 1016 Cedar St. (427-2000). Outstanding vegetarian restaurant and one of the best bargains in town. All-you-can-eat buffets include the $3.25 "lunch special" (available anytime) and the $5 complete buffet (also available anytime). Curries galore. Open daily 11am-9pm.

SIGHTS AND ACTIVITIES

The **Boardwalk** is the most awesomely loud, fun, tacky thing on the Pacific this side of L.A. The three-block-long strip of 25 amusement park rides, guess-your-weight booths, shooting galleries, and caramel apple vendors provides a free diversion from the beach. Highly recommended is the Big Dipper ($3), a 1924 wooden tower roller coaster (open daily Memorial Day-Labor Day; weekends the rest of the year).

The **Santa Cruz Beach** (officially named Cowell Beach) itself is broad and sandy, and generally packed with students. If you're seeking solitude, try the banks of the San Lorenzo River immediately east of the boardwalk. If you've got a hankerin' to **get nekkid,** head for the **Red White and Blue Beach.** Take Rte. 1 north to just south of Davenport and look for the line of cars to your right ($7 per car).

Along the coast south of Santa Cruz Beach chills the **Santa Cruz Surfing Museum** (429-3429). The main room of the lighthouse displays vintage wooden boards, early wetsuits, and surfing videos, while the tower contains the ashes of Mark Abbott, a local surfer who drowned in 1965 and to whom the museum is dedicated (open Mon. and Wed.-Fri. noon-4pm, winter Sat.-Sun. noon-4pm; free).

The 2000-acre **University of California at Santa Cruz (UCSC)** campus lies 5 mi. northwest of downtown. The campus is accessible by public bus, auto, and bicycle. (From the Metro Center, bus #1 leaves every 15 to 30min. on Mon.-Fri. 6:30am-12:45am, Sat.-Sun. 7:30am-12:45am.) Then-governor Ronald Reagan's plan to make UCSC a "riot-proof campus" (i.e., without a central point where radicals could inflame a crowd), when it was built in the late 60s, resulted in stunning, sprawling grounds. Santa Cruz is famous for leftist politics supplemented by a curriculum offering such unique programs as "The History of Consciousness."

Entertainment and Nightlife

Carding at local bars is stringent. The Boardwalk bandstand offers free Friday night concerts. *Good Times* and UCSC's *City on a Hill* are informative free weeklies.

Kuumbwa Jazz Center, 320-2 Cedar St. (427-2227). Great jazz, renowned throughout the region. Under 21derlings are welcome in this small, low-key setting. The big names play here on Mon. ($12-17); Fri. is the locals' turn (about $5). Rarely sold out. Most shows around 8pm.

The Catalyst, 1011 Pacific Ave. (423-1336). This concert hall draws national acts, college favorites, and local bands. Boisterous, beachy bar and dance club with pool, grill, deli, and bar. Sandwiches ($2-5). Cover for local bands $1 until 9pm; cover for bigger acts $5-20. Must be 21. Shows at 9:30pm. Open daily 9am-2am.

Blue Lagoon, 923 Pacific Ave. (423-7117). Relaxed gay/straight bar. Giant aquarium contributes pleasantly flickering light. Sun.-Wed. videos, dancing, Thurs.-Sat. DJ. Cover $1-3. Drinks about $1.75-3. Open daily 4pm-2am.

SAN FRANCISCO BAY AREA

■ San Francisco

Perched atop an arrestingly beautiful site and overlooking one of the world's greatest natural harbors, San Francisco has learned from the diverse teachings of its residents. The city that evokes images of gold, cable cars, LSD, and gay liberation possesses a cosmopolitan character unknown outside of a few world capitals.

History has taught the city to be tolerant. It began in 1776 as the Spanish mission *San Francisco de Asis.* In 1848, gold was discovered in the Sierra Nevada's foothills. Over 10,000 people passed through the Bay Area to get to the gold and a city was born. The city's growth was neither smooth nor stable. In its early days, San Francisco was the sin and murder capital of America, a thriving center of casinos, brothels, and opium dens. It took a natural disaster to wipe out these manmade disasters. A 8.3

earthquake rocked the city on April 18, 1906, setting off three days of fire and looting. Unfazed, residents rebuilt their city within three years. The 1936 and 1937 openings of the Golden Gate and Bay Bridges ended the city's isolation from the rest of the Bay Area. The city served as home to Jack Kerouac and the Beat Generation in the 1950s. In the 60s, Haight-Ashbury became the hippie capital of the cosmos, and in the 70s, the gay population emerged as one of the city's most visible groups.

Native San Franciscans think of their city as a group of neighborhoods which pack an amazing level of diversity into a small area. San Francisco is one of the most racially heterogeneous cities in the U.S.: 47% white, 30% Asian, 13% Latino, and 10% black. Today, the city continues to rest on the appreciation of differences between its residents. Playing off this variety, San Francisco has become one of the global meccas of cheap cuisine and cutting-edge nightlife. Whatever your fancy, San Francisco's vital *esprit* and liberal attitude is sure to satisfy it.

PRACTICAL INFORMATION

Tourist Office: Visitor Information Center; Hallidie Plaza, 900 Market St. (391-2000), at Powell, beneath street level in Benjamin Swig Pavillion at the exit of the Powell St. BART stop. Multilingual staff. Open Mon.-Fri. 9am-5:30pm, Sat. 9am-3pm, Sun. 10am-2pm. Phone inquiries accepted Mon.-Fri. 8:30am-5pm.

American Youth Hostels Travel Center, 308 Mason St. (788-2525), between Geary and O'Farrell. A great resource for budget travelers, they stock maps, books, earplugs, and more. AYH/HI 10% discount. They make hostel reservations for you. Open April-Oct. Mon.-Sat. 10am-6pm, Nov.-March Tues.-Sat. 1am-6pm.

Airport: San Francisco International Airport (SFO; 761-0800) is located on a small peninsula in San Francisco Bay about 15mi. south of downtown via U.S. 101. SFO has luggage lockers ($2 first 4hr., $4 entire day). **SamTrans** (800-660-4287) runs two buses downtown. (Bus #7F; 35min.; runs 6am-midnight, 9am-4pm less frequently; $2.50. Bus #7B; 55min.; 5:43am-1:16am; $1.)

Trains: Amtrak (800-872-7245), 1707 Wood St. in Oakland (open daily 6:45am-10:45pm; to L.A. $75). Free buses shuttle passengers to downtown. They have a desk in the Transbay Terminal. **CalTrain** (800-660-4287) runs south from San Francisco to Palo Alto ($3.50), San Jose ($4.75), and Santa Cruz. The 4th and Townsend depot is served by **MUNI buses** #15, 30, 32, and 42.

Buses: Greyhound (800-231-2222) serves the **Transbay Terminal,** 425 Mission St. (495-1575), between Fremont and 1st downtown (open 5am-12:35am; to L.A. $39). The terminal is a regional transportation hub; buses from **Golden Gate Transit** (Marin County), **AC Transit** (East Bay), and **samTrans** (San Mateo County) all stop here. **Green Tortoise** (800-867-8647; in San Francisco 956-7500) offers overnight service complete with meals, beds, and a mellow attitude to destinations along the coast including L.A. ($30) and Seattle ($49).

Taxis: Yellow Cab, 626-2345. **Luxor Cabs,** 282-4141. For both, $1.70 plus $1.80 per additional mi. Rides to downtown from SFO cost about $25. 24-hr. service.

Car Rental: Budget (928-7864, reservations 800-527-0700) has several conveniently located branches, including Pier 39 and 321 Mason St. in Union Sq. Compacts are about $30 per day, $150 per week. Must be over 21. Unlimited miles.

Ride Boards: Berkeley Ride Board (510-642-5259). **San Francisco State University** (469-1842, in the SFSU student union; open Mon.-Fri. 7am-10pm, Sat. 10am-4pm). **KALX Radio** (642-5259) broadcasts a ride list (Mon.-Sat. 10am and 10pm). Call them to put your name and number on the air for free.

Crisis Lines: Rape Crisis Center, 647-7273. **United Helpline,** 772-4357.

Emergency: 911.

Post Office: 101 Hyde St. at Golden Gate. Open Mon.-Fri. 7am-5:30pm, Sat. 8am-3pm. **ZIP code:** 94142. General Delivery Mon.-Sat. 10am-2pm. **Area code:** 415.

ORIENTATION

San Francisco is 403 mi. north of Los Angeles and 390 mi. south of the Oregon border. The city proper lies at the north tip of the peninsula that separates San Francisco Bay from the Pacific. From the south, the city can be reached by car via **U.S. 101,** via

A **B** **C** **D**

Alcatraz

Pier 39

San Francisco Bay

1

FISHERMAN'S WHARF

Maritime Museum

Beach St.

Beach St.

Ghirardelli Square

Bay St.

Van Ness Ave.

Polk St.

Larkin St.

Hyde St.

Leavenworth St.

Taylor St.

Mason St.

Powell St.

Stockton St.

Bay St.

Francisco St.

Chestnut St.

2

Lombard St.

Lombard St.

TELEGRAPH HILL

Tattoo Art Museum

Filbert St.

Union St.

Washington Square

Coit Tower

Jones St.

POWELL-HYDE CABLE CAR LINE

POWELL-MASON CABLE CAR LINE

NORTH BEACH

Montgomery St.

Sansome St.

Battery St.

RUSSIAN HILL

Broadway

Broadway Tunnel

Broadway

City Lights Bookstore

Columbus Ave.

Pacific Ave.

3

Jackson St.

Jackson St.

Justin Herman Plaza

Ferry Building

Washington St.

Mason St.

Stockton St.

Transamerica Pyramid

Clay St.

Embarcadero Center

Clay St.

Grace Cathedral

NOB HILL

Sacramento St.

CHINATOWN

California St.

The Embarcadero

CALIFORNIA ST CABLE CAR LINE

California St.

Jones St.

Pine St.

Pine St.

Embarcadero Station

4

Van Ness Ave.

Bush St.

FINANCIAL DIST.

Sutter St.

Taylor St.

Mason St.

Market St.

Fremont St.

Beale St.

Main St.

Post St.

Union Square

Greyhound Terminal

Polk St.

Larkin St.

Hyde St.

Geary St.

Maiden Lane

Montgomery St. Station

2nd St.

1st St.

Folsom St.

O'Farrell St.

POWELL-HYDE CABLE CAR LINE

Powell St.

Ellis St.

TENDERLOIN

Visitor Information Center

3rd St.

SOUTH OF MARKET

Eddy St.

Powell St. Station

Museum of Modern Art

5

Turk St.

Mission St.

Ansel Adams Center

4th St.

Folsom St.

Market St.

Old Mint

Howard St.

80

City Hall

CIVIC CENTER

Main Post Office

5th St.

South Park

2nd St.

Civic Center Station

Folsom St.

MOMA, Opera House

Mission St.

7th St.

6th St.

Howard St.

Harrison St.

3rd St.

6

Van Ness Ave.

Howard St.

8th St.

9th St.

Folsom St.

Bryant St.

Brannan St.

Townsend St.

9th St.

12th St.

10th St.

11th St.

7th St.

N

7

13th St.

101

San Francisco Downtown

280

0   250 yards

0   250 meters

I-5 to **I-580,** or via **Rte. I.** If approaching from the east on I-580 or I-80, go over the Bay Bridge into downtown. From the north, U.S. 101 leads directly into the city over the Golden Gate Bridge (toll $3). If you are driving from L.A., the City by the Bay is a 6-hr. drive up I-5, an 8-hr. drive via U.S. 101, and a 9½-hr. jaunt up the coast along Rte. 1. U.S. 101 might offer the best marriage of speed and vistas, but is often plagued by heavy traffic. If you have the time, try Rte. 1, regarded by many as one of the most beautiful roads in the country.

San Francisco radiates outward from its docks (on the northeast edge of the peninsula just inside the lip of the bay). Most visitors' attention still gravitates to this area. Many of San Francisco's most common attractions are found within a wedge formed by **Van Ness Ave.** (running north-south), **Market St.** (running northeast-southwest), and the **Embarcadero** (curving along the coast). Market St. takes a diagonal course and interrupts the regular grid of streets.

At the top of this wedge lies **Fisherman's Wharf** and slightly below, around **Columbus Ave.,** is **North Beach.** The focal point of North Beach is **Telegraph Hill,** topped by Coit Tower. Across Columbus begin **Nob Hill** and **Russian Hill,** home to some of the oldest money in the nation. Below Nob Hill and North Beach, and north of Market, the largest **Chinatown** in North America covers about 24 square blocks between Broadway to the north, Bush to the south, Powell to the west, and Kearny to the east. The heavily developed **Financial District** lies between Washington to the north and Market to the south, east of Chinatown and south of North Beach. Down Market from the Financial District, you pass through downtown, centered on **Union Sq.** and then, beyond Jones, the **Civic Center.** Below Market lies **South-of-Market Area (SoMa),** largely deserted during the day but home to much of the city's nightlife. SoMa extends inland to 10th, at which point the **Mission** begins and spreads south. The **Castro,** center of the gay community, abuts the Mission at 17th and also extends south.

On the north end of the peninsula, Van Ness leads to the commercially developed **Marina. Fisherman's Wharf** lies to the east, the prison/tourist attraction **Alcatraz Island** reposes to the north, and to the west lie the **Presidio** and the **Golden Gate Bridge.** Inland from the Marina rise the wealthy hills of **Pacific Heights.** Farther west is the rectangular **Golden Gate Park,** bounded by Fulton to the north and Lincoln to the south. At its east end juts a skinny panhandle bordered by hippie-trippie **Haight-Ashbury.** North of Golden Gate Park is **Richmond,** with a large Chinese and Russian-American population.

GETTING AROUND

A **car** here is not the necessity it is in L.A. **Parking** in the city **sucks** and is very expensive. On steep hills, make sure your wheels point towards the curb. *Always* set the emergency brake. Think twice about attempting to use a **bike** to climb up and down San Francisco's many hills. Golden Gate Park is a more sensible location for biking. Even **walking** in this city is an exciting exertion—some of the sidewalks are so steep they have steps cut into them. There are many **walking tours** of the city; some even promise "no steep hills." **City Guides** (332-9601) has free summer tours. The $2 *San Francisco Street and Transit Map* is a valuable purchase.

The **Municipal Railway,** or **MUNI** (673-6864), operates buses, cable cars, and subway/trolleys (bus $1, seniors and ages 5-17 35¢). MUNI passports are valid on all MUNI vehicles, including cable cars (1 day $6; 3 days $10; 7 days $15). **MUNI buses** run frequently throughout the city. **MUNI Metro** runs streetcars along five lines.

Cable cars were named a national historic landmark in 1964. Of the three lines, the California (C) line is by far the least crowded; it runs from the Financial District up Nob Hill. The Powell-Hyde (PH) line, however, might be the best, for it has the steepest hills and the sharpest turns. Powell-Mason (PM) runs to Fisherman's Wharf. (All lines run daily 6:30am-12:30am. $2, seniors $1; 3-hr. unlimited transfers.)

Bay Area Rapid Transit (BART; 992-2278) does not serve the *entire* Bay Area, but it does operate modern, carpeted trains along four lines connecting San Francisco with the East Bay, including Oakland, Berkeley, Concord, and Fremont. Unfortunately, BART is not a local transportation system within the city (trains run Mon.-Sat. 6am-1:30am, Sun. 8am-1:30am; one way 80¢ to $3). Maps and schedules are available at all stations. All stations and trains are wheelchair accessible.

ACCOMMODATIONS

There are a tremendous number of reasonably priced and convenient places to stay in San Francisco, but the Tenderloin and the Mission can be particularly unsafe.

Hostels

Pacific Tradewinds Guest House, 680 Sacramento St. (433-7970), between Montgomery and Kearny in the **Financial District.** Simply fabulous, darlings. 30 beds. No TV. Laundry ($4, they do it), kitchen, free tea and coffee. No smoking. No curfew. 14-day max. stay. $16 per night. Reservations advised.

Globetrotter's Inn, 225 Ellis St. (346-5786), at Mason **downtown.** On the border of the Tenderloin; visitors should be cautious in the area. Comfortingly small and intimate. Large kitchen, common room, piano, and TV. Washer/dryer and linen provided. Check-in summer 8am-11pm; winter 8am-1pm and 5-11pm. No curfew. $12 per night; $75 per week. Call to reserve and confirm 2 days ahead.

India House, 1430 Larkin St. (673-7790), between California and Sacramento, in Nob Hill. A new hostel with a pleasant, congenial atmosphere. Free Sat. night keg parties. Kitchen and patio for BBQin' and socializin'. 30 beds. $12 per night.

San Francisco International Student Center, 1188 Folsom St. (255-8800 or 487-1463), at 8th in **SoMa.** With bay windows, brick walls, and a big couch, this hostel prides itself on cleanliness and coziness. Only 17 rooms. Great massage showerheads. Registration 9am-11pm. No curfew. $13 per night.

Fort Mason Hostel (HI-AYH), Bldg. 240, Fort Mason (771-7277), in the **Marina.** Beautiful location. Free-standing fireplace and sturdy bunks give it that campground charm. Movies, walking tours, kitchens, laundry. Free parking. No smoking. Registration 7am-2pm and 3pm-midnight daily. Come early. Be sure to have valid photo ID. IBN reservations available. $13 per night, $14 in the summer.

Green Tortoise Guest House, 494 Broadway (834-1000), at Kearney in the colorful and relatively safe border of **North Beach** and **Chinatown.** Clean, fully furnished rooms in an beautiful old Victorian building. Friendly atmosphere. Lockers under each bed; bring your own lock. Sauna, laundry (wash $1.25, dry 75¢), internet, kitchen, and complementary continental breakfast. 21-day max. stay. Dorm bed $17 (Nov.-May $15), private single $20, private double $39 (Nov.-May $35).

Hostel at Union Square (HI-AYH), 312 Mason St. (788-5604), 1 block from **Union Sq.** Third largest hostel in the country. Caution in this neighborhood is advised. Management is very safety-conscious and works hard to foster a sense of community. TV room, kitchen, common rooms. $14 per night, nonmembers $17. Key deposit $5. 24-hr. desk. Quiet time midnight-7am. IBN reservations available.

Interclub Globe Hostel, 10 Hallam Place (431-0540), off Folsom in **SoMa.** Caters to an adventurous Euro-clubbing crowd. Pool table, some fairly wild parties, and the Globe Café, which serves breakfast and dinner. Free sheets, blankets and pillows. $16 per night. $10 reservation deposit. **International passport required.**

Hotels

Many budget-range hotels are in unsavory areas. In terms of cleanliness and helpfulness, you often get what you pay for. It's best to call several weeks ahead to reserve.

Adelaide Inn, 5 Isadora Duncan (441-2261), at the end of a little alley off Taylor near Post, 2 blocks west of Union Sq. One of the most charming of the city's many "European-style" hotels. Large windows and kitchenettes. Continental breakfast included. Doors always locked. Office usually closes at 9pm. 18 rooms. Shared bathrooms. Singles $42, twin beds or doubles $48-52. Reservations encouraged.

Golden Gate Hotel, 775 Bush St. (392-3702), between Powell and Mason. Charming 1913 hotel with tasteful antiques and bay windows. Beautiful rooms. Friendly, multi-lingual staff. Rooms $65, with bath $99. Continental breakfast included.

Nob Hill Pensione, 835 Hyde St. (885-2987), between Bush and Sutter. Newly renovated, super-snazzy, super-friendly hotel is an incredible bargain. HBO, continental breakfast, and nightly wine tasting all free. Rooms $20-30 in winter, $30-40 in summer. Not surprisingly, it's *very* popular; reservations recommended.

The Amsterdam, 749 Taylor St. (673-3277 or 800-637-3444), between Bush and Sutter. Beautiful rooms in a central location. Some rooms have jacuzzi and private deck. Charming turn-of-the-century feel. Kitchen and patio. Continental breakfast included. Singles $45, with bath $60; doubles $50, with bath $69.

Commodore International Hotel, 825 Sutter St. (923-6800 or 800-338-6848), between Jones and Leavenworth. 113 spacious rooms, each with a different design and named after a different "hidden" treasure of San Francisco. Get ready for Neo-Deco overload. Room with a queen bed $69, with 2 queen beds $79.

Sheehan Hotel, 620 Sutter St. (775-6500 or 800-848-1529), at Mason. Excellent location. International students galore. Cable TV, phone, pool. Continental breakfast included. Singles $49, with bath $69; doubles $55-75. $10 per additional person. Children under 12 free with parents. 15% discount with Countdown card.

Temple Hotel, 469 Pine St. (781-2565), between Montgomery and Kearny. Decent, well-maintained hotel. Room decor is *so* 1967. Singles $30-40, doubles $35-45 per person. Weekly rates $112 for one, $147 for two.

The Red Victorian Bed and Breakfast Inn, 1665 Haight St. (864-1978). The Red Vic is more a cosmic understanding than a hotel. 18 fantab-fab rooms. Fresh breakfast included. Check-in 3-6pm. 2-night stay usually required on weekends. Discounts on stays longer than 3 days. Doubles $86-200. Reserve well in advance.

Harcourt Residence Club, 1105 Larkin St. (673-7720), at Sutter. One of the city's most popular residence clubs offers rooms by the week or by the month. Price includes maid service, 2 meals, Sunday brunch, and mailbox service. TV room, laundry, and sundeck. Office hours 9am-5pm. Weekly rates $140-225 per person.

Hotel Essex, 684 Ellis St. (474-4664, within CA 800-44-ESSEX/443-7739, outside CA 800-45-ESSEX/453-7739), at Larkin. Newly renovated; one of the best budget hotels around. Color TVs and phones. 24-hr. reception. Staff speaks French and German. Singles $39, with bath $49; doubles $44, with bath $59. Weekly rates: singles $175, with bath $225; doubles $225, with bath $250.

FOOD

San Francisco's 4000 restaurants offer a bewildering array of culinary wonderment. For the latest finds, consult Jim Wood's reviews in the *Examiner.*

The Mission

Even the most substantial appetites will be satisfied by the Mexican, Salvadoran, and other Latin American restaurants located on 24th St. After a burrito or some raw cuttlefish, nearby Castro St. is a great place for an evening coffee or drink.

La Cumbre, 515 Valencia St. (863-8205) between 16th and 17th. Mouth-watering steak is grilled to perfection and deftly made into superlative burritos while-U-watch ($2.75). Open Mon.-Sat. 11am-10pm, Sun. noon-9pm.

New Dawn Café, 3174 16th St., at Guerrero. An intense sensory experience prepared with zest by a 57-year-old drag queen. Badass homefries $5.25, vegetarian chili $3.50. Open Mon.-Thurs. 8:30am-2:30pm, Wed.-Sun. 8:30am-8:30pm.

Amira, 590 Valencia St. (621-6213). Arabic food in a setting fit for a sheik. Entrees $7-12. Open Tues., Thurs., Sun. 5-10pm, Wed. 5-11pm, Fri.-Sat. 5pm-midnight.

Mission Grounds, 3170 16th St. (621-1539). A popular café. Sit outside and enjoy a delicious Mexican chocolate drink ($1.65). Open daily 7am-10pm.

Taquería San Jose, 2830 Mission St. (550-0856), at 24th. Don't be put off by the fast-food-style menu; loving verve goes into the cooking. Soft tacos with your choice of meat, from magnificent spicy pork to brains or tongue ($1.80). Open Sun.-Thurs. 8am-1am, Fri.-Sat. 8am-4am.

Chinatown

Chinatown is filled with downright cheap restaurants; in fact, their multitude and incredible similarity can make a choice nearly impossible. Many feel the city's Chinese food is among the best in the world. Pick any restaurant and go buckwild!

Gam Moon Vegetarian Restaurant, 909 Grant Ave. (362-9888), at Jackson. Taking the fake meat trend to a new level (vegetarian eel, $5.50), Gam Moon offers outstanding, healthy food for ridiculously low prices. Daily specials (served with steamed rice) $3.50, entrees $4-6. Open daily 11am-9:30pm.

House of Nanking, 919 Kearny St. (421-1429), between Columbus and Jackson. Eat and nank to your heart's desire. *Mu-shu* vegetables $5, onion cakes $1.75. Tsing Tao beer sauce is essential. Open Mon.-Sat. 11am-10pm, Sun. 4-10pm.

Brandy Ho's, 217 Columbus Ave. (788-7527), at Pacific. The paintings of peppers on the wall are a warning: yes, the food is friggin' spicy! Order mild or extra mild if you're feeling timid enough to be sitting up in your room. Open Sun.-Thurs. 111:30am-11pm, Fri.-Sat. 11:30am-midnight.

Yuet Lee, 1300 Stockton St. (982-6020), at Broadway. Not much on atmosphere, but the yummy seafood makes up for that. Many exotic seasonal specialties, like abalone with duck feet $6.50. Open Wed.-Mon. 11am-3am.

North Beach

North Beach has excellent cafés, bakeries, and delis, but what truly sets it apart from other neighborhoods is its profusion of great Italian restaurants.

Tommaso's, 1042 Kearny St. (398-9696). Some of the best pizza in the known universe. The super deluxe, piled high with mushrooms, peppers, ham, and Italian sausage, is enough for two ($18.50). Open Tues.-Sat. 5-10:30pm, Sun. 4-9:45pm.

Sodin's Green Valley, 510 Green St. (291-0499), at Grand. Popular family restaurant. *Ravoili Alla Casa* ($8.25). Open Mon.-Fri. 5-10pm, Sat.-Sun. 5pm-midnight.

Mario's Bohemian Cigar Store, 566 Columbus Ave. (362-0536). Hip café at Washington Sq. First-rate grub $2-6. Mon.-Sat. 10am-midnight, Sun. 10am-11pm.

Richmond

Some locals claim that the popular and authentic Chinese restaurants in Richmond are better than the ones in Chinatown.

The Red Crane, 1115 Clement St. (751-7226), between Funston and 12th, is an award-winning Chinese and seafood restaurant. Locals wax ecstatic over the Szechuan eggplant ($5). Lunch special Mon.-Fri. $3.50. Open daily 11:30am-10pm.

The Blue Danube, 306 Clement St. (386-1446). A great café to read, write, or do yer 'rithmetic. Gardenburger with sprouts $4. Mysterious yet tasty espresso eggs $4. Open Mon.-Thurs. 7am-11:30pm, Fri.-Sat. 7am-12:30am, Sun. 7am-10:30pm.

New Golden Turtle, 308 5th Ave. (221-5285), at Clement. Like the food in heaven, only with more ginger. Lemon grass chicken ($8) or flambé BBQ quail ($5). Veggie options abound. Open Tues.-Sun. 11am-11pm, Mon. 5-11pm.

Civic Center

Petite restaurants dot the entire Civic Center area, and **Hayes St.** offers an extensive selection of cafés. In the summer, load up on produce at the **farmer's market** in the UN Plaza (every Wed. and Sun.). Use caution in this area at night.

Nyala Ethiopian Restaurant, 39A Grove St. (861-0788), east of Larkin. Nyala's Ethiopian and Italian cuisine is excellent. Buffet Mon.-Sat. 11am-3pm ($5) and 4pm-closing ($7). Open Mon.-Thurs. 11am-9pm, Fri.-Sat. 11am-11pm.

Ananda Fuara, 1298 Market St. (621-1994), at 9th. Vegetarian sandwich shop emphasizing raw, unbridled sensuality. Great sandwiches $5-6. Open Mon.-Tues. and Thurs.-Sat. 8am-8pm and Wed. 8am-3pm.

Millenium, 246 McAllister St. (487-9800), between Larkin and Hyde. All vegan, all the time. And in an *hotel restaurant?* The food astounds (entrees $7-13). Open Tues.-Fri. 11:30am-2:30pm, 5-9:30pm, Sat.-Sun. 5-9:30pm.

CALIFORNIA

Haight-Ashbury

The Haight has many great bakeries and ethnic restaurants with reasonable prices.

Crêpes on Cole, 100 Carl St. (664-1800), at Cole. The tastiest crêpes in the city. Varieties from chocolate to cheddar and salsa ($3-4). Open daily 7am-10:30pm.

Ganges, 775 Frederick St. (661-7290). Delicious vegetarian Indian food draws locals to this intimate restaurant. 11-15 curry dishes ($6 each) prepared daily. Live music Fri.-Sat. from 7:15pm. Open Tues.-Sat. 5-10pm. Reservations most wise.

Cha Cha Cha, 1801 Haight St. (386-5758). Thought to be the best restaurant in the Haight. Nationwide publicity has resulted in long waits; be prepared to wait up to 2hr. Fried bananas in black bean sauce are droolingly good ($4.50). Entrees $6-13. Open Mon.-Fri. 11:30am-4pm and 5-11pm, Sat.-Sun. 5-11:30pm. No reservations.

Tassajara Bread Bakery, 1000 Cole St. (664-8947), at Parnassus. The scrumptious foccacia with pesto, artichoke hearts, feta, and garlic ($2.75) should not be missed. Open Mon.-Thurs. 7am-9pm, Fri.-Sat. 7am-10pm, Sun. 8am-9pm.

Castro

Inexpensive cuisine is hard to locate in this trendy area—a café might be your best bet. Many restaurants serve a primarily gay crowd.

Bagdad Café, 2295 Market St. (621-4434), at Noe. Supreme people-watching ops and some of the best burgers around ($5-6). Breakfast served all day. Open 24hr.

Hot 'n' Hunky, 4039 18th St. (621-6365). Hysterical staff. 50s decor. Burgers ($5) funk a mad groove. Open Sun.-Thurs. 11am-midnight and Fri.-Sat. 11am-1am.

No-Name Sushi, 314 Church St. at 15th. Insanely popular, cramped, and damn fine food. Standard and far-out sushi options $7-11. Open Mon.-Sat. noon-10pm.

Marina and Pacific Heights

Pacific Heights and the Marina abound in high-quality restaurants serving tasty, fresh food. They love the ultra-chic, but anyone can find a great meal for under $10.

Leon's Bar-B-Q, 1911 Fillmore St. (922-2436), between Pine and Bush. At the southern end of yuppified Fillmore, Leon's has been serving up Cajun jambalaya ($6) and the like since 1963. Dinner plates with ribs or seafood and fixin's for $8-15.50. Open daily 11am-9:30pm for table service and for take out.

Sweet Heat, 3324 Steiner St. (474-9191). This spunky little place serves south-of-the-border food to a health-conscious crowd. Delicious veggie burrito in whole wheat tortilla ($4.25). Open Sun.-Thurs. 11am-11pm, Fri.-Sat. 11am-midnight.

La Méditerranée, 2210 Fillmore St. (921-2956), by Sacramento. Hearty portions for reasonable prices ($7-9). Open Mon.-Thurs. 11am-10pm, Fri.-Sat. 11am-11pm.

SIGHTS

Any resident will tell you that this city is not made of landmarks or "sights," but of neighborhoods. If you blindly rush from the Golden Gate Bridge to Coit Tower to Mission Dolores, you'll be missing the point—the city itself. Whether defined by ethnicity, tax brackets, topography, or a shared spirit, these neighborhoods present offbeat bookstores, Chinatown *dim sum,* Pacific Heights architecture, SoMa's nightlife, Japantown folk festivals, Golden Gate Park's Strawberry Hill, North Beach's Club Fugazi, and Haight-Ashbury's charmingly anachronistic crunchiness. As Frank Lloyd Wright said, "What I like best about San Francisco is San Francisco." Nobody really knows what Frank meant by this; maybe he was high at the time.

Downtown and Union Square

Now an established shopping area, **Union Sq.** has a rich and somewhat checkered history. During the Civil War, Unionists made the square their rallying ground. Their placards, reading "The Union, the whole Union, and nothing but the Union," gave the area its name. When the Barbary Coast (now the Financial District) was down and dirty, Union Sq.'s Morton Alley was dirtier. After the 1906 earthquake and fire destroyed most of the flophouses, a group of merchants moved in and renamed the area **Maiden Ln.** in hopes of changing the street's image. Surprisingly enough, the switch worked. Today Maiden Ln.—extending two blocks from Union Square's eastern side—is home to chi-chi shops and ritzy boutiques.

One of Maiden Ln.'s main attractions is the **Circle Gallery** (989-2100), 140 Maiden Ln. The only Frank Lloyd Wright building in San Francisco, the gallery sells some *very* expensive art (open Mon.-Sat. 10am-6pm, Sun. noon-5pm; free). Rise to the occasion by taking a free jaunt on the outside elevators of the **Westin St. Francis Hotel** on Powell St. at Geary. As you swiftly rise, the Bay Area spreads out before you. Live it up as you're going down. The "elevator tours" offer an unparalleled view of the Golden Gate. Kitsch sinks in at the funky lobby of the **Hotel Triton,** 342 Granite St. (394-0500), where every room is decorated according to a different motif.

Financial District

Here is where business-suited bankers bustle buoyantly by boulevards bordered by the Bay Area's biggest buildings. Unless corporate America or steel skyscrapers get you going, there's not much to attract the casual visitor.

At the foot of Market St. is **Justin Herman Plaza** and its famous geodesic **Vallaincourt Fountain.** The area is often rented out by bands or for rallies during lunch from noon to 1:30pm. One such free lunchtime concert, performed by U2 in the fall of 1987, resulted in the arrest of lead singer and madcap non-conformist Bono for spray painting "Stop the Traffic—Rock and Roll" on the fountain.

Connected to the $300-million complex is the **Hyatt Regency** hotel (788-1234). Its 17-story atrium, dominated by a four-story geometric sculpture, is worth a peek. The glass elevator up the building's side leads to the 20th floor and the **Equinox Revolving Rooftop Restaurant and Lounge.** From the revolving cocktail lounge, you can catch a dazzling view the bay. Buy a drink and dawdling time for as little as $3 (open Mon.-Fri. 4-11:30pm, Sat. noon-1am, Sun. 10am-11:30pm).

Designed by William Pereira and Associates as a show of architectural virtuosity, the 853-foot **Transamerica Pyramid,** on Montgomery St. between Clay and Washington (take MUNI bus #15), was never actually meant to be built. The Montgomery Block, a four-story brick building, once stood in its place. The Montgomery's in-house bar lured the likes of Mark Twain, Robert Louis Stevenson, and Jack London.

Golden Gate Ferries (332-6600) sends boats on the scenic voyage to Larkspur and Sausalito. (Fare to Sausalito $4.25, ages 6-12 $3.20, under 5 free; to Larkspur $2.50, ages 6-12 $1.90. Seniors and people with disabilities travel ½-price.)

South-of-Market (SoMa)

During the day the area fills with workers from the encroaching Financial District. At night, SoMa is the place for hip young professionals to dine at chic restaurants before hitting San Francisco's club scene. SoMa is one of the easiest areas of the city in which to park your car, but lock it securely and don't leave valuables inside. Take SamTrans bus #1A or 1L (weekends and holidays) or #1C, 22D, 10L, or 10T (8-10am and 4-6pm only) or take MUNI bus #9x, 12, 14, 15, 26, 27, 30, 45, or 71.

Civic Center

The Civic Center is a collection of gigantic buildings arranged around two massive plazas. Parking is easy on the streets around the plazas. Take MUNI Metro to "Civic Center/City Hall" or MUNI bus #5, 16X, 19, 21, 26, 42, 47, or 49. Likewise, take J, K, L, M, or N lines to Van Ness station or Golden Gate Transit bus #10, 20, 50, or 70.

The palatial **San Francisco City Hall,** modeled after St. Peter's Cathedral, is the centerpiece of the largest gathering of Beaux Arts architecture in the U.S. The city hall was the site of the 1978 murder of Mayor George Moscone and City Supervisor Harvey Milk, the first openly gay politician to be elected to public office in the United States. At the eastern end are the library and UN Plaza, at the western end are the Opera House and Museum of Modern Art.

In the evenings, the $33-million **Louise Davies Symphony Hall,** 201 Van Ness Ave. (431-5400), at Grove, rings with the sounds of the **San Francisco Symphony** (open Mon.-Fri. 10am-6pm). Next door, the **War Memorial Opera House,** 301 Van Ness Ave. (621-6600), between Grove and McAllister, hosts the well-regarded **San Francisco Opera Company** (864-3330) and the **San Francisco Ballet** (865-2000). The opera house is under repair until October '97; until then, all shows will take place in the Orpheum Theater on Grove. Call for details. Also in the block of Van Ness between Grove and McAllister is the **Veteran's Building** (252-4000). Between the Opera House and the Veteran's Building lies **Opera Plaza.** (Tours of these buildings leave every hr. from the Grove St. entrance to Davies Hall Mon. at 10am-2pm. $3, seniors and students $2. For more info, call 552-8338.)

The Mission

Founded by Spanish settlers in 1776, the Mission is home to some of the oldest structures in the city, as well as its newest cafés and clubs. Colorful **murals** (the best are around Mission and 21st) celebrate local ethnic history, while numerous *taquerías* and bakeries testify to today's prominent Latino presence. The area is also home to a significant lesbian community. The Mission is ideal for daytime walks, but be cautious at night. The district, south of Civic Center, is roughly bordered by 16th to the north, Noe to the west, Army to the south, and U.S. 101 to the east. The Mission is laced with MUNI bus routes, including #9, 12, 22, 26, 27, 33, and 53.

Extant for over two centuries, **Mission Dolores,** at 16th and Dolores in the old heart of San Francisco, is considered the oldest building in the city. The mission was founded in 1776 by Father Junípero Serra and was named in honor of St. Francis of Assisi, as was San Francisco itself. The mission, however, sat close to a marsh known as *Laguna de Nuestra Señora de los Dolores* (Laguna of Our Lady of Sorrows) and despite Serra's wishes, gradually became known as *Misión de los Dolores*. Exotic bougainvillea, poppies, and birds-of-paradise bloom in the cemetery, which was featured in Hitchcock's *Vertigo*. (Open daily 9am-4pm. Masses Mon.-Fri. 7:30am and 9am, Sun. 8am and 10am, Mass in Spanish Sun. noon. $1.)

Get a buzz and come to **Good Vibrations,** 1210 Valencia St. (974-8980), the nationally famous do-it-yourself autoerotica superstore. Includes a tasteful display of antique vibrators (open daily 11am-7pm).

La Galería de la Raza, 2857 24th St. (826-8009), at Bryant, is small but shows excellent exhibitions of Latino art by local and international artists. The gift shop next door sells impressive pieces of folk art (open Tues.-Sat. noon-6pm; free). The **Mission Cultural Center,** 2868 Mission St. (821-1155), between 24th and 25th, hosts a theater, art exhibitions, and cultural events throughout the year. (Gallery open Tues.-Fri. 10am-9:30pm, Sat. 10am-4pm. Free. Box office 695-6970.)

Castro

Much of San Francisco's gay and lesbian community calls the Castro home. Many say the scene has mellowed considerably from the wild days of the 70s, but Castro St. remains a proud and assertive emblem of gay liberation. Most of the action takes place along Castro St. to the south of Market St.

Perhaps the best way to see the Castro is in the reflection of a mug of cappuccino, but for a more conventional way around, **Cruisin' Castro** gives **walking tours** of Castro St. (daily 10am). Guide Trevor Hailey, a member of the Castro community since 1972, is consistently recognized as one of San Francisco's top tour guides. (Tours are $30, including brunch at the famed Elephant Walk Restaurant, at the "gayest four corners on earth." Call Trevor at 550-8110 for reservations.) MUNI bus #24 runs along Castro St. from 14th to 26th. Down the street, **The Names Project,** 2362 Market St. (863-1966), sounds a more somber note. This is the headquarters of an organization that has accumulated over 12,000 3 ft. by 6 ft. panels from over 30 countries for the **AIDS Memorial Quilt.** Each panel is a memorial to a person who has died of AIDS. (Open Mon.-Fri. noon-5pm. Quilting bee Wed. 7-10pm.)

Where else but in San Francisco, and in the Castro in particular, would you find a shrine to her fabulousness, Barbra Streisand? **Hello Gorgeous!,** 549A Castro St. (864-2678), at 18th and 19th, is kitsch at an all-time high. A Streisand mannequin moves along a truck and Babs sings "Funny Girl" on the period TV set. Sign the fan letter on the way out (open Mon.-Thurs. 11am-7pm, Fri.-Sat. 11am-8pm, Sun. 11am-6pm; $2).

West of Castro, the peninsula swells with several large hillocks. On rare fogless nights, you can get a breathtaking view of the city from **Twin Peaks,** between Portola Dr., Market St., and Clarendon Ave. South of the peaks on Portola Dr. is **Mount Davidson,** the highest spot in San Francisco (938ft.).

Haight-Ashbury

It's in the 60s and sunny every day in Haight-Ashbury. Originally a quiet lower-middle-class neighborhood, the Haight's large Victorian houses—perfect for communal living—saw a huge hippie influx in the mid- and late-1960s. The hippie voyage reached its apogee in 1966-67 when Janis Joplin, the Grateful Dead, and the Jefferson Airplane all made love and music here. During 1967's "Summer of Love," young people converged on the grassy panhandle for the celebrated "be-ins." Today, walking around the Haight is kind of like seeing a film adaptation of a Jane Austen novel; the costumes seem right and the actors are fairly convincing, but you can't shake the fact that it's 1997. The huge Gap at the corner of Haight and Ashbury especially spoils the effect. Many of the bars and restaurants are remnants of yesteryear, with faded auras and live-in regulars, and you're sure to run into some characters who don't know the 60s are over, wandering the streets in various shades of purple haze. The Haight is great for browsing; bookstores abound, as do vintage clothing stores and cafés, but take heed at night. MUNI buses #6, 7, 16x, 43, 66, 71, and 73 all serve the area, while Metro line N runs along Carl St., four blocks south.

The former homes of several counterculture legends still survive: for an introduction, check out **Janis Joplin's** old abode at 112 Lyon St. between Page and Oak; the **Grateful Dead's** house at 710 Ashbury St. at Waller; or the **Charles Manson** mansion at 2400 Fulton St. at Willard.

The **Red Vic Movie House,** 1727 Haight St. (668-3994), between Cole and Shrader, is a collectively owned and operated theater that shows foreign, student, and recently run Hollywood films. **Wasteland,** 1660 Haight St. (863-3150), is an immense used clothing store, deserving of notice for more than its great façade and window displays (open daily 11am-7pm). **Reckless Records,** 1401 Haight St. (431-3434; open Mon.-Sat. 10am-10pm, Sun. 10am-8pm) and **Recycled Records,** 1377 Haight St. (626-4075; open daily 10am-10pm) have kickass selections.

Resembling a dense green mountain in the middle of the Haight, **Buena Vista Park** has, predictably, a reputation for free-wheeling lawlessness. Enter at your own risk, and once inside, be prepared for those doing their own thing and doing enough of it to kill a small animal. Northeast of the Haight at Hayes and Steiner, lies **Alamo Sq.,** the vantage point of a thousand postcards. Climb the gentle slope and you'll understand why it's a photo fave—a string of lovely Victorian homes (the "Painted Ladies") is presented with the metropolitan skyline as a backdrop. Far out.

Golden Gate Park

This is where native San Franciscans spend Sundays. Frederick Law Olmsted—designer of New York's Central Park—said it couldn't be done when San Francisco's 19th-century elders asked him to build a park to rival Paris's Bois de Boulogne. But engineer William Hammond Hall and Scottish gardener John "Willy" McLaren proved him wrong. Hall designed the 1000-acre park—gardens and all—when the land was still just shifting sand dunes, and then constructed a mammoth breakwater along the oceanfront to protect the flora from the sea's burning spray.

To get to the park from downtown, hop on bus #5 or 21. Bus #44 passes right by the major attractions and serves 6th Ave. to California Ave. to the north, and the MUNI Metro to the south. Most of the park is bounded by Fulton St. to the north, Stanyan St. to the east, Lincoln Way to the south, and the Pacific Ocean to the west.

Park Headquarters (666-7200), where you can procure information and maps, is in McLaren Lodge at Fell St. and Stanyan, on the eastern edge of the park (open Mon.-Fri. 8am-5pm; inexplicably closed weekends and holidays).

Golden Gate Park offers a variety of intriguing museums, flowery gardens, cultural events, windmills, tea gardens, and buffalo herds to keep even the most MTV-afflicted visitor interested. Many people enjoy spending the whole day here. The **Conservatory of Flowers** (752-8080), erected in 1879, is the oldest building in the park. The delicate and luminescent structure is modeled after Palm House in London's Kew Gardens and houses scintillating displays of tropical plants. (Open daily 9am-6pm; Nov.-April 9am-5pm. $1.50, seniors and ages 6-12 75¢, under 6 free. Free daily 9:30-10am and 5:30-6pm, on the 1st Wed. of month, and on holidays.) The **Strybing Arboretum,** on Lincoln Way at 9th (661-1316), southwest of the academy, is home to 5000 varieties of plants. The **Garden of Fragrance** is designed especially for the visually impaired; the labels are in Braille and the plants are chosen specifically for their texture and scent. (Open Mon.-Fri. 8am-4:30pm, Sat.-Sun. 10am-5pm. Tours daily 1:30pm, Thurs.-Sun. 10:30am. Free.) Near the Music Concourse on a path off of South Dr., the **Shakespeare Garden** contains almost every flower and plant ever mentioned by the herbalist of Stratford-upon-Avon (open daily dawn-dusk; in winter closed Mon.; free). In the middle of Stow Lake, **Strawberry Hill** is covered with strawberry fields forever. Rent a boat ($9.50-14.50 per hr.), or cross the footbridge and climb the hill for a dazzling view of the San Francisco peninsula. At the intersection of Lincoln Way and South Dr., the **Japanese Cherry Orchard** blooms intoxicatingly during the first week in April.

Created for the 1894 Mid-Winter Exposition, the elegant **Japanese Tea Garden** is a serene collection of dark wooden buildings, small pools, graceful footbridges, and carefully pruned flora. Buy tea and cookies for $2.50 and watch the giant carp circle the central pond. (Open daily 9am-6:30pm; Oct.-Feb. 8:30am-dusk. $2, seniors and ages 6-12 $1, under 6 free. Free 9-9:30am and 6-6:30pm, and holidays.) In the northwest part of the park, the **Dutch Windmill** turns and turns again. The powerhouse, built in 1905 to pump water for the emerging park, measures 114 ft. from sail to sail.

What could be more American than a herd of **buffalo**? A dozen of the shaggy beasts roam a spacious paddock at the western end of John F. Kennedy Dr., near 39th Ave. On Sundays traffic is banned from park roads, and bicycles and in-line skates come out in full force.

Richmond

Historically a neighborhood of first- and second-generation immigrants, Richmond has served as a traditional home to the Irish-, Russian-, and now Chinese-American communities. "Inner Richmond," the area east of Park Presidio Blvd., has a large Chinese population, earning it the nickname "New Chinatown."

Lincoln Park, at the northwest extreme of San Francisco, is Richmond's biggest attraction in area and worthiness (MUNI bus #1 or 38). The grounds around the park also offer a romantic view of the Golden Gate Bridge. Take the **Land's End Path,** running northwest of the cliff edge, for an even better look. Southwest of Lincoln Park sits the precarious **Cliff House,** the third of that name to occupy this spot. The nearby **National Park Service Visitors Center** (556-8642), dispenses information on the wildlife of the cliffs area, as well as on the history of the present and previous Cliff Houses. (Open daily 10am-5pm. Free.)

Scope out **Seal Rocks,** often occupied by sleek aquatic fauna. Don't feed the coin-operated binoculars—simply have a free look at the visitor's center. **Ocean Beach,** the largest and most popular of San Francisco's beaches, begins south of Point Lobos and extends down the northwestern edge of the city's coastline. The undertow along the point is so strong that swimming is prohibited and even wading is dangerous. Swimming is allowed at **China Beach** at the end of Seacliff Ave. on the eastern edge of Lincoln Park. The water is my-T-cold here too, but the views of the Golden Gate Bridge may be worth it (lifeguards on duty April-Oct.).

The Presidio and the Golden Gate Bridge

Established in 1776, the **Presidio** is a sprawling preserve that extends all the way from the Marina in the east to the wealthy Sea Cliff area in the west. The preserve also supports the southern end of San Francisco's world-famous Golden Gate Bridge, and used to support the troops of the U.S.'s 6th Army. (Take MUNI bus #28, 29, or 76 to the preserve.) The national park is ideal for biking, jogging, and hiking.

At the northern tip of the Presidio (and the peninsula), under the tower of the Golden Gate Bridge, **Fort Point** (556-1693) stands guard over the entrance to San Francisco Bay. The fort was built in 1853 as one of a series of bunker defenses designed to protect San Francisco from invasion by the British during the tense dispute over the Oregon boundary. (Museum open Wed.-Sun. 10am-5pm. Free 1hr. walks with presentation 11am and 3pm. Grounds open sunrise-sunset.)

The **Golden Gate Bridge,** the rust-colored symbol of the West's bounding confidence, sways above the entrance to San Francisco Bay. Built in 1937 under the direction of chief engineer Joseph Strauss, the bridge is a breathtaking masterpiece from any angle on or around it. The bridge's overall length is 8981 ft.; the main span is 4200 ft. long. The stolid towers are 746 ft. high. Built to swing, the bridge was undamaged by the '89 quake. If you bike or walk across, be prepared for some wary glances—the Golden Gate is the most popular site for suicides in the world. Just across the bridge, **Vista Point** is just that, providing a stunning view of the city.

Marina, Pacific Heights, and Presidio Heights

Hit hard by the '89 rumbler, yuppie-ville has been rebuilt quickly, with more well-kept gardens and aerobics studios than ever. **Fillmore, Union,** and **Chestnut St.** bustle in the evenings, when they resemble your average Muffy and Buffy frat party, but the area can be enjoyed best for its magnificent waterfront view of the Golden Gate Bridge during the day. Most everything is overpriced, but the beautiful parks, homes, and views warrant a glance. Buffy, fetch the flip-phone.

Presidio Heights and Fort Mason are home to a wide variety of museums. The **Palace of Fine Arts,** Baker St., between Jefferson and Bay, is west of Fort Mason. The beautiful domed structure and the two curving colonnades are reconstructed remnants of the 1915 Panama Pacific Exposition, which commemorated the opening of the Panama Canal and signalled San Francisco's recovery from the great earthquake. The grounds of the Palace are some of the best picnic spots in the city. On summer days performances of Shakespeare are sometimes given in the colonnade section. For information on the nearby **Exploratorium,** see page 770.

Centered around Union and Sacramento, Pacific Heights boasts the greatest number of **Victorian buildings** in the city as well as the best view of the Golden Gate. The **Octagon House,** 2645 Gough St. (441-7512), at Union, was built in 1861 with the belief that such architecture would bring good luck to its inhabitants; the house's survival of the many earthquakes and fires that have swept the city shows more than good fortune. (Open 2nd Sun. and 2nd and 4th Thurs. of all months except Jan. noon-3pm; group tours by arrangement available on any weekday.)

Fisherman's Wharf and Ghirardelli Square

East along the waterfront is the most popular tourist destination in San Francisco. Stretching from Pier 39, in the east, to Ghirardelli Sq., in the west is "Fisherman's Wharf," home to ¾-mi. of porcelain figurines, enough t-shirts to have kept Washington's army snug, and enough salt-water taffy to have made them all violently ill.

Easily visible from boats and the waterfront is **Alcatraz Island.** Named in 1775 for the *alcatraces* (pelicans) that flocked to it, this former federal prison looms over San Francisco Bay, 1½ mi. from Fisherman's Wharf. In 1934, Alcatraz was brought under federal purview and used to hold those who had wreaked too much havoc in other prisons. Of the 23 men who attempted to escape, all were recaptured or killed, except for five who were "presumed drowned" although their bodies were never found. The film *Escape from Alcatraz* relates the story of the Anglin Brothers, who undertook the most likely escape. They managed to swim away from Alcatraz, but

CALIFORNIA

were presumed drowned as some of their clothes and belongings later washed up on Angel Island. In 1962, Attorney General Robert Kennedy closed the prison, and the island's existence was uneventful until 1969, when about 80 Native Americans occupied it as a symbolic gesture, claiming the rock as their property under the terms of a broken 19th-century treaty. Alcatraz is currently a part of the **Golden Gate National Recreation Area,** the largest park in an urban area in the United States, administered by the National Park Service. The **Red and White Fleet** (546-2700 for reservations, 800-229-2784 for info) runs boats to Alcatraz from Pier 41. Once on Alcatraz, you can wander by yourself or take a kitschy 2-hr. audiotape-guided tour, full of clanging chains and the ghosts of prisoners past. (Boats depart every ½hr. from Pier 41; summer 9:15am-4:15pm, winter 9:45am-2:45pm. Rides $6.75, seniors $5, ages 5-11 $3.50; tours cost $3.25 extra, ages 5-11 $1.25 extra. Passengers can remain on the island until the final 6:30pm ferry departs.) Reserve tickets in advance through Ticketron (392-7469) for $1 extra or confront long lines.

Back on the mainland, **Pier 39** (981-7437), built on pilings that extend several hundred yards into the harbor, was designed to recall old San Francisco; in reality, it looks more like a Dodge City scene from a Ronald Reagan Western (shops open daily 10:30am-8:30pm). Toward the end of the pier is **Center Stage,** where mimes, jugglers, and magicians wow you with their unadulterated jocundity.

If you want to pay big bucks to gawk at the harbor with 400 other lemmings, then you should head for the **tour boats and ferries** dock west of Pier 39. The **Blue and Gold Fleet** (705-5444) offers 1¼-hr. tours on 400-passenger sight-seeing boats. The tours cruise under the Golden Gate, past Angel Island, Alcatraz, and Treasure Island, and provide sweeping views of the skyline. (Tours begin at 10am, last boat 5:30pm. $15, seniors, ages 5-18, and military $8.) The Red and White Fleet (see info above) at Pier 41 offers both tours and ferry rides. The 45-min. Bay Cruise leaves from Piers 41 and 43½ and goes under the Golden Gate Bridge and past Alcatraz and Angel Island. ($16, over 62 and ages 12-18 $12, ages 5-11 $8; ask about the multi-lingual narratives.) Like the Jungle Cruise at Disneyland, both cruises are fully narrated.

The **Maritime National Historic Park** (929-0202), at the Hyde St. Pier where Hyde meets Jefferson, displays the *Balclutha,* a swift trading vessel that plied the Cape Horn route in the 1880s and 90s and was featured in the first Hollywood version of *Mutiny on the Bounty.* (Open daily 9am-6pm, last ticket sold at 5:30pm. $3, ages 12-17 $1, over 61 and under 12 free.)

Ghirardelli Sq. (GEAR-ah-dch-lee), 900 N. Point St. (information booth 775-5500; open daily 10am-9pm), is the most famous of the shopping malls in the area around Fisherman's Wharf and rightfully so—it houses some of the best chocolate in the world. Today, the only remains of the machinery from Ghirardelli's original **chocolate factory** (transformed from a uniform factory in the 1890s by Domingo Ghirardelli's family) are in the rear of the **Ghirardelli Chocolate Manufactory,** an old-fashioned ice-cream parlor. Ghirardelli Sq. is now a popular destination, with an elegant mermaid fountain. (Stores open Mon.-Sat. 10am-9pm, Sun. 10am-6pm.)

North Beach

As one walks along Stockton St. or Columbus Ave., there is a gradual transition from shops selling ginseng to those selling provolone. In the 50s this area was home to the bohemian Beats who moved in alongside the traditional Italian residents of the neighborhood. North Beach maintains a sense of serenity while being an entertaining, energetic, and popular place for locals and travelers both day and night.

Lying between Stockton and Powell is **Washington Sq.,** North Beach's *piazza* and the wedding site of Joe DiMaggio and Marilyn Monroe. Across Filbert, to the north of the square, is the **Church of St. Peter and St. Paul** (421-0809), beckoning tired sight-seers to take refuge in its dark, wooden nave. In the square itself is the **Volunteer Firemen Memorial,** donated by Mrs. Lillie Hitchcock Coit, who was rescued from a fire as a girl. Coit's most famous gift to the city is **Coit Tower** (362-0808), also known as "the candle," which stands a few blocks to the east of the memorial. The tower sits on Telegraph Hill, the steep mount from which a semaphore signalled the arrival of ships in Gold Rush days. Rumor has it the tower was built to resemble a fire nozzle, but its other nickname gives a cruder approximation: "coitus tower." (Open daily 10am-7pm; Oct.-May 9am-4pm. Elevator fare $3, over 64 $2, ages 6-12 $1, under 6 free. Last ticket sold ½hr. before closing.) There is very limited parking, so leave your car on Washington St. and walk up the **Filbert Steps** that rise from the Embarcadero to the eastern base of the tower. The walk is short, allows excellent views, and passes by many attractive Art Deco buildings.

North Beach Bohemianism came to national attention when Ferlinghetti's **City Lights Bookstore**, 261 Columbus Ave. (362-8193), published Allen Ginsberg's anguished and ecstatic dream poem *Howl*. Banned in 1956, the book was found "not obscene" after an extended trial, but the resultant publicity turned North Beach into a must-see for curious tourists. Says a clerk, "We're more than a bookstore—we're on to something!" Whatev. (Store open daily noon-midnight.)

Nob Hill and Russian Hill

This area is where the rich walk their foofy dogs. Before the earthquake and fire of 1906, Nob Hill attracted the mansions of the great railroad magnates. Today, Nob Hill remains one of the nation's most prestigious addresses. The streets are lined with many fine buildings, and the aura is that of idle and settled wealth. Sitting atop a hill and peering down upon the hoi polloi can be a pleasant afternoon diversion. **Grace Cathedral**, 1051 Taylor St. (776-6611), the biggest Gothic edifice west of the Mississippi, crowns Nob Hill. The castings for its portals are such exact imitations of Ghiberti's on the Baptistery in Florence that they were used to restore the originals.

Nearby Russian Hill is named after Russian sailors who died during an expedition in the early 1800s and were buried on the southeast crest. At the top of Russian Hill, the notorious snaking curves of **Lombard St.** (between Hyde St. and Leavenworth) afford a fantastic view of the city and harbor—that is, if you dare to allow your eyes to stray from the road. The switchbacks were installed in the 1920s by homesick Genoans to allow horse-drawn carriages to negotiate the extremely steep hill.

Nihonmachi (Japantown)

Partly prodded by discrimination, Japanese immigrants moved here after the 1906 quake, which heavily destroyed this part of town. Today, Nihonmachi is one of the largest Japanese enclaves in the world outside of Japan (the largest is in São Paulo, Brazil, of all places). Nihonmachi is less tourist-oriented than Chinatown, catering more to its 12,000 Japanese residents. This small neighborhood 1.1 mi. from downtown San Francisco is bounded on its east side by Fillmore, on its west side by Laguna, by Bush to the north, and by the Geary Expressway to the south. Take MUNI buses #2, 3, and 4 to Buchanan or #38 to Geary. Nihonmachi is centered around the **Japanese Cultural and Trade Center** at the corner of Post and Buchanan. Similar to the Tokyo Ginza, the five-acre center includes Japanese *udon* houses, sushi bars, and a massage center/bathhouse. Japan gave the 12,000 Japanese-Americans of San Francisco the **Peace Pagoda**, a magnificent 100-ft. tall, five-tiered structure that graces the heart of Japantown. The **Kabuki 8 Complex**, 1881 Post St. (931-9800) at Fillmore, shows current films, and during early May it is the main site of the San Francisco International Film Festival (see page 772).

Chinatown

The largest Chinese community outside of Asia (over 100,000 people), Chinatown is also the most densely populated of San Francisco's neighborhoods. Chinatown was founded in the 1880s when, after the gold had been dug and the tracks laid, bigotry fueled by unemployment engendered a racist outbreak against what was then termed the "Yellow Peril." In response, Chinese-Americans banded together for protection in a small section of the downtown area. As the city grew, speculators tried to take over the increasingly valuable land, especially after the area was leveled by the 1906 earthquake. The Chinese were not to be expelled, however, and Chinatown, which has gradually expanded, remains almost exclusively Chinese. **Grant Avenue** is a sea of Chinese banners, signs, architecture, and tourist kitsch.

Watch fortune cookies being shaped by hand in the **Golden Gate Cookie Company,** 56 Ross Alley (781-3956; huge bag of cookies $3; with uproarious sexy fortunes $4), between Washington and Jackson, just west of Grant. This famous alleyway has been a filming site for many well-known movies including *Big Trouble in Little China, Karate Kid II* (starring Noriyuki "Pat" Morita), and *Indiana Jones and the Temple of Doom*. Nearby **Portsmouth Sq.,** at Kearny and Washington, made history in 1848 when Sam Brennan first announced the discovery of gold at Sutter's Mill from the square. Now the square is filled with Chinese men playing lively card games. A stone bridge leads from this square to the **Chinese Culture Center,** 750 Kearny St., 3rd floor of the Holiday Inn (986-1822; open Tues.-Sat. 10am-4pm), which exhibits Chinese-American art and sponsors two **walking tours** of Chinatown. The **Chinese Historical Society,** 650 Commercial St. (391-1188), between Kearny and Montgomery, relates the tale of Chinese immigrants through informative tomes and snappy artifacts, including a 1909 dragon head (open Tues.-Sat. noon-4pm; donation).

At Grant and Bush stands the ornate, dragon-crested **Gateway to Chinatown.** The dragon motif is continued on the lampposts that line Chinatown's streets. Some of Chinatown's noteworthy buildings include **Buddha's Universal Church** (720 Washington St.), the **Kong Chow Temple** (855 Stockton St.), and **Old St. Mary's,** (660 California St. at Grant), built in 1854 from granite cut in China.

Museums

Exploratorium, 3601 Lyon St. (563-7337, recording 561-0360) near the **Marina.** *Scientific American* calls it the "best science museum in the world," and it deserves this heady moniker. This mega-cool warehouse is like a mad scientist's penny arcade, scientific funhouse, and experimental lab all put together. Displays range from interactive tornadoes to computer finger-painting and giant bubble-makers. You could easily spend the day romping among the hundreds of interactive exhibits. Open Sun.-Tues. and Thurs.-Sat. 10am-6pm, Wed. 10am-9:30pm. From Labor Day-Memorial Day, open Tues. and Thurs.-Sun. 10am-5pm, Wed. 10am-9:30pm. $9, students and seniors $7, ages 6-17 $5. Free on the first Wed. of every month. Within the Exploratorium dwells the **Tactile Dome** (561-0362), a pitch-dark maze of tunnels, slides, nooks, and crannies designed to help refine your sense of touch. The Dome is sometimes home to chemically enhanced youths looking to expand their minds. Claustrophobes and darkaphobes should stay away (open Mon.-Fri. 10am-5pm; $10; advance reservations required).

California Academy of Sciences (221-5100), in **Golden Gate Park** is one of the nation's largest institutions of its kind. The **Steinhart Aquarium** (home to members of over 14,000 aquatic species) is more lively than the natural history exhibits. The **Space and Earth Hall** lets you experience the great quake of 1906 firsthand, as an exhibit recreates the earthquake, which hit 8.3 on the Richter Scale. The **Far Side of Science** shows over 150 of Gary Larson's zaniest cartoons. **Morrison Planetarium** (750-7138) re-creates the heavens ($2.50, seniors and students $1.25). Academy open daily 9am-6pm. $7, $5 with MUNI Fast Pass or transfer, seniors and ages 12-17 $3, 6-11 $1.50. Free 1st Wed. of the month.

M. H. de Young Memorial Museum (750-3600), in **Golden Gate Park,** takes visitors through a 21-room survey of American painting, from the colonial period to the early 20th century. The **Asian Art Museum** (668-7855) in the west wing of the building is the largest museum outside Asia dedicated entirely to Asian artwork. The museum's beautiful collection includes rare pieces of jade and porcelain, in addition to 3000-year-old works in bronze. Both open Wed.-Sun. 10am-4:45pm. Admission to both $6, $3 with MUNI Fast Pass or transfer, seniors $4, ages 12-17 $2, under 12, 1st Wed. of the month, and Sat. 11am-noon free.

Museum of Modern Art, 151 3rd St. (357-4000), between Mission and Howard in **SoMa,** displays an impressive collection of 20th-century European and American works. The museum's new $60 million complex in the **Yerba Buena Gardens** is one of the largest building projects ever undertaken by an American museum. Open Tues.-

Wed. and Fri.-Sun. 11am-6pm, Thurs. 11am-9pm. $7, students and over 61 $3.50, ½-price Thurs. 6-9pm. 1st Tues. of the month free.

Ansel Adams Center, 250 4th St. (495-7000), at Howard and Folsom in **SoMa,** houses a permanent collection of the eponymous master's work. $4, students $3. Open Tues.-Sun. 11am-5pm, and until 8pm on first Tues. of every month.

The Martin Lawrence Gallery, 465 Powell St. (956-0345), in **Union Sq.,** sells and displays the works of pop artists like Andy Warhol and Keith Haring. Open Mon.-Sat. 9am-9pm, Sun. 10am-6pm; free.

San Francisco Women Artists Gallery, 370 Hayes St. (552-7392), between Franklin and Gough near the **Civic Center.** Exhibits women's photographs, paintings, prints, and crafts. Open Tues.-Sat. 11am-6pm, Thurs. until 8pm.

Cable Car Powerhouse and Museum, 1201 Mason St. (474-1887), at Washington in **Nob Hill.** The building is the center of the cable-car system. Check out the operation from a gallery or view displays to learn more about the cars, some of which date back to 1873. Open daily 10am-6pm; Nov.-March 10am-5pm; free.

Tattoo Art Museum, 841 Columbus Ave. (775-4991), in **North Beach.** Tattoo memorabilia, including exhibits on different techniques. $50 buys a glowing rose on the hip. Open Mon.-Thurs. noon-9pm, Fri.-Sat. noon-10pm, Sun. noon-8pm.

Fort Mason, east of the Marina. The army's former embarkation facility has been converted into a center for non-profit organizations. The Fort Mason Center houses many small museums with adjoining gift shops. The **African-American Historical and Cultural Society Museum** (441-0640), Building C, #165, focuses on contemporary African arts and crafts (open Wed.-Sun. noon-5pm; donation requested). **Museo Italo Americano** (673-2200), Building C #100, displays work created by artists of Italian heritage (open Wed.-Sun. noon-5pm; $2, students and seniors $1). The **Mexican Museum** (441-0404), Building D, offers free tours, exhibits, and educational workshops (open Wed.-Sun. noon-5pm; $4, seniors and students $2, under 10 free). The **Magic Theater** (441-8822), Building D, founded in 1967 by John Lion, is renowned for hosting Sam Shepard as its playwright-in-residence from 1975 to 1985. The Magic Theater continues to stage contemporary American plays (Oct.-July Wed.-Sun.).

ENTERTAINMENT AND NIGHTLIFE

San Fran nightlife is the freshmaker. Call the **Entertainment Hotline** at 391-2001 or 391-2002. The *Bay Guardian* and *SF Weekly* always have a thorough listing of dance clubs and live music. The excellent free monthly *Oblivion* gives a complete rundown of what's up in the **gay** community. **Sports** enthusiasts should see the **Giants** and the **49ers** play baseball and football at nearby **3Com/Candlestick Park** (467-8000), 8 mi. south of the city on the Bayshore Fwy. (U.S. 101).

Bars and Cafés

Nightlife in San Francisco is as varied as the city's personal ads. Everyone from "dominant duo looking for a third" to "shy first-timer" can find places to go on a Saturday (or even a Wednesday) night.

Café du Nord, 2170 Market St. (861-5016), between Church and Sanchez in the **Castro.** Painfully hip. Huge bar. Pool tables 75¢. Live music nightly, excellent jazz. No cover before 9pm. Happy hour 4-7pm. Open daily 4pm-2am. Min. age 21.

Noc Noc, 557 Haight (861-5811) in the **Haight.** The Everyclub: hang with goths, raver-chicks, Haight hippies, and Eurotrash. Intimate corners make this a good place for a tête-a-tête. Never a cover. Pints $2.50 until 8pm. Open daily 5pm-2am.

Muddy Waters, 521 Valencia St. (863-8005), in the **Mission.** Hang with the laid-back, or just be a dork and use the computer. Cappuccino $1.50, mocha $2. Open Mon.-Fri. 6:30am-midnight, Sat.-Sun. 7:30am-midnight.

Brainwash, 1122 Folsom St. (861-FOOD/3663 or 431-WASH/9274). On the **SoMa** club A-list. Where to go to socialize while spinning your dirty Calvins. Free live music Wed.-Sat. nights. Open Sun.-Thurs. 7:30am-11pm, Fri.-Sat. 7:30am-1am.

Vesuvio Café, 255 Columbus Ave. (362-3370), in **North Beach.** You can watch poets and chess players from a balcony in this beat bar or you can hide from them in some dark corner. Drinks average $3.25-6. Open daily 6am-2am.

Tosca, 242 Columbus Ave. (986-9651), in **North Beach.** No-frills, red vinyl bar with cappuccino, opera on the juke, and a quietly cool attitude that makes other bars look like they try too hard. Open Mon.-Fri. 5pm-1am, Sat.-Sun. 5pm-2am.

Danny's, 684 Commercial St. (392-5331), off Kearny in **Chinatown.** More than unassuming, it's downright self-effacing. Pool table and rarely functional Ms. Pac Man (kind of) lighten up the decor. Open Mon.-Fri. 2pm-2am.

Clubs

The San Francisco club scene rages hardcore. Underage clubbers will be pleased to know that most places do not card hard, unless otherwise noted. For a line into local nightlife, pick up a *Guardian* or try the **"be-at" line** (626-4087; 24hr.).

DNA Lounge, 375 11th St. (626-1409), at Harrison in **SoMa.** Both hip live music and funkalicious jammin'. The best night for dancing is Wed. Funk, house, and soul. Cover usually doesn't exceed $10. Open daily until 4am. Must be 21 and up.

Club DV8, 540 Howard St. (957-1730), in **SoMa.** Three floors of dance mania. Music from house to gothic, but the crowd is all hip-o-rama. For the best dancing, stick to the 3rd floor "osmosis." Cover free-$10. Open Tues.-Sun. 8pm-4am.

Cesar's Latin Palace, 3140 Mission St. (648-6611), in the **Mission.** *Huge* Latin dance hall. If you don't know what salsa is, this is the place to learn. Over 1000 people show up on weekends. Dance yo' ass off. Open Thurs.-Sun. 'til dawn.

Slims, 333 11th St. (621-3330), between Folsom and Harrison in **SoMa.** Epicenter of the big SoMa blues 'n' jazz scene. Legendary house for American roots music, rock, and "world beat." Open nightly. Must be 21 and up.

3D's (Don's Different Ducks), 668 Haight St. (431-4724), at Pierce in the **Haight.** Shake it to reggae, funk, jazz, and hip-hop. No cover. Open noon-2am. 21+.

Gay and Lesbian Clubs

Gay nightlife in San Francisco rocks. Most of the popular bars can be found in three areas—the Castro, Polk St., and SoMa. Most "straight" dance clubs in San Francisco feature at least one gay night a week. The absolutely best guide to gay San Francisco is the free monthly *Oblivion,* available at most gay and lesbian stores. Also consult the staffers at the **Gay Switchboard** (510-841-6224). While a woman in a gay club may cause merely apathy, a man in a lesbian club may cause some hostility.

Litterbox, 683 Clementina Alley (431-3332), between Howard and Folsom at 8th in **SoMa.** May well be the snazziest damn club around. Mixed alternaqueer crowd of hipsta lesbians and gay men. Cover $5-6. Beer $3-4. Open roughly 9am-2pm.

The Café, 2367 Market St. (861-3846), in the **Castro.** One of San Francisco's most popular dance spots. Hoppin' music and pool, pinball, and cruisin'. No cover. $1.25 beers Mon. 5pm-2am. Open daily 11:30am-2am.

The Box, 715 Harrison St. (695-9688), between 3rd and 4th in **SoMa.** Described by some as "the best place to be on Thursdays," The Box pumps funk and soul for a young queer crowd once a week. Beer $3. Cover $6. Open Thurs. 9pm-2:30am.

Baby Judy's Discothèque and Leisure Lounge, 527 Valencia St. (863-9328), at the Casanova between 16th and 17th in the **Mission.** Very bizarre. Anything-goes crowd chills by the bar or bops to just about anything. Open Wed. 10pm-2am.

The Stud, 399 9th St. (863-6623), in **SoMa.** This legendary bar/club recreates itself every night of the week. Cover varies. Open daily 5pm-2am.

Seasonal Events

Chinese New Year Celebration (982-3000), Feb. 7-22 in Chinatown.

Cherry Blossom Festival (563-2313), 2 weekends in April; Japantown.

San Francisco International Film Festival (929-5000), mid-April to mid-May. The oldest film festival in North America.

San Francisco Examiner Bay to Breakers (777-7770), mid-May. The largest road race (7.1 mi.) in the United States, done in inimitable San Francisco style.

19th San Francisco International Lesbian & Gay Film Festival (703-8650), mid-late June. The world's largest presentation of lesbian and gay media.
Lesbian-Gay Freedom Parade (864-3733), late June.

∎ San Jose

In 1851, San Jose was deemed too small to serve as California's capital and Sacramento assumed the honors. It's not small anymore. San Jose (pop. 855,000) is the fastest-growing city in California, thanks to its many assets: outstanding weather, a booming high-tech industry, two pro sports teams, and an excellent location. Much of its current growth is a result of its status as the heart of the computer chip factory known as the Silicon Valley. Therein lies San Jose's problem. The economic boom that quadrupled the city's population in a mere ten years never allowed it to acquire cultural and aesthetic refinements to match its size. Compared to Berkeley and San Francisco, San Jose is an upstart adolescent. It's a great place to live—the third-safest city in the U.S., according to the FBI—but not a great place to visit.

PRACTICAL INFORMATION

Visitor Information: Convention and Visitor Bureau, 333 W. San Carlos St. #1000 (977-0900). Decent maps (free-$4). The view from their board room is one of the best in the city. Extremely helpful staff. Open Mon.-Fri. 8am-5pm.

San Jose International Airport: 1661 Airport Blvd. (277-4759, touchtone only). Serviced by most major domestic airlines. From I-880, take Coleman Ave. to Airport Blvd. and turn right; from U.S. 101, take Guadalupe Pkwy. to Airport Pkwy. and turn right. Or, take Santa Clara County Light Rail to Metro/Airport station and transfer to the free light rail shuttle (inquire at info booths about the shuttles).

Amtrak: 65 Cahill St. (287-7462; info, 800-USA-RAIL/872-7245). To Los Angeles ($75) and San Francisco ($9).

CalTrain: 800-660-4287; TDD 415-508-6448. San Francisco to San Jose with stops at peninsula cities. $4.50 one way, $8 roundtrip. Over 64, under 12, and disabled ½-price. Operates hourly Mon.-Thurs. 6am-10pm, Fri. 6am-midnight, Sat. 7am-midnight, Sun. 8am-10pm.

Greyhound: 70 S. Almaden Ave. (800-231-2222), at Santa Clara. The station feels reasonably safe, even at night. To L.A. ($31) and S.F. ($7). Luggage lockers for ticketed passengers only. Open daily 5am-midnight.

Santa Clara County Transit System: 4 N. Second St. (321-2300). Ultra-modern and air-conditioned. $1.10, ages 5-17 55¢, over 64 and people with disabilities 35¢. Day passes cost double regular fare. Exact change only.

Ride Board: San Jose State Student Union (924-6350). Open Mon.-Thurs. 7am-10pm, Fri. 7am-5pm, Sat. 10am-5pm; summer Mon.-Fri. 8am-4:30pm.

Crisis Lines: Rape Crisis, 287-3000. **Poison Control,** 800-662-9886. Both 24hr.

Hospital: San Jose Medical Center, 675 E. Santa Clara St. (998-3212), at 14th. Emergency room (977-4444) open 24hr.

Emergency: 911.

Post Office: 105 N. 1st St. Open Mon.-Fri. 9am-5:30pm. **ZIP Code:** 95113.

Area Code: 408.

THE WAY TO SAN JOSE

As Dionne Warwick knows, this third-largest city in California, the 11th largest city in the U.S.A., lies on the southern end of San Francisco Bay, about 40 mi. from San Francisco (via Hwy. 101 or I-280) and Oakland (via I-880). From San Francisco, take Hwy. 280 South rather than 101 South—101 is full of traffic snarls at all hours of the day, especially during rush hour (early mornings and late afternoons). For information on reaching San Jose from San Francisco on **CalTrain,** see p.238. San Jose is centered around the plaza and mall area near east-west **San Carlos St.** and north-south **Market St.** The area south of First St., or **SoFA,** has the most bars, restaurants, and clubs. The **Transit Mall,** the center of San Jose's transit system, runs north-south along 1st and

2nd in the downtown area. **San Jose State University's** grassy grounds cover several blocks between S. 4th and S. 10th downtown.

ACCOMMODATIONS AND CAMPING

County parks with **campgrounds** surround the city. It doesn't resemble a cone-shaped bra, but **Mt. Madonna County Park** has 117 campsites in a beautiful setting, occupied on a first-come, first-camped basis. (*Let's Go* does not recommended that you mount Madonna.) **Joseph D. Grant County Park** (reservation line: 358-3751; open Mon.-Fri. 10am-3pm) offers 20 campsites and 40 mi. of horse and hiking trails. **Saratoga,** 20 minutes southwest of San Jose on Rte. 85, offers a number of sites and trails in the wooded and lovely **Sanborn County Park.** These can be pricey. You may want to stay in the wonderful hostel instead.

Sanborn Park Hostel (HI-AYH), 15808 Sanborn Rd., Sanborn County Park (741-0166), in Saratoga, 13mi. west of San Jose. If you take a bus or train into town, call the hostel between 5-11pm, and they will pick you up. Situated in a lovely old log building with 39 beds. Surrounded by redwoods; peaceful and clean. Piano, kitchen, and fireplaces. Usually has vacancies. Open daily 5-11pm. Check-out 9am. Curfew 11pm. Special wheelchair facilities (room & shower), but call ahead to reserve them. $8.50, non-members $10.50, under 18 ½-price.

San Jose State University, 375 S. 9th St. (924-6180), at San Salvador, in Joe West Hall. Rooms rented in summer through mid-Aug. Call before noon. Some university affiliation is required to stay there, though you don't have to be affiliated with SJSU. Singles $26, doubles $41.

Park View Motel, 1140 S. 2nd St. (297-8455). 41 rooms. Kitchenettes and a pool. Generally pretty quiet. Swimming pool. Comfortable and centrally located. Check-in after 11am. Rates vary, summer weekdays singles $45, doubles $55.

FOOD

Most of San Jose's cheap eats cluster along S. 1st and on San Pedro by San Pedro Square. Asian and Mexican restaurants are especially tasty and inexpensive options. A **farmer's market** at the Pavilion, at S. 1st and San Fernando, sells Brentwood's peaches and the San Joaquin Valley's sweet corn (open Thurs. 10am-2pm May 25-Nov. 16). The places listed below are all in downtown San Jose.

White Lotus, 80 N. Market St. (977-0540), between Santa Clara and St. John. One of few vegetarian restaurants in the area. Omnivores will enjoy the food too. Lots of great choices; lotus vermicelli "salad" and imperial roll ($5.75), steamed plantain with coconut milk makes a great dessert ($2). Open Tues.-Fri. 11am-2:30pm and 5:30-9pm, Sat. 11am-10pm, Sun. 11am-9pm.

La Guadalajara, 45 Post St. (292-7352). Since 1955 this lunch counter has been serving delicious Mexican food and pastries. Jumbo burritos ($2.50) and combo plates ($4) are a bargain. Open Mon.-Sat. 8am-7pm, Sun. 8am-5pm.

Sal and Luigi's Pizzeria, 347 S. 1st St. (297-1136). Sal split for Florida 30 years ago, but students still flock to Luigi and this well-known hole-in-the-wall. Medium pizza $8.50. Gnocchi and ravioli $7. Open Tues.-Thurs. 11am-11pm, Fri. 11am-midnight, Sat. noon-midnight, Sun. 4-10pm.

Lan's Garden, 155 E. San Fernando St. (289-8553), at 4th. Whether you want adventurous cuisine (squid with pineapple, $6) or tamer fare, this Vietnamese restaurant won't disappoint. Huge *pho* noodle soup ($4) is their specialty. Lunch specials (Mon.-Fri. 11am-3pm) $4.25, most dinner entrees $6-7. Open later than most places in town; open Sun.-Thurs. 9:30am-midnight, Fri.-Sat. 9:30am-3am.

House of Siam, 55 Market St. (279-5668). A cozy, elegant Thai eatery that serves super-spicy dishes of both the flesh and fleshless varieties. Dinner and a *Singha* (the beer that don't ask no questions and don't tell no lies) $10. Open Mon.-Fri. 11am-3pm and 5-10pm, Sat.-Sun. 11:30am-10pm.

SIGHTS

San Jose does not have a wealth of sights, but some of the main attractions are bizarrely intriguing. However, if you're looking for a grand tour of the Silicon Valley, forget it—**the Silicon Valley doesn't exist.** The computer companies are scattered throughout the Santa Clara Valley in the suburbs of San Jose and are *very* wary of visitors (industrial sabotage, maybe?). Built on farmland from the 70s on, the anonymous-looking buildings, often shielded behind black glass, hint at the companies' attitude towards tourists. Head to the Tech Museum in San Jose for a technological grasp of this region, but if you want to say you've "been there," you can drive by the garage where David Packard and Bill Hewlett started computer behemoth **Hewlett-Packard** (367 Addison Ave., 5 blocks south of University Ave. in Palo Alto).

In San Jose, start with the **Winchester Mystery House,** 1525 S. Winchester Blvd. (247-2101), at I-880 and I-280, west of town. This highly popular and entertaining tourist spot was the home of Sarah Winchester, heir to the Winchester rifle fortune. The Victorian estate is filled with oddities: stairs leading to ceilings, doors opening to walls, and tourist traps. Visit to discover the mysterious motive behind Winchester's order that construction continue on her home without cease. The hours, like the architecture itself, are subject to change, but tours (65min.) usually start every 10-15 min. from 9am-8pm ($13, over 64 $10, ages 6-12 $7, under 6 free). The **Egyptian Museum and Planetarium** (formerly the **Rosicrucian Museum**) 1342 Naglee Ave. (947-3636), at Park, houses the West Coast's largest collection of Egyptian artifacts, including a walk-in tomb. It's spooky and worth a visit. The collection belongs to the mystical order of the Rosy Cross, but their name is no longer associated with the museum, for reasons shrouded in the murky mist of the past. (Open daily 9am-5pm. Admission is an eerie $6, seniors and students $4, youth 7-15 $3.50.)

Originally called "The Garage" in honor of the humble beginnings of such technological powerhouses as Hewlett-Packard and Apple, the **Tech Museum of Innovation,** 145 W. San Carlos St. (279-7150), should not be missed. This is truly a museum of innovation, with lots of excellent hands-on exhibits. Other exhibits deal with robotics, DNA engineering, and space exploration, including an opportunity to drive the Mars Rover (open July 1-Labor Day Mon.-Sat. 10am-6pm, Sun. noon-6pm, rest of year Tues.-Sun. 10am-5pm; students $6, over 64 and ages 6-18 $4, under 6 free).

Founded in 1857, **San Jose State University (SJSU),** 1 Washington Sq. (924-5000), is the oldest public college in California. The campus is centered around San Carlos and 7th, east of downtown. For information on campus events, call the 24-hr. events line (924-6350) or, in summer, pick up a copy of the *Summer Times,* a weekly publication of the *Spartan Daily,* the campus newspaper.

ENTERTAINMENT & SEASONAL EVENTS

For information on things to see and do in San Jose, look for *Metro,* a periodical hip enough to make San Jose seem interesting. It's published weekly and available free on street corners downtown. The Student Union (924-6350) at SJSU has an amphitheater that often hosts concerts and other performances. Hockey fans may want to check out the **San Jose Sharks,** the city's own NHL team, at the San Jose Arena. Call 287-4275 for tickets. Soccer aficionados can catch Eric Wynalda and the **San Jose Clash,** the city's new MLS representative, at Spartan Stadium, on 7th off I-280. Call 408-985-4625 for tickets. **SoFA,** south of 1st, is home to most of the city's nightlife.

Dos Locos, 150 S. 1st St. (993-9616), in the mall-like Pavillion, attracts a devoted college and local following. Sharks players are known to come here after games. Famous for 32-oz. schooner margaritas ($6.50) because, as they say, "size does matter." Outdoor seating. Happy hour Mon.-Fri. 4-7pm. Open daily 11:30am-2am.

Katie Bloom's Irish Pub and Restaurant, 150 S. 1st St. (294-4408). It's clear why "pub" comes before "restaurant" in the name and why "Irish" comes before both. Drink $2.50 imported beers with locals while Oscar Wilde and James Joyce watch from the walls. Punkers rejoice! The jukebox features (along with some Irish bands) the Clash, Ramones, and Sex Pistols. Some crap too. Bar open daily 11am-1:30am. Food served Mon.-Wed. 11am-2pm, Thurs.-Fri. 11am-2pm and 6-9pm.

Gordon Biersch, 33 E. San Fernando St. (294-6785). California cuisine and American fare (entrees $6-8). Three great beers brewed here ($3 for a ½-liter), making barging through throngs of yuppies worth it. Live jazz, blues, and swing Wed.-Sat. nights. Open Sun.-Wed. 11am-11pm, Thurs. 11am-midnight, Fri.-Sat. 11am-1am.

Film fans might want to visit **Camera,** 366 S. First St. (998-3005), the coolest theater in town. The *Rocky Horror Picture Show* is screened every Sat. at midnight. There's another Camera at 288 S. 2nd (998-3005), at San Carlos. The annual **Blues Festival** (924-6261) in May is the site of the largest free blues concert in Northern California.

If you're in town at the right time, you can catch some funky **seasonal events.** In early Sept., head to the **SoFA Street Fair** (295-2265, south of 1st, between San Carlos and Reco). There are cool vendors and bands—not your average San Jose crowd (noon-9pm). On Sept. 30 or Oct. 1, buzz downtown to the **San Pedro Square Brew-Ha-Ha** (279-1775), which has beer tasting and fun for all (noon-7pm).

■ Near San Jose: Santa Clara

This commercially focused small town is known as the site of Mission Santa Clara and two Paramount-owned theme parks. To reach Santa Clara, take U.S. 101 to the De La Cruz exit and follow the signs to the Santa Clara University.

Mission Santa Clara, 500 El Camino Real, was the first California mission to honor a woman—Clare of Assisi—as its patron saint. Initially located in 1771 on the Guadalupe River, it moved to its present site in 1825. In 1851, **Santa Clara University** was established in the old mission. The beautiful structures have been restored several times and are surrounded by a rose garden and 200-year-old olive trees.

Paramount's Great America theme park (988-1776), on U.S. 101, is one of the nation's largest. Rides are themed after Paramount movies—there's the *Top Gun* Jet-coaster and the *Days of Thunder* Racetrack. (Open Mar.-Oct. Sun.-Thurs. 10am-9pm, Fri.-Sat. 10am-11pm. $28, over 54 $19, ages 3-6 $14. Parking $5.) Paramount recently bought **Raging Waters** (654-5450), 1½ mi. east of U.S. 101 at the Tully Rd. exit, the area's best collection of waterslides. Great on a hot day, but expect huge crowds and killer prices (open daily May-Sept. 10am-7pm; $19, under 42in. $15).

■ Berkeley

Although the peak of its political activism occurred in the 60s and 70s, U.C. Berkeley still deserves it's funky, iconoclastic reputation. Telegraph Ave.—the Champs-Elysées of the 60s—remains the home of street-corner soothsayers, hirsute hippies, countless cafés, and itinerant street musicians. Berkeley is also home to some of the best food in the Bay, thanks to the presence of a sizable professional population willing to pay for the freshest and tastiest seasonal ingredients. Alice Waters' Chez Panisse is the landmark home of California Cuisine.

PRACTICAL INFORMATION

Tourist Office: Berkeley Convention and Visitors Bureau, 1834 University Ave. (549-7040), at Martin Luther King, Jr. Way. Open Mon.-Fri. 9am-5pm. **24-hr. Visitor Hotline** 549-8710. **U.C. Berkeley Visitor Center,** 101 University Hall, 2200 University Ave. (642-5215). Open Mon.-Fri. 9am-5pm.

Public Transportation: Bay Area Rapid Transit (BART; 465-2278) stops at Shattuck Ave. and Center St., close to the western edge of the university, about 7 blocks from the Student Union. $2 to downtown San Francisco. The **Perimeter Shuttle** (642-5149; 25¢) connects the BART station with the university campus (shuttles run Sept.-June Mon.-Fri. 7am-7pm every 8min.). **Alameda County Transit (AC Transit;** 800-559-4636 or 839-2882) buses #15, 40, 43, and 51 all run from the BART stop to downtown Oakland. ($1.25; seniors, ages 5-12; and disabled 60¢; under 5 free; transfers 25¢, valid for 1hr.).

Post Office: 2000 Allston Way (649-3100). Open Mon.-Fri. 8:30am-6pm, Sat. 10am-2pm. **ZIP code:** 94704. **Area code:** 510.

Berkeley lies across the bay northeast of San Francisco, just north of Oakland. Reach the city by **BART** from downtown San Francisco or by car (**I-80** or **Rte. 24**). Crossing the bay by BART ($2-2.20) is quick and easy; driving in the city is difficult and frustrating. The choice is yours.

ACCOMMODATIONS

It is surprisingly difficult to sleep cheaply in Berkeley. Do it as a daytrip. The **Bed and Breakfast Network** (540-5123) coordinates 20 B&Bs in the East Bay.

Travel Inn, 1461 University Ave. (848-3840), 2 blocks from the North Berkeley BART station, 7 blocks west of campus. Renovated rooms are clean and comfy. All have TVs and phones. Free parking and coffee One queen $40, two queens $60.

YMCA, 2001 Allston Way (848-6800), at Milvia. Recently renovated. Prices include tax and use of pool, bed, phone, and basic fitness facilities. All share hall baths. No curfew. 14-day max. stay. Singles $25, rooms for couples $30.

Golden Bear Motel, 1620 San Pablo Ave. (525-6770), at Cedar. Located further away from campus but has recently painted bedrooms and clean white bedspreads. Singles $49, doubles $46-59.

FOOD

Berkeley is a relatively small area with a wide range of excellent budget eateries. For Berkeley's best food, head downtown to **Shattuck Ave.** or north to **Solano Ave.**

Anne's Soup Kitchen, 2498 Telegraph Ave. (548-8885), at Dwight. *The* place for breakfast in Berkeley. Special includes 2 whole-wheat pancakes with bacon and eggs or with homefries ($3.55). Open Mon.-Fri. 8am-7pm, Sat.-Sun. 8am-5pm.

Hana Sushi Buffet, 1722 University Ave. (841-9500). The best Japanese lunch deal in the Bay Area. All-you-can-eat lunch buffet of fresh sushi, tempura, and noodles $7; dinner buffet $10. Open Mon.-Sat. 11am-2:30pm, daily 5:30-9pm.

Café Fanny, 1603 San Pablo Ave. (524-5447). Alice Waters' most recent venture. Lots of standing room and benches near the outdoor trellis. Famous for bowls of *café au lait* ($2). Open Mon.-Fri. 7am-3pm, Sat. 8am-4pm, Sun. 9am-3pm.

Plearn, 2050 University Ave. (841-2148), at Shattuck, 1 block west of campus. Constant winner of best Thai in the Bay Area. Curries $7. Plentiful vegetarian options. Lunch specials 11:30am-3:30pm for $4.25. Open daily 11:30am-10pm.

Blondie's Pizza, 2340 Telegraph Ave. (548-1129). Try this popular student hangout if only for the peace poppy atmosphere. Pizza and coke special $2. Open Mon.-Thurs. 10:30am-1am, Fri.-Sat. 10:30am-2am, Sun. noon-midnight.

SIGHTS

In 1868, the private College of California and the public Agricultural, Mining, and Mechanical Arts College coupled to give birth to the **University of California.** Because Berkeley was the first of the nine University of California campuses, it is permitted the nickname "Cal." The school has an enrollment of over 30,000 students and more than 1000 full professors. Berkeley also boasts more Nobel laureates per capita than any other city. Berkeley's uniqueness has made it home to a student body of unparalleled diversity, although some have grumbled about the increasing "Asianization" of the school—Cal's student population is 35% Asian-American.

The staff at the **Visitor Information Center,** 101 University Hall, 2200 University Ave. (642-5215; open Mon.-Fri. 8:30am-4:30pm), provides free maps and information booklets (guided campus tours last 1½ hrs. Mon., Wed., Fri. 10am and 1pm).

Sather Tower (much better known as the **Campanile,** Italian for "bell tower"), a 1914 monument to Berkeley benefactor Jane Krom Sather, is the most dramatic campus attraction. It was modeled after the clock tower in Venice's St. Mark's Sq. You can ride to the observation level of the 307-ft. tower for a stupendous view (50¢). The tower's 61-bell carillon is played most weekdays at 7:50am, noon, and 6pm. The **University Art Museum (UAM)**, 2626 Bancroft Way (642-0808), at College, holds a diverse and enticing permanent collection and hosts different exhibits yearly. Check out the new galleries housing Asian art. Within the museum, the **Pacific Film Archives (PFA;** 642-1124), with one of the nation's largest film libraries, is a uniquely rich museum of cinematic art. (Open Wed. and Fri.-Sun. 11am-5pm, Thurs. 11am-9pm. $6; free Thurs. 11am-noon and 5-9pm.)

The **Lawrence Hall of Science** (642-5132), a concrete octagon standing above the northeast corner of campus, competes with San Francisco's Exploratorium for honors as the finest science museum in the Bay Area. Take bus #8 or 65 from the Berkeley BART station; it's a 1-hr. walk from campus (open Mon.-Fri. 10am-5pm, Sat.-Sun. 10am-5pm; $5, seniors, students, and ages 7-18 $4, ages 3-6 $2).

The **Botanical Gardens** (642-3343), on Centennial Dr. in Strawberry Canyon, contain over 10,000 varieties of plant life. Berkeley's Mediterranean climate, moderated by coastal fog, provides an outstanding setting for this 33-acre garden (open daily 10am-4pm; free, parking permit $1 for 2 hrs.). The **Berkeley Rose Garden** on Euclid Ave. at Eunice St. north of campus, contains a lovely collection of roses. Built by the WPA during the Depression, the garden spills from one terrace to another in a vast semicircular amphitheater (open May-Sept. dawn-dusk).

The **Judah Magnes Museum,** 2911 Russell St. (849-2710), displays a leading collection of Judaica (open Sun.-Thurs. 10am-4pm; free). The **Julia Morgan Theater,** 2640 College Ave. (box office 845-8542), is housed in a beautiful former church designed by its namesake and notable for its graceful and unusual mix of materials.

People's Park, on Haste St., one block off Telegraph, is a kind of unofficial museum. A mural depicts the 60s struggle between the city and local activists over whether to leave the park alone or to develop it commercially. During the conflict, then-governor Ronald Reagan sent in the National Guard, an action that led to the death of a Berkeley student. Three years ago, despite heated protests, the city and the university bulldozed part of the park to build beach volleyball courts, basketball courts, and restrooms. The park is patrolled by police officers 24hr.

Tilden Regional Park is part of the extensive East Bay park system. Hiking, biking, running, and riding trails crisscross the park and provide impressive views of the Bay Area. **Lake Anza** is a popular swimming spot and is overrun with screaming kids ($2, lake open 10am-dusk during summer).

ENTERTAINMENT

Hang out with procrastinating students in front of or inside the **Student Union** (642-4636). **The Underground** (642-3825) contains a ticket office, an arcade, bowling alleys, **foosball tables,** and pool tables (open summers Mon.-Fri. 8am-6pm, Sat. 10am-6pm; winter Mon.-Fri. 8am-10pm, Sat. 10am-6pm). The **Bear's Lair,** 2425 Bancroft (843-0373), is *the* popular campus hangout on sunny Friday afternoons, when quarts of beer go for $2.75 (open Mon.-Thurs. 9am-10pm, Fri. 10am-midnight, Sat.-Sun. 10am-10pm; summer 10am-6pm daily). **Café Milano,** 2522 Bancroft Way (644-3100), is perhaps the hippest contender in the Telegraph café-a-thon. Lively discussions about everything from O'Neal (Shaquille) to O'Neill (Eugene). (Open Mon.-Fri. 7am-11pm, Sat. 7am-midnight, Sun. 8am-11pm.) **921 Gilman,** 924 Gilman St. (525-9926), at 8th, is a legendary all-ages punk club. Green Day, Operation Ivy, and Crimpshrine all played before they made the big time. Bring the kiddies! (Cover $3-5.) **Jupiter,** 2181 Shattuck Ave. (843-8277), is across the street from the BART station. Table-bowling, beer garden, and terrific pizza ($6 for a loaded 8-in. pie) will keep you busy. Exotic international beers flow from Euro-taps (open Mon.-Thurs. 11:30am-1am, Fri. noon-2am, Sat.-Sun. noon-11pm; live music Fri.-Sun., no cover).

■ Near Berkeley: Palo Alto

This burg is a well-manicured and wealthy high-tech hub. However, it is Stanford University that really puts Palo Alto on the map. The **Stanford University Information Booth** (723-2560) is across from Hoover Tower (open daily 9am-5pm). **CalTrain** chugs to San Francisco ($3.75) from the station at 95 University Ave. (323-6105), at Alma (open Mon.-Fri. 5am-10pm, Sat. 6:30am-10pm, Sun. 7am-10pm). **SamTrans** drives to Frisco ($2.50) and the airport ($1). **Area code:** 415.

Stanford University was founded in 1885 as a secular, co-educational school by Jane and Leland Stanford in honor of their 16-year-old son Leland, Jr., who had died of typhoid on a family trip to Italy. The colonnaded Main Quadrangle is the center of campus and the site of most undergrad classes. Zoom around campus on the free **Marguerite Shuttle** (Mon.-Fri. 6am-6pm; every 10min.). Tours leave from the steps of Memorial Hall daily at 11am and 3:15pm, and last for one hour (free). The student guides ooze jocundity and are skilled at walking backwards.

Sleep tight at the **Hidden Villa Ranch Hostel (HI-AYH)**, 26870 Moody Rd. (949-8648), about 10 mi. south of Palo Alto. (28 beds. Open daily 4:30-9pm Sept.-May. Closed in summer. Beds $10.) The **Mango Café**, 435 Hamilton Ave. (325-3229), dishes out the bombest Caribbean cuisine ($5-6. Open daily 11:30am-8:30pm.)

■ San Mateo Coast

Route 1, the **Pacific Coast Highway**, winds along the San Mateo County Coast from San Francisco to the Big Basin Redwoods State Park. This expanse of shore is scattered with beautiful, isolated, sandy beaches. Although most people find it too cold for swimming (even in summer), the sands offer a royal stroll along the water's edge. State beaches charge $4, with admission valid for the entire day at all state parks—keep your receipt. About 2 mi. south of Pacifica (take samTrans bus #1L) is **Gray Whale Cove State Beach**, a privately owned **nudist** beach off Rte. 1. You must be 18 and pay $5 to join the fun (but where do you keep your ID?).

If you like pamphlets, you'll love the **San Mateo County Coast Convention and Visitor Center**, Seabreeze Plaza, 111 Anza Blvd., Ste. 410 (800-28-VISIT/288-4748), in Burlingame (open Mon.-Fri. 8:30am-5pm). **San Mateo County Transit (samTrans)**, 945 California Dr. (800-660-4287), has service from Burlingame to Half Moon Bay ($1, seniors 25¢, ages 5-17 50¢). **Area code:** 415.

Half Moon Bay is an old coastal community 29 mi. south of San Francisco. Locals complain that it's becoming too commercialized, but visitors won't notice the change. The fishing and farming hamlet of **San Gregorio** rests 10 mi. south of Half Moon Bay. **San Gregorio Beach** is a delightful destination; walk to its southern end to find little caves in the shore rocks (open 8am-sunset; day use $4, seniors $3). To find a less-frequented beach, visit **Unsigned Turnout, Marker 27.35.** It's difficult to find without aid; keep an eye out for mysteriously vacant cars parked along the highway. A trip up Rte. 84 will take you into **La Honda**, where Ken Kesey (author of *One Flew Over the Cuckoo's Nest*) lived with his merry pranksters in the 60s, before it got too small and they took off across the U.S. in a psychedelic bus. A few decades ago, residents of **Pescadero** created the **olallieberry** (oh-LA-la-behr-ee) by crossing a blackberry, a loganberry, and a youngberry. Pick a peck at **Phipp's Ranch**, 2700 Pescadero Rd. (879-0787), in Pescadero (mid-June to July 10am-7pm. 85¢ per lb.) The **Pescadero Marsh** shelters such migratory birds as the elegant blue heron, often seen poised on its spindly legs. **Año Nuevo State Reserve** (379-0595), 7 mi. south of Pigeon Point and 27 mi. south of Half Moon Bay, is the mating place of the 15-ft.-long **elephant seal**. December to March is breeding season, when males compete for beach space next to the more pleasingly hideous females. To see this unforgettable show (Dec. 15-Mar. 31), you must make reservations (8 weeks in advance recommended) by calling Destinet (800-444-7275), since access to the park is limited. Tickets go on sale Nov. 15 and are generally sold out by the end of the month, so plan ahead (The park is open daily 8am-sunset; last permits issued 4pm.) Nestled inside the peninsula, the

Burlingame Museum of Pez Memorabilia, 214 California Dr. (347-2301), a block from the train station, will revive your childhood love affair with Pez. Like all the pleasures of youth, it's free (open Tues.-Sat. 10am-6pm).

The **Pigeon Point Lighthouse Hostel (HI-AYH;** 879-0633), 6 mi. south of Pescadero on the highway and 20 mi. south of Half Moon Bay, near the lighthouse, is almost an attraction in itself. This 52-bed beauty operates a hot tub in the old lightkeeper's quarters. (Check-in 4:30-9:30pm. Doors locked at 11pm. Check-out and chores completed by 9:30am. Closed 9:30am-4:30pm. Dorm-style beds $11-14. You must reserve 48hr. ahead.) **Point Montara Lighthouse Hostel (HI-AYH;** 728-7177) is a 45-bed facility on windswept Lighthouse Point, 25 mi. south of Frisco, 4 mi. north of Half Moon Bay. (Check-in 4:30-9:30pm. Curfew 11pm-7am. $9-14.)

The **Flying Fish Grill,** 99 San Mateo Rd. (712-1125), on Rte. 92 close to Rte. 1 at the southwest corner of Main, in Half Moon Bay, is an inexpensive, tasty way to sample the delicious seafood of the coast. Fishburger and fries ($4.35) or a pint of clam chowder ($4.25) will satisfy a seafarer's appetite (open Tues.-Sun. 11am-8pm).

■ Marin County

Home of Dana Carvey, 560 acres of spectacular redwood forest, and Jerry Garcia's eternal memory, Marin County (mah-RIN) boasts a bizarre blend of outstanding natural beauty, trendiness, liberalism, and wealth. Much of Marin can be explored in a daytrip from San Francisco by car, bus, or ferry. Muir Woods National Monument with its coastal redwoods, Marin Headlands, Mt. Tamalpais (tam-uhl-PAY-iss) State Park, and the Point Reyes National Seashore offer trails for mountain bikers and hikers looking for a day's adventure or a two-week trek.

PRACTICAL INFORMATION

Tourist Office: Marin County Visitor Information, at the end of Avenue of the Flags (472-7470), San Rafael. Open Mon.-Fri. 9am-5pm. **Sausalito Chamber of Commerce,** 333 Caledonia St. (331-7262). Open Mon.-Fri. 9am-noon and 1-5pm.

Public Transportation: Golden Gate Transit (455-2000; 923-2000 in San Francisco). Daily bus service between San Francisco and Marin County via the Golden Gate Bridge, as well as local service in Marin. Buses #10, 20, 28, 30, and 50 provide service to Marin from San Francisco's Transbay Terminal at 1st and Mission. The **Golden Gate Ferry** (923-2000) provides transportation between Sausalito or Larkspur and San Francisco from the Ferry Bldg. at the end of Market St. Mon.-Fri. $2.50, Sat.-Sun. $4.25; seniors, youths, and disabled ½-price.

Taxis: Radio Cab (800-464-7234) serves all of Marin County.

Car Rental: Budget, 20 Bellam Blvd. (457-4282), San Rafael. $27 per day, up to 150mi. Will rent to ages 21-25 for a $10 surcharge.

Post Office: San Rafael Main Office, 910 D St. (453-1153). Open Mon.-Fri. 8:30am-5pm, Sat. 10am-1pm. **ZIP code:** 94915. **Area code:** 415.

ACCOMMODATIONS AND CAMPING

HI-Marin Highlands (HI-AYH), 331-2777. Located in historic 1907 buildings in the Marin Headlands, 6mi. south of Sausalito and 10mi. from downtown San Francisco. Those with cars coming from the north should take the Sausalito exit off U.S. 101 and follow the signs into the Golden Gate Recreation Area. From San Francisco, take U.S. 101 to the Alexander Ave. exit. Beautiful location. Game room, pool table, kitchen, common room, and laundry facilities. Bring a lock for their lockers. Check in 9:30am-11:30pm. Hostel closed (except for check-in) 9:30am-3:30pm. $11-12. Children under 13 ½-price. Reservations recommended.

Point Reyes Hostel (HI-AYH), 663-8811, sits 6mi. off Limantour Rd. in the Pt. Reyes National Seashore. By car, take the Seashore exit west from Rte. 1, then take Bear Valley Rd. to Limantour Rd. and drive 6mi. into the park. The hostel is spread between two cabins on a spectacular site. Hiking, wildlife, bird-watching, and Limantour Beach are all within walking distance. Registration 4:30-9:30pm. Closed 9:30am-4:30pm. Members and nonmembers $10-12. Chore expected.

Marin Headlands, northwest of the Golden Gate Bridge. 15 campsites; most are primitive. Two sites have running water; one site, Kirby Cove, has a cooking area. Reserve as much as 90 days in advance by calling the **visitors center** (331-1540; 9:30am-noon). Permits are required; sites are free. The Golden Gate Youth Hostel (see above) allows use of showers and kitchen ($2 each). Free outdoor cold showers available at Rodeo Beach (in the Headlands).

Mt. Tamalpais State Park, 801 Rte. 1 (388-2070). 16 walk-in campsites ($14; first come, first served), a group camp, and **Steep Ravine,** an "environmental camp" with cabins ($30 for up to 5 people) and tent sites ($9). Tent sites with fire pits, no showers. Cabins have wood-burning stoves but no running water or electricity. Make cabin reservations 90 days in advance (Destinet 800-444-7275) or get there early. Reservation fee $6.75.

FOOD

Eco-head Marinites take their fruit juices, tofu, and non-fat double-shot cappuccino very seriously. A fun, cheaper option is to raid the area's many organic groceries and picnic in one of Marin's countless parks.

Mama's Royal Café, 387 Miller Ave. (388-3261), in Mill Valley. A local fave. Looks like gramma's attic after an explosion. Try the Enchilada El Syd ($6) or the Groove Burger ($5.45). Huge breakfast selection. Brunch with live music Sat. and Sun. Open daily 8:30am-2:30pm, 6-10pm.

Café Reyes, (663-9493), on U.S. 1 in Pt. Reyes Station. Way hip restaurant serving burgers and Mexican chow. Excellent coffee $1. Open daily 8am-9pm.

The Depot Bookstore and Café, 87 Throckmorton Ave. (383-2665), in Mill Valley. One of the best people-watching places around. Marinites sip mocha ($2) and munch on tasty veggie roll-ups ($3). Open daily 7am-10pm.

SIGHTS

Marin's attractions range from the excellent hiking trails that criss-cross the county's parks and beaches to unique shopping and dining opportunities in the pleasant towns of Tiburon and Sausalito. **Sausalito** lies at the extreme southeastern tip of Marin. A complicated, bizarre, and somewhat showy houseboat community occupies the harbor, fostering such personalities as the **Pope of Soap,** a man who builds sculptures out of soap bubbles and then puts the unsuspecting inside of them.

The undeveloped, fog-shrouded hills just to the west of the Golden Gate Bridge comprise the **Marin Headlands.** The **Marine Mammal Center** (289-7325) offers a sobering look at the rehabilitation of beached marine mammals (open daily 10am-4pm; donation requested). Nearly all of the gorgeous headlands are open to hikers, and camping is allowed in designated areas.

Muir Woods National Monument, a 560-acre strand of primeval coastal redwoods, is located about 5 mi. west along Rte. 1 off U.S. 101. The **visitors center** (388-2595) will help you find a trail suited to your abilities. Nearby are **Muir Beach** and **Muir Beach Lookout** (open daily sunrise-9pm). Adjacent to Muir Woods is the isolated, largely undiscovered, and utterly beautiful **Mount Tamalpais State Park.** The heavily forested park has a number of challenging trails that lead to the top of **Mount Tam** (the highest peak in the county) and to a natural stone amphitheater.

Encompassing 100 mi. of coastline along most of the western side of Marin, the **Point Reyes National Seashore** juts into the Pacific from the eastern end of the submerged Pacific Plate. Sir Francis Drake Blvd. runs from San Rafael through Olema, where it crosses Rte. 1, all the way to Pt. Reyes itself. In summer, an explosion of colorful wildflowers attracts surging crowds. **Limantour Beach,** at the end of Limantour Rd., west of the seashore headquarters, is one of the area's best beaches.

San Rafael, the largest city in Marin County, lies along U.S. 101 on the bay. Architecture buffs can check out the **Marin Civic Center,** 3501 Civic Center Dr. (499-7404), off U.S. 101. Frank Lloyd Wright designed this unusual but functional open-air building which looms over the highway. An information kiosk in the lobby supplies brochures; phone ahead for the tour (open Mon.-Fri. 9am-5pm).

WINE COUNTRY

Only about 5% of California's wine is made in "Wine Country," the collective term for the Napa, Sonoma, and Russian River Valleys, but this relatively small output does not dissuade millions of visitors from coming here. Wine Country is where the premier Californian wines are produced, the names that are highly regarded by connoisseurs both in the U.S. and abroad. Napa is better known; Sonoma is older and less crowded. In the Russian River Valley, you'll receive the most personal attention. The valleys themselves are beautiful and rural, and generally 15 degrees warmer than the bay. Green fields of gnarled grape vines stretch in all directions and scenic mountain views tower along the horizon. In spite of the area's natural beauty, you will not forget for long that wine is the focus here. This is a place after Robert Louis Stevenson's own heart, where "the stirring sunlight and the growing vines make a pleasant music for the mind, and the wine is bottled poetry."

Wine Country is a one- to two-hour drive from San Francisco; it might be wiser to make it a daytrip than to stay here and endure the steep hotel prices. For those in shape, Wine Country's flat, scenic terrain makes it easy to get around via bike; rental shops abound throughout the valleys.

■ Napa Valley

While not the oldest, the Napa Valley is certainly the best-known of America's wine-growing regions. The gentle hills, fertile soil, ample moisture, and year-round sunshine are ideal for viticulture. Charles King planted vines brought from Europe in the late 1850s, but producers were crippled by Prohibition, when the grapes were supplanted with figs. The region did not begin to reestablish itself until the 1960s. During the 70s attention focused on Napa's rapidly improving offerings as those in the know started recommending an occasional California bottle. In 1976, a bottle of red from Napa's Stag's Leap Vineyard beat a bottle of Château Lafitte-Rothschild in a blind taste test at a Paris salon. American wine was a big boy now, and tourists from across the country started flocking to the California valley. Today, local vineyards continue to reap national and international awards, and a tasting carnival goes on from sunrise to sunset, dominating life in the valley's small towns. Besides **Napa,** the towns of **Calistoga, St. Helena,** and **Youngtville** are convenient, though expensive, bases for exploring.

PRACTICAL INFORMATION

Visitor Information: Napa Visitor Center, 1310 Town Center (226-7459; fax 255-2066; www.napavalley.com/nvcvb.html), on 1st. Ancient staff and a wide brochure collection. Open daily 9am-5pm, phones closed Sat.-Sun. Stop by for free tasting tix and a free copy of *Inside Napa Valley* for maps, winery listings, and a weekly events guide (also available in many stores). There are Chambers of Commerce in **St. Helena,** 1010A Main St. (963-4456; open Mon.-Fri. 10am-noon), and in **Calistoga,** 1458 Lincoln Ave. (942-6333; open daily 10am-3pm).

Greyhound: 2 per day through the valley. The bus stops in Napa at 9:45am and 6pm in front of Napa State Hospital, 2100 Napa-Vallejo Hwy. Also stops in Youngtville, St. Helena, and Calistoga. Closest bus station is Vallejo (643-7661).

Local Transportation: Napa City Bus ("VINE" or Valley Intercity Neighborhood Express—the things people will do to get a cute acronym), 1151 Pearl St. (800-696-6443 or 255-7631; TDD 226-9722). Provides transport throughout the valley and to Vallejo. Fare $1, seniors and disabled 50¢, ages 13-18 75¢; 1 transfer free. Buses run Mon.-Fri. 6:45am-6:30pm, Sat. 7:45am-6pm. **Napa Valley Transit** (800-696-6443) runs along Rte. 10 from Napa to Calistoga. Fares vary within area, from $1-2.50; student, senior, and disabled discount fares available.

Car Rental: Budget, 407 Soscol Ave. (224-7845), Napa. $35 per day. Must be 21 with credit card. $10 per day surcharge for those 21-25.

Bicycle Rental: St. Helena Cyclery, 1156 Main St. (255-3377), Napa. Bikes $25 per day, including maps, helmet, lock, and picnic bag. Open Mon.-Sat. 9:30am-5:30pm, Sun. 10am-5pm.

Crisis: Red Cross, 257-2900. **Emergency Women's Service,** 255-6397. 24hr. **Disabled Crisis,** 800-426-4263. **Sexual Assault Crisis Line,** 258-8000. 24hr.

Hospital: Queen of the Valley, 1000 Trancas St. (252-4411).

Emergency: 911.

Police: 1539 First St. (253-4451).

Post Office: 1625 Trancas St. (255-1621). Open Mon.-Fri. 8:30am-5pm. **ZIP Code:** 94558.

Area Code: 707.

ORIENTATION

Rte. 29 runs through Napa Valley from **Napa** at the south to **Calistoga** in the north, passing **St. Helena** and **Yountville.** The **Silverado Trail,** parallel to Rte. 29, is a more scenic and less crowded route than the highway. Napa is 25 minutes away from Sonoma on **Rte. 12.** If you're planning a weekend trip from San Francisco, avoid Saturday mornings and Sunday afternoons; the roads are packed with like-minded people. Try to visit the valley on weekdays. From the city, take U.S. 101 over the Golden Gate, then Rte. 37 east to Rte. 121 north, which will cross Rte. 12 north (to Sonoma) and Rte. 29 (to Napa). It is always a good idea to steer clear of tour buses. If you're in shape, consider seeing Napa by bicycle (see Practical Information, above).

Vin Friends and Influence People

For starters, most wines are recognized by the grape-stock from which they're grown—**white** grapes produce Chardonnay, Riesling, and Sauvignon; **reds** are responsible for Beaujolais, Pinot Noir, Merlot, and Zinfandel. **Blush** or **rosé** wines issue from red grapes which have had their skins removed during fermentation in order to leave just a kiss of pink. White Zinfandel comes from a red grape often made skinless—the wine is therefore rose in colour. Between us, though, blush is not the wine of choice among the wine-tasting elite; it's for plebes and picnics. **Dessert** wines, such as Muscat, are made with grapes that have acquired the "noble rot" *(botrytis)* at the end of picking season, giving them an extra-sweet flavor.

When tasting, start with a white, moving from dry to sweet (dry wines have had a higher percentage of their sugar content fermented into alcohol). Proceed through the reds, which go from lighter to fuller bodied, depending on tannin content. Tannin is the pigment red wine gets from the grape skin—it preserves and ages the wine, which is why reds can be young and sharp, but grow more mellow with age. It's best to end with dessert wines. One should cleanse one's palate between each wine, with a biscuit, some *fromage,* or fruit. Don't hesitate to ask for advice from the tasting-room pourer. Tasting proceeds thusly: stare, smell, swirl, swallow (first three steps are optional). You will probably encounter fellow tasters who slurp their wine and make concerned faces, as though they're trying to cram the stuff up their noses with the back of their tongues. These chaps consider themselves serious tasters, and are aerating the wine in their mouths to better bring out the flavor. Key words to help you seem more astute during tasting sessions are: dry, sweet, light, crisp, fruity, balanced, rounded, subtle, rich, woody, and complex. Feel free to banter these terms about indiscriminately. *Sally forth, young naïfs!*

ACCOMMODATIONS AND CAMPING

B&Bs and most hotels are a budget breaking $60-225 per night. A few resorts have rooms under $40, but they go fast and are inaccessible without a car. If you do have a car, it's better to stay in Santa Rosa, Sonoma, or Petaluma, where budget accommodations are more plentiful. Without a reservation or a car, plan on camping.

Triple S Ranch, 4600 Mountain Home Ranch Rd. (942-6730). Beautiful setting in the mountains above Calistoga. Take Rte. 29 toward Calistoga, and turn left past downtown onto Petrified Forest. Light, woody cabins. The best deal in the valley. Pool, restaurant, and bar. Check-in 3pm. Check-out noon. Singles $42. Doubles $54. $7 per additional person. Call in advance. Open April-Dec.

Silverado Motel, 500 Silverado Trail (253-0892), near Soscol in Napa. Clean, fresh, newly remodeled rooms with kitchenette, cable TV, and a subtle edge. More personality than a chain-motel. Non-smoking rooms available. Registration noon-6pm. Singles and doubles $40 Sun.-Thurs., $65 on weekends.

Bothe-Napa Valley State Park, 3801 St. Helena Hwy. (942-4575; for reservations, call DESTINET, at 800-444-7275), north of St. Helena on Rte. 29. Often full, so call ahead to avoid a long, unnecessary drive. Park open 8am-sunset. 49 campsites. Hot showers (3min. 25¢) will kick you right in the pants. Sites $16, seniors $14, vehicles $5. Crisp swimming pool $3, under 18 $1. Call for reservations.

Napa County Fairgrounds, 1435 Oak St. (942-5111), Calistoga. First-come, first-camped. Dry grass in a parking lot with showers and electricity. $18 covers 2 adults. Closed late June-early July for county fair. Check-out noon. Open 24 hrs.

FOOD

Sit-down meals are often expensive, but Napa and its neighbors support numerous delis where you can buy inexpensive picnic supplies. Keep an eye out for the many **Safeway** stores.

Curb Side Café, 1245 1st St. (253-2307), at Randolph, Napa. Sandwich place with tasty breakfasts. Pancake special: 4 buttermilk pancakes, 2 eggs, and ham or sausage $6. Sublime sandwiches $5-6. Open Mon.-Sat. 8am-3pm, Sun. 9:30am-3pm.

Calistoga Natural Foods and Juice Bar, 1426 Lincoln (942-5822), Calistoga. One of few natural foods stores around. Organic juice bar and sandwich bar—select the ingredients for the perfect sandwich. 3 items for $4, 4 or more items $4.50. Open Mon.-Thurs. 9:30am-6pm, Fri.-Sat. 9:30am-8:30pm, Sun. 10am-6pm.

Ana's Cantina, 1205 Main St. (563-4921), St. Helena. A locals' bar with nightly music and great Mexican food. Combo platters $6. No cover. Open 10am-2am.

Taylor's Refresher, 933 Main St. (963-3486), on Rte. 29 across from the Merryvale Winery, near the heart of wine country. A burger stand with vegetarian and traditional burgers ($2.75), Mexican dishes, and ice-cream cones. Outdoor seating in beautiful picnic area. Open Sun.-Thurs. 11am-7pm, Fri.-Sat. 11am-8pm.

WINERIES

There are more than 250 wineries in Napa County, nearly two-thirds of which are in Napa Valley. The valley is home to wine country's heavyweights; vineyards include national names such as Inglenook, Christian Brothers, and Mondavi. Many wineries now charge for wine tastings, but free tours and tastings are still available. The fee is usually small ($3-6) and includes a tour with three or four tastes. The majority of smaller wineries require that visitors phone ahead to ensure that someone is around to pour the wine. The wineries listed below (from south to north) are among the valley's larger operations and have established tour programs that attract large numbers of neophytes every day. Visitors unfamiliar with U.S. drinking laws should be forewarned: you must be 21 or older to purchase or drink alcohol, which includes tastings at vineyards. And, yes, they do card. Vineyards in Napa often do not allow picnicking. All except the two noted have full wheelchair access.

Clos Du Val Wine Company, Ltd., 5330 Silverado Trail (259-2200), Napa. Take Oak Knoll Rd. to Silverado Trail. An outdoor picnic area with whimsical drawings by Ronald Searle. Tasting room open all day, but call in advance to make sure there's room. $3 charge. Open daily 10am-5pm. Tours by appointment.

Domaine Chandon, 1 California Dr. (944-2280), Yountville. One of the finest tours in the valley; can be given *en français* if prior arrangements are made. Owned by Moët Chandon of France (the people who make Dom Perignon), this is the place to learn the secrets of making sparkling wine. 45-min. tours hourly 11am-5pm. Tastings by the glass ($3-5; includes bread and goat cheese). Open daily 11am-6pm; Nov.-April Wed.-Sun. 11am-6pm.

Stag's Leap Wine Cellars, 5766 Silverado Trail (944-2020), Napa. The tiny vineyard that beat Europe's best. Call a week in advance to arrange a tour. Superb tasting ($3 for 5-6 wines and you can keep the glass!). Open daily 10am-4pm.

Hakusan Sake Gardens, 1 Executive Way (800-HAKUSAN/425-8726 or 258-6160), Napa. Take Rte. 29 south to the Rte. 12 intersection, turn left on North Kelly, then left onto Executive Way. A pleasant self-guided tour through the Japanese gardens provides a delightful respite from the power-chugging at the vineyards. Generous, free pourings of *Hakusan Sake,* known as *Haki Sake* to locals. Usually open 9am-6pm, but call first as hours vary.

Goosecross Cellars, 1119 State Ln. (944-1986), in Yountville off Silverado Trail. Small winery with wonderful wine and pleasant staff. Free wine tasting class on Sat. at 11am. Tastings daily 10am-5pm ($3).

Robert Mondavi Winery, 7801 St. Helena Hwy. (963-9611), 8mi. north of Napa in Oakville. The best free tour with tasting for the completely unknowledgeable. Spanish-style buildings, beautiful grounds. Spirited tour takes visitors through crepuscular catacombs and past towering stacks of oak barrels filled with mellowing wine. It's a good idea to call ahead; they book up fast, especially in the summer. Open daily 9am-5pm; Oct.-April 11am-4:30pm.

Vichon Winery, 1595 Oakville Grade (800-VICHON-1/842466-1 or 944-2811). Take a left off of Rte. 29 north at the Carmelite Monastery sign. The gorgeous view of the valley merits the detour. Picnic tables available for wine-purchasers. Free tasting. Tours Sat.-Sun. 11am, 1pm, and 3pm. Reservations requested. Open daily 10am-4:30pm.

Domaine Carneros, 1240 Duhig Rd. (257-0101). Go north on Rte. 29, turn right on Rte. 121, and go 2½mi. Picturesque estate modeled after a French château. Sparkling wine $4 per glass. No free tastings. Tour and film are free. 30min. on the hour from 11am-4pm. Open daily May-Oct. 10:30am-6pm; winter 11am-4pm.

Beringer Vineyards, 2000 Main St. (963-4812 or 963-7115), off Rte. 29 in St. Helena. The first vineyard to offer tours, and everyone's favorite. Very reminiscent of *Falcon Crest.* Free tours include Rhine House, a landmark mansion, and a tasting session. To avoid the crowds and taste Beringer's better wines, try the reserve room on the second floor of the Rhine House. Generous samples in the reserve room cost $2-3. Open daily 9:30am-5pm in winter, 10am-6pm in summer.

Sterling Vineyards, 1111 Dunaweal Lane (942-3344), in Calistoga, 7mi. north of St. Helena (go right on Dunaweal from Rte. 29 north). Perhaps the most visually arresting of the valley's vineyards. Aerial tram to vineyard, tour, and tasting $6. Terrace for picnicking May-Oct. Open daily 10:30am-4:30pm.

NOT DRINKING

Napa does have non-alcoholic attractions. Ten mi. south of Napa is 160-acre **Marine World Africa USA** (643-6722), an enormous zoo-oceanarium-theme park (which is often mobbed on summer weekends). To get there, take Rte. 29 south to Rte. 37 west, and follow the signs. Bring a picnic and plan to spend the whole day, especially if bringing a child or two along. Although the park suffers from a mild case of artificiality, patrons are encouraged to interact with the animals. Visitors can ride the elephants, and are allowed to pet many of the other animals at specific times. All proceeds benefit wildlife research and protection programs. (The park is accessible by BART Mon.-Sat.; call 415-788-2278 for more information. You can also take the Blue and Gold fleet from Pier 39 in San Francisco; call 415-705-5444 for more information. Park open daily 9:30am-6pm. $27, seniors $23, ages 4-12 $19, under 3 free. Parking is $4. Rides cost extra. Wheelchair and stroller access.)

Robert Louis Stevenson State Park (942-4575), on Rte. 29, 4 mi. north of St. Helena, centers around the abandoned bunkhouse where the Scottish writer, sick and penniless, spent a rejuvenating honeymoon in 1880. He gathered information for *Silverado Squatters* in the area, and eventually patterned Spyglass Hill in *Treasure Island* after looming Mt. St. Helena (open daily 8am-sunset). The **Silverado Museum,** 1490 Library Ln. (963-3757), off Adams in St. Helena, is a labor of love by a devoted collector of Stevensoniana. See manuscript notes from *Master of Ballantrae* and *Dr. Jekyll and Mr. Hyde* (open Tues.-Sun. noon-4pm; free).

Farther to the north, 2 mi. outside Calistoga, the **Old Faithful Geyser of California** (942-6463; not to be confused with its more famous namesake in Wyoming), on Tubbs Ln. off Rte. 128, spurts boiling water 60 ft. into the air. The 3500°F jet appears on average every 50 minutes in summer and every 30 minutes in winter; the ticket vendor will tell you the estimated time of the next spurt. (Open daily 9am-6pm; winter 9am-5pm. Admission $5, seniors $4, ages 6-12 $2. Bathrooms not wheelchair accessible, but those in wheelchairs admitted free.)

Calistoga is also known as the "Hot Springs of the West." Sam Brannan, who first developed the area, promised to make the hot springs the "Saratoga of California," but he misspoke and promised instead to make them "The Calistoga of Saratina." His cottage is now the base for the **Sharpsteen Museum,** 1311 Washington St. (942-5911), which traces the town's development (open daily 10am-4pm; in winter noon-4pm; free but donations are encouraged).

The 110°F hot springs of Calistoga are not very refreshing during the hot days of summer. For a cool swim, head to **Lake Berryessa** (966-2111), 20 mi. north of Napa (take Rte. 29 north to Rte. 128 east). The lake has cool water for swimming and sailing, and 169 mi. of shoreline for sunbathing.

The annual **Napa Valley Wine Festival** (252-0872) takes place in November. **Napa Valley Fairgrounds** hosts a month-long summer fair in August, with wine-tasting, rock music, juggling, a rodeo, and rides. Music lovers can catch **Music-in-the-Park,** downtown at the riverfront, for free jazz concerts in summer. Contact Napa Parks and Recreation Office (257-9529) for more information. In the summer, try the **Napa farmer's market** (252-7142), at the corner of Pearl and West for a truly fresh sampling of the valley's other produce (open 7:30am-noon).

■ Sonoma Valley

The sprawling Sonoma Valley is a quieter (and less expensive) alternative to Napa. **Sonoma,** the largest town in the Sonoma Valley, takes pride in its beautiful, expansive eight-acre town plaza. It is surrounded by art galleries, novelty shops, and vintage clothing stores, yet—with a playground, plum trees, and a pond—it's the perfect place for a "rural" picnic. **Petaluma,** west of Sonoma, is distinguished by its odd mix of architecture, unflinchingly juxtaposing nearly every 20th-century genre.

PRACTICAL INFORMATION

Visitor Information: Sonoma Valley Visitor Bureau, 453 E. 1st St. (996-1090), in Sonoma Plaza. Open daily 9am-7pm. Plenty of maps ($1.50-2.25). Look around town for a copy of *The Review,* a free weekly with extensive winery listings. **Petaluma Visitor Center,** 799 Baywood Dr., Ste. 1 (769-5644), at Lakeville. Open June-Sept. Mon.-Fri. 9am-6pm, Sat.-Sun. 10am-6pm. Shorter hours off-season.

ATM: 35 Napa St. at 1st, in Sonoma. In Petaluma at 101 Western Ave.

Bus: Sonoma County Transit (576-RIDE/7433 or 800-345-7RIDE433) serves the entire county, including Santa Rosa in the north. Bus #30 runs between Sonoma and Santa Rosa (Mon.-Fri., 3 on Sat.; $1.90, students $1.55, over 60 and disabled 95¢, under 6 free). Within Sonoma, bus fare 80¢, students 60¢, seniors and people with disabilities 40¢. County buses stop when flagged down. Buses operate Mon.-Fri. 7am-6pm. 2 buses run daily between San Francisco and Sonoma—call

Golden Gate Transportation for more information (541-2000 or 415-923-2000 in S.F., TDD 257-4554). Rte. 80 buses run from San Francisco to Santa Rosa ($4.50), stopping in Sonoma County. Bus #40 goes from Sonoma to Petaluma ($1.60). An 18-and-under "Cruisin' Pass" for unlimited summer rides is available for $15.

Volunteer Wheels: 800-992-1006. Door-to-door for people with disabilities.

Taxi: Sonoma Valley Cab (996-6733). 24-hr. service.

Bicycle Rental: Bicycle Factory, 110 Kentucky St. (763-7515), downtown Petaluma. Bikes $8 per hr., $22 per day. Must leave major ID or credit card as deposit. **Sonoma Valley Cyclery,** Broadway (935-3377), Sonoma. $6 per hr., $28 per day. Open Mon.-Fri. 10am-6pm, Sat. 10am-6pm, Sun. 10am-4pm.

Laundromat: Launder Land, 122 Petaluma Rd. (763-3042).

Auto Safety/Road Conditions: 800-424-9393.

Crisis Lines: Sonoma Valley Crisis Line, 938-HELP/4357. 24-hr. referrals. **Rape Crisis Hotline,** 545-7273. 24hr. **Poison Control,** 800-523-2222. **Disabled Crisis,** 800-426-4263. **Red Cross,** 577-7600.

Hospital: Sonoma Valley, 347 Andrieux St. (935-5000), Sonoma. **Petaluma Valley,** 400 N. McDowell Blvd. (778-1111), Petaluma.

Emergency: 911.

Police (non-emergency): **Sonoma,** 996-3602. **Petaluma,** 778-4372.

Post Office: Sonoma, 617 Broadway (996-2459), at Patten. Open Mon.-Fri. 8:30am-5pm. **ZIP Code:** 95476. **Petaluma,** 120 4th St. (769-5350). Open Mon.-Fri. 8:30am-5:30pm, Sat. 10am-2pm. **ZIP Code:** 95476.

Area Code: 707.

ORIENTATION

Sonoma Valley runs between **Sonoma** in the south and **Glen Ellen** in the north, with **Rte. 12** traversing its length. The center of downtown Sonoma is Sonoma Plaza, a park which contains City Hall and the visitor center. **Broadway** dead-ends in front of City Hall at Napa St. The numbered streets run north-south and grow higher in number as they radiate out. **Petaluma** lies to the west and is connected to Sonoma by **Rte. 116** (follow the signs closely), which becomes **Lakeville St.** in Petaluma. Lakeville St. intersects **Washington St.,** the central downtown road. The valley is small enough to tour by bicycle if you're fit and can handle the heat. Keep your eyes peeled when using the roads; the local signposting is dreadful.

ACCOMMODATIONS AND CAMPING

Pickings are pretty slim for lodging; if you can't find a vacancy in your price range, try the cheaper motels along U.S. 101 in Santa Rosa or Petaluma.

Motel 6, 1368 N. McDowell Blvd. (765-0333; fax 765-4577), just off Hwy. 101 in Petaluma. TV, "cooling system," and pool. Quiet, spacious, and almost tastefully decorated. Check-out noon. $33 singles; second person $6, third and fourth persons $3 each. Tykes 17 and under free.

Sugarloaf Ridge State Park, 2605 Adobe Canyon Rd. (833-5712), near Kenwood. 50 sites. By far the most beautiful place to camp in Sonoma Valley. Pretty views and open field for frisbee. Drive carefully up the mountain road. Flush toilets, running water, no showers. Sites $16. Call DESTINET (800-444-7275) to reserve.

San Francisco North/Petaluma KOA, 20 Rainsville Road (763-1492 or 800-992-2267), Petaluma. Take Penngrove exit, make a right turn onto Stony Pt. to Rainsville. Campground has over 300 sites. Rec hall with activities, petting zoo, pool, hot showers, store, and jacuzzi. Overrun with families and screaming kids. RV and trailer park with cabins ($37). Some tent sites separated from trailers ($27 for 2; $5 per additional adult, $2 per additional child).

FOOD

Fresh produce is seasonal and available directly from the area farms or through roadside stands and farmer's markets. Obtain a free *Farm Trails* map from the Sonoma Valley Visitor Bureau. Those in the area toward the end of the summer should ask about the ambrosial **Crane Melon,** grown nowhere else in the world but on the Crane Farm north of Petaluma. The **Sonoma Market,** 520 W. Napa St. (996-0563), in the Sonoma Valley Center, is an old-fashioned grocery store with deli sandwiches ($3-4.25) and very fresh produce. For inexpensive fruit (cantaloupe 59¢, apples 39-50¢ per lb.) head to the **Fruit Basket,** 18474 Sonoma Hwy. (996-7433). **Safeway,** 477 W. Napa (996-0633), is open 24 hours.

Fay's Garden Court Café and Bakery, 13875 Sonoma Hwy./Rte. 12 (935-1565). Quite possibly the best restaurant in the valley for the price. Delicious sandwiches and pasta meals ($7-8). Open daily 7am-2pm.

Ford's Café, 22900 Broadway (938-9811), near Rte. 12 and Rte. 121 intersection in Sonoma. Where the locals go for breakfast. Cheese omelette $5. Breakfast served until 11:30am. Open Mon.-Fri. 5am-2pm, Sat.-Sun. 6am-2pm.

Quinley's, 310 D St. (778-6000), at Petaluma. Great standard food at great prices. Newly remodeled burger counter first opened its doors in 1952. Listen to 50s tunes and enjoy your meal outdoors while sitting at the bar or picnic tables. Half-pound burger with all the fixins $2.75. Four-scoop shake or malt $1.75. Open Mon.-Thurs. 11am-10pm, Fri.-Sat. 11am-11pm, Sun. 11am-9pm. No credit cards.

Sonoma Cheese Factory, 2 Spain St. (996-1931). A deli run wonderfully wild. Forget the *vino* for now—try Sonoma's other produce and cheese-taste (free). Some varieties made in the back room. Take your toothpick and start sampling. Sandwiches $3.50-6.50. Open Mon.-Fri. 8:30am-6pm, Sat.-Sun. 8:30am-6:30pm.

The Chocolate Cow, 452 1st St. (935-3564), across from the visitor bureau. The air is thick with chocolate, the walls are crammed with bovinalia, and the ice cream is Ben and Jerry's. They sell chocolate pasta. Open daily 10am-9:30pm.

WINERIES

Sonoma Valley's wineries, located near Sonoma and Kenwood, are less tourist-ridden and offer more free tasting than Napa's. Near Sonoma, signs will point you to the different wineries; in Kenwood they are harder to find.

Ravenswood, 18701 Gehricke Rd. (938-1960), off Lovall Valley in Sonoma. Produces some of the valley's best *vino,* strongly recommended by the locals. The picnic area and the view alone are worth the trip. Summer weekend BBQs ($4.75-8.75). Free tasting and tours by appointment. Open daily 10am-4:30pm.

Château St. Jean, 8555 Sonoma Hwy./Rte. 12 (833-4134), Kenwood. Brief self-guided tour of holding tanks. Expansive winery in a Mediterranean-villa setting. Lookout tower with balcony. Tasting daily 10am-4:30pm.

Buena Vista, 18000 Old Winery Rd. (252-7117), off E. Napa. The oldest winery in the valley. Fine wines and an interesting self-guided tour of their famous old stone buildings, preserved as Mr. Haraszthy built them in 1857, when he allegedly founded the California wine industry. Beautiful grounds with trellises, berries, and great views. Shakespearian plays staged here Aug. and Sept. Picnic area and tasting room open daily 10am-5pm. Free tasting downstairs; vintage wine and champagne tasting upstairs for small fee. The under-21 set can taste Johannesburg Riesling grape juice for free. Tours Mon.-Fri. 2pm, Sat.-Sun. 11:30am and 2pm.

Glen Ellen Winery, 14301 Arnold Dr. (939-6277), 1mi. from Glen Ellen in Jack London Village. Gorgeous grounds, complete with roaming peacocks. Picnic tables available. Free tours at 11am and 2pm. Open daily 10am-5pm.

Sebastiani, 389 E. 4th St. (938-5532), a few blocks from the northwest corner of Sonoma's central plaza. This giant mass-producer draws 250,000 visitors per year, and is a good place to get an introduction to the noble drink. 20-min. tour of the sepulchral aging rooms 10:30am and 4:20pm. Free tasting daily 10am-5pm.

SIGHTS AND SEASONAL EVENTS

Local historical artifacts are preserved in the **Sonoma State Historic Park,** at E. Spain and 1st, in the northeast corner of town. Within the park, an adobe church stands on the site of the **Sonoma Mission** (938-9560), the northernmost and last of the Spanish

Sparkling Wine Supernova

What is sparkling wine? What is champagne? You'll see both terms plastered on the bubbly in your favorite liquor store, but why? If the French had their way, only their stuff would be called champagne, but Prohibition interfered with their plans. In 1923, France convinced all wine-producing countries to sign a mandate to limit use of the "champagne" label exclusively to grapes from Champagne, France. The U.S., under Prohibition at the time, never signed the bill. After Prohibition was repealed, the California wineries could still freely call their product champagne. In the 1950s, the U.S. government permitted usage of the term "champagne" only if it were preceded by "California" in letters of the same size. Most bubbly producers follow this rule today. However, European-owned wineries, such as Domaine Chandon, call the product "sparkling wine" out of respect to their parent owners. So, the next time someone tells you champagne supernova should correctly be called "sparkling wine supernova," you can fight back by explaining that it should actually be "California champagne supernova."

missions. Built in 1826 when Mexico was already a republic, the mission houses a remnant of the original California Republic flag, the rest of which was burned in the 1906 earthquake/fire. (Open daily 10am-5pm. $2; seniors and ages 6-12 $1, under 6 free; includes Vallejo's Home and Petaluma Adobe, see below.)

General Vallejo's Home (938-9559), ¾ mi. northwest of Sonoma's Central Plaza on Spain, is the Gothic-style home of the famed Mexican military and civil leader. Later, the general went on to serve as mayor of Sonoma and a California senator. The house still contains its original furnishings (no, they were not destroyed in the earthquake/fire of 1906). The grounds are garnished by a serene picnic area designed in part by Vallejo and his *esposa* ($2, children $1; open daily 10am-5pm).

To find the **Jack London State Park** (938-5216), take Rte. 12 north about 4 mi. to Arnold Lane and turn left (follow the signs). At the turn of the century, hard-drinkin' and hard-livin' Jack London (author of *Call of the Wild* and *White Fang*) bought 140 acres in Glen Ellen, determined to create his dream home. Today, the land he purchased belongs to the State Park bearing his name. London's hopes for the property were never realized—the estate's main building, the Wolf House, was destroyed by arsonists in 1913. Only the chimney and fireplaces, made of volcanic stone, remain. London died three years after the fire and is buried in the park. The nearby **House of Happy Walls,** built by his widow, is now a two-story museum devoted to the writer. The park offers several vistas of the valley as well as the scenic **Beauty Ranch Trail,** which passes by the lake, winery ruins and silos, and several quaint cottages (park open daily 9:30am-sunset; museum open daily 10am-5pm; $5 per car.)

Just south of the city center, **Traintown** (938-3912), the self-acclaimed "most well-developed scale railroad in the U.S.," offers a 20-minute steam engine tour through a 10-acre park. Young 'uns will love the petting zoo. (Open June-Sept. daily 10am-5pm, Oct.-May Fri.-Sun. 10am-5pm. $3.50, children and seniors $2.50.) Farther south, just past the junction of Rtes. 37 and 121, lies **Sears Point Raceway** (938-8448). The track revs up for auto and motorcycle racing year-round, including major international competitions. The dusty, exhaust-filled atmosphere stand in contrast to the chi-chi wineries farther north. Call for a schedule of events ($8-45.)

Just past Glen Ellen on Rte. 12 lies the village of **Kenwood.** Kenwood has a surprising number of excellent but reasonably priced restaurants, including **The Vineyards Inn** at Rte. 12 and Adobe Canyon Rd. The town heats up on July 4, when runners gather to vie for bragging rights in the **Kenwood Footrace,** which features a tough 10-k course winding through the hills and vineyards. A chili cook-off and the **World Pillowfighting Championships** will help you pass the rest of the day. There's nothing like two people straddling a metal pipe over a mud pit and beating the hell out of each other with wet pillows to get the blood racing.

CALIFORNIA

Nearby **Petaluma** merits a visit, not just for its cheap accommodations, but for its magnificent old buildings. Virtually untouched by the 1906 earthquake, the area is home to Spanish churches, Art Deco banks, and long hotels with manual elevators.

NORTHERN CALIFORNIA

■ Avenue of the Giants

About 6 mi. north of **Garberville** off U.S. 101, the **Avenue of the Giants** winds its way through a 31-mi.-long canopy of the largest living creatures this side of sea level. The tops of the mammoth trees cannot be seen from inside a car—pull over and get out to avoid straining your neck, wrecking your vehicle, and looking ridiculous. A slow meander through the forest is the best way to experience the redwoods' grandeur. The less crowded trails are found in the northern section of the park around **Rockefeller Forest,** which contains the largest grove of old-growth redwoods (200+ years) in the world. Be sure to pay your respects to the **Dyerville Giant,** located in the redwood graveyard at Founder's Grove, about midway through the Avenue of the Giants. It is difficult to appreciate the height of the trees while standing next to the upright trunk. However, because the Dyerville Giant rests on its side, over 60 human body-lengths long, it is possible to fully appreciate its size. Its **root ball** kicks it three stories high. The **Garberville Chamber of Commerce,** 733 Redwood Dr. (923-2613; open daily 10am-5pm), will supply you with a free list of businesses on the Avenue, most of which you can safely dismiss as tourist traps. The **Eel River Redwoods Hostel,** 70400 U.S. 101 (925-6469), 16 mi. south on U.S. 101 in Leggett, is the place to hang your hat. This hosteling wonderland is located in an aromatic redwood grove right on the South Fork Eel River and provides access to a sauna, a jacuzzi, and a swimming hole (inner tubes provided). If you're traveling by bus, ask the driver to stop at the hostel or get off at **Standish Hickey State Park;** the HI-AYH hostel is a ½-mi. walk north from there ($12, nonmembers $14).

■ Redwood National Park

Redwood National Park gives new meaning to the word "lush." The ferns grow the height of humans and the redwood trees the size of skyscrapers. You almost expect a dinosaur to tromp by at any moment. The redwoods here are the last remaining stretch of the old-growth forest which used to blanket 2 million acres of Northern California and Oregon. However, the park ain't just about redwoods—wildlife runs rampant, too. While a simple tour of the appropriate sights and the Drive-thru Tree will give visitors a few thrills and ample photo ops, it will also provide an overdose of fellow tourists. A less thorough, but more memorable way to experience the park is to head down one of the less-traveled hiking paths into the quiet of the woods, where you can see the redwoods as they have been for thousands of years. As you listen to the quiet sounds of the creaking trees and burbling brooks, and inhale the wonderful mix of salty ocean air and trees, imagine a time when the only tourists were the wee furry forest animals.

PRACTICAL INFORMATION

Tourist Office: Redwood National Park Headquarters and Information Center, 1111 2nd St., Crescent City (464-6101; open daily 9am-5pm). **Redwood Information Center** (488-3461; open daily 9am-5pm), on U.S. 101, 1mi. south of Orick. **Crescent City Chamber of Commerce,** 1001 Front St., Crescent City (464-3174) provides cartloads of info. Open Mon.-Fri. 8am-7pm, Sat.-Sun. 9am-5pm; Labor Day-Memorial Day Mon.-Fri. 9am-5pm.

Buses: Greyhound, 1125 Northcrest Dr. (464-2807), in Crescent City. 2 buses per day going north and 2 going south. Buses can supposedly be flagged down at 3

places within the park: at the **Shoreline Deli** (488-5761), 1mi. south of Orick on U.S. 101; at **Paul's Cannery** in Klamath on U.S. 101; and the **Redwood Hostel.** Beware capricious drivers who may ignore you. Call the Greyhound station directly preceding your stop and ask the attendant to make the driver aware of your presence. Open Mon.-Fri. 7-10am and 5-7:35pm, Sat. 7-10am and 7-7:45pm. **Emergency:** 911.
Post Office: 751 2nd St. (464-2151), in **Crescent City.** Open Mon.-Fri. 8:30am-5pm, Sat. noon-3pm. **ZIP code:** 95531. Another office at 121147 U.S. 101 in **Orick.** Open Mon.-Fri. 8:30am-noon, 1-5pm. **ZIP code:** 95555. **Area code:** 707.

Crescent City, with park headquarters and a few basic services, stands at the park's northern end. The small town of Orick is situated at the southern limit and harbors an extremely helpful ranger station, a state park headquarters, and a handful of motels. **Rte. 101** connects the two, traversing most of the park. **Orick** in the south, **Klamath** in the middle, and **Crescent City** in the north provide basic services and are home to a few motels.

ACCOMMODATIONS

A most pleasant pad is the **Redwood Youth Hostel (HI-AYH),** 14480 U.S. 101, Klamath (482-8265), at Wilson Creek. This hostel, housed in the historic Victorian DeMartin House, combines ultramodern facilities with a certain ruggedness. Its 30 beds and kitchen, dining room, and laundry facilities are all wheelchair accessible. There's a separate stove for vegetarians, a dozen recycling bins, two sundecks overlooking the ocean, staple foods for sale, and a laundry service. (Check-in 4:30-9:30pm. Curfew 11pm. Closed 9:30am-4:30pm, so you'll have to be an early riser. $10, under 18 with parent $5. Linen $1. Couples rooms available.) Reservations are recommended, and must be made by mail three weeks in advance.
    Camp Marigold, 16101 U.S. 101 (482-3585 or 800-621-8513), in Klamath, has cabins with kitchens ($34 for 2 people) and is the best budget place in the area, after the Redwood Hostel. The well-kept, woodsy cabins are a pleasant alternative to the mundane budget-motel look. The **Park Woods Motel,** 121440 Rte. 101 (488-5175), in Orick, has clean, bare-bones rooms for the lowest prices in town ($35 for 1 or 2 people, and a 2-bedroom unit with full kitchen is only $40). **El Patio,** 655 H St. (464-5114), in Crescent City, offers decent rooms with a wood-paneled early 70s look. All rooms have TVs (singles $25, doubles $28; $2 key deposit).

FOOD

The best option for eating is probably to stop by the reasonably priced **Orick Market** (488-3225; open daily 8am-7pm) to stock up on supplies, and then find a spot by the ocean or the trees. **Alias Jones,** 983 3rd St. (465-6987), is known for serving hearty portions. For breakfast, try a cinnamon roll the size of a cake ($1.75) or a fruity muffin ($1.45; open Mon.-Fri. 7am-5:30pm, Sat. 7am-3pm). **Torero's,** 200 U.S. 101 (464-5712), dishes out filling, flavorful Mexican food in a not-so-authentic environment (lunch specials $5, entrees $4-8; open daily 11am-8pm). The **Palm Café,** Rte. 101 in Orick (488-3381), dishes out basic diner food to locals. (Burgers $4.25. Positively delicious homemade fruit pies $2. Open daily 4:45am-8pm.)

SIGHTS

You can see Redwood National Park in just over an hour by car, but why rush? The park is divided into several regions, each of which have unique attractions and information centers. Get out and stroll around—the redwoods are coolest when it's just you and the trees. The National Park Service conducts a panoply of organized activities for all ages. Pick up a detailed list of Junior Ranger programs and nature walks at any of the park's ranger stations or call the **Redwood Information Center** (488-3461) for details. Hikers should take care to wear protective clothing—**ticks** and **poison** oak thrive in these deep, dark places. Also be on the lookout for the cool but deadly black bears and mountain lions that inhabit the southern region of the park.

Orick Area The Orick Area covers the southernmost section of the park. Its **visitors center** lies about 1 mi. south of Orick on U.S. 101 and ½ mi. south of the Shoreline Deli (the Greyhound bus stop). The main attraction is the **tall trees grove,** a 2½-mi. trail which begins 6 mi. from the ranger station. If you're driving, you'll need a **permit** (available at the visitors center; free). A minimum of three to four hours should be allowed for the trip. From the trailhead at the end of Tall Trees Access Rd. (which is accessible by Bald Hills Rd. off U.S. 101 just north of Orick, it's a 1.3-mi. hike down (about 30 min.) to the tallest redwoods in the park and, in fact, to the tallest known tree in the world (367.8 ft., one-third the height of the World Trade Center). Orick itself (pop. 650) is a friendly town, overrun with souvenir stores selling "burl sculptures" (wood carvings pleasing to neither eye nor wallet). Nevertheless, the town provides some useful amenities. Along U.S. 101 are a **post office** and some motels. **Patrick's Point State Park** lies 15 mi. south of Orick along U.S. 101 and offers one of the most spectacular views on the California coast. Campers, boaters, and nature enthusiasts may want to spend a day or two here before heading north to the redwoods (camping $16).

Prairie Creek Area The Prairie Creek Area, equipped with a **ranger station** and **state park campgrounds,** is perfect for hikers, who can experience 75 mi. of trails in the park's 14,000 acres. The **James Irvine Trail** (4.5mi. one-way) winds through magnificent redwoods, around clear and cold creeks, past numerous elk, through **Fern Canyon** (famed for its 50-ft. fern walls and crystalline creek), and by a stretch of the Pacific Ocean. The trail starts at the Prairie Creek Visitors Center. The less ambitious can elk-watch too, as elk love to graze on the meadow in front of the ranger station. The **Elk Prairie Trail** (1.4mi. one way) skirts the prairie and can be made into a loop by joining the nature trail. Elk may look peaceful, but they are best left unapproached. **Revelation** and **Redwood Access Trails** were designed to accommodate people with disabilities. **Big Tree Trail** is an easy walk, and its 306-ft. behemoth is a substitute for those who don't want to make the long trek to the tallest tree in the world.

Klamath Area To the north, the Klamath Area consists of a thin stretch of park land connecting Prairie Creek with Del Norte State Park. The main attraction here is the rugged and beautiful coastline. The **Klamath Overlook,** where Requa Rd. meets the Coastal Trail, is an excellent **whale-watching site.** The mouth of the **Klamath River** is a popular fishing spot (permit required) during the fall and spring when salmon spawn and during the winter when steelhead trout do the same. The town of Klamath has gone so far as to name itself the "Salmon and Steelhead Capital of the World." Sea lions in the spring and harbor seals in the summer congregate near the **Douglas Memorial Bridge,** or the part of it that survived a 1964 flood. Two golden bears guard each end of the bridge. **Coastal Drive** passes by the bridge and then continues along the ocean for 8 mi. of incredible views. The **Yurok Loop** (1mi.) is the best way for hikers to see the shoreline.

Crescent City Area Crescent City calls itself the city "where the redwoods meet the sea." In 1964, a wrathful Mother Nature took this literally, when a *tsunami* caused by oceanic quakes brought 500mph winds and leveled the city. Nine blocks into the town, the powerful wave was still two stories high. The **Crescent City Visitors Center,** in the Chamber of Commerce at 1001 Front St. (464-3174), has lots o' brochures (open Mon.-Fri. 8am-7pm, Sat.-Sun. 9am-5pm; Labor Day-Memorial Day Mon.-Fri. 9am-5pm). The **Battery Point Lighthouse** (464-3089), on a causeway jutting out of Front St., houses a **museum** open only during low tide (open Wed.-Sun. 10am-4pm, tide permitting; $2, children 50¢).

Hiouchi Area This inland region sits in the northern part of the park along Rte. 199 and contains several excellent hiking trails. The **Stout Grove Trail** can be found by traveling 2 mi. north of Jedediah State Park on U.S. 101, and then 3 mi. along South Fork Rd., which becomes Douglas Park Dr. It's an easy ½-mi. walk, passing the park's widest redwood (18ft. in diameter). The path is also accessible to people with disabilities; call 458-3310 for arrangements. Just 2 mi. south of Jedediah State Park on U.S. 101 lies the **Simpson-Reed Trail.** A tour map (25¢ from the ranger station) will guide you on this pleasant trek. The **Howland Hill Road** skirts the Smith River as it travels through redwood groves. This scenic stretch of road (no RVs or trailers allowed) begins near the Redwood Forest information center and ends at Crescent City. **Six Rivers National Forest** (457-3131) lies directly east of Hiouchi. The Smith River rushes through rocky gorges as it winds its way from the mountains to the coast. This last wild and scenic river in California is the state's only major undammed river. Consequently, its salmon, trout, and steelhead fishing is heavenly.

■ Sacramento Valley and the Cascades

Sleepy Sacramento is set in the heart of even sleepier farm country that extends northward for hundreds of miles. The quality of life here is vastly different than along the fast-paced coast, and such a Middle-America atmosphere comes as a welcome break to many who tire of the rigors of urban life. The expanse of farmland is interrupted to the northeast where both ancient and recent volcanic activity has left behind a surreal landscape of lava beds, mountains, lakes, waterfalls, caves, and recovering forest areas. The calm serenity of the Cascades matches that of the farm country, but its haunting beauty draws visitors in a way the Central Valley cannot.

Sacramento is the Charlie Brown of California. As the indistinctive capital of a highly distinctive state, its residents don't give it no respect. In mock tribute of Sacramento's location in the middle of farm country, locals have dubbed it "Sacratomato" and "Excremento." Info! Get your fresh-roasted info at the **Sacramento Visitors Bureau,** 1421 K St. (264-7777; open daily 8am-5pm)! A 20-min. drive west leads to **Davis,** a quaint town with 45,000 bicycles, a branch of the University of California, wonderful public transportation—and not much else. Don't go out of your way to come to **Chico.** The pervasive sense of tranquility is deceptive, however; beneath the placidity lurks Chico State, where partying is the one true god.

Lassen Volcanic National Park is accessible by **Rte. 36** to the south, and **Rte. 44** to the north. Both roads are about 50 mi. from **Rte. 5.** In 1914, the earth radiated destruction as tremors, streams of lava, black dust, and a series of huge eruptions ravaged the land, climaxing in 1915 when Mt. Lassen belched a 7-mi.-high cloud of smoke and ashes. Eighty-two years later, the destructive power of this eruption is still evident in the strange, unearthly pools of boiling water and the stretches of barren moonscape. Don't come between October and May or you'll be stuck in a snowdrift. **Lassen National Park Headquarters,** in Mineral (595-4444), is an infogasm.

You can see the rugged snow-capped top of **Mt. Shasta** (14,162ft.), just off I-5, from as far as 50 mi. away. It's that big. Those who live around it will tell you no one just visits the mountain—people are called to it. Shasta Indians believed a great spirit dwelled within the giant volcano, and modern day spiritualists are drawn to the mountain by its mystical energy. Thousands of New Age believers converged here to witness the great event of Harmonic Convergence, which climaxed when a resident turned on her TV set and saw an angelic vision displayed on the screen. Climbers come to challenge the slopes, while overstressed yuppies are attracted by the fragrant air and peaceful atmosphere. **Shasta-Trinity National Forest Service,** 204 W. Alma St. (926-4511 or 926-4596, TDD 926-4512), will charge your New Age info-crystals and give out maps. The **Alpenrose Cottage Hostel,** 204 Hinckley St. (926-6724), has a fabulous assortment of herb gardens and wacky guests. ($13 per night, $75 per week. Reservations recommended.) The **area code** for the region is 916.

■ Gold Country

In 1848 California was a rural backwater of only 15,000 people. That same year, sawmill operator James Marshall frantically scrawled in his diary: "This day some kind of mettle...found in the tailrace...looks like goald." In the next four years, 90,000 49ers from around the world headed for California and the 120 mi. of gold-rich seams called the Mother Lode. Sadly, few prospectors struck it rich. Miners, buoyed by dreams of instant wealth, worked long and hard, yet most could barely squeeze sustenance out of their fiercely guarded claims. Although gold remains in them thar hills, today the towns make their money mining the tourist traffic. Gussied up as "Gold Rush Towns," they solicit tourists traveling along the appropriately numbered Rte. 49, which connects dozens of small Gold Country settlements.

Unsuspecting **Calaveras County** turned out to be literally sitting on a gold mine—the richest part of the Mother Lode—when the big rush hit. Over 550,000 pounds of gold were extracted from the county's earth. Calaveras County hops with small towns. **Angels Camp,** at the juncture of Rtes. 4 and 49, is the county hub and population center, but it isn't very big. Scattered throughout the rest of the county are **Alteville, Copperopolis, Sheep Ranch, San Andreas,** and other wee burgs. Just south of Angels Camp is **Tuttletown,** Mark Twain's one-time home, now little more than a historic marker and a grocery store. **Mokelumne Hill,** 7 mi. north of San Andreas, is not a ghost town but rather a ghost story town—this town's modern claim to fame is an affinity for spooky tales.

About 20 mi. due east of Angels Camp lies **Calaveras Big Trees State Park** (795-2334; open dawn-dusk; day use $5). Here the *Sequoiadendron giganteum* (Giant Sequoia) reigns over all. **Mercer Caverns** (728-2101), 9 mi. north of Angels Camp off Rte. 4, offers 1-hr. walking tours of its various crepuscular concavities. ($5. Open daily Memorial Day-Sept. 9am-5pm. Oct.-May open weekends only 11am-4pm.)

Stanislaus National Forest features 900,000 acres of the pine trees, craggy peaks, dozens of cool topaz lakes, and wildflower meadows. Here, peregrine falcons, bald eagles, and burly bears roam the hills and skies. In addition to great hiking trails, fishing, and campsites, Stanislaus offers a chance for a bit of solitude—something its better-known neighbor, Yosemite, doesn't have. Beware of poison oak, rattlesnakes, mountain lions, and horse crap. **Park headquarters** (532-3671) are located in Sonora at 19777 Greenly Rd. (open summer 8am-5pm).

Every gold miner's life was rough, but none had it rougher than those who worked the **northern** half of the Mother Lode. Here, granite peaks kept a judo death grip on the nuggets, while merciless winters punished persistent miners for their efforts. Today, the small towns of the Northern Gold Country (**Nevada City, Coloma,** and **Placerville**) are far removed from the less authentic "Main Street" scenes of the Southern Gold Country, and the natural beauty of this region handsomely rewards exploration. If you're lucky, you may catch a glimpse of a wiry, bushy-bearded prospector leading his donkey into the sunset.

Pannin' fer Goald I: Theory

It's easy and fun to pan for gold. Once you're in Gold Country, find one of many public stretches of river. You'll need a 12- or 18-inch gold pan, which will be easily found at local stores. Dig in old mine tailings, at turns in the river, around tree roots, and at the upstream ends of gravel bars where heavy gold may settle. Swirl water, sand, and gravel in a tilted gold pan, slowly washing materials over the edge. Be patient, and keep at it until you are down to black sand, and—hopefully—gold. Gold has a unique color. It's shinier than brassy-looking pyrite (Fool's Gold), and it doesn't break down upon touch, like mica, another common glittery substance. Later, we'll practice this technique.

■ Lake Tahoe

As soon as settlers rolled into California in the late 18th century, Tahoe became a playground for the wealthy. After roads were cut into the forested mountain terrain in the 1940s, more affordable motels opened and today, members of all tax brackets can enjoy Tahoe's pure blue waters, tall pines, and high-rises silhouetted by the deep auburn glow of the setting sun. Tahoe is an outdoor adventurist's dream in any season, with miles of hiking, biking, and skiing trails, long stretches of golden beaches, rock-climbing opportunities, lakes stocked with fish, and hair-raising whitewater activities from which to choose.

PRACTICAL INFORMATION

Tourist Office: South Lake Tahoe Visitors Center, 3066 Lake Tahoe Blvd. (541-5255), at Lion's. Open Mon.-Fri. 8:30am-5pm, Sat. 9am-4pm. **Lake Tahoe/ Douglas Chamber of Commerce,** 195 U.S. 50 (588-4591), in Zephyr Cove, NV. See what happens when casinos help decorate. Open Mon.-Fri. 9am-6pm, Sat.-Sun. 9am-5pm. **Visitors Bureau,** 950 North Lake Blvd. (581-6900), in Tahoe City.

Buses: Greyhound, 1098 U.S. 50 (702-588-4645), in Harrah's Hotel Casino in Stateline, NV. To San Francisco (4 per day, $21) and Sacramento (4 per day, $19). All rates subject to seasonal price changes. No lockers. Open daily 8am-noon, 2:30-6pm. **Tahoe Casino Express** (800-446-6128) provides shuttle service between the Reno airport and Tahoe casinos (6:15am-12:30am; $17, roundtrip $30).

Public Transportation: Tahoe Area Regional Transport (TART), 581-6365. Connects the west and north shores from Tahoma to Incline Village. 12 buses daily 6:10am-6:23pm ($1.25). **South Tahoe Area Ground Express (STAGE),** 542-6077. 24-hr. bus service around South Tahoe, service to the beach every hr.

Taxis: Sierra Taxi, 577-8888. Available 24hr.

Car Rental: Enterprise Rent-a-Car, (702-586-1077), in the Horizon in Stateline, NV. Must be 21 with credit card. $29 per day, $160 per week. Unlimited mileage.

Bicycle Rental: Anderson's Bicycle Rental, 645 Emerald Bay Rd. (541-0500), convenient to the west shore bike trail. Mountain bikes $20 ½-day, $25 full day. Deposit (usually ID) required. Open daily 9am-6pm.

Post Office: Tahoe City, 950 N. Lake Blvd. (583-3936), Ste. 12 in the Lighthouse Shopping Center. Open Mon.-Fri. 8:30am-5pm. **ZIP code:** 96145. **South Lake Tahoe,** 1046 Tahoe Blvd. (544-2208). Open Mon.-Fri. 8:30am-5pm. **ZIP code:** 96151. **Area code:** 916 in CA, 702 in NV.

Lake Tahoe is located 118 mi. northeast of Sacramento and 35 mi. southwest of Reno. **U.S. 50** (also called Lake Tahoe Blvd.), **Rte. 89,** and **Rte. 28** overlap to form a ring of asphalt around the lake. The versatile Rte. 89 is also known as W. Lake Blvd. and Emerald Bay Rd. Rte. 28 masquerades as N. Lake Blvd. and Lakeshore Dr.

ACCOMMODATIONS AND CAMPING

The strip off U.S. 50 on the California side of the border supports the bulk of Tahoe's 200 motels. Others line Park Ave. and Pioneer Trail off U.S. 50, which are quieter. The Forest Service provides up-to-date information on camping. **Bayview** is the only free campground for miles (544-5994; 2-night max.; open June-Sept.). Reservations for all sites, except Bayview, are essential. (Call Destinet, 800-365-2267.)

Peach Tree Inn, 3520 Lake Tahoe Blvd. (544-1177 or 800-556-2500), in S. Lake Tahoe. Adorable motel with (you got it) peach decor and clean rooms. Heated pool and cable TV (I want my MTV). Rooms $25-35 Fri.-Sat., $35-45 Sun.-Thurs.

El Nido, 2215 Lake Tahoe Blvd. (541-2711), in S. Lake Tahoe. Squishy beds with quilts give it that homey feel. TV, VCR, hot tub, pool, and casino shuttle to Stateline. Singles $39 Mon.-Fri., $49 Sat.-Sun. 10% senior discount, off-season discount.

Lake Shore Lodge, 3496 Lake Tahoe Blvd. (544-2834), in S. Lake Tahoe. Light, airy rooms are cheap, but beware of seasonal and weekend rate increases. TV and pool. Singles $20, doubles $28 Mon.-Thurs.; $35/$48 Fri.-Sat.

> ### Pannin' fer Goald II: Practice
> Swish. Swish. Swish swish. "Dammit." Swish. Swish swish swish. Swish. "Dammit!" Swish. Swish swish swish swish swish. Swish. *"Goald!!!"*

Nevada Beach (544-5944), 1mi. from Stateline on U.S. 50. Flush toilets and drinking water; no showers. Sites ($16) 300ft. from the shore. Open June-Labor Day.

D.L. Bliss State Park, (525-7277), Rte. 89, a few mi. west of Emerald Bay. Hot showers, blissful beach. 14-day max. stay. 168 sites; $14, near-beach sites $19. Open June to Labor Day. Arrive early to stake your claim.

FOOD

The casinos offer perpetually low-priced buffets, but there are restaurants along the lakeshore with reasonable prices, similarly large portions, and much better food.

Margarita's Café, 2495 Lake Tahoe Blvd. (544-6907), in S. Lake Tahoe. Amazing Mexican cuisine. Excellent combos ($7). Open Wed.-Mon. 11:30am-9pm.

Killer Chicken, 2660 Lake Tahoe Blvd. (544-9977), in S. Lake Tahoe. True to its name, this "anti-chain" serves great chicken sandwiches ($6-7). Whole chickens done Jamaican Jerk or Cuban Roast ($13). Open daily 11:30am-"til we close."

Seedling Café, 7081 N. Lake Tahoe Blvd. (546-3936), across from Agate Bay on Rte. 28 in Tahoe Vista. Happy veggie restaurant serving a great hummus sandwich ($7). Drum circle every other Tues. Entrees $8-11. Open daily 11am-9pm.

The Bridgetender, 30 W. Lake Tahoe Blvd. (583-3342), in Tahoe City. No lack of burger variety ($4-6). Watch the Truckee River go by or marvel at the graffiti in the men's room. Hopping night spot. Open daily 11am-10pm, bar open til 2am.

ACTIVITIES

Lake Tahoe supports numerous beaches. On the south shore, **Pope Beach,** off Rte. 89, is wide and shaded by pines (less traffic on the east end). **Nevada Beach** is close to the casinos off U.S. 50, offering a quiet place to reflect on your losses. **Zephyr Cove Beach** is a favorite spot for the younger well-oiled college crowd. On the west side, **Chambers Beach** draws the same bouncy types. **Meeks Bay,** 10 mi. south of Tahoe City, is more quiet. The North Shore offers **Hidden Beach** (just south of Incline Village) and **Kings Beach** (just across the California border on Rte. 28). The **nude beach** near Hidden is said to be a local gay and lesbian hangout.

Would-be **cyclists** without wheels are requited in the Tahoe-Truckee area. Bike rental places give all sorts of good advice. Rentals run $5 per hr., $20 per full day. Several paved bike trails circle the lake. **Angora Ridge** (4mi.) is a moderate mountain bike trail accessible from Rte. 89 that meanders past Fallen Leaf Lake to the Angora Lakes. For serious mountain bikers, **Mr. Toad's Wild Ride** (3mi.) is a strenuous, winding trail that climbs to 9000 ft. It can be reached from U.S. 50 or Rte. 89, with parking located off the major roads.

Hiking is one of the best ways to explore the beautiful Tahoe Basin. Detailed information, including trail maps for all types of hikes, is available at the visitors center. The **Lake of the Sky Trail** (0.6mi. roundtrip) leads to the **Tallac Historic Site,** which features a look at turn-of-the-century Tahoe life (i.e., old casinos). More experienced hikers may want to try the West and the South Shore trails. **Backcountry** aficionados must obtain a free **Wilderness Permit** for any hike into the Desolation Wilderness. Magnificent **Emerald Bay,** in the lake's southwest corner, has Tahoe's only island, **Fannette** (the most photographed sight in the area).

River rafting is an exciting and refreshing way to appreciate the Tahoe scenery. Unfortunately, the quality (and existence) of rafting on the American and the Truckee Rivers depends on the amount of snowfall during the preceding winter. Consequently, late spring and early summer are the best times to hit the rapids. If water levels are high, keep a look out for raft rental places along the Truckee. (For more information, call 583-RAFT/7238 or 581-2441.) If droughts make conventional rafting scarce, all need not be lost. Floating around in an **inner tube** is popular with many would-be rafters. Make sure tubes are permitted on the body of water you select, don't go alone, and always know what lies downstream before you shove off.

In the summer, **Windsurf North Tahoe,** 7276 N. Lake Tahoe Blvd. (546-2369), in Tahoe rents windsurfing equipment ($15). They also offer lessons for even the most timorous first-timers (open July-Oct.). Rent a wetsuit: the average temperature of the lake remains a chilly 39°F year-round. Most drowned bodies are never recovered, one tourist leaflet cheerfully reveals, because the cold prevents the decomposition that usually makes corpses float to the surface. In fact, the Native Americans who used to live around Lake Tahoe "buried" their dead in the lake; changes in water temperature and current movements have, on occasion, brought these perfectly preserved bodies to the surface.

Tahoe is a **skiing** mecca, and there are approximately 20 ski resorts in the Tahoe area. Check the visitors center for prices and maps. Pick up a copy of *Ski Tahoe* (free) at visitors centers for valuable coupons and more information. **Alpine Meadows** (583-4232), **Squaw Valley** (583-6985), and **Heavenly** (702-586-7000) are modern classics. For **nordic** enthusiasts **Hope Valley** (694-2266) has 11 trails of varying difficulty (free!). Take Rte. 89 south from S. Lake Tahoe and turn left on Rte. 88.

SIER'RA NEVADA

The Sierra Nevada is the highest, steepest, and perhaps the most visually stunning mountain range in the contiguous United States. Thrust skyward 400 million years ago by plate tectonics and shaped by erosion, glaciers, and volcanoes, this enormous hunk of granite stretches 450 mi. north from the Mojave Desert to Lake Almanor near Lassen Volcanic National Park. The heart-stopping sheerness of Yosemite's rock walls, the craggy alpine scenery of Kings Canyon and Sequoia National Parks, and the abrupt drop of the Eastern Sierra into Owens Valley are unparalleled sights.

Temperatures in the Sierra Nevada are as diverse as the terrain. Even in the summer, overnight lows can dip into the 20s. Check local weather reports. Normally, only U.S. 50 and I-80 are kept open during the snow season. Exact dates vary from year to year, so check with a ranger station for local road conditions, especially from October through June. Come summer, protection from the high elevations' ultraviolet rays is necessary; always bring sunscreen, and a hat is a good idea.

■ Yosemite National Park

In 1868 a young Scotsman named John Muir arrived in San Francisco and asked for directions to "anywhere that's wild." He was pointed toward the Sierra Nevada and a lifetime of conservationism. In 1880 he succeeded in securing national park status for **Yosemite National Park.** Today, few of the park's 3.5 million annual visitors know of his efforts, but most leave with an appreciation and love for the awe-inspiring granite cliffs, thunderous waterfalls, lush meadows, and thick pine forests. The park covers 1189 sq. mi. of mountainous terrain. **El Capitán, Half Dome,** and **Yosemite Falls** lie in the Yosemite Valley, carved out by glaciers over thousands of years. Unless you like to hang out with mobs of Midwesterners and their screaming kids, you should duck out quickly. Little Yosemite Valley, accessible by hiking trails, offers two spectacular waterfalls: **Vernal** and **Nevada Falls. Tuolumne Meadows** (pronounced ta-WALL-um-ee), in the northeastern corner of the park, is an Elysian expanse of alpine meadows surrounded by granite cliffs and rushing streams. **Mariposa Grove** is a forest of giant sequoia trees at the park's southern end.

PRACTICAL INFORMATION

Tourist Office: A map of the park and a copy of the informative *Yosemite Guide* are available for free at visitors centers. Wilderness **permits** are available at all visitors centers; write ahead and reserve in advance. **General Park Information** (372-0265; 24-hr. recorded information 372-0200; TTY users 372-4726). Open Mon.-Fri. 9am-5pm. **Campground information:** 372-0200 (recorded). **Yosemite Valley Visitors Center,** Yosemite Village (372-0229). Open daily 8am-9pm mid-June to Labor Day; winter 8am-5pm.

Tour Information: Yosemite Lodge Tour Desk (372-1240), in Yosemite Lodge lobby. Open daily 7:30am-6pm. **Incredible Adventures** (800-777-8464) leads 1- and 3-day hiking tours of the park, leaving from San Francisco, for $75-150. Meals, equipment, and transportation included. Tours leave Wed. and Sun.

Equipment Rental: Yosemite Mountaineering School, Rte. 120 (372-8344 or 372-1244), at Tuolumne Meadows. Sleeping bags $4 per day, backpacks $4 per day, snowshoes $11 per day. Climbing shoes rented to YMS students only. Driver's license or credit card required. Open daily 8:30am-5pm.

Post Office: Yosemite Village, next to the visitors center. Open June-Aug. Mon.-Fri. 8:30am-5pm, Sat. 10am-noon; Sept.-May Mon.-Fri. 8:30am-12:30pm and 1:30-5pm. **ZIP code:** 95389. **Area code:** 209.

Yosemite lies 200 mi. east of San Francisco and 320 mi. northeast of Los Angeles. It can be reached by taking **Rte. 140** from Merced, **Rte. 41** north from Fresno, and **Rte. 120** east from Manteca or west from Lee Vining.

Park admission is $3 if you enter on foot, bicycle, or bus or $5 for a 7-day vehicle pass. Yosemite runs public **buses** that connect the park with Merced and Fresno, home of GBK. **Yosemite VIA,** 300 Grogan Ave., Merced 95340 (742-5211 or 800-VIA-LINE/842-5463), makes two roundtrips per day from the Merced Amtrak station to Yosemite ($20, roundtrip $33; discount for seniors). **Yosemite Gray Line** (YGL; 722-0366), connects with **Amtrak** (800-USA-RAIL/872-7245) in Merced. The free **shuttle bus** has knowledgeable drivers and broad viewing windows (daily at 10-min. intervals from 9am to 10pm, and every 20 min. from 7:30-9am).

ACCOMMODATIONS, CAMPING, AND FOOD

Lodgings in Yosemite Valley are monopolized by the **Delaware North Co. Room Reservations,** 5410 E. Home, Fresno 93727 (252-4848; TTY users 255-8345).

Yosemite Lodge, in Yosemite Valley west of Yosemite Village. Small, sparsely furnished cabins under surveillance by deer. To catch cancellations, inquire before 4pm. Singles and doubles $56, with bath $73.

Yosemite is camping country. Most of the campgrounds are crowded, and many are choked with trailers and RVs. Reservations are required from April to November and must be made through Destinet (800-444-4275) up to four months ahead.

Camping Inside Yosemite Valley

Sunnyside, at the west end of Yosemite Valley past the Yosemite Lodge Chevron station. Near the climber's camp. Water, toilets, and tables. $3 per person. Often fills up early with reservation-less visitors. Open year-round.

Backpacker's Camp, 1½mi. east of Yosemite Village across the river, behind North Pine Campground. Must have a wilderness permit and be a backpacker without a vehicle to camp here. Unadvertised. Low on facilities, high on camaraderie. Fishing is popular. 2-night max. stay. $3 per person. Open May-Oct.

Lower Pines, in the busy eastern end of Yosemite Valley. This is the designated **winter camping** spot and the only one in the valley which allows **pets.** Commercial and crowded, it has toilets, water, showers, and tables. Sites $15.

Camping Beyond Yosemite Valley

Hodgdon Meadow, on Rte. 120 near Big Oak Flat entrance. Suitable for winter camping or for finding solitude year-round. Water, tables, and toilets. Sites $12.

Wawona, Rte. 41 in the southern end of the park. 100 sunny sites along the beautiful Merced River. Tables, toilets, and water. No showers. Pets allowed. Sites $10.

Porcupine Flat, off Rte. 120 east. RV access to front section only. Pit toilets, potable stream water. 52 sites. $6 per site. Open June or July-Sept.

Bring your own food for a campfire feast. Overpriced groceries are available from the **Yosemite Lodge, Wawona,** or the **Village Stores** (open daily 8am-10pm; Oct.-May 8am-9pm). You'd be better off buying supplies before coming to the park.

SIGHTS AND THE OUTDOORS

By Car or Bike You can see a large part of Yosemite from the bucket seat, but the view is better if you get out. The *Yosemite Road Guide* ($3.25 at every visitors center) is keyed to the roadside markers and outlines a superb tour of the park—it's almost like having a ranger tied to the hood. The drive along **Tioga Road** (Rte. 120 east) reveals one panorama after another. Driving west from the Pass brings you to **Tuolumne Meadows,** its open, alpine spaces, and shimmering **Tenaya Lake.** A drive into the heart of the valley leads to thunderous 2425-ft. **Yosemite Falls** (the highest in North America), **Sentinel Rock,** and **Half Dome.** For a different perspective on the valley, drive to **Glacier Point,** off Glacier Point Rd. Hovering 3214 ft. above the valley floor, this gripping overlook is guaranteed to impress the most jaded of travelers. Half Dome rests majestically across the valley, and the sight and sound of **Vernal Falls** and **Nevada Falls** shatter the silence.

A short hiking trail through the giant sequoias of **Mariposa Grove** begins off Rte. 41 at the **Fallen Monarch,** a massive trunk lying on its side, and continues to the 209-ft., 2700-year-old **Grizzly Giant,** and the fallen **Wawona Tunnel Tree.** Ancient Athens was in its glory when many of these trees were saplings.

Cyclists can pick up brochures indicating the safest roads at the visitors center. Roads are fairly flat near the villages, more demanding farther afield. Those near **Mirror Lake,** open only to hikers and bikers, guarantee a particularly good ride, and the valley roads, filled with traffic, are easily circumvented by the bike paths. For further information on bike routes, contact the bike rental stands at Yosemite Lodge (372-1208) or Curry Village (372-1200).

Day Hiking To experience Yosemite the way it was meant to be, travel on foot. Day-use trails are usually fairly busy, sometimes positively packed, and occasionally (i.e. July 4th weekend) the site of human traffic jams. A colorful trail map with difficulty ratings and average hiking times is available at the visitors center for 50¢. Misty **Bridalveil Falls** is an easy ¼-mi. walk from the shuttle stop. The **Mirror Lake Loop** is a level, 3-mi. walk to the glassy lake, which is silting up to become a meadow. These two trails, as well as pretty **Lower Yosemite Falls,** are wheelchair accessible.

The wildflower-laden **Pohon Trail** starts from Glacier Point, crossing Sentinel River (spectacular Sentinel Falls, the park's second largest cascade, lies to the north) on its way to Taft Point and other secluded lookouts. For a taste of "real" rock climbing without requisite equipment and training, Yosemite day hikers scramble up **Lembert Dome** above Tuolumne Meadows.

The world's best climbers come to Yosemite to test themselves at angles past vertical. If you've got the courage, you can join the stellar Yosemite rock climbers by taking a lesson with the **Yosemite Mountaineering School** (372-1335 or 372-8435; Sept.-May 372-1244; open 8:30am-5pm). The basic **rock-climbing classes,** offered daily in summer (usually mid-April to Oct.), teach you the basics on the ground, then take you 80 ft. up a cliff and introduce you to bouldering and rappelling (lesson prices depend on demand; $60 for three or more, $120 for individual courses).

■ Beyond Yosemite Valley

Most folks never leave the valley, but a wilder, lonelier Yosemite awaits those who do. Preparation is key before a backcountry adventure; obtain a **topographical map** of the region you plan to explore and plan your route. **Backcountry camping** is prohibited in the valley (you'll get slapped with a stiff fine if caught), but it's generally permitted along the high-country trails with a free **wilderness permit** (call 372-0310 for general information). Each trailhead limits the number of permits available. Reserve by mail between March 1 and May 31 (write Wilderness Center, P.O. Box 577, Yosemite National Park 95389), or take your chances with the 50% quota held on 24-hr. notice at the Yosemite Valley Visitors Center, the Wawona Ranger Station, and Big Oak Flat Station. Popular trails like **Little Yosemite Valley, Clouds Rest,** and **Half Dome** fill their quotas regularly. To receive a permit, you must show a planned itinerary. Many hikers stay at the undeveloped mountain campgrounds in the high country for the company and for the **bear lockers,** used for storing food. Hikers can also store food in hanging bear bags or in rentable plastic **canisters** from the Yosemite Valley Sports Shop ($3 per day). Canisters may be mandatory on more popular hiking routes (check with rangers).

A free shuttle bus to **Tuolumne Meadows** will deposit you at the heads of several trails. The **Pacific Crest Trail** follows a series of awe-inspiring canyons. South Yosemite is home to the **Giant Sequoia and Mariposa Grove,** the park's largest. Some trails continue as far as Washington State. Several **high country hikes** provide access to truly spectacular areas. For a taste of "real" rock-climbing without requisite equipment and training, Yosemite day hikers scramble up **Lembert Dome** above Tuolumne Meadows. This gentle incline riddled with foot and hand holds is nonetheless a solid granite face. The 4-mi. approach to **Cathedral Lakes,** a great spot for a secluded nap and daydream, from the west end of the meadows is another worthwhile hike. It begins at the Cathedral Lake parking lot at the west end of Tuolumne Meadows. The 7-mi. roundtrip trail winds through dense forest en route. For those with more rigorous adventures in mind, a tough scramble past **May Lake** up to the peak of **Mt. Hoffman** (10,850ft.) provides a totally dope 360° view.

■ Mono Lake

As fresh water from streams and springs drains into the "inland sea" of Mono Lake, it evaporates, leaving behind a mineral-rich, 13-mi. wide expanse that Mark Twain called "the Dead Sea of the West." The lake derives its lunar appearance from remarkable towers of calcium carbonate called *tufa,* which form when calcium-rich freshwater springs well up in the carbonate-filled salt water. At over 700,000 years old, this lake remains the Western Hemisphere's oldest enclosed body of water.

The town of **Lee Vining** provides the best access to Mono Lake and the ghost town of **Bodie.** Lee Vining is located 70 mi. north of **Bishop** on U.S. 395 and 10 mi. west of the Tioga Pass entrance to **Yosemite.** For tasty granola info-nuggets, see the **Mono Lake Visitors Center and Lee Vining Chamber of Commerce** (647-6595 or 647-6629; open daily 9am-9pm; Labor Day-Memorial Day 9am-5pm), on Main St. in Lee Vining. **Greyhound** (647-6301 or 800-231-2222; open daily 8am-9pm), in the Lee Vining Market, goes to L.A. ($42; 11am) and Reno ($30; 2:15am). Buy your ticket at the next stop, because they don't sell them here. **Area code:** 619.

Hotel accommodations are often scarce on Friday afternoons and holidays. At any time, lodging and meals are going to be expensive. There are six **Inyo National Forest campgrounds** ($0-8) within 15 mi. of town; these may fill quickly during peak times. Head west from town on Rte. 120. The **Lee Vining Market** is the town's closest thing to a grocery store (647-6301; next to the laundromat on Main St.).

In 1984, Congress set aside 57,000 acres of land surrounding Mono Lake and called it the **Mono Basin National Forest Scenic Area** (647-6525). **South Tufa Grove,** 10 mi. from Lee Vining, harbors an awe-inspiring collection of calcium carbonate formations. (Take U.S. 395 south to Rte. 120, then go 4mi. east and take the Mono Lake Tufa Reserve turn-off 1mi. south of Tufa Grove.) The **Mono Lake Committee** offers excellent guided canoe tours of the lake that include a crash course on Mono Lake's natural history, ecology, and conservation. Arrange tours through the visitors center ($12, ages 4-12 $6). **June Lake,** a canyon carved by glaciers and now filled with water, is 10 mi. south of Lee Vining on U.S. 395. If you have time, take the scenic loop along Rte. 158. The sparkling lake and its surrounding ring of mountains are prized by visitors as a wayward slice of the Alps more beautiful than the original.

Tucked away in the high, God-forsaken desert, **Bodie** is a real ghost town, even if it does charge admission ($5; dogs $1; self-guide booklet $1). Described in 1880 as "a sea of sin, lashed by the tempests of lust and passion," the town was home to 10,000 people, 65 saloons, and one homicide per day. Bodie is accessible by a paved road off U.S. 395, 15 mi. north of Lee Vining, and by a dirt road from Rte. 167 out of Mono Inn (open daily 8am-7pm; Labor Day-Memorial Day 9am-4pm).

■ Mammoth Lakes

Home to one of the most popular ski resorts in the United States, the town of Mammoth Lakes is rapidly transforming itself into a giant, year-round playground. Mountain biking, rock-climbing, and hiking now complement the traditional wintertime pursuits. Mammoth is an outdoor lover's dream—spectacular peaks overlook a town where every establishment seems to exist solely for the excursionist's benefit.

Practical Information Mammoth Lakes is on **U.S. 395** 160 mi. south of Reno and 40 mi. southeast of the eastern entrance to Yosemite National Park. **Rte. 203** runs through the town as **Main St.** The **Visitors Center & Chamber of Commerce** (934-2712 or 800-367-6572), east off U.S. 395, north of town at the National Forest Visitors Center, taps into Mammoth's big, hairy info subculture (open July-Sept. daily 6am-5pm; Oct.-June Mon.-Sat. 8am-5pm). **Greyhound** (213-620-1200) stops in the parking lot behind McDonald's on Main. One bus daily to Reno ($32; 1:30am) and L.A. ($42; 12:30pm). The **post office** (934-2205) is on Main St., across from the visitors center (open Mon.-Fri. 8:30am-5pm). **ZIP code:** 93546. **Area code:** 619.

Accommodations, Camping, and Food There are nearly 20 Inyo Forest public campgrounds in the area, at **Mammoth Lakes, Mammoth Village, Convict Lake,** and **Reds Meadow.** All sites have piped water. Call the Mammoth Ranger District (924-5500) for more info. Reservations taken for all group sites ($20-55), as well at nearby Sherwin Creek, through Destinet (800-280-2267). In-doorsy types should seek the **ULLR Lodge** (934-2454). Turn left from Main St. onto Minaret Rd. It's a chalet-esque place with sauna and a shared kitchen. (Dorm style rooms $12-16.) For a bite to eat, **Angel's** (934-7427), at Main and Sierra, is almost unanimously recommended among locals for da BBQ (open Mon.-Fri. 11:30am-10pm, Sat.-Sun. 5-10pm).

Sights There's plenty to see in Mammoth Lakes, but unfortunately most of it is accessible only by car. **Devil's Postpile National Monument,** an intriguing geological oddity, was formed when lava flows oozed through Mammoth Pass thousands of years ago and then cooled to form columns 40 to 60 ft. high. A pleasant 3-mi. walk away from the center of the monument is **Rainbow Falls,** where the middle fork of the San Joaquin River drops 140 ft. past dark cliffs into a glistening green pool. From U.S. 395, the monument can be reached by a 15-mi. drive past Minaret Summit on paved Rte. 203. To save the monument area from being completely trampled, rangers have introduced a shuttle service between a parking area and the monument center, which *all* visitors must use between 7:30am and 5:30pm. (Drivers have free access 5:30pm-7:30am. Shuttle lasts 45min. Roundtrip $7, ages 5-12 $4.)

Although there are over 100 lakes near town (60 of them within a 5-mi. radius), not one actually goes by the name of "Mammoth Lake." The mile-long **Lake Mary** is popular for boating, fishing, and sailing. **Lake Mamie** has a picturesque picnic area, and many short hikes lead to **Lake George,** where granite sheets attract climbers.

You can ride the **Mammoth Mountain Gondola** (934-2571) during the summer for a spectacular view of the area (open daily 9:30am-5:30pm; roundtrip $10, children $5; $20 per day for gondola ticket and trail use). **Obsidian Dome** lies 14 mi. north of Mammoth Junction and 1 mi. west of U.S. 395 on Glass Flow Rd. (follow the sign to "Lava Flow"). Hot-air balloons, climbing walls, mountain bike paths, and even dogsled trails attract visitors to Mammoth. You can evaluate your options at the **Mammoth Adventure Connection** (934-0606 or 924-5683), in the Mammoth Mountain Inn. Courageous cyclists can take the gondola to the top of **Mammoth Mountain Bike Park,** where the ride starts at 11,053 ft. and head straight down the rocky ski trails. Helmets are required. A **ropes course** ($40 adults, $10 youth program) and **climbing wall** ($5 per climb or $15 per hr.) are the latest attractions at Mammoth (open July 1-Labor Day; call 924-5638 for reservations).

The **skiing** season extends from mid-Nov. to June. **Mammoth Mountain** lift tickets can be purchased at the **Main Lodge** at the base of the mountain on Minaret (934-2571; open Mon.-Fri. 8am-3pm, Sat.-Sun. 7:30am-3pm), at **Stormriders** at Minaret and Canyon (open daily 8am-9pm), or at **Warming Hut II** at the end of Canyon and Lakeview (934-0787; open Mon.-Fri. 8am-3pm, Sat.-Sun. 7:30am-3pm). A free **shuttle bus** transports skiers between lifts, town, and the Main Lodge. The Forest Service can provide information on the area's cross country trails.

CALIFORNIA

ALASKA

Alaska's beauty is born of extremes. By far the largest of the 50 states, it comprises one-fifth of the land mass of the United States. The 33,000-mi. coastline stretches 11 times the distance from New York to San Francisco. Nineteen Alaskan peaks reach over 14,000 ft. and several glacial ice fields occupy areas larger than the state of Rhode Island. Alaska has the highest mountain in North America (20,320-ft. Mt. McKinley, or "Denali"), the largest American National Park (13-million-acre Wrangell-St. Elias National Park), the hugest carnivore in North America (the Kodiak brown bear), and the greatest collection of bald eagles in the world. At the height of summer, Alaska becomes the "Land of the Midnight Sun," where you can play softball at 2am; in spring and fall, shimmering curtains of spectral color—the *aurora borealis*—dance like smoke over the dark horizon; in the depths of winter Alaska is land of the noonday moon, when large portions of the state never see the sun.

The first humans to colonize North America crossed the Bering Strait into Alaska via a now-sunken land bridge. Russian-sponsored Danish navigator Vitus Bering was the first European to arrive, bringing in his wake a wave of Russian fur traders who exhausted the fur supply within a century. When Secretary of State James Seward negotiated the United States's acquisition of the territory from Russia for a trifling $7,200,000 (about 2¢ per acre) in 1867, he became the laughingstock of the nation. The purchase of seemingly worthless frozen land was commonly called "Seward's Folly," but within 20 years Alaska showed its worth in a series of massive gold strikes. In 1968, long after the gold rush had slowed to a trickle, the state's fortunes rebounded yet again, with the discovery of "black gold" (oil) on the shore of the Arctic Ocean. By 1981, $7,200,000 worth of crude oil flowed through the Trans-Alaska pipeline from the Arctic oil field every four-and-a-half hours.

PRACTICAL INFORMATION

Capital: Juneau.
Alaska Division of Tourism, 33 Willoughby St., 9th Floor; P.O. Box 110801, Juneau 99811-0801 (465-2010; fax 465-2287). Open Mon.-Fri. 8am-5pm. **Alaska Public Lands Information Center** and **National Park Service,** 605 W. 4th Ave. #105, Anchorage, 99501 (271-2737), in the Old Federal Bldg. Help in crossing any and all wilderness areas. Branch offices in Fairbanks, Ketchikan, and Tok. Open daily 10am-5:30pm. **Alaska State Division of Parks,** 3601 C St., Suite 200, Anchorage 99510 (269-8400). Info on camping and other activities at all state parks. Open Mon.-Fri. 11am-5pm.
Time Zones: Alaska (most of the state; 4hr. behind Eastern); Aleutian-Hawaii (western Aleutian Islands; 5hr. behind Eastern). **Postal Abbreviation:** AK. **Area Code:** 907.
Sales Tax: None.

CLIMATE

No single climatic zone covers the whole state. Fairbanks, the Interior, and parts of the Bush can experience 95°F hot spells in summer, -50°F temperatures in winter, and less than eight inches of precipitation annually. Farther south, the climate is milder and rainier. Anchorage and other southcentral coastal towns are blessed with the Japanese Current, which has a moderating effect on the climate. Average temperatures for Anchorage range from 13°F in January to 57°F in July. In the southeast, temperatures are even milder and rain even more frequent; the region is covered with a cold-temperate rainforest.

TRAVEL

Driving in Alaska is not for the faint of heart. Roads reach only a quarter of the state's area, and many of the major ones remain in deplorable condition. "Frost heaves" from melting and contracting permafrost cause potholes and incredible dips in the road. Radiators and headlights should be protected from flying rocks with wire screens, and a full-size spare tire and a good set of shocks are essential. Winter can actually offer a smoother ride. At the same time, the danger of avalanches and ice is cause for major concern. Anyone venturing onto Alaska's roads should own a copy of *The MILEPOST,* available for $19 from Vernon Publications, Inc., 3000 Northup Way, #200, Bellevue, WA 98004 (800-726-4707; fax 206-822-9372).

Alaska's road and rail networks cover little of the massive state, and it is no mystery why one in 36 Alaskans has a pilot's license. Air travel is often a necessity, albeit an exorbitantly expensive one (the hourly rate usually exceeds $100). Several intrastate airlines, almost exclusively based at the Anchorage airport, transport passengers and cargo to virtually every village in Alaska: **Alaska Airlines** (to larger Bush towns and Cordova; 800-426-0333); **ERA Aviation** (southcentral; 243-6633); and **Reeve Aleutian Airways** (Aleutians; 243-4700). Many other charters and flight-seeing services are available. Write **Ketchum Air Service Inc.,** P.O. Box 190588, Anchorage 99519 (243-5525), on the North Shore of Lake Hood, to ask about their charters. One-day flights and overnight or weekend trips to isolated lakes, mountains, and tundra usually range from $165 up.

AlaskaPass offers unlimited access to Alaska's railroad, ferry, and bus systems; a 15-day pass sells for $649, a 30-day pass for $899. A pass allowing travel on 21 non-consecutive days over a 45-day period costs $949. The pass extends from Bellingham, WA to Dutch Harbor on the Aleutian Islands, and is a good deal for those who want to see a lot of the region in a short time. Call 800-248-7598 for details.

■ Ketchikan

Ketchikan is the first stop in Alaska for northbound cruise ships and ferries that expel flocks of ambitious tourists and would-be cannery workers. One might conclude that the crowds and notoriously bad weather (the town averages nearly 14 ft. of rainfall a year) would make Ketchikan an unpleasant place to visit. Its location is the key: the city provides access to Prince of Wales Island, Metlakatla, and most notably, Misty Fjords National Monument.

Practical Information The **Southeastern Alaska Visitors Center (SEAVC)** (228-6214), on the waterfront next to the Federal building, has info on Ketchikan and the entire Panhandle, especially good on the outdoors (open May-Sept. daily 8:30am-4:30pm; Oct.-April Tues.-Sat. 8:30am-4:30pm). The **Ketchikan Visitors Bureau,** 131 Front St. (225-6166 or 800-770-3300), is on the cruise ship docks (open May-Sept. daily 7am-5pm; limited winter hours). **Alaska Marine Highway** (225-6181) ferries dock north of town on N. Tongass Hwy. A ferry runs from the **airport** to just above the state ferry dock every 15min. summer, every 30min. otherwise ($2.50). **Alaska Airlines** (225-2145 or 800-426-0333), in the mall on Tongass Ave., has flight info from Ketchikan. Daily flights to Juneau are $124 (open Mon.-Fri. 9:30am-5pm). The **post office** (225-9601) is next to the ferry terminal (open Mon.-Fri. 8:30am-5pm); **General Delivery ZIP Code:** 99901. **Area Code:** 907.

Accommodations, Camping, and Food Besides hostels, rooms here are expensive. The **Ketchikan Reservation Service** (225-3273) provides info on B&Bs (singles from $50-75). **Ketchikan Youth Hostel (HI-AYH),** (225-3319) at Main and Grant St. in the basement of the First Methodist Church, has no beds, although foam mats on the floor are reasonably comfortable if you have a sleeping bag. Clean kitchen, common area, two showers, tea and coffee. (Strict lockout 9am-6pm. Lights out at 10:30pm, on at 7am. Curfew 11pm. Call ahead if arriving on a late ferry. 3-day max. stay subject to availability. Open June 1-Sept. 1. $8, nonmembers $11. Reservations advisable.) SEAVC (228-6214) provides info and reservations for Forest Service campgrounds, including **Signal Creek Campground,** 6 mi. north of the ferry terminal

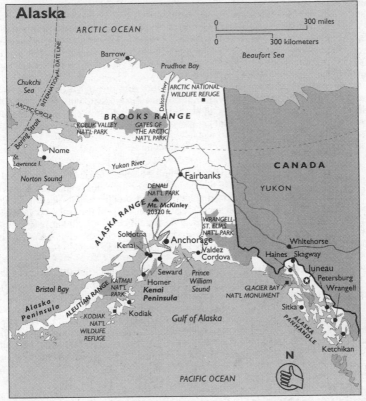

Alaska

ARCTIC OCEAN

0   300 miles

0   300 kilometers

Beaufort Sea

Barrow

Prudhoe Bay

Chukchi
Sea

ARCTIC NATIONAL
WILDLIFE REFUGE

BROOKS RANGE

KOBUK VALLEY
NAT'L PARK

GATES OF
THE ARCTIC
NAT'L PARK

Dalton Hwy

Nome

Yukon River

CANADA

St.
Lawrence I.

Norton Sound

DENALI
NAT'L PARK

Fairbanks

YUKON

Mt. McKinley
20320 ft.

Soldotna

WRANGELL-
ST. ELIAS
NAT'L PARK

Kenai

Anchorage

Valdez
Cordova

Whitehorse

Haines   Skagway

Bristol Bay

KATMAI
NAT'L
PARK

Seward

Homer

Prince
William
Sound

GLACIER BAY
NAT'L MONUMENT

Juneau

Petersburg

Wrangell

Kenai
Peninsula

Sitka

Alaska
Peninsula

KODIAK
NAT'L
WILDLIFE
REFUGE

Kodiak

Gulf of Alaska

Ketchikan

N

PACIFIC OCEAN

ALASKA

on Tongass Hwy., which features attractive views and pleasant nature trails (water; pit toilets; $8).

The supermarket most convenient to downtown is **Tatsuda's,** 633 Stedman, at Deermount St., just beyond the Thomas Basin (225-4125; open daily 7am-11pm). The **5 Star Café,** 5 Creek St. (247-7827), serves a daily soup for $2.50 and delicious scones for $2 (open Mon.-Sat. 7:30am-5:30pm, Sun. 9am-5pm).

Sights and the Outdoors   When you say "Ketchikan" you might as well say "totems galore." The **Saxman Native Village,** 2½ mi. southwest of Ketchikan on Tongass Hwy ($8 by cab), is the largest totem park in Alaska. The village has a traditional house, dancers, and an open studio where artisans carve new totems (open weekdays 9am-5pm and on weekends when a cruise ship is in).

The **Totem Heritage Center,** 601 Deermount St. (225-5900), houses 33 well-preserved totem poles from Tlingit, Haida, and Tsimshian villages. It is the largest collection of authentic, pre-commercial totem poles in the U.S. Only a handful are on display ($3, under 13 free, Sun. afternoon free; open daily 8am-5pm). Across the creek, at the **Deer Mountain Fish Hatchery** (225-6760), a self-guided tour explains artificial sex, salmon style (open daily 8am-4:30pm).

While most of "historic downtown" is unremarkable, the colorful stretch of houses perched on stilts along **Creek Street** is worth a look. This picturesque area was once a thriving red-light district where, as tour guides quip, sailors and salmon went upstream to spawn. Women in black fishnets and red-tasseled silk still beckon passersby into **Dolly's House,** 24 Creek St. (225-6329), a brothel turned museum. Antiques are set amid secret hideaways where Dolly kept money, bootleg liquor, and respectable customers during police raids. Hours vary with cruise ship arrivals; typically open 'til 2:30 or 4:30pm. Call ahead ($3).

A good dayhike from Ketchikan is 3001-ft. **Deer Mountain.** Walk up the hill past the city park on Fair St.; the marked trailhead branches off to the left just behind the dump. A steep but manageable ascent leads 2½ mi. up the mountain. The trail then runs above treeline along a steep ridge. At the peak, clear skies open upon a mountain-and-lake vista extending into Misty Fjords.

Many of the boats and planes continually buzzing through Ketchikan's harbor travel to nearby **Misty Fiords National Monument.** Only 20 mi. from Ketchikan, this region of narrow waterways and old-growth forests, home to both whales and mountain goats, invites hikers and kayakers to play in a huge, rugged wilderness.

■ Juneau

In October 1880, in a move he probably regretted later, Tlingit Chief Kowee led Joe Juneau and Richard Harris to the gleaming "mother lode" in the hills up from Gold Creek. The next summer would bring boatloads of prospectors to dig in the mines. Juneau today is one of the most spectacular capital cities in the United States. Victorian mansions crowd against log cabins, and state office buildings compete for space with frame houses. Monolithic Mt. Juneau looms large over the city. Accessible only by water and air, Juneau retains its small-town friendliness.

Practical Information   **Davis Log Cabin,** 134 3rd St. (586-2201 or 586-2284), at Seward St., is a visitors center (open Mon.-Fri. 8:30am-5pm, Sat.-Sun. 9am-5pm; Oct.-May Mon.-Fri. 8:30am-5pm). **National Forest and National Park Services,** 101 Egan Dr. (586-8751), at Willoughby, in Centennial Hall, provides info on, and reservations for, Forest Service **cabins** in **Tongass National Forest. Juneau International Airport,** 9 mi. north of Juneau on Glacier Hwy., is served by Alaska Air, Delta Airlines, and local charters. **Alaska Marine Highway,** 1591 Glacier Ave. (800-642-0066 or 465-3941; fax 277-4829) docks at the Auke Bay terminal 14 mi. from the city on the Glacier Hwy. To: Bellingham, WA ($226), Ketchikan ($74), Sitka ($26), and Haines ($20). Lockers (25¢ for 48hr.) are limited and fill quickly. The **post office's main office** is at 709 W. 9th St. (586-7987; open Mon.-Fri. 9am-5pm, Sat. 6am-3pm for parcel pick-up only.) **ZIP Code:** 99801. **Area code:** 907.

Accommodations, Camping, and Food   Two words: phone ahead. The **Alaska Bed and Breakfast Association,** P.O. Box 3/6500 #169, Juneau 99802 (586-2959), can help you find a room downtown from $65.

Juneau International Hostel (HI-AYH), 614 Harris St. (586-9559), at 6th atop a steep hill, is a beautiful facility in a prime location with an astoundingly rigid management. (Laundry facilities. Lockout 9am-5pm. Non-negotiable 11pm curfew. All 48 beds $10. Frequently fills; make reservations with a $10 deposit mailed in advance. No phone reservations. 3-day max. stay if they're full.) **Inn at the Waterfront,** 455 S. Franklin (586-2050), over the Summit Restaurant, was once a Gold Rush brothel and now has 14 clean, comfortable rooms (a few shared baths; singles $51, doubles $60. Breakfast included). If you're outdoorsing it, try **Mendenhall Lake Campground,** on Montana Creek Rd. Take Glacier Hwy. north 9 mi. to Mendenhall Loop Rd.; continue 3½ mi. and take the right fork. If asked, bus driver will let you off within walking distance (2 mi.) of camp. (60 sites. Fireplaces, water, pit toilet, picnic tables, free firewood. 14-day max. stay. Sites $8, Golden Age $4. Reserve for an extra $7.50 by calling 800-280-CAMP/2267.)

Armadillo Tex-Mex Café, 431 S. Franklin St. (586-1880), dishes out fantastic food to locals and tourists alike (open Mon.-Sat. 11am-10pm, Sun. 4-10pm). For a $5.50 breakfast feast of heavily embellished pancakes, make for the **Channel Bowl Café** (586-6139), across from Juneau A&P on Willoughby Ave. (open daily 7am-2pm). The **Thane Ore House Salmon Bake,** 4400 Thane Rd. (586-3442), is a few mi. outside of town, but "Mr. Ore" will pick you up at your hotel. All-you-can-eat salmon, halibut, ribs, and fixings are $18.50 (open May-Sept. daily 11:30am-9pm).

Sights The **Alaska State Museum,** 395 Whittier St. (465-2901), leads you through the history, ecology, and culture of Alaska's four major indigenous groups (Tlingit, Athabascan, Aleut, and Inuit) with excellent exhibits. The museum also houses the famous "First White Man" totem pole, a carved likeness of Abraham Lincoln. ($3, seniors and students free; open Mon.-Fri. 9am-6pm, Sat.-Sun. 10am-6pm; Sept. 18-May 17 Tues.-Sat. 10am-4pm.) The hexagonal, onion-domed **St. Nicholas Russian Orthodox Church,** on 5th St. between N. Franklin and Gold St. holds rows of icons and a glorious altar. Services, held Saturday at 6am and Sunday at 10am, are conducted in English, Old Slavonic, and Tlingit. Tours are open to the public ($1 donation requested; open daily 9am-5pm).

The **Alaska Brewing Co.,** 5429 Shaune Dr. (780-5866), offers free tours complete with a free sample of its excellent award-winning brews. To reach the brewery, take the hourly city bus to Lemon Creek, turn onto Anka Rd. from the Glacier Hwy., and Shaune Dr. is the first on the right. (Tours on the ½-hr. Tues.-Sat. 11am-4:30pm; Oct.-April Thurs.-Sat. 11am-4:30pm.)

Juneau is a prime hiking center in southeast Alaska. If you're looking for the best view of Juneau, go to the end of 6th St. and head up the steep, 4-mi. trail to the summit of **Mt. Roberts** (3576 ft.). The recent addition of a **tramway** means that you'll have to deal with many who didn't sweat for the view. The trams run every half hour from a terminal on the cruise ship dock (463-3412; $16).

The 38 glaciers of the **Juneau Icefield** cover an area larger than Rhode Island. The most visited glacier is the **Mendenhall Glacier,** about 10 mi. north of downtown Juneau. The 9½-mi. **Montana Creek Trail,** near Mendenhall Glacier, is a local favorite. So is the **Perseverance Trail,** which starts at the end of Basin Rd. and leads to the ruins of the Silverbowl Basin Mine and booming waterfalls.

The slopes of the **Eaglecrest Ski Area,** 155 S. Seward St., Juneau 99801 (586-5284 or 586-5330), on Douglas Island, offer alpine skiing in winter ($24 per day, children grades 7-12 $17, up to 6th grade $12; full equipment rental $20, children $14). Boat tours of **Tracy Arm** are well worth the money (about $100). **Temsco Helicopters,** Juneau Airport (789-9501), offers a one-hour flight to the Mendenhall Glacier, including a one and a half-hour glacier landing ($142 per person).

▓ Wrangell-St. Elias National Park

The **largest national park in the U.S.,** Wrangell-St. Elias is so vast that the 22 largest National Parks from the lower 48 states could all fit within its boundaries (Yellowstone, Glacier, Grand Canyon, Grand Teton, Yosemite, Everglades…). Nine peaks tower more than 14,000 ft. within the park, including the second highest mountain in the U.S. (18,008 ft. **Mt. St. Elias**). If you have any time at all to spend in Alaska, spend it here; even among its vast and pristine park brethren, Wrangell-St. Elias stands out because it is little known and uncrowded, features spectacular wilderness and wildlife, and can be enjoyed on a tight budget.

Two roads provide park access: the **McCarthy Rd.** and the **Nabesna Rd.,** which enters from the northern park boundaries. The **visitors center** (822-5234) is 1 mi. off Richardson Hwy. Mile 105.1 on the side road toward **Copper Center** (open in summer daily 8am-6pm; winter Mon.-Fri. 8am-5pm). There are also **ranger stations** in **Chitina** (CHIT-na; 823-2205; open daily 10am-6pm) and in **Slana** on the northern park boundary (822-5238; open daily 8am-5pm).

Outdoors Most travelers head into the park via the Edgerton Hwy., eventually arriving in **McCarthy.** To reach McCarthy, the hub of the park, and its sister town **Kennicott,** turn onto the Edgerton Hwy. at its junction with the Richardson Hwy. (33mi. south of Glenallen) and follow the Edgerton east. After 33 mi. of blessed pavement you'll reach **Chitina,** a sleepy town with a single café, the **It'll Do Café** (open daily 6am-10pm), a general store (823-2111; open daily 7am-8pm), and a ranger station (see above). From Chitina, the **McCarthy Road**—arguably the roughest road in Alaska—follows the old roadbed of the **Copper River and Northwestern Railway** for 58 mi. to the Kennicott River. The only way across the raging river is by a hand-operated **tram** (a metal "cart" with two seats, running on a cable). McCarthy is an easy ½-mi. walk from the opposite side of the river. **Backcountry Connections** (822-5292 or 800-478-5292 in Alaska) offers a car-sparing McCarthy shuttle ($49 one way, $70-88 roundtrip; $35 one way from Chitina, $60-70 roundtrip). Vans depart Monday through Saturday from Glenallen (7am) and Chitina (8am), depart from McCarthy (4pm), then go back through to Chitina (7:30pm) and Glenallen (8:30pm). **Wrangell Mountain Air** (see below) flies to McCarthy daily from Chitina for those who would rather not tackle the highway ($60 each way).

Rooms at the **McCarthy Lodge** (554-4402), in downtown McCarthy, are expensive ($95 single, $105 double). **Camping** is $10 in the lot just west of the river (before you cross to go to McCarthy) and free at the lot half a mile farther back toward Chitina (pit toilets, no water). Camping is prohibited in all areas on the eastern side of the Kennicott River except on land north of Kennicott.

If you go **flightseeing** anywhere in Alaska, do it here. On **Wrangell Mountain Air** (800-478-1160 for reservations), based in downtown McCarthy, flights come with a variety of destinations, durations, and prices ($40-100). **McCarthy Air** (800-245-6909), also in McCarthy, offers comparable flights and rates. The two companies are very competitive, so make sure to compare rates before you sign on.

Mountain biking is an excellent way to explore the area. At **St. Elias Alpine Guides** (277-6867) you can rent bikes ($30 per day, $35 with shocks) and take the Old Wagon Trail to Kennicott (5 mi.), then continue on a trail that takes you alongside Root Glacier and within view of the Erie Mine (4 more mi.). **Copper Oar** (522-1670), at the end of the McCarthy Rd., offers a two-hour whitewater trip down the Kennicott River for $45.

Most **hikers and trekkers** use the McCarthy Road or McCarthy as a base. The park maintains no trails, but miners and other travelers from decades past have established various routes and obscure roads that follow the more exciting pathways. The most common route, a 16-mi. hike out past Kennicott to the Root Glacier, follows road-bed and glacial moraine with three moderate stream crossings and makes a long daytrip or an easy two-day hike. For any overnight trip, the park service requests a written itinerary; though it's not required, it's in your best interest.

■ Anchorage

Only 80 years ago, cartographers wasted no ink on the modest tent city that is now Alaska's foremost metropolis. Approximately half the state's population, about 250,000 people, lives in the unflatteringly nicknamed "Los Anchorage." The city achieved its comparatively monstrous size by serving as the headquarters of three economic "projects": the railroad, the war, and the pipeline. Anchorage doesn't stand a chance against her physically stunning sister cities. While the wilderness occasionally encroaches on the city, it cannot save Anchorage from being, in the end, an eyesore with a bad rap.

Practical Information   The **Log Cabin Visitor Information Center,** W. 4th Ave. (274-3531), at F St., dispenses lots of maps, including the 25¢ **Bike Trails** guide (open June-Aug. daily 7:30am-7pm; May and Sept. 8am-6pm; Oct.-April 9am-4pm). The **Anchorage International Airport** (266-2525) is serviced by 8 international and 15 domestic carriers, including **Delta** (249-2110 or 800-221-1212), **Northwest Airlines** (266-5636 or 800-225-2525), **United** (800-241-6522), and **Alaska Airlines** (800-426-0333). Nearly every airport in Alaska can be reached from Anchorage, either directly or through a connecting flight in Fairbanks. **Alaska Railroad,** 411 W. 1st Ave. (265-2494, 800-544-0552 out of state), runs to Denali ($95), Fairbanks ($135), and Seward ($50). In winter, 1 per week to Fairbanks; no service to Seward. For more info write to Passenger Service, P.O. Box 107500, Anchorage. (Ticket window open Mon.-Fri. 5:30am-5:30pm, Sat.-Sun. 5:30am-1:30pm.) **Alaskon Express** (800-544-2206) sends buses daily to Seward ($39), Valdez ($65), and Portage train station ($29), and every other day to Haines ($185) and Skagway ($205). **Homer Stage Lines** (272-8644) rolls to Homer ($45) Mon., Wed., and Fri. **Alaska Direct** (277-6652) connects to Whitehorse, YT (3 per week, $145).

  Alaska Marine Highway, 333 W. 4th St. (272-7116), in the Post Office Mall, has no terminal, but ferry tickets and reservations (open Mon.-Fri. 8am-4:30pm). **Affordable Car Rental,** 4707 Spenard Rd. (243-3370), across from the Regal Alaskan Hotel, charges $35 per day with unlimited mi. You must be at least 21 with a major credit card. The **hospital** is located at 2801 DeBarr Ave. (264-1224). Call 911 in an **emergency** or 786-8400 for the **police**. The **post office** (279-3062), W. 4th Ave. and C St. on the lower level in the mall, is open Mon.-Fri. 10am-5:30pm, Sat. 10am-4pm. **General Delivery ZIP Code:** 99510. The **area code** is 907.

  The **downtown area** of Anchorage is laid out in a grid. Numbered avenues run east-west, and addresses are designated East or West from **C Street.** North-south streets are lettered alphabetically west of **A Street,** and named alphabetically east of A Street. The rest of Anchorage spreads out along the major highways. The **University of Alaska Anchorage** campus lies on 36th Ave., off Northern Lights Blvd.

Accommodations, Camping, and Food

Both **Alaska Private Lodgings,** 1010 W. 10th Ave. (258-1717), and **Stay With a Friend,** 3605 Arctic Blvd. #173 (278-8800), can refer you to B&Bs. **Anchorage International Youth Hostel (HI-AYH),** 700 H St. (276-3635), at 7th, has a fantastic location on the edge of downtown. (Write or call at least a day ahead for reservations. Wheelchair accessible. Lockout noon-5pm. Curfew 1am; check-in til 3am. 3-night max. in summer. Pay by 11am. $15, nonmembers $18; photo ID required.) The spacious, friendly **Spenard Hostel,** 2845 W. 42nd Pl. (248-5036), provides an ideal departure point for the airport. Take bus #7 or 36 out Spenard to Turnagain Blvd. 42nd Pl. is the 1st left from Turnagain. (3 kitchens, free local phone calls, common rooms with TV, bike rental, no curfew, no lockout. Chore requested. 6-day max. Beds $12.)

  Excellent camping opportunities await in nearby **Chugach State Park** (354-5014); two of the best areas are **Eagle River** (688-0998; $15) and **Eklutna** (EE-kloot-nah; 694-2108; $10), respectively 12.6 mi. and 26½ mi. northeast of Anchorage along Glenn Hwy. **Centennial Park,** 5300 Glenn Hwy. (333-9711), is north of town off Muldoon Rd.; look for the park sign. Take bus #3 or 75 from downtown. (90 sites for tents and RVs. Showers, pay phones, and water. 7-day max. Noon check-out. Sites $13, Alaskans or Golden Age $11. Open May 1-Sept. 30.) **John's Motel and RV Park,** 3543 Mt. View Dr. (277-4332), is only 2 mi. from downtown (50 RV sites; full hookups $20).

  Being the large city that it is, Anchorage presents budget travelers with the most affordable and varied culinary fare in the state. Check out **Twin Dragon,** 612 E. 15th Ave. (276-7535), near Gambell, for one of the town's finest treats: a lunch buffet of marinated meats and vegetables, lightly barbecued on a giant, circular grill ($6.25). This new spot has become a favorite among Anchorage's knowledgeable diners (open daily 11am-midnight). Or try **Maharaja's,** 328 G St. (272-2233) between 3rd and 4th Ave., where the spicy lunch buffet ($8) provides a feast for all senses. Dinner is served Sun.-Thurs. 5:30-9:30pm, Fri.-Sat. 5:30-10pm. At **Blondie's Café** (279-0698), at the corner of 4th and D St., the all-day breakfast includes 3 hotcakes for $4.25 (open daily 5am-midnight).

Sights and Activities

Close to town off Northern Lights Blvd., **Earthquake Park** recalls the 1964 Good Friday earthquake. The quake was the strongest ever recorded in North America, registering 9.2 on the Richter scale. You can walk, skate, or bike to the **Tony Knowles Coastal Trail,** an 11-mi. paved track that skirts Cook Inlet on one side and the backyards of Anchorage's upper-crust on the other.

  The **Anchorage Museum of History and Art,** 121 W. 7th Ave. (343-6173), at A St., features permanent exhibits of Native Alaskan artifacts and art, as well as national and

ALASKA

international art exhibits. A traditional dance series runs three times per day in summer ($4), and a summer film series shows at no extra cost. ($5, seniors $4.50, under 18 free; open daily May 15-Sept. 15 9am-6pm; Sept. 16-May 14 Tues.-Sat. 10am-6pm, Sun. 1-5pm.) The **Alaska Aviation Heritage Museum,** 4721 Aircraft Dr. (248-5325), provides a fun look at Alaska's pioneer aviators. Take bus #6 to the airport; the museum in summer is within easy walking distance ($5.75, seniors $4.50, youths $2.75; open daily 9am-6pm, winter Tues.-Sat. 10am-4pm). Trek to the **Alaska Experience Theater,** 705 W. 6th Ave. (276-3730), to vicariously experience 40 minutes of Alaskan adventures on the inner surface of a hemispherical dome ($7, children $4; every hr. 9am-9pm).

Railway Brewing Company (277-1996), in the railroad depot on 421 W. 1st., offers six tasty creations at affordable prices (pints $3.25, 6-beer sampler $4.50). The popular **Glacier Brewhouse,** 737 W. 5th (274-BREW/2739), pours a smaller selection of more expensive brews (pints $4) in a mammoth restaurant. The food is even pricier (nachos $7). Anchorage's leading gay and lesbian bar is the **Blue Moon,** 530 E. 5th Ave. (277-0441), near the Sheraton (bar open Mon.-Thurs. 1pm-2am, Fri. 1pm-3am, Sat. 3pm-3am, Sun. 3pm-2am). In midtown, Alaskans party at **Chilkoot Charlie's,** 2435 Spenard Rd. (272-1010), at Fireweed. Take bus #7 or 60. Six bars fill this huge space, in addition to a rockin' dance floor and a quiet lounge (open Mon.-Thurs. 10am-2:30am, Fri.-Sat. 10am-3am, Sun. noon-2:30am). Less overwhelming and more intriguing is **Mr. Whitekey's Fly-by-Night Club,** 3300 Spenard Rd. (279-SPAM/7726). The house special promises you anything with Spam at half-price when you order champagne, free with Dom Perignon (bar open Tues.-Sat. 4pm-2:30am).

Climb 2 mi. to the summit of **Flattop Mountain** near Anchorage. To reach the trailhead, hop on bus #92 to the intersection of Hillside Rd. and Upper Huffman Rd. From there walk ¾ mi. along Upper Huffman Rd., then go right on Toilsome Hill Dr. for 2 mi. Trail signs at the park entrance point the way up the 4,500-ft. mountain.

A cornucopia of less crowded trails branch from the **Powerline Trail,** which is accessible from the same parking lot as Flattop Trail. The **Middle Fork Loop** provides a 7½-mi. roundtrip to **Little O'Malley Peak,** a taller cousin of Flattop with similarly splendid views and considerably fewer hikers.

The Iditarod: A Pretty Long Race

And you thought walking to school in winter was rough. For the first three weeks of March each year, dog mushers race their teams 1100 mi. from Anchorage to Nome in the **Iditarod Trail Sled Dog Race.** The trail, made famous in 1925 when mushers ferried life-saving diphtheria serum to stave off an epidemic in Nome, crosses two mountain ranges, the Yukon River, and the frozen Bering Sea. The race, once a **rollicking good time Alaska-style,** has come under fire in recent years by animal-rights activists because of the hardships suffered by sled dogs, some of which inevitably die en route to Nome. Still, the city turns out in force for the ceremonial start of the race in Anchorage on March 3. (Just outside town, the teams are unceremoniously loaded onto trucks and ferried to the actual starting line.) For more information, contact the Iditarod Trail Committee, P.O. Box 870800, Wasilla, AK 99687 (376-5155).

■ Denali

Established in 1917 to protect wildlife, **Denali National Park** is also the home of Denali (Athabascan for "The Great One"), the tallest mountain in North America. Also known as **Mt. McKinley,** Denali boasts the greatest vertical relief in the world from base to summit; even mighty Mt. Everest rises only 10,000 ft. from its base on the Tibetan Plateau. Denali's 18,000 ft. of rock and ice scrape toward the sky with hardly a hill intervening. The peak's top is visible only for about 20% of the summer, but even if you can't see the peak, you can still experience the park's tundra, taiga, and wildlife.

Practical Information The Park **entrance fee** is $3, families $5. All travelers stop at the **Denali Visitor Center** (683-1266), 0.7 mi. from Rte. 3 for orientation. It is also headquarters of the **shuttle-bus** (see below). Also at the center are **maps**, shuttle-bus schedules, free permits for backcountry camping, and the indispensable publication *Alpenglow* (free). (Center open summer daily 7am-8pm. Lockers 50¢.)

Only the first 14 mi. of the park road is accessible by private vehicle; the remaining 71 mi. of dirt road can be reached only by a bus. **Shuttle buses** leave the visitors center daily (5:30am-2:30pm). Go for the less frequent, 11-hour roundtrip Wonder Lake bus if you can, as the best views of Denali are beyond Eielson. Some shuttle bus tickets may be reserved in advance (800-622-7275), but more are available each day on a first come, first served basis. **Camper buses** ($15) move faster, transporting *only* people with **campground permits** and **backcountry permits.** However, camper buses will stop to pick up dayhikers along the road. Camper buses leave the visitors center five times daily. The final bus stays overnight at Wonder Lake and returns at 7am. You can get on and off these buses **anywhere along the road;** flag the next one down when you want to move on or back. This is a good strategy for dayhiking and convenient for Park explorers.

Eielson Visitors Center, 66 mi. into the park, is staffed by helpful rangers and is accessible by shuttle bus (open summer daily 9am-dusk). For info write to **Denali National Park and Preserve,** P.O. Box 9, Denali Park, AK 99755 (683-1266).

Denali National Park can be easily reached by air, road, or rail. The best place to catch a flightseeing tour is **Talkeetna.** The **George Parks Hwy.** (Rte. 3) connects Anchorage (240 mi. south of Denali) and Fairbanks (120 mi. north), and offers direct access to the Denali Park Rd. Several bus companies have service connecting Denali with Anchorage and Fairbanks. **Parks Highway Express** (479-3065) charges $20 per person from Anchorage or Fairbanks to Denali. **Moon Bay Express** (274-6454) has one bus daily to Anchorage ($35, $60 roundtrip). **Fireweed Express** (452-0251) provides daily van service to Fairbanks ($25). The **Alaska Railroad,** P.O. Box 107500, Anchorage 99510 (683-2233, out of state 800-544-0552), makes stops at Denali station 1½ mi. from the entrance.

In an **emergency** call 683-9100. Denali's **post office:** (683-2291), next to the Denali Hotel, 1 mi. from the visitors center (open Mon.-Fri. 8:30am-5pm, Sat. 10am-1pm; Oct.-May Mon.-Sat. 10am-1pm). **ZIP code:** 99755. **Area code:** 907.

Accommodations, Camping, and Food The **Denali Hostel,** (683-1295) is 9.6 mi. north of the park entrance. Take a left on Otto Lake Rd.; it's the second house on the right about 1.3 mi. down. They offer bunks, showers, kitchen facilities, and morning shuttles into and out of the park (beds $22). Seven **campgrounds** within the park line Denali Park Rd. Most have water and some form of toilet (sites $6-12). You must have a permit to camp inside the park. 40% of the sites at 4 of the park's 7 campgrounds can be reserved in advance by calling 800-622-7275 or 272-7275; the remainder are issued daily on a first come, first served basis—arrive early. Hikers waiting for a backcountry permit or a campsite can find space in **Morino Campground** ($6), next to the hotel.

Food in Denali is expensive. Try to bring groceries into the park with you. Meager provisions in the park are available at **Mercantile Gas and Groceries,** 1½ mi. along Denali Park Rd. (683-2215; open daily 7am-10pm). The **Lynx Creek Grocery** (683-2548) has similarly priced items 1 mi. north of the park entrance and is open 24 hr. **Lynx Creek Pizza** (683-2547), 1 mi. north of the park entrance, has imposing Italian and Mexican favorites ($7-8.25) and good pizza (open daily 11am-11pm).

Exploring the Backcountry Denali National Park has no trails, and is not a park that can be covered in one day. Although dayhiking is unlimited, only two-twelve hikers can camp at one time in each of the park's 43 units. Select a few different areas in the park in case your first choice is booked. The first third of the park is taiga forest and tundra which is hellish to hike—imagine walking on old wet mattresses with bushes growing out of them. The last third of the park is infested with mosquitoes in July and biting "no-see-ums" in August. The prime hiking and back-country camping spots are in the middle third. Rangers at the backcountry desk will not give recommendations for specific areas—they want to disperse hikers as widely as possible. No matter where you camp, keep within the zone for which you signed up. To keep from getting lost, pick up **topographic maps** ($2.50) at the visitors center. Before you leave the visitors center, rangers will give you a short introduction to bear management, and you must watch five brief **backcountry simulator programs.** Most zones require that you carry a black, cylindrical **bear-resistant food container,** available free at the backcountry desk.

■ Alaska Highway

Built during World War II, the Alaska Highway maps out an astonishing 2647km route between Dawson Creek, BC, and Fairbanks, AK. After the Japanese attack on Pearl Harbor in December 1941, worried War Department officials planned an over-land route, out of range of carrier-based aircraft, to supply U.S. Army bases in Alaska. The U.S. Army Corps of Engineers completed the daunting task in just 34 weeks.

In recent years, the U.S. Army has been replaced by an annual army of over 250,000 tourists, most of them RV-borne senior citizens from the U.S. In July, the busiest month, travelers will face crowded campgrounds and nearly impassable RV caravans. If you're willing to take the time, there are countless hiking, fishing, and wildlife viewing opportunities off the highway. If your priority is to beat the quickest path to the Alaska border, however, you're best off taking an alternate route.

Before setting out on your epic Northwestern journey, pick up a copy of the free pamphlet *Help Along the Way* at a visitors bureau, or contact the Department of Health and Social Services, P.O. Box 110601, Juneau, AK 99811-0601 (907-465-3030); the pamphlet includes an exhaustive listing of emergency medical services and emer-gency phone numbers throughout Alaska, the Yukon, and British Columbia, plus tips on preparation and driving. Mileposts along the highway were put up in the 1940s and are still used as mailing addresses and reference points, although the highway has been reconstructed and rerouted so many times that they no longer reflect mileage accurately. Kilometer posts were installed in the mid-1970s and recalibrated in 1990; the distances they report are more accurate.

■ Fairbanks

Fairbanks' university, its omnipresent tourism industry, and its endless strip malls can't hide the rough-and-ready flavor of this frontier town poised on the arctic. Men noticeably outnumber women, the streets are filled with 4WD steeds, and any of the roads leading out of town will take you to utter wilderness in minutes. Through frigid winters and swarms of vicious hybrid mosquitoes, Fairbanks residents persevere and enjoy everything from Shakespeare in the Park to moose hunting.

Practical Information Convention and Visitors Bureau Log Cabin, 550 1st Ave., Fairbanks 99701 (456-5774 or 800-327-5774), distributes the free Visitor's Guide and offers free local calls (open daily 8am-8pm; Labor Day-Memorial Day Mon.-Fri. 8am-5pm). **Alaska Public Lands Information Center (APLIC),** 250 Cushman St. #1A, Fairbanks 99707 (456-0527), has exhibits and info on different parks and pro-tected areas of Alaska (open daily 9am-6pm; in winter Tues.-Sat. 10am-6pm). Fair-banks is also home to the headquarters of the **Gates of the Arctic National Park,** 201 1st Ave. (456-0281; open Mon.-Fri. 8am-5pm) and the **Arctic National Wildlife Ref-uge,** 101 12th Ave., Room 266 (456-0250), in the U.S. District Court Building (open Mon.-Fri. 8am-4:30pm). The **airport,** 5mi. from downtown on Airport Way, is served by: **Delta** (800-221-1212), to the lower 48; **Alaska Air** (452-1661), to Anchorage ($39) and Juneau ($268); and **Frontier Flyer Services** (474-0014), to smaller Bush towns such as Bettles ($113). **Alaska Railroad,** 280 N. Cushman St. (456-4155), next to the *Daily News-Miner* building, runs one train daily from mid-May to mid-Sept. to

Nenana ($36), Anchorage ($135), and Denali National Park ($50; depot open Mon.-Fri. 7:30am-4:30pm, Sat.-Sun. 7:30am-noon). **Parks Highway Express** (479-3065) runs 6 buses per week to Denali ($20, roundtrip $40) and Anchorage ($40, roundtrip $75). The **Municipal Commuter Area Service (MACS)** (459-1011), at 6th and Cushman St., runs two routes through downtown and the surrounding area. ($1.50; seniors, high school students, and disabled 75¢; under 5 free. Day pass $3. Transfers good within 1hr. of stamped time.) In an **emergency**, call 911. The **post office** at 315 Barnette St. (452-3203) is open Mon.-Fri. 9am-6pm, Sat. 10am-2pm (**General Delivery ZIP Code:** 99707). **Area code:** 907.

Anchorage is 358 mi. south via the **George Parks Hwy.**, and Prudhoe Bay is 480 mi. down dangerous, gravelly **Dalton Hwy.** Delta Junction is 97 mi. southeast of Fairbanks on the **Richardson (Alaska) Hwy.** Most tourist destinations lie on one of four thoroughfares: **Airport Way, College Rd., Cushman Blvd.,** and **University Way.** The city center lies in the vicinity of South Cushman, north of Airport Way.

Accommodations, Camping, and Food

For info on bed and breakfasts, go to the visitors bureau, or call or write **Fairbanks B&B,** 902 Kellum St., Anchorage (452-4967). **Grandma Shirley's Hostel,** 510 Dunbar St. (451-9816), beats out all other hostels to earn the title of überhostel of Fairbanks. Take the Steese Expressway to Trainor Gate Rd., go right and follow to E St., take a left, and finally right onto Dunbar St. (showers, common room, free bike use; coed room with 9 beds, $15). **Alaska Heritage Inn Youth Hostel (AAIH),** 1018 22nd Ave. (451-6587), sports a common room with TV and a picnic area (15 beds; $12, non-members $15, $3 linen charge first night).**Tanana Valley Campground,** 1800 College Rd. (456-7956), is somewhat noisy, but grassy and secluded for its in-town location (5 spots with power hookup available; sites $12; tentsites for travelers on foot $6). With two or more people, **Chena River State Campground,** off of Airport way on University Ave., is worth the $15 per night fee.

For an artery-blocking good time, look no further than Airport Way or College Rd. For healthier fare, try **Souvlaki,** 112 N. Turner (452-5393), across the bridge from the visitors center. Succulent stuffed grape leaves are 3 for $1.15, salad in a pita is $3, and they do take-out (open Mon.-Fri. 10am-9pm, Sat. 10am-6pm; in winter Mon.-Sat. 10am-6pm). The superb, family-run **Gambardella Pasta Bella,** 706 2nd Ave. (456-3417), offers subs from $4 and excellent eggplant parmesan or pasta à la carte for $6.50 on the lunch menu (open daily 11am-5pm and 5:30-10pm).

Sights and Entertainment

One of Fairbanks's proudest institutions and main attractions is the **University of Alaska-Fairbanks (UAF),** at the top of a hill overlooking the flat cityscape. The **University of Alaska Museum** (474-7505), a ten-minute walk up Yukon Dr., features exhibits ranging from displays on the aurora borealis to a 36,000 year-old bison recovered from the permafrost. ($5, seniors $4.50, 13-18 $3, families $12.50. Open daily 9am-7pm; May and Sept. 9am-5pm; Oct.-April noon-5pm.) Weekdays at 10am, the university offers free, two-hour tours of the campus beginning in front of the museum. The **Large Animal Research Station** is also worth a visit, and its tours offer a chance to see baby musk ox and other animals up close. (Tours Tues. and Sat. at 11am and 1:30pm, and on Thurs. at 1:30pm only. $5, seniors $4, students $2, families $10.) You can also grab your binoculars and view the big beasts from the viewing stand on Yankovitch Rd.

Well worth the 9 mi. trip north along the Steese Hwy., **Gold Dredge #8** is only $10 for a day of panning. Not only do you have a good chance of earning your money back in gold, but fossilized fragments of mammoths and mastodons abound.

UAF students and everyone else head for the legendary **Howling Dog Saloon** (457-8780), 11½ mi. down Steese Hwy., at the intersection of the Old and New Steese Highways, for live rock-and-roll. Look for a colorful wooden structure in the middle of nowhere encircled by pickup trucks (open May-Oct. daily 9pm-5am).

ALASKA

HAWAI'I

Hawai'i, 2400 miles off mainland America, is the most geographically isolated place in the world. This unique position has made Hawai'i a place apart, both in landscape and lifestyle. Here, as nowhere else, you will find lush vegetation, seemingly endless beaches, towering surf, and sultry breezes that keep the weather wonderful year-round. Acres of untainted tropical forest border luxurious resort areas and bustling urban enclaves. Meanwhile, active volcanoes fill the horizon and release billows of grey ash into the air. If it sounds Elysian, that's because it *is*.

The state's cultural geography is as varied as that of the land. Hawai'i is one of the most ethnically diverse regions in the world. The state serves as a bridge between East and West as well as North and South, and as a remarkably vital nexus of Asian and Western influences with the native Polynesian culture. This diverse ethnic heritage expresses itself in the arts, literature, and cuisine of Hawai'i's residents.

132 islands comprise the Hawaiian chain, though only seven are inhabited. Honolulu, the cosmopolitan capital, resides on the island of **O'ahu**, as do most of the state's residents and tourists. The **Big Island** (officially called Hawai'i) is famed for its Kona coffee, macadamia nuts, volcanoes, and black sand beaches. **Maui** boasts the historic whaling village of Lahaina, fantastic windsurfing, and the dormant volcanic crater of Haleakala. The garden isle of **Kaua'i**, at the northwestern end of the inhabited islands, ranks first for sheer beauty. **Moloka'i**, once stigmatized because of its leper colony, is the friendliest spot in the islands. On tiny **Lana'i**, exclusive resorts have replaced pineapples as the primary commodity. The seventh populated isle, **Ni'ihau**, is closed to most visitors, supporting just a few hundred plantation families who still converse in the Hawaiian language. In the words of Twain, the islands present "the loveliest fleet of islands that lies anchored in any ocean."

For more comprehensive coverage of Hawai'i, please see *Let's Go: California*.

PRACTICAL INFORMATION

Capital: Honolulu.
Hawai'i Visitors Bureau, 2270 Kalakaua Ave., 7th fl., Honolulu 96815 (923-1811). Open Mon.-Fri. 8am-4:30pm. The ultimate source. **Camping and Parks: Department of Land and Natural Resources,** 1151 Punchbowl St., Room 131, Honolulu 96813 (587-0300). Open Mon.-Fri. 8am-3:30pm. Info and permits for camping in state parks, and trail maps. **National Park Service,** Prince Kuhio Federal Bldg., #6305, 300 Ala Moana Blvd., Honolulu 96850 (541-2693). Permits are given at individual park headquarters. Open Mon.-Fri. 7:30am-4pm.
Time Zone: Hawai'i (3hr. behind Pacific in spring and summer; 2hr. otherwise).
Postal Abbreviation: HI.
Area Code: 808.
Sales Tax: 4.167%; hotel rooms 10.167%. **Road Tax:** $2 per day for rental cars.

GETTIN' AROUND AND SLEEPIN' AROUND

From Los Angeles and San Francisco, tickets on many major carriers start at $300 roundtrip and go up from there. **Cheap Tickets** (947-3717 in Hawai'i; 800-234-4522 on the mainland) in Honolulu, offers low fares. Regular **ferry** service runs only from Maui to Moloka'i and Lana'i. **Cruise ships** and private fishing boats will carry passengers to the other islands, but their prices are often exorbitant. **Airlines** are faster, more convenient, cheaper, and often offer special deals on car rentals. The major inter-island carriers, **Hawaiian Airlines, Aloha Airlines,** and **Mahalo Air** can jet you quickly (about 30min.) from Honolulu to any of the islands. Travel agents, such as **Hawai'i Travel Wholesalers,** 1188 Bishops St., Ste. 2810, (538-1900) sell inter-island coupons at significantly lower prices (Hawaiian and Aloha, $38, Mahalo, $28, though rates fluctuate frequently) HTW also offers air, room, and car economy packages for those who want convenience at a discount. Most local travel agents carry individual

Hawaii

N ←

PACIFIC OCEAN

Kilauea
Wailua
Lihue
KAUAI
Poipu

Na Pali Coast
Waimea
NIIHAU

OAHU
Waimea Bay
Wai-a-lua
Mākaha
La'ie
Kāne-'ohe Bay
Honolulu
Pearl Harbor
Wai-kiki Beach

MOLOKAI
Kalaupapa N.P.
Mauna Loa
Kaunakakai
Garden of the Gods
Lanai City
LANAI

D. T. Fleming Beach Park
Kaanapali
Iao Valley State Park
Kahului
Kihei
Lahaina
MAUI
KAHOOLAWE

Hookipa Beach Park
Keanae
Waianapanapa State Park
Hana
Oheo Stream (Seven Pools)
Haleakala Crater

HAWAII
(The Big Island)
Waimea
Kohala Mts.
Mauna Kea Hilo
Mauna Loa
KONA
VOLCANOES NATIONAL PARK
Kilauea Caldera
Kalapana Black Sand Beach
Naalehu
Kailua-Kona
Kealakekua Bay
Hapuna Beach Park

50 miles
50 km
0
0

Oahu

N ←

PACIFIC OCEAN

Ka-'ena Point
Waimea Bay
Wai-mea
La'ie
Hau-'ula
Puna-lu'u
KOOLAU RANGE
Wai-Kāne
Kai-lua
Kāne-'ohe Bay
Wai-'alae Beach Park
Wai-mānalo
Wai-mānalo Bay
Mauna-lua Bay
Hanauma Bay Beach Park

Honolulu
Diamond Head
Wai-kiki Beach
Honolulu Harbor

Wai-a-lua
Wahi-a-wā
Ka-mehameha Hwy.
Pearl City
WAIANAE RANGE
Mākaha
Nānā-kuli
U.S.S. Arizona Memorial
Pearl Harbor Entrance

10 miles
10 kilometers
5
5
0
0

83
99
80
803
930
93
72
61
63
1
78
H1

HAWAI'I

Mahalo Air coupons for $34-38 apiece. Check the miscellaneous section of the classified ads in the *Star-Bulletin* or *Advertiser* for individuals selling these coupons at cut-rate prices. Inter-island flights are often extremely scenic, particularly in the early morning or late afternoon.

Despite rumors to the contrary, reasonable room rates do exist on the islands. **Sands and Seaside Hotels** (800-451-6754), manages some of the cheapest resort hotels on Kaua'i, Maui, and the Big Island, ($59 per night and up) and is the only locally owned chain of hotels on the islands. **Hostels** are one of the best bets for cheap accommodations. Many run airport shuttles and sightseeing trips and offer discounts on car rentals, inter-island flights, and activities. Another alternative are the **bed and breakfast organizations** which offer rooms in private homes. **B&B Honolulu,** 3242 Kaohinani Dr., Honolulu 96817 (595-7533 or 800-288-4666; fax 595-2030) operates throughout the state. (Prices start from about $40 for a double room with breakfast.) **Camping** is Hawai'i's best deal ($0-3 per night). It's also a great way to truly experience the islands' natural beauty. The national campgrounds on Maui and the Big Island require no permit, but they do enforce a 3- or 5-day max. stay. Free **camping permits** are required for the popular state parks (applicants must be at least 18 years old; available from the Dept. of State Parks in Honolulu). Camping is limited to five nights per 30 days. Sites are open Friday through Wednesday on O'ahu, daily on the other islands.

O'AHU

O'ahu bears the mixed blessing of being the cultural, economic, and tourist center of Hawai'i. O'ahu can be roughly divided into four sections. **Honolulu** and its suburbs constitute the metropolitan heart of the island. The **North Shore,** from Kahuku to Kaena Point, is the most rural part of the island and home to some mighty big waves. The **Windward Coast** (on the east), lies between sculpted mountains and colorful reefs. The **Leeward Coast** (on the west) is raw and rocky. The slopes of two now-extinct volcanic mountain ridges, **Wai'anae** in the west and **Ko'olau** in the east, make up the bulk of Oahu's 600 sq. miles. The narrow inlets of **Pearl Harbor** push in at the southern end of the valley between the two ridges. Honolulu spreads along six mi. of oceanfront southeast of Pearl Harbor, hemmed in by the Ko'olau Range. Three mi. east of downtown, **Waikiki Beach** extends outward toward the volcanic crater of **Diamond Head,** the island's southernmost extremity. Honolulu continues around Diamond Head to Koko Head in **Hawai'i-kai.**

■ Honolulu

Honolulu is City Lite. It's got all the trappings of a major city: industry, transportation centers, skyscrapers, and traffic. There are all-night restaurants, housing developments, and a Chinatown. But Honolulu isn't hopelessly citified: you can actually see tropical fish in the harbor, there's a beautiful beach almost the entire length of the city, and the local news anchors wear Aloha shirts on Friday. Waikiki in particular is considered by many to be too crowded. A traveler who does not leave this section of O'ahu will see only a small segment of what Hawai'i has to offer.

Practical Information Visitors info is available at the **Hawaii Visitors Bureau,** 2270 Kalakaua Ave., 8th Floor (923-1811; open Mon.-Fri. 8am-5:30pm). **Buses** (848-5555) cover the entire island, but different lines start and stop running at different times (fare $1). **Sida,** 439 Kalewa St. (836-0011), runs a taxi service. **Enterprise,** 445 Seaside Ave. (922-0090), in Waikiki, or at the airport (836-7722; 800-325-8007) rents to those over 21 for about $26 per day (open Mon.-Fri. 8am-6pm, Sat.-Sun. 8am-1pm). Honolulu's **post office** is at 3600 Aolele Ave. (423-3990; open Mon.-Fri. 7:30am-8:30pm, Sat. 8am-4pm). **ZIP code** is 96820. **Area code:** 808.

Honolulu International Airport is 20 minutes west of downtown, off the Lunalilo Freeway (H-1). The **Nimitz Hwy.** (Rte. 92) will take you all the way to Waikiki. Buses #19 and 20, among others, go the 9 mi. to Waikiki, but you won't be able to bring your luggage unless it can fit on your lap. **Airport Motorcoach** (839-0911) offers continuous service from Waikiki to the airport ($7; call 6:30am-10:30pm). **EM Tours and Transportation** (836-0210) will pick up at any time ($7).

Accommodations Honolulu, especially Waikiki, caters to affluent tourists, but there *are* bargains. Guests must show an airline ticket to stay at **Interclub Waikiki,** 2413 Kuhio Ave. (924-2636. Female or mixed dorms. Laundry, refrigerators, and outdoor grill. No curfew; reception open 24 hr. Check-out 10am. Bunks $15, doubles $45. Key deposit $10.) Single-sex rooms and free use of snorkeling gear are available at **Hale Aloha (HI-AYH),** 2417 Prince Edward St. (926-8313), in Waikiki, 2 blocks from the beach; take Waikiki #8 bus to Kuhio and Uluniu. (Beds guaranteed 3 nights although you might be allowed to stay longer. 24-hr. check-in. Check-out 11am. No lockout or curfew. Dorm bunks $15, doubles $35. Sleep sack rental $1. Key deposit $5. Make reservations.) Small and peaceful, though somewhat remote is **Honolulu International (HI-AYH),** 2323A Seaview Ave. (946-0591). 1½ mi. north of Waikiki. Take bus #6 from Ala Moana Shopping Center to Metcalf and University Ave. (Kitchen, locker, and clean single-sex facilities. Beds guaranteed for 3 nights. Reception open 8am-noon and 4pm-midnight. Check-out 10am. Lights out 11pm; rooms locked noon-4:30pm. $12.50, nonmembers $15.50. Reservations recommended.) A converted hostel now houses **Kim's Island Hostel,** 1946 Ala Moana Blvd., Suite 130 (942-8748). Take bus #19 or #20 to the Hilton Hawaiian Village, cross Ala Moana, turn right and go about half a block. Each room has A/C, bathroom, sink, fridge, and TV. Cooking facilities available. (24-hr. check-in. 10am check-out. First night $11, each additional night $15; $95 per week, $350 per month. Singles $45 per night or $275 per week. $20 deposit includes linens.) **B&B Pacific Hawaii,** 19 Kai Nani Place (262-6026), will book B&B rooms all over the island from $45 per couple.

Food and Nightlife The **Kapahulu, Kaimuki, Moili'ili,** and **downtown** districts are all within 10 min. of Waikiki by bus, and with a good map, you can walk from one district to the next quite easily. Small Chinese and other Asian food counters serve excellent, authentic, and affordable lunches and *dim sum* all over Chinatown, especially on **Hotel Street.** A variety of ethnic restaurants, including Hawaiian, Japanese, Thai, and French, are located between the 500 and 1000 blocks of **Kapahulu Avenue.** The **Rainbow Drive-In,** 3308 Kanaina Ave. (737-0177), at Kapahulu, has served tasty cuisisne at rock-bottom prices (sandwiches $2) since 1961 (open daily 7:30am-9pm). When the sun goes down, **World Café,** 500 Ala Moana Blvd. (599-4450), on Restaurant Row, has the best dance mixes in town and kickin' drink specials. ($2 beer, Fri. and Sat.; $3 cover. Open Mon.-Thurs. 4pm-3am., Fri. 4pm-4am, Sat. 7pm-4am., Sun. 8pm-2am.)

Sights The **Iolani Palace** (538-1471), at King and Richard St., the only royal residence ever built in America, was first the home of King Kalakaua and his sister Queen Liliuokalani. (45-min. tours begin every 15 min. Wed.-Sat. 9am-2:15pm. $6, ages 5-12 $1. Under 5 not admitted.) At the corner of Beretania and Richard St. stands Hawaii's postmodern **State Capitol,** an architectural mosaic of Hawaii's landscape (open Mon.-Fri. 9am-4pm; free). The "Westminster Abbey of Hawai'i," **Kawai'ahao Church,** at Punchbowl and King, was built from bits of coral in 1842. Services are held in Hawaiian at 8am and 10:30am on Sundays. For a complete guide to Honolulu's historic district, pick up the **Capitol District Walking Tour** from the Hawai'i Visitor Bureau.

On December 7, 1941 a stunned nation listened to reports of the Japanese bombing of the U.S. Pacific Fleet in **Pearl Harbor.** Today, the **U.S.S. Arizona National Memorial** (422-2771) commemorates that event. The **visitor center** is open Mon.-Sun. 7:30am-5pm, with the last program starting at 3pm. Take bus #20 from Waikiki,

#50, 51, or 52 from Ala Moana, or the $2 shuttle (839-0911) from the major Waikiki hotels. Tickets to the memorial are free, but plan ahead because 2-hr. waits are not unusual.

Visitors of all ages flock to the Waikiki Beach area for rest, relaxation, sun, surf, nightlife, romance, and tacky souvenirs. Originally a marshy swampland and hide-away for Hawaiian royalty, Waikiki's wetlands were drained into the Ala Canal to launch the island's tourist industry. Farthest to the east is the **Sans Souci Beach,** in front of the Kaimona Otani Hotel. The **Queen's Surf Beach,** closer to downtown, attracts swimmers, skaters, and an increasing number of in-line roller-skaters. If you seek more secluded beaches, head east on Diamond Head Rd. (a moped will do) until you hit Kahala Ave. For a break from sun and surf, hike the 1 mi. into the **Diamond Head Crater.** To get there, take bus #58 from Waikiki. Bring a flashlight to guide you through a pitch-dark section of the tunnel. The view of Waikiki is spectacular, and if you go on the right day, you might catch a rainbow arching over the U.S. military base in the center of the crater.

O'ahu's Windward (East) Coast is as refreshing as a long, cool drink after a hot Honolulu afternoon. This 40-mi. string of sleepy towns is colored in vibrant shades of green and blue by the dramatic Ko'olau Mountains on one side and the Pacific Ocean on the other. Drive the **Kamehameha Hwy.** (Rte. 83) to take in the dazzling land-scape and marvel at views which match any glossy postcard. Bus #55 (Circle Island) from Ala Moana Center delivers the experience for only $1.

Fruit vendors, plate lunches, and shaved ice are plentiful on the Windward Coast. You might try **Ka'a'awa Country Kitchen and Grocery,** 51-480 Kamehameha Hwy. (237-8484), Ka'a'awa. Open up and say a'a'a! This mom-and-pop country drive-in has kept the locals of Ka'a'awa satisfied for more than 30 years. The teri-beef ($4.50) is tasty, as are the "Hawaiian Nutrition" unique alternatives ($5.50; open Mon., Wed., Fri., 5:30am-6pm, Tues. 5:30am-2pm, Sun. 6am-5pm. No credit cards).

■ Windward and Southeast O'ahu

O'ahu's Windward (East) Coast is as refreshing as a long, cool drink after a hot Hono-lulu afternoon. This 40-mi. string of sleepy towns is colored in vibrant shades of green and blue by the dramatic Ko'olau Mountains on one side and the Pacific Ocean on the other. Drive the **Kamehameha Hwy.** (Rte. 83) to take in the dazzling landscape and marvel at views which match any glossy postcard. Bus #55 (Circle Island) from Ala Moana Center delivers the experience for only $1.

ACCOMMODATIONS AND CAMPING

While the Windward Coast is postcard-perfect, the accommodations picture is not as pretty. Affordable options are hard to come by. One possibility is **camping** in one of the county parks along the coast such as **Mala'ekahana State Recreation Area, Bellows Field State Park,** and **Kahana Beach State Park.** Be wary when putting up your tent, however, as campground crime has supposedly occurred in the area, though less so in recent years. Also make sure that you secure the necessary permits from the state and county offices in Honolulu before setting up camp. Another option for those who want to experience a rural Hawaiian lifestyle is **Countryside Cabins,** way out at 53-224 Kamehameha Hwy. (237-8169), which provides 15 rustic cabins with kitchens, fridges, bathrooms, and linen. The cabins are connected by a maze of paths through a dense garden of local vegetation. One bedroom $30, two bedrooms $45.

FOOD

Frankie's Drive-Inn, 41-1610 Kalaniana'ole Hwy. (259-7819), Waimanalo. Plate-lunch paradise since 1953. Plates $4. Serves up the native delicacy Hawaiian spam and eggs for $3.25. Open Mon.-Fri. 9:30am-4:30pm. Sat. 9:30am-3:30pm.

Bueno Nalo, 41-865 Kalaniana'ole Hwy. (259-7186), Waimanalo. Piñatas, chile lights, and a black velvet painting of a matador. What else could you want in a Mexican restaurant? They also have excellent south-of-the-border cuisine at reasonable prices (entrees $5-10). Open daily 11:30am-9pm.

Ka'a'awa Country Kitchen and Grocery, 51-480 Kamehameha Hwy. (237-8484), Ka'a'awa. Open up and say a'a'a. Take your chow across the street and enjoy it by the surf of Swanzy Beach Park. This mom-and-pop country drive-in has kept the locals of Ka'a'awa satisfied for more than 30 years. The teri-beef ($4.50) is tasty, as are the "Hawaiian Nutrition" unique alternatives ($5.50). Open Mon., Wed., Fri., 5:30am-6pm, Tues. 5:30am-2pm, Sun. 6am-5pm. No credit cards.

SIGHTS AND ACTIVITIES

Hanauma Bay to Waimanalo Beach

From Waikiki, take **Kalaniana'ole Hwy.** (Rte. 72) east to **Koko Head Crater.** Some of the friendliest and most colorful fish in the Pacific reside in **Hanauma Bay,** formed where the ocean has washed away the crater's eastern wall. This park, with federally protected waters, is the best spot for **snorkeling** in O'ahu. For the clearest underwater trip, come early in the morning. On display are such interesting and brightly colored creatures as octopi, spiny lobster, convict tangs, damselfish, Moorish idols, and large schools of sunburned vacationers. Snorkel rentals are available at the beach. (Complete set $6, prescriptive lens set $10. Deposit of rental car keys, major credit card, or $30 required. Rentals open 8am-4:30pm.) For those unwilling to make the trek to the bay from the parking lot, a trolley is available for 75¢ one-way. (The park is open Thurs.-Tues. 6am-7pm, Wed. noon-7pm. Free.)

A 10-minute walk to the left of the bay brings you to the less well-known **Toilet Bowl.** Locals climb into the large volcanic tube when it's full and get flushed up and down as waves fill and empty the chamber through natural lava plumbing. When the surf's high, swimmers should be cautious; the sides are rocky and the ocean is always unpredictable. One mi. farther on Kalaniana'ole Hwy., a similar mechanism causes the **Halona Blowhole** to release its spray. The dramatic effect is dependent upon tidal conditions and can vary from a weak squirt to a full-blown Old Faithful spout. From here, the island of Moloka'i, 20 mi. away, is easily visible, and on a clear day, you might spy as many as three of the neighboring islands. Blowhole is also beautiful at night as the moon backlights the mist and sparkles coldly on the Pacific.

Sandy Beach, 25 minutes from Waikiki and just beyond Halona, is a primo spot for bodysurfing, boogie-boarding, and people-watching. The beach serves as the center of the Hawaiian summer surf circuit. The beach is expansive and pleasantly sandy, but the summer swells burst onto the shore with spine-crushing force, making swimming a serious hazard for all but the most expert beachgoer. While you're there, you may also catch hang-gliders landing on the grassy field behind the beach.

The landscape undergoes a dramatic change at **Mokapu Point,** with one twist of the highway taking you from the semi-arid hills around Hanauma Bay to the vertical shades of green provided by the **Ko'olau Mountains. Makapu'u Beach,** 41-095 Kalaniana'ole Hwy., is a prime place to bodysurf. Before swimming, check the flags hoisted by the lifeguards. Red flags mean danger, no swimming. Across from Makapu'u lies **Sea Life Park** (259-7933), a minor-league Sea World, with performing penguins and the world's only "wholphin," a whale-dolphin hybrid. Look in *Oahu This Week* and other such publications to find coupons that will make the price less painful. ($20, seniors $16, ages 4-12 $10. Open daily 9:30am-5pm.)

Farther down the road is **Waimanalo Beach Park,** with its long, graceful white crescent and the two offshore **islands** of **Manana** and **Kaohika'ipu** resting in impossibly turquoise waters. Turn down Aloilo St. by the McDonald's for a more secluded section of beach. The best novice bodysurfing is found at **Sherwoods** and, on weekends, at **Bellows Air Force Base.** Both are on Kalaniana'ole off the road to Kailua; neither one provides lifeguards. If you thought the only polo in Hawai'i was in the outlet stores, think again. The **Waimanalo Polo Club,** across from the Waimanalo McDonald's on Kalaniana'ole Hwy., fires up chukkers every Sunday at 2pm ($5).

HAWAI'I

Kailua Beach to Laie

Kailua Town and nearby **Kailua Beach Park** are *the* places to go for prime **beach** area unadulterated by large hotels. Kalaniana'ole ends by intersecting **Kailua Road.** Follow this road toward Kailua Town and Kailua Beach Park (450 Kawailoa Rd.). This is excellent **windsurfing** territory, as the enthusiastic beach locals will attest. The sandy beach and strong, steady onshore winds are perfect for windsurfers of all abilities. If you left your rig at home, nearby companies rent equipment. **Kailua Sailboard Company,** 130 Kailua Rd. (2 blocks from the park, 262-2555), rents "standard" longboards for $30 per day (harness $5 extra) and Bic Ace tech shortboards for $35 per day (open daily 9am-5pm). They also offer three-hour beginner lessons for $39 at 10:30am and 2pm daily. When the winds are blowing, those left on shore may cringe as they are pelted with powdery sand (particularly perilous to contact lens wearers). If you can bear the grit, this is a great place to swim.

White sand and emerald green waters make nearby **Lanikai Beach** (Mokulua Dr. east of Kailua) the best place on O'ahu to savor the **sunrise.** (Kailua Rd. in the other direction takes you to **Kane'ohe** via Kamehameha Hwy.) Grab your snorkel gear and swim or wade out into the bay; better yet, use an inner tube and float around effortlessly. Flora enthusiasts should visit the free **Haiku Gardens,** 46-316 Haiku Rd. (247-6671), where many weddings are held (open daily sunrise to sunset). The **Ulupo Hei'au,** 1200 Kailua Rd., next to the YMCA, was supposedly built by the legendary *menehunes,* a mischievous little people. The temple still stands as a platform of black lava rock overlooking the Kawainui marsh. Smooth stones lead across the jagged lava of the *heiau* and down the far side to the roots of a great **banyan tree,** where a natural spring wells up.

Look for the **Valley of the Temples,** 47-200 Kahekili Hwy., a burial ground that holds the serene **Byodo-In Temple.** A replica of a temple in Uji, Japan, it was built in 1968 to commemorate the 100th anniversary of Japanese immigrants' first arrival in Hawaii. Stroll through the tropical gardens and by the running stream filled with 10,000 brightly colored Japanese carp. Ring the three-ton brass bell to bring happiness and the blessings of the Buddha (open daily sunrise to sunset; $2).

Approaching the North Shore on the Kamehameha Hwy., you will reach **Kualoa Regional Park** and **Chinaman's Hat,** an island named for its conical shape. Much of *Karate Kid II* was filmed on the island, which must have made local favorite Pat Morita pretty giddy. North of here, **Swanzy Beach State Park, Ka'a'awa Beach Park, Kahana Bay Park,** and **Punalu'u Beach** possess secluded stretches of sand shared only with the wind and the waves. Right around the bend from **Punalu'u** is the entrance to **Sacred Falls Park,** a scenic 50-ft. waterfall in a dramatic, narrow canyon. The falls are a two-mi. walk from the parking lot. The trail crosses a stream twice and takes about an hour each way. The falls and the refreshing pool underneath make the hike worthwhile. Stick to the trail, though—hikers have gotten lost in recent months. Provision yourself for the hike at the trailside fruit stand run by a group of brothers who own a farm about half-mi. up the trail.

Past **Laie,** the land gives way to abandoned sugar plantations. Shrimp and corn are now the crops of choice and can be sampled fresh at a number of roadside stands. Rounding the island's northern tip at Kahuku, you will also see strange two-armed windmills gyrating on the hillside—it's nothing extraterrestrial, just another experimental energy project. The **Polynesian Cultural Center,** 55-370 Kamehameha Hwy. (293-3333), staffed by Mormon students from adjacent Brigham Young University, is the home of an overpriced "living museum," which seeks to capture the flavor of seven Polynesian cultures. You can see authentic natives here as well as the same tourists you left in Waikiki (adults $26, children $14).

■ North Shore and Central O'ahu

As the stunningly verdant home to cane fields and surfers, it is hard to believe that the North Shore is on the same island as Honolulu. One-week stops sometimes become decade-long sojourns along this gorgeous stretch of coastline. Many O'ahu locals who

work in Honolulu come home to the "country" of the North Shore and its more traditional Hawaiian way of life. The pace is slow and peaceful in the summer—you can
spend a day counting the different blues of the sky and ocean. Surf and adrenaline
both rise during the winter as the world-famous breaks **Sunset, Waimea,** and **Pipeline,** turn the North Shore into a surfing mecca. The best things to see here are those
you stumble across on your own—secluded bays free from footprints, coral reefs full
of brightly colored fish, or perhaps the perfect wave.

ACCOMMODATIONS

North Shore accommodations are few and far between. If you're coming in the winter, book early or you'll be squeezed out by the zealous hordes arriving to challenge
the surf. **Thomsen's Bed and Breakfast,** 59-420 Kamehameha Hwy. (638-7947), is an
especially beautiful (and popular) place to say. Located in a comfortable 2-story home
near Sunset Beach, this studio apartment above a garage has cable TV, phone, kitchenette, and private bath. ($65 per night for 2 people, $350 per week. Winter fills up
6-8 months in advance.)

FOOD

Kua Aina Sandwich, 66-214 Kamehameha Hwy. (637-6067), Hale'iwa. Crowds line
up at lunch time for giant burgers on kaiser rolls ($4.60). The mahi and ortega sand-
wich ($5.40) is a taste extravaganza. Open daily 11am-8pm. No credit cards.

Coffee Gallery, 66-250 Kamehameha Hwy. (637-5571), in the North Shore Marketplace. Relaxed atmosphere and jazzy patio assures that lunch can, and often does,
turn into an afternoon's affair. The owner will pause from his grinding to explain
how it's really the fog which makes Kona coffee so good. Humongous pastries,
rich slabs of pie, great vegetarian menu, and the deservedly popular yogurt fruit
cup (any of these from $1.50-6). Open Mon.-Fri. 6am-9pm, Sat.-Sun. 7am-9pm.

Kelea Kafé, 59-254 Kamehameha Hwy. (638-5960). Enjoy a selection of sandwiches
($3.25-4.50) and fruit smoothies ($3) on aqua picnic tables under a canopy of broken surfboards. Operates under the auspices of the Hawaiian Healing Center, and
even sells clothes! Look for the 25-ft. tall sculpture of Maui rising from the earth.
Open daily 10am-6pm in summer, 8:30am-8:30pm in winter.

SIGHTS AND ACTIVITIES

Surfing is king on the North Shore, but there's still plenty to do here even if you don't
know the difference between Mr. Zog's Sex Wax and K-Y jelly. The action on the
North Shore centers around **Hale'iwa.** Once a plantation town, Hale'iwa is now
enlivened by surf shops and art galleries. The signs welcoming artistic surfer visitors
to Hale'iwa prompted community outrage when stolen this past year. Luckily, they
were found, and Hale'iwa's equanimity has been restored. **Surf-n-Sea,** 62-595 Kamehameha Hwy. (637-3008), rents snorkeling gear ($9.50 per day), windsurfing equip-
ment ($12 first hr.; $3.50 per additional hr.), surfboards ($5 first hr.; $3.50 per
additional hr.), and boogie-boards ($3 first hr.; $2 per additional hr.), and gives surfing
and sailboarding lessons (open daily 9am-6pm). To the north of Hale'iwa is **Waimea
Beach Park,** where locals and Budweiser-emboldened tourists jump off a high rock
formation into the sea. The beach shares its name with **Waimea Valley** (638-8511),
an 1800-acre nature preserve with tropical gardens and a 45-ft. waterfall extravaganza. Performers dive off the cliffs daily at 11:15am, 12:45, 2:15, 3:45, and 3:45pm
(also 5pm in the summer). Admission to the park is almost as steep as the falls ($20,
ages 6-12 $10, under 6 free, free for people in wheelchairs and their pushers; open
daily 10am-5:30pm.) They also offer free guided nighttime strolls offered the day
before and the day of the full moon. For free round-trip shuttle service from Waikiki
call 988-8276. About ¼ mi. north of Waimea on Pupukea Rd. lies **Pu'u O Mahuka
Hei'au,** the largest temple of its kind on the island—it was used for human sacrifices
until 1794. The serene setting and spectacular panorama of Waimea Bay and surrounding countryside make the winding trip over camouflaged speed bumps worth

the sacrifice. Turn right off Kamehameha onto Pupukea Rd. at the Foodland and follow the signs that say "State Monument."

Back on Kamehameha Hwy., another few minutes drive will bring you to breathtaking **Sunset Beach** and the **Banzai Pipeline,** infamous winter wavelands of the world. During the summer, the surf disappears and these big beaches are excellent for swimming. Not far past Sunset, on Kamehameha Hwy., sits a 25-ft. wooden **statue** of the god Maui rising out of the earth. Next to the sculpture is the **Hawaiian Trading Post,** operated by a guy whose name also happens to be Maui. Even if you don't have something to trade, stop in and check out the shrine in the garage and the merchandise ranging from old typewriters and foreign coins to Polynesian idols and woven hats. Maui (the store owner, not the god) will also explain to you the peril to Sunset Beach that lies behind all the bumper stickers. For a bird's eye view, you can fly (or fall 10,000ft.) with **Skydive Hawai'i,** Rte. 930, Dillingham Airfield. (Tandem jumping $225. Call 521-4404 or 637-9700 for reservations.) A cheaper and lower-altitude option for the aerial perspective is **The Original Glider Rides,** (677-3404), at the other end of the airfield. The 20-min. ride affords a fantastic perspective of the whole North Shore. If the winds are good, you can get up high enough to see Honolulu. Check in with the original Mr. Bill ($60 single or $90 for 2 passengers). If you prefer, head to secluded, beautiful, and windy **Makuleia Beach.**

Rte. 82 winds through Wahi'awa, another plantation town and home to tattoo parlors and the **Sacred Healing Stones,** which became so popular in the first part of this century they had to be enclosed in a concrete, cubical "temple" for their protection. On the way, take a poke around the unapologetically commercial **Dole Pineapple Pavilion,** 64-1550 Kamehameha Hwy. (621-8408). Displays offer the visitor a crash course on the ins and outs of the pineapple business. Be sure to drink some of the delicious free pineapple juice flowing from the plastic pineapple towering in the corner of the store. You can also eat next door at the **Helemano Plantation,** 64-1510 Kamehameha Hwy. (622-3929), a non-profit organization that provides residences and jobs for people with mental disabilities (fab Chinese buffet $8.25).

MAUI

The majority of the island's two million visitors per year laze on the beaches of the island's resort areas; with little effort, therefore, you can enjoy Maui's handiwork on cool mountain trails and empty stretches of sand without the company of tourist crowds. Known as "the Valley Isle" and consisting of two mountains joined by an isthmus, Maui offers lush tropical jungles that spill right to the edge of sheer seaside cliffs, acres of windblown sugarcane, and verdant pine-scented mountainsides. The island's visitors are just as varied, including a mellow windsurfing contingent and scores of lobster-red Midwestern tourists with their screaming kids. Residents proclaim "Maui no ka oi," (Maui is the best) and they are right. Just about everyone can find the Hawai'i they seek here. Locals advise visitors to "eat, drink, and be *Maui.*"

Practical Information Visitors should visit the **Visitor Information Kiosk** (872-3893), at the Kahului Airport terminal. (Open daily 6:30am-9pm.) **Trans Hawaiian** (877-7308) offers hourly service between Kahului Airport and the major Lahaina-Ka'anapali for $13; reservations are necessary only for return (runs 8am-5:30pm as needed). The **Lahaina Express** provides free transport between the Ka'anapali Resorts and Lahaina. Get the schedule in the *Lahaina Historical Guide* (available at the tourist stands in Lahaina). **Department of Parks and Recreation,** War Memorial Gym, 1580 Ka'ahumanu Ave. (243-7389), between Kahului and Wailuku, has information and permits ($3) for county parks. (Open Mon.-Fri. 8am-4pm. You may have to knock on the window.) **Ferries** are an ideal way to go from Maui to Moloka'i and Lana'i. Going by boat is more exciting and cheaper than flying. The **Maui Princess** (661-8397) runs daily from Lahaina to Kaunakakai (Moloka'i) at 7:30am and 5:15pm, and from Moloka'i, to Lahaina at 5:45am and 3:30pm. Crossing takes about 1¾ hr.

and costs $25 each way. **Expeditions** (661-3756) runs daily between Lahaina and Manele, Lana'i, $25 one way. **Resort Taxi** (661-5285) offers a $10 ride into Kahului or Wailuku from the airport. **Rent a car** at **Regency,** Kahului Airport (871-6147); it's the only option for those under 21. ($25 per day, $8 per day extra if under 25. Open daily 8am-8pm.)

Maui's highways follow the shape of the island in a broken figure-eight pattern. The **Kahului Airport** sits on the northern coast of the isthmus. To the west lie **Kahului** and **Wailuku** ("water of destruction"). **Rte. 30** leads to hot and dry **Lahaina** ("cruel sun") and **Ka'anapali** ("Ka'ana cliff"), the major resort area. **Rte. 34** leads counterclockwise around the same loop from the isthmus through West Maui's remote and spectacular scenery. Circling the slopes of Haleakala southbound along the eastern loop, **Rte. 31** runs past **Kihei** and **Wailea** (water of *Lea,* "the canoe maker's goddess"). **Rte. 36** meanders through rainy terrain, over 56 one-lane bridges and 600 hairpin curves to **Hana. Rte. 40** or **Rte. 37** will lead you to **Rte. 377,** and then **Rte. 378,** which heads up 10,023-ft. to **Mt. Haleakala.**

Accommodations The **Banana Bungalow Hotel and International Hostel,** 310 N. Market St. (244-5090), in Wailuku, has uncrowded rooms and numerous facilities including a TV room, laundry, hot tub, hammocks, volleyball court and kitchen. (Bunks $15, singles with double bed $32, doubles $39. Key deposit $5.) Another option is the **Northshore Inn,** 2080 Vineyard St. (242-8999), a relaxed place with a kitchen, TV, laundry and fridges in every room. Movies play nightly at 9pm. (Hostel bunks $15, singles $30, doubles $41.)

Haleakala Featuring a fantastic volcanic crater, **Haleakala National Park** is open 24 hr. and costs $4 per car for a seven-day pass. The **Park Headquarters** (572-9306), about 1 mi. up from the entrance, provides camping **permits,** displays on Haleakala wildlife, and funky postcards (open daily 7:30am-4pm). **Haleakala Visitors Center,** near the summit, has a few exhibits on the region's geology, archaeology, and ecology, and one of the best views of the crater (open daily sunrise-3pm). **Haleakala Crater Campground,** P.O. Box 369, Makawao, HI 96768 (572-9306), 4 mi. from Halemauu parking lot, has camping and cabins within the crater. The park allocates cabins by a highly competitive lottery. You must apply three months prior to your visit. Holua and Paliku areas also serve as campgrounds. Free camping permits are issued at park headquarters. (1 mi. up from park entrance; 2-night max. stay in cabins, 3 in campgrounds.)

Hana The **Hana Coast** spans from the Keanae Peninsula to Kaupo. The **Hana Highway,** leading to the Hana coast, may be the world's most beautiful stretch of road; carved from cliff faces and valley floors, its alternate vistas of smooth sea and lush terrain are made only somewhat less enjoyable by its tortuous curves. Be prepared to spend an entire day on the trip. Wild ginger plants and fruit trees laden with mangos, guavas, and bananas perfume the air of the twisted drive.

THE BIG ISLAND

The Big Island, officially known as Hawai'i, emerged from the confluence of five major volcanoes on top of a hot spot in the Pacific Plate. Two are still active: "Long Mountain," **Mauna Loa** (13,677ft.), and **Kilauea** (4000ft.), home of **Halemaumau Crater.** Kilauea is currently in its 51st phase of eruption without showing any signs of exhaustion, and crowds flock daily to the island to tread on newly created earth. Although the eruptions are powerful, the volcanoes do not emit dangerous ash clouds. The lava flow is quick only near the summit and in underground lava tubes. **Hilo** and **Kailua-Kona,** on opposite sides of the island, are the main tourist towns.

The two mountains in **Volcanoes National Park** continue to spout and grow, adding acres of new land each year. **Kilauea Caldera,** with its steaming vents, sulfur

HAWAI'I

fumes, and periodic "drive-in" eruptions, is the star of the park, although the less active **Mauna Loa** and its dormant northern neighbor, **Mauna Kea,** are in some respects more amazing. Each towers nearly 14,000 ft. above sea level and drops some 16,000 ft. to the ocean floor. Mauna Loa is the largest volcano in the world, while Mauna Kea, if measured from its ocean floor base, would be the tallest mountain on earth (park entrance $5 per car, valid for 7 days). The **visitors center** in **Kilauea** (967-7311), just inside the park gates, has exhibits and info on ranger-led walks. Trails of varying difficulty lead around Kilauea and to the summit of Mauna Loa; speak to a ranger before setting out. (Open daily 7:45am-5pm.)

Staying in the volcano area is expensive because of the limited number of hotels. From Hilo, take Rte. 11 almost to the National Park, turn right at Haunani Rd. in Volcano Village, then left on Kalani Holua Rd, 2 mi. from the visitors center, to the **Holo Holo Inn,** 19-4036 Kalani Holua Rd., (967-7950), which offers several large, clean rooms (bunk $15; call after 4:30pm and reserve in advance). **My Island Volcano B&B,** on Old Volcano Rd. (967-7216), has beautiful rooms in a historic mission-style home (singles $35, with bath $40, doubles $55, with bath $65). Also try the **Namakani Paio** cabins, in an *ohia* forest. (Check-in after 3pm; singles or doubles $32; $15 key deposit). In **Volcanoes National Park** (967-7311), find free campsites at **Kipuka Nene, Namakani Paio** (near Kilauea Crater), and **Kamoamoa** (on the coast)—each with shelters and fireplaces, but no wood. (Free; 7-day max; no reservations; register with the visitor center by 4:30pm.)

The lush **Waipi'o Valley,** 8 mi. down Rte. 24 from Honoka'a, is regarded as one of the most beautiful places in Hawai'i. This 2000-ft. gorge is the crowning point of a series of breathtaking canyons between Waipi'o and Pololu. The vertical green walls of the valley are gilded by silver cascades and the flat valley floor is organized by taro fields. Home to 10,000 people in the 19th century, the valley today only has around 50 residents, all of whom live without electricity and a water source (water must be brought in from Hilo). Resident *'ohanas* (families) live much like their ancestors did, cultivating their gardens and fishing in the Waipi'o River.

Pat Morita: A Life in Film

You and I can travel and see some of the most exotic places in the world, and never run out of popcorn. Now that's civilization!

Noriyuki "Pat" Morita

Noriyuki "Pat" Morita was not always the renowned thespian he is today. His early life was marred by struggle. Pat was in a hospital as a youth for nine years as he battled spinal tuberculosis, and upon his release, he and his family were interned in a detention camp for Japanese-Americans during WWII. But through all the tears, Pat's indomitable spirit prevailed, and soon he landed a part as the original Arnold during the first few years of "Happy Days." Times were tough after he left the show. He had a bit part as "Ah Chew" on "Sanford and Son" (1973-4), and though he became the first Asian-American to star in a prime-time television show ("Mr. T and Tina," 1976), the show was yanked after five episodes. The 80s were Pat's salad days; his role as Mr. Miyagi in "The Karate Kid" earned him an Academy Award nomination and nationwide adulation. Soon thereafter, he became the second Asian-American to star in a prime-time television show, "Ohara," though it failed to survive the 1987 season. Recent times have seen Pat serve as the spokesman for both Colgate toothpaste *and* First Hawaiian Bank, where he jumps out of things and shouts, "YES," the bank's slogan. Of late, he's won the Integrity Award at the First Annual Minority Motion Picture Awards, married actress Evelyn Guerrero, and starred in a Shiatsu massage video which rocketed to the top of the video charts in 1993. Definitive film roles include "Midway" (1976); "Karate Kids" II, III, and Next (1986, 1989, 1994); "American Ninja V" (1991); "Even Cowgirls Get the Blues" (1994), and "Timemaster" (1995). Wax on, wax off, Pat, Hawaii's theatrical native son.

The **Waipi'o Lookout,** at the end of Rte. 240 on the edge of the valley, offers one of the most striking panoramas in the islands, but a trek into the valley will give you a much better sense of its amazing beauty. The steep drive into the valley requires 4WD; the hike is as steep as it looks but only takes 25 minutes. The hike up takes 40 minutes, but feels 10 times as grueling as the way down—water breaks are key. You can also reach the valley via the **Waipi'o Valley Jeep Shuttle** (775-7121), which you can catch at the top of the valley. Purchase tickets and check in at the **Waipi'o Woodworks Art Gallery** (775-0958), ½ mi. from the Waipi'o Valley lookout. Reservations are highly recommended. (Open Mon.-Sat. 8am-4pm; tour is $30, under 11 $15. Write P.O. Box 5128, Kukuihaele, 96727 for more information.)

KAUA'I

Anything nature does, Kauai can do better. The splendor of the Garden Isle is unsurpassed anywhere in the Hawaiian archipelago. The beaches are more graceful, the mountains more outrageous, and the waterfalls have more water and fall. When producers of such films as *Raiders of the Lost Ark, King Kong,* and *Jurassic Park* sought out a primeval paradise, they ended up on Kauai.

The land of **Hanalei,** on the north coast, was made famous in by Peter, Paul, and Mary in their fattie-fueled song "Puff the Magic Dragon." If you squint, you may be able to make out the shape of a dragon from Hanalei Beach. **Lumahai Beach** is probably on the postcard you'll send home. After visiting it, you'll see that pictures can't do it justice. The northwest side of the island, the **Na Pali Coast** is a true natural wonder. Sheer cliffs are interrupted only by empty white sand beaches washed by the bright blue seas. **Hanakapiai Beach** lies 2 mi. in, and a marvelous waterfall lies another 2 mi. up Hanakapiai Valley. The mind-blowing **Kalalau Valley** lies at the end of 11 steep and cliffside miles but is said to be one of the most beautiful places on earth. The wild coastal areas beyond **Haena** are accessible only by hiking or by kayak.

The **Hawai'i Visitors Bureau,** Lihu'e Plaza Bldg., 3016 Umi St. #207 (245-3971), at Rice in Lihu'e, has the fun and informative Kaua'i Illustrated Pocket Map. Write for their vacation planner, a directory of services, events, and coupons. (Open Mon.-Fri. 8am-4pm.) Camping is the best option on Kauai. Evaluate your options at the **Kaua'i County Parks Office,** 4444 Rice St., Moikeha Bldg., Ste. #150, Lihu'e (241-6670). They have permits for camping in county parks ($3 per person/night; open Mon.-Fri. 7:45am-4:30pm.) Permits are also available from rangers onsite ($5). The **Division of State Parks,** 3060 Eiwa St. #306, (274-3444), in the State Office Bldg. at Hardy in Lihu'e, has even more info on camping in state parks. (Permits issued Mon.-Fri. 8am-4pm.)

If you can't stand to camp, try another island or try the **Kaua'i International Hostel,** 4532 Lehua St. (823-6142 or 800-858-2295), in Kapa'a. This popular hostel is located across the street from the beach and several restaurants, and the friendly backpacker crowd and staff make this a great base for exploring the island. It offers a full kitchen, cable TV, pool table, laundry facilities, co-ed and single-sex dorms, and fantastic, choose-your-own-adventure daytrips to many of Kaua'i's hidden spots. ($20; bunk $16 per night, private room $40 per night. Key deposit $10; check out 10am. Office open daily 8am-10pm.)

HAWAI'I

CANADA

O Canada! The second largest country in the world, Canada covers almost 10 million square km (3.85 million square mi.); only Russia looms larger. Still, only twenty-six million people inhabit Canada's 10 provinces and two territories; well over half the population crowds into either Ontario or Québec. Framed by the Atlantic coastline in the east and the Pacific Ocean in the west, Canada extends from fertile southern farmlands to frozen northern tundra.

The name Canada is thought to be derived from the Huron-Iroquois word "kanata," meaning "village" or "community." This etymology reveals the dependence of early settlers on the Native Canadians as well as the country's origins in a system of important trading posts. The early colonists, the French and English, were relatively distant and culturally distinct. Each population has fought to retain political dominance, but it was only in the 1970s that ethnic and linguistic differences between the two communities flared briefly into quasi-terrorist acts of violence. Native Canadian concerns and a rapidly increasing "allophone" population—neither English nor French—have also become intertwined in the cultural struggle. Inter-regional tensions have been exacerbated by divergent economic foundations; bankrupt fisheries have drained the Maritime provinces while the West Coast booms with trans-Pacific trade.

For crucial info on travel in Canada, see Essentials, in the front of this book.

THE NATIVES AND THE NEWCOMERS

Canada was first settled around 25,000 years ago when a stream of Siberian hunter-nomads flowed over the Asian-Alaskan land bridge in search of better lands. Their descendants flooded the continent, fragmenting into disparate tribes. Arriving Europeans stepped up inter-tribal warfare by trading guns for fur, and by exchanging aid in preexisting conflicts for native knowledge of the local terrain.

Such bargains proved a raw deal for the tribes. As the English and French became more familiar with the land, they squeezed the Native Canadians out by force and by less-than-just land agreements. Natives found themselves confined to large settlements such as Moose Factory in Ontario or Oka in Québec. Recently, the Assembly of First Nations, the umbrella aboriginal organization, has taken legal action to secure compensation for lands that were taken from the tribes.

The first Europeans known to explore the area were the Norse, who apparently settled in northern Newfoundland around the year 1000. England came next; John Cabot sighted Newfoundland in 1497. When Jacques Cartier claimed the mainland for the French crown in 1534 upon landing on the gulf of the St. Lawrence River, he touched off a rivalry that persisted until Britain's 1759 capture of Québec in the Seven Years' War. Four years later, all of French North America was ceded to the English. Britain eventually came to possess a colony split into what one governor of Canada called "two nations warring in the bosom of a single state."

The movement to unify the British North American colonies gathered speed after the American Civil War, when U.S. military might and economic isolationism threatened the independent and continued existence of the British colonies. On March 29, 1867, Queen Victoria signed the British North America (BNA) Act, uniting Nova Scotia, New Brunswick, Upper Canada, and Lower Canada (now Ontario and Québec). Though still a dominion of the British throne, Canada had its country—and its day: the BNA was proclaimed on July 1, Canada Day.

IN RECENT HISTORY

The past 130 years have witnessed the increase of Canadian territory and clout, though not without turbulence. After consolidation, a Conservative ascent financed economic growth and encouraged mass settlement in the west by building an important cross-continental railway; the country quickly grew to encompass most of the land it covers today. Participation in World War I earned the Dominion international respect and a charter membership in the League of Nations; it joined the United Nations in 1945 and was a founding member of the North Atlantic Treaty Organization in 1949. The Liberal government of the following decade created a national social security system, a national health insurance program, and a national flag. Pierre Trudeau's government repatriated Canada's constitution in 1981, freeing the nation from Britain in constitutional legality (Canada is a constitutional monarchy that operates on a parliamentary system). Free to forge its own alliances, the country signed the North American Free Trade Agreement (NAFTA) in 1992, under the leadership of Prime Minister Brian Mulroney.

Mulroney will go down in Canadian history as the leader who almost tore the nation apart in an effort to bring it back together. His numerous attempts to negotiate a constitution that all ten provinces would ratify (Canada's present constitution lacks Québec's okay) consistently failed, flaring century-old regional tensions and spelling the end of his government. Riding on a wave of backlash, the 1993 election saw conservative support collapse to a mere two seats in the Commons and the election in Québec of a separatist government at both federal and provincial levels.

The question of Québec still drives recent politics. An October 1996 referendum negged separation by a mere 1.2% margin—another referendum seems likely in the future. Separatist leaders hope to capitalize on the votes of the older generation, who grew up fighting for a separate nation; the younger generation tend to cite as their primary concern the economic advantages of remaining Canadian.

LANGUAGE

Canada has two official languages, English and French, but there are numerous other native languages. Inuktitut is widely spoken in the Northwest Territories; most Natives also speak English. *Québécois* pronunciation of French can be perplexing, but natives are generally sympathetic toward attempts to speak their language. The *Québécois* are also less formal than European French-speakers; you might be corrected if you use the formal *vous.*

THE ARTS

Most Canadian literature has been written post-1867. The opening of the northwest and the Klondike Gold Rush (1898) provided much fodder for the adventure tale— Jack London penned stories of wolves and prospectors based on his Rush-time experience. In the Maritimes, L.M. Montgomery authored *Anne of Green Gables* (1908), about one of the world's most characterful redheads. In the *Deptford Trilogy*, novelist/playwright Robertson Davies chronicled the roving Canadian identity.

Canada also boasts three of the world's most authoritative cultural and literary critics: Northrop Frye, Hugh Kenner, and Marshall McLuhan. Prominent contemporary authors include Margaret Atwood, best known for the futuristic bestseller *The Handmaid's Tale,* and Sri Lankan-born poet and novelist Michael Ondaatje, whose *The English Patient* received the prestigious Booker Prize.

Canada's contribution to the world of popular music includes a range of artists such as Neil Young, Joni Mitchell, Bruce Cockburn, Rush, Cowboy Junkies, Bare Naked Ladies, k.d. lang, Bryan Adams, Crash Test Dummies, Sarah McLachlan, and the band Tragically Hip. Recent chart-toppers include teeny-bopper *cum* "angry woman" Alanis Morisette, country goddess Shania Twain, and Céline Dion, who's everything she is because we loved her. Catch them on MuchMusic, the Canadian version of MTV. Canada is also home to *Québécois* folk music, and to several world-class orchestras, including the Montréal, Toronto, and Vancouver Symphonies.

On the silver screen, Canada's National Film Board (NFB), which finances many documentaries, has gained worldwide acclaim. The first Oscar given to a documentary film went to the NFB's *Churchill Island* in 1941. Since then, *Québécois* filmmakers have caught the world's eye with Oscar-nominated movies like *Le declin de l'empire americain*, directed by Denys Arcand, who also directed the striking *Jesus de Montréal;* art flick *Léolo* was deemed a classic by critics. François Girard provoked gasps with his *Thirty-two Short Films about Glenn Gould*, and actress Sheila McCarthy shone in *I Have Heard the Mermaids Singing*.

THE MEDIA AND SPORTS

The Toronto *Globe and Mail* is Canada's national newspaper, distributed six days a week across the entire country. Every Canadian city has at least one daily paper; the weekly news magazine is *Maclean's*. The publicly-owned Canadian Broadcasting Corporation (CBC) provides two national networks for both radio and TV, one in English and one in French. A host of private networks serve limited areas; CTV broadcasts nationally. Cable and satellite enable access to U.S. television networks.

Many famous television actors and comedians are of Canadian origin, including Dan Aykroyd, Mike Myers of *Saturday Night Live* and *Wayne's World* fame, Michael J. Fox (*Family Ties, Back to the Future*), newscaster Peter Jennings, *Jeopardy* host Alex Trebek, universal heartthrob Jason Priestly, and William Shatner (Captain James T. Kirk himself). The Canadian comedy troupe SCTV spawned the careers of big-time laughmasters Martin Short, John Candy, and Rick Moranis.

On the field, Canada is best known for sports appropriate to its northern latitudes. Winter sports include curling, ice skating, skiing, and, of course, the ultimate winter sport in Canada, ice hockey. Some of Canada's other popular sports are derived from those of the aboriginal peoples. Lacrosse, the national game, was played long before the colonists arrived—it is a little-known fact that basketball is also a Native Canadian original. Finally, sports played in the U.S. have crossed the border. There is a Canadian Football League (CFL), and the Toronto Blue Jays won the 1992 and 1993 baseball World Series, beating Americans at their own game.

THIS YEAR'S NEWS

This year was one of Canadian constitutional convalescence. After facing a nail-biting referendum on separation in Québec, and after almost a decade of Conservative-led misattempts to reshape Canada's constitution, the country settled down under Prime Minister Jean Chrétien, who ran for office promising to put constitutional reform on the back burner. Still, separatist leaders in Québec continue to keep the issue, and its high emotions, at the forefront.

Former Prime Minister Brian Mulroney would not go gentle into the night after his party's defeat in 1993; in an unprecedented *cause celèbre*, the former Prime Minister sued the federal government for $50 million this year, crying libel when he was publicly linked to illegal profits from an Air Canada business transaction. The likelihood of an out-of-court settlement did not stave off disgusted communal uproar at the notion of a former Prime Minister suing his own debt-plagued nation.

"Safe" Canada also had a bit of a wake-up call this year when an intruder broke through several levels of security at 24 Sussex Dr., the Prime Minister's official residence, and made it right up to Jean Chrétien's bedroom. The Prime Minister's wife Aline, wielding a heavy candlestick holder, locked the bedroom door and protected her husband while he called the RCMP, Canada's domestic security service. The incident sparked a thorough and embarrassing review of RCMP safety procedures and shocked a citizenry accustomed to a high degree of civility and safety. Still, even this incident did not stop the United Nations from awarding Canada its number one spot for the "best overall quality of life" in 1996, a distinction the country has received consistently for the past decade.

Nova Scotia

Four distinct geographies dominate Nova Scotia: the rugged Atlantic coast, the lush agricultural Annapolis Valley, the calm coast of the Northumberland Strait, and the magnificent highlands of Cape Breton Island. Each offers uniquely breathtaking scenery, and all are complemented by the province's diverse cultural landscape. Nova Scotia's population collectively embodies the Canadian ideal of a cultural "mixed salad." Around 1605, French colonists joined the indigenous Micmac Indians in the Annapolis Valley and on the shores of Cape Breton Island. During the American Revolution, Nova Scotia declined the opportunity to become the 14th American state, establishing itself as a refuge for fleeing British loyalists. Subsequent immigration waves infused Pictou and Antigonish Counties with a Scottish flavor.

PRACTICAL INFORMATION

Capital: Halifax.
Economic Renewal Agency, Tourism Nova Scotia: Historic Properties, P.O. Box 456, Halifax B3J 2R5. **Check-in Nova Scotia** (800-565-0000 from Canada or the continental U.S.) will make lodging reservations.
Drinking Age: 19.
Time Zone: Atlantic (1hr. ahead of Eastern). **Postal Abbreviation:** NS.
Provincial Sales Tax: 11%, plus 7% GST.

▓ Atlantic Coast

Gulf Stream waters crash onto the rocky Atlantic Coast, setting the pace of life on the shore. Follow Nova Scotia's **Lighthouse Route** south on Hwy. 3 from Halifax to coastal villages where boats and lobster traps are tools of a trade, not just props for tourists. **MacKenzie Bus Lines** (902-543-2491) runs between Halifax and Yarmouth, at the tip of the peninsula, with few stops (call for details Mon.-Sat. 9am-5pm).

The quintessential Nova Scotia lighthouse overlooks **Peggy's Cove,** off Hwy. 333, 43km southwest of Halifax. No public transportation serves the town, but most bus companies offer packages which include a stop there. These buses, along with throngs of cars during the summer and cruise lines arriving on Wednesdays and Sundays, make a mockery of the cove's declared population of 60. Arrive early to avoid the crowds, and wake up with espresso ($1.25) and fresh baked goods from **Beales Bailiwick** (902-823-2099; open May-Oct. daily 9am-dusk).

Return to Hwy. 3 and head south for about 50 km to find **Mahone Bay,** a slightly larger town quaint enough to attract proportional crowds. The **tourist office,** 165 Edgewater St. (902-624-6151), is open daily 10am-5pm. The **Wooden Boat Festival** (902-624-8443), a celebration of the region's ship-building heritage, includes a boat-building contest and race (lucky participants are supplied with wood and glue), and a parade of old-style schooners. Avast, ye scurvy dog! **Mug & Anchor Pub,** 634 Main St. (902-624-6378), tames a matey's appetite for seafood and draft beer beneath wooden beams laden with a collection of coasters. Specialties include meat pie ($8), fish and chips ($4), and seafood pasta dishes ($8). (Kitchen open Sun.-Thurs. 11am-9pm, Fri.-Sat. 11am-10pm. Bar open daily 11am-midnight.)

The undefeated racing schooner Bluenose, which graces the Canadian dime and the Nova Scotia license plate, saw its start in the shipbuilding center of **Lunenburg,** 11 km east of Mahone Bay on Hwy. 3. Explore the schooner and exhibits at the **Fisheries Museum of the Atlantic** (902-634-4794), on Bluenose Dr. by the harborfront. (Open daily 9:30am-5:30pm; Oct. 15-May Mon.-Fri. by appointment. $6, families with children under 17 $15.) Several bed and breakfasts dot the roadsides in this area, but don't aim for bargains; **Margaret Murray's Bed and Breakfast,** 20 Lorne St. (902-634-3974), is as reasonable as it gets. (Singles $30, doubles $40. Includes full breakfast and parking. Reservations highly recommended.) The **tourist office** (902-634-8100 or

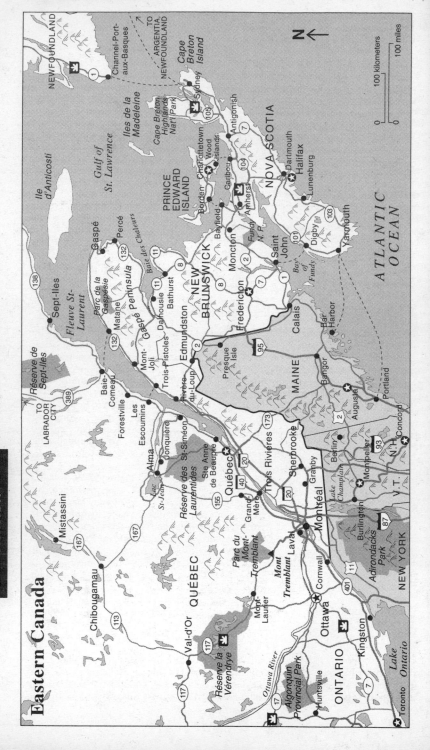

Eastern Canada

634-3656), does its thing in the new blockhouse on Blockhouse Hill Rd. (open mid-May to late Oct. daily 9am-8pm).

From Lunenburg, follow the signs 16km to **Ovens Natural Park** (902-766-4621), west on Hwy. 3 then south and east on Hwy. 332. The park features a spectacular trail along a cliff to a set of natural seacaves, the "ovens" from which the area takes its name, as well as the region's best **campground**. Steeped in lore that extends from Native Canadian legends to tales of the Nova Scotia Gold Rush (when a town arose here, only to fold six years later when things didn't pan out), the park attains an almost spiritual quality, assisted by efforts not to overpackage it for tourists. The campground consists of 65 sites (some overlook the ocean) with access to the caves, free hot showers, a heated saltwater swimming pool, flush toilets, a restaurant, and a store; half are kept unreserved and allotted to early arrivals. (Sites $16, with water and electricity $18, with full hookup $20. Open mid-May to mid-Oct.)

Hwy. 332 continues along the shore and into the town of **East LaHave,** where a **cable ferry** runs across the LaHave River to **LaHave** (on the ½hr. 6am-midnight, by demand midnight-6am; 50¢ fare per car or person). The **LaHave Bakery** (902-688-2908) beckons about 1000 ft. from the ferry dock on the left. Follow the mouthwatering smell of cheese-and-herb bread ($2.75) inside to check in for a night at the **LaHave Marine Hostel (HI-C).** Located upstairs in a homey apartment with a wood-burning stove, the hostel is run by the bakery proprietor; call ahead or arrive during bakery hours. (Bakery open daily 9am-6:30pm; mid-Sept. to June 10am-5pm. Hostel has 9 beds. $10, nonmembers $12. Open June-Oct.)

Yarmouth The port of **Yarmouth,** 339 km from Halifax on the southwestern tip of Nova Scotia, has a major **ferry terminal,** 58 Water St., from which boats shuttle across the **Bay of Fundy** to Maine (open daily 8am-5pm). **Marine Atlantic** (902-742-6800 or 800-341-7981 from the continental U.S.) provides service to Bar Harbor, ME (1 per day; 6-7hr.; $52, car $68, bike $11.50). **Prince of Fundy Cruises** (800-341-7540 from Canada or the continental U.S.) sails from Yarmouth to Portland, ME. (May-Oct. daily 10am; 10 hr.; early May to mid-June US$58, ages 5-14 US$29, car US$80, bike US$7; mid-June to mid-Sept. US$78/$39/$98/$10. Add $3 passengers' tax.) Car rental agencies keep busy in Yarmouth; reserve ahead. **Avis,** 42 Starr's Rd. (902-742-3323), and at a desk in the ferry terminal, rents cars for $43 per day (plus $10 for insurance) with 200 free km (15¢ per additional km); must be 21. The **information center,** 288 Main St., uphill and visible from the ferry terminal, houses both **Nova Scotia Information** (902-742-5033) and **Yarmouth Town and County Information** (902-742-6639; both open daily 8am-7pm). If you're staying around, crash at the **Ice House Hostel** (902-649-2818), overlooking Darling Lake 15 km from Yarmouth on Rte. 1; take Old Post Rd. The small (soon to be not-so-small—they're expanding) two-story building will give you a genuine feel for cabin life. (4 beds, shared bath, kitchen. $8.50, nonmembers $10. Open June-Sept.)

■ Halifax

The British erected the Halifax Citadel in 1749 to counter the French Fortress of Louisbourg on the northeastern shoulder of Cape Breton Island. Never captured or attacked during the era of the colonial empires, the Citadel has seen more French tourists than it has French soldiers. A horrific event mars Halifax's placid history, however. In 1917, miscommunication between a Belgian relief ship and a French ship carrying picric acid and 400,000 tons of TNT resulted in a collision in Halifax Harbor. One hour later, the largest synthetic explosion before the advent of the atomic bomb rocked the city. Approximately 11,000 people were killed or injured, and windows were shattered up to 50 mi. away. Long recovered, Halifax (pop. 320,000) has grown to be the largest city in Atlantic Canada. The city's universities and active nightlife draw young people from throughout the province and beyond.

CANADA

PRACTICAL INFORMATION

Tourist Office: Halifax International Visitors Center, 1595 Barrington St. (490-5961). Call for additional locations. Open daily 8:30am-7pm. For reservations, contact **Tourism Nova Scotia,** P.O. Box 519, B3J 2L7 (800-565-0000).

Student Travel Office: Travel CUTS (494-2054; fax 494-2230), on the 3rd floor of the Dalhousie University Student Union Building. Open Mon.-Fri. 9am-4pm. Rideboard posted near the cafeteria.

Airport: Halifax International, 40km from the city on Hwy. 102. The **Airbus** (873-2091) runs to downtown (20 per day 7:45am-10:45pm; $11, round-trip $18; under 10 free with adult). **Ace Y Share-A-Cab** (429-4444) coordinates shared cab rides to the airport 5am-9pm. Phone 3hr. ahead of pick-up time. Fare $18 ($30 for 2) from anywhere in Halifax. From the airport to town $20.

Trains: VIA Rail, 1161 Hollis St. (429-8421), at South St. in the South End near the harbor. To: Montréal ($147, student or senior $132, under 12 $73; discounts Sept. to mid-Dec. and mid-Jan. to mid-June). Open daily 9am-5:30pm.

Buses: Acadian Lines and **MacKenzie Bus Line** share a terminal at 6040 Almon St. (454-9321), near Robie St. (To get downtown, take bus #7 or #80 on Robie St., or any of the 6 buses on Gottingen St. 1 block east of the station.) MacKenzie travels down the Atlantic coast to Yarmouth (1 per day, 6hr., $40); ask about stops at small towns en route. Acadian covers most of the remainder of Nova Scotia and Canada: Annapolis Royal (2 per day, 3-5hr., $25); Charlottetown, PEI (2 per day, 8½hr., $47); North Sydney (3 per day, 6-8hr., $47). 25% senior discounts, 50% discount for kids 5-11, under 5 free with adult. Station open Sun.-Fri. 6:30am-midnight, Sat. 6:30am-11pm; ticket office daily 7am-7pm.

Public Transportation: Metro Transit (421-6600; open Mon.-Fri. 7:30am-10pm, Sat.-Sun. 8am-10pm). Efficient and thorough. Pick up route maps and schedules at any info center. Fare $1.30, seniors 95¢, ages 5-15 80¢; fare from Sackville $1.50. Buses run daily roughly 7am-midnight.

Ferries: Dartmouth-Halifax Ferry (421-6600), on the harborfront. 15-min. crossings depart from both terminals every 15-30min. Mon.-Fri. 6:30am-11:30pm; every 30min. Sat. 6:30am-11:30pm, Sun. noon-5:30pm. Fare $1.20, seniors and ages 5-12 90¢.

Taxi: Aircab, 456-0373. **Ace Y Cab,** 429-4444. $2.40 base fee, $1.50 per mi.

Car Rental: Rent-a-Wreck, 2823 Robie St. (454-2121), at Almon St. $33 per day with 200 free km; 12¢ per additional km. Insurance $12 per day, ages 21-25 $14. Must be 21 with credit card. Open Mon.-Fri. 8am-5pm, Sat. 8am-1pm.

Bike Rental: Pedal and Sea, 1253 Barrington St. (471-1616), outside the hostel. Mountain bikes $6 per hr., HI members $5; $13/$11 per ½-day; $22/$15 per day; $80/$60 per week. Open mid-May to mid-Oct. daily 9am-6pm.

Crisis Lines: Sexual Assault, 425-0122. **Crisis Centre,** 421-1188. Both 24hr. **Gayline:** 423-7129. Operates Thurs.-Sat. 7-10pm.

Emergency: 4105.

Post Office: Station A, 6175 Almon St. (494-4712), in the North End. Open Mon.-Fri. 8am-5:15pm. **Postal code:** B3K 5M9. **Area code:** 902.

Barrington St., the major north-south thoroughfare, runs straight through downtown. Approaching the Citadel and the Public Garden, **Sackville St.** cuts east-west parallel to **Spring Garden Rd.,** Halifax's shopping thoroughfare. Downtown is flanked by the less affluent **North End** and the mostly quiet and arboreal **South End,** on the ocean. Downtown traffic doesn't get too hectic, but parking is difficult.

ACCOMMODATIONS AND CAMPING

You'll have no trouble finding affordable summer accommodations in Halifax, except during major events, such as the Tattoo Festival or the Moosehead Grand Prix (see Entertainment below). Plan well in advance for those times.

Halifax Heritage House Hostel (HI-C), 1253 Barrington St. (422-3863), a 3-min. walk from the heart of downtown, 1 block from the train station. Immaculate rooms with access to TV lounge, kitchen, and laundry facilities. 1st-floor rooms enjoy a low people-to-bathroom ratio. Get the security access code if you'll be out past 10pm. Office closed noon-3pm. Check-in 3-11pm. $14, nonmembers $17, non-Canadian nonmembers $18. Free linen. IBN reservations available.

Technical University of Nova Scotia, M. M. O'Brien Bldg., 5217 Morris St. (422-2495), at Barrington St. Refinished brick dorms right downtown. Free laundry facilities and parking. Kitchen access. Check-in 8am-midnight. Singles $26, doubles $21 per person; students with ID $21/$19; under 10 free with adult. Reservations recommended July-Aug. Open May-Sept.

Dalhousie University (494-8840; 494-2108 after 8pm), Howe Hall on Coburg Rd. at LeMarchant, 3km southwest of downtown. "Dal" is usually packed; arrive early. Laundry and recreation facilities costs extra. Open 24hr. Singles $29, doubles $43 (breakfast and parking included); students $20/$32 ($5 extra for breakfast); under 11 free. July-Aug. make reservations 1 week in advance. Open early May-late Aug.

Gerrard Hotel, 1234 Barrington St. (423-8614), between South and Morris St. Subdued live-in clientele and elaborate rooms. Kitchen access, free parking, pool, laundry, game room. Check-in Mon.-Fri. 8am-8:30pm, Sat. 8am-7:30pm. Singles $30, with private bath $49; doubles $44/$54. $5 per extra person.

Wood Havens Park (835-2271), in Hammond's Plain, a 20-min. drive north on Rte. 102, has the closest campsites in the Halifax area. Take Exit 3 on Rte. 102 to Rte. 213 and follow the signs. 95 sites; $15, with hookup $18.50; open May-Oct.

FOOD

Downtown venues provide many options for appeasing the demons of hunger. Pubs peddle cheap grub and inner peace, but their kitchens often close down around 10pm. For fresh local produce and baked goods, visit the **farmer's market** (492-4043), in the old brewery on Lower Water St. (open May-Sept. Sat. 7am-1pm).

Granite Brewery, 1222 Barrington St. (423-5660). A microbrewery with some of the best pub food around. Produces 3 labels; the "Peculiar" is strangely appealing ($2.55). Try it with the smoked salmon club sandwich ($7) or the hearty beef and beer stew ($5). Open Mon.-Sat. 11:30am-12:30am, Sun. noon-11pm.

Lawrence of Oregano, 1726 Argyle St. (425-8077). Unlike his Arabian cousin, this Lawrence never made it to the silver screen. Called "Larry O's" by the regulars. Satisfying Italian and seafood dishes around $5; daily specials $3-4. Open Mon.-Tues. 11am-2am, Wed.-Sun. 11am-3:30am. Kitchen closes at 9pm.

Mediterraneo Café, 1571 Barrington St. (423-6936). Somber, long-haired students converse over Middle Eastern dishes. Coffee's filled twice for 90¢, so relax and stay a while. Tabouli with 2 huge pita pockets $3; falafel sandwich $3; filling daily specials $3.25-5. Open Mon.-Fri. 7am-8:30pm, Sat.-Sun. 9am-8:30pm.

SIGHTS

The star-shaped **Halifax Citadel National Historic Park** (426-5080), in the heart of Halifax, and the old **Town Clock,** at the foot of Citadel Hill, are Halifax traditions. A walk along the fortress walls affords a fine view of the city and harbor. Small exhibits and a one-hour film inside the fortress will fill you in on the relevant history. Come any day between June 15 and Labor Day at 11:40am to see the pageantry of preparation for the **noonday cannon firing.** (Open June 15-Labor Day daily 9am-6pm; Labor Day-Oct. and mid-May to mid-June 10am-5pm. In summer $5, seniors $3.75, ages 6-16 $2.50; off season $3/$2.25/$1.50. Under 5 free with adult.)

The **Halifax Public Gardens,** across from the Citadel near the intersection of South Park and Sackville St., make a relaxing spot for a lunch break. The Roman statues, Victorian bandstand, gas lamps, exquisite horticulture, and overfed loons on the pond are very properly British. (Open daily 8am-sunset.) From July through September, watch for concerts on Sunday afternoons at 2pm. Reconstructed early-19th-century architecture covers the **Historic Properties** district (429-0530), downtown on lower Water St. Unfortunately, the charming stone-and-wood façades are only sheep's clothing disguising wolfishly overpriced boutiques and restaurants. Museums in Halifax don't stack up to the competition elsewhere in Nova Scotia, though the **Maritime Museum of the Atlantic,** 1675 Lower Water St. (424-7490), has an interesting display on the Halifax Explosion. (Open Mon.-Sat. 9:30am-5:30pm, Sun. 1-5pm. $4.50.)

Point Pleasant Park, 186 car-free wooded acres at the southern tip of Halifax (take bus #9 from Barrington St. downtown), remains one of England's last imperial holdings, leased to the city of Halifax for 999 years at the bargain rate of 1 shilling per year. Inside the park, the **Prince of Wales Martello Tower,** an odd fort built by the British in 1797, stands as testimony to one of Prince Edward's two fascinations: round buildings and his mistress—both of which he kept in Halifax.

ENTERTAINMENT AND NIGHTLIFE

The **Neptune Theatre,** 5216 Sackville St. (429-7070), presents the area's most noteworthy professional stage productions. (Performances Sept. to mid-May. Tickets $20-30.) At **Wormwood's Dog and Monkey Cinema,** 2015 Gottingen St. (422-3700), Canadian and international art films have been known to prompt sell-outs and sizable lines; get there early to beat the intellectual masses. (Tickets $7. Shows daily around 7 and 9:30pm; matinees on Sun.)

The Nova Scotia International Tattoo Festival (420-1114; 451-1221 for tickets), is possibly Halifax's biggest summer event. Presented by the Province of Nova Scotia and the Canadian Maritime Armed Forces, the festival runs through the first week of July, featuring international musicians, bicyclists, dancers, acrobats, gymnasts, and military groups. At noon, the Metro area overflows with free entertainment. Later, a two-hour show, featuring over 2000 performers, takes place in the Halifax Metro Centre. (Show tickets $11-25, seniors and kids under 13 $2 off.) The **DuMaurier Atlantic Jazz Festival** (492-2225 or 800-567-5277) fests for a week in mid-July with both ticketed and free concerts throughout the city. For ten days in mid-August, **Buskerfest** (429-3910) brings street performers to Halifax from around the world. The **Atlantic Film Festival** (422-3456) wraps up the festival season with a showcase of Canadian and international films at the end of September.

To put it bluntly, Halifax boasts one of Canada's most intoxicating nighttime scenes. Numerous pubs and clubs pack the downtown area, making bar-hopping common and recommended. Pick up a free copy of *The Coast* for a listing of special goings-on. The un-domelike amalgam known as **The Dome** (that's the **Liquordome** to locals) houses eating and drinking establishments which draw young people to daily drink specials and dancing. Inside, **Lawrence of Oreganos** and **My Apartment** have combined kitchens to form **The Atrium** (cover $2-4; open daily noon-3:30am). At the **Seahorse Tavern,** 1665 Argyle St. (423-7200), purple-haired students meet lawyers in a dark basement room with carved woodwork and live music on summer Sunday nights. (Open Mon.-Wed. noon-1am, Thurs.-Sat. noon-2am.) The **Lower Deck** (425-1501), in the Historic Properties, offers excellent Irish folk music along with nautical pub decor. (Cover $2-4. Open Mon.-Sat. 11am-12:30am, Sun. 9pm-midnight.) Huge and always packed, **Peddler's Pub** (423-5033), in Barrington Place Mall on Granville St., is favored for good pub food, including wings ($4.50) and steamed mussels ($4). (99¢ food specials Fri. after 4pm. Open Mon.-Sat. 10am-midnight, Sun. noon-8pm.) **J.J. Rossy's,** 1887 Granville St. (422-4411), across the street from Peddler's, attracts nocturnal crowds with a dance floor and tremendous drink specials—during the "power hours" (Wed.-Sat. 10-11pm and midnight-1am) a draft falls to 70¢ and shots plummet to $1.25. Rossy's also offers a $4.50 all-you-can-eat lunch special on Fridays, noon-2pm. (Cover Thurs.-Sat. after 8pm $2.50. Open Mon.-Sat. 11am-2am; kitchen until 10pm.) **Birdland,** 2021 Brunswick St. (425-0889), at Cacross Cogswell St. from downtown, caters to an alternative crowd with live bands three or four nights per week. (Cover $3-15. Open Mon.-Sat. 4pm-3:30am, Sun. 8pm-3:30am.) **The Studio** (423-6866), at Barrington St. and Spring Garden Rd., is a primarily gay and lesbian club with some of the city's best techno dance music. ($2 cover Fri.-Sat. after 10pm. Open Mon.-Sat. 4pm-2am, Sun 6pm-2am.)

New Brunswick

Powerful South Indian Ocean currents sweep around the tip of Africa and ripple thousands of miles through the Pacific before coming to a spectacular finish at New Brunswick. Here, in the Bay of Fundy are the world's highest tides which sometimes reaching a staggering 48 ft. Away from the ocean's violent influence, vast unpopulated stretches of forest swathe the land in timeless wilderness. Over two centuries ago, British Loyalists, fleeing in the wake of the American Revolution, came to rest on the shores of the bay. Disgruntled by the distant government in Halifax, the colonists complained and were granted self-government by the Crown, and the province of New Brunswick was born. Much earlier, in the 17th century, French pioneers established the farming and fishing nation of *l'Acadie* on the northern and eastern coasts; today, the traditions of the French and British cultures live on in everything from cuisine to language. Although over a third of the province's population is French-speaking, English is far more widely used.

PRACTICAL INFORMATION

Capital: Fredericton.
Department of Economic Development and Tourism, P.O. Box 12345, Fredericton E3B 5C3, distributes free publications including the *Official Highway Map, Outdoor Adventure Guide, Craft Directory, Fish and Hunt Guide,* and *Travel Guide* (with accommodation and campground directory). Call **Tourism New Brunswick** (800-561-0123) from anywhere in Canada.
Drinking Age: 19.
Time Zone: Atlantic (1hr. ahead of Eastern). **Postal Abbreviation:** NB.
Provincial Sales Tax: 11%.

■ Saint John

The city of Saint John was founded literally overnight on May 18, 1783, by the United Empire Loyalists, a band of about 10,000 American colonists loyal to the British crown. Saint John's long Loyalist tradition shows through in its architecture, festivals, and institutions; the walkways of King and Queen Squares in central Saint John (never abbreviated in order to prevent confusion with St. John's, Newfoundland) were laid out to resemble the Union Jack. Yet not all is royal about the city parks—one end of the Loyalist Plaza has been converted into a sand pit for "Beach Volleyball on the Boardwalk." Now home to 125,000 people, Canada's oldest incorporated city rose to prominence in the 19th century as a major commercial and shipbuilding port. Saint John's location on the Bay of Fundy ensures cool summers and mild winters, though it often makes the city foggy and wet; locals joke that Saint John is where you go to get your car, and body, washed for free.

PRACTICAL INFORMATION

Tourist Office: Saint John Visitors and Convention Bureau, 15 Market Sq. (658-2990), on the 11th floor of City Hall at the foot of King St. Open Mon.-Fri. 8:30am-4:30pm. The **City Center** info center (658-2855), at Market Sq., is open mid-June to Labor Day daily 9am-8pm; off-season daily 9am-6pm.
Trains: Via Rail (642-2916), has a station in Moncton; take an SMT bus from Saint John, then catch a train in Moncton. A train ticket to Saint John or a Canrail pass will cover bus fare. Call for prices and schedules.
Buses: SMT, 300 Union St. (648-3555), provides service to: Moncton (2 per day, 2hr., $20); Montréal (2 per day, 14hr., $80); Halifax (2 per day, 8hr., $54). Station and ticket office open daily 7:30am-9pm.
Public Transportation: Saint John Transit (658-4700), runs until roughly 11:30pm. Fare $1.35, under 14 $1. June 15-Sept., their 3-hr. guided tour of historic Saint John leaves from Loyalist Plaza and Reversing Falls. $16, ages 6-14 $6.

Ferry: Marine Atlantic (636-4048 or 800-341-7981 from the continental U.S.), on the Lancaster St. extension near the mouth of Saint John Harbor. Take the "West Saint John" bus, then walk 10min. Crosses to Digby, NS (1-3 per day; 3hr.; $23, seniors $20.75, ages 5-12 $11.50, bike $11.25, car $50; mid-Sept. to Oct. and May-June $17.75/$16/$9/$8.75/$44; Jan.-April $16.75/$15/$8.50/$5.50/$42.50).

Taxi: Royal Taxi, 800-561-8294. **Diamond,** 648-8888. Both open 24hr.

Car Rental: Downey Ford, 10 Crown St. (632-6000). $20 per day with 100 free km; 10¢ per additional km. Insurance $10; ages 21-24 must be able to cover a hefty $1500 deductible. Must be 21 with major credit card. Open Mon.-Fri. 7am-6pm, Sat. 8am-5pm, Sun. 9am-5pm.

Weather: 636-4991. **Dial-a-Tide:** 636-4429.

Crisis Lines: Provincial Crisis Line, 800-667-5005. **Rape Crisis Line,** 658-1791. **Emergency:** 911.

Post Office: Main Office, 125 Rothesay Ave. (800-565-0726). Open Mon.-Fri. 7:30am-5:15pm. Most other local post offices located inside drug stores. **Postal code:** E2L 3W9. **Area code:** 506.

Saint John's busy downtown (Saint John Centre) is bounded by **Union St.** to the north, **Princess St.** to the south, **King Sq.** on the east, and **Market Sq.** and the harbor on the west. Find free three-hour parking outside the city's malls. Fort Latour Harbor Bridge (toll 25¢) on Hwy. 1 connects Saint John to West Saint John, as does a free bridge on Hwy. 100.

ACCOMMODATIONS AND CAMPING

Finding lodging for under $35 per night is difficult, especially in summer. In West Saint John, a number of nearly identical motels on the 1100 to 1300 blocks of **Manawagonish Rd.** charge $35-45 for a single. Call Saint John Transit for directions by bus (see Practical Information above); by car, avoid the bridge toll by taking Hwy. 100 into West Saint John, turn right on Main St., and head west until it turns into Manawagonish Rd.

Saint John YMCA/YWCA (HI-C), 19-25 Hazen Ave. (634-7720); from Market Sq., it's 2 blocks up Union St. on the left. Drab, bare, but clean rooms. Access to YMCA recreational facilities, pool, and work-out room. Open daily 5am-11pm; guests arriving on the evening ferry can check in later. $25, nonmembers and nonstudents $30. Reservations recommended in summer.

Hillside Motel, 1131 Manawagonish Rd. (672-1273), in a quiet residential neighborhood within 10min. of downtown. Standard motel comforts include TV and private baths. 1 bed $38, 2 beds $50; Sept.-April $35/$45.

O'Neill's Bed and Breakfast, 982 Manawagonish Rd. (672-0111). Exudes Irishness. Few frills, but clean and well-kept. 3 doubles available (1 has twin beds); 1 person $44, 2 people $49. Full breakfast included.

Rockwood Park Campground (652-4050), at the southern end of Rockwood Park 2km north of uptown off Hwy. 1; take the "University" bus to the Mount Pleasant stop, then walk 5min. Tents in a partly wooded area. Showers included. Sites $13, with hookup $15; weekly $60/$80. Open mid-May to Sept.

Anglican Centre, 230 Hawthorne Ave. Extension (634-8732). A retreat house situated at the southern entrance to Rockwell Park, the Anglican Centre welcomes travelers when not filled with retreaters. A variety of clean, attractive rooms, under $15 per person. Reservations required.

University of New Brunswick at Saint John (648-5755), on Tucker Park Road. If you're willing to drive 10-20min. out of Saint John, the university's Sir James Dunn Residence Hall offers new, neat, furnished rooms to summer visitors. Check-out 11am. Singles $24, doubles $35; students $13, $12 per person in a double. Reservations required. Office open Mon.-Fri. 8am-4pm.

FOOD

For cheap food, fresh from the butcher, baker, fishmonger, produce dealer, or cheese merchant, visit **City Market,** 47 Charlotte St. (658-2820), between King and Brunswick Sq. The market may also be the best place to look for **dulse,** a local specialty not found outside New Brunswick, which consists of sun-dried seaweed from the Bay of Fundy; it can best be described as "ocean jerky." A $1 bag is more than a sample. (Market open Mon.-Thurs. 7:30am-6pm, Fri. 7:30am-7pm, Sat. 7:30am-5pm.) **Reggie's Restaurant,** 26 Germain St. (657-6270), provides fresh, homestyle renditions of basic North American fare. The sandwiches ($2-4), made with famous smoked meat from Ben's Deli in Montréal, may not fill you up, but the breakfast special will: two eggs, sausage, homefries, toast, and coffee for $3.50, served 6-11am. (Open Mon.-Wed. 6am-6pm, Thurs.-Fri. and Sun. 6am-7pm, Sat. 6am-5pm.)

SIGHTS AND ENTERTAINMENT

Saint John's main attraction is **Reversing Falls,** a natural phenomenon caused by the powerful Bay of Fundy tides (for more on the tides see Fundy National Park, below). Though the name may suggest 100-ft. walls of gravity-defying water, the "falls" are actually beneath the surface of the water. At high tide, patient spectators see the flow of water at the nexus of the Saint John River and Saint John Harbor slowly halt and change direction. More amazing than the event itself may be the number of people captivated by it. The appropriately named **Reversing Falls Tourist Centre** (658-2937), at the west end of the Hwy. 100 bridge (take the west-bound "East-West" bus), distributes tide schedules and shows a thrill-a-minute 12-min. film on the phenomenon. (Screenings every ½hr.; $1.25, kids under 12 free. Center open mid-June to mid-Oct. daily 8am-8pm.) **Jet boat rides** (634-8987) through the rapids are the latest in Reversing Falls excitement.

The oldest independent brewery in Canada, **Moosehead Breweries,** 49 Main St. (635-7020), in West Saint John, waits at the end of many a devoted enthusiast's pilgrimage. (Free 1-hr. tours with samples mid-June to Aug. 9:30am and 2pm. Tours limited to 25 people; avoid heartbreak by making reservations 2-3 days in advance.) The **New Brunswick Museum** (643-2300) features neither moose nor brew, but it does house a 45-ft. Right Whale skeleton among multiple exhibits. (Open Mon.-Fri. 9am-9pm, Sat. 10am-6pm, Sun. noon-5pm. $5.50, seniors $4.50, students/kids $3, families $12; Wed. 6-9pm free.)

Pick up a brochure at any tourist info center for the city's three self-guided **walking tours** (each about 2hr.). **The Victorian Stroll** roams past some of the old homes in Saint John, most dating to the late 1800s; **Prince William's Walk** details commerce in the port city; **The Loyalist Trail** traces the places frequented by the Loyalist founders. All three heavily emphasize history, architecture, and nostalgia. **Trinity Church,** 115 Charlotte St. (693-8558), on the Loyalist Trail tour, displays amazing stained-glass windows and the Royal Coat of Arms of George III's House of Hanover. It was stolen ("rescued") from the old Boston Council Chamber by Loyalists fleeing the American Revolution (tours and viewing Mon.-Fri. 9am-3pm).

Fort Howe Lookout, originally erected to protect the harbor from dastardly American privateers, affords an impressive view of the city and its harbor. To visit the lookout, walk a few blocks in from the north end of the harbor and up the hill; look for the wooden blockhouse atop the hill (open 24hr.; free). Live naturally at the **Irving Nature Park** (653-7367), in West Saint John off Sand Cove Rd. (free).

■ Fundy

Fundy National Park, occupying 260 sq. km of New Brunswick's coast an hour's drive southeast of Moncton on Hwy. 114, is characteristically New Brunswickian in that its main attractions are its natural wonders. Approximately every 12 hr., the world's largest tides draw back over 1 km into the Bay of Fundy, allowing visitors to explore the vast territory uncovered by the ebbing tide. Don't get caught too far out

CANADA

without your running shoes though; the water rises 1 ft. per min. when the tide comes in. When you're not fleeing the surf, Fundy's extensive hiking tails, forests, campgrounds, and recreational facilities should keep you occupied.

Practical Information **Park Headquarters** (887-6000), P.O. Box 40, Alma, E0A 1B0, consists of a group of buildings in the southeastern corner of the Park facing the Bay, across the Upper Salmon River from the town of Alma. The area includes the administration building, the assembly building, an amphitheater, and the **visitors reception center,** which sits at the park's east entrance. (Open daily 8am-10pm; Sept. to mid-Oct. and mid-May to mid-June Mon.-Fri. 8:15am-4:30pm, Sat.-Sun. 10am-6pm.) **Wolfe Lake Information** (432-6026), the other visitors center, lurks at the northwest entrance off Hwy. 114. (Open daily 8am-9pm; mid-May to mid-June and Sept. to mid-Oct. 10am-6pm.) No public transportation serves Fundy. The nearest bus depots are in Moncton and Sussex. The park extracts an entrance fee of $3 per day from mid-June to Labor Day. The free and invaluable park newspaper *Salt and Fir*, available at the entrance stations and info centers, includes a map of hiking trails and campgrounds, and a schedule of programs and activities.

Fundy weather can be unpleasant for the unprepared. Evenings are often chilly, even when days are warm. It's best to always bring a wool sweater or jacket, as well as a can of insect repellent for the warm, muggy days. **Weather** forecasts are available from the info centers by calling 887-6000. **Area code:** 506.

Camping, a Hostel, and Food The park operates four **campgrounds** totaling over 600 sites. Getting a site is seldom a problem, but landing one at your campground of choice may be a little more difficult. The park accepts no reservations; all sites are first come, first served. **Headquarters Campground,** closest to facilities, is usually in highest demand. When the campground is full, put your name on the waiting list, and sleep somewhere else for the night. Return the next day at noon when the names of those admitted for the night are read. (Sites $11, with hookup $17. Open mid-June to Labor Day.) The only other campground with facilities, **Chignecto North Campground,** off Hwy. 114, 5 km inland from the headquarters, puts the forest and distance between campsites for more privacy. (Sites $10, with hookup $15-17. Open mid-May to mid-Oct.) **Point Wolfe Campground,** scenically located along the coast 7 km west of headquarters, stays cooler and more insect-free than the inland campgrounds (sites $10; open July to mid-Aug.). All three campgrounds have showers and washrooms. The **Wolfe Lake Campground,** near the northwest park entrance a minute's walk from the lake, offers primitive sites with no showers or washrooms (sites $8; open mid-May to mid-Oct.). Year-round wilderness camping is also available in some of the most scenic areas of the park, especially **Goose River** along the coast. The campsites, all with fireplaces, wood, and an outhouse, carry a $2 per person per night permit fee. Call 887-6000 to make the required reservations one or two weeks in advance.

The **Fundy National Park Hostel (HI-C)** (887-2216), near Devil's Half Acre about 1 km south of the park headquarters, has a full kitchen, showers, and a common room with TV. Ask the staff for the lowdown on park staff nightlife. (Check-in 8-10am and 5-10pm. $9.50, nonmembers $11.50. Open June-Aug. Wheelchair accessible.) For a cheap, home-cooked meal, try **Harbor View Market and Coffee Shop** (887-2450), on Main St. in Alma. Dinner specials are $6, and the breakfast special of two eggs, toast, bacon, and coffee runs $3. (Open daily 7am-10pm; Sept.-May daily 7:30am-9pm. Restaurant open Mon.-Sat. 7:30am-7pm, Sun. 8am-7pm.)

Activities The park maintains about 104 km of park trails year-round, about 35 km of which are open to mountain bikes. Hoof it or rent a bike from **Eastern Outdoors** (887-1888), in downtown Alma ($7 for 1hr., $10 for 3hr., $15 for 5hr., $20 1 day, $50 5 days). *Salt and Fir* contains detailed descriptions of all trails, including where you'll find waterfalls and ocean views. Though declining in numbers, deer are still fairly common, and thieving raccoons run thick around the campsites. Catching a glimpse of a peregrine falcon will require considerable patience, but the moose come out to be seen around dusk.

Most recreational facilities operate only during the summer season (mid-May to early Oct.), including free daily interpretive programs designed to help visitors get to know the park. Park staff lead beach walks, evening programs, and weekly campfire programs. Visit the park in September and October to catch the fall foliage and avoid the crush of vacationers. Those seeking quiet, pristine nature would be wise to visit in the chillier off season.

■ Near Fundy: Kouchibouguac

Unlike Fundy's rugged forests and the high tides along the Loyalist coast, **Kouchibouguac National Park** shows off warm lagoon waters, salt marshes, peat bogs, and white sandy beaches. Bask in the sun along the 25 km stretch of barrier islands and sand dunes, or swim through canoe waterways that were once highways for the Micmacs. Rent canoes ($6.50 per hr., $27 per day), kayaks ($4.75 per hr.), and bikes ($5 per hr., $22 per day) at **Ryans Rental Center** (876-3733), in the park between the South Kouchibouguac Campground and Kellys Beach. (Open early June to early Sept. daily 8am-9pm; late May to early June Sat.-Sun. 9am-5pm.) The park operates two campgrounds in the summer, neither with hookups. **South Kouchibouguac** has 219 sites ($15) with showers, and **Côte-à-Fabien** has 32 sites ($13) and no showers. Off-season campers take advantage of primitive sites within the park and several commercial campgrounds just outside of the park. Kouchibouguac (meaning "river of the long tides" in Micmac) charges those over five years of age a daily fee of $3, ages 6-16 $1.50. The **park information centre** sits at the park entrance, on Hwy. 117 just off Hwy. 11, 90-km north of Moncton (open 10am-6pm). The park administration (876-2443) is open year-round (Mon.-Fri. 8:15am-4:30pm).

Prince Edward Island

Prince Edward Island, now more commonly called "P.E.I." or "the Island," began as St. John's Island. In 1799, residents renamed the area for Prince Edward, son of King George III, in thanks for his interest in the territory's welfare. Almost too conveniently, the change cleared up the exasperating confusion between the island and St. John's, Newfoundland; St. John, Labrador; and Saint John, New Brunswick.

The smallest province in Canada attracts visitors hoping to share in the relaxing beauty made famous by Lucy Maud Montgomery's novel *Anne of Green Gables*. The fictional work did not exaggerate the wonders of natural life on the island; the soil, made red by its high iron-oxide content, complements the ubiquitous green crops and shrubbery, turquoise waters, and purple roadside lupin. On the north and south shores, some of Canada's finest beaches extend for miles. Relentlessly quaint, Island towns seem to exist more for visitors than for residents, consisting mainly of restaurants and shops. From lawn bowling, a favorite of the older set, to nightly public parties (Celtic music is big here), P.E.I. comes alive during the summer.

PRACTICAL INFORMATION

Capital: Charlottetown.
Drinking Age: 19.
Time Zone: Atlantic (1hr. ahead of Eastern time). **Postal Abbreviation:** P.E.I.
Provincial Sales Tax: 10%.
Tourist Office: P.E.I. Visitor Information Centre, P.O. Box 940, C1A 7M5 (368-4444 or 800-463-4734), by the waterfront in Charlottetown. Open daily 9am-10pm; Sept.-May 9am-5pm. The **Charlottetown Visitors Bureau,** 199 Queen St. (566-5548), hides inside City Hall. Open Mon.-Fri. 9am-9pm.

CANADA

Beach Shuttles: Beach Shuttle, 566-3243. Picks up at the **P.E.I. Visitor Information Centre** at 178 Water St. (call for additional points) and drops off in Cavendish. 2 per day June and Sept., 4 per day July-Aug.; 45min.; $9, $14 roundtrip.

Ferries: Marine Atlantic (855-2030; 800-341-7981 from U.S.), in Borden, 56km west of Charlottetown on the TCH. To: Cape Tormentine, NB (every hr. on the ½-hr. 6:30am-1am, 45min., roundtrip $8, cars $19.50, not including driver). **Northumberland Ferries** (566-3838 or 800-565-0201 from P.E.I. and Nova Scotia), in Wood Islands 61km east of Charlottetown on TCH. To: Caribou, NS (8-14 per day, 1½hr., $9.25). Both ferries collect only round-trip fares and only when leaving P.E.I. Thus, it is cheaper to leave from Borden than from Wood Islands, no matter how you come over.

Taxis: City Cab, 892-6567. Open 24hr. Service from Borden ferry to downtown Charlottetown $45.

Bike Rental: Shaw's Hotel Cycle Rental, Rte. 15 (672-2022). $6 per hr., $14.50 per day. Open June-Oct. 10am-6pm. **MacQueens,** 430 Queen St. (368-2453). Road and mountain bikes $20 per day, $80 per week. Must have credit card or $75 deposit. Open Mon.-Sat. 8:30am-5pm.

Crisis Line: Crisis Centre, 566-8999. 24hr.

Emergency: Charlottetown Police, 368-2677. **Royal Canadian Mounted Police,** 566-7111.

Post Office: 135 Kent St. (566-4400). Open Mon.-Fri. 8am-5:15pm. **Postal code:** C1A 7N1. **Area code:** 902.

Queen St. and **University Ave.** are Charlottetown's main thoroughfares, straddling **Confederation Centre** along the west and east, respectively. The most popular beaches, **Cavendish, Brackley,** and **Rustico Island,** lie on the north shore in the middle of the province, opposite but not far from Charlottetown.

ACCOMMODATIONS AND CAMPING

B&Bs and **country inns** crowd every nook and cranny of the province; some are open year-round, but the most inexpensive are closed during the off season. Avoid frustration by calling ahead. Rates hover around $28 for singles and $35 for doubles. Fifteen farms participate in a provincial **Farm Vacation** program, in which tourists spend time with a farming family. Call the **Tourist Industry Association of P.E.I.** (566-5008) for info, or pick up a brochure at the visitors center.

The **Charlottetown International Hostel (HI-C),** 153 Mt. Edward Rd. (894-9696), across the yard from the University of P.E.I. in a large green barn one long block east of University Ave., a 45-min. walk from the bus station. The green and white sign marking the turnoff leads to neat, spacious rooms, friendly staff, and diverse clientele. (Kitchen facilities, showers, TV lounge. Bike rentals $8.50. 3-night max. stay. Check-in 7-10am and 4pm-midnight. Curfew midnight. $13, nonmembers $16. Blanket rental $1. Open June-Labor Day.) The University of P.E.I. runs a B&B in **Marion Hall.** (July-Aug. singles $28.50, doubles $37, breakfast included; May-June $26/$32.) **Bernadine Hall,** open for most of the summer, is another option. (July-Aug. singles $34.50, doubles $42, breakfast included; May-June $32/$37.) Students receive a $5 discount on all U.P.E.I. rates. Check-in for all locations takes place at Blanchard Hall. **Midgell Centre** (961-2963), Rte. 2 in Midgell (the big, green buildings with a white cross in front), is a Christian retreat center that welcomes travelers to its neat, comfy cabins in the summer. (Kitchen facilities and showers available; sleeping bags recommended. $14; open June-Aug.; reservations required.)

Prince Edward Island National Park (672-6350 or 963-2391) operates three campgrounds during the summer (148 primitive, secluded sites $12; 330 sites with showers, toilets, kitchen access, laundry facilities $15; 80 sites with hookup $19) and one off-season campground (primitive sites $8). The many other provincial parks that offer camping, as well as the plentiful private campgrounds scattered throughout the Island, ensure that there will always be a campsite available. (Open seasons vary, but expect to find a campground open from mid-June to Sept.)

FOOD

The quest for food on P.E.I. boils down to the search for a cheap **lobster.** At market, the coveted crustaceans go for $4-6 per lb. Fresh seafood, including the world famous **Malpeque oysters,** is sold along the shores of the island, especially in North Rustico on the north shore. **Fisherman's Catch,** near the Stanley Bridge west of Cavendish, peddles incredibly fresh, cheap seafood from a shack across the lake from the Fiddle 'n' Vittles restaurant. Ask the staff about oyster-shucking supplies and for a demo. (Lobster cooked or uncooked from $6 per lb. Oysters in the shells $2.50 per lb. Open mid-June to early Sept. daily 10am-8pm.) The back of the *P.E.I. Visitor's Guide* lists fresh seafood outlets. For the freshest food around, shop the **Charlottetown Farmers' Market** (368-4444), on Belvedere St. opposite U.P.E.I. (open July-Sept. Sat. 9am-2pm and Wed. 10am-5pm).

The cosmopolitan young clientele at **Café Soleil,** 52 University Ave., Charlottetown (368-8098), takes time out from postulating to partake of U-build deli sandwiches ($3.50). (Bakery open Mon.-Sat. 7am-7pm; restaurant open Mon.-Sat. 9am-11pm, Sun. 9am-2pm.) For non-aquatic fare, including vegetarian dishes a-plenty, stop by **Shaddy's,** 44 University Ave., Charlottetown (368-8886), a local favorite that serves Lebanese and Canadian cuisine. All-you-can-eat lunch (Mon.-Fri. 11:30am-2pm) goes for $6. (Open Mon.-Fri. 7:30am-11pm, Sat. 9am-11pm, Sun. 10am-10pm.)

SIGHTS AND ENTERTAINMENT

The Island at Large

Green Gables House (672-6350), off Rte. 6 in Cavendish near Rte. 13, has become a mecca for adoring Lucy Maud Montgomery readers—a surprising number make the pilgrimage all the way from Japan. Green Gables can get very crowded between late July and September, so it's best to arrive in the early morning or the evening (peak hours 11am-4pm). Tours are available in English and French. (Open daily 9am-8pm; mid-May to late July and early Sept. to Oct. daily 9am-5pm; Nov. to mid-May by request, 894-4246. $2.50.)

Prince Edward Island National Park (672-2259 or 963-2391), the most popular Canadian national park east of Banff, consists of a 32-km coastal strip embracing some of Canada's finest beaches and over a fifth of P.E.I.'s northern coast. Wind-sculpted sand dunes and salt marshes rumple the park's terrain. The park is home to many of the Island's 300-odd species of birds, including the endangered **piping plover.** Park campgrounds, programs, and services operate mid-June to Labor Day; **Cavendish campground** stays open until late September. (Sites $15, entrance $4 per day.) Snag a copy of the park guide *Blue Heron* at the entrance kiosks.

The stretches of beach on the **eastern coast** of PEI are considerably less touristed than those in the west. **Lakeside,** a beach 35 km east of Charlottetown on Rte. 2, is often near-deserted on July and August weekdays (unsupervised). For the romantic equestrian in you, trot along the surf atop a sturdy steed from **Gun Trail Ride** (961-2076), located right beside the golf course ($8 per hr., with trail guide $9, June-Labor Day daily 9am-6pm). **Basin Head Beach,** 95 km east of Charlottetown, makes a relaxing day trip; over seven mi. of white sand ensures that you won't have to rumble with other visitors for turf (unsupervised).

Charlottetown

The province's capital prides itself on being the "Cradle of Confederation." Delegates from the British North American colonies met in 1864, inside the brownstone **Province House** (566-7626), on the corner of Great George and Richmond St., to discuss the union which would become the Dominion of Canada in 1867. Both the modern and the historical chambers of the legislature are open for viewing. (Open daily 9am-8pm; mid-Oct. to June Mon.-Fri. 9am-5pm. Free.) Adjoining the Province House, the modern performing arts complex at **Confederation Centre for the Arts** (628-1864), on the corner of Queen and Grafton St., contains theaters, exhibits, and an art gallery.

CANADA

The Centre conducts guided tours July to August. (Box office open daily 9am-9pm; Sept.-June daily noon-5:30pm.) Every summer, a musical production of **Anne of Green Gables** takes the Mainstage as part of the Charlottetown Festival. (Performances July to early Sept. Mon and Wed.-Fri. 8pm; tickets $22-30. Matinees Wed. and Sat. 1:30pm; tickets $17-25. For ticket info, call 566-1267 or 800-565-0278). Proof that some Islanders aren't so reverent when it comes to *her,* **Annekenstein 6** (566-1267) jives the girl and the island; call for details. In the summer, moving **P.E.I. House Parties** (800-461-4734) are all the rage. Local musicians perform traditional music across the island for anyone who will pay to party ($5, kids under 12 $2; refreshments included).

Québec

Home to 90% of Canada's French-speaking citizenry, Québec continues to fight for political and legal recognition of its separate cultural identity. Originally populated by French fur trading settlements along the St. Lawrence River, Québec was ceded to the British in 1759. Ever since, anti-federalist elements within *québecois* society have rankled under control of the largely Anglicized national government. French is spoken by 95% of Québec's population; all signs are printed in French, as required by provincial law. The failure of the 1990 Meech Lake Accord to recognize Québec as a "distinct society" and the more recent election of the Bloc Québecois, a separatist party, to the status of official opposition in the federal government signal uncertain times ahead for the province. Visitors will likely never notice these underlying tensions—the majority of the struggle goes on behind closed doors in Ottawa—but the entire country wonders if this province will choose to stay a part of the whole.

PRACTICAL INFORMATION

Capital: Québec City.
Tourisme Québec: C.P. 20,000, Québec G1K 7X2 (800-363-7777; 514-873-2015 in Montréal). Open daily 9am-5pm. **Canadian Parks Service, Québec Region,** 3 Buade St., P.O. Box 6060, Québec GIR 4V7 (800-463-6769; 418-648-4177 in Québec City).
Time Zone: Eastern. **Postal abbreviation:** QU.
Drinking Age: 18.
Sales Tax: 6.5% on goods and services, plus a 7% GST.

ACCOMMODATIONS INFORMATION

For assistance in locating accommodations throughout the province, try the following organizations.

Vacances-Familles, 5972 Sherbrook E., Montréal H1N 1B8 (514-251-8811 or 800-465-2711). A lodging network with discounts of 10-40% on accommodations throughout Canada, primarily in Québec. Owned by the Canadian Automobile Association (CAA). Household membership $43 for the first year.
Camping: Association des terrains du camping du Québec (Camping Association of Quebec), 2001 de la Metropole St., office 700, Longueil, Québec J4G 1S9 (514-651-7396 or 800-363-0457), and **Fédération québecoise du camping et de caravaning,** 4545, ave. Pierre-de-Coubertin, Stade Olympique, C.P. 1000, succursale "M," Montréal H1V 3R2 (514-252-3003).
Hostels: Regroupement Tourisme Jeunesse (HI-C), at the Fédération address (514-252-3117). For reservations in any Québec hostel and a few in neighboring Ontario call 800-461-8585 at least 24hr. in advance, with a credit card.

▓ Montréal

This island city, named for the Mont-Royal in its midst, has been coveted territory for over 300 years. Wars and sieges have brought governments in and out like the tide, including a brief takeover by American revolutionaries in late 1775. Amidst it all, Montréal has grown into a diverse city with a cosmopolitan air seen in few other cities on the continent. Above and beyond the Québecois and English cultures which often still chafe, the city hosts large enclaves of Chinese, Italians, and Greeks. Whether you credit the international flavor or the large student population of the city, it is hard not to be swept up by the energy, vibrancy, and fun which course through Montréal's *centre-ville*.

PRACTICAL INFORMATION

Tourist Office: Infotouriste, 1001, rue de Square-Dorchester (873-2015 or outside Montréal 800-363-7777), on Dorchester Sq. between rue Peel and rue Metcalfe. Metro: Peel. Free city maps and guides, and extensive food and housing listings. Open in summer daily 7:30am-8pm; Labor Day-June 9am-6pm. A branch office in **Old Montréal,** 174, rue Notre-Dame Est at Place Jacques Cartier. Open late June to early Sept. daily 9am-7pm; early Sept.-Oct. 9 9am-5pm; Oct. 10-Easter Thurs.-Sun. 9am-5pm; Easter-late June daily 9am-5pm.

Youth Travel Office: Tourisme Jeunesse, 3603, rue St-Denis (252-3117). Métro: Sherbrooke. Free maps, hostel info, travel gear, and advice. A non-profit organization that inspects and ranks all officially recognized youth hostels in Québec. Open Mon.-Wed. 10am-6pm, Thurs.-Fri. 10am-9pm, Sat. 10am-5pm. **Travel CUTS,** McGill Student Union, 3480, rue McTavish (398-0647). Métro: McGill. Specializes in budget travel for college students. Open Mon.-Fri. 9am-5pm.

Consulates: U.S., 1155, rue St-Alexander (398-9695). Open Mon.-Fri 8:30am-12:30pm; for visas 8:30am-noon. **U.K.,** 1000, rue de la Gauchetière Ouest, ste. 4200 (866-5863). Open for info Mon.-Fri. 9am-5pm; for consular help call the British High Commission in Ottawa (613-237-1303 for passports, 613-237-2008 for visas). **France,** 1 Place Ville-Marie, 26th fl. (878-4385). Open 8:30am-noon.

Currency Exchange: Currencies International, 1250, rue Peel (392-9100). Métro: Peel. Open in summer Mon.-Wed. 8:30am-8pm, Thurs.-Fri. 8:30am-9pm, Sat. 8:30am-6pm, Sun. 9am-5pm; in winter Mon.-Wed. 8:30am-7pm, Thurs.-Fri. 8:30am-8pm, Sat. 8:30am-6pm. **Thomas Cook,** 625, bl. René-Lévesque Ouest (397-4029). Métro: Square-Victoria. Open Mon.-Wed. 9am-5pm, Thurs.-Fri. 9am-6pm. Another office, at 777, rue de la Gauchetiere (Métro: Bonaventure), is open daily 7am-9pm. Most bank machines are on the PLUS system and charge only the normal transaction fee for withdrawals abroad; ask your bank about fees.

Airports: Dorval (633-3105 for info), 20-30min. from downtown by car. From the Lionel Groulx Métro stop, take bus #211 to Dorval Shopping Center, then transfer to bus #204. Handles flights from U.S. and within Canada. **Autocar Connaisseur-Grayline** (934-1222) runs a minivan to Dorval from 777, rue de la Gauchetiere, at University St., stopping at any downtown hotel if you call in advance. Vans run Mon.-Fri. every ½hr. 5:10-7:20am and every 20min. 7:20am-11:10pm, Sat.-Sun. every ½hr. 5:10am-11:10pm. $9, under 5 free. Taxi downtown $30. **Mirabel International** (476-3010), 45min. from downtown by car. Handles all flights from outside U.S. or Canada. Grayline buses service Mirabel daily $14.50; call for schedule. Taxi downtown $60.

Trains: Central Station, 895, rue de la Gauchetière Ouest, under the Queen Elizabeth Hotel. Métro: Bonaventure. Served by **VIA Rail** (989-2626 or 800-561-9181). To: Québec City (3-4 per day, 3hr., $44); Ottawa (4 per day, 2hr., $36); Toronto (6 per day, 4-5½hr., $84). Ticket counter open daily 6:15am-8pm. Also, **Amtrak** (800-872-7245). To: New York (2 per day, 10hr., US$48-76) and Boston (2 per day, 13hr., US$70-83). Amtrak ticket counter open daily 5:45am-5pm. Baggage check $2; open Tues.-Sun. 7:30am-7pm, Mon. 8am-7pm for baggage pick-up.

Buses: Voyageur, 505, bd. de Maisonneuve Est (842-2281). Métro: Berri-UQAM. Voyage to: Toronto (7 per day, 6½hr., $70); Ottawa (18 per day, 2½hr., $27.30); Québec City (18 per day, 3hr., $35.50). Buses to Ontario leave from **Dépanneur**

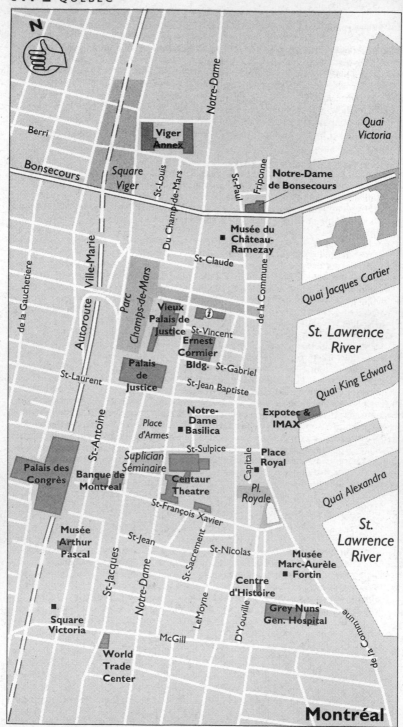

Montréal

Beau-soir, 2875, bl. St-Charles (630-4836). Ride **Greyhound** (287-1580) to New York City (7 per day, 8¾hr., $89) or Boston (3 per day, 7½hr., $70).

Public Transportation: STCUM Métro and Bus, 288-6287. A generally safe and extremely efficient network. The four Métro lines and most buses operate daily 5:30am-12:30am; some have night schedules as well. Get network maps at the tourist office, or at any Métro station booth. Maps have locations of shops and malls as well, especially useful for navigating the **underground city.** Downtown ticketing is rampant so take the Métro. Buses are a well integrated part of the system; transfer tickets from bus drivers are good as subway tickets. Fare for train or bus $1.75, 6 tickets $7.50.

Taxis: Taxi Pontiac, 761-5522. **Champlain Taxi Inc.,** 273-2435. Both operate 24hr. at the city's regulated rates. $2.25 base fare.

Car Rental: Via Route, 1255, rue MacKay (871-1166), at Ste-Catherine. $37 per day with 200 free km; 12¢ per additional km. Insurance $16 per day, ages 21-24 $19 per day. Must be 21 with credit card. Open Mon.-Fri. 7am-9pm, Sat. 7:30am-5pm, Sun. 9am-9pm.

Driver/Rider Service: Allo Stop, 4317, rue St-Denis (985-3032). Matches passengers with member drivers; part of the rider fee goes to the driver. To: Québec City ($15), Ottawa ($10), Toronto ($26), Sherbrooke ($9), New York City ($50), or Boston ($42). Riders and drivers fix their own fees for rides over 1000mi. Annual membership fee required ($6, drivers $7). Open Mon.-Tues. 8am-6pm, Wed.-Fri. 8am-7pm, Sat.-Sun. 9am-6pm.

Bike Rental: Cycle Pop, 978, Rachel Est (524-7102). Métro: Mont-Royal. 21-speeds $20 per day, $50 for the weekend. Open Mon.-Wed. 9:30am-6pm, Thurs.-Fri. 9:30am-9pm, Sat.-Sun. 9:30am-5pm. Credit card or $250 deposit required.

Hotlines: Tel-aide, 935-1101. **Sexual Assault,** 934-4504. **Suicide-Action,** 723-4000. All three open 24hr. **Rape Crisis,** 278-9383. Open Mon.-Fri. 9:30am-4:30pm. **Gay Info,** 768-0199. Open Fri.-Sat. 7:30-10:30pm.

Emergency: 911.

Post Office: Succursale (Postal Station) "B," 1250, rue University (395-4539), at Cathcourt. Open Mon.-Wed. 8am-5:45pm, Thurs.-Fri. 8am-9pm, Sat. 9:30am-5pm. **Postal code:** H3B 3B0. **Area code:** 514.

Two major streets divide the city, making orientation convenient. The **boulevard St-Laurent** (also called "The Main") stretches north-south, splitting the city and streets east-west (traffic here runs one way: north). The Main also serves as the unofficial French/English divider; English **McGill University** lies to the west while slightly east is **St-Denis,** a parallel two-way thoroughfare which defines the **French student quarter** (also called the *quartier latin* or the student ghetto). **Rue Sherbrooke,** which is paralleled by de Maisonneuve and Ste-Catherine downtown, runs east-west almost the entire length of Montréal. Parking is often difficult in the city, particularly during winter when snowbanks narrow the streets and slow traffic. Meters cost 25¢ for 10 min. downtown, and $30 parking tickets are common. Take the **Métro** to avoid the hassle. Montréal's population is 85% Francophone, but most are bilingual. Speak French if you know it.

ACCOMMODATIONS AND CAMPING

The **Québec Tourist Office** is the best resource for info about hostels, hotels, and *chambres touristiques* (rooms in private homes or small guest houses). B&B singles cost $25-40, and doubles run $35-75. The most extensive B&B network is **Bed & Breakfast à Montréal,** P.O. Box 575, Snowdon Station, H3X 3T8 (738-9410; fax 735-7493), which recommends that you reserve by phone, fax, or mail. (Singles from $35, doubles from $55; $15 per night deposit upon confirmation. Leave a message if the owners are out.) The **Downtown Bed and Breakfast Network,** 3458, ave. Laval, H2X 3C8 (289-9749 or 800-267-5180), near Sherbrooke, lists about 80 homes downtown. (Singles $40, doubles $55. Open in spring and summer daily 9am-9pm; in fall and winter 9am-6pm.) Virtually all B&Bs have bilingual hosts.

Many of the least expensive *maisons touristiques* and hotels cluster around rue St-Denis, ranging from quaint to seedy. The area, which abuts Vieux Montréal, flaunts lively nightclubs and a number of funky cafés and bistros. Two blocks east of St-Denis, **Hotel Le Breton**, 1609, rue St-Hubert (524-7273; Métro: Berri-UQAM), around the corner from the bus station, is a gem in the city's budget accommodation crown. Although the neighborhood is not particularly wholesome, the 13 rooms are clean and comfortable and have TV and A/C. (Singles $40-55, doubles $45-70.) The hotel fills up quickly—make reservations.

Montréal Youth Hostel (HI-C), 1030, rue MacKay (843-3317). Métro: Lucien-L'Allier. Airport shuttle drivers will stop here if asked. Relatively new, large, and extremely convenient location in a hotel, complemented by great service. The friendly, upbeat staff will give you the nightlife lowdown in addition to their own free tours and outings. Rooms have 2-6 beds (250 total). Kitchen, laundry facilities, carpet, A/C, and extensive ride board. Some parking. 1-week max. stay; in winter 10 days. Open 24hr. $16, Canadian nonmembers $18, non-Canadian nonmembers $20.56. Private doubles $20/$25/$24.56 per person. New café with kitchen facilities and limited food. Linen $1.75. Reservations by credit card accepted with 24-hr. notice. IBN reservations available.

Collège Français, 5155, ave. de Gaspé, H2T 2A1 (495-2581). Métro: Laurier, then walk west on Laurier and ½ block north on Gaspé. Clean and well-located. Young clientele, though not young enough to be in *collège* (elementary school). Free parking during off-school hours. Open July-Aug. 24hr.; Sept.-June Mon.-Fri. 7:30am-1am, Sat.-Sun. 7:30am-2am. Prices vary from $13, depending on the number of beds in the room (4-7) and whether there's a private shower. Summer breakfast $3.25. In July-Aug., more beds located at the inconvenient 1391, rue Beauregard Longueuil (Métro: Longueuil, then take bus #71 up Taschereau and Ségin).

Marbel Guest House, 3507, boul. Décarie, H4A 3J4 (486-0232). Métro: Vendôme. 3-room duplex in a residential neighborhood. Fully equipped kitchen, living room with color TV, laundry facilities, backyard barbecue. The seventh-night stay is free. Singles $25. Doubles $35. Breakfast $5. Reservations accepted.

McGill University, Bishop Mountain Hall, 3935, rue de l'Université, H3A 2B4 (398-6367). Métro: McGill. Follow Université through campus (bring your hiking boots; it's a long haul). Ideally located singles. Desk open Mon.-Fri. 7am-10:30pm, Sat.-Sun. 8am-10pm; a guard will check you in late at night. Kitchenettes and payphones on each floor. Common room with TV and laundry facilities. Ask for Gardner building, where the views are best. $36.75, students $28. $51.50 for 2 nights. Weekly $150. Full breakfast $5, served Mon.-Fri. 7:30-9am. Reservations (1-night deposit) needed July- Aug. Open May 15-Aug. 15.

Université de Montréal, Residences, 2350, rue Edouard-Montpetit, H2X 2B9, off Côte-des-Neiges (343-6531). Métro: Edouard-Montpetit. Located on the edge of a beautiful campus; try the East Tower for great views. Laundry facilities. Phone and sink in each room. Desk open 24hr. Singles $37.60, students $26.20. Cafeteria open Mon.-Fri. 7am-7pm. Open early May to mid-Aug.

Maison André Tourist Rooms, 3511, rue Université (849-4092). Métro: McGill. Mme. Zanko will spin great yarns for you in her old, well located house—but only if you don't smoke. Guests have been returning to this bastion of European cleanliness and decor for over 30 years. Singles $26-35, doubles $38-45; $10 per additional person. Reservations recommended.

YMCA, 1450, rue Stanley (849-8393), downtown. Métro: Peel (right across the street from station). 331 rooms. Co-ed. Access to newly renovated Y facilities. Rooms tiny but neat and impeccable. TV and phone in every room. Singles for men $35, for women $38; doubles $54; triples $62; quads $71. Students and seniors $2 off. Cafeteria open daily 7am-8pm. Usually fills up June-Aug; no reservations June-Sept.

YWCA, 1355, rue René-Lévesque Ouest (866-9941). Métro: Lucien l'Allier. Clean, relatively safe rooms in the heart of downtown. Women only. Newly renovated. Access to Y facilities. Kitchen, TV on every floor. Doors lock at 10pm but the desk will buzz you in at night. Singles $38, with semi-private bath $43, with private bath

$48; doubles $54, with semi-private bath $64. Key deposit $5. Reservations accepted.

Manoir Ambrose, 3422, rue Stanley (288-6922), just off Sherbrooke. Somewhat upscale both in price and appearance. 22 rooms with Victorian decor. Singles from $40, doubles from $50. Continental breakfast included.

Hotel de Paris, 901 Sherbrook E. (522-6861). In cahoots with the pricier Dansereau Mansion, the Hotel has been painting, hammering, sweeping, and setting up a kitchen, all to bring you a brand new 50-bed hostel, expected to open in late 1996 or 1997. Inaugurate a single-sex or co-ed dorm room, or the solitary double, available for guests staying at least three nights (beds $15, double $40).

Those with time, a car, and a good map can camp at **Parc d'OKA** (479-8337), 45 min. from downtown; take Autoroute 20 west to 13 north to 640 west, which eventually becomes the park road. There are 850 beautiful sites on the **Lac des Deux Montagnes.** (Sites $17.50, beachside $18.50, with hookup $23.) For slightly more private sites in the campground closest to the city, try **KOA Montréal-South,** 130, bl. Monette, St-Phillipe J0L 2K0 (659-8626), 15 mi. from the city; follow Autoroute 15 south over Pont Champlain, take Exit 38, turn left at the stop sign, and go straight for about 1 mi. (1.6km)—it's on your left. (Sites for 2 $18, with hookup $22.50. $3.25 per each additional person up to 6, $1.75 if that person be a child.) KOA has a pool, laundry facilities, a small store, free showers, and a daily shuttle to and from Montréal. If these don't wet your camping whistle, try the dramatic (there's a theater here, folks) **Camping Pointe-des-Cascades,** 2 ch. du Canal, Pte. des Cascades (455-9953). Take Autoroute 40 west, Exit 41 at Ste. Anne de Bellevue, junction 20, and west to Dorion. In Dorion, follow "Théâtre des Cascades" signs. (140 sites, many near water. Sites for 4 $20, with hookup $25.)

FOOD

Restaurants pack in along **bd. St-Laurent** and on the western half of **Ste-Catherine,** with prices ranging from affordable to astronomical. In the Latin Quarter, scout out energetic **rue Prince Arthur,** which vacuum-packs Greek, Polish, and Italian restaurants into a tiny area. (See Sights, p. 848, for details on ethnic neighborhood dining.) Here maître-d's stand in front of their restaurants and attempt to court you toward their cuisine. The accent changes slightly at **ave. Duluth,** where Portuguese and Vietnamese establishments prevail. **Rue St-Denis,** the main thoroughfare in the French student quarter, has many small cafés and eateries that cater to student pockets. If you'd like wine with that, you can save money by buying your own at a *dépanneur* or the **SAQ** (Sociéte des alcohols du Québec) and bringing it to an unlicensed restaurant; they're concentrated on the **bd. St-Laurent,** north of Sherbrooke, and on the pedestrian precincts of **rue Prince Arthur** and **rue Duluth.**

French-Canadian cuisine is unique but generally expensive. When you're scrounging for change, look for *tourtière,* a traditional meat pie with veggies and a thick crust, or *crêpes québecois,* stuffed with everything from scrambled eggs to asparagus with *béchamel* (a cream sauce). Wash it down with *cidre* (hard cider). Other Montréal specialties include French bread (the best on the continent), smoked meat, Matane salmon, Gaspé shrimp, lobster from the Iles de la Madelene, and *poutine,* an omnipresent goo of French fries *(frites),* cheese curds, and gravy. Jewish cuisine is to be had in the delis and bakeries on bd. St-Laurent, north of downtown. Savory bagels spring forth from the brick ovens at **La Maison de l'Original Fairmount Bagel,** 74, rue Fairmount Ouest (272-0667; Métro: Laurier; open 24hr.). A food mall with 58 vendor shops, markets, and restaurants, **Le Faubourge** sits on Ste-Catherine at St-Mathieu.

You'll be charged 13% tax for meals totaling more than $3.25. All restaurants are required by law to post their menus outside, so shop around. Consult the free *Restaurant Guide,* published by the Greater Montréal Convention and Tourism Bureau (844-5400), which lists more than 130 restaurants by type of cuisine (available at the tourist office; see Practical Information, above). When preparing your own grub, look for produce at the **Atwater Market** (Metro: Lionel-Groulx); the **Marché Maison-neuve,** 4375, rue Ontario Est (Métro: Pie-IX); the **Marché St-Jacques** (Metro: Berri-UQAM, at the corner of Ontario and Amherst); or the **Marché Jean-Talon** (Métro: Jean Talon). For info on the markets, call 937-7754. (Call Mon.-Wed. and Sat. 7am-6pm, Thurs. 7am-8pm, Fri. 7am-9pm, Sun. 7am-5pm. All markets open Sat.-Wed. 8am-6pm, Thurs.-Fri. 8am-9pm.)

Café Santropol, 3990, rue Duluth (842-3110), at St-Urbain. Métro: Sherbrooke, then walk north on St-Denis and west on Duluth. "Bienvenue à la planète Santropol!" A student hangout, complete with an aquarium and an outdoor terrace for schmooz-ing. Cream cheese, cottage cheese, yogurt, and nuts are staples on the eclectic menu. Huge veggie sandwiches with piles of fruit $6-8. Open Mon.-Thurs. 11:30am-midnight, Fri. 11:30am-2am, Sat. noon-2am.

Etoile des Indes, 1806, Ste-Catherine Ouest (932-8330), near St-Matthieu. Métro: Guy-Concordia. Split-level dining room with tapestries covering the walls. The best Indian fare in town. Dinner entrees $7-17; daily lunch specials $7 (11:30am-2:30pm). The brave should try their bang-up bangalore phal dishes. Open Mon.-Fri. 11:30am-2:30pm and 5-11pm, Sat. noon-2:30pm and 5-11pm, Sun. 5-11pm.

Dunn's, 892, Ste-Catherine Ouest (866-3866). Arguably the best smoked meat in town, served in monstrous slabs tucked between bread and slathered with mus-tard. Sandwiches $4-8; larger meat plates $8-10. Famed for its strawberry cheese-cake ($4). Open 24hr.

El Zaziummm, 51 Roy Est (844-0893), a St. Laurent side street. Spicy Mexican cui-sine and sly, sweet alcoholic beverages; the food and funkiness distract you while the drinks strike silently with a kick like a mule. Entrees $7-11. Open Mon.-Fri. 11am-11pm, Sat.-Sun. 11am-11:30pm.

Wilensky's, 34, rue Fairmount Ouest (271-0247). Métro: Laurier. A great place for a quick lunch. Pull out a book from Moe Wilensky's shelf, note the sign warning "We always put mustard on it," and linger. Hot dogs $1.70; sandwiches $2. Open Mon.-Fri. 9am-4pm.

Da Giovanni, 572, Ste-Catherine Est (842-8851). Métro: Berri. Serves generous por-tions of fine Italian food; don't be put off by the lines or the diner atmosphere. The sauce and noodles are cooked up right in the window. Open Sun.-Wed. 6:30am-11pm, Thurs. 6:30am-midnight, Fri.-Sat. 6:30am-1am.

Au Pain Doré, 5214 Cote des Neiges, near rue Jean Brillant. An answer to the ques-tion "Oh where, oh where can I get some French baked goods?" Also offers a selec-tion of cheeses (brie, havarti, cheddar, and more). Baguettes $1.50-4. Open Mon.-Fri. 9am-7pm, Sat.-Sun. 8am-5pm.

SIGHTS

On the Streets

Montréal has matured from a riverside settlement of French colonists into a hip metropolis. Museums, Vieux Montréal (Old Montréal), and the new downtown are fascinating, but Montréal's greatest asset is its cultural vibrancy. Wander aimlessly and often—but *not* through the high-priced boutiques touted by the tourist office. A small **Chinatown** orients itself along rue de la Gauchetière, near Vieux Montréal's

---

Smoked Meat on Rye

Any true Montrealian will agree that Smoked Meat—a spicy, salty, greasy cured beef brisket—is a delicacy not to be compared with anything else in the world. The great landmark **Ben's Delicatessen,** 990, boul. de Maisonneuve, in the heart of downtown, is often said to be the originator of this artery clogging delicacy, which resembles pastrami or even corned beef. The story has it that Ben Kravitz, a native Lithuanian, longed for the briskets of his native land and, in an effort to recreate them, invented Smoked Meat. A proper Smoked Meat sandwich is served hot with mustard on seedless rye, with fries, vinegar, a half-sour pickle, and a black cherry soda. (At Ben's, that'll run you about $6.)

Place d'Armes. Between 11:30am and 2:30pm, most of its restaurants offer mouth-watering Canton and Szechuan lunch specials ranging from $3.50 to $5. Baklava abounds in **Little Greece,** a bit farther than you might care to walk from downtown just southeast of the Outremont Métro: stop around rue Hutchison between ave. Van Horne and ave. Edouard-Charles. At the northern edge of the town's center, **Little Italy** occupies the area north of rue Beaubien between rue St-Hubert and Louis-Hémon. Walk east from Métro Beaubien and look for pasta. For a **walking tour** approach to the city, stick to the downtown area. Many attractions between Mont Royal and the Fleuve St-Laurent are free, from parks (Mont Royal and Lafontaine, see below) and universities (McGill, Montréal, Concordia, Québec at Montréal) to architectural spectacles of all sorts.

Walk or bike down **bd. St-Laurent,** north of Sherbrooke. Originally settled by Jewish immigrants, this area now functions as a sort of multi-cultural welcome wagon, home to Greek, Slavic, Latin American, and Portuguese immigrants. **Rue St-Denis,** home to the city elite at the turn of the century, still serves as the **Latin Quarter's** mainstreet (Metro: Berri-UQAM). Jazz fiends command the street at the beginning of July during the annual **Montréal International Jazz Festival** (871-1881), with over 350 free outdoor shows. Also visit **rue Prince-Arthur** (Métro: Sherbrooke), which has street performers in the summer, **Carré St-Louis** (Métro: Sherbrooke), with its fountain and sculptures, and **Le Village,** a gay village in Montréal from rue St-Denis Est to Papineau along rue Ste-Catherine Est.

Museums

The **McGill University** campus (main gate at the corner of rue McGill and Sherbrooke; Métro: McGill) runs up Mont Royal and boasts Victorian buildings and pleasant greens in the midst of downtown. More than any other sight in Montréal, the university illustrates the impact of British tradition on the city. The campus also contains the site of the 16th-century Native-American village of Hochelaga and the **Redpath Museum of Natural History** (398-4086), with rare fossils and two genuine Egyptian mummies. (Open in summer Mon.-Thurs. 9am-5pm; Sept.-June Mon.-Fri. 9am-5pm. Free.) Guided tours of the campus are available (daily 9am-4pm with 1-day advance notice; call 398-6555).

About 5 blocks west of the McGill entrance, Montréal's **Musée des Beaux-Arts** (Fine Arts Museum), 1379-80, rue Sherbrooke Ouest (285-1600 or 285-2000; Métro: Peel or Guy-Concordia), houses a small permanent collection that touches upon all major artistic periods and includes Canadian and Inuit work; inquire about their impressive visiting exhibits. (Open Tues. and Thurs.-Sun. 11am-6pm, Wed. 11am-9pm. Permanent collection free. Temporary exhibits $10, students and seniors $7, under 12 $3; ½-price Wed. 5:30-9pm, but permanent collection closed then.) The **McCord Museum of Canadian History,** 690, rue Sherbrooke Ouest (398-7100; Métro: McGill), presents textiles, costumes, paintings, prints, and 700,000 pictures spanning 133 years. (Photographic archives open by appointment only; contact Nora Hague. Open Tues.-Sun. 10am-5pm. $5, students $2, seniors $3, families $8. Free Thurs. 6-9pm.) The relatively new **Centre Canadien d'Architecture,** 1920, av. Baile (939-7026; Métro: Guy-Concordia), houses one of the world's most important collections of architectural prints, drawings, photographs, and books. (Open Tues.-Wed. and Fri.-Sat. 11am-6pm, Thurs. 11am-8pm; in winter also open Sun. 11am-6pm. $5, students and seniors $3, under 12 free. Students free all day on Thurs., everyone free Thurs. 6-8pm.) **Musée d'Art Contemporain** (Museum of Contemporary Art), 185, Ste-Catherine Ouest at Jeanne-Mance (847-6226 or 847-6212; Métro: Place-des-Arts), has the latest by *québecois* artists, as well as textile, photography, and avant-garde exhibits. (Open Tues.-Sun. 11am-6pm, Wed. also 6-9pm. $5, seniors $4, students $3, families $12, under 12 free. Wed. 6-9pm permanent exhibits free, temporary exhibits ½-price.) Outside of the downtown museum circuit, the **Montréal Museum of Decorative Arts,** 2929, rue Jeanne-d'Arc (259-2575; Metro: Pie-IX), houses is home to innovatively designed decorative pieces dating from 1935 to the present, from the functional to the ridiculous. (Open Fri.-Sun. 11am-5pm; $3, students under 26 $1.50, under 12 free.)

Great Big Green Places

Olympic Park, 4141, ave. Pierre-de-Coubertin (252-4737; Métro: Viau), hosted the 1976 Summer Olympic Games. Its daring architecture, uncannily reminiscent of the *U.S.S. Enterprise,* includes the world's tallest inclined tower and a stadium with one of the world's only fully retractable roofs. Despite this, baseball games *still* get rained out because the roof cannot be put into place with crowds in the building (small goof, really). (Guided tours in English daily 12:40 and 3:40pm; more often May-Sept. $5.25, ages 5-17 $4.25, under 5 free.) Take the *funiculaire* to the top of the tower for a panoramic view of Montréal and a guided tour of the observation deck. (Every 10min. Mon.-Thurs. 10am-9pm, Fri.-Sun. 10am-11pm; off season daily 10am-6pm. $10.25, kids $7.75.) The most recent addition to Olympic Park is the **Biodôme,** 4777, ave. Pierre-de-Coubertin (868-3000). Housed in the former Olympic Vélodrome, the Biodôme is a "living museum" in with four complete ecosystems have been reconstructed: the Tropical Forest, Laurentian Forest, the St-Laurent marine ecosystem, and the Polar World. The goal is environmental awareness and conservation; the management stresses repeatedly that the Biodôme is *not* a zoo, but a means for people to connect themselves with the natural world. (Open in summer daily 9am-8pm, off season 9am-6pm. $9.50, students and seniors $7, ages 6-17 $5, under 6 free.) In the summer, a train will take you across the park to the **Jardin Botanique** (Botanical Gardens), 4101, rue Sherbrooke Est (872-1400; Métro: Pie-IX), one of the most important gardens in the world. The Japanese and Chinese areas house the largest *bonsai* and *penjing* collections outside of Asia. (Gardens open in summer daily 9am-8pm; Sept.-June daily 9am-6pm. $7, students and seniors $5, ages 6-17 $3.50, under 6 free; 30% less Sept.-April.) Package tickets for the Biodôme and the Gardens allow you to save money and split a visit up over a two-day period. Parking in the complex begins at $5.

Montréal's more natural approach to a park, **Parc du Mont-Royal,** Centre de la Montagne (844-4928; Métro: Mont-Royal), climbs up to the mountain from which the city took its name. From rue Peel, hardy hikers can take a foot path and stairs to the top, or to the lookouts on Camillien-Houde Pkwy. and the Mountain Chalet. The 30m cross at the top of the mountain commemorates the 1643 climb by de Maisonneuve, founder of Montréal. In winter, *montréalais* congregate here to ice-skate, toboggan, and cross-country ski. In summer, Mont-Royal welcomes joggers, cyclists, picnickers, and amblers. (Officially open 6am-midnight.) **Parc Lafontaine** (872-2644; Métro: Sherbrooke), bordered by Sherbrooke, Rachel, and Papineau ave., has picnic facilities, an outdoor puppet theater, seven tennis courts (hourly fee), ice-skating in the winter, and an international festival of public theater in June.

The Underground City

Montréal residents aren't speaking cryptically of a sub-culture or a hideout for dissidents when they rave about their Underground City. They literally mean *under the ground;* 29km of tunnels link Métro stops and form a subterranean village of climate-controlled restaurants and shops—a haven in Montréal's sub-zero winter weather. The ever-expanding network connects railway stations, two bus terminals, restaurants, banks, cinemas, theaters, hotels, two universities, two department stores, 1700 businesses, 1615 housing units, and 1600 boutiques. Somewhat frighteningly hailed by the city as "the prototype of the city of the future," these burrows give the word "suburban" a whole new meaning. Enter the city from any Métro stop, or start your adventure at the **Place Bonaventure,** 901, rue de la Gauchetière Ouest (397-2205; Métro: Bonaventure), Canada's largest commercial building, with a mélange of shops, each selling products imported from a different country. The tourist office supplies city guides that include treasure maps of the tunnels and underground attractions. (Shops open Mon.-Wed. 9:30am-6pm, Thurs.-Fri. 9:30am-9pm, Sat. 9:30am-5pm, Sun. 9am-noon.) Poke your head above ground to see **Place Ville-Marie** (Métro: Bonaventure), a 1960s office-and-shopping complex. Revolutionary when first built, the structure triggered Montréal's architectural renaissance.

Back in the underworld, ride the train that made it all happen, the Métro, to the McGill stop and enjoy some of the underground city's finest offerings. Here, beneath the Christ Church Cathedral, 625, Ste-Catherine Ouest, waits **Promenades de la Cathédrale** (849-9925), where you can not only shop but enjoy theatrical presentations in the complex's central atrium (call for details). Three blocks east, passing through **Centre Eaton,** of grand department store fame, the **Place Montréal Trust** is famous for its modern architecture and decadently expensive shopping area. Still, there's no charge for an innocent peek around.

Vieux Montréal (Old Montréal) and Fleuve St-Laurent Islands

In the 17th century, the city of Montréal struggled with Iroquois tribes for control of the area's lucrative fur trade, and erected walls encircling the settlement for defense. Today the remnants of those ramparts do no more than delineate the boundaries of Vieux Montréal, the city's first settlement, on the stretch of river bank between rues McGill, Notre-Dame, and Berri. The fortified walls that once protected the quarter have crumbled, but the beautiful 17th- and 18th-century mansions of politicos and merchants retain their splendor. Take the Métro to Place d'Armes, or get off at Bonaventure and check out **Cathédrale Marie Reine du Monde (Mary Queen of the World Cathedral),** at the corner of René-Lévesque and Mansfield (866-1661), before walking to the port. A scaled-down replica of St. Peter's in Rome, the church was built in the heart of Montréal's Anglo-Protestant area. (Open Mon.-Fri. 6:30am-7:30am, Sat. 7:30am-8:30pm, Sun. 8:30am-7:30pm.)

The 19th-century basilica **Notre-Dame-de-Montréal,** 116, rue Notre-Dame Ouest (842-2925), towers above the Place d'Armes and the memorial to de Maisonneuve. Historically a center for the city's Catholic population, the neo-Gothic church once hosted separatist rallies. It seats 4000 and is one of the largest and most magnificent churches in North America. (Shuffle around silently for free; concerts are held here throughout the year.) After suffering major fire damage, the **Wedding Chapel** behind the altar re-opened in 1982, complete with an enormous bronze altar. (Open in summer daily 7am-8pm; Labor Day-June 24 7am-6pm. Free guided tours 8:30am-4:30pm.)

From Notre-Dame walk next door to the **Sulpician Seminary** (the seminary of Old Saint-Sulpice), Montréal's oldest building (built in 1685) and still a functioning seminary. The clock over the facade is the oldest public timepiece in North America and has recorded the passage of over 9.3 billion seconds since it was built in 1700 (do the math). A stroll down rue St-Sulpice will bring you to the old docks along the **rue de la Commune,** on the banks of the Fleuve St-Laurent. Proceed east along rue de la Commune to **rue Bonsecours.** At the corner of rue Bonsecours and the busy rue St-Paul stands the 18th-century **Notre-Dame-de-Bonsecours,** 400, rue St-Paul Est (845-9991; Métro: Champ-de-Mars), founded on the port as a sailors' refuge by Marguerite Bourgeoys, leader of the first congregation of non-cloistered nuns. Sailors thankful for their safe pilgrimage presented the nuns and priests with the wooden boat-shaped ceiling lamps in the chapel. The church also has a museum in the basement and a bell tower with a nice view of Vieux Montréal and the Fleuve St-Laurent. (Chapel open May-Oct. daily 9am-4:30pm, Nov.-April 10am-3pm. Free. Tower and museum open the same hours. $4, under 4 50¢.)

Opening onto rue St-Paul is **Place Jacques Cartier,** site of Montréal's oldest market. Here the modern European character of Montréal is most evident; cafés line the square and street artists strut their stuff during the summer. Visit the grand **Château Ramezay,** 280, rue Notre-Dame Est (861-3708; Métro: Champ-de-Mars), built in 1705 to house the French viceroy, and its museum of Québecois, British, and American 18th-century artifacts. (Open May-Aug. daily 10am-8pm, off season 10am-4:30pm. $5, students and seniors $3, families $10. Guided tours available Wed. and Sun. noon and 2pm.) The **Vieux Palais de Justice,** built in 1856 in Place Vaugeulin, stands across from **City Hall. Rue St-Jacques** in the Old City, established in 1687, is Montréal's Wall Street.

There are many good reasons to venture out to **Ile Ste-Hélène**, an island in the Fleuve St-Laurent just off the coast of Vieux Montréal. The best is **La Ronde** (872-6222 or 800-361-7178; bus #167), Montréal's popular amusement park, especially when you go in the afternoon and buy an unlimited pass. (Open June-Labor Day Sun.-Thurs. 11am-11pm, Fri.-Sat. 11am-midnight. Tickets start at $30.) From late May to July on Thursday and Saturday or Sunday at 10pm, La Ronde hosts the **International Fireworks Competition** (872-8714). If you don't want to pay the park's steep fee, skygaze from crowded Pont Jacques-Cartier or Mont-Royal, above the city.

Le Vieux Fort ("The Old Fort," also known as the **David M. Stewart Museum;** 861-6701), was built in the 1820s to defend Canada's inland waterways. Now primarily a military museum, the fort displays artifacts and costumes detailing Canadian colonial history. (Open in summer Wed.-Mon. 10am-6pm; Sept.-April Wed.-Mon. 10am-5pm. 3 military parades daily June-Aug. $5, students, seniors, and ages 7-17 $3, under 6 free, families $10.) Take the Métro under the St-Laurent to the Ile Ste-Hélène stop.

The other island in Montréal's Parc des Iles is **Ile Notre-Dame,** where the recently opened **Casino de Montréal,** 1, ave. de Casino (392-2746 or 800-665-2274), awaits those who wish to push their luck on nearly 2000 slot machines. Don't bet against the house sticking to its dress code. T-shirts and running shoes are allowed only between June 1 and Labor Day; athletic wear, shorts, and jeans in any size, shape, or color are taboo. (Open daily 11am-3am. Free. *Minimum age 18 to enter and to gamble.* Parking free, with shuttles from the parking lot every 10-15min.)

Whether swollen with spring run-off or frozen over during the winter, the **Fleuve St-Laurent** (St. Lawrence River) can be one of Montréal's most thrilling attractions, although the whirlpools and 15-ft. waves of the **Lachine Rapids** once precluded river travel. No longer—now Old Port of Montréal cruises (842-3871) depart from the clock tower pier mid-May to mid-Oct. at noon and 2:30pm. (3 per day., 2hr., $20, students and seniors $18, ages 6-12 $10, under 6 free, families $42.) Jet-boating tours of the Lachine Rapids (284-9607) leave five times a day from the Old Port. (May-Sept. 10am-6pm. 1½-2-hr. $48, seniors $43, ages 13-19 $38, ages 6-12 $28.) For a more intimate introduction to the river, contact **Rafting Montréal,** 8912, boul. LaSalle (983-3707), in LaSalle. Two 1½-hr. (2hr. with preparation and travel) white water trips are available, at differing levels of shock-induction. They also offer 1½-hr. "hydrojet" trips, and will send a shuttle to pick you up downtown. Reservations are necessary. (Rafting $34, students and seniors $28, ages 6-12 $17. Hydrojet $40/$30/$20. Open May to late Sept. daily 9am-6pm.Trip frequency decreases off season.)

ENTERTAINMENT

Like much of the city, Vieux Montréal is best seen at night. Street performers, artists, and *chansonniers* in various *brasseries* set the tone for lively summer evenings of clapping, stomping, and singing along. The real fun goes down on St-Paul, near the corner of St-Vincent. For a sweet Sunday in the park, saunter over to **Parc Jeanne-Mance** for bongos, dancing, and handicrafts (May-Sept. noon-7pm).

The city has a wide variety of theatrical groups: the **Théâtre du Nouveau Monde,** 84, Ste-Catherine Ouest (866-8667; Métro: Place-des-Arts) and the **Théâtre du Rideau Vert,** 4664, rue St-Denis (844-1793), stage *québecois* works (all productions in French). For English language plays, try the **Centaur Theatre,** 453, rue St-François-Xavier (288-1229; 288-3161 for ticket info; Métro: Place-d'Armes), which performs most works mainly October to June. The city's exciting **Place des Arts,** 260, boul. de Maisonneuve Ouest (842-2112 for tickets), houses the **Opéra de Montréal** (985-2258), the **Montréal Symphony Orchestra** (842-9951), and **Les Grands Ballets Canadiens** (849-8681). **The National Theatre School of Canada,** 5030, rue St-Denis (842-7954), stages excellent student productions during the academic year. **Théâtre Saint-Denis,** 1594, rue St-Denis (849-4211), hosts traveling productions like *Cats* and *Les Misérables.* Check the *Calendar of Events* (available at the tourist office and reprinted in daily newspapers), or call **Ticketmaster** (790-2222; open Mon.-Sat. 9am-9pm, Sun. noon-6pm) for ticket info. **Admission Ticket Network** (790-1245 or 800-

361-4595) also has tickets for various events. (Open daily 8am-11pm. Credit card number required.)

Montréalais are rabid sports fans, and their home team support runs deep. In order to see professional sports, call well in advance to reserve tickets. The **Expos,** Montréal's baseball team, swing in Olympic Stadium (see Sights, above; for Expos info call 846-3976). Between October and April, be sure to attend a **Montréal Canadiens** hockey game; the **Montréal Forum,** 2313, Ste-Catherine Ouest (Métro: Atwater), is the shrine to hockey and **Les Habitants** (nickname for the Canadiens) are its acolytes. Be advised, however, that these are turbulent times at the Forum. The Habs have gone from a league championship in 1993 to missing the playoffs (virtually unheard of) only two seasons later. Games usually sell out; call for tickets as early as possible. Dress at games can be unusually formal. Jacket and ties are not uncommon. The t-shirt-clad, jeans-ripped, hat-on-backwards, beer-drinking American-style fan is somewhat unwelcome here. (For ticket info, call 790-1245.) *Montréalais* don't just like to watch; the one-day **Tour de l'île,** consisting of a 64km circuit of the island, is the largest participatory cycling event in the world, with 45,000 mostly amateur cyclists pedaling their wares. (Call 521-8356 if you wanna be a player. Registration for the ride in early June must be completed in April.) During the second weekend in June, the **Circuit Gilles-Villeneuve** on the Ile Notre-Dame hosts the annual **Molson Grand Prix,** a Formula One race (392-0000 or 800-567-8687), and in August, **Tennis Canada** brings the world's best tennis players to Jarry Park. The tournament features men and women in alternating years and will host men in 1997. (Metro: De Castelnau; 273-1515 ticket info.)

NIGHTLIFE, NIGHTLIFE, AND NIGHTLIFE

Montréal has some hip, hop, happening nightlife. Even in the dead of winter, the bars are full. Should you choose to ignore the massive neon lights flashing "films érotiques" and "château du sexe," you can find lots and lots of nightlife in Québec's largest city—either in **brasseries** (with food as well as beer, wine, and music), in **pubs** (more hanging out and less eating), or the multitude of **dance clubs.** In the gay village of Montréal there are plenty of clubs for both women and men. (Métro: Papineau or Beaudry).

Though intermingled with some of the city's hottest dance venues, the establishments of **rue Ste-Catherine Ouest** and nearby side streets tend to feature drink as the primary entertainment (Metro: Peel). Downstairs at 1107, rue Ste-Catherine Ouest, the **Peel Pub** (844-6769) provides live rock bands and good, cheap food nightly, but more noted are its exceptional drink prices. Here waiters rush about with three pitchers of beer in each hand to keep up with the mötley crüe of university students and suited types. Happy hour (Mon.-Fri. 2-8pm) floods the joint with $6 pitchers and 9¢ wings. Another location is at 1106, boul. de Maisonneuve (845-9002). (Both open daily 11am-3am.) For slightly older and more subdued drinking buddies, search the side streets and the touristy English strongholds around **rue Crescent** and **Bishop** (Métro: Guy), where bar-hopping is a must. **Déjà-Vu,** 1224, Bishop (866-0512), near Ste-Catherine, has live bands each night at 10pm, and excellent atmosphere (happy hour 3-10pm; no cover; open daily 3pm-3am). Set aside Thursday for a night at **D.J.'s Pub,** 1443, Crescent (287-9354), when $12 gets you drinks for the night after 9pm (open Mon.-Fri. noon-2pm, Sat.-Sun. noon-3am). **Sir Winston Churchill's,** 1459, Crescent (288-0616), is another hotspot. (No cover; open daily 11:30am-3am).

Rue Prince Arthur at St-Laurent is devoted solely to pedestrians who mix and mingle at the outdoor cafés by day and clubs by night. **Café Campus,** 57, Prince Arthur (844-1010), features live rock and other genres. (Cover up to $8. Open Sun.-Fri. 8pm-1am.) **The Shed Café,** 3515, St-Laurent (842-0220; open Mon.-Fri. 11am-3am, Sat.-Sun. 10am-3am) and **Angel's,** 3604, St-Laurent (282-9944; open Thurs.-Sat. 8pm-3am) host a primarily student clientele, charge little or no cover, and cluster within a few blocks of **St-Laurent** (Métro: St-Laurent or Sherbrooke). Farther up St-Laurent on the corner of rue Bernard (farther than most people care to walk), lies **Eugene Patin,**

Bassin Louise
Côte d'Abraham
175
Côte Dinan
Parc de l'Artillerie
McMahon
Côte du Palais
St-André
440
Av. Dufferin
Porte Saint-Jean
St-Jean
St-Flaven
Ste-Famille
Porte Kent
Dauphine
Côte de la Fabrique
Musée du Séminaire
St-Pierre
Ste-Anne
D'Auteuil
Ste-Ursule
Ste-Anne
Notre-Dame Basilica
Musée des Ursulines
Buade
Musée du Fort
Musée de la Civilisation
Parc de l'Esplanade
des Ursulines
St-Louis
du Trésor
Place d'Armes
Côte de la Montagne
Notre-Dame
175
Grand Allee
Porte Saint-Louis
Château Frontenac
Parc des Gouverneurs
Place George-V
Côte de la Citadelle
Av. Ste-Geneviève
Av. St-Denis
Terrasse Dufferin
Av. George-VI
Parc des Champs-de-Bataille
Citadelle
Av. Ontario
Av. du Cap Diamante
Boulevard Champlain
Fleuve Saint-Laurent

Vieux-Québec

5777, St-Laurent (278-6336), one of the city's hidden jewels (cover until 2am $5; open Wed.-Sat. 10pm-3am).

French nightlife also parleys in the open air cafés on **rue St-Denis** (Métro: UQAM). Rockin' dance club by night, **Bar Passeport**, 4156, rue St-Denis (842-6063), at Rachel, doubles as a store by day (no cover; open daily 10pm-3am).

■ Québec City

Dubbed the "Gibraltar of America" because of the stone escarpments and military fortifications protecting the port, Québec City sits high on the rocky heights of Cape Diamond where the Fleuve St-Laurent narrows and joins the St. Charles River. Passing through the portals of North America's only walled city is like stepping into the past. Narrow streets and horse-drawn carriages greet visitors to the Old City; there are enough sights and museums to satisfy even the most voracious history buff. Along with the historical attachment, Canada's oldest city boasts a thriving French culture—never assume that the locals speak English. Acutely aware of their history and intensely devoted to their culture, local Québecois exude an energetic, cosmopolitan spirit and a refreshingly positive, upbeat outlook on life.

PRACTICAL INFORMATION

Visitor Information: Centre d'information de l'office du tourisme et des congrés de la Communauté urbaine de Québec, a.k.a. "that place with an uncommonly long name," 60, rue d'Auteuil (692-2471), in the Old City. Accommodations listings, brochures, free maps, and friendly bilingual advice. Ask for the annual *Greater Québec Area Guide.* Free local calls. Open June-Labor Day daily 8:30am-

8pm; April-May and Sept.-Oct. Mon.-Fri. 8:30am-5:30pm; mid-Oct. to March Mon.-Fri. 8:30am-5pm. **Maison du tourisme de Québec,** 12, rue Ste-Anne (800-363-7777), deals specifically with provincial tourism, distributing accommodations listings for the entire province and free road and city maps. Budget Rent-a-Car and some bus tours have desks here. Open daily 8:30am-7:30pm; Labor Day to mid-June 9am-5pm.

Youth Travel Office: Tourisme Jeunesse, 2700, boul. Laurier (800-461-8585), in Ste-Fo, in Place Laurier. Sells maps, travel guides, ISICs, and HI-C memberships, and health insurance. Makes reservations at hostels in Québec or Ontario. (Open Mon.-Wed. 10am-6pm, Thurs.-Fri. 10am-9pm, Sat. 9am-5pm, Sun. noon-5pm.)

Airport: The airport is far out of town and inaccessible by public transport. Taxi to downtown $22. By car, turn right onto Rte. de l'aéroport and then take either bd. Wilfred-Hamel or, beyond it, Autoroute 440 to get into the city. **Maple Leaf Sightseeing Tours** (649-9226) runs a shuttle service between the airport and the major hotels of the city. (Mon.-Fri. 5 per day to airport and 8 per day from the airport, 8am-5:30pm; Sat.-Sun. 4 per day to and from the airport, 10am-3pm. $8.75, under 12 free.)

Trains: VIA Rail, 450, rue de la Gare du Palais in Québec City (524-3590). To: Montréal (3 per day, 3hr., $44; *40% discount with 5-day advance purchase).* Open Mon.-Fri. 6am-8:30pm, Sat.-Sun. 7am-8:30pm. Nearby stations at 3255, ch. de la Gare in Ste-Foy (658-8792 or 653-6427; open Mon.-Fri. 6am-9pm, Sat.-Sun. 7:30am-9pm) and 5995, St-Laurent Autoroute 20, Lévis (833-8056). Open Thurs.-Mon. 4-5am and 8-10:30pm, Tues. 4-5am, Wed. 8-10:30pm. Reservations 800-561-9181 in Canada or the U.S.

Buses: Orlean Express, 320 Abraham Martin (525-3000). Open daily 5:30am-1am. Outlying stations at 2700, ave. Laurier, in Ste-Foy (651-7015; open daily 6am-1am), and 63, Hwy. Trans-Canada Ouest (Hwy. 132), in Lévis (837-5805; open 24hr). To Montréal (every hr. 6am-9pm and 11pm, 3hr., $35.50) and Ste-Anne-de-Beaupré (2 per day, 25min., $5). Connections to U.S. via Montréal or Sherbrooke.

Public Transportation: Commission de transport de la Communauté Urbaine de Québec (CTCUQ), 270, rue des Rocailles. 627-2511 for route and schedule info. Open Mon.-Fri. 6:30am-10pm, Sat.-Sun. 8am-10pm. Buses operate daily 5:30am-12:30am although individual routes vary. $1.85, students $1.45, seniors and kids $1.25; advance-purchase tickets $1.50/95¢/95¢; under 6 free.

Taxis: Coop Taxis Québec, 525-5191. $2.25 base, $1 each additional km.

Driver/Rider Service: Allo-Stop, 467, rue St-Jean (522-0056), will match you with a driver heading for Montréal ($15) or Ottawa ($29). Must be a member ($6 per year, drivers $7). Open daily 9am-5pm.

Car Rental: Pelletier, 900, bd. Pierre Bertrand (681-0678). $39 per day; 500 km free, 50¢ each additional km, $15 insurance. Must be 25 with credit card deposit of $350. Open Mon.-Fri. 7:30am-8pm, Sat.-Sun. 8am-4pm.

Bike Rental: Promo-Vélo (522-0087), located in a tent in the tourist center parking lot on Rue d'Auteuil. 1hr. $6, 4hr. $14, 1 day $23; credit card deposit of $40 required. Open daily May-Oct. 8am-9pm, weather permitting.

Crisis Lines: Tél-Aide, 683-2153. Open daily noon-midnight. **Viol-Secours** (sexual assault line), 522-2120. Counselors on duty Mon.-Fri. 9am-4pm and on call 24 hrs. for emergencies. **Center for Suicide Prevention,** 522-4588. Open 24hr. **Vet-Médic,** 647-2000. **Weather,** 640-2736. **Tides,** 648-7293.

Emergency: Police, 911 (city); 623-6262 (province). **Info-santé,** 648-2626. 24-hr. service with info from qualified nurses.

Post Office: 3, rue Buade (694-6102); also at 300, rue St-Paul (694-6175). **Postal code:** G1R 2J0. **Postal code:** G1K 3W0. Both open Mon.-Fri. 8am-5:45pm. **Area code:** 418.

Québec's main thoroughfares run through both the Old City *(Vieux Québec)* and outside it, generally parallel in an east-west direction. Within **Vieux Québec,** the main streets are **St-Louis, Ste-Anne,** and **St-Jean.** Most streets in Vieux Québec are one way, the major exception being rue d'Auteuil, which borders the walls and is the best bet for parking. Outside the walls of Vieux Québec, both St-Jean and St-Louis continue (St-Jean eventually joins Chemin Ste-Foy and St-Louis becomes **Grande Allée**). **Bd. René-Lévesque,** the other major street outside the walls, runs between St-

Jean and St-Louis. The Basse-ville (lower town) is separated from the Haute-ville (upper town, Old Québec) by an abrupt cliff roughly paralleled by rue St-Vallier Est.

ACCOMMODATIONS AND CAMPING

For Bed and Breakfast referrals, contact Montréal-based Breakfast á Montréal (see p. 843), or **Le Transit,** 1050 Turnbull Ave., Québec City G1R 2X8 (647-6802; call 8am-noon or 4-8pm). Singles run $50, doubles $65-75. Hosts are usually bilingual. If parking is a problem (usually the case in Old Quebec) and you have to make use of the underground parking areas, ask your host about discount parking passes. Most places offer them, which means paying $6 rather than $10 for a 24-hr. pass.

You can obtain a list of nearby campgrounds from the Maison du Tourisme de Québec (see Practical Information), or by writing tourisme Québec, c.p. 979, Montréal, Québec H3C 2W3 (800-363-7777; open daily 9am-5pm).

Auberge de la Paix, 31, rue Couillard (694-0735). While it lacks many facilities, the friendly staff and big, clean mattresses make it worthwhile. Offers great access to the restaurants and bars on rue St.-Jean. An open, casual atmosphere; no locks on the doors. Large coed rooms. 56 beds; 2-8 per room, but most have 3-4. Curfew 2am with all-day access. Beds $18. Breakfast of toast, cereal, coffee, and juice included (8-10am). Kitchen open all day. Linen $2 for entire stay. Reservations necessary July-Aug.

Centre international de séjour (HI-C), 19, rue Ste-Ursule (694-0755), between rue St-Jean and Dauphine. Follow Côte d'Abraham uphill from the bus station until it joins ave. Dufferin. Turn left on St-Jean, pass through the walls, and walk uphill, to your right, on Ste-Ursule. If you're driving, follow St-Louis into the Old City and take the second left past the walls onto Ste-Ursule. The rooms are cramped, but a diverse, youthful clientele and a fabulous location make it a solid choice. 300 beds. Laundry, microwave, TV, pool, ping-pong tables, living room, kitchen, smoking room (open 7:30am-11pm), cafeteria in basement. Breakfast served 7:30-10am ($4). Check-out 10am, check-in starting at noon. Doors lock at 11pm, but front desk will let you in if you flash your key. One bed in a 2-bed room $19, in a 3- to 8-person room $15, in an 10- to 16-person room $13; nonmembers pay $3 more; ages 9-13 $8; under 8 free. HI-C memberships sold. Usually full July-Aug., so make reservations or arrive early. IBN reservations available.

Au Petit Hôtel, 3, ruelle des Ursulines (694-0965), just off of rue Ste-Ursule. This tidy little hotel is a great deal for two people, with a TV, free local phone, private bath, and refrigerator in each room. Audaciously combines a downtown location with free parking. May-Oct. $50 for 1 or 2 occupants, continental breakfast included; Nov.-May $40-45.

Montmartre Canadien, 1675, ch. St-Louis, Sillery (681-7357), on the outskirts of the city, in the Maison du Pelerin; a small white house behind the main building at 1671. Take bus #25 or 1. Clean house in a religious sanctuary run by Assumptionist monks overlooking the Fleuve St-Laurent. Relaxed, almost ascetic setting—don't expect to meet tons of exciting new people here. Mostly used by groups. Common showers. Dorm-style singles $15. Doubles $26. Triples $36. Beds in 7-person dormitory $11; groups of 20 or more $13 per person. Breakfast (eggs, cereal, bacon, and pancakes...mmm!) $5. Reserve 2-3 weeks in advance.

Manoir La Salle, 18, rue Ste-Ursule (692-9953), opposite the youth hostel. Clean private rooms in this ornate Victorian mansion fill quickly, especially in summer. Reservations recommended. Resident felines add eccentricity. Reservations necessary. Singles $25-30. Doubles $60.

Tim House, 84, rue Ste-Louis (694-0776). Adjacent to the Au Petit and run by the same folks, this is loveliness in action, B&B-style. The third-floor rooms have shared baths; a delectable breakfast is included. Free parking. Rooms $45-50, slightly less off season.

Municipal de Beauport, Beauport (666-2228). Take Autoroute 40 east, Exit 321 at rue Labelle onto Hwy. 369, turn left, and follow the signs marked "camping." Bus 800 will also take you to this campground on a hill (it overlooks the Montmorency River). Swimming pool and canoes ($7 per hr.) are available, as are showers ($1 per 8min.) and laundry. 135 sites. $16, with hookup $20; weekly $85/$120. Open June-Labor Day.

CANADA

FOOD

In general, rue Buade, St-Jean, and Cartier, as well as the **Place Royale** and **Petit Champlain** areas offer the widest selection of food and drink. The **Grande Allée,** a 2km strip of nothing but restaurants on either side, might seem like heaven to the hungry, but its steep prices make it a place to visit rather than to eat. Still, there are a few exceptions; see the Vieille Maison, below.

Don't be fooled into thinking that your best bet for a simple and affordable meal is to line up behind one of the many fast-food joints which proliferate throughout the city. Traditional *québecois* food is not only appetizing, but usually economical. One of the most filling yet inexpensive meals is a *croque-monsieur,* a large, open-faced sandwich with ham and melted cheese (about $5), usually served with salad. Be sure to try *québecois* French onion soup, slathered with melted cheese and generally served with bats of French bread or *tourtière,* a thick meat pie. Other specialties include the *crêpe,* stuffed differently to serve as either an entree or a dessert. The **Casse-Crepe Breton,** 1136, St-Jean, offers many choices of fillings in their "make your own combination" crepes for dinner ($3-6), as well as scrumptious dessert options ($2.25-$3; open daily 7:30am-1am). Finally, seek out the French-Canadian "sugar pie," made with brown sugar and butter. Experience culinary excellence at the **Pâtisserie au Palet d'Or,** 60, rue Garneau (692-2488), a quaint French bakery where $2.75 will get you a salmon sandwich and $1.50 a crisp, golden baguette. (Open daily 8am-7pm, later in summer to meet rising pastry demand.) Remember that some of these restaurants do not have non-smoking sections.

For those doing their own cooking, **J.A. Moisan,** 699, rue St-Jean (522-8268), sells groceries in an old country-style store (open daily 8:30am-10pm). **Dépanneurs** are like corner stores, selling milk, bread, snack food, and booze.

Café Mediterranée, 64, bd. René Lévesque Ouest (648-1849). Take bus #25 or walk for about 10min. outside the walls. Elegant surroundings for a Mediterranean buffet. Enjoy vegetable platters, *couscous,* spicy chicken dishes—or all three—the ideal, filling lunch. Soup, dessert, coffee, and all-you-can-eat entrees for $8. Open Mon.-Sat. noon-2pm. Arrive early for the best of the buffet. Reservations recommended.

Kyoto, 560, Grande Allée (529-6141). By night an expensive Japanese restaurant with authentic garden decor, by day a cheap buffet with authentic garden decor. Buffet $6.50 Mon.-Fri. 11:30am-2pm. Also open daily 5:30-9pm.

La Fleur de Lotus, 38, Côte de la Fabrique (692-4286), across from the Hôtel de Ville. Cheerful and unpretentious. Thai, Cambodian, Vietnamese, and Japanese dishes $8.75-14. Open Mon.-Wed. 11am-10:30pm, Thurs.-Fri. 11am-11:30pm, Sat. 5-11:30pm, Sun. 5-10:30pm.

Chez Temporel, 25, rue Couillard (694-1813). Stay off the tourist path while remaining within your budget at this genuine *café québecois,* discreetly tucked in a side alley off rue St-Jean. Besides the usual café staples, it offers exotic liquor drinks ($4.50). Linger as long as you like. Open Sun.-Thurs. 7am-1:30am, Fri.-Sat. 7am-2:30am.

Restaurant Liban, 23, rue d'Auteuil (694-1888), off rue St-Jean. Great café for lunch or a late-night bite. Tabouli and hummus plates $3.50, both with pita bread. Excellent falafel ($4.25) and baklava ($1.75). Open 9am-4pm.

SIGHTS

Inside the Walls

Confined within walls built by the English, Vieux Québec (Old City) contains most of the city's historic attractions. Monuments are clearly marked and explained; still, you'll get more out of the town if you consult the *Greater Québec Area Tourist Guide,* which contains a walking tour of the Old City (available from all tourist offices; see Practical Information, above). It takes one or two days to explore Vieux Québec by foot, but you'll learn more than on the many guided bus tours, and you'll tone those legs on the roller coaster roads to boot.

CANADA

Begin your walking tour of Québec City by climbing to the top of **Cap Diamant** (Cape Diamond) to see what you can see. Just north is **Citadelle,** the largest North American fortification still guarded by troops—who knows why? Anyway, don't attack it. Visitors can witness the **changing of the guard** (mid-June to Labor Day daily 10am) and the **beating of the retreat** (July-Aug. Tues., Thurs., and Sat.-Sun. 6pm). Tours are given every 55 min. (Citadelle open daily 9am-6pm; Sept. and May-June 9am-4pm; mid-March to April and Oct. 10am-3pm; Nov. to mid-March by reservation only. $4.50, seniors $4, ages 7-17 $2.25, disabled and under 7 free.)

Beat your own retreat from Citadelle by taking **Promenade des Gouverneurs** downhill to **Terrasse Dufferin.** Built in 1838 by Lord Durham, this popular promenade offers excellent views of the Fleuve St-Laurent, the Côte de Beaupré (the "Avenue Royale" Highway), and Ile d'Orléans across the channel. The promenade passes the landing spot of the European settlers, marked by the **Samuel de Champlain Monument,** where Champlain secured French settlement by building Fort St-Louis in 1620. Today, the promenade offers endless fascinating performers of all flavors—clowns, bagpipers, and banjo and clarinet duos.

At the bottom of the promenade, towering above the *terrasse* next to rue St-Louis, sits immense, baroque **le Château Frontenac** (691-2166), built in 1893 on the ruins of two previous châteaux and named for Comte Frontenac, governor of *Nouvelle-France.* The château was the site of two historic meetings between Churchill and Roosevelt during World War II, and is now a luxury hotel. The hotel is the budget traveler's nemesis, but you can still take a guided tour of Québec's pride and joy. (Tours leave daily on the hr. May to mid-Oct. 10am-6pm, mid-Oct. to April Sat.-Sun. 12:30-5pm. $5.50, seniors $4.50, ages 6-16 $3.50, under 6 free.)

Near Château Frontenac, between rue St-Louis and rue Ste-Anne, lies the **Place d'Armes.** *Calèches* (horse-drawn buggies) that congregate here in summer provide a certain air that grows especially strong in muggy weather. A carriage will give you a tour of the city for $56, but your feet will do the same for free. From the Place d'Armes, the pedestrian and artist-choked rue du Trésor leads to rue Buade and the **Notre-Dame Basilica** (692-2533). The clock and outer walls date back to 1647; the rest of the church has been rebuilt twice, most recently after a fire in 1922. (Open daily 6:30am-6pm. Tours in multiple languages, mid-May to mid-Oct. daily 9am-4:30pm.) In addition to the ornate gold altar and impressive religious artifacts (including a chancel lamp given to the congregation by the cheery Louis XIV), the basilica is home to a 3D historical **sound and light show** (692-3200; call for showtimes, which vary by season; $7, ages 12-17 $4.50, under 12 free). Notre-Dame, with its odd mix of architectural styles, contrasts sharply with the adjacent **Seminary of Québec,** an excellent example of 17th-century *québecois* architecture. Founded in 1663 as a Jesuit training ground, the seminary became the *Université de Laval* in 1852. The **Musée du Séminaire,** 9, rue de l'Université (692-2843), lies nearby. (Open in summer daily 10am-5:30pm; Sept.-June Tues.-Sun. 10am-5pm. $3, students and seniors $2, ages 12-16 $1, under 12 free.)

The **Musée du Fort,** 10, rue Ste-Anne (692-2175), presents a sound and light show that narrates the history of Québec City and the series of six battles fought between 1629 and 1775 for control of it. (Open daily 10am-5pm; in winter Mon.-Fri. 11am-3pm, Sat.-Sun. 11am-5pm. $5.50, seniors $4.50, ages 7-25 $3.50.)

The all-too-exciting **post office,** 3, rue Buade, now called the **Louis St-Laurent Building** (after Canada's second French Canadian Prime Minister), was built in the late 1890s and towers over a statue of Monseigneur de Laval, the first bishop of Québec. Across the Côte de la Montagne, a lookout park provides an impressive view of the Fleuve St-Laurent. A statue of Georges-Etienne Cartier, one of the key French-Canadian fathers of the Confederation, presides over the park.

Outside the Walls

From the old city, the **promenade des Gouverneurs** and its 310 steps lead to the **Plains of Abraham,** otherwise known as the **Parc des Champs-de-Bataille.** General James Wolfe's British troops and General de Montcalm's French forces clashed here in 1759; both leaders died during the decisive 15-min. confrontation, won by the British. The Plains currently host drill fields and the **Royal Québec Golf Course.**

At the far end of the Plains of Abraham you'll find the **Musée du Québec,** 1, ave. Wolfe-Montcalm (643-2150), which contains (shockingly!) a collection of *québecois* paintings, sculptures, decorative arts, and prints. The **Gérard Morisset pavilion,** greeting you with the unlikely *ménage à trois* of Jacques Cartier, Neptune, and Gutenberg, houses the Musée's permanent collection. The renovated old "prison of the plains," the **Baillarce Pavilion,** incarcerates temporary exhibits. (Open Thurs.-Tues. 10am-5:45pm, Wed. 10am-9:45pm; Labor Day-May Tues. and Thurs.-Sun. 11am-5:45pm, Wed. 11am-8:45pm. $5.75, seniors $4.75, students, disabled persons and escorts $2.75, under 15 free. Free Wed. except June-Aug.) The pavilion is also home to that map-wielding species known as the **visitor reception center** (648-4071). At the corner of la Grande Allée and rue Georges VI, right outside Porte St-Louis, stands **l'Assemblée Nationale** (643-7239), built in the style of French King Louis XIII's era and completed in 1886. View debates from the visitors gallery. Anglophones and Francophones both have recourse to simultaneous translation earphones. (Free 30min. tours daily 9am-4:30pm; Labor Day-May Mon.-Fri. 9am-4:30pm. Call ahead to ensure a space.)

For the Stairmaster-less, a *funiculaire* (cable car; 692-1132) connects Upper Town with Lower Town and **Place Royale,** the oldest section of Québec. (Operates June-Labor Day daily 8am-midnight. $1, under 6 free.) This way leads to **rue Petit-Champlain,** the oldest road on the continent. Many old buildings along the street have been restored or renovated and now house craft shops, boutiques, cafés, and restaurants. The **Café-Théâtre Le Petit Champlain,** 68, rue Petit-Champlain (692-2613), presents *québecois* music, singing, and theater. From here, just continue west (right, from the bottom of the *funiculaire*) to reach the Plains of Abraham.

From the bottom of the *funiculaire* you can also take rue Sous-le-Fort and then turn left to reach **Place Royale,** built in 1608, where you'll find the small but beautiful **l'Eglise Notre-Dame-des-Victoires** (692-1650), the oldest church in Canada, dating from the glorious year of 1688. (Open in summer Mon.-Sat. 9am-4:30pm, closed on Sat. if a rite of passage is occurring; Oct. 16-April Mon.-Sat. 9am-noon, Sun. 7:30am-1pm. Guided tours mid-May to mid-Oct. Free.) The houses surrounding the square have been restored to late-18th-century styles. Considered one of the birthplaces of French civilization in North America, the Place Royale is now the site of fantastic outdoor summer theater and concerts. Giant phone booths, satellites, videos, and recreated moon landings celebrate Québec's past, present, and future at the **Musée de la Civilisation,** 85, rue Dalhousie (643-2158), also along the river. The museum targets French Canadians, though English tours and exhibit notes are available. (Open daily 10am-7pm; early Sept. to late June Tues.-Sun. 10am-5pm, Wed. 10am-9pm. $6, students $3, seniors $5, ages 12-16 $1, under 12 free.)

ENTERTAINMENT AND NIGHTLIFE

The raucous **Winter Carnival** (626-3716) breaks the tedium of northern winters and lifts spirits in mid-February; the **Summer Festival** (692-4540) boasts a number of free outdoor concerts in mid-July. In early August, the **Plein Art** (694-0260) exhibition floods the Pigeonnier on Grande-Allée with arts and crafts. **Les nuits Black** (849-7080), Québec's burgeoning jazz festival, bebops the city for two weeks in late June. But the most festive day of the year is June 24, **la Fête nationale du Québec** (Saint-Jean-Baptiste Day; 681-7011), a celebration of *québecois* culture with free concerts, a bonfire, fireworks, and five million roaring drunk francophones.

The Grande Allée's many restaurants are interspersed with *Bar Discothèques,* where the early 20s mainstream crowd gathers. **Chez Dagobert,** 600 Grande Allée (522-0393), saturates its two dance floors while plentiful food and drink pour onto the streetside patio; it is *the* place to be seen. (No cover. Outside bar open daily 11am-3am, inside club 10pm-3am.) Down the block at **O'Zone,** 564 Grande Allée (529-7932), the tempo is a little slower and more pub-like (open daily 11am-3am).

Québec City's young, visible punk contingent clusters around rue St-Jean. **La Fourmi Atomik,** 33, rue d'Auteuil (694-1463), features underground rock, with reggae-only Mondays and rap-only Wednesdays. (No cover. Open daily 1pm-3am; Oct.-May 2pm-3am. 18+.) At **L'Ostradamus,** 29, rue Couillard (694-9560), you can listen to live jazz and eavesdrop on deep discourse in a smoke-drenched pseudo-spiritual ambience with artsy Thai decor. ($1-3 cover when band is playing. Open daily 5pm-3am.) A more traditional Québec evening awaits at **Les Yeux Bleux**, 1117½, rue St-Jean (694-9118), a local favorite where *chansonniers* perform nightly. (No cover. Open daily 8pm-3am.) The gay scene in Québec City isn't huge, but neither is it hard to find. **Le Ballon Rouge, 811,** St-Jean (647-9227), near the walls of the Old City, is a popular dance club where dimly lit pool tables coexist with neon rainbows. (No cover. Open daily 10:30pm-3am.) Farther from downtown at 157 Chemin Ste-Foy, **Studio 157** (529-9958), caters to a crowd of women only.

■ Near Québec City

Ile-d'Orléans on the St-Laurent is untouched by Québec City's public transport system, but its proximity to Québec (about 10km downstream) makes it an ideal side trip by car or bike. Take Autoroute 440 Est., and cross over the only bridge leading to the island (Pont de l'Ile). A tour of the island covers 64 km. Originally called *Ile de Bacchus* because of the multitudinous wild grapes fermenting here, the Ile-d'Orléans remains a sparsely populated retreat of several small villages and ongoing strawberry fields. The **Manoir Mauvide-Genest,** 1451, ch. Royal (829-2630), dates from 1734, and is now a private museum flaunting crafts and traditional colonial furniture. (Open June-Aug. daily 10am-5:30pm; Sept. to mid-Oct. weekends by reservation. $4, ages 10-18 $2, families $10.)

Exiting Ile-d'Orléans, turn right (east) onto Hwy. 138 (bd. Ste-Anne) to view the splendid **Chute Montmorency** (Montmorency Falls), which are substantially taller than Niagara Falls. In winter, vapors from the falls freeze completely to form a frozen shadow of the running falls. About 20 km along Hwy. 138 lies **Ste-Anne-de-Beaupré** (Orléan Express buses link it to Québec City, $5). This small town's entire *raison d'être* is the famous **Basilique Ste-Anne-de Beaupré,** 10018, ave Royale (827-3781). Since 1658, this double-spired basilica has contained a miraculous Statue and the alleged forearm bone of Saint Anne (mother of the Virgin Mary). Every year, more than one million pilgrims come here in the hopes that their prayers will be answered—legend has it that some have been quite successful. (Open early May to mid-Sept. daily 8:30am-5pm.) In the winter months (Nov.-Apr.), go to Ste-Anne for some of the best skiing in the province (lift tickets $41 per day). Contact **Parc du Mont Ste-Anne,** P.O. Box 400, Beaupré, G0A IE0 (827-4561), which has a 625m/2050ft. vertical drop and night skiing to boot. And that's not all. You will also find here a **gondola** (800-463-1568), which climbs to 800m, affording a fabulous view of the St-Laurent River valley. (July-Labor Day daily 11am-5pm, Labor Day-snowfall Sat.-Sun. $8, ages 14-20 $6, seniors and ages 7-13 $4.50.)

Ontario

First claimed by French explorer Samuel de Champlain in 1613, Ontario soon became a center of English influence within Canada. Hostility and famine in Europe drove hordes of Scottish and Irish immigrants to this territory. They asserted control in 1763 during the Seven Years War with a takeover of New France. Twenty years later, a flood of Loyalist emigres from the newly formed United States streamed into the province, fortifying its Anglo character. Now serving as a political counterbalance to French Québec, this populous central province raises the ire of peripheral regions of Canada due to its high concentration of power and wealth. In the south, world-class Toronto shines—multicultural, enormous (3 million plus, by *far* the largest city in sparse Canada), vibrant, clean, and generally safe. Yuppified suburbs, an occasional college town, and farms surround this sprawling megalopolis. In the east, national capital Ottawa sits on Ontario's border with Québec. To the north, layers of cottage country and ski resorts give way to a pristine wilderness that is as much French and Native Canadian as it is British.

PRACTICAL INFORMATION

Capital: Toronto.
Ontario Ministry of Culture, Tourism, and Recreation: Customer Service Branch, 800-668-2746. Open Mon.-Sat. 9am-8pm, Sun. 10am-5pm; Sept.-May Mon.-Fri. 9am-6pm, Sat.-Sun. 10am-5pm. Send written requests to Ontario Travel, Queen's Park, Toronto, ON M7A 2R9. Free brochures, guides, maps, and info on special events.
Drinking Age: 19.
Time Zone: Eastern. **Postal Abbreviation:** ON.
Sales Tax: 8%, plus 7% GST.

■ Toronto

Once a prim and proper Victorian city where even window-shopping was prohibited on the Sabbath, the city dubbed the world's most multicultural by the United Nations is today one of the hippest and most accessible urban areas in North America. Toronto has spent millions in recent decades on spectacular public works projects: the world's tallest "free-standing" structure (the CN tower), the biggest retractable roof (the Sky Dome), outstanding lakefront development, and significant sponsorship of arts and museums. Cosmetically, Toronto's skyscrapers and neatly gridded streets are strikingly reminiscent of New York, a resemblance which has not gone unnoticed—or unexploited—by Hollywood. But New York it is not, and, legend has that two film crews learned this the hard way. One crew, after dirtying a Toronto street to make it look more like a typical "American" avenue, went on coffee break and returned only to find their set spotless again, swept by the ever-vigilant city maintenance department. Another crew, filming an attack scene, was twice interrupted by Torontonians hopping out of their cars to "rescue" the actress.

PRACTICAL INFORMATION

Tourist Office: Metropolitan Toronto Convention and Visitors Association (MTCVA), 207 Queens Quay W (203-2500 or 800-363-1990), at Harborfront Centre. Open Mon.-Fri. 8:30am-6pm, Sat.-Sun. 9:30am-6pm; in winter Mon.-Fri. 8:30am-5pm, Sat. 9am-5pm, Sun. 9:30am-5pm. **Ontario Travel** (800-668-2746) has info on Ontario. Open Mon.-Fri. 10am-9pm, Sat. 10am-6pm, Sun. noon-5pm.
Student Travel Office: Travel CUTS, 187 College St. (979-2406), just west of University Ave. Subway: Queen's Park. Smaller office at 74 Gerrard St. E. (977-0441). Subway: College. Both open Mon.-Fri. 9am-5pm.
Consulates: U.S., 360 University Ave. (595-1700). Subway: St. Patrick. Consular services Mon.-Fri. 8:30am-1pm. **Australia,** 175 Bloor St. E., 3314 (323-1155). Subway: Bloor St. Open for info Mon.-Fri. 9am-5pm; visas 9am-1pm and 2-4pm. **U.K.,** 2800 Bay St. (593-1267). Subway: College. Open Mon.-Fri. 8:30am-5pm.
Currency Exchange: Toronto Currency Exchange, 313 Yonge St. (598-3769; open 9am-7pm), and 2 Walton (599-5821; open 8:30am-5:30pm), gives the best rates around. **Royal Bank of Canada,** 200 Bay St. Plaza (974-5151 for info; 974-5535 for foreign exchange), has exchange centers at Pearson Airport (905-676-3220; daily 5am-11:30pm) and around the city. **Money Mart,** 688 Younge St. (924-1000), has 24-hr. service and some fees. Subway: Bloor/Younge.
Airport: Pearson International (247-7678), about 20km west of Toronto via Hwy. 427, 401, or 409. Take Bus #58 west from Lawrence W. subway. **Pacific Western Transportation** (905-564-6333) runs buses every 20min. directly to downtown hotels ($12.50, roundtrip $21.50) and every 40min. to Yorkdale ($7.25), York Mills ($8.30), and Islington ($6.75) subway stations (all buses 5am-midnight). **Hotel Airporter** (798-2424) transports to select airport hotels ($12, roundtrip $20).
Trains: All trains chug from **Union Station,** 65 Front St. (366-8411), at Bay and York. Subway: Union. **VIA Rail** (366-8411) cannonballs to Montréal (5-7 per day, 5hr., $84) and Windsor (4-5 per day, 4hr., $63). **Amtrak** (800-872-7245) blasts off to New York City (1 per day, 12hr., US$61-93) and Chicago (6 per week, 11hr.,

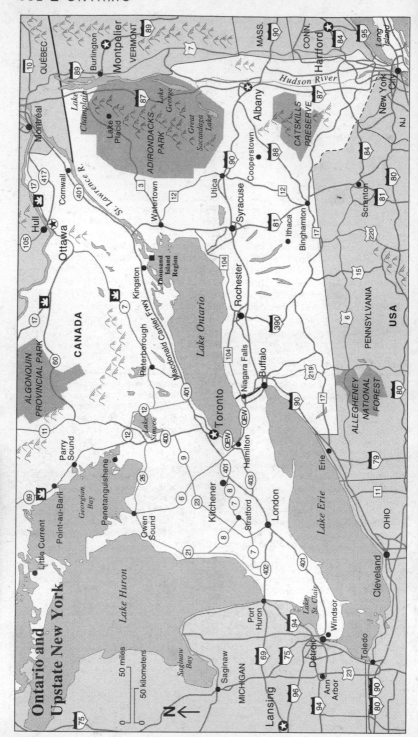

Ontario and
Upstate New York

US$93). Ticket office open Mon.-Sat. 6:45am-9:30pm, Sun. 8am-8:30pm; station open daily 6am-midnight.

Buses: Voyageur (393-7911) and **Greyhound** (367-8747) operate from 610 Bay St., just north of Dundas. Subway: St. Patrick or Dundas. Voyageur has service to Montréal (5-6 per day, 7hr., $64). Greyhound goes to Calgary (3 per day, 49hr., $244), Vancouver (3 per day, 2½ days, $285), and New York City (3 per day, 11hr., $79). No reservations; show up 30min. prior to departure. An advance-purchase, unlimited ticket can be used anywhere in Canada for 7 days ($212); a 15-day pass sells for $277. Ticket office open daily 5:30am-1am.

Ferries: Toronto Island Ferry Service (392-8194, 392-8193 for recording). Ferries to Centre Island, Wards Island, and Hanlans Point leave from Bay St. Ferry Dock at the foot of Bay St. Service daily every ½hr.-1hr. 8am-midnight. Roundtrip $4, seniors, students, and ages 15-19 $2, under 15 $1.

Public Transportation: Toronto Transit Commission (TTC) (393-4000). A network of 2 subway lines and numerous bus and streetcar routes. After dark, buses are required to stop anywhere along a route at a female passenger's request. Subway approximately 6am-2:25am; then, buses cover subway routes. Free transfers among subway, buses, and streetcars, but only at stations. Fare $2 (5 tokens $8), seniors with ID ½-price, under 13 50¢ (10 for $4). Mon.-Sat. 1-day unlimited travel pass $6.50.

Taxis: Co-op Cabs, 504-2667. $2.50 base fee, $1.25 per km. 24hr.

Car Rental: Wrecks for Rent, 77 Nassau St. (585-7782). Subway: Spadina or Bathurst. $29 per day with 100km free, 9¢ each additional km. Ages 23-25 pay $3 per day surcharge, ages 21-23 $5. Open Mon.-Fri. 8am-6pm, Sat. 9am-4pm.

Driver/Rider Service: Allo-Stop, 609 Bloor St. W (531-7668). Matches riders with drivers. Membership for passengers $6, for drivers $7 for a full year. To: Ottawa ($24), Montréal ($26), Québec City ($41), New York ($40). Open Mon.-Wed. 9am-5pm, Thurs.-Fri. 9am-7pm, Sat.-Sun. 10am-5pm.

Bike Rental: Brown's Sports and Bike Rental, 2447 Bloor St. W. (763-4176). $17.50 per day, $35 per weekend, $46.50 per week. $200 deposit or credit card required. Open Mon.-Fri. 9:30am-6pm, Sat. 9:30am-5:30pm.

Hotlines: Rape Crisis, 597-8808. **Services for the Disabled,** 314-0944. **Toronto Gay and Lesbian Phone Line,** 964-6600. Open Mon.-Sat. 7-10pm.

Emergency: 911.

Post Office: Toronto Dominion Centre, 66 Wellington St. W. (360-7105). **Postal code:** M5K 1AO. General Delivery at Postal Station A, 25 The Esplanade, Toronto M5W 1A0 (365-0656). Open Mon.-Fri. 6am-2pm. **Area code:** 416 (city), 905 (outskirts).

ORIENTATION

The city maps available at tourism booths only show major streets and may prove inadequate for getting around. A better bet is to buy the indispensable *Downtown and Metro Toronto Visitor's Map Guide* with the yellowish-orange cover, available in drug stores or tourist shops. The *Ride Guide,* free at all TTC stations and tourism information booths (see Practical Information, above), shows the subway and bus routes for the metro area.

Toronto's streets lie in a grid pattern. Addresses on north-south streets increase towards the north, away from Lake Ontario. **Yonge St.** is the main north-south route, dividing the city and the streets perpendicular to it into east and west. Numbering for both sides starts at Yonge St. and increases as you move away in either direction. West of Yonge St., the main arteries are **Bay St., University Ave., Spadina Ave.,** and **Bathurst St.** The major east-west routes include, from the water north, **Front St., Queen St., Dundas St., College St., Bloor St.,** and **Edlington St.**

Toronto's traffic gets crowded—avoid rush hour (4-7pm). The city has done a great deal in the last few years to combat transportation problems and their efforts have resulted in some traffic regulations. A flashing green light means that you can go straight or turn left freely—the opposing traffic has a red light. Parking on the street is hard to find and usually carries a one-hr. limit, except on Sundays when street spaces are free and abundant. You can also park for free at night, but your car must

CANADA

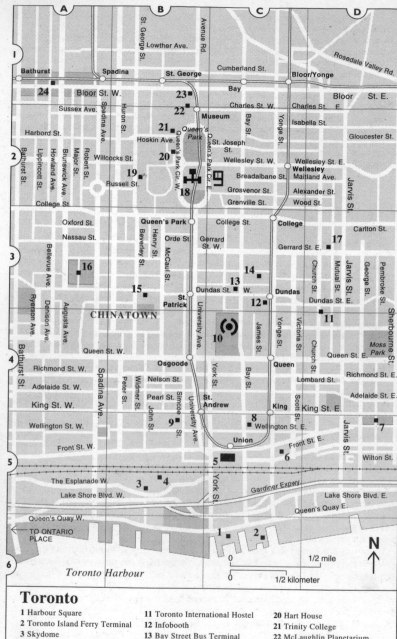

Toronto

1 Harbour Square
2 Toronto Island Ferry Terminal
3 Skydome
4 CN Tower
5 Union Station
6 O'Keefe Centre
7 St. Lawrence Market
8 Post Office
9 Roy Thomson (concert) Hall
10 Toronto City Hall

11 Toronto International Hostel
12 Infobooth
13 Bay Street Bus Terminal
14 World's Biggest Bookstore
15 Art Gallery of Ontario
16 Kensington Market
17 Neill-Wycik College-Hotel
18 Ontario Provincial Parliament
   Building
19 Knox College

20 Hart House
21 Trinity College
22 McLaughlin Planetarium
23 Royal Ontario Museum
   (ROM)
24 The Annex

○──○ Subway Line and Station

be gone by 7am. Parking officials enforce regulations zealously—don't tempt them. Day parking generally costs inbound daytrippers $2-4 at outlying subway stations; parking overnight at the subway stations is prohibited. If you park within the city, expect to pay at least $12 for 24 hr. (7am-7am), although some all-day parking lots downtown on King St. sell unguarded spots for $3-5.

NEIGHBORHOODS

Downtown Toronto splits into many distinctive and decentralized neighborhoods. Thanks to zoning regulations that require developers to include housing and retail space in commercial construction, many people live downtown. **Chinatown** centers on Dundas St. W. between Bay St. and Spadina Ave. Formerly the Jewish market of the 1920s, **Kensington Market,** on Kensington Ave., Augusta Ave., and the western half of Baldwin St., is now a largely Portuguese neighborhood with many good restaurants, vintage clothing shops, and an outdoor bazaar of produce, luggage, spices, nuts, clothing, and shoes. A strip of old factories, stores, and warehouses on **Queen St. West,** from University Ave. to Bathurst St., contain a fun mix of shopping from upscale, uptight boutiques to reasonable used book stores, restaurants, and cafés. The ivy-covered Gothic buildings and magnificent quadrangles of the **University of Toronto** occupy about 200 acres in the middle of downtown. The law-school cult flick *The Paper Chase* was filmed here because the campus supposedly looked more Ivy League than Harvard, where the movie was set. **The Annex,** Bloor St. W. at the Spadina subway, has an artistic and literary ambiance and excellent budget restaurants dishing up a variety of ethnic cuisines (see Food, below). This is the best place to come at night when you're not sure exactly what you're hungry for; afterwards, stay and hit the nightclubs. **Yorkville,** just north of Bloor between Yonge St. and Avenue Rd., was once the crumbling communal home of flower children and folk guitarists. Today, if you can afford the upscale shops (Tiffany's, etc.), you probably don't need to read this book. **Cabbagetown,** just east of Yonge St., bounded by Gerrard St. E., Wellesley, and Sumach St., takes its name from the Irish immigrants who used to plant the green, leafy vegetable in their yards. Today, professionals inhabit its renowned Victorian housing, along with quite probably the only crowing rooster in the city. The **Gay and Lesbian Village,** located around Church and Wellesley St., offers fine dining and outdoor cafés.

The **Theatre District,** on Front St. between Sherbourne and Yonge St., supports enough venues to feed anyone's cultural and physical appetites. Music, food, ferry rides, dance companies, and art all dock at the **Harborfront** (973-3000), on Queen's Quay W. from York to Bathurst St., on the lake. The three main **Toronto Islands,** all accessible by ferry (see Practical Information, above), offer beaches, bike rentals, and an amusement park. East from the harbor, the beaches along and south of Queen's St. E. between Woodbine and Victoria, boast tons of shops and a very popular boardwalk. Farther east still, about 5km from the city center, **Scarborough Bluffs,** a rugged, 16-km. section of cliffs, climb up from the lakeshore.

Three more ethnic enclaves lie 30 to 40 min. from downtown by public transit. **Corso Italia** surrounds St. Clair W. at Dufferin St.; take the subway to St. Clair W. and bus #512 west. You'll find **Little India** at Gerrard St. E. and Coxwell; ride the subway to Coxwell, then take bus #22 south to the second Gerard St. stop. Better known as **"the Danforth," Greektown** is on Danforth Ave. at Pape Ave. (subway: Pape). All three have bilingual street signs, cater to locals, and are worth the ride.

ACCOMMODATIONS AND CAMPING

Avoid the cut-rate hotels concentrated around Jarvis and Gerrard St. The University of Toronto provides cheap quality sleep for budget travelers; contact the **U. of Toronto Housing Service,** 214 College St. (978-8045), for $35-45 rooms (open Mon.-Fri. 8:45am-5pm; reservations recommended). You can call the visitors bureau to obtain a room; the **Downtown Association of Bed and Breakfast Guest Houses** (690-1724) places guests in renovated Victorian homes (singles $40-60), while the **Metropolitan**

B&B Registry (964-2566) handles locations all over the city (singles from $35). Because it is difficult to regulate these registries, you should always visit a B&B before you commit.

Toronto International Hostel (HI-C), 90 Gerrard St. W. (971-4440), a few blocks from the bus station. Subway: College or Queen's Park. This newly relocated hostel occupies several floors of the Toronto Residence, a dorm-like building affiliated with the U of T Hospital. Great central location with a kitchen, laundry facilities, pool, and fitness center. Rooms have 2 beds each. $22.50, nonmembers $27; linen provided. 24-hr. access. Check-in after 11am, check out by 10am. Reservations recommended.

Neill-Wycik College Hotel, 96 Gerrard St. E. (977-2320 or 800-268-4358). Subway: College. Small, clean rooms, some with beautiful views of the city. Kitchen on every floor, but no utensils. Singles $33, doubles $44.50. Family rooms available. Check-in after 4pm; check-out 10am. Lockers available. Students, seniors, and HI members get a 20% discount. Open early May to late Aug.

Knox College, 59 St. George St. (978-0168, Mon.-Thurs. 10am-5pm). Subway: Queen's Park. U of T's most coveted residence has huge rooms with wooden floors surrounding an idyllic courtyard in the heart of campus. Many rooms refinished by the crew of TV's *Class of '96;* some, though, are a little ragged. Common rooms and baths on each floor. Singles $28, students $22.40; doubles $40. Call to reserve months in advance, or chance it on short notice. Open June-Aug.

Allenby Bed and Breakfast, 223 Strathmore Blvd. (461-7095). Subway: Greenwood. Spacious rooms with private-use kitchens and bathrooms in a quiet neighborhood. Subway stop next door adds convenience, not noise. Light breakfast. Long-term and group stays encouraged. Singles $45, doubles $55.

Hotel Selby, 592 Sherbourne St. (921-3142 or 800-387-4788). Subway: Sherbourne. A registered historic spot and a thriving guest house, Hotel Selby has seen some changes since Hemingway knew it. Totally refurbished, including cable TV, A/C, laundry facilities, and phones. Special period suites are set up to capture the splendor of the 1920s Selby. Some private baths. Singles from $59; Jan.-April $49.

YWCA-Woodlawn Residence, 80 Woodlawn Ave. E. (923-8454), off Yonge St. Subway: Summerhill. 115 rooms *for women only* in a nice neighborhood. Breakfast, TV lounges, and laundry facilities. Small, neat singles $45, doubles $60; private bath available. Beds in basement dormitory $20; linen $3. 10% senior discount. Office open Mon.-Fri. 7:30am-11:30pm, Sat.-Sun. 7:30am-7:30pm.

Indian Line Tourist Campground, 7625 Finch Ave. W. (905-678-1233; off season 661-6600, ext. 203), at Darcel Ave. Follow Hwy. 427 north to Finch Ave. and go west. The closest campground (30min.) to metropolitan Toronto; near Pearson Airport. Showers, laundry. Gatehouse open 8am-9pm. Unwooded sites $16, with hook-up $20. Open May 10 to early Oct. Reservations recommended July-Aug.

Glen Rouge Provincial Park, 7450 Hwy. 2, a.k.a. Kingston Rd. (392-8092), 30min. east of Toronto in the suburbs. Accessible by public transportation; call for directions. 127 sites. Showers, toilets. Near hiking, pool, tennis courts, and beach. $16, with water and electricity $22.

FOOD

A burst of immigration has made Toronto a haven for good international food rivaled in North America only by New York City. Over 5000 restaurants squeeze into metropolitan Toronto; you could eat out at a different place every night for the next 15 years. Some of the standouts can be found on **Bloor St. W.** and in **Chinatown.** For fresh produce, go to **Kensington Market** or the **St. Lawrence Market** at King St. E. and Sherbourne, 6 blocks east of the King subway stop. **Village by the Grange,** at the corner of McCaul and Dundas near the Art Gallery of Ontario, is a vast collection of super-cheap restaurants and vendors—Chinese, Thai, Middle Eastern, you name it (generally open 11am-7pm). "L.L.B.O." posted on the window of a restaurant means that it has a liquor license.

Shopsy's, 33 Yonge St. (365-3333), at Front St. 1 block from Union Station. The definitive Toronto deli. 300 seats, snappy service. If you're feelin' frisky, try the "Hot and Topless" Reuben ($7.75). Shopsy's Hot Dog $3.85. Open Sun. 8am-11pm, Mon.-Wed. 7am-11pm, Thurs.-Fri. 7am-midnight, Sat. 8am-midnight.

Country Style Hungarian Restaurant, 450 Bloor St. W. (537-1745). Hearty stews, soups, and casseroles. Meals come in small (more than enough) and large (stop, lest I burst) portions. Entrees $4-9. Open daily 11am-10pm.

Real Peking Restaurant, 355 College St. (920-7952), at Augusta Ave. The effort some Chinese restaurants put into decorations goes into the food here. Understanding servers will explain the menu. Entrees $6.50-8.50. Lunch specials $4.25 (noon-3pm). Open Mon.-Thurs. noon-10pm, Sat. 5-11pm, Sun. 4-10pm.

Bagelworks, 326 Bloor St. W. (92-BAGEL/922-2435), at Spadina St. Fast becoming a Toronto institution, the original Bagelworks (other locations at 1946 Queen St. E. and 1450 Yonge St.) serves up gourmet bagels in a stylishly decorated café close to U of T and swingin' Spadina. Specialty bagels like Sourdough, Black Pepper or Sundried Tomato as well as old favorites (60¢, 6 for $3.25). Tues. from 7-8pm bagels are $3.60 per dozen. Open summers Mon.-Fri. 7am-6pm, Sat. 7am-5pm, Sun. 8am-5pm.

Mr. Greek, 568 Danforth Ave. (461-5470), at Carlaw. Subway: Pape. A friendly, bustling café serving shish kabobs, salads, steak, chicken, Greek music, and wine. Family atmosphere, fast service. Gyros or souvlaki $6.70. Open Sun.-Thurs. 10am-1am, Fri.-Sat. until 4am.

By The Way Café, 400 Bloor St. W. (967-4295). Subway: Spadina. Formerly vegetarian, this Mediterranean restaurant and café now apologizes for its use of chicken, but they need not apologize for the food. Outdoor patio seating available. Veggie burger $8. Open Mon.-Fri. 11am-1am, Sat.-Sun. 10am-2am.

Saigon Palace, 454 Spadina Ave. (968-1623), at College St. Subway: Queen's Park. Popular with locals. Great spring rolls. Beef, chicken, or vegetable dishes over rice or noodles $4-7. Open Mon.-Thurs. 9am-10pm, Fri.-Sat. 9am-11pm.

Mövenpick Marché (366-8986), in the BCE Place at Yonge and Front St. A 22,000-sq.-meter market/restaurant. Browse through and pick a meal from the various culinary stations, including a bakery, wine shop, pasta, seafood, and salad counters, and grill. Yuppie extravagance at its finest, and not too hard on the budget. Entrees run $5-8. Open daily 9am-2am.

The Old Fish Market Restaurant, 12 Market St. (363-FISH/3474), just off the Esplanade. Somewhat pricey but excellent seafood (lunch $6-14, dinner $10-30). Look for special deals: daily noon-2pm ½-price oyster special, 6 for $3.50; Mon. night all-you-can-eat mussels $8; ½-price menu nightly 5-8pm. Open Mon.-Thurs. 11:45am-2:30pm and 5-10pm, Fri. 11:45am-2:30pm and 5-11pm, Sat. 8:30-11am, 11:30am-3pm, and 4:30-11pm, Sun. noon-3pm and 4-10pm.

The Organ Grinder, 58 the Esplanade (364-6517). Subway: Union. Jingles dance forth from the 1925 theater pipe organ, assembled from pieces of over 50 pipe organs. Pizzas $7-9. Open Sun.-Thurs. 11:30am-11pm, Fri.-Sat. 11:30am-midnight.

The Midtown Café, 552 College St. W. (920-4533), sounds alternative music while you play pool or just relax. On weekends, eat from the large *tapas* menu $2.50-3.50. Sandwiches $3.50-5. Open daily 10am-2am.

SIGHTS

A walk through the city's diverse neighborhoods can be one of the most rewarding (and cheapest) activities in Toronto. Signs and streetside conversations change languages while an endless stream of food aromas wafts through the air. For a more organized expedition, the **Royal Ontario Museum** (586-5513 or 556-5514) operates seven free **walking tours.** (Tours June Wed. 6pm, July-Aug. Wed. 6pm and Sun. 2pm. Destinations and meeting places vary; call for specific information.) The **University of Toronto** (978-5000) conducts free one-hour walking tours of Canada's largest university (and alma mater of David Letterman's band leader, Paul Schaffer). The tours, available in English, French, Portuguese, or Hindi (call ahead for the last two), meet at the map room of Hart House. (Tours June-Aug. Mon.-Fri. 10:30am, 1pm, and 2:30pm.)

Other guided trips within the city revolve around architectural themes, sculptures, or ghost-infested Toronto haunts (contact the visitors bureau for info; tours $10).

Modern architecture aficionados should visit the curving twin towers and two-story rotunda of **City Hall** (392-7341), at the corner of Queen and Bay St. between the Osgoode and Queen subway stops; pick up a brochure for a self-guided tour (open 8:30am-4:30pm). In front of City Hall, **Nathan Phillips Square** is home to a reflecting pool (which becomes a skating rink in winter) and numerous special events. Call the **Events Hotline** (392-0458) for info. A few blocks away, the **Toronto Stock Exchange**, 2 First Canadian Place (947-4676), on York between Adelaide St. W. and King St. W., exchanges over $250 million daily as Canada's leading stock exchange. (Presentations Tues.-Fri. 2pm. Visitors center with viewing gallery open Mon.-Fri. 9am-4:30pm.) The Ontario government legislates in the **Provincial Parliament Buildings** (325-7500; subway: Queen's Park), at Queen's Park in the city center. (Building open Mon.-Fri. 8:30am-6pm, Sat.-Sun. 9am-4pm; chambers close 4:30pm. Parliament in session March-June and Oct.-Dec. Mon.-Wed. 1:30-6pm, Thurs. 10am-noon and 1:30-6pm. Free guided tours Mon.-Fri. by request, Sat.-Sun. every ½hr. 9am-4pm except during lunch. Free gallery passes available at main lobby info desk 1:30pm.) At 553m, the **CN Tower** (360-8500; subway: Union) towers as the tallest free-standing structure in the world. The ride to the top is pricey ($12, seniors $9, children $7, $3 additional to go to the Space Deck; open daily 9am-11pm), but the view is worth it. The **Horizons** bar at the top is a great youth hang-out. Straight out of a fairy tale, the 98-room **Casa Loma** (923-1171 or 923-1172), Davenport Rd. at 1 Austin Terrace, near Spadina a few blocks north of the Dupont subway stop, is a classic tourist attraction. Secret passageways and an underground tunnel add to the magic of the only real turreted castle in North America. (Open daily 9:30am-5pm last entrance at 4pm. $8, seniors and ages 13-17 $5, ages 4-13 $4.50, under 3 free with parent.)

Check out an autopsy of a mummified Egyptian at the **Royal Ontario Museum (ROM)**, 100 Queen's Park (586-5551; subway: Museum), which houses artifacts from ancient civilizations (Greek, Chinese, and Egyptian), a bat cave (not *the* Bat Cave), and preserved, stuffed animals. (Open Mon. and Wed.-Sat. 10am-6pm, Tues. 10am-8pm, Sun. 11am-6pm. $8, seniors, students, and children $4; free Tues. for seniors, and Tues. after 4:30pm for everyone. Includes the **George R. Gardiner Museum of Ceramic Art** across the street.) There was an old lady who lived in a shoe, but it probably wasn't the shoe-shaped glass-and-stone edifice that is the **Bata Shoe Museum**, 327 Bloor St. W. (979-7799; subway: St. George). Even the shoe-indifferent will find the collection of footwear from many cultures and ages fascinating: Hindu ivory stilted sandals, Elton John's sparkling silver platform boots, and two-inch slippers once worn by Chinese women with bound feet. (Open Tues.-Wed. and Fri.-Sat. 10am-5pm, Thurs. 10am-8pm, Sun. noon-5pm. $6, seniors and students $4, 5-14 $2, families $12, 1st Tues. of every month free.) The **Art Gallery of Ontario (AGO)**, 317 Dundas St. W. (979-6648; subway: St. Patrick), 3 blocks west of University Ave., houses an enormous collection of Western art from the Renaissance to the 1990s, concentrating on Canadian artists. (Open Tues.-Sun. 10am-5:30pm, Wed. until 10pm;

"Wake Up, Morris: We're There"

At 1,815 feet, 5 inches, Toronto's CN Tower stands as the **world's tallest free standing structure,** a colossal beast hovering over the downtown region and visible from nearly every corner of the city. Built in the mid-1970s, the Canadian National Tower took 1,537 construction workers and $63 million to build. The structure weighs a massive 130,000 tons (the same weight as 23,214 large elephants) and uses 80 miles of post-tensioned steel. The world's longest metal staircase rests in the tower's center with 2,570 steps—those with visions of athletic grandeur may attempt the climb twice yearly, when the tower opens its stairwell to benefit the United Way and World Wildlife Fund.

early Sept.-late May Wed.-Sun. 10am-5:30pm, holiday Mon. 10am-5:30pm. $7.50, students and seniors $4, under 12 free, families $15. Wed. 5-10pm free. Seniors free Fri.)

The **Holocaust Education and Memorial Center of Toronto,** 4600 Bathurst St. (635-2283), on the Bathurst bus route near the Joseph Latimer Library, runs a museum and two audio-visual presentations portraying the lives of Jews in Europe before, during, and after WWII. The collection soberly commemorates the six million people murdered by Germany's Nazi regime. (Open daily 9am-4pm. Free.)

The **Hockey Hall of Fame,** 30 Yonge St. (360-7765), on the concourse level of BCE at Front St., celebrates Canada's favorite sport. Head first to the Bell Great Hall, where plaques of hockey greats such as Bobbys Orr and Clarke grace the walls; then be sure to catch the exhibits, including a goalie mask collection and a replica dressing room. Flick a few pucks or test your goal-tending on the interactive video games. (Open Mon.-Sat. 9am-6pm, Sun. 10am-6pm. $9.50, seniors and children $5.50. Wheelchair accessible.)

The **Upper Canada Brewing Company,** 2 Atlantic Ave. (534-9281; subway: King or St. Andrews, then take the King streetcar west to Atlantic and Jefferson), gives free tours and tastings. (Tours Mon.-Sat. 1, 3, and 5:30pm, Sun. 1 and 3pm; reservations required. Open Mon.-Sat. 10am-8pm, Sun. 10am-6pm.)

Toronto crawls with **biking** and **hiking** trails. For a map of the trails, write the **Metro Parks and Property Department,** 55 John St., 24th fl., station 1240, M5V 3C6 or call 392-8186. The **Parks and Recreation Department** (392-1111) has info on local facilities and activities (open Mon.-Fri. 9am-4:30pm). It might not be the Caribbean, but the **beaches** on the southeast end of Toronto now support a permanent community in what was once a summer resort. A popular "vacationland," the **Toronto Islands Park** has a boardwalk, bathing beaches, canoe and bike rentals, a frisbee golf course, and an amusement park. The park is located on a 4-mi. strip of connected islands just opposite downtown. Ferries leave from the Bay Street Ferry Dock at Bay St. (15-min. ferry trip; 392-8193 for ferry info).

The **Ontario Science Center,** 770 Don Mills Rd. (696-3127), at Eglington Ave. E., presents more than 650 interactive exhibits, showcasing man's greatest innovations. (An Omnimax theater is slated to open in Jan. 1997. Though farther from downtown than most sights, the center is within the range of public transportation. Open Sat.-Thurs. 10am-6pm, Fri. 10am-9pm. $8, youths 11-17 $5.50, seniors and ages 5-16 $5.) The **Metro Toronto Zoo** (392-5900), Meadowvale Rd. off Exit 389 on Hwy. 401N, houses over 6400 animals in a 710-acre park that features sections representing the world's seven geographic regions. (Open late May to late June 9am-7pm, late June-Labor Day 9am-7:30pm; call for off season hours. Last entry 1hr. before closing. $12, seniors and ages 12-17 $9, ages 4-11 $7, $2 less in winter; parking $5.)

ENTERTAINMENT

The monthly *Where Toronto,* available free at tourism booths, gives the arts and entertainment run-down. Before you buy tickets, contact **T.O. Tix** (596-8211); they sell ½-price tickets for theater, music, dance, and opera on performance day. Their booth at 208 Yonge St., north of Queen St. (subway: Queen) at Eaton's Centre opens at noon; arrive before 11:45am for first dibs. (Open Tues.-Sat. noon-7:30pm, Sun. 11am-3pm.) **Ticketmaster** (870-8000) supplies tickets for many Toronto venues, although sometimes it has a hefty service charge.

Ontario Place, 955 Lakeshore Blvd. W. (314-9811 or 314-9900 for a recording), features cheap entertainment in the summer. Top pop artists like R.E.M. perform here in the new **Molson Amphitheatre** (260-5600); Ticketmaster handles tickets. ($17.50-50. Park open mid-May to early Sept. daily 10:30am-midnight. Call for events schedule.) Be ready to crane your neck for the IMAX movies in the six-story **Cinesphere** (870-8000; $6-9, seniors and kids $3-6; call for screening schedule.)

Roy Thomson Hall, 60 Simcoe St. (872-4255; subway: St. Andrews), at King St. W., is both Toronto's premier concert hall and the home of the **Toronto Symphony Orchestra** (593-4828). Buy tickets ($19-50) at the box office or by phone. (Mon.-Fri. 10am-6pm; off season Mon.-Fri. 9am-8pm, Sat. noon-5pm; year-round Sun. 3hr. before performances. Ask about discounts.) Rush tickets for the symphony ($10) are available at the box office on concert days (Mon.-Fri. 11am, Sat. 1pm). The same ticket office serves **Massey Hall,** 178 Victoria St. (593-4828; subway: Dundas), near Eaton Centre, a great hall for rock and folk concerts and musicals. The opera and ballet companies perform at **O'Keefe Centre,** 1 Front St. E. (393-7469 or 872-2262 for tickets; ballet from $15, opera from $27), at Yonge. Rush tickets for the last row of orchestra seats go on sale at 11am (from $10); a limited number of ½-price tickets are available for seniors and students. Selected shows have seats at student dress rehearsals. ($12. Box office open Mon.-Sat. 11am-6pm, or until 1hr. after curtain.) Next door, **St. Lawrence Centre,** 27 Front St. E. (366-7723), stages excellent drama and chamber music recitals in two different theaters. Ask for possible student and senior discounts. (Box office open Mon.-Sat. 10am-6pm; in winter Mon.-Fri. 10am-8pm.) **Canadian Stage** (367-8243; box office 368-3110) puts up superb performances of summer Shakespeare amid the greenery of **High Park,** on Bloor St. W. at Parkside Dr. (subway: High Park). Year-round performances include new Canadian works and time-honored classics. Bring something to sit on or perch yourself on the 45° slope which faces the stage. ($5 donation requested. Call for schedule.)

Film fans looking for good classic and contemporary cinema choose the **Bloor Cinema,** 506 Bloor St. W. (532-6677), at Bathurst, or the **Cinémathèque Ontario,** 317 Dundas St. W. (923-3456), at McCaul St. Fans of Asian film should check out the **Golden Classics Cinema,** 186 Spadina Ave. (504-0585), for retrospectives.

Canada's answer to Disneyland awaits at **Canada's Wonderland,** 9580 Jane St. (832-7000), about one hr. from downtown but accessible by public transportation. Splash down the water rides or try your stomach on the backwards, looping, and suspended roller coasters. (Open late June-Labor Day daily 10am-10pm; open in fall Sat.-Sun. and in May daily; closing times vary. $33.50, seniors and ages 3-6 $16.50.)

Groove to the rhythms of old and new talents—in all, more than 1500 artists from 17 countries—at the ten-day **Du Maurier Ltd. Downtown Jazz Festival** (363-5200), at Ontario Place in late June. Also in June, the **Toronto International Dragon Boat Race Festival** (364-0046) continues a 2000-year-old Chinese tradition. The race finishes at Toronto's Center Island. The celebration includes traditional performances, foods, and free outdoor lunchtime concerts. From mid-August through Labor Day, the **Canadian National Exhibition (CNE)** (393-6050), the world's largest annual fair, brings an international carnival atmosphere to Exhibition Place. (Open daily 10am-midnight. $9.50, seniors $4.50, children $3; call for info on discount days.)

From April to October, the **Toronto Blue Jays** (341-1111, 341-1234 for tickets) play ball at the **Sky Dome,** Front and Peter St. (subway: Union, follow the signs). Most games sell out, but the box office usually has some obstructed view seats before the game (tickets $6-23). Scalpers sell tickets for far beyond face value; latecomers wait until the game starts and then haggle like mad. To get a behind-the-scenes look at the modern, commercialized Sky Dome, take the tour (341-2770; Mon.-Fri. 10am-6pm, Sept.-June Mon.-Fri. 10am-4pm, event schedule permitting; $9, seniors and under 16 $6). For info on concerts and other Sky Dome events, call 341-3663. Hockey fans should head for **Maple Leaf Gardens,** 60 Carlton St. (977-1641; subway: College), to see the knuckle-crackin', puck-smackin' **maple leaves.** Tours of the gardens leave daily at 11am, 1, 2:30, and 4pm, and require a ticket.

NIGHTLIFE

Early in the summer of 1996, the Toronto City Council passed a law prohibiting smoking in all public establishments, including restaurants, clubs, and bars. Protest against this radical law ensued, and the council is still debating how strictly it ought to be enforced. Along with this conservative measure, some of Toronto's clubs and pubs remain closed on Sundays because of liquor laws. The city shuts down alcohol distribution daily at 1am, so most clubs close down then. Nevertheless, Toronto maintains a fantastic nightlife scene. The most interesting new clubs are on trendy **Queen St. W., College St. W.,** and **Bloor St. W.** The gay scene centers around

Wellesley and **Church St.** Two comprehensive free entertainment magazines, *Now* and *Eye,* come out every Thursday.

Brunswick House, 481 Bloor St. W. (964-2242), between the Bathurst and Spadina subway stops. Teeming with students. Beer hall atmosphere, with long benches and little round tables. Beer $3.75—ouch! Thurs. means $6.50 pitchers; Fri. $2 domestic bottles. Open Mon.-Sat. noon-2am.

Lee's Palace, 529 Bloor St. W. (532-7383), just east of the Bathurst subway stop. Crazy creature art depicts a rock 'n' roll frenzy. Live music nightly downstairs; DJ dance club, the **Dance Cave,** upstairs. Pick up a calendar of bands. Box office opens 8pm, shows begin 10pm. Downstairs open daily noon-1am; cover $3-12. Upstairs open Tues. and Thurs.-Sat. 8pm-3am; cover after 10pm $4.

The Madison, 14 Madison Ave. (927-1722), at Bloor. Subway: Spadina. Blonde wood, 2 pool rooms, 1 large patio, and 2 small patios, 16 beers on tap. Victorian exterior. Pints $4.80. Wings $2.70. Open Mon.-Sat. 11am-2am, Sun. noon-1am.

Second City, 110 Lombard St. (863-1111), in the old firehall at Jarvis St., 2 blocks east and 2 short blocks south of Queen's Park subway stop. One of North America's wackiest, most creative comedy clubs. Spawned comics Dan Akroyd, John Candy, Gilda Radner, Martin Short, a hit TV show (SCTV), and the legendary "Great White North." Free improv sessions Mon.-Thurs. 10:15pm. Mon.-Thurs. dinner 6pm, show 8:30pm; Fri.-Sat. dinner 5 and 8:30pm, shows 8 and 11pm. Dinner and theater from $33, students $30. Theater only $13-20/$10; first come, first served behind the dinner tables. Sun. "best of" 8pm $11. Reservations required.

Sneaky Dee's, 431 College St. W. (603-3090 or 603-1824), at Bathurst. A hip Toronto hotspot tapping the most inexpensive brew (60oz. pitcher of Ontario microbrewery draught $8.50). Mon.-Fri. before 6pm, domestic beer goes for $2.50 per bottle. Pool tables in back. DJ and dancing upstairs daily 9:30pm. Open Sun.-Thurs. 11am-4am, Fri.-Sat. 11am-5am.

College St. Bar, 574 College St. W. (533-2417). A brick interior and mellow atmosphere. Mostly Italian food; dinner entrees $8-10. Live music; Wed. jazz and Sun. blues/funk pack the place (10:30pm both nights). Open Mon.-Fri. noon-1am, Sat. 4pm-1am, Sun. 11:30am-1am.

Woody's/Sailor, 465-467 Church St. (972-0887), by Maitland. *The* established gay bar in the Church and Wellesley area. Neighborhood atmosphere; walls are lined with art nudes and photos of locals. Come to relax and hang out before heading to the clubs, but don't miss the raunchy Mr. Woody (and now Miss Woody) contests on the weekends. Bottled beer $4. Open daily noon-3am.

Aztec, 2 Gloucester St. (975-8612), at Yonge. Subway: Wellesley or Bloor/Yonge. Toronto's premier gay dance club offers disco music beneath two huge bronze suns for a mixed crowd of men and women. Open daily 11am-2am. **Tango,** the women's club downstairs, has pool tournaments, live performances, and a cozier bar atmosphere. Drinks in either bar run $2.75-4.

■ Near Toronto

As beautiful as its name is strange, **Onation's Niagara Escarpment** passes west of Toronto as it winds its way from Niagara Falls to Tobermory at the tip of the Bruce Peninsula. Along this rocky 724-km ridge, the **Bruce Trail** snakes through parks and private land; hikers are treated to spectacular waterfalls, the breathtaking cliffs along **Georgian Bay,** and unique flora and fauna, including an old growth forest. Because the escarpment is registered as a UN world biosphere reserve, future land development is limited to that which can exist symbiotically with the natural environment. For maps and Escarpment info, write or call the **Niagara Escarpment Commission,** 232 Guelph St., Georgetown L7G 4B1 (905-877-5191). Specifics on the Bruce Trail can be obtained by contacting the **Bruce Trail Association,** P.O. Box 857, Hamilton L8N 3N9 (905-529-6821).The area is unreachable by public transportation, but **The Canadian Experience** (800-668-4487) organizes phenomenal escapes into the Ontarian countryside. However, guides Kellie and Larry Casey Shaw, an Olympic skier and a former pro hockey player respectively, recently had a baby, so their tours are postponed at this time.

■ Stratford

Filling the coffers since 1953, the **Stratford Shakespeare Festival** has proven to be the lifeblood of this picturesque town. Stratford-born scribe Tom Patterson founded the festival, which opened its inaugural season with Sir Alec Guiness in the title role of *Richard III*. Since then, the town and the festival have become inextricably intertwined. Today only a few of the plays are Shakespeare each year, and enthusiasts of all types of drama are likely to find something to their tastes amid the dozen or so plays produced each season. The **Stratford Festival** runs from May, when previews begin, through late October. During midsummer madness (July-Aug.), up to six different shows play per day (none on Mon.). Matinees begin at 2pm and evening performances at 8pm in each of three theaters: the crown-shaped **Festival Theatre,** the vaudevillesque **Avon Theatre,** and the intimate **Tom Patterson Theatre.** Complete info about casts and performances can be obtained by phone (363-4471 or 800-567-1600) or by writing the **Stratford Festival,** P.O. Box 520, Stratford N5A 6V2. Tickets are expensive ($30-60), but a few good deals lower the stakes. For every performance, a number of **rush tickets** are sold at 9am on the morning of the show at the Festival Theatre Box Office, ½ hr. before the show by phone, and at the appropriate theater ($15-40). Seniors and students enjoy discounts at certain designated midweek matinee performances ($16.75-20). Students can also purchase $20 tickets two weeks prior to any performance for any day except Saturday. During previews, seniors can claim unsold seats for $20. Tickets to some theater performances go for ½-price on Tuesdays. (Box office open Mon.-Sat. 9am-8pm, Sun. 9am-5pm.)

There is much more to Stratford than its annual festival, not the least of which is the town's tranquility and charm. Placid Lake Victoria (Avon River) sits at the middle of town and offers beautiful views and bridges for romantic evening strolls. Monday and Friday evenings from 6:30-8pm look for free **Jazz on the River** (mid-June to early Sept.). For a longer walk try the **Avon Trail,** which crosses Stratford at the T.J. Dolan Natural Area, near the intersection of John and Centre St.

The **Tourism Stratford Information Center,** 1 York St. (273-3352 or 800-561-7926), on the river, will send a free visitors guide if you call ahead, and they're just as willing to help walk-ins (open Mon.-Sat. 9am-8pm, Sun. 9am-5pm).

The **Festival Accommodations Bureau** (273-1600) can tell you where to go when now spurs the lated traveler apace to gain the timely inn, guest home ($31-45), or B&B ($50-120). The **Burnside Guest Home,** 139 William St., Stratford N5A 4X9 (271-7076), is the budget traveler's best bet for lodging and offers a great view of Lake Victoria. The room charge includes a hearty breakfast. (B&B rooms $40-60; student rooms $25. Reserve in advance.) Campsites at the **Wildwood Conservation Area** (519-284-2292), on Hwy. 7, 11km southwest of Stratford, may have bugs, but they also have access to a beach, pool, and marina. The area can get cramped; trailers often outnumber tents 30 to one. (430 sites. $17, with hookup $21.50.)

To get to Stratford, take **VIA Rail** (273-3234 or 800-361-1235) or **Cha-Co Trails** (271-7870), a bus company owned by Greyhound. Both operate out of a depot on Shakespeare St. Service to Toronto (2hr., $25), London (1hr., $12), or Kitchener (½hr., $10) costs the same and takes an equal amount of time by train or bus.

■ Ottawa

Legend has it that Queen Victoria chose this as Canada's capital by closing her eyes and poking her finger at a map. But perhaps political savvy and not blind chance guided the Queen to this once-remote logging town, which, as a stronghold for neither French nor English interests, became a perfect compromise capital. Today, faced with the increasingly tricky task of forging national unity while preserving local identities, Ottawa continues to play cultural ambassador to its own country.

At the turn of the century, Prime Minister Sir Wilfred Laurier called on urban planners to polish Ottawa into a "Washington of the North." The carefully groomed and cultured façade which resulted has contributed to Ottawa's reputation for being somewhat boring. An evening stroll through Byward Market will challenge this notion. Rest assured that, behind the theaters, museums and parks, there is plenty of action both before and after quitting time in the capital.

PRACTICAL INFORMATION

Tourist Office: National Capital Commission Information Center, 14 Metcalfe St. (239-5000 or 800-465-1867 in Canada), at Wellington opposite the Parliament Buildings. Open daily 8:30am-9pm; early Sept. to early May Mon.-Sat. 9am-5pm, Sun. 10am-4pm. Provides free maps and the helpful *Ottawa Visitors Guide.* For info on Hull and Québec province, contact the **Association Touristique de l'Outaouais,** 103 rue Laurier, Hull (819-778-222 or 800-265-7822), at rue St. Laurent. Open mid-June to Sept. Mon.-Fri. 8:30am-8pm, Sat.-Sun. 9am-5pm; off season Mon.-Fri. 8:30am-5pm, Sat.-Sun. 9am-4pm. **Gayline-Telegai,** 238-1717. Info on local bars and special events. Open daily 7-10pm.

Police: Ontario Provincial Police, 592-4878; infoline 800-267-2677. **Ottawa Police,** 230-6211; infoline 236-0311.

Student Travel Agencies: Travel CUTS, 1 Stewart St., #203 (238-8222), at Waller, just east of Nicholas 2 blocks north of the Université d'Ottawa; also on the 1st level of the Unicentre, Carleton Univ. (238-5493). Experts in student travel, youth hostel cards, cheap flights, and VIA Rail. Open Mon. and Wed.-Fri. 9am-5pm, Tues. 9am-4pm. **Hostelling International-Canada (HI-C), Ontario East Region,** 75 Nicholas St. (569-1400). Youth hostel passes, travel info, and equipment. Open Mon.-Fri. 9:30am-5:30pm, Sat. 9:30am-5pm.

Embassies: U.S., 100 Wellington St. (238-5335), directly across from Parliament. Open daily 8:30am-5pm. **U.K.,** 80 Elgin St. (237-1530), at the corner of Queen St. Open Mon.-Fri. 9am-5pm. **Australia,** 50 O'Connor St. #710 (236-0841), at Queen St. Open for visas and info Mon.-Fri. 9am-noon and 2-4pm. **New Zealand,** 99 Bank St. #727 (238-5991). Open Mon.-Fri. 8:30am-4:30pm. **Ireland,** 170 Metcalfe St. (233-6281). Open Mon.-Fri. 10am-1pm and 2:30-4pm. **France,** 42 Sussex Dr. (789-1795). Open for info Mon.-Fri. 9:30am-1:30pm.

American Express: 220 Laurier W. (563-0231), between Metcalfe and O'Connor St., in the heart of downtown. Open Mon.-Wed. 8:30am-5:30pm, Thurs.-Fri. 8:30am-7:30pm, Sat. 9am-4pm.

Airport: Ottawa International (998-3151), 20min. south of the city off Bronson Ave. Take bus #96 from MacKenzie King Bridge. **Tourist info** (998-3151) available daily 9am-9pm in arrival area. Kasbary Transport, Inc. runs **shuttles** (736-9993) between the airport and 11 hotels; the Novotel is near Ottawa Int'l Hostel. Call for pick-up from 15 other hotels. Daily every ½hr. 5am-1am; call for later pick-up. $9; students with ID, seniors, and ages 6-18 $4; under 6 free. Group rates available.

Trains: VIA Rail, 200 Tremblay Rd. (244-8289 or 800-561-3949), off Alta Vista Rd. To: Montréal (4 per day, 2hr., $36, students $32); Toronto (4 per day, 4hr., $76/68); Québec City via Montréal (3 per day, 7hr., $66/59). Ticket office open Mon.-Fri. 5am-9pm, Sat. 6:30am-9pm, Sun. 8:30am-9pm.

Buses: Voyageur, 265 Catherine St. (238-5900), between Kent and Lyon. Services primarily eastern Canada. To: Montréal (on the hr. 6am-10pm, 2½hr., $26). **Greyhound** (237-7038) buses leave from the same station, bound for western Canada or southern Ontario. To: Toronto (7 per day, 5hr., $56). For service to the U.S. you must first go to Montréal or Toronto; the Québec City-bound must go through Montréal. Station open daily 5:30am-12:30am.

Public Transportation: OC Transport, 1500 St. Laurent (741-4390). Excellent system. Buses congregate on either side of Rideau Centre. $1.85 or 2 80¢ tickets; peak hours (Mon.-Fri. 3-5:30pm) $2.10; express (green buses) $2.70; seniors $1.60; under 5 free. For info on the blue **Hull City Buses,** call 819-770-3242.

Taxis: Blue Line Taxi, 746-8740. $2 base fare, $1.90 per km. 24hr.

Driver/Rider Service: Allostop, 238 Dalhousie (562-8248), at St. Patrick. To: Toronto ($24), Québec City ($29), Montréal ($10), and New York City ($50). Membership ($7) required. Open Mon.-Wed. 9am-5pm, Thurs.-Fri. 9am-7pm, Sat.-Sun. 10am-5pm. There is also an active **rideboard** on the 2nd floor of the University of Ottawa's University Center.

Bike Rental: Rent-A-Bike-Vélocationo, 1 Rideau St. (241-4140), behind the Château Laurier Hotel. $7 per hr., $16 for ½-day, $20 per day. Tandems $15 per hr., $50 per day. Maps, locks, helmets free. 2-hr. escorted tours $14. Family deals available. Open mid-May to Oct. daily 9am-7:30pm. Credit card required. All new roads in Ottawa are required to have a bicycle lane.

Crisis Lines: Ottawa Distress Centre, 238-3311, English-speaking. **Tel-Aide,** 741-6433, French-speaking. **Rape Crisis Centre,** 729-8889. All 3 open 24hr.

Emergency: 911.

Post Office: Postal Station B, 59 Sparks St. (844-1545), at Elgin St. Open Mon.-Fri. 8am-6pm. **Postal code:** K1P 5A0. **Area code:** 613 (Ottawa); 819 (Hull).

ORIENTATION

Rideau Canal divides Ottawa into the eastern lower town and the western upper town. West of the canal, Parliament buildings and government offices line **Wellington St.,** one of the city's main east-west arteries, which runs directly into the heart of downtown and crosses the canal. **Laurier** is the only other east-west street which permits traffic from one side of the canal to the other. East of the canal, Wellington St. becomes **Rideau St.,** surrounded by a fashionable shopping district. North of Rideau St. lies the **Byward Market,** a shopping area which hosts a summertime open-air market and much of Ottawa's nightlife. **Elgin St.,** a primary north-south artery, stretches from the **Queensway** (Hwy. 417) to the War Memorial just south of Wellington in front of **Parliament Hill. Bank St.,** parallel to Elgin three blocks to the east, services the town's older shopping area. The canal itself is a major access route; in winter, thousands of Ottawans skate to work on this, the world's longest skating rink; in summer, power boats breeze by regularly. Bike paths and pedestrian walkways also line the canals. Parking is painful downtown; meters often cost 25¢ for 10 min. Residential neighborhoods east of the canal have longer limits and the police ticket less often than on main streets.

Hull, Québec, across the Ottawa River, is most notable for its less strict drinking laws, including an 18-year-old drinking age. Many bars and clubs rock nightly until 3am. Close to Gatineau Provincial Park, Hull connects to Ottawa by several bridges and the blue Hull buses from downtown Ottawa (see Practical Information).

ACCOMMODATIONS AND CAMPING

Clean, inexpensive rooms and campsites are not difficult to find in Ottawa except during May and early June, when student groups and conventioneers come to claim their long-reserved rooms, and during the peak of the tourist season in July and August. A complete list of B&Bs can be found in the *Ottawa Visitors Guide;* **Ottawa Bed and Breakfast** (563-0161) represents ten B&Bs in the Ottawa area (singles $50, doubles $50-75).

Ottawa International Hostel (HI-C), 75 Nicholas St., K1N 7B9 (235-2595), in downtown Ottawa. The site of Canada's last public hanging, this trippy hostel now "incarcerates" travelers in the former Carleton County Jail. Rooms contain 4-8 bunks and minimal storage space. Communal showers (hot only in the thermal sense), kitchen, laundry facilities, large lounges, and a cast of friendly, personable regulars. Centrally located. International crowd. Many organized activities (biking, canoeing, tours). IBN reservations available. 130 beds. In winter, doors locked 2-7am. $16, nonmembers $20. Parking $5 first day, $3 each additional.

University of Ottawa Residences, 100 University St. (564-5400), in the center of campus, an easy walk from downtown. From the bus station, take bus #1, 7, or 11 on Bank St. to Rideau Centre and walk up Nicholas to the U of O campus. From the train station, catch bus #95 west. Clean dorm rooms in a vast concrete landscape. Hall showers. Free local hall phone. Access to University Center (with bank machines). Check-in 4:30pm; they'll store luggage until then. Free linen, towels.

Singles $32, doubles $40; students with ID $21.50/$35. Continental breakfast $2. Open early May to late Aug. Parking $7 per day, $4 per ½-day.

Centre Town Guest House Ltd., 502 Kent St. (233-0681), just north of the bus station, a 10- to 15-min. walk from downtown. Clean rooms in an aging but comfortable house. Free breakfast (eggs, cereal, bacon, toast) in a cozy dining room. Singles from $25, doubles from $35, 2 twin beds $50. Monthly rates from $400. Reservations recommended. Parking available.

YMCA/YWCA, 180 Argyle St. (237-1320), at O'Connor St. Close to the bus station; walk left on Bank St. and right on Argyle. Nicely-sized (though unattractively decorated) rooms in a modern high-rise. Free local phones in every room. Kitchen with microwave available until 11pm. Guests can use gym facilities. Front desk open Mon.-Thurs. 7am-11pm, Fri.-Sat. 24hr. Singles with shared bath $42, with private bath $48.50; doubles $49. Weekly and group rates available. Payment must be made in advance. Cafeteria open Mon.-Fri. 7am-6:30pm, Sat.-Sun. 8am-2:30pm; breakfast $4. Indoor parking evenings 4:30pm-8:30am $2.75; day parking available.

Gatineau Park (456-3016 for reservations; 827-2020 for info), northwest of Hull, has three rustic campgrounds within 45 min. of Ottawa: **Lac Philippe Campground,** 248 sites with facilities for family camping, trailers, and campers; **Lac Taylor Campground,** with 34 "semi-wilderness" sites; and **Lac la Pêche,** with 36 campsites accessible only by canoe. Camping permits for Taylor and Philippe ($16, seniors $8) are available at the campground entrance. Pay for a site at La Pêche ($13) on Eardley Rd. All sites available mid.-May to mid.-Oct. All the campgrounds are off Hwy. 366 northwest of Hull; watch for signs. Map available at visitors center. (Open daily 9am-6pm, in winter Sat.-Sun. 9am-6pm.) From Ottawa, take the Cartier-MacDonald Bridge, follow Autoroute 5 north to Scott Rd., turn right onto Hwy. 105, and follow it to 366. To reach La Pêche, take Hwy. 366 to Eardley Rd. on your left.

FOOD

Fans of the cholesterol-rich breakfast find friends in Ottawa; the ubiquitous greasy spoon scene revolves around the worship of eggs, potatoes, meat, toast, and coffee. **Copacabano,** 380 Dalhousie St. (241-9762), offers a particularly artery-wrenching rendition of this stand-by: homefries, 3 pieces of bacon, ham or sausage, 2 eggs, toast, and coffee ($2; open 24hr.). During the summer, occasional street music surrounds the fresh fruit, vegetables, and flowers of the lively open-air **Byward Market,** on Byward St. between York and Rideau St. (open daily 8am-6pm). After eating, relax and linger at the Dutch **Café Wim,** 537 Sussex Dr. (241-1771), which serves sumptuous Colombian coffee ($1.45), decadent desserts ($2-6), creative sandwiches ($5-7), and bar fare (open daily 7:30am-1am). Sweeten your palate with one of 40 homemade Italian gelato flavors at **Belmondo,** 381 Dalhousie St. (746-2983).

Sunset Grill, 47 Clarence St. (241-9497). Sit on the huge outdoor terrace and grapple with a huge club sandwich ($8). Lively colors, perky staff, and California-style food melt the worries away. Open Sun.-Mon. 11am-11pm, Tues.-Sat. 11am-1am.

Las Palmas, 111 Parent Ave. (241-3738). Outstanding Mexican grub heaped high; "like eating in a Mexican funhouse during a fiesta." Hot means *hot* here. Dinners $7-13. Open Mon.-Thurs. and Sat. 11:30am-10:30pm, Fri. 11:30am-midnight.

Royal Star, 99 Rideau St. (562-2772), in the Byward Market Mall (entrance at 96 George St.). Killer lunch buffet ($7) with over 100 selections of Szechuan, Cantonese, Polynesian, and Canadian favorites. Open for lunch Mon.-Fri. 11am-3pm.

Mamma Grazzi's Kitchen, 25 George St. (241-8656). Quiet, intimate quarters bathed in the aroma of Italian specialties and thin-crust pizza ($6-12). Be patient; it's worth the wait. Open Sun.-Thurs. 11:30am-10pm, Fri.-Sat. 11:30am-11pm.

The International Cheese and Deli, 40 Byward St. (241-5411). Deli and Middle Eastern sandwiches to go. Vegetable *samosa* $1.25; turkey and cheese $4; falafel on pita $2.30. Open Sat.-Thurs. 7am-6pm, Fri. 7am-8pm; in winter opens at 8am.

Father and Sons, 112 Osgoode St. (233-6066), at the eastern edge of the U of O campus. Student favorite for a menu of tavern-style food with some Lebanese dishes thrown in. Try the falafel platter or a triple-decker sandwich (both $7). Spicy specials served daily 8-11pm; Mon. after 7pm and Sat. all day 15¢ wings. Open Mon.-Sat. 7am-2am, Sun. 8am-1am. Kitchen open until midnight.

SIGHTS

Though overshadowed by Toronto's size and Montréal's cosmopolitan color, Ottawa's status as capital of Canada is shored up by its cultural attractions. Since the national museums and political action pack tightly together, most sights can be reached by foot. **Parliament Hill,** on Wellington at Metcalfe St., distinguished by its Gothic architecture, towers over downtown. Warm your hands and heart over the **Centennial Flame** at the south gate, lit in 1967 to mark the 100th anniversary of the Dominion of Canada's inaugural session of Parliament. The Prime Minister can occasionally be spotted at the central parliament structure, **Centre Block,** which contains the House of Commons, Senate, and Library of Parliament. On display behind the library, the original bell from Centre Block is the only part of the original 1859-66 structure to survive the 1916 fire; according to legend, the bell crashed to the ground after chiming at midnight on the night of the flames. The carillon of 53 bells that replaced the old bell hangs in the **Peace Tower.** The bells range from ½ ounce to several tons; the tower is currently under renovation, and the bells hang mute. Free, worthwhile tours of Centre Block (in English or French) depart every 30 min. from the white **Infotent** by the visitors center. (Group reservations, 996-0896. Public info, 992-4793. Open in summer Mon.-Fri. 9am-5pm; early Sept. to mid-May daily 9am-4:30pm. Last tour begins 40min. before closing time.) When Parliament is in session, you can watch Canada's government officials squirm on the verbal hot seat during the official **Question Period** in the **House of Commons** chamber (Mon.-Thurs. 2:15-3pm, Fri. 11:15am-noon). Those interested in trying to make a statuesque soldier giggle should attend the **Changing of the Guard** (993-1811), on the broad lawns in front of Centre Block (late June-late Aug. daily 10am, weather permitting). At dusk, Centre Block and its lawns transform into the set for *A Symphony of Sound and Light,* which relates the history of the Parliament Buildings and the nation (mid-May to July 9:30 and 10:30pm, Aug. to early Sept. 9 and 10pm; performances alternate between French and English). A five-min. walk west along Wellington St., the **Supreme Court of Canada** (995-5361) cohabitates with the Federal Court. (Free 30-min. tours every ½hr. Open daily 9am-5pm; Sept.-April hours vary.)

One block south of Wellington, the recently renovated **Sparks Street Mall,** hailed as an innovative experiment in 1960, when it was one of North America's first pedestrian malls, now houses a slew of banks and upscale retail stores. The **Rideau Centre,** south of Rideau St. at Sussex Dr., is the city's primary shopping mall as well as one of the main OC Transport stations. Glass encloses the sidewalks in front of Rideau St.'s stores to make them bearable during the winter months.

East of the Parliament Buildings at the junction of Sparks, Wellington, and Elgin St. stands **Confederation Sq.** with its enormous **National War Memorial,** dedicated by King George VI in 1939. The structure symbolizes the triumph of peace over war, an ironic message on the eve of World War II. **Nepean Point,** several blocks northwest of Rideau Centre and the Byward Market behind the National Gallery of Canada, provides a panoramic view of the capital. The Governor-General, the Queen's representative in Canada, resides at **Rideau Hall** (998-7113). Free tours leave from the main gate at One Sussex Dr. (998-7114; 800-465-6890 for tour info). Dress up for the open house on New Year's Day or Canada Day and they'll even let you see the interior. Otherwise, gawk from **24 Sussex Dr.,** the Prime Minister's residence.

Ottawa's reputation for respecting cultural difference extends beyond the whole French-English thing. Many nationalities integrate well here; ethnically-grouped neighborhoods, somewhat sparse, include a small **Chinatown** around Somerset St. between Kent St. and Bronson Ave. From downtown, walk south on Elgin St.; go west on Somerset until fruit stands line the streets and the French on signs turns to Chinese (about a 20-min. walk). **Little Italy** is just around the corner on Bronson Ave., stretching south from Somerset to the Queensway (Hwy. 417).

Museums and Parks

Ottawa contains many of Canada's huge national museums. Most are wheelchair accessible; call for details. **The National Gallery,** 380 Sussex Dr. (990-1985), a spectacular glass-towered building adjacent to Nepean Pt., holds the world's most comprehensive collection of Canadian art as well as outstanding European, American, and Asian works. The building's exterior is a parody of the neo-Gothic buttresses of the facing Library of Parliament. (Open in summer Wed.-Mon. 10am-6pm, Tues. 10am-8pm; Oct.-May. Wed.-Sun. 10am-5pm. Permanent collection free; special events $8, students and under 18 free, seniors $5.) The **Canadian Museum of Contemporary Photography,** 1 Rideau Canal (990-8257), between the Chateau Laurier and the Ottawa Locks, allows a frozen glimpse of modern Canadian life. (Open in summer Fri.-Tues. 11am-5pm, Wed. 4-8pm, Thurs. 11am-8pm; Sept.-April Wed. 11am-5pm, Thurs. 11am-8pm, Fri.-Sun. 11am-5pm. Free.)

A sand-dune-like structure across the river in Hull houses the **Canadian Museum of Civilization,** 100 Laurier St. (776-7000). Admire the architecture but beware overly ambitious exhibits that attempt to put 1000 years of Canadian history into perspective. Don't miss the breathtaking films shown at **CINEPLUS** (776-7010 for showtimes), capable of projecting both IMAX and OmniMax. (Open June Fri.-Wed. 9am-6pm, Thurs. 9am-9pm; July-Aug. Sat.-Mon. 9am-6pm, Tues.-Fri. 9am-9pm; in winter Tues.-Sun. 9am-5pm. Museum $5, seniors and ages 13-17 $3.50, under 13 $3; free Sun. 9am-noon. CINEPLUS $8, seniors and kids $5.) The **Canadian Museum of Nature,** 240 McLeod St. (996-3102), at Metcalf, explores the natural world from dinosaur to mineral through multi-media displays. (Open in summer Fri.-Wed. 9:30am-5pm, Thurs. 9:30am-8pm; Sept.-April Fri.-Wed. 10am-5pm, Thurs. 10am-8pm. $4, students $3, seniors and ages 6-16 $2; Thurs. ½-price until 5pm, free 5-8pm.)

Canadian history buffs could easily lose themselves in the **National Library Archives,** 395 Wellington St. (995-5138), at Bay St., which houses oodles of Canadian publications, old maps, photographs, letters, and historical exhibits. (Open daily 9am-9pm.) Liberal Prime Minister William Lyon Mackenzie King governed Canada from the elegant **Laurier House,** 335 Laurier Ave. E. (992-8142), for most of his lengthy tenure. Admire at your leisure the antiques King accumulated, as well as the crystal ball he used to consult his long-dead mother on matters of national import. (Open in summer Tues.-Sat. 9am-5pm, Sun. 2-5pm; call for Oct.-March hours. Free.)

Farther out of town, the **National Museum of Science and Technology,** 1867 St. Laurent Blvd. (991-3044), at Smyth, lets visitors explore the wonderful world of tech and transport with touchy-feely exhibits. The museum entrance is on Lancaster, 200m east of St. Laurent; take bus #85 or 148 from downtown. (Open in summer Sat.-Thurs. 9am-6pm, Fri. 9am-9pm; Sept.-April closed Mon. $6, students and seniors $5, ages 6-15 $2, under 6 free; free Thurs. 5-9pm.) The **National Aviation Museum** (993-2010), at the Rockcliffe Airport off St. Laurent Blvd. north of Montréal St., illustrates the history of human flight and displays more than 100 aircrafts; take bus #95 and transfer to #198. (Open in summer daily 9am-5pm, Thurs. 9am-9pm; Labor Day-April closed Mon. $5, students and seniors $4, ages 6-15 $1.75; free Thurs. 5-9pm.)

Ottawa has managed to skirt the traditional urban vices of pollution and violent crime; the multitude of parks and recreation areas may make you forget you're in a city at all. A favorite destination for Ottawans who want to cycle, hike, or fish, **Gatineau Park** (see Accommodations, above) extends 356 sq. km into the northwest. Artificial **Dow's Lake** (232-1001), accessible by the Queen Elizabeth Driveway, extends off the Rideau Canal 15 min. south of Ottawa. **Dow's Lake Pavilion,** 101 Queen Elizabeth Driveway, near Preston St., rents pedal boats, canoes, and bikes. (Open daily 11:30am-1am. Rentals by the ½hr. and the hr.; prices vary.)

ENTERTAINMENT

The **National Arts Centre,** 53 Elgin St. (996-5051; 755-1111 for tickets), at Albert St., houses an excellent small orchestra and theater company and frequently hosts international entertainers (box office open Mon.-Sat. noon-9pm). **Odyssey Theatre** (232-

8407) puts on open-air comedy at **Strathcona Park,** at the end of Laurier Ave. at Charlotte St., well east of the canal. The shows are bawdy enough that they don't recommend using the children's discount. (Shows late July to late Aug. Tues.-Sun. 8:30pm. $18, students and seniors $15, under 12 $6.)

Ottawans seem to celebrate just about everything, even the bitter Canadian cold. During the first three weekends of February, **Winterlude** (239-5000) lines the Rideau Canal with ice sculptures illustrating how it feels to be an Ottawan in the winter (frozen). For a week in mid-May, the **Tulip Festival** (567-5757) explodes in a colorful kaleidoscope of more than 100,000 blooming tulips around Dow's Lake. Music fills the Ottawa air during the **Dance Festival** (237-5158), in mid-June, and the **Jazz Festival** (594-3580), in mid-July, both of which hold free recitals and concerts, as well as pricier events. Labor Day weekend, the folks on Parliament Hill lend some of their bombast to the **Hot Air Balloon Festival** (243-2330), when hundreds of beautiful balloons from Canada, the U.S., and Europe take to the friendly skies.

For an escape from the city hubbub, seek out the **beaches,** west of town by way of the Ottawa River Pkwy. (follow the signs). **Mooney's Bay,** one popular strip of river bank, is 15 min. from Ottawa by car.

NIGHTLIFE

Hull, Québec remains the place for the dedicated nightlifer. Right across the border, where the legal drinking age is 18, establishments grind and gnash until 3am every night of the week. Over 20 popular nightspots pack the **Promenade du Portage** in Hull (a.k.a The Strip), just west of **Place Portage** government office complex. The capital also has its own share of excitement, especially in the **Byward Market** area. Though Ottawa clubs close at 1am (many at 11pm on Sun.), many are coverless, making them worth more than a look. **Château Lafayette,** 42 York St. (241-4747), the oldest tavern in Ottawa, lures the budgeteer with $3 pints; regulars are the kind of hard-core beer drinkers who pound a beer, slam the mug down on the bar, and say "Mr. Keeper, I'll hava 'nuther." (Open Mon.-Sat. 11am-2am, Sun. noon-2am.) **Heart & Crown,** 67 Clarence St. (562-0764), packs in a rowdier crowd eager to open wallets and gullets for $5.50 pints of Harp and Guinness on tap. (Open Mon.-Wed. 11am-1am, Thurs.-Fri. 11am-2am, Sat. 10am-2am, Sun. 10am-1am.)

On a musical note, Ottawa caters to both listeners and dancers. Land on the **Reactor,** 18 York St. (241-8955), for bright lights and dance music. (Open daily 4pm-1am.) Experience life, the universe, and a bit of everything else at **Zaphod Beeblebrox,** 27 York St. (562-1010), in Byward Market, a popular alternative club famous for their $5.50 Pangalactic Gargle Blasters. (Cover up to $10 on Tues. and Thurs.-Sat. when live bands play. Open Mon.-Fri. 4pm-2am, Sat.-Sun. noon-2am.) The show must go on, and it has done so every single night for the last decade at **The Rainbow Bistro,** 76 Murray St. (241-5123), a dark, smoky blues joint that often draws acts from Chicago and New Orleans. (Music starts 9pm. Cover $0-10. Sat. afternoon matinee 3:30-7pm; $1. Open daily 4pm-2am.) A popular gay pub, **The Market Station,** 15 George St. (562-3540), sits above a happening, subterranean dance cavern called **The Well.** (Thurs.-Sat. cover $2. Market Station open Mon.-Tues. 3pm-1am, Wed.-Sun. noon-1am; Well open Wed.-Sat. 9pm-1am, in summer also Tues. 9pm-1am. 19+.) A slightly older crowd (25-35) congregates in the bars on Elgin St.

■ Algonquin Provincial Park

The wilder Canada of endless rushing rivers and shimmering lakes awaits in Algonquin Provincial Park, about 250 km west of Ottawa. From the city, take Hwy. 417 (the Queensway) west to Renfrew exit, then follow Hwy. 60 west to the park. For info and camping permits, visit the **East Gate Information Center** (705-633-5572; open in summer daily 8am-4pm; Labor Day-May 8am-4pm). Tents and trailers crowd the Hwy. 60 Corridor (permits $16 per night per site). To experience the "essence of Algonquin," pierce the park interior (permits $5 per person per night). **Algonquin**

Reservation Network (705-633-5538), handles reservations for 1200 sites on the corridor (free showers, bathrooms, no hookups) and limitless primitive campsites in the interior, accessible only by hiking or canoe. Several outfitting stores in the park area rent backcountry gear; closest to the eastern entrance, **Opeongo Algonquin Outfitters** (613-637-2075), on Rte. 60 on Opeongo Lake, is about 15 min. into the park. (Tents $6-10 per night, sleeping bags $3.50-5.50, canoes $15-25. Open in summer daily 8am-8pm; Sept.-June 8am-6pm.)

Alberta

Alberta's glitter is concentrated in the west of the province; the icy peaks and turquoise lakes of Banff and Jasper National Parks reign as Alberta's most prominent landscapes. To the east, less sublime vistas of farmland, prairie, and oil fields fill the yawning expanses. Alberta boasts thousands of prime fishing holes, world-renowned fossil fields, and centers of Native American culture. Calgary caught the world's eye when it hosted the XV Winter Olympics in 1988, and is annual host to the wild and woolly Stampede.

PRACTICAL INFORMATION

Capital: Edmonton.
Visitors Information: Alberta Tourism, Commerce 10155 102 St., 3rd fl., Edmonton T5J 4L6 (427-4321 or 800-661-8888). Contact **Parks Canada,** 220 4th Ave. SE, Suite 552, Calgary T2G 4X3 (292-4401), for info on Waterton Lakes, Jasper, Banff, and Wood Buffalo provincial parks. **Alberta Wilderness Association,** P.O. Box 6398, Station D, Calgary T2P 2E1 (283-2025; fax 270-2743). Distributes info for off-highway adventurers.
Emergency: 911 in most areas; some rural areas may not have 911 service.
Time Zone: Mountain (2hr. behind Eastern).
Postal Abbreviation: AB.
Provincial Sales Tax: None.
Drinking Age: 18.
Traffic Laws: Mandatory seatbelt law.
Area Code: 403.

▓ Edmonton

When western Alberta's glitz and glamour were distributed, Edmonton was apparently last in line. Not one to wallow in its reputation for drabness, the city continues to improve its cultural offerings. The Oilers have made Edmonton a minor mecca for hockey fans while music, art, and performance festivals draw summer crowds. Add the largest mall in the world and an exotic plant conservatory, and Edmonton becomes an urban oasis after the overpowering splendor of the nearby Rockies.

Practical Information Edmonton Tourism, City Hall, 1 Sir Winston Churchill Sq. (496-8423), at 102A Ave. west of 99 St., has info, maps, and directions (open Victoria Day-Labor Day Mon.-Fri. 9am-4pm, Sat.-Sun. 11am-5pm; in winter Mon.-Fri. 9am-4pm). **Greyhound,** 10324 103 St. (420-2412) runs to Calgary (nearly every hr. 8am-8pm, plus a midnight run, $33), Jasper (4 per day, $47), Vancouver (5 per day, $113), and Yellowknife (1 per day Mon.-Fri.; in winter 3 per week, $177). The station is open daily 5:30am-midnight. **VIA Rail,** 10004 104 Ave. (422-6032 for recorded info, 800-561-8630 for reservations), in the CN Tower, offers service to Jasper and Vancouver, but none to Calgary. **Edmonton Transit** (496-1611 for schedule info). Buses and light rail transit **(LRT)** run frequently throughout the city. LRT is free in the downtown area Mon.-Fri. 9am-3pm and Sat. 9am-6pm (between Grandin Station at 110 St. and 98 Ave. and Churchill Station at 99 St. and 102 Ave.). Otherwise,

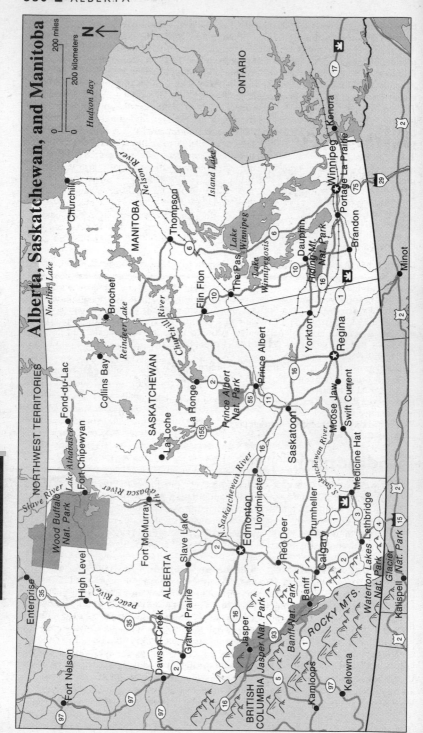

Alberta, Saskatchewan, and Manitoba

fare is $1.60, over 65 and under 15 80¢. No bikes are allowed on buses; none on LRT during peak hours (Mon.-Fri. 7:30-8:30am and 4-5pm). For a taxi, call **Yellow Cab,** 462-3456, or **Alberta Co-op Taxi,** 425-8310. In an **emergency,** dial 911. The **post office,** 9808 103A Ave. (495-4105), sits adjacent to the CN Tower and is open Mon.-Fri. 8am-5:45pm. Edmonton's **postal code** is T5J 2G8; the **area code** is 403.

Accommodations, Food, and Sights Take bus #1 or 2 to reach the **Edmonton International Youth Hostel (HI-C),** 10422 91 St. (429-0140), off Jasper Ave. The small building, low water pressure, and lack of TV make this a rather rustic urban hostel. It does have A/C, common room, snack bar, showers, kitchen, and laundry facilities (open daily 8am-midnight; $12.50, nonmembers $17). You can also try **St. Joseph's College** (492-7681), on 89 Ave. at 114 St. near the University of Alberta. Take bus #43, or take the LRT and get off at University. The rooms here are smaller, quieter, less institutional, and cheaper than those at the university nearby. In summer, make reservations; rooms fill up fast. (Check-in Mon.-Fri. 8:30am-4pm. Singles $21, weekly $130. Single with full board $34, or pay for meals separately: breakfast $3.25, lunch $4.50, dinner $6.50.) **The Travel Shop,** 10926 88 Ave. (travel 439-3096, retail 439-3089) also serves as the regional office for **Alberta Hostels.** A travel agency with camping and hiking gear, the Travel Shop serves youth and students and will make international and local hostel reservations (open Mon.-Wed. and Fri.-Sat. 9am-6pm, Thurs. 9am-8pm).

Edmonton is awash in coffee shops. Escape the flood at **Carson's Cafe,** 10331 Whyte (82) Ave. (432-7560), a classy but cozy restaurant in the middle of the Old Strathcona district. The selection is small, but daily specials and creative seasonings add diversity to the menu. Feast on anything from grilled chicken teriyaki sandwiches ($7) to burgers ($5-6.25) from 11am to 11pm daily. **Chianti's,** 10501 Whyte (82) Ave. (439-9829), oozes Italian flavor. Daily specialty wines and an expanse of pasta and seafood dishes (pastas $7-8, $6 Mon.-Tues.; veal $10-11) are lip-smackin' good (open Mon.-Thurs. 11am-11pm, Fri.-Sat. 11am-midnight, Sun. 4-11pm).

Take a breather at the refreshing **Fort Edmonton Park** (496-8787) on Whitemud Dr. at Fox Dr. Buses #32 and 39 stop near the park. At the far end of the park sits the fort, a 19th-century "office building" for Alberta's first entrepreneurs, ruthless whiskey traders. Park volunteers dressed as schoolmarms and general-store owners greet visitors. ($6.50, seniors and ages 13-17 $5; discounts for HI members. Park open Victoria Day to late June Mon.-Fri. 10am-4pm, Sat.-Sun. 10am-6pm; late June to Labor Day daily 10am-6pm.) After visiting the fort, stop at the **John Janzen Nature Centre** next door to pet the salamanders and take hikes through birch groves. (Free. Open Mon.-Fri. 9am-6pm, Sat.-Sun. 11am-6pm; in winter Mon.-Fri. 9am-4pm, Sat.-Sun. 1-4pm.) From the fauna of the Nature Centre, turn to the flora of the **Muttart Conservatory,** 9626 96A St. (496-8755). Bus #51 whisks you to Muttart. Plant species from around the world live here in the climate-controlled comfort of four ultramodern glass and steel pyramids. ($4.25, seniors and youth $3.25, kids $2. Open Sun.-Wed. 11am-9pm, Thurs.-Sat. 11am-6pm.)

Capitalism's Mothership

The **West Edmonton Mall** (444-5200) envelops the general area of 170 St. and 87 Ave. When the Milky Way's largest assembly of retail stores first landed, it seized 30% of Edmonton's retail business, choking the life out of the downtown shopping district. The Über-mall boasts a water park, an amusement park, and dozens of pathetically caged exotic animals, as well as over 800 stores, 110 eating establishments, twice as many submarines as the Canadian Navy, a full-scale replica of Columbus's *Santa Maria,* a 14-story roller coaster, and an indoor bungee jumping facility (don't forget the golf course and ice skating rink). Take bus #10 to The Mall (open Mon.-Fri. 10am-9pm, Sat. 10am-6pm, Sun. noon-5pm). Touring Western Alberta without passing through its hallowed halls is almost as insulting as claiming that Canadians drink watery beer. One final note: remember where you park. The world's largest mall has the world's largest parking lot.

CANADA

■ Calgary

The name Calgary is derived from Gaelic for "clear running water," but it was oil that built this city at Alberta's gateway to the Rockies. Founded in the 1870s by Mounties trying to stop the illegal whiskey trade, Calgary got its big break with the discovery of black gold, Texas tea. With the 1988 Winter Olympics, the Calgarian economy hit the big time again. But no matter how urbane Alberta's largest city may become, it retains a close tie to its roots and its original claim to fame—the "Greatest Outdoor Show on Earth," the **Calgary Stampede.**

PRACTICAL INFORMATION AND ORIENTATION

Visitors Information: For drop-in info, go to the **Visitor Service Center** near the Calgary Tower at 131 9th Ave. SW (263-8510; open daily 8:30-5pm). For the cost of a local call, the **Talking Yellow Pages** provides a wide range of info. Dial 521-5222 and the appropriate 4-digit code, listed in the front of the Yellow Pages (general visitors info is code 8950).

Buses: Greyhound, 877 Greyhound Way SW (265-9111 or 800-661-TRIP/8747). Frequent service to Edmonton (10 per day, $33), Banff (4 per day, $18), and Drumheller (3 per day, $19). Seniors 10% off. Free shuttle bus from C-Train at 7th Ave. and 10th St. to bus depot (almost every hr. on the ½hr., 6:30am-7:30pm).

Public Transportation: Calgary Transit. Downtown Information and Sales Centre, 240 7th Ave. SW. Bus schedules, passes, and maps. Open Mon.-Fri. 8:30am-5pm. Fare $1.50, ages 6-14 90¢, under 6 free. Exact change required. Day pass $4.50, children $2.50. Book of 10 tickets $12.50, children $8.50. **Information line** (262-1000) open Mon.-Fri. 6am-11pm, Sat.-Sun. 8:30am-9:30pm.

Taxi: Checker Cab, 299-9999. **Yellow Cab,** 974-1111. Both 24hr.

Car Rental: Rent-A-Wreck, 4201 MacLeod Trail SE (228-1660). Cars start at $40 per day, 200km free, 12¢ each additional km. Must be 21 with a credit card. Open Mon.-Fri. 8am-7:30pm, Sat.-Sun. 8am-7pm.

Bike Rental: Budget Car Rental, 140 6th Ave. SE (226-1550). $12 per day. Must be 18 with credit card. **Sports Rent,** 9250 Macleod Trail (292-0066). $20 per day.

Hospital: Calgary General, 841 Centre Ave. E (268-9111).

Emergency: 911.

Post Office: 207 9th Ave. SW (974-2078). Open Mon.-Fri. 8am-5:45pm. **Postal Code:** T2P 268.

Area Code: 403.

Calgary is divided into quadrants: **Centre Street** is the east-west divide; the **Bow River** divides the north and south sections. The rest is simple: avenues run east-west, streets run north-south. Pay careful attention to the quadrant distinctions (NE, NW, SE, SW) at the end of each address.

ACCOMMODATIONS AND FOOD

Lodging costs skyrocket when packs of tourists Stampede into the city's hotels. You cannot reserve too early for stays in July. Contact the **B&B Association of Calgary** (531-0065) for info on B&Bs. Prices for singles start around $35, doubles around $50. **Calgary International Hostel (HI-C),** 520 7th Ave. SE (269-8239), is conveniently located several blocks east of downtown with access to the 3rd St. SE C-Train station and public buses. The pleasant, modern facility resembles a ski lodge. Make reservations for the Stampede *far* in advance. (Wheelchair accessible. Open 24hr. $14, nonmembers $19.) Bookings for the **University of Calgary,** in the NW quadrant, are coordinated through **Kananaskis Hall,** 3330 24th Ave. (220-3203), a 12-min. walk from the University C-Train stop (open 24hr.). The university is out of the way, but accessible via bus #9 or the C-Train. U of C offers clean rooms at competitive prices. Rooms are available May to August only. 22 rooms are set aside for students with ID (singles $30, doubles $38). More lavish suites with private bathrooms are approximately $35. Popular with conventioneers, U of C is often booked solid. **Regis Plaza**

Hotel, 124 7th Ave. SE (262-4641), boasts a friendly management and clean, comfortable rooms. If you're feeling ascetic, try an inside room with no TV, bath, or windows for $31.35. Doubles start at $55.

Downtown's food offerings are concentrated in the **Stephen Avenue Mall,** 8th Ave. S between 1st St. SE and 3rd St. SW. Good, reasonably priced food is also readily available in the **"+15" Skyway System.** Designed to provide indoor passageways during bitter winter days, this futuristic mall-in-the-sky connects the second floors of dozens of buildings throughout downtown Calgary; look for the blue and white "+15" signs on street level. At **Satay House,** 206 Centre St. S (290-1927), large portions of authentic Vietnamese cuisine are one of the best deals in Chinatown. The house special offers a taste of everything for $5.50 (open Mon.-Fri. 11am-10pm, Sat.-Sun. 10am-11pm). **4th Street Rose,** 2116 4th St. SW (228-5377), is all about California. The house specialty is a "pro-size" Caesar salad ($4.50), but the pizzas and pastas are also great (open Mon.-Thurs. 11am-1am, Fri.-Sat. 11am-2am, Sun. 10am-midnight). **Island Experience,** 314A 10th St. NW (270-4550), makes Caribbean treats borrowed from India (open Mon.-Wed. 11:30am-10pm, Sun. noon-8pm).

SIGHTS, ENTERTAINMENT, AND THE STAMPEDE

Visit the remnants of Calgary's 15 min. of Olympic fame at the **Olympic Oval** (220-7954), an enormous indoor speed-skating track on the University of Calgary campus (open daily 7am-11pm; in winter 9am-9:30pm). The **Glenbow Museum,** 130 9th Ave. SE (268-4100), has it all—from rocks and minerals, to exhibits of native Canadian lifestyles, to the art of Asia, to the history of the Canadian West. ($5; seniors, students and kids $3.50, under 7 free. Open daily 9am-5pm.) **Prince's Island Park** is loaded with biking and running trails and can be reached by footbridges from either side of the Bow River. Many evenings in summer at 7pm, Mount Royal College puts on free Shakespeare in the park (call 240-6359 for info).

Calgary's other island park, **St. George's Island,** is accessible by the river walkway to the east and is home to the marvelous **Calgary Zoo** (232-9300). The Canadian Wilds exhibit re-creates the sights, sounds, and, yes, smells of Canada's wilderness. The squeamish may be content to stroll through the **botanical gardens** or visit the **children's zoo.** ($7.50, seniors $5.50, kids $3.75; seniors $2 on Tues. Gates open daily 9am-6:30pm; in winter daily 9am-4pm. Grounds open until 8:30pm, in winter until 5:30pm.) The **Devonian Gardens,** 317 7th Ave. SW (263-3830), on the top floor of the Toronto Dominion Sq. retail center, are 2½ acres of sculptures, fountains, waterfalls, bridges, and over 20,000 plants representing 138 local and tropical species (free; open daily 9am-9pm).

For an easy-to-find good time, rock down to **"Electric Avenue,"** the stretch of 11th Ave. SW between 5th and 6th St., and pound back bottles of local brew with oodles of young Calgarians. **The King Edward Hotel,** 438 9th Ave. SE (262-1680) serves up live music and dancing nightly. The Eddy brings in bluesmen including Buddy Guy, Clarence "Gatemouth" Brown and Matt "Guitar" Murphy. Cover depends on acts, but usually ranges $3-5. (Great blues Mon.-Sat. 11am-2am. Jazz on Sat. afternoons and Sun. 7pm-1am; jam sessions Sat. 2:30-7pm and Sun. 7pm-1am.)

Drawing millions every summer from across Canada and the world, the Stampede is worth a special visit. Make the short trip out to **Stampede Park,** just southeast of downtown, for steer wrestling, saddle bronc, bareback, and bull riding, pig racing, **wild cow milking,** and the famous chuckwagon races, involving four horses per wagon and nerves of steel. For info and ticket mail-order forms, write **Calgary Exhibition and Stampede,** Box 1860, Station M, Calgary T2P 2L8, or call 800-661-1260 (261-0101 in Calgary). Tickets are $16-42. Same-day rush tickets are $8 (youth $7, seniors and kids $4). Plan now. The Stampede takes place July 4-13 in 1997.

CANADA

■ Banff National Park

Banff is Canada's best-loved and best-known natural preserve. It offers 6600 sq. km (2543 sq. mi.) of peaks, canyons, white foaming rapids, brilliant turquoise lakes, dense forests, and open meadows. One of Canada's most popular vacation destinations, the town of Banff has exploded in a riot of Hard Rock Café Banff t-shirts. Fortunately, Banff's priceless beauty really does grow on trees, offering an expansive diversity of environments and experiences.

PRACTICAL INFORMATION AND ORIENTATION

Visitors Information: Banff Information Centre, 224 Banff Ave. Includes **Banff/ Lake Louise Tourism Bureau** (762-8421) and **Canadian Parks Service** (762-1550). The most efficient, informative, and well-organized info center in Western Canada. Open in summer daily 8am-8pm; Oct.-May 9am-5pm.

Buses: Greyhound, 100 Gopher St. (800-661-8747). From the Brewster terminal. 4 per day to: Lake Louise ($10), Calgary ($18), and Vancouver ($97).

Public Transportation: Banff Explorer (760-8294), operated by the town, runs 2 routes stretching from the Banff Springs Hotel ($1.50) to the hostel and Tunnel Mountain Campground ($1, children 50¢). Exact change required. Operates mid-June to mid-Sept. daily 9am-9pm.

Taxis: Legion Taxi, 762-3353. 24hr. **Lake Louise Taxi,** 522-2020.

Emergency: Banff Warden Office, 762-4506. Open 24hr. **Police:** (762-2226; non-emergency 762-2228), on Railway St. by the train depot.

Post Office: 204 Buffalo St. (762-2586). Open Mon.-Fri. 9am-5:30pm. **Postal Code:** T0L 0C0.

Area Code: 403.

Banff National Park hugs the Alberta-British Columbia border, 120km west of Calgary. The **Trans-Canada Hwy.** (Hwy. 1) runs east-west through the park connecting it to Yoho National Park to the west; **Icefields Parkway** (Hwy. 93) connects Banff with Jasper National Park to the north and Kootenay National Park to the southwest. Greyhound links the park to major points in Alberta and British Columbia. Civilization in the park centers around the towns of Banff and **Lake Louise,** 55km northwest of Banff on Hwy. 1. The **Bow Valley Pkwy.** (Hwy. 1A) parallels Hwy. 1 from Lake Louise to 8km west of Banff.

ACCOMMODATIONS, CAMPING, AND FOOD

Finding a cheap place to stay in Banff is easy if you reserve ahead. Check the list in the back of the *Banff and Lake Louise Official Visitor's Guide,* available free at the Banff Townsite Information Centre. Mammoth modern hostels at Banff and Lake Louise anchor a chain of hostels stretching from Calgary to Jasper. For reservations at any rustic hostel, call Banff International at 762-4122.

Banff International Hostel (BIH) (HI-C), Box 1358, Banff T0L 0C0 (762-4122), 3km from Banff Townsite on Tunnel Mountain Rd., among a nest of condominiums and lodges. Clean rooms with 2-4 bunk beds. Take the Banff Explorer from downtown, or join the pack of hostelers hoofing it. Café, laundry facilities, hot showers. Wheelchair accessible. Accommodates 154. Linen free. Open all day. No curfew. $17, nonmembers $22.

Castle Mountain Hostel (HI-C) (762-4122), on Hwy. 1A, 1½km east of the junction of Hwy. 1 and 93 between Banff and Lake Louise. Recently renovated. 36 beds. The only rustic with running water and electricity. $11, nonmembers $16.

Lake Louise International Hostel (HI-C), Village Rd. (522-2200), ½km from Samson Mall in Lake Louise Townsite. 100 beds. Cafeteria, full service kitchen. Wheelchair accessible. $18.50-22.50, nonmembers $25-29.

Mosquito Creek Hostel (HI-C), 103km south of the Icefield Centre and 26km north of Lake Louise. Propane gas and heat. Close to Wapta Icefield. Sleeps 38. Fireplace, full-service kitchen. Call BIH for reservations. $11, nonmembers $16.

Rampart Creek Hostel (HI-C), 34km south of the Icefield Centre. Rampart's proximity to several famous ice climbs (including Weeping Wall, 17km north on Icefields Parkway) makes it a favorite of winter mountaineers. Sleeps 30 in rustic cabins. Sauna, full service kitchen, wood-heated bathtub. $10, nonmembers $15.

Hilda Creek Hostel (HI-C), 8½km south of the Icefield Centre on the Icefields Pkwy. Excellently situated at the base of Mt. Athabasca. Some of the Icefield's best hiking and skiing lie just behind the hostel on Parker Ridge. Wood-burning sauna, full service kitchen. Propane heat and light. $10, nonmembers $15.

None of the park's popular camping sites accepts reservations, so arrive early. Many campgrounds reserve sites for bicyclists and hikers; inquire at the office. Rates range from $8 to $22, depending on the season and type of site. Park facilities include (from south to north): **Tunnel Mountain Village** (over 1100 sites), **Two Jack Main** (458 sites), **Johnston Canyon** (132 sites), **Castle Mountain** (43 sites), **Protection Mountain** (89 sites), **Lake Louise** (405 sites), **Mosquito Creek** (32 sites), and **Waterfowl** (116 sites). There is a chain of campgrounds connecting Banff to Jasper with large, fully hooked-up campgrounds as anchors.

Restaurants in Banff generally serve expensive, mediocre food. Luckily, the Banff **(Café Aspenglow)** and Lake Louise **(Peyto's Café)** International Hostels and the Banff YWCA serve affordable meals for $3-7. Shop at **Safeway** (762-5378), at Marten and Elk St., just off Banff Ave. (open daily 8am-10pm; in winter 9am-9pm). Some of the bars offer reasonably priced daily specials.

OUTDOORS

Hike to the **backcountry** for privacy, intense beauty, over **1600km** of trails, and trout that bite anything. Pick up the complete *Backcountry Visitors' Guide* at info centers (see Practical Information). You need a **permit** to stay overnight; get one at the info centers for $6 per person per day, up to $30 per person, or $42 per year.

Two easy trails are within walking distance of Banff. **Fenland** winds 2km through an area frequented by beaver, muskrat, and waterfowl. Follow Mt. Norquay Rd. out of Banff and look for signs across the railroad tracks on the left side of the road (the trail is closed in late spring and early summer due to elk calving). The summit of **Tunnel Mountain** provides a spectacular view of the Bow Valley and Mt. Rundle. Follow Wolf St. east from Banff Ave. and turn right on St. Julien Rd. to reach the head of the steep 2.3km trail.

About 25km out of Banff toward Lake Louise along the Bow Valley Parkway, **Johnston Canyon** is a popular half-day hike. The 1.1km hike to the canyon's lower falls and the 2.7km trip to the upper falls consist mostly of a catwalk along the edge of the canyon. Don't stop at the falls, though: keep on the more rugged trail for another 3.1km until you get to seven cold water springs known as the **Inkpots.**

You and your car will enjoy the **Tunnel Mountain Drive,** which begins at the intersection of Banff Ave. and Buffalo St. and proceeds 9km past Bow Falls and up the side of Tunnel Mountain. Turn right onto Tunnel Mountain Rd. to see the **hoodoos,** long,

---

Head-Smashed-In Buffalo Jump

Coveted as a source of fresh meat, sustenance, tools, and shelter, the buffalo was the victim of one of history's most innovative forms of mass slaughter: **the buffalo jump.** While warriors maneuvered the herd into position, a few extremely brave young men, disguised in coyote skins among the buffalo, would spook hundreds of nearly-blind bison into a fatal stampede over a 10m cliff. When successful, the buffalo jump created an instant all-you-can-eat-or-use buffet at the bottom of the cliff. Head-Smashed-In Buffalo Jump was named about 150 years ago in memory of a young thrill-seeking warrior who was crushed against the cliff by a pile of buffalo as he watched the event from below. The town sits west of Fort Macleod on Rte. 785, about 30km west of Hwy. 2.

CANADA

finger-like projections of limestone once part of the cliff wall and thought by indigenous Canadians to encase sentinel spirits.

After the steep 5.3km (and 2-3hr.) hike up **Sulfur Mountain,** you can enjoy a free ride down. The **Sulfur Mountain Gondola** charges nothing for the trip downhill. The gondola runs trips to the top as well—for a price ($10, ages 5-11 $4, under 5 free; open daily 8am-9pm). The **Summit Restaurant** (762-2523), perched atop Sulfur Mountain, serves an "Early Morning Lift" breakfast special. The gondola and the trail start close to the Upper Hot Springs pool and travel 700m up to the summit.

Fishing is legal virtually anywhere you can find water, but you can't use bait (only lures) and you must hold a National Parks fishing permit, available at the info center ($6 for 7 days, $13 for an annual permit good in all Canadian National Parks). The 7km trail to **Borgeau Lake** offers both hiking and fishing with some privacy—and a particularly feisty breed of brook trout. Closer to the road, try **Herbert Lake,** off the Icefields Pkwy. between Lake Louise and the Columbia Icefield, or **Lake Minnewanka,** on Lake Minnewanka Rd. northeast of Banff Townsite, rumored to be the home of a half-human, half-fish Indian spirit. The road also passes **Johnson Lake,** where the sun warms the shallow water to a swimmable temperature.

Kootenay River Runners (604-347-9210) offers half- and full-day rafting trips for $49 and $75 respectively, as well as a more boisterous full-day trip on the **Kicking Horse River** for $75. For tickets call 762-5385. The day-long trip offered by **Alpine Rafting Company** (800-663-7080; $75) includes a steak barbecue lunch. A full day of rafting on the Kicking Horse River (transportation included) for $45 is offered by the **Banff International Hostel** (see Accommodations, above).

Those 1600km of summer hiking trails also provide exceptional cross-country skiing while **Sunshine Mountain, Mount Norquay,** and **Lake Louise** divide the downhill crowd. **Performance Ski and Sports,** 208 Bear St. (762-8222) rents downhill skis ($17 for 1 day, $45 for 3 days), cross-country skis ($11, $29), snowboards ($28, $74), telemarking skis and boots ($18, $48), and snowshoes ($8, $21).

■ Jasper National Park

Before the Icefields Pkwy. was built, few travelers dared venture north of Banff into the untamed wilderness of Jasper. Those bushwhackers who returned came back with stunning reports, and the completion of the Parkway in 1940 paved the way for the masses to appreciate Jasper's astounding beauty. The only conspicuous traces of Jasper's tourist trade are the blue and white signs advertising "approved accommodations" and the imitation totem pole at the VIA Rail station. It keeps its back turned to the town in a gesture of good taste.

Practical Information The staff at the **Park Information Centre,** 500 Connaught Dr. (852-6176) will lavish you with trail maps and info (open daily 8:30am-7pm; early Sept. to late Oct. and late Dec. to mid-June 9am-5pm). **VIA Rail** (800-561-8630), on Connaught Dr., runs 3 trains per week to Vancouver ($147), Edmonton ($87), and Winnipeg ($232). 10% discount for seniors and students, 50% for kids. Coin-operated lockers cost $1 for 24hr. **Greyhound** (852-3926), in the VIA station, runs buses to Edmonton (4 per day, $45), Kamloops ($47), and Vancouver ($86). **Brewster Transportation Tours** (852-3332), in the VIA station, journeys daily to Banff ($42) and Calgary ($56). **Heritage Taxi,** 611 Patricia (852-5558), offers a flat rate of $10 between town and Whistler's Hostel, and $16 to the Maligne Canyon Hostel. If need be, call the **local police** or the **RCMP** at 852-4848, or an **ambulance** at 852-3100. The **post office** is at 502 Patricia St. (852-3041), across from the townsite green. (Open Mon.-Fri. 9am-5pm. **Postal Code: T0E 1E0.**) The **area code** is 403.

All of the above addresses are found in **Jasper Townsite,** which is near the center of the park, 362km west of Edmonton and 287km northwest of Banff. **Hwy. 16** transports travelers through the northern reaches of the park, while the **Icefields Parkway** (Hwy. 93) connects to Banff National Park in the south.

Accommodations and Camping   Hotels in Jasper Townsite are expensive. You may be able to stay cheaply at a **B&B** (singles $45-55, doubles $50-70). Most are located in town near the bus and train stations. HI-C runs a shuttle service connecting all the Rocky Mountain hostels and Calgary with rates from $9 to $59, depending on how far you're going. For reservations at any rustic hostel and info on winter availability, call **Jasper International Hostel** at 852-3215.

Jasper International Hostel (HI-C) (852-3215), on Sky Tram Rd., 5km south of the townsite off Hwy. 93. The park's most modern (and crowded) hostel. Bring your own food. Accommodates 69. Curfew midnight. $15, nonmembers $20.

Maligne Canyon Hostel (HI-C), 11km east of the townsite on Maligne Canyon Rd. Small, recently renovated cabins on the bank of the Maligne River. Gas heat without electricity or running water. Accommodates 24. $9, nonmembers $14.

Mt. Edith Cavell Hostel (HI-C), on Edith Cavell Rd., off Hwy. 93A. Propane light, pump water, and immediate access to Mt. Edith Cavell. The road is closed in winter, but the hostel welcomes anyone willing to ski 11km from Hwy. 93A. Accommodates 32. $9, nonmembers $14.

Athabasca Falls Hostel (HI-C) (852-5959), on Hwy. 93, 30km south of Jasper Townsite, 500m from Athabasca Falls. Electricity but no running water. Huge dining/recreation room with woodstove. Accommodates 40. $9, nonmembers $14.

Beauty Creek Hostel (HI-C), on Hwy. 93, 87km south of Jasper Townsite. Near the stunning Sunwapta River and close to the Columbia Icefields with several hiking trails of its own. Sleeps 24. $9, nonmembers $14.

Most campsites are primitive. They are also first come, first served, so get there early. For detailed info, call 852-6176. From north to south, sites include: **Whistlers** (782 sites), **Snaring River** (56 sites), **Pocahontas** (140 sites), **Wapiti** (366 sites), **Wabasso** (238 sites), and **Wilcox Creek** (46 sites). Sites run $10-19.

Food   **Super A Foods,** 601 Patricia St. (852-3200), satisfies all basic grocery needs (open Mon.-Sat. 8am-11pm, Sun. 9am-10pm). Groups and 10-day backpackers will love the selection of bulk foods at **Nutter's,** 622 Patricia St. (852-5844), not to mention the deli meats, canned goods, and freshly ground coffee (open daily 9am-11pm). **Mountain Foods and Café,** 606 Connaught Dr. (852-4050), makes an excellent stop for breakfast or lunch featuring an extensive selection of sandwiches and sandwich-like concoctions (bagelwich, anyone?) with a constantly shifting mix of ingredients (open daily 7am-11pm). **Scoops and Loops,** 504 Patricia St. (852-4333), dishes out sandwiches, pastries, sushi, udon noodles, and ice cream (open Mon.-Sat. 10am-11pm, Sun. 11am-10pm).

Outdoors   **Mt. Edith Cavell** will shake you to the bone with the thunderous roar of avalanches off the Angel Glacier. Take the 1.6km loop **Path of the Glacier** to the top, or hike through **Cavell Meadows.** Edith rears her enormous head 30km south of the townsite on Mt. Edith Cavell Rd. Because Mt. Edith Cavell has become one of Jasper's most popular attractions, the road to the top is now regulated. Check at the info center for times when you can travel up and down.

Intrepid hikers should attempt the three-faced **Mystery Lake Trail,** leading east, 11km uphill from the pools. **Maligne Lake,** the second largest glacier-fed lake in the Canadian Rockies, is located 48km southeast of the townsite at the end of Maligne Lake Rd. You can enjoy every water sport imaginable in Maligne's vivid turquoise waters. **Whitewater Rafting (Jasper) Ltd.** (852-7238) offers several rafting trips from $40; a two-hr. trip down the Maligne River costs $48. **Boat rental** is available at **Pyramid Lake** (852-4900; canoes $10 for 1hr., $7 each additional hr., $25 per day; $20 and a valid ID required for deposit) and **Maligne Lake,** 626 Connaught Dr. (852-3370; canoes $10 per hr., $45 per day; ID required for deposit).

The **Jasper Tramway** (852-3093) sits off Hwy. 93, 2km from Jasper. The longest and highest tramway in Canada offers a panoramic view of the park as it rises 2km up the side of **Whistlers Mountain.** The gondola draws crowds and packs the parking lot ($15, ages 5-14 $8.50, under 5 free; open April-Oct. 8:30am-10pm). Or make the steep 7km hike to the top, feel studly, then take the tram ride down ($7.50) to spare your quadriceps. No matter how you go, bring sunglasses and a warm jacket.

Rent **fishing** equipment and get tips on good spots at **Currie's,** in The Sports Shop, 414 Connaught Dr. (852-3654; rod, reel, and line $10; one-day boat rental $25, $18 if rented after 2pm, $12 after 6 pm). Cruise down the ski slopes of **Marmot Basin** (852-3816), near Jasper Townsite. A full-day lift ticket costs $35 (youth $29, juniors $14, seniors $24). Ski rental is available at **Totem's Ski Shop,** 408 Connaught Dr. (852-3078). A full rental package (skis, boots, and poles) runs $9 per day. The **Jasper Climbing School,** 806 Connaught Dr. (852-3964), offers an introductory three-hr. rappelling class ($25) for those who want a closer look at the imposing cliffs surrounding Jasper. **Caving** is a little-talked-about and extremely dangerous pursuit, and is not permitted in the national parks without a permit; one should try it only with an experienced guide. Ben Gadd (852-4012), author of *Handbook of the Canadian Rockies,* leads tours to the **Cadomin Caves** (flat rate of $250 for 10-20 people). You don't need a permit since the caves are outside the National Park.

British Columbia

British Columbia attracts so many visitors that tourism has become the province's second-largest industry, after logging. Despite excellent year-round skiing, most tourists arrive in the summer and flock to the beautiful cities of Vancouver and Victoria and to the pristine lakes and beaches of the warm Okanagan Valley. Heading north, thick forests, low mountains, and occasional patches of high desert are interrupted only by supply and transit centers like Prince George and Prince Rupert.

British Columbia's parks are popular with hikers, mountaineers, cyclists, rafters, and skiers. On Vancouver Island, the coastal rainforests of Strathcona and Pacific Rim Parks are beautiful and largely untrammeled. In the southeastern part of the province, Glacier, Yoho, and Kootenay Parks allow visitors to escape into some of Canada's most amazing outdoor country.

PRACTICAL INFORMATION

Capital: Victoria.
Tourism British Columbia, 1117 Wharf St., Victoria, BC V8W 2Z2 (604-387-1642 or 800-663-6000). **Parks Canada,** 220 4th Ave. SE #552, Calgary, AB T2G 4X3 (403-924-2200). **BC Parks,** 1610 Mt. Seymour Rd., North Vancouver, BC V7G 1L3 (604-666-0176).
Time Zone: Pacific and Mountain. **Postal Abbreviation:** BC.
Provincial Sales Tax: 7%.
Drinking Age: 19.
Traffic Laws: Mandatory seatbelt law.
Area Code: 604.

■ Vancouver

Western Canada's largest city has joined the post-industrial age. Electronics and international finance are supplanting timber and mining as the city's economic base. Vancouver is Canada's gateway to the Pacific, hosting scores of immigrants from China, Hong Kong, and the Far East. With nature walks among 1000-year-old virgin timber, wind-surfing, and the most technologically advanced movie theater in the world all downtown, Vancouver offers an astounding range of things to do.

PRACTICAL INFORMATION AND ORIENTATION

Visitors Information: Travel Infocentre, 200 Burrard St. (683-2000). Full info on accommodations, tours, and activities spanning much of BC. Courtesy phones for reservations. Open daily 8am-6pm. **Parks and Recreation Board,** 2099 Beach Ave. (257-8400). Open Mon.-Fri. 8:30am-5pm.

VIA Rail, 1150 Station St. (800-561-8630, in U.S. 800-561-3949). Sky Train stop. 3 trains per week to: Jasper ($147) and Edmonton ($204). Open Mon. and Thurs. 8am-8pm, Tues.-Wed., Fri., and Sun. 8am-3:30pm, Sat. 12:30-8pm.

BC Rail, 1311 W. 1st St. (651-3500), just over the Lions Gate Bridge at the foot of Pemberton St. in North Vancouver. Take the BC Rail Special Bus on Georgia St. or the SeaBus to North Vancouver, then bus #239 west. Daily trains to: Garibaldi ($26), Whistler ($30), Williams Lake ($115), Prince George ($171), and points north. Open daily 6am-8:30pm, phones on 8am-8pm.

Greyhound, 1150 Station St. (662-3222), in the VIA Rail Station. Bus service to the south and across Canada. To: Calgary (6 per day, $98), Banff (5 per day, $96), Jasper (3 per day, $86), and Seattle (5 per day, $30). Open daily 5:30am-12:30am.

Pacific Coach Lines, 1150 Station St. (662-7575). Buses serve southern BC, including Vancouver Island, in conjunction with Greyhound. Service to Victoria ($22.50, roundtrip $42) includes ferry and service into downtown Victoria.

Public Transportation: BC Transit Information Centre (521-0400). Fare $1.50, rates rise during rush hr.; students, seniors, and kids 75¢. Day passes $4.50/$2.25; available at 7-11 and Safeway stores, Skytrain stations, and the Travel Infocentre.

BC Ferries (669-1211 for general info, 685-1021 for recorded info, 943-9331 for Tsawwassen ferry terminal). To Victoria, the Gulf Islands, Sunshine Coast, Mainland, and Vancouver Island ($6.50, ages 5-11 $3.25, car and driver $31.50-33.50, motorcycle and driver $20, bike and rider $9). Ferries to Nanaimo on Vancouver Island leave from Horseshoe Bay, approximately 10km northwest of Vancouver.

Taxis: Yellow Cab (681-3311). **Vancouver Taxi** (255-5111). Both 24hr.

Car Rental: ABC Rental, 255 W. Broadway (873-6622). $35 per day, unlimited mileage. $209 per week; $13 per day for collision coverage. Must be 21 with credit card. Open Mon.-Fri. 7:30am-6:30pm, Sat.-Sun. 7:30am-5pm.

Bicycle Rental: Bayshore Bicycles, 745 Denman St. (680-2453). Convenient to Stanley Park. Practically new bikes $5.60 per hr., $20 for 8hr., $25 overnight. Open May-Sept. daily 9am-9pm. Winter hours vary with daylight hours.

Help Lines: Vancouver Crisis Center, 872-3311. **Rape Crisis Center,** 255-6344. Both 24hr. **Gay and Lesbian Switchboard,** 1170 Bute St. (684-6869). Open daily 7-10pm. **Poison Control,** 682-5050.

Emergency: 911. **Police:** 312 Main St. (665-3535), at Powell.

Post Office: Main branch, 349 W. Georgia St. (662-5725). Open Mon.-Fri. 8am-5:30pm. **Postal Code:** V6B 3P7.

Area Code: 604.

Vancouver looks like a mitten with the fingers pointing west (brace for an extended metaphor) and the thumb to the north. South of the hand flows the Fraser River and beyond the fingertips lies the Georgia Strait. Downtown is on the thumb. At the thumb's tip lie the residential **West End** and **Stanley Park.** Burrard Inlet separates downtown from North Vancouver; the bridges over False Creek (the space between the thumb and the rest of the hand) link downtown with **Kitsilano** ("Kits"), **Fairview, Mount Pleasant,** and the rest of the city. East of downtown, where the thumb is attached, lie **Gastown** and **Chinatown.** The **airport** lies south, on the pinkie; the University of British Columbia lies on top of the fingers at **Point Grey.** Kitsilano and Point Grey are separated by the north-south **Alma Ave.** The major highway approaches, Hwy. 99 and the Trans-Canada Hwy., enter the city from the south and east.

ACCOMMODATIONS AND CAMPING

Greater Vancouver is a warren of bed and breakfast accommodations. The visitors bureau has an extensive list of B&Bs. Several private agencies also match travelers

British Columbia and the Yukon Territory

NATIONAL PARKS
1 Banff
2 Glacier
3 Jasper
4 Kluane
5 Kootenay
6 Mt. Revelstoke
7 Pacific Rim
8 Yoho

PROVINCIAL PARKS
9 Atlin
10 Garibaldi
11 Kwadacha Wilderness
12 Mt. Edziza
13 Mt. Robson
14 Muncho Lake
15 Spatsizi Plateau Wilderness
16 Stone Mountain
17 Strathcona
18 Tweedsmuir
19 Wells Gray
20 Willmore Wilderness

Beaufort Sea

ALASKA

Inuvik

Fort Mcpherson

Arctic Red River

Dawson City

YUKON TERRITORY

Carmacks

Ross River

Haines Junction

Whitehorse

Carcross

Johnson's Crossing

Skagway

Haines

Watson Lake

NORTHWEST TERRITORIES

Juneau

Alaska Hwy.

Fort Nelson

Casslar Highway

Meziadin Jct.

BRITISH COLUMBIA

Dawson Creek

ALBERTA

Masset

Port Clements

Tlell

Queen Charlotte

Sandspit

QUEEN CHARLOTTE ISLANDS

Prince Rupert

Prince George

Edmonton

Barkerville

Quesnel

Williams Lake

Cariboo Highway

Cache Creek

Revelstoke

Salmon Arm

Penticton

Port Hardy

Garabaldi

Lytton

Yale

Hope

PACIFIC OCEAN

Vancouver Island

Nanaimo

Vancouver

Victoria

WASHINGTON

CANADA

0   150 miles
0   150 kilometers

N

with B&Bs, usually for a fee; get in touch with **Town and Country Bed and Breakfast** (731-5942) or **Best Canadian** (738-7207).

Vancouver Hostel Downtown (HI-C), 1114 Burnaby St. (684-4565). The hub of BC hosteling, perched between downtown and the West End. 225 beds. 4 bunks to a room and a vast array of facilities and services. Free shuttle to Vancouver Hostel Jericho Beach. Open 24hr. $17.50, nonmembers $21. Private doubles $40. Reservations are a must in summer.

Kingston Hotel, 757 Richard St. (684-9024; fax 684-9917), between Robson and Georgia. Classy but not pricey. Recently renovated. Breakfast included. Coin laundry and sauna. 10% student and senior discounts. Singles $40-60. Doubles $45-75.

Vancouver International Hostel Jericho Beach (HI-C), 1515 Discovery St. (224-3208), in Jericho Beach Park. Turn north off 4th Ave., following signs for Marine Dr., or take bus #4 from Granville St. Superlative view of the city. 285 beds in dorm rooms and 9 family rooms. $15, nonmembers $19. Reservations crucial.

Paul's Guest House, 345 W. 14th Ave. (872-4753), south of downtown. Take bus #15. Vancouver's best B&B deal. Clean, cheap, and cheerful. If Paul can't put you up in one of his warm and welcoming rooms, he'll try to arrange your stay at another B&B. Tidy, cozy rooms. Shared baths. Full breakfast included. Prices are negotiable; tell them you want a "reasonable" rate.

Richmond RV Park, 6200 River Rd. (270-7878), near Holly Bridge in Richmond. Take Hwy. 99 to Westminster Hwy., then follow the signs. Clearly the best deal within 13km of downtown. Offers little privacy, but there are washrooms and the showers are great. Sites $15.50, with hookup $20.50. Open April-Oct.

Hazelmere RV Park and Campground, 18843 8th Ave. (538-1167), in Surrey. Off Hwy. 99A, head east on 8th Ave. Quiet sites on the Campbell River, 10min. from beach. Showers 25¢ for 4½min. Washrooms. Sites for 1-2 people $18, with full hookup $24, $2 each additional person, $1 each additional child aged 7-12.

FOOD

Vancouver's international restaurants serve some of the best food in town. Its **China-town** is the second largest in North America (only San Francisco's is larger), and the Indian neighborhoods along Main, Fraser, and 49th St. serve exquisite fare. The **Granville Island Market,** southwest of downtown under the Granville Bridge, off W. 4th Ave. across False Creek, intersperses trendy shops, art galleries, and restaurants with countless produce stands. Take bus #50 from Granville St. downtown (complex open daily 9am-6pm; Labor Day-Victoria Day Tues.-Sun. 9am-6pm).

Cactus Club Café, 1136 Robson St. (687-3278); also at 4397 W. 10th (222-1342). Trendy café and night spot. Irreverent menu cartoons, alcohol-themed foods, and a number of vegetarian items. Jack Daniels' soaked ribs $9.45. Open Sun.-Wed. 11am-midnight, Thurs.-Sat. 11am-1:30am.

WaaZuBee Cafe, 1622 Commercial Dr. (253-5299), at E. 1st St. Sleek, metallic decoration, a utensil chandelier, and ubiquitous artwork. Smoked chicken fettuccine $10, Thai prawns $7. Open Mon.-Sat. 11:30am-1am, Sun. 11:30am-midnight.

Nuff-Nice-Ness, 1861 Commercial Dr. (255-4211), at 3rd. Nuff food at a nice price in a Jamaican deli. Jerk chicken with salad and rice $6.25; beef, chicken, or veggie patties $2. Open Mon.-Fri. 11:30am-9pm, Sat. noon-9pm, Sun. 1pm-8pm.

Rumble In Vancouver

According to Hollywood producers, Vancouver is exactly like New York City—except that it's cleaner and cheaper. Not only was it a most unBronx-like locale for Jackie Chan's *Rumble in the Bronx,* but all three *Look Who's Talking* movies, *Stakeout, Jumanji,* **Happy Gilmore,** and **The X-Files** can all claim Vancouver as their true home. But while the cameras roll through fairly regularly, Canada's relative lack of glamour makes it only a temporary home. The only stargazing nearby is in the mountains on clear winter nights, and Canada's most famous television show, *LA Law,* spent years disguising its true Canuck identity.

CANADA

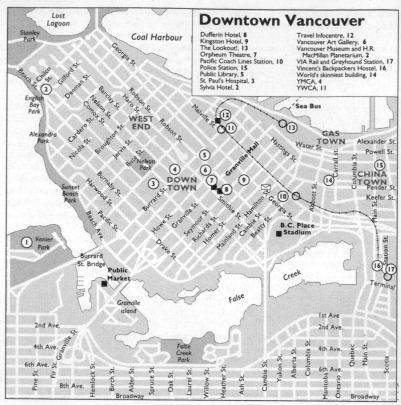

Downtown Vancouver

Dufferin Hotel, 8
Kingston Hotel, 9
The Lookout!, 13
Orpheum Theatre, 7
Pacific Coach Lines Station, 10
Police Station, 15
Public Library, 5
St. Paul's Hospital, 3
Sylvia Hotel, 2

Travel Infocentre, 12
Vancouver Art Gallery, 6
Vancouver Museum and H.R.
  MacMillan Planetarium, 2
VIA Rail and Greyhound Station, 17
Vincent's Backpackers Hostel, 16
World's skinniest building, 14
YMCA, 4
YWCA, 11

Phnom Penh, 244 E. Georgia (682-1090), near Main St. Take bus #3 or 8 from downtown. Big portions of tasty Cambodian-style noodles $5-7, Vietnamese entrees $6-13. Phnomenal jellyfish salad $10.75. Open Wed.-Mon. 10am-9pm.

Hamburger Mary's, 1202 Davie St. (687-1293), at Bute. Neo-50s sensibility, late hours, big portions, and allegedly the best burgers in town. Burger varieties (including veggie) $5-8. Open Sun.-Thurs. 6am-3am, Fri.-Sat. 6am-4am.

The New Japanese Deli House Restaurant, 381 Powell (662-8755), in Japantown. Lunch and dinner specials ($8-9) provide more than ample servings of their exceptional fare. Open Mon. 11:30am-3pm, Tues.-Thurs. 11:30am-8pm, Fri. 11:30am-9pm, Sat. noon-9pm.

SIGHTS AND ACTIVITIES

Expo '86 brought attention and prestige to Vancouver and paved the way for its transformation into one of Canada's hippest places. The **main grounds,** between Granville and Main St., are now devolving into office space, housing for seniors, and a cultural center. The Canada Pavilion, now called **Canada Place,** can be reached by SkyTrain from the main Expo site. The shops and restaurants inside are outrageously expensive, but the promenades around the complex are terrific vantage points for gawking at one of the more than 200 luxury liners that dock here annually.

The real big-screen star of Expo '86 is the **Omnimax Theatre,** part of **Science World,** 1455 Quebec St. (268-6363), on the Main St. SkyTrain stop. The 27m sphere is one of the largest, most technologically advanced spherical theatres in the world. **Science World** also features hands-on exhibits for kids. (Both $12, seniors and kids $8; only Science World $9/$5.50; under 4 always free. Science World open daily summer 10am-6pm; call for winter hours. Tickets for the Omnimax alone can be purchased after 4pm for $9; shows Sun.-Fri. 10am-5pm, Sat. 10am-9pm.)

The **Lookout!**, 555 W. Hastings St. (689-0421), offers 360° views of the city. Tickets are expensive!, but they're good for the whole day. ($7!, seniors $6!, students $4! ½price with HI membership or receipt from Vancouver International Hostel.) Come back for the night skyline (open daily 8:30am-10:30pm, in winter 9am-9pm).

The **Vancouver Art Gallery**, 750 Hornby St. (682-5621), in Robson Sq., has a small but innovative collection of classical and contemporary art and photography. Free tours are frequently given for large groups; just tag along. ($9.50, seniors and students $5.50, under 12 free; Thurs. 5-9pm free, but donations requested. Open Mon.-Wed. and Fri. 10am-6pm, Thurs. 10am-9pm, Sat. 10am-5pm, Sun. noon-5pm.)

Gastown is named for "Gassy Jack" Deighton, the glib con man who opened Vancouver's first saloon here in 1867. Today the area overflows with touristy craft shops, nightclubs, restaurants, and boutiques. Take the time to stroll along **Water St.** Gastown is a fairly long walk from downtown or a short ride on bus #22 along Burrard St. to Carrall St. It is bordered by Richards St. to the west, Columbia St. to the east, Hastings St. to the south, and the waterfront to the north. Just east of Gastown is **Chinatown.** The neighborhood teems with restaurants, shops, bakeries, and (gasp) Chinese street signs, and is reachable on foot or by bus #22.

Established in 1889 at the tip of the downtown peninsula, 1000-acre **Stanley Park** is a testament to the genius of Vancouver's urban planners. Surrounded by a seawall promenade, the thickly wooded park is laced with **cycling** and **hiking** trails. It contains a few restaurants, tennis courts, an outdoor theater, **Malkin Bowl,** and beaches with lifeguards and restrooms. The **Brockton Oval,** on the park's small eastern peninsula of Brockton Point, is a cinder running track, with hot showers and changing rooms. **Lost Lagoon,** an artificial lake next to the Georgia St. entrance, is brimming with fish, birds, and the rare trumpeter swan. On the eastern side of the park, the **Vancouver Aquarium** (682-1118) features orcas and Beluga whales in a sideshow revue. Weather permitting, the aquarium stages several performances per day. ($11, seniors and students $8.50, under 12 $6.50. Open daily 9:30am-8pm.)

Reach **Vanier** (van-YAY) **Park** by ferry ($1.75, youth $1; ferries daily, every 15min. 10am-8pm) or by bus #22 and visit the circular **Vancouver Museum,** 1100 Chestnut St. (736-4431), fronted by an abstract fountain. The museum displays artifacts from native cultures in the Pacific Northwest as well as several rotating exhibits. ($5; students, seniors, and under 18 $2.50; families $10. Open daily 10am-6pm; Oct.-April Tues.-Sun. 10am-5pm.) In the same building, the **H. R. MacMillan Planetarium** (738-7827) runs up to four different star shows per day, as well as **laser shows** set to music. (Star shows $6.50, kids and seniors $5; laser shows $7.75, seniors free on Tues. Call for showtimes.) The adjacent **Gordon Southam Observatory** and its 50cm telescope is also open to the public. (Free. Open Sat.-Sun. noon-5pm and 7-11pm; call ahead after noon at 738-2855 to check times.)

Kitsilano Beach (731-0011), known to Vancouverites as "Kits," on the other side of Arbutus St. from Vanier, is a local favorite with a heated outdoor saltwater pool, lockers, and a snack bar ($3.65, seniors $1.80, children $2.35). For less crowding, more students, and free showers (a winning combination), visit **Jericho Beach.** A great cycling path at the edge of the road leads to the westernmost edge of the UBC campus. Bike and hiking trails cut through the campus and crop its edges.

The high point of a visit to the **University of British Columbia (UBC)** is its **Museum of Anthropology,** 6393 NW Marine Dr. (822-3825 for a recording, 822-5087 for an operator). To reach campus, take bus #4 or 10 from Granville. The high-ceilinged glass and concrete building houses totems and other massive sculptures crafted by the indigenous peoples of the Northwest coast. The *Guide to the UBC Museum of Anthropology* ($1), available at the entrance desk, is worth picking up. Hour-long guided walks will help you find your way through the museum. ($6, seniors and students $3.50, families $15, under 6 free; Tues. after 5pm free. Open in summer Mon. and Wed.-Sun. 10am-5pm, Tues. 10am-9pm; Sept.-June closed Mon.) UBC also has a pool open to the public (except in summer) in the **Aquatic Centre**

(822-4521), a free **Fine Arts Gallery** (822-2759), free daytime and evening concerts (822-3113), and a geology museum (822-5586; museums and pool open Mon.-Fri. 8:30am-4:30pm).

Granville Mall, on Granville Ave. between Smythe and Hastings St., is a pedestrian and bus mall that caters to young professionals on their power-lunch hours, theater-goers, leather lovers, and avid music collectors. Mallrats going through withdrawal should head a few blocks west, to the **Harbour Centre,** 555 W. Hastings St. If you're dying to fill your matching luggage set with chic purchases, there's always the ritziest mall west of Long Island: the **Park Royal Shopping Centre** on Marine Dr. in West Vancouver. Take bus #250, 251, or 252 on Georgia St. downtown.

ENTERTAINMENT AND NIGHTLIFE

To keep abreast of Vancouver's lively entertainment scene, pick up a copy of the weekly *Georgia Straight* or the monthly *AF Magazine,* both free at newsstands and record stores. The renowned **Vancouver Symphony Orchestra (VSO)** (684-9100) plays in the **Orpheum Theater,** 884 Granville St. (280-4444). The VSO often joins with other groups such as the 53-year-old **Vancouver Bach Choir** (921-8012) to present a diverse selection of music. Vancouver theater is praised throughout Canada. The **Arts Club Theatre** (687-3306) hosts big-name plays and musicals. The **Theatre Under the Stars** program (687-0174), in Stanley Park's Malkin Bowl, plays a summer season of musicals. The annual **Vancouver Shakespeare Festival** in Vanier Park often needs volunteers, who work in exchange for free admission to the shows (June-Aug.). Ask at the visitors center for details. **UBC Summer Stock** (822-2678) puts on four plays in summer at the **Frederick Wood Theatre.**

The famed **Vancouver Folk Music Festival** (734-6543) jams in mid-July in Jericho Park. (Tickets $28 per evening, $42 per weekend day; $75 per weekend if purchased before June 22, $90 if purchased before July 19, $112 after July 19. Prices higher at the gate.) For more details, write to the festival at Box 381, 916 W. Broadway, Vancouver V5Z 1K7. The annual **Du Maurier International Jazz Festival Vancouver** (682-0706), in the third week of June, features over 500 performers and bands such as Randy Wanless's Fab Forty and Charles Eliot's Largely Cookie. Write to 435 W. Hastings, Vancouver V6V 1L4 for details.

> **Purple Onion,** 15 Water St. (602-9442) in Gastown. Two rooms with both live music and DJ, and music to please anyone of any musical preference. Groovin'. Cover $3-6. Open Mon.-Thurs. 8pm-2am, Fri.-Sat. 7pm-2am, Sun. 7pm-midnight.
>
> **Luv-A-Fair,** 1275 Seymour St. (685-3288), at Drake downtown. Trendy dance space pipes hip-hop and alternative music into the ears of clubsters. Tuesday's 80s night is a huge weekday draw. Open Mon.-Sat. 9pm-2am, Sun. 9am-midnight.
>
> **Celebrities,** 1022 Davie St. (689-3180), at Burard downtown. Popular with Vancouver's gay crowd, it usually draws all types. Thurs. is Devil's Disco night, Fri. is talent show, Sun. is retro. Open Mon.-Sat. 9pm-2am, Sun. 9pm-midnight.
>
> **The Town Pump,** 66 Water St. (683-6695), in Gastown. A pub-style club, one of Vancouver's few remaining venues for showcasing up-and-coming or up-already progressive and alternative bands. Cover varies. Open Tues.-Sat. noon-2am.

■ Victoria

Victoria is a city of diverse origins and interests. Trading posts featuring Native American arts and crafts live harmoniously next to American classics like the Gap. There's an English pub on every corner and East Asian restaurants, teahouses, markets, and stores in every neighborhood. Downtown, new age stores and tattoo parlors stake their ground aside tourist traps and more authentic craft shops.

Practical Information   Tourism Victoria, 812 Wharf St. V8W 1T3 (953-2033), at the corner of Government St., offers pamphlets and bus, boat, and nature tours and is also a Ticketmaster outlet (open daily 8:30am-7:30pm; in winter 9am-5pm). **Pacific Coach Lines (PCL)** and its affiliate, **Island Coach Lines,** 700 Douglas St. at Belleville (800-661-1725 or 385-4411) run to Nanaimo (7 per day, $16.10) and Vancouver (on the hr. 6am-8pm, $22.50). **BC Ferries** (656-0757 for a recording; 386-3431 for an operator 7am-10pm) float between Swartz Bay and Tsawwassen. (20 per day, 7am-9pm. $6.50, bikes $2.50, cars $25.) **Washington State Ferries** (381-1551) run from Sidney, BC to Anacortes, WA via the San Juan Islands. **BC Transit** (382-6161) offers city bus service with major connections downtown at the corner of Douglas and Yates St. (Single-zone travel $1.50, multi-zone—north to Sidney and the Butchart Gardens—$2.25, students $1.50, seniors $1, under 5 free.) Buy day passes ($5, seniors and students $4) at 7-11, Money Mart, Shoppers Drug stores, or the tourism office. In an **emergency,** call 911. Find the **post office** at 905 Gordon St. V8W 3P9 (381-6114). Open Mon.-Fri. 9am-5:30pm, Sat. 9:30am-5pm. **Postal Code:** V8W 1L0. Victoria's **area code** is 604.

Hwy. 1, the **Trans-Canada Hwy.,** leads north and reaches the rest of Vancouver Island; **Hwy. 14** leads west to **Port Renfrew** and **Pacific Rim National Park.** Victoria enfolds the Inner Harbour; **Government St.** and **Douglas St.** are the main north-south thoroughfares, running through downtown.

Accommodations, Camping, and Food
Victoria Youth Hostel (HI-C), 516 Yates St. V8W 1K8 (385-4511), at Wharf St. downtown, holds 108 beds and extensive facilities in the remodeled Victoria Heritage Building. Family rooms are available. (Desk open 7am-midnight. Curfew 2:30am. $15, nonmembers $19.) **Renouf House Bunk & Breakfast,** 2010 Stanley Ave. (595-4774; fax 598-1515), take bus #10 or walk, offers private rooms and bunks. The staff organizes kayaking tours of the islands (breakfast included; bunks $18.25; singles $33.25-$55; doubles $45-$65). **Goldstream Provincial Park,** 2930 Trans-Canada Hwy. (391-2300; 800-689-9025 for reservations) hosts great short hiking trails and swimming (150 sites; $15.50). **Thetis Lake Campground,** 1938 Trans-Canada Hwy. (478-3845), 10km north of the city, has peaceful, removed sites ($19 for 2 people, 50¢ per additional person).

Hop over to **John's Place,** 723 Pandora St. (389-0711), for Canadian fare with a Thai twist and a little Mediterranean thrown in. The *Goong Nam Prik Pow* (sautéed tiger prawns in curry sauce; $11) is John's favorite. (Open Mon.-Thurs. 7am-10pm, Sat. 7am-11pm; Sun. brunch 8am-3pm, dinner 5-10pm.) Imagine Judy Jetson meeting the 50s in a wacky gas station and you've got **Pluto's,** 1150 Cooke St. (385-4747). Blessed by the budget fairy, Pluto's lies far from the bustle of downtown (open Sun.-Thurs. 8am-11pm, Fri.-Sat. 8am-midnight). At **Milky Way,** 128-560 Johnson St. (360-1113), cheap prices for a multi-course meal make it one of the better bargains in town while the star-studded decor makes it one of the more entertaining (open daily 7am-11pm). Go to **Ferris' Oyster and Burger Bar,** 536 Yates St. (360-1824), for a menu that runs from tofu hot dogs ($4) and burgers ($5) to the $3 oyster shooter—a raw oyster with salsa and a half-shot of vodka or tequila to kill any bacteria (open Sun.-Thurs. noon-10pm, Fri.-Sat. noon-11pm).

Sights and Nightlife
A trip through the **Royal British Columbia Museum,** 675 Belleville St. (387-3014 recording; 387-3701 operator) will remind you of why you came to Canada, with excellent exhibits on the biological, geological, and cultural history of the province. ($5.35, seniors $3.20, youth $2, under 5 free. Open daily July-Sept. 8 9:30am-7pm; Sept. 9-June 30 10am-5:30pm.) **Thunderbird Park** and its many totems loom large behind the museum. Free tours leave daily from the main steps of the **Parliament Buildings,** 501 Belleville. (20-23 tours per day in summer; in winter on the hr. Open Mon.-Fri. 8:30am-5pm, Sat.-Sun. for tours only.)

Beacon Hill Park, off Douglas St. south of the Inner Harbour, is a flowering oasis just blocks from downtown that pleases walkers, bikers, and the picnic-inclined. More adventurous mountain bikers can try tackling the **Galloping Goose Trail,** a

CANADA

60km trail from downtown Victoria to the west coast of the island. Snaking through cities, rainforests, and canyons, it's open to cyclists, walkers, and horses.

By sea, Victoria is a hub for a number of the sailing, kayaking, and whale-watching tours available on Vancouver Island. **Oak Bay Marine Group** at the Oak Bay Marina (598-3369) rents deep sea fishing charters for $6 per hr., minimum 4 hr. After a few days of hiking, biking, and visiting museums, unwind with a tour of the **Vancouver Island Brewery,** at 2330 Government St. (361-0007). Tours start at 1 and 3pm Wednesday through Saturday and include free samples.

Victoria is lousy with pubs. For pints that come with live music, **Harpo's Cabaret,** 15 Bastion Sq. (385-5333), at Wharf St., brings in an eclectic array of bands ranging from blues and jazz to neo-hippie rock acts. The **Drawing Room,** 751 View St. (920-7797), is considerate enough to offer a lounge, with easy chairs, pool tables, and a wall-to-wall carpet for dancers fleeing the frenzied techno/alternative/house music playing next door (open Tues.-Thurs. 8pm-2am, Fri.-Sat. 9pm-2am).

The **Victoria Symphony Society,** 846 Broughton St. (385-6575), performs regularly under conductor Peter McCoppin. For the last week and a half of June, Victoria keys up for jazz during **JazzFest,** as over a dozen performers play venues throughout the city (388-4423). And from mid-July to mid-August, Victoria goes Elizabethan/Jacobean with the **Annual Shakespeare Festival** in the Inner Harbour (360-0234).

■ Glacier National Park

Major A.B. Rogers won a $5000 salary bonus and immortality when he discovered a route through the Columbia Mountains, finally allowing Canada to build its first transcontinental railway. The railway was a dangerous enterprise; more than 200 lives were lost to avalanches during its first 30 years of operation. Today, **Rogers Pass** is at the center of Glacier National Park, and 1350 sq. km of national park commemorate the efforts of explorers who bound British Columbia to the rest of Canada. Glacier hosts over 400 of the big guys.

Practical Information The Trans-Canada Hwy.'s many **scenic turn-offs** offer picnic facilities, bathrooms, and historical plaques. *Footloose in the Columbias* ($1.50), available at the **Rogers Pass Information Centre** (837-6274) on the highway in Glacier, gives a detailed description of the park. The center has enough computerized info, scale models, and exhibits to warrant a visit (open daily 7am-9pm; winter hours vary). **Park passes** are required if you don't drive straight through ($4 per day, $35 per year, good in all Canadian national parks). Prices in the park often change; for updates or general info about Glacier National Park, write the Superintendent, P.O. Box 350, Revelstoke V0E 2S0, or call 873-7500.

Glacier lies on the Trans-Canada Hwy., 350km west of Calgary and 723km east of Vancouver. **Greyhound** (837-5874) makes four trips daily from Revelstoke ($10). In an emergency, call the **Park Warden Office** (837-6274; open daily 7am-5pm; winter daily 7am-11pm; 24hr. during avalanche control periods). The **area code** is 250.

Accommodations, Camping, and Food There are two campgrounds in Glacier: **Illecillewaet** (ill-uh-SILL-uh-watt) and **Loop Brook.** Both offer flush toilets, kitchen shelters with cook stoves, and firewood (sites for both $13; open mid-June to Sept.). Illecillewaet stays open in winter without plumbing; winter guests must register at the Park Administration Office at Rogers Pass. **Backcountry campers** need a backcountry pass ($6), and must register with the Administration Office beforehand and pitch their tents at least 5km from the pavement. You'd do well to drop by a supermarket in Golden or Revelstoke before you enter the park.

Outdoors The Trans-Canada Hwy. cuts a thin ribbon through the center of the park, affording spectacular views of over 400 glaciers. More than 140km of challenging trails lead from the highway, inviting rugged mountain men and women to penetrate the near-impenetrable. Try to visit the park in late July or early August, when brilliant explosions of mountain wildflowers offset the deep green of the forests. Glacier receives measurable precipitation every other day in summer, but the clouds of mist that encircle the peaks and blanket the valleys only add to the park's astonishing beauty. Avoid exploring the park in winter, as near-daily snowfalls and the constant threat of avalanches often restrict travel to the Trans-Canada Hwy.

Eight popular **hiking trails** begin at the Illecillewaet campground, 3.4km west of Rogers Pass. The easy 1km **Meeting of the Waters** trail leads to the impressive confluence of the Illecillewaet and Asulkan Rivers. The 4.2km **Avalanche Crest** trail offers spectacular views of Rogers Pass, the Hermit Range, and the Illecillewaet River Valley; the treeless slopes below the crest testify to the destructive power of winter snowslides. From early July to late August, the park staff run daily **interpretive hikes** beginning at 9am (for info contact the center). Come prepared for a four- to six-hr. tour with a picnic lunch, a rain jacket, and a sturdy pair of walking shoes. Regulations prohibit biking on the trails in Glacier. The park's glacial meltwaters—a startling milky-aqua color due to sediment suspended in the current—do not support many fish; determined anglers can try their luck with the cutthroat in the **Illecillewaet River** (get a permit, $6 for 7 days, at the info center).

■ Prince Rupert

Most visitors come to Prince Rupert either for fishing or ferries. An afternoon in a guided fishing boat costs upwards of $100; pass the hours before your ship comes in browsing the 15 downtown blocks. The **Traveler's Information Centre** (624-5637), at 1st Ave. and McBride St. (open May 15-Labor Day daily 9am-9pm; winter Mon.-Fri. 10am-5pm), offers stacks of info and a map for a less-than-riveting self-guided tour. More impressive is the small **Museum of Northern British Columbia** that shares the same building (open in summer 9am-8pm). The only major road into town is **Hwy. 16,** or McBride at the city limits, which curves left and becomes 2nd Ave. downtown. **Prince Rupert Bus Service** (624-3343) provides local service downtown Mon.-Sat. ($1, seniors 60¢; day pass $2.50/$2). The #52 bus runs about every ½hr. 7am-10pm, from 2nd Ave. and 3rd St. to within a 5-min. walk of the ferry terminal. Or try **Skeena Taxi** (624-2185; open 24hr.).

Alaska Marine Highway (627-1744), at the end of Hwy. 16 (Park Ave.), runs ferries north from Prince Rupert along the Alaskan panhandle, including Ketchikan (US$38, car US$75) and Juneau (US$104, car US$240). **BC Ferries** (624-9627), next door, serves the Queen Charlotte Islands (6 per week; $22.25, car $85) and Port Hardy (every other day; $100, car $206). Vehicle reservations are required 3 weeks in advance. Ferry-goers may not leave cars parked on the street. Some establishments charge a daily rate for storage; check with the ferry company or the info center. The **post office** (624-2136) is on 2nd Ave. and 3rd. St. General delivery mail goes to the main office (open Mon.-Fri. 8:30am-4:30pm), but only **substations** sell stamps and postal supplies. The most convenient is in the **Shoppers Drug Mart** at 3rd Ave. and 2nd. St. (open Mon.-Fri. 9:30am-9pm, Sat. 9:30am-7pm, Sun. 11am-6pm). **Postal code:** V8J 3P3. The **area code** is 604.

Nearly all of Prince Rupert's hotels are within the six-block area defined by 1st Ave., 3rd Ave., 6th St., and 9th St. Everything fills when the ferries dock, so call a day or two ahead. **Pioneer Rooms,** 167 3rd Ave. E (624-2334), is well-kept and clean, but noise could be a problem for singles blocked off only by curtains ($20, singles with door $25, doubles $30). **Park Ave. Campground,** 1750 Park Ave. (624-5861 or 800-667-1994), the only campground in Prince Rupert, sits less than 2km east of the ferry terminal via Hwy. 16. Some sites are forested, others have a view of the bay, and all are well-maintained (sites $9, RV sites $16; reservations recommended).

Cow Bay Café, 100 Cow Bay Rd. (627-1212), around the corner from Eagle Bluff B&B, cooks up everything from smoked salmon tarts ($6.50) to jambalaya ($7.50) to shrimp quesedillas ($8). Gaze out at the harbor and thank your lucky stars that you found this place (open Tues. noon-2:30pm, Wed.-Sat. noon-2:30pm and 6-9pm). **Galaxy Gardens,** 844 3rd Ave. W. (624-3122) stands out in the surprisingly large Chinese restaurant crowd (open daily 11am-10pm). The bar at the **Commercial Inn,** 901 1st Ave. (624-6142), sports authentic local color in the form of tipsy fishermen and other down-to-earth folks (open Mon.-Fri. 11am-1am, Sat.-Sun. noon-2:30am), while **Breaker's Pub,** 117 George Hills Way (624-5990), in Cow Bay, offers pool tables and expensive beers. ($4 for a pint on draft. Bar open Mon.-Thurs. 11:30am-midnight, Fri-Sat. 11:30am-1am, Sun. noon-midnight; kitchen closes earlier.)

Tiny **Service Park,** off Fulton St., offers panoramic views of downtown (which isn't any more attractive from above) and the harbor beyond. Take in an even broader view from a trail leading up the side of **Mt. Oldfield,** to the east of town. The trailhead is about 6km from downtown on Hwy. 16—consider renting a bike to get there if you don't have a car. The **Butze Rapids** and **Tall Trees** trails depart from the same location. Ambitious bikers can cycle 16km down the road to **Diana Lake Park,** which features a picnic area set against an enticing lake.

Yukon Territory

Native Americans recognized the majesty of this land when they dubbed the Yukon River "Yuchoo," or Big River. Gold-hungry white settlers streamed in at the end of the 19th century, interested in the yellow metal turned up by the Big River's tributaries, and left almost as quickly when the rushes didn't pan out. Although the Yukon and Northern British Columbia were the first regions of North America to be settled some 20,000 years ago, today they remain largely untouched and inaccessible. With an average of only one person per 15 sq. km, the loneliness of the area is overwhelming—as is its sheer physical beauty, a reward for those willing to deal with unpredictable winter weather and poor road conditions.

■ Whitehorse

Named for the once-perilous **Whitehorse Rapids,** this was often the rest stop where the bone-weary Cheechako ("newcomer") of the 1898 Gold Rush paused to wring himself out after successfully navigating the rapids. Prospectors then continued on across Lake Laberge and down the Yukon along with the floating armada of expectant gold seekers headed for Dawson City and the Klondike. In the warmer months, Whitehorse is still a good base for exploring the vast surrounding wilderness.

Practical Information   The **Whitehorse Visitor Reception Centre** (667-7545), sits in the new Tourism and Business Center at 100 Hansen St. (open Mon.-Sat. 8am-6pm, Sun. 10am-6pm). You can also get info by writing to **Tourism Yukon,** P.O. Box 2703, Whitehorse, YT Y1A 2C6. **Canadian Airlines** (668-4466, for reservations 668-3535), **NWT Air** (800-661-0789), and **Royal Air** (800-663-9757) all fly to Calgary, AB (4 per day, $568), Edmonton, AB (4 per day, $568), and Vancouver, BC (5 per day, $466). **Greyhound,** 2191 2nd Ave. (667-2223) runs to Vancouver, BC ($292), Edmonton, AB ($228), and Dawson Creek, BC ($164). Desk open Mon.-Fri. 8am-5:30pm, Sat. 10am-1pm, Sun. 4-8am. **Alaskon Express** (tickets at the Westmark Hotel, 668-3225), at 2nd Ave. and Wood St., runs in the summer to Anchorage (3 per week, US$190), Haines (3 per week, US$85), Fairbanks (3 per week, US$165), and Skagway (daily, US$54). Call 911 in an **emergency.** There is no main post office in Whitehorse. **General services** is 211 Main St. (668-5847; open Mon.-Fri. 8am-6pm, Sat. 9am-5pm). **General delivery** is at 3rd and Wood, in the Yukon News Bldg. (open Mon.-Sat. 7am-7pm). **General Delivery Postal Code** for last names beginning with letters A-L is Y1A 3S7; for M-Z it's Y1A 3S8. The **area code** is 403.

Accommodations, Camping, and Food   Call the **Northern Network of Bed and Breakfasts** (993-5649), in Dawson City, to reserve a room in a Klondike household. **High Country Inn (HI-C)**, 4051 4th Ave. (667-4471), has doubles for $25 per person, private singles starting at $45, and private quads for $115. **Roadhouse Inn**, 2163 2nd Ave. (667-2594), adjacent to the Roadhouse Saloon, has shared rooms for $19 per person, plus a $5 refundable deposit for sheets and towels. Private rooms are $50, plus $5 per additional person. Camping in Whitehorse is limited. **Robert Service Campground** (668-3721), 1km from town on South Access Rd. on the Yukon River, is a convenient stop for tenting folk, but has no RV sites (48 sites, $10.50). Rest your rig at the **High-Country RV Park** (667-7445), at the intersection of the Alaska Hwy. and South Access Rd. ($18-21 for 2 people, $3 each additional person; tents $12).

No Pop Sandwich Shop, 312 Steele (668-3227), at 4th Ave., is popular with White-horse's small suit-and-tie crowd. Enjoy a Beltch (BLT and cheese, $4.50) or a veggie sandwich ($4.25), but don't think of asking for anything carbonated (open Mon.-Thurs. 7:30am-8:30pm, Fri. 7:30am-9:30pm, Sat.-Sun. 10am-8:30pm). The **Klondike Rib and Salmon Barbeque**, 2116 2nd Ave. (667-7554), lets you sample northern salmon without breaking the bank (open daily 6am-10pm).

Sights and Activities The restored *S. S. Klondike* (667-4511), on South Access Rd., is a dry-docked 1929 sternwheeler that recalls the days when the Yukon River was the city's sole means of survival. Pick up a ticket from the info booth at the entrance to the parking lot for a fascinating video and guided tour. ($3.25, kids $2.25, families $7.50. Open June 1-Sept. 15 daily 9am-7:30pm.) The **Whitehorse Rapids Fishway** (633-5965), at the end of Nisutlin Dr., 2km southeast of town, allows salmon to bypass the dam and continue upstream in the **world's longest salmon migration** (open daily mid-June to mid-Sept. 8am-10pm; free). **Miles Canyon** lies 2km south of town on Miles Canyon Rd. off South Access Rd. Once the location of the feared Whitehorse rapids, this dammed stretch of the Yukon now swirls silently under the first bridge to span the river's banks. (Note: Large RVs may have trouble maneuvering on the small access road to the parking lot.) The **MV Schwatka** (668-4716), on Miles Canyon Rd. off South Access Rd., floats you through Miles Canyon. (2hr. $17, kids 6-11 $8.50, under 6 free. Cruises June 15-Aug. 15 daily 2pm and 7pm; early June and Aug. 16-Sept. 10 2pm only.) **Taste of 98** (633-4767) also offers motorized raft trips of various lengths. **Up North Boat and Canoe Rentals**, 86 Wickstrom Rd. (667-7905), across the river from downtown, lets you paddle 25km to Jakkimi River for $20 per person (cost includes pick-up and return to Whitehorse; trip takes about 4hr.).

▨ Dawson City

Of all the insanity ever inspired by the lust for the dust, the creation of **Dawson City** ranks among the most extreme. For 12 glorious, crazy months, from July 1898 to July 1899, Dawson City, on the doorstep of the Arctic Circle and 1000 miles from any other settlement, was the largest Canadian city west of Toronto. These days, legions of RV travelers, a sizeable international crowd, and a swarm of college students migrate north in the summer and create a remarkably lively atmosphere. Almost 100 years after its moment in the midnight sun, Dawson City is again the jewel of the Yukon.

Practical Information The **Visitor Reception Centre** (993-5566), at Front and King St., offers historic movies and extensive information (open mid-May to mid-Sept. daily 8am-8pm). For info, write Box 40, Dawson City, YT Y0B 1G0. The **North-west Territories Visitors Centre** (993-6167) is across the street and has plenty of advice on driving the Dempster Hwy. (open daily late May to early Sept. 9am-9pm). **Norline Coaches Ltd.** (993-6010), at the Gas Shack Chevron Station on 5th Ave. and Princess St., run buses to Whitehorse thrice per week (twice in winter) for $73. Call for an **ambulance** at 993-4444; the **police** at 993-5555 (if no answer 1-667-5555). The **post office** (993-5342) is at 5th Ave. and Princess St. (Open Mon.-Fri. 8:30am-5:30pm, Sat. 8:30am-12:30pm.) **Postal Code:** Y0B 1G0. **Area code:** 403.

Accommodations, Camping, and Food   Dawson City River Hostel (HI-C) (993-6823) lies across the Yukon river from downtown; take the 1st left when you come off the (free) ferry. An array of amenities complements the brand-new log cabins ($13, nonmembers $15; tent sites $8 for one person, $6 each additional person). Not only is **The Bunkhouse** (993-6164), at Front and Princess St., brand new and very clean, it's also in a great location (singles $45; doubles $50, with bath $60).To get to the **Yukon River Campground,** ride the ferry to the west side of Dawson City and take the 1st right. The roomy, secluded sites are a haven for budget travelers who want to nestle down in nature (water and pit toilets; RVs welcome, but no hookups available; sites $8).

The breakfast special at **Klondike Kate's** (993-6527), at 3rd and King St., should satisfy even the hungriest Sourdoughs ($4 for 2 eggs, bacon or sausage, home fries, and toast). Kate's is open mid-May to mid-Sept. daily 7am-11pm. Visits **Nancy's** (993-5633), at Front St. and Princess, for a veggie sandwich on fresh, super-thick bread or delicious German-style sausage (open daily 7am-10pm, in winter until 8pm).

Sights and Entertainment   The **Dawson City Museum** (993-5291), on 5th St. south of Church, elaborates on regional history and exhibits the full range of Yukon history, from mastodons to sluice boxes to modern mining machinery ($3.50, seniors $2.50, students and kids $1; open daily 10am-6pm). At the **Jack London Cabin,** on 8th Ave. and 5th, admission is free and the great Californian author's life and times in the Yukon are recounted daily during readings at noon and 2pm. Be sure to catch the thoroughly entertaining **Robert Service readings** given at his nearby cabin. Performances of witty and unpretentious ballads by the Yukon Bard are given in front of the cabin where he penned them on 8th Ave. at Hanson ($6, under 8 $3; shows daily at 10am and 3pm).

Diamond Tooth Gertie's, at 4th and Queen, was Canada's first legal casino and should be proof enough that Dawson is no movie set: for a $4.75 cover you can try your hand at roulette, blackjack, and if you dare, play "Texas hold 'em" against local legends like Johnny Caribou and No Sleep Filippe. Or just take in one of three nightly floor shows at 8:30, 10:30pm, and 12:30am (open nightly 7pm-2am).

Further out of town, the goldfields of **Bonanza** and **Eldorado Creeks** yielded some of the richest lodes discovered in the Klondike. Nearly 16km of maintained gravel road follows Bonanza Creek to the former site of **Grand Forks,** chewed up when the dredges came through. Along the way are **Gold Dredge #4,** the huge machine used to thoroughly mine Bonanza Creek after the rush was over, and **Discovery Claim,** the site of the first discovery of gold by George Carmack on August 16, 1896. For modern day fortune hunters, many businesses let you pan gold for around $5. Anyone can pan for free at the confluence of the Bonanza and Eldorado Creeks (you need your own pan, available at local hardware stores). Panning anywhere else along the creeks could lead to a *very* unpleasant encounter with the owner/miner of the claim you're jumping.

No, Ma'am, That's Not an Olive in Your Martini...

For Capt. Dick Stevenson, the discovery of a **pickled human toe** in a cabin in the Yukon meant one thing: a damn fine cocktail. The drink became famous and spawned the **Sourtoe Cocktail Club,** an institution with a history as peculiar as its name. Aspiring initiates buy a drink of their choice and pay a small fee ($5) to Bill "Stillwater Willie" Boone (Dick's replacement as keeper of the sourtoe), who drops the chemically preserved (er, pickled) toe in the drink. Then it's bottoms up, and the moment the toe touches your lips, you've become one of the club's 12,000-plus proud members. Listening to Stillwater Willie explain the club's sordid history and philosophize about life in the Yukon is itself worth the $5, but the fee includes a certificate, membership card, and pin. Inquire at the **Pleasure Island Restaurant** (993-5482), on Front St. between King and Queen, for initiation times and location.

■ Kluane National Park

Kluane, a Tutchone Native word meaning "place of many fish," is also Canadian wilderness at its most rugged, unspoiled, and beautiful. The "Green Belt" along the eastern park boundary supports the greatest diversity of plant and animal species in northern Canada. Beyond the Kluane Range loom the glaciers of the Icefield Range, home to Canada's highest peaks, including the tallest, 19,850-ft. **Mt. Logan.** The Alaska Hwy., near the northeastern boundary of the park, provides an easy way to see the park's eastern edge and glimpse a few of the spectacular peaks beyond.

Practical Information Pick up plenty of free info at the **Haines Junction Visitor Centre,** on Logan St. in Haines Junction (Canadian Park Service 634-7209; Tourism Yukon 634-2345; open mid-May to mid-Sept. daily 8am-8pm), or at the **Sheep Mountain Visitor Centre** (600/700-6116), at Alaska Hwy. Km 1707 (open June to mid-Sept. daily 9am-5pm). **Emergency numbers** in Haines Junction include: **medical,** 634-4444; **fire,** 634-2222; and **police,** 634-5555 (if no answer, call 1-403-667-5555). The **post office** (634-2706) is in Madley's General Store. (Open Mon., Wed., and Fri. 9-10am and 1-5pm, Tues. 9am-5pm, Thurs. 9am-noon and 1-5pm. Store open Mon.-Fri. 9am-5pm.) The **Postal Code** is Y0B 1L0. **Area code:** 403.

Kluane's 22,015 sq. km are bounded by the Kluane Game Sanctuary and the Alaska Hwy. to the north, and the Haines Hwy. (Hwy. 3) to the east. The town of **Haines Junction** is at the eastern park boundary, 158km west of Whitehorse. **Alaska Direct** (800-770-6652, 668-4833 in Whitehorse) runs three buses per week from Haines Junction to Anchorage (US$125), Fairbanks (US$100), Whitehorse (US$20), and Skagway (US$55).

Camping, Accommodations, and Food Haine's Junction offers clean but forgettable highway hotels; B&Bs and the several area campgrounds are the best options. **Kathleen Lake Campground** (634-2251), 27km south of Haines Junction off Haines Rd., is close to good hiking and fishing and has water, flush toilets, fire pits, firewood, and "campfire talks" (sites $10; open June-Oct.). The Yukon government runs four campgrounds, all with water and pit toilets (sites $8; call Tourism Yukon at 634-2345 for more info). The closest to Haines Junction is beautiful **Pine Lake,** 7km east of Haines Junction on the Alaska Hwy. Seekers of an indoor bed should skip the motels and march straight to **Laughing Moose Bed and Breakfast,** 120 Alsek Crescent (634-2335; singles $55, doubles $65; shared bath).

Haines Junction restaurants offer (yawn) standard highway cuisine. For groceries, head to **Madley's General Store** (634-2200) at Haines Rd. and Bates (open in summer daily 8am-9pm; Oct.-April 8am-6:30pm). At the **Village Bakery and Deli** (634-2867), on Logan St. across from the visitors center, you can sate your sweet-tooth with a scrumptious $1.50 cinnamon bun (open May-Sept. daily 9am-9pm).

Outdoors in the Park Kluane has few developed trails, but the existing ones give ample opportunity to surround yourself with utter wilderness. For a warm-up try the easy **Dezadeash River Loop** (DEZ-dee-ash), beginning at the Kluane RV Park just west of Haines Jct. The flat, forested 4km stroll includes a lookout deck where you can scope the valley for moose and bear. Rather than drive to the RV park, take the **Wetlands River Trail** which begins from the nearby day use area, and hike through Ducks Unlimited protected wetlands to reach the **Dezadeash River Trail.** The 15km **Auriol Trail** can take only four to six hr. but is also an excellent overnight hike. Starting from Haines Hwy., the trail cuts through boreal forest and leads to a subalpine bench in front of the Auriol Range. The **King's Throne Route** and **Sheep Mountain Ridge Walk** (starting near the Sheep Mountain Visitor Centre) offer more challenging terrain and the best views available on a day hike.

The park also offers many **"routes"** that follow no formal trail and are not maintained by the park. These are reserved for more experienced hikers. *All overnight hikers are required to register at one of the visitors centers to pay user fees ($5 per*

CANADA

person per night; a season pass is $50). The park strongly encourages dayhikers to register, especially in the **north end** and **Slims Valley** section of the park where trails are not as well marked and bear activity is more frequent.

The **Kluane Park Adventure Centre** (634-2313) is the central booking office for outdoor activities in and around the park (open daily 8am-8pm). The center rents **canoes** for $30 per day. For $100, travelers can ride the class III and IV rapids on the Tatshenshini River from Copper Mine, BC to Dalton Post, YT; the center also offers a two-hr. scenic interpretive float trip illustrating the park's ecology, fauna, and geology for $25.

■ Carcross

Carcross, short for "Caribou Crossing," sits on the narrows between Bennet and Nares Lakes, surrounded by snow-capped peaks and boasting a population of around 400. The native Tagish people hunted caribou at the crossing until the early 1900s when the herds were obliterated. Carcross also served as a link in the gold seekers' famous Chilcoot route from Skagway to the Yukon River and as a supply depot for the construction of the Alaska Highway. On the Klondike Hwy. (Hwy. 2), Carcross is 74km south of Whitehorse and 106km north of Skagway, AK.

Practical Information The **Carcross Visitor Reception Centre** is inside the White Pass and Yukon Railroad depot (821-4431; open mid-May to mid-Sept. daily 8am-8pm). **Atlin Express** (604-651-7617) runs buses from Carcross to: Atlin, BC ($21, seniors $18, ages 5-11 $10.50, under 5 free); Whitehorse ($26/$20/$13/free); and Tagish ($15/ $13/$7.50/free). **Emergency numbers** include: **ambulance,** 821-3333; **fire,** 821-2222; and **police,** 821-5555 (if no answer call 667-5555). The **post office** is the white building with red trim on Bennett Ave. (open Mon., Wed., Fri. 8am-noon and 1-4pm, Tues. and Thurs. 10-11:45am; **postal code:** Y0B 1B0). The **area code** is 403.

Accommodations, Camping, and Food History buffs will love the **Caribou Hotel** (821-4501), the **oldest operating hotel in the Yukon.** The original structure was destroyed in a 1909 fire; the present building was erected shortly thereafter (no phones, no TVs, shared bath; singles and doubles $35). **Spirit Lake Lodge** (821-4337), 7km north of town on Hwy. 2, maintains forested tent sites overlooking the lake (sites $6.50, showers $3, firewood $3 per bundle) and rooms (single $35, doubles $55, no TVs or phones). The **Spirit Lake Lounge** is also a popular after-hours spot for locals, particularly in winter. The Yukon Government maintains 14 secluded sites ($8) with drinking water, firewood, and pit toilets at **Carcross Campground,** 1km north of town on Hwy. 2.

The restaurant at the **Caribou Hotel** has standard food and prices (entrees $5-7; open daily 7am-8pm). Herbivores can get inexpensive meals for $5-9 at the **Spirit Lake Restaurant** (821-4337), in the Spirit Lake Lodge (open daily 8am-9:30pm). Groceries are available for cheap at **Montana Services** (821-3708), at the Chevron station on Hwy. 2 (open May-Sept. daily 7am-11pm, Oct.-April 8am-8pm).

Sights and Outdoors Area hiking is excellent. The most popular hike is the **Chilcoot Trail,** a moderately difficult three-day adventure from Skagway over a formidable mountain pass that ends at the far end of Lake Bennet. The lake's two-mi. sandy beach is popular with locals in July and August. An astounding view of the Yukon rests partway up **Montana Mountain,** but it's a view you have to suffer for. To get there follow Hwy. 2 south, take the first right after crossing the bridge, then the first left, and then follow until the road becomes impassable. Scramble up the rest of the way past lichen, snow, and boulders to a spectacular view.

Visitors to the Yukon Territory should come to Carcross just to check out **The Barracks** (821-4372) and the **Chilcoot Trading Post** (821-3621), two shops which sell all

Yukon-made crafts, clothing, and souvenirs, just across the railroad tracks from the reception center (open daily 9am-5pm).

Frontierland (667-1055), 1km north of the Carcross Desert (the exposed, sandy bottom of a glacial lake), presents a wildlife gallery of mounted animals in life-like settings, including the **largest bear ever mounted,** and Heritage Park, featuring live Yukon wildlife such as lynxes and Dall sheep. (Museum and park $6, kids $4; gallery or park alone $3.50/$2.50. Open mid-May to mid-Sept. daily 8am-5:30pm.)

Appendix

■ Climate

Average Temp in °F Rain in inches	January		April		July		October	
	Temp	Rain	Temp	Rain	Temp	Rain	Temp	Rain
Atlanta	51°	4.9"	73°	4.4"	89°	4.7"	74°	2.5"
Chicago	29°	1.6"	59°	3.7"	83°	3.6"	64°	2.3"
Dallas	54°	1.7"	84°	3.6"	98°	2.0"	80°	2.5"
Honolulu	80°	3.8"	83°	1.5"	88°	0.5"	87°	1.9"
Las Vegas	56°	0.5"	77°	0.2"	105°	0.5"	82°	0.3"
Los Angeles	67°	3.7"	71°	1.2"	84°	0.0"	79°	0.2"
New Orleans	62°	5.0"	79°	4.5"	91°	6.7"	79°	2.7"
New York	38°	3.2"	61°	3.8"	85°	3.8"	66°	3.4"
St. Louis	38°	1.7"	67°	3.6"	89°	3.6"	69°	2.3"
Seattle	45°	5.9"	58°	2.5"	74°	0.9"	60°	3.4"

In general, if you want to **convert Fahrenheit temperatures to Celsius**, simply divide the Fahrenheit number by 2 and then subtract 14. (For example, 80 degrees Fahrenheit would be 26 degrees Celsius.) That will give you a rough estimate, which should be good enough for general climate concerns. If you're hard-core about either math or weather, go for the real thing: C=5/9F - 18. Phew.

■ Measurements

Although the metric system has made considerable inroads into American business and science, the British system of weights and measures continues to prevail in the U.S. The following is a list of U.S. units and their metric equivalents:

1 inch = 25 millimeter (mm)
1 foot (ft.) = 0.30 meter (m)
1 yard (yd.) = 0.91m
1 mile = 1.61kilometer (km)
1 ounce = 25 gram (g)
1 pound (lb.) = 0.45 kilogram (kg)
1 quart = 0.94 liter (L)

1mm = 0.04 inch (in.)
1m = 3.33 foot (ft.)
1m = 1.1 yard (yd.)
1km = 0.62 mile (mi.)
1g = 0.04 ounce (oz.)
1kg = 2.22 pound (lb.)
1 liter = 1.06 quart (qt.)

COMPARATIVE VALUES OF U.S. UNITS OF MEASUREMENT:

1 foot   = 12 inches
1 yard   = 3 feet
1 mile   = 5280 feet
1 pound   = 16 ounces (weight)
1 cup   = 8 ounces (volume)
1 pint   = 2 cups
1 quart   = 2 pints
1 gallon   = 4 quarts

It should be noted that gallons in the U.S. are not identical to those across the Atlantic; one U.S. gallon equals 0.83 Imperial gallons.

■ Official U.S. Holidays in 1997

New Year's Day: Wed. Jan. 1
Martin Luther King, Jr.'s Birthday: Mon. Jan. 20
Presidents Day: Mon. Feb. 17 (observed)
Memorial Day: Mon. May 26
Independence Day: Fri. July 4
Labor Day: Mon. Sept. 1
Columbus Day: Mon. Oct. 13
Veterans Day (Armistice Day): Tues. Nov. 11 (observed)
Thanksgiving: Thurs. Nov. 27
Christmas Day: Thurs. Dec. 25.

■ Official Canadian Holidays in 1997

New Year's Day: Wed. Jan.1
Easter Monday: Mon. Mar. 31
Victoria Day: Mon. May 19
St. Jean: Tues. June 24 (in Quebec)
Canada Day: Tues. July 1
Thanksgiving: Mon. Oct. 13
Remembrance Day: Tues. Nov. 11
Christmas Day: Thurs. Dec. 25
Boxing Day: Fri. Dec. 26.

■ Where's the Party?

New Year's Day (Jan. 1): Rose Bowl, Pasadena, CA; Orange Bowl, Miami, FL
St. Patrick's Day (Mar. 17): St. Pat's Day Parade, New York City, NY.
Mardi Gras (Feb. 1-11): New Orleans, LA; Mobile, AL.
Independence Day (July 4): Boston, MA and Washington D.C. have great fireworks!
Labor Day (Sept. 1): wherever the tourists are not.
Thanksgiving (Nov. 27): Macy's Parade, New York City, NY.
New Year's Eve (Dec. 31): Times Square, New York City, NY.

■ Electricity

Electricity is 110V AC in the U.S. and Canada, only half as much as that of most European countries. Visit a hardware store for an **adapter** (which changes the shape of the plug) and a **converter** (which changes the voltage). Do not make the mistake of using only an adapter, or you'll fry your appliances. Travelers who heat-disinfect their **contact lenses** should consider switching to a chemical disinfection system.

■ Doodle Space:

■ Mileage

	Atlanta	Boston	Chic.	Dallas	DC	Denver	L.A.	Miami	New O.	NYC	Phila.	Phnx.	St. L	San F.	Seattle	Trnto.	Vanc.	Mont.
Atlanta		1108	717	783	632	1406	2366	653	474	886	778	1863	560	2492	2699	959	2825	1240
Boston	22 hr		996	1794	442	1990	3017	1533	1542	194	333	2697	1190	3111	3105	555	3242	326
Chicago	14 hr	20 hr		937	715	1023	2047	1237	928	807	767	1791	302	2145	2108	537	2245	537
Dallas	15 hr	35 hr	18 hr		1326	794	1450	1322	507	1576	1459	906	629	1740	2112	1457	2255	1763
DC	12 hr	10 hr	14 hr	24 hr		1700	2689	1043	1085	229	139	2350	845	2840	2788	526	3292	665
Denver	27 hr	38 hr	20 hr	15 hr	29 hr		1026	2046	1341	1785	1759	790	860	1267	1313	1508	1458	1864
L.A.	45 hr	57 hr	39 hr	28 hr	55 hr	20 hr		2780	2005	2787	2723	371	1837	384	1141	2404	1285	2888
Miami	13 hr	30 hr	24 hr	26 hr	20 hr	39 hr	47 hr		856	1346	1214	2368	1197	3086	3368	1564	3505	1676
New O.	9 hr	31 hr	18 hr	10 hr	21 hr	26 hr	30 hr	17 hr		1332	1247	1535	677	2331	2639	1320	2561	1654
NYC	18 hr	4 hr	16 hr	31 hr	5 hr	35 hr	45 hr	23 hr	27 hr		104	2592	999	2923	2912	496	3085	386
Phila.	18 hr	6 hr	16 hr	19 hr	3 hr	33 hr	44 hr	23 hr	23 hr	2 hr		2511	904	2883	2872	503	3009	465
Phoenix	40 hr	49 hr	39 hr	19 hr	43 hr	17 hr	8 hr	47 hr	30 hr	48 hr	44 hr		1503	753	1510	2069	1654	2638
St. Louis	11 hr	23 hr	6 hr	13 hr	15 hr	17 hr	35 hr	29 hr	13 hr	19 hr	16 hr	32 hr		2113	2139	810	2276	1128
San Fran.	47 hr	60 hr	41 hr	47 hr	60 hr	33 hr	7 hr	59 hr	43 hr	56 hr	54 hr	15 hr	45 hr		807	2630	951	2985
Seattle	52 hr	59 hr	40 hr	40 hr	54 hr	25 hr	22 hr	65 hr	50 hr	55 hr	54 hr	28 hr	36 hr	16 hr		2623	146	2964
Toronto	21 hr	11 hr	10 hr	26 hr	11 hr	26 hr	48 hr	29 hr	26 hr	11 hr	13 hr	48 hr	14 hr	49 hr	48 hr		4563	655
Vancvr.	54 hr	61 hr	42 hr	43 hr	60 hr	27 hr	24 hr	67 hr	54 hr	57 hr	56 hr	30 hr	38 hr	18 hr	2 hr	53 hr		4861
Montreal	23 hr	6 hr	17 hr	28 hr	12 hr	39 hr	53 hr	32 hr	31 hr	7 hr	9 hr	53 hr	23 hr	56 hr	55 hr	7 hr	55 hr	

EXPLORE THE EAST COAST WITH HOSTELLING INTERNATIONAL

New York

Miami Beach

Washington, DC

Boston

With Hostelling International you can visit some of America's exciting East Coast cities for a budget price. They're priced to fit a student's budget and are great places to meet people from all over the world. You can stay at a landmark building on the trendy Upper West Side of Manhattan, a highrise in the heart of the Nation's Capital, a historic masterpiece in Miami's Art Deco District, just two blocks from the ocean, or a handsomely refurbished turn-of-the-century guest house in the center of Boston, the Hub of New England. For reservations call:

New York City .... (212) 932-2300
Washington, DC .... (202) 737-2333
Miami Beach .... (305) 534-2988
Boston .... (617) 536-9455

HOSTELLING INTERNATIONAL

The new seal of approval of the International Youth Hostel Federation.

HOSTELLING INTERNATIONAL®

Index

A

AAA (American Automobile Association) 39
Abraham Lincoln's Birthplace National Historic Site, KY 266
Acadia National Park, ME 77
Adirondacks, NY 185–186
AIDS 17
Air Canada 33
Air Travel
  From Asia, South Pacific, South Africa 29
  From Europe 29
airline ticket consolidators 35
airlines
  international 29
Alabama 352–360
  Birmingham 355
  Mobile 358–360
  Montgomery 352–355
Alamo Car Rental 41
Alamo, TX 530
Alamogordo, NM 666
Alaska 803–813
  Alaska Highway 812
  Anchorage 808
  Denali National Park 810
  Fairbanks 812–813
  Juneau 806
  Ketchikan 804
  Wrangell-St. Elias National Park 807
Alaska Airlines 33
Alaska Hwy, AK 812
Alaska Public Lands Information Center 803
Alaska State Museum 807
Alaskan National Park Service, 803
AlaskaPass 804
Albany, NY 176–177
Alberta 879–888
  Banff Nat'l Park 884
  Calgary 882
  Edmonton 879

Jasper Nat'l Park 886
Albuquerque, NM 661–664
Alcatraz Island, CA 767
alcohol 14
Alexandria Bay, NY 188
Algonquin Provincial Park, ONT 878
Allegheny National Forest, PA 209
Alliance, NE 487
Amana Colonies, IA 481–482
Amarillo, TX 534–536
America West 33
America's largest swamp 381
Americade 45
American Express 9, 11, 12, 39, 43, 55
American Indian Art Museum, WY 568
American Motorcyclist Association 45
American Police Hall of Fame and Museum, FL 339
American Quarter Horse Heritage Center and Museum, TX 535
American Red Cross 15
Amish World, PA 205
Amtrak 37
Anaheim, CA 733
Anchorage, AK 808
Anheuser-Busch Brewery, MO 497
Ann Arbor, MI 407–409
Annapolis, MD 217
Apache Junction and the Superstition Mountains, AZ 649
Apache Trail, AZ 649
APEX 33
APLIC Fairbanks 812
Apostle Islands, WI 449–451
Appalachian Mountains Club (AMC), NH 79

Appalachian Trail 79, 257, 294
Appendix 904
Arapahoe National Forest, CO 587
Aravaipa Canyon, AZ 650
Arches National Park, UT 57, 623–624
Arcosanti, AZ 646
Arctic National Wildlife Refuge, AK 812
Arizona 631–654
  Canyon de Chelly National Monument 637–638
  Flagstaff 642–644
  Grand Canyon National Park 631–636
  Jerome 645
  Lake Powell, Page, and Rainbow Bridge 639–640
  Navajo and Hopi Reservations 636–639
  Petrified Forest and Meteor Crater 641
  Phoenix 646–649
  Sedona 645–646
  Sunset Crater, Wupatki, and Walnut Canyon 640
  Tombstone 653–654
  Tucson 650–652
Arizona-Sonora Desert Museum, AZ 652
Arkansas 385–391
  Hot Springs National Park 390–391
  Little Rock 385–388
  The Ozarks 388–390
armadillo races, TX 517
Arthur Bryant's, Kansas City, MO 57, 502
Ashe, Arthur 242

Asheville, NC 292
Ashland, OR 701
Aspen, CO 591–592
Astoria, OR 699
Astrodome, TX 526
Astronauts Memorial, FL 332
Atchafalaya Basin, LA 381
Athens, GA 312–313
Atlanta, GA 304–312
Atlantic City, NJ 189
Atlantic Coast, NS 829–831
ATMs (automatic teller machines) 11
Audubon House, FL 346
Audubon Park, LA 375
Austin, TX 517–520
auto transport companies 43
Avenue of the Giants, CA 790
Avery Island, LA 385
Avis Car Rental 41

B

Badlands National Park, SD 57, 470–471
baked in Telluride 601
Baltimore, MD 213–217
Bandelier National Monument, NM 658
Banff Nat'l Park, AB 884
Banzai Pipeline, HI 822
bar containing collection of 3,500 animal heads, horns, and antlers 531
Bar Harbor, ME 77
Bardstown, KY 265
Basque Museum and Cultural Center, ID 544
bat guano 666
Bata Shoe Museum, ONT 868
Baton Rouge, LA 381
Battleship Park, AL 359

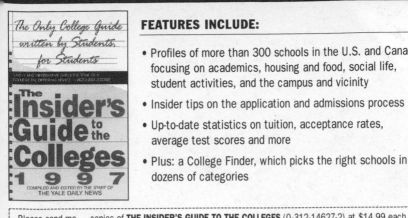

★ 1997 Reader Questionnaire ★

Fill this out and return it to **Let's Go, St. Martin's Press,**
175 5th Ave. NY, NY 10010

Name: _____ **What book did you use?** _____

Address: _____

City: _____ **State:** _____ **Zip Code:** _____

How old are you? under 19 19-24 25-34 35-44 45-54 55 or over

Are you (circle one) in high school in college in grad school employed retired between jobs

Have you used Let's Go before? yes no

Would you use Let's Go again? yes no

How did you first hear about Let's Go? friend store clerk CNN bookstore display advertisement/promotion review other

Why did you choose Let's Go (circle up to two)? annual updating reputation budget focus price writing style other: _____

Which other guides have you used, if any? Frommer's $-a-day Fodor's Rough Guides Lonely Planet Berkeley Rick Steves other: _____

Is Let's Go the best guidebook? yes no

If not, which do you prefer? _____

Which part of Let's Go do you feel needs most to be improved, if any (circle up to two)? packaging/cover practical information accommodations food cultural introduction sights practical introduction ("Essentials") directions entertainment gay/lesbian information maps other: _____

How would you like to see these things improved?

_____

_____

How long was your trip? one week two weeks three weeks one month two months or more

Have you traveled extensively before? yes no

Do you buy a separate map when you visit a foreign city? yes no

Have you seen the Let's Go Map Guides? yes no

Have you used a Let's Go Map Guide? yes no

If you have, would you recommend them to others? yes no

Did you use the internet to plan your trip? yes no

Would you buy a Let's Go phrasebook adventure/trekking guide gay/lesbian guide

Which of the following destinations do you hope to visit in the next three to five years (circle one)? Australia China South America Russia other: _____

Where did you buy your guidebook? internet chain bookstore independent bookstore college bookstore travel store other: _____

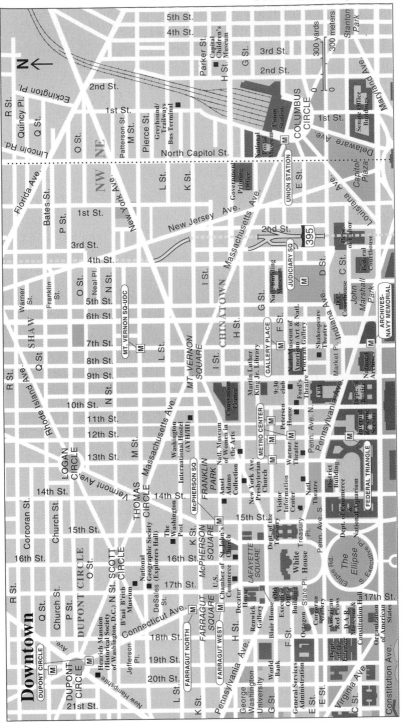

Downtown Washington, D.C.

Central Washington, D.C.

Klingle St.

Adams Mill Rd.

MT. PLEASANT

16th St.

14th St.

CLEVELAND PARK

Washington National Cathedral

Klingle St.

Cathedral Ave.

National Zoo

Irving St.

Colur

Harva

15th St.

Woodley Rd.

WOODLEY PARK-ZOO

Calvert St.

Euclid St.

GLOVER PARK

Massachusetts

Calvert St.

Vice Presidential Mansion

ADAMS-MORGAN

Florida A

Observatory

La. U.S. Naval Observatory

37th St.

Ave.

Rock Creek Park

Rock Creek Pkwy.

Waterside Dr.

KALORAMA CIRCLE

Columbia Rd.

EMBASSY ROW

Whitehaven Park

Dumbarton Oaks Park

U St.

U ST/CAP

R St.

Montrose Park

Rock Creek

DUPONT CIRCLE

Florida

New Hampshire Ave.

16th St.

15th St.

Georgetown University

Wisconsin Ave.

28th St.

Q St.

SHERIDAN CIRCLE

Q St.

Ave.

20th St.

DUPONT CIRCLE

M

P. St.

LC CI

14th St.

34th St.

GEORGETOWN

30th St.

R St.

P. St.

DUPONT CIRCLE

M

Connecticut Ave.

SCOTT CIRCLE

THOMAS CIRCLE

MCPHERSO SQUARE

C&O Canal

26th St.

M St.

23rd St.

NEW DOWNTOWN

FARRAGUT NORTH

FARRAGUT SQUARE

MCPHER

M

White hurst Fwy.

Key Br.

WASHINGTON CIRCLE

66

FOGGY BOTTOM-GWU

M

FARRAGUT WEST

M

K St.

Pennsylvania Ave.

H St.

New Yo

LAFAYETTE SQUARE

METRO

George Washington Pkwy.

Theodore Roosevelt Memorial

Rock Creek Pkwy.

JAUREZ CIRCLE

GWU

G St.

FOGGY BOTTOM

18th St.

White House

15th St.

ROSSLYN

M

Theodore Roosevelt Island

Virginia Ave.

F St.

E St.

17th St.

The Ellipse

E St.

DOWN

ROSSLYN

66

Roosevelt Bridge

50

Constitution Ave.

FEDERAL TR

14th

50

66 50

SMITHS

George Washington Pkwy.

Lincoln Memorial

Washington Monument

U.S. Holocaust Memorial Museum

ARLINGTON CEMETERY

M

Memorial Bridge

Independence Ave.

Kutz Br.

Raoul Wallenberg Pl.

East Basin Dr.

C St.

Memorial Dr.

Lady Bird Johnson Park

Columbia Island

Ohio Dr.

West Potomac Park

Tidal Basin

Outlet Br.

Maine

Visitors Center

Potomac River

Jefferson Memorial

Fra Me

ARLINGTON CEMETERY

395

East Pot

VIRGINIA

Jefferson Davis Hwy.

395

1

Pentagon

PENTAGON

M

Central Washington, D.C.

The Mall Area, Washington, D.C.

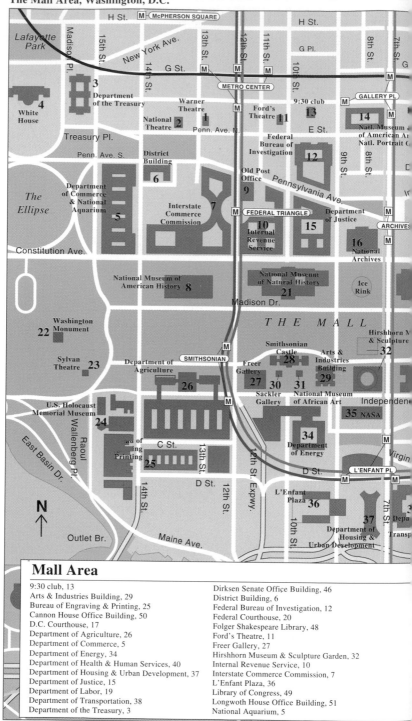

Mall Area

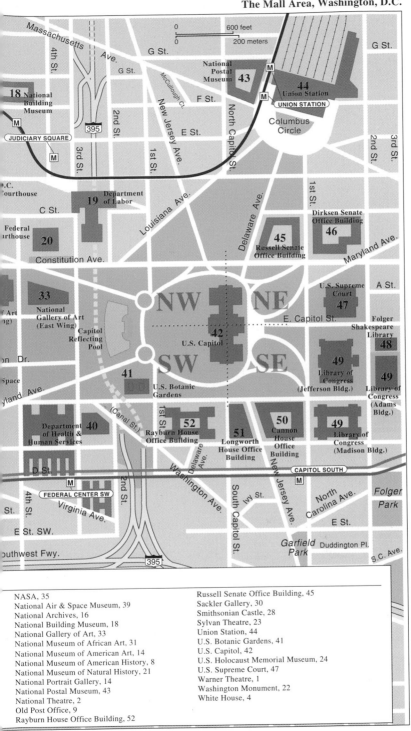

White House Area, Foggy Bottom, and Nearby Arlington

Prospect St.
GEORGETOWN
Old Stone House
N St.
Olive St.
M St.
33rd St.
31st St.
Rock Creek
24th St.
L St.
C&O Creek
South St.
Whitehurst Fwy.
26th St.
25th St.
WASHIN
CIRC
29
K St. (under expressway)
FOGGY BOTTOM-GWU
66
M
Potomac River
Thompson Boat Center
Watergate Hotel
JUAREZ CIRCLE
24th St.
FOC
BOT
Francis Scott Key Br.
Fort Myer Dr.
N. Lynn St.
N. Moore St.
N. Kent St.
19th St.
Theodore Roosevelt Memorial
Watergate Hotel Complex
Rock Creek Pkwy.
Kennedy Center for the Performing Arts
ROSSLYN
M
Theodore Roosevelt Island
T
D
Wilson Blvd
George Washington Pkwy.
ROSSLYN
Fairfax Dr.
Arlington Ridge Rd
66
Theodore Roosevelt Br.
66 50
N. Nash St.
Mead Dr.
50
50
NW
SW
I
M
Marine Corps War Memorial (Iwo Jima Statue)
George Washington Memorial Pkwy.
12th St.
Netherlands Carillon
Arlington Memorial Br.
Ericsson Memorial
ARLINGTON
Ladybird Johnson Park
Columbia Island
M
Memorial Dr.
ARLINGTON CEMETERY
Jefferson Davis Hwy.
Grave of President John F. Kennedy
Arlington House
Robert E. Lee Memorial
Visitor Center
ARLINGTON NATIONAL CEMETERY
Lyndon B. Johnson Memorial
Tomb of the Unknown Soldier
VIRGINIA
0   1500 feet
0   500 meters
Pentagon, National Airport

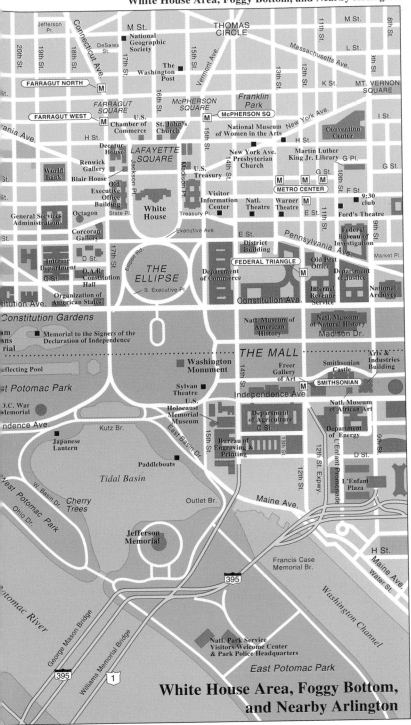

White House Area, Foggy Bottom, and Nearby Arlington

Metrorail System, Washington, D.C.

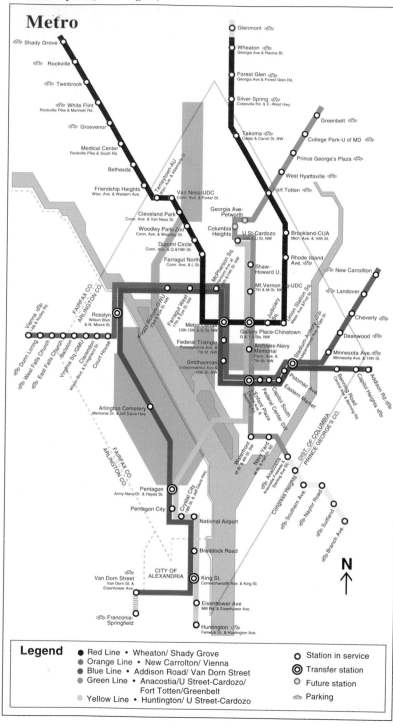

Metro

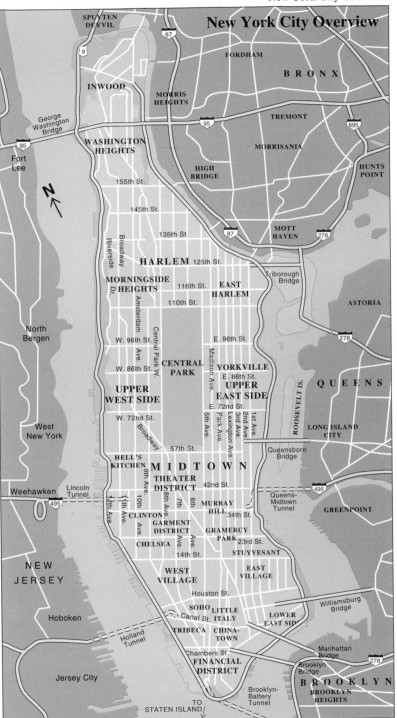

New York City Subways

Subways

Stops are not served by all trains at all times. Refer to Transit Authority map for descriptions of express, local, and limited service.

LEGEND

K,B   Line
168 St Terminal

Downtown Manhattan

FDR Drive

Williamsburg Br.

Lewis St.

Jackson St.

Water St.

Columbia St.

Willett St.

Montgomery St.

Madison St.

Clinton St.

Avenue D

Pitt St.

Clinton St.

East Broadway

Avenue C

Ridge St.

Rivington St.

E. 13th St.

E. 12th St.

E. 11th St.

E. 10th St.

E. 9th St.

E. 8th St.

Avenue B

Clinton St.

Suffolk St.

LOWER EAST SIDE

E. 2nd St.

E. Houston St.

Norfolk St.

Essex St.

Ludlow St.

Avenue A

EAST VILLAGE

NOHO

Stanton St.

F, J, M, Z

First Avenue

E. 1st St.

Orchard St.

Allen St.

Eldridge St.

Forsyth St.

Delancey St.

Broome

Grand

Hester St.

St. Marks Pl.

E. 7th St.

E. 6th St.

E. 5th St.

E. 4th St.

E. 3rd St.

Second Avenue

Stuyvesant St.

40

F

Chrystie St.

B, D, Q

The Bowery

Third Avenue

39

COOPER SQUARE

33

The Bowery

Broome St. J, M

Elizabeth St.

LITTLE ITALY

30

Baxter St.

E. 15th St.

E. 14th St.

L

Mott St.

Spring St.

Kenmare St.

L, 4, 5, 6

Fourth Ave.

38

Jones St.

Bond St.

Mulberry St.

Cleveland Pl.

Cent

6

42

41

Astor Pl.

Lafayette St.

36

Shinbone Al.

4, 6

Lafayette St.

Crosby St.

6

UNION SQUARE

N, R

43

University Pl.

Broadway

N, R

W. 3rd St.

6

Great Jones

31

B, D, F, Q

N, R

Mercer St.

Greene St.

Wooster St.

SOHO

Howard St.

N, R

L, 4, 5, 6

New York University

Spring St.

A, C, E

Canal St.

29

Lispenard St.

Fifth Avenue

47

W. 12th St.

W. 11th St.

E. 8th St.

Washington Mews

Waverly Pl.

37

Washington Sq. N.

Washington Sq. S.

La Guardia Pl.

Prince St.

Thompson St.

44

W. 10th St.

W. 9th St.

Washington Square Park

Bleecker St.

Sullivan St.

C, E

W. 15th St.

Macdougal Alley

Macdougal St.

W. Houston St.

W. 14th St.

46

Avenue of the Americas (6th Ave.)

Waverly Pl.

Washington Pl.

A, B, C, D, E, F, Q

Minetta La.

Ave. of the Americas (Sixth Ave.)

F, L, Q

(6th Ave.)

W. 13th St.

Milligan Pl.

Patchin Pl.

45

Gay St.

Jones St.

Cornelia St.

Bedford St.

Downing St.

1, 9

Varick St.

TRIBECA

N. Moore St.

1, 2, 3, 9, L

SHERIDAN SQUARE

1, 9

Carmine St.

Commerce St.

Hudson St.

Spring St.

Dominick St.

Broome St.

A, C, E, L

Seventh Ave.

GREENWICH VILLAGE

Grove St.

34

St. Luke's Pl.

Clarkson St.

Leroy St.

W. Houston St.

King St.

Charlton St.

Vandam St.

Watts St.

Desbrosses St.

8th Ave.

W. 4th St.

Christopher St.

W. 10th St.

35

Barrow St.

Morton St.

Greenwich St.

W. Washington St.

West Side Hwy.

ABINGDON SQUARE

Bank St.

W. 11th St.

Charles St.

Perry St.

9th Ave.

Little W. 12th St.

Gansevoort St.

Horatio St.

Jane St.

W. 12th St.

Bethune St.

West St.

Holland Tunnel

10th Ave.

W. 14th St.

Eighth Ave.

Greenwich Ave.

N ←

Midtown Manhattan

East River

Queensboro Bridge

Queens-Midtown Tunnel

FDR Dr.

First Ave.

Second Ave.

TURTLE BAY

United Nations

E. 56th St.
E. 55th St.
E. 54th St.
E. 53rd St.

Third Ave.

Citicorp Center

59

58
57

Second Ave.

E. 52nd St.
E. 51st St.
E. 50th St.
E. 49th St.
E. 48th St.
E. 47th St.
E. 46th St.
E. 45th St.
E. 44th St.
E. 43rd St.

E. 42nd St.
E. 41st St.
E. 40th St.

Third Ave.

E. 39th St.
E. 38th St.
E. 37th St.
E. 36th St.
E. 35th St.

E. 34th St.
E. 33rd St.

Lexington Ave.

Park Ave.

Madison Ave.

Fifth Ave.

Grand Central Terminal

New York Public Library

MURRAY HILL

Empire State Building

Bryant Park

W. 40th St.

GARMENT DISTRICT

HERALD SQUARE

N,R

1,2,3,9

Broadway

Seventh Ave.

Eighth Ave.

TIMES SQUARE

Port Authority Bus Terminal

General Post Office

A,C,E

COLUMBUS CIRCLE

A,B,C,D,
1,2,3,9

New York Convention & Visitors Bureau

N,R

Carnegie Hall

Museum of Modern Art

Rockefeller Center

B,D,F,Q

B,D,E

C,E

Ninth Ave.

Dyer Ave.

Tenth Ave.

Lincoln Tunnel

HELL'S KITCHEN

Eleventh Ave.

Twelfth Ave.

Grand Army Plaza

N,R

Central Park South

B,Q

E. 60th St.
E. 59th St.
E. 58th St.
E. 57th St.

W. 60th St.
W. 59th St.
W. 58th St.
W. 57th St.
W. 56th St.
W. 55th St.
W. 54th St.
W. 53rd St.
W. 52nd St.
W. 51st St.
W. 50th St.
W. 49th St.
W. 48th St.
W. 47th St.
W. 46th St.
W. 45th St.
W. 44th St.
W. 43rd St.
W. 42nd St.
W. 41st St.

W. 39th St.

W. 38th St.
W. 37th St.
W. 36th St.
W. 35th St.
W. 34th St.

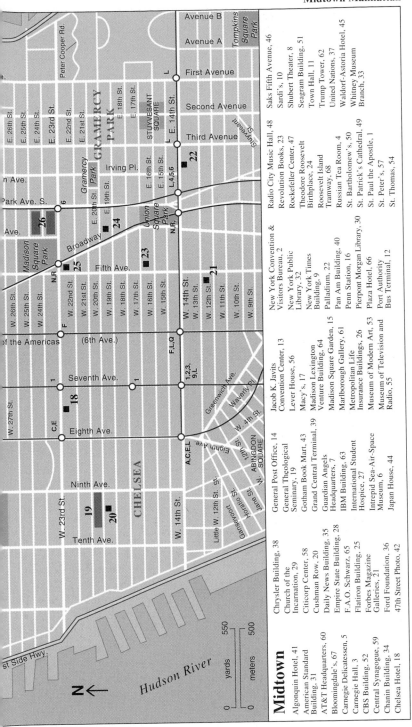

Uptown Manhattan

Uptown